Gay Histories and Cultures

Garland Reference Library of the Social Sciences (Vol. 1002)

Advisory Board

The Encyclopedia of Lesbian and Gay Histories and Cultures
Volume II

Gay Histories and Cultures: An Encyclopedia

George E. Haggerty
Editor

John Beynon
Douglas Eisner
Assistant Editors

Garland Publishing, Inc.
A member of the Taylor & Francis Group
New York and London
2000

Published in 2000 by
Garland Publishing Inc.
A Member of the Taylor & Francis Group
19 Union Square West
New York, NY 10003

10 9 8 7 6 5 4 3 2 1

Library of Congress Cataloging-in-Publication Data

Gay histories and cultures : an encyclopedia / George E. Haggerty, editor; John Beynon, Douglas Eisner, assistant editors.
     p. cm. — (Encyclopedia of lesbian and gay histories and cultures ; v. 2) (Garland
  reference library of the social sciences ; vol. 1002)
  Includes index.
  ISBN 0-8153-1880-4 (alk. paper)
    1. Gay men—Encyclopedias. 2. Homosexuality, Male—Encyclopedias. I. Series. II.
  Haggerty, George E.

HQ75.13 .G37 1999
306.76'6'03 21—dc21
                                           99-040905

Printed on acid-free, 250-year-life paper
Manufactured in the United States of America

Contents

This book is dedicated to the memory of

William A. H. Kinnucan
(1949–1998)

"('twas all he wished) a friend"

Introduction

Bonnie Zimmerman and George E. Haggerty

The Encyclopedia of Lesbian and Gay Histories and Cultures in two volumes is the latest, and we hope the richest, in a long line of publications that attempt to open up for contemporary readers the complex history and wide cultural diversity of lesbian and gay life. Unlike earlier endeavors, however, which tended to limit the kinds of questions that could be asked about the past, these volumes try to avoid the stigma conventionally attached to "homosexuality" and look instead at examples of same-sex desire in different cultures at different times. They are the product of an age in which self-definition is challenged by cultural urgency of various kinds and when lesbian and gay concerns have moved out from the shadows into the bright light of national and international politics. What better moment to undo the misconceptions of the past and to reclaim the histories and cultures that have been denied us? In doing so, we hope to be seen not as appropriating the past but rather as making it available for all sorts of purposes, including but not limited to an increase in present-day awareness. Too often we have been told by others who we are or where we came from. It is time not just to claim our place in history and culture but also to negotiate with the histories and cultures to which we might most closely relate.

History

The study of homosexuality can be said to have begun in 1869, when a generation of medical doctors established the profession of sexology, the medical and supposedly scientific study of sex. Among its earliest objects of study was "in-version"—a term that signified a range of behaviors and attitudes that would later be classed under the term *homosexuality*. Inversion redefined same-sex desire as an aspect of human personality or essential being, not a sin-laden act against nature. Many of the most prominent figures of early sexology—such as Richard von Krafft-Ebing and Havelock Ellis—described the invert, or homosexual, in excruciating and, from the perspective of today, stigmatizing or, as contemporary lesbian scholar Lillian Faderman put it, morbidifying, detail. A century later, the prominent French historian and theorist Michel Foucault would point to this construction of the modern homosexual as a signal moment in the history of sexuality.

Although homosexuality became known as "the love that dare not speak its name," in fact, even in the nineteenth century there were many names used for homosexuality: some, like *bugger, sodomite,* and *tribade,* referring to the specific sexual behaviors that men and women performed with members of their own gender, and others, like *homosexual, invert,* and *Urning,* referring to the identities that were being constructed around these behaviors. The shift from behavior to identity was also to have an unexpected impact: the beginnings of a political movement based upon that identity. Among the early generations of sexologists were several individuals who themselves identified as homosexuals and directed their scholarly activity toward both the elimination of prejudice and discrimination and the demand for equal human rights. These individuals—including Karl Maria Ulrichs, Edward Carpenter, Magnus Hirschfeld, and Anna Rüling—were pioneers in uniting scholarship and activism, as their descendants would do several generations later.

The period between roughly 1900 and 1930 was one of considerable intellectual activity in the areas of sexology and literature, particularly. But economic crisis and political repression in the United States and Europe would drive nascent gay and lesbian communities, with their potential for scholarly research and creative activity, underground. Although individuals produced monumental work, in general academic institutions generally avoided and suppressed gay and lesbian scholarship. These individuals have become heroic role models: Alfred Kinsey, for example, with his groundbreaking sexological studies, and Jeannette Foster, who self-published an extraordinary study of lesbianism in literature. With the exception of Kinsey, these figures were unable to generate an ongoing academic movement or produce individual scholars to carry on their work. Before lesbian and gay studies could become a reality, something else needed to happen. That "something else" was the gay liberation movement, which burst into public consciousness in 1969 when the patrons of the Stonewall Inn in New York City's Greenwich Village fought back against a police raid. Although political activism and organizing had existed throughout the 1950s and 1960s and had accelerated at the end of the latter decade, the three nights of what has become known as the Stonewall Rebellion galvanized a new generation. Inspired by the civil rights movement in particular, and with experience in that movement as well as in the student, antiwar, and women's liberation movements, gay and lesbian activists organized and mobilized their own movement to end the social, political, and cultural oppression of homosexuals.

Many of these activists were students in universities. They sought to bring their academic work to the service of activism and to apply their political consciousness to their scholarly work. In the same way that African American studies grew out of the civil rights and black power movements, and women's studies out of the women's liberation movement, so did gay and lesbian studies have its beginnings in the gay liberation movement. At that time, very few academics had the psychological and material security to be openly gay or lesbian and to focus their scholarly work on the study of homosexuality. Lesbian and gay professors had long lived more or less comfortably in closets within the ivory towers; however, the growing gay and lesbian movement impelled some professors and graduate students to begin to organize within professional institutions and associations.

Gay and lesbian scholars first began to organize caucuses within professional associations in the early 1970s. For example, the gay caucus of the Modern Language Association first met in 1973 and soon organized large and enthusiastic sessions at the annual MLA meetings throughout the 1970s. Caucuses were also formed in 1974 in the American Anthropological Association and the American Sociological Association. The Lesbian and Gay Caucus in the MLA and its more scholarly counterpart, the Gay Studies Division, continue to thrive, as do the caucuses of the AAA and the ASA. Similar caucuses and divisions exist within the professional associations of historians, musicologists, art historians, psychologists, and so on. These caucuses and divisions have played an important part in opening up the academic profession to new scholarship and new ways of thinking, thus being directly responsible for much of the knowledge collected in this encyclopedia.

A second important source of knowledge came from outside formal academic institutions. From the early 1970s until the present, groundbreaking work has been done by scholars and writers not affiliated with any institutions. These independent scholars worked without financial resources or public recognition, at least until their books and articles were finally published. For some, the Gay Academic Union, founded in New York City in 1974, provided solidarity and support. The GAU, while ostensibly open to both men and women, did, like many other political groups, became a primarily male organization. Lesbians turned to other venues, including lesbian feminist collectives, women's studies programs, and feminist newspapers and journals, to produce their work.

By the mid-1970s, both gay men and lesbians in the United States had produced a substantial body of important work. Jonathan Ned Katz had published *Gay American History,* a collection of primary documents that would shape a generation of scholars; Beth Hodges had produced two journal issues on lesbian writing and publishing (one in *Margins* and the other in the influential lesbian feminist journal *Sinister Wisdom*); and under the leadership of John deCecco, the *Journal of Homosexuality* had been established as the first scholarly journal in Gay and Lesbian Studies. By 1981, we would also have seen Carroll Smith-Rosenberg's paradigm-building article, "The Female World of Love and Ritual" (published in the first issue of what would become the premier feminist scholarly journal, *Signs*), John Boswell's rewriting of the history of oppression, *Christianity, Social Tolerance, and Homosexuality,* independent scholar J. R. Roberts' *Black Lesbians: A Bibliography,* and Lillian Faderman's *Surpassing the Love of Men.* Lesbian and gay scholarship was making its mark on the map.

This energy emerged in several places at once, not only in the United States. French social and cultural theorists like Michel Foucault and Guy Hocquenghem used the political urgency of the student uprisings of 1968 to retheorize gay liberation from a post-Marxist perspective, while Luce Irigaray and Monique Wittig revised Lacanian psychoanalysis in ways that offered new paradigms for discussing gender and sexuality in a cultural context. The Australian Dennis Altman published *Homosexual Liberation and Oppression,* which investigated the social and personal consequences of internalized homophobia. In England, Mary McIntosh and Kenneth Plummer considered the ways in which homosexual identities are socially constructed; at the same time, Jeffrey Weeks traced the emergence of lesbian and gay identities. All produced foundational work that helped to give direction to the early gay liberation movement as well as to academic inquiry in the area of lesbian and gay studies. At the same time, artists, writers, and filmmakers throughout North America, Europe, and beyond were producing impressive accounts of lesbian and gay experiences, as dozens of entries in these volumes will attest.

In the 1980s, lesbian and gay scholarship would become formalized as a field of study in the United States, Canada, and a number of European countries, most particularly the United Kingdom and the Netherlands. At times Europe has taken the lead: indeed, the conference "Homosexuality, Which Homosexuality?" held in Amsterdam in 1987 holds the distinction of being the first international lesbian and gay academic conference of the contemporary era. Gay

and lesbian studies is thoroughly institutionalized in the Netherlands and is growing in strength throughout Europe, Australia, and New Zealand.

In the United States, at the turn of the millennium, gay and lesbian scholarship is growing in all fields of academic endeavor. It is no longer marginal but now occupies a central place in academic publishing, curricula, and conferences. Not only are lesbian and gay scholars increasingly able to identify as such in the classroom and in scholarly work, but lesbian, gay, bisexual, and queer ideas and theories are addressed with respect by heterosexual colleagues. Lesbian and gay studies programs have emerged at several prominent institutions, and students there are as likely to take a course on the "homosexual" as on the "heterosexual" past. Like ethnic studies and women's studies previously, lesbian and gay studies has left an indelible mark on what we are permitted to know.

This encyclopedia offers accounts of the most important international developments in lesbian and gay history and attempts to assess the state of lesbian and gay culture around the world. This makes it possible to see what kinds of issues and concerns lesbian and gay scholars have had in common around the world. It also suggest how deeply varied has been the experience of those who are attracted to members of their own gender at different times and in different cultures. From one perspective, these differences are so great that no term like *gay* or *queer* or even *homosexual* can encompass them. To see sexual identity as a lens through which to view an impossibly broad range of human experience is to risk obscuring specific and very important differences; but not insisting on this perspective is to be in danger of overlooking profoundly suggestive similarities that make connections across time and space.

Methodology

For many readers of these volumes, an immediate question may be raised as to why there are separate volumes on lesbian histories and cultures and gay histories and cultures. Some encyclopedias and reference works are co-sexual, while others have focused on either one or the other, most often concentrating on lesbian issues separately from gay male. For this publication, the editors chose to develop separate volumes, edited independently but with close cooperation and communication.

Why should lesbian and gay histories and cultures be organized and written as separate volumes? We have done so first because this assures that both histories receive full and unbiased attention. Historically, lesbianism has not always been addressed equally within gay studies. It has been assumed that lesbianism is more difficult to identify historically, more hidden and silenced, less accessible to the scholar. While it is true that chroniclers and historians have addressed female lives less thoroughly in general than male lives, these assumptions may flow less from what exists than from what we have looked for and the questions we have asked. Focusing an entire volume on lesbian histories and cultures assures that full attention be paid to recovering and collecting a full range of information that currently exists.

Moreover, as these two volumes will demonstrate, the difference of gender has always been significant in the conceptualization and experiences of lesbianism and male homosexuality and in the experiences of individuals and communities. Lesbians and gay men have shared many aspects of life—those that flow from self-affirmation and those that flow from resistance to heterosexism and homophobia—but they have also developed in profoundly different ways. Lesbians are marked as female and gay men as male, no matter what the rhetoric about inversion, and in patriarchal systems, gender matters. Feminism, in particular, has been a potent force in lesbian lives from at least the nineteenth century to the present. The more public presence of male homosexuality has often led to different emphases within legal and political movements. The degree to which male lives are recorded while female lives are ignored or suppressed affects the historical record. The fields of lesbian studies and gay studies have, until very recently, developed in an independent, though related, fashion. For these reasons, and many others, we believe that at this time readers will be best served by separate volumes. In the future, editors may choose a different strategy.

Definitions

The most difficult question, of course, is that of definition. What do we mean by "gay" and "lesbian"? Are we only documenting evidence of homosexual behavior? Are there rules of inclusion/exclusion for different kinds of sexual behavior or identity? How do we relate to the "state of alliance" that exists in many contexts, especially in North America, between "lesbian," "gay," "bisexual," and "transgender" identities, or to the reconditioned umbrella term *queer,* which has preoccupied both the academy and many outside it over the last ten years? It would be disingenuous for the editors to say that the question of sexual behavior and self-definition—that is, did she or didn't he—did not often influence inclusion or that the issue of sexual identity did not figure prominently in the entry lists suggested and reviewed by advisory editors and by specialists in certain fields. But neither editor sees "homosexuality" as a transhistorical or transcultural condition that can be analyzed in, say, classical Greece, modern Japan, and the last twenty-five years in this history of the United States in anything like similar terms. In fact, one of the intentions of the entries included is to demonstrate the range of difference within what we loosely call lesbian history and culture and gay history and culture.

At the same time, none of us can ignore that we live in a culture in which the past has been appropriated to various ends. Those of us who are lesbian and gay have participated in this appropriation as much or as little as our nonlesbian and nongay contemporaries. The effect of this appropriation is that for better or worse we have a very rich lesbian and gay heritage that itself needs to be documented in a volume such as this. In other words, while there may be no proof that Alexander the Great or Sor Juana Inés de la Cruz were what we would call "gay" or "lesbian," gay culture and lesbian culture in the twentieth century has used such figures in defining itself, and it would be a mistake to ignore this rich layering of historical detail. In this sense, the encyclopedia is archaeological: a figure, a movement, or a sexual practice might be included for its own sake, of course, but it might also be included because it has been central to lesbian or gay history and mythology. This is not the same dynamic as "strategic essentialism," whereby historical understanding is sacrificed for an urgent political end; rather, it is a "practical constructionism," which tries to use historical and cultural difference to tell the story of lesbian and gay culture today as well as other stories about other cultures at other times.

For a similar reason we do not call this an encyclopedia of queer culture. "Queer" has had an important recent function in challenging the notion of sexual identity and insisting on a coalition between and among lesbian, gay, bisexual, and transgendered subjects, as well as people of color, sympathetic straights, and others. At the same time, it has created political difficulties of its own. For some, it suggests that sexual identity is the only basis from which to resist hegemonic culture. For others, it seems to dismiss the possibility of those gay and lesbian identities that have produced a rich intellectual and political culture. Queer theory, which was hailed as an answer to the seeming dead end of identity politics, has had to be rethought in light of challenges from grassroots activists as well as the rigorous self-questioning of the theorists themselves. Many of these issues are discussed in entries collected herein. It seems to us, however, that as happy as we might be to "queer" the past, we have not yet reached the point at which the differences that "lesbian" and "gay" imply can be completely ignored. On the other hand, in answer to queer theorists like Michael Warner and others who argue against the minoritizing stigma of lesbian and gay identity and suggest "queer" as an alternative identity that can resist institutionalization and various separatist or assimilative moves in an aggressively generalizing attempt to challenge the ascendancy of the normal, we offer this encyclopedia. If it does anything, it shows that the "normal" is nothing more than a fiction that has been challenged in various ways in various cultures at various times with varying success. In this sense, then, it is an encyclopedia of queer histories and cultures after all.

How to Use the Encyclopedia

This encyclopedia is intended for a wide audience, including students, scholars in all fields, and the general public, who is interested in the state of lesbian and gay research. All efforts have been made to write entries in "user-friendly" language, avoiding jargon and technical language that would place a barrier between the experts and their readers. At the same time, the authors have maintained a high level of scholarship, in-

corporating both passionate engagement and scholarly objectivity. The encyclopedia addresses areas of academic and political controversy, attempting always to address multiple points of view and varied theoretical perspectives. In particular, the authors and editors have worked hard to pay close attention to the inclusivity of race, class, and ethnicity.

The editors are particularly proud of the exceptional group of authors who have contributed entries to these volumes. These include some of the most famous names in the field of lesbian and gay studies as well as junior faculty and graduate students who will carry it forth into the future, independent scholars and writers like those who initiated this field, and the political and community activists who have maintained the important connection between scholarship and activism. These authors position themselves everywhere along the continuum of sexualities: lesbian, gay, bisexual, heterosexual, transgender, and queer. Readers will find both similarities and differences in the selection and treatment of topics in the two volumes. In a minority of cases, entries may overlap. The editors suggest that in the case of general topics—for example, sexology or history or individual countries—readers turn to the entries in each volume for a full treatment. It will prove instructive to see how a topic remains similar, or changes subtly, depending on who writes the entry and from what perspective. Other topics may appear in one volume and not the other: this is not necessarily a sign that an entry is only of interest to one group or the other. The editors found that to limit certain topics to one entry allowed them to cover many more topics over the range of two volumes. In every case, the editors hope that the two volumes are complementary in ways that will benefit users of either volume.

The reader will find that in the places where topics overlap, the entries together create a quilt or web of knowledge, one entry bordering on or leading to many others. For the student who is focused on one very specific question, each entry gives a general overview; for the browser it will lead to many additional topics and questions to be addressed in other entries.

To assist the reader in seeing the connections among the various entries included here, each is followed by a list of cross-referenced entries that relate to or expand it. In addition, each entry includes a bibliography with the most important and easily accessible titles. In the case of biographies, these include secondary rather than primary texts. Complete books are listed where possible; in addition, major articles are included. It is possible to use the book to study various topics in lesbian and gay studies. To assist the reader, we include a guide to the entries by topic. We also think, however, that these are volumes in which to browse: what better way to spend a few hours than to wend a path through a past (or a present) that is both foreign and familiar.

Readers will note that the encyclopedia does not insist upon rigid consistency in the use of certain terms. Authors have been free to use lesbian, gay, homosexual, bisexual, or queer as is appropriate to the particular requirements of their topics. Entries may also use cultural designations interchangeably, either because of personal preference or historical and political context. Different entries on related topics may emphasize different aspects of the subjects; once again, the editors have insisted upon factual consistency and accuracy while permitting individuality and even a touch of idiosyncracy.

No encyclopedia can be truly comprehensive. We could not include every topic, survey every historical period and every region of the world, or include every individual whose life included same-sex relationships. Biographical entries, in particular, needed to be selective, especially since we have included living figures. There has been an explosion of prominent figures who have "come out of the closet" in recent years, and were everyone to be included, this encyclopedia would be seriously imbalanced toward the present. Moreover, it is difficult to know who will have a long-lasting influence in the future. In considering these problems, the editors have chosen those figures who were the first in their particular fields, or who have already had unquestionable influence and notoriety. The editors recognize that our choices will be controversial, that while anyone will have chosen certain figures, in other cases, different choices might have been made.

The entries as a group move across the disciplines, across historical periods, and across cultures and nations. Some are general and expansive, others limited and particular. The editors have worked hard with the members of the advisory board to make the selections comprehensive, and both the range of fields and the entries within various fields have been the product of much thought and debate. The contributors have also worked to expand fields and define areas in a way that has made our work easier. We are grateful for the tireless efforts of everyone involved with this project.

Neither the editors nor the contributors intend these volumes to codify knowledge in the fields of lesbian and gay history and culture. These are by their natures ever-changing, and there will always be debate about what constitutes them as fields and how they are best represented historically. We hope that these volumes will participate in these debates and even provoke them. Of course, we also think that the debates will be more informed as the result of the wealth of material that is included here. There will always be a certain amount of fragmentation of information and gaps in the knowledge of these fields precisely because secrecy resulting from persecution and ignorance masquerading as science have been so strong a part of their representation historically. If lesbian and gay history and culture as told by lesbian and gay subjects (or those who identify with them) has had to struggle to find its place in contemporary letters, then this encyclopedia represents a new stage, attempting as it does to open up questions that previous encyclopedias of homosexuality considered closed.

Acknowledgments by George Haggerty

I find myself with a number of people to thank. My assistant editors, John Beynon and Doug Eisner, made several years of arduous work seem like fun, and editorial assistants Sukanya Banerjee, Jon Lewis, and Cheli Reutter were energetic and enthusiastic assistants without whom the work would surely have foundered. Especially helpful was Jens Geirsdorf, who worked as assistant editor for illustrations and put in long hours tracking down images and procuring rights. Other U. C. Riverside students (and former students), such as Jon Adams, Todd Black, David Gere, Julia Gardner, John Ison, John Jordan, Maura Keefe, Craig McCarroll, Lisa Nelson, Will Peterson, Rebecca Rugg, and Ashley Stockstill have supported the volume with valuable contributions in their fields of specialty as well as with their ideas and suggestions.

I am grateful to the scholars who agreed to serve on the advisory board, and I benefited from their advice in a number of ways throughout the editing process. The range of fields and specialties within each field bears their stamp, and I thank them all for giving their time and energy to this project.

For the hundreds of scholars who have contributed to this volume, I have nothing but awed respect. That such an august body of contributors could produce such lucid and challenging essays, surpassing my expectations, has been the single most rewarding feature of this project. I have a more intimate knowledge of the field of gay studies now, of course, and I am more than ever impressed by the sheer brilliance of people working in the field.

I have worked with a number of editors at Garland, and each of them has been enormously encouraging about this project. Gary Kuris first persuaded me to take on this project, and I will always feel especially grateful to him for the wit and irony that got this project off on the right foot. Marianne Lown saw us through the long years of soliciting writers and dealing with the first entries, and Richard Steins, though coming to this project much later, has been an encouraging presence for this difficult final phase. Leo Balk, vice president, and Joanne Daniels, senior editor, have also been directly involved in this project and have always given the best advice.

I have also had generous support from the Committee on Research at the University of California, Riverside. Such research support has made it possible to complete this project in a timely manner, and it has also enabled me to have research assistance without which I would have been severely handicapped.

Editing an encyclopedia has a way of making demands on one's friends, and I have been lucky to have had such support from colleagues and friends. At the University of California, Riverside, I would thank Byron Adams, Greg Bredbeck, Jennifer Brody, Richard Godbeer, John Ganim, Stephanie Hammer, Parama Roy, and Carole-Anne Tyler. Katherine Kinney and Geoff Cohen have been willing to listen endlessly to an editor's woes; Sue-Ellen Case and Susan Foster helped to create a community out of which a work like this could emerge. Friends like Bob Glavin, Bill Kinnucan, Davitt Moroney, Christian Boyer, and Mark Steinbrink helped me to keep my purpose clear; and my sister Pat was full of sisterly wisdom.

Bonnie Zimmerman and I have worked together in the past, and I have both admired her abilities and benefited from her sage advice before now. For this project, however, her work on *Lesbian Histories and Cultures* has been a constant inspiration. Bonnie has offered me endless help as an editor and unflagging support as a friend. I have enjoyed working with her on this project.

My greatest debt is to Philip Brett. Philip has been there all along, and without his example I would probably not be a scholar in this field at all. He has encouraged this project from the start and even welcomed it into our home, where it has been able to flourish.

Finally, I would like to remember one friend who taught me how easy it could be to be gay and how much difference it could make. For thirty years he was the friend I could turn to in any difficulty. He celebrated the start of this project and would have partied at its completion. He died, though, before it was finished. I miss him, but I feel his presence in many little things. Let this one big thing be for him. I dedicate this volume to the memory of Bill Kinnucan.

Contributors

Julie Abraham, the author of *Are Girls Necessary?: Lesbian Writing and Modern Histories* (1996), teaches English and women's studies at Emory University.

Byron Adams, professor of music at the University of California, Riverside, is a gay composer and musicologist. His articles and reviews have appeared in *Music and Letters, MLA Notes, Current Musicology,* and *The Music Quarterly,* as well as in *Vaughan Williams Studies* (1996).

Jon Adams is completing a Ph.D. in English at the University of California, Riverside. He is interested in the representations of masculinity in the twentieth century.

Robert Aldrich, associate professor of economic history at the University of Sydney, has written *The Seduction of the Mediterranean: Writing, Art, and Homosexual Fantasy* (1993) and other works in European history, colonial history, and gay studies.

David Aldstadt, a doctoral candidate in nineteenth- and twentieth-century French literature, cinema, and critical theory and a graduate teaching and research associate at the Ohio State University in Columbus, has conducted workshops on the cinema of John Waters and served as a volunteer at the Harvey Milk Institute in San Francisco.

Blake Allmendinger is an associate professor in the English department at the University of California, Los Angeles. His most recent book is *Ten Most Wanted: The New Western Literature* (1998).

Dennis Altman is professor in the School of Politics at La Trobe University in Bundoora, Australia. His publications include *Homosexual: Oppression and Liberation* (1993) and *The Homosexualisation of America, The Americanisation of the Homosexual* (1982).

Edward Alwood is a former correspondent with CNN and is the author of *Straight News: Gays, Lesbians, and the News Media* (1998). He has written for a variety of publications, including *The Christian Science Monitor.* He is working on a Ph.D. in mass communications at the University of North Carolina, at Chapel Hill.

Sasha Anawalt is the author of *The Joffrey Ballet: Robert Joffrey and the Making of an American Dance Company* (1996).

James D. Anderson is professor of library and information science at Rutgers University, where he has chaired the President's Select Committee for Lesbian and Gay Concerns since 1987. Since 1980 he has been national communications secretary for Presbyterians for Lesbian and Gay Concerns.

Robert W. Anderson is currently studying English and American literature at the University of California Riverside, where he is pursuing an M.A. with an emphasis on queer theory.

David Appell has written extensively on travel and is editor of *Access Gay USA* (1998) and the

Hot! series of gay and lesbian language phrase-books (BabelCom). He is also senior editor at Arthur Frommer's *Budget Travel* magazine.

Dawn Atkins is the editor of *Looking Queer: Body Image and Identity in Lesbian, Bisexual, Gay and Transgender Communities* (1998). She was the founder and director (1988–1994) of the Body Image Task Force (BITF) and has presented over a hundred body-image workshops. She has an M.A. in anthropology and is currently a doctoral candidate in anthropology at the University of Iowa.

Robert Atkins, art historian and editor in chief of the Arts Technology Entertainment Network, is author of *ArtSpeak: A Guide to Contemporary Ideas, Movements, and Buzzwords* (1997) and *ArtSpoke* (1993), its modern art companion. He co-curated *From Media to Metaphor: Art About AIDS,* the first traveling museum exhibition about AIDS, and is founding editor of *TalkBack! A Forum for Critical Discourse*, the first American on-line journal about on-line art.

Paul Attinello, founding co-editor of the *Newsletter* of the Gay and Lesbian Study Group of the American Musicological Society and co-founder of the Society of Gay and Lesbian Composers, has published numerous academic and journalism articles, stories, and poems. He teaches in the music department at the University of Hong Kong.

Mark Bailey is a recent graduate of Ohio Wesleyan University, where he studied politics and government and economics. He now lives in Washington, D.C.

Stephen Banfield is Elgar Professor of Music at the University of Birmingham. His publications include *Sensibility and English Song*, 2 vols. (1985).

Leonard Barkan is University Professor of the Humanities at New York University and director of the New York Institute for the Humanities. His books include *The Gods Made Flesh: Metamorphosis and the Pursuit of Paganism* (1986) and *Transuming Passion: Ganymede and the Erotics of Humanism* (1991). His forthcoming volume is entitled *Unearthing the Past: Archaeology and Aesthetics in the Making of Renaissance Culture.*

Brett Beemyn, assistant professor in African American studies and the director of Leadership 21, a multicultural leadership program at Western Illinois University, is the co-editor of *Queer Studies: A Lesbian, Gay, Bisexual, and Transgender Anthology* (1996) and the editor of *Creating a Place for Ourselves: Lesbian, Gay, and Bisexual Community Histories* (1997). Currently he is completing a history of the lesbigay communities of Washington, D.C.

Matthew Bell is a Ph.D. candidate at Tufts University. His dissertation, tentatively titled "The Oedipal Negative: Narrating Homosexuality in the 20th Century," discusses the impact of Freudian conceptions of sexual identity on film, the novel, and narrative theory.

David Bergman is professor of English at Towson University. His latest books include the volume of poetry *Heroic Measures* (1998) and the anthology of gay short stories *Men on Men 7: Best New Gay Fiction* (1998).

Aaron Betsky, curator of architecture and design at the San Francisco Museum of Modern Art, is the author of eight books, the most recent of which is *Queer Space: The Spaces of Same-Sex Desire* (1995). He is also editor at large at *Architecture* magazine and contributes to many design journals. He teaches widely and is a visiting professor at the California College of Arts and Crafts.

John Beynon is a doctoral candidate in English at the University of California, Riverside. His dissertation explores questions of taste, desire, and masculinity in eighteenth-century England.

Paal Bjorby is associate professor of Nordic literature at the University of Bergen. His research interests include the nineteenth- and twentieth-century novel, with specific emphasis on the relationship between science and literature and the meeting between feminism and queer theory.

Todd Black is a doctoral candidate in French at the University of California, Davis, and *lecteur* in American literature at the Université de

Cergy-Pontoise in France. His dissertation considers same-sex desire in French Renaissance poetry.

Mark Blasius teaches in the Department of Social Sciences at La Guardia Community College.

Thomas Maurer Boellstorff is a Ph.D. candidate in the Department of Social and Cultural Anthropology at Stanford University.

Jacqueline Boles is a professor in the Department of Sociology at Georgia State University. Her publications include "The Social Organization of Transvestite Prostitution and AIDS" and "Sexual Identity and HIV: The Male Prostitute."

Dário Borim Jr., a literary critic and writer from Minas Gerais, Brazil, with a Ph.D. from the University of Minnesota, has published in the anthology *Bodies and Biases: Sexualities in Hispanic Cultures and Literature* (1996) and in the journals *Chasqui, Quadrant*, and *Brasil/Brazil.*

Daniel Boyarin, Taubman Professor of Talmudic Culture at the University of California at Berkeley, has written extensively about the history of Jewish sexuality. His most recent work is *Unheroic Conduct: The Rise of Heterosexuality and the Invention of the Jewish Man* (1997).

Gregory W. Bredbeck, associate professor of English at the University of California, Riverside, specializes in the literature of the English Renaissance and twentieth-century England and America. His publications include *Sodomy and Interpretation: Marlowe to Milton* (1991) and "B/O: Barthes's Text/O' Hara's Trick" (*PMLA*, March 1993).

Philip Brett, professor and chair of music at the University of California, Riverside, has published *Benjamin Britten's* Peter Grimes (1983) and *Queering the Pitch: The New Gay and Lesbian Musicology* (1994).

Joseph Bristow, professor of English at the University of California, Los Angeles, is the author of several books, including *Sexuality* (1997).

James F. Buckley teaches in the English department at Ohio State University in Mansfield, Ohio.

He works on Melville and other topics in nineteenth-century American literature and culture.

Robert J. Buckley works as a consultant and trainer on universal design and disability issues and is honorary research fellow at the Centre for Middle Western and Islamic Studies, University of Durham, and a fellow of the Royal Society for the Promotion of Health. He holds a doctorate in Islam in modern Turkey from the University of Durham.

Vern L. Bullough is a State University of New York distinguished professor emeritus and currently a visiting professor at the University of Southern California. He is the author, co-author, and editor of approximately 50 books, 150 refereed articles, and several hundred other articles.

Ramsay Burt, senior research fellow in dance at De Montfort University, England, wrote his doctoral dissertation on representations of masculinity in dance. This formed the basis for his first book, *The Male Dancer: Bodies, Spectacle, Sexualities* (1995). His second book, *Alien Bodies: Representations of Modernity, "Race" and Nation in Early Modern Dance,* was published in 1998.

José Ignacio Cabezón, associate professor of philosophy at the Iliff School of Theology in Denver, has published extensively in the area of Indo-Tibetan Buddhist philosophy and in Buddhism, sexuality, and gender studies.

Lionel Cantú is a Ph.D. candidate in the social relations program at the University of California, Irvine. He is currently completing his dissertation research, funded by the Social Science Research Council's Sexuality Fellowship Program and the Ford Foundation, which examines the lives of queer immigrants to the United States and how sexuality influences migratory processes.

James Carmichael, associate professor of library and information studies at the University of North Carolina at Greensboro, is the editor of *Daring to Find Our Names: The Search for Lesbigay Library History* (1998).

Robert L. Caserio directs graduate studies in English at Temple University. He is the author of

Plot, Story and the Novel: From Dickens and Poe to the Modern Period (1979) and of *The Novel in England 1900–1950: History and Theory* (1998); currently he is at work on a book entitled *Citizen Queen: Gay Fictions and Democratic Dogmas.*

David Chambers is the Wade H. McCree Collegiate Professor of Law at the University of Michigan. His principal field is family law.

John Champagne is an assistant professor of English at Penn State University, the Behrend College. A novelist as well as a critic, Champagne has published in such journals as *boundary 2, The Journal of Homosexuality*, and *Cinema Journal*. His most recent book is *The Ethics of Marginality: A New Approach to Gay Studies* (1995).

Cheryl Chase is the executive director of the Intersex Society of North America. As part of the project of undermining the Western epistemology of sex and gender, she is presently working, with historian Alice Dreger on a book that juxtaposes medical narratives of hermaphrodites with their personal narratives.

Don Clark, a San Francisco psychologist, is the author of *Loving Someone Gay* (1997, rpr. 1997).

Fabio Cleto teaches English literature at the University of Bergamo (Italy). His teaching and research interests include queer issues, gender and sexuality, critical theory, and the politics of representation. He has published essays on biography and authorship, on turn-of-the-century literary writing, and on British cultural materialism and queer theory, and is currently editing a volume on the theory and history of camp.

John M. Clum is professor of English and professor of the practice of drama at Duke University. He is the author of *Acting Gay: Male Homosexuality in Modern Drama* (1994) and numerous essays on modern drama and is currently writing *Razzle Dazzle: Musical Theater and Gay Culture.* He is also a director and playwright.

Bud Coleman is an assistant professor in the Department of Theatre and Dance at the University of Colorado at Boulder. A widely published director/choreographer, he has a Ph.D. from the University of Texas at Austin.

Gary David Comstock, University Protestant Chaplain and visiting associate professor of sociology at Wesleyan University, is author of *Unrepentant, Self-Affirming, Practicing: Lesbian/Bisexual/Gay People Within Organized Religion* (1996) and *Violence Against Lesbians and Gay Men* (1991). He is also co-editor of *Que(e)rying Religion: A Critical Anthology* (1997).

Peter J. Conradi is a member of the faculty of human sciences at Kingston University in Kingston-upon-Thames, England.

Robert J. Corber is the author of *In the Name of National Security: Hitchcock, Homophobia, and the Political Construction of Gender in Postwar America* (1994), which was named outstanding book on the subject of human rights by the Gustavus Myers Center, and *Homosexuality in Cold War America: Resistance and the Crisis of Masculinity* (1997).

María Dolores Costa, assistant professor of Spanish, California State University, Los Angeles, received her Ph.D. from the University of Massachusetts. She specializes in modern Spanish literature.

Rob Cover is completing a Ph.D. in cultural and media theory at Monash University, Australia. He has been involved in several queer political organizations.

Julie M. Cox is a graduate student at the University of Nebraska–Lincoln, where she studies sex, gender, and sexuality in literature and film.

Christopher Craft, assistant professor of English at the University of California, Santa Barbara, is the author of *Another Kind of Love: Male Homosexual Desire in English Discourse, 1850–1920* (1994) and is currently working on a study of ocular fetishism in Victorian culture.

Russell Crofts is completing his doctoral dissertation on Victorian concepts of the multiple self at the University of Sussex. He is co-editor, with

Jenny Bourne Taylor, of *Lady Audley's Secret* by Mary Elizabeth Braddon (1998).

Arnaldo Cruz-Malavé, associate professor of Spanish and director of the literary studies program at Fordham University, is author of *El primitivo implorante: El "sistema poético del mundo" de José Lezama Lima* (1994) and of numerous articles on the intersections of nationalisms and sexualities in Caribbean and U.S. Latino literatures.

Brian Currid is a graduate student in the Department of Music at the University of Chicago and is completing a dissertation on popular music in Germany from 1924 to 1945. He has published articles on house music, race, and voice in American film and on the politics of world music stardom.

Joseph Dalton is the executive director of Composers Recordings, Inc., and a voting member of the National Academy of Recording Arts and Sciences. He was an editor at *EAR* magazine and a cofounder of the AIDS Music Emergency Network, a project of LIFEbeat.

James Darsey, associate professor of communication at Northern Illinois University in DeKalb, Illinois, is a founding member of the Caucus on Gay and Lesbian Concerns of the National Communication Association and was an associate editor for and contributor to *Queer Words, Queer Images: Communication and the Construction of Homosexuality* (1994). He is the author of *The Prophetic Tradition and Radical Rhetoric in America* (1997), which was nominated for the 1998 gay, lesbian, bisexual book award of the American Library Association.

Michael Davidson, professor of literature at the University of California, San Diego, is the author of *San Francisco Renaissance Poetics and Community at Mid-Century* (1991) and *Ghostlier Demarcations: Modern Poetry and the Material Word* (1997). He is also the author of eight books of poetry.

Thomas DeFrantz is assistant professor of theater arts at the Massachusetts Institute of Technology and an archivist of the Alvin Ailey American Dance Theater.

William DeGenaro is a Ph.D. student in the English department at the University of Arizona.

Kimberly Wilson Deneris is a Ph.D. student in the English department at the University of Utah.

Dennis Denisoff is the author of *Erin Mouré: Her Life and Works* (1995), editor of *Queeries: An Anthology of Gay Male Prose* (1993), and co-editor of *Perennial Decay: The Aesthetics and Politics of Decadence* (forthcoming).

Doug DiBianco teaches in the music department at Eastern Illinois University in Charleston.

Patrick Dilley is a Ph.D. candidate at the University of Southern California, where he studies queer theory and college student development. He also chairs "Reclaiming Voice," an annual conference on qualitative and ethnographic research.

Andre Dombrowski has completed his M.A. in the history of art at the Courtauld Institute in London. He is interested in issues of masculinity and homosexuality in British and German painting of the nineteenth and twentieth centuries.

James M. Donovan has a doctorate in psychological anthropology, specializing in the psychobiology of spirit possession trance. He did his field-work in Rio de Janeiro, Brazil, among the Candomble cult. He is presently on leave from his duties as librarian at the Tulane Law School.

Julie Dorf is the executive director and founder of the International Gay and Lesbian Human Rights Commission (IGLHRC).

Alexander Doty is associate professor of English at Lehigh University. He has written *Making Things Perfectly Queer: Interpreting Mass Culture* (1993), and co-edited *Out in Culture: Gay, Lesbian, and Queer Essays on Popular Culture* (1995).

David D. Doyle Jr. is a doctoral candidate in American history at the City University of New York and is writing his dissertation on the dandy in nineteenth-century America.

Jennifer Doyle is co-editor of *Pop Out: Queer Warhol* (1996). She received her Ph.D. in literature from Duke University and is currently an assistant professor of English at the University of California, Riverside.

Alice Dreger holds a Ph.D. in history and philosophy of science and is assistant professor of science and technology studies at the Lyman Briggs School of Michigan State University. She is also adjunct assistant professor in the Center for Ethics and Humanities in the Life Sciences at MSU.

Robin Duff has a B.A. in speech and drama and is assistant head of the English department and a secondary school teacher in Christchurch New Zealand, where he has been active in the gay rights movement—locally and nationally—since the early 1970s.

Thomas Dukes, associate professor of English at the University of Akron, has written on Elizabeth Bowen, E. M. Forster, and Christopher Isherwood, among others.

Derek Duncan teaches in the Italian department at the University of Bristol. He has published a number of articles on twentieth-century Italian fiction and AIDS literature and is currently working on a study of Italian masculinities and national identity.

Steven M. DuPouy has a Ph.D. in Hispanic literatures. He has published articles on Manuel Puig, Fernando Vallejo, and Jaime Manrique, among other Latin American authors. He resides in Atlanta, Georgia.

Richard Dyer teaches film studies at the University of Warwick. He is the author of *Stars* (1998), *Heavenly Bodies: Film Stars and Society* (1987), *Now You See It: Studies on Lesbian and Gay Film* (1996), *Only Entertainment* (1992), *The Matter of Images: Essays on Representations* (1993), and *White* (1997).

James Eby, an associate professor in the English department at James Madison University in Harrisonburg, Virginia, is also Samaritan Education Facilitator for the Mid-Atlantic district of the Metropolitan Community Church. He reviews for the *Lambda Book Report*.

Douglas Eisner teaches at Fullerton College. He has published essays on AIDS in literature and early gay novels and is currently working on a project exploring the ambivalence of sexual identification in American novels of the 1940s–1960s.

Andrew Elfenbein, associate professor of English at the University of Minnesota–Twin Cities, is the author of *Byron and the Victorians* (1995) and the *Romantic Genius: The Prehistory of a Homosexual Role* (1999).

Greger Eman, who since 1988 has been editor of the gay and lesbian magazine has published work on the lesbian journalist Klara Johanson, an anthology by homosexual and bisexual parents, *Loved Children* (1996), and *The Secret Power of Sympathy* (1998), a history of Stockholm's gays and lesbians.

Marc Epprecht is a lecturer, Department of History, University of Zimbabwe, Harare.

Brad Epps is John L. Loeb Associate Professor in the Humanities at Harvard University. He is the author of *Significant Violence: Oppression and Resistance in the Narratives of Juan Goytisolo, 1970–1990* (1996), as well as numerous articles on literature, film, and art in Spain, Latin America, France, and Catalunya.

John Nguyet Erni, associate professor in the Department of Communication, University of New Hampshire, is the author of *Unstable Frontiers: Technomedicine and the Cultural Politics of "Curing" AIDS* (1994) and numerous articles on media and cultural studies, queer theory, and the politics of HIV/AIDS. He is currently working on a book about HIV/AIDS in Asia, globalization, and sexual politics.

Kristin G. Esterberg, assistant professor of sociology at the University of Massachusetts at Lowell, is the author of *Lesbian and Bisexual Identities: Constructing Communities, Constructing Selves* (1997).

Jessica R. Feldman, associate professor of English at the University of Virginia, is the author of *Gender on the Divide: The Dandy in Modernist Literature* (1993).

Josep-Anton Fernández, who teaches Catalan literature and lesbian and gay studies at Queen Mary and Westfield College, University of London, is currently preparing two books: one on questions of sexuality and national identity in Catalan gay fiction and the other on issues of legitimation, identity, and postmodernism in contemporary Catalan culture.

Willow Fey is writing his Ph.D. on the Radical Faeries as a graduate student in studies in religion at the University of Queensland, Australia. He lives in an owner-built, straw-bale house with his lover, two Jersey cows, half a dozen chooks, a border collie, and an organic veggie garden full of faeries.

Jennifer Fisher received her master's degree in dance from York University in Toronto and has recently completed her Ph.D. in dance history and theory from the University of California, Riverside. She is a regular contributor of dance criticism to the *Los Angeles Times*.

David William Foster, Regents' Professor of Spanish, Humanities, and Women's Studies at Arizona State University, has held Fulbright teaching appointments in Argentina, Brazil, and Uruguay. His most recent publications include *Violence in Argentine Literature: Cultural Responses to Tyranny* (1995), *Cultural Diversity in Latin American Literature* (1994), *Contemporary Argentine Cinema* (1992), and *Gay and Lesbian Themes in Latin American Writing* (1991).

Raymond-Jean Frontain, associate professor of English and interdisciplinary studies at the University of Central Arkansas, is the editor of *Reclaiming the Sacred: The Bible in Gay and Lesbian Culture* (1997).

Joshua Gamson teaches sociology at Yale University. He is the author of numerous articles on sexuality, social movements, and contemporary culture, and of the books *Claims to Fame: Celebrity in Contemporary America* (1994) and *Freaks Talk Back: Tabloid Talk Shows and Sexual Nonconformity* (1998).

Ramon García has a Ph.D. in literature from the University of California at San Diego. He has published criticism, poetry, and short stories in the following journals and anthologies: *New Chicano Writing #1* (1992), *The Americas Review, Story, Best American Poetry 1996* (1996), *The Paterson Review, POESIdA: An Anthology of Poetry from the United States, Latin America and Spain,* and *Aztlan: A Journal of Chicano Research Studies.*

David Garnes is a senior reference librarian at the University of Connecticut. He is a frequent contributor to a variety of anthologies, including *Gay and Lesbian Biography* (1997); *Gay and Lesbian Literature,* Vol. II (1997); *Liberating Minds* (1997); *Connecticut Poets on AIDS* (1996); *Telling Tales Out of School* (1998); and *A Loving Testimony: Remembering Loved Ones Lost to AIDS* (1995).

Gustavo Geirola graduated from the University of Buenos Aires in 1977 and from Arizona State University in 1995. He works as an assistant professor at Whittier College in California.

Marc Geller, a photographer in San Francisco, has documented gay life for two decades.

David Gere is assistant professor in the Department of World Arts and Cultures at UCLA. A longtime dance critic, he has written extensively about dance and AIDS and earned his Ph.D. in dance history and theory from the University of California, Riverside.

Christian A. Gertsch is a senior lecturer in the English department of the University of Berne, Switzerland. He is particularly interested in male role-playing as portrayed in queer literature.

Jens Richard Giersdorf is currently writing his dissertation in dance history and theory at the University of California, Riverside, on the construction of corporeal identities in East Germany around the reunification in 1990. His research focuses on the creation of an ideal socialist body and the citizens' resistance to the state's surveillance and disciplining. His performance reviews, interviews, and articles have appeared in *Tanz Aktuell, Morgenpost, Theater* magazine, and *DAZ*.

Richard Godbeer is a specialist in colonial American history at the University of California, Riverside.

Juan M. Godoy, a Barcelona native, is an assistant professor of Spanish at San Diego State University and the author of *Cuerpo, deseo e idea en la poesía de Luis Antonio de Villena* (forthcoming).

Terry Goldie is the Robarts Chair of Canadian Studies at York University, where he teaches postcolonial literatures, literary theory, and gay studies. He is the author of *Fear and Temptation: The Image of the Indigene in Canadian, Australian and New Zealand Literatures* (1989) and co-editor (with Daniel David Moses) of *An Anthology of Canadian Native Literature in English* (1998). At present he is completing a book tentatively titled *Homotextual Possibilities in Canadian Fiction.*

James N. Green is assistant professor of Latin American history at California State University, Long Beach, and a member of the editorial board of Latin American Perspectives. His first book, *Beyond Carnival: Homosexuality in Twentieth-Century Brazil,* is forthcoming.

Ellen Greenblatt is the assistant library director for technical services at Auraria Library, University of Colorado at Denver. She served as list-owner of QSTUDY-L, the queer studies electronic discussion list for four years, and is a co-editor of the book *Gay and Lesbian Library Service* (1990).

Larry Gross is a professor of communication at the Annenberg School of the University of Pennsylvania and cochair of the Philadelphia Lesbian and Gay Task Force. He has also served as cochair of the Gay, Lesbian, and Bisexual Studies Interest Group of the International Communication Association and of the Society of Lesbian and Gay Anthropologists. He is the author of *Contested Closets: The Politics and Ethics of Outing* (1993) and associate editor of *The International Encyclopedia of Communications* (1989).

Jay Grossman teaches courses on American literature, poetry, and gay studies at Boston University.

James Haines holds a Ph.D. from Columbia University and has been senior lecturer of American studies and English at the University of Oulu (Finland) since 1974. His current gay studies research centers on homosexuality and religion.

David M. Halperin has been appointed Collegiate Professor in the Dept. of English Language and Literature, University of Michigan, Ann Arbor. He is the author of *One Hundred Years of Homosexuality* (1990) and *Saint Foucault* (1995), and an editor of *Before Sexuality* (1990), *The Lesbian and Gay Studies Reader* (1993), and *GLQ: A Journal of Lesbian and Gay Studies.*

Stephanie Hammer, associate professor of comparative literature at the University of California, Riverside, is currently writing a book on Schiller, masculinity, and cultural studies.

Kylie Hansen completed a Ph.D. and served as a postdoctoral fellow at Washington University, focusing on the ways in which Henry James was able to stage the theater in his own life and in his writing. She currently works for the Saint Louis Symphony Orchestra and is pursuing an independent creative writing project.

Mark J. Harris is a graduate student in jurisprudence and social policy at the University of California, Berkeley. His interests include international law and international relations, constitutional law, and human rights.

Dan Healey is a Ph.D. candidate in history at the University of Toronto. He was a volunteer at the London Lesbian and Gay Switchboard from 1989 to 1991.

Adam Hedgecoe is studying for a Ph.D. at the Department of Science and Technology Studies at University College, London. He has research interests in the philosophy of medicine and medical ethics.

Gert Hekma works in gay and lesbian studies at the Department of Sociology of the University of Amsterdam.

Laurence R. Helfer is an associate professor of law at Loyola Law School in Los Angeles. He has written, taught, and lectured extensively on issues concerning lesbian and gay rights and international law.

Gilbert Herdt is a professor in the Department of Human Development at the University of Chicago. He specializes in Melanesia and other Pacific cultures.

Ralph Hexter, professor of classics and comparative literature at the University of California, Berkeley, has published on Homer, both ancient and medieval Latin literature, and more widely on the reworking of the "classical tradition" in later periods.

Bret Hinsch, associate professor of history, National Chung Cheng University, Chiayi, Taiwan, is author of *Passions of the Cut Sleeve: The Male Homosexual Tradition in China* (1990).

Patrick Holland has been at the University of Guelph since 1980 teaching, among other things, gay literature and queer theory. His book *Tourists with Typewriters* (co-authored with Graham Huggan) includes a study of gay travel writing.

Michael M. Holmes teaches early modern English literature at Brock University, Canada. He is the author of articles dealing with gender and sexuality in the work of Derek Jarman, Aemilia Lanyer, and Christopher Marlowe.

F. Valentine Hooven III, born a war baby and raised an Air Force brat, has written and illustrated for many gay magazines. His books include *Beefcake: The Muscle Magazines of America, 1950–1970* (1995) and *Tom of Finland: His Life and Times* (1994). His latest work is *Glad Rags and Stud Duds: Sex and Politics in the Clothing of the American Male.* Hooven lives and works in Hollywood.

Robert H. Hopcke is the author of five books, including *Jung, Jungians and Homosexuality* (1989), and was a co-editor of *Same-Sex Love: A Path to Wholeness* (1993). A psychotherapist in private practice, Hopcke is the founding director of the Center for Symbolic Studies in Berkeley, California.

Patrick Hopkins teaches in the Department of Philosophy at Washington University in St. Louis.

Robert Howes, a sublibrarian in the University of Sussex Library, Brighton, England, is interested in Portuguese and Brazilian history and culture and in the literature of the lesbian and gay communities in those countries.

Hans Tao-Ming Huang is working on a Ph.D. dissertation currently entitled "Articulating Queer Diaspora: Gay Identity, Taiwanese-ness, and Geopolitics of Male Homosexual Desire/Identification" in media studies at the University of Sussex, Britain. He is the co-editor (with Kuan-Hsin Chen) of *Trajectories: Toward a New Internationalist Cultural Studies* (forthcoming).

Arthur J. Hughes is a lecturer in the Spanish section of Arizona State University, modern languages and literatures, where he has just completed a Ph.D. on the novels of Terenci Moix, a contemporary Catalan writer.

Michael Hurley is associate professor in the Department of Media and Text, University of Technology, Sydney, Australia.

Jörg Hutter a sociologist, engaged in scientific research and teaching at the University of Bremen since 1985 and participated in the foundation and institutionalization of the Bremen Department of Gay and Lesbian Studies in 1995.

Stephen Infantino has published *Photographic Vision in Proust* (1992), as well as several articles on narrative and visual art. He is currently working on the arrival of surrealism in the New World and its impact on Abstract Expressionism in New York from 1938 to 1945.

John M. Ison, who is pursuing a doctorate in English at the University of California, Riverside, has published numerous stories, poems, criticism, and journalism in the gay press.

Peter A. Jackson, Ph.D., is research fellow in Thai history within the Australian National University's Research School of Pacific and Asian Studies. His main interest is Thai cultural history, particularly reforms in Buddhist teaching and practice and transformations in patterns of sexuality and gender in the twentieth century.

Dominic Janes is based at Pembroke College, Cambridge University, where he works on cultural history. Having published on the subject of wealth and religion (*God and Gold*, 1998), he is now examining sexual taboos in western European culture from antiquity to modernity.

Valerie Jenness, an assistant professor in the Department of Criminology and Law and in the Department of Sociology at the University of California, Irvine, studies the links between deviance and social control (especially law), gender, and social change (especially social movements). She is the author of *Making It Work: The Prostitutes' Rights Movement in Perspective* (1993), *Hate Crimes: New Social Movements and the Politics of Violence* (1997), and articles on the politics of prostitution, AIDS, civil liberties, hate-crimes and hate crime law, and the gay/lesbian movement and the women's movement in the United States.

James W. Jones, professor of German at Central Michigan University, has published on a variety of topics in German gay and lesbian history, including the study *"We of the Third Sex": Literary Representations of Homosexuality in Wilhelmine Germany* (1990). He is currently completing a history of gay and lesbian literature in Weimar Germany.

John Bryce Jordan, a doctoral candidate in dance history and theory at the University of California, Riverside, is investigating attitudes toward the male dancer in Restoration and eighteenth-century England.

Mark Jordan, Asa Griggs Candler Professor of Religion at Emory University, has written *The Invention of Sodomy in Christian Theology* (1997) and other works on the relation of homosexuality and Christianity.

Jeffrey Kahan, a lecturer at the University of California, Riverside, wrote his Ph.D. dissertation on Shakespeare forgeries.

Arnie Kantrowitz, former vice president of the Gay Activists Alliance, is a professor of English at the College of Staten Island, City University of New York, and the author of *Under the Rainbow: Growing Up Gay* (1996).

Simon Karlinsky, professor emeritus of Slavic languages and literatures, University of Califor-

nia, Berkeley, is the author of *The Sexual Labyrinth of Nikolai Gogol* (1992); *Marina Tsvetaeva: The Woman, Her World and Her Poetry* (1966); and *Russian Drama: From Its Beginnings to the Age of Pushkin* (1985).

Steven Kates (Ph.D., York University, Canada) is assistant professor of marketing at the University of Northern British Columbia in Canada. His research interests include identity issues pertaining to consumer behavior research.

Maura Keefe is a choreographer, dancer, and historian currently working on her Ph.D. in dance history and theory at the University of California, Riverside. During the summer, Keefe is a scholar in residence at Jacob's Pillow Dance Festival. Her interview with Mark Morris appeared in the literary journal *Salmagundi* in the Winter 1994/95 issue.

James Kelley is a doctoral student in English literature at the University of Tulsa. His dissertation explores the often conflicting legitimizing narratives of male homosexuality in Anglo-American literature of the 1920s and 1930s.

Jacinta Kerin is currently pursuing a Ph.D. in bioethics at Monash University in Melbourne. Her area of research regards philosophy of science, postmodernism, and the ontology of sexual difference.

Sister Ann R. Key, Mistress of Propaganda, has helped shape media representation of the Sisters of Perpetual Indulgence, Inc., since 1995. Her alter ego, Deacon Dyke, is a (Bible) packin', pious pillar of the lesbian and bi community of Sin Francisco.

Terence Kissack is a doctoral candidate in history at the Graduate School and University Center of the City University of New York. He is currently at work on a study of the politics of homosexuality in the turn-of-the-century anarchist movement in the United States.

George Klawitter did his graduate studies in Renaissance literature at the University of Chicago and has published *Richard Barnfield: The Complete Poems* (1990) and *The Enigmatic Narrator: The Voicing of Same-Sex Love in the*

Poetry of John Donne (1994). He teaches at St. Edward's University in Austin, Texas.

Jay M. Kohorn, a graduate of the UCLA School of Law, is presently assistant director of the California Appellate Project, a nonprofit public interest law firm created to administer the indigent defense program for the state appellate courts.

Charles Krinsky is a Ph.D. candidate in the program in comparative culture at the University of California, Irvine, where he has taught courses on lesbian and gay politics and culture.

Dejan Kuzmanovic is a Ph.D. candidate in English at Rice University. His dissertation explores the interdependencies between various notions of "influence" and "homosexuality" in a number of literary and cultural discourses in Britain from the 1890s through the 1930s.

Nimisha Ladva is a Ph.D. student in English at the University of California, Irvine, and is writing a dissertation on migrancy and representation in postcolonial fiction and film.

Frederic Lagrange, Maître de Conférences en Langue et Littérature Arabe, Université de Paris VIII, wrote a doctoral thesis on "Poètes et Musiciens en Egypte au Temps de la Nahda." He is currently working on homosexuality in modern Arabic literature.

Lambda Rising is a gay bookstore in Washington, D.C. The staff of the bookstore composed the entry on "Lambda."

Michael Lambert is senior lecturer in classics at the University of Natal, Pietermaritzburg, KwaZulu Natal, South Africa. His research interests include gender and sexuality in antiquity, comparative ancient Greek and traditional Zulu ritual, and Roman love poetry.

Alycee J. Lane, an assistant professor in the Department of English at the University of California, Santa Barbara, is currently revising for publication her dissertation, titled "Homosexuality and the Crisis of Black Cultural Particularity."

Christopher Lane, associate professor of English at Emory University, is the author of *The*

Ruling Passion: British Colonial Allegory and the Paradox of Homosexual Desire (1995) and *The Burdens of Intimacy: Psychoanalysis and Victorian Masculinity* (1998), as well as editor of *The Psychoanalysis of Race* (1998).

Norman Laurila started "A Different Light" Bookstore in 1979. There are branches in Los Angeles, San Francisco, and New York. He currently serves as treasurer or the American Booksellers Association and sits on the board of directors of the American Booksellers Foundation for Free Expression (ABFFE).

D. S. Lawson is associate professor of English at Lander University in Greenwood, South Carolina, where he also serves as director of honors and international programs. His scholarly work has included publications on AIDS theater and writing pedagogy as well as studies of such figures as David Leavitt, James Merrill, Paul Russell, Kevin Killian, Joe Orton, John Guare, and David Storey. He is an actively publishing poet.

William L. Leap is professor of anthropology and a member of the core faculty in women's/gender studies at American University. He is author of *Word's Out: Gay Men's English* (1996), editor of *Beyond the Lavender Lexicon* (1996), and co-editor of *Out in the Field: Reflections of Lesbian and Gay Anthropologists* (1996). He is cochair of the American Anthropological Commission on Lesbian/Gay/Bisexual/Transgendered Concerns.

John Alan Lee has taught at the University of Toronto for thirty years. In 1974, he was the first Canadian academic to "go public," and has published many books and articles on gay topics.

Arthur S. Leonard, a professor at New York Law School, is a founder of the Lesbian and Gay Law Association of Greater New York and edits the newsletter "Lesbian/Gay Law Notes." A graduate of Cornell University and Harvard Law School, he has focused his research and publications on lesbian and gay legal issues and AIDS law and is co-author of the leading law school textbook on AIDS.

Maurice van Lieshout, formerly a lecturer in gay literary studies at the University of Amsterdam, has published several books and articles on gay history, literature, subcultures, and lesbian and gay youth. Currently he is working as the chief editor of *0/25*, a Dutch monthly about youth and related policy.

Michael Lobel, a critic and historian of twentieth-century art, has written on the work of Andy Warhol, Roy Lichtenstein, and designer Hasi Hester.

Scott Long is advocacy coordinator of the International Gay and Lesbian Human Rights Commission. He taught American literature for four years at the University of Budapest and for two years held a Fulbright professorship of literature in Romania.

Christoph Lorey, a professor of German at the University of New Brunswick, Fredericton, Canada, is the editor of *The International Fiction Review* and co-editor of *Queering the Canon: Defying Sights in German Literature and Culture* (1998). His recent book publications include *Lessings Familienbild* (1992) and *Die Ehe im klassischen Werk Goethes* (1995).

Michael Lucey teaches in the departments of French and comparative literature at the University of California, Berkeley, and also in Berkeley's program in lesbian, gay, bisexual, and transgender studies. His research focuses on French, English, and American literature and culture of the nineteenth and twentieth centuries; he is the author of *Gide's Bent: Sexuality, Politics, Writing* (1995).

Wim Lunsing, who received his M.A. in Japanese studies from the University of Leiden and his Ph.D. in social anthropology from Oxford Brookes University, is currently associate research professor in the Department of Asian Studies at the University of Copenhagen. He writes about sexuality and gender in contemporary Japan.

Michael A. Lutes is a reference/government documents librarian at the Hesburgh Library, University of Notre Dame. He is a freelance writer in the field of gay studies and an avid collector of gay antiquarian books.

William MacGregor holds a Ph.D. in art history from the University of California at Berkeley.

The recipient of both a Getty predoctoral and a Killam postdoctoral fellowship, he is currently completing a book on prints and visual literacy in ancien régime France.

Robert L. Mack, assistant professor of English at Vanderbilt University, has edited both the *Arabian Nights' Entertainments* (1995) and a collection of *Oriental Tales* (1992) for Oxford University Press; he has also edited a volume on Thomas Gray (1997).

Ed Madden is an assistant professor of English at the University of South Carolina, where he teaches courses on British literature, modernism, and creative writing. He has published essays on Victorian poetry, AIDS literature, Radclyffe Hall, and Havelock Ellis, and he is currently completing a book on the figure of Tiresias in modernist literature.

Donald Mager is assistant professor at Johnson C. Smith University, where he is director of the liberal arts program. His volumes of poetry are *To Track the Wounded One* (1986), *Glosses* (1992), *That Which Is Owed To Death* (1999), and *Borderings* (1998).

Armando Maggi is assistant professor of Italian at the University of Pennsylvania. His areas of specialization are Renaissance culture and contemporary literature.

Jan Magnusson is a librarian and Ph.D. student in comparative literature at the University of Gothenburg. He works on the life and work of Paul Andersson, a Swedish poet of the 1950s, and is also on the editorial board of *Lambda Nordica*.

Mark Markell, associate professor of special education at St. Cloud University, works on sexuality education, sexual orientation, and gender issues in education.

Fredric Markus lives in Minneapolis, where he works as a community activist.

Richard Martin, curator of the Costume Institute at the Metropolitan Museum of Art, is adjunct professor of art history and archaeology at Columbia University and adjunct professor of art at New York University. His books include *Fashion and Surrealism* (1989), *Contemporary Fashion* (1995), and *Gianni Versace* (1997).

Robert K. Martin, professor of English at the Université de Montréal, is the author of *The Homosexual Tradition in American Poetry* (1979) and *Hero, Captain, Stranger: Male Friendship, Social Critique, and Literary Form in the Sea Novels of Herman Melville* (1986), as well as editor of *The Continuing Presence of Walt Whitman* (1992) and co-editor of *Queer Forster* (1997) and *American Gothic: New Interventions in a National Narrative* (1998).

Alan Mason, an investment management professional and a freelance musicologist in San Francisco, is a Ph.D. candidate in ethnomusicology at the University of California at Berkeley.

Lawrence D. Mass, M.D., is a cofounder of Gay Men's Health Crisis and was the first writer to cover the AIDS epidemic in any press. He is the author of a memoir, *Confessions of a Jewish Wagnerite: Being Gay and Jewish in America* (1994), and the editor of three anthologies: *Dialogues of The Sexual Revolution*, Volumes I and II (both 1990), and *We Must Love One Another or Die: The Life and Legacies of Larry Kramer* (1997).

Craig McCarroll received his M.A. in English at the University of California, Riverside. He is interested in AIDS narratives and the rhetoric of health.

Stephen McClatchie is assistant professor of musicology at the University of Regina and has published articles on Britten, Mahler, and Wagner in such journals as *Cambridge Opera Journal, 19th-Century Music*, and *Notes*. From 1996 to 1998, he was co-editor of the *Gay and Lesbian Study Group Newsletter* of the American Musicological Society.

Ian McCormick is senior lecturer in English studies at Nene College of Higher Education. He is the editor of *Secret Sexualities: A Sourcebook of 17th and 18th Century Writing* (1997).

Elliott McEldowney has investigated twentieth-century American theories of addiction through its appearance in novels, film, and popular culture. He is interested in the figure of the addict and the ways the abjection of addiction mirrors cultural phobias around deviant sexuality.

Alan McKee, Ph.D., who lectures in the Department of Media Studies at Edith Cowan University, has published in *Screen, Cultural Studies, and Continuum*. His research interests include social justice, false consciousness, and gay pornography.

Richard McKewen is a J.D./Ph.D. candidate in performance studies at New York University. He has taught at the University of Louisville, the United Arab Emirates University, and the City University of New York.

Beatrice Medicine (Standing Rock Lakota), associate professor emeritus of anthropology at California State University, Northridge, is the author of numerous articles and co-editor of *The Hidden Half: The Lives of Plains Indian Women* (1983).

David Menasco is a graduate student in interdisciplinary social science at California State University, San Francisco. His baccalaureate degree includes a dual major in psychology and interdisciplinary social science and a minor in human sexuality studies.

Richard Meyer, an assistant professor in the Department of Art History at the University of Southern California, has written *Outlaw Representation: Censorship and Homosexuality in American Art, 1934–1994* (forthcoming).

Wendy Michallat, a Ph.D. student of French at the University of Nottingham, England, researching a thesis on francophone *banden dessinée* of the 1950s, is a published cartoonist who has illustrated several academic publications.

Kitty Millet, assistant professor of comparative literature at California State University at Long Beach, has published on testimonial writings in Latin America, indigenous women's narration of the Southern Cone, and Holocaust survivor narratives. She has publications forthcoming on Goethe, the cultural history of German wine, post-1945 Judaism, Thomas Mann, Gustave Flaubert, and Djelal Kadir.

Zoran Milutinović, Ph.D., assistant professor of comparative literature and literary theory, University of Belgrade, is the author of two books and numerous articles dealing with twentieth-century drama and drama theory.

Framji Minwalla is an assistant professor in the theater department at Dartmouth College.

Richard D. Mohr, professor of philosophy at the University of Illinois, is the author of *Gays/Justice: A Study of Ethics, Society, and Law* (1990).

Leland Monk, who teaches literature and film at Boston University, is the author of *Standard Deviations: Chance and the Modern British Novel* (1994) and essays about Austen, Forster, James, and Lytton Strachey.

Liora Moriel, a doctoral candidate in comparative literature at the University of Maryland, was chair and spokeswoman (1991–1993) for the Society for the Protection of Personal Rights, produced the International Women's Music Festival (1986) and Laila Lohet/Hot Night (1994), and coproduced the Europe-Israel conference for LGB Jews in 1994.

Davitt Moroney, a musician born in Britain of Italian and Irish parentage, studied at the University of London (King's College) before moving to America for his Ph.D. (University of California, Berkeley). He has lived in Paris since 1980 and divides his time between making records, giving recitals, and teaching. His lover, Christian Boyer, is actively involved with the political work of the Paris Gay and Lesbian Center.

Cynthia Morrill, Ph.D., is museum writer, research and communications, at UCR/California Museum of Photography. Included in her dissertation, "Paradigms Out of Joint: Feminist Science Fiction and Cultural Logic," is the chapter "Stranger in a Strange Land: Bron Helstrom in Samuel R. Delany's *Triton*."

Mitchell Morris, who teaches in the Department of Musicology at UCLA, has spoken and published on many aspects of gay and lesbian studies in music, including popular music and opera.

Kevin Moss teaches Russian at Middlebury College. He is the editor of *Out of the Blue: Russia's Hidden Gay Literature* (1997).

Luiz Mott, professor of anthropology at Federal University of Bahía (Brazil), is the founder of Grupo Gay da Bahia and Centro Baiano Anti-Aids, as well as author of *O Lesbianismo no Brasil* (1987) and several papers about sodomites in Luso-Brazilian history.

Mbogo Murage, a journalist from Nairobi, Kenya, is a commentator on social and cultural issues. A graduate of the School of Journalism, University of Nairobi, and of the University of Michigan, he is the deputy chief subeditor of Nation Newspapers, Nairobi, and has written a weekly column as the newspaper's national radio and television critic.

Michael John Murphy, M.A., holds degrees in art history from the University of Iowa and Washington University (St. Louis). He is revising his master's thesis for publication before undertaking doctoral work in the histories of American visual culture.

Robert Murphy is a graduate of Yale College and of New York University School of Law. He has written about Tom Stoddard and gay legal history for the New York University legal history colloquium, the *NYU Law Review*, and *POZ* magazine.

Timothy F. Murphy is associate professor in the medical humanities program at the University of Illinois College of Medicine at Chicago. His most recent publication is *Gay Science: The Ethics of Sexual Orientation Research* (1997).

Seigo Nakao, associate professor of Japanese language, culture, and literature at Oakland University, Michigan, is the author of *The Random House Japanese-English Dictionary/English-Japanese*.

Serena Nanda, professor of anthropology at John Jay College of Criminal Justice (CUNY), is the co-editor of *Cultural Anthropology* (6th ed., 1998) and *American Cultural Pluralism and Law* (1996), and the author of *Neither Man nor Woman: The Hijras of India* (2d ed., 1990). Her research interests are culture and law, gender, and visual anthropology.

Peter M. Nardi is professor of sociology at Pitzer College/The Claremont Colleges. He is co-editor of *In Changing Times: Gay Men and Lesbians Encounter HIV/AIDS* (1997) and *Social Perspectives in Lesbian and Gay Studies: A Reader* (1998). He is also the special features co-editor of the international journal *Sexualities*.

Ethan Nasreddin-Longo is assistant professor of music at the University of California, Riverside.

Lisa K. Nelson is a graduate student in English at Columbia University working in American studies and queer/cultural theory.

Emile Netzhammer is chair and associate professor in the communication department at Buffalo State College. He received his Ph.D. from the University of Utah in 1987.

Matthew Guy Nichols is a Ph.D. candidate in the Department of Art History at Rutgers University.

Guillermo Nuñez-Noriega is in the anthropology department at the University of Arizona. He has published *Sexo entre varones. Poder y resistencia en el campo sexual* (1994).

Connell O'Donovan is a freelance writer and historian living in Santa Cruz, California.

Baden Offord teaches Australian and Asian studies at Southern Cross University, Australia, and is presently completing his Ph.D. on "Homosexual Rights as Human Rights in Australia, Indonesia and Singapore."

Harry Oosterhuis, assistant professor of history at the University of Maastricht, Netherlands, has published *Homosexuality and Male Bonding in Pre-Nazi Germany* (1991) and (with James Steakley) *Gay Men and the Sexual History of the Political Left* (1995). His next book will be about Richard von Krafft-Ebing.

Salvador A. Oropesa, associate professor, Kansas State University, writes extensively on Mexican and Spanish literatures. He has written

a book on Ariel Dorfman and a forthcoming one on Antonio Muñoz Molina.

Ricardo Ortiz is assistant professor of critical and cultural theory at Georgetown University. He has published several articles on gay Latino writers, including Reinaldo Arenas, John Rechy, and Arturo Islas, and is currently writing a book on Cuban-American literature entitled *Diaspora and Disappearance.*

Mustafa Fatih Ozbilgin, from Turkey, is completing a Ph.D. from Bristol University. His current research is on sex equality in financial services sectors in Britain and Turkey.

Matthew Parfitt is assistant professor in the Division of Humanities and Rhetoric in the College of General Studies at Boston University. He received his Ph.D. in English from Boston College, and he writes on Robert Frost, hermeneutics, and literature of the World War I era.

Robert Patrick wrote gay plays from 1964 (*The Haunted Host*) through at least 1997 (*Hollywood at Sunset*), told how it all started in a novel in 1994 (*Temple Slave*), and in 1996 received the Robert Chesley Foundation Award for Lifetime Achievement in Gay Playwrighting.

Eugene J. Patron is a freelance writer who originated a weekly gay-interest column in the *Miami Herald* and has contributed to more than forty publications on five continents, including *The Advocate, The Harvard Gay and Lesbian Review, Lambda Book Report,* and *Genre.*

Will Petersen, who holds a B.A. in music from the University of California, Riverside, is an editor/broadcast journalist living in Belgrade, Yugoslavia.

Daniel F. Pigg is an associate professor of English at the University of Tennessee at Martin, where he teaches courses on medieval and Renaissance English literature. He has published widely on medieval English literature.

George Piggford is the co-editor of *Queer Forster* (1997) and the author of essays in *Modern Drama* and *Mosaic*. He is assistant professor of English at Tufts University

Kirk Pillow teaches at Hamilton College and specializes in Kant and Hegel's aesthetic theories and philosophies of mind.

Kenneth Pobo, associate professor of English at Widener University, has eight collections of poems, the most recent being *Cicadas* and *Apple Trees* from Palanquin Press.

Howard Pollack, a pianist and musicologist, is professor of music at the University of Houston. He has authored four books including *Aaron Copland: The Life and Work of an Uncommon Man* (1999).

Todd Porterfield is an assistant professor of art history at Princeton University.

Murray Pratt is a researcher in contemporary French language, literature, and culture, with a special interest in lesbian and gay studies. He has published on Roland Barthes, Hervé Guibert, and AIDS in France; he is currently working at Warwick University, Coventry, England.

Antonio Prieto, who holds a Ph.D. in Latin American studies from Mexico's National University and an M.A. in performance studies from New York University, has written several essays on border-crossing performance art and gay Chicano performance. He is currently lecturer at Stanford University's Department of Spanish and Portuguese, and Information Activist for DataCenter's Information Services Latin America (ISLA).

Brian Pronger, assistant professor at the Faculty of Physical Education and Health, University of Toronto, is the author of *The Arena of Masculinity: Sports, Homosexuality, and the Meaning of Sex* (1991). He also writes on the science and culture of physical fitness.

Shane S. Que Hee, professor in the Department of Environmental Health Sciences, UCLA School of Public Health, is president of the Lesbian/Gay Health and Health Policy Foundation in Los Angeles.

Vincent Quinn, a lecturer in English at the University of Sussex, England, has published work on eighteenth-century British culture and on contemporary lesbian and gay writing.

Diane Raymond is professor of philosophy and chair of the women's studies department at Simmons College in Boston. She is the author of *Existentialism and the Philosophical Tradition* (1990) and co-author (with Warren Blumenfeld) of *Looking at Gay and Lesbian Life* (1993). In addition, she has published essays in feminist theory, bioethics, and queer theory. She is currently working on a book-length project on feminist revisionings of autonomy.

Christopher Reed has published widely on the Bloomsbury group. His books include *A Roger Fry Reader* (1996) and *Not at Home: The Suppression of Domesticity in Modern Art and Architecture* (1996). He is on the art history faculty of Lake Forest College.

Diane Reynolds teaches women's studies at Simmons College in Boston.

Robert Rhyne, assistant professor of French and francophone studies at the University of Southwestern Louisiana (Lafayette), has recently published an article on Paul Valéry's "Art de travailler" in the *Bulletin des Études Valéryennes* and is currently preparing his dissertation (Stanford) on French symbolist author Paul Valéry for publication.

Simon Richter, associate professor of German at the University of Pennsylvania, is the author of *Laocoon's Body and the Aesthetics of Pain* (1992). His article "The Ins and Outs of Intimacy: Gender, Epistolary Culture and the Public Sphere" won the Max Kade Award for best article in *The Germany Quarterly* (1996).

R. Jeffrey Ringer, Ph.D., professor of speech communication at St. Cloud State University in Minnesota, edited the book *Queer Words, Queer Images: Communication and the Construction of Homosexuality* (1994) and continues his research into gay male relationships.

Michael Rocke is an adjunct professor at Syracuse University in Florence. His publications include *Forbidden Friendships: Homosexuality and Male Culture in Renaissance Florence* (1996).

Carlos Antonio Rodríguez-Matos is associate professor of Spanish at Seton Hall University.

He edited *POESIdA: An Anthology of AIDS Poetry from the United States, Latin America, and Spain/Antología de poesía del SIDA escrita en los Estados Unidos, Hispanoamérica y España* (1995).

Eric Rofes has taught education and queer studies at the University of California at Berkeley's graduate School of Education and at Bowdoin College. He is the author of ten books, including *Dry Bones Breathe: Gay Men Creating Post-AIDS Identities and Cultures* (1998).

David Román, associate professor of English at the University of Southern California, is the author of *Acts of Intervention: Performance, Gay Culture, and AIDS* (1998) and coeditor (with Holly Hughes) of *O Solo Homo: The New Queer Performance* (1998).

Stephen Rooney is a postgraduate research student at the University of Sussex. He is currently completing his doctoral thesis on representations of male homosexuality in British literature of the 1950s and 1960s.

Vernon A. Rosario, a psychiatry resident at the Neuropsychiatric Institute of the University of California, Los Angeles, is the editor of *Science and Homosexualities* (1996) and author of *The Erotic Imagination: French Histories of Perversity* (1997).

Wilhelm von Rosen, Dr. Phil., senior researcher and archivist at the National Archives of Denmark, took part in the Copenhagen Gay Liberation Front in the early 1970s. He was co-editor of the gay magazine *Pan* (1977–1981), and he has written books and articles on gay politics and Denmark's gay history.

Terry Rowden is assistant professor of English at the University of Colorado at Boulder, where he teaches African American literature and gay and lesbian studies. He has published essays on James Baldwin and Carl Van Vechten and is currently completing a book on community and sexuality in modern African men's fiction.

Parama Roy is associate professor of English at the University of California, Riverside, where she teaches postcolonial theory and literatures and Victorian studies. She is the author of *Indian Traffic: Subjects in Question in Colonial and Postcolonial India* (1998) and is currently working on a project on gastropoetics and diaspora.

Sandip Roy-Chowdery grew up in Calcutta and is currently the editor of *Trikone*, a quarterly magazine on South Asian lesbian, gay, and bisexual issues, which is published in San Jose, California.

Rebecca Ann Rugg is a student in the dramaturgy and dramatic criticism program at the Yale School of Drama.

Miles D. Samson, associate professor of art history at Worcester Polytechnic Institute, works on the dissemination of modern design and theory in America, gender issues in cultural production, and architecture and design between 1870 and 1930. He has published on Lewis Mumford and the German architectural avant-garde.

Nancy San Martin is a Ph.D. candidate in history of consciousness at the University of California, Santa Cruz. Her research interests include queer theory, nineteenth- and twentieth-century nationalism, and U.S. narratives.

Ritch C. Savin-Williams is professor of clinical and developmental psychology at Cornell University. Recent books include *Gay and Lesbian Youth: Expressions of Identity* (1990), *The Lives of Lesbians, Gays, and Bisexuals: Children to Adults* (1996), and *. . . And Then I Became Gay: Young Men's Stories* (1998). He is currently writing a book on the relations sexuality minority youth have with their families.

Marc Schachter is a doctoral candidate in literature at the University of California, Santa Cruz, working in queer theory and pre- and early modern studies.

Lawrence R. Schehr, professor of French and head of the Department of Foreign Languages and Literatures at North Carolina State University, is the author of *Flaubert and Sons: Reading of Flaubert, Zola and Proust* (1986); *The Shock of Men* (1995); *Alcibiades at the Door: Gay Discources in French Literature* (1995); *Rendering French Realism* (1997); *Parts of an Andrology on Representation of Men's Bodies* (1997); and co-editor of *Articulations of Difference: Gender Studies and Writing in French* (1997).

Udo Schüklenk, B.A. (Hons), Ph.D. (Monash), is a German philosopher. He is course leader of the University of Central Lancashire's Centre for Professional Ethics' M.A. in Bioethics Program.

David Serlin is a writer, composer, and doctoral candidate in American studies at New York University, where he is currently completing a dissertation on sexuality and medical technology during the Cold War. He is a co-editor of *Policing Public Sex: Queer Politics and the Future of AIDS Activism* (1996), and a co-editor of the forthcoming anthology *Artificial Parts and Practical Lives: Histories of Modern Prostheses*.

Juan Antonio Serna teaches Spanish at Arizona State University in Tempe. He works on contemporary literature and film.

Gayle Seymour, assistant professor of art history at the University of Central Arkansas, has published an essay on the artist Simeon Solomon entitled "Simeon Solomon and the Biblical Construction of Marginal Identity in Victorian England" in Volume 33 of the *Journal of Homosexuality*.

Nayan Shah, assistant professor of history at the State University of New York at Binghamton, is writing a book on the politics of public health in San Francisco's Chinatown and has written articles on sexuality and the South Asian diaspora.

Anthony Shay, who holds a Ph.D. in dance history and theory from the University of California at Riverside, has received five NEA fellowships in choreography. He founded and serves as artistic director and choreographer for the AVAZ International Dance Theatre, which specializes in dances and music of the Middle East, Central Asia, and Eastern Europe.

W. Anthony Sheppard is assistant professor of music at Williams College, where he teaches courses in twentieth-century art and popular musics, opera, and Asian musics. His forthcoming book is on modernist music theater and his current research is focused on cross-cultural musi-

cal encounters between Japan and the United States.

Ken Sherill, chair of the political science department at Hunter College, City University of New York, specializes in public opinion and political participation. He has been an expert witness in such landmark cases as *Romer v. Evans* (Colorado Amendment 2) and *Equality Foundation v. Equal Rights, Not Special Rights* (Cincinnati Issue 3).

Charley Shively, professor of American studies, University of Massachusetts, Boston, has written two books on Walt Whitman. He has served as a Fulbright professor in Mexico and Ecuador.

Ana Sierra is associate professor in the department of modern languages at Seton Hall University. Her publications include *El mundo como voluntad y representacion: Borges y Schopenhauer* (1997) and a variety of articles on Latin American literature.

Roger Simpson is associate professor in the School of Communications, University of Washington. A historian and ethicist, he is co-author of *An Evening in the Garden of Allah: A Gay Cabaret in Seattle* (1996).

Prods Oktor Skjaervo is Aga Khan Professor of Iranian Studies, Harvard University. His interests range over the entire field of pre-Islamic Iranian civilization, about which he has published over 100 articles and book reviews. He wrote an article on homosexuality in Middle Persian literature for Claude J. Summers's *The Gay and Lesbian Literary Heritage* (1995).

Mathew Sloan is a Ph.D. candidate in sociology at the University of Wisconsin–Madison. His research interests include gender politics and the welfare state.

James Smalls teaches art history at Rutgers University. He has written extensively on queer issues, gender, and race in European and American art of the nineteenth and twentieth centuries.

Bruce Smith is professor of English at Georgetown University and author of *Homosexual De-*

sire in Shakespeare's England (1991) and *The Acoustic World of Early Modern England* (1999).

Raymond A. Smith is research associate, HIV Center for Clinical and Behavioral Studies, New York State Psychiatric Institute and Columbia University and editor of *The Encyclopedia of AIDS: A Social, Political, Cultural, and Scientific Record of the HIV Epidemic* (1998).

Nicholas Derek Southey is senior lecturer in the Department of History at the University of South Africa. Co-editor of the *Historical Dictionary of South Africa*, he works on religion and society as well as on homosexuality in South African history.

Scott Speirs is a graduate student at Tufts University working on queer theory and Victorian literature.

Stephen Sposato is a writer and librarian (Chicago Public Library). He majored in English at the honors tutorial college of Ohio University and has an M.L.S. from the University at Buffalo.

Edward Stein is the editor of *Forms of Desire: Sexual Orientation and the Social Constructionist Controversy* (1994) and author of *Without Good Reason: The Rationality Debate in Philosophy and Cognitive Science* (1998) and the forthcoming *Sexual Desires: Science, Theory and Ethics*.

Marc Stein, who received his Ph.D. in history from the University of Pennsylvania, is a visiting assistant professor at Colby College. His forthcoming book is entitled *City of Sisterly and Brotherly Loves: The Making of Lesbian and Gay Communities in Greater Philadelphia, 1945–72*.

Sister Phyllis Stein the Fragrant is currently Mistress of Ceremonies (President) of the San Francisco Mother House. She is also the Mistress of Sistory (historian). As such, she religiously locks herself away in a tiny, tiny room all in the name of ensuring the preservation of the order's history. (Men all over the Bay Area sigh with relief.)

Terry S. Stein, M.D., professor of psychiatry at Michigan State University in East Lansing, is the former chair of the American Psychiatric Associa-

tion's committee on gay, lesbian, and bisexual issues and a past president of the Association of Gay and Lesbian Psychiatrists. He has written and edited numerous publications on mental health issues of lesbians, gay men, and bisexual persons.

Mark Steinbrink is a writer and teacher who has written about Leonard Bernstein and David Hockney for publications such as *Life, Saturday Review,* and *New York* magazine. He has also written a book and an opera libretto about Bernstein's love affair with Tom Cothran and recently had his portrait painted by David Hockney.

Simon Stern, an assistant professor of English at the University of Utah, is completing a study of authorship and literary property in eighteenth-century England, focusing on Henry and Sarah Fielding.

Michael R. Stevenson, professor of psychological science and director of the Diversity Policy Institute at Ball State University, spent 1993–1994 in Indonesia as a Fulbright Senior Scholar and 1995–1996 in Washington, D.C., as an American Psychological Association Senior Congressional Fellow. He is book review editor for the *Journal of Sex Research* and serves on the editorial boards of the *Journal of Men's Studies* and the *Journal of Psychology and Human Sexuality.*

Brett Stockdill is a queer educator and activist currently doing AIDS research and teaching sociology at UCLA.

Kathryn Bond Stockton, associate professor of English at the University of Utah, has published *God Between Their Lips: Desire Between Women in Irigaray, Brontë, and Eliot* (1994) and *Heaven's Bottom: Essays on Debasement in "Black" and "Queer" Fictions* (forthcoming).

Rodger Streitmatter, author of *Unspeakable: The Rise of the Gay and Lesbian Press in America* (1995), teaches journalism at American University in Washington, D.C.

Robert S. Sturges teaches gender studies, opera, and medieval literature at the University of New Orleans, and he is finishing a book entitled

Chaucer's Pardoner and Gender Theory: Bodies of Discourse.

Claude J. Summers is the William E. Stirton Professor in the Humanities and professor of English at the University of Michigan–Dearborn. He has published widely in Renaissance literature and gay studies, including *Gay Fictions: Wilde to Stonewall* (1990) and *The Gay and Lesbian Literary Heritage: A Readers' Companion to the Writers and Their Works, from Antiquity to the Present* (1995).

Edward Summers, a librarian in the education and social sciences library at the University of Illinois Urbana–Champaign, received his M.L.S. from Rutgers University in 1996.

Michael Sweet is clinical assistant professor of psychiatry, University of Wisconsin–Madison, and a practicing psychotherapist. He has published articles on queer aspects of classical South Asian culture and on Buddhist studies and is presently working on a translation and study of two Buddhist meditation texts.

Holger Szesnat is lecturer in biblical studies at Pacific Theological College, Suva, Fiji. He recently completed a Ph.D. in theological studies at the University of Natal (South Africa).

Fiona Tasker, Ph.D., is lecturer in psychology at Birkbeck College, University of London, England. Her publications include papers on gay and lesbian families, and she co-authored *Growing Up in a Lesbian Family: Effects on Child Development* (1998).

Richard Taylor is professor of politics at the University of Wales, Swansea. He has edited Eisenstein's *Selected Works* (4 vols., 1988–1996) in English and written widely on Russian and Soviet cinema.

Alex Robertson Textor is a doctoral candidate in American culture at the University of Michigan, where he studies histories of sexual dissidence and theories of citizenship.

Gary C. Thomas is associate professor in the Department of Cultural Studies and Comparative Literature and the Graduate Program in Comparative Studies in Discourse and Society at the University of Minnesota.

Wesley Thomas (Navajo, born of Mud Clan and Edge of Water Clan, from Mariano Lake, New Mexico) is currently an A.B.D. doctoral student in cultural anthropology at the University of Washington. A regular consultant on traditional Navajo cultural elements, a frequent lecturer in academic and nonacademic settings in the United States and abroad and in Native and non-Native communities, and a consultant to the National Museum of the American Indian, Museum of New Mexico and others. A poet, photographer, and weaver, he is currently writing his dissertation, "Gendering Navajo Bodies." He has also co-edited the book *Two-Spirit People: Native American Gender Identity, Sexuality, and Spirituality* (1997).

Jacqueline Thomason is a radical feminist and an activist for peace and social justice. A lesbian mother of a gay son, she holds a Ph.D. in philosophy from the University of Massachusetts at Amherst and an M.A. in feminist psychology from the New College of California.

Stuart Timmons is an investigative journalist and author who covers gay and HIV politics and medicine for a variety of national magazines. His biography of Harry Hay, *The Trouble with Harry Hay: Founder of the Modern Gay Movement*, appeared in 1990.

John Tinker studied English at the University of California at Berkeley and received his Ph.D. in English from Stanford University. He is currently working on a book on William Beckford.

Jeffrey Tobin is a cultural anthropologist who wrote his dissertation at Rice University on "Manly Acts: Buenos Aires 24 March 1996." He is currently teaching in the Department of World Arts and Cultures at UCLA.

Robert Tobin, associate professor of foreign languages at Whitman College, teaches courses in German and gay and lesbian studies. His research interests include the age of Goethe and the early twentieth century.

Daniel Torres, associate professor of Spanish at Ohio University, is a specialist on colonial and contemporary Spanish-American literature and has published books on García Márquez, José Emilio Pacheco, and the Spanish American baroque, as well as a novel and a collection of short stories. He is currently working on a book-length project that examines queer poetry from Argentina, Cuba, Chile, and Puerto Rico.

Daniel C. Tsang has done research that focuses on moral panics over sex and gangs. He is a social sciences bibliographer and occasional lecturer at the University of California, Irvine, where he hosts a weekly interview program, "Subversity," on KUCI, 88.9 FM public radio. He also writes for the *Orange County Weekly*.

Hans Turley is assistant professor of English at the University of Connecticut. His forthcoming book is entitled *Rum, Sodomy, and the Lash*.

Carole-Anne Tyler, associate professor of English and chair of the program in film and visual culture at the University of California, Riverside, is the author of the forthcoming book *Female Impersonation*.

Nancy C. Unger teaches American history at Santa Clara University, specializing in the Progressive era. Her biography *Fighting Bob La Follette: The Righteous Reformer* is forthcoming.

Alejandro Varderi, associate professor of Spanish at Borough of Manhattan Community College, City University of New York, has written *Severo Sarduy y Pedro Almódovar: del barroco al kitsch en la narrativa y el cine postmodernos* and *Anatomía de una seducción: reescrituras de lo femenino*. He is currently working on a novel and a study of kitsch in Spanish-American narrative.

Paul L. Vasey received his Ph.D. (anthropology) in 1997 from the University of Montréal. His research focuses on the evolutionary implications of female homosexual behavior in Japanese macaques.

Margaret R. Vendreyes, who received her Ph.D. from Princeton in 1997, has been doing research on black American art and artists since 1982. She has just completed a monograph on Richmond Barthé and studies cross-cultural aesthetic and social concerns in the art and life of artists.

Bruce Vermazen is a professor of philosophy at the University of California, Berkeley, a translator, and the musical director of the San Francisco Starlight Orchestra.

Martin Vodražká is a classically trained singer working and living in Prague, Czech Republic.

Eibhear Walshe, a lecturer in the department of English, University College, Cork, Ireland, is the editor of *Sex, Nation and Dissent in Irish Writing* (1997).

Rae N. Watanabe is instructor of English at Leeward Community College in Pearl City, Hawaii.

Thomas Waugh, an author most recently of *Hard to Imagine: Gay Male Eroticism in Photography and Film from Their Beginnings to Stonewall* (1996), has taught film studies as well as interdisciplinary curriculum on queer culture and HIV at Concordia University, Montréal, since 1976. He has published in such periodicals as *Jump Cut, The Body Politic*, and *Cineaction!*

Cynthia Weber is associate professor of political science at Purdue University. Her focus on international relations and gender/queer theory is best expressed in her book *Faking It: U.S. Hegemony in a Post-Phallic Era* (1999).

Jonathan Weinberg, a painter and an associate professor in art history at Yale University, is the author of *Speaking for Vice: Homosexuality in the Art of Charles Demuth, Marsden Hartley and the First American Avant-Garde* (1993).

Barry Weller teaches at the University of Utah and edits the *Western Humanities Review*. In addition to collaborating on editions of Byron's dramas (1991) and Elizabeth Cary's *Tragedy of Mariam, the Fair Queen of Jewry* (1994), he has published articles on Renaissance, nineteenth- and twentieth-century literature in various journals and collections, including, recently, *Novel Gazing: Queer Readings in Fiction* (1997).

J. A. White, Ph.D., is an assistant professor of English at Morgan State University in Baltimore, Maryland.

Lloyd Whitesell received his Ph.D. in music at State University of New York at Stony Brook, where he now teaches. His research interests include Benjamin Britten, the subject of his dissertation, and other topics in lesbian and gay music.

Matthew Williams, author of numerous articles on race, media, and sexuality, attended Goddard College and is currently putting together the sprucemountain.org on-line arts project.

Matthew W. Wise is a music librarian at New York University and has performed with the Lesbian and Gay Big Apple Corps, BAC Symphonic Band, and Hot Lavender Swing Band.

Christopher S. Wood, who teaches art history at Yale University, is the author of *Albrecht Altdorfer and the Origins of Landscape* (1993) and writes on the history and theory of art history.

Gregory Woods, professor of gay and lesbian studies at the Nottingham Trent University, England, is the author of *Articulate Flesh: Male Homoeroticism and Modern Poetry* (1987) and *A History of Gay Literature: The Male Tradition* (1998).

Les K. Wright is assistant professor of humanities and English and liberal arts program director at Mount Ida College in suburban Boston. He edited and contributed to *The Bear Book: Readings in the History and Evolution of a Gay Male Subculture* (1997), is curator of the Bear History Project, was a founding member of the Gay and Lesbian Historical Society of Northern California, and has published numerous articles on bears, gay history, and German and American cultural studies.

Lawrence L. Wu is professor and former associate chair in the Department of Sociology at the University of Wisconsin–Madison. He and four other sociologists were authors of an amicus brief in support of same-sex marriage in the recent Hawaii Second Circuit Court and Hawaii Supreme Court cases on same-sex marriage.

Danny Yatim is an Indonesian psychologist and AIDS counselor based in Jakarta.

Christine Yared, J.D., is assistant professor at Grand Valley State University, School of Criminal Justice, where she has developed the course "Sexual Orientation, Law and Policy." She is also president of the Lesbian and Gay Community Network of Western Michigan and has published and presented articles addressing legal issues for gays and lesbians.

Heather Zwicker, associate professor in the Department of English, University of Alberta, works at the intersection of postcolonial, queer, and feminist theories and literatures.

Subject Guide

Tom of Finland
Twombly, Cy
Warhol, Andy

Asian-American
Asians in North America
Chinese Bachelor Society

Black Studies
African American Gay Culture
Black Power Movement

Chicano/Latino
Cantina Culture
Chicano and Latino Gay Cultures

Classics
Alexander the Great
Artemedorus
Athens
Dionysus
Elegiac Poetry
Etruscans
Ganymede
Hadrian
Hippocratic Corpus
Homer
Mythology
Orpheus
Petronius
Philo of Alexandria
Plato
Priapus
Rome, Ancient
Scythians
Sparta
Thebes

Dance
Ailey, Alvin
Ballet (British)
Ballets Russes
Ballets Trockadero de Monte Carlo
Béjart, Maurice
Beloved
Bennett, Michael
Cunningham, Merce

Dance: Concert Dance in America
Dance and AIDS
Dancing Boys
Diaghilev, Sergey
Dove, Ulysses
Goode, Joe
Joffrey Ballet
Jones, Bill T.
Kirstein, Lincoln
Morris, Mark
Nijinsky, Vaslav Fomich
Nureyev, Rudolf Hametovich
Rousseve, David
Taylor, Paul
Tune, Tommy
Voguing

Economics
Boycott
Business
Keynes, John Maynard
Marketing

Education
Children's Books
Education: Theory and Pedagogy
Gay Studies
Schools
Sex Education
Student Organizations

Fashion
Fashion
Gernreich, Rudi
Klein, Calvin
Leyendecker, J. C.

Film
Almodóvar, Pedro
Anger, Kenneth
Araki, Gregg
Bogarde, Dirk
Broughton, James
Carné, Marcel
Cukor, George
Davies, Terence
Eisenstein, Sergey Mikhailovich
Fassbinder, Rainer Werner

Film
Film: New Queer Cinema
Film Stars
Hawkes, Howard
Haynes, Todd
Hitchcock, Alfred
Jarman, Derek
Laughton, Charles
Leander, Zarah
Marais, Jean
Mineo, Sal
Pasolini, Pier Paolo
Riggs, Marlon
Rosa von Praunheim
Russo, Vito
Schlesinger, John
Smith, Jack
Van Sant, Gus
Visconti, Luchino
Waters, John
Whale, James

Gay Culture
Adult Bookstores
Bathhouses and Sex Clubs
Bear Culture
Black and White Men Together, National
    Association of
Camp
Castro
Circuit Party Scene
Clone
COC
Community Centers
Disco and Dance Music
Drag Balls
Faggot
Fairy
Flowers and Birds
Gay
Gay Families
Gay Language
Gay Relationships
Gentrification
Kissing
Lambda
Leathermen
Queen
Queer Skinheads
Radical Faeries
Sisters of Perpetual Indulgence

Switchboards, Gay
Sydney Gay and Lesbian Mardi Gras
Trade
Trick

Geography
Africa: Precolonial sub-Saharan Africa
Alexandria
Amsterdam
Argentina
Australia
Bangkok
Berlin
Brazil
Canada
China
Czech Republic
Denmark
Egypt, Ancient
England
Finland
Florence
France
Germany
Greece
India
Indonesia
Iran
Ireland
Israel and Palestine
Italy
Japan
Kenya
London
Los Angeles
Mediterranean
Melanesia
Mexico
Miami
Morocco
Netherlands
New York City
New Zealand
Paris
Portugal
Russia
San Francisco
Singapore
Slovenia
South Africa
Spain

Sweden
Taiwan
Thailand
Tunisia
Turkey
United States
Washington, D.C.
Yugoslavia
Zimbabwe

History
Aelred of Rievaulx
Aestheticism
Alan of Lille
Albert the Great
Blunt, Anthony
Boy Scouts
Buggery
Burton, Sir Richard Francis
Casement, Roger
Cohn, Roy M.
Colonial America
Colonialism
Dandy
Edward II
Effeminacy
Feminism
Fops
Galen of Pergamon
Gay Activists Alliance (GAA)
Gay Liberation
Gay Liberation Front
Gilles de Rais
Hay, Harry
Henri III
Ibn Sina
Inquisition
Italian Renaissance
James I
Juan II of Castille
Lawrence, T. E.
Leopold and Loeb
Libertine and Libertinism
Ludwig (Louis) II, King of Bavaria
Marches on Washington
Mattachine Society
Mollies
Molly Houses
Montesquieu, Count Robert de
Nazism and the Holocaust
Nicolson, Harold

Orléans, Monsieur Philippe, duc d'
Peter Damian
Pink Triangle
Piracy and Pirates
Renaissance Neoplatonism
Rhodes, Cecil John
Röhm, Ernst
Sandow the Magnificent
Sodomy
Sodomy Trials
Stonewall
Théophile de Viau
Vere Street Coterie
War
Winckelmann, Johann Joachim
YMCA

Journalism
Advocate
AIDS in the U.S. Media
Arvin, Newton
Body Politic
Christopher Street
Gay and Lesbian Press
Gay Community News
Journalism
Kreis, Der
Media
Morris, Jan
ONE Magazine
Shilts, Randy
Talk Shows

Law
Bentham, Jeremy
Bowers v. Hardwick and *Romer v. Evans*
Civil Rights (U.S. Law)
Code Napoléon
Domestic Partnership
European Commission of Human Rights
Gay Rights in the United States
Hate Crimes
Homosexual Panic
Immigration, U.S.
International Law
Legal Organizations
Lewd and Lascivious Conduct
Nameless Sin (or Crime)
Natural Law
Paragraph 175

Kleist, Heinrich von
Kliuev, Nikolai
Kuzmin, Mikhail
Lampião
Lautréamont, Comte de
Lezama Lima, José
Libraries and Archives
Lorrain, Jean
Love Poetry, the Petrarchan Tradition
Malouf, David
Mann, Thomas
Manrique Ardila, Jaime
Marlowe, Christopher
Matthiessin, F. O.
Maupin, Armistead
McAlmon, Robert
McKay, Claude
Medieval Latin Poetry
Melville, Herman
Merrill, James
Mishima, Yukio
Moix, Terenci
Monette, Paul
Montaigne, Michel de
Montherlant, Henry de
Mujûn
Mystery and Detective Fiction
Nava, Michael
Navarre, Yves
Novo, Salvador
O'Hara, Frank
Orton, Joe
Owen, Wilfred
Pater, Walter Horatio
Penna, Sandro
Penteado, Darcy
Perlongher, Néstor
Persian (Iranian) Literature and Culture
Pessoa, Fernando
Peyrefitte, Roger
Piñera, Virgilio
Platen, August Graf von Hallermund
Preston, John
Price, Reynolds
Proust, Marcel
Puig, Manuel
Purdy, James
Rabe, David
Radiguet, Raymond
Raffalovich, Marc-André
Ramos Otero, Manuel
Renault, Mary

Rimbaud, Arthur
Rochester, John Wilmot, Earl of
Rodríguez Matos, Carlos A.
Rolfe, Frederick William
Russian Literature
Saba, Umberto
Sade, Donatinen-Alphonse-François, Marquis de
Saint, Assoto
Saki
Salinas, Pedro
Sánchez, Luís Rafael
Sarduy, Severo
Sargeson, Frank
Schuyler, James
Settembrini, Luigi
Shakespeare, William
Spanish Literature
Strachey, (Giles) Lytton
Takahashi, Mutsuo
Tennyson, Alfred
Thurman, Wallace
Tondelli, Pier Vittorio
Townsend, Prescott
Trevisan, João Silvéro
Tyler, Parker
U.S. Literature
U.S. Literature: Contemporary Gay Writing
Van Vechten, Carl
Verlaine, Paul
Vidal, Gore
Villaurrutia, Xavier
Violet Quill
Walpole, Horace
White, Edmund
White, Patrick
Whitman, Walt
Wilde, Oscar Fingal O'Flahertie Wills
Williams, Tennessee
Williams, William Carlos
Wilson, Sir Angus
Yourcenar, Marguerite
Zapata, Luís

Music
Barber, Samuel
Benjamin, Arthur
Berners, Gerard Tyrwhitt-Wilson, Baron
Bernstein, Leonard
Blitzstein, Marc
Britten, (Edward) Benjamin
Bussotti, Sylvano

Cage, John
Choruses and Marching Bands
Copland, Aaron
Corelli, Arcangelo
Corigliano, John
Cowell, Henry
Davies, Peter Maxwell
Del Tredici, David
Epstein, Brian
Falla, Manuel de
Gay American Composers
Griffes, Charles Tomlinson
Harrison, Lou
Henze, Hans Werner
Ireland, John
Kohs, Ellis Bonoff
Lully, Jean-Baptiste
McPhee, Colin
Moran, Robert
Music and Musicians 1: Classical Music
Music and Musicians 2: Popular Music
Musical Theater
Opera
Opera Queens
Partch, Harry
Pears, Sir Peter
Porter, Cole Albert
Poulenc, Francis
Rorem, Ned
Saint-Saëns, Camille
Schubert, Franz Peter
Sims, John Reed
Sondheim, Stephen Joshua
Strayhorn, Billy
Susa, Conrad
Szymanowski, Karol
Tchaikovsky, Pyotn Ilich
Thomson, Virgil
Tippett, Sir Michael Kemp
Wagner, Richard

Philosophy
Fichte, Hubert
Kant, Immanuel
Schopenhauer, Arthur
Wittgenstein, Ludwig Josef Johann

Photography
Athletic Model Guild
Beaton, Cecil
Bruce of Los Angeles
Day, F. Holland
Eakins, Thomas
French, Jared Blandford
French, Jim
Gloeden, Baron Wilhelm von
Hujar, Peter
Lynes, George Platt
Mapplethorpe, Robert
Michals, Duane
Mizer, Bob
Photography
Quaintance, George
Ritts, Herb
Tress, Arthur
Weber, Bruce
White, Minor
Zane, Arnie

Politics
Activism, International
Activism, U.S.
Altman, Dennis
Anarchism
Antigay Initiatives and Propositions (U.S. Law)
Censorship
Chambers, Whittaker
Gay and Lesbian Alliance Against Defamation
    (GLAAD)
Gay Left
Guevara, Ernesto "Che"
Hoover, J. Edgar
Human Rights Campaign
Identity Politics
Jorgensen, Christine
Mahlsdorf, Charlotte von
Marches and Parades
Marches on Washington
McCarthyism
Milk, Harvey (1930–1978)
Minority Standing
NAMBLA: North American Man/Boy Love
    Association
National Gay and Lesbian Task Force
Outing
Owles, Jim
Parents and Friends of Lesbians and Gays
    (PFLAG)
Political Asylum
Politics, Global
Queer

Queer Nation
Queer Politics
Rainbow Flag
RFSL
Rustin, Bayard
U.S. Government Surveillance
Voting Behavior
Wittman, Carl

Popular Culture

Cabaret, Variety, and Revue Entertainment
Comic Strips and Books
Cowboy Culture
Crisp, Quentin
Divine
Resorts and Beaches
Somerville, Jimmy
Sylvester
Television
Tourism and Travel
Vampires

Pornography

Pornography

Psychology

Counseling
Ferenczi, Sándor
Hooker, Evelyn
Jung, Carl Gustav
Perversion
Psychiatry and Homosexuality
Psychological and Psychoanalytic Perspectives
  on Homosexuality
Psychotherapy
Sexual Orientation Therapy

Religion

Adelphopoiêsis
Augustine of Hippo
Bible
Buddhism
Canon Law
Catholicism
Christianity
Clergy
David and Jonathan
Hinduism

Islam
Islamic Mysticism
Josephus Flavius
Juan de la Cruz, San
Judaism
Metropolitan Community Church
Monasticism, Christian
Papacy
Pastoralia and Penetentials
Paul, Saint
Quakers
Religion and Religiosity
Religious Organizations
Religious Right
Sodom
Thomas Aquinas

Science

Animal Sexual Behavior
Evolution
Gender
Mass, Lawrence
Scientific Approaches to Homosexuality
Turing, Alan

Sex Practice

Masturbation
Pederasty
Phone Sex
Safer Sex
Sex Practice: Anal Sex
Sex Practice: Fisting
Sex Practice: Oral Sex
Sex Practice: Watersports and Scar
Tearooms

Sexology

Androgyny
Bisexuality
Bloch, Iwan
Carpenter, Edward
Cory, Donald Webster
Ellis, Havelock
Freud, Sigmund
Hermaphroditism
Hirschfeld, Magnus
Homophile Movement
Homosexuality
Inversion

Kama Sutra
Kertbeny, Karl Maria
Kinsey, Alfred C.
Krafft-Ebing, Richard von
Moll, Albert
Phallus
Sadomasochism
Sex Practice: Watersports and Scat
Sexology
Sexual Orientation
Symonds, John Addington
Third Sex
Transgender
Uranianism
Westphal, Carl Friedrich Otto

Sociology
Aging
Alcohol and Drugs
Assimilation
Class
Coming Out
Couples
Crime and Criminality
Friendship
Gay Bashing
Homophobia
Hustlers
Incest
Librarians
Machismo
Masculinity
Military
Misogyny
Mukhannath
Neighborhoods: Gay Neighborhoods in the
   United States
Oppression
Parenting
Prisons, Jails, and Reformatories
Recruitment Myth
Sexual Abuse
Sexual Violence
Sociology of Gay Life

Stereotype
Suicide
Transsexualism
Transvestism

Sports
Gay Games
Physical Culture
Richards, Renee
Soccer
Sports

Theater
Albee, Edward
Beaumont and Fletcher (Francis Beaumont and
   John Fletcher)
Beck, Julian
Caffé Cino
Coward, Noël
Fierstein, Harvey
Fitch, Clyde
Hart, Lorenz
Inge, William
Jewel Box Revue
Kabuki
Kushner, Tony
Ludlam, Charles
McNally, Terrence
Parnell, Peter
Patrick, Robert
Pomo Afro Homos
Theater: Premoderna and Early Modern
Wilson, Lanford

Theory
Barthes, Roland
Deleuze, Gilles
Essentialist-Constructionist Debate
Foucault, Michel
Hocquenghem, Guy
Queer Theory

Abû Nuwâs (c.747–762 to c.813–815)

An emblem of homoerotic Arabic poetry, Abû Nuwâs is one of the most celebrated poets of the early Abbasid age. Al-Hasan (b. Hâni' al–Hakamî) was born in al-Ahwâz (Iran) between A.D. 747 and 762, and died in Baghdâd between 813 and 815. His father might have been a soldier in the army of the last Umayyad caliph Marwân II, and his grandfather was a *mawlâ* (emancipated servant) of al-Garrâh (b. 'Abdallah al-Hakamî), a governor of Khurasân of southern Arabian descent, which accounts for Abû Nuwâs's avowals of disdain toward Arabs of northern origin (thus indirectly, if not openly, aiming at the family of the Prophet and caliphs, all of the northern tribe of Quraysh, a most provocative stance). His mother is said to have been the owner of a tavern in Basra and her morals the object of much jest. Two anecdotes quoted by Ibn Manzûr allude to Abû Nuwâs's being a *mu'âjir* in his youth, a term that could be understood as an escort for rich and refined literati. The same author presents three versions of Abû Nuwâs's encounter with the poet Wâliba (b. al-Hubâb), a lover of wine and beardless youths. All versions agree that the latter was charmed by Abû Nuwâs's wit and beauty and decided to take him to al-Kûfa to effect his formation as a poet. Wâliba was generous enough to send him to the desert to master the subtleties of the language. After Wâliba's death, the young poet, besides studying Koranic sciences, *hadîth* (sayings attributed to the Prophet Muhammed), and grammar, became a disciple of the famous transmitter of poetry Khalaf al-Ahmar. Ibn Manzûr mentions that when Abû Nuwâs asked his master for authorization to compose verses, Khalaf ordered him first to learn a thousand poems. Having learned them, recited them

before Khalaf for many nights, and asked again for the right to compose, Khalaf enjoined him to forget those verses before he would be able to compose. This Abû Nuwâs dutifully did while drinking wine in a monastery. This parable on poetic creation also underlines Abû Nuwâs's formidable intelligence, acknowledged by all the learned men of his time. He joined the caliphal court in Baghdâd as a protégé of the Iranian clan of Al Nawbakht, and became acquainted with the caliph Harûn al-Rashid's son, al-Amîn, who shared his taste for wine, young and available male servants, and hunting. Although Abû Nuwâs had to flee to Egypt as a result of composing a eulogy to the Al Barmak, a family of viziers to Hârûn al-Rashid who were put to death after losing the caliph's favor, he lived the most brilliant period of his life upon returning to Baghdâd during his friend al-Amîn's reign (809–813). The circumstances of his death are unknown.

Abû Nuwâs's poetic production is particularly renowned for three themes: hunting, drinking wine, and *mujûn* (libertinism), the last two often connected. His devotion to homoerotic themes and his often scandalous life made him an emblem to the classical figure of the *mâjin* (ribald) and *lûti* (active dominant sodomist). Many anecdotes and verses in this field were seseqently attributed to a character who had become mythical, although such attribution should be treated with skepticism. As a former handsome young boy and object of desire for older men, in his poetry he portrays himself as a man in turn attracted by adolescent youths, to whom he can give only the passive role in a sexual encounter. Abû Nuwâs does not praise the male body as much as an androgynous beauty, as evidenced in the *ghulâmiyyât* (servant girls dressed up as boys to please lovers of both sexes. In many pieces), the poet falls for a stereotypically described boy, one of those "eternally young ones before whom Time is in debt, and reaches them no more than as much as they wish," who plays at being unattainable, and with whom he will or will not suceed. Those boys are usually court servants, objects of gifts, and sometimes Christians of Arab or Byzantine descent. Fashionable *mujûn* includes witty and ironical allusions to the Muslim (or Christain) faith, in a way often close to blasphemy, as when the poet assimilates his penetration of a Christian boy as an act of *jihâd* against the infidel. Short pieces offer light and humorous longings of a lover of slender waists:

> In the hammam appears what pants hide
> So rise in your naked glory, cast a glance and care for nothing
> You shall see the arse ending the back of a slender nice looking one
> They all murmur to each other their admiration [at this sight]
> Isn't the hammam a place of utter beatitude?
> Even if some of its charm is spoilt by those who won't leave their towels. . . .
>
> *Frédéric Lagrange*

Bibliography

Bey, Hakim. *O Tribe That Loves Boys: The Poetry of Abû Nuwâs*. Amsterdam: Entimos Press, 1993.

Montgomery, James E. "For the Love of a Christian Boy: A Song by Abû Nuwâs." *Journal of Arabic Literature* 27 (1996): 115–124.

———. "Revelry and Remorse: A Poem by Abû Nuwâs." *Journal of Arabic Literature* 25 (1994): 123–132.

Wagner, Ewald. "Abû Nuwâs." In *Encyclopedia of Islam*.

Wormhoudt, Arthur. *The Diwân of Abû Nuwâs*. Oskaloosa, Iowa: William Penn College, 1974.

See also Arabic Literature; Mujûn; Mukhannath; Nuzhat al-Albaab; Persian Literature

Ackerley, J. R. (1896–1967)

J. R. Ackerley is best known for *My Father and Myself* (1968), a memoir in which Ackerley interweaves the separate stories of his gay life, his father's extramarital heterosexual life, and his father's bisexuality. Because the protagonists of the book failed to tell their stories to each other, Ackerley's interweaving seeks to repair the lamentable fact that "two intelligent people, . . . parent and son," whose lives represent a century of English cultural conventions, "should have gone along together . . . without ever reaching the closeness of an intimate conversation." The memoir shows how heterosexual and homosexual persons have a mutual stake in freeing eros and intimacy from constraint.

Freedom and success in love depend upon intimacy, whose prospects in turn depend, Ackerley suggests, upon widespread, indeed global, sociohistorical and political conditions. Ackerley's *Hindoo Holiday: An Indian Journal* (1932) records Ackerley's employment, in 1923, as a secretary to an elderly gay maharajah of an Indian native state. The native ruler and the English secretary achieve an interracial, anti-imperialist intimacy based on their common dedication to illicit eros. But their friendship cannot withstand the imperialism-intensified homophobia of the ruler's countrymen and of Ackerley's compatriots.

Nevertheless, there are tensions in *Hindoo Holiday*'s portrayal of friendship that escape sociohistorical and political intelligibility, just as there are tensions in *My Father and Myself* that evade therapeutic repair. This is because friendship and sexual love have a stubbornly perplexing character throughout Ackerley's work that evokes the limits even of liberated eros and of candid intimacy. Having found no all-absorbing intimate homosexual relation in his life, in 1946 Ackerley became exclusively attached to a pet Alsatian bitch. The responsibilities of his relation to his dog are recounted in the memoir *My Dog Tulip* (1956) and are novelized in *We Think the World of You* (1960), where interspecies affection is weighed against homosexual, heterosexual, and bisexual human eros. Both books brilliantly dramatize a constraint that appears to be inherent in all love, no matter how free, honest, and unashamed love's forms might become.

Ackerley's career began in 1925, when his autobiographical play, *The Prisoners of War*, about homosexuality in a World War I internment camp, had a brief success in London. Ackerley joined the Talks Department of the BBC in 1928, and from 1935 to 1959 he was arts editor of the BBC magazine *The Listener*. Ackerley's work is influenced by the writers T. E. Lawrence and David Garnett, and Ackerley's writing and editorial activity influenced many contemporaries, among them E. M. Forster, whom he encouraged to write gay stories (and whose *A Passage to India* receives a gay rewriting in *Hindoo Holiday*), and Christopher Isherwood.

Robert L. Caserio

Bibliography

Ackerley, J. R. *My Father and Myself*. New York: Coward-McCann, 1969.

Parker, Peter. *Ackerley: A Life of J. R. Ackerley*. London: Constable, 1989.

See also Bloomsbury; Forster, E. M.; Isherwood, Christopher; Lawrence, T. E.

Acosta–Posada, Juan David (1954–)

Juan David Acosta-Posada is an excellent example of a writer who is also a culturally aware gay activist of the 1980s and 1990s. Acosta-Posada was born in Cali, Colombia, in 1954. Since 1969, he has lived in Philadelphia, where he has become the most visible gay Latino leader, particularly in the areas of AIDS, human rights, and other issues important to the Latino community. He is the founder and director of Gay and Lesbian Latino AIDS Education Initiative (GALAEI), started in 1989. He is also a founding member of the Latin American Writers' Collective and its literary magazine, *Desde este lado (From This Side)*, cofounded with Puerto Rican lesbian filmmaker and writer Frances Negrón Muntaner. As an active member of Latino Lesbian and Gay Organization (LLEGO), Acosta-Posada has been instrumental in bringing cultural and literary issues into the annual national meetings of the most important Latino gay and lesbian organizations in the United States, helping to bridge the gap between activism and the general culture and academia. Acosta-Posada's articles on Latino, gay, and AIDS issues appear frequently in the Philadelphia press. His poems have appeared in periodicals such as the *Painted Bride Quarterly* and the *Evergreen Chronicles*, and in the anthologies *American Poetry Confronts the 1990s*, *Shouting in a Whisper: Latino Poetry in Philadelphia*, and *POESIdA: An Anthology of AIDS Poetry from the United States, Latin America and Spain*.

Acosta-Posada's poetry is intensely—aggressively—lyrical and personal, as if it longed to (re)create a private/intimate pastoral space: a *locus amenus* within the madding crowd of sociopolitical and health problems so bravely faced by the Latino/gay/AIDS activist and poet. His first book, *Grasping for Light* (dated 1989, the year GALAEI was founded) centers on the experience(s) of love and loss, and words (poetry), the three themes intertwined from the first to the last poem of the collection. Words mark the existence of both love and absence, and they both survive through poetry. Language substitutes nature as the source of imagery; writing is possible only *locus amenus*; and like the Garden of Eden, it contains/creates both the fruit and the snake, love and grief, everything transformed into words: poems are "the geography of love," "Words leaning half naked into the afternoons," "poems, like a flock of paper birds."

Through his personal and professional involvements, Acosta-Posada has seen many friends and clients die. His second collection of poetry, *Migrations to Solitude* (1993), tells of such unending loss using motifs similar to those used to express the loss of love: nature and language. Significantly enough, in the face of ravaging death, it is nature that is given a privileged space: the function of (re)constructing love and grief given to language in *Grasping for Light,* "the way winter & weather impersonate our loss." Throughout these poems, nature and language struggle to hold on to such space/function. It is also the struggle between rage/grief and poetry, tension that characterizes so much of AIDS-related artistic production. "How do I make the earth sing? Sing?," proposes and opposes the poem "Sur." The collection ends with a sensual vision of summer and the all-conquering sun: "The sun's naked heat undressing our thirst, and rowing towards me still." But it is a vision of the past ("we were both sixteen") made possible by language. The only way the poet can make the earth sing (the sun rise) is through words; and thanks to them, anger and grief are both conquered and "constructed" (a word from *Grasping*) or "impersonalized" (a word from *Migrations*). There is no way out . . . for the poet.

The third collection is titled *Songs to Survive the Body* (1993). Although AIDS is not the focus of the book, it is a generating force. As the poet explains in a letter, "I discerned in the late eighties a preoccupation with the body and desire as a problem in the age of AIDS. [From 1987 on], I became more conscious of the body, alienation, desire, hunger, and death, as central elements in the poems written after that year." *Carlos A. Rodríguez-Matos*

Bibliography

Negrón Muntaner, Frances, ed. *Shouting in a Whisper: Latino Poetry in Philadelphia*. Santiago de Chile: Asterión, 1994.

Rodríguez-Matos, Carlos A., ed. *POESIdA: An Anthology of AIDS Poetry from the United States,*

A

Latin America and Spain. New York: OLLAN-TAY, 1995.

See also Activism; AIDS; Poetry

ACT UP (AIDS Coalition to Unleash Power)

> LIBERTY
> AND
> JUSTICE
> FOR ALL*
>
> *Offer not available to anyone with AIDS
> (Flier by Ken Woodard for ACT UP New York's
> U.S. Civil Rights Commission demonstration
> in 1988 [Crimp 67])

The direct-action AIDS organization ACT UP (AIDS Coalition to Unleash Power) was formed by a group of angry queer activists in New York City in 1987. They were angry because tens of thousands of people had already died of AIDS, yet the response of the government, the mass media, the medical establishment, and other institutions was characterized by genocidal neglect. By the time ACT UP started, members of the group had watched while friends and lovers had died of AIDS. Many people in ACT UP were themselves living with HIV/AIDS.

They refused merely to sit back and die. ACT UP is self-described as follows: "A diverse, nonpartisan group of individuals united in anger and committed to direct action to end the AIDS Crisis. We meet with government and health officials; we research and distribute the latest medical information. We protest and demonstrate; we are not silent" (Carter 1). Within a short time, there were ACT UP chapters in various cities across the country and in Europe, Australia, and Canada.

Since the 1980s, ACT UP has utilized creative, confrontational, direct-action tactics targeting multiple aspects of the AIDS crisis, including exorbitant drug prices, inadequate government funding for research and prevention, sluggish medical research, inaccessible clinical drug trials, negligent AIDS service organizations, and biased media coverage. These tactics have included phone and fax zaps in which an agency, corporation, or other group is bombarded with hundreds of simultaneous phone calls and faxes. ACT UP chapters have engaged in marches, rallies, and "die-ins"—sit-ins in which people symbolically die to call attention to the ever-increasing number of AIDS deaths.

In other protests, ACT UP has occupied the offices of agencies and corporations, disrupting business as usual and using the media to publicize the

ACT UP protesters. Photo by Marc Geller.

AIDS crisis. In the late 1980s, ACT UP New York targeted Wall Street at least three times as a way to highlight the prioritization of profits over human lives. In 1989, after first posing as tourists to conduct surveillance, ACT UP members entered the New York Stock Exchange using counterfeit ID badges. They then chained themselves to the banister leading to the VIP landing and unfurled a banner reading, "Sell Wellcome" (Burroughs Wellcome is the manufacturer of the AIDS drug AZT). The activists used portable foghorns to drown out the 9:30 A.M. opening bell and dropped fake $100 bills imprinted with the words "Fuck your profiteering. We die while you play business" onto the stock exchange floor.

A central element of ACT UP's work has been forcing government agencies such as the National Institutes of Health to develop more rigorous research programs on HIV/AIDS, improve treatments, and make those treatments more affordable. One early success of ACT UP was to force the Food and Drug Administration (FDA), a federal agency that approves drugs and sets prescribed doses, and Burroughs Wellcome, one of the largest pharmaceuticals in the world, to acknowledge (after a year's delay) studies showing that the antiviral drug AZT was just as effective at 600 mg/day as at 1,200 mg /day. This halved the price of AZT and reduced the likelihood of the sometimes toxic side effects of the drug.

ACT UP has been particularly innovative in developing art, video, street theater, and agitprop (agitational propaganda) to call attention to the inequities of the AIDS crisis. In 1987, ACT UP's float in New York City's annual gay pride parade, trimmed with barbed wire and driven by a man in a Ronald Reagan mask, represented an AIDS quarantine camp. Surrounding it on the street were internment camp guards wearing gas masks and yellow rubber gloves.

Members of ACT UP realized that to fight AIDS, they would have to fight the homophobia that undergirded the epidemic. In true queer fashion, ACT UP has not just exposed antiqueer bigotry but publicly embraced the right to be queer. This includes speaking openly and explicitly about lesbian and gay male sex, publicly displaying homosexual affection, distributing thousands of condoms and dental dams, and unfurling banners promoting safer sex at major league baseball games, the Republican national convention, and other public events. ACT UP has often used video and art to expose the injustice of the AIDS crisis and boldly promote positive

images of homosexuality. ACT UP popularized the pink triangle, which homosexuals were forced to wear in Nazi German concentration camps during the Holocaust, as a symbol of queer pride. Notably, the pink triangle has been reversed to point upward as a symbol of hope and resistance. The organization's mission to emphasize the value of queer lives and vocally defy the status quo is encapsulated in the slogan SILENCE = DEATH, which appears below the pink triangle.

As in other movements, there has been considerable infighting around issues relating to race, class, and gender in several ACT UPs, including Chicago, Los Angeles, New York, and San Francisco. A significant number of ACT UP members, typically but not exclusively white gay men, have been reluctant to focus on how racism and sexism are connected to AIDS. Simultaneously, they have frequently been reluctant to accept the leadership of women and people of color—many of whom have had prior activist experience. In some ACT UPs, this faction has maintained that race and gender are not integrally linked to AIDS and that time spent on these issues would be better spent focusing on AIDS treatment issues and finding a cure.

While some ACT UP members have been reluctant to focus energy on fighting racism and sexism, other members have argued strongly that systemic racial and gender oppression are part and parcel of the AIDS crisis. People-of-color caucuses were formed in many ACT UP chapters to do educational outreach in communities of color. These caucuses have put together educational workshops to challenge racism within the organization, sponsored conferences on AIDS in communities of color, and worked with community-based organizations to improve AIDS services. Most of these caucuses are now defunct, with many of the members having left the organizations to work elsewhere.

One of the primary goals of ACT UP has been to expose the distorted, and often bigoted, coverage of AIDS by the mass media. For example, in 1988, ACT UP New York's art group, Gran Fury, produced a chilling poster printed in English and Spanish in response to a *Cosmopolitan* article (January 1988 issue) that asserted that heterosexual women had little to fear from AIDS:

AIDS: 1 in 61
One in every sixty-one babies
in New York City is born with AIDS
or born HIV antibody positive.

A

So why is the media telling us
that heterosexuals aren't at risk?
Because these babies are black.
These babies are Hispanic.

Ignoring color ignores the facts of AIDS.
STOP RACISM: FIGHT AIDS (Crimp 42).

Women, particularly lesbians, have criticized perceptions of AIDS as a gay male disease, pushing for more research on, and services for, women with HIV/AIDS. Women in ACT UP led several protests—disrupting conferences and sitting in at the Centers for Disease Control (CDC)—against the CDC definition of AIDS, which did not include the primary manifestations of AIDS in women for several years. Women's caucuses have challenged the portrayal of women as "vectors of transmission" (to men and to children) rather than people actually at risk for HIV infection themselves. Creating programs for women has meant simultaneously reconceptualizing women as whole people rather than just childbearers and wives and confronting the male-centered health-care system. Significantly, lesbians in many ACT UP chapters have stimulated internal dialogues on race, class, and gender and have played a central role in pushing for collective action around these and related issues, such as AIDS among prisoners and injection drug users.

In one action illustrating ACT UP's creativity and determination, ACT UP Chicago led a protest against the failure of the Cook County Board of Commissioners to establish an AIDS ward for women at Cook County Hospital. ACT UP's Women's Caucus, supported by People with Immune System Disorders (PISD) Caucus and the People of Color Caucus, created a symbolic AIDS ward by placing sixteen mattresses, wrapped in sheets covered with slogans about women and AIDS, in the center of a busy intersection, blocking traffic. The women lay down on the beds and refused to move. Over one hundred people were arrested in the demonstration. The AIDS ward was opened the next day.

ACT UP has faced considerable resistance from different groups. Some members of the gay and lesbian community consider their in-your-face tactics to be excessive and counterproductive. The mass media have often painted ACT UP as irrational and extremist. In addition, ACT UP's strong critique of the oppression it believes to be entrenched in U.S. social institutions and culture has alarmed political authorities at various levels. This alarm has some-

times translated into government attempts to destablilize the organization.

While not as severe as the political repression targeting movements of the 1960s and early 1970s, ACT UP has faced repression including police violence, FBI surveillance and harassment, and the use of the judicial system to intimidate ACT UP members. The writer George M. Carter says that "incidents of police brutality include physical assault and verbal abuse sustained by AIDS activists in Chicago, Philadelphia, New York and elsewhere. This affects AIDS activism directly. The point of AIDS demonstrations is lost in the story of violence while activists continue to face the threat of police brutality" (18–19).

FBI files released under the Freedom of Information Act show that ACT UP has been the subject of "Domestic Terrorism" and "Civil Unrest" investigations since its birth in 1987. A campaign of harassing phone calls and death threats targeted ACT UP women nationally, and multiple felony charges were filed against the Houston Three (members of ACT UP/New York) at the 1992 Republican Party convention. Echoing government attempts to divide earlier movements, a grand jury was used to divide queer/AIDS activists in Colorado and to indict three members of ACT UP/Denver on felony charges in 1993 for their participation in an action protesting the AIDSphobia and homophobia of the Catholic Church.

ACT UP's queer political response to the AIDS crisis has been very successful. The combination of extensive educational programs and social protest has been integral in raising awareness in the gay, lesbian, and bisexual community and broader society, increasing government AIDS budgets, opening up experimental trials, and making treatment more accessible. ACT UP chapters in several cities have been key players in the formation of clean-needle exchanges and improved AIDS programs and services for women and for prisoners. ACT UP has played a crucial role in the empowerment of People with AIDS (PWAs) and queers. They have exposed what they consider the inefficiency and greed of pharmaceuticals and the insurance industry, as well as the calculated negligence of the government.

On a broader level, ACT UP has provided a model for confrontational queer political struggles against homophobia and other oppressions. ACT UP has exposed the concrete ways in which homophobia has driven the AIDS crisis; challenged the idea that being gay, lesbian, bisexual, or transgendered is bad; and linked AIDS to other issues such as housing, incarceration, sexism, racism, poverty, and militarism. ACT UP has confronted not only the specific institutions and policies that fuel the AIDS crisis but also the underlying beliefs that promote neglect and allow hundreds of thousands to die. Exploding myths about homosexuality, asserting their queerness, and making links to other communities hit by AIDS have been key parts of ACT UP's work.

Since 1991, various factors have contributed to a reduction in the ranks of ACT UP. Many members have died, while others are simply burned out after years of physically and emotionally draining work. Some ACT Upers have moved into paid positions in the ever-expanding AIDS service industry. A lack of interest in society in general and the news media in particular as well as an increasingly conservative political climate have also made AIDS activism increasingly difficult. By 1997, many ACT UP chapters were defunct, but the organization persisted in some cities and continued to "ACT UP" against AIDS. "After we kick the shit out of this disease, I intend to be alive to kick the shit out of this system, so that this will never happen again," –the late Vito Russo, ACT UP New York member (Crimp 302).

Brett Stockdill

Bibliography

ACT UP/New York—Women and AIDS Book Group. *Women, AIDS and Activism.* Boston: South End Press, 1992.

Arno, Peter S., and Karyn L. Feiden. *Against the Odds: The Story of AIDS Drug Development, Politics and Profits.* New York: Harper Collins, 1992.

Carter, George M. *ACT-UP, the AIDS War and Activism.* Westfield, N.J.: OpenMagazine Pamphlet Series, 1992.

Corea, Gena. *The Invisible Epidemic: The Story of Women and AIDS.* New York: Harper Collins, 1992.

Crimp, Douglas. *AIDS Demo Graphics.* Seattle: Bay Press, 1990.

Gamson, Joshua. "Silence, Death, and the Invisible Enemy: AIDS Activism and Social Movement Newness." *Social Problems* 36 (1989): 351–367.

Kramer, Larry. *Reports from the Holocaust: The Making of an AIDS Activist.* New York: St. Martin's Press, 1989.

McKenzie, Nancy F., ed. *The AIDS Reader: Social, Political, Ethical Issues.* New York: Penguin, 1991.

Patton, C. *Inventing AIDS.* New York: Routledge, 1990.

See also Activism; AIDS; AIDS Organizations, U.S.; Gran Fury; Lesbians and Gay Men; Nazism and the Holocaust; Pink Triangle

Activism, International

In the age of globalization and rapid-fire movement of both information and money, when distances contract and national borders appear increasingly irrelevant, the distinction between local and international activism may seem difficult to maintain. Local activists often take an international perspective and call on the examples—or the resources—of other countries to reinforce their domestic message; news of victories or defeats on a local level may spread worldwide and have a global impact. On closer inspection, though, inequities of power and resources still prevent many groups from working in a transnational arena; other groups possessing such resources may likewise be reluctant to enable the participation of others.

However, a number of activist organizations are specifically dedicated to working on gay, lesbian, bisexual, and transgendered issues on an international scale—whether regional, subregional, or global.

The oldest such group is the International Lesbian and Gay Association (ILGA), founded in 1978 in Coventry, England, as the International Gay Association. ILGA is currently a federation of approximately 300 organizations, which holds a World Conference for its members every two years and distributes an English-language bulletin for its members via its administrative office in Brussels, Belgium. In 1997, ILGA changed its structure to increase regional power and representation. Where formerly positions in its governing secretariat had been distributed among member groups, an Executive Board representing all world regions as well as two secretaries general (one male, one female) now manage the organization between world conferences. The organization has no paid staff but maintains an active presence on the Internet.

The International Lesbian Information Service (ILIS) was formed in the late 1970s by a number of women reportedly responding to sexism and lack of lesbian representation in the then International Gay Association. ILIS is now located in the Netherlands, where a group of dedicated women (all volunteers) have produced a newsletter since 1984 in English and Spanish, containing current news and information from lesbians around the world. The group maintains contacts with lesbians from over sixty countries. In 1986, the group held its first and only international conference in Geneva for approximately 200 lesbians from about forty countries. The conference was disrupted by issues of racism and militarism, yet regional efforts were launched at this event, and many contacts were made between key lesbian activists still organizing in the movement today. ILIS has maintained its modest goals (with a very modest budget) of increasing communication and information about lesbians worldwide and strategically participating in certain international events such as the UN World Conference on Women and the Gay Games.

The International Gay and Lesbian Human Rights Commission (IGLHRC) is a U.S.-based organization advocating worldwide against human rights violations on the basis of sexual orientation, gender identity, or HIV status. IGLHRC was formed in 1991 to bridge the gap between the mainstream human rights movement and the growing lesbian, gay, bisexual, and transgender movements worldwide. With twelve staff members and offices in New York and San Francisco, IGLHRC monitors, documents, and mobilizes responses to human rights violations in partnership with thousands of grassroots organizations in over 120 countries. The organization produces regular action alerts in three languages, mobilizing responses to urgent situations that need international attention. IGLHRC also provides support to asylum seekers; provides technical assistance to grassroots lesbian, gay, bisexual, transgender, and other sexual minority groups in developing countries; and produces human rights reports.

The International Gay and Lesbian Youth Organization (IGLYO), formerly the Union of Gay and Lesbian Youth, has functioned since 1983 as a loose group of lesbian and gay youth activists who hold an annual conference and produce a newsletter.

Other organizations of gays and lesbians are also becoming more international in focus. The World Congress of Gay and Lesbian Jewish Organizations has a membership nearing 300, advocating for greater inclusion of lesbian and gay issues in mainstream Jewish international institutions. The Universal Fellowship of Metropolitan Community Churches, founded in 1968, also has over 300 churches, primarily in the United States, but with 30 churches in other countries.

Iranian demonstrators at the International Lesbian and Gay Activism Convention in Stockholm, Sweden (1989). Photo by Marc Geller.

Some organizations of bisexuals and transgendered people are taking a more international scope, notably Female-to-Male International. An international bisexual conference is held every three years, although no formal international organization has grown from it. Participants in both these groups are largely drawn from the United States and Europe but do include some representation of other parts of the world.

Finally, some mainstream international organizations contain gay, lesbian, bisexual, or transgendered components. Amnesty International, for example, hosts an international network of "members for gay and lesbian concerns," who press that organization to improve its generally languid record of response on sexual-orientation issues.

Significant regional networks of gays and lesbians also exist. ILGA has held regional conferences in eastern and western Europe and in Latin America. Since the early 1980s, lesbians have been meeting as part of annual feminist conferences for Latin America and the Caribbean, called the Encuentros Feministos; in 1987, these subgatherings were formalized as a separate conference, the Encuentros Lesbianas Feministas, held approximately at three-year intervals. The Asian Lesbian Network (ALN) was formed in 1991 after the first Asian lesbian conference in Thailand. A loose network of lesbians from ten Asian countries, as well as of Asian lesbians living outside the continent, ALN holds biennial conferences and as of 1998 is formalizing its constitution and membership.

Numerous conflicts and contradictions not only inhibit but inhere in the effort to create international coalitions. Economic, racial, and even linguistic privileges have been particularly divisive. As the examples above suggest, conferences have been a primary venue for sharing strategies and building alliances—including not just meetings organized around activism but events such as pride festivals, international gay and lesbian film festivals, and even the Gay Games. However, travel itself is a privilege that many activists working on a local level do not enjoy. And activists may find themselves further excluded by the language in which international conferences are held—usually, though not uniformly, English. The burgeoning of the Internet is sometimes taken to promise activists more democratic access to information, but computers, Internet service providers, and even electricity are hardly evenly distributed; gay and lesbian Internet resources are still dominated by the developed North.

Still, significant advances have been achieved by working at an international level. Although efforts by ILGA to obtain consultative status at the United Nations have been stymied by right-wing U.S. opposition and allegations of "pedophile influences," it has recently won similar status at the Council of Europe. In 1995, IGLHRC helped organize a global grassroots campaign for lesbian participation in the UN World Conference on Women in Beijing. This significantly raised the visibility of issues of sexuality and sexual orientation within UN structures. In the 1990s, major international nongovernmental organizations, including Amnesty International and Human Rights Watch, have also slowly begun to respond to the most egregious abuses committed against people owing to their sexual orientation.

Arguably, however, the most significant outgrowth of the still nascent international gay, lesbian, bisexual, and transgendered movement has not been its effect on these established institutions but the slow building of an international consciousness—an awareness of both the need for, and the continuing

difficulty of, solidarity between activists divided not only by distance but by barriers of culture, identity, and access to power. This process is gradual and certainly still unfinished. Yet as it goes on, it will ensure that the groundbreaking struggles of local activists can become known and understood in wider circles, which in turn can give those struggles new effect, new respect, and new meaning.   Scott Long
Julie Dorf

Bibliography

Dorf, Julie, and Gloria Cariega Pérez. "Discrimination and the Tolerance of Difference: International Lesbian Human Rights." In *Women's Rights, Human Rights: International Feminist Perspectives*. Julie Peters and Andrea Wolper, eds. New York: Routledge, 1995.

Hendriks, Aart, Rob Tielman, and Evert van der Veen, eds. *The Third Pink Book: A Global View of Lesbian and Gay Liberation and Oppression*. New York: Prometheus Books, 1993.

ILIS Newsletter. International Lesbian Information Service, Nieuwezijds Voorburgwal 68–70, 1012 Amsterdam.

Reinfelder, Monika, ed. *Amazon to Zami: Towards a Global Lesbian Feminism*. London: Cassell, 1996.

Rosenbloom, Rachel, ed. *Unspoken Rules: Sexual Orientation and Women's Human Rights*. London: Cassell, 1996.

Wilets, James. "International Human Rights Law and Sexual Orientation." *Hastings International and Comparative Law Review* 18:1 (Fall 1994).

See also Activism, U.S.; AIDS; Gay Games; International Law; Metropolitan Community Church; Politics (Global); Youth

Activism, U.S.

As a means of effecting change and raising consciousness, the dynamic of activism as utilized by gay, lesbian, bisexual, and transgender people (as well as people with AIDS) has contributed greatly to the creation of most contemporary gay communities and gay identities. There have been innumerable and widely diverse interpretations of gay activism during the last half-century, but the association of activism with sexual identity is itself a concept virtually unknown before the twentieth century.

The 1948 study by Dr. Alfred C. Kinsey, *Sexual Behavior in the Human Male*, put homosexuality

A squarely in the American public's consciousness for the first time, and his use of sexuality as a group identifier enabled homosexuals to view themselves as members of an identifiable minority. Defining a shared identity and examining how society discriminated against homosexuals was a core focus of the earliest homophile groups in the 1950s, such as the Mattachine Society and the Daughters of Bilitis.

Whether to seek acceptance of homosexuals as a distinct group deserving of equal legal protection or to take a more assimilationist approach—presenting homosexuals as virtually "normal" and "well adjusted" to fit into society—was an ideological struggle that divided the membership of many of these homophile groups. The first public gay protests in the mid-1960s were something of a hybrid of the two strategies. Calling for an end to witch-hunts targeting gay federal employees and military personnel, protesters outside the White House, State Department, and Independence Hall in Philadelphia dressed in suits and ties (skirts for women) in a conscious attempt to look like the average American.

The civil rights and black power movements of the 1950s and 1960s were pivotal in shifting the ideology and strategies of virtually all contemporary minority rights struggles. Achieving equality and strengthening group identity became a matter of asserting rights and reclaiming cultural identity, rather than simply seeking the acceptance of mainstream society.

In the struggle to attain full equality for homosexuals, the 1969 Stonewall riots were quickly seized upon by a new generation of gay activists as the kind of self-definitional moment after which nothing would be the same again. Previous nonconfrontational appeals for society to accept homosexuals were traded for loud, direct public actions demanding the rights which were being withheld from gays and lesbians. Activism quickly expanded beyond being the tool of a handful of dedicated activists to become a popular form of gay community liberation. The increased exposure given to gay issues in mainstream media was seized upon by gay activists to exert pressure on various targets, and the media itself came under fire for slanted reporting.

Many of the activist groups that formed in the months and early years following the Stonewall riots cultivated a new, positive, collective gay identity by staging public demonstrations of "gay power" and "gay pride." But there was an increasing divergence of opinion among these groups as to their specific agendas and goals, including the repeal of sodomy laws, ridding gay establishments of Mafia connections, protecting homosexuals in the workplace, ending police harassment, and deciding whether and how to support other "liberation" and grassroots movements—the women's movement, the Black Panthers, the antiwar movement—all competing for the attention and energies of the gay community.

Lobbying city and state governments to enact laws protecting homosexuals from discrimination was another focus of gay activists in the early to mid-1970s. While initially gays met with notable success, such as the passing of a human rights ordinance in cities like Ann Arbor (1972) and Minneapolis (1975), singer Anita Bryant led a successful campaign in 1977 to repeal a similar ordinance in Dade County (Miami). Extensive media attention given to the public vote against gay rights in Miami put gay activists on the defensive, and they suddenly had to fight to protect recently won rights. The attack by Bryant and her religious fundamentalist supporters on the idea of gays and lesbians as a group needing protection from discrimination would be repeated by conservatives over the next decade who portrayed gay rights activists as fighting for special rights for homosexuals. The 1978 slaying of openly gay San Francisco City Supervisor Harvey Milk and police attacks on gay protesters in the city's Castro neighborhood in 1979 further heightened awareness of the precarious inroads gays and lesbians had made toward being accepted by society.

After the initial terror of the unknown that accompanied the arrival of the AIDS epidemic in the early 1980s, the gay community challenged the inadequate response of government, the scientific community, and the medical industry to the crisis of HIV and AIDS. ACT UP (AIDS Coalition to Unleash Power) was particularly successful in staging direct public demonstrations and protests—a die-in (bodies prone on the pavement) on Wall Street and phone zaps (jamming) of corporate switchboards—in an effort to have these issues addressed.

Recognizing the power of advertising, ACT UP made considerable use of graphic images and succinct messages (particularly the pink triangle and the "Silence = Death" equation) in attracting the public's attention. Commanding that attention was also the aim of the direct-action group Queer Nation, whose members chanted, "We're here! We're Queer! Get Used to Us!" Born of the same grassroots activism of ACT UP, Queer Nation sought

ACT UP shouting down Dr. Louis Sullivan, Secretary of Health and Human Services (1990). Photo by Marc Geller.

both figuratively and literally to acquire space for gay concerns by staging actions in the late 1980s and early 1990s such as "kiss-ins" in malls and challenging prohibitions against same-sex dancing at Disney World.

In the 1990s gay activism continued to organize around gay rights issues and promoting greater visibility of gays and lesbians in all areas of society. A two-year tourism boycott by gays and lesbians of the state of Colorado was launched in 1993 after a statewide voter referendum voided all municipal gay rights legislation. In New York City and elsewhere, school curricula that include discussions of nontraditional family structures, such as gay and lesbian parents, remain a contentious issue. The right of gay and lesbian couples to adopt children and the campaign to have states sanction marriage between same-sex partners is likely to preoccupy gay activists for some years to come.

After the 1992 election of the relatively gay-friendly Clinton administration, there was a shift in some of the energies of gay activists from public actions to focusing on internal gay community debates over sociocultural currents. Particularly volatile in the late 1990s was the issue of promiscuity and fidelity (including the quest for legalized gay marriages), as related to continued high rates of HIV infection, bathhouse shutdowns, and the extent to which overt sexual expression is celebrated in the gay male community.

Within the broader concept of gay activism are a number of activist movements with more specific foci: activism directed toward lesbian issues, bisexual issues, and transgender issues; activism pairing sexuality with co-constructs of identity such as race and ethnic background; activism on campuses and in the workplace, as well as within the labor movement. Growing popular use of the Internet has made it possible for activists to broadcast information electronically to the gay community and readily coordinate actions.

Yet these activist movements often take as much issue with their perceived lack of visibility within the gay community as they do with mainstream society. The lesbian community has expressed considerable frustration over the lack of attention given to women's health issues, especially after the prominent role lesbians have played and continue to play in confronting the AIDS epidemic. Activists have also been challenging gay community organizations on the gender, racial, and overall diversity imbalance of having predominately white gay men in leadership roles.　　*Eugene Patron*

Bibliography

Alwood, Edward. *Straight News: Gays, Lesbians and the News Media*. New York: Columbia University Press, 1996.

D'Emilio, John. *Sexual Politics, Sexual Communities: The Making of a Homosexual Minority in the United States, 1940–1970*. Chicago: University of Chicago Press, 1983.

Jennings, Kevin. *Becoming Visible*. Boston: Alyson, 1994.

Kepner, Jim. *Our Movement Before Stonewall*. Los Angeles (self-published), 1994.

Shilts, Randy. "1990: The Year of the Queer." *Advocate* 567 (January 1, 1991): 32–39.

Stryker, Susan and Jim Van Buskirk. *Gay by the Bay*. San Francisco: Chronicle, 1996.

Taylor, Paul. "AIDS Guerrillas." *New York Magazine* 23 no. 44 (November 12, 1990): 62–73.

Teal, Donn. *The Gay Militants*. New York: Stein and Day, 1971.

See also ACT UP; Activism, International; AIDS; AIDS Organizations, U.S.; Gay Left; Hay, Harry; Mattachine Society; Queer Nation; Stonewall Rebellion

Adelphopoiêsis

Adelphopoiêsis is a liturgical rite that originated in the early Greek-speaking Christian churches. (The equivalent rite in the Slavic spiritual churches was called *bratotvorenia*.) The Greek term means literally "brother-making" or "friend-making," and the rite has typically been understood as a ceremony establishing a special kinship between the persons joined by it. Some scholars have argued that the rite developed as an adaptation of pre-Christian forms of nonbiological kinship, such as brotherhood-in-arms. The Christian rite was certainly used on occasion to seal a peace between warring parties or to strengthen social relations outside family lines. Other scholars have seen the rite as a continuation of certain kinds of adoption practiced in the Roman Empire for dynastic and economic reasons. But the

Christian rite of *adelphopoiêsis* did not have fixed legal consequences, say, for inheritance. Indeed, perhaps in the majority of cases, the rite seems to have served as a public enactment of some special affection between two Christians. John Boswell proposed that the *adelphopoiêsis* served in some cases as something like a church-approved lesbian or gay marriage. Arguing both from the content of the rite and from historical accounts of same-sex couples joined by it, Boswell held that ordinary Christians would sometimes not have been able to distinguish the practice of the rite of *adelphopoiêsis* from standard Christian marriage ceremonies. Boswell's reinterpretation has not been generally accepted.

Mark D. Jordan

Bibliography

Boswell, John. *Same-Sex Unions in Premodern Europe*. New York: Villard Books, 1994.

See also Couples; Friendship

Adult Bookstores

The combination adult bookstore/video arcade provides for the rental, purchase, and consumption of pornography. One of the few commercial spaces not strictly either heterosexual or homosexual, the typical adult bookstore features a mélange of products promising to satisfy a variety of sexual aims. In this particular instance, it is ironic that in many localities the goals of capitalism take precedence over so-called community values; certain consumers need to locate homoerotic merchandise, and, given the threat of shame or ostracism involved, must be able to do so without having to ask for help. The space of the porno shop is thus polymorphously perverse, rendered increasingly so by capitalism's commodification of even "aberrant" sexual desires.

Adult bookstores are located in both urban and rural environments, usually concentrated in downtown areas or along rural highways. Most customers are men; while more women appear to be visiting such establishments recently, they are usually accompanied by men. Bookstores are typically divided into a front area that sells magazines, novels, videos, lubricants, and sexual novelties such as dildos, penis pumps, and blow-up dolls, and a back area featuring an adult movie arcade in which customers sometimes have sex. (It is a testament to the puritanical strains in U.S. society that even during such a severe health crisis such as AIDS, the only place to purchase a safe and effective lubricant in many towns and cities has been an adult bookstore.)

The arcade is spatially separated from the remainder of the shop and usually requires an admission fee. It is rare to find women in the video arcade. One of the consequences of the explosion of the home video porno market has been the escalating homoeroticization of the arcade. Given the falling price of VCRs, many people now watch porno films at home. As a result, arcade customers tend to be searching for homoerotic contact—the primary exception being people who don't have access to VCRs or video rentals, or people who wish to view pornography without being detected by other members of their household.

Like many spaces in which consensual homoerotic activity may occur, adult bookstores blur the distinction between public and private. Theoretically open to the public, like tearooms they are spaces where private activities transpire. Some shops advertise themselves as private clubs and require the purchase of a membership. The fee must be sufficiently low to attract customers who may visit only a single time and high enough to discourage customers who might exploit the shop's cruising potential without actually purchasing anything.

In addition to purchasing commodities, visitors to the adult bookstore sometimes develop conventional social relationships. The space around the counter seems to be a particularly active area, especially if the clerk invites conversation. Depending on the store and its community, some customers might exchange pleasantries and discuss other aspects of their life such as their job, particularly the "regulars," who in smaller communities are likely to recognize one another from other (homoerotic) social settings. These factors challenge the view that those attending the bookstore are simply interested in sex. *John Champagne*

Bibliography

Champagne, John. "Stop Reading Films!: Film Studies, Loose Analysis, and Gay Pornography." *Cinema Journal* (Fall 1997): 76–97.

See also Bathhouses and Sex Clubs; Pornography; Tearooms

Advocate

The oldest continually produced gay publication in the United States, the *Advocate* was founded in 1967. Originally titled the *Los Angeles Advocate*, it became gay America's first all-news publication as well as the first to operate as a commercial enterprise financed entirely by advertising and circulation revenue. Founder Dick Michaels surreptitiously printed his first several issues on a printing press in the offices of the ABC Television Network, where his lover worked in the mailroom. In 1970, Michaels shifted from monthly to biweekly publication and dropped "Los Angeles" from the title to become the *Advocate*. He then transformed his local newspaper into a national one that published gay news from across the country.

In 1974, former Wall Street investment banker David B. Goodstein paid Michaels $1 million for the *Advocate* then spent another $2 million converting it into a cultural magazine subtitled "Touching Your Lifestyle." Redesigned with a bold, modern look, the *Advocate* documented the myriad dimensions of the gay culture, including gay America's enormous impact on such diverse subjects as men's fashion and the disco music craze. The magazine also moved gay publishing into the mainstream, becoming one of the dozen fastest-growing magazines in the country.

In the late 1970s, Goodstein began to place more emphasis on news, changing the *Advocate*'s subtitle to "America's Leading Gay Newsmagazine." A major force in this transition was reporter Randy Shilts, who joined the staff in 1976 and undertook such blockbuster projects as documenting the explosion of gay bars and bathhouses into a big business with annual receipts of $120 million and the emergence of a national gay health crisis as the incidence of venereal disease soared to epidemic proportions. In 1978, Shilts left the *Advocate* to work in the mainstream press.

When the AIDS epidemic erupted in 1981, Goodstein was so skeptical about what caused the disease and how it was spread that he opted not to sound the alarm, even though his magazine's eighty thousand circulation was triple that of any other gay publication. The *Advocate* did not advocate that gay men wear condoms during anal intercourse until 1983—a full two years after some other gay newspapers had published that advice.

The *Advocate* did, however, take the lead in attracting big-ticket advertising to gay publishing. In 1982, it landed Absolut vodka as the first major national advertiser in the gay press. The magazine's momentum waned in 1985 when publisher Goodstein died of colon cancer.

When a spate of glossy gay magazines emerged in the early 1990s, the *Advocate* unveiled a slick new look highlighted by its switch from newsprint to glossy paper. The redesign helped the magazine reap the benefits of dozens of mainstream advertisers seeking to attract the affluent gay dollar. Among gay glossies, the *Advocate* was the most news-oriented. It was during an *Advocate* interview in 1992 that candidate Bill Clinton promised that, if elected, he would lift the ban against gay men and lesbians serving in the armed forces.

Rodger Streitmatter

Bibliography

Streitmatter, Rodger. "The *Advocate*: Setting the Standard for the Gay Liberation Press." *Journalism History* 19:3 (Autumn 1993): 93–102.

———. *Unspeakable: The Rise of the Gay and Lesbian Press in America*. Boston: Faber and Faber, 1995.

Thompson, Mark, ed. *Long Road to Freedom: The* Advocate *History of the Gay and Lesbian Movement*. New York: St. Martin's Press, 1994.

See also Bookstores; Journalism; Shilts, Randy

Aelred of Rievaulx (1110–1167)

Aelred takes his name from the Cistercian monastery of Rievaulx in northeastern England, which he served for some years as abbot. A powerful spiritual writer, he is rightly regarded as one of the founding theologians of the Cistercian movement, which sought a more ascetic practice of the Christian monastic life. Aelred enters the history of homosexuality in part because of biographical facts, in part because of certain themes in his theological writings. Aelred himself describes his passionate attachments to men, and he confesses that he was particularly afflicted with sexual temptations. His biographer conceded when challenged that Aelred was sexually active as a young man and perhaps even notoriously so. The least strained conclusion is that Aelred had some sexual experiences with other men when young. Moreover, there are in Aelred's writings many passages that strike modern readers as homoerotic. His treatise "On Jesus at the Age of Twelve" encourages quite graphically the practice of devotion to the body of the young savior. In other writings, Aelred addresses equally strong devotion to the body of the crucified Jesus. At the same time, in many other passages Aelred explicitly condemns as sin genital contact between members of the same sex. Whether or how far Aelred should be counted a closeted homosexual or a gay writer depends almost entirely on how those terms are defined.

Mark D. Jordan

Bibliography

McGuire, Brian Patrick. *Brother and Lover: Aelred of Rievaulx*. New York: Crossroad, 1994.

See also Alan of Lille; Albert the Great; Augustine of Hippo; Christianity; Thomas Aquinas

Aestheticism

The terms *aestheticism* and *homosexual* were both coined in the nineteenth century and each had a notable impact on the others' formulation. This relation did not attain public recognition until Oscar Wilde's trials in 1895, when the dandy-aesthete's image and epigrammatic wit became familiar signifiers of homosexuality. By that time, however, aestheticism itself had already passed its peak in popularity. Overlapping with the decadent movement, the pre-Raphaelite movement, and the notion of *l'art pour l'art* (art for art's sake), aestheticism is a theory of art and life that entered primarily French and British culture during the second half of the nineteenth century, although its influence can also be found in other parts of the world including Canada, Germany, Italy, Latin America, Russia, and the United States. Aestheticism's principal tenet is that the worthiest of human endeavors is the full appreciation of beauty, which is an end in itself and which need not address utilitarian, political, moral, or other concerns. With advocates encouraging people to try to sustain such a temperament during every waking moment, aestheticism became signified by an amazing array of items, including literature, art, fashion, household goods, decor, poses, and terminology. This cultural production became known as the aesthetic movement.

Aestheticism arose from theories dating at least as far back as Immanuel Kant's *Critique of Aesthetic Judgment* (1790) and his claim that the ideal aesthetic experience demanded the "disinterested" contemplation of an object without any consideration of its practical or moral value. The argument for beauty's autonomy from cultural and political dictates made its earliest aestheticist appearance in the preface to *Mademoiselle de Maupin* (1835), in which French author Théophile Gautier argues in favor of the "spiritual" utility provided by beauty and one's maximum experience of diverse pleasures over the practical utility that so many critics were demanding from art. The novel's hero, D'Albert, offers an erotic enactment of Gautier's argument by searching for new sensations that he locates in the sexual encounters among himself, his mistress, and the cross-dressing eponymous heroine. Both aestheticism and its association with uncommon sexual acts were later developed in French literature by Charles Baudelaire, Joris-Karl Huysmans, Gustave Flaubert, and others, although their representations of same-sex desire were often more objectifying and titillating than sympathetic.

The notion that the appreciation of beauty is the most valuable human capability did, however, encourage positive conceptions of male-male desire, most apparently in England. Predating a number of texts now in the aestheticist canon, such as Gautier's *L'Art moderne* (1856), Baudelaire's *Les Fleurs du mal* (1857) and *Salon de 1859* (1859), Algernon Swinburne's *Poems and Ballads* (1866), and Walter Pater's *Studies in the History of the Renaissance* (1873), the first recorded use of the term *aestheticism* in England is George Brimley's 1855 review of Alfred Tennyson's poem "The Lotos-Eaters." While not suggesting sexual unconventionality, Brimley criticizes the poem for its lack of moral emphasis and its focus on the external environment, rather than God and society. Swinburne introduced a more full-bodied aestheticism to England when he used its arguments in an essay defending Baudelaire's work. He could not have been surprised by the critical attacks against his own later *Poems and Ballads*, which highlights a decadent image of sexual desire in such pieces as "The Leper," "Hermaphroditus," and "Anactoria."

The most influential articulation of aestheticism's principles as a theory of art and life is in Pater's collection of essays, *The Renaissance*. The disinterestedness of aesthetics, as described by Kant, means that appreciation demands the experience of sensual pleasure while disregarding the actual object that causes such pleasure; it can thereby be used to sanction same-sex admiration of the physical body. In the essay "Winckelmann," from *The Renaissance*, Pater defines such admiration as a necessity for the appreciation of beauty when he argues that Winckelmann's romantic friendships with beautiful men reflect the same developed sensibility that led him to appreciate fully Greek sculpture without any sense of corruption or shame. Not only an advo-

cation of same-sex pleasure, Pater's *Renaissance* reinforces a history of positive conceptions of such enjoyment extending back at least as far as the Hellenic model of *paiderastia*, in which an older, educated man admires and instructs a younger man who reciprocates the affection in part by offering a heightened sensuality signified by his physical beauty.

Critics and parodists also encouraged the association of aestheticism with homosexuality. W. H. Mallock's *New Republic* (1877) caricatures Pater as Mr. Rose, an aesthete attracted to young men. Vernon Lee incorporates lesbian desire into her novel *Miss Brown* (1881) to articulate notably both an elitist and a sympathetic model of aestheticism. W. S. Gilbert's play *Patience* (1881), Robert Hichens's novella *The Green Carnation* (1894), various pieces by Ada Leverson, and George Du Maurier's numerous cartoons in *Punch* magazine also use suggestions of same-sex male desire to poke fun at aestheticism. At the same time, these products of popular culture helped extend aestheticism's credo and its own positive image of male-male attraction to a broader audience. Wilde, however, was aestheticism's greatest marketer, as well as one of its most important authors. He infused a homoerotic aestheticism into many of his works, including *The Picture of Dorian Gray* and *Salome*. Even his children's stories such as "The Happy Prince" combine aestheticism, uncommon affections, and a Paterian notion of sympathy in their critique of utilitarian, bourgeois values.

Other authors and artists from England and elsewhere who participated in aestheticism include Gabrielle d'Annunzio, Aubrey Beardsley, Max Beerbohm, Sergey Diaghilev, Henry James, Lionel Johnson, Mikhail Kuzmin, Marc-André Raffalovich, Rainer Maria Rilke, John Symonds, Arthur Symons, and James McNeill Whistler. A sympathetic strain of aestheticism's parodic formulations extends into such twentieth-century camp texts as Ronald Firbank's *Concerning the Eccentricities of Cardinal Pirelli* (1926) and Christopher Isherwood's *Mr. Norris Changes Trains* (1935).

Dennis Denisoff

Bibliography

Dellamora, Richard. *Masculine Desire: The Sexual Politics of Victorian Aestheticism.* Chapel Hill, N.C.: University of North Carolina Press, 1990.

Gautier, Théophile. *Mademoiselle de Maupin.* 1835. Paris: Bibliothèque-Charpentier, 1924.

A

Pater, Walter. *The Renaissance*. Cleveland: Meridian, 1967.

See also Dandy; Decadence; Diaghilev, Sergey; English Literature; Firbank, Ronald; French Literature; French Symbolism; German Literature; Greek Love; Homosexuality; Isherwood, Christopher; James, Henry; Kant, Immanuel; Kuzmin, Mikhail; Pater, Walter; Pederasty; Raffalovich, Marc-André; Symonds, John Addington; Tennyson, Alfred Lord; Wilde, Oscar; Wincklemann, Johann Joachim

Africa: Precolonial sub-Saharan Africa

The most ancient depiction of homosexual practices in sub-Saharan Africa comes from the San (Bushmen), a classless hunter/gatherer people once scattered in small migratory groups throughout southern Africa. One of the many paintings they left behind on rock faces shows a group of men apparently engaged in anal or intracrural (between-the-thighs) intercourse. This dates from at least 2,000 years ago.

The communitarian San were gradually displaced or assimilated by more complex societies that spread throughout the continent over the past two millennia. Their enormous diversity makes generalization of limited values. Nonetheless, three features of premodern cultures that affected attitudes toward homosexual relationships and practices appear to have been fairly consistent across the continent. First, wealth tended to be measured in people attached to a household rather than in land holdings or conspicuous consumption. This made heterosexual marriage and reproduction a material as well as moral imperative. Second, societies tended to be very homosocial, with strict sexual divisions of labor and space. Third, the notion of community extended beyond the living to include ancestral spirits. Strange or eccentric behavior in individuals could be explained as their being possessed by such spirits.

The political economy of heterosexuality derived from the fact that, unlike in most of Europe or east Asia, land was abundant and shortage of people was the principal constraint on food and other production. As a result, children were not only considered as wealth and prestigious in their own right but were also a means to acquiring further wealth and prestige. Daughters in particular were valued for their labor and for the "income" they brought to the family upon marriage Indeed, bride-price accumulated from several daughters not only enriched a family but was also a means of advancing the prospects of sons, who could then afford to marry upward. Many daughters also served the political interests of a family in that they could be given as reward to loyal male clients or to establish interfamily alliances.

Sons, meanwhile, were generally required to marry before they were given their own fields, cattle, and the social status of manhood. Wives who did not subsequently get pregnant could be divorced, would lose the social status of womanhood, and would invite shame (and the possible expense of reimbursing bride-price) upon their family.

Heterosexual marriage resulting in successful pregnancy was thus the vocation that children were taught from earliest years. For a man or woman to forgo this and at the same time to elicit condemnation of family and community for the love of another of the same sex was an absurd and dangerous life choice, and in some cases there were explicit prohibitions against it, including the death penalty. The Orientalist stereotype of a "Sotadic (or torrid) zone" where homosexuality was unknown or highly discouraged is therefore largely correct empirically, if homosexuality is understood as a lifelong identity or persistent condition.

The second generalization about sub-Saharan African societies, however, is that pronounced homosociality created conditions for widespread homosexual "play." Homosociality meant that boys and girls, as well as men and women, conducted their daily lives in largely separate spheres. They typically had different crops, separate fields, separate huts, and their own institutions, games, duties, rituals, and so on. As a result, erotic touching between same-sex friends of the same age was considered quite normal and in no way threatening to future heterosexual relations. Indeed, homosexual sex play was often regarded as appropriate "training" for future heterosexual marriage, preferable to heterosexual mixing that could result in illegitimate pregnancies and political complications.

Homosociality was especially pronounced in pastoral, hunting, or militarized societies. In these, men in groups could be away from home for long periods of time. Among the Azande (of the present-day Central African Republic) and Zulu (southeastern South Africa), pederastic "marriages" among warriors were said to have been condoned in part to keep the men from developing mixed loyalties while they remained in the army. Among the Nuba (southwestern Sudan), homosexual relations between comrades-in-arms were said to have been "widespread" owing to fear of the enfetterment and supposed loss of virility that love and marriage to women could entail. The term "widespread" was also applied to homosexual relations among Tutsi and Hutu male youths, particularly at the royal court, where women were excluded.

Situational explanations of homosexual behaviors should be treated with great caution. It is a fact, however, that young men in the more stratified societies often lacked access to women and so turned to each other for intimate companionship and sexual release. Heterosexual contact could be restricted by decree or taboo, by men's inability to afford bride-price, and by the practice of polygyny on such a grand scale by elite old men that marriageable women were simply not available. The risks of adultery could be so high—death or mutilation in the Azande case—that taking boys as *badiya ngbanga* (court lovers) was a "very sensible" alternative. A similar situation among the Kololo/Lozi of western Zambia was rued by David Livingstone. Such behavior in no way invited stigma or precluded moving on to heterosexual marriage when circumstances allowed.

Legitimate, nonsexual friendships among men may also have acted as a cover for otherwise forbidden or inconceivable homosexual love. Reflective of this, contemporary gays and lesbians in Zimbabwe have coopted the word *sahwira* to denote a loving homosexual relationship. The all-important appearance of heterosexual virility for men could also be maintained regardless of reality through the custom of "raising seed," a practice found throughout the continent. By this, a man who was impotent or uninterested in consummating his marriage to a woman could invite a brother or friend to impregnate her. The children and prestige that ensued belonged to the husband, who was then free to pursue his sexual preferences without compromising his social standing.

In rare cases, revulsion at the idea of heterosexual sex was so strong that individuals resisted the intense social and economic pressures to marry. The third generalization about premodern cultures was that such defiance could be explained by spirit possession. A woman possessed of a male spirit could legitimately marry another woman, could remain unattached, and could dress and behave as a man. Similarly, a man possessed by a female spirit did not attract condemnation but could be an accepted part of the community. The Konso of Ethiopia had no fewer than four words for such "effeminate" men,

while among the Langa of Uganda, *jo apele* (impotents) were married by men, dressed as women, and purportedly simulated menstruation.

A man so possessed could in some cases win considerable respect if his ability to commune with powerful ancestors was thought to be effective. The first Portuguese to visit Angola found that such transvested "sodomites" were an apparently respected caste of *jin bandaa* or *quimbanda* (medicine men). Kirby also writes of an ancient tradition of "medicine men" among the Ovambo in Angola and Namibia. One of their ritual functions was to entice men who showed evidence of sexual uncertainty to come out, as it were, charging their clients for the service.

Male homosexuality with ritual connotations appears to have crossed the Atlantic with the slave ships in the sixteenth century to become a part of African-American culture: African "sodomites" were tortured and burnt at the stake during the Portuguese and Spanish Inquisitions in their colonial territories. The early-twentieth-century ethnographer Gunther Tessman also noted that anal intercourse among the Fang or Pangwe of Cameroon was imputed to have magical qualities in some cases, allowing the active partner to draw "medicine" for acquiring wealth from a friend who desired to share.

Colonialism and capitalism, as they spread throughout Africa at the turn of the nineteenth century, had contradictory effects on African sexuality. On the one hand, colonial rule put an end to many of the taboos, military traditions, and grand polygyny that once favored homosexual "play" in some societies. Christian ideologies and colonial laws meanwhile offered new injunctions against "unnatural acts," turning what had formerly been play into a crime punishable by death, a hundred lashes, or five years in prison. Colonial rule also weakened old men's monopoly on marriageable women. Young men and women were able to gain independent access to cash and hence to abscond from parental control or pay their own bride-price. In some of the new urban centers, a culture of conspicuous heterosexual consumption emerged in response to this freedom and against the other "emasculating" tendencies of colonial racism.

On the other hand, colonial regimes demanded vast amounts of cheap labor and set about to procure it in ways that frequently abetted homosexual behavior. Above all, they encouraged or compelled men to migrate to work while leaving the women and children behind in the rural areas. When the men had ceased to be useful, they were sent back to the "labor reserve," where women's labor supposedly maintained hearth and home. This benefited capital by justifying African men's less-than-subsistence wages, lack of pensions, or injury compensation; scrimping on building a proper urban infrastructure; and frustrating development of an organized, politically conscious proletariat.

In South Africa, where the migrant labor system became the most entrenched, cities and industrial centers were as much as 90 percent male. The men were typically housed in vast hostels or compounds where access to prostitutes let alone wives was extremely limited. The former, in short supply and high demand, tended to suffer from high rates of venereal disease. Entanglement with prostitutes was thus costly both in financial and health terms. For a migrant worker to take a town wife or prostitutes undermined his ability to maintain a rural household—the real source of his social standing and his only real insurance against injury, unemployment, and old age.

Under these circumstances, a common practice emerged of men taking young boys as "wives." Throughout southern Africa this was known as "mine marriage" (*bukhontxana, izinkotshana, ngochane*). The husband used the boy for sexual gratification as well as other domestic work. In return, the boy expected gifts and protection in a dangerous, alienating environment. Eventually, when the "wife" had saved a bit and was confident enough, he could leave the "marriage," possibly to acquire a "wife" of his own.

Male prostitution also emerged in the early years of colonial rule. This derived in part from the understanding that intracrural sex with males was safer than vaginal sex with prostitutes. From the sketchy testimony of repeat offenders in the colonial courts, it also appears that the anonymity of urban centers enabled the emergence of a gay minority—men who were exclusively homosexual by preference.

Thus traditions of homosexual behaviors and "sexual inversion" existed throughout sub-Saharan Africa prior to the coming of Europeans. The homosexual practices and identities that arose in the early colonial period also reflected indigenous expressions of sexuality in a rapidly changing context, rather than imitations of exotic behaviors, as some African chauvinists now declare.   *Marc Epprecht*

Bibliography

Bleys, Rudi C. *The Geography of Perversion: Male-to-Male Sexual Behaviour outside the West and the Ethnographic Imagination, 1750–1918.* New York: New York University Press, 1995.

Epprecht, Marc. "'Good God Almighty, What's This!' Homosexual "Crime" in Early Colonial Zimbabwe." In *African Homosexualities*, Stephen O. Murray and William Roscoe, eds. New York: St. Martin's Press, 1998.

———. "The 'Unsaying' of Homosexuality among Indigenous Black Zimbabweans: Mapping a Bias in a Patriarchy in Turmoil." Unpublished paper, University of Zimbabwe, 1997.

Evans-Pritchard, Edward E. "Sexual Inversion among the Azande." *American Anthropologist* 72 (1970): 1428–1434

———. *The Azande.* Oxford: Clarendon, 1971.

Garlake, Peter. *The Hunter's Vision.* London: British Museum, 1995.

Glasser, Clive. "The Mark of Zorro: Sexuality, Gender Relations and the Tsotsi Subculture on the Witwatersrand." *African Studies* 51:1 (1992): 47–67.

Herskovits, Melville. "A Note on 'Woman Marriage' in Dahomey." *Africa* 10 (1937): 335–341.

Junod, Henri. "Unnatural Vice in the Johannesburg Compounds." In *The Life of a South African Tribe,* vol. 1. New York: University Books, 1962.

Kendall. "Women in Lesotho and the (Western) Construction of Homophobia." In *Culture, Identity and Sexuality: Cross-cultural Perspectives on Women's Same-Sex Erotic Friendships.* Evelyn Blackwood and Saskia Wieringa, eds. New York: Columbia University Press, 1998.

Kirby, P. R. "A Secret Musical Instrument: The Ekola of the Ovakuanyama of Ovamboland." *South African Journal of Science* 38 (1942): 345–51.

Krige, Eileen J. "Woman-Marriage with Special Reference to the Lovedu." *Africa* 44 (1975): 11–36.

Livingstone, David and Charles. *Narrative of the Expedition to the Zambesi.* London: John Murray, 1865.

Maquet, Jacques. *The Premise of Inequality in Rwanda.* London: Oxford University Press, 1961.

Moodie, T. D., with V. Ndatse. *Going for Gold: Men's Lives in the Mines.* Berkeley: University of California Press, 1994.

Nadel, Siegfried. *The Nuba.* Oxford: Oxford University Press, 1947.

———. *A Black Byzantium: The Kingom of Nupe in Nigeria.* Oxford: Oxford University Press, 1951.

Oosterhof, J. "Sodomy and Sea and the Cape of Good Hope during the 18th Century." *Journal of Homosexuality* 18:2 (1988).

Sweet, James H. "Male Homosexuality and Spiritism in the African Diaspora: The Legacies of a Link." *Journal of the History of Sexuality* 7:2 (1996): 184–202.

See also Colonialism; Kenya; South Africa; Zimbabwe

African American Gay Culture

Although it is difficult to pinpoint something as untraceable as the emergence of a culture, there can be little argument that the beginnings of a recognizable tradition of African American gay men's culture can be found in the explosion of black creativity that has come to be called the Harlem Renaissance. The number of major figures in this movement considered to have been either gay or bisexual is startling. They include most notably Countee Cullen, Alain Locke, Claude McKay, Wallace Thurman, Richard Bruce Nugent, and, arguably, Langston Hughes. Nugent's short stories "Sadji" and "Smoke, Lilies, and Jade" are generally considered to be the premier texts in African American gay literature, and Wallace Thurman's novel *Infants of the Spring* offers the first explicit representation of a gay black man in African American literature.

Although a number of gay black writers achieved public recognition, most notably Willard Motley and Owen Dodson, James Baldwin was the first African American writer to consistently present homosexual themes and characters in his work. But his depictions of black gay men cannot be read as in any way celebratory. He was soon followed, however, by science fiction writer Samuel Delany, who more explicitly and positively explored alternative sexualities although more often than not leaving black men out of the picture until relatively late in his career. The emergence of a self-defined and self-consciously black gay aesthetic can be seen with the publication of two landmark anthologies of gay black men's writing—*In the Life: A Black Gay Anthology* (1986), edited by Joseph Beam, and *Brother to Brother: New Writings by Black Gay Men* (1991), edited by Essex Hemphill. Most of the directions taken in subsequent gay black men's writing can be discerned in the work collected in these volumes as well as in that promoted and generated by the black gay writers collective Other Countries, established in New York City in the early 1980s.

It is not surprising that literature would be an area in which gay black expressiveness would first reveal itself. Less expected, however, is the extent to which the black church has also served as a sanctuary in which many gay men could lead relatively open lives and express their personalities despite the church's putative rejection of homosexuality as a sin. The commonplace and often satirized notion of the black church as a haven for "sissies" was reflected in the rejection of Christianity that was one of the key components of black nationalism in the 1960s, as evidenced by the homophobic pronouncements regularly issued by such key nationalist figures as LeRoi Jones (Amiri Baraka) and Eldridge Cleaver. Unfortunately, this homophobia has been taken up wholesale in the discourse of Afrocentricity into which black nationalism has metamorphosed and the often Afrocentrically inspired notions of community that one finds in much rap music. Relying on historically and anthropologically falsified images of a monolithically heterosexual "Africa," Afrocentricity keeps in circulation the notion of the "unnaturalness" of black homosexuals consistently challenged by modern gay black men's writing, art, and filmmaking.

Until the emergence of the contemporary gay black scene, those gay black men who chose to live uncloseted lives and still function within the public sphere were usually forced to compromise by wielding influence through the mediation of a more acceptably heterosexual figure as can be seen most obviously in the lives and careers of civil rights activist Bayard Rustin, who strategically avoided the spotlight throughout his career, and jazz composer Billy Strayhorn, much of whose work was presented to the public as having been created by his mentor, Duke Ellington. Marlon Riggs's documentary *Tongues Untied* and the controversy surrounding its broadcast on national television, Riggs's sequel, *Black Is . . . Black Ain't*, and Jennie Livingston's *Paris Is Burning* brought gay black men's culture unprecedented prominence and decisively signaled the end of black gay invisibility.

As Riggs wrote of his own success, "Negro faggotry *is* in vogue." The popularity of E. Lynn Harris's best-selling novels *Invisible Life* and *Just As I Am* with both heterosexual and gay black readers and the success of the transgendered performer RuPaul indicate the extent to which gay black expression has, however problematically and

A

stereotypically for now, entered the mainstream of American popular culture. This is especially apparent when RuPaul's multimedia omnipresence is contrasted with that of some of the similarly gender-ambiguous performers who preceded "him," such as Little Richard and the disco superstar Sylvester.

Much of the work of contemporary gay men has been both to clarify the real continuities and to articulate the real differences between gay black men's culture and the African American and the often racist gay white communities between which African American gay men are uncomfortably situated. Keith Boykin's *One More River to Cross: Black and Gay in America* is a particularly important attempt to articulate this position. Only within the climate created by post-Stonewall gay activism and the rise of the disco movement of the 1970s and the flooding into the commercial mainstream of gay style and sensibilities was the ground set for the emergence of black gay men's culture and the sensitive and unapologetic representation of gay black men's lives. This emergence was slowed down but not destroyed by the onset of the AIDS epidemic, which hit the gay black community especially hard for reasons related primarily to the way in which information about the crisis was structured and disseminated. Black males make up only 6 percent of the U.S. population, yet as many as 23 percent of those with the disease have been African American men.

Although much still needs to be done, it is a long road that leads from the tragic image of the gay black hustler presented in Shirley Jackson's 1967 documentary *Portrait of Jason* to the self-loving expressiveness of contemporary songwriter and performer Blackberri.   *Terry Rowden*

Bibliography

Beam, Joseph, ed. *In the Life: A Black Gay Anthology*. Boston: Alyson, 1986.

Hemphill, Essex, ed. *Brother to Brother: New Writings by Black Gay Men*. Boston: Alyson, 1991.

See also Ailey, Alvin; Baldwin, James; Beam, Joseph; Black and White Men Together; Black Power Movement; Cullen, Countee; Delaney, Samuel R.; Disco; Dove, Ulysses; Hemphill, Essex; Hughes, Langston; Jones, Bill T.; McKay, Claude; Pomo Afro Homos; Riggs, Marlon; Rousseve, David; Rustin, Bayard; Saint, Assoto; Strayhorn, Billy; Sylvester; Thurman, Wallace; Voguing

Aging

Gay gerontology has become a well-established field of research only in the past two decades. Prior to 1980, scholarly research on aging was almost oblivious to the existence of older gays and lesbians. Even today there are college texts devoid of any reference to gay aging, making these elders invisible to generations of graduate therapists and counselors in fields serving seniors. With no shortage of popular mythology about the "sorry state" of old homosexuals, fictional literature often supports such a gloomy view. Meanwhile, the "liberated" gay subcultures of North America (and often elsewhere) remain youth-obsessed, and many younger homosexuals consider the "elders of their tribe" to be unfortunate figures, lonely and bitter at best, predators on youth ("chicken hawks") at worst.

Much of the gay media that has mushroomed since 1970 is heavily slanted toward youth. Advertising in gay community newspapers is heavily weighted with images of gays and lesbians under thirty. In gay novels and periodicals, younger gay and lesbian readers are often subtly—and sometimes not so subtly—exposed to an image of their own future in which thirty is old and forty is "over the hill." Although there are some positive images, such as the aging gay detective Dave Brandsetter in Joseph Hansen's mysteries, major gay novels like Andrew Holleran's 1996 novel, *The Beauty of Men*, still portray gay aging as a frightening prospect.

A counterculture of gay aging has slowly emerged to battle these myths with positive images of older lesbians and gay "daddies." With a little effort, it is possible to obtain gay pornography featuring older models. More gay autobiographies and journals are available, providing histories of a positive gay maturity, such as Alan Helms's *Young Man from the Provinces* (1994) or the controversial but charmingly camp writings of Quentin Crisp. However, in the gay subculture of bars, discos, baths, and other specifically gay facilities, most men find it a severe disadvantage to show signs of aging. Some gay telephone dating lines compel users to classify themselves by age, and those in the older categories often do not get messages.

Early scientific research on gay aging varies in its conclusions. Some studies supported the argument that homosexuals adjust well to age, while others argued theories such as "accelerated aging"—the notion that homosexuals experience the effects of aging at an earlier chronological age than do heterosexuals. Indeed, age forty was often the baseline

Growing old gracefully. Photo by Marc Geller.

for recruiting a "scientific" sample of "older homosexuals." Forty is still the base recruiting age of many gay organizations for elders, such as Prime Timers.

One of the consequences of the period immediately after Stonewall was a variety of attempts to compensate for previous antigay images by actually suggesting that homosexuals enjoyed "advantages" over heterosexuals in adjusting to old age. Theories such as "crisis competence" argued that homosexuals who survived to old age had overcome more life crises than most heterosexuals, and so were better able to deal with stresses of aging. Today a more moderate position is usual: on key issues of health, friendship, and satisfaction with life, older homosexuals do not appear to differ significantly from the general population.

Gays and lesbians in most metropolitan urban centers have worked to build "institutionally complete" communities, in which a range of services from food stores, restaurants, travel agencies, and physicians to legal, accounting, and counseling services are available from gay-positive suppliers. The "gay yellow pages" of such cities list a wide range of services; yet services for older homosexuals remain glaringly underdeveloped. Remarkably few gay urban subcultures offer a range of programs for

gay seniors even remotely comparable to services available for heterosexuals (or gays who pass as straight). There are few travel programs for elders and even fewer gay and lesbian retirement facilities. In 1996, the friends of Harry Hay, one of the early heroes of gay liberation, were compelled to issue an international appeal in the *Journal of Homosexuality* for funds to help Hay and his lover with the poverty that besets many gay elders.

The majority of gay elders now over fifty were teenagers or young adults in the 1930s to 1960s, a period in which it was risky and rare to be openly gay. Gays and lesbians of that period tended to absorb a hatred of homosexuality from the dominant heterosexist culture and thus frequently failed to develop pride in their own gay identity. In spite of gay liberation, many of these elders have remained closeted and self-effacing. Large numbers of gay elders have not found gay liberation particularly helpful to their own lives, remaining isolated from gay community organizations, where they expect to feel unwelcome. Some even resent the way gay liberation destroyed the underground gay culture of pre-Stonewall days.

The Stonewall generation of gay and lesbians now reaching middle age spent their young adulthood becoming more comfortable with their sexual orientation. Many learned to expect and demand social rights and services equal to those of heterosexuals. Meanwhile, a paradoxical mix of events ranging from gay pride days to "respectable" campaigns for AIDS relief has made society at large somewhat more tolerant of homosexuals. Large numbers of middle-aged gays today have marched, protested, and served as activists and leaders in gay communities. As gay and lesbian elders in the new millennium, they are not likely to settle for the second-class status imposed on the older homosexuals of the 1980s and 1990s.

While many aspects of gay life are still changing, some have remained the same for centuries. One of the most interesting is the love relationship between two gays or lesbians of widely different chronological ages—the intergenerational relationship. Modern gerontology clearly distinguishes between chronological and other measures of age (e.g., biological, psychological). Sometimes a person of twenty-five or thirty prefers the company of someone much older who has the benefit of years of experience and qualities of maturity, wisdom, and stability not commonly found among young people. Meanwhile, an older person may feel much younger than his years in comparison with the energy levels, sports and hobbies, and lifestyle interest of his peers.

The intergenerational partnership that results when such individuals meet can greatly benefit both. Unfortunately, the ageism still widespread in gay communities has tended to devalue these partnerships, applying labels such as "sugar daddy" for the elder and "gold digger" for the younger, as if the only purpose of these relationships were economic. Partnerships such as those between novelist Christopher Isherwood and artist Don Bachardy, which began when Isherwood was near fifty and Bachardy only eighteen and which endured until Isherwood's death more than thirty years later, demonstrate that much more than money is involved.

In addition, the near absence of gay and lesbian elders from the communal experience of younger homosexuals deprives them of suitable role models. Typical young heterosexuals have no lack of elders on which to pattern their adjustment to basic life issues such as education, work, vocation, friendship, marriage, and aging. The younger heterosexual can see what it is like to become a parent, teacher, manager, or spouse. Many younger homosexuals are denied these guides to growth and development. One of their teachers may be gay, but no one in the class is likely to know it. Perhaps the person who represents their vocational ideal is gay and even mentioned in the history books; but the fact of being gay has almost always been erased from the official history. It remains for older gays, especially those who have lived a happy and successful life, including full acceptance of their sexuality, to provide younger gays with role models wherever possible.

The burst of interest in and publishing about gay gerontology during the 1980s has subsided, and there is presently a lull in research that cannot be entirely explained by a general cutback in funding. Lee's *Gay Midlife and Maturity* was the last sociological contribution to the field. Only three psychotherapeutic studies have been published since, and nothing of a general nature that would bring the problems of gay aging to the attention of growing gay communities, much less attract the scientists in gerontology. Symptomatic of the lull, a second edition of Berger's *Gay and Gray* (1982) was published in 1996 with a new foreword, but the rest of the book is the 1982 version, which is based on 1970s research. Research remains to be done to examine both the condition of today's elders and the changes coming as "liberated" generations of gays and lesbians approach retirement.   *John Alan Lee*

Bibliography

Berger, Raymond M. *Gay and Gray*, 2d ed. Binghamton, N.Y.: Haworth, 1996.

Brecher, Edward M., et al. *Love, Sex, and Aging.* Boston: Little, Brown, 1984.

Grube, John. "Natives and Settlers." In Lee, *Gay Midlife and Maturity.*

Lee, John Alan, ed. *Gay Midlife and Maturity.* Binghamton, N.Y.: Haworth, 1991.

———. "A Conversation with Don Bachardy." *Christopher Street* 112 (1987).

See also Bear Culture; Couples; Crisp, Quentin; Gay Relationships; Isherwood, Christopher; Pederasty

AIDS

Acquired Immunodeficiency Syndrome (AIDS) is a disorder characterized by a severe suppression of the immune system that renders the human body susceptible to a variety of normally manageable infections, cancers, and other illnesses. The syndrome is caused by the Human Immunodeficiency Virus (HIV), a retrovirus of unknown origin that primarily infects and destroys white blood cells (particularly a type known as T lymphocytes, or T cells), which help clear disease-causing microbes from the bloodstream. In addition, HIV directly infects other cells in the central nervous system, the digestive tract, and other sites in the body. There are actually two different versions of HIV: HIV-1 and the far less common and somewhat less harmful HIV-2, found mainly in West Africa. In the absence of further clarification, the generic use of the term HIV almost universally refers to HIV-1, although both versions can cause AIDS.

While commonly referred to as being of epidemic proportions, AIDS is pandemic as it is found throughout the world. By 1996, approximately half a million AIDS cases had been reported in the United States, with another quarter-million people believed to be infected with HIV. The comparable worldwide estimates are some five million AIDS cases and twenty million HIV infections. In the developed world, as many as 50 percent of people with HIV/AIDS have been gay men.

Pathology and Treatment

Once introduced into the human body, HIV replicates inside white blood cells using an enzyme called reverse transcriptase. The virus releases new copies of itself into the bloodstream and, in the process, kills the cell. The multiple newly created copies of the viruses then infect additional white blood cells, continuing the cycle and spreading the infection. AIDS is not a single disease per se but a diagnostic category created by the U.S. Centers for Disease Control and Prevention (CDC). For individuals with HIV who are thirteen years or older, a diagnosis of clinical AIDS is made when there is an abnormally low count of one type of T cell (the CD4 cell). The drop in T cell count can occur in one of two ways: the absolute count per cubic millimeter of blood can drop from the normal range of 600 to 1,000 down to below 200, or CD4 cells can account for less than 14 percent of all lymphocytes.

An AIDS diagnosis can also be made whenever a person with HIV experiences one or more of 25 "AIDS-defining illnesses." Among the most common illnesses are opportunistic infections caused by protozoa, fungi, bacteria, or other viruses that are normally held in check by the immune system but that an immunocompromised body is unable to combat. The chief opportunistic infections are *Pneumocystis carinii* pneumonia, cytomegalovirus, *Mycobacterium avium* complex, herpes, tuberculosis, toxoplasmosis, histoplasmosis, salmonellosis, candidiasis, cryptosporidiosis, cryptococcosis, coccidiodomycosis, and, in women, microsporidiosis. A variety of cancers, including lymphoma, Kaposi's sarcoma, and, in women, invasive cervical cancer, are also associated with AIDS. Further, severe loss of lean body mass (wasting) can result from the direct infection by HIV of the gastrointestinal tract. Direct HIV infection of the nervous system can cause encephalopathy (dementia), peripheral neuropathy, and other neurological complications. The immediate cause of death in people with AIDS is usually related to the effects of an opportunistic infection or cancer rather than to HIV itself. Effects of opportunistic infections are wide-ranging and can cause such severe conditions as loss of motor control, blindness, neuropathy, hearing impairment, and seizures.

The course of disease progression from initial HIV infection to clinical AIDS varies dramatically among individuals, owing to a range of factors in the genetic and immunological makeup of the infected individual, the particular strain of HIV with which he or she is infected, and the quality of primary health care, as well as other possible but as yet unknown biochemical cofactors. Shortly after infection with HIV, many people experience "seroconversion syndrome," characterized by acute flulike symptoms as HIV first overwhelms the immune system before being brought back under control. A period of clinical latency typically follows during which most people are asymptomatic or have relatively minor symptoms such as night sweats, diarrhea, and skin rashes.

The clinical latency period can range from around two years to over fifteen, with the mean time around ten years. Research has indicated that, despite the appearance of general health, the body's immune system itself is at nearly constant war with HIV, with billions of new T cells and billions of new copies of the virus being created daily. As blood tests indicate declining immune function, many individuals are put on prophylactic medications designed to ward off the opportunistic infections to which they are becoming increasingly susceptible. While a small percentage of individuals with HIV seem never to progress to AIDS at all, the vast majority develop AIDS-defining illnesses over time.

As of late 1998, there was no "cure" for AIDS in the sense of a treatment that could completely neutralize HIV or totally eliminate it from the body. The first antiretroviral drug approved for use against HIV was the highly toxic substance zidovudine, or AZT. By 1996, however, standard therapy against HIV had become the combined use of three antiretroviral drugs. The most commonly used antiretroviral drugs were five nucleoside analogs reverse transcriptase inhibitors (AZT, ddI, ddC, 3TC, and D4T) and the three protease inhibitors (saquinivir, indinavir, and ritonavir). In early tests, the combined use of nucleoside analogs, protease inhibitors, and other antiretroviral drugs, all of which attack the virus at different points in its replication cycle, produced a dramatic lowering in the level of HIV, or "viral load," detectable in the blood of many patients.

As of mid-1998, protease inhibitors had realized much of their promise, with the death rate from AIDS in some areas dropping by as much as 60 to 80 percent and the occurrence of new opportunistic infections also greatly diminished. However, early concerns that multiple-drug-resistant strains of the virus might begin to be transmitted were beginning to be borne out; by mid-1998 there were at least two known cases of an individual becoming newly infected with a strain of HIV which is already resistant to all available antiviral drugs. Further, there is increasing evidence that the antiviral medications themselves may exact a heavy toll on people with AIDS, including liver damage, redistribution of

A body fat from limbs to torso, and cardiac conditions. And, finally, while it appears to be possible to dramatically reduce viral load, total reversal of infection, or "eradication of the virus" remains purely theoretical, in part because HIV is able to remain in latent form in certain cells.

In addition to antiretroviral combination therapy, a wide variety of prophylactic regimens and other treatments for opportunistic infections and cancers are standard for people with AIDS, notably drugs like acyclovir for the suppression of herpes and Bactrim or other antibiotics to prevent pneumonia. Research has been undertaken toward a vaccine for HIV as well as toward other "immune-based" therapies aimed at boosting the body's own defenses rather than at attacking HIV directly. A variety of complementary or alternative treatments are also frequently employed, such as holistic, traditional Chinese, and Ayurvedic medicines.

Transmission and Prevention

HIV is transmitted by three principal routes: from mother to child, through blood-to-blood contact, and via sexual contact. Maternal transmission can occur *in utero,* during delivery through the birth canal, or through breast milk. Evidence has emerged that the use of antiretroviral therapy during pregnancy can reduce the risk of maternal transmission from about one in four to fewer than one in ten.

Blood-to-blood transmission occurred in numerous cases early in the epidemic through direct transfusion of infected blood or blood products, notably the clotting factors needed by hemophiliacs. However, since the institution of routine screening for HIV in 1985, blood transfusions have rarely caused HIV transmission in the United States. Blood-to-blood transmission also occurs, albeit very rarely, as a result of accidental exposures such as blood splashes in health-care settings.

The most common mode of blood-to-blood HIV transmission occurs through the sharing of unsterilized hypodermic needles and syringes by injecting drug users. HIV is transmitted not just on the tip of the needle but also in the syringe itself, since a small quantity of blood normally backs up into the syringe after all the drug has been injected. Because in many parts of the world, the supply of needles and syringes is tightly controlled by prohibitionist drug laws, many injecting drug users are forced to share their "works" with others, essentially inoculating themselves with the virus and causing very high rates of transmission that could largely be eliminated by making needles freely available. In the absence of needle-exchange programs, some public health outreach efforts have focused on teaching at-risk populations to clean drug paraphernalia with bleach, although the actual effectiveness of such cleaning methods has been seriously questioned. Injecting drug users frequently pass along the virus not only to their drug-using partners but also to their sexual partners and, directly or indirectly, to their children.

Sexual transmission, by far the most common mode of transmission, can occur whenever the HIV-infected bodily fluids of one person have direct contact with the mucous membranes or the broken skin of an uninfected person. The most infectious bodily fluids are blood, semen, and vaginal/cervical secretions, all of which have been proven to transmit the virus. Although HIV has been isolated in saliva, tears, and certain other bodily fluids, it is usually found in quantities so low that these and other secretions probably cannot normally transmit the virus. The mucous membranes most commonly implicated in HIV transmission are those of the rectum and the vagina, although transmission does sometimes occur through the mouth, the urethra, and, in uncircumcised men, the head of the penis. Because HIV must be introduced directly into the bloodstream for infection to occur, and because the virus dies quickly outside the human body, the risk of infection through routine casual contact or less intimate sexual behaviors appears to range between minimal and nonexistent.

Over time, a rough hierarchy of sexual risk behaviors has been discerned. The highest risk is posed by anal or vaginal intercourse, particularly for the receptive partner. Oral sex poses a lower but nonetheless significant risk, again particularly for the receptive partner. Other sexual behaviors, such as kissing and frottage (nonpenetrative rubbing), are considered low- or perhaps even no-risk. The presence of cuts, tears, or lesions (such as those caused by sexually transmitted diseases) in mucous membranes or skin can significantly increase the risk of transmission by providing HIV more ready access into the body. Epidemiological evidence suggests (although it cannot conclusively prove) that the great majority of HIV-positive gay men were infected through receptive anal intercourse; the remainder may have been infected through insertive anal intercourse, receptive oral sex, heterosexual contact, injecting drug use, or by other routes.

Of all sexual behaviors, receptive anal intercourse creates the most efficient route for sexual transmission of HIV. This is because the mucous membranes of the rectum are relatively delicate and thus easily torn during intercourse, providing multiple points of entry for the virus from the semen of the infected partner into the bloodstream of the uninfected one. Studies have demonstrated that sexual transmission of HIV can be almost completely prevented by the consistent and correct use of latex condoms with water-based lubricants during anal or vaginal intercourse. (Animal-skin condoms prevent pregnancy but not HIV transmission, while oil-based lubricants can cause latex to crack.)

HIV prevention campaigns, particularly within the gay community, have been built largely upon the singular message that condoms must be used for each and every act of intercourse with a partner who is known to be HIV-positive or whose HIV status is unknown. In practice, however, sustaining "safer sex" over a lifetime has proven to be a difficult challenge for many people, particularly when individuals are under the disinhibiting and judgment-impairing influence of alcohol or other drugs. Further, outreach campaigns to gay men have often overlooked particular subpopulations, such as closeted men and bisexual men, or promoted messages that were ineffective for certain ethnic or racial subpopulations. In addition, there are practical concerns, such as that condoms are sometimes not available during impromptu sexual encounters, sometimes rupture or slip off during intercourse, and, for many people, create a psychological barrier to full sexual intimacy with a regular partner.

While fellatio poses little or no risk to the partner on whom it is being performed, the partner who is performing the fellatio definitely can become infected, especially if the act is taken to the point of ejaculation into the mouth. This risk can be essentially eliminated if a condom is worn, but condom use during oral sex is widely considered to radically diminish the quality of the experience for both partners. Alternatively, the active partner may avoid putting the head of the penis in his mouth, although this also reduces the intensity of the experience. Most commonly, the partners may attempt to withdraw the penis before ejaculation. Even if successfully enacted, however, the withdrawal strategy leaves open the possibility of contact with pre-ejaculatory fluid, which is probably also capable of transmitting HIV. Another popular form of oral sex among gay men, oral-anal contact, or "rimming," has not been demonstrated to cause HIV transmission but does present a high risk of exposure to intestinal parasites and other microbes that can cause serious illness, particularly in the immunocompromised.

Overall, the risk of HIV transmission through oral sex appears to be considerably lower than anal or vaginal intercourse because, among other factors, of the relative impermeability of the mucous membranes of the mouth and the presence of HIV-inhibiting substances in the saliva. Nonetheless, it is absolutely clear that oral sex can transmit the virus. It is also possible that cases of transmission via oral sex have been undercounted because standard epidemiological practice has been to assume that any HIV-positive person who has had unprotected intercourse became infected that way rather than through oral sex.

Because it represents such a gray area, oral sex has been the source of stormy controversy within the gay male community. Proponents of a "harm-elimination" model have argued that, since there is some level of risk involved, all unprotected oral sex must be avoided. Their counterparts from the "harm-reduction" perspective have emphasized the relative unlikeliness of this route of transmission and the need to focus attention on reducing incidents of unprotected anal intercourse.

Emergence in the Gay Community

In the developed world, AIDS was first identified among gay men in major urban centers; in the developing world it has primarily afflicted heterosexuals. The first signs of the epidemic were detected in 1981 by officials at the U.S. Centers for Disease Control and Prevention, who noted an unusual increase in incidence of *Pneumocystis carinii* pneumonia and Kaposi's sarcoma, two previously rare conditions that are among the most common AIDS opportunistic infections. Because of its perceived concentration among gay men, the syndrome now called AIDS was initially known as "gay cancer" or "Gay-Related Immune Deficiency" (GRID).

It soon became clear that the new syndrome was most commonly found among men associated with a "fast-lane" lifestyle including heavy drug use and frequent sex with multiple partners in gay bathhouses and other public sex environments. Some early theories of causation centered around the use of nitrate inhalants ("poppers") and other street drugs. Other theories recognized the possibility of sexual transmission.

The new syndrome was soon running rampant through such large gay male communities as New

York's Greenwich Village and San Francisco's Castro district. Because of the long clinical latency period between HIV infection and the appearance of first symptoms, many thousands of gay men were infected long before the first AIDS cases were identified. In the early to mid-1980s, entire social networks of gay men began simultaneously to take sick and begin dying. Amid such a siegelike atmosphere, gay communities throughout the developed world soon developed self-help networks and service agencies, preeminently Gay Men's Health Crisis (GMHC) in New York City, to provide treatment information, palliative care, support services, and safer-sex education.

The early years of the epidemic were most thoroughly documented by *San Francisco Chronicle* reporter Randy Shilts in his 1987 book, *And the Band Played On*. From the perspective of Shilts and many others, the epidemic was allowed to spiral out of control because of the hostility and indifference of the government and the society at large alongside mass denial from within some sectors of the gay community. Few mainstream politicians and policymakers were willing to grapple with the sensitive issues of sexuality inevitably raised by the epidemic. Indeed, President Ronald Reagan (1981–1989) did not even publicly mention AIDS by name until

1987. At the same time, many gay leaders, still influenced by the 1970s ethos of sexual liberation and deep suspicion of officialdom, initially refused to support bathhouse closure or endorse safer-sex practices.

Eventually, it became clear that grassroots prevention efforts had succeeded in effectuating mass behavioral changes that dramatically curbed the rate of new infections among gay men. One San Francisco study, for instance, found a 90 percent drop in sexual risk behaviors among gay men between 1978 and 1985. The best available data on overall rates of HIV infection among gay men in the U.S., from studies conducted by the University of California at San Francisco, indicate that between 1987 and 1997 the prevalence of HIV among gay men in New York, Los Angeles, San Francisco, and Chicago dropped by about two-thirds, from as high as 50 percent to around 15 percent, although the drop was more marked among white men than among men of color.

Despite an ever-expanding death toll in the gay community—as well as among hemophiliacs, injecting drug users, and some other populations—public attention to the AIDS epidemic was scant until 1985, when film star Rock Hudson died of AIDS. The connection of the disease to a high-profile, heterosexually perceived celebrity is widely regarded

Participants in a 1991 AIDS Memorial in San Francisco. Photo by Marc Geller.

as being the catalytic event that brought AIDS to the forefront of national debate. As fears of a "heterosexual epidemic" spread, however, antigay attitudes became more pronounced and numerous right-wing public figures called for coercive public health measures such as mandatory HIV testing, aggressive contact tracing, and involuntary quarantine for all those who tested positive. Many conservative religious leaders continued to describe AIDS as divine retribution for sexual transgressions. Rather than being perceived as the innocent victims of a viral infection, many gay (and, particularly, bisexual) men with AIDS were instead regarded as potential vectors of incurable disease into the general population.

In an explosive response fueled by fear and rage, gay men, along with lesbian, bisexual, and heterosexual allies, began expanding their efforts beyond support services and prevention activism to outspoken protest through demonstrations and direct actions. In 1987, the flagship of AIDS protest organizations, ACT UP (AIDS Coalition to Unleash Power) was launched in New York City. In short order, new chapters were formed throughout the United States, Canada, and western Europe that undertook dramatic street protests aimed at government officials, public health agencies, and pharmaceutical companies. Among the goals of ACT UP and other protest groups were increased funding for treatment and research, faster drug approval processes, and expanded prevention efforts. ACT UP maintained a commitment to radical democratic practices that made it extraordinarily flexible and innovative but also highly decentralized and organizationally chaotic.

Inevitably, the impact of the AIDS epidemic was also powerfully felt in the social and cultural realms. Gay male fiction, poetry, dance, performance art, music, theater, and other arts became suffused with images of pain, loss, decay, and death. At points, gay male arts and artists became nearly synonymous with AIDS. Among the landmark works of AIDS-related gay literature have been Larry Kramer's *The Normal Heart* and *Reports from the Holocaust: The Making of an AIDS Activist*; Paul Monette's *Borrowed Time: An AIDS Memoir;* Tony Kushner's *Angels in America* plays; Andrew Holleran's *Ground Zero*; and Terence McNally's *Love! Valour! Compassion!* AIDS-themed works in the visual arts have been produced by gay artists such as photographer Robert Mapplethorpe, Keith Haring, and the Gran Fury art collective. Other prominent gay artists grappling with AIDS have

been dancer/choreographer Bill T. Jones and performance artist David Wojnarowicz. Among the most common artistic images evoking the epidemic are red ribbons worn for AIDS awareness, the massive AIDS Memorial Quilt, and the pink triangle symbol above the slogan "Silence = Death."

In retrospect, the late 1980s represented the high-water mark of AIDS activism. By the early 1990s, AIDS was increasingly becoming "normalized." While the feared large-scale heterosexual epidemic never fully materialized in the developed world, the 1991 disclosure by basketball star Magic Johnson that he had tested HIV-positive had an impact comparable to that of Rock Hudson's disclosure six years earlier. AIDS became somewhat destigmatized as people became less concerned about contracting HIV through casual contact. With many of their goals realized and their ranks depleted by ongoing death, ACT UP and other protest groups grew moribund.

On the political front, high hopes that the administration of President Bill Clinton would launch a Manhattan Project to find a cure for AIDS went unfulfilled, although Clinton did pay far more attention to HIV/AIDS than had either Reagan or Bush. Overall, however, the epidemic began to level off among gay men even as it became ever more thoroughly entrenched among poor urban populations of color. By the mid-1990s, advances in the treatment of opportunistic infections and other AIDS complications had helped to foster a sense that AIDS was becoming a chronic, manageable, perhaps survivable disease. The introduction of protease inhibitors in 1996 magnified this sense, even leading some to predict that the epidemic was slowly grinding to a halt, or at least that the "crisis" phase of AIDS had passed.

While undeniably optimistic, many AIDS professionals also saw dangers in the more relaxed attitude of many gay men toward the risk of HIV infection. Evidence emerged that some older gay men were relapsing into earlier unsafe behaviors, while other young gay men, who had not witnessed the effects of AIDS firsthand, were forming a second wave of new infections. Some forward-looking researchers raised concerns that the epidemic might become worse than ever if mutant strains of HIV developed that were multiply drug resistant, more easily transmitted, and/or more virulent. In 1997, journalist Gabriel Rotello sparked a huge controversy with his book *Sexual Ecology*, which argued that 1970s-style patterns of sex with larger numbers of partners will always create biological conditions that promote epidemics of sexually transmitted disease, whether caused by HIV or other microbes.

Whether or not AIDS continues in the direction of becoming a chronic, manageable illness, the epidemic has made an indelible impact on the course of gay history. Surfacing at a time when gay men and lesbians were making their first tentative forays onto the public scene, AIDS forced a societywide recognition that homosexuality was a common phenomenon and that virtually everyone had relatives, friends, or acquaintances who were gay. Despite many significant backlashes against the gay community, the social response to AIDS has on the whole been balanced, with the most extreme and coercive proposals of right-wing forces rarely enacted.

Yet if the epidemic has forced a beneficial recognition of the reality of homosexuality and begrudging acceptance of gay communities in the United States and other developed countries, it has come at a high cost. The human toll of the AIDS epidemic in terms of pain, suffering, death, and mourning has been incalculable among gay men and all others affected by so devastating a disease. The deeper scars left upon the collective psyche of the community can only be guessed at now but will continue to be felt for decades to come.

Raymond A. Smith

Bibliography

Baker, R. *The Art of AIDS*. New York: Continuum, 1994.

Bayer, Ronald. *Private Acts, Social Consequences: AIDS and the Politics of Public Health*. New York: Free Press, 1989.

Cohen, P. T., M. A. Sande, and P. A. Volberding, eds. *The AIDS Knowledge Base*. Waltham, Mass.: Medical Publishing Group, 1990.

Burkett, Elinor. *The Gravest Show on Earth: America in the Age of AIDS*. Boston: Houghton Mifflin, 1995.

Fan, Hung, Ross Conner, and Luis Villarreal. *The Biology of AIDS*, 2d ed. Boston: Jones and Bartlett, 1991.

Fee, Elizabeth, and Daniel M. Fox. *AIDS: The Burdens of History*. Berkeley, Calif.: University of California Press, 1988.

Grmek, Mirko D. *History of AIDS: Emergence and Origin of a Modern Pandemic*. Princeton, N.J.: Princeton University Press, 1990.

Joseph, Stephen C. *Dragon Within the Gates: The Once and Future AIDS Epidemic*. New York: Carroll and Graf, 1992.

Kübler-Ross, Elisabeth. *AIDS: The Ultimate Challenge*. New York: Macmillan, 1987.

McKenzie, M. F. *The AIDS Reader: Social, Political, Ethical Issues*. New York: Meridian, 1991.

Miller, James. *Fluid Exchanges: Artists and Critics in the AIDS Crisis*. Toronto: University of Toronto Press, 1992.

Panem, Sandra. *The AIDS Bureaucracy*. Cambridge, Mass.: Harvard University Press, 1988.

Perrow, Charles, and Mauro F. Guillen. *The AIDS Disaster: The Failure of Organizations in New York and the Nation*. New Haven: Yale University Press, 1990.

Rotello, Gabriel. *Sexual Ecology: AIDS and the Destiny of Gay Men*. New York: Dutton, 1997.

Shilts, Randy. *And the Band Played On: Politics, People, and the AIDS Epidemic*. New York: St. Martin's Press, 1987.

Sontag, Susan. *AIDS and Its Metaphors*. New York: Farrar, Straus, and Giroux, 1988

Vaid, Urvashi. *Virtual Equality: The Mainstreaming of Gay and Lesbian Liberation*. New York: Anchor Books, 1995.

Vaucher, A. R. *Muses From Chaos and Ash: AIDS, Artists, and Art*. New York: Grove Press, 1993.

See also ACT UP; AIDS in the U.S. Media; AIDS Literature; AIDS Organizations, U.S.; AIDS Performance; Dance and AIDS; Gran Fury; Haring, Keith; Kramer, Larry; Kushner, Tony; McNally, Terrence; NAMES Project AIDS Memorial Quilt; Sexually Transmitted Diseases

AIDS in the U.S. Media

From 1980 to 1985, the U.S. media's coverage of the AIDS epidemic was sporadic; in 1985–88, it soared to a high level of public hysteria and panic; 1987–92 marked a focused attention on treatment issues; and the coverage since 1992 can best be described as the moment of normalization. The urgency about the epidemic has disappeared in the media because of the significant decline of coverage since 1992, while the clinical, social, and political uncertainties surrounding it continue domestically and globally.

Research suggests that the coverage of AIDS in the U.S. media can generally be characterized in the following ways:

1. The language of reporting tends to be euphemistic (as in 1994, "the exchange of bodily fluids"), mystifying (as in "guilty victims," "general population"), and sometimes inaccurate (as in the "AIDS test").
2. Short-lived and often decontextualized reporting triggered by specific and highly "newsworthy" events (such as the stories concerning Rock Hudson, Kimberly Bergalis, Magic Johnson, and Greg Louganis, as well as blood contamination stories) outweighs in-depth and analytical reporting.
3. Reporting latches onto and perpetuates fixed social and symbolic hierarchies (e.g., innocent/guilty, heterosexual/homosexual, exposed/closeted, First World/Third World).
4. By convention and by myth, AIDS is still linked to homosexuality as a *foundation* (as both cause and effect) of the crisis.
5. The image of gay men infected with the virus is consistently cast in stereotypical ways: (a) they are "burned out" by their own fast-lane lifestyle; (b) they are abandoned by their friends and families; (c) they are terrorized and devastated by their own sickness; (d) some of them continue to engage in "dangerous" sex; and (e) others regret and denounce their "former lifestyle."
6. Time and timeliness preoccupy journalists, who often turn to rhetorical constructs such as projections, statistical speculations, and doomsday scenarios in their reporting.
7. Journalists depend heavily on a small group of medical authorities to shape and control reporting.
8. AIDS activism is often confused with, and collapsed into, gay and lesbian activism.

On television, scientific documentaries continue to serve the important function of translating dense scientific information into the vernacular. But in television and film, the single most important format by which AIDS is represented is the genre of gay melodrama. Such films and television programs as *An Early Frost* (1985), *Our Sons* (1991), *Long Time Companion* (1991), *Philadelphia* (1994), and *It's My Party* (1996) all chronicle and dramatize the sociopsychological transformation of largely middle-class white gay men by means of AIDS. Many of them underemphasize the politics of gay life. None of them portrays the experiences of gay minorities. Of late, television films like *A Place for Annie* (1994) and *A Mother's Prayer* (1995) have worked to "de-gay" the crisis by shifting its focus to infants and children with AIDS and the struggle of their (typically single) mothers.

Alternative media images of AIDS have proliferated side by side with dominant images. They work to remap the crisis by presenting a more complex depiction of gay men with AIDS (as in *The Living End* [1992] and *Zero Patience* [1994]), the experience of women and minorities (as in *Doctors, Liars, and Women: AIDS Activists Say No to Cosmo* [1988] and *Tongues Untied* [1989]), a multitude of safer-sex practices (as in *Safer Sex Shorts* [1990]), and activist interventions through graphic arts (such as Gran Fury). Such alternative representations of AIDS can alter our perception of the crisis now and for the future.   *John Nguyet Erni*

Bibliography

Kinsella, James. *Covering the Plague: AIDS and the American Media.* New Brunswick, N.J.: Rutgers University Press, 1989.
Treichler, Paula A. *How to Have Theory in an Epidemic: A Cultural Chronicle of AIDS.* Durham, N.C.: Duke University Press, 1997.

See also AIDS; AIDS Organizations AIDS Performing; Gran Fury; Media; Television

AIDS Literature

That so many autobiographies, novels, plays, poems, short stories, and memoirs have been written about AIDS puts it in the very top ranks of literature about disease. This is all the more remarkable, given that this literature has been produced in fewer than twenty years, whereas plague, cancer, syphilis, and other illnesses have had all of human history in which to find their scribes. The meaning of AIDS is contested in these works; it has been tied to personal and cultural immorality but also to personal heroism and social criticism. Because AIDS has struck many gay men in developed countries, its literary meanings must be considered in the context of literary traditions regarding homosexuality. Those traditions involve many problematic and objectionable representations that linger over contemporary writing about gay men almost as much as AIDS itself. Consequently, much contemporary writing by gay men is at pains to resist literary representations that denigrate homosexuality, doing so to imagine a future at once less vulnerable to the epidemic and more favorable to gay people. In large measure that resis-

Atance takes the form of portraying gay men not as hapless victims or as predatory creatures but as valuable people actively involved in determining their own futures.

It was not always to the advantage of homosexuality or AIDS that AIDS writing sometimes drew on traditional ways of writing about homosexuality. For example, in the 1987 short story "Porphyria's Lover," by Ferroll Sams, the narrator is a duplicitous bisexual man whose liaisons with men are anonymous, manipulative, and ultimately fatal. His high school lover commits suicide, in part because of the narrator's coldness: "I am not queer and never will be." Nevertheless, he becomes famous in San Francisco's bathhouses as "Roscoe," the pet name he uses for his penis. But his sexual prowess is a cover for a predatory nature. Acting out an urban legend, Roscoe kills a man by inserting a greased hamster into his anus. For Roscoe, homosexuality means anonymity and deceit: "You can't really trust anybody in this world." In the end, he contracts an HIV infection, infects his wife, who in turn infects their child, who ultimately dies with AIDS. Roscoe kills the interior designer who had befriended him and his wife, and—that done—contemplates whether to end his own life with a bullet before the police arrive or whether to die in jail all the while intimidating his jailers with HIV-infected saliva. As portrayed in this story, homosexuality is a profound evil, leading to vice and death. Every named gay man in the story dies, and a few others besides. In literary traditions of this kind, AIDS functions merely as another means to secure the death of gay men, as another consequence of the evil of homosexuality.

More favorable to gay men was writing about AIDS that overlaid the epidemic onto that paradigmatic gay literary form—the coming-out story. Paul Reed's *Facing It* (1984) was the first U.S. novel to look at AIDS in a sustained way. That novel prefigured many of the themes that subsequently occupied AIDS writing. Even so, it relied on certain stock conventions regarding homosexuality. One of the key dramas of *Facing It* is whether the protagonist's family will reunite with their son after he is diagnosed with AIDS. Both Andrew's parents reject homosexuality, and AIDS doesn't make things better. "To be involved in that kind of situation, and now this too," his mother worries. Even Andrew wonders whether his AIDS is a judgment on his worth: "It's like punishment, that's how I feel sometimes. Like God has waved his hand and said that we must pay." Andrew's father, Chuck Stone, has disowned his son

and refuses a reconciliation, calling Andrew the greatest disappointment of his life: "Andy is not my son anymore, no matter what's happening." This "stone chucker's" own brother had committed suicide because of his homosexuality, thus invoking an all too typical ending to the narrative life of gay men. Throughout the novel, AIDS becomes a problem to be managed and sometimes a secret to be kept, like homosexuality before it. Indeed, there is a closeted gay man in the novel who obstructs AIDS research, in part to throw suspicion away from his sexual orientation. It is only when an old friend threatens to expose his "houseboys" that he agrees to fund AIDS research. Blackmail has also been a staple of writing about homosexuality.

If this novel drew on conventions of gay literature in dealing with family acceptance and the closet, it also drew on the gains of activism to portray gay people positively. It presents Andrew Stone, who has AIDS, in a loving relationship with David Markham, who takes up AIDS journalism to make inroads against the indifference of the public to gay people. Andrew's sister, Beth, offers criticism of the "family values" that in fact work against family love. Some physicians are also shown as being in common cause with gay men facing down the epidemic, and despite Andrew's death, there is room for hope that all these struggles have not been in vain. There are in this novel the stirrings of activism and community among gay men—and their allies—that are necessary to the dignity and health of gay men.

In the early years of the epidemic, many writers tried to eulogize the growing number of dead, and they adopted elegiac traditions of mourning, in ways that had not been done publicly for gay men before. For example, novelist and essayist Andrew Holleran wrote a number of essays in *Christopher Street* that are at pains to resist cultural mythologies about gay men as moral abominations. By contrast, Holleran pictured his circle of friends as cultured, accomplished, and vibrant. For example, he said of his friend 0.: "0. included, invited, charmed, cooked for, and amused so many people that, going uptown to have dinner there, one always felt a bit like a child on Christmas morning—one never knew what would be under the tree. He was merely the best of hosts—that's all." The deaths of men Like O., Emie Mickler, and George Stambolian leave Holleran bereft, and such is the overriding tone of his 1988 anthology, *Ground Zero*, and 1996 novel, *The Beauty of Men*. He even goes so far as to say that "anger is subsumed, lost, in sadness." If there is absence of anger on the part of some men toward the epidemic, it is because they have long been accustomed to ill treatment, and because they are not quite sure what to do about the epidemic. The immediate task at hand, then, is to offer testimonial to the lives of gay men lost to AIDS, to give some sense, as novelist George Whitmore put it in the title of his essays on AIDS, that *Someone Was Here.*

Whether this elegiac approach was adequate to the epidemic became one of the central questions of AIDS literature. Critic Douglas Crimp rejected the notion that creating artistic works that express human suffering is the only way (besides, perhaps, helping to raise money for research) that artists should respond to the epidemic. On the contrary, he proposed an activist aesthetic that would directly engage many of the assumptions by which the epidemic—and gay men—are understood. No dramatist exemplifies this approach more unrelentingly than Larry Kramer. His 1985 play *The Normal Heart* was a scorching indictment of social malevolence toward gay people and the indifference gay people show toward their own lives and responsibilities. Kramer not only asserts a gay history ("I belong to a culture that includes . . . Plato, Socrates, Aristotle, Alexander the Great, Michelangelo, Leonardo da Vinci"), he also rallies gay people to the cause of fighting AIDS by comparing the epidemic to the Holocaust ("Yes, everybody has a million excuses for not getting involved. But aren't there moral obligations, moral commandments to try everything possible? Where were the Christian churches, the Pope, Churchill?")

In *The Normal Heart,* Kramer was unsparing in his criticism of society at large and of gay men in particular—whom he accused of complicity in their own suffering because they refused to raise their voices against political indifference. For Kramer, as for other authors, the fight against AIDS was inescapably a fight for gay dignity and self-respect. Urging gay men to overcome their complacency, Ned Weeks, the principal character in *The Normal Heart*, observes in a defiant tone, "It's all there—all through history, we've been there; but we have to claim it, and identify who was in it, and articulate what's in our minds and hearts and all our creative contributions to the earth. And until we do that, and until we organize ourselves block by neighborhood by city by state into a united visible community that fights back, we're doomed." The path from lamentation to rage is a short one in the first decade of gay writing about AIDS. Kramer continued to repeat these same sorts of recriminations in his essays, *Reports from the Holocaust* (1988), and his play, *The Destiny of Me* (1992).

One of the central problematics of AIDS literature of this kind was whether a fight against AIDS also meant a fight against gay sex. For example, in *The Normal Heart*, Dr. Emma Brookner encourages Ned Weeks to "tell gay men to stop having sex." That suggestion, meaningful at a time when there was no clear indication of how AIDS was acquired, was bound to grate because it ran contrary to the learned pride of gay men and to the primacy of sex in gay culture, especially when that message continued long after it became clear that latex barriers were as much protection from HIV as most gay people needed. Brookner's counsel recalls moralistic "solutions" to the "problem" of homosexuality. Some writers avoided this kind of problem by writing about the past or by moving AIDS to the edge of the drama. For example, Allan Hollinghurst's 1988 novel, *The Swimming Pool Library*, was set in the time just before AIDS, "the last such summer of its kind there ever was to be." Hollinghurst was then free to tell a psychologically acute and sexually rich tale of gay lives prior to the epidemic Other writers focused on gay lives in the present that were not swallowed up in the epidemic, to indicate that gay men would survive and flourish, the epidemic notwithstanding. Christopher Bram's 1989 *In Memory of Angel Clare* described a circle of friends *after* the death of one of their members. For writers like these it was important that AIDS not be taken as a refutation of gay life, even if AIDS did reconfigure the meaning of the past and expectations of the future.

One writer exemplifying both elegiac and activist themes is Paul Monette, who, in the 1988 memoir *Borrowed Time*, takes the reader almost day by day through the account of losing his lover, Roger Horwitz, to AIDS, despite endless medications, clinic visits, hospitalizations, and experimental treatments. Monette, infected with HIV himself, opens the memoir this way: "I do not know if I will live to finish this." In some ways such memoirs should be read as attempts to create a verbal equivalent of the epidemic as gay men experience it. Certainly that is the effect as Monette describes the fears and harrowing experiences of the epidemic, matters he likens more than once to living on the barren moon. Contrary to their expectations of a lifetime together, Paul and Roger face their own mortality even as they watch their circle of friends

A fall sick and die. They are not, however, impassive about their futures. Positioned by their intellects and social standing, Paul and Roger try to stave off illness by searching out state-of-the-art medical care: "Life was about survival and challenge—so *meet* it." Toward that end, they pursue any experimental drug that might help, but Roger dies nevertheless. One of Monette's observations about the need to express love to the dying serves equally well as the motive for this kind of memoir: "Loss teaches you very fast what cannot go without saying."

Part of what cannot go without saying, for Monette, is a study of the lives of gay men and their living through the epidemic in U.S. society. In his 1990 novel, *Afterlife*, Monette describes how AIDS structures the lives of a circle of Los Angeles AIDS "widowers" who knew full well the meaning of AIDS. They had all "watched the disengagement of the brain, when the men with the tubes in their arms couldn't remember they were dying anymore. No more than they could remember being alive, or who the figure was sitting weeping softly by the bed." In consequence, they bond together, an improbable group, but one that knows flashes of hatred for those who haven't been touched by AIDS. In fact, virtually all of the novel's gay characters are HIV-infected. Golden boy Sonny Cevathos finds answers to his infection and looming illness in the vagaries of New Age channeling. After fits and starts, Steven Shaw finds love with Mark Inman, and both are happy to be "not alone, because time was very short." Dell Espinoza, by contrast, takes vengeance on homophobic society as an AIDS terrorist; he assassinates Mother Evangeline, a TV preacher who says Jesus would never have cured a man with AIDS. After killing Mother Evangeline, Dell then takes his own life. This novel is a mourning of the coming of AIDS ("The old life, the lost one, was all that made any sense") and a chronicle of its central place in the lives of gay men, but it is also a novel in which gay men can struggle toward outlooks other than cynical bleakness. In this context, Dell's behavior seems less part of a political program than a spasm of rage against prominent social figures who feed their ambitions on hatred of gay men.

Monette's poetry in *Love Alone* (1988) and Michael Lynch's poetry in *These Waves of Dying Friends* (1989) are elegiac in their own way as they struggle to express the enormity of loss in the epidemic, but they also express political objections to the treatment of gay men in society. Monette, for example, asserts the value of gay men in his "Brother of the Mount of Olives" by asking all "far brothers" to "pray that my friend and I be still together / just like this at the Mount of Olives blessed / by the last of an ancient race who loved / youth and laughter and beautiful things so much / they couldn't stop singing and we were the song." But idyllic prayers won't go very far in meeting the political needs of gay men, and so Monette also rails against society with unvarnished anger. In "Manifesto" he writes: "we need / the living alive to bucket Ronnie's House / with abattoirs of blood hand in hand lesions / across America need to trainwreck the whole / show till someone listens." In "Yellow Kitchen Gloves," Lynch describes a demonstration of AIDS activists outside the U.S. Supreme Court. The demonstrators write the names of dead PWAs on latex gloves they don to mock the police monitoring the demonstration. Lynch issues a cry to the troops: "We want you all beside us on these steps, / this other dancefloor, / gloved fists in the air / defying the empowered who deny / our lives and deaths, our fucking, and our hate." Gloved in the dignity of the dead, the demonstrators are not immobilized by mourning; they demand a reckoning with heterosexist oppression. It turns out therefore that elegy and activism can coincide in the same literary and political projects.

Tony Kushner's drama *Angels in America* (1992 and 1994) also frames AIDS as a question of the survival and dignity of gay men. Before larger questions about the social fate of gay men as a whole can be answered, it must first be settled whether Louis Ironson will leave his lover, Prior Walter, who is diagnosed with AIDS: "K.S., baby. Lesion number one. Lookit. The wine-dark kiss of the angel of death." After consulting a rabbi and grappling with his own conscience, Louis does in fact leave Prior: "I have to find some way to save myself." For his part, Prior is tempted by an angel into accepting a vision of the world as static and unchanging, a world in which there would be no AIDS. Prior rejects this world, because it is the world of change and challenge and, yes, disease that is ultimately important to human beings: "If I can find hope anywhere, that's it, that's the best I can do. It's so much not enough so inadequate but. . . . Bless me anyway, I want more life." When Louis wants to reunite with Prior, Prior has learned a thing or two from AIDS about endurance and will not take him back. Though their relationship does not stand the test of AIDS, they remain friends, which is a victory in its own right because AIDS not only alienated gay men from society, it also threatened to alienate them from one another. The will of gay men to survive the epidemic is evident in Prior's closing remarks: "This disease will be the end of many of us, but not nearly all, and the dead will be commemorated and will struggle on with the living, and we are not going away. We won't die secret deaths anymore. The world only spins forward. We will be citizens." While *Angels* is primarily concerned with individual relationships, it does invoke the necessity of a political consciousness for the well-being of gay men.

Because of their links with the epidemic, writing about sex and drug use must either confront AIDS directly or find some narrative technique to contain its effects. AIDS has an entrenched place in the lives and perceptions of gay men, whether or not it is mentioned directly. Just as earlier gay writers had to resist pathological interpretations of homosexuality, contemporary writers must struggle to resist facile equations of AIDS with immorality and with death. There are many different literary fronts in a battle of this kind. Writing that has as its task the blessing of the dead does not necessarily interfere with a vigorous political literature inasmuch as both work to improve the social standing of gay men. As the record has shown, illness is not only brute suffering but it can be the occasion of personal and social growth. At its best, AIDS writing is both the record of and the spur to that progress. Reflecting the demographics of the groups most affected by the epidemic and those positioned to write about it, most writing about AIDS has been done thus far by white gay men. By comparison, writing that reflects the lives of other groups affected by AIDS is not as well developed. Essex Hemphill's anthology *Brother to Brother* does contains short fiction about AIDS from an African American perspective, and the 1992 anthology *Positive Women* collects first-person narratives about AIDS from women around the world. Imagining the full range of social progress will, of course, require contributions from men and women of all ethnicities and sexual orientations.

Poet James Dickey has observed that writing about AIDS becomes highly problematic when it moves from a single, powerful instance to numbing mass death. AIDS literature is now at a crossroads precisely because the epidemic has taken such a toll. AIDS has lost much of its shock value. As critic John Clum has observed, the fortifying memories that gay men have of a time without AIDS have faded as a new generation of gay men came of age with AIDS taken for granted. As it is unclear that there is any treatment for AIDS on the horizon, the hope of a future without AIDS proves a receding goal, though from time to time optimism along these lines does appear in the medical literature. It is not surprising that Larry Kramer has declared more than once that the war against AIDS has been lost. Whether he is right or not, for the time being AIDS is here to stay. This impasse in overcoming the epidemic may have contributed to the sprees of vengeance that occur in Robert James Baker's *Tim and Pete* (1992). In that novel, a gang of AIDS terrorists stalk conservative politicians whom they plan to kill for failing to take the epidemic, and gay men, seriously. This novel augurs many of the challenges ahead for AIDS literature: how to break the stranglehold of AIDS on the lives of gay men when neither the past nor the future offers clear refuge from the epidemic.   *Timothy F. Murphy*

Bibliography

Avea, Thomas. *Life Sentences: Writers, Artists, and AIDS*. San Francisco: Mercury House, 1994.

Bram, Christopher. *In Memory of Angel Clare*. New York: 1989.

Campos, Rafael. *What the Body Told*. Durham, N.C.: Duke University Press, 1996.

Crimp, Douglas, ed. *AIDS: Cultural Analysis, Cultural Activism*. Cambridge, Mass.: MIT Press, 1988.

Gunn, Thom. *The Man with Night Sweats*. New York: Faber and Faber, 1992.

Hemphill, Essex, ed. *Brother to Brother*. Boston: Alyson, 1991.

Holleran, Andrew. *Ground Zero*. New York: Morrow, 1988.

Kramer, Larry. *Reports from the Holocaust: The Making of an AIDS Activist*. New York: St. Martin's Press, 1989.

Kushner, Tony. *Angels in America*, Parts I and II. New York: Theatre Communication Group, 1992, 1994.

Lynch, Michael. *These Waves of Dying Friends*. New York: Contact II Publications, 1989.

Miller, James, ed. *Fluid Exchanges: Artists and Critics in the AIDS Crisis*. Toronto: University of Toronto Press, 1992.

Monette, Paul. *Borrowed Timer: An AIDS Memoir*. New York: Harcourt Brace Jovanovich, 1988.

———. *Love Alone: Eighteen Elegies for Rog*. New York: St. Martin's Press, 1988.

Murphy, Timothy F., and Suzanne Poirier, eds. *Writing AIDS: Gay Literature, Language, and Analysis*. New York: Columbia University Press, 1993.

Reed, Paul. *Facing It*. San Francisco: Gay Sunshine Press, 1984.

Rodriguez Matos, Carlos A. *POESIdA*. Jackson Heights, N.Y.: Ollantay Press, 1995.

Sergios, Paul A. *One Boy at War: My Life in the AIDS Underground*. New York: Knopf, 1993.

White, Edmund, and Adam Mars-Jones. *The Darker Proof: Stories from a Crisis*. New York: NAL/Plume, 1988.

Whitmore, George. *Someone Was Here: Profiles in the AIDS Epidemic*. New York: New American Library, 1988.

Wojnarowicz, David. *Close to the Knives: A Memoir of Disintegration*. New York: Vintage, 1991.

See also AIDS; AIDS Performance; Christopher Street Dance and AIDS; Fiction; Hemphill, Essex; Kramer, Larry; Kushner, Tony; Monette, Paul; Sexually Transmitted Diseases; White, Edmund

AIDS Organizations, U.S.

AIDS knows no boundaries, nor do the organizations that have arisen in response to the AIDS crisis. The Centers for Disease Control (CDC) National AIDS Clearing House has a database with information on about nineteen thousand organizations in the United States. This database, while incomplete, gives a sense of the scope of AIDS organizations.

Types and Examples of AIDS Organizations

The 1983 Denver principles addressing the rights of people with AIDS (PWAs) and the responsibilities of all of us mapped out the basic principles and strategies that continue to form the basis for AIDS organizations.

Activist organizations have pressured, advocated, demonstrated, performed, mourned, and threatened to achieve change. They have educated themselves and others about the complexities of biomedicine, immunology, research methodologies, finance, and corporate politics. Probably the most well known of the activist organizations—the AIDS Coalition to Unleash Power (ACT UP)—celebrated its tenth year of activism and advocacy in March 1997. ACT UP describes itself as "a diverse, non-partisan group of individuals united in anger and committed to direct action to end the AIDS crisis."

It is a loose coalition of organizations with a common mission that share information and may coordinate actions. From its inception ACT UP has advocated changes in the way research for new drugs is done and demonstrated against excessive corporate profits on AIDS drugs. Harm reduction through needle exchange, condom availability, and accurate information about HIV transmission has also been on the ACT UP agenda. One of ACT UP's greatest strengths has been the ability of its members to develop areas of expertise, to disseminate the information rapidly, to develop policy based on it, and to create public actions to help put the policy into action. This strength has also been instrumental in weakening ACT UP. As individuals developed expertise, they often moved on to create or participate in nonprofit organizations that focused on that particular expertise. Many of the human service, legal, treatment action, and arts organizations discussed here were created by and are staffed by people who developed their skills in ACT UP. Thus, while ACT UP's power as an organization may have lessened over the years, its methods and commitments have spread through other organizations so that the work continues, often in different forms.

Affinity groups are small groups, typically six to fifteen people who work together around a particular philosophy, a shared degree of willingness to risk arrest and police violence, and a commitment to a particular set of issues. These groups are often long term. Affinity groups can frequently execute fast, dramatic, and highly effective actions. Examples of affinity groups are the Marys, the Treatment Action Group (TAG), and City AIDS Action, all in New York City. One of the most moving and dramatic actions by the Marys was a funeral procession for one of their members who had died from AIDS extending from New York City to Washington, D.C., with a memorial service at the White House.

TAG and City AIDS Action carry on the ACT UP tradition of excellent research and policy development and powerful political action. Their focus is on treatment developments and making these available to all PWAs. There are also many small, short-term (sometimes existing for one action or event), and politically radical groups. Bad Cop, No Doughnut, and Slut Nation in San Francisco have done effective and informative zap actions, for example.

Other AIDS activist organizations include Parents and Friends of Lesbians and Gays (PFLAG), which has expanded its mission to address AIDS issues politically and socially, and Mothers Voices, a grassroots organization of mothers organized specifically to address the AIDS crisis. A large number of organizations have arisen to address the monumental health needs of PWAs. In every state, new organizations have grown up or existing ones have been extended to provide services to PWAs. These range from the National Institutes of Health (NIH) to churches and other community institutions to community-based organizations working on needle exchange and medical marijuana.

Project Inform, a nonprofit, volunteer organization, was founded in 1985 "to collect, review, and distribute information on experimental drug treatments for HIV/AIDS." Project Inform has been a source of information not only for PWAs but also for physicians who treat PWAs. Project Inform's information gathering and analysis have literally saved the lives of many PWAs who otherwise would not have had information about treatment choices or an appropriate standard of care. The American Foundation for AIDS Research (AmFAR) funds scientific research on AIDS prevention and treatment, as well as social research, policy analysis, and advocacy for public policies on legal and ethical issues relating to AIDS and HIV.

Organizations such as Planned Parenthood, the American Red Cross, and the Visiting Nurses Association have interpreted or reinterpreted their mission to enable them to provide information and services related to HIV and AIDS. Sadly, the hospice movement has had to grow in order to provide services including housing, food, and basic care for PWAs to facilitate death with dignity. The AIDS pandemic has raised numerous legal issues such as fair treatment in the workplace, appropriate care, services in prisons, and provision of services by government organizations. Hundreds of legal organizations have sprung up to meet this need. When a PWA becomes ill, basic services such as food and shelter are addressed by churches and other social institutions that have expanded their existing services and by organizations such as Project Open Hand, developed especially to meet the needs of PWAs. Project Open Hand in Atlanta, Chicago, and San Francisco, for example, delivers daily meals and bags of groceries weekly to the homes of PWAs. Other service organizations provide one-on-one care for PWAs, including practical support and companionship.

The complexity of the needs of PWAs and the fragmentation of health and social services led to the creation of organizations whose primary mission has been to coordinate information and ser-vices in a particular geographic area. This service has been needed equally, though for different reasons, in urban and rural environments. In rural areas, the need for coordinating information and services is driven by the relative scarcity of services, the relative lack of information and awareness of AIDS, and special issues about confidentiality that arise in a small community.

Women with HIV and AIDS are underserved both as women and when they are also poor and/or women of color. The initial, symptom-based definition of AIDS excluded most women because women have different symptoms from men. Similarly, drug testing and research protocols tend to exclude women. Transmission methods may be different for women than for men, and women have different issues and constraints about safe sex than do men. Women frequently have family obligations that make it more difficult for them to receive treatment and in general to obtain the level of care that they need. It is therefore critical that research, policy, treatment protocols, and services for women be integrated into all organizations and that organizations specifically address the needs of women with AIDS. ACT UP was instrumental in changing the CDC definition and thus making social services benefits available to women with AIDS. Women Alive, in Los Angeles, is an organization "committed to providing support, a sense of community, and a powerful voice for women living with HIV/AIDS."

People living in poverty, especially the homeless, also have special issues. They often do not have access to community services. As drug treatments becomes more costly and more complex, the poor and homeless are less likely to have access to information about available treatments or the drugs themselves. This lack of access may be because they cannot afford treatment or are deemed by the medical establishment to be unable to maintain the complex protocols required for successful use of new drugs. This population is likely to be excluded from research protocols in which new drugs are first made available. Expansion of outreach for human services such as the delivery of meals and groceries to this group is one of the challenges presented to AIDS organizations. The Center in Oakland, California, is an example of an organization that serves the poor and homeless.

The many social, cultural, and economic issues faced by people of color also affect them in relationship to AIDS and HIV. Blacks Educating Blacks About Sexual Health Issues (BEBASHI) is an edu-

A cational organization that provides information about sexual health issues, particularly AIDS, to the black, Hispanic, and other minority communities.

Men and women with AIDS in prison face extraordinary barriers to maintaining health and obtaining appropriate medical and other services. Condoms are not available—indeed, they are often forbidden—and the level of health services is poor or nonexistent. The People With AIDS Coalition (PWAC) in New York City has led the way in providing support to PWAs in prison and giving them a voice through PWAC publications.

Children and youth are another group with special needs. The schools have become a battling ground between AIDS organizations and others who want to teach youth about AIDS transmission and prevention, on the one hand, and those who place moral strictures against sexual activity above the need to save lives through preventive measures such as condom use.

The arts community has been especially hard hit by AIDS. At the same time, artists use their work to provide information about AIDS and to sustain PWAs with community arts programs. Visual AIDS provides venues for showing the work of artists with AIDS and coordinates Day Without Art to communicate the impact of the AIDS crisis on the arts. Day Without Art honors artists who have died from AIDS and those who are living with AIDS. It began with the shrouding of public art and in recent years expanded to provide oppportunities for artists living with AIDS to present their work to the public. In 1998, more than 5,000 organizations and institutions worldwide participated in Day Without Art. Visual AIDS's archival program documents the work of artists with AIDS. The Actors fund provides services to PWAs in the entertainment community. AIDS Art Alive uses the visual arts to promote positive responses to the AIDS crisis.

With so many services and organizations, and rapid change continuing to occur, there is a need for coordinating policy as well as services. The SF AIDS Foundation is "actively involved in a number of key federal issues, including funding for the Ryan White CARE Act, AIDS housing, health-care reform (Medicaid), research and treatment, and issues related to confidentiality." The foundation coordinates with other organizations to advocate within federal and state programs. There is a wide range of government organizations from the various county, state, and federal Departments of Health and Human Services, including the National Institutes of Health and the Centers for Disease Control, to the organizations that distribute and manage Ryan White funds.

Direction and Issues

AIDS organizations have been characterized by their ability to adapt to new information and emerging needs. As the AIDS crisis continues, the toll of death and dying has often helped people to recommit to working against this pandemic. It has also at times exhausted individuals and depleted organizations. While the promise of new drugs has given hope, the efficacy and long-term impact of these drugs is still unknown, and their availability is in practice severely limited. These advances in treatment, and the insufficient information about them, have also dulled the general awareness of the continuing monumental level of this crisis.

As AIDS organizations mature, they have of necessity become more aware of the general issues of delivering health and human services to all people. Ideally, this knowledge will lead to coalition building with other activist and human services organizations. We can see this trend, for example, in the work of the PWAC organizations. A major challenge to AIDS organizations is to maintain high levels of activism, research, and service; to expand the political agenda to ensure that the needs of all PWAs are addressed; and to continue to fight for the rights of all PWAs and people infected with HIV. The added challenge is to do this in the face of the continuing tragedy of large numbers of people dying of AIDS; the ignorance, indifference, and at times the seeming hostility of the U.S. government; and a corporate culture that too frequently values greed above life.

Jacqueline Thomason

Bibliography

Altman, Dennis. *Power and Community: Organizational and Cultural Responses to AIDS.* London: Taylor and Francis, 1994.

Burkett, Elinor. *The Gravest Show on Earth.* New York: Picador, 1995.

Smith, Raymond, ed. *Encyclopedia of AIDS: A Social Political, Cultural, and Scientific Record of the HIV Epidemic.* Chicago: Fitzroy Dearborn, 1998.

Stoller, Nancy E. *Lessons from the Damned: Queers, Whores, and Junkies Respond to AIDS.* New York: Routledge, 1998.

Web Sites

CDC/NAC Resources and Services Data Base. Online at http://www.cdcnac.org/cgi/databases/rdir/nac_complex.cgi.

The Living With Group Resource List. Online at http://www.tiac.net/users/geneva/LWG/Resources.html.

SF AIDS Foundation. Online at 2. CDC/NAC Resources and Services Data Base: Online at http://www.cdcnac.org/cgi/databases/rdir/nac_complex.cgi.

See also ACT UP; AIDS; Parents and Friends of Lesbians and Gays (PFLAG); Sisters of Perpetual Indulgence

AIDS Performance

Since the earliest days of the AIDS epidemic, performance has proven to be one of the most effective means of galvanizing people in the fight against the disease. Shortly after reports of the first fatalities in the early 1980s, and with growing concern and anxiety about the emerging health crisis, artists and community activists began to produce benefit performance events to raise funds for direct support for those afflicted and to educate others who might be at risk. These events were often held in nontraditional theater venues such as community centers, bars, and cabarets. Performance was also an important component of early public gatherings meant to commemorate the dead, such as memorial services, candlelight vigils, and marches.

The first plays to address AIDS include *One*, Jeff Hagedorn's one-person drama produced by Chicago's Lionheart Theater in 1983; *Warren*, Rebecca Ranson's multicharacter play, produced by Atlanta's Seven Stages Theatre in 1984; and *The A.I.D.S. Show*, a collaborative production at San Francisco's Theatre Rhinoceros in 1984. *One* and *Warren* were both produced as AIDS fund-raisers, education campaigns, and memorials. Productions of these plays often helped launch local AIDS service organizations throughout the United States. Early AIDS plays, like early AIDS activism, were directly linked with lesbian and gay politics and the lesbian and gay theaters that emerged after Stonewall.

The first plays produced in New York City were *Night Sweat* by Robert Chesley and *Fever of Unknown Origin* by Steven Holt. Both these plays, however, failed to galvanize New Yorkers. It was not until 1985, with the premieres of William Hoffman's *As Is* and Larry Kramer's *The Normal Heart*, that AIDS theater crossover into the mainstream. Both these plays were produced by prestigious theater venues, guaranteeing critical reviews in the national media. *As Is,* produced by the Circle Repertory Company, was the first AIDS play to be staged on Broadway. *The Normal Heart*, produced by the New York Shakespeare Festival at the Public Theatre, remains to this day the most controversial AIDS play. Unlike earlier plays that set out to represent the psychosocial issues of people with AIDS and their supporters, Kramer's play focuses on the institutional networks of power—government, medical science, media—that ignored AIDS in the years 1981–84. Perhaps more than any other play, *The Normal Heart* brought national attention to AIDS. The play has been produced throughout the United States as well as internationally.

Larry Kramer, who helped found the Gay Men's Health Crisis (GMHC), the AIDS service organization that he also criticizes in *The Normal Heart*, went on to help found the AIDS Coalition to Unleash Power (ACT UP) in 1987, a direct-action group committed to ending the AIDS crisis. ACT UP, which grew to have chapters throughout the world, demonstrated its own form of street theater influenced by agitprop performance, calling attention to a diverse range of AIDS issues and protesting an equally diverse group of individuals and institutions. Performance was instrumental to these demonstrations and protests. Throughout the late 1980s and up through the early 1990s, ACT UP was the most visible and influential site of AIDS activist performance. Already by this time, however, people with HIV and AIDS had formed specific theater ensembles and had begun staging their own works. Companies such as Artists Confronting AIDS, founded in Los Angeles by Michael Kearns and Jim Pickett, and New York City's HIV Ensemble were designed to provide people with HIV and AIDS an opportunity to convey their AIDS experiences through performance and in the theater.

Beginning in the late 1980s and continuing throughout the 1990s, emerging and established playwrights and performers began to write and produce AIDS plays for regional and national stages. Gay playwrights such as Harry Kondoleon, David Greenspan, Scott McPherson, Terrence McNally, Harvey Fierstein, and Craig Lucas were among the first dramatists to address AIDS in their work. Solo performers and performance groups such as Charles Ludlam and the Ridiculous Theatre, Michael Kearns, Ron Vawter, Luis Alfaro, Tim Miller, Pomo Afro Homos, and David Drake had also begun to explicitly discuss and reference AIDS, many as early as the mid-1980s. The proliferation of AIDS

A performance in the late 1980s also included plays and other productions by women. Paula Vogel, Diamanda Galas, Cheryl West, and Sarah Schulman were among the first women playwrights and performers to join Rebecca Ranson and write about AIDS. Nonetheless, despite the diversity of style, content, and form that these plays and performances displayed, nearly all these works focused on gay men with AIDS.

The late 1980s also saw the proliferation of community-based AIDS educational theater initiatives designed to educate individuals and populations living on the margins or entirely outside of white gay male culture. Productions such as San Francisco's Asian AIDS Project's *Love Like This* Theater Program or Los Angeles's Teatro Viva! were successful in their outreach efforts to specific communities underaddressed or neglected by more mainstream AIDS service organizations and outside the representational framework of AIDS theater. Like the AIDS performances of the early 1980s, these efforts invested in educating audiences in HIV prevention.

AIDS theater returned to the national spotlight in 1992 and 1993 with the premieres in Los Angeles, London, and New York City of Tony Kushner's two-part play *Angels in America*, which linked AIDS issues with U.S. national politics. The play won various prestigious awards including the 1993 Pulitzer Prize for drama. Kushner, like Larry Kramer before him, used the international attention generated by his play to speak out about AIDS in the media. With the success of *Angels in America*, Kushner emerged as one of the most outspoken and influential voices in the fight against AIDS. In the wake of *Angels* and with the recent commercial success of such plays as Paul Rudnick's *Jeffrey*, Terrence McNally's *Love! Valour! Compassion!*, and Jonathan Larson's *Rent*, AIDS theater entered the mainstream. Commercialization, while never the goal of AIDS performance, brings new opportunities for artists and audiences. Rather than seeing these works as the culmination of AIDS theater, one must remember that community-based AIDS theater continues to be performed in smaller venues and that these works still matter in the ongoing struggle against AIDS.   *David Román*

Bibliography

AIDS: Cultural Analysis, Cultural Activism. Ed. Douglas Crimp. Cambridge, Mass.: MIT Press, 1991.

Román, David. *Acts of Intervention: Performance, Gay Culture, and AIDS.* Bloomington: Indiana University Press, 1998.

See also AIDS; *AIDS Quilt Songbook*; Kramer, Larry; Kushner, Tony; Ludlum, Charles; McNally, Terrence; Names Project AIDS Memorial Quilt; Pomo Afro Homos

AIDS Quilt Songbook

The *AIDS Quilt Songbook* was conceived and organized by baritone William Parker (1943–1993) as a singer's response to the AIDS epidemic. Although the first songs were written specifically for baritone, Parker saw the project as infinitely expandable in reflecting the manner of the NAMES Project AIDS Memorial Quilt, capable of embracing a mixture of vocal and instrumental forces. The first performance, in Alice Tully Hall, by Parker, Kurt Ollmann, William Sharp, and Sanford Sylvan on June 4, 1992, was billed as the *AIDS Quilt Songbook–1992*, Parker's open-ended conception of the piece. Composers in the *Songbook* range from established figures—both gay and straight—such as Ned Rorem, William Bolcom, Lee Hoiby, and John Harbison, to younger figures, many of whom likely will not live to fulfill their promise. Some of the songs are to texts by the composers themselves (Fred Hirsch, Richard Thomas); others are settings of the poetry of James Merrill, Kabir (translated by Robert Bly), David Bergman, and others. Boosey and Hawkes has published a score of the original eighteen songs (#VAB-303), fifteen of which were also recorded by their creators (Harmonium Mundi HMN 907602); profits from both are donated to the AIDS Resource Center.

As Parker wished, composers have continued to add to the *Songbook*: new songs were commissioned for a performance in Minneapolis on December 1, 1992 (Parker's last public performance before his death), and later recorded. *Heartbeats: New Songs from Minnesota for the AIDS Quilt Songbook* (Innova 500) includes these eight new songs, as well as seven from the original *Songbook*; it widens the work's perspective by addressing issues of women living with AIDS and includes more women composers and performers. Several of the new songs transcend a narrow definition of art song: Janika Vandervelde's "Positive Women," for example, calls for a narrator, a solo violinist, and a women's choir.

The subject matter of the *Songbook*'s songs varies in the specificity of its confrontation with the disease: some poems are allusive or metaphorical; others are more literal and include quite graphic symptomatic descriptions. The poetic forms are similarly diverse, encompassing both sonnets and unrhymed prose. Almost all present a gay male perspective. The musical settings demonstrate a wide variety of musical styles, from Broadway patter ("AIDS Anxiety") and atonal angularities ("The 80s Miracle Diet") to neoromantic lyricism ("Walt Whitman in 1989").   *Stephen McClatchie*

Bibliography

Baker, Rob. *The Art of AIDS*. New York: Continuum, 1994.

Kellow, Brian. "Art in the Age of AIDS." *Opera News* 56 (June 1992): 40–43.

Mass, Lawrence. "Musical Quilts." *Gay and Lesbian Study Group Newsletter* 2, no. 2 (October 1992): 11–13.

McCalla, James, and Karen Pierce. "Review of *The AIDS Quilt Songbook* [CD and score] and *Heartbeats: New Songs from Minnesota for the AIDS Quilt Songbook*." *Gay and Lesbian Study Group Newsletter* 5, no. 2 (October 1995): 20–24.

See also AIDS Performance; Names Project AIDS Memorial Quilt; Rorem, Ned

AIDS Writing in France

The HIV/AIDS epidemic in France has resulted in both the highest infection figures of any western European country (35,773 cases of AIDS in 1995) and in profound social and cultural perturbations and reevaluation, affecting the ways in which homosexuality in particular figures in the national consciousness. As in the United States, the epidemic has also been experienced as affecting other socially excluded groups such as drug users and sex workers. Official reactions to the threat moved through stages of dismissiveness and inaction, to well-intentioned campaigns that urged *solidarité* and targeted the young but still failed to counter conservative attitudes around issues such as public (homo-)sexuality and condom use. For instance, in 1988 a poster campaign advocating condom use was deemed too sensitive to be shown in the Paris subway.

Artistic representations and responses in the 1980s and 1990s have therefore been made within a context of political and social debate: equally, the reconfiguration of sexual and social mores in France led to innovative responses. With the right seizing on AIDS as an excuse to restrict newly acquired liberties won by gay men, the earliest texts in which AIDS figured were such works as *Danger de vie* by Michel Simonin, published in 1986; Jean-Paul Aron's essay, first published in the *Nouvel Observateur* in 1987, "Mon sida"; and Guy Hocquenghem's *Ève* (1987). In short, writers have been concerned with claiming a voice and an identity, the right to speak publicly about AIDS and homosexuality in the first person.

Hervé Guibert (1955–1991), the most notable author to write about discovering he was HIV-positive and becoming ill with AIDS, did so indirectly through the genre of autofiction, a self-writing practice that is neither wholly true nor wholly invented, which he had already put to use in earlier texts about his sexuality. The 1990 publication of Guibert's *À l'ami qui ne m'a pas sauvé la vie* attracted much publicity, mainly for "betraying" the secret of Michel Foucault's AIDS-related death by writing about the last days of the philosopher using a changed name. However, as Ralph Sarkonak has shown in his *Texte* article, Foucault appears more as an opportunity for Guibert to advance his project of exposing the body in pain and writing into death. The text opens with a veiled declaration of Guibert's HIV-positive status, at the same time holding out the possibility (later proving vain) that he has found a cure.

Further criticism of Guibert, together with questions about Cyril Collard's 1989 book and film *Les Nuits fauves*, came from campaign group Act Up–Paris, who objected to their representations of gay men as self-regarding narcissists and/or murderers (Collard for his depiction of the semiautobiographical bisexual character Jean, who has unprotected sex with his girlfriend, Laura; Guibert for plotting to drip blood into the wineglass of Bill, the American who offered the illusory cure).

Later works by Guibert continued to foreground the dynamics of self-revelation, performative identity, risk, and writing the body; worth special mention are *Le Paradis* (1992), a fantastic travelogue inscribing all sense of self and identity with radical epistemological doubt, a video diary entitled "La Pudeur et l'impudeur" (first shown 1992) documenting transcendental moments, daily struggles, and a Russian roulette scene of his failed suicide, and a harrowingly terse hospital diary written toward the end of his life, *Cytomégalovirus* (1992).

Other writers to use the *témoignage*, or witnessing, form in experimental and often therapeutic ways include Alain-Emmanuel Dreuilhe, in his metaphorization of the struggle against disease written partly in a North American context, *Corps à*

A *corps* (1987); Barbara Samson, who, in *On n'est pas sérieux quand on a dix-sept ans* (1994), offers the account of how, as an anorexic, she is seduced by HIV-positive Antony, and her struggle to come to terms with her changed HIV-status and use her life affirmatively; and *Cargo vie* (1993), by Belgian-born author Pascal de Duve, who during a sea voyage, both explores his own illness and revisits his past, poetically embracing a new love affair for the virus VÍH relationship to replace his affair with "E," who abandoned him. A related trope, which Ross Chambers calls "accompaniment witnessing," offering accounts of the tender/vicious relationships between those ill with AIDS and their lovers, and exploring issues of duty, mourning, and responsibility beyond the trite *solidarité* of poster campaigns, includes *L'Accompagnement* (1994) by René de Ceccatty, Yves Navarre's *Ce sont amis que vent emporte* (1990), and Michel Manière's *À ceux qui l'ont aimé* (1992). Françoise Baranne's *Le Couloir* (1994) provides the perspective of a professional carer, while *Les Quartiers d'hiver* (1990) by Jean-Noël Pancrazi is a more general elegy to a lost community, marking the devastation to Paris's gay scene caused by the ravages of the epidemic.

Later generations of French authors pick up on and radicalize the developments of new forms of identity and relationships found in the works of their predecessors. Guillaume Dustan's *Dans ma chambre* (1996) controversially documents the unfolding dramas among a group of sexually adventurous friends on the Paris scene, while Vincent Borel, in *Un Ruban noir* (1995) combines elements of rave culture, alternative medicine, and ecological cosmographics to explore forms of social organization that favor an AIDS-positive outlook. One self-conscious literary text to cast further doubt on the ability of dominant paradigms of individual identity to "resist infection" is *Le Fil* (1994) by Christophe Bourdin, the opening section of which implicates the reader in the minutiae of personal defenses against contamination that fail to prevent the virus's infiltration of text and body alike.   *Murray Pratt*

Bibliography

Boulé, Jean-Pierre. *Hervé Guibert: Voices of the Self.* Liverpool: Liverpool University Press, 1999.
Boulé, Jean-Pierre, and Murray Pratt, eds. *French Cultural Studies.* October 1998.
Lévy, Joseph, and Alexis Nouss. *Sida—fiction, Essai d'Anthropologie Romanesque.* Lyon: Presses Universitaires de Lyon, 1994.
Maxence, Jean-Luc. *Les Écrivains sacrifiés des années sida.* Paris: Bayard, 1995.
Pratt, Murray. "Imagining Positive Geographies: French AIDS Writing in the 1990's as Refusing and Destabilising the Psycho-Social Untouchable Body." *Mots Pluriels* 1, no. 3 (1997).
———. "'A Walk along the Side of the Motorway?': AIDS and the Spectacular Body of Hervé Guibert." In *Gay Signatures.* Owen Heathcote, Alex Hughes, and James Williams, eds. Oxford: Berg, 1998, pp. 155–72.
Sarkonak, Ralph, ed. *Le Corps textuel d'Hervé Guibert, "Au jour le siècle 2."* L'Icosathèque (20th), no. 15, *La Revue des lettres modernes.* Paris: Lettres Modernes, 1997.

See also: ACT UP; AIDS; AIDS Literature; AIDS Organizations, U.S.; Foucault, Michel; Guibert, Hervé; Hocquenghem, Guy; Navarre, Yves

Ailey, Alvin (1931–1989)

This African American dancer and choreographer was founder of the Alvin Ailey American Dance Theater. Born in Rogers, Texas, the only child of working-class parents who separated when he was an infant, Ailey and his mother moved to Los Angeles in 1942. Shy from his itinerant Texas life and already aware of his homosexuality, Ailey turned to dance when a high school classmate introduced him to Lester Horton's Hollywood studio in 1949. Horton, an openly gay white man from Indianapolis, Indiana, had created a multiracial school and concert company that performed his challenging choreography. Under Horton's tutelage, Ailey developed as a dancer and learned the essentials of stage design, music awareness, costuming, and storytelling.

Ailey poured himself into study and developed a weighty, smoldering performance style that suited his athletic body. He moved to New York in 1954 to dance with partner Carmen De Lavallade in the Broadway production of Truman Capote's *House of Flowers.* Performing success led Ailey to found his own dance theater company in 1958.

The Alvin Ailey American Dance Theater began as a repertory company of seven dancers devoted to both modern dance classics and new works created by Ailey and other young artists. Successful from the start, the company's first concert premiered Ailey's masterful *Blues Suite* (1958), set in and around a barrelhouse, which depicts the desperation and joys of life on the edge of poverty in the South.

Alvin Ailey. Courtesy of Alvin Ailey American Dance Center Archives.

dance imagery that acknowledged male and female homosexuality in abstract work he made for the American Ballet Theater (*The River*, 1970) and his own company (*Streams*, 1970). These two dances include sections that recognize a sensual, intimate bond between men and women in dances of same-sex partnering framed by opposite-sex encounters. Among his later works, *For "Bird"—With Love* (1984) included an extended lyrical section for five men that described a nurturing connection among the musicians of Charlie Parker's quintet.

Ailey carefully guarded his public persona of masculine virility dissociated from homosexuality. He suffered a nervous breakdown in 1980, which some associates attributed to pressures surrounding administering his world-famous company; his career as a choreographer, which produced over fifty ballets for an international roster of companies; and his status as a figurehead statesman of African-American artistry. He died of AIDS in New York City. His company and its associated school, which was incorporated in 1967, continued under the direction of former star dancer Judith Jamison and remains the most celebrated and active company of American modern dance artists.   *Thomas DeFrantz*

Bibliography

Ailey, Alvin, with A. Peter Bailey. *Revelations: The Autobiography of Alvin Ailey*. New York: Birch Lane Press, 1995.
Dunning, Jennifer. *Alvin Ailey: A Life in Dance*. New York: Addison Wesley, 1996.

See also African-American Gay Culture

Early performances of the unequivocal masterpiece *Revelations* (1960) established Ailey's company as the foremost dance interpreter of African-American experience. The dance quickly became the company's signature ballet, eclipsing previous concert attempts at dancing to sacred black music. *Revelations* depicts a spectrum of black religious worship, including richly sculpted group prayer ("I've Been Buked"), a duet of trust and support for a minister and devotee ("Fix Me, Jesus"), a ceremony of ritual baptism ("Wade in the Water"), a moment of introverted, private communion ("I Wanna Be Ready"), and a final, celebratory gospel exclamation, "Rocka My Soul in the Bosom of Abraham."

Although Ailey maintained an affable, closeted public persona, his work consistently encouraged male homosexual spectatorship in its varied depictions of glamorous masculinity, as in the hypermasculine working men of *Blues Suite*, and the sensitive but sensually deprived religious archetypes of *Revelations* and *Hermit Songs* (1961), set to the Leontyne Price recording of Samuel Barber's song cycle. The extravagant costume and setting design of works like *Quintet* (1968), *Flowers* (1971), and *The Mooche* (1974) fit a prevalent mold of campy excess enjoyed by some gay audiences. Ailey created

Alan of Lille (c.1120–1203)

Alan of Lille was a student and teacher in the Parisian schools, then a churchman with various ecclesiastical duties, including conducting public controversies with heretics. He wrote extensively and in a variety of genres on the principal topics of Christian theology. One of his earliest works is a mixture of prose and poetry entitled the *Complaint of Nature*. It presents an allegorical "dream" or vision in which the goddess Nature bewails human sexual deviations. Instead of following the reproductive cycles set by divine plan, human beings have fallen into sterile practices, including same-sex copulation. Although Alan's work has often been read as an attack on male sodomy or even clerical sodomy, it is concerned on its surface with a wider variety of sex-

A ual practices. It links sexual deviation with the greed of prostitution and seems to hint at what we would call bisexuality and masturbation. Moreover, a number of anomalies in the allegory suggest that Alan does not mean it to be taken literally. He may be suggesting, for example, that nature will always fall into sexual irregularity until it is instructed by Christian theology and aided by divine grace. Alan's later, explicitly theological works condemn same-sex desire or activity in terms typical of twelfth-century theology.   *Mark D. Jordan*

Edward Albee. Photo by Marc Geller.

Bibliography

Jordan, Mark D. *The Invention of Sodomy in Christian Theology*. Chicago: University of Chicago Press, 1997.

Ziolkowski, Jan. *Alan of Lille's Grammar of Sex*. Cambridge, Mass.: Mediaeval Academy of America, 1985.

See also Aelred of Rievaulx; Albert the Great; Augustine of Hippo; Christianity; Paul, Saint; Thomas Aquinas

Albee, Edward (1928–)

Grandson by adoption of his namesake, the famous, powerful theatrical impresario, American playwright Edward Albee rose to fame in the lively Off-Broadway theater of the 1950s with a series of one-act plays. One of those, *The Zoo Story* (1958), has distinct homoerotic overtones in the Central Park meeting of an uptight middle-class man and a volatile stranger. This cautious glimpse of homosexuality and transgression of the gender order was daring in the 1950s. The title character of *The American Dream* (1960) is a scantily clad hustler. The homoerotic overtones in Albee's early work were combined with scathing attacks on conventional heterosexual marriage and an alarming amount of sort of misogyny that was part of the pre-Stonewall gay stereotype.

In the early 1960s Albee moved to Broadway, first creating a sensation with his lengthy full-length dark comedy, *Who's Afraid of Virginia Woolf?* (1962), which depicts two grotesque, unhappy heterosexual couples. Martha, the most memorable character, is a heavy-drinking, sexually promiscuous woman who constantly excoriates her husband for not being as powerful as her beloved father. Martha's camp humor and extreme behavior, coupled with her and her husband's inability to have children, have led some critics and directors to see her as a man in drag and, thus, the central couple as two gay men rather than a man and a woman. Such a heterosexist reading, denied by the playwright, blunts and limits Albee's satire. The Pulitzer Prize committee denied the prize to *Who's Afraid of Virginia Woolf?* because it did not foster American values (the prize went to a musical, *How to Succeed in Business Without Really Trying*).

Albee did receive the Pulitzer two years later for *A Delicate Balance*, which was successfully revived on Broadway in 1996. Like his previous work, *A Delicate Balance* mixes social satire with existential meditation on the meaningless void that human behavior and language futilely try to deny. Amid the barren, terrified heterosexual couples is the comic character Claire, another Albee female gargoyle, who takes the play into the realm of camp.

For a number of years Albee alternated original works with adaptations of novels by James Purdy, Carson McCullers, and others. Often these works, too, had homoerotic overtones, e.g., *The Ballad of the Sad Cafe* (1964) and *Malcolm* (1965). Along with Tennessee Williams and William Inge, Albee was subjected to homophobic attacks from a number of mainstream critics. *Tiny Alice* (1964), which is filled with homosexual innuendo, inspired a flurry of nasty critical jibes, including Philip Roth's description of the play's language as "pansy rhetoric."

After a series of disasters in the 1970s and 1980s (*The Lady From Dubuque* [1979], *The Man Who Had Three Arms* [1983]), Albee had a major success with *Three Tall Women* (1991), whose central character is a dying woman who has spurned her gay son.

A number of basic themes permeate all of Albee's work: spiritual nihilism, death, marriage as a battleground, the cruelty and indomitability of women, the sacrificed son, and the often denied but omnipresent homoerotic dimension of relations between men. He is most interested in those moments when the surface of social intercourse becomes disrupted by the irrational, even the spiritual.

John M. Clum

Bibliography

Bigsby, C.W.E. *A Critical Introduction to Twentieth Century American Drama, Volume II: Williams, Miller, Albee.* Cambridge: Cambridge University Press, 1984.

Clum, John M. *Acting Gay: Male Homosexuality in Modern Drama.* New York: Columbia University Press, 1994.

Green, Charles Lee. *Edward Albee: An Annotated Bibliography, 1968–1977.* New York: AMS Press, 1980.

Kolin, Philip C., and J. Madison Davis, eds. *Critical Essays on Edward Albee.* Boston: G. K. Hall, 1986.

Wasserman, Julian, ed. *Edward Albee: An Interview and Essays.* Houston: University of St. Thomas Press, 1983.

See also Inge, William; Kushner, Tony; Purdy, James; Theater Premodern and Early Modern; Williams, Tennessee

Albert the Great (c.1200–1280)

Albert of Lauingen, who even during his lifetime was called Albert "the Great," rose to fame as a theologian and early leader of the Dominican order. He had a long and various career as university teacher, religious superior, and bishop. Best known today as the mentor of Thomas Aquinas, Albert is properly appreciated in his own right for his commitment to integrating Christian theology with the full range of scientific and philosophical knowledge available to him. The most impressive evidence of this is a set of commentaries or paraphrases on the whole corpus of Aristotle. Albert did not admit the project of integration into his views on same-sex desire. Ignoring medical teaching on the possible physiological causes for same-sex activity, Albert condemns "sodomitic sin" as a deadly contravention of the purposes for which God created genital organs. The sin, which is found especially in the powerful and well educated, overwhelms reason by the very intensity of its desire. It is almost never uprooted, Albert adds, and it spreads quickly from one person to another. Although he never defines exactly what he

means by "sodomy," Albert seems to have in mind chiefly sexual relations between men, since he allows in one place that female masturbation may not be so serious a matter.

Mark D. Jordan

Bibliography

Jacquart, Danielle, and Claude Thomasset. "Albert le Grand et les problèmes de la sexualité." *History and Philosophy of the Life Sciences* 3 (1981): 73–93.

Jordan, Mark D. *The Invention of Sodomy in Christian Theology.* Chicago: University of Chicago Press, 1997, 114–135.

See also Aelred of Rievaulx; Alan of Lille; Augustine of Hippo; Christianity; Paul, Saint; Sodomy; Thomas Aquinas

Alcibiades Boy at School
(L'Alcibiade fanciullo a scola)

An anonymous text published in Venice circa 1650, *L'Alcibiade* is considered one of the most obscene works of Italian literature. It has been attributed to the friar Antonio Rocco, a prominent figure of the so-called Accademia degli incogniti (Academy of the Unknown), notorious for its libertine ideology and its strong anticlericalism. Since the Academy of the Unknown was composed of the most affluent members of Venetian society, it could afford to ignore the constant threats of the Catholic Church. *L'Alcibiade* is structured as a dialogue between a teacher and his student in ancient Greece.

Filotimo, a renowned Athenian teacher, attempts to convince Alcibiades, his beautiful young disciple, to let him penetrate him. Although the adolescent allows his mentor to kiss and to caress him, he denies Filotimo his virgin ass. To accomplish his desire, the master performs an ironic reversal of the relationship among rhetoric, sodomy, and the Bible. In *L'Alcibiade*, Genesis 19 hovers as an unspoken reference; even the term "Sodom" remains absent from the text. Rocco does not allow the Bible to articulate its mythic discourse against homosexuality. Being aware of the powerful and destructive force inherent in any myth, the author "silences" the biblical narration. Rocco sees sodomy as the quintessential expression of man's "natural" desire for power. In "Amore è puro interesse" ("Love Is Sheer Interest"), a discourse delivered to the Academy of the Unknown, Rocco makes

A

it clear that for him love is nothing but a longing for power.

"When one loves," Rocco states, "one loves oneself and not the other." In *L'Alcibiade* sodomite love is intrinsically ironic; that is, it constantly distances itself from its own articulation. Because its goal is the fulfillment of a desire for power, sodomite discourse interprets, falsifies, and nullifies any previous discourse. As Rocco writes at the beginning of his text, the best way of imparting one's own knowledge is to stick it (one's "knowledge") into one's interlocutor's ass. The teacher's rhetoric is infused with puns and irony. For instance, to convince his beautiful pupil to give in to his desire, Filotimo states that the expression "contra naturam" has been misinterpreted. "Cunt being called 'natura,' " the teacher argues, "asshole has been called 'contra naturam,' simply because it is on the side opposite cunt" (51). The teacher also stresses that vagina is called "natura" not because the ass is "contra naturam," but only because the vagina generates man. According to the master, the act of giving birth is usually called "natura." However, Filotimo hastily adds that desire is multifaceted. Man does not look for pleasure only to generate other human beings. Every kind of desire is natural. The master also reminds his pupil that man's desire for a boy is superior to that for a woman because a man and a boy are more similar to each other. Moreover, articulating a modern-sounding argument in favor of homosexuality, the master says that Sodom had been burned not because it supported sodomite practices but because it was inhospitable.

Armando Maggi

Bibliography

Dall'Orto, Giovanni. " 'Socratic Love' as a Disguise for Same-Sex Love in the Italian Renaissance." *Journal of Homosexuality* 16, nos. 1–2 (1988): 38–59.

Maggi, Armando. "The Discourse of Sodom in a Seventeenth-Century Venetian Text." *Journal of Homosexuality* 28 nos. 3–4 (1997): 25–43.

See also Italian Literature; Italian Renaissance, Sodomy

Alcohol and Drugs

Alcohol and drugs are here grouped together on the basis of their shared social function in enhancing recreational activities and their ability to lead to chemical dependency. Scientific studies in the early twentieth century sought to establish a correspondence between alcoholism and homosexuality, to demonstrate how the one led to the other, or vice versa. In reality, alcohol and drug use by gay men corresponds generally to that of American society as a whole, with two notable exceptions: the central role the gay bar continues to play in gay culture and, for some, the continuing importance placed on sex and its enhancement through alcohol and drug use as a hallmark of gay life or identity.

Alcohol is a physical depressant that creates an initially euphoric state as the drinker's inhibitions are relaxed, and allows for a more spontaneous sexual arousal. Larger quantities cause portions of the brain to shut down, deadens the nervous system (dulls sense of pain), and causes loss of balance, blurred vision and speech, impaired judgment, or unconsciousness. Taken to such a degree as to cause alcohol poisoning, it may cause permanent brain damage or induce a coma, a heart attack, and death. Prolonged use of alcohol (alcohol abuse) often leads to the onset of alcoholism (the loss of the ability to control one's drinking), which may include additionally the symptoms of irritability, extreme mood swings, blackouts (memory loss), lack of ability to concentrate, decreased motor skills, alcohol-induced psychosis and other personality transformations, and a wide range of ensuing social, family, and health problems.

The term *drug,* as used here, describes a variety of mood-altering chemical agents of a narcotic or otherwise potentially physically additive nature, which serve, at least initially, a similar recreational (social or sexual) activity function as alcohol. These include stimulants (amphetamines, cocaine), depressants (barbiturates, alcohol), hallucinogens (LSD, psilocybin, marijuana), and narcotics (morphine, heroin, opium, methadone), and their "designer drug" derivatives. Each drug has the potential to become addictive (physically or psychologically habit-forming), and each, in turn, may follow its own trajectory to the addict's self-destruction.

Drinking and/or recreational drug use often play a key role in the social behavior of gay men, whether in a bar cruising situation, or socializing with friends at home, over dinner, at a bar, or at a party. Few latitudinal studies have been undertaken to explore the myriad subcultures of gay social groups, cliques, gay extended families, and their variant drug and alcohol use. Until recently, most studies addressed the issue of alcoholism and the problem drinker. More recent research affirms the expected patterns: moderate and light drinkers tend to socialize with each other in a wide range of social settings; heavy drinkers and alcoholic drinkers tend to organize their social life around drinking with other heavy drinkers; and abstinent or "recovering" alcoholics tend to socialize with others in recovery and/or around Alcoholics Anonymous–related activities. Some gay men do not drink or use drugs at all, also for a variety of reasons—religious, medical, social, or personal.

Recent studies have found that being in or out of a primary relationship has no long-term bearing on the amount of alcohol and drug use. Light users who may have drunk a bit more while frequenting the bars while single tend to use less when they leave such social situations. Similarly, heavy drinkers tend to drink just as heavily coupled as they did while single, perhaps doing so at home or among a private circle of friends rather than at the bars.

The gay bar remains a venerable institution in the gay community. For a very long time it was the only social space in which homosexual men could meet; in many ways, it mirrored the traditional English pub as the urban dweller's public "front parlor." In many places outside major cities, the gay bar still serves this unique role, and the bartender is often both respected as an authority figure or confidant and revered as a sexual icon. In places with a sufficiently large gay population, other venues for socializing have developed, Metropolitan Community Church parishes or AIDS support organizations being the most often cited. Where alternate social outlets exist, lighter drinkers tend to become involved in community or leisure activities. Nevertheless, the gay bar as social locus and the degree of social activity organized around bars or drinking (as compared with heterosexual society) remains relatively high. For this reason, the recovering alcoholic often substitutes AA meetings and social activities for the bar, thus allowing him to remain socially connected to the gay community. In many places MCC and/or AA are the *only* social alternative to the gay bar.

Les Wright

Bibliography

Weinberg, Thomas S. *Gay Men, Drinking, and Alcoholism.* Carbondale, Ill.: Southern Illinois University, 1994.

See also Circuit Party Scene; Metropolitan Community Church

Alexander the Great (356–323 B.C.E.)

Alexander III of Macedon, commonly known as "the Great," the son of Philip II and Olympias, conquered the vast area from Asia Minor in the west to modern-day Afghanistan and India in the east. His expedition of conquest (334–324 B.C.E.), designed as revenge for the Persian attempts to invade Greece in 490 and 480/479 B.C.E., resulted in the destruction of the Persian Empire of Darius III and in the export of Greek language and culture to countries as far-flung as Egypt and Bactria.

Alexander attempted publicly to fuse aspects of Greek and Persian culture. From 330 B.C.E. his court dress comprised both the traditional Macedonian hat and cloak as well as the Persian crown, tunic, and girdle, symbols of the absolute monarchy he perpetuated.

In 327 B.C.E. he married Roxane, the captured daughter of a Bactrian noble, and, in 324 B.C.E., one of the daughters of Darius III, in a mass marriage ceremony at Susa. His friend and almost certainly his lover, Hephaestion, married another daughter of Darius in the same ceremony.

Hephaestion, a Macedonian noble who held several commands during the expedition, was one of the elite corps surrounding Alexander. Later, the Cynic philosophers claimed that Alexander was defeated only once—by Hephaestion's thighs. His sudden death at Ecbatana in 324 B.C.E. plunged Alexander into uncontrollable grief, reminiscent of Achilles' grief for Patroclus in Homer's *Iliad*. The manes and tales of all horses were shorn (as Achilles had done), music was forbidden, and the male population of a neighboring tribe was massacred as a sacrifice to Hephaestion's spirit. Alexander planned a gigantic funeral monument, to be built with bricks from the breached walls of Babylon, but there is no evidence that this plan was ever fulfilled. Zeus Amun's oracle decreed that Hephaestion could be worshiped as a hero.

Alexander's attitude to same-sex sexual relations seems typical of the Greek mores of his age, but his passionately enduring love for Hephaestion undeniably surpassed his infatuation with Roxane and his desire for the young Persian eunuch Bagoas. By Roxane, he had a son, who was murdered, together with his mother, in 311 B.C.E.. After Alexander's death, his empire was divided among his generals, who established ruling dynasties in their respective spheres of influence (for example, the Ptolemies in Egypt).

Representations of Alexander, especially sculpture and coinage, tend to depict an idealized youth, with an Apollo-like mien. In fact, by 331 B.C.E.,

A

Battle of Issus. *Detail of Alexander the Great. Mosaic. Museo Archeologico Nazionale, Naples, Italy (Art Resource, NY).*

Alexander, who considered himself a descendant of Hercules, began to portray himself as a son of Zeus Amun. His favorite sculptor, Lysippus, was responsible for one of the most famous portraits of Alexander, with his head inclined toward the left and his hair swept back from a middle parting. In 1995 a Greek archaeologist claimed to have found the tomb of Alexander at Al-Maraqi, near his favorite oracle of Zeus Amun at Siwa, in Egypt, but this has been hotly disputed. *Michael Lambert*

Bibliography

Renault, Mary. *The Persian Boy*. Harmondsworth: Penguin, 1974.

Scott-Kilvert, Ian, trans. *The Age of Alexander. Nine Lives by Plutarch*. Harmondsworth: Penguin, 1985.

See also Alexandria; Egypt, Ancient; Greece, Ancient; Plato; Rome, Ancient

Alexandria

Named after its founder, Alexander the Great, Alexandria was established in 331 B.C.E. near the western mouth of the Nile, after Egypt had been wrested from Persian rule. Under the Ptolemies, the Macedonian dynasty that ruled Egypt after Alexander's death, Alexandria became Egypt's capital, its major port, and the intellectual center of the Mediterranean world.

Designed as a Greek city-state with its own citizenship, coinage, and laws, Alexandria developed into a vibrant, multi-cultural city with strong Jewish and Egyptian communities that did not enjoy the full citizenship intended for the original Greek settlers and their descendants. Under Roman rule, Alexandria became the second-largest city in the Roman Empire, with a population of more than 500,000.

Under the Ptolemies, the museum and library at Alexandria became the primary research centers in the ancient world, where major discoveries (such as the existence of the ovaries) were made in the fields of medicine, mathematics, and geography, and where the great epics of Homer were arranged in books and edited.

A new style of literary composition (the Hellenistic or Alexandrian), characterized by innovative versification, the subjective expression of sexual desire and emotion, as well as by arcane subject matter, was inspired by the scholar-poets, such as Callimachus (third century B.C.E.), who catalogued the library's contents and complied a bibliography of Greek literature. The library eventually contained about 500,000 papyrus rolls—approximately 100,000 modern books.

Alexandrian love poetry is of particular interest; poets like Asclepiades and Meleager wrote exquisitely shaped love epigrams, addressed to both sexes, which profoundly influenced Roman love poets like Catullus and Propertius. Although Alexandrian erotic poetry is predominantly bisexual, love for boys is celebrated in the poems that make up book twelve of the Palatine or Greek anthology, which contains some of the gems of Alexandrian same-sex poetry.

The association of Alexandria and homosexual poetry has been continued in the modern era by another Alexandrian-born Greek poet, Constantine Cavafy (1863–1933), whose lyric poems capture the homoerotic sensuousness of his Hellenistic forbears. Other authors, like Lawrence Durrell, have attempted to capture the decadent languor of a city Durrell describes as "princess and whore, the royal city and the *anus mundi.*"

The later history of Alexandria is one of conquest, decline, and renaissance. Roman rule, which began with the defeat and suicide of Cleopatra VII (69–30 B.C.E.), the last of the Ptolemies, was followed by that of the Byzantine Greeks. The Arab conquest (C.E. 641) eventually led to the decline of the great port into a small fishing village, as the Arabs established a new capital at Fustat, now part of old Cairo. Under the sultan Muhammad Ali in the early nineteenth century, Alexandria was transformed into a bustling, commercial port again, with the cosmopolitan air of the ancient city. The Egyptian revolution and Gamal Ab-del Nasser's expulsion of British and French citizens in 1957 led to the depletion of the foreign community, especially the Greeks and the Jews who had given the city its special character.
Michael Lambert

Bibliography

Cavafy, Constantine P. *Collected Poems.* London: Hogarth, 1975.
Durrell, Lawrence. *The Alexandria Quartet.* London: Faber, 1985.
Forster, E. M. *Alexandria: A History and a Guide.* London: Whitehead Morris, 1922.

See also Alexander the Great; Cavafy, Constantine P.; Durrell, Lawrence; Egypt, Ancient

Alger, Horatio (1832–1899)

Born in 1832 to the Reverend Horatio Alger Sr., an outspoken abolitionist and Unitarian minister, and his wife, Olive Augusta Alger, herself a popular writer and lifelong fighter in causes of women's suffrage, Horatio Alger was a leading American writer of tales for young people. His stories about *Ragged Dick* (1868) and *Tattered Tom* (1871) established the pattern for more than a hundred rags-to-riches stories in the American literary tradition. Initially, serialized in *Student and Schoolmate,* a magazine for both boys and girls, his overnight literary sensations took nineteenth-century America by storm. In an era of national expansion, Alger heroes left the farm to seek their fortunes; they always returned in time to save the old homestead from the clutches of villainous squires. Critics describe his work as bristling with the energy of a young and developing nation with pioneers ever moving toward unknown frontiers.

The repressed fact about these wholesome narratives was Alger's own dark secret. Found guilty of a "crime of no less magnitude than the abominable and revolting crime of unnatural familiarity with boys," Alger left Brewster, New York, where he had hoped to follow in his father's footsteps, and moved to New York City, where he began to write. This scandal emerged after an archival discovery made by a biographer in the early 1970s. Details of earlier biographers confirmed his interest in lower-class boys and his devotion to the real-life subjects of his many novels. Since these discoveries, the myth of an American success has had to be rewritten with the centrality of pederasty in mind. The most successful attempts at this rewriting are listed below. The classic American boy's story must be understood as a tale of desire.
Craig McCarroll

Bibliography

Moon, Michael. "The Gentle Boy from the Dangerous Classes": Pederasty, Domesticity, and Capitalism in Horatio Alger." *Representations* 19 (Summer 1987): 87–110.
Schamhorst, Gary, and Jack Bales. *The Lost Life of Horatio Alger.* Bloomington, Ind.: Indiana University Press, 1985.

See also Fiction; Pederasty; U.S. Literature

Almodóvar, Pedro (1949–)

The Spanish filmmaker Pedro Almodóvar was born in Calzada de Calatrava (Ciudad Real, Spain) and

Pedro Almodóvar gets a kiss from his star Rossy de Palma. Photo by Marc Geller.

moved to Madrid in 1967. After Franco's death in 1976, he joined other artists and intellectuals to celebrate a new era of cultural and social freedom, known in Madrid as the *movida*. He performed in a rock n' roll band wearing heavy makeup, fishnets, and skirts, wrote stories for *La luna* magazine disguised as the porn star Patty Diphusa, and made super 8 shorts with titles like *Sex Comes, Sex Goes* (1977) and *Fuckfilms . . . Fuck . . . Fuck Me . . . Tim* (1978). These films were connected to the American underground of Kenneth Anger, Jack Smith and John Waters, Hollywood melodramas, and comic books. The films were screened in homes, night clubs, and the cafeteria of the Alphaville cinemas, with the director improvising a live sound track filled with camp humor and Spanish pop music.

Almodóvar's shorts and personal displays, cheerfully celebrated by the audience, anticipated the blissfulness of his feature-length films, which may be seen as the expression of a postmodern carnival or Baroque saturation framed by Spanish, Latin American, and North American popular culture. Hence, from *Pepi, Lucy, Bom and Other Girls on the Heap* (1980) to *The Flower of My Secret* (1995), the blend of romantic music such as the Castellan *cuplé*, the Caribbean bolero, and the Mexican *ranchera* alludes to Almodóvar's celebration of sentimentality. On the other hand, the recycling of Hollywood films from the 1940s and 1950s brings to his movies the Spanish nostalgia for the MGM and Twentieth-Century Fox productions that en-

livened, with the glowing red lips of their stars, the darkness of Franco's dictatorship.

With this strategy, the director enhances the lives of transvestites, transsexuals, homosexuals, lesbians, and heterosexual women, and reenacts the clash of gender and moral conflicts of Spanish society by means of an excessive mise-en-scène. In this sense, *The Law of Desire* (1987) subverts sexual and religious codes, and unifies through first-degree kitsch Spanish popular culture, in the scene where Tina's home altar, cluttered with all types of paraphernalia, becomes the deadly backdrop for Pablo and Antonio's last sexual encounter performed to the rhythm of the bolero "Lo dudo" (I Doubt It). Moreover, the film deconstructs machismo by presenting melodrama within an exclusive male domain.

Conversely, *Women on the Verge of a Nervous Breakdown* (1988) brings melodrama back to feminine territory and delves more deeply into the emotional conflicts of heterosexual couples that unfolded in *What Have I Done to Deserve This?* (1984). In this way, Pepa's appearance signifies the determination of any Spanish woman for being acknowledged in the masculine world, without giving away the seductive power of the full feminine attire.

In subsequent works like *High Heels* (1991), *Kika* (1993), and *Live Flesh* (1997) Almodóvar has further used and, it may be argued, abused popular culture. However, aside from the aesthetic value that in light of a postmodern sensibility such reiteration might have, his remain powerful tools in the process of subverting an increasingly conservative society and making more audible the voices at the margins of phallic discourse.   *Alejandro Varderi*

Bibliography
Smith, Paul Julian. *Desire Unlimited: The Cinema of Pedro Almodóvar*. London: Verso, 1994.

Vidal, Nuria. *El cine de Pedro Almodóvar*. Barcelona: Destino, 1989.

See also Anger, Kenneth; Film; Film: New Queer Cinema; Smith, Jack; Spain; Waters, John

Altman, Dennis (1943–)
An international commentator on gay politics and cultures and professor of politics at La Trobe University, Melbourne, Australia, Dennis Altman has written and edited eleven books including a novel, *The Comfort of Men* (1993), his autobiography, *Defying Gravity* (1997), and five others on gay politics.

Altman's *Homosexual Oppression and Liberation* (1971) was the first book internationally to describe and theorize the emerging gay liberation movement in the United States and elsewhere. It is difficult to overestimate its contemporary political importance in the context of a hundred years of writing by homosexuals attempting to change how homosexuality was perceived and represented. Since 1971, Altman's books and articles have anticipated, charted, and in many ways defined some of the major issues facing gays and sexual politics and their relationships to feminism, the state, and wider political cultures.

Altman has systematically addressed cultural, political, and sexual issues that have to do with the impact of HIV on gay men both locally and internationally. He writes in a personalized voice that combines his own experience, wide research, and participant observation. The resulting writing has involved an informed, sometimes passionate voice in dialogue with the traditions of radical sexual politics, liberalism, and socialism.   *Michael Hurley*

Bibliography

Altman, Dennis. *Coming Out in the Seventies*. Sydney: Wild and Woolley, 1979.
———. *Homosexual Oppression and Liberation*. New York: Outerbridge and Dienstfrey, 1971.
———. *The Homosexualisation of America: The Americanisation of the Homosexual*. New York: St. Martin's Press, 1982.
———. *Rehearsals for Change*. Melbourne: Fontana/Collins, 1980.
Altman, Dennis, et al. *Homosexuality, Which Homosexuality?* London and Amsterdam: GMP Publishers and Uitgeverij An Dekker/Schorer, 1989.
Hurley, Michael. *A Guide to Gay and Lesbian Writing in Australia*. Sydney: Allen & Unwin and the Australian Lesbian and Gay Archives, 1996.

See also AIDS; Australia; Homosexuality; Oppression; Sociology of Gay Life

American Indian/Alaskan Native Gender Identity and Sexuality

The categorization of gender identity and sexuality within Native communities in the Americas is complex. Self-identity in the United States according to censuses have yielded almost two million Natives in about 545 tribal groups speaking a variety of Native languages and exhibiting varied cultural contours. It is exceedingly difficult to generalize because each Native nation is unique—culturally and linguistically.

In the past, several attempts have been made by non-Native researchers to address Native gender and sexuality issues. And only recently, Native people themselves have begun to provide some clarification about Native gender and sexuality. From that we have learned, gender is primarily a process and is not considered static.

The key issue being discussed at present is the long-standing indigenous cultural recognition of gender categories beyond man/boy and woman/girl. Some people have labeled additional genders as "alternative" genders. Within diverse Native contexts, however, there are no "alternative" genders. There are, instead, additional markers that are part of the continuum of gender categories.

In each of the tribal groups in the United States, tribal languages designate specific gender categories. For example, in the Navajo nation, which is located in the American Southwest, a specific term is used within traditional cultural settings to classify a male-bodied person who functions in the role of a woman. That person is referred to as *na'dleeh*. A female-bodied person who functions in the role of a man is referred to as *dilbaai*. Another example, within Lakota culture, is the use of the term *winkte* when referring to a male-bodied woman. Thus, each tribe in North America has its own explanation about how gender markers are created, established, and used.

Beginning in the sixteenth century, the male-bodied and female-bodied persons briefly described above were labeled by European military colonists and missionaries as *berdaches*. This term and its underlying concept has been forced on Native people since then, and has proliferated in use through introductory textbooks in Western educational systems. The word *berdache* was never part of Native conversations until contemporary times. Recently, both Native and non-Native people have challenged the use of this label as a catchall for gay, lesbian, bisexual, and transgendered Natives. By the late 1980s, a new term had evolved. The new term "two-spirit," is not intended to mark a new category of gender. Instead, "two-spirit" is an indigenously defined pan–Native North American term that bridges Native concepts of gender diversity and sexualities and those of Western cultures.

"Two-spirit" is used by some people who formerly referred to themselves as either gay or lesbian. Also, the word is used by some tribal members who no longer have their cultural information avail-

A able to help or define their gender identity or mark themselves linguistically with a tribal term.

In very few Native communities are tribal members defined as gay, lesbian, two-spirit, or by their specific tribal gender term, which does not refer to a man or a woman. There is flexibility in how gender markers are used, and this varies from one tribal group to another. Thus, gender identity or sexuality changes according to what environment someone is in at any given moment. For example, when one is a participant in a religious event on a reservation, a specific tribal term is used, for example, *na'dleeh, dilbaaí,* or *winkte.* But when one leaves the reservation and returns to an urban area, he or she may be referred to as a gay or a lesbian. Furthermore, this same person could be labeled as a two-spirit when not within his or her own reservation but in another Native community or at a gathering of Native people. In addition, Native people who no longer have a direct relationship with their heritage might use this label, or they might simply refer to themselves as gay or lesbian.

To complicate the Western view of gender and sexuality, sexuality in Native cultures often has different tribal or cultural definitions. Within the very few traditional Native settings where the basic cultural rules are abided by, a sexual relationship between a male-bodied woman and a heterosexual man is viewed as a heterosexual relationship. This type of relationship is, however, viewed as homosexual in Western cultures. The same is true for a relationship between a female-bodied man and a heterosexually defined woman: their relationship in Native cultures is seen as heterosexual. Gender status is the deciding factor in how these relationships are defined. In most traditional Native communities, gender supersedes the physical sex of a person's body.

The way gender and sexuality are defined within traditional Native communities in the United States is obviously different from how relationships are constructed within the broader Euro-American cultures. For example, some Native sexual relationships are defined and established in ways that preclude bisexuality. In these communities, bisexuality is seen to exist only if one is unable to acknowledge the importance and function of traditionally expanded categories of gender status and role.

The world of engenderment—the ways in which genders are conceived, assigned, and lived—is extremely varied among American Indian, Alaskan Native, and First Nations (Canadians) societies. There has been little analysis of indigenous words,

which are contextually placed within a lexicon of the attributions of gender by speakers of Native languages. Rather, there is increasingly a designation of terms for those individuals who fit third- or fourth-gender categories—be they males or females in their outward appearances. Outsiders who attribute meaning and gender categories for the occupants of these gender roles often utilize these terms. Even though the gender researchers often state that they have checked their words with their "informants," there is seldom a referral to reconfirm the linguistic connotation of these appellations. It was thus encouraging in the late 1990s to note that emic analyses are beginning to occur in the field of naming, designating, and attributing the range of gender occupancies in some aboriginal groups. This direction is significant, for it is an attempt to deal with the permutations of gender-specific categories within indigenous total cultural frameworks, rather than subsuming them under "gay and lesbian studies" alone. These new attempts should also focus upon the ways in which terms are shared in a given cultural group and the ways in which they are seen to differ in the ordinary usage in this cultural group. This latter caveat is necessary in order to give meaning to the cultural construction of gender. *Wesley Thomas (Navajo)*
Beatrice Medicine (Standing Rock Lakota)

Bibliography

Jacobs, Sue-Ellen, Wesley Thomas, and Sabine Lang, eds. *Two-Spirit People: Native American Gender Identity, Sexuality, and Spirituality.* Urbana: University of Illinois Press, 1997.

Trexler, Richard C. *Sex and Conquest: Gendered Violence, Political Order, and the European Conquest of the Americas.* Ithaca, N.Y.: Cornell University Press, 1995.

Williams, Walter L. *The Spirit and the Flesh: Sexual Diversity in American Indian Culture.* Boston: Beacon Press, 1986.

See also Anthropology; Berdache; Canada; Gender

Amsterdam

This medieval city experienced its greatest expansion and its Golden Age in the seventeenth century, when it considered itself to be the center of the world. The first signs of subcultures of sodomites are to be encountered in the latter part of that century, and they became abundant with the large-scale persecutions of sodomites in the Dutch Republic

Amsterdam Canal Parade. Photo by Jan Carel Warffemius.

novel in Dutch, *Pijpelijntjes,* by Jacob Israël de Haan, providing detailed information on gay life in Amsterdam. The book provoked a scandal, and De Haan lost his jobs as a teacher and as a journalist for the socialist daily newspaper.

All the while, a gay and lesbian bar culture was slowly developing, but it was fervently persecuted by the police. Gay bars were the targets of raids both before and during World War II. Although the German occupiers did introduce their antihomosexual legislation in the Netherlands, they undertook little to enforce it. The few Dutch gays to be prosecuted under this law had had sexual relations with German soldiers. Soon after the war, a significant subculture of bars and dance halls unfolded in Amsterdam. Lesbians played a key role in this expanding subculture, often acting as bartenders. The most celebrated example was the butch dyke Bet van Beeren of 't Mandje, a bar frequented by gay men, lesbians, sailors, and prostitutes. The DOK, the largest gay dance hall in the world at its inception in 1952, brought Amsterdam world fame. The first leather bar, Argos, in the 1950s and the first gay sauna in the 1960s bolstered Amsterdam's reputation as it became an important travel destination gay British and French men.

The COC, the Dutch homophile movement, was launched in Amsterdam in 1946 and enjoyed its heyday during the sexual revolution of the 1960s and early 1970s. As early as the late 1950s, Amsterdam had already become a gay capital, with a burgeoning subculture and a strong political movement. Halfway through the 1970s, lesbian and gay groups queered sexual politics. In the late 1970s, a whole network of gay groups sprang up alongside the COC, in trade unions, political parties, universities, medicine, and many other walks of life. AIDS hit Amsterdam slightly later than other gay centers, and the response of the gay movement and the government was more prompt. Sex venues and darkrooms were not shut down, because they were regarded not just as places for virus transmission but for safe-sex education as well. An important institution has been the homosexual help organization—the Schorer Foundation—founded in 1967 and growing wings during the AIDS epidemic of the 1980s. Amsterdam's gay reputation has been ebbing since the 1980s, although one new impulse in the 1990s has come from kinky sex parties. Yet as other western European cities began to generate sexual infrastructures similar to those Amsterdam had developed earlier, the city relinquished its head start. The

beginning in 1730. Cruising took place in taverns, on squares, on city walls, in churches, and underneath the very city hall, in front of which sodomites were being executed for the crime of sodomy (anal penetration). In the late eighteenth century some tribades (lesbians) were persecuted as well.

Little is known about the *verkeerde liefhebbers* (wrong lovers) in the first part of the nineteenth century, but their underworlds surfaced toward the end of the century. Police began actively harassing homosexual spaces and doctors began writing their case histories. At the close of the nineteenth century, an antivice organization published a list of brothels that also included the addresses of six or so homosexual meeting places. From 1897 onward, the Amsterdam physicians Arnold Aletrino and Lucien von Römer took up the cause of homosexual emancipation. Both belonged to the Dutch section of the Wissenschaftlich-humanitéres Komitee (Scientific Humanitarian Committee), founded in 1912 in The Hague. In 1901, Aletrino defended the rights of "uranians" before the fifth congress of criminal anthropology in Amsterdam, facing an audience of staunch adversaries, among them Cesare Lombroso. The year 1904 saw the appearance of the first gay advantages it can still boast are its tolerant social climate, compact urban structure, and architectural beauty.

Lesbians have been consistently marginal in Amsterdam's subculture. The first exclusively lesbian bar opened in 1970, but later efforts to establish similar venues met with little success. The predominant features of lesbian life at present are circles of friends meeting at home or on sports fields. A few small, mostly mixed bars are the visible part of the lesbian scene, and some discos and bars feature monthly lesbian parties. In the gay movement, where lesbian women were largely absent up to the 1960s, they gained an equal place in the 1980s and 1990s. Today equal homosexual rights have been virtually secured in the Netherlands, and both the national and the city government have resolved to pursue policies of nondiscrimination toward gays and lesbians. Some major incidents, such as gay bashing at the national pride day in nearby Amersfoort in 1982 and the murder of a gay man cruising in an Amsterdam park in 1985, gave a strong boost to homosexual politics in the Netherlands.

In many cities, including Amsterdam, the police force is now required to learn about gays and lesbians and to protect gay cruising places. At the Amsterdam city hall, a deputy mayor and a city official have been charged with shaping a form of homosexual emancipation that emphasizes lesbian visibility, and the city council has several openly gay or lesbian members. The city authorities have strongly endorsed the 1998 Amsterdam Gay Games. While gay and lesbian emancipation is thus a prominent feature of Amsterdam politics, city officials still show little awareness that their city is a major gay tourist attraction and little willingness to promote this attribute. Much to the contrary, they are extremely wary of Amsterdam's "bad" reputation as a city of sex and drugs. A planned campaign to advertise Amsterdam as a gay capital was initially called off, owing to adverse reactions from commercial interests, but has since been resumed. Amsterdam may be a gay capital, but its gay institutions and opportunities do not enjoy universal endorsement from politicians or from the public at large. *Gert Hekma*

Bibliography

Hekma, Gert. *De roze rand van donker Amsterdam. De opkomst van een homoseksuele kroegcultuur, 1930–1970*. Amsterdam: van Gennep, 1992.

van der Meer, Theo. *Sodoms zaad in Nederland. Het ontstaan van homoseksualiteit in de vroegmoderne tijd*. Nijmegen: SUN, 1995.

See also C.O.C.; Haan, Jacob Israel de Netherlands

Anarchism

Anarchism, a variety of socialism, was forged in the political and economic struggles of the mid-nineteenth century. By 1900 it could claim millions of adherents around the world. The Russian Revolution of 1917 and the rise of fascism in the 1930s cut deeply into anarchist ranks. Since that time anarchism has subsisted as an intellectual and cultural tradition rather than a mass movement. Though they differ on tactics and goals, all anarchists uphold the sovereignty of the individual and reject representational politics. Inspired by their ideals, anarchists have formulated trenchant critiques of religion, law, marriage, and other social relations.

Throughout its history anarchism has provided a home for sexual dissidents. During its heyday, anarchist journals such as *Revista Blanca*, *Mother Earth,* and *The Free Comrade* published articles sympathetic to homoeroticism. Benjamin R. Tucker and Emma Goldman were among the few public figures to defend Oscar Wilde during his sexual show trial of 1895. (Historian George Woodcock argues that the fury unleashed toward Wilde was, in part, a function of Wilde's political writings.) In the early 1900s, Goldman and Alexander Berkman gave public lectures on the subject of homosexuality. Less well-known anarchists such as John William Lloyd, E. Armand, and John Henry Mackay wrote extensively on same-sex eroticism.

In the late 1960s anarchism reemerged as a strong influence in gay and lesbian politics. In Paris in 1968, graffiti appeared on walls calling for the liberation and multiplication of homosexual desires, and Murray Bookchin's work circulated in New York's Gay Liberation Front. The direct-action tactics and decentralized structure of gay liberation and lesbian-feminist groups, and more recently ACT UP and WHAM (Women's Health Action and Mobilization), were anarchistic in form if not always in inspiration. In the post-1960s era, periodicals such as the *Arrow: Bulletin of the Mackay Society* continued in the now venerable tradition of anarchist sexual agitprop. Contemporary radical feminists, such as Bonnie Haaland, who are critical of social purity crusaders, identify themselves as anarchists. And today in many cities, anarchist bookstores continue to be some of the few places that carry literature that dispassionately—and sometimes passionately—examines intergenerational eroticism, sadomasochism, and other marginalized sexual practices.

Anarchism has also influenced in the world of gay and lesbian arts and letters. Henry James's novel *The Princess Casamassima* was one of the many works of the late nineteenth and early twentieth centuries to feature anarchists. The bohemian demimonde of the period was suffused with anarchist imagery and influences: the Decadent writers and artists of Europe were identified as anarchists by both supporters and detractors; the anarchists Leonard Abbott and Helena Born celebrated the expansive sexuality found in Walt Whitman's poetry; and Margaret Anderson and George Sylvester Viereck (who would later become a Nazi sympathizer) were but two of the Greenwich Village literary avant-garde who flirted with anarchism. In the post–World War II era, the work of Paul Goodman, the rather less-well-known authors of "queer zines," and others have kept alive anarchist thought and practice in the realm of sexuality, politics, and the arts.   *Terence Kissack*

Bibliography

Sonn, Richard D. *Anarchism*. New York: Twayne, 1992.

Haaland, Bonnie. *Emma Goldman: Sexuality and the Impurity of the State*. Montreal: Black Rose Books, 1993.

See also ACT UP; Decadence; Gay Liberation Front; Goodman, Paul; James, Henry

Androgyny

"When you meet a human being, the first distinction you make is 'male or female?' and you are accustomed to make the distinction with unhesitating certainty," Freud tells us in his famous 1932 essay on femininity. Because it confounds just such confident participation in our sex-gender system, androgyny, from the Greek *andro* (male) and *gyne* (female), has been both valorized and vilified over the years, together with its sometime synonym, *hermaphroditism*, or *intersexuality*. Whereas intersexuality is most often understood as a relatively rare biological hybrid of male and female, androgyny usually is imagined as a potential in all of us, a psychological composite of masculinity and femininity

that for some of its advocates necessarily expresses itself in bisexuality, rather than hetero- or homosexuality. In the West, the androgyne has often figured the wholeness or totality of one who seems to transcend the limitations of having only one sex or sexuality, at once both and neither. Writers and other artists—from the romantic poets Coleridge and Shelley to feminist modernist Virginia Woolf—therefore frequently have claimed that the great mind is androgynous, rather than expressive of a single gender. Philosophers too have embraced androgyny, perhaps especially those interested in the religious occult, including traditions in which Christ is represented as having feminine as well as masculine qualities. For psychologist Carl Jung, who was fascinated by alchemy and hermeticism, the healthy psyche was androgynous, integrating female anima and male animus so as to fully realize human potential. Like Jung, idealizers of androgyny have found support in the Western tradition of mysticism (as well as in Jung himself), but more recently, they have turned to non-Western cultures for recognition of the legitimacy and even special powers of the androgynous or transgendered, from the Indian hijra to the Siberian shaman, the Native American berdache or winkte to the Polynesian mahu. Nevertheless, the most often cited source for the value of androgyny is still Plato's *Symposium*. According to Aristophanes, one of the characters in that Platonic dialogue, the perfection of the androgynes threatened even the power of Zeus himself. Zeus therefore split them—together with the two single-sexed and homosexual beings whose union was evidently equally disturbing to the gods and generally forgotten by Plato's later readers. Ever since, human beings have been searching for their missing half; it is this comedy of love and lack that finally allayed Zeus's fears.

The belief that androgyny is a liberation from limiting and polarized gender and sexual roles led to its embrace by both feminists and gay liberationists in the early 1970s. Carolyn Heilbrun opened her influential feminist text on the topic, *Toward a Recognition of Androgyny* (1973), by arguing that androgyny "suggests a spectrum upon which human beings choose their places without regard to propriety or custom" (xi). In a chapter in the equally important *Homosexual Oppression and Liberation* (1972) entitled "Liberation: Toward the Polymorphous Whole," Dennis Altman called for "freedom from the surplus repression that prevents us from recognizing our essential androgynous and erotic natures" (83), including our "bisexual potential" (94),

A a sentiment echoed by Gayle Rubin in her much-cited 1975 essay, "The Traffic in Women": "The dream I find most compelling is one of an androgynous and genderless (though not sexless) society, in which one's sexual anatomy is irrelevant to who one is, what one does, and with whom one makes love" (204). However, androgyny quickly came under fire from some of the very feminists who had endorsed it, including lesbian feminist Adrienne Rich, who excluded her poem about it, "The Stranger," from her collected poems and later wrote a critique of it in *Of Woman Born* (1976). For Rich and others, androgyny had come to be complicit with, rather than critical of, patriarchy. Androgyny seemed to be a personal, rather than political, solution to the problems of the sex-gender system, and in any case, it did not recognize gender inequity as crucial to that system's institutions and functioning. The androgyne, as the word itself suggested, was most often a man perfected through the addition of some femininity; this only reinscribed the masculine as the norm and ideal and consolidated the construction of the sexes as opposite and complementary without exposing that fabrication. As feminists pointed out, by the late 1970s and early 1980s, androgyny was little more than a fashion statement that signified a generalized eroticism congruent with new youth ideals of gender. The basic heterosexual appeal (and sexism) of male glam and heavy metal rockers and of female body-builders was generally supported, rather than subverted, by their assimilation of some cross-gender elements of character, costume, or physique, as long as it was not explicitly bisexual, as with David Bowie, or too "butch" and potentially lesbian, as with Bev Francis, one of the lead female weightlifters in the film *Pumping Iron II*.

At about the same time as androgyny fell out of favor with feminists, it also ceased to function as an ideal in the gay movement, which in response to Michel Foucault's *History of Sexuality* and other postmodern critiques of sexuality and gender began to question the whole notion of "liberation" to which androgyny was tied. The initial gay enthusiasm for androgyny owed something to its similarity to early homophile movement notions of homosexuals as a "third sex" of "uranians" or "inverts" combining the masculine and the feminine (which owed much to the work of sexologists and psychoanalysts such as Magnus Hirschfeld and Freud). As lesbians and gay men began to struggle against the medical establishment's view of such "gender dysphoria" as a sign of poor mental health and gender inadequacy, rather than androgynous wholeness, they increasingly rejected drag, butch-femme roles, and other forms of gender-crossing and combining. Lesbian and gay movement theorists, like feminists, began to stress the Foucaultian notion that gender identities were social constructs and the psychoanalytic idea that they were impossible ideals, locating differences within as well as between the sexes that made calls for the androgynous addition of gender difference seem naive. More recently, however, there has been a revalorization of drag and cross-dressing as self-reflexive examples of the social construction of gender and as critiques of the gender binary, an argument made by both "queer theorists" and members of the gender community, including transvestites, drag queens, drag kings, transsexuals (pre-, post-, and nonoperative), intersexuals, she-males, boy-chicks, transgenderists, gender-benders, those who engage in genderfuck, and others who now identify themselves as "transgendered," neither male nor female (or sometimes both). In *Vested Interests* (1992) Marjorie Garber asserts that such practices only constitute "a space of possibility" and are "not an instantiated 'blurred' sex as signified by a term like 'androgyne' or 'hermaphrodite'" (11), yet for her and other queer theorists such as Judith Butler and Foucault, the gender and sex crossings and combinings we now identify with "transgender" have a privileged status, as androgyny once did. For some they move beyond an androgyny that imagined only two genders, as Kate Bornstein implies in *Gender Outlaw* (1994) when she calls for what she believes transgender implies, "the ability to freely and knowingly become one or many of a limitless number of genders for any length of time, at any rate of change" (52). For others, however, among them lesbian feminist critic Biddy Martin, they are only manifestations of a new, queer androgyny, a refusal of sexual difference through the defensive disavowal of femininity and the limitations of having a sexed body. Such androgyny is impossible because it abolishes identity along with gender, according to Francette Pacteau, in "a narcissistic 'caress' in which the subject annihilates itself" (82).

Carole-Anne Tyler

Bibliography

Bornstein, Kate. *Gender Outlaw: On Men, Women, and the Rest of Us.* New York: Routledge, 1994.
Butler, Judith. *Gender Trouble: Feminism and the Subversion of Identity.* New York: Routledge, 1990.

Devor, Holly. *Gender Blending: Confronting the Limits of Duality*. Bloomington, Ind.: Indiana University Press, 1989.

Garber, Marjorie. *Vested Interests: Cross-Dressing and Cultural Anxiety*. New York: Routledge, 1992.

Heilbrun, Carolyn. *Toward a Recognition of Androgyny*. New York: Norton, 1973.

Herdt, Gilbert, ed. *Third Sex, Third Gender: Beyond Sexual Dimorphism in Culture and History*. New York: Zone Books, 1994.

Hirschfeld, Magnus. *Die transvestiten*. 1910. Michael Lombardi-Nash, trans. *Transvestites: An Investigation of the Erotic Drive to Cross-Dress*. Amherst, N.Y.: Prometheus Books, 1991.

Martin, Biddy. "Extraordinary Homosexuals." *Differences* 6 no. 2-3 (Summer–Fall 1994): 100–125.

Pacteau, Francette. "The Impossible Referent: Representations of the Androgyne." In *Formations of Fantasy*. Victor Burgin, James Donald, and Cora Kaplan, eds. New York: Methuen, 1986, pp. 62–84.

Weil, Kari. *Androgyny and the Denial of Difference*. Charlottesville, Va.: University Press of Virginia, 1992.

See also Altman, Dennis; Berdache; Bisexuality; Effeminacy; Essentialist-Constructionist Debate; Feminism; Foucault, Michel; Freud, Sigmund; Gay Liberation; Gender; Hermaphroditism; Hijras of India; Hirschfeld, Magnus; Homophile Movement; Homosexuality; Intersexua/Intersexuality; Inversion; Jung, Carl; Masculinity; Music and Musicians 2 (Popular Music); Oppression; Plato; Postmodernism; Psychological and Psychoanalytic Perspectives on Homosexuality; Queer Theory; Sexology; Sexual Orientation; Third Sex; Transgender; Transvestism; Uranianism

Anger, Kenneth (1930?–)

An American filmmaker and writer, Anger is one of the first important underground filmmakers of the post–World War II era. His first major film, *Fireworks* (1947), portrays a young man's homoerotic dreams, including cruising public rest rooms, being brutalized by sailors, and connecting with another sailor. The film is dreamy and deeply interiorized and has clear influences in European and American modernist art film. After a nearly a decade living in Europe, Anger came back to the States and produced the work that he is most known for, particularly *Scorpio Rising* (1963).

Scorpio Rising is considered by many to be the most representative film of the 1960s underground. The film focuses on motorcycles and motorcycle culture in thirteen sections, depicting men fixing and polishing their bikes, getting dressed in leather and other bike gear, attending a party, driving recklessly, and crashing. Each section's soundtrack is a pop song from the early 1960s, and this film is the first to use this technique. The film is also littered with pop imagery: movie star stills, comic book images, and kitsch items that help place the film in a more postmodern bricolage tradition. The homoeroticism in the film is intense, created by cut shots from man's face to man's face, or from face to crotch. One section includes a party with drag queens, men kissing, and the stripping of one man and squirting him with mustard. The film also explores the uncomfortable relationship among masculinity, homosexuality, and fascism through a sequence of "Scorpio" speaking in front of a Nazi flag, ambivalently and humorously splicing it with footage of a film of Jesus.

Anger finished ten films and also wrote the widely popular *Hollywood Babylon* books.

Douglas Eisner

Bibliography

Haller, Robert. *Kenneth Anger*. Minneapolis: Walker Art Center, 1980.

Moon, Michael. "A Small Boy and Others: Sexual Disorientation in Henry James, Kenneth Anger, and David Lynch." In *Comparative American Identities*. Hortense Spillers, ed. New York: Routledge, 1991.

Suárez, Juan A. *Bike Boys, Drag Queens, and Superstar: Avant-Gard, Mass Culture, and Gay Identities in the 1960s Underground Cinema*. Bloomington: Indiana University Press, 1996.

See also Film; Smith, Jack; Tearooms

Animal Sexual Behavior

It is probably incorrect to speak of homosexual animals or animal homosexuality, because virtually nothing is known about the cognitive aspects of sexuality in nonhuman species (hereafter, animals). In contrast, male homosexual behavior involving courtship, pair bonding, mounting, and other forms

A

of genital contact has been noted in numerous animal species independent of hormonal or neurological manipulation. Some of these interactions involve clear sexual elements, since erections and ejaculation are sometimes observed. Isolated anecdotes concerning male sexual behavior exist for numerous species in nature, but very few studies have focused on this behavior and attempted to place it within a larger constellation of social and sexual behaviors. To date, the most detailed studies of male homosexual behavior in animals have been on birds (razorbills, pukekos, greylag geese), primates (bonobos, mountain gorillas), and domestic livestock (pigs, sheep, goats).

Some of the first systematic studies of male homosexual behavior were conducted toward the end of the Victorian era. During the 1890s, research on pigeons argued erroneously that an absence of opposite-sex partners and artificial confinement could "force" males to choose same-sex mates. The use of caged subjects meant that homosexual interactions were invariably characterized as abnormal products of captivity, unlikely to be found in "nature." Moreover, male choice of same-sex mates was seen as Hobson's choice: that is, a choice made for want of any female alternatives. These early investigations may have helped foster the paradigm of homosexual behavior as an abnormal phenomenon. This viewpoint is still widespread among zoologists today.

With the emergence of sociobiology in the 1970s, a paradigmatic shift occurred that resulted in some zoologist's reconceptualizing homosexual behavior as an adaptation produced by natural selection. Within this theoretical framework, homosexual behavior was often depicted as socially beneficial, a perspective cheered by gay activists. Indeed, a number of researchers have demonstrated that homosexual activity among male animals sometimes serves various social roles including dominance demonstration, tension regulation, reconciliation, and alliance formation. More often than not, however, sociobiology was unsuccessful in establishing supporting evidence for the many adaptive hypotheses it generated to explain homosexual interactions. It may well be that sexual stimulation provides sufficient motivation in and of itself for animals to engage in homosexual behavior. Homosexual behavior in animals serves a social function and provides sexual stimulation at the same time.

Opponents of gay rights frequently claim that homosexual behavior is unnatural and use erroneous notions about animal behavior to support such opinions. While the logic that equates all that is "natural" with all that is socially desirable is faulty, its popular folk appeal is undeniable. Knowledge concerning male homosexual behavior among animals can be of value to those interested in negating such claims and placing human homosexuality within a larger, cross-species perspective. For instance, while homosexual behavior is widespread among male animals, aggression specifically directed to individuals who engage in such behavior appears to be a uniquely human invention lacking any counterpart in nature.   *Paul L. Vasey*

Bibliography

Dagg, Anne I. "Homosexual Behaviour and Female-Male Mounting in Animals—A First Survey." *Mammal Review* 14 (1984): 155–185.

Vasey, Paul L. "Homosexual Behavior in Primates: A Review of Evidence and Theory." *International Journal of Primatology* 16 (1995): 173–204.

See also Homosexuality; Sexual Orientation

Anthropology

Anthropology seeks to understand the different ways in which humans live their lives as social beings. It has traditionally been distinguished from psychology and sociology, the two social sciences that arose alongside it in the late nineteenth century, by an emphasis on culture and society (versus the individual psyche) on the one hand, and by an emphasis on comparative, qualitative data on the other. Anthropology is divided into four subfields: physical anthropology (the study of human biological adaptation and variation, particularly through the study of prehistoric human remains [paleontology] or present-day primates [primatology]), archaeology (the study of material remains and artifacts), linguistic anthropology (the study of language and its relationship to human social life), and social/cultural anthropology (the study of society and culture). Most work on homosexuality, bisexuality, and transgenderism within anthropology has taken place within the last of these four subfields, social/cultural anthropology.

Social/cultural anthropology developed from an earlier social science known as "ethnology," which gained prominence in the mid-nineteenth century. Ethnology was concerned with the comparative search for human universals and/or evolutionary sequences of social and cultural phenomena. Understanding the lives of "primitives" was thought to shed light on the early history of "civilized" peoples: Primitives were seen as living fossils whose physique and lifeways provided a glimpse into the past. Of particular interest to ethnologists were "primitive" marriage and kinship, since many were concerned with the status of women in industrial society, and so in a sense the study of sexuality has always been integral to anthropology (see Morgan). Most ethnologists, however, did not travel for even short periods to "primitive" places, relying instead on the written accounts of travelers, missionaries, and colonial officials. The discipline of anthropology took its current form in the first decades of the twentieth century, particularly through the work of Bronislaw Malinowski and Franz Boas—who, in contrast to the ethnologists, emphasized firsthand experience with other cultures through extended periods of fieldwork.

Social/cultural anthropology is primarily concerned with "culture," a highly contested term that many authors would provisionally define as those ways of thinking, patterns of social interaction, and sets of power relations within which human beings live their lives and understand their existence. Human beings enter the world with a highly underdeveloped cognitive system relative to other animals, and the vast majority of human behavior is learned rather than genetically transmitted. While there are human instincts and universal aspects to human cognition (which can be seen, for instance, in linguistic universals), these universal aspects of human existence only become manifest in the specific milieu in which a child grows up. Human beings are fundamentally social animals and their cognitive development depends upon particular cultural contexts.

Social/cultural anthropology (hereafter "anthropology") is the study of these varied contexts. Its primary methodology is participant observation, the process of structured involvement in (and critique of) the life of a community or communities. Its primary product is ethnography, the written record of some aspect of a culture or cultures. In addition to participant observation, anthropologists sometimes use techniques such as interviews and focus groups, and they also rely extensively on the analysis of texts and historical data in cases where these exist. In addition to ethnographies, anthropologists sometimes produce reports, films, music, performance art, or fiction and are frequently involved in various forms of political activism. Since anthropologists seek to understand the ways of thinking of a particular group of people, an important aspect of the anthropologist's work is to call into question his or her own cultural assumptions. This is the case even when the anthropologist is studying a culture that is in some respect his or her "own." Anthropologists strive to make this self-critique as complete as possible, calling into question even such foundational concepts as "person," "power," "cognition," "sexuality," and, of course, "culture" itself. It must be noted, however, that self-critique can never be complete. (It is impossible to be completely aware of one's own assumptions, and thus collaboration and peer critique are vital.) Additionally, the internal critique of anthropology is a relatively recent development, gaining a foothold only in the 1980s.

Early anthropology remained closely intertwined with colonialism and thus emphasized the study of exotic "others," often with the explicit goal of enabling colonial powers to better understand and control their colonies. Sexuality in general and homosexuality in particular played a key role in this process. One of the best analyses of the relationship between same-sex practices and early anthropology is Rudi Bleys's *The Geography of Perversion* (1995). Bleys shows how early ethnologists built on the ostensible distinction between "innate" and "acquired" homosexuality to portray homosexuality as merely incidental in the West, but endemic to the "Orient." Homosexuality could thus serve as a crucial conceptual barrier distinguishing colonizer from colonized. In the "Terminal Essay" of his 1885 translation of the *Thousand and One Arabian Nights,* Sir Richard Burton provides a classic formulation of this paradigm in his notion of the "Sotadic Zone," stretching from the Mediterranean through India, and China to the New World, wherein "the vice [of pederasty] is popular and endemic, held at the worst to be a mere peccadillo."

Beginning in the 1920s, Malinowski and a new generation of anthropologists like Margaret Mead and Ruth Benedict began using anthropology to challenge evolutionary models from ethnology as well as colonialism and Freudian psychoanalysis. Under the banner of the "culture and personality" movement, they used notions of *cultural relativity* to argue that a unilinear narrative of savagery to civilization was grounded in a racist framework that failed to appreciate the multiple ways in which it was possible to become a person and live in society. They also sought to critique established gender norms in the West by comparing them with radically

A different gender norms outside the West (Benedict, Mead). One important way they did this was by showing that Freud's ostensibly universal narrative of childhood development, centered around the Oedipus complex, was in fact but one culturally specific variant of how people came to understand themselves as individuals (Malinowski). Sexuality was a frequent theme in this work and the existence of homosexuality in "other" cultures was catalogued with a rather tolerant attitude. However, homosexuality (or bisexuality, or transgenderism) was rarely the focus of study, and homosexuality in the West itself was left to sociologists studying "social deviance."

In the 1950s and 1960s, reeling from the horrors of World War II and thesis of essential human evil that arose in its aftermath, the *structural-functionalist* school gained ascendancy in many social sciences, including anthropology. Structural-functionalists built on the work of Emile Durkheim and A. R. Radcliffe-Brown, among others, to develop a theory of society as an organism with constituent elements that contributed to the smooth functioning of the whole. Under this theoretical framework "normal" gender roles (like most dominant elements of culture) were valorized as structurally necessary, while "deviant" gender roles and sexualities were stigmatized as diseases of the body politic. From the mid-1960s, however, a growing body of work in feminist anthropology (and feminism more generally) challenged structural-functionalist explanations of gender inequality, exposing the conceptual incoherencies of this work as well as the role it played in legitimating the status quo oppression of women (Rosaldo and Lamphere, Reiter). While nonheterosexual sexualities were rarely addressed by these feminists, their work laid the foundations for the anthropological study of homosexuality, bisexuality, and transgenderism.

Anthropological studies of homosexuality itself began to blossom in the 1970s. Kath Weston's 1993 essay "Lesbian/Gay Studies in the House of Anthropology" provides a comprehensive review up to the early 1990s. The pioneering work in this field is usually seen to be Esther Newton's pathbreaking study of female impersonators, *Mother Camp* (first published in 1972), though other important research had begun ten years before Newton's. In the decade following Newton's work, the majority of anthropological studies of homosexuality fell into a pattern Weston dubs "ethnocartography," the search for "evidence of same-sex sexuality and gendered ambigu-ity in 'other' societies" (Weston, *Families* 341). Weston notes that this approach was characterized by severe theoretical lacunae: "many an author opens with an obligatory nod to Foucault before presenting research findings, but more commonly, the researcher's theoretical perspectives remain embedded in apparently straightforward reports from the field. In effect, the absence of theory becomes the submersion of theory. Lurking between the lines are functionalist explanations, ethnocentric assumptions, and ad hoc syntheses of philosophically incompatible schools of thought" (Weston, *Families* 344). In this respect, what Weston terms "the 'salvage' anthropology of indigenous homosexualities" parallels the "gay history" movement of the 1980s which attempted to uncover an ostensibly "hidden" history of homosexuality. Where gay history looked for comrades across time, gay anthropology searched through space. While the gay history movement brought to light previously little-known data (as did "ethnocartography" in anthropology), by subsuming this data under a rubric of "gay history" it assumed the data represented the "same" phenomenon and thus took as given precisely the point that should have been the goal of inquiry. More recent work in "gay history" has largely moved beyond these limitations by using a more sophisticated analytical framework to ask how particular same-sex identities, communities, and practices were understood by the participants themselves (see, for instance, Kennedy and Davis, Chauncey).

In general, this "documentary rush" in both history and anthropology was occasioned by the political climate of the 1970s and 1980s, in which a newly emergent gay and lesbian movement faced the charge that it was a decadent "lifestyle" occasioned by a particular conjunction of decadent morality and soulless consumerism. Documenting the existence of homosexualities across time and space was seen as countering this claim by showing how same-sex desire could be found in social and economic circumstances radically different from the contemporary West. In some cases, this work was also used to argue for a transhistorical, universal homosexuality rooted in biology rather than the familial psychodrama of the dominant psychoanalytic paradigm.

Beginning in the mid-1980s, however, a growing chorus of academics and activists began to argue against this trend, building upon the theoretical framework of Michel Foucault to claim that homosexualities were "socially constructed" rather than reflecting genetic or hormonal essences. The "essentialist/social constructionist" debates are beyond the scope of this article, except to note that anthropological data were used primarily (but not exclusively) to support the "social constructionist" side of the controversy. This makes sense in the context of social/cultural anthropology's own focus on culture and difference.

Despite these contributions, anthropology has had a somewhat marginal place in the emerging field of lesbian/gay/bisexual/transgender (hereafter LGBT) studies in the 1980s and 1990s. One reason for this has been LGBT studies' emphasis on theoretical advances over substantive research. While anthropology has had a strong theoretical component from its beginnings, it has lagged behind other fields of inquiry in this respect in the second half of the twentieth century. With a few exceptions, contemporary anthropologists draw their theoretical paradigms largely from other disciplines (e.g., history, literary theory, and philosophy). While this interdisciplinary standpoint has been highly fruitful, it has not aided the entry of anthropology into LGBT studies. In addition, anthropological fieldwork is an extremely time-consuming and difficult process, whether undertaken in one's "own" culture or "another" culture, in one's own country or abroad. Since there is little funding available for LGBT-themed anthropological research, and even fewer job positions for anthropologists working on these topics, there are to this day remarkably few in-depth ethnographies of LGBT communities (but see Parker, Weston [*Families*], Carrier, Shokeid, Prieur).

Nevertheless, we can identify three hopeful trends as LGBT anthropology enters the twenty-first century. First, there is a growing body of work which "anthropologizes" the West. Instead of documenting the existence of LGBT communities in exotic "other" places, these works turn the anthropological gaze onto the West itself, examining how LGBT identities vary in different contexts and how they are related to other aspects of Western cultures such as kinship, class, and race. Kath Weston's study of kinship in LGBT communities (*Families We Choose*) and Moshe Shokeid's study of Judaism and LGBT identity (*A Gay Synagogue in New York*) are excellent examples of this trend. Second, while most anthropological LGBT studies have focused on gay male identities and communities, a growing number of works are examining transgenderism, bisexuality, and lesbianism, though transgenderism has received more attention than either lesbianism or bisexuality to this point. Finally, a growing number of works eschew the traditional search for non-Western "indigenous" or "traditional" homosexualities to ask instead how growing numbers of individuals outside the West transform the ostensibly Western terms *gay, lesbian,* and *bisexual* so that they become seen as locally relevant. In Indonesia, for example, this process results in new identities and a complex sense of global community that can be reduced neither to a simplistic universal "queer planet" nor to a narrative of cultural loss and the eclipse of "native" authenticity by modernization (Boellstorff).

Anthropology, then, has an important role to play in the developing field of LGBT studies. On the level of data, anthropological techniques can help us understand how LGBT identity and community are lived "on the ground" by people around the world, including those who produce few or no magazines, films, and other sorts of documents. This allows us to link the theoretical advances of LGBT studies to the practices of everyday life. While beyond the scope of this entry, LGBT anthropology (often in conjunction with medical anthropology) also plays an important role in HIV/AIDS prevention by demonstrating the culturally specific ways in which risk, sex, and disease are conceptualized in different LGBT communities (Bolton and Singer, ten Brummelhuis and Herdt).

On the level of theory, anthropology helps us to understand the diversity of beliefs and practices behind terms like "lesbian" and "gay," and how this diversity is related to factors of economics, power, family, religion, gender, and nation. Anthropology can help us understand how the very category of "sexuality" contains crucial cultural assumptions about what it means to be a person, and how other groups of people may understand sex and personhood differently. Finally, anthropology can play a crucial role in "making strange" heterosexuality itself, showing its historical and cultural instability and the ways in which its coherence depends on the oppression of LGBT communities. Not only new LGBT identities but new heterosexualities can be charted through anthropological methods.

Thomas Maurer Boellstorff

Bibliography

Benedict, Ruth. *Patterns of Culture.* New York: Mentor Books, 1934.

Bleys, Rudi. *The Geography of Perversion: Male-to-Male Sexual Behavior Outside the West and the Ethnographic Imagination, 1750–1918.* New York: New York University Press, 1995.

A

Boellstorff, Thomas Maurer. *The Gay Archipelago: Translocal Sexualities in Indonesia.* Forthcoming.

Bolton, Ralph, and Merrill Singer, eds. *Rethinking AIDS Prevention: Cultural Approaches.* Amsterdam: Gordon and Breach, 1992.

Burton, Sir Richard Francis. *A Plain and Literal Translation of the Arabian Nights.* 10 vols. Printed by the Kama Shastra Society for private subscribers of the Burton Club only, 1885–86. Facsimile edition. Denver: Press of the Carson-Harper Co., 1899–1901. Reprinted in 7 vols., New York: Limited Editions Club, 1934.

Carrier, Joseph. *De Los Otros: Intimacy and Homosexuality Among Mexican Men.* New York: Columbia University Press, 1995.

Chauncey, George. *Gay New York: Gender, Urban Culture, and the Making of the Gay Male World, 1890–1940.* New York: Basic Books, 1994.

Kennedy, Elizabeth Lapovsky, and Madeline D. Davis. *Boots of Leather, Slippers of Gold: The History of a Lesbian Community.* New York: Routledge, 1993.

Leap, William. *Word's Out: Gay Men's English.* Minneapolis: University of Minnesota Press, 1996.

Malinowski, Bronislaw. *Sex and Repression in Savage Society.* London: Routledge & Kegan Paul, 1927.

Mead, Margaret. *Sex and Temperament in Three Primitive Societies.* 1935. New York: Morrow Quill Paperbacks, 1980.

Morgan, Louis Henry. *Systems of Consanguinity and Affinity of the Human Family.* Smithsonian Contributions to Knowledge. Vol. 17. Washington, D.C.: Smithsonian Institution, 1871.

Newton, Esther. *Mother Camp: Female Impersonators in America.* Chicago: University of Chicago Press, 1972.

Parker, Richard G. *Bodies, Pleasures, and Passions: Sexual Culture in Contemporary Brazil.* Boston: Beacon Press, 1991.

Prieur, Annick. *Mema's House, Mexico City: On Transvestites, Queens, and Machos.* Chicago: University of Chicago Press, 1998.

Reiter, Rayna R., ed. *Toward an Anthropology of Women.* New York: Monthly Review Press, 1975.

Rosaldo and Lamphere, eds. *Woman, Culture and Society: A Theoretical Overview.* Stanford, Calif.: Stanford University Press, 1974.

Shokeid, Moshe. *A Gay Synagogue in New York.* New York: Columbia University Press, 1995.

Taylor, Timothy. *The Prehistory of Sex: Four Million Years of Human Sexual Culture.* New York: Bantam Books, 1996.

ten Brummelhuis, Han, and Gilbert Herdt, eds. *Culture and Sexual Risk: Anthropology and AIDS.* Amsterdam: Gordon and Breach, 1995.

Weston, Kath. *Families We Choose: Lesbians, Gays, Kinship.* New York: Columbia University Press, 1991.

———. "Lesbian/Gay Studies in the House of Anthropology." *Annual Review of Anthropology* 22 (1993): 339–367.

See also Arabian Nights; Bisexuality; Burton, Sir Richard Francis; Gay Families; Homosexuality

Antigay Initiatives and Propositions (U.S. Law)

Although gay men and lesbians have made numerous social and political gains in the United States since the struggles of early homophile organizations and the Stonewall riots of 1969, progress has not come without resistance from mainstream and conservative elements of the American public. More recently this resistance to the gay rights movement has become a well-organized and powerful effort by the right wing to scapegoat gays and lesbians for perceived "social ills," to ensure the continued criminalization of homosexuality, and to legalize discrimination against gays and lesbians.

Beginning in the 1970s gays and lesbians made major gains in the arena of gay rights by repealing the sodomy laws of various states and securing local ordinances protecting them from employment and housing discrimination. The first organized backlash or countermovement to gay rights advances began in 1977 with a fundamentalist Christian-based campaign in Dade County, Florida. Led by former beauty queen and Christian music entertainer Anita Bryant, the group successfully repealed a local ordinance protecting gay and lesbian employees from discrimination. This right-wing victory encouraged religious conservatives across the country to organize at a grassroots level in opposition to both gay and women's rights movements.

During the 1980s conservative Christian elements (led most notably by Jerry Falwell of the Moral Majority and the Christian Coalition's Pat Robertson) joined forces with social conservatives of the Republican Party. This new coalition of right-wing conservative groups, known collectively as the New Christian Right (NCR), became a major influence within the Republican Party and a bellwether for the political climate of the 1990s.

A presidential election year, 1992 was particularly important for both sides of the battleground over gay rights. While gays and lesbians were gaining greater visibility and clout within the Democratic Party and the Clinton/Gore campaign, they were also the target of scapegoat politics within the Republican Party and a poorly veiled rhetoric of "family values." Stopping "the gay agenda" became a battle cry of the NCR, which capitalized on a national discomfort with homosexuality in particular and a growing sentiment against affirmative action policies in general.

In November 1992, adversarial organizations of the gay rights movement and the NCR met head-on in the electoral battlefields of Oregon and Colorado as the residents of those states voted on similar initiatives that in effect would have banned state and local authorities from prohibiting discrimination based on sexual orientation. Although the initiatives were similar in intent, they differed radically in tone.

In Colorado the initiative, sponsored by Colorado for Family Values (CFV), tested a fairly new strategy of "special rights." "Special rights" was here used by gay rights opponents to refer to gay rights advocates' demand for equal protections under the law. Specifically, the CFV claimed that gays and lesbians were an elite class and did not need legal protections; thus they proposed to exclude "homosexual, lesbian, or bisexual orientation, conduct, practices, or relationships" from a minority or "protected status" and claims of discrimination.

Oregon's Measure 9 was backed by the Oregon Citizen's Alliance (OCA) formed in 1986, and the proposition had some precedent. In 1988 the OCA sponsored an anti-gay rights initiative, Measure 8, which sought to overturn a gubernatorial executive order that prohibited employment discrimination based on sexual orientation in state government. The initiative passed despite projections that it would fail and caught most opponents off guard. By 1992, however, Measure 8 was found unconstitutional by a state court. Compared to Colorado, the OCA's new proposition used more caustic language and tactics in their move to legalize homophobia by requiring that "homosexuality, pedophilia, sadism, and masochism" be excluded from a protected status

and that the state discourage these activities and teach through its institutions that they are "abnormal, wrong, unnatural, and perverse."

Oregon's and Colorado's election results surprised many. Oregon's, Measure 9, was rejected by 57 percent of the voters, but Colorado's Amendment 2 passed with an approval rate of 53.4 percent, making Colorado the first state in the country to legalize discrimination against gays and lesbians. The immediate response to the passage of Amendment 2 was a court injunction preventing its implementation and a national boycott of Colorado costing an estimated $40 million in convention business alone. The issue was eventually taken to the courts to decide its constitutionality.

In *Romer v. Evans,* first the Colorado Supreme Court in 1994 and then the U.S. Supreme Court in 1996 (6–3) ruled Amendment 2 to be unconstitutional. While the court decision was a victory for gay rights, the success of Amendment 2 among Colorado's voters continues to reverberate across the country as antigay initiatives have spread at every level of government. That a certain level of intolerance toward gays and lesbians has been deemed acceptable by Americans is perhaps best exemplified in the recent passage of the Defense of Marriage Act.

The Defense of Marriage Act (DOMA) was proposed and passed to "protect" the heterosexual institution of marriage. The bill was created in response to Hawaii's same-sex marriage case, which would legalize same-sex marriages in Hawai'i and would then presumably carry the same weight in other states. DOMA defines marriage for federal purposes as a legal union between one man and one woman and protects states from having to recognize same-sex marriages recognized by other states. The bill became law on September 11, 1996, as promised by President Clinton.

The future of antigay initiatives and the antigay countermovement seems assured for at least the foreseeable future. There is hope, however, as the Employment Non-Discrimination Act (ENDA), proposing to add sexual orientation to employment discrimination protections, came remarkably close to passing the Senate. In addition, the increasing visibility of gays, lesbians, and bisexuals and the political efforts of organizations such as the Human Rights Campaign Fund and the Lambda Legal Defense and Education Fund have increased the level of social tolerance and acceptance of sexual minorities across the country.   *Lionel Cantú*

A

Bibliography

Gallagher, John. "High Drama: The Supreme Court Takes a Powerful Stance on Gay Rights." *Advocate* 710 (June 25, 1996): 24.

People for the American Way. 1996. http://www.pfaw.org.htm.

See also Censorship; Religious Right; Same-Sex Marriage; U.S. Government; U.S. Law: Discrimination; U.S. Law: Equal Protection; Voting Behavior

Arabian Nights

The Eastern or "Oriental" tales known collectively in the English tradition as the *Arabian Nights' Entertainments* or, alternately, *The Thousand and One Nights*, were first translated from their original Arabic sources into French by the Orientalist Antoine Galland at the beginning of the eighteenth century (1702–1717). The collection, which even in its earliest Western version consisted of some twelve volumes, was translated from French into English almost immediately by an anonymous "Grub Street" translator. This edition of the stories—read and enjoyed by writers such as Alexander Pope, Thomas Gray, and Horace Walpole—remained the most popular version in English well into the nineteenth century. Later translations and editions of the collection, each of which grew larger and more ambitiously inclusive in their retelling, prominently included those of Dr. Jonathan Scott (1811), E. W. Lane (1839–1841), John Payne (1882–1884), and Sir Richard Burton (1885–1888). It is owing largely to Burton's supposedly "unexpurgated" translation, originally published by private subscription in a limited edition of ten monumental volumes, that the *Nights* has subsequently enjoyed a reputation for being a collection of ribald or erotic tales, set within the sexually ambiguous confines of the "mysterious East." While earlier translators such as Galland attempted to impose a certain decorum on the bawdier aspects of their source texts, Burton chose rather to emphasize the erotic nature of many of the stories included in the collection. His extended and often overwhelming footnotes to the *Nights*, which pretended in a pseudoscientific manner to explain the anthropological and sociological ramifications of the text, are likely to strike modern readers as a bizarre and highly idiosyncratic mixture of racism and sexual fetishism. Burton believed that much of the Islamic world lay within a so-called "sotadic zone"—a geographically proscribed area extending from the shores of the Mediterranean well into the Middle East—within which homosexual behavior (between men) was the norm. In fact, of course, the Koran itself on several occasions characterizes homosexuals as "great transgressors," and under Islamic law sodomy was punishable by castration and death. The injunctions included in the Koranic suras did not, however, prevent homosexual behavior from becoming fashionable in certain circles of Islamic culture in the thirteenth and fourteenth centuries, and several stories in Burton's version of the *Nights* reflect this popularity or (at least) tolerance. Foremost among those tales that include casual reference to the attractions of young boys for mature men are those featuring the historical figure of Abu Nowas, or Abû Nuwâs, a ninth-century poet patronized in the court of the Caliph al-Amîn (e.g., "Abu Nowas with the Three Boys and the Caliph Harun Al–Rashid"). Other collections of Arabic stories and folktales generically related to the *Nights* and known as *kutub al-bah* were more specifically dedicated to erotic and pornographic stories. Ahmad ibn Yusuf al-Tayfashi's *Nuzhat al-Albab* (Delight of the Hearts), for example, is a work from the early thirteenth century that shows a particular interest in narratives involving homosexuals and pederasts.

Robert L. Mack

Bibliography

Burton, Richard Francis. *The Book of the Thousand and One Nights: A Plain and Literal Translation of the Arabian Nights' Entertainments*. 10 vols. London, 1885.

Irwin, Robert. *The Arabian Nights: A Companion*. London: Press, 1994.

See also Abû Nuwâs; Arabic Literature; Persian (Iranian) Literature and Culture

Arabic Literature

As in all culture-related subjects, words are controversial, and much debate has been aroused around the use of the term *homosexuality* concerning classical, premodern, and present-day Arab societies. It is probable that the widespread modern Arabic term *shudhûdh jinsi* (sexual deviationism) and the more politically correct but still seldom found term *mithliyya jinsiyya* (homosexuality) coincide with the Western notion of homosexuality, but these are both recent and modern terminologies that have no equivalent in local dialects or in classical Arabic. The classical language has no word to cover the wide spectrum of same-sex attraction and sexuality, using such specialized terms as *liwât* (anal sex), *lûti* (active sodomite who prefers boys to women, thus not concerning what modern terminology would qualify as occasional bisexual), *ma'bûn* (passive sodomite), *mukhannath* (effeminate passive sodomite), *mu'âjir* (passive male prostitute), *dâbb* (active sodomite who likes raping his victims in their sleep regardless of their age), and *musâhiqa* (lesbian).

Indeed, the classical Arabic concept of *adab* and the Western word *literature* have been covering approximately identical fields of meaning for only a century. Moreover, Arabic literature covers over fifteen hundred years, and although the linguistic alterations have nothing in common with their equivalents in Western languages, notions and words do change, especially when confronted with other civilizations. It is therefore natural that research on same-sex eroticism in Arabic literature has been very cautious with its vocabulary, preferring to *homosexuality* terms such as *homoeroticism* or *same-sex sexuality,* or even *homosensuality*. It should also be stressed that male-male relationships are far more documented than lesbianism, thus orienting the general tone of this article.

A few basic notions concerning homoeroticism in classical Arabo-Islamic societies must be stressed: first, this culture's recognition of male beauty, even in the eyes of other males, and this beauty's ability to cause *fitna* (disorder). The Koran depicts the effect of Prophet Yûsuf's (Joseph) beauty on the women of Egypt, who were so seized by his charm that, at his mere sight, they cut their hands with knives they had been given to peel fruit, and exclaimed, "He is not a human being, he must be a noble angel." Yûsuf will subsequently become a rhetorical cliché depicting young male beauty in love poetry. The Koranic paradise is filled with elements to which men are naturally inclined but are lawful only in the Other Life: wine that "causes no intoxication" (56:19), served by lads "eternally young" and "if looked at seem scattered pearls" (56:17, 76:19).

A second point is the admittance that a grown man's attraction for a handsome adolescent is a natural tendency (even for theologians as Imâm Ibn Hanbal [d. 855]), and that the unforgivable sin lies in its *realization* as a sexual practice. Third, man-to-man attraction is not a mere sexual phenomenon but is also related to love, passion, and their subsequent dangers. Authors concerned with the effects of pas-

sion on man such as Ibn Hazm (d. 1064) in his *Tawq al-hamâma* (The Dove's Necklace) or Ibn al-Jawzi (d. 1201) in his *Dhamm al-hawä* (Condemnation of Passion) do not treat man-to-man passions differently from heterosexual ones and depict similar consequences. When preparing his *Masâri' al-'ushshâq,* an anthology of anecdotes about lovers stricken by death over losing their beloved, al-Sarrâj (d. 1106) also includes homosexual tragic love affairs scattered among heterosexual anecdotes. A fourth point: whereas man-to-boy attraction is a commonplace of poetry and prose literature, grown man-to-grown man attraction is often underplayed, and is almost uniquely acknowledged in *mujûn* (ribaldry) and *sukhf* (obscenity) related literature.

The effeminates, female-identified men who participated in pre-Islamic and early Islamic social life as singers and entertainers, freely mingling with high-rank women, are mentioned in both *hadîth* (sayings attributed to the Prophet) and later compilations of anecdotes, such as al-Isfahânî's (d. 967) "Book of Songs." But the taste for the male adolescents' beauty becomes for classical authors a sign of "civilization," as opposed to "beduoinity," the less refined taste for slave girls that was practiced by an earlier nomad culture. This contrast is expressed in in al-Jâhiz's (d868) epistle "Mufâkharat al-jawâri wa-l-ghilmân" (an imaginary controversy between a lover of young boys [*ghilmân*] and a lover of slave-girls [*jawârî*], each one using poetry verses and anecdotes as arguments). The *ghilmân* that the boy-loving character is referring to are not free adolescents, but servants attached to a noble house and often exchanged as presents. When the girl-loving character argues that in referential seventh-century poetry, one has never heard of a man dying for his love of a boy, the *lûtî* answers that if such seventh-century poets had had the chance of a glance at some of the high-priced, handsome servants of present days, they would have cast their beloved from a high mountain and left them to the dogs. He adds that those early poets were unrefined Bedouins, unaware of life's pleasures, eating hedgehogs and lizards' grease, whereas educated and refined people of our times (*udabâ' wa-zurafâ'*) have produced the most delicate poetry about boys, both in the fields of seriousness and jest.

Abû Nuwâs (d. 815?), one of the most celebrated poets of the Abbasid period, illustrates an age of self-confidence in which Arabo-Islamic society lovingly tolerates the transgression of its values, allowing the poet to celebrate his earthly love of

A heavenly pleasures, chasing boys for a kiss, admiring naked bodies at the *hammâm* (bath), drinking wine served by fifteen-year-old Christian boys, or by *ghulâmiyyât*, slave girls dressed as boys with short cut hair, a stratagem invented by the mother of the caliph al-Amîn (reigned 809–813) to force him to look at females.

The depiction of both the lover and the beloved as males in Arabic poetry should not, however, always be taken as homoerotic. While homoerotic allusions are a standard cliché in Abbasid and Andalusian poetry, they can also be a cover for heterosexual love, since mentioning a free woman's name is an insult to her family and a far greater danger for the poet than boasting of his love of slave boys. The use of masculine in love poetry becomes a convention, still followed in present-day popular love songs (by Umm Kulthûm for instance), that allows for all combinations of lovers. Sûfi (mystical) medieval poets such as Ibn al-Fârid (d. 1234) make extensive use of chaste, homoerotic clichés, like describing a beloved who, if looked upon by Jacob, the latter would have forgotten the beauty of Joseph. But the true beloved of the Sûfis is no less than God himself.

Homoeroticism is also found in works standing at the inner or outer limits of the classical notion of *adab* (for the *adîb* has the right to write and read about lower subjects [*bâtil, sukhf*] to rest his mind from seriousness, but the language used has to be that of *adab*). The *mujûn* poetic tradition of chaste homoeroticism would be found, for instance, in the famous treatise on eroticism by the Maghriban mineralogist Ahmad al-Tîfâshî (d. 1253) "Nuzhat al-albâb fî mâ lâ yûjad fî kitâb" (The promenade of hearts in what is to be found in no other book), which is ripe with piquant and often hilarious anecdotes on the underworld of active and passive homosexuals, their argot, their classifications of the male organ according to shape and size, and their witty (often blasphemous) replies when scorned by heterosexuals or men of religion.

At the outer limits of *adab* lies "popular" literature, such as the shadow plays that were popular in Egypt under the Mamluk age. The only remains of this type of production is a highly literary rendition of it by Ibn Dâniyâl (d. 1310) in three shadow plays, two of which, "Tayf al-khayâl" (The Imaginary Shadow) and "Al-mutayyam wa-l-yutayyim" (The Man Stricken by Passion and the Little Orphan/The Cause of Passion) expose a character's rowdy life, full of homosexual adventures, until final repentance and death. This image of homosexual attraction as a possible entrapment in a youth's formation is repeated in many stories of the *Arabian Nights,* in which the recurrent pederast Maghriban sheikh chanting his love of the young fifteen-year-old hero is nothing but a common ambush on the path initiating a boy to manhood.

But whether homoeroticism is to be found in its chaste and often symbolic version, or, on the contrary in its coarsest expression in amusing anecdotes, it is a natural phenomenon in classical literature. If a tragic tone is to be found, it is because unrewarded love is tragic, never because of its homosexual nature.

In contrast, the invisibility of same-sex relationships in modern Arabic literature is somehow puzzling. There is no Proust, Wilde, or Gide among modern novelists, the works of whom could be read in such a light. "Homosexual" characters are rare, although not necessarily depicted in derogatory terms. The first obviously "gay" character in a modern Arabic novel is the character Kersha in Egyptian novelist Naguib Mahfouz's *Zuqâq al-midaqq* (Midaq Alley, 1947). Kersha is a sixtyish coffee-shop owner who unwisely invites his younger and effeminate lovers to free glasses of tea at his place, to the knowledge of the whole neighborhood, until his crazed wife (and mother of five) decides to make a public scandal, sweeps her dazzled boy-loving husband out of the coffee shop, and insults him before a company of amused customers. But when the Sheikh Darwish, the café's local Sûfi, draws the moral of the scene, he simply declares, "This is an old evil, that is called in English homosexuality, but it is not love. True love is for the Family of the Prophet." Such a conclusion, which should not be mistaken for Mahfouz's view on homosexuality, does not seem far from the medieval mystical conception: if homosexuality is not true love, it is not because it is against nature but because true Love is reserved to God. Other novels by Mahfouz portray homosexuals, such as Ridwân in the last part of the trilogy *Al-Sukkariyya* (1957). This character is a young and handsome youth who uses his beauty to seduce an aging pasha and soon becomes a prominent figure in a right-wing monarchist party.

The homosexual in contemporary Egyptian novels or short stories is seldom a central character, with one of the few exceptions being "Al-raqsa al-mubâha" (The Permitted Dance, 1981), a short story by Yahyä al-Tâhir 'Abdallah in which a small boy caught being sodomized by a friend his age is killed by his father because of the shame brought upon the family, while the friend is expelled from the village. The homosexual is usually just another typical character of the popular *hâra* (quarter) of Cairo, such as in Gamâl al-Ghitâni's novel *Waqâ'i' hârat al-Za'farânî* (Incidents in Zafarani Alley, 1975), in which we find Samîr, a shy young man who secretly visits popular *hammâms* at night to get sodomized by 'Ewês, the Upper Egypt stud who works all night through and can satisfy seven customers in succession, although he has vague fears that practicing sex only with men might diminsh his attraction to females.

Since the modern Egyptian novel is more preoccupied with society as a whole, and characters tend to be mere representative archetypes of this society's diversity, there is little place for the individual, and the questionings triggered by his sexual preferences or identity are avoided. Only in the indirect free style of Yûsuf Idrîs's (d. 1991) short story "Abû al-rigâl" (The He-man, 1987), the reader enters the mind of Sultân, the aging leader of a group of gangsters, who finds himself confronted by the unbearable fantasy of being raped by one of his subordinates, al-Tôr (the Bull). He remembers his village's effeminate miller, Shâhîn, who payed boys to sodomize him in the cornfields, and, in the ambiguous conclusion of the story, imagines himself becoming another Shâhîn after a whole life as the most manly male of the community. The reader is given no basis for deciding whether his sexual fantasy of proposing himself to al-Tôr is realized or merely imagined, but the clear impression left by the story is that allowing oneself to be possessed by another male leads to general mockery and loss of social status..

Such a feeling is beautifully depicted by the Syrian playwright Sa'dallah Wannûs (d. 1997) in *Tuqûs al-ishârât wa-l-tahawwulât* (The Rites of Signs and Transformations, 1994), a play set in an imaginary nineteenth-century Damascus in which an effeminate male prostitute, Semsem, reveals to 'Abbâs, a famous braggart who has already used his services, that his best friend and feared braggart, al-'Afsa, is a closeted homosexual dying of love for him. Al-'Afsa confesses his love to his friend, who uses him sexually and swears to keep it secret. But burned by his love, al-'Afsa is slowly transformed into an effeminate creature, while 'Abbâs gets disgusted with him and explains that his attraction to him was merely sexual, and that his pleasure was to have taken posession of a man universally considered a braggart. Al-'Afsa boasts about his love for 'Abbâs around the city, his lover rudely rejects him, and he consequently commits suicide. This interesting work depicts the homosexual relationship as casual for the active partner, and it presents a dialectical conflict between a fantasy of virility and domination, and another of femininity and need for affection. Sa'dallah Wannûs makes 'Abbas and al-'Afsa's ulfulfilling love affair a tragedy that unlike in classical literature is a consequence not of passion but of homosexuality.

Various explanations can be proposed for the absence of homoerotic themes in modern literature, as compared with classical. And though the moral standards of Arab societies have changed since the colonial confrontation with the West, one point remains: the common feeling that unveiling one's inability to conform to standards or, worse, demanding a space of freedom to practice one's own moral standards is a far greater offense than discretely satisfying one's taste as long as one keeps quiet about it. This is what Stephen O. Murray has rightly named "the will not to know," and it is a clear reason for the lack of a "gay" movement comparable to what has appeared in the West. But any society needs to create its own secret "space of transgression," and the relative absence of homosexuality in the Arabic literary field still needs to be studied. It is partly explainable by censorship and the close relationship between the act of writing and local cultural dicta which enforce a kind of silence on these matters. The present moral code of Arab society is a mixture of traditional Islamic morals and European colonial fascination and distaste for the "Oriental vice." The rejection of homosexuality in modern Arab societies is mainly based on rigorous sexual standards that however stringently imposed do not go so far as to disrupt the aesthetic appreciation of the classical expressions of same-sex love. At the same time Arab societies seem to have started delegating this "function of transgression" to the Western world, with which contact is nowadays constant, therefore ridding itself of the task of producing its own transgression and consumming an imported transgression, both delightful and easy to condemn when necessary as examples of a moral failure of the West. But as modern Arabic literature is starting to break the wall of silence and increasingly include sexuality in its narrative discourse, homosexuality will perhaps also find in it a greater expression.

Frédéric Lagrange

Bibliography

Murray, Stephen O., and Will Roscoe, ed. *Islamic Homosexualities*. New York: New York University Press, 1997.

Schmitt, Arno. *Bio-Bibliography of Male-Male Sexuality and Eroticism in Muslim Societies.* Berlin: Verlag Rosa Winkel, 1995.

Wright, J. W., and Everett K. Rowson, eds. *Homoeroticism in Classical Arabic Literature.* New York: Columbia University Press, 1997.

See also Abû Nuwâs; *Arabian Nights Beloved*; Islam; Morocco; Persian (Iranian) Literature and Culture; Turkey

Araki, Gregg (1960–)

A sharp-witted writer-director-cinematographer, Gregg Araki is one of a few underground gay filmmakers to emerge in the 1990s. Struggling for artistic originality, Araki, a Japanese American and graduate of the University of Southern California's School of Cinema-Television, demands that contemporary audiences negotiate with AIDS as it has come to transform gay sex into metaphors of suicide and cautions against risk, rather than just say no to male-male desire. Concerns with sexual identity, self-disclosure, and subversiveness resonate urgently in Araki's work, which borrows paradigmatic motifs of his predecessor, French filmmaker Jean-Luc Godard.

Like Godard, Araki uses jump cuts, intertitles, blackouts, handheld cameras, and eccentric points of view to appropriate and transform conventions and images of standard Hollywood productions into narratives that exploit them to their own sovereign end. In each of the films that his "teenage apocalypse" trilogy comprises, Araki is clearly marking out a space and an opportunity for gay men to represent themselves in a way that had previously been unimaginable. *Living End, The Doom Generation,* and *Nowhere* formally articulate his association with the gay underworld through allusion and appropriation of gay and camp iconography. His characters' anticipation of adult sex is repeatedly marred by the prospect of the inevitable approach of illness and death.

The contemporary dystopia that AIDS has created is central to the suspended animation of *Living End,* a film that explores inner emotions condemned to unspeakable states, fragmentation, and ennui mirrored in the desolate, postindustrial California landscape. As for drama, two gay HIV-positive lovers bash back at some of the more diabolical evil and oppressive members of society (namely, gay bashers) and have what Araki terms "a lot of cathartic fun along the way." Like all of his films, *Living End*

received both independent and mainstream attention, but this notice has not always secured critical acclaim. One critic warned, "For those who haven't walked out before the closing credits (of [*The*] *Doom Generation*), good luck searching for meaning—you'll find mostly blood and epithets." This review exemplifies the controversy imparted to depictions of gay sexuality in the late twentieth century. An outlaw on the run himself, Araki is an unquestionably dynamic filmmaker who, when he refuses to temper himself, contributes to our world in cinematically and socially meaningful ways.

Craig McCarroll

Bibliography

Yutani, Kimberly. "Gregg Araki and the Queer New Wave." In *Asian American Sexualities: Dimensions of the Lesbian and Gay Experience.* Russell Leong, ed. New York: Routledge, 1996, 175–180.

See also AIDS; Asians in North America; Film: New Queer Cinema

Architecture

There appears to be a natural affinity between same-sex desire and architecture. Throughout the ages, gay men and women have made places for themselves whose elaborate articulation stood in contrast to their more functional surroundings. To a certain extent, this ability came from the simple fact that they had to. Living in societies in which the expression of their most body-based social relations was usually taboo, gay men and women had to come up with ways of representing themselves in and to the world through everyday objects and spaces. Architecture allowed them to make a home for themselves in a hostile world. It also allowed them to erect within that domain a place that fixed in physical form the artifices through which they acted out their self-constructed personae.

This process was further helped by the dissolution of class structures as the Industrial Revolution took hold in Western culture. If middle-class men and women had to erect their own space separate from the land in both time and place, then gay middle-class men and women had to do so in a self-conscious manner, because they could depend on few of the mass-produced spaces of collectivity, such as cultural or entertainment institutions that marked the territory of the middle-class city.

As a result, much of the architecture associated with same-sex desire is interior. The association of gay men with the professions of hairdressing and decorating may be more than a cliché. Excluded by temperament or discrimination from professions that our culture judges to be the realm of men asserting power over the world, gay men and women instead became masters of accepting the world as given and making it into a mirror of themselves and their lives. As such, it could become a stage set on which they could act out an alternative manner of living. Their ability to do so became, in the late nineteenth century, one of the few sellable talents or trades in which they could engage. This profession also situated them midway between activities usually associated with men, such as building and planning, and those to which women were assigned, such as the arrangement of the domestic interior and decorating. This fitted the "in-between" or "third sex" position to which our society assigned gay men and women.

The first examples of such interiors appeared in England, France, and Germany in the first few decades of the nineteenth century. The grand interiors of Charles Percier (1764–1838), Pierre-François Fontaine (1762–1853), and Thomas Hope (1769–1831) provided encampments of domesticity within the puritan neoclassicism then holding sway over popular taste. They presented the interior as a light, fabric-based version of the proportions and decorative systems that schools and governments had only then standardized. Ephemeral and modern, yet filled with associations, these spaces were adaptable cells for self-expression.

Against such formal preoccupations, the more eclectic activities of two of the century's greatest collectors of art, decor, and architecture, King Ludwig of Bavaria (reigned 1845–1866) and William Beckford (1759–1844), presented the interior as the museum of the soul. Their grand palaces brought together furnishings from all over the world and provided time to allow their inhabitants to invent personal heritages, status, and other myths. Though both Ludwig and Beckford used professional architects, decorators, and stage-set designers, their complex visions were syncretic expressions of a life lived on a domestic stage, rather than monuments reflecting established values, proportions, and ways of living.

A third element that layered into the emergence of such interiors as the flexible reflection of grand styles and an eclectic gathering of disparate elements into a personal stage set was the interest in the rediscovery of the body that lurked under or within Victorian conformity. With the interiors of the aesthetic movement, such as those of C.R. Ashbee (1863–1942), a delight in the materiality of highly worked and refined material became a reflection of an attempt to posit a kind of sensuality that would still delight in its own ability to act—its, as it was then defined, masculinity.

Together, these three strands of design created a fairly coherent set of models for domestic interiors that led to a proliferation and elaboration of such spaces when mass production put the designed environment within the reaches of the middle classes. Great gay designers such as Elsie De Wolfe (1865–1950) led the way in developing these themes in ever more elaborate and refined ways. Eventually, their contributions became so powerful that they overwhelmed architecture, making interiors much more popular than the exterior forms that modernist styles and economic logic had reduced to abstract shells.

Postmodern architects such as Charles Moore (1925–1993) accepted this delight in (personal) history, lightness, play, and sensuality and brought it out of the closet of the home into the arena of public buildings at exactly the same time (the 1960s) when gay liberation movements made it possible for men and women to express their same-sex desires in public.

It was also at this time that the ways in which same-sex desire had carved places of sensuality and sense out of the forgotten corners of the city coalesced into strategies for community building. The cruising grounds that first appeared in the seventeenth century—the baths and bars that became the focal points of gay communities, and the protective ghettos where gay men and women gathered—came together in urban neighborhoods. Picking up on techniques developed by hippies and urban squatters, gay men and women were among the first to reclaim the inner city, fix it up, and create an artificial community.

In the 1980s, AIDS devastated such communities and depleted the ranks of gay designers. At the same time, popular culture became so adept at adopting the techniques and sensibilities pioneered by gay men and women that it became difficult to distinguish the spaces of same-sex desire. The urban redevelopment that gay men and women had helped pioneer cleared out the spaces of sexual congress hidden within the city, while making urban beautification a badge of class rather than sexual orientation.

Self-proclaimed queers reacted by engaging in aggressive attempts to take back the city, make themselves felt, and in general mark the presence of the body in the urban and interior environment. This work took the form of art projects and political actions but left few lasting monuments.

It is unclear how the spaces of same-sex desire will transform themselves to meet the challenges of sprawl, assimilation, and technological dispersion of place while continuing to answer the need to protect gay men and women from discrimination and bigotry. Yet the history of invention that has made the spaces of same-sex desire engines of spatial transformation through self-conscious artifice promises continual contributions to our ability to make our own space.

Aaron Betsky

Bibliography

Betsky, Aaron. *Queer Space: Architecture and Same Sex Desire.* New York: Morrow, 1997.

See also Aestheticism; Beckford, William; Johnson, Philip; Ludwig II

Arcidiácono, Carlos (1929–)

Carlos Arcidiácono is best known for the novel *Ay de mí, Jonathan* (Woe Is Me, Jonathan [1976]), which was published at the same time as the military takeover in Argentina that sponsored the so-called dirty war against subversion, which contained a virulent dimension of gaybashing.

Ay de mí, Jonathan details the hermetic closeting of gay culture that military masculinism brought with it and of the social and existential isolation of an individual who finds no lines of communication open to him to the hegemonic sexual code. The novel is characterized by the sort of pathos to be found in U.S. writing before the emergence of a gay pride mentality. However, it is difficult to overestimate the sense of absolute isolation and abiding psychological terror associated with being gay in Argentina during the years of terror following the 1976 coup, which *Ay de mí, Jonathan* anticipates so eerily.

Yet the novel is not all pathos. In his closeted exile, the narrator recalls with campy wit the manifestations of gay culture that did survive, more or less clandestinely, throughout the period of the 1960s and 1970s. That period began with the gay persecutions of Juan Domingo Perón's second government in the 1950s, followed by the halcyon days of prosperity and enormous cultural openings be-

fore the 1966 military coup (probably the last great era of dynamic cultural production in Buenos Aires), the brief reprise of the sixties in 1973, and the vertiginous descent into social dissolution and draconian tyranny that began in 1974 and led to the 1976 coup. Argentina was not to have cultural democracy again until 1981, but the period since has never regained the excitement of the early 1960s. Still, gay culture, whether openly identified or, more often, simply known to be such without public comment, exercised considerable influence on cultural production. In this sense, Arcidiácono's novel, held to be the first openly gay text in Argentina, provides an important midcentury sketch of gay life.

David William Foster

Bibliography

Costa Picazo, Rolando. "Carlos Arcidiácono." *Latin American Writers on Gay and Lesbian Themes: A Bio-Biographical Sourcebook.* David William Foster, ed. Westport, Conn.: Greenwood Press, 1994, 22–24.

Foster, David William. *Gay and Lesbian Themes in Latin American Writing.* Austin: University of Texas Press, 1991, pp. 107–110.

See also Argentina

Arenas, Reinaldo (1943–1990)

When he committed suicide in December 1990, during the last stages of his bout with AIDS, Reinaldo Arenas was little known outside primarily Latin American and European literary and academic circles. There he was already regarded as one of the lions of the "postmodern" Latin American literary movement, a prolific writer the majority of whose many works remained unpublished until after his escape from Cuba during the 1980 Mariel boat lift. The decade he lived in the United States before his death saw the appearance of several works that had been composed and then suppressed in Cuba during the preceding decade. These included *Farewell to the Sea* (1984), the third and perhaps best of his five-novel sequence (or "pent-agony") of fictional autobiography, and *El Central* (1981), a long poem recounting his experiences in forced labor at a large Cuban sugar plantation in the early 1970s. While homosexual themes figure prominently in *Farewell to the Sea*, drafts of which were confiscated and destroyed by Cuban authorities over the course of the 1970s, Arenas's homosexuality was merely a convenient excuse for government harassment and persecution; his more threatening subversive power lay in his unflinching commitment, evident in all his work, to artistic and personal freedoms in which for him the erotic was always directly implicated.

His most vocally critical work could take forms as elaborately allegorical as the Orwellian nightmare vision of *The Assault* (1994), the surreal conclusion to the pent-agony, or as direct and literal as accounts of his own persecution and imprisonment by the Cuban government in his posthumously published memoir, *Before Night Falls* (1993). The publication of the English translation of his memoir effectively introduced Arenas to an Anglophone (and gay) readership, and spurred the republication of other of his literary works. These include three important early works, the first two installments of the pent-agony, *Singing from the Well* (1987), and *The Palace of the White Skunks* (1990), as well as the *Illfated Peregrinations of Fray Servando* (1994), his earliest fully conceived, and by all accounts his best, novel, which first appeared in France in the early 1970s as *Hallucinations*. Arenas's belated rise to prominence after his death also renewed interest in the one major novel he wrote to reflect his experience of immigrating and accommodating to the United States, *The Doorman* (1987).

Born to abject rural poverty in 1943 near the town of Holguín in Cuba's Oriente province, Arenas never lost touch with the basic elemental factors of his experience: nature, sex, and language. From the earliest images in *Singing from the Well* to those that haunt the last passages of his memoir as he declines into illness, Arenas held steadfast to his commitment to personal freedom, especially in the forms of artistic and sexual expression. Arenas's last important public gesture, however, was a significantly political one: he left a suicide note to be published after his death in select journals, in English and Spanish, in which he demands that readers consider his death not as the result of AIDS or of spiritual despair but exclusively as the result of his dehumanization at the hands of the government in place on the island. This note, which is included as an epilogue to his memoir, concludes with a confirmation of his faith in Cuba's eventual freedom and with the assurance that, if only in death, Arenas could also, and at last, declare himself "free."   *Ricardo Ortiz*

Bibliography

Epps, Brad. "Proper Conduct: Reinaldo Arenas, Fidel Castro, and the Politics of Homosexuality." *Journal of the History of Sexuality* 6, no. 2 (1965): 231–82.

Soto, Francisco. *Reinaldo Arenas: The Pentagonía*. Gainesville, Fla.: University Press of Florida, 1994.

See also AIDS Literature; Cuban Literature; Cuban Writing in Exile

Argentina

Although Argentina differs from other Latin American societies in which the concept of nation emerged under the aegis of military institutions (e.g., Chile or revolutionary Cuba since 1959)—the Argentine independence movement was led by burghers dissatisfied with Spanish centrist controls over commerce—Argentine social history has, in fact, been dominated by the military, which, like the Catholic Church, has traditionally constituted quasi-political institutions. Argentina had its first military coup only in 1930, and the political life of the country has been dominated ever since by an overtly masculinist institution that has repeatedly assumed control over the government to safeguard and enforce ideologies associated with male privilege, including those of gender, class, and ethnicity.

As a consequence, a strong and explicit version of homophobia has long characterized Argentine society. The founding text of Argentine fiction, Esteban Echeverría's long short story *El matedoro* (The Slaughterhouse), which was probably written in 1839 but not published until 1874, ends with a homosexual rape scene, as male agents of one political faction assert their authority by attacking the body of what they take to be a token representative of the opposition. In Echeverría's story, it is clear that an overdetermined schism between political agendas includes an overdetermined physical aggression against a token body of opposition in which male-male rape is a legitimate form of social control and an intelligible assertion of the superiority of one band, thanks to its ability to "feminize" and penetrate an exemplar of the opposing band (in the story, the victim asserts, in turn, his moral superiority by willing his own elliptic-like death rather than submit to the humiliating invasion of his body by his tormentors).

Echeverría's story—in addition to inaugurating, along with the tradition of narrative fiction in Argentina, and one insistently marked by political analysis, the representation of political difference in terms of masculine vs. feminine, sexual aggressor

A vs. sexual victim, master vs. slave—articulates what continues to be a dominant sexual ideology in Argentina: the Mediterranean scheme whereby the inserter retains his masculine and heterosexist privilege. It can never be a question for the political toughs in *El matadero* that they will become feminized or homosexualized by penetrating the body of another man. Yet the insertee is, by the act of subjugation, rape, and attending signs of humiliation, feminized and made into a sexually deviant body that lacks masculinist/heterosexist authority and bears the sign of the loser in the struggle for political survival and authority. The cultural reflexes of this strain in Argentina have yet to be tracked and analyzed adequately, although novelists and cultural theoretician David Viñas has made many suggestions on what texts and aspects will have to be taken into account in such a study.

That the toughs in Echeverría's story are associated with the paramilitary forces of the early nineteenth century underscores how homophobia in the Argentine military tradition has included literal and displaced male-male rape as a strategy of ideological control. Recent scandals concerning the treatment of recruits even during the period following the return to democracy and attempts to restructure military authority has led both to abandonment of universal conscription and the introduction of women into a new career army.

Though references to the record of homophobia in Argentina can be teased out of the cultural record prior to the 1950s, they become increasingly explicit with the second presidency of Juan Domingo Perón (1952–1955). They attain insistent force in the context of the so-called dirty war against subversion after the military coup in 1976. This coup, which established the Process of National Reconstruction, asserted the primacy of the well-constituted Catholic, patriarchal family, and sexual mores were of special concern to its agents. Relying on the concept of public decency rather than personal sexual acts (although it was assumed that lapses in public decency were to be equated with pernicious private behavior), the military regime persecuted an array of signs that it considered to be evidence of sexual deviancy, one major cluster of which was attributed to male homosexuality: flamboyant clothing, long hair, overt body language, preference for certain types of music in certain types of public or semiclandestine spaces, and a generalized nonmasculinist persona.

The stridency of police persecution and the repeated willingness to confuse gender deviancy with political insubordination and even revolutionary conduct (homosexuals joined women and Jews in receiving sadistically enhanced forms of torture after detention) led eventually to the inclusion of a specifically gay and lesbian component to the public struggle of resistance against the military's intrusion into every aspect of personal and public life. The Argentine Frente de Liberación Homosexual (Argentine Liberation Front) was founded in 1971 and dissolved at the time of the 1976 coup, but its leaders and new elements regrouped as part of the protest movements that gained public support in the early 1980s. The Comunidad de Homosexuals Argentinos (Community of Argentine Homosexuals) worked throughout the period of the transition to constitutional democracy in 1981, and it eventually won the nominal support of President Carlos Menem in the early 1990s, with the result that its present-day descendants have managed to amass a considerable amount of symbolic, if not directly political, support fifteen years into the current period of institutional normalcy.

At the present moment, the major concern among Argentine gays and lesbians is for the right to public visibility, including legitimate civil status for the recipients of sex-change operations. Although Buenos Aires has numerous gay bars and openly sells publications advertising locations and activities (in Argentina "gay" includes lesbians, and despite profound political and historical differences, there is a sustained attempt at a unified front), public gayness continues to be harassed by the police, often violently, and gay meeting places are extremely circumscribed as to their from-the-street identification. Visibility here means the freedom to manifest gayness publicly in a way that would bring rights of individuals into conformity with current rights for gay-marked cultural products—at least as far as publications, film, theater, and the like go; sex shops and their accoutrements still remain banned under the same concept of public decency that affects gay individuals.

As regards sex-change operations, while the majority of them appear to be performed abroad (a clinic in Chile is often spoken of and has been featured on at least one television program), the police edict still in force regarding public decency penalizes individuals for the act of cross-dressing, and individuals have been unsuccessful in approaching the Civil Registry to have their sexual identity and, usually, their official name altered. This forces them to continue to use a registration card that identifies them as a man, including an appropriately attired photographic image.

The intense interest in transgendering continues to reiterate the ideology whereby homosexuality is a matter of the passive or the insertee, and thus the identification of oneself as a homosexual means reinscription as a woman. Nevertheless, Argentina is a country with a long tradition of Freudian and Lacanian psychoanalysis, and alternative, more "medicalized" interpretations of homosexuality exist, running the gamut from homosexual machos (a 1995 controversy over whether or not there were homosexuals on the national all-stars soccer team) to efforts at a gay politics that emulates North American identity politicos and the "Queer" movement.

The prospects for gay liberation are bright in Argentina, beginning with a fine record in the suspension of moral censorship of culture and the possibilities that the economy offers for the empowerment of alternative lifestyles. In this sense, Argentina seems willing to make good on the traditional constitutional guarantees of the individual rights. Yet a remaining virulent substratum of homophobia evinces itself in gay bashing, the absence of institutional guarantees for individuals publicly marked as gay, and a persistent veil of silence in most quarters about anything having to do with the homoerotic.

David William Foster

Bibliography

Acevedo, Zelmar. *Homosexulidad; hacia la destrucción de los mitos.* Buenos Aires: Ediciones del Ser, 1985.

Gregoric, Luis. *Literatura y homosexualidad y otros ensayos.* Buenos Aires: Editorial Legasa, 1985.

Jáuregui, Carlos. *La homosexualidad en la Argentina.* Buenos Aires: Ediciones Tarso, 1978.

Jockl, Alexandro. *Ahora, los gay.* Buenos Aires: Ediciones de la Pluma, 1984.

See also Arcidiácono, Carlos; Perlongher, Néstor; Puig, Manuel

Armah, Ayi Kwei (1939–)

The gay novelist Ayi Kwei Armah began his education in Ghana, where he won a scholarship to the United States to attend Groton School. He went on to Harvard, graduating summa cum laude in sociology, after which he worked for his M.A. at Columbia University. He lectured briefly at the University of Massachusetts and later worked as a translator in France and Algeria; he has also taught in several universities in African countries such as Tanzania and Lesotho. Armah has written a number of short stories and several essays, though his fame justifiably rests on his five novels written so far: *The Beautyful Ones Are Not Yet Born* (1968), *Fragments* (1970), *Why Are We So Blest?* (1972), *Two Thousand Seasons* (1973), and *The Healers* (1978).

Armah's works can be described as postcolonial in that they deal with the problems of African countries and their failure to build a united and prosperous nation since independence. The causes are both internal and external, as the leaders and elite who have taken over after independence imitated and perpetuated structures inherited from colonial patrons. The problems are analyzed on the level of the relationship of the individual to society, as well as in personal and emotional relationships with smaller units such as family and friends. The estrangement that results from this leads to frustration and a feeling of being an outsider in a structure that, like the patriarchy and its institutions, seems immovable and monolithic.

Usually Western-educated, the typical early Armah protagonist becomes disillusioned with the corruption, greed, and shortsightedness of political leaders and sinks into despair at being unable to make a meaningful change. On the personal level, the protagonist finds himself unable to fulfill the expectations of family, whose members see the educated child as a means of acquiring material and economic comforts. This implied betrayal of the spirit of independence—sacrifice, honesty, and the common good—necessary to acquire material wealth makes the struggle tragic.

In later works, Armah widens his scope, seeing in the relationship between dominant countries and ex-colonies the seeds of a disease that incapacitates the latter from initiating new beginnings. This examination takes on racial and sexual overtones when the African student fails in his attempts to establish genuine friendships with white friends, who either use him to work through their sexual hang-ups (Mrs. Jefferson, Aimée) or reaffirm Western hegemony of intelligence and the complicity of non-Western intellectuals (Mike) in *Why Are We So Blest?*

In *Two Thousand Seasons*, possibly his most daring and controversial novel, Armah turns to premodern African history in an attempt to explain the creation of a colonized mentality, identifying reciprocity as "the way" of black people and seeing its

A loss as due to the influence of other cultures. Reciprocity extends to all aspects of life: education, politics, sex, and religion, insofar as it sets the standard for communal relations, and its abandonment paves the way for the debasement of traditions. Patriarchy and its institutions are seen as consequences of deviation from the way, the result of incorporating power and hierarchical notions into traditions that used to be based on consensus. Sexuality, like other social norms (leadership, professional training, commerce), must conform to a system that stresses power and domination, male over female or white over black, in a reversal of what used to be unregulated and liberal structures in which same-sex desire had free play among other sexual relations. This divergence from the path occurs even before the European conquest of Africa, as earlier contact with Arab peoples prepared the ground for what will turn out to be the most decisive period of brainwashing and the corruption of culture: the European merchants and the attendant slave trade.   *Arthur J. Hughes*

Bibliography

Anyidoho, Kofi. "Literature and African Identity: The Case of Ayi Kwei Armah." In *Literature and African Identity*. Bayreuth, Germany: Bayreuth University, 1986, 23–42.

Fraser, Robert. *The Novels of Ayi Kwei Armah*. London: Heinemann, 1980.

Jackson, Tommie Lee. *The Existential Fiction of Ayi Kwei Armah, Albert Camus, and Jean-Paul Sartre*. Lanham, Md.: University Press of America, 1997.

Oforiwaa, Yaa. *The Wisdom of the Ages: Themes and Essences of Truth, Love, Struggle in the Works of Ayi Kwei Armah and Kiarri T-H Cheatwood*. Richmond: Native Sun, 1995.

Wright, Derek. *Ayi Kwei Armah's Africa: The Sources of His Fiction*. London: Hans Zell Publishers, 1989.

———. *Critical Perspectives on Ayi Kwei Armah*. Washington D.C.: Three Continents Press, 1992.

See also Africa, Precolonial sub-Saharan; Colonialism

Art History

It can be argued that art history found its very origins in a homosexual impulse. The writings of Johann Joachim Winckelmann (1717–1768)—often considered the first systematic study of the history of art—are infused with a clandestine attraction to the beautiful male body. Winckelmann's famous description of the Apollo Belvedere evokes the god's love for a male youth, lingering on the sculpture's features as if describing a lover:

> a mouth shaped like that whose touch stirred with delight the loved Branchus. The soft hair plays about the divine head as if agitated by a gentle breeze, like the slender waving tendrils of the noble vine; it seems to be anointed with the oil of the gods, and tied by Graces with pleasing display on the crown of the head.

Winckelmann's private passion had a public influence on the formation of the neoclassical style, helping to shift for a time the central theme of art from the female to the male nude. His writings' combination of scholarship and empathic description continues to be the model for much art historical description. Winckelmann had a strong influence on the romantic art critic Walter Pater (1839–1894), who noticed as early as 1867 that Winckelmann's "Hellenism was not merely intellectual." However, where Winckelmann tied the greatness of the classical age to its superior morality—a morality that exalted pederasty—Pater insisted on the autonomy of art from questions of ethics. Perhaps Pater's own homosexuality made him wary of moral systems that sought to put limits on experience and feeling. A distrust of the state's interference in matters of art and life may in part explain the art-for-art's-sake creed of the criticism of Joris-Karl Huysmans (1854–1900), Oscar Wilde (1848–1907), and their fellow aesthetes. It is ironic that the claim of art's autonomy so essential to a later puritanical modernist art history had its roots in the homoeroticism of the decadent movement.

The earliest studies of homosexuality and art have focused on biography. Long before Winckelmann, Giorgio Vasari (1511–74) made a reference to the artist whose preference for boys supposedly earned him the nickname Il Sodoma (1477–1549). Gay studies under the influence of Michel Foucault continued to debate whether such a preference was considered crucial to the formation of identity prior to the modern period. Certainly the late-nineteenth-century construction of homosexuality (and heterosexuality) produced, and was itself produced through, new forms of historical interpretation that emphasized the role of sexual orientation in determining character. A new sense of difference and group identification as a kind of species—a "third sex"—encouraged the search for great homosexuals of the past and the creation of a tradition of inversion. The supposed propensity of great artists for the love of boys was used as a defense by early advocates of homosexuality. For example, John Addington Symonds (1840–1893) stressed the importance of Michelangelo's love for Tommaso de' Cavalieri in his biography of the Renaissance artist. Yet if Symonds projected his own conception of sexual identity onto his hero, he corrected the bowdlerization of Michelangelo's poetry and letters by earlier scholars intent on superimposing their own morality on the artist's life.

The single most influential study of homosexuality and art, Sigmund Freud's *Leonardo da Vinci and a Memory of His Childhood* (1910), comes from outside the discipline of art history. Although this essay has been much maligned by the art historical establishment for its mistranslations and essentialism, Freud's interpretation of the origins of the mysterious smile of the Mona Lisa in Leonardo's supposed homosexuality and his ambivalent relationship to his mother continues to exert a powerful hold on literary studies if not on art history itself. Indeed, despite its origins in Winckelmann's love of masculine beauty, the art historical discipline has been slow to embrace gay studies. Perhaps popular misconceptions about the supposedly "effeminate" nature of art appreciation and the perversion of artists have made certain art historians unwilling to risk an approach that might cast aspersions on their already suspect heterosexuality. At the same time, art history's truck with objects of enormous monetary value encourages a conservative approach. For a long time, when homosexual themes were raised, it was usually to explain particular classical allusions in terms of larger philosophical and moral ideas.

It was not until the advent of gay liberation that the question of homosexuality and art has been discussed openly and in depth in mainstream art history. Prior to the Stonewall riots, art critics could not entirely ignore the issue in the work of such important contemporary artists as Andy Warhol, David Hockney, and Francis Bacon, but it was usually dismissed as unimportant to the ultimate significance of the work of art. For the first time in such essays as Donald Posner's "Caravaggio's Homoerotic Early Works" (1971) or in Kermit Champa's "Charlie Was Like That" (1974), established art historians dealt with homosexuality; however, both these essays are permeated with a sense of distaste for their artist's

subject matter. At the same time, these critics unwittingly followed in Freud's footsteps in seeing homosexuality as the psychic key to the artist's entire production spilling uncontrollably into all his work no matter what his ostensible subject. Barbara Haskell's catalog for the 1980 Marsden Hartley retrospective at the Whitney Museum of Art in New York City, was among the first if not *the* first major monographs to deal with the question of a visual artist's homosexuality in a nonjudgmental and balanced manner. Kenneth J. Dover's *Greek Homosexuality* (1978), although not ostensibly an art history book, used extensive visual sources to discuss the ways in which same sex relationships were essential to classical life and art. Another landmark was James Saslow's *Ganymede and the Renaissance* (1986). This study departs from the biographical mode to explore the implications of the Ganymede myth for the Western visual tradition. Saslow differentiates the question of homosexual content from gay identity, discussing the use of the myth by both homosexual and heterosexual artists.

In contrast to Saslow's measured and systematic approach, Cecile Beurdeley's *L'Amour bleu* (1977) and Emmanuel Cooper's *Sexual Perspective* (1986) offer a broad, impressionistic overview of gay and lesbian art. The usefulness of these books is limited because they never really grapple with problems of historical definition and identity. They fail to ask or answer several crucial questions. How do we decide that a work of art is about homosexuality? Should such a discussion be limited to works of art that overtly depict homosexual themes or to works by known homosexuals? To what degree is the sexual identity of an artist crucial to an understanding of his art? What is the role of the viewer in determining a gay theme? A picture that concerns homosexuality might be read differently depending on the knowledge of its audience. For example, Marsden Hartley's *Portrait of a German Officer* (1914) depicts Karl von Freyburg, a soldier Hartley loved and who was killed in the early stages of World War I. Freyburg is represented not by how he actually looked but by juxtaposing numbers, letters, and elements of his uniform in a collage-like composition. Given the abstract nature of the picture, it is likely that only Hartley's friends understood its homosexual significance. But merely identifying the theme of the painting in terms of Hartley's love only raises more questions. What does it mean to represent homosexuality in 1914 in the United States? Why would an artist risk disgrace by painting such a

A theme? How does it relate to other depictions by contemporary artists and artists in the past? Is there such a thing as a homosexual iconography—a set of symbols or themes that can be decoded if we have the key?

A growing number of scholars have begun to focus on the kinds of complex problems raised by the representation of homosexuality. The *Bibliography of the Gay and Lesbian Art* (1994), published by the Gay and Lesbian Caucus of the College Art Association, lists over a thousand entries, but this number is misleading. The actual number of scholarly works is still relatively small and for the most part consists of essays rather than sustained book-length studies. This is changing, however. Two important anthologies are *Homosexuality and Homosexuals in the Arts* (1992), edited by Wayne Dynes and Stephen Donaldson, and *Gay and Lesbian Studies in Art History* (1994), edited by Whitney Davis. The College Art Association's *Art Journal* has devoted two special issues that highlight gay/queer issues—*We're Here: The Gay and Lesbian Presence in Art* (1996) and *How Men Look* (1997). Several art historians, including Whitney Davis, Ann Gibson, Jonathan Katz, Kobena Mercer, Richard Meyer, Michael Plante, Christopher Reed, Kenneth Silver, Patricia Simons, and James Smalls, have made gay/queer studies essential to their work.

The overwhelming number of works on art and homosexuality focuses on the nineteenth and twentieth century. Given the postmodernist conviction that homosexuality was in fact "constructed" in the modern period, this is not surprising. But the phenomenon has been fueled by the AIDS crisis and the so-called cultural wars. The work of Robert Mapplethorpe, in particular, has generated the largest attention because of the attempts to censor the retrospective, *A Perfect Moment* (1988) and the notoriety given Mapplethorpe's photography by Senate Foreign Relations Chairman Jesse Helms. Among the vast literature on Mapplethorpe, Kobena Mercer's "Sin Head Sex Thing: Racial Difference and the Homoerotic Imaginary" (1991) stands out for its discussion of homoeroticism, class, and race—issues rarely discussed together in art history. Mapplethorpe's notoriety has fueled interest in the tradition of male nude photography, which is surveyed by Allen Ellenzweig in *The Homoerotic Photograph* (1992). There has also been an enormous amount of scholarly interest in the work of individual artists who have died from AIDS/HIV, including Keith Haring and David Wojnarowicz, as well as in the

AIDS collectives Gran Fury and the NAMES Project. Certainly, some of the best work in art history and gay/queer studies concerns AIDS/HIV. Douglas Crimp's writings on the ways in which the AIDS crisis has been conceptualized by the media and the art world insists that questions of sexuality and gender are essential to the processes of representation itself. In turn, the representation of AIDS/HIV impacts the society's response in terms of research and in terms of helping those who live with the disease. AIDS/HIV has had an immediate and devastating effect on art history, taking the lives of artists, curators, and faculty including one of the most profound writers on art and gender, Craig Owens. Owens was particularly interested in defining what he saw was a postmodernist shift in the nature of identity and the role of art. He sought to link gay/queer studies with feminism, identifying shared concerns and conflicts that are still rarely addressed.

Presently, gay/queer studies in art history seems to be moving in several different directions. Writers such as Charlotte Furth, Kazuo Hanazaki, and Bret Hinsch have begun to focus on cultures outside the West, in periods other than the modern. Postmodernism has introduced a shift away from questions of identity and authorship to the ways homosexuality functions in society in terms of broader power relationships and prejudices. Literary critic Eve Kosofsky Sedgwick, who insists that the question of homo-heterosexuality definition is paramount for understanding modern culture, has had an enormous influence on recent work, for example, Abagail Solomon-Godeau's *Male Trouble*: *A Crisis in Representation* (1997). A postmodernist fear of categories and a distrust of the hegemonic nature of the academy informed the University Art Museum at Berkeley's *In a Different Light* (1995), the first survey of gay and lesbian art to be sponsored by a mainstream American museum. The curators, Nayland Blake and Lawrence Rinder—both artists rather than academics—attempted to create a fluid conception of sexuality and content that could be called "queer" rather than gay or lesbian, and would not be dependent on individual sexual orientation. But *In a Different Light*'s ahistorical approach in which works of art and artifacts of the last fifty years were grouped according to broad social categories without regard to chronology or movement had the unintended effect of essentializing "queerness." To be queer is not to be free from historical and cultural forces that constructed gay identities in the first place.

Whether essentialist or constructivist, historical or ahistorical, approaches to the question of homosexuality and art share a common fault—they rarely have much to say about form, that is, what works of art look like, their particular qualities of composition, color, and style. An exception are the various attempts to define a camp sensibility beginning with Susan Sontag's famous "Notes on Camp" (1964), as well as later attempts to define gay and queer style as in the *Extended Sensibilities* (1982) exhibit of gay and lesbian contemporary art. In any case, such attempts to classify queer art by broad stylistic and/or symbolic characteristics are different from a close analysis of the way particular works express potentially dangerous content through their structure and medium. If homosexuality was there in the beginning of art history, it was in Winckelmann's longing for a beautiful male god who was, after all, only stone. What role does this aesthetic transformation have in homosexual imaginary? How is form—simultaneously distant and seductive, abstract and real—made over into desire?

Jonathan Weinberg

Bibliography

Blake, Nayland, Lawrence Rinder, and Amy Scholder, eds. *In a Different Light: Visual Culture, Sexual Identity, Queer Practice.* San Francisco: City Lights Books, 1995.

Davis, Whitney, ed. *Gay and Lesbian Studies in Art History.* New York: Harrington Park Press, 1994.

Saslow, James. *Ganymede and the Renaissance: Homosexuality in the Renaissance.* New Haven: Yale University Press, 1986.

———, ed. Bibliography of *Gay and Lesbian Art.* New York: Gay and Lesbian Caucus of the College Art Association, 1994.

Weinberg, Jonathan. *Speaking for Vice: Homosexuality in the Art of Charles Demuth, Marsden Hartley, and the First American Avant-Garde.* New Haven: Yale University Press, 1993.

See also Aestheticism; Bacon, Francis; Cadmus, Paul; Caravagio, Michelangelo Merisi da; Demuth, Charles; Freud, Sigmund; Ganymede; Gran Fury; Hartley, Marsden; Hockney, David; Leonardo da Vinci; Mapplethorpe, Robert; Michelangelo, Buonarroti; NAMES Project; Owens, Craig; Pater, Walter; Il Sodoma; Symonds, John Aldington; Warhol, Andy; Winckelmann, Johann Joachim; Wojnarowicz, David

Artemidorus (c.138–160 C.E.)

Artemidorus of Daldis was a dream interpreter who traveled widely through the Greco-Roman world, collecting and categorizing, with admirable objectivity, his clients' dreams. His surviving work, the *Oneirokritika* (On the Interpretation of Dreams) is extremely valuable for an understanding of the construction of gender and sexuality in antiquity.

He divides dreams of sexual intercourse into three broad categories: "*kata phusin*" and "*kata nomon*" (in accordance with nature and convention), "*para nomon*" (against convention), and "*para physin*" (against nature). In the first category are grouped, inter alia, dreams of sex with one's wife or one's slaves (male or female); in the second, dreams of incest; in the third, dreams of necrophilia and bestiality. Artemidorus' interpretations reflect the commonly perceived link between sex and the status of the penetrator—a dream about penetrating one's male slave is a good one (in the predictive sense), but a dream about being penetrated by a social inferior (a slave, one's son, a poor man) is inevitably bad.

The *Oneirokritika* thus illustrates how male-initiated penetrative sex (the sexual object or choice being irrelevant) was considered "natural" or "conventional," and highlights one of the central debates in Greek philosophy, that between "nature" and "convention." Dreams against nature include dreams of lesbian penetration, necrophilia, and bestiality, whereas dreams of incest are included in the category of dreams against convention. The arbitrariness of these categories suggests that "*physis*" (nature) is a cultural category as well, constructed by the society of Artemidorus and his clients.

Michael Lambert

Bibliography

Foucault, Michel. *The History of Sexuality.* Vol 3. *The Care of the Self.* Trans. Robert Hurley. New York: Random House, 1988.

Winkler, J. J. *The Constraints of Desire.* London: Routledge, 1990.

See also Greece; Rome

Arvin, Newton (1900–1963)

Leading critic of American literature, Newton Arvin spent most of his professional career at Smith College. He was forced to retire in 1960 after a "pornography" scandal, involving photos of young men.

Arvin's most important works include his *Whitman* (1938), one of the most enduring works of socialist criticism in American literature, and his critical biography, *Herman Melville* (1950). In both these studies Arvin struggled to express his sense of the importance of homosexuality to the great figures of what F. O. Matthiessen was calling the "American renaissance." The task of confronting these subjects was complicated by Arvin's own attempt at marriage (to a former student) and his gradual emergence as an "out" man seeking to integrate life and work.

Arvin's Whitman is fully engaged in the political struggles of mid-nineteenth-century America, struggles that offered an analogy to the literary and political conflicts of the 1930s, when Arvin was active in left-wing causes such as support for the Republicans in the Spanish Civil War. Arvin is also remarkably open about Whitman's sexuality and its place in his poetry. "Whitman's homosexuality," he writes, "cannot be denied," but he struggles to integrate a sexuality seen in the discourse of his time as "abnormal" with Whitman's role as a democratic poet.

The portrait Arvin paints of Melville is less anguished in part because he can now locate his study of the author of *Moby-Dick* in the context of a social concept of the "different," in which Melville's homosexual figures are the object of scorn and hatred. Arvin identifies the search for a friend as Melville's continuing theme, and he is particularly acute in portraying the pain caused by Melville's marriage and links to heterosexual society. These shifts in critical method are a product of, among other things, his love affair with Truman Capote, who brought Arvin to a much more openly gay life and to a greater understanding of contemporary literature.

Although Arvin's biographical method is now somewhat unfashionable, his early explorations of desire and identity assure him a permanent place in American literary criticism.   *Robert K. Martin*

Bibliography

Martin, Robert K. "Scandal at Smith." *Radical Teacher* 45 (Winter 1994): 4–8.

See also Capote, Truman; Matthiessen, F. O.; Melville, Herman; Whitman, Walt

Ashbery, John (1927–)

John Ashbery is a luminary of the New York school of poets, along with gay poets Frank O'Hara and James Schuyler. Although not closeted in his social life, Ashbery has always resisted being labeled as a gay poet, preferring to be regarded—if necessary—as a poet who happens to be gay. Increasingly, however, critics within gay studies are reading him, against his wishes, as the former. Once biographers set to work, connections between the events in his life are likely to be made with individual poems. Such connections, it seems, will never be authorized by the author himself.

The concept of camp is certainly likely to prove useful in any analysis of how Ashbery's poems can so suddenly veer from mere whimsy to performative—even melodramatic—seriousness. It is also possible to link his insistently paradoxical view of reality to the potential obliquity of a gay subcultural viewpoint. The tones of his voices are generally opposed to bourgeois small-mindedness and suburban narrowness. Indeed, his tones can veer into a lofty (and often European-sounding) aestheticism that gives the impression of being deliberately off-putting to the provincial American reader.

Ashbery's refusal to take part in the identity politics of post-Stonewall gayness eventually begins to look mannered. There is a deliberateness, some would even say a perversity, about the areas he has chosen not to write about. For example, it is not uninteresting to read a New York poet, gay or not, who has had so little to say about AIDS.   *Gregory Woods*

Bibliography

Bergman, David. "Choosing Our Fathers: Gender and Identity in Whitman, Ashbery, and Richard Howard." In *Gaiety Transfigured: Gay Self-Representation in American Literature*. Madison: University of Wisconsin Press, 1991, 44–63.

Woods, Gregory. "Ashbery's Abnormalcy." *PN Review* 99 (September–October 1994): 70–71.

See also O'Hara, Frank; Schuyler; James; U.S. Literature

Asians in North America

Gay Asian activism is tied directly to the social protest movements of the 1960s. Even before the Stonewall riots of 1969, individual gay Asians were active in the civil rights movement. One of them, Kiyoshi Kuromiya, of Philadelphia, would later be featured in Arthur Dong's documentary *Out Rage '69* (1995). Kuromiya eventually became an AIDS activist and edited the Critical Path AIDS Project's newsletter. In 1996, he was a plaintiff in an ACLU lawsuit against the Communications Decency Act.

In February 1975, this writer, who had attended radical gay meetings in Berkeley in the late 1960s, penned the first coming-out essay by a gay Asian American in *Bridge* magazine, an Asian American publication from Manhattan.

It was not until the late 1970s that queers of Asian heritage in North America began organizing into groups. The first such co-gender group started meeting in the summer of 1979 in Boston. The Boston Asian Gay Men and Lesbians (BAGMAL) was founded by Chua Siong-huat, a Malaysian immigrant. A few months after forming BAGMAL, Chua marched to the Washington Monument during the first National March on Washington for Gay and Lesbian Rights in October 1979. The event was preceded by a National Third World Lesbian and Gay Conference at Howard University, where the first loose, national network Lesbian and Gay Asian Collective was formed by the dozen or so activists present.

Tana Loy, a Chinese American lesbian, spoke October 13, 1979, on "Who's the Barbarian?" before a plenary session of the Third World Conference; the next day, Margaret Cornell, a lesbian poet of Japanese/European background, spoke before the thousands gathered at the Washington Monument on "Living in Asian America." For the first time in North America, Asian Americans "came out" publicly by marching through Washington's Chinatown that Sunday, carrying a large banner proclaiming, "We're Asians, Gay & Proud."

Shortly thereafter, Richard Fung, a Chinese Canadian born in Trinidad, who had attended the Washington, D.C., events, organized Gay Asians Toronto, another pioneering group. These early pioneers challenged conventional Asian perspectives that viewed homosexuality as a decadent, foreign import and frowned on any public display of taboo sexualities.

Fung set out to document the growing movement and soon became the preeminent video documentarian of queer Asian political activism. Independent video productions he directed ranged from *Orientations* (1984), an early talking-heads video about gay and lesbian Asians in North America, to *Dirty Laundry* (1996), a dramatic account of a Chinese Canadian gay man seeking his "roots."

Chua himself was profiled in Fung's 1990 *Fighting Chance*, the first video to record the lives of Asians with AIDS or seropositivity. In the video,

Chua refused to apologize for getting AIDS, proclaiming he would change nothing in his behavior.

In his writings, Chua, who succumbed to AIDS in 1994, argued "there is nothing wrong really with being a sexual object if you can also be a sexual subject." He explained that "the Asian gay man and the Asian lesbians are our subjects," since "we see the world through their eyes."

In the 1980s and 1990s, as the gay movement proliferated, more and more gay Asian groups started up. Asian Lesbians of the East Coast formed in 1983, while on the West Coast, Asian women organized around the publication *Phoenix Rising*. Trikone, a South Asian group from Palo Alto, Calif., bridged domestic American culture and that of the home countries. In San Francisco, the Gay Asian Pacific Alliance was formed, and in Los Angeles, the Gay Asian Project became the Gay Asian Pacific Support Network. The first West Coast Asian/Pacific Lesbian and Gay Conference was held July 18, 1987, in West Hollywood, California, and the first North American Conference for Lesbian and Gay Asians was held August 19–21, 1998, in Toronto, Canada. In the 1990s, a Gay Vietnamese Alliance was formed in Orange County, Calif.; *Doi Dien,* a literary publication in Vietnamese and English, also appeared in California.

Asian queers soon became more and more visible, not just in West Hollywood, where clubs (such as Buddha Lounge) began catering to their needs, but also nationally, culminating in a large delegation of Asian marchers at the 1993 March on Washington (which carried the same banner from the 1979 march).

Published anthologies include *Between the Lines* (1987), a Pacific Asian Lesbians of Santa Cruz collection; *A Lotus of Another Color* (1993), a South Asian compilation; *The Very Inside* (1994), another lesbian collection; *Asian American Sexualities* (1996), derived from a special issue of Amerasia Journal; and *CelebAsian: Shared Lives* (1996), an oral history from Gay Asians Toronto.

Queer Asians also emerged on the Internet, facilitating the coming-out process for thousands. Computer dating and sex on the Web became an easy way for Asians to discard traditional inhibitions while coming out. Gay Asian home pages, listservs, and other Internet resources have proliferated during the late 1990s.

While a few from Asia have attained asylum in the United States based on a fear of persecution, it would be wrong to oversimplify and consider the Asian societies as sites of pure traditional values and the United States as the land of tolerance and acceptance.   *Daniel C. Tsang*

Bibliography

CelebAsian: Shared Lives, An Oral History of Gay Asians. Toronto: Gay Asians Toronto, 1996.

Chung, C., A. Kim, and A. K. Lemeshewsky, eds. *Between the Lines: An Anthology.* Santa Cruz, Calif.: Dancing Bird Press, 1987.

Gay Insurgent no. 6 (Summer 1980). Philadelphia. Essays by Tana Loy, Michiyo Cornell, Richard Fung, and Daniel Tsang.

Leong, Russell, ed. *Asian American Sexualities: Dimensions of the Gay and Lesbian Experience.* New York: Routledge, 1996.

Lim-Hing, Sharon, ed. *The Very Inside: An Anthology of Writings by Asian and Pacific Islander Lesbians and Bisexual Women.* Toronto: Sister Vision, 1994.

Ratti, Rakesh, ed. *A Lotus of Another Color: An Unfolding of the South Asian Gay and Lesbian Experience.* Boston: Alyson, 1993.

Tsang, Chun-tuen, Daniel. "Gay Awareness." *Bridge: An Asian American Perspective* 3, no. 4 (February 1975): 44–45.

See also AIDS; Activism; Araki, Gregg

Assimilation

Assimilation has not only been the goal of much of the activism of gays and lesbians in this century; it has also constituted the horizon of much theorizing in gay and lesbian studies. Yet the concept itself is rarely analyzed explicitly. Conceptual investigations of assimilation catalyze two sorts of questions—one ontological, seeking to understand the "nature" of sexuality, including homosexuality; the other political, interrogating the relationship between assimilation and social justice. The political may emerge from analysis of the ontological or may bracket that question entirely as unknowable or uninteresting or both. Eve Sedgwick's distinction between "minoritizing" and "universalizing" discourses is useful here. Minoritizing views see the homosexual subculture as "small, distinct, [and] relatively fixed" (Sedgwick 1). In contrast, a universalizing strategy frames the homo/heterosexual relationship as only part of a spectrum of historically and culturally constituted sexualities.

Like Foucault, Sedgwick notes (but cannot explain) the "sudden, radical condensation of sexual categories" of the late nineteenth century. For Foucault, that period's discourses produced sexuality itself as well as a "reverse discourse" by which "homosexuality [begins] to speak in its own behalf" (101). This historicized understanding of sexuality may lead one to suspect that assimilation—from the ancient Greeks, whose social organization included erotic relationships between adult and younger men; to the varieties of sexual expression documented by anthropologists; to the erotic, lifelong relationships between women up to the early twentieth century—constitutes a cultural norm. Freud's own antiminoritizing view posits universal bisexuality and mutable sexual desire. Kinsey's well-known research on gay men (and later on lesbians) revealed that a significant number of people who identified as heterosexual had had same-sex sexual experience and few people exclusively homosexual or heterosexual. Indeed, he urged that "homosexual" and "heterosexual" be employed only as adjectives, to describe acts—not persons.

Whereas both Freud and Kinsey believed that their new understandings entailed full political assimilation, others argue that homosexuality's ontological status is separable from the normative question of social treatment and that homosexuality has always existed as a discrete, immutable category. Boswell, for example, uses classical materials to defend his claim that "gays" existed even in pre- and early Christianity. Kirk and Madsen describe homosexuality as a "condition," and a condition, they maintain, is "not subject to solution: it is simply an aspect of life that must be accommodated" (10–11). Likewise, earlier sexologists of the late nineteenth century (e.g., Havelock Ellis and Magnus Hirschfeld) struggled to invent nonperjorative labels like "third sex" or "invert" to suggest the distinctiveness of homosexuality; Ellis even likened homosexuality to another "condition," namely, color blindness.

Political differences do not attach themselves neatly to these distinctions. For a minoritizing view like radical feminism, gender oppression and not sexuality organizes culture; indeed, radical feminists argue that patriarchal ideology has effaced the extent to which women's culture has assimilated lesbianism's multiple manifestations. If gender oppression inevitably privileges men, then political organizing between gay men and lesbians will not serve women. In contrast, other minoritizing views insist that choice of sexual partner, though significant, is the only generalizable distinction (and is morally irrelevant) between homosexuals and heterosexuals.

Thus, social and political assimilation logically follows. Kirk and Madsen comment on "the enormous preponderance of gays, who are, except for what they like to do in bed, just like everyone else" (352), and they recommend a political public relations agenda that single-mindedly emphasizes sameness: "We want [heterosexuals] to realize that we look, feel, and act just as they do" (379).

Opponents of political assimilation have insisted on the contagiousness and immorality of homosexuality. For those opponents, to afford gays and lesbians access to social institutions currently exclusionary—marriage, the military, adoption, insurance, and the like—is not assimilation but rather the destruction of those very institutions. This view must, however, live with the apparent implication that these institutions—including heterosexuality—are incredibly fragile. But the minoritizing view also lives with a dilemma of sorts, that homosexuality is a defining characteristic of a significant (and mostly unchanging) number of people, that that characteristic is identified by those people as an (if not the) important identity marker, and that that characteristic ought not to matter legally or socially. A further irony resides in the political reality that legal victories have depended on the minoritizing argument that homosexuals are a discrete, insular group and that homosexuality (analogous to race) is immutable. Finally, the universalizing view does not entail obvious consequences for political thinking about assimilation. To seek only assimilation, for example, refuses to question those institutions that, like marriage and the military, may be problematic for reasons that go beyond their heterosexism. For this reason many feminists have insisted on the importance of a feminist analysis of any political strategy of assimilation. Further, if sexuality falls on a "spectrum" rather than a binary, demanding inclusion privileges those who most resemble the heterosexual norm and also reinscribes that very binary. Indeed, does not the very notion of "assimilation" suggest a norm to which one assimilates? In the last analysis, defenders of the universalizing view tend to reject the notion of an a priori politics and to embrace in place of "ideological rigor" (Sedgwick, 13) an ad hoc politics that deploys whatever strategies—assimilationist or separatist—that further an antihomophobia agenda.   *Diane Raymond*

Bibliography

Boswell, John. *Christianity, Social Tolerance, and Homosexuality: Gay People in Western Europe from the Beginning of the Christian Era to the Fourteenth Century.* Chicago: University of Chicago Press, 1980.

Faderman, Lillian. *Surpassing the Love of Men.* New York: Morrow, 1982.

Foucault, Michel. *The History of Sexuality.* Volume I. Trans. Robert Hurley. New York: Vintage Books, 1978.

Kirk, Marshall, and Hunter Madsen. *After the Ball: How America Will Conquer Its Fear and Hatred of Gays in the '90s.* New York: Doubleday, 1989.

Sedgwick, Eve. *Epistemology of the Closet.* Berkeley: University of California Press, 1990.

See also Ellis, Havelock; Foucault, Michel; Freud, Sigmund; Gay Relationships; Hirschfeld, Magnus; Homosexual Panic; Inversion; Kinsey, Alfred; Recruitment Myth; Same-Sex Marriage; Sexology; Third Sex

Athens

Most of the evidence for ancient Greek "homosexuality" is derived from Athenian literary and artistic evidence, mainly vase paintings. Because the term *homosexuality* as we know it was conceptualized only in the late nineteenth century, it reflects a sexual taxonomy unknown to the Athenians, and it thus cannot accurately describe the Athenian experience. As the literary evidence was produced exclusively by men of the upper, educated classes largely for male audiences, our view of same-sex relations between men is conditioned by the ideology of this class.

In Plato's *Symposium*, Pausanias, the lover of Agathon, distinguishes between custom regarding male same-sex love in Athens and in other Greek city-states. Athenian custom is described as *poikilos* (complex) because the lover (*erastes*) is encouraged and praised, whereas the beloved (*eromenos*) is closely protected by his father and his tutor, and is teased by his friends.

Athenian custom, argues Pausanias, subjects good and bad *erastai* to a moral competition. The *eromenos* who surrenders quickly, because of either the wealth or the reputation of his *erastes,* is a victim of Aphrodite Pandemos (vulgar love); the *eromenos,* however, who desires excellence and recognizes that his *erastes* can contribute to his moral and intellectual development, exemplifies the far nobler Aphrodite Ourania (heavenly love).

This ambivalence discussed by Pausanias reflects attitudes to male same-sex love implied in

A other works, for instance, the comedies of Aristophanes, where the anally penetrated man becomes a target of abuse. To be passive and penetrated was clearly a mark of shame in a society where honor and shame largely motivated moral behavior.

The position of the younger *eromenos* who "yields" was thus potentially dishonorable, if he did not respect the social code. The younger male, who would become an Athenian citizen and a member of the city's lawmaking assembly, could not, by his behavior, flout the prevailing concept of masculinity by being publicly passive and thus "feminine." Furthermore, behaving like a prostitute could eventually result in disenfranchisement. Hence the ambivalent position of the *eromenos,* who was watched and teased; hence the fact that no extant vase paintings of the period depict citizen men being penetrated anally, but several depict women being so penetrated. Face-to-face intercrural (between the thighs) intercourse was regarded with approval, but oral and anal sex were regarded as activities for women, barbarians, and satyrs, beneath the dignity of an Athenian citizen. This was, of course, the public ideology; as in every society, practice in private presumably differed.

There have been other interpretations of these relationships, however. Influenced by the examples of Dorian Crete and Sparta, as well as by comparative studies in anthropology, some scholars have suggested that same-sex behavior in classical Athens could be the relic of an Indo-European initiation ritual. Initiatory elements are undeniably present in the educative nature of the relationship between *erastes* and *eromenos,* as Plato conceptualizes it, but there is no convincing Athenian evidence for Dorian-style initiatory practices. The unavailability of citizen women before marriage and the arranged marriage system have also been offered as explanations.   *Michael Lambert*

Bibliography

Dover, Kenneth. *Greek Homosexuality,* 2d ed. London: Duckworth, 1989.
Halperin, David. M. *One Hundred Years of Homosexuality and Other Essays on Greek Love.* New York: Routledge, 1989.

See also Greece, Ancient; Pederasty; Plato; Sparta

Athletic Model Guild

Bob Mizer of the Athletic Model Guild (1922-1992) was the standard-bearer of the American physique photographers whose voluptuous mail-order glossies and coy little magazines made the 1950s a golden age of gay eroticism. He came to maturity as postwar gay networks were beginning to crystallize and in 1945 set up the Athletic Model Guild in Hollywood. Ads in straight bodybuilding magazines soon established a lively mail-order trade in the smiling "athletes" whose erotic appeal was camouflaged by muscular development.

At first frontal nudes were the staple product, but after a few scrapes with the law and outraged parents, Mizer became the high priest of the posing strap, from scallop-shaped codpieces to improvisations with washcloths. In 1953 Mizer launched the era of small gay physique magazines when the U.S. Post Office clamped down on suspect advertising in the straight magazines. *Physique Pictorial,* the most brazen of the new pocket-size, mass-distributed mags, offered mainly black-and-white photos of Mizer's volatile stable of movie extras, G.I.s, drifters, and hustlers recruited from Tinseltown bus stations and gyms. All were fleshed out by titillating biographies, and readers were urged to order sets. The bodybuilding alibi was sometimes forgotten as Mizer thinned out the champions with amateurs who were slim or pudgy, hairy, tattooed, even sometimes fey. When the legendary AMG courtyard setting, complete with open shower stall, grew stale, rear-projected backdrops of waterfronts and Roman temples sufficed, along with Mizer's characteristic phallic props and fetish costumes.

PP always had room for graphics as well, fantasy narratives by Tom of Finland and George Quaintance, that could be even more suggestive than the photos. Alongside this bulging gallery ran Mizer's editorial fulminations on censorship, hypocrisy, and human rights. Although the artisanal AMG and *PP* were surpassed by the increasingly commercial competition, Mizer was virtually alone in using a pop culture platform to break through the complacency of the closet.

In 1958, Mizer joined the industry shift toward mail-order cinema and soon led the embryonic "physique movie" market, unrivaled for his variety, ingenuity, and output. His unmistakable flair in the wrestling and posing subgenres and in unselfconscious plots of prison delinquents and Polynesian harems made him the true precursor of post-Stonewall gay porn.

Mizer went frontal with everyone else in the late sixties, but a younger, more entrepreneurial generation fed the hardcore explosion in the theater circuit of the 1970s. The VCR put finishing touches to the AMG studio around 1981, but until his death Mizer maintained his small, kinky niche in the market (anus shots and spanking).

However much AMG was to be recycled in the nostalgia of postmodern gay culture, its achievement belonged to the fifties, when its clash between unabashed lustfulness and campy ghetto irony, between innocence and experience, epitomized Eisenhower's America. Mizer brought to physique culture, despite the enforced alibi and paranoia, an unapologetic celebration of flesh, community, and ambiguous masculinity in an age when erotic consumerism had not yet colonized gay desire.

Thomas Waugh

Bibliography

Mizer, Robert. *Physique: A Pictorial History of the Athletic Model Guild*, Winston Leyland, ed. San Francisco: Gay Sunshine Press, 1982.

Hooven, F. Valentine III. *Beefcake: The Muscle Magazines of America 1950–1970*. Cologne: Benedikt Taschen, 1995.

Waugh, Thomas. *Hard to Imagine: Gay Male Eroticism in Photography and Film from Their Beginnings to Stonewall*. New York: Columbia University Press, 1996.

See also Body Image; Bruce of Los Angeles; Photography; Physical Culture; Quaintance, George; Tom of Finland

Auden, W. H. (1907–1973)

Born in York, England, Wystan Hugh Auden graduated from Oxford University in 1928. His father was a doctor, his mother a nurse. After a year in the "cabaret" Berlin of 1929, he taught school in Scotland and England until 1935. As a noble gesture he married Thomas Mann's daughter, Erika, to help her escape Nazi Germany in 1938. The marriage was never meant to last, and by January 1939, Auden had settled in New York City with a Brooklyn boy of eighteen, Christopher Kallman. The relationship lasted until Auden's death in 1973, although there was little sex between the couple after the early years.

In prewar literature Auden soon became a star, even though he was not yet thirty. He published *The Spender Orators* in 1932 and an expanded edition of *Poems* in 1933. His literary group included Stephen Spender, C. Day Lewis, and Christopher Isherwood.

Although he accepted early on his homosexuality, Auden veiled it so that the gentlest of his love poems, e.g., "Lullaby" (1937), passed through the straight world as a tenderness between a man and a woman. Lighthearted poems like "Heavy Date" and "Law Like Love" were similarly accepted as celebrations of heterosexual love; few readers realized that the object of Auden's affections was Kallman. To readers who knew the details of Auden's household, the poems were doubly appreciated, and Auden's influence on so important a gay voice as James Merrill eventually afforded the deceased poet a chance to come back to life via a Ouija board in *The Changing Light at Sandover*, a book-length poem published by Merrill in 1982, a decade after Auden's death.

In addition to his lyric poems, Auden tried his hand at plays and opera librettos, but his only real success in these genres was *The Rake's Progress*, which he and Kallman wrote for Igor Stravinsky in 1951. His ten plays, eight documentary film scripts, and eight librettos were published in 1988 in two volumes by Princeton University Press, edited by Edward Mendelson. His collaboration with Benjamin Britten on a libretto resulted in estrangement for the pair. Auden's opinions were seldom sought on literary matters, and he did not make a name for himself in criticism, being content to create primary material. His corpus was uniformly good throughout his long career, and he was forever lauded. His 1939 poem "In Memory of W.B. Yeats" was even credited with bringing the rise of fascism to the attention of Europe and America.

Although Auden enjoyed dividing his time between New York City and Austria, he longed for England in his final years and returned to his native country, a move that did not bring him the adulation he expected from the young bucks at Oxford, who considered him a quaint if famous old duffer. He died in Vienna and is buried at Kirchstetter. After his death some early campy verse, including the circulated limerick "A Day for a Lay," was incorporated into his established canon.

George Klawitter

Bibliography

Callan, Edward. *Auden: A Carnival of Intellect*. New York: Oxford University Press, 1983.

Davenport-Hines, Richard. *Auden*. London: Heinemann, 1995.

See also Britten, Benjamin; English Literature; Isherwood, Christopher; Merrill, James

Augustine of Hippo (354–430)

Aurelius Augustine, who died as bishop of Hippo Regis, is the single most influential theologian of Latin Christianity. A pagan professor of rhetoric who was baptized only at the age of thirty-three, Augustine composed a large body of writings that would become foundational texts in many areas of theology. His influence is particularly strong in Christian sexual morality, since he wrote often and explicitly on marriage, chastity, and virginity. He describes his own struggles with lust and diagnoses the root sin underneath present human misery as a sin of disordered desire (*libido*). In Augustine, one finds stated very clearly the principle that human genitals are to be used only within permanent, monogamous marriages open to producing children. Augustine concludes from this principle that sexual activity between members of the same sex is "against nature," by which he means not only that it is deeply sinful but that it violates the divine plan for human reproduction. Augustine was also one of the first theologians to identify the story of the Sodom (Genesis 19) with male homosexuality. He teaches that the Sodomites wanted to rape Lot's guests, visitors to their city. This is why Lot offered up his daughter instead, since it is better for men to violate women than to violate other men. During the Middle Ages passages from Augustine were cited, combined, and even rewritten as authoritative justifications for the canonical prohibitions of same-sex activity.   *Mark D. Jordan*

Bibliography

Brown, Peter. *The Body and Society: Men, Women, and Sexual Renunciation in Early Christianity.* New York: Columbia University Press, 1988.

See also Aelred of Rievaulx; Alan of Lille; Albert the Great; Christianity; Sodomy; Thomas Aquinas

Australia

Australia's eighteen million people are governed by a federal political system. With Tasmania's decriminalization of homosexuality in 1997, homosexual practices are now legal in all six Australian states and the two territories. The age of consent varies from state to state, and some states also have antidiscrimination legislation of various kinds, including that protecting transgenderists in New South Wales.

The head of state is the governor general, who is appointed by the queen on the advice of the federal government, headed by the prime minister. There is a strong popular movement for a republic.

After the white invasion in 1788, the indigenous Aboriginal peoples were dispossessed of their land by the doctrine of *terra nullius*. This doctrine was overturned in the early 1990s by the High Court's Mabo decision, which has been a source of intense political conflict over land rights ever since. Australia has had a long history of immigration. English is the dominant language. Most Australians live on the east coast, in and around three state capital cities (Sydney, Melbourne, Brisbane) and the national capital (Canberra). These cities, along with Adelaide and Perth, have strong lesbian and gay communities.

Shifts in social perceptions of homosexuality in Australia can be marked by contrasting the harsh punishments meted out for sodomy in nineteenth-century colonial court cases and media representations of homosexuality and cross-dressing in the 1950s, on the one hand; with the emergence of the women's liberation and the homosexual civil rights movements in Australia at the end of the 1960s, the (slow) legalization of homosexuality in the various states, the national televising of the Sydney Gay and Lesbian Mardi Gras since 1994, and government and community partnership in response to the HIV/AIDS epidemics. However, twenty-five years of relatively liberal censorship regulations of same-sex desire in film and video are currently under challenge. "Homosexual panic" has emerged as a legal defense in cases of antigay violence and murder.

Recent discussions of the Australian colonial period have uncovered a wealth of information concerning same-sex practice at that time. Some of the most interesting of these studies, such as Robert French, *Camping by a Billabong* (1993) and Robert Hughes, *The Fatal Shore* (1987), have painted a rich and complex picture of both colonial history and culture. In more recent years, Australia has had an important role in international social reform. Works like Germaine Greer's *The Female Eunuch* (1970) and Dennis Altman's *Homosexual: Oppression and Liberation* (1971) have been milestones in the sexual liberation movement and are still cited today with awe and respect.

The historical existence and status of same sex practices among indigenous Australians has been a matter of anthropological dispute and is beyond the scope of this entry. An issue of *Gay Perspectives* (11 [1993]), edited by Robert Aldrich, has recorded a serious and informative discussion by the Gays and Lesbians Aboriginal Alliance. In addition, contemporary Aboriginal gay and lesbian experiences, which form a culture that is distinct from the dominant gay and lesbian culture in Australia, emerge in the historical and cultural work of Dino Hodge, *Did You Meet Any Malagas? A Homosexual History of Australia's Tropical Capital* (1993) and of Wayne King, *Black Hours* (1996).

Mardi Gras began in 1978 as a rally organized by the Gay Solidarity Group in solidarity with a request from San Francisco's Gay Freedom Day Committee. It was timed to coincide with international commemorations of Stonewall and resulted in a police riot with the arrest of fifty-three men and women. It is now a monthlong cultural festival culminating in a parade watched by a street audience of 500,000–750,000, followed by a dance party of 20,000. The festival is opened on the steps of Sydney's Opera House and on the World Wide Web. Events are held in all major Sydney cultural venues in the city's premier festival, which is a major international tourist attraction for Asian, European, and North American gays and lesbians and contributes significantly to the local economy. All states now have annual gay and lesbian pride events, and both Melbourne and Sydney have major queer film festivals. The national televising of the Sydney Gay and Lesbian Mardi Gras in 1994 was marked by political controversy; however, it received the highest ratings of any television show ever in Australia and has been televised annually since.

National gay publications include the monthly glossy magazines *Campaign* (1975) and *outRage* (1983). The Sydney-based *Lesbians on the Loose* is the major lesbian publication, though a new glossy lesbian magazine, *Lip*, has emerged from Melbourne. Each city has free "coalitionist" (gay, lesbian, transgender, bisexual) newspapers.

The increasing cultural and economic commodification of gayness and lesbianism on television and in tourism is significantly affecting social attitudes generally in the major cities. However, as Ana Kokkinos' film *Only the Brave* (1995) and Christos Tsiolkas's novel *Loaded* (1995) indicate, relative gay equality has occurred largely separately from the ways racial, ethnic, and social differences are played out in relation to same-sex desires. This same issue is addressed in the film *The Adventures of Priscilla, Queen of the Desert* (1993). Commodification includes the recycling of international body imagery in the local gay and lesbian media and involves close representational, and some political, links with U.S. concepts of gayness.

These links have often been parodied as well as celebrated, with Mardi Gras costumes including not only Ron Muncaster's superbly glamorous creations but also Jackie Kennedy Onassis's dress post-assassination and a bar and lounge room cult following for *The Golden Girls* television program. The older British connection remains in a preference for politicized forms of camp, wit, and irony. Parades in the 1980s saw an Elton John contingent in trademark sunglasses and "poofter" T-shirts on the day he married in Sydney, and Imelda Marcos lamenting her shoe collection post–Cory Aquino. Even so, links with British traditions of law reform, politics, and to some extent high culture have generally receded, though culturally older British and European reference points still have some resonance (Oscar Wilde, Radclyffe Hall, opera, sundrenched youth), which increases once popular music and television are brought into play (*Absolutely Fabulous*). Australia, in turn, exported the lesbian cult television series *Prisoner* to the United States and Britain.

Cultural commodification has also influenced the shaping of community and community organizations in the major cities. Direct action and campaigning have generally given way to political lobbying and an increasing reliance on the law for various reforms. Violence and discrimination against gays and lesbians are still significant problems. There have been no major, regular national political meeting grounds since the demise of national gay and lesbian conferences in 1986.

The HIV and AIDS epidemics though small by international standards have hit hard in Melbourne and Sydney. About 15 percent of gay men are HIV-positive, and AIDS in Australia has been experienced largely by gay men (about 85 percent of infections and deaths). Early and close collaboration among gay communities, the federal government, and state governments ("the partnership") saw extensive preventative educational campaigns, including widespread condom distribution and free needle exchanges. Australia's public health system has provided relatively easy access to health care and treatment, though emerging shifts in the funding of health services indicate this situation may change for people with HIV.   *Michael Hurley*

Bibliography

Carbery, Graham. *A History of the Sydney Gay and Lesbian Mardi Gras.* Melbourne: Australian Lesbian and Gay Archives, 1995.

French, Robert. *Camping By a Billabong: Gay and Lesbian Stories from Australian History.* Sydney: BlackWattle Press, 1993.

Hodge, Dino. *Did You Meet Any Malagas? A Homosexual History of Australia's Tropical Capital.* Darwin: Little Gem Publications, 1993.

Hughes, Robert. *The Fatal Shore.* London: Collins, 1987.

King, Wayne. *Black Hours.* Sydney: Angus & Robertson, 1996.

Matthews, Jill Juius, ed. *Sex in Public: Australian Sexual Cultures.* Sydney: Allen & Unwin, 1997.

Thompson, Denise. *Flaws in the Social Fabric: Homosexuals and Society in Sydney.* Sydney: George Allen & Unwin, 1985.

Timewell, Eric, Victor Minichiello, and David Plummer, eds. *AIDS in Australia.* Sydney: Prentice Hall, 1992.

Wotherspoon, Garry. *City of the Plain: History of a Gay Sub-Culture.* Sydney: Hale & Iremonger, 1991.

See also Altman, Dennis; Australian Literature; Malouf, David; Sydney Gay and Lesbian Mardi Gras; White, Patrick

Australian Literature

Gay and lesbian writing has expanded rapidly in Australia during the 1990s. For the first time, such publications saw crossover success, not just in terms of mainstream publishing but as national bestsellers: Tim Conigrave's posthumous autobiography, *Holding the Man* (1995); Christos Tsiolkas's first "wog poofter" novel, *Loaded Sydney* (1995); and Robert Dessaix's *Night Letters* (1996). Dorothy Porter staked a large popular claim to revivifying narrative poetry with *Akhenaten* (1992) and *A Monkey's Mask* (1994).

About 50 percent of current queer writing is published by mainstream publishers and 50 percent by independent gay and lesbian feminist presses, mainly BlackWattle, Sybylla, and Spinifex. Major publishing houses now publish half the fiction; previously this was the case only for nonfiction (histories, autobiographical essays, and life stories). There has been significant Australia (Arts) Council support through writers' grants and publishing and event subsidies.

Arguably, the best stylists are those women writers who developed a strong poetics of narrative in the 1980s. Though their output is relatively small, it is carefully considered and robustly wrought: Kathleen Mary Fallon, Susan Hampton, Helen Hodgman, Jan McKemmish, and Finola Moorhead in the novel and experimental prose, Dorothy Porter and Pam Brown in poetry. Few writers have demonstrated the sustained grasp of traditional narrative seen in Andrea Goldsmith's novels or Bron Nichol's *Reasons of the Heart* (1993). New stylists among the women writers include Kirsty Machon, who wrote *Immortality* (1997). Major popular successes in fiction include Claire McNab's Detective Inspector Carol Ashton series and Jenny Pausacker's romances. The anthology has been the major form of publishing in Australian queer writing, which has a distinct preference for short fiction.

Two of Australia's best-known writers internationally, Patrick White (1912–1990) and David Malouf (1934–), have written on homoerotic and homosocial themes. White, winner of the 1973 Nobel Prize in literature, disdained "gay writing" as a genre, but *The Twyborn Affair* (1979) is a major exploration of queer sensibilities, and he discusses his attitudes to homosexuality and gayness in his autobiography, *Flaws in the Glass* (1981). Malouf's 1975 novel *Johnno* is a homosocial classic relying on a self-reflexive narrative of repressed homoeroticism. Robert Dessaix is emerging nationally as a writer of similar literary stature with his 1994 autobiography, *A Mother's Disgrace,* and in 1996 a novel, *Night Letters.*

Both Barbara Hanrahan (1939–1991) and Elizabeth Jolley (1923–) have extensively explored friendships and love between women in their fiction, often creating a neo-Gothic landscape of desire. Hanrahan's fiction clearly has a queer point of view embedded in a tapestry of densely textured prose. Jolley disclaims lesbianism, but as Bronwen Levy notes, "this does not mean her work may not be read from a lesbian-feminist perspective or, perhaps more broadly, for its lesbian themes."

Same-sex friendship, love, and sexual desire have a long history in Australian writing, especially in fiction. Homosociality in the name of "mateship" and masculinist adventure has been an intrinsic part of national myths, complicating a homosexual reading of literary history. While female friendship has been depicted in historical representations of women, it has rarely been part of national legend. Examples of cross-dressing and transgender practices also abound. While much of the nineteenth-century writing is indeterminate from contemporary gay, lesbian, transgender, and bisexual identity perspectives, this indeterminacy has as much to do with how same-sex desire was understood as with codings caused by repression. As a consequence, the sparse body of criticism on nineteenth-century same-sex desire is very uneven, descriptively and analytically.

Rosa Praed (1851–1935), for example, resisted medicalizations of desire as "homosexual" in her novels, relying more on spiritualist notions to explore friendship, female bonding, and Wildean male desire (*Affinities* [1886]; *The Scourge Stick* [1898]). Marcus Clarke briefly depicts love between young men in prison and its outcome in *For the Term of His Natural Life* (1870, 1885). Challenges to the sexually "innocent" male friendships of Henry Kingsley's *The Recollections* (1859) and of the critically acclaimed novels of Martin Boyd (1893–1972) can be seen as peaking in the surreal horror of the novel and film *Wake in Fright* and in the revisionist narratives of national maturity seen in the charged homoeroticism of Clem Gorman's play *A Manual of Trench Warfare* (1978), the film *Gallipoli,* and the sexually parodic landscapes of painter Juan Davila. In this context Patrick White's *The Twyborn Affair* (1979) may be seen as a powerful literary riposte to notions of "innocent" masculinity. It was a myth long queried by other writers (Barbara Baynton, Ada Cambridge) but not so clearly in terms of the vagaries of sexual desire, same-sex and otherwise.

Before David Stevens's New York premiere of *The Sum of Us* in 1990, there had been no major commercially successful Australian plays on gay male themes since the premiere in 1976 of Steve J. Spear's *The Elocution of Benjamin Franklin* and, before that, Peter Kenna's *A Hard God* in 1973. Alex Harding's 1988 musical, *Only Heaven Knows,* played at the Opera House in 1995. Photographer William Yang's slide monologues, especially *Sadness* (1992), have been critically well received. Barry Lowe and Stephen Dawson are both critically and popularly successful with gay audiences. Only Spears and Kenna have received major critical discussion.

Much of the best innovative writing is ephemeral or occurs at the margins in performance, polemic, art criticism, cultural journalism, and commentary. The extensive, internationally celebrated cabaret work of Robyn Archer and the plays of Sandra Shotlander and Sara Hardy have served lesbian feminist themes well. However, neither of Shotlander's major plays—*Framework* or *Is That You, Nancy?*—has been given mainstream production, and lesbianism has tended to be submerged in feminism. Archer and feminist theater in the 1970s created a major lesbian and feminist audience nationally, with key creative and collaborative support from Chris Westwood.

Critical discussion of gay and lesbian writing is increasing, yet it has received little sustained attention in the professional journals and there are no book-length studies other than Michael Hurley's *A Guide to Gay and Lesbian Writing in Australia* (1996).   *Michael Hurley*

Bibliography

Dessaix, Robert. "Introduction." In *Australian Gay and Lesbian Writing: An Anthology.* Melbourne: Oxford University Press, 1993.

Dunne, Gary. "Our Own Bookshelf: Publishing Australian Gay Writing." In *Gay Perspectives 11: More Essays in Australian Gay Culture.* Robert Aldrich, ed. Sydney: Sydney University Press, 1993.

Levy, Bronwen. "Theorising Sexualities: The Deferral of Lesbianism." In *Literature and Opposition.* Chris Worth, Pauline Nestor, and Marko Pavlyshyn, eds. Melbourne: Monash University Press, 1994.

See also Australia; Malouf, David; White, Patrick

Autobiographical Writing

The autobiographical impulse operates in the forefront of modern gay literature. From the days of shame and confession to those of pride and avowal, the voice of the first person singular has been the most authentic witness to the homosexual experience. From the recriminations of Oscar Wildes' *De Profundis*, written in prison and addressed to the feckless Alfred Lord Douglas, to the postmodern riffs of David Wojnarowicz's HIV-infected *Close to the Knives* (1991), queer autobiography has insistently asserted a silenced people's right to self-expression.

Although there are notable precedents from earlier times—such as the acknowledgments of secular friendships in Saint Augustine's *Confessions*, or memories of sexual assault in Jean-Jacques Rousseau's—the most important autobiographical texts have been written during the century that redefined homosexuality as a fixing of personal identity.

A Early in the twentieth century the new model for homosexual autobiography was the sexological case study—confessions of sickness rather than sin. For instance, Claude Hartland's *The Story of a Life* (1901) had the subtitle *For the Consideration of the Medical Fraternity*. Yet far from being a medical book, it turns out to be a moving narrative of subjection and resistance to oppression.

Several French novelists brought the subject of their own homosexuality into the foreground of modernism. André Gide's *Si le grain ne meurt* (If I Die, 1921) set a high standard of frankness in its account of his introduction to Arab boys. The autobiographical novels of homosexual writers like Marcel Proust and Jean Genet paved the way for the later work of Christopher Isherwood in the United States, Hubert Fichte in Germany, and Julien Green in France. These were followed, in turn, by a wave of post-gay liberationist novelists like Renaud Camus, John Rechy, and Edmund White.

No amount of fiction can compare with the authenticity of a first-person account of oppression. This is one of the central tenets of all writing about the Holocaust, for instance. Indeed, there is no better book about the gay men who were forced to endure that catastrophe than Pierre Seel's *Moi, Pierre Seel, deporté homosexuel* (1994; *I, Pierre Seed, Deported Homosexual: A Memoir of Nazi Terror,* 1995). Other writers have had less appalling, but no less important, tales to tell. For instance, Peter Wildeblood's *Against the Law* (1995) offers a classic insider's account of a public scandal, the notorious "Montague case" of 1954.

Many autobiographical moments attest to their authors' bravery and honesty. Michael Davidson's *The World, the Flesh, and Myself* (1962) opens with the arresting (and arrestable) sentence, "This is the life-history of a lover of boys." Quentin Crisp's *The Naked Civil Servant* (1968) is a magnificent narrative of effeminacy triumphant over pre-Stonewall values of intimidation and shame.

During the AIDS epidemic, the coincidental development of video technologies enabled people with AIDS even more dispassionately to record their ways of living and dying. The camcorder vies with traditional writerly methods in the exemplary career of Hervé Guibert, who continued to record the progress of his illness until the eve of his death, shocking French society into closer attention than it wanted to pay.

Gregory Woods

Bibliography

Buckton, Oliver S. *Secret Selves: Confession and Same-Sex Desire in Victorian Autobiography.* Chapel Hill: University of North Carolina Press, 1998.

See also Augustine of Hippo; Camus, Renaud; Crisp, Quentin; Fichte, Hubert; Genet, Jean; Gide, André; Guibert, Hervé; Isherwood, Christopher; Proust, Marcel; Rechy, John; U.S. Literature: Contemporary Gay Writing; White, Edmund; Wilde, Oscar; Wojnarowicz, David

B

Bacon, Francis (1909–1992)

As Great Britain's most successful artist of the post-war period—a time when abstraction came to dominate the cultural landscape—Francis Bacon was paradoxically dedicated to the human form. However, his adherence to the figure, generally to the male body, did not produce realist portraiture at all. Rather, Bacon's paintings—though rooted in his everyday personal life and peopled with friends as well as lovers—are nonetheless essays on the dark side of the human condition: horror, pain, death, and lust. Bacon worked from the real, but in his art the distinction between life and representation, high culture and low, order and disorder, revelation and concealment is empty.

Born in 1909, Bacon never attended an art school but was an autodidact. Leaving his home in Dublin at the age of sixteen, he traveled to Paris and Berlin, the gay centers of Europe between the wars. Having established himself as an interior decorator, he did not think of himself as a painter until the end of World War II, even destroying most of the work he had completed before 1944.

Throughout his career, Bacon was interested in depicting flesh: crucified, captive, bound, tortured, and screaming. He sought inspiration from a wide variety of sources like Sergey Eisenstein's film *Battleship Potemkin*; Eadweard Muybridge's photos of naked men wrestling; and old masters' paintings. He at once adopted traditional modes like the triptych or the gold frame, then perversely used the back of the primed canvas as his painting surface. In 1951–1965 he worked on his famous series of Pope Portraits, based on reproductions of Velázquez's *Portrait of Pope Innocent X*, although Bacon never went to see the original. In the mid-1960s, he met George Dyer, who became his lover and the subject of a number of portraits like *George Dyer, Riding a Bicycle* (1966), or *Triptych—In Memory of George Dyer,* completed after Dyer's suicide in 1971.

Bacon never publicly acknowledged his homosexuality, although he frequently revealed his intimacy with other men. His art is not only homoerotic; it challenges the image and power of the masculine, revealing hesitancies and insecurities foreign to traditional representations of maleness. This acknowledgment of a pervasive ambivalence toward the masculinity that was often his subject gives Bacon's art an aura of mystery, undermining the "closet" from within it. Although he gave many interviews, he rarely discussed his personal life, and though he wished to avoid being considered a homosexual artist only, he never shied away from portraying his lovers. In Bacon's art, opposites merge: the real and the iconic, love and violence, heterosexuality and homosexuality; a world built on distinctions and polarities is made fluid, contingent, and relative.

In his famous *Study of George Dyer in a Mirror* (1968), Bacon threw a splash of white paint at the canvas. This jarring intrusion into the picture plane can be read as pure abstraction; as a protest against pictorial naturalism; as a declaration of authorial presence (rather like a signature); or, especially given its location at crotch level, as ejaculate. Typically for Bacon, meaning here is once again ambivalent, though no less evocative and affective for being so.

When Bacon died in April 1992, he was one of Europe's most celebrated artists.

Andre Dombrowski

B

Bibliography

Alphen, Ernst van. *Francis Bacon and the Loss of Self*. London: Reaction Books, 1992.

Deleuze, Gilles. *Francis Bacon: Logique de la sensation*. Paris: Éditions de la Différence, 1984.

Francis Bacon. Exhibition catalogue. Tate Gallery, London: Thames and Hudson, 1985.

Francis Bacon 1909–1992. Exhibition catalogue. Haus der Kunst, Munich: Ostfildern-Ruit: Hatje, 1996.

Francis Bacon Symposium: "Where Men Are Close," organized by Bernhart Schwenk, Hubertus Gassner, Munich, Nov. 8–9, 1996.

Sylvester, David. *The Brutality of Fact: Interviews with Francis Bacon*. London: Thames and Hudson, 1987 (1975).

See also Art History; Eisenstein, Sergei

Baldwin, James (1924–1987)

The U.S. novelist James Baldwin was born on August 2, 1924, in New York City's Harlem. One of his early teachers at Frederick Douglass Junior High School was the noted Harlem Renaissance poet Countee Cullen, who directed the school's literary club and encouraged Baldwin to write. Early in his career, Baldwin brought himself to the attention of the most famous black writer of the period, Richard Wright, who then used his influence to promote Baldwin's career. This relationship ended acrimoniously with the publication of Baldwin's essay "Everybody's Protest Novel," in which he attacked the kind of protest fiction for which Wright was famous. However, this essay and the controversy it generated established Baldwin as a major figure and set the stage for his eclipsing of Wright as America's foremost African American writer with his first collection of essays, *Notes of a Native Son* (1955). This book and Baldwin's other essay collections represent for most critics the heart of his achievement as a writer.

Although he had sympathetically addressed the issue of homosexuality in his early essay "The Preservation of Innocence" (1949), it is in his fiction that Baldwin deals with the issue of homosexuality and bisexuality in ways that make him one of the most important figures in the tradition of gay literature. Not only is homosexuality a constant theme in Baldwin's novels; Baldwin was the first nationally known African American writer to present himself publicly as homosexual or bisexual and to incorporate consistently that perspective into his

work. This forthrightness led to the homophobic attacks that Baldwin received from black militants such as LeRoi Jones (Amiri Baraka) and Eldridge Cleaver and the consistent critical undervaluing of his fiction. From his first novel, *Go Tell It on the Mountain* (1953), to his last, *Just Above My Head* (1979), with the notable exception of the atypical *If Beale Street Could Talk* (1974), a self-consciously heterosexual romance that many critics feel Baldwin wrote in an attempt to win back the popular audience he had lost by the mid-1970s, all of Baldwin's novel deal to some extent with homosexuality and bisexuality. *Giovanni's Room* (1956), despite the problematic, perhaps even homophobic particulars of its representation of homosexuality, is generally considered to be one of the founding texts of the American tradition of gay fiction.

Although for much of his career Baldwin displayed a certain ambivalence about specifying his own sexual identity, his influence on black gay male novelists such as Larry Duplechan, Steven Corbin, E. Lynn Harris, and Darieck Scott has been obvious and inestimable, and in the last years of his life he developed closer ties to the gay community and often spoke out on issues pertaining to homosexuality. Baldwin died on November 30, 1987, in St. Paul de Vence, France.   *Terry Rowden*

Bibliography

Leeming, David. *James Baldwin: A Biography*. New York: Knopf, 1994.

See also African American Gay Culture; Cullen, Countee Harlem Renaissance; U.S. Literature: Contemporary Gay Writing

Ballet (British)

The English ballet critic Arnold Haskell wrote in 1934, "Of the outstanding male dancers that I know, and I know them all, not one is effeminate in manner, and very few indeed are not thoroughly normal" (Haskell 299). In Britain at the time, homosexuality was a prosecutable offense, and ballet's respectability depended on disassociating it from any tainting connection with homosexuality, a situation that still persists to some extent at the end of the twentieth century. It is generally acknowledged that there are connections between homosexuality and the world of professional dance as a whole and with ballet in particular. It is curious, however, that this subject has received little serious attention. In western Europe and North America the profession of male dancing went into a decline during the nineteenth century, but there is no evidence that prejudice against the male dancer had anything to do with sexuality until the beginning of the twentieth century. At that time Sergey Diaghilev, by presenting Vaslav Nijinsky in a series of ballets that showcased his talents, reintroduced the male dancer to the ballet stages of London, Paris, and New York and other leading Western cities. Since that time ballet has attracted a large, metropolitan gay audience, and many gay men have sought careers in the dance world. Richard Dyer suggests that "gay men have been balletomanes for everything from the fact of ballet's extreme escapism from an uncongenial world to its display of the male physique, and to its reputation as an area of employment in which gay men could be open and safe." In Britain, while homosexuality was a prosecutable offense, ballet's escapism was the principal means for the expression of gay identities through camp spectacle. Since the liberalization of the law on homosexuality in the 1960s and the advent of the gay liberation movement, increasing numbers of dance artists used performance as a means through which to explore and make statements about the changing nature of gay identities. By the time of his death in 1929, Diaghilev had made ballet in London into a forum that in effect created and supported the idea of the artistic, homosexual man, and defined a homosexual aesthetic sensibility. Books about the Diaghilev period and many biographies of dancers and choreographers provide useful information about homosexual lifestyles and social groups at that time. Anton Dolin writes about his seduction by Diaghilev in a first-class sleeping compartment between Paris and Monte Carlo, and his subsequent, brief relationship with him. The Bloomsbury group, some of whom were homosexual and who were liberal in their attitudes toward homosexuality, were supporters of Diaghilev before and after World War I. In the 1920s the largely homosexual Eton and Oxford circle of Harold Acton and Oliver Messel became advocates of the ballet. By the mid-1920s the young dancer and choreographer Frederick Ashton was learning ballet and moving in upper-middle-class London society homosexual. His biographer reveals that Ashton frequented parties on the fringe of the Bloomsbury group, where, with his friend William Chappell, he used to do a popular impromptu cabaret including a male-male tango that later became incorporated in his ballet *Façade* (1931) as the "Popular Song." Where there are male-male duets in Ashton's ballets—in *Façade, Cinderella,* and *Enigma Variations*—these are not explicitly homoerotic but can be seen as double-coded—signifying homosexuality to those who know the code but apparently nothing sexual to those who don't. A formative experience for the thirteen-year-old Ashton was seeing a performance by the great ballerina Anna Pavlova. He famously recalled: "She injected me with her poison and from the end of that evening I wanted to dance" and, in effect, to be a ballerina. Later in life he created cross-dressing roles for himself and for others in his ballets. These too can be seen as double-coded—acceptably referring to the popular tradition of the pantomime dame but also appealing to a camp sensibility. This enforced compromise with hegemonic heterosexual values has also characterized the few British ballets of the mid-century that attempted to draw seriously on homosexual experience.

It has been said that Antony Tudor's *Undertow* (1945) established a genre of homosexual ballets. It explores the destruction of a sensitive young man's psyche—rejected by sexually predatory parents, unable to form a relationship with a young, naive girl, and finally led on by a sadistic group of youths. Homosexuality as such is not explicitly present, but the young man conforms to a homosexual stereotype of the marginal outcast who comes to an obligatory unhappy end. It is significant that *Undertow*, like Ashton's *Illuminations* (1949)—set to Benjamin Britten's song cycle inspired by Rimbaud's poetry and his relationship with Verlaine—was made for an American and not an English ballet company. The role of Verlaine was cast as a ballerina who represents Profane Love and is a dominating and castrating figure. The creation of several aggressive female figures in mid-twentieth-century homosexual ballets has caused some feminist writers to accuse these choreographers of misogyny. Graham Jackson has argued, however, that, although these female roles are undeniably stereotypical, they are neither malicious nor hostile: "Like Tennessee Williams' Blanche or Alma or even Maggie Smith, they are icons worshipped for their ambivalence, their toughness-through-vulnerability, and of course, their self-dramatizing glamour."

Changing attitudes toward homosexuality since the 1960s have had surprisingly little effect on the way homosexual experience has been represented by British ballet choreographers. The one possible exception is the work of Matthew Bourne. His ver-

B sion of *Swan Lake* (1995) cast the swans, traditionally a female corps de ballet, as men—not camp men en pointe wearing tutus but powerfully masculine and potentially dangerous birds. These swans are unambiguously presented as objects of gay male desire, while the young prince's infatuation with their leader results in several homoerotic male-male duets. Yet the ballet as a whole showed the young prince as mentally unstable in ways that conform to the stereotype of the sad young man who comes to a predictably sad end. It has been largely within the area of modern and postmodern dance and physical theater that new ways of representing gay experience have developed. Lindsay Kemp, who first came to prominence in the 1970s, has created theatrical spectacles that present sexual dissidents as uncompromising outlaws. In works like *The Maids* (1973)—after Genet's play—and *Cruel Garden* (1977)—based on the life of Spanish poet and dramatist Federico García Lorca—his performance works combine an overcharged, intense artificiality and excess. Kemp's exploration of queer sensibilities allows an appeal to a shared recognition of socially oppressive codes and structures.

At a time when most British gay theater and film practitioners supported the idea of presenting "positive images" to foster tolerance, Michael Clark and Lloyd Newson have attained international recognition for specifically queer dance works that have asserted sexual dissidence in ways that break with earlier humanistic approaches. Clark, who had been a highly regarded student at the Royal Ballet School, confounded expectations by dropping out, dancing for a contemporary dance company, then performing on the experimental fringes. He says a formative experience as a student was dancing all night to punk rock in London new wave clubs, and his choreography has invariably combined the stylistic elegance derived from his ballet training with the calculated provocation and anarchic nihilism of punk rock. By displaying bare bottoms in some pieces and dancing a solo naked, except for a fur muff held over his genitals, Clark's explicitly homoerotic choreography takes pride in difference through a postmodern use of irony and pastiche that breaks with the work of an older generation whose work was never overtly gay.

Since the mid-1980s, Lloyd Newson's company, DV8 Physical Theater, has developed a performance style that blurs dance, theater, and performance art to present disturbing performances about gender and sexuality. Often working with an all-male cast, Newson develops his work from improvisations based on the dancers' experiences and reactions to specific themes and issues concerning gender and sexuality. Thus DV8's major work to date, *Dead Dreams of Monochrome Men* (1988), took as its starting point the life of British homosexual mass murderer Dennis Nilson, presenting a disturbingly dystopian picture of metropolitan gay lifestyles. *MSM* (1993) dealt with men seeking anonymous sex with other men in public lavatories, while *Enter Achilles* (1995) showed a group of men, most of whom were not specifically gay-identified, drinking and becoming violent in a British pub. DV8's intentions seem to be not only to legitimize present-day gay experience but also to appeal to the nonqueer world through common experiences of the restrictions of gender ideologies.

It would be a mistake to judge too harshly the work of choreographers who were gay and grew up in the first half of the twentieth century if their work is less explicit about gay identities and sensibilities than the work of later generations who came to maturity during the gay liberation period or have had to come to terms with the AIDS crisis. The 1980s and 1990s have seen the publication of biographies and autobiographies that have explicitly documented the private lives of older generations of choreographers who were homosexual. Some commentators have warned against using these to reinterpret ballets as if their only subject matter was homosexuality. Most of Ashton's ballets, it has been argued, are about love—a universal experience that transcends sexuality. Other voices have been raised against the ghettoization of gay dance as if it were something relevant only to gay people. Newson, for example, has consistently asserted that the pieces he makes with all-male casts are not exclusively about homosexual experience but focus on the problematic nature of socially and psychologically constructed masculine identities. It is clear however, that British ballet and, more recently, modern and postmodern dance have been an area in which dancers and choreographers have been less isolated as homosexuals than in other creative fields, and have been able to explore aspects of gay identities with a degree of openness, though nevertheless in circumscribed ways.

Ramsay Burt

Bibliography

Dolin, Anton. *Last Words.* London: Century, 1985.

Dyer, Richard. *Only Entertainment.* London: Routledge, 1992.

Haskell, Arnold. *Balletomania*. London: Victor Gollancz, 1934.

Jackson, Graham. *Dance as Dance*. Toronto: Catalyst, 1978.

See also Ballets Russes; Bloomsbury Group; Britten, Benjamin; Diaghilev, Sergey; Nijinsky, Vaslav Fomich; Rimbaud, Arthur; Verlaine, Paul

Ballets Russes

Sergey Diaghilev (1872–1919) was neither a dancer, a choreographer, nor a composer, but there is little question that he had more effect on twentieth-century classical dance than any other single individual. His principal talent was his ability to synthesize volatile artistic ingredients, thus transforming classical ballet into a vital, modern art. Diaghilev nurtured several of the most significant choreographers of the twentieth century—Michel Fokine, Vaslav Nijinsky, Léonide Massine, Bronislava Nijinska, and George Balanchine—providing them with commissioned scores from Stravinsky, Ravel, and Satie, and uniting them with such prominent visual artists as Picasso, Braque, Gris, Matisse, Chirico, Benois, and Bakst. Impresario Diaghilev and his Ballets Russes literally shaped the history of twentieth-century Western dance.

Born into Russian provincial aristocracy, Diaghilev was sent to St. Petersburg to study law; instead, he fell in with a group of avant-garde writers and artists. After cofounding and serving as editor of a progressive art magazine, *The World of Art* (1898–1904), Diaghilev discovered his true calling when he organized a series of exhibitions of modern Russian painting, one of which he took to Paris in 1906. Finding a European audience hungry for Russian art, he subsequently arranged concerts of Russian music at the Paris Opera (1907), and then the first performances of Modest Mussorgsky's opera *Boris Godunov* (1908) outside Russia.

But in 1909 Diaghilev irrevocably changed the course of dance when he brought Russian ballet to Paris. Diaghilev did not simply import concert dance as it had been performed in Russia; rather, he gathered together the best in Russia and forged new collaborations. The brilliant technique of dancers Michel Fokine, Anna Pavlova, and Vaslav Nijinsky was combined with the startling scenography of Benois and Bakst and the diatonicism of Russian composers Igor Stravinsky and Sergey Prokofiev. The robustness of Ballets Russes productions with their brilliant colors and exotic Orientalism took Europe by storm.

Even though the 1909 dance performances were originally intended for only one summer, their phenomenal success led to a second engagement the following spring, and in 1911 a company was formed, the Ballets Russes. A new soloist with the Imperial Russian Ballet at the Maryinsky Theater in St. Petersburg, Vaslav Fomich Nijinsky (1888?–1950), became Diaghilev's lover while both still lived in Russia. Diaghilev saw himself not only as the brilliant young man's romantic partner but as his mentor and protector. As a principal dancer of the Ballets Russes, Nijinsky created a sensation in a series of roles created for him, the Poet in *Les Sylphides* (1909), the title role in *Petrushka* (1911), and the Rose in *Le Spectre de la rose* (1911), all choreographed by Fokine. Encouraged by Diaghilev, Nijinsky began to choreograph: Debussy's *L'Après-midi d'un faune* (1912) and *Jeux* (1913), and Stravinsky's *Le Sacre du printemps* (1913). These radical works rejected the strictures of classical ballet, and their unorthodox choreographic aesthetic has since earned them the accolade of being ballet's first "modern" dances.

During the 1913 South American tour of the Ballets Russes, Nijinsky angered Diaghilev when he married a fellow dancer, Romola de Pulszky. The Hungarian ballerina was a minor dancer but well-to-do; at the time the couple were married, neither could speak the other's language. After being fired from the Ballets Russes, Nijinsky established his own company, but it failed in London. Diaghilev hired his former lover for the 1916 Ballets Russes's tour of the Americas, during which Nijinsky choreographed Richard Strauss's *Till Eulenspiegel*. But then the great dancer, only twenty-seven years old and in his physical prime, began to unravel mentally. Settling in St. Moritz, Switzerland, Nijinsky gave his last performance—a solo in a Swiss hotel in 1919. Thereafter moving from one mental institution to another, Nijinsky never recovered. He died in 1950, leaving behind his wife and two daughters.

Nijinsky was modern ballet's first male superstar, remarkable in that his professional performing career lasted only seven years outside Russia. His physical prowess found expression in his soaring leaps, and his troubled personality fueled his impassioned acting. Not only did he elevate the importance of the male dancer by his three-dimensional characters in traditional nineteenth-century ballets that focused on female characters, Nijinsky also

B

made a case for (and choreographed) ballets that featured male characters.

When Diaghilev removed Nijinsky from the company, he promoted Léonide Massine (1895–1979) to principal dancer, company choreographer, and his lover. Massine excelled in character roles and as a choreographer found popular success in comic (*Gaîté Parisienne*, 1938) and symphonic ballets (*Beethoven's Seventh Symphony*, 1938), as well as cubist experimentations (*Parade*, 1917). Massine left Diaghilev in 1921 but returned in 1925, only to leave again three years later.

Diaghilev's last great male protégé and lover was Serge Lifar (1905–1986). Trained in Kiev, he joined the Ballets Russes in 1923 and was promoted to premier danseur in 1925, where he created roles in George Balanchine's *Apollon musagète* (1928) and *Prodigal Son* (1929), among others. Upon Diaghilev's death in 1929, Lifar took over production at the Paris Opera Ballet, revitalizing the company and reestablishing its artistic prominence.

Despite the company's name—it never performed in Russia—Diaghilev continued to engage Russian émigré dancers, even though he turned to commissioning French painters and composers to collaborate with his in-house choreographers, especially after the Russian Revolution cut the company off forever from its homeland. In 1921, verging on financial insolvency, the company was invited to take up residency in Monte Carlo, the only permanent base they ever had. When Diaghilev, suffering from diabetes, died in Venice in 1929 at the age of fifty-seven, a protracted struggle ensued over the future of the company.

The second Ballets Russes was formed in 1932 by René Blum, impresario at the Casino de Monte Carlo, and Wassily G. Voskresensky (also known as Col. W. de Basil), a sometime officer of the Russian Army who had a passion for ballet. Bitter copyright fights plagued the company, and the organization split in 1936, becoming Col. W. de Basil's Ballets Russes (later renamed the Original Ballet Russe) and Ballet Russe de Monte Carlo, under the direction of René Blum. The third generation came in 1938, when Léonide Massine joined forces with Blum, while Fokine was invited back to Basil's Ballets Russes. The Massine-Blum enterprise lasted until 1943; later Massine organized Ballet Russe Hightlights, which toured in 1945 and 1946. Basil's Original Ballet Russe ceased operations in 1952.

Always on the verge of bankruptcy, the Ballets Russes was not only the conduit by which nine-teenth-century ballet discovered its voice of modernity for the twentieth century; it was also the most popular dance company in the world. Most of the century's premier international ballet companies trace their lineage to the Ballet Russes: George Balanchine, Léonide Massine, and Michel Fokine settled in America; Anton Dolin, Alicia Markova, Marie Rambert, and Ninette de Valois shaped the British dance scene; and Serge Lifar became director of the Paris Opera Ballet. The Ballets Russes promoted superb male dancers, showcasing them in sensuous works that often challenged the accepted notions of gender and sexuality. *Bud Coleman*

Bibliography

Buckle, Richard. *Diaghilev*. New York: Atheneum, 1979.

Garafola, Lynn. *Diaghilev's Ballets Russes*. New York: Oxford University Press, 1989.

Garcia-Marquez, Vicente. *The Ballets Russes: Colonel de Basil's Ballets Russes de Monte Carlo, 1931–1952*. New York: Knopf, 1990.

Kochno, Boris. *Diaghilev and the Ballets Russes*, trans. Adrienne Foulke. New York: Harper & Row, 1970.

See also Ballet (British); Diaghilev, Sergey; Nijinsky, Vaslav Fomich

Ballets Trockadero de Monte Carlo

While men have probably been dancing on their toes ever since the pointe shoe was developed in the 1830s, the first company of men performing as ballerinas *en pointe* occurred on August 31, 1972, at the tiny Jean Cocteau Theatre in New York City's East Village. Led by Larry Ree (Madame Ekathrina Sobechanskaya), the five men in the Trockadero Gloxinia Ballet Company sought to evoke the glamour of late-nineteenth-century Russian ballet. Armed with more attitude than dance technique, the Gloxinia nevertheless attracted a following. In 1974, three members of the troupe, chafing under the restricted aesthetic of the Gloxinia (their ballets never contained male characters), decided to form their own troupe. Established by Peter Anastos (b. 1948), Antony Bassae (1943–1985), and Natch Taylor (b. 1948), Les Ballets Trockadero de Monte Carlo made its debut at the Westside Discussion Group, a homophile organization on West 14th Street.

The new company was more interested in parody and satire than in the glorification of the drag ballerina. Within their first month, Arlene Croce wrote a glowing review in *The New Yorker* and soon the Trocks—as they were affectionately known—were playing in larger Off-Off-Broadway theaters. In 1976 the company signed with a management firm, began to tour, and qualified for the National Endowment for the Arts Dance Touring Program. It is now a professional company with a full-time teacher, and the technical proficiency of its dancers has risen to match their comic expertise.

The majority of the ballets that the Trockadero perform are the traditional "warhorses" in the classical ballet repertory: *Swan Lake* Act II, *Giselle* Act II, *Les Sylphides,* Pas de Quatre. Because the Trocks stick faithfully to original choreography, humor arises in how the dance is performed and who performs it. For instance, the Trock preparation for a step might be exaggerated, or the movement might begin with the wrong point of initiation, or a muscled preparation may lead up to nothing more than a single pirouette. William Zamora's (1952–1986) Zamarina Zamarkova was so arthritic you could swear you heard her joints creak as he moved. Sanson Candelaria's (1941–1986) incomparable Tamara Boumdiyeva, although possessing solid dance technique, nevertheless always appeared a little rattled. And Rusty Curcio was built like a muscular fire hydrant, making his Ludmila Bolshoya look as if she'd pulled a plow in the old country.

Tamara Boumdiyeva as the Princess Aspica. Photo by John L. Murphy.

Original choreography performed by the Trocks pinpoints specific choreographers: Anastos's *Go for Barocco* is a deconstruction of George Balanchine; Anastos's *Yes, Virginia, Another Piano Ballet* targets Jerome Robbins; Shawn Avrea's *Phaedra Monotonous #1148* skewers Martha Graham; and Roy Fialkow's *I Wanted to Dance With You at the Cafe of Experience* dissects Pina Bausch. The Trocks have performed in forty-one of the fifty states and in Washington, D.C., in addition to international tours that have taken them to over one hundred cities in eleven countries, on six continents. Not only is the Trockadero the only financially successful comedic dance company, but it is also the oldest all-male dance ensemble in America. As many dance companies established in the dance boom of the 1970s folded in the 1990s, the Trocks became international celebrities. The Trocks are a nonprofit organization, yet they have never applied for private or government grants and exist without a board of well-heeled patrons. That they have been able to survive financially, completely dependent on box office receipts alone, makes them unique. The success of the company is also not linked to one performer, choreographer, or artistic director: Bassae left the Trocks in 1976 to form his own company, Les Ballets Trockadero de La Karpova (1976–1983); Anastos left in 1978 to pursue a career as a freelance choreographer; and Taylor was voted out by the board in 1990. Tory Dobrin, a dancer who joined the company in 1980, assumed responsibility for aesthetic matters when he was appointed associate director in 1991. The two links of continuity are General Director Eugene McDougle and Company Archivist Anne Dore Davids, who began working with the Trocks in the second month of their existence.

The world of Les Ballets Trockadero de Monte Carlo is total artifice: they are based in New York, not Monte Carlo; most of the dancers are Americans despite their faux Russian names; men assume the roles of ballerinas; and they perform *Swan Lake* with a cast of ten instead of one hundred. But their knowledge of dance history, various styles of dance, and comedic timing are anything but artificial.

Bud Coleman

Bibliography

Coleman, Bud. "Ballerinos on Pointe: Les Ballets Trockadero de Monte Carlo." Kim Grover-Haskin, ed. *Choreography and Dance: An International Journal,* 1997.

Croce, Arlene. "The Two Trockaderos." In *Afterimages*. New York: Vintage, 1979.

See also Ballets Russes; Camp; Dance and AIDS; Jewel Box Review; Transvestism

Bang, Herman (1857–1912)

A man does not become a poet because he is above his times but because he is a full and living expression of the times, because he has suffered with it, fought with it and understood it. (Herman Bang: *Realisme og Realister*, 1880, *Realism and Realists*)

Herman Joachim Bang, who was born in Adserballe, Denmark, and died in Ogden, Utah, was a novelist, short story writer, stage director, journalist, literary critic, acclaimed lecturer in Scandinavia, Germany, and Russia, and a central figure in Scandinavian literature of the Modern Breakthrough period during the latter part of the nineteenth century. Because he is seen as an unsurpassed renewer of the Danish novel tradition, his work has remained a focal point of literary critical interest. Importantly, Bang staged the transition from realism/naturalism to impressionism, for which he was praised by French painter Claude Monet. His experimentation with narrative objectivity resulted in a distinct style characterized by its cameralike focus and dramatic-scenic presentation, where nothing is explained, reported, or analyzed, and everything takes place before the eyes of the reader.

Bang arrived from the Danish provinces, via Sorö Academy, in Copenhagen in the late 1870s, where he created a position for himself as a pathbreaking journalist and critic by importing the modern Parisian feuilleton style. More important, he reviewed contemporary French literature, Émile Zola in particular, thus establishing himself as a purveyor of literary modernity. Both his journalism in general and his critical and theoretical writings in particular served as laboratories for his own subsequent fiction writing.

Bang sought the position as leader of Danish modernity but met with derision as well as lampooning in the Danish press, largely caused by his studied and rather provocative dress and lifestyle. His appearance—perfumed, with makeup (coal under his eyes to evoke suffering), and in the latest of cosmopolitan (French) chic (tight pants, silk socks—deep red for lecture tours)—spelled effemi-

nacy and decadence, and hinted strongly of increasingly popularized notions of degeneracy. He was attacked as shrill, affected, and hysterical. The quest to spearhead the gathering of young, radical voices in Danish literature quickly derailed. His notoriety grew with the spreading perception of his sexually anomalous nature. The impact of his homosexuality on his sense of self and his authorship as well as on his public career as critic, lecturer, and successful stage director (Copenhagen before and after 1900, and Paris in the early 1890s at the avant-garde Théâtre de l'Œuvre) cannot be overestimated. Bang lived in constant fear of blackmail, exposure, scandal, police surveillance, and deportation (from Germany, Austria, and Czechoslovakia). It is difficult to say precisely when Bang became acquainted with German views on homosexuality, like those of Otto Westphal, Karl Heinrich Ulrichs, and Richard von Krafft-Ebing. He never broached the topic in his writing other than obliquely, whereas in letters he referred to his predicament as a burden and a disease. It is doubtful he ever distanced himself from common notions of degeneracy or current medical/psychiatric claims about homosexuality, as can be deduced from his essay "Gedanken zum Sexualitätsproblem" (Thoughts on the Problem of Sexuality, 1909), wherein he describes his understanding of homosexuality. The essay was dictated to his German doctor in Berlin after Bang fled police harassment in Copenhagen and was published posthumously in German.

Bang became a master of masks and poses in his public persona and in his writings, both critical and fictional. His view of life and his aesthetics were to a large degree based on popularized versions of positivism and determinism, a sort of Darwinism via Zola. It is especially his understanding of sexuality as a forceful drive, as unmitigated lust and power, combined with a disillusioned view of love that remained the structuring perspective in his work. His was a tragic view of life. His literary characters struggle in vain against the law of the sexual drive in the wake of which would always follow loss, betrayal, alienation, brutality, egotism, loneliness, demoralization, deceit, lies, prejudice, and injustice. Yet another side to his writing balances what may seem to be overriding pessimism, and that is Bang's sense of humor and his pre-Wildean camp. Furthermore, and in spite of the tendency to minimize his social/political awareness, Bang, especially in *Stuk* (1887), produced a scathing critique of the rise of capitalism: financial, social, political fraud, increasing number of investment schemes and failures with their parallels in a spreading spiritual hollowness and vulgar commercialism that was the modern metropolis of Copenhagen. In *Tine* (1889) and *Ludvigsbakke* (1896, trans. Ida Brandt, 1928) as well as in several of his brilliantly executed short stories, he exhibits understanding for the position of women under patriarchal repression (neglected, abused, sacrificed).

His authorship was off to an auspicious beginning with the naturalist bildungsroman *Haablöse slaegter* (Lost Generations, 1880). Confiscated by the police and censored, it was an immediate scandal, owing to its daring depictions of sex, drugs, and dangerously seductive femmes fatales. But what unnerved critics and readers more was the young author's unmistakably effeminate, subjective style. Furthermore, the book's unnaturally anxious, nervous dwelling on modish decadence, on Darwinian notions of heredity, degeneracy, and a family in decline were deplored. The book deserves attention as it can lay claim to be one of the first major European decadent novels. Not only in its tone but particularly in the self-analysis attempted in the portraits of the two main male characters, the novel represents a watershed in Scandinavian literature as the attempt to tell of a sexual nature and accompanying identity conflict that cannot be named. The novel is the story of anti-education, of anti-character, becoming the story of Bang's particular and perhaps rather naive notion of otherness. It is a naturalist case study of degeneracy à la Zola, Daudet, Musset, and Feuillet and meant to be a warning to its readers. But it is also Bang's coming-out story, such as it could be told in that genre at that time.

The attempt to explore and perhaps propose a self that is "new" and "complex," capable of expressing a truth that must not speak openly, meets with disappointing defeat in *Digte* (Poems, 1891), *Mikaël* (1905), *and De udon faedreland* (1906, Those Without a Country, 1928). Next to *Haablöse slaegter*, *Digte* and *Mikaël* are the two texts in which Bang, albeit masked with appropriate noun changes, reveals familiar, late-nineteenth-century notions of homosexuality as well as hints of his personal encounters with such a love. In *Digte* he is at his most direct in describing his passion for the German actor Max Eisfeld and the latter's betrayal of him: a naked and pessimistically deterministic sizing up of the impossible pairing of love and sexual desire. In *Mikaël* the love of an older artist for a younger, beautiful adopted son further explores the themes of jealousy, pain, and inevitable betrayal. *Mikaël*, though stylistically reaching back to pre-impressionist aesthetics, remains Bang's "gay" novel. In tandem can be read his correspondence with the much younger Fritz Boesen, whom he "discovered" and sought to form as an actor (*Breve til Fritz* [*Letters to Fritz,* 1952]). *Paal Bjørby*

Bibliography

Bjørby, Paal. "The Prison House of Sexuality: Homosexuality in Herman Bang Scholarship." *Scandinavian Studies* 58 (1986): 223–55.

———. "Herman Bang's 'Franz Pander': Narcissism and the Nature of the Unspoken." *Scandinavian Studies* 62 (1990): 449–67.

Driver, Beverly. "Herman Bang's Prose: The Narrative as Theatre." In *Mosaic: Scandinavian Literature: Reality and Visions.* R. G. Collins and Kenneth McRobbie, eds. New Views: A Mosaic Series in Literature, Vol. 11. Winnipeg: University of Manitoba Press, 1971, 79–90.

See also Decadence; Denmark; Kraft-Ebbing, Richardson; Westphal, Otto Wilde, Oscar

Bangkok

Bangkok, Thailand's capital city of almost ten million inhabitants, has the largest gay scene in Southeast Asia, with some one hundred commercial venues (bars, saunas, restaurants, gift shops, etc.) catering to a homosexual clientele and twenty-three Thai-language magazines oriented toward the local gay readership. The northern city of Chiang Mai and the resorts of Pattaya and Phuket also have significant but far smaller concentrations of gay venues. However, while boasting of an increasingly diverse commercial scene, Bangkok lacks the community focus and activist organizations found in Western gay centers. The absence of antihomosexual laws and the generally tolerant religious and moral climate mean that Thailand's gay men have not had to mobilize to achieve basic rights, and the Bangkok scene has emerged over the past four decades as part of a process of cultural liberalization rather than as the commercial parallel of a political gay movement.

The scene began in the 1960s with the establishment of several gay bars in the Patpong district in response to demand from an emerging local middle class and visiting American servicemen on leave from active duty in Southeast Asia. The fifteen-year period until the mid-1980s saw a relatively stable

B

number of about a dozen bars operating in the central entertainment district; but with the Thai economy's take off in the late 1980s and several years of sustained high growth, the number of venues expanded rapidly to current levels, which have stabilized in recent years. The market for these newer gay venues is overwhelmingly local, but it is also supported by Western tourists and growing intra-Asia gay tourism from countries such as Singapore, Maylasia, and Taiwan with less liberal policies toward homosexuals.

Despite rapid growth and the emergence of a wealthy middle class, the majority of Thais remain impoverished. These economic disparities are reflected in the divisions within the Bangkok scene, where venue cover charges and drink prices are often greater then the legislated minimum daily wage. In the early 1990s the Soi 2 and Soi 4 areas of the Patpong district emerged as vibrant centers of the city's gay night life, patronized by growing numbers of fashionable, fun-seeking gay men. However, the participation in this scene is restricted largely to a wealthier minority, with many poorer homosexual men continuing to use public parks, shopping malls, and cheap cinemas as informal meeting places. Marked economic disparities combined with cultural expectations that middle- and upper-class homosexual men should marry have produced a third major division within the scene, with a large commercial sex sector of host bars servicing a local clientele of often married gay men.

While many poorer gay men can afford to socialize only at informal venues and participate in the gay scene only as sex workers rather than as clients, the proliferation of Thai-language gay magazines in the past decade has disseminated representations of an affluent, independent, and glitzy gay lifestyle to all sectors of the population. Cheap secondhand copies of these Bangkok-based publications, affordable to even the poorest laborers, are sold throughout the country from sidewalk stalls, permitting vicarious participation in the scene by men from all socioeconomic backgrounds. The expensive Bangkok scene is thus now the focus of a much larger "imagined gay scene" extending throughout the metropolis and beyond into the countryside.

Peter A. Jackson

Bibliography

Allen, Eric. *The Men of Thailand: Guide to Thailand for Gay Men.* 5th ed. Bangkok: Floating Lotus Communications, 1995.

Jackson, Peter A., and Eric Allyn. "The Emergence of Thai Gay Identity." In *Dear Uncle Go: Male Homosexuality in Thailand.* Peter A. Jackson, ed. Bangkok: Bua Lang, 1995.

See also Thailand; Tourism

Barba Jacob, Porfirio
(Miguel Angel Osorio, 1883–1942)

Miguel Angel Osorio was born in Antioquia, Colombia, and died in Mexico City. His ambiguous identity can be symbolized by his use of pseudonyms such as Main Ximenez, Ricardo Arenales, and, his best-known, Porfirio Barba Jacob. His best poems are "La estrella de la tarde" (The Afternoon Star), "Canción de la vida profunda" (Song of the Deep Life), "Elegía de septiembre" (September Elegy), "Un hombre" (A Man), "Los desposados de la muerte" (The Bridegrooms of Death), "El son del viento" (The Sound of the Wind), "Canción de la soledad" (Song of Solitude), "Balada de una loca alegría" (Tune of a Wild Joy), "La reina" (The Queen), and "Futuro" (Future).

The most common themes in Barba Jacob's poetry are homosexuality, the quest for a space, an existentialist emptiness of soul, conflict with the oppressor, and the vulnerability of human beings. A modernist poet, he uses metaphor to break the rules of heterosexist society; and in his own life, he never denied his homosexuality but instead confronted dominant bourgeois values, which demanded he follow established canons. Metaphor in his poetry allows the reader to defamiliarize Barba Jacob, as poet and individual, and to perceive him as a double figure, one who faces a cultural crisis and one who enters wholeheartedly into a struggle against the heterosexual tide of his time.

Barba Jacob used metaphoric language to protest against Colombian patriarchal society because it attempted to control his sexual desires. Nevertheless, he did not allow this society to castrate him either emotionally or ideologically. Therefore, he challenged the world that marginalized him as a subversive individual because of his breaking of traditional norms. In his homoerotic poetry one can perceive the Greek concepts of eros and thanatos. Eros surfaces when his love for the beautiful male becomes a way to attain wisdom and perfection. Thanatos inspires his obsession with the fleeting nature of time. In sum, Barba Jacob expresses through his poetry his desire to attain immortality by framing, in language, perfect beauty and perfect love.   *Juan Antonio Serna*

Bibliography

Arango L, Manuel Antonio. *Tres figuras de Hispanoamerica en la generación de vanguardia o literatura de postguerra*. Bogotá: Procer, 1967, 49–69.

Mejía Gutiérrez, Carlos. *Porfirio Barba Jacob: Ensayo biográfico*. Centenario de nacimiento 1883–1983. Medellín, Colombia: Imprenta Municipal, 1982.

Puerta Palacios, M. C. *Miguel Angel Osorio o Porfirio Barba Jacob: Su vida y poesía*. Medellín, Colombia: Tipografía Especial, 1984.

Serna, Juan Antonio. "Barba Jacob Porfirio." In *Latin American Writers on Gay and Lesbian Themes: A Bio-Critical Sourcebook*. David William Foster, ed. Westport, Conn.: Greenwood Press, 1994, 53–55.

———. "La metáfora: elemento de transgresión en la poesía de Barba Jacob." *Revista de Estudios Colombianos* 14 (1994): 18–24.

See also Greece

Barber, Samuel (1910–1981)

Although the bright promise of the American composer Samuel Barber's early career gradually dimmed toward a tragic conclusion, his musical achievement ranks with that of Aaron Copland and Charles Griffes, and it easily surpasses that of most other American composers. Despite a few unfortunate lapses, such as the overtly Stravinskian *Capricorn* Concerto (1944) and the acerbic Second Symphony (1944, later withdrawn), Barber had the courage to resist the strictures of modernism and compose music of inimitable beauty and power. His expressive range as a composer was deep but not wide; the aching nostalgia that pervades much of Barber's music rarely degenerates into self-indulgence. Barber's habitual introspection mars his two grand operas, *Vanessa* (1957) and *Anthony and Cleopatra* (1966), for the composer's fluent technique and melodic invention cannot entirely disguise his inherent indifference to the delineation of character. Aside from the problematic operas, Barber's response to literature was often insightful; his songs bear comparison with those of Strauss and Wolf, and his *Knoxville: Summer of 1915* for soprano and orchestra (1947) is an eloquent distilla-

tion of the emotions found in James Agee's prose poem.

Barber was born in West Chester, Pennsylvania, into a wealthy and cultured family; his aunt Louise was a famous contralto whose husband, Sidney Homer, was a noted composer. Encouraged by his family, Barber embarked on a musical career, studying composition, piano, and voice at the Curtis Institute in Philadelphia. While a student at Curtis, Barber met a young Italian composer, Gian Carlo Menotti, with whom he formed an intimate friendship; the two shared a house from 1943 to 1974. Beginning in 1933 with the favorable reception of his *Dover Beach* (1931) for baritone and string quartet, Barber's fame increased with each new score. His success was crowned by many honors: the Bearns Prize; the American Prix de Rome; and two Pulitzer prizes, in 1958 and 1962. In 1938, the famed conductor Arturo Toscanini conducted the premiere of two of Barber's finest scores, the *First Essay* for orchestra (1937) and the beloved Adagio for strings (1936).

After serving in the Army Air Force during World War II, Barber produced several beautifully wrought scores, such as the Sonata for Piano (1959), written for Vladimir Horowitz (1904–1989). A postwar change of musical fashion had already begun to set in, however, and Barber's music was often criticized as old-fashioned. The disastrous premiere of *Anthony and Cleopatra* at the Metropolitan Opera in 1966 provided the pretext for a torrent of vituperative and covertly homophobic critical abuse against the now hapless composer. Barber never recovered fully from his public humiliation; his final years were clouded by illness and depression.

Byron Adams

Bibliography

Broder, Nathan. *Samuel Barber*. New York: Schirmer, 1954.

Heymann, Barbara B. *Samuel Barber: The Composer and His Music*. New York: Oxford University Press, 1992.

See also Copland, Aaron; Griffes, Charles Tomlinson; Music and Musicians I (Classical music)

Barnfield, Richard (1574–1620)

Richard Barnfield, one of the most talented minor English poets of the Elizabethan period, was born at Norbury Manor in Staffordshire, England, the eldest

B son of Richard and Mary Skrymsher Barnfield. The Barnfield and Skrymsher families were prosperous farmers who aspired to membership in the landed gentry. The poet was educated at Brasenose College, Oxford, receiving a B.A. in 1592. He is best known for *The Affectionate Shepherd* (1594), which includes three pastoral poems that recount the love of Daphnis for a younger man named Ganymede; and *Cynthia. With Certaine Sonnets, and the Legend of Cassandra* (1595), which features twenty homoerotic sonnets in which Daphnis yearns for Ganymede, followed by a pastoral ode in which the shepherd, frustrated by Ganymede's rejection, is now in love with a woman named Eliza.

Until the recent biographical discoveries of Andrew Worral, it had been thought that after Barnfield retired from his poetic labors in the 1590s, he married, lived as a gentleman farmer, and died in 1627. But Worral has shown that the death registered in 1627 and the will executed soon thereafter were those of the poet's father. Moreover, legal documents of 1598 systematically deprived the poet of his rights to inherit the Barnfield estates in favor of his younger brother, Robert. Worral has established that the poet died not in 1627, but in February 1620, apparently a bachelor and perhaps estranged from his family.

In the preface to *Cynthia*, Barnfield, probably responding to criticism of the homoeroticism in his earlier book, offers a disclaimer: "Some there were, that did interpret *The affectionate Shepheard*, otherwise then (in truth) I meant, touching the subject thereof, to wit, the love of a Shepheard to a boy; a fault, the which I will not excuse, because I never made," he writes; and he adds: "Onely this, I will unshaddow my conceit: being nothing else, but an imitation of *Virgill*, in the second Eglogue of *Alexis*." It is difficult to determine whether Barnfield's explanation reflects simple naïveté or whether it is a bluff designed to conceal anxiety. Barnfield was well aware of the transgressiveness involved in Daphnis's love for a youth suggestively named Ganymede: "If it be sinne to love a Lovely Lad; / O then sinne I" (ll. 9–10), the shepherd announces early in the poem. Indeed, throughout the work Barnfield challenges the condemnation of homoeroticism as sinful; and his appeal to classical precedence, especially to Virgil's hugely influential second eclogue, illustrates how classical literature—particularly the pastoral—could authorize homoeroticism in the English Renaissance. Moreover, the inclusion of the homoerotic sonnets in *Cynthia*

should warn against accepting the disclaimer at face value.

Barnfield's accounts of Daphnis's homoerotic longing for Ganymede are, along with works by Christopher Marlowe and William Shakespeare, among his era's most explicit and sympathetic treatments of same-sex love. The twenty sonnets of *Cynthia* are particularly interesting for their possible influence on Shakespeare's greater sonnet sequence.

Claude J. Summers

Bibliography

Barnfield, Richard. *The Complete Poems*. George Klawitter, ed. Selinsgrove, Pa.: Susquehanna University Press, 1990.

Worral, Andrew. "Richard Barnfield: A New Biography." *Notes and Queries* n.s. 39 (Sept. 1992): 370–71.

See also English Literature; Love Poetry, the Petrarchan Tradition; Marlowe, Christopher; Shakespeare, William

Barr, James (Fugaté) (1922–1995)

James Barr was an American novelist, playwright, and essayist whose two books, *Quatrefoil* (1950) and *Derricks* (1951), were among the first post–World War II works of gay fiction to be published. Although they are often ignored by literary critics, both gay and straight, they are fascinating portrayals of male homosexuality at the beginning of the Cold War.

Barr's fiction revolves around what we could call "masculine" homosexual lives during and after World War II. *Quatrefoil*, for example, is the story of naval officer Phillip Froelich's romance with Commander Tim Danelaw. Taking place almost completely in the military, the novel is, in Samuel Steward's words, "a wonderful treatise on how to live happily in the closet in 1950." Although the novel ends tragically, with Danelaw dying in a plane crash, therefore reinforcing the notion that gay male couples are always doomed, the work is remarkably lacking in self-loathing. Even Danelaw's death, because it's an accident, seems less dire than the fates of many other gay male protagonists in the novels of the period.

Despite the lack of critical interest in Barr, *Quatrefoil* has been a popular novel not just in the 1950s but also in the 1980s and '90s, when Alyson Publications reprinted it. *Derricks* is a collection of short stories that take place mostly in rural areas of the Midwest. Barr also wrote a number of articles for the 1950s homophile publication, the *Mattachine Review,* that document gay life in both the military and the rural Midwest. Not much is known about Barr's life, but he has written a number of autobiographical essays that detail a rural upbringing.   *Douglas Eisner*

Bibliography

Barr, James. "Facing Friends in a Small Town." *Mattachine Review* 1, no. 1 (1955): 9–12.
———. *Quatrefoil.* 1950. Intro. Samuel Steward. Epilogue James Barr. Boston: Alyson, 1991.

See also Mattachine Society; U.S. Literature: Contemporary Gay Writing

Barthé, James Richmond (1901–1989)

James Richmond Barthé was born in Bay St. Louis, Mississippi, into a family of devout Roman Catholic Creoles. Barthé was an introverted child drawn to fairytales and day dreams, preferring copying figures in local newspapers and magazines like *Physical Culture* rather than his studies, which ended at age fourteen. At sixteen, Barthé left home to take a job as a houseboy for a well-heeled New Orleans family. While living in the midst of finery, his artistic models expanded to include the romantic and neoclassical nineteenth-century fine art in his employer's collection.

In 1924, a gift from his parish priest made possible the first year of evening classes at the Chicago Art Institute School. A classroom exercise with portraiture in clay brought the soft-spoken, handsome artist public attention as a sculptor in the 1927 Negro in Art Week held in Chicago. By that time, Barthé had completed three years of evening instruction under painters Charles Schroeder at the School and privately with Archibald J. Motley Jr. Thereafter, Barthé's attention turned from painting to sculpture for the remainder of his career.

Barthé's move to Manhattan in 1929 at the height of the Harlem Renaissance, and just months before the stock market collapsed, was at the insistence of his friend Richard Bruce Nugent, an openly homosexual actor-illustrator. Barthé eventually settled in a studio apartment on the edge of Greenwich Village, and associated with bohemian circles that welcomed him without undue emphasis on his race and encouraged his interest in figurative art. Subsequently, Barthé enjoyed a market for his art that allowed him to tap into his rich imagination. He remains the only black American artist to concentrate on the male nude.

Dominated by actors, dancers, writers, and artists, many of whom were homosexuals, Barthé's list of friends and patrons reads like a Who's Who of the pre–World War II homosexual world. Notable figures, like Lyle Saxon, the New Orleans journalist and historian; Winifred Ellerman, the wealthy novelist who published under the name Bryher; Edgar Kaufmann Jr., heir to the famous Pittsburgh mercantile empire; and Carl Van Vechten, stage critic turned photographer who documented the era's African America, promoted and commissioned Barthé's sculpture. But one of the most lasting and profitable

Richmond Barthé, Feral Banga (Benga: Dance Figure), 1935, *Bronze (19 in.). Newark Art Museum (Art Resource, NY).*

B

friendships was with the undisputed black American arbiter of taste, Alain Locke. Locke, who favored bright, young, and gay men, convinced his own benefactor, wealthy dowager Charlotte Mason, to support Barthé once he arrived in New York City in 1929.

Today, considered the most broad-minded of the New Negro artists, Barthé was an unfailing advocate of racial integration and social assimilation, and used his sophisticated expressions of race, religion, and sexuality in sculpture to assert that advocacy. Barthé was also his generation's most elusive public figure. He invited the scorn of African Americans involved in the civil rights struggle by choosing his themes with personal rather than political interests in mind. In keeping with the social and moral restrictions of his day, Barthé never publicly revealed his sexual orientation. He was well aware of the centrality of racist stereotypes to the reception of black American art, and his carefully controlled public identity required considerable personal restraint. Barthé's art was his voice.

Margaret Rose Vendreyes

Bibliography

Bearden, Romare, and Harry Henderson. *A History of African-American Artists from 1792 to the Present.* New York: Pantheon, 1993.

Mathews, Marcia M. "Richmond Barthé, Sculptor." *South Atlantic Quarterly* 74 (1975): 324–39.

See also African American Gay Culture; Harlem Renaissance; Van Vechten, Carl

Barthes, Roland (1915–1980)

It is not immediately clear what case can be made for the inclusion of Roland Barthes in this volume. Known as the French philosopher, writer, and intellectual whose work in linguistics, culture, and literature defines the evolution from abstract structuralist logic to poststructuralist discourse, he rarely addressed questions of homosexuality directly in his writing, with the exception of the short text "Incidents"—a Moroccan travel diary—published posthumously and comprising a series of diary extracts describing his encounters in the form of brief meditations on questions of language, sexuality, and desire. However, it is characteristic of Barthes's attitude to homosexuality, and of his work in general, that his discourse on the subject is instead an indirect one, pieced together from fragments and

snatches. Yet as commentators have revealed throughout the 1990s, homosexuality can be seen to figure behind and within much of his theoretical work (it is atopically spaced by his desire), while Barthes's relation to his own sexuality, and the possibility of its expression and concealment, functions as an uncompleted autobiographical project through which his writing is often filtered.

In *Roland Barthes by Roland Barthes*, he refers to "the Goddess H(omo)" (although "H" also refers to "hashish"), commenting on how "difference" becomes a "more," which enhances life and moves it toward its textualization. Barthes's mistrust of occupying any fixed identity in language—a dynamic that generates much of this fragmented, autotheoretical text—leads him toward an ethics of partiality, digression, deferral, and the mask, which—as Andreas Bjørnerud has shown—provides an alternative model of sexual identity to the dominant one of "coming out." Instead, Barthes proposes a sexuality that escapes essentialist definition and instead favors the multiple and mobile patterns of flirting and cruising as identifications through which the homosexual emerges as relational, respectful (*bienveillant*), and dynamic.

Consequently Barthes's theorization of homosexuality not only valorizes transience and seduction but also enacts this by writing in the discourses of other writers or texts. His preface to Renaud Camus's cruising notebook, *Tricks*, his essays on reversals or inversions (*le renversement*) in Marcel Proust, together with the network of sexual metaphors, figures, and vocabulary across his writing offer Barthes the possibility of elaborating a marginal, eroticized, and figurative writing of homosexuality within the feint of formal criticism. By doing so he both avoids the distortions of rigid sense making within the operations of language and prolongs the dynamic *jouissance* of desiring, displacement, and differentiation with and against the other into the stylistics of his own readings and writing. Barthes's militancy lies in his imaginative disappropriation of the aggressivity of identity, which imagines a plural space for a liberated gay erotics in both text and life.

Murray Pratt

Bibliography

Barthes, Roland. *Incidents.* Berkeley: University of California Press, 1992. (1987).

———. *Roland Barthes by Roland Barthes.* New York: Hill and Wang, 1977. (*Roland Barthes par Roland Barthes*, 1975).

———. *The Rustle of Language.* Oxford: Basil Blackwell, 1986. (*Le Bruissement de la langue: Essais critiques* IV, 1984).

Bjørnerud, Andreas. "Outing Barthes: Barthes and the Quest(ion) of (a Gay) Identity Politics." *New Formations* 18 (Winter 1992): 122–41.

Knight, Diana. *Barthes and Utopia: Space, Travel Writing.* Oxford: Oxford University Press, 1997).

Miller, D. A. *Bringing Out Roland Barthes.* Berkeley: University of California Press, 1992.

Pratt, Murray. "From 'Incident' to 'Texte': Homosexuality and Autobiography in Barthes's Late Writing." *French Forum* 22, no. 2 (May 1997): 21–34.

Schehr, Lawrence. *The Shock of Men: Homosexual Hermeneutics in French Writing.* Stanford, Calif.: Stanford University Press, 1995.

Worton, Michael. "Cruising (Through) Encounters." In *Gay Signatures: Gay and Lesbian Theory, Fiction and Film in France 1945–1995.* Owen Heathcote, Alex Hughes, and James Williams, eds. Oxford: Berg, 1998, 29–50.

See also France; French Literature; Proust, Marcel

Bathhouses and Sex Clubs

Although gay men have claimed the baths of ancient Turkey, Rome, and Greece as primeval sites of same-sex desire and activity, recuperating a history of sexuality as it might have unfolded at these baths is as tricky as recovering the histories of sexual identity, desire, and behavior throughout classical antiquity. Nevertheless, gay men and women of the West have considered the baths in light of their erotic appeal since at least the eighteenth century. Nineteenth-century Europe was dotted with bathhouses in cosmopolitan centers, and men could conceivably have met there and had sexual encounters. The Victorian preoccupation with hygiene and the perpetually clean body gave rise to numerous bathhouses in both Europe and North America, largely in response to a concern with providing immigrants and the poor with places in which to bathe. In 1852, for instance, the New York Association for the Improvement of the Condition of the Poor opened a bath, and by the later nineteenth century, more followed, catering to working-class as well as well-to-do clienteles. Among Jewish immigrants, the ritual bath, or *mikvah,* also served as a place in which to perform religious ablutions.

By the 1890s, baths were certainly frequented by gay men searching for sexual encounters or associations with like-minded men. In fact, along with bars, bathhouses were among the first spaces in which gay men could develop social relations with other gay men. As George Chauncey has noted, "While the baths attracted men in the first instance because of the sexual possibilities they offered— and, indeed, fostered a distinctive sexual culture— they encouraged the cultivation of broader social ties as well (208)." The earliest known case of homosexual activity at bathhouses in New York City was recorded in 1910 when a thirty-eight-year-old man and his sixteen-year-old companion were caught by an attendant. Both were charged with sodomy, a court case ensued, both pleaded guilty, and the elder gentleman was sentenced to three to five years in the state penitentiary.

A series of raids on bathhouses in New York and San Francisco during the early decades of the twentieth century indicate that public baths had gained a widespread reputation as hotbeds of homosexual activity among men. In 1916, thirty-seven patrons and employees of New York's Ariston baths were arrested, and twenty-five of them were later convicted and sent to prison. In 1929, the Lafayette Baths of New York were raided, and a European visitor published an eyewitness account of the raid in a German gay magazine. The visitor noted the American policemen's brutality toward the patrons and wrote, "I would place the blame for this on the terrible furtiveness and phony shame which prevails here in America" (quoted in Bérubé 195). Although many Europeans were delighted to attend the by-now famous baths of New York, Chicago, and San Francisco during the earlier twentieth century, their shock at the oppressive response to gay male culture indicates how homosexual identities were shaped by differing cultural and national patterns of (in)tolerance.

These early baths included both mainstream establishments that turned a blind eye to their homosexual patrons and their activities as well as bathhouses run and frequented nearly exclusively by gay men. Those baths that fell into the latter category were among the first commercial enterprises run by and for gay men. Allan Bérubé has surmised that gay bathhouses led gay men to seek relationships (sexual and otherwise) with other gay men, thus fostering a new sense of self-acceptance. By World War II, bathhouses and similar places like the YMCA were the destinations for thousands of gay servicemen coming to port cities like San Francisco, and

B for a while, public and military officials seemed to accept that, like brothels, bathhouses would serve a provisionally useful purpose. By the 1950s and 1960s, however, a newly repressive environment in the United States led to a resurgence of raids on bathhouses. The names of those who attended the baths were published in local newspapers, but despite such crackdowns, more and more bathhouses catering to gay men opened in the early 1960s.

After Stonewall, an environment emerged in which the bathhouses could be celebrated precisely because they fostered sexual experimentation and promiscuous relations among men, but the baths continued to serve a variety of social and cultural purposes as well. A chain of "Club Baths" emerged in various cities across the United States around 1970. These and other new bathhouses featured larger pools, clean facilities, and video rooms, and could serve upwards of a thousand men at a time. Performers such as Bette Midler, Tiny Tim, and Barry Manilow performed at gay bathhouses in New York, and evenings devoted to cabaret acts, country-and-western entertainment, and, of course, disco helped the baths to appeal to a wide variety of gay men. By the mid-1970s police raids on baths were less frequent, while legislation decriminalizing consensual adult sex chipped away at the legal rationales for attacking the bathhouses. Many baths also provided routine VD checkups for their patrons, often in cooperation with local municipal health officials.

Nevertheless, conservative political trends and the sexual panic fostered by AIDS led to a backlash against gay bathhouses throughout the 1980s. In February 1981, Toronto's police force raided the city's six gay bathhouses after undercover policemen had been infiltrating the baths for the previous six months. Patrons were forced to leave the premises, line up, and stand outdoors in the snow wearing only their towels. Over three hundred men were arrested. These raids led to massive protests the following day, and three thousand demonstrators marched on the police station that had conducted the raids as well as on the Ontario Parliament. Later, a city-sponsored investigation condemned the police force's actions and confirmed the right of men to engage in consensual sex. This event led to a mobilization of Toronto's gay community that has continued to counter police crackdowns on consensual sex among men in public parks and restrooms.

In New York and San Francisco, on the other hand, the cities' attacks on gay sex establishments would lead to the closure of many bathhouses, sex clubs, and backroom bars by the mid-1980s. As physicians and writers like Larry Kramer, Joseph Sonnabend, David Goodstein, and Michael Callen began to speculate on the connections between the presence of immunosuppression and the numbers of partners with which urban gay men had sex, risk came to be inextricably associated with promiscuity. Promiscuous behavior became the target for early AIDS prevention, and the bathhouse was singled out as an obvious site of sexual promiscuity. In 1984, Randy Shilts would condemn the bathhouses in an essay for the *New York Native* in which, with outrage, he described bathhouses as "unprecedented in that they were businesses created solely for the purpose of quick multiple sexual acts, often accomplished without speaking so much as one word." (quoted in Bayer 29–30). On the other hand, many gay activists rallied behind the gay bathhouses as sites and symbols of gay liberation and sexual difference. Thus a furious rift developed within the gay community over the status of the bathhouses. Those who favored their closure often presented moralistic arguments attacking the commercial nature of the sexual encounter in the baths. (In this respect, the efforts to close bathhouses and eradicate the activity that took place within them echoes similar efforts to close brothels and regulate prostitutes' behavior at the turn of the century.) But others remarked that businesses such as hotels also served to facilitate commercial, sexual transactions.

The debate also circulated around whether gay bathhouses should be considered private or public establishments. While the opponents of the bathhouses argued that commercial establishments were necessarily public spaces and could be regulated or closed in the best interests of the public good, others argued that gay bathhouses were sites in which only those unlikely to find them offensive would attend. Bathhouses already restricted their clientele to legal-aged men and often provided their patrons with private rooms or cubicles. Furthermore, they argued that unsafe and promiscuous behavior could occur anywhere—whether in the privacy of one's home or the semiprivacy of a public rest room. Driving gay male sex out of commercial establishments would drive many gay men into less safe public environments. Conceivably, bathhouses could even serve as venues where men might receive safe-sex education as well as condoms, lubricants, and other safe-sex items.

While San Francisco Director of Public Health Mervyn Silverman had originally favored allowing the bathhouses for both civil rights and public health reasons, Mayor Dianne Feinstein and others finally swayed him to close six bathhouses and four gay sex clubs as public nuisances. Although the city's decision spurred a series of protests concerning gay men's rights to engage in consensual sex and to associate freely with one another, San Francisco's bathhouses have remain closed well into the late 1990s. Sex clubs—locations in which the traditional amenities of the bathhouses are absent and the men remain (more or less) clothed—have since opened in the city, but often with quite strict regulations concerning the nature of the sexual activity that patrons can engage in there.

New York's history of bathhouse closures is closely intertwined with that of San Francisco's. Many of the same figures emerged making the same arguments when suggestions were made to close the baths in New York. Although David Sencer, the city's commissioner of health, remained firm in insisting that there was no compelling reason to close the bathhouses, Governor Mario Cuomo and the State Health Department moved independently to gather evidence of promiscuous activity in the baths and focused on the threat AIDS posed to the wives and children of bisexual bathhouse patrons. In New York, gay activists Michael Callen and Larry Kramer both emerged as major gay spokesmen in favor of closing the baths to save gay men from the consequences of their own desires and behaviors. On November 7, 1985, a court order mandated the closure of the Mineshaft, a cruisy gay men's bar with a backroom. Soon thereafter the city's famed St. Mark's Baths was closed down.

Surprisingly, although debates over the fate of gay men's bathhouses occurred in places as diverse as Minnesota, Buffalo, and Los Angeles, gay men's sex establishments in these locations were not forced to close during the mid-1980s AIDS panics. In more recent years, Los Angeles municipal authorities have attempted to relocate or permanently close sex clubs and bathhouses, asserting alleged violations of city zoning laws.

In New York, both commercial and private sex clubs have replaced the baths as places for men to gather and have sex, while in 1995, the West Side Club opened as a "private gay men's club," complete with exercise equipment and cubicles. Soon after opening, ten policemen without warrants raided the club, but the club's owner has since worked to comply with the city's regulations. In the wake of New York's efforts at gentrification, however, many gay

male commercial sex clubs that had operated since 1984 have been shut down for a variety of reasons, from tax-code and zoning violations to evidence of oral sex on their premises. The recent wars on gay commercial sex establishments have been fueled largely by a handful of gay journalists and activists who in 1995 formed Gay and Lesbian HIV Prevention Activists (GALHPA). Members of GALHPA have used the mainstream press as a way of attacking bathhouses particularly and gay male promiscuity more generally. In response to this sexual backlash, alternative organizations like the AIDS Prevention Action League and Community AIDS Prevention Activists have formed to work with the owners and patrons of sex clubs in making such venues safe places to have sex. A more radical contingent of academics and activists called Sex Panic decries any attempt to curb gay sexual expression and works to undermine the oversimplified equation of public sex with unsafe sex.   *John Beynon*

Bibliography

Bayer, Ronald. *Private Acts, Social Consequences: AIDS and the Politics of Public Health.* New York: Free Press, 1989.

Bérubé, Allan. "The History of Gay Bathhouses." In *Policing Public Sex: Queer Politics and the Future of AIDS Activism.* Dangerous Bedfellows, eds. Boston: South End Press, 1996, 187–220.

Betsky, Aaron. *Queer Space: Architecture and Same-Sex Desire.* New York: Morrow, 1997.

Chauncey, George. *Gay New York: Gender, Urban Culture, and the Making of the Gay Male World 1890–1940.* New York: Basic Books, 1994.

See also Activism, U.S.; AIDS; Kramer, Larry; Shilts, Randy; United States

Bazille, Jean-Frédéric (1841–1870)

Frédéric Bazille contributed to the formation of impressionist painting. From 1862 to his death in 1870, he produced approximately sixty-five oil paintings. Many are now in Paris and Montpellier, the rest scattered in public and private collections throughout the world.

Born to a bourgeois Protestant family, Bazille studied medicine and painting in Montpellier, then moved to Paris in 1862, where his interest in the former gave way to the latter. In the Swiss artist Charles Gleyre's Paris teaching studio, Bazille befriended

B Monet and Renoir, and together with Manet, Sisley, Morisot, Cézanne, and Degas, they helped forge impressionist painting. Pissarro called him "one of the most gifted among us." In the 1860s, they sought governmental and art-critical success for their fresh and ostensibly unmediated depictions of subjects from modern life. In handsome, saturated colors, Bazille incisively drew and firmly modeled his subjects, placing him among the more figural of the impressionist painters, Degas and Caillebotte.

Like his friends, Bazille had mixed success. To the salons of 1866, 1868, 1869, and 1870, he submitted two paintings, and each time only one was accepted. When both his 1867 offerings were rejected, he joined his colleagues in petitioning the government and in projecting an independent exhibition free of governmental control; that would come to fruition in the eight impressionist exhibitions held from 1874 to 1886.

Until very recently, scholars have uncritically assumed the homosociality of Bazille's world, while skirting questions of sexuality in his life and work. They have recounted his family's financial support and encouragement as proof of harmonious relations, exacting from the dead artist and his work the same deal that he may have implicitly negotiated with his family—good career support from them, respectable conduct from him. In fact, Bazille traveled between two worlds: the supportive and heterosocial world of his family's provincial bourgeoisie and the more urbane homosociality of his Paris milieu, which included the poets Rimbaud and Verlaine, whom he drew and painted.

Bazille worked side by side with Monet and Renoir. They lacked Bazille's family support, so he shared his studio and apartment with them. He bought Monet's ambitious *Women in the Garden* (Paris, Musée d'Orsay, 1867), and he painted Renoir nattily dressed and seated in a provocative pose (Paris, Musée d'Orsay, 1867). In contrast to the informality and ease of Bazille's atelier life represented in his *Studio on the Rue de la Condamine* (Paris, Musée d'Orsay, 1870) is *The Family Gathering* (Paris, Musée d'Orsay, 1867), one of his most outstanding and disconcerting achievements. It is a group portrait of members of his nuclear and extended family, shaded and contained beneath the branches of a large chestnut tree on one of the family's estates. The compression of the space and the severity of the light, the line, and the gazes of the figures complicates the novelist Zola's estimation that Bazille "loves his own time."

Bazille's homosociality extends to two of his most provocative pictures, depictions of unclothed boys and men in nature. *Fisherman with a Net* (Zurich, Rau Foundation for the Third World, 1868) features a robust nude young man, seen from behind, poised to cast, improbably, a net in a stream. In the middle distance, a younger man, seated on the grass, removes his last article of clothing. The picture was refused entry into the Salon of 1870. As technically complicated as the tour de force portrait of his biological family, the *Summer Scene* features eight male figures stripping down to swimwear or already stripped to bathe, wrestle, and lounge by a stream. Traditionally, the male nude was painted as a student exercise or in a mythological drama, and scenes of female nudes required even fewer pretexts for the delectation of the human body. Bazille turned those traditions on their heads. His broad and vigorous technique was coded as manly, and he painted a man's world, a sort of regendering of Monet's *Women in the Garden* (1867) and an inspiration to, among others, Thomas Eakins's *The Swimming Hole* (Fort Worth, Amon Carter Museum, 1883–1885). Bazille's other entry for the Salon of 1870 was rejected: *La Toilette* (Montpellier, Musée Fabre), by contrast, features three female figures, among them a stripped white woman and a half-nude black slave, a concentration of Orientalist clichés that connoted a lesbian encounter.

Although Bazille's father had purchased a substitute for his son, the artist volunteered for military duty in 1870, and, after a brief station in French Algeria, was sent to fight in the Franco-Prussian War, where he died on the battlefield at the age of twenty-eight.

Todd Porterfield

Bibliography

Bajou, Valérie. *Frédéric Bazille, 1841–1870*. Aix-en-Provence, France: Edisud, 1994.

Bazille, Frédéric. *Frédéric Bazille: Correspondance*. Guy Barral and Didier Vatuone, eds. Montpellier, France: Les Presses du Languedoc, 1992.

Brettell, Richard R. "Thomas Eakins and the Male Nude in French Vanguard Painting, 1850–1890." *Thomas Eakins and the Swimming Picture*. Doreen Bolger and Sarah Cash, eds. Fort Worth: Amon Carter Museum, 1996.

Champa, Kermit Swiler. *Studies in Early Impressionism*. New Haven: Yale University Press, 1973.

Montpellier, Musée Fabre. *Frédéric Bazille: Prophet of Impressionism*. John Goodman, trans. Brooklyn: Brooklyn Museum of Art, 1992.

Schulman, Michel. *Frédéric Bazille, 1841–1870.* Paris: Éditions de l'Amateur, 1995.

Tinterow, Gary, and Henri Loyrette. *Origins of Impressionism.* New York: Metropolitan Museum of Art, 1994.

See also Art History; Eakins, Thomas; Rimbaud, Arthur; Verlaine, Paul

Beam, Joseph Fairchild (1954–1988)

Joe Beam was the editor of *In the Life: A Black Gay Anthology* (1986), believed to be the first anthology of solely black, specifically gay writing ever to reach publication. During his lifetime he published work in the *Advocate, New York Native, Gay News, Gay Community News,* and *Black Heart,* among other publications; he was also a columnist for *Au Courant* and a contributing editor of *Blacklight.* He also served as a board member of the National Coalition of Black Lesbians and Gays. He was editing another anthology, *Brother to Brother,* at the time of his death from AIDS-related complications in Philadelphia in 1986.

His vision of a liberated black gay subjectivity inspired his mother, Dorothy Beam, to complete the anthology, assisted by others—most notably, poet Essex Hemphill—while his legacy in words serves as an inspiration to a new generation of queers of color as they battle the double-edged sword of racism and homophobia, both from within and from without black culture: "I dare myself to dream of a time when I will pass a group of brothers on the corner, and the words 'fucking faggot' will not move the air around my ears; and when my gay brother approaches me on the street that we can embrace if we choose. I dare us to dream that we are worth wanting each other." *Matthew Williams*

Bibliography

Beam, Joseph, ed. *In the Life: A Black Gay Anthology.* Boston: Alyson Publications, 1986.

See also African American Gay Culture; Hemphill, Essex

Bear Culture

Bear as a gay male self-identity developed in the late 1980s and 1990s. In part a response to the AIDS epidemic and in part a manifestation of the aging baby-boomer generation, gay men who first chose the term *bear* sought a masculine self-image, suggesting a large or husky body, a prevalence of body hair, and a generally friendly and sanguinary attitude. "Coming out" as a bear follows a strategy similar to the "coming out" of the 1970s gay liberation movement. A striking parallel may be found between bears-as-attitude and the utopian ideals of the original gay liberation movement. Early bears proudly proclaimed being "average," masculine gay men, neither effeminate queens nor hypermasculine leathermen. In fact, many of them were former clones, now heavier and graying at the temples.

A bear subculture rapidly developed along three trajectories, all emanating from San Francisco—the underground press, private sex parties, and the newly emergent medium of electronic communications. Originally a local 'zine, *BEAR* magazine's commercial success became an overnight sensation. As bear images proliferated in the gay press, an entire new niche of bear-oriented publications and pornography developed as well. Word-of-mouth broadcast of "bears" via computer bulletin boards, and then the Internet, spread the concept even more rapidly. Bear spaces, particularly bars and private sex parties, occurred where various subsubcultures within gay male communities, including "chubbies," radical fairies, bikers, blue-collar men, rural men, computer geeks, and fetishists, came together. The need for bears to socialize often led to the founding of bear clubs.

The rise of bear clubs, sometimes as not-for-profit charity organizations and often modeled on the motorcycle (social) clubs, led to a new conformity among the membership. By 1997, the first decade of bears, there were some 140 bear and bear-friendly clubs worldwide, primarily in the United States and Canada, but also in Great Britain, Germany, Belgium, Italy, Israel, Japan, Australia, New Zealand, and elsewhere. A social calendar of regional social conventions (e.g., Octobearfest in Denver, Orlando Bear Bust, Bear Pride Weekend in Chicago, European Big Men's Convergence in Brussels are among the best known) is capped by the annual International Bear Rendezvous every February in San Francisco. The widely popular "bear contests," originally staged as camp parodies of beauty pageants, have become a stock-in-trade of many clubs and are considered serious competitions, much along the lines of the leather competitions.

B

The official organizing within the bear subculture expanded rapidly, and numerous clubs rose and fell within a few years. As the subculture enters its second decade, it is not clear how extensive a club scene will survive. The bear, as successor to the leather man and the clone, represents a renewed effort for some gay men to develop a personal sense of masculinity, of overcoming the core paradox of being both gay and a man in a society that defines these terms as mutually exclusive.   *Les Wright*

Bibliography

Wright, Les, ed. *The Bear Book: Readings in the History and Evolution of a Gay Male Subculture.* Binghamton, N.Y.: Haworth Press, 1997.

See also Aging; Body Image; Clone; Community Centers; Leatherman; San Francisco

Beat Generation

The Beat Generation refers to a group of writers and artists who emerged in New York City during the late 1940s and established a counterculture beachhead there and in San Francisco during the 1950s. Although the phrase "Beat Generation" has been applied to painters and musicians of the period, the movement is primarily associated with writers such as Allen Ginsberg, William Burroughs, Jack Kerouac, Herbert Hunke, Peter Orlovsky, Gregory Corso, Bob Kaufman, and Diane DiPrima. As a literary movement, the Beats extended several strains of modernism—particularly dada and surrealism—that stressed spontaneity and psychological catharsis. Their openly romantic, often vatic works contested the then-reigning New Criticism, with its emphasis on impersonality, irony, and formal control. As a cultural movement, the Beats set themselves against the conservative mood of the Eisenhower era, adopting an adversarial relationship to the politics of consensus, consumerism, and middleclass heterosexuality. In works such as Ginsberg's "Howl," Kerouac's *On the Road*, and Burroughs's *Naked Lunch*, American Cold War paranoia and suburban normalcy were satirized, and a participatory ethos of sexual excess, personal confession, and spontaneity were celebrated. The fame of these works turned their authors into pop culture icons and inaugurated a series of Beat revivals that continue in the present day.

Although the origins of the term "Beat" have been hotly debated, most commentators refer to Kerouac's 1948 remark to John Clellon Holmes: "So I guess you might say we're a *beat* generation." In a 1958 *Esquire* article, Kerouac explained that "beat" refers to a quality of world-weariness, of being "down and out but full of intense conviction." "Beat" also implies beatitude, a quality of mystical attentiveness that Kerouac identifies with hobos, Zen mystics, black jazz musicians, and the lumpen underclass who live at the margins of American society. Kerouac sees his Beat compatriots as "solitary Bartlebies staring out of the dead wall window of our civilization . . . taking drugs, digging bop, having flashes of insight, experiencing the 'derangement of the senses.' "

Perhaps the Beats' most enduring legacy to American society was a lifestyle revolution that found its popular expression in the "beatnik," a media stereotype of the hipster that appeared in numerous television sitcoms. The bohemia represented in Kerouac's novels or Ginsberg's poems offered a lively alternative to the cult of normalcy being diagnosed by popular sociologists or depicted in the TV series *Ozzie and Harriet*. The Beats seized upon the possibilities of the media, appearing on television talk shows and writing for popular magazines like *Esquire* and *Playboy*. Although the Beats never aligned themselves with traditional political parties and movements, their belief in the personal as political resonated with many social movements of the 1960s and 1970s.

It is in the area of gender and sexuality that the Beats posed the greatest challenge to Cold War normalcy, but there was a cost to their sexual liberation. Although women were associated with the Beat movement (Joanne Kyger, Diane DiPrima, Carolyn Cassedy), the core group consisted of homosexual or bisexual males, for whom women were often irritating domestic encumbrances or sexual surrogates. Although Beats engaged in same-sex liaisons, they configured their sexual identity largely through heterosexual models. A kind of macho ethos pervaded their relationships, most famously in Kerouac's depiction of himself and Neal Cassedy in *On the Road*. Although Cassedy, Burroughs, and Kerouac maintained heterosexual domestic households at various times, they had sexual contacts with both men and women outside their marriages. Moreover, their representations of homosexual lifestyles were often marked by comments that seem homophobic by today's standards. Burroughs's excoriation of "high teacup queens" in *Naked Lunch* or Kerouac's assertion in a letter to Cassedy that "I consider queerness a hostility, not a love" suggests that homosexuality among the Beats was a contested site for masculine identity. To some extent, this phobic response reflected the pervasive 1950s attitude toward gays, but the openness with which the Beats treated such relationships diagnosed fractures in the edifice of compulsory heterosexuality.

At a recent symposium, Allen Ginsberg spoke for many of his Beat colleagues by defining himself not as "gay" but "queer," the former referring to males who desired sex only with other gay men. "Queer," for Ginsberg, implied desire for other heterosexual males, and many of his poems celebrate acts of private initiation rather than communitarian sexual solidarity:

> Sweet Boy, Gimme Yr Ass
> lemme kiss your face, lick your neck
> touch your lips, tongue tickle tongue end
> nose to nose quiet questions
> ever slept with a man before? (613)

In early poems like "Transcription of Organ Music" (1955), Ginsberg speaks positively of heterosexual initiation as well ("the door to the womb was open to admit me if I wished to enter"), but in his later poems, his anxiety about women is more frontal:

> Woman
>   herself, why have I feared
>   to be joined true
>   embraced beneath the Panties of Forever
> in with the one hole that repelled me 1937 on?
>   (285)

Such misogyny and masculinism have understandably come under attack by feminists and gay rights activists, but Barbara Ehrenreich has argued that the Beats provided significant lifestyle alternatives to the 1950s nuclear family. She points out that in Kerouac's novels, women are permitted a degree of independence and autonomy that contests traditional gender roles, and that domestic labor is seldom configured around the breadwinner male but rather the working woman. Further, within Beat writings female sexuality is encouraged, and same-sex relationships among men pose no threat to masculine identity. Although she does not focus specifically on homosexuality, Ehrenreich implies that within the bohemian counterculture of the 1950s, possibilities for more open and complex sex/gender relationships were being acted out and new possibil-

ities for family and community being envisioned. The fame of works like *On the Road* and "Howl" helped sustain interest in those lifestyles, turning them from the bohemian margins to the cultural mainstream in ways that we are only now beginning to understand.   *Michael Davidson*

Bibliography

Davidson, Michael. *The San Francisco Renaissance: Poetics and Community at Mid-Century*. Cambridge: Cambridge University Press, 1989.

Ehrenreich, Barbara. *The Hearts of Men: American Dreams and the Flight from Commitment*. Garden City, N.Y.: Anchor/Doubleday, 1983.

Nicosia, Gerald. *Memory Babe: A Critical Biography of Jack Kerouac*. New York: Grove Press, 1983.

Watson, Steven. *Birth of the Beat Generation: Visionaries, Rebels and Hipsters, 1944–1960*. New York: Pantheon, 1995.

See also Burroughs, William Seward; Gay; Ginsberg, Allen; masculinity; Queer; San Francisco; U.S. Literature

Beaton, Cecil (Walter Hardynine, 1904–1980)

Cecil Beaton was a British photographer, set designer, and costume designer. For much of his career, Beaton was the most famous photographer and designer in the world. His fascination with photography and theater began when at the age of eight, he saw a picture postcard of the actress Lily Elsie.

In the 1920s Beaton became a successful photographer of celebrity portraits, and in 1932 he began to focus on fashion photography as well. In the United States, his work appeared in *Vogue* and *Vanity Fair* magazines. In many of Beaton's early photographs, his subjects were posed in front of elegant and sometimes surrealistic sets. His later photographs, including many portraits of the British royal family, were less elaborate but equally stylish.

Beaton first designed for the theater in 1926, but it was not until ten years later that he found commercial success in this field. He became a renowned designer of costumes and sets for both films and theater. His greatest triumph as a designer came when he created the costumes for the theater and film versions of *My Fair Lady* (1956, 1964).

Beginning in 1961, Beaton published a series of collections of excerpts from his diaries. In the

B third of these, *The Happy Years* (1972; U.S. title, *Memoirs of the 40s*), he told the story of his love affair with film star Greta Garbo. Although most of Beaton's romances were with men, this affair—which seems to have been largely nonsexual and unrequited—lasted from 1946 to 1952. Beaton was knighted in 1972.   *Charles Krinsky*

Bibliography

Vickers, Hugo. *Cecil Beaton: A Biography.* New York: Primus/Donald I. Fine, 1985.
———. *Loving Garbo: The Story of Greta Garbo, Cecil Beaton and Mercedes de Acosta.* London: Jonathan Cape, 1994.

See also Film Fashion; Film Stars; Photography

Beaumont and Fletcher (Francis Beaumont [c.1594–1616] and John Fletcher [1579–1625])

According to Aubrey's *Lives,* in 1608, the English dramatists Francis Beaumont and John Fletcher "lived together on the Banke Side, not far from the Play-house, both batchelors; lay together; had one wench in the house between them, which they did so admire; the same cloathes and cloake, &c., betweene them" (quoted in Chambers, vol. 3, 217). Aubrey, however, cannot always be trusted. One other biographical note makes reference to two-thirds of this ménage à trios: in Thomas Shadwell's play, *Bury-Fair* (1689), a character named Oldwit recalls eating and drinking with Fletcher and his maid, Joan, but did not mention Beaumont living with them. There is reference to a John Fletcher marrying a Joan Herring on November 3, 1612, at St. Saviour' s, Southwark, on Bank Side. Biographers remain uncertain whether this is a reference to John Fletcher, the playwright.

Despite Shadwell's reference to Fletcher's apparent heterosexual, domestic bliss and the marriage notification that seems to support the claim, Aubry's reference to a close personal relationship between Beaumont and Fletcher has persisted: J. St. Leo Strachey noted that they "lived and worked together, their thoughts no less in common than the cloak and bed . . . we think of them as of two minds so married that to divorce or disunite them were a sacrilegious deed" (vii); Leigh Hunt discreetly hints that "Nothing is known of their personal habits . . . except they were intimate."

Their work is filled with sexual taboos, particularly on the theme of incest, which features promi-nently in *A King and No King* (1619). Dyce describes their collaborations as full of "unblushing licentiousness. In this respect they sinned more grievously than their contemporary playwrights" (quoted in Hunt xi). M. C. Bradbrook described their plays as "deeply disturbed" (x).

John Dryden states that Fletcher wrote two or three plays "very unsuccessfully" before teaming up with Beaumont. It was often thought that the first play they wrote together was *The Woman Hater* (c.1606), but that play is now thought to be substantially by Beaumont. In 1647 and 1679, various actors and publishers issued collections in which they attributed fifty-three plays to this tandem. The number has since been revised downwards. According to Chambers, the two definitely wrote seven plays together: *Philaster, A Maid's Tragedy, A King and No King, Four Plays in One, Cupid's Revenge, The Coxcomb,* and *The Scornful Lady.* Beaumont is accorded the famous *The Knight of the Burning Pestle,* one of the finest plays of the era.

After Beaumont' s death, Fletcher continued to write plays, completing six on his own and nine in collaboration with other playwrights. Most famously, he collaborated with William Shakespeare on *Henry VIII, Cardinio,* and the homoerotically charged *The Two Noble Kinsmen.* Confusion and controversy reign over Fletcher's hand in twelve other plays.   *Jeffrey Kahan*

Bibliography

Bradbrook, M. C., ed. *Beaumont & Fletcher: Select Plays.* London: J. M. Dent, 1962.
Chambers, E. K. *The Elizabethan Stage.* Vol. 3. Oxford: Clarendon Press, 1923.
Hunt, Leigh, ed. *Beaumont and Fletcher.* London: Henry G. Bohn, 1862.
Strachey, J. St. Leo, ed. *The Best Plays of the Dramatists Beaumont and Fletcher.* Mermaid Series. London: T. Fisher Unwin, 1893.

See also English Literature; Friendship; Shakespeare, William; Theater: Premodern and Early Modern

Beck, Julian (1925–1985)

Dedicated to breaking boundaries and opening "the jails of the body," Julian Beck attended New York's Thomas Mann High School and Yale University before dropping out. He met Judith Malina in 1943 and became a painter, and they formed the Living Theater in 1947.

Beck made no separation between his own life and that of the stage or among the traditional functions of director, stagehand, and audience or even among stage, house, and surrounding community. Their first productions (1951) were in his apartment with plays by Paul Goodman, Gertrude Stein, Bertoldt Brecht, and Federico García Lorca. John Ashbery's *Some Heroes* (1952) disturbed many with its open homosexuality.

Living Theater productions have transformed many people's lives. *The Connection* (1959) by Jack Gelber, *The Brig* (1963) by Kenneth H. Brown, *Frankenstein* (1965), *Antigone* (1966), *Paradise Now* (1968), *Seven Meditations on Sado-Masochism* (1974), *The Heritage of Cain* (1975)—all have aimed, Beck wrote, "to increase conscious awareness, to stress the sacredness of life, to break down the walls."

Jailed twelve times and arrested many more, Beck fused art with anarchism. He served a year in a U.S. prison fighting the IRS and over two years in Brazil for opposing the dictator there.

Malina bore Beck two children, but the couple never passed themselves off as "heterosexual" or "homosexual," as their view of universal liberation fought against labels. On stage the nudity of their productions sometimes aroused astonishment. In *Paradise Now*, actors and audience both could remove their clothing; in *New Haven* (1968), a group followed the lines, "The theater is in the street. . . . Free the theater. Free the street. Begin."

Charles Shively

Bibliography

Biner, Pierre. *The Living Theater.* New York: Avon Books, 1972.

Paradise Now: Collective Creation of the Living Theater. New York: Random House, 1971.

Silvestro, Carlo, ed. *The Living Book of The Living Theater.* Greenwich, Conn.: Graphic Society, 1971.

See also Ashbery, John; García Lorca, Federico; Goodman, Paul; Sadomasochism

Beckford, William (1760–1844)

Writer, art collector, and builder William Beckford was born into a wealthy and politically influential family at Fonthill, near Bath, England. His father, twice lord mayor of London, died in 1770, leaving one of the largest fortunes in England to his only legitimate son. Beckford's guardianship was then shared by William Pitt and Lord Chancellor Thurlow, two of the most powerful politicians of the age. Elected to Parliament for Wells in 1784, Beckford arranged through Thurlow later in the same year to be elevated to a peerage as Lord Beckford of Fonthill. To prevent Beckford's elevation, one of Thurlow's most vigorous political enemies, Lord Loughborough, planted rumors in the press that Beckford had been seen through a keyhole at Powderham Castle sodomizing William "Kitty" Courtenay, Loughborough's fifteen-year-old nephew with whom Beckford had been engaged in a passionate relationship for several years. Although the keyhole scene appears to have been without basis in fact, Beckford's peerage was revoked. For the first time in British politics, mere rumors of homosexuality resulted in the exclusion of a politician from public life. Beckford spent the remaining sixty years of his life ostracized by polite society.

The tensions between male homosexuality and an active participation in British political life can be seen in much of Beckford's literary work. In 1783 his family convinced him to suppress the publication of *Dreams, Waking Thoughts and Incidents*, a highly stylized account of his travels through the Low Countries, Germany and Italy, in part because it contained thinly veiled raptures on homoerotic passions that his guardians believed would interfere with his political career. Beckford published his most widely read work, *Vathek*, in 1786. Originally written in French and then translated into English under Beckford's supervision, *Vathek* tells the story of an Oriental caliph's pursuit of sensuous pleasures and infernal powers, which, on an autobiographical level, can be read as Beckford's reflections on his love affair with Courtenay. Like much of his work, this tale thematically as well as stylistically expresses an emerging homosexual sensibility and a nostalgic longing for inclusion in the society that has become increasingly intolerant of homosexuality. Beckford cultivated this divided sensibility throughout his long life, and in his final published work, *Recollections of an Excursion to the Monasteries of Alcobaça and Batalha* (1835), a memoir of his travels in Portugal in the 1790s, he presents a fantasy of himself as a flamboyant homosexually identified man engaging in polite society and wielding political influence without taking on the normative manliness of the period.

In addition to his fame as author of *Vathek*, Beckford is also well known as the eccentric builder

B of a gargantuan Gothic folly, Fonthill Abbey, and as the owner of one of the most spectacular art collections in England. *John Tinker*

Bibliography

Alexander, Boyd. *England's Wealthiest Son: A Study of William Beckford.* London: Centaur Press, 1962.

Fothergill, Brian. *Beckford of Fonthill.* London: Faber and Faber, 1979.

See also Architecture; English Literature; Pederasty; Walpole, Horace

Béjart, Maurice (1927–)

Choreographer, director, and dancer Maurice Béjart (Maurice Jean Berger) was born on January 1, 1927, in Marseilles, France. He studied philosophy and, following the example of his father, Eastern religion, adopting the Muslim faith during a trip to Iran. Béjart turned to dance after he finished his studies, achieving his first engagement as a dancer at the opera in Marseilles in 1945. He founded his first dance company (Ballets de l'Étoile) in 1957. In 1959, Béjart choreographed Stravinsky's *Sacre du printemps* in Brussels and founded the Ballet du XXe Siècle (Ballet of the Twentieth Century). He stayed in Brussels with his company until 1987, when he moved to Lausanne, Switzerland, renaming his troupe Béjart Ballet Lausanne. In cooperation with Léopold Sédar Senghor, the president of Senegal, Béjart founded a Mudra school in Dakar, Senegal, which he led from 1972 until 1988. In July 1992 the choreographer reduced his company from fifty-eight dancers to twenty-four and, because of financial cutbacks, renamed it Rudra Béjart Lausanne. Béjart also founded Rudra École-Atelier, a multidisciplinary ballet school in Lausanne.

Each year since 1954, Béjart has created several pieces, mostly evening-length works, many of which are autobiographically motivated. Béjart returns repeatedly to certain themes, literary figures, and historical figures in his work. Love, death, and redemption; Faust, Don Juan, and Sebastian; and Mahler, Offenbach, Rimbaud, and Malraux are fixed points in Béjart's oeuvre. He re-creates with his work what he calls *spectacle total*—offering a variation on Wagner's *Gesamtkunstwerk*. Béjart is well known not only for his impressive group choreographies, but also for his exceptional creations for male solo dancers. *Jens Richard Giersdorf*

Bibliography

Assman, Claudia. "Forschungslabor der Tänzerausbildung." *Ballet International/tanz Aktuell* (April 1996): 50–51.

Christout, Marie Françoise. *Maurice Béjart.* Paris: Seghers, 1972.

Stengele, Roger. *Who's Béjart.* Brussels: J. Verbeeck, 1972.

See also Dance: Concert Dance in America

Beloved

The "beloved" forms a central literary concept, highly developed during the medieval Islamic period and still popular in our own times, in the urbanized societies of the Middle East and Central Asia. Encountered throughout the literatures of Persian, Ottoman, and Chaghatay (Uzbek) Turkish, Urdu, and Arabic, among others, this concept manifests itself through highly charged, homoeroticized images and metaphors. The beloved is characterized through such highly eroticized and theatrical tropes of wanton allurement as disheveled locks, torn garments, intoxication symbolized by a wine cup in hand, and appearing at the bedside of the feverish lover. (See, for example, the poems of Hafez, c.1320–1390.) Generally the beloved does not represent an actual personage (except as an historical youth such as Ayyaz, the paramour of Sultan Mahmoud of Ghazna, a symbol of idealized love in Persian literature), but rather an idealized handsome youth inspired by the presence of thousands of Turkish slaves who served as cupbearers (*saqi*) and pages in royal courts and informal, all-male social gatherings as well as in Mamluk (slave) armies throughout the Middle East. These youth are depicted in the miniature paintings of the period that pictorially embody the literary images found in the poetry they illustrate.

Ambiguity regarding the actual gender of the beloved remains obscured by at least three factors. First, the Persian and Turkish languages are grammatically ungendered; the pronouns for "he" and "she" are the same. The attributes referring to the beloved such as "moon-faced" (*mahchehreh*), "disheveled locks" (*zolf-e-parishan*), "graceful cypress" (*sarv-e naz*), and "bow-shaped eyebrows" (*abru-kamari*) that suffuse this vast literature may be applied either to a youthful male or female. Second, beginning at the end of the eighteenth, and particularly toward the end of the nineteenth, century, a large body of this classical Middle Eastern literature was translated by individuals such as A. J. Arberry and Gertrude Bell, who, either from societal pressure or personal impulse, translated this poetry in terms of females as the beloved, a practice continued by many natives of the area in modern times because of their awareness of the homophobic attitudes found in the West. Only recently have important scholars such as Schimmel, Southgate, and Hillmann seriously questioned such translations, and the attitudes they represent, providing sorely needed scholarly corrective measures to counteract decades of deliberate obfuscation in translations reflective of historic anachronistic homophobic attitudes. Third, Sufism (Islamic mysticism) constitutes another type of ambiguity. In Sufi poetry, God is represented as a fabulously beautiful, unattainable youth (*shahid,* witness): the Ultimate Beloved. Sufi poetry such as that by Jallal-ad-Din Rumi (1207–1273) extols the quest of union with the Beloved and the utter annihilation that ensues for the seeker. A major issue in literary scholarship is discerning the degree of Sufi elements in poems by famous classical poets such as Sa'di (c.1215–c.1290) and Hafez. The issue of ambiguity in the representation of the beloved focuses on the question: to what degree did these poets celebrate the earthly and the heavenly that constitutes a major area of analysis of classical literatures of the Middle East. Always foregrounded in this poetry is the concept of the beloved, that beautiful, unattainable, provocative youth. *Anthony Shay*

Bibliography

Arberry, A. J. *Classical Persian Literature.* London: George Allen and Unwin, 1958.
———. *Fifty Poems of Hafiz.* Richmond and Surrey, U.K.: Curzon Press, 1993 (1947).
Hillmann, Michael C. "Persian Classicism, Aesthetics of Decoration, and Ambivalence." In *Iranian Culture: A Persianist View.* Lanham, Md.: University Press of America, 1990, 65–90.
Murray, Stephen O. "Medieval Persian and Turkish Tropes." In *Islamic Homosexualities: Culture, History, and Literature.* Stephen O. Murray and Will Roscoe, eds. New York: New York University Press, 1997, 132–41.
Schimmel, Annemarie. *As Through a Veil: Mystical Poetry in Islam.* New York: Columbia University Press, 1982.
Southgate, Minoo S. "Men, Women, and Boys: Love and Sex in the Works of Sa'di." *Iranian Studies* (17) 1984: 413–52.
Surieu, Robert. *Sarv-e Naz: An Essay on Love and the Representation of Erotic Themes in Ancient Iran.* Geneva: Nagel, 1967.
Wafer, Jim. "Vision and Passion: The Symbolism of Male Love in Islamic Mystical Literature." In *Islamic Homosexualities: Culture, History, and Literature.* Stephen O. Murray and Will Roscoe, eds. New York: New York University Press, 1997, 107–31.

See also Abû Nuwâs; Androgyny; Arabic Literature; Islam; Mujûn; Nuzhat Al-Albaab; Persian (Iranian) Literature and Culture

Benjamin, Arthur (1893–1960)

The Australian-English composer Arthur Benjamin possessed an adventurous and generous spirit that enabled him to assimilate influences as disparate as Brahms, Gershwin, and Jamaican popular music. Benjamin's love of popular culture, while admirable and foresighted, did his career considerable harm during his lifetime and has muted his posthumous reputation. He was further damaged by courageously rejecting modernist fashions and by composing a piece of genuine popular music, the *Jamaican Rhumba* (1938). His ambitions as an opera composer were thwarted in part by the operatic successes of his erstwhile piano student Benjamin Britten, but Vaughan Williams had warm praise for Benjamin's grand opera, *A Tale of Two Cities* (1950).

Benjamin began his career as a pianist at six; at eighteen he was a composition pupil of Stanford's at the Royal College of Music in London. He served in World War I, first in the Royal Fusiliers and later in the Royal Air Force. After a brief stint teaching in his native Australia, Benjamin left for England in 1925, teaching piano at the Royal College of Music. In 1938, Benjamin accepted a post as conductor of the C.B.R. Symphony Orchestra in Vancouver, Canada. He returned to England in 1945, living in London with his partner, Jack Henderson, and concentrating on his compositions. In addition to his musical gifts, Benjamin was a lovable and flirtatious man who once listed his hobbies as cooking, bridge, and sunbathing. *Byron Adams*

Bibliography

Arundell, Dennis. "Benjamin's Operas." *Tempo* 15 (1950–1951): 15–21.
Howells, Herbert. "Obituary." *Tempo* 55 (1960–1961):2.

Keller Hans. "Arthur Benjamin and the Problem of Popularity." *Tempo* 15 (1950–1951): 4–15.

See also Australia; Britten, Benjamin

Bennett, Michael (1943–1987)

Michael Bennett (born Michael Bennett DiFiglia in Buffalo, New York) is best known for his work as the creator of the musical *A Chorus Line*, which ran from 1975 to 1990 on Broadway and won the New York Drama Critic's Circle Award, the Tony Award, and the Pulitzer Prize. This hugely successful show grew out of workshops funded by Joseph Papp's New York Shakespeare Festival and made innovations in the genre of musical theater. Bennett worked consistently to expand the roles of Broadway dancers, and he choreographed movement that required acting skill and emphasized the individuality of performers, especially chorus members. *A Chorus Line* is a backstage story dealing with the lives of dancers and allowing each the individuality and characterization that Bennett sought in his choreography throughout his career. Particularly notable in *A Chorus Line* is the gay character Paul, whose monologue about being seen by his parents while performing in a gay drag revue was the cause of some controversy and homophobic protest when the show toured outside New York.

Bennett left high school in 1960 to join the European tour of *West Side Story* as Baby John and to dance with choreographer Jerome Robbins, who became one of his major artistic influences. On that tour, Bennett also met Robert Avian, his lifelong collaborator, friend, and lover. His early Broadway career was encouraged by Bob Fosse, and his talent for fixing troubled shows earned him a reputation as a "show doctor." Before *A Chorus Line,* he choreographed *Promises, Promises* (1968), *Company* (1970), and *Follies* (1971), and after *A Chorus Line,* he choreographed *Ballroom* (1979) and *Dreamgirls* (1981). Michael Bennett died of AIDS in 1987.

Rebecca Rugg

Bibliography

Flinn, Denny Martin. *What They Did for Love: The Untold Story Behind the Making of* A Chorus Line. New York: Bantam, 1989.

Mandelbaum, Ken. A Chorus Line *and the Musicals of Michael Bennett*. New York: St. Martin's Press, 1989.

See also Dance: Concert Dance in America; Dance and AIDS Musical Theater

Benson, E. F. (1867–1940)

Writer Edward Frederick Benson was a typical product of Victorian public education, which encouraged intimate friendships and strong feelings between young men but condemned any physical expression of those feelings. His upper-middle-class upbringing made him intensely reticent about sexuality. He never married and throughout his life enjoyed intimate friendships with men but always professed that the sexual aspect of such relations repelled him. Benson certainly cultivated homoerotic romantic feelings and physical admiration for male beauty, but there is no reliable evidence of his sexual encounters with men. However, Benson was well acquainted with late Victorian and Edwardian homosexual circles. While still in Cambridge, he struck up a friendship with Oscar Wilde and Lord Alfred Douglas, and in 1894, while studying archaeology in Greece, he explored Egypt with Douglas and Reggie Turner. In later years, he was a frequent visitor to Capri, one of the homosexual meccas of the period. Benson's contacts with homosexual subculture became more intermittent after 1919, when he took permanent residence in Rye, Sussex, where he was elected mayor three times between 1934 and 1937 and where he died in 1940.

Benson was a fast and prolific writer. He published over 100 books, including biographies, memoirs, and works on sports and politics, but most of his writings were fiction, ranging from sentimental romances, to ghost stories, to public school and university novels to comedies of manners. While reviewers occasionally slighted his novels as trivial and cliché-ridden, the general readership loved them, and Benson quickly became a best-selling author. Particularly popular were his social comedies, especially the six "Lucia Novels," in which he satirized, unrelentingly but affectionately, the intellectual pretensions, egotism, and snobbery of high society. The over-the-top, camp quality of these novels earned them a cult following among gay readers.

Homoeroticism is mostly absent from Benson's society novels, except for the frequent appearance of effete male characters, but his public school and university novels, in particular *David Blaize* (1916), *David of King's* (1924), and *The Inheritors* (1930), radiate with ubiquitous yet suppressed homoeroticism. Sexual urge is represented in these novels, however, as a "bestial" temptation that must be resisted if the friendship between men is to survive. Homoerotic feeling is also strong in *Raven's Brood* (1934), a remarkable novel in Benson's opus both for choosing its heroes among farm workers and for its heavy atmosphere of barely controlled sexuality. It also contains the only one among Benson's numerous characters who comes close to being openly homosexual. Benson also wrote a biography of Socrates' beautiful, young companion Alcibiades, whose predilection for "unnatural vice" he could hardly deny. He insisted, however, that Socratic love, ennobled by Plato's idealist renunciation of the body, led to "noble friendships untainted by physical indulgence." Benson subscribed to standard Victorian sanitization of Greek homoeroticism as asexual, either because he feared homophobic bigotry or because he truly believed in the necessity of physical denial in preserving the pure ideal value of male friendships.   *Dejan Kuzmanovic*

Bibliography

Masters, Brian. *The Life of E. F. Benson*. London: Chatto & Windus, 1991.

Palmer, Geoffrey, and Noel Lloyd. *E. F. Benson: As He Was*. Luton, U.K.: Lennard, 1988.

See also Effeminacy; English Literature; Greece; Plato; Wilde, Oscar

Bentham, Jeremy (1748–1832)

Jeremy Bentham is perhaps best known for his perverse wish to have his body preserved as a lasting "auto-icon" after his death; his latter-day followers still gather around his remains housed in a glass box in University College London. His major contributions to English liberal political thought and philosophy, however, secure his place in intellectual history. Bentham was a philosopher who carefully analyzed English legal history and proposed a wide-scale reform of England's legal system based on an ethics of utilitarianism: the maximizing of pleasure and diminishing of pain. Rather than rely on the ideas of a natural state of human nature in which an original contract determined proper human behavior, Bentham argued that one should measure the possible harmful effects that individual actions might have on society. He determined that in the absence of harm to others, the state should not legislate individual and social behavior. Ensuring the greatest amount of happiness for the majority

of a citizenry was the only legitimate role of the state.

Although Bentham never published a full study of sodomy, his works were profoundly shaped by his struggles to understand England's long tradition of prosecuting sodomites. Louis Crompton has observed that in Bentham's several hundred pages of notes addressing sodomy and its condemnation in England, Bentham "made himself the spokesman of a silent and invisible minority" (Byron, 26). In Bentham's analysis, same-sex desire and activity constituted no social harm, and thus the horrific punishments of social ostracism, the pillory, and the gallows were wholly unjustified responses to sodomitical behavior.

Such arguments amount to a unique and unprecedented critique of homophobia at a time when the very notion of homophobia, as described in the critical work of Crompton and Eve Kosofsky Sedgwick, was only just emerging. Bentham characterized violent reactions against sodomy as "blind hatred." Bentham's position against irrational hatred was elaborated in his criticisms of the lexicon that was then used to discuss same-sex desire. "It is by the power of names, of signs originally arbitrary and insignificant," Bentham wrote in 1814, "that the course of the imagination has in great measure been guided" (quoted in Crompton, Byron, 9).

Perhaps Bentham's most innovative contribution to a critique of homophobia was his discussion of same-sex desire as a matter of taste. While to contemporary ears such a discussion might seem to trivialize the history of homosexual desire and its suppression, in Bentham's day taste was a highly charged and contested notion that encapsulated more than the development of refined sensibilities. Taste was very much at the heart of political and aesthetic debates, so that to address sexual desire as entwined in the dynamics of taste was to situate homoerotics within a larger sociopolitical context. "To destroy a man there should certainly be some better reason than mere dislike of his Taste, let that be ever so strong," surmised Bentham, suggesting that men had rights to different tastes at a time when conformity to cultural standards were mandated by English nationalism.

If Bentham's early versions of gay liberation never gained the kind of strength necessary to decriminalize sodomy in England during his own era, certainly his utilitarian philosophies were instrumental in liberalizing English law and politics. Michel Foucault's anti-humanist writings about social regulation and control are also indebted to Bentham's discussion of the Russian panopticon, a kind of peniten-

B tiary that ensured the absolute surveillance of the imprisoned. Foucault's elaboration on the social ramifications of the panopticon in his 1975 study *Discipline and Punish* later informed his discussions of the ways in which institutions and discourse were mobilized to construct and control a variety of sexual identities and perversions that emerged in the late eighteenth century.   *John Beynon*

Bibliography

Crompton, Louis. "Jeremy Bentham's Essay on 'Paederasty': An Introduction." *Journal of Homosexuality* 3 (1978): 384–85.
————. *Byron and Greek Love: Homophobia in 19th-Century England.* Berkeley: University of California Press, 1985.
Foucault, Michel. *Discipline and Punish: The Birth of the Prison.* Trans. Alan Sheridan. New York: Pantheon, 1978.

See also Foucault, Michel; Homophobia; Sodomy; Sodomy Trials

Berdache

In numerous historic Native American cultures cross-dressing and breaching of gender norms was celebrated. The berdaches were not aberrant personalities but considered integral, productive, and revered members of their communities. In some instances they were looked on as shamans or deities. Many participated in same-sex relationships sexually and emotionally. Male and female berdaches have been documented in over 130 tribes from every region of the United States.

Early French explorers referred to these tribal members as *bardache*, while the Spanish called them *bardaxa* or *bardaja*, which later became the term *berdache*. The word, which had its earliest origins in the Persian language as *bardag*, signified a boy or adolescent kept by a man as a male catamite or slave. After the term was imported into European Romance languages in the sixteenth century, it denoted a male engaged as a passive partner in anal sex. The European concept of the berdache was primarily oriented toward homosexuality or sodomy. The essential focus of the berdache phenomenon in Native American society was of the androgynous male in gender roles. Many tribes accepted sexual diversity within the community and assimilated more than two gender options. The belief held in common among tribes was that all persons were made that way by design of the spirits. Their philosophy maintained that certain individuals were cast into alternative gender roles different from those of men and women. The social identity of the berdache was created by the guiding spirit taking precedence over the biological sex of the person. Often it was believed that the spirit gods or goddesses would appear to such people in their dreams, requesting that they take up the cloak of the berdache. Such persons were often believed to be divine entities given up by the spirit world.

Berdaches were highly respected and considered especially gifted within the tribal unit. Many communities honored them with sacred rituals, gave them special ceremonial roles in religious rituals, and knew them as shamans or healers. Because they could observe the world through both feminine and masculine perspectives, the berdaches were recognized as prophets or seers. Owing to their multidimensional gender roles, the berdaches were acknowledged as creative people who worked diligently to assist tribe and family. The berdache personality went beyond "sexual preference" or "orientation," incorporating a vast army of skills, attitudes, and behaviors. The European colonists, including the Spanish in Latin America and the English in North America, repudiated the traditions of gender crossing and annihilated the berdache traditions. The customs and beliefs of the berdache had to go underground and often disappeared in many tribal cultures. During the last twenty years, a number of gay Native American groups have tried to revive the traditions of the berdache.

While discussion of the berdache has frequently been limited to Native American populations, a similar role has also been observed in other regions around the world. The tradition of alternative gender roles with a homosexual component has been observed in cultures in East and Southeast Asia, Polynesia, Siberia, Africa, and the Middle East.   *Michael A. Lutes*

Bibliography

Brown, Lester, ed. *Two Spirit People: American Indian Lesbian Women and Gay Men.* New York: Haworth Press, 1997.
Lang, Sabine. *Men as Women, Women as Men: Changing Gender in Native American Culture.* Austin: University of Texas Press, 1998.
Roscoe, Will. *Changing Ones: Third and Fourth Genders in Native North America.* New York: St. Martin's Press, 1998.

———, ed. *Living the Spirit: A Gay American Indian Anthology*. New York: St. Martin's Press, 1989.

———. *Zuni Man-Woman*. Albuquerque, N.M.: University of New Mexico Press, 1991.

Whitehead, Harriet. "The Bow and the Burden Strap: A New Look at Institutionalized Homosexuality in Native North America." In *The Lesbian and Gay Studies Reader*. Henry Abelove, Michèle Aina Barale, and David M. Halperin, eds. New York: Routledge, 1993, 498–527.

Williams, Walter. *The Spirit and the Flesh: Diversity in American Indian Cultures*. Boston: Beacon Press, 1986.

See also American Indian/Alaska Native Gender Identity and Sexuality; Anthropology; Hijras of India; Third Sex; Transgender

Berlin

The Berlin of the 1920s is still one of the historical markers of gay liberation. But the emancipated Berlin that Christopher Isherwood so famously described in his *Berlin Stories* was framed by less liberated periods for gay people. It was not before the turn of the eighteenth century that the death penalty for homosexual activities was changed to imprisonment, physical punishment, and exile. In 1871, this punishment achieved legal force for the entire German nation with the installation of paragraph 175. Although punishment for gay sex was carried out by the German state long before paragraph 175, this law marks the beginning of 124 years of legal discrimination against gay men. In its wording, paragraph 175 defined any sexual activities between men as well as between men and animals as perverse sexual offenses and provided for imprisonment of six months up to four years and the loss of citizenship.

Physicist and scholar of sexual science Magnus Hirschfeld (1868–1935) was one of the first who fought for an alteration of paragraph 175. In 1897 he founded the Wissenshaftliche-humanitäres Komitee (WhK, Scientific-Humanitarian Committee) in Berlin. In addition to contemporary theories on homosexuality, the WhK published in its *Jahrbuch für sexuelle Zwischenstufen* (Annual Journal for Intermediate Stages) one of the first debates with the developing field of psychoanalysis. Also in 1897 in Berlin, Adolf Brand (1874–1945) published the first issue of *Der Eigene* as an anarchistic literary journal. The journal changed its focus in September 1898 to become the first gay journal in the world by publishing on an irregular basis essays, nude male photography and prints. *Der Eigene* became a part of the extensive gay movement in Berlin after World War I.

In 1919, the first gay German silent movie, *Anders als die Anderen* (Different from Others), was shown in Berlin's Apollo Theater. The establishment of numerous *Freundschaftsbünde* (federation of friends) in Berlin became a model for a mass movement in Germany after the war. Elaborate balls were held and lively bars for gay men, lesbians, and transvestites flourished. Over a hundred gay bars and restaurants could be counted by 1933 in Berlin. Homosexuality was chic and avant-garde. In 1924 the UfA Studios near Berlin produced *Wege zu Kraft und Schönheit* (Ways to Strength and Beauty), a film by the gay director Nikolas Kaufmann, which illustrated the nudist culture and the emerging German *Ausdruckstanz* (modern dance scene).

The most vivid sign of the end of this liberal period for gay men and lesbians was the plunder and destruction of Hirschfeld's Institute for Sexual Science by the Nazis on May 6, 1933, right after Adolf Hitler became chancellor of Germany. The already ongoing persecution of homosexual men and women reached a peak after Hitler ordered a purge of the SA (the Nazi paramilitary organization) on June 30, 1934. Ernst Röhm, the openly homosexual leader of the SA, was arrested and executed along with other top SA leaders, many of whom were homosexual. Although the purge of the SA was political and designed to eliminate a potential threat to Hitler, the SA leaders' "perversion" was touted as one excuse for the executions. Two years after Röhm's execution, a law was passed that legalized the imprisonment of homosexuals without trial. In 1936 the Nazis created a department (*Reichszentrale zur Bekämpfung der Homosexualität und Abtreibung*) in Berlin that was specifically organized for the elimination of homosexuals. Only very few gay men could remain in their positions, such as director and choreographer Hanns Niedecken-Gebhard, who was responsible for the opening show of the Berlin Olympics in 1936. All other gay men were deported and often murdered in concentration camps if they could not escape into exile.

The destruction of the Nazi system after World War II allowed a short renaissance of Berlin's prewar gay life. The first gay bar opened in war-torn Berlin in the summer of 1945. The first drag ball took place in the fall of 1945 in the American sector.

B The Federal Republic of Germany reinstated the Nazi version of paragraph 175 in West Germany and in West Berlin and kept it until 1969, when paragraph 175 was changed to punish only adults who engage in same-sex activities with minors under the age of twenty-one. On the other side of the Wall, the German Democratic Republic adopted the original 1871 version of paragraph 175 until 1968, when it substituted a law that punished only same-sex sexual activity with minors under the age of eighteen. This new law was finally deleted from East German law books in 1989.

As a result of the contrasting laws in divided Berlin, the gay movement developed in different ways in the western and eastern sectors. Gay life in West Berlin was marked by the open fight against the antigay laws. The controversy around Rosa von Praunheim's movie *Nicht der Homosexuelle ist pervers, sondern die Situation in der er lebt* (The Homosexual Isn't Perverse, but the Situation in Which He Lives) initiated the founding of Homosexuelle Aktion Westberlin (HAW) at Berlin's cinema Arsenal in August 1971. Praunheim and Volker Eschke became the key figures in an attempt to form a gay movement mirroring the North American liberation movement. The annual gay pride parade in Berlin is still called Christopher Street Day Demonstration.

In contrast to the U.S. movement, however, the West German gay movement defined itself as considerably more left-wing in its political agenda and included in its program a vehement critique of capitalism. All members of HAW were required to be a member of other political organizations or parties to avoid constituting a gay ghetto. HAW included not only gay men but also lesbians in the fight against government regulations. Yet as in many other cities, this union did not last very long, and the lesbians eventually split from the male-dominated movement. Continuous controversies over political agendas weakened and scattered many gay organizations, so that by the mid-1980s the political work of those organizations focused on community work and the fight against paragraph 175. Nonetheless, the gay movement was still strong enough to influence the depiction of the AIDS crisis in West German media and other public domains in a positive way. This treatment of AIDS on West German TV could be followed on the other side of the wall in East Berlin. However, owing to the secluded situation of East Berlin, AIDS never became a similar issue there.

For gays and lesbians in East Berlin, the difficulty of becoming visible in a doctrinaire state that focused entirely on the heterosexual family as the breeding cell of socialism remained the main focus. Similar to the developments in West Berlin, the screening of Praunheim's film on West German television in 1973 initiated the founding of the Homosexuelleninitiative Berlin (HIB) in East Berlin, the first organization of gays and lesbians in the socialist countries. All meetings had to be disguised as private parties or excursions to avoid punishment by the state. When the East German government detected these activities, the HIB moved its meetings to Charlotte von Mahlsdorf's private museum on the edge of East Berlin. But their 1978 meetings were also prohibited there, and East Berlin's gay movement had to continue its work inside (and under the protection of) the Protestant church.

During the 1980s, the East German government changed its attitude toward homosexuality. As a result, the Berlin-based organization Schwule in der Kirche (Gays in the church) began publishing the first gay newspaper in East Germany in 1986. State-sponsored gay meetings were held at cafés and restaurants. Books and articles about gay experiences could be published. On November 9, 1989, the night the Berlin Wall came down, Heiner Carow's movie *Coming Out*, the first East German feature about a gay man, premiered in Berlin. Finally, in 1994 any remaining antigay laws were stricken from German law books. After a forty-year division, the gay movement in reunited Berlin had to refocus its political agenda. The gay scene still has to overcome difference in the politics of desire in the former western and eastern parts of Berlin.

Jens Richard Giersdorf

Bibliography

Grau, Günter, ed. *Hidden Holocaust?: Gays and Lesbian Persecution in Germany 1933–45*. Chicago: Fitzroy Dearborn, 1995.

Persky, Stan. *Then We Take Berlin*. Woodstock, N.Y.: Overlook Press, 1996.

Plant, Richard. *The Pink Triangle: The Nazi War Against Homosexuals*. New York: Henry Holt, 1986.

Schulze, Micha. *Schwule Hauptstadt*. Berlin: Elephanten Press, 1992.

Soukup, Jean Jacques, ed. *Die DDR. Die Schwulen. Der Aufbruch. Versuch einer Bestandsaufnehme*. Gleichen-Reinhausen, Germany: Waldschlößchen, 1990.

Starke, Kurt. *Schwuler Osten. Homosexuelle Männer in der DDR*. Berlin: Ch. Links Verlag, 1994.

Steakey, James D. *The Homosexual Emancipation Movement in Germany.* New York: Arno Press, 1975.

Sternweiler, Andreas, and Hans Gerhard Hannesen, eds. *Goodbye to Berlin: 100 Jahre Schwulenbewegung.* Berlin: Verlag Rosa Winkel, 1997.

Stümke, Hans-Georg. *Homosexuelle in Deutschland: Eine politische Geschichte.* München: Verlag C. H. Beck, 1989.

Stümke, Hans-Georg, and Rudi Finkler. *Rosa Winkel, Rosa Listen. Homosexuelle and 'Gesundes Volksempfinden' von Auschwitz bis heute.* Reinbeck: Rowohlt, 1981.

See also AIDS; Brand, Adolph; Germany; Hirschfeld, Magnus; Isherwood, Christopher; Mahlsdorf, Charlotte von; Nazism and the Holocaust; Paragraph 175

Berners, Gerald Tyrwhitt-Wilson, Baron (1883–1950)

The English composer Sir Gerald Hugh Tyrwhitt-Wilson, later the fourteenth baron Berners of the English peerage, was surely one of the most unusual in the annals of twentieth-century English music. Unabashedly eccentric, Berners was a country gentleman who had the pigeons on his estate dyed different colors; but at the same time, he was a skilled composer of songs, film music, and music for ballets. In addition to his activities as a composer, Berners nurtured ambitions as a painter and a novelist. Berners's gentle landscapes were heavily influenced by Corot and the impressionists; his novels, such as *Count Omega* (1941) and the privately printed and suggestively titled *The Girls of Radcliffe Hall* (1937) are elegantly written and quietly, subversively, queer. His homosexuality was subsumed under the antic mask of his eccentricities, his title, and his wealth, all of which gave him the freedom to compose and live as he chose.

Berners's music aims for charm and often hits the mark; the expert elegance of his ballet scores elicited praise from Stravinsky, who doubtless detected traces of his beloved Tchaikovsky in Berners's music. Berners's first ballet, *The Triumph of Neptune,* was a great success upon its production in 1926 by Diaghilev's Ballets Russes. Sacheverell Sitwell's scenario concerns the adventures of a plucky sailor, Tom Tug, who travels to Fairyland through the agency of a transparently phallic magic telescope. Sitwell's scenario was a paean to the lively sailors of the British Navy, a subject that understandably inspired some of Berners's finest music. Several ballets for Frederick Ashton followed upon this early triumph, but none came up to the high standard set by *The Triumph of Neptune.* Despite signal achievement as a film composer in the 1940s, including a beautiful score for *Nicholas Nickleby* (1946), Berners was depressed by the gritty postwar world and ended his days alone and in silence.   *Byron Adams*

Bibliography

Berners, Gerald Hugh Tyrwhitt-Wilson, Baron. *First Childhood* and *Far from the Maddening War.* Oxford: Oxford University Press, 1983.

Lambert, Constant. *Music Ho!: A Study of Music in Decline.* London: Faber and Faber, 1934.

See also Ballet (British); Ballets Russes; England

Bernstein, Leonard (1918–1990)

"I'm gayish in the way that I'm Jewish," said Leonard Bernstein, provocatively, late in life. Though married for many years to the actress Felicia Montaleagre, the New York Philharmonic conductor and prolific composer of American theater scores (among them *West Side Story, On the Town, Wonderful Town, Candide, Mass*) and orchestral works (three symphonies and several ballets among others) nevertheless had numerous sexual relationships with men throughout his life.

After first bursting onto the national music scene in November 1944, when, at age twenty-six he stepped in at the last moment for an ailing Bruno Walter and conducted a brilliant—and widely publicized—performance of the New York Philharmonic, the conductor remained more or less constantly in the public eye throughout his lifetime. With his varied and wide-ranging output of compositions, concert work, conducting, television shows, books, and political causes, he achieved a stature in the world of serious music unique for an American.

Despite his professional successes, Bernstein's personal life remained conflicted, and in the fall of 1976 he and his wife separated because of an ongoing romantic liaison the conductor was then having with Thomas Cothran, a young man he had met five years previously in San Francisco, and who later died of AIDS.

While living with Cothran for a short time in a New York hotel, Bernstein composed a touching and little-known gay love song that he inserted in his "An American Songfest," written for the American Bicentennial. Entitled "To What You Said" and based on an obscure (and then only recently discovered) poem by Walt Whitman, the piece includes the line: "I kiss my comrade lightly on the lips at parting, and I am one who is kissed in return," then goes on to say: "I introduce the new American salute / Behold love choked, correct, polite, always suspicious: / Behold the received models of the parlor. / What are they to me? / what, to these young men that travel with me?"

"The received models of the parlor" continued to mean a lot to the conductor, however, and despite the post-Stonewall Zeitgeist of increasing openness about homosexuality, Bernstein never quite managed to come out of the closet. Even the Whitman song is curiously "love choked." The ravishing melody on which it is built is heard only in the orchestra and in a humming chorus of soloists; the baritone soloist never really does more than declaim Whitman's stirring text. Bernstein's declaration of a "new American salute"—open love among men—is even here in a very real way muted.

At the end of 1976, Bernstein returned to his wife and shortly thereafter she was diagnosed with cancer, from which she died in 1978. Overcome with guilt, the composer told friends that he had tortured his wife to death by running off with a man.

In 1983, Bernstein collaborated with librettist Stephen Wadsworth on an opera called *A Quiet Place*. One of the characters is a troubled bisexual named Junior; many at the time of the opera's premiere (and since) have drawn a comparison with the composer.

Despite Bernstein's enormous conflict over his sexuality—always a source of confusion for him (as well as a topic of conversation among those who knew him and of speculation among those who didn't)—in the end it probably mattered little to the millions of appreciative music lovers touched by his genius.

A story going around New York shortly before Bernstein died told of two blue-haired, Jewish ladies at a Friday afternoon New York Philharmonic matinee speaking of the conductor:

"I hear he sleeps with men," one of them allegedly whispered to the other.

"Incredible!" responded her friend. "Is there anything that man can't do?"   *Mark Steinbrink*

Bibliography

Burton, Humphrey. *Leonard Bernstein*. New York: Doubleday, 1994.

See also Music and Musicians 1 (Classical Music)

Bible

The Judeo-Christian Bible speaks neither of homosexuals nor of homosexuality, if one understands these terms to pertain to an exclusive attachment, often sexual in expression, to members of one's own gender. Indeed, no reliable English-language translation of the Bible uses either word. Concerned, rather, with cultic purity, passages like Leviticus 18:22 and 20:13 denounce the religious practices of the Canaanites, who inhabited the land that the ancient Israelites claimed had been promised to them by Yahweh, and who employed male prostitutes and worshiped phallic stocks and stones in an attempt to ensure the fertility of the land. Similarly, Paul's imprecations in Romans 1:27 and 1 Corinthians 6:9–10 are directed against local practices to which Jewish Christians in Rome and Corinth were in danger of succumbing. Only in the European Middle Ages, after the threat of rival religions had faded while the decontextualized written strictures remained, were the latter interpreted as denouncing outright any instance of male same-sex activity.

Indeed, ancient Judaism proves to have been strongly phallocentric. Circumcision is, according to Abraham's covenant with Yahweh, the sign that one has been chosen by God (Genesis 17:8–11). Boaz's cupping his kinsman "under the thigh" appears to be a euphemism for grabbing hold of the other man's genitals, the ancient equivalent of sealing a bargain with a handshake (Ruth 4:7–18). Looking upon his father's genitals, however, ensures that the descendants of Noah's son Ham will be displaced by the Israelites (Genesis 9:21–27). Elsewhere enforced circumcision proves an aggressive ploy: in Genesis 34, two of Jacob's sons lure Schechem and other friendly natives into voluntarily undergoing the rite only to massacre them as they are recovering from the surgery, while David is charged by King Saul with securing one hundred Philistine foreskins if he wants to marry the royal princess (1 Samuel 18:25–27). The Bible expresses no analogous interest in female genitalia.

When freed of modern bias, the Bible proves surprisingly homoerotic. The Hebrew Testament evinces a frank admiration of male beauty. Saul, David, and Absolom are all praised for comeliness, the latter's name indicating in medieval culture a male so conscious of his attractiveness that he is reduced to effeminate vanity (as, for example, Absalon in Chaucer's "Miller's Tale" who is proud of his hair, effeminate in his dress, and "somedeel squamious of farting"). Celebration of the Bridegroom's sexual desirability in The Song of Solomon is voiced by a female character, but the litany of his body parts—surely one of the most erotic portions of biblical canon—was for centuries necessarily read aloud by a male lector.

Most provocative are the narrative episodes that inscribe male same-sex desire and/or love. Genesis 19:1–11 and Judges 19:14–30 record parallel incidents in which locals incur the wrath of God or society by attempting to rape male visitors; the visitors' hosts (in the first instance, Abraham's nephew, Lot), mindful of the ancient code extending hospitality to travelers that leaves a host responsible for his guests' safety, offer the randy crowds their virgin daughters or concubine instead. A modern reader's difficulty with the sexual politics of the Sodom episode is captured in A. E. Housman's witty refusal of A. J. Symons's request to print certain of his lyrics in an anthology of 1890s verse: "To include me in an anthology of the nineties would be just as technically correct, and just as essentially inappropriate, as to include Lot in a book on Sodomites: in saying which I am not saying a word against sodomy, nor implying that intoxication and incest are in any way preferable." Himself the seemingly platonic lover of Shropshire lads and eulogizer of athletes dying young, Housman coyly places himself in the Sodomite camp while underscoring the excesses of presumptively normal heterosexual behavior represented by the biblical story. The Sodom episode has fostered the development of a gay literary tradition—which includes Paul Russell's Boys of Life and Tony Kushner's Angels in America, as well as numerous erotic short stories like Jon Paarl's "Snow Angel"—in which angelic visitation results in sexual epiphany or apocalypse.

Other episodes hint at relationships or practices so common that they do not require elaboration. Joseph may have been purchased by Potiphar for pederastic purposes; the judge Samuel may have been, in youth, a homosexual temple prostitute; and the prophet Daniel may have been involved in a sexual relationship with the master of Nebuchadnezzar's palace. The Roman centurion who asks that Jesus cure his servant seems to speak with a lover's concern in Matthew 8:5–13 and Luke 7:2–10. And the mysterious young man who flees the scene of Jesus' arrest without his loincloth in Mark 14:51–52 seems to have been engaged in a sexual rite that the arrest party interrupted.

But the most prominent instances of male same-sex love are the couples David and Jonathan in the First Book of Samuel, and Jesus and John the "beloved disciple" in the Gospel according to Saint John. Each narrative suggests a fully developed emotional relationship that includes gestures of physical intimacy and extraordinary grief on the part of the surviving partner on the death of his beloved. The similarities in lineage and name—Jesus being a descendant of David, and John being a variant of Jonathan—suggest conscious design on the part of the gospel's author who understood David's relationship with Jonathan to be a crucial part of the ancient warrior-psalmist's identity.

Historically the Bible has been something of a Rorschach test, inviting interpretations that reveal as much about the interpreter as about the text itself. Conservative readers, on the one hand, who fear the suggestiveness of certain biblical texts, have moved to limit their potential for signification; for example, the author(s) of the biblical books of Chronicles and first-century C.E. Jewish historian Flavius Josephus carefully rewrote the David narrative to remove any hint of Israel's great king's amorous relations with the son of his political rival. More liberal readers, on the other hand, have often resorted to drastic methods in reclaiming the Bible from orthodoxy's misinterpretation and censorship. Christopher Marlowe is supposed to have asserted that "all they that love not Tobacco and Boies were fooles" and that "St John the Evangelist was bedfellow to Christ and leaned alwaies in his bosome, that he used him as the sinners of Sodoma," using the Bible to offer so provocative a challenge to Elizabethan orthodoxy that he may have been assassinated, in part, for his subversiveness. Likewise the Marquis de Sade's 120 Days at Sodom, the earl of Rochester's Sodom, or the Quintessence of Debauchery, and Gore Vidal's Live from Golgotha exploit well-defined spaces in the Bible for cultural disruption, appropriating biblical motifs to turn the Bible against the upholders of its purported morality.

Raymond-Jean Frontain

Bibliography

Boswell, John. *Christianity, Social Tolerance and Homosexuality: Gay People in Western Europe from the Beginning of the Christian Era to the Fourteenth Century*. Chicago: University of Chicago Press, 1980.

Comstock, Gary David, and Susan E. Hengking, eds. *Que(e)rying Religion: A Critical Anthology*. New York: Continuum, 1997.

Frontain, Raymond-Jean, ed. *Reclaiming the Sacred: The Bible in Lesbian and Gay Culture.* Binghamton, N.Y.: Harrington Park–Haworth Press, 1997.

Helminiak, Daniel A. *What the Bible Really Says About Homosexuality.* San Francisco: Alamo Square Press, 1994.

Horner, Tom. *Jonathan Loved David: Homosexuality in Biblical Times.* Philadelphia: Westminster Press, 1978.

Jordan, Mark D. *The Invention of Sodomy in Christian Theology.* Chicago: University of Chicago Press, 1997.

See also Christianity; David and Jonathan; Housman, A. E.; Kushner, Tony; Marlowe, Christopher; Pederasty; Rochester, John Wilmot, Earl of; Sade, Marquis de; Sodom; Vidal, Gore

Bisexuality

Bisexuality, which is generally defined as being sexually and emotionally attracted to women and men, did not begin to be recognized as a distinct identity category by researchers until the turn of the twentieth century. Previously, bisexuality was seen as simply a transitional stage for individuals who would eventually recognize themselves as heterosexual or homosexual, or it was believed that bisexuality did not really exist; that is, anyone who engaged in same-sex relationships was homosexual, regardless of the extent to which he or she might also pursue other-sex relationships. But as sexologists encountered more and more people in the early twentieth century who had been involved with both women and men throughout their lives, it became increasingly difficult to deny the existence of bisexuality. The landmark studies by Alfred Kinsey and his colleagues in the late 1940s and early 1950s, which showed that human sexual behavior was more accurately reflected along a continuum rather than as a hetero/homosexual dichotomy, added further weight to the "naturalness" of bisexuality.

Although a few early-twentieth-century writers and artists such as Bessie Smith, Virginia Woolf, and Richard Bruce Nugent were openly bisexual, most bisexuals did not visibly differentiate themselves from either heterosexuals or lesbians and gay men. Recognizing the potential risks for anyone known to be involved in same-sex sexual relationships, some bisexuals, like some lesbians and gay men, passed as heterosexual; they kept their interest in people of the same sex hidden while foregrounding their attraction to people of the other sex, often through marriage. Given their bisexuality, though, these were more than marriages of convenience, and in some cases, the spouses knew of their partners' attraction to members of the same sex. Other bisexuals joined lesbians and gay men in creating same-sex social networks and group institutions such as bars, private parties, and cruising locations in cities across the United States in the early and mid-twentieth century. By establishing spaces where they could find emotional support, make friends, and meet potential partners, lesbians, gay men, and bisexuals forged cultures that enabled them to develop a positive self-identity and a sense of community belonging.

Behaviorally bisexual women and men also helped establish the Mattachine Society, the Daughters of Bilitis, and other homophile groups in the 1950s and 1960s, but they did not always receive support from the lesbian and gay members of these organizations. For example, when Martha Shelley, the principal organizer of the New York Daughters of Bilitis, was dating a male leader of the Student Homophile League, she remembers that other activists thought "it was a scandal. . . . [B]ut at the same time, because the two of us were so blatant and out there in public being pro gay, they certainly couldn't afford to throw us out." In contrast, bisexuality was not only accepted in the sexual liberation movement of the late 1960s and early 1970s but was often celebrated. Both radical gay-dominant groups like the Gay Liberation Front and organizations that consisted mainly of heterosexually identified "swingers" such as the Sexual Freedom League encouraged sexual fluidity and experimentation, believing that people should be free to love regardless of gender. This kind of supportive space enabled bisexuals to come out and find others like themselves prior to forming their own organizations.

The first specifically bisexual groups in the United States developed in large cities during the early and mid-1970s. The National Bisexual Liberation Group and the Bi Forum began in New York City in 1972 and 1975, respectively; the San Francisco Bisexual Center opened its doors in 1976; and Chicago's BiWays formed in 1978. Other early bisexual organizations were started in Los Angeles, Detroit, and Minneapolis. But except for the Bisexual Center, the first groups were predominantly male, and all had disbanded by the early 1980s, as bisexual men devoted more of their time to AIDS activism.

While male-dominated bisexual organizations were beginning to fold, bisexual women were creating groups to support each other and to counter the hostility they received within many lesbian communities. Most had been active themselves in lesbian groups until being excluded for their involvement with men, as lesbian separatism and a dichotomous view of sexuality became more entrenched in the late 1970s. Yet despite their rejection of an exclusive lesbian politics, they remained committed to feminism, and feminist principles were central to groups like the Boston Bisexual Women's Network, Chicago Action Bi-Women (both formed in 1983), and the Seattle Bisexual Women's Network (1986).

A national bisexual movement began to take shape when a call for a bisexual contingent for the 1987 March on Washington for Lesbian and Gay Rights brought together seventy-five people from around the country and laid the groundwork for the establishment of the North American Bisexual Network. The movement further took shape at the first national bisexual conference, which was held in San Francisco in 1990. The following year, the name was changed to BiNet U.S.A., and, reflecting the influence of feminism, it developed a consensus decision-making process and a leadership structure consisting of six elected national coordinators and numerous regional organizers in different parts of the country. And in direct contrast to the male-dominated groups of the 1970s, the organization has had about equal numbers of women and men in leadership roles. During its first ten years, BiNet has fought biphobia in the dominant society and increased the visibility of bisexuals, with members appearing on television talk shows and being quoted in the mainstream and lesbian and gay press. The organization has also educated national lesbian and gay rights organizations about the importance of using bi-inclusive language and recognizing the involvement of bisexuals in the sexual liberation struggle. One major victory was convincing lesbian and gay organizers to include bisexuals by name in the 1993 March on Washington, the first time that bisexuals have been acknowledged in a national political action. Another important step forward came when the National Lesbian and Gay Task Force rewrote its mission statement to encompass bisexuals and transgendered people explicitly in its work and elected a self-identified bisexual to its board of directors for the first time in 1997. In addition, BiNet is represented at the National Policy Roundtable sponsored by the Task Force.

But perhaps the bisexual movement's most significant progress has been on the local level. In the 1990s, the number of bisexual organizations in the United States had grown tremendously, from several dozen groups established primarily on the coasts to more than three hundred located in every region of the country. As a result, bisexuals have created supportive communities throughout the country, not just in major cities or at traditionally liberal universities. At the same time, the names and charters of many local lesbian and gay organizations, newspapers, and conferences have been changed to include bisexuals, as more bi-identified individuals have come out and, mirroring the national political scene, sought to have their involvement recognized. Many groups formed in the1990s have simply referred to themselves as "queer" to be inclusive of bisexuals and transgendered people and often to challenge heteronormativity.

The 1990s have also witnessed a boom in the number of resources by and for bisexuals, including books such as *Bi Any Other Name: Bisexual People Speak Out, Plural Desires: Writing Bisexual Women's Realities,* and *Bisexuality: The Psychology and Politics of an Invisible Minority;* publications like *Anything That Moves,* the first national bisexual magazine; and regular regional, national, and international conferences. In recent years, bisexuality has similarly received widespread attention in popular culture; in fact, not since the early 1970s, when "bi chic" was the rage in the news media, has bisexuality been the subject of so much attention. Contributing to this coverage has been the visibility of bisexual artists and celebrities such Ani Difranco, Jill Sobule, Tom Robinson, Sophie B. Hawkins, Joan Osborne, Me'Shell Ndege'Ocello, and Sandra Bernhard.

Because of the prominence of bisexuality, people growing up in the 1990s often have a wider range of accepted identity options than previous generations. As a result, many youth today identify as bisexual when they first begin to acknowledge their sexuality, rather than initially coming out as lesbian or gay, as was the case for many bisexuals during the 1970s and 1980s.   *Brett Beemyn*

Bibliography

The Bisexual Anthology Collective, ed. *Plural Desires: Writing Bisexual Women's Realities.* Toronto: Sister Vision: Black Women and Women of Colour Press, 1995.

Firestein, Beth A., ed. *Bisexuality: The Psychology and Politics of an Invisible Minority.* Thousand Oaks, Calif.: Sage, 1996.

B

Garber, Marjorie. *Vice Versa: Bisexuality and the Eroticism of Everyday Life.* New York: Simon and Schuster, 1995.

Tucker, Naomi, ed. *Bisexual Politics: Theories, Queries, and Visions.* New York: Harrington Park Press, 1995.

See also Homosexuality; Kinsey, Alfred; Mattachine Society; Sexology

Black and White Men Together, National Association of

Although often vilified as a collection of self-hating blacks and exoticizing white racists, especially in its earlier days, the organization black and White Men Together has for almost two decades been one of the best-known, most often criticized, and most misunderstood collectives in the contemporary gay world. In its statement of purpose, the association describes itself as "a gay interracial organization committed to fostering supportive environments wherein racial and cultural barriers can be overcome and the goal of human equality realized." If its success at creating these utopian spaces is indeed debatable, the group's popular image bears little relation to its reality. As Mike Smith, the group's founder, said, "We hurt when non-interracialists poke fun at us. And we resent their assigning us their racial hang-ups" (quoted in Bean 70).

Started in San Francisco in 1980 by Smith, a white man, to more systematically facilitate contacts with black men with whom he sought to pursue sexual and social relationships, the organization remains, as Thom Bean writes, "the most identifiable beacon in the gay community for men of all colors who want to experience cross-cultural communication and relationships" (Bean 70). As they have described their goals, "We are committed to fostering respect, honesty, and communication and understanding between and among people of different races and cultural backgrounds" (Bean 70).

To "emphasize the multi-racial inclusivity of their membership," (Bean 70), many of the affiliates have changed their names to reflect this evolution away from the bi-racial impetus of its founder. Now headquartered in Washington, D.C., the National Association of Black and White Men Together (NABWMT) is a collective nationwide network of affiliated and developing chapters in over thirty cities that identify themselves as Black and White Men Together (BWMT), Men of All Colors Together (MACT), or People of All Colors Together (PACT), in keeping with the cultural dynamics of their respective areas. This acronymical diversity highlights NABWMT's goal of fostering discussions and awareness of transracial and transcultural attraction and the issues that pertain to them, rather than BWMT's earlier goal of functioning simply as a minimally politicized social club.

Terry Rowden

Members of BWMT in the 1980s. Photo by Marc Geller.

Bibliography

Bean, Thom. " 'A Matter of Personal Pride': A Conversation About Black and White Men Together." *Outlook* (Summer 1990): 70–71.

http://members.aol.com/nabwmtocc/intron.html (National Association of Black and White Men Together)

See also African American Gay Culture; Community Centers

Black Power Movement

The black power movement was a period of African American activism between the years 1965 and

1975 that evolved from black people's nonviolent struggle, waged during the 1950s, for civil rights and against racial segregation in the South (the civil rights movement). Unlike the civil rights movement, through which activists sought to reform American society, the Black Power Movement was a struggle in which activists fought to radically transform America's social, political, and economic structure. They came to believe that racial justice could not be achieved under the system as it was configured, and that consequently black people needed to wage a new American Revolution that would effect black liberation.

Several factors contributed to the evolution of the black power movement. One was that the young activists involved in the civil rights movement were becoming increasingly frustrated with the recalcitrance of Southern whites as well as with the influence that white liberals exerted over the civil rights movement agenda. Moreover, the activists were beginning to consider inadequate the reform-oriented, integrationist politics of the civil rights movement elite. This agenda, many argued, did not really effect any real changes in the lives of black people. And for the younger activists, nothing spoke more eloquently about the inadequacy of the elite's politics than the increasing number of urban riots that occurred throughout the 1960s—another factor that contributed to the evolution of the black power movement.

While the nonviolent protests forged in the South by the Student Nonviolent Coordinating Committee (SNCC), the Congress of Racial Equality (CORE), and Dr. Martin Luther King Jr.'s Southern Christian Leadership Conference (SCLC) certainly had an impact on the lives of Northern urban blacks and indeed radicalized them, the Southern-based civil rights movement did not, to any significant degree, materially change their lives. As the movement scored a number of victories in terms of voting rights and the desegregation of public facilities, the lives of urban blacks were continuing to deteriorate. High unemployment, crime, substandard housing and public education, police brutality, disease, and high infant mortality greatly diminished the quality of black urban life. Although police brutality was often what sparked urban riots, it would nevertheless become clear that the riots themselves

Mississippi marchers entering Jackson on June 26, 1996. AP/Wide World Photos.

B proved to be protests against the horrible conditions within Northern ghettos.

The civil rights movement also did not fully address the needs of Northern blacks. As a Southern-based movement, it specifically addressed the lives of Southern blacks and the apartheid system under which they lived. But what did speak to Northern blacks' concerns was the fiery rhetoric of Malcolm X, organizer for and minister within the Nation of Islam, which was located primarily in Northern urban centers. Malcolm not only indicted whites for the conditions under which black people lived in both the Northern ghettos and the South, but he also preached to black people his philosophy of black nationalism. Since black people live in and are relegated to the ghetto, he argued, they should own and control the politics and economics of the ghetto. Moreover, as long as whites continued to own and to control black people's housing, businesses, and schools, Malcolm predicted that black people's quality of life would continue to deteriorate and black people themselves would continue to rebel against the conditions under which they lived.

Malcolm's influence over young blacks, especially those active in the civil rights movement, was another factor that contributed to the evolution of the black power movement. His speeches and black nationalist ideology further radicalized young activists looking for ways to make the movement a more broad-based struggle.

The frustrations of the young civil rights activists erupted in 1966 when, after the assassination of NAACP leader James Meridith—who started his own march from Memphis, Tennessee, to Jackson, Mississippi, "as an individual act to assert all blacks' rights to move across the South unmolested"—movement leaders decided to join together to complete Meridith's symbolic journey. But the coming together was fraught with tension, much of which was rooted in the competing political interests and perspectives of the older and younger civil rights activists. During the march, Willie Ricks of SNCC began promoting the slogan "Black Power," much to the chagrin of the older civil rights movement leadership. The march itself resulted in several arrests, and after their release the marchers staged a rally in Greenwood, Mississippi. Here, SNCC leader Stokely Carmichael told supporters, "This is the twenty-seventh time I have been arrested. I ain't going to jail anymore. What we gonna start saying now is 'Black power.' " Ricks immediately took advantage of Carmichael's proclamation and yelled to the audience, "What do we want?" Their response: "Black Power!"

From this moment, the slogan "Black Power" took on a life of its own and became the subject of intense critique and debate throughout American society. Some condemned it as an expression of "racism in reverse," while others embraced it as an expression of black political and economic self-determination. Black power came to be defined in a variety of ways during the 1960s, so that there is no definite meaning of the term nor any one agreed-upon black power ideology. Thus what black power meant depended on who was using the term. (President Richard M. Nixon, for example, would himself appropriate the slogan and define it in terms of black capitalism.) Whatever the case, the slogan became the impetus not only for asking new questions about how blacks could achieve equality within American society but also for thinking beyond the civil rights integrationist agenda. Many young black activists began thinking more in terms of black liberation and the complete overhaul—politically, socially, culturally, and economically—of American society. Black power thus "completed the evolution from integrationist to black nationalist ideologies" that were beginning to be articulated in the early 1960s in reaction to the reform-oriented civil rights movement agenda.

The various pronouncements regarding black power, and the creation of black power organizations and programs, had a profound impact during this time on other political movements. The idea of self-determination and people power resonated, for example, with women's rights, Chicano, and new left activists. It resonated, too, with gays and lesbians, as is clearly illustrated by the "gay power" slogan chanted at the historic Stonewall riots (1969). Until this moment, gays and lesbians had been leading their own quiet struggle for civil rights, primarily through the Mattachine Society and the Daughters of Bilitis. Stonewall catapulted the struggle in a much more radical direction; gay organizations, like the Gay Liberation Front (GLF), formed with the express purpose of achieving "gay power" within American society. As did many black power movement activists, the organizers of the Gay Liberation Front believed that American society needed to be radically transformed. Only by creating a completely different America could gays and lesbians, GLF argued, be truly liberated (GLF often worked in coalition with the Black Panther Party, which at the time was considered the most influential black power organization in the United States). Like the black power slogan, the meaning of "gay power" depended on who was using the term. Its very articulation, nevertheless, speaks to the influence of black power activism on the gay and lesbian struggle.

Political repression, the expansion of the black middle class, the successful election of black politicians, the deterioration of urban centers, and ideological incoherence and battles among black militants are just some of the many factors that contributed to the demise of the Black Power Movement. The "organic center fell apart," writes historian Vincent Harding. By the mid-1970s, new challenges faced black communities that the term and the politics of black power no longer seemed to answer.   *Alycee Jeanette Lane*

Bibliography

Adam, Barry D. *The Rise of a Gay and Lesbian Movement*. Boston: G. K. Hall, 1987, 75–82.

Allen, Robert L. *Black Awakening in Capitalist America*. New York: Doubleday, 1969.

Carson, Clayborne. *In Struggle: SNCC and the Black Awakening of the 1960s*. Cambridge, Mass.: Harvard University Press, 1981.

D'Emilio, John. *Sexual Politics, Sexual Communities: The Making of a Homosexual Minority in the United States, 1940–1970*. Chicago: University of Chicago Press, 1983.

Dreva, Jerry. "Huey Speaks." *The Great Speckled Bird* 3 (October 4, 1970): 4, 7.

Lane, Alycee J. "Newton's Law." *BLK* (March 1991): 11–15.

Marable, Manning. *Race, Reform, and Rebellion*. Jackson, Miss.: University Press of Mississippi, 1991, 86–148.

Van DeBurg, William L. *New Day in Babylon: The Black Power Movement and American Culture, 1965–1975*. Chicago: University of Chicago Press, 1992.

Wittman, Carl. "A Gay Manifesto." *The Great Speckled Bird* 3 (November 23, 1970): 3–4, 18–19.

See also Activism; African American Gay Culture; Civil Rights (U.S. Law); Gay Left; Gay Liberation; Gay Liberation Front; Mattachine Society; Rustin, Bayard; Stonewall

Blitzstein, Marc (1905–1964)

Too often typed as left-wing political propaganda, Marc Blitzstein's musical and dramatic achievements were unjustly ignored in the period immedi-

ately following his death. A revival of interest in the 1980s and 1990s, however, has allowed a reassessment of Blitzstein as a major voice in American theater.

Born into a middle-class Jewish family in Philadelphia, Blitzstein studied at the Curtis Institute with both Nadia Boulanger and Arnold Schoenberg. Unquestionably homosexual, in 1933 he nevertheless married Eva Goldbeck, who encouraged his leftist political sympathies; following her death in 1936 Blitzstein's erotic life was exclusively gay. After an early period of modernist classical composition, Blitzstein repudiated this approach in favor of one that combined the classical with the commercial style of "proletarian" music.

From this point on his compositions, usually theater pieces, reflect his left-wing political convictions both musically and verbally. Blitzstein was a Communist Party member by 1938; the trade-union opera *The Cradle Will Rock* (1937) was the first major product of this affiliation. Its original production, by Orson Welles and John Houseman, is legendary: Federal Theatre Project funding having been withdrawn literally at the last moment (a move widely understood as the government's attempt to censor left-wing material), the producers led the waiting audience on foot to another theater, hired shortly before curtain time, where Blitzstein played through the score on a borrowed piano. The actors, forbidden to appear on stage, performed their roles from the audience.

When the United States entered World War II, Blitzstein joined the Air Force, where his major duty was the composition of the choral *Airborne Symphony* (1946). During the war Blitzstein also entered his only long-term relationship with another man, Bill Hewitt; it lasted until 1948. After the war, Blitzstein became disillusioned with the Communist Party's attempts to dictate the kind of music he should write. He left the party in 1949, and from that point on his theater pieces, while still dealing with social issues and making use of popular musical idioms, became less doctrinaire. The opera *Regina* (1949), for example, based on Lillian Hellman's play *The Little Foxes*, is concerned with the industrialization of the American South but treats this theme by examining a realistically drawn family rather than through the ideological stereotypes of his agitprop works. Also dating from this period is Blitzstein's English translation of Brecht and Weill's *Threepenny Opera* (1954), including the popular songs "Mack the Knife" and "Pirate Jenny."

B

In 1964 Blitzstein took a working vacation in Martinique, where he died of injuries sustained in a gay bashing at the hands of three sailors he had picked up in a waterfront bar.

Although Blitzstein, like most important gay cultural figures of his period, remained publicly closeted, on a personal level he was comfortable with his sexual orientation and honest about it with his friends. Among his early works are settings of several implicitly homoerotic lyrics by Whitman. Blitzstein also explored the possibility of including homosexual characters in his librettos: an early version of the agitational opera *No for an Answer* (1941) includes a sympathetic, explicitly gay man (whose sexuality had to be rendered more ambiguously in the final version), and Blizstein's notes for his musical *Reuben Reuben* (1955) refer to the villain as a repressed homosexual. Indeed, the sympathy with the oppressed that motivates his major theatrical works may be understood as conditioned in part by his own status as homosexual outsider.

Blitzstein's musical works include *A Blitzstein Cabaret: Songs and Scenes from Theater Works of Marc Blitzstein* with Helene Williams, Ronald Edwards, and Leonard Lehrmann (Premier PRCD 1005); *Concerto for Piano and Orchestra* (first movement) with Michael Barrett and the Brooklyn Philharmonic, conducted by Lukas Foss (*Gay American Composers*, vol. 2. CRI CD750); *The Cradle Will Rock* with Patti LuPone, conducted by Michael Barrett (TER CDTEM2 1105); and *Zipperfly and Other Songs* with William Sharp, Karen Holvik, and Stephen Blier (KOCH 3–7050–2 H1).

Robert S. Sturges

Bibliography

Blitzstein, Marc. *The Cradle Will Rock*. New York: Random House, 1938.

Gordon, Eric A. *Mark the Music: The Life and Work of Marc Blitzstein*. New York: St. Martin's Press, 1989.

See also Gay American Composers; McCarthyism; Theater: Premodern and Early Modern; Whitman, Walt; United States

Bloch, Iwan (1872–1922)

A German Jewish psychiatrist, Bloch worked as a dermatologist and sexual scientist in Berlin. His academic career stretched over fields ranging from medical history and cultural history to sex research. Bloch favored a multicausal explanation of homosexuality. He believed the major reason for the widespread occurrence of homosexuality was the seduction of children and teenagers by adults. He also pointed to young homosexuals' unsuccessful sexual encounters with members of the opposite sex as a serious cause. Bloch suggested that gay men develop erogenous zones around the anus over time. In his theory homosexuality was nurtured and not a result of biological causes, as Hirschfeld suggested.

Bloch believed originally that homosexuality was preventable and could be successfuly treated. He published basic rules designed to "prophylax homosexuality," stressing the need to keep youth away from homosexual adults, literature, pictures, and bars. Bloch was a strong supporter of paragraph 175 in German law, which declared homosexual acts among adults illegal under all circumstances. He thought that each living homosexual was a potential source for many more homosexuals.

In 1908 Bloch fundamentally changed most of his views on homosexuality, largely influenced by psychiatric evaluations of highly intelligent and educated professionals, including some of his doctor colleagues. He discriminated subsequently between a "real homosexuality," which was inborn, and a "pseudohomosexuality," which was adapted behavior. Bloch argued at this point that most homosexuals were healthy, suffered from no genetic disorder, and were psychologically and physiologically normal. He wrote that the stress-related problems he diagnosed in many homosexuals were a consequence of social isolation and discrimination, rather than a consequence of their homosexuality. Subsequently Bloch joined forces with other psychiatrists who suggested abolishing paragraph 175. He proposed that famous and well-known closeted public figures come out as homosexuals to counter societal prejudices. *Udo Schüklenk*

Bibliography

Bloch, I. "Die Homosexualität in Köln am Ende des 15 Jahrhunders." *Zeitschrift für Sexualwissenschaft* 1 (1908): 528–35.

Egger, B. *Iwan Bloch und die Konstituierung der Sexualwissenschaft als eigene Disziplin*. Medical dissertation. Düsseldorf, 1987.

See also Paragraph 175; Sexology

Bloomsbury Group

Deriving its name from the London neighborhood surrounding the British Museum, Bloomsbury was a coterie of mainly homosexual or bisexual English writers and artists active in the first half of the twentieth century. Its lasting contributions are in the fields of art and literature: Bloomsbury represents the core of English postimpressionism and modernism.

The specific characteristics of Bloomsbury are notoriously difficult to define. Its descendant Quentin Bell has asserted that it has "the dimensions of a whirlpool" and "the character of a beast that is half chameleon and half hydra." This indefiniteness and fluidity should be seen as one of the group's significant features. Civilized conversation and friendship, which often took on sexual overtones, were the spirits that guided Bloomsbury. Hailing from the middle and upper classes, the Bloomsberries formed a cultural elite in the London of the 1910s and 1920s. They tended to be passionately loyal to each other but could be viciously exclusive when perceived "outsiders" attempted to enter their circle.

The antecedents of the group may be found in turn-of-the-century Cambridge, where many of the men associated with Bloomsbury originally met as undergraduates. Most were members of the Apostles, a secret society that encouraged candid talk among its largely homosexual membership, including the future Bloomsberries E. M. Forster, Roger Fry, John Maynard Keynes, Desmond MacCarthy, Lytton Strachey, Saxon Sydney-Turner, and Leonard Woolf. Three slightly older Apostles influenced the intellectual outlook of the group: Goldsworthy Lowes Dickinson, whose skeptical, Platonist philosophy of tolerance had a lifelong impact on Forster and Fry; Oscar Browning, whose acid wit and theatricality influenced most of the male Bloomsberries (and who, like Dickinson, was homosexual); and, most important, G. E. Moore, whose *Principia Ethica* (1903) outlines a moral philosophy rooted in personal affection.

The Bloomsbury group began when two Cambridge undergraduates, Thoby and Adrian Stephen, introduced their sisters, Vanessa and Virginia, to their Apostolic friends. The four siblings moved into 46 Gordon Square in Bloomsbury after the 1904 death of their father, Sir Leslie Stephen, forming the nucleus of Old Bloomsbury along with Keynes; Strachey; Virginia's future husband, Leonard Woolf; Strachey's cousin Duncan Grant; and Clive Bell, who would marry Vanessa in 1906. Virginia and Vanessa hosted Thursday evening "at homes" where discussions freely ranged through a wide variety of intellectual topics of great interest to the sisters, who had been denied a formal, sustained education by their father. A new topic of conversation emerged in 1908, when one evening Strachey, pointing to a stain on Vanessa's dress, said, "Semen?" Virginia Woolf later recorded, "With that one word all barriers of reticence and reserve went down. . . . Sex permeated our conversation. The word bugger was never far from our lips." Afterward, the informal get-togethers of Bloomsbury encouraged discussions of sexuality in all its forms.

The year 1910 was a watershed. Virginia, amid bouts of insanity that would plague her until her death by suicide, was hard at work on her first novel, *The Voyage Out* (1914). Forster entered the Bloomsbury circle more fully in 1910, the publication year of his *Howards End*. The pivotal event occurred in December: the English Post-Impressionist Exhibition, presided over by Roger Fry and put together through the efforts of Fry, Clive Bell, Desmond MacCarthy, and Lady Ottoline Morrell, Bloomsbury's primary benefactor. The exhibit introduced Cézanne, Van Gogh, and Gauguin to a wide English public and caused such a sensation that Virginia Woolf later asserted, "On or about December 1910 human character changed." Influenced by the exhibition, Grant and Vanessa Bell emerged as important English postimpressionist artists. Clive Bell and Fry championed the postimpressionist emphasis on form over content and became the most influential English art critics of the early twentieth century.

As the notoriety of Bloomsbury increased, so did opposition to its broad liberalism, class snobbery, and homosexual character. The men of Bloomsbury gave D. H. Lawrence sexually implicit nightmares of "black beetles," and Ezra Pound derisively referred to them as the "Bloomsbuggers." Bloomsbury also met resistance to its pacifist position during World War I. During this period the Bells bought Charleston farmhouse in Sussex, in many ways the country home of Bloomsbury. Their sexual arrangements might now be termed "queer": Duncan Grant, who had been courted by Strachey and Keynes, lived at Charleston as the lover of both Vanessa Bell and David Garnett. In a bizarre twist, Garnett eventually married Angelica, the daughter of Duncan and Vanessa. Keynes, whose early life was almost entirely homosexual, lived intermittently at Charleston before his marriage to the ballerina Lydia Lopokova. Visitors included the Woolfs, the homosexual Strachey, and his romantic friend, the painter Dora Carrington.

B In the decade following World War I, three Bloomsberries reached the height of literary fame: Forster, with *A Passage to India* (1924), Virginia Woolf, with *Mrs. Dalloway* (1925) and *To the Lighthouse* (1927), and Strachey, whose irreverent biographies, particularly *Eminent Victorians* (1918), epitomize Bloomsbury's rejection of Victorian prudery and earnestness. Heirs to the traditions of aestheticism and decadence, the Bloomsberries utilized the camp mode of Oscar Wilde in texts such as Strachey's biographies, Woolf's sapphic *Orlando* (1928), Keynes's *Economic Consequences of the Peace* (1919), Clive Bell's *Old Friends* (1956), and Forster's early, undergraduate writing and late biographies. Forster, Woolf, and to a certain extent Strachey (see his "Monday June 26th 1916") were modernists: they desired to move beneath surfaces and into the mysteries of the unconscious. This desire is paralleled in Bloomsbury's postimpressionism, with its emphasis on subjective perception. The group was thus united not just by common values but also by a set of shared artistic and literary aesthetics.

Strachey's death in 1932, Fry's in 1934, and Virginia Woolf's 1941 in suicide signaled the end of the Bloomsbury group, followed in the 1950s by the nadir of its reputation. Concurrent with the sexual revolution, popular interest in Bloomsbury rose in the 1960s and reached something of a peak in the 1970s, although recent biographies and films such as *Carrington* (1995) suggest continued widespread interest. The 1990s witnessed a boom in scholarly interest, most notably S. P. Rosenbaum's ongoing, encyclopedic study. *George Piggford*

Bibliography

Bell, Quentin. *Bloomsbury*. New ed. London: Weidenfeld & Nicholson, 1986.

Edel, Leon. *Bloomsbury: A House of Lions*. New York: Avon, 1980.

Palmer, Alan, and Veronica Palmer. *Who's Who in Bloomsbury*. New York: St. Martin's Press, 1987.

Rosenbaum, S. P., ed. *The Bloomsbury Group: A Collection of Memoirs and Commentary,* rev. ed. Toronto: University of Toronto Press, 1995.

———. *Edwardian Bloomsbury: The Early Literary History of the Bloomsbury Group*. Vol. 2. New York: St. Martin's, 1994.

———. *Victorian Bloomsbury: The Early Literary History of the Bloomsbury Group*. Vol. 1. New York: St. Martin's, 1987.

Stansky, Peter. *On or About December 1910: Early Bloomsbury and Its Intimate World*. Cambridge, Mass.: Harvard University Press, 1996.

See also The Bloomsbury Group and Art; Forster, E. M.; Grant, Duncan; Keynes, John Maynard; London; Strachey, Lytton; Wilde, Oscar

The Bloomsbury Group and Art

Of the artists and critics most closely associated with the Bloomsbury group, only one—painter Duncan Grant—can be described as a male homosexual. A cousin of Lytton Strachey and lover of John Maynard Keynes, Grant was central to Bloomsbury's artistic contingent of homosexual men. As a lifelong domestic companion of the painter Vanessa Bell, Grant was also central to Bloomsbury's artistic contingent, which was headquartered at Charleston, a Sussex farmhouse now open as a museum of Bloomsbury art and design. Clive Bell, a prominent art critic and Vanessa's husband, shared Charleston with Grant and Bell. The painter and critic Roger Fry was a frequent visitor and admirer of Grant's work.

Grant, the youngest member of the original Bloomsbury group, was also its only man not to attend Cambridge University. Roger Fry's aesthetic theory, which dismissed Victorian narrative painting in favor of modernist styles that seemed sensual and free, attracted Grant's attention around 1910, and he quickly became the group's most celebrated painter. Grant immediately adapted this modernist style to the representation of homoerotic themes. Though only the subtlest of this work was exhibited during his lifetime, Grant produced innumerable homoerotic sketches and paintings throughout his long and prolific career. His early homoerotic work draws heavily on the precedent of the aesthetic movement (writers such as Walter Pater and John Addington Symonds), which posited the lands around the Mediterranean as paradises of unfettered sensuality. The classicized nudes in Grant's paintings of around 1910 can be compared quite closely with the work of photographers such as Wilhelm von Gloeden, who was well know in England. Like other artists at midcentury—David Hockney is the most famous example—Grant in his later work often drew on nudist and physical magazines to create his homoerotic images. Grant continued to paint until shortly before his death in 1978 at the age of ninety-three. A selection of late homoerotic work was published in 1989.

For many in the highly cerebral Bloomsbury group, Grant seemed the quintessential artist: intuitively talented and spontaneously sensual. Bloomsbury's advocacy of the aesthetic doctrine of formalism, which values art for the intrinsic aesthetic impact of abstract form rather than for subject matter, precluded self-conscious consideration of the themes of Grant's imagery. Without explicitly endorsing his iconography, however, the Bloomsbury critics' praise for the sensuality of his style encodes the group's acceptance of his sexuality. "The quality of his paint is often as charming as a kiss," Clive Bell wrote in one review, specifying, "there is something Greek about him, too; not the archeological Greek of Germany, nor yet the Graeco-Roman academism of France, but rather that romantic, sensuous Hellenism of the English literary tradition." Only recently have historians initiated analyses of Grant's work that go beyond formal issues. The most thoughtful study of Grant's painting is Simon Watney's *The Art of Duncan Grant*.

Christopher Reed

Bibliography

Bell, Clive. "Duncan Grant." In *Since Cézanne*. London: Chatto and Windus, 1922, 105–12.
Reed, Christopher. "Making History: The Bloomsbury Group's Construction of Aesthetic and Sexual Identity." In *Gay and Lesbian Studies in Art History*. Whitney Davis, ed. New York: Haworth Press, 1994.
Turnbaugh, Douglas Blair. *Private: The Erotic Art of Duncan Grant*. London: Gay Men's Press, 1989.
Watney, Simon. *The Art of Duncan Grant*. London: John Murray, 1990.

See also Aestheticism; Art History; Bloomsbury Group; Forster, E. M.; Gloeden, Wilhelm von; Grant, Duncan; Hockney, David; Keynes, John Maynard; Pater, Walter Horatio; Strachey, Lytton; Symonds, John Addington

Blunt, Anthony (1907–1983)

Anthony Blunt was born in Hampshire, England, and was educated at Marlborough, a distinguished public school, and Trinity College, Cambridge. He became a fellow of the college in 1932. A distinguished art historian, he was surveyor of the queen's pictures until 1972 and was awarded a knighthood in 1956. He died of a heart attack in London on March 26, 1983.

Blunt came to public attention in November 1979, when Prime Minister Margaret Thatcher announced to the House of Commons that Blunt had confessed in 1964 to working as a Soviet spy. His knighthood was withdrawn, and Blunt became the subject of a great deal of press attention for a while.

Blunt's espionage, such as it was, started during his Cambridge days in the 1930s. At that time some British intellectuals had a certain sympathy for the Communist cause based more on an almost romantic idealism than on full understanding of conditions in the Soviet Union. For some, this sympathy led to collaboration with the Soviet authorities, which included passing on intelligence material. Cambridge appears to have been a hotbed of such activity, with a number of British traitors having attended the university during the 1930s or after.

Unlike Kim Philby, Blunt appears not to have been active as a spy. His contribution likely consisted of acting as a "talent scout," notifying more willing agents of students and others he met who seemed inclined to sympathize with the cause and who might be recruited to spy for the Soviet Union. During World War II, Blunt worked for British Intelligence and may have been in a position to pass on secrets to the Soviets, though it must be remembered that Britain and the Soviet Union were officially allies at the time.

After the war Blunt returned to art history and talent scouting, with his only active involvement apparently assisting the defection of Guy Burgess and Donald Maclean in 1951. In 1964, following the defection of Kim Philby, Blunt was interrogated and confessed his role in spying for the Soviet Union. In return for the confession he was granted immunity from prosecution and continued as surveyor of the queen's pictures.

The press emphasized Blunt's homosexuality in its coverage of his unmasking by Prime Minister Thatcher. This served only to enforce existing prejudices that saw homosexuality as a security risk in and of itself. Even after homosexual acts between consenting adult males in private were decriminalized during the 1960s, a complete ban was maintained on known or suspected homosexuals in the higher ranks of the civil service, the armed forces, and the intelligence services. Homosexuals, the reasoning went, were open to blackmail and thus represented a security risk. Blunt's homosexuality was given as evidence in support of this prejudice, though there was never any suggestion that Blunt had been blackmailed into cooperating with the communists.

B On the contrary, Blunt's private life seemed to have conformed more with another stereotype. Rather than being the homosexual in danger of blackmail, Blunt seems to have been the stereotypical upper-class, intellectual aesthete, whose sexuality would be known to a group of close friends and tolerated by them, with the watchword always discretion.

The last four years of his life appear to have been lonely and the subject of occasional controversy, particularly his expulsion from a number of learned societies. It seems, if anything, to have been a tragic life. His espionage work, though largely unimportant, completely overshadowed other achievements, leaving him known as Anthony Blunt traitor, rather than art historian. Further, his homosexuality was wrongly construed as having influenced his espionage and thus enforcing the existing official prejudice. Yet the truth is that while there may have been a link between Blunt's homosexuality and his interest in art history, the only link to his espionage activities was one to a political-romantic idealism and naïveté common in British intellectual circles during the 1930s.

Robert J. Buckley

"Mirror, mirror . . . ". Photo by David Hawe.

Bibliography

Higgins, Patrick. *Heterosexual Dictatorship: Male Homosexuality in Post-War Britain*. London: Fourth Estate, 1996.

See also England; McCarthyism

Body Image

The term "body image" involves an individual's experiences and conception of the body, such as attitudes toward physical appearance, eating disorders, weight obsession, and appearance discrimination. For many years clinicians assumed that body-image difficulties affected only women. Yet it has become clear that men—especially gay men—are increasingly affected by similar concerns. Body-image problems can result in lowered self-esteem, isolation, and self-abuse or neglect; symptoms include eating disorders, steroid abuse, and bodily injury resulting from overexercise.

Lowered self-esteem may also contribute to intimacy problems, unsafe sexual activity, and tolerance for abusive relationships. Discrimination between gay men on the basis of looks can also result in isolation and a divided community that may not have the resources to combat societal homophobia.

As early as 1979, one study found that homosexual males differed from heterosexual males in both their perception of their physical appearance and how their physical appearance was perceived by others. In the early 1980s, psychological research began to focus on males with eating disorders. Some found sexual dysfunction and conflicted homosexuality among men with eating disorders, while another study said that such men showed "atypical gender role behavior." These researchers seem to have confused gender behavior and homosexuality in a way that reinforced the stereotype of gay men as effeminate.

Studies in the 1980s found gay men to be more concerned with their own and other men's appearance, less accepting of their bodies, and more likely to be dieting or suffering from eating disorders than straight men. One study found gay men prone to binge eating; feeling fat or being terrified about becoming fat; abusing diuretics, taking laxatives, and vomiting; dissatisfied with their bodies, fearing maturity, and feeling ineffectual. Among men who exercised, it was found that gay men where more likely to work out for their appearance and straight men to develop strength.

In the 1990s, the situation may have worsened. Several studies have since found gay men to be not only more unhappy with their bodies than straight men but even more dissatisfied than straight women.

Yet despite this research and the increasing seriousness of the problem, it was not until the 1990s that gay men began to write about it. *Outweek*, a national gay magazine, published two articles on the issue within three months of each other. Only in the last couple of years have major works addressed to the gay community focused on the possible impact of gay culture in perpetuating these problems. Michelangelo Signorile's book, *Life Outside* (1997), indicted gay men's culture for its "body fascism." In 1998, Dawn Atkins's *Looking Queer: Body Image and Identity in Lesbian, Bisexual, Gay and Transgender Communities* became the first book to address directly the issue and include the writings of several gay men about a variety of body-image issues.

One of the primary explanations for women's body-image problems has been seen to be a male-dominated culture that sets unrealistic ideals of beauty and then teaches women that men will value them only if they meet these standards. In heterosexual relationships, women are taught that men value them for their appearance and that they should value men for their power and wealth. It may be that that gay culture's body-image problems are the result of the internalization of these ideals combined with homophobia. In other words, gay men are taught that to be valued by other men, they must achieve an ever increasingly unrealistic ideal of beauty, and that they must also desire this in other men. They may also be expected to value other men and be valued for their own wealth as well. This double bind may be part of the reason that many gay men feel worse about their bodies than straight women.

AIDs and HIV may have complicated the situation. The destructiveness of this disease can be disfiguring, and the fear of contagion may be expressed in terms of looks. Even more dangerous, the appearance of health may sometimes be mistaken for health itself, with the result that some gay men might believe that someone who "looks good" will be HIV-negative. Though neither muscle tone nor clear skin protects against HIV, they may be mistaken as doing so. In addition, someone with low self-esteem because of body-image conflicts may be unwilling to insist on safe sex with his partners. Body-image dissatisfaction can also lead to relationship difficulties. For example, gay men may not trust their partners to value them for more than their appearance, and this can then result in lowered trust and intimacy in relationships. Gay men whose negative body image results in lowered self-esteem may remain in abusive relationships. And since the aging body is feared, men may fear losing relationships as they age. Older and/or disabled gay men may be neglected by their community rather than valued. Consequently, the community may lose the experience of these men.

Research with people of color and women have shown that alternative communities that support diversity in appearance can improve body-image satisfaction, self-esteem, and community bonds. Body-image dissatisfaction is not simply the result of being gay but of cultural influences from both outside and within the gay culture. Gay culture could resist these negative ideals, thereby providing a source of positive body image and self-esteem and support for gay relationships. At this time, however, body-image dissatisfaction and appearance discrimination remain major problems among gay men.

Dawn Atkins

Bibliography

Atkins, Dawn, ed. *Looking Queer: Body Image and Identity in Lesbian, Bisexual, Gay and Transgender Communities.* New York: Harrington Park Press, 1998.

Blotcher, Jay. "A Matter of Gravity: How the Queer Community Trims the Fat." *Outweek* (January 23, 1991): 38–43.

Brand, Pamela A., Esther D. Rothblum, and Laura J. Solomon. "A Comparison of Lesbians, Gay Men, and Heterosexuals on Weight and Restrained Eating." *International Journal of Eating Disorders* 11, no. 3 (1992): 253–59.

Deaux, Kay, and Randel Hanna. "Courtship in the Personals Column: The Influence of Gender and Sexual Orientation." *Sex Roles* 11, no. 5/6 (1994): 363–75.

Fichter, M. M., and C. Daser. "Symptomatology, Psychosexual Development and Gender Identity in 42 Anorexic Males." *Psychological Medicine* 17, no. 2 (1987): 409–18.

Herzog, David B., Dennis K. Norman, Christopher Gordon, and Maura Pepose. "Bulimia in Men: A Series of Fifteen Cases." *Journal of Nervous and Mental Disease* 174, no. 2 (1986): 117–19.

———. "Sexual Conflict and Eating Disorders in 27 Males." *American Journal of Psychiatry* 141 (1984): 989–90.

Prytula, Robert E., Christopher D. Wellford, and Bobby G. DeMonbreun. "Body Self-Image and Homosexuality." *Journal of Clinical Psychology* 35, no. 3 (1979): 567–72.

Siever, Michael D. "Sexual Orientation and Gender as Factors in Socioculturally Acquired Vulnerability to Body Dissatisfaction and Eating Disorders." *Journal of Consulting and Clinical Psychology* 62, no. 2 (1994): 252–60.

Signorile, Michelangelo. *Life Outside.* New York: Harper Collins, 1997.

See also Aging; Clone; Fashion; Physical Culture

The Body Politic. *Photo by Michelle Power.*

Body Politic

From 1971 to 1987, the *Body Politic* encapsulated gay male culture in Toronto, much of gay culture in the rest of Canada, and a good part of gay culture in the balance of North America. The magazine's first issue records a brief presented in 1971 by "The August 28th Gay Day Committee" to the federal government. Many believed Canada had "decriminalized homosexuality" in the late 1960s but much remained to be done. Thus the *Body Politic* began as a record of and promoter of Canadian gay activism. Yet while early issues depict many lesbians at gay liberation events, few were ever part of the *Body Politic* "collective." As feminism became more powerful and the sexism of even gay males more obvious, the female contributions became somewhat threatened and self-justifying.

Politicized travelogues, such as Tim McCaskell's account of Basque gays, showed international interests, but the latter were more generally evident through philosophical excursions on gay existence: social construction vs. genetic; mainstreaming vs. separate communities: psychotherapy, families, etc. Some of the many reviews of books and films were specifically Canadian, but most were North American, such as discussions of the boycotts of the 1980 film *Cruising.* Ed Jackson, a member of the collective from the second issue, makes the case that the *Body Politic*'s early approach to AIDS offered a Canadian example that should have had international influence. There was also international history, such as prepublication excerpts from James Steakley's *The Homosexual Emancipation Movement in Germany* (1975) and John D'Emilio's *Sexual Politics, Sexual Communities: The Making of a Homosexual Minority in the United States 1940–1970* (1983). By the early 1980s the magazine featured a section on "world" news, but by that time all the articles had become less theoretical and less overtly activist.

The most important moments were local but potentially had international appeal. In the police raids on Toronto bathhouses in 1980, the *Body Politic* exemplified the potential for a gay community magazine as observer, recorder, and activist. Perhaps less important locally but with a larger philosophical dimension was Gerald Hannon's "Men Loving Boys Loving Men." After much soul-searching the collective published this quite positive view of pedophilia. Hannon interviewed a number of men and a few of their young lovers and simply recorded the result. The effect was not only police raids and a court case but also the animosity of many *Body Politic* supporters, especially lesbians who saw simply more adult males exerting sexual power. The novelist Jane Rule, however, offered a different response:

> By writing for *The Body Politic*, I refuse to be a token, one of those who doesn't really seem like a lesbian at all. If the newspaper is found to be obscene, I am part of that obscenity. And proud to be, for, though my priorities and the paper's aren't always the same, I have been better and more thoughtfully informed about what

it is to be homosexual in this culture by *The Body Politic* than by any other paper.

By the time the *Body Politic* ceased publication in 1987, it had lost much of its original energy, and the many advertisements for gay businesses seemed a far cry from the gritty little rag of 1971. The entity continues, with two members of the early collective still on the board of directors, as Pink Triangle Press, which publishes a periodical, *Xtra*, providing community news and comment in Toronto, Vancouver, and Ottawa. Originally an events flyer distributed in the *Body Politic*, now its activist parent is no more, while the child, less serious and thoughtful, more flirtatious and concerned with fashion and fun, flourishes. For many old gay liberationists, that is a philosophical statement in itself.   *Terry Goldie*

Bibliography

Jackson, Ed, and Stan Persky, eds. *Flaunting It! A Decade of Gay Journalism from the* Body Politic. Toronto: Pink Triangle Press, 1982.

See also Bathhouses and Sex Clubs; Canada; Gay and Lesbian Press; Journalism

Bogarde, Dirk (1921–1999)

Dirk Bogarde's long and illustrious career contained more references to homosexuality than any mainstream movie star in the English-speaking world. Born Derek Jules Gaspard Ulric Niven van den Bogaerde, his many films include *Darling* (1956), *The Damned* (1969), and *Death in Venice* (1971), but three roles in particular have earned Bogarde a lasting place in gay cinematic history.

In the first, Basil Dearden's *Victim* (1961), Bogarde plays a closeted and blackmailed lawyer. Bogarde once reflected that "it was the first film in which a man said 'I love you' to another man. I wrote that scene in. I said, 'There's no point in half-measures. We either make a film about queers or we don't'" (in Russo 126). In the second, Joseph Losey's *The Servant* (1963), Bogarde manipulates James Fox in a sadomasochistic power game. Film critic Leonard Maltin called Losey's production both "an insidious story of moral degradation" and "a superb story of brooding decadence" (Maltin 1147).

In the third, Bogarde plays the long-suffering if separated former husband of a tragic songstress in Ronald Neame's *I Could Go on Singing* (1963). Bogarde was used to playing opposite the gay community's most flamboyant thrushes, as he costarred with the cult sensation Sylvia Syms in *Victim*. But that experience could not have prepared him for the hazing rites of tantrums and insecurities that became the shooting schedule on Neame's musical drama. For Bogarde's leading lady was none other than Judy Garland, playing a mirror image of herself. On the first day of filming, Bogarde called her "Miss Garland"; by the last, Bogarde and most of the crew called her "It." A few years after Garland's death, Bogarde mused sadly that she "wore out" all her friends.

Bogarde's steely gaze and imperious manner suited his roles; he could convey British imperialism or post-Wildean effete snobbery without stretching his acting muscles too tightly. Bogarde was knighted in 1992.   *John Ison*

Bibliography

Maltin, Leonard, ed. *Leonard Maltin's Voice and Video Guide 1995*. New York: Signet, 1995.

Manvell, Roger. "Dirk Bogarde." *International Films and Filmmakers: Actors and Actresses*. Nicholas Thomas, ed. Detroit: St. James, 1992, 112–14.

Russo, Vito. *The Celluloid Closet: Homosexuality in the Movies*. Rev. ed. New York: Harper and Row, 1987.

See also Film; Film Stars; Visconti, Luchino

Bookstores

The first known gay and lesbian bookstore was New York's Oscar Wilde Memorial Bookshop (1967). It was quickly followed in the post-Stonewall period (1969) by Glad Day Bookshop in Toronto (1971) and Boston (1979); Giovanni's Room in Philadelphia (1973), Lambda Rising in Washington, D.C. (1974), Baltimore (1984), Rehoboth Beach, Del. (1991), and Norfolk, Va. (1996); and A Different Light in Los Angeles (1979), New York (1983), and San Francisco (1986). In the last fifteen years a number of other stores have opened throughout North America (Atlanta, Minneapolis, Chicago, Seattle, Vancouver, and Montreal, to name a few). The original five companies mentioned above are still in business, while many others survived only a short time. Other well-known stores can be found in London (Gay's the Word, 1979), Amsterdam (Intermale, 1984; Vrolijk, 1984), Berlin (Prinz Eisenherz, 1978), and Paris (Les Mots à la Bouche, 1980).

B Gay and lesbian bookstores were instrumental in helping both to define and to educate the community in the early years. The printed word was extremely important in exploring who gay men and lesbians were and what their shared goals should be. Reading gay and lesbian books was also a large part of the coming-out process, helping to reassure and educate during a confusing and stressful time.

The stores for many years were all but the only reliable source of gay and lesbian books; as they developed a loyal following the stores provided a well-known outlet for new books. Without gay and lesbian booksellers the majority of the books published for, by, and about gay men and lesbians would never have been written, let alone published. As more titles were published, the stores became more successful, and that in turn led to more books being published. A store might have carried a few thousand titles at the end of the 1970s, while today there are upwards of twenty thousand titles to stock. Many gay and lesbian writers owe their success to the dedication and enthusiasm of gay and lesbian booksellers. Unlike the average general bookstore where each title has a limited life span (often as short as three months), gay and lesbian bookstores are much more likely to stock a book as long as it remains in print. Gay and lesbian bookstores ensure the survival of an important backlist of titles that have long since vanished from the rest of the marketplace.

Most gay and lesbian bookstores also function as focal points or resource centers for the community. They sponsor in-store events, readings, author signings, music, art displays, and writing classes, and they provide, usually free of charge, bulletin boards, community event flyers, tickets, and specialty newspapers.

Along with the success of the stores and the increase in titles came a certain legitimacy for gay and lesbian publishing and bookselling. Not surprisingly it is now common to find well-stocked gay and lesbian sections in most comprehensive general bookstores throughout the United States.

The irony of the success of gay and lesbian bookstores in mainstreaming gay and lesbian titles is that the stores now face ferocious competition from national chain superstores, which seriously threaten the survival of gay and lesbian bookstores. This same threat has already had a destructive impact on feminist bookstores and on numerous small presses. Gay and lesbian bookstores are an essential part of the intellectual and political life of the community. Their future survival will depend on the community's committed loyalty and support.

Norma Laurila

Bibliography

Stryker, Susan, and Jim Van Buskirk. *Gay by the Bay: A History of Queer Culture in the San Francisco Bay Area.* San Francisco: Chronicle Books, 1996.

See also Gay and Lesbian Press; Journalism; Marketing

Bowers v. Hardwick and *Romer v. Evans*

In a 1986 landmark decision on the limitations of the right of privacy, the U.S. Supreme Court held that the U.S. Constitution contains no fundamental right to engage in "homosexual sodomy," even in the privacy of one's own bedroom.

The case *Bowers v. Hardwick* resulted from the arrest of Michael Hardwick for engaging in oral sex with another consenting adult male in the bedroom of Hardwick's home. He was charged with violating the Georgia sodomy statute that makes all oral-genital and anal-genital sexual acts punishable by up to twenty years in prison. When the district attorney decided not to go forward immediately with the case but to hold it over Hardwick's head for possible future prosecution, Hardwick sought protection in Federal District Court, arguing that the statute was unconstitutional.

Hardwick's lawyers, along with other civil liberties attorneys, agreed that the facts were unusually good for a privacy challenge. The case featured a confluence of the privacy of the bedroom, the sanctity of the home, and the intimately personal nature of decisions about relationships that, many argued, should be none of the government's business. Over the years the Supreme Court had issued a number of important opinions that found a right of privacy implicit in various sections of the Constitution, although that right is nowhere explicitly in the text.

The District Court dismissed Hardwick's case for failure to state a valid claim. The U.S. Court of Appeals reversed the District Court's decision, holding that Hardwick's fundamental rights of privacy and intimate association were implicated by the statute. Finally, the State of Georgia took the case to the U.S. Supreme Court, which again reversed, validating the Georgia law.

The Hardwick case is, at its core, about the power of language. By focusing on the words *homo-*

sexual and *sodomy* to describe Hardwick's relationship and intimate lovemaking, Justice Byron White, writing for the 5-to-4 majority, framed the question of Georgia's right to outlaw such conduct with a cold objectification that instantly devalued both the sex act and the relationship. He rejected any factual similarity to the high court's previous privacy decisions, finding support for Georgia's law in its citizens' moral disapproval of homosexuality and his belief in the state's role as guardian of traditional morality.

Chief Justice Warren Burger, writing a separate concurring opinion, went further, basing his condemnation specifically on religious ideology. His opinion used phrases such as "the infamous crime against nature," an offense of "deeper malignity" than rape, a heinous act "the very mention of which is a disgrace to human nature," and "a crime not fit to be named."

Justice Harry Blackmun's dissent evinced an understanding of the dangers inherent in making historical tradition the measure of human rights: "A State can no more punish private behavior because of religious intolerance than it can punish such behavior because of racial animus." *Hardwick* is also about the Supreme Court's powerful inclination to rest its decisions more on existing social consensus than on any newly evolving sense of social justice. At the time of the *Hardwick* ruling, only about half the states had decriminalized sodomy within their own jurisdictions, and there had been no nationwide concerted effort to educate the public or to gain general respect and acceptance for lesbians and gay men. The "coming-out" process had not yet achieved the necessary critical mass of openly gay and lesbian family members, fellow employees, friends, and acquaintances to break down society's myths, stereotypes, and deeply rooted phobias.

For example, Justice Lewis Powell, the swing vote in *Hardwick,* waffled before joining the majority. (Years later he repudiated that decision.) More important, that decision was based purely on legal theoretics about the importance of states' rights and the power of each state to control its own criminal law. According to him, he did not personally know anyone who might actually be affected by the case. The several gay people close to him remained silent about themselves, never revealing the human face of the issue. The litigation itself was not designed to focus on the human face but on what Hardwick's attorney, Harvard professor Lawrence Tribe, believed to be compelling legal arguments. An important lesson gay and lesbian litigators took from *Hardwick* is the essential imperative, in every case, no matter how complex or difficult the legal theories, of instilling in the judges empathy for the client.

Ten years later (1996), the U.S. Supreme Court had an opportunity to decide another case of historical landmark proportion for the gay and lesbian communities. In *Romer v. Evans* the state of Colorado attempted to reverse its own state supreme court, which had invalidated a new state constitutional amendment known as Amendment 2, adopted by Colorado voters in a 1992 statewide referendum. Amendment 2 essentially repealed all existing state and local sexual orientation antidiscrimination laws and prohibited any governmental entity in the state from ever protecting the rights of gays and lesbians in the future. The amendment did not affect countless laws prohibiting discrimination on the basis of age, marital status, political affiliation, physical or mental disability, or any other enumerated category.

By the time the Court decided *Romer,* the shift in society's attitudes had been dramatic. The HIV epidemic had propelled masses out of the closet, the entertainment industry was bringing a more realistic and benign face to the public consciousness, and corporate employers were banning discrimination, granting domestic partner benefits, and supporting gay and lesbian/bi/transgender employee groups. In essence, the closet doors were opening wide.

The Court itself was now less of a stranger to the humanity of gays and lesbians. It had, for just one example, heard openly lesbian attorney Mary Dunlap argue the "Gay Olympics" case (*San Francisco Arts & Athletics, Inc. v. International Olympic Committee*), in which the defendant, the U.S. Olympic Committee, claimed an exclusive trademark bestowed by Congress in the word *Olympics.* The U.S. Supreme Court agreed, holding that the defendants had the legal prerogative to grant use of the word to an event such as the Special Olympics and prohibit its use by the Gay Olympics. The Gay Games, as the event was subsequently called, continues to be one of the largest and most respected amateur athletic competitions in the world. The point is that the Court was now hearing cases depicting real people with real lives and compelling stories in nonsexual contexts.

Thus, when deciding *Romer,* the justices had an opportunity to follow a new, albeit still evolving, consensus that recognized the legitimized status gays and lesbians had achieved in our national human diversity. As in *Hardwick,* the power and sym-

B bolism of language was not lost on the justices. By using throughout the opinion the words *gay* and *lesbian* rather than just the clinical *homosexual,* Justice Anthony Kennedy, writing for six justices, implicitly recognized gays and lesbians as whole human beings with identities beyond the inescapable sexual allusion attached to the words used by Justice Antonin Scalia in the dissent.

In *Romer,* the constitutional theories did not center on privacy but the equal protection clause of the Fourteenth Amendment ("no person shall be denied the equal protection of the laws"). Because, as a practical matter, most laws do discriminate in some way, the U.S. Supreme Court had adopted the standard that if a law does not affect a "fundamental right" or target a "suspect" classification (such as race), the law will be upheld "so long as it bears a rational relation to some legitimate end."

The Supreme Court agreed with the Colorado court, holding that the breadth of the amendment's consequences and the narrowness of its focus on only one group revealed its motive to be hostility toward that single group. Justice Kennedy, writing for the majority, explained that the "desire to harm a politically unpopular group cannot constitute a legitimate governmental interest." He stressed that "it is not within our constitutional tradition to enact laws of this sort."

By deciding that the statute was not rationally related to a legitimate end, the Court did not have to cross the more difficult bridge of elevating gays and lesbians to a specially protected "suspect" class, a move that could have created a significant societal backlash. The dissenting justices, now numbering three, suggested that what the majority saw mistakenly as animus was really a "Kulturkampf" (culture war) and argued passionately that the Court's earlier *Hardwick* decision mandated that states do have the right to single out "homosexuality" "for disfavorable treatment." Significantly, while majority opinions often respond to issues raised in dissents, the *Romer* majority did not engage the *Hardwick* question at all.

Postscript: On November 28, 1998, the sodomy law of Georgia was overturned, not by the U.S. Supreme Court on federal constitutional grounds, but by Georgia's own state supreme court based on the state's constitutional right of privacy *(Powell v. the State,* Case no. S98A0755). The decision has no value as precedent any place in the United States except Georgia. However, the decision is significant, if not in some ways ironic.

First, this was not a gay-related case. The facts involved a heterosexual defendant who was charged with raping his wife's niece. The jury acquitted him of the charges related to force and lack of consent, convicting him only of consensual sodomy. The more poignant irony, however, is related to the legal strategy in Hardwick's case. Hardwick's attorneys had gone directly into the federal court system and avoided the state courts, in part to access the body of federal privacy law which, they believed, was lacking in their own state. However, the right of privacy had actually been "birthed" in 1905 by the Georgia Supreme Court in the landmark decision of *Pasevich v. New England Life Ins.,* 122 Ga. 190. This case and its progeny led the court in *Powell* to the conclusion that the fundamental constitutional right of privacy screens from governmental interference a non-commercial sexual act that occurs without force in a private home between persons legally capable of consenting . . . .; that the police power of the state is limited and subject to this privacy principle absent a compelling public purpose for the criminal statute; and that the state's desire to further "social morality" does not supply the compelling public purpose. The decision applies equally to heterosexual and homosexual situations and will likely prove quite influential in future sodomy-law reform efforts.

Legal scholars also enjoyed the amusing coincidence of the defendant's name with that of the justice of the Supreme Court who was the swing vote in Hardwick.   *Jay M. Kohorn*

Bibliography
"Developments—Sexual Orientation and the Law." *Harvard Law Review* 102 (1989): 1508.

Henderson, L. "Legality and Empathy." *Michigan Law Review* 85 (1987): 1574.

Case References
Bowers v. Hardwick, 478 U.S. 186 (1986).

Powell v. the State, Case no. S98A7055 (1998).

Romer v. Evans, 116 S.Ct. 1620 (1996).

San Francisco Arts & Athletics, Inc. v. International Olympic Committee, 107 S.Ct. 2971 (1987).

See also Civil Rights (U.S. Law); Homosexual Panic; International Law; Lewd and Lascivious Conduct; Nameless Sin (or Crime); U.S. Law: Discrimination; U.S. Law: Equal Protection; U.S. Law: Privacy

Bowles, Paul (1910–)

Born in New York City into an upwardly mobile family, Paul Bowles first exhibited there his precocity as a fantasist and builder of imaginary worlds as a child, much to the disdain of his father, an ambitious dentist. By the time he matriculated at the University of Virginia, he was somewhat familiar with European modernist activity, not only in writing but also in music, art, and sculpture; and he achieved early success with the publication of some experimental poetry in an avant-garde magazine. He disappeared abruptly from the university, making his way to Paris; there, Gertrude Stein met and took a liking to him but discouraged him from writing poetry. Back in America, Bowles turned his attention to music. Befriended by Aaron Copland and his circle of European-influenced modernists, he worked at being a composer. (Several of Bowles's compositions of the 1930s have recently been recorded and are now available on CD.) The letters that reflect the young man's close friendships are playful and sexually suggestive but hardly explicit; Bowles has remained extremely discreet about his sexual orientation, perhaps because he has preferred to express "deviance" through a series of elaborated displacements: music, including the recording of traditional North African forms; exotic travel writing (*Their Heads Are Green and Their Eyes Are Blue*, 1957); taut, existentialist novels starting with *The Sheltering Sky* (1949); and oral translations of Moroccan autobiographical fiction, suggestive of sexually different cultural forms and practices.

In 1938 Bowles married the bisexual Jean Auer, who achieved literary success in her own right; the unconventional marriage lasted until 1973, when his wife died in mysterious circumstances. In 1947 he achieved major recognition with the much-anthologized "Pages at Cold Point," an intense story that probes a father-son relationship to the edge of incest. That same year the Bowleses moved to Tangier, and Bowles has made his home there ever since. Although four novels followed *The Sheltering Sky*, none consolidated Bowles's reputation as a novelist. His fame now is in his connection with Tangier, where he became a cult presence during the Beat period: William Burroughs, Allen Ginsberg, Jack Kerouac, Joe Orton, Tennessee Williams, Truman Capote, and Jean Genet made pilgrimages—to name a few. Bowles translated accounts of both Genet and Williams by one of his young Moroccan friends, Driss ben Hamet Charhardi (Larbi Layachi), and between 1964 and 1992 alternative presses in the United States and England published at least fifteen translations of the orally recorded accounts of three such protégés.

Readers will remember Bowles for *The Sheltering Sky*, which Bernardo Bertolucci later directed as a film in which Bowles himself made a cameo appearance. Many others will associate him with the decades of the fifties and sixties, and with the evocation of liberatory "zones" such as Tangier, offering scope for lifestyle experimentation. And although homosexuality is no more than a muted suggestion in some of his works, attentive gay readers will locate subtle, nuanced psychological differences with sexual implications.   *Patrick Holland*

Bibliography

Green, Michelle. *The Dream at the End of the World: Paul Bowles and the Literary Renegades in Tangier*. New York: HarperCollins, 1991.
Sawyer-Laucanno, Christopher. *Paul Bowles: An Invisible Spectator*. New York: Ecco Press, 1990.

See also Beat Generation; Burroughs, William Seward; Capote, Truman; Copland, Aaron; Genet, Jean; Ginsberg, Alan; Morocco; Orton, Joe; Tunisia; Williams, Tennessee

Boycott

Boycotts have been a traditional means for consumers to voice their grievances and dissatisfactions with market-oriented organizations in the United States, Canada, and abroad. In this manner, gay and lesbian consumers are no different from their heterosexual counterparts. Homophobic actions by companies have often been challenged by gay and lesbian consumers, who have withheld their purchases and brand loyalty.

Perhaps the most famous boycott in recent history was directed against the Adolph Coors Company, based in Colorado. During the late 1970s, it was reputed that the ultra-conservative German Coors family fired gay and lesbian employees for their sexual orientation. In retaliation, gay bars in Canada and the United States refused to serve any Coors products on their premises. Coors denied all allegations and in 1978 added sexual orientation to its antidiscrimination policy. Since that time, the Coors company has funded numerous compassionate AIDS initiatives and has an active gay employees group, even though the Coors family also funds several right-wing causes including the Heritage Foundation, which supports reintroduction of sodomy laws and mandatory AIDS testing for public employees.

Yet boycotts are a double-edged sword, for in recent years, the Christian fundamentalist right-wing movement in the United States has adopted the same means of expressing disapproval of companies that actively solicit gay and lesbian customers or provide same-sex domestic partnership benefits to employees. Levi-Strauss Company, the blue jeans manufacturer, and Bank of America were both targeted by the Christian right when they announced that they would no longer help to fund the Boy Scouts of America because of that organization's homophobic policy of denying gay men the opportunity to be scout leaders. Both companies maintained their stance, and neither reported any significant decline in sales or profits resulting from these decisions.

Some companies have responded adaptively to gay and lesbian public opinion. For example, American Airlines personnel were accused of being insensitive to gays, lesbians, and persons living with AIDS during flights to and from the March on Washington in April 1993. By 1997, a concerted effort by gays and lesbians was made to demonstrate support for the antidiscrimination policies subsequently adopted by the airline, especially after AA was accused of promoting the "homosexual agenda" by members of the Christian right. Other companies such as Cracker Barrel Old Country Stores of Leba-

non, Tennessee, have also been boycotted by gays and lesbians, owing to discriminatory employment practices.

Overall, the boycott has had mixed success for both the gay and lesbian political movement and its enemies. While some companies have been quick to apologize and acknowledge wrongdoing, others have maintained their hostility to gay and lesbian consumers and/or employees or changed policies only after recognizing the lucrative potential of the market they stood to lose. *Steven M. Kates*

Bibliography

Baker, Daniel, B., Sean O'Brien Strub, and Bill Henning in association with the National Gay and Lesbian Task Force Policy Institute. *Cracking the Corporate Closet*. New York: Harper Business, 1995.

Kates, Steven. *20 Million New Customers! Understanding Gay Men's Consumer Behavior*. Binghamton, N.Y.: Harrington Park Press, 1998.

See also Boyscouts; Business; Marketing

Boy Scouts

Lord Robert Baden-Powell, lieutenant general in the British Army and Boer War hero, founded the Boy

Activists protest a showing of the film Basic Instinct *(1991). Photo by Marc Geller.*

Scouts in 1908. Two years later the Boy Scouts were established in the United States. They were given a charter by the U.S. Congress in 1916, and they file an annual report of their activities to a joint committee of Congress each year.

A few biographers have intimated that Baden-Powell was gay, but corroborating or substantive evidence has yet to be revealed. Tim Jeal, author of *The Boy-Man: The Life of Lord Baden-Powell*, points to evidence from Powell's diaries and correspondence that led him to conclude Baden-Powell was a repressed homosexual. Also noted was Baden-Powell's long-standing relationship with Kenneth McLaren, with whom he served in the British Army and frequently bunked. Since the late 1970s two other authors have made similar allusions to Baden-Powell's sex life: Pierre Brendon's *Eminent Edwardians* (1979) and Michael Rosenthal's *The Character Factory: Baden-Powell and the Origins of the Boy Scout Movement*.

Since its inception the Boy Scouts of America forbade homosexuals serving as leaders or troop members. The National Executive Board of Directors of the Boy Scouts of America (BSA) reaffirmed by unanimous vote at its February 1992 meeting that the BSA would continue to deny admittance to avowed homosexuals as leaders or members of the organization. The decision was based primarily on the principle of the organization upholding "traditional family values," whereby homosexuality does not present a role model consistent with the principles of boy scouting. The Boy Scouts strongly emphasize traditional family values as a key component of a healthy society. This belief is derived from the Boy Scout oath:

> On my honor I promise I will do my best to do my duty to God and my country, and to obey the scout law, to help other people at all times, to keep myself physically strong, mentally awake, and morally straight.

The Boy Scouts' refusal to admit homosexuals, atheists, agnostics, and girls is based on the interpretation of this oath; they claim they have the right to exclusionary practices owing to the private nature of the organization. The message they seek to convey is that homosexual behavior is not compatible for a person who commands attention as role model and moral leader. Article VIII of the Boy Scout by-laws states, "Our member standards have been developed to ensure that we have the best possible individuals in our organization, and the enforcement of these standards should not be construed to suggest that any individual in question is not a decent citizen."

A former Boy Scout reminisces (1993). Photo by Marc Geller.

B The ban on admittance of homosexuals to the Boy Scouts has been called into question over the last twenty years. The chief legal issue under debate is whether the organization is in actuality a nontax-supported institution, private in nature as contended, or operated as a business, subject to state and local antidiscrimination statutes.

The Boy Scouts of America states that each of its units or chapters must be owned and operated by a sponsoring or charter organization. Some of these may be tax-supported institutions such as police or fire organizations, while religious organizations sponsor the largest proportion of scout groups. Because some chapters are chartered by tax-supported institutions, make free use of public facilities, and may be legally defined as a "public accommodation," the question has been raised whether they are subject to governmental antidiscrimination regulations. Or are the Boy Scouts exercising their First Amendment rights and freedom of association standards, under the guise of a private organization, when excluding homosexuals?

The first legal case to test the merits of these issues was *Curran v. Mount Diablo (California) Council of the Boy Scouts of America* (1981). Timothy Curran had earned twenty-two merit badges and achieved Eagle Scout status, but he was denied the position of adult leader after the local council became aware of his sexual orientation. Curran sued the Boy Scouts, claiming that their policy violated the California Unruh Civil Rights Act. The issue at hand in the Curran case was whether the Boy Scouts of America could be declared a "business establishment," defined more broadly than a "place of public accommodation," subject to state antidiscrimination regulations. The trial court disagreed, but the appellate court concurred and reversed the ruling. In 1998 the California State Supreme Court ruled that the Boy Scouts did not violate the Unruh Civil Rights Act and should be considered a private club, which could exclude individuals whose views or orientations were incompatible with the group.

When the Boy Scout council discovered in 1992 that El Cajon, California, police officer and scout leader Chuck Merino was gay, it dismissed him. The organization stated Merino no longer provided a "morally straight" role model for its troops. A key difference between Curran's and Merino's lawsuit was that Merino worked in Police Explorer Post, chartered by the El Cajon Police Department, supported by tax dollars. The merits of *Merino v. BSA* were argued under the premise of the Unruh

Act again, with the question of state tax dollars supporting a program (BSA) with discriminatory policies. While the lower court agreed with Merino's lawsuit, the Fourth District Court of Appeals again ruled that the Boy Scouts of America shall be considered a private group, not subject to state law.

Other lawsuits across the nation have had dissimilar results. James Dale, of Fort Monmouth, N.J., was an Eagle Scout and assistant scoutmaster with Troop 73 of Matawan, N.J., and held thirty merit badges. In 1990 his membership was terminated by the Monmouth Council owing to his homosexuality. In 1998 a New Jersey appeals court ruled that the Boy Scouts of America should be treated as a "public accommodation" and that the BSA failed to prove gay men are inappropriate role models for service.

Comparable court cases are being filed nationally and at human rights commission offices in Chicago, Illinois, and Washington, D.C. The Illinois courts will also decide whether the city of Chicago, which maintains numerous Cub, Boy, and Explorer posts around the city with tax dollar support can legally retain ties with an organization that discriminates against gay men.   *Michael A. Lutes*

Bibliography

Friess, Jim. "Scouts' Dishonor." *Advocate* 737 (July 8, 1997): 39–41.

Jeal, Tim. *The Boy-Man: The Life of Lord Baden-Powell.* New York: Morrow, 1990.

Mirken, Bruce. "Boy Scout Confidential." *Advocate* 593 (Dec. 31, 1991): 52–56.

Rosenthal, Michael. *The Character Factory: Baden-Powell and the Origins of the Boy Scout Movement.* New York: Pantheon, 1986.

Salzman, Allen. "The Boy Scouts Under Siege." *American Scholar* 61, no. 4 (1992): 591–97.

Taylor, Larry. "How Your Tax Dollars Support the Boy Scouts of America." *Humanist* 55, no. 5 (Sept.–Oct. 1995): 6–13.

Wilhelm, Maria. "He's Gay, But a California Eagle Scout Says His Adult Leader Application Should Be Judged on Its Merit." *People Weekly* 20 (Nov. 7, 1983): 139–40.

See also Boycott; U.S. Law: Equal Protection

Brand, Adolph (1874–1945)

This essayist and publisher of writings promoting the "Love Between Friends" (*Freundesliebe*) was also a leader in the German homosexual emancipation movement from 1900 to 1933. Brand co-founded in 1903 the Gemeinschaft der Eigenen (translated either as "Community of the Special" or "Community of Self-Owners").

Rejecting Magnus Hirschfeld's theory of homosexuals as a "third sex," the Gemeinschaft promoted a revival of the Greek "ideal," namely, an erotic bond between thoroughly masculine males of different ages. Such an ideology proved attractive to men who would not see themselves as "women's souls in men's bodies" (as Hirschfeld proposed), to men who were married yet enjoyed "friendships" with young men, and to men who rejected "modern society" as too restrictive, too feminized, too socialist, and too egalitarian.

The masculine refuge of male-male friendship was populated by handsome, well-built young men, in fiction and in fact. Many of them posed naked in various natural settings for the photographs Brand published in the magazines he edited, *Eros* (1930–1932) and *Race and Beauty* (1926–1930). He is chiefly remembered as the publisher-editor of the Gemeinschaft's journal *Der Eigene* (The Self-Owner), published from 1898 through 1931, with some interruptions. Subtitled for most of its years "A Journal for Masculine Culture," the magazine included essays on politics, history, art, and literature, as well as short stories, poems, artwork, and personal ads.

The pictorial and written content of his publications brought Brand more than once before German courts. In 1916 and 1920, he was unsuccessfully charged with selling pornography. He did receive an eighteen-month prison sentence, however, for his libelous accusation in 1907 that the German Chancellor, von Bülow, was homosexual.

While the Gemeinschaft was clearly culturally conservative, it was by no means protofascist. Brand himself sounded the anti-Nazi alarm in several of his final essays for *Der Eigene*. The Nazis did not persecute him personally, probably because he was married, not Jewish, and, after his library and archives had been confiscated, not a threat. Adoph Brand died on February 26, 1945, when his Berlin home was destroyed in a bombing raid.

James W. Jones

Bibliography

Hohmann, Joachim S., ed. *Der Eigene: Ein Blatt für männliche Kultur. Eine Querschnitt durch die erste Homosexuellenzeitschrift der Welt.* Frankfurt: Foerster, 1981.

Oosterhuis, Harry, ed. *Homosexuality and Male Bonding in Pre-Nazi Germany.* Hubert Kennedy, trans. New York: Harrington Park Press, 1991.

See also Berlin; Carpenter, Edward; Couples; Friendship; Hirschfeld, Magnus; Masculinity; Sexology; Symonds, John Addington

Brazil

After the United States, Brazil is the country with the most gays, lesbians, and transvestites. Most Brazilian gays disagree with the famous estimate by Alfred Kinsey that 10 percent of all men are predominantly or exclusively homosexual. Rather, they consider that realistically 20 percent of all Brazilian men are predominantly homoerotic, which represent more than thirty million people. Although, as described below, the situation for Brazil's gays is extremely difficult, Brazil has South America's most effervescent gay scene. The movement is the largest and the most dynamic, but, unfortunately, deaths from AIDS and the number of gays murdered have reached catastrophic proportions.

The tradition of homosexuality in Brazil has roots that predate the discovery of America by Europeans. When the first Portuguese colonizers arrived in Brazil in 1500, they encountered and recorded much evidence of the practice of male and female homosexuality among many tribes in the Amazon River basin, along the coast, and in the hinterlands. Among the Tupinambá, the main Amerindian ethnic group, gays were called *tibira* and lesbians, *Haçoaimbeguira*. Among the Gaicurus of central Brazil, transvestite Indians received the name *cudinos*. New World natives were first called *berdaches* in Brazil in the second half of the sixteenth century. Equally important documents indicate that African slaves brought from the kingdoms of Angola and Benin practiced homoerotic acts, and transvestism was also observed among these ethnic groups. Already in 1591, Francisco Manicongo, a black transvestite *quimbanda* from Angola, was accused of practicing sodomy with other black slaves.

Since the Middle Ages, the king of Portugal was responsible for the persecution of sodomy, considered the "vilest, dirtiest and most dishonest sin which provoked divine wrath and caused droughts, floods, earthquakes and plagues to be sent to earth." With the establishment of the Inquisition in Portugal (1536), the Court of the Holy Office was responsi-

B ble for the persecution of sodomites, who after Jews were the most numerous victims of Catholic intolerance. White and mixed-race settlers were the main casualties of the Inquisition in Brazil. Over a hundred denunciations were leveled against Luso-Brazilian sodomites, and twenty-five received sentences that resulted in the confiscation of their property, flogging, exile to Africa, or forced labor on galley ships. In 1591, a Portuguese lesbian, Felipa de Sousa, was imprisoned in Salvador, the capital of Brazil, whipped in the public square, and exiled from the area. Her name is honored as the title of the annual award given by the San Francisco, California–based International Gay and Lesbian Human Rights Commission. In the seventeenth century two sodomites were executed in Brazil: a Tupinambá Indian in Mananhão and a young black slave in Sergipe.

With the end of the Inquisition in 1821 and Brazil's independence from Portugal and because of the influence of the Napoleonic Code, sodomy ceased to be a crime in the country. Nevertheless, homophobia remained strongly rooted in Brazilian tradition. During the nineteenth century, "pederasts" were imprisoned by the police and accused of "offending modesty." Today it is common for parents to state unabashedly: "I would rather have a son who was a thief than a *veado* [faggot]," or "I would rather have a daughter who was a prostitute than a *sapatão* [dyke]." Many adolescents are used to calling out, "Death to faggots."

Research indicates that of all Brazilian social minorities, homosexuals are the main victims of discrimination and are rejected by up to 80 percent of those polled. More than 60 percent of those interviewed state that they wouldn't vote for a homosexual candidate, while only 4 percent would refuse to vote for a black candidate. Antihomosexual discrimination is registered at all levels of society. At home, gay and lesbian youth are insulted by their parents and siblings. They suffer physical violence. Many find prostitution the only way to avoid starving to death. Companies and businesses administer psychological tests to screen out closeted homosexuals. There are registered incidents of serious discrimination against gays and lesbians in public and private schools. Homosexuals are denied access to certain commercial establishments and even shopping centers. Between 1980 and 1996 fourteen death squads operated in Brazil against homosexuals. More than 1,468 homosexuals were murdered in this period: 75 percent gay men, 22 percent transvestites, and 3 per-

cent lesbians. In 1996 alone, 126 homosexuals were murdered, representing an average of one every three days. Only 10 percent of these crimes ever go to trial. Usually the criminals (police, hustlers, clients of transvestites) receive light sentences because they allege "legitimate defense of honor." Numerous gays have emigrated from Brazil owing to homophobia, and the first homosexual to receive political asylum in the United States because of persecution as a result of sexual orientation was a gay man from Rio de Janeiro.

Lampião, the first Brazilian homosexual newspaper, was founded in 1978. In February 1979, Somos: Grupo de Afirmaçno Homossexual (We Are: Group of Homosexual Affirmation), the pioneering group of gay militancy, came into being. The first gathering of Brazilian homosexuals took place in 1980. That same year, Grupo Gay da Bahia, the oldest continually functioning group in Latin America, was founded. The group led several crucial campaigns that included the fight for the exclusion of homosexuality from the classification of diseases in 1985. Laws prohibiting discrimination based on sexual orientation have now passed in seventy-three cities and two Brazilian states. In 1995 the Brazilian Association of Gays, Lesbians, and Transvestites was founded. The Brazilian National Congress has begun to debate a proposed law to grant domestic partnership to people of the same sex. According to several recent polls, this proposal has the support of 45 percent of Brazilians, but it faces stiff opposition from the Catholic hierarchy and representatives of evangelical churches.

Cultural expressions of homosexuality include the pioneering poem by Gregório de Matos (1695), describing the passion of a lesbian, and Adolfo Caminha's *O Bom Crioulo*, an 1895 romance with a homoerotic theme. In 1906, Pires de Almeida published *O Homossexualismo: A Libertinagem no Rio de Janeiro*, a major study of the subject with strong influences of sexologists such as Albert Moll and Kraft-Ebing. *O Terceiro Sexo* (The Third Sex), by Odilon Azevedo (1930), a biography of a radical, separatist lesbian who wants to destroy men's power in Brazil, is the first work of fiction in the Portuguese language to address the subject of female homosexuality. Some famous historical figures said to have been homosexual are the governor general of Brazil, Diogo Botelho (1607), writers Olvao Bilac (1865–1918) and Mário de Andrade (1893–1945), the Brazilian inventor of the airplane, Santos Dumont (1873–1932), and Empress

Leopoldina (1797–1826).   *Luis Mott*
                        Translation by James N. Green

Bibliography

Trevisan, Jono S. *Perverts in Paradise*. London: Gay Men's Press, 1986.

Mott, Luiz. *Epidemic of Hate: Violations of the Human Rights of Gay Men, Lesbians and Transvestites in Brazil*. San Francisco: IGLHRC, 1996.

———. *O lesbianismo no Brasil*. Porto Alegre, Brazil: Mercado Aberto, 1987.

Parker, Richard. *Bodies, Pleasures and Passions*. Boston; Beacon Press, 1991.

See also Berdache; Caminha, Adolfo; Inquisition; Krafft-Ebing, Richard von; *Lampião*; Portugal; Transvestism

Britten, (Edward) Benjamin (1913–1976)

The English composer Benjamin Britten was born in Lowestoft, Suffolk, to a middle-class family. His prodigious musical talent, extraordinary productivity, and ailing constitution were evident from an early age. Dawning awareness of attraction to other boys caused him private anguish; reconciliation with his sexual identity apparently remained an effort well into adult life. After graduating in 1934 from the Royal College of Music, London, the composer produced incidental music for a documentary film unit. There he met poet W. H. Auden, who for a while became his artistic collaborator, as well as mentor in matters personal and political. This included a campaign on Auden's part to overcome Britten's inhibitions against a fully passionate sexual life. Under Auden's influence, Britten left for America in 1939, where he toured, performing with his new friend, the tenor Peter Pears. This relationship became serious; on their return to England in 1942, the two began living together in London. The overwhelming success of his opera *Peter Grimes* (1945) gave Britten international recognition, and he was able to establish his own touring opera company. In 1947, Britten and Pears moved to the town of Aldeburgh, on the Suffolk coast, where they founded an annual arts festival. Their performing partnership lasted until Britten's affliction with heart trouble in 1973; a substantial number of his works were written for Pears to sing. Over the course of this relationship, Britten developed a series of intense paternalized attachments to young boys. These affairs never disturbed his relationship with Pears, who remained the emotional mainstay of his life.

Britten composed nearly one hundred major works of all sorts, including fifteen operas, and is one of the few twentieth-century opera composers whose works have found a lasting place in the repertoire. His style integrates a riveting sense of drama, vivid orchestration, chiseled structures, and glowing melody; familiar tonal courses and generic designs are freshly reworked, darkly unraveled, or held in ambivalent counterpoise. He was gifted at finding compelling musical form for the most challenging, unexpected literary material. Often drawn to the words of homosexual or bisexual authors, among them Michelangelo, Shakespeare, Arthur Rimbaud, Herman Melville, E. M. Forster, Wilfred Owen, Henry James, and Thomas Mann, Britten traces a scattered and diverse tradition of male love through the high literary canon. Yet the homoerotic themes in his chosen texts are usually veiled or subterranean.

Britten's relationship with Pears was an open secret in British musical circles. In contrast to Auden's insolent frankness, they conformed to the model of discretion whereby one's homosexuality was relegated to the private sphere, making no demands for public acknowledgment. Closet accommodations thus shaped the composer's work to a great extent; but he managed to explore in covert ways issues relating to his private experience of sexuality throughout his career. In the youthful, American period, the steamy visions of Rimbaud in *Les Illuminations* (1939) merge in a jungle of surreal images; Britten's selection from the love sonnets of Michelangelo (1940) hint only once at the gender of the beloved. Both are further camouflaged by settings in the original language. In the period of fame, Philip Brett has outlined an evolution of Britten's thought, from a focus on the effects of social oppression, to the metaphysical implications of power and desire, then turning inward to magical worlds of fantasy, followed by a period of ascetic severity, and culminating in important statements of personal disclosure.

The sexual element in the story of the fisherman Peter Grimes was forgone for a more general portrait of a social outcast, the eccentric individual against the crowd. Grimes's brutal ways prove fatal for his boy apprentices, but the heartless condemnation of the borough folk is no less villainous; it is Grimes's internalization of their judgment that misshapes his psyche and compels him to suicide. In the operas *Billy Budd*

B

(1951) and *The Turn of the Screw* (1954), Britten treats the erotic element with irony, as a deeply ambiguous symbol of desire and dread. The representation of an alternative love destroyed by a powerful taboo provides a cathartic experience that straddles differences within the audience, whose members will be both spellbound and uncomfortable for different reasons. It is important to note how many of Britten's works center on children, as creatures of beauty, fragile innocence, and inscrutable powers. The discourse on homosexuality in his music is inextricable from intergenerational love. But if he was able to achieve personal resolution concerning his homosexual nature, the same was not true for his pedophilic inclinations. The appearance of such a subjectivity in his work is rarely free of self-laceration; glimpses of young male flesh are accompanied by fearful reflexive aspersions of destructiveness and corruption.

In the orchestral song cycle *Nocturne* (1958) and the opera *A Midsummer Night's Dream* (1960), Britten sublimates homoerotic desire, translating it into dreamy, twilit pleasures and magical, rarefied soundscapes. The blurred, suspended quality he creates accommodates a multitude of individual fantasies by dissolving or veiling their exact objects. The love of male youth and beauty infusing Owen's texts for *War Requiem* (1961) is overshadowed by the work's harrowing pacifist message. Under the extreme stress of warfare, the lyric personae seek to erase themselves or retreat into an airless limbo. At the same time, this enforced sacrifice is excoriated, in a voice purified by outrage at enforced killing, social hypocrisy, and human loss. Britten's last opera, *Death in Venice* (1973), stands as his most overt profession of sexual identity. The aging writer's fateful encounter with the beautiful boy is cast as an achingly private, inward drama. His climactic recognition of the possibility of love is offset by his inability to make it real before he dies.

Britten encountered some adverse reactions to his success, his sexuality, and his commitment to pacifism; but he received great public honor while living in relative openness for his time. His works provide an eloquent record of personal conflict; while in his understated but determined refusal to be completely silenced by the closet, he reflects an emergent claim for a public homosexual identity.

Lloyd Whitesell

Bibliography

Brett, Philip. "Britten's Dream." In *Musicology and Difference: Gender and Sexuality in Music Scholarship*. Ruth Solie, ed. Berkeley, Calif.: University of California Press, 1993, 259–80.

———. "Eros and Orientalism in Britten's Operas." In *Queering the Pitch: The New Gay & Lesbian*. Philip Brett, Elizabeth Wood, and Gary Thomas, eds. New York: Routledge, 1994, 235–256.

———, ed. *Benjamin Britten: Peter Grimes*. Cambridge: Cambridge University Press, 1983.

Carpenter, Humphrey. *Benjamin Britten: A Biography*. New York: Scribner's, 1992.

Emslie, Barry. "*Billy Budd* and the Fear of Words." *Cambridge Opera Journal* 4 (1992): 43–59.

Evans, Peter. *The Music of Benjamin Britten*, rev. ed. New York: Oxford University Press, 1996.

McClatchie, Stephen. "Benjamin Britten, *Owen Wingrave,* and the Politics of the Closet: or, 'He shall be straightened out at Paramore.'" *Cambridge Opera Journal* 8 (1996): 59–75.

Mitchell, Donald, and Philip Reed, eds. *Letters from a Life: Selected Letters and Diaries of Benjamin Britten*. Berkeley, Calif.: University of California Press, 1991.

Palmer, Christopher, ed. *The Britten Companion*. Cambridge: Cambridge University Press, 1984.

See also Auden, W. H.; England; English Pastoral Composers; Music and Musicians 1 (Classical Music); Opera

Bronzino, Agnolo (1503–1572)

Agnolo Bronzino, who started out as a pupil of Jacopo da Pontormo and later became court painter to Duke Cosimo I de' Medici, was the premier portraitist of midsixteenth-century Florence. He was also an accomplished poet. Recent scholarly attention to his burlesque verse—a genre characterized by equivocal meanings and erotic, often obscene subtexts to which members of Florence's court and intellectual circles, such as Benedetto Varchi, would have been alert—has detected a wealth of more or less latent homoerotic references (see critical edition edited by Petrucci Nardelli). In one memorable early poem, "Del Pennello," Bronzino gives bawdy praise to his "tool," slipping knowingly between two close spellings, one for paintbrush, the other for penis. With the Counter-Reformation, such allusions appear to have been increasingly camouflaged in his literary work. The nickname "Bronzino" itself (his given name was Agniolo, or Angelo, di Cosimo di

Agnolo Bronzino, Portrait of Cosimo I de' Medici as Orpheus, *c.1538–1540. Philadelphia Museum of Art: Gift of Mrs. John Wintersteen.*

Mariano) has been suspected of encoding a homosexual allusion, given that *il bronzo* was an alloy of copper and tin, elements that together in the burlesque code signified "anus." Alternatively, it may simply refer to the painter's reddish hair.

The homoerotic subtext in Bronzino's burlesque poetry (in his more serious lyric verse, he addressed himself in amorous terms to a lady) has given some of his interpreters license to read a similar set of allusions, or sensibility, into his striking portraits of eroticized male sitters, young and old. Among the more provocative of Bronzino's portraits are his *Andrea Doria as Neptune* (McCorquodale, fig. 40) and *Cosimo I de' Medici as Orpheus* (Philadelphia Museum of Art), in which the use of a mythological guise provides an occasion to portray the sitter, duly idealized, in the nude. In the former, a low-hanging swatch of drapery partially exposes the admiral's genitals, suggesting an equivalence between virility and heroism. The conceit of the latter, which was painted to commemorate the young duke's wedding, turns on the curious adaptation of the muscular *Belvedere Torso* as a model for the body of the sitter, turned to show a three-quarter's rear (and hence passive) view, who coyly fondles a phallic if delicate violin bow—in sum, a seemingly counterintuitive strategy for making claims about the duke/Orpheus's prowess as a great lover of *women*. More characteristic of Bronzino's approach to portraying handsome, well-born youths are his *Portrait of a Young Man* in the Metropolitan Museum of Art in New York City and his *Portrait of Ludovico Capponi* in the Frick Collection in New York, whose virility is asserted by—and savored for—their frontal stances, heavy-lidded gazes, and jutting codpieces.   *William B. MacGregor*

Bibliography

[Bronzino, Agnolo.] *Rime in burla*. Franca Petrucci Nardelli, ed. Rome: Istituto della Enciclopedia Italiana, 1988.

McCorquodale, Charles. *Bronzino*. New York: Harper and Row, 1981.

Pilliod, Elizabeth. "Bronzino's Household." *Burlington Magazine* 134 (1992): 92–100.

See also Art History; Florence; Italian Renaissance; Italy; Michelangelo Buonarroti

Broughton, James (Richard) (1913–)

American poet, playwright, and filmmaker James Broughton is identified with the movement sometimes called the San Francisco Renaissance, which flourished from 1945 to 1952 and also included Kenneth Rexroth and Robert Duncan. Influences on Broughton's poetry include Duncan, Whitman, Blake, nursery rhymes, and, in his later works, Allen Ginsberg and other Beat poets. Broughton's poems combine simple language with formal experimentation to express emotions ranging from optimism to defiant anger. They celebrate the human spirit as a force of nature but also depict the social and psychological constraints that impede personal liberation.

Though Broughton has stated that he considers himself chiefly a poet, he is also an influential figure among American avant-garde filmmakers. His films are odes to the enlivening power of love and sex. The earliest of them focus on the joys of heterosexuality, and it was not until *Together* (1976) that he created an entirely gay-themed film. This was the first of several collaborations between Broughton and his life partner, artist Joel Singer.

Besides poems and films, Broughton has written plays and other works, including *The Androgyne Journal* (1977; revised edition, 1991), comprising autobiographical prose poems and *Coming Unbuttoned: A Memoir* (1993). *Coming Unbuttoned* tells the stories of his life, travels, work, and love affairs with men and women. (From 1962 until their divorce in 1978, Broughton was married to Suzanne Hart.) It begins with his California childhood and ends on Christmas Eve 1976, when Broughton and Singer celebrated their relationship in a marriage ceremony.   *Charles Krinsky*

Bibliography

Broughton, James . *Coming Unbuttoned: A Memoir*. San Francisco: City Lights Books, 1993.

Murray, Raymond. *Images in the Dark: An Encyclopedia of Gay and Lesbian Film and Video*, rev. ed. New York: Plume, 1996.

Peters, Robert. *Where the Bee Sucks: Workers, Drones and Queens of Contemporary American Poetry*. Santa Maria, Calif.: Asylum Arts, 1995.

See also Film; San Francisco

Bruce of Los Angeles

Bruce of Los Angeles, American physique photographer, whose real name was Bruce Bellas (1909–1974), was both sculptor and ethnographer of the eroticized American male.

Equal parts chronicler of the sport of bodybuilding, photographic artist-technician, and carnal visionary, Bruce made his mark in both studio and natural settings, in both shimmering black and white and lurid Kodachrome, in both formal poses that sculpted titanic champions and informal portraits that recorded illicit interactions. Only occasionally taking up the pseudoclassical plaster pillars of tradition, Bruce registered a documentary preference for corrals, motorcycles, navy yards, and the vinyl flotsam of suburbia.

Unlike Bob Mizer, who seldom left the Athletic Model Guild (AMG) compound, Bruce toured the country in search of his models. In the process he gathered an underground erotic travelogue and also distributed his more risqué wares one step ahead of the U.S. Post Office. Somehow Bruce always ended up in New Orleans during Mardi Gras, and there his camera never slept.

Alongside his mail-order success, Bruce founded in 1956 his own bimonthly physique magazine, *The Male Figure*. He soon made his mark in the emerging eight-millimeter movie business as well: such works as *Cowboy Washup* and *Big Gun for Hire* offered even more erotic playfulness than the stills.

Bruce's photo sessions often ended in discarded posing straps and rearing hard-ons, leaving a whole new product line to be marketed after his death. But it is the discreet pinups and performances that are more fitting emblems of the pre-Stonewall decades, when dreams came in glossy 8 by 11's and muscle sculptures camouflaged American men in heat.   *Thomas Waugh*

Bibliography

Bruce of Los Angeles. *Bruce of Los Angeles*. Jim Dolinsky, ed. Berlin: Bruno Gmänder Verlag, 1990.

See also Athletic Model Guild; Photography; Physical Culture

Buddhism

The historical and cultural diversity of the Buddhist tradition, which has a history of more than 2,500 years and today a global geographical span, makes it impossible to identify a single "Buddhist" view regarding homosexuality. Same-sex relations have been viewed differently in different places and at different times, and yet underlying this diversity of opinions (and perhaps allowing for it) is a fundamental neutrality on the issue of homosexual love.

Buddhism was founded as a contemplative/monastic religion in northern India by Siddhartha Gautama, who, believed to have attained the state of human perfection known as enlightenment (*bodhi*) at about the age of thirty, spent the next fifty years teaching his method to monastic and lay followers. Central to the tenets of the religion is the belief in the importance of moral discipline (*sila*), the epitome of which is considered to be the life of the fully ordained monk (*bhiksu*) or nun (*bhiksuni*), a life that entails, among other things, strict celibacy. The emphasis on sexual abstinence was more practical than metaphysical. On the one hand, sexual activity (and especially procreation) was seen as a distraction to the religious life. On the other, it was seen as aggravating the already strong human tendency to desire, the elimination of which was seen as necessary to the attainment of enlightenment. Hence, the Buddha's chief concern was to set forth the boundary of what constitutes sexual activity, rather than to distinguish between forms of sexual activity (e.g., homo/heterosexual). For example, in the *Vinaya*, the texts dealing with the monastic discipline, the breaking of the vow of celibacy is described in strictly physiological terms—for men, the insertion of the male organ into any one of three orifices (mouth, anus, or vagina) of a woman, man, or animal, whether living or dead—with no moral distinction drawn among the various objects. Hence, when homosexuality is condemned in the *Vinaya* texts, it is condemned more for being an instance of sexuality than for being a form of sexuality involving partners of the same sex. Various Indian Buddhist texts do disparage the figure of the *pandaka*, a category of human beings that includes men with so-called passive homosexual leanings. But this condemnation has more to do with the *pandaka's* effeminacy—his taking on the sex roles of women—than with the fact that he engages in same-sex relations. Indeed, for the active (top) partner, same-sex relations were seen to be neither abnormal nor a threat to one's status as a normative male.

In another genre of Indian Buddhist literature, the *Jataka*, that recounts episodes of the Buddha's former lives, there appears to be more overt homoerotic sentiment. As Jones has shown, in those texts the Buddha's intimacy to his closest disciple, Ananda, during the Buddha's own lifetime is explained in moving, and at times even sexually implicit, terms, as in the case when the two were, in a former life, deer, who "always went about together . . . ruminating and cuddling together, head to head, nozzle to nozzle, horn to horn" (Jones 114).

Reference to lesbian relations is more infrequent in the Indian Buddhist texts, although the *Vinaya*, for example, prescribes a relatively lenient punishment for nuns who engage in mutual masturbation. More material is to be found in China, though mostly in fiction. Hence, the hero of *Dream of the Red Chamber* is delighted when he stumbles upon two nuns in sexual embrace, and in the lesbian classic *Love of the Perfumed Companion*, two women vow before the Buddha to be reborn as husband and wife.

Of course, for both monks and nuns, the monastic life provided a socially sanctioned means of escape from unwanted marriage, as well as access to same-sex partners (whether for friendship or sexual relations). In Tibet, Goldstein has documented the preponderance of homosexual relationships between the *ldab ldob*, the working monks of large monasteries, although homosexual relations were by no means restricted to this segment of the monastic population. In Japanese Buddhism the ethos was even more favorable to same-sex love, as exemplified in the texts that ex-tolled the love between older monks and young temple acolytes (*chigo*). Kukai, the founder of Japanese esoteric Buddhism, is ascribed with having brought the practice of homosexuality from China, and this is considered one of his many accomplishments. A short text, said to have been revealed by him to a monk as a boon for his prayers, describes techniques for seducing a *chigo* and various positions for anal intercourse. Perhaps the most important work extolling homosexual love in Japan is the seventeenth-century classic of Ihara Saikaku, *The Great Mirror of Male Love*, in which "the norm is the unabashed and enthusiastic enjoyment of male love, as if it were somehow outside the confines of Buddhist stricture" (see Schalow, *The Great Mirror*).

Although at times ambivalent about same-sex love, the Buddhist tradition has also been at times laudatory. This range of views is possible because of Buddhism's essentially neutral stance on homosexuality. For most Buddhist traditions, the concern has been and continues to be focused on sexuality in general, with same-sex relations being seen as no better and no worse than heterosexual ones.

This same attitude has made it possible for many contemporary gay men and women in Western countries to embrace the Buddhist faith without feeling their gay and lesbian sexual identities threatened. In the United States gay Buddhists have also been at the forefront of responding to the AIDS crisis. In San Francisco, for example, the first hospice established for people with AIDS is said to have been founded by members of the Hartford Street Zen Center.   *José Ignacio Cabezón*

Bibliography

Cabezón, José Ignacio. *Buddhism, Sexuality and Gender*. Albany: State University of New York Press, 1992.

———. "Homosexuality and Buddhism." In *Homosexuality and World Religions*. Arlene Swidler, ed. Valley Forge, Pa.: Trinity Press International, 1993.

Childs, Maggie. "Chigo Monogatari." *Monumenta Nipponica* (1978).

Golstein, Melvyn. "A Study of the Ldab Ldob." *Central Asiatic Journal*, 9 (1964): 134.

Jones, John Garrett. *Tales and Teachings of the Buddha*. London: George Allen and Unwin, 1979.

Schalow, Paul Gordon. *The Great Mirror of Male Love by Ihara Saikaku*. Stanford, Calif.: Stanford University Press, 1989.

B ————. "The Priestly Tradition of Homosexual Love in Japanese Buddhism." In *Buddhism, Sexuality and Gender*. J. I. Cabezón, ed.

See also China; India; Japan; Religion and Religiosity; Thailand

Buggery

This term is used mainly in a legal context to describe anal penetration in either homosexual or heterosexual sex, although it can also be used to denote anal intercourse with animals. It is derived from the verb "to bugger," an insulting corruption of "Bulgarian" that was originally applied to members of an eleventh-century eastern European sect. The usage spread until it was used against other heretical groups, as well as moneylenders. "Bugger" acquired its association with sexual deviancy when these heretics (especially the Albigenses) were subsequently accused of the "unnatural" practice of sodomy. The religious and financial connotations of the word gradually declined until "bugger" simply meant anyone who indulged in anal intercourse. As their original meanings suggest, however, "bugger" and "buggery" are part of a complex cultural history in which the construction of sexual desire is intermingled with questions of religious orthodoxy and national identity. In this instance, dissident religious beliefs have supposedly combined with foreign decadence to produce a "deviant" form of sexual pleasure. As a result, practitioners of buggery are often said to have been corrupted by overseas influence, while state propagandists in England and North America have been able to insist that anal sex is an import that has no place in their "native" traditions. A similar mixture of religious and sexual associations adheres to "sodomy," which was used interchangeably with "buggery" in sixteenth- and seventeenth-century England. Both words occur frequently in court documents and in tracts attacking sexual misbehavior, but recent Renaissance historians have argued that the terms were used indiscriminately to describe both heterosexual and homosexual intercourse. It was only with the rise of homosexual subcultures in the eighteenth century that "buggery" began to be associated primarily with same-sex unions; yet even now, it can still be used in a legal context to describe heterosexual anal sex, which in some countries is subject to the same prohibitions as homosexual intercourse. The word also crops up in popular cultural discussions of such texts as *Lady Chatterley's Lover* (D. H. Lawrence, 1928; published 1960) and *Last Tango in Paris* (Bernardo Bertolucci,

1973), both of which feature famous instances of heterosexual anal sex. In a homosexual context, it would be exciting to see "bugger" and "buggery" reappropriated in the same way that dyke, fag, queer, and fruit have been, but this seems unlikely. Virginia Woolf used "bugger" provocatively as a challenge to polite speech: "At Duncan [Grant]'s show, we met the Bugger boys, Joe [Ackerley], Morgan [Forster], William [Plomer]; and savoured the usual queer scent" (*The Diary of Virginia Woolf* 120); but nowadays "bugger" exists only in British English as a mild swear word, and it is rarely encountered in North America, except in a technical or legal context. Even in England it is unlikely to reappear as a term of empowerment, given that its popular usage is largely restricted to upper-middle-class military circles, which are the least likely to use it in a celebratory, nonderogatory fashion.
Vincent Quinn

Bibliography

Moran, Leslie. *The Homosexual(ity) of Law*. London: Routledge, 1996.

Woolf, Virginia. *The Diary of Virginia Woolf*. Anne Olivier Bell, ed. Vol. 5. London: Hogarth Press, 1984.

See also England; Gay Language; Sexual Practice: Anal Sex; Sodomy

Burroughs, William Seward (1914–1997)

William S. Burroughs, born on February 5, 1914, in St. Louis, Missouri, grew up in upper-class privilege in the suburbs of St. Louis. His grandfather's fotune from the invention of the Burroughs adding mchine kept his family secure before, during, and after the Great Depression.

He was sent to a series of private schools and went on to graduate from Harvard University (which he hated) with an A.B. in 1936. Throughout a series of failed graduate school attempts—at Harvard, 1938; University of Vienna, 1937; Mexico City College, 1949–1950—and a brief stint in the army, he was supported by a steady income in trust from his parents. He tried making money as an advertising copywriter in New York City in the early 1940s and later as a bartender, exterminator, and private detective. The financial cushion of his trust fund helped lead eventually to experimentation with drugs and small-time crime in New York City.

Burroughs became addicted to morphine and heroin in 1944 while living in New York. He also met and befriended Allen Ginsberg and Jack Kerouac there. The friendship of these three men formed the basis for the Beat circle of writers, artists, and musicians. As the elder statesman of the Beat trinity, Burroughs played the role of pedagogue and guide to the younger Ginsberg and Kerouac, introducing them to junky Manhattan and to Rimbaud. Burroughs's writings are significantly different from the works of both other celebrated writers, though. His early works are explorations of addiction, recovery, and relapse; he examined the culture of addiction in ways that were amazing and shocking to audiences in 1950s America. He pushed the limits of novelistic content and the form of the novel itself. In a piece written several months after his death, *Harper's* called him "the last of [America's] revolutionary modernists" (Passaro).

Burroughs published the novel *Junky: Confessions of an Unredeemed Drug Addict*, which was released in America in 1953, under the pen name Bill Lee. It is an autobiographical treatment in a hard-boiled, film noir style. After the early hard-boiled narrative of *Junkie*, he turned to a much more formally experimental style in *Naked Lunch*, marked by fragmentary and disordered narrative pieces, "routines," or grotesque and violent comic meditations, and an almost complete abandonment of stable character development. *Naked Lunch* was held on obscenity charges when it was published in America in 1962 and cleared of charges in 1966; its publication virtually marked the end of the American judicial system's use of obscenity laws to suppress literary works.

Burroughs was married twice and pursued male lovers during both marriages. He and his wife Joan Vollmer moved to Mexico City to avoid drug possession prosecution charges in the United States. While in Mexico City, on September 6, 1951, he accidentally shot and killed her during a "William Tell" stunt in a bar, and was bailed out by his parents. This incident was followed by six years of traveling/living in Tangier, Morocco, then in Paris. It should not be surprising that Burroughs, like many gay men of his time, married disastrously. Joan's death seems to have freed him to both write about and to explore his homosexuality. In the introduction to *Queer*, Burroughs relates two stories that seem to encapsulate the novel: the protagonist's recovery from addiction which has the effect of recovering his homosexual desires, and the novel "is motivated and formed by an event which is never

mentioned, in fact is carefully avoided: the accidental shooting death of my wife, Joan, in September 1951." He goes on to claim, "I am forced to the appalling conclusion, that I never would have become a writer but for Joan's death and to a realization of the extent to which this event has motivated and formulated my writing." This complex knot of addiction and sexuality compelled Burroughs to write for the rest of his life.

Burroughs is perhaps the last homosexual to whom one should look for useful, positive, or affirmative narratives of gay male sexuality. He is very much a product of his historical moment and Midwest suburban upbringing. He strongly disliked most gay men, although the detail with which he describes them suggests he spent more than a little time cruising—and perhaps being rejected in—gay bars. In *Junkie* he writes,

> In the French Quarter there are several queer bars so full every night the fags spill out on to the sidewalk. A room full of fags gives me the horrors. They jerk around like puppets on invisible strings, galvanized into hideous activity that is the negation of everything living and spontaneous. The live human being has moved out of these bodies long ago. But something moved in when the original tenant moved out. Fags are ventriloquists' dummies who have moved in and taken over the ventriloquist. The dummy sits in a queer bar nursing his beer, and uncontrollably yapping out of a rigid doll face. (*Junkie* 72)

Despite the critical sting and homophobia of this early passage (in which the butch Midwesterner meets the urban queen), Burroughs discusses, details, and explores gay male sexuality in virtually all his novels. Many of those come to feature an almost utopic (for Burroughs) vision of the queer youth as terrorist: subversive, violent, sexual, tough. Burroughs also maintained an affectionate correspondence, alternately literary, philosophical, and sexual, with Allen Ginsberg that lasted many years.

After undergoing an apomorphine cure with a doctor in London in 1957, Burroughs claimed to be cured of addiction, although there were instances of relapse. From 1974, when he returned to New York, he made a living by teaching, writing, and giving readings. He received the National Institute of Arts and Letters and American Academy award in litera-

B ture in 1975 and was made a member of that organization in 1983. He moved to Lawrence, Kansas, in 1981, where he continued to write and paint until his death on August 2, 1997.

Burroughs is perhaps most well known to contemporary audiences as an aged figure in popular culture—his appearances in Gus Van Sant's *Drugstore Cowboy* (1989); in a wide range of pop music videos; with spoken recordings with artists like Kurt Cobain, R.E.M., and Laurie Anderson; and in Nike commercials—in which his immaculately dressed aging body seemed less important than his voice, an ironic monotone verging on oracular. That these appearances celebrated Burroughs as a celebrity rather than as a writer, painter, addict, or homosexual was the point; he became a ghostly relic of the Beat trinity and was willing to sell himself and his image as he aged. Yet even a firm like Nike could not contain the subversive potential of Burroughs. His voice and image remained seductive and weirdly disturbing even as it was peddling sneakers. Burroughs had before his death become a signifier for a system of knowledge and codes that we can only call *cool*. And as America continues to be consumed with the idea of consuming what is cool, this always disruptive presence in the popular culture indicates his success in queering it.

Elliott McEldowney

Bibliography

Lydenberg, Robin. *Word Cultures: Radical Theory and Practice in William S. Burroughs' Fiction.* Urbana: University of Illinois Press, 1987.

McNally, Denis. *Desolate Angel: Jack Kerouac, the Beat Generation, and America.* New York: McGraw-Hill, 1979.

Miles, Barry. *William Burroughs: El Hombre Invisible, A Portrait.* New York: Hyperion, 1993.

Morgan, Ted. *Literary Outlaw. The Life and Times of William Burroughs.* New York: Henry Holt, 1988.

Mottram, Eric. *William Burroughs: The Algebra of Need.* London: Marion Boyars, 1977.

Passaro, Vince. "The Forgotten Killers." *Harper's Magazine.* 296: 1775 (April 1998): 71–76.

Tytell, John. *Naked Angels: The Lives and Literature of the Beat Generation.* New York: McGraw-Hill, 1976.

See also Beat Generation; Ginsberg, Allen; New York City; Queer; Rimbaud, Arthur; U.S. Literature: Contemporary Gay Writing

Burton, Sir Richard Francis (1821–1890)

Richard Burton began his career in the Bombay Army of the East India Company. In his seven-year sojourn in the Indian subcontinent, he cultivated his gift for languages and for "native" disguise. He was to become an explorer of considerable renown, best known for making a pilgrimage in disguise to the holy Islamic cities of Mecca and Medina. He helped to establish the Anthropological Society in London, a body that shared his long-standing interest in the explicit ethnographic documentation of "exotic" sexual codes and practices, including polygamy, pederasty, clitoridectomy, infibulation, and male circumcision. This interest in sexual anthropology may have been triggered by what he described as his official investigation of three brothels in Karachi offering the services of boys and eunuchs, and popular with the company's troops. Though there has been much speculation—fueled substantially by Burton himself—about the report that supposedly resulted from the investigation, there is little reason to believe that such a document ever existed.

In 1885 Burton fulfilled his long-cherished dream of publishing a "complete and unexpurgated" translation of the *Alf Laylah wa Laylah* (rendered as *The Book of the Thousand Nights and a Night*). The copiously annotated translation, which eventually encompassed seventeen volumes, was notable not only for its unreserved descriptions of a variety of sexual acts between men and men, women and women, and men and women, but perhaps even more for the now famous Terminal Essay that formed part of the tenth volume. This ethnographic essay sought, among other things, to provide a map of what Burton called the Sotadic Zone, within whose borders "le Vice" was "popular and endemic, held at worst to be a mere peccadillo." The Zone encompassed the Mediterranean region; West Asia; portions of India, China, and Japan; the South Sea Islands; and the Americas. Burton insisted that male same-sex eroticism was caused or facilitated by "geographic and climatic" rather than racial characteristics, though the terms seem to function with a deliberate emptiness in his analysis. Toward the end of his treatise, for instance, there are extensive descriptions of the activities of sodomitical communities in decadent urban settings like Paris and London, both outside the Sotadic Zone proper. Elsewhere in his essay Burton speculated on other proximate causes for the prevalence of male same-sex eroticism, including the demands of religious ritual, restricted access to women, and the irregular biological/neurological constitution of the male pederast. Encyclopedic in scope, provocative and prurient, and to a certain degree free of heterosexual moralizing, the essay has assumed the status of a classic of Victorian sexology.

Over his lifetime Burton translated several volumes of Indian and North African erotica, including the *Kamasutra* (1883) and the *Ananga Ranga* (1885). Among the last of these was *The Perfumed Garden of Cheikh Nefzaoui*, translated from a French version of the Arabic original. At his death, Burton was engaged in a new and more fully annotated translation from the Arabic, which was rumored to include a lengthy final chapter on same-sex erotic practices. There has been considerable confusion—as well as prurient conjecture—about the details of this enterprise, including the putative section on "le Vice." The manuscript was burned, along with several other papers, by Isabel Burton in the days following her husband's death.   *Parama Roy*

Bibliography

Bleys, Rudi C. *The Geography of Perversion: Male-to-Male Sexual Behaviour Outside the West and the Ethnocentric Imagination, 1750–1918.* New York: New York University Press, 1995.

Brodie, Fawn. *The Devil Drives: A Life of Sir Richard Burton.* New York: Norton, 1967.

Burton, Richard. *First Footsteps in East Africa.* 2 Vols. Isabel Burton, ed. 1856; New York: Dover, 1987.

———. "Terminal Essay." *The Book of the Thousand Nights and a Night.* Vol. 10. Privately printed by the Burton Club. London: Kamashastra Society, 1885.

Said, Edward W. *Orientalism.* New York: Random House, 1978.

See also Africa: Precolonial sub-Saharan Africa Anthropology; *Arabian Nights*; Arabic Literature; Colonialism; India; Islam; *Kama sutra*; Pederasty

Busi, Aldo (1948–)

Since the publication of his first novel, *Seminario sulla gioventù*, in 1984, Aldo Busi has established himself as one of Italy's most prominent, prolific, and controversial writers. Busi's work is difficult to categorize. His first three books published in rapid succession might be called novels, although they defy conventional expectations of the genre. This is also true of his subsequent work, which includes

travel writing, a version of Boccaccio's medieval classic *The Decameron*, a compilation of his responses to problem-page letters, and a screenplay. On a personal level he is also difficult to pin down. A media celebrity in Italy, he is considered both charming and outrageous, someone who courts publicity but who is equally skeptical of his celebrity status. He is also famous for his homosexuality, but his vitriolic social commentary is as often directed at the conventions of gay society as at the morality of the heterosexual middle class.

The dominating aspect of almost all Busi's writing is the narrative voice, which may or may not be that of Busi himself. The Busi of the novels can be arrogant, bombastic, and self-obsessed yet also honest, intelligent, and insightfully critical of the world around him. His voice can be that of the urbane educated intellectual or appear to emanate from the conservative peasant culture of Busi's origins. Neither is definitive but rather a part of the complex linguistic tapestry that his writing constitutes and the motor of his often convoluted sense of plot.

This "auto-profanation," as Busi calls it, is also expressed through his work's tortured eroticism. Graphic descriptions of mostly homosexual sex abound, never gratuitous or sentimentalized but used as a means of understanding the nature of social relations. It is this aspect of his writing that has on occasion proved so shocking to his readership. This is clearest in the travel narrative *Sodomie in corpo 11*. He launches into a punishing yet informative sexual schedule, and the knowledge he acquires offers all sorts of insights into the diverse societies he visits.

It is language, however, that transforms this knowledge, and Busi is insistent that the true role of literature is to reveal the potential of language. His work displays great semantic richness, merging standard Italian forms with dialect and popular language that, like the content of his work, is jarring and challenging. His inventiveness in disrupting conventional language is instrumental in conveying his deforming vision of a corrupt society.

Busi's linguistic virtuosity is the aspect of his work that has attracted the most critical attention in Italy, but it is also a barrier to its successful translation. Similarly, Busi's concerns are not always amenable to an Anglo-American gay readership. He is not at all interested in writing about "gay" issues such as "coming out" or even AIDS. For Busi, homosexuality is a provocation, an often solitary chal-

B

lenge to all aspects of the status quo, and a focus through which to chart his adventures in language.

Derek Duncan

Bibliography

Bacigalupo, Massimo. "Aldo Busi: Writer, Jester and Moral Historian." In *The New Italian Novel*. Zygmunt G. Baranski and Lino Pertile, eds. Edinburgh: Edinburgh University Press, 1993, 35–42.

See also Italian Literature; Italy

Business

Since the seventeenth-century "Molly Houses," commercial activities and establishments have been vital aspects of gay community, identity, and culture. It is not an overstatement to claim that a thriving consumer culture and business community has accompanied and even, to some extent, inspired gay liberation's progress during the last half of the twentieth century. There are many examples of the symbiotic relationship between gay culture and business: urban "ghettos," gay and lesbian movies, RSVP luxury cruises, and perhaps most significantly, with its campy excess and extravagance, the Lesbian Gay Pride Day festival itself.

Before and after the Stonewall riots of 1969, gay bars emerged as key institutions in modern gay communities. The bar served many social, leisure, and political purposes. First, in its most obvious role, it allowed gay men and lesbians to socialize and establish same-sex contacts in a relatively safe environment. It also served as a nexus for a web of social relations and the patterning of behavior. Bars were used as a conduit for information about gay current events, health issues, and politics. From approximately the 1950s to the present, gay neighborhoods with coffeehouses, bookstores, and music rooms flourished in large urban North American cities. These businesses were very much embedded within social relations at the time and were part and parcel of relatively more positive and supportive social networks for gay men and lesbians. In a profound sense, businesses such as these were deemed part of gay and lesbian communities and contributed to the richness and diversity of the gay cultural and urban milieu.

Still, the relationship between gay culture and business has developed beyond private social networks of gay men and the traditional bar culture. A qualitative, anthropological stream of work pioneered within the consumer research literature by researchers Russell Belk, John Sherry Junior, Melanie Wallendorf, and Elizabeth Hirschman is useful when exploring the relationships among business, consumer culture, and gay culture. Goods, services, and businesses assume symbolic deep meanings, both idiosyncratic and shared. These meanings are important in facilitating the framing and understanding of everyday experience, the establishment of personal and social identity, and the expression of resistances to class, racial, or sexual oppression.

Over the last three decades, the relationship between gay culture and business has become stronger and significantly more complex and nuanced by the incorporation of coded gay consumer symbols and images in mainstream advertising. Correspondingly, a plethora of gay consumer styles emerged that were readily catered to by clothing and jewelry businesses: "club kids," drag, leather, "jock," clone, and more conservative looks, among others. In terms of overall self-presentation and appearance, the gay social identity assumed a number of diverse but related consumer manifestations, including the popular butch "clone" look, which involved wearing tight blue jeans, a T-shirt, and the adoption of particular grooming practices such as a short mustache. This particular style was emblematic of the gay machismo that developed during the 1970s. It is not surprising, then, that simultaneously, mainstream companies such as International Male, Benetton, and Calvin Klein have advertised using either provocative or homoerotic images extensively, reaping profits from an emerging gay consumer segment with a collective awareness of itself as a social movement.

The business side of gay culture naturally has its critics. The activities of marketing and advertising may be considered products of many different discourses that incorporate elements of gay identity, community, and experience. Advertising in particular may have a mirroring function and impact on how gays and lesbians think of themselves. Critics have asserted that advertising has tended to promote the image of gays as male, white, and good-looking, at the expense of anyone else who is gay and does not quite fit that stereotype. Such pervasive images are thought to reinforce the alienation of lesbians, blacks, Latinos, Asians, and other ethnic groups from the remainder of the gay communities.

The relationship between gay culture and business may be understood, then, as something of a paradox. On the one hand, as leftist critics maintain, business interests cater to the most affluent of the gay community's members: mainly white males in urban centers. Thus, the targeting of affluent gay white males, it is argued, is not in the best interests of the political "diversity agenda" of the entire gay community. On the other hand, these businesses, as agents of capitalism, do provide a measure of choice and freedom in which people may at will express their preferences, building lives outside the traditional nuclear family structure.

Perhaps there is no grander conflation of business, consumer culture, and gay culture than many of the annual Gay and Lesbian Pride Day Festivals held worldwide. Pride festivals were originally political, as opposed to commercial, in nature, but there has been a significant shift in character and emphasis of this celebration. The Lesbian and Gay Pride Day in Toronto, for example, has attracted approximately seven hundred thousand participants during its recent years. These large numbers give businesses the opportunity to sell a wide array of products within a festive atmosphere in which many may spend freely. During the Toronto festival (which, like its counterparts in most major cities in North America, has come to resemble a huge vendor's fair), participants are offered the opportunity of buying a wide variety of products: food, drinks, toys (such as waterguns), calendars, CDs, arts and crafts, magazines, books, jewelry, clothes, and many other items. Many of these products feature important symbols of gay sensibility and pride in their design, such as the rainbow flag or pink triangle on hats, items of clothing, and keychains.

The pride parade itself may be considered a pageant of gay consumer semiotics, with its flamboyant excess of drag, camp, leather, and other gay clothing styles. Indeed, the festival has become an unparalleled opportunity for gays and lesbians alike to out on their gay apparel and display it for all to see in a fabulous display of pride—and consumer pageantry.   *Steven M. Kates*

Bibliography

Altman, Dennis. *The Homosexualization of America, the Americanization of Homosexuality*. New York: St. Martin's Press, 1982.

D'Emilio, John. *Sexual Politics, Sexual Communities: The Making of a Homosexual Minority in the United States, 1940–1970*. Chicago: University of Chicago Press, 1983.

Hebdige, Dick. *Subculture: The Meaning of Style*. New York: Routledge, 1979.

Kates, Steven. *20 Million New Customers! Understanding Gay Men's Consumer Behavior*. Binghamton, New York: Harrington Park Press, 1998.

Peñaloza, Lisa. "We're Here, We're Queer and We're Going Shopping: A Critical Perspective on the Accommodation of Gays and Lesbians in the U.S. Marketplace." In *Gays, Lesbians, and Consumer Behavior: Theory, Practice, and Research Issues in Marketing*. Daniel L. Wardlow, ed. New York: Haworth Press, 1996, 9–42.

See also Bathhouses and Sex Clubs; Bookstores; Boycott; Fashion; Marketing Molly Houses

Bussotti, Sylvano (1931–)

Sylvano Bussotti is an Italian avant-garde composer and artist. Born into an artistic, cosmopolitan family, he was encouraged to express himself muscially from an early age. He began to study violin when he was five, piano under Luigi Dallapiccola from the age of nine, and composition from the age of thirteen. In 1957 Bussotti met Heinz-Klaus Metzger, one of the most brilliant of Theodore Adorno's students, and within a year they were lovers; Metzger's political aesthetics were a major influence on Bussotti's early scores. Bussotti attended the Darmstadt courses in 1958, meeting John Cage and Pierre Boulez and writing his first mature works including the homoerotic song cycle *pièces de chair II* (1958–1960). The works of this period, including *sette fogli* (1959) and *siciliano* (1962), represented an attack on formalism through deconstructions of notation and linearity. The decadent and controversial *la passion selon Sade* (1964) joined music, theater, lighting, and costumes in a tangle of symbolic seductions. Starting with the *rara requiem* (1969–70), works including the ballet *Bergkristall* (1974) and the operas *Le Racine* (1980) and *L'Ispirazione* (1988) were more traditionally composed and notated. He was artistic director of the La Fenice opera in Venice in 1975–1983 and increasingly involved in direction and design of grand opera; he became music director for the Venice Biennale but was fired in 1991 after producing a series of controversial performance that included, among other things, the hiring of a famous prostitute to appear on stage. It was too outrageous even for the jaded Italian public. Sexual politics abound in Bussotti's works but with little distinction between gay and straight; a polymorphous expression of sensuality is his chief tool in dissolving the rigidity of modernism.   *Paul Attinello*

Bibliography

Bucci, Moreno. *L'opera di Sylvano Bussotti: musica, segno, immagine, progetto, il teatro, le scene, i costumi gli attrezzi ed i capricci dagli anni quaranta al Bussottioperaballet* [exhibition catalogue]. Milano: Electa, 1988.

Bussotti, Sylvano. *I miei teatri: diario segreto, diario pubblico, alcuni saggi*. Palermo: Edizioni Novecento, 1982.

See also Cage, John; Italy; Music and Musicians 1: Classical Music; Opera

Byron, George Gordon, Lord (1788–1824)

Byron's poems sold better than those of any previous English poet; his life embraced scandal of every variety; members of both sexes threw themselves at his feet; and he died at thirty-six in Greece—not quite in battle, but close enough. Yet these startling facts hardly convey all he meant to nineteenth-century readers. As the Italian patriot Giuseppe Mazzini wrote, "Never did 'the eternal spirit of the chainless mind' make a brighter apparition amongst us." In Europe and the Americas, young and old, men and women, Protestants and Catholics, aristocrats and laborers—all found in him not merely a new poetry but a new ferocity of emotion that made whatever they had previously known of human experience look bland.

Even Byron was taken aback by his success, which no one could have predicted at his birth. Although he was from a good family, his father died when he was three, leaving him and his mother to a life of relative poverty in Aberdeen, Scotland. He also faced the serious and lifelong disability of a clubfoot. Through a series of unlikely deaths, he became the Sixth Baron Byron when he was ten years old and inherited the decaying ancestral estate of Newstead Abbey when he came of age. Despite his title and his education at England's elite institutions, including Harrow (1801–1805) and Cambridge University (1805–1808), he never quite made up for the marginality of his childhood, or at least so he felt. He compensated by bragging frequently about his aristocratic rank and by doing everything that respectable men of the middle ranks were not supposed to do, such as having sex with pretty boys.

George Gordon Byron, the sixth Baron Byron. Artist: Thomas Phillips (1835). National Portrait Gallery, London.

Byron belonged to the venerable aristocratic tradition in which boys and women were equally acceptable as passive partners in sex. The all-male schools he attended encouraged his early homosexual experiments. Although Byron had several passionate heterosexual flings as a young man, he loved no one in his life more than John Edleston, a choirboy he met at Cambridge. He wrote several love poems to Edleston, which he later published with the exotic female name "Thyrza" as a mask for the boy, and concluded Canto II of *Childe Harold's Pilgrimage* (1812) with a passionate lament over Edleston's death. In 1821, Byron recalled his "violent, though *pure*, love and passion" for Edleston as part of the "romance of the most romantic period" of his life (*Letters and Journals*, 8:24).

Byron emphasized the purity of his love for Edleston because in the early nineteenth century, British behavioral codes were making pedophilia less socially acceptable than ever before. Although in the aristocratic tradition, pedophilia like Byron's was not considered sexually deviant, new bourgeois norms frowned on sex between men and sex between adults and those considered to be children. Those convicted of sodomy faced, at best, complete loss of reputation and, at worst, hanging. Such treatment guaranteed that Byron kept his actual sex with boys for times when he was far from England. His journey between 1809 and 1811 to Portugal, Spain,

Greece, and Albania gave him plenty of chances to indulge. His most detailed affairs were with two youths, Eustathius Georgiou and Nicolo Giraud, whom he treated far more lightly than he did Edleston. On leaving Georgiou, for example, he wrote, "Our *parting* was vastly pathetic, as many kisses as would have sufficed for a boarding school, and embraces enough to have ruined the character of a county in England" (*Letters and Journals*, 2:6).

Byron's life changed drastically in 1812, when, having returned from his travels, he published an account of them in *Childe Harold's Pilgrimage* that made him England's most famous poet. He increased his fame in the following years by writing verse tales supposedly based on what had happened to him in the Near East. These short and violent poems featured solitary, alienated heroes haunted by memories of erotic misdeeds, whose details Byron kept conveniently vague. Byron's readers assumed that he modeled his heroes on himself, and many found themselves gripped as never before by his representation of the dark side of the soul. From the standpoint of revealing his sexuality, his poems are ambiguous. None features an overt treatment of love between men, although one, "Lara" (1814), flirts with it in the form of the love between the hero and his page, a woman disguised as a man. Nevertheless, in each case, the hero has an undisclosable secret that makes him a rebel against society and prevents anyone from knowing him fully. From a post-Stonewall vantage, despite the overt heterosexuality of Byron's stories, the heroes look like closeted homosexuals whose homosexuality is never spoken by the text.

Byron meanwhile indulged in several scandalous affairs, including one with his half-sister Augusta Leigh and another with Lady Caroline Lamb, who disguised herself as a male page in the vain hope of holding his fancy. In 1815, he bowed to social pressure by marrying a woman of indisputable respectability, Annabella Millbanke. It was a serious mistake. She walked out on him one year later, and English society buzzed with speculation. Given Byron's reputation, no rumor was too scandalous, and Lady Caroline Lamb, to get revenge on Byron for having spurned her, made sure that homosexuality was one of the top contenders. Byron's sin was less that he indulged in scandalous behavior than that, whatever he had done, he had become a subject for common gossip. Faced with what he felt was overwhelming social ostracism, Byron left England forever in 1816. After a summer with Percy and Mary Shelley in Switzerland that inspired Mary with the idea for *Frankenstein*, Byron settled in Italy.

There he flourished as never before. He shelved for the most part his earlier, melodramatic style, and his poetry took new directions that dealt more openly with his sexuality. In his masterpiece, the satirical epic *Don Juan*, he lambastes English sexual hypocrisy. Even though his hero is a famously mythic heterosexual, he laces the work with homosexual innuendo and a gossipy, campy wit that looks forward to Oscar Wilde. In the closet drama *Sardanapalus*, he features a hero who enters in a dress, his head crowned with flowers, and who rebels against the martial ethos of his society. Such works, especially *Don Juan*, scandalized Byron's English readers more than ever, but also brought him his widest audience.

By 1823 Byron had grown restless and longed for a new field of action. He found it in Greece's struggle for independence from Turkey and traveled there to aid the troops. On arriving, a quagmire of competing factions quickly dispelled his romantic illusions, but he also met Loukas Chalandritsanos, a beautiful youth of fifteen. Byron's last three poems describe his passion for Loukas and his frustration that Loukas, unlike Byron's earlier pages, did not love him back. A fever and incompetent doctors ended Byron's life on April 19, 1824. Although nineteenth-century writings about him sometimes hinted at his pedophilia, the full details of his sexual life remained hidden until Louis Crompton's pioneering *Byron and Greek Love* in 1985.

Andrew Elfenbein

Bibliography

Byron, George Gordon, Lord. *Byron's Letters and Journals*. Leslie A. Marchand, ed. 13 vols. London: John Murray, 1973–1982.

———. *The Complete Poetical Works*. Jerome J. McGann and Barry Weller, eds. 7 vols. Oxford: Clarendon, 1980–1993.

Crompton, Louis. *Byron and Greek Love: Homophobia in Nineteenth-Century England*. Berkeley: University of California Press, 1985.

Rutherford, Andrew, ed. *Byron: The Critical Heritage*. London: Routledge & Kegan Paul, 1970.

See also England; English Literature; Greece Pederasty

C

Cabaret, Variety, and Revue Entertainment

Recent research argues that gay-oriented performances have been a constant in American entertainment at least since the early nineteenth century. Evolved from minstrel shows and a gay subculture, female impersonation, a popular mode of gay performance, entered variety theater in San Francisco by the 1860s and eastern cities in the 1870s. By the 1890s, the homosexual presence was overt in clubs in New York's Bowery.

While New York's Harlem and Greenwich Village supported a gay culture of theater, music, and club acts by 1910, in other cities, entertainment venues catering to gay and lesbian audiences emerged later in Depression-era speakeasies. After Prohibition, cabarets and nightclubs provided venues for gay performances.

Middle-class theaters and clubs in America and some European cities in the nineteenth century shaped powerful and damaging effeminate stereotypes that persist in entertainment today. At the turn of the century, Paris revues offered such freakish caricatures. In the twentieth century, homosexual performers in variety, revue, and cabaret entertainment have gradually become the creators of those images, balancing the demeaning portrayals in movies, television, and popular entertainment.

Songs and characters of the minstrel show, America's premier antebellum entertainment, gave white men avenues to desire black men and made "currency out of the black man" for the white males in the audience, it is argued. The appeal of minstrelsy paralleled the birth of a gay male subculture in New York City and elsewhere. Moreover, the minstrel characters—men and women played by men—allowed the tracing of homoerotic desire between the performer and the male observer. In England, the music halls, the emergent mid-nineteenth-century entertainment, fostered the dame, a man in woman's costume, who sang popular songs laden with social and sexual commentary, a counterpart to the minstrel wench.

The wench and dame roles evolved into the fixed characters of the twentieth-century female-impersonator repertoire, the dame and the prima donna. The dame and the prima donna have been viewed as constructions of gender in which sexuality could be commented upon by the impersonator and considered by the audience.

The intimate cabaret was born at the end of the nineteenth century, especially in Germany, France, and Holland, of a quest for entertainment that distilled from popular amusements to convey a political or social message. But between the wars, the "amusement cabaret," scorned by those in political cabaret, offered venues with gay performers that attracted gay audiences. In Weimar Berlin by the late 1920s, numerous gay cabarets, such as the Alexander-Palais, encouraged a gay subculture and attracted a tourist trade.

Female impersonation, legitimated by theater and vaudeville, entertained and, in a subtle, nonpolitical way, provoked audience members to consider their political and social worlds. Important performers in the early decades of the century included Karyl Norman, Jean Malin, and Francis Renault. Julian Eltinge, who led musical, minstrel show, and vaudeville bills after 1906, was the model for serious but humorous impersonation of women that flourished in cabarets in the 1920s. In contrast, Bert Savoy offered the model of the loud-mouthed prostitute. Barbette, an acrobat, performed a strip on the

C trapeze in vaudeville and circuses in Europe. Other popular impersonators of the 1920s and 1930s included Ray Bourbon, Lester LaMonte, Francis David, Gita Gilmore, Harvey Lee, and Ricky Renee.

In the United States, as Prohibition fostered a largely unregulated underworld entertainment scene in the 1920s, speakeasies seeking new ways to appeal to their middle-class clients played on the fascination with gay culture. Increasingly, the speakeasies depended on gay entertainers, who joined the casts of Depression-era cabarets, touring shows that offered programs for presumably straight service clubs and roadhouses, as well as carnivals and bump 'n grind burlesque. In the thirties, the Clam House, a famous Harlem club that catered to gays and lesbians, featured Gladys Bentley, "a 250-pound, masculine, dark-skinned lesbian, who performed all night in a white tuxedo and top hat" (Garber, 324). In New York and some other cities, gay men attended African American clubs that often featured famous black entertainers. The Harlem Renaissance (1917–1937) powerfully melded African American and lesbian and gay cultures through the nightclub and cabaret performances of such singers as Mabel Hampton, Alberta Hunter, Bessie Jackson, Jackie "Moms" Mabley, Bessie Smith, and Gertrude "Ma" Rainey.

Through the thirties and into the postwar years, gay cabaret, based largely on female impersonation, survived in a circuit that included Chicago, Kansas City, New Orleans, Miami, San Francisco, Seattle, and other cities.

In 1938, two New York gay men, Doc Benner and Danny Brown, produced the first Jewel Box Revue. The cabaret company played the Jewel Box Club in Miami in the winter and toured during the summer. The promoters vowed "to bring back female impersonation as a true art," but also insisted on a strong comic flair in what often were lavish song-and-dance revues. The Jewel Box was popular at such clubs as the Apollo in New York, the Turf Club in Denver, and the Garden of Allah in Seattle. It closed in 1973. In Miami, "Babe" Baker's Revue supported a large cast of female impersonators and other entertainers.

In World War II, gay men frequently impersonated women for revues for service personnel. Members of the Women's Army Corps were generally banned from taking part in soldier revues, making it possible for gay men to volunteer for parts that allowed them to explore gender roles, make contact with other gay men, and find ways to be physically affectionate with other men. Comic routines interlaced contemporary movies with impersonations of Carmen Miranda, the Andrews Sisters, Gypsy Rose Lee, and Mae West, all spiced with "campy asides, double entendres, gestures and tones of voice that created parallel gay meanings for their acts" (Bérubé 67–97).

Scholars identify several roles of the gay cabaret and drag show after World War II. The venues offered entertainment, rather than political or overt sexual expression, sometimes keeping police at a distance. The entertainment also attracted heterosexual tourists and residents, giving them more knowledge about homosexuals. Protected somewhat from police harassment, clubs provided gathering places for lesbians and gay men and indirectly fostered a group consciousness, if not a political awareness.

Conventional gay cabaret faltered in some cities in the fifties and early sixties, victim of television, the changing economics of entertainment venues, and greater police harassment. Clubs cut back on costly backup music and installed sound systems using recordings. Female impersonators who were talented singers were replaced by glamorous drags, who simply moved their lips to recordings. Principal centers for such shows were New York, Chicago, New Orleans, Kansas City, San Francisco, and Los Angeles. At the same time, entertainment took on a political edge characteristic of turn-of-the-century Paris cabarets. In San Francisco, the Black Cat Cafe staged satirical operas that made political statements about repressive police actions.

Baths, small clubs, and theaters featured gay artists increasingly in the 1970s. While drag, focused on glamour and female superstars, remained, club acts increasingly commented on themes from institutional hypocrisy to coming-out experiences. Political activism from the late 1960s on fostered a parallel growth in gay entertainment venues.

Roger Simpson

Bibliography

Baker, Roger. *Drag: A History of Female Impersonation on the Stage.* London: MacDonald, 1968.

Bérubé, Allan. *Coming Out Under Fire: The History of Gay Men and Women in World War II.* New York: Free Press, 1990.

Chauncey, George. *Gay New York: Gender, Urban Culture, and the Making of the Gay Male World 1890–1940.* New York: Basic Books, 1994.

Garber, Eric. "A Spectacle in Color: The Lesbian and Gay Subculture of Jazz Age Harlem." In

Hidden from History: Reclaiming the Gay and Lesbian Past. Martin Bauml Duberman, Martha Vicinus, and George Chauncey Jr., eds. New York: New American Library, 1989.

Lott, Eric. *Love and Theft: Blackface Minstrelsy and the American Working Class.* New York: Oxford University Press, 1995.

Moore, F. Michael. *Drag! Male and Female Impersonators on Stage, Screen and Television.* Jefferson, N.C.: McFarland, 1994.

Newton, Esther. *Mother Camp: Female Impersonators in America.* Chicago: University of Chicago Press, 1979.

Paulson, Don, with Roger Simpson. *An Evening at the Garden of Allah: A Gay Cabaret in Seattle.* New York: Columbia University Press, 1996.

Senelick, Laurence, ed. *Cabaret Performance.* Vol. 1. New York: PAJ Publications, 1989. Vol. 2. Baltimore: Johns Hopkins University Press, 1993.

See also Camp; Jewel Box Revue; Harlem Renaissance; Theater; Transvestism

Cadmus, Paul (1904–)

This American painter was born on December 17, 1904, in New York City. Both his parents were commercial artists. He studied at the National Academy of Design and at the Art Students League with Joseph Parnell. His first mature works were completed in 1931–1933 in Europe, where he traveled with the artist Jared French. In 1937 Cadmus joined French and his wife, Margaret, to form the photographic team PAJAMA. Cadmus and French were frequent models for George Platt Lynes's highly charged homoerotic photographs.

Cadmus said that he owed "the start of [his] career really to the Admiral who tried to suppress it," referring to the Navy's removal of *The Fleet's In!* (1934) from an exhibition of government-sponsored paintings at the Corcoran. Although it was left unsaid at the time, the Navy was probably less worried by the painting's depiction of "enlisted men consorting with a party of streetwalkers" than its inclusion of a homosexual pickup. Slightly downstage from the interchanges between women and men, an elegantly dressed gentleman with red tie and painted lips offers a cigarette to a smiling seaman. The suppression of the picture only made it more famous: "For every individual who might have seen the original," *Esquire* claimed, "at least one thousand saw it in black and white reproduction."

A fat man puts a hand on the shoulder of a half-dressed youth in *Y.M.C.A. Locker Room* (1933); a pretty boy negotiates with a sailor in *Shore Leave* (1933); and a gentleman with long fingernails looks over his shoulders knowingly as he enters a bathroom in *Greenwich Village Cafeteria* (1934). These paintings remind us that "cruising" was often enacted through the surreptitious exchange of glances and gestures while it was hoped "straights" were not paying attention.

Cadmus takes the moral role of satirist in the picture *What I Believe* (1947–1948) and *Bar Italia*

Paul Cadmus, YMCA Locker Room, *1934. Courtesy DC Moore Gallery, NY.*

C

(1952–1953). Yet the way in which Cadmus's male figures seem to burst out of their clothing belies his claim of cool detachment. Lewis Mumford suggested that Cadmus "lingers too lovingly on the flesh he would chastise." His obsession with the male body caused the censorship of the post office mural *Pocahontas and John Smith* (1938), in which the rescue of John Smith is obscured by an emphasis on the buttock and genital regions of the Indians.

The logic of closet—hiding or selectively revealing homosexuality, depending on different audiences—recedes in his later work. *The Bath* (1951) explores the theme of all-male domestic life, and Cadmus's love for his companion, singer Jon Andersson, is frankly expressed in *Artist and Model* (1973) and *The Haircut* (1986).

Cadmus's so-called magic realism fell out of favor in the late fifties. However, gay liberation caused a resurgence of interest in Cadmus, although he is ambivalent about what he sees as the resultant marginalization of his work. Cadmus's long career was the subject of the PBS documentary *Paul Cadmus, Enfant Terrible at 80*, and his ninetieth birthday was celebrated by several gallery and museum exhibitions.   *Jonathan Weinberg*

Bibliography

Cadmus, Paul, Margaret French, and Jared French. *Collaborations*. Santa Fe, N.M.: Twelvetree Press, 1992.
Kirstein, Lincoln. *Paul Cadmus*. New York: Chameleon Books, 1992.

See also Art History; French, Jared Blandford; Lynes, George Platt

Caffe Cino

This New York City coffeehouse and later the city's first café theater, which flourished from 1959 to 1967, spawned the Off-Off Broadway movement in that city. Under founder Joseph Cino, then managers Charles Stanley, Michael Smith, and Albert Zuckerman, Caffé Cino produced over two hundred plays and introduced gay playwrights Doric Wilson (who later founded the first gay theater, T.O.S.O.S.), Lanford Wilson (*Talley's Folly*), William M. Hoffman (*As Is*), and Robert Patrick (*Kennedy's Children*). Other playwrights who were presented include Tom Eyen, H. M. Koutoukas, Paul Foster, Robert Heide, Jean-Claude Van Itallie, David Starkweather, Jeff Weiss, Ronald Tavel, Sroen Agenoux, George Birsima, and

many others. The Caffé also premiered *Dames at Sea* and works by Sam Shepard, John Guare, Oliver Haley, and Diane DiPrima. Featured directors included Tom O'Horgan, Marshall Mason, and John Vacarro. In 1985, Lincoln Center Library and Museum of the Performing Arts curators Richard Buck and Magie Dominic mounted an exhibition entitled "Caffé Cino and Its Legacy, an American Cultural Landmark". Though it did plays of many kinds, Caffé Cino is especially remembered as the first venue for unapologetic plays about gay characters.   *Robert Patrick*

Bibliography

Patrick, Robert. "Caffe Cino." *Los Angeles Theatres* (Nov. 1994): 12–13, 18, 20–21.
———. "Where Plays Began." *Other Stages* 1, no. 10 (Feb. 1979): 26–27.

See also New York City; Patrick, Robert; Theater; Wilson, Lanford

Cage, John (1912–1992)

"The enfant terrible of twentieth-century music" is how Marjorie Perloff and Charles Junkerman describe John Cage in their anthology devoted to the composer. It fits well enough without quite suggesting the range of this chameleonlike musician, thinker, writer, one time artist, and mycologist. He upset the musical establishment in almost every possible way, but, he followed the majority of homosexual musicians of his era in remaining silent about his sexuality even after the 1960s; yet his partnership with Merce Cunningham might be called one of the most significant artistic collaborations of the century.

Thomas S. Hines, who interviewed Cage in his last years, has been able to fill in the details of the early life. The son of a male inventor and a woman with feminist leanings, Cage grew up in the Los Angeles area, graduated from Los Angeles High School and Pomona College, and then in 1930 took the familiar path for American artists to Paris. In this foreign atmosphere his interest in all the arts— and his sexuality—flourished. He returned to the United States in 1931 with a lover, an aspiring artist named Don Sample, with whom he lived for a number of years in a nonexclusive relationship. Feeling that his sexual life was chaotic (did his later musical ideas of chance and indeterminacy owe something to his cruising episodes along the Palisades in Santa Monica?), he began to have affairs with women, eventually marrying the highly artistic Xenia Andreevna Kashevaroff. It was also during the Los Angeles years that he began to focus increasingly on music, rather than art, and studied with Richard Bühlig, Henry Cowell, and even the European master-composer Arnold Schoenberg. A year in New York got him introduced into the Virgil Thomson circle, which he took by storm, having a short affair with the architect Philip Johnson. In 1938 Cage and Xenia moved to Seattle, where they met a teenaged dancer named Merce Cunningham, whose effect on Cage led at length to a painful breakup with Xenia: he moved to New York with Cunningham in 1942, the year he wrote *Credo in Us.*

The influences on Cage were as multifarious as his inventive compositional ideas. For the art and persona of Marcel Duchamp he had a similar reverence as for Schoenberg, the one disrupting the authority the other represented. Among composer forebears it was Erik Satie who most engaged him (this formed a link between him and Virgil Thomson, whom he abandoned after having contributed critical parts to the first biography). James Joyce provided an admired literary model; Thoreau the independent-minded attitudes suitable to an American artist. In the 1940s, after the breakup with Xenia and an abortive spell of psychoanalysis, came his famous involvement with Zen Buddhism.

James Pritchett insists on separating Cage from the various images projected onto him (of philosopher-in-music, inspired jester, etc.) in order to view him as a composer. An early preoccupation with numerical systems was combined with a revolutionary concentration on percussion—noise was to be as important a part of Cage's music as traditionally musical sounds had been for others. The prepared piano, an instrument defamiliarized by the doctoring of its strings, was part of this percussive phenomenon, in which pitch was indeterminate and rhythm the organizing parameter. Later, through Zen and the *I Ching,* the notion of controlled chance operation emerged. Also important was the idea of using the world of sound that already exists—the structure being in the person listening. Cage's most famous composition, *4'33"* (1952), inspired by Robert Rauschenberg's *White Painting,* places the onus on the listener to create a world of sound out of silence. A performer (or performers) on any instrument(s) "play" a silent three-movement work. It was at this stage that Cage left the ordinary music lover behind in bewilderment as he pursued increasingly wild ideas supported by the New York artistic world of Rauschenberg, Robert Motherwell, Jasper Johns, Cy Twombly, Mary Caroline Richards, fellow composer Morton Feldman, and of course Merce Cunningham, many of whom were, like him, discreet homosexuals. A further step in the application of chance was to take it beyond the compositional process to ensure a different performance solution each time—the concept of indeterminacy as exemplified in *Winter Music* (1958) and later works. There followed experimentation with electronic sounds, superimposed pieces, and "happenings." Typical of this phase are gargantuan show stoppers like *HPSCHD* (1969), in which seven harpsichordists played computer-realized excerpts of musical classics to the accompaniment of electronic tapes, film, slides, and colored lights. One thread that held these experiments together was Cage's belief that art was not separate from life, and that the artist's role was to make audiences more aware of the actual world in which they lived rather than removing them from it as high art had traditionally tried to do.

Cage's own influence on the world of music is still hard to assess. An unlikely association in which sexual attraction may have played a part was a friendship with the young Pierre Boulez (1925–), whom Cage met when he returned to Paris in 1949 on a Guggenheim. It became clear that the effect of Boulez's highly calculated serialist manipulations of the period were not so different from those Cage could achieve by chance manipulations. The American's example, then, may have helped to arrest the flight toward total serialism that was a strong element of the European agenda, and to bring the avant garde on both sides of the Atlantic closer together. On the whole, Cage's effect on artists working outside music has been arguably more lasting.

Reactions to Cage are as multifarious and contradictory as the phenomenon of the man himself. Many influential Cage admirers see him as a proto-postmodernist, deconstructing "classical music" by bringing it closer to life and eliminating its authority figures and modes of operation. The static orientalist patterns of *Sonatas and Interludes* (1946–1948) can be heard, moreover, as heralding the longer sustained repetitive schemes of Philip Glass and Steve Reich. Others would view Cage contrarily as an (if not *the*) arch-modernist. Lydia Goehr has pointed out that *4'33"* needs concert-hall ambiance and etiquette to make it work. Richard Taruskin in a debunking obituary essay sees "Cage's radical conceptions as much intensifications of traditional practices, including traditional power relations, as departures from them." One observer will hear or see his performances as profoundly anticapitalistic and antibourgeois, another as traditional art-for-art's sake tyranny. George E. Lewis has gone so far as to portray Cage's insistent distancing of his own chance and indeterminacy experiments from the great American indeterminate art of jazz improvisation as a form of cultural racism.

Denial of effects in music of life as a homosexual are traditional in the field: Cage never mentioned his sexuality, and his devotees, who, judging from the e-mail forum devoted to him, are often straight white males with apolitical new-age outlooks, and are either nonplussed or angered by suggestions of any such connection. Jonathan Katz has made a promising start by invoking the title of Cage's most famous book, *Silence,* to show how it not only signified a symptom of oppression but also became, through the Zen-inspired philosophy of nonintervention and nonexpressionism, a chosen form of resistance. As Cage said (in *For the Birds,* 231), relating his involvement with noise to black power (with gay liberation a subtext?), "Today, we must identify ourselves with noises instead [of harmony and counterpoint with its rules of good and bad], and not seek laws for the noises, as if we were blacks seeking power! Music demonstrates what an ecologically balanced situation could be—one in which whites would not have more power than blacks, and blacks no more than whites." But the contradiction of Cage's remaining hidden, along with most other composers, undermines his proclamations about destroying the power system entirely. New ideas about Cage as homosexual artist will surely follow as the inconsistencies and incongruities that surround his life and work are further explored and clarified. A good place to start would be his collaborative partnership with Cunningham, which exemplifies many things that musical critics, typically single-minded in their approach, have omitted to notice.   *Philip Brett*

Bibliography

Cage, John. *Silence.* Middletown, Conn.: Wesleyan University Press, 1961.
——— (in conversation with Daniel Charles). *For the Birds.* Boston: Marion Boyars Inc., 1981.
Hines, Thomas S. "Then Not Yet 'Cage': The Los Angeles Years, 1912–1938." In *John Cage: Composed in America.* Marjorie Perloff and Charles Junkerman, eds. Chicago: University of Chicago Press, 1994, 65–99.
Jones, Caroline A. "Finishing School: John Cage and the Abstract Expressionist Ego." *Critical Inquiry* 19 (1993): 643–47.
Katz, Jonathan. "John Cage's Queer Silence or How to Avoid Making Matters Worse." *GLQ* 5.2 (1999).
Kostelanetz, Richard. *Conversing with Cage.* New York: Limelight, 1988.
Lewis, George E. "Improvised Music after 1950: Afrological and Eurological Perspectives." *Black Music Research Journal* 16 (1996): 91–111.
Perloff, Majorie, and Charles Junkerman, eds. *John Cage: Composed in America.* Chicago: University of Chicago Press, 1994.
Pritchett, James. *The Music of John Cage.* Cambridge: Cambridge University Press, 1993.
Taruskin, Richard. "No Ear for Music: The Scary Purity of John Cage." *The New Republic* (March 15, 1993).

See also Cunningham, Merce; Johnson, Philip C.; Music and Musicians 1: Classical Music; Rauschenberg, Robert

Calva Pratt, José Rafael (1953–)

Calva was born in Mexico City and attended the Iberoamericana University. He has published short stories in *Comunidad* (Community), *La Palabra y el Hombre* (The Word and the Man), and *Tierra Adentro* (Inland). He is currently working as a freelance writer for the Mexican newspapers *Unomásuno* (Oneplusone) and *Vaso Comunicante* (Communicating Vessel), and he is a regular contributor to the literary magazine *Alta Fidelidad* (High Fidelity). Calva lives in Washinghton, D.C., where he coordinates a narrative workshop and does research on contemporary music. His best-known books are *Variaciones y fuga sobre la clase media* (Mexican Middle Class Diversities and Escape), published in 1980 by the University of Veracruz; *Utopía gay* (Gay Utopia), published in 1983 by Editorial Oasis; and *El jinete azul* (The Blue Horseman), published in 1985 by Editorial Katún.

Calva's novels have made him a founding, central figure in gay and lesbian studies. They emphasize social criticism of urban societies and the marginalization of women and other minority groups. He also addresses such topics as homosexual spaces (bathhouses, cruising areas), uses of onanism, feminization through language, homosocial desire, uses of the body, the dynamics of sexual need, urban decadence, misogyny, a demythification of sexual roles, the problematics of identity, and love and nature as means of deconstructing contemporary society.   *Juan Antonio Serna*

Bibliography

Bermúdez, María Elvira. "*Utopía gay* descontaminar por la risa." *Revista mexicana de cultura* 16 (June 12, 1983): 10.

Cohen, Sandro. "*Utopía gay*: Que nadie se ofenda." *Casa de tiempo* 31–32 (July–Aug.1983): 82–83.

Foster, David William. *Gay and Lesbian Themes in Latin American Writing*, 136–139. Austin: University of Texas Press, 1991.

Schnider, Luis Mario. "El tema homosexual en la nueva narrativa mexicana." *Casa del tiempo* 5, nos. 49–50 (Feb.–Mar. 1985): 82–86.

See also Chicano and Latino Gay Cultures; Mexico

Caminha, Adolfo (1867–1897)

Brazilian novelist and critic Adolfo Caminha was forced to resign from a promising naval career because of his relationship with an army officer's wife, and he died in obscurity in Rio de Janeiro, age twenty-nine. He published some poems and stories, a travel book, three novels, and a collection of literary criticism.

Although probably not homosexual himself, Caminha wrote Latin America's first major novel explicitly about homosexuality. *Bom-Crioulo* (Good-Darkie), published in 1895, describes the relationship between a black sailor, Amaro, or Bom-Crioulo, and a young white cabin boy, Aleixo, whom he seduces on board a Brazilian warship. They rent a room in downtown Rio, where they live together while on leave. The idyll ends when Bom-Crioulo is transferred to another ship and Aleixo, left alone, is seduced by the Portuguese washerwoman who owns the rooming house. Bom-Crioulo's frustration and jealousy explode when he learns of this betrayal, which leads to the tragic denouement.

The novel was attacked by hostile reviewers when it appeared and was largely forgotten after Caminha's death. Renewed critical interest in the 1940s led to the publication of a new edition in 1956. Since then there have been successive Brazilian editions, and the novel is now recognized as a naturalist work. To date it has been translated into English, Spanish, and French.

Bom-Crioulo touches on all the major questions of Brazilian society—race, gender, class, nationality, and slavery as well as sexuality. Nevertheless, as Caminha made clear when defending his book, it is essentially about homosexuality. It is perhaps the first modern novel in which the central protagonist is portrayed as exclusively homosexual rather than bisexual. Caminha uses the negative language of the day but counterbalances this with a detached, nonjudgmental authorial attitude, deliberately refusing to suggest any cause for his hero's sexual orientation. His portrayal of jealousy is masterly, lifting Bom-Crioulo to a level where he has been compared with Othello. His works besides *Bom-Crioulo* include *Cartas literárias* (1895); *No país dos ianques* (1894); *A normalista (cenas do Ceará)* (1893); *Tentação* (1896); *Um livro condenado* (1896); and *Trechos escolhidos, por Lúcia Miguel Pereira* (1960).   *Robert W. Howes*

Bibliography

Azevedo, Sânzio de. *Adolfo Caminha (vida e obra)*. Fortaleza, Brazil: Casa de José de Alencar, 1997.

Bueno, Eva Paulino. "Caminha, Adolfo (Brazil; 1867–97)." In *Latin American Writers on Gay and Lesbian Themes: A Bio-critical Sourcebook*. David William Foster, ed. Westport, Conn.: Greenwood Press, 1994, 94–100.

Enciclopédia de literatura brasileira. Direção: Afrânio Coutinho, J. Galante de Souza. Rio de Janeiro: Minestério da Educação, Fundação de Assistência ao Estudante, 1990, vol. 1, p. 370.

Foster, David William. "Adolfo Caminha's *Bom-Crioulo*: A Founding Text of Brazilian Gay Literature." In his *Gay and Lesbian Themes in Latin American Writing*. Austin: University of Texas Press, 1991, 9–22.

Ribeiro, João Felipe de Saboia. *O romancista Adolfo Caminha, 1867–1967*. Rio de Janeiro: Editora Pongetti, 1967.

See also Brazil

Camp

The slipperiness of camp, that signpost of contemporary popular culture and of pre-Stonewall queerdom, has constantly eluded critical definitions and has proceeded in tandem with the discursive existence of camp itself. Described, in the wake of Susan Sontagís landmark essay "Notes on 'Camp' " (1964, later collected in *Against Interpretation*), as sensibility, taste, style, aesthetic discourse, or cultural economy, camp hasn't lost its relentless power

C to frustrate all efforts to stably pinpoint it. Recent studies therefore tend to avoid the pitfalls of essentializing or deterministic definitions, taking into account the performative and provisional existence of camp as both theory and field of reference, by analyzing it in terms of its circulation within culture and its production through "camp effects" or, to cite another most influential essay by unfolding the multilayered and contradictory *uses* of camp at different times and by different communities (Andrew Ross, "Uses of Camp," 1988, reprinted in *Camp,* ed. Fabio Cleto).

In this sense camp reveals how it is closely intertwined with "queer," being at once an adjective, a sometimes capitalized noun, and a both transitive ("to camp something up") and intransitive verb ("camping"). In its verbal form, camp enacts its duplicitous existence as mode of performance—which Sontag calls "deliberate camp," or the ironical, excessively and consciously "dressing up" of self-love and flaunting—and as a mode of perception (Sontag's favorite "naive camp"), where the camp(ing) up) observer perceives a failed seriousness or the artificiality of what passes for natural, and thus dethrones such seriousness and debunks its constructedness, its being "in drag"—i.e., its being an act of performance. Victor Mature, Luchino Visconti, Marylin Monroe, Oscar Wilde, the Queen Mother, and Divine, to name a few, can thus find a "queer" common campground.

The history of the term, along with its wide range of reference, is excitingly troublesome. On the one hand, with the shaping role perception plays—irrespectful of intentions and original contexts—in determining the camp effect, examples can be drawn from all places and times, with instances such as Petronius and Pontormo, Caravaggio and the Versailles court in seventeenth-century France, and the transvestite molly houses in eighteenth-century England—whose affinities with our century's drag underworld signal them as protocamp cases—forming an extended history of camp (histrionically mapped in Mark Booth's *Camp*). On the other hand, we should remember that the word "camp" itself is of unknown origins, and while it was in use among British aristocratic cliques in the second half of the nineteenth century, it may well be arbitrary to extend its modern meaning to earlier ages. "Camp" was first recorded in print, in a dictionary of Victorian slang in 1909, as meaning "actions and gestures of exaggerated emphasis," and it later gained currency in the slang of theatricals, high so-

ciety, the fashion world, show business, and the underground city life. Indeed, the word found some clandestine circulation in high culture, and has been used since the 1920s to describe a literary style exemplified by Oscar Wilde, Max Beerbohm, Ronald Firbank and Carl Van Vechten. These writers' works are regarded as literary enactments of precisely those strategies—aestheticism, aristocratic detachment, irony, theatrical frivolity, parody, effeminacy, and sexual transgression—traced in the drag urban scene which will appear in the first public discussion of camp (Christopher Isherwood's 1954 *The World in the Evening*) and find their seminal study in Esther Newton's *Mother Camp* (1972; both partly reprinted in *Camp,* ed. Fabio Cleto).

Given the stereotypical merging of theatricality, male homosexuality, and the aesthetic sense, the main early twentieth-century use of camp has in fact been identified in a male homosexual lingo deployed on both verbal and non-verbal axes, as a way to communicate among those "in the know," while (for survival reasons, both legal and psychological) excluding those whose "*norm*-ality," homophobic or otherwise, couldn't be part of this outlaw, yet proximate, community. In this sense, camp has been claimed since the 1970s (most notably by Richard Dyer, whose "It's So Camp as Keeps Us Going" is collected in *Camp*) to constitute the major aspect of pre-Stonewall gay culture, coinciding with the rise of a "gay sensibility"—that catch-phrase of early identity politics described by Jack Babuscio in "Camp and the Gay Sensibility" (1977, also reprinted in *Camp*). Camp theatricality would indeed be induced by the role-playing activity necessitated by passing for straight, and camp-coded signs and innuendoes would conceivably be invoked by a necessity for clandestine recognition and communication among "peer queers," though such indirectness might be abandoned in favor of outrageous bitchiness when camp was deployed on the "safer grounds" of the drag underworld.

While acknowledging camp as possibly the singlemost defining characteristic of male pre-Stonewall gay culture, recent queer criticism shows that camp has been used as a subversive and survivalist tool by other marginal formations, most notably within the lesbian butch/femme working class culture (about which we owe many insights to Sue-Ellen Case in "Toward a Butch/Femme Aesthetic," 1988, reprinted in *Camp*), or within the tradition (outlined in Pamela Robertson's *Guilty Pleasures*) of queer heterosexual ("anti-straight") women which, from Mae West in the 1920s to Madonna in the 1980s, identified in the female mimicry of camp a deconstructive send-up of their performative status as women and as objects of male desire and representation. Under the sign of queer performativity, in fact, the 1970s images of butch or clone negations of gay effeminacy have also become themselves camp effects; and rather than a synonym of pre-Stonewall gay culture, camp is now regarded as a pre-second wave, constructivist feminist theory enactment of anti-essentialism consciously masquerading as selfhood.

The very instability of camp allowed for an even bigger shift in its uses during the pop revolution of the sixties. If the esoteric nuances of camp explained its virtual absence from "proper" language—an absence contrasting with its earlier circulation as an open secret—by 1964 Sontag's essay disseminated camp as the cipher for contemporary culture, as a refined (and, most infamously, apolitical) aesthetic taste for the vulgar and the mode of appreciation for kitschy middle-class pretensions, and she thereby captured the mass media's attention and turned camp into a popular fad. From the very publication of her essay to the most recent gay reclaiming of camp, gay critics have accused Sontag of turning a basically homosexual mode of self-performance into a degayified "taste," a simple matter of ironically relishing an indulgence in what is "so bad it's good." Such critics claim that defining camp as an objective and neutral style which can be appropriated and reoriented by dominant culture allows the mainstream to indulge in a form of nostalgia, which paradoxically elides the historical existence of the object of nostalgic desire, just as it elides camp's origins within a homosexual subculture, as well as the subversive politics inscribed in this previous mode of circulation.

It is reasonable, though, to exempt Sontag's essay from at least the charge of transforming camp into something different than it was at her time. As brilliantly recounted by Andrew Ross, camp had in fact significantly rearticulated itself in the postwar years, and came to include the subtly transgressive taste for forgotten cultural forms which characterized young countercultures such as the Teds and Mods (witness the Mods' relish for Victoriana and the Union Jack), or in the flea market fashion of the time. It also included popular cultural forms such as rock music (especially with androgynous or transgressive stars, as in the case of the Kinks, the New York Dolls, Mick Jagger, Dusty Springfield, and David Bowie), Andy Warhol's pop art and his superstars, the cult for the great stars of silent cinema, and the appreciation of "low" culture (snobbish precisely because practiced by highly refined, "cultured" people) such as television and trashy films. In short, rather than something which removes the gay elements of camp—which, in the words of Daniel Harris, would bring about "the death of camp"—Sontag's essay can be seen as part of a wider process of opening camp to the public sphere, signaling a different relation between the dominant and deviant in end-of-millennium culture.

During the 1960s and 1970s the campy bricolage of upper-class snobbish dress codes, theatrical transgressivity, and effeminacy were taken up by working-class juvenile countercultures and by glam rock stars, but we shouldn't forget that censorship was undergoing a severe critique at the time, and that homosexuality and the drag scene were themselves in the process of coming out. The underground scene was gaining access to an unprecedented visibility. Andy Warhol brought drag queens to superstardom, and pop art was moving from the supermarket to the highbrow galleries. In that extraordinary dialectic of progressive and reactionary positions, in short, society at large was getting a little queerer (as charted in David Van Leer's *The Queening of America*), while at the same time, with gay attempts at assimilation to the mainstream, homosexuality was willing to give up some of its queerness.

Of course, this means acknowledging that in the process camp may have lost to some degree its cutting edge for gay culture, its uses for gay political resistance, as well as its potential for co-optation as a fashionable phenomenon that was basically inoffensive to the power and production structures. But as Carole-Anne Tyler acutely argues in "Boys Will Be Girls" (also reprinted in *Camp*), even in its "original" setting camp did not necessarily, for instance, further progressive politics. For camp is the twin brother (or sister) of queer transgression and the carnivalesque, and as such cannot be straightened into "correctness," political or otherwise: its reliance on stereotypes, its flirtings with the society of the spectacle and the capitalist structures of production, or, in other words, its dependency on the subverted *normality*, always already make it an ambiguous cultural formation and political tool, haunted by the shadow of complicity and containment.

If we are looking for a gay political significance within this most recent, postmodernist scenario, we

C

have to look at the gay activism of the Radical Faeries, ACT UP, and Queer Nation, which, after the 1970s refusal of camp within first-wave gay activism as a self-derogatory attitude and a politically ineffective weapon (discussed in Andrew Britton's "For Interpretation: Notes Against Camp," reprinted in *Camp*), have been reclaiming the confrontational discourse of queerness and camp as a useful way to fight the homophobic and reactionary stances that surfaced in the aftermath of 1960s and 1970s liberationist euphoria. The significance of camp in recent years also seems to have moved into the realm of academic discourse, as evidenced by the use of cognate terms such as "performativity" and "queer." As the manifold critical perspectives that have intervened on the issue in the latest twenty years (for example, lesbian and gay studies and queer theory, but also cultural studies, feminist theory, film studies, psychoanalysis, aesthetics, and cultural history) echo—and are legitimated by—the definitional instability or variously localized uses of camp, any claim to camp as an exclusive property of academic discourse by gay studies can be framed as a form of survivalist identity politics, which in fact surreptitiously emerge in some deployments of self-alleged "queer" theory (most notably in *The Politics and Poetics of Camp*, ed. Moe Meyer), and which should, for good or bad, be valued as such.   *Fabio Cleto*

Bibliography

Bergman, David, ed. *Camp Grounds: Style and Homosexuality.* Amherst: University of Massachusetts Press, 1993.

Booth, Mark. *Camp.* London: Quartet, 1983.

Cleto, Fabio, ed. *Camp: Queer Aesthetics and the Performing Self—A Reader.* Edinburgh: Edinburgh University Press, 1999.

Core, Philip. *Camp: The Lie That Tells the Truth.* New York: Delilah, 1984.

Harris, Daniel. *The Rise and Fall of Gay Culture.* New York: Hyperion, 1997.

Kiernan, Robert F. *Frivolity Unbound: Six Masters of the Camp Novel.* New York: Continuum, 1990.

Meyer, Moe, ed. *The Politics and Poetics of Camp.* New York: Routledge, 1994.

Mizejewski, Linda. *Divine Decadence: Fascism, Female Spectacle, and the Makings of Sally Bowles.* Princeton: Princeton University Press, 1992.

Robertson, Pamela. *Guilty Pleasures: Feminist Camp from Mae West to Madonna.* Durham, N.C.: Duke University Press, 1996.

Sontag, Susan. *Against Interpretation and Other Essays.* New York: Farrar, Straus and Giroux, 1966.

Van Leer, David. *The Queening of America: Gay Culture in Straight Society.* New York: Routledge, 1995.

See also ACT UP; Caravaggio; Divine; Drag Balls; Effeminacy; Film Stars; Firbank, Ronald; Isherwood, Christopher; Mollies; Molly Houses; Music and Musicians 2: Popular Music; Petronius; Pontormo, Jacopo da; Postmodernism; Queer; Queer Nation; Radical Faeries; Van Vechten, Carl; Visconti, Luchino; Warhol, Andy; Waters, John; Wilde, Oscar

Camus, Renaud (1946–)

Born in Chamalières, France, Renaud Camus studied philosophy, law, and political science in France and at Oxford. His first published literary works are a series of four novels, appearing under various names: *Passage* (Renaud Camus, 1975), *Échange* (Denis Duparc, 1976), *Travers* (Renaud Camus and Tony Duparc, 1978), and *Été* (Jean-Renaud Camus and Denis Duvert, 1982). Among the first postmodern French novels, these works are influenced by theorist Roland Barthes's ideas about fragmentation, seduction, and writing. These novels introduce literary games, narrative strategies, and textual interconnections to undercut the continuity and purported completeness of the works. With *Tricks* (1979), whose preface was written by Barthes, Camus amorally explores the idea of the one-night stand as a valid literary topos and an autobiographical device. In *Buena Vista Park* (1980), *Notes achriennes* (1982), and *Chroniques achriennes* (1984), Camus develops his views on the inscriptions and hermeneutics of homosexuality in the modern world. In the same period, Camus published two historical novels, *Roman roi* (1983) and *Roman furieux* (1987). Important and informative on his views of homosexuality in modern life are such works as *Journal d'un voyage en France* (1981) and the excellent *Journal romain* (1987), the record of a one-year stay in Rome, as well as the subsequent journals, which are records of the life, aesthetic interests, and moral commentaries of this openly gay man. Camus's strength comes from his militant refusal to cast moral aspersions on sexual behavior, to define homosexuality as something secondary to the dominant praxes of heterosexuality, and, most important, to see sex as anything other than innocent behavior. *Lawrence R. Schehr*

Bibliography

Baetens, Jan. *Les Mesures de l'excès: Essai sur Renaud Camus*. Paris: Impressions Nouvelles, 1992.

Schehr, Lawrence R. *The Shock of Men: Homosexual Hermeneutics in French Writing*. Stanford, Calif.: Stanford University Press, 1995.

See also French Literature; Paris

Canada

In Canada, as in all other countries, sexuality is a physical fact organized in social terms. Thus the title of the best book on the subject in Canada is *The Regulation of Desire: Homo and Hetero Sexualities* (1996), by Gary Kinsman. But Canada also has its peculiarities as a remnant of British imperialism now part of the American economic empire. In the law, Canada began with British statutes against sodomy and eventually developed its own regulations primarily shaped by changes in both British and American laws.

Most recent histories of Canadian sexualities commence with the Native nations that predate European settlement, but terms associated with homosexuality such as *berdache* and *two-spirited* are interpreted in ways more concerned with modern needs than with accurately depicting past cultures. The first historical figure generally acknowledged to be homosexual was Alexander Wood (1772–1844). Arriving in 1793 from his native Scotland, he became a successful merchant and magistrate, but his sexuality caused such scandal that he was for a period forced to return to Britain and even became the object of an attack by a pamphlet. Yet the *Dictionary of Canadian Biography* records, "At his death the *British Colonist* called him one of Toronto's 'most respected inhabitants.'" His name is honored on two Toronto streets, one of them now, appropriately, home to Buddies in Bad Times, Toronto's lesbian and gay theater. A play on his life, titled *Molly Wood*, by John Wimbs and Christopher Richards, was produced in 1994, as the general Canadian nationalist interest in recovering a forgotten past is now extending to important gay ancestors. Significantly, Wood's combination of success and scandal seems a typical Canadian compromise.

As in both Britain and the United States, of course, there was much persecution of homosexuals. An extreme case was that of Everett George Klippert, declared a dangerous sexual offender in 1966. Many elements came together in this conviction, including regionalism (Klippert was first arrested in the Northwest Territories) and class (he was a mechanic's helper), but its extreme homophobia crystallized various energies that were already developing. The Association for Social Knowledge (ASK) began in Vancouver in 1964. Similar but usually less well organized groups existed elsewhere, such as the Canadian Council on Religion and the Homosexual, but it was ASK that coalesced as the most useful gay resource, including publicizing Klippert's case.

Yet few gay Canadians have ever heard of Klippert. As Canada moved toward the law reform of 1969, which removed the most general proscriptions against homosexuality, Prime Minister Pierre Elliott Trudeau made the very quotable assertion, "The State has no business in the bedrooms of the nation." This might have provided the flavor of Canada's sexual coming-of-age at the time the Stonewall riots were happening in the United States. What seems like a coincidence, or at most a similar response to the Zeitgeist of the sixties, once again led to an American event becoming the dominant metaphor in Canada. Thus the period of gay liberation throughout North America is "after Stonewall."

Gay developments in Canada have tended to be quietly Canadian. A classic example is Jim Egan, who began his activism with antihomophobic letters and articles in 1949. He continued to confront Canadian heterosexism, usually in ways that the general populace ignored, until 1995, when he became national news as he and his partner, Jack Nesbitt, reached the supreme court with an attempt to gain the shared pension benefits available to heterosexual couples. While their claim was denied, the majority of the court agreed the situation was discriminatory. Their story is recorded in a documentary film, *Jim Loves Jack*.

Another Canadian significant in the struggle for gay rights is Gerald Hannon. From 1971 gay news magazine *The Body Politic* developed a reputation for radical but also innovative and thoughtful analysis of gay culture. The magazine had various problems with censorship, but its most disastrous encounter was a result of Hannon's piece on "man-boy love" in 1977. In the following years Hannon became well respected as a journalist on gay issues, including a number of pieces for "Canada's national newspaper," *The Globe and Mail,* and he became a

C part-time journalism instructor at Ryerson University. Then in 1996, claims were made that he had supported in class the National Association for Man-Boy Love. Soon after a newspaper revealed that Hannon was a part-time prostitute, which led to the loss of his position.

Hannon received significant support from the local gay community, much from *Xtra*, the Toronto gay newspaper that began as a small-events calendar and came with *The Body Politic*. After the demise of the latter, it expanded to the point where it is joined by sister papers in Vancouver and Ottawa. Yet it also has a much more established and less intellectual approach than its parent had. Regardless of its opposition to oppression of individuals such as Hannon, it reflects the general mainstreaming of gay society in Canada.

The aforementioned Buddies in Bad Times, under the artistic direction of Sky Gilbert, tries to maintain an opposition to conservative values, whether gay or straight. The same could be said of the artist Attila Richard Lukacs, whose homoerotic paintings of Nazi skinheads have sold well but also draw animosity. Still, in many ways they seem to be an exception. One of Canada's best-known and best-loved authors, Timothy Findley, has long been known to be gay, his companion always prominent in his life, but his general demeanor seems to have deflected any of the homophobia felt by Gilbert and Lukacs. Recently the popular fiddler Ashley MacIsaacs has been very open about his sexual practices, and it remains to be seen whether this will destroy the usual Canadian acceptance of idiosyncrasies that remain assuredly safe.

Many more names deserve mention but particularly in the theater, where the gay writers include the most important Native and Quebec playwrights, Tomson Highway and Marcel Tremblay, and arguably the most prominent of recent English-Canadian dramatists, Brad Fraser. Parliamentary politics has been much more closeted, but Svend Robinson, Canada's first openly gay politician, ran for the leadership of Canada's third major party, the New Democrats, in 1995. He did not win, but his strong showing, with significant support from major labor unions, might be seen as a demonstration of an acceptance of gays in Canada greater than that in the United States. Gay culture is similar throughout North America, but Canadians are at once less flamboyant and yet more generally respectful of difference than their American neighbors. The Canadian gay comic Scott Thompson, now on American television, used to do a bit in which he demonstrated what it means to be a Canadian by blowing his nose on a handkerchief that resembled a Canadian flag. Then he would say, "Now you can't do that in the States." Anyone who can understand at least a few of these layers of irony has a sense of what it means to be a gay Canadian. *Terry Goldie*

Bibliography

Kinsman, Gary. *The Regulation of Desire: Homo and Hetero Sexualities.* Toronto: Black Rose, 1996.

Maynard, Stephen. *Of Toronto the Gay: Homosexuality, Policing, and the Dialectics of Discovery, Urban Toronto, 1890–1930.* Chicago: University of Chicago Press, 1998.

See also American Indian/Alaskan Native Gender Identity and Sexuality; Asians in North America; Berdache; *Body Politic*

Canon Law

"Canon law" refers properly to the bodies of law developed within the older Christian churches, including the Orthodox, or eastern, groups, but the term is often restricted to the law systematized in the Latin-speaking churches of Europe. Today the most elaborate and most widely applied code of canon law is the Roman Catholic. Its codification is the result of centuries-long efforts to harmonize and adapt a great variety of materials—the canons of church councils or assemblies, passages from major theologians' rulings or regulations by bishops of important cities, and decisions from church courts. The major collections of Latin church law from the twelfth century on have included laws against same-sex relations. Typical punishments for the laity included excommunication and exile; for the clergy, deposition and perpetual confinement to a monastery. These punishments were mitigated only somewhat in early modern legislation, such as is the decrees *Cum primum* and *Horrendum* of Pius V (1566–1572). Contemporary Catholic law is embodied in two successive codifications, promulgated in 1917 and 1983. In the first, a layperson convicted of sodomy is automatically deemed "of infamous" and made subject to further sanctions (can. 2357). Members of the clergy who are so convicted can also be suspended, stripped of church offices, and expelled from the clerical state (can. 2358–2359). The 1983 code retains the provisions but omits specific mention of "sodomy," speaking inclusively of "external sin against the sixth commandment" (can. 1395). *Mark D. Jordan*

Bibliography

Brundage, James A. *Law, Sex, and Christian Society in Medieval Europe*. Chicago: University of Chicago Press, 1987.

See also Christianity

Cantina Culture

The cantina is a place and a business where people go to socialize while drinking alcoholic beverages. The standard cantina has room for around fifty people. It has a jukebox, a bar, and tables, although some include groups that play popular music, or a television set (showing sports events or porno films). Some of them offer *botana* or tapas (elaborate snacks). There are plenty of cantinas in rural and urban Latin America, where they continue to be major (sometimes the main) scenarios of homosociality and popular culture. Although the acceptance of women in cantinas can vary according to local legislation, the clientele are almost exclusively adult males. In some Mexican cantinas, one can find female prostitutes and male transvestites. All these features set the cantinas in contrast to *bares* (bars) and *Lady's Bar*, similar to their U.S. counterparts.

In general, cantinas have a certain degree of tolerance for unconventional masculine behavior: confessions of love, pain, sadness, or family problems. The cantinas are also spaces where men *se rajan* (open themselves up) to other men and confess, letting other people see intimate dimensions of their lives. It is in this sense a space where masculine subjectivities get activated, transformed, discharged, and reproduced.

In this context of tolerance of emotion, alcohol, and homosociality, homoerotic encounters may take place. There is a complex array of signs through which men express their affections and their homoerotic desires to other men: through conversation that is heavy in body contact, through body language (like eye contact), and through subtle (and not so subtle) glances at the genitals of other men while urinating.

The communal character of the urinal or the lack of barriers (when there are individual urinals) is complicit. No explicit sexual practices take place (although a quick touch may happen); nevertheless, exhibitionism and voyeurism are common and disguised as "drunken behavior" or a poetic expression of masculinity. At least in northern Mexico, for example, a "real man" should not be prudish while uri-

nating, so the custom is to open completely the trouser and not hide one's genitals. Such encounters are dangerous, of course, and homophobic violence is always a possibility.

Cantinas are not "gay bars" or "gay places"; on the contrary, some people consider them more related to macho behavior. Although in all of them there is certain room for homoeroticism, some cantinas are visited more than others by openly homosexual people than others or are known as easy places to meet for sexual experiences. Some cantinas can function too as meeting places for the *gente de ambiente*.

Little research has been done on cantinas, despite their importance in Latin American societies. However, the cantinas have been privileged scenarios in film production, particularly Mexican. Their significance to the social organization of emotions, the gender order, the homoerotic experience, the popular culture, and even the imagining of Mexicans by insiders and outsiders, particularly American (as a stigmatized "drunken Other"), is still insufficiently explored.   *Guillermo Nuñez-Noriega*

Bibliography

Carrier, Joseph. *De Los Otros: In Homosexuality among Mexican Men*. New York: Columbia University Press, 1995.

See also Mexico

Capote, Truman (1924–1984)

Born Truman Steckfus Persons on September 30, 1924, in New Orleans, Truman Capote would become among the first—perhaps the first—major author to use television to promote his work and life as salable commodities. While his initial success on the talk-show circuit brought fame to him and his writing, celebrity and alcohol would in the end contribute to the decline in his critical reputation and his life.

The product of an unsuccessful marriage, Capote grew up largely in a household of bizarre relatives in Alabama, later being educated in Northern boarding schools; he did not attend college. Capote enjoyed early success with a series of stories belonging to what might be called the Southern-Gothic-romantic school including *Other Voices, Other Rooms* (1948) and *The Grass Harp* (1951). The darker *Other Voices* suggests an affinity with Tennessee Williams, for example, while *The Grass Harp* suggests kinship with Carson McCullers's novel and play, *The Member of the Wedding*, and some stories of Eudora Welty. Capote's early stories undercut possible sentimentality; if love wins out in the end, it does so only after kindhearted people have paid dearly. He returned to this mode twice in his later career with *A Christmas Memory* (1966) and *The Thanksgiving Visitor* (1968).

Capote became most famous for the novella *Breakfast at Tiffany's* (1958), which made for an influential and successful Audrey Hepburn film, and the triumphant "nonfiction novel" (his term) *In Cold Blood* (1966), also an acclaimed Richard Brooks movie. These two works show Capote's intelligence and imagination at their best: he is at once sympathetic and unsparing in his portraits of both the social-climbing Holly and the killers of the innocent farm family, respectively.

These books and their film versions projected Capote to a high level of celebrity, as did his famous Black and White Ball in 1966. Unfortunately, as described in Gerald Clarke's excellent biography, Capote could not handle his insecurities about himself as a man and a writer, which led him to self-destruction through drink, drugs, the wrong men, and, finally, the betrayal of his friends in his last fiction, the unfinished and cruel *Answered Prayers* (1986). Capote finished his life largely alone except for such stalwart friends as Joanne Carson, who found him dead on August 25, 1984.

Had drink and drugs not poisoned the last twenty years of his life, Capote might have become the contemporary Proust he wanted to be. Despite his failure to develop much as a writer after the mid-1960s, however, Capote does not deserve to be forgotten. As much for his early- and middle-period prose, Capote merits attention as an "obvious" gay writer who made a place for himself in high society and on television, a visible gay presence in millions of middle-class homes. Although it is impossible to estimate his suffering because of homophobia, we can credit Capote with being a good writer who also pioneered gay celebrity at a time when that took courage.   *Thomas Dukes*

Bibliography

Christensen, Peter G. "Truman Capote." In *Contemporary Gay Authors*. Emmanuel S. Nelson, ed. Westport, Conn.: Greenwood, 1993.

Clarke, Gerald. *Capote*. New York: Ballantine, 1988.

See also Fiction; U.S. Literature: Contemporary Gay Writing

Caravaggio (b. Michelangelo Merisi, 1571?–1610)

Greatly influential during his lifetime and in the early years of the seventeenth century, the painter Caravaggio was all but forgotten for three hundred years. Then in 1955, an exhibition of his work in Milan, followed by the publication of Walter F. Friedlander's *Caravaggio Studies* in 1955, initiated an intense revival of interest in his work. Today he is regarded as one of the greatest artists of all time. Much of Caravaggio's life, however, remains clouded in ambiguity and controversy, including the nature of his sexuality, although there is a notable presence of homoeroticism in his work.

Caravaggio was born Michelangelo Merisi in Milan, probably in 1571. Although the early years of his life are not well documented, it is known that he was the son of Fermo Merisi, steward and architect to the Marquis of Caravaggio. In 1582, the young and talented Caravaggio was apprenticed to the artist Simone Peterzano. Some time after 1588, Caravaggio left Milan for Rome and eventually enjoyed the patronage of Cardinal Francesco del Monte. During this period he produced several paintings of androgynous young men, including the celebrated *Young Boy with a Basket of Fruit* and *Young Bacchus*.

In 1597 Caravaggio was commissioned to paint a cycle of the life of St. Matthew in the Contarelli Chapel in Rome, a series of works that established his reputation. In these paintings Caravaggio's nontraditional style becomes clearly evident: the realistic depiction of the subjects (harsh and muscular

Caravaggio (1571–1610), Young Boy with a Basket of Fruit. *Galleria Borghese, Rome, Italy. Alinari Art Resource, NY.*

figures presented in ungainly, nonelegant poses) and the unusual use of darkness and light (known as chiaroscuro, or, more specifically, tenebrism, a dramatic illumination of form out of shadow). The effect of these paintings on a public used to seeing highly idealized renderings of religious themes was immediate and powerful.

Although Caravaggio at this point began to enjoy the social privileges and advantages accorded an esteemed artist, his personal life appears to have been tumultuous, perhaps the result of a violent, egomaniacal temperament. Several arrests are on record—for brawling, libel, and assaults with weapons—and in 1606, himself wounded, he fled Rome after the murder of an opponent in a sports game.

During the next four years, Caravaggio took up residence in Naples, Malta, and Sicily, where he was generally received as a celebrated artist, but he continued to live on the edge of violence. In 1610, after a characteristically frenetic attempt to return to Rome (where a pardon had in fact been granted him), he died, most likely of pneumonia, at Port' Ercole, a Spanish possession in the Papal States.

What is known of Caravaggio's homosexuality? The only contemporary supporting documentation comes from a libel trial in 1603, where a principal, one G. Battista, is described in an account as Caravaggio's *bardassa* (kept boy). As Howard Hibbard notes in his biographical and critical study, *Caravaggio*: "Whether Caravaggio was essentially or exclusively homosexual is far from certain. . . . Although we do not need to presume that Caravaggio's pictures with homoerotic content are necessarily more confessional than others, there is a notable absence of the traditional erotic females. . . . In his entire career he did not paint a single female nude" (Hibbard 97).

Perhaps the early paintings of adolescent boys most argue for a homoerotic interpretation of the artist's sensibility. Although mostly executed during his patronage under Cardinal del Monte (a known admirer of young men and admittedly a possible influence on Caravaggio's choice of subjects), these paintings nevertheless convey a palpable and unmistakable gay eroticism. While there has been controversy relating to the gender of the subjects of some of these early paintings, that fact in itself is of relevance. The Renaissance idea of "homosexuality" (not a defined term or concept in that era, as it is to modern scholars) usually assumed androgyny as a primary indication of same-sex interest.

Whatever the content of these and later paintings, Caravaggio's technique was as original and intense as his defiance of convention. As Hibbard further writes: "He was the only Italian painter of his time to rely more on his own feelings than on artistic tradition, while somehow managing to remain within the great mainstream of the Renaissance. From this point of view, he is an important precursor of Rembrandt and even of modern art" (Hibbard 1983, vii).

David Garnes

Bibliography

Friedlander, Walter F. *Caravaggio Studies*. Princeton, N.J.: Princeton University Press, 1955.

Hibbard, Howard. *Caravaggio*. New York: Harper & Row, 1983.

Shreve, Jack. "Caravaggio." In *Gay & Lesbian Biography*. Detroit: St. James Press, 1997.

See also Art History; Italian Renaissance; Italy; Rome

Carné, Marcel (Albert) (1909–)

Marcel Carné is a French film director whose best-remembered films are the dramas he directed from screenplays written by poet Jacques Prévert. Products of the Carné-Prévert collaboration include *Quai des brumes* (Port of Shadows, 1938), *Le Jour se lève* (Daybreak, 1939), and *Les Enfants du paradis* (Children of Paradise, 1945). The term "poetic realism" has often been used to describe Carné's films, particularly those made before World War II, in which narratives about ordinary people are visualized using heightened imagery and elaborate sets and lighting. The protagonists of these films are men and women—alienated and persecuted criminals or social outcasts—who find fleeting salvation through love until they are separated by fate and society. Carné's biographer has written that his films focus on the "relations between illusion and disenchantment, blindness and enlightenment." As was the case with other gay directors of his era, severe limitations were placed on Carné's ability to express homoeroticism in his films. There have been very few homosexual characters or themes in Carné's films, but those few have been portrayed without the use of clichés.

After World War II Carné's reputation as a director declined, especially in France. Beginning in the 1940s there was widespread questioning of his decision to remain and work in occupied France. In the 1950s François Truffaut and other young film critics reacted against the artifice and fatalistic

C

social vision of Carné's films. There was also an undercurrent of heterosexism in many of their criticisms. The reputation of Carné's early films has again risen since the 1960s, however, and the director has received a number of honors since his retirement in 1977.   *Charles Krinsky*

Bibliography

"Marcel Carné." In *World Film Directors*. Vol. 1. John Wakeman, ed. New York: H. W. Wilson, 1987, 193–97.

Turk, Edward Baron. *Child of Paradise: Marcel Carné and the Golden Age of French Cinema*. Cambridge, Mass.: Harvard University Press, 1989.

See also Film; France

Carpenter, Edward (1844–1929)

While Edward Carpenter was at one time one of the most widely recognized names in both political and sexual theory in England, today he is all but forgotten. His memory lives on primarily as an influence, with his socially progressive views of sexuality and social order forming a basis for the writings of E. M. Forster; his educational work can still be seen in the English extension colleges—now popularly known as the "red bricks."

Carpenter was born the son of a former naval commander who became a lawyer and an investor in British and American railroads, and a mother who patterned herself after the stereotypical image of the Victorian housewife and spent her time tending to young Edward and his six sisters. Carpenter's life initially followed the rather banal trajectory predicted by such privileged origins. He was educated at Oxford and Cambridge, and in 1868 became a lecturer at Trinity Hall, Cambridge. He was elected a clerical fellow during his second year and ordained deacon.

Rifts soon emerged in this otherwise orthodox career path. Carpenter's family raised him in the liberal doctrines of the Broad Church, and the young deacon found himself in conflict with the more restrictive Anglican doctrine he was charged to uphold. In 1871 he resigned as deacon and reverted to an exclusive lecturer position. During this time of crisis Carpenter also began a romance with Andrew Beck, the future master of Trinity Hall. Beck later denied the affair to save his career, another aspect of the situation that deeply disillusioned Carpenter.

The aftermath of this period of crisis seems to have been a formative period for Carpenter. In the following years he began to emulate Walt Whitman, and to pattern his own poetry after the liberational erotic and democratic patterns of *Calamus*. During this period Carpenter also began his systematic embrace of British socialist thought that before had surfaced only sporadically in his writing. Also as a result of these transitions, Carpenter accepted a position in the University Extension program started by James Stuart of Cambridge, and moved to Sheffield to start a university designed primarily to educate women and members of the laboring class.

Following the death of his parents in 1880 and 1881, Carpenter resigned his teaching position and began in earnest his life as a writer. He moved to Millthorpe, a retreat he bought in rural Sheffield, and commenced a systematic study of Eastern religions, in particular the Bhagavad Gita. He also completed an epic poem cycle in the style of Whitman entitled *Towards Democracy*. He became active in groups such as the Progressive Association and the Fabians and met other progressives like William Morris, Havelock Ellis, and Olive Schreiner. In 1891, after returning from a journey to India, the most decisive event of his postuniversity life happened: he met George Merrill, a younger man raised in the slums of Sheffield, who subsequently became his life partner. The relationship between the two men is viewed by many critics as the basis of the Alec-Scudder relationship in Forster's *Maurice*.

Though Carpenter was a prodigious writer, his reputation rests largely on three important radical texts dealing with sex and gender relations. *Love's Coming of Age* (1896) is a collection of three pamphlets published by the Labour Press in Manchester in 1894. They document the theoretical relationship between the hierarchy of man-woman in modern England and the hierarchy of master-serf in feudal systems. *The Intermediate Sex* (1906) is an expansion of a pamphlet on "homogenic love" Carpenter wrote in 1894. It explores the phenomenon of "Uranism"—Carpenter's term for homosexuality—and adopts a quasi-Darwinist stance to explore the Uranist as the evolution of a new type of social and sexual being. *Intermediate Types Among Primitive Folks* (1914) expands the work in *The Intermediate Sex* by exploring the role of Uranists in ancient, non-European countries. The essay attempts to demonstrate that Uranists in all cultures other than repressive industrial ones occupy spaces of spiritual and social divination.   *Gregory W. Bredbeck*

Bibliography

A Bibliography of Edward Carpenter. Sheffield, England: Sheffield City Libraries, 1949.

Carpenter, Edward. *Selected Writing*, Vol. 1, *Sex*. London: Gay Men's Press, 1984.

———. *Towards Democracy*. London: Gay Men's Press, 1985.

Jones, Gareth Stedman. *Outcast London*. Oxford: Clarendon Press, 1971.

Pierson, Stanley. *Marxism and the Origins of British Socialism: The Struggle for a New Consciousness*. Ithaca, N.Y.: Cornell University Press, 1973.

Rowbotham, Sheila, and Jeffrey Weeks. *Socialism and the New Life: The Personal and Sexual Politics of Edward Carpenter and Havelock Ellis*. London: Pluto Press, 1977.

Weeks, Jeffrey. *Sex, Politics and Society: The Regulation of Sexuality Since 1800*. London: Longman, 1981.

See also Ellis, Havelock; Evolution; Forster, E. M.; Sexology; Third Sex; Whitman, Walt

Casement, Roger (1864–1916)

An Irish rebel against British imperialism in the cause of home rule, Casement was tried and executed for treason by the English. During his trial, the prosecution and Scotland Yard unofficially circulated Casement's diaries, which record his secret homosexual life. Although they never appeared in the trial, the diaries enabled the prosecution to immobilize Casement's supporters and to sabotage Casement's appeal for clemency. Thus Casement's death is a gay martyrdom as well as an Irish nationalist one.

Before 1912, Casement's anti-imperialism, directed at powers other than Britain, was approved by Casement's employer: the British Foreign Office. In 1904 Casement painstakingly reported Belgian atrocities against natives of the Congo. This controversial report's publication gained Casement an appointment as consul general at Rio de Janeiro and an assignment in 1909 to investigate exploitation of natives by rubber cartels in Brazil's Putumayo district. Casement's Putumayo report earned him knighthood in 1911.

In 1912 Casement resigned from the Foreign Office. In the same year Sir Edward Carson formed the Ulster Volunteer militias to resist home rule. A nationalist Irish volunteer movement, instigated partly by Casement, sprang up in reaction.

When the world war stalled home rule, Casement initiated a daring plot. He went to Germany to procure armaments for an Irish rebellion against England and to incite Irish prisoners of war to return to Ireland as rebels. However, owing to lack of response from the Irish POWs and to tepid German support, Casement's plot failed. Sexual passion perhaps contributed to the failure. Casement had taken to Germany a new lover, Adler Christensen, whose flamboyance made the Germans suspect both men. And Christensen's indiscretions helped keep Casement under the thumb of British intelligence. When Casement landed in Ireland from a German U-boat in April 1916, he was arrested almost immediately.

Casement's nationalist supporters have insisted that their martyr was not gay, and that the sex diaries were forged by Scotland Yard to smear Casement and Ireland. Since 1957, however, sympathetic biographers have authenticated Casement's memoranda. Nevertheless, their biographies marginalize Casement's eros and scapegoat Christensen. A study of Casement that deals more openly with homosexuality remains to be written.

So does a study of Casement's impact on literature. His trial echoes that of Oscar Wilde. Sir Edward Carson had prosecuted Wilde; Casement's prosecutor was an Ulster volunteers friend of Carson's. Novelist Joseph Conrad met Casement in the Congo, perhaps represented him in *Heart of Darkness* (1902), and praised his Congo report. Casement haunted poet William Butler Yeats. And novelist James Joyce's fascination with the earlier home rule advocate Charles Stewart Parnell, who was tainted by forged allegations of anti-imperialist terrorism and who was undone by a trial involving heterosexual scandal, has a homosexual complement in Casement. The hero of Joyce's *Finnegans Wake* (1924–1939) is tried for crimes that include anti-imperialist and homosexual activity, and his trial involves claims of forged evidence and alibis. In the *Wake*, because of Casement, a heterosexual center of interest in Joyce's earlier works gains a homosexual twin.

Robert L. Caserio

Bibliography

Caserio, Robert L. "Casement, Joyce, and Pound: Some New Meanings of Treason." In *Quare Joyce*. Joseph Valente, ed. Ann Arbor, Mich.: University of Michigan Press, 1998.

Reid, B. L. *The Lives of Roger Casement*. New Haven: Yale University Press, 1976.

See also English Literature; Ireland; Wilde, Oscar

Castro

Known worldwide as the premier "gay hometown," the Castro is a roughly thirty-four-block neighborhood in the geographic center of San Francisco. Originally known as Eureka Valley and demarcated by the original Most Holy Redeemer Church parish boundaries of 16th, Dolores, 22nd, and Douglass Streets, the Castro takes its name from the commercial corridor that runs south from the intersection of Castro and 18th Streets.

White homesteaders first settled the Eureka Valley in the 1880s, supplanting the Mexican landowners based near Mission Dolores. Germans, Scandinavians, and Finns also settled there. By the 1920s it had become a predominantly Irish-Catholic, blue-collar neighborhood. The Castro movie theater was built during this time, and "sunny Eureka Valley" served as an early suburban neighborhood to downtown.

Following World War II, San Francisco reputedly became a "haven for homosexuals," as the city's homosexual population had increased dramatically. Thriving (by 1950s standards) gay enclaves could be found along Polk Street, Nob Hill, the Tenderloin, North Beach, and South of Market. The "white flight" to the suburbs further out in the 1950s led to a dramatic drop in real estate prices and numerous empty buildings in the Castro, making it increasingly attractive as a cheap area for homosexuals to live in. The first gay bar in the Castro, the Missouri Mule, opened in 1963.

As Haight-Ashbury's 1967 summer of free love (and experimental drugs) gave way to serious social problems in that district, numerous gay hippies migrated over the hill to settle down in the Castro, attracted by the low rents. During this second-wave, hippie-era migration, several more gay bars were established (e.g., Toad Hall, Twin Peaks, Midnight Sun), and several restaurants and two sex venues (Castro Baths and Jaguar bookstore) opened.

San Francisco's homosexual community had already been energized by the 1964 California Hall police raid. Following the spirit of Stonewall (1969) and gay liberation, an angry and apparently self-confident, predominantly male, new "gay" generation—expressing itself in a self-conscious and sex-positive "clone" look and sensibility—formed the third wave of gay newcomers, transforming the Castro virtually overnight. The 1970s saw gay urban pioneers move in to stay, buying and fixing up the old Victorian houses, re-creating an entire parallel gay

Castro Street, San Francisco, showing the Castro Theater (1987). Photo by Marc Geller.

society with a complete, self-contained commercial and community infrastructure. The Castro became the world's first gay city-within-a-city.

The mainstream press, the gay press, popular songs, Armistead Maupin's *Tales of the City*, and word of mouth fueled this lavender gold rush. At decade's start, there were approximately 90,000 gays in San Francisco; by 1977, there were about 120,000, and by 1978, 150,000. The Castro Street Fair began in 1974, and the first lesbian club, Full Moon Coffeehouse, operated between 1974 and 1978. A Mardi Gras–like atmosphere prevailed along Castro Street.

Into this $25 million to $30 million annual gay economy in the Castro, Harvey Milk migrated and opened a camera shop. Milk called himself "the mayor of Castro Street," and after three unsuccessful bids, won a seat as city supervisor in the first district-based elections in 1977. Milk's political vision and personal charisma were central in shaping the transformation of the Castro as a gay community. Milk and then-mayor George Moscone were assassinated by fellow supervisor and Irish-Catholic ex-cop Dan White. The aftermath—an extremely lenient sentence for White, the gay backlash "White Night Riots," and police counterattack on the Castro's Elephant Walk bar—entrenched and further validated the political will of a gay Castro.

Just as the Castro seemed to have come into its own, rumors and then mysterious deaths by some "gay cancer" spread through the community. The neighborhood became a ground zero for the AIDS epidemic. By 1984 Castro Street was nearly a ghost town, businesses boarded up, and fear gripped the community as hundreds, then thousands of gay men died. There was even talk of AIDS eradicating the Castro entirely. Once again, however, the gay community rallied to the challenge, establishing many needed support services, the KS/AIDS Foundation, and the NAMES Project among them. ACT UP cum Queer Nation became the new political activism.

With 1991 widely celebrated as the "Year of the Queer," the Castro entered a fourth-generation of queer influx, with many more lesbians, as well as bisexuals, transgenders, and queers of color claiming the neighborhood as their own, even as they perceived it as an established older gay white male residential neighborhood. Less affluent queers have settled into cheaper neighborhoods surrounding the Castro. Even as franchises move onto Castro Street, and the city has developed it as a tourist site, the Castro will remain, at least for a while, a unique city-within-a-city.   *Les Wright*

Bibliography

"The *Bay Area Reporter* Celebrates Twenty-Five Years: The Persistence of Vision" (special anniversary edition). *Bay Area Reporter* 26, no. 14 (2d section): 33–68.

Hippler, Mike. *. . . So Little Time: Essays on Gay Life*. Berkeley: Celestial Arts, 1990.

Murray, Stephen O. *American Gay*. Chicago: University of Chicago Press, 1996.

———. "Components of Gay Community in San Francisco." In *Gay Culture in America*. Gilbert Herdt, ed. Boston: Beacon, 1992, 107–46.

See also Clone; Neighborhoods; San Francisco

Catholicism

Catholicism represents that segment of the Christian community that looked to the bishop (later pope) at Rome as its leader. During the early medieval period, largely through the missionary efforts of monks loyal to the Roman pontiff, areas in western Europe that had constituted the Roman Empire looked to Rome as did converts from migrating Germanic tribes. It was not until the eleventh and twelfth centuries, however, when an effective administrative and legal structure under papal control began to emerge, that the pope had much more than moral authority over his constituents.

The state of early papal authority was often very dependent on the support of kings and emperors. This meant that even though the basis of Christian doctrine was essentially agreed upon through the decisions of councils and decrees from the pope, there was often ambiguity in interpreting and a general inability by the pope to settle disagreements.

In theology the Catholic Church essentially followed Augustine as supplemented by Jerome, Ambrose, and other western fathers. The Augustinian position on sex was that the ideal life was one in which Christians abstained from sex altogether. Yet recognizing the biblical injunction to be fruitful and multiply, Augustine allowed sexual activity for those unable to abstain, but the only justification was for procreation. As to the proper physical position, the female lay on the bottom on her back, and the only orifice to be penetrated by the penis was the vagina. Neither fingers nor other orifices were to be used. All other sexual activity was regarded as sinful.

C Accordingly, same-sex relationships involving actual contact were deemed sinful. This is important to emphasize because one of the major contemporary controversies in the historical field is over how hostile the Western church was to same-sex contacts. Such controversy has come about largely owing to the work of the late John Boswell, who in his book *Christianity, Social Tolerance, and Homosexuality* argued that the Catholic Church was not particularly homophobic before the thirteenth century. To mount such an argument, Boswell attempted to reinterpret the edicts of the Christian emperor Justinian and the subsequent compilation of Roman law codes that formed the basis for church, or canon, law. He also ignored the writings of the church fathers, who are nearly unanimous in their condemnation of same-sex relations, almost all the penitential literature, the Benedictine rules for monks, the enactments of Charlemagne and other western European emperors—the list could go on. This does not mean that there was a lack of homoeroticism in early medieval literature, for it has been amply documented by many scholars. It also does not mean that there were not highly erotic and sexual same-sex relationships. We know that they either existed or were feared to exist because of their periodic denunciation by clerics such as Peter Damian in the eleventh century, who accused such individuals of avoiding punishment by confessing their sins to supportive clerics.

What is true for males was also true for females. Augustine condemned female eroticism in a letter to a community of nuns written circa 423. Some of the penitentials refer to lesbian love, which periodically is mentioned negatively by many women writers such as Hildegard of Bingen.

Sometimes the Catholic medieval attitudes seem especially fearful of the sequelae of same-sex eroticism, often equating it with witchcraft or heresy. Condemnation of it became a mainstay of canon law, which, in the early Middle Ages, had been rather unarticulated but developed rapidly—and homophobically—after the year 1000. It is even possible to claim, as some have, that the Catholic Church was the bulwark of hostility to homosexuality in much the same way as its opposition to contraception and abortion, even though its opposition and strictures have often been ignored.

Not until the last part of the twentieth century were challenges mounted to traditional Catholic ideas about same-sex relationships. One of the first

was by Jesuit John J. McNeill in *The Church and the Homosexual* (1976), who, after pointing out the erroneous assumptions about sexuality inherent in Catholic doctrine, concluded that sexual relations (including same-sex ones) could be morally justified if they were true expressions of human love. In retaliation the Catholic Church imposed a blanket silence on his further discussion of the issue, claiming that he gave a false impression that the church was changing its position. It surely was not, as evidenced by a 1986 document issued by Cardinal Joseph Ratzinger, prefect of the Congregation for the Doctrine of Faith, a position that allowed him to speak authoritatively on such matters. In that document, Ratzinger stated that the inclination toward same-sex behavior was not a sin but a tendency ordered toward an intrinsic moral evil, and thus the inclination itself was an objective disorder requiring special concern and pastoral attention. Moreover, living out this orientation was not a morally acceptable option. Perhaps the best summary of current attitudes can be found in the revised Catechism of the Catholic Church published in English in 1994. This recognized the widespread existence of homosexual "tendencies" in people and then issued a call for those who have them to remain chaste.

Vern Bullough

Bibliography

Boswell, John. *Christianity, Social Tolerance, and Homosexuality: Gay People in Western Europe from the Beginning of the Christian Era to the Fourteenth Century.* Chicago: University of Chicago Press, 1980.

Bullough, Vern L., and James Brundage, eds. *Handbook of Medieval Sexuality.* New York: Garland, 1996.

Fox, Thomas C. *Sexuality and Catholicism.* New York: Braziller, 1995.

McNeill, John J. *The Church and the Homosexual.* Boston: Beacon Press, 1976.

See also Augustine of Hippo; Peter Damian; Thomas Aquinas

Cavafy, Constantine P. (1863–1933)

A Greek poet born in the Egyptian city of Alexandria, Constantine Cavafy was at home as an outsider: exile was the nature of his being. Consequently, when he thought of his homosexuality as an exiling force, he did not feel any the worse for it. To be homosexual was to participate even more fully in the nature of his cultural marginality. In his early years he spent five years in England and three in Constantinople. Otherwise, he spent his life in Alexandria. His poems on modern life are rooted in that city. The poems on ancient subjects are as wide-ranging as the Greek diaspora itself.

Cavafy was in no great hurry to promote his work: the fourteen poems that made up his first collection were privately published when he was forty-one; within five years he added another seven poems to the same collection. That is the full extent of his public poetry during his lifetime. He preferred to circulate his poems in folders to trusted friends and valued readers.

Only the most superficial readings of his poetry—and there have been a number of them—can evince a Cavafy who hated his homosexuality. In actuality, he connected his desires with everything he valued most in the world at all levels between the carnal and the spiritual. He is one of the great poets of mortality. If he is depressive about sex, it is not because he is homosexual, but because he is subject to Time. One of his main themes is *carpe diem* (sieze the day), and what depresses him the most is that any opportunity to experience male beauty, literally, in the flesh might be missed and might never arise again. One should not store up regrets for a time when the beauty of youth has faded. Many of the poems carry the same insistent message: young men who desire each other should waste no time creating the opportunity—in a rented room or mere darkened corner—to make love. Making love is the creation of beauty. Art follows later, when the artist remembers past encounters and revives them for posterity.

Cavafy was the first great laureate of urban queer lifestyles. He is particularly good on the thrills and hesitancies of cruising. Moreover, because of his cultural position within the Greek diaspora, he was better able than any other writer to assert real links, rather than sentimental wish fulfillments, between ancient Greek pederasty and modern adult homosexuality. His classical elegies and his modern Alexandrian street scenes share one homoerotic ethos.

Cavafy's work was introduced to English-speaking readers by E. M. Forster's essay on him in *Pharos and Pharillon* (1923). Another English admirer was Lawrence Durrell, in whose *Alexandria Quartet* Cavafy figures as a character of major importance, if not in a particularly positive light. More important, he exerted a strong influence on later generations of Greek gay and bisexual poets, such as Yannis Ritsos and Dinos Christianopoulos.

Gregory Woods

Bibliography

Bien, Peter. "Cavafy's Homosexuality and His Reputation Outside Greece." *Journal of Modern Greek Studies* 8, no. 2 (1990): 197–211

Jusdanis, Gregory. *The Poetics of Cavafy: Textuality, Eroticism, History*. Princeton, N.J.: Princeton University Press, 1987.

Lilly, Mark. "The Poems of Constantine Cavafy." In *Gay Men's Literature in the Twentieth Century*. London: Macmillan, 1993, 33–52.

See also Alexandria; Durrell, Lawrence; Forster, E. M.; Love Poetry, the Petrarchan Tradition

Cellini, Benvenuto (1500–1571)

Benvenuto Cellini, who served successive popes, the king of France, and Duke Cosimo I de' Medici, was the premier mannerist practitioner of gold-smithing and sculpture in sixteenth-century Italy. Cellini also stands out as one of the early-modern artists about whose same-sex attractions and affections relatively a lot is known, thanks in part to the libertine, swashbuckling life he led. The most thorough and accessible account of the homoerotic dimension of his life and art is by James Saslow. Official court documents record Cellini's conviction on two separate occasions, in 1523 and 1557, in Florence for homosexual sodomy. While he received a lenient fine of twelve measures of flour in the earlier case, his sentence in 1557 (for pleading guilty to habitually sodomizing his young apprentice over a five-year period and sleeping "in the same bed with him as though he were a wife") condemned him to four years imprisonment in his own house. Under these circumstances, Cellini, at fifty-six, dictated his famous autobiography (first published in the eighteenth century) to a fourteen-year-old assistant, which retains in its written form much of the popular Florentine dialect in which it was spoken. Benedetto Varchi, a high-profile Florentine intellectual and notorious sodomite with whom Cellini was a close friend since childhood, encouraged him to keep the colloquial style.

Though his sodomy convictions per se are passed over in silence in his autobiography, numerous passages indicate—despite his repeated protestations of innocence and his anecdotes about his heterosexual exploits—that Cellini's attractions for and relations with his young male shop assistants figured prominently not only in his private life but in his public reputation at the time. His accuser on a third occasion—a prostitute whose "very pretty" son worked for a time in his studio and served as a model—was clearly banking on the authorities' recognition of his reputation as a pederast when she sought to blackmail him for one hundred crowns for seducing the "little apprentice lad." Cellini, however, succeeded in getting the youth to admit that he had not "sinned" with him and evaded the charges. By far the most cited public accusation Cellini tells of facing down was leveled at him—before his patron, Cosimo de' Medici, no less—by Baccio Bandinelli, a rival sculptor in Florence, during an acrimonious debate between them over the relative merits of their sculpted works for the duke. Cellini's skillful retort to being called an "ugly sodomite" (*soddomitaccio*) by Bandinelli was greeted by much laughter: "[Would] that I understood so noble an art as you allude to; they say that Jove used it with Ganymede in paradise, and here upon this earth it is practiced by some of the greatest emperors and kings. I, however, am but a poor humble creature, who neither have the power nor the intelligence to perplex my wits with anything so admirable" (Cellini, 357).

The work that sparked this exchange was Cellini's restoration of an antique marble torso that he proposed to Duke Cosimo as a Ganymede, a homoerotic myth in which—to go by the references to it in his autobiography and verse—he invested special significance. Other male nude figures he carved in marble that are noteworthy for their homoerotic theme and treatment are his *Narcissus* and *Apollo and Hyacinth*, both in the Museo Nazionale del Bargello, Florence.   *William B. MacGregor*

Bibliography

[Cellini, Benvenuto.] *The Life of Benvenuto Cellini, Written by Himself*, 3d ed. John Addington Symonds, trans. London: Phaidon, 1949.

Greci, Luigi. "Benvenuto Cellini nei delitti e nei processi fiorentini ricostruiti attraverso le leggi del tempo." *Quaderni dell'archivio di antropologia criminale e medicina legale* 2 (1930): 1–79.

Pope-Hennessy, John. *Cellini*. New York: Abbeville, 1985.

Saslow, James M. *Ganymede in the Renaissance: Homosexuality in Art and Society*. New Haven: Yale University Press, 1986.

See also Art History; Bronzino, Agnolo; Florence; Ganymede; Italian Renaissance

Censorship

The official suppression of expression was probably not new when Plato specified that in his Republic, poets would be permitted to show their work only after approval by the appointed censors and guardians of the law. But it was only after the invention of the printing press, in the fifteenth century, that censorship became a prime concern for civil and religious authorities. During the upheavals of the Reformation, both Catholic and Protestant authorities censored materials considered dangerous. The Catholic Church's Index of Prohibited Books, first published in 1559, went through fifty editions before being discontinued in the twentieth century.

The popular media have consistently raised the specter of unrest and misbehavior among the "lower orders"—children, women, the lower classes. The suspect media—newspapers, novels and theater, in the nineteenth century; movies, radio, comic books, television, and the Internet, in the twentieth—are seen by some as a threat to norms of belief, behavior, and morality. The feared power of verbal or, especially, visual depictions of violence and sexuality seems to reside in their representation of precisely those behaviors and options authorities wish to deny to those they control, protect, and fear.

Images of violence remain ubiquitous although repeatedly denounced by moral authorities. Images of sexual behavior, in contrast, have been hedged around with legal proscriptions that criminalize many explicit sexual images, and authorities have often prosecuted those who produce or distribute and even, on occasion, those who consume them. Homosexuality, "the crime not to be named among Christians," in the famous words of eighteenth-century British jurist William Blackstone, has been the most unmentionable sexuality.

In the United States Anthony Comstock lobbied for the passage of An Act for the Suppression of Trade in, and Circulation of, Obscene Literature and Articles of Immoral Use, which President Grant signed in 1873. Comstock became a symbol of America's fear of uncontrolled sexuality, just as his unique position as special agent of the U.S. Post Office for over forty years made him its moral policeman. For the most part, however, media in the United States have adopted formal or informal codes of self-censorship, such as the Motion Picture

Production Code that governed Hollywood from the 1930s through the early 1960s. Even after the demise of the code, producers tread warily into controversial territory, and thus in movies, as in novels, the line uttered in *Boys in the Band* long rang true: "Show me a happy homosexual and I'll show you a gay corpse."

The first significant victory of the gay movement was the 1958 Supreme Court decision requiring the Post Office to distribute the gay magazine *One*. In the decades since, the emergence and strength of the movement owed much to an independent gay press that told the stories mainstream media censored. The insistent visibility of the gay movement gradually shredded the veil of media censorship as gay people demanded their place on the public stage.

By the mid-1990s gay characters were relatively common in movies and television, and even noncontroversial, as long as they were not depicted in a sexual situation. Episodes of popular TV series showing physical intimacy between lesbians or, even more rarely, gay men, invariably set off storms of protest. When right-wing politicians used homoerotic images as pretexts for mounting attacks on arts funding, liberals wrapped their responses in the First Amendment and avoided defending the artworks themselves. Across the political spectrum, the consensus regarding the sexuality of gay people seems to follow the Clinton administration's policy for gays in the military: "Don't ask, don't tell."

Larry Gross

Bibliography

Kendrick, Walter, *The Secret Museum: Pornography in Modern Culture*. New York: Viking, 1987.

Russo, Vito. *The Celluloid Closet: Homosexuality in the Movies*. New York: Harper & Row, 1987.

Waugh, Thomas. *Hard to Imagine: Gay Male Eroticism in Film and Photography from Their Beginnings to Stonewall*. New York: Columbia University Press, 1996.

See also Catholicism; Gay and Lesbian Press; Media; Plato; Pornography; Television

Cernuda, Luis (1902?–1963)

Poet Luis Cernuda was born in Seville some time between 1902 and 1904. The uncertainty is possibly due to Cernuda himself, who, like Federico García Lorca, tended to understate his age. About 1924, he read André Gide, who made him conscious of his own homosexuality and reconciled him to it. In 1927, he met Lorca, later his close friend. Cernuda remembered that, when they met, "Something that I scarcely knew or that I didn't want to recognize began to draw us together." In 1931, he published *Los placeres prohibidos* (The Forbidden Pleasures), a book unprecedented in Spanish literature because of its openness about the poet's homosexuality.

Cernuda's first love affair after the brief encounters of youth began in 1931 and figures in several poems, for example his "Apología pro vita sua." Serafín was a teenage boy of the Madrid streets whom Lorca met at the Café Universal. Lorca was attracted to his natural intelligence and self-assurance and, a few days later, sent him to Cernuda with a note: "Dear Luis it is my pleasure to introduce you to Serafín I hope you will be able to help him out, A hug from Federico." Luis lived with Serafín for a year and was devastated by the breakup.

In 1934, Cernuda discovered Friedrich Hölderlin's poetry, from which he gained an admiration for the ideals of Hellenic paganism and nostalgia for its disappearance.

In 1938, fleeing the Spanish Civil War, Cernuda left for Britain, remaining until 1947 and teaching in Glasgow, Cambridge, and London. In 1940, Cuban friends got him a job and a residence permit, but he declined the offer in order to remain with his lover, a young Scottish student he met in Glasgow.

Later, he left Britain to teach at Mount Holyoke College in Massachusetts. During the summer vacation of 1949, he visited Mexico for the first time. Each year he returned, and in 1951 he met the great love of his life, called "X" in Cernuda's essay "Historial de un libro" (Dossier of a book): "I kept returning to Mexico each summer, and during the 1951 vacation, prolonged by a request for a semester's leave from Mount Holyoke, I met X, the inspiration for *Poemas para un coerpo* [Poems for a body], which I then began to write. Given my age, this could have been ridiculous. But also I knew, if excuses are necessary, that there are moments in life that require from us a surrender to fate, total and without reservations, a leap into emptiness, trusting in the impossible that we won't break our skulls. I think that at no other time was I, if not so in love, in love so well." In November 1952, he resigned from Mount Holyoke and moved to Mexico. In "Historial de un libro," Cernuda said: "As if possessed by a devil, I did not hesitate to throw aside a worthy job, a decent position, and an adequate salary, not to speak of residence in a welcoming country, where life offers a maximum of comfort and convenience. But love drew me toward Mexico." He remained in Mexico until his death, in 1963, of a heart attack.

Cernuda differs from Lorca, the other great gay Spanish poet of the early twentieth century, in his representation of homosexuality. Lorca defends freedom to love in all its manifestations. Cernuda speaks of gay love as if heterosexual love were something lower, or not even acceptable. His openness brought critical neglect during his lifetime, but ironically has now resulted in his recognition as one of the most important poets of twentieth-century Spain.

Juan M. Godoy translated by Bruce Vermazen

Bibliography

Silver, Philip. *"Et in Arcadia Ego": A Study of the Poetry of Luis Cernuda.* London: Tamesis Books, 1965.

See also García Lorca, Federico; Spain; Spanish Literature

Chambers, Whittaker (1901–1961)

An editor of *Time* magazine in the forties, Whittaker Chambers is best known as the former communist who accused Alger Hiss of passing classified documents to the Soviet Union while in the State Department. Chambers edited several Communist Party publications, including *New Masses* and the *Daily Worker*, before going underground in 1935 to spy for the Soviet Union. He broke with the party in 1938, disillusioned by the Stalinist terror. Brilliant but emotionally unstable, he became militantly anti-communist and began warning the FBI about communist infiltration of the government. Because of his penchant for self-dramatization, it is difficult to know how much of his story about the party's underground activities was true and how much of it was an embellishment intended to inflate his own importance.

Chambers's homosexuality played a central but still largely unacknowledged role in the Hiss case. Chambers worried that Hiss's lawyers would use his homosexuality as part of their defense strategy, and in 1949, shortly before Hiss's perjury trial was to begin, he made a written confession to the FBI. Hiss's lawyers did in fact consider using Chamber's homosexual past, but they eventually abandoned the idea,

afraid that it might expose Hiss's gay stepson, Timothy Hobson, who had received a dishonorable discharge from the navy. Moreover, Chambers's FBI statement seemed to confirm the link between communism and homosexuality in Cold War ideology. He claimed that he did not become actively homosexual until he went underground, and that he became a "model" husband and father upon his break with the party.

Robert J. Corber

Bibliography

Chambers, Whittaker. *Witness.* New York: Random House, 1950.

Weinstein, Allan. *Perjury: The Hiss-Chambers Case.* New York: Knopf, 1978.

See also Cohn, Roy M.; Hoover, J. Edgar; McCarthyism; United States

Cheever, John (1912–1982)

Novelist and short-story writer John Cheever, whose *Collected Stories* earned him a Pulitzer Prize in 1979, was known as the "Chekhov of suburbia." He pioneered the subgenre known as "the *New Yorker* short story." Like John Updike, whose work he envied and admired, Cheever detailed the messy lives of the East Coast upper middle class in clean, ironic prose.

Although he won many prizes in the 1950s, including a Guggenheim fellowship and an O. Henry award for his short fiction, Cheever did not win fame as a novelist until he wrote his third novel, *Bullet Park* (1969). Subverting the realism of his magazine style, Cheever combined fantasy and moral fable to reveal the corrupt undertone of a suburban existence. His second novel, *Falconer* (1977), told the story of a man's imprisonment. With its publication, he secured his place in late-twentieth-century American letters. Many of his stories became motion pictures, most notably "The Swimmer" (1964), the tale of an aging man's sexual identity.

The theme of sexual confusion recurred throughout Cheever's oeuvre, but Cheever's clever, understated prose masked the deep pain resulting from the ambivalence. His fiction chronicled the vagaries of heterosexual love, yet homosexual desire (usually coded as narcissistic, as in the case of "The Swimmer") also appeared with startling frequency.

Cheever's bisexuality was revealed in Scott Donaldson's 1988 biography, *John Cheever*, and confirmed by the posthumous publication of *The*

Journals of John Cheever in 1991. His sexual doubts complicated an already troubled life marked by alcoholism, marital infidelity (with women and men), and depression. Cheever married Mary Winternitz in 1941, fathering three children with her (Benjamin, Fred, and Susan, who later wrote a harrowing memoir of her father). He longed for male companionship yet rejected the possibility of an openly homosexual life. His sense of propriety covered a profoundly internalized homophobia. "Lunching with friends who talked of their tedious careers in lechery," Cheever wrote in his journal, "I thought: I am gay, I am gay, I am at last free of all this. This did not last for long" (347).

However, in a 1980 *Journal* entry, Cheever could finally admit, after decades of turmoil, that his feelings had historical origins: "In the thirties and forties men seemed to fear homosexuality as the earlier mariners feared sailing off the end of the ocean in a world supported on a turtle's back" (358). Two years later, cancer ended his life.

"I can tell a story," Cheever once said. "I can do . . . little else."   *John Ison*

Bibliography

Cheever, John. *The Journals of John Cheever.* Robert Gottlieb, ed. New York: Alfred A. Knopf, 1991.

Donaldson, Scott. *John Cheever: A Biography.* New York: Random House, 1988.

See also Fiction; U.S. Literature: Contemporary Gay Writing

Chicano and Latino Gay Cultures

One of the most notable social phenomena to emerge from the civil rights mobilizations in the United States during the sixties was the Chicano movement, which at its height spanned roughly from 1965 to 1975. The word *Chicano* was and is still used by the Mexican-Americans as a self-empowering label for their community, which was led by charismatic of activists like César Chávez, Dolores Huerta, and Rodolfo "Corky" Gonzales. The word *Latino* emerged in the eighties in an attempt to acknowledge the rapidly growing immigrant population of Central and South Americans, but this term is also meant to include older immigrants such as Puerto Ricans and Cubans. Indeed, today many Chicanos and Chicanas prefer Latino or Latina as labels that are more inclusive.

The role that gays and lesbians played within these communities was initially dismissed, a result of the pervasive homophobia of a "macho-centric" social structure associated with Hispanic cultures. In the case of the Chicanos, many key activists and artists remained in the closet in order to conform to an image of family values perpetuated to resist the negative portrayal of Mexican-Americans in the media. The creation of allegedly "positive" stereotypes, however, grossly simplified that community's complex social component. Within early Chicano cultural production, men were macho heroes, women their faithful, enchilada-baking sidekicks, and gays simply did not exist. Interestingly, the first novel to be penned by a Mexican-American (before the word *Chicano* became widespread) during the sixties was John Rechy's *City of Night* (1963), a groundbreaking account of a gay hustler's life. Rechy's controversial novels, including *Numbers* (1967) and *The Sexual Outlaw* (1977), were initially not accepted among the canon of Chicano literature, but they have now been accorded their rightful place by Chicano critics such as Juan Bruce-Novoa. Lesbian and gay and Chicanos and Chicanas have thus been subjected to ethnic as well as sexual oppression both within and without their community.

Attitudes began to change toward the late seventies. The Chicano movement's initial thrust had been lost because of internal ideological disagreements, and in this period of transition, women and gays began to aggressively assert their presence. The new critical climate, made possible by the emergence of a new generation of university-educated, middle-class Chicanos and Chicanas, was open to internal differences as well as to a quest for allegiance with other oppressed communities. Activist organizations that developed in the late seventies included the Gay Latino Alliance (GALA) in San Francisco and the Gay and Lesbian Latinos Unidos (GLLU) in Los Angeles. These organizations were also first to stress an outreach to the diverse Latin communities in the United States. With the advent of the AIDS crisis, Latinos in the Bay Area began organizing as early as 1983 with Community United in Response to AIDS/SIDA (CURAS), which later evolved into VIDA, Proyecto Contra SIDA.

A watershed for the airing of gay issues within the Chicano community was the play *Reunion* by young Filipino-American playwright Edgar Poma. *Reunion* is the story of a Chicano youth who comes out to his family by inviting his boyfriend to meet

C them. Poma wrote the piece as a class project at Berkeley for Chicano playwright Carlos Morton, and the work had its first performance in the spring of 1980. In August 1981 openly gay director Rodrigo Reyes from San Francisco directed the one-act version of the play for the Mission Cultural Center. The next month, Reyes and his cast were part of a sexuality seminar in the eleventh International Chicano/Latino Theater (TENAZ) Festival, where scenes of *Reunion* were performed to much controversy. Although many Chicano participants at the time argued that such themes were not "appropriate" for the community, the moment was decisive in furthering Chicano/Chicana queer issues. In spite of internal disagreements, a first-of-its-kind formal statement against sexism and homophobia in the Chicano community was issued at the festival's closing. A longer, two-act version of *Reunion* was staged in the spring of 1983 by the San Francisco Teatro Gusto group under the direction of Hank Tavera, and this time Reyes was featured as one of the main characters.

Hank Tavera and Rodrigo Reyes have been instrumental in furthering gay issues within the Latino community and in promoting AIDS awareness. Tavera is the co-founder (in 1986) and co-chair of the National Latina/o Lesbian, Gay and Bisexual Organization (LLEGÓ) with headquarters in Washington, D.C., and of LLEGÓ California. He has been the artistic director of the annual National AIDS Theater Festivals (since 1989), the Performing Arts Show of Latino/a Gay, Lesbian, Bisexual and Transgender Artists (since 1991), and the Latino/a AIDS Theater Festival (since 1993) of San Francisco.

In the area of literature, Chicana lesbians such as Cherríe Moraga and Gloria Anzaldúa were the trailblazers of the early eighties, placing themselves in the vanguard of the community's literary production. The first collection of homoerotic Chicano poetry—*Ya Vas, Carnal*—was published in 1985 by three San Francisco–based poets: Francisco X. Alarcón, Juan Pablo Gutiérrez, and Rodrigo Reyes. Alarcón went on to be the most acclaimed of Chicano gay poets, with such works as *Body in Flames/Cuerpo en Llamas* (1990), and *De Amor Oscuro/Of Dark Love* (1991). After John Rechy, Chicano novelist Arturo Islas dealt with gay themes in his works *The Rain God: A Desert Tale* (1984) and *Migrant Souls* (1990). Poet Gil Cuadros eloquently addressed Chicano queerness in his *City of God* (1994). These two writers, along with director Rodrigo Reyes, recently died as a result of AIDS-related illness.

Gay and lesbian Latino and Latina artists and activists have been at work in Los Angeles as well. In 1988 a group of gays and lesbians founded VIVA! in Los Angeles, an arts group that explicitly addresses gender issues and promotes AIDS-prevention awareness through activism and theater. Members Luis Alfaro, Mónica Palacios, and Beto Araiza have used performance pieces filled with humor and irony (such as *Deep in the Crotch of My Latino Psyche* [1992]) to explore lesbian and gay sexuality. Alfaro—a 1997 McArthur fellow—is a community worker and performance artist whose work addresses the intersections of class, race, sexuality, and ethnicity. His 1994 piece *El Juego de la Jotería* uses poetry and autobiographical skits to subvert the stigmatized labelings of *joto* (queer), and it critiques the obstacles that gay Latinos encounter when seeking alliances with the white gay community. Indeed, many gay Chicanos have made it a point to confront white gays with their often unacknowledged racism.

In the same vein, San Antonio–based artist David Zamora-Casas uses the paintbrush and the stage to perform his highly baroque and personal take on queerness. In theater proper, Chilean-American Guillermo Reyes has emerged as a leading Latino playwright with sharply parodic works like *Men on the Verge of a His-Panic Breakdown*. Cuban-American Eduardo Machado is another playwright, the author of an epic tetralogy, *Floating Islands*. The work—spanning forty years of history and running six hours in its 1994 production—addresses the complex interactions of race and sexuality with the Cuban diaspora. Ricardo Bracho of San Francisco is one of the first gay Chicano playwrights to fully address queer issues in his work, as shown in the recent production of his play *The Sweetest Hangover and Other STDs* (1997). Also from the Bay Area is the comedy group Latin Hustle, founded by Jaime Cortez, Al Luján, and Lito Sandoval.

Transgender Chicanos and Chicanas have attained popularity and respect within much of the community, as in the cases of San Francisco's Teresita la Campesina and Los Angeles's Vaginal Creme Davis (who has African American roots as well). Drag performers thrive in gay Latino clubs such as New York City's La Casita and San Francisco's Esta Noche.

Gay and lesbian Chicanos and Chicanas have made important headway in academia, thus securing spaces for the study of hitherto neglected identities. The largest Chicano/Chicana academic association—

the National Association of Chicana and Chicano Studies—has a prominent *joto* caucus. Some notable academics addressing gender issues are Yvonne Yarbro-Bejarano and Tomás Almaguer. Almaguer has authored a key essay that examines the complexities of gay Chicano identity formations (1989).

Other leading queer Latino/Latina artists are Cuban-American performance artist Marga Gómez and Guatemalan-American visual artist Alex Donis. Novelists Jaime Manrique, the Colombian-American author of *Twilight at the Equator* (1997), and Rafael Campo, the Cuban-American author of *The Poetry of Healing: A Doctor's Education in Empathy, Identity and Desire* (1997), are new key voices for the gay Latino communities in the nineties. In the field of academia, cultural critics Sylvia Molloy, David Román, and José Esteban Muñoz have made essential contributions to the study of queer Latino texts and performances.

That gay issues still spark controversy is shown by an incident surrounding a 1997 window display by Alex Donis. The display (titled *My Cathedral*) showed images of religious, political, and media figures engaged in same-sex French kisses (Madonna kissing Mother Teresa, Fidel Castro kissing John F. Kennedy, Pope John Paul II kissing Gandhi, for example). It was shown in the Galería de la Raza, a community gallery located in the Mission district, a predominantly Latino neighborhood of San Francisco. A few days after the show's opening, the gallery windows featuring the display were broken by anonymous assailants, leading to a heated debate on queer issues within the community.

Gay, lesbian, bisexual, and transgender in the Chicano and Latin communities have come a long way, from being systematically ignored by their own people and doubly discriminated by the mainstream society, to figuring prominently in their communities' cultural and political debates. Likewise, they have been striving to raise awareness within the white lesbian and gay community of the need to tackle issues of race and ethnicity in addition to the ones pertaining to gender.   *Antonio Prieto*

Bibliography

Almaguer, Tomás. "Chicano Men: A Cartography of Homosexual Identity and Behavior." *differences* 1:1 (1989): 75–100.

Bruce-Novoa, Juan. *Retrospace: Collected Essays on Chicano Literature.* Houston: Arte Público Press, 1990.

Foster, David, ed. *Chicano/Latino Homoerotic Identities.* New York: Garland, 1999.

Román, David. "Teatro Viva! Latino Performance and the Politics of AIDS in Los Angeles." In *Acts of Intervention. Performance, Gay Culture and AIDS.* Bloomington: Indiana University Press, 1998.

See also AIDS Performance; Cuadros, Gil; Islas, Arturo; Machismo; Manrique Ardilla, Jaime; Mexico; Rechy, John

Children's Books

Before the 1980s, many young gay men and lesbians gravitated to books that flouted traditional gender roles such as Tomie DiPaola's *Oliver Button Is a Sissy*, Louise Fitzhugh's *Harriet the Spy*, and Munro Leaf's *Ferdinand the Bull*. While many of the most prominent authors and illustrators of books for children and young adults have been rumored to be gay, the theme of homosexuality was almost entirely absent from this expanding field. Children's books that address gay and lesbian issues emerged in numbers only in the late 1980s as the growing number of gay and lesbian families sought sympathetic and age-appropriate materials for use with their children.

Young adult books that addressed lesbian and gay themes appeared before children's books, in the late 1960s and 1970s. These included John Donovan's *I'll Get There. It Better Be Worth the Trip* (1969), Isabelle Holland's *The Man Without a Face* (1972), Rosa Guy's *Ruby* (1973), Lynn Hall's *Sticks and Stones* (1974), and Sandra Scoppettone's *Trying Hard to Hear You* (1974) and *Happy Endings Are All Alike* (1978). Although these were considered landmark books for bringing homosexuality into the rapidly expanding field of young adult literature, most of the books' treatments of the subject have been considered disturbing, ominous, and inappropriately linked to homophobic violence.

A dramatic shift occurred in the late 1970s and early 1980s. The publication of young adult novels such as Deborah Haautzig's *Hey Dollface* (1978), Nancy Garden's *Annie on My Mind* (1982), and B. A. Ecker's *Independence Day*, and nonfiction books such as Frances Hanckel and John Cunningham's *A Way of Love, A Way of Life* (1979), Ruth Bell's *Changing Bodies, Changing Lives* (1980), and Fayerweather Street School's *The Kids' Book of Divorce* (1981) presented more complex and detailed treatments of lesbian and gay issues and

C avoided the earlier, seemingly mandatory homophobic violence.

The founding of the pioneering gay-owned Alyson Publications led to the publishing of teen-focused books such as *Young, Gay & Proud* (1980), Aaron Fricke's autobiographical *Confessions of a Rock Lobster* (1981), Ann Heron's edited collection of writings by lesbian and gay youth, *One Teenager in Ten* (1983), and Frank Mosca's novel *All-American Boys* (1983). Since that time, countless young adult books have appeared that include lesbian, gay, and bisexual characters and themes.

Before the 1980s, the children's section of libraries offered no materials explicitly involving homosexuality. In the early 1980s, several books were published—usually by small feminist or gay presses—that indirectly or explicitly discussed lesbian and gay families. These included Meredith Tax's *Families* (1981), Susanne Bosche's *Jenny Lives with Eric and Martin* (1983), and Jane Severance's *Lots of Mommies* (1983).

Alyson Publications took the lead again in the late 1980s and introduced "Alyson Wonderland," a line of gay-themed books for children. They published a range of materials, including coloring books (Michael Willhoite's *Families* [1991] and Sarita Johnson-Calvo's *A Beach Party with Alexis* [1993]), fairy tales (Johnny Valentine's *The Duke Who Outlawed Jelly Beans* [1991] and *The Day They Put a Tax on Rainbows* [1992]), and Dr. Seuss–inspired stories (Valentine's *One Dad, Two Dad, Brown Dad, Blue Dad* [1993] and *Two Moms, the Zark, and Me* [1995]).

Perhaps most controversial have been Leslea Newman's *Heather Has Two Mommies* (1989) and Michael Wilhoite's *Daddy's Roommate* (1990), which both became targets of Christian right censorship campaigns and were discussed widely in the mainstream press and at local school boards throughout the nation. They rose to the top of annual lists of books most challenged in the nation's libraries and remained there for several years. One event illustrates the historic role these two books have played in efforts to address lesbian and gay issues in schools. When Jon Nalley was elected to the New York City school board as an openly gay man, he took the oath of office with his hand held over these two books. *Eric Rofes*

Bibliography

Brogan, Jim. "Gay Teens in Literature." In *The Gay Teen: Educational Practice and Theory for Lesbian, Gay, and Bisexual Adolescents.* Gerald Unks, ed. New York: Routledge, 1995.

Stewig, John Warren. "Self-Censorship of Picture Books About Gay and Lesbian Families." In *Open Lives, Safe Schools: Addressing Gay and Lesbian Issues in Education.* Donovan R. Wallings, ed. Bloomington, Ind.: Phi Delta Kappa Educational Foundation, 1996.

See also Education: Theory and Pedagogy; Gay Families

China
Dynastic China

The civilization of China emerged from prehistory during the first half of the second millennium B.C. in the valley of the Huang Ho (Yellow River), spreading gradually southward. Over the centuries China has exercised extensive influence on Korea, Japan, and Southeast Asia. Inasmuch as Chinese society has traditionally viewed male homosexuality and lesbianism as altogether different, their histories are separate.

Zhou Dynasty

As with many aspects of Chinese civilization, the origins of homosexuality are both ancient and obscure. The fragmentary nature of early sources, the bias of these records toward the experiences of a tiny social elite, and the lack of pronouns differentiated by gender in ancient Chinese all frustrate any attempt to recapture an accurate conception of homosexuality in China's earliest periods. Only with the Eastern Zhou dynasty (722–221 B.C.) do reliable sources become available.

During the latter part of the Zhou, homosexuality appears as a part of the sex lives of the rulers of many states of that era. Ancient records include homosexual relationships as unexceptional in nature and not needing justification or explanation. This prosaic acceptance indicates that these authors considered homosexuality among the social elite to be fairly common and unremarkable. But because the political, ritual, and social importance of the family unit made procreation a necessity, bisexuality became more accepted than exclusive homosexuality, a predominance continuing throughout Chinese history.

The Eastern Zhou produced several figures who became so associated with homosexuality that later generations invoked their names as symbols of homosexual love, much in the same way that Europeans looked to Ganymede, Socrates, and Hadrian. These famous men included Mizi Xia, who offered his royal lover a half-eaten peach, and Long Yang, who compared the fickle lover to a fisherman who tosses back a small fish when he catches a larger one. Subsequent references to "sharing peaches" and "the passion of Lord Long Yang" became classical Chinese terms for homosexuality. Rather than adopt scientific terminology, with associations of sexual pathology, Chinese literateurs preferred the aesthetic appeal of these literary tropes.

Homosexual Emperors of the Han Dynasty

Although the unification of China with the fall of the Zhou induced fundamental changes in China's political and social order, homosexuality seems to have continued in forms similar to those it took in the previous dynasty. In fact, the Former Han dynasty (206 B.C.–A.D. 9) saw the high point of homosexual influence at the Chinese court. For 150 years, bisexual or exclusively homosexual emperors ruled China. The Han dynastic history discusses in detail the fabulous wealth and powerful influence of male favorites and their families, analogous to that of imperial consorts. The comprehensive Han history, *Records of the Historian (Shi ji),* even includes a section of biographies of these favorites, the author noting that their sexual charms proved more effective than administrative talents in propelling them to the heights of power.

Several early Han emperors, such as Gaozu (r. 206–194 B.C.) and Wu (r. 140–86 B.C.) favored more than one man with their sexual attentions. This behavior paralleled the heterosexual polygamy popular at court and among wealthy families. Some of the imperial male favorites had special talents in fields such as astrology and medicine that originally brought them to the ruler's attention, while others obtained favor solely through their sexuality. The desire to catch the emperor's eye at any cost, and thereby win substantial material rewards, fueled intense sartorial competition as courtiers vied with one another to dazzle the Son of Heaven with ornate clothing.

Dong Xian

The most famous favorite of the Han, Dong Xian, exemplifies the rewards and dangers that could come to one of these men. He became the beloved of Emperor Ai (r. 6 B.C.–A.D. 1), the last adult emperor of the Former Han, and rose to power with his lover. The Han dynastic history records that Emperor Ai presented him with an enormous fortune and lists an extensive array of offices he held. Since Emperor Ai lacked sons or a designated heir, he proposed during his reign to cede his title to Dong Xian. Although his councillors had firmly resisted the notion, nevertheless on his deathbed Ai handed over the imperial seals to his beloved. This unorthodox succession lacked the support of the most powerful court factions, and so Dong Xian found himself compelled to commit suicide. The resulting political vacuum left the kingmaker Wang Mang in control, and after a short period of nominal regency through child emperors, Wang Mang declared the overthrow of the Han dynasty. Thus the homosexual favoritism that helped shape the political topography throughout the former Han was also present in its destruction.

One incident in the life of Dong Xian became a timeless metaphor for homosexuality. A tersely worded account relates how Emperor Ai was sleeping with Dong Xian one afternoon when he was called to court. Rather than wake up his beloved, who was reclining across the emperor's sleeve, Ai took out a dagger and cut off the end of his garment. When courtiers inquired after the missing fabric, Emperor Ai told them what had happened. This example of love moved his courtiers to cut off the ends of their own sleeves in imitation, beginning a new fashion trend. Ever since then, Chinese authors have used "cut sleeve" as a symbol of homosexuality.

The periods of disunity following the Han produced a wider range of source materials that reflect the presence of homosexuality in classes other than the uppermost elite. Famed literary figures such as the "Seven Worthies of the Bamboo Grove" admired one another's good looks quite openly, and the contemporaneous accounts in *A New Account of Tales of the World (Shishuo xinyu)* substantiate the wide diffusion of homosexuality in post-Han society. Honored poet Pan Yue and master calligrapher Wang Xizhi both fervently admired male beauty. And the greatest intellectual force of the third century, Xi Kang (223–262), had a male lover.

Male Prostitution

During this period male prostitution also becomes evident and is both celebrated and denigrated in verse. During the Jin dynasty (265–420), poet Zhang Hanbian wrote a glowing tribute to a fifteen-year-old boy prostitute, Zhou Xiaoshi, in which he presents the boy's life as happy and carefree, "inclined toward extravagance and festiveness, gazing around at the leisurely and beautiful." A later poet, Liang dynasty (502–57) figure Liu Zun, tried to present a more balanced view in a poem entitled "Many Blossoms." In this piece he shows the dangers and uncertainty associated with a boy prostitute's life. His Zhou Xiaoshi "knows both wounds and frivolity / Withholding words, ashamed of communicating." Although these poems take opposite perspectives on homosexual prostitution, the appearance of this theme as an inspiration for poetry points to the presence of a significant homosexual world complete with male prostitutes catering to the wealthy.

Of course, homosexuality also continued among the social elite. Emperors such as Wei Wen (r. 220–27), Jin Diyi (r. 336–71), Liang Jianwen (r. 550–51), and several Tang dynasty rulers all had male favorites. These powerful men often preferred boys or eunuchs, although they sometimes also favored grown men.

By the Song dynasty (960–1280) a broadening of literary accounts makes available detailed information beyond the lives of emperors and literary figures. One source estimates that at the beginning of the dynasty in the Song capital alone there were more than ten thousand male prostitutes inhabiting a maze of brothels known as "mist and moon workshops." A love of sensuality continued throughout the dynasty. A source describing the fall of the Song notes "clothing, drink, and food were all that they desired. Boys and girls were all that they lived for."

The high profile of male prostitution led the Song rulers to take limited action against it. Many Confucian moralists objected to male prostitution because they saw the sexual passivity of a prostitute as extremely feminizing. In the early twelfth century, a law was codified that declared that male prostitutes would receive one hundred strokes of a bamboo rod and pay a fine of fifty thousand cash. Considering the harsh legal penalties of the period, which included mutilation and death by slicing, this punishment was actually quite lenient. And it appears that the law was rarely if ever enforced, so it soon became a dead letter.

The revival and transformation of Confucian doctrine in the movement now referred to as Neo-Confucianism had influence far beyond metaphysics. On a practical level the movement enforced a more rigid view of the status of women and of sexual morality. In general, Confucians became more intolerant of any form of sexuality taking place out-side of marriage. This was all part of an attempt to strengthen the family, held by Confucians to be the basic unit of society. The Song law prohibiting male prostitution came as an early response to this new social ethos. Legal intervention peaked in the Qing dynasty (1644–1911), when Emperor Kang Xi (r. 1662–1723) took steps against the sexual procurement of young boys, homosexual rape, and even consensual homosexual acts.

A law codified in 1690 specifically prohibited consensual homosexuality as part of an overall series of laws designed to strengthen the family. Although laws against rape of males were actively enforced, as demonstrated in a substantial body of Qing case law, it seems that the traditional government laissez-faire attitude toward male sexuality prevented enforcement of the law against consensual homosexual acts. After 1690 homosexuality continued as an open and prominent sexual force in Chinese society.

Flowering of the Ming Period

By the Ming dynasty (1368–1644) homosexuality had attained a high degree of representation in literature, erotic art, scholarship, and society as a whole. The rise of literacy and inexpensive printing generated a demand for popular literature such as *Golden Lotus* (*Jin ping mei*), depicting in colloquial language all forms of sexual conduct, and for erotic prints that presented homosexuality visually. A thirst for knowledge of homosexual history led to the compilation of the anonymous Ming collection *Records of the Cut Sleeve* (*Duan xiu pian*), which contains vignettes of homosexual encounters culled from nearly two millennia of sources. This anthology is the first history of Chinese homosexuality, perhaps the first comprehensive homosexual history in any culture, and still serves as our primary guide to China's male homosexual past.

In Fujian province on the South China coast, a form of male marriage developed during the Ming. Two men were united, the older referred to as an "adoptive older brother" (*qixiong*) and the younger as "adoptive younger brother" (*qidi*). The younger *qidi* would move into the *qixiong's* household, where he would be treated as a son-in-law by his husband's parents. Throughout the marriage, which often lasted for twenty years, the *qixiong* was completely responsible for his younger husband's upkeep. Wealthy *qixiong* even adopted young boys who were raised as sons by the couple. At the end of each marriage, which was usually terminated because of the familial responsibilities of procreation, the older husband paid the necessary price to acquire a suitable bride for his beloved *qidi*.

As China entered the Qing era, homosexuality continued to maintain a high profile. Besides several prominent Ming and Qing emperors who kept male favorites, a flourishing network of male brothels, and a popular class of male actor-prostitutes dominating the stage, Qing popular literature expanded on the homosexual themes explored during the Ming. The famous seventeenth-century author Li Yu wrote several works featuring male homosexuality and lesbianism. The greatest Chinese work of prose fiction, *Dream of the Red Chamber* (*Honglou meng*), features a bisexual protagonist and many homosexual interludes. And the mid-nineteenth century saw the creation of *A Mirror Ranking Precious Flowers* (*Pinhua baojian*), a literary masterpiece detailing the romances of male actors and their scholar patrons.

Western Influences

The twentieth century ushered in a new age for all aspects of Chinese society, including homosexuality. Within a few generations, China shifted from a relative tolerance of homosexuality to open hostility. The reasons for this change are complex and not yet completely understood. First, the development of a colloquial *baihua* literary language removed many potential readers from the difficult classical Chinese works, which contained the native homosexual tradition. Also, the Chinese reformers early in the century began to see any divergence between their own society and that of the West as a sign of backwardness. This led to a restructuring of Chinese marriage and sexuality along more Western lines. The uncritical acceptance of Western science, which regarded homosexuality as pathological, added to the Chinese rejection of same-sex love. The end result is a contemporary China in which the native homosexual tradition has been virtually forgotten and homosexuality is ironically seen as a recent importation from the decadent West.

People's Republic of China (PRC)

Although early Chinese communists preached sexual liberation, after assuming power in 1949 they declared homosexuality a sign of bourgeois decadence. Some homosexuals were punished by "reeducation" in labor camps, where they were subjected to anal rape and other forms of abuse. Openly gay life came to an abrupt end.

Because communist orthodoxy saw homosexuality as a symptom of bourgeois decay, it was considered virtually eradicated by the new proletarian society. For decades the PRC leadership declared homosexuality to be extremely rare or even denied its existence outright. Western psychologists, however, noted that the official reporting of impotence is much higher in mainland China than in the West. It seems that many Chinese men, unfamiliar with the concept of homosexuality, interpreted their sexuality solely according to relations with women. Lack of sexual desire for women was considered "impotence," not homosexuality.

Since the death of Mao Zedong in 1976, economic reforms have allowed Chinese society to become much more prosperous, open, and pluralistic. A few Chinese scholars now admit the existence of homosexuality and AIDS in China, and have begun to conduct research, although finding venues for publication is still very difficult. Gay subcultures have begun to emerge in major cities, particularly Shanghai and Guangzhou. Because of rising economic inequality, much of the new gay life involves prostitution and other forms of exploitation.

Preoccupied with rising crime and corruption, Chinese police now generally ignore gay people. Nevertheless, fear of discovery and lack of privacy tend to limit the quality and duration of homosexual relationships. And for the vast majority of Chinese living in the conservative countryside, making homosexual contacts is extremely difficult.

Hong Kong

As a British territory, Hong Kong adopted many aspects of British law, including the criminalization of sodomy. Until recently the Hong Kong police actively sought out and persecuted homosexuals. But as part of the legal reforms in preparation for the return of Hong Kong to China in 1997, sodomy laws were repealed despite considerable opposition from many local people. Prior to the decriminalization of sodomy, Hong Kong already had a sizable gay community. Now that homosexuality is legal, several bars publicly provide a center for Hong Kong gay life. But the universal uncertainty about life in post-1997 Hong Kong has led some gay people to emigrate; the majority who remain in Hong Kong face unclear prospects.

Taiwan

Today Taiwan has the most openly gay life in the Chinese world. There has never been a sodomy law in Taiwan. And unlike mainland China or Hong

Kong, there has never been systematic persecution of homosexuals in Taiwan, although police would still occasionally raid bars and saunas.

Soldiers frequenting Taipei's New Park were an important early nucleus of homosexual activity. One of Taiwan's most respected novelists, Pai Hsien-yung, raised the issue of homosexuality with the general public in his controversial novel, *Crystal Boys* (*Niezi*), which served as the basis for a 1986 film of the same title. The AIDS crisis focused widespread public attention on gay life, resulting in general public awareness of the existence of homosexuals in Taiwan.

During the 1990s Taiwanese rapidly reformed their authoritarian political system to become one of the most democratic countries in Asia. Liberal social attitudes emphasizing tolerance and pluralism have grown out of political reform and economic prosperity. Taiwan now has a monthly glossy magazine (*G&L*) for gays and lesbians, several radio talk shows devoted to gay issues, widely distributed books on gay issues, and the beginnings of gay campus and political organizations. Both major opposition parties now publicly endorse gay rights. Liberal Taiwanese often refer to homosexuals as "comrades" (*tongzhi*), a self-consciously ironic appropriation of communist jargon associated with sexual oppression.

Although the situation for homosexuals in Taiwan is rapidly improving, the attitudes of many Taiwanese remain conservative. Some younger Taiwanese have begun resisting heterosexual marriage. But traditionally the goal of marriage was procreation rather than personal fulfillment. As in mainland China and Hong Kong, most homosexuals in Taiwan still endure tremendous pressure to marry. The rising conflict between the new Western-style gay life and traditional Chinese patrilineal values continues to intensify.   *Bret Hinsch*

Bibliography

Hinsch, Bret. *Passions of the Cut Sleeve: The Male Homosexual Tradition in China*. Berkeley: University of California Press, 1990.

See also Asians in North America; Chinese Bachelor Society

Chinese Bachelor Society

Bachelor society was considered a form of social organization peculiar to Chinese immigrants in North America. From the mid-nineteenth century to World War II, white politicians and social critics characterized Chinese in the United States and Canada as inscrutable aliens living in mysterious clan networks of single men. Nineteenth-century political morality and twentieth-century sociology established the chief features of bachelor society: single male workers, female prostitutes, and transient life. In nineteenth-century travelogues and political commentary, the image of bachelor life was that of dissolute men trapped in a culture of vice, which included frequenting opium dens, gambling houses, and brothels. Critics of Chinese immigration observed the absence of nuclear families as evidence that Chinese men had no commitment to permanent residence and assimilation to North American societies.

Twentieth-century sociologists and historians have attributed the persistence of a Chinese bachelor society to immigration restrictions, antimiscegenation laws, and migratory labor patterns. Many men left wives and children in China because labor recruitment and business opportunities favored the migration of men. Prohibitions on the immigration of single women and hostility to Chinese immigration in general exacerbated an already skewed gender ratio. Limited opportunities for conjugal marriage, sociologists argued, resulted in "sexual maladjustment" of men who sought female prostitution. This interpretation of "deviant heterosexuality" presumed that Chinese men were frustrated by the denial of prerogatives of marriage and family life in North America.

Historians and artists recently have sought to reevaluate and explore textual evidence of male-to-male sexual possibilities. Historical studies have engaged in a reinterpretation of homosexuality as traced in medical, legal, and political documents, often retrieved from problematic accusations. For instance, in investigations of Chinese immigration conducted by the U.S. Congress (1877) and the Canadian Royal Commission (1885), white physicians and merchants testified that Chinese men engaged in "habitual" anal intercourse that exacerbated the spread of syphilis. In both Canadian and U.S. courts, Chinese men were prosecuted for sodomy and gross indecency in instances involving white men and boys. Although this evidence was initially employed to confirm worries about the deviance and depravity of Chinese men, historians have weighed the conditions of knowledge and the politics of accusation with the possibilities of social and sexual contact. Ethnographic and literary interpretation indicate that the possibilities of homosexual relations within Chinese bachelor society fascinated, amused, and horrified both white and Chinese American communities. One sociologist made an inventory of the variety of slang insults and jokes in interviews with Chinese laundry workers that considered effeminate males or literally "dead penis" as men who were unresponsive to women and who desired other men. In the literary analysis of fin-de-siècle English-language fiction, the opium den was a strategic site of sexual transgression where the sharing of opium pipes suggested homoerotic and oral exchange.

These interpretive interventions of sexual acts and male homoerotic companionship have recast the possibilities of deviant subjectivity. The exploration of deviant heterosexuality and homosexuality in bachelor society exposed the implicit presumption that heterosexual conjugal marriage represented the perpetuation of Chinese American community and assimilation to North American society. However, the subjectivity of the men involved and the diverse cultural meanings of their emotional and physical relations may continue to defy easy categorization.

Nayan Shah

Bibliography

Fung, Richard. "Burdens of Representation, Burdens of Responsibility." In *Constructing Masculinity*. Maurice Berger et al., eds. London: Routledge, 1995, 291–99.

Fung, Richard, director. *Dirty Laundry*. Canada. Videotape, 30 minutes. 1996. Distributed by NAATA and V-Tape.

Siu, Paul C.P. *The Chinese Laundryman: A Study in Social Isolation*. John Kuo Wei Tchen, ed. New York: New York University Press, 1987.

Ting, Jennifer. "Bachelor Society: Deviant Heterosexuality and Asian American Historiography." In *Privileging Positions: The Sites of Asian American Studies*. Gary Okihiro et al., eds. Pullman: Washington State University Press, 1995, 271–79.

See also Asians in North America; China; Immigration, U.S.

Choruses and Marching Bands

Few Americans today realize just how frequently community music ensembles have been organized in this country to promote political and social causes and to instill cultural confidence in disenfranchised populations. For example, during their heyday in the nineteenth century, town bands were often employed to underscore rallies of the abolitionist, suffragist, and temperance movements. Dozens of New York trade-union bands reportedly marched in the first Labor Day parade of 1882; and several radical choruses were active in Chicago and Milwaukee well into the 1950s. The abundance and popularity of regional folk-heritage choirs and polka, klezmer, and salsa bands attest to the importance of such musical groups as expressions of ethnic pride and solidarity. So it is not surprising that choruses and marching bands became important voices for the gay rights movement during the latter part of the twentieth century.

One of the earliest of such groups was Women Like Me, a lesbian chorus founded in New York City by composer Roberta Kosse. Established primarily to perform Kosse's own compositions, the most famous being an oratorio, *The Return of the Great Mother*, the chorus sang from 1971 to 1980, growing to approximately forty voices by 1977.

After borrowing instruments and music from a Salvation Army post in New York, Hester Brown started the Victoria Woodhull All-Women's Marching Band in 1973. Named for a nineteenth-century feminist and presidential candidate, the Woodhull Band played popular tunes with themes of love, women, and patriotism for the first Susan B. Anthony Day celebration and three of the city's Gay Liberation Day parades. Although not exclusively a lesbian ensemble, their theme song was *When the Dykes Go Marching In*.

Responding to a friend's challenge to stage a Bicentennial folk-opera that would tell the history of women in song, Catherine Roma assembled the Anna Crusis Women's Choir in Philadelphia in 1975, the name being a pun on the musical term *anacrusis*. The choir performed the opera *American Women : A Choral History* at several East Coast colleges, often accompanied by a lecture from the work's compiler, Roma's friend and noted historian Ann Dexter Gordon. Having recently celebrated its twentieth anniversary, this early feminist choir remains a leader in the performance of new music written by, about, and for women.

Conductor Donald Rock, envisioning a chorus that would "dig music as well as each other," founded the first gay men's ensemble, the Gotham Male Chorus, in late 1977. Specializing in a repertoire of plainchant and Renaissance polyphony, the Gotham invited women to join in 1980, becoming the nation's first lesbian and gay chorus, the Stonewall Chorale.

Certainly the most prolific and charismatic leader in the gay community music movement was Jon Sims, a 31-year-old music teacher who in 1978 formed the San Francisco Gay Freedom Day Marching Band and Twirling Corps. Originally conceived by Sims as merely a way to add more sound and color to the city's annual pride parade, the band also represented a positive political statement against the homophobic attacks of Anita Bryant and the Briggs Initiative. Later that same year Sims founded the second of five music organizations, the San Francisco Gay Men's Chorus, which debuted by singing a Mendelssohn hymn at City Hall on the evening of the George Moscone and Harvey Milk assassinations. Within a year there were choruses and bands forming in Los Angeles, New York, Chicago, and Seattle; and when the San Francisco Chorus, under the baton of Dick Kramer, toured a dozen U.S. cities in 1981, it acted as a catalyst for the founding of many more lesbian and gay music ensembles.

As the number of these otherwise isolated groups increased, many sought nationwide alliances to provide leadership, support, and inspiration. The Sister Singers Network was the first to develop in 1981, fostering communication and cooperation among women's and lesbian choruses. Today the Network utilizes a matrix organizational model to link a membership of forty-five choruses and several affiliated composer/arrangers, to exchange music, and to produce regional, national, and international women's choral festivals.

The Gay and Lesbian Association of Choruses (GALA) was established in September 1982 by 14 choruses performing in San Francisco as part of the first Gay Games. Growing to encompass more than 140 men's, women's, and mixed choruses throughout North America, Europe, and Australia, GALA promotes excellence in the choral arts among its member by distributing promotional publications; maintaining membership, repertoire, and performance databases; and holding annual leadership conferences and festivals. Many of the larger GALA member choruses have attracted broad audiences and have been quite successful at commissioning new choral works and producing commercial recordings. Not without their adversaries, however, the choruses fought to win a lawsuit in 1986 that fi-

nally allowed them to use the word *gay* in their names when performing at conventions of the American Choral Directors Association.

By October 1982 seven bands had organized to form the Lesbian and Gay Bands of America (LGBA), which now includes dozens of marching, concert, and jazz bands in sixteen U.S. cities, as well as Vancouver and Melbourne. In addition to its networking and leadership missions, LGBA exists to promote "music as a medium of communication" and to stimulate "public interest in the unique art form of community band music," which it achieves through semiannual conferences and festivals. Similar to the GALA choruses, the LGBA member bands communicate through a quarterly newsletter, an electronic mailing list, and a series of linked Web pages. The massed bands and their auxiliary drill corps, sometimes numbering more than three hundred performers, have played in many of the nation's major concert halls and have provided music for the two most recent marches on Washington, three Gay Games, and President Clinton's inaugural parade in 1993.

Unfortunately, in this age of mass-media entertainment and declining support for the arts, many community music ensembles are struggling to survive, despite the fact that they have been important vehicles for social and political protest in the past.

Matthew W. Wise

Bibliography

Attinello, Paul. "Authority and Freedom: Toward a Sociology of the Gay Choruses." In *Queering the Pitch: The New Gay and Lesbian Musicology*. Philip Brett, Elizabeth Wood, and Gary C. Thomas, eds. New York: Routledge, 1994, 315–46.

Baker's Biographical Dictionary of Musicians, 8th ed., s.v. "Sims, Jon Reed."

Gordon, Eric A. "GALA: The Lesbian and Gay Community of Song." *Choral Journal* 30, no. 9 (1990): 25–32.

See also Marches and Parades; Sims, John

Christianity

Christianity collectively represents a variety of beliefs and practices based on a tradition centered around Jesus of Nazareth ("the Christ"), who is believed to have lived c.3 B.C.–A.D. 33. Since the original churches were congregational, each tended to reflect the values or assumptions of the social and cultural community in which it found itself, and these differences continue to exist. By about A.D. 200, the church had come to recognize the texts making up the New Testament as a single canon, although some groups included texts that others labeled as Apocrypha. After some hesitation the Hebrew Scriptures known to Christians as the Old Testament were taken from Judaism as divinely inspired.

From this point onward, Christian doctrines were elaborated by groups of intellectuals, known collectively as the fathers of the church, or patristic rite, and including Origen, Clement of Alexandria, Tertullian, Athanasius, and Basil. Differences among the interpretations were decided, after Christianity became a legal religion in the Roman Empire in the fourth century, by a series of councils, the first of which was called by the emperor Constantine. Those groups who disagreed either compromised or went their own way, helping to explain the continuing variety of Christian interpretations.

The church fathers (and the councils supporting them) pieced together the often contradictory and ambiguous scriptural statements about sex and homosexuality into a consistent doctrine. Though the church fathers based their exegesis on the Bible, they were inevitably influenced by philosophical and religious currents of their own time or region, especially Greek stoicism and Neoplatonism, and by rival mystery cults such as Manicheanism and Gnosticism. Inevitably there were differences on such sexually related topics as divorce, celibacy, and so forth, but the dominant voice in the Latin tradition came to be what today is known as the Roman Catholic Church. Most of the powerful opposition came from Greek and other linguistic groups that gave rise to the Orthodox, Coptic, Nestorian, Armenian, and other churches.

Particularly influential in the West was St. Augustine (d. 430), one of the great scholars of the ancient world. Educated in the Neoplatonic and Stoic ideals of his teachers, he had converted as a student to Manicheanism, one of rival religious groupings to Christianity. Manicheanism regarded intercourse leading to procreation as particularly evil because it caused other souls to be imprisoned in bodies, thus continuing the cycle of good versus evil, a theme emphasized by Zoroastrianism, from which Manicheanism had derived.

Augustine strove for some twelve years to free his body of its material desires and become one of the elect, those who successfully lived the stringent life of the true believer. In this he was not particularly successful since he had a mistress and a child. He reported in his autobiography that he prayed each day for God to give him chastity and continence, but always added silently with a wish at the end that God not do that yet.

Dissatisfied with the way his life was going, Augustine had a religious crisis that resulted in conversion to Christianity, the religion of his mother; now miraculously he found he could control his sexual desires and in fact no longer desired a wife. He rose quickly in the Christian Church, becoming bishop of Hippo and writing prolifically on every aspect of Christian doctrine, in the process interpreting and integrating into Western Christianity Neoplatonic, Stoic, and even Manichean beliefs. He continued to feel that continence and celibacy were the proper way to live but had to recognize that the Hebrew Bible emphasized marriage and reproduction. He felt, however, that the necessary need to reproduce should be done without lust. Sexual intercourse could be justified only in terms of reproduction, and Augustine specified that the proper way to do this was with the woman on her back and the penis in the vagina. No other position was acceptable, and no other bodily part could be used.

This became the policy of the Western Church; taken literally, it condemns homosexuality and lesbianism, although comparatively little about same-sex relations was discussed in the patristic literature. What discussion did take place emphasized that homosexuality in the West was considered to be on the level of adultery, a serious sin, while the Eastern traditions generally classified it as equivalent to fornication, a much less serious sin.

In the West the church took control of sexual issues by the eighth century and attempted both to teach the public about its position and to enforce it. The Augustinian position was affirmed and amplified by St. Thomas Aquinas, who held that homosexual activities were more sinful than other sins of lust because they were also sins against nature. Much of canon law that emerged in the twelfth century laid down the importance of controlling sex.

Increasingly, deviance from the church's code on sexual preference was equated with deviance from accepted church doctrine, that is, homosexuals and lesbians could be regarded as proponents of heresy. Sodomy came to be regarded as the most heinous of sexual offenses, even worse than incest, and as civil law began to take over from canon law, it could be punished as a capital crime.

The trend toward civil control of sexuality was accentuated by the development of Protestantism in the sixteenth century, although the Protestants were more accepting of heterosexual sex, but not much different from the Catholic Church on homosexuality and lesbianism. Martin Luther, for example, regarded homosexuality as being derived from the devil; those involved in it should be treated accordingly. John Calvin was not quite so hostile; he simply reemphasized that homosexuality was a sin against nature. Interestingly, one of the charges that both sides of the Catholic-Protestant quarrel brought against the other was that of sodomy. Sodomy, in fact, became one of the accusations even within religious congregations when something horrible was believed to be going on. The dissolution of the Jesuit order in 1773 was preceded by accusations of sodomy, just as similar charges had encouraged the breakup of the Knights Templar several centuries earlier.

No real changes took place in Christian attitudes until the twentieth century, when a number of churches, led by the Quakers, the Anglicans, and the Unitarian-Universalists in the period following World War II, modified their stand on homosexuality and lesbianism. Gradually most of the mainline Protestant churches changed, although ordination to the ministry of homosexual or lesbian individuals remained controversial. Pentecostal and fundamentalist Christians, however, were slow to change, and one result of this was the founding of the Metropolitan Community Church, which emphasized that since God created men and women homosexuals and lesbians, he loved them. Even among Christian churches that failed to modify their stands officially, however, special homosexual groups and organizations such as Dignity emerged, and this particular association has received a lot of support from within the Catholic Church, which is not true of some of the other groups nominally identified with particular religious groupings.

In sum, Christian religions of all traditions had been hostile not only to homosexuality and lesbianism but to sexuality in general. Protestants have been only slightly less hostile than Catholics. In general, those Christians in the Eastern traditions were less hostile than those in the West. The source of these attitudes was not so much biblical or uniquely Christian but a reflection of undercurrents of thought in existence at the time Christianity emerged on the world scene. These extraneous ideas about sex and homosexuality were incorporated into Christian teachings by theologians and canon lawyers who then erected a belief system on them, and from the church they were communicated to the public at large. When Christian churches ceased to have any real enforcement power over secular laws, the penalties if anything increased, simply because what had become a sin, without any attempt to rethink the issues, became a crime, although some sexual activities were also recognized as illnesses. Only when these extraneous ideas are effectively challenged, as they have been in the last decades of the twentieth century, have the churches rethought their attitudes and concepts about sexuality, including lesbianism and homosexuality, and realized that much of what they accepted as the Christian tradition had little biblical foundation but instead was based on philosophies and beliefs that we no longer accept.

Vern L. Bullough

Bibliography

Bailey, Derrick Sherwin. *Homosexuality and the Western Christian Tradition*. London: Longmans, Green, 1955.

Bullough, Vern L. *Sexual Variance in Society and History*. Chicago: University of Chicago Press, 1976.

See also Augustine of Hippo; Catholicism; Religion and Religiosity; Religious Organizations; Religious Right; Sodomy; Thomas Aquinas

Christopher Street

The *Advocate*, over the last three decades, has been the American gay community's *New York Times*, *Newsweek*, or even, redundantly, its *GQ*. But *Christopher Street*, until recently America's most popular and prestigious gay literary journal, did not change much from its founding in 1975 to its demise in 1997.

Printing the Walt Whitmans and the Henry Jameses of its age (and outing those long-dead historical figures in ad campaigns), publisher Charles Ortleb's *Christopher Street* modeled itself after the *New Yorker.* The homospecific works of Tennessee Williams and James Purdy, as well as groundbreaking post-Stonewall prose by legendary Violet Quill members Edmund White, Andrew Holleran, and Felice Picano, found a home between *CS*'s pages.

Ortleb's journal promoted a vision of gay literature that was as urbane as it was erotic; the ideal *CS* contributor resembled an openly gay John Cheever, minus the guilt. Michael Denneny, an editor and author, praised this influential vision: "Without our storytellers and poets, we would never be able to recognize ourselves and regain through the realm of the imagination the reality of our lives."

As long as "we" spent "our lives" on Fire Island, that is. As *CS* entered its final years, many (especially people of color) voiced legitimate concerns over the Anglocentrism and class bias of Ortleb's journal. Although *Christopher Street* continued to run paeans to Manhattan's bent bourgeoisie, other journals (including "'zines") offered alternatives. Still, when the magazine folded in 1997, many felt that an important voice had been silenced.

John M. Ison

Bibliography

Denneny, Michael. "Further Down the Road." In *First Love/Last Love: New Fiction from Christopher Street*. Michael Denneny, Charles Ortleb, and Thomas Steele, eds. New York: G. B. Putnam, 1985.

See also Fiction; Gay and Lesbian Press; James, Henry; Journalism; Violet Quill; White, Edmund; Whitman, Walt; Williams, Tennessee; U.S. Literature: Contemporary Gay Writing

Circuit Party Scene

The circuit party scene is an informal network of large gay dance parties in various U.S., Canadian, European, and Australian cities. The calendar of subsequent events comprises a "circuit" of parties that can be attended throughout the year. Dance music, drug use, the AIDS epidemic, gym-body aesthetics, even gay-focused niche marketing all intersect to form a distinct subculture with its own cultural codes, conduct, and argot.

From relative obscurity as a small gay subculture in the mid- to late 1980s, circuit parties became more widely known as the number of events rapidly expanded in the 1990s. Gay and then mainstream media began to focus on the circuit scene as concern rose about large-scale drug use and reports of unsafe sex. While many observers and critics have labeled the circuit scene as irresponsible hedonism, the popular self-definition of the circuit is based around a defense of sexual and personal freedoms. As proclaimed in *Circuit Noize*, a publication devoted to the circuit scene, "A circuit party gives us the chance to escape the pressures of our day-to-day existence and to enter the altered world where man-to-man sex is not only accepted, but is celebrated."

The roots of circuit are in a hard-core dance club scene that developed in the early 1980s as the full force of the AIDS epidemic hit major gay urban centers such as New York and Los Angeles. Seeking to escape the fears and stress brought on by the widespread sickness and death around them, a small number (perhaps two to three thousand) of gay men in both cities turned to all-night dance parties at clubs such as the Saint in New York and Probe in LA. So-called club drugs such as ecstasy and crystal methamphetamine (usually called "crystal"), newly popular in the European "rave" scene, were employed to further the sense of escape and lessen personal inhibitions.

Many of these men also began turning to body-building as both a physical and psychological counterweight to the physical wasting syndrome that was then a near inevitable consequence of AIDS. The long-standing gay male fascination with representations of masculinity and the prescription of steroids by doctors to combat AIDS-related wasting syndrome fueled a heightened idealizing of muscle development. An increased sense of tactile touch sensation experienced under the influence of drugs also promoted muscularity as the preferred and even required aesthetic for entrance and acceptance into the dance party scene.

In the mid-1980s, the major AIDS service organizations (ASOs) in such cities as New York, Los Angeles, and Miami developed large-scale dance parties as vehicles both to raise funds and to foster an uplifting response to the AIDS crisis. The annual Morning Party thrown by New York's Gay Men's Health Crisis (GMHC) and the White Party thrown by Health Crisis Network in Miami first attracted hundreds and then thousands of gay men. By the early 1990s ASOs in other cities as well as independent party promoters also established parties to benefit AIDS treatment and care. As men from different cities began traveling from one dance event to another, the concept of a "circuit" of events that could be followed took hold.

A parallel exists between the concurrent development of the circuit scene among gay men and the rave scene among adolescents. Both groups often self-describe themselves as "misunderstood" by general society. Both groups look to circuit and rave events as "tribal" gathering, where drugs are used to heighten a sense of bonding among participants. Forms of coded argot used to refer to drug use and the conduct of dancing have developed (separately) within the circuit and rave scenes, with the circuit having a particular focus on phrases to describe sexual activity.

Use of a tribal metaphor to describe the circuit scene is often coupled with an expression by participants of deriving a form of "spiritual" nourishment they have not found elsewhere. It is not surprising that the image of three thousand men jammed onto a dance floor, swaying with their hands in the air and singing along to a popular song is very analogous to that of a gospel music revival at a Southern Baptist worship service. The analogy is one that circuit participants not only recognize but actively celebrate when seeking to validate the dynamic of circuit events. As male pornography star and performer Tom Collins told *Genre* magazine, "Straight people may go to church for their spirituality, but Circuit events are my form of church and the DJs are my priests."

In 1996 the circuit came under increased mainstream media scrutiny after a handful of near-fatal drug overdoses during GMHC's Morning Party on Fire Island. Similarly, gay media have also turned a critical eye on the circuit as part of the evolving debate on promiscuity, sexual identity, and continued high rates of HIV infection. The role of AIDS service organizations in promoting circuit events has also become an issue of concern, with the drug use and sexual conduct at the parties viewed as contrary to the aims of HIV/AIDS prevention efforts. Additionally, the emphasis on gym body culture in the circuit—which some have termed "body fascism"—has triggered a debate on the gay community's preoccupation with hypermasculine gender roles. This external pressure has led to a self-moderating campaign by circuit party promoters, DJs, and media, with the focus on controlling excessive drug use at circuit events.

As the number of circuit events increases (with a greater emphasis on corporate sponsorship), there is evidence of a schism developing between celebrating the increased size of the "tribe" and a sense of losing the closer-knit fraternization and interaction of the earlier, more closed scene. Some ancillary parties to the main circuit events have become member or invitation only; this recalls the entrance policies of the New York and L.A. clubs that birthed the scene.

The demographic composition of circuit parties has somewhat expanded beyond the hegemony of white, professional males. However, the cost of traveling to circuit events and the cost of the events themselves still exclude many men of color and the less affluent.

Eugene Patron

Bibliography

Collins, Tom. Interview. *Genre*, 42 (October 1996): 36.

Hart, Christian. "The Circuit: Drugged Out Party Boys, or Neo-Tribal Spirituality?" *Circuit Noize* 11 (Winter 1997): 30.

Lewis, Lynette A., and Michael W. Ross *A Select Body: The Gay Dance Party Subculture and the HIV/AIDS Pandemic*. London: Cassell, 1995.

Rofes, Eric. *Reviving the Tribe: Regenerating Gay Men's Sexuality and Culture in the Ongoing Epidemic*. Binghamton, N.Y.: Harrington Park/Hawthorn Press, 1996.

Signorile, Michelangelo. *Life Outside: The Signorile Report on Gay Men: Sex, Drugs, Muscles, and the Passages of Life*. New York: HarperCollins, 1997.

See also Alcohol and Drugs; Body Image; Disco and Dance Music; Music and Musicians 2: Popular Music

Civil Rights in the U.S. Law
Current Status

Current federal civil rights law bars private-sector discrimination in housing, employment, and public accommodations on the basis of race, national origin, ethnicity, gender, religion, age, and disability, but not sexual orientation. From the beginning of gay activism at least up until the AIDS crisis, securing civil rights protections was the main focus of the gay movement. Indeed, in this period, if one mentioned gay rights, one was presumed to be talking of legislated civil rights protections against discrimination in employment, housing, and public accommodations.

But gays' record of success in this area has been checkered at best. Between 1981 and 1996, nine states passed civil rights protections for gays covering at least employment: California, Connecticut, Hawaii, Massachusetts, Minnesota, New Jersey, Rhode Island, Vermont, and Wisconsin. In addition, some hundred municipalities and counties around the country offer such protections. In general, though, these local and state provisions are weak in scope, enforcement mechanisms, and effects, as were such local protections against racial discrimination prior to the enactment of the federal 1964 Civil Rights Act and its considerably strengthened enforcement mechanisms in 1972. Once passed, local gay ordinances have frequently been overturned through referendum initiatives, ranging from Anita

Bryant's 1977 "Save Our Children" campaign in Miami through Cincinnati's 1993 Amendment 3. Every year since the late 1970s, a federal gay civil rights bill has been introduced in Congress. The versions of the bill from the early 1990s onward are very weak in their protections and enforcement mechanisms. They cover only employment discrimination, prohibit gay affirmative action, and eliminate the use of what has historically has been the most effective mechanism for establishing the existence of discrimination—statistical analyses of hiring pools and workplace practices. Only "smoking gun" evidence of a specific intention to discriminate—the sort of evidence a lawyer never finds—could launch a case under current drafts of the legislation. In the 1990s, the national gay civil rights bill has usually been referred to as ENDA (Employment Non-Discrimination Act). Even in its weakened forms, ENDA's passage appears remote—off perhaps a generation or two.

General Arguments for Civil Rights Legislation

Frequently debates over gay civil rights legislation have operated merely as stand-ins for referenda over whether "gay" is considered good or not. Principled opposition to civil rights legislation flows from a belief that it illegitimately restricts the workings of individual independence, especially in the form of free enterprise. Admittedly such legislation does impinge on employers' ability to contract with whomever they want; but such legislation promotes other values, ones that stand behind independence and make having it valuable in the first place. These values include self-respect, self-sufficiency, general prosperity, and individual flourishing.

People cannot have much self-respect or maintain a solid sense of self if they are subject to whimsical and arbitrary actions of others. Work, entertainment, and housing are major modes through which people identify themselves to themselves. People thrown out of work frequently compare this loss to the loss of a family member, especially to the loss of a child. Here the comparison is not simply to the intensity of the emotion caused by the loss but to the nature of the loss: what was lost was a central means by which one constituted one's image of oneself. Work is also a chief means by which people identify themselves to others. In America, one's job is tantamount to one's social identity, and job discrimination is a chief mode of expatriation from the national experience.

Civil rights legislation also helps people meet the general expectation that each individual is primarily responsible for fulfilling his or her own basic needs and that government becomes an active provider only when all else fails. Civil rights legislation helps unclog channels between an individual's efforts and the fulfillment of the individual's needs. For it is chiefly through employment, in conjunction with access to certain public accommodations and housing, that people acquire the things they need to assure their continued biological existence—food, shelter, and clothing. These are also the chief means by which people acquire those various culturally relative needs that maintain them as credible players in the ongoing social, political, and economic "games" of the society into which they have been born—say, needs for transportation and access to information. Civil rights legislation then helps people discharge their presumptive obligation to meet through their own devices their basic biological needs and other needed conditions for human agency.

Civil rights legislation also promotes general prosperity. Such legislation tends to increase the production of goods and services for society as a whole. By eliminating extraneous factors in employment decisions, such legislation promotes an optimal fit between a worker's capacities and the tasks of his prospective work. Both workers and their employers are advantaged, because workers are most productive when their talents and the requirements of their jobs mesh. Across the business community as a whole, such legislation further enhances the prospects that talent does not go wasting and that job vacancies are not filled by second bests.

Further, human resources are wasted if one's energies are constantly diverted and devoured by fear of arbitrary dismissal. The cost of life in the closet is not small, for the closet permeates and largely consumes the life of its occupant. In the absence of civil rights legislation for gays, society is simply wasting the human resources that are expended in the day-to-day anxiety—the web of lies, the constant worry—that attends leading a life of systematic disguise as a condition for continued employment.

Finally, employment makes up a large part of what happiness is. To a large extent, happiness is job satisfaction. When one's employment is of a favorable sort, one finds a delight in its very execution—quite independently of any object that the job generates, whether product or wage. To permit discriminatory hiring practices is to reduce happiness generally by barring access to one of its main sources.

Fundamentalists claim that God opposes civil rights for gays. Photo by Marc Geller.

Civil rights legislation also promotes individual flourishing—not merely by enhancing the prospect that individuals' needs are met but more so by expanding the ranges of individual choice. Such legislation withdraws the threat of punishment by social banishment, loss of employment, and the like from the arsenal of majoritarian coercion, so that individual lives need not be molded by social conventions and by the demands of conformity set by others. The result of such legislation is that the means by which one lives shall not be permitted to serve as instruments for the despotism of custom.

In the absence of civil rights legislation, lesbians and gay men are placed in the position of having to make zero-sum trade-offs between the components that go into making a full life, trade-offs, say, between a reasonable personal life and employment, trade-offs that the majority would not tolerate for themselves even for a minute.

Civil Rights and Democratic Processes

As an invisible minority, gay men and lesbians also need civil rights protections to have reasonably guaranteed access to an array of fundamental rights that virtually everyone would agree are supposed to pertain equally to all persons in a constitutionally regulated representative democracy. An "invisible minority" is a minority whose members can be identified only through an act of will on someone's part, rather than merely through observation of the members' day-to-day actions in the public domain.

First, such civil rights legislation is necessary for gays having equitable access to civic rights. "Civic rights" are rights to the impartial administration of civil and criminal law in defense of property and person. In the absence of such rights, there is no rule of law. But an invisible minority historically subjected to widespread social discrimination has reasonably guaranteed access to these rights only when the minority is guaranteed nondiscrimination in employment, housing, and public services. For the fair administration of law—the working of the police and the courts—casts the private into the public realm in consequence of the requirements that trials be open to the press and public and that defendants have access to witnesses against them. It is unreasonable to expect people to give up that by which they live, their employment, their shelter, their access to goods and services and to loved ones in order for judicial procedures to be carried out equitably, in order to demand legal protections from the police and to press cases in the courts. If the judiciary system is to be open and fair, it is necessary that gays be granted civil rights. Otherwise judicial access becomes a right only for the dominant culture.

Widespread social prejudice against lesbians and gay men also eclipses their political rights. In the absence of gay civil rights legislation, gays are—over the range of issues that most centrally affect their minority status—effectively denied access to the political rights of the First Amendment, that is, freedom of speech, freedom of press, freedom of assembly, freedom of political association, and freedom to petition for the redress of grievances, all of which in order to be effective require of their bearer a public presence.

A gay person who has to laugh at and manufacture fag jokes in the workplace to deflect suspicion in an office that routinely fires gay employees could hardly be said to have freedom to express his or her views on gay issues. Such a person could not reasonably risk appearing in public at a gay rights rally or circulate a petition protesting the firing of a gay worker. Nor would such a person likely try to persuade workmates to vote for a gay-positive city councilman, nor sign a letter to the editor protesting abusive reportage of gay issues and events, or advocating the discussion of gay issues in schools. Such a person is usually so transfixed by fear that it is highly unlikely that he or she could even be persuaded to write out a check to a gay rights organization.

A person who is a member of an invisible minority and who must remain invisible, hidden, and secreted with respect to his or her minority status as a condition for maintaining a livelihood is not free to be public about that minority status or to incur suspicion by publicly associating with others who are open about their similar status. And so such a person is effectively denied all political power—except the right to vote. But voting aside, he or she will be denied the freedom to express views in a public forum and to unite with or organize other like-minded individuals in an attempt to compete for votes that would elect persons who will support the policies advocated by his or her group. Such a person is denied all effective use of legally available means of influencing public opinion prior to voting and all effective means of lobbying after elections are held. If First Amendment rights are not to be demoted to privileges to which the dominant culture has access, then invisible minorities subject to widespread social discrimination will have to be guaranteed protection from those forces that maintain them in their position of invisibility. Civil rights protections take a very long step in that direction.

Richard D. Mohr

Bibliography

Burstein, Paul. *Discrimination, Jobs, and Politics: The Struggle for Equal Employment Opportunity in the United States since the New Deal.* Chicago: University of Chicago Press, 1985.

The Editors of the *Harvard Law Review. Sexual Orientation and the Law.* Boston: Harvard University Press, 1990.

Mohr, Richard D. *Gays/Justice: A Study of Ethics Society, and Law.* New York: Columbia University Press, 1988, chap. 5–7.

Rubenstein, William B., ed. *Lesbians, Gay Men, and the Law.* New York: New Press, 1993.

See also U.S. Law: Discrimination; U.S. Law: Equal Protection

Class

Perhaps no issue is more contentiously debated in gay political discourse today than the relationship between gay liberation and class struggle. Embracing the myths of a classless society and equal opportunity, some gays envision a liberation that will culminate in their full assimilation into capitalist mainstream culture. While these gays struggle to attain gay marriage and military service, queers influenced by Marxism in particular argue that such things as the causes of homophobia, the increased media visibility of homosexuals, and the efficacy of "coming out" as a political strategy are virtually unintelligible outside of an examination of class politics. They believe a gay liberation inattentive to class inequalities is both unjust and destined for failure.

In his *History of Sexuality*, Michel Foucault argues that sexuality "induces specific class effects" (127). A number of theorists—Jeffrey Weeks, John D'Emilio, and Nicola Field among them—have attempted to articulate some of the links between class and homosexuality. Field, for example, critiques the idea of a gay sensibility. Defined by Michael Bronski as "a distinct political, artistic, and social identity" shared by modern homosexuals, this gay sensibility is allegedly evidence of the creation of "a separate culture that reflects their attitudes, moods, thoughts, and emotions as an oppressed group" (10–11). According to Field, this myth obscures the relationship between a contemporary gay identity and capitalism. Attempting to unite individuals with competing class interests and varying social relationships, gay sensibility has become a "shared consumer taste, a predilection for certain

C forms of art, decor, clothing, food and drink." This in turn has led both to the development of a queer market ready to be exploited by business interests and the reduction of a gay liberation to a set of "meager single-issue demands which reflect the very few common interests of a fictional cross-class 'community' " (37). Field suggests that what often passes for a gay lifestyle "is in fact a distilled replica of a traditional middle-class lifestyle" (75).

John D'Emilio's "Capitalism and Gay Identity" remains a watershed attempt to theorize modern homosexuality. D'Emilio suggests that the development of a modern gay identity "is associated with the relations of capitalism; it has been the historical development of capitalism—more specifically, its free-labor system—that has allowed large numbers of men and women in the late twentieth century to call themselves gay, to see themselves as part of a community of similar men and women, and to organize politically on the basis of that identity" (5). D'Emilio suggests that capitalism's continuing expansion has necessarily been accompanied by both an expansion of wage labor *and* a diminishing of the importance of the family; as the institution of wage labor has expanded, some subjects have been capable of freeing themselves from economic dependency on the family. Over time, the family has thus gradually lost its importance as a unit of production.

This reduction of the economic importance of the family has in turn made it possible for sexuality to be freed from the obligations of procreation. D'Emilio concludes that "[i]n divesting the [family] of its economic independence and fostering separation of sexuality from procreation, capitalism has created conditions that allow some men and women to organize a personal life around their erotic/emotional attraction to their own sex. It has made possible the formation of urban communities of lesbians and gay men and, more recently, of a politics based on sexual identity" (7). For Field, this politics based on sexual identity is precisely the problem, for it substitutes consumption for production, transforming lesbians and gays into a "discrete social group and potential market sector." The "failure" of gay liberation is thus its refusal to "relocate sexual liberation within the politics of class" and its inability to theorize the relationship between homophobia and capitalism.

Weeks, Field, and D'Emilio have discussed some of the ways in which coming out as a political strategy presumes a certain class privilege. They argue that the process of coming out is predicated on a number of material factors not always available to working-class homosexuals in particular, including financial independence from one's family, work and living spaces secured against the threat of homophobic violence, and recourse to the existing legal means of challenging homophobia.

Despite this important work, however, class remains largely undertheorized. For example, capitalism exploits gender and racial differences in an effort to code subjects into interior positions in a hierarchized division of labor, assigning to women and racial minorities low-paying jobs, and socializing them into the (inferior) roles most conducive to capitalism. How might sexuality fit into this equation? Obviously, the less "visible" the markers of homosexuality, the more difficult it becomes to use (homo)sexual difference as a means of assigning subjects positions within the division of labor. Given this, as well as the fluidity of the boundaries that delimit who "is" and "is not" a homosexual, the analogy of sexuality to race and gender seems false. And yet there are a number of occupations historically "open" to particular (and particularly visible) stylizations of gay and lesbians identity. This suggests that capitalism may be extremely adept at exploiting our own desires to stabilize homosexual identities. In any case, much more work of a historical nature in particular needs to be done in this area.

Michael Warner attributes the failure to theorize class sufficiently to both a reluctance within social theory to examine questions of sexuality and to the predominance of literary studies in determining the shape of gay studies. This predominance has led to an exploration of the textual representation of sexuality at the expense of a rethinking of the social. To this we might add that some theorists use important Marxist concepts in a somewhat doctrinaire manner, applying nineteenth-century ideas with insufficient attention both to recent developments in capitalism and to Marx's own reluctance to dehistoricize his own materially based analyses. For example, Field does little to expand our understanding of the relationship between homophobia and capitalism, simply attributing homophobia to the need to maintain divisions among workers, and to keep the family at "the centre of our social, political, and economic system" (7). This formulation fails to pay sufficient attention to the changing role of the family under capitalism pointed to by D'Emilio.

Additionally, Field's astute critique of gay consumer culture is nonetheless undertheorized around questions of gay consumption in particular. Noting the "close connection between consumer culture and the most visible spaces of gay culture: bars, discos, advertising, fashion, brand-name identification, mass-cultural camp, 'promiscuity,' " Warner argues that post-Stonewall urban gay men "demand of theory a more dialectical view of capitalism than many people have imagination for"; as Matthew Tinkcom has argued, for Marx, "every moment of production is simultaneously one of consumption, and attempts to exclude one from the other are frequently simplifications of the workings of commodity circulation." Some very recent and exciting work by such scholars as Robyn Wiegman, Dennis Allen, and David T. Evans attempts to retheorize gay and lesbian identity through a Marxism attentive to recent trends in multinational capitalism in particular, and extends a class-based critique to the formation of the discipline of gay and lesbian studies itself.

Unfortunately, some academic queers consistently refuse to interrogate their own disciplinary power and privilege and the cultural and financial capital they wield, dismissing as "bourgeois self-consciousness" the attempt to understand this privilege. A version of Marxism that fails to interrogate one's own location in the division of labor seems highly suspect at a moment when, as Field notes, "rather than describing an economic and material relationship—which is what work and production are about—'working class' has been bandied about in an attempt to gain political currency" (5).

The urgent task for queer theory of class is not simply the description but the *production* of a link between subjectivity and politics. How might attempts to resist normative notions of sexual subjectivity be harnessed in the service of social justice and a more equitable distribution of goods and resources? What kinds of new social relationships are possible when sexuality has been freed from the demands of procreation? It is only through (political) struggle that attempts to resist heteronormative definitions and regulations of sexuality can be articulated alongside class-based forms of resistance to capitalism.   *John Champagne*

Bibliography

Allen, Dennis. "Lesbian and Gay Studies, A Consumer's Guide." *Genders* 26 (1997): 23–50.

Bronski, Michael. *Cultural Clash: The Making of Gay Sensibility*. Boston: South End Press, 1984.

Champagne, John, and Elayne Tobin. " 'She's Right Behind [Y]ou': Gossip, Innuendo, and Rumor in the (De)Formation of Gay and Lesbian Studies." *Genders* 26 (1997): 51–82.

D'Emilio, John. "Capitalism and Gay Identity." In *Making Trouble*. New York: Routledge, 1992, 3–16.

Evans, David T. *Sexual Citizenship: The Material Construction of Sexualities*. London: Routledge, 1993.

Field, Nicola. *Over the Rainbow: Money, Class, and Homophobia*. London: Pluto Press, 1995.

Foucault, Michel. *The History of Sexuality*. Vol. 1, *An Introduction*. Trans. Robert Hurley. New York: Vintage, 1990.

Tinckom, Matthew. "Working Like Homosexual: Camp Visual Codes and the Labor Gay Subjects in the MGM Freed Unit." *Cinema Journal* 35, no. 2 (Winter 1996): 24–42.

Warner, Michael, ed. *Fear of a Queer Planet*. Minneapolis: University of Minnesota Press, 1993.

Weeks, Jeffrey. *Sexuality and Its Discontents*. London: Routledge and Kegan Paul, 1985.

Wiegman, Robyn. "Queering the Academy." *Genders* 26 (1997): 3–22.

See also Business; Coming Out; Foucault, Michel; Gay Left; Gay Studies

Clergy

Homosexual desire and behavior have a long but fiercely secret history in the various groups of Christian clergy (the only clergy treated here). Christianity itself has always condemned homosexual activity, and Christian churches often found themselves in cultures that condemned it with equal or greater force. In the vast majority of times and places, Christians were taught that their salvation depended on repenting of same-sex desire. Even stricter standards applied to the clergy, especially when celibacy became compulsory in the Western churches after the eleventh century. With a few and very recent exceptions, no Christian denomination will ordain a practicing homosexual as a church leader, and many want no "out" lesbians or gays as members. It is hardly surprising, then, that church institutions and homosexual priests or ministers themselves impose a rigorous silence on cases of homosexuality in the clergy. This silence makes it impossible to construct anything like a comprehensive history or even an adequate contemporary survey, even though it is generally admitted that many of the most prominent Christian clergy have been and continue to be homosexual. Historically, there are some records of priests

C or (later) ministers accused of homosexual behavior. These records are found in the proceedings of church courts, for example, or in chronicles and histories, both secular and religious. Inferences can also be drawn from official prohibitions or precautions against homosexual activity. More interesting but more difficult to interpret is the evidence from polemical texts. Religious reformers frequently paint pictures of widespread homosexual practices among the ordinary clergy or (perhaps especially) among members of religious orders, and Protestant polemicists sometimes made this a general charge against the Catholic practice of celibacy. Equally colorful and equally ambiguous is the evidence of popular literature, which frequently accuses priests and pastors of unbridled homosexual lust. But no combination of these kinds of evidence will permit generalizations about the extent or kinds of homosexual practice in the clergy. The same is true of modern attempts to survey acts or attitudes. No large-scale survey of the clergy has gotten honest responses about homosexuality. More targeted inquiries into self-selected populations have been conducted, but these obviously cannot provide reliable statistical generalizations. The case of the Roman Catholic priesthood is particularly telling in this regard. There is an enormous body of anecdotal, journalistic, and clinical evidence suggesting that homosexual activity is not uncommon among Catholic priests. Indeed, the deep homosociality of Catholic clerical institutions seems particularly attractive to some homosexual men. But attempts to quantify this evidence have yielded contradictory results. Sipe estimates that 10 to 12 percent of all Catholic priests engage in homosexual acts, while Wolf reports that his group of informants estimates homosexual priests at between 40 and 60 percent of all priests. All sources agree that the percentage of homosexuals reported in the Catholic clergy has increased markedly since the late 1970s, and some assume that at least a third of American Catholic priests under forty-five are homosexually active. But these figures and the analogous figures for other denominations are at best educated guesses. For the moment, and despite some small steps toward public discussion, homosexuality in the clergy remains the secret topic it always has been.

Mark D. Jordan

Bibliography

Sipe, A. W. Richard. *A Secret World: Sexuality and the Search for Celibacy*. New York: Brunner/Mazel, 1990, chap. 6.

Wolf, James G., ed. *Gay Priests*. San Francisco. Harper & Row, 1989.

See also Catholicism; Christianity; Religion and Religiosity

Clone

Used to express pride, self-parody, or as a pejorative, the gay male "clone" may be viewed either as a sociopolitical phenomenon of the gay liberationist generation of the 1970s and 1980s or, as sociosexual iconography, an archetypal gay male icon originating with that generation.

The Christopher Street or Castro Street clone "look" was an urban street fashion that became synonymous with the 1970s urban gay lifestyle, particularly in New York and San Francisco, and reached its zenith and self-parody with the disco group Village People. At a time when mainstream fashion pursued a sanitizing version of hippie dress (long hair, platform heels, pantsuits and leisure suits, wide ties, wide lapels, jewelry for men), the clone look portrayed an image of the "liberated gay man" as sexually charged and archetypically all-American.

The basic look consisted of a body-hugging ensemble—plaid shirt or tight-fitting T-shirt, tight-fitting 501 (button-up fly) blue jeans, sneakers or construction boots, a hat or cap, an earring, and facial hair, usually a mustache. The uniformity of the look and the fact that the look was worn as a uniform (to signal "gay and proud") led to the epithet "clone," as if every individual were an exact copy of some original "liberated gay man"—5'9", 29-inch waist, 29 years old, gay white male (GWM).

The clone look embraced a range of variations. The early hippie clone (hip-hugger jeans, long hair, and full beard) gave way over time to ubiquitous cropped haircuts and a preponderance of mustaches. With the newer trend of gym-toned bodies, variations highlighted the sculpted male form—athletic shirts, polo shirts (preferably bearing the trademark Izod alligator), with gym shorts, cutoffs, or fatigue or painter's pants. The color-coded hanky—in the rear pocket—was adopted from the leather culture. Outerwear might include a zippered sweatshirt, a letter jacket, or a leather jacket.

The original intent of the clone look was to express a newfound pride and self-confidence, to advertise oneself as sexual and sexually available, and to identify oneself publicly as a member of this new quasi-ethnic homosexual minority. At the time, those celebrating their newfound freedom were oblivious to the group-think culture it was creating as well as to its exclusionary effect on lesbians and queers of color. It would take the next generation to begin building a new queer multiculturalism out of the rubble of the old homophobic order that the clone generation had tried to dismantle.

The clone look was embraced as a middle-of-the-road, yet distinctly gay and gay-positive, fashion semiotics. It contrasted with then-popular images of homosexuals as drag queens (wearing dresses and women's makeup), fluffy-sweater queens ("smart" casual attire, typically including cashmere sweaters), or leather queens (perceived by some as hypermale "drag"), but was a continuation of (or posthippie-era return to) the "all-American" look of the 1950s and 1960s, of chino pants, polo shirt, penny loafers, and (the telltale gay signifier) white socks.

The look became synonymous with the 1970s urban fast-lane lifestyle of drugs, disco, and bathhouse sex. With the advent of AIDS, the look came to symbolize a tainted, self-absorbed urban gay white male subculture, whom some blamed for the epidemic. A decade after the onset of AIDS, the clone look would reemerge in new variations—the ACT UP look (shaven head, goatee, baseball cap worn backwards, tattoos, and/or body piercings) would become a predominant look of the youth culture of the 1990s, and an exaggeratedly gym-toned body (often helped by steroids), clean-shaven head and body (associated with the "Chelsea" or "boy-toy" look) would colonize the mainstreamed gay consumer culture of the 1990s.   *Les Wright*

Bibliography

Fischer, Hal. *Gay Semiotics: A Photographic Study of Visual Coding among Homosexual Men.* San Francisco: NFS Press, 1977.

See also Body Image; Castro; Fashion; Gay

COC

A Dutch chapter of the German Wissenschaftlich-humanitäres Komitee (Scientific Humanitarian Committee) was founded in 1912 by the Dutch esquire J. A. Schorer. In 1940, shortly before Germany invaded the Netherlands, the homosexual monthly *Levensrecht* (Right to Live) saw the light. Its editors went underground for the duration of the war and revived the journal shortly thereafter. Their initiative resulted in the founding of the Shakespeare Club in Amsterdam in 1946, which was renamed Center for Culture and Recreation (COC) three years later. It soon spawned chapters in other Dutch cities. Its most prominent representative was left-wing activist Nico Engelschman, who worked under the pseudonym Bob Angelo. The club organized social events and lobbied the authorities to exercise toleration toward gay men and lesbians. Its politics were prudent in view of the adverse climate. The preferred term was "homophile," because it played down the sexual aspect of gay and lesbian life.

In the fifties, the COC went on to establish an International Committee for Sexual Equality (ICSE), the forerunner of the International Gay and Lesbian Association (ILGA). A panel of psychiatrists, priests, and other professionals was set up in the Netherlands to initiate a scholarly debate on homosexuality. This group, which brought together Protestants, Catholics, and non-Christians, was very successful in that its members achieved high visibility in discussions on homosexuality in the sixties. They assumed tolerant stances, and this paved the way for homophile emancipation in political parties, churches, and social organizations.

The COC grew by leaps and bounds in the sixties and opened itself up to the public. Its new leader, Benno Premsela, became the homosexual voice in the media, making his first open television appearance in 1964. By enlisting the aid of the leading contemporary Dutch novelist, Gerard Reve, and by allying itself with the booming Dutch Society for Sexual Reform (NVSH), the COC paved the way for a broad-ranging debate on homosexuality. The distinction in the ages of consent for homosexual and heterosexual sex under criminal law was eliminated in 1971, and two years later gays and lesbians were allowed to join the armed forces and the COC gained statutory recognition. It had renamed itself the Dutch Society for Integration of Homosexuality COC in 1971 to highlight its more political stance. The word *recreation* was dropped, because any separate social organization of homosexuals was now deemed superfluous. However, when the COC subsequently failed to develop a perspective on either the content of homosexuality or the conditions of integration, its political role began to weaken. In the seventies, new radical groups and separate organizations of gays and lesbians in political parties, trade unions, and universities put an end to the monopoly of the COC as the "mother church" or "national home" of all Dutch homosexual men and women. Yet it remains the biggest organization of gays and lesbians in the Netherlands, with some eight thousand members and with chapters in up to fifty cities and towns. It is still the recipient of most of the subsidies earmarked for gay and lesbian emancipation by local and national government.

Though it retains a key place among the wide array of gay and lesbian organizations, it no longer plays the leading role it did in the sixties, and other groups and individuals have taken over its central position in gay and lesbian debates. In recent discussions on gay genes, same-sex marriage, and pedophilia, for instance, the COC has remained largely invisible. It has turned into a bureaucratic organization focused more on internal than external dynamics. At its fiftieth anniversary celebrations in 1996, the hot news on the COC was its financial and organizational predicament. The COC has shown itself incapable of formulating its place in a postmodern Dutch society that perhaps tolerates but fails to accept gay and lesbian desires. *Gert Hekma*

Bibliography

Tielman, Rob. *Homoseksualiteit in Nederland. Studie van een emancipatiebeweging.* Amsterdam/Meppel: Boom, 1982.

Warmerdam, Hans, and Pieter Koenders. *Cultuur en Ontspanning. Het COC 1946–1966.* Utrecht: Rijksuniversiteit Utrecht/Homostudies, 1987.

See also Amsterdam; Netherlands

Cocteau, Jean (1889–1963)

Born in Maisons-Lafitte into a wealthy Parisian family, Jean Cocteau achieved fame for his films, plays, drawings, and poetry. Though he was not an exceptional student at the Lycée Condorcet, Cocteau took to the theater early; in later years he lovingly recalled his "fever of crimson and gold." Cocteau had family approval when actor Édouard de Max, friend of Oscar Wilde and peer of Sarah Bernhardt, took him under his wing. It was de Max who sponsored the Cocteau's poetry reading at the Théâtre Femina when he was eighteen, an event that brought him instant literary renown. Cocteau met and befriended Marcel Proust, Vaslav Nijinsky, Colette, Simone de Beauvoir, Jean-Paul Sartre, and Amedeo Modigliani. In agreeing to collaborate on a ballet, Sergey Diaghilev commanded: "Astonish me!" Cocteau long honored this challenge. Their *Parade* (1917), with music by Erik Satie and sets by Pablo Picasso, is considered a major achievement of twentieth-century ballet.

At the beginning of his career, Cocteau was associated with older mentors, including de Max, Comtesse Anna de Noailles, and Igor Stravinsky, with whom he created the opera-oratorio *Oedipus Rex* (1927), only one of his reworkings of the Oedipus story. Later he drew inspiration from a series of mostly younger men, many of them lovers. At a time when his poetry was criticized for being derivative, Cocteau met the young poet and novelist Raymond Radiguet, who inspired him to write *Plain-Chant* (1923). (When Radiguet died of typhoid at the age of twenty, a grieving Cocteau began using opium, then published the essay "Opium" in 1930.) His quest to improve artistically is evidenced by the figure of "The Poet" and the concept of "Poetry" that occupies much of his work, such as the film *The Blood of a Poet* (1930). The mythical poet Orpheus inspired a 1927 play and 1950 film (both named *Orpheus*) and nicely combined the theme of poetry with the theme of death, another primary Coctelian concern. The figure of the Angel of Death recurs in his work, as does the guardian angel Heurtebise. It seems only natural that death preoccupied him: not only did Cocteau lose Radiguet, but his young friend Jean Desbordes was tortured to death by the Gestapo after Germany overran France in World War II. The German occupiers also killed other friends like John LeRoy and aviator Roland Garros (shot down in his plane). Despite the deaths of these young men, Cocteau did not ally himself with the Resistance; his productions continued during the

Jean Cocteau, St. Peter Sleeping in Herod's Prison. *Wall painting. Chapel of St. Pierre, Villefranche-sur-Mer, France. SEF/Art Resource, NY.*

occupation. He considered himself an anarchist, with allegiance to no government, always attempting to avoid politics in his life as in his art. He focused instead on finding the perfect vehicle for perhaps his greatest inspiration, actor Jean Marais.

Though critics portray Cocteau as cultivating a private mythology, gay readers will sympathize with his expression of a more widely shared homosexual experience. Homosexual themes are usually disguised or sublimated in his work. Certainly his most accomplished novel, *Enfants Terribles* (1929), the story of some children who retreat into an imaginary world, can be read as a retreat from a heterosexist society. And though the love object in *Plain-Chant* is gendered female, the inspiration is undoubtedly Radiguet (Cocteau also sketched his friend). Cocteau was familiar with and engaged many of the paradigms and stereotypes of homosexuality of his day, including the problematic mother-son relationship, the narcissistic homosexual, and the Freudian notion of sexual retardation. Cocteau's plays have even been convincingly compared to those of Tennessee Williams in terms of the female roles.

Cocteau remained independent of artistic movements such as surrealism (whose leader, André Breton, loathed homosexuals, including Cocteau). Though he was friends with many of the most high-profile homosexuals of his day, André Gide disliked him, as the publication of his journals proved. Cocteau's only major work to deal overtly with homosexuality, the early "novel" *The White Paper* (1930), is often read as a response to Gide's *Corydon* (1924). Cocteau published the book anonymously, though the illustrations of a later edition were clearly his. Also of note to a modern gay audience is Cocteau's role in supporting Jean Genet—he testified in court when Genet faced a life sentence—and Genet's work (including illustrations for *Querelle of Brest,* 1948).

Cocteau is well known for reinterpreting Greeks myths and dramas, such as his adaptation of *Antigone* (1922) and his most successful version of the Oedipus story, *The Infernal Machine* (1934). Other major works include his plays *The Human Voice* (1930) and *Intimate Relations* (1938), the film *Beauty and the Beast* (1946), and the poetry collection *Opera* (1927). Cocteau also published criticism, including a book about Picasso and one about "Les Six," a group of French composers. In addition to his drawings, musical compositions, and acting, Cocteau also designed the frescoes for several churches, including the Chapel of St. Pierre, Ville-franche-sur-Mer, where he is buried. Cocteau died only hours after learning of the death of his friend, singer Edith Piaf.   *Stephen Sposato*

Bibliography
Brown, Frederick. *An Impersonation of Angels: A Biography of Jean Cocteau*. New York: Viking, 1968.
Gilson, Rene. *Jean Cocteau: An Investigation into His Films and Philosophy*. Ciba Vaugh, trans. New York: Crown, 1969.
Steegmuller, Francis. *Cocteau: A Biography*. Boston: Little, Brown, 1970.

See also Diaghilev, Sergey; Film; France; French Literature; Genet, Jean; Gide, André; Maraís, Jean; Nijinsky, Vaslav; Proust, Marcel; Williams, Tennessee

Code Napoléon

Enacted in March 1804, the Code Napoléon embodies the civil law of France. Originally titled the "Code Civil," it was renamed the "Code Napoléon" when Napoléon Bonaparte became emperor.

The *cahiers* of 1789 demanded uniformity in French law, while the French revolutionaries sought to simplify over four hundred legal codes used in the republic. Napoléon was a strong proponent of the project and civil liberties. He appointed a commission of four members to draft the civil code under the auspices of Jean-Jacques Regis de Cambacérès, a known homosexual. Napoléon presided over more than half of the sessions devoted to the section of the Council of State considering the final draft of the legal code.

The reform of the penal laws pertaining to homosexuality and sodomy were not due to the actions of Cambacérès but were actually the result of omission by the Constituent Assembly of 1791. Changing philosophical trends of the eighteenth century and critiques of the old regime by authors such as Voltaire and Becarria played an identifiable role.

During September and October 1791, the French Constituent Assembly adopted the new criminal code. The guidelines held in principle that offenses against morality or religion that did not harm individuals or society should not be subject to prosecution by secular authorities. This legal precedent became the guiding ethic for the Code Napoléon.

Napoléon's progressive attitude toward homosexuality contrasted with other early-nineteenth-century political figures and permitted him to let

C stand the decision of the Constituent Assembly to omit sodomy as a sexual offense. This reflected beliefs of enlightened thinkers of the day. For the first time in modern history homosexuality, when it did not use force or violate public decency, was no longer a punishable offense. The Code Napoléon became the model for further repeals of repressive medieval laws throughout the civilized world.

The final version of the French statutes summarized the laws into 28 codes, 2,281 succinct articles, entailing 115,000 words in all. The Code Napoléon was divided into three sections: persons, property, and acquisition of property. Its chief importance lies in the civil rights it enumerated and guarantees of equality for all in the eyes of the law.

After 1810 many Germanic states including Bavaria, Württemburg, and Hanover modeled their legal principles upon the Code Napoléon. The influence of the code was quite widespread in both Old and New World Catholic countries such as France, Belgium, Germany, Luxembourg, southern Italy, the French-speaking cantons of Switzerland, Brazil, and Mexico. Owing to the influence of the Code Napoléon, nearly all the Catholic states of western Europe abandoned medieval sodomy laws. Meanwhile, in the Protestant sphere of Europe only the Netherlands experienced a similar shift in attitude because of its temporary annexation by France under Napoléon. The Code Napoléon was also adopted into the statutes of the state of Louisiana. Attempts at sexual reform in the twentieth century led countries such as Denmark, Portugal, and Poland to adapt the tolerant principles of the Code Napoléon into their national legal systems. *Michael A. Lutes*

Bibliography

Merrick, Jeffrey and Bryan Ragan Jr., eds. *Homosexuality in Modern France.* New York: Oxford University Press, 1996.

Rees, J. Tudor and Harvey Usill. *They Stand Apart: A Critical Survey of the Problem of Homosexuality.* London: Heinemann, 1955.

Ulrichs, Karl. *Riddle of "Man-Manly" Love: The Pioneering Work on Male Homosexuality.* Buffalo, N.Y.: Prometheus Books, 1994.

See also France; sodomy

Cohn, Roy M. (1927–1986)

Roy M. Cohn, the controversial chief counsel of Senator Joseph McCarthy's investigating committee, began his career as an anticommunist at the unprecedentedly young age of twenty when on the very day he passed the New York bar exam, he was appointed an assistant district attorney. Cohn quickly developed a reputation as a brilliant strategist, and he helped shape the case against atomic spies Julius and Ethel Rosenberg. He later claimed that he and Judge Irving Kaufman were in constant contact throughout the trial plotting strategies, although his tendency to inflate his importance may have led him to misrepresent his relationship with the judge, which would have been grounds for a mistrial. But Cohn is best known for his role in the McCarthy witch hunts. As McCarthy's chief counsel, Cohn helped formulate the senator's sensationalistic charges, including that the State Department harbored known homosexuals.

Speculation about Cohn's homosexuality first surfaced during the McCarthy hearings when he tried to obtain preferential treatment for G. David Schine, who had been drafted into the army. Even after Cohn entered private practice in the late 1950s, the media continued to speculate about his homosexuality, contributing to his notoriety as an unethical celebrity lawyer. This speculation was troubling because it allowed the media to misrepresent the homophobia of the McCarthy era. In 1985, when Cohn revealed that he had contracted the AIDS virus and was dying, the media treated his illness as just punishment for his role in the McCarthy witch hunts. In focusing obsessively on Cohn's refusal to acknowledge that he was homosexual, despite his impending death from "the gay plague," the media diverted attention from those who were responsible for the persecution of homosexuals during the McCarthy era and focused it instead on gay homophobia.

Robert J. Corber

Bibliography

Hoffman, Nicholas von. *Citizen Cohn.* New York: Doubleday, 1988.

Zion, Sidney. *The Autobiography of Roy Cohn.* Secaucus, N.J.: Lyle Stuart, 1988.

See also McCarthyism; United States

Colonial America

Our understanding of sodomy as a sexual category and as a social phenomenon in colonial America will always be tentative because only sparse and fragmentary evidence has survived. The attitudes of colonists toward sodomitical behavior as it occurred in their communities are much more elusive than official viewpoints, legal and theological, promulgated through sermons, laws, and judicial decisions. Even more obscure is an understanding of the ways in which people attracted to persons of the same sex viewed their own physical impulses.

Early American ministers, who provided the official lens through which colonists were supposed to view sexual impulses, condemned all nonmarital sex as "unclean" and disorderly. But they made a clear distinction between illicit sex performed by a man and a woman and that between either two persons of the same sex or a human being and an animal. Those who engaged in sodomy or bestiality disrupted the natural order and crossed scripturally ordained boundaries between sexes and species. Such behavior was thus much more sinful and disorderly than extramarital sex between a man and a woman. The clergy defined sodomy as an act involving two persons of the same sex, but the notion of sexual orientation had no place in their discourse; nor did they evoke desire as an independent agency that gave rise to sexual acts. They explained sodomy just as they did all other sinful acts, sexual and nonsexual: it was driven by the innate corruption of fallen humanity and embodied disobedience to God's will. Sodomy did spring from a particular frame of mind, but that mental state was not specifically sexual.

Sodomy was a capital offense in colonial America, but actual prosecutions for sodomy were unusual, and only three men are known to have been executed for the crime in British North America (Richard Cornish in Virginia in 1624, William Plaine in New Haven in 1646, and John Knight in New Haven in 1655), plus one execution in New Amsterdam (Jan Quisthout in 1660). Courts usually insisted on proof of actual penetration as grounds for execution; neither intent nor physical intimacy short of penetration would suffice. This was consistent with the treatment of sodomy in official discourse as a specific physical act rather than as a form of desire. But establishing that penetration had taken place was no easy matter, and so the court could usually find only that relations to some degree sodomitical had taken place. In such cases, the accused would be given a warning, fined, or whipped, but not executed. Colonists were often reluctant to invoke official sanctions against men in their communities whom they knew were practicing sodomy. Some of these men may have been protected by their local status and power. Reluctance to tear the

fabric of community life by taking formal action against an established citizen and employer may also have counterbalanced disapproval of an individual's sexual proclivities. Legal prosecution became desirable only if the behavior became socially disruptive and so outweighed his worth as a citizen.

Others may have neglected to act against sodomitical behavior because they were slow to recognize or label it as such. At least some of the men prosecuted for sodomy had sought to penetrate men whose age and status placed them in a position subordinate to themselves, usually servants; their sexual impulses were articulated in the context of power relations. Sexual advances made by a master toward a male servant could be understood in terms of the power dynamic between the two individuals; there was no compelling need to treat the sexual act as distinct from the broader relationship or to label it explicitly as sodomy. Those unable or unwilling to do so may well have been disturbed by what they saw but were unable to respond because the behavior was undefined.

New Englanders who did identify and condemn sodomy often may have been deterred by the rigorous demands of the legal system from taking formal action against offenders. Informal measures by local magistrates or church elders constituted an attractive alternative to the expensive and often intractable legal system. Addressing the behavior through nonjuridical channels was, moreover, less direful than invoking capital law and so would have appealed to those who wanted to proceed against offenders but did not want to endanger the lives of those involved. Local responses to sodomy ranged from outright condemnation to a live-and-let-live attitude that did not go so far as to condone such behavior but did enable peaceful cohabitation, especially if the individual concerned was an otherwise valued member of the local community. The weight of opinion does not appear to have rested with those actively hostile to sodomy.

Neighbors and acquaintances clearly recognized that some men did have an ongoing sexual interest in members of the same sex, even though the persistent and specific impulse that they identified was not acknowledged in official discourse. In identifying a particular inclination toward sodomitical behavior within certain individuals, they did not go so far as to invoke a "homosexual" identity as such; but some villagers and townspeople do seem to have posited an ongoing erotic predilection that transcended the acts themselves. While religious and le-

C gal statements match the paradigm of premodern sexual discourse as focused on *acts* rather than *identity*, popular perceptions of sodomy sometimes appear to have been closer to the latter, though we should take care not to invest them with a twentieth-century sensibility. Some of those men drawn to sodomy were clearly troubled by religious guilt, while others rejected wholesale the spiritual system that condemned their behavior.

No evidence has emerged thus far to suggest that colonial cities provided a sodomitical subculture such as London offered by the early eighteenth century. Men who wanted to have sex with other men in early America had to rely on more tenuous networks and chance encounters. Such individuals might face the disapproval of their neighbors, or even prosecution and the possibility of execution. Yet early Americans were generally pragmatic in their responses to sodomy, focusing on practical issues rather than moral absolutes. Whatever their leaders' expectations, they viewed and treated sodomy on their own terms.   *Richard Godbeer*

Bibliography

Godbeer, Richard. " 'The Cry of Sodom': Discourse, Intercourse, and Desire in Colonial New England." *William and Mary Quarterly* 52 (1995): 259–86.

Talley, Colin L. "Gender and Male Same-Sex Erotic Behavior in British North America in the Seventeenth Century." *Journal of the History of Sexuality* 6 (1996): 385–408.

See also Christianity; Sodomy; Sodomy Trials; United States

Colonialism

This term defines the political repercussions of one country's imposing its values, culture, and administration on another. Contemporary critics generally prefer this word to *imperialism,* which designates the period of European expansion (roughly 1830–1914) following the abolition of slavery in their colonies by Britain, France, and, later, Spain. *Colonialism* refers to diverse forms of appropriation with a much longer history. Linked etymologically to "culture" (via the root *colonia,* Latin for "settlement"), *colony* suggests a powerful relationship between policies of economic expansion and cultural domination.

Homosexuality has a complex relation to this history, of which only a fraction can be outlined here. From the 1850s on, ethnographers and anthropologists such as Paolo Ambrogetti, Claude Ancillon, Sir Richard Burton, A. Kocher, Henry Junod, H. Quedenfeldt, Georg Schweinfurth, and Herman Soyaux studied male and female homosexuality in many parts of the world, using their data to endorse sexological claims about British and European culture. Much of this ethnography strove either to vindicate or to clarify Britain's and Europe's rapacious colonial policies.

Within the empires themselves, many white men and some women devoted themselves to service and duty, perhaps using the empire to offset laws and restrictions that late-Victorian society imposed on homosexuals and independent women. Sir Roger Casement exemplifies a radical lineage of homosexual men and women in Africa: he endorsed the antislavery movement in the Belgian Congo, and later in Peru, while recording in his *Black Diaries* his many interracial affairs with the Congolese; Britain executed Casement in 1916 for his role in Ireland's Easter Rebellion. Yet Casement's radical politics and sexuality were atypical. In southern Africa, General Sir Hector Macdonald, Cecil Rhodes, Leander Starr Jameson (Rhodes's companion), Viscount Alfred Milner, Field Marshal Earl Kitchener, and Baron Robert Baden-Powell, among many others, greatly influenced Britain's colonial policies. Macdonald, who gained national recognition for his military service in the Sudan and the 1899 and 1900 Boer wars, shot himself in 1903 after he was caught having sex with four Sinhalese boys in Ceylon; the incident greatly influenced Britain's subsequent policies on interracial relationships. Kitchener's power also derived from his brutal military policies in the Sudan, his reputation later tarnished slightly by his handling of the Boer wars and ensuing military policies in India. Recent biographies of these men identify either love letters written to close male companions, claims of self-imposed chastity, or statements that successful colonial duty can obtain only from confirmed bachelorhood. Kitchener insisted that his "Band of Boys" be unmarried; his group of elite servicemen included Macdonald and Colonel Oswald Fitzgerald, Kitchener's companion for at least ten years, who drowned with Kitchener in 1916 when HMS *Hampshire* struck a mine during World War I.

It is relatively easy to identify these men's emphasis on intense same-sex friendships but harder to assess the role and meaning of homosexual desire in Britain's and Europe's empires, and thus to bridge the complex interpretive gap among colonial policies, ethnographic material, and contemporaneous literature by Rudyard Kipling, H. Rider Haggard, G. A. Henty, John Buchan, and A. E. W. Mason. Some, like Maj. Gen. Frank M. Richardson, have sought to resuscitate Rhodes and Kitchener as important representatives of gay history, using these and other men as proof that male homosexuals were vital components of Britain's imperial past. To be sure, the military reputation of both men—and their simultaneous resistance to marriage—makes their influence over Queen Victoria paradoxical to say the least (Kitchener was her "special favorite" from 1888 on). This paradox suggests that expressions of male and female homosexuality were more diverse in fin-de-siècle Britain and its empire than Britain's severe proscriptions against effeminacy in men suggest; these proscriptions surfaced with considerable vehemence in Oscar Wilde's second trial in 1895.

The complexity of Rhodes's and Kitchener's political positions derives in part from their loyalty to Britain's Purity movement, which aimed to curb homosexuality, prostitution, vagrancy, abortion, and the availability of contraception in Britain and its colonies. That such men actively encouraged punishment for same-sex relationships in Britain and its empire suggests a complex relationship to their own desire (much of which was either unpronounced or represented in nonsexual terms) that surpasses hypocrisy and bad faith.

Ronald Hyam has used these and other examples to claim that Britain's empire represented a field of "sexual opportunities," and that men and women fled the mother country to sustain same-sex friendships and relationships in its colonies. Similar arguments could be made of other European empires (particularly the French and German), though these countries' proscriptions against homosexuality and interracial contact in their colonies did not exist to the extent favored by Britain's empire. Generally, such arguments about sexual opportunity tend not only to downplay the material factors involved in colonial administration and to paint the colonial past in rather nostalgic ways but also to simplify the complex interplay among homosexuality, patriotic identification, and partial sublimation that appeared to sustain these people abroad. Such arguments also ignore the context of homosexuality in each colonized country, whose postcolonial conceptions of homosexuality owe much to British legislation that has remained after these countries' independence. Yet Hyam has usefully identified the

impact on all but a few of Britain's colonies of Lord Crewe's 1909 circular on interracial heterosexual relationships: Crewe's circular aimed to prohibit sexual contact between (primarily) British men and indigenous women, but Hyam argues convincingly that the circular was also implicitly designed to restrict same-sex interracial contact.

Not surprisingly, many critics are ambivalent about whether Macdonald, Kitchener, Rhodes, and other colonials were homosexual, seeing these figures' military loyalty and racism as the logical culmination of white men's sexual tourism elsewhere— for instance, in North Africa, the Near East, and various Mediterranean resorts, including Capri. Considering the ethnographic material published between 1850 and 1920, we find such arguments reasonable, yet the relation between colonialism and tourism is complex and not self-evident. Recent work on European tourism clarifies its importance for homosexual men and women, suggesting that literature and culture produced at the time would not have flourished had the resorts not existed as places free of persecution and imaginative foci for a diverse set of sexual fantasies. Robert Aldrich has assessed the importance of Capri for lesbians such as Romaine Brooks, Renée Vivien, Checca Lloyd, and Kate and Saidee Wolcott-Perry. André Gide's *The Immoralist* (1902) and Thomas Mann's *Death in Venice* (1912) also exemplify these fantasies, the former novel complicated by its protagonist's involvement with Tunisian boys in the context of France's colonial relationship to North Africa.

Since in both novels the protagonists' homosexuality emerges only from their distance from France and Germany, respectively, and their encounters with boys they consider different, even exotic, it is relatively easy to link these protagonists with their wider cultures' perspectives on foreign countries and cultures; some critics even dismiss these characters as merely sexual manifestations of their cultures. Yet such readings downplay the very homosexuality violently alienating these protagonists from their countries. If applied to men such as T. E. Lawrence and Jean Genet, the claims above would misunderstand how both writers struggled to renounce their national origins and to identify with the colonized on the basis of—among other things—shared sexual attraction. General claims about sexual tourism implicitly frown on interracial desire as irrevocably compromised or even shaped by colonial policies.

Other critics have begun to assess the differences in style and structure between adventure fic-

C tion and travel memoirs, the latter genre often clarifying an author's varied observations, shifting loyalties, and sexual perspectives. British and European women's relationships to colonialism emerge most clearly in this genre, and writers such as Mary Kingsley and Nina Mazuchelli—describing themselves as "lady pioneers"—aimed to supplement the observations of their male counterparts. As Sara Mills has shown, however, these writers often succumbed to narrative patterns and exoticizing tendencies closely resembling colonial stereotypes. In her *Travels in West Africa* (1897; reprinted Virago, 1965), for instance, Kingsley provides the following observations about African women: "The comeliest ladies I have ever seen are on the Coast. Very black they are, blacker than many of their neighbours, always blacker than the Fans [Fanny Po tribeswomen]" (223). Here and elsewhere, Kingsley's alignment with conventionally male judgments seems to add a "lesbian" dimension to her appraisal of foreign women: "The Fanny Po ladies . . . are not the most beautiful women in this part of the world. Not at least to my way of thinking. I prefer an Elmina, or an Igalwa, or a M'pongwe or—but I had better stop and own that my affections have got very scattered among the black ladies on the West Coast, and I no sooner remember one lovely creature whose soft eyes, perfect form and winning, pretty ways have captivated me than I think of another" (72).

The difficulty facing critics and historians of colonialism stems partly from conservative *and* radical dimensions of homosexual desire. Desire may confirm—and even derive from—unequal material conditions; it may also undermine them, leading to more democratic arrangements. Critics and readers must neither idealize the desire nor the men and women who experienced and acted on it, but rather analyze homosexuality's complex affinity with—and occasional rejection of—national and cultural identifications.   *Christopher Lane*

Bibliography

Aldrich, Robert. *The Seduction of the Mediterranean: Writing, Art, and Homosexual Fantasy.* New York: Routledge, 1993.

Ballhatchet, Kenneth. *Race, Sex and Class under the Raj: Imperial Attitudes and Policies and Their Critics, 1793–1905.* New York: St. Martin's, 1980.

Bleys, Rudi C. *The Geography of Perversion: Male-to-Male Sexual Behavior Outside the West and the Ethnographic Imagination, 1750–1918.* New York: New York University Press, 1995.

Boone, Joseph A. *Libidinal Currents: Sexuality and the Shaping of Modernism.* Chicago: University of Chicago Press, 1998.

Bristow, Joseph. *Empire Boys: Adventures in a Man's World.* New York: HarperCollins, 1991.

Hyam, Ronald. *Empire and Sexuality: The British Experience.* Manchester, England: Manchester University Press, 1990.

Lane, Christopher. *The Ruling Passion: British Colonial Allegory and the Paradox of Homosexual Desire.* Durham, N.C.: Duke University Press, 1995.

McClintock, Ann. *Imperial Leather: Race, Gender, and Sexuality in the Colonial Conquest.* New York: Routledge, 1995.

Moodie, Dunbar. "Migrancy and Male Sexuality on the South African Gold Mines." *Journal of Southern African Studies* 14 (1988): 228–56.

Young, Robert J. *Colonial Desire: Hybridity in Theory, Culture and Race.* New York: Routledge, 1995.

See also Africa: Precolonial sub-Saharan Africa; Boy Scouts; Burton, Sir Richard Francis; Casement, Roger; Friendship; Forster, E. M.; Genet, Jean; Gide, André; Lawrence, T. E.; Mann, Thomas; Rhodes, Cecil; Tourism; Wilde, Oscar

Comic Strips and Books
Mainstream Strips

Two widely distributed strips have highlighted gay men. Lynn Johnston's "For Better or for Worse" spent March 1993 telling of a teenager's efforts to tell friends and family about his orientation. Reaction was vociferous, and she says Lawrence's future appearances will not focus on this issue. No stranger to controversy, Gary Trudeau's "Doonesbury" introduced the first gay comic strip character, Mark Slackmeyer, in 1977, and another, Andy, who later died of AIDS. Liberal Slackmeyer is currently in a relationship with a fierce conservative, and the couple has enjoyed much recent exposure in the strip.

Mainstream Books

D.C. Comics initiated gay and lesbian subtext a half-century ago when readers began wondering about the true relationship between Batman and Robin, or among the Amazons on Wonder Woman's Paradise Island. Perhaps the first overtly gay hero

For Better or Worse. *Courtesy of United Media.*

was Extraño, an effeminate Hispanic whose name means "Strange," introduced in *Millennium* (#2, 1987) and continued in *New Guardians*. *New Guardians* was soon canceled, although not before another of its members had died of AIDS.

Element Lad of the *Legion of Super-Heroes* discovered that the woman he loved was actually a man taking an alien sex-change drug (#31, 1992). (Transsexual themes also appear in *Camelot 3000* [1988] and Neil Gaiman's *Sandman* "A Game of You" story arc [1991].) A lesbian relationship between Shrinking Violet and Lightning Lass is occasionally implied. These "adult" Legion themes vanished when the D.C. Universe was rewritten following the Zero Hour storyline (#61, 1994).

The other mainstream publisher, Marvel, has been less prolific but more deliberate. Much publicity accompanied the "coming out" of *Alpha Flight*'s Northstar (#106, 1992). Introduced in *Uncanny X Men* (#120, 1979), creator John Byrne confirmed that Northstar was designed from his inception to be gay (see cryptic response from Byrne to this writer's letter in *AF* #18, 1985). But Northstar was never a reader favorite, although we would later attribute his irritating paranoid personality to having been oppressed as a homosexual. Also, revelations that he is half elf (#50) do little to emphasize a message of the acceptability of homosexuality among normal humans. His own four-issue miniseries mentions his homosexuality only obliquely.

Substantive mainstream presentation of gay themes in the future seems most likely in D.C.'s adult-oriented Vertigo titles. Several less-than-mainstream producers have not shied away from overt lesbian content, although their goal seems less the examination of alternative lifestyles than the titillation of the largely male, adolescent readership. Hardly the worst offender, Image Comics' increasingly popular *Spawn*, now getting MTV exposure,

depicts heaven as a male-free but hardly passionless environment, leading the main character to inquire of the angels why they all look like "exotic dancers."

Gay Strips

Many local gay newspapers include a comic strip. For instance, New Orleans's *Impact* features Ron Williams's "Quarter Scenes," which puts a unique local spin on gay and lesbian topics. Formerly the *Advocate* included Howard Cruse's "Wendel" (formally ending in #537, 1989), "Leonard & Larry" by Tim Barela, and work by Donelan. Interestingly, this national news magazine no longer carries any cartooning work, be it comics or editorials.

Gay Books

Gay Comix (later *Gay Comics*) debuted in 1980 and has sporadically appeared through #23 (summer 1996). The title features gay, lesbian, and transgender artists originally emphasizing autobiographical themes, with later expansion to more diverse topics. The series is also an excellent source of notices and announcements leading to other nonmainstream gay-related comics materials.   *James M. Donovan*

Bibliography

McCloud, Scott. *Understanding Comics: The Invisible Art.* Northampton, Mass.: Kitchen Sink Press, 1993.

See also Gay and Lesbian Press; Media

Coming Out

"Coming out" borrows vocabulary from the tradition of the debutante ball in which affluent young women, having reached a certain age, are publicly presented. In certain African tribes, "coming out" has described an event in which girls, upon reaching

C marriageable age, come out of the little hut in which they have been confined. Such analogies reinforce the notion that coming out is a single life event, usually associated with puberty, marking an irreversible transition from privacy and concealment to public presence and exposure. Though the phrase has been used in gay and lesbian circles to describe "a courageous act," it is most commonly and appropriately conceived as a lifelong process through which gay men and lesbians work toward an integrated homosexual identity and toward incorporating that identity into their public lives.

The question, even posing the question, of the etiology of homosexuality has been controversial from the earliest days of the homophile rights movement, but as the battle between essentialists and constructivists rages, there is mounting evidence that there are significant biological components to homosexuality. If so, coming out may come to be seen as psychological reconciliation with biological nature. In other words, homosexuality may be, to a significant degree, biological while homosexual identity may be largely constructed. In any case, coming out is a complex process, often conceived as occurring in stages, marked by a large number of events, and defying any clear laws of linear and inexorable progress. Coming out is a socialization process characterized by ambivalence and "affiliation cycles" (Goffman).

The gay and lesbian analog to the little hut has been the metaphorical closet. The metaphor, though it has lost much of its power through overuse, is enormously suggestive. "Coming out of the closet" suggests escape from a cramped, crowded, dark space, the locus of many childhood fears, the repository of anything not fit for public display, including whatever skeletons one's personal history might hold. At the same time, the closet may have been a favorite hiding place, a secret playground, or a refuge from punishment. One of the great camp instances of coming out involves the good witch Glinda the Good, in *The Wizard of Oz,* calling the Munchkins forth from just such safe hiding: "Come out, come out, wherever you are," now a staple on T-shirts and banners at pride parades. Coming out is an issue in gay and lesbian life because the signs of homosexuality tend to be, in contrast to race, ethnicity, and gender, invisible. Among the earliest American homophile liberation organizations, the Mattachine Societies were so named out of a recognition of the kinship between gay men and lesbians in the twentieth century and masked figures of early European courts. Having a stigma that places gays and lesbians among the discreditable rather than the discredited, they may choose between "passing," by which one may enjoy freedom from persecution (and sometimes prosecution), and coming out. Passing, though, publicly maintaining one's heterosexual "normalcy," comes at the expense of maintaining a public sense of shame at what one secretly is and enormous psychic energy spent maintaining the mask and worrying over the ever-present possibility that one may be found out.

Early studies of coming out were often limited to the perspective of "northern-industrial societies." In fact, recent work on gay and lesbian history and cross-cultural studies of homosexuality have forced more and more precise distinctions between homosexuality and contemporary gay and lesbian identity. Inasmuch as contemporary northern industrial societies may be unique in their social placement of homosexuality, coming out as presented here may be an experience unique to gays and lesbians living in the cultural dynamic created by those societies.

Though "the closet" is treated as a singular entity, there are in fact many loci for coming out—to oneself, to other gay people, to close friends and family members, to colleagues, to the world at large—and within each of these arenas, there are degrees of coming out ranging from unarticulated knowledge of the "Don't ask, don't tell" variety to "In your face."

Coming Out As an Intrapersonal Process

Coming out involves, first, a willingness to recognize the possibility that one may be homosexual. Many coming-out stories express an initial unwillingness to acknowledge this possibility. Males and females alike tell of struggling with the attempt to reconcile their sexual attractions with the most egregious stereotypes of gays and lesbians, often their only referents for the terms. This first step can be enormously lonely as it is really the prerequisite for seeking help.

The gay and lesbian community has become increasingly visible in recent decades, even making a presence in mainstream media. This has helped to dispel some stereotypes or at least to diminish their hegemony, and it has made it easier for gays and lesbians in the process of coming out to find positive, affirming, healthy models, social support, and resources to facilitate "identity acceptance," "identity pride," and "identity synthesis" (Cass). Coming out groups are a standard feature in many large urban gay community centers and on many college campuses. Gays and lesbians have also been in the vanguard in taking advantage of the Internet, in some ways a remarkably democratic mass medium. There are a number of resource sites, many of them linked under the umbrella "queer resources directory," or "qrd," and a number of these sites are devoted to coming-out information and advice.

Though positive gay and lesbian images and resources are more visible and available than ever before, the anxieties and stresses associated with coming out are still formidable. In the model proposed by Craig O'Neill and Kathleen Ritter, coming out represents a kind of rebirth, which must be preceded by a symbolic death in which one loses one's former self, may lose acceptance from family and others, and may lose a sense of belonging. For many the potential losses are overwhelming, as indicated by the fact that between 30 and 40 percent of gay and lesbian teenagers make a serious attempt at suicide, a figure corroborated by Department of Health and Human Services statistics indicating that, of the roughly five thousand adolescent and early-adult suicides in the United States each year, 30 percent are related to emotional turmoil over sexual orientation.

For most, the coming out process not only involves rethinking one's own identity but rethinking one's understandings of "gay" and "lesbian." Once upon a time, this struggle occurred over images inherited from unenlightened religion, science, and social lore: "I'm not a sissy, I can't possibly be homosexual," or "I'm not a diesel dyke, I can't be a lesbian." Recently the arena has become more complicated, and outcoming gays and lesbians find themselves with challenges to identity from the enlightened, politically correct, academic left as well.

This largely personal process of coming out, redefining oneself and redefining what it means to be gay or lesbian, is mediated and made social in the coming-out story, a staple of gay and lesbian literature. From Donald Webster Cory's (pseud.) *The Homosexual in America* to *Generation Q*, gays and lesbians of every generation have felt the need to provide public "maps" to the possibilities in coming out, and many more have testified that they found valuable direction therein.

The synthesis, by most accounts, is never complete, probably because the lifelong struggle is against "internalized homophobia." The negative lessons about the worthlessness of homosexuals that are uncritically accepted early in life and that society continues to project through policies of unequal treatment and tolerance of homophobia and hate crimes are deep-seated and corrosive.

Coming Out As a Social Process

Some have defined the stages of coming out as an ever-expanding circle in which one operates as an openly gay or lesbian individual. In the early stages, this usually means to close, sympathetic friends and/or to family. Often these steps are taken before one has made one's way into the gay and lesbian community or before one has established a very secure place there; consequently, there is a high sense of risk associated with these decisions. Coming out to family may be particularly difficult, raising fears, not always unfounded, of excommunication. Sometimes parents especially are "excused" for reasons of their perceived infirmity: "It would just kill them if I told them." Such decisions invariably create barriers to close family relationships and often make the gay or lesbian in effect a half-member of the family. Considerable attention has been given in recent years to factors that affect the decision to come out to family and its outcomes. Among the findings: high-quality parental attachment makes coming out easier and contributes to positive outcomes, while strong traditional family values, especially among ethnic and racial minorities, makes coming out difficult and often with unsatisfactory results. Highly visible groups like Parents and Friends of Lesbians and Gays (PFLAG) have aided both gays and lesbians and their families and friends through this process, and self-help books for every conceivable party to the process have become a minor publishing industry.

AIDS has added a tragic element of near necessity to the coming-out equation. Too many gay men especially have been forced out of the closet by disease.

It has also become increasingly possible in recent years to make the decision to come out at work. More and more corporations have adopted official nondiscrimination policies; some have company-sanctioned employee groups; and a few are even beginning to provide benefits for domestic partners.

Coming Out As a Political Stratagem

Perhaps it was gay activist Arthur Bell who once opined that things might have been easier if gays and lesbians had been born lavender. Certainly there would never have been the temptations of the closet or the ability of society to deny homosexuals by

C reason of invisibility. Long before feminism provided the phrase "The personal is political," gays and lesbians understood this, and coming out especially has always been recognized as a deeply personal act with profoundly political consequences. In the early 1970s, this was captured in the call to arms "Out of the closets and into the streets!" Today, this awareness is reflected in the titles of many gay and lesbian publications, as for example, *Outlines, Outwrite, Out/Look,* and *Outweek,* and *OUT.*

Nowhere is the political aspect of coming out more apparent than in the National Coming Out Project sponsored by the Human Rights Campaign. As part of this project, October 11 is annually designated as National Coming Out Day. In its literature, the Human Rights Campaign appeals to well-established findings that show that those who personally know gay men or lesbians are much more likely to support gay and lesbian issues than are those who do not believe they know personally any gay men or lesbians.

Though the Human Rights Campaign is on solid ground when it makes claims for the positive political effects of coming out, it is also true that increased visibility of the gay and lesbian community has created a political backlash. As gays and lesbians and their issues have become more visible, groups loosely gathered under the umbrella of the radical Christian right have campaigned vigorously against what they see as "the gay agenda" and "special rights" for gays and lesbians.

Outing is another arena in which coming out becomes intensely political. Outing refers to public revelation of someone's sexual orientation without his or her consent and usually against his or her will. The most frequent targets are closeted public figures who might serve as good role models or use their position to influence public opinion and politicians openly working against gay and lesbian causes while secretly leading gay or lesbian lives. The debate over outing reached a peak in the late 1980s. Outing as a political tactic has been extremely divisive within the gay and lesbian community.

The political aspects of coming out make clear that it is central not only to the personal identity of gays and lesbians but to their political identity as well; just as "passing" exists as an option at the personal level, there have always been those in the gay and lesbian movement who have recommended assimilationism at the political level. The assimilationist model has generally held that gays and lesbians are and should be different from straight society only in the area of sexual orientation, which is essentially a private matter. Therefore, gays and lesbians should work for protection against the possible repercussions of having their sexual orientation exposed but otherwise should simply seek to blend, that is, disappear into the surrounding societal landscape. The assimilationist position is taken up anew in each generation by clear-eyed, hard-headed, self-styled pragmatists who believe they have discovered the arts of disguise and the ancient uses of the mask.

James Darsey
(with research assistance from
Jeffrey Martin and Lucila Gonzalez)

Bibliography

Cass, Vivienne C. "Homosexual Identity Formation: A Theoretical Model." *Journal of Homosexuality* 4 (1979): 219–35.

Eichberg, Rob. *Coming Out: An Act of Love.* New York: Penguin, 1991.

Fairchild, Betty, and Nancy Hayward. *Now that You Know: What Every Parent Should Know About Homosexuality.* New York: Harcourt Brace, 1989.

Gershen, Kaufman, and Raphael Lev. *Coming Out of Shame: Transforming Gay and Lesbian Lives.* New York: Main Street Books, 1997.

Goffman, Erving. *Stigma: Notes on the Management of Spoiled Identity.* Englewood Cliffs, NJ: Prentice–Hall, 1963.

Gross, Larry. *Contested Closets: The Politics and Ethics of Outing.* Minneapolis: University of Minnesota Press, 1993.

Jandt, Fred E., and James Darsey, "Coming Out as a Communicative Process." In *Gayspeak: Gay Male and Lesbian Communication.* James W. Chesebro, ed. New York: Pilgrim Press, 1981, 12–27.

Jay, Karla, and Allen Young, eds. *Out of the Closets: Voices of Gay Liberation.* Twentieth Anniversary Edition. New York: New York University Press, 1992.

Mohr, Richard D. Gay Ideas: *Outing and Other Controversies.* Boston: Beacon Press, 1992.

O'Neill, Craig, and Kathleen Ritter. *Coming Out Within.* New York: HarperCollins, 1992.

Saks, Adrien, and Wayne Curtis, eds. *Revelations: Gay Men's Coming-Out Stories.* Boston: Alyson, 1994.

See also AIDS; Assimilation; Class; Community Centers; Cory, Donald Webster; Essentialist-Contructionist Debate; Evolution; Marches and Parades; Mattachine Society; Outing; Parents and Friends of Lesbians and Gays (PFLAG); Politics, Global; Religious Right

Community Centers

Since 1970, lesbian and gay community centers throughout the United States have played a central role in initiating grassroots political action and the delivery of social services to lesbians, gay men, bisexuals, and transgender people. Born in the heyday of gay liberation, the community services center movement was inspired by early activists' realization that a homophobic culture had produced a gay population with human services needs. Early centers were formed to promote the social and cultural development of local communities and to heal the wounds of individual community members.

By 1996, seventy-five lesbian and gay community centers existed in the United States, "act[ing] as engines of progressive social change." Centers range from start-up ventures operating out of founders' homes to modest volunteer groups renting a few rooms in an office building, to large multipurpose agencies with budgets over $1 million that own their own building and employ dozens of paid staff members. While most centers are nestled in urban areas such as Atlanta, Baltimore, Cleveland, and San Diego, suburban (Woodbury, N.J.; Garden Grove, Calif.; White Plains, N.Y.) and rural (Caribou, Me.; Scottsbluff, Neb.) centers also exist.

The two largest centers, in New York and Los Angeles, illustrate two distinct ways that centers have evolved. The Lesbian and Gay Community Services Center in New York was established in 1983, long after a significant number of that city's lesbian and gay social service agencies had been founded. Hence it initially functioned as the hub of social and political organizing for the city and provided meeting and recreational space for dozens of community groups. In the late 1980s, the center began to address social service gaps in the local

Officers of the Lesbian and Gay Community Services Center, New York City (1995); from left to right, Judith E. Turkel, Esq., president; Odell Mays II, treasurer; Richard D. Burns, Esq., executive director; and Janet Weinberg, co-chair. Photo courtesy Lesbian and Gay Community Services Center, Inc.

C community by delivering direct social services, including programs focused on substance-abuse counseling, AIDS bereavement, children of lesbian and gay parents, gender identity support, and youth activities. By 1996, the agency had a budget approaching $4 million and sixty staff members, and had begun an ambitious capital campaign to raise funds to renovate and expand their building, a former high school, in Greenwich Village.

The Los Angeles Gay and Lesbian Community Services Center was founded in 1971, inspired in part by the community services center model developed by minority and disenfranchised populations in U.S. urban centers in the 1960s. A variety of gay-oriented human services programs were pioneered in the center's early years, including peer support groups, a gay male sexually transmitted disease clinic, and programs for homeless and runaway youth. In the mid-1980s, with the arrival of the AIDS epidemic, the center intensified its effort to "take care of its own" and dramatically expanded its service delivery system to include HIV testing, counseling, prevention, lesbian social activities, a twenty-four–bed youth shelter, addiction counseling, and an expanded mental health clinic. Only with the acquisition of a new 44,000-square-foot building in 1992 and an additional 33,000-square-foot site in 1996 did the center begin to increase dramatically its social programming and offer expanded meeting space to community groups. "L.A. Gay and Lesbian Center" became the agency's official name at this time. By 1996, the L.A. center had a budget approaching $20 million, employed 240 full-time staff, and owned several buildings in Hollywood.

In 1994, center directors from New York, Los Angeles, Denver, Minneapolis, and Dallas formed the National Association of Lesbian and Gay Community Centers. This network promotes a range of collaborative efforts among centers and provides support, guidance, and consultation to new developing centers.   *Eric Rofes*

Bibliography

Burns, Richard, and Eric Rofes. "Gay Liberation Comes Home: The Development of Community Centers Within Our Movement." In *The Sourcebook on Lesbian and Gay Healthcare.* Michael Shernoff and William Scott, eds. Washington, D.C.: National Lesbian and Gay Health Foundation, 1988, 24–29.

National Association of Lesbian and Gay Community Centers. *National Directory of Lesbian & Gay Community Centers.* New York: Lesbian and Gay Community Services Center, 1996.

Osborne, Torie. *Coming Home to America: A Roadmap to Gay and Lesbian Empowerment.* New York: St. Martin's Press, 1996, 141–59.

See also Los Angeles; New York City; San Francisco

Copland, Aaron (1900—1990)

Composer, pianist, conductor, and writer Aaron Copland was born in Brooklyn, N.Y., the son of Russian Jewish immigrants. He found his most important teacher, Nadia Boulanger, in Paris (1921–1924). She helped guide his understanding of Europe's master composers, while encouraging his determination to assert his American identity.

On his return to the States, he won important friends, notably the conductor Serge Koussevitzky. The modernity of *Music for the Theatre* (1925), the *Piano Concerto* (1926), and the *Piano Variations* (1930) befuddled and sometimes scandalized the concert-going public but spoke deeply to an elite. Even as he continued to write challenging pieces like the *Piano Sonata* (1941), some more accessible works—including *El Salón México* (1936); ballet scores for Eugene Loring (*Billy the Kid*, 1938), Agnes de Mille (*Rodeo*, 1942), and Martha Graham (*Appalachian Spring*, 1944); the patriotic *Fanfare for the Common Man* and *A Lincoln Portrait* (both 1942); and film music for *Our Town* (1940) and *The Red Pony* (1948)—made him by midcentury the best-known American concert composer of his time. For some of his later scores—including the *Piano Fantasy* (1957), *Connotations* (1962), and *Inscape* (1967), whose title derived from the writings of Gerard Manley Hopkins—he adapted Schoenberg's twelve-tone method of composition.

Working within the tradition of European art music, though indebted to jazz and the folk musics of the Americas as well, Copland produced a vibrant body of work deeply resonant of American life in style and content. Exceptionally generous, he also helped the careers of numerous composers as teacher, benefactor, concert organizer, critic, and friend.

Copland came to terms with his homosexuality, which he believed a natural phenomenon, early in life, his understanding of the matter shaped in part by Whitman, Freud, Ellis, and Gide. His celebrated mentorship of young composers sometimes assumed a homoerotic dimension and he enjoyed quasi romances with such protégés as Israel Citkowitz, Paul Bowles, and Leonard Bernstein.

From 1932 to the early 1940s, he had an ongoing romantic relationship with Victor Kraft (1915–1976), a bisexual musician and photographer; they remained lifelong friends after the romance ended. Other such relationships included those with dancer-writer Erik Johns (b. 1927), who wrote the libretto for his opera, *The Tender Land* (1954), and composer John Brodbin Kennedy (b. 1931).

Copland lived a relatively open life for someone of his generation, treating his homosexuality with serenity and humor. Composer David del Tredici writes, "Aaron showed me that it was OK to be making music and be gay." At the same time, he remained highly discreet about his private life; when Bernstein urged that he "come out," he responded, "I'll leave that to you, boy."

Copland believed that his sexuality informed his work, but like his Jewish background, only indirectly. Homosexual subtexts can be detected in certain pieces, but his work emphasizes more general issues and concerns (including sexual freedom); as both man and artist, he exemplifies the engaged homosexual sensitive to the joys, fears, and aspirations of his fellow citizens.   *Howard Pollack*

Bibliography

Copland, Aaron, and Vivian Perlis. *Copland: 1900 Through 1942*. Boston: Faber and Faber, 1984.
———. *Copland Since 1943*. New York: St. Martin's Press, 1989.
Pollack, Howard. *An Uncommon American: Aaron Copland and His Music*. New York: Holt, forthcoming.

See also Dance: Concert Dance in America; Ellis, Havelock; Freud, Sigmund; Gide, André; Music and Musicians 1: Classical Music; Whitman, Walt

Corelli, Arcangelo (1653–1713)

Eighteenth-century descriptions of this Italian composer and violinist character note "the mildness of his temper and the modesty of his deportment." Corelli's influence on European instrumental music was fundamental, despite his small output of only six published collections: forty-eight trios sonatas (Opus I—IV, 1681–1694), twelve sonatas for solo violin and continuo accompaniment (Opus V, 1700), and twelve string concertos (Opus VI, 1714). These works, reprinted many dozens of times during the eighteenth century, were considered perfect models by French, English, and German composers, who published many collections imitating them.

Corelli never married, and his sponsors included patrons who moved in known homosexual circles. They included Cardinals Ottoboni and Pamphili, Queen Christina of Sweden, and several of the private "academies" devoted to the arts, with all-male membership. Henry Colburn's *Musical Biography*, drawing on eighteenth-century sources, stresses that Corelli "lived in great intimacy with Carlo Cignani and Carlo Marat." The nature of this relationship is unclear.

On the other hand, his partnership from 1682 until his death with the violinist Matteo Fornari (an employee of Cardinal Pamphili) is better documented. Corelli "became devoted" to him and "from then on was rarely to be absent from his side" (Talbot). Their closeness is reflected in the publication of two fine trio sonatas dedicated to them by their younger contemporary Giuseppe Valentini (in his *Villegiature armoniche*, Opus 5, Rome, 1707), entitled *La Corelli* and *La Fornari*. For nearly twenty years, they lived together at the Roman palazzo of Cardinal Pamphili. Many of the trio sonatas which form the main part of Corelli's output must be the musical result of this relationship. Corelli died a rich man, bequeathing to Matteo Fornari all his violins and his musical manuscripts (and it was Fornari who oversaw the posthumous publication of the Opus VI concertos). Corelli is buried in the Pantheon in Rome, next to the painter Raphael.

Davitt Moroney

Bibliography

Colburn, Henry. *Musical Biography*. Vol. 1. London: 1814, 280–291.
Talbot, Michael. "Corelli, Arcangelo." In *The New Grove Dictionary of Music and Musicians*. London: Macmillan, 1980.

See also Italy; Music and Musicians 1: Classical Music

Corigliano, John (1938–)

John Corigliano is an American composer, born and educated in New York City. In 1964, his violin sonata won first prize at the Spoleto Festival Chamber Music Competition, launching a career that was furthered four years later by a Guggenheim fellowship. Since then, Corigliano has received frequent commissions from performers (James Galway, *Pied*

C *Piper Fantasy*), symphonies (Chicago Symphony, Symphony No. 1), and other groups, such as the Metropolitan Opera (*The Ghosts of Versailles*). His film score for Ken Russell's *Altered States* was nominated for an Academy Award in 1980.

Although Corigliano's works reveal a conservative idiom, they encompass a wide variety of styles and techniques. They tend to be basically tonal and lyrical, but with interpolations of other styles such as tone clusters (the rats in the *Pied Piper Fantasy*), microtones (*Altered States*), or quotation/pastiche (Oboe concerto, *The Ghosts of Versailles*), often used for dramatic effect. Corigliano sees this eclecticism as advantageous, since it allows him to begin each piece without predetermined ground rules.

Corigliano's First Symphony (1990) was directly inspired by his "feelings of loss, anger, and frustration" as the AIDS epidemic took its toll on friends and colleagues. According to the composer, the symphony's structure was modeled on the AIDS Quilt: each movement is dedicated to a particular friend and is based on some musical quotation connected with that person. The third movement also includes melodic remembrances (originally settings of verses by William M. Hoffman) of other friends lost to AIDS; Corigliano later restored Hoffman's words in his "vocalization" of this movement for mezzo-soprano, male chorus, and small chamber ensemble (*Of Rage and Remembrance*, 1990). Corigliano resists being labeled as a "gay composer," arguing that apart from these two more overtly political works, his sexuality has little to do with his compositions. The critical reception of his work—particularly the symphony and *The Ghosts of Versailles*—however, has often been tinged by homophobic overtones.   *Stephen McClatchie*

Bibliography

Baker, Rob. *The Art of AIDS*. New York: Continuum, 1994.

Mass, Lawrence. "Musical Quilts." *Gay and Lesbian Study Group Newsletter* 2, no. 2 (October 1992): 11–13.

The New Grove Dictionary of American Music. S.v. "Corigliano, John." By Dale Cockrell.

See also Gay American Composers

Cortázar, Julio (1914–1984)

A member of the well-known Latin American narrative "boom" of the 1960s and 1970s, Argentine Julio

Cortázar is an emblem of his generation: political activist, literary critic, translator (mainly of Edgar Allan Poe), anthologist (not unexpectedly of Pedro Salinas), and Parisian exile. His novels and short stories show how experimental writing assumes the multiple cultural trends of the sixties. However, neither Cortázar nor any other member of the Latin American boom have been examined in terms of the literary, cultural, and political connotations of sexual "deviance."

Beginning with his most famous novel, *Rayuela* (Hopscotch, 1963), the homoerotic triangle, with its inherent compulsory heterosexuality and homosexual panic, constitutes the narrative frame that defines the main character's wanderings through the novel. La Maga in Paris and Talita in Buenos Aires, like many women in Cortázar's short stories, work as proxies through whom Horacio Oliveira, the bohemian bachelor hero, can veil his homoerotic desire for other actual or hypothetical partners, many of them his own narcissistic double. As a mirror of himself, La Maga is the visible form of his own repressed homoeroticism. The equivocal game between the narrator and the protagonist in *Rayuela*, as in many of Cortázar's short stories, allows the reader to contemplate the extent to which the position of the narrator, as an invisible figure behind the performance of the plot, is concealing his or her homosexual desire, as in the famous "Las babas del diablo" (later the basis of the acclaimed film *Blow Up*).

Cortázar also addresses such complex erotic relations as: incest ("Los venenos" [Poisons], "Cartas de mamá" [Mother's Letters]), narrative identification with women (as in "Carta a una señorita en Paris" [Letter to a Young Lady in Paris], or in the gay short story "Los buenos servicios" [Good Services]), homosexual secrecy ("Sobremesa" [Sitting on after the Meal]), and the demonization of women, especially mothers (as in "La salud de los enfermos" [The Patient's Health] and "La Señorita Cora" [Miss Cora]).

As in the Sartrean philosophical model, Cortázar probes sexual and racial identity, male militant solidarity ("Reunión"), and terrorist aggression ("El perseguidor" [The Pursuer]), by means of the homoeroticism implied by the look between two men ("Las puertas del cielo" [Sky's Doors]). "Las armas secretas" (Secret Arms) is one of his best short stories, where he paradoxically works both through the reinscription of the "male fantasies" and how the culture in capitalism enforces the ignorance around the central point of male/female homosexual desire. Unfortunately, this critical approach to Cortázar's work has not yet been developed.

Gustavo Geirola

Bibliography

Cortázar, Julio. *Cuentos completos*. Madrid: Alfaguara, 1994.

———. *Hopscotch*. Gregory Rabassa, trans. New York: Pantheon, 1966.

———. *Rayuela*. Buenos Aires: Editorial Sudamericana, 1963.

See also Argentina; Salínas, Pedro

Cory, Donald Webster (1913–1986)

Using the name "Donald Webster Cory," American sociologist Edward Sagarin wrote *The Homosexual in America* (1951), a pioneering study of gay men in American society. Sagarin, a gay man who was a husband and father (he would remain married until his death), decided to write this book after a long struggle for self-acceptance. In it he argues that homosexuals are in most respects like heterosexuals, that any problems in social and psychological adjustment they experience result from discrimination rather than homosexuality itself, and that they share the "caste-like status" of ethnic, religious, and racial minorities. Though when Sagarin wrote *The Homosexual in America* he was a businessperson who had not completed college, it combines careful cultural analysis with persuasive appeals for legal, medical, and social reform.

By 1954, however, Sagarin's view of homosexuality had undergone a dramatic transformation. Though he still favored protection of gay peoples' civil rights, in writings and statements he argued for the medical model of homosexuality, characterizing it as a psychopathology. In his mid-forties Sagarin returned to school, subsequently receiving a Ph.D. in sociology and joining the faculty of the City College of New York. By 1966 he stopped writing as Cory, but under his own name produced several highly critical studies of homosexuality, never publicly acknowledging that he had written Cory's works or that he was himself homosexual.

The Homosexual in America's argument that gay people are an oppressed minority whose civil rights deserve protection gave impetus to the homophile movement. In contrast, Sagarin's later work increasingly expressed a regressive view of homosexuality.

Charles Krinsky

Bibliography.

Cory, Donald Webster. *The Homosexual in America: A Subjective Approach*. Introduction by Dr. Albert Ellis. New York: Greenberg, 1951.

———. *The Lesbian in America*. Introduction by Dr. Albert Ellis. New York: Citadel, 1964.

D'Emilio, John. *Sexual Politics, Sexual Communities: The Making of a Homosexual Minority in the United States, 1940–1970*. Chicago: University of Chicago Press, 1983.

Marotta, Toby. *The Politics of Homosexuality*. Boston: Houghton Mifflin, 1981.

See also Homophile Movement; United States

Counseling

Counseling has not been a standard part of the repertoire of human interaction for quite as long as homosexuality, but almost. Informal counseling has been with us since the first person brought his or her unsureness to another person with the hope of understanding, compassion, and assistance in finding her or his way. Certainly if the person to whom the unsureness was brought listened with care, asked clarifying questions, and made suggestions, counseling was under way.

For as long as the word *counseling* has been used, however, it has been confused (sometimes intentionally) with a process of giving direction(s). "I counsel you to . . ." can easily mean "The best course of action is . . . ," "You should . . . ," or "The appropriate action is . . ." Counseling has also been confused at times with consoling or hand holding when disaster strikes. As the world became more complex, specialization in formal counseling followed. It might be *vocational, educational, medical, pastoral, marital*, or *legal*, for instance. In some places the state sets standards and licenses the right to give formal counseling.

While both directions and solace are needed and welcome at times, they do not offer the lasting value of genuine counseling for unsure people. The prejudice against homosexuality that has existed in many parts of the world for many years made many developing gay males and lesbians very unsure. While it was often much too dangerous to breathe a word of these feelings to anyone, counsel was sometimes sought informally from a trusted friend or relative and sometimes formally from someone presumed to be a trustworthy professional counselor. Not infrequently, since prejudice had poisoned the

C entire culture, the results were harmful. It is devastating to self-esteem to be told that one must become someone other than the person one is if one wants to be considered of worth in human society.

The death grip of prejudice came loose during Word War II as people from various nations and cultures mixed and began to comprehend how relative the sacred local values and prejudices were. In addition, thousands of the hundreds of thousands of men from different places, battle-frightened and sex-starved, mixed together in unfamiliar emotional territory, discovering that they shared a secret homosexual desire. Many shared sexual affection with one another and some fell in love in a miracle that could not have happened in their hometowns.

That period was the beginning of enormous changes in the fabric of human societies. Antique assumptions could be questioned. Optimism was in the air. Liberation had found meaning beyond war.

Citizens assumed to be inferior or second class because of popular prejudice became restless and joined in communication and union with one another. An Association for Humanistic Psychology took root near the end of the 1950s in the United States. In the 1960s the human potential movement, drawing on a vast array of disciplines, came into being with the aim of questioning all previous assumptions about human psychology and human behavior. And in June 1969, the days of rioting in the streets of Greenwich Village in New York City, known as the Stonewall Rebellion, served notice to the world that gay men and lesbians were ready to forcefully demand full civil rights as first-class citizens.

Prejudice had decreed that homosexual inclinations were pathological and that individuals who admitted to such feelings and indulged in homosexual behavior were both emotionally disturbed and criminal. Such prejudice was based on an observation that such persons were not "normal." And that was true, because such individuals did not fit the statistical norm or average of the entire population. They were not common, ordinary, or of the majority. The presumptive circular reasoning betrayed the prejudice that had infected the society. If one could be categorized as belonging to a minority, one was inferior because one was not normal, trustworthy, or average.

This pervasive prejudice had permeated the fields of psychological counseling and psychotherapy that had their ancestral roots in the birth of psychoanalysis at the end of the Victorian era. To his credit, Sigmund Freud, father of psychoanalysis and explorer of the unconscious mind, did not share the belief that those primarily homosexual in orientation were either pathological or criminal. But his followers and other prominent pioneers in the new fields of counseling did carry that prejudice into their work.

It was not until 1963 that a nongay American woman psychologist was permitted to publish a modest scientific study that flatly contradicted the years of professional observations and opinion based on prejudice about homosexuality that had filled the counseling journals and textbooks. It was not until 1972 that a nongay American male psychologist was able to publish a book challenging the professionals' prejudice about homosexuality while contributing an important concept that he named *homophobia*. And it was not until 1977 that a gay American male clinical psychologist, licensed and in private practice, was permitted to publish a book declaring gay identity a healthy ability (to love fully someone of the same gender) rather than a disability.

Near the end of 1973 the American Psychiatric Association, amid much political tumult in the fields of psychotherapy and counseling, had removed the listing of homosexuality, per se, from its influential official *Diagnostic and Statistical Manual*. Some members of the organization forced a follow-up polling of the membership (using professional views influenced by personal views) that produced a very close vote but affirmed the official action of the organization. The American Psychological Association in January 1975 issued a more comprehensive statement of support for lesbians and gay men. Sixteen years later, in 1991, the American Psychoanalytic Association finally managed to issue its first statement opposing discrimination against gay men and lesbians.

As legal and political climates changed, counselors in private practice who had been in danger of losing the recognition of their professional organizations as well as their state-granted licenses began to appear. As they found one another, they formed gay-affirmative professional organizations and gained political clout. It then become safer for gay counselors employed by agencies and institutions to appear, swept along in what has become a flood of respectable research appearing in professional journals, supporting gay identity as well as gay-affirmative psychotherapy and counseling.

The unsure gay man or lesbian may now, at last, safely seek the assistance of a counselor if that counselor is gay-affirmative. Such a counselor may or may not be primarily homosexual in orientation, but if she or he is gay-affirmative by declaration, she or he believes that homosexuality is not merely to be accepted but must be appreciated—not as good as, but rather a gift accepted at some cost in a world still far from free of prejudice. The gay-affirmative counselor knows that while there is no need to address the question of whether or not to *be* gay, there may be some need to help a client find the way to be the best (gay) person he or she can be.

Professional counseling has come of age and recognizes the needless damage done by prejudice. It recognizes that human differences are better examined and appreciated than feared and pathologized. It is not the counselor's job to steer the client toward *average* or *normal*. The counselor's job is to be empathic, offer careful listening, ask informational questions, and offer suggestions. It is the client, arriving for counseling with unsureness about his or her path, who must ultimately identify the best path and the probable destination.

Don Clark

Bibliography

Clark, Don, *Loving Someone Gay*. Millbrae, Calif.: Celestial Arts, 1977.
Hooker, Evelyn A. "The Adjustment of the Male Overt Homosexual." *Journal of Projective Techniques* 21, nos. 17–31 (1957).
Weinberg, George, *Society and the Healthy Homosexual*. New York: St. Martin's Press, 1972.

See also Freud, Sigmund; Psychiatry; Psychological and Psychoanalytical Approaches to Homosexuality; Psychotherapy

Couperus, Louis (1863–1923)

Louis Couperus is one of Holland's most famous and productive writers. His novels about society life in The Hague and the Dutch East Indies were, and still are, extremely popular. Homoeroticism is a theme in some of his other major novels. *Noodlot* (Footsteps of Fate, 1890), admired by Oscar Wilde, portrays a platonic friendship between an androgynous dandy and his earthy but weak-minded friend. The story, composed like a tragedy, explicitly refers to Ibsen's *Ghosts* (1881). Criticism was directed against the main character's "unhealthy" emotions and especially against the fatalistic philosophy expressed in this novel.

Couperus's most outspoken homosexual novel is *De Berg van Licht* (Mountain of Light), published in three volumes in 1905–1906. In this high point of fin-de-siècle decadent literature, Couperus sketches a psychological portrait of Heliogabalus, Roman emperor from 218 to 222. Initially, the masses, described by Couperus as an autonomous force, adore the sixteen-year-old androgynous boy. However, in his relation and wedding (!) with a muscular Roman gladiator, Heliogabalus becomes more and more feminine. Together with his mercilessly decadent lifestyle, this leads to the crowd's aversion and the cruel death of Heliogabalus and his followers.

Couperus, who was married to his cousin Elisabeth Baud, was a dandylike aesthete with at least a strong interest in other men. Like many other homosexual artists of his day, he was very drawn to the Mediterranean and classical antiquity. For many years he and his wife lived in Nice and Italy.

Maurice van Lieshout

Bibliography

Bastet, Frédéric. *Louis Couperus: Een biografie*. Amsterdam: Querido, 1987.
Couperus, Louis. *Verzameld Werk*. 50 volumes. Utrecht, Netherlands: Veen, 1986–1996.

See also Dandy; Decadence; Mediterranean; Netherlands; Wilde, Oscar

Couples

Formal records of the existence of male couples can be found in the Western world throughout recorded history, and long-term coupling between males has taken many different forms. In some cultures, social conventions demand that the couple meet certain requirements, such as age differentiation (e.g., an older man and a youth) or class-differentiation (e.g., master and slave, noble and commoner). Sometimes, these conventions would be combined and were occasionally even inscribed into myth, as in the story of the Greek god Zeus taking the beautiful mortal youth Ganymede as his cupbearer.

In many historical cases of couplings between men, it would be expected that the junior or subordinate partner would invariably be cast into the "feminine" role as the receptive partner in anal intercourse, thereby allowing the senior or dominant partner to retain his "masculine" identity. Parallel to such socially sanctioned and rigidly structured forms of male coupledom, however, have been sexual and emotional partnerships among men who related to one another as equals within the relationship. Some of the most famous examples from antiquity were Achilles and Patroclus, noble Greek warriors in the *Iliad*, and the youths David and Jonathan of the Bible.

Historian John Boswell has argued that a substantial historical record suggests the ubiquity of male couples throughout European history. However, Boswell argues that this legacy has been overlooked not only owing to outright censorship but also because phrases such as "friend" and "brother" were often used to denote "lover" and thus have been misinterpreted by scholars. Although his findings have been challenged, Boswell claimed that the official church blessings conferred on male "friends" were in fact consecrations of marriage-type unions. Boswell also notes that among the upper classes in premodern Europe, marriages between men and women were as often about inheritance and dynastic considerations as about love between partners, and as such were frequently arranged by families. By contrast, since no children would result from male-male couplings, such partners were generally much freer to choose their own mates, and such relationships were, perhaps ironically, more reflective of contemporary ideals of romantic love than male-female pairings.

Since the emergence of the modern notion of homosexual identity in the nineteenth century, same-sex coupledom has largely been constructed as a parallel to opposite-sex coupledom. Popular belief, insofar as it encompassed the idea of male couples at all, held that in such couples one partner was the "husband" in the relationship, while the other was the "wife" (a distinction also played out in the "butch-femme" dichotomy found among lesbians). In this reckoning of male coupledom, the "husband" would not only be the head of the household and make important decisions but also dominate as the "active," "penetrative," or "top" partner in anal intercourse.

Whatever the popular perception of male couples, the reality among individual couples was inevitably more complex and variable. Since Stonewall an increasing resistance has developed to the idea that gay men should conform to what were perceived as heterosexual norms. More gay men became "versatile" in that they would have both penetrative and receptive anal intercourse, while also rejecting monogamy as a restraint on sexual liberation. Sexually "open" relationships, in which both partners were free to have sex with others, became commonplace. In fact, ongoing studies have revealed that male couples are significantly more likely than other couples to maintain open relationships. Even while eschewing sexual exclusivity, however, many couples maintained powerful emotional commitments to each other and built lives together.

Empirical study of gay male couples has been limited, and it is impossible to provide reliable statistics as to how many gay men are members of same-sex couples. In the late 1960s, researchers Alan Bell and Martin Weinberg found that 51 percent of white gay men and 58 percent of black gay men reported being in a relationship. In another research cohort of 439 gay men in New York City, interviewed throughout the early 1990s, 44 percent of Caucasian men and 58 percent of ethnic minority men were in primary relationships.

Despite the lack of hard statistics, certain patterns particular to such couples have been discerned. Perhaps the best-known study was conducted by two gay male researchers who were themselves a couple. The researchers, David McWhirter and Andrew Mattison, identified several stages through which gay male couples progress: blending, nesting, maintaining, collaborating, trusting, and renewal. McWhirter and Mattison also noted, however, that social sanctions often forced gay male couples to "improvise" their relationships by, for instance, living apart or even having one or both partners maintain a parallel marriage to a woman.

On a different note, psychiatrist Richard Isay has argued that gender similarities between two male partners may tend to cause same-sex relationships to burn out more quickly than opposite-sex relationships, in which an inherent mystery and tension may be maintained because the partners face each other across the gender divide. Isay has suggested that many successful long-term same-sex couples are marked by "complementarity" rather than similarity between the partners in some characteristic other than gender, such as age, race, class, education, or occupational status. Anecdotally, same-sex couples do seem to cross such dividing lines more often than heterosexual couples, although it is not clear that this is because of complementarity or for other reasons, such as having a comparatively smaller pool of potential partners, or because homosexual couples, already violating one major taboo, are less concerned about other forms of social propriety.

The onset of the AIDS epidemic in 1981 created enormous difficulties for many male couples.

In some couples, both partners were HIV-infected and have had to face the prospect that either or both might soon take ill or die. In other couples, one partner might be HIV-positive while the other remained HIV-negative; these couples faced the dilemma of maintaining long-term safer-sex practices while facing the possible decline of the HIV-positive partner. In some cases, men abandoned their partners in time of illness, but the AIDS epidemic has also proven a testimony to the closeness of many partners and the strength of their commitment to each other. Some of the most striking works of art produced by gay men during the epidemic, writings by Paul Monette in memory of his partner, Roger Horwitz, have focused on the love within couples and the tremendous grief and loss faced by surviving partners.

Among couples in which both partners were HIV-negative, a significant number have chosen to "close" relationships that had formerly been sexually open, believing that this would enable them to continue to practice unprotected sex at least with each other. But the monogamy tactic has proven far from fail-safe, and by the 1990s some suspected that the main venue for new HIV infections among gay men had shifted from the "backroom" to the "bedroom," meaning that many men found it easier to implement self-protective sexual behaviors with casual partners than with long-term partners with whom they felt emotionally connected.

Even beyond the uncertainties raised by the ongoing AIDS epidemic, the future of gay male coupledom is unclear. An "assimilationist" perspective would argue that as homosexuality becomes increasingly destigmatized, same-sex couples will inevitably become more similar to opposite-sex couples. This movement is evidenced by the dramatic expansion of domestic partnership rights afforded by many private companies and city governments in the United States, by the movement for full marriage rights for same-sex partners, and by the increasing tendency of lesbian and gay couples to raise children. A "liberationist" perspective would decry what it sees as this movement back toward heterosexual norms and calls for the perpetuation of sexual non-monogamy and other socially transgressive but uniquely gay male characteristics of relationships.

While the liberationist model appears to be gradually eroding and same-sex couples are becoming less unusual in society and in popular culture, there also seems to be an absolute outer limit to the degree to which same-sex couples can ever resemble opposite-sex couples. Aside from the fact that same-sex couplings are inherently nonprocreative, the coupling of two individuals of the same gender will tend to lead to an intensification of intrinsic gender-specific characteristics rather than their mitigation. Insofar as men and women remain different, then male-male couples will inevitably be distinct from both female-female couples and male-female couples. *Raymond A. Smith*

Bibliography

Bell, Alan, and Martin Weinberg. *Homosexualities: A Study of Diversity Among Men and Women.* New York: Simon and Schuster, 1978.

Berger, R. M. "Men Together: Understanding the Gay Couple." *Journal of Homosexuality* 19, no. 3 (1990): 31–49.

Boswell, John. *Same-Sex Unions in Premodern Europe.* New York: Villard, 1994.

Cabaj, R. P. "Gay and Lesbian Couples: Lessons on Human Intimacy." *Psychiatric Annals* 18, no.1 (1988): 21–25.

Duffy, S. M., and C. E. Rusbult. "Satisfaction and Commitment in Homosexual and Heterosexual Relationships." *Journal of Homosexuality* 12, no. 2 (1986): 1–23.

Isay, Richard. *Being Homosexual: Gay Men and their Development.* New York: Avon, 1989.

Kurdek, L. A., and J. P. Schmitt. "Relationship Quality of Gay Men in Closed or Open Relationships." *Journal of Homosexuality* 12, no. 2 (1985): 85–99.

Mattison, Andrew M., and David P. McWhirter. "Stage Discrepancy in Male Couples." *Journal of Homosexuality* 14 (1987): 88–99.

McWhirter, David P., and Andrew M. Mattison. *The Male Couple.* Englewood Cliffs, N.J.: Prentice-Hall, 1984.

Powell-Cope, G. M. "The Experiences of Gay Couples Affected by HIV Infection." *Qualitative Health Research*, 5, no. 1 (1995): 36–62.

See also Assimilation; Domestic Partnership; Love Poetry, the Petrarchan Tradition; Monette, Paul; Same-Sex Marriage

Coward, Noël (1899–1973)

Noël Coward's life and career approximates the status of myth: a poor young Englishman from the suburbs of London becomes a celebrated actor, singer, composer, lyricist, playwright, director, screenwriter, cabaret artist, painter, fiction writer, and

C above all, international celebrity whose long hoped-for knighthood is delayed for decades because, according to some accounts, he had an affair with a prince (Prince George, Duke of Kent). Coward was an expert at self-presentation; from the young, self-made sophisticate and rebel against stuffy respectability of the 1920s, to the celebrator of "London Pride" and British values during World War II, to the aging sophisticate of his 1950s Las Vegas act and television specials, to Sir Noël, "the Master," in his later years.

Born of lower-middle-class parents (his mother ran a boardinghouse), and in show business from childhood, Coward was a model of a new kind of social mobility for England. By the 1920s, when he had achieved the aura of writer prodigy and matinee idol, he was a model of sophistication and chic decadence for his generation of affluent young people. Part of that image was a decidedly gay style: Coward was the first public personality since the Oscar Wilde scandal a generation before to reflect and mainstream aspects of gay behavior while, of course, being cautious about exposure of his own homosexuality. Laws against homosexual acts were fervently enforced in England between Wilde and the Wolfenden Act, although the sexual orientation of leading theater personalities like matinee idol and composer Ivor Novello, producer Binkie Beaumont, actor John Gielgud, and Coward fell under the category of "open secret." Coward may have been gay, but above all he was a celebrity and, like his dear friend Marlene Dietrich, who was with him at his last public appearance, Coward lived to maintain his public image. His two volumes of memoirs, testaments to his self-absorption, never mention his romantic or sex life with men or weave fictions about romances with women. Unlike Cole Porter or Lorenz Hart, who dallied with rough trade and male prostitutes, Coward had long-term loving relationships, first with Jack Wilson, who became his business manager, then with singer Graham Payn. Still, while Coward was one kind of icon of sophistication for straight society, he was another for gay men in London and New York.

Design for Living (1931) is the first of Coward's plays to tiptoe into the dangerous waters of same-sex desire. Written for Coward and the American star husband and wife team of Alfred Lunt (a bisexual) and Lynn Fontanne, the play chronicles the bisexual triangle of Otto, an artist, Leer, a successful playwright (one of Coward's many self-portraits), and Gilda, the object of both their affections. The play hints that Otto and Leo were lovers before they met Gilda and ends with the three of them in a menage, superbly documented by the famous publicity photo of pajama-clad Coward, Lunt, and Fontanne intertwined on a sofa. In *A Song at Twilight* (1964), an aging playwright discusses his youthful homosexual affair. The play is Coward's vehicle for expressing his views of the newly burgeoning homosexual politics.

Coward's most important contribution to gay culture during his lifetime was as a model for one form of gay style: elegant, witty, tasteful, and always at least a bit camp. *John M. Clum*

Bibliography

Castle, Terry. *Noel Coward and Radclyffe Hall: Kindred Spirits.* New York: Columbia University Press, 1996.

Clum, John M. *Razzle Dazzle: Musical Theater and Gay Culture.* New York: St. Martin's, 1999.

Coward, Noël. *Diaries.* London: Weidenfeld and Nicholson, 1982.

———. *Future Indefinite.* London: Heinemann, 1954.

———. *Present Indicative.* London: Heinemann, 1937.

Fischer, Clive. *Noël Coward: A Biography.* New York: St. Martin's, 1992.

Hoare, Philip. *Noël Coward: A Biography.* New York: Simon and Schuster, 1995.

See also English Literature; Hart, Lorenz; Musical Theater; Porter, Cole Albert; Wilde, Oscar; Wolfenden Report

Cowboy Culture

Because men outnumbered women on the western frontier, the area was populated in the nineteenth and early twentieth centuries by numerous homosocial societies. Among these groups—which included railroad laborers, miners, and lumberjacks—cowboys were both the best known and the least understood. Dime novels, formula westerns, films, TV series, advertising, and other forms of popular media have represented cowboys as icons of manliness. The historical record, however, challenges traditional and widely accepted definitions of manliness, suggesting that cowboys played complex roles in all-male societies to compensate for the scarcity or absence of women.

On trail drives, chuckwagon cooks functioned as caretakers, nurses, and confidants. Paradoxically, by performing domestic tasks, cooks earned higher wages and greater authority than cowboys, who carried out rougher and more dangerous jobs. At social gatherings, held in small frontier communities, cowboys sometimes wore "heifer" brands, acting as female partners in square dances. Lacking women to couple with, men made a virtue of necessity, crossdressing and thus gaining, among a group of unpartnered men, increased popularity. Other aspects of culture addressed the problem of male sexual identity. During roundups cowboys branded and castrated calves, afterward eating the testicles. By consuming organs that were anatomical indications of maleness, they enhanced their sense of their own virility. At the same time, they called attention to their enforced symbolic castration, enacting their status as men stranded on ranches outside society and therefore cut off from women.

References to same-sex encounters are nonexistent in literature of the middle and late nineteenth century. Formula westerns, however, begin to explore the homoerotic nature of male friendships and rivalries in the decades that follow. Interactions between heroes and villains are characterized by close physical contact and emotional intensity. Typically, heroes are forced to choose between civilization, represented by the women they love, and the cult of the phallus, symbolized by villains who pack loaded guns. Although their aggression and rough independence seem to suggest they are masculine, other characteristics also type cowboy heroes as feminine. The archetypal cowboy is well spoken and chivalrous. His dandylike qualities at times make him seem almost effeminate.

More recent works portray cowboys as latent or overt homosexuals. The writings of John Rechy and James Leo Herlihy depict the cowboy as sexual outlaw, as gay male prostitute. Andy Warhol and Gus Van Sant question the cowboy's alleged "straight" identity in subversive, outrageous films. Gay men have adopted the roles and assumed the costumes of cowboys, often facetiously, in disco music (the Village People), leather bars, rodeos, and even pornography. Such kinds of carnival represent critiques of dominant heterosexual myths and traditions as well as subversive examples of gay male empowerment.

Blake Allmendinger

Bibliography

Allmendinger, Blake. *The Cowboy: Representations of Labor in an American Work Culture.* New York: Oxford University Press, 1992.

———. *Ten Most Wanted: The New Western Literature.* New York: Routledge, 1998.

See also Rechy, John; Van Sant, Gus; Warhol, Andy

Cowell, Henry (Dixon) (1897–1965)

A composer of boundless enthusiasm for new musical experiences and experimentation, Cowell played a vital role in promoting American music during the 1920s and 1930s. He was instrumental in developing a wider interest in the music of Charles Ives and of South American composers and in publishing contemporary compositions. Cowell was also an important teacher, directly inspiring such composers as John Cage and Lou Harrison.

Cowell was incredibly prolific and inventive. In his early experimental piano works he employed tone clusters, (e.g., striking the keyboard with the forearm) and explored the sonic possibilities of playing directly on the strings. Cowell's concept of "elastic form" prefigured the compositional use of indeterminacy, and his interest in correlating rhythm with harmony was also prophetic. (On Cowell's experimental techniques, see his 1930 *New Musical Resources*.) Cowell's interest in non-Western musics was inspired by the multicultural environment of the San Francisco area and his contact with the famous world music guru and composition teacher Charles Seeger. Later in life, he became something of a global tourist, composing works influenced by his multiple musical encounters.

In 1936, Cowell was arrested for engaging in homosexual sex with a seventeen-year-old. Seeking leniency, Cowell confessed his guilt and pledged to suppress his homosexual inclinations. After a vicious press campaign against him, he was sentenced to fifteen years. He was paroled in 1940 and pardoned in 1942, enabling him to participate in a government cultural program aimed at strengthening U.S. relations with Latin America. (On Cowell's arrest, see Hicks.) Cowell's arrest and subsequent psychological "rehabilitation" appears to have somewhat diminished his legendary exuberance and musical experimentation.   *W. Anthony Sheppard*

Bibliography

Cowell, Henry. *New Musical Resources.* New York: Knopf, 1930. 2d ed., with notes and an essay by David Nicholls. Cambridge: Cambridge University Press, 1996.

Hicks, Michael. "The Imprisonment of Henry Cowell." *Journal of the American Musicological Society* 44, no. 1 (Spring 1991): 92–119.

C

See also Cage, John; Gay American Composers; Harrison, Lou

Crane, Hart (1899–1932)

Born in 1899 in Garrettsville, Ohio, Harold Hart Crane (he later dropped the "Harold" in order to use "Hart," his mother's maiden name) grew up in Cleveland. At age eighteen he moved to New York, the city that exercised great fascination for him as a site of modern energy and sexual possibility. Largely self-educated, Crane read voraciously, immersing himself in the poets and novelists who engaged him. He was aware of his homosexuality at an early age but found it difficult to integrate with his family, from which he fled repeatedly, or with the literary elite who failed to understand his attempt to work within a homosexual tradition even as he adapted it to the modern world. His first published poem, "C 33," written when he was sixteen, was a tribute to Oscar Wilde in prison. Many of Crane's earliest models were French symbolists (he published translations of three poems of Laforgue) who helped him make a shift from late romanticism to modernism. Other works, such as "Episode of Hands," display the warm feeling and praise of male friendship that made him an admirer of Whitman against modernist disdain.

Crane's first book, *White Buildings* (1926), established the young poet as a major force in contemporary American poetry. Allen Tate's introduction sets the binary terms by which Crane is usually understood: he writes "abstractly [and] metaphysically" (that is, he is a modernist like Eliot) but his work is "confined to an experience of the American scene." Crane's poetry is often seen as the product of a search for an adequate American modernism. It might also be argued that he constantly sought a reconciliation between the myth of America and the reality of his life as a gay man. The poignancy of that position of alienation is evident in a number of the poems that dramatize positions of suffering and loss, from the moth and the flame of "Legend" to the black man in "Black Tambourine" or the incarnation of modernism's "meek adjustments" in "Chaplinesque." Other poems point to ways out of this sense of decadent despair, particularly "For the Marriage of Faustus and Helen," with its attempt to go beyond a European mythology and tradition of patriarchal aggression, and "Voyages," the set of six love poems for Emil Opffer. These poems, which conclude the volume, locate desire in absence, employing Crane's dense verse to evoke the sensual world ot the lovers.

Although Crane made the obligatory 1920s trip to Paris, he remained an American, not a permanent exile. His greatest work is *The Bridge,* a long poem that is an answer to T. S. Eliot's *The Waste Land.* Crane's poem interweaves the poet's contemporary experience with the journey of Columbus and the rites of an Appalachian spring. The "Cape Hatteras" section has an epigraph from Whitman and occupies the central position in the poem, using Whitman's male comradeship as the basis for a renewal after the destruction of war. Whitman points the speaker toward the second half of the poem, which seeks to incorporate suffering and desire, taking a subterranean route that balances the transcendental and Platonic quest for ideal completion.

After the publication of *The Bridge* in 1930, Crane received a Guggenheim grant that took him to Mexico and enabled him to explore the world of native Indian mythology and to pursue his quest for an incarnate love. A sexual relationship with Peggy Baird seemed to offer him the possibility of what he depicted as "healing" in his last poem, "The Broken Tower." Returning with Baird to the States, after a long evening in which he was beaten by sailors he had attempted to seduce, Crane jumped overboard and was drowned. His *Collected Poems* were edited the following year (1933) by Waldo Frank.

Robert K. Martin

Bibliography

Crane, Hart. *The Complete Poems and Selected Letters and Prose of Hart Crane.* Brom Weber, ed. Garden City, N.Y.: Doubleday, 1966.

Edelman, Lee. *Transmemberment of Song. Hart Crane's Anatomies of Rhetoric and Desire.* Stanford, Calif.: Stanford University Press, 1987.

Martin, Robert K. *The Homosexual Tradition in American Poetry.* Austin: University of Texas Press, 1979.

Yingling, Thomas E. *Hart Crane and the Homosexual Text. New Thresholds, New Anatomies.* Chicago: University of Chicago Press, 1990.

See also U.S. Literature; Whitman, Walt; Wilde, Oscar

Crime and Criminality

Homosexuals have been subject to criminal prosecution because of their sexuality in most of recorded history. Prior to independence in 1776, residents of the American colonies of Great Britain were subject to English statutory and common law rules dating from the reign of Henry VIII (1509–1547). Under those laws, anal intercourse (defined as penile penetration of the anus, and described variously as "sodomy," "buggery," or the "crime against nature," and normally classed together with "bestiality," or sex between humans and animals) was a serious felony regardless of the genders of the participants, even if consensual and performed in private. Before the English Reformation of the sixteenth century, sex crimes had normally been the subject of church law rather than the province of the civil government, and as such the "unnatural" sex acts were usually classed as *malum in se* (intrinsically wrong) rather than *malum prohibitum* (wrong only because declared so by legislation). These were capital offenses.

Under the common law, solicitation to engage in sodomy was also a serious crime. Oral intercourse was generally proscribed as dissolute, lewd, or promiscuous conduct, as was prostitution. The sodomy laws were not applicable to sex between lesbians, because at least one party had to possess a penis to perform the criminal act, but lesbians were nonetheless subject to prosecution under the other sex crimes laws, and in some cases lesbians were prosecuted as witches or heretics. The common law also condemned all sexual activity outside of marriage, prohibiting fornication, public lewdness, and open and notorious cohabitation of unmarried persons of the opposite sex.

After the adoption of the U.S. Constitution in 1789, the U.S. Supreme Court declared that the English statutes and common law rules that had governed the colonies remained in effect as state common law unless or until replaced by the states. During the first century of U.S. history, the states did adopt "crime against nature" statutes and other sex crimes laws, although in many jurisdictions solicitation to engage in criminal conduct remained a common law crime. By the time of the adoption of the Fourteenth Amendment to the Constitution in 1868, every state had criminalized sodomy, either through statute or judicial construction of the common law. The nineteenth-century statutes did not explicitly describe the prohibited conduct, which was normally called "crime against nature."

Although sodomy laws are frequently cited as the fundamental laws marking homosexuals as criminals, it is noteworthy that prior to the midtwentieth century they were not normally restricted to same-sex conduct, were usually restricted in their application to anal sex, and were frequently interpreted as not applying to lesbian sex. Further, the other sex laws that might be applied to homosexual conduct, such as lewdness laws, were also generally applicable to heterosexual conduct. The history of criminalization focused primarily on homosexual conduct is more of a twentieth-century phenomenon in the United States, tracking the evolving social construction of "homosexual" as a classification of persons. In addition, it is worth noting that homosexuals were rarely prosecuted for consensual sodomy, because most of such conduct took place in private beyond normal police detection. Sodomy laws were more important as agents of stigmatization. (When the American Civil Liberties Union studied sodomy law convictions in Georgia in the 1980s, it found that most of those imprisoned under the statute had engaged in heterosexual sodomy in a public place or incident to prostitution.)

At mid-twentieth century, the American Law Institute, a law reform organization comprising of leading judges, professors, and practitioners, undertook a study of American criminal law that culminated in the drafting of a *Model Penal Code*. The *Code* was responsive to criticisms that American criminal law was based on old common law concepts and obscurely worded Victorian-era statutes that failed adequately to communicate with the precision required by court interpretations of the due process clause exactly what was prohibited. The *Code* was also responsive to efforts by criminologists to reduce the intrusiveness of state regulation of private conduct. (A similar law reform effort was underway in England with particular reference to sex crimes laws. A parliamentary committee under the chairmanship of Lord Wolfenden produced recommendations similar in many respects to those of the *Model Penal Code*.)

The *Code* drafters determined that "crime against nature" was inadequately precise as a description of prohibited conduct and that, in any event, it was no business of the government what consenting adults did in private, so long as nobody was injured and no element of commerce was involved. Consequently, the *Code* replaced the common law terminology with "deviate sexual intercourse," which is defined as sexual contact between the penis and the anus, the penis and the mouth, or the mouth and the vagina. Thus, the act of "deviate sexual intercourse" applies essentially to anal or oral sex and makes no distinction between the

C genders of participants. The *Code* recommends that such conduct be penalized only when consent is lacking, if it takes place in public, or if minors are involved. Reflecting continuing concern about public order, however, the drafters of the *Code* recommended penalizing public solicitation to engage in deviate sexual intercourse, even if the sexual conduct were to be performed in private.

In 1960, Illinois became the first state to adopt the recommendations of the *Code* with respect to sex crimes. Through the following two decades, proposals to adopt the *Model Penal Code* were debated in many state legislatures, leading to reform of the sex crime laws in most of the states. However, many states refused to go as far as the *Code* recommended in deregulating private sexual conduct. In New York, for example, while adopting the terminology of the *Code*, the legislature retained the offense of deviate sexual intercourse for *unmarried* adults regardless of gender, while reducing the penalty by reclassifying the act as a misdemeanor, and also retained penalties for soliciting or loitering with the intention of soliciting deviate sexual intercourse. By the mid-1970s, about half the states had decriminalized consensual sodomy between adults acting in private. The states most resistant to sex law reforms were in the Southeast and the Midwest.

The budding movement for lesbian and gay rights took to the courts beginning in the late 1960s to challenge the constitutionality of the remaining criminal penalties for private, consensual sex. Some cases attacked the laws in jurisdictions that had not adopted *Model Penal Code* language by contending that they violated due process through lack of specificity. Although this argument achieved initial success, ultimately the U.S. Supreme Court ruled that the common law terms had acquired specific meanings through generations of judicial interpretation. As the new constitutional right of privacy theory emerged, embraced by the Supreme Court in cases concerning birth control and abortion, challenges to sodomy laws, including those outlawing deviate sexual intercourse, proceeded under these theories. In addition, because some states had removed all penalties for heterosexual intercourse while retaining penalties for homosexual intercourse, some challenges relied on theories of equal protection of the laws.

These court challenges have been successful in some states but notably unsuccessful in the federal courts. In 1976, the U.S. Supreme Court rejected a challenge to the Virginia sodomy law in *Doe v. Commonwealth's Attorney for City of Richmond*, af-

firming without written opinion a decision by a special three-judge federal district court. Early in the 1980s new federal constitutional challenges arose in Texas and Georgia, in both cases achieving some success in the lower federal courts but ultimately foundering in the Supreme Court. In *Baker v. Wade*, a federal district judge found in 1982 that the Texas sodomy law, which then prohibited only homosexual conduct, violated both the rights of privacy and equal protection, but this decision was reversed by the court of appeals. Meanwhile, a challenge to the Georgia sodomy law (which penalized all sodomy regardless of the genders of participants) stemming from the 1982 arrest of a gay man in his bedroom by an intruding police officer who had observed the commission of oral sex, achieved success in the court of appeals, and the state brought the case to the Supreme Court.

Ruling on June 30, 1986, in *Bowers v. Hardwick*, the Supreme Court upheld the Georgia sodomy law against the right of privacy challenge. The opinion by Justice Byron White asserted that the long history of penalization of homosexual sodomy placed such conduct outside the sphere of traditionally protected privacy derived from the due process clause of the Fourteenth Amendment. A week later, the court denied review in *Baker v. Wade*.

Prior to the failure of *Hardwick*, sexual law reform advocates had won victories in several state courts over the previous decade, most notably New York, Iowa, Pennsylvania, and Massachusetts. Before the *Hardwick* decision, most of these state court rulings were based on those courts' interpretations of federal constitutional requirements. After *Hardwick*, state litigation proceeded exclusively using state constitutional theories, with mixed success. The most important victories for sodomy law opponents came in Kentucky and Tennessee, with important intermediate-level victories in Texas, whose statewide impact was blunted by the refusal of the state's supreme court to deal with the merits of these challenges.

The combined result of legislative reform efforts and litigation was that by the mid-1990s, an overwhelming majority of the U.S. population lived in states where consensual sodomy was no longer a crime, and in some of the other states retaining sodomy laws, the crime had been reduced to a misdemeanor.

Early experience in states such as Illinois and California, where sodomy law reform was achieved legislatively, showed that repealing sodomy laws was just the first step in liberating homosexuals from the bonds of the criminal law. Solicitation and loitering statutes continued to be applied to the public activities primarily of homosexual men, and here reform ultimately counted as much on policy decisions of law enforcement agencies as on court decisions. In some states, however, courts were willing to accept the argument that once the underlying sexual act had been decriminalized, it was improper for the states to penalize solicitation to commit the now-lawful act; in some others, courts were willing to entertain the proposition that unequal enforcement of solicitation laws targeted on homosexual males violated constitutional equality requirements.

Combined with evolving social attitudes toward homosexuality, these legal developments led to a dramatic lessening of police harassment targeted on publicly visible gay life in many parts of the country, although such enforcement efforts still carried a significant threat in much of the South, the Midwest, and many rural areas elsewhere. Although sodomy laws remain on the statute books in about twenty states, most arrests of homosexuals under sex crime statutes involve sexual activity in public places, most prominently public rest rooms and parks.

The *Model Penal Code*, contrary to its British analog, did not recommend ending the ban on prostitution, which remains illegal in all states except Nevada, where the legislature has given local communities the option to allow licensed and heavily regulated prostitution confined to brothels. In England, by contrast, private acts of prostitution are not subject to criminal law, although public solicitation activities and organized brothels remain criminalized. Occasional legal challenges to the constitutionality of prostitution statutes have all been unsuccessful, the courts finding that the introduction of a commercial element into the sexual transaction takes it outside the domain of constitutional privacy.

Arthur S. Leonard

Case References

Baker v. Wade, 553 F.Supp. 1121 (N.D.Tex. 1982), *reversed en banc*, 769 F.2d 289 (5th Cir. 1985), *cert. denied*, 478 U.S. 1022 (1986).

Bowers v. Hardwick, 478 U.S. 186 (1986).

Doe v. Commonwealth's Attorney for City of Richmond, 403 F.Supp. 1199 (E.D.Va. 1975), *summarily affirmed*, 425 U.S. 901 (1976).

See also Bowers v. Hardwick and Romer v. Evans; Buggery; Civil Rights in the U.S.; Prisons, Jails, and Reformatories; Sodomy; Sodomy Trials; Wolfenden Report

Crisp, Quentin (1908–)

Fabulist, cult figure, wit. Diva. Nonagenarian (he of the blue-rinsed, once-henna'd hair). "A stately old homo of England." American in his heart. A resident alien now in New York. On income tax forms a "retired waif," after a stunning career as transient, illustrator (often unemployed), designer of book covers, freelancer, teacher of tap dancing, nude model for life-drawing classes (the first job "in which I understood what I was doing"), writer (kangaroo poem, unread novels, window-dressing volume, autobiography, book of manners, and now occasional pieces on film and lifestyles, not to mention selected diaries, about to appear), and homosexual exhibitionist extraordinaire.

There would be no *Naked Civil Servant* (the title to his memoirs) without a call: "My function in life was . . . to render what was almost clear blindingly conspicuous." The "rest of England" (outside of the already faithful West End) "was straightforward missionary country . . . densely populated by aborigines who had never heard of homosexuality." Therefore, Quentin Crisp, from the suburb of Sutton, son of "middle-class, middlebrow" parents, schooled in middling ways at Derbyshire ("a cross between a monastery and a prison") took upon himself the role of camp christ. (He was born on Christmas day.)

His was a clarity yoked to suffering. He courted the visible production of a bruise. Bruising, the seen result of cruising the streets as an open effeminate queer, became the sign of a message getting through; his wounds the sign that he, like any martyr worth his cause, was outing regularity regimes and the systematic failure of their forcings. His bruise was the badge of *their* defeat. The bruise was also, strangely, the sign of a tension between an effeminate dream and Quentin's cause: the dream, he would say, of THE GREAT DARK MAN. For the "problem that confronts homosexuals is that they set out to win the love of a 'real' man." "If they succeed," however, "they fail." If they win the love of a man, he cannot be what they would deem a "real man." Against this dream, Crisp plays the socialist. He redistributes the wealth of his sex to those whose *unloveliness* serves as the sign that he is choosing to love them as paupers. (About a man he called Barn Door—a great dark thing—he makes the remark:

C

"Because he had never known a world in which he had the upper hand, I became his slave.")

And so, as a spoiler of a dream he might have held, Quentin Crisp, as camp-christ-effeminate-queer-there-is-no-great-dark-man, makes us see that if "health consists of having the same diseases as one's neighbors," "the prophylactic is, never to conform at all." *Kathryn Bond Stockton*

Bibliography

Crisp, Quentin. *The Naked Civil Servant*. New York: Plume, 1968.

———. *Manners from Heaven: A Divine Guide to Good Behavior*. New York: Harper & Row, 1984.

See also Autobiographical Writing; Effeminacy; England; English Literature

Cuadros, Gil

Gil Cuadros published one important collection of short fiction and poetry entitled *City of God* (1994). Cuadros's poetry and short stories add to the body of work that deals, in an autobiographical mode, with AIDS. Along with David Wojnarowicz's *Close to the Knives*, Cuadros's *City of God* stands as one of the most disturbing, raw, and unsentimental accounts of the disease. His writings complicate the image of Chicanos in Los Angeles fiction in general and in Chicano literature as a genre dealing with issues of identity. Los Angeles in Cuadros's work appears as a political dystopia where a Chicano community and a Chicano self battle a history of violence. Cuadros's writings offer no easy solution to the "problem" of sexual or ethnic identity. Gay identity is politicized by race, ethnicity, and class, and Chicano identity is de-idealized by the dissolution of cultural myths such as Aztlán, the family, heroism, and masculinity. *Ramón García*

Bibliography

Cuadros, Gil. *City of God*. San Francisco: City Lights, 1994.

Rodríguez Matos, Carols A., ed. *POESIdA: An Anthology of AIDS Poetry from the United States, Latin American and Spain*. Jackson Heights, N.Y.: Ollantay Press, 1995.

Wolverton, Terry, ed. *Blood Whispers: L.A. Writers on AIDS*. Los Angeles: The Los Angeles Gay and Lesbian Community Services Center and Silverton Books, 1994.

See also AIDS; Chicano and Latino Gay Culture; Wojnarowicz, David

Cuban Literature and Culture

In *Machos, Maricones and Gays*, his recent study of homosexuality in Cuba since the 1959 revolution, Ian Lumsden reports that, as of 1990, "the only novel with homosexual content published in Cuba since 1959" had been "out of print for twenty-five years despite its universal acclaim as a literary masterpiece." That novel, José Lezama Lima's 1966 baroque epic *Paradiso*, has recently enjoyed cultural resuscitation in Cuba, not least through its prominent invocations in Senel Paz's popular 1990 novella, *El Lobo, El Bosque y El Hombre Nuevo*, and in *Strawberry and Chocolate*, the popular 1992 film based on Paz's novella and directed by the legendary Tomás Alea Gutierrez.

Little that can be termed a "gay" literature emerged in the years intervening between the publication and subsequent suppression of *Paradiso* in the late 1960s and the relaxation of state policy toward the open expression of homosexual themes in art and literature since the early 1990s. Ironically, at the point in the late 1960s that the Castro government began to suppress homosexual themes in its literary output (through measures as extreme as the internment in work camps of any suspected homosexuals), Cuba could boast one of the most impressive lineups of gay writers in Latin America, from Lezama Lima to Severo Sarduy to Virgilio Piñera to Reinaldo Arenas. None of these writers, prominent as they were, could hope to publish anything explicitly gay if they stayed in Cuba; of the four, Sarduy had already defected in the early 1960s; Lezama and Piñera died in Cuba, silenced and frustrated, the 1970s; and Arenas saw much of his creative work confiscated and destroyed, and himself frequently incarcerated, until his own departure from Cuba in 1980. Perhaps the only gay-themed Cuban novel to rival Lezama's in ambition and in brilliance, Arenas's *Farewell to the Sea,* was composed in Cuba, confiscated, destroyed, recomposed there, then smuggled out of Cuba, finally to be published first in Spain in 1982.

If Paz's 1990 novella marks the turning point in Cuba's regrettable official history with regard to open literary expression of homosexual themes, it also bears witness to the resilience of an underground gay sensibility in Cuba through those very difficult decades. It may be Lezama's most remarkable legacy that, in the face of impossible odds, his name nevertheless achieved adjectival status for those among his compatriots devoted to his work; Diego, Paz's gay protagonist in *El Lobo,* celebrates with his newfound straight communist friend an *almuerzo lezamiano,* a "lezamian feast" worthy of the sumptuous literary inheritance Lezama left for all Cubans, and all lovers of literature, to enjoy, freely.

Testimonies to the struggles faced by gay and straight writers alike in Cuba can be found in a variety of texts, from literary autobiographies and memoirs by Reinaldo Arenas (*Before Night Falls,* 1993), Guillermo Cabrera Infante (*Mea Cuba,* 1994), and Heberto Padilla (*Self-Portrait of the Other,* 1990), to more general studies, such as Lumdsen's *Machos, Maricones and Gays* (1996), Marvin Leiner's *Sexual Politics in Cuba* (1994), and Allen Young's *Gays Under the Cuban Revolution* (1984). *Ricardo Ortiz*

Bibliography

Lumsden, Ian. *Machos, Maricones and Gays.* Philadelphia: Temple University Press, 1996.

Leiner, Marvin *Sexual Politics in Cuba.* Boulder, Col.: Westview Press, 1994.

Young, Allen. *Gays Under the Cuban Revolution.* Madrid: Editorial Playor, 1984.

See also Arenas, Reinaldo; Cuban Writing in Exile; Lezama Lima, José; Piñera, Virgilio; Sarduy, Severo

Cuban Writing in Exile

Two historical events have had the most significant influence on the emergence of sexuality as a dominant theme in literary writing by Cuban exiles and Cuban Americans. The first is the 1980 Mariel boat lift, which emptied Cuba's prisons and streets of people suspected of or actively persecuted for being homosexual. The dramatic increase of lesbian and gay Cubans in the community already in exile in the United States forced that community to address for the first time its own deeply homophobic attitudes. After Mariel, the 1984 release of *Improper Conduct,* Nestor Almendros's film documentary of the Cuban regime's forced detention of homosexuals in work camps in the late 1960s, again challenged the exile community to rethink its own intolerance of homosexuality in the face of its vocal condemnation of such practices on the island.

A more subjective but no less compelling account of life especially for gay men in Cuba's prisons may be found in novelist Reinaldo Arenas's landmark autobiography, *Before Night Falls* (1993). Arenas, himself a *marielito,* became perhaps the most noted Cuban exile writer of his time, as a combined result both of his well-publicized 1990 suicide during the late stages of his struggle with AIDS and of the publication and translation into English of his varied and substantial body of literary work, much of it deeply critical of Cuban homophobia on and off the island. In addition to Arenas, other Cuban writers of note who have gone into exile have published memoirs that to varying degrees take up the issue of Cuba's repressive treatment of its artists and itsqueers. These include Guillermo Cabrera Infante, whose essays collected in the volume *Mea Cuba* (1994) recount the artistic and personal struggles in Cuba of such figures as the novelist José Lezama Lima and the playwright Virgilio Piñera, as well as Arenas himself. Another is the poet Herberto Padilla, whose memoir *Self-Portrait of the Other* (1990) offers an even more intimate account of these writers' struggles, chiefly because Padilla himself remained in Cuba with them until1980, while Cabrera Infante went into exile in Brussels and London in the mid-1960s.

In the 1990s, gay and nongay Cubans writing in exile have been increasingly drawn to homosexual themes and homoerotic effects in their work. These texts run the gamut of literary genres. Relatively mainstream, successful novelists like Oscar Hijuelos (in *The Mambo Kings Play Song of Love,* 1989) and Cristina García (in *Dreaming in Cuban,* 1992) have either inflected their work with subtle homoeroticism or woven minor gay characters into their stories. Playwrights whose work has commanded serious critical attention, but less popular success, like Eduardo Machado (the *Floating Islands* Plays, 1991) and Dolores Prida (*Beautiful Señoritas and Other Plays,* 1991) have featured homosexual themes quite prominently in their theatrical work. Other fiction writers, like Achy Obejas (*We Came All the Way From Cuba So You Could Dress Like This?,* 1994 and *Memory Mambo,* 1996) and Elías Miguel Muñoz (*Crazy Love,* 1987, and *The Greatest Performance,* 1991), struggled in the 1990s to find a wider audience; they have, however, foregrounded lesbian and gay themes quite prominently in their work. Among Cuban American poets, the prominent "queer" voice belongs to Rafael Campo, an accomplished formalist whose published collections of verse (*The Other Man Was Me,* 1993, and *What the Body Told,* 1996) also quite explicitly and movingly describe the poet's experiences as a gay Cuban American, and as a doctor devoted to the care of people with AIDS.

In the mid-1990s, popular Cuban exile cultural figures like cabaret singer Albita Rodríguez (*No Se Parece a Nada*, 1995), comedian Marga Gómez (*A Line Around the Block*, 1996), and performance artist Carmelita Tropicana (*Milk of Amnesia*, 1994) have, to varying degrees, enjoyed both critical and even some commercial success with material, song lyrics, and written performance pieces that highlight issues of sexual and national identity simultaneously. And while he left behind no conventionally written texts, Pedro Zamora's real-life "performance" on MTV's 1994 installment of *The Real World* can certainly be read as the poignant symbolic inscription of one young gay man's battle with both bigotry and AIDS. MTV's hour-long "memorial" to Zamora on the occasion of his death explores in detail his Cuban family's struggle first to accept his homosexuality and later to educate the Cuban exile community against its persistent homophobia.

As a result of, and alongside, this remarkable boom in Cuban exile literary and cultural production on issues of sexuality, critical and scholarly work in the United States on Cuban and Cuban exile culture has also notably increased. While there is nothing explicitly gay about *Life on the Hyphen* (1994), Gustavo Pérez-Firmat's recent study of Cuban American culture, Pérez-Firmat's reading in that text of Desi Arnaz as both a sexual and cultural icon exhibits an admirable sexual openness that at least begins the work of relaxing some of the more rigidly held of conventional Cuban sexual attitudes. Academic critics working more closely within the space of "queer" studies, like José Esteban Muñoz and José Quiroga, have published provocative and influential articles in various journals and anthologies on figures like Carmelita Tropicana and Virgilio Piñera. The social and cultural situations of lesbian and gay Cubans on and off the island remain remarkably fluid; sociological and anthropological work by scholars like Ruth Behar (*Bridges to Cuba*, 1995), Marvin Leiner (*Sexual Politics in Cuba*, 1994), and Ian Lumsden (*Machos, Maricones and Gays*, 1996) has contributed valuable knowledge and insight to the work of more conventional writers, artists, and critics.

The "Cuban" situation is fluid and continues to evolve. It is clear that issues of sexual identity and sexual politics will continue to provide Cubans on both sides of the divide with at least one point of common, and compelling, concern, discussion, and struggle. The 1995 success in the United States of Cuban director Tomás Alea Gutierrez's film *Strawberry and Chocolate* suggests the possibility of posing complicated political questions in sexual terms; such a development could well transform the general discussion of U.S.-Cuban relations, a discussion that, at the time of this writing, remains hopelessly stalemated.   *Ricardo Ortíz*

Bibliography

Ortíz, Ricardo L. "Cuban-American Literature." In *New Immigrant American Literature: A Sourcebook to Our Literary Multicultural Heritage*. Alpana Sharma Knippling, ed. Westport, Conn.: Greenwood, 1996, 187–206.

Pérez-Firmat, Gustavo. *Life on the Hyphen: The Cuban-American Way*. Austin: University of Texas Press, 1994.

See also Arenas, Reinaldo; Lezama Lima, José; Piñera, Virgilio

Cukor, George (1899–1983)

It might seem odd that the only place the man who directed such elegant films as *Gaslight* (1944) and *My Fair Lady* (1964) ever came out in public during his lifetime was in the gay porn magazine *Stallion*. But coming out first within the gay community seems fitting for someone who directed many films that became key gay cult texts: *Dinner at Eight* (1933), *Sylvia Scarlett* (1936), *Camille* (1937), *The Women* (1939), *The Philadelphia Story* (1940), *Born Yesterday* (1950), *A Star Is Born* (1954), and *Travels with My Aunt* (1972), to name some of the most famous. The "woman's director" label that was often used to dismiss Cukor as a lightweight auteur inside and outside the film industry actually indicates his most crucial connection with gay culture, as time and again this director appeared to reveal a rapport with such important-to-gay-culture stars as Joan Crawford, Greta Garbo, Katharine Hepburn, Judy Garland, Judy Holliday, Rosalind Russell, Tallulah Bankhead, and Jean Harlow.

While this fabled rapport was true to a great extent (recall the stories about Vivien Leigh and Olivia de Havilland having secret meetings with him about their parts after the director had been fired from *Gone with the Wind*), Cukor biographer Patrick McGilligan also reveals that the director was often ambivalent about his homosexuality and about the idea of being identified with women actors or characters. A film like *The Women* is a good example of how complexly and contradictorily Cukor could express his feminine homosexuality (he disliked the term *gay*) in his films, as the film moves between high-spirited campy and witty comedy, mean-spirited misogyny, tender sisterly dramatic interludes, and conventional gender role sentiments. Besides his connection to women stars and characters, Cukor's often theatrical style and themes; his interest in costuming, decor, and aesthetic details; and his concern with fostering glamour and chic in a number of his films have also endeared him to many gay men—even though they may not know his name, only the titles of his films and the names of stars he directed. *Alexander Doty*

Bibliography

Clarens, Carlos, with John Hofsess. "The Secret Life of George Cukor." *Stallion*, August 1983.

McGilligan, Patrick. *George Cukor: A Double Life.* New York: St. Martin's Press, 1991.

See also Film; Film Stars; Whale, James

Cullen, Countee (1903–1946)

Countee Cullen is the poet whose work is generally credited with inaugurating the literary discourse of the Harlem Renaissance. Although the exact place of his birth is open to conjecture, Cullen is believed to have been born in Louisville, Kentucky, in 1903. In 1918 he was informally adopted by Reverend Frederick A. Cullen, a prominent Methodist pastor and political figure, and his wife, Carolyn. Frederick Cullen's homosexuality was more or less an open secret in Harlem at the time, which led to much speculation about the exact nature of his very close relationship with the young Countee. A gifted student, Cullen earned a bachelor's degree Phi Beta Kappa from New York University and a master's degree in English and French from Harvard. These credentials set him up beautifully to play the role in 1920s black literary culture for which he was soon drafted. His personal reticence and gentility as well as his commitment to formal conservatism when coupled with his desire to explore racial themes made him an ideal representative and figurehead for the more conservative wing of race-conscious Harlem Renaissance writers and intellectuals, most notably W.E.B. Du Bois. These conflicting impulses were satirized by Wallace Thurman in his portrait of Cullen as DeWitt Clinton in *Infants of the Spring*.

Cullen published four volumes of poetry: *Color* (1925), *Copper Sun* (1927), *The Ballad of the Brown Girl* (1927), and *The Black Christ and Other Poems* (1929), and edited the influential collection *Caroling Dusk: An Anthology of Verse by Negro Poets* (1927). He also wrote a popular column, "The Dark Tower," for *Opportunity* magazine. Additionally, he published a translation of *Medea* (1935), wrote children's books, and worked with the novelist Arna Bontemps on a musical adaptation of Bontemps's novel *God Sends Sunday* that was later presented on Broadway as *Saint Louis Woman*. In 1934 he published his only novel, *One Way to Heaven*. Later, with his career in decline, he taught French, English, and creative writing at Frederick Douglass Junior High School in New York City, where his best-known student was a young James Baldwin.

Although he married twice, his first wife being the daughter of Du Bois, and none of Cullen's work deals explicitly with homosexual themes, he is widely believed to have been primarily homosexual. The most significant relationship of his life, one that caused much speculation that, to his credit, Cullen never seriously tried to quiet, seems to have been with the Harlem schoolteacher Harold Jackman, with whom for much of his adult life Cullen was inseparable. *Terry Rowden*

Bibliography

Early, Gerald, ed. *My Soul's High Song: The Collected Writings of Countee Cullen, Voice of the Harlem Renaissance.* New York: Doubleday, 1991.

See also African American Gay Culture; Harlem Renaissance

Cunningham, Merce (1919–)

Breaking with a half-century of modern dance, which treated the body as a vehicle for expressing the deepest truths of the human psyche, Cunningham questioned the need for weighty psychological concerns to motivate choreography. Instead, he proposed that movement was in and of itself fascinating, beautiful, and sufficient.

Inspired by John Cage, an early teacher who became his lifelong partner, Cunningham is most famous for his use of chance procedures as a compositional tool. Rather than rely on narrative or emotional experience to generate and sequence movement, Cunningham created charts listing the variables of choreography: body parts and their movements, areas of the stage, durations, and the like. Then flipping coins to select from the charts, Cunningham assembled sequences he would learn bodily and teach to his dancers. The results were highly structured and demanding dances, which disrupted habits and forced performers into new, sometimes nearly impossible sequences. For Cunningham, these chance procedures also took on a spiritual significance related to his interest in Eastern philosophies. By giving up control of part of the creative process, he hoped to work against the glorification of artist as creative genius in favor of a more workmanlike humility. While Cunningham could not escape the reverence shown to choreographic innovators, the method did produce dances less centered on the choreographer's personality than had previous modern dance approaches.

While Cunningham is best known for his use of chance, in many instances he seems to generate movement phrases more traditionally. Nonetheless, his aesthetic choices remain profoundly shaped by the unlikely combinations, difficult transitions, and unpredictable sequences his experiments with chance produced. His dances never build to a climax; instead, each moment is treated equally, leaving spectators free to decide where to invest their attention. Cunningham has repeatedly stressed this active role of the spectator, eschewing any one intended meaning that the spectator must decode. Interestingly, Cunningham rarely includes opportunities for improvisation in his dances, preferring set choreography. Even this set material remains mutable, however, with the sections of some dances being randomly reordered just before the performance, while virtually all his dances become excerpted and recombined in "Events." Originally an adaptation to the demands of nontraditional performance spaces such as art galleries or school gymnasiums, Cunningham's Events rearrange and overlap dances from the repertory into unique programs of continuous movement.

Supporting his choreographic approach, Cunningham developed a precise, highly variable movement vocabulary. His dances explore the body as a system of joints, combining movements of the spine, arms, and legs in a vast array of permutations. This demands not only the flexibility and precision of other dance techniques but also a mental agility to learn and remember complex sequences unsupported by musical or emotional logics. Freed from the demands of conventional elegance or emotional expressivity, his vocabulary also welcomes moments of awkwardness and more pedestrian activities.

Together, Cunningham and Cage developed a startling model of artistic collaboration, giving each participant broad freedoms and equal status. This model understands music, dance, and stage decor as independent, sharing the time and space of the performance but requiring no further coordination. The company often brings all three parts together for the first time in performance after rehearsing separately. Unpredictable resonances and vivid synchronicities inevitably result. The freedom of this collaborative method has attracted visual artists and musicians of the first rank, which in turn has drawn audiences and patrons from the worlds of music and visual art. These interdisciplinary connections provided crucial sources of funding for the early company, which benefited from the generosity of individual artists and from the systems of patronage for music and visual art not yet developed in the modern dance community.

Only the second man to dance in Martha Graham's pioneering dance company, Cunningham began working in a modern dance world dominated by women artists. While Graham reintroduced men into modern dance as archetypes of masculinity, Cunningham's less psychological model of dance making deemphasizes the gender of the dancing body. His dancers cultivate a matter-of-fact performance quality, and contact between them is businesslike rather than intimate. While a few of his works include same-gender couples, partnering more typically involves a man lifting or supporting a woman. The few examples of men partnering other men only highlight Cunningham's lack of interest in exploring explicitly homosexual themes, consistent with his determination not to make dances about himself. His near-exclusive use of cross-gender couples remained almost invisible in its familiarity until the increasing attention to gender and sexuality across the 1970s and 1980s began to make his choice appear oddly conservative.

Though some have criticized Cunningham's lack of an overt political voice, his politics are perhaps better understood as a way of being in the world, emphasizing personal freedom and peaceful coexistence, instantiated in his collaborative model. His methods were liberating for generations of artists and audiences, opening up creative possibilities and fostering a reconsideration of the nature of art and its relation to life. It is impossible to account fully for Cunningham apart from his collaboration with Cage, and that intense artistic partnership cannot be divorced from their personal one except by the willfully blind eye. Their long relationship has made them artistic heroes and gay father figures to many subsequent dancers and musicians.

After limited critical attention in his early career, Cunningham has become recognized as one of the twentieth century's most influential dance artists. In his later career Cunningham has continued to innovate, investigating videodance and computer-assisted choreography.   *John Bryce Jordan*

Bibliography

Cunningham, Merce. *The Dancer and the Dance: Conversations with Jacqueline Lesschaeve.* New York: Marion Boyars, 1985.

Foster, Susan Leigh. *Reading Dancing: Bodies and Subjects in Contemporary American Dance.* Berkeley, Calif.: University of California Press, 1986.

Klosty, James, ed. *Merce Cunningham.* New York: Saturday Review Press, 1975.

Kostelanetz, Richard, ed. *Merce Cunningham: Dancing in Space and Time: Essays 1944– 1992.* Chicago: A Cappella Books, 1992.

Vaughan, David. *Merce Cunningham: Fifty Years.* New York: Aperture, 1997.

See also Cage, John; Dance: Concert Dance in America; Johns, Jasper; Rauschenberg, Robert

Czech Republic

The first recorded laws against homosexual acts in Czech history existed during the fourteenth century, when Charles IV, who ruled from Prague what was then the Holy Roman Empire, implemented a law in 1353 that punished homosexual sex acts with death. There are no extant records that the ruling punished anyone. The law was subsequently removed in 1787, during the reign of Joseph II, when Bohemia and Moravia, the two regions that the modern Czech Republic comprises, were part of the Hapsburg Empire. Nevertheless, there are no instances throughout this or any of the subsequent periods in Czech history when a Czech gay culture was visible.

The moment that such a culture first appeared was in 1931, when a circle of Prague writers and intellectuals including poet Jiří Karásek ze Lvovic (1871–1951, né Josef Jiří Karásek) started the gay-themed magazine *Glas* (Voice). Owing to financial

reasons, the magazine folded after only a few issues, reappearing in 1933 as *Nový Glas* (New Voice). It failed once again. Following this brief flowering of a Czech gay culture, there was another long period of invisibility, for obvious reasons—this was the exact moment in Czech history when the nation was fighting for its survival against Hitler's Germany. The Germans seized Czechoslovakia in 1939, bringing Hitler's ideas of a pure race to the Czech and Slovak nations. One need hardly be reminded of the Nazi's attitude toward homosexuals.

Following World War II, Czechoslovakia established a brief democracy in 1945 that fell prey to communist rule in 1948. The totalitarian regime reinstated laws condemning homosexual activities, punishing those who committed them with five to six years of imprisonment. No one appears to have been actually punished by this ruling. In 1961, condemnation of homosexual behavior was again abolished, as a result of the strenuous work of Czech sexologists, who removed homosexuality from the list of diseases and subsequently influenced the legislators drafting new laws on sexual conduct. The regime did retain the paragraph (244) of the law, however, that left heterosexual and homosexual sex on unequal footing: the age of consent for homosexuals was eighteen, but only fifteen for heterosexuals.

Despite this apparent tolerance of gay people in Czech society, any same-sex culture remained invisible. Even though the former regime did not actively speak out against homosexuals, as in the Soviet Union, it did limit information on the topic from being spread and prevented gay people from meeting together. The state police, which kept lists of homo-

Jan Lany, Czech gay activist, Lambda Prague (1991). Photo by Marc Geller.

sexuals, used these lists to blackmail them into keeping contacts with the police. These lists were officially scrapped in the early 1990s.

This censorship of homosexual life continued during the early 1980s. It was not possible to publish texts that were homosexual in content or even place a "lonely hearts" ad in a newspaper. This began to change during the second half of the decade as Czech society began to become more liberal. In 1987, more information about homosexuality began to appear in the mass media as the AIDS crisis forced the general public to become aware of safe-sex issues. Nevertheless, the Czech gay community was rather ill equipped to deal with the crisis. By 1988, there was only one gay and lesbian group, the Prague-based Lambda, but its activities were limited to internal social gatherings. Most Czech gays and lesbians, particularly those who lived outside of the capital, were still living under the overriding fear of getting into trouble with the totalitarian regime. They choose to marry and live outwardly "heterosexual" lives rather than face the danger of public exposure or participation in clandestine activities that were available only to those gays and lesbians living in Prague.

The first Czech gay and lesbian political activist group, the Movement for Equality of Homosexual Citizens (HRHO), was founded in 1990 during the wake of the now-famous Velvet Revolution. In the same year, HRHO supported an openly gay man, Jiří Hromada, in his campaign to be elected to the federal parliament. As a result of their efforts during 1990, the infamous paragraph 244 was finally removed when legislators, working in conjunction with HRHO in drafting the new penal code, amended the existed law, making the age of consent fifteen for both homosexuals and heterosexuals. The following year, Lambda and HRHO were incorpo-

rated in a new organization, the Association of Organizations of Homosexual Citizens (SOHO).

It has been mostly through SOHO's efforts that a huge network of gay and lesbian organizations has been started throughout the Czech and Slovak republics. Its most successful work thus far has been to establish nationwide support groups and safe-sex education programs in response to the continuing AIDS/HIV crisis. In addition, they have helped to foster the growth of an increasingly visible gay and lesbian community by supporting gay-friendly discos and clubs, establishing several gay- and lesbian-themed magazines and newspapers, and sponsoring gay pride events throughout the country. In 1995, SOHO introduced a domestic partnership bill into the Czech legislature. It was voted down, despite a 1994 poll that indicated 78 percent of Czech people supported the law.

Despite such laudable advances in Czech society for sexual minorities, there is still a regrettable lack of openly gay and lesbian citizens in the republic.

Will Petersen
Martin Vodražká

Bibliography

Brzek, Antonín, and Jaroslava Pondělíčková-Mašlová. *Třetí Pohlaví* (The Third Sex). Prague: Scintia Medica, 1992.

Fanel, Jiří. "Gay Historie: Svět Gayu V Kultuře" (Gay History: World Gay Culture). Martin Vodražká, trans. *SOHO Review* 7, no. 6 (June 1997): 24–25.

Stehlíková, Dzamila, Ivo Procházka, and Jiří Hromada. *Homosexuality, Society and AIDS in the Czech Republic*. Prague: ORBIS Publishing House, 1996.

See also Nazism and The Holocaust; Russia; Slovenia

D

Damata, Gasparino (1918–198?)

Damata, a Brazilian writer and gay activist whose real name was Gasparino de Mata e Silva, published a novel, three collections of stories, and three anthologies. The anthologies of gay prose, *Histórias do amor maldito* (1967), and poetry, *Poemas do amor maldito* (1969), were milestones in creating a gay identity in Brazil, as was the pioneering gay newspaper, *Lampião* (1978–1981), which Damata helped found.

Damata's early fiction was inspired by his experiences of seaboard life. In *Queda em Ascensão* (Fall in Ascension, 1951), the friendship between the narrator, a Brazilian sailor, and an American soldier reaches a dramatic conclusion when the former fails to reciprocate the soldier's tentative declaration of love. The reticence of the relationship and the first-person narrative give a confessional tone.

In *Os solteirões* (The Confirmed Bachelors, 1976), homosexuality becomes the major theme. Set in Rio de Janeiro in the 1960s, the stories in this collection describe the lives, relationships, and attitudes of young working-class hustlers, soldiers, middle-class boys, and older homosexuals. The relationships are governed by inequalities of wealth, power, social skills, and age, with the attractiveness and poverty of the younger men set against the experience and loneliness of the older ones. The attitudes show a struggle for identity and self-esteem interspersed with cynicism, self-interest, and misogyny, with moments of tenderness and vulnerability. The lively, colloquial style of the narrative and the detached stance of the author raise these stories above their bleak subject matter. The best, "Muro de silêncio" (Wall of Silence) and "O voluntário" (The Volunteer), have been translated into English.

Robert W. Howes

Bibliography

Damata, Gasparino. *Histórias do amor maldito. Seleção de Gasparino Damata*. Rio de Janeiro: Record, 1967.

———. *Poemas do amor maldito. Seleção de Gasparino Damata e Walmir Ayala*. Brasília: Coordenada Editora de Brasília, 1969.

———. *Queda em Ascensão: romance*. Rio de Janeiro: Edições O Cruzeiro, 1951.

———. "Revenge" and "Wall of Silence." In *Now the Volcano: An Anthology of Latin American Gay Literature*. Winston Leyland, ed. San Francisco: Gay Sunshine Press, 1979, 98–144.

———. *A sobra do mar*. Rio de Janeiro: Ministério da Educação e Cultura, Serviço de Documentação, 1955.

———. *Os solteirões*. Rio de Janeiro: Pallas, 1976.

———. "The Volunteer: A Novella." In *My Deep Dark Pain Is Love: A Collection of Latin American Gay Fiction*. Winston Leyland, ed. San Francisco: Gay Sunshine Press, 1983. 171–224.

See also Brazil; Daniel, Herbert; Lampião

Dance: Concert Dance in America

The critic Clive Barnes noted in 1974 that many of the twentieth century's great male dancers and choreographers have been homosexual or bisexual. "Why then," he asked, "is the dance world so coy and mealy-mouthed about dealing with the subject on stage?" On the other hand, for fellow critic Marcia Siegel even the veiled discussion was loud enough when she proclaimed the same year that "so much dance these days is primarily a homosexual pitch." Any discussion concerning the (re)presenta-

Dtion of homosexuality on the concert dance stage is inextricably linked to one's definition of dance. If dance is physical poetry, it is then an art of metaphor and abstraction. Isadora Duncan embraced this theory that dance evokes rather than states: "If I could write it, I wouldn't have to dance it." Nevertheless, even in this poetic realm, to what extent does the gay choreographer or gay dancer's own sexuality manifest itself is his work? Russian ballet dancer Mikhail Baryshnikov contends that dancers are not blank slates, that "all the experiences" of the dancer's life, "all the images that his body has accumulated, these come up as colors in the dancing, giving it sparkle and complexity. They come out through the eyes, through the pores." A further complication of dance analysis is that audience members can "see" homoerotic content where it was neither constructed nor implied. Despite this analytic quagmire, it is still possible to celebrate the accomplishments of queer dancers, choreographers, and impresarios who have shaped dance in America.

While many a country established its own national ballet company—Paris Opera Ballet (1661), Royal Danish Ballet (1722), Royal Swedish Ballet (1773), Bolshoi Ballet (1776), to name a few—there seemed little room in a democracy for an art form that began in the courts of Europe, and whose very organization of dancers into principals and corps de ballet reinforced the notion of a classed society. Not only was dance looked on as undemocratic, it was also viewed as effete and romantic, and therefore unmasculine. By the end of the nineteenth century, American audiences preferred their dance performed by women in extravaganzas like *The Black Crook* (1866) and its numerous successors, and in leg shows like Lydia Thomas and her British Blondes. But beginning with the tours of Anna Pavolva (1910) and the Ballets Russes de Sergey Diaghilev (1916–1917), American audiences could witness world-class dance, including virtuosic male dancers, on their own soil.

One of the earliest attempts at an indigenous showcase for the American male dancer occurred in 1933, when Ted Shawn (1891–1972) trained an ensemble of eight men to tour as Ted Shawn and His Men Dancers. Utilizing Native American, folk dance, and sports movement, a great deal of Shawn's choreography was aggressively "masculine," showcasing his dancers as laborers, athletes, and warriors. When Shawn dissolved the company in 1940, they had performed over 1,250 times in 750 cities before over a million people.

Despite the contributions of Shawn's company, early-twentieth-century American dance was dominated by tours of Russian dancers until the formation of the School of American Ballet in 1933, co-founded by Lincoln Kirstein (1907–1996) and George Balanchine (1904–1983), dedicated to the creation of an American ballet tradition. Interestingly, the first generation of American classical ballet was given financial stability by two homosexual men who were neither dancers nor choreographers: producers Lincoln Kirstein and Oliver Smith.

Kirstein and Balanchine formed the American Ballet Company (1934–1935), the forerunner of the New York City Ballet (founded in 1948). As general director (a post he held until 1989), Kirstein worked behind the scenes of NYCB securing funding, devising ballet scenarios, and writing endless scholarly articles promoting dance, freeing Balanchine from administrative duties. It is generally acknowledged that Kirstein is one of the most important men in the American dance scene, forever altering dance in this country by enticing Balanchine to America.

Oliver Smith (1918–1994) had already established himself as a set designer on Broadway when he was asked to serve as co-artistic director (with dancer Lucia Chase) of Ballet Theatre in 1945; the company became American Ballet Theatre in 1957. With former members of the Mordkin Ballet (1937–1940), Ballet Theatre was formed in 1940 to provide a venue for original American classical ballet. Even though ABT and NYCB were both committed to creating an American expression within the classical ballet tradition, both followed the example set by Diaghilev's Ballets Russes in showcasing male dancers, acknowledging that male dancers were capable of being much more than escorts to the ballerinas. And it wasn't long before choreographers began to explore male/male eroticism.

This foray into homosocial worlds was not embraced by all. Critic Marcia Siegel was disturbed by "A whole series of ballets [which] could be grouped under the title 'The Making of a Homosexual,'" which began with Antony Tudor's *Undertow* (1945) for ABT. Siegel lists Jerome Robbins's *The Cage* (1951) in this group even though it concerns a tribe of female insects who castrate and kill men after copulation. Siegel was not only responding to the repertoire of ABT and NYCB but to any company that turned their men into sex objects, pointing out that no one could "be unaware of the sexuality of modern ballet's strong, sleek, handsome men showing you thighs, buttocks, and bulging baskets."

Even dances with no apparent sexual tension nevertheless can be interpreted through an erotic lens, given the display of the dancing body. The number of gay choreographers who included varying degrees of homoerotic content to their dances continued to expand, including Paul Taylor (Paul Taylor Dance Company, established 1955); Robert Joffrey and Gerald Arpino (Joffrey Ballet, established 1956); Alvin Ailey (Alvin Ailey American Dance Theater, established 1958); and Lar Lubovitch (Lubovitch Dance Company, established 1968). Concurrently with this trend was the 1961 defection of Soviet dancer Rudolf Nureyev to the West. His astonishing athleticism, sensuous musicality, and above all his commanding charismatic stage presence brought the male dancer to a prominence he had not enjoyed since the glory days of the Ballets Russes in the teens and twenties.

With the 1960s and a loosening of some puritanical strictures concerning the body and displays of the flesh, and the beginnings of the gay rights movement with the Stonewall riots in 1969, the next generation of gay choreographers approached homoeroticism far more openly than had been the norm.

The dawn of the 1970s did not mean, however, that "elder statesmen" choreographers did not learn to speak in a bolder language. Jerome Robbins's *The Goldberg Variations* (1971) was hailed by dance critic Tobi Tobias for containing "one of the most beautifully subtle inventive treatments of a male-male duet." And the homoerotic work of two prominent British choreographers appeared in the repertoire of American dance companies: Frederick Ashton's *Death in Venice* (1973) and Kenneth MacMillan's *The Wild Boy* (1982). Openly gay, many choreographers in this second wave were often quite explicit in their depiction of same-sex love and lust, including Mark Morris (Mark Morris Dance Group, established 1980); Bill T. Jones and Arnie Zane (Bill T. Jones/Arnie Zane & Company, established 1982); Stephen Petronio (Stephen Petronio Company, established 1984); and Peter Pucci (Peter Pucci Plus Dancers, established 1986). But most agree with Mark Morris that the issues are never more important than artistic skill: "My concern is whether it's a good dance. You can do anything you want, it just has to be good."

When Mikhail Baryshnikov defected to the West in 1974, the world of dance was bolstered again by a male superstar. But within a decade, this dance boom was undermined by the deaths of dancers, choreographers, and audience members who had contracted the AIDS virus. The deaths of Michael Bennett (1943–1987), Robert Joffrey (1928–1988), Arnie Zane (1947–1988), Alvin Ailey (1931–1989), Edward Stierle (1978–1991), and Rudolf Nureyev (1938–1993) were but a few of the scores who perished from this incurable disease. Lar Lubovitch organized thirteen New York–based companies for the 1987 "Dancing for Life" AIDS benefit, an event that annually raises money for research, education, and patient care.

Bill T. Jones inadvertently caused a critical maelstrom when the HIV-positive choreographer premiered *Still/Here* (1994). The work was the result of a series of workshops Jones conducted with terminally ill people of all races, ages, and occupations searching for "the resourcefulness and courage necessary to perform the act of living." *New Yorker* dance critic Arlene Croce launched a national debate when she refused to review the piece, stating that victim art was outside the purview of criticism. Despite the arguments and controversy, *Still/Here* is considered one of the landmarks of twentieth-century dance.

As many choreographers explored the capacities of male and female bodies to execute the same movements—jumping, turning, lifting—others were intrigued by the cultural construction of gender. Perhaps the most dramatic exploration of gender is the work of Les Ballets Trockadero de Monte Carlo, an all-male company formed in 1974. Established by Peter Anastos (b. 1948), Antony Bassae (1943–1985), and Natch Taylor (b. 1948), the Trocks present a burlesque of the staid conventions of classical ballet by performing the female roles in drag. With a thorough knowledge of dance history and dance styles, solid dance technique, and brilliant comic timing, the company parodies gender as well as its stylization in ballet and modern dance. Internationally popular, not only is the Trockadero the only financially successful comedic dance company, but it is the oldest all-male dance ensemble in America.

Romanticism shaped nineteenth-century ballet, thrusting woman and her idealization into the limelight. The Ballets Russes moved the male dancer front and center, not only to display his physical virtuosity but also to present him as a sexual object. Oblique references to male homosexuality on the dance stage became more overt in the 1960s as gay liberation made the exploration of same-sex desire more culturally acceptable. For many, the wordless

D

art form of dance is the perfect medium to explore the emotions of life and the possibilities of the human body.   *Bud Coleman*

Bibliography

Hanna, Judith Lynne. *Dance, Sex and Gender*. Chicago: University of Chicago Press, 1988.

Kirstein, Lincoln. *Dance: A Short History of Classic Theatrical Dancing*. New York: Dance Horizons, 1969.

Provenzano, Jim. "Mark Morris on the Move." *Advocate* (March 24, 1992): 72–74.

Siegel, Marcia B. *Watching the Dance Go By*. Boston: Houghton Mifflin, 1977.

Tobias, Tobi. "Ballet Partners—Matches Not Made in Heaven." *New York Times*, August 17, 1975, 1, 6.

See also Ailey, Alvin; Ballet (British); Ballets Russes; Ballets Trockadero de Monte Carlo; Bennett, Michael; Cunningham, Merce; Dance and AIDS; Diaghilev, Sergey; Dove, Ulysses; Goode, Joe; Joffrey Ballet; Jones, Bill T.; Kirstein, Lincoln; Morris, Mark; Nureyev, Rudolf Hametovich; Rousseve, David; Taylor, Paul

Dance and AIDS

Two dancers—two men—enter the stage from opposite wings, walking slowly toward each other until they meet face to face. Their fingers touch. Their arms arc straight overhead to form an inverted V. And as they turn to face the audience, their forearms glide down to rest on each other's shoulders.

These are the opening moments of the duet from Lar Lubovitch's *Concerto Six Twenty-Two* (1986), a six-minute piece—set to Mozart's Clarinet Concerto—that has become synonymous with AIDS in its U.S. performances. Why has this particular choreographic statement taken on such a heavy mantle? Medical sociologist Paula Treichler offers an explanation, arguing that AIDS is both an epidemic disease and an "epidemic of signification." (Signification here refers to the science of semiotics founded by Charles Sanders Peirce in the late 1800s as a way of conceptualizing the manner in which meaning is communicated via linguistic or visual "signs.") As Treichler explains, the meanings of AIDS far supersede its etiology as a biological disease, encompassing notions that are socially, not scientifically, constructed—such as the idea that AIDS afflicts only gay men, or that it is a punishment meted out by an angry God. Nowhere is Treichler's theory of the social construction of AIDS more vividly demonstrated than in theatrical dance, where the very body of the dancer is capable of spewing an enormous number of seemingly disconnected signs.

Consider, for example, the complex chain of meanings built on Lubovitch's unprepossessing duet. The starting point is a highly common if unspoken presumption: that all male dancers are homosexual. (This is a peculiarly Western notion forged in the crucible of American Puritanism.) A priori, the male dancer is coded as gay. As a result of the AIDS epidemic, however, this coding is further layered upon, the male dancer signifying not only homosexuality but also AIDS. This is based on the view, especially prevalent in the 1980s, that homosexual men are the most strongly at risk for the syndrome. Thus the depiction of two men in a relationship of tender affection catalyzes an inexorable chain of significations extending all the way from the male dancer to homosexuality to AIDS. In 1992, Jennifer Dunning, a dance critic for the *New York Times,* wrote: "Today, almost all dances for men are interpreted as alluding to AIDS, whether the choreographer meant to or not."

Such dance makers as Rick Darnell (of the High Risk Group), Joe Goode, Neil Greenberg, Tracy Rhoades, and David Rousseve have used these chains of meaning to their advantage, purposefully manipulating bodily significations of AIDS in their work. Their "outness" as gay men translates into outness as choreographers dealing with AIDS. Others—Lubovitch, for example—seem somewhat surprised by the interpretations imposed on their work but are not resistant to them. Lubovitch, in fact, chose to feature his duet at the 1987 Dancing for Life benefit held at Lincoln Center's New York State Theater, the first large-scale AIDS benefit sponsored by dancers (and Lubovitch's brainchild).

But not all dance figures have been comfortable with the linkages connecting male dancers to AIDS. New York City Ballet artistic director Peter Martins, for example, willingly signed up his company to participate in the Dancing for Life benefit, but not before telling the press that he didn't know of any dancers stricken with the disease. (That dozens of dancers in major American companies were then ill was already an open secret in the dance world.) Some major dance figures, such as postmodern choreographer Arnie Zane, have bravely chosen to reveal their AIDS diagnoses publicly, while others, such as Rudolf Nureyev, Robert Joffrey, and Alvin Ailey, denied their AIDS-related illnesses literally up to the moment of death.

Remarkably, despite widespread reluctance to link AIDS and dance, several durable AIDS organizations have been born from within the national dance community, among them the AIDS Oral History Project founded by Lesley Farlow of the New York Public Library Dance Collection in 1987; the Parachute Fund, a Bay Area emergency fund established in 1988 in memory of dancer Joah Lowe; Legacy Oral History Project, created by Bay Area dancer/choreographer Jeff Friedman in 1988; and Dancers Responding to AIDS, established by New York dancer Hernando Cortez in 1991 and honored with the *Dance Magazine* Award in 1997.

David Gere

Bibliography

Dunning, Jennifer. "Choreographing Deaths of the Heart in a Singular Age." *New York Times*, March 22, 1992.

Gerard, Jeremy. "Creative Arts Being Reshaped by the Epidemic." *New York Times*, June 9, 1987.

Gere, David, ed. "Dance and AIDS." *Dance/USA Journal* 9, no. 4 (Spring 1992).

Kisselgoff, Anna. "Dance: 13 Companies in 'Dancing for Life,' an AIDS Benefit." *New York Times*, October 7, 1987.

Lubovitch, Lar. *Concerto Six Twenty-Two.* Videotape, produced by the BBC, 1989.

Ricketts, Wendell. "Words from the Front: The Death of Rudolf Nureyev Has Refocused Attention on AIDS in the Dance Profession. But Why Are So Many Industry Leaders Tap Dancing Around the Issue?" *Spin* (May 1993): 73–75.

Schnitt, Diana. "AIDS Deaths Among Professional Dancers." *Medical Problems of Performing Artists* 5, no. 4 (December 1990): 128–30.

Treichler, Paula A. "AIDS, Homophobia, and Biomedical Discourse: An Epidemic of Signification." *AIDS: Cultural Analysis/Cultural Activism.* Douglas Crimp, ed. Cambridge, Mass.: MIT Press, 1988.

See also AIDS; AIDS Performance; Ailey, Alvin; Dove, Ulysses; Goode, Joe; Joffrey Ballet; Nureyev, Rudolf Hametovich; Rousseve, David

Dancing Boys

The informal, and occasionally formal, institution of the dancing boy—the term used by most Western writers in their descriptions of the Islamic world—has been attested for centuries by European observers throughout the Middle East, North Africa, and Central Asia, as well as the Indian subcontinent and throughout the Islamic areas of Southeast Asia such as Indonesia and the southern Philippines. These individuals have been called by a variety of names: *bachchec* [*batcha*], literally "child" in Persian and some Turkish languages, *luti* (itinerant performer), *raqqas* (dancer) in many regions, *kocek* (little) and *tavsan* (rabbit) in Ottoman Turkey, *khawal* in Egypt, as well as less specific designations such as *khanith* and *mukhannas* [*mukkannath*] (from the same Arabic root) in many areas of the Arab world, and *hajira* in Pakistan and India, which also generally designated passive, sometimes castrated homosexuals who were, in many instances, expected to dance and entertain. The specific terms used for these entertainers depend on the linguistic and cultural areas in which they were found. These generally young dancers invariably had in common that they were viewed by their contemporaries as being available as passive sexual partners, generally for financial reward. Although many sources stress the extreme youth of these performers, it is known that these men danced well into their late twenties and even much later. The word *dancer* might be better rendered as *performer,* because these two young males, who were often highly skilled in their art, sang, played instruments, performed gymnastic and highly acrobatic movements, mimed, clowned, and acted, as well as danced.

Descriptions of these young men and their dance performances most often appear in the journals of European travelers, whose shocked but breathless accounts display a homophobic sensibility familiar to readers of Orientalist European descriptions, ever anxious to portray the "depraved morality" and "degenerate" populations of the Islamic world in an unfavorable light. Missed by many of these observers, as well as by their more anthropologically trained modern counterparts, is that the dress and behavior of these entertainers had a comedic as well as erotic component that also played an important role in their performances. Comic sartorial ambiguity was as entertaining to Islamic audiences as the sight of Tony Curtis and Jack Lemmon dressed in flapper drag in *Some Like It Hot* is to contemporary audiences. The audiences for these performances were fully aware that the performers were male, which constituted one of their chief attractions for their eager clientele. In fact, in

D cities such as Istanbul, Cairo, and Tehran, where female dancers also attracted audiences, male dancers never lost their popularity.

Like young male actors who undertook female roles in Renaissance Europe owing to the proscription against women appearing public performances, young men throughout the Islamic world acted out the part of seductive or comic dancers in all-male gatherings, where the presence of women in male public spaces was unthinkable in a proper Muslim environment. A popular misconception both in the writings of Europeans in historical descriptions and carried forth in recent works, not only by aficionados of belly dancing but by scholars as well, is that these boys were attempting to pass themselves off as, or were disguised as, females and that their dancing was female dancing. This anachronistic reasoning originates from the notion that men had no access to women in the Islamic world and thus had to substitute boys. Such misconceptions may be readily dismissed when it is seen that throughout the Middle East, men and women dance alike (see, for example, the video film "Dancing," program 3, Morocco; Shay), and that the majority of these young men wear clothing that consciously and ambiguously utilized elements of both male and female garb. (A photograph [Jonas 113] of a male dancer from Luxor, Egypt, states that the "dancers are impersonating women." The dancer in question, however, sports a mustache, a bare chest, and primarily male garments.)

The dancing most commonly performed by professional, public performers is the solo improvised dance of the largely urban milieu, with its unlimited (within specific stylistic parameters) movement vocabulary and frequently erotic content. This dance genre has many local variations, the best known of which is Egyptian belly dancing.

Historically in large cities such as Tehran, Istanbul, Bukhara, Kabul, and Cairo, bands of these performers, usually accompanied by older men (often themselves formerly boy dancers) who served as musicians, plied their trade. Highly organized along guild lines, these bands in Istanbul have been describes by Turkish dance historian Metan And as servicing specific areas of the city, while Medjid Rezvani describes the composition of a group of performers for early-twentieth-century Tehran. Many observers such as And and Rezvani comment that the public musicians and dancers of the Islamic world originated from the Jewish and Christian minorities because public entertaining was an improper profes-

sion for a Muslim. While true for specific cities such as Shiraz, verifying such claims is difficult since few, if any, official records of this despised class exist.

Lest one think that this institution of professional male entertainer has disappeared, films of at least two professional male dancers were taken in Afghanistan just prior to the Soviet invasion of 1979, where the author also saw such performers in 1976. Wikan and Murray note that the *khanith* of Oman publicly danced. *Lutis* were common in rural Iran until the 1979 revolution, as were performances in both rural and urban areas of the *siyah-bazi* (comic blackface theater) in which at least one male performer dresses as a female (*zan-push*) and dances.   *Anthony Shay*

Bibliography

Afghan Village. Outtake footage of a 12-minute dance scene provided by Smithsonian Institute archives. 1972.

And, Metin. *Dances of Anatolian Turkey.* New York: Dance Perspectives 3 (1959): 3.

Beeman, William O. "Mimesis and Travesty in Iranian Traditional Theatre." In *Gender in Performance.* Laurence Senelick, ed. Hanover, NH: University Press of New England, 1992, 14–25.

"Dancing" (Video series in eight parts). Created by Rhoda Grauer. Produced by Thirteen/WNET and RM Arts, 1993.

Hanna, Judith Lynn. *Dance, Sex, and Gender.* Chicago: University of Chicago Press, 1988.

Jonas, Gerald. *Dancing: The Pleasure, Power, and Art of Movement.* New York: Abrams, 1993.

Loeb, Laurence D. "Jewish Musicians and the Music of Fars." *Asian Music* 4, no. 1 (1972): 3–13.

Mortensen, Inge Demant. *Nomads of Luristan: History, Material Culture, and Pastoralism in Western Iran.* London: Thames and Hudson, 1993.

Murray, Stephen O., and Will Roscoe. *Islamic Homosexualities: Culture, History, and Literature.* New York: New York University Press, 1997.

Pictorial History of Turkish Dancing. Ankara: Dost Yayinlari, 1976.

Rezvani, Medjid. *Le Théâtre et la danse en Iran* (Theater and Dance in Iran). Paris: G. P. Maisonneuve et Larose, 1962.

Shay, Anthony. "Choreophobia: Iranian Solo Improvised Dance in the Southern California Diaspora." Ph.D. diss., University of California, Riverside, 1997.

See also Hijras; Khanith; Mukhannath

Dandy

The dandy we must regard as the exquisite butterfly of cultural history—once sighted, difficult to pin down. Just as we do not know the origin of the word *dandy*, the larger phenomenon of dandyism resists definition and even circumscription. We may study it most narrowly as a phenomenon of Regency England. The fashionable world, "high society," expanded as the son of George III ascended to the regency in 1811; novels, select clubs, arts of the toilette, slang, entertainments—all created together a dandyism personified by George Bryan ("Beau") Brummell. He set the standard for the many dandies of the era, creating himself as a refined, superlatively well-dressed, and original man of considerable means and endless leisure. Nevertheless, Brummell's person, actions, and bons mots were always shadowed by tragedy and mendacity. He died a pauper, his pose shattered by poor health and loneliness.

To focus thus narrowly on a few decades and one man is to miss the central quality of dandyism: its protean nature. Metamorphosis and pose are at its ever-changing "core." We may regard the phenomenon in its widest sense as a mythical form, a culture's personified answer to the questions it poses about the ability of human character to bridge or annul the very binaries by which it is organized. Beginning with Siva in Hindu mythology and extending to twentieth-century artistic "personalities" such as Fred Astaire, dandies occupy the space *outside* a society's opposing categories such as male and female, revolution and repression, material excess and spiritual ascesis, nature and artifice, inner self and outer world. To trace the dandy more widely is, then, to consider figures across national boundaries—especially those between England and France—and across centuries.

The phenomenon expands and changes even more when we consider that in addition to creating themselves as works of art, dandies often have been artists themselves—writers, dancers, choreographers, painters, sculptors, actors, composers, and musicians. There exists a rich literature of dandyism in which actual dandies mirror in fictional figures their own already "made-up" and paradoxical selves of delicate strength, cold passion, voracious abstention. Dandyism becomes a hall of mirrors. Just as Oscar Wilde, for example, played the part of himself in everyday life and created the consummate dandy, Lord Henry Wotton, in *The Picture of Dorian Gray*, so many dandies deliberately blurred the distinction between art and life.

Important expressions of the dandy's androgynous form, his code of lawlessness, her sensitive cruelty, his exquisitely sociable aloofness may be found in Barbey D'Aurevilly's *Du Dandysme and de G. Brummell* and Charles Baudelaire's *Le Peintre de la vie moderne* (The Painter of Modern Life). These writings crossed the Channel, establishing the intrinsic foreignness of the dandy (in England, dandyism was a matter of "bon ton," in France, of "le high life") and its need for continual translation.

And translated it was. We may follow the movement of nineteenth-century French dandyism back to England, then on to many modernist cultures, American among them. For example, Willa Cather, Wallace Stevens, and Vladimir Nabokov all worked self-consciously in the tradition of nineteenth-century French dandyism, translating, rewriting, and reconceiving literary dandyism at the same time as they practiced a local version of it in their own lives of exquisite superiority, refinement, and intensity.

Jessica R. Feldman

Bibliography

Carassus, Emilien. *Le Mythe du dandy*. Paris: Armand Colian, 1971.

Feldman, Jessica. *Gender on the Divide: The Dandy in Modernist Literature*. Ithaca: Cornell University Press, 1993.

Moers, Ellen. *The Dandy: Brummell to Beerbohm*. 1960. Lincoln, Neb.: University of Nebraska Press, 1978.

O'Flaherty, Wendy. *Asceticism and Eroticism in the Mytholgy of Siva*. London: Oxford University Press, 1973.

See also Aestheticism; Crisp, Quentin; Decadence; Effeminacy; Wilde, Oscar

Daniel, Herbert (1946–1992)

Brazilian writer Herbert Daniel is best known for his work on AIDS education and sexual awareness. In *Sexuality, Politics, and AIDS in Brazil*, he denounced the perils of a social epidemic of fear and prejudice instigated by religious, judicial, and medical discourses on AIDS. Until his death, before he could coordinate the Eighth International Conference on AIDS in Geneva, Daniel was a relentless defender of open dialogue on all forms of sexuality. His autobiographical writings, especially *Passagem* (1982), reveal that Daniel reclosaged himself and became a guerrilla against Brazil's military dictatorship. After participating in the kidnapping of two ambassadors in 1970, he escaped two death sentences. Following a seven-year exile in Portugal and France, Daniel faced other conflicts. He scrutinized his relationship with orthodox factions of the left, for which homosexuality is taboo and an insignificant case of bourgeois decadence.

His social consciousness and intellectual honesty also prompted him to attack the homosexual ghetto. He questioned the idea that homosexuals are marginal because they are born different beings, a fabrication of marginality that contributes to the commercialization of products or otherwise, for a preposterously peculiar "race." According to Daniel, humans cannot be separated into heterosexuals and homosexuals (or even bisexuals), since these identities do not account for the enormous variety, blending, and crisscrossing between two such polarities. Daniel urged us not to ignore individual diversity that results from sexual aspects and circumstances like love, desire, pleasure, self-image, eroticism, fantasy, action, and gender-based appearance. Furthermore, he challenged the notion that gays are necessarily on the side of the oppressed. They can be oppressors of other groups or of themselves in the workplace, for instance, or even at sites for sexual entertainment. *Passagem* and *Meu corpo* both describe experiences in gay Paris saunas between 1975 and 1981, where wealthy gays' prejudice against nonwhite, poor, old, ugly, or other "repulsive people" takes the form of abusive sex, humiliation, and hate-graffiti. *Dario Borim*

Bibliography

Borim, Dario. "Herbert Daniel." In *Latin American Writers on Gay and Lesbian Themes: A Biocritical Sourcebook*. David W. Foster, ed. Westport, Conn.: Greenwood, 1994, 129–34.

Daniel, Herbert. *Passagem para o proximo sonho*. Rio de Janeiro: Codecri, 1982.

Daniel, Herbert, and Richard G. Parker. *Sexuality, Politics, and AIDS in Brazil: In Another World?* London: West Palmer, 1993.

See also Brazil; Damata, Gasparino

Dante Alighieri (1265–1321)

Dante is one of the greatest of medieval poets and, with Petrarch and Boccaccio, one of the founders of Italian literature. Dante wrote both in Latin and in Italian, in a number of genres, including autobiography (*Vita Nuova*), literary criticism (*Convivio, De vulgari eloquentia*), and political philosophy (*De monarchia*). His masterpiece, the *Divine Comedy*, envisions the poet's pilgrimage through hell, purgatory, and heaven. The *Comedy* is much more than a catalogue of vices and virtues, though Dante does incorporate traditional categorizations of sin—if only to transform them. Dante meets sodomites twice in the course of his pilgrimage. In hell, the sodomites are confined to the seventh circle, the circle of the violent. Sodomy is understood as violence against God's creation. Those guilty of it appear together with blasphemers, who do violence to God in speech, and usurers, who violate the nature of money. Sodomites are sentenced to run naked over burning sand under a steady rain of fire. As he makes purgatory his way, Dante is hailed by one of them (*Inferno* 15), who turns out to be his old teacher, Brunetto Latini (c.1220–1294), an eminent Florentine man of letters. The meaning of Brunetto's appearance has been much disputed. Some readers think that Dante means to teach that unrepented acts of sodomy are enough to damn someone, whatever talents or achievements he might have.

Others find that Dante here repeats the clichés linking the teaching of literature with pederasty, or that he means to remark on the sterility of the classicizing culture that Brunetto espoused. It is notable that Brunetto names as a fellow sufferer the Roman grammarian Priscian, a required author in literary education. Yet other readers find here the assertion that sodomy is particularly a sin of the learned and professional classes. Two further figures named by Brunetto are a professor of law and a bishop, respectively. It is best to take the disagreements over Brunetto as a caution against misusing a complex literary work like the *Comedy* as straightforward evidence for anyone's sexual practices. Dante is not interested in "outing" Brunetto or even in pronouncing some simple condemnation about sodomy. Evidence of the complexity of his purposes is found later on in the *Comedy* itself, when Dante encounters penitent sodomites. They are found not among those being purged of anger but among those doing penance for their lusts (*Purgatorio* 26). The sodomites and those guilty of heterosexual deviations move in two interlocking groups, each calling out the name of its sin. Here no sodomite speaks to Dante, and the only figure mentioned in connection with the sin is Julius Caesar, neither a Christian nor a contemporary. The reader of this canto does hear the voices of two poets who do penance of heterosexual lusts. The prominence of heterosexual lust might mean that Dante wants to keep a discreet silence about sodomy. It may equally well suggest that he feels no need to join in the exaggerated denunciations of the sin to be found in some medieval theologians.

Mark D. Jordan

Bibliography

Holsinger, Bruce. "Sodomy and Resurrection: The Homoerotic Subject of the *Divine Comedy*." In *Premodern Sexualities*. Louise Fradenburg and Carla Freccero, eds. New York: Routledge, 1996, 243–74.

See also Italian Literature; Sodomy

David and Jonathan

The narrator of the biblical First Book of Samuel emphasizes the special relationship between Jonathan, who is the son of King Saul, and David, the harp-playing shepherd-turned-soldier described as "ruddy, and withal of a beautiful countenance, and goodly to look to" (1 Samuel 18:1). "The soul of Jonathan was knit with the soul of David," the narrator records, "and Jonathan loved him as his own soul" (1 Samuel 18:1). Later, when Saul's murderous jealousy causes David to flee the court, the two friends suffer a poignant parting at which "they kissed one another, and wept one with another, until David exceeded" (1 Samuel 20:41). Jonathan's death alongside his father in battle with the Philistines occasions from David a powerful lament: "The beauty of Israel is slain upon the high places; how are the mighty fallen! . . . I am very distressed for thee, my brother Jonathan; very pleasant hast thou been unto me: thy love was wonderful, passing the love of women" (2 Samuel 1:19–26). While the biblical text does not state that David fails to recover emotionally from this loss, his career seems to climax when he is crowned king upon the deaths of Saul and Jonathan. Subsequently his moral life disintegrates, and he grows increasingly passive, both politically and domestically, until his death.

Historically, the David and Jonathan story has provided biblical Judeo-Christianity's most influential justification of homoerotic love. Oscar Wilde used David and Jonathan to exemplify "the love that dare not speak its name," and reference to their relationship has proven an effective means of alluding to a sexual and psychological reality that—for various reasons at various times—could not be otherwise named. Vernacular renditions of David's elegy for Jonathan functioned, in part, as a religiously sanctioned means of expressing male same-sex desire, while David and Jonathan's weeping at parting—iconographically related to John the Beloved's tenderly laying his head on Jesus' bosom—permitted the representation of physical and emotional intimacy between men in religious art. David's relationship with Jonathan allowed Abraham Cowley to exalt male friendship in *Davideis* (1656), while D. H. Lawrence—deeply conflicted about his own homosexual desires—was psychologically indebted to the depiction of "man-for-man love" in *The Books of Samuel* and dramatized David and Jonathan's swearing their covenant in his play *David* (1926). In nineteenth- and early-twentieth-century English-language texts, the phrase "passing the love of women" functioned as a code for male same-sex love when more open expression would have been met with disdain and possibly even prosecution.

The homosexual nature of David and Jonathan's relationship has been more explicitly asserted by modern writers. In André Gide's *Saul* (1896), a psychological drama of sexual repression and emotional disintegration, the title character is jealous of his son's relationship with the comely young shepherd whom he himself covets. The Bible-imbued ethos of American black culture permitted James Baldwin to use the David and Jonathan story subtly to dissect the discovery of same-sex desire in his short story "The Outing" and, in *Giovanni's Room* (1956), to explore the tragic consequences of a man's inability to accept the strange package that love sometimes arrives in. Activist Wallace Hamilton makes explicit the homoerotic possibilities of the biblical narrative in his novel *David at Olivet* (1979).

This literary tradition has been reinforced by two fifteenth-century sculptural representations of David as the slayer of Goliath. The bronze David of Donatello depicts a beautiful naked youth standing over the severed head of the defeated Philistine giant, on whose helmet is depicted a Triumph of Cupid, the plume on which rises suggestively along the interior of the naked boy's inner thigh toward his buttocks. As Richard Howard astutely comments in *The Giant on Giant-Killing* (1976), Donatello's statue suggests that David's power was entirely erotic, the older man being slain by the boy's beauty, not by martial prowess or with divine assistance. Michelangelo's famous white marble colossus, on the other hand, has become the symbol of adult male beauty, one effectively appropriated by gay men in both pre- and post-Stonewall culture.

Conservative writers have attempted to contain the homoerotic resonance of David and Jonathan's relationship. The compilers of the biblical Books of Chronicles, for example, deleted the episodes of David's affection for Jonathan, and in *The Jewish Antiquities* (early first century C.E.), historian Josephus carefully emphasized that Jonathan "revered [David] for his virtue." More recently, novelist Joseph Heller has an irrepressibly heterosexual

David and Jonathan are represented in the two top panels this thirteenth-century illuminated manuscript: in the first Jonathan warns David of imminent danger; in the second, they embrace and part. Pierpont Morgan Library/Art Resource, NY.

David complain that "most likely it was that line about Jonathan, love, and women near the end of my famous elegy that is more to blame than anything for the malicious gossip about the two of us," protesting finally, "I am David the King, not Oscar Wilde" (*God Knows*, 1984). Such efforts to defeat the text's suggestiveness, however, seem only to prove how strong those suggestions are.

Raymond-Jean Frontain

Bibliography

Frontain, Raymond-Jean. "James Baldwin's *Giovanni's Room* and the Biblical Myth of David." *CEA Critic* 57, no. 2 (Winter 1995): 41–58.

———. "'Ruddy and goodly to look at withal': Drayton, Cowley, and the Biblical Model for Renaissance Hom[m]osexuality." *Cahiers Elisabethains* 36 (October 1989): 11–24.

Horner, Tom. *Jonathan Loved David: Homosexuality in Biblical Times.* Philadelphia: Westminster Press, 1978.

Lerner, Anne Lapidus. *Passing the Love of Women: A Study of Gide's "Saul."* Lanham, Md.: University Press of America, 1980.

Pebworth, Ted-Larry. "Cowley's *Davideis* and the Exaltation of Friendship." In *The David Myth in Western Literature.* Raymond-Jean Frontain and Jan Wojcik, eds. West Lafayette, Ind.: Purdue University Press, 1980, 96–104.

See also Baldwin, James; Bible; Elegiac Poetry; Gide, André; Michelangelo Buonarroti; Wilde, Oscar

Davies, Peter Maxwell (1934–)

Sir Peter Maxwell Davies is an English composer and conductor who studied with Goffredo Petrassi (1957), and with Milton Babbitt and Roger Sessions (1962–1964). With Harrison Birtwistle and Alexander Goehr, he founded New Music Manchester, an ensemble to perform their works and those of the continental avant-garde. He also cofounded the contemporary ensemble Pierrot Players in 1967, later renamed The Fires of London, which disbanded in 1987. Davies is prolific, writing numerous stage and concert works for various combinations. Among the most important are *Prolation* (orchestra, 1959), *Taverner* (opera, 1962–68), *Revelation and Fall* (stage work, 1965–66), *Notre Dame des fleurs* (mini-opera, 1966), *Worldes Blis: Motet for Orchestra* (1966–69), *Eight Songs for a Mad King* (voice and

ensemble, 1969), film music for Ken Russell's *The Devils* (1970), four symphonies (1973–1976, 1980, 1984, 1989), *A Mirror of Whitening Light* (chamber orchestra, 1976–1977), *Salome* (ballet, 1978), and *Resurrection* (opera, 1988). Numerous concerti for solo instruments and orchestra include those written for the Scottish Chamber Orchestra, where he has been associate composer and conductor since 1985. The early works are characterized by bizarrely imaginative expressionism, references to medieval Anglo-Saxon culture, and enraged alienation from sentiment and conformity; since the 1980s, many works have been calmer and more traditional but still characteristically intellectual. Davies's works often exhibit strong political engagement; a few works (*Dark Angels* [voice and guitar, 1974] and *The Lighthouse* [chamber opera, 1980]) focus on men alone, and the brutal satire of the early works could be read as a sublimated response to being gay in a straight society.

Paul Attinello

Bibliography

Griffiths, Paul. *Peter Maxwell Davies.* London: Robson, 1982.

Pruslin, Stephen, ed. *Peter Maxwell Davies: Studies from Two Decades.* London: Boosey and Harks, 1979.

See also Music and Musicians 1: Classical Music

Davies, Terence (1945–)

Gay British filmmaker Terence Davies was born in Liverpool in 1945. The youngest of ten children, Davies grew up in a working-class Catholic family. To escape poverty and his abusive father, he turned to film and fell in love with the American musical. Davies dropped out of school at fifteen to act, but prudence made him return and study to become an accountant. When he was twenty-seven, Davies abandoned prudence, quit his accounting job, and began drama school.

He immediately began to use film to express his sense of alienation as a young gay man, but he couldn't forget the powerful images of *Singing in the Rain* and Doris Day in *Young at Heart*. The British Film Institute produced three of Davies's short films: *Children* (1976), *Madonna* (1980), and *Death and Transfiguration* (1983). The trilogy traced the life of Robert Tucker, a gay man tortured by poverty, an abusive father, and an oppressive Catholic upbringing. The films were autobiographical, a series of translations of Davies's childhood traumas onto the screen. The morose shorts were a hit in the gay community, and they garnered critical acclaim as they traveled the festival circuit, but their length and format (16 millimeter, black and white) made them anything but commercially accessible.

Davies's first two full-length films combined autobiography, social criticism, and the musical. His approach was minimalist, as well as personal and unflinchingly noncommercial as he continued to translate the working-class Britain of his youth onto the screen. *Distant Voices, Still Lives* (1988) was a dark, antinostalgic melodrama that graphically chronicled the domestic violence of Davies's youth; the film captured the International Critics Award at Cannes that year. Davies's camera remained for the most part in the home, suggesting the family's confinement. Smatterings of bright color and oxymoronic show tunes developed an escapist theme. His next effort, *The Long Day Closes* (1992), was slightly more optimistic. This time, the family is without a cruel patriarch (Davies's own father died in 1955, and *The Long Day Closes* takes place in 1955–1956). His precocious, gay, eleven-year-old protagonist struggles to fit in at a new school and escapes his troubled world by going to the movies and listening to the BBC. Again, Davies uses pop culture to develop a theme of escapism amid the rainy, pub-filled streets of pre-Beatles Liverpool.

In 1995, Davies—by now an art house favorite—adapted John Kennedy Toole's *Neon Bible* into his most accessible and entertaining film. He declared himself finished with autobiography and made a film about a World War II–era working-class family in the American South's Bible Belt. However, the stock Terence Davies characters—abusive father, ineffectual mother, precocious boy—make their return. The young protagonist has already escaped his confining home and remembers coming-of-age thanks to a visit from his aunt May (wonderfully played by Gena Rowlands), an out-of-work singer whom the boy finds glamorous.

Davies, in his limited dealings with the press, presents a somewhat sad persona, not unlike his semiautobiographical characters. But he stresses his dedication to honesty and vision and its importance to his work.   *William DeGenaro*

Bibliography

Dixon, Wheeler Winston. "The Long Day Closes: An Interview with Terence Davies." In *Re-Viewing British Cinema, 1900–1992*. Wheeler Winston Dixon, ed. Albany, N.Y.: State University of New York Press, 1994.

Williams, Tony. "The Masochistic Fix: Gender Oppression in the Films of Terence Davies." In *Fires Were Started: British Cinema and Thatcherism*. Lester Friedman, ed. Minneapolis: University of Minnesota Press, 1993.

See also Film; Film: New Queer Cinema

Day, F. Holland (1864–1933)

If groundbreaking photographer F. Holland Day had never taken a single photograph, he would still belong in this encyclopedia. Born to Boston wealth, young Day was a flamboyant decadent aesthete who idolized Oscar Wilde. He traveled to England and got to know Wilde and, among others, Lord Alfred Douglas, George Santayana, and the brilliant but doomed Aubrey Beardsley. Returning to the United States, he formed a publishing house and brought their works to a stunned American public. He also mentored a young immigrant from Lebanon who was not only strikingly handsome—portraits of him are among Day's earliest photographs—but strikingly talented as well. (Kahlil Gibran would write and illustrate the immensely influential *The Prophet*.)

Fortunately, Day did take up a camera. A picturalist, he created photographs that enhanced the reputation of photography as at art by the rather backhanded method of using soft focus, chiaroscuro lighting, and historical costumes to echo the look of paintings. His photos were among the first to portray African Americans (mostly his chauffeur and family) with dignity, but it was his religious images that brought him fame. Those works today seem a little strange, juxtaposing naked men and hothouse Christian sentiment, but art critics were as yet unaffected by Freud and Jung; they loved his work. His writhing St. Sebastians and moody Crucifixions (he often played the role of Jesus himself) sold only as sex and religion can.

Wilde's trial and imprisonment (1895–1900) cast a lurid light on "homosexuals"—a word that had just been invented. Beardsley escaped by dying of tuberculosis, but many others saw their lives and careers wrecked. Day's religious works were now eschewed because he was seen to be a member of that tainted brethren, despite the fact that no hint of scandal ever attached to Day personally. To cap things off, a fire swept his New York City studio in 1904, destroying virtually all his negatives up to that point.

Being wealthy, he could be artistically independent of the public's opinion. Weathering the blows, he continued to produce, yet he was strongly affected. He became a recluse and his photography too changed dramatically. He withdrew in art as well as life; gone are the intimate close-ups of nude young men. Men, young and naked, are still there, but now his camera is placed at a distance. Gone too are the Christian motifs. Although the subjects continued to be religious, he now evoked the myths of Greece and Rome. Day knew Wilhelm von Gloeden, who also created fantasies of the ancient world, but those hard-edged shots of plebeian boys drowsing semi-aroused in the Sicilian sunshine could not have been more different from Day's work. He photographed the gods and heroes themselves, but circumspectly. Often the figure in an F. Holland Day photograph is just a small part of a dreamy landscape and so softly focused as to be little more that a wistful blur. One does not approach the gods too closely lest they turn on one.

F. Valentine Hooven III

Bibliography

Doty, Robert, ed. *Photography in America*. New York: Greenwich House, 1974.

Ellenzweig, Allen. *The Homoerotic Photograph: Male Images from Durieu/Delacroix to Mapplethorpe*. New York: Columbia University Press, 1992.

Waugh, Thomas. *Hard to Imagine*. New York: Columbia University Press, 1996.

See also Aestheticism; Gloeden, Wilhelm von; Photography; Wilde, Oscar

Decadence

In its most general sense, *decadence* (Latin: *de*, down, and *cadere*, to fall) refers to a person or society's loss of health, power, morals, or economic growth, as well as any appreciation or support of such changes. Major prenineteenth-century literary discussions of decadence include Charles-Louis le Secondat, Baron de La Brède et de Montesquieu's *Considérations sur les causes de la grandeur des Romains et de leur décadence* (1734), Edward Gibbon's *The History of the Decline and Fall of the Roman Empire* (1776–1788), and the works of the Marquis de Sade. The first known use of the term *decadence* in English is in Thomas Carlyle's *History of the French Revolution* (1837).

During the nineteenth century, *decadence* acquired an aesthetic meaning applied to both lifestyle and literature, where literature is defined as decadent either because of its representation of a decadent lifestyle or because of its structural deformation and its seemingly excessive refinement of style, form, and/or language. Most decadent authors were not decadent; that is, their literature did not accurately reflect their lives. Major decadent authors include Théophile Gautier, Charles Baudelaire, Joris-Karl Huysmans, Algernon Swinburne, Oscar Wilde, Fedor Sologub, Rachilde, and Gabriele D'Annunzio. While these authors would not feel comfortable being grouped together under the roof of one decadent hothouse, they all imply or assert a belief that art has no moral or political responsibility, and attend instead to the appreciation of beauty through the unique mind of each individual. Didactic art that enforces conventional notions of morality, social growth, and the natural as healthy were seen as lacking individuality, and were challenged through a valorization of immorality, lethargy, and what was regarded as the unnatural and artificial. The correlation of same-sex desire with these qualities is apparent in works such as Gautier's *Mademoiselle de Maupin* (1835), Baudelaire's *La Fanfarlo* (1847), Jean Lombard's *L'Agonie* (1888), Huysmans's *À Rebours* (1884), Catulle Mendès's *Lesbia* (1887) and *Méphistophéla* (1890), and Swinburne's "Anactoria," "Fragoletta," and "Hermaphroditus" in his *Poems and Ballads* (1866).

The best-known decadent visual artists—Gustave Moreau, Félicien Rops, and Aubrey Beardsley—all died in 1898, and the movement has often been depicted as ending at roughly that time. However, recent scholars of decadence, focusing on the strategic aims of its proponents, have shown that the issues that concerned decadent authors and artists and the methods they used to address them have not disappeared with the vogue for decadent mainstays such as scrawny, pallid aristocrats; artificial vegetation; and the view of same-sex desire as deviant. Despite the conventional affiliation of pose and artifice with decadence, conscious self-fashioning was not an exclusively decadent strategy. The gestures became decadent when the subterfuge was acknowledged through such things as exaggerated physical gestures or excesses in literary form. Celebrating the artifice in all of us, proponents of decadence from Gautier to Wilde to neo-Gothic queers realized, to varying degrees, that exposing the fact that society often identified individuals by how they consciously presented themselves threatened to undermine the essentialist models of identity from which those in power drew their authority. The line of conflict addressed by decadents was (and is) not between the artificial and the natural (as has often been claimed) but between the celebration of artifice and its denial. Artifice, the decadents argue, is a part of the semiotic systems through which we understand ourselves as individuals and, as such, is not secondary or subordinate to any "natural" aspects of such comprehension. As the queer T-shirt of the hour puts it, "So what if it *is* a choice?"

Dennis Denisoff

Bibliography

Constable, Liz, Dennis Denisoff, and Matt Potolsky, eds. *Perennial Decay: On The Aesthetics and Politics of Decadence*. Philadelphia: University of Pennsylvania Press, 1999.

Felski, Rita. *The Gender of Modernity*. Cambridge, Mass.: Harvard University Press, 1995.

See also Aestheticism; Sade, Marquis de; Wilde, Oscar

Del Tredici, David (1937–)

David Del Tredici is an American composer and pianist who, as a child prodigy, excelled at piano and debuted with the San Francisco Symphony at age sixteen. He studied piano with Bernhard Ambromowitsch and Robert Helps. At the encouragement of French composer Darius Milhaud, he devoted himself to composition, studying with Seymour Shifrin at the University of California, Berkeley and with Roger Sessions and Earl Kim at Princeton. His early works include *Fantasy Pieces* (1960), anthologized in the recording *Gay American Composers*, and a series of settings of James Joyce. In 1968, he turned to the *Alice in Wonderland* writings of Lewis Carroll and began a series of large orchestral/vocal works including *Pop-pourri* (1968), *An Alice Symphony* (1969), *Final Alice* (1976), and *Child Alice* (1977–1981), a portion of which, *In Memory of a Summer Day*, received the Pulitzer Prize in music in 1980. Through the progression of these independent works, he reintegrated functional tonality into contemporary composition and became known as the leader of the neoromanticism movement. In the later 1990s, Del Tredici turned for inspiration to a diversity of sources, most prominently contemporary gay poets. His orchestral song cycle *Gay Life* (1996),

commissioned by Michael Tilson Thomas and the San Francisco Symphony, sets to music Federico García Lorca, as well as Allen Ginsberg, Paul Monette, and other American poets. *Love Addiction* (1997), another song cycle, sets texts by the gay performance artist John Kelly. Actively involved in the body electric movement, Del Tredici has spoken movingly in interviews to the gay press about his recovery from alcoholism and sex addiction.

Joseph R. Dalton

Bibliography

Galvin, Peter. "Silent Nights: Renowned Classical Composer David Del Tredici Talks About Life, Loneliness and Sexual Addiction." *Advocate*, August 22, 1995.

Schwarz, K. Robert. "Composers' Closets Open for All to See." *New York Times*, June 19, 1994.

Wierzbicki, James. "David Del Tredici." In *The New Grove Dictionary of American Music*. Saide Hitchcock, ed. London: Macmillan, 1986.

See also García Lorca, Federico; Gay American Composers; Ginsberg, Allen; Monette, Paul

---

Delany, Samuel R. (1942–)

This highly influential, multiple-award-winning science fiction writer, literary critic, and radical pornographer published his first novel, *The Jewels of Aptor* (1962), at the age of twenty. A trilogy, *The Fall of Towers: Captives of the Flame* (1963), *The Towers of Toron* (1964), and *City of a Thousand Suns* (1963), quickly followed. His *Ballad of Beta-2* (1965), in which the novel's protagonist, Jonny, engages in a quest to find the meaning of the a particular folk ballad, introduced Delany's ongoing theoretical interest in music (in his youth Delany was a Greenwich Village folk singer) and mythology. Later works, such as *Babel-17* (1966) and *The Einstein Intersection* (1967), both winners of the Nebula Award, demonstrated Delany's rapidly developing skills as a novelist capable of rendering complex characters and adept at exploring and challenging the theoretical foundations of the social sciences, particularly anthropology and linguistics. With his Hugo Award–winning short stories "Aye, and Gomorrah . . ." (1967) and "Time Considered as a Helix of Semi-Precious Stones" (1969), Delany established his interest in using science fiction to explore sexuality, particularly homosexuality. *Nova* (1968) reestablished Delany's interests in mythology and storytelling with its presentation of Prometheus and Grail stories within the context of a splendid space opera. Noted by some as a prototype for cyberpunk, *Nova* followed the exploits of Delany's characteristic protagonist, a sympathetic criminal outcast, and displayed his increasing range as a literary stylist. Delany's first collection of short stories, *Driftglass* (1971), was soon followed by his first pornographic novel, *The Tides of Lust* (1973), republished in 1994 under the title *Equinox. Dalgren* (1975) and *Triton* (1976) marked Delany's return to science fiction.

Although a best-seller and the recipient of praise, *Dalgren's* difficult stream-of-consciousness narrative was found wanting by some critics. *Triton* offered a return to a more conventional writing style; it also included, embedded within the narrative and presented in the form of two appendixes, Delany's current theoretical thought on science fiction as a paraliterary genre. If *Dalgren* may be understood as Delany's meditation on the modernist novel, particularly the work of James Joyce, *Triton* may be seen as Delany's first meta-critical text, as much about the misadventures of Bron Helstrom as about science fiction itself.

Following a six-year gap, Delany published *Stars in My Pocket Like Grains of Sand* (1984), a complex future history of a galactic civilization. In the 1980s Delany published his four-novel *Nevèrÿon* series, a complex treatment of sword and sorcery. This deeply thought investigation of race, gender, sexuality, and class as complex symbolic systems presents in each novel a series of linked stories. His most recent works include *They Fly at Çiron*, a fantasy; *The Mad Man*, a work of gay male pornography; and *Atlantis: Three Tales*.

Delany's critical work is considerable. A frequent contributor to the *New York Review of Science Fiction* and *Science-Fiction Studies*, Delany has published several critical volumes, including *The Jewel-Hinged Jaw* (1977), *The American Shore* (1978), *Starboard Wine* (1984), and *Silent Interviews* (1994).   *Cynthia Morrill*

Bibliography

Delany, Samuel R. *The Motion of Light on Water: Sex and Science Fiction Writing in the East Village, 1957–1965*. New York: Arbor House, 1988.

———. *Silent Interviews*. Hanover, N.H.: Wesleyan University Press, 1994.

———. *Trouble on Triton: An Ambiguous Heterotropia*. 1976. Hanover, N.H.: Wesleyan University Press, 1996.

See also African American Gay Culture

Deleuze, Gilles (1925–1995)

Gilles Deleuze became known in France as a political activist and philosopher during the demonstrations of May 1968. By the time of Deleuze's death in 1995, his philosophical activism had come to be frequently associated in Paris with gay politics. In fact, the French gay men's magazine *GAIHEBDO's* routine interviews with Deleuze and his "longtime friend," the late Félix Guattari, often cited him in the definition of French gay identity. Yet Deleuze was survived by a wife and children and rejected identifying himself either as gay or straight.

Deleuze's lack of visibility as a "queer French philosopher" stems partly from his own reticence to provide details about his private life and partly from his philosophical orientation. His desire to be "imperceptible" in French culture is underscored in the essay "I Have Nothing to Admit." Addressed and appended to the 1973 publication of Michel Cressole's *Deleuze*, the essay is Deleuze's response to Cressole's charge that Deleuze was an intellectual who took "advantage of the experiments of others—homosexuals, drug addicts, alcoholics, masochists, madmen, etc." (112).

Yet Deleuze's essay reveals how his relationship with Guattari had affected the writing of *Anti-Oedipus* and reflected his "philosophy of desire":

> And then, there was my meeting Félix Guattari, the way we got along and completed, depersonalized, singularized each other—in short how we loved. That resulted in *Anti-Oedipus*, which marked a new progression. . . . So they try to untangle what is undiscernible or to determine what belongs to each of us. But since everyone, like everyone else, is multiple to begin with, that makes for quite a few people. (114)

In the passage, Deleuze implies that if people are "multiplicities," the notion that one could be identified through only one form of desire is both inaccurate and dishonest. Deleuze imagines the philosophical project begun with Guattari, then, as a liberation of desire. Thus he describes his encounter with Guattari as one formed by multiple desires that inflects the history of philosophy.

For Deleuze, the history of philosophy becomes a place for this symbolic and sexual revolu-

D

tion. Expressed in homoerotic terms, philosophy is an important site for desire's liberation. Thus philosophy must be the site for "screwing":

> But what really helped me to come off at that time was, I believe, to view the history of philosophy as a screwing process or, what amounts to the same thing, an immaculate conception. I would imagine myself approaching an author from behind, and making him a child, who would indeed be his and would, nevertheless, be monstrous. That the child would be his was very important because the author had to say, in effect, everything I made him say. But that the child be monstrous was also a requisite because it was necessary to go through all kinds of decenterings, slidings, splittings, secret discharges which have given me much pleasure. (117)

Foucault once stated that Deleuze had "the only philosophical mind" in France and that Deleuze's work was a philosophical derailing of fascism. Deleuze's rethinking of philosophy as "screwing" suggests that Deleuze, like Foucault, saw multiplicities in sexual desire and identity as forms of political and philosophical activism.   *Kitty Millett*

Bibliography

Cressole, Michel. *Deleuze*. Paris: Éditions Universitaires, 1973.

Deleuze, Gilles. "I Have Nothing to Admit." Janis Forman, trans. *Semiotext(e)* 2, no. 3 (1977): 111–16.

———. *Venus in Furs*. Boston: Zone, 1990.

Deleuze, Gilles, and Félix Guattari. *Anti-Oedipus/Capitalism and Schizophrenia*. Minneapolis: University of Minnesota Press, 1983.

———. *A Thousand Plateaux/Capitalism and Schizophrenia*. Minneapolis: University of Minnesota Press, 1987.

Deleuze, Gilles, and Claire Parnet. *Dialogues*. New York: Columbia University Press, 1987.

Foucault, Michel. *Deleuze*. Minneapolis: University of Minnesota Press, 1989.

Grosz, Elizabeth. "Bodies and Pleasures in Queer Theory." In *Who Can Speak? Authority and Critical Identity*. Judith Roof and Robyn Wiegman, eds. Urbana: University of Illinois Press, 1995.

See also Foucault, Michel; France; French Literature; Sadomasochism

Demuth, Charles (1883–1935)

Charles Demuth, American painter, was born in Lancaster, Pennsylvania. At the age of five he contracted a hip disease that left him lame and dependent on his mother, Augusta, with whom he lived for much of his life. He studied painting at the Pennsylvania Academy of Art with Thomas Anschutz and William M. Chase, but it was during extended stays in Paris in 1907 and 1912–1914 that he came directly in contact with cubism, which was so important for his later precisionist style. In Paris he first met his close friend Marsden Hartley, and he frequented Gertrude Stein's salon.

On return to the United States in 1914, he became closely associated with the artists in photographer and editor Alfred Stieglitz's circle. He also was friendly with French painter Marcel Duchamp, whose notorious *Fountain*—a urinal signed "R.Mutt" and rejected by the Society of Independent Artists in 1917—was the subject of Demuth's poem "For Richard Mutt." Influenced by Duchamp's dadaist gestures and a general mania for "Freudian" imagery, Demuth punned on the male genitalia in pictures like *Paquebot "Paris"* (1921–1922).

Demuth addressed different audiences with three different genres of work: small figure paintings (including literary illustrations, erotica, and vaudeville studies), still lifes, and larger, more heraldic semiabstract pictures (cityscapes and poster portraits). These later works were attempts to speak in a modernist language that would impress Stieglitz's stable of artists. Almost all the poster portraits depict members of Stieglitz's circle: Arthur Dove (1924), John Marin (1926), Georgia O'Keeffe (1923–1924), and William Carlos Williams (1928). The poster portrait of Williams, *The Figure Five in Gold,* is Demuth's most famous painting. Demuth also did a poster portrait of the female impersonator Bert Savoy (1926).

Demuth's watercolors of homosexual encounters were made for a private audience. From 1915 to 1918 he executed a series of pictures of bathhouses culminating in *Turkish Bath with Self-Portrait* (1918), in which the artist and two other men seem to size up one another's physical endowments. Likewise, in the later *Two Soldiers Urinating* (1930), two men compare genitals, while in *Three Sailors on the Beach* (1930), a figure thrusts his penis into the mouth of another sailor in broad daylight.

Demuth's erotic watercolors share with his public illustrations for *Nana* (1916), *The Turn of the Screw* (1918), and *The Beast in the Jungle* (1919) a general pessimism about love. Although the illustrations do not take on male homosexuality directly, almost all concern the destructive consequences of sexual relationships. The deathlike man shrouded in a towel in *Turkish Bath* suggests that homosexual relationships were not exempt from this unhappiness. However, the scatological release of the later *Three Soldiers Urinating* expresses the liberating potential of homoerotic desire.

When told about an investigation of vice in his hometown, Demuth supposedly said that he was "going home to speak for vice." There in Lancaster, it was waiting for Demuth's defense. His paintings make the case that clandestine desire permeates American life.   *Jonathan Weinberg*

Bibliography

Haskell, Barbara. *Charles Demuth*. New York: Whitney Museum of American Art in association with Harry N. Abrams, 1987.

Weinberg, Jonathan. *Speaking for Vice: Homosexuality in the Art of Charles Demuth, Marsden Hartley and the First American Avant-Garde*. New Haven: Yale University Press, 1993.

See also Art History; Duchamp, Marcel Hartley, Marsden

Denmark

In Denmark during the Middle Ages sodomy was a sin dealt with solely by the ecclesiastical courts of the Catholic Church according to canon law. The Inquisition did not have jurisdiction in Denmark, nor was the prohibition against sodomy received in secular law as in central and southern Europe. After the Reformation in 1536, the secular law courts handled sodomy on the legal basis of the Bible (God's Law). This practice, prescribing death at the stake, was codified in the *Danske Lov* (Danish Lawbook) of 1683. Few of the known cases concerned sex with a man or a boy. Only one execution (1613) is documented; two other purported executions are uncertain (1628). The vast majority of sodomy cases concerned bestiality. Sodomy was seen as a transgression of God's will, punished by the secular state to prevent the wrath of God from causing floods, famine, and military catastrophe.

There is evidence of one case of sodomy with a man or a boy in the eighteenth century. During the trial, however, it became clear that anal penetration had not occurred. A seventy-two-year-old rural artisan was sentenced to two years at hard labor and ex-

pulsion from the province of Jutland for having regularly had intercourse between the thighs with a boy from the time the boy was eight years old. The then eighteen-year-old boy was acquitted. Although the trial was conducted in a local court, the sentencing was decided by the central administration in Copenhagen. In its opinion the trial ought not to have taken place. The local vicar was blamed for not having dealt with the matter discreetly. The politics of the government was to keep such instances of carnal transgression between males from public knowledge. Until the 1830s the authorities unofficially banned rumored pederasts from a town or province (*consilium abeundi*) if admonitions and warnings did not stop the behavior. The politics of silence was successful. In eighteenth-century Denmark sodomy and other sexual activities between men had no social significance, and genital sex between men probably occurred only to a small extent.

In 1814 the authorities in Copenhagen discovered a small group of men socially organized around pederasty and recruitment of military personnel as its central activity. The key figures were immigrants from France and Germany, and most of the others were in the theater. They secretly received official warnings, and one was banned to the Danish West Indies. This seems to have been the end of the group. There was no historical continuity to Copenhagen's early pederast subculture of the 1850s.

From the 1830s on, sodomy with men or boys was no longer dealt with administratively but handled by the courts like any other crime. There were twelve cases (involving twenty-one men and boys) between 1835 and 1866, when a new criminal code was adopted. Until the 1850s these cases were characterized by violence, force, and rape, and several of them occurred in the Christianshavn jail in Copenhagen. Between 1801 and 1850 the population of Copenhagen grew from approximately 100,000 to about 150,000. Thus the capital of Denmark had the size required among the cities of northern Europe to sustain a sodomitical or pederast subculture able to grow on a scale that would secure generational and historical continuation. In 1856 the army abandoned the fortifications around the capital, and these vast grounds did not become part of the jurisdiction of the Copenhagen Police Department until 1864. Certain parts of the fortifications became a nightly meeting place for pederasts and have served as such for homosexuals to this day.

A few decades after the emergence of the social role of the pederast in Denmark and of a modest pederast subculture in Copenhagen, pederasts and psychiatrists in Germany developed the medical and emancipatory model of congenital contrary sexuality—later "homosexualism"—which soon spread to the rest of the northern European and North American culture. From the 1870s recurring homosexual scandals in the Danish press and in the courts attested to a growing social panic and a growing homosexual subculture culminating in the so-called Great Morality Affair of 1906–1907, triggered by the adoption in 1905 of a statute making male (homosexual) prostitution a crime. After the turn of the century, the far larger and far more developed homosexual subculture of Berlin with its extensive male prostitution served as an important inspiration for individual homosexuals in Denmark, as well as for their antihomosexual opponents.

Under the criminal code of 1866, sodomy was punished with eight months at hard labor for attempt, one year for sodomy with an adult man or woman, and up to four years for sodomy with boys under fifteen years. Gross indecency (mutual masturbation) was an activity not foreseen by legislators. Court practice consequently established that it was not a crime unless one of the parties was under fifteen years. By 1912 the courts had raised the age of consent in such cases to eighteen years.

The sentencing in 1907 of a number of men of the Copenhagen bourgeoisie for sodomy—and for sex with minors—provoked the medical establishment, whose certificates on congenital homosexuality as an extenuating circumstance had been set aside by the court. Medical experts in alliance with the legal establishment and with the modern and urban opinion makers succeeded in influencing the Royal Commission on a New Civil Criminal Code. Its report of 1912 proposed the abolition of sodomy as a criminal category. The preparation of the new civil criminal code lasted until 1930. The code took effect in 1933 and established a homosexual age of consent of eighteen years (fifteen for heterosexuals). Motions in parliament to set the age of consent at twenty-one years and to punish not only the male prostitute but also the homosexual customer were countered in two articles in 1924 and 1925 in juridical journals by psychiatrist Sophus Thalbitzer. His articles provided scientific legitimation for the rejection of these motions. It was not known at the time that Thalbitzer was a member of the governing body of the Wissenschaftlischehumanitäres Komitée, the principal organization in Germany for homosexual emancipation.

In the period between the two world wars, homosexuality was less of a public issue than before World War I and after World War II. In 1924 the so-called Nekkab Association, which had organized drag balls and other social activities with a large presence of homosexuals, was declared illegal and banned by the supreme court. From this period also dates the first taverns and bars in Copenhagen catering to a largely (from the 1930s exclusively) homosexual clientele.

A general expectation of extended liberties in civil society generated by the resistance movement during World War II, the end of the German occupation, and the U.N. Declaration of Human Rights inspired a group of young homosexual men (notably Axel Axgil and Helmer Fogedgaard) to found in 1948 the first and still extant national organization for homophiles in Denmark, the Forbundet af 1948 (Association of 1948). The Forbundet af 1948 immediately began publication of the first Danish periodical for homosexuals, *Vennen* (The Friend). Homosexuality now became more visible. The comparatively unrestrained cruising activities in the urban space of Copenhagen (the Town Hall Square) and a probably real increase in homosexual prostitution attracted increasingly hostile public attention. The antihomosexual climate of the 1950s made it virtually impossible for the Forbundet af 1948 to pursue actively a homosexual political agenda. Until the mid-1960s the association concentrated on organizing social activities and counseling homosexuals.

In 1950, under a new police superintendent, the vice squad of the Copenhagen Police Department was reorganized. During the following fifteen years the police harassed the homophile subculture to prevent prostitution, cruising in public areas (cottaging), and sex with minors. A major scandal in 1955 touched on the leadership of the Forbundet af 1948. As a consequence the association's position was severely weakened, both within the homophile subculture and without. During the following ten years the political profile of the homophile subculture was formed by two "independent" periodicals, *Vennen*, now privately owned, and *Eos*, which were edited by the homophile activists Martin Elmer and Kim Kent, respectively.

Homosexual prostitution was seen in light of the theory that heterosexual boys and youths who sold their sexual services would themselves become homosexual (the theory of seduction). Furthermore, the cause and the extent of homosexual prostitution was explained by the demand of older homosexuals for boys and young men. To counter the supposed homosexual demand for young prostitutes, the government introduced a bill in 1961 that made it a criminal offense to obtain through payment a sexual relationship with someone of the same sex under twenty-one years. The so-called ugly clause was in effect for four years and then abrogated. When introduced in parliament the bill had already met with strong opposition from politicians of all parties and the press. There had been seventy-nine convictions under the clause, but the clause's symbolic significance was of far greater importance; it became the widely known shorthand for harassment by the police, legal discrimination, and societal oppression of homosexuals.

In the 1960s the general climate of fear that had characterized the 1950s lightened and was succeeded by the beginning of a more permissive society. Increasing international communication and wider cultural perspectives began to admit to the country the relevance of non-European cultures. "The homosexual problem" became less of an issue in light of the diversity of sexual behavior found in descriptions of cultures across the world. In 1967 homosexual prostitution was legalized by the same statute that also legalized pornography.

The Stonewall riots in New York City in 1969 inspired the formation of the Gay Liberation Front (Copenhagen and Arhus) and the Lesbian Movement, which gradually influenced the Forbundet af 1948 to adopt a policy that did not seek to legalize homosexuality in terms of the general value system, which saw homosexuals as a pitiful minority that should not be unnecessarily discriminated against. In 1977 the Forbundet changed its name to Association of Queer Men and Lesbians. (The Danish word *bøsse* is better translated as "queer" than "gay.") The association began a campaign for the lowering of the age of consent, which was subsequently changed, in 1976, from eighteen to fifteen years.

From the outbreak of AIDS in the early 1980s, the Danish health authorities cooperated more closely and extensively with the Association of Queer Men and Lesbians than did health officials in most other countries. By decision of parliament in 1987, the politics of the prevention of AIDS was based on "voluntariness, anonymity, open, direct, and honest information, the individual's sense of confidence when dealing with the health authorities, and the desire to avoid discrimination in any form."

In the 1970s the Association of Queer Men and Lesbians began to lobby for a change of the marriage law to allow individuals of the same sex to marry legally. In 1984 the conservative minority government was compelled by the center-left majority in parliament to appoint a Royal Commission on the Situation of Homosexuals in Society. Four of its twelve members were homosexuals, two representing the Association of Queer Men and Lesbians. The commission was asked to recommend measures to eliminate discrimination against homosexuals and to improve their situation in society, including regulation of lasting relationships. The draft by the Royal Commission of a bill on registered partnership between persons of the same sex was passed by parliament in 1989. According to opinion polls in 1988 and 1989, the majority of Danes supported the introduction of registered partnership as a matter equality and equal value. Arguments in favor or against based on nature, God, family, or the homosexual as a "naturally different type of person" were largely absent. They had lost their power of persuasion in the modern Danish welfare state.

Homosexuality in Denmark was largely a local variety of the modern western European–American social division of gender into three sexes. The comparatively swift dismantling of the social drama connected with the "third sex," as it can be seen in the changes in the regulation of homosexuality in Denmark after 1965, is probably a reflection of the small size of the population and its homogeneity, advanced urbanization, a welfare system that makes the individual materially independent of the family, and an electoral system of proportional representation.

Wilhelm von Rosen

Bibliography

Bech, Henning. "Report from a Rotten State: 'Marriage' and 'Homosexuality' in Denmark." In *Modern Homosexualities: Fragments of Lesbian and Gay Experiences*. Kenneth Plummer, ed. Routledge: London, 1992, 134–47.

———. *Månens Kulør. Studier i dansk brøssehistorie 1628–1912* (The Moon's Color. Danish Gay History 1628–1912). Copenhagen: Rhodos, 1993.

———. "A Short History of Gay Denmark 1613–1989: The Rise and the Possibly Happy End of the Danish Homosexual." *Nordisk Sexologi* 12 (1994): 125–36.

von Rosen, Wilhelm. "Sodomy in Early Modern Denmark: A Crime Without Victims." In *The Pursuit of Sodomy: Male Homosexuality in Renaissance and Enlightenment Europe*. Kent

D

Gerard and Gert Hekma, eds. New York: Harrington, 1989, 177–204.

See also Bang, Herman; European Commission of Human Rights; Germany; Same-Sex Marriage; Sexology; Sodomy

Diaghilev, Sergey (1872–1929)

Russian cultural arbiter, art critic, and, later, ballet impresario, Sergey Diaghilev spent his childhood and adolescence in the provincial town of Perm. In 1890, he moved to the capital, St. Petersburg, hoping to pursue a career in music. He settled at the home of his father's older sister, prominent feminist Anna Filosofova. His aunt Anna's son, Dmitry ("Dima") Filosofov, became Diaghilev's first lover, a relationship that was to last ten years. Together with Dima and Dima's erstwhile classmates, Diaghilev organized an educational circle—The World of Art—the name that was also given to the epochal journal that Diaghilev and Dima began to coedit in 1898. The participants formed the circle because they were dissatisfied with the way literature and the arts were perceived and written about in Russia.

Russia was an absolute monarchy that censored books and periodicals. Censorship was somewhat relaxed after the 1860s, the decade of the abolition of serfdom and other fundamental reforms of Alexander II. But that decade also left the country another inheritance: domination of criticism by radical utilitarian critics. From the 1860s to the 1890s, Russian critics demanded that all literature and other arts be topical, realistic, and politically relevant, completely ignoring such values as originality or profundity.

Diaghilev and Filosofov's journal, *World of Art*, broke this utilitarian monopoly. The journal was not concerned with art for art's sake but declared its artistic independence from reigning orthodoxies and party lines. The journal totally changed the artistic outlook of Russian culture, leading to rediscovery of the church architecture and frescoes of the Middle Ages, the rococo art of the eighteenth century, and the romantic painters and poets of the early nineteenth century—all of them heretofore condemned by the utilitarians for lack of realism and ideological content. The journal also inaugurated a new approach to the great Russian writers of the nineteenth century, examining their work as art and not only as propaganda.

But by 1903, the journal had lost its financial support and Diaghilev lost his cousin/lover to a determined woman, poet Zinaida Gippius, who deliberately broke up their relationship. During the first decade of the twentieth century, Diaghilev specialized in exporting exhibitions of Russian art and festivals of Russian music and opera to the West. In 1908, he met a promising young dancer, Vaslav Nijinsky, whose earlier lover had deliberately foisted him off on Diaghilev. The ensuing relationship led to Diaghilev's full-time involvement with ballet, which he exported to Paris and London, featuring the work of innovative choreographer Michel Fokine and centered on Nijinsky, whom in the course of their five-year relationship Diaghilev developed into one of the greatest male dancers ever seen and a choreographer of immense originality (he staged Debussy's *Afternoon of a Faun* and *Jeux* and Stravinsky's *Rite of Spring*).

When Diaghilev began his ballet projects, that art was in a state of decline. Diaghilev's *Ballets Russes* brought it to amazing new heights and pioneered the synthesis of the visual, the musical, and the choreographic. Diaghilev knew how to attract the best Russian dancers, artists, and composers of the day, enabling him to develop a new aesthetic that impacted the course of ballet for the rest of the century wherever it was danced.

After five years, Nijinsky deserted Diaghilev to marry a young Hungarian he barely knew whom he met on an ocean crossing. Diaghilev reacted by firing him from the company and replacing him with a sixteen-year-old dance student, Léonid Massine (Myasin), who though heterosexual was willing to become Diaghilev's lover for the sake of his career. By the time Massine deserted Diaghilev seven years later, he had become one of the best-known choreographers in Europe.

In the 1920s, Diaghilev's *Ballets Russes* was based in Paris, where he commissioned scores from French and English composers as well as Russians (e.g., Igor Stravinsky, Sergey Prokofiev); the sets and costumes were designed by such artists as Picasso, Georges Roualt, and Giorgio de Chirico; and choreographers included Bronislava Nijinska and George Balanchine. Some of their ballets staged for Diaghilev are still danced today. During his last decade, Diaghilev had affairs with three young men whose talents he had helped nuture: dancer Anton Dolin (born Patrick Healy Kay), dancer and choreographer Serge Lifar, and composer and conductor Igor Markevich. In 1929, after twenty years of creative activity in the West, Diaghilev died in Venice, where he was buried.

Simon Karlinsky

Bibliography

Buckle, Richard. *Diaghilev*. New York: Atheneum, 1984.

Karlinsky, Simon. "A Cultural Educator of Genius." In *The Art of Enchantment: Diaghilev's Ballets Russes, 1909–1922*. Nancy Van Norman Baer, ed. San Francisco: Universe Books, 1989.

See also Ballets Russes; Kirstein, Lincoln; Nijinsky, Vaslav; Russia

Dionysus

Dionysus, also known as Bacchus, son of Zeus and Semele, daughter of Kadmos, king of Thebes, was the Greek god of wine, emotional and sexual ecstasy, the theater, and, eventually, the afterlife. Rescued from the womb of his mother as she was being destroyed by one of Zeus's thunderbolts, Dionysus was sewn into his father's thigh from where he was born again. The decipherment of the Linear B tablets (the earlier form of Greek, inscribed on clay tablets) confirms that Dionysus was known in Minoan-Mycenaean civilization and thus belongs to the formative years of Greek religion, although he was traditionally regarded as a late Thracian or Phrygian import.

In Greek vase painting, Dionysus is depicted either as a bearded, mature man or as a beardless, effeminate youth, with flowing black locks, often accompanied by a retinue of maenads or bacchants (his female followers) and satyrs (goat-men with impressive phalluses). In Euripides' *Bacchae*, his female followers indulge in *sparagmos*, the ripping apart and perhaps even the eating of a live animal, which may have been a feature of some Dionysian rituals. For repressing these rites, Pentheus, king of Thebes, attired in women's clothing to spy on the maenads, is dismembered by his mother and her sisters.

Ritualized transvestism and an ambiguous atmosphere of elation and menace, wine and blood, are features of some Dionysiac rituals, reflecting the god's essential ambiguity, revealed in his love life— he rescues the abandoned Ariadne on Naxos, but Nonnus's *Dionysiaca* describes his affairs with youths, especially his passion for the beautiful Ampelos ("the vine"). *Michael Lambert*

Bibliography

Burkert, W. *Greek Religion*. Cambridge, Mass.: Harvard University Press, 1985.

Kirk, Geoffrey. *The Bacchae by Euripides*. Upper Saddle River, N.J.: Prentice-Hall, 1970.

See also Athens; Greece, Ancient; Mythology; Orpheus; Sparta; Thebes

Disco and Dance Music

The ways that the queer community locates itself within mass culture are complex and contradictory, and disco and dance music and the club cultures that are their primary site of consumption are no exception. The sort of community that circulates around disco and dance music has two forms. First, the disco moment is a utopic present-tense miming of forms of national imagination. In this mode, the Sister Sledge disco "anthem," "We Are Family," imagines "gay" as a "we," a communal affect, a minority able to express itself within the realm of commodity culture.

At the same time, disco and dance music produce history. The forms of African American dance music that predominate in the queer scene were, since the moment of their inception, all about the production and transformation of historical narrative. New York DJs invented "disco," characterized by its 4/4 thump, its extensive use of polyrhythm, and its dramatic use of (usually female) vocals, by mixing elements from an established tradition of black popular styles. Club, garage, house, deep house, techno—all of these dance musics in the "family tree" of disco continue to work on that tradition and thereby produce something of a queer historical narrative, by which the queer hyperpresent tense of the club sounds and feels always like the acoustic reverberations of gay boys past. Already in the 1970s, this historical production was operative, as shown by this passage from Andrew Holleran's 1978 novel, *Dancer from the Dance*:

> There was a moment when their faces blossomed into the sweetest happiness ... when everyone came together in a single lovely communion that was the reason they did all they did; and that occurred about six-thirty in the morning, when they took off their sweat soaked T-shirts and screamed because Patty Joe had begun to sing, "Make me believe in you, show me that love can be true. . ." (Or because the discaire had gone from Barrabas' "Woman" to Zulema's "Giving Up," or the Temptations' "Law of the Land." Any memory of those days is nothing but a string of songs.)

This force of this tribal moment, recounted by Holleran as nostalgia, is displaced by the critical

D potential in remixing histories of dance music that occurs daily on the dance floor. A synchronic communal fantasy in this alternative version is replaced by a more insistently localized critique of the ways in which gay community itself has developed inside commodity capitalism; that is, in the history of ever-emerging dance music "movements," the "string of songs" that symbolizes gay history is remixed, and the issues of difference within queer culture come to the surface again in new and provocative ways. In house music, a form of post-disco dance music made popular in the mid-1980s in Chicago clubs, narratives of the history of style and specific relationships to place and agency take the fore in the style and content of the music itself. While disco aimed at universal pop consumption, house focused on local moments of community performance. Reclaiming dance music for forms of queer black subculture, these moments serve as a lived-out critique of the production of a queer communal "we" in gay politics.

While it is important to acknowledge the black origins of disco and dance music, the strategic essentialism that operates through the consumption and production of African American queer dance music(s) in the queer community as a whole functions only insofar as its liberatory moment is dialectically produced. This occurs within the confines of a racializing regime that produces the gay/black "Ms. Thing" as social fantasy. In Sandra Bernhard's miming of a white boy's coming-out narrative in *Without You I'm Nothing*, we see how the "disco" itself—where the music, the throbbing rhythms transform the blandness of white straight America into gay glamour—is a geography of racial production. The white "protagonist" of this narrative is entering a gay disco for the first time. As he enters the space of the club: "Somebody hands you a tambourine. Suddenly, in the corner of the disco, you see a big black man with a gold lamé capped head looming above the crowd. He has a blonde Afro, red lipstick smeared across his face. He's a black angel. There to take you higher. You feel like Columbus crossing the Atlantic. You discover the new world. You feel free. Thank God almighty, free . . . at last. Do it Sylvester, do it girl!" Bernhard here literalizes the racial logic of disco by her mobilization of a language of discovery as well as by the racial impersonation that the end of her narrative enacts (free at last, do it, girl . . .)." This production of race in the spaces and sounds of disco continues throughout the history of clubs and dance music in the post-Stonewall queer "community," illustrating how it is not incidental to that formation but definitive.

As the "Africanness" of the rhythms of disco and other forms of dance music determine the fantasy of "underground," of "community," the pleasures of the black diva further illustrate how not only the operation of race but its appearance in/as gender is at issue in the gay disco moment. Gloria Gaynor, Donna Summer, The Weather Girls, Ultra Naté—the black diva is a staple of disco and dance music more generally. In one of the classic diva moments in disco history, Gaynor's "I Will Survive," we hear an amazing portrayal of despair in a love gone wrong, followed by a confident refusal of pity. Not only do the lyrics operate within the semantic locus of the historically constituted blues woman; the ways these lyrics are orchestrated into a soundscape evokes the very materiality of the proud diva: it is this racially marked affect that circulates through every moment of diva-nity on the dance floor. The queer performativity of that white boy in the disco is thus possible only inside the matrix of meanings that race and gender provide, while, in the practices of lip-synching and dance, comments on that racializing regime of gender by ironizing its effects and queering its content.

Disco and dance music, then, illustrate not only the ways in which queer "community" and performativity are possible but also, in both the gay black critique of white forms of communal imaginings and the contradictory moment of queering the technologies of race and gender, disco and dance musics more generally have been and remain central to the politics of everyday queer culture. *Brian Currid*

Bibliography

Berlant, Lauren, and Elizabeth Freeman. "Queer Nationality." In *Fear of a Queer Planet: Queer Politics and Social Theory*. Michael Warner, ed. Minneapolis: University of Minnesota Press, 1993.

Bradby, Barbara. "Sampling Sexuality: Gender, Technology, and the Body in Dance Music." *Popular Music* 12 (1993): 155–76.

Currid, Brian. " 'We Are Family': House Music and Queer Performativity." In *Cruising the Performative: Interventions into the Representation of Ethnicity, Nationality, and Sexuality*. Sue-Ellen Case, Philip Brett, and Susan Leigh Foster, eds. Bloomington, Ind.: Indiana University Press, 1995.

Dyer, Richard. "In Defense of Disco." In *On Record: Rock, Pop, and the Written Word*. Simon Frith and Andrew Goodwin, eds. New York: Pantheon, 1990.

Patton, Cindy. "Embodying Subaltern Memory: Kinesthesia and the Problematics of Gender and Race." *The Madonna Connection*. Cathy Schwichtenberg, ed. San Francisco: Westview Press, 1992.

Thomas, Anthony. "The House the Kids Built: Dance Music's Gay Black Roots." *Outlook: National Lesbian and Gay Quarterly* 5 (1989): 28.

See also African American Gay Culture; Music and Musicians 2: Popular Music; Somerville, Jimmy; Sylvester

Divine (b. Harris Glenn Milstead, 1946–1988)

The major vehicle for director John Waters' celebration of the outsider, Divine sashays her way through numerous Waters films from early shorts through *Hairspray* (1988). In *Multiple Maniacs* (1970), she's a thief who runs a freak show of perversions, gets a "rosary job" in a church, eats the heart of her disaffected lover, is raped by a fifteen-foot lobster, and is shot to death by the National Guard.

This extraordinary, swaggering performance is followed by the role of the world's filthiest person in *Pink Flamingos* (1972). Antisocial, living in an isolated trailer, she shoplifts meat by placing it in her crotch, enjoys a castration, gives her son a blow job, and licks her competitors' furniture. Asked about her politics, she replies, "Kill everyone now. Condone first degree murder. Advocate cannibalism. Eat shit. Filth are [sic] my politics. Filth is my life."

In *Female Trouble* (1974), Divine is a wayward schoolgirl who turns to a life of crime and pre-Madonna voguing. Failing to receive cha-cha heels, she knocks over the family Christmas tree, curses her parents, and proceeds to get raped (by a character also played by Divine). She eventually strangles her daughter for becoming a Hare Krishna and performs a one-woman show that includes an amazing backflip attempt on a trampoline. She is eventually put to death in the electric chair.

His mellifluous baritone voice, his extraordinary physical presence, and the sheer apoplectic force of his performances mark Divine as one of the great, and still underappreciated, actors of his generation.   *Doug DiBianco*

Divine on a good *hair day. Penguin/Corbis-Bettman.*

Bibliography

Jay, Bernard. *Not Simply Divine*. New York: Simon & Schuster, 1994.

See also Camp; Film; Film Stars; Waters, John

Dixon, Melvin (1950–1992)

The African American writer Melvin Dixon was born in Stamford, Connecticut. He earned a BA at Wesleyan University in 1971 and a Ph.D. from Brown University in 1975. During his career he published two critical, well-received collections of poetry. *Change of Territory* (1983) is an autobiographical and somewhat self-consciously cosmopolitan poem cycle in which Dixon charts and geographically metaphorizes his own intellectual development. The posthumously published *Love's Instruments* (1995) offers similarly place-oriented poems as well as meditations on gay themes including Dixon's own struggle with AIDS, most notably in the poems "One by One," "Heartbeats," and "Turning Forty in the 90s." The volume also includes the often cited and controversial essay "I'll Be Somewhere Listening for My Name," with its opening line, "As gay men and lesbians, we are the sexual niggers of our society."

In addition to his creative writing, Dixon was a productive academic and translator. His major achievement in this field was the definitive translation of the complete poems of Senegalese poet Léopold Sédar Senghor. Dixon also wrote an influential work of literary criticism, *Ride Out the Wilderness: Geography and Identity in Afro-American Literature* (1987). At various points in his career he taught at Williams College, Fordham University, Columbia University, and finally at the graduate school and at Queens College, City University of New York (CUNY).

Dixon is perhaps best known for his two novels, *Trouble the Water* (1989) and *Vanishing Rooms* (1991). Although he briefly alludes to an emotionally formative adolescent homosexual encounter between the protagonist, Jordan, and his best friend in *Trouble the Water*, it is in *Vanishing Rooms* that Dixon offers his most extensive consideration of gay issues. In this novel set in Greenwich Village, through the alternating first-person narrative voices of three characters—Jesse, a black dancer struggling with the emotional aftermath of the gay bashing and murder of Metro, his white lover; Ruella, a female dancer in love with Jesse; and fifteen-year-old Lonny, one of the white youths responsible for Metro's death—Dixon examines with an often startling directness the issues of interracial relationships, violence against gay men, and the psychosexual dynamics of relationships between gay men and heterosexual women. The stylistic and thematic variety that characterizes these two novels as well as Dixon's other achievements as a creative writer and scholar led many critics to herald him as a potentially major figure on the American and African American literary and intellectual scene. This promise was cut short, however, by Dixon's death from an AIDS-related illness in 1992.

Terry Rowden

Bibliography

Nelson, Emmanuel. "Melvin Dixon (1950–1992)." In *Contemporary Gay American Novelists*. Westport, Conn.: Greenwood, 1993.

See also African American Gay Culture; AIDS Literature

Domestic Partnership

Domestic partnership is a generic term for all the forms of legal and institutional recognition of same-sex couples other than recognition through formal marriage. At present, the most extensive legal recognition of "domestic partnerships" has occurred in Norway, Denmark, the Netherlands, Sweden, and Iceland. The legislature in each of these countries has passed laws permitting same-sex couples to register their relationship with the state. After the couples affirm an enduring commitment to each other, they are treated for purposes of all financial aspects of their relationship in a manner that is fully or nearly identical to the treatment of opposite-sex married (and divorcing) couples. Many hundreds of lesbian and gay male couples have now registered. Even these countries, however, fail to treat registering same-sex couples identically to married couples in some significant respects. All deny to same-sex unions the name of "marriage." Moreover, registered same-sex couples are not provided the opportunities for legal adoption or other legal aspects of parenting that are accorded opposite-sex married couples.

No American state as yet provides the same degree of legal recognition for same-sex couples that these Scandinavian countries do. Still, several forms of recognition have begun to occur. Hawai'i has recently become the first state to permit same-sex couples to register as partners and obtain some

Domestic partners inside San Francisco City Hall. Photo by Marc Geller.

of the benefits accorded to married couples. In addition, many cities with large gay and lesbian populations, such as San Francisco, Chicago, Madison, and Ann Arbor, have adopted ordinances that permit same-sex couples to register as domestic partners. Because the benefits of marriage are largely created by state law, however, these local governments lack the authority to extend most marital benefits to same-sex couples. Thus, in many cities with registration ordinances, the registration is wholly symbolic, representing simply a forward-looking public recognition of same-sex relationships. Some cities have nonetheless reached beyond symbolism and permitted registered same-sex couples who are city employees to obtain health and other employment-related benefits for their partners.

State courts in the United States have also begun to recognized same-sex partners in at least some contexts. When a long-term unmarried opposite-sex couple separates, courts in most American states now enforce agreements between the partners regarding the division of property and the provision of financial support. In many states, a partner in a same-sex couple has been able to obtain similar enforcement from a court. Similarly, in a landmark decision, New York's highest court held that a gay male partner was entitled to remain in a rent-controlled apartment after the death of his partner, who was the tenant of record under a statute that provided rights of succession only to members of the tenant's "family." Of even wider significance, courts in several states now permit the lesbian partner of the mother of a child to become an equal legal parent of the child through adoption. In these contexts, courts typically do not use the term "domestic partner," but the consequences of their actions are much the same as legislative acts that do use the label.

Large numbers of private employers in the United States are also beginning to treat their gay and lesbian employees with domestic partners in the same manner that they treat their married employees. Hundreds of corporations in the United States, including such large employers as IBM, Microsoft, and Disney, now provide health insurance and other benefits to the same-sex domestic partners of their employees. So also do a growing number of institutions of higher learning, including Harvard, Stanford, the University of Michigan, and the University of Iowa.

A few lesbian and gay scholars have opposed legal recognition for any sorts of couple relationships, believing that the state should not be in the business of defining familial relationships. Most gay advocates, however, have strongly favored efforts toward legal recognition of domestic partners. Where there has been debate and disagreement among gay advocates, it has been over whether the efforts to obtain a right to legal marriage should be given a higher priority. Those who push for the right to marry believe that state recognition of domestic partnership rather than marriage continues to relegate gay men and lesbians to second-class status. They believe that only by being permitted to marry will gay men and lesbians be accepted as full citizens within the country. Those who favor a strategy of domestic partnership also have principled and pragmatic reasons. The reason of principle is that they perceive "marriage" to be irredeemably infected by its history as an institution built on gendered hierarchy, with one partner subordinate to the other and with one often subjected to serious abuse. The reason of strategy is simply that many believe that calling same-sex unions "domestic partnerships" will be more acceptable politically to heterosexual Americans and thus that progress toward attaining legal entitlements for same-sex couples will occur more quickly by this route. *David Chambers*

Bibliography

Eskridge, William N. Jr. *The Case for Same-Sex Marriage: From Sexual Liberty to Civilized Commitment.* New York: Free Press, 1996.

Mohr, Richard. *Gays/Justice: A Study of Ethics, Society, and Law.* New York: Columbia University Press, 1988.

Whitacre, Diane. *Will You Be Mine?: Domestic Partnership, San Francisco City Hall, February 14, 1991.* San Francisco: Crooked Street Press, 1992.

See also Business; Denmark; Netherlands; Same-Sex Marriage; Sweden

Doty, Mark (1948–)

Currently teaching creative writing at the University of Utah in Salt Lake City, Mark Doty has also taught at Sarah Lawrence College, Brandeis University, and the University of Iowa Writer's Workshop. To date he has published four books of poetry—*Turtle, Swan* (1987), *Bethlehem in Broad Daylight* (1991), *My Alexandria* (1993), and *Atlantis* (1995)—and one memoir of his lover, Wally Roberts, entitled *Heaven's Coast* (1997). His work has garnered such prestigious prizes as the National Book Critics Circle Award, the *Los Angeles Times* Book Award, and grants from the National Endowment for the Arts and the Guggenheim and Ingram Merrill Foundations.

Much of Doty's recent work reflects joint inspiration from the death of his lover from AIDS and his seaside home, for both seem to contain the hope and loss that finds central focus in Doty's poetry and prose. Especially in the later works, Doty turns toward a concentration on the body, on bodies, and the myriad ways in which they dissolve, dismember, and age. Both the sea and the progression of Wally's disease seem apt metaphors for the gravity the writing seeks to measure in the dissolution of bodies, simultaneously acknowledging the body as mere vehicle, yet bemoaning its loss. The body, however, is not merely Wally's; it is also that of a wounded seal or dog, the barnacled and decaying or weatherwracked boat, the shell of a gull-eaten crab. This body can be adorned and celebrated, as in drag, or covered with a blanket or snow or a quilt before being sent to the crematorium, but still it disappears, always, and the importance in Doty's poetry lies in the letting go of the body in favor of the soul, which places as much faith in the unrecovered body of a lost city as it does in knowing life and love.

Jon Adams

See also AIDS Literature; U.S. Literature: Contemporary Gay Writing

Dove, Ulysses (1950–1996)

U.S. choreographer and dancer Ulysses Dove's presence in the dance world remains vivid as his dances continue to be performed by companies in Europe and the United States. Dove started his career as a dancer, performing with the Merce Cunningham Dance Company and the Alvin Ailey Dance Company. Dove's choreography draws on the very disparate styles of Cunningham, with his pure-dance form of composition, and Ailey's emotional expressivity. Dove tempered passion with exquisite technical demands. Although his training is primarily as a modern dancer, he is probably best known for his freelance choreography for various ballet companies in Europe and America. Among his commissions were pieces for the New York City Ballet, American Ballet Theatre, the Joffrey Ballet, the Royal Swedish Ballet, and the Paris Opera Ballet. One of his best-known works, *Vespers*, was made for Ailey's company. The large-group piece, based

on his memories of growing up in a churchgoing family, honors the strength and passion of African American women. The piece commissioned by the Royal Swedish Ballet, *Dancing on the Front Porch of Heaven*, is a signature work. Performed to music of Arvo Part, the dance, for three men and three women, mourns the passing of friends and family. Most of the dance is performed with desperate urgency, at breakneck speed, except for a poignant and tender duet between two men, drawing on partnering techniques quite unfamiliar to a ballet audience. Dove knew he was ill while creating the choreography, but he had not begun to fail visibly. Because he worked so long as a freelance choreographer, when he became incapacitated with AIDS, like so many other dancers and artists, he had insufficient healthcare coverage and was supported by the Actors' Fund. In 1996, a gala performance of his choreography *For the Love of Dove* was given to benefit the fund, with half of the money raised earmarked for helping people in dance. The performance brought together dance companies never before seen on the same program, demonstrating a respect for both Dove and his choreography. Dove died one week before the performance, leaving a too-small legacy of dances from his short but impressive career.

Maura Keefe

Bibliography

Kisselgoff, Anna. "For the Love of Dove." *New York Times*, June 19, 1996, C11–12.

Solomons Jr., Gus. "Dove Ascending." *Dance Magazine* (May 1992): 54–56.

See also Ailey, Alvin; Cunningham, Merce; Dance and AIDS; Joffrey Ballet

Drag Balls

Drag balls are a combination of masked balls, theatrical performance, and fashion show in which cross-dressing plays an integral role. They are masked balls that have been assimilated into gay subculture. Drag balls, like their earlier incarnation, the masked ball, allow for an obscuring of identity. The primary difference between the two is that masked balls were traditionally assumed to be for heterosexual audiences, whereas drag balls were not.

Since 1717, when Swiss entrepreneur John James Heidegger introduced for-profit masquerade balls to London, masked balls have provided an outlet for expressions of behavior deemed unconventional at best, immoral and criminal at worst. However, within a context that encouraged performance and masquerade, the masked ball allowed for experimentation with gender roles because women could dress as men, and men as women, and "innocently" pursue homosexual relationships.

Those who did not have the means to attend the exclusive masked balls could participate in the annual Mardi Gras, or Carnival, celebrations that marked the beginning of the Christian Lent season. Mardi Gras (literally, Fat Tuesday) was a time for secular excesses that preceded a religious period of self-denial in preparation for the Christian celebration of Easter. These celebrations continue to this day in cities such as New Orleans and Paris, and have maintained the tradition of masquerade, including frequent cross-dressing.

When sexologists began to study homosexuality, they sometimes worked on theories of "inversion." "Inverts," who frequently cross-dressed, were assumed to be homosexual. Theatrical cross-dressing began to take on an entirely different interpretation, and clubs where female and male impersonators performed soon became associated with gay communities.

As gay ghettos developed in areas such as New York's Greenwich Village and Left Bank Paris, social activities that had previously been the realm of mainstream society changed to conform with a growing sense of cohesive identity. The masked balls that had provided an opportunity for overt cross-dressing and gender role reversal outside of theatrical settings became homosexual-sponsored drag balls.

The drag balls of Harlem have been documented in Langston Hughes's autobiography, *The Big Sea* (1940), and more recently in Jennie Livingston's film *Paris Is Burning*, released in 1991. Participants compete with one another in military, collegiate, and feminine drag categories, often performing stylized "street" dances called "voguing."

Julie M. Cox

Bibliography

Bullough, Vern L., and Bonnie Bullough. *Cross Dressing, Sex, and Gender*. Philadelphia: University of Pennsylvania Press, 1993.

Garber, Marjorie. *Vested Interests: Cross-Dressing and Cultural Anxiety*. New York: Routledge, 1992.

Miller, Neil. *Out of the Past: Gay and Lesbian History from 1869 to the Present*. New York: Vintage, 1995.

See also Hughes, Langston; Sexology; Sydney Gay and Lesbian Mardi Gras; Transvestism; Voguing

Duchamp, Marcel (1887–1968)

Marcel Duchamp was born in Blainville, France, and died in Paris. He spent a considerable amount of his adult life in New York City. As an artist, Duchamp was often claimed as a surrealist, but although he clearly had affinities with surrealism, he opposed the commercialism as well as the often doctrinaire cultural politics of the movement.

Within art-historical criticism, Duchamp tends to be associated with the end of modernism and the rise of postmodernism. His work embodies this split in innumerable ways. Two artistic practices in particular are worth considering as part of the artist's relation to lesbian, gay, and other sexually dissident cultures: the Duchampian "readymades" and Duchamp's alter ego, Rrose Sélavy. In both of these contexts reiteration produces effects of variation and variability in Duchamp's works.

The readymades were mass-produced objects purchased in stores. Duchamp titled and signed the objects and introduced them as his works of art. Sometimes the artist retouched these objects slightly, calling specific attention to their status as reproductions or altered versions of an "original." Very often, the titles he gave them surprisingly reconfigure utilitarian relationships to the objects displayed. Perhaps the most famous of the readymades was Duchamp's 1919 rendering, with a mustache, of a postcard of Leonardo da Vinci's *Mona Lisa*, which he entitled *L.H.O.O.Q.* Certainly, Duchamp's readymades provoke viewers' considerations of the relationships between form and function, object and purpose, original and copy. At the same time, they call into question the authorial role: why and how does the artist's proclamation of their status as "art" render or produce them as actual, bona fide "art" objects? This kind of open critique also inspires a rethinking of the arbitrariness of categorization and authorization in realms outside visual art. In this capacity, Duchamp's readymades dovetail suggestively with lesbian and gay cultural resistances to the imposition of singular meanings and restrictive taxonomies on the field of sexual dissidence.

Duchamp's alter ego, Rrose Sélavy, was invented in 1920, and he continued to invoke the persona until the early 1940s. "Rose" was a popular name in 1920, and with the added letter it comes close to sounding like "eros"; "Sélavy" can be pronounced as a contraction of "*c'est la vie*": the name therefore produces the statement "eros, that's life." Not only was it affixed to many of the readymades, but also, as "Rrose," Duchamp posed for Man Ray in drag, displaying exaggerated feminine mannerisms in many of the resulting photographs, though not passing particularly well as a woman. Considered from a range of feminist perspectives, Duchamp's tendency to see Rrose Sélavy as his "muse" can be seen as representing an assimilation of an abstract "feminine" as a territory for the critically transgressive. But since he was openly disdainful of feminism, this move is clearly problematic. Still, as Amelia Jones has argued, the alter ego of Rrose Sélavy also ruptures the seamless authority of the status of the modernist artist. Duchamp enacts this rupture in a manner that furthermore makes him accessible to viewers' interpretations across the divide of gender binarisms. For such reasons, there has been a resurgence of critical and biographical interest in Duchamp at the tail end of the twentieth century.

Alex Robertson Textor

Bibliography

Jones, Amelia. *Postmodernism and the En-Gendering of Marcel Duchamp*. Cambridge: Cambridge University Press, 1994.

Judovitz, Dalia. *Unpacking Duchamp: Art in Transit*. Berkeley: University of California Press, 1995.

Tomkins, Calvin. *Duchamp: A Biography*. New York: Henry Holt, 1996.

See also Art History; France; Postmodernism

Dürer, Albrecht (1471–1528)

Albrecht Dürer, the outstanding German artist of the Renaissance, was married and never publicly accused of homosexual behavior. Still, several of his works evince an interest in the theme of homosexual desire. And several comments in letters by Dürer and his friends hint at bisexuality.

In contemporary Italian culture, artists and humanist scholars were frequently associated with homosexuality, both jocularly and accusingly. Neoplatonic poets and thinkers in particular introduced homophilic as well as misogynist themes into their works. It is likely that Dürer, the son of a goldsmith, was introduced to the possibility of "learned homosexuality" by his friend Willibald Pirckheimier, a Nuremberg patrician and scholar who had studied in

Italy. Dürer himself visited Venice twice, in 1494–1495 and again in 1506–1507.

In a drawing dated 1494, Dürer depicts the murder of Orpheus for the sin of pederasty, at the hands of the scorned Thracian women. The episode is recounted in Ovid (*Metamorphoses* XI, 1ff). Dürer shows Orpheus on his knees, defending himself from the blows of the women, while a very small boy runs away. A banner in the tree above identifies the figure as "Orpheus, the first sodomite." Dürer's drawing is based on an engraving by an anonymous north Italian master. A similar boy escapes in Dürer's woodcut *Hercules;* in some traditions Hercules, too, was associated with homosexuality. In the woodcut print from about 1496, *The Men's Bath,* Dürer shows six nearly nude men lounging in an open-air bathhouse. The four main figures are believed to bear the facial features of Dürer, Pirckheimer, and the brothers Stephan and Larenz Paumgartner. They are joined by two musicians. The genitals of the "Dürer" figure are directly juxtaposed to a waterspout with a spigot in the shape of a rooster. The woodcut is sometimes interpreted as an allegory of the four humors; it may also reflect actual contemporary customs in Nuremberg.

Undated woodcut by Albrecht Dürer (1471–1528) titled The Men's Bath *depicted a medieval scene at an open-air bath. Corbis-Bettman.*

A drawn portrait of Pirckheimer by Dürer in Berlin, from about 1503, is inscribed probably in Pirckheimer's hand, and in Greek: "With erect penis, into the man's anus." Dürer's letters to Pirckheimer from Venice are filled with crude allusions to the latter's heterosexual activity, both with Nuremberg patrician wives and with prostitutes. However, in a letter of September 8, 1506, Dürer wrote: "O if you were here, what handsome Italian lancers you would find!" It is clear that Dürer's wife, Agnes, and Pirckheimer hated each other. In a letter of October 13, 1506, to Pirckheimer, Dürer made obscene and demeaning references to his own wife. Dürer's relations with Agnes, whom he married in 1494 and with whom he had no children, were said by his friends to be bad.

It is possible that homosexuality, for Dürer and Pirckheimer, remained a matter for rakish, misogynist wit and sophisticated mythological allusions. Pirckheimer had been married; moreover, Pirckheimer had many political enemies, and if he had been known to have engaged in any homosexual activity, this would certainly have been used publicly against him.

Dürer was notoriously vain of his appearance. In a letter to Pirckheimer of March 19, 1507, Lorenz Behaim mocked Dürer for his fastidiously groomed beard, and he observed that Dürer's "boy"—*il gerzone*, presumably his apprentice—loathed that beard. But there is also evidence that Dürer was hoping to attract women with his beard. In a letter of October 13, 1506, Dürer seems to refer to an earlier letter in which Pirckheimer had reported that the "whores and pious women" alike in Nuremberg had been asking after Dürer. And in a letter of May 23, 1507, Behaim reports that, according to Dürer's horoscope, he is an *ingeniosus amator* (an ingenious lover), and that because Venus is turned to the moon, he "desires many women."

Christopher S. Wood

Bibliography

Rosasco, Betsy. "Albrecht Dürer's 'Death of Orpheus': Its Critical Fortunes and a New Interpretation of its Meaning." *IDEA: Jahrbuch der Hamburger Kunsthalle* 3 (1984): 19–40.

Wind, Edgar. " 'Hercules' and 'Orpheus': Two Mock-Heroic Designs by Dürer." *Journal of the Warburg and Courtauld Institutes* 2 (1938/39): 206–18.

See also Art History; Orpheus

Durrell, Lawrence (1912–1990)

Born in Jullunder, India, Durrell has a personal history that reflects the tensions and desires on which he would focus for the rest of his life. His father, a British civil engineer, would always be part of the colonial regime in India; his mother, an Irish national, likewise would juxtapose her cultural difference so that Durrell would redistribute the legacy of colonization, war, and fascism along an axis of sexual desire. In his writing, Durrell suggests that sexual desire counteracts the boundaries of history. Often linked creatively to Henry Miller and Alfred Perles, Durrell represents a particular point in Anglo-American arts and letters when the novel ruptured under the weight of erotic intensity.

Although he was not gay, Durrell's books, plays, letters, and poetry exhibit diverse sexual orientations that come about through his characters' identification with particular times and places. Thus Alexandria, Geneva during World War II, and Cairo are places where characters explore their desires and are, thus, constantly caught in a tangle of ever-changing combinations. Their desires, furthermore, demand this sexual multiplication. They are sexually active in a kind of heady atmosphere in which the sensuality of the locations elicit their responses.

Most of the literary criticism concerning Durrell's work derives from the sixties and reflects an emphasis on Durrell's preoccupation with eros and thanatos. Secondary materials focus on Durrell's characters' restatement of sexual desire as the desire for death. We see this direction particularly in literary criticism concerning the novel *Sebastian*, a spin-off of Durrell's famous *Alexandria Quartet*. However, in *Sebastian*, Durrell experiments with the Lacanian theory of the "death drive." In fact, both gay and straight characters discuss Lacan's theory implicitly and explicitly throughout the text. Thus Durrell's exploration of the three male characters, Affad, Schwarz, and Mnemides, gives the beginning of a fiction-based theory of masculine desire. For example, in the homosexual character of Mnemides, sexual desire is reimagined as a release of pent-up energy: "I cried out and dropped the phone, but it was done . . . I dreamed of him. I was on fire. Finally, . . . I capitulated and asked him to come. I could not wait, I was in a frenzy of capitulation" (14). By following Lacan, Durrell posits that desire leads to death because death is the conduit to a pre-Oedipal passivity.

The problem with Durrell's texts is that they are complicated now by a world caught up in the destructive power of AIDS. Eros and Thanatos as

D tropes of the forgotten innocence of liberated desires seem rather dated, then, when the watchword of today's queer communities must be "safe sex." However, Durrell's texts should not be sidelined because of our lack of cultural currency for understanding them. His work still offers a point of departure for imagining a sexual objectivity grounded in passion and possibility. *Kitty Millet*

Bibliography

Pinchin, Jane L. *Alexandrian Still: Forster, Durrell, Cavafy*. Princeton, N.J.: Princeton University Press, 1977.

Pine, Richard. *The Dandy and the Herald*. New York: St. Martin's Press, 1988.

Ragland-Sullivan, Elie. *Jacques Lacan and the Philosophy of Psychoanalysis*. Urbana, Ill.: University of Illinois Press, 1986.

Wickes, George, ed. *Lawrence Durrell and Henry Miller: A Private Correspondence*. New York: Dutton, 1963.

See also Alexandria; Colonialism

E

Eakins, Thomas (1844–1916)

American painter Thomas Eakins belongs to a generation of American artists that has recently begun to assert an increasingly important place in U.S. lesbian and gay history.

His most direct link to that history is as a member of a circle of Philadelphia area bohemians who clustered around Walt Whitman. Eakins painted a portrait of Whitman in 1887–1888—the only portrait of himself that Whitman actually admired. Like Whitman's poetry, in some of Eakins's paintings, most notably *The Swimming Hole* (c.1883–1885) and *The Wrestlers* (1899), we find frankly homoerotic celebrations of the male body and athletic culture. This segment of his oeuvre looks like a distinctly American utopia in which men might enjoy each other without the threat of either prohibition or diminishing labels. Other works, most notably the 1875 portrait of the surgeon Samuel Gross, *The Gross Clinic* (for which Eakins is most famous), describe a much more ambivalent, even anxious relation to the spectacle of the male body.

Of special interest to those interested in the history of sexuality in the United States are Eakins's photographs, which include numerous studies of the male nude. These photographs may be the artist's most direct and least complicated legacy to something we might want to call a distinctly American gay culture.

As an artist Eakins is famous for having led the battle to use naked models in his classes, even when women students were present. In fact, Eakins pioneered the education of women in the arts, believing that even though she may not have a man's natural tendencies to greatness, woman ought to be taught in exactly the same manner. His attitudes about men and women and his affection for the naked body inspired his rivals to generate devastating rumors about his sexual practices. His brother-in-law was instrumental in spreading the story that Eakins had an incestuous and sodomitical relationship with his own sister. These rumors, together with his arrogant personality, his insistence on teaching from naked models, and his tendency to introduce the spectacle of his own body to his students, led to his expulsion from the Philadelphia Academy for Fine Arts in 1886.

Though embittered by this experience, Eakins held fast to his principles and continued to paint and explore photography.

Among his most famous works are *The Gross Clinic, William Rushing Carving His Allegorical Figure of the Schuykill River, The Swimming Hole,* and *Agnew Clinic.*   *Jennifer Doyle*

Bibliography

Davis, Whitney. "Erotic Revision in Thomas Eakins's Narratives of Male Nudity." *Art History* 13, no. 3 (September 1994): 301–41.

Foster, Kathleen, and Charyl Leibold. *Writing About Thomas Eakins: The Manuscripts in Charles Bregler's Thomas Eakins Collection.* Philadelphia: University of Pennsylvania Press, 1989.

Hatt, Michael. "Muscles, Morals, Mind: The Male Body in Thomas Eakins's Salutat." In *The Body Imaged.* Kathleen Adler and Marcia Pointon, eds. Cambridge: Cambridge University Press, 1993, 57–69.

See also Art History; Whitman, Walt

E Education

This article presents some of the reasons why lesbian and gay teachers may choose to disclose or hide their sexual orientation. In addition, the closely related topic of the benefits and problems associated with discussing the topic of homosexuality in schools is addressed. In many schools the issue of lesbian and gay teachers disclosing their sexual orientation has been, and continues to be, controversial. Most lesbian and gay educators do not reveal their sexual orientation to their students, colleagues, or administrators because disciplinary action may be taken against those that do. Some school districts still terminate teachers who reveal their lesbian or gay orientation on the grounds of "immorality." Similarly, the issue of discussing homosexuality in elementary and secondary schools remains contentious; many educators do not discuss homosexuality with their students. Throughout history, homosexuality has been considered a sin, a mental disorder, and/or a crime. Some people still consider homosexuality abhorrent and not an appropriate topic to discuss with elementary or secondary students. In many school districts, especially small ones, healthy discussion of homosexuality remains nonexistent.

The employment of openly lesbian and gay teachers at the elementary and secondary school level has received much attention in districts across the United States. Lesbian and gay teachers not only need to decide if they will reveal their sexual orientation; they also need to decide to whom they will reveal it: students, colleagues, parents, and/or administrators. If a teacher reveals her or his sexual orientation to any person in a school, this may mean revealing that orientation to all people associated with the school. Teachers who are lesbian or gay and disclose their sexual orientation may be more accepting of themselves and others than lesbian or gay teachers who do not disclose their orientation. It has been found that gay men are more likely to reveal their sexual orientation publicly than lesbians. This is not surprising, owing to the fact that when lesbians reveal their sexual orientation they must deal not only with the potential homophobic backlash, as gay men do, but they must also deal with possible accompanying sexism.

There are additional positive reasons for teachers to reveal their sexual orientation in the school environment. The experience of being a gay or lesbian person may also foster a substantial respect for individual and alternative living. Moreover, even though disclosing one's sexual orientation can be stressful, there are lesbian and gay teachers who have found that the benefits of revealing it outweigh the accompanying stress. The reasons why many lesbian and gay teachers remain silent about their sexual orientation or, in some cases, actively pretend to be heterosexual depend on the individual and the situation. A lesbian or gay teacher may not disclose her or his sexual orientation because of fear of verbal harassment, feelings of vulnerability, fear of being denied promotion, and fear of losing a teaching position (this fear is more prevalent in small rural communities than suburban or urban ones). Suburban and rural teachers are less likely to reveal their sexual orientation than urban teachers, and when they do disclose it, they report experiencing more job-related stress. Even tenured teachers, may still feel fearful of disclosing their orientation from fear of professional, social, or physical repercussions.

Although only lesbian and gay teachers need to decide if, when, to whom, and how they will disclose their sexual orientation, all teachers need to decide how they will go about doing so. Follett and Larson wrote a point/counterpoint article addressing the topic of English teachers discussing homosexuality with their students. Follett notes that since it is estimated that 10 percent of the population is lesbian or gay, it is important for teachers to discuss homosexuality so that students who identify themselves as lesbian or gay or may identify themselves as such in the future know they are not alone. Lesbian and gay students are known to experience low self-esteem and commit suicide and drop out of school at a greater rate than other students. Follett also writes that it is equally important for teachers to discuss homosexuality for students who have lesbian or gay relatives and friends. Follett continues by stating that teachers have no other moral option but to discuss the sexual orientation of the authors they read in an open and honest manner. In contrast to Follett, Larson states that teachers have no reason to discuss authors' sexual orientation unless the literature they are studying has something to do with homosexuality. Larson also contends that since adolescents are bombarded with sex messages from the mass media, teachers should not add to this type of information.

If teachers do choose to discuss homosexuality with their students, they need to present the topic carefully so that the discussion does not leave heterosexual students disengaged. Careful preparation may also prevent the discussion from turning into a platform for homophobic responses. Teachers need to be careful to provide a safe environment for all students to discuss the topic of homosexuality.

Lesbian and gay teachers should weigh the advantages and disadvantages of disclosing their sexual orientation in their specific situations. Even though the benefits of revealing one's orientation may outweigh the stress, in some schools it may also mean job termination. Also, all teachers need to decide when and how and at what risk to their safety and job security they can discuss the issue with their students. Dealing with gay and lesbian issues and confronting homophobia in the classroom must be more than lesbian and gay teachers' concern; the issue of homophobia must involve them as well as heterosexual teachers and students. To whatever level it is possible, all teachers are responsible for discussing homosexuality in a healthy manner so that all their students will feel safe.   *Marc Markell*

Bibliography

Berg, A., J. Kowaleski, C. Le Guin, E. Weinauer, and E. A. Wolfe. "Breaking the Silence: Sexual Preference in the Classroom." *Feminist Teacher* 4 (1989): 29–32.

Follett, R., and R. Larson. "Bait/Rebait: It Is Dishonest of English Teachers to Ignore Homosexuality of Literary Figures Whose Works They Teach." *English Journal* 71 (1982): 18–21.

Harbeck, K. M. "The Homosexual Educator: Past History/Future Perspectives." Paper presented at the Annual Meeting of the American Educational Research Association, San Francisco, Calif. (March 27–31, 1989). (ERIC Document Reproduction No. ED 322 016.)

Juul, T. P. "Community and Conformity: A National Survey Contrasting Rural, Suburban, and Urban Lesbian, Gay Male, and Bisexual Public School Teachers." Paper presented at the Annual Meeting of the American Educational Research Association, San Francisco, Calif. (April 18–22, 1995). (ERIC Document Reproduction No. ED 383 687.)

———. "Tenure, Civil Rights Laws, Inclusive Contracts and Fear: Legal Protection and Lives of Self-Identified Lesbians, Gay Men, and Bisexual Public School Teachers." Paper presented at the Annual Meeting of the Northeastern Educational Research Association, New York, N.Y. (October 26–28, 1994). (ERIC Document Reproduction No. ED 377 565.)

Kissen, R. M. "Teachers Talk About Their Lives." Paper presented at the Annual Meeting of the American Educational Research Association, Atlanta, Ga. (April 12–16, 1993). (ERIC Document Reproduction No. ED 363–556.)

Koski, F. "Queer Theory in the Undergraduate Writing Course." Paper presented at the Conference on College Composition and Communication, Washington, D.C. (March 23–25, 1995). (ERIC Document Reproduction No. ED 391 160.)

Rofes, E. "Queer, Education, Schools, and Sex Panic." Paper presented at the Annual Meeting of the American Educational Research Association, San Francisco, Calif. (April 21, 1995). (ERIC Document Reproduction No. ED 383 270.)

Schneider-Vogel, M. "Gay Teachers in the Classroom: A Continuing Constitutional Debate." *Journal of Law and Education* 12 (1986): 285–318.

See also Schools

Edward II (1284–1327)

Edward II probably would not be a part of gay and lesbian history were it not for the play by Renaissance playwright Christopher Marlowe that describes the English king's affections for his minion Gaveston. Indeed, the image of Edward as a homosexual is almost entirely the invention of the late sixteenth and seventeenth centuries, and this image has since become canonical.

Edward II, also known as Edward of Caernarfon, was born in 1284. The son of Edward Longshanks and Eleanor of Castile, he ascended to the throne at the age of twenty-three in 1307 upon the death of his father. England in the fourteenth century experienced tremendous population and economic fluctuation that, combined with tremendous financial outlays for a war with France, resulted in a series of confrontations between Longshanks and his subjects that left the monarchy seriously debased. The propertied classes and the clergy were subject to an unprecedented level of taxation to offset the expenses of war. As a monarch, Edward II did little to alleviate any of these problems, and material conditions under his reign reached an all-time low.

Augmenting the financial problems of Edward's reign was a general lack of prudence in his selection of advisers. He relied on close and even affectionate bonds with Peter Gaveston and Hugh

Despenser, which outraged many of the magnates who had a valid claim to access to the monarch. In 1308 the magnates, led by Thomas, Earl of Lancaster, extracted a protracted and more specific coronation oath from Edward that bound the king more firmly to English common law, and in 1311 they sought to limit his freedom of action through ordinance. This series of actions, combined with the murder of Gaveston in 1312, turned Edward into a hardened and obstinate ruler. In 1322, facing renewed threats of rebellion stemming from livestock diseases and harvest blights that left the country starving, Edward renounced all the restrictive ordinances. The magnates acted quickly to complete the overthrow of Edward and, aided by his queen, Isabelle, forced him to abdicate his throne in 1327 and allow the ascent of Edward III.

There is nothing to indicate that during his own time Edward was deposed for any other reason than his abysmal lack of political skill. The images of him as a sodomite that appear in the Renaissance may have a basis in fact, but they also probably only derive from the late-sixteenth and seventeenth-century concern with sexual decorum and with the prospect that King James I was, himself, a sodomite. For the representation of Edward as a homosexual, readers must turn to Jacobean writers such as John Taylor, whose *Briefe remembrance of All the Englishe Monarchs* recounts in Edward's voice how "Peirce Gaveston, to thee my love combinde: My friendship to thee scarce left me a friend," or to Michael Drayton, Francis Hubert, or Ben Jonson, all of whom wrote similar Renaissance accounts of the king.　　　*Gregory W. Bredbeck*

Bibliography

Bredbeck, Gregory W. *Sodomy and Interpretation: Marlowe to Milton.* Ithaca, N.Y.: Cornell University Press, 1991.

Prestwich, Michael. *The Three Edwards: War and State in England, 1272–1377.* 1980. New York: Routledge, 1992.

See also Marlowe, Christopher

Effeminacy

The popular imagination often associates effeminacy with the supposedly telltale audible and physical signs of a man's homosexuality. Pejorative terms like "faggot" in the United States and "poof'" in the United Kingdom invoke a well-known stereotype of the gay man as a limp-wristed, lisping, mincing individual who deviates from the male norm because he embodies femininity, not masculinity. This stereotype takes for granted that femininity encompasses such qualities as delicacy, fragility, sensitivity, and weakness, whereas masculinity manifests courage, invulnerability, mastery, and strength. As a result, the stigma of effeminacy strives to separate male homosexuality from male heterosexuality. In other words, if gay men have discarded their manhood in favor of femininity, then straight men have exclusive rights over masculinity. The stereotype assumes that no one should regard effeminacy as an authentic or appropriate masculine behavior.

Given the hostility toward effeminacy in modern culture, it is relatively unusual to encounter affirmative representations of femininity in men. Yet there have been notable instances of celebrities and writers making the effeminate man into an inspiring and powerful icon. Quentin Crisp's famous autobiography, *The Naked Civil Servant* (1968), throws important light on how and why some men might develop an effeminate identity when confronted by a deeply homophobic society. In 1979, Manuel Puig published *The Kiss of the Spider Woman,* featuring Molina, an effeminate man who identifies with women film stars and opera divas, expressing a strong desire to lie and die in the arms of a real heterosexual man. Crisp's and Puig's explorations of effeminacy have important implications for the emergence of transgender identities. Yet the links are not automatic between effeminacy and male-to-female transsexuality and between effeminacy and male-to-female cross-dressing. Effeminacy does not necessarily describe the styles of femininity that male-to-female transsexuals and male cross-dressers express.

In some circumstances, effeminacy can form part of an acceptable masculinity. Rock singers like David Bowie and Mick Jagger on occasion adopted effeminate styles that proved central to their commercial marketing as hip, progressive, trendy performers. Part of their success, however, relied on distancing their effeminate mode of dress and use of women's cosmetics from the stigma of male homosexuality.

What, then, gave rise to this widespread connection between effeminacy and male homosexuality? Why does this connection endure in many representations of gay men in film, literature, and television? Part of the answer lies in how some gay men have for hundreds of years developed effeminate mannerisms to distinguish their homosexual identity. Although homosexual subcultures sometimes express disdain toward effeminate men, it remains the case that gay male meeting places and friendship networks frequently celebrate effeminate gestures, turns of phrase, and styles of dressing. Especially important here are the links with camp and drag. Gay men often use types of body language, tones of voice, and word choices that would be generally understood as effeminate. Although effeminacy has been a significant part of gay life, there has been a comparatively small number of investigations into what it has meant in both past and present cultures.

One of the few comprehensive surveys of effeminacy appeared in *The Archives of Sexual Behavior* (1975). This study needs to be viewed with caution because it fails to challenge the stereotype of the gay man upon which its analysis depends. Four behavioral scientists devised a series of sixty-seven questions about a man's gait, gesture, posture, and speech to assess exactly where he might rate on an "effeminacy scale." "Does he speak," they asked, "with breathy, seductive tones?" "Does he move sinuously?" "When he sits, does he double-cross his legs, that is, at both knee and ankles?" Even though these scholars produced a mechanical tabulation of behaviors, their questions reveal much about what is still generally presumed to come under the category of effeminacy. From a sample of thirty-two men, the researchers found that half were homosexual. Since the gay sample displayed a much greater tendency toward effeminacy than their heterosexual counterparts, the researchers speculated on the prevalence of these behaviors in the homosexual community. "Effeminacy," they argued, "can be a cue which signals sexual availability to men and sexual unavailability to women." Further, they inferred that some effeminate responses "seemed to express castration anxiety," since many of the behaviors were narcissistic in their attention to the body, involving "hair preening, self-caressing, and self-cuddling." From this perspective, effeminacy becomes a pathological condition that reveals the difficulties gay men experience when engaging in what sexologists call "sexual signaling." They quote psychoanalyst Helene Deutsch, who argues that, since gay men cannot connect with women, they have a tendency to invest the whole of their male bodies with female narcissism. By all accounts, their research suggests that gay men suffer badly from effeminacy, since effeminate behavior reveals that male homosexuality lacks the phallic strength to relate sexually toward a woman.

Effeminacy has always defined femininity in men. The *Oxford English Dictionary* states that *effeminacy* was first used in 1602; the adjective *effeminate* has an older lineage, dating from 1430. Yet *effeminacy* had several other meanings during the late Middle Ages and the Renaissance. On the one hand, it illustrated types of moral and physical weakness, while on the other it suggested forms of self-indulgence and voluptuousness. In 1652, for instance, an "effeminate stomach" meant a delicate constitution. By comparison, writer George Puttenham in 1589 juxtaposed the words *amorous* and *effeminate,* indicating that they had similar connotations. Moreover, the term *effeminate* was sometimes employed as a noun to describe sodomy; the Douay Bible of 1609 records that "effeminates were in the land" (1 Kings 14: 24). These examples disclose that by the seventeenth century, effeminacy related to diverse phenomena, from physical debility to sexual intercourse between men.

During the eighteenth century, the meanings of *effeminacy* diversified even further. By this time, the word was often linked with ideas about luxury and immorality. Social historian Kathleen Wilson observes that in the 1750s, the British aristocracy's "feckless pursuit of self-interest" led to attacks on the effeminacy of the nation. "Effeminacy," Wilson argues, "denoted a degenerate moral, political, and social state that opposed and subverted the vaunted 'manly' characteristics—courage, aggression, martial valor, discipline and strength—that constituted patriotic virtue." This view of effeminacy arises in John Brown's *Estimate of the Manners and Principles of the Times* (1757–58), where he deplores "the luxurious and effeminate Manners of the higher ranks." In his study of English nationalism, Gerald Newman claims this attack on effeminacy "was to become one of the favorite hobbyhorses of social analysis for the next generation." Newman claims that Brown's hated "Town Effeminacy" defined a "creeping system of moral rot," where old-fashioned values such as honesty and hospitality mere corrupted by luxurious London society that had no regard for principle and tradition.

In the nineteenth century, the meanings of *effeminacy* were as various as before. But literary scholars generally agree that effeminacy became firmly—if not exclusively—linked to male homosexuality when Oscar Wilde was tried for "gross indecency" in 1895. Prior to that time, according to gay critic Alan Sinfield, Wilde's effeminate manners and flamboyant dress presented him as a dandified aesthete, not necessarily as a man with homosexual tastes. It is mistaken, Sinfield claims, to assume that in the years leading up to the trials, satirical portraits of Wilde's mannerisms insinuated male same-sex desire. Instead, Wilde was often under attack as an avant-garde artist who readily mocked the more conservative values of his day. Only when Wilde stood on trial did the public associate a man who adopted the image of an aesthete with the figure of the homosexual. Although the word *homosexual* was not popularly understood until the early twentieth century, Wilde became the first famous icon of the effeminate queer: the stereotype widely familiar to twentieth-century culture. *Joseph Bristow*

Bibliography

Bristow, Joseph. *Effeminate England: Homoerotic Writing after 1865.* New York: Columbia University Press, 1995.

Sinfield, Alan. *The Wilde Century: Effeminacy, Oscar Wilde and the Queer Moment.* London: Cassell, 1994.

See also Camp; Crisp, Quentin; Dandy; Film; Film Stars; Music and Musicians 2 (Popular Music); Opera; Puig, Manuel; Queen; Sodomy; Television; Transsexualism; Transvestism; Wilde, Oscar

Egypt, Ancient

It is difficult to find evidence for ancient Egyptian male same-sex sexual relationships and attitudes toward them, as the Egyptian textual and pictorial records are either notoriously reticent on sexual matters or ambiguously allusive.

Fragmentary papyri record the power struggle between two deities, Seth (the destructive brother of the god Osiris and the goddesses Isis and Nepthys) and Horus, son of Isis and Osiris. In one account, Seth arranges to seduce Horus and ejaculates between his loins; in another, he compliments Horus on his buttocks and tries to penetrate him anally. In the former account, Seth believes he has defeated Horus because he has "performed an aggressive act against him" (Manniche 57). Clearly, anal penetration is also regarded as an act of aggression by one male against another. In the mythological record, this male same-sex relationship is constructed in terms of victory and humiliation, in common with attitudes toward anal intercourse in the ancient Mediterranean basin, where the active penetrator was regarded as quintessentially masculine, whereas the passive recipient was regarded was an object of unmasculine shame.

From these accounts of divine behavior in which the evil Seth is associated with same-sex Eros, it would seem that ancient Egyptian attitudes toward male same-sex sexual relationships were negative. This appears to be confirmed by one of the statements in the New Kingdom (c.1550–1070 B.C.E.) *Book of the Dead,* which has been interpreted as "I have not practiced homosexuality" (Robins 72): such a confession would have aided the dead man's rebirth in his "second life," for it would have demonstrated that he was not sterile during his "first life."

Egyptian mythology and iconography constantly highlight divine and human fertility, the very essence of Egyptian life, dramatically reinforced by the annual flooding of the Nile. Male potency was personified in the form of the god Min, depicted as a mummiform deity with an erect phallus. Rather like Seth, Min humiliates an enemy by raping him anally and eventually becomes assimilated to the cult of Horus as "Min-Horus-the-victorious," conqueror of Seth. Fertility and power relations are thus symbolized by the phallus. This is confirmed by the interpretations of some of the erotic dreams listed in the dream book for men, which has survived: if a man dreams that his phallus has become large, the dream is a good one as it signifies that the man's possessions will multiply.

Apart from the mythological record, a fragmentary papyrus dating from the New Kingdom gives an account of the love affair between Pharaoh Neferkara (or Pepi II) of the Old Kingdom (c.2649–2150 B.C.E.) and his general, Sasenet. The pharaoh used to slip out of his palace at night, signal to his lover by throwing a brick and kicking his foot on the ground, then wait for the ladder that was lowered to him. Thanks to the gossiping observer, we know that the pharaoh spent four hours with his lover, then returned to the palace, in which there was no wife, for four hours before dawn. That the divine pharaoh had to sneak around at night suggests that male same-sex relationships (certainly in the Old Kingdom) were regarded as improper.

Evidence of pharaonic sexual ambiguity could be suggested by some of the sculptures of the controversial Akhenaton (c.1353–1335 B.C.E.), depicted with breasts and rounded female hips in the image of his wife, Nefertiti. However, the sculptures could imply an attempt to unify male and female in the pharaoh's person. Such an attempt would be in keeping with Akhenaton's reduction of Egyptian polytheism to one unifying principle: the sun. Furthermore, the blending of male and female in the mythological tradition was not unknown. The goddess Anat, wife of Ra, the sun god, is a warrior goddess, "clad as men and girt as women" (Manniche 54): significantly, Seth attempts to rape her. Seth thus displays violent desire for the beautiful Horus and the masculinized goddess, Anat; the sex of the object of desire is not an issue, but the manner in which he expresses it is inextricably connected with relations of power and dominance. Such relations are evident in the love spells from Greco-Roman Egypt, preserved on papyri dating from the second century B.C.E. until the fifth century C.E. While most of these spells are directed at women by men, a small number of them are aimed at women by women and at men by men. The language of these spells reflects the same desire for complete domination and control of the loved one revealed in the heterosexual spells; same-sex desire is thus constructed in the same way as heterosexual desire, reflecting the traditional patriarchal pattern of hierarchical rather than reciprocal relationships. *Michael Lambert*

Bibliography

Manniche, L. *Sexual Life in Ancient Egypt.* London: Kegan Paul International, 1987.

Robins, G. *Women in Ancient Egypt.* London: British Museum Press, 1993.

See also Alexandria; Greece, Ancient; Rome, Ancient

Eisenstein, Sergey Mikhailovich (1898–1948)

Sergey Eisenstein is generally regarded as the greatest filmmaker to emerge from the golden age of Soviet cinema. His major completed films are *The Strike* (1924), *Battleship Potemkin* (1925), *October* (1927), *The Old and the New* (originally titled *The General Line*, 1929), *Alexander Nevsky* (1938), and the first two parts of the proposed trilogy *Ivan the Terrible* (1943–1946). Known to his colleagues simply as "the Master," he influenced them through his films, his theoretical writings, and his teaching at the State Film Institute in Moscow.

The subject of Eisenstein's sexuality is problematic; there are plenty of anecdotes but little or no hard evidence. This is likely to remain the case until such time as his diaries are made available more widely to interested scholars in Russia and abroad.

Part of the problem lies in the Byzantine Russian attitudes toward homosexuality, reinforced by its illegality during the Stalin period, when to be in any way different was to be suspect, and to be dangerous, and therefore, of course, also vulnerable. Although Eisenstein frequently and openly examined his relationship with his own parents and with substitute father figures like the theater director Vsevolod Meyerhold, he never openly analyzed his own sexuality. The student of Eisenstein's personality is therefore left with only scattered clues, from the high camp of *Ivan the Terrible* (especially in the color sequence) to the numerous phallocentric drawings dating from this time in Mexico and subsequently.

One anecdote from a reliable source tells how, after the international success of *Battleship Potemkin,* Eisenstein consulted a psychiatrist about his "problem." The psychiatrist told him he had to make a choice between his sexuality and his art; Eisenstein allegedly chose to repress his sexuality and indulge in his art. The latter he certainly did; the former cannot be proved or disproved in our present state of knowledge.

There is no doubt that Eisenstein married Pera Attasheva in 1934, shortly after homosexual activity was outlawed in the USSR. This was in all probability a cover; they never lived together and, as far as we know, the marriage was never consummated. Attasheva acted as a mother substitute, housekeeper, and secretary but never as a conventional wife. Rumor has it that the great love of Eisenstein's life was his assistant director, Grigori Alexandrov, who accompanied him on his tour abroad from 1929 to 1932 across western Europe, to the United States and to Mexico.

Although we can discern clues to Eisenstein's sexuality from various sequences in his films, from the tumescent guns of *Battleship Potemkin,* through some scenes cut from the release version of *October* to a number of scenes in *Ivan the Terrible,* the drawings furnish the most consistent evidence. Not, of course, the published drawings, but the thousands upon thousands of explicitly erotic drawings that he penned from the time of his trip to Mexico until the end of his life. A small sample of these is to be found in the Ivor Montagu collection at the British Film Institute in London, but the overwhelming bulk are still held in private collections in Russia, conveniently obscured from public inspection.

In a diary entry written during the 1919–1921 civil war, when he was working as a set designer with the Red Army, Eisenstein asked his diary why he was always creating masks to conceal his true identity. Given the way the political situation in general, and specifically for homosexuals, developed in the USSR, it is scarcely surprising that he continued to create a network of masks for the rest of his life.

Richard Taylor

Bibliography

Christie, I., and R. Taylor, eds. *Eisenstein Rediscovered*. London: Routledge, 1993.

Eisenstein, Sergei. *Selected Works.* Richard Taylor, ed. 4 vols. London: British Film Institute, 1988–1996.

Lövgren, Håkan. *Eisenstein's Labyrinth: Aspects of a Cinematic Synthesis of the Arts.* Stockholm: Almqvist and Wiksell, 1996.

See also Film; Russia; Russian Literature

Elegiac Poetry

Celebrating the pain of losing what one values or desires the most, the elegy is the generic meeting place of Eros and Thanatos, of passion and death. Because the beloved is by nature the "not-self" or "other" that cannot be fully known or completely possessed, there is an elegiac dimension to all passion, loss through death signaling but the final, unbridgeable distance between the lover and the object of his affections. Historical circumstances, however, have made the elegy a particularly poignant expression of male same-sex desire.

The elegy enters gay literature through both the heroic narrative and the poetic pastoral tradition. Heroic narrative is homosocial, the presence of a male companion rather than a female beloved inspiring the hero to fight bravely and, conversely, the loss of that companion suggesting the fragility of all heroic accomplishment. Thus in the Sumerian legend *Gilgamesh* (3000 B.C.E.), while Gilgamesh's relationship with Enkidu allows him to defeat Humbaba, the giant of the Cedar Forest, and build the city of Uruk, on which Gilgamesh's glory rests, his subsequent loss of Enkidu causes him to question the meaning of his own existence and drives him to cross boundaries that no mortal has ever trespassed. Similarly, in Homer's *Iliad*, the Greek Achilles defeats Trojan hero Hector and wins glory, but only after the loss of his friend Patroklus arouses within him the pathological fury that makes him invincible. In biblical narrative, David enjoys with Jonathan a love "passing the love of women" (2 Samuel 1: 26); his career falls off in emotional intensity and heroic accomplishment after the death of his "brother." Their narratives allow Gilgamesh, Achilles, and David to speak haunting elegies on the deaths of their companions for which there is no parallel in the heroic world inspired by the loss of a female beloved.

Although concerned with the leisured world of bucolic existence rather than with the frenetic world of heroic accomplishment, the pastoral offers no less an occasion for elegiac song. The natural world is dominated by seasonal change, making the pastoral lover acutely aware of both the transience of human affection and of the aging process that must inevitably destroy the sweet bloom of youth. In the natural cycle, perfection holds but for an hour, the freshness of spring passing all too quickly into the passionate rage of summer, which in turn lapses into the chill of autumn, and diminishes into the cold sterility of winter. Likewise a beloved boy's beauty. His body, figured in pastoral poetry as the world of nature, is at first a marvel of sensual delights to be tasted, smelled, touched, savored, and celebrated. But as he passes from young adulthood into full physical maturity, his freshness fades and he falls from perfection. The unbridgeable distance between self and other, and between the adult lover and the ephemeral beauty of a beloved boy, figures the nostalgia for perfection that is at the heart of pastoral. The elegy enters pastoral tradition in Theocritus' *Idyll* 13, in which Heracles (Hercules) lapses into madness on losing golden-haired Hylas; Apollo, in Ovid's *Metamorphoses*, similarly loses both Narcissus and Hyacinthus.

Classical pastoral's elegization of the beautiful youth is burlesqued in Christopher Marlowe's *Hero and Leander*, christianized in both John Milton's "Lycidas" and Renaissance depictions of martyred St. Sebastian, but survives in Gerard Manley Hopkins's "Felix Randall" and the lyrics of A. E. Housman lamenting athletes dying young. The pastoral combines with the heroic in Walt Whitman's "Drum Taps" for the beautiful young men killed during the American Civil War, and in the homoerotic elegies for "Soldier Boys" killed during World War I.

There are two reasons why the elegy should be so heavily appropriated by male voices lamenting the loss of a male friend or beloved. First, as Michel Foucault argues, Christian interdiction of homosexual courtship and marriage has centered homosexual relations on the transitory sexual act itself, making gay literature a literature of memory; the elegy, by definition, is the primary poetic form and/or richest literary mode of remembrance and commemoration. Thus, an elegiac note pervades Marcel's description of Albertine in Proust's *Remembrance of Things Past*, colors von Aschenbach's pursuit of Tadzio in Thomas Mann's *Death in Venice*, and dominates the lyrics of Constantin Cavafy ("Body, remember").

And, second, during periods when the open expression of male same-sex desire is discouraged, conventions of grieving allow the expression of intense emotion—even of homoerotic feeling—that would otherwise be unseemly in a man. Byron may have been able publicly to lament the loss of his schoolboy love, John Edelstone, only by fictionalizing him as "Thyrza," but Thomas Gray—who laments the loss of Richard West in "Sonnet on the Death of Richard West" and, less directly, "Elegy in a Country Churchyard"—and Alfred Tennyson—who records in *In Memoriam* the three-year drama of his coming to accept the death of Arthur Henry Hallam ("him [whom] I loved, and love / For ever")—created the most popular poems of their respective generations, initial audiences little suspecting how their celebration of elegiac loss figures "physical longing and frustrated physical desire" (Haggerty 89).

Likewise, writing in the elegiac mode is sometimes the only way that a man ambivalent about his own sexuality can allow himself to express desire for another man. For Norman Page, Walter Pater's "looking freely and unashamed" "over a beautiful, youthful but dead [male's] body" in the Paris morgue is psychologically analogous to A. E. Housman's linking "youth and love and beauty with death and corruption" in *A Shropshire Lad*: "A dead young man does not constitute—and even more importantly does not appear to constitute—a temptation, except to a sentimental regret that camouflages the sexual attraction" (189). Similarly, Milton, unable to act on his attraction to Charles Diodati while the latter was alive, elegized him in *Epitaphium Damonis*, further distancing himself from troublesome homoerotic feeling by writing in Latin. *The Waste Land* has been read as T. S. Eliot's encoded elegy for Jean Verdenal, a flier whom Eliot met in Paris and who died aged twenty-six during World War I. And James Baldwin's novels function as extended elegies narrated by the surviving member of a male-male relationship who is able to articulate love only after the death of his "brother" when he himself no longer

feels threatened by such feeling. In each case, the death of the beloved precludes any possibility of the lover's acting on his desire, making verbal expression of that desire finally "safe."

"My thoughts are crowded with death"—the opening line of Thom Gunn's "In Time of Plague"—summarizes the mood both of his *The Man With Night Sweats* (1992) and of much gay literature composed since the AIDS pandemic instilled new urgency in elegiac writing. Paul Monette's extraordinary outpouring of grief in *Love Alone: Eighteen Elegies for Rog* (1988) is but the best-known collection of poetic elegies. Novels like Christopher Bram's *In Memory of Angel Clare* (1989) and Peter Cameron's *The Weekend* (1994) examine the emotional paralysis of AIDS "widows"; Dale Peck's *Martin and John* (1993), which depicts John's agonized search for coherence after the loss of Martin renders their shared world incoherent, is perhaps the most powerful novel yet to emerge. Terrence McNally's *Andre's Mother* (1988) dramatizes a memorial service at which a surviving lover exorcises his resentment of his dead partner's mother's persistent silence, while Andre's death leaves his mother with no choice but finally to let go of the son whom she never allowed herself to know. Tony Kushner's Pulitzer Prize– and Tony Award–winning *Angels in America* (1990–1993), which opens with a funeral service and includes a scene in which Ethel Rosenberg prays kaddish for Roy Cohn, is a meditation on how one is able to achieve the blessing of "More Life" in the face of unwarranted early death. And in the transcendent final scene of the film *Longtime Companion* (1990), the ferry that, during the sexually rambunctious 1970s, brought gay weekenders to Fire Island is transformed into Charon's ferry that in Greek mythology carried the souls of the dead over the river Styx.

Ironically, loss is the one experience that recent American audiences seem willing to allow gay lovers. Arnold's disturbing sexuality was dignified and made palatable for the Broadway audiences of Harvey Fierstein's *Torch Song Trilogy* (1981) by his transformation on the death of his lover Alan into a grieving widow. And the most moving scene in the commercially popular film *Four Weddings and a Funeral* (1994) comes when Matthew recites an elegy by "another splendid bugger"—W. H. Auden's "Stop all the clocks" (from his *Twelve Songs*)—at his lover's funeral. The gay couple, significantly, is allowed the sole funeral of the film's title, but none of the four weddings. *Raymond-Jean Frontain*

E

Bibliography

Crompton, Louis. *Byron and Greek Love: Homophobia in 19th-Century England.* Berkeley: University of California Press, 1985.

Frontain, Raymond-Jean. "James Baldwin's *Giovanni's Room* and the Biblical Myth of David." *CEA Critic* 57, no. 2 (Winter 1995): 41–58.

Fussell, Paul. "Soldier Boys." In *The Great War and Modern Memory.* New York: Oxford University Press, 1975, 270–309.

Haggerty, George E. "*O lachrymarum fons*: Tears, Poetry, and Desire in Gray." *Eighteenth-Century Studies* 30 (1996): 81–95.

Miller, James. "Dante on Fire Island: Reinventing Heaven in the AIDS Elegy." In *Writing AIDS: Gay Literature, Language, and Analysis.* Timothy F. Murphy and Suzanne Poirier, eds. New York: Columbia University Press, 1993, 265–305.

Page, Norman. *A. E. Housman: A Critical Biography.* New York: Schocken, 1983.

Peter, John. "A New Interpretation of *The Waste Land*." *Essays in Criticism* 19, no. 2 (April 1969): 140–75.

Shawcross, John T. "Milton and Diodati: An Essay in Psychodynamic Meaning." *Milton Studies* 7 (1975): 127–63.

Staten, Henry. *Eros in Mourning: Homer to Lacan.* Baltimore: Johns Hopkins University Press, 1995.

Woods, Gregory. "AIDS to Remembrance: The Uses of Elegy." In *AIDS: The Literary Response.* Emmanuel S. Nelson, ed. New York: Twayne, 1992, 155–66.

See also Arabic Literature; Auden, W. H.; Baldwin, James; Cavafy, Constantine P.; David and Jonathan; English Literature; Fierstein, Harvey; French Literature; German Literature; Gilgamesh Epic; Gray, Thomas; Gunn, Thom; Homer; Housman, A. E.; Kushner, Tony; Mann, Thomas; Marlowe, Christopher; Monette, Paul; Pater, Walter; Proust, Marcel; Tennyson, Alfred

Ellis, Havelock (1859–1939)

"Like breathing a bag of soot": such were the objections to the frank examinations made by this British writer, who spanned the domains of literature, medicine, and modern sexology. More honored now, and more infamous then, for his work in sexology than his literary criticism (essays on Hardy, for example;

editions of Ibsen, Vasari, and then-forgotten dramatists such as Marlowe), Ellis authored, among many books, the seven-part voluminous *Studies in the Psychology of Sex,* one part of which was *Sexual Inversion.* First published in Germany in the German language (1896), *Sexual Inversion* ran into trouble in its English debut. Not the least of these was the sale and destruction of the whole first English edition by the family of Ellis's co-collaborator, John Addington Symonds, followed by, in its next appearance, a dramatic lawsuit against a London bookseller carrying it.

By its final version, the controversial volume began with definitions, conceiving "sexual inversion" ("sexual instinct turned by inborn constitutional abnormality toward persons of the same sex," Ellis, Vol. 1, Part 4.1) as a narrower term than "homosexuality" ("which includes all sexual attractions between persons of the same sex [for example, prison inmates] . . . phenomenon of wide occurrence among all human races and among most of the higher animals"). By means of these distinctions, not only did Ellis introduce the term *homosexuality* to the English public (coined by fellow Victorian Richard Burton), he also made it possible to strike a middle path between Krafft-Ebing, who stressed the inborn nature of inversion, and Schrenk-Notzing, who argued that it was largely acquired (by suggestion) and amenable to treatment. As his title suggests, Ellis wished to stress the congenital elements of what he called "true sexual inversion." To this end, he offered characteristically extensive examples of both homosexuality and inversion, ranging over various groups of people (Albanians, Greeks, Eskimo), over various times (ancient Rome in one instance, modern prisons in another) and "among men of exceptional intellect" (Muret, Michelangelo, Whitman, Verlaine). He then examined leading theories of his day, followed by actual case histories for which he supplied limited analysis and from which he drew limited conclusions.

Ellis is said to have been painfully shy, though enormously generous with advice and attention to those who called on him; received as messianic (in both looks and wisdom); though passive, chronically dyspeptic and impotent; devoted to many women in his life—the likes of feminist writer Olive Schreiner, birth-control advocate Margaret Sanger, and his seemingly lesbian wife, Edith—though himself, in the eyes of many biographers, a latent homosexual. Ellis is now often compared to Freud. (Both men admired each other and politely disagreed throughout intermittent correspondence.) The result of this correlation is usually to present Ellis as a sex pioneer who, unlike Freud, lacked modern methods and wrote as if manifest and latent content were identical. Yet, in the area of *sex reform*, Ellis, in the eyes of many commentators, established the most persuasive rationales for decriminalization and sex-positive views of any writer of his day.

Kathryn Bond Stockton

Bibliography

Brome, Vincent. *Havelock Ellis: Philosopher of Sex.* London: Routledge and Kegan Paul, 1979.
Ellis, Havelock. *Studies in the Psychology of Sex.* New York: Random House, 1936.

See also Freud, Sigmund; Michelangelo Buonarroti; Sexology; Symonds, John Addington; Verlaine, Paul; Whitman, Walt

England

Social attitudes in England over the centuries have been, to a considerable extent, a subset of those prevalent across the Christian West. Above all, Scriptural authority has been a habitual companion for repression. Nevertheless, insular attitudes to homosexuality have repeatedly shown a differing pattern from those widely held on the Continent. The main divergence lies in greater moderation in England in the period up to 1700 and greater intolerance in the period after. This division more or less corresponds to the emergence of a homosexual identity as opposed to the identification of same-sex acts. It appears that the English disliked secret deviant behavior but abhorred unavoidable deviant ideas. This phenomenon expressed itself in a tradition of hypocrisy in which a blind eye was sometimes turned unless the issue were made public. At that point earlier complicity was denied by an over-the-top display of horror and detestation lest accusations of involvement should be leveled.

If we assume that a standard proportion of human populations have same-sex desires, then the materials we are studying represent the tip of an erotic iceberg that has risen significantly out of the opaque waters only in the last one hundred years. The situation with regard to evidence for lesbianism is even worse than for homosexual men, since woman-to-woman desire was perhaps less disapproved of but also less well recognized than its male counterpart. The reason for this was the long exclu-sion of women from positions of importance in society. Women's matters were, therefore, not thought of as very significant, and as with the concerns of the poor, frequently went unreported until recent times. A further complication of the pre-modern period is disentangling same-sex acts and homosexual identities, with the mainstream view being that the latter were slow to emerge. Gay identities as such do not appear clearly in early sources, but that does not mean there were no people who were not well aware that their desires were for their own gender. A further problem is caused by our understanding of "friendships." In previous centuries "friends" would often write to each other in emotional tones that would be read in modern society as indicating sexual interest. However, it may be we who are exceptional in doubting the sincerity of Platonic emotional bonds.

Wider public perception is what changes over time, and the story of gay men and women in history is really that of the way that they were viewed. The narrative, for England, as for most of the West, is largely a depressing tale of incomprehension and repression. Accusations of same-sex behavior were made toward a number of medieval monarchs including William II and Richard I. Although it was Edward II, killed by having a red-hot poker shoved up his backside, who has achieved the greatest notoriety. Late medieval and early modern society was implacably hostile to homosexual behavior. Sodomy was made a capital offense in England in 1533, based on the biblical authority of the destruction of Sodom and Gomorrah and of the Mosaic Laws of Leviticus, but taking the jurisdiction away from church courts. This legislation did not cover lesbian behavior since penetration was the key issue.

The image of the sodomite conjured up such diabolical associations that people who engaged in some same-sex activity might well not have applied it to themselves. A sodomite was an extreme sexual deviant. The authorized version of the Bible, for example, gave "sodomitess" as an alternative word for "whore." The general notion was of debauchery to which everyone, in theory, was vulnerable. For the Puritan John Rainolds, homosexuality was a sin to which "men's natural corruption and viciousness is prone." There was no sense that there could be different rules for different people. And yet there were not many prosecutions, mainly because the law was narrow and specific to penetrative activity and, second, because of the relative infrequency of "moral" executions for crimes such as heresy, to which sodomy was often associated, when compared with Continental Europe.

The active sexual position (insertion) was the only one conceivable. Men who were passive were seen as freaks. Emotions as well as lusts were engaged, as we might expect, and are most famously attested by Shakespeare's sonnets, which were written partly to a youth and partly to a woman. More explicit imagery appears in the writings of Marlowe, especially in his play on the life of Edward II. The man-to-youth paradigm was less upsetting than an association of equals because the adult male kept his active sexual role, thus not upsetting expected behaviors of men and women. This can be compared to attitudes prevalent in ancient Rome.

By the seventeenth century, however, new forms of behavior and identity slowly become visible. From this era come the first references to "male stews" in London (taverns where rent boys would entertain clients). Sodomites in satire were now young men about town with a mistress on one arm and a catamite on the other. Sodomy was associated with luxury, decadence, and extravagance often sliding into rape and incest. The period saw the recognition of religious nonconformism and has been seen as the point of origin for a pluralist society. The appearance of a homosexual identity is related to the rise of the individual. But that identity was imposed by society at large and was strongly negative, focusing not on the active libertine side of the phenomenon but on the passive and effeminate, and therefore detested, catamite.

Nevertheless, the increase in urbanization created greater anonymity and sexual opportunity. Popular places for assignations through the eighteenth century were parks and coffeehouses. Sunday was the main night for action when the "molly houses" (male brothels) were most frequented. Most clients had wives and participated only occasionally. Although there was a lack of organized police, there was still great danger of blackmail and public exposure. The origins of specialized gay argot dates from this period, functioning as a way of communicating group identity that was impenetrable to outsiders.

In continental Europe the peak of executions for sodomy occurred during the wars against heresy and witchcraft in the sixteenth and seventeenth centuries. In England, by contrast, there were few executions in this period. Enlightenment thinking, although abhorring femininity, went against the death penalty in sodomy cases. The great European powers liberalized during the eighteenth century. France went the furthest in 1791 by decriminalizing same-sex relations entirely, a move preserved in the 1810 Napoleonic Code. By contrast, in England there was a dramatic rise in executions through the end of the eighteenth and into the early nineteenth century when there were two or so executions per year, and this was in an age when executions for other reasons were in decline. Although few of the potential "one in ten" were killed, those that were served as examples, inspiring terror in others. Repression was part of Protestant English identity, in proud opposition to the supposed immorality of Roman Catholics in general and the French in particular.

The number of executions was still relatively low because of the difficulty of conviction. If proof of penetration and emission were missing, then the charge of sodomy failed and conviction was for "assault with intent to commit sodomy," the penalty being the pillory and imprisonment, both of which could lead to death. Women, particularly prostitutes, were involved in abusing those shackled in the pillory, thus demonstrating their superiority over the detested sodomites. The screaming of the mob for blood contrasts with the silence of polite society, in which the subject of homosexual behavior was completely taboo. Jeremy Bentham was exceptional in recognizing homophobia as a social phenomenon and not simply as a natural part of the world order. English Enlightenment thinking most often produced merely "rational" explanations for persecution, such as the supposed robbing of women of their rights and the threat to population levels. Among the masses, "superstition," as expressed in the death penalty of Leviticus 20:13, continued to be the motor of hatred. Sex was to be for procreation, and all other sexual acts, including masturbation, were evil and inspired by the devil.

The media were particularly homophobic and ardent in condemning the "foreign vice" on the rare occasions that it surfaced from the conspiracy of silence. The vogue for classics was stemmed in the realm of high ideas by the ideological power of Anglican theology. Suspect Greek texts were translated into Latin, and Latin ones into Italian. However, the elite would know originals even if translations were incomplete or dramatically bowdlerized. Lord Byron was not the only aristocrat to court scandal with his voyages abroad in search of freedom and sexual opportunities. All of this was grist for the mill of the popular culture of homophobia, since same-sex behavior could be condemned as a vice of the rich and educated, who then were stung into an attempt at self-repression so as to retain their status as leaders of society, morally as well as economically and politically.

The year 1861 saw the repeal of the death penalty for sodomy. This was not a liberal measure, but rather a recognition that a very high standard of proof had been required and successful prosecution was difficult. Replacement was by the Offences Against the Person Act, which enacted penal servitude of between ten years and life. During these later years of the nineteenth century, the word *homosexual* made its appearance, and lawmakers were made aware of the dangers not simply of a sexual act but of a whole class of persons. In 1887 a late-night amendment was tacked on to a bill of other public health measures that established the offense of gross indecency, penalizing any gay sexual act with up to two years in prison, with or without hard labor. This legislation was much broader in scope than the previous. Britain was the only country in Europe with such a sweeping statute. The importance of this move should be seen in the context of Britain as an imperial power. Such attitudes were exported across the globe's many "pink bits."

Yet the greater prominence of antigay legislation in the law codes was simply a reflection of the rising profile of lesbians and homosexuals in society. This was the period when lesbian couples began to appear in gay and lesbian sources, especially in a butch/femme configuration. Gay male sexuality, in the universities as well as among the aristocracy and in the brothels of London, was forced into the public gaze by the scandal (in both contemporary and modern terms) of the downfall of Oscar Wilde. The violent press reaction resulted in a precise stereotyping of the homosexual as exotic, luxurious, artistic, and effeminate. For decades, Wilde's name was not to be mentioned in polite society. In 1898, Havelock Ellis's *Sexual Inversion*, which alleged that a considerable number of prominent Renaissance figures were "inverts", was banned under the 1857 Obscene Publications Act. Scholarship did not approach the subject again for decades.

Positive homosexual identities were restricted to minor and marginal milieus in the early twentieth century. *Queer* and *Sapphist* were the main terms used in middle-class contexts, with a wide range of slang below. The social upheavals of the twenties, including the fashion of a boyish look for women, made some impact. Radcliffe Hall, a woman of private means, published the pioneering lesbian novel *Well of Loneliness* (1928) and was duly prosecuted for obscenity, arousing the same level of controversy as did the great trials of D. H. Lawrence's *Lady Chatterley's Lover* in 1960. There were large sales, but the media rushed in for the kill; *Sunday Express* writer James Douglas famously asserted that it were better to give a child a vial of prussic acid than a copy of the book, "because while poison kills the body, moral poison kills the soul." Prosecution came under the Obscene Publications Act. The judge referred to "acts of the most horrible, unnatural and disgusting obscenity" and ordered all copies destroyed.

But the overall effect of this repression was a great rise in public perception of lesbianism, with active public debate as to whether these people were born with a particular sexuality or learned it, and whether gay sexuality was a criminal or a medical issue. There was a certain degree of positive interest among rebellious students in the thirties, as in the division in Oxford, for example, between hearties and aesthetes. But while there was some tacit acceptance of homosexuality in universities or in the theater, it was still highly dangerous to be open about such desires. Nöel Coward was camp and very popular, but his style was closeted coquetry and contrasts, in retrospect, with Radcliffe Hall's honesty. London was the great center of English gay life, as it had been for centuries. Lyons Corner House on Leicester Square was then known as the "Lilypond." The end of the thirties and the advent of World War II threw large numbers of people together in single-sex environments. Extraordinary procedures understandably failed to weed out homosexuals from the armed forces, save for such instances as when Quentin Crisp turned up in his habitual semidrag and was, unsurprisingly, declared unsuitable for service because he was "suffering from sexual perversion." Many men in the service would indulge in same-sex activity, not thinking themselves homosexual but simply without access to women.

With postwar society came the desire for security and the reassertion of traditional family life. There was even a brief attempt to ban the Kinsey Report (1948). The defection of Guy Burgess and Donald Maclean to the USSR in 1951 seemed to confirmed the suspicion that communism and homosexuality were related, and that deviants were not to be trusted since they were susceptible to blackmail. The number of arrests for homosexual offenses shot up. It was, however, becoming clear that

E homosexuals were to be found throughout the establishment, and that gay men were not all obviously effeminate nor lesbians butch, and that some of them were even married. Science found the phenomenon puzzling. Medical treatments prescribed at the time included aversion therapy with emetics, electric shocks, and lobotomies. These alarming regimes were frequently forced on patients and offenders, including Alan Turing, the mathematician who broke the German codes in World War II. He committed suicide after hormone treatment, a condition of a probation sentence, led to depression.

The first signs of a shift in atmosphere came from the BBC, whence a number of words of the gay argot, Polari, entered more general usage following camp radio comedies, especially the duologues between Kenneth Williams and Hugh Paddick on *Round the House.* More surprisingly, a new direction appeared in a Church of England report asking for a reexamination of the law. This was followed by the Wolfenden Committee (1954–1957), which recommended in a report that homosexual acts in private over the age of twenty-one not be punished, but that male prostitution should be made specifically illegal, as had not previously been the case. The media were violently negative in their response, regarding the report as a "buggers' charter."

The committee, however, was not "pro" homosexual. The belief was that there were very few inverts, that is, biological mistakes, but that others could "catch" homosexuality from them. The intention was that, by removing the danger of prosecution, individuals would be persuaded to come forward for medical and psychological assistance toward a "cure." However, MPs reacted with horror to the idea that this malady might no longer be suppressed, and they expressed fears that it would grow like a "cancer," "killing off normal life" and reducing society to a "bestial state." The Sexual Offences Act, 1959, made male prostitution illegal but ignored the other recommendations of the Wolfenden Committee. Meanwhile, social changes lagged behind Parliament, as has often been the case. Unofficial gay bars were springing up with increasing frequency, although raids were just as frequent. In 1964 the director of public prosecutions, however, urged a scaling down of persecution. This was the age of Joe Orton, Francis Bacon, and Benjamin Britten, when lauded public figures were known to be homosexual, even if their sexuality was still officially a matter of disgrace.

This anomaly was partially addressed by the Sexual Offences Act, 1967, which emerged under Prime Minister Harold Wilson as an element in a wave of liberalization on personal morality issues. Finally, after a dramatic and hard-fought passage through Parliament, partial decriminalization of gay sex acts established in law the main conclusions reached by the Wolfenden Committee a decade earlier. Nevertheless, the atmosphere of the reform was still way behind the rapidly changing youth climate of the times. Events in America, such as the Stonewall riots of June 27, 1969, had their impact in Britain, although the emerging gay community was for many years small, isolated, and viewed as extremist. The first meeting of the Gay Liberation Front took place in the London School of Economics on October 13, 1970. The first gay pride march took place on Saturday July 1, 1972. It was promoted as a "carnival parade" and over one thousand people participated in such activities as traveling the London Underground in drag.

In 1973 homosexuality was finally taken off the register of psychological diseases. Two years later the *Rocky Horror Picture Show* played in London and Thames Television made the *Naked Civil Servant,* based on the biography of England's "stately homo," Quentin Crisp. A survey suggested that 85 percent of viewers failed to find it shocking. The midseventies saw the opening of big gay clubs, Bang being the premier. The leather clone look came in from New York. Gay culture was American-dominated in clothes and music, although a different tone was set by British glamrock, which found its most remarkable expression in David Bowie. In March 1977 the *Sunday Mirror* ran a positive article on a number of "respectable" gay men, arguing that "gays are probably Britain's most powerful and vocal minority group." Camp images of gay men were being challenged by muscle-clad butch. It seemed as though real progress was being made.

The 1980s, however, in England as in America, saw a series of setbacks. The country swung politically to the right. Gay men started becoming ill in 1981 from what would later be recognized as HIV-related illnesses. On July 4, 1982, Terrence Higgins died and Britain had its first death from the disease that would come to be called AIDS. Paranoia reigned in the popular press. Prime Minister Margaret Thatcher, particularly after her third election victory in 1987, reasserted what she called "Victorian values," exploiting and furthering a decline in public support for gay lifestyles. Clause 28 was added to the Local Government Bill, stating that "a local authority shall not intentionally promote homosexuality or publish material with the intention of promoting homosexuality and shall not promote the teaching in any maintained school of the acceptability of homosexuality as a pretended family relationship." There was substantial protest at the measure, including by lesbians who disrupted the House of Lords from the public gallery and later broke onto a BBC TV news set.

The power of the Conservatives was beginning to decline with the changing fortunes of the British economy. Progress in European Community legislation was beginning to make itself felt. In 1994 the age of gay sexual consent was reduced from twenty-one to eighteen. Three years later the Labour Party returned to power and England saw an openly gay man, Chris Smith, in the cabinet, after the general election witnessed a number of other openly gay candidates elected. The death of Diana, Princess of Wales, in 1997 highlighted her charitable interests, prominent among which were trusts for those with AIDS, thus helping to break taboos surrounding discussion of a disease that was far more than a "gay plague," but that often was still perceived as such.

By the late nineties, England remained in many ways a sexually repressive society, although liberated to a remarkable degree from the situation a century ago. The strongest divide in social attitudes concerning homosexuality remained between the young and the old, which gives hope for improvement over time. Nevertheless, the state still clings tenaciously to its long tradition of making moral decisions concerning such issues as drug use and sexuality. Legal changes may come in from Europe, although even across the European Community, gay relationships are still undervalued compared with those between heterosexuals. The Church of England and other religious groups remain suspicious of liberalization. Will there be the first-ever era of general toleration, indifference, or even enthusiasm? The fate of lesbians and gay men in England is in the balance.   *Dominic Janes*

Bibliography

Bray, Alan. *Homosexuality in Renaissance England.* New York: Columbia University Press, 1995.

Crompton, Louis. *Byron and Greek Love: Homophobia in 19th-Century England.* London: Faber and Faber, 1985.

Higgins, Patrick. *Heterosexual Dictatorship: Male Homosexuality in Postwar Britain.* London: Fourth Estate, 1996.

Hyde, Harford Montgomery. *The Other Love: An Historical and Contemporary Survey of Homosexuality in Britain.* London: Heinemann, 1970.

Jivani, Alkarim. *It's Not Unusual: A History of Lesbian and Gay Britain in the Twentieth Century.* London: Michael O'Mara Books, 1997.

Power, Lisa. *No Bath but Plenty of Bubbles: An Oral History of the Gay Liberation Front, 1970–73.* London: Cassell, 1995.

Sanderson, Terry. *Mediawatch: The Treatment of Male and Female Homosexuality in the British Media.* London: Cassell, 1995.

Spencer, Colin. *Homosexuality: A History.* London: Fourth Estate, 1995.

Weeks, Jeffrey. *Sex, Politics and Society Since 1800.* London: Longman, 1981.

See also AIDS; Bacon, Francis; Bentham, Jeremy; Bible; Britten, (Edward) Benjamin; Buggery; Byron, George Gordon, Lord; Camp; Coward, Noël; Crisp, Quentin; Ellis, Havelock; European Commission of Human Rights; France; Gay Liberation Front; Inversion; Kinsey, Alfred; Leathermen; London; Mollies; Molly Houses; Orton, Joe; Paris; Queer; Sodom; Sodomy; Sodomy Trials; Turing, Alan; Wilde, Oscar; Wolfenden Report

English Literature

Gay or queer criticism has signaled, from the outset, that its project entails not the examination of a circumscribed canon of gay-centered or gay-identified texts but a rereading of the way in which the entire body of Anglo-American literature—and beyond—delineates among other things the boundaries of sexual identity, the norms of sexual behavior, the grotesque and classically desirable body, and the terms of social inclusion and exile. Ignoring such questions makes the scope of a single essay on the topic perilously indefinite. However, what follows merely attempts, rather pragmatically, to mark some of the places in the canon of British literature where discussion of same-sex desire has already begun and might proceed further; it focuses particularly on the period before there is a stable vocabulary for sexual orientation or a perceived category of men whose identities, rather than actions, are to be seen as "homosexual." This historical division is not meant to imply that such an identification is or could be—much less should be—stabilized even after the late nineteenth century.

The high literary culture of the Middle Ages was emphatically international, so it is somewhat misleading to limit discussion of medieval English literature to purely native texts. One influential French text—cited, for example, by Chaucer in *The Parlement of Foule*—is Alan of Lille's twelfth-century *De Planctu Nature* (The Complaint of Nature), in which a personified Nature laments that sodomy undoes the very basis of the physical universe. Moreover, homosexuality is bad grammar: the man who "is made woman is both predicate and subject, he becomes likewise of two declensions, he pushes the laws of grammar too far."

When medieval English culture even acknowledges that sexual relations between men exist, such relations are designated as "sodomy," and mentioned primarily for purposes of denunciation; "sodomites" have the same relation to sodomy that adulterers have to adultery: their respective actions mark them, but they have no relation to a preexisting classification of those who perform them as "sodomite" or "adulterer." The definition of sodomy, however, is notoriously flexible and, as nearly all critics (following Michel Foucault) have said, "utterly confused." Since the term extends to most nonprocreative sexual behavior, even between men and women, its application specifically to intercourse between men becomes noteworthy. *Clannesse* (Cleanness or Purity), a fourteenth-century poem of about 1,800 lines by the anonymous writer usually known as the Pearl Poet, offers an unusually extended and explicit account of the events leading up to the destruction of Sodom; the male inhabitants of Sodom are said to fornicate "on femmalez wyse" ("in female fashion," line 696)—presumably meaning that one partner is passive, though the phrase seems to lesbianize both. The demand of the Sodomites that they be allowed to instruct Lot's angelic visitors in their form of love ("That we may lere hym of lof, as oure lyst biddez," line 843) is of course treated as unspeakable filth, but the sensual attractiveness of the angels is treated in surprising, even amorous detail: "They were beardless youths, beautiful both to behold, / They had long hair, like lovely, luxurious silk, / And their skin where it showed, was as soft as a rose. / Their eyes shimmered" (Casey Finch's modern translation, lines 789–92). Allen J. Frantzen argues that the poet's attention to "the sights, sounds, and smells of sodomy," which is franker than that of any other Middle English text, effectively "queers" the poem, even against the grain of its ostensible moral discourse (452).

A more famous work attributed to the Pearl Poet is *Sir Gawain and the Green Knight*, whose complicated courtly games and exchanges of power also, though differently, put the alignment of sexual roles in question. One of these courtly games entails Sir Gawain's trading what he has "won" for the hunting spoils of his host, Sir Bertilak; Gawain's winnings are kisses from Bertilak's wife, which he faithfully renders to her husband. "The kisses were seductive, erotic in their first instance; are they now?" Carolyn Dinshaw asks (206). While she and another recent critic of the poem, David Lorenzo Boyd, diverge in their answers to this question, both their analyses (like Frantzen's of *Cleanness*) point to heterosexuality itself as "produced" by the poem, rather than simply given; the otherness of homosexuality underwrites this production.

In the Prologue to Geoffrey Chaucer's *The Canterbury Tales*, the Pardoner is paired with the Summoner, who "bar to hym a stif burdoun," a phrase that ostensibly means that he supplied the bass harmony (burden) to the Pardoner's song, "Come hither, love, to me!" but since "burdoun" can also mean an erect penis, it may also suggest anal intercourse. Chaucerian critics have long pointed out this pun but, until the advent of an explicitly gay criticism, have stopped short of discussing the hypervirile Summoner as an active homosexual partner, perhaps on the tacit assumption that only the masculinity of the passive Pardoner has been compromised. However the Summoner understands his own activity, he is in no way inhibited from using his tale to impute sodomy to his rival, the Friar. The portrait and narrative fortunes of Absolon in "The Miller's Tale" also metaphorically associate effeminacy with sodomy. The parish clerk Absolon's fastidious dress and dainty manners make him an improbable suitor for Alisoun, the frisky, down-to-earth wife of an old carpenter. She rewards his wooing by sticking her ass out the window for Absolon to kiss, "ful savoury," in the nocturnal darkness. Absolon recoils, "For wel he wiste a womman hath no berd" (For well he knew a woman has no beard). He borrows a heated ploughshare from the smith down the street and returns for revenge; when his successful rival, Nicholas, decides to join in the fun by sticking his own ass out the window and letting a fart fly, Absolon strikes him "amydde the ers" with the glowing iron and henceforth forswears the pursuit of women. This parody of anal rape that climaxes "The Miller's Tale" evokes a grimmer historical parallel: in 1327 the murderers of the homosexual king Edward II inserted a red-hot poker up his rectum.

John Boswell's historical work, especially *Christianity, Social Tolerance and Homosexuality,* has influenced a whole generation of younger medieval scholars, who are now exploring the range of literary texts on which a gay critical perspective might prove illuminating. Nevertheless, the English Renaissance presents, even at first glance, a far broader and more varied field of inquiry. A rhetoric of friendship that could both veil and express same-sex desire, a language of classical allusion that gave at least specious authority to the representation of errant sexuality, a transvestite theater in which all the women's parts were played by boys of tradition may have all contributed to the possibilities of expressing a wider spectrum of sexual feeling between men than at any period before the late nineteenth century. By 1603 the English had a king, James I of England who openly embraced and showered endearments on his male favorites; his Lord Chancellor, Sir Francis Bacon (1561–1626), though married, also lived in unabashedly sexual intimacy with his manservants. The abundance of resources for investigating gay literary and social history only multiplies the perplexities of definition and classification that treating early-modern materials entails, and a broad survey can do no more than gesture toward some of the areas of discussion that have been pursued with interpretive subtlety and dense historical detail by scholars including Stephen Orgel, Jonathan Goldberg, Gregory Bredbeck, Bruce Smith, and Valerie Traub; Alan Bray's groundbreaking work, *Homosexuality in the English Renaissance,* though often challenged, remains an indispensable starting place for social history.

One of the defining figures of the Elizabethan theater, Christopher Marlowe (1564–1593), was daringly transgressive in both his religious and sexual attitudes. In 1593 an informant named Richard Baines denounced his blasphemous opinions to the Privy Council; among a long litany of heresies about Moses and Jesus as impostors, Marlowe is quoted as saying "that St John the Evangelist was bedfellow to Christ and leaned alwaies in his bosome, that he used him as the sinners of Sodoma; That all they that love not Tobacco & Boies were fooles." The document was clearly intended to get Marlowe in trouble—which doesn't necessarily mean Marlowe didn't say the things it reports; Marlowe's gleeful intention to shock seems visible through Baines's pious, tale-bearing horror. In any case, Marlowe's poetry, both dramatic and nondramatic, is suffused with homoerotic feeling. His long but unfinished narrative poem *Hero and Leander* evokes its heroine, Hero, in her role as priestess of Venus, encrusted with elaborate garments and headdress, but for purposes of description strips Leander naked, and the poet virtually runs his finger over Leander's body: "Even as delicious meat is to the tase, / So was his neck in touching, and surpass'd / The White of Pelops' shoulder. I could tell ye / How smooth his breast was, and how white his belly." Later, as Leander swims across the Hellespont, Neptune caresses him; when Leander protests, "You are deciev'd, I am no woman, I," the sea god only smiles knowingly.

Marlowe's *Edward the Second* famously depicts King Edward's love for his favorite, Piers Gaveston; the opening scene brilliantly captures Gaveston's mixture of affection for the king and self-serving ambition, as well as the piquant character of the entertainments with which he plans to stimulate Edward's erotic appetites: as one part of the "Italian masques" Gaveston will provide: "Sometime a lovely boy in Dian's shape, / With hair that gilds the water as it glides, / Crownets of pearl about his naked arms, / And in his hands an olive-tree, / To hide those parts which men delight to see" (I, i, 61–68).

It has required centuries of collective cultural effort to keep Shakespeare's *Sonnets* (published in 1609) from seeming homosexual; the effort begins with John Benson's 1640 edition of the *Sonnets,* which changed the gender pronouns of the earlier sonnets. Edmond Malone's was the first scholarly edition of the *Sonnets* (1780); it restored the original pronouns and gave the poems wider currency. (The romantic poets were among the newly appreciative readers of the *Sonnets,* but Coleridge had to lean heavily on Sonnet 20 to reassure himself that "that very worse of all possible vices" never "entered even [Shakespeare's] imagination." He also asserts that none of the plays do much as alludes to that "disposition," much less to "the absurd and despicable act.") The first 126 of the 154 sonnets are addressed to a young man, called in Sonnet 20 "the Master Mistris of my passion"; popular mythology about Shakespeare has preferred to focus on sonnets 127–152, which are primarily concerned with the "Dark Lady," but a man, who may be the friend ad-

E dressed in the earlier sonnets, also appears in these poems as both a "better angell" (144) and a rival. The primary strategy for making these poems safe for a heterosexual readership has been decontextualization; when "Shall I compare thee to a summer's day?" (Sonnet 18) is anthologized, it is seldom pointed out that the poem is addressed to a man. The specific character of the relationship between Shakespeare and the young man whom most of the sonnets address remains a topic of debate; the first seventeen sonnets, after all, urge the young man to marry and perpetuate his beauty by begetting children, and the most obvious reading of Sonnet 20 seems to assign "thy love's use" (intercourse) to "women's pleasure." However, even if one implausibly supposes that marriage and fatherhood are incompatible with same-sex relations, the emotional tone of the sonnets is hard to mistake or—despite the efforts of earlier generations of critics—to assign solely to an unusually fervid rhetoric of (nonsexual) male friendship. Except for Richard Barnfield's poems—which have struck most readers as unambiguously homosexual—no comparable sequence of sonnets addressed to a man exists in English; the Italian parallel of Michelangelo's sonnets addressed to Tommaso de' Cavalieri hardly fortifies the argument for avoiding an erotic reading of the first 126 *Sonnets*. In *Some Versions of Pastoral,* William Empson suggests that Parts I and II of *Henry IV* replay the situation of the *Sonnets*, with the desirable young man as Prince Hal and "Shakespeare" self-caricatured as the aging, physically gross, phallically deflated "Fal[l]-staff."

The only character in Shakespeare's plays who is explicitly labeled a male passive partner is Patroclus in *Troilus and Cressida*. The bitter Thersites calls him "Achilles' brach [bitch]" (II, i, 114), "Achilles' varlot" (V, i, 15), and "his masculine whore" (V, i, 17). Thersites' venomous disposition has allowed critics to regard these epithets as slanders, but the venom may reside mainly in Thersites' evaluation of Achilles and Patroclus' intimacy; a long tradition, extending back at least as far as Plato's *Symposium,* had cast them in the roles of lovers.

It is frequently argued, especially by scholars of a Foucauldian bent, that while English men and women of the Middle Ages and early-modern periods recognized discrete acts of "sodomy," or heterodox and presumably contingent choices of sexual objects, they did not perceive homosexual men or women as constituting separate human types—at the very least until a visible homosexual subculture emerges in London at the end of the seventeenth century. It took the form of "molly houses," that is, gathering places where campy, cross-gendered styles of behavior could find free expression—and where, as Randolph Trumbach has argued, the first "queens" might have been found. (An even stronger—almost nominalist—position would defer acknowledgment of the "homosexual" until the late nineteenth century, when a medicalized, scientific vocabulary for sexual orientation comes into currency and the term itself is first used.) It nevertheless seems that, without a vocabulary to describe such inclinations, Shakespeare recognized that there were temperaments whose emotional intensity centered on their affection for members of the same sex; among the ways in which he registers this perception is by giving the same name, Antonio, to two characters in different plays who might plausibly be characterized in these terms. The better known is the title character of *The Merchant of Venice*; much of the play revolves around the tacit contest between Antonio and Portia for Bassanio's affections—in conventional terms, friendship vs. love. Antonio financially sponsors Bassanio's courtship of Portia, in the process indenturing himself to Shylock; Portia sees that if Antonio dies as a consequence of his act of friendship for Bassanio, his idealized image will always come between her husband and herself, and undertakes to free Antonio from Shylock's claims. Antonio, meanwhile, anticipates the prospect of death with a kind of emotional abandon: "Pray God Bassanio come / To see me pay his debt, and then I care not!" (III, iii, 35–36). Some of his language may, moreover, encode what seems, at least in hindsight, a kind of gay self-hatred: "I am a tainted wether of the flock, / Meetest for death; the weakest kind of fruit / Drops earliest to the ground, and so let me" (IV, i, 114–16). In less complicated ways the sea captain and sometime pirate Antonio in *Twelfth Night* seems equally self-abnegating in his devotion to Sebastian (the male half of the play's androgynously paired twins, Sebastian and Viola). A third Antonio makes an appearance as one of the conspirators in *The Tempest*, paired (reunited?) with another courtier named Sebastian, and thus invites speculation about whether the nomenclature embodies for the playwright some private code.

Even more conspicuous is the frequent recourse of Shakespeare's comedies to plots in which the women characters dress as men, thus aligning the gender of the "disguise" with the gender of the boy actor playing the woman's role. It can be argued that both the theatrical practice and the plots foreground the instability of gender, and these cross-dressed figures seem to have a sexual glamour that disrupts the socially sanctioned channels of desire and that manifests itself, almost indifferently, in either a male or a female body—in the case of Sebastian and Viola in both. On the other hand, these situations also have a specifically homoerotic dimension. Among other things, they dramatize the tensions of one-sided same-sex desire. For example, in *Twelfth Night* and *As You Like It,* "Cesario" (Viola/boy actor) and "Ganymede" (Rosalind/boy actor) ache with unexpressed longing for older male figures; it is particularly noteworthy that "Ganymede"—whose name functions in the Renaissance virtually as a synonym for a male beloved, and in some contexts specifically for "catamite," the passive sexual partner—should here be presented as the active, desiring party. "Ganymede" is so charged as a signifier in both classical (cf. Marlowe's *Tragedy of Dido*) and contemporary contexts that Rosalind's choice of this pseudonym hardly seems neutral.

Cross-dressing also figures prominently in such romance narratives as Sir Philip Sidney's *Arcadia* (1593). Musidorus tells his friend Pyrocles that loving a woman will make him effeminate, and when Musidorus next sees him, Pyrocles is disguised as an Amazon named Zelmane; Pyrocles' masquerade produces the sexual heat in both women and men, and the erotic atmosphere of *Arcadia* seems more notable for its pervasiveness than for the specific vectors of desire. Musidorus' argument that you become like what you love—hence, that heterosexual desire feminizes men—is not unique to the period but recurs in the antierotic rhetoric of the Puritans and others. The converse argument—that loving men makes a man masculine—is not advanced, at least in sexual terms, but the denigration of love contributes to the idealization of friendship.

In interpreting either instances of representation or items of biographical information, one frequently confronts the indeterminate—and perhaps always arbitrary—boundary between friendship and erotic feeling, but the category of "friendship" seems to have been particularly capacious in the sixteenth century. Even the term *paederastice* (pederasty) could be presented as a synonym for friendship. In the January eclogue of Spenser's *Shepheardes Calender* (1579), the rustic speaker Colin Clout describes another shepherd, Hobbinol, who seeks his love "with dayly suit: / His clownish gifts and curtsies I disdaine, / His kiddes, his cracknelles [biscuits], and his early fruit," but the commentary that accompanies the first edition (attributed to E. K., probably Spenser's acquaintance, Edmund Kirke) draws additional attention to this male suitor who distracts Colin from his quest for Rosalind's love: "In thys place seemeth to be some savour of disorderly love, which the learned call paederastice; but it is gathered beside his meaning." Having guaranteed that the reader will consider this meaning by disclaiming it, the commentary goes on to cite Plato and Xenophon, among others, in support of the opinion that "paederastice [is] much to be preferred before gynerastice, that is the love whiche enflameth men with lust toward woman kind," as long as "such love is . . . meant, as Socrates used it: who sayth, that in deede he loved Alcybiades extremely yet not Alcybiades person, but hys soule. . . . But yet let no man think, that here I stand . . . in defence of execrable and horrible sinnes of forbidden and unlawful fleshlinesse." This deeply anxious language conveys almost as much distaste for male lust for women as for "unlawful fleshlinesse" between men. Spenser himself may have been more relaxed about the matter. When Scudamour, in Book IV, Canto x, of *The Faerie Queene* (1596), narrates his journey to the Temple of Venus the "lovers lincked in true harts consent" whom he finds wandering its precincts include famous pairs of friends, like Hercules and Hylas, Jonathan and David, Theseus and Pirithous, Pylades and Orestes, and Damon and Pythias. Their "desire" is of course said to be grounded on "chast vertue," but their affiliation with the worship of Venus (who, the canto later hints, is androgynous) suggests how elusive—or permeable—the boundaries between love and friendship may be. In the case of Hercules and Hylas (whose name is frequently paired with "Ganymede" as a classical euphemism for a male beloved), the erotic connotations of the pairing are particularly hard to evade.

The pastoral convention also licenses the representation of same-sex desire in Richard Barnfield's *The Affectionate Shepherd* (1594). The sexual disposition of other Renaissance poets—Andrew Marvell (1621–1678), for example—remains even more elusive; in his lifetime his political opponents accused him of impotence and sodomy—an all-purpose canard—but William Empson, discussing Marvell's poems concerned with Damon the mower, finds textual reasons for concluding that "the poet . . . is in love with Damon" and comments that to his knowledge no "other poet has praised the smell of a farm hand" (15).

In the final decades of the seventeenth century the characteristic style of the Restoration "rake" was bisexual, libertine swagger; such rakes figure not only in contemporary anecdote but in such plays as Aphra Behn's *The Amorous Prince*, Thomas Otway's *The Soldier's Fortune*, and Nathaniel Lee's *The Princess of Cleve*. This style finds fullest literary expression in the poems of John Wilmot, the earl of Rochester (1647–1680). In "The Disabled Debauchee," the speaker tells his mistress, "Nor shall our love-fits, Chloris, be forgot, / When each the well-looked linkboy strove t'enjoy, / And the best kiss was the deciding lot / Whether the boy fucked you, or I the boy." Although one of his lyrics proclaims "Love a woman? You're an ass! ... / There's a sweet, soft page of mine / Does the trick worth forty wenches," his poems more frequently rehearse the humiliations and disappointments of heterosexual intercourse (e.g., in "The Imperfect Enjoyment") than they renounce them. On the other hand, scholars have grown increasingly confident in attributing to Rochester the play *Sodom, or The Quintessence of Debauchery*, in which such dignitaries as King Boloxinon, Prince Prickett, and Borastus the Buggermaster General promulgate the superiority of "buggery" and encourage experiments with its permutations—until at the farce's conclusion divine intervention restores heterosexual hegemony.

By the end of the seventeenth century another bisexual king, William III, was sharing the English throne; he was rumored to have brought Joost van Keppel (eventually made earl of Albemarle) over from Holland to be his lover, and his sexual interest in boys as well as women was widely known. Moreover, as indicated earlier, the late seventeenth and early eighteenth centuries saw the emergence of a protogay subculture in London, focused on "molly houses." Stephen Orgel suggests in Sir John Vanbrugh's comedy *The Relapse* (1697) that the "unabashed overtness and singlemindedness" of the matchmaker Coupler's sexual appetite makes the first dramatic character "who would be recognizable as gay in the modern sense" (61).

The increased visibility of sodomites predictably evoked lamentations over the moral decay of the English, and the century to follow was especially notable for its literary elaboration of homophobic stereotypes. Initially, the theatrical figure of the fop, though effeminate in style, was not necessarily coded as a sodomite, but as Randolph Trum-

bach indicates, between 1720 and 1750 such dramatic characters as Fribble in Garrick's *Miss in Her Teens* (1747) began more clearly to signal deviance from a heterosexual norm. In his *Epistle to Dr. Arbuthnot* (1735), Alexander Pope's portrait of Sporus, "that mere White Curd of Ass's milk," is an exercise in poisonous overkill: "Amphibious Thing! that acting either Part, / The trifling Head, or the corrupted Heart! / Fop at the Toilet, Flatt'rer at the Board, / Now trips a Lady, and now trips a Lord." (The classical Sporus was Nero's castrated catamite; Pope's contemporary target is Lord Hervey.)

Although the all-male milieus of Defoe's novels, from the castaway island of *Robinson Crusoe* to the pirate ship of *Captain Singleton*, have elicited critical attention to their sexual dynamics, their homosexual implications remain at most below the surface. On the other hand, in Chapters 34 and 35 of Tobias Smollett's *Roderick Random* (1748), the perfumed, bejeweled, ornately dressed sea captain, who wears his hair in flowing ringlets, is an unambiguous portrait of a sodomite; he is attended by his private surgeon, Simper, and his valet, Vergette, ("tiny penis"). In the early decades of the eighteenth century, highly publicized prosecutions of sodomy, a growing body of denunciatory polemics, and the notoriety of cross-dressed masquerades and carnivals that provided opportunities for unorthodox sex may all have contributed to the context of Smollett's mid-century satire; G. S. Rousseau presents *Satan's Harvest Home* (1749), a tract detailing "Reasons for the growth of Sodomy," as a nonfictional counterpart to the episode from Smollett's novel.

The figures who later in the century gathered around Horace Walpole (1717–1797) and Thomas Gray (1716–1771) were almost certainly more aware of their inclinations and perhaps more disposed to act on them. At Eton College, Walpole, Gray, Richard West, and Thomas Ashton formed the so-called Quadruple Alliance, which they sustained through much of their adult lives. Gray's elegiac poetry of the 1740s and 1750s, including his "Ode on a Distant Prospect of Eton College," "Elegy Written in a Country Churchyard," and a memorial sonnet on the death of Richard West, expresses a Housman-like feeling for the lost beauties of youth, and particularly of young men; less ambiguously, in the 1760s Gray fell in love with the Swiss student Charles-Victor de Bonstettin.

Gray's friend Walpole essentially invented the Gothic novel. Feminist criticism has long found opportunities in this genre to explore displaced representations of female sexuality, but some of its features—the fascination with emotional extremity and "unspeakable secrets," the representation of physical and psychological claustrophobia—may also speak metaphorically to the condition of unexpressed same-sex desire, while its deployment of exotic locales or romanticized medievalism promises at least imaginative escape from a confining present. Walpole's *The Castle of Otranto* (1764), the founding work of Gothic fiction, which is dominated by melodramatic paternal tyranny, and his drama *The Mysterious Mother* (1768), which represents mother-son incest, cast the most lurid possible light on ordinary familial arrangements.

William Beckford (1760–1844) contributed an Orientalist cast to Gothic fiction through his fantasy *Vathek* (1786). Its celebration of sensuality and pederastic focus on the child Gulchenrouz go further than *The Castle of Otranto* in exposing the tacitly homosexual underpinnings of Gothic narrative; his projected sequel to *Vathek* would have more explicitly depicted transgressive sexuality. Beckford himself may have been the most notoriously homosexual literary figure of the eighteenth century (though he lived on till 1844); although born into a rich and socially influential family, he became an outcast when his correspondence with his cousin, William Courtenay ("Kitty"), was made scandalously public in 1784; thereafter he either traveled in Europe or lived among a closed circle of friends at his architecturally Gothic estate, Fonthill Abbey. Matthew G. Lewis's *The Monk* (1795) was yet another crucial addition to the Gothic canon by a sexually heterodox (if not unquestionably homosexual) author; it harks back to Renaissance theatrical conventions of cross-dressing to present the mutual attraction of two ostensibly male characters—whose "problem" is resolved when one is revealed to be a woman.

When George Gordon (1788–1824), Lord Byron, began his travels on the Continent, Beckford's Portuguese retreat, Cintra, near Lisbon, was among the first places he (and later his barely fictional alter ego, Childe Harold) visited, and he began composition of *Manfred* after "Monk" Lewis paid him a visit in Switzerland, during which Lewis extemporized translations of Goethe's *Faust*. Although a suppressed stanza of *Childe Harold's Pilgrimage* expresses conventional horror at Beckford's behavior ("Gainst Nature's voice seduced to deed accurst") and Byron's journal expresses distaste for *The Monk* as conveying "the *philtred* ideas of a jaded voluptuary," Byron, who was bisexual, may well have felt an affinity with both these figures. To shield himself from the intensity of Regency homophobia (see Louis Crompton's *Byron and Greek Love*), he developed a coded language for corresponding with his college friends John Cam Hobhouse and Charles Skinner Matthews about homosexual involvements during his early travels in Greece. At Cambridge his affections centered on a chorister named John Edleston. His early poem "The Cornelian" expresses the intensity of their bond; so do a series of lyrics ostensibly addressed to "Thyrza," the same name under which he mourned Edleston's death in 1811 at the age of nineteen. If the middle years of Byron's life were crowded with often scandalous heterosexual affairs, in the last year of his life, once again in Greece, he fell in love a fifteen-year-old boy named Lukas; though second-person pronouns veil the gender of their addressee, Byron's final poems, "Love and Death" and "Last Words on Greece," allude to this affair.

Thomas Lovell Beddoes (1803–1849) was another romantic poet who left England for the Continent and presumably found Switzerland and Germany more accommodating to his personal inclinations, although an unhappy love affair with a German actor may have prompted his suicide. His plays, *The Bride's Tragedy* and *Death's Jest-Book*, indicate the continued attractions of Gothic atmosphere and conventions to sexually heterodox writers. Some of his elegiac writing may more directly express his feelings for other men, but the genre of elegy seems always to have licensed a more passionate rhetoric of affection between men than other poetic occasions would allow. The emotional outpourings of Alfred Lord Tennyson's *In Memoriam A. H. H.* (1850) make these poems read as among the "gayest" of the nineteenth century, though there is nothing in the biographical record to suggest that Tennyson (1809–1892) was ever sexually intimate with another man. Nevertheless, in this sequence of poems, which grieves over the early death of his college friend Arthur Henry Hallam, Tennyson speaks of himself as "widow'd" and mourns the loss of Hallam's physical presence as well as his companionship. *In Memoriam* was influenced by Tennyson and Hallam's shared enthusiasm for Shakespeare's *Sonnets*, and in 1839 Henry Hallam, Arthur's father, had written, in his *Introduction to the Literature of Europe*, "Notwithstanding the frequent beauties of these sonnets, . . . it is impossible not to wish that Shakspeare had never written them. There is a weakness and folly in all excessive and mis-placed affection." It seems unlikely that Tennyson was completely unaware of the sexual implications of either Shakespeare's sonnets or the tradition of Theocritean elegy which *In Memoriam* also invokes; at least two of his Cambridge contemporaries, Richard Monckton Milnes and Arthur Buller, had bisexual adventures, and the homosexual Edward Fitzgerald, best known for his translation of *The Rubáiyát of Omar Khayyám* (1859), became one of his close friends.

Not surprisingly, some members of Tennyson's family and circle were uneasy about how his elegies might be received by the general public; although the Oxford classicist Benjamin Jowett commented that the "love of the sonnets which [Tennyson] so strikingly expressed was a sort of sympathy with Hellenism," Tennyson's son Hallam dropped this revealing sentence from his memoir of his father. Nineteenth-century expressions of enthusiasm for the art and philosophy of ancient Greece often suggested—and sometimes deliberately signaled—homosexual sympathies, especially in academic milieus; the aesthetics of homosexual German classicist Johann Joachim Winckelmann (1717–1768) have paved the way for this identification, and not surprisingly, Walter Pater's *The Renaissance* (1873) includes a heartfelt appreciation of Winckelmann. Other contributions to the genre of Hellenophilic-homophilic writing include John Addington Symonds's *A Problem in Greek Ethics* (1873; published 1883) and the Cambridge don Goldsworthy Lowes Dickinson's *The Greek View of Life* (1896), though the latter was more discreet and partial in its defense of homosexuality.

The fervent religious language of the Victorian period could also serve both to accommodate and to veil intensities of same-sex desire, like those that find expression in John Henry (later Cardinal) Newman's early poetry. The mutual attachment of Newman (1801–1890) and Hurrell Froude (1803–1836), another leader of the Oxford Movement, was widely known and sometimes sneered at. Froude died before Newman actually broke with the Church of England, and Newman's later affections centered on the Rev. Ambrose St. John, with whom he asked to be buried. Later in the century, Gerard Manley Hopkins (1844–1889) fell in love with another Oxford student, Digby Mackworth Dolben, and recorded his passion in his diary and two poems that remained unpublished until 1948. It is impossible to distinguish the religious enthusiasm that Hopkins shared with Dolben from the current of erotic feeling that supported it; as Richard Dellamora says, "Dolben and Hopkins both sought to resolve the problem of illicit desire" by focusing "on the real but transcendent body of Christ" (47). The larger project, in the cases of both Newman and Hopkins, would be to investigate the ways in which sublimated desire shapes theological or imaginative writings less legibly connected to their emotional ordeals.

If Victorian novels present few, if any, frankly homosexual male characters, they abound in sexually ambiguous figures (like Frederick Fairlie in Wilkie Collins's *The Woman in White,* 1859–1860) and male pairings whose basis is never clearly specified (one of the characters in Dickens's *Pickwick Papers,* 1836–1837, refers to Alfred Jingle's partner, Job Trotter, as "that servant, or friend, or whatever he is—you know"). Above all, there are the bachelors, barred forever from marriage by "a mysterious imperative (physical debility, hereditary curse, secret unhappy prior marriage, or simple extreme disinclination)" (Sedgwick, 174); in London they hang out in clubs with other "single gentlemen," but often enough they head for the outposts of British empire, perhaps in quest of the notorious "Sotadic Zone" described in the "Terminal Essay" to Sir Richard Burton's translation of *The Arabian Nights* (1885).

In *David Copperfield* (1849–50) Steerforth flirts outrageously with the title character, whom he calls "Daisy"—though schoolboy homosexuality always carries the alibi of immaturity. However, in Dickens's last novels, *Our Mutual Friend* (1864–1865) and the unfinished *Mystery of Edwin Drood* (1870) more adult versions of same-sex desire rise almost to the surface—but sometimes in murderous forms, as though avenging their repression. On the other hand, the banter between Eugene Wrayburn and Mortimer Lightwood—a same-sex couple who happily share living quarters at the beginning of *Our Mutual Friend*—already anticipates the tone of Jack and Algernon's exchanges in *The Importance of Being Earnest*.

The traumatic event that shaped the conditions of male homosexual life for the next eighty years was the passage of the Labouchère amendment to the 1885 Criminal Law Amendment Act, which made "any act of gross indecency" between men, whether in public or private, punishable by two years' hard labor. Ironically, but not accidentally, the passage of this law coincided not only with an increasingly well-established homosexual subculture in London but with the proliferation of texts that celebrated male camaraderie, defended ancient Greek mores, and at least obliquely celebrated "masculine love" (one of John Addington Symonds's terms). If Symonds's poetry is minor, his essays defending homosexuality (*A Problem in Greek Ethics*, 1873, and its sequel, *A Problem in Modern Ethics*, 1891); his critical writings on such topics as Greek poetry, Renaissance art, Michelangelo, and Whitman; and above all, his *Memoirs* (1889–1893; published in 1984) make him a crucial figure. Together with Walter Pater's *Studies in the History of the Renaissance* (1873), his selective scrutiny of Western culture implicitly stakes out a "tradition" of same-sex desire. Pater (1839–1894) wrote with more density, elegance, and discretion, but his aesthetic allegiances and the character of his sensibility spoke no less clearly to his contemporaries than Symonds's more direct and intellectually available productions; in his historical novel *Marius the Epicurean* (1885), set in the court of the Roman emperor Marcus Aurelius, the passion of friendship is rarified but unmistakably erotic. The poetry and fiction of Algernon Swinburne (1837–1909) evoke such sexually transgressive areas as sadomasochism, flagellation (*Love's Cross-Currents*, *Lesbia Brandon*), and lesbianism ("Anactoria," "Sapphics," etc.), but only occasionally suggest genital contact between males; more "queer" perhaps than gay, Swinburne nevertheless ostentatiously compromised his masculinity in the eyes of conventional society.

Nearly all the homosexual or bisexual writers of the late nineteenth century equivocated—arguably, were forced to equivocate—about their sexuality, but the contradictions in Oscar Wilde's life (1854–1900) and art are—like his martyrdom, as the most famous victim of the Labouchère Amendment—especially conspicuous. He is the figure who dominates imaginings, both straight and gay, of fin-de-siècle homosexuality. Of the works Wilde wrote before his trial and imprisonment, "The Portrait of Mr. W. H." (1889) most overtly engages homosexual themes. It embeds a sustained interpretation of Shakespeare's *Sonnets*—more particularly, of Shakespeare's relation to their dedicatee and "onlie begetter"—in a novella. It is characteristic of Wilde that even within this already fictional framework, "proof" for the existence of Willie Hughes—the charismatic boy actor whose name is inferred from the punning language of the *Sonnets*—depends on a counterfeit portrait. Another beautiful boy—actor Cyril Graham—has provided both the "Willie Hughes" hypothesis and the forgery; years after Graham's suicide, his friend Erskine, still smitten and grieving, retells the circumstances to the narrator, so the mirrorings, projections, and relays of desire in the novella's complicated plot cast further doubt on the empirical basis of its venture into literary history.

In *The Picture of Dorian Gray* (1891) the sexual character of Basil Hallward's and Sir Henry Wotton's attraction to Dorian is tacit but, in the cultural milieu of the 1890s, not especially hard to decipher; how far Dorian's own transgressions are homosexual is even more conjectural. The sexual content of such plays as *The Importance of Being Earnest*—whose "Bunburyist" male protagonists find opportunities to go on holiday from Victorian respectability—seems even more deeply encoded. While *The Importance of Being Earnest* mocks the "nominalism" of Victorian marriage—its stipulation that the bridegroom bear a certain name or label—"Lord Arthur Savile's Crime: A Study in Duty" presents heterosexual conventionality as literally murderous: the protagonist must kill before he can marry. It would of course be hasty to attribute Wilde's witty equivocations solely to the wish to maintain a deniable relation to his "unspeakable" sexual desires. As William A. Cohen argues, the indeterminacies of Wilde's plays and fiction have at least as much to do with his understanding of the literary, but the "balance struck in Wilde's work between the literary and the sexual was eventually upset" when "the Crown insisted on deciphering the connotativeness that Wilde argued was formative of literature." After the failure of his libel suit against the marquess of Queensbury and his own prosecution for "gross indecency," Wilde wrote *De Profundis* (1897), his letter from Reading Gaol—addressed to Lord Alfred Douglas but clearly framed for a wider readership—in which he explores his situation as wounded lover, suffering artist, and homosexual outcast. Nevertheless, the different moments of Wilde's career remain difficult to integrate. A study of Wilde by novelist Neil Bartlett, half biography, half meditation on his place in gay iconography and culture, is aptly titled *Who Was That Man?*

As the narrative of literary history reaches the late nineteenth century, the scholar has far greater access to biographical information—even if the bearings of that information are not always self-evident—and the critic encounters a body of writing that is self-consciously (if not always self-declaratively) gay-identified. The interpretive task becomes how, nonreductively, to understand the specific terms in which that identification expresses itself—

E not merely in an understanding of sexual behavior or sexually differentiated human type but in an interrogation of Anglo-American society's capacity, or incapacity, to incorporate diversely constituted realms of experience; that is, at the moment when homosexuality is named as such, issues of sexual orientation become inextricably—and explicitly—involved with questions of race, class, and gender hierarchy. With Wilde and with those who follow him, the kind of brief notation this overview can afford seems increasingly unsatisfactory, and the sheer number of writers and topics that invite consideration threatens to overwhelm any possibility of compact narrative. The following paragraphs enumerate a few of the figures of whom any discussion of homosexual or gay writing in the twentieth century would need to take fuller account.

In the wake of Wilde's ordeal, much writing by homosexual authors expressed a relation to mainstream English life that could easily be assimilated to—or pass as—a less particularized form of social critique. Samuel Butler's *The Way of All Flesh* (posthumously published in 1903) concentrates its satiric vitriol on the repressions of family life and the hypocritical respectability of late Victorian England. The strategy of E. M. Forster's early novels is similar, but it is young women like Lilia Theobald, Lucy Honeychurch, and the Schlegel sisters (in *Where Angels Fear to Tread, A Room with a View,* and *Howards End*) who enact vicarious rebellions against or liberations from rigid social expectations. The homosexual subtext comes closer to the surface in Forster's short fiction, where true life is always elsewhere, on the other side of the confining hedge, and *The Longest Journey* (1907), in which the Pan-like Stephen Wonham and other male figures beckon Rickie Elliott to break free of his dreary marriage (already mediated by a crush on his wife's late fiancé). *A Passage to India* (1924) suggests the possibility of alliances across cultural barriers, but such unions are erotically, if fatally, actualized only in such posthumously published stories as "The Life to Come" and "The Other Boat." *Maurice* (1914) writes the happy ending to a homosexual love story that the other novels withhold, but significantly remained unpublished until 1971.

Homosexual desire is even more thoroughly disguised in the short stories of H. H. Munro ("Saki"; 1870–1916) and the novels of Somerset Maugham (1874–1965), though Maugham's choice to depict scenarios of escape in *The Moon and Sixpence* (1919), based on Gauguin's life in the South

Seas, and *The Razor's Edge* (1945) may be significant; *Of Human Bondage* (1915) draws on one of Maugham's homosexual affairs but transposes the sex of his lover. His plays and those of Noël Coward (1899–1973) dominated the English stage in the 1920s; both playwrights sustain the tradition of Oscar Wilde, epigrammatically needling English pieties in a style of satire evidently compatible with mainstream success. Coward's choice of topics was more daring than Maugham's, especially in *The Vortex* (1924) and *Design for Living* (1933), and his career as a dramatist extended over several decades, though his later plays are more conservative in subject matter and sometimes patriotically celebratory; his short fiction of the 1960s more directly addresses homosexual themes.

By contrast, the far less discreet fiction of the short-lived Ronald Firbank (1886–1926) animates multiple worlds of sexual and social improvisation, in which orthodox heterosexuality comes to seem like the exception rather than the norm. He is also the most modernist and stylistically adventurous of gay male writers; his economical, elliptical narratives deflate the conventions of late-nineteenth-century realism—as though these conventions themselves embodied an arbitrary moral dispensation and an unjust distribution of political power. The writings of Frederick William Rolfe ("Baron Corvo"; 1860–1913), notably *Hadrian the Seventh* (1904) and *The Desire and Pursuit of the Whole* (1909–1910; published 1934), are less formally innovative than Firbank's but display a similar high-camp sensibility. The Lucia novels of E. F. Benson (1867–1940) from the 1920s and 1930s offer a more asexual style of campiness—though his earlier novels, which center on life at Cambridge, do carry a homoerotic charge.

In *A Shropshire Lad* (1896) and later volumes of poetry, A. E. Housman (1859–1936) was able to use the well-established conventions of classicizing elegy to express not only a melancholy sense of the transience of natural beauty but also his sexual feelings for young men. However, the massive loss of life in World War I redeployed these conventions on a wider scale and produced a literary outpouring of grief that made poems by both homosexual and heterosexual authors seem overwhelmingly homoerotic; Rupert Brooke (1887–1915) and Wilfred Owen (1893–1918) were casualties of the war, while Siegfried Sassoon (1886–1967) survived it. T. E. Lawrence's *Seven Pillars of Wisdom* (1935) also emerges from the conflicts of World War I; his rape by Turkish soldiers is conveyed in veiled language, and his attraction to the young Salim Ahmed is signaled mainly by the dedicatory poem, but the politics and ethics of the book may say as much about Lawrence's alienation from military and sexual hegemonies of the British Empire as its more autobiographical elements. During this period the pacifist Lytton Strachey (1880–1932) more slyly subverted English complacencies by reappropriating the past in a series of witty, revisionary biographies: *Eminent Victorians* (1918), *Queen Victoria* (1921), and *Elizabeth and Essex* (1928)—especially the last, in which Queen Elizabeth I's androgynous enactment of monarchy is given full play. Strachey was a charter member of the Bloomsbury group, whose other homosexual or bisexual figures as painter Duncan Grant, economist John Maynard Keynes, Virginia Woolf, and Vita Sackville-West.

The representation of homosexual experience by writers who were not—predominantly at least—homosexual also plays an important role in twentieth-century English literature. Thanks perhaps to filmmaker Ken Russell, the nude wrestling scene ("Gladiatorial") in *Women in Love* (1920) is D. H. Lawrence's best-known depiction of male mutual attraction. Gerald Crich had biographical counterparts in critic John Middleton Murry, Katherine Mansfield's husband, to whom Lawrence was presumably drawn, and in a Cornish farmer, William Henry Hocking, with whom Lawrence's involvement was probably more physical. Homoeroticism may loom larger in Lawrence's fiction than it did in his life. There are homosexual episodes or elements throughout his novels (e.g., *Aaron's Rod* [1922], *Kangaroo* [1923], and *The Plumed Serpent* [1926]), and same-sex attraction is also a recurrent motif of the short stories. The case for bisexuality, which Birkin voices explicitly in *Women in Love*, are cumulatively advanced by these writings.

Evelyn Waugh's homosexual experiences, like those of Charles Ryder in *Brideshead Revisited* (1945), were apparently confined to his years at Oxford, but the relationship between Charles Ryder and Sebastian Flyte is one of the most widely circulated images of a homosexual affair—acceptable, perhaps, to a mainstream readership because Charles "outgrows" the friendship and Sebastian is doomed. Waugh's queenier characters, Anthony Blanche in *Brideshead* and Ambrose Silk in *Put Out More Flags* (both probably based on Brian Howard), are less sympathetically treated but memorable. Homosexuals figure prominently, and often as objects

of hostility, in the writings of Wyndham Lewis (1886–1957); on the other hand, *The Lion and the Fox* (1926) is a full-length study of Shakespeare as homosexual artist, and Lewis not only saw homosexuality as "natural" but thought that the homosexual's outsider status gave him a useful vantage point on the limitations of power politics.

Among the most influential English writers of the century have been the émigrés Christopher Isherwood (1904–1986) and W. H. Auden (1907–1973). Isherwood's early fiction reflects his experiences in pre–World War II Berlin, but the autobiographical *Christopher and His Kind* (1976) more directly describes the homosexual milieu that drew Isherwood to Germany. In 1939 Isherwood moved to the United States and settled in Los Angeles; beginning in the 1950s his later novels focus on the situations of homosexual protagonists in a variously hostile or resistant heterosexual world. Auden, Isherwood's sometime literary collaborator, visited Berlin more briefly; he wrote and taught in England during the 1930s—passionately embracing, then growing disillusioned with left-wing politics. Like Isherwood, he emigrated to the United States in 1939 but settled in New York. He brilliantly distilled the artistic resources and intellectual ambitions of the English poetic tradition, reaching back across several centuries to recuperate a wider range of formal possibilities. Auden's lifetime relationship with Brooklyn-born Chester Kallman, like Isherwood's with Don Bachardy, was woven into his later work; Auden also worked with Kallman on the libretto for Stravinsky's *The Rake's Progress* and for several other operas. A later British émigré, poet Thom Gunn (b. 1929), who moved to California in 1954, has also had a substantial impact on gay writing in America; *The Man with Night Sweats* (1992) arguably incorporates the most powerful poetry to emerge from the AIDS crisis

Poet Stephen Spender (1909–1995), Auden and Isherwood's friend and ally, remained behind in England; his leftist political commitments proved more enduring than theirs, but he moved away from the homosexual friendships depicted, in part, in his novel *The Temple* (1929; published 1988) and married twice, in 1936 and 1939. His early poems addressed to or concerned with homosexual lovers have moved in and out of various editions of his *Collected Poems*, but whether part of his official poetic canon or not, they remain of interest. Other significant homosexual writers of the 1930s and 1940s are short-story writer and novelist Denton Welch

E (1915–1948) and T. H. White (1906–1964), best known for his revision of the Arthurian legends, beginning with *The Sword in the Stone* (1939). The novels of John Cowper Powys (1872–1963)— among them *Wolf Solent* (1929), *Weymouth Sands* (1934), and *A Glastonbury Romance* (1955)—offer an unusually broad array of human types; if not simply homosexual, Powys was, like many of his characters, sexually heterodox in ways that elude straightforward description. In addition, any survey of the 1940s and 1950s seems incomplete without mention of Mary Renault's *The Charioteer* (1953), in which homosexual soldiers and conscientious objectors struggle to reconcile conflicting impulses toward sexual fulfillment and heroic action—or inaction—during World War II.

Beginning with *The Wrong Set* (1949), the short stories and later the novels of Angus Wilson (1913–1991) pungently portrayed the social attitudes of post–World War II Britain. The protagonists of *Hemlock and After* (1952) and *As If by Magic* (1973) are, respectively, a bisexual novelist and a gay scientist, but often Wilson's homosexual characters mingle matter-of-factly with others who embody a broad cross section of English society. Fantastic elements ("the romantic side of familiar things," he said, quoting Dickens) complicate the realism of his satire, which targets the impostures and the self-delusions of the English intelligentsia as well as the frustrated aspirations of social progressivism. The plays of Joe Orton (1933–1967) express a similar disillusionment with the postwar welfare state in more gleefully assaultive and surreal forms. *Entertaining Mr. Sloane* (1963), *Loot* (1966), and *What the Butler Saw* (1967) exploited the anarchic potential of bedroom farce and theatrical drag, among other traditions of the British stage, before Orton's murder by his lover, Kenneth Halliwell, elevated him to mythic status and all but overshadowed his accomplishments as a playwright. Alan Bennett (b. 1934), a onetime member of the *Beyond the Fringe* troupe, supplied the screenplay for *Prick Up Your Ears* (1987), a film biography of Orton—a possibly ironic conjunction, since Bennett's drier style of dramatic wit maintains a link with the earlier, more genteel tradition represented by homosexual playwrights like Noël Coward and Terrence Rattigan and, in a play like *The Madness of King George*, with the revisionary historical writing of Lytton Strachey. Bennett's plays about Kim Philby (*An Englishman Abroad*) and Sir Anthony Blunt (*A Question of Attribution*) resonate with episodes of twentieth-century history in which the homosexual affiliation of British spies has figured.

In 1957 the Wolfenden Committee, a royal commission appointed to investigate the law against homosexuality, issued a report recommending decriminalization of consensual homosexual relations in private. It was not until 1967, however, that Parliament finally enacted this reform, thus ending the era begun by passage of the Labouchère Amendment in 1885. Quentin Crisp's autobiography, *The Naked Civil Servant* (1968), gives some idea of what it meant for a flamboyant homosexual to live through the era of official persecution. Another noteworthy memoir, posthumously published in the same year, was J. R. Ackerley's *My Father and Myself,* which brackets his own homosexual experiences with his father's (mostly) heterosexual but bigamous existence; Ackerley's earlier memoir, *My Dog Tulip* (1965), only tacitly gay-identified, had been devoted to an Alsatian bitch, who was the great love of his life.

Among the contributions to the gay novel that have attracted the most attention in recent years are Andrew Harvey's *Burning Houses* (1986), Patrick Gale's *Kansas in August* (1988), Alan Hollinghurst's *The Swimming-Pool Library* (1988), Neil Bartlett's *Ready to Catch Him Should He Fall* (1990), and Hanif Kureishi's *The Buddha of Suburbia* (1990). Kureishi's screenplays for *My Beautiful Laundrette* (1986) and *Sammy and Rosie Get Laid* (1988) are equally significant additions not only to gay literature but to an emergent literature that dramatizes the collisions of race, ethnicity, class, and sexuality in postcolonial Britain. *Was* (1992), by science-fiction writer Geoffrey Ryman (born in Canada but now living in London), reimagines, from various historical vantage points, lives of those connected with the novel and film of *The Wizard of Oz*, including an actor dying of AIDS. The stories of Adam Mars-Jones, *Monopolies of Loss* (1992), also address the AIDS crisis.

As even this brief outline of English literary history suggests, writing about male homosexuality—and writing by male homosexual authors—has never been a wholly separate or separable phenomenon but always intimately intertwined with the major developments within the British cultural tradition; it continues to be so.   *Barry Weller*

Bibliography

Bartlett, Neil. *Who Was That Man? A Present for Oscar Wilde.* London: Serpent's Tail, 1988.

Boswell, John. *Christianity, Social Tolerance and Homosexuality: Gay People in Western Europe from the Beginning of the Christian Era to the Fourteenth Century.* Chicago: University of Chicago Press, 1980.

Boyd, David Lorenzo. "On Lesbian and Gay/Queer Medieval Studies." *Medieval Feminist Newsletter* 15 (1993): 12–15.

Bredbeck, Gregory. *Sodomy and Interpretation: Marlowe to Milton.* Ithaca, N.Y.: Cornell University Press, 1991.

Bristow, Joseph. *Effeminate England: Homoerotic Writing after 1865.* New York: Columbia University Press, 1995.

Caserio, Robert. *The English Novel 1900–1950: Theory and History.* New York: Twayne, 1998.

Cohen, William A. *Sex Scandal: The Private Parts of Victorian Fiction.* Durham, N.C.: Duke University Press, 1996.

Craft, Christopher. *Another Kind of Love: Male Homosexual Desire in English Discourse, 1850–1920.* Berkeley: University of California Press, 1994.

Crompton, Louis. *Byron and Greek Love: Homophobia in 19th-Century England.* Berkeley: University of California Press, 1985.

Dellamora, Richard. *Masculine Desire: The Sexual Politics of Victorian Aestheticism.* Chapel Hill, N.C.: University of North Carolina Press, 1990.

Dinshaw, Carolyn. *Getting Medieval: Sexualities and Communities, Pre- and Postmodern.* Durham, N.C.: Duke University Press, 1999.

———. "A Kiss Is Just a Kiss: Heterosexuality and Its Consolations in *Sir Gawain and the Green Knight.*" *Diacritics* 24, nos. 2–3 (1994): 205–26.

Dowling, Linda. *Hellenism and Homosexuality in Victorian Oxford.* Ithaca, N.Y.: Cornell University Press, 1994.

Empson, William. "Natural Magic and Populism in Marvell's Poetry." In *Using Biography.* Cambridge, Mass.: Harvard University Press, 1984.

———. "They That Have Power." In *Some Versions of Pastoral.* New York: New Directions, 1960.

Frantzen, Allen J. "The Disclosure of Sodom in *Cleanness.*" *PMLA* 111.3 (May 1996): 451–64.

Goldberg, Jonathan. *Sodometries: Renaissance Texts, Modern Sexualities.* Stanford, Calif.: Stanford University Press, 1992.

Haggerty, George E., and Bonnie Zimmerman, eds. *Professions of Desire: Lesbian and Gay Studies in Literature.* New York: MLA, 1995.

Howard, Donald R. *The Idea of the Canterbury Tales.* Berkeley: University of California Press, 1976.

Kopelson, Kevin. *Love's Litany: The Writing of Modern Homoerotics.* Stanford, Calif.: Stanford University Press, 1994.

Kruger, Steven F. "Claiming the Pardoner: Toward a Gay Reading of Chaucer's Pardoner's Tale." *Exemplaria* 6, no. 1 (1990): 115–39.

Lane, Christopher. *The Ruling Passion: British Colonial Allegory and the Paradox of Homosexual Desire.* Durham, N.C.: Duke University Press, 1995.

McFarlane, Cameron. *The Sodomite in Fiction and Satire, 1660–1750.* New York: Columbia University Press, 1997.

Orgel, Stephen. *Impersonations: The Performance of Gender in Shakespeare's England.* Cambridge: Cambridge University Press, 1996.

Rousseau, G. S. "The Pursuit of Homosexuality in the Eighteenth Century." In *'Tis Nature's Fault: Unauthorized Sexuality during the Enlightenment.* Robert Maccubbin, ed. Cambridge: Cambridge University Press, 1987, 132–68.

Sedgwick, Eve Kosofsky. *Between Men: English Literature and Male Homosocial Desire.* New York: Columbia University Press, 1985.

Smith, Bruce R. *Homosexual Desire in Shakespeare's England: A Cultural Poetics.* Chicago: University of Chicago Press, 1991.

Traub, Valerie. *Desire and Anxiety: Circulations of Sexuality in Shakespearean Drama.* New York: Routledge, 1992.

Trumbach, Randolph. "Sodomitical Subcultures, Sodomitical Roles, and the Gender Revolution of the Eighteenth Century." In *'Tis Nature's Fault: Unauthorized Sexuality during the Enlightenment.* Robert Maccubbin, ed. Cambridge: Cambridge University Press, 1987, 109–21.

See also Ackerley, J. R.; AIDS Literature; Alan of Lille; *Arabian Nights*; Auden, W. H.; Autobiographical Writing; Barnfield, Richard; Beckford, William; Benson, E. F.; Bloomsbury Group; Burton, Sir Richard Francis; Byron, George Gordon, Lord; Coward, Noël; Crisp, Quentin; Decadence; Durrell, Lawrence; Fiction; Fairbank, Ronald; Fops; Forster, E. M.; Goeth, Johannes Wolfgang von ; Grant, Duncan; Gray, Thomas; Gunn, Thom; Housman, A. E.; Isherwood, Christopher; James I; Keynes, John Maynard; Lawrence, T. E.; Libertine and Libertinism; Marlowe, Christopher; Michelangelo Buonarroti; Orton, Joe (John Kingsley); Owen, Wilfred; Pater, Walter Horatio; Plato; Renault, Mary; Rochester, John Wilmot, Earl of; Rolfe, Frederick William ("Baron Corvo"); Saki (Hector Hugh Munro); Shakespeare, William; Strachey, Lytton; Symonds, John Addington; Tennyson, Alfred; Theater: Premodern and Early Modern; Walpole, Horace; Whitman, Walt; Wilde, Oscar; Wilson, Sir Angus; Winckelmann, Johann Joachim

English Pastoral Composers

The nationalist phase of English art music, roughly from 1880 to 1940 and known as the English musical renaissance, entailed a certain strain of homoeroticism that is difficult to insist upon yet distinctive. To understand the sensibility, certain areas must be cordoned off. Aggressive self-expression burst out only later, most notably in the operas of Benjamin Britten (*Peter Grimes*, 1945; *Billy Budd*, 1951). The creative suppression that preceded this dates back at least to high Victorianism, whose rectitude perhaps explains one seam of that suppression, resistance to Liszt and to Wagner's *Tristan* and hence to the whole notion of musical libido. Chromatic abandon was simply not cricket; composers such as Bax, Bridge, and Bantock who espoused it were marginalized, and the diatonic positivism of *Die Meistersinger* was altogether preferred, as a glance at Hubert Parry's "Blest pair of sirens" or any of Stanford's works immediately demonstrates. Another vein of suppression was probably in play, though it has never been considered: the posthumous denigration of Tchaikovsky, more or less contemporaneous with the disgrace of Oscar Wilde in 1895.

In the wake of these inhibitions, certain English composers developed a keepsake mentality, frustrated yet potent, that came to characterize a generation's music. Three representatives may be considered: Roger Quilter (1877–1953), John Ireland (1879–1962), and George Butterworth (1885–1916). Butterworth was probably homosexual, Ireland and Quilter certainly were. None of the three found a long-term or stable sexual partner. All of them excelled at composing songs, inscribing fulfillment in the perfection of the small-scale and containable while counterbalancing that with the powerful erotic yearning of the English lyric poetry they chose to set to music. Quilter took his cue from the already established salon tradition of women songwriters such as Maude Valérie White and Liza Lehmann and refined it exquisitely (*Songs of Sorrow*, 1907, to Dowson poems). It is not difficult for a late-twentieth-century audience to hear their overblown Victorian sentimentality as camp. Ireland learned much of his stance from Elgar, a heterosexual partly immune from the suppressions described above yet still deeply inhibited about romantic passion, which he sublimated into secrecy, memory, and nostalgia within friendship (*Enigma Variations*, 1899). Musical symbols, motives, vignettes, and juxtapositions play themselves out with suggestive and often frustrated or sentimental passion in both men's large-scale music. Ireland's two violin sonatas (1908 and 1917) perhaps represent the apogee of this aesthetic.

On the smaller scale, Ireland and Butterworth made some of the best musical settings of poems from A. E. Housman's *A Shopshire Lad* (1896). Something in these poems attracted many other English composers, including Ivor Gurney and C. W. Orr: it was probably the lad's homoerotic aura and fatalism rather than the rural nostalgia conventionally laid at their door. Nevertheless, with the simple poems and the simple lad went the contemporaneous English folk revival, musically encapsulated in Butterworth's modal tunes and harmonies, a rustic analogue presumably as sexy to him and his followers as it was restrained and unfulfilled. One notices that even Butterworth leaves the folksiness behind when he approaches real homoerotic passion, as in "On the Idle Hill of Summer" and the orchestral rhapsody *A Shropshire Lad* (1912), based on his song "Loveliest of Trees." Here the rural landscape becomes the consoling background for implicitly dramatic, indeed tragic, musical narration (the lad, like Butterworth the soldier in World War I, will die). But since such consolation betrays a self-hating conclusion—that nature gives the genetic matrix and nature takes away the life that cannot deal with it—the English pastoral aesthetic remains problematic in this context, just as it has been in many others. *Stephen Banfield*

Bibliography

Banfield, Stephen. *Sensibility and English Song.* 2 vols. Cambridge: Cambridge University Press, 1985.

See also Britten, Benjamin; Housman, A. E.; Ireland, John; Tchaikovsky, Pyotr Ilich

Epstein, Brian (1934–1967)

In 1961, Brian Samuel Epstein was the manager of the record department of his father's furniture store in Liverpool, England. In response to customers' requests for a record that the Beatles had made in Germany, Epstein went to hear them perform at a local club, the Cavern; he became their manager a few weeks later. It was Epstein who advised the Beatles to wear suits instead of leather jackets and blue jeans, introduced them to record producer George Martin, fired drummer Pete Best and hired Ringo Starr as his replacement, and negotiated the Beatles' first contract with a major record company. Epstein continued to manage the Beatles' careers until his death.

Building on his success with the group, Epstein became the best-known rock-and-roll manager of the mid-1960s, steering the careers of Gerry and the Pacemakers and many other performers. During his lifetime, Epstein was the subject of newspaper articles and television documentaries, in many of which he was called "The Fifth Beatle." The contrast between his personal manner and those of the Beatles was much commented upon; Epstein, a closeted gay man, was personally reticent and soft-spoken.

After his death from a drug overdose at age thirty-two, Epstein became the subject of several fictionalized characterizations. In particular, his relationship with John Lennon has been the subject of speculation. Christopher Munch's critically acclaimed film *The Hour and the Times* (1991) presented a fictional account of a flirtation between Epstein and Lennon during a weekend vacation in Barcelona, Spain, that the two actually took in 1963.

Charles Krinsky

Bibliography

Coleman, Ray. *The Man Who Made the Beatles: An Intimate Biography of Brian Epstein*. New York: McGraw-Hill, 1989.

Epstein, Brian. *A Cellarful of Noise*. New York: Doubleday, 1964.

See also Music and Muscians 2: Popular Music

Esenin, Sergey (1895–1925)

Sergey Esenin was born into a peasant family in a village in the Russian province of Ryazan. He attended the traditional gymnasium, which was followed by several years at a teachers' college. At the age of seventeen, Esenin wrote to a young woman infatuated with him that he had not yet decided whether the great love of his life would turn out to be a man or a woman. Handsome, ingratiating, and thoroughly opportunistic, Esenin came to St. Petersburg in 1915, where he made a tremendous hit with his early poems about his native Ryazin countryside and voiced a touching compassion for wild and domestic animals mistreated and tortured by humans. To further his literary ambition, he used his personal charm, his peasant origins (very fashionable at the time), and, where necessary, his appeal to gay men. His brief liaisons with gay poets Riurik Ivnev and Leonid Kannegiser opened many literary doors to him. The fashion for literary *paysannerie* had been launched earlier by Nikolai Kliuev, a powerful and openly gay poet who enjoyed great popularity. In April 1915, Esenin wrote Kliuev an admiring letter and, as a memoirist put it, Kliuev came to St. Petersburg and "took over Esenin, becoming his sole possessor."

For the next two years, the two poets lived together as lovers. In response to the fad for peasant culture, they affected fantastic and identical folk costumes straight out of opera, gave joint poetry recitals, and filled their poems and personal speeches with incomprehensible words from remote village dialects. The masquerade was so successful that it brought them to the attention of the imperial court. By 1916, Esenin had become a protégé of Empress Alexandra, reciting his poetry at court and planning to dedicate his next book to her.

But only two years later, Esenin lent his support to the October Revolution. Like Kliuev and the rest of his circle, Esenin saw in Lenin a new peasant czar who would restore patriarchal ways and religious piety in the Russian countryside and protect village life from modernization and Westernization. Esenin welcomed the October Revolution with a series of baroque, visionary poems in which he equated Russia giving birth to worldwide revolution with nature yielding a harvest, a cow producing a calf, and the Virgin Mary giving birth to Christ. Culminating with the utopian narrative poem "Inonia," this series remains a unique poetic statement that mingles remnants of an ancient fertility cult with a vision of cosmic revolutionary changes.

It took Esenin several years to realize that his vision of the revolution as a peasant utopia was misguided. When he did, he changed his peasant garb to elegant Western attire. During and after his relationship with Kliuev, Esenin also had a number of affairs with women, some of whom bore his children. But he left each woman after less than a year, at times after battering her. More substantial was his four-year affair with poet Anatoly Marienhof, who described their life together in his book *A Novel Without Lies* and to whom Esenin addressed the beautiful homoerotic poem "Farewell to Marienhof." When Marienhof started courting a young actress, Esenin, in revenge, married the famed American dancer Isadora Duncan, whom he supposedly impressed by slugging her at a party after one of her Moscow performances.

With Duncan he traveled widely. It was a rude shock to Esenin to learn that in Western Europe and America he and his poetry were totally unknown. His resentment led to heavy drinking, furniture-smashing brawls in hotels from Paris to Chicago, and repeated, well-publicized beatings of his aging, overweight, adoring wife. She apparently enjoyed (or at least tolerated) this behavior, which she called "Russian love," though she had to cover the results with heavy makeup and veils. After he walked out on Duncan nine months later, he declared in an interview: "I married her for her money and for a chance to travel."

An archetypal instance of the violent, alcoholic, doomed poet, Esenin returned to Russia after his breakup with Duncan and embarked on a self-destructive course that led to his suicide two years later. The poetry he wrote in his last years was a poetry of despair: he could find no place for himself in the new Soviet society, and the only people with whom he could identify were the alcoholics and derelicts of Moscow's skid row. He went to see Kliuev shortly before his death, but his suicide note was a poem addressed to a young Jewish poet, Wolf Ehrlich, who had spent the night with him a few days earlier.   *Simon Karlinsky*

Bibliography

McVay, Gordon. *Isadora and Esenin.* Ann Arbor, Mich.: Ardis, 1980.

See also Kliuev, Nikolai; Russia; Russian Literature

Essentialist-Constructionist Debate

According to an influential and widely held metaphysical thesis, some classes of entities in the world constitute natural kinds. Natural kinds are groupings that play an explanatory role in scientific explanation and that exist independent of human thought. The chemical elements are natural kinds; they play a role in chemical explanations (e.g., why an explosion occurs), and they existed before humans did. The debate between essentialists and so-cial constructionists about sexual orientation (which was central to the formation of lesbian and gay studies and which has roots in history, sociology, and long-standing debates in philosophy) is, at heart, about whether the categories of sexual orientation refer to natural kinds or whether they are simply the creation of human culture.

Were there gay men, lesbians, heterosexuals, and bisexuals in ancient Greece or among the indigenous cultures of New Guinea? Questions like these gave rise to the debate between essentialists and constructionists. No one denies that people in every culture have sex with people of the same gender (or sex) while others have sex outside their gender. The question is whether classification in terms of the gender of the people whom one sexually desires captures some basic fact about her. Constructionists say no, pointing to the differences among how various cultures view sex and sexual desire. For example, they note that in Attic Greece, a person's social status was important to how the culture viewed his sexual interests. In terms of law and social custom, a citizen was allowed to penetrate but not be penetrated by noncitizens (i.e., slaves, children, women, and foreigners) and was not allowed to penetrate or to be penetrated by other citizens. For constructionists, this historical evidence indicates that it is anachronistic to apply our categories of sexual orientation to the Greeks. Insofar as the various sexual orientations are types that apply to humans, constructionists say they came to do so only after we developed the categories to refer to them.

Essentialists, on the other hand, claim that what historical and cultural variation there is does not conflict with the existence of the basic human types—heterosexual, homosexual, and (maybe) bisexual. That some cultures may not recognize these types does not prove that these types, are not genuine natural kinds. Just as people had blood types before blood types were discovered, essentialists would argue that even though people in other cultures may not have known about sexual orientation does not entail that the categories of sexual orientation fail to apply to them.

The debate between essentialists and constructionists is often understood as reducing to whether sexual orientation is the result of a person's genetic makeup or her environment. As typically discussed, this question of nature versus nurture is based on a false dichotomy. No human trait is strictly the result of genes or of environmental factors; all human traits are the result of both. There are genetic factors that affect even the most seemingly environmental traits (e.g., what kind of music a person likes). On the other hand, developmental and environmental factors contribute to the development of even the most seemingly genetic traits (e.g., eye color). Although every human trait is affected by genetic and environmental factors, there does seem to be some variance in degree: that my eyes are hazel is more tightly constrained by genetic factors than that I like classical music more than contemporary. In this context, the nature-nurture debate concerns where sexual orientation fits on the continuum between eye color and taste in music.

Given this, the commonly held view that essentialism entails that sexual orientation is strongly constrained by genetic factors and constructionism entails that sexual orientation is primarily shaped by the environment is shown to be mistaken. In general, it is possible for a category to refer to a natural kind of human without its being the case that a person fits into that category by virtue of her genes. For example, being a person who is immune to polio is a natural kind, but whether or not one is a member of this group involves the presence of certain antibodies in the bloodstream, which is not genetic. With respect to sexual orientation, if a simplistic version of the Freudian theory of the origins of male sexual orientation were true and a man has his particular sexual orientation by virtue of his relationship with his parents—namely, whether or not he has a resolved Oedipal complex—then essentialism would be true. Once a boy has settled into a particular Oedipal status, he has a naturally determined sexual orientation: he has the psychological makeup of a heterosexual or homosexual. If this theory (or a structurally similar psychological theory) were true, then sexual orientations would be natural kinds, but they would not be primarily genetic. This shows that essentialism does not entail nativism. The same example suffices to show that if sexual orientation is primarily environmental, constructionism need not follow. While essentialism does not entail nativism and environmentalism does not entail constructionism, nativism does entail essentialism. If a person's sexual orientation is primarily determined by genetic factors, then there are natural kinds associated with sexual orientations by virtue of the genes responsible for sexual orientation. If this were the case, constructionism would be false. This is not to say that constructionism is in fact false but rather that constructionism and essentialism are empirical theses.

Edward Stein

Bibliography

Halperin, David. *One Hundred Years of Homosexuality and Other Essays in Greek Love.* New York: Routledge, 1990.

Stein, Edward, ed. *Forms of Desire: Sexual Orientation and the Social Constructionist Controversy.* New York: Routledge, 1992

See also Evolution; Gender; Greece; Homosexuality; Queer; Scientific Approaches to Homosexuality

Etruscans

The Etruscans established their civilization between the rivers Tiber and Arno (in what is now Tuscany, Italy) and by c. 500 B.C.E. their settlements extended as far as the Po valley in the north and Campania in the south. Where the Etruscans originated has been a long-standing scholarly controversy; current scholarship favors an indigenous origin. However, their non–Indo-European language and certain aspects of Etruscan religion, for example, hepatoscopy—the science of peering at the liver and/or entrails of a sacrificed beast to discern favorable or unfavorable omens—is of Eastern influence, if not origin. In the power struggle with neighboring Rome, the Etruscans provided a dynasty of Roman kings, the Tarquins, expelled in c. 509 B.C.E.. By the third century B.C.E., the Etruscans had been completely subsumed by the Romans, whose culture (especially religion) they deeply influenced.

In their politically independent cities, the Etruscans forged a vibrant culture. In the absence of any extant literature, Etruscan art is of supreme importance for interpreting the manner in which the Etruscans constructed gender and sexuality. Tomb statuary suggests a relaxed and tolerant attitude toward women (certainly in the upper classes). Vase painting, mostly of Attic origin, celebrates all varieties of human sexual activity. A fresco in the Tomb of the Bulls in Tarquinia (mid-sixth century B.C.E.) depicts a naked male couple engaged in anal intercourse. Tomb paintings of Etruscan banquets portray scantily clad men and youths, male dancers, and musicians; naked camp deities and heroes on silver and bronze mirrors, and nude male dancers on bronze candelabras suggest a positive attitude toward same-sex relations and the homoerotic.

Michael Lambert

E

Bibliography

Brendel, O. J. *Etruscan Art*. New York: Penguin, 1978.

Hallett, Judith. "Roman Attitudes Toward Sex." In Michael Grant and Rachel Klitzinger, eds. *Civilizations of the Ancient Mediterranean: Greece and Rome*. Vol. 2. New York: Scribner, 1988, 1265–1278.

See also Greece, Rome

European Commission of Human Rights

The European Commission of Human Rights is one of the two main supranational courts (the other being the European Court of Human Rights) available to citizens and governments of not only the fifteen member states of the European Union but also the thrity-three states that make up the Council of Europe (as of January 1997). Both courts have frequently considered cases concerning homosexuality, under the terms of the European Convention on Human Rights (signed November 4, 1950, effective as of September 3, 1953). To date, the commission has rendered decisions in over fifty such cases, while the court has dealt with fewer than thirty.

The nature of the two courts differs considerably from that of the United States or Canadian Supreme Courts. They have in general functioned over the years in a consensual fashion, imposing on national governments only those changes of law that have been already adopted by a large majority of the member states. In practice, therefore, their effect has rarely been to open new legal perspectives for gay Europeans but rather to encourage those remaining countries that have not yet reformed their laws to do so.

The main clauses of the convention invoked by gay plaintiffs are Articles 3 ("no one shall be subjected to . . . inhuman or degrading treatment . . ."), 8.1 ("everyone has the right to respect for his private and family life . . ."), and 14 ("The enjoyment of the rights and freedoms set forth in this Convention shall be secured without discrimination on any ground such as sex, race, colour, language, religion, political or other opinion . . . or other status"). The main clause invoked by governments in support of continued discriminatory legislation is Article 8.2 ("There shall be no interference by a public authority with the exercise of this right except such as is in accordance with the law and is necessary in a democratic society in the interests of national security, public safety or . . . for the prevention of disorder or crime, for the protection of health and morals").

The earliest cases were all considered by the commission (nine, between 1955 and 1967, concerning men who had been imprisoned in Germany and Austria for consensual sexual activity with other men). The prevailing view then was that governments had the right "to punish homosexuality" under Article 8.2. More recently, the commission's famous decision in 1982 upholding the British courts' conviction of the publisher of *Gay News*, and of Denis Lemon, the newspaper's editor, on charges of "blasphemous libel" (the case concerned the publication of a poem by Professor James Kirkup describing the homoerotic feelings of a Roman soldier looking at Jesus Christ on the cross), continued to rely on the traditionally restrictive interpretation of Articles 7, 9, 10, and 14 of the convention, but would not consider the case in terms of Article 8.

A change of attitude appeared only following the liberalization of laws in several European countries. In 1977–1978 applications were made to declare illegal Great Britain's discriminatory ages of consent in England and Wales (twenty-one for male homosexual activity versus sixteen for heterosexual or lesbian activity) and the total ban on homosexual activity in a British dependent territory, Northern Ireland. In the former case the commission upheld Britain's laws (although the age has since been lowered to eighteen, retaining a discriminatory difference). In the latter case, on the other hand, which was brought by Jeffrey Dudgeon, the commission's 1980 decision upheld that the Northern Ireland prohibition "breaches the applicant's rights to respect for private life under article 8[.1]".

This decision, upheld in 1981 by the European Court, constituted a turning point in legal protection for European gays. Similar judgments have since been given in 1988 and 1993 in cases brought by Senator David Norris against the Republic of Ireland and by Alecos Modinos against Cyprus, respectively.

Further progress in the international protection of gay rights in Europe is unlikely to come from new interpretations of the convention by the judges of the commission and the court. Rather, it will depend on changes of legislation in individual states since only the existence of such new laws can provide the consensual basis on which changing interpretation of the convention may occur.

Although the cases that have been brought before the court and the commission have sometimes dealt with more detailed gay matters (the right to marry or to adopt, and the bid for nondiscriminatory inheritance laws, for example, almost all of which claims have been rejected as "manifestly ill-founded"), the vast majority of cases have dealt with the far more basic question of the legitimacy of laws criminalizing all male homosexual activity. The protection offered to gay European citizens by the convention, as interpreted by the commission and the court, is thus still very limited, often reduced to a legal lowest common denominator. The current ambiguous position has been summarized as follows: "Criminalization of private same-sex sexual activity between no more than two persons who are both over 21 and are not in the armed forces violates Article 8, but every other kind of sexual orientation discrimination has so far been held to be consistent with the Convention" (Wintemute, 248).

Governments have sometimes been notoriously pernicious in their defenses. The British government claimed in 1980 that criminalizing homosexual activity does not constitute sexual orientation discrimination since it applies uniformly to all men, heterosexual as well as homosexual. While the commission rejected this line of argument here, it was willing to accept it in other contexts, declaring that gay people are free to marry since a woman can marry a man even if she is a lesbian. But neither the commission nor the court has so far accepted that the fundamental question here does not concern sexual orientation discrimination but sexual discrimination: a woman can marry a man, but a man cannot do so.

Governments have also usually been slow in implementing new legislation in accordance with the commission's judgments. Nevertheless, significant progress has occurred. The Republic of Ireland finally complied with the 1988 *Norris* decision, but only in 1993. The *Dudgeon* case led to a series of reluctant changes in the legislation of British dependent territories, in Scotland (1980), Guernsey (1983), Jersey (1990), the Isle of Man (1992), and Gibraltar (1993), all of which had had particularly repressive antigay laws.

As a result of these changes and the subsequent *Modinos* decision, laws criminalizing all sexual activity between men have been totally removed from the twenty-three member states that, until 1989, formed the Council of Europe. Since that date ten eastern European countries have also joined the council. All except Romania have decriminalized homosexual activity (and this country has been formally requested by the Parliamentary Assembly of the Council of Europe to legalize homosexual relations between consenting adults in private). Among the countries waiting to join the council, Croatia and Montenegro have already liberalized their laws in anticipation of joining, as have to some extent Albania, Serbia, Russia, and Ukraine. The other potential members whose laws maintain a strict prohibition of all homosexual activity are Armenia, Azerbaijan, Belarus, Bosnia and Herzegovina, Georgia, Macedonia, and Moldova. It is on these nations that the future effects of the European commission's and court's decisions concerning the illegality of legislation criminalizing homosexuality could have the most forceful results in coming years, because the overwhelming consensus among existing members is against them.

Further change may also be precipitated, however, by appeals to the still higher level of international protection against sexual orientation discrimination provided by the International Covenant on Civil and Political Rights of the United Nations (signed on December 16, 1966, effective as of March 23, 1976). This has since been ratified by 125 nations, 74 of which (excluding the United States) allow their citizens to address the UN court directly. Article 26 of this text has recently been successfully invoked in front of the UN Human Rights Committee in the case *Toonen v. Australia* (1994), which could eventually have far-reaching effects on the 28 countries that have signed the UN International Covenant, do allow their citizens to address the court directly, but still have laws forbidding all homosexual activity. This could directly affect at least one member country of the Council of Europe, as well as several potential members. In this way, the European court and commission could in future years find themselves overtaken by a higher level of international law protecting basic gay rights.

Davitt Moroney

Bibliography

Tatchell, Peter. *Europe in the Pink: Lesbian and Gay Equality in the New Europe.* London: GMP Publishers, 1992.

Wintemute, Robert. *Sexual Orientation and Human Rights: The United States Constitution, the European Convention, and the Canadian Charter.* Oxford: Clarendon Press, 1995.

See also Code Napoléon; Denmark; Netherlands; Sweden; U.S. Law: Equal Protection; Wolfenden Report

E

Evolution

Scientists have long treated homosexuals as people whose bodies and actions are badly in need of explanation. One way scientists have tried to explain homosexuality is via appeal to evolutionary theories. Most of these intellectual efforts have been aimed at showing homosexuality to be a sign of deviance or degeneration—that is, as an evolutionary evil. Lately, however, a number of theorists have instead been interested in imagining why homosexuals could be good for the human species, evolutionarily speaking. As Vernon Rosario has noted in *Science and Homosexualities*, regardless of this political shift, the basic goal has remained the same, namely, to make sense of homosexuality via "final causes"—that is, via appeal to evolution.

Evolutionary theories are those that posit cumulative changes in species. Most also account for the emergence of new species. Many people associate the word *evolution* strictly with Charles Darwin and his revolutionary book, *Origin of Species* (1859), but there were evolutionary theories before Darwin's and there have been many more since. Darwin's long-lived innovation was to posit natural selection as the key to evolution. Natural selection is said to occur when environmental conditions favor one variant trait over another. If that variation is genetic and it is reproductively advantageous—that is, if it somehow enables the possessor ultimately to leave behind more offspring than peers who lack that variation—then, according to natural selection theory, over time the species will come to exhibit that trait consistently. In other words, the trait will have been "naturally selected" and the species will have "evolved" with regard to that trait.

Darwin could not account for all he saw simply with his natural selection theory, so he developed a corollary theory called "sexual selection," which states that a trait may be "selected" directly by a mate. For example, a peahen might choose as a mate a peacock who has particularly spectacular coloration. Such a favored peacock would leave more offspring than a less-favored peacock, and over time, peacocks would presumably become relatively more colorful. By contrast, if natural selection operated alone, bright coloring would presumably be "selected out" of the gene pool because it makes individuals visible to predators. Like natural selection, sexual selection could theoretically result in cumulative species change over time. Most evolutionists still adhere to versions of Darwin's theories, although some also employ other explanatory hypotheses.

Homosexuality would seem hard to explain via natural selection or sexual selection because it would appear to be reproductively disadvantageous. Nevertheless, late-nineteenth- and early-twentieth-century theorists did use evolutionary theory to explain how homosexuality could arise "by mistake." Most presumed that humankind had a hermaphroditic past—that progenitors of humans were physically bisexual (double-sexed). They also assumed that "ontogeny recapitulates phylogeny"—that during its own personal development (ontogeny), each individual passed through (recapitulated) all the evolutionary stages that the species itself had passed through (phylogeny). Therefore, if a man or woman acted "hermaphroditic" by having the body of one sex but the desires "natural" to the other, he or she was thought by evolutionists to be an example of arrested development or degeneration. He or she simply had failed, for whatever reason, to reach the pinnacle of human sexuality (heterosexuality).

As evidence of this degeneration, late-nineteenth-century medical and scientific professionals pointed out that gay men often seemed effeminate and lesbians virile (i.e., hermaphroditic). Lesbians were said typically to possess large clitorises—a serious sign of hermaphroditism. As Margaret Gibson has documented, scientists also believed that the prevalence of "hermaphroditic" genitalia and homosexual relations among the "lower races" (like people indigenous to Africa and New Zealand) further proved the association of homosexuality, hermaphroditism, and degeneration. Julian Carter has noted that "the atavistic qualities of sexual perversion were not [considered] unique to homosexuality; fetishists, adulterers, sadists, masochists, and prostitutes [and nonwhites] were all explained as evolutionary failures, throwbacks, and threats."

Some early gay rights activists tried to use evolutionary theory to explain why the homosexual should be seen as a normal, natural, nonthreatening variation. For example, in his circa 1908 privately published book, *History of Similisexualism*, Xavier Mayne (pseudonym for Edward Stevenson) declared, "Between a protozoan and the most perfect development of the mammalia, we trace a succession of dependent intersteps. . . . A trilobite is at one end of Nature's workshop: a Spinoza, a Shakespeare, a Beethoven is at the other." Why, then, have we "gone on insisting that each specimen of sex in humanity must . . . follow out [one of] two programmes only, or else be thought amiss, imperfect, and degenerate[?] Why have we set up masculinity and femininity as processes that have not perfectly logical and respectable inter-steps?" Mayne suggested that the homosexual (or what he called the "intersex") is just one of those natural, normal intersteps. But as long as desire for females was seen as the purview of the male, and desire for males as the purview of the female, the homosexual was bound to be constructed as a hermaphroditic developmental anomaly dangerous to the success of the human species.

Since the 1970s, some sociobiologists have attempted to explain homosexuality in a way that makes it natural and good for the human species. (Sociobiologists try to explain human behavior via evolutionary theory.) For example, in *On Human Nature*, Edward O. Wilson imagined that "homosexuals may be the genetic carriers of some of mankind's altruistic impulses." This altruism link would keep gayness in the human gene pool: homosexuals would help out their reproducing heterosexual kin who would, via the extra help, leave more offspring than the gay-kin-less peers. The gay-kin progeny would presumably carry and pass on some of the "gay" genes and keep the gay-altruism link going. Some scientists have tried to find empirical support for these sociobiological theories, for example, by trying to show that gay people are indeed more altruistic than straight people or by trying to find "gay" genes. Others have tried to come up with alternative explanations for why homosexuality should exist in an evolutionary world. Some, for example, propose that greater individual plasticity (e.g., in terms of individual potential sexual orientation) is likely to be favored, given that environments can change suddenly. (Rigid genomes are risky.) Others have suggested we stop trying to explain gay people—that doing so only feeds into a system that says they are in need of "normalizing" explanations.

Alice Dreger

Bibliography

Rosario, Vernon A., ed. *Science and Homosexualities*. New York: Routledge, 1997.

Futuyma, Douglas J., and Stephen J. Risch. "Sexual Orientation, Sociobiology, and Evolution." *Journal of Homosexuality* 9 (1983–1984): 157–68.

See also Androgyny; Hermaphroditism; Scientific Approaches to Homosexuality

F

Faggot

This abusive slang for male homosexual developed in the United States near the turn of the century but has since been exported to other countries. *Faggot* (or *fagot*, or its shortened form, *fag*) largely replaced its predecessors, *fairy* and *queer*, as an insult expressing hostility and disgust, becoming the put-down of choice for heterosexuals, appearing unabashedly in movies throughout the 1980s. It can, but need not necessarily, imply the effeminate or the flamboyant (as in the term *flaming faggot*). It certainly suggests the visible, a perceived failure in the enactment of an individual's heterosexuality/masculinity.

The words first appeared in print as a reference to homosexuals as early as 1914, in Jackson and Hellyer's *Vocabulary of Criminal Slang*, in the sentence "All the fagots (sissies) will be dressed in drag at the ball tonight." The diminutive *fag* first appeared in 1923, in Nels Anderson's *The Hobo* in the following sentence: "Fairies or Fags are men or boys who exploit sex for profit, the vague nature of which manages to almost completely elide the homosexual nature of its subject."

Its etymology as a slang term has been highly contested, with various root words and linguistic pathways suggested by different theorists. Some have argued that the slang usage draws on the word's meaning as a bundle of sticks, twigs, or small branches of trees bound together, especially as these faggots were used in burning heretics and witches at the stake, seeking to connect male homosexuals with the ostracized, outcast, and scapegoated. This suggestion has been hotly debated and (somewhat persuasively) dismissed as myth. A more plausible suggestion is the word's use as a term of abuse or contempt for women, a use that continued well into the twentieth century.

Or, alternately, the word's use in reference to underclassmen, typically adolescent boys, who performed duties for seniors in British public schools, related to the definition of the word as hard work, toil, or drudgery. Given the word's connotations of effeminacy and the extent to which institutionalized homosexuality was viewed as endemic within the British school system, it seems likely that these connotations had some resonance in the word's growth as a popular slang phrase. However, we should be wary of declaring a definitive pathway for the slang's development or of closing down alternate meanings.

In recent years, some activists have attempted to reclaim *faggot*, along with other pejorative words, by using it reflexively with humor and a degree of ironic distance. This seeks to neutralize the homophobic force of slang terms by preempting their use. Hence *fag* and other abusive slang appeared frequently on colorful stickers worn by member of direct-action groups like Queer Nation. Whether such an effort of reclamation will succeed or spread to the gay and lesbian community at large remains to be seen.

Scott Speirs

Bibliography

Grahn, Judy. *Another Mother Tongue*. Boston: Beacon, 1984.

Rodgers, Bruce. *The Queen's Vernacular*. San Francisco: Straight Arrow Books, 1972.

See also Fairy; Gay; Mollies; Queen; Queer Nation

Fairy

This slang for a male homosexual, especially one displaying signs of effeminacy, was especially pop-

Fular during the first half of this century. The word stems from the Old French *faerie* or *faierie*, referring to either a small, supernatural creature or its homeland. In the nascent decades of male homosexual urban culture in the United States, *fairy* designated the most obvious type of homosexual, those transvestite sex workers whose mode of dress resembled female prostitutes. The term became part of a communal language and aided the emergence of a communal identity, at the same time serving to signify the male prostitute's availability and character to others in the know. Eventually, its use spread to refer to any male homosexual, not merely prostitutes. With its associations of the delicate, diminutive, and mystical, *fairy* was a less pejorative term than *queer*, or the later *faggot* or *fag*. With the emergence of the gay liberation movement in the late 1960s, *fairy* was largely replaced by *gay*, which was seen as a less derogatory term of self-identification.

The Radical (alternately, Sacred) Faeries is a movement that adopted the word for its name. Begun in the 1970s, the Radical Faeries are based on the philosophies of early gay rights activist Harry Hay, which combines elements of New Age spiritualism, hippie counterculture, and political activism. The movement sought to redefine gayness by rejecting bourgeois notions of heteronormative masculine behavior. Using neopagan rituals and favoring a loosely organized, nonhierarchical structure, Faeries meet in gatherings and form faerie circles as a means of celebration, worship, and consciousness raising.   *Scott Speirs*

Bibliography

Chauncey, George. *Gay New York*. New York: Harper Collins, 1994.

Timmons, Stuart. *The Trouble with Harry Hay*. Boston: Alyson, 1990.

See also Faggot; Gay; Queer; Radical Faeries

Falla, Manuel de (1876–1946)

Spanish composer Manuel Maria de Falla y Matheu was the eldest son of a cultured and prosperous couple who resided in the Andalusian city of Cádiz. Falla's parents made sure that their three children had the best tutors at home, including excellent training in music. At twenty, Falla enrolled as a student at the Real Conservatorio de Música in Madrid, where he completed the demanding course in piano in just two years. He later fell under the sway of the noted composer and musicologist Felipe Fedrell, who encouraged Falla to explore Spanish folk music. In 1907, Falla journeyed to Paris, where he impressed leading French composers such as Dukas, Ravel, and Debussy. While in Paris, Falla was entranced by the music and aesthetics of impressionism and worked hard to perfect his mastery of orchestration. This seven-year period of study in Paris bore fruit in 1915 with the creation of the gipsy ballet *El amor brujo* and the completion in the same year of a set of "symphonic impressions" for piano and orchestra entitled *Noches en los jardines de España*. Falla's next large work, the ballet *El sombrero de tres picos*, was written for Diaghilev's Ballets Russes; it successfully premiered in London on July 22, 1919, with choreography by Diaghilev's then lover Léonid Massine and decor by Picasso. Falla settled in Granada in 1920, living with his sister, María del Carmen. Falla's serene life was shattered by the convulsions of the Spanish Civil War. The deleterious effect of the war on the composer's precarious physical and mental health eventually necessitated an escape from Spain. Falla and his sister emigrated to a remote part of Argentina in 1939, where he worked on his final work, the "scenic cantata" *Atlántida*. This massive score was left unfinished at the composer's death and was later completed by Falla's disciple Ernesto Halffter.

Igor Stravinsky once characterized Falla's nature as "the most unpityingly religious I have ever known." Yet Falla never composed a note of religious music, and his style is often as overtly erotic as that of Ravel. Like the reclusive Ravel, Falla's sexual predilections are difficult to determine with any certainty. Thus evidence of any homosexuality is circumstantial. Falla was a lifelong bachelor with no documented love affairs with members of either sex. Aside from his sister and the lesbian harpsichordist Wanda Landowska, he seems to have had no interest in women whatsoever. Falla collaborated enthusiastically with both Diaghilev and Massine on *El sombrero de tres picos*, making a protracted automobile tour through Spain with them in search of inspiration for the ballet. Falla's home in Granada was a meeting place for gay Spanish artists and intellectuals, such as his intimate friend Federico García Lorca. Lorca's murder by the Nationalists in 1936 and the stringent homophobia of Franco's regime may well have contributed to Falla's decision to settle in Argentina. Finally, there is his music: so sensuous, so coruscating, so elegant, and, at times, so very campy.   *Byron Adams*

Bibliography

Crichton, Ronald. *Falla.* London: British Broadcasting Corporation, 1982.

Pahissa, Jaime. *Manuel de Falla: His Life and Works.* Jean Wagstaff, trans. Westport: Hyperion Press, 1979.

Trend, John Brande. *Manuel de Falla and Spanish Music.* New York: Alfred A. Knopf, 1934.

See also Diaghilev, Sergey; Lorca, Federico García; Music and Musicians 1: Classical Music

Fashion

"In the fashion business," wrote James Brady, former publisher of *Women's Wear Daily* and *Harper's Bazaar,* in *Super Chic* (1974), "the suggestion of homosexuality is never far below the surface." In *Fashion and the Unconscious* (1953), psychologist Edmund Bergler posited that contemporary style is driven by "a fashion-hoax, unconsciously perpetrated by homosexuals." In her influential book *The Beautiful People* (1967), *New York Times* reporter Marylin Bender said of her time, "American fashion turns increasingly homosexual. And the public senses it. 'Fashion is being taken over by the pansy boys. We're being made to look like Lolitas and lion tamers. All those boots and helmets,' protests Barbara Tuchman, the writer of history." Thus claimed the reporter and the writer of history; their account, however malicious, probably begins with a truth. Bender continues, "There are no statistics to prove that Seventh Avenue has more homosexuals than Wall Street.... The homosexual doesn't have to camouflage himself on Seventh Avenue. He can flaunt. Desperate manufacturers are known to say, 'I'll get myself a fairy designer.'"

As an art and business of self-expression, striving for beauty, and perhaps even idealization of women, fashion is a favored enterprise of homosexual men. But lesbian feminist artist Zoe Leonard photographed a runway fashion show from below to look up the dresses and see underwear in her politically driven art of 1990. Lesbian attraction is also suggested in some fashion photography, and homoeroticism is a leitmotif of menswear advertising and promotion.

Fashion's intimate connection with the body, its innate physical and metaphorical relationship with sexuality, and its pursuit of beauty have captivated many, especially gay men. Bergler argued that fashion was neurotic, implicit aggression imposed on women customers. But fashion is volitional in the manner of consumerism, not a conscious and subliminal edict of fashion designers, whether gay, lesbian, or straight.

Fashion's inflammatory arena of sexual incorporation arouses issues of modern fashion's privileged relationship to the body and fashion's ubiquitous, powerful role in culture. In the traditional paradigm of fashion—ignoring menswear—its primary purpose is to render women beautiful or to feel beautiful by apparel. But fashion also promotes comfort and self-confidence as well; not every dress is for an upward-aspiring, man-hunting Cinderella, nor is it to achieve heterosexual desire. Fashion designers can be male or female, gay, bisexual, or straight. Their supposed "psychological" motives are not wholly homogeneous. Homosexual men have been great designers: both Christian Dior and Cristobal Balenciaga, the leading figures of mid-century Paris fashion; Yves Saint Laurent and Jean Paul Gaultier in successor generations in Paris; and Giorgio Armani and Gianni Versace in Italy. Personal style and self-expression among these designers and others have varied as globally as any human behavior: New York milliner Mr. John was deliberately campy and aestheticized; married but misogynist designer Charles James fulfilled the cliché of the fashion designer who exalted a female silhouette in ballgown but otherwise scorned most women; Halston affected a narcissistic grand style; John Bartlett is an "out" menswear designer of late-century forthrightness.

As an industry of beauty and appearances, fashion has customarily allowed the gay designer to touch the female body. If Dior was on some level always reaching for his mother's fin-de-siècle grace, he or his fitters were nonetheless in immediate contact with his clients' bodies. Unlike the painter or composer who works on an artist-determined plane, the fashion designer works directly on or about the human body. Like the cliché of the attractive gay hairdresser to women, the gay man who makes a woman proud may be a perfect and unthreatening complement of interest and indifference. In ready-to-wear clothing, the design process is abstracted from the client; in haute couture, the garment is custom-made to the client by the designer and requires physical contact. In the intermediate range, many women traditionally employed dressmakers who were other women to assist in fit and alterations.

In the American ready-to-wear industry, located on and eponymous with New York's Seventh Avenue, the cliché was that manufacturers were straight and they hired gay male (or, in rare instances, women) designers. Never automatic, though sometimes plausible as a distinction between those attracted to business and those drawn to tactile and creative skills, this stereotype can no longer describe a fashion system in which designers have assumed most of the prerogatives of the manufacturers. Designers lead many fashion houses; Pierre Bergé as businessman and Saint Laurent as designer founded the Saint Laurent house; today, Todd Oldham and his lover/partner preside over their fashion business.

As fashion is no longer conceived solely as a business of women's garments but of apparel for men, women, and children, and more important of "lifestyle" and identity through body-related products but expanding into other product as well, fashion is little touched by fetishes and claims of psychological games. Much puritanical taboo about fashion and the body has been diminished, and both fashion and fashion advertising have been overt in sexuality of multiple inferences. Conversely, menswear, once staid, has opened itself to a number of influences from women's fashion, including many of the same designers. Armani, for example, began as a menswear designer and only later became a womenswear designer, reversing the usual practice.

Are gay men more disposed to fashion as consumers because they are gay? Awareness of oneself as a sex object may promote acuity to clothing and style, but most supposedly "gay" styles are little more than distilled forms of menswear conventions.

As fashion is so effectively the juggernaut of contemporary consumption and identity, it becomes ever more a field of the physical body collateral with the social body. Homoerotic advertising, a spectrum of personal and cultural identities, and gay and straight creative endeavor may simply be part of contemporary fashion as an imaginative process and as a forward business system, but seldom as an impulse of perverse or perverted affliction as once was thought.   *Richard Martin*

Bibliography

Bender, Marilyn. *The Beautiful People.* New York: Coward-McCann, 1967.

Bergler, Edmund. *Fashion and the Unconscious.* New York: Robert Brunner, 1953.

Francis, Mark, and Margery King, et al. *The Warhol Look: Glamour, Style, Fashion.* New York: Little Brown, 1997.

Martin, Richard. "Out and in Fashion." *Artforum.* May 1995.

————. "The Gay Factor in Fashion." *Esquire Gentleman.* 1:1(Spring, 1993): 135–40.

See also Body Image; Clone; Klein, Calvin; Leathermen; Leyendecker, J. C.; Versace, Gianni

Fassbinder, Rainer Werner (1945?–1982)

Fassbinder was the enfant terrible of the German New Wave cinema of the 1970s, an actor, writer, and director who gave new meaning to the term "polymorphously perverse." In an astoundingly prolific career of just under thirteen years, Fassbinder made forty-one feature films before he died of a drug and alcohol overdose at the age of thirty-seven. Strongly gay-identified, he defied social convention even as he recorded its devastating effects on the human heart. His most enduring films—*Angst essen Seele auf* (Fear Eats the Soul, 1973) and *Die Ehe der Maria Braun* (The Marriage of Maria Braun, 1976)—explore an individual's negotiation of class and cultural differences in postwar Germany by setting passionate explorations of love, betrayal, or loss before a politically charged backdrop. All his films, however, reflect an "out" gay sensibility: His were not movies encoded with a homosexual subtext—no green on Thursdays— but stories filtered through a queer lens.

Fassbinder's personal life was a veritable game, set, and match of contradictions. He was a disheveled, fleshy, pockmarked mess, a tyrant by turns sadistic and arrogant, yet people of all genders and races were drawn to his charismatic genius. Openly gay, he still married a woman at least once and had a female companion at the time of his death. He lived a fast life and became addicted to drugs early on, yet the more dissipated he became, the more disciplined and focused he became, and some of his most mature and complex films were created at a time when Fassbinder, personally, was at his worst. He wanted to be remembered for his work, yet the wildly controversial performance that was his life eclipsed his art.

It can be difficult to separate the genuine details of Fassbinder's life from the myth. He was born on May 31, 1945 or 1946, in Bad Wörishofen, in Bavaria; various accounts cite the director himself as the source of the later birth date, but others suggest that he subtracted a year from his true age to perpetuate the myth of the wunderkind. Fassbinder's parents divorced when he was about six years old. His father pursued his own life; his mother, charitably described as chronically unwell, or, less charitably, an emotional wreck, left him to fend for himself. The predominant image of Fassbinder's childhood is that of a young boy crushed by his parents' divorce, escaping into the darkness of a theater to be mesmerized and somehow comforted by Hollywood melodrama playing on the screen. A second vignette presents Fassbinder several years later, in the gay bars of Cologne, as teenage bar slut, or even pimp, notably for a young and already outrageous Udo Kier. These images crystallize the defining moments of Fassbinder's early life.

By the time he was twenty-one, Fassbinder had become involved in writing plays. For fifteen months, his theatrical playground was the Action Theater, where he produced, directed, and sometimes acted in company productions; for another two years, it was his famed "anti-theater" group, which he founded with Peer Raben. Fassbinder once said that he "learned to make films by making them," but he clearly learned about the dynamics of dramatic structure, along with the practical considerations of working with actors, by working in theater.

A year later, in 1969, Fassbinder wrote, directed, and acted in his first feature film, *Liebe ist kälter als der Tod* (Love Is Colder Than Death). He would make three other features and two short films in that year. And that was just the beginning. For the next twelve years, Fassbinder browbeat or manipulated members of his company, which included lovers, friends, roommates, and even his mother, into collaborating on film after film; he wrote, directed, and sometimes acted in as many as four feature films in one year and still worked in theater, demanding that all keep up with him. And most of them did.

The 1978 death of Fassbinder's lover Armin Maier, whom the director is generally considered to have driven to suicide, was the beginning of the end for the director. Fassbinder was devastated by Maier's death, but by then it was attention paid too late. Always prone to depression, his outlook soured considerably and his addictions worsened. Yet in his final four years he completed the epic *Berlin Alexanderplatz*, all fifteen hours' worth; the dark satire suggested by *Lola* (1981); and the deeply moving story of a has-been actress's plunge into drug addiction, a masterpiece in the tradition of *Sunset Boulevard* as well as *Lost Weekend*: *Die Schusucht der Veronika Voss* (Veronica Voss) (1981). Unfortunately, he died on June 10, 1982, before the premiere of his final film, *Querelle*.

Fassbinder's life also melded the personal with the political. He produced four films with gay, lesbian, or transgendered subjects and made the then-radical determination that none of these films would actually be about homosexuality and the allegedly unhappy state of being homosexual. Fassbinder's first queer story, made in 1972, was actually a lesbian film: *Die bitteren Tränen der Petra von Kant* (The Bitter Tears of Petra von Kant). An elegant, beautifully photographed film about a lesbian couple and their maid caught up in a series of nasty power games, it has been hailed as a moving tale of lesbian passion and trashed as the clueless work of a male voyeur. There is some truth to both these statements; but set against such a film as *The Killing of Sister George* (1968), *Bitter Tears* is far more entertaining and bitchy rather than oppressive in its sadistic leanings. Fassbinder's poignant, multilayered 1975 drama, *Faustrecht der Freiheit* (Fox and His Friends), a story of a working-class man financially comfortable thanks to lottery winnings who falls in love with a manipulative upper-class lover, was a welcome antidote to *Boys in the Band* (1970) in that conflicts arose out of class differences and personal flaws rather than sexuality. In both these films, Fassbinder examines the relationship among love, power, and desire without pathologizing the characters who establish that dynamic in their romantic relationships.

In the 1979 film *In einem Jahr mit 13 Monden* (In a Year of Thirteen Moons), Fassbinder gives an account of the last five days of a male-to-female transsexual who has had surgery only to please her lover, who then rejects her. *Thirteen Moons* is actually Fassbinder's pessimistic examination of what happens when traditional binary definitions of identity fail; it has probably the only scene ever filmed in which a gay gang queer-bashes the main character because they don't understand who she/he is. Eventually Elvira/Elvin, rejected by old friends and an ex-wife, dies of an overdose, although it is unclear whether her death is a suicide or an accident.

Querelle (1982), Fassbinder's last film, is a steamy yet uninvolving story set in the port city of Brest about an amoral sailor, a murderer in hiding (Brad Davis), who falls in love with another man wanted for murder yet eventually betrays him to the police. The sets and lighting are garish and deliberately artificial, but the end to which such a striking effect has been created is unclear. Convoluted messages about the relationship between sex and death are lost to an audience that finds it difficult to care about the characters. Some critics felt that Fassbinder's demons had finally overtaken him and that he had simply lost his grip while he was making the movie; others insisted that Fassbinder was staking

F out new territory as a filmmaker. His untimely death is doubly sad because his fans will never know whether *Querelle* was an aberration or the beginning of a new phase in his work.

Fassbinder's queer work was far ahead of its time: he created sentimental gay characters and brutal ones, endearing gay characters, and even a master manipulator or two. The bottom line is that Fassbinder—one gay man, one gay voice—created characters who expressed little truths about all our lives. *J. A. White*

Bibliography

Katz, Robert. *Love Is Colder Than Death: The Life and Times of Rainer Werner Fassbinder.* New York: Random House, 1987.

Lensing, Leo A., and Michael Töberg, eds. *Rainer Werner Fassbinder: The Anarchy of the Imagination: Interviews, Essays, Notes.* Krishna Winston, trans. Baltimore: Johns Hopkins University Press, 1992.

Rayns, Tony, ed. *Fassbinder.* London: British Film Institute, 1976.

Thomsen, Christian Braad. *Fassbinder: The Life and Work of a Provocative Genius.* London: Faber and Faber, 1997.

See also Film; Germany; Transexuality

Feminism

Any discussion of the relationship between gay men and feminism must begin with the acknowledgment that both terms are contested and historically specific. The material relations of class and race as well as ideological difference complicate and fracture both categories. So, for example, both Andrea Dworkin and Gayle Rubin call themselves feminists but are in violent disagreement with each other over the imperatives that arise from that position. Dworkin has criticized gay male sadomasochism and pushed for censorship laws, while Rubin identifies herself as a member of the S/M community and has defended the right of sexual expression. Likewise, "gay man" is a malleable construct. It would stretch the term past usefulness to lump together Roy Cohn, James Baldwin, and Oscar Wilde under the same category without noting that they are as different from one another, perhaps more so, than similar. Without too much violence to the complexities of the terms under consideration or their relationship to each other, however, it can be said that both feminism and "gayness" are sites of struggle over the boundaries of gendered and sexualized identities, power, and pleasure. Both terms name communities of interest as well as political and cultural traditions and practices. While there is no necessary connection between the respective projects, there are commonalities. As such, feminism and gay men have enjoyed a conflicted but fruitful relation to each other.

Though there was some overlap between the homosexual rights movement and the women's movement in the late nineteenth and early twentieth centuries—as, for example, in Germany—the two camps remained largely separate prior to the 1960s. This historic separation arose not only out of ideological differences but from the very different social positions of men and women, the latter not enjoying the full rights of suffrage and property in most Western countries until the second third of the twentieth century. The different material interests of men and women determined, and continues to condition, the possibility for an alliance between feminists and gay men. Furthermore, the misogynist attitudes of some male homosexuals, clearly illustrated in the cultural politics of the Community of the Special, the "masculinist" branch of the pre–World War II German homosexual rights movement, prevented cooperation. It is notable, however, that such early homosexual rights activists as Edward Carpenter allied themselves publicly with the women's rights movement, drawing support and inspiration of the struggles of women to liberate themselves from sexist oppression.

Sexuality and gender were reconstituted as areas of explicit political contest in the second half of the 1960s. Almost simultaneously, gay liberation and second-wave feminism emerged across the Western world. While formal reform, such as sex-blind access to credit and the repeal of antisodomy laws, remained part of the agenda of both movements, increasingly the political agenda moved to the level of culture with the aim of redefining sexuality and gender. In fact, the distinction between sex, or biological difference, and gender, the meanings ascribed to that difference, was forged in this period by women in the radical feminist movement and gay liberationists. It was in this redefinition, both in explicit theoretical work and lived life experience, that feminists and gay men found common ground.

The connections and conflicts between the two movements can be seen in the history of New York's Gay Liberation Front (1969–1971). Many women in the GLF operated at the intersection of both movements. Some gay men in the GLF embraced the feminist analysis of patriarchy and began to call themselves "effeminists," believing their interests as gay men were best served by identifying wholly with women's liberation. More generally, male GLF members were critical of the masculinist codes and aesthetics of gay male culture. Public subversion of gender codes, in the form of dress and social behavior, was lauded by many gay males in the front. Both men and women joined consciousness-raising groups, a form of political self-education crafted by radical feminists in groups such as the Red Stockings. The alliance was formalized in the GLF's manifesto, which stated that the "current system denies us our basic humanity in much the same way as it is denied to blacks, women, and other oppressed minorities; the grounds are just as irrational. Therefore, our liberation is tied to the liberation of all peoples."

Despite the best of intentions—and the willful resistance of some men—the alliance between male gay liberationists and feminist women in the GLF was short-lived. The possibility for tension can be seen in the grammatical structure of the manifesto quoted above. Who is the subject—the author making the statement, which collectively pledges itself to serve the interests of like-situated "oppressed minorities," which explicitly includes "women"? Are not lesbians women? And if so, why the need for a gay liberation manifesto to list them separately? While this discursive analysis may seem forced, it illustrates the tendency for women in a mixed-sex group of being decentered as political subjects. Certainly this contradiction was foregrounded by women in the GLF, who almost as a body denounced the sexism of the front, left the group, and began to pour their energies into lesbian-feminist efforts—some of them becoming separatists, explicitly rejecting the notion that men can ever act outside their interests as men, a sex/gender class.

Of course, the paradox of simultaneously seeking to transcend and act from difference has long haunted and spurred both gay male and feminist politics—and this paradox has been the site of intellectual and practical work. The effort to acknowledge difference was no doubt the impetus behind the decision on the part of the GLF to name "women" as a separate category. Without careful attention to the way in which interests of men and women can come into conflict, a gay male feminist politics remains problematic.

While the cautionary tale of the GLF was to be reenacted again and again in the decades since the 1960s, the richness of feminist thought continues to seduce gay male theorists and activists. It would be impossible to write a history of gay male activism, whether during the gay rights campaigns of the late 1970s or the now too-long history of AIDS activism, without acknowledging the decisive contributions of feminist women both as allies and as sources of critical analysis. Nor is the importance of this connection confined to serving a narrow identity politics. As Craig Owens, drawing on the insights of the work of Eve Kosofsky Sedgwick, has argued, "Homophobia is not primarily an instrument for oppressing a sex minority; it is, rather, a powerful tool for regulating the entire spectrum of male relations" (Owens, 221). It is the open-ended promise of the conjunction of gay male and feminist politics that makes inevitable a continued if conflicted exchange.

Terence Kissack

Bibliography

Ehrenreich, Barbara. *The Hearts of Men: American Dreams and the Flight from Commitment*. New York: Doubleday, 1983.

Jackson, Ed, and Stan Persky, eds. *Flaunting It!: A Decade of Gay Journalism from the* Body Politic. Toronto: New Star Books, 1982.

Kissack, Terence. "Freaking Fag Revolutionaries: New York's Gay Liberation Front, 1969–1971." *Radical History Review* 62 (Spring 1995): 104–34.

Owens, Craig. "Outlaws: Gay Men in Feminism." In *Men in Feminism*. Alice Jardine and Paul Smith, eds. New York: Methuen, 1987, 219–32.

Preston, John, and Joan Nestle, eds. *Sister and Brother: Lesbians and Gay Men Write About Their Lives Together*. San Francisco: Harper Collins, 1994.

Steakley, James. *The Homosexual Emancipation Movement in Germany*. Salem: Ayer, 1982.

Weeks, Jeffrey. *Coming Out: Homosexual Politics in Britain from the Nineteenth Century to the Present*. London: Quartet Books, 1990.

See also Act Up; Activism, U.S.; Carpenter, Edward; Gay Liberation; Gay Liberation Front; Owens, Craig; Sadomasochism

Ferenczi, Sándor (1873–1933)

Sándor Ferenczi worked as a doctor and psychoanalyst in Budapest, Hungary. For a short period after World War II, he was a professor of psychoanalysis

F

and published important works about the interdependence between psychoanalytical techniques and theories.

In his academic works, Ferenczi claimed there was a direct link between pathological paranoia and homosexuality, arguing that homosexuality plays a major role in the pathogenesis of paranoia. Ferenczi even suggested that homosexuality might be nothing other than a form of paranoia. His articulation of the alleged nexus between latent homosexuality and paranoia was the direct result of lengthy discussions with Sigmund Freud. Ferenczi ascribed central importance to the Freudian mechanism of projection (which is, in the case of homosexuality, the projection of one's own homosexual desires onto other men).

Ferenczi distinguished between object and subject homoeroticism. In the former case, homosexuals were described as predominantly interested in men and boys, and having a male identity. They were characterized as harboring hatred or antipathy toward women, resulting from the suppression of aggressive sexual urges directed toward their mothers. Ferenczi believed that psychoanalytical treatment could help reverse the sexual orientation of such men. Conversely, subject homoeroticism was held to manifest as "passive" homosexuality, where the individual identifies as a woman, both within and outside the context of sexual intercourse. He prefers masculine men as sex partners and maintains friendships with women. Ferenczi considered this type of homosexuality to be a developmental anomaly, somehow constitutive, and essentially irreversible. This distinction between subject and object homoeroticism also derives from Freudian thought, and applies heterosexual sex-role stereotypes to homosexuality.   *Jacinta Kerin*

Bibliography

Ferenczi, Sándor. "Über die Rolle der Homosexualität in der Pathogenese der Homosexualität." *Schriften zur Psychoanalyse.* Vol. 1. Frankfurt am Main: Fischer, 1982.

Till, Wolfgang. "Die Schule Freuds-Sándor Ferenczi." In *Homosexualität: Handbuch der Theorie—und Forschungsgeschichte.* Rüdiger Lautmann, ed. Frankfurt am Main: Fischer, 1993, 173–75.

See also Bloch, Iwan; Ellis, Havelock; Hirschfeld, Magnus; Kertbeny, Karl Maria; Kinsey, Alfred; Krafft-Ebing, Richard von; Moll, Albert; Sexology; Westphal, Carl Friedrich Otto

Fichte, Hubert (1935–1986)

Hubert Fichte was born in Perleberg, Germany, in 1935, during the early years of the Nazi regime. In fact, studies about this openly gay German novelist and critic usually emphasize his literary preoccupation with the Marquis de Sade, voodoo, and the S/M leathermen's movement as an exclusively creative rebellion against his experience as a *Mischling* (a person of "mixed blood") in Nazi Germany. But this focus on Fichte's early history ignores the profound philosophical nature of his work and its centrality to any program of queer aesthetics. Fichte's artistic project unites the core concepts of German Enlightenment philosophy with the identity of the sexual transgressor. Thus his philosophical "bent" derives from an aesthetic experience of oppression: he was a German subject who was politically, imaginatively, and sexually excluded from German culture. As such a subject, he found it necessary to produce "a transgressive aesthetic experience" in order to question even the imagined orientation of communities built on any form of exclusion.

Until the time of his death in 1986, Fichte remained a sexual outsider both in gay and straight communities. Although he self-identified as gay, his lifelong companion was the female photographer Leonore Mau. Furthermore, his perspective of a sexual transgressor offers a queer aesthetics, unrecognizable to many Western "epistemologies of the closet." In fact, his last work in progress, the nineteen-volume *History of Sensitivity*, emphasized the idea of a queer aesthetics and made the product of that experience a radically singular identity of exclusion. This exclusion permits Hubert Fichte to see in gay male identity the opportunity not to identify with a community, because identification would be a reinstatement of the aesthetic project he resolutely rejects.

This desire to produce a transgressive art and identity is noted particularly in the essay "Revolution as Restoration," translated in *The Gay Critic*. In the essay, a study of the French poet Rimbaud, Fichte traces Rimbaud's "breakdown of language before the presence of Africa!" (248). Rimbaud's loss of language suggests for Fichte a singular loss of the productive nature of the imagination. Since Rimbaud's unscrupulous behavior in Africa imitates Europe's experiences with the Third World, Rimbaud has abandoned his transgressive status to act as Europeans have historically acted in Africa.

Fichte's reimagination of Rimbaud's poetic revolution, then, is "a double denial of responsibility:

once in respect to his own influential work, and once in regard to his own actions in Africa" (249). He indicates that Rimbaud's aesthetic revolution was lost the moment Rimbaud participated in a European aesthetic experience of Africa. When Rimbaud loses sight of his transgressive identity and "acts like a European," then his poetics become part and parcel of "[a] further consequence of the European idea of revolution, and its restorative application in the countries of the Third World" (Fichte 250).

Fichte's gay aesthetic experience is predicated on a ritual form of isolation, an isolation he construes as central to his work on the S/M movement and his "poetic ethnology" of the Marquis de Sade. Since the subject of his aesthetic experience does not desire to reproduce a gay reality, the experience becomes a queer aesthetic; it is queer because of the subject's lack of desire for reproduction—both literally and symbolically.   *Kitty Millet*

Bibliography

Fichte, Hubert. *The Gay Critic*. Kevin Gavin, trans. Ann Arbor: University of Michigan Press, 1996.

———. *Homosexualität und Literatur: Polemiken.* Frankfurt am Main, Germany: S. Fischer, 1987–1988.

———. *Jean Genet.* Frankfurt am Main, Germany: Qumran, 1981.

Teichert, Torsten. *Herzschlag aussen: die poetische Konstruktion des Fremden und des Eigenen in Werk von Hubert Fichte.* Frankfurt am Main, Germany: Fischer Taschenbuch Verlag, 1987.

Weinberg, Manfred. *Akut, Geschichte, Struktur: Hubert Fichtes Suche nach der verlorenen Sprache einer poetischen Welterfahrung.* Bielefeld, Germany: Aisthesis, 1993.

See also German Literature; Rimbaud, Arthur; Sade, Donatien-Alphonse-Françoise, Marquis de

Fiction

Minority literatures typically distinguish themselves from works that merely represent the minority. For example, Jewish literature distinguishes itself from literature about Jews, and African American literature from the more general representations of blacks. But making such a distinction has been particularly difficult for gay fiction, both theoretically and practically. In general, heterosexuals have pre-ferred to remain silent about homosexuals; consequently, most of the writing that explicitly represents homosexuals—even when that representation is hostile and stereotyped—was written by homosexuals. Moreover, if we consider the narrowest definition of gay fiction—fiction written by, for, and about gay people—we can immediately see the theoretical problems. There is first the problem of defining *gay* and whether it is a synonym of *homosexual, sodomite,* and *queer.* Can we rightly speak of people or fiction before the second half of the nineteenth century as *gay* or *homosexual* since the medical concept of homosexuality had not yet been constructed? For example, is *The Satyricon* by Petronius (c.27–66), in which same-sex relations and affections are explicitly related, to be considered a part of homosexual fiction when the characters organize their behavior along a very different model of sexual desire? There is also the problem of defining *fiction,* since much of recent gay fiction is highly autobiographical. But even if we put aside these theoretical questions, there are the practical issues of how do we know whether an author has engaged in homosexual relations, how can we determine whether a work was intended for a gay readership, and how can we decide—short of an explicit erotic scene—whether characters and actions are homosexual? These issues are more problematic for gay fiction than for Jewish or African American fiction because the stigma of such labels was greater, government suppression was greater, and consequently the tactic of hiding and encoding such identities was so much more highly developed. Moreover, because so few authors until after World War II represented explicitly homosexual characters or scenes, there was all the more reason to conflate fiction *about* homosexuality with gay or homosexual fiction.

Any of the existing structures to discuss gay fiction distort the complexity of the literary and cultural dynamics that inform individual works. Not only does historical context affect the reading of works, but nationality, class, as well as genre affect what sorts of experiences can be represented and how explicitly they can be described. Moreover, the temperament of the individual artist can determine his or her willingness and ability to write. Finally, the state of gay literary criticism makes it difficult to develop clear and convincing general statements about gay fiction. For example, early writers of gay fiction disparaged any works that represented male characters who continued having sex with both men

F and women. Roger Austen, in what was one of the first studies of American gay literature, termed such representations as "playing the game," which became the title of his book. "Playing the game" was succumbing to the prejudices of heterosexuals by making the character not entirely gay. Since Austen's study, critical opinion has swung in the opposite direction; the books that Austen saw as "playing the game" are now viewed by many writers as breaking down the binarism between heterosexuality and homosexuality, a binarism that is necessary for the maintenance of heterosexuality. As one can see, any attempts at fixing classification or periodization must be regarded skeptically.

Most fiction that attempts to thematize male same-sex relations before the twentieth century is usually highly encoded and exclusive. For example, same-sex relations are a common part of the pastoral tradition and prose pastoral romance, yet there is no critical consensus on how to handle such works, which typically use cross-dressing as a narrative device to explore and confuse gender. In such works as Longus's *Daphnis and Chloe* (third century A.D.), Honoré d'Urfe's *L'Astrée* (1627), Jorge de Montemayor's *La Diana*, or Philip Sidney's *Arcadia* (1590, 1593), cross-dressing allows either people of the same sex to fall in love or people of different sexes to confront same-sex attractions. Such works were given license to explore these issues because they were clearly distinguished from histories and other genres that purported to be factual. A more explicitly homosexual work, *A Vision of Love Revealed in Sleep* (1871), by painter Simeon Solomon (1841–1905), uses the dream vision as a means to explore such issues without raising police suppression or censorship. Whether we consider such early pastoral works homosexual fiction or not, twentieth-century writers have used pastoral elements as though they were. Frederick William Rolfe (1860–1913), who wrote under the pseudonym Baron Corvo, borrows from the pastoral tradition in his last novel, *The Desire and Pursuit of the Whole* (written between 1909 and 1910 but not published until 1934). In the novel, a man rescues Zildo, a girl whom he raises as a boy. As a boy, Zildo wins back his lost patrimony and is able in return to save her ailing and increasingly feminized rescuer. Similarly, André Gide titled his most explicit work about homosexuality *Corydon* (1924), after the pastoral character. Even outside the European tradition, transvestite disguise appears as a means to explore questions of gender and sexuality. In *The Change-*

lings, an elaborate court tale of twelfth-century Japan, a brother and sister are raised as girl and boy, respectively. The sister appears in court as a man who marries. After "his" wife becomes pregnant by a man, her brother assumes her role as husband, confusing the illicit lover.

An outgrowth of the pastoral tradition with its simplified characters, convoluted plots, and fantastic occurrences is what Robert F. Kiernan calls the camp novel or what Northrop Frye has called an *anatomy* or Menippean satire, a work characterized by placing more emphasis on ideas than on characterization, or a work such as Plato's *Symposium*, in which characters sit around discussing ideas. Oscar Wilde's dialogues published in *Intentions* (1891) are one form of this campy prose composition. The satire of Wilde, Robert Hitchen's *The Green Carnation* (1894), is a more traditionally novelistic version of this mode. The master of the form was Ronald Firbank (1886–1926), who, in a series of novels beginning with *Vainglory* (1915) and ending with the posthumously published *The Artificial Princess* (1934), produced works of startling originality, outrageous humor, and biting insight. Firbank's novels are noted for their dialogue, which overshadows their rudimentary and scandalously sexual plots as in *Flower Beneath the Foot* (1924), which recounts how Laura de Nazianzi gives up court society to join the lesbian Convent of the Flaming Hood. Interestingly, both gay men and lesbians used the camp novel. Firbank influenced Ivy Compton-Burnett (1884–1969), Jane Bowles (1917–1973), and Brigid Brophy (1929–), as well as Alfred Chester (1929–1971), whose novel *Exquisite Corpse* (1967) is a remarkable extension of the mode, John Ashbery (1927–), and James Schuyler (1923–1991), whose *A Nest of Ninnies* (1969) carries on the tradition.

As in the pastoral, the release from realism and the invitation to express the abject and the horrible allows Gothic fiction to explore—albeit often in highly masked ways—sexual drives not otherwise allowed expression. It is not surprising that several of its earliest practitioners, including William Beckford (1760–1844), Matthew "Monk" Lewis (1775–1818), and Horace Walpole (1717–1797), were men either accused of sodomy in their lifetime or who expressed deeply romantic attachments to other men. Walpole in his novel *The Castle of Otranto* (1764) is credited with starting the Gothic craze. Today Clive Barker and Anne Rice carry on the Gothic tradition but have made its homosexual content quite explicit.

Rice has achieved great popularity perhaps because, by situating her homosexual characters as vampires, she has placed them outside the human and the mortal. Between Beckford and Rice, such important Gothic works as Oscar Wilde's *The Picture of Dorian Gray* (1891) and Henry James's *The Jolly Corner* (1908) and *The Turn of the Screw* (1898) explored transgressive sexuality. The handling of homoerotic material in Wilde and James is so subtle and disguised, however, that it remains a subject of debate.

Yet another way that fiction writers have found space to write about same-sex relations is by setting their novels in exotic or primitive places. Herman Melville's *Typee* (1846) and *Omoo* (1847) are set in the Pacific Islands, far from civilization. In *Moby-Dick* (1851), Queequeg, as a native, can free Ishmael from the repressions that had marked his life. Yet shipboard, while providing an all-male space for exploring same-sex eroticism, does not provide the same openness as does the tropics. In *Billy Budd*, Melville's last work (not published until 1924), the British man-of-war shows the destructiveness of homosexual desire when molded in the crucible of European systems of justice and values. Charles Warren Stoddard (1843–1909), in his *Island of Tranquil Delights* (1904), also found that removing his narrative from the constraints of Euro-American culture gave him the room to approach homoerotic experiences. The ship as a site where suppressed homoerotic desires get expressed can be found in Robert Ferro's first novel, *The Others* (1977).

Foreign countries are frequently used by writers in the Euro-American tradition as a site for releasing repressed sexual desires. Polynesia is only one place in what English writer, explorer, and anthropologist Sir Richard Burton (1821–1890) described as the "Sotadic Zone," a ring roughly developing from the equator, in which native people give expression to same sex-desires. This Sotadic Zone spans southern Europe, North Africa, Asia, as well as the Pacific, confounding both racial and sexual otherness. An entire literature was developed around Europeans, whose homosexual desires are aroused or released when brought into contact with these peoples. André Gide's *The Immoralist* (1902) treats the homosexual awakening of a married European visiting North Africa. Paul Bowles (1910–), American composer and author, has written about such sexual awakenings in Morocco and the Caribbean. The protagonist of *Totempole* (1965) by playwright and novelist Sanford Friedman (1928–)

finds his sexual self when confined to a prisoner-of-war camp with Koreans.

Still another way that fiction has found to deal with same-sex relations in a manner that distances the material sufficiently from contemporary life to make it safe and acceptable to a general readership is to place it in different historical periods—ancient Greece or Rome. Walter Pater (1839–1894) sets his novel, *Marius the Epicurean* (1885), in Rome, far from the late Victorian world. One of Holland's greatest novelists, Louis Couperus (1863–1923), wrote *Mountain of Light* (1905–1906) and *The Comedians* (1917) set in third- and first-century Rome, respectively. *Mountain of Light* concerns the life of the emperor Heliogabalus, who marries one of his centurions. Since World War II, historical fiction of the classical world has been a particularly useful genre. Mary Renault's (1905–1983) novels, from *The Last of the Wine* (1956) through *Funeral Games* (1981), were enormously popular with the general public though they contained explicit and positive representations of same-sex love among her ancient Greek characters. Similarly, Marguerite Yourcenar (1903–1987), in *Memoirs of Hadrian* (1951), found in the Roman Empire a way to speak about same-sex desire in a time of stringent repression. It seems more than coincidental that in the fifties, these two women—both attached to other women, and exiles from their country—should find in the voices of the classical world of male-male desire the medium of their most powerful expression. Today Steven Saylor (1956–), both in his mystery novels and in his erotic novels (under the name of Aaron Travis), continues the use of classical settings for the exploration of gay experience.

Toward the turn of the century, as the figure of the homosexual became better established in legal and medical discourse, the problem novel *about* the homosexual begins to appear. The first explicitly gay-themed novel in the United States was Alan Dale's *A Marriage Below Zero* (1889), a novel about the wife in an unconsummated marriage who finds her husband first in the arms of another man, and then later, dead on the floor of his Paris hotel room from an overdose of laudanum. *A Marriage Below Zero* establishes one of the basic patterns of the gay novels: they end in death, especially suicide. Perhaps the most famous American gay novel of the first third of this century is *Imre: A Memorandum*, written by Edward Prime-Stevenson under the pseudonym of Xavier Mayne. It ends happily, if ambiguously, with its protagonists moving off together

F toward "Rest." The kind of self-conscious defense of homosexuality and homosexual love found in *Imre* is a staple of gay fiction. Among its many examples are Blair Nile's *Strange Brothers* (1931), Foreman Brown's *The Better Angel* (1933), and Patricia Nell Warren's *The Front Runner* (1974) and *The Fancy Dancer* (1976).

French fiction, like pastoral romance, begins exploring same-sex relationships through the device of cross-dressing. Théophile Gautier's *Madame de Maupin* (1835) concerns a woman who enters male society by dressing as a man. Honoré de Balzac's short story "Sarrasine" (1830) is about a man who falls in love with a transvestite performer. In Vautrin, Balzac created a gay male character who appears in various volumes of his *Comédie humaine* (1842–1848). Vautrin represents the stereotype of homosexual as thief. Toward the end of the nineteenth century, a different stereotype emerged in French literature—the homosexual as aesthete. This pattern is established in Joris-Karl Huysmans's *À Rebours* (1884), whose title is translated as either *Against the Grain* or *Against Nature*. Its protagonist, Des Esseintes, isolates himself in his country home to surround himself with exquisite sensations. These two figures—the aesthete and the criminal—play themselves out in much twentieth-century French fiction, particularly by such major figures as Marcel Proust (1871–1922), André Gide (1869–1951), and Jean Genet (1910–1986), as well as Jean Cocteau (1889–1963). In Proust, Gide, and Genet, homosexuality is marked by, among other features, a tendency to exquisite sensation and the underworld. Genet, in particular, in prose that aspires to an aristocratic elegance of manner, tells the stories of pimps, prostitutes, petty thieves, and murderers.

In fact, Continental representations of homosexuality often rest on the way the search for the beautiful is also a search through the abject, the deadly, and the criminal. Nowhere is this more clearly developed than in what is perhaps the most famous German novella about homosexuality, Thomas Mann's *Death in Venice* (1912), in which the author, Gustav Aschenbach, falls in love with a Polish boy, Tadzio, whom he follows to his death. In the process, Aschenbach is stripped of all his dignity and self-control. Mann's eldest son, Klaus Mann (1906–1949), an openly homosexual writer, intellectual, and antifascist activist, continued his father's pessimistic attitude toward the fate of his gay characters. In the work of Pier Paolo Pasolini (1922–1975), Italy's most important openly homo-

sexual writer and filmmaker, exploitation of lower-class boys is a recurrent theme as it was in his life. In the United States, this tradition of writing about the gay demimonde is represented by the works of William S. Burroughs (1914–1997), John Rechy (1934–), particularly in his novels *City of Night* (1963) and *Numbers* (1967), Hubert Selby Jr., in *Last Exit to Brooklyn* (1964), and Bruce Benderson (1952–) in his collection of short stories *Pretending to Say No* (1990) and *User* (1994).

In Spanish, both the literature from Spain and from Spanish-speaking America has been often experimental or surrealistic in the twentieth century. Some of the difficulty of these works is a result of political repression. The treatment of homosexuality in the novels of Cubans José Lezama Lima (1910–1976) and Virgilio Piñera (1912–1979) is obscured by the Castro regime's suppression of homosexuality. The more straightforward and lyrical works of Reinaldo Arenas (1943–1990) faced even more opposition from the government. Arenas was able eventually to escape Cuba after having been jailed, but he committed suicide in the United States after contracting HIV. Government repression of homosexuals is a theme of the most celebrated Latin American gay novel, Manuel Puig's *Kiss of the Spider Woman* (1976), in which the political activist Valentin and the effeminate Molina come to share more than their political and social views. Juan Goyotisolo (1931–), who was born in Barcelona but has lived most of his life in France or Morocco, represents homosexuality as a force in opposition to the sterile, oppressive, joyless state of Spanish life in novels whose structure and style are extremely challenging.

In the United States, gay fiction has gone through several stages of development. There are extremely strong homoerotic themes in Melville's fiction, particularly *Billy Budd* (1924), *Moby-Dick* (1851), and *Pierre* (1852), the subject of James Creech's important study *Closet Writing/Gay Reading* (1993). But since Melville lived in an age before the construction of the medical classification of homosexuality and because Melville's work is highly encoded, it remains a subject of controversy whether to regard him as a homosexual writer. As mentioned above, the first American novel dealing explicitly with sexual relations between men is Alan Dale's *A Marriage Below Zero* (1889), which does not portray homosexuality positively. But in a homophobic culture that would prefer complete silence about homosexuality even as it condemns any deviance from heteronormative behavior, any representation of homosexuality, even disparaging references to it, may be an advance, creating—if nothing else—visibility.

Most of the early works that explicitly dealt with same-sex desire in a positive manner were published privately, in small editions, under anonymity or pseudonyms. John Addington Symonds's *A Problem of Greek Ethics* (1891), a long essay, was published privately in an edition of only fifty copies. The first complete edition of Gide's *Corydon* was published privately and anonymously in 1925 in an edition of twenty-one copies. Edward Prime-Stevenson's *Imre: A Memorandum* (1906) was published privately in an edition of 125 copies in Naples, Italy, by a typesetter who, it has been speculated, probably knew no English. Clearly, these works were meant not for large audiences but for intimate friends who would understand and be sympathetic to the sentiments of the works. The small number of copies printed and their anonymity indicate that the authors were anxious about the legal consequences of publishing such work.

Fiction representing homosexuals appeared sporadically during the first quarter of the twentieth century, but toward the end of the Roaring Twenties, and in the early thirties, a number of important works appeared in quick succession. At the height of gay visibility in the early thirties, this efflorescence of gay visibility was dubbed "the pansy craze." Although the pansy craze mostly involved theater and popular music, a number of books appeared at this time, including André Tellier's *Twilight Men* (1931), Blair Niles's *Strange Brother* (1931), Wallace Thurman's *Infants of the Spring* (1932), Kennilwoth Bruce's *Goldie (*1933), and *The Young and the Evil* (1933) jointly authored by Parker Tyler (1904–1974) and Charles Henri Ford (1913–). *Better Angel* is the first homosexual novel with a truly happy ending. The highly autobiographical book was written by Forman Brown (1900–1996), and it narrates the early stages of his relationship with "lifelong friend and partner" Harry Burnett. It is essentially a love story, as its title, drawn from one of Shakespeare's sonnets, suggests. But unlike virtually all the fiction written at the time, this love story ends with the lovers together. Whereas *Better Angel* was the only novel by Brown (Richard Meeker), and one of the few books he wrote, Tyler and Ford went on to have distinguished literary careers, Tyler as one of the first film critics, authoring the groundbreaking study *Screening the Sexes: Homosexuality in the Movies* (1972), and Ford as an avant-garde poet and a leading American surrealist. *The Young and the*

Evil can be said to be the first *gay* novel, meaning a novel about gay life, by gay authors, for an ostensibly gay audience. The novel is free, as almost no other book of the period is, of moralizing about, apologizing for, or explanation of gay life. In fact, the inspiration for the book and many of its passages were derived from the letters Tyler sent Ford about life in New York while Ford was living in Mississippi. It is this openness and unwillingness to censor materials or to assume a heterosexual readership that makes the book so important in the history of the gay American novel, but it is also the reason it had to be published in France by the Olympia Press, a publisher known for its erotica.

The relationship between letter writing and gay fiction needs comment. Letters are the first written medium in which homosexuals can directly address one another in fairly explicit terms. As *The Young and the Evil* shows, when gay writers looked for a way to express gay life without translating it into straight terms, they found inspiration from letters. But *The Young and the Evil* is not in the form of an exchange of letters. However, Christopher Isherwood's *A Meeting by the River* (1967) is an epistolary novel. It concerns two men—Patrick, who is gay and becoming a Hindu priest, and his brother, Oliver, a bisexual, who wishes to bring Patrick back to England. The novel is made up of Patrick's journal and Oliver's letters to their mother, Oliver's wife, and his male lover. *A Meeting by the River* demonstrates the difference between the way men involved in a sexual relationship talk to each other and the way those engaged in heterosexual relations communicate. After Stonewall, novelists have continued to use the letter as a way of establishing that their works are not going to translate experiences for heterosexual readers. Edmund White's *Nocturnes for the King of Naples* (1979) is a novel addressed to a young man's dead lover. Published in the same year, Andrew Holleran's *Dancer from the Dance* is framed by letters between two gay friends. Richard Zimler (1956–) structures his novel *Unholy Ghosts* (1996) as a 250-page letter to his ex-lover.

The Great Depression brought a temporary halt to the development of the gay novel, and it was not until after World War II that an entirely new generation of gay writers emerged. The two most famous of these authors were Gore Vidal (1925–) and Truman Capote (1924–1984), but one should not forget Tennese Williams (1911–1983), whose short fiction is as good as his writing for the theater and an important if overlooked contribution to gay litera-

F ture. Of these writers, Vidal created the greatest controversy with his novel *The Pillar and the City* (1948), in which the gay protagonist, unable to create the romantic idyll of innocent love when he meets his childhood friend after the war, ends up either murdering or else raping him, depending on the ending (Vidal published two). Despite some advances in this novel, it is much more conservative with its dark conclusion than other works written at the same time. Nevertheless, the *New York Times* refused to accept advertisements for the book, and Vidal credits a nearly decade-long critical blackout on his novels with causing him to turn his attention to writing for television, the movies, and the theater. Capote published *Other Voices, Other Rooms* (1948), a haunting tale in the Southern Gothic manner then in vogue. Another Southern novel of importance is the *Bitterwood Path* (1949) by Thomas Hal Phillips (1922–).

The fame of these writers has overshadowed several other valuable contributions made in the late forties and early thirties. John Horne Burns (1916–1953) wrote what many critics of the time regarded as the finest book to come out of World War II, *The Gallery* (1947), which has one explicitly gay section but whose entire structure revolves around homosexual soldiers. Burns went on to write two other novels before his untimely death from exposure. *Lucifer with a Book* (1949), about a veteran who goes to teach at a boys' preparatory school after the war, tells about his involvement with one of his students and with a female faculty member.

Like Burns, Fritz Peters (1913–1979) wrote both a book about soldiers and one on education. *The World Next Door* (1948) takes place in a veterans' mental hospital where the protagonist, during a psychotic episode, is forced to fellate one of the orderlies. He admits to a homosexual affair although he maintains a generally heterosexual orientation. *Finistere* (1951), one of his most famous books of the period, is about a teacher who has a love affair with one of his students, who commits suicide. Other novels about the war include Loren Wahls's *The Invisible Path* (1950) and James Barr's *Quatrefoil* (1950). Calder Wilingham brought army life and education together in his novel *End Life as a Man* (1947), which takes place in a military academy.

At the end of this wave of novels about homosexuality, in which there is a great deal more fluidity in sexual roles than has been generally realized, appears James Baldwin's (1924–1987) *Giovanni's Room* (1956), about an American who falls in love with a young Italian who, as the novel closes, is being executed for murdering a gay man. *Giovanni's Room* caused a sensation not only for the explicitness of its erotic obsession, the haunting lyricism of its prose, but also because its author, the leading African American essayist of his day, had penned a novel exclusively about Europeans and European Americans. In two other novels, *Another Country* (1962) and *Just Above My Head* (1979), Baldwin writes about black men attracted both to women and to men. Baldwin is not, however, the first African American author to write about same-sex love. Wallace Thurman (1902–1934) in *Infants of the Spring* (1932) gives a straightforward account of gay black life in Harlem. In 1926, Richard Bruce Nugent (1906–1989) wrote what is the first published gay African American story, "Smoke, Lilies, and Jade." Thurman and Nugent shared quarters from time to time and were members of the Harlem Renaissance. Since Baldwin, a number of important African American fiction writers have emerged including Samuel R. Delany (1942–), Melvin Dixon (1950–1992), Larry Duplechan (1956–), and Randall Kenan (1963–).

During the sixties many different sorts of gay fiction were attempted. William S. Burroughs (1914–1997) in *Naked Lunch*, first published in the United States in 1962, and in subsequent books created a drug-induced nightmare world of teenage boys. John Rechy (1934–), in *City of Night* (1963), wrote about the world of hustlers and drag queens. James Purdy (1927–) is a difficult writer to characterize, although his work grows out of the Southern Gothic tradition, which is metaphysical anti-realist and yet grittily real. *Eustace Chisholm or the Works* (1967) is a remarkable book set in Chicago, bringing together the very wealthy and the utterly destitute. Alfred Chester (1928–1971) created the surrealist masterpiece *Exquisite Corpse* (1967) before succumbing to madness. In contrast to these works of low-life and dreamlike reality, Christopher Isherwood (1904–1986) wrote three novels in the sixties—*Down There on a Visit* (1962), *A Meeting by the River* (1967), and, especially, *A Single Man* (1964)—that set the tone for a great deal of later gay writing. *A Single Man* follows one day in the life of a British English professor living in California. George, who is not remarkable, has lost his lover of many years. He is at once seemingly ordinary and terribly isolated. In the plainest of styles and without apology, Isherwood tells the story of how a middle-class, middle-aged white gay man lives.

Emerging in the late seventies and early eighties was a group of writers known as the Violet Quill. The group included Edmund White (1940–), Andrew Holleran (1943–), and Felice Picano (1944–). Their work continued the project Isherwood started. In addition, these writers wished to go beyond the conclusion of previous gay novels, which typically ended unhappily with death, alcoholism, or addiction. To be sure, these novels do not escape the darker side of gay life. Particularly in White's *A Boy's Own Story* (1982), Holleran's *The Beauty of Men* (1996), and Picano's *Late in the Season* (1981), these writers discuss the lives of middle-class gay men in a straightforward, unapologetic way. Their work rarely describes low life—the world of hustlers, pimps, or drug dealers—although the use of hallucinogen is a frequent element of their work; rather, they write about the world of consultants, bankers, and art dealers. Two other writers of importance emerged in the late seventies: Larry Kramer (1935–), whose 1979 satire, *Faggots,* caused an enormous stir and whose nonfictional writing on AIDS has been of singular importance, and Paul Monette (1945–1995), whose novels and memoirs about AIDS have put a human face on the epidemic.

The generation of writers that emerged after Stonewall has created two of the most important subgenres of gay fiction—the coming-out story and the AIDS story. The coming-out story is essentially a comic tale of self-identification, an offshoot of the bildungsroman, the novel of education in which a young man comes of age and forms himself into an adult. The classic bildungsroman has its hero develop sexually by having affairs with both good and bad women and usually involves a move from the country to the city. It is interesting to note that Edmund White wrote one of the finest coming-out novels, *A Boy's Own Story,* but an imitation of the classic bildungsroman, *Caracole* (1985), a book without any gay characters. The AIDS novel is essentially a tragic tale, also of self-realization, but one of approaching death and reconciliation.

One of the challenges of gay fiction has been to find an alternative to one of the classic structuring devices of heterosexual fiction—the wedding plot. Typically, the marriage of the two principal characters forms the "happy" ending of many novels and plays. This does not mean that there are no gay stories in which a couple is happily united, but because so far gay men cannot get married, these unions do not resolve the tension between the individual and society; they do not constitute the final step in integrating the young person into the ongoing, self-perpetuating social system. Perhaps creating such an ending is one of the challenges of gay writing today.

David Bergman

Bibliography

Austen, Roger. *Playing the Game: The Homosexual Novel in America.* Indianapolis: Bobbs-Merill, 1977.

Gifford, James. *Daynesford's Library: American Homosexual Writing, 1900–1913.* Amherst: University of Massachusetts Press, 1995.

Woodhouse, Reed. *Unlimited Embrace: A Canon of Gay Fiction, 1945–1995.* Amherst: University of Massachusetts Press, 1998.

Woods, Gregory. *A History of Gay Literature: The Male Tradition.* New Haven: Yale University Press, 1998.

See also Arenas, Reinaldo; Argentina; Ashbery, John; Baldwin, James; Barr, James; Beckford, William; Bowles, Paul; Burroughs, William Seward; Burton, Sir Richard Francis; Capote, Truman; Cocteau, Jean; Coming Out; Couperus, Louis; Delany, Samuel R.; Dixon, Melvin; English Literature; Firbank, Ronald; Ford, Charles Henri; French Literature; Genet, Jean; German Literature; Gide, André; Goyotisolo, Juan; Isherwood, Christopher; Italian Literature; James, Henry; Kramer, Larry; Lezama Lima, José; Mann, Thomas; Melville, Herman; Monette, Paul; Pasolini, Pier Paolo; Pater, Walter Horatio; Petronius; Piñera, Virgilio; Plato; Proust, Marcel; Puig, Manuel; Purdy, James; Rechy, John; Renault, Mary; Rolfe, Frederick William ("Baron Corvo"); Schuyler, James; Spanish Literature; Symonds, John Addington; Thurman, Wallace; Tyler, Parker; U.S. Literature: Contemporary Gay Writing; Vidal, Gore; Violet Quill; Walpole, Horace; White, Edmund; Wilde, Oscar; Williams, Tennessee; Yourcenar, Marguerite

Fiction: New Queer Narrative

Around 1980 two gay men, Bruce Boone and Robert Glück, were talking about how to describe their writings, which at that point were heavily influenced by the Language poets. Boone said, "How about New Narrative? What a stupid name" (qtd. in Jackson, 26). A genre was born. New Narrative became at least marginally canonized as a critical term when, in 1984, Steve Abbott published his article "Notes on

F Boundaries: New Narrative," which describes a loose but discernible group of writers including Boone, Glück, Kathy Acker, Dennis Cooper, Michael Amnasan, and Dodie Bellamy. Since the late 1980s the names associated with this school have grown in number to include, among others, Sarah Schulman, Bo Huston, Gary Indiana, Kevin Killian, the Canadian collective Dumb Bitch Deserves to Die, Dorothy Allison—the list could continue. Schulman, reviewing Killian's *Bedrooms Have Windows* in 1986, provided an early recognition that something was afoot in terms of "an evolving literary movement": "This trend consists of gay men and lesbian writers who are informed by the last 30 years of the avant-garde but [who] show feelings, don't think they're better than other people and put words together in a way that everyone can understand, even while using unusual rhythms and word orders" (Shulman, 60). She ends her statement not with a summation of the genre but with an ironic jab at the Bush administration: "It's a kinder, gentler avant-garde."

As with any genre, school, or modality, what is in and what is out, as well as what is definitive and what is extraneous, are highly debatable. But these writers seem to share certain traits. Most of the New Narrative's practitioners hail from the urban centers of San Francisco, Los Angeles, and New York—and a few from Montreal—and most reside there as a result of personal diasporic movements from smaller towns. All are familiar with postmodern theorists such as Jacques Derrida, Georges Bataille, and Paul Virilio, and many label their art "abject," a term derived from Julia Kristeva. Most of them stress an interrelatedness between prose and other modes of writing as well as other media; David Wojnarowicz, for example, earned his primary artistic fame as a photographer, while Vaginal Creme Davis, in addition to writing, plays in the bands Pedro, Muriel, and Esther; the Afro Sisters; and Cholita; edits the 'zine *Fertile LaToya Jackson*; and directs and stars in such videos as *That Fertile Feeling* and *It All Started in Black*. Most if not all New Narrative—particularly in recent years—also incorporates violence and pornographic sex, elements of shock that are repeated structurally in a reliance on pastiches, cut-and-paste techniques, and nonlinear narratives. And most if not all New Narrative writers owe a debt to the counterculture literary journals of the 1980s, such as *Soup* and *Little Caesar*, and the flourishing 'zine scene of the 1990s; this writing has not, until recently, benefited from mainstream publishing support. But what perhaps most unifies the genre (if it can be called that) is that while not all its practitioners would accept the labels gay or lesbian, all their writings eschew the boundaries that typify heterosexuality as it is normatively constructed in Western culture; hence, in recent years, the genre has frequently been called the New Queer Narrative.

Although the looseness of the school makes a reading list difficult to compile, certain texts are almost universally acknowledged to be part of the New Narrative canon. Dennis Cooper's *Frisk*, which explores the erotics of murder, anal mutilation, and teenage desire, is generally conceded to be quintessential. Sarah Schulman's novel *After Delores*, to provide another example, filters the conventions of hard-boiled detective fiction through the lifestyles of younger lesbians in modern New York City to tell of a nameless lesbian's obsessive desire for a lost lover. Gary Indiana's novel *Horse Crazy* also explores the dynamics of obsession, telling of the narrator's self-destructive and humiliating obsession for Gregory Burgess, a beautiful young conceptual artist in the East Village of New York City. Dennis Cooper's anthology *Discontents* and Amy Scholder and Ira Silverberg's anthology *High Risk* provided excellent cross sections of the large portion of this writing that happens in the format of essays, short stories, and memoirs.

Gregory W. Bredbeck

Bibliography

Abbott, Steve. "Notes on Boundaries: New Narrative." *Soup* 4 (1984); reprinted in Steve Abbott. *View Askew: Postmodern Investigations.* San Francisco: Androgyne Books, 1989, 39–55.

Cooper, Dennis, ed. *Discontents: New Queer Writers.* New York: Amethyst, 1992.

Jackson, Earl Jr. "Bruce Boone." In *Contemporary Gay American Novelists: A Bio-Bibliographical Critical Sourcebook.* Emmanuel S. Nelson, ed. Westport, Conn.: Greenwood Press, 1993, 25–28.

Killian, Kevin. *Bedrooms Have Windows.* New York: Amethyst Press, 1989.

Scholder, Amy, and Ira Silverberg, eds. *High Risk: An Anthology of Forbidden Writings.* New York: Plume, 1991.

Schulman, Sarah. "Lust on Long Island." *Outweek* 29 (October 1989): 60.

See also Fiction; Sadomasochism; U.S. Literature: Contemporary Gay Writing

Field, Edward (1924–)

Poet Edward Field is noted for the directness of his style and the unadorned way he deals with homosexuality. Field was born in Brooklyn to Jewish immigrant parents, and his poetry grows out of his urban experience, particularly the bohemian milieu—with its leftist politics—that flourished in Manhattan and Paris. Although his first book of poems only suggested his sexual orientation, he came out openly in *Variety Photoplay* (1967), which featured wildly campy retellings of old movies. In *A Full Heart* (1977), he further defined his erotic and spiritual nature.

During World War II, Field flew twenty-five bombing missions over Europe. He attended New York University on the GI bill, where he met gay Jewish novelist and critic Alfred Chester. Since Chester's death in 1971, Field has sought to revive his reputation, editing several volumes of his works. In the fifties, Field worked as an actor and temp typist, and in 1963 he published *Stand Up, Friend, with Me*, which won the Lamont Poetry Prize and established him as an important poet. A Guggenheim fellowship, the Prix de Rome, and the Shelley Memorial Award followed. He wrote the narration for the Academy Award–winning documentary *To Be Alive* (1964). With Neil Derrick, his companion of thirty-five years, he has written several novels under the name of Bruce Elliot, including *The Potency Clinic* (1978) and *Village* (1982). Field's other collections of poetry include *Eskimo Songs and Stories* (1973), *Stars in My Eyes* (1978), *New and Selected Poems* (1983), and *Counting Myself Lucky* (1992), winner of the Lambda Literary Award.   *David Bergman*

Bibliography

Bergman, David. "Edward Field." *Dictionary of Literary Biography,* vol. 105.

See also U.S. Literature: Contemporary Gay Writing

Fierstein, Harvey (1954–)

Raspy-voiced actor, performance artist, and playwright Harvey Forbes Fierstein was born in Brooklyn and received a B.F.A. in art from the Pratt Institute in New York City in 1973. His early career was as a drag queen in a variety of New York City area clubs in the 1970s. He appeared as an asthmatic lesbian in Andy Warhol's only play, *Pork*, in 1971 at the age of sixteen. His early, unpublished plays, *Freaky Pussy, Flatbush Tosca,* and *Cannibals Just Don't Know Better*, are set in the drag subculture.

Fierstein's best-known work has come with his Broadway success, *Torch Song Trilogy* (1982), for which he received Tony awards for both best actor and best play. He also won another Tony for best book of a musical for *La Cage aux Folles* (1983). His play *Spookhouse* was produced Off-Broadway in 1984. He returned to Broadway as star and playwright in 1987 with *Safe Sex*. In 1989 the musical *Legs Diamond* featured a book Fierstein coauthored with Charles Suppon.

In addition to appearing in the stage and screen versions of his own plays, Fierstein has continued his career as a performer in the films *Garbo Talks* (1984), *The Harvest* (1993), *Mrs. Doubtfire* (1993), *Bullets Over Broadway* (1995), and *Independence Day* (1996); in the Off-Broadway revival of Robert Patrick's groundbreaking play *The Haunted House* (1991); in cabaret performances at such venues as New York's Bottom Line and the 92d Street Y; on his compact disc *This Ain't Gonna Be Pretty* (1995); and as the voice of a gay male secretary on the television cartoon series *The Simpsons*.   *D. S. Lawson*

Bibliography

Brelin, Christa. "Harvey Fierstein." *Contemporary Authors,* vol. 129. Susan M. Trotsky, ed. Detroit: Gale, 1990, 144–46.

Clum, John M. *Acting Gay: Male Homosexuality in Modern Drama.* New York: Columbia, 1992.

Cohen, Jodi R. "Intersecting and Competing Discourse in Harvey Fierstein's *Tidy Endings.*" *Quarterly Journal of Speech* 77 (May 1991): 196–207.

de Johng, Nicholas. *Not in Front of the Audience: Homosexuality on Stage.* London: Routledge, 1992.

Gross, Gregory D. "Coming Up for Air: Three AIDS Plays." *Journal of American Culture* 15 (Summer 1992): 63–67.

Lawson, D. S. "Harvey Fierstein." *The Gay and Lesbian Literary Heritage.* Claude J. Summers, ed. New York: Henry Holt, 1995, 273–74.

Powers, Kim. "Fragments of a Trilogy: Harvey Fierstein's Torch Song." *Theatre* 14, no. 2 (Spring 1983): 63–67.

Scott, Jay. "Dignity in Drag." *Film Comment* 25 (January–February 1989): 912f.

See also Films; Theater: Premodern and Early Modern; Transvestism

F

Film

There are three major, sometimes overlapping, approaches to understanding the concept of "gay film": (1) the history of gay film representation, (2) the history of gay work in film production, and (3) the history of gay film spectatorship.

Gay Representation

Who the gay characters are in films and how they are portrayed are complicated issues. For one thing, should only "obvious," or so-called denotatively coded, figures be considered in a history of gay representation in film? That is, are the only gay or homosexual characters the ones who are named as such by the dialogue or by the visual presentation of certain sexual and affectional behavior? What of those characters whom people understand as gay on the basis of what is often considered more connotative coding, like voice quality, dress and other style codes, or (sub)cultural in-jokes and references?

While it is clear Harvey Fierstein's character, Arnold Beckhoff, is gay in *Torch Song Trilogy* (1988, Paul Bogart) because he works as a drag queen and has sex with men, what about the two killers in Alfred Hitchcock's *Rope* (1948)? Nothing is ever said about them, nor do we see them in a romantic or sexual situation. But the stylish way they dress, their apartment's tasteful interior decor, their refined and soft-spoken voices, and something about their body language and close proximity to each other when they are alone have convinced many people that they are homosexual characters, while other viewers don't see it this way. So where someone would begin a history of gay representation would depend on how he or she decodes "homosexuality" or "gayness" in films. Questions of decoding are perhaps more important in relation to mainstream films than in relation to documentary, independent, or avant-garde films, as films in these last three categories tend to be more explicit about naming homosexuality or about showing romantic and sexual material.

Vito Russo's *The Celluloid Closet* is the most famous English-language survey of the history of both denotatively and connotatively coded gays (and lesbians) in mainstream and independent films from 1895 to 1987. Beginning with an Edison short of two men dancing, *The Gay Brothers* (1895), and ending with crossover-into-mainstream independent films like *My Beautiful Laundrette* (1986, Stephen Frears), Russo's book covers 1930s sissies; 1940s noir queer sidekicks; 1960s and 1970s tormented,

killer, or comic gays; and 1980s nonthreatening, "just like heterosexuals" gays. Overall, he suggests that the history of gay (and lesbian) representation in mainstream films has been far from stellar and riddled with misinformation and negative images of every sort, including the recent "gay as AIDS victim" stereotype. Independent films have a better track record of portraying "idiosyncratic gay vision[s]" for Russo (274).

Beyond mere listing and labeling, Russo is concerned with providing a critical commentary on the quality of gay representation in film. Like that of many other critics, much of this commentary is informed by an approach that considers representation in terms of "positive" and "negative" images; that is, in terms of how stereotyped an image is or is not. Many have questioned this approach to analyzing the history of representation, however, because of a tendency to too narrowly and conservatively define what constitutes a "positive image." Besides this, not everyone agrees on what a stereotyped image is: for example, might not the drag queens in *The Adventures of Priscilla, Queen of the Desert* (1995, Stephan Elliott) be pejoratively understood as stereotypic by one group, positively viewed as complex characters by another group, and considered rather limited, if not fully negative, "types" by a third group?

Gay Production

There are three aspects of gay film production history: invisible, closeted, and open. The first two categories are most often associated with mainstream ("Hollywood") filmmaking, while the last is largely concerned with documentary, independent, and avant-garde filmmaking. Though we may never know who they were or what they contributed, it is safe to say there have been thousands of gays involved in making all types of films over the years. These people constitute the "invisible" history of gays and film production. The closest we usually can get to tapping into this history is having a "queer feeling" when we see or hear something in a film and thinking: "A gay guy *must* have had something to do with that." More and more of this invisible history has been moving into the ranks of closeted gay film production history as people come out or are "outed." As a result, we have cases like those of director George Cukor and actor Rock Hudson where their work will be reconsidered as part of the history of gay film production after public revelations of their homosexuality.

An exemplary article concerned with the invisible and the closeted histories of gay production is Matthew Tinkcom's "Working Like a Homosexual: Camp Visual Codes and the Labor of Gay Subjects in the MGM Freed Unit." In this piece, Tinkcom places certain classic MGM musicals—most notably *Yolanda and the Thief* (1945, Vincente Minnelli) and *The Pirate* (1948, Vincente Minnelli)—within the history of gay film production by considering both gay spectatorial responses to the campiness of these musicals as well as the presence of gay workers on these films who were out to coworkers but not to the public. By and large, the methodologies Tinkcom uses to discuss gay production history during Hollywood's "golden age" are still useful for constructing a more recent history of gay production in mainstream films, as most gay film workers on both sides of the camera remain invisible or closeted. Currently, the best single source for the history of openly gay film production is Richard Dyer's *Now You See It: Studies on Lesbian and Gay Film and Video*. Dyer traces the history of gay mainstream, documentary, independent, and avant-garde production from *Anders als die Andern* (1919, Richard Oswald) to what he calls the "affirmation" and "post-affirmation" fiction and documentary films of the 1970s and 1980s that followed the Stonewall rebellion.

Gay Spectatorship

Because of the often connotatively coded, subtextual, invisible, or closeted aspects of gay representation and production, gay spectatorship often becomes an important source for constructing histories of gay film. Armed with gossip, rumor, and that vague thing called "gay sensibility," viewers often brave ridicule and other attempts to discredit their spectatorship as they "queer" films, characters, performers, directors, and other film workers. Approaching the idea of "gay film" from the perspective of spectatorship offers the most inclusive (though some would say the least rigorous) history of gay film, as it would take in *The Sound of Music* (1965, Robert Wise) as well as *Fireworks* (1947, Kenneth Anger), Maria Montez as well as Ian McKellen, Alfred Hitchcock as well as Gregg Araki, and Joel Cairo (*The Maltese Falcon*, 1941, John Huston) as well as Andrew Beckett (*Philadelphia*, 1993, Jonathan Demme). As is suggested by Montez's name in the list above, a spectatorship history of gay film would include women as well as men, and it also would break down many of the distinc-

tions between gay and lesbian film histories, as a number of gay men count as part of their queer popular culture history such people, characters, and films as Marlene Dietrich, Dorothy Arzner–directed works, Mrs. Danvers (*Rebecca*, 1940, Alfred Hitchcock), the two lead characters in *Heavenly Creatures* (1995, Peter Jackson), and Sadie Benning's short films.

Selected Timeline for a History of Gay Representation and/or Production

1895   William Dickson directs *The Gay Brothers* for the Edison Studios. The short film depicts two men dancing, while a third plays a violin.

1914   *A Florida Enchantment*, directed by Sidney Drew, centers on male and female sex and gender reversals.

1915   Fatty Arbuckle (*Miss Fatty's Seaside Lovers*) and Charles Chaplin (*A Woman*) are two of the many comedians to don drag during the silent period.

1916   Mauritz Stiller's *Vingarne*, the story of an artist and his male model (remade in 1924 as *Mikael* by Benjamin Christiansen).

1919   *Anders als die Andern* (Richard Oswald), perhaps the first film to discuss homosexuality openly.

1923   Alla Nazimova's adaptation of Oscar Wilde's *Salome* has a largely gay and lesbian cast.

1930s   Vito Russo dubs this the decade of the "sissies," as actors like Franklin Pangborn, Edward Everett Horton, and Eric Blore make careers out of playing effeminate supporting characters. A number of Hollywood films of the period contain brief bits by sissy characters.

1930   Jean Cocteau's *Blood of a Poet* and Melville Webber and James Sibley Watson's *A Lot in Sodom* begin gay experimental and avantgarde film production.

1940s   A period of homosexually coded noir, war, musical, and western characters. There is often a thin line between crime partnership, military camaraderie, song-and-dance teaming, and buddy-bonding adventure and homosexual longing in films like *The Maltese Falcon* (1941, John Huston), *Anchors Aweigh* (1945, George Sidney), *A Walk in the Sun* (1946, Lewis Milestone), *Gilda* (1946, Charles Vidor), *Red River* (1948, Howard Hawks), and *Rope* (1948, Alfred Hitchcock). This "don't ask, don't tell" situation has con-

F tinued to the present in most mainstream and independent male-bonding films.

1947 Kenneth Anger's first film, *Fireworks*, begins what is to become one of the most influential bodies of work in the American gay avant-garde. *Fireworks* is followed by *Eaux d'artifice* (1953), *Scorpio Rising* (1962–1963), *Kustom Kar Kommandoes* (1965–1966), and *Invocation of My Demon Brother* (1969), among other films.

1950 Jean Genet's short film *Un Chant d'amour*, set in a prison, is a lyrical representation of sadomasochistic eroticism.

1961 Sympathetically portrayed openly gay characters in the mainstream British films *A Taste of Honey*, directed by Tony Richardson, and *Victim*, directed by Basil Dearden.

1962 Unsympathetically portrayed homosexuality in the American film *Advise and Consent*, directed by Otto Preminger.

1964 Jean Delannoy's *That Special Friendship* offers a complex and sensitive representation of adolescent homosexuality.

mid-1960s–1970s Many different lines of representation and filmmaking run parallel in the United States. Much of this work is done in the wake of the developing gay rights movement and the Stonewall rebellion: mainstream films that usually comically trivialize or melodramatically demonize gay characters (*The Sergeant*, 1968, John Flynn; *Reflections in a Golden Eye*, 1967, John Huston; *The Detective*, 1968, Gordon Douglas; *Caprice*, 1967, Frank Tashlin); independent fiction and documentary films that are made "by and for" gays (*A Very Natural Thing*, 1973, Christopher Larkin; *Word Is Out*, 1977, Mariposa Film Group; *Gay U.S.A.*, 1977, Arthur Bressan); "underground" avant-garde films (the works of Curt McDowell, Tom Chomont, Andy Warhol, Gregory Markopoulos, Jack Smith, and even John Waters, to some extent) that were often designed to shock and antagonize both straight and queer viewers; and last, but not least, pornography.

1969 German director Rosa von Praunheim's first film, *Schwestern der Revolution* (Sisters of the Revolution), is released. Its radical "in your face" style and politics marks most of the director's subsequent films such as *Nicht der Homosexuelle ist pervers, sondern die Situation in der er lebt* (It Is Not the Homosexual Who Is Perverse, but the Situation in Which He Finds Himself), 1970; and *Armee der Liebenden oder Aufstand der Perversen* (Army of Lovers, or Revolt of the Perverts), 1978.

1970 *The Boys in the Band*, directed by William Friedkin, becomes the first Hollywood film in which all the principal characters are homosexual. The question of whether the film was positive, negative, both, or neither in its representation of gays and gay life is still being debated.

1973 *That Certain Summer*, directed by Lamont Johnson, is a landmark American made-for-television movie about a father's coming out to his son.

1977 British television's *The Naked Civil Servant*, based on the autobiography of Quentin Crisp, is broadcast.

1978 Edouard Molinaro's farce *La Cage aux Folles* opens to great success. It is followed by sequels in 1980 and 1985. Remade with even greater box office success as *The Birdcage* (1996, Mike Nichols).

1980 William Friedkin's *Cruising* raises the hackles of a number of gays for its use of the S/M scene as the setting for a story about a serial killer of gays. Director Frank Ripploh's *Taxi zum Klo* offers a "politically incorrect" view of gay life in Germany.

1982 What Russo calls a "mini-cycle of so-called gay films" are made by studios, including *Making Love* (Arthur Hiller), *Victor/Victoria* (Blake Edwards), and *Partners* (James Burrows).

mid-1970s–1980s Outside America, mainstream and independent feature films with gay central characters are being made: Germany's *Fox and His Friends* (1975, Rainer Werner Fassbinder); Egypt's *Alexandria . . . Why?* (1978, Youssef Chahine); Spain's *The Deputy* (1978, Eloy de la Iglesia); Holland's *The Fourth Man* (1983, Paul Verhoeven); England's *Another Country* (1984, Marek Kanievska) and *My Beautiful Laundrette* (1986, Stephen Frears); and Mexico's *Dona Herlinda and Her Son* (1986, Jaime Hermosillo).

1985 *Buddies*, directed by Arthur Bressan Jr., is the first feature film about AIDS. The same year sees the broadcast of the American made-for-television AIDS film *An Early Frost* (John Erman). Documentaries *Before*

Stonewall (Greta Schiller, Andrea Weiss, and John Scagliotti), *Silent Pioneers* (Lucy Winer, Harvey Marks, Pat Snyder, and Paula DeKoenigsberg), and *The Times of Harvey Milk* (Robert Epstein) are released. The latter film wins the Academy Award for best feature documentary.

1990s A group of independent American films achieve international film festival, critical, and art house success and are dubbed "New Queer Cinema" by critic B. Ruby Rich. Tom Kalin's *Swoon* (1991), Todd Haynes's *Poison* (1991), Gregg Araki's *The Living End* (1992), Christopher Munch's *The Hours and the Times* (1992)—Rich's four cornerstones of the movement—are joined by films like *Paris Is Burning* (1990, Jeannie Livingston), *Edward II* (1991, Derek Jarman), *Young Soul Rebels* (1991, Issac Julien), and *My Own Private Idaho* (1991, Gus Van Sant). By mid-decade, New Queer Cinema as a critical and marketing category had been pretty much subsumed within the more general independent film ("indie") category.

1993 *Philadelphia* (Jonathan Demme) becomes the first American mainstream film to center its narrative on gay men and AIDS.

1995–1996 *The Adventures of Priscilla, Queen of the Desert* (1995, Stephan Elliott), *To Wong Foo, Thanks for Everything, Julie Newmar* (1995, Beeban Kidron), and *The Birdcage* (1996, Mike Nichols) show that drag queens can garner critical and box office success.

Alexander Doty

Bibliography

Doty, Alexander. *Making Things Perfectly Queer: Interpreting Mass Culture*. Minneapolis: University of Minnesota Press, 1993.

Dyer, Richard. *Now You See It: Studies on Lesbian and Gay Film*. London: Routledge, 1990.

Murray, Raymond. *Images in the Dark: An Encyclopedia of Gay and Lesbian Film and Video*. Philadelphia: TLA Publications, 1994.

Olson, Jenni. *The Ultimate Guide to Lesbian and Gay Film and Video*. New York: Serpent's Tail, 1996.

Russo, Vito. *The Celluloid Closet*, rev. ed. New York: HarperCollins, 1987.

Tinkcom, Matthew. "Working Like a Homosexual: Camp Visual Codes and the Labor of Gay Subjects in the MGM Freed Unit." *Cinema Journal* 35, no. 2 (1996): 24–42.

See also Anger, Kenneth; Araki, Gregg; Camp; Crisp, Quentin; Cukor, George; Fassbinder, Rainer Werner; Fierstein, Harvey; Film: New Queer Cinema; Film Stars; Genet, Jean; Haynes, Todd; Jarman, Derek; Musical Theater; Russo, Vito; Smith, Jack; Van Sant, Gus; Warhol, Andy; Waters, John

Film: New Queer Cinema

What came to be called "New Queer Cinema," or the "Queer New Wave," began with a group of American films that received high-profile press coverage after they had successful screenings and won awards at the Sundance, Toronto, and Berlin film festivals of 1991 and 1992. Critic B. Ruby Rich, who championed these films, is generally credited with coining the term "New Queer Cinema" and with naming the "four exemplars of the movement: Tom Kalin's *Swoon* (1991), Todd Haynes's *Poison* (1991), Gregg Araki's *The Living End* (1992), and Christopher Munch's *The Hours and the Times* (1992). For most critics, two qualities that distinguish these independently produced films from other gay and lesbian films past and present is their assumption of a queer audience as well as their desire to break from traditional narrative forms.

For many directors, audience and form were related. In discussing the difference between newer "queer" films and other then-recent films with gay content, Todd Haynes remarked, "[F]ilms like *Longtime Companion* [and] *An Early Frost*—films which stick to narrative forms so completely—I think are really heterosexual" (Petit 39). For New Queer directors like Haynes, the form you put your film into indicates the type of audience you are addressing: conventional forms called out to heterosexual(ized) viewers, while nontraditional forms connected with queer viewers. Perhaps more immediately striking to most audiences and critics were these films' "fuck you" attitude and content that included things like "appropriating negative stereotypes and exploitation for their own ends" (Grundmann 25). Unconcerned with so-called positive images, and appearing to revel in "political incorrectness," New Queer Cinema films were often hotly debated in gay and lesbian press.

Of course, as with any movement, New Queer Cinema had its own progenitors. The two decades before New Queer Cinema witnessed the growth of gay and lesbian independent and avant-garde filmmaking in many countries in the wake of the 1970s gay liberation politics. In their subjects and their

F

Bruce la Bruce in a contemplative mood. Photo by Marc Geller.

forms, most of these works offered alternatives to conventional straight films: *Taxi zum Klo* (1981, Frank Ripploh), *She Must Be Seeing Things* (1987, Sheila McLaughlin), *Seduction: The Cruel Woman* (1985, Elfi Mikesch and Monika Treut), *Born in Flames* (1983, Lizzie Borden), and films by Derek Jarman, Ulrike Ottinger, Rosa von Praunheim, John Greyson, Jan Oxenberg, Barbara Hammer, John Waters, and Andy Warhol, among others. Even before these films, there was the American gay underground (with Kenneth Anger's *Fireworks* [1947], and *Scorpio Rising* [1963], and Jack Smith's *Flaming Creatures* [1963] as perhaps the most influential underground works for New Queer Cinema), and Jean Genet's only attempt at directing, *Un Chant d'amour* (1950). Also influential for New Queer Cinema (as well as for many of the films and directors above) were pornography and "exploitation" films with their explicit sexuality and taboo-breaking subjects.

Considering the breadth of its influences, it is not surprising to discover that one early point of contention about defining New Queer Cinema centered on the fact that the films receiving the most attention from critics, distributors, and exhibitors were invariably gay feature-length fiction films—and largely white gay films at that. Added to this critique were complaints about the America-centrism

of the movement—at least in terms of what films were included by critics and in promotional material. After all, hadn't *Paris Is Burning*, the 1990 documentary about Harlem drag balls, directed by lesbian Jennie Livingston, been the toast of the Berlin Film Festival? And what about late 1980s–early 1990s films from British directors like Derek Jarman (*The Garden*, 1990; *Edward II*, 1991) and Isaac Julien (*Young Soul Rebels,* 1991), or German director Monika Truet (*The Virgin Machine*, 1989; *My Father Is Coming,* 1991), Canadian Bruce LaBruce (*No Skin Off My Ass,* 1990), or the Austrian-German film *Flaming Ears* (1992, Angela Hans Scheirl, Dietmar Schipek, and Ursula Purrer)? Were Jarman and Truet disqualified because they had directed films before the 1990–1992 watershed period and, therefore, were not exactly "new"? Besides all this, why was a video like Marlon Riggs's *Tongues Untied* (1989) being overlooked, when it daringly mixed documentary and fiction in its examination of black gay men's lives?

With time, many films like those listed above made their way into the ranks of an expanded New Queer Cinema (and Video), along with the non-feature-length, not-always-fictional works of Sadie Benning, Pratibha Parmar, Su Friedrich, Jerry Tartaglia, John Greyson, and others. But even with a more inclusive list of directors and films, some critics were not convinced that the "queer" in New Queer Cinema was really appropriate. Cherry Smith felt that most of what was being called New Queer Cinema was really only repackaged lesbian, gay, or "lesbian and gay" work that did little to radically question or challenge traditional sexual and gender categories. Besides this, not everyone was eager to be included in New Queer Cinema. For example, Gus Van Sant was never comfortable being called a gay or queer director ("new" or otherwise). He actively resisted this kind of categorization in interviews, even though his *Mala Noche* (1985), the gritty story of a man in love with a straight Mexican teenager, was one of the films that paved the way for New Queer Cinema, while *My Own Private Idaho* (1991) seemed to many critics a model of how New Queer Cinema and mainstream filmmaking might meet.

Van Sant's desire not to be pigeonholed as a "gay" or "queer" director—that is, not to be restricted to gay, lesbian, or queer subjects—brings up another critical question related to defining New Queer Cinema: Can it be queer cinema without queer subject matter? While it seems to be a given that directors of New Queer Cinema films must be queer, would nonqueer material directed by these people still qualify the resulting films as New Queer Cinema? While the predominant response to this question from critics and audience appears to have been no, some people, particularly filmmakers, have asked "Why not?" Don't films like Su Friedrich's *First Comes Love* (1991) and Todd Haynes's *Safe* (1995) present queer perspectives on heterosexuality and straight gender roles, among other topics?

In one way, the desire of some New Queer Cinema directors to tackle nonqueer (and, sometimes, more "mainstream" material) has contributed to the waning of the movement in recent years. But perhaps a more important reason why New Queer Cinema isn't surviving as a distinct movement has something to do with the overall growth of the American independent ("indie") film scene, which has by and large absorbed its queer contingent. These days, one is as likely to hear a film like *Watermelon Woman* (1996, Cheryl Dunye) discussed as an American indie as one is to find it cited as another example of New Queer Cinema. But while you rarely hear the term used anymore to describe or publicize films, there is the occasional rough-and-ready independent film with attitude, like *Go Fish* (1994, Rose Troche), *Super 8½* (1994, Bruce LaBruce), and *Totally F***ed Up* (1994, Gregg Araki), that is still connected to the movement.

Alexander Doty

Bibliography

Grundmann, Roy. "The Fantasies We Live By: Bad Boys in *Swoon* and *The Living End.*" *Cineaste* 19, no. 4 (March 1993): 25–29.

"New Queer Cinema." *Sight and Sound* 2, no. 5 (September 1992): 30–41.

Petit, Sarah. "Reel to Real: A Conversation Between Jennie Livingston and Todd Haynes." *Outweek* 94 (1991): 34–41.

Rich, B. Ruby. "A QUEER: From Toronto to Berlin to New York: The Work Is Out—A New Gay Cinema Is Here." *Village Voice* 37, no. 12 (March 18–24, 1992).

———. "Reflections on a Queer Screen." *GLQ: A Journal of Lesbian and Gay Studies* 1, no. 1 (1993): 83–91.

Smyth, Cherry. *Lesbians Talk Queer Notions.* London: Scarlet Press, 1992.

See also Araki, Gregg; Film; Gay Liberation; Haynes, Todd; Van Sant, Gus; Waters, John

Film Stars

Theorizing the relationship between film stars and gay men is problematic. Any opinion sets up essentializing traps about homosexual subjectivity that demands a careful attention to changing historical conditions to be persuasive. Nevertheless, few would dispute that film stars occupy an "absolutely central importance," according to gay film critic Richard Dyer, "in gay ghetto culture," for this culture feels "a peculiarly intense degree of role/ identity conflict and pressure, and an (albeit partial) exclusion from the dominant articulacy of, respectively, adult, male, heterosexual culture." Dyer's explanation is useful for defining a pre-Stonewall gay identity shaped by shame, concealment, and societal oppression, an identity that found vicarious fulfillment in watching the Hollywoodized lives of glamorous cinematic icons. Living in a homophobic world where gay marriage was impossible and true love unlikely, gays could identify with a (usually female) star as she fell in love with a gorgeous leading man, rose in class, changed wardrobe, and suffered exquisitely in mink.

The emotional transsexualization that occurred in the gay male film spectator established a clear, if controversial, bond between homosexuals and women. It is no accident that they often shared the same favorite stars: Ruth Chatterton, Joan Crawford, Bette Davis, Lana Turner. If the homosexual was a member of the "third sex," possessing the soul of a woman within the body of a man (an identity endorsed by Havelock Ellis if dismissed by Sigmund Freud), then he could share a soulful sisterly union with his biologically different cohorts. They both could vicariously enjoy the antics of Joan Crawford in her various cinematic personae: the gold-digging shop girl with a heart of gold (in the thirties); martyred mom (in the forties); murderous gangster's moll or menopausal old maid (in the fifties). When Crawford went Gothic, however, in *What Ever Happened to Baby Jane?* (1962), many homosexuals and women took distinctly opposing sides. Molly Haskell, in her protofeminist film study *From Reverence to Rape* (1974), condemned "the very idea" of *Baby Jane* and its abject, freakish view of older women.

But gay Gothic spectatorship found an ally in gay camp taste. Camp, defined by Philip Core as "the lie that tells the truth" and Christopher Isherwood as "expressing what is basically serious to you in terms of fun and artifice and elegance," made a style out of a substance. In other words, "bad was good" in camp discourse. Camp taste applauded film actresses for their excessive behavior rather than their innate (and, therefore, indeterminate) "talent." Sensing a repressive antieroticism and homophobia within a film acting "standard" that stressed tasteful restraint, gay camp spectators often found a liberating, transgressive potential within the ludicrous, the absurd, or the over-the-top.

For instance, gay camp spectators rejected the subdued, if beautiful, Elizabeth Taylor of *Father of the Bride* in favor of her blowzy viragoes of *Who's Afraid of Virginia Woolf?, X, Y & Zee,* and *The Driver's Seat.* (When Liz told a macho mechanic twenty years her junior, "If you think you're going to have sex with me, you're very much mistaken!" in *The Driver's Seat,* she ruined her legitimate film career but gained a respect in camp circles that eluded her gender-conformist cinematic coevals who had retired gracefully years before.) Other camp favorites included *Valley of the Dolls, Mommie Dearest* (Faye Dunaway in a career-crippling turn as a Kabuki Joan Crawford!), and *Showgirls* (heterosexuality as sequined nightmare).

Feminists referred to camp spectatorship as a form of misogyny, but it might be more accurate to call it a politically astute expression of misanthropy. Appropriating African American critic bell hooks's "oppositional gaze" theory of film watching, one might say that camp opened up resistant "spaces of agency" for homosexuals whose lives would never be fairly or respectfully represented on the Hollywood screen. Camp taste permitted a derision that might seem "one note," but it also allowed a critical gaze at a hegemonic hetero-normativity that burlesqued, erased, or eliminated the filmic gay image.

If this theory seems conservative, if not fatalistic, then it may be a discouraged response to the relentlessly capitalistic, and increasingly monopolistic, Hollywood industry. Things never seem to change in Hollywood; the late film historian Vito Russo's *Celluloid Closet* theory remains valid as the industry enters the new millennium In his groundbreaking work Russo traced the reappearance of the onscreen homosexual after the breakdown of the moralistic Hays Code and noted a bitter irony: gay visibility did not guarantee justice. Faced with the choice of vicarious satisfaction in a hetero love story or humiliation in a "sensitive" drama about homosexual suicide, many gays preferred to watch Shirley MacLaine as a call girl (in films too numerous to mention) than watch Shirley MacLaine as a dead lesbian (in *The Children's Hour*).

After Stonewall, gay rights advances promised more balance but not necessarily better box office. Audiences squirmed when "straight acting" (but really straight) Michael Ontkean made love to hot het-in-real-life Harry Hamlin in *Making Love*, but they cheered when Julie Andrews played a fag in drag in *Victor/Victoria.* As the millennium approached, the only gay-themed films that avoided a "box-office poison" label were those jolly entertainments that replicated a heterosexual paradigm. *The Birdcage,* for example, reassured straights that gays, too, believed in marriage, monogamy, and male dominance. Film star Robin Williams could play a poof without threatening his masculinity because his "boyfriend" acted like a girl, and a fifties girl at that, never asking to go further than first base on a date. Mainstream audiences could relax, and gays could contemplate the future with jaundiced eyes.

Or gays could imagine alternatives. Russo, in his revised edition of *The Celluloid Closet,* gave up on Hollywood and encouraged a growing avant-garde to represent homosexual interests onscreen. Thanks in part to Russo's and other film critics' encouragement, a new "queer cinema" emerged: directors Marlon Riggs, Tom Kalin, Todd Haynes and Gregg Araki shocked, titillated, amused, and satisfied homo spectators with their refreshingly honest, if no less entertaining, images of gays. Unfortunately, this new cinema made stars of the *filmmakers* behind the camera. Recognizable faces, such as Craig Chester's, reappeared with startling frequency in these movies, but no "stars" came forth. The "New Queer Cinema" reinvented the "auteur theory" of filmmaking fashionable in the late fifties and early sixties. Queers had their own Federico Fellini, if not their own Marcello Mastroianni.

A discussion of the homosexuality (suspected or openly admitted) of Hollywood's stars deserves a mention. From the silent era, homosexual actors such as Ramon Navarro and Rudolph Valentino fueled heterosexual passions in the peanut gallery while exchanging love tokens to each other (such as personally autographed dildoes) offscreen. Rock Hudson, the king of the women's picture, changed heterosexual America's perception of homosexuality and AIDS when his orientation and medical condition were made public. Although they have not been permitted on-camera rolls in the hay with their true loves, gay performers Rupert Everett and Ellen DeGeneres have found mainstream acceptance and healthy paychecks. Yet Hollywood and homosexuality remain strange bedfellows, with the former res-

olutely clinging to the position of controlling, withholding "top." *John M. Ison*

Bibliography

Bergman, David. "Introduction." In *Camp Grounds:
Style and Homosexuality*. David Bergman, ed.
Amherst, Mass.: University of Massachusetts
Press, 1993.

Dyer, Richard. "Charisma." In *Stardom: Industry of
Desire*. Christine Gledhill, ed. London: Routledge, 1991.

hooks, bell. "The Oppositional Gaze." In *Reel to
Real: Race, Sex and Class at the Movies*. London: Routledge, 1996.

Russo, Vito. *The Celluloid Closet: Homosexuality
in the Movies*, rev. ed. New York: Harper and
Row, 1987.

See also Araki, Gregg; Camp; Ellis, Havelock; Film;
Film: New Queer Cinema; Freud, Sigmund; Haynes,
Todd; Riggs, Marlon; Russo, Vito; Television

Finland

Though it lies geographically just to the east of the
Scandinavian peninsula and 93 percent of its 5.1
million inhabitants speak a Finno-Ugric language
(Finnish), Finland is both governmentally and culturally one of the five Scandinavian (more properly
Nordic) democracies and maintains close consultative relations at the ministerial level with its western
neighbors: Sweden, Norway, Denmark, and Iceland.
Finland is also a member of the European Union.

Finland was recognized as an eastern province
of the Kingdom of Sweden by the pope in 1216. In
1908 the province achieved a measure of autonomy
as a grand duchy when it was ceded to the czar of
Russia as a result of the Napoleonic Wars. During
the period of unrest in the newly erected Soviet
Union following the Russian Revolution of 1917,
Finland claimed complete independence on December 6, 1917. The immediately following Civil
War (January 27–May 16, 1918) determined that
the new republic would follow the capitalist road to
development.

Though Finland has yet to follow the lead of its
Scandinavian neighbors and grant legal recognition
to same-sex couples, constitutional reforms adopted
in the mid-1990s guarantee homosexual individuals
a full measure of legal equality with the heterosexual majority. A glance at history will show that the
legal position of Finnish homosexuals has undergone considerable improvement, and that Finnish
law has been slow to follow changes in societal attitudes and practices.

Homosexual acts—both male and female—
first became a civil offense on Finnish soil (with a
maximum penalty of two years' imprisonment) in
1889. The courts continued to follow "enlightened"
scientific thinking so that by 1952, in a case that became the subject of a novel by Kim Benz, a rural
schoolteacher received a reduced sentence for submitting to castration. In 1971 homosexual acts became legal, though the age of consent was set at
eighteen (versus sixteen for heterosexuals), and the
"encouragement of homosexuality" was made illegal. Following the proposal of a 1993 law reform
commission, the "encouragement" clause was removed from Finland's current criminal code and sixteen has been set as the common age of consent for
both heterosexuals and homosexuals. In addition,
sexual orientation has been added as a protected category to already existing antidiscrimination laws.

There have also been moves toward equality in
other areas of Finnish society. A 1993 sexological
study revealed significant softening of antigay and
lesbian attitudes among the general population from
1971 to 1992—a trend that continues, particularly
among the young. In 1981 homosexuality was removed from the Finnish classification of mental illnesses. By the mid-1980s even state-owned radio
and television channels were broadcasting gay and
lesbian–positive programming, in spite of the then-
existing "encouragement" clause.

But acceptance has been slower in the church:
as the result of a 1993 radio interview interpreted as
suggesting that homosexuals need not remain celibate, Archbishop John Vikström was accused of
heresy—the first heresy charge against the head of
the Finnish state Lutheran Church (to which 86 percent of the population belongs) since the seventeenth century. Although large numbers of laity and
clergy joined the complaining parishioner, Vikström
was eventually acquitted by both ecclesiastical and
civil courts (where charges had been filed under the
"encouragement" clause).

In its 1992 decision to overturn a deportation
order against a male asylum seeker living in partnership with a Finnish man, the Finnish Supreme Court
referred to European human rights agreements protecting "family life and the sanctity of the home,"
but same-sex partnership legislation has yet to be
debated in full parliament. Although the current
minister of justice is on record as opposing gay and

lesbian partnerships as "not part of Finnish culture," individual members' bills received more and more support throughout the 1990s. So it appears likely that before the turn of the millennium, same-sex couples who wish to register with their local authorities will be granted legal recognition of their relationships, though under the current climate it is unlikely that the right of adoption will be extended to homosexual couples.

Finnish homosexuals began to organize for improved legal rights by the 1940s, but only in the late 1960s had groups of any strength developed. Since 1974, SETA (Seksuaalinen tasavertaisuus SETA ry.), with branches in most Finnish cities, has been the main organization working on behalf of sexual minorities (including homosexuals, transvestites, and transsexuals). Serving members primarily through its social and educational functions, SETA publishes a magazine as well as a monograph series, both in Finnish.

Though a number of master's theses on homosexual topics have appeared since the mid-1980s (particularly in sociology, psychology, and theology) and a handful of doctoral theses written by Finns on topics of gay and lesbian interest have been accepted at Finnish and foreign universities, it is only at the University of Helsinki's Karoliina Institute for Women's Studies that a course on homosexuality is regularly taught. An eclectic collection of scholarly articles, interviews, personal essays, and poems edited by Kai Sievers and Olli Stålström in 1984 remains the most accessible general work on homosexuality for most Finns.

Owing partly to educational efforts and an open attitude toward the distribution of condoms, Finland is fortunate in having a relatively low rate of HIV infection. Of the HIV-positive cases in Finland, fewer than half can be traced to homosexual transmission, so AIDS is not viewed as primarily a "gay disease" (in part because the country's first successful AIDS play dealt with heterosexual transmission and tourism). Though there are AIDS support centers in all major cities, Finland's only AIDS ward is located in the capital, Helsinki.

The Finnish authors best known abroad who have written on homosexual themes are Gunnar Björling (1887–1960), Tove Jansson (b. 1914), Christer Kihlman (b. 1930), and Edith Södergran (1892–1923). It is perhaps only incidental that all are members of the country's 6 percent Swedish-speaking minority. The Finnish homosexual best known abroad, Finnish-speaking artist Tom of Fin-

land (1920–1991)—creator of hunky leatherman drawings based on American, not Finnish, models—remained virtually unknown to most Finns until after his death, but a retrospective of his work staged shortly thereafter by one of Finland's most reputable galleries became the subject of much (favorable) media attention.

James Haines

Bibliography

Benz, Kim. *Kastroitu* (Castrated [a novel]). Jyväskylä: Gummerus, 1989.

Haavio-Mannila, Elina, and Osmo Kontula. "Seksuaaliset vähemmistöt" (Sexual Minorities). In *Suomalainen seksi: Tietoa suomalaisten sukupuolielämän muutoksesta* (Finnish Sex: Facts about Change in the Sex Lives of the Finns). Porvoo: Werner Söderström, 1993, 238–68.

Sievers, Kai, and Olli Stålström, eds. *Rakkauden monet kasvot: Homoseksuaalisesta rakkaudesta, ihmisoikeuksista ja vapautumisesta* (The Many Faces of Love: On Homosexual Love, Human Rights, and Freedom). Espoo: Weilin+Göös, 1984.

See also Denmark; European Commission of Human Rights; Sweden; Tom of Finland

Firbank, Ronald (Arthur Annesley) (1886–1926)

English author Ronald Firbank was obsessed with the possibility of achieving immortality through his fiction, and he constructed a fictional monument to memorialize what he himself predicted would be an all-too-brief life. Firbank's fiction often provides the only evidence we have to deduce some of the intimate details and circumstances of the author's life. Shy, sickly, socially isolated, and more than a little paranoid, Firbank was among the most self-effacing of men. His modernist aesthetic committed him to blurring the boundary between art and life; the difficulty with discussing his life apart from the imaginative work he produced was deliberately imposed by Firbank himself.

An infatuation with Evan Morgan was intertwined with his literary interest in pyramids, sphinxes, and Egyptology. Brigid Brophy reports in her critical biography of Firbank that the author perceived a resemblance between Morgan and the mummy of Ramses; Firbank insisted on taking Morgan to the British Museum to see "the original." According to Brophy, Firbank fell in love with Morgan at first sight, an experience he attributed to reincarnation; it may well have been the only time that Firbank fell in love.

Firbank was an intrepid traveler, but his narratives are set in the far more exotic locales of fantasy. In the 1924 preface to *The Flower Beneath the Foot*, Firbank wrote, "I suppose the Flower Beneath the Foot is really Oriental in origin, although the scene is some imaginary Vienna. The idea came in Algeria while writing *Santal*. . . . Ah, the East. . . . I propose to return there, someday, when I write about New York." When asked by Siegfried Sassoon what his favorite country was, Firbank replied, "Lotus Land, of course!"

"I always know instinctively when the Mrs. has on her spiked garters," a servant remarks in *Valmouth*. We do not know whether Firbank himself ever wore spiked garters, but his fascination with masochism is evident in his frequent and enthusiastic references to flagellation and bondage. Certainly Firbank deserves to be one of the great fetishists of literature. His conversion to Roman Catholicism is indistinguishable from his literary subversion of it. His interests included but were not limited to lesbians, nuns who "wield discipline," an entire calendar of saints and martyrs (both historical and invented), and flowers—some of whom have speaking parts in his novels. Firbank presents himself as such a fetish in *Prancing Nigger* when he appears as an orchid, "the Ronald Firbank, a dingy lilac blossom of rarity untold."

Writing books may not have been easy for Firbank, but publishing them proved nearly impossible. He published eight works at his own expense prior to Carl Van Vechten's U.S. publication of *Prancing Nigger* in 1924. (The novel was published under Firbank's chosen title, *Sorrow in Sunlight*, several months later in Britain.) Firbank's last completed work, *Concerning the Eccentricities of Cardinal Pirelli*, was rejected for publication. In it, the Spanish cardinal baptizes a puppy at a high-society black mass. The puppy celebrates "communion" by fornicating with his police-dog father at the altar. Cardinal Pirelli also cruises the streets in drag; holds conversation with St. Teresa of Avila whenever he has more than four or five glasses of wine, and dies in the sacristy wearing nothing but a miter on his head, overcome by the exertion of pursuing a coyly elusive altar boy.

It does not help much to rescue Firbank and his works from the charges of "anachronism," which many critics have used to dismiss him as a minor talent. We should understand "anachronism" as a euphemism alluding to Oscar Wilde's fin-de-siècle art-for-art's sake aesthetics. Critics' failure to recognize Firbank as a modernist innovator is partly due to the fact that Firbank was tremendously influenced by Wilde—indeed, he was obsessed with Wilde in the role as homosexual art-martyr. Firbank was not only a literary disciple of Wilde and heir to Wilde's aesthetics; he also suffered from the sense of paranoia common to many homosexual men living under Britain's repressive antisodomy laws. While we know that Firbank enhanced his personal appearance with powder and rouge, Brophy attributes Firbank's "literary transvestism," as well as his interest in lesbians, to the persecution of male homosexuals in Great Britain.

Firbank's literary transvestism corresponds to an aesthetic in which only the "artifice" of fiction—or the making of an autonomous fictional world—permits certain identities to really appear. In this last sense, the fairy-tale quality of Firbank's novels can no longer be dismissed as mere anachronistic whimsy, nor can Firbank himself be dismissed as a mere imitator of Wilde.   *Kimberly Wilson Deneris*

Bibliography

Brophy, Brigid. *Prancing Novelist: A Defence of Fiction in the Form of a Critical Biography in Praise of Ronald Firbank*. New York: Harper and Row, 1973.

Firbank, Ronald. *Five Novels*. New York: New Directions, 1981.

———. *Three More Novels*. New York: New Directions, 1986.

See also Van Vechten, Carl; Wilde, Oscar

Fitch, Clyde (1865–1909)

American playwright Clyde Fitch was born in Schenectady, New York, to an old New England family. Educated at the Holderness School in New Hampshire and Amherst College, he moved to New York City in late 1880 to make his way as a writer. Early success came with the play *Beau Brummell*, which attracted a large audience and proved to be the first of a long string of popular works Fitch wrote for the stage. His best-known plays include *The Girl with the Green Eyes* (1902), *Her Own Way* (1903), *The Truth* (1907), the posthumously produced *The City* (1909), and historical works such as *Captain Jinks* (1901) and *Nathan Hale* (1899).

Fitch also collaborated with novelist Edith Wharton to bring her best-selling 1905 novel, *The House of Mirth,* to the stage. Throughout his career Fitch wrote with startling speed—often completing many plays in one year. By the first decade of the twentieth century, he stood as one of the most popular living playwrights in the United States. In all, over sixty-two of his plays were produced.

Fitch's plays remain very much a reflection of their period, specifically in upholding the assumptions of the Northeastern turn-of-the-century ruling elite. His work invariably supports New York's class system, rewards patriotic sentiment, and reaffirms the traditional moral values of the day. Much like the plays of his mentor, Oscar Wilde, Fitch's work remained focused on polite upper-class society and rarely ventured into any uncomfortable directions, such as the many problems associated with New York's dramatic urbanization around the turn of the century.

In his work, Fitch portrayed women and their concerns vividly and accurately. Thus fashionable society almost always constituted his most loyal audience. Fitch's personal direction and production of his plays was also the key to his success. He not only brought the plays to the stage but personally coached the actors and closely supervised the decoration of all sets and costumes. Many women attended Fitch's plays as much to learn about the latest trends in interior design and fashion as to see the play itself.

In his personal life, Fitch cultivated the image of the "aesthete," or "new dandy." George (Beau) Brummell, J.-K. Huysmans, and especially Oscar Wilde served as his models. As in his plays, houses and decoration were important in his life: he built and lavishly decorated a succession of homes culminating in a townhouse on East 40th Street and a country house, Quiet Corner, in Greenwich, Connecticut. Throughout his life Fitch experienced a number of attractions and loving unions with other men. While he conceptualized these relationships as romantic friendships, he also had a clear awareness of the sexual element. Thus in this knowledge of his "temperament" the playwright combined elements of both the nineteenth and the twentieth centuries.

Fitch died suddenly in the summer of 1909 at the age of forty-four while at the height of his fame. Unfortunately, his literary reputation did not long survive him, and by the 1920s his plays were declining in popularity. As a result, surprisingly little has been written on this once famous playwright.

David D. Doyle Jr.

Bibliography

Moses, Montrose J., and Virginia Gerson. *Clyde Fitch and His Letters*. Boston: Little, Brown, 1924.

See also Dandy; Theater: Premodern and Early Modern

Flandrin, Hippolyte (1809–1864)

In art history, French painter Hippolyte Flandrin is always mentioned in the same breath as his mentor, J.A.D. Ingres (1780–1867). It was Flandrin who kept closest to Ingres's quality of linear purity and insistence on perfection through reviving artistic methods and subjects of the past. Both were influenced by the art of Raphael and had an uncanny way of mixing modernity with tradition.

Flandrin was one of seven children born into a middle-class family from Lyons. Two of his brothers were also accomplished artists. Hippolyte became the most famous of the three and gained a reputation as a painter of mythological scenes and religious subjects. Influential nineteenth-century art critic Théophile Gautier (1811–1872) equated Hippolyte's purity of line and color with purity of emotions and devotion of purpose. Flandrin himself was devotedly religious, and most of his works were spiritual in content. Many were commissioned by churches such as Saint-Paul in Nîmes, and Saint-Germain-des-Prés and Saint-Vincent-de-Paul in Paris.

Flandrin was not a homosexual and did not intentionally grapple with the homoerotic as an expressive motif. Nevertheless, an intense focus on the beautiful youthful male nude draws erotic attention to many of his secular images. Unlike Ingres, who became a celebrity by applying a purity and abstraction of line to the female figure, Flandrin's use of the same was concentrated almost exclusively on the youthful male subject. According to the artist himself, it was a form of beauty born out of his reading and knowledge of Homer, Plutarch, Tacitus, and Virgil that dictated the creation of his nonreligious works—the majority of which feature secluded youthful nude males situated in calm environments. In most of these paintings, the viewer's attention is drawn to the subject's genital area by strategic placement of some compositional device intended to hide it. This is pronounced in his painting *Theseus Recognized by His Father* (1832; Paris, École Nationale Supérieure des Beaux-Arts), where a rack of meat is conspicuously positioned in front

Hippolyte Flandrin's Figure d'Étude *Louvre, Paris. Scala/Art Resource, NY.*

of Theseus' genital area to draw our attention to it. This *cache-sexe* device, plus the fact that Theseus is completely nude and surrounded by clothed figures, gives a heightened erotic aspect to a mythological scene of dramatic recognition.

Between 1833 and 1836, Flandrin produced several noteworthy paintings with homoerotic overtones. One of these, *Polytes, Son of Priam Observing the Movements of the Greeks Near Troy* (1833–1834; Saint-Étienne, Musée d'Art et d'Histoire), shows a nude male youth sitting in profile atop a classically decorated pedestal while looking out of the picture frame and into the distance. The prominent curve of the figure's back and formal focus on the interplay between form and line communicate a quality of hushed beauty and purity. In conjunction with the work's implicit eroticism, a religious spiritualism suffuses this canvas. One unusual detail is the rendering of the figure's pubic hairs with a shocking and jarring realism that appears to be at odds with the overall idealized quality of the painting. This feature reveals to what extent Flandrin had

gone in blending the real with the ideal, the erotic with the contemplative, a poeticized romanticism with an incongruous realism, and classicalized form with a sense of pious emotion. Most of Flandrin's figures express "a perfect peace" and mix Virgilian lyricism with a striking realism in detailing of the head, hands, and feet.

Flandrin's most popular and recognizable work is his *Figure d'Étude* (Nude Young Man Seated on a Rock) (1835–1836; Paris, Louvre). Characteristic of Flandrin, this work uses the nude male youth to showcase a stylistic purity of line, modeling, and color. The work is not only erotically suggestive in its concentration on the purity and beauty of the male form but is also mysterious in its calm, meditative quality and aura of poetic lyricism. Critics praised the almost hyperreal rendering of the figure's hands and feet and gave them a spiritual interpretation. Critics also noted the work's geometric composition (a circle within an equilateral triangle) and gave that a sacred significance as well. The subject's fetal pose was a unique invention in the history of art and has been repeated by a variety of artists ranging from Edgar Degas to Robert Mapplethorpe. It is a pose whose main purpose was to highlight the male body as an object of spiritual and erotic contemplation. The painting has, in its own right, become a classic gay icon of sorts.

James Smalls

Bibliography

Camille, Michael. "The Abject Gaze and the Homosexual Body: Flandrin's *Figure d'Étude I.*" In *Gay and Lesbian Studies in Art History*. Whitney Davis, ed. New York: Haworth Press, 1994, 161–88.

Foucart, Jacques, et al. *Hippolyte, Auguste et Paul Flandrin*. Paris: Éditions de la Réunion des Musées Nationaux, 1984.

See also Art History; France; French Literature; Homer

Florence

Since the Renaissance in the fifteenth and sixteenth centuries, when this city was one of the most dynamic cultural centers of Europe, Florence has had lasting fame as a community hospitable to homosexuality. In modern times this reputation has rested largely on the figures of prominent native artists of the period who had presumed or documented same-sex inclinations—men such as Donatello, Leonardo da Vinci, Benvenuto Cellini, and Michelangelo, all of whom produced artworks that are homoerotically suggestive. For their contemporaries, the fame, or rather infamy, of Florence for sodomy (which was understood mainly but not exclusively as sexual relations between males) had little to do with particular individuals but reflected a generalized practice and ethos, and it was noted as such by many observers both in Italy and elsewhere. Florentines' proclivities were evidently so familiar to Europeans across the Alps that in sixteenth-century Germany a popular term for "to sodomize" was *florenzen*, while a sodomite was dubbed a *Florenzer.*

Renaissance Florence was far from being a haven of tolerance for sodomy, however, despite its well-justified reputation for extensive homosexual activity. Although contradictory attitudes abounded, officially this sexual practice always remained both a serious crime and a nefarious sin. Preachers such as Bernardino of Siena in the 1420s and Girolamo Savonarola in the 1490s reasserted the church's an-

cient condemnation of sodomy and terrorized Florentines with the threat of divine punishment, and both staged dramatic bonfires of "vanities" to help drive home their message of doom against sodomites. More significantly, fifteenth-century civic authorities, like those in many other Italian cities, perceived in sodomy an increasing menace to public order, moral decency, and population growth, and they took unprecedented measures to control and repress it.

In 1432 the Republic of Florence created a special judiciary commission, the "Office of the Night," to pursue and prosecute sodomy. This was probably the first and one of the very few institutions ever created with this specific scope in the history of Europe. Through a combination of effective methods of detection (anonymous denunciations, hired spies, and incentives to encourage confession), rapid summary proceedings, and reduced, relatively mild penalties (mostly monetary fines, raised with successive convictions), the Office of the Night carried out an exceptionally systematic and widespread persecution of sodomy. In just seventy years, up to 1502 when this magistracy was abolished, approximately seventeen thousand men and adolescents were incriminated for same-sex sexual relations, and some three thousand were convicted. These extraordinary numbers, especially for a small city of forty thousand inhabitants, far exceed those currently known for any other city. They attest both to the pervasiveness of sexual activity between males in Florence—in the later fifteenth century probably the majority of the city's men were publicly incriminated at least once during their lifetimes—and equally to the determination of many civic leaders and a large segment of the community to police it.

One unintended legacy of this effort of surveillance and prosecution is perhaps the richest and most detailed historical record of homosexual experience surviving for any premodern society, which is enhanced by a wealth of sermons, poems, tales, and anecdotes on homoerotic themes. All this information throws important light on questions having to do with the social contours, behavioral conventions, and cultural meanings of same-sex sexuality in the Western past.

Sex between males in Florence almost always involved an older partner, usually a physically mature adult over the age of eighteen, who took the so-called active, or penetrating, sexual role with a younger partner, normally an adolescent between the ages of thirteen and eighteen or twenty, who assumed the so-called passive, or receptive, role. Relations in which these sexual roles were reversed or reciprocated were rare and limited to adolescents, while sex between two adult men was both practically unknown and considered reprehensible. These conventions were linked to contemporary notions of life stages, gender values, and masculine status. According to prevailing conceptions, the receptive sexual role, denigrated as womanly, was appropriate only for boys who were not yet completely formed men but shameful for older youths and men who had acquired the physical and social traits that defined manhood. Males could, however, assume the dominant sexual role with other males without jeopardizing their status as virile men. For most people, moreover, homosexual relations represented only temporary or occasional transgressions, common especially in the long period of adolescence and bachelorhood before marriage, and they did not preclude either concurrent or subsequent sexual relations with women. While same-sex eroticism formed part of the life experience at one time or another of many, if not most, Florentine men of the Renaissance, this did not foster the creation of discrete categories of social "deviants" or distinctive sexual "identities." Sexual encounters were on the whole casual and often mercenary, procured on the streets or in taverns, brothels, public baths, and workshops, although more durable and committed relationships, sometimes characterized as "marriages," are also documented. Despite the amorphous nature of the same-sex social environment, wide-ranging networks and coteries of friends and acquaintances with similar erotic desires were common, and at times they even organized forms of resistance against repression.

By the mid-sixteenth century the urgency that for 150 years had animated Florentine efforts to police sodomy, especially same-sex sexual activity, had subsided. Sodomy continued to be a serious crime during the period of the grand duchy under the Medici dynasty (1532–1737), but the last important law against it was issued in 1542, and by the following decade prosecutions had become and remained few and sporadic. Some of the later Medici rulers themselves were reputed or acknowledged to be attracted erotically to young males, particularly Gian Gastone, whose failure to produce an heir brought the dynasty to an end. On the whole, however, little is known about homosexuality in the early-modern city. Under Ferdinand III, the third of

the enlightened Austrian successors to the Medici, Tuscany was among the first European states after the French Revolution to repeal its laws against sodomy, in 1795. Throughout the nineteenth and early twentieth centuries, Florence continued to attract a good deal of elite homosexual tourism and colonization, probably as much for its often romanticized past as for its contemporary pleasures.

Michael Rocke

Bibliography

Rocke, Michael. *Forbidden Friendships: Homosexuality and Male Culture in Renaissance Florence.* New York: Oxford University Press, 1996.

See also Art History; Cellini, Benvenuto; Italian Renaissance; Leonardo da Vinci; Michelangelo Buonarroti

Flowers and Birds

Flowers and birds have played an important role in both the language and the cultural symbolism of homosexuality. Although it is difficult to trace much of the ephemera (floral names of drag queens, for example), floral imagery appears consistently in a variety of cultural, mythological, historical, and literary representations of homosexuality. Bird imagery seems less central in Anglo-American culture, though it may be more common in other traditions.

In Western culture, the connection between flowers and homosexuality may be traced in part to classical mythology and the association of flowers with the transient beauty of young men—as, for example, in the *Iliad*, in which young men dying in battle at Troy are compared to poppies whose heads are severed by the plow. Several young men in Greek mythology were transformed into flowers at their untimely deaths: Adonis (from whose blood sprang the anemone), Attis (the violet), Narcissus, and Hyacinth (transformed into the flowers that bear their names). Connected to larger themes of transience and loss, such floral metaphors of transformation and male beauty inform much of the Western literary tradition of pastoral elegies. That Narcissus was in love with the image of himself and that Hyacinth was the beloved of Apollo suggest the further connection of the floral with love between men—a connection exploited by the Uranian and decadent poets of the nineteenth century. The associations among male beauty, tragic death, and floral imagery was revived in the twentieth century in the

F homoerotic poetry of World War I and, to a lesser extent, in recent writing about AIDS. The visible lesions of Kaposi's sarcoma, for example, are metaphorized as flowers in recent writing by Felice Picano, Reginald Shepherd, and Abraham Verghese.

In the nineteenth century, floral literature in general was at its height, but by the end of the century, the floral would be firmly linked with homosexuality. Victorian England was obsessed with flowers, staples of both home decoration and literature, and charmed by the idea of a "language of flowers," a custom of associating flowers with particular meanings. This tradition was codified in sometimes contradictory "dictionaries" and gift books of the period, and was based on an inaccurate understanding (which continues to this day) of the *sélam*, or a secret floral code used in Turkish customs. By 1855, when poet and sexologist Marc-André Raffalovich published a collection of poems titled *Tuberose and Meadowsweet*, this "language" was already a sentimentalized and nostalgic representation of romantic courtship. Because of its connotations of secrecy, it was easily appropriated by gay writers searching for language through which to figure their own desires. In most floral dictionaries, tuberose represented "dangerous pleasures." Raffalovich called it a flower "whose name I may not tell," prefiguring by almost a decade Lord Alfred Douglas's "love that dare not speak its name."

Prefiguring fin-de-siècle decadence, Baudelaire's *Fleurs du Mal* (1867) had begun a resistance to traditional romantic or sentimental symbolism by aligning the literary flower with evil. By the end of the century, hothouse flowers and orchids had begun to signify the decadent cult of artificiality. (Orchids, etymologically linked to testicles, were the subject of Darwin's study of artfully evolved fertilization.) As demonstrated in W. S. Gilbert's satire *Patience* (1881), a young man carrying a lily or poppy symbolized the poetic dandy or aesthete. Hothouse flowers represented the triumph of the aesthetic, the cultural, and the unnatural over the sentimental and the natural—establishing or substantiating sexual stereotypes of aestheticism, cultural privilege, and unnaturalness.

Late Victorian homoerotic writing was full of flowers, much of it linking aestheticism with homoerotic classical myths. Oscar Wilde would repeatedly address Lord Alfred Douglas as Hyacinth and Narcissus, and both Douglas and Raffalovich would write of Narcissus as an image of modern love. According to Neil Bartlett, not only would Wilde refer to two young men in 1895 (the year of his trials) as "flowers of the narcissus kind," but floristry itself was identified as one of the professions characteristic of sexual "criminals" arrested on the streets of Paris. In 1911, Uranian poet John Gambrill Nicholson published *A Garland of Ladslove* — "ladslove" being the name of a common herb but clearly a pun in a book of pederastic poems. In other literature of this century, floral symbolism is central to the high-camp style of Ronald Firbank, and it reaches a criminal apotheosis in the work of Jean Genet.

Other than the decadent orchid, two other flowers have been tied historically to homosexuality in Anglo-American cultures: the green carnation and the pansy, and to a lesser extent, the pansy's relatives, the hearts-ease or viola and the violet, a flower connected with lesbianism. Robert Hitchens published *The Green Carnation* in 1894, a parodic novel about Wilde and Douglas, which pointed to Wilde's reputation for wearing the dyed flower—emblem of the aesthete, the dandy, or the homosexual. Since the early part of this century, "pansy" has been commonly used as a name for a homosexual or an effeminate man. Some linguists suggest that the word is a corruption of *nancy*, a nineteenth-century euphemism for an effeminate man or homosexual and slang for catamite. Robert Scully's *The Scarlet Pansy*, a camp novel of gay life before and during World War I, was published in 1933. (In it one character asks the effeminate protagonist whether he makes sexual contacts by using "the language of flowers," to which he replies, "Yes, dearie, scarlet pansies!") Like *queer*, the term *pansy* was originally an invective, though it has sometimes been appropriated, as in the slogan Pansy Power, or in the name of the gay punk rock band Pansy Division. The related violet became most clearly an emblem of lesbianism after the appearance of Edouard Bourdet's play *La Prisonnière*, performed in 1926 on Broadway as *The Captive*, in which female lovers exchange the flower.

Since midcentury, several flower names have been employed as slang for male homosexuals or effeminate men: daisy, lilac, daffodil (British slang), buttercup (American). "Lily-white boys" earlier in this century could refer to cowardly men or male lovers. In dictionaries of slang, one also finds that a "daisy chain" or, infrequently, a "floral arrangement" may represent a homosexual orgy. The association of flowers with homosexuality also seems to further an equation of homosexuality with effeminacy. "Flowerdew" was the name of an effeminate character played by Peter Sellers early in his career. The florist, like the hairdresser and the interior designer, continues to appear as a stereotypical homosexual role in film and television.

Floral imagery has also been used in heterosexual and homosexual erotica to metaphorize the body. Historically, the rose has been linked to female genitalia, and in the florid prose of gay pornography, the anus is commonly compared to a flower, often a rosebud. This image, echoing as it does the long tradition connecting the "flower" of youth with the hymen or virginity (common in English literature since the sixteenth century), alludes to the "deflowering" of a virgin. In traditional Japanese culture, the chrysanthemum was also linked to the anus, and a "chrysanthemum tryst" symbolized gay anal sex.

One might draw further comparisons to other horticultural and botanical images of sexual desire, such as the "forbidden fruit" of Eden, the "apple of Sodom," or the calamus reed that figures so significantly in the homoerotic poetry of Walt Whitman. Like other homoerotic figures of Greek myth, Calamus was transformed into a plant after the drowning of his male lover, Carpus. Algernon Charles Swinburne called Uranian poet John Addington Symonds and his associates "Calamites," adapting the term to echo "catamite," derived from a Latin form of Ganymede, cupbearer to Zeus. In Western culture both "catamite" and "Ganymede" have come to signify a young man or boy who takes a receptive role in homosexual relations or is the object of pederastic desire.

Through the story of Ganymede, bird imagery may also be traced to classical mythology: disguised as an eagle, Zeus abducted the boy Ganymede. Ganymede was sometimes depicted riding on a cock, implying a link between the bird and pederasty or sodomy. In ancient Greece, where the rooster was a symbol of virile sexuality, an older man who wished to seduce a boy might give him a cock as a gift, as represented in classical art. The partridge also has a cultural association with homosexuality since, according to ancient natural historians who focus on the bird's rampant sexuality, partridges are likely to practice male-male sex when the female is nesting.

Although *bird* and *chick* are dated terms for a woman (*bird* traceable to Middle English), *chicken,* in twentieth-century slang, refers to an adolescent male; an older romantic or erotic pursuer of young men is called a "chicken hawk." Originally, *chicken* referred more specifically to young runaways who were likely to be "preyed" upon by homosexual men, but now the term refers more generally to intergenerational affairs. In American underworld slang earlier in the twentieth century, a *cock* referred to a boy used as a sexual decoy for extortionists. Of course, "birds and bees" remains a euphemism for sexual intercourse, but more interestingly, a "bird's nest" may represent (female) genitalia or pubic hair—in texts as diverse as *Romeo and Juliet,* in which climbing a bird's nest suggests sex, and Djuna Barnes's *Nightwood,* in which a gay man (who calls himself a "lame duck" and a "queer bird") speaks of making a bird's nest (of pubic hair) in his stomach.

The association of homosexuality with birds is more common in Spanish and Latin American cultures, in which homosexual men are frequently referred to as birds—*pájaros* or *pajaritos* (birds, or little birds) in Latin America, *pato* (duck) in Cuba, and *aves* (wings) in Costa Rica. The phrase *plumas de una misma ala* (feathers of the same wing, equivalent to the English birds of a feather) may be used to refer to gay men as a group. Spanish poet Luís Cernuda utilizes these associations in his poem "The Eagle/Aguila," referring to the abduction of Ganymede. *Faygeleh,* an endearment in Yiddish meaning "little bird," has come to be used pejoratively for gay men in American Jewish cultures.

In Western literature, birds have often been used as a symbol of transcendence or aspiration; in gay literature, such an association may have roots in Plato's *Symposium,* in which pederastic love is tied to the "heavenly" or Uranian Aphrodite. Tennessee Williams uses bird imagery in his plays to represent loss (often lost youth or opportunities) and forbidden or thwarted desires—the image of the legless bird in *Orpheus Descending,* for example. More recently, bird imagery, like floral imagery, has been reduced to simple stereotype: the flamboyant plumage and flightiness (and perhaps refined lunacy) of drag queens in the film *The Birdcage,* the American adaptation of *La Cage aux Folles.*   *Ed Madden*

Bibliography

Bartlett, Neil. *Who Was That Man? A Present for Mr. Oscar Wilde.* London: Serpent's Tail, 1988.

Fussell, Paul. *The Great War and Modern Memory.* London: Oxford University Press, 1975.

Harris, Amy. "The Flowers of Pestilence: Flower Imagery in AIDS Discourse and the Literature of Disease." *Harvard Gay and Lesbian Review* 3, no. 2 (1996): 26–31.

Leupp, Gary. *Male Colors: The Construction of Homosexuality in Tokugawa Japan.* Berkeley: University of California Press, 1995.

Madden, Ed. "Say It With Flowers: The Poetry of Marc-André Raffalovich." *College Literature* 24, no. 1 (1997): 11–27.

Partridge, Eric. *A Dictionary of Slang and Unconventional English.* Paul Beale, ed. New York: Macmillan, 1984.

Richter, Alan. *Dictionary of Sexual Slang.* New York: Wiley, 1993.

Roland, Beryl. *Birds with Human Souls: A Guide to Bird Symbolism.* Knoxville, Tenn.: University of Tennessee Press, 1978.

Seaton, Beverly. *The Language of Flowers: A History.* Charlottesville, Va.: University Press of Virginia, 1995.

Smith, Page, and Charles Daniel. *The Chicken Book.* Boston: Little, Brown, 1975.

See also Aestheticism; AIDS; Arabic Literature; Cernuda, Luis; Dandy; Decadence; Firbank, Ronald; Ganymede; Genet, Jean; Greece, Ancient; Pederasty; Plato; Raffalovich, Marc-André; Symonds, John Addington; Whitman, Walt; Wilde, Oscar; Williams, Tennessee

Jack Megoot, the fop in Benjamin Hoadley's play The Suspicious Husband. *Courtesy University of Waterloo Library.*

Fops

Vain and preoccupied as they were with fashion and self-presentation, seventeenth- and eighteenth-century dandies, known at the time as fops, provide significant insight into the now familiar association between effeminacy and homosexuality. Foppish characters appear in Roman and medieval texts and later become targets of disparagement for Renaissance satirists such as John Marston and Michael Drayton. Fops (at times known as *beaus*), however, really come into their own on the Restoration English stage in comedies such as George Etherege's *Man of Mode; or, Sir Fopling Flutter* (1676); Aphra Behn's *The Town Fop; or, Sir Timothy Tawdrey* (1676); John Crowne's *Sir Courtly Nice; or, It Cannot Be* (1685); Colly Cibber's *Love's Last Shift; or, the Fool in Fashion* (1695–1696) and *The Careless Husband* (1704); and John Vanbrugh's *The Relapse* (1696). In these texts, fops are not unsympathetically characterized by polished manners, social nobility, verbal ingenuity, cynicism, monomania, sartorial extravagance, and Francophilia. Often, these fellows' penchant for epigrammatic speech foreshadows Wildean wit. In *Love's Last Shift*, for in

"renews the shame / Of *J.* the first, and *Buckingham*" (12), a reference to England's first Stuart king and his handsome beloved. Another anonymous piece, *Satan's Harvest Home* (1749), expounds at even greater length on the slippery slope of foppish kissing between men. Originally imported from Italy, this transgressive habit is "the first *Inlet* to the detestable Sin of *Sodomy*" (52).

In 1747, David Garrick added fuel to the fire with his two-act farce, *Miss in her Teens: Or, the Medley of Lovers.* Garrick's character Mr. William Fribble soon became the literary namesake of "a Species too despicable for Correction" (32). Capitalizing on the homophobic anti-Fribble sentiments unleashed by Garrick's play, that same year Nathaniel Lancaster published a prose satire, *The Pretty Gentleman*, in which he uses the language of Platonic friendship to draw foppery's "*Mollifying Elegance*" (6) into a sodomitical orbit, "molly" at the time being a common term for a male homosexual. Drawing on Milton's council of the devils in *Paradise Lost*, Garrick, in his mock-epic *The Fribbleriad* (1761), portrays a "PANFRIBBLERIUM" (7) of mincing, conspiratorial fops whose gender is demonically neuter (2) and whose substandard poetry is written "in namby-pamby feet" (6).

Posed with "kimbow'd arm, and tossing head" (15), Garrick's devilish fop Pattypan is a direct ancestor of twentieth-century representations of weak-wristed pansies. Putting aside the homophobia that motivates such representations, we note that one of the most significant aspects of fops, then as now, is their denaturalization of gender. On stage, on page, and in life, fops remind us of culture's role in legitimating and demonizing certain desires, behaviors, and identities. *Michael M. Holmes*

Bibliography

Haggerty, George E. *Men in Love: Masculinity and Sexuality in the Eighteenth Century.* New York: Columbia, 1999.
Satan's Harvest Home. 1749. Facsimile reprint. New York: Garland, 1985.

See also Dandy; Effeminacy; Mollies; Molly Houses

Ford, Charles Henri (1913–)

Charles Henri Ford, a prominent and influential surrealist artist and poet, was born in Brookhaven, Mississippi. He entered the literary scene in 1929 as founder and editor of *Blues: A Magazine of New Rhythms,* which published important modernists like Ezra Pound and William Carlos Williams in its yearlong existence. Ford spent most of the early 1930s writing poetry in Paris, in expatriate communities with artists and writers like Jean Cocteau, Gertrude Stein, and Pavel Tchelitchew. The latter, a Russian painter, would become Ford's companion.

While in Paris, Ford published his poetry in journals like *New Review* and *Front*, and collections like *Americans Abroad: An Anthology.* Ford lived briefly with Djuna Barnes in Morocco, where he typed her novel *Nightwood* for her. With his friend Parker Tyler, he cowrote *The Young and the Evil*, a gay-themed novel about artists and bohemians in Greenwich Village. The Obelisk Press published the book in Paris in 1933, but it was banned in America, where the novel didn't see publication until Arno Press, in 1975, included it in its Homosexuality: Lesbians and Gay Men in Society, History, and Literature series.

Ford returned to America in 1934 with Tchelitchew; the two lived together first in America, then in Italy, until Tchelitchew died in 1957. During the late 1930s and 1940s, Ford published six collections

of poetry and continued to expand the circle of contemporary poets with whom he associated (William Carlos William, e.e. cummings). Critics loved Ford's original style and voice but acknowledged that his poems lacked any recognizable form or structure. Ford set out to introduce America to surrealism, editing a collection of prose called *A Night With Jupiter* and founding and editing *View* (1940–1947), a journal devoted to surrealist art and literature that published, among others, Wallace Stevens and Randall Jarrell.

Since the early 1950s, Ford has published little poetry, devoting most of his time to art. Exhibitions of his painting and photography have appeared around the world, and he has continued to introduce the public at large to new forms of expression. Always open to new ideas, Ford became interested in multimedia art and directed two underground films, *Poem Posters* (1966) and *Johnny Minotaur* (1972). *William DeGenaro*

Bibliography

Ford, Hugh. *Published in Paris: American and British Writers, Printers, and Publishers in Paris, 1920–1939.* New York: Macmillan, 1975.

See also Cocteau, Jean; Tyler, Parker; Tchelitchew, Pavel; U.S. Literature

Forster, E(dward) M(organ) (1879–1970)

Forster remains one of the most influential English writers of the twentieth century. Best known for his novels, Forster was also an important literary critic and essayist. His homosexuality was not public knowledge until after his death, although it was well known to many friends and provided the most sustained subject matter of his work.

Forster was born into a middle-class family. His father, a descendant of the liberal, evangelical Clapham Sect, died when Forster was an infant. He was brought up mainly by his overprotective mother, Lily (née Whichelo), who remained a strong influence on him until her death in 1945. The other significant maternal figure for Forster was his great-aunt Marianne Thornton, who upon her death left him a legacy that enabled him to enjoy a moderate income and attend Cambridge University.

After his repressive home life—only occasionally enlivened by the erotic stimulus of a series of garden boys—and miserable years at public school, Cambridge, which Forster attended from 1897 to

1901, was a revelation. He was elected to the Apostles, a secret society that fostered explicit discussion of sexuality. Until the end of his life, Forster remained loyal to many of his Apostolic brothers, a number of whom, including Roger Fry, John Maynard Keynes, Lytton Strachey, and Leonard Woolf, became, like Forster, closely associated with the Bloomsbury group. At Cambridge Forster tentatively explored his homosexual inclinations with a fellow undergraduate, Hugh Meredith.

Forster found quick success as a writer after graduation, first with a series of mythological short stories, then with four novels. *Where Angels Fear to Tread* (1905) and *A Room with a View* (1908) deal with the encounter between English suburbanites and passionate Italians. Although the plots of these novels are ostensibly heterosexual, there are important homosexual subtexts and narrative eruptions. *The Longest Journey* (1907) portrays a hero unable to sustain the homoerotic friendships that he forms as a Cambridge undergraduate and instead enters into a conventional world of marriage and bourgeois values, with tragic consequences. The last of his Edwardian novels, *Howards End* (1910), is unique in Forster's canon in its concentration on two sisters, modeled loosely on Virginia Woolf and her sister, Vanessa Bell. Its famous motto, "Only connect," became a touchstone of Forster's faith in human relationships across class, ethnicity, and race.

Forster's novels brought him considerable success, enabling him to meet other writers, including D. H. Lawrence, with whom he had a long and difficult friendship. But he was unhappy with the limitations imposed on his writing by the norms of a prudish and homophobic society. He was also anxious to translate his sexual desires into practice. The crucial event was a 1913 visit to the reformer Edward Carpenter, whose theory of the "intermediate" sex provided Forster with a liberating model of sexual desire. Forster later believed that his explicitly homosexual novel, *Maurice,* had been "conceived" when George Merrill, Carpenter's working-class lover, touched his backside. *Maurice* was completed by 1914, though Forster revised it throughout his life; it was not published until 1971. The novel follows the eponymous, middle-class hero through two homosexual romances: the first at Cambridge under the influence of the Platonic idealism of John Addington Symonds and the second with a gameskeeper modeled on Merrill.

Forster did not fully consummate his homosexual desire until 1916. His first important sexual relationship was with an Alexandrian tram conductor, Mohammed el Adl, whom he met in Alexandria during World War I. For Forster, as for other homosexual men of his generation, the "Orient" provided a space for alternate sexualities, continuing his attraction to the "South" expressed in the Italian novels. Greek poet Constantine Cavafy became Forster's guide to the multiple nationalities of the city and to the celebration of male beauty. Forster's collection of essays on Alexandria, *Pharos and Pharillon* (1923), contains a tribute to Cavafy.

His experiences in Alexandria and an earlier visit to India to see Syed Ross Masood (with whom he had long enjoyed a romantic friendship) prepared Forster for a second trip to India in 1921–1922 that would lead to the writing of his last novel. In *A Passage to India* (1924) two men—an Indian and an Englishman—explore the possibilities of friendship against a backdrop of colonial misrule and accusations of sexual assault. Ultimately, the novel judges their friendship to be impossible under colonialism.

After the resounding success of *A Passage to India,* Forster became a major cultural figure, writing and broadcasting on a wide variety of topics. His *Aspects of the Novel* (1927) established him as an important literary critic. Forster also became one of the most vocal opponents of fascism. He clearly articulated his liberal humanist philosophy in "What I Believe" (1938), in which he defended personal affection against nationalism, stating, "If I had to choose between betraying my country and betraying my friend I hope I should have the guts to betray my country." He wrote two biographies: *Goldsworthy Lowes Dickinson* (1934), a tribute to his friendship with a homosexual don at Cambridge, and *Marianne Thornton* (1956), the life of his great-aunt. A great lover of music, he collaborated on the libretto of Benjamin Britten's opera *Billy Budd* (1951), based on Melville's homoerotic novella of shipboard desire. The fiction that Forster wrote after *A Passage to India* was explicitly homosexual and was not published until after his death, as *The Life to Come and Other Stories* (1971).

Forster's most significant relationship, with Robert Buckingham, began in the 1930s and lasted until Forster's death. Forster quickly grew attached to Buckingham, a London policeman, who became intimate with Forster's circle of literary, homosexual friends, including Christopher Isherwood and J. R. Ackerley. The relationship was complicated by Buckingham's marriage in 1932, but Forster, Buckingham, and his wife, May, quickly settled into "domestic intimacy." When Forster suffered the last of his strokes in his rooms at Cambridge, he was brought to the Buckinghams' home, where he died.

The posthumous publications brought Forster new fame as a homosexual writer but also contributed to a marginalization of his work. Yet in the 1980s and 1990s popular film adaptations of five of his six novels introduced him to a new, wider audience.

Robert K. Martin
George Piggford

Bibliography

Beauman, Nicola. *Morgan: A Biography of E. M. Forster*. London: Hodder & Stoughton, 1993.

Furbank, P. N. *E. M. Forster: A Life*. 2 Vols. New York: Harcourt, 1977, 1978.

Herz, Judith Scherer, and Robert K. Martin, eds. *E. M. Forster: Centenary Revaluations*. London: Macmillan, 1982.

Martin, Robert K., and George Piggford, eds. *Queer Forster*. Chicago: University of Chicago Press, 1997.

Stone, Wilfred. *The Cave and the Mountain: A Study of E. M. Forster*. Stanford, Calif.: Stanford University Press, 1966.

Summers, Claude J. *E. M. Forster*. New York: Ungar, 1983.

See also Alexandria; Bloomsbury Group; The Bloomsbury Group and Art; Britten, (Edward) Benjamin; Cavafy, Constantine P.; Keynes, John Maynard; Melville, Herman; Strachey, (Giles) Lytton; Symonds, John Addington

Foucault, Michel (1926–1984)

The genius of philosopher Michel Foucault lies in his persistence in challenging basic assumptions about the nature of human knowledge. More specifically, his broad, historical scope allowed him to determine how ideas evolved out of power struggles within society and its institutions. As a "skeptic," according to Alan Sheridan, Foucault avoids traditional philosophical categories in his writings; therefore, it is difficult to align his poststructuralist theories with any traditional school of thought. His early influences from phenomenology, Marxism, and psychoanalysis were obvious and unoriginal, given the context of intellectual turmoil in postwar France. His ethical stance as an "engaged" philosopher was typical of the existentialism of his early teacher Jean-Paul Sartre. The unique blending of Georges Can-guilhem's philosophy of science, Nietzsche's radical critique of positivism, and the Frankfurt School's critical inquiry into fascism made Foucault's thought diverse, original, and insightful. A sixties-style Parisian philosopher, active in political organizations such as the Group for the Information of Prisoners (GIP), Foucault tried to demystify the invisible strategies of power and their deployment in complex arrangements surrounding individuals. His self-proclaimed goal was "to create a history of the different modes, by which . . . human beings are made subjects" (*The Foucault Reader* 7). According to Foucault, a human being's subjectivity is formed out of modes of manipulation that objectify, categorize, and exclude, namely, through the use of scientific categories as exemplified by such terms as "sexual deviant" and "homosexual."

Nineteenth-century sexologists such as Havelock Ellis were operating out of a "divide and conquer" strategy toward the so-called deviant; they delineated categories of sexual differentiation to such an extent that they constructed a coherent identity for homosexual. Sexuality became an epistemological foundation on which knowledge of the self and the other could be grounded. This strategy, instead of repressing instincts, proliferated modes of self-expression by which the "sodomite" was elevated from his identification with "unlawful and unnatural" actions to the status of a "species" with a "hermaphroditic soul." Foucault's thesis on the modern formation of the subject provides incontrovertible appeal for historians of the various liberation movements of the 1960s.

Foucault developed a unique style of questioning where philosophy itself became suspect and viewed as derivative of different power interests. He historicized abstract truths by asking how they came to be used within specific institutions, such as the family, prisons, hospitals, government, and so on. For example, Foucault tried to unhinge the humanist belief that man was a natural entity whose sexuality was a result of unchecked forces at war with culture; instead, he argued for a construction hypothesis that placed sex at the center of an interlocking grid of institutional discourses on power.

Although he left no autobiography, interest in his modern lifestyle has made Foucault the subject of numerous biographies and controversies since his death from AIDS in 1984. In his memoir, *À l'Ami qui ne m'a pas sauvé*, novelist Hervé Guibert attacked Foucault for infecting him with HIV. Many have come to Foucault's defense, claiming that, while the philosopher was aware of his illness and impending death, it was not known in the early 1980s how the disease was transmitted. Traveling and changing jobs frequently, Foucault discovered the sex clubs of San Francisco when he was a professor at Berkeley. He didn't bother to hide his preference for S/M and even made it the subject of much reflection.

Foucault's life ended with a certain closure when he published the second and third volumes of *The History of Sexuality* in the early 1980s. What he wrote prior to this moment helped to underline and foreshadow the importance of his advanced reflections on sexuality. Already in 1960, with the defense and publication of his doctoral dissertation, *Madness and Civilization*, a work that brought him international attention, he proposed an analysis of sexuality based on the same principles. Three years later, he published *The Birth of the Clinic*, in which he detailed how the hospital sprang out of the eighteenth-century context. A work on surrealist writer Raymond Roussel, his first and only foray into literary analysis, followed.

The year 1968 was a watershed for Foucault, who returned from a teaching position in Tunisia soon after the student revolts in Paris. Reports indicate that he may not have participated in the actual demonstrations. Foucault preferred to refine his method of analysis and his understanding of the workings of power. From *The Order of Things* (1966) to *The Archeology of Knowledge* (1969), Foucault set a course to develop the human sciences and to purge humanism's anthropomorphic method of analysis. Consequently, he could treat all human thought as a discourse, or a material practice grounded in historical conditions. His interpretation of the past is similar to an archaeologist's strata in the earth, in which each layer exposes a system complete within itself. For Foucault, history is divided into three distinct periods: the Renaissance, the classical age, and the modern age. Each contains its own convincing mode of gaining knowledge, which Foucault calls an episteme, not a worldview but a structuring of knowledge. With such a discontinuous view of history, Foucault upsets the notion of causality that is the basis of traditional historiography.

Foucault, in his inaugural lecture to the Collège de France, where he assumed the position of professor of history of systems of thought in 1970, moves away from an archaeology in which discourses are closed systems to a genealogy in which discourses are used as practices of violent intervention into reality. *Discipline and Punish* uses Jeremy Bentham's panopticon as a model of how discourse is used within the prison colony. Here, he extrapolates from these new panoptic "technologies of organization and control" to define how power is manipulated in other, related institutions.

After such an extensive study of the uses of power and knowledge in his earlier books, Foucault's volumes on *The History of Sexuality* conclude his career as a major twentieth-century thinker. This French philosopher, in his two decades as a scholar, masterfully delineated how human sexuality emerged as an historical construct and is continually dominated by power interests that manipulate it for their own purposes.   *Robert Rhyne*

Bibliography

Halperin, David. *Saint Foucault: Towards a Gay Hagiography*. New York: Oxford University Press, 1995.

Miller, James. *The Passion of Michel Foucault*. New York: Simon and Schuster, 1993.

Rabinow, Paul, ed. *The Foucault Reader*. New York: Pantheon, 1984.

See also Bentham, Jeremy; Ellis, Havelock; Essentialist-Constructionist Debate; Guibert, Hervé; Paris; Sadomasochism; San Francisco; Sexology

France

France is often hailed as the first European nation to decriminalize homosexuality. With the Penal Code of 1791 and the Code of Municipal Police and Correctional Police, established by the Constituent Assembly of 1791 two years after the French Revolution, sodomy and crimes against nature, the intertwined rubrics under which same-sex sex acts had been punished during the ancien régime, were removed from the law books. Likewise, the Penal Code of 1810, established under Napoléon, contained no mention of sodomy. However, despite this progressive legislative past, France has a history of repression of sodomy and homosexuality that stretches from the Middle Ages to the twentieth century. The early consolidation of the French nation occurred in part through the mobilization of sentiments against sodomy, and during World War II the Vichy government collaborated in the deportation of homosexuals to German concentration camps.

In 1209, at the instigation of Innocent III, nobles from the Île-de-France and northern France undertook a crusade against the Albigensians, a religious sect popular in Languedoc (now southern France). The Albigensians were depicted by church propaganda as *bougres*, a term of complicated provenance first linked with heresy and subsequently with sodomy. Although the accuracy of the association of the Albigensians with sodomy is not verifiable, it is clear that the accusations of sodomy were effective in building support for military action against them, which provided an occasion for the expansion of the lands and power of the French monarchy. A century later, accusations of sodomitical practices were instrumental in Philip the Fair's successful attempt to gain control of the wealth of the Knights Templar, despite the fact that investigations conducted outside France into the charges of sodomy found them to be without substance.

By the fifteenth century, the Renaissance was under way in the city-states of the Italian peninsula. The limited success of French armed incursions during the Wars of Italy (1494–1516) were met with the tremendous success of Italian culture imported into France, including, according to some propagandists, the vice of sodomy. The sixteenth century may have seen the popularization of homosexuality, particularly among nobles who found a life of debauchery at the court, and among artists and humanists influenced by the recently disseminated works of ancient Greek philosophers such as Plato. If there was such an efflorescence of homosexual practice and culture, it happened alongside continuing persecution of sodomites. Men and women were burned alive in France for crimes against nature throughout the Renaissance and into the eighteenth century.

Political propaganda about deviant sexuality probably reached its apogee in France under the rule of Henry III, the last of the Valois kings. Henry's predilection for pageantry, manifested alternately in public scenes of self-flagellation and sumptuous transvestism, was the target of criticism by both Protestant reformers and hard-line Catholics, as were the wealth and power he lavished on the handsome young men—known as *mignons*—who were his favorites. Henry was assassinated in 1587.

By the seventeenth century, the Counter-Reformation was well under way in France. However, the church's austere moral reforms were met with growing anticlerical sentiment, and some freedom of expression existed for political satirists and champions of corporeal pleasures, as long as their work did not become politically threatening or anger the wrong people. Denis Sanguin de Saint-Pavin, for example, could write verses celebrating the pleasures of boy-love and be known as the King of Sodom by his contemporaries, and face no criminal charges. Théophile de Viau, on the other hand, known for his militant atheism and his satires of religious and political figures, found himself accused of crimes against nature, the church, and his king for scandalous writings ascribed to him.

The potential relationship between such historical personages and something one might call a homosexual or bisexual subculture in early-modern France is not easy to determine. Nonetheless, it appears possible that some nobles, often as united in their contempt for women as in their erotic interest in boys and other men, formed something of a homosexual subculture in the French courts under Louis XIII and Louis XIV. Various period accounts attest, for example, to the formation in 1678 of a society requiring of its adherents the pursuit of relationships with other men and sexual abstinence from women except for the purposes of procreation. When Louis XIV heard of the existence of this society, which had as its device a knight treading on a woman, he banished numerous participants including his son, the count of Vermandois.

Whereas satirists, pamphleteers, and historians of the seventeenth century paint a vivid, and probably exaggerated, portrait of homosexual court culture, police records from the eighteenth century offer us a view of Parisian homosexuality among commoners and noblemen alike. Using patrols, informants, and undercover agents known as *mouches* (flies), the Parisian police tracked hundreds of homosexual men, known as *pédérastes* or *infâmes*. Detailed police reports, depositions, and diaries enable us to trace the public geography of Parisian homosexual culture in the eighteenth century, with its favorite taverns and cruising areas. From these accounts, it seems that at least one segment of the emergent working-class homosexual subculture was characterized by feminine and aristocratic dress and comportment.

Contemporaneous with ongoing police surveillance and harassment of *infâmes*, debates on the subject of pederasty and the law took place in Enlightenment philosophy. Voltaire, for example, asserted that sodomy should not be subject to legal control, but he nonetheless considered it worthy of moral condemnation because it did not serve the public interest through procreation. Whatever the ambivalences of Enlightenment thought on sodomy, it is clear that the movement was in part responsible for the removal of crimes against nature from the French law books in 1791. If postrevolutionary

F France had no laws specifically criminalizing sexual relations between members of the same sex, however, there was nonetheless a category of public offense against decency often used in efforts to curb cruising and male prostitution.

The July Monarchy (1830–1848) seems to mark a period of relative fluidity in gender and sexuality in France, despite uninterrupted police harassment of homosexuals, but with the Second Empire (1848–1871), there was a move toward more fixed sexual identities. The accelerating production of legal and medical studies of homosexuality through the nineteenth century and into the twentieth were central to the consolidation of a modern homosexual identity in France, as were the contributions to public debates about homosexuality made by homosexual men themselves. Authors such as Marcel Proust, André Gide, and Jean Cocteau were instrumental in representing different models of homosexuality to a broad public.

During the years leading up to World War II, there were still no laws specifically criminalizing homosexuality. It wasn't until the establishment of the Vichy government, after the German invasion of France, that the French penal system established a discrepancy between heterosexual and homosexual ages of consent, reintroducing the concept of "acts against nature" in the penal code. These additions occurred in the context of a "national revolution" organized around "Work, Family and Fatherland" meant to address the moral decay ostensibly responsible for France's ignominious defeat at the hands of the Germans. Additionally, the government collaborated in the deportation of homosexuals, resulting in their internment in camps where more than half of them died. After the liberation of France, the Vichy laws against homosexuality were confirmed by the De Gaulle government, and thus in France as well as elsewhere homosexuals liberated from the camps sometimes risked reincarceration. Only in the last few years has the French government acknowledged the deportation of homosexuals, and as recently as 1994 gay activists were refused the right to place a wreath at the national memorial to the deportation during official ceremonies.

In the years after the war, homosexuality was categorized, along with tuberculosis, prostitution, and alcoholism, as a social plague, and the government was empowered to undertake "all appropriate measures to combat homosexuality." The beginnings of the modern gay rights movement in France occurred in parallel with the proliferation of such antihomosexual legislation. *Arcadie*, the longest-lived of the early homosexual publications, first appeared in 1954; it was followed by the formation of a related social organization. Conservative in its approach (the magazine contained no erotic images or stories and even refrained for two decades from protesting discriminatory laws), *Arcadie* was nonetheless banned from public display, advertisement, or sale to minors.

Following the social unrest of 1968, the landscape of the gay rights movement changed enormously in France, and *Arcadie*'s assimilationist politics were largely superseded. In 1971, the Front homosexuel d'action révolutionnaire (FHAR) emerged from discussions following zaps conducted by lesbians and gay men in cooperation with the Mouvement de libération des femmes (MLF). FHAR's agenda included free and legal abortion and contraception, rights for all sexualities, and the rights of minors to sexual self-determination. The group, despite its revolutionary Marxist leanings, was nonetheless rebuffed by the French Communist Party, which would remain skeptical of homosexual liberation until the eighties. The Socialist Party, however, would assert as early as 1976 that homosexuality was normal and announce its intention to repeal discriminatory laws if elected to power.

In 1973, the FHAR was dissolved. The alliance between the FHAR and the MLF had already crumbled under accusations that the FHAR was misogynist and the MLF heterosexist. Schisms along varying axes of difference continued to plague the gay rights movement throughout the seventies. FHAR's successor, the Groupe de libération homosexuelle (GLH), was composed largely of former members of FHAR and young activists expelled from *Arcadie* for their radical views. It would quickly be divided into three sects, each with a different agenda, and by the late seventies it too was defunct.

In 1979, a "homosexual summer school" was organized, attended by representatives from various different lesbian and gay organizations. From this summer school a group, the Emergency Committee against Homosexual Repression (Comité d'urgence antirépression homosexuelle, or CUARH), emerged. CUARH undertook to address employment, adoption, and age-of-consent discrimination, among other issues. The group's numerous marches, conferences, and dances attracted enormous attention, and CUARH was eventually successful in gaining the support of the majority of leftist political parties for its agenda. In the first years of the eighties, after a decade of political activism by assorted gay and lesbian rights groups and heated debate at all levels of government, and with the rise of the Socialist Party to power, the discriminatory laws against homosexuals were repealed.

The great political victories of 1981 and 1982 occurred alongside the first rumors in France of a "gay cancer" striking homosexual men in the United States. At first, these reports were seen by many gay activists as an attempt to repathologize homosexuality in the wake of recent political gains. As the decade progressed, however, the reality of the AIDS epidemic became apparent, and numerous organizations emerged to address the tragedy. At first, groups such as Aides struggled to separate the fight against AIDS from homosexuality; but with the passage of time it became apparent to many that the struggle against homophobia and the fight against AIDS were linked. In 1989, ACT UP–Paris, modeled on the New York ACT UP affiliate, was formed. Coalitional in nature, comprised of men and women, concerned to address a wide range of social issues (mostly relating to AIDS) while retaining a militant gay perspective, and committed to direct action, ACT UP–Paris is in some ways reminiscent of the revolutionary French homosexual movements of the early seventies.

While AIDS has had a devastating effect on gay men, as well as hemophiliacs, Haitians, and IV-drug users in France, the gay community today is more visible than it has ever been before. In 1977, France had its first gay pride parade. In 1988, there were one thousand marchers. In 1995, there were sixty thousand. Political goals such as the right to engage in legally sanctioned domestic partnerships have become popular causes alongside the fight against AIDS. Political and social groups for gay men and lesbians have proliferated throughout France, as have lesbian and gay community centers. Whether these developments represent the maturation of the gay liberation movement in France, the domestication of a once-revolutionary homosexuality, or a complicated hybrid of the two is subject to debate.   *Marc Schachter*

Bibliography

Courouve, Claude. *Vocabulaire de l'homosexualité masculine.* Paris: Payot, 1985.

Lever, Maurice. *Les Bûchers de Sodome: histoire des "infâmes."* Paris: Fayard, 1985.

Martel, Frédéric. *Le Rose et le noir: les homosexuels en France depuis 1968.* Paris: Éditions du Seuil, 1996.

Merrick, Jeffrey, and Bryant T. Ragan, eds. *Homosexuality in Modern France.* New York: Oxford University Press, 1996.

Mossuz-Lavau, Janine. *Les Lois de l'amour: les politiques de la sexualité en France de 1950 à nos jours.* Paris: Payot, 1991.

Poirier, Guy. *L'Homosexualité dans l'imaginaire de la Renaissance.* Paris: Champion, 1996.

Rey, Michel. "Parisian Homosexuals Create a Lifestyle, 1700–1750: The Police Archives." In *'Tis Nature's Fault: Unauthorized Sexuality during the Enlightenment.* Robert Purks MacCubbbin, ed. New York: Cambridge University Press, 1987.

Seel, Pierre. *I, Pierre Seel, Deported Homosexual: A Memoir of Nazi Terror.* New York: Basic Books, 1995; *Moi, Pierre Seel, déporté homosexuel.* Paris: Calmann-Levy, 1994.

Stambolian, George, and Elaine Marks, eds. *Homosexualities and French literature: Cultural Contexts, Critical Texts.* Ithaca, N.Y.: Cornell University Press, 1979.

See also AIDS Organizations; ACT UP; Code Napoleon; Henry III; French Literature

French, Jared Blandford (1905–1988)

Painter and photographer Jared Blandford French may rightfully be called the greatest American symbolist artist of the twentieth century. Although, because of his reticence, less well known, French was associated with some of the best-known gay artist figures of the 1930s and 1940s: artist George Tooker, patron Lincoln Kirstein, artist Paul Cadmus, photographer George Platt Lynes, writer Glenway Westcott, curator Monroe Wheeler.

In 1926, while at Amherst College, French met artist Paul Cadmus, who became a love interest and lifelong friend. In the thirties, after leaving a Wall Street job, French and Cadmus toured Europe. On his return to America, French began to produce murals for the Public Works of Art Project (PWA precursor), in the style of American scene artists like Reginald Marsh and Cadmus. French's 1937 marriage to artist Margaret Hoening marked the beginning of the 1937–1945 photographic collaboration of Paul Cadmus and Jared and Margaret: the PA-JAMA group. PAJAMA photographs featured its members and other prominent gay figures at Fire Island, Provincetown, Rome, and London. The Fire Island beach photographs in turn influenced French's painting subjects of the 1940s and 1950s.

In the 1940s French's easel painting is marked by a shift toward symbolism, akin to European surrealism and visually similar to the work of Belgian painter René Magritte. French's use of the egg tempera medium reflects an interest in the styles of quattrocento Italy, while his stoic figures owe a debt to ancient Greek sculpture and Egyptian wall painting. His carefully composed spatial geometries and occasional use of pointillism owe much to the work of French painter Georges Seurat and Renaissance painter Piero della Francesca. French produced a personal synthesis of symbolism and realism in images that place emotionally detached human figures in improbable or impossible physical environments. The result is a conceptually abstract art founded on the natural and the representative that produces a familiar yet eerily disconcerting experience.

The motivation of much of French's symbolism stems from the artist's familiarity with the writings of psychologist Carl Jung. Jung proposed that modern society's reliance on reason and science had resulted in a loss of the sensual and the spiritual. French's employment of timeless mythical and spiritual symbols echoes Jung's theory of an archetypal unconscious that reaches across both physical and temporal distances. Jung's theory that the reconciliation of this unconscious with the subject's ego would result in a more complete self helps explain the many dualities, binaries, and parallel compositions in French's painting.

In the 1960s French debuted a new imagery of weird, biomorphic shapes, predicting the organisms of alien life-forms ubiquitous in 1990s science fiction films, and recalling the experiments of late Japanese ukiyo-e prints. From within these amorphous shapes emerge barely discernible limbs, heads, and torsos like some genetics experiment gone awry. With this work French reached beyond his previous allegorical figures to their formative, primal essences; however, the dramatic shift in style was not appreciated by critics. French retired to Rome, in seclusion until his death.

Michael J. Murphy

Bibliography

Grimes, Nancy. *Jared French's Myths.* San Francisco: Pomegranate, 1993.

Morrin, Peter. "Pajama Game: The Photography Collection of Paul Cadmus." *Arts Magazine* 53 (December 1978): 118–19.

See also Cadmus, Paul; Jung, Carl; Kirstein, Lincoln; Lynes, George Platt

French, Jim (1946?–)

When the U.S. Supreme Court ended the ban on depictions of male frontal nudity in 1967, it was a disaster for homoerotica. The market was flooded with shots of every scrawny street kid willing to bare his all for a nickel bag. For the next few years, only a couple of photographers developed reputations for beautiful pictures of beautiful men who happened to be naked, most notably Roy Dean and Jim French.

With his then-partner, Lou Thomas (who went on to edit the FirstHand stable of publications and died of AIDS in 1989), French formed Target Studio, featuring his own work and that of others. Throughout the seventies, while the older physique studios were failing to adapt, Target flourished, eventually combining with several others into the conglomerate known today as Colt Studios.

As a photographer, French is amazingly versatile, shooting models who vary in type from sun-streaked preppy to tattooed biker, modulating his technique to suit. He is equally at home with formal studio setups and a variety of outdoor locations, particularly Hawaii's tropical glens and beaches. French works hard to make it look easy, but despite his incredible range and his avoidance of any artsy mannerisms that might make his work instantly identifiable, a French photograph usually gives itself away because of its impeccable craftsmanship.

By the late nineties, Roy Dean was a name known only to fans of vintage homoerotica, but Jim French had become the most successful homoerotic photographer of the last third of the century. And he did it the hard way—with talent.

F. Valentine Hooven III

Bibliography

French, Jim. *Man.* New York: Jim French, 1972.

Stanley, Wayne, ed. *The Complete Reprint of Physique Pictorial.* Cologne: Benedikt Taschen, 1997.

Waugh, Thomas. *Hard to Imagine.* New York: Columbia University Press, 1996.

See also Photography

French Literature

Before the Renaissance, the recorded instances of homosexuality in French literature are rather scarce. As Simon Gaunt has shown, allusions to a queer sexuality have to be made through a denial of Christian chastity, virtue, celibacy, or virginity, as if such topics could be evoked only through some silent, negative definition, whereas, the great sexual topic of the age, cuckoldry, could be directly evoked. In the *Vie de Saint Alexis*, Gaunt shows that Alexis refuses heterosexual coupling, fearing that "if he has sex, he will 'lose God.' " In the little-known hagiographic life of Ste. Euphrosine, Gaunt demonstrates that this saint's attempt to protect her virginity at all costs, pushing her even to cross-dressing, is a mechanism that queers the model and provides a homosexual subtext. This topos of cross-dressing, threatening to the stability of gender, appears both in the *Roman d'Énéas* and in the public imaginary of the "pucelle d'Orléans," Joan of Arc. The twelfth-century *Roman d'Énéas* has a striking passage in which Lavine has confessed her love for Énéas to her mother, who cannot brook the person in question and rants about the dubious morals of Énéas: "This hypocrite is of such a nature that he cares not a fig for women; he prefers the love of boys; he does not want to eat the meat of a female pigeon; he prefers male flesh; he would rather hold a boy in his arms than you or any other woman; he does not know how to make love to a woman; he would not speak at the little door; he likes young men's cherries too much. . . . You will never get anything from him, as I think, from a traitor, from a sodomite." The results will be dire if Lavine pursues her love: "The end of the world would soon come if all the men in it were like this in the entire universe . . . there would be no more children and the world would end before a hundred years were up." Thus sodomy is not only an individual peccadillo but something that can thwart the master plan for the survival of the human race. Two centuries later, the epicene figure of Joan of Arc becomes part of the French collective unconscious as the female warrior of God, dressed as a man, confounding gender and role in late medieval society. This figure will go on to inspire many writers including at least two twentieth-century authors, Jean Anouilh (*L'Alouette*) and Michel Tournier (*Gilles et Jean*). The latter associates Joan with her admirer, the infamous Gilles de Rais, whose trial and condemnation focused in part on his repeated acts of sodomy. Elsewhere in the Middle Ages, there are scattered references to homoeroti-

cism, including, as Byrne Fone points out, a poem by Peter Abelard, "David's lament for Jonathan," that invokes the homophilic friendship of the two biblical characters.

The Renaissance Through the Enlightenment

As Guy Poirier and Maurice Lever amply demonstrate, discourses on, or rather, against, homosexuality, sodomy, tranvestism, and other such vices abound in religious tracts, especially those dealing with the confessional, medical texts, and juridical documents, as these codes develop in the Renaissance. Such discourses continue as late as the eighteenth century and will be consolidated into the familiar medical and psychological treatises of the nineteenth century, as Michel Foucault shows in his *History of Sexuality*. As Poirier also shows, stories of sodomy are found in travel narratives and specifically those dealing with the discovery of the New World: Jean de Léry, André Thevet, and René de Laudonnière, among others, all invoke images of sodomites, transvestites, and other figures of that ilk.

In literature, the Renaissance brings us such figures as Étienne de la Boétie and his dearest friend, Michel de Montaigne. The latter, who would ever mourn the former's early death, writes an impassioned essay entitled "De l'Amitié," in which he finds their friendship superior to the love of women. If classic Greek pederasty is blamable for Montaigne because of the age difference, there is nothing better than the friendship between two real men. Indeed, it was only after La Boétie's death that Montaigne got married.

Joachim Du Bellay and Pierre de Ronsard criticize the practices of Henri II, who surrounded himself with favorites. Du Bellay contents himself with references to a "foreign vice" and "Ganymede." But Ronsard goes all out: "Eux [the favorites], pour avoir argent, lui prêtent tour à tour / Leurs fessiers rebondis, et endurent la brèche. / Ces culs, devenus cons, engouffrent plus de biens/que le gouffre de Scylle" [To get money, the favorites lend him their rounded butts and put up with the breach. / These assholes become cunts, engulf more goods than the gulf of Scylle]. In an apostrophe to the king in another sonnet, Ronsard exhorts him to "fuck mouths, assholes, cunts" and elsewhere; using the same compare-and-contrast strategy, Ronsard writes: "Assholes are now more open than cunts." Ronsard's satirical criticisms are not so much a criticism of debauchery or sodomy as a satiric attack on the king as

F head of state. References to lesbianism as such are uncommon in the Renaissance, but poet Pontus de Tyard does write an "Elegy for a lady in love with another lady." However, as Joan de Jean points out, allusions to sapphism in writers from Louise Labé on, including such diverse authors as Mlle de Scudéry and, much later, Germaine de Staël, in her famous novel, *Delphine*, are a means of staging "her accession to authorship through an identification with the original woman writer." In the middle of the seventeenth century, Madeleine de Scudéry was "known to her contemporaries as Sappho" (DeJean 96), and DeJean convincingly demonstrates the extent to which gynocentric female bonding is central in Mlle de Scudéry's *Femmes illustres*, dating from 1642.

While references to sapphism remain rare, there had already been a very overt inscription of the male body as the scene of sodomy twenty years earlier in the work of Théophile de Viau. One of the libertines of the 1620s, this poet was roundly accused of being a sodomite. In 1623, Beurdeley tells us, Viau, tried in absentia, was condemned to be burned at the stake. Viau's poetry follows the very matter-of-fact anatomical description found in Ronsard and Du Bellay's satirical verse on the favorites (*mignons*) of Henri III. In a plaint to Phyllis, Viau acknowledges that he got syphilis, and that if he survives, "je fais voeu désormais de ne foutre qu'un cul," or, as Michael Taylor translates, he vows, "I'll never fuck anything but ass."

If the depiction of homosexuality of all sorts culminated in the eighteenth century with the writing of the Marquis de Sade, his was not the only work that engaged the subject. Bryant Ragan points out a long list of pornographic texts, including works by Mirabeau, whom Ragan calls "the consummate pornographer-philosophe." In works like *Erotika Biblion* and *Hic-et-Haec*, Mirabeau engages homosexuality according to the specific physical activity: sodomy, sapphism, socratization (finger fucking). If in his own pornographic text, *Les Bijoux indiscrets*, Denis Diderot kept the world heterosexual, in his novel *La Religieuse*, he evokes a rather lubricious mother superior in a convent who has her sights set on the hapless heroine of the novel. Providing comfort and succor in listening to Suzanne's tales of mistreatment, the mother superior gets sexually aroused and leads Suzanne into exchanges of kisses and caresses. Somewhat critically, Voltaire used buggery and fascination with male buttocks in his satire *Candide*. Though Voltaire and the other

philosophes may have had personal revulsion to the act of sodomy, by and large, they preached tolerance. As Beurdeley notes, Voltaire says, in "The Price of Justice and Humanity," "When not accompanied by violence, sodomy should not fall under the sway of criminal law, for it does not violate the right of any man." Voltaire's position was ambiguous, to say the least. Using the expression "an infamous crime against nature," he still was known for his epigram, "Once a scientist, twice a sodomite," and wrote verse to his friend Frederick II, king of Prussia, in which he imagined the latter "beneath or on top of Nicomedes." Voltaire's position probably epitomizes the point at which a personal distaste (or, revulsion) for sodomy was outstripped by a belief in the less-than-sinful nature of such an act and a proactive belief in the rights of man, including the right to privacy. Somewhat ambiguously, yet quite evocatively, Diderot goes even further than Voltaire in his *Supplément au voyage de Bougainville,* which casts doubt, as Larivière remarks, on contemporary mores as being rather unnatural when compared with what the noble savages do.

Jean-Jacques Rousseau describes a personal experience with a homosexual proposition in his *Confessions*, as he finds himself the favorite of a Moor he meets in Turin. One day, the Moor, no longer able to control himself, let go and had an orgasm in front of Jean-Jacques, who, amazed, saw the man's seminal fluid shoot out and to the ground. It is of course in the works of the Marquis de Sade, including *Juliette*, *Justine*, and *Les 120 Jours,* that homosexuality becomes the watchword of the day. Generally the characters are initiated into sexual activities, with all orifices being indiscriminately used as receptacles by all manner of agent and device. After initiation, Sade's narrators argue in favor of unbridled freedom for homosexual and heterosexual activity. Indeed, Sade's characters' revulsion at the idea of procreation per se leads to the favoring of sodomy of all sorts. As the novels develop, simple orgies give way to complex geometric scenarios, male members become ever larger, and the level of violence increases until carnage, fornication, sodomy, and death all intermingle in a flow of desire and blood.

While various pamphlets accused Queen Marie-Antoinette of all sorts of sexual peccadilloes, and while the chevalier d'Eon was found one night stripped naked, supposedly after having lusted after a military man, the turning point for the representation of homosexuality probably came with the decriminalization of sodomy in the French legal code ushered in by Cambacérès. In the early decades of the nineteenth century, aside from the work of Germaine de Staël, male impotence and epicene characters were more prominent than depictions of homosexuality. It is really only with the development of realist narrative by Stendhal and especially Balzac that homosexuality comes once again to the fore.

The Nineteenth Century

Among the first authors to use the device of a recurring character, appearing in several works, Honoré de Balzac creates his most powerful character, Vautrin, who appears in *Le Père Goriot* [Old Goriot], and then reappears in *Illusions perdues* [Lost Illusions], *Splendeurs et misères des courtisanes* [Splendors and Miseries of Courtesans], as well as in an eponymous play. Paris's leading criminal who eventually becomes head of the secret police, Vautrin is also a homosexual. Balzac presents the character sympathetically in *Old Goriot* through various mechanisms, including an emblematic sign that legitimizes his domicile as a "Boarding House for Both Sexes and Others." Vautrin's arrest, which involves the beginnings of a rape scenario as Vautrin is slipped a narcotic and stripped, is not perceived as justice getting its due but rather as a betrayal. Escaped from the hands of justice and disguised as a minor order priest, Abbé Herrera, Vautrin befriends the hapless Lucien de Rubempré in *Lost Illusions* and tries to push him toward success, though Lucien will fail in the end and commit suicide. Vautrin's attitude toward Lucien is maternal and loving, and Balzac underlines the homoerotic attraction of the older to the younger man. While there is no blatant description of Lucien accepting a homophile relation with Vautrin, there is also no attempt to hide the matter. Elsewhere in *La Comédie humaine*, in works like "Sarrasine" and "La Fille aux yeux d'or" [The Girl with the Golden Eyes], Balzac is quite direct: in the former story, studied extensively by Roland Barthes in his epoch-making *S/Z*, the title character is in love with "La Zambinella," whom he thinks is a woman, but who is actually a castrato protected by a cardinal; in the latter, the title character, Paquita Valdès, again, loved by a man, is killed by her protectress and lover, the Marquise de San Réal. Balzac seems to conceive of homosexual relations in a classical way, with an inequality built into the relationship. Still, from a contemporary perspective, Balzac's development of

such material, and especially in the character of Vautrin, has a humanizing, inclusive effect.

The middle of the century brought experiments with sexual identity. Most notably, Théophile Gautier's important novel, *Mademoiselle de Maupin,* explored changing sexual identity as a reflection of social conditioning, of disguise and travesty, and of perception. With Gautier's work, one might say that the notion of the individual psychology that Balzac, for example, was developing in a character such as Vautrin was seconded by the beginnings of social construction: a woman/a man is she or he who is perceived to be a woman or a man. And behavior may follow that is more appropriate to the perceived individual than to the innate essential being. Walking around in men's clothes, George Sand therefore can be said to impersonate, if not incarnate, male homosexual desire with her lovers, Musset and Chopin. Gustave Flaubert, of course, during his trip to Egypt, bluntly writes of his personal homosexual experiences, a fact denied by Sartre in his monumental reading of Flaubert's life and works before the publication of *Madame Bovary.* Sartre does not believe him. No matter: with Frédéric and Deslauriers in *L'Éducation sentimentale,* where there are also notions of female homoeroticism relating to the characters of La Vatnaz and Rosanette and with the title characters in *Bouvard et Pécuchet,* Flaubert tests the waters of homophilic relationships between men who fail with women. In keeping with the nineteenth-century belief that anything can be described as long as it takes place in a trip to the "East," Flaubert mentions same-sex bonding among army buddies in his story of Carthage, *Salammbô.*

In her masterful article, "Lesbian Intertextuality," Elaine Marks provides a "Who's Who" of French lesbianism, both insofar as characters are concerned as well as the real-life literary figures themselves. Perhaps the greatest monument to an evolving lesbian sexuality can be found in Baudelaire's poems about "damned women," included in *Les Fleurs du mal.* As Dominique Fisher notes, Baudelaire at one point had intended to call the entire anthology *Les Lesbiennes.* In poems like "Lesbos" and "Femmes damnées," Baudelaire tries to create a lesbian poetics distant from the imprisoning leer of male heterosexual desire, even if such an attempt is doomed to fail. In fact, all destabilizing features of Baudelaire's verse aside, it is the constant—canonic—fetishizing of the female body that makes the description of lesbianism resistant to any self-generative poetics and any inscription of identity.

One version of lesbian poetics was given by Pierre Louÿs in his *Chansons de Bilitis* (1894) and *Aphrodite* (1896), but these works also seem to be primarily subjected to the male gaze. Twenty years earlier, in his exploration of the life of a family under the Second Empire, Émile Zola put lesbianism center stage in one of the best known of his works, *Nana* (1889). He had already written about lesbian loves between Suzanne Haffner and the Marquise d'Espanet in his earlier *La Curée* (1871). In Nana's sapphic scenes with Satin, we are called upon, with some mixture of fetishistic interest and voyeuristic desire, to examine the bodies of these two women. But cast in the circle of degeneration that marks these novels, Zola's vision of lesbianism remains a heterosexual male fantasy of two women. Later in his career, as Vernon Rosario explains so well, Zola was contacted by an individual proposing a naturalist writing and reading of *Memoirs of an Invert*. Zola never wrote his own version of that novel and kept the contact to an epistolary exchange. In Zola's wake, Joris-Karl Huysmans, somewhere between naturalism and decadence, alludes to homosexuality in the dissipative narrative *À Rebours*, whose main character, Jean Des Esseintes, like Proust's Baron de Charlus several decades later, was based in part on the "notorious" aesthete Robert de Montesquieu, author of the precious work *Les Hortensias bleus* (Blue Hydrangeas). Late in the nineteenth century, the decadents and their circle made homosexuality a common topic in works like Jean Lorrain's *Monsieur de Bougrelon* and *Le Vice Errant*, works by the mystic Sâr Péladan, and the novels of Rachilde in the early years of the twentieth century.

In a separate category are the loves, lives, and poetry of Paul Verlaine and Arthur Rimbaud. As an adolescent, the younger Rimbaud wrote to the older, married, and ultimately alcoholic Verlaine, and eventually they began a tempestuous relationship that reached its nadir with Verlaine's imprisonment after he shot Rimbaud. Verlaine wrote numerous poems detailing the glories of same-sex love, both in Sodom and in Gomorrah. Most remarkable are, in what Charles Minahen calls "erotic scriptings," poems that celebrate homosexual sex acts: "Car voici que ta belle gaule, / Jalouse aussi d'avoir son rôle, / Vite, vite gonfle, grandit, / Raidit ... Ciel! la goutte, la perle / Avant-courrière, vient briller / Au méat rose" (Your lovely staff also jealous to play its role, quickly swells, grows, stiffens. Heavens! The drop, the pearl, forerunner, comes to shine at the pink

meatus). Perhaps best known in its unrivaled celebration was the sonnet written by Verlaine and Rimbaud together, "Sonnet du trou du cul" (Sonnet of the Asshole), with its images of delicate flora, of a mouth coupled to its sucker, and with its famous last three lines, written by Rimbaud: "C'est l'olive pâmée et la flûte câline / C'est le tube où descend la céleste praline / Chanaan féminin dans les moiteurs éclos" (It is the olive that fainted and the playful flute / It is the tube where the celestial praline comes down / Feminine Canaan in open moistness).

Modernism

Significantly, the century itself seemed to bring a new change with the works of André Gide and, a few years later, those of Marcel Proust. Gide published his narrative *L'Immoraliste* in 1900; charged with a homoerotic atmosphere though devoid of explicit sexual encounters this work set the tone for the works to come. In later works such as *Si le Grain ne meurt*, Gide details his attraction to and love of North African adolescents, and in his masterful novel, *Les Faux-Monnayeurs*, Gide provides a complicated portrait of the epitome of the gay uncle, Édouard. As much as his fiction provided the confessional model for much early and mid-twentieth-century homosexual narratives, including works by authors as different as Marcel Jouhandeau (in works like *Tirésias*) and Jean-Paul Sartre, it is Gide's groundbreaking *Corydon* that may be his most important work. First published in a small privately printed edition then expanded and republished in the 1920s, *Corydon* is nothing less than a defense and illustration of homosexuality. If Gide rails against what he perceives—in an author like Proust—to be effeminate homosexuality, he makes strong arguments, grounded in the natural and the biological, for more manly, i.e., Greek, homosexuality. To many, *Corydon* seems quaint today, but it is one of the first reasoned arguments from an internationally known literary figure that engages the subject head-on.

Writing in the 1920s, René Crevel had the distinction of being surrealism's only openly gay writer, for Louis Aragon revealed and renewed his own homosexuality in his waning years after the death of his wife. The climate was not at all propitious for a gay man, for the surrealists' leader, André Breton, condemns male homosexuality vituperatively. Despite that hostility, Crevel stood up proudly and openly in this circle as a gay man, and in fiction and in fictional narratives about his own tempestuous relations with his lover Eugene Mac-Cown. Most notably, in works like *Mon Corps et moi* and *Babylone*, Crevel makes an impassioned appeal for true liberation that goes beyond the acceptance or the blind eyes of tolerance, as he calls for what amounts to a "de-heterosexualization" of memory itself.

The sprawling work of Marcel Proust (1871–1922), *À la Recherche du temps perdu*, translated poetically by Scott Moncrieff as *Remembrance of Things Past* but more correctly rendered as *In Search of Lost Time*, is a multi-stranded epic reading of Third Republic France, the development of the bourgeoisie, the increased remoteness of the aristocracy, and the aesthetic development of the narrator as an author in the making. Proust's novel is also a detailed study of the depiction of male and female homosexuality in various levels of society. For Proust, homosexuality is connected to the ambiguity of the modern world: the nameless "friend of Mlle Vinteuil," who is her lover, participates in an act of profanation of M. Vinteuil, the father, who is also a composer. Yet much later, it is that same nameless individual who helps decipher Vinteuil's greatest score, a septet left unpublished at the time of his death. Perhaps the best-remembered homosexual character is the Baron de Charlus, member of Proust's most aristocratic fictional family, the Guermantes. As we follow Charlus through the book, we see him early on as part of a false rumor of heterosexuality, wherein he is supposed to be the lover of Odette Swann, then later on, as the admirer of the narrator, still naive about Charlus's nature and intentions, and the participant in a chance encounter with Jupien, a tailor. This encounter, situated at the beginning of the volume entitled *Sodome et Gomorrhe* (Cities of the Plain), is also the locus at which Proust expatiates on the creatures of Sodom and Gomorrah. Many have seen this thirty-page disquisition as the quintessence of Proustian homophobia, but others have seen it as the poetics of a bringing to language that which had no language of its own. Later scenes involve Charlus's sponsoring of a young musician of whom he is fond and an incident in a gay brothel in which Charlus is whipped. In addition to this strand, which amounts to an episodic view of the life of one homosexual man, Proust presents situations in which various characters, among which his great friend (and Charlus's nephew) Saint-Loup, are revealed to have a hidden homosexual life. Proust's reading of Gomorrah as well includes numerous characters reputed to have had, or to be suspected of having, lesbian affairs and incurring thereby, at one point or another, the wrath, the interest, and especially the jealousy of some of the male protagonists.

Colette's *Claudine*, protagonist in several novels, evolves from a schoolgirl to a mature woman and has both male and female lovers during the course of her journey; she approaches both with a *naturalezza* second to none and is not afraid to mix stories of female homosexual love—the relations between Claudine and Aimée, for example—with those of male homosexual love—the stories about Claudine's stepson Marcel. And her work *Le Pur et l'impur* breaks new ground in its revealing discussions of lesbianism untainted by any moralizing tone and in its sympathetic discussions of real women and not just fictional creations. Jean Cocteau forms, with Gide and Proust, the third anchor in the development of the representation of male homosexual desire in modern French writing. In a series of works from the late twenties and early thirties, Cocteau provided textual and visual illustrations of homoeroticism, including films and drawings, as well as theater, novels, essays, poetry, and letters. Equally important for Cocteau was the famous anonymous book, *Le Livre blanc*, written during this same era; it depicts the narrator's loves and especially his unrequited love for the archetypal Coctelian fallen angel, Dargelos. Cocteau eventually illustrated an edition of this "anonymous" book, just as he would provide in later years illustrations for some of Jean Genet's work. But Cocteau's absent signature on *Le Livre blanc* remains the index pointing to its author.

Existentialism and After

During the modern era, Jean-Paul Sartre and Simone de Beauvoir, with their characteristic fervor and commitment, engaged the topic of homosexuality. In her most influential book, *The Second Sex*, Beauvoir engaged the subject of lesbianism head-on. If today much of that work seems somewhat old-fashioned in its approach, we must remember that Beauvoir's project necessarily had a double-indemnity clause built in: she was not only trying to argue about the normalization and acceptance of lesbian sex from a reasonably dispassionate point of view; she had to do so from within the discourses permitted by the patriarchy, by phallocentric discourses, and by a male-dominated world. Her life partner, Sartre, endlessly returned to the subject of

F homosexuality in his writings, whether in his philosophical tome, *L'Être et le néant* (Being and Nothingness), where he uses the "tolerance" and "acceptance" of homosexuality as an illustration of bad faith, or in his literary endeavors, including *La Nausée*, with its touching portrait of the self-taught man who is also a pedophile, *Huis-Clos*, with its portrait of the self-loathing lesbian Inès Serrano, condemned to Second Empire hell for all eternity, or *Les Chemins de la liberté*, where the ambiguous gay character Daniel Serrano has to choose between bad faith and engagement.

One of Sartre's most important projects was a series of literary biographies, and in his most influential, *Saint Genet, comédien et martyr*, he took up the case of writer Jean Genet, who had been condemned to prison for a series of crimes and who, while in prison, wrote works like *Notre Dame des fleurs*, *Miracle de la rose*, and *Querelle*, the last of which was turned into a film by German director Rainer Werner Fassbinder. Poetic, masturbatory flights of fancy, Genet's narratives are extraordinary solo recitals of homosexual desire, criminality, and betrayal in worlds untouched by the niceties of bourgeois manners or the propriety of middle-class rationalization and two-facedness. Genet's world has no room for such tolerance; it lives at the margins of a world where the center has been evacuated of its validity. In later works, such as the play *Les Bonnes*, Genet evokes more than a hint of lesbianism mixed with incest, but after his release from prison, he turned his attention to the political in a broader sense. Again, as the margins become the focus and as the Greek model is replaced by a more widely cast net, a writer like Raymond Queneau can, in *Zazie dans le métro*, introduce the idea of gender bending as the title character's uncle is portrayed as a *danseuse de charme*, a transvestite exotic dancer. And homosexuality makes an appearance in the languorous world of Francophone Egypt in the novels of an Egyptian writing in French, Albert Cossery (1913–), who has introduced episodes with homosexual content in works like *The House of Certain Death*.

Aside from Beauvoir's analysis of lesbianism, the subject fared less well in French writing of the mid-twentieth century, with the notable exceptions of Violette Leduc's work, including *La Bâtarde* and *Thérèse et Isabelle*, Françoise Mallet-Joris's lesbian love story, *Le Rempart des Béguines*, and that of Marguerite Yourcenar, known more as a writer who was a lesbian than as a writer who wrote on the subject of lesbianism. She did, however, produce a prose poem in 1936 entitled "Sappho ou le suicide," and (male) homosexuality is invoked in her *Mémoires d'Hadrien*. More recently, aside from Marguerite Duras's best-seller *L'Amant*, Monique Wittig has provided the single most important figure of lesbian poetics in her works, such as *Les Guérillères* (1969), written largely with the use of the pronoun *elles*, and marking a separatism that would be reinscribed in *Le Corps lesbien* (1973). Like René Crevel and Guy Hocquenghem, and like Adrienne Rich in her essay on compulsory heterosexuality, Wittig offers a radical critique of all that smacks of acceptance, tolerance, integration, and assimilation in her influential essay "The Straight Mind."

From Structuralism to the Age of AIDS

Two theorists, Michel Foucault and Roland Barthes, both of whom came to prominence during the 1960s, had a profound impact on the writing about contemporary homosexuality. Foucault's concept of an episteme in which discursive praxes formed the possibilities of what could and could not be enunciated was seminal in the formulation of the concept of social constructivism. In particular, in *The History of Sexuality*, Foucault talks about the invention of the homosexual as an individual during the nineteenth century, a being that goes beyond the simple act of sodomy. Author Hervé Guibert fictionalizes Foucault, who was also one of France's earliest prominent victims of AIDS, in the character of Muzil in the novelist's autobiographical fiction, *À l'Ami qui ne m'a pas sauvé la vie*. Guibert's Muzil is the voice of philosophical reason and skepticism, an openly gay man in his private life, yet his family had problems dealing with his sexuality even after his death. Much of Guibert's own production, both before and after his own diagnosis of AIDS, engages a frank, matter-of-fact approach to homosexuality. In works like *Les Chiens* and *Fou de Vincent*, as well as in his post-AIDS narrative *Le Protocole compassionnel*, Guibert sees homosexuality and AIDS as parts of human existence, neither to be blamed nor excused.

In his own autobiography, Roland Barthes invokes the Goddess "H," and one of her avatars is homosexuality. More openly, in the posthumously published work, *Incidents*, Barthes constructs a fragmentary narrative about travel in the so-called sotadic (or torrid) zone of North Africa. Delicately evoking sexual and sensual experiences, Barthes creates a text in which homosexual desire figures the play of the signifiers, to use an expression that Barthes himself would have employed. Barthes's influence on gay studies was also felt in his study of Balzac's story "Sarrasine," mentioned above, and in his influential introduction to Renaud Camus's narrative *Tricks.* Camus is one of the most important contemporary French writers engaging matters relating to homosexuality. In a series of novels, essays, and diaries, including *Journal romain, Chroniques achriennes, Buena Vista Park, Notes achriennes, Aguets, Vigiles,* and *P.A.,* among others, Camus, subtle observer of mores and manners, argues for the innocence of sex, the amorality of the sexual encounter, and the freedom essential to the effective living of one's life as a gay individual. Camus proposes strategies for deghettoizing homosexuality, neologisms for doing the same, including *achrien,* his word for homosexual, and a renewal of manners and etiquette to dedramatize, demystify, and reintegrate homosexual men and women into the fabric of society. Defying convention, Tony Duvert has written boldly about gay pedophilia in works like *L'Enfant au masculin* (1980) and *Un Anneau d'argent à l'oreille* (1982).

Taking his clues from the work of Foucault, Barthes, and Gilles Deleuze, among others, writer Guy Hocquenghem, first in *Le Désir homosexuel* and then in a series of novels and essays, including *La Beauté du métis, La Dérive homosexuelle,* and *Le Gai Voyage,* provided the motive force for the French gay liberation movement, and by that, for a liberation of writing itself. In an echo of earlier surrealist writer René Crevel, Hocquenghem seeks total liberation of the body and mind from heterosexual paradigms. Work like that of Yves Navarre, Dominique Fernandez, and others helped normalize the depiction of homosexuality during the last years before the onset of the AIDS epidemic. To date, however, the final militance has come with the inscription of that epidemic in writing. Hocquenghem's militance was echoed later in the work of Guibert, Thierry de Duve, and, perhaps most notably, Cyril Collard, whose book *Les Nuits fauves,* later turned into a movie directed by the author, was a serious examination of the ramifications of homosexuality and AIDS in an amoral world that had to accept the reality that liberated homosexuality was here to stay.

Lawrence R. Schehr

Bibliography

Barthes, Roland. *S/Z.* Paris: Seuil, 1970.

Berthier, Philippe. "Balzac du côté de Sodome." *L'Année balzacienne* (1979): 147–77.

Fisher, Dominique D., and Lawrence R. Schehr. *Articulations of Difference.* Stanford, Calif.: Stanford University Press, 1997.

Fone, Byrne R. S., ed. *Hidden Heritage: History and the Gay Imagination. An Anthology.* New York: Irvington, 1981.

Fradenburg, Louise, and Carla Freccero, eds. *Premodern Sexualities.* New York: Routledge, 1996.

Hocquenghem, Guy. *Le Désir homosexuel.* Paris: Éditions Universitaires, 1972.

Larivière, Michel. *Les Amours masculines: Anthologie de l'homosexualité dans la littérature.* Paris: Lieu Commun, 1984.

Lever, Maurice. *Les Bûchers de Sodome.* Paris: Fayard, 1985.

Lucey, Michael. *Gide's Bent.* New York: Oxford University Press, 1995.

Merrick, Jeffrey, and Bryant T. Ragan Jr., eds. *Homosexuality in Modern France.* New York: Oxford University Press, 1996.

Poirier, Guy. *L'Homosexualité dans l'imaginaire de la renaissance.* Paris: Honoré Champion, 1996.

Povert, Lionel. *Dictionnaire Gay.* Paris: Jacques Grancher, 1994.

Schehr, Lawrence R. *Alcibiades at the Door.* Stanford, Calif.: Stanford University Press, 1995.

———. *Parts of an Andrology.* Stanford, Calif.: Stanford University Press, 1997.

———. *The Shock of Men.* Stanford, Calif.: Stanford University Press, 1995.

Stambolian, George, and Elaine Marks, eds. *Homosexualities and French Literature: Cultural Contexts/Critical Texts.* Ithaca, N.Y.: Cornell University Press, 1979.

Stewart, William. *Cassell's Queer Companion: A Dictionary of Lesbian and Gay Life and Culture.* London: Cassell, 1995.

Sutherland, Alistair, and Patrick Anderson, eds. *Eros: An Anthology of Male Friendship.* New York: Citadel Press, 1963.

Waller, Margaret. *The Male Malady: Fictions of Impotence in the French Romantic Novel.* New Brunswick, N.J.: Rutgers University Press, 1993.

Young, Ian. *The Male Homosexual in Literature: A Bibliography.* 2d ed. Metuchen, N.J.: The Scarecrow Press, 1982.

See also AIDS Literature; Barthes, Roland; Cocteau, Jean; Crevel, René; Deleuze, Gilles; Essentialist-

Constructionist Debate; Fassbinder, Rainer Werner; Foucault, Michel; France; French Symbolism Friendship; Genet, Jean; Gide, André; Guibert, Hervé; Hocquenghem, Guy; Montaigne, Michel de; Montesquieu, Count Robert de; Proust, Marcel; Rimbaud, Arthur; Sade, Marquis de

French Symbolism

An aura of controversy surrounds the French symbolists. On the one hand, the symbolist period (1850–1920) has been described as a "golden age of French poetry" (Robert Cohn). On the other, it was a narcissistic distraction from reality or a disillusionment at the possibility that poetry can be directly apprehended by a "general public" (Henri Peyre). Disregarding personal taste, most concur that French symbolism, hermetic and ambitious in scope, produced some great poets, such as Charles Baudelaire, Arthur Rimbaud, Paul Verlaine, Stéphane Mallarmé, and Paul Valéry. What unites their disparate styles is curiously the use they made of poetry in their lives. Perhaps owing to a "disturbed childhood" (Charles Chadwick), except in Verlaine's case, each lost a parent at an early age. They precociously developed their imaginations to compensate for a lack of structure. Instead of retreating from the world, they wanted to bring to the world the psychic and spiritual resources of their dreamworld.

The modernist strain in symbolism grew out of a need to reject the realist assumptions that "art imitates reality" and a desire to validate the artist's visions in an "art for art's sake" poetics. Contrary to a commonly held assumption, this shift to a new poetics did not confine the poetic experience to the poem but expanded it to equate the axis of reception with that of the poem's creation. For this reason, Valéry, the last symbolist, viewed symbolist poetics as a "hesitation" between the field of writing and reading. Symbolism is difficult to define because the symbol, like irony, lacks a textual code and can only be contextually understood by the reader. As a "poetry of effects," inspired by Edgar Allan Poe, the symbolists chose to evoke, not to describe, the object of their poetic reflection. According to Mallarmé, "To name is to destroy the object; to suggest is to create."

In his sonnet "Correspondances," Baudelaire (1821–1867) fixed his theoretical aim on the concept that objects are symbols of ideal forms lying beneath reality. With the 1857 publication of his volume of poetry *Les Fleurs du mal* (The Flowers of Evil), Baudelaire was put on trial for endangering "public morals" in a number of his poems that were inspired by his interest in lesbians.

Rimbaud (1854–1891), adding to Baudelaire's mysticism, compared the poet to a seer whose Promethean mission was not just to discover the symbols beneath reality but to steal the sacred fire from God and illuminate the path for others. Verlaine (1844–1896) invited the sixteen-year-old poet to Paris in 1871, at which time the beginning of their physical intimacy coincided with a "poetic revolution" that changed the course of French poetry. They challenged the establishment with their "free verse" poems on modern themes. Rimbaud outstepped his senior in the art of versification, creating lines with an uneven number of syllables. Further, Rimbaud did not impose a strict number of lines for the same poem. In addition to technical innovation, he experimented with drugs and alcohol to achieve his famous "deregulation of the senses." His poetry from *Une Saison en enfer* (A Season in Hell) to *Illuminations* became increasingly hallucinatory. Their feverish lives brought Rimbaud to the brink of isolation in Abyssinia and Verlaine to insanity and prison after a murder attempt on the younger poet.

Verlaine made music an important definition of symbolism in his famous poem "Art poétique"; later, he coined the term *poète maudit* to describe Stéphane Mallarmé (1842–1898), whose verse is reputed to be the most difficult in the French language. Profoundly serious about the aims of poetry, Mallarmé was a painstaking craftsman. To create was to accept the impossible quest for the perfect form.

Valéry (1871–1945), Mallarmé's most brilliant disciple, is one of the most-quoted spokesmen of symbolist theory and a laborious practitioner. He produced such great works as "The Cemetery by the Sea" and "The Young Parque," along with a series of critical works. His symbolist rejection of reality led him to abandon his poetry during a twenty-year hiatus to conduct a private investigation into the nature of the mind and the function of poetry.

Symbolism was a nineteenth-century literary reaction against the arbitrariness and naïveté in the romantic dreamworld and against the cold, Parnassian idiom. Philosophically, it was a revolt against positivism and an attempt to establish a metaphysics with transcendental claims for literature. Its repercussions found adherents in America and Belgium whose contributions to symbolism include the dramatic works by Maurice Maeterlinck, poetry by André Fontainas, and novels by Joris-Karl Huysmans.

Robert Rhyne

Bibliography

Chadwick, Charles. *Symbolism*. Methuen: London, 1971.

Cohn, Robert Greer. *The Poetry of Rimbaud*. Princeton: Princeton University Press, 1973.

Peyre, Henri. *Qu'est-ce que le symbolisme?* Paris: Presses universitaires de France, 1974.

Wilson, Edmund. *Axel's Castle: A Study in the Imaginative Literature of 1870–1930*. New York: C. Scribner's Sons, 1931.

See also French Literature; Howard, Richard; Rimbaud, Arthur; Verlaine, Paul

Freud, Sigmund (1856–1939)

Something happened around 1890, something that John C. Fout has called "a 'new,' historically specific stage in the history of sexuality" (389). It is quite clear that our reading of what exactly happened around 1890 will be contingent in large measure on our assessment of Freud's "discovery" of the Oedipus complex, and thus of psychoanalysis, just at this time. The key to understanding the development of Freud's Oedipal model is the "invention of homosexuality," or rather, the "invention of heterosexuality" in his lifetime. Freud's original hysteria (or "seduction") theory was as much about men as about women, and he said as much openly. It is well known that what most aroused the ire of the Viennese medical audience that heard Freud's first lecture on his return from the French psychologist Jean-Martin Charcot was that it was about male hysteria. In his first model, Freud reconstructed (or invented) memories of child abuse not only for female patients but for boys as well—including his brother—as a means of accounting for his own male hysteria. Six of the eighteen cases mentioned in the paper on which the seduction theory is based, "The Aetiology of Hysteria" (1896), are cases of boys, not girls. In one of the most famous of his letters to his friend Wilhelm Fliess, Freud writes: "Unfortunately my own father was one of these perverts and is responsible for the hysteria of my brother (all of whose symptoms are identification) and those of several younger sisters" (Freud and Fliess 230–31; see also 264).

This theory implicated Freud himself quite directly, a point that enables us to propose an explanation for otherwise quite startling developments. Freud invented the Oedipus complex as a self-diagnosed male hysteric, a representation that further configured him as female and thus according to the "inversion" model then current as queer. This transpires clearly in his letter to Fliess of October 3, 1897, where he refers to "resolving my own hysteria" (Freud and Fliess 269). Freud's apparent renunciation of all sexual contact early in his forties takes on a new meaning in this light. He would not be the first married man not meant to be of the marrying kind, for whom celibacy ends up being the only psychologically tolerable solution. His famous fainting incident with Jung in 1912 was interpreted by Freud himself in a famous letter to his follower Jones as powerful evidence for continuing homoerotic desire on his own part. Interestingly enough, this diagnosis was current in the psychoanalytic establishment itself, albeit discreetly so. In 1951 James Strachey, Freud's English translator, wrote to Ernest Jones, "I was very much interested by your account of the suppressed passages in the Fliess letters. It is really a complete instance of *folie à deux*, with Freud in the unexpected role of hysterical partner to a paranoiac" (quoted in Masson 216). This is easily decoded as "with Freud in the unexpected role of female partner to a male," hysteria naming the characteristically female neurosis, while paranoia represents the characteristic male (homosexual) neurosis. This diagnosis in the correspondence was, moreover, explicitly associated both by Strachey and by Jones with Freud's "bisexuality," by which they, writing in the 1950s, meant not the theory of androgyny but precisely what we mean with this word, sexual desire for both male and female objects.

It is striking how many scholars and interpreters of Freud have recently been talking about the powerful homoerotic content in some of Freud's early writings, notably in his letters to Fliess, and in the text produced at about the same time, *The Interpretation of Dreams*. The association of homoerotic desire with the "feminized" men included in the category of hysterics was a commonplace of fin-de-siècle culture.

That the "seduction" theory disclosed Freud's own homoerotic inclinations becomes clear if we look more deeply into his understanding of the hysteria that the Oedipus model effaces and represses—the hysteria that Freud had diagnosed in himself.

F It should not be understood that the hysterogenic sexual event was necessarily homosexual. As it is eminently clear, in the cases of male hysteria including Freud's own there was often a female sexual abuser. Sprengnether writes of Freud's interpretation of an incident in which the Wolf Man's sister had played with his penis: "Freud's comment on this episode reveals the extent to which he associates it with the kind of sexual humiliation he had experienced at the hands of his own nannie. He characterized the Wolf Man's memory of this event as 'offensive to the patient's self-esteem,' and one that elicits a counterfantasy in which he takes the aggressive role" (72). It is the sexual passivity of the male that "feminizes" (and paradoxically homosexualizes), not the gender of the active subject. This transfer takes place within Freud's reading of the Wolf Man. The reality (or fantasy) of female sexual aggression directed at the boy is translated into a "feminine" desire directed at his father. Freud writes: "The boy had travelled, without considering the difference of sex, from his Nanya to his father" (*Standard Edition* XVII:46), the same journey that Freud took in his own psyche, from the nanny to the father, thus representing for us via the Wolf Man his own feminized and thus homosexual desire.

This interpretation receives strong support from a famous passage of *The Interpretation of Dreams*, in which Freud repeats a story that his father told him of having had his hat knocked off his head by a gentile who demanded that he get off the sidewalk. The boy Freud asked the father what he had done and received the reply that he had gone into the gutter and picked up the hat. The man Freud, reporting this incident, writes of his disappointment with this "unheroic conduct on the part of the big, strong man" (*Standard Edition* IV:197). In a brilliant interpretation, McGrath argues that the hat in the story would have been understood by Freud as a symbol for the phallus, so "the knocking off of his father's hat could have directly symbolized to him the emasculation of Jakob Freud" (McGrath 64; see *Standard Edition* V:361). Psychoanalytic historian Samuel Slipp has remarked that "Freud's early oedipal experience with a dominant mother and a passive father probably led him to the conclusion that male homosexuality was due to lack of resolution of the Oedipus complex and failure to identify with the father" (6). What seems to be missing from his account is the obvious logical conclusion to which it inexorably leads, namely, that Freud himself identified as "a homosexual." That is the only way that

Freud's experience could have "led him" to such a "conclusion."

Freud wrote to his friend Wilhelm Fliess: "I am looking forward to our congress as to the slaking of hunger and thirst. I bring nothing but two open ears and one temporal lobe lubricated for reception" (Freud and Fleiss 193). The various interpreters of Freud who have focused at the same time on the homoerotic content of Freud's early writings complement one another and together yield the possibility of a powerful hypothesis with regard to the question of the origins of the Oedipus complex. Freud was engaged in what can only be described as a highly erotic relationship with his friend. They exchanged the most intimate of letters and had "congresses." The next sentence of the letter quoted above includes a reference to "male and female menstruation in the same individual," that is, to the bisexuality theory. The association seems hardly coincidental.

Didier Anzieu makes the startlingly pungent observation that Freud's love letters to his fiancée, Martha, were "a kind of dress rehearsal for his later correspondence with Fliess" (Freud and Fliess 22), and indeed the tone of these two bodies of correspondence is remarkably alike. Freud had written to Martha, "The sweet girl . . . came towards me [and] strengthened the faith in my own value and gave me new hope and energy to work when I needed it most" (qtd. in Anzieu 22). Later he was to write to Fliess, "When I think of the many weeks when I felt uncertain about my life, my need to be with you increases greatly" (Freud and Fliess 89).

What is at stake in the suppression of the male hysteric and of the desire for the father in the shift to the Oedipal theory is the suppression of Freud's own homoeroticism. Freud was motivated in his relationships with men, and especially with Fliess, by acknowledged homoerotic desires, associated as they were at the time with both fantasies of "inversion" and of all-male procreation. To what extent these desires found physical satisfaction we will never know, although the possibility seems rather improbable. The Oedipus complex is an inexorably heterosexual, even heterosexist concept. It was gradually unfolding itself and its full heteronormative purport, moreover, approximately at the same time as the rift with Fliess was opening and then widening, finally resulting in what Freud later refers to as an overcoming of Fliess as well as an overcoming of "a bit of unruly homosexual investment" (Freud and Ferenczi 221). The friendship was largely over by August

1901, although it could plausibly be argued that at that point it was Fliess who was motivated by homosexual panic to separate from Freud and not the other way around. Freud still seems in this period to be affirming the value of homoeroticism; it is only in the next decade that he will finally claim to "overcome" it. The year 1910 is crucial—as crucial as 1897. In 1910, as we shall see, Freud was claiming (in letters to Ferenczi) that he had been recently "occupied with overcoming Fliess" (Freud and Fliess 221), that is, with repressing his own homoerotic desire. And in 1910 he was writing the classic study of male paranoia, "The Psychotic Dr. Schreber." An adequate explanation of these developments will, therefore, necessitate an understanding of how they are imbricated in each other.

According to Anzieu's reading, the invention of psychoanalysis was intimately connected with Freud's repudiation of his "homosexuality." Anzieu—like Schur and McGrath—understands this event, however, as a freeing of Freud from Fliess's pernicious influence so that he would be free to develop his own theories. The inexorability of this explanation is questionable. Once it is questioned, other possibilities arise almost of themselves. Freud explained his breakup with Breuer to Fliess: "If Breuer's masculine inclination were not so odd, so faint-hearted, so contradictory, as is everything emotional in him, he would be a beautiful example of the kinds of achievements to which the androphile current in men can be sublimated" (Freud and Fliess 447). What Freud is saying here, astonishingly, is that if Breuer had been more open and direct about his homoerotic nature, he would have been a worthier friend for Freud to hang on to. Can there be much doubt that a message is being sent to Fliess as well, just as Freud is acknowledging the unbridgeable rift between them (August 7, 1901)? Freud never quite got over his love for Fliess, even according to Jones. Why did Freud feel comfortable with (sublimated) homoeroticism early in the 1890s but later feel that he had to "overcome [repress]" it, "overcome" Fliess, and produce a theory in which repudiation of passivity—of femininity—is projected as the "bedrock" of the psyche?

The "official" view of the link between Freud's break with Fliess and his discovery of Oedipus is summed up by Schur: "He recognized that his patients' fantasies rather than early seductions were the most frequent etiological factor of their hysteria; he uncovered the ubiquitous role of infantile sexuality and especially the Oedipal conflict in normal and abnormal development. He now knew that he had

solved one of the great riddles of nature. With this conviction he also achieved an inner independence. Simultaneously the critical part of him reasserted itself in relation to Fliess" (Freud 139).

Freud indeed abandoned the seduction theory/trauma theory of hysteria (the fantasy of his own "seduction") at the same time he was beginning to separate from Fliess. In the letter that first announces Oedipus, there is already a strong—if indirect and ironic—indication of the skepticism about Fliess's theories that would eventually be one of the major causes of their break. Schur and McGrath both date the beginnings of the "collision course" to the fall of 1897. The final breakup was, of course, not until 1900. But during all this period, when Freud struggled with his growing ambivalence about Fliess and Fliess's theories and about his own theories of seduction and the Oedipal complex, what was constantly at stake was the tension between a theory of sexuality that would heterosexualize him via the repression of homoeroticism and a theory of sexuality that implicated him homoerotically and that was mapped over a heartfelt (if unconsummated) homoerotic relationship.

In short, not only was the new theory of psychoanalysis essentially an act of repression/overcoming, but the Oedipus model itself ought to be interpreted as a repression of homoerotic desire. The fundamental ideas of human sexual development in Freud are a sort of screen or supervalent thought for a deeper but very threatening psychic constituent that Freud had found in his own hysteria but that then panicked him: the desire for "femaleness," for passivity, to be the object of another man's desire, even to bear the child of another man. The analysand that Freud came to disbelieve was thus himself.

The real question underlying the invention of the heteronormatizing Oedipus model is: What was the source of this panic? The answer is that it was occasioned by a nexus of historical forces that included the pathologizing of the "homosexual," an appellation that had only recently become available, and the racialization of the Jews. Freud panicked at the discursive configuration imposed on him by three deeply intertwined cultural events: the racialization/gendering of anti-Semitism, the fin-de-siècle production of sexualities, including the "homosexual," and the sharp increase in contemporary Christian homophobic discourse (the "Christian Values" movement). These discourses produced a perfect and synergistic match between homophobia and anti-Semitism. By identifying himself as hyster-

F ical and as Fliess's eromenos (or "female" partner in a "Greek" relationship), Freud had been putting himself into the very categories that the anti-Semitic discourse of the nineteenth century would put him in: feminized, pathic, queer—Jewish.

In the second half of the 1890s, Freud realized (consciously or not) the deeply problematic implications of his position. Charcot had, of course, referred to the special propensity of Polish Jews to hysteria. An American Jewish doctor of the time wrote: "The Jewish population of [Warsaw] alone is almost exclusively the inexhaustible source for the supply of specimens of hysterical humanity, particularly the hysteria in the male, for all the clinics of Europe" (Fishberg, quoted in Gilman, "Image" 405). By focusing on hysteria, especially in light of his own self-diagnosed hysteria, Freud was fashioning a self-representation that collaborated with one of the most tenacious of anti-Semitic topoi—that Jews are a third sex: men who menstruate. The topos of the Jewish man as a sort of woman is a venerable one going back at least to the thirteenth century in Europe, where it was ubiquitously maintained that Jewish men menstruate.

The ideal Jewish male of eastern Europe was the pale, sedentary, studious Yeshiva bokhur (that is, a young man studying the Talmud), whose wife (and he did always end up with one) was ideally robust, energetic, and economically active. If, as Freud writes, after discovering the heteronormativizing power of Oedipus, the etiology of homosexuality is "masculine women, women with energetic traits of character, who were able to push the father out of his proper place" (*Standard Edition* XI:99), that is, it seems, exactly the sort of mother Freud had, as well as a father who had indeed been pushed out of his "proper place." More to the point, Galician Jewish culture in general had such mothers and fathers.

For the emancipated Jew this effeminization of Jewish men would have been transvalued into something negative and shameful, especially as two discourses were intensifying at the end of the century, the discourses of misogyny and homophobia. These two discourses are, moreover, profoundly related at this time, owing to the associations of male homosexuality with passivity, i.e., with femaleness, and hatred of femaleness was raised to a fever pitch such as it seems not to have known before just this time. Misogyny thus returns, in a much more complex guise, however, as a motive force in Freud's ideation.

The shift in Freud's thinking records the subjectivity of a person living and experiencing the invention of heterosexuality in his lifetime, and he invented himself as that new type of man, the heterosexual, by repressing his own homoerotic desire. "Heterosexuality," as its tenets have been ventriloquized by David Halperin, involves the strange idea that a "normal" man will never feel desire for another man.

Two particular events of the century's end may very well have been instrumental in focusing Freud's attention on the dangers that his own theories posed to him: the Oscar Wilde trials in 1895 and the discourse of and around Otto Weininger with his claim of an essentially female Jewishness. In 1902 and 1906 there were sensational "homosexual" scandals in Germany as well. Traditional Jewish male passivity—associated with queerness—would have become very problematic in such an environment.

There was even an anti-Semitic homoerotic movement in Germany, Hans Blüher's Bund, which promoted an ideal of the homosexual as supermanly, not degenerate and effeminate like the queer Jew. As Garber has written, "Here, too, definitions of 'homosexuality' cross with stereotypes of Jewish male identity, for the 'homosexual' could be either supermale, especially manly and virile, and therefore associating only with other men (rather than with polluting and 'effeminizing' women), or, on the other hand, a 'degenerate' 'aesthete,' blurring the boundaries of male and female" (227). Mosse notes that Benedikt Friedländer, a Jewish homosexual rights advocate, was careful to claim that all the "effeminate" homosexuals were in the other movement, that of Magnus Hirschfeld. Friedländer was associated as well with the most vicious of anti-Semitic racists. It would not be entirely wrong to suggest that it was passivity and effeminacy that were more problematic at this period than homoeroticism itself, i.e., homophobia is, at this time, almost subsumed under misogyny, to which anti-Semitism bears then a strong family connection as well.

Gilman has provided a vitally important piece of information by observing how thoroughly Jewishness was constructed as queer in fin-de-siècle Mitteleuropa: "Moses Julius Gutmann observes that 'all of the comments about the supposed stronger sexual drive among Jews have no basis in fact; most frequently they are sexual neurasthenics. Above all the number of Jewish homosexuals is extraordinarily high.' This view is echoed by Alexander Pilcz, Freud's colleague in the Department of Psychiatry at the University of Vienna, who noted that 'there is a relatively high incidence of homosexuality among the Jews'" (Gilman, "Sigmund" 59–60). The literary locus classicus for this association is, of course, Proust, for whom both

Jews and queers are the "accursed race." Both of these conditions constitute, for Proust, "incurable diseases" (Garber 226; Sedgwick). All the features that construct the figure of the homosexual construct the Jew as well, namely, hypersexuality, melancholia, and passivity. It was this factor and the hysterization of the Ostjude that led to the relative abandonment of hysteria together with its etiology in childhood seductions, that is, fantasies of seduction of the son by the father, and to the production of the inexorably heteronormative Oedipus narrative: "To say to a man 'You are hysterical' became under these conditions a form of saying to him 'You are not a man' " (Showalter, "Hysteria" 291). Since within this culture, male hysteria and homosexuality are both symptoms and products of gender inversion, there is a slip page between them: the Jew was queer and hysterical—and therefore not a man. In response, the normatively straight Jewish Man was invented to replace the bent Ostjude, and his hysteria—his alternative gendering—was the first victim: "All psychoanalytic theory was born from hysteria, but the mother died during the birth" (Etienne Trillat, quoted in Showalter, "Hysteria" 291). The Oedipus complex is Freud's family romance of escape from Jewish queerdom into Gentile, phallic heterosexuality.

With the shift in the discourse of sexuality in the 1890s, with homosexuality identified as a Jewish problem—not least via Magnus Hirschfeld's prominence, with the growing homophobia and anti-Semitism—indeed with the virtual identity of these two discourses—in the Christian Values movement documented by John Fout, Freud needed desperately to hide this dimension of his personality. As Fout has observed of one of the leading exponents of the "moral purity" (family values) movement in Germany, "Adolf Stoecker was a rabid anti-Semite, and many of the moral purity attacks on Hirschfeld were of a fundamentally anti-Semitic character—homosexuals were always depicted as outside the bounds of society." Freud had good reason to be scared: the persistent association of Jews with homosexuals and homosexuals with Jews was to turn not half a century later into the most murderous practice against both that the world has ever known. In 1928 a typical Nazi newspaper referred to the "indissoluble joining of Marxism, pederasty, and systematic Jewish contamination" (*Völkischer Beobachter*, qtd. in Moeller 400), and in 1930 Wilhelm Frick, soon to be minister of the interior of the Nazi government, called for the castration of homosexuals, "that Jewish pestilence" (Mosse 158). The Oedi-

pus complex, the fantasy of a masculinity rendered virile through both its moments, the desire for the mother (not the father) and violent hostility toward the father, provided Freud with the psychosocial/cultural cover for his dread.

The later association of Freud with homophobic discourse needs to be understood historically. American psychoanalysts, themselves homophobes, emphasized systematically those aspects of Freud's theories that could be made into a general homophobic psychology. The work of Freud himself suggests that he was anything but a homophobe.

Daniel Boyarin

Bibliography

Abelove, Henry. "Freud, Male Homosexuality, and the Americans." In *The Lesbian and Gay Studies Reader*. Henry Abelove, Michéle Aina Barale, and David M. Halperin, eds. New York: Routledge, 1993, 381–91.

Anzieu, Didier. *Freud's Self-Analysis*. P. Graham, trans. Preface by Masud R. Khan. Madison, Conn.: International Universities Press, 1986.

Biller, Peter. "Views of Jews from Paris around 1300: Christian or Scientific." *Studies in Church History* 29 (1992): 187–207.

Boyarin, Daniel. "The Colonial Drag: Zionism, Gender, and Colonial Mimicry." In *Dimensions of (So-Called) Postcolonial Studies*. Kalpna Seshadri-Crooks and Fawzia Alzal-Kahn, eds. Durham, N.C.: Duke University Press, 1998.

———. "What Does a Jew Want?: The Phallus as White Mask." *Discourse* 19.2 (1997): 21–52.

Brenkman, John. *Straight Male Modern: A Cultural Critique of Psychoanalysis*. New York: Routledge, 1993.

Dijkstra, Bram. *Idols of Perversity: Fantasies of Feminine Evil in Fin-de-Siècle Culture*. New York: Oxford University Press, 1986.

Ellenberger, Henri F. *The Discovery of the Unconscious: The History and Evolution of Dynamic Psychiatry*. New York: Basic Books, 1970.

Fout, John C. "Sexual Politics in Wilhelmine Germany: The Male Gender Crisis, Moral Purity, and Homophobia." *Journal of the History of Sexuality* 2.3 (1992): 388–421.

Freud, Sigmund, and Sándor Ferenczi. *The Correspondence of Sigmund Freud and Sándor Ferenczi: Vol. I. 1908–1914*. E. Brabant and P. Giampieri-Deutsch, eds. Ingeborg Meyer-Palmedo and Peter T. Hoffer, trans. Introduc-

F

tion by Andre Haynal. Cambridge: Harvard University Press, Belknap, 1993.

Garber, Marjorie. *Vested Interests: Cross-Dressing and Cultural Anxiety.* New York: Routledge, 1992.

Gilman, Sandor L. "The Image of the Hysteric." In *Hysteria beyond Freud.* Sandor L. Gilman, ed. Berkeley: University of California Press, 1993, 345–452.

———. "Sigmund Freud and the Sexologists: A Second Reading." In *Reading Freud's Reading.* Sandor L. Gilman, Jutta Birmele, Jay Geller, and Valerie D. Greenberg, eds. Literature and Psychoanalysis. New York: New York University Press, 1994, 47–76.

Halperin, David M. *One Hundred Years of Homosexuality and Other Essays on Greek Love.* New York: Routledge, 1990.

Heller, Peter. "A Quarrel over Bisexuality." In *The Turn of the Century: German Literature and Art, 1890–1915.* Gerald Chapple and Hans H. Schulte, eds. *Modern German Studies,* vol. 5. Bonn: Bouvier, 1981, 87–116.

Hertz, Neil. "Dora's Secrets, Freud's Techniques." *Diacritics* 13 (1983): 65–76.

Jones, Ernest. "The Young Freud." In *The Life and Work of Sigmund Freud.* New York: Basic Books, 1953.

Major, Rene. "Revolution of Hysteria." *International Journal of Psychoanalysis,* 55 (1974).

Masson, Jeffrey Moussaieff. *The Assault on Truth: Freud's Suppression of the Seduction Theory.* Harmmondsworth, England: Penguin, 1985.

Masson, Jeffrey Moussaieff, ed. and trans. *The Complete Letters of Sigmund Freud to Wilhelm Fliess, 1887–1904.* Cambridge, Mass.: Harvard University Press, 1985.

McGrath, William J. *Freud's Discovery of Psychoanalysis: The Politics of Hysteria.* Ithaca, N.Y.: Cornell University Press, 1986.

Moeller, Robert G. "The Homosexual Man Is a 'Man,' the Homosexual Woman Is a 'Woman,' "Sex, Society, and the Law in Postwar West Germany." *Journal of the History of Sexuality* 4.3 (1994): 395–429.

Mosse, George L. *Nationalism and Sexuality: Middle-Class Morality and Sexual Norms in Modern Europe.* Madison: University of Wisconsin Press, 1985.

Ramas, Maria. "Freud's Dora, Dora's Hysteria: The Negation of a Woman's Rebellion." *Feminist Studies* 6.3 (1980): 472–510.

Robinson, Paul. *Freud and His Critics.* Berkeley: University of California Press, 1993.

Schur, Max. *Freud Living and Dying.* New York: International Universities Press, 1972.

Sedgwick, Eve Kosofsky. *Epistemology of the Closet.* Berkeley: University of California Press, 1990.

Senelick, Laurence. "The Homosexual as Villain and Victim in Fin-de-Siècle Drama." *Journal of the History of Sexuality* 4.2 (1993): 201–29.

Showalter, Elaine. "Hysteria, Feminism, and Gender." In *Hysteria beyond Freud.* Sandor L. Gilman, ed. Berkeley: University of California Press, 1993, 286–344.

———. *Sexual Anarchy: Gender and Culture at the Fin de Siècle.* New York: Penguin Books, 1990.

Slipp, Samuel. *The Freudian Mystique: Freud, Women, and Feminism.* New York: New York University Press, 1993.

Sprengnether, Madelon. *The Spectral Mother: Freud, Feminism, and Psychoanalysis.* Ithaca, N.Y.: Cornell University Press, 1990.

See also Germany Psychiatry and Homosexuality; Psychological and Psychoanalytic Perspectives on Homosexuality; Judaism; Psychotherapy; Sexology

Friendship

Images of friendship in Western history and literature typically have been male-dominated (such as Damon and Pythias or Jonathan and David). For centuries, men's bravery, loyalty, and heroism were celebrated as signs of the ideal form of friendship. Women were often viewed and belittled as not capable of "true" friendship—of having friendships that were a pale imitation of men's. French philosopher Michel de Montaigne, for example, wrote in his sixteenth-century essay "Of Friendship" that women's capacity and soul were neither adequate nor firm enough for the sacred bond of friendship. Yet he described male friendship as souls mingling and blending "with each other so completely that they efface the seam that joined them."

By the mid- to late-nineteenth century, however, both women's and men's friendships in America were described in romantic terms. Research by Carroll Smith-Rosenberg and Lillian Faderman discovered romantic friendships between women, and Anthony Rotundo and Karen Hansen uncovered similar examples of men's romantic friendships with each other. These friendships could be erotic but not necessarily sexual; a certain degree of affectionate desire was allowed. However, as same-gender sexual relationships started to be defined in pathological terms by the end of the nineteenth century, labels of perversion (as well as the newly created medical word "homosexual") were applied to same-gender romantic friendships. Romantic friendships, especially for men, soon ended or became hidden. True friendship, in the early twentieth century would be seen as something women were more capable of experiencing. Continuing into the contemporary era, the ideal form of friendship is usually described with more "female" language: intimacy, trust, caring, disclosing, and nurturing. The poems of Sappho and the biblical story of Ruth and Naomi have been praised as classic exemplars of the depth of women's friendships.

Most academic research on friendship has perpetuated the idea that men, as a category, have friendships based on instrumental, "side-by-side" interactions, while women's friendships are expressive and "face-to-face." Men tend to describe their friendships in terms of doing activities, and women emphasize talking about feelings and disclosing personal information. But these categorical differences have begun to be refuted as studies emerge uncovering the diversity within categories of gender linked to other characteristics such as race, class, and sexual orientation.

For many gay men and lesbians, friendships are inextricably part of the narrative histories and coming-out stories. Friends are often described in terms of family and intimacy—ways that are not as deeply expressed especially by heterosexual men. In the face of opposition by the larger culture and sometimes by family of origin, many gay men and lesbians imbue their friendships with more intense meanings and weave them into alternative kinship structures. Gay and lesbian friendships, as a result, can have salient political, social, psychological, and even language implications. Lesbians and gay men, for example, have signaled recognition of each other with code phrases and songs that use family and friendship terminology: "Are you a member of the family?," "He's a friend of Dorothy," "We are Family," and other kinship expressions ("daddy," "sisters," or "auntie").

Friendships take on political power as they challenge the constraints imposed by American culture's social institutions of family, marriage, and sexuality. Organizing friendship networks and alternative kinship structures more openly—and in ways that uncover the arbitrariness of many of our social norms—is unquestionably a politically empowering act. Friendships can become political movements when they provide the power and identity that are often minimalized in lesbians' and gay men's lives by the dominant culture. They become the mechanisms for learning about gay and lesbian identity and cultures, for entering gay and lesbian communities, for organizing into resistance groups, and for maintaining personal identities within an otherwise nonsupportive social environment.

Gay and lesbian friendships also raise questions about the complex ways people structure their lives in terms of sexual attraction, intimacy, and gender roles. The stories people relate about making friends are similar to the kinds of stories people often tell about meeting their lovers—and not just among those whose friends are their ex-lovers. The intensity of first meetings, the emotional connections, the sharing of feelings and personal fears, and the physical attractions are all components of the "how we became friends" stories, just as they are parts of the "how I met my lover" narratives. Attraction and sexuality are inextricably linked to friendship formation among lesbians and gay men in ways that do not typically play out among same-sex heterosexual friendships.

In two studies of gay friendship, gay men and lesbians were asked to describe one *best* friend (not a casual or close friend) who was not a current lover. The combined results showed that around 78 percent of the gay men and 72 percent of the lesbians responded that their best friend was of the same gender and sexual orientation as themselves; almost 4 percent of gay men reported having a best friend who is a lesbian and around 5 percent of lesbians claim a gay male best friend. Nearly 18 percent of the gay men and 23 percent of the lesbians described their best friend as heterosexual or bisexual (in the case of lesbians, mostly women; for the gay men, about evenly split between men and women).

For the approximately three-fourths of the respondents whose best friend was of the same gender and sexual orientation, lesbians were twice as likely as gay men (34 percent versus 17 percent) to report that their best friend was an ex-lover. Almost 56 percent of the gay men and 48 percent of the lesbians said they had been sexually involved with their best friend in the past, but twice as many gay men as lesbians (63 percent versus 34 percent) responded that they had ever had sex with their casual friends. The

F numbers were higher when they were asked whether they had ever been sexually attracted to their best friend.

These findings raise provocative questions, often untapped in friendship research, that need to be addressed more explicitly. If attraction and sexuality are elements of friendships—something that has yet to be studied in any depth, particularly among heterosexual same-gender friendships or in straight-gay friendships—what are the political, social, and psychological implications? What is the role of attraction in friendships when that attraction goes against societal constraints? Do heterosexual men who bond with each other in some powerful way (such as the recurrent stories one hears about wartime friendships or sees in numerous male buddy movies) also feel erotic attraction? Are they holding sexual feelings in abeyance? What does it mean, for example, when a lesbian is close friends with a heterosexual man or a gay man? Does this challenge one's sexual orientation identity in such a way that it becomes necessary to deny that friendship or not even look for one?

In other words, one cannot come away from reading the research and personal stories about gay and lesbian friendships without being challenged to reconstruct the ways we think about all kinds of friendship, to organize our social institutions, and to understand the meaning of gender and sexuality in contemporary American society. And as important, we cannot help but radically rethink how we conceptualize our own personal stories of love and friendship in a social world that often places barriers and creates resistance to alternative ways of living. Such is the personal and political importance of lesbian and gay friendships. By looking closely at the way gay men and lesbians organize their friendships into alternative forms of families and communities, we come to understand more about the culture's constructions of gender, heterosexuality, and sexuality.

Peter M. Nardi

Bibliography

Faderman, Lillian. *Surpassing the Love of Men: Romantic Friendship and Love Between Women from the Renaissance to the Present*. New York: Morrow, 1981.

Hansen, Karen. " 'Our Eyes Behold Each Other': Masculinity and Intimate Friendship in Antebellum New England." In *Men's Friendships*. Peter Nardi, ed. Newbury Park, Calif.: Sage, 1992, 35–58.

Nardi, Peter M. "Sex, Friendship, and Gender Roles Among Gay Men." In *Men's Friendships*. Newbury Park, Calif.: Sage, 1992, 173–85.

———. "That's What Friends Are For: Friends as Family in the Gay and Lesbian Community." In *Modern Homosexualities: Fragments of Lesbian and Gay Experience*. Ken Plummer, ed. London: Routledge, 1992, 108–20.

Nardi, Peter M., and Drury Sherrod. "Friendship Survey: The Results." *Out/Look* 2, no. 4 (1990): 86.

———. "Friendship in the Lives of Gay Men and Lesbians." *Journal of Social and Personal Relationships* 11 (1994): 185–99.

Rotundo, E. Anthony. *American Manhood: Transformations in Masculinity from the Revolution to the Modern Era*. New York: Basic Books, 1993.

Rubin, Lillian. *Just Friends: The Role of Friendship in Our Lives*. New York: Harper and Row, 1985.

Smith-Rosenberg, Carroll. "The Female World of Love and Ritual: Relations between Women in Nineteenth-Century America." *Signs* 1 (1975): 1–29.

Weinstock, Jacqueline, and Esther Rothblum. *Lesbian Friendships for Ourselves and Each Other*. New York: New York University Press, 1996.

Weston, Kath. *Families We Choose*. New York: Columbia University Press, 1991.

See also Couples; Masculinity; Montaigne, Michel de; Same-Sex Marriage

G

Galen of Pergamon (c.130–c.200 C.E.)

Galen was an influential physician and medical writer under the Roman Empire. A critical systematizer of the work of his predecessors, Galen produced an enormous body of writings on most medical topics, theoretical and practical. Translations of parts of his corpus became a principal source for medieval Arabic and then medieval Latin medicine, carrying forward his authority for more than a millennium. There is no focused presentation of same-sex desire or activity in Galen; he tends to regard it as one variety of erotic life. He mentions it in passing when discussing the physiological effects of intercourse or in giving therapeutic instructions. Galen does have a doctrine about the gradation of sex differences between men and women. The various mixtures of male and female seed, together with the placement of these seeds in the uterus, will produce persons along a scale of combinations of male and female characteristics and sexual desires. Among these will be effeminate men and masculine ones. But Galen does not insist, with his near predecessor Soranus, that clitoridectomy should be performed to correct the "pathology" of masculine women. Nor does Galen insist (as Soranus does) that a man can desire to be penetrated by another man only if he is suffering from a pathological condition.

Mark D. Jordan

Bibliography

Brooten, Bernadette J. *Love Between Women: Early Christian Responses to Female Homoeroticism.* Chicago: University of Chicago Press, 1996, chap. 5.

See also Rome, Ancient; Scientific Approaches to Homosexuality

Ganymede

Ganymede was a beautiful young boy, son of the king of Troy, whom Zeus loved; he was carried off to Olympus by an eagle (in some versions, the metamorphosed Zeus himself) and served as cupbearer to the gods. Along with Orpheus, Ganymede forms the mythological grounding in the Greek and Roman tradition for the practice of love between mature men and young boys; and one Latin form of the name became the now largely obsolete term *catamite*, referring to the passive partner in a pederastic act. (He also came to be identified with the zodiacal sign Aquarius.) In the earliest references to the story (Homer, *Iliad* 20.231–35), there is no mention of a sexual relationship. But by Plato's time the myth is proverbial for its connection to man-boy love, whether viewed as an abomination (*Laws* 1.636d) or as the highest form of spirituality (*Phaedrus* 255c).

The principal sources for the enormous diffusion of Ganymede in postclassical literature and art are, as with so many other mythological tales, Virgil and Ovid, both of whom recount the story in a positive tone. In Virgil's *Aeneid*, the myth is narrated very beautifully as it is said to be stitched in gold on a cloak awarded to the winner of epic games (5.250–57), though the opening lines of the poem allude obliquely to the boy's abduction as a cause of the Trojan War. Ovid in the *Metamorphoses* declares that in Ganymede the king of the gods finally found "something he would prefer to be rather than the thing he was" (10.155–161).

Through the Middle Ages and the Renaissance the story is narrated, depicted, and interpreted widely. Ganymede becomes a hero within a subculture of same-sex erotic practice in the High Middle

G

Correggio's "Rape of Ganymede." Vienna, Kunsthistorisches Museum. Foto Marburg/Art Resource, NY.

in a series of Jupiter's Loves, appear to have less direct autobiographical significance.

In the arts of more recent times, Ganymede retains his exemplary status as the figure of both spiritual rapture and erotic excitement. Goethe's lyric poem "Ganymed," which sets the experience as a dramatic monologue of Sturm und Drang ecstasy, was set to passionate music by Schubert as well as Hugo Wolf and many others. Danish sculptor Bertel Thorwaldsen (1770–1844) created many marble versions of the boy. In the twentieth century, notable versions of the myth have been created by poets W. H. Auden, William Rose Bent, and William Plomer, as well as by artists Jean Arp, Giorgio de Chirico, and Robert Rauschenberg.

Leonard Barkan

Bibliography

Barkan, Leonard. *Transuming Passion: Ganymede and the Erotics of Humanism.* Stanford, Calif.: Stanford University Press, 1991.

Boswell, James. *Christianity, Social Tolerance, and Homosexuality.* Chicago: University of Chicago Press, 1980.

Reid, Jane Davidson. *The Oxford Guide to Classical Mythology in the Arts.* New York: Oxford University Press, 1993.

Saslow, James. *Ganymede in the Renaissance.* New Haven: Yale University Press, 1986.

See also Auden, W. H.; Goethe, Johannes Wolfgang von; Greece, Ancient; Plato; Rome, Ancient; Schubert, Franz Peter

García Lorca, Federico (1898–1936)

Spanish poet and playwright Federico García Lorca was born into a prosperous Andalusian family. His joyful attitude, passion, and enormous charm made him the center of the group. He was taken prisoner and murdered by anti-Republican rebels at the beginning of the Spanish Civil War and has since become the most translated Spanish author in history, surpassing even Cervantes.

When he was eleven, his family moved to Granada, where, at the age of sixteen, he became part of the Club de Arte de Granada, an informal, bohemian group with several gay members, and within which homosexuality did not have to be hidden. When he was about twenty-one, Lorca acquired a first edition of the new Spanish translation of Oscar Wilde's *De Profundis.* He also read Verlaine, and by this time he had begun to think of himself as bisexual.

Ages as well as an exemplum of sublime rapture to a Renaissance Neoplatonism that often hedged between an abstract ideal of male love and practices that individuals wished to conceal or reinterpret in a nonsexual vein.

Among the major artistic expressions of the story, some are explicitly connected to the erotic lives of the artists, including Michelangelo's drawings of Ganymede made for his beloved Tommaso Cavalieri, Benvenuto Cellini's two statues of the boy, and various references in the work of Christopher Marlowe (e.g., *Hero and Leander*, 1.141–150, 2.153–225). Other versions, including Dante's Ganymede dream in the *Purgatorio* (9. 16–33) and Correggio's painting

From the time of his first acquaintance with Salvadore Dalí (1923), Lorca was fascinated by the eighteen-year-old's beauty, personality, and talent. Dalí responded to Lorca's charisma and genius, and an intense but short-lived relationship developed. In 1925, Lorca met eighteen-year-old Emilio Aladrén, a promising sculptor whom Lorca's friends disliked, and they became lovers in 1927. That same year, Lorca met gay poets Vicente Aleixandre and Luís Cernuda, later his great friends. Lorca admired Cernuda's courage in writing openly about his sexuality in reactionary Spain. Soon, Aladrén, the great love of Lorca's life, threw the poet into a serious depression by beginning an affair with a woman he later married.

Lorca, at his friends' suggestion, tried to recover by going to New York City in 1929, where he studied English at Columbia University and began writing *Poeta in Nueva York* (Poet in New York, 1940). At a party, he met Hart Crane, with whom he shared an intense interest in sailors. (Like Jean Cocteau, Lorca illustrated some of his poems with his own drawings of mariners.) After nearly a year, he went to Cuba briefly, and then returned to Spain. In Havana, he began *El Público* (The Public, 1930), the first Spanish play to explore the theme of male homosexuality, even containing clear allusions to sadomasochism. The central figure, Gonzalo, denounces the duplicity that prevents people from living in accord with their own sexuality. Two days at sea from Cuba to Spain, he began his "Oda a Walt Whitman" (Ode to Walt Whitman, 1934), privately published in Mexico four years later. The poem idealizes Whitman and criticizes "effeminate" gay men who "corrupt" others. Lorca's use of the pejorative *marica* (gay man) and his evocation of homosexuals in figures of rats, mud, and sewers suggest that he is decrying in others what he fears in himself.

In 1933, Lorca fell in love with twenty-year-old Rafael Rodríguez Rapún, the new secretary of La Barraca, a theater group, headed by Lorca, that toured rural Spain presenting classic Spanish theater. Though straight, Rodríguez Rapún succumbed to the poet's magical personality. Two years later, the relationship gone bad, Lorca expressed his unhappiness in "El soneto de la carta" (The Sonnet of the Letter) and "El poeta dice la verdad" (The Poet Tells the Truth), two of the *Sonetos del Amor Oscuro* (Sonnets of Dark Love). Like Lorca, Rodríguez Rapún died at the hands of the fascists early in the Spanish Civil War.

An unpublished gay-themed work now lost is one completed act of *La destrucción de Sodoma* (The Destruction of Sodom), intended to round out a trilogy together with the very succesful dramas *Bogas de sangre* (Blood Wedding, 1932) and *Yerma* (1934).

Juan M. Godoy
Bruce Vermazen, trans.

Bibliography

Gibson, Ian. *Federico García Lorca: A Life.* New York: Pantheon Books, 1987.

Sahuquillo, Angel. *Federico García Lorca y la cultura de la homosexualidad.* Alicante, Spain: Instituto de Cultura "Juan Gil-Albert," 1991.

Walsh, John K. "The Social and Sexual Geography of *Poeta en Nueva York.* In *"Cuando yo me muera . . .": Essays in Memory of Federico García Lorca.* Lanham, Md.: University Press of America, 1988.

See also Cernuda, Luis; Spain; Spanish Literature

García Marquez, Gabriel (1928–)

In the second half of the twentieth century, and because of the country's undeclared civil war (1948–1965), Colombian narrative as well as theater began to respond to public events by means of a series of exceptional literary works that were internationally recognized. García Marquez's influence in Latin American narrative and film is enormous. His faith in the Cuban revolution promoted and goes on promoting a controversial debate within the Latin American intelligentsia.

In his early works García Marquez, using a Faulknerian model, placed his plots and characters in a mythical city called Macondo. His most famous novel, *Cian años de soledad* (One Hundred Years of Solitude, 1967), is the culmination of a long process of dealing with that imaginary city, characters, and situations, focusing on the civil war, the sociopolitical effects of modernization, and the massacre of workers in the exploitative banana industry.

Cien años is a fantastic metaphor of Latin America from the colonial period to the present. Even though *Cien años*, like García Marquez's other novels and short stories, invokes many cultural analyses, little attention has been paid to sexual dissidence and its political consequences in his text.

The genealogy of the Buendía family and the final incest in which they are involved captivated critics who emphasized the system of reproduction (in content as well as in form) and the main characters' presence and deeds. But in doing this, the theoretical

G

perspectives seem to echo endlessly the novel instead of exploring what falls beyond the heterosexual compulsion of both the surface of the novel and their own theoretical preconceptions. In fact, the reading of textual surface and the critical obsession for absorbing the whole novel into a totalitarian narrative logic opposes, in a fascist way, the excess implicit in the exultant foundation of Macondo and its decadent end as a failure of the national decency discursive apparatus. On the contrary, the reading of various textual details, especially on the topic of nonreproductive sexuality, would allow one to speculate on other cultural and historical perspectives that the novel envisions. In these terms, the novel represents not a utopia but all that is repressed by the patriarchy and the nation, promptly and paradoxically dislocated and simultaneously liberated by modernity. In no small way the omniscience of the narrator supports and encourages the totalitarian perspective by means of which the story (the history) is told.

Despite the cancellation of the marginal voices, it is still possible to read how an alternative cultural and political project could emerge. It is worth noting that Macondo is the result of the incest and the homosexual panic linked to the crime. Even if the reader decides to focus on the main characters and the lineal plot, the repercussions of this event will reappear in many situations and will affect many characters when they are read, avoiding the essentialist viewpoint and fostering the subject-position examination. In *Cien años*, as in many other works by García Marquez, it is possible to hear, under a sort of heterosexual simulacrum or semblance, both the (un)veiled homoerotic sexuality's voice and many narrative fascinations with the (white) exuberant male body. In fact, this also occurs in the homoerotic plot of *Crónica de una muerte anunciada* (Chronicle of a Death Foretold, 1981) and in the multiple changes and transformations of binary sexual (op)positions in *El amor en los tiempos del cólera* (Love in the Time of Cholera, 1985).

Gustavo Geirola

Bibliography

Bell-Villada, Gene H. "Banana Strike and Military Massacre: One Hundred Years of Solitude and What Happened in 1928." In *From Dante to Garcia Marquez.* Gene H. Bell-Villada and Antonio Gimenez, eds. Williamstown: Williams College, 1987, 391–403.

Jaramillo Zuluaga, J. Eduardo. "Desire and Decorum in the Twentieth-Century Colombian Novel." In *Bodies and Biases: Sexualities in Hispanic Cultures and Literatures.* David W. Foster and Roberto Reis, eds. *Hispanic Issues,* vol. 13. Minneapolis: University of Minnesota Press, 1996, 37–78.

Ludmer, Josefina. *Cien años de soledad: una interpretacion.* Buenos Aires: Ediciones Tiempo Contemporaneo, 1972.

See also Argentina; Brazil; Cuban Writing in Exile; Mexico

Gay

This word has largely replaced *homosexual* as the preferred term both for declaring oneself attracted to members of the same sex and designating others as so inclined. *Gay* can be used when talking of either men or women, although some women, justifiably feeling that *gay* too often becomes synonymous with *male* to the point of excluding, or at least obscuring, any sense of women, prefer the term *lesbian.* Hence the frequent coupling of *gay* and *lesbian.* In the 1960s and 1970s, *gay* supplanted the earlier *homosexual,* deemed by many activists to be too clinical, retaining the taint of the pathological, coming as it did from the scientific/medical discourses of psychology and sex research. In contradistinction to *homosexual, gay* was thought to express the growing political consciousness of the gay liberation movement and soon suggested an entire lifestyle.

The word *gay* derives from the French *gai* (merry, exhilarating), the use of which may be traced back to the twelfth century, with some linguists suggesting a link to the Old High German *wahi* (pretty). The word's English usage initially referred to a person's actions or character—lighthearted, exuberantly cheerful, and merry. However, by the seventeenth century the word had developed an additional sense, referring to an addiction to sensual pleasures, or one of loose or immoral life, as in the expressions "gay dog" or "gay Lothario." Used to describe a woman, *gay* took on the meaning of a life of prostitution. The word's evolution to a term for homosexuals cannot help but retain these connotations of immorality and promiscuity in addition to its more positive meanings; however, *gay* has also long been a term for something brilliantly colored or showy, a connotation of flamboyance that might explain the wordmen who popularized the use of the word as a camp phrase to describe anything homosexual. The interplay of the word's various connotative senses creates a dizzying dichotomy that neatly encapsulates the culturally vexed position of the individuals it came to describe.

Because of its early, innocuous meaning (the unproblematic use of *gay* by many to refer solely to a lissome attitude continued well into the 1970s), *gay* initially functioned, like other slang terms, as a double entendre, a means for homosexual men to signal their sexuality to other homosexuals while simultaneously concealing that aspect of their identity from the uninitiated and the culture at large. Though it has not been located in print prior to 1935 (in Noel Ersine's *Dictionary of Underworld Slang*, where the term *gay cat* is defined as a homosexual boy), *gay* was likely used much earlier. Certainly, its circulation was well under way by 1938, when, in the movie *Bringing Up Baby*, Cary Grant—in response to a question as to why he is dressed in a woman's frilly bathrobe—shouts, "Because I just turned gay all of a sudden!" By the time of the Stonewall riots, *gay* was the dominant term of expressing their sexual identity for a group of younger, more overtly political homosexual activists, who formed groups such as the Gay Liberation Front.

Its use increased throughout the 1970s and 1980s, a watershed occurring in 1987, when, after negotiations with the Gay and Lesbian Alliance Against Defamation (GLAAD), the *New York Times,* which had previously refused to print the word *gay* outside of direct quotations, adopted a policy allowing the term to be used without restraint.

In recent years, some members of the community have rejected *gay* in favor of *queer.* The reasons for this change are threefold: first, it represents a defiant attempt to reclaim so-called pejorative terms like *faggot, pansy,* and *queer* with an ironic and humorous distance, as part of a confrontational politics aimed at heightening gay visibility; second, it represents a rejection of *gay* at a time when some believe that the gay movement is becoming too mainstream, compromising its initial liberationist impulses in favor of mainstream acceptance and practical political gains; third, *queer* is thought by some to be a more inclusive term, less exclusively aligned with men than *gay* and able to include other individuals with nonheteronormative sexual identities, such as bisexuals, transsexuals, pedophiles, and even gay-friendly heterosexuals who reject the term *straight* and its connotations. However, it seems unlikely that *gay* will decrease in popularity any time soon. If Ellen DeGeneres's

1997 statement, "Yep! I'm Gay," on the cover of *Time* magazine is any indication, it may become instead even more ubiquitous.   *Scott Speirs*

Bibliography

Chauncey, George. *Gay New York: Gender, Culture, and the Making of the Gay Male World 1890–1940.* New York: Basic Books, 1994.

Rodgers, Bruce. *The Queen's Vernacular: A Gay Lexicon.* San Francisco: Straight Arrow Books, 1972.

See also Camp; Flowers and Birds; Gay Liberation Front; Gay and Lesbian Alliance Against Defamation (GLAAD), Queer; Stonewall

Gay Activists Alliance (GAA)

New York City's Gay Activists Alliance (GAA) was founded in December 1969 by disgruntled members of the Gay Liberation Front (GLF). Activists such as Donn Teal, Arthur Bell, Marty Robinson, Jim Owles, and Kay Tobin were unhappy with the GLF's expansive, radical political agenda. The GLF, formed in the aftermath of the Stonewall riots, was a self-proclaimed "militant coalition of radical and revolutionary homosexual men and women." In addition to pursuing gay and lesbian rights, the GLF supported the Black Panther Party, radical feminists, and the anti–Vietnam War movement. GLF broadsides called for the overthrow of patriarchy, racism, and capitalism—seeing each as constitutive elements in a "System" that oppressed sexual minorities. GAA members were put off by what journalist Ralph Hall called the "politically articulate dogmatists" who dominated GLF meetings. The break was not complete. While GAA members rejected the politics of the New Left, they embraced the counterculture's atmosphere of social and sexual dissidence.

A number of specific events led to the GAA bolt. In the fall of 1969, then GLF members Robinson and Owles threw their energies into the city's mayoral campaign. They confronted candidates, demanding that they speak to the issue of gay and lesbian civil rights. This media-savvy political intervention, soon named "zapping," became a signature GAA political tactic. Instead of finding their efforts lauded, however, Robinson and Owles were criticized by some GLFers for cooperating with the System, playing by the rules instead of trying to change them. Robinson and Owles were also deeply upset

G

by the GLF's support for the Black Panther Party—whose spokespeople, like many late-sixties activists, liberally peppered their oratory with the word *faggot,* meant to convey the craven, debased nature of the opposition. While some GLFers argued that *faggot* was merely a metaphor, albeit an offensive one, GAAers insisted that rhetoric mattered. Further, they argued, GLF's limited resources should not be used to support causes other than gay liberation. When the GAA wrote up its bylaws, it included a clause that stated that the alliance "will not endorse, ally with, or otherwise support any political party, candidate for public office, and/or any organization not directly related to the homosexual cause." The GAA was to be a single-issue interest group pursuing an identity politics agenda. GAAers sought the repeal of repressive sex laws and acted to ensure civil rights for gays and lesbians.

In 1971 the GAA rented an empty firehouse. The "Firehouse" rapidly became a cultural center for the gay community—serving a largely male audience drawn from the burgeoning gay neighborhoods that surrounded it. Self-identified gay writers, filmmakers, and artists presented their work in a supportive environment. The Firehouse was also the site for numerous dances. Unfortunately, the GAA's best-known community-based project was destroyed in a fire in 1974. To date, the perpetrators have not been apprehended; suspicions have fallen on alienated GAA members and homophobes. Despite the Firehouse's destruction, its spirit lives on in the numerous community centers that continue to serve sexual and gender minorities. *Terence Kissack*

Bibliography

Marotta, Toby. *The Politics of Homosexuality.* Boston: Houghton Mifflin, 1981.

See also Community Centers; Gay Liberation; New York City; Owles, Jim

Gay American Composers

A series of compact discs produced by the New York City–based nonprofit label Composers Recordings, Inc., "Gay American Composers" (CRI CD 721), released in May 1996 was the first recording of out and predominately living homosexual composers. It featured music of Chester Biscardi (1948–), Conrad Cummings (1948–), Chris DeBlasio (1959–1993), David Del Tredici (1937–), Lou Harrison (1917–), Robert Helps (1928–), William Hibbard (1939–

1989), Lee Hoiby (1926–), Jerry Hunt (1943–1993), Robert Maggio (1964–), and Ned Rorem (1923–). The selections were drawn from the label's catalogue with nine of the composers performing their own works. The program was stylistically broad and inclusive, drawing on neoromanticism (DeBlasio, Rorem, Maggio), serialism (Del Tredici, Hibbard), minimalism (Cummings), and experimentalism (Hunt). The disc was released during a period of increased attention to gay music in both academia and popular journalism. Rather than a commissioned essay by a queer musicologist, the booklet notes to the collection consisted of brief essays by each of the composers, often with revealing personal histories and differing views on the relationship between sexuality and music.

"Gay American Composers," Vol. 2 (CRI CD 750), released in May 1997, focused on deceased homosexual composers from the early and midcentury, many of whom were founders of the American school of music. Included were orchestral, chamber, electronic, and solo piano compositions again drawn from a catalogue featuring Samuel Barber (1910–1981), Marc Blitzstein (1905–1964), John Cage (1912–1992), Aaron Copland (1900–1990), Henry Cowell (1897–1965), Alwin Nikolais (1910–1993), Harry Partch (1901–1974), Virgil Thomson (1896–1989), and Ben Weber (1916–1979). Liner notes were by the label's executive director, Joseph R. Dalton, who conceived and produced the series.

A third volume of lesbian composers includes music of Ruth Anderson (1928–), Eve Beglarian, Jennifer Higdon (1962–), Paula Kimper–Annea Lockwood (1939–), Pauline Oliveros (1932–), and Nurit Tilles (1952–), and the Canadian improvisation duo of Marilyn Lerner and Lori Freedman. Like the previous volumes, the disc will feature a wide variety of instrumental combinations and musical styles including a "love duet" from Kimper's lesbian-themed opera *Patience and Sarah* and original liner notes by the composers.

The CRI collections followed on the notoriety of two more commercially oriented collections of classical music also aimed at gay audiences but issued by major labels. *OUT Classics* (BMG, 1995) featured mainstream orchestral works by composers who, according to the liner notes and the marketing tag, "just happen to be gay." Included was music by Barber, Bernstein, Britten, Chopin, Copland, Saint-Saëns, Schubert, and Tchaikovsky. *Sensual Classics, Too* (Teldec, 1995) was an easy-listening collection targeted to gay male audiences but featuring a generic program of romantic orchestral music. Typical of much gay marketing in the mid-1990s, the cover art of both these collections accentuated male flesh and bulging muscles. CRI's artwork for its first volume followed in this vein and drew considerable criticism even while the recording and liner notes were recognized as substantial and revealing.

CRI's first release was widely reviewed in mainstream print media as well as numerous regional gay publications. Alex Ross wrote in the *New York Times*: "Any packaging can be justified by the product it contains, and CRI's disk turns out to be a thoughtful, playful cross section of American styles from the last half-century. It's a useful way of showing composers to be human, even if their music nimbly escapes the strictures of social identity." K. Robert Schwarz wrote in *OUT* magazine: "To CRI's credit, the provocative question posed on the back cover—'Is there a gay sensibility to American classical music?'—was answered with a resounding 'no' by the disc itself." Elaine Belsito wrote in *Windy City Times,* "These are blue-ribbon compositions that showcase the breadth of contributions made by gay composers in 20th century American classical music."

The introduction to the liner notes of *Gay American Composers,* Vol. 2, reads in part: "In the relatively short history of American classical music, it is a curious and extraordinary phenomenon that so many important composers were also homosexuals. . . . May this collection help new audiences and new generations to recognize the important gay thread within the marvelous history of American music, and therefore to recognize also that American music has become a part of gay history."   *Joseph R. Dalton*

Bibliography

Brett, Philip, Elizabeth Wood, and Gary C. Thomas, eds. *Queering the Pitch: The New Lesbian and Gay Musicology*. New York: Routledge, 1994.

See also Barber, Samuel; Bernstein, Leonard; Blitzstein, Marc; Britten, Benjamin; Cage, John; Copland, Aaron; Cowell, Henry; Del Tredici, David; Harrison, Lou; Partch, Harry; Rorem, Ned; Saint-Saëns, Camille; Schubert, Franz Peter; Tchaikovsky, Pyotr Ilich; Thomson, Virgil

Gay and Lesbian Alliance Against Defamation (GLAAD)

The Gay and Lesbian Alliance Against Defamation (GLAAD) is a national organization dedicated to promoting the fair and accurate representation of gay, lesbian, bisexual, and transgender individuals in the media. To accomplish this goal, GLAAD monitors occurrences of defamation in the media; trains gay, lesbian, bisexual, and transgender organizations to work effectively with the media; provides accurate information regarding gay, lesbian, bisexual, and transgender people to media professionals; and promotes gay, lesbian, bisexual, and transgender visibility. In addition, GLAAD publishes the *Media Guide to the Lesbian and Gay Community* and the *GLAAD Bulletin,* and sponsors the annual GLAAD Media Awards to honor those who have worked to further the cause of gay, lesbian, bisexual, and transgender individuals.

GLAAD was founded in 1985 in New York City by a group of gay writers dissatisfied with the media's coverage of the AIDS crisis. Originally called the Gay and Lesbian Anti-Defamation League, the fledgling organization ran into problems when the Anti-Defamation League of B'nai B'rith threatened to sue it for copyright infringement. The group subsequently changed its name to the Gay and Lesbian Alliance Against Defamation. GLAAD gained its first media attention on November 14, 1985, when it held a meeting in New York's Greenwich Village to discuss the media's poor representation of gays and lesbians, particularly in light of the AIDS crisis. More than seven hundred people attended the event. A little more than a year later, on December 1, 1986, the group organized its first demonstration at the *New York Post* to protest what it considered that paper's sensationalistic coverage of AIDS; more than five hundred demonstrators attended. In early 1987, Wall Street lawyer and gay activist Craig Davidson was appointed as GLAAD's first executive director. The Los Angeles chapter of GLAAD was established a year later. Together, the New York and Los Angeles chapters formed the nucleus of a growing network of independent, city-based GLAAD chapters throughout the nation. By 1993, chapters had been established in Atlanta, Dallas, Denver, Kansas City, San Diego, San Francisco, and Washington, D.C., and total membership exceeded ten thousand members. In 1994, the New York and Los Angeles chapters voted to merge and become a national organization. Public relations executive William Waybourn was hired by the GLAAD board of directors as managing director in 1995 to coordinate the transition. In 1996, the Washington, D.C., and San Francisco chapters also voted to merge with the national organization. Waybourn left GLAAD in early 1997, and former entertainment industry exec-

G utive Joan M. Garry took over as executive director with plans to merge the Kansas City and Atlanta chapters into the national structure in late 1997.

Over the years, GLAAD's efforts have had an impact on the media. For example, the *New York Times* changed its editorial policy in 1987 to allow the use of the word *gay* after meeting with members of GLAAD. In 1989, the Nynex Yellow Pages, which serve most of New England, included a section on gay and lesbian services as a result of a two-year campaign by GLAAD. In 1990, GLAAD protested an insensitive remark made by CBS commentator Andy Rooney regarding AIDS, resulting in the network's suspension of Rooney, and in 1996, GLAAD persuaded the Partnership for a Drug-Free America to alter a public service announcement that seemed to imply that homosexuality was worse than drug addiction.

As a result of its media relations efforts and growing clout in the entertainment industry, GLAAD was named as one of Hollywood's one hundred most powerful groups by *Entertainment Weekly* in 1992.

Mark Bailey

Bibliography

Alwood, Edward. *Straight News: Gays, Lesbians, and the News Media.* New York: Columbia University Press, 1996.
"A Brief Introduction to GLAAD." *Gay and Lesbian Alliance Against Defamation.* <http://www.glaad.org/glaad/history.html> (Aug. 8, 1997).
Hays, Constance L. "Listing Is Won in Yellow Pages by Gay Group." *New York Times,* Jan. 18, 1989, B3.
Levere, Jane L. "Group to re-edit TV Commercials." *New York Times,* Jul. 12, 1996, D5.
Meers, Erik. "Executive Action." *Advocate* (July 8, 1997): 49–50.

See also AIDS; Gay and Lesbian Press; Journalism; Media

Gay and Lesbian Press

The American gay and lesbian community that began to emerge after World War II spawned a new genre of alternative journalism. This specialized press created a forum for issues that establishment presses refused to cover, while simultaneously advocating for gay rights. Its history has been convulsive, partly because of society's hostility toward gay people and partly because of other external forces.

A precursor of the gay press was founded in 1924 when Henry Gerber, a Chicago postal worker, formed the Society for Human Rights and produced two issues of *Friendship and Freedom.* When the police learned of the activities, they arrested Gerber, who was fired from his job, and destroyed all copies of the newsletter.

The earliest extant copies of a lesbian or gay publication are of *Vice Versa,* a lesbian magazine founded in Los Angeles in 1947. The editor was a woman using the pseudonym Lisa Ben, an anagram for "lesbian." Ben produced twelve copies of each issue on her manual typewriter and distributed them in lesbian bars. She published nine issues of the magazine, which consisted mainly of her own short stories, poems, and personal essays.

The first widely distributed gay publication was *ONE,* founded in Los Angeles in 1953. The second and third were the San Francisco–based *Mattachine Review,* founded in 1955 for gay men, and *The Ladder,* founded in 1956 for lesbians. The three monthly magazines consisted largely of personal essays. *ONE* provoked lively debates about gay rights; *Mattachine Review* and *The Ladder* urged readers to accommodate the norms of heterosexual society. The magazines had a total circulation of seven thousand but a readership of many times that number. All three survived more than a dozen years. *ONE* fought federal postal censors and in a 1958 U.S. Supreme Court case won the right for homosexual-oriented materials to be sent through the mail.

In the 1960s, the lesbian and gay press shifted toward militancy, with the same women and men editing the magazines also organizing the first demonstrations for gay rights at the White House and Independence Hall. Toward the end of the decade, many of the dozen publications adopted counterculture values by incorporating explicit language and homoerotic images into their editorial mix and by advocating sexual promiscuity, drug use, and opposition to the Vietnam War. In 1967 the first true gay newspaper appeared when the *Los Angeles Advocate* was founded with an all-news format.

After the Stonewall rebellion ignited the modern phase of the gay and lesbian liberation movement, the number and circulation of publications exploded. By 1972, some 150 magazines and newspapers boasted an aggregate circulation of 250,000. The most visible were the "wild and woolly" tabloids defined by titillating images, anarchistic concepts, and language designed as much to shock as to illuminate. Titles of the revolutionary journals communicate a sense of what they stood for: *Gay Flames* and *Come Out!* in New York City, *Gay Sunshine* in San Francisco, *Gay Liberator* in Detroit, *Killer Dyke* in Chicago. Many of the publications were short-lived.

In the mid-1970s, the gay and lesbian press entered a less overtly political phase as it concentrated on exploring the dimensions of the culture. Publications plumbed the breadth and depth of topics ranging from sex and the gay sensibility in art and literature to spirituality, personal appearance, women's music, "dyke" separatism, lesbian mothers, and the rising popularity of gay bathhouses. The most prominent of the publications was the *Advocate*, an upscale lifestyles magazine for gay men that Wall Street multimillionaire David B. Goodstein created by revamping the *Los Angeles Advocate*.

At the end of the decade, the gay and lesbian press once again shifted its focus, this time in response to an antihomosexual campaign led by conservative political and religious forces. In an effort to convince mainstream America that gay people were an oppressed minority group that deserved civil rights, publications developed a new degree of professionalism. Many began to look and read very much like conventional newspapers, following Associated Press style and presenting both the gay and the antigay perspectives on issues.

In the early 1980s, the gay and lesbian press confronted an even more formidable enemy when AIDS began devouring gay men at an alarming rate. Publications such as the *New York Native* and *Washington Blade* distinguished themselves by reporting and crusading against the disease, often breaking new developments before mainstream news organizations with far more resources. Gay newspapers such as the *San Francisco Sentinel* and *Bay Area Reporter*, on the other hand, did not sound the alarm to the same degree, partly because they opted for a state of denial and partly because they were reluctant to oppose the sexual liberation that had traditionally been a large part of defining gay liberation.

AIDS and the hysteria that it spawned continued to dominate the lesbian and gay press in the late 1980s, propelling the genre into a new radicalism. The leader of the era was *OutWeek,* a New York–based weekly that burst into the the national spotlight when it "outed" closeted men and women such as publishing tycoon Malcolm Forbes. Other publications joined the trend to create a press that paralleled the radical organizations of ACT UP and Queer Nation and their demands for more money to support AIDS research and treatment, as well as an end to second-class citizenship for gay people.

In the early 1990s, yet another chapter in the genre's history unfolded as increased visibility of gay people spurred a spate of glossy lifestyle magazines. *Out,* based in New York City, led this new phase, with the upscale magazine's sophisticated design and superficial editorial content attracting a large stable of mainstream advertisers.

In the context of alternative media, the vital statistics of the lesbian and gay press today are impressive. Publications number some 900 titles with a total circulation surpassing 2 million. Since 1947, when the first lesbian magazine was founded, more than 2,600 publications have been produced in the United States.   *Roger Streitmatter*

Bibliography

Miller, Alan V., compiler. *Our Own Voices: A Directory of Lesbian and Gay Periodicals, 1890–1990.* Toronto: Canadian Gay Archives, 1990.

Streittmatter, Rodger. *Unspeakable: The Rise of the Gay and Lesbian Press in America.* Boston: Faber and Faber, 1995.

See also *Advocate*; Christopher Street; *Gay Community News*; Mattachine Society; *ONE* Magazine

Gay Bashing

Verbal and physical attacks directed at lesbians and gay men because of their sexual orientation are often referred to as gay bashing, homophobic violence, antigay and lesbian violence, or violence against lesbians and gay men. Verbal gay bashing includes the disparaging remarks of politicians and religious leaders directed at the general gay population, as well as the insults and harassment by individuals directed at specific lesbians or gay men. Physical gay bashing includes arson and property damage to gay institutions, such as community centers and bars, as well as individual assaults on targeted lesbians or gay men.

Propaganda campaigns and speeches against gay people by such well-known figures as U.S. Senator Jesse Helms, Anita Bryant, Jerry Falwell, and Pat Robertson and the murder of gay San Francisco Supervisor Harvey Milk by fellow Supervisor Dan White have received widespread attention by the news media, but studies and surveys of gay people have been conducted showing that gay bashing is

G

At an antibashing demonstration (1990). Photo by Marc Geller.

also a common everyday occurrence practiced by ordinary citizens.

Approximately 90 percent of lesbians and gay men surveyed in the United States report that they have been the targets of verbal gay bashing by individuals. Most perpetrators are teenage men who mirror the racial makeup of society, usually act with others, and attack with equal frequency victims who are alone, in pairs, and in groups of three or more. Most often perpetrators are strangers to the their victims, but in many other cases they are fellow students and fellow employees. Verbal attacks most often occur outside of gay recreational establishments, but they are also reported often in nongay neighborhoods, in high school, and at work. Gay men report higher rates of attacks than lesbians, and people of color report higher rates than white people. The language most often used condemns homosexuality, and references to God, religion, or the Bible are common also.

Over one-half of surveyed lesbians and gay men have been the victims of physical violence because of their sexual orientation. Most perpetrators of physical violence are young men in their teens and twenties who mirror the racial makeup of society. Most often they are strangers to their victims and are lone assailants who attack victims who are alone. As with verbal attacks physical attacks most often occur outside of gay recreational establishments, but they are also reported often in or outside of victims' homes. In the workplace, the more open

gay people are about their sexual orientation, the more likely they are to be attacked. Gay men report higher rates of violence than women, but the rates for people of color compared with white people vary across surveys.

In descending order of occurrence, the kinds of physical attacks most often reported by victims are being chased or followed; having objects thrown at them; being punched, hit, kicked, or beaten; having their property destroyed; being spit at; being sexually assaulted; and being attacked with a weapon. In approximately 40 percent of reported incidents, victims are outnumbered by their attackers. Other advantages commonly used by perpetrators are to frighten the victim with excessively violent threats, to surprise or attack the victim from behind, to attack in a location in which no help can be summoned, and to be larger than the victim. In most physical attacks, perpetrators do not use any language. When language is used, perpetrators typically disparage homosexuality and/or boast of heterosexuality.

The rate of physical violence directed at lesbians and gay men because of their sexual orientation is higher than the rate of criminal violence experienced by the general population. One study that focused on yearly reports of criminal violence in large cities found that victimization is two times greater for lesbians and four times greater for gay men than that reported by women and men in the general population. Since lesbians and gay men in this study reported only homophobic violence and not violent crimes unrelated to sexual orientation, their overall rate of victimization would presumably be even higher and the comparison more striking.

Victims of antigay violence are less likely than crime victims in general to report incidents to the police. The reason most often given for not reporting is previous experience with or perception of the police as antigay. Among the general population, police-related reasons are given less frequently, and these are based on anticipated indifference rather than fear of hostility or abuse. The reason for not reporting given most often by crime victims in general is that they themselves do not consider the crime important enough. This reason is given least frequently by victims of antigay violence.

Comparisons with national crime statistics for perpetrators of violent crimes in general show that perpetrators of antigay violence tend to be younger and are more often male and strangers to their victims. Perpetrators of antigay violence are less likely than perpetrators in general to attack lone victims and are more likely to attack in groups. Concerning the race, white perpetrators of antigay violence attack lesbians and gay men of color more frequently than white perpetrators of violent crimes in general attack people of color.

Psychiatric and law enforcement professionals observe that perpetrators of antigay violence do not typically exhibit what are customarily thought of as criminal attitudes and behaviors. They are often described as "average kids from ordinary backgrounds." Many conform to and are models of middle-class respectability. Systematic reviews of cases of perpetrators who have been apprehended reveal a paucity of criminal backgrounds or histories of psychological disorders. Although attacks are often motivated by hatred or disapproval of lesbians and gay men, a more common interest especially among younger perpetrators is adventure, excitement, and recreation. Antigay attacks occur most often at those times when teenagers socialize with each other—on weekend nights and during summer. To relieve boredom, a suggested "Let's go out and get some fags" is followed by a visit to the nearest area known for gay residency or socializing. Lesbians and gay men are often targeted less because of the perpetrators' personal dislike or disapproval of them, and more because they are a socially disapproved of and marginalized group that lacks police protection.

Within many communities gay bashing is a sport, tradition, or rite of passage among male teenagers sanctioned and sometimes admired by peers and elders. Unlike other criminal acts viewed as antisocial, gay bashing is often socially accepted and approved. When attackers are apprehended, police officers often side with them against the victim. Although there is some evidence of change within the legal system, juries and judges have often acquitted or imposed minimum penalties on perpetrators who have caused serious injury or death.

Research on antigay murder has found that victims are often "overkilled," as in the brutal murder of Matthew Shepard in Wyoming in 1998. Multiple stabbing and excessive mutilation are common; knives are used much more often than in homicide in general; and a number of victims have been stabbed, mutilated, and strangled after being fatally shot. Homicide detectives and physicians in hospital emergency rooms concur that physical attacks against gay men are the most heinous and brutal of any that they encounter.   *Gary David Comstock*

Bibliography

Aurand, Steven K., Rita Addessa, and Christine Bush. *Violence and Discrimination Against Philadelphia Lesbian and Gay People: A Study by the Philadelphia Lesbian and Gay Task Force*. Philadelphia, December 1985.

Comstock, Gary David. *Violence Against Lesbians and Gay Men*. New York: Columbia University Press, 1991.

Peeples, Edward Jr., Walter W. Tunstall, Everett Eberhardt, and Commission on Human Relations, City of Richmond. *A Survey of Perceptions of Civil Opportunity Among Gays and Lesbians in Richmond, Virginia*. Richmond, 1985.

See also Homophobia; Homosexual Panic; Milk, Harvey; Sexual Orientation

Gay Community News

A lesbian and gay newspaper published in Boston, Massachusetts, *Gay Community News* was founded in June 1973 as a local, community-based mimeographed newsletter. It soon became an influential sixteen- to twenty-page weekly newspaper providing local, national, and international news and features to a large national audience. Unlike the vast majority of U.S. lesbian and gay periodicals, *GCN* was produced by and oriented toward both lesbians and gay men. A strong advocate for radical social change, the newspaper developed explicit commitments to feminism, antiracism and multiracialism, awareness of class issues, support and advocacy for prisoners, sexual liberation, the fight against AIDS, and alliances with other progressive movements. The number of *GCN* subscribers peaked in the 1980s at approximately four thousand, although thousands more copies of the newspaper were printed each week for newsstand and bookstore sales and free distribution. Estimates of *GCN*'s weekly readership reached as high as sixty thousand.

Dependent on subscription, advertising, and fund-raising income, *GCN* was produced for most of its history by a democratic and nonhierarchical collective of grassroots lesbian, gay, bisexual, and transgendered volunteers, who together made up the newspaper's decision-making "membership." Many *GCN* staff and volunteers became important local and national activists, writers, artists, lawyers, community service administrators, and scholars, leading the newspaper to acquire a reputation as a training school for lesbian and gay leadership. Celebrated and criticized for exploring conflicts within lesbian and gay communities, *GCN* was also seen by some as strong and by others as weak because of its own internal divisions. The goal of having *GCN* serve as a newspaper for all lesbians staff and gay men simultaneously supported and conflicted with the vision of the newspaper as a progressive political forum.

In 1979, *GCN* was reorganized as a nonprofit corporation, the Bromfield Street Educational Foundation, which also sponsored the Lesbian and Gay Prisoner Project. In July 1982, *GCN*'s offices, which it shared with *Fag Rag*, a gay male liberation publication, and Glad Day Bookstore, a gay business, were destroyed by arson. Although members of a ring of "fire buffs," firefighters, security guards, and police officers were convicted on charges related to setting the *GCN* fire and more than two hundred other fires, some activists affiliated with the newspaper suspected that antigay activists, the landlord, redevelopers, and other police officers may have been involved. The fire exacerbated *GCN*'s long-standing financial problems, which worsened with local competition from *Bay Windows*, national competition from the *Advocate*, the withdrawal of local advertisers opposed to *GCN*'s politics and national orientation, and the increasingly conservative cultural climate. Facing financial crisis, in 1992 *GCN* suspended publication, returning the following year as an occasional newspaper and in 1997 as a quarterly magazine. After the San Francisco–based quarterly *OUT/LOOK* ceased publication in 1992, the Bromfield Street Educational Foundation also became the sponsor of the *OutWrite* conference of lesbian, gay, bisexual, and transgendered writers. The foundation continued to support the prisoner project, developed a local reading series, and established Q-Pos, a queer progressive organizing school.   *Marc Stein*

Bibliography

Alwood, Edward. *Straight News: Gays, Lesbians, and the News Media.* New York: Columbia University Press, 1996.

Bronski, Michael. *Culture Clash: The Making of Gay Sensibility.* Boston: South End Press, 1984.

Streitmatter, Rodger. *Unspeakable: The Rise of the Gay and Lesbian Press in America.* Boston: Faber and Faber, 1995.

Vaid, Urvashi. *Virtual Equality: The Mainstreaming of Gay and Lesbian Liberation.* New York: Doubleday, 1995.

See also Gay and Lesbian Press

Gay Families

The discovery of gay families has recently graced national newspapers, magazines, and television programming; social science and legal journals; and clinicians' notebooks. Issues that have been discussed include the many gaps in our knowledge, the significance of studying gay and lesbian families for theories of families, the health of families, and public policies that affect both gay lesbian individuals and families. Perhaps most perplexing to all concerned is the question of what constitutes a gay family. Heterosexist notions of family suggests that lesbian and gay families consist of two same-sex parents and their child(ren). This definition, however, is not sufficiently inclusive of other family norms. All families are potentially gay, if by that we mean a family with at least one gay, lesbian, or bisexual member. The following vignettes bring into sharp relief issues involved in defining lesbian and gay families.

A bisexual woman with a history of serial relationships with women and men legally marries a man. Her early adolescent niece lives with them much of the time. Several years later the woman invites a lesbian with whom she would like to be sexually involved to move into the home. The lesbian joins her lover's household, creating a four-member family (three adults and one child).

Two gay men in their thirties have lived together for eight years. They invite other single gay males to join their family as adults with whom they are sexually involved. The couple anticipates that eventually these males will move out of their family to create other families, with whom they may be involved. Currently, they have a three-member family (three adults) and have no interest in including children in their family.

A gay male couple, one thirty-five and the other sixty-five, have been together for eight years. Anticipating his earlier death, the older legally adopted the younger to ensure full legal rights for the couple. They have had a church wedding ceremony; bought a house together; regularly entertain both gay and straight couples; and have dogs, cats, birds, fish, rabbits, and no children.

A lesbian gave birth to a son whom she conceived through alternative insemination. The child lives part of the week with his two mothers and the other part of the week with the gay male sperm donor/father and his male lover. The family intends to add another child to their extended household, with the other women becoming pregnant with sperm from the nonbiological father.

A lesbian and her female ex-lover are raising their daughter. The three do not live together. The daughter is the biological child of the ex-lover, but her nonbiological mother has physical and legal custody.

Two gay men who have lived together for over ten years have opened their home to foster children. They consider their immediate family to include themselves, their foster children, and the mother of one of the men who lives with them.

A lesbian couple adopted a newborn baby girl in an open adoption. Because of state law, only one of the women could have legal custody. The daughter continues to have regular contact with her birth mother after the adoption. When the girl was five, her two mothers separated; she lives with the mother who has legal custody. The girl remains close with her other adoptive mother and her birth mother. Shortly thereafter, her legal mother took as her lover a woman who has three adopted sons. The girl thinks of herself as having three step-siblings and four moms: a birth mother, two real mothers, and a stepmother.

A gay man in his sixties who lives alone has spent every Sunday and holiday for the last ten years with his chosen family—another gay man and two lesbians. The four rely on one another for emotional and financial support. They vacation together, plan elaborate holiday meals together, and speak to each other on the phone or in person nearly every day.

A group of gay street kids relies on an older gay man, whom they call "the mother," for emotional support, small loans, and an occasional overnight stay. "The mother" has helped literally hundreds of street kids in this way, providing whatever he can in the way of food, shelter, and support.

Three siblings, two sixteen-year-old identical twins and an eighteen-year-old sister, are "out" in the local high school. Their father remains married to their mother, although he currently lives with his male lover of two years. The children report that their mother is now "hanging out all the time with her feminist friends," and they believe she may also be gay.

A gay college junior, the only child of a wealthy East Coast couple, disclosed to his parents that he is gay and has AIDS. The couple do not re-

veal the son's status to his grandparents or other extended family members but declare their commitment to him. He dies two weeks later and no one is told the real cause of death.

As these vignettes make clear, sexual minority families vary in composition, structure, function, and longevity. They may or may not include children; they may be—but are most likely not—legally recognized; and they may include chosen kin. Lesbian and gay family members may not even live together. Research on lesbian, gay, and bisexual families has only begun to recognize this diversity. At the same time, policy debates about domestic partnerships and same-sex marriage are now addressing some of the thorny legal issues faced by sexual minority families.   *Ritch Savin-Williams and*
Kristin G. Esterberg

Bibliography

Borhek, Mary V. *Coming Out to Parents: A Two-Way Survival Guide for Lesbians and Gay Men and Their Parents*, 2nd ed. Cleveland: Pilgrim, 1993.

Demo, David A., and Katherine R. Allen. "Diversity within Lesbian and Gay Families: Challenges and Implications for Family Theory and Research." *Journal of Social and Personal Relationships* 13 (1996): 415–34.

Laird, Joan. "Lesbian and Gay Families." In *Normal Family Processes*, 2nd ed. Froma Walsh, ed. New York: Guilford, 1993, 282–328.

Martin, April. *The Lesbian and Gay Parenting Handbook*. New York: Harper, 1993.

Murphy, Bianca, and Lourdes Rodrígues-Nogués, eds. *Lesbian and Gay Parenting: A Resource for Psychologists*. Washington D.C.: American Psychological Association, 1995.

Savin-Williams, Ritch C., and Kenneth M. Cohen, eds. *The Lives of Lesbians, Gays, and Bisexuals: Children to Adults*. Fort Worth: Harcourt Brace, 1996.

Savin-Williams, Ritch C., and Kristen G. Esterberg. "Families and Sexual Orientation." In *Handbook of Family Diversity*. David H. Demo, Katherine R. Allen, and Mark A. Allen, eds. Forthcoming.

Weston, Kath. *Families We Choose: Lesbians, Gays, Kinship*. New York: Columbia Univesity Press, 1991.

***See also** Adelphopoiêsis*; Couples; Friendship; Gay Relationships

Gay Games

An international festival of athletic competition and the arts, the Gay Games were launched in 1982 and are held quadrennially as a celebration of the international gay community. The first and second games were held in San Francisco, the third in Vancouver, the fourth in New York, and the fifth in Amsterdam. The games are overseen by the Federation of Gay Games, based in San Francisco. The stated purpose of the federation is to "ensure that the original principles of the Gay Games, inclusion and participation, are maintained at each Games. The federation chooses the site for each Gay Games, works with the host organization in its production of the upcoming Gay Games, and reaches out to the international lesbian and gay community to promote both the Gay Games' concept and event."

The games were founded by a physician and former Olympic decathalete, Tom Waddell, and organized by a mostly volunteer group called San Francisco Arts and Athletics. The 1982 games involved 1,300 male and female athletes in sixteen sports. At the 1994 Games 10,870 athletes participated in more than thirty sports, with 55,000 spectators at the closing ceremonies. Like the ancient games of Olympia, the athletic competitions of the Gay Games are complemented by festivals of the arts. In her opening address to the 1986 games,

novelist Rita Mae Brown highlighted the meaning of the games: "These games are not just a celebration of skill, they're a celebration of who we are and what we have become . . . a celebration of the best in us."

Tom Waddell said that the games were "conceived as a new idea in the meaning of sport based on inclusion rather than exclusion." Anyone is welcome to compete regardless of race, sex, age, nationality, sexual orientation, religion, or athletic ability. In keeping with the masters movement in sports, athletes compete with each other in their own age group. Many of the sports are officially sanctioned by their respective national masters organizations. Athletes participate not as representatives of their respective countries but as individuals on behalf of cities and towns. To date there have been no minimum qualifying standards in any events.

The games have been used by gay activists for ideological purposes. Historically, homosexuality has been associated with pathology, and the rise of AIDS in homosexual communities has reinforced that association. Many of those who spoke at the 1986 games said that the games emphasized a healthy image of gay men and lesbians. Brown also said in her opening address that the games "show the world who we really are. We're intelligent people, we're attractive people, we're caring people,

"Yves with Flag." Photo courtesy John Hawe.

we're *healthy* people, and we are proud of who we are."

The original organizers of the Gay Games experienced considerable legal difficulties. Before the 1982 games, the United States Olympic Committee (USOC) filed a court action against organizers of the Gay Games, which were going to be called the "Gay Olympic Games," successfully arguing that the organizers were impinging on their exclusive rights to the use of the word *Olympic* granted the USOC by the U.S. Congress in 1978. Although the USOC had allowed the "Rat Olympics," "Police Olympics," and "Dog Olympics," it took exception to the term "Gay Olympic Games." Two years later, the vastly wealthy USOC continued its harassment of the Gay Games and filed a suit to recover legal fees in the amount of $96,600. A lien was put on the house of Tom Waddell, a member of the 1968 U.S. Olympic team, who at the time of the punitive legal action was dying of AIDS and financially exhausted.

Just as the Sacred Olympic Games and Pythian Games of ancient Greece were celebrations that gave expression to Hellenistic values of the time, so, too, the Gay Games celebrate and express the contemporary spirit of gay communities. *Brian Pronger*

Bibliography

Coe, Roy. *A Sense of Pride: The Story of Gay Games II.* San Francisco: Pride Publications, 1986.

Labreque, Lisa. *Unity: A Celebration of Gay Games IV and Stonewall.* San Francisco: Labreque Publications, 1994.

Pronger, Brian. *The Arena of Masculinity: Sports, Homosexuality and the Meaning of Sex.* New York: St. Martin's Press, 1990.

Also look for information on the Internet. At the time of writing there is a Gay Games Web page: http://www.gaygames.org/games.htm

See also Physical Culture; Sports

Gay Language

Language is a central and critical component of gay culture, just as is the case for other domains of human experience. Whether gay men are interacting with friends at an all-gay dinner party, signaling gay identity to a colleague or new acquaintance at the office or in some other public place, applying for medical services at a public health clinic, or disclosing newly discovered gay desires to a parent, super-visor, or (straight) spouse, language helps to shape the content and context of the social moment and helps to regulate other details of the social exchange.

Two features of gay language use have become closely linked to stereotypic images of gay men in U.S. popular culture: mincing or lisping pronunciation of certain consonant sounds, for example, turning "boys" into *boyth* and "swim" into *thwim*; and exaggerated, heightened qualities of sentence intonation that give statements more dramatic changes in pitch level than are ordinarily the case in spoken English. More widely attested, perhaps, is the use of certain words and phrases that appear to be gender-neutral but take on specialized meaning each time they appear in gay language settings, for example, *friends of Dorothy* (a collective reference to a person's gay friends), *chicken* (a sexually desirable but underaged young man), and *faabulous* (anything that enlivens or brightens an otherwise dull evening). Also prominent in gay speech settings are certain narrative styles (how people tell gay-centered stories) and turn-taking strategies (how people share responsibilities for speaking and listening during conversations); metaphors, images, and other forms of indirect referencing; spatial relationships between speakers and listeners; gestures and body posture, as well as the strategic use of pauses, hesitations, and silence.

Example: *At Sunday Brunch*

Source: "Gay Men's English" (Leap 52)

(Note: The notation S1, S2, etc. distinguishes each of the different speakers who participated in this conversation.)

1 S1: Did you see the costume on Miss Louisiana? Imagine—she dressed up like a crawfish!

3 S2: Well the contestants were supposed to wear something typical of their home state.

5 S3: And it's difficult to walk out on stage dressed like a bayou.

6 S4: I wouldn't mind being by-you, that's for sure.

7 S5: Maybe she should have dressed up like a Creole princess.

8 S6: Or like David Duke.

9 S2: Now, there is a road kill for you—all over the pavement.

10 S3: But his face is so cute—and the way he wears his hair!

11 S1: Yeah, but what comes out his mouth isn't so cute. All that trash makes him ugly.

13   S5: She could have worn a David Duke costume.

14   S2: I have a triangle-shaped hat. Maybe I could have gone as David Duke.

16   S1: Pointed at the top of your head?

17   S2: And a white sheet to match (*pause*) Ralph Lauren.

18   S7: 200 thread count.

19   S8: 200 thread count Ralph Lauren.

20   S2: And embroidered eyeholes.

21   S4: Do you really think anyone will take that man seriously?

This example shows how one group of gay men incorporated some of these features into conversation during an all-gay Sunday brunch. (See further discussion in Leap, "Gay Men's English" 51–55; *Word's Out* 16–23.) Some of the guests were members of the same gay choral group or had met on previous occasions; others knew no one at the party other than the host. One of the functions served by this exchange (which took place over coffee and dessert) was the transformation of strangers into friends through the joint discovery of areas of common interest and appeal. The shared recollections of the recently televised Miss America pageant (lines 1–7) were particularly effective in that regard (all the men had seen the telecast, or were familiar with what the contest entails), and so were opportunities for creative verbal play that arose during the constructed discussion of *gay clan attire* (lines 13–20).

Note also that, aside from the possible allusion to same-sex desire in line 10, there is nothing in the content or structure of this conversation that could be considered specifically or uniquely "gay." At the same time, the interweaving of sarcasm (lines 3–4, 16) exaggeration (lines 5, 13), misogyny (lines 1–2, 7), parody and satire (lines 8, 14–15, 17–20), and political commentary (lines 11–12, 21) produces a package of meanings that would be unlikely to emerge in a heterosexually centered speech setting. Moreover, the conversation was not dominated by one or two voices, or controlled through competitive turn-taking, in the sense that it is more generally attested in male speech. Instead, speakers made every effort to insure that the exchange was highly cooperative: opportunities for speaking were widely shared, and potentially disruptive or divisive statements (line 4, line 16) were simply disregarded.

Besides being a useful resource in all-gay social settings, gay language can be equally important in settings where the participants' gay identities have not been fully disclosed. In those instances, the introduction of a carefully coded gay image or metaphor, or the particular use of gesture, silence, or some other nonverbal ploy, allows individual speakers opportunities to "out themselves"—the disclosure process that gay men at an earlier time referred to as "dropping pins"—without having to make explicit statements in that regard. And while gay language offers avenues out of "the closet," it also helps gay men maintain a "closeted" stance, if they so desire, by identifying linguistic features that they must never employ in public settings.

To date, most gay language research has focused on the speech of gay men who come from English-language backgrounds. Much less clear, however, is the extent to which "gay languages" have been spoken, or are still used, in speech communities not traditionally associated with English or other Western language traditions. Unfortunately, the increased frequency of international gay tourism, voluntary and forced relocation from homelands to urban centers, transnational migration patterns, and the expansion of transglobal communication and media are all leading to widespread diffusion of Western ways of talking about same-sex desire and identities. With that diffusion comes a growing eradication and/or reconstruction of corresponding vocabulary, metaphor, and conversational practices that may have been present in third world settings at earlier times. Common concerns about health, safe sex, and death raised by the AIDS pandemic also cut across national and cultural boundaries and give additional incentives for the incorporation of a unifying discourse of male-centered, same-sex experience into local language traditions.

Yet it seems unlikely that a single, internationalized "gay language" will emerge out of this process of international convergence. Much of the vocabulary and forms of nonverbal communication that were essential to urban gay life in the United States during the 1930s and 1940s are unknown to today's younger gay men. At the same time, younger urban gay men in the western United States who are from English-speaking, low-income backgrounds have incorporated into their gay language skills a narrative style that blends, rather than distinguishes, the contrasts in tense reference (e.g., present, past, and future) that are habitually maintained in the English of older gay men (and many heterosexual persons) in these cities. Similar class/age–based contrasts are reported for Polari, an aggregate of gay English varieties found in Great Britain, with sailors and maritime personnel speaking the code quite differently from persons associated with the theater or some other more upscale profession. Such internal diversity is only one component of the wide range of expressions given to male same-sex desire cross-culturally. To be consistent with the lived experiences of its speakers, gay language will remain a pluralized code, reflecting the details of male same-sex desire that are relevant to each speech setting.

William Leap

Bibliography

Cox, Leslie J., and Richard J. Fay. "Gayspeak, the Linguistic Fringe: Bona Polari, Camp, Queerspeak, and Beyond." In *The Margins of the City.* Stephen Whittle, ed. Hants, U.K.: Ashgate, 1994, 103–28.

Goodwin, Joseph P. *More Man Than You'll Ever Be: Gay Folklore and Acculturation in Middle America.* Bloomington, Ind.: Indiana University Press, 1989.

Leap, William. "Gay Men's English: Cooperative Discourse in a Language of Risk." *New York Folklore* 19 (1993): 45–70.

———. *Word's Out: Gay Men's English.* Minneapolis: University of Minnesota Press, 1996.

Manalansan, Martin F. " 'Performing' the Filipino Gay Experience in America: Linguistic Strategies in a Transnational Context." In *Beyond the Lavender Lexicon.* William Leap, ed. Newark: Gordon and Breach, 1995, 249–66.

Murray, Stephen O. "Stigma Transformation and Relexification in the International Diffusion of Gay." In *Beyond the Lavender Lexicon.* William Leap, ed. Newark: Gordon and Breach, 1995, 297–317.

Murray, Stephen O., and Manuel Arboleda. "Stigma Transformation and Relexification: 'Gay' in Latin America." In *Male Homosexuality in Central and South America.* Stephen O. Murray, ed. Gai Saber Monograph No. 5. New York: Gay Academic Union, 1997, 129–38.

Olivier, Gerrit. "From ADA to ZELDA: Notes on Gays and Language in South Africa." In *Defiant Desire: Gay and Lesbian Lives in South Africa.* Mark Gevisser and Edwin Cameron, eds. Johannesburg: Raven Press, 1994, 219–24.

Simes, Gary. "The Language of Homosexuality in Australia." In *Gay Perspectives: Essays in Australian Gay Culture.* Robert Aldrich and Garry Wootherspoon, eds. Sydney: University of Sydney, 1992, 31–58.

See also Coming Out; Faggot; Fairy; Flowers and Birds; Queer

Gay Left

In 1895, the year of Friedrich Engels's death, Oscar Wilde, the great aesthete, critic, playwright, and notorious homosexual, first published in book form his essay "The Soul of Man Under Socialism" in which he praised socialism as the only form of government committed to the abolition of private property and the consequent liberation of all humankind. The historical coincidence of Engels's death and Wilde's essay serves as a powerful synecdoche for the puzzling, uneasy, sometimes tortured, and contradictory relationship of the gay and lesbian liberation movement to the political left.

According to the *Oxford English Dictionary* the use of "left" in a political sense originates with the French National Assembly of 1789, in which the nobility was seated to the president's right and the Third Estate, representing progressive, democratic politics, to his left. The term "left" in a political context has, over the years, expanded to include progressive politics around the world. By this definition, "gay left" might seem as redundant as "gay Republican" has in the United States historically seemed oxymoronic. For many, any advocacy of gay and lesbian rights is leftist.

Though there is no necessary connection between Marxist orthodoxy and leftist politics, there has been, in the twentieth century, a tendency to associate the two, and Marxist groups have often been able to define the proper parameters of left-wing ideology. In this situation, though gay and lesbian Marxists have persisted in the pursuit of an analysis sympathetic to homosexuality and based on Marxist principles, this effort must proceed without the benediction of Marx and Engels, whose opinions on the subject, insofar as they were expressed in private correspondence, were "distinctly unsympathetic" (in Hekma et al.).

Internationally, to the degree that the Left has been identified with the political and economic theories of Marx and Engels, there has been a confusion of policies regarding sexual orientation and behavior emanating from leftist governments. In the former Soviet Union and in China, homosexuality has been consistently punished, suppressed, and denied. In 1996, it was the Socialist Party in France that introduced into the National Assembly a bill that would legalize same-sex marriages, though it

G has been noted that those same French Socialists have been scandalously reticent regarding AIDS policy, reflecting deeply rooted homophobia and racism. In the United States, the career of gay liberation has been visible and sustained only in the post–World War II period, a period marked by the New Left, a Left self-consciously revisionist and eclectic, further confounding any sense of the relationship between theory and practice.

What is clear is that gay men and lesbians have invariably suffered under the political sway of the right, whether in Nazi Germany or in Pat Robertson's evangelical vision of America. In contrast, they have at least been able to hope for indifference or tolerance, if not embrace, from the political left. Most often history suggests that gay men and lesbians are, ironically, better off under the large umbrella of a struggling and oppressed left than with a successful, powerful one.

The relationship of gay and lesbian politics to the political left becomes even more tangled when social constructionist theories of gay and lesbian identity force a separation of identity and homosexuality. Though there is no question that homosexuality has always been with us, historians and others now debate whether or not the same can be said for an identity that bears any meaningful correspondence to what we today call "gay" and "lesbian." John D'Emilo, expanding on work by Michel Foucault and Jeffrey Weeks, employs a Marxist analysis to argue that two conditions of industrial capitalism—wage labor and commodity production—created the space in which modern gay and lesbian identity emerged. Whether such an analysis is politically leftist depends, as Hegel's students discovered about his reading of history, on whether one emphasizes the liberating aspect of capitalism compared with past history or its oppressiveness compared with an ideal future world.

Early Associations: Gays, Lesbians, and the Left

Homosexual rights activists, beginning with Magnus Hirschfeld's inauguration of the Scientific-Humanitarian Committee, generally recognized as the world's first homosexual rights organization, have remarkably often cast their lot with the politics of socialism. In England at the turn of the twentieth century, Edward Carpenter wrote widely popular treatises espousing socialism and very liberal views on sexuality. W. H. Auden and other homosexuals were drawn to the Communist Party in the 1920s and 1930s. Anthony Blunt and Guy Burgess were the two most famous British spies for the USSR of World War II. The precise link between the sexuality of these men and the attractions of communism is still to be articulated, but Malcolm Muggeridge once posed in print the fatuous hypothesis that the defection of Blunt and Burgess had less to do with the seductiveness of Marxism than with the natural gifts of homosexuals as actors combined with a grudge against society for having been deprived of the satisfaction of parenthood, this combination resulting in "an instinctive sympathy with effort to overthrow [society]." After the war, Burgess and Blunt went into exile in the Soviet Union, but most homosexuals who flirted with communism during the period were so disillusioned by Stalinism, including its antihomosexual component, that they rejected communism and returned to the fold. In Auden's case this included reconversion to Christianity.

World War II and the rise of fascism in Western Europe effectively destroyed the early homosexual rights movement there. The movement would find a sustained and visible theater of operations only in the United States after the war.

The Gay Left in the United States

The career of the gay left in the United States parallels the broad contours of the history of the American Left considered generally. The "old," Marxist left was never without partisans who, for ideological or personal reasons, worked to advance the cause of homosexuals. "Red Emma" Goldman's lectures on lesbianism and free love in the early 1900s provide a prominent example. Early leaders of the post–World War II homophile movement, most notably Harry Hay, received much of their training in organizing and strategy while members of the Communist Party U.S.A. The program of Hay's first homosexual organization was to use left politics as a vehicle to gain rights for homosexuals. Bachelors for Wallace was dedicated to the support of the Progressive Party candidate for president of the United States, Henry Wallace, in the 1948 election.

The 1950s saw homosexuality and communism linked by the political right in the United States. Though McCarthyism is most commonly remembered as an anticommunist witch-hunt, it was as virulent in its attacks on suspected homosexuals as it was on "reds" and "fellow travelers." The San Francisco Renaissance and the emergence of the Beat Generation during these years, led by such figures as Robert Duncan, Jack Spicer, Allen Ginsberg, and Jack

Kerouac, mingled homosexuality and vaguely leftist politics (Allen Ginsberg did, reportedly, on meeting Che Guevara, offer to fellate the revolutionary leader and theorist) in an aesthetic and literary enterprise.

In the political tempest of the 1960s, almost all radical political reform in the United States was cast in the patois of revisionist Marxism. The thought of Frankfurt School thinkers such as Herbert Marcuse was particularly influential, and as the gay liberation movement at the end of that decade eclipsed the homophile movement, it was perhaps inevitable that it, too, should adopt this vocabulary. After all, just as early leaders of the homophile movement had been schooled by the "Old Left," many leaders of the gay liberation movement had come up through the ranks of the "New Left." There was the Gay Activists Alliance and the Gay Liberation Front, the Gay Theater Collective, part of the People's Theater Collective of San Francisco in the 1980s, and the Gay People's Union of Milwaukee in the 1970s; *The New Gay Liberation Book* (1979) carried an epigraph from Karl Marx; and the activist group Red Butterfly hoped in the late 1960s to develop "an extended analysis of gay liberation and the family" based on Friedrich Engels's *The Origin of the Family, Private Property, and the State,* Wilhelm Reich's *The Sexual Revolution,* and "the literature of various women's liberation groups." The most honest appraisals, though, could not ignore the homophobic realities of history or of the moment; "free sex" and "free love" were to be free only for heterosexuals. Carl Wittman's widely reprinted "Refugees from Amerika: A Gay Manifesto," while it aped the forms and language of communism, denied that gays, as a group, were either Marxist or communist: "Neither capitalist nor socialist countries have treated us as anything other than non grata so far." Chicago Gay Liberation's 1970 "Working Paper for the Revolutionary Working People's Constitutional Convention" similarly noted the oppression of gays and lesbians by Marxist groups and vowed not to work with such groups any longer.

The relationship of the gay and lesbian left to the black left in the United States has been especially problematic. At the height of Black Panther visibility, Eldridge Cleaver declared homosexuality "a sickness, a disease like baby-killing or wanting to be president of GM." Huey Newton later offered a startling reappraisal: "Whatever your personal opinions and your insecurities about homosexuality and the various liberation movements among homosexuals and women (and I speak of the homosexuals and women as oppressed groups), we should try to unite with them in a revolutionary fashion. . . . I know through reading and through my life experience, my observations, that homosexuals are not given freedom and liberty by anyone in the society. Maybe they might be the most oppressed people in the society." The debate between coalition politics, which would include alliances with blacks, environmental activists, antinuclear activists, Latinos, and others, and identity politics, which stresses the uniqueness of gay and lesbian issues and the necessity for looking after their own, has been a perennial one in the gay and lesbian movement.

In the last twenty-five years, as American politics has settled into unexciting routines, the gay and lesbian movement has largely followed suit. The most prominent gay and lesbian organizations on the scene today are dedicated to participation in mainstream politics or the regular processes of the judicial system. The leftist press has continued to give greater attention to gay and lesbian issues than those issues receive in the mainstream press. Probably the most consistently leftist of the gay and lesbian publications in the United States is *Gay Community News* of Boston. The *Guardian,* a self-described "independent radical newsweekly" published by the Institute for Independent Social Journalism, provided regular sympathetic coverage to gay and lesbian issues until it ceased publication. Other publications from the left such as *In These Times, Mother Jones,* and the *Socialist Review* continue to do so. Gays and lesbians have often received their most enthusiastic political support from left, independent candidates including Angela Davis of the Communist Party U.S.A., Lenora Fulani, the Socialist Workers Party, and the New Alliance Party.

Against the relatively mundane political background of the 1980s and 1990s, there are momentary examples of radical resistance. Organizations like ACT UP, Queer Nation, Lesbian Avengers, and Radical Faeries are colorful and may be popularly considered the contemporary gay left and endorsed by the Left, though their leftist, as opposed to radical, credentials are tenuous. Urvashi Vaid has provided a genuinely leftist analysis of contemporary gay and lesbian politics for our time, and Tony Kushner has advocated what he calls "a socialism of the skin." Kushner directly engages a cohort of gay neoconservatives, including Bruce Bawer and Andrew Sullivan, who are engaged in a crusade against a chimerical and monolithic "gay left orthodoxy."

G

The International Gay Left

The post–World War II gay and lesbian rights movement in the United States has been the catalyst and model for the international movement. As Dennis Altman has noted, not only has gay and lesbian liberation resulted in the "homosexualization of America" but also the "Americanization of the homosexual." Groups and events all over the world have borrowed Stonewall, the rainbow flag, and other American symbols of the movement.

The "Americanization" of the movement does not mean that the politics of gay and lesbian liberation around the world is without local peculiarities, and it is clear that gay men and lesbians have, in some cases, been able to avoid the deep-seated, sexually suspicious Puritanism of the United States and to use indigenous political ideologies and local custom to their advantage. In the aftermath of the Sandinista revolution in Nicaragua, the new government refrained from making any laws specifically targeted at homosexuals, and officials of the Sandinista government professed a commitment to the equal rights of all Nicaraguans, including gays and lesbians. The minister of health under the Sandinistas, Dora Maria Tellez, was widely believed to be lesbian. The policy in practice, though, was really a version of "Don't ask, don't tell," and because homosexual activity, particularly among men in Nicaragua, while very common, tends to be more about machismo and specific behaviors than about identity and politics, there is a weak base for agitation for homosexual rights. One of the first acts of the Chamorro government, which succeeded the Sandinistas, was the proscription by law of even favorable public discussion of homosexuality.

Leftist governments, from Stalin's Soviet Union to Mao's China have been a source of disillusionment and disappointment to advocates for gay and lesbian rights. The situation that has been the most visible (and to many, the most disappointing) in the United States has been that of gays and lesbians in postrevolutionary Cuba. Cuba under Castro has conformed to Marxist orthodoxy in holding homosexuality, along with prostitution, to be a bourgeois perversion destined to disappear in a liberated society. Gay men are referred to as *escoria* (feeders on carrion) and are under constant risk of discovery by Committees for the Defense of the Revolution, though recent scholarship has sought to complicate this picture, especially for Cuba since the 1970s. In 1992 President Fidel Castro declared that homosexuality was "a natural human tendency that must simply be respected," though this declaration has hardly meant the transformation of Castro's Cuba into gay paradise.

The only country in the world today in which gays and lesbians are constitutionally guaranteed full equality under the constitution is South Africa, where the ruling African National Congress decided against collaboration with the Communists in the late 1920s.

James Darsey

Bibliography

Altman, Dennis. *The Homosexualization of America*. Boston: Beacon Press, 1983.

Arguelles, Lourdes, and B. Ruby Rich. "Homosexuality, Homophobia, and Revolution: Notes Toward an Understanding of the Cuban Lesbian and Gay Male Experience." In *Hidden from History: Reclaiming the Gay and Lesbian Past*. Martin Baum Duberman, Martha Vicinus, and George Chauncey Jr., eds. New York: New American Library, 1989, 441–55.

Bawer, Bruce, ed. *Beyond Queer: Challenging Gay Left Orthodoxy*. New York: Free Press, 1996.

Birken, Lawrence. "Homosexuality and Totalitarianism." *Journal of Homosexuality* 33 (1997).

Berlandt, Konstantin. "Been Down So Long It Looks Like Up to Me." In *The Sixties Papers*. Judith Clavir Albert and Stewart Edward Albert, eds. New York: Praeger, 1984, 450–55.

Darsey, James. "From 'Commies' and 'Queers' to 'Gay Is Good.' " *Gayspeak: Gay Male and Lesbian Communication*. James W. Chesebro, ed. New York: Pilgrim Press, 1981, 224–47.

———. "From 'Gay Is Good' to the Scourge of AIDS: The Evolution of Gay Liberation Rhetoric, 1977–1990." *Communication Studies* 42 (1991): 43–66.

D'Emilio, John "Capitalism and Gay Identity." In *Making Trouble: Essays on Gay History, Politics, and the University*. New York: Routledge, 1992, 3–16.

———. *Sexual Politics, Sexual Communities: The Making of a Homosexual Minority in the United States, 1940–1970*. Chicago: University of Chicago Press, 1983.

Fernbach, David. "Toward a Marxist Theory of Gay Liberation." *Socialist Revolution* 28 (April/June 1976): 29–41.

Gay Left Collective, ed. *Homosexuality: Power and Politics*. London: Allison & Busby, 1980.

Hekma, Gert, Harry Oosterhuis, and James Steakley, eds. *Gay Men and the Sexual History of the*

Political Left. New York: Harrington Park Press, 1995.

Jay, Karla, and Allen Young, eds. *Out of the Closets: Voices of Gay Liberation.* New York: Pyramid, 1972.

Katz, Jonathan. *Gay American History: Lesbians and Gay Men in the U.S.A.* New York: Crowell, 1976.

Kushner, Tony. "A Socialism of the Skin (Liberation, Honey!)." In *Thinking About the Longstanding Problems of Virtue and Happiness.* New York: Theatre Communications Group, 1995, 19–32.

Lancaster, Roger N. *Life Is Hard: Machismo, Danger, and the Intimacy of Power in Nicaragua.* Berkeley: University of California Press, 1992.

McCubbin, Bob. *The Gay Question: A Marxist Appraisal.* New York: World View Publishers, 1979.

Meyer, Gerald. "Gay and Lesbian Liberation Movement." *Encyclopedia of the American Left.* Mari Jo Buhle, Paul Buhle, and Dan Georgakas, eds. Urbana: University of Illinois Press, 1992, 257–65.

Mitchell, Pam, ed. *Pink Triangle: Radical Perspectives on Gay Liberation.* Boston: Alyson, 1980.

Morton, Donald, ed. *The Material Queer: A Lesbigay Cultural Studies Reader.* Boulder, Colo.: Westview, 1996.

Nathan, Debbie. "Cuban Homosexuals in Chicago: Refugees from the Revolution." *The [Chicago] Reader.* (June 12, 1981): 1:1ff.

Phillips, Eileen, ed. *The Left and the Erotic.* London: Lawrence and Wishart, 1983.

Rowbotham, Sheila, and Jeffrey Weeks. *Socialism and the New Life: The Personal and Sexual Politics of Edward Carpenter and Havelock Ellis.* London: Pluto, 1977.

Ruan, Fan-fu, and Yung-mei Tsai. "Male Homosexuality in Contemporary Mainland China." *Archives of Sexual Behavior* 17 (1988): 189–99.

Teal, Donn. *The Gay Militants.* New York: Stein and Day, 1971.

Timmons, Stuart. *The Trouble with Harry Hay: Founder of the Modern Gay Movement.* Boston: Alyson, 1990.

Tyburn, Susan. *Breaking the Chains: The Struggle for Gay Liberation and Socialism (An International Socialist Pamphlet).* Toronto: International Socialists, 1979.

Vaid, Urvashi. *Virtual Equality: The Mainstreaming of Gay and Lesbian Liberation.* New York: Anchor, 1995.

Workers World Party. *In the Spirit of Stonewall.* New York: World View, 1979.

Young, Allen. "The Cuban Revolution and Gay Liberation." *Out of the Closets: Voices of Gay Liberation.* Ed. Karla Jay and Allen Young. New York: Pyramid, 1972, 206–28.

See also ACT UP; Altman, Dennis; Auden, W. H.; Black Power Movement; Blunt, Anthony; Carpenter, Edward; China; Essentialist-Constructionist Debate; Foucault, Michel; France; Gay Liberation, Gay Liberation Front; Germany; Ginsberg, Allen; Guevara, Ernesto "Che"; Hay, Harry; Hirschfeld, Magnus; Homophile Movement; McCarthyism; Nazism and the Holocaust; Politics, Global; Queer Nation; Radical Faeries; Rainbow Flag; Religious Right; Russia; South Africa; Stonewall; Wilde, Oscar; Wittman, Carl

Gay Liberation

"Gay liberation" is a term that in contemporary culture has come to mean anything relating to the advancement of gay and lesbian rights. This generalization, however, has tended to elide the very specific social history of the term. Gay Liberation as a phrase and concept originally surfaced in the late 1960s. It was a component of the New Social movements or the New Left movements of the late 1960s, and was in theory and form—if not in practice—closely aligned with women's liberation, black liberation, and the yippie and hippie movements. During this time, gay and lesbian underground journalists started a newspaper called *Rat* that helped to popularize and disseminate the phrase.

Gay liberation as a philosophy was characterized by a radical embrace of social revolution and Marxist philosophy. It arose in opposition to earlier civil rights movements, such as the homophile movement, which suggested that social acceptance of homosexuals was the primary goal of activism. Liberationists, in contrast, believed that society itself needed radical restructuring and that accommodation was a conservative and counterproductive goal. The period between 1968 and 1971 produced a vast canon of radical tracts designed to explicate this view of gay liberation, many of which have been helpfully collated by Karla Jay and Allen Young in *Out of the Closet: Voices of Gay Liberation.* The manifesto written by the Chicago Third World Gay Revolution and Gay Liberation Front is exemplary; as it states:

G

While to us as individual gay people gay represents potential for love with equality and freedom, that's only the first level of gay is good. . . . A higher level of gay is good is as a tool to break down enforced heterosexuality, sex roles, the impoverished categories of straight, gay, and bisexual, male supremacy, programming of children, ownership of children, the nuclear family, monogamy, possessiveness, exclusiveness of "love," insecurity, jealousy, competition, privilege, individual isolation, ego-tripping, power-tripping, money-tripping, people as property, people as machines, rejection of the body, repression of emotions, anti-eroticism, authoritarian anti-human religion, conformity, regimentation, polarization of "masculine" and "feminine," categorization of male and female emotions, abilities, interests, clothing, etc., fragmentation of the self by these outlines, isolation and elitism of the arts, uniform standards of beauty, dependency on leaders, unquestioning submission to authority, power hierarchies, caste, racism, militarism, imperialism, national chauvinism, cultural chauvinism, domination, exploitation, division, inequality, and repression as the cultural and politico-economic norms, all manifestations of non-respect and non-love for what is human (not to mention animals and plants)—maybe even up to private property and the state.

Gay is not a person, nor is it a thing; rather, "Gay is the revolution."

Gay in these tracts symbolizes a process that works directly against the objectification and individuation of desire and identity. It is a form of revolution that can resist quantification into specific contents and that, thereby, could form a constellation of disparate revolutionary impulses. As Carl Wittman, a Berkeley activist, stated in 1969, "Chick equals nigger equals queer. Think about it." This attention to radical Marxist ideas of revolution led liberation theorists to sometimes extreme but always fascinating commentaries on the relationship between power, identity, eroticism, and sex. The lesbian activist Katz, writing in *Come Out!* in the final days of 1970, labeled sex not as a system of pleasure, but as the institutionalization of phallic imperialism. As she sees it,

Sex is an institution. In an oppressive society like Amerika, it reflects the same ideology as other major institutions. It is goal-oriented, profit and productivity oriented. It is a prescribed system, with a series of correct and building activities aimed toward the production of a single goal: climax.

It's also a drag. For women, in a culture based on our oppression, heterosexual sex is a product we have had to turn out. To encourage us, we are given two minutes of this, a few moments of that, a couple of minutes of something else . . . all aimed towards the Great Penetration and the Big Come. There is great pressure to have an orgasm. Sex without orgasm is a failure, it's a drag, it's incomplete, and very very sad. (Just like marriage is not real until it is "consummated.") Because of phallic imperialism built upon Freud's ignorance of the female body, orgasm is supposed to come from intercourse. That's just terrific for boys, but since our orgasm-producing organ is the clitoris, external to the vagina—contradicting capitalist sexist physiology—many women don't produce the appropriate orgasm through heterosexuality. By that criteria, they are frigid.

Because Katz defines sex as an economic system of capitalistic (re)production, and because (re)production in sex *as it is defined in capitalism* is contingent on the cross-gendered acts of penetration and orgasm (but really only *male* orgasm) that define the physical activities of heterosexuality, she comes to the astonishing but entirely congruent conclusion—lesbians do not have sex: "For me, coming out meant an end to sex. It's dead and gone in my life. I reject that institution totally. Sex means oppression, it means exploitation." In contrast to sex, Katz defines the physical interactions of women together as sensuality: "Sensuality is formless and amorphous. It can grow and expand as we feel it. It is shared by everyone involved."

The establishment of gay liberation as a political activist movement was propelled primarily by the Stonewall riots. Late on the night of Friday, June 27, 1969, New York City police staged one of their routine raids on a gay bar in Greenwich Village, the Stonewall Inn. The First Division of the New York City Police Department reportedly had staged five similar raids in the preceding three weeks, but this time the patrons fought back. *Rat* reported the events: "The crowd took charge. . . . Soon pandemonium broke loose. . . . The orgy was taking place. Vengeance vented against the source of repression."

Craig Rodwell, a participant in the riots and the owner of the Oscar Wilde Bookstore on Christopher Street, recalls,

> There was a very volatile political feeling, especially among young people. And when the night of the Stonewall riots came along, just everything came together at that one moment. People quite often ask, "What was special about that night . . . ?" There was no one thing that was special about it. It was just everything coming together, one of those moments in history where, if you were there, you just knew that this is IT. This is what you've been waiting for.

Historical accounts of the riot tend to be conflicted. There are the stories like Rodwell's, which suggest an apocalyptic consciousness to the day. As Allen Ginsberg said to a reporter from the *Village Voice*, "The guys [at the riot] were so beautiful—they've lost that wounded look that fags all had 10 years ago." The account in *Rat* says, "Strangely, no one spoke to the crowd or tried to direct the insurrection. Everyone's heads were in the same place." There are others, however, who recall the riots being started by a group of prostitutes, pimps, and addicts, with no real gay community involvement until at least a day later. Still others suggest that a substantially heterosexual hippie resistance initiated the event. There is also, of course, the omnipresent explanation: a spontaneous outpouring of grief over the death of Judy Garland, whose funeral took place the afternoon of the riots. Even the date varies, depending on the memory and on the choice between pinpointing the eruption as very late Friday or very early Saturday, and neither is there agreement on how long the riots lasted, though three days seems to be generally agreeable.

The effects of the riots, however, are well documented—and one particularly important one is the rift it engendered between homophile activists and gay liberation activists. Immediately after the riots, the Mattachine Society of New York (MSNY), one of the oldest homophile groups in America, organized an "action committee" to respond to and capitalize on the energy of the riots and called a community meeting at their organizational headquarters, Freedom House. Michael Brown, a New Left sympathizer and younger member of the group, volunteered to head the committee. The meeting resulted in a series of propositions, one of which was to stage a demonstration to protest police harassment. Brown, who considered the course to be far

too minimal and weak, began recruiting other New Left sympathizers to join the committee. The committee decided to separate from MSNY and to form a new organization, the Gay Liberation Front (GLF).

At the same time that Brown was separating from MSNY, two other New Left sympathizers, Bill Katzenberg and Charles Pitts, organized a meeting that sought to unite members of Students for a Democratic Society (SDS) who wanted to address gay and lesbian issues from a leftists perspective. Along with Susan Silverman, who was an early leftist force in the women's liberation movement, they held a meeting on July 24, 1969, at the Alternate University in lower Manhattan. Pitts recruited Pete Wilson, one of the few established homophile activists interested in radical theories of sex, to attend the meeting, and Wilson in turn brought many members of the now disenfranchised action committee of MSNY. This final coalescence of leftist thinkers formed the full nucleus of the GLF.

The new group staged a rapid-fire series of radical sex protests. They distributed leaflets at Kew Gardens in Queens to protest the efforts of neighborhood crusaders who were harassing and driving out gay men who were "cruising" for sex. They convened a "protest hang out" on Christopher Street and also picketed at the United Nations to commemorate the West German decriminalization of sodomy. The demonstrations differed not only in degree, but in kind, from earlier MSNY strategies. The radical attempts to raise social consciousness motivated the final separation between MSNY and GLF and established the group as its own entity.

GLF's rise as a political group was rocky and brief. By December of 1969, many of its members were expressing hostility toward the New Left ideal that motivated its formation. Many homosexuals in the group felt that the allegiance to a broad minority politics obscured the specific concerns of homosexuals. Perhaps the germinal event for these internal fissures was GLF's vote to support the Black Panthers—a group of New Left black activists who also publicly espoused a strong antihomosexual viewpoint. At this time a group of members of the GLF broke from the group and wrote a constitution for a new organization, the Gay Activists' Alliance (GAA). Similarly, many lesbians in the GLF felt that the group, dominated by men, was hostile to the minority concerns of women. A number of the lesbians in the GLF separated and formed their own alliance, The Radicalesbian Collective. Also at this time, the women's political action committee of the GLF offi-

G cially changed its name to Gay Women's Liberation Front and started holding its own meetings.

The simultaneous uprising of the Gay Activists' movement and the Gay Women's movement severely limited the authority of the GLF and also formed the basic structure of political activism that is still in place in America. Both groups formed as a response to alienation from both older, more conservative political organizations and the radical politics of the New Left movement. GAA members felt that the messages of accommodation preached by older homophile groups did little to champion a positive image of gay people, but at the same time sought goals of social reform and civil rights that found little support in New Left political programs. Members of the GWLF had originally split from the earlier women's movement because of its intense homophobia, but also found the sometimes violent misogyny of New Left movements to be just as unacceptable. It is this reaction against both the homophile movement and the New Left that crystallized a definitive split between gay male activism and lesbian activism in America—a split that still informs much contemporary political thought.

It was, moreover, this second wave of activists who helped to propel gay activism into a national movement. While activist groups relating to gay and lesbian issues existed in the 1960s in most major urban centers, the GAA specifically sought to motivate the growth of activism in all areas of America, including rural and agricultural areas. They established a National Gay Movement Committee that assigned more seasoned workers to help gay people in smaller towns form alliances. By 1973 the GAA was well on its way to achieving the goal of bringing liberational consciousness—at least as a known concept, if not an accepted practice—to all areas of America and some of Canada and Europe. And while radical activist groups had existed in other urban areas of the nations, most notably in the San Francisco Bay area and in Los Angeles, it was GAA who first instilled the idea of a national, rather than a local, agenda for gay activism.

The dominance of GAA was quickly supplanted, however, by yet another emerging activist group, the National Gay Task Force (NGTF). Unlike GAA, which specifically rejected the Mattachine philosophy of accommodation and embraced radical stances of consciousness work, NGTF sought to blend several aspects of gay liberation and earlier trends of accommodation together. Whereas Mattachine philosophies sought tolerance of homosexuals, NGTF sought acceptance. Whereas liberation philosophies posited homosexuals as essentially different from heterosexuals and indicative of a new social order, NGTF promoted homosexuals as important and productive members of society. Suturing the rift between Mattachine homophiles and liberationist radicals, while at the same time implicitly rejecting both, NGTF formed what in many ways is the basic and immutable structure of the modern gay civil rights movement.

NGTF's final reform of activism is also perhaps its most important. Moving away from tactics of demonstration and civil disobedience, the group instead formed strategic courses of legal intervention and institutional lobbying. One of its earliest and most important victories occurred in 1973, when NGTF members completed successful negotiations with the American Psychiatric Association to declassify homosexuality as a pathology. In 1974, NGTF successfully boycotted the ABC and NBC television networks to protest stereotypical portrayal and gays and lesbians in several shows. Working with the American Civil Liberties Union, the NGTF also launched a series of legal challenges that addressed issues of gay and lesbian paternity, the right for homosexuals to serve in the armed forces, and states restrictions on sodomy and other forms of consensual adult activity. In a mere two years NGTF succeeded in setting the parameters for the entire two decades of gay and lesbian politics to follow.

NGTF's rise to authority is perhaps the most important historical event for understanding the precise importance and dimensions of gay liberation. While by 1973 liberationist tactics had all but disappeared, their effects remained visible in the very ability of NGTF to exist. In retrospect, the importance of gay liberation might not rest so much in its specific content as in the effect it had on altering a trajectory of political progression. By using leftist politics as a means of dislodging the assumptions of homophile activism as championed by the Mattachines, gay liberation also opened up the space for the broad reconceptualization of political intervention that resulted in the NGTF. And in so doing, gay liberation became the unintentional source—or at least the cause—of virtually every dominant legal and political assumptions of the gay and lesbian movement today. *Gregory W. Bredbeck*

Bibliography

Jay, Karla, and Allen Young. *Out of the Closet: Voices of Gay Liberation.* 20th anniversary edition. New York: New York University Press, 1994.

Marotta, Toby. *The Politics of Homosexuality.* Boston: Houghton Mifflin, 1981.

Teal, Donn. *The Gay Militants.* New York: Stein and Day, 1971.

Weiss, Andrea, and Greta Schiller. *Before Stonewall: The Making of a Gay and Lesbian Community.* Tallahassee, Fla.: The Naiad Press, 1988.

See also Activism, U.S.; Assimilation; Black Power Movement; Gay Activists Alliance (GAA); Gay Left; Gay Liberation Front; Gay and Lesbian Press; Gay Rights in the United States; Homophile Movement; Mattachine Society; National Gay and Lesbian Task Force; Queer Politics; Stonewall; Wittman, Carl

Gay Liberation Front

Formed in the aftermath of the 1969 Stonewall riots, New York City's Gay Liberation Front (GLF) was, in the words of one of its manifestos, "a militant coalition of radical and revolutionary men and women committed to fight the oppression of the homosexual as a minority group and to demand the right to the self-determination of our own bodies." New York's GLF was among the first of the hundreds of gay liberation groups that spread across the United States in the late 1960s and early 1970s. During these years, Gay Liberation Fronts were started in big cities like Philadelphia, Los Angeles, and Chicago and in college towns such as Tallahassee, Florida, and Austin, Texas. By the fall of 1970 a London GLF had formed.

Gay Liberationists were not the first organized gay and lesbian rights activists. In the 1950s and 1960s, homophile groups such as the Mattachine Society and the Daughters of Bilitis pushed for the integration of homosexuals into society. Though homophile groups had become increasingly militant by the late 1960s, for the most part they remained wed to a politics of respectability. GLF activists, often ignorant of the hard work their predecessors had done, were critical of what they saw as the homophile movement's timid reform efforts. Calling themselves "revolutionaries," GLFers sought to transform society, not gain admittance to it.

In adopting this oppositional stance, gay liberationists threw their lot in with the Movement, the loosely defined coalition of Black Power, feminist, and New Left groups that was so much a part of the landscape of the late 1960s and early 1970s. The Gay Liberation Front participated in anti–Vietnam war demonstrations, Black Panther Party rallies, and actions undertaken by radical feminists. Unfortunately, GLFers found that their presence at Movement rallies was not always appreciated. GLF activists were often hurt by the homophobic rhetoric and actions of Movement activists.

Internal debates over ideology, gender, and race contributed to the breakup of many Gay Liberation Fronts. New York's GLF very early broke up into quasi-independent "cells," reflecting the members' complex identities and commitments. By the early 1970s, for example, many of the women in the GLF had broken off to form lesbian-feminist organizations. By 1972 the last New York City GLF cells folded. Very few of the other GLF outlasted their predecessor.

Despite their brief lives, New York's Gay Liberation Front and its sister fronts were influential. The reams of propaganda published and distributed by the GLFs reached hundreds of thousands and provided a language of resistance and community that still resonates. The history of Queer Nation—the first chapter of which was founded in New York City in the 1990s—recapped GLF's history almost to the letter. The discussions at both Queer Nation and GLF meetings were loud, circular, divisive, and inspiring. For better and for worse, the conjunction of the politics of the sixties and the politics of homosexuality as embodied in the Gay Liberation Front are still with us today.   *Terence Kissack*

Bibliography

Kissack, Terence. "Freaking Fag Revolutionaries: New York's Gay Liberation Front, 1969–1971." *Radical History Review* 62 (Spring 1995).

Weeks, Jeffrey. *Coming Out: Homosexual Politics in Britain from the Nineteenth Century to the Present.* London: Quartet Books, 1990.

See also Black Power Movement; Feminism; Gay Liberation; Mattachine Society; Queer Nation; Stonewall

Gay Men's Health Crisis (GMHC)

The Gay Men's Health Crisis was the first and has remained the largest AIDS information, service, and advocacy organization in the world. The six cofounders were Nathan Fain, Larry Kramer, Lawrence Mass, Paul Popham, Paul Rapoport, and Edmund White. Officially established January 4,

G 1982, in Larry Kramer's living room in New York City, GMHC was the outgrowth of the NYU Fund for Kaposi's Sarcoma and Opportunistic Infections (KSOI), the first appeals for which were likewise made in Kramer's home by NYU dermatology chief Dr. Alvin Friedman-Kien.

GMHC was immediately and hugely successful within the gay community, thanks largely to its first president, Paul Popham, a former Green Beret who was a magnet for the white middle-class gay men who summered in Fire Island Pines and were its first principal constituency. By contrast, gay movement and community activists tended to keep their distance. They were the ones who had fought so hard for civil liberties and were suspicious of anything having to do with Kramer, who had written *Faggots*, a blisteringly satirical novel about gay life, or with official medicine, which had a long history of pathologizing homosexuality. Likewise keeping its distance was the *New York Times*, which ran a front-page story on a viral epidemic among Lippizaner stallions but had yet to give such attention to an epidemic that the Centers for Disease Control had designated as "the most important new public health problem in the United States." Similarly, the newspaper of record did not even mention GMHC's first benefit, an event with the Circus at Madison Square Garden that featured such stars as Leonard Bernstein and that was the largest and best-attended explicitly gay event in history up to that time.

Despite its huge budget and expansive, pioneering, and standard-setting achievements, especially in the areas of crisis intervention, individual and group counseling, and legal services, GMHC has frequently been the butt of criticism for conservatism, most sensationally and persistently from cofounder Kramer, who eventually resigned and whose legendary feuds with the organization's leadership he dramatized in his play *The Normal Heart*.

According to Rodger McFarlane, pioneering former executive director of GMHC and architect of some of its most innovative programs and policies, "What's historically important about GMHC is that it provided the model for hundreds of other health agencies and advocacy groups, nationally and internationally, and for other diseases as well as AIDS. It has set new standards for consumer response to disease and health care in America and throughout the world."   *Lawrence D. Mass*

Bibliography

Andriote, John. *Victory Deferred*. Chicago: University of Chicago Press, 1999.

Kayal, Philip M. *Bearing Witness: Gay Men's Health Crisis and the Politics of AIDS*. Boulder, Colo.: Westview Press, 1993.

Kramer, Larry. *Reports from the Holocaust*. New York: St. Martin's Press, 1994.

See also AIDS; AIDS Organizations, U.S.; Bernstein, Leonard; Kramer, Larry; Mass, Lawrence; Sexually Transmitted Diseases; White, Edmund

Gay Relationships

Human relationships occur as humans interact with one another within historical, material, and cultural conditions. The form that these relationships take is

GMHC at the March on Washington (1993). Photo by Marc Geller.

greatly influenced by the beliefs and ideologies present in the society in which they form. Throughout various periods of history, dominant beliefs and ideologies have accommodated, prohibited, encouraged, or tolerated intimate "gay" relationships between men resulting in three different forms: age-differentiated, status-differentiated, or egalitarian relationships.

Age-differentiated relationships are relationships between people of different ages, sometimes between adult men and young boys but also between adult men. Status-differentiated relationships are those where one partner engages in one type of behavior (such as active) while the other consistently engages in an often stigmatized complementary behavior (such as passive). The male-male relationships of ancient Greece and Rome were both age- and status-differentiated. Adult men regularly had sexual intercourse with unwilling prepubescent boys (only slave boys in Rome), with men taking the active role. Such relationships were possible within a system of beliefs where pleasure was reserved for men and passivity in men was scorned. Other societies where age-differentiated relationships existed include Melanesia, Japan, and Sudan. Status-differentiated relationships have existed in Oman and Pakistan, where the *khanith* and the *hijra,* respectively, played the stigmatized role of the receptive partner.

In the Northern Hemisphere, particularly the United States and Europe, egalitarian gay relationships have begun to emerge. In these relationships, one's sexual attraction for the same sex is an important part of one's identity, resulting in the desire to develop intimate sexual relationships not so different from heterosexual marriages. The age or sexual role played by one's partner does not limit one's choice of partners, and each partner enters the relationship willingly. Although a tremendous stigma is still placed on one who publicly acknowledges his or her homosexuality, most gay men pursue such relationships.

In the early stages of the contemporary gay movement, some gay writers encouraged gay men to be wary of imitating heterosexual relationships. They encouraged gay men to avoid exclusiveness, promises about the future, and inflexible roles. Influenced by feminism, these writers saw heterosexual marriage as oppressive and unnecessary. Instead, they advocated that gay men create their own social structures for their relationships, defining for themselves with whom and how they should live. As a result, men experimented with open relationships and communal living arrangements. But the presence of AIDS in the latter part of the twentieth century has complicated such arrangements.

Most of the research conducted on gay couples in the 1970s demonstrated that many gay couples were open—allowing the partners to have sexual relations with people outside the relationship. But once the HIV virus was linked to AIDS, gay men were advised to reduce their number of sex partners. Then an increasing number of gay men began to develop monogamous relationships. Additionally, the problems faced by partners of people with AIDS (lack of medical coverage, hospital visitation policies, conflicts over inheritance) highlighted the unequal treatment of gay relationships, resulting in increased demands for equal treatment. Thus, to ensure equal treatment, the contemporary gay movement has begun to advocate for the institutionalization of gay relationships by demanding the legalization of gay marriage.

In addition to the legal level, social scientists have begun to compare gay and lesbian to heterosexual relationships, which will result in institutionalization on a social level. Once models of gay relationships are developed and confirmed, therapists and instructors will potentially teach these models as they do heterosexual models, making them a standard part of the culture.

Recent research on gay couples has found that gay and lesbian relationships are more able to achieve equality between partners than are heterosexual couples and are more able to resist traditional sex roles within their relationships. However, the continued stigmatization of homosexuality causes problems. Gays and lesbians receive less family support than other couples, and issues with family members are among the problems most often cited by gay couples.

Although there has been an increased interest in monogamy among gay men, there are still couples who successfully create and maintain alternative forms of relationships. These include various forms of nonmonogamy, sexual friendships, communal promiscuity, and couples who live separately. Some of these forms (particularly nonpossessive love) are explored by Radical Faeries—a collective of men who join together in circles to explore the spirituality of being gay.

One model of egalitarian relationships was developed by David McWhirter and Andrew Mattison. In their model, they argue that most gay couples' relationships pass through six different stages, each of which has its own characteristics. The blending stage is characterized by limerance—the intense emotional feelings of togetherness—and high sexual activity. The nesting stage is characterized by home and compatibility building as well as a decline in limerance. In maintaining, the third stage, the couple begins to establish a balance between individualization and the intensity of togetherness experienced in the earlier stages. In the collaborating stage the couple experiences a new sense of security, releasing the partners to develop independent interests while still being supported. In the fifth stage, trusting, partners merge money and possessions and may begin to take the relationship and each other for granted. The final stage is the renewing stage. By the time the couple has reached this stage, they have generally reached their personal goals, expect their relationship to be permanent, and begin to develop concerns about personal health and security as well as the death of their partner.

Although each couple's relationship is different, McWhirter and Mattison postulate that the first four stages occur within the first ten years of a relationship. Stage five generally occurs between ten and twenty years, with stage six occurring after twenty years. The value of the model, however, comes not from comparing chronological ordering. The model allows gay couples who are experiencing difficulties the possibility of comparing their relationship to others. In many cases the model demonstrates that their difficulties are actually common occurrences in the life of a contemporary male-male relationship.   *R. Jeffrey Ringer*

Bibliography

Berger, Raymond M. "Men Together: Understanding the Gay Couple." *Journal of Homosexuality* 19, no. 3 (1990): 31–49.

Blumstein, Phillip, and Pepper Schwartz. *American Couples*. New York: Morrow, 1983.

Hay, Harry. *Radically Gay: Gay Liberation in the Words of Its Founder*. Will Roscoe, ed. Boston: Beacon Press, 1960.

McWhirter, David. P., and Andrew M. Mattison. *The Male Couple*. Englewood Cliffs, N.J.: Prentice-Hall, 1984.

Murray, Stephen O., and Will Roscoe. *Islamic Homosexualities: Culture, History and Literature*. New York: New York University Press, 1997.

Patterson, David G., and Pepper Schwartz. "The Social Construction of Conflict in Intimate Same-Sex Couples." In *Conflict in Personal Relationships*. Dudley Cahn, ed. Hillsdale, N.J.: Lawrence Erlbaum, 1994.

Veyne, Paul. "Homosexuality in Ancient Rome." In *Western Sexuality*. Philip Aries and Andre Bejin, eds. Oxford: Basil Blackwell,1985, 26–35.

See also AIDS; Couple; Feminism; Friendship; Gay Families; Hijras of India; Japan; Khanith; Melanesia; Radical Faeries; Same-Sex Marriage

Gay Rights in the United States

The American people's attitudes toward the rights of lesbians and gay men can be characterized as a combination of a distaste for homosexuality per se, a dislike of homosexuals as a group, along with an evolving tolerance for the rights of lesbians, gay men, and bisexuals.

Few systematic data exist about attitudes toward homosexuals and homosexuality prior to the 1970s. From 1973 until 1991, between two-thirds and three-quarters of the American people have said they thought same-sex sexual relations to be "always wrong." Since 1991, disapproval rates declined to the point that, in 1996, only 56 percent thought it "always wrong." In the earlier period, between 10 and 15 percent said homosexual relations were "not wrong at all"; by 1996, that percentage nearly doubled—to 26 percent.

Homosexuals may well be the single most systematically disliked group of citizens in the United States. Between 1984 and 1994, about 30 percent of the American people said they had the coldest possible feelings toward lesbians and gay men. By 1996, this percentage had dropped to only 20 percent—a substantial change. Similarly, between 1984 and 1994, an absolute majority of Americans characterized their feelings toward lesbians and gay men as being more cold and distant than as warm and close. In 1996, only 44 percent characterized their feelings in those terms. The mean rating of respondents' warmth to gay people rose from 30.0 degrees in 1984 to 37.7 in 1992 and reached 39.9 degrees in 1996. While some might find this increase to be gratifying, researchers have been hard-pressed to find another group of citizens toward whom their fellow Americans hold as cold feelings.

As a rule in public opinion research, public attitudes toward social groups are more stable than are public attitudes on specific policy issues. Generally, people infer from their feelings toward groups in society to positions on public issues. Many people operate in terms of self-interest—and the overwhelming majority of Americans do not think of themselves as being lesbian, gay, or bisexual. In some cases, having acquaintances, friends, or relatives who belong to a social grouping may result in warmer, more charitable feelings toward that group and translate into support for public policies perceived as benefiting that group. During the mid-1980s, roughly a quarter of Americans said they had friends or acquaintances who were homosexual. A decade later, the comparable figure rose to 50 percent or more. This should lead one to expect a substantial liberalization of public attitudes. Before examining some specific data, some words of cautions should be raised. First, the overall levels of negative attitudes toward gay people and toward homosexuality did not decline in proportion to the increase in the percent of the population who said they knew a gay person. Second, one cannot be certain of the direction of causality between liberalized attitudes and knowing gay people. The correlational data demonstrate that liberalized attitudes on gay rights issues is associated with saying that one knows a gay person. Quite possibly, the questionnaire items measure realizing that one knows gay people; that is, one must know that one knows a gay person, and many Americans appear not to realize that they, in fact, encounter gay people every day. Quite possibly, saying that one knows a gay person is more a measure of the respondent's openness to diversity than it is a measure of the nature of the respondent's acquaintances.

While the gay rights movement was an outgrowth of the seemingly radical youth culture of the 1960s and 1970s, and was strongly influenced by the civil rights movement, the antiwar movement, and the feminist movement, by the 1990s, the major public issues surrounding the rights of gay people had focused on questions that are matters of everyday life for most Americans (at least for heterosexual Americans). Notably—after the radical demand for the right to assert one's sexuality publicly and not to be forced into a life of hiding and deception—the major issues have been demands for freedom from discrimination in employment and in housing and for the right to domesticity, including marriage, adoption, and inheritance.

The American people have shown increasingly high levels of support for the rights of gay men and lesbians in the areas of employment and housing. For the past twenty years, a clear majority of Americans have supported equal rights in terms of job opportunities. In 1996, 50 percent more Americans (84 percent) think that gay people should have equal rights in terms of job opportunities than in 1977, when only 56 percent thought so. However, when the question becomes whether or not there should be a law to protect homosexuals against job discrimination, majority support remains, but at lower levels (ranging from 52 percent in 1983 to 60 percent in 1996). The most recent trend data on support for equal rights for gay people in terms of housing confirms the extraordinarily high levels of support shown for employment rights. Eighty percent of the American people think that there should be "equal rights for gays in terms of housing."

The issue of same-sex marriage may well pose the greatest threat to hegemonic heteronormative assumptions about the cultural necessity of conventional heterosexual relationships and family structure. More than thirty years have passed since the passage of the Civil Rights Act of 1964 and the Supreme Court decision in *Loving v. Virginia,* which declared unconstitutional antimiscegenation laws that forbade marriage between persons of different races in 1967. Nevertheless, at least one American in six thinks that there should be a law prohibiting interracial marriages. Thus, it is not surprising that the prospect of same-sex marriage should arouse intense opposition in the public. The most recent data show that 35 percent of Americans think there should be "equal rights for gays in terms of legally sanctioned gay marriages," a 25 percent increase in a five-year period. Nevertheless, almost two out of three Americans oppose same-sex marriages.

Intriguingly, while Americans are opposed to extending the symbolic recognition of marriage to same-sex couples, majorities support extending certain tangible benefits associated with marriage. Since May 1996, just over 60 percent of Americans have favored inheritance rights for gay spouses. Support for equal rights for gay spouses in terms of Social Security benefits has increased substantially. In May 1996, just weeks before the passage of the Defense of Marriage Act (DOMA), which prohibited same-sex couples from marrying and claiming federal benefits such as Social Security, 48 percent of Americans supported these rights. By June 1997, support had increased to 57 percent, indicating that roughly one-fifth of those who had opposed these rights now supported them.

Analysis of these data leads to the conclusion that all trends in public opinion toward lesbians and gay men are toward growing acceptance of the rights of gay people, as well as toward increased tolerance of homosexuals and homosexuality. Never-

G

theless, there has been greater acceptance over time of specific equal rights for gay people than there has been of general approval of the role of gay people in society.
*Kenneth Sherrill and
Alan S. Yang*

Bibliography

Data sources: General Social Survey, 1973–1996, conducted by the National Opinion Research Center, University of Chicago. National Election Studies conducted by the Center for Political Studies at the University of Michigan and made available by the ICPSR. Yankelovich and Princeton Survey Research Associates data made available through ICPSR.

Sherrill, Kenneth. "On the Political Power of Lesbians, Gay Men, and Bisexuals." *PS: Political Science and Politics* (September 1996).

———. "Homosexuality and Civil Liberties," American Political Science Association, 1987.

Yang, Allan S. "Attitudes toward Homosexuality." *Public Opinion Quarterly* (Fall 1997).

See also Homosexual Panic; U.S. Law: Equal Protection

Gay Studies

In the past twenty years scholarly research in the field of gay and lesbian studies has experienced exponential growth. Previously ignored in academic circles, queer studies is now expanding from interdisciplinary origins to recognized programs on campuses around the United States. Scholarship in gay studies covers a broad spectrum of interests including the history of sexual identities, gay and lesbian rights movement, community structure, and subcultures within gay society. Coming to fruition in the 1990s, the field is marked by a zeal similar to the development of African American studies and women's studies.

Academic research on the topic of homosexuality has been fostered by both political and personal motives. Some writers such as Jeffrey Escoffier have questioned "whether as an academic discipline it should or can exist without structural ties to gay and lesbian political struggles." Others point to the efforts of pioneering academicians, historians, and authors who strongly believed in justice through knowledge. Most of the founders of gay and lesbian studies followed in the footsteps of Magnus Hirschfeld and were gay and lesbian rights activists.

Prior to coinage of the term *gay studies,* individual such as Heinrich Hoessli, Karl Ulrich, John Addington Symonds, and Edward Carpenter conducted the first research on same-sex love. The researchers focused on finding historical factors that would validate their sexual feelings and prove to society that same-sex love could be an affirming experience.

Heinrich Hoessli (1784–1864), was the premier gay scholar and homosexual rights advocate. His book *Eros: Die Männerliebe der Griechen* (Eros: The Male Love of the Greeks, 1836–1838) gathered literary materials from ancient Greece and medieval Islam that exhibited cases of love between men. Karl Heinrich Ulrichs's (1825–1895) encyclopedic *Forschungen zur Mannmännlichen Liebe* (Research on Love Between Males, 1864–1870) studied the ethnography, history, and literature of homosexuality.

Far broader in scope was the work of the Wissenschaftlich-humanitäre Komitee (Scientific-Humanitarian Committee), which published the journal *Jahrbuch für sexuelle Zwischenstufen* (Yearbook for Sexual Intergrades). Published in twenty-three volumes, the yearbook covered a broad spectrum of homosexuality, including extremely valuable bibliographies of historical and contemporary literature. Working under the tutelage of Magnus Hirschfeld, the committee posited homosexuality was a constant and stable phenomenon throughout history.

Richard von Krafft-Ebing's *Psychopathia Sexualis* (1886) presented a view of homosexuality as sexual abnormality. In the meantime, homosexual apologetics were presented by Albert Moll's *Berühmte Homosexuelle* (Famous Homosexuals, 1910). In Italy Paolo Mantegazza (1831–1910) compiled anthropological materials on the subject in *Gli amori degli uomini* (Sexual Relations of Mankind, 1886). Later Iwan Bloch (1872–1922) attacked the concept of innate homosexuality in *Beiträge zur Ätiologie der Psychopathia Sexualis* (Contributions to the Etiology of Psychopathia Sexualia, 1902). Psychopathic dimensions were established by writings of Sigmund Freud's *Drei Abhandlungen zur Sexualtheorie* (Three Essays on the Theory of Sexuality, 1905).

In Britain, John Addington Symonds was a leader in the field of homosexual research. Two privately printed titles, *A Problem in Greek Ethics* and *A Problem in Modern Ethics,* introduced the English-speaking reader to the gay research of Karl Ulrichs and Walt Whitman. Meanwhile, Andrew

Dickson White's comprehensive analysis and dismissal of the Sodom legend was inserted into his two-volume *History of Warfare of Science with Christendom* (1896), while Marc-André Raffalovich published *Uranisme et unisexualité* (Uranism and Unisexuality), containing German bibliographical and literary materials. Edward Irenaeus Prime-Stevenson published the key work, *The Intersexes,* in Naples in the early twentieth century. The book collected gay folklore and studied socio-historical roots of European homosexuality.

Just as German-language research on homosexuality was ignored in the United States, it was also ignored during organizational endeavors in 1924 and 1925. An amateur effort to create a gay rights group at the University of Chicago died; the university's prestigious school of sociology failed to address the issue of homosexuality, while engaging many other issues of "deviancy."

In 1938 Alfred C. Kinsey began conducting a massive series of interview studies that provided the material for his *Sexual Behavior in the Human Male.* The book challenged the medical model of sexual pathology and advocated the concept of homosexuality as an expression sexual pluralism. The Kinsey studies, by challenging established scientific thought and raising public consciousness of homosexuality, acted as a driving force for the development of gay and lesbian studies.

Research during the middle of the twentieth century was performed outside the walls of academia by the Mattachine Society, ONE Inc., medical consulting facilities, or scholars in private libraries. Materials were published in specialized journals with limited availability and duration. This impeded the creation of an academic tradition with scholarly credentials. Until Stonewall, each generation of gay men and lesbians had to restart the job of reconstructing a history and heritage of same-sex love. The first regular college courses to adopt an approach sympathetic to homosexuality and uphold scholarly aspirations seem to have been offered by Rosalind Regelson at New York and Yale Universities in the late 1960s.

The gay intelligentsia coalesced in the Gay Academic Union, with a founding conference held at John Jay College in New York City in November 1973. A new gay studies journal was created named *Gai Saber.* The early 1970s also witnessed the approval of a homophile studies course at the University of Nebraska, taught by Louis Crompton. In July 1972, Sacramento State University offered the first gay studies program.

Through the efforts of gay scholar John Boswell, the Lesbian and Gay Studies Center was opened at Yale University. Soon afterward the governing board of the City College of San Francisco approved the first gay and lesbian studies department. Also in the 1980s Martin Duberman began the process of creating the Center for Lesbian and Gay Studies (CLAGS) at the graduate school of the City University of New York; it was formally established in 1991.

With the formalization of gay studies curricula, patterns have emerged in schools of thought. During the early 1970s there was a search for historical authenticity, proceeded by ongoing issues of social construction of identity, race, and culture.

Michael A. Lutes

Bibliography

Abelove, Henry, Michele Barale, and David Halperin, eds. *Lesbian and Gay Studies Reader.* New York: Routledge, 1993.

Bunzl, Maatti. "Between Oppression and Affirmation: Historical Ethnography of Lesbian and Gay Pasts." *Anthropological Quarterly* 68, no. 2 (April 1995): 121–28.

Dynes, Wayne R. "Queer Studies in Search of a Discipline." *Academic Questions* 8, no. 4 (Fall 1995): 34–52.

Knapper, Karl Bruce. "Queer Subjects: Lesbian and Gay Studies." *Socialist Review* 25, no. 1 (Winter 1995): 25–29.

Minton, Henry L., ed. "Gay and Lesbian Studies." *Journal of Homosexuality* 24, no. 1–2 (1992): 1–202.

Nardi, Peter, and Beth Schneider, eds. *Social Perspectives in Lesbian and Gay Studies.* New York: Routledge, 1998.

Roscoe, Will. "Strange Craft, Strange History, Strange Folks: Cultural Amnesia and the Case for Lesbian and Gay Studies." *American Anthropologist* 97, no. 3 (September 1995): 448–53.

See also Activism, U.S.; Bloch, Iwan; Carpenter, Edward; Education: Theory and Pedagogy; Freud, Sigmund; Hirschfeld, Magnus; Hössli, Heinrich; Kinsey, Alfred; Krafft-Ebing, Richard von; Mattachine Society; Moll, Albert; *ONE* Magazine; Raffalovich, Marc-André; Symonds, John Addington

Geldzahler, Henry (1935–1994)

This American critic, curator, and early advocate of pop art, was born in Antwerp, Belgium, on July 9,

1935, the son of a diamond broker, and he immigrated to New York City in 1940. Trained as an art historian at Yale and Harvard Universities, he was the first curator of twentieth-century art at the Metropolitan Museum of Art, where his most controversial show was *New York Painting and Sculpture: 1940–1970*.

An "incurable aesthete," Geldzahler was not handsome, but he was a favorite subject of artists, making of himself, according to Francesco Clemente, "an image as good as a great painting." Henry's *pose* was that of an openly homosexual man, which, in contrast to many of his museum colleagues, was no pose at all.

During the 1960s, Geldzahler was among Andy Warhol's coterie at the Factory, and he was the lone actor in one of Warhol's earliest films, in which he merely smokes a cigar. Supposedly, Geldzahler gave Warhol the suggestion for his *Disaster Series* (1963). Geldzahler was one of David Hockney's closest friends, and the subject of numerous of his paintings including the "marriage portrait," *Henry Geldzahler and Christopher Scott* (1969), and his reverie on art history, *Looking at Pictures on a Screen* (1977).

In 1977 Geldzahler became New York City commissioner of cultural affairs and the first openly gay commissioner in the city's history. Retiring from politics in the 1980s, he once more took up the role of glamorous patron, participating in the meteoric rise of Keith Haring and Jean-Michel Basquiat. He died of cancer on August 16, 1994.

Jonathan Weinberg

Bibliography

Geldzahler, Henry. *Making It New: Essays, Interviews and Talks*. New York: Turtle Point Press, 1994.

See also Haring, Keith; Hockney, David; Warhol, Andy

Gender

Gender is a concept that exists in fields from biology to linguistics and sociology and refers to the "sex" of an individual. In spite of the fundamental nature of the concept, gender has become an increasingly contentious topic. For this article, *gender* may be discussed as a biological category and as an issue within social, psychological, and cultural discourse.

In biology the issue of gender is at its clearest. At its simplest, this consists of assigning each human being to a biological category consisting of male or female. Even at this level, the notion is more complex than it might appear. What, for instance, should be the basis on which we decide the gender to which someone belongs? Traditionally the decision has been made on the basis of the appearance of the external genitalia. Advances in medical understanding have placed this basis of assignment under considerable strain with the possibility of surgery to completely transform the appearance of external genitalia. This method of assignment also fails to take adequate account of the significant number of live births each year where babies are born with "ambivalent" genitalia, often possessing some of the genital characteristics of each sex. More sophisticated biological mechanisms have become available to judge the appropriate gender of an individual. The most common of these is the examination of chromosomes, where generally females have two X chromosomes while males possess both an X and a Y. Even this is less certain than is popularly believed. There are cases, for example, of males seeking gender-reassignment treatment who had two or even three X chromosomes and one Y chromosome. Other yet more sophisticated biochemical indicators have been proposed at various times, often in an attempt to prevent "cheating" in sports events, though none of these have proved fool-proof and straightforward.

At a biological level, then, the concept of gender gets progressively less straightforward the further we look into it. This might cause us to question just how fundamental this category ought to be. Things are further complicated at the biological level when we understand that a fetus always begins its development as a female, only transforming into a male fetus after several weeks in the womb.

More significant than biological notions of gender, for most of us at any rate, are social, cultural, and psychological notions. Not only are these the notions with which most of us come into daily contact, but they are, perhaps because of their influence on daily life, more hotly disputed than biological notions.

All these notions relate to the influence that an individual's assigned or presumed biological gender identification should have on his or her character, behavior, and life changes. Socially and culturally, there are considered to be appropriate ways in which individuals of each gender should behave. Such social and cultural notions, often strongly held and forming the basis of widespread prejudice, include a number of ideas. In the West, for example, this complex of notions would include the following: men are strong and unemotional, competitive and work-orientated, sexually and physically aggressive, sexually attracted to women. On the other hand, women are caring and noncompetitive, physically weak, submissive and deferential to men, fall in love with and are sexually attracted to men.

Such gender-based notions also arise in the field of psychology. Men are thought to be analytical, while women are intuitive. Men are oriented toward tasks, goals, and mechanisms, while women are oriented toward the needs of individuals and relationships.

Such preconceptions of gender role, behavior, and inclination are clearly sources of prejudice against and the stigmatizing of sexual minorities. Gay men are sexually attracted to men, not women, while lesbians are attracted to women. Bisexuals are attracted, in some degree, to individuals belonging to each gender group. Transsexuals, transvestites, and transgendered people challenge gender stereotypes in more fundamental, and thus more threatening, ways in the eyes of the wider society.

There is a long-running dispute over the extent to which such social notions of gender are learned from existing social norms or are biologically determined. If they are biologically determined, then those who violate such social gender norms are rebelling against nature, which can lead to greater condemnation. If such norms are socially learned, however, then those who transgress them are merely rebelling against society, challenging it to change its norms. Whichever way these norms are viewed, the reaction of society to those who transgress such gender roles tends to be overwhelmingly hostile.

It may thus be argued that the notion of gender, and more specifically social and cultural notions of behaviors and attitudes appropriate to different genders, are at the root of the oppression experienced by different sexual minorities. Not only members of sexual minorities but also all people committed to the personal integrity of the individual and to freedom of choice for the individual have a vested interest in removing much of the rigidity from social and cultural conceptions of gender.

Regardless of issues of sexual orientation, the above stereotypes based on social and cultural norms associated with gender roles suggest that for men, being violent is appropriate and understandable behavior, as is a lack of relationship building and relationship-maintenance skills. For many, these stereotypes are increasingly difficult to accept and may encourage behaviors that are not in the best interests of individuals, or of the wider society.

At the root of all such gender stereotypes is a particular mind-set that relates most readily to a binary universe, that is, a universe consisting of black and white, of direct opposites, without intermediate stages. This leads to an insistence on the appropriateness of "either/or" assumptions. An individual must be either male or female, aggressive or passive, competitive or nurturing, and so on.

This represents too simplistic an understanding of the universe; a more helpful approach would be to move toward accepting that in addition to either/or we accept the possibility of "both/and" as an alternative. This would mean, for example, that where an individual is born with "ambivalent genitalia," rather than imposing surgery on the child to force conformance to our either/or universe, accepting the individual as being, or having, elements of both male and female should be accepted.

The case of ambivalent physical features is an extreme, though valid, one. The both/and approach is far more powerful at the social and cultural level. Here we would recognize the ability of the individual to be both aggressive and caring, as the situation demands. Individuals could be active in some circumstances and passive in others. This would enable each of us to give full expression to all the aspects of our personality, rather than having to concentrate on those elements that seemed to be the most in keeping with prevailing social norms for our physical gender.

Such an approach and understanding would lead, almost inevitably, to a greater degree of tolerance within society, and would certainly benefit those whose sexual orientation is presently stigmatized by the wider culture. *Robert J. Buckley*

Bibliography

Brown, Jan. "Is She or Isn't She." *Ultra Fit* 5, no. 5.
Herdt, Gilbert. *Third Sex, Third Gender*. New York: Zone Books, 1994.

See also Evolution; Feminism; Hermaphroditism; Scientific Approaches to Homosexuality; Transgender; Transsexualism; Transvestism

Genet, Jean (1910–1986)

One of the most brilliant French novelists, dramatists, and essayists of the mid-twentieth century,

G Jean Genet is also famous for his criminal escapades, his homosexuality, his insistence on his outsider status, and his involvement with various political movements, in particular the Black Panthers and the Palestinians. Born in Paris, the son of Camille Gabrielle Genet and an unknown father, Genet was abandoned by his mother seventh months after his birth and raised in a foster home in the French countryside. He received a standard French education through age thirteen, at which time he was apprenticed as a typographer. He fled after ten days. After a series of other placements, flights, and petty crimes, he was imprisoned for the first time at age fifteen in an institution for children located in Mettray, where he stayed until age eighteen, when he enrolled in the army. He stayed in the army until 1936, serving in the Middle East and North Africa. In 1936 he deserted, traveling throughout Europe and finding himself in many irregular situations and in a number of prisons. He was back in France in 1937, and would be in and out of prison numerous times over the next several years for a variety of petty crimes, including stealing books by authors such as Marcel Proust. In the prison of Fresnes in 1942, Genet wrote a poem entitled "Le condamné à mort" (The Man Condemned to Death), which he also arranged to have printed. At the same time, he worked on *Notre-Dame-des-fleurs* (Our Lady of the Flowers), which became his first novel, originally published clandestinely in 1943. Both the poem and the novel describe homosexual rituals of prison life; both celebrate the figure of a murderer. On the level of syntactic and poetic complexity, both works are stunningly accomplished. *Notre-Dame-des-fleurs* further demonstrates the complicated narrative structure that was typical of Genet's prose writing: the novel tells of the complicated imaginings spun out of the mind of a narrator in prison. The fantasies reveal in a disjointed way bits of the narrator's life but also recount the stories of a number of imagined characters. The boundaries between fantasy and reality seem to become permeable. Various temporal moments blend together. Characters move between various imagined levels of narration.

If some of the material for *Notre-Dame-des-fleurs* (and for the next several books Genet would write) seems clearly drawn from his own life, the poetic and narrative complexity of these books makes them difficult to read as primarily autobiographical. They are profound reflections on the identities of the most socially marginal groups of people, on prejudicial forms of sexual identity, and on what happens when these identities and the experiences of people who live them are aestheticized, put into literary language for consumption by the better-heeled, more socially accepted people around them. In *Pampes funèbres* (Funeral Rites), for instance, Genet would describe his aesthetic project as "the art of using shit and getting you to eat it."

Genet wrote an amazing amount between 1942 and 1947. "The Man Condemned to Death" was followed by other poems. *Notre-Dame* was followed by *Miracle de la rose* (Miracle of the Rose) (which recounts the experience of Mettray), *Pompes funèbres* (Funeral Rites, which pays controversial homage to a resistance fighter, Jean Decarnin, whom Genet had loved and who was killed during the final days of the Occupation), *Querelle de Brest* (Querelle, which tells the imagined story of a naval lieutenant's fascination with the beautiful sailor Querelle and of Querelle's murderous and queer sexual adventures), and *Journal du voleur* (The Thief's Journal, which recounts Genet's European wanderings after he deserted the army in 1936, and part of his life in Paris).

Genet's important career as a writer for the theater also began during these years, most notably with the publication and first production of *Les Bonnes* (The Maids) in 1947. At this time he would also be befriended by many important figures in the Parisian literary establishment, including Jean Cocteau and Jean-Paul Sartre. Cocteau and Sartre would, in 1948, petition the French president for an official pardon for Genet's criminal past, claiming his work placed him in the pantheon of French literature along with other poet-criminals such as Villon and Verlaine. Sartre wrote a lengthy study of Genet, entitled *Saint Genet*, that the Gallimard publishing house printed as the first volume of what it inexactly called Genet's *Oeuvres complètes* (Complete Works), which were published in five volumes between 1951 and 1979. A sixth volume of interviews and articles was published in 1991.

From the granting of his official pardon in 1949 through 1955, Genet wrote and published little. In 1950 he directed a short film, *Chant d'amour* (A Song of Love), based on some of the same material as in his first novels and poems. In 1955 Genet began writing and publishing again, and in the next several years he produced three complex plays, *Le balcon* (The Balcony), *Les Nègres* (The Blacks), and *Les paravents* (The Screens). He rewrote *Le balcon* in particular many times. Like his novels, it has many levels, plays within plays, confused identities, and intermixed locales of action: a brothel and a city in revolt. It could be said to investigate the theatricality, fantasy, ceremony, and illusion that underpin many manifestations of social and political power. *Les Nègres*, first produced in Paris under the direction of Robert Blin in 1959, was a notable success. It too is formally complicated, with different plots happening on- and offstage. An investigation of racism and the psychology and politics of racially motivated violence—with clear reference to the struggles for independence then under way in many African nations—*Les Nègres* too relies heavily on ritual and ceremony. An American production was mounted in 1961 in New York City, including in the cast James Earl Jones, Cicely Tyson, and Maya Angelou, and would run with success for four years. Epic in its proportions, and theatrically perhaps the most challenging and radical of Genet's plays, *Les paravents* deals with the struggle to bring an end to the colonial order in an unspecified Arab country. Given the range of emotions surrounding the recent Algerian revolution (France had withdrawn from Algeria in 1962), the first Parisian production of *Les paravents* was the scene of riots and many other disturbances.

Genet also wrote important essays (one on Alberto Giacometti, for instance) during the late 1950s and early 1960s. The mid-1960s are another period when he wrote little. In 1964, his friend Abdallah Bentaga committed suicide. Genet had known Bentaga, a circus acrobat, since 1955. Their relations had cooled in the early 1960s, and Genet had taken up with a race-car driver, Jackie Maglia. Speaking of the nature of his relations, Genet said in 1964, "Of course I've made love with all the boys that I've taken an interest in. But my interest has not only been in making love. I've made an effort to recreate with them the adventure I've lived, whose symbol is bastardy, betrayal, a refusal of society, and finally, writing, which is to say a return to society by other means." Bentaga's suicide so upset Genet that he told his friends he would renounce literature.

In the late 1960s Genet traveled a great deal. He covered the 1968 Democratic National Convention in Chicago for *Esquire* magazine, in spite of having been denied a visa to the United States because of "sexual deviancy." He entered the United States again illegally in the spring of 1970, touring and speaking with the Black Panthers for two months. In October he traveled to the Middle East to visit Palestinian refugee camps, spending several months there. He returned several more times in the next few years. Throughout the seventies he published a number of short texts about the Black Panthers and the Palestinians.

In September 1982, Genet found himself in Beirut at the moment of the massacres in Sabra and Shatila, two Palestinian camps. He visited Shatila shortly after the massacres, spending four hours. In October in Paris he would write "Quatre heures à Chatila" (Four Hours at Shatila), an important text of political testimony.

Genet was treated for throat cancer in 1979. In 1983, spurred by his experience at Shatila, he returned to writing in earnest, working on *Un Captif amoureux* (Prisoner of Love), which tells of his experiences with the Black Panthers and the Palestinians, using all the theoretical and poetical complexity that were his trademark. Genet had corrected one set of proofs of his final book before he succumbed to cancer in April 1986. *Un Captif amoureux* was published the next month.   *Michael Lucey*

Bibliography

Durham, Scott, ed. "Genet: In the Language of the Enemy." *Yale French Studies* 91 (1997).

Genet, Jean. *L'Ennemi déclaré. Textes et entretiens. Oeuvres complètes*, Vol. 6. Albert Dichy, ed. Paris: Gallimard, 1991.

White, Edmund. *Genet: A Biography*. New York: Knopf, 1993.

See also Cocteau, Jean; France; French Literature; Proust, Marcel; Theater

Gentrification

Gay men and lesbians have played a major role in the economic and cultural revitalization of many urban areas during the past fifty years. Often, the initial revitalization of a neighborhood will lead to a process of gentrification. Property values rise, leading to a displacement of poorer residents and small businesses as the area becomes more affluent. Examples of gay-driven revitalization and gentrification of neighborhoods can be found in most large and medium-sized U.S. cities, as well as major cities in Canada, the United Kingdom, and Australia, and to a lesser extent in various western European metropolises.

Revitalization and gentrification are both the spatial and social reconstruction of an urban area. While economic opportunity based on undervalued real estate is a key force behind accelerated gentrification, the early neighborhood revitalization pro-

G cess finds individuals and groups migrating to a geographic area that is tolerant of diverse cultural expression and interaction. This securing of a safe space is essential for any group of people (whether their associations are based on identity constructs of race, ethnic background, or sexuality) seeking to interact as a community.

The need for the realization of safe spaces is particularly acute for gays and lesbians, for whom there are few geographies free of hostility toward an open display of their sexuality. Interestingly, the areas that have been the most susceptible to gay gentrification tend to be working-class neighborhoods, generally in economic decline but with homes and buildings of architectural merit.

The populations in these areas are themselves to varying degrees marginalized from the mainstream. Essentially lacking private economic capital and a corresponding social status viewed as needing to be protected, residents have little incentive to be exclusionary of others. In the case of the late 1980s gentrification of the South Beach area of Miami Beach, the resident population was mostly poor refugees from Cuba and Jewish retirees, many having immigrated from Europe decades earlier. While these residents may not condone homosexuality, the sight of two men or two women holding hands is largely unthreatening compared with the institutionalized oppression they experienced in their own lives.

Given that many gay men and lesbians have experienced strained relations with their families because of their sexuality, acquiring property to refurbish as a home or business becomes an important reassertion of place and belonging. The establishing of gay-owned and -operated shops, bars, and cultural institutions within an area is also an important reinforcement of a shared gay identity and allows for the visible defining of gay space, often notable for being gay male–dominated. Lesbians generally have fewer economic resources than gay men to apply toward the gentrification process, but basic characteristics of gender also play a role in the spatial re-creation of a neighborhood, with men tending to emphasize external markings of territory and women, the construction of internal social networks.

The political clout of the gay community in San Francisco is perhaps unmatched anywhere, and is often cited as having been made possible by economic and social forces arising from gay-driven gentrification of the city's Castro neighborhood. Yet the basic economic dynamic of successful gentrification serves to attract more established (usually nongay) property developers, merchants, and more affluent residents. Protecting historic properties from destruction, controlling spiraling rents, and preserving the "flavor" and quality of life of an area become part of an ever-more-consuming struggle for a community. The threat of displacement faced by the original residential population as the first wave of gentrification unfolded becomes amplified and in turn may force less affluent gays and lesbians also to move away. *Eugene Patron*

Bibliography

Bell, Davis, and Gill Valentine. *Mapping Desire: Geographies of Sexuality.* London: Routledge, 1995.

Betsky, Aaron. *Queer Space: Architecture and Same-Sex Desire.* New York: Morrow, 1997.

Bouthilette, Anne-Marie, Gordon Brent Ingram, and Yolanda Retter. *Queers in Space: Communities, Public Places, Sites of Resistance.* Seattle: Bay Press, 1997.

Castells, Manuel. *The City and the Grassroots.* Berkeley: Edward Arnold, 1983.

Chauncey, George. *Gay New York: Gender, Urban Culture and the Making of the Gay Male World, 1890–1940.* New York: Basic Books, 1994.

Knoop, Lawrence. "Gentrification and Gay Neighborhood Formation in New Orleans: A Case Study." In *Homo Economics.* Amy Gluckman and Betsy Reed, eds. New York: Routledge, 1997.

Smith, Nail, and Peter Williams, eds. *Gentrification of the City.* Boston: Allen and Unwin, 1986.

Whittle, Steven, ed. *The Margins of the City: Gay Men's Urban Lives.* Brookfield: Ashgate, 1994.

See also Castro; Community Centers; Neighborhoods; San Francisco

Géricault, Théodore (1791–1824)

The art and life of Théodore Géricault have become synonymous with romanticism. Unlike neoclassicism, which is defined by a specific style and approach to subject matter, romanticism is a movement in art, literature, music, and theater (lasting from around 1750 to 1850) that was based on a profoundly new way of thinking about life and death. Romanticism sought out and glorified the irrational, the emotionally intense, the subjective, the unpredictable, and the unusual. In art, experimentation with peculiar subject matter, lighting, coloration, and approaches to form was preferred.

Although he produced many works in a variety of media, Géricault is best known for his oil on canvas masterpiece of 1819, *Raft of the Medusa* (Paris, Musée du Louvre). This work broke the conservative rules of neoclassicism in several ways. *Raft* was most significant in that it redefined what kinds of subject matter were appropriate for grand history painting by choosing a theme of topical interest and putting it on a monumental scale. The painting measures approximately 16 feet by 23 feet, and each figure is twice life-size. The full story of the *Raft of the Medusa* is a real-life tragedy that took place off the coast of Senegal in 1816. What occurred became a public scandal that brought into question the ethics and politics of the Bourbon restoration government (1815–1830).

Raft is a painting in which an array of male bodies sprawl across the canvas in physical and psychological torment. Statuesque and classical male forms are presented in positions that evoke tender pathos in varying states of life and physical decay. The tension depicted between the living and dead men aboard the doomed craft suggests a homoerotic charge. The erotic and the morbid are linked in an image that juxtaposes masculine physical charge with limp, effeminate enervation. The black man who caps the composition possesses a muscular physique that evokes reference to Michelangelo's heroic male nudes. It is his muscularity amid the dead and dying below him and his frantic gesturing to a rescue ship barely visible on the horizon that draws our eye to him and to his comrades supporting him from below. The interracial chain of mingled male bodies becomes the "equivalent of one single body in the state of transformation" from dead and limp to life and vitality. The combining of the morbid, erotic, and political was an idea embraced by romanticism and, in Géricault's case, was underscored by a series of still-life studies for *Raft* showing severed human limbs and decapitated heads (*Study of Two Severed Heads,* National Museum, Stockholm, c.1819; and *Study of Feet and Hands,* Musée Fabre, Montpellier, c.1819).

Most art histories prefer not to talk much about Géricault's sexuality or sexual orientation when considering his works of art. Even though the label "gay" cannot be applied in the modern sense of awareness to Géricault, a homoerotic sensibility does seem to permeate his choices of theme and their presentation. Throughout his career, Géricault was master of the heroic single figure and produced many studio studies called *académies* of men in various states of rest or engaged in strenuous physical activity (for example, S*tudy of a Nude Man Pulling*

Géricault's Raft of the Medusa (Le Radeau de la Méduse), *Louvre, Paris. Art Resource, NY.*

G *on a Rope*, Musée Bonnat, Bayonne, c.1816). In all these, a pronounced muscularity is evident.

Géricault's art is unique in that it highlights the potent primacy of masculinity and ideas of heroic action that had been associated with the earlier art and thought processes of neoclassicism. The idea of men engaged in battle with the irrational and uncontrollable forces of war predominates in Géricault's images of military soldiers on and off the battlefield (for example, *The Wounded Cuirassier*, Musée du Louvre, Paris, Salon of 1814; *The Chasseur of the Imperial Guard*, Musée du Louvre, Paris, Salon of 1812). Underscoring this focus on the world of men and the tense, erotic charge between them is the fact that Géricault's art is marked by a nearly complete absence of women. His compositions generally comprise an all-male cast that consists of brawny males who confront the harsh elements of nature, animals, and one another. The artist produced many drawings and watercolors of muscular men attempting to control horses and bulls (e.g., *The Bull Market*, Fogg Art Museum, Harvard University, 1817–1818; *Race of the Barbieri Horses*, Musée du Louvre, Paris, 1817). The struggle between men and animals is a favorite theme throughout Géricault's body of works, a pairing derived from classical sources and serving as visual metaphor of man's destiny in attempting to harness the uncontrollable and potentially destructive forces of physical, emotional, and sexual energies in himself and in nature.

Throughout his personal and creative life, Géricault the man and the artist struggled as hard as the males he represented against the destructive forces of nature. However, nature finally triumphed in 1824 when Géricault died at the premature age of thirty-two from a painful illness aggravated by a serious horse-riding accident. *John Smalls*

Bibliography

Bryson, Norman. "Gericault and Masculinity." In *Visual Culture: Images and Interpretations.* Norman Bryson, Michael Ann Holly, and Keith Moxey, eds. Hanover: Wesleyan University Press, 1994, 228–59.

Crow, Thomas. *Emulation: Making Artists for Revolutionary France.* New Haven: Yale University Press, 1995, 279–99.

Eitner, Lorenz. *Géricault: His Life and Work.* London: Orbis, 1983.

Nochlin, Linda. "Gericault, or the Absence of Women." *October* 68 (Spring 1994): 46–59.

See also Art History; French Literature; Masculinity; Michelangelo Buonnaroti

German Literature

Scattered references to sodomy appear in such literary German medieval texts as Heinrich von Veldeke's *Eneit*, Hartman von Au's *Erec*, and Ulrich von Lichtenstein's *Frauenbuch*. Nonetheless, histories of gay German literature usually begin with eighteenth-century art historian Johann Joachim Winckelmann. His sense of aesthetics and history profoundly influenced many subsequent writers. Goethe specifically pointed out the centrality to aesthetics of Winckelmann's erotic glorification of the male youth as depicted in ancient Greek sculpture.

In Classics departments, eighteenth-century writers felt free to discuss male-male desire. Christoph Meiners and Alexander von Humboldt wrote academic essays on same-sex love in ancient Greece. Christoph Martin Wieland introduced readers to Greek love in a parodic poem called "Juno and Ganymede." The earliest known novel that centers on an explicitly male-male love affair, *Ein Jahr in Arkadien: Kyllenion* (One Year in Arcadia: Kyllenion, 1805), by August duke of Sachsen-Gotha, takes place in a Greek environment.

The cult of friendship in eighteenth-century German literature usually makes it difficult to decipher the signals of sexuality. Among the authors whose texts seem ambiguous to modern readers are Klopstock, Gleim, Jacobi, Lenz, Heinse, Goethe, Ramdohr, and Kleist. Traditionally, academic scholars have denied any possible homosexual interpretations, while gay readers have just as resolutely read a great deal of homosexuality into them. But even in the eighteenth century, some readers objected to the effusive declarations of friendship and love because they sounded as though they were crossing the bounds of decorum and becoming physical. Johannes Friedel claims in his *Briefe über die Galanterien von Berlin* (Letters on the Galantries of Berlin, 1782) that sodomitical subcultures in Germany used the conventions of the cult of friendship to disguise their relationships.

The cult of friendship between men died out in the early nineteenth century, presumably because of anxieties about its possible homosexual implications. At this time, writers like historian Johannes Müller and poet August von Platen, clearly recognized in their own time as sodomitical, began to appear. At the request of Heinrich Hössli, Swiss author

Heinrich Zschokke published in 1821 a novella called *Eros*, about male-male desire gone awry.

By the mid-nineteenth century, the boundary lines delineating modern structures of homosexuality began to emerge. Political activists from Karl Heinrich Ulrichs to Magnus Hirschfeld demanded legal rights for members of "the third sex," female souls in male bodies or vice versa. Physicians, psychiatrists, and sexologists identified natural causes of homosexuality. One of the earliest novels with a clear notion of a third-sex theory is Adolf von Wilbrandt's (1837–1911) *Fridolins heimliche Ehe* (Fridolin's Secret Marriage, 1875), in which a major character is depicted as a female soul in a male body. Other early literary works that openly discuss male homosexuals from the medico-legal perspective—or at least with it in mind—include Ludwig Dilsner's play *Jasminblüthe* (Jasmine Flower, 1898), Hans Fuchs's many fictional and nonfictional works, and Otto Julius Bierbaum's (1865–1910) novel, *Prinz Kuckuck* (1907). In Hermann Bahr's play, *Die Mutter* (The Mother, 1891), Franz Wedekind's *Frühlings Erwachen* (Spring Awakening, 1891), Robert Musil's *Verwirrungen des Zöglings Törless* (Confusions of Young Törless, 1906), and many of Hermann Hesse's and Thomas Mann's writings, one also sees depictions of medico-legal understandings of homosexuality.

Almost at the same time as the emergence of medico-legal understandings of homosexuality, a reaction against these models of identity also appeared in literary circles. At times misogynistic, the *Gemeinschaft der Eigenen* (Community of the Special) around Benedikt Friedländer and Adolf Brand promoted male bonding and a less explicitly sexual homosociality, rejecting what they considered to be the pathologized homosexual identity. Anarchist poet John Henry Mackay, who wrote in German despite his English name, contributed some of his work to the community's journal, *Der Eigene* (The Special, 1896–1931) and wrote a number of longer works about male-male desire. Even more important for literary history than Mackay, the circle around poet Stefan George overlapped extensively with the Gemeinschaffder Eigenen.

Klaus Mann, the son of Thomas Mann, explicitly and implicitly discussed homosexuality in many of his works and attempted to demonstrate the importance of leftist thought for sexual politics in his essay "Homosexuality and Fascism." As the twentieth century progressed, Hans Henny Jahnn (1894–1959) became one of the more prominent gay literary voices. Wolfgang Koeppen (1906–1995) continues in *Tod in Rom* (Death in Rome, 1954), a discussion about Italy, death, homosexuality, and art that Thomas Mann had begun. Hubert Fichte (1935–1986) makes homosexuality a central part of his writings, which consist of criticism, fiction, and anthropological observations. For Josef Winkler (1953–), the double suicide of two young gay male teenagers in Italy is the central experience around which his writing revolves. Other contemporary gay writers include Ronald Schernikau and Alexander Ziegler. In the cinematic world, gay voices like Rainer Maria Fassbinder are heard ever more strongly.

AIDS has also left its stamp on German writing. Some works, by Christoph Geiser, Christoph Klimke, and Mario Wirz, movingly mourn the losses caused by AIDS. Poet Stefan Reichert writes in the tradition of the Holocaust survivor, Paul Celan, whose works he also edited. Wolfgang Max Faust produced a literary work that left much up to chance—a diary, containing news clippings and daily insights, called *Dies alles gibt es also* (This all exists, therefore, 1993). Authors like Detlev Meyer and Napoleon Seyfarth, as well as the filmmaker Rosa von Praunheim, have confronted AIDS with a corrosively and subversively ironic, bitterly campy humor.

The gay and lesbian literary scene is thriving in Germany today. As gay and lesbian scholarship develops, more and more gay writers of the past are being uncovered. At the same time, new insights from queer theory are allowing fascinating new accounts of such seemingly straight authors as Wieland, Lichtenberg, Goethe, Kleist, Hölderlin, Jean Paul, Wagner, Nietzsche, Brecht, and Kafka. All of German literature may soon have a place in the queer imagination.   *Robert Tobin*

Bibliography

Derks, Paul. *Die Schande der heiligen Päderastie: Homosexualität und Öffentlichkeit in der deutschen Literatur, 1750–1850*. Berlin: Verlag Rosa Winkel, 1990.

Jones, James. *"We of the Third Sex": Literary Representations of Homosexuality in Wilhelmine Germany*. New York: Lang, 1990.

Kuzniar, Alice A. *Outing Goethe and His Age*. Stanford, Calif.: Stanford University Press, 1996.

Ooosterhuis, Harry, ed. *Homosexuality and Male Bonding in Pre-Nazi Germany*. London: Harrington Park Press, 1991.

G

See also AIDS; Brand, Adolph; Fassbinder, Rainer Werner; Fichte, Hubert; Friendship; Ganymede; Goethe, Johannes Wolfgang von; Greece, Ancient; Hirschfeld, Magnus; Kleist, Heinrich von; Mann, Thomas; Platen, August Graf von Hallermund; Rosa von Praunheim; Third Sex; Wagner, Richard; Winckelmann, Johann Joachim

Germany

German gay men and women experienced, on the one hand, one of the worst persecutions in history, and on the other hand, one of the most liberated periods in the history of gay life. When men-loving Frederick the Great came to the Prussian throne in 1740, sex between two men was still officially punished by the death penalty. The first written testimony of such a punishment is dated from 1704, when two men who confessed their sexual offense were executed. Prussia changed this law before the turn of the eighteenth century and demanded imprisonment, physical punishment, and exile for any homosexual activities. The newly installed paragraph in German law books received the infamous number 175 and achieved legal force for the entire German nation in 1871. The fight against laws that legalized discrimination against gays was manifold. The Wissenschaftlichehumanitäres Komitee (WhK, Scientific-Humanitarian Committee), founded in 1897 by physicist and scholar of sexual science Magnus Hirschfeld (1868–1935), was the first political organization that fought for equal rights for gay men and women and an alteration of the paragraph 175. Between 1897 and 1907, the WhK proposed five petitions to alter paragraph 175, so that it was reworded to apply only in three situations: cases of nonconsensual sex between persons of the same sex, homosexual contact with minors under the age of sixteen, and same-sex sexual contacts in public space. The Reichstag (legislature) denied all these petitions, even though some of them were signed by famous and influential persons like August Bebel, leader of the Social Democratic Party. In addition to contemporary theories on homosexuality, the WhK published in its Jahrbuch für sexuelle Zwischenstufen (Annual Journal for Intermediate Stages) one of the first debates with the developing field of psychoanalysis.

From 1907 until 1909, the German Empire was shaken by several scandalous court cases on the matter of homosexuality. These trials, known as the Eulenburg Affair, drove the gay movement into a deep crisis. For instance, Adolph Brand (1874–1945), publisher of the gay journal Der Eigene, was imprisoned for one and a half years in 1907 as a result of the trials. Although Der Eigene had been published as early as 1897 in Berlin as an anarchistic literary journal, it changed its focus entirely in September 1898 and became the first gay journal in the world. The journal published not only essays but also nude male photography and prints. The first annual volume, published in 1906, was followed by a long break because of World War I. In 1919, Der Eigene celebrated a comeback because of the newly developing gay mass press in Berlin and elsewhere in Germany. The same year, Hirschfeld founded the Institut für Sexualwissenschaften (Institute for Sexual Science). Also in 1919, the silent movie Anders als die Andern (Different from Others) was shown in Berlin. The opening-night screening of the first gay German movie was followed by a discussion with director and cast. The success of the movie and its discussions continued as it toured throughout Germany as well as larger cities all over Europe. Freundschaftesbünde (federations of friends) and unions for gay men and lesbian women were founded in small towns, and advertisements for gay meetings and gay bars were posted in magazines. Business owners advertised in gay publications using their real names instead of pseudonyms. The gay movement was now highly political and affirmed that the Weimar Republic supported the liberation and acceptance of gay men after the breakdown of the German Empire. The political agenda was linked to large social events, such as elaborate balls and an active bar scene for gay men, lesbians, and transvestites. During this period, homosexuality achieved an avant-garde status, particularly when theater, cabaret, dance, and the fine arts were influenced by gay artists and gay themes. The scandalous Anita Berber and her gay partner Sebastian Droste depicted in their famous performance Tänze des Lasters, des Grauens und der Ekstase (Dances of Vice, Horror, and Ecstasy), lust, love, urban decay, homosexuality, and drug culture. Even homophobic playwright and director Bertolt Brecht used gay characters in his plays. In 1924, the UfA studios produced Wege zu Kraft und Schönheit (Ways to Strength and Beauty), a film by gay director Nikolas Kaufmann, which illustrated the nudist culture and the emerging German modern dance scene.

With the German economy already weakened by disastrous inflation, this short period of gay liberation was brought to an end when Adolf Hitler became chancellor of Germany in 1933. The unrestricted persecution of homosexual men and women began after Hitler eliminated the *Sturmabteilung* (SA), his paramilitary followers, on June 30, 1934. Ernst Röhm, the leader of the SA and a homosexual, was arrested and executed. Röhm's homosexuality was used as one excuse for his murder and for the elimination of the entire SA-elite and Hitler's other political enemies. Hitler asserted his political and moral control over the German public by eliminating his enemies under the guise of "cleaning" the German nation from the homosexual leader of the SA and his "companions."

Two years after Röhm's execution, a law was passed that legalized the imprisonment of homosexuals without trial. In 1936, the Nazis created a department (Reichszentrale zur Bekämpfung der Homosexualität und Abtreibung) specifically organized for the elimination of homosexuals. Numerous gay men were exiled, deported, or murdered in concentration camps. The collapse of the Nazi system after World War II brought a short period of hope for the gay community in Germany. However, the Federal Republic of Germany, founded in 1949, reinstated the 1936 Nazi version of the paragraph 175. It was changed in 1969 to punish only adults who engage in same-sex sexual activities with minors under the age of twenty-one. Gay life in West Germany was marked by open conflict over these antigay laws.

The scandal in connection with the screening of Rosa von Praunheim's movie *Nicht der Homosexuelle ist pervers, sondern die Situation in der er lebt* (It Isn't the Homosexual Who is Perverse, but the Situation in Which He Lives) at the Berlin Film Festival in 1971 was the initiation of a gay movement in West Germany that mirrored the gay liberation in North America. On the other side of the Wall, the East German government repressed any gay activity by labeling it as decadent and as destructive to the socialist family. In 1950, the German Democratic Republic adopted the original 1871 version of paragraph 175, but later stopped implementing this law. In 1968, the East German government also substituted for paragraph 175 a law that punished only same-sex sexual activity with minors under the age of eighteen. Although several gay bars existed, East German gay life rarely appeared in public places before the 1980s. Even in the eighties, politically active gay groups were connected to the Protestant church or the Communist Party. Only two years before the fall of the Wall in 1989, the East German government changed its attitude toward homosexuality and tried to incorporate homosexual men and women into society. Any law that punished homosexuals was deleted from East German law books in 1989. On November 9, 1989, the night the Wall fell, Heiner Carow's movie *Coming Out*, the first East German feature film about a gay man, premiered in Berlin. The reunification of Germany in 1993 and the abolishment of antigay laws in 1994 did not reunite German gay men. Most gay men returned to their gay networks after a brief period of East-West encounters. It will take years until the obvious or hidden differences between the gay men of former East and West Germany disappear. But these conflicts between gay Eastern and Western Germans is endemic in the rest of the German society as well.

Jens Richard Giersdorf

Bibliography

Baumann, J. *Paragraph 175*. Berlin: Neuwied,1968.

Grau, Günter, ed. *Hidden Holocaust?: Gay and Lesbian Persecution in Germany 1933–45*. Chicago: Fitzroy and Dearborn, 1995.

Persky, Stan. *Then We Take Berlin*. Woodstock: Overlook Press, 1996.

Plant, Richard. *The Pink Triangle*: *The Nazi War Against Homosexuals*. New York: Henry Holt, 1986.

Soukup, Jean Jacques, ed. *Die DDR.D Schwulen. Der Aufbruch. Versuch einer Bestandsaufnahme*. Gleichen-Reinhausen, Germany: Waldschlächen, 1990.

Stark, Kurt. *Schwuler Osten. Homosexuelle Männer in der DDR*. Berlin: Ch. Links Verlag, 1994.

Steakley, James D. *The Homosexual Emancipation Movement in Germany*. New York: Arno Press, 1975.

Sternweiler, Andreas, and Hans Gerhard Hannesen, eds. *Goodbye to Berlin: 100 Jahre Schwulenbewegung*. Berlin: Verlag Rosa Winkel, 1997.

Stümke, Hans-Georg. *Homosexuelle in Deutschland: Eine politische Geschichte*. Munich: Verlag C. H. Beck, 1989.

Stümke, Hans-Georg, and Rudi Finkler. *Rosa Winkel, Rosa Listen. Homosexuelle und 'Gesundes Volksempfinden' von Auschwitz bis heute*. Reinbeck, Germany: Rowohlt, 1981.

See also Brand, Adolph; German Literature; Hirschfeld, Magnus; Nazism and the Holocaust; Paragraph 175; Rosa van Praunheim; Röhm, Ernst

G

Gernreich, Rudi (1922–1985)

This American fashion designer, born in Austria, immigrated to Los Angeles, California, in 1938. During the 1960s, Gernreich was the most celebrated American fashion designer in the world. His designs were marked by bold colors, striking patterns, and geometric silhouettes. Gernreich's designs were functional, helped to free women from the constraining styles of the 1950s, and were influenced by the fashions of the street. Among his innovations were the braless swimsuit; the topless swimsuit; the transparent "no-bra bra"; unisex fashion; and the thong, or thigh-baring, swimsuit for men and women.

In July 1950, Gernreich met Harry Hay, founder of the early gay rights group, the Mattachine Society, when both attended a dance recital. From 1950 to 1952, Gernreich and Hay were lovers, and Gernreich became one of the seven original members of the society. He advised Hay and acted as recording secretary at meetings. He resigned from the Mattachine Society in 1953, along with all the founding members, when more conservative members temporarily gained control of the group.

During his lifetime, Gernreich did not comment publicly on his homosexuality or lesbian and gay rights, because, as he put it, "It's very simple. It's bad for business." After his death, however, the American Civil Liberties Union announced that the estates of Gernreich and his surviving life partner of thirty-one years, Oreste Pucciani, provided funds for litigation and education in the area of lesbian and gay rights.   *Charles Krinsky*

Bibliography

Moffit, Peggy, and William Claxton. *The Rudi Gernreich Book*. New York: Rizzoli, 1991.

Timmons, Stuart. *The Trouble with Harry Hay: Founder of the Modern Gay Movement*. Boston: Alyson Publications, 1990.

See also Fashion; Hay, Harry; Mattachine Society

Gide, André (1869–1951)

One of the most imposing figures on the French literary scene from the late-nineteenth through the mid-twentieth centuries, André Gide was in his early years a relatively little-known author of symbolist writing, moving in avant-gardist, somewhat elite literary circles. He began earning a broader reputation for himself through a number of texts that he called *récits* (short novels of relatively simple narrative construction): *La Porte étroite* (Straight Is the Gate, 1909), the story of a heterosexual love frustrated by sexual fears and religious devotion, was one of his first popular successes. By the 1920s Gide's reputation and controversial status had grown considerably. In the 1920s, the relation of homosexuality to literature was the source of much discussion in Paris, with Marcel Proust and Gide being the names most often mentioned. Proust's *Sodome et Gomorrhe* (Cities of the Plain), the volume of *Remembrance of Things Past* that opens with a reflection on the nature of the homosexuality of certain of the novel's characters, had been published in 1921 and 1922. Gide would publish *Corydon* in 1924. *Corydon* is a set of four dialogues between two imaginary characters on the nature and social utility of homosexuality—in particular, of what Gide called *pédérastie*, the attraction of a mature man to adolescents and young men. In 1925, Gide published the one book of his that he chose to label a novel, *Les Faux-Monnayeurs* (The Counterfeiters), whose central character, the novelist Édouard, is such a pederast. In the same year, Gide published a memoir of the early years of his life, *Si le grain ne meurt* (If It Die), which discussed openly his childhood sexual experimentation with boys and also sexual experiences he had with Arab boys while traveling in North Africa in his twenties.

Thanks to the publication of these books by Gide and Proust, one can see a wide variety of reactions to male homosexuality reflected in the literary press of the 1920s, including disdainful refusal to discuss the subject, outright condemnation, moralizing condescension, reluctant tolerance, and even evenhanded or enthusiastic acceptance. Proust, who died in 1922, had never been open about his own homosexuality. Gide's openness won him both a devoted following and great notoriety. References to him as a dangerous corrupter of youth, for instance, would be frequent in attacks throughout the rest of his life.

Some of Gide's earliest writing, while never broaching same-sex sexuality explicitly, certainly seemed to edge toward the subject. His rhapsodic *Les Nourritures terrestres* (Fruits of the Earth, 1897) is addressed to an imaginary youth named Nathanaël, advising him to learn to profit from sensuous experience, to be open to his desires, to learn to emancipate himself. The book also presents the figure of an older mentor figure, Ménalque, who at a certain point, gazing through a window at a cozy family scene involving father, mother, and son, utters the famous Gidean phrase, "Families, I hate you!" Ménalque expresses a desire to steal the son from the family and to encourage him to wander in search of himself.

Ménalque also figures in Gide's *L'Immoraliste* (The Immoralist, 1902), as a person who encourages for the protagonist, Michel, a life of exploration rather than one of stability. In this case, the advice is offered between two trips to North Africa. On the first, Michel is traveling with his new wife and spends a long time in Biskra recovering from a bout of tuberculosis. While there he becomes fascinated by the young boys of the town. In the middle section of the book, Michel and his wife are back in France, and Michel lives his structured, propertied, bourgeois life in a state of restless frustration. In the third part of the book, Michel and his wife undertake a repeat voyage to North Africa. This time, his wife is ill. She succumbs to her illness while in North Africa, partly owing to the neglect of her husband, who remains alone in North Africa at the end of the book, cared for by a young Arab boy.

Rachilde, in her review of the book when it was published, would use the word *uraniste* to describe its protagonist. Whether or not *L'Immoraliste* had a homosexual subtext was a question many other critics never posed. In his journal entry for November 26, 1915, Gide recounts a conversation with older French novelist Paul Bourget, who asks Gide: "Now that we're alone, tell me, Mr. Gide, if your Immoralist is or is not a pederast." Gide replies, taken aback, "He is doubtless more of an unavowed homosexual. . . . There are quite a lot of them." Still, whatever rumors may have circulated about Gide's personal life, references to homosexuality or homosexual subtexts in his writing remained sufficiently discrete as to pass unperceived until, perhaps, the publication of *Les Caves du Vatican* (Lafcadio's Adventure), 1914; also translated as *The Vatican Swindle* and *The Vatican Cellars*). Lafcadio is a dynamic young man who, at a certain point in the novel, recalls several explicitly homoerotically charged moments from his past. When this installment of the book appeared in the journal *La Nouvelle Revue Française*, which Gide helped found and of which he was one of the most important collaborators, Paul Claudel, an important Catholic poet and dramatist of the time, wrote to Gide and to others at the *NRF* that publishing such a text was scandalous and suggested that Gide must have "frightful"

morals. In his letter to Gide, he asked point-blank whether Gide was a pederast. Gide responded indirectly, unable or unwilling to make a frank avowal at this point, even though he was also unwilling to make any changes to the text of the book.

Gide's reticence at this point in his life was related to his devotion to his wife. In 1895 he married his cousin, Madeleine Rondeaux, a marriage that apparently remained unconsummated. Gide considered it a deep spiritual commitment, yet one that did not preclude sexual encounters elsewhere. Finally in 1918, there would be a major crisis in that marriage. Whereas Gide's encounters with men had been mostly fleeting and solely sexual, in 1917–1918, Gide formed an abiding attachment to a friend of the family, the young Marc Allégret. Gide and Allégret traveled to England and spent the summer there in 1918. Madeleine expressed her feelings of betrayal by rereading and then burning Gide's correspondence with her, one Gide had imagined her carefully preserving for posterity as one facet of his ongoing project of self-portraiture. The discovery of what Madeleine had done threw Gide into a long depression, subsequent to which he began to assume the openness about his sexual identity that characterizes his published work of the 1920s.

The 1920s mark as well a new level of political activity in Gide's life. In 1925 he took a long trip through the French colonies in central Africa, and upon his return published *Voyage au Congo* (Travels in the Congo), which was critical of many aspects of French colonialism. In 1936 he traveled to the Soviet Union as a guest of the government, only to publish a disillusioned *Retour de l'U.R.S.S.* (Return from the U.S.S.R.) upon return. In the early 1930s he attempted a trilogy of feminist narratives—*L'École des femmes* (The School for Wives), *Robert,* and *Geneviève*. He never finished the final volume and remained dissatisfied with his results.

Gide spent most of World War II in southern France and then in North Africa. He was awarded the Nobel Prize in literature in 1947. In 1952, the year after his death, the Vatican banned all his writing.

In 1932, Gide began publishing his *Journal.* This project of making public his space of private reflections continued even after his death, with the publication of the final pages he had been working on *Ainsi soit-il* (So Be It, 1952). It was dedicated to his daughter, Catherine, born in 1923, whose mother was Elisabeth van Rysselberghe. *Ainsi soit-il* continued to reflect openly on, among other things, Gide's sex life. Consistent in these reflections, and legible in the last pages of *Ainsi soit-il,* as in *Corydon* and in various pages of his *Journal*, is his refusal to associate himself, with his pederastic practices, with those he called "inverts." In fact Gide regularly insisted on the barrier of disgust that for him separated men of these two types.

A new edition of Gide's *Journal* was published in 1996, including for the first time many manuscript pages Gide himself had chosen to exclude from earlier published versions.   *Michael Lucey*

Bibliography

Ahlstedt, Eva. *André Gide et le débat sur l'homosexualité de L'Immoraliste* (1902). *Si le Grain ne meurt* (1926). Göteborg, Sweden: Acta Universitatis Gothoburgensis, 1994.

Anglès, Auguste. *André Gide et le premier groupe de la Nouvelle Revue Française: Une inquiète maturité, 1913–1914*, vol. 3. Paris: Gallimard, 1986.

Gide, André. *Journal 1887–1925*. Eric Marty, ed. Paris: Gallimard (Pléiade), 1996.

Lucey, Michael. *Gide's Bent: Sexuality, Politics, Writing.* New York: Oxford University Press, 1995.

Painter, George D. *André Gide: A Critical Biography*. New York: Atheneum, 1968.

See also France; French Literature; Proust, Marcel

Gilbert and George

The British artistic duo of Gilbert Proesch (born in 1943 in the Dolomites, Italy) and George Passmore (born in 1942 in Devon, England). The two met and began working together in 1967 while students at St Martin's School of Art in London. Soon after graduation, in order to emphasize the collaborative nature of their artistic project, they dropped their surnames and adopted a uniform style of dress (similar but never-matching business suits). Declaring themselves "living sculptures," they began to stage a series of theatricalized performances. These included The Meal (with the painter David Hockney) and Singing Sculpture, in which the artists, their faces covered in metallic paint, robotically mouthed the words to a recording of the English music-hall tune "Underneath the Arches."

While they have produced a wide variety of works—artist's books, postcard assemblages, films,

Gilbert and George. England, 1980. Photography. Tate Gallery, London/Art Resource, NY.

and performances—Gilbert and George are perhaps best known for their distinctive photo pieces, which they began producing in the 1970s. These large black-and-white photographic collages, often underlaid in flat areas of primary color (reminiscent of stained glass), are presented in gridded black frames. The photo pieces depict the two artists in a variety of stylized scenes that treat issues of politics, religion, and sexuality; series have included *Dirty Words, Modern Fears*, and *The Sexual Pictures* (which utilized pictographic rather than photographic imagery). These works often foreground homosexual themes, from the aestheticization of youthful male beauty to the coupling of the artists themselves. That coupling extends to the domestic sphere, as Gilbert and George share a house together in London.   *Michael Lobel*

Bibliography

Richardson, Brenda. *Gilbert and George* (exhibition catalog). Baltimore: Baltimore Museum of Art, 1984.

Wolf Jahn. *The Art of Gilbert and George, or an Aesthetic of Existence*. David Britt, trans. New York: Thames and Hudson, 1989.

See also Art History; Hockney, David; Photography

Gilgamesh, Epic of

The Epic of Gilgamesh recounts the heroic acts attributed to a king who lived around 2700 B.C.E. in what is present-day Iraq. Independent episodes that circulated orally throughout ancient Mesopotamia were eventually united and put down in cuneiform on twelve clay tablets. The most complete version, dating from around 1700 B.C.E., was found among the ruins of the library of the Persian king Assurbanipal. The poem is a powerful meditation on how lawless sexual impulses must be channeled in the service of civilization and, paradoxically, on the fragility of any erotic—in this case, specifically homoerotic—relationship.

The wild man Enkidu is created by the gods to contain the threat offered by Gilgamesh's sexual exploitation of his people. Enkidu's initial "civilizing" by a temple prostitute anticipates the effect he will have on the seemingly unconquerable Gilgamesh. That the men are fated to meet is suggested by a series of dreams forewarning Gilgamesh of the imminent arrival of "a strong companion able to save a friend." Enkidu is prophesied to be Gilgamesh's "equal" whom Gilgamesh will love "like a wife." At their first meeting, they wrestled, then "kissed one another/and were friends." From the outset the text sacralizes their relationship, imbuing it with a cosmic dimension.

The men support each other both physically and emotionally, functioning as the two halves of a single great hero rather than as separate entities in the adventures that establish their heroic fame. They conquer nature by defeating Humbaba, the giant of the cedar forest, whose timbers are necessary to build the great city of Uruk, with which Gilgamesh's name—and the poem—is associated. They assert the completeness of their relationship when Gilgamesh refuses the invitation of Ishtar, Goddess of Love, to become her consort; and, when she seeks revenge, he and Enkidu further insult her by defeating the Bull of Heaven and flinging its genitals in her face. The poem suggests that heterosexual domesticity, however essential for biological continuity, is less necessary as a civilizing force, and less noble spiritually, than male heroic coupling. Rather than remaining at home with wives and children to enjoy the fruits of the earth, as Sidori advises Gilgamesh to do, the heroic male couple takes to the road, each man inspiring and reinforcing the other's efforts. Gilgamesh is the first great representation of a homosocial world to survive in which women threaten to exhaust the male physically and emotionally, whereas his bond with another male allows both men to channel their energies for the good of civilization.

But Gilgamesh is also the first great poem in which Eros struggles against Thanatos. To avenge the heroes' insult to Ishtar, the gods decree that Enkidu must die. Gilgamesh grieves magnificently, even excessively, dressing Enkidu's body for burial as a bride and initially refusing to release his friend's corpse. Eventually he builds a splendid monument to his friend and composes a haunting elegy. The loss of Enkidu challenges Gilgamesh's understanding of the meaning of life itself and sends him on a frustrated search for immortality that only further emphasizes the fragility of human existence.

The destruction of Assurbanipal's library and the death of the text's ancient tongues caused the Gilgamesh poem to be lost for over two thousand years. Its themes, however, survived within the collective unconscious of the Middle Eastern and Western worlds. The male couple continued—and continues still—to be elevated to heroic, even mythic proportions; witness the examples of David and Jonathan, Achilles and Patroclus, Roland and Oliver, and—in American popular culture—the Lone Ranger and Tonto, Batman and Robin, or Starsky and Hutch. And the elegy remains an essential part of the homoerotic cultural tradition as one man's grief for the irrecoverable loss of his partner is transformed into verbal art.

Raymond-Jean Frontain

Bibliography

Dynes, Wayne R., and Stephen Donaldson, eds. *Homosexuality in the Ancient World*. New York: Garland, 1992.

Gilgamesh: Translated from the Sin-leqi-unninni Version. John Gardner and John Maier, trans. and eds., with the assistance of Richard A. Henshaw. New York: Knopf, 1984.

Halperin, David M. "Heroes and Their Pals." In *One Hundred Years of Homosexuality and Other Essays on Greek Love*. New York: Routledge, 1990, 75–87.

See also David and Jonathan; Elegiac Poetry; Greece, Ancient; Persian (Iranian) Literature and Culture

Gilles de Rais (1404–1440)

Born in Champtocé, France, to Guy II de Laval and Marie de Craon, Gilles, at the death of his parents eleven years later, inherited a number of important lands and the title of Baron de Rais. He was then placed in the care of his maternal grandfather, Jean de Craon, from whom he would inherit a small medieval empire. In 1429 he was charged with leading the troops of Joan of Arc as her companion-in-arms. After several years of fighting against the English, Joan of Arc's execution at Rouen, and the death of Jean de Craon in 1432, he left public life to devote himself to satanism and the rape and murder of children, most of whom came from the villages surrounding his many domains, including Champtocé and Tiffauges.

While some of those sacrificed were young girls, the vast majority of his victims were boys chosen either by him or by his companions from among the alms seekers who came to his castles. Some of his companions were young nobles whose fortunes had been lost during the war, while others, like Poitou, who testified against him at his trial, had been in his service since childhood and had also had sexual relations with him. Although he would at times violate the child before killing him, Gilles took the greatest pleasure in the torture and brutal murder of his victims: he would often decapitate them or have them decapitated and then sit on their dying bodies to ejaculate at the moment of passing. He would sometimes keep the heads of the most beautiful boys, comparing them to those of previous victims; the head judged the most beautiful would be given the prize of a kiss. Depending on the source, it is estimated that his victims numbered between two hundred and six hundred.

Ironically, Gilles's condemnation and execution in 1440 resembled the martyrdom of a saint more than the death of a hated criminal, since his great repentance on the scaffold was seen as an example of the power of God. After being assured by a priest that he would go to heaven, he asked his magician and accessory to his crimes, François Prelati, to pray for his soul. He was then strangled before being burned at the stake, and since his body was not consumed by the flames, his family members were given permission to collect the remains for burial in hallowed ground.

The myth and mysticism of Gilles de Rais found their echoes in the fables of Perrault and in Huysmans' novel *Là-bas*. In the former the essentially heterosexual tale of the murderous husband Blue-Beard, based perhaps on a medieval king who had nothing to do with Gilles de Rais, effaces all elements of homosexual desire and pederasty. In the latter he is viewed by the fictional author Durtal as a misogynist—which might explain the assimilation

to the historical Blue-Beard—sodomite and medieval mystic. *Todd Black*

Bibliography

Bataille, Georges. *Le Procès de Gilles de Rais*. Paris: Jean-Jacques Pauvert, 1965.

See also France; French Literature; Piracy and Pirates

Ginsberg, Allen (1926–1997)

The American poet Allen Ginsberg was one of the most visible and influential authors of the second half of the twentieth century. He was a central figure in the Beat movement of the 1950s, instrumental in encouraging the careers of both Jack Kerouac and William Burroughs, and he subsequently became one of the most prominent hippies not to be a rock star. Committed to the principle of openness—inherited from his radical Jewish parents, Naomi and Louis, as well as from his poetic master, Walt Whitman—he made little or no distinction between his personal and public lives. With Ginsberg's life and poetry, the personal was political.

Openness meant refusing to rewrite after the heat of the inspired moment. He associated the editing impulse with debilitating inhibition and sexual repression. More than most who used the phrase, he was willing to "let it all hang out." His was a knowing exhibitionism that was to become one of the key behavioral styles of 1970s gay liberation. By investing so much weight in the principle of spontaneity, Ginsberg gave up any ambition to produce polished work. At its best his poetry, like Whitman's, achieves its own completeness, at once expansive and concise. While individual lines are concise, lim-

Allen Ginsberg in 1989. Photo by Marc Geller.

ited by the measure of his own breathing, the poems as a whole are often rambling and capacious.

Although the reluctance to edit and select led to the publication of many poems that are weak by conventional literary-critical standards, Ginsberg wrote several of the most powerful and memorable long poems in twentieth-century American literature. His status as a major poet will be assured by *Howl* (1956), that incontinent manifesto of youthful revolt, and *Kaddish* (1961), his terrifying elegy on the madness and death of his mother. Moreover, the volume *Planet News* (1968) ranks with anything by the likes of Norman Mailer in voicing a countercultural response to the war in Vietnam. The volume *The Fall of America* (1972), while uneven in texture and baggy in structure, nevertheless offers a broad-screen survey of the nation at one of the most troubled moments in its history.

The hip status of *Howl* was ensured by an obscenity trial focused on the line "who let themselves be fucked in the ass by saintly motorcyclists, and screamed with joy." The objection was to the joy, rather than the pain the heterosexist establishment expected. More of the same species of joy was expressed in later poems, either on particular lovers, such as Neal Cassady and Peter Orlovsky, or on passing encounters with the generality of desirable manhood.

Politically, Ginsberg was best known for his resistance to U.S. involvement in the Vietnam War but also for a more general abhorrence of his nation's massive military-industrial complex. His espousal of the principles of gay liberation was influentially outspoken, but somewhat in the manner of straight men in the counterculture: his interest was in the liberating of gay men and not much concerned with lesbian women; his participation in the so-called sexual revolution was oddly resistant to the skeptical analyses of feminist women. In the later years his failure to develop as a significant voice in the AIDS crisis was a disappointment to many readers.

Gregory Woods

Bibliography

Miles, Barry. *Ginsberg*. New York: Simon and Schuster, 1989.
Schumacher, Michael. *Dharma Lion*. New York: St. Martin's Press, 1992.
Woods, Gregory. "Allen Ginsberg." In *Articulate Flesh: Male Homo-eroticism and Modern Poetry*. New Haven: Yale University Press, 1987, 195–211.

See also Beat Generation; Burroughs, William Seward; Gay Left; Gay Liberation; U.S. Literature: Contemporary Gay Writing

Girodet, Anne-Louis (1767–1824)

Anne-Louis Girodet-Trioson was a French neoclassical painter of historical and mythological scenes. Girodet is considered an important yet transitional figure between the rational components of neoclassicism and the flights of fantasy that define romanticism. At age eighteen, he entered as a pupil into the studio of renowned neoclassical painter Jacques-Louis David (1748–1825). Of all David's students, Girodet was the most learned and gifted. He was also one of the most competitive and rebellious. On entering the studio, he quickly demonstrated his grasp of the tenets of neoclassicism but soon proceeded to violate the principles he had been taught and to embark on a quest to distinguish himself from his contemporaries. Instead of deriving subject matter from Roman histories, as Davidian neoclassicism had dictated, he turned to Greek myths for inspiration. As opposed to a neoclassical emphasis on linearity, sculptural form, and masculine physical virtues, he chose instead to play with these elements and reverse their expected effects. In his quest to be original and forge a new aesthetic sensibility, the homoerotic played a significant role. He set out on this quest with his most famous work, *The Sleep of Endymion* (Louvre, 1791). This painting was a success with the general public and critics alike when it was exhibited in Paris in 1793. Nothing like it had ever been seen before, and it was to have a lasting effect on how the male body was represented in subsequent art. It was praised as a tour de force in its novel treatment of a conventional myth, for its mysterious, innovative lighting effects, and for its dreamy, lyrical, and nocturnal mood. *The Sleep of Endymion* highlights the theme of androgyny and provokes an erotic response from the viewer to the youthful male body. The image exploits feminine qualities and bestows them on the male nude figure. The curly ringlets that suggestively fall about Endymion's shoulders are complemented by the overall elongation of form and marmoreal quality of the flesh. The stiff, rigid angularity of David's male figures is gone, replaced by a passive and indolent reclining pose typically associated with the female nude. The subject is the shepherd boy Endymion asleep in a hidden alcove atop the mythical Mount Latmos. The moon goddess, Selene, appears in the

Girdodet's Sleeping Endymion. *Louvre, Paris. Scala/Art Resource, NY.*

guise of moonbeams, while an overgrown hybrid figure of Cupid (the boy-god of love) and Zephyr (personification of the West Wind) eagerly part the foliage so that the moonrays can shine through, penetrate, and inhabit the supple body of the sleeping youth.

Throughout his long and bitter career, Girodet chose to concentrate on subjects that engaged in the confusion and conflating of masculine and feminine characteristics. His works exhibit a timeless and dreamlike feminized delicacy. In works such as his *Scene of a Deluge* (Louvre, 1806), stoic masculinity is deliberately undermined by overwhelming forces and is placed under serious threat of annihilation. In his turbulent and exotic *Revolt at Cairo* (Versailles, 1810), a charged homoerotic energy between men emerges from a physical and emotional contrast set up between men of different races and psychological dispositions. After 1810, Girodet's production of large-scale paintings slowed considerably, and his efforts were directed almost exclusively toward translating and illustrating classical literature. The images accompanying these texts are referred to as his "anacre-

onic" drawings, which concentrate on rendering classical stories of hetero- and homosexual love through a feminine lightness, curvilinearity, and delicacy of line.

Although his actions were discrete, rumors circulated within art circles of Girodet's notorious homosexual affairs. Even the artist's biographer, P. A. Coupin, claims to have destroyed, upon the artist's death, several letters written by Girodet for fear that they "revealed too much of the artist's inner life." Girodet did manage, however, to sublimate his homoerotic desires into much of his art. By so doing, he was one of the earliest visual artists of the modern era to successfully create a meaningful link between homoerotic desire and art production and serving as a foundation for the subsequent modernist notion of the artist as agent of a cultural, aesthetic, and sexual avant-garde.   *James Smalls*

Bibliography

Davis, Whitney. "The Renunciation of Reaction in Girodet's *Sleep of Endymion.*" In Norman Bryson, Michael Ann Holly, and Keith Moxey, eds. *Visual Culture: Images and Interpreta-*

tions. Hanover, NH: Wesleyan University Press, 1994, 168–201.

Levitine, George. *Girodet-Trioson: An Iconographical Study*. New York: 1974.

See also Art History; Greece, Ancient

Gloeden, Baron Wilhelm von (1856–1931)

Wilhelm von Gloeden, son of a Prussian baron, grew up while Bismarck was uniting Germany under the kaisers. He was not happy in that milieu, judging by his photographs, which extolled everything Greek and Roman *except* swords, helmets, or anything militaristic. After studying art at Weimar, he used "weak lungs" as an excuse to flee the damp, cold north for Teorima, a Sicilian city ringed with Greek and Roman ruins.

After his father was disgraced in 1890 (over an alleged forgery), Gloeden began to offer his "pictural-ist" photographs commercially. His naked youths were festooned with enough classical allusions to appeal safely to turn-of-the-century art movements—especially the decadents. By 1895, he was so successful that Teorima had become a stop on the Grand Tour, visited by Vanderbilts and Rothschilds, Eleanora Duse, the king of Siam, and, of course, Oscar Wilde.

Although the best of his efforts impart an eerie sense of seeing actual photographs of ancient Rome, generally Gloeden kitsched up "Greek" shots with Persian rugs, Asian tiger skins, and young men whose tanned hands and feet, contrasting sharply with their pale, naked limbs, showed clearly they were normally dressed from wrist to ankle. But Gloeden was not really re-creating the classical world; his true interest was in the "noble näiveté and quiet greatness" of those beggar boys with their cracked toenails, street-urchin bravado, and eyes like wounded deer. His triumph at that is the reason he is admired today.

World War I brought a four-year hiatus in his sales, and, after it ended, the passion for "Greek Dreams" was over. Baron von Gloeden's death in 1931 came barely in time to spare him the sight of fascists smashing his plates and burning his prints in 1933. His heroic assistant, Pancracio Bucini, saved eight hundred of the plates; fortunately, prints of his *"griechisten Traums"* already resided in treasured collections around the world.   *F. Valentine Hooven III*

Bibliography

Ellenzweig, Allen. *The Homoerotic Photograph*. New York: Columbia University Press, 1992.

Sternweiler, A., and H. G. Hannesen, *Goodbye to Berlin? 100 Jahre Schwulenbewegung*. Berlin: Verlag Rosa Winkler, 1997.

Waugh, Thomas. *Hard to Imagine*. New York: Columbia University Press, 1996.

Weiermair, Peter. *Wilhelm von Gloeden*. Cologne: Benedikt Taschen Verlag, 1993.

See also Germany; Greece, Ancient; Mediterranean; Photography; Wilde, Oscar

Goethe, Johannes Wolfgang von (1749–1832)

In a discussion about sodomite and historian Johannes Müller, Goethe observed that, although Greek love was against nature, it was also as old as nature, meaning that it was both in and against nature. In his own life, Goethe seems to have dwelled primarily on those aspects of same-sex desire that were in nature. He defended art historian Johann Joachim Winckelmann, who was known for his predilection for male beauty. Although the chronicling of Goethe's heterosexual love life has a long and distinguished tradition in German literary criticism, an understanding and appreciation of male-male desire reveals itself throughout his writings.

Goethe became aware of widespread male-male sexual activity first in Italy, where he observed "the love of men among themselves," as he wrote to the duke of Weimar on December 29, 1797. In one of "The Venetian Epigrams," he intimates knowledge of male-male sex, claiming, "Boys I have also loved." "The Roman Elegies" also refer occasionally to male-male sexual acts. A little-known essay published in 1788 on Italian theatrical transvestitism, "Women's Roles on the Roman Stage, Played by Men," does not deal specifically with male-male sexuality but does contribute to Goethe's sense of the queerness of Italy. Later in life, Goethe made extensive use of homoerotic themes in the *West-Eastern Divan*, a collection of poetry inspired by ancient Persian literature. In his own commentary on the *Divan*, Goethe asserts that he could not ignore "the tender feeling for the beauty of a growing boy" in the poem, emphasizing the homoerotic slant of this ancient literature.

Goethe's two most famous male protagonists in his novels both had homoerotic experiences in their youths. Werther, who famously kills himself because of heterosexual love, was initially entranced

Johann Heinrich Tischbein's portrait Goethe in the Campagna *(1787). Staedelisches Kunstinstitut, Frankfurt am Main, Germany. Foto Marburg/Art Resource, NY.*

with the beauty of a young male friend, as the reader finds out in *The Letters from Switzerland* (1796), a little-known sequel that relates events from Werther's youth. In *Wilhelm Meister's Journeyman Years* (1832), Wilhelm recounts the central event from his childhood, the drowning of the fisherman's son, a young boy with whom Wilhelm was in love.

Rarely does Goethe use male-male sexuality in a derogatory way. In *Faust II*, however, Mephistopheles, who is homosexually tinged throughout the play, ends up leering at the boy angels. This can obviously provoke homophobic laughs, but his leering is not entirely negative because Mephistopheles is, by his own account, "a part of that power that always desires evil and always does good." Thus his homosexuality is good in the larger picture of the cosmos.

Homosexuality has a clear presence throughout Goethe's works. Since Goethe has become the most canonical poet in the German tradition and the most uplifting representative of Germany, one can conclude that homosexuality has a place in, although

perhaps also against, the German canon and the image of modern Germany.   *Robert Tobin*

Bibliography

Kuzniar, Alice A., ed. *Outing Goethe and His Age.* Stanford, Calif.: Stanford University Press, 1996.

See also German Literature; Persian (Iranian) Literature and Culture; Winckelmann, Johann Joachim

Gogol, Nikolai (1809–1853)

Nikolai Gogol was a Russian fiction writer and playwright. Two events from Gogol's childhood determined both his personality and his artistic vision. The first was the close personal attachment to his younger brother, Ivan, who died when Gogol was ten: this set in motion the writer's lifelong search for an equally ideal male friend and companion. The second was his mystically minded mother's instilling in him her variant of fundamentalist Christianity that emphasized the hellfire and retribution that await sinners; this led Gogol to fight against and to conceal his homosexual impulses.

From age twelve to nineteen, Gogol attended an all-male boarding school in the town of Nezhin. There he began writing prose and poetry for the school's literary journal, enjoyed great success in the school's theatricals, especially when playing the parts of comical women, and formed a sentimental attachment to an older fellow student. Gogol moved with this friend to St. Petersburg in 1928, only to find that his love was not reciprocated.

At this time, Gogol made his literary debut with some derivative poetry and a book-length romantic narrative poem, *Hanz Kuechelgarten,* which he published at his own expense and which was a failure. Then, realizing that his own native Ukrainian heritage was a valuable literary asset within the romantic trends of the time, he wrote eight novellas about a fairy-tale-like Ukraine of olden times. They were brought out in two volumes (1831 and 1833), under the general title *Evenings on a Farm Near Dikanka.* This work made Gogol a national celebrity and opened all literary doors to him by the time he was twenty-four.

In the first of the *Dikanka* novels, *St. John's Eve,* Gogol had already sounded his cardinal theme, which was to reverberate through his writings until the end. Love for a woman, marriage, or heterosexual desire invariably leads to death, catastrophe, or assorted dangers for the male protagonist. A happy ending in a tale or a play by Gogol consists of a man's escape from impending matrimony (as happens in the novella *The Nose* and a play, *Marriage*). The illogicality of this pattern was wrapped up in a colorful operatic merriment in Gogol's early works and in absurdist or surrealistic horror in the later ones. Like Lautramont (Isidore Ducasse) and Lewis Carroll, Gogol was an absurdist and a surrealist long before these categories were invented.

Gogol's next cycle of novellas, *Mirgorod* (1834), consisted of a rural idyll, a comic social satire, a military romance, and a supernatural horror story. Despite their thematic and generic variety, these tales are all variations on the same theme: the happy existence of one or more men is ruined when they come under the sway of a sexually active female. Two of the *Mirgorod* tales—the satire and the horror story—come close to depicting homosexual situations. The apex of Gogol's narrative art was reached in his cycle of tales set in St. Petersburg, written in 1835–1841. Here, Gogol abandoned the Ukrainian setting and the supernatural forces of his earlier work and developed the great myth of a solitary, powerless man facing the impersonal, inhuman metropolis, a theme that Balzac and Dickens were independently investigating at the same time.

The satirical comedy *The Inspector General* (1836) brought Gogol huge success. In it, he parodies the love interest, obligatory in comedies, by having the young protagonist make the lunatic offer to marry both the wife and the daughter of the town mayor. To the horror of the politically conservative Gogol, the play was interpreted as an indictment of all the institutions of the Russian Empire. In his panic, Gogol fled Russia and settled in Rome, where he was to stay for the next twelve years. In Italy, the writer's inhibitions were loosened to the point where he allowed himself to love openly the young nobleman Iosif Vielhorsky, who, however, died of consumption a year after he and Gogol met.

During his stay in Rome, Gogol completed the two comedies he had begun in Russia, *Marriage,* a headlong attack on the entire institution of matrimony, and *The Gamblers,* where the cardsharp protagonist comes to grief for loving a specifically—marked—female deck of cards named Adelaida Ivanovna. Gogol's popular novel *Dead Souls* (1841) uses the formula of Spanish, French, and English picaresque novels (such as *Tom Jones* by Henry Fielding); Gogol's *picaro* had no interest in sexual adventures, so usual for this genre. Like *The Inspector General* earlier, *Dead Souls* was read by many as a call to reform society and free the serfs.

Outraged by his readers' interpretations, Gogol published a volume of essays, *Selected Passages from Correspondence with Friends* (1846), in which he spoke his political mind openly: slavery and social stratification were justified in the Bible, and any reform or political change was an offense against Christianity. Gogol expected to be acclaimed as Russia's moral preceptor and prophet for this book; instead, he brought down upon himself the wrath of every political faction in the country. In January 1852, Gogol confessed his sexual orientation to a bigoted priest, who prescribed abstinence from food and sleep, so as to cleanse Gogol's "inner filth." Gogol died of starvation on February 21, 1852.

Despite his popularity and wide influence (on Fyodor Dostoyevsky, for example, it was enormous), much of Gogol's work was misread in the nineteenth century. Mid-nineteenth-century critics saw him as a photographic realist, the originator of the humanitar-

G ian trend in Russian literature. Even his contemptuous treatment of the protagonist of *The Overcoat* was mistaken for a model of compassion and social awareness. His complexity and originality, as well as his fantasy and surrealistic humor, were noted by other Russian writers (rather than critics) of the early twentieth century, such as Andrey Beli, Aleksey Remizov, and Vladimir Nabokov.   *Simon Karlinsky*

Bibliography

Fanger, Donald. *Dostoevsky and Romantic Realism: A Study of Dostoevsky in Relation to Balzac, Dickens and Gogol.* Cambridge, Mass.: Harvard University Press, 1965.

Karlinsky, Simon. *The Sexual Labyrinth of Nikolai Gogol.* Cambridge, Mass.: Harvard University Press, 1976.

Setchkarev, Vsevolod. *Gogol: His Life and Works.* New York: New York University Press, 1965.

See also Friendship; Mediterranean; Russia; Russian Literature

González-Torres, Felix (1957–1996)

Just eight years after his first solo show in New York in 1987, Cuban-born American artist Felix González-Torres was accorded an unusual midcareer exhibition at the Solomon R. Guggenheim Museum. The show surveyed his entire output of conceptualist objects, installations, and projects. Less than one year later, in early 1996, he died of HIV-related complications.

González-Torres was born in Guaimaro, Cuba, and moved to New York City in 1979, where he studied photography at the Pratt Institute and International Center of Photography, earning undergraduate and graduate degrees, respectively, from these institutions. He also participated in the theory-driven Whitney Museum of American Art's independent study program. It was there he was exposed to the postmodernism of such writers as Roland Barthes and Michel Foucault, and to the budding art world debate about social power relations embodied in such systems of representation as advertising and visual art. His sensibility was formed by such thinking and by the related work of slightly older, so-called postfeminist artists such as Jenny Holzer and Barbara Kruger.

In 1987, he joined the collective Group Material, which organized huge group exhibitions devoted to themes such as homelessness (1988) and AIDS (1988–1989). Collective members regarded these installations as artworks themselves. González-Torres remained part of the group for the rest of his life, while he continued to produce his own, less didactic art.

Language often plays a key role in González-Torres's work. His early New York shows comprised black prints featuring cryptic, white time-line texts running along the bottom. The entries spanned the public and private realms, typically alluding—as in the case of one untitled 1987 work—to AIDS and genocide, civil rights and good times: "Alabama 1964 . . . Safer Sex 1985 . . . Disco Donuts 1979 . . . Cardinal O'Connor 1987 . . . Klaus Barbie 1944 . . . Napalm 1972 . . . C. O. D." With their nonlinear chronologies and sparse compositions, such prints invoke the constructed nature of history and encourage viewers to project their own histories—or her-stories—onto them.

González-Torres applied this format to his first public artwork, a 1989 billboard on New York's Christopher Street commemorating key events in gay history for the twentieth anniversary of the Stonewall rebellion. Afterward he produced numerous billboards, among the most moving a black-and-white photo of an empty, rumpled bed that refers to the death of his lover in 1991.

His art has taken many forms, united less by a refined, minimalist look than by the thinking underlying each of his series of works. Two of the most extensive are the "candy spills" and the "stacks." The former are piles of wrapped hard candies intended as portraits of subjects in a color that evokes them and in spills that correspond to their weight. The latter are stacks of prints. Some bear words and/or images, including one that chronicles actual deaths through captioned photos. Viewers are invited to take both candy and prints, evoking a gift economy entirely foreign to the contemporary art world.   *Robert Atkins*

Bibliography

Spector, Nancy. *Felix González-Torres* (exhhibition catalog). New York: Solomon R. Guggenheim Museum, 1995.

See also Cuban Writing in Exile

Goode, Joe (1951–)

Based in San Francisco, Joe Goode is an "out" gay dance-theater artist known for performances of passion, poignancy, and surprising humor. As artistic director of the Joe Goode Performance Group, founded in 1986, he has dealt with subjects ranging from gender and effeminacy to the deep mourning of a generation coping with AIDS—all with a sharp sense of irony that he identifies as a key to his gay sensibility. In a chapbook created to celebrate the company's tenth anniversary, Goode identifies four themes running throughout his work: body and location, gender, disaster and epiphany, and the inappropriate person. He sings (as does his company of six men and women), intoning mellifluous texts to hypnotic effect. Heavily influenced by Contact Improvisation, he crafts movement that places his dancers in interdependent physical relationships, requiring them to bear one another's weight, or to live upended, or sideways. His is a total theater, encompassing an operatic range of artistic genres and exploring a phantasmagoria of gay themes.

Born in Presque Isle, Maine, Goode moved to Hampton, Virginia, at the age of seven. Escaping his working-class upbringing, he earned a B.F.A. in drama from Virginia Commonwealth University in 1973 and subsequently moved to New York City to become an actor, director, and choreographer. In New York he studied dance with Merce Cunningham and Viola Farber. In 1979, he relocated to the Bay Area and danced with the Margaret Jenkins Dance Company for four years. His first major independent piece, *The Ascension of Big Linda into the Skies of Montana* (1986), won two Isadora Duncan awards for its evocative, layered narrative and audacious site-specific staging. Other significant works include *29 Effeminate Gestures* (1987), a solo broadcast on PBS's *Alive From Off Center* in 1989; *The Disaster Series* (1989), in which physical disasters—flood, earthquake, dust bowl—are construed as metaphors for societal and bodily dissolution; *Remembering the Pool at the Best Western* (1990), a philosophical rumination on AIDS and life after death; *Convenience Boy* (1993), inspired by the disposable culture of gay and lesbian street hustlers; and the *Maverick Strain* (1996), a site-specific work that likens the lone cowboy to the survivor of AIDS. *David Gere*

Bibliography

Goode, Joe. *Joe Goode Performance Group: Ten Years Old.* San Francisco: Joe Goode Performance Group, 1996.

Ross, Janice. "San Francisco's Joe Goode: Working Hard to Be the Bad Boy of Modern Dance." *Dance Magazine* (January 1989): 46–50.

Joe Goode Performance Group, Remembering the Pool at the Best Western. *Left to right: Joe Goode, Liz Burritt. Photo by Bill Pack.*

———. "Twenty-Nine Strategic Gestures: Joe Goode in the Context of American Dance." In *Joe Goode Performance Group: Ten Years Old*. San Francisco: Joe Goode Performance Group, 1996, 42–45.

Shank, Theodore. "Joe Goode's Performance Life-Style: An Interview with Theodore Shank." *Theatre Forum* 5 (September/Fall 1994): 71–77.

See also AIDS Performance; Cunningham, Merce; Dance and AIDS

Goodman, Paul (1911–1972)

Paul Goodman was an American novelist, poet, political analyst, and utopian thinker. In "Being Queer" (1969), he claims that "remarkable political values" in "queer life" had "usefully simplified my notions of what a good society is." Rooted in his own queer life (bisexual, twice married in common law, the father of three; a conscientious objector in World War II; and by 1951, three times fired from academic employment because of affairs with students), Goodman achieved celebrity when his *Growing Up Absurd* (1960) became a best-seller. The book excoriates American business, politics, and culture for preventing Americans from achieving authentic adulthood—the keystone for a good society. Americans typically surrender their meaningful maturation, Goodman argues, in exchange for a stunting submission to corporate capitalism and for an infantilizing capitulation to the authority of technology and media. Thinking in a characteristically antithesis-laden way, Goodman identifies maturity with radical individuation on the one hand and with wholehearted commitment to community on the other. In that same paradoxical fashion, *Growing Up Absurd* offers youth a model of adult life in Jean Genet and in the heroes of "the exclusive homosexuality" that shapes Genet's novels. Goodman approvingly describes Genet's protagonists as "ignorant and self-destructive kids [who] glow with nobility and religious significance."

Goodman's antinomic thought is expressed in his double political stance: he calls himself both an anarchist and a "neolithic conservative." The identification with Genet is anarchistic; but in *Growing Up Absurd* Goodman's simultaneous hostility to the Beats is conservative: he attacks their rebellion for evading adult responsibility and intellectual and artistic excellence. Routinely Goodman criticizes the left, even as he is a spokesman for it: he dis-

sented from black power and from post-Stonewall gay nationalism because he believed both movements betrayed libertarian coalition building. Yet despite his praise of liberating coalitions, Goodman insists that personal and political aims keep within narrow limits: "Our mistake is to arm anybody with collective power"; "The aim of politics is to increase autonomy and so it is mostly undoing." He laments patriotism's decline and American democracy's becoming defunct; but his anarchist formula for a replacement—dignified individual practices of crafts and professions, and the cultural evolution of "unique prerogatives and lots of borders to cross"—strikes a note that is provocatively antiegalitarian.

Goodman's literary vocation encapsulates his social thought's paradoxes. In the novel *Parents' Day* (1951), his portrayal of a teacher's erotic passion for a high school student mingles convention-bound shame and radically defiant sexual politics. In *The Empire City* (1942–1959), a neglected masterpiece of experimental fiction that is a key link between surrealism and postmodernist writing, Goodman says that he "undertook the task of not giving up *any* claims of culture and humanity, but my characters . . . turn out to be far out of this world." Yet Goodman loves the very form of literature precisely because it takes us away from immediate worldliness. He justifies the study of literary form in itself, independent of historical or political relevance, in *The Structure of Literature* (1954) and *Speaking and Language* (1971), where he praises literature for resisting "positivistic clarity" and for bringing life's shadows "into the foreground."

Robert L. Caserio

Bibliography

Goodman, Paul. *Crazy Hope and Finite Experience*. Taylor Stoehr, ed. San Francisco: Jossey-Bass, 1994.

———. *Format and Anxiety*. Taylor Stoehr, ed. Brooklyn: Autonomedia, 1995.

See also Beat Generation; Black Power Movement; Gay Left; Gay Liberation; Genet, Jean

Goytisolo, Juan (1931–)

Juan Goytisolo has become a canonical writer by studiously questioning—and even attacking—the canon. This paradox, by which dissent is co-opted and resistance reappropriated, bears on other aspects of Goytisolo's work as well. His critiques of capitalism, communism, racism, heterosexism, and Western thought in general are caught in a web of complicity that complicates any simple assessment. This, he knows, and his novels, essays, interviews, travelogues, and two-volume autobiography—*Cofo redado* (*Forbidden Territory* [1985]) and *En los reinos de taifa* (*Realms of Strife* [1986])—provide eloquent testimony to the power of established codes and the difficulty, yet necessity, of liberational projects.

Goytisolo is arguably the contemporary Spanish writer most explicitly concerned with freedom: sexual, artistic, political. Championing the cause of the persecuted, oppressed, and marginalized, he positions himself in a heterogeneous line of dissidence that includes the Marquis de Sade, Lawrence of Arabia, Jean Genet, the Sufi mystics, José María Blanco White, Américo Castro, Luis Cernuda, and St. John of the Cross. Professing no religious affiliation himself, he is a passionate advocate of Islamic culture, as important to Spanish history as it is denigrated and denied. He is also profoundly interested in questions of homosexuality, often autobiographically inflected, though he refuses the role of advocate, at least in any organized sense. He is thus not quite a "gay" writer, not only because he presents himself as attached to his wife, Monique Lange (recently deceased), and hence as implicitly bisexual, but also because even when he presents himself, insistently, as desiring other men (virtually always non-Western and poor), he remains suspicious of the gay and lesbian movement. This suspicion is the result of his disillusionment with communism, especially in Cuba, where in the mid-sixties homosexuals were targeted by the revolutionary regime as "improper." The problem, according to Goytisolo, is that *any* organized movement can become dogmatic, obsessed with proper lines and averse to the supposedly free play of creativity. Such a position is, of course, prone to dogmatism itself. And yet, the turns of freedom, authority, individuality, and community are, along with a deep appreciation of language, what makes this writer so compelling.

Juan Goytisolo Gay (his mother, killed during the Spanish Civil War, was Julia Gay) was born in 1931 in Barcelona to a prosperous family of Basque descent. His early years are marked by war and then by the fascist dictatorship of Francisco Franco, where Catholicism and a Castilian-oriented nationalism haunted by dreams of imperial grandeur combined to create, for Goytisolo, a climate of austerity, fear, and (self-)censorship. Goytisolo's first literary endeavors, from *Juegos de manos* (1954) to *La resaca* (1958) and *La isla* (1961), are written in loose accordance with the principles of social realism, striving to reflect and express a brutal, unjust social reality in clear, unobtrusive, objective terms. Marxism and Sartrean existentialism condition his understanding of literature as engagement. In the fifties, Goytisolo moved to Paris as a self-declared exile and met Jean Genet, whose influence he deemed crucial to his artistic and personal transformation. Disaffected with a writing that keeps form in check, in 1966, with *Señas de identidad* (*Marks of Identity*), he initiated a rupture with realism that is radicalized in *Reivindicación del Conde don Julian* (*Count Julian* [1970]), perhaps the most sweeping literary assault on Spain ever written. That this assault entails the symbolic violation of women renders its much-celebrated "revolution" problematic (the representation of women later becomes the focus of reflection in *La saga de los Marx*, 1993). Problematic too is his representation of Arab men and of gays, where guilt, shame, and abjection, reworked along Genetian lines, become forms of radical resistance.

Goytisolo, however, is hardly one to avoid problems. His writing from 1970 on is confrontational, fragmentary, and demanding, refracting more than merely reflecting the violence of civilization. Texts such as *Juan sin tierra* (*Juan the Landless* [1975]), *Makbara* (1980), and *Paisajes depués de La batalla* (*Landscapes after the Battle* [1982]) waver deliriously between political commitment and aesthetic autonomy and map the collisions of globality and locality, the conflictive, yet promising, infolding of Paris, Marrakech, Pittsburgh, and Havana. In *Las virtudes del pájaro solitario* (*The Virtues of the Solitary Bird* [1988]) and *La Cuarentena* (*Quarantine* [1991]), Goytisolo plunges into a cross-cultural, highly eroticized, heterodox recuperation of Christian and Sufi mysticism. In both, death and transcendence figure prominently, *Las virtudes* (*Virtues*) being a dense and provocative allegory in which AIDS is bound to the Inquisition, the Holocaust, the Gulag, and other modes of political persecution. *El sitio de los situous* (1995) and *Las semanas del jardín* (1997) focused on ethnic strife and "matricide" (the assault on collective memory) in Bosnia, pushing at the limits of authority, authorship, and property. Here as elsewhere identity—sexual, ethnic, national, or otherwise—is not simply reaffirmed or rejected but is instead a problem, a question that concerns "us" all.

Brad Epps

G

Bibliography

Epps, Brad. *Significant Violence: Oppression and Resistance in Juan Goytisolo*. New York: Oxford University Press, 1996.

Pope, Randolph. *Understanding Juan Goytisolo*. Columbia, S.C.: University of South Carolina Press, 1995.

Six, Abigail Lee. *Juan Goytisolo: The Case for Chaos*. New Haven: Yale University Press, 1990.

Ugarte, Michael. *Trilogy of Treason: An Intertextual Study of Juan Goytisolo*. Columbia, Mo.: University of Missouri Press, 1984.

See also Cernuda, Luis; Genet, Jean; Islamic Mysticism; Lawrence, T. E.; Sade, Marquis de; Spain; Spanish Literature

Gran Fury

Gran Fury was founded in 1988 as a self-described "band of individuals united in anger and dedicated to exploiting the power of art to end the AIDS crisis." The collective consisted of several fine and commercial artists as well as a hairdresser, a costume designer, an architect, a filmmaker, and a nurse. The very heterogeneity of the group's constitution underscored its activist—rather than expressly artistic—commitments and training. The group took the name Gran Fury, in reference both to their own rage in the midst of the AIDS epidemic and, more ironically, to the particular model of Chrysler sedan that New York City police use as squad cars.

Though organized as an autonomous group, Gran Fury worked in close alliance with the New York chapter of the AIDS Coalition to Unleash Power (ACT UP), producing imagery and agitprop to accompany the latter group's demonstrations, and serving, in the words of Douglas Crimp and Adam Rolston, as ACT UP's "unofficial propaganda ministry and guerrilla graphic designers" (16). In creating graphic work for ACT UP demonstrations, Gran Fury considered not only how the work would function within the moment of the action but, equally, if not more important, how it would "read" in coverage by the mainstream press. The impact of Gran Fury's work thus extended into its subsequent reproduction on television news programs and in local newspapers.

Gran Fury produced its protest work in a variety of media, including billboard signs, bus shelter advertisements, mock newspapers, and music videos. What is more, the collective simulated the glossy look and pithy language of mass-market advertising to seduce their audience into dealing with issues of AIDS transmission, research, funding, and government (non)response, issues that might otherwise be avoided or rejected out of hand. In catching viewers off-guard, Gran Fury sought to shock them into a heightened awareness of the AIDS crisis.

A graphic from 1989 entitled *Kissing Doesn't Kill* exemplifies the attention-getting strategies exploited by Gran Fury's work. Designed as an advertisement to be affixed to the side of a city bus, *Kissing Doesn't Kill* offers three interracial couples dressed in high-contrast colors and posed against an expanse of white monochrome. Each of the couples is kissing. Both the brightly patterned clothing worn by the figures and the overall visual style of the image simulate Benetton's well-known "Colors of the World" ad campaign. At a quick first glance, one may think one has encountered yet another in that would-be provocative (but ultimately vacant) series of advertisements. It takes only another moment, however, to notice the differences this image has propelled into the space of advertising and to recognize that its agenda has nothing to do with boosting retail sales of Italian sportswear. Two of the three couples are of the same sex and a banner caption extending above the entire image declares "Kissing

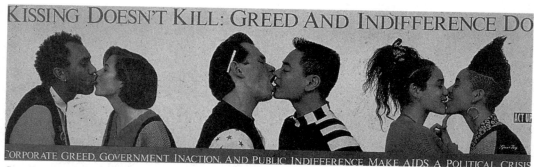

Gran Fury, Kissing Doesn't Kill: Greed and Indifference Do (1989).

Doesn't Kill: Greed and Indifference Do." In smaller type, a caption below the image reads, "Corporate Greed, Government Inaction, and Public Indifference Make AIDS a Political Crisis."

Kissing Doesn't Kill mimics the codes of consumerist pleasure and visual seduction to capture the viewer's attention and direct it to the AIDS crisis. Equally important, it affirms the power of sexual desire and physical affection in the face of an ongoing epidemic, insisting that lesbians and gay men fight the efforts of the larger culture to position their sexuality as deviant. *Kissing Doesn't Kill* also challenges misinformation about AIDS, rejecting early accounts (and rumors) that erroneously named kissing as a risk behavior and saliva as a likely fluid of HIV transmission. The graphic, like all of Gran Fury's work, located the root cause of the AIDS crisis not in HIV infection but in larger social forces— the government, the corporate culture, the mainstream public—that ignored or exploited the terms of the epidemic.

The work of Gran Fury courted as wide a consumer audience as possible. "We are trying to fight for attention as hard as Coca-Cola fights for attention," observed Gran Fury member Loring McAlpin of the group's mass-market ambitions. Throughout the course of its relatively brief career (the collective disbanded in 1992), Gran Fury exploited the force of art and graphic design to propel its activist message into the public sphere. By tying visual images to a larger politics of protest and intervention, Gran Fury insisted that, within the context of AIDS, "art is not enough." *Richard Meyer*

Bibliography

Crimp, Douglas, and Adam Rolston. *AIDS Demo Graphics*. Seattle: Bay Press, 1990.
Jacobs, Karrie. "Night Discourse." In *Angry Graphics: Protest Posters of the Reagan/Bush Era*. Steven Heller and Karrie Jacobs, eds. Salt Lake City: Peregrine Smith Books, 1991.

See also ACT UP; Activism, U.S.; AIDS; Art History

Grant, Duncan (1885–1978)

Duncan Grant was the preeminent painter of the circle of artists and intellectuals known as the Bloomsbury group. The youngest of Bloomsbury's founding generation, Grant was also its only man not to attend Cambridge University. His initial connection to the group was based on his homosexuality, which created a passionate bond first between Grant and his cousin, Lytton Strachey, and then with Strachey's friend John Maynard Keynes. Together these three gay men were central to Bloomsbury's initial cohesiveness. In the teens, Grant became the lifelong domestic companion of another Bloomsbury painter, Vanessa Bell. Charleston, the Sussex farmhouse they shared with Clive Bell, a prominent art critic and Vanessa's husband, is today open as a museum of Bloomsbury art and design, and offers the best insight into the range of Grant's work.

Like others in Bloomsbury, Grant was deeply affected by the aesthetic theory of Roger Fry, which dismissed Victorian narrative painting in favor of modernist styles that seemed sensual and free. Grant was attracted to Fry's ideas on their first publication around 1910, and he immediately adopted a modernist style for his representations of homoerotic themes. Though only the subtlest of this work was exhibited during his lifetime, Grant produced innumerable homoerotic sketches and paintings throughout his long and prolific career. His early homoerotic work draws heavily on the precedent of the aesthetic movement (writers such as Walter Pater and John Addington Symonds), which posited the cultures of the Mediterranean as paradises of unfettered sensuality. The classicized nudes in Grant's paintings of around 1910 can be compared quite closely to the work of photographers such as Wilhelm van Gloeden, who was well known in England. Like other gay artists at midcentury—David Hockney is the most famous example—Grant in his later work often drew on nudist and physique magazines to create his homoerotic images. Grant continued to paint until shortly before his death in 1978 at the age of 93. A selection of late homoerotic work was published in 1989.

For many in the highly cerebral Bloomsbury group, Grant seemed the quintessential artist: intuitively talented and spontaneously sensual. Bloomsbury's advocacy of the aesthetic doctrine of formalism, which values art for the intrinsic aesthetic impact of abstract form rather than for subject matter, precluded self-conscious consideration of the themes of Grant's imagery. Without explicitly endorsing his iconography, however, the Bloomsbury critics' praise for the sensuality of his style encodes the group's acceptance of his sexuality. "The quality of his paint is often as charming as a kiss," Clive Bell wrote in one review, specifying that "there is something Greek about him, too; not the archeological Greek of Germany, nor yet the

Bathing. *Oil on canvas (1911). Tate Gallery, London/Art Resource, NY.*

Graeco-Roman academicism of France, but rather that romantic, sensuous Hellenism of the English literary tradition." Only recently have historians initiated analyses of Grant's work that go beyond formal issues, the most thoughtful of which is Simon Watney's *The Art of Duncan Grant*.

Christopher Reed

Bibliography

Bell, Clive. "Duncan Grant." In *Since Cézanne*. London: Chatto and Windus, 1922, 105–12.

Reed, Christopher. "Making History: The Bloomsbury Group's Construction of Aesthetic and Sexual Identity." In *Gay and Lesbian Studies in Art History*. Whitney Davis, ed. New York: Haworth Press, 1994.

Turnbaugh, Douglas Blair. *Private: The Erotic Art of Duncan Grant*. London: Gay Men's Press, 1989.

Watney, Simon. *The Art of Duncan Grant*. London: John Murray, 1990.

See also Bloomsbury Group; The Bloomsbury Group and Art; Gloeden, Baron Wilhelm von; Hockney, David; Keynes, John Maynard; Pater, Walter Horatio; Strachey, (Giles) Lytton; Symonds, John Addington

Gray, Thomas (1716–1771)

Thomas Gray was born in London and educated at Eton and Cambridge. His best-known work—"Elegy in a Country Churchyard"—has been popular since its publication in 1751. Gray was uncomfortable with the fame that the poem brought him; he spent most of his life in retirement in Cambridge, and in 1757 he refused the poet laureateship. The "Elegy" features a misunderstood poet who dies after seeming to be "crossed in hopeless love." Early commentators read the "Elegy" in the light of Gray's relationship with his school friend Richard West, whose death in 1742 seriously affected the poet; contemporary gay critics have argued that the poem investigates the boundaries between male friendship and homoerotic desire. A similar theme is present in Gray's "Sonnet on the Death of Mr Richard West" and in his Latin elegy for West, "De Principiis Cogitandi" (The Principles of Thought). Gray's English poetry contains frequent references to Latin and

Greek homoerotic texts, and his letters and unpublished manuscripts display a similar interest in Greek and Latin homosexuality. He wrote commentaries on many of Plato's Dialogues, and his letters use classical poetry to express his emotional dependence on male friends. These letters display a wit that is often lacking in Gray's poetry. Besides Richard West, his most important friendships were with Horace Walpole and Charles-Victor de Bonstetten, a Swiss nobleman. Gray's works—particularly his letters—are an important link between the ethical classicism of the early eighteenth century and the more emotionally inflected Hellenism of the Romantic period.   *Vincent Quinn*

Bibliography

Gray, Thomas. *The Correspondence of Thomas Gray*. Paget Toynbee and Leonard Whibley, eds. 3 vols. Oxford: Clarendon Press, 1935. Rev. H. W. Starr, 1971.

———. *Gray, Collins and Goldsmith: The Complete Poems*. Roger Lonsdale, ed. London: Longman, 1969.

Haggerty, George E. "*O lachrymarum fons*: Tears, Poetry, and Desire in Gray." *Eighteenth-Century Studies* 30 (1996): 81–95.

See also Elegiac Poerty; English Literature; Friendship

Greece, Ancient

The origins of male same-sex sexual relations in ancient Greece are unclear. That these relations existed is evident from mythology, art, literature, and graffiti found in the agora of Athens.

A fragment of the historian Ephorus (c.405–330 B.C.E.) contains an interesting account of the ritualized abduction of younger men by older, practiced on Dorian Crete in the seventh century B.C.E. In this ritual, the lover informs the boy's friends three or four days in advance that he is going to abduct him; if the lover is worthy, it is customary for the boy's friends to help the lover capture him; however, if the lover is unworthy, the boy's peers protect him from the older man's advances. When captured, the boy, who should be "exceptionally manly and decorous," is taken to the *andreion* (the men's mess) of his abductor, where he is given presents, before being taken away into the country for two months. The friends, who were present at the capture, join the lover and the young man as they feast and hunt and then return to the city, where the boy is presented with a military habit, a cup, and an ox (among other gifts) before being released. The boy then sacrifices the ox to Zeus, entertains his friends at a feast, and reveals the facts "about his intimacy with his lover." If he feels that he was captured against his will, he can avenge himself at this feast and rid himself of his lover.

Scene of pederasty on a Greek Vase. Amphora 206. Bibliothéque Nationale, Paris. Art Resource, NY.

G Employing models of initiation such as that established by such early authorities on rituals of initiation as Arnold van Gennep, author of *Rites of Passage,* some scholars have argued that the characteristic elements of an initiation are present in Ephorus's account. Anthropological studies testify to the almost universal practice of present giving in initiation rituals: gifts like the military habit, cup, and ox could thus signify the boy's initiation into those institutions (the army, the men's mess) and religious practices (sacrifice) that characterized Dorian manhood. ("Dorian" refers to one of the Greek tribes speaking a particular Greek dialect with a particular social organization [e.g., Sparta].) The older man thus initiates the younger into manly pursuits (like hunting and feasting) and, presumably, sexual relationships. Evidence of extensive initiatory practices in the most important Dorian community on mainland Greece (Sparta), where boys at the age of twelve received lovers chosen from among the respectable young men, would suggest that male same-sex sexual relationships were common initiatory features of a highly conservative, militaristic society in which sexes were rigidly separated.

Although it is unlikely that Dorian Greeks exported initiation rites of the above kind to other Greek linguistic and religious groups (such as the Ionians associated with Athens), there are unmistakable initiatory features in the relationships between older men and younger, so well attested in the art and literature of classical Athens. In the works of Plato and Xenophon especially, the lover (*erastes*) was supposed to be a model of courage and morality for the beloved (*eromenos*), who was required to be the chaste recipient of the lover's advances, not the initiator. In Attic vase paintings, sexual contact seems restricted to intercrural sex (mutual masturbation between the thighs) in a standing position, face-to-face. Anal intercourse may well have occurred in reality (as it did among the Dorian Greeks), but Athenian ideology seems to have associated anal intercourse with women, and hence with passivity and unmasculine shame. In Aristophanic comedy, the language of insult reflects this demarcation between active and passive; "bugger," "wide-arsed," and "tank-arsed" are thus used of effeminate men. Oral-genital contact was associated with the alien behavior of satyrs, who were part man and part animal, and would thus have been taboo for Athenian citizens.

For the *eromenos,* the situation was particularly difficult as he was technically the passive recipient of a man's attentions, yet he could not appear to behave passively and so align himself with a male prostitute, a woman, or a slave. The Athenian citizen was expected to be active, assertive, and dominant; consequently, considerable anxiety surrounded the behavior of the *eromenos,* lest he be seen to be transgressing the hierarchical gender boundaries.

In contrast to the initiation model, some scholars, for example, Dover, have attempted to understand Athenian same-sex sexual relationships in the context of the institution of arranged marriages and the position of women. An Athenian citizen could not have had a love affair with a citizen woman before marriage, which was a contract between a man of about thirty and a girl in her early teens; prostitutes and slave women were readily available and exploited, but not every prostitute was an educated *hetaira* like Pericles' Aspasia, and some Athenian men wanted more from relationships than sex. Consequently, for emotional and intellectual stimulation in addition to erotic passion, Athenian men turned to each other.

In other city-states in Greece, such as Thebes, attitudes toward male same-sex relationships were not as complicated or as well documented as those of Athens. The Sacred Band of Thebes was a battalion composed of 150 pairs of male lovers, maintained at state expense and stationed on the battlefield in couples, which greatly contributed to its military successes. The famous Theban general Epaminondas was killed in battle with his lover beside him. Greek military commanders seemed to have had a penchant for men. The greatest commander of them all, Alexander, made no secret of his intense love for Hephaestion, and even Athenian playboy general Alcibiades attempted to seduce philosopher Socrates, if Plato's account is to be believed.

Whether Greece can be regarded as the mother of Western gay relationships is highly debatable, as the Greeks did not possess a conceptual and/or linguistic category corresponding to our current use of the nineteenth-century term *homosexual* or anything remotely suggestive of the word *gay.* However, in Plato's *Symposium*, Aristophanes' amusing account of the origin of male-female, male-male, and female-female relationships implies that for some Athenians, at any rate, attempts at categorizing people on the basis of their sexual orientation did exist. Generally speaking, the Greeks categorized sexual acts, focusing on penetration rather than people: in this way, ancient Greece apparently constructed sexuality differently from the modern West, thus challenging the essentialist notion that sexuality is an ahistorical constant. *Michael Lambert*

Bibliography

Dover, Kenneth J. *Greek Homosexuality.* 2d ed. London: Duckworth, 1989.

Halperin, David M. *One Hundred Years of Homosexuality and Other Essays on Greek Love.* New York: Routledge, 1990.

See also Athens; Friendship; Homosexuality; Pederasty; Plato; Sparta; Thebes

Griffes, Charles Tomlinson (1884–1920)

Charles Tomlinson Griffes was one of the most gifted American composers of his generation, and his gay sensibility pervades his music. Griffes forged a formidable compositional technique that eschewed the commonplaces of German romanticism then favored by most American composers, creating an inimitable style derived from the experiments of Scriabin, Debussy, Ravel, and Schoenberg. Griffes was unique among American composers of his day for showing an interest in non-Western music, including the Japanese and Arabic folk songs he incorporated into several of his works.

Born in Elmira, New York, to an intellectually undistinguished family of modest means, Griffes exhibited as a child both unusual musical gifts and an unaccountably refined taste in art and literature. He began piano lessons with his sister but soon became the pupil of Mary Selena Broughton, who taught piano at Elmira College. In 1903, Broughton provided the financial support for Griffes to study piano and composition in Germany. The young composer responded with alacrity to the enlightened atmosphere of Berlin.

On returning to America in 1907, Griffes became the director of music at the Hackley School for Boys in Tarrytown, New York. He escaped from Tarrytown to New York City as often as possible, becoming part of a bohemian set of artists, singers, and dancers, as well as honing his considerable skills as a seducer of firemen, trolley conductors, and Irish policemen. Despite the considerable demands of his mundane teaching position and financial difficulties created by his grasping family, Griffes created a series of remarkable scores: *Roman Sketches* (including *The White Peacock*) for piano; *Three Poems of Fiona MacLeod* for voice and orchestra; *The Pleasure Dome of Kubla Khan* for orchestra. Perhaps his perfect achievement is the Sonata for Piano (1918), a taut work of enormous emotional power.

Griffes read Oscar Wilde, Edward Carpenter, and other pioneer gay intellectuals and came to believe that his homosexuality was perfectly natural and enjoyable. His secret sexual diaries, written in German, survived his sister Marguerite's posthumous destruction of his papers (which she thought too compromising) and became a primary source for George Chauncey's history of early-twentieth-century urban America—*Gay New York.* Thus Griffes managed to preserve a substantial slice of the gay history of his time and place; his early death remains an irreparable tragedy for American music.

Byron Adams

Bibliography

Anderson, Donna K. *Charles T. Griffes: A Life in Music.* Washington, D.C.: Smithsonian Institution Press, 1993.

Chauncey, George. *Gay New York: Gender, Urban Culture and the Making of the Gay Male World, 1890–1940.* New York: HarperCollins, 1994.

Maisel, Edward. *Charles T. Griffes: The Life of an American Composer.* New York: Knopf, 1984.

See also Carpenter, Edward; Gay American Composers; New York City; Wilde, Oscar

Guevara, Ernesto "Che" (1928–1967)

Among the texts by Ernesto "Che" Guevara, Argentine revolutionary, this article refers mainly to those that illustrate his sexual politics and the homosexual panic, namely, *Pasajes de la guerra revolucionaria* (*Passages on the Revolutionary War*, 1969), *La guerra de guerrillas* (*Guerrilla Warfare*, 1960), and *Diario en Bolivia* (*Bolivian Diary*, 1968). These texts, as many others, give us the base to explore how Guevara tries and fails to promote a new subject (the New Man), and has to deal with a long Christian and Western tradition that has designed a specific sexual politics by means of assembling a perverse structure.

Since Guevara's revolutionary idea is established, first, on the prominent figure of Ignacio de Loyola and the formation of the Compañía de Jesús as a model for the *guerrillero* and the *revolucionario*, and, second, on the homoerotic colonial and later national paradigm of *gaucho malo* (rebellious Argentinean cowboy) and the "*cimarrón*" (resistant black slave), it is possible to explore from these sources how the notion of revolution he had in mind was based on the unstable relation between "the *pre*scription of the most intimate male bonding and the *pro*scription of homosexuality" (Sedgwick).

To achieve their goals, Ignatius and Che will execute the same sort of exclusion of children, women, and old people. Their "militia Christi" require young, good-looking, healthy, and vigorous male soldiers, very well trained in observing a blind obedience to the Chief/Master/Commander and able to confront the social corruption of the world. Once they are selected (they are chosen by Christ or the Commandant), once they have given up their families and abdicate their rights to deal with their properties, once they are trained to be the endless reproduction of the same, they operate, via the imitation of the Master, as a perfect institutional mechanism. For achieving their goals, they have to encourage obedience, poverty, and chastity as the columns of the whole edifice of soldiers/robots working at the service of the Father. Soldiers have to give up individualism and promote their subjectivity as an isolated subject (subject to the Master), as a portable unity working mechanically in a legal and emotional uprooting.

While Che is attentive to the young male peasants and always observes their bodies and beauty, especially their youth, single state, and physical virtues, he categorizes women as "*enanas, viejas, cotudas, madres feroces, delatores*" (dwarves, old, goitered, ferocious mothers, betrayers) and so forth. At stake in such formulations are the "male fantasies" of fatherhood, the consideration of the other as a bestial, ignorant, and stupid enemy, the fear of women, the community of males tied by homoerotic feelings, and the rejection of the sensual pleasures, the fascination with the statuary of the male body, the consecration of obedience as a fatal machine inside the subject, or rather as a subject itself.

In his own fashion, Che Guevara tries to destroy capitalism while using the same ideological devices that capitalism promotes in its purest and religious form: fascism. His journey against the sins of capitalism enforces the sacrifice of the body, the renunciation of pleasures, and the promotion of Death, and all these fantasies finally work to recompense heroism, glory, and fame.   *Gustavo Geirola*

Bibliography

Anderson, Jon Lee. *Che Guevara: A Revolutionary Life*. New York; Grove Press, 1997.

Barradas, Efrain. "El Che, narrador: Apuntes para un estudio de Pasajes de la guerra revolucionaria." In *Literatures in Transition: The Many Voices of the Caribbean Area: A Symposium*. Upper Montclair, N.J.: Montclair State College, 1982, 137–45.

See also Catholicism; Gay Left; Inquisition

Guibert, Hervé (1955–1991)

One of the most important French novelists of the 1980s, Hervé Guibert was catapulted to celebrity shortly after the publication of his 1990 novel *À l'Ami qui ne m'a pas sauvé la vie* (To the Friend Who Did Not Save My Life). In the early pages of this novel about a narrator named Hervé who is struggling to cope with the early stages of HIV disease, the narrator recounts the death from AIDS-related causes of a friend named Muzil. This friend was easily recognized by many as a thinly disguised portrait of the philosopher Michel Foucault, with whom Guibert had been close friends. It had never been publicly acknowledged that Foucault had died from AIDS-related disease, and certain people found Guibert's "betrayal" of this "secret" to be scandalous. The scandal was aired on French television when Guibert, himself notably ill, appeared on the popular cultural program *Apostrophes* on March 16, 1990. His appearance on that program won him great popularity and many new readers, who wrote to encourage him not to give up writing, as he had suggested he might. His subsequent AIDS novel, *Le protocole compassionnel* (The Compassion Protocol, 1991) enjoyed great success. He died on December 27, 1991, weakened by HIV-related conditions and having attempted to commit suicide a few days earlier. Before his death, he completed several more books: *Mon valet et moi* (My Valet and Me, 1991), *L'Homme au chapeau rouge* (The Man in the Red Hat, 1992), *Cytomégalovirus: Journal d'hospitalisation* (Cytomegalovirus: A Hospital Diary, 1992), and *Le Paradis* (Paradise, 1992). He also completed a video for French television, *La pudeur ou l'impudeur* (Modesty or Immodesty), which became the subject of further controversy. It showed in great detail a body (Guibert's) ravaged by HIV disease; it showed a suicide attempt as well, making some reluctant to allow it to be screened. In the end it was shown on late-night French television on January 30, 1992.

Earlier works in Guibert's career include a short S/M narrative entitled *Les Chiens* (The Dogs, 1982). He collaborated on the screenplay for Patrice Chéreau's film *L'Homme blessé* (The Wounded Man). Guibert was also a photographer and photography critic, writing regularly for the French newspaper *Le Monde* from 1977 to 1985.

Much of the material for Guibert's fiction writing was drawn from his own life. Friends and relatives became characters and reappeared from book to book. The precise relation between fictional retelling and autobiography remains open to question throughout Guibert's career. He kept an extensive journal—as yet unpublished—and said that his novels often grew out of his writing in that journal. He wrote about the family origins of sexuality and his discomfort with kinship ties in a book called *Mes Parents* (My Parents, 1986), and about obsessive relations to love objects in *Fou de Vincent* (Crazy about Vincent, 1989). *À l'Ami qui ne m'a pas sauvé la vie* and *Le Protocole compassionnel* are remarkable portraits of someone living with AIDS just as AZT and ddI are beginning to be used as treatments. More than that, these novels—and Guibert's writing more generally—investigate the kinds of relations (friendship, networks of acquaintances, desire, love) that structure and support the lives of gay men of his time and place, even as those relations are often granted no recognition by larger social institutions.   *Michael Lucey*

Portrait of Thom Gunn (1998). Photo by Marc Geller.

Bibliography

"Hervé Guibert." Jean-Pierre Boulé, ed. *Nottingham French Studies* 34, no. 1 (1995).

See also AIDS Literature; AIDS Writing in France; Foucault, Michel; France; French Literature

Gunn, Thom (1929–)

Although Thom Gunn was born in Gravesend, England, and educated at Cambridge University, he has been associated with the United States and in particular with the Berkeley poetry scene for so long that he has become in fact an American poet. He arrived in 1954 to pursue graduate study at Stanford, where Yvor Winters was his primary teacher. Thereafter he took a teaching position in San Antonio for one year, at the end of which he returned to the West Coast, where he has remained, teaching at the University of California, Berkeley. In his early books, Gunn established himself as an accomplished versifier, using traditional meters and rhymes, in poems characterized by motorcycles, sex, and leather. His early poems carry a subtle homoeroticism, and mainstream readers thrilled to young bikers with or without knowing that Gunn is gay. In some of the early poems he seems to tease the reader with his ambiguous sexuality, e.g., the refrain line "I know you know I know you know I know" in "Carnal Knowledge." *Fighting Terms,* his first book of poems, appeared in 1954 and *The Sense of Movement* in 1956, both evoking the good life of carefree abandon that both straight and gay readers enjoyed as a prelude to the social experiments of the 1960s.

The necessity to hide behind dense metaphor for his personal sexuality began to erode after Gunn's drug poems in the early 1970s. *Moly* (1971) uses as its title a word Gunn culled from Homer's drug-of-choice for Ulysses' men. Along with the drug highs, his poetry reflects also the lows, especially in the collection *Jack Straw's Castle* (1976). Poems like "Fever" and "The Geysers" weave in and out of consciousness. In mid-career Gunn began to loosen up in metrics, and some of the pieces that emerge in his later career are gently untethered, e.g., "Smoking Pot on the Bus" and "At the Barriers," the latter written in memory of fellow San Francisco poet Robert Duncan. He continues, however, to publish in both metered and free verse.

Gunn responded in the 1980s with occasional pieces on the AIDS crisis, but it was not until 1992 that he published an entire book devoted to the disease, *The Man With Night Sweats.* His emphasis in this collection is on the suffering self, but he does include remarkable poems in which an individual

G finds solace within a community, e.g., "Courtesies of the Interregnum" and "Death's Door."

In addition to his eleven volumes of verse, Gunn has published a collection of literary essays, *The Occasions of Poetry*. He has been awarded numerous prizes over the years including the MacArthur Prize, a Guggenheim Fellowship, and the Lenore Marshall/Nation Poetry Prize. His *Collected Poems* appeared in 1994.

George Klawitter

Bibliography

Gunn, Thom. "My Life up to Now." *Thom Gunn: A Bibliography*. Compiled by Jack Hagestrom and George Bixby. London: Bertram Rota, 1979, 11–26.

Parini, Jay. "Rule and Energy: The Poetry of Thom Gunn." *The Massachusetts Review* 13 (1982): 134–51.

Woods, Gregory. *Articulate Flesh: Male Homo-Eroticism in Modern Poetry*. New Haven: Yale University Press, 1987.

See also AIDS Literature; Elegaic Poetry; English Literature; Love Poetry, The Petrarchan Tradition

H

Haan, Jacob Israël de (1881–1924)

Author of the first modern Dutch gay novel, *Pijpelijntjes* (Scenes from Ade Pijp, an Amsterdam working-class district [1904]). Although De Haan was familiar with the concept of the third sex as described by Magnus Hirschfeld and De Haan's friend, writer and physician Arnold Aletrino, he presents a homosexual relation as something that needs no explanation. The publication of *Pijpelijntjes* aroused a scandal, and De Haan lost his job as an editor and later also his teaching job. In his second novel, *Pathologieën de ondergangen van Johan van Vere de With* (Pathologies: The Destructions of Johan van Vere de With [1908]), the protagonist comes to accept his feelings by reading unspecified scientific studies of homosexuality. In many respects, *Pathologieën* has the characteristics of a "coming-out" story, culminating in the development of a modern homosexual identity. Both novels depict explicitly homosexual scenes and, in the case of *Pathologieën,* some heavy sadomasochism.

De Haan, who also wrote short stories, critical reviews, judicial studies, and journalism, achieved greatest fame as a "Jewish" poet, although the homosexual content of his poems now seems to be as important as the Jewish. His prose was forgotten until the mid-1970s, when new editions became available.

De Haan's life is almost as remarkable as his work. The son of a rabbi, he first became a socialist and later an orthodox Jew. Just before World War I he left Holland for Palestine, where he joined the Zionist movement. When he later dissociated himself from its political goals, he was murdered by extreme Zionists who spread the rumor that the murder was a homosexual killing perpetrated by Arabs.   *Maurice van Lieshout*

Bibliography

Bittremieux, C. "Bijeen biografie van J.I. de Haan." *Tirade* 12 (1968): 137–147.

Delvigne, Rob Ross, Leo. "Mythologieen rondom Jacob Israel de Haan." *Revisor* 4.2 (1977): 68–70.

Haan, Jacob Israël de. *Pathologieën*. 1908. Den Haag, Kruseman, 1975.

———. *Pijpelijntjes*. 1904. Amsterdam: Nijgh & Van Ditmar, 1991.

———. *Verzamelde Gedichten* (*Collected Poems*). 2 vols. Amsterdam: Van Oorschot, 1952.

Lieshout, Maurice van. "De 'ondergangen' van 'een zuiver homosexueelen jongen.'" In *Deugdelijk Vermaak*. Eweg, E., ed. Amsterdam: Huis aan de Drie Grachten, 1987, 136–50.

See also Amsterdam; Hirschfeld, Magnus; Netherlands

Hadrian (76–138 C.E.)

Hadrian was a Roman emperor of Spanish provincial background. Apart from his military achievements and fair treatment of the provinces that resulted in a more stable empire, with the notable exception of Judaea, Hadrian was something of a Renaissance man, interested in law, finance, art, literature, music, mathematics, and religion. An indefatigable traveler, he incorporated in his villa near Rome many architectural memories of his travels.

Although married to Sabina, Hadrian fell passionately in love with a young Bithynian named Antinous. On a journey to Egypt in 130 C.E., Antinous drowned under mysterious circumstances in the Nile. Inconsolable, Hadrian deified him in numerous guises, founded an Egyptian city in his honor (Antinopolis), and immortalized his sensual beauty in many statues scattered throughout the Roman Empire; for example, a colossal statue in the Sala Rotonda of the Vatican depicts Antinous as the god Dionysus.

In an age when the concept of mutual love within a heterosexual marriage was growing in importance and male same-sex relationships seemed to be confined to sexual passions for slave boys, Hadrian's relationship with Antinous reflects something of the world of classical Athens and of Alexander the Great's obsession with Hephaestion. One of the features of Hadrian's villa at Tibur is a circular island surrounded by a moat on which a beautiful, miniature villa was built; here Hadrian probably retired to seek solace and perhaps to write the poem on the soul that Marguerite Yourcenar used to introduce her evocative *Memoirs of Hadrian*.   Michael Lambert

Bibliography

Lambert, R. *Beloved and God*. New York: Viking, 1984.

See also Alexander the Great; Rome, Ancient; Yourcenar, Marguerite

Handel, George Frideric (1685–1759)

Though a native German, Handel lived most of his life in and around London, with important excursions to Italy during his formative years. He early attained the status of English cultural icon and darling of the Christian choral establishment, with a cult following (the Handelians) and eventually brisk commercial appeal. Discourses constructing the familiar myth of "Handel" in music history, biography, and criticism circulated even before his death and have since worked to mystify the material realities of his life and to naturalize a nonsexually "pure" or unambiguously heterosexual image. However, in the absence of even a scrap of reliable evidence indicative of a heterosexual Handel (a man of "normal masculine constitution," in the words of Paul Henry Lang's attempted reification), this has proved a Sisyphean and in the end fruitless task. Underpinned by a combination of scholarly cowardice and homosexual panic, and with the reputation of this ubiquitously adored composer hanging in the balance (not to mention the profitable industry grown up around him), the discourse framing Handel's sex-

George Frideric Handel at the clavier. Portrait by Sir J. Thornhill. Corbis-Bettman.

uality, on those few occasions when speech has displaced silence, amounts to a tissue of prevarication, distortion, and omission, including statements by early biographers that may be read as evidence. Thus around Handel has been constructed the first biographical closet (of many to come) for a major composer in the West. Owing to the vicissitudes of the closet, Handel's as well as those of his commentators, precise knowledge concerning the composer's sex life may never be available. What can be known and studied are the discursive and ideological effects of the struggle, continuing to the present day, to maintain this great figure in a state of disembodied transcendence.

When examined without prejudice, the record of the composer's lived experience reveals ample evidence of a homoerotically inclined man. Handel lived virtually his entire life in the company of demonstrably homosexual men, in precisely those subcultural venues most closely associated with them. Of particular interest in this regard are his various stays with Gian Gastone in Florence, Cardinal Ottoboni in Rome (cf. Arcangelo Corelli and Agostino Steffani), with Lord Burlington and his boyfriend William ("Kentino") Kent at Chiswick House outside London, and his contacts within the theater and opera milieu of London itself. Like the so-called real history of the librettist Pietro Metastasio that Joseph Spence claims to have discovered in Italy, a candid sociosexual history of these venues and of Handel's involvement with them, as antidotes to a firmly entrenched mythology, remains to be written.

More than simply the discursive and material histories of a man, "Handel" is also the composer's entire corpus of artistic work, including the political economy of its production, reception, and (ongoing) circulation. Handel's operas, oratorios, and other texts constitute a rich field of social discourse, a theater of human power and desire virtually every aspect of which intersects with a homosexual problematic: from the composer's mere association with music (an "effeminizing" pursuit, equated by many in Handel's time with sodomy itself), to the highly politicized controversies surrounding his turn from "Italian" opera to "English" oratorio. Like the struggles over the representation of Handel's life, those surrounding the production and reception of his work actively participate in the defining ideological contests—involving the politics and erotics of manhood, nation, and patriarchy—of the Enlightenment and the modern West. *Gary C. Thomas*

Bibliography

Brett, Philip. "Musicality, Essentialism, and the Closet." In *Queering the Pitch: The New Gay and Lesbian Musicology*. Philip Brett, Elizabeth Wood, and Gary C. Thomas, eds. London: Routledge, 1994, 9–26.

Burrows, Donald. *Handel*. New York: Schirmer Books, 1994.

Rousseau, G. S. "The Pursuit of Homosexuality: 'Utterly Confused Category' and/or Rich Repository?" In *'Tis Nature's Fault: Unauthorized Sexuality during the Enlightenment*. Robert Purks Maccubbin, ed. Cambridge: Cambridge University Press, 1985, 132–68.

Thomas, Gary C. " 'Was George Frideric Handel Gay?': On Closet Questions and Cultural Politics." In *Queering the Pitch: The New Gay and Lesbian Musicology*. Philip Brett, Elizabeth Wood, and Gary C. Thomas, eds. London: Routledge, 1994, 155–203.

See also England; Music and Musicians 1: Classical Music; Opera

Haring, Keith (1958–1990)

Keith Haring was born in Kutztown, Pennsylvania, on May 4, 1958. He began his formal art education in Pittsburgh, then moved to New York City in 1978 to study at the School of Visual Arts. Over the following decade, Haring developed one of the most universally recognized artistic styles of the late twentieth century. Eschewing academic traditions of perspective and modeling, he drew and painted with thick contours to create simplified, cartoonlike forms. Using this bold, graphic style, he introduced a unique lexicon of highly expressive images, in-

One of Keith Haring's more famous ACT UP posters (1989). Courtesy The Estate of Keith Haring.

cluding barking dogs, glowing babies, flying saucers, and dancing, gesticulating figures. Haring's inventive combination of the primitive and the futuristic was heavily influenced by both the graffiti art and downtown dance clubs of New York City, and seemed to illustrate the gritty vitality of the modern urban environment. He is credited with expanding the tradition of pop art by synthesizing fine art with urban street culture.

Accessibility and immediacy were always central to Haring's personal credo as an artist. He sought to reach a broad and popular audience by placing his high-impact graphic symbols in the public domain. Haring's subway drawings from the early 1980s represent his first significant achievement of this goal. Inspired by New York City's conspicuous graffiti, Haring drew chalk outlines on countless empty advertising billboards that lined the city's subway tunnels. Other simple public interventions exposed a vast, unsuspecting audience for his emerging style.

By the mid-1980s Haring's underground work had caught the attention of many art dealers and collectors. His art was promoted as a pop variation of the neoexpressionism movement, and his professional career accelerated rapidly. He exhibited in galleries and museums worldwide. Haring's growing success allowed him to work in the public arena on a far more ambitious scale than ever before. He accepted numerous international commissions to design outdoor sculpture and large-scale public murals, including painting a portion of the Berlin Wall in 1986. The democratic impulse that formed much of Haring's art also prompted the 1986 opening of his Pop Shop in New York City, which sold his designs in the form of small, collectible objects. As Haring himself stated of this enterprise, "I wanted it to be a place where not only collectors could come, but also kids from the Bronx" (Gruen 148).

The immense popular appeal of Haring's art also lent itself to the numerous social and political causes that the artist advocated throughout his career. Many of these efforts, like his antidrug *Crack Is Wack* mural of 1986, spoke to the social ills that plagued the urban communities from which his art originally derived. Haring learned he was HIV-positive in 1987. A great deal of his later work was fueled by this awareness and the mounting number of deaths exacted by the AIDS virus, particularly in New York City's artistic communities. Haring employed the instant legibility and expressive intensity of his signature style to help provoke public re-

sponse to the epidemic. His highly effective graphics were used by activist groups such as ACT UP. Haring died of AIDS-related complications on February 16, 1990; he was thirty-one years old.

Matthew Nichols

Bibliography

Gruen, John. *Keith Haring: The Authorized Biography*. London: Thames and Hudson, 1991.
Sussman, Elizabeth. *Keith Haring*. New York: Whitney Museum of American Art, 1997.

See also Activism, U.S.; AIDS; Art History

Harlem Renaissance

Although the dates for the Harlem Renaissance are contested, this first period of African American cultural modernity is generally considered to have taken place during the interwar years of 1919–1939, peaking just before the onset of the Depression in 1929. Whatever the exact dates that one might settle on, however, there is little doubt that few periods in African American history have been as dominated by the works and personalities of gay men, lesbians, and bisexuals.

As one component of the "great migration" of blacks from the South to urban areas in the North, it is not surprising that Harlem would become a mecca for gay men and lesbians, given the difficulty of finding affordable lodging for a family in the notoriously exploitative housing market of 1920s Harlem and the relative ease with which people unencumbered by familial obligations could migrate from the South. Among those Harlem Renaissance figures widely believed to have been gay, lesbian, or bisexual can be included Richmond Barthé, Gladys Bentley, Casca Bonds, Mae Cowdery, Countee Cullen, Augustus Dill, Angelina Weld Grimké, Alexander Gumby, Langston Hughes, Alain Locke, Claude McKay, Richard Bruce Nugent, Wallace Thurman, and Eric Walrond.

These figures revealed their homosexuality with varying degrees of openness, and the homosexual dynamics of their lives are becoming clearer only as archival work is being done on the letters and private journals that are in many cases only now becoming available for critical scrutiny. This recuperative work is being done often over the strenuous objections of family members and literary executors dedicated to maintaining the figure's sexual "respectability." The Langston Hughes estate's legal response to gay filmmaker Isaac Julien's "meditation," *Looking for Langston*, which prohibited the use of any of the poet's work in the film, is a particularly pertinent case in point. These repressive efforts are buttressed by the fact that, despite the often tortured efforts of some critics to drag seemingly innocuous and resolutely neutered poems and works of fiction out of the closet and into the uncozy confines of the queer canon, there are, not surprisingly, few texts from the period that represent same-sex attraction with any real explicitness.

One of the few Harlem Renaissance texts whose homoerotic dynamics are relatively transparent is Richard Bruce Nugent's short story "Smoke, Lilies, and Jade," which appeared in the short-lived journal *Fire!!* (1926), edited by Wallace Thurman. This impressionistic account of a youth's attraction for another youth called Beauty was included for the express purpose of shocking the black bourgeoisie, and nothing was more likely to achieve this purpose with Du Bois's "talented tenth" than a depiction, however stylized, of homosexual love. Nugent, in fact, would become the emblem for male homosexuality during the period with his thinly disguised portrait in Thurman's roman à clef, *Infants of the Spring* (1932), as Paul Arbian, a character whose transgressively camp lifestyle culminates in the suicide that would soon become standard in literary and cinematic representations of "queers."

Although explicit literary representations of same-sex desire were rare during this period, other places in popular culture were somewhat more accommodating. One of the few homosexually suspect entertainers to achieve public recognition in the years preceding the Harlem Renaissance was the "male impersonator" Florence Hines, a star of the minstrel stage about whom practically nothing is known. Because female performers were rare and, in fact, often banned from the rough-and-tumble world of the minstrel stage, her presence, even in drag, was noteworthy. Hines's performances marked the entry into the public sphere of the kind of ambiguously gendered black female figure later represented by such women as Gladys Bentley, the sexually parodic Josephine Baker, and the flagrantly transgendered poet and "person" about town Mae Cowdery, who would achieve real prominence during the Harlem Renaissance. As Bruce Kellner has reported of Bentley, "She dressed openly in tailor-made drag and made no secret of either her name or her homosexuality, even marrying her lover in a civil ceremony in Atlantic City" (Keller 31). Bent-

ley's performances as well as those of other cross-dressing performers, most notably a "male Gloria Swanson," made the Clam House, along with Edmond "Mule" Johnson's Edmond's Cellar, one of the most notable queer cabarets of the period. Equally well known were the "integrated transvestite costume balls" held at the Manhattan Casino (Rockland Palace) and the Savoy Ballroom.

If the heterosexuality of these women was merely called into question by their sartorial choices and social antics, the celebrated blues singers such as Ma Rainey, Bessie Smith, and Alberta Hunter who emerged during the twenties and thirties were, even in their own time, often known to be sexually attracted to and involved with other women. According to Bruce Kellner, "Bessie Smith once had to bail [Ma Rainey] out of jail in Chicago, following a particularly indecent drinking and stripping party with a group of young women" (Kellner 294). Perhaps because male homosexuality was subject to greater policing and social scrutiny, few homosexual or bisexual men of any real prominence exhibited their desires as openly as did these women. In fact, the sexually freewheeling nature of blues lyrics was one of the few places where homosexual desire could be forthrightly expressed in such songs as "B. D. Woman's Blues," "The Boy in the Boat," "Freakish Man Blues," "Prove It on Me Blues," "Sissy Man Blues," and "Two Old Maids in a Folding Bed."

Gay black novelist Steven Corbin's *No Easy Place to Be* (1989) offers an interesting and wide-ranging depiction of the "queer" dynamics of the period.   *Terry Rowden*

Bibliography

Corbin, Steven. *No Easy Place to Be*. New York: Simon and Schuster, 1989.

Kellner, Bruce, ed. *The Harlem Renaissance: A Historical Dictionary for the Era*. Westport, Conn.: Greenwood Press, 1984.

See also African American Gay Culture; Barthé, James Richmond; Cullen, Countee; Hughes, Langston; McKay, Claude; Rustin, Bayard; Thurman, Wallace; Transvestism

Harrison, Lou (1917–)

An American composer born in Portland, Oregon, Harrison lives in Aptos, California, with partner William Colvig, with whom he has collaborated in the construction of many musical instruments. Harrison studied briefly though significantly with Henry Cowell in San Francisco during the year 1934–1935, and then later with Arnold Schoenberg in Los Angeles, supporting himself by various means—some musical, some not—while pursuing composition. In 1943 he moved to New York and inaugurated an association with Virgil Thomson. During this period he wrote for several publications including the *New York Herald Tribune*. Closely following his 1951 move back to California, Harrison won several prestigious awards including two Guggenheim fellowships in 1952 and 1954 and a Fromm Foundation Award in 1955. He has taught extensively, notably at Mills College between 1937 and 1940, and since 1968 at San Jose State University.

Many factors distinguish Harrison as a composer—his interest in the Esperanto language, his delight in the building of musical instruments, and his explicit and passionate concern with peace and pacifism. His oeuvre is extraordinary in its breadth of idioms, ranging from pantonality, diatonicism, and non-Western modality to Ivesian bricolage. In terms of composition, identity, and nationalism, Harrison is distinguished by his awareness of the Pacific, as well as the Atlantic, Rim, an awareness that perhaps has participated in creating an out-of-the-mainstream image for himself. In 1961, Harrison received a Rockefeller fellowship for the study of Asian music, a grant that enabled him to travel to Korea, where he worked with Lee Hye-Ku and Liang Tsai-Ping.

While not utterly within the Europe-centered mainstream of American composition, a movement characterized by such figures as Elliott Carter, Milton Babbitt, Roger Sessions, and Walter Piston, he is very much cast in an American mold exemplified by Charles Ives and, of course, Harrison's own teacher, Henry Cowell, both of whose innovative and inventive approaches to composition can be viewed as precursors—directly and indirectly—to the work of Harrison. Cowell and Ives are certainly inspirations for Harrison, as is the work of visionary composer Harry Partch. Partch's treatise, *Genesis of a Music*, written in 1949, was an important text for Harrison.

Harrison has long been fascinated with the Javanese ensemble, largely comprised of bronze idiophones known as gamelan. In Harrison's works involving Javanese gamelan, one not infrequently encounters notions of cultural hybridity reified musically. In his *Main Bersama-Sama* (1978), for gamelan and French horn, there is from the outset a joining of European-American and Javanese elements clearly seen in the instrumentation. To match the tuning of the gamelan, the horn's valves are placed in a particular position. But the evidence of hybridity goes further insofar as the cyclical form of the work approximates Javanese notions of time and musical structure. Other works that evidence this brand of hybrid thinking are the *Concerto in Slendro*, which approximates a Javanese tuning system but does not incorporate a gamelan, and the memorable Double Concerto for Violion and Cello with Javanese Gamelan (1981–1982).

Ethan Nasreddin-Longo

Bibliography

Miller, Leta E., and Fredric Lieberman. *Lou Harrison: Composing a World*. New York: Oxford University Press, 1998.

See also Cowell, Henry (Dixon); Music and Musicians I: Classical Music; Gay American Composers Project; Partch, Harry; Thomson, Virgil

Hart, Lorenz (1895–1943)

In the spring of 1919, when composer Richard Rodgers was introduced to lyricist Lorenz Hart, a partnership began that would ultimately revolutionize the American musical stage. Together, Rodgers and Hart wrote twenty-seven musicals for the New York theater, including *A Connecticut Yankee* (1927), *On Your Toes* (1936), *Babes in Arms* (1936), *I'd Rather Be Right* (1937), *The Boys from Syracuse* (1938), *Too Many Girls* (1939), *Pal Joey* (1940), and *By Jupiter* (1942), as well as eight scores for Hollywood musicals and songs interpolated in other Broadway shows. Their best-known songs—"Manhattan," "My Heart Stood Still," "Ten Cents a Dance," "Where or When," "My Funny Valentine," "The Lady Is a Tramp," "I Could Write a Book," "Bewitched, Bothered and Bewildered"—became the standard by which their successors would be measured. Hart's witty, intricately rhymed, topical lyrics crystallized an upheaval in the conventions of songwriting for the musical theater; his work spurred the transition from revue-style theatrical music, typified by vaudeville and the Ziegfeld Follies, to the modern, "integrated" book musical, realized in *Oklahoma!* (Rodgers/Hammerstein, 1943).

Hart's habits were as unconventional as his lyrics, and he became both notable and notorious for several of them: cigar smoking, drinking, and cultivating friendships with pimps and gay men. His sexual identity remains somewhat indeterminate, obscured by his own secrecy, by his public proclamations of love for certain women, and by his biographers (Nolan calls Hart sexually "ambivalent"); nonetheless, the biographical material and individual accounts suggest that he was more or less homosexual. His increasing unreliability and drinking in the late 1930s and early 1940s led Rodgers to pursue a working relationship with Oscar Hammerstein. Hart died of pneumonia during a wartime blackout on November 17, 1943.   *Matthew Bell*

Bibliography

Marx, Samuel, and Jan Clayton. *Rodgers & Hart: Bewitched, Bothered, and Bedeviled.* New York: Putnam, 1976.

Nolan, Frederick. *Lorenz Hart: A Poet on Broadway.* New York: Oxford University Press, 1994.

See also Musical Theater

Hartley, Marsden (1877–1943)

American painter, critic, and poet, born Edmund Hartley in Lewiston, Maine, on January 4, 1877. After his mother died in 1885, he was shuttled between his father and his older sister. Hartley felt that his mother's death left him "alone on the doorstep of the world." Yet he later felt sufficiently part of his father's new family to exchange "Edmund" for "Marsden," his stepmother's maiden name. He studied at the Cleveland School of Art and the National Academy of Design in New York City. As a young man he was part of a circle of followers of Walt Whitman that included Whitman's biographer, Horace Traubel. His earliest extant painting is of Whitman's house in Camden (1905). His poetry, which was published in *The Dial* and *Poetry*, was heavily influenced by Whitman. In 1909 he met Alfred Stieglitz, who became his dealer for most of his professional career.

Hartley's displaced childhood established a pattern for the remainder of his life. As an adult, he never stayed in one location for more than a year, participating in the American expatriate life of Paris, Berlin, and Mexico. He alluded both to his wandering and to his homosexuality in a letter to Mabel Dodge Luhan: "I belong to a less specialized species, to commoner elements. I must never do more, at most than walk in as graciously as possible, sit a little, and pass out again for there is always the quality of wonder in being really not quite anywhere at all times."

To the degree that Hartley expressed his homosexuality, it was almost always in the context of death. His synthetic cubist *Portrait of a German Officer* (1914), in which military regalia are loosely assembled to suggest a body, was one in a series of memorials to Karl von Freyburg, a German soldier whom Hartley loved. The painting's personal significance does not so much erase its militarism as focus forbidden desire on the man in uniform as potential enemy and ultimate other.

With the U.S. entry into World War I, Hartley abandoned the pro-German style of the War Motif Series. From 1916 to 1930, his career went through a long period of uncertainty during which he mostly concentrated on landscapes. A turning point was another memorial, *Eight Bells Folly* (1933), dedicated to his friend, the gay poet Hart Crane. Death also haunts Hartley's *Archaic Portraits* (1940–1941), a response to the fatal sea accident of Alty Mason, with whom Hartley became enamored in Nova Scotia. Alty's father, mother, brother, and sister became, in *Fisherman's Last Supper* (1940–1941), an ideal of Christian love. That love merges with homosexual desire in Hartley's *Christ Held by Half-Naked Men* (1940–1941). Hartley fantasized in the Mason family the possibility of ideal home, parents, and lover. He wrote that Alty had pledged "to build a house and live in it with him, as he was such a dear even though he had spells of drinking hard, but even then he was more delightful." Hartley died in Ellsworth, Maine, on September 2, 1943.

Jonathan Weinberg

Bibliography

Ludington, Townsend. *Marsden Hartley: The Biography of an American Artist.* Boston: Little, Brown, 1992.

Weinberg, Jonathan. *Speaking for Vice: Homosexuality in the Art of Charles Demuth, Marsden Hartley and the First American Avant Garde.* New Haven: Yale University Press, 1993.

See also Art History; Crane, Hart; Whitman, Walt

Hate Crimes

Violence against homosexuals and people presumed to be homosexual has been documented for as long as the lives of gay men and lesbians have been documented. For example, John Boswell documented violence against gay men and lesbians in western Europe from the beginning of the Christian era to

H the fourteenth century. In *Gay American History*, which covers a period of more than four hundred years, Jonathan Ned Katz documented a history of violence directed at individuals because of their sexual orientation, identity, or same-sex behavior. Historically, such violence has often represented state policies and has been perpetrated by representatives of the state as well as private citizens. More recently, the National Gay and Lesbian Task Force (1991) documented literally thousands of incidents of violence against gay men and lesbians in the United States throughout the latter part of the twentieth century. These data led the Reagan administration's Justice Department to commission a report on bias violence in 1987, which concluded that "the most frequent victims of hate violence today are blacks, Hispanics, Southeast Asians, Jews, and gays and lesbians. Homosexuals are probably the most frequent victims" (cited in Vaid 11). As Virginia Apuzzo, former executive director of the National Gay and Lesbian Task Force, proclaimed, "To be gay or lesbian in America is to live in the shadow of violence" (cited in Comstock 1991:54).

Reports such as these reveal that violence against gays and lesbians continues to take a variety of forms, from symbolic to fatal assaults; and they implicate a range of perpetrators, from intimates to strangers to institutions such as the state, religion, and medicine. Moreover, documented cases of antigay and lesbian violence throughout history and across societies illustrate that physical, psychological, and symbolic violence against gays and lesbians crosses racial, ethnic, religious, nationality, and age boundaries. Despite an undeniable history of violence against gays and lesbians, however, systematic and reliable information on the causes, manifestations, and consequences of antigay and lesbian violence is scant. Only since the late 1980s has empirical work on the epidemiology of violence against gays and lesbians accumulated. These studies reveal that the majority of gay men and lesbians report that they have experienced actual violence or the threat of it because of their sexual orientation (i.e., having objects thrown at them and being chased, punched, hit, kicked, and/or beaten); gays and lesbians of color are at an increased risk for violent attack because of their sexual orientation and their race/ ethnicity; and most antigay and lesbian violence goes unreported because of fear of abuse by police, fear of public disclosure, and the perception that law enforcement officials are homophobic. Compared with gay men, lesbians report higher rates of verbal harassment by family members and a greater fear of "antigay" violence, as well as a higher rate of victimization in nongay-identified public settings and in their homes and a lower rate of victimization in school and public gay-identified areas. Finally, studies suggest that the typical perpetrator of antigay and lesbian violence is young, white, and male.

Defined by sexism, heterosexism, and at times racism, classism, anti-Semitism, and ageism, antigay and lesbian violence has been greeted with an array of legal and extralegal responses designed to bring attention to and curb violence directed at gays and lesbians. At the federal level, the Hate Crimes Statistics Act of 1990 recognized "crimes that manifest evidence of prejudice based on race, religion, *sexual orientation*, or ethnicity" as a new category of criminal behavior: hate crime. At the state level, by 1995 thirteen states had adopted hate crime legislation that includes provisions for "sexual orientation" as a protected status. These laws have in effect created a new category of criminal conduct: antigay and lesbian violence.

Just as recent legal reform has defined violence against gays and lesbians as criminal, a plethora of community-based activism has defined antigay and lesbian violence as a social problem in need of remedy. Most notably, throughout the 1980s and the 1990s gay- and lesbian-sponsored antiviolence projects emerged and proliferated in the United States and abroad. As extensions of the gay and lesbian movement in the United States and abroad, these organizations documented and publicized the incidence and prevalence of antigay and lesbian violence, established crisis intervention and victim assistance programs, sponsored public education campaigns, and undertook surveillance efforts in the form of street patrols. Combined, these activities comprised an "unprecedented level of organizing against violence" (National Gay and Lesbian Task Force 22) that has ensured that antigay and lesbian violence has "finally taken its place among such societal concerns as violence against women, children and ethnic and racial groups" (Comstock 1). As Urvashi Vaid, former director of the National Gay and Lesbian Task Force, noted in her book on the gay and lesbian movement:

> From 1982 to today, the movement has won near-universal condemnation of gay bashing from governmental, religious, and civil bodies. We got gay-bashing classified as a crime motivated by prejudice and hate, secured the pas-

sage of bias-penalty bills, produced studies into the causes and solutions to homophobic violence, and secured funding for a range of service programs.

This is evident in a 1988 case involving the beating death of an Asian American gay man. A Broward County, Florida, circuit judge jokingly asked the prosecuting attorney, "That's a crime now, to beat up a homosexual?" The prosecutor answered, "Yes sir. And it's also a crime to kill them." The judge replied, "Times have really changed" (Hentoff).

Valerie Jenness

Bibliography

Boswell, John. *Christianity, Social Tolerance, and Homosexuality*. Chicago: University of Chicago Press, 1980.

Comstock, Gary. *Violence Against Lesbians and Gay Men*. New York: Columbia University Press, 1991.

Fout, John C. *Forbidden History: The State, Society, and the Regulation of Sexuality in Modern Europe*. Chicago: University of Chicago Press, 1992.

Hentoff, Nat. "The violently attacked community in America." *Weekly Newspaper of New York*, September 25, 1990.

Herek, Greogry, and Kevin Berrill T. *Hate Crimes: Confronting Violence Against Gay Lesbian and Gay Men*. Newbury Park, Calif.: Sage Publications, 1992.

Island, David, and Patrick Letellier. *Men Who Beat the Men Who Love Them: Battered Gay Men and Domestic Violence*. New York: Hawthorne Press, 1991.

Jenness, Valerie, and Kendal Broad. *Hate Crimes: New Social Movements and the Politics of Violence*. Hawthorne, N.Y.: Aldine de Gruyter, 1997.

Jenness, Valerie, and Ryken Grattet. "The Criminalization of Hate: A Comparison of Structural and Polity Influences on the Passage of 'Bias-Crime' Legislation in the United States." *Sociological Perspectives* 39 (1996): 129–54.

Katz, Jonathan Ned. *Gay American History: Lesbians and Gay Men in the U.S.A.* New York: Crowell, 1976.

National Gay and Lesbian Task Force. *Anti-Gay and Lesbian Violence, Victimization, and Defamation in 1990*. Washington, D.C.: National Gay and Lesbian Task Force Policy Institute, 1991.

Renzetti, Claire. *Violent Betrayal: Partner Abuse in Lesbian Relationships*. Newbury Park, Calif.: Sage Publications, 1992.

Vaid, Urvashi. *Virtual Equality: The Mainstreaming of Gay & Lesbian Liberation*. New York: Anchor Books, 1995.

See also Activism, U.S.; Civil Rights (U.S. Law); Gay Bashing; Homophobia; National Gay and Lesbian Task Force; Oppression; U.S. Law: Equal Protection

Hawks, Howard (1896–1977)

While from all accounts, Howard Hawks was neither homosexual nor bisexual, his oeuvre contains some of the most entertaining queer films ever made. It has become a critical commonplace to split the films Hawks directed into two categories: adventure and comedy. But there is queerness on both sides of the great divide. The adventure films are largely hymns to the primacy of male bonding, with the occasional deep-voiced straight woman (Ann Dvorak, Frances Farmer, Lauren Bacall, Angie Dickinson) competing for attention by acting like one of the boys. The sexual dynamics set up in films like *A Girl in Every Port* (1928), *Scarface* (1932), *The Road to Glory* (1936), *Only Angels Have Wings* (1938), *Red River* (1948), *The Big Sky* (1952), and *Rio Bravo* (1959) move between the homoerotic and the bisexual, with a little masculinization of the lead women characters tossed in sometimes.

The two most audacious films of the adventure lot are *Red River* and *The Big Sky*. Among other things, both films homosexualize Oedipus, by having their "father and son" narrative tensions erupt not over rivalry for a woman or over gaining phallic mastery but over the men's repressed affection for each other. At one point toward the end of *Red River*, the straight woman has had enough. Shooting at Tom Dunson (John Wayne) and Matthew Garth (Montgomery Clift) to stop them fighting, Tess Millay (Joanne Dru) yells, "Anyone with half a mind would know you two love each other!" The relationship between Jim Deakins (Kirk Douglas) and Boone (Dewey Martin) in *The Big Sky* is also described at one point by using the term "love"—and lest you mistake the form of that love, at least on the part of Boone, all you need to do is observe the adoring way Boone looks at Deakins during the course of the film. But then, "Papa" Hawks's camera came to look adoringly at the "sons" in his later films: Dewey Martin (*The Big Sky* and *Land of the*

H *Pharaohs*, 1955), Ricky Nelson (*Rio Bravo*), James Caan (*Red Line 7000*, 1965, and *El Dorado*, 1967), and Jorge Rivero (*Rio Lobo*, 1970).

Hawks's comedies offer queerness that is most often based on so-called gender reversals: men acting feminine or effeminate and women acting masculine or butch. To some degree, *Bringing Up Baby* (1938), *His Girl Friday* (1940), *Ball of Fire* (1941), *A Song Is Born* (1948), *I Was a Male War Bride* (1949), *Gentlemen Prefer Blondes* (1953), and *Man's Favorite Sport* (1964) can be understood as gender-reversal comedies. With the exceptions of *Ball of Fire* and its remake, *A Song Is Born*, the gender play in these films isn't fully recontained by the final fadeout. Adding to the queerness for viewers "in the know" is the knowledge that most of these films star gay, lesbian, or bisexual (or rumored-to-be-so) performers: Cary Grant, Barbara Stanwyck, Danny Kaye, Rock Hudson. Grant's character in *Bringing Up Baby* actually leaps in the air at one point, clad in a woman's fluffy dressing gown, shouting, "Because I just went gay all of a sudden!" while his character in *I Was a Male War Bride* spends much of the film in drag trying to pass for the French equivalent of a WAC. But in many ways, *Gentlemen Prefer Blondes* is Hawks's most queer-friendly work, with feminized male leads, a butch-femme pair of female leads (Jane Russell and Marilyn Monroe), the swimsuit-clad American Olympics team served up as a beefcake chorus line (in the "Is There Anyone Here for Love?" number), and a general air of bisexual joie de vivre (the Russell and Monroe characters marry the male leads yet also renew their vows to each other by exchanging a tender look in the last shot of the film). Classical Hollywood cinema doesn't get much better than this.

Alexander Doty

Bibliography

Mast, Gerald. *Howard Hawks, Storyteller*. New York: Oxford University Press, 1982.

Wood, Robin. *Howard Hawks*. Revised. London: BFI, 1983.

See also Film; Film Stars

Hay, Harry (1912–)

Radical activist and theoretician Henry "Harry" Hay is most commonly known as the father of gay liberation for founding the Mattachine Society in 1950. But beyond political rights, Hay has agitated for awareness of the social purpose of homosexuals as their best political strategy. Gays are distinguished as much by their consciousness as by their sexuality, he argues, and this different outlook constitutes their social value.

He was born in Worthing, England, on April 7, 1912, of American parents. Rebellion against his upper-crust background—Hay's father developed South African gold mines for Cecil Rhodes—stimulated Hay's populist identity. At age eleven, in a Los Angeles school library, he discovered the writings of Edward Carpenter, which strongly informed his lifelong obsession with homosexuality as an "intermediate type" with a social purpose. Hay's Stanford University education was curtailed after a year by ill health. Working in Hollywood allowed for affairs with many actors, but his liaison with Will Geer pushed him toward membership in the American Communist Party and, ultimately, marriage to Anita Platky from 1938 to 1951.

During the 1948 presidential campaign of Henry Wallace, Hay drafted a prospectus designating homosexuals as a cultural minority and calling for their mobilization. In 1950 fashion designer Rudi Gernreich became Hay's first recruit; while teaching a Marxist class, he met Chuck Rowland and Mattachine's other founders. The society, which Hay named after a medieval troupe of male dancers, held underground discussion groups in a cell structure modeled on the Masons. The steady growth of Mattachine and Hay's public gay identification soon led to his divorce.

Previous gay organizations worked in isolation and with little result. Mattachine's success included instigating ONE Institute, which in turn produced *ONE* magazine, the forebear to the American gay press. After successfully fighting a sexual entrapment charge, Mattachine's legend exploded and a nationwide network developed. In an internal witch-hunt, McCarthyist elements forced Mattachine's Red founders to resign in 1953.

Later, Hay turned his eye to anthropological studies of gay roles. In 1963 he published in *ONE Quarterly* a lost 1883 report by a U.S. surgeon general describing homosexual behavior among Plains Indians. Hay's article became one of the earliest berdache citations, and he inspired many contemporary gay anthropologists. That same year, Hay met optical engineer John Burnside, who became his life partner. The couple boostered campaigns from the Council on Religion and the Homophile to the Gay Liberation Front, of which Hay served as the first L.A. chapter president.

In 1979 Hay helped convene the first Radical Faerie conference. Manifestations of this neopagan movement had been evident previously, but Hay's efforts secured the Faeries in the forefront of the gay men's spirituality movement.

Their vow of anonymity obscured Hay and his Mattachine confreres to historians. Jonathan Ned Katz broke the silence in 1975 by profiling Hay's story in *Gay American History*, and others followed. In 1990, Hays became the subject of a full-length biography, and six years later his writings were anthologized. Hay's charismatic presence and fiercely original ideas continue to be sought by new gay generations.   *Stuart Timmons*

Bibliography

Hay, Harry, and Will Roscoe. *Radically Gay: Gay Liberation in the Words of Its Founder*. Boston: Beacon, 1996.

Timmons, Stuart. *The Trouble With Harry Hay: Founder of the Modern Gay Movement*. Boston: Alyson, 1990.

See also Carpenter, Edward; Gay Liberation; Gernreich, Rudi; Mattachine Society; McCarthyism; Radical Faeries

Haynes, Todd (1965–)

His career is only about a decade old, but Todd Haynes has already established himself as one of the most eclectic of the so-called New Queer Cinema directors. The suppressed (by Richard Carpenter) cult classic *Superstar: The Karen Carpenter Story* (1988) contains most of the elements found within Haynes's later films: observations on stardom, concern about women and "cultural sicknesses," camp genre play, critiques of straight middle-class family life, and insights into male homosexuality troubled by straight culture or self-oppression. Haynes's trademark blankly ironic, or coolly detached, tone and style (which, in this film, includes having Barbie and Ken dolls as "actors") asks viewers to take responsibility for their intellectual and emotional responses.

When *Poison* (1991) won the Grand Jury Prize at the Sundance Film Festival, Haynes found himself at the forefront of what some critics and publicists dubbed "New Queer Cinema." Actually, only one of the three interwoven narratives in this film—an S/M prison story inspired by the works of Jean Genet—received New Queer Cinema critical atten-

tion and accolades. But as it turned out, the other stories—one about a child who kills his abusive father to protect his mother (and then flies away), the other an AIDS-metaphoric reworking of a 1950s mad scientist film—indicated where Haynes would go in his subsequent works.

The brilliant short *Dottie Gets Spanked* (1994) is a humorously painful account of a boy whose obsession with a Lucille Ball–like sitcom star marks the first evidence of his homosexuality for his family and schoolmates. Oppressed by his nervous father, supported by his mother, and taunted by other children, the boy bravely carries out his diva worship. *Safe* (1995) takes up *Poison*'s "mad scientist" story's interest in social responses to illness (or here, perhaps, illness as a response to society) with the story of Carol, an upper-middle-class housewife who develops a puzzling immunity disorder that causes her body to react against elements in her everyday life. Moving to Wrenwood, a resortlike treatment center in New Mexico, Carol becomes increasingly cut off from her family and her former life, while also becoming more isolated from the staff and the other patients at Wrenwood. With his typical ambiguity, Haynes never lets us know for certain what Carol is suffering from (is it chronic fatigue syndrome? allergies? psychosomatic rebellion against her sterile life? AIDS?), or whether we should see her New Age–style treatment at Wrenwood as helpful or harmful.

Haynes' most recent film, *Velvet Goldmine* (1998), employs a complex (post)modernist narrative to examine the glitter and glam rock scene of the 1970s. In its focus on star-fan relationships, the film suggests that the queerness of this scene was simultaneously a matter of surface image and absolutely essential to its cultural impact.

                      Alexander Doty

Bibliography

See also Film; Film: New Queer Cinema; Genet, Jean; Music and Musicians 2: Popular Music; Warhol, Andy

Hemphill, Essex (1957–1995)

U.S. poet and cultural critic Essex Hemphill was born on April 16, 1957, in Chicago, but his family soon moved to Washington, D.C., where he grew up. After attending the University of Maryland and the University of the District of Columbia, he published

H the chapbook *Earth Life* (1985) and followed it with another, *Conditions,* in 1986. His best-known work is the collection *Ceremonies: Prose and Poetry* (1992). In that book Hemphill offers poetic reflections on the condition of black gay men, autobiographical essays, and critiques of Robert Mapplethorpe's photographs of black men and Jennie Livingston's documentary *Paris Is Burning.* Hemphill and Marlon Riggs are the two figures whose emergence can be read as marking the beginning of the renaissance of black gay expression that occurred during the 1980s. Like Riggs, Hemphill achieved recognition not only as a creative writer but also as a cultural critic and activist.

Perhaps more than any other black gay writer of his generation, Hemphill was committed to interrogating and complicating received ideas about both homosexuality and blackness as experience by African American men. Keenly sensitive to the dynamics and positionality of black gay men in relation to the black family and, by extension, the black community, as well as to the white gay community, Hemphill explores the problematics of these issues with an explicitness and level of self-disclosure unprecedented in African American literature. As he wrote, "What is most clear for black gay men is this: we have to do for ourselves *now,* and for one another *now*, what no one has ever done for us."

Hemphill's work appeared in the landmark anthology of black gay writing *In the Life: A Black Gay Male Anthology,* edited by Joseph Beam; Hemphill himself edited the sequel, *Brother to Brother: New Writings by Black Gay Men* (1991), after Beam's death, a task and friendship that he memorialized in his poem "When My Brother Fell." Despite, or perhaps because of, the consistently provocative and engaged tone of his work and its centrality in the ongoing attempt to articulate modern gay black sensibility, Hemphill is one of the most anthologized of contemporary gay black poets. This centrality is reflected in the fact that he is the last writer presented in the canon-defining *Norton Anthology of African American Literature* and is thereby presented as the representative voice of both gay black identity and implicitly of the future of African American writing.

Not surprisingly, in the last years of his life Hemphill took on an iconic status within both black and white gay cultural circles. He appeared in the films *Looking for Langston, Out of the Shadows, Tongues Untied,* and *Black Is . . . Black Ain't* and was in constant demand as a speaker until his death from an AIDS-related illness on November 4, 1995. Even after his death, however, Hemphill generated controversy, owing to an acrimonious exchange between his family and black gay activists who accused the family of refusing to fully acknowledge his homosexuality at the funeral and memorial services.
Terry Rowden

Bibliography

Hemphill, Essex. *Ceremonies: Prose and Poetry.* New York: Penguin, 1992.

See also African American Gay Culture; Mapplethorpe, Robert; Riggs, Marlon

Henri III (1551–1589)

The fourth son of Henri II and Catherine de Medici, the future Henri III was given at birth the title duc d'Angoulême and the names Alexander-Édouard. In 1573 he was elected king of Poland. After assuming the throne in January 1574, he occupied it less than five months when, at the death of his older brother, Charles IX, he fled Poland to be crowned king of France. In 1575 he wedded Louise of Lorraine. The years of his reign correspond to a period of civil unrest that included France's religious wars and an opulent court life that was criticized by his enemies.

Henri was most criticized for his effeminacy and the love of his favorites, called *mignons.* These elegant nobles, who ranged in age from sixteen to thirty, were his constant companions and lovers. Some of them he married off to wealthy noblewomen, and one, the duc de Joyeuse, to his sister-in-law. Among his *mignons* were the duc d'Épernon, Saint-Luc, Saint-Mégrin, Maugeron, and Jacques de Levi, called Quelus, referred to mockingly as Culus (*cul* in French meaning "ass"). It was the death of these last three in a duel that became famous as "the quarrel of the *mignons*" in 1578 that inspired many poets, including Ronsard, to depict the episode poetically to console their grieving king, but the duel was more often portrayed satirically:

> Samson force aux cheveux avait,
> Et Maugeron l'eust au derrière.
> Fuiant, Riberac ne devait
> Le poursuivre en telle manière.

> (Samson's strength was in his hair
> And Maugeron's in his rear.

As he fled, Riberac wouldn't dare
To try to catch him there.)

In addition to their sexual relationship, both Henri and his *mignons* were known for their cross-dressing, which included, on one occasion, disguising themselves as Amazons. The *mignons* were often described as *"frisé et fraisé"*—a designation that emphasized their unnaturally curly hair and thick ruffled collars—and compared to women.

In spite of the negative image French history would associate with the last Valois king, Henri III was an able military leader, a liberal patron of the arts, and founder of the religious Order of the Holy Spirit. Moreover, with the help of his mother, Catherine, he conducted a successful foreign policy and outwitted his harshest critics, the Catholic League, by naming himself their leader.

Henri III was assassinated by a Dominican monk named Jacques Clément in August 1589, leaving as his successor the recent convert to Catholicism, Henri of Navarre.   *Todd Black*

Bibliography

l'Estoile, Pierre de. *Registre-Journal du Règne de Henri III*. Vol. 2 (1576–1578). Madeleine Lazard and Gilbert Schrenck, eds. Geneva: Droz, 1996.

Poirier, Guy. *L'Homosexualité dans l'imaginaire de la Renaissance*. Paris: Champion, 1996.

See also France; French Literature

Henze, Hans Werner (1926–)

This German composer and conductor studied music in Brunswick, against his parents' wishes, and composed from the age of twelve without formal training; as a teenager he was interested in the modernism banned by Hitler's Third Reich. In 1944 he was drafted into the German army, serving in Poland before being transferred to a propaganda film unit. In 1946 he returned to his musical education, studying in Heidelberg with Wolfgang Fortner and writing his first acknowledged compositions. He attended music courses at Darmstadt from 1946 to 1960, viewed at first as a young, innovative star but later (after Pierre Boulez and Karlheinz Stockhausen rose to power) as a reactionary; aggressively Marxist critic Heinz-Klaus Metzger handed out pamphlets at Henze's performances that purported to expose Henze as a political and aesthetic fraud. This ambiguous political and aesthetic position—being regarded as avant-garde by the bourgeoisie but as a tool of—establishment by the avant-garde—has haunted Henze's career; it was part of the reason, along with his increasing distaste for postwar Germany, to move permanently to Italy in 1953. He was professor of music in Salzburg (1962–1967) and Cologne (1980–1991), and first composer in residence for the Berlin Philharmonic (1990); he is founder and has been director of the important Munich Biennale for contemporary music theater since 1988. Henze is the most flexible and facile of modern composers, having written an opulent variety of stage and concert works in different styles. His numerous operas include *König Hirsch* (1955, revised as *Il Re cervo*, 1962), *Elegy for Young Lovers* (1961), and *The Bassarids* (1965–66), both to librettos by Auden and Kallman; the political comedies *Der junge Lord* (1964) and *The English Cat* (1980–1982); an allegory for multiple stages and orchestras, *We Come to the River* (1976); and *Das verratene Meer* (1990), based on a story by Mishima. Among his other explicitly political works are *Versuch über Schweine* (1968), the cantata *Das Floss der Medusa* (1968), the recital for four musicians based on a slave narrative *El Cimarrón* (1970), the bizarre "show for 17" *Der langwierige Weg in die Wohnung der Natascha Ungeheuer* (1971), the "anthology" cantata *Voices* (1973), and the ballet *Orpheus* (1978). Most of these works oppose downtrodden proletariat and rich oppressor, employing massive irony with tragic consequences. Other important works include eight symphonies (1947–1993), five string quartets (1947–1976), the remarkable Second Piano Concerto (1967), and numerous concerti, keyboard works, chamber works, cantatas, and ballets. Frequently accused of being a "limousine Marxist" whose powerfully expressed political convictions don't prevent him from living well, Henze has been relatively open about his sexuality for most of his career, without presenting it in association with a political or cultural context; references to being gay appear in *Heliogabalus Imperator* (1972) and *La Miracle de la rose* for clarinet and ensemble (1981).   *Paul Attinello*

Bibliography

Henze, Hans Werner. *Music and Politics: Collected Writings 1953–81*. Peter Labanyi, trans. London: Faber and Faber, 1982.

Rexroth, D., ed. *Der Komponist Hans Werner Henze: ein Buch der Alten Oper.* Frankfurt: Frankfurt Feste, 1986. Mainz: Schott, 1986.

See also Music and Musicians 1: Classical Music; Opera

Hermaphroditism

Individuals who arrive in the world with sexual anatomy that fails to be easily distinguished as male or female are labeled "intersexuals" or "hermaphrodites" by modern medical discourse. About one in a hundred births exhibit some anomaly in sex differentiation, and about one in two thousand is different enough to raise the question "Is it a boy or a girl?"

The concept of physical sex, in popular usage, refers to multiple characteristics, including karyotype (organization of sex chromosomes), type of gonadal differentiation (e.g., ovarian or testicular), external genital morphology, configuration of internal reproductive organs, and pubertal sex characteristics such as breasts and facial hair. These characteristics are assumed and expected to be concordant in each individual—either all male, or all female. Intersexual bodies are those that break this concordance. Because of the assumption of concordance, an observer, once having attributed male or female sex to another, assumes the values of other, unobserved characteristics. Thus a person with a beard and a deep voice is attributed male sex and assumed also to have a penis and testes in a scrotum, and XY karyotype. Some of these characteristics have discrete, nonbinary values (like the number of coins in a purse), while others have continuously distributed values (like the position of a speedometer needle); none is strictly binary. The configuration of the sex chromosomes, for example, can take on such discrete values as XXY, XO, XYY, and XXXY, in addition to XX and XY, and can even vary from cell to cell in a single individual. The morphology of the external genitals is continuously distributed—infants are born with phalluses that range in size from zero to several centimeters, with urinary meatuses (pee holes) located anywhere from the tip to positions along the shaft's underside, to the shaft's base, in the perineum. Most people labeled female have a small phallus, called a clitoris; most people labeled male have a large phallus, called a penis. In medical discourse a phallus whose size lies between these extremes causes the genitals to be labeled ambiguous, and their owner intersexed, or hermaphroditic.

Since the early 1960s, nearly every major city in the United States has had a hospital with a standing team of medical experts who intervene in these cases to assign—through drastic surgical means—male or female status to intersex infants. The fact that this system for enforcing the boundaries of the categories "male" and "female" has existed for so long without drawing criticism or scrutiny from any

Hermaphrodites protesting medical decisions. Photo courtesy of author.

quarter is an indication of the extreme discomfort that sexual ambiguity excites in our culture. Pediatric genital surgeries literalize what many might otherwise consider a purely theoretical operation—the attempted production of normatively sexed bodies and gendered subjects through what amount to constitutive acts of violence. Intersex people began, during the mid-1990s, to politicize intersex identities (including through organizations like the Intersex Society of North America), thus transforming intensely personal experiences of violation into collective opposition to the medical regulation of bodies that queer the foundations of heteronormative gender identifications and sexual orientations.

Cheryl Chase

Bibliography

Chase, Cheryl. "Hermaphrodites with Attitude: Mapping the Emergence of Intersex Political Activism." *GLQ* 4 (1998): 189–211.

Dreger, Alice Domurat. *Hermaphrodites and the Medical Invention of Sex.* Cambridge, Mass.: Harvard University Press, 1998.

Kessler, Suzanne J. "The Medical Construction of Gender: Case Management of Intersexual Infants." *Signs: Journal of Women in Culture and Society* 16, no. 1 (1990): 3–26.

See also Gender; Transsexualism

Hijras of India

The *hijras* are an alternative gender role in India. *Hijras* are male devotees of the Indian mother goddess Bahuchara Mata. As religious devotees, *hijras* dress and act like women and undergo surgical removal of their genitals. This "operation," called *nirvan* or (rebirth), defines *hijras* as vehicles of the creative power of the mother goddess, as neither man nor woman, or alternately, as sacred, female, men. In this capacity, *hijras* traditionally perform for childbirth and at weddings, conferring blessings of fertility and prosperity in the goddess's name. In addition to this religious role (and contrary to its requirements), *hijras* also engage in sexual relations with men in the receiver role, most frequently as male prostitutes.

The cultural construction of *hijras* as an alternative gender is based on the hermaphrodite or biologically intersexed person. Most frequently glossed as eunuch or "intersexed," the *hijra* role emphasizes male sexual impotence, rather than the erotic attraction of same-sexed persons. As "man minus man" or female sacred men, *hijras* transform the negative quality of male impotence into a positive female creative power through emasculation. *Nirvan* is a form of denial of (any) sexual desire and activity, and the *hijras'* powers (like other ascetics) derive from the renunciation of sexuality.

It is widely believed in India that *hijras* expand their community by making successful claims on intersexed infants whom they discover in the course of their performances, during which they inspect the genitals of the male infant. Contrary to this belief, research supports the view that *hijras* join the community in their youth from many motives: a desire to more fully express their feminine gender identity, including pleasure gained from the receptor role in sexual relations with men, under the pressure of poverty or ill treatment by parents and peers for feminine behavior, or after a despairing lifestyle as a male prostitute on their own.

Hijras live mainly in communal households, to which members contribute most of their earnings in return for food, shelter, pocket money, and protection. *Hijra* households are governed by strict rules, and sanctions for disruptive behavior such as drinking, theft, or laziness range from mild ridicule to ostracism. Seniority underlies *hijra* social organization, regulating behavior between elders (*gurus*) and junior members (*chelas*) of the community. There is no caste or other social distinctions within *hijra* households or communities.

Hijra gender identity grows out of traditional Hindu concepts of the possibility of sex and gender alternatives and transformations and also out of the historical role of eunuchs in Mogul courts. Some *hijras* today also identify with Western transsexualism and gay culture. Despite repressive efforts by the British raj and the postindependent Indian state, the *hijra* community demonstrates a millennia-old ability to survive economically and culturally by incorporating modern cultural elements into an age-old role.

Serena Nanda

Bibliography

Hiltelbeitel, A. "Siva, the Goddess, and the Disguises of the Pandavas and Draupadi." *History of Religions* 20 (1980): 147–74.

Nanda, Serena. *Neither Man nor Woman: The Hijras of India.* Belmont, Calif.: Wadsworth, 1990.

See also Anthropology; Berdache; Hinduism; India; Transgender

H

Hinduism

To understand how Hinduism treats homosexuality, it is first necessary to understand how Hinduism views gender. While Western thought has always treated gender as binary—male or female—Hinduism recognizes the existence of a third sex for those who were sexually anomalous or sexually ambiguous. This class of person basically included those whose sexual practices did not result in procreation. The Sanskrit term *napumsaka* (one who is unmanly) was often used to describe the third sex and included those who derived sexual gratification from fellatio and anal sex. *Nari shandi*, on the other hand, was a woman who was breastless and sterile. Medical treatises like the *Caraka Samhita* and *Susruta* also had many interesting theories about the causes of anomalous sexual behavior. For example, lesbianism is apparently caused by the mother having been in a "superior" position during intercourse. The *Susruta* also claims that two women can approach each other sexually and ejaculate semen (*sukra*), producing a boneless thing. The Jain religion, which was born out of Hindusim, carried the concept of sexuality a step further by arguing that psychological sexuality was independent of physical gender, so that a biological male could have psychologically female sexuality, that is, a desire to have sex with men.

However, we should not be led to believe that just because there was a category like "third sex," people who belonged to that category led lives free of all forms of social stigma. The Laws of Manu specify that a virgin who has sex with another virgin must be fined two hundred pennies, pay double the bride price, and receive ten lashes. But a mature woman who does it to a virgin will have her head shaved or have two fingers cut off and be made to ride a donkey through town. Yet it is worth noting that the Laws of Manu comprise a social regulatory text, not scripture. As a result, while specific instances of homosexuality, especially those transgressing caste boundaries, were punishable, there were similar punishments for comparable heterosexual transgressions. For example, Kautilya's *Arthashastra* prescribes the same punishment for a man who has sex with a woman "against the order of nature" as that prescribed for a man who has intercourse with another man. Homosexuality itself did not acquire the stigma of religious sin.

In fact, it is hard for it to acquire that stigma when the texts and epics are replete with examples that, if not directly about homosexuality, are clearly about gender bending. Certainly there seems to have been a far less rigorous separation between what was masculine and what was feminine. The god Siva is commonly represented as Ardhanariswara—a form that is half man, half woman. His most powerful symbol is the phallus, but it is usually set in the *yoni* (vagina). The Tantric school of Hinduism conceptualizes the Supreme Being as one complete sex with male and female sexual organs. So male devotees often imitate a woman to realize the woman in them. It is also believed in Tantra that the serpentine power of enlightenment lies coiled in the perineum and can be aroused through anal penetration.

In other examples of gender bending the god Vishnu transformed himself into a beautiful nymph, Mohini, and had a child with Siva, while the god Krishna took on the form of a beautiful woman and married the demon Araka to destroy him. Krishna's son Samba was known to cross-dress, often as a pregnant woman. Researcher Giti Thadani has shown that in Vedic times (before 1500 B.C.), there was a strong tradition of dual feminine deities embodying women-centered kinship structures whose bonds are not derivative of procreative sexuality.

In the Hindu epic Ramayana, the monkey god Hanuman witnesses the many wives of the demon king Ravana embracing each other at night and clinging amorously to each other under the influence of wine. In the other great epic, the Mahabharata, written by Vyasa around 500 B.C., the warrior Arjuna is cursed with the loss of his manhood and spends a year in female attire living with the ladies of the court and teaching them singing and dancing.

Of course, *hijras* have always held a special place in Hindu culture. *Hijras* have been defined as hermaphrodites, transsexuals, and eunuchs, but they are usually men who give up their genitals in homage to their goddess, Bahuchara Mata, and live in female attire mostly in small groups consisting of a guru and her disciples. The *hijras* say that when king Rama of the Ramayana went into exile for fourteen years, he was followed by his weeping citizens. At the edge of the forest, he asked all the men and women to return home. But the *hijras*, being neither men nor women, did not return home. So when Rama came back fourteen years later, he found them still waiting. Greatly touched, he promised they would one day rule the world.

Male transvestism has been a form of devotion in many Hindu sects. In the Sakhibhava sect, Krishna may not be worshiped directly. Instead, devotees aim to worship him through his consort Radha. They imitate feminine gestures and even simulate menstruation. In medieval times many mystic poets like Chaitanya and Kabir envisaged themselves as women in love. Meanwhile the Sufi saints who formed the bridge between Hinduism and Islam were well known for their homosexual traditions. In fact, the sixteenth-century Sufi poet Lal Hussein was so inseparable from a young Hindu boy named Madho that they became known by a single name—Madho Lal Hussein—and they are buried next to each other in Lahore. The nineteenth-century Bengali mystic Ramakrishna often donned female clothes and acted as a woman. He also raised many eyebrows by dancing naked amid young male disciples.

Yet despite these many instances, modern Hindus are often unaware of the broad spectrum of sexuality their culture encompasses. It survives today in intricate carvings in the temples of Khajuraho and Orissa, showing same-sex sexual acts. It survives in the eight-step guide to fellatio in the Kama Sutra. it comes to light in the careful excavations of researchers who have been translating the forgotten and omitted portions of ancient Sanskrit texts. It is hard to give this spectrum of human sexuality the simple modern label "gay" or "lesbian," but it is obvious even to a casual student that Hinduism has had a rich culture of alternate sexuality—a culture that was most striking in its absence of guilt in regard to homosexual behavior.   *Sandip Roy*

Bibliography

Kavi, Ashok Row. "A Guiltless Homosexual Tradition." *Trikone* 11, no. 3 (1996): 8–9.

Kripal, Jeffrey. *Kali's Child: The Mystical and Erotic in the Life and Teachings of Ramakrishna.* Chicago: University of Chicago Press, 1995.

Kumar, Mina. *Some Indian Lesbian Images.* Toronto: The Very Inside (Sister Vision Press), 1994.

Mukherjee, Subodh. "Homosexuality in India: A Personal Quest for Historical Perspective." *Trikone* 5, no. 1 (1990): 1–3.

Nanda, Serena. *Neither Man nor Woman: The Hijras of India.* Belmont, Calif.: Wadsworth, 1990.

Ratti, Rakesh. *A Lotus of Another Color.* Boston: Alyson Publications, 1993.

Sikand, Yogi. "Martyr for Gay Love." *Bombay Dost* 4, no. 4 (1996): 7, 18.

Zwilling, Leonard, and Michael Sweet. "In Search of the Napumsaka." *Trikone* 11, no. 3 (1996): 14–15.

See also Gender; Hijras of India; India; Islamic Mysticism; Kama Sutra; Religion and Religiosity; Third Sex

Hine, Daryl (1936–)

Born in Burnaby, British Columbia, Daryl Hine attended McGill University and lived in Paris before attending the University of Chicago, where he taught classics and assumed editorship of the prestigious magazine *Poetry* in 1968, a position he held for a decade. In that same year, *Minutes*, his first substantial volume of poems, appeared. Since then Hine has had a faithful following among poetry lovers, especially those with a taste for classical learning, formal elegance, and wit. While Hine's earlier volumes were allusively erotic, the poems were never explicitly homosexual. Hine chose to write of his own homosexual awakening and early romantic experience in a verse autobiography, *In and Out*, which he first published in a small-press edition in 1975. It relates how he fell in love while at McGill, and how he tried to suppress consciousness of his sexual difference through Catholic practice and discipline. Harold Bloom, one of the most influential American critics, warmly praised *In and Out,* and publisher Alfred A. Knopf brought it before a wider audience in 1989. Meanwhile, the appearance of *Academic Festival Overtures* (1985) gave explicit poetic attention to Hine's adolescent experience of sexuality. In his more mature poems, Hine chose a subtle, gently ironic mode to communicate the young male's tangled process of identifying, repressing, and then accepting his sexuality. The poems he produced in this mode are scintillating and yet touched with profound feeling. Though they will never reach a wide audience, they are among the best American classicist poems of the last half-century.   *Patrick Holland*

Bibliography

Howard, Richard. *Alone with America: Essays on the Art of Poetry in the United States Since 1950.* New York: Atheneum, 1969.

See also Canada; Love Poetry, the Petrarchan Tradition

Hippocratic Corpus

The Hippocratic corpus is the body of Greek medical writings traditionally ascribed to Hippocrates of Cos (c.460–c.370 B.C.E.). In fact, the sixty-odd writings of the collection were composed by authors

H holding rather different views and over the course of at least two centuries. Same-sex desire receives no systematic treatment in the Hippocratic writings. It sometimes figures, as it did in Greek societies, just as a fact of male erotic life. In the famous Hippocratic Oath, the (male) physician swears not to engage in sexual activities with women or men, slave or free, during his house calls. At other times the writings repeat popular myths about the causes of gender inversion or reversal. The men of Scythia are said to be effeminate, for example, because they cut the blood vessels behind their ears. The surgery is meant to alleviate swelling in the joints, but it has the unintended effect of rendering them impotent, hence (the author reasons) like women in their behavior. (Another echo of this myth can be heard in Aristotle.) The most interesting Hippocratic teaching about same-sex desire comes in the doctrine of mixed-sex constitutions or physiologies. Different mixtures of male and female "seed" at conception produce offspring of different sexual temperament. Weakness in the father's seed and strength in the mother's will produce either an androgyne, literally a "man-woman," or else a mannish woman. This doctrine would be considerably developed by later medical writers.   *Mark D. Jordan*

Bibliography

Cadden, Joan. *Meanings of Sex Difference in the Middle Ages: Medicine, Science, and Culture.* Cambridge: Cambridge University Press, 1993, 15–21.

See also Androgyny; Gender; Greece; Inversion; Scientific Approaches to Homosexuality

Hirschfeld, Magnus (1868–1935)

Reformer, activist, sexologist, author, and physician, Magnus Hirschfeld spent most of his career battling legal strictures against homosexuality in his native Germany and challenging the notion of a pathological homosexuality throughout the world.

A student of endocrinology and a proponent of temperance, divorce reform, and legalized abortion, Hirschfeld began his career in sexology pseudonymously with the 1896 publication of *Sappho and Socrates*. Based on the experiences of a homosexual patient who committed suicide the night before his wedding, this treatise was the first of numerous publications designed to increase public awareness and acceptance of homosexuality.

Throughout his career, Hirschfeld's theory of a hormonal etiology for homosexuality was closely linked with his political activities. He created the Scientific-Humanitarian Committee (Wissenschaftlich-Humanitäre Komitee) in 1897 to protect homosexuals from legalized abuses. Moreover, in serving as an expert witness in hundreds of trials and testifying to the congenital nature of homosexuality, he saved many men from prison sentences imposed under the Weimar Republic's paragraph 175. However, his controversial testimony in the Eulenburg scandal—ironically designed to illustrate the hypocrisy of antisodomy statutes in a monarchy riddled with sodomites—damaged Hirschfeld's credibility and his political gains. During the scandal fomented by anti-imperialists and Social Democrats, close associates of Kaiser Wilhelm II, including Prince Philipp von Eulenburg, were publicly labeled homosexuals by journalist Maximilian Harden. Unfortunately, Hirschfeld's corroborating testimony in Harden's libel trial discredited Eulenburg and the monarchy, helped fuel antigay and nationalist factions, and nearly ruined efforts to repeal paragraph 175.

From 1899 to 1923, Hirschfeld and the committee published the *Yearbook for Sexual Intermediaries (Jahrbuch für sexuelle Zwischenstufen)*, which provided materials of interest to homosexuals, transvestites, androgynes, hermaphrodites, and other sexually liminal types. Hirschfeld's theory of intermediaries drew from the third-sex theory popularized by Karl Heinrich Ulrichs in the 1860s. Both suggested that the homosexual was an intermediary type between male and female heterosexuals, exhibiting the physical attributes of one sex while manifesting the emotional characteristics, behaviors, and drives of the other. Aware of the incredible diversity of human sexual behaviors, Hirschfeld hypothesized the existence of more than forty-three million types of intermediaries.

Truly a pioneer in his field, Hirschfeld was the first to undertake an extended study of cross-dressing. His *Transvestites* proposed an understanding of cross-dressing as a phenomenon apart from homosexuality, fetishism, masochism, and masturbation, categories under which it had been subsumed in previous scientific discourses. In addition, Hirschfeld began the first scholarly sexological journal, *Journal of Sexual Science*, and he was the first to disseminate and interpret thousands of sexological questionnaires. The data gathered from these appear in *Die Homosexualität des Mannes und des Weibes*, which has not been translated into English. World-renowned during the first decades of the twentieth century, he presided over four meetings of the World League for Sexual Reform and, in 1919, founded the Institute for Sex Research (Institut für Sexual wissenschaft), a medical, counseling, and research center and library.

Undeterred by Nazism and the opposition of some contemporaries, Hirschfeld saw the medicalization of homosexuality and the use of accessible, didactic materials aimed at the lay public as effective means toward political and social change. Tragically, the virulent homophobia and anti-Semitism that nearly cost Hirschfeld his life in a 1921 assault virtually obliterated his institute in 1933, when his expansive library was summarily ravaged and burned. During this attack, Hirschfeld was on a world lecture tour collecting ethnographic materials on Eastern sexualities and genders. In exile after the tour, he settled in Nice, hoping to build a smaller version of the institute with his partner Karl Giese. This last project was unrealized at Hirschfeld's death on his sixty-seventh birthday.

Nancy San Martin

Bibliography

Hirschfeld, Magnus. *Transvestites: The Erotic Drive to Cross Dress*. Michael A. Lombardi-Nash, trans. 1910. Buffalo: Prometheus, 1991.

Wolff, Charlotte. *Magnus Hirschfeld: A Portrait of a Pioneer in Sexology*. London: Quartet, 1986.

See also Ellis, Havelock; Freud, Sigmund; Germany; Kinsey, Alfred; Krafft-Ebing, Richard von; Scientific Approaches to Homosexuality; Sexology; Ulrichs, Karl Heinrich

Hitchcock, Alfred (1899–1980)

No, Alfred Hitchcock never said he was gay or bisexual, but he made enough films with queer characters to reveal a deep and abiding interest in nonstraight sexuality. Granted, these characters aren't openly named as gay, lesbian, or bisexual, but they have been read as such by many viewers: Handel Fane in *Murder!* (1930), the General in *The Secret Agent* (1935), Mrs. Danvers in *Rebecca* (1940), Charlie Oakley in *Shadow of a Doubt* (1943), Brandon and Philip in *Rope* (1948), Bruno Anthony in *Strangers on a Train* (1951), Norman Bates in *Psycho* (1960), Marnie Edgar in *Marnie* (1964), and Bob Rusk in *Frenzy* (1972). Still, Robin Wood cau-

tions viewers against becoming too eager to name the queers in Hitchcock films, lest they succumb to heterosexist and homophobic stereotyping as they decode what he calls the "supposed to be" gay, lesbian, and bisexual characters in Hitchcock films. Wood does not say there aren't queerly coded characters in these films but that he'd like to encourage viewers also to name as queer such positively presented characters as Caldicott and Charters in *The Lady Vanishes* (1938) and André Latour in *The Paradine Case* (1947), while reconsidering their queering of figures like Charlie Oakley, Norman Bates, and Bob Rusk.

Once we get beyond naming, however, a nagging question still remains: Is Hitchcock homophobic? More precisely, to what degree do his films reveal an understanding of gays, lesbians, and other queers that falls within the negative terms of dominant culture? In Hitchcock-directed films, are the gay, lesbian, and bisexual characters seen as being psychologically ill, criminal, emotionally stunted, and sinful (to put things in the terms of the Catholicism within which the director was raised) because they are queer? John Hepworth was among the first critics to brand Hitchcock a notorious homophobe, calling the director "a supreme fag baiter," among other things. More recently, many critics have come to feel that, taken individually or as a group, Hitchcock's films contain homophobic elements as well as material that suggests how cultural pressures and constraints might be understood as the cause of criminality and psychosis in queers.

Besides his roster of read-as-queer characters, Hitchcock has a connection to gay, lesbian, and bisexual cultures through some of the actors he chose to work with: Ivor Novello, Cary Grant, Montgomery Clift, Judith Anderson, Marlene Dietrich, Anthony Perkins, Raymond Burr, Tallulah Bankhead, John Gielgud, and others. Donald Spoto's popular biography *The Dark Side of Genius: The Life of Alfred Hitchcock* is full of material chronicling how the director alternated between fascination and resistance while working with these queer performers.

Apart from queer characters and actors, however, many Hitchcock films are most interesting to gay, lesbian, and bisexual viewers for what they say about heterosexuality. In a recent poll of lesbian, gay, and otherwise queer critics, curators, and film- and video-makers, *Vertigo* (1958) was selected as the best film of all time. Simultaneously romantic and disturbing, *Vertigo* presents obsessive desire in a way that many queers can identify with, while still

H allowing them to be thrilled by the film's exposure of heterosexual patriarchy as sick, sick, sick.

Alexander Doty

Bibliography

Hepworth, John. "Hitchcock's Homophobia." In *Out in Culture: Gay Lesbian and Queer Essays on Popular Culture.* Corey Creekmur and Alexander Doty, eds. Durham, N.C.: Duke University Press, 1995, 186–96.

Olson, Jenni. *The Ultimate Guide to Lesbian and Gay Film and Video.* New York: Serpent's Tail, 1996.

Spoto, Donald. *The Dark Side of Genius: The Life of Alfred Hitchcock.* New York: Ballantine, 1983.

Wood, Robin. "The Murderous Gays: Hitchcock's Homophobia." In *Hitchcock's Films Revisited.* New York: Columbia University Press, 1989, 336–57.

See also Film; Film: New Queer Cinema; Film Stars; Homophobia

Hockney, David (1937–)

In the popular press and public imagination—as well as in the more rarefied realms of art world journals—few twentieth-century artists have garnered as much long-lasting and positive attention as Los Angeles–based British painter David Hockney. His distinctive style and uninhibited use of color have embellished an enormous range of medias—from painting and drawing, to etchings, photographic collages, printing, and stage design. Hockney's paintings—from *A Big Splash* (1967) to *Mulholland Drive: The Road to the Studio* (1980)—have made the freeways, swimming pools, and gardens of Los Angeles, since the mid-1970s his adopted home, into icons of the modern imagination, while his stage designs and paintings have graced major opera houses and museums around the globe.

Hockney has been successful from the very beginning of his career. In 1961, while still a student at the Royal College of Art in London, he was taken up by London art dealer John Kasmin, and two of his drawings were bought that year by the Museum of Modern Art in New York. Two years later, one year out of art school, he had his first one-man show in London and soon became known in England as the "King of Pop." In 1974, he had a retrospective at the Musée des Arts Décoratif, part of the Louvre Museum, in Paris. The next year, he did his first opera stage designs for a production of Igor Stravinsky's *The Rake's Progress* at the Glyndebourne Festival in England, and has been creating celebrated set designs for major opera houses ever since.

Throughout his career, Hockney has been unapologetically open and candid about his homosexuality. In 1960, while still at the RCA, the artist began creating overtly homoerotic paintings, known generically now as the "Love Paintings." Works such as *Queer* (1960), *Doll Boys, The Most Beautiful Boy in the World* (1961), and *We Two Boys Together Clinging* (1961) were explicitly homosexual at a time before such themes were widely portrayed. Often numbered and coded to represent the initials of the painter's boyfriends, the "Love Paintings" were influenced by gay nudist magazines—published in Los Angeles—then becoming available in London.

These magazines, like *Physique Pictorial*, contained photos of naked or nearly naked young men awkwardly posed while doing everyday things—taking a shower, standing around a pool, leaning against a garden planter. And they inspired in Hockney both a desire to see the place where they were published and to paint the subjects portrayed therein. The artist created a work called *Domestic Scene, Los Angeles*—depicting two boys in a shower—two years before actually going to California.

Two years later, in 1963, Hockney visited Los Angeles for the first time. "It was really the promise of the things I saw in those magazines that attracted me there," says the painter in his broad, lower-middle-class Yorkshire accent. After arriving he even visited the place where the magazines photos were shot. "It seemed to me like a very seedy Alexandria," he declared. As his art school friend, painter Ron Kitaj, put it, at first Los Angeles for Hockney quite simply "meant boys."

After arriving in Southern California, Hockney said he felt immediately at home in this "sunny land of movie stars and beautiful, semi-naked people," and he decided to make himself the painter of that city. "I immediately loved the light in Southern California," he said, seated comfortably by the fire, playing with his two pet dachshunds, at his estate in the Hollywood Hills. "It seemed to me that you could see more clearly here. It's so bright, things seem somehow more in focus than they do in Europe. And you can also live your own life in America. Even live out your wildest fantasies and no one bothers you." While in Los Angeles, Hockney began creating the paintings of boys and swimming pools, alone or in combination, that were to become hallmarks of his style and of the popular imagination for years to come.

The early 1960s—the period of the "Love Paintings"—was the painter's most militantly gay period. As time went by, however, the militancy quieted and in the works of the later 1960s, 1970s, and beyond, homosexuality was treated as just a natural part of life.

Early in 1974, Jack Hazon's semi-documentary film *A Bigger Splash* appeared, treating the artist's devastating breakup with his young American lover, Peter Schlesinger, in forthright and open terms. *A Bigger Splash* was uncommonly explicit about homosexuality for the time and was considered inspirational and revolutionary to some while disgusting to others. Did Hockney worry that being so openly gay might have a detrimental effect on his career? "Well, no quite frankly," he responded, inviting the listener on a tour of his studio, a large industrial building with fluted skylights on his property not far from his house. "Being gay has always seemed like the most natural thing in the world to me. It's never seemed like a problem or something to be hidden. I don't know why. Perhaps it's because I grew up in World War II when they were dropping bombs on everybody all around me." (Hockney did alternate service as a conscientious objector when he reached draft age.) "The world as a result has always seemed to me a little mad. And I've always felt at an angle to it. So being gay always just seemed like part of that. Though I have to say that I feel rather saner than most of the people around me most of the time."

"Besides," he went on, signaling to his two dachshunds, which follow him everywhere, "I've never really thought of my career as such. It's my life that I'm interested in. And how can you hope to have an interesting life if you're not honest about who you are? Doing creative things that interest me, that's what I'm concerned with. And fortunately, I've been able to do that throughout my entire life. I've been very lucky in that regard. No matter how much money I've made or haven't made is inconsequential. I've been able to work on the things I've wanted and support myself doing it. Therefore, I'm a rich man." Throughout his career, Hockney, a gregarious and personable man with a keen and highly developed interest in friendship, has always done lots of paintings of his friends and lovers. It is, he says, a way of getting to know them better.

The AIDS epidemic, in consequence, has had a devastating effect on his personal life. "I've lost so many friends over the years," he admits. "I couldn't even watch *A Bigger Splash* today. In fact, I haven't watched it in twenty years. And now I wouldn't dare. It would be too sad. Too many of my friends are gone. AIDS and my deafness have made me a much lonelier man. But fortunately I can still work. As long as I can do that I'm all right. Otherwise it's just too depressing."

Hockney, who wears two hearing aids and in his early sixties is almost completely deaf, says he will no longer do designs for the theater. "I can't hear what's happening on the stage anymore," he has explained, arranging prints and artists proofs on a large table in the center of his huge work space. "I have to fill in the music in my mind. It can be frustrating." Neither, he says, does he go out much anymore. "Restaurants and most public places are too difficult for me. I can't hear what people are saying. Neither can I smoke—at least in California. Which seems tyrannical, but there's nothing to do about it. So instead I stay home—hardly ever go out—and have my friends visit me here. The place is big enough that guests can stay for weeks and never seem underfoot. Otherwise, I work. All the time. From morning to night. After all, Love, when all is said and done, what else is there?"

The "Love Paintings" and boys in pools, so lovingly and poetically painted; the unapologetic boldness of *A Bigger Splash*; the uncomplicated candor of Hockney's public sexuality—all have served as groundbreaking expressions of homosexual self-acceptance—beacons of openness—in the later part of the twentieth century, helping gay men over two generations find the courage to be themselves.

Mark Steinbrink

Bibliography

Livingstone, Marco. *David Hockney*. New York: Holt, 1981.

See also Art History; Athletic Model Grid; Los Angeles

Hocquenghem, Guy (1946–1988)

Both as novelist and critical thinker, Guy Hocquenghem's writing raises pertinent questions about how gay identity is and can be thought of from the perspective of France's "intellectual revolution." Rejecting the dominant normative concept of personhood as an ideological invention that circumscribes and determines experience, his theoretical writing valorizes passion and catastrophe over causal logic

H and humanism. The shifting positions he adopts in his work are not easily summarized, characterized by a refusal of consistency themselves, but one recurring theme is Hocquenghem's suspicion of the signifier "homosexual" as a fixed identity position. For him, the label "gay," together with pride and affirmation politics, functions as a compromise with dominant concepts that aim to produce and commodify sexuality and desire in socially containable and ultimately unchallenging ways. Instead he projects alternative forms of social organization (including the dynamics or aesthetics of cruising and an investigation into the ways in which the concept of pedophilia is deployed) in a way that is something akin to a more radical version of what later emerges as queer.

Hocquenghem's published work, coming in the aftermath of May 1968 and continuing until shortly before his death in 1988, can be roughly grouped into theoretical texts and fictional writing. Following his organization and dialogue with the Front Homosexuel d'Action Révolutionnaire (FHAR, or the Homosexual Front for Revolutionary Action) in identifying homophobia as systematic within French society, Hocquenghem wants "homosexuality" to be understood not as a recuperable rights claim but as a "permanent questioning" of social norms. Drawing on ideas similar to Deleuze and Guattari's *L'Anti-Oedipe* (Anti-Oedipus, 1972), his first major publication, *Le Désir homosexuel* (Homosexual Desire, 1972), refers less to *individual* desire than to the polymorphous flows of desire, which society, by inducing paranoia, guilt, and anxiety, uses to channel and regulate human sexual activity. In this text, alongside later theoretical texts such as *La Dérive homosexuelle* (Homosexual Drift, 1977) and *Comment vous appelez-vous déjà? Ces hommes que l'on dit homosexuels* (What Is It You Call Us Again? These Men Known as Homosexuals, 1977), cowritten with Jean-Louis Bory, Hocquenghem's critique is coupled with a valorization of the anus over the phallus, as a site that offers a celebratory challenge to the property and propriety necessary to maintain the doxa of individual self. While not fully able to account for the ways in which homosexuality is produced precisely *as* an identity at specific historical junctures, Hocquenghem's approach usefully points to the collusions among state, capital, family, and psyche in defusing and regulating desire as a key moment of society's organization of energy into forms of production/procreation.

Later essays build on these arguments in an investigation into French obsessions with statehood,

in *La Beauté du métis* (The Beauty of the Mixed, 1979) and in the more philosophically sustained text, cowritten this time with René Schérer, *L'Âme atomique* (The Atomic Soul, 1986). This later volume mobilizes the aesthetics of the baroque (including allegory, contradiction, and digression) to question the totalizing and universalizing tendencies of contemporary thought and society. Fictional texts include fantastical, defamiliarizing histories such as *La Colère de l'agneau* (The Wrath of the Lamb, 1985) and *Les Voyages et aventures extraordinaires du frère Angelo* (The Travels and Extraordinary Adventures of Brother Angelo, 1988), together with the polysemous and antitotalizing global novel *L'Amour en relief* (Love in Relief, 1982). Perhaps his most extraordinary piece of fiction is *Eve* (1987), a thriller written in the midst of France's AIDS epidemic that aims at exposing and confronting genetic dictatorships behind sociofamilial organization and the individual through a reconfiguration of the myth of genesis.

Murray Pratt

Bibliography

Marshall, Bill. *Guy Hocquenghem*. London: Pluto Press, 1996.

———. "Reconsidering 'Gay': Hocquenghem, Identity Politics and the Baroque." In *Gay Signatures*. Owen Heathcote, Alex Hughes, and James Williams, eds. Berg: Oxford, 1998, 51–71.

Martel, Frédéric. *Le Rose et le noir*. Paris: Éditions du Seuil, 1996.

Morrey, Douglas. "Sida-topies: Provocative communities in Guy Hocquenghem's *Eve* and Vincent Borel's *Un Ruban noir*." In *French Cultural Studies*. Jean-Pierre Boulé and Murray Pratt, eds. 1998.

See also Barthes, Roland; Deleuze, Gilles; Foucault, Michel; France; French Literature; Gay; Homosexuality; Queer

Homer

Homer may or may not have been a historical individual. He is credited with the authorship of two great ancient Greek epics, the *Iliad* and the *Odyssey*. Twentieth-century scholarship believes these two texts reflect a long tradition of oral composition; bards working in the tradition learned a vast array of formulas they used to tell traditional stories, inventing the poems anew at least in some details at every telling. The two poems must have attained more or less their present form by the eighth century B.C.E. and started to circulate as texts attributed to Homer not long thereafter, thanks to the importation and adaptation of alphabetic writing.

As traditional epics, the poems memorialize earlier generations of legendary heroes and gods. The *Iliad* details events of the tenth and last year of the Trojan War, traditionally dated to the early twelfth century B.C.E. The ostensible aim of the Greek expedition was to recover Helen, whom the Trojan prince Paris had seduced and abducted from his Greek host and Helen's husband, Menelaus of Sparta, but the tale likely recalls elements of many a Bronze and early Iron Age siege. Troy, for example, the great walled city strategically located in northwestern Asia Minor, was sacked and rebuilt many times during the second millennium. The *Odyssey* tells the story of the homecoming (*nostos*) of Odysseus, one of the most notable of the Greek captains (whom the Latin tradition knows as Ulysses). Odysseus wanders on seas and amid exotic, sometimes monstrous peoples for ten years after the sack of Troy until he finally reaches his home island, Ithaca. He has been absent some twenty years, and his hall is filled with his wife Penelope's unruly suitors, who threaten his family and in particular his son, Telemachus. The epic ends only after a disguised Odysseus and Telemachus rout the suitors and Penelope recognizes Odysseus.

Penelope and Odysseus are a remarkable couple, celebrated by the poet for their "like-mindedness" (*homophrosune*). The significant responsibility given Penelope in this early work of Greek literature seems to indicate that women were less restricted in archaic Greece than in, for example, classical Athens. Of homoeroticism there is little (or no) trace in the *Odyssey*. In book three Odysseus' son Telemachus, seeking word of his absent father, visits Nestor. He is bunked with Nestor's son Peisistratos, who accompanies him on the next stage of his quest, to the Spartan court of Menelaus and Helen. The most that can be said about this incident is that it may reflect an assumption that Peisistratos and Telemakhos, both unmarried youths in their late teens, would prefer to sleep together than alone, and if additional pleasures for guest and a member of the host's family ensued, this was nothing that needed to be either said or denied.

In contrast, at the center of the *Iliad* is one of the most celebrated of all male-male friendships, the comradeship of Achilles, the "best of the Achaeans [Greeks]," and Patroklos. It is not suggested that Achilles has abandoned attachments to women (see, for example, the concluding lines of *Iliad* 9). Indeed, the crisis in the Greek camp that precipitates the events of the *Iliad* is, like the Trojan War itself, the result of intemperate heterosexual passion: Agamemnon, the Greek commander-in-chief, is forced to give up his Trojan concubine, considered booty, and demands that Achilles yield his concubine to him. Achilles, whose wrath is announced as the theme of the poem in its opening line, gives up his girl (Briseis), then withdraws from the Greek campaign. Only the death of Patroklos, filling in for Achilles and in Achilles' own armor, brings the Greek hero back to the battlefield, and then not to help the Greeks so much as to avenge his comrade's death at the hand of Hector, son of the king of Troy. Achilles mourns Patroklos' death, kills Hector, and defiles Hector's body, but nothing truly assuages his grief.

Homer does not speak about Achilles and Patroklos as "lovers." The quality of their relationship is notable, in the poem comparable in its depth only to that of Hector and Andromache. They both wish that after their deaths their bones be buried together (Il. 23.83 and 239–48), and so, tradition has it, they were (Od. 24.79). Classical Greeks looking back and reading through the perspective of their own times assumed they were lovers (e.g., Aeschines, *Against Timarchus* 142), and fragments of the lost Myrmidons of Aeschylus refer to kisses and lovemaking. Since Athenian male-male contact was modeled on a strict lover/beloved dichotomy, there was active debate about which of the two Homeric heroes played that role, a debate that could go either way since Homer provided (as the Athenians saw it) mixed signals, making Patroklos older but Achilles the greater fighter (and with "shaggy breast"). In Shakespeare's Troilus and Cressida the couple is presented in crudely sexual terms.

Ralph D. Hexter

Bibliography

Aeschines. *The Speeches*. Charles Darwin Adams, trans. Cambridge, Mass.: Harvard University Press, 1919.

Dover, K. J. *Greek Homosexuality*. Revised. Cambridge, Mass.: Harvard University Press, 1989.

Halperin, David "Heroes and Their Pals." *In One Hundred Years of Homosexuality*. New York: Routledge, 1990, 75–87.

Homer. *The Iliad*. Robert Fagles, trans. London: Penguin, 1990.

———. *The Odyssey*. Robert Fitzgerald, trans. New York: Vintage: 1990.

H

See also Athens; Friendship; Greece; Sparta

Homophile Movement

The homophile movement constituted the first wave of organized political activity in the United States aimed at securing civil rights for homosexuals and lesbians. In the 1950s, homosexual rights activists eager to combat the stereotype of the sex-obsessed homosexual began using the term *homophile* as a euphemism. The suffix was meant to suggest that homosexuality was an emotional as well as a sexual attraction and that homosexuals did not differ significantly from heterosexuals. The term was officially adopted by the movement in the early 1960s.

The early homophile movement was deeply influenced by the Communist Party's nationalistic approach to the "Negro question." Although the party's policy on homosexuality mirrored that of the government during the Cold War—it expelled homosexuals on the grounds that they could be blackmailed by its enemies—it provided homosexual rights activists with a powerful model. Henry Hay, Chuck Rowland, and Bob Hull, who in 1951 founded the Mattachine Society, the first homophile organization, were members of the Communist Party, relying heavily on the knowledge and organizing skills they had acquired as party activists. They formed discussion groups that sought to empower homosexuals by teaching them to see themselves as an oppressed minority with their own distinct culture. Membership remained small until adopting a party strategy, the society organized a demonstration protesting police entrapment, an oppressive practice directly affecting the mass of gay men.

Another influential figure in the early homophile movement was Edward Sagarin, who wrote under the pseudonym Donald Webster Cory. His pioneering study of the similarities between gays and other oppressed minorities, *The Homosexual in America* (1950), provided homosexual rights activists with a less militant approach. Unlike Hay, Rowland, and Hull, he did not see the value of building a separate homosexual culture in which gays and lesbians could take pride. Deeply influenced by Gunnar Myrdal's landmark study of racism, *The American Dilemma* (1944), he argued that the homosexual's problems stemmed from societal disapproval and that education and policy reform would improve his situation. In his view, the practices and forms of identity (frequenting gay bars, cruising in public places, and so on) homosexuals had created in response to their oppression were pathological and should be repudiated. Like Myrdal, Sagarin believed deeply in the myth of the American melting pot, and he was convinced that if homosexuals simply demonstrated that they did not differ significantly from heterosexuals, then like other minoritized groups, they would eventually gain acceptance by mainstream Americans.

Sagarin's influence on the homophile movement was ultimately greater than that of the more radical founders of the Mattachine Society. In the context of the McCarthy witch-hunts, Hay, Rowland, and Hull's links to the Communist Party were a liability that made the movement doubly vulnerable to political repression. Although the three activists had broken with the party because of its policy on homosexuals, questions about their politics persisted, leading some members of the Mattachine Society to propose requiring a loyalty oath. Their party affiliation aside, the three's emphasis on the importance of building a homosexual culture may have asked too much of rank-and-file activists. Men and women constantly made aware of their differences from mainstream American society were understandably reluctant to risk further marginalization by embracing those differences. Sagarin, by contrast, offered a way of achieving equality that accentuated the similarities rather than the differences between homosexuals and heterosexuals. With the ascendance of his approach, the homophile movement shifted its priorities and goals, focusing on educating a hostile public rather than engaging in militant political action.

Although leaders withheld information about the movement's radical origins, Hay, Rowland, and Hull's political vision (their emphasis on the distinctiveness of homosexual culture, their goal of building a mass movement, their political militancy) remained a vital, if marginalized, force in the movement. Whereas Hay and Hull distanced themselves from the movement following the repudiation of their ideas by the Mattachine Society, Rowland became a writer for *One*, the most widely circulated of the magazines associated with the movement. Frustrated by the movement's political timidity, he advocated the use of more confrontational tactics. Even after he left the magazine in 1955, *One* continued to publish articles expressing a variety of viewpoints intended to spark controversy. Editorials regularly attacked the medical model of homosexuality. A monthly column reported on oppressive police practices such as bar raids and shakedowns. And writers debated whether the homosexual subculture was a source of strength and courage or a destructive force that instilled shame and self-hatred. In refusing to adopt a party line, *One* may have been more effective than official movement organizations in shaping the consciousness of average gays and lesbians.

In the 1960s, a new generation of activists, deeply influenced by the civil rights movement, proved more receptive to Hay, Rowland, and Hull's vision of a militant mass movement. In opposition to their leaders, these activists began to experiment with more confrontational tactics designed to attract the attention of the media. They picketed government agencies that expelled homosexuals and lesbians, lobbied for legislation barring discrimination, and organized demonstrations against police harassment. More interested in gaining the support of gays and lesbians than that of heterosexuals, they also tried to build a national organization of homophile groups modeled on the civil rights movement. But they were unable to overcome the ideological differences and organizational rivalries that had long divided the movement. The Daughters of Bilitis, an organization of lesbians founded in 1956, understandably resented the focus on issues such as sodomy laws that primarily affected gay men and discouraged its members from participating in the coalition. Other groups continued to believe in the efficacy of education and resented the new militancy. Although at a conference in 1968 the movement officially adopted the confrontational motto "Gay Is Good," the show of unity was largely symbolic. The disaffection of organizations such as the Daughters of Bilitis indicated that differences over strategy were greater than the radicals realized. Following the Stonewall rebellion of 1969, the movement collapsed, displaced by gay liberation.

Robert J. Corber

Bibliography

Adam, Barry D. *The Rise of the Gay and Lesbian Movement.* Boston: Twayne, 1987.

D'Emilio, John. *Sexual Politics, Sexual Communities: The Making of a Homosexual Minority in the United States, 1940–1970.* Chicago: University of Chicago Press, 1983.

Cory, Donald Webster. *The Homosexual in America.* New York: Greenberg, 1951.

Katz, Jonathan Ned. *Gay American History: Lesbians and Gay Men in the U.S.A.,* rev. ed. New York: Meridian, 1992.

Marotta, Toby. *The Politics of Homosexuality: How Lesbians and Gay Men Have Made Themselves a Political and Social Force in Modern America.* Boston: Houghton Mifflin, 1981.

See also Activism; Cory, Donald Webster; Gay Liberation; Hay, Harry; Mattachine Society; McCarthyism; *ONE* Magazine; Stonewall Rebellion

Homophobia

Homophobia is the fear or hatred of gay people and homosexuality. The term is usually used without regard to gender, although in some instances "lesbophobia" and "antilesbianism" are employed to denote enmity toward lesbians in particular. Homophobia is sometimes distinguished from heterosexism and heterocentrism, which refers to "a belief system that values heterosexuality as superior to and/or more 'natural' than homosexuality." In this context, heterosexism and heterocentrism are used to describe more subtle expressions of prejudice while homophobia is employed with specific reference either to psychological reactions against homosexuality or overt discrimination against gay people, motivated by hatred. However, a number of commentators have pointed out that homophobia and heterosexism exist on a continuum of antigay attitudes and behaviors, and homophobia is often used to designate any form of antihomosexual bias.

The word *homophobia* was coined around 1969 but gained wider currency after the publication of George Weinberg's *Society and the Healthy Homosexual* (1972), which included detailed and insightful discussion of the topic. Weinberg defined homophobia as "the dread of being in close quarters with homosexuals—and in the case of homosexuals themselves, self-loathing . . . revulsion toward homosexuals and often the desire to inflict punishment at retribution." Weinberg, a psychotherapist, focused primarily on the psychological dimensions of homophobia, characterizing it as an irrational fear of homosexuality. The concept was soon expanded to include cultural prejudices against homosexuals and has been described as "any of the varieties of negative attitudes which arise from fear or dislike of homosexuality" or "any belief system which supports negative myths and stereotypes about homosexual people." Since Weinberg's groundbreaking study,

H several theories attempting to explain the psychological origins of homophobia have been advanced. One theory, influenced by the work of American psychoanalyst Harry Stack Sullivan (1892–1949), associates homophobia with "homosexual panic," extreme fear of homosexuality in oneself. Another theory identifies homophobia as an element of erotophobia, a general fear of sexuality.

Internalized homophobia refers to gay people's absorption, from the larger society, of negative ideas about homosexuality. Studies conducted during the 1990s suggest that those who hold such beliefs tend to have lower self-esteem and less enduring or satisfactory relationships than do other gay men and lesbians. They are also less likely to be open about their sexual orientation, more prone to suffer from depression, and less inclined to maintain ties to gay community institutions. Researchers have also pointed to internalized homophobia as a cause of increased use of alcohol and drugs among gay men and lesbians. It has been identified with high suicide rates among gay and bisexual teenagers, failure to take effective safer-sex precautions among young gay men, and increased emotional stress among HIV-positive gay men.

Institutionalized homophobia occurs when antigay intolerance and discrimination are made part of established social systems and institutions. Examples include school curricula that do not incorporate discussion of gay issues, immigration and tax laws that do not treat same-sex partners equally with legally recognized spouses, legal prohibitions against consensual homosexual behaviors, and corporations that do not provide domestic partnership benefits for unmarried couples or fail to offer such benefits on an equal basis with those given to married people. The English language's lack of widely accepted positive terms for same-sex partners, and its abundance of pejorative labels for lesbians and gay men, are also evidence of systemic homophobia.

Suzanne Pharr, Barbara Smith, and other social critics have argued that homophobia intersects in important ways with other forms of discrimination such as sexism, racism, and classism—despite apparent differences in the social and state mechanisms that reproduce these inequalities. Pharr contends that homophobia supports sexism because condemnation of gay people who do not conform to gender expectations helps maintain rigidly conventionalized roles for women and men. She concludes that this cultural homophobia has significant economic consequences for women because antilesbian censure of women who do not fit "traditional" gender categories limits their abilities to achieve parity in the workplace, whatever their sexual orientations. Smith focuses on the relative lack of public outrage that followed a 1982 police raid on Blues, a New York City bar frequented by African American, working-class lesbians. She asserts that scant media coverage of the incident indicated a refusal to recognize the connections that exist among homophobia, racism, sexism, and classism. She goes on to state that such blindness about the relationships among oppressions confirms homophobia as the one prejudice that is acceptable even to otherwise progressive people. To counteract ingrained homophobia, Smith recommends education that "focuses in a positive way upon issues of sexual identity, sexuality, and sexism" as well as bridge-building among civil rights, feminist, gay rights, and other social activists.

Homophobia has had significant impact on social understanding of, research about, and medical treatment of AIDS. For example, it contributed to the slowness of government agencies, during the Reagan and subsequent administrations, in acknowledging the AIDS crisis and initiating research and information programs. Cultural critic Simon Watney has argued that homophobia is the reason that AIDS is often equated with homosexuality in public discourses; biased assumptions about homosexuality lead to the false conclusion that a natural correspondence exists between two supposed illnesses. Similarly, efforts to educate the public about HIV transmission have often characterized AIDS as a gay disease instead of focusing on the behaviors by which the virus is communicated. In other instances, the fact that gay men are at high risk for HIV is ignored in educational materials aimed at heterosexuals. Homophobia is also responsible for both the common misconception that lesbians are at high risk for AIDS and the lack of media attention paid to lesbians who are HIV-positive.

Assessing the prevalence or demographic distribution of individuals' homophobic attitudes is difficult. However, research indicates that, in the United States, men are more likely to hold antigay beliefs than are women, and that both men and women express greater antipathy toward gay men than toward lesbians. According to one study, young adults are often less homophobic than are older people. Women and men who have openly gay people among their coworkers, friends, or relatives also have comparatively low rates of homophobia. This seems to suggest that greater visibility for gay people and issues may be an important first step in combating antihomosexual prejudice.

Charles Krinsky

Bibliography

Abelove, Henry, Michèle Aina Barale, and David M. Halperin eds. *The Lesbian and Gay Studies Reader*. New York: Routledge, 1993.

Berkman, Cathy S., and Gail Zinberg. "Homophobia and Heterosexism in Social Workers." *Social Work* 42, no. 4 (July 1997): 319–32.

Ficarrotto, Thomas J. "Racism, Sexism, and Erotophobia: Attitudes of Heterosexuals Toward Homosexuals." *Journal of Homosexuality* 19, no. 1 (January 1990): 111–16.

Pharr, Suzanne. *Homophobia: A Weapon of Sexism*, 2d ed. Berkeley: University of California Press, 1997.

Rothblum, Esther D., and Lynne A. Bond, eds. *Preventing Heterosexism and Homophobia*. Thousand Oaks, Calif.: Sage, 1996.

Sears, James T., and Walter L. Williams, eds. *Overcoming Heterosexism and Homophobia: Strategies That Work*. New York: Columbia University Press, 1997.

Sedgwick, Eve Kosofsky. *Between Men: English Literature and Male Homosocial Desire*. New York: Columbia University Press, 1985.

Weinberg, George. *Society and the Healthy Homosexual*. New York: St. Martin's, 1972.

See also AIDS; Gay Bashing; Gay Rights in the United States; Gender; Hate Crimes; Homosexuality; Psychological and Psychoanalytic Perspectives on Homosexuality; U.S. Law: Discrimination

Homosexual Panic

"Homosexual panic" is the popular label for a theory frequently advanced by criminal defendants (almost always males) seeking to excuse their violent crimes against lesbians or gay men. The most prominent form of the theory suggests that individuals who are latent homosexuals may, spurred by fear of their own homosexuality, have a violent response to others whom they perceive to be homosexual. Variations on this theory may be advanced in support of three defensive arguments: (1) that the defendant was insane at the time of the attack, and thus not criminally responsible for his actions; (2) that the defendant suffered from diminished capacity at the time of the attack, and thus did not have the mental state necessary for conviction on the most serious charges; or (3) that the defendant acted reasonably to defend himself from a homosexual advance.

Although American jurisdictions differ in their formulation and degree of recognition of insanity as a defense for murder or other serious violent crimes, most jurisdictions allow defendants to introduce evidence that they were incapable of distinguishing right from wrong owing to mental illness or defect and thus should not be held criminally responsible for their actions. Defendants acquitted by reason of insanity are normally committed to mental institutions until such time as their mental illness or defect is found to be cured or ameliorated such that they no longer present a risk to others in the community.

The use of the homosexual panic theory in support of an insanity defense can be criticized in light of the American Psychiatric and Psychological Associations' findings that homosexuality is not a mental illness. Only recently, however, has the American Psychiatric Association removed from its diagnostic lexicon the concept of a mental illness stemming from personal discomfort with sexual orientation. It is still possible to find cases in which psychiatrists or psychologists testify as expert witnesses for the defense, contending that because of "homosexual panic," the defendant did not appreciate what he was doing at the time of the attack.

A diminished capacity defense may be used to negate an element of the crime charged against the defendant. Evidence of "homosexual panic" might persuade the court that the defendant's murderous activity was actually a "heat of passion" response to the victim's provocation, resulting in an acquittal from murder charges but a conviction for manslaughter, which normally carries a shorter prison term. The same theoretical problems underlying use of the homosexual panic theory to support an insanity defense would logically pertain to its use in a diminished capacity case.

The most frequent use of a homosexual panic defense does not rely on an argument that the defendant is a latent homosexual whose fear of his own sexuality causes his severe reaction to homosexuals. Rather, defendants may argue that they acted reasonably in self-defense when subjected to a homosexual advance. When "psychological" explanations are offered in such cases, they may rely on an argument that the defendant's "macho" personality (or, by contrast, insecurity about his masculinity) leads

H him to overreact to a homosexual advance by responding with deadly force.

The law permits somebody subjected to an unwelcome sexual advance to respond with reasonable force necessary to repel the advance. Response with deadly force normally requires that the defendant have reasonably believed that he was in danger of death or serious physical injury. Under these doctrines, defendants may argue that they were attempting to repel a forcible homosexual rape.

Because there are no surviving witnesses to most murders other than the defendant, the defendant's version of what happened may be the only version offered to the court. This provides an opportunity for the defendant to fabricate a homosexual panic defense based on a fictional provocation, or to treat an innocent provocation as forcible or coercive. Unfortunately, the normal skepticism of courts toward murder defendants' stories is sometimes abandoned when the story concerns a homosexual advance, especially if there is independent evidence that the victim was gay or had made homosexual advances toward other people in the past.

No appellate court in the United States has explicitly adopted the homosexual panic theory as a complete defense to a serious, violent crime against a victim who is or is perceived to be gay. However, the defense appears to have been successfully used in many cases to persuade juries to acquit defendants, or to convict them of less serious offenses than charged by the prosecution. If the court allows the defendant to introduce testimony about the victim's homosexuality, accompanied by psychiatric or psychological testimony about the defendant, the jury is free to draw its own conclusions about the defendant's psychological state, relying on individual jurors' own beliefs about homosexuality. Although the prosecution may request the court to instruct the jury about the problems with relying on such evidence, unless the court entirely excludes the evidence, its impact on the jury's deliberations cannot be fully circumscribed. Furthermore, jurors may not be questioned afterward by the court about their reasons for their verdict. However, courts may set aside jury verdicts that appear to have been severely tainted by the introduction of prejudicial, nonrelevant evidence.

Homosexual panic theories may be even more significant at an earlier stage in criminal proceedings, when a prosecutor is determining whether to bring charges and what level of offense to charge. Prosecutors may offer suspected murderers lenient plea bargains, either because of their own belief in homosexual panic theories or because they believe that the court will allow such testimony on behalf of the defendant and that it will cause most jurors to sympathize with the defendant.

The homosexual panic theory has become more controversial among courts as lesbian and gay community groups have organized to combat anti-gay violence and have educated courts and law enforcement officials. There is a trend toward disallowing evidence concerning the homosexuality of the victim or psychiatric or psychological evidence in support of homosexual panic theories unless there is corroborative evidence about the circumstances of the attack. But in many jurisdictions such evidence is still introduced, and juries may, as a consequence, acquit defendants of murder charges in favor of less serious manslaughter charges.

Arthur S. Leonard

Bibliography

Bagnall, Robert G., Patrick C. Gallagher, and Joni L. Goldstein. "Burdens on Gay Litigants and Bias in the Court System: Homosexual Panic, Child Custody, and Anonymous Parties." 19 Harv. Civ. Rts.-Civ. Lib. L. Rev. 497 (Summer 1984).

"Developments in the Law—Sexual Orientation and the Law, II. Gay Men and Lesbians in the Criminal Justice System, B. Gay Men and Lesbians as Victims in the Criminal Justice System." 102 Harv. L. Rev. 1508, 1541 (May 1989).

Dressler, Joshua. "When 'Heterosexual' Men Kill 'Homosexual' Men: Reflections on Provocation Law, Sexual Advances, and the 'Reasonable Man.' " Standard, 85 J. Crim. L. & Criminology 726 (Winter 1995).

Mison, Robert B. "Comment, Homophobia in Manslaughter: The Homosexual Advance As Insufficient Provocation," 80 Calif. L. Rev. 133 (January 1992).

See also Civil Rights (U.S. Law); Homphobia; U.S. Law: Discrimination

Homosexuality

The word *homosexuality* appeared in print for the first time in German (*Homosexualität*) in 1869. It was coined by an obscure Austro-Hungarian writer and translator, Karl Maria Kertbeny (1824–1882). Kertbeny's family was from Bavaria in what is now

Germany, and his surname was originally Benkert, but he grew up in Budapest, and he eventually adopted an inverted, Hungarianized version of his German surname, although he continued to write in German.

Kertbeny claimed (not very convincingly) to be "sexually normal" himself. Nonetheless, he participated in a lobbying campaign to persuade the North German Federation, a newly formed union of previously independent states led by Prussia, to omit article 143 of the Prussian penal code, which criminalized sexual relations between men, from its own penal code, a draft of which was being circulated at the time. In 1869, accordingly, Kertbeny published in Leipzig, some months apart, two anonymous pamphlets that took the form of open letters to the Prussian minister of justice, and it was in these two texts that the word *homosexuality* made its historic debut. Kertbeny argued that a number of great men had been homosexual, that the condition was innate, not acquired, and that it was therefore pointless to criminalize it. His effort was unsuccessful: the penal code of the North German Federation retained the old Prussian law as article 152, and in 1871 that article was incorporated into the new penal code of the German Empire as paragraph 175, which criminalized "unnatural lewdness" (*widernatürliche Unzucht*) between men. The law remained in force for the next hundred years, strengthened by the Nazis in 1935 and retained by West Germany until 1969.

The word *homosexuality,* then, was originally a pro-gay coinage, invented for the purpose of political activism. It did not retain that character for long, although some time passed before it entered the languages of Europe. The word itself would have been entirely forgotten had it not been for Gustav Jaeger, a zoologist and a friend of Kertbeny. Jaeger decided to employ *homosexuality* in 1880, in the second edition of a work entitled *Entdeckung der Seele* (*The Discovery of the Soul*), where it attracted the attention of the great forensic sexologist Richard von Krafft-Ebing. Krafft-Ebing in turn borrowed the word from Jaeger in 1887, for the second edition of his massive encyclopedia of sexual deviance, the *Psychopathia Sexualis*, and he employed it with increasing frequency and freedom in the many later editions of that vastly influential work. That is how the word acquired its medical and forensic connotations, mutating from a gay-friendly affirmation into a clinical designation.

Homosexuality appears in the writings of late-nineteenth-century and early-twentieth-century sexologists and psychiatrists, notably Sigmund Freud, as well as in the writings of the early homosexual activists, but it did not begin to achieve wider currency in Europe until the Eulenburg affair, a homosexual scandal at the court of the German emperor, in 1907–1908. Hostile French newspapers, eager to publicize the details of the scandal but requiring a word that sounded scientific and clinical enough to be used in print without outraging contemporary standards of decency, fixed upon the German term and imported it into French usage. It appears in a French dictionary, the *Larousse mensuel illustré*, as early as December 1907. Less than a year later, Edward Westermarck, writing in English for a scholarly audience in *The Origin and Development of the Moral Ideas*, could already refer to "what is nowadays commonly called homosexual love." And in 1914 George Bernard Shaw used the adjective *homosexual* without further explanation in the *New Statesman*, a mass-circulation newspaper.

Despite these signs of increasing currency, *homosexuality* and its derivatives were slow to enter the vocabulary of even educated people in England and the United States. When a Swiss friend asked the future English novelist J. R. Ackerley in 1918, "Are you homo or hetero?" Ackerley was mystified; as he recalls in his memoirs, "I had never heard either term before." Another English novelist, T. C. Worsley, reports that in 1929 "the word [*homosexual*] . . . was not in general use, as it is now. Then it was still a technical term, the implications of which I was not entirely aware." Both writers were gay men who either had received or shortly would receive a university education at Cambridge. It was not until the 1950s that *homosexuality* entered popular English and American usage, largely as a result of the Kinsey reports.

But what did the word mean? *Homosexuality* originally referred to a sexual drive directed toward persons of the same sex as the sex of the person who was driven by it (from *homo*, a Greek prefix for "same" or "like," and *sexus*, Latin for "sex/gender"). It did not initially figure in a binary system of sexual classification as the polar opposite of heterosexuality, however. For example, in the draft of a private letter in May 1868, Kertbeny indicated that the adjectives *homosexual* and *heterosexual* constituted merely two of the four terms he had devised to map out exhaustively the spectrum of human sexual object-choice as he understood it. In his published pamphlets of 1869, moreover, he did not use *heterosexual* at all, referring instead to the opposite of *ho-*

H *mosexual* as *normalsexual*. As a result, the meaning of *heterosexuality* continued to shift, sometimes signifying a sexual perversion, and being defined as late as 1923 by Merriam-Webster's *New International Dictionary* as a "morbid sexual passion for one of the opposite sex." It was the earlier consolidation of the meaning of *homosexuality* that ultimately helped to stabilize the definition of *heterosexuality,* which is historically and conceptually dependent on *homosexuality* for its current meaning.

Unlike other late-nineteenth-century terms for aspects of same-sex sexual desire or behavior, such as "contrary sexual feeling," "sexual inversion," "Uranism," and "the third sex," *homosexuality* was not coined to interpret the phenomenon it described or to attach a particular psychological or medical theory to it. Perhaps that is the secret of its success: different writers, with very different notions about sex and gender, found the term easy to adapt to their own ideological purposes. It may also explain why the term, which began life as a purely descriptive, conceptually empty category, so quickly absorbed from those who used it a number of quite specific substantive notions about the nature of same-sex sexual desire and behavior, thereby becoming a repository for a number of very different ideological perspectives. In any case, the single word *homosexuality* has come to condense a variety of mutually conflicting ideas about same-sex sexual attraction and an assortment of conceptual models for understanding it. This broad range of possible meanings is what helps to make *homosexuality* such an irresistible, powerful, and ambiguous term nowadays. For that reason, it is less useful to insist on any one definition of *homosexuality* than it is to describe and to account for the conceptual incoherence that has now become inseparable from both the term and the category.

The modern concept of *homosexuality* is distinguished by its unprecedented absorption and combination of at least three different, previously uncorrelated concepts: (1) a psychiatric notion of perverted or pathological *psychosexual orientation,* derived from nineteenth-century medicine, an essentially psychological concept that applies to the inner life of the individual and does not necessarily presume same-sex sexual behavior; (2) a psychoanalytic notion of same-sex sexual object-choice or desire, derived from Freud and his co-workers, which is a category of erotic intentionality and does not necessarily imply the existence of a permanent sexual orientation, let alone a deviant or pathological one (since, according to Freud, most normal individuals make an unconscious homosexual object-choice at some point in their fantasy lives); and (3) a sociological notion of sexually *deviant behavior,* derived from nineteenth- and twentieth-century forensic inquiries into "social problems," which focuses on nonstandard sexual practice and does not necessarily refer to erotic psychology or sexual orientation (since same-sex sexual behavior, as, for example, Kinsey understood it, is not the exclusive property of those with a homosexual sexual orientation, nor is it necessarily pathological, since it is widely represented in the population). So neither a notion of orientation, a notion of object-choice, nor a notion of behavior alone is sufficient to generate the modern definition of homosexuality; rather, the notion seems to depend on the unstable conjunction of all three. *Homosexuality* is at once a psychological condition, an erotic desire, and a sexual practice.

Hence, *homosexuality* is capable of being conceived in both universalizing and minoritizing terms. Some of the time, that is, *homosexuality* may be understood to represent an actual or potential element in everyone's experience, whatever her or his sexual orientation (this is the universalizing model), whereas the rest of the time *homosexuality* may be considered a distinctive characteristic possessed only by a minority of homosexual individuals (the minoritizing model). The relation between homosexual identity and gender identity is similarly vexed. Some of the time *homosexuality* appears as the logical extension and intensification of an integrated gender identity: according to such an outlook, it is the most womanly women, those who are the most closely identified with other women and with their gender, who are lesbians, whereas gay men embody the values of patriarchal masculinity and male supremacism at their most extreme. But at other times homosexuality appears as a betrayal of gender identity: according to this latter outlook, the true lesbian is butch, aggressive, masculine, whereas the typical gay man is effeminate— a fairy, a sissy, a queen. All these views are likely to be held, in uneasy combination and to differing degrees, by the same person, and none is likely to achieve a sufficient degree of ascendancy over the others to destroy their plausibility and eliminate their appeal once and for all. Hence the state of conceptual crisis surrounding notions of sexuality today.

At the same time as it absorbs earlier notions about sex and gender, *homosexuality* as a concept and a category also cuts across previous sexual classifications as well as previous ways of making sense of same-sex sexual contacts. For thousands of years European cultures, which had observed and evaluated different modalities of love, including same-sex love, did not systematically distinguish or conceptualize sexual relations between persons of the same sex as a single, discrete, homogeneous entity in contradistinction to sexual relations between persons of different sexes. The very notion of homosexuality, by contrast, implies that same-sex sexual feeling and expression, in all the many different forms they take, constitute a single thing, called *homosexuality,* that can be thought of as a single integrated phenomenon, and is distinct and separate from *heterosexuality*. This development marks a radical departure and reflects a distinctively modern concept and experience of sexuality.

In many premodern societies, the sameness or difference of the sexes of the persons who engaged in a sexual act was less important than the extent to which sexual acts either violated or conformed to the precepts of religion or to the norms of conduct deemed appropriate to individual sexual actors by reason of their gender, age, and social status. In particular, sexual acts were often categorized in terms of a hierarchy of sexual (or phallic) roles, according to which the sexually insertive or "active" partner was thought to demonstrate, by virtue of penetrating the sexually receptive or "passive" partner, masculine precedence, power, and authority—even if she was a woman. The asymmetrical gesture of sexual (or phallic) penetration organized the sexual act around a polarity of active and passive roles and produced a series of distinctions between the sexual partners in terms of gender, power, penetration, activity/passivity, and social status.

Where the emphasis on asymmetry, polarity, and hierarchy is so marked, notions of *homosexuality* can have little place, because such notions assimilate *both* partners in a same-sex sexual contact to *the same status*, regardless of their sexual role, social identity, or gender style. That is precisely the sort of categorical collapse that traditional European notions of sexual hierarchy and asymmetry resisted. Instead, earlier sexual discourses looked at same-sex sexual behavior either from the point of view of the partner whose sexual role conformed to his or her gender role and social status or from the point of view of the partner whose sexual role violated his or her gender role and social status. Discourses of pederasty or sodomy are typical of the former approach; discourses of inversion are typical of the latter.

Pederasty or sodomy views the sexual pursuit of adolescent males by adult males from the point of view of the senior partner, for it is he who is thought to experience the greater share of erotic feeling in the relation. The junior partner enters the erotic scene as the object of his older lover's desire, not as an erotic subject in his own right. For example, fourteenth- and fifteenth-century Italian usage applies the terms *sodomy* and *sodomite* only to the "active" partner in sodomitical relations. Although love, emotional intimacy, and tenderness are not necessarily absent from the relation, the distribution of erotic passion and sexual pleasure is assumed to be more or less lopsided, with the older, "active" partner being the subject of desire and the recipient of the greater share of pleasure from a younger partner who feels no comparable desire and derives no comparable pleasure from the contact, and whose motivation to participate in a sexual encounter must be supplied by his older lover in the form of gifts, money, or threats. As an erotic experience, pederasty or sodomy refers to the "active" partner only. Although European communities punished sodomy, often savagely, they tended to regard the "active" male partners merely as morally depraved rather than as different, abnormal *types* of people.

By contrast, inversion was regarded as an abnormality and an invert as an abnormal type of person. Inversion applied to those who reversed, or "inverted," their proper sex and gender roles by taking up roles or identities or personal styles associated with the opposite sex. A desire to be sexually penetrated combined with effeminate mannerisms on the part of a man, or sexual aggression and penetration combined with masculine traits on the part of a woman were seen as markers of inversion. A male whose motivation to participate in an act of sodomy as the "passive" partner was sexual, who did not need to be offered gifts or money, who willingly pursued "active" male partners was considered a different *kind* of being, an invert. Premodern terms for inverts included *catamite* and *pathic* in the case of men, *tribade* in the case of women, *inversion* itself being a late-nineteenth-century coinage.

The originality of *homosexuality* as a category and a concept can be seen more clearly in this light. Earlier discourses, whether of sodomy or inversion, referred to only one of the partners—to the "active"

H partner in the first case, to the effeminate male or masculine female in the second. The other partner, the one who was not motivated by sexual desire in the first case, the one who was not gender-deviant in the second, did not qualify for inclusion in the category. *Homosexuality* applies to both partners, whether active or passive, whether gendered normatively or deviantly. The hallmark of *homosexuality,* in fact, is the refusal to distinguish between same-sex sexual partners or to rank them—by treating one of them as more (or less) homosexual than the other. Kinsey can be taken as representative of this modern outlook. Dismissing the tendency of some men to define their own sexual identity according to a role-specific, pre-homosexual model—to consider themselves straight because they only received oral sex from other men and never performed it themselves—Kinsey wrote that all "physical contacts with other males" that result in orgasm are "by any strict definition . . . homosexual." According to Kinsey, it doesn't matter who sucks whom.

Thus, *homosexuality*—both as a concept and as a social practice—significantly rearranges and reinterprets earlier patterns of erotic organization, and as such it has a number of important practical consequences. First of all, under the aegis of homosexuality the significance of gender and of gender roles for categorizing sexual acts and sexual actors fades in significance. Thus, one effect of the concept of "homosexuality" is to detach sexual object-choice from any necessary connection with gender identity, making it possible to ascribe "homosexuality" to women and to men whose gender styles and outward appearance or manner are perfectly normative.

This conceptual transformation has not been either total or absolute. Many people nowadays, both gay and nongay, continue to draw a direct connection between gender deviance and homosexuality. Despite the dominance of the categories of homosexuality and heterosexuality, "active" women and "passive" men, as well as effeminate men and masculine women, are still considered somehow *more* homosexual than other, less flamboyantly deviant persons who also make homosexual object-choices. Here we can discern the force with which earlier, prehomosexual sexual categories continue to exert their authority within the newer conceptual universe of homo- and heterosexuality. In some quarters, it still matters a lot who sucks whom. Nonetheless, one effect of the modern homo/

heterosexual model has been to downplay the taxonomic significance of gender identities and sexual roles.

The homo/heterosexual model has other consequences. Homosexuality translates same-sex sexual relations into the register of sameness and mutuality. Homosexual relations no longer necessarily imply an asymmetry of social identities or sexual positions, nor are they inevitably articulated in terms of hierarchies of power, age, gender, or sexual role (which, again, is not to deny that such hierarchies may continue to function meaningfully in a lesbian or gay male context). Homosexual relations are not necessarily lopsided in their distribution of erotic pleasure or desire. Rather, like heterosexual romantic love, the notion of homosexuality implies that it is possible for sexual partners to bond with one another not on the basis of their difference but on the basis of their sameness, their identity of desire and orientation and sexuality. Homosexual relations cease to be compulsorily structured by a polarization of identities and roles (active/passive, insertive/receptive, masculine/feminine, or man/boy). Exclusive, lifelong, companionate, romantic, and mutual homosexual love becomes possible for both partners. Homosexual relations are not merely organized according to the requirements or prescriptions of large-scale social institutions, such as kinship systems, age-classes, or initiation rituals; rather, they function as principles of social organization in their own right and give rise to independent and freestanding social institutions.

Homosexuality is now set over against heterosexuality. Homosexual object-choice, in and of itself, is seen as marking a difference from heterosexual object-choice. Homo- and heterosexuality have become more or less mutually exclusive forms of human subjectivity, different *kinds* of human sexuality, and any feeling or expression of heterosexual desire is thought to rule out the likelihood of any feeling or expression of homosexual desire on the part of the same individual. Sexual object-choice attaches to a notion of sexual orientation, such that sexual behavior is seen to express an underlying and permanent psychosexual feature of the human subject. Hence, people are routinely assigned to one or the other of two sexual species on the basis of their sexual object-choice and orientation.

In short, homosexuality is more than same-sex sexual object-choice, more even than conscious erotic same-sex preference. Homosexuality is the specification of same-sex sexual object-choice in and of itself as an overriding principle of sexual and social difference. Homosexuality is part of a new system of sexuality, which functions as a means of personal individuation: it assigns to each individual a sexual orientation and a sexual identity. As such, homosexuality introduces a novel element into social organization, into the social articulation of human difference, into the social production of desire, and ultimately into the social construction of the self.   *David Halperin*

Bibliography

Adam, Barry D. "Structural Foundations of the Gay World." *Comparative Studies in Society and History* 27 (1985): 658–671. Reprinted In *Queer Theory/Sociology*. Steven Seidman, ed. Oxford: Blackwell, 1996. 111–26.

Bray, Alan. *Homosexuality in Renaissance England.* London: Gay Men's Press, 1982.

Chauncey, George Jr. "From Sexual Inversion to Homosexuality: The Changing Medical Conceptualization of Female Deviance." In *Passion and Power: Sexuality in History*. Kathy Peiss and Christina Simmons, eds. Philadelphia: Temple University Press, 1989, 87–117.

Davidson, Arnold I. "Sex and the Emergence of Sexuality." *Critical Inquiry* 14 (1987/88): 16–48.

Féray, Jean-Claude. "Une Histoire critique du mot homosexualité." *Arcadie* 28, nos. 325–28 (1981): 11–21, 115–24, 171–81, 246–58.

Foucault, Michel. *The History of Sexuality.* Volume 1, *An Introduction.* Robert Hurley, trans. New York: Random House, 1978.

Halperin, David M. *One Hundred Years of Homosexuality and Other Essays on Greek Love.* New York: Routledge, 1990.

Herzer, Manfred. "Kertbeny and the Nameless Love." *Journal of Homosexuality* 12, no. 1 (1985): 1–26.

Katz, Jonathan Ned. *The Invention of Heterosexuality.* New York: Dutton, 1995.

Kennedy, Hubert. *Ulrichs: The Life and Works of Karl Heinrich Ulrichs, Pioneer of the Modern Gay Movement.* Boston: Alyson, 1988.

Kinsey, Alfred C., Wardell B. Pomeroy, and Clyde E. Martin. *Sexual Behavior in the Human Male.* Philadelphia: W. B. Saunders, 1948.

Rocke, Michael. *Forbidden Friendships: Homosexuality and Male Culture in Renaissance Florence.* New York: Oxford University Press, 1996.

Sedgwick, Eve Kosofsky. *Epistemology of the Closet.* Berkeley: University of California Press, 1990.

See also Ackerley, J. R.; Freud, Sigmund; Inversion; Kertbeny, Karl Maria; Kinsey, Alfred C.; Krafft-Ebing, Psychological and Psychoanalytical Approaches to Homosexuality; Richard von; Paragraph 175; Pederasty; Sexology; Sodomy; Third Sex

Hooker, Evelyn (1907–1996)

American psychologist who was one of the early pioneers in the depathologization of homosexuality. Hooker was responsible for breakthrough studies on male homosexuality in the 1950s and 1960s, in which she proved that gay men were no more likely to be mentally ill than straight people. All previous studies of male homosexuality had collected their data either from men who had been arrested for soliciting or from men either institutionalized or in outpatient psychological care because of their homosexuality. Realizing that this approach practically guaranteed a population with numerous psychological problems, Hooker designed her study around "normal" gay men, whom she recruited in part through the Mattachine Society in Los Angeles. She concluded that the psychological profiles of gay men not in therapy were indistinguishable from a similar group of straight men, and that homosexuality did not necessarily imply pathology. In the 1960s, she turned to investigating the social life of gay urban men, describing how they created a social identity and structures to allow for their self-acceptance. In 1967, she was appointed chair of a National Institute of Mental Health committee on homosexuality; this committee's final report, which reinforced the Kinsey studies' assertions that sexuality existed across a continuum, argued that homosexuals should not be discriminated against in employment and implied that tolerance for those people who identified as gay was the best social policy.

A documentary film of Hooker's life and work received wide critical attention. Her work, along with Kinsey's, paved the way for the pre-Stonewall homophile movement's many successes in combatting discrimination and prejudice, and she was an active writer for the *Mattachine Review*.

Douglas J. Eisner

Bibliography

D'Emilio, John. *Sexual Politics, Sexual Communities: The Making of a Homosexual Minority in*

H

the United States, 1940–1970. Chicago: University Chicago Press, 1983, 117, 141, 217.

Hooker, Evelyn. "Adjustment of the Male Overt Homosexual." *Mattachine Review* (December 1957): 32–39, and (January 1958): 4–11.

———. "Male Homosexuals and Their 'Worlds.'" In *Sexual Inversion: The Multiple Roots of Homosexuality*. Judd Marmor, ed. New York, 1965, 83–107.

National Institute of Mental Health. *Final Report of the Task Force on Homosexuality*. Washington, D.C.: GPO, 1969.

See also Counseling; Kinsey, Alfred; Mattachine Society; Psychological and Psychoanalytic Perspectives on Homosexuality

Hoover, J. Edgar (1900–1972)

J. Edgar Hoover first gained prominence for his role in the Palmer raids of the early twenties. As head of the General Intelligence Division of the Justice Department, he supervised the roundup and deportation of foreign-born radicals ordered by Attorney General A. Mitchell Palmer following the great strike wave of 1919. When Attorney General Harlan Fiske Stone reorganized the FBI in 1924, he rewarded Hoover for his role in the Red scare by appointing him director, a position that he held until his death in 1972. Hoover had been trained in political countersubversion rather than law enforcement, and thus his appointment legitimated the Right's tendency to confuse radicalism with crime. Hoover's lifelong obsession with the Red menace led him, ironically, to transform the FBI into a mirror reflection of the KGB. The McCarthy witchhunts of the 1950s would have been impossible without his willing cooperation. He identified the Communists and fellow travelers subpoenaed by Congress and enforced the blacklist that prevented those who refused to name names from finding employment.

Throughout his career Hoover's political enemies circulated rumors that he and Assistant Director Clyde Tolson were lovers, but he was able to silence those enemies by threatening to release incriminating information about their private lives. After his death, photographs of Hoover and Tolson in drag surfaced, intensifying speculation about their homosexuality. This speculation raises troubling questions for scholars of gay history and culture. The Right has treated Hoover's homosexuality as a dirty secret, the

Left, as further evidence of his insidiousness. But other lessons can be drawn from Hoover's career. For as a closeted gay man who persecuted other closeted gay men, Hoover provides a particularly tragic example of the double life that gay men led before gay liberation.

Robert J. Corber

Bibliography

Gentry, Curt. *J. Edgar Hoover: The Man and His Secrets*. New York: Norton, 1991.

Rogin, Michael. "Political Repression in the United States." In *Ronald Reagan, the Movie, and Other Episodes in Political Demonology*. Berkeley: University of California Press, 1987, 44–80.

See also McCarthyism

Hössli, Heinrich (1784–1864)

Swiss businessman and writer who was an early promoter of the theory that homosexuality was innate, natural, and not to be judged. Although he later found out that his own son was homosexual, his interest in the subject was initially sparked by the cruel form of execution applied to a jurist from Bern who had murdered his presumably homosexual partner in a crime of passion. Hössli successfully encouraged popular writer Heinrich Zschokke (1771–1848) to write a novella about the scandal called *Der Eros, oder über die Liebe* (Eros, or on Love), which appeared in 1824. Hössli was, however, unsatisfied with Zschokke's treatment of the subject and eventually produced his own seven-hundred-page treatise on homosexuality called *Eros; über die Männerliebe* (Eros; on the Love of Men), which came out in two volumes in 1836 and 1838. Although the style is turgid and the evidence Hössli's work—primarily citations of ancient Greek literature—does more to document the existence of male-male desire in ancient cultures than to prove that such desire is inborn, Hössli's book was an important first step in the German-speaking world of the nineteenth century, both for the sexologists, who were attempting to research the biology of homosexual desire, and the homosexual emancipation movement, which was trying to decriminalize homosexuality.

Robert Tobin

Bibliography

Hössli, Heinrich. *Eros. Die Männerliebe der Griechen, ihre Beziehung zur Geschichte, Erziehung, Literatur und Gesetzgebung aller Zeiten.* 3 vols. Berlin: Rosa Winkel, 1996.

Steakley, James. *The Homosexual Emancipation Movement in Germany*. New York: Arno Press, 1975.

See also German Literature; Greece, Ancient; Sexology

Housman, A(lfred) E(dward) (1859–1936)

Contemporary critics of Housman's poetry noted more than once the homosexual connotations of verse that was perceived by many to reflect universal notions of love, compassion, and friendship. Housman would not have seen this universalism as entirely inappropriate, even if his unreciprocated lifelong love for heterosexual Moses Jackson reminded him of the more general cultural infringements on his desire. As students, Housman and Jackson shared rooms at Oxford (along with other classmates) and later worked in the same office in London, sharing lodgings with Jackson's brother Adalbert. Housman's desires may have been reciprocated by Adalbert, to whom poems XLI and XLII in *More Poems* are both tributes.

It was not until Jackson emigrated to India in 1887—returning to London two years later to marry, without inviting Housman to the wedding—that the poet began writing seriously. There is reason to believe that Housman was a member of the Order of Chaeronea, an 1890s homosexual society in which his brother Laurence participated. Housman's first collection, *A Shropshire Lad* (1896), was followed by *Last Poems* (1922), appropriately titled as they were compiled for Jackson who, now in Vancouver, British Columbia, was on the verge of death. The collection's publication over thirty years after Jackson had left England emphasizes both the poet's undying love for his former friend and the poignant futility of such lines as "Because I liked you better / Than suits a man to say, / It irked you, and I promised / To throw the thought away" (XXXI). Subsequent publications include *More Poems* (1936) and *Additional Poems*, the latter appearing as part of Laurence's memoir of his brother, *A.E.H.* (1937), the title of which brings to mind Tennyson's *In Memoriam: A.H.H.* Housman was also considered to be the top Latin scholar of his time in the English-speaking world, and in 1931, he published a collection of bawdy passages from Latin authors. He also had a fairly extensive collection of literary pornography.

A Shropshire Lad was in part a reaction to Oscar Wilde's trials in 1895 and the suicide of a homosexual Woolwich naval cadet described in the newspapers later that same year. Housman in fact sent Wilde an autographed copy of the collection. The homoeroticism of the poems is not explicit, but the constant focus on male figures and the usually ambiguous genders (only eight of the sixty-three pieces are overtly heterosexual) encourage homosexual readings.

On a more subtle level, Housman's poems frequently present a man's affection for another who has died (usually a soldier). This mortal chasm adds resonance to the isolation and lack of fulfilment that Housman experienced not only in his love for Jackson but also with regard to homosexual desire in general. The poet took part in a convention that allowed a greater acceptance of elegiac representations of love and attraction between men, when sexual consummation was seen as no longer a threat. Housman's "lads" are "in love with the grave" (*Last Poems*, IV), the context of war offering an all-male society seen as an appropriate topic for poetry and the elegiac genre making acceptable an eroticization of that context; after all, "who would not sleep with the brave?" (*Last Poems*, VI).

While couching most of his depictions of same-sex attraction within elegies, Housman does on occasion refer to physical fulfilment, or "answered passions" (*More Poems*, XII). He also uses challenges to a general range of social biases to attain an acceptable voice for articulating his personal sense of oppression. The opening verse in *More Poems* dedicates the collection to "all ill-treated fellows," while the narrator of poem XII in *Last Poems* describes himself as "a stranger and afraid / In a world I never made." It is when Housman addresses this broader scope that his voice becomes most forceful: "let God and man decree / Laws for themselves and not for me; / And if my ways are not as theirs / Let them mind their own affairs" (*Last Poems*, XII).

Dennis Denisoff

Bibliography

Bayley, John. *Housman's Poems*. Oxford: Clarendon Press, 1992.

Housman, A. E. *Collected Poems*. New York: Holt, Rinehart and Winston, 1965.

Jebb, Kieth. *A. E. Housman*. Bridgend, U.K.: Seren, 1992

See also Elegaic Poetry; English Literature; Friendship; Love Poetry, the Petrarchan Tradition; Wilde, Oscar

Howard, Richard (1929–)

Richard Howard is as close as one comes to a complete man of letters. A poet, translator, essayist, critic, and editor, he has quite literally surrounded himself with books throughout his adult life. Adopted as a baby by a rich Jewish family in Cleveland, Ohio, he attended Columbia University and the Sorbonne. A resident of New York since the fifties, he has made himself an integral part of the intellectual and cultural life of that city as the editor of various journals and book series and as a teacher. In 1997, he was appointed professor at Columbia University.

In ten volumes of poetry, Howard has consistently shown himself to be a master of literary form and dramatic characterization in works demanding, varied, and subtle. His third volume, *Untitled Subjects* (1969), a series of dramatic monologues that form an impressionist history of nineteenth-century British artistic and intellectual life, won the Pulitzer Prize in poetry. *Like Most Revelations* (1994) was nominated for a National Book Award. Sometimes criticized for the intellectuality of his verse, Howard is a man who is able to feel ideas and find in thought a richly emotional life grounded in history and specific cultural settings.

As perhaps this century's most distinguished translator from the French with well over a hundred books to his credit, he has been honored with the P.E.N. Translators Medal, the 1983 American Book Award for his translations of Baudelaire's *Les Fleurs du mal*, and the Ordre National du Mérite from the French government.

In 1969, he published *Alone with America,* a critical study of the poets of his generation, a collection that highlighted such gay, lesbian, or bisexual writers John Ashbery, Edward Field, Allen Ginsberg, Paul Goodman, Daryl Hine, William Meredith, James Merrill, Howard Moss, Frank O'Hara, Sylvia Plath, Adrienne Rich, and May Swenson.

David Bergman

Bibliography

Bergman, David. "Choosing Our Fathers: Gender and Identity in Whitman, Ashbery, and Richard Howard." *American Literary History* 1:2 (Summer 1989): 383–403.

Lynch, Michael. "The Life below the Life." In *The Gay Academic*. Louie Crew, ed. Palm Springs: ETC Publishers, 1978, 178–92.

See also U.S. Literature: Contemporary Gay Writing

Hughes, Langston (1902–1967)

U.S. writer Langston Hughes was born in Joplin, Missouri, but he spent most of his early years in Lawrence, Kansas. He moved to New York City in 1921, ostensibly to attend Columbia University, where he lasted for one year, but in fact to take advantage of the creative ferment that was beginning there. His famous poem "The Negro Speaks of Rivers" had been published the previous year in *The Crisis*, the official journal of the NAACP, to much acclaim, and Hughes quickly came to the attention of Harlem intellectuals. Soon he was one of the most heralded black writers in the country, second only to Countee Cullen in terms of the expectations that his talent generated. Unlike Cullen, however, these expectations did not go unfulfilled, and over the next four decades Hughes would be one of the most productive, successful, and well-known black writers in America, consistently creating works of fiction, poetry, drama, and history. His commitment to legitimizing distinctively African American cultural forms, most notably jazz and blues, and offering representations of black life beyond W.E.B. Du Bois's "talented tenth" earned him both praise and condemnation over the course of his life.

His reticence about his sexuality was legendary, and colleagues and friends tended to view him as simply asexual. Little in his work deals explicitly with homosexual themes or issues, even after writers like James Baldwin had proven that such work was not necessarily career-destroying and could be rendered acceptable to a mass audience, nor does he discuss homosexuality in either of his autobiographies, *The Big Sea* (1940) and *I Wonder As I Wander* (1956).

Although he probably would not approve and there is little textual or biographical justification for it, Hughes has taken on a surprising prominence in the work of contemporary black gay artists and in the discourse of black gay culture. His contemporary status as a gay icon may, however, reflect our inability to imagine asexuality as a "real" sexual identity more than it does any substantial evidence relating to his sexual practices. The construction of the "gay Langston" was sparked most notably by the reception and circulation of British filmmaker Isaac Julien's oblique meditation on Hughes and the Harlem Renaissance, *Looking for Langston*, and the controversy generated when the Hughes estate demanded that all the writer's work be deleted from the film.

Of course, the erotic unreality of the image of Hughes that has been constructed over the years may also reflect the refusal of most critics and biographers to seriously question the sexless persona that Hughes presented. This reluctance is obvious, for instance, in Arnold Rampersad's otherwise exemplary two-volume biography. Hughes died in 1967 in New York City. *Terry Rowden*

Bibliography

Rampersad, Arnold. *The Life of Langston Hughes*. 2 vols. New York: Oxford University Press, 1986–1988.

See also African American Gay Culture; Baldwin, James; Cullen, Countee; Harlem Renaissance

Hujar, Peter (1934–1987)

The square is the quietest of geometric shapes. A square format allows a wilder mix of interior elements without loss of control of the overall picture. Not surprising, then, that the square has been popular with photographers, like WeeGee and Diane Arbus, who are drawn to the more unsettling images of modern life. Peter Hujar's photographs, beginning with his documenting of the mounds of dusty skeletons in Sicilian catacombs back in the 1950s, usually unsettle. They are most often square.

Although a fashion photographer for the establishment (a star pupil of Richard Avedon) and a little old for the "Don't trust anyone over thirty!" generation, in the sixties Hujar began recording the gay life of Greenwich Village. He snapped the most famous image of the Stonewall era, a jubilant band of male and female hippy homos marching through the streets, which became a rallying poster for the emerging gay rights movement of the seventies.

Despite that, Hujar was not particularly political. His work is much more often personal rather than journalistic. His best portraits and nudes are an intense combination of the lyrical and the classical, taken in the privacy of his studio. He meticulously rendered every mundane detail of face and figure but infused them with a sweet, transcendent calmness that is partly the influence of his square formats but is mostly the art of Peter Hujar.

F. Valentine Hooven III

Bibliography

Duberman, Martin. *Stonewall*. New York: Dutton, 1993.
Ellenzweig, Allen. *The Homoerotic Photograph: Male Images from Durieu/Delacroix to Mapplethorpe*. New York: Columbia University Press, 1992.

See also Photography; Stonewall

Human Rights Campaign

Founded in Washington, D.C., in 1980 by Steve Endean as the Human Rights Campaign Fund (HRCF), the Human Rights Campaign (HRC) is the nation's largest gay and lesbian political organization, claiming more than two hundred thousand members in 1997. According to its mission statement, HRC is dedicated to an "America where lesbian and gay people are ensured of their basic rights—and can be open, honest and safe at home, at work and in the community." Originally formed as a political action committee (PAC) to support gay-friendly political candidates, the Human Rights Campaign has broadened its role significantly under the leadership of Steve Endean (1980–1983) and executive directors Vic Basile (1983–1989), Tim McFeeley (1989–1995), and Elizabeth Birch (1995–present). In addition to HRC's campaign fund-raising activities, which enabled it to donate more than one million dollars to candidates for federal office in 1996, the organization also lobbies the federal government in support of gay and lesbian civil rights and increased AIDS and women's health research, organizes and trains grassroots volunteers, conducts public opinion research, and sponsors the National Coming Out Project to promote honesty and openness about homosexuality. Over the years, HRC lobbying efforts have helped pass important legislation such as the Americans with Disabilities Act, the Ryan White Comprehensive AIDS Resources Emergency (CARE) Act, and the Hate Crimes Statistics and Hate Crime Sentencing Enhancement Acts; HRC continues to lobby in support of the Employment Non-Discrimination Act, a bill it helped introduce in 1994. To emphasize its many facets and to discourage public perception of HRC as simply a PAC, the Human Rights Campaign dropped the word "fund" from its name in 1995. *Mark Bailey*

Bibliography

Birch, Elizabeth. "The Human Rights Campaign: So Much More Than a Fund." *HRC Quarterly* (Fall 1995): 2–3.
Chibbaro, Lou, Jr. "HRCF Board Votes to Drop the 'F.'" *Washington Blade* (October 6, 1995): 19.

"HRC's Mission." *The Human Rights Campaign* (pamphlet). <http://www.hrc.org/hrc.mission.html> (August 8, 1997).

Keen, Lisa. "Elizabeth Birch to Take Helm at HRCF." *Washington Blade* (November 25, 1994): 1f.

See also Activism, Politics, U.S.; Global

Hustlers

In the rialto areas of most large cities, male prostitutes (hustlers) lounge against the street lights, sit along the curbs, and stand at the edge of the pavement as they signal their availability to passersby. These hustling areas are frequently located near gay bars, but some are in working-class neighborhoods, particularly those having a large immigrant population. Like their female counterparts, hustlers sell sex, companionship, and sometimes affection. Their customers are primarily gay men but also include straight- and bisexual-identified men and a few women.

The term *hustler* (Dutch for "shake" or "jog") connotes a person who works energetically to obtain money. The term was associated with the game of pool before it became the name given to male prostitutes. Until the beginning of the AIDS pandemic, there was little academic interest in male prostitution; however, since the mid-1980s a dramatic increase in research on male sex workers has occurred.

Both male and female prostitution thrived in societies around the world: in ancient Greece, Rome, Japan, and China and in Southeast Asia, Europe, the United States, parts of Africa, and South America today. Currently, many of the prostitutes are children sold into sexual service by their destitute parents.

There is a rich literature about and by hustlers, including *The Sins of the City of the Plain* (1881), *The Happy Hustler: My Own Story* (1975), *Calamus: Male Homosexuality in Twentieth Century Literature* (1982), and John Rechy's (1963) *City of Night* and *The Sexual Outlaw* (1977).

A substantial body of social science studies of male prostitution has developed. Many of these studies are flawed owing to (1) small and/or unrepresentative samples, (2) the obvious bias of the investigator, and (3) problems associated with developing rapport with men engaged in an illegal and stigmatized activity. The more successful researchers "hung out" in hustling areas and got to know the hustlers personally. Their findings are based on an intimate understanding of the experiences of the sex workers.

Most of the earlier studies viewed hustlers as pathological; terms like "neurotic," "psychotic," and "sociopath" were used freely. These studies focused on the sexual orientation of the hustlers, and the latency model was used to explain their choice of occupation. For example, one researcher has argued that hustlers were latent homosexuals "in denial."

Eventually, researchers began to view hustling as an occupation and the hustler as a worker. These researchers studied how hustlers were recruited and trained and strategies they used to survive in a hostile and stigmatized work environment. Albert Reiss described the strategies that a sample of working-class heterosexual-identified hustlers used to maintain their heterosexual self-image.

G. W. Levi Kamel, a former hustler, described the imaging styles (courtship activities designed to impress the client with the hustler's erotic value) hustlers used to recruit customers. He identified three hustling images: trade (hypermale, aggressive), jock (athletic, androgynous), and chicken (young, feminine). He argued that hustlers' imaging styles are closely related to their self-identified sexual orientation so that, for example, those who identified as heterosexual adopted a trade image, and bisexuals adopted a jock image.

Recent studies of male sex workers from several major cities in the United States including San Francisco, New York, New Orleans, and Atlanta have found that they (1) self-identify in all three sexual orientation categories, (2) are primarily either African American or white, (3) are primarily young adults (17–30), (4) are polydrug users, and (5) often use condoms with customers but are less likely to with recreational partners.

Most hustlers are poor, with slightly less than high school education, and they engage in risky sexual behavior with paying and recreational partners. Many are homeless and live literally on the street. Police surveillance and HIV education are usually sporadic. The police generally use methods close to entrapment to make arrests, and the hustlers are often denied medical treatment and other assistance after they are apprehended.

There are also a few studies of transvestite (drag queen) and/or transsexual prostitutes. Only a few studies report on actual HIV rates among male prostitutes, and those find that homosexual-identified and transvestite sex workers have higher HIV rates than heterosexual or bisexual-identified hustlers, in large part because the transvestite and homosexual-identified hustlers engage in more receptive anal intercourse with both recreational and paid partners.

Some evidence suggests that fewer young American men are choosing hustling because of fear of AIDS, the dominance of violent drug dealers in street life, and the increased acceptability of homosexuality. The hustling scene that so characterized many urban neighborhoods like the Times Square area in New York City may be disappearing; however, the "action" is shifting to more exotic environments, especially in Southeast Asia.

While female prostitutes and their advocates have supported a number of organizations that work for the decriminalization of prostitution, organizations for hustlers have not flourished. The Gay Men's Health Crisis started one organization, Coalition for Safer Hustling (CASH), in 1993, but it ceased operation in 1996 owing to lack of funds.

Since the beginnings of an identifiable gay subculture, hustlers have been part of the scene, though little recognized. In contrast to call men and escorts, they are usually not welcome in gay clubs or the homes of their customers. One still sees them standing on the street corner, trying to attract the attention of a cruising motorist. They have been part of the city for five hundred years; will they still be in the next five hundred?   *Jacqueline Boles*

Bibliography

Boles, J., and K. Elifson. "Sexual Identity and the Male Prostitute." *Journal of Sex Research* 31 (1994): 39–46.

———. "The Social Organization of Transvestite Prostitution and AIDS." *Social Science and Medicine* 19 (1994): 85–93.

Bullough, Vern. *The History of Prostitution.* New York: New York University Press, 1964.

Kamel, G. *Downtown Street Hustlers: The Role of Dramaturgical Imaging Practices in the Social Construction of Male Prostitution.* Ph.D. diss., University of California, San Diego. 1983.

McNamara, R. *The Times Square Hustler: Male Prostitution in New York City.* Westport, Conn.: Praeger, 1995.

Pleak, R., and H. Meyer-Bahlburg. "Sexual Behavior and AIDS Knowledge of Young Male Prostitutes in Manhattan." *Journal of Sex Research* 27 (1990): 557–87.

Polsky, N. *Hustlers, Beats and Others.* Chicago: Aldine, 1967.

Rechy, John. *City of Night.* New York: Grove Press, 1963.

———. *The Sexual Outlaw: A Documentary.* New York: Grove Press, 1977.

Saul, J. *The Sins of the City of the Plain.* London, 1881.

Saxon, G. (pseud.) *The Happy Hustler: My Own Story.* New York: Warner Paperback Library, 1975.

Waldorf, D., S. Murphy, D. Lauderback, C. Reinarman, and T. Marotta. "Needle Sharing Among Male Prostitutes: Preliminary Findings of the Prospero Project." *Journal of Drug Issues* 20 (1990): 309–34.

See also Gay Men's Health Crisis (GMHC); Rechy, John; Trade

I

Ibn Sina (Avicenna) (980–1037)

Ibn Sina, known in Europe as Avicenna, was an Islamic philosopher and theologian whose writings decisively influenced medieval Christian thought. Like other Islamic men of letters, Ibn Sina was also a physician, and his most studied work proved to be his *Qanun* or *Canon of Medicine*. The *Canon* was a standard textbook in European medical schools from the thirteenth century through at least the sixteenth, attracting dozens of commentators and critics. In the *Canon*, Ibn Sina discusses same-sex desire in several passages. He distinguishes between active or insertive desire and passive or receptive desire. Insertive copulation he treats along with heterosexual activity as a general topic in hygiene, even while he recognizes that it is prohibited by Islamic law. Receptive desire, the desire to be "passive" in anal intercourse, Ibn Sina regards as a pathological condition. He reports that some authorities considered it to have physical causes. The reference is to a doctrine that goes back to Greek medicine, holding that some men are attracted to anal intercourse because of an abnormal arrangement of their seminal ducts. This abnormality makes it difficult or impossible to ejaculate except when they are penetrated. But the anatomical hypothesis is then confused with a claim that the desire also derives from a psychological aberration. Whatever he holds about possible cause or causes, Ibn Sina rejects the suggestion of his predecessor, ar-Razî, that medical therapy can cure someone of this condition.   *Mark D. Jordan*

Bibliography

Rosenthal, Franz. "Ar-Razî on the Hidden Illness." *Bulletin of the History of Medicine* 52 (1978): 45–60.

See also Arabic Literature; Islam; Persian (Iranian) Literature and Culture

Identity Politics

Whether or not one subscribes to the Foucauldian premise that modern institutions such as medicine and the law do not simply "prohibit" but also "produce" the homosexual as the necessary if evil twin of a normative heterosexuality, it is still evident that people who engage in homoerotic activity are often the object of (a sometimes murderous) reprobation. What is less certain is how to remedy this situation and to what particular end. For some gays and lesbians, an answer is to be found in what since the 1970s has been termed "identity politics."

Identity politics refers to the use of an identity—sexual, gender, religious, ethnic, racial—as a means of arguing for political power, recognition, and legitimacy, usually in the form of increased rights. If politics is the struggle to alter existing relations of power in one's favor, identity politics uses identity as both a rationale for altering such relations and a tool with which to do so. Borrowing its logic from civil rights discourse and representational politics, identity politics argues that gays and lesbians represent a constituency held together by a shared set of concerns. Sometimes these concerns are understood to result from something intrinsic to homosexuality—a uniquely homosexual "essence," or some biological factor thought to link all gay men and lesbians. Other times, they are understood to be the product of specific historical factors, the argument being that culturally specific prohibitions against homosexuality have produced common interests among people who engage in homosexual acts. Both cases assume, however, that, as a legitimate political constituency, this group is deserving of political representation and "equal" rights.

Critiques of identity politics often attempt to show that identity is always a fiction, or at the very least, a mutable historical construction, not something "essential," transhistorical, or cross-cultural. For example, psychoanalytic feminists have noted that identities are precarious and provisional; sexual and gender identity are superimposed by culture onto human beings, and they are never fully achieved and always subject to the disruptive power of the unconscious. This makes it difficult to speak of either homosexuality or heterosexuality as anything other than provisional arrangements of desire.

Poststructuralist critics have gone to some lengths to deconstruct sexual identity. Pointing out that the line dividing "homosexuality" from "heterosexuality" is necessarily contingent on a variety of cultural, social, and historical factors, such critics attempt to render it impossible to answer the question of what precisely constitutes a homosexual. A variety of political theorists have noted that, as a group, homosexuals are as divided as they are united, crossed by competing identities including those of race, class, and gender. There is thus no necessary reason for people who engage in homosexual activity to form a constituency around homosexuality in particular; those who can afford to form a constituency are usually the relatively privileged—white, male, middle class.

Some queer political activists have argued pragmatically that, owing to their relatively small numbers, gays and lesbians will be treated as an "expendable" constituency. Queer Marxist critics have suggested that gay liberation as it is constituted around the question of identity is actually an intrabourgeois struggle and not an attempt to alter existing relations of production. Identity politics often fails to note, for example, the link between systemic homophobia and capitalist exploitation. Finally, some critics have argued against identity politics through a more general critique of a politics based on individual rights. According to such critics, identity politics is too dependent on liberal individualism. It thus promises not a radical alteration of existing power relations but a simple reshuffling that leaves existing political structures largely intact.

Defenders of identity politics sometimes argue that, while identity is a fiction, it has proved historically necessary and politically efficacious. By providing a "fictive" collectivity around which to resist the censure of homoeroticism, gay identity is a myth that has significantly improved the lives of many. Identities are necessary for the producing of political affiliations. The critique of identity politics tends to foreclose possibilities for political agency. Some theorists have countered, however, that the reverse is true—that acts of affiliation produce identifications, and that the myth of identity tends to thwart possibilities for political agency by dangerously equating "being" or even "style" with rational political action.

Other writers have, in turn, warned that some critiques of identity politics too readily assume that political subjects that act through identity necessarily fall for its lure. When it does not imagine that it refers to an already existing constituency, gay identity politics assumes that the use of the term *gay* will produce or fabricate a constituency, and with that constituency, a certain moral obligation to act. Identity politics, then, deploys a fictive identity as a means of producing political affiliations and accompanying ethical imperatives. What remains to be charted, however, are the historical effects of that deployment—effects whose ends are beyond the agency of any individual who calls him- or herself gay.

Interestingly, there appears to be little traffic between popular endorsements of identity politics and its critique. For many people who call themselves gay, the prospect of a gay liberation that does not necessarily seek to liberate gays in particular seems unimaginable. Yet some historians have argued that gay liberation began precisely as an attempt to call into question the Maginot Line dividing hetero- from homosexual desire. As long as (at least) two definitions of homosexuality compete—homosexuality as naming a potential in all human beings and homosexuality as defining a discrete category of persons—identity politics will seem both divisive and efficacious.

Despite the lingering cultural prohibitions against homoeroticism, it is probably also true that some gay people today live better lives than they would have in the past. But are gays as a whole better off? A certain version of identity politics assumes that the phrase "gays as a whole" is intelligible. Critics of identity politics would argue that such a phrase is a fiction whose necessity and efficacy must be argued rather than simply assumed.

John Champagne

Bibliography
Butler, Judith. *Gender Trouble*. New York: Routledge, 1990.

Champagne, John. *The Ethics of Marginality: A New Approach to Gay Studies*. Minneapolis: University of Minnesota Press, 1995.

Field, Nicola. *Over the Rainbow: Money, Class and Homophobia*. London: Pluto Press, 1995.

Foucault, Michel. *The History of Sexuality*. Volume 1, *An Introduction*. Robert Hurley, trans. New York: Vintage, 1980.

Fuss, Diana. *Essentially Speaking*. New York: Routledge, 1989.

Phelan, Shane. *Identity Politics, Lesbian Feminism and the Limits of Community*. Philadelphia: Temple University Press, 1989.

Sedgwick, Eve Kosofsky. *The Epistemology of the Closet*. Berkeley: University of California Press, 1990.

Warner, Michael, ed. *Fear of a Queer Planet*. Minneapolis: University of Minnesota Press, 1993.

Weeks, Jeffrey. *Sexuality and Its Discontents*. London: Routledge and Kegan Paul, 1985.

See also Bisexuality; Civil Rights (U.S. Law); Essentialist-Constructionist Debate; Gay Liberation; Gender; Politics, Global; U.S. Law: Equal Protection; Queer

Immigration, U.S.

The freedom of movement, one of the most basic of human rights, is a freedom denied to gay men and lesbians throughout the world through the immigration policies of numerous nations. This article focuses on U.S. immigration policy and its treatment of "homosexuality."

"Homosexuals" were first targeted by U.S. immigration policy in 1952 with the McCarran-Walter Immigration Act, also known as the Immigration and Nationality Act (INA). According to section 212(a) subsections 1182 (a) (4) and (9) of the INA, "aliens" (i.e., persons not citizens or nationals of the United States) could be denied entry if they were found to be "afflicted with psychopathic personality, or sexual deviation" or "convicted of a crime involving moral turpitude." In 1967 the U.S. Supreme Court determined in *Boutilier v. INS* that the subsection was meant to prohibit all homosexuals from immigration to the United States. Immigration became even more exclusive in 1987, when Congress enacted a law preventing the immigration of those infected with HIV. In a surprising turnaround in 1990, however, Congress dropped the exclusion of gays based on the old "public health" and moral reasoning of the INA (Editors of the *Harvard Law Review* 1990).

Currently, gay and lesbian immigrants continue to be overtly discriminated against by U.S. immigration policies and laws by the following means: family definition, HIV status, and political asylum.

Immigrants who apply for U.S. residency based on a family petition must be the parent, child, sibling, or spouse of a U.S. citizen. While seven countries currently permit same-sex partners to immigrate (Australia, Canada, Denmark, New Zealand, Norway, Sweden, Netherlands), in the United States, gay relationships are not recognized as a legitimate means by which a "spouse" can claim citizenship rights for a partner. Proponents of gay rights argue that binational couples (i.e., gay and lesbian citizens and their "alien" partners) have the right to maintain loving and supportive relationships that they demand be recognized as legitimate by the state, i.e., same-sex marriage and/or that the definition of family be extended to include gay and lesbian families.

Individuals who are HIV-positive are still excluded from immigrating to the United States, though this exclusionary policy may be waived for heterosexual spouses. Several national and international organizations have publicly denounced this ban including the National Commission on AIDS, the Centers for Disease Control, the American Medical Association, and the World Health Organization.

While the INS has officially recognized sexual orientation and HIV serostatus as membership in a persecuted class for granting political asylum, this status is granted only rarely and only for immigrants from specific countries who can demonstrate "well-founded" fears of persecution. Countries that fit such a definition include Cuba, Brazil, Mexico, and several Islamic countries (LLDEF 1995; "Queer Immigration" 1996).

At the forefront of gay rights and immigration reform today are the Lesbian and Gay Immigration Rights Task Force, Inc. (LGIRTF), the Lambda Legal Defense and Education Fund, and the International Lesbian and Gay Association.   *Lionel Cantú*

Bibliography

Editors of the *Harvard Law Review*. *Sexual Orientation and the Law*. Cambridge, Mass.: Harvard University Press, 1990.

Lambda Legal Defense and Education Fund (LLDEF). "Basic Immigration Law Concepts." 1995 (pamphlet).

———. "Queer Immigration." 1996 (pamphlet). http://qrd.tcp.com/qrd/www/world/immigration/lgir tf.html

I *See also* AIDS; Australia; Canada; Denmark; Netherlands; Sweden; U.S. Law: Equal Protection

Incest

In its narrowest sense, incest describes sexual activity categorically prohibited between two people because they are closely related by blood. Freud's Oedipus theory posited a structurally innate incestuous desire on the part of the prepubescent son for his mother and a murderous jealousy of his father as sexual rival. Contemporary mental health professionals broadly define incest as any "inappropriate" sexual or sexualizing relationship between blood relatives, or between a child and any emotionally close or other adult authority figure. As in all sexual abuse, the informing dimension is the profound psychic trauma caused by the transgressive act rather than the act per se. Incest is never about love but rather about the perpetrator's exercise of power. Incest is perhaps the most traumatizing sexual abuse and remains society's "last taboo." The vigorous assertion of the taboo nature of incest would logically bear out the prevalence of the activity that recent research has revealed, rather than the traditional notion of a one-in-a-million rate of occurrence.

In the majority of cases involving gay men, the incest referred to is that of being sexually abused during childhood. The impact of incest in the lives of gay men is threefold: all incest victims share in the trauma, gay men suffer additionally as men (men are understood by definition as not-victims), and they suffer as homosexuals (sexual trauma to nonheterosexuals is minimized or discounted in our society). The underlying trauma is the violation of trust by a trusted family member. Victims are often further traumatized by not being believed (only a "monster" would do such things, not a beloved relative). Males are typically held to be responsible for having encouraged the incest; hence the trauma of the victim being blamed as well as having his masculinity called permanently into question. Gay men may suffer from a further sense of blame, that they are being held accountable by society. Male children who appear weak, effeminate, or presumed to be gay are sometimes sexually abused for that very reason.

The child victim of incest usually emerges as an adult survivor. The effects of the trauma and ensuing survival techniques that the child victim develops may include loss of childhood memories, healthy social contact, control over one's body or intimacy (adult sexual relationships may either be un-

conscious reenactments of the victim/perpetrator dynamic or may be avoided altogether), and may lead to development of social masks or a false persona, chemical dependency problems, emotional numbing, compartmentalization, split or multiple personalities, habitual suicidal feelings, pervasive all-or-nothing thinking, and a profound, lifelong inability to trust others.

Treatment approaches for gay male adult victim/survivors of incest and other sexual abuse were developed during the 1980s and 1990s. Recovery begins with the conscious recognition of past abuse (either the return of repressed memories or an emotional "unfreezing") and is typically predicated on shifting the psychological focus from a "victim" to a "survivor" mentality. The enormous anguish caused by Freud's later recant of his theory, as "merely" childhood fantasies (because both Freud and his society rejected this reality), only added to the burden, until recent empirical breakthroughs and a loosening of moral strictures against investigating this "last taboo" have allowed progress again to be made. Psychological scarring during childhood is never completely eradicated. Recovery from incest trauma often takes a lifetime, but recovery has become possible for more and more victims.

Les Wright

Bibliography

Lew, Mike. *Victims No More: Men Recovering from Incest and Other Sexual Child Abuse.* New York: HarperCollins, 1990.

See also Freud, Sigmund; Pederasty; Sexual Abuse; Sexual Violence

India

Since the Vedic period (c.1200–600 B.C.E.), which began with the migration of Sanskrit-speaking Aryans to India, phenomena that might today be categorized as homosexuality have been inextricably linked in Indian thought to a third sex/gender defined in terms of culturally nonnormative behavioral, biological, and gender-role traits. Masculinity was to a large extent equated with sexual potency, which engendered powerful anxieties about impotence and the concomitant creation of rituals for the restoration or maintenance of potency. In these rituals we see the first appearance of the term *napumsaka*, literally "not-a-male." A *napumsaka* was probably an animal with hermaphroditic or androgynous traits, sacrificed in potency rituals; the term was later applied to humans. The late Vedic period also saw the development of a three-gender grammatical system: female, male, and *napumsaka*, the latter defined as "neither feminine nor masculine," a rubric still applied to third-sex persons in India. Other terms originally referring to impotent men came to be associated with equivocal sexuality: the *kliba*, for example, was a dancer described as impotent and longhaired—two characteristics associated with women. By not fulfilling the expected male role of procreator and for taking on feminine qualities, such persons were held in contempt in the highly patriarchal Vedic world. Later grammarians (c.300 B.C.E.) discussed the third grammatical gender (*napumsaka*) in terms of impotent men (*sanda*) and *pandakas* (longhaired dancing transvestites like the *klibas*), in contemporary Buddhist literature, *pandakas* are portrayed as homosexuals. Still later, in medical texts of the first through fourth centuries C.E., third-sex persons were viewed as males with congenital sexual abnormalities or dysfunctions, which included receptive homosexual behavior and effeminacy.

In Buddhist and Jain treatises spanning the fourth century B.C.E. to the tenth century C.E., third-sex persons are dealt with primarily in the context of their capacity to be monks or lay disciples. The Buddhists rejected as monks those whom they considered to be congenital members of the third sex; such gender-atypical persons were considered to be homosexually voracious, likely to disrupt and bring discredit on the monastic order. They were also considered to be incapable of the discipline necessary even for lay religious practice. A few sculptural representations of Hindu ascetics or monks engaging in male-male sex suggest a popular association of same-sex sexuality with male renunciants. The Jains viewed third-sex persons as possessing both male and female libidos, and thus as hypersexual, but eventually came to accept them as monastics and members of the lay community. In the Hindu epics and myths there are many references to gods and heroes who are androgynous, or who change gender (e.g., Ardharnarisvara, Sikandin, Arjuna). In classical Indian literature, third-sex persons are associated with prostitution and dancing and depicted as having low social status.

In the Kama Sutra (fourth century C.E.), third-sex persons are portrayed as either masculine or feminine, earning their living as masseurs (for the "masculine" types) or as prostitutes (for the "feminine"), and as receiving sexual gratification by performing fellatio. This text also speaks of urban male sophisticates (*nagarikas*) who, for mutual pleasure, engage in sexual activity with each other.

There is little information on the third sex or male homosexuality during the twelfth to seventeenth centuries, when Muslims of central Asian ethnicity came to dominate most of India. One Islamic source indicates that Hindus regarded anal intercourse with loathing, considering it to be a foreign vice. In later periods of Muslim rule, from the end of the Moghul period in the eighteenth century to the local dynasties that survived until independence in 1947, third-sex persons, now called by the Persian-derived term *hijra*, were often patronized by the courts. Most were castrated and employed as servants in the women's quarters, as cooks and nursemaids. Some who lived outside the courts were organized into guilds, which received government grants of property and permission to solicit money in specified districts by performing as singers and dancers. The special privileges granted to *hijras* were rescinded by the British, who saw these "eunuchs" as criminal elements engaging in unnatural vice; that some were prostitutes is attested to by the accounts of European residents. The *hijras*, whose numbers are estimated at anywhere from fifty thousand to over a million, remain a visible presence in modern India. Many worship Bahuchara, a form of the mother goddess, although others are Muslims or religiously syncretic. They are organized into familylike houses led by a guru "mother," maintain secrecy about their way of life, have their own argot, and earn their living by begging at birth and marriage ceremonies and by prostitution. Most are biological males who cross-dress and have been ritually castrated; they are universally derided but also believed by many to possess special powers of conferring or blighting potency.

There are also effeminate uncastrated males (*jankhas* or *zenanas*) who cross-dress and are receptive homosexuals, and who may perform as singers and dancers. In addition, there is an extensive public cruising scene, mainly among lower-class men who are characterized as either *gandu* (receptive anal or oral partners) or *londebaaz* (insertive partners). With the recent emergence of a large middle class, Western tourism, and media influence, a "gay" identity has developed involving same-sex orientation but not necessarily cross-dressing or other transgender characteristics. Gay culture is primarily found in Bombay and other large cities; it includes bars, magazines, support groups, and other institutions.

Gay themes have been treated in fiction, journalism, and films. The AIDS epidemic has also spurred organizations advocating civil rights and social services for gays and *hijras*, although "sodomy" remains illegal under the Indian penal code inherited from the British, and gay men, lesbians, and *hijras* are often harassed by the police. However, India has never had the kind of organized persecution of homosexual or transgendered people found in the Judaeo-Christian West.

Michael J. Sweet

Bibliography

Cohen, Lawrence. "The Pleasures of Castration: The Postoperative Status of Hijras, Jankhas and Academics." In *Sexual Pleasure, Sexual Culture*. Paul R. Abramson and Steven D. Pinkerton, eds. Chicago: University of Chicago Press, 1995, 276–304.

Gautam, Siddhartha. *Less Than Gay: A Citizen's Report on the Status of Homosexuality in India.* New Delhi: AIDS Bhedbhav Virodhi Andolan, 1991.

Jaffrey, Zia. *The Invisible: A Tale of the Eunuchs of India.* New York: Pantheon, 1996.

Nanda, Serena. *Neither Man nor Woman: The Hijras of India.* Belmont, Calif.: Wadsworth, 1990.

O'Flaherty, Wendy Doniger. *Women, Androgynes, and Other Mythical Beasts.* Chicago: University of Chicago Press, 1980.

Ratti, Rakesh, ed. *A Lotus of Another Color.* Boston: Alyson, 1993.

Sweet, Michael J., and Leonard Zwilling. "The First Medicalization: The Taxonomy and Etiology of Queerness in Classical Indian Medicine." *Journal of the History of Sexuality* 3, no. 4 (1993): 590–607.

Vatsyasyana. *The Complete Kama Sutra.* Alain Daniélou, trans. Rochester, Vt.: Park Street Press, 1994.

Zwilling, Leonard, and Michael J. Sweet. "'Like a City Ablaze': The Third Sex and the Creation of Sexuality in Jain Religious Literature." *Journal of the History of Sexuality* 6, no. 3 (1996): 359–84.

———. "The Evolution of Third Sex Constructs in Ancient India: A Study in Ambiguity." In *Empowerment: Gender Constructs in Indian Religion and Society.* Julia Leslie, ed. (forthcoming).

See also Buddhism; Effeminacy; Gender; *Hijras* of India; Hinduism; Islam; Kama Sutra; Third Sex

Indonesia

The history of same-sex sexuality among the more than 3,700 inhabited islands of Indonesia, the world's fourth most populous nation, is immense. Many islands boast traditions of male-to-female transgenderism (e.g., the Bissu of south Sulawesi, men who dress as women for certain ritual functions) or socially recognized male same-sex sexual behavior. For instance, in east Java there is a long-standing tradition of the *warok-gemblak* relationship in traditional Javanese drama, where adult male actors (the *Worok*), usually married, nevertheless take a younger man (the *gemblak*) as an understudy and sexual partner for a period of several years. But the current status of same-sex practices and identities in Indonesia is defined primarily by its gay and lesbian movement. Under conditions ranging from grudging tolerance to open bigotry, a growing movement of Indonesian men and women reaches halfway across the world to appropriate the concepts "gay" and "lesbian," transforming them through magazines, weekly meetings, and the practices of daily life to interpret their experiences. This movement, the oldest and largest gay and lesbian movement in Southeast Asia, is remarkable for the ways in which its members reject "traditional" sexualities in favor of the ostensibly Western terms *lesbian* and *gay*. But these concepts are not thrust on the movement; instead, Indonesians adapt notions of gay and lesbian sexuality so that they become seen as authentically Indonesian. This process of active transformation cannot be understood independently of the worldwide changes in mass media, technology, and capitalism at the end of the twentieth century; but it must also be emphasized that Indonesians have a long history of appropriating ideas from elsewhere, as the examples of Islam, Hinduism, Buddhism, capitalism, and nationalism make clear.

Prior to the beginnings of the organized movement in 1982, men with same-sex interests who did not participate in "traditional" same-sex sexualities met primarily in public spaces, particularly parks or waterfront areas. These remain the primary locus of same-sex social activity for men in Indonesia whether or not they identify as "gay," since few gay or lesbian organizations have the resources to rent office or community space. The importance of public spaces also reflects that few men live in homes or apartments large enough to provide any degree of privacy; even when such conditions exist, the anonymity of a park or beach is usually preferred when seeking the company of other men with same-sex interests. Women, whose ability to travel alone in public spaces is highly restricted—particularly at night—tended to meet each other through friendship networks, particularly in the context of parties and get-togethers at home. Secrecy continues to be a constant concern for women, since the home environment is filled with household members from whom same-sex interests must be hidden. Open discrimination in the form of arrests, police beatings, and the like is rare in Indonesia, but the government's rhetoric of "the Indonesian family" has no place for gay or lesbian Indonesians. Most gay and lesbian Indonesians list their greatest concerns as bringing shame to their family or being expelled from it, feeling that they are sinning or are rejected by Allah (89 percent of Indonesians are Muslim); the pressure to marry; and feeling that they are rejected by society. It is primarily toward these concerns that the gay and lesbian movement directs its energies.

In March 1982, the first Indonesian lesbian and gay organization, Lambda Indonesia (LI), was formed by three Indonesian gay men as a forum for gay men and lesbians to communicate with one another, especially those living in small towns. LI was also the first gay and lesbian movement organization established in Asia. (From the beginnings of the movement until the present, gay men have dominated its membership and leadership.) LI aimed to develop gay pride and provide guidance and support for fellow gays and lesbians. In mid-1987, activists in Surabaya founded the Kelompok Kerja Lesbian dan Gay Nusantara (KKLGN, Nusantara Lesbian and Gay Working Group), which became the umbrella organization for gays and lesbians throughout the archipelago. In its initial manifesto, KKLGN listed its two primary purposes as follows:

- Providing a means for Indonesian lesbians and gay men to get in touch with one another, to read positive things about ourselves and in general to express ourselves artistically or otherwise.
- Facilitating the formation of similar groups or the emergence of individual activists in other localities.

Currently, KKLGN publishes the periodical *GAYa Nusantara*, which provides detailed information about the gay and lesbian world. *Nusantara* means "archipelago," a term used by Indonesians to describe the diversity of this multicultural nation, whereas *gaya* literally means "style" or " à la" but as

a play on words also means "gay." Thus, *GAYa Nusantara* has a double meaning: "archipelago style" and "the gay archipelago." Gay and lesbian Indonesians see their movement as a gay archipelago linking groups in various cities throughout the country in a national network. This network is then envisioned as part of a global archipelago of gay and lesbian communities. Perhaps gay men and lesbians elsewhere in the world have something to learn from this highly sophisticated and flexible way of conceptualizing the relationship between organizations and cultures that are neither identical nor absolutely different.

The HIV/AIDS epidemic came late to Indonesia, but there is no indication that the archipelago will be spared. Current data (1997) indicate that about 550 Indonesians have HIV or are sick with AIDS, but even the government estimates that this figure is low by a factor of 100 owing to difficulties in testing and a lack of knowledge that the test exists, as well as the meaning of negative or positive results. Approximately 80 percent of known cases can be attributed to sex between men, but, once again, these statistics must be regarded as highly tentative.

Many gay and lesbian organizations have survived by performing HIV/AIDS education, gaining the double benefit of a "cover" and, in many cases, funding from transnational HIV/AIDS agencies. One result is that the epidemic has become a major mediator between "Western" gay and lesbian sexualities and the Indonesian movement, influencing the ways by which the movement—as well as Indonesian society at large—perceive gay and lesbian sexuality. But since lesbians are not seen as at risk for HIV infection by development agencies, the influence of these agencies further marginalizes lesbians, rendering their communities and identities invisible to much of Indonesian society.

Since the early 1990s, the gay and lesbian movement in Indonesia has undergone a remarkable expansion. *GAYa Nusantara* is now one of several gay and lesbian magazines (e.g., *Buletin Paraikatte* in Ujung Pandang, *Jaka-Jaka* in Yogyakarta, *Gaya Betawi* in Jakarta); however, only *GAYa Nusantara* publishes on a regular basis and has a sustained national readership. In addition, the number of gay and lesbian organizations has exploded; at last count there were twenty-eight organizations in places as far-flung as Medan, Pekanbaru, and Ambon. The first lesbian organization, Chandra Kirana, appeared in Jakarta around 1992 and published the magazine *Gaya Lestari* until 1994; there are now informal lesbian networks in many cities, including Surabaya, Denpasar, and Ujung Pandang. In December 1993, sixteen gay and lesbian groups established a stronger network as a result of the First Indonesian Lesbian and Gay Congress held in Yogyakarta. A second congress was held in Bandung in December 1995, and a third congress took take place in Denpasar, Bali, in December 1997.

Tom Boellstorff
and Danny Yatim

Bibliography

Oetomo, Dede. "Gender and Sexual Orientation in Indonesia." In *Fantasizing the Feminine in Indonesia.* Leslie Sears, ed. Durham, N.C.: Duke University Press, 1996.

See also Buddhism; Hinduism; Islam

Inge, William (1913–1973)

Much to the chagrin of Tennessee Williams, his colleague, erstwhile mentor and friend, and, briefly, lover, William Inge was a phenomenally successful playwright who could boast of four major Broadway hits in the 1950s: *Come Back, Little Sheba* (1950), *Picnic* (1953), *Bus Stop* (1955), and *The Dark at the Top of the Stairs* (1957). All were made into Hollywood films. In addition, Inge wrote the hit film *Splendor in the Grass* (1961).

Unfortunately for Inge, his personal life was a misery. He grew up in the Kansas he depicted so powerfully in his plays. He was a schoolteacher before he became an arts critic for a St. Louis newspaper. This Midwestern beginning made him deeply fearful of any exposure of his homosexuality. He spent years in psychoanalysis trying unsuccessfully to cure himself of his sexuality and his alcoholism. He committed suicide in 1973.

Many of the most powerful moments in Inge's plays center on sexual repression: the alcoholic Doc's attraction for the young female boarder and ambiguous feelings toward her boyfriend in *Come Back, Little Sheba* and the repressed desire of the spinster schoolteacher Rosemary in *Picnic* are typical, powerful Inge moments. Some have read the anguish of the suicidal Jewish boy, Sammy, in *The Dark at the Top of the Stairs* as a figure of homosexual panic. In the 1950s as part of his psychoanalysis, Inge wrote two one-act plays, *The Tiny Closet* and *The Boy in the Basement*, which are powerful expressions of the fear of exposure of homosexuality and the anguish of the closet.

When Inge created overtly homosexual characters in his plays in the 1960s, he was brutally excoriated by New York critics as one of the corrupting homosexual triumvirate (with Williams and Albee).

John M. Clum

Bibliography

Clum, John M. *Acting Gay: Male Homosexuality in Modern Drama.* New York: Columbia University Press, 1994.
Shuman, R. Baird. *William Inge.* Boston: Twayne, 1989.
Voss, Ralph F. *A Life of William Inge: The Strains of Triumph.* Lawrence, Kans.: University of Kansas Press, 1989.

See also Albee, Edward; Theater: Premodern and Early Modern; Williams, Tennessee

Inquisition
Spain

The Spanish Inquisition was established in 1478 by royal authority with the approval of the pope. Its principal task was to investigate heresy and apostasy in the territories controlled by the Spanish crown. A papal inquisition with jurisdiction over the whole church had grown since the 1230s. The Spanish agency was not so much a branch of the papal inquisition as a supplement to it. Issues of heresy and apostasy were particularly urgent for the Spanish monarchy because of the large numbers of new converts to Christianity from Islam and Judaism. Like the papal original, the Spanish Inquisition managed a large bureaucracy that operated according to complicated legal procedures. Inquisitors were allowed to use torture as a means of extracting confessions, and they could also impose a variety of sentences, including fines, confiscations, imprisonment, and exile. In capital cases, the Inquisition handed over or "relaxed" its prisoners to the civil authority for execution. The crime of "sodomy" was not originally within the sometimes jurisdiction of the Spanish Inquisition, even though the papal inquisitors had been authorized to deal with it since 1451. "Sodomy" was typically taken to include male-male copulation, bestiality, and any genital contact between men and women other than insertion of the penis into the vagina. Lesbian activity was more problematic for church lawyers, who sometimes counted it as sodomy and sometimes not. The Spanish Inquisition seems to have been reluctant at first to accept such cases. In 1509, responding to prosecutions from Seville, the agency's governing body, the Suprema, ruled that sodomy was to be left to the secular courts, for which it was already a capital crime. But in 1524, the Suprema joined with its officers in Saragossa to request papal authority to prosecute sodomy. Clement VII granted permission for the Spanish inquisitors to pursue sodomites, with two stipulations. The papal ruling was technically only for part of the Spanish possessions, the Kingdom of Aragon, and it furthermore required that sodomites be tried not according to standard inquisitorial procedure but according to civil laws. The inquisitors of Aragon and some territories made use of this papal license for more than a century, although always with jurisdictional and procedural confusions. Between 1570 and 1630, there were nearly one thousand sodomy trials before the Aragonese inquisition, and as many men were executed for sodomy as for heresy. (During the same decades, the Spanish civil courts were executing many more sodomites.) Among those executed for sodomy by the Inquisition, there is a disproportionate number of clergy, foreigners, and the socially marginalized. Many cases involve rape or coerced intercourse. Before 1589, a number of adolescents were executed on the charge. After 1633, the Spanish Inquisition ceased treating sodomy as a capital case, though it continued to try cases and to impose lesser sentences.   *Mark D. Jordan*

Bibliography

Haliczer, Stephen. *Inquisition and Society in the Kingdom of Valencia, 1478–1834.* Berkeley: University of California Press, 1990, 302–13.

Monter, William. *Frontiers of Heresy: The Spanish Inquisition from the Basque Lands to Sicily.* Cambridge: Cambridge University Press, 1990, 276–99.

Portugal

When the medieval inquisitions shut down, the Iberian peninsula obtained the permission from Rome to install the Courts of the Holy Office of the Inquisition in Spain in 1478 and in Portugal in 1536.

Like the medieval Inquisition, the main goal of the so-called Modern Inquisition was the fight against heresies. In Portugal, the New Christians were the main scapegoats. They were descendants of Jews who had been forcibly baptized but secretly continued Jewish rituals within their homes. More than 80 percent of the victims of the Portuguese Inquisition were descendants of Jews. The second-most-persecuted group by the Holy Office were sodomites, popularly known as *sodomitigos* or *fanchonos*.

Under Afonsine and Manueline laws, sodomy already carried the death penalty by burning at the stake and was considered as heinous a crime as regicide and treason. Portuguese law stated, "Above all other sins, the vilest, dirtiest and most dishonest is Sodomy and no other is as abhorrent to God and the world that the mere mention of this sin without any other act is already so serious and abhorrent that it putrefies the air and because of it God sent the flood over the earth, destroying Sodom and Gomorrah and the Knights Templar."

The Inquisition had jurisdiction over persecuting "perfect sodomy," that is, the penetration of and ejaculation into the anus, whereas it was the privilege of the king or the bishop to repress heterosexual anal penetration. After 1646 the Inquisition excluded lesbianism from the definition of perfect sodomy, turning over *sodomia faeminarum* to secular jurisdiction.

During its nearly three hundred years in operation, the Portuguese Inquisition registered in the Index of Abominations 4,419 denunciations against men suspected of having practiced the "abominable and perverted sin of sodomy." Of those denounced, 447 were arrested and underwent a formal trial—62 percent in the seventeenth century, the period of greatest antihomosexual intolerance in the Iberian peninsula. Thirty of the sodomites considered "most perverted and incorrigible" were burned at the stake. The rest were condemned to rowing the king's galley ships or to temporary or perpetual exile in Africa, India, or Brazil. Most sodomites who were imprisoned had their property seized and were publicly whipped until blood flowed. The relatives of the sodomites sentenced in the Inquisition lost their civil rights for three generations.

Among the sodomites who were victims of the Inquisition, 85 percent were whites; the rest were blacks, Amerindians, Moors, and people of mixed racial background. The overwhelming majority worked providing services or as skilled laborers, and 25 percent were clerics. Among the sodomites denounced and/or imprisoned by the Inquisition, some were famous in Luso-Brazilian history, such as the count of Vila Franca, Senhor de Belas; the bishop of Ivora, Dom Jono Coutinho; Garcia de

I

Noronha, captain of Ormuz e Malaca; the governor general of Brazil, Diogo Botelho; and Crist\vao Cabro, the governor of Cabo Verde.

Portuguese Inquisitional documents can be found in the National Archive of the Torre do Tombo in Lisbon, which contains the largest and richest archive about homosexuality of the period, with biographical details and descriptions of the homoerotic preferences of each sodomite and his partners. This documentation affords the vividly colorful reconstruction of the rich and frenetic gay subculture in Lisbon and other cities in the kingdom and overseas, where *fanchonos* and *sodomitigos*, some cross-dressing and using makeup, used feminine names and even organized parties and dances known as the "dances of the *fanchonos*."

Luiz Mott, translated by James N. Green

Bibliography

Mott, Luiz. "Slavery and Homosexuality." *Quarterly, National Association of Black and White Men Together* 24 (Winter 1985).
"Pogode Portugues: a subcultura gay em Portugal nos tempos inquisitioriais." *Revista Ciéncia e Cultura* 40, no. 20 (1988): 120–39.
Vainfas, Ronaldo. *Trópico dos Pecados*. Rio de Janeiro: Editora Campus, 1989.

See also Brazil; Catholicism; Portugal; Sodomy; Spain

International Law

The significance of public international law, and international human rights law in particular, to gay men and lesbians is a phenomenon of the last two decades. Although no international treaties expressly mention the words "homosexuality" or "sexual orientation," international courts and tribunals have begun to interpret the treaties to protect certain aspects of lesbian and gay conduct and identity. As a result, international law is emerging as a distinct source of legal rights to which sexual minorities can sometimes turn when their national governments refuse to recognize or protect their basic liberties. The decisions of these tribunals have also helped to buttress claims by advocates that respecting the dignity of lesbians and gay men should be an accepted part of the broader international human rights movement.

The development of international human rights as a distinct component of public international law emerged in the years immediately following World War II. The 1945 United Nations Charter and the 1948 Universal Declaration of Human Rights committed the member countries of the United Nations to promote and protect fundamental rights and freedoms shared by all human beings. The International Covenant on Civil and Political Rights and the International Covenant on Economic, Social, and Cultural Rights, both finalized in 1966, further clarified these rights and freedoms and established monitoring bodies of human rights experts to help ensure compliance by national governments. Additional UN human rights conventions provide detailed prohibitions against torture and race and sex discrimination, and protect children's rights. Finally, human rights treaties have also been adopted on a regional level in Europe, the Americas, and Africa.

The most significant developments in lesbian and gay human rights have occurred in Europe under the European Convention on Human Rights. In the 1981 landmark case of *Dudgeon v. United Kingdom*, the European Court of Human Rights ruled that Northern Ireland's criminal ban on homosexual sodomy between consenting adults in private violated the right to respect for private life protected by the convention. The court specifically rejected the government's argument that majoritarian moral sentiments provided a sufficient justification for upholding the law, stating that "although members of the public who regard homosexuality as immoral may be shocked, offended, or disturbed by the commission by others of private homosexual acts, this cannot on its own warrant the application of penal sanctions when it is consenting adults alone who are involved." The court did not, however, consider whether the sodomy statute also violated the convention's nondiscrimination right.

After the British government repealed the sodomy statute in response to *Dudgeon*, advocates for lesbians and gay men brought additional cases under the European Convention, hoping that other favorable rulings would be forthcoming. In some ways, this has come to pass. In 1988, the court refused to uphold Britain's criminal ban on consensual sodomy, and it reached the same decision in 1993 in a case against Cyprus. Yet in other respects, the hoped-for expansion of the *Dudgeon* case has not occurred. It is the European Commission of Human Rights, a tribunal that screens claims before they can be appealed to the European Court, that has limited the convention's applicability to gay and lesbian concerns.

The commission has rejected challenges to numerous laws that discriminate against lesbians and gay men. These include a statute that prohibits homosexuals from serving in the armed forces, a law that denies the ability of same-sex partners to continue an apartment lease after one of them dies, and an immigration policy permitting the deportation of one partner in a same-sex relationship if one of them is a foreign national. In the past, the commission repeatedly upheld statutes that impose a higher age of consent for gay men as compared with heterosexuals or lesbians, but in 1997, in the case of *Sutherland v. United Kingdom*, it upheld a challenge to the United Kingdom's unequal age of consent laws, concluding that the laws discriminate against gay men and violate their right to respect for private life.

European advocates have been more successful at achieving law reforms by invoking human rights principles at the national level. As a result of their efforts, general antidiscrimination laws including sexual orientation have been enacted in Norway, Ireland, Slovenia, France, Denmark, Sweden, and the Netherlands. Incitement to hatred against gays and lesbians is now a criminal offense in Norway, Sweden, Denmark, and Ireland. Belgium, Estonia, France, Germany, Iceland, Latvia, and Luxembourg equalized the age of consent for sexual relations within the last decade, and a dozen or so European nations permit lesbians and gay men to serve in the armed forces. Finally, Denmark, Norway, Sweden, and Iceland permit same-sex couples to marry and enjoy rights comparable to married heterosexual couples. Law reform efforts are by no means complete, however, and many European countries continue to discriminate against lesbians and gay men in numerous aspects of their public and private lives.

Given this patchwork of legal protections and the limited relief available under the European Convention, advocates and litigants have turned their attention to the European Court of Justice, the judicial arm of the fifteen-member European Community (EC). They have asked the court to rule that an European Unity (EU) directive prohibiting discrimination "on grounds of sex" in employment matters encompasses discrimination on the basis of sexual orientation. In February 1998, in a ruling that surprised and angered lesbian and gay rights advocates, the court in *Grant v. Southwest Trains*, rejected this claim, ruling that British Rail could legally provide free travel passes to its employees' unmarried heterosexual partners, but could deny those same passes to its employees' same-sex partners. In a second pending case, *Perkins v. Regina*, the court will soon consider whether the employment directive prohibits governments from dismissing a member of the armed forces because of his homosexuality.

Although the human rights dimension of sexual orientation has been a frequent subject of both European litigation and European politics, no other region of the globe had until recently experienced similar developments. That outlook changed unequivocally in April 1994, when the UN Human Rights Committee, the body of eighteen independent experts that reviews complaints filed by individuals under the International Covenant on Civil and Political Rights, decided the case of *Toonen v. Australia*. The committee unanimously concluded that the sodomy statutes in force in the Australian state of Tasmania violated the right to be free from arbitrary interference with one's private life and the right to nondiscrimination protected by the covenant. In a significant and controversial aspect of its ruling, the committee also concluded that the word *sex* in the covenant's nondiscrimination clauses "is to be taken as including sexual orientation."

The Australian federal government responded to the committee's decision by enacting the Human Rights (Sexual Conduct) Act of 1994, which effectively prohibits the criminal persecution of consensual homosexual conduct in private. In May 1997, the Tasmanian parliament, bowing to national and international pressure, finally repealed the statutes entirely.

Two important trends can be discerned from the recent experience of lesbians and gay men seeking the protection of international human rights laws. First, although international challenges to sodomy statutes have been the most successful cases thus far, they provide only limited protection and concern primarily the private lives of lesbians and gay men. Cases seeking to overturn legal hurdles that sexual minorities face in the public realm—such as discrimination in employment, recognition of marriages and domestic partnerships, and freedom of expression and association—have been far less successful. As a result, advocates have developed new strategies to achieve greater legal protection, including bringing test cases based on the fact that discrimination on the basis of sexual orientation is a form of sex discrimination. Given the recent rejection of this argument by the European Court of Justice, it remains to be seen how successful this strategy will be.

Second, what began as an exclusively European phenomenon is now spreading to the rest of the world. Advocates for lesbian and gay equality can now argue with increasing force that the link between

I sexual orientation and human rights is not limited to one region but rather is part of a global system for protecting basic individual liberties. International advocacy and litigation in other parts of the world is now likely to increase, particularly because the UN Human Rights Committee is authorized to hear complaints from individuals in more than 85 countries and to receive government reports from more than 130 countries.   *Laurence R. Helfer*

Cases

Dudgeon v. United Kingdom, 45 Eur. Ct. H.R. (ser. A) (1981), reprinted in 4 Eur. Hum. Rts. Rep. 149 (1981).

Norris v. Ireland, 142 Eur. Ct. H.R. (Ser. A) (1988), reprinted in 13 Eur. Hum. Rts. Rep. 186 (1991).

Modinos v. Cyprus, 259 Eur. Ct. H.R. (Ser. A) (1993), reprinted in 16 Eur. Hum. Rts. Rep. 485 (1993).

Sutherland v. United Kingdom, App. No. 25186/94.

Grant v. Southwest Trains, Ltd., Case No. 1784/96.

Perkins v. Regina, Case No. 279/96.

Toonen v. Australia, Comm. No. 488/1992, UN GAOR Hum. Rts. Comm., 49th Sess. Supp. No. 40, vol. II at 226 (1994), reprinted in1 Int'l Hum. Rts. Rep. 97 (1994).

Bibliography

Heinze, Eric. *Sexual Orientation: A Human Right.* Dordrecht, NL: Martinus Nijhoff, 1995.

Helfer, Laurence R., and Alice M. Miller. "Sexual Orientation and Human Rights: Toward a United States and Transnational Jurisprudence." *Harvard Human Rights Journal* (1996).

International Lesbian and Gay Human Rights Commission. *Unspoken Rules: Sexual Orientation and Women's Human Rights* (1995).

Sanders, Douglas. "Getting Lesbian and Gay Issues on the International Human Rights Agenda." 18 *Human Rights Quarterly* 67 (1996).

Wintemute, Robert. *Sexual Orientation and Human Rights: The United States Constitution, the European Convention, and the Canadian Charter.* Oxford: Clarendon, 1995.

See also Denmark; European Commission of Human Rights; France; Germany; Ireland; Netherlands; Slovenia; Sweden

Inversion

Inversion as a term to describe homosexual desire entered British scientific discourse in 1897, when Havelock Ellis and John Addington Symonds published their book *Sexual Inversion*. The term probably circulated in English thought for at least some time before that as well, but Ellis and Symonds's book marks its most major and respected articulation as a psychological term.

Ellis, who wrote the majority of the tract, defines "congenital sexual inversion" as "sexual instinct turned by inborn constitutional abnormality towards persons of the same sex." The tract further draws a distinction between "homosexual love," which is "sexual attraction between persons of the same sex, due merely to the accidental absence of the natural objects of sexual attraction," and inversion. Homosexual love is "of universal occurrence among all human races and among most of the higher animals," whereas inversion "is a comparatively rare phenomenon."

This formulation introduces several notions that are of extreme importance in the history of sexual thought. First, the distinction between homosexual love and inversion marks a line between desire and identity. Homosexual love or desire may be felt by anyone and may be largely environmental. Inversion, on the other hand, is a unique constitutional identification that constitutes a specific subpopulation of people. Ellis's definition therefore foreshadows two major modes of thought regarding sexuality. "Homosexual love" anticipates Freudian ideas of desire, in which every person is subject to polymorphous patterns of desire and experiences an essential bisexuality; inversion looks forward to civil rights discourses, which seek to view homosexuals as a unique status or class in society.

The most important part of the definition of sexual inversion, however, is the insistence that true inversion is congenital—that is, biologically or hereditarily predetermined. Prior to Ellis's theorization, the dominant theories of sexuality posited deviances as the effect of degeneration—that is, as the effects of disease and decay on the healthy system. In such a schema, sexual differences are inherently pathological. For Ellis, inversion is inherently a predisposition of the general constitution of the subject, and this hereditary predisposition "either appears spontaneously from the first, by development or arrest of development, or it is called into activity by some accidental circumstance." Ellis's theory in many ways marks the first successful attempt to pry sexuality from the discourses of pathology and to open a space for the invert as a healthy, unique, individual classification.

In its own time, Ellis's work as a sexual theorist was enormously influential. *Sexual Inversion* appeared as a part of a massive, multivolume study, *Studies in the Psychology of Sex*, which contained comparative anthropological studies of topics ranging from masturbation to urolagnia. However, the cultural authority of inversion theory quickly diminished in the 1920s, owing primarily to the rise of Freudian psychoanalysis as the preferred discourse of treatment for psychological abnormalities in the wake of World War I.   *Gregory W. Bredbeck*

Bibliography

Ellis, Havelock, and John Addington Symonds. *Sexual Inversion*. London: Wilson and Macmillan, 1897.

See also Ellis, Havelock; Freud, Sigmund; Homosexuality; Masturbation; Sexology; Symonds, John Addington; Third Sex

Iran

Often incorrectly perceived in the West as Arab, Iran actually derives its name from the word *Aryan*, testifying to its claim to an Indo-European heritage and language. While there is a small ethnic Arab minority (along with Turks, Azeris, Kurds, and others), most Iranians are Farsi-speaking ethnic Persians. Farsi, though written in Arabic script, is Indo-European and not Semitic in origin.

Located in southwestern Asia, Iran has always been strategically significant to foreign powers. Known in antiquity as Persia, the region was conquered by the Arabs in the seventh century C.E., and the predominantly Zoroastrian populace rapidly converted to Islam. (Today, approximately 90 percent of the population follows the Shiite sect of Islam, 10 percent Sunni Islam, and there remains a dwindling number of Zoroastrians, Christians, Jews, and Baha'i.) Later conquerors would include Turks, Mongols, and Russians. In the modern era, with the discovery of oil in the region, Great Britain, the United States, the USSR, and Germany have all vied for control of the region.

Despite Islamic injunctions against male-male sex acts, during the premodern era homosexual love was celebrated by Persian poets such as Rumi, Hafiz, and Omar Khayyám. In the classical poetry of these authors, homosexual relationships almost always consisted of an older man (the active, or "masculine," partner) falling in love with a beautiful young boy (always the passive, or "feminine," partner). In fact, "Khurasan love," named for the province where Khayyám was born, was a common euphemism for pederasty. Probably as a result of the inaccessibility of women to men within the highly sexually segregated Iranian society, pederasty and male-male sex acts were tolerated, provided that a certain level of discretion was maintained and provided that patriarchal values were reinscribed through the gendering of one participant as "male" and the other as "female."

A similar view of homosexual acts has continued into the modern era, with some modifications. In the 1950s, the U.S.-backed Pahlavi government instituted and enforced a widespread modernization and Westernization program. In the following decades, a more "Western" style of homosexuality began to appear alongside the traditional *bachebazi* (literally, boyplay). Gay bars began to appear in the capital, Tehran, and male hustlers began to ply their trade openly. Encouraged by gay Westerners living and working in Iran, a small gay rights movement even started to develop.

The overthrow of Shah Pahlavi in 1979 and the rise of the Ayatollah Khomeini resulted in hostility toward the West and many Western institutions and influences. For political reasons, the new Islamic regime labeled homosexuality as uniquely Western in origin, and in the turbulent years immediately following the revolution, many homosexuals were executed as enemies of Islam and society. While many people may have been executed solely for their homosexuality, most were found guilty of a whole list of crimes of which homosexuality was but one. Homosexuality was often included on lists of charges simply as further proof of the criminal's supposed degeneracy. The widespread persecution and execution of homosexuals ceased in the mid-1980s, and recent reports from Iran currently indicate the presence of a growing underground homosexual community.   *Richard McKewen*

Bibliography

Chebel, Malek. *Encyclopédie de l'amour en Islam: Éroticism, beauté et sexualité dans le monde arabe, en Perse et en Turquie.* Paris: Éditions Payot & Rivages, 1995.

Kafi, Hélène. "Tehran: Dangerous Love." In *Sexuality and Eroticism Among Males in Moslem Societies.* Arno Schmitt and Jehoeda Sofer, eds. New York: Haworth Press, 1992, 67–69.

See also Activism, International; Arabic Literature; Beloved; Dancing Boys; Islam; Islamic Mysticism; Persian (Iranian) Literature and Culture

Ireland

In 1993, after a lengthy civil rights campaign, the Irish Parliament (Dail) finally passed a bill decriminalizing homosexuality, that is, between adult males and thus ending a lengthy era of official unease with sexual difference in Irish society. The original British law outlawing homosexuality, the so-called Labouchère Amendment (1885), had been incorporated into Irish law in 1922, as part of the creation of an independent Irish state, and this resulted in religious and social intolerance for homosexuality until the start of a gay liberation movement in the early 1970s. The Labouchère Amendment had already been repealed in Britain in 1967, but it took another twenty-six years for this Victorian statute to be removed from Irish law. (The Labouchère Amendment, nicknamed the "Blackmailers Charter," sentenced Oscar Wilde, Ireland's most celebrated gay writer, to prison in 1895.)

In cultural terms, when religious and judicial codes refused legitimacy and public space for same-sex desire, it is difficult to classify or trace a lesbian and gay culture or identify one before the 1970s. Postcolonial countries like Ireland have particular difficulty with homosexuality because colonialism generates a gendered power relationship and sees the colonizing power (Britain) as masculine and dominant and the colonized (Ireland) as feminine and passive. Therefore, in Irish cultural discourse, silencing sexual difference became an imperative, and thus Ireland provides a striking example of this kind of postcolonial censorship. Gay rights campaigner David Norris argues persuasively that the history of the prosecution of same-sex desire in Ireland is intertwined with the history of colonization. In spite of this, some Irish writers did manage to write about gay and lesbian identity and explored dissident sexualities within their works, most notably Oscar Wilde (1854–1900), poet Eva Gore-Booth (1870–1926), actor and dramatist Michael MacLiammoir (1899–1978), and novelist Kate O'Brien (1897–1974).

For Irish lesbians, the issue of identity was more complicated because of the lack of a public identity, even a criminalized one. (It is said that Queen Victoria had objected to the criminalization of lesbianism on the grounds that it did not exist!) There was more than one attempt (1895 and 1922) to make lesbianism a crime, but this never made the statute books, and so Irish lesbians were both outside the law and at the same time rendered invisible by lack of official recognition, or condemnation.

The only Irish lesbian writer directly banned by the Irish government was Kate O'Brien, for her 1941 novel, *The Land of Spices*, a controversial banning that led to a public outcry and a parliamentary debate. What is significant about this incident of censorship is that *The Land of Spices* was banned for referring to homosexual rather than lesbian desire. This lack of an official identity for Irish lesbians can be seen as something of a mixed blessing, with little cultural visibility but a greater freedom from prosecution and a consequent imaginative freedom and openness, and this is reflected in the writings of contemporary Irish lesbians.

The whole process of challenging the law began in 1980, when Joycean scholar and activist David Norris brought a case against the Irish government, arguing that the criminalization of his own sexuality was an infringement on his constitutional rights as an Irish citizen. In 1988, having lost his case in the Irish courts, Norris and his attorney, Mary Robinson (now president of Ireland), brought their case to the European Court of Human Rights and won. However, it took the Irish government another five years to act on this case and reform the law. (For a full account of gay law reform in Ireland, see Kieran Rose's excellent *Diverse Communities*.)

As a result of this alteration in legal status, contemporary Irish lesbian and gay culture has been experiencing a distinct sense of empowerment and revitalization. More specifically, in TV, drama, literature, film, and popular culture, a modern Irish lesbian and gay identity has come into its own, and thus one can observe an appropriation of Irish literary, linguistic, and dramatic forms to express a lesbian and gay identity. This gay sensibility within contemporary Irish culture is found in dramas like Gerry Stembridge's *The Gay Detective*, in the Wet Paint Theatre's education project *Tangles*, in short story collections like David Marcus's *Alternative Loves* or Mary Dorcey's *Noises from the Woodshed*, in Irish language Ceili's or Gay-li's, the gay rights group GLEN, the free newspaper *Gay Community News,* and the *Out-To Play* lesbian and gay theater project. All these creative and political projects reflect a new confidence for the contemporary Irish lesbian and gay imagination. Most significantly, in the poetry of Irish-language writer Cathal O'Searcaigh, we find a remaking of a contemporary Irish gay imagination through the traditions of Gaelic poetry.

A distinct difference between Irish lesbian and Irish gay writing has emerged. Men writing from or about a sexually dissident perspective in Ireland have traditionally occupied a more public space, especially in theater, and therefore have tended to be more circumspect in their representation of sexual otherness. Women, on the other hand, have occupied a different literary space, using letters and diaries, and then novels and short stories to develop a lesbian sensibility, often more radical and subversive but less widely known. Writers like Emma Donoghue and Mary Dorcey are part of this contemporary lesbian sensibility in Ireland and in the universities, centers for women's studies have facilitated the emergence of Irish lesbian and gay literary and cultural studies, as seen in the 1997 collection of essays *Sex, Nation and Dissent in Irish Writing*.

Eibhear Walshe

Bibliography

Collins, Eoin, and Ide O'Carroll. *Lesbian and Gay Visions of Ireland*. London: Cassells, 1995.

Donoghue, Emma. *Stir-Fry*. London: Hamish Hamilton 1994.

Dorcey, Mary. *The River That Carries Me*. Galway, Ireland: Salmon, 1995.

Marcus, David. *Alternative Loves*. Dublin: Martello, 1994.

Norris, David. "Homosexual People and the Christian Church." *Crane Bag* 5, no. 1 (1981).

Rose, Kieran. *Diverse Communities*. Cork, Ireland: Cork University Press, 1994.

Walshe, Eibhear. *Sex, Nation and Dissent in Irish Writing*. Cork, Ireland: Cork University Press, 1997.

See also Casement, Roger; Colonialism; European Commission of Human Rights; International Law; Wilde, Oscar

Ireland, John (1879–1962)

English composer John Ireland was unusual among twentieth-century British composers in rejecting the legacy of German symphonists, preferring the French impressionism of Debussy and Ravel. This led to the creation of a series of lapidary songs such as the once popular "Sea-Fever," and elegant piano pieces, such as "The Island Spell" and "The Holy Boy." At its best, Ireland's music is a fetching combination of French sensibility and English pastoralism, but his creamy harmonic idiom, closer to Delius than Debussy, is in constant danger of clotting into a series of cloying and affected mannerisms.

Psychologically crippled by the tyranny of the closet, Ireland's life was one of almost unrelieved gloom. Despite passionate homoerotic attachments to choirboys and male friends, he tried several times to woo social normalcy by courting various women. This ill-advised strategy culminated in a disastrous attempt at marriage in 1927, which was annulled shortly after an unconsummated wedding night. After this semipublic humiliation, Ireland sank ever deeper into depression. Although his chronic alcoholism was an open secret in English musical circles, Ireland was allowed to remain as a composition teacher at the Royal College of Music; his famous pupil, Benjamin Britten, recorded in his diary that Ireland was often drunk during lessons. Ireland virtually stopped composing in the 1940s, and his later years were marked by illness, blindness, and profound melancholy.

Byron Adams

Bibliography

Banfield, Stephen. *Sensibility and the English Song*. Cambridge: Cambridge University Press, 1985.

Longmire, John. *John Ireland: Portrait of a Friend*. London: John Baker, 1969.

See also Britten, Benjamin; English Pastoral Composers

Isherwood, Christopher (1904–1986)

Born Christopher William Bradshaw Isherwood on August 26, 1904, in High Lane, Cheshire, England, into a family of landed gentry, Isherwood was educated at Repton School and Corpus Christi, Cambridge. After leaving the university without a degree in 1925, he frankly acknowledged his homosexuality to himself and to his mother, and renewed his friendship with W. H. Auden, his former classmate at St. Edmund's preparatory school, with whom he was to share an unromantic sexual relationship for some ten years. Isherwood published his first novel, *All the Conspirators*, in 1928, but its low sales prompted a brief attempt to study medicine at King's College, London. After visiting Berlin in 1929, he decided to move there. Living in Berlin from 1930 to 1933, he came to feel liberated from the sexual and social inhibitions that stifled his development in England. In Berlin, he revised his second novel, *The Memorial* (1932), and translated his experience of the demimonde into what would eventually become the unsurpassed portrait of pre-Hitler Germany, the *Berlin Stories* (comprising *The Last of Mr. Norris* [1935] and *Good-bye to Berlin* [1938]).

Disillusioned with English insularity and with left-wing politics, Isherwood and Auden emigrated to the United States in 1939. Declaring himself a pacifist, Isherwood settled in Los Angeles, where he supported himself by writing film scripts. In 1940, the influence of a Hindu monk and surrogate father, Swami Prabhavananda, prompted his conversion to Vedantism. He became a U.S. citizen in 1946. In 1971, he publicly revealed his homosexuality and became an active participant in the American gay liberation movement. He died of cancer on January 4, 1986, survived by the artist Don Bachardy, his partner of thirty-three years.

Isherwood's homosexuality had a major influence on his art. His interest in certain psychological predicaments and in recurring character types and themes, as well as his fascination with the antiheroic hero, his rebellion against bourgeois respectability, his identification with the excluded, and his ironic perspective, are probably all directly or indirectly related to his homosexuality. Homosexuality features in all his work, including the celebrated *Berlin Stories*, but it is treated most explicitly in his later novels, beginning with *The World in the Evening* (1954), which presents perhaps the earliest sympathetic portrait of a gay activist in Anglo-American literature. Isherwood's masterpiece is *A Single Man* (1964), which traces one day in the life of a gay, middle-aged English professor grieving at the death of his lover of many years. The book is at once a classic of gay literature and a profound meditation on death and decay. It vigorously asserts a minority consciousness, thereby anticipating the gay liberation movement, but also places this consciousness within a larger context of spiritual transcendence. In *Christopher and His Kind* (1976), a revisionist reinterpretation of his experience in the 1930s, Isherwood makes clear that homosexuality was one of the central aspects of his life, and that the homophobia of the Western world necessarily invested his sexuality with political significance.

Homosexuality was not only Isherwood's nature but also his way of protesting the "heterosexual dictatorship." Perhaps the finest Anglo-American novelist of his generation, Isherwood was also a courageous teacher who unashamedly expressed solidarity with his "kind."   *Claude J. Summers*

Bibliography

Finney, Brian. *Christopher Isherwood: A Critical Biography*. New York: Oxford University Press, 1979.

Summers, Claude J. *Christopher Isherwood*. New York: Ungar, 1980.

See also Auden, W. H.; English Literature; Los Angeles

Islam

According to the teachings of Islam, sexual intercourse between males is a sin, and its only concern with this aspect of human sexuality is therefore to determine who should be punished and the nature of the punishment.

Islamic law is based only to some extent on the Qur'an, the word revealed by God to the prophet Muhammad. This is not a legal text, however, and does not touch on all aspects of human behavior. The explicitly Qur'anic law is called the *shari'a*, while the basis for most of Islamic law is tradition (*hadith*). The injunctions against homosexuality derived from the Qur'an are based on interpretations of passages referring to Lot and his family, who lived in Sodom before they were warned by an angel to leave that city, which was about to be punished for its sins. Thus, the common Arabic word for the sin of Sodom is *liwat*, derived from the name of Lot. In one of these Qur'anic passages male sodomy seems to be blamed for the punishment of the city, namely, Surah 26:165–175, where Lot's family are said to have left their wives and come unto males, whence the destruction of Sodom. Of texts not connected with Lot, Surah 4:16 contains an instruction to punish two males from the community of believers who have sexual relations. The nature of the punishment is not stated, but since the possibility is allowed for that they may repent and mend their ways, in which case they are to be let be, it was concluded that the Prophet considered this a lesser crime than, for instance, heterosexual "fornication" (Arabic *zina*), which was to be punished with a hundred whiplashes (Surah 24:2). This allegedly lenient attitude of the Prophet is also reported in stories from the Prophet's life (*akhbar*), but according the *hadith*, all sexual acts between males are criminal, although the punishment is not set.

In the punishment of homosexual offenses, a distinction was often made as to whether the offender was free or unfree, married (*muhsan*) or not. Thus, Ibn al-Jawzi of the Hanbalite school reports the Prophet to have said that male sodomy made the throne of God itself tremble, and Hanbalite scholars, quoting Surah 26, maintained sodomy should be punished with death by stoning; the official Hanbalite position was that sodomy was to be treated like fornication, and a free married man must be stoned to death, while if free and unmarried, his crime was punished only with one hundred lashes. According to a different *hadith*, however, both married and unmarried offenders should be put to death. This was one of the positions of the Shafi'ites; the other was that a married man should be stoned, while the unmarried should be whipped and deported. Lawyers from the Hanafite school, on the other hand, quoted a *hadith* according to which a Muslim could suffer capital punishment only because of fornication, apostasy, or homicide, and since they did not consider sodomy to be fornication, it should not be punished in the same way but rather with imprisonment or flagellation or both. There are numerous reports throughout the history of Islam of cruel punishments inflicted on men accused of sodomy, which show that the former view often prevailed. Clear proof of sodomy (and other sexual offenses) had to be produced, however; usually it required the testimony of four trustworthy Muslim men or the four times repeated confession of the offender. There was also severe punishment for false accusations ("slander of fornication"), which helped reduce the number of actually imposed penalties. The ambiguous attitude to sexual intercourse between males is reflected in the rules for ablutions necessary before praying: in paragraph 349 of his "Clarification of Questions," Khomeini states a definition of "ejaculator" (requiring specific ablution procedures) that includes all kinds of intercourse.

Nonsexual or spiritual love, however, or admiration for unbearded young males is cited even in connection with the Prophet himself, although he allegedly warned against the dangers of temptation, and, according to Surah 56:17–18, they serve as cupbearers in paradise.

Studies of Islamic homosexuality have little to say about the evolution of attitudes throughout the centuries, on a scholarly, theological, or sociological level, though anecdotal material is relatively abundant, and male relationships are frequent literary topics. From this it has been concluded that sexual relations between older and younger men were never uncommon and therefore must have been tolerated to varying degrees at different times. Especially the arrival of the Abbasid army, with its notoriously pedophile leader, al-Amin, is reported to have brought about an increase in male-male sexual relationships. Female relationships are also reported at various times from various places, and sexual relationships between women were also condemned in the *hadith*.

Male prostitutes and cross-dressers (*mukhannath*) are frequently mentioned by travelers in Muslim countries; apparently they were not to be punished as severely as homosexuals but were nevertheless expelled from the towns under dire threat of punishment were they to return.

In modern times Islamic law has been modified, sometimes relaxed, especially under the influence of Western law (notably British and French/Italian), and partly again reintroduced with a vengeance. Not infrequently it is left to the judge to determine the punishment, a procedure referred to as *ta'zir*. The most progressive of Muslim countries is probably Turkey, whose gender-neutral law has provisions only for the protection of minors (under fifteen) and against sexual harassment. At the other end of the spectrum, in the penal code of the present Iranian regime, some forms of sodomy are still (or again) punishable by death, for a non-Muslim even for rubbing his penis between the thighs or buttocks of a Muslim (without penetration). In other countries the death penalty is applied only when the offense is aggravated by rape and/or murder. Life imprisonment is the penalty for aggravated sodomy on a blood relative in Iraq.

It is not in the nature of Islam to "love the sinner, but hate the sin"; on the contrary, while the sin is widely condoned, the sinner must be punished—if caught. The *Bismillah* ("In the name of God the compassionate and merciful)," recited millions of times a day by Muslims all over the world, in the interpretation of conservative Muslims, does not induce tolerance and acceptance; eliminating offenders such as homosexuals constitutes an act of compassion for the rest of society, which is thereby purified and protected from their offenses.

Prods Oktor Skjaervo

Bibliography

Khomeini, Ruhollah Mousavi. *A Clarification of Questions: An Unabridged Translation of Resaleh Towzih al-Masael.* J. Boroudjerdi, trans. Boulder: Westview Press, 1984.

Schild, Maarten. "Islam." In *Sexuality and Eroticism Among Males in Moslem Societies.* Arno Schmitt and Jehoeda Sofer, eds. 179–87.

Schmitt, Arno, and Jehoeda Sofer, eds. *Sexuality and Eroticism Among Males in Moslem Societies.* New York: Harrington Park Press, 1992.

Sofer, Jehoeda. "Sodomy in the Law of Muslim States." In *Sexuality and Eroticism Among Males in Moslem Societies*. Arno Schmitt and Jehoeda Sofer, eds. 131–49.

See also Arabic Literature; Beloved; Iran; Islamic Mysticism; Indonesia; Mukhannath; Persian (Iranian) Literature and Culture; Sodomy

Islamic Mysticism

Muslim authors frequently include references to love of young men in their prose and poetry, and mystical writers (Sufis) are no exception. The difference between mystical writers and others rather lies in the deeper meaning they imparted to this theme. Since their aim was to express their relationship with God, descriptions of male relationships were used metaphorically to express the mystical relationship between the Sufi and the ultimate reality. The metaphor of male love takes on different forms in the literature, among which is the standard theme of the poet's love for young beardless males, the *shahid*, or "witness," of the divine beauty—hence he is also called an "idol"—but also love for women. The fact that some Sufis occasionally moved this love down from the spiritual to the material level is unimportant in this context; it has even been suggested that some poets intended to blur the distinction between erotic and spiritual love. The theme of the love for the young man is often accompanied by other themes: it often takes place in musical gatherings in which drinking of wine is also indulged in, which further indicates that the mystics' concern is not with this world, in which both activities were condemned. Rather, the gathering of the mystics reflects paradise, the drinking of wine divine intoxication, and the beautiful young servant boy the Divine beloved, hence the necessity of his presence.

The love theme has several aspects. One is the beauty of the beloved, another the suffering of the poet from the beloved's torturing him, which can cease only when the beloved kills him, usually by beheading. The latter aspect clearly indicates that the lover has entered "the mystery that is beyond human comprehension" (Wafer 109). Since the beauty of the beloved is a reflex of that of the Divine, the revelation of the beloved's complete beauty (or body), which the poet seeks, is likely to overwhelm the beholder, as in the case of Sultan Mahmud, who, on learning that his slave boy Ayaz had gone to the bath, rushed after him and, beholding the boy's naked body, fell into a swoon. Persian poet Farid-al-din Attar's description of how Mahmud explained his weakness shows clearly the transcendence of the situation: "As long as I only saw your face, I knew nothing of your limbs; now that I see all your limbs, I have become quite wretched. My soul was already on fire with love of your face, but now a hundred new fires have ignited me, and I don't know which of your limbs I should love more" (Wafer 124).

Presumably because the young man is the reflection of God himself, sex and sexual relief are not usually part of the relationship, although the need for close physical contact with the beloved is often expressed. Also, since in male sexual relationships the youth was necessarily the passive one, we see that the metaphor hardly leaves room for sex, altogether, and one wonders if the motif of suffering and death—as well as the whirling dance of the dervishes—may not have originated from the necessary suppression of sexual impulse in the man-God relationship. Another way out of this quandary was for the Sufi to take the passive role vis-à-vis God. This then led to the image of the Sufi—or his soul—as a bride, who is ultimately enjoyed by her bridegroom, sitting in God's lap naked, so that they can see each other's private parts. This imagery is even connected with the notion of God's dual attributes of *jamal* (beauty and kindness) and *jalal* (power and majesty), so that one poet describes the virgin soul's penetration by God as the expression of his *jalal*.

Prods Oktor Skjaervo

Bibliography

Murray, Stephen O., and Roscoe, Will, eds. *Islamic Homosexualities: Culture, History, and Literature*. New York: New York University Press, 1997.

Schimmel, Annemarie. *As Through a Veil: Mystical Poetry in Islam*. New York: Columbia University Press, 1982.

———. "Eros—Heavenly and not so Heavenly—In Sufi Literature and Life." In *Society and the Sexes in Medieval Islam*. A. Lutfi al-Sayyid Marsot, ed. Malibu, Calif.: Undena, 1979, 119–41.

———. *Mystical Dimensions of Islam*. Chapel Hill, N.C.: University of North Carolina Press, 1975.

Wafer, Jim. "Vision and Passion. The Symbolism of Male Love in Islamic Mystical Literature." In *Islamic Homosexualities. Culture, History, and Literature*. Stephen O. Murray and Roscoe Will, eds. 107–31.

See also Arabic Literature; Beloved; Islam; Persian (Iranian) Literature and Culture

Islas, Arturo (1938–1991)

A year before his death from AIDS-related causes in 1991, Arturo Islas told an audience of his colleagues, students, and admirers at Stanford University that he saw his life as one lived on a bridge between cultures, languages, sexes, and religions, and between his profession as an educator and his vocation as a writer. The author of three of the finer novels in the Chicano/a literary canon, *The Rain God* (1984), *Migrant Souls* (1991), and *La Mollie and the King of Tears* (1993, posthumous), Islas was also a successful and beloved professor of English at Stanford, where he received his undergraduate and graduate degrees. In *The Rain God* and *Migrant Souls*, Islas wove in elegant, lyric prose a largely autobiographical account of his familial and cultural roots in El Paso, Texas, where he was born and where he grew up. These two novels also document, through the character of Miguel (Chico) Angel, Islas's own struggles with his sexual and cultural identity, his commitment to both the traditional sensibilities of his family in Texas and the secular cosmopolitanism of university life in the San Francisco Bay Area, and his long history of illness. The ribald and playful *La Mollie* represents Islas's stylistic and tonal departure from the more melancholic earlier novels, an artistic experiment Islas did not live to see through to its fulfillment. Critical work on Islas by both Chicano/a and gay scholars is ongoing, but perhaps the best-known study of Islas is José David Salvídar's account in a chapter of *The Dialectics of Our America,* which describes Islas's struggle to sell his first novel to the Anglo-dominated U.S. publishing industry.   *Ricardo Ortiz*

Bibliography

Saldívar, José David. "The Hybridity of Arturo Islas's *The Rain God.*" In *The Dialectics of Our America: Queer Readings, Hispanic Writings*. Emile Bergman and Paul Julian Smith, eds. Durham, N.C.: Duke University Press, 1991, 105–20.

See also AIDS Literature; Chicano and Latino Gay Cultures

Israel and Palestine

In May 1998 Dana International, Israel's disco diva, won the Eurovision songfest that had, in previous years, catapulted Sweden's ABBA and Canadian Celine Dion to international prominence. The fact that Dana International won was not a sensation—Israeli singers had won twice before, back to back in 1970—but the fact that Dana International is an out, loud, and proud transsexual was sensational. Hundreds celebrated at Rabin Square in the heart of Tel Aviv; weeks later, thousands poured into the streets in protest when the annual Wigstock event was cut short by police sent to reinforce the Sabbath closing time in accordance with Orthodox Jewish practice (for observant Jews, a day begins at sundown, not dawn). In between, Dana International was treated to a hero's welcome in the Knesset (parliament) and crowned as Israel's roving ambassador by Tourism Minister Moshe Katsav. Then she flew to Europe to perform at gay pride events and launch an international career.

Meanwhile, in Israel, Pride Week in June was heralded by the strong showing of lesbian Michal Eden: she placed second in the progressive Meretz Party's election of candidates for the Tel Aviv city council. Then, on the hottest day in memory, thousands of gay men and lesbians marched and motorcaded through downtown Tel Aviv in the country's first-ever parade, signaling that the community was finally out of the closet.

It was not always so. Before 1991, Israel's lesbians, gay men, bisexuals, and transsexuals were deeply closeted and formed only ad hoc communities that centered on bars that catered to them only once a week in Tel Aviv, the metropolitan center in which one in six Israelis resides. In 1991, Israel's lesbigay rights umbrella organization, the Society for the Protection of Personal Rights (SPPR), decided to expand its board from five to nine members to ensure participation by a wider cross section, including one Arab and three from the geographical periphery of Haifa (north) and Beersheba (south). A concerted effort was initiated to bring lesbian, gay, and bisexual (LGB) issues to the attention of the media and the mainstream public, under the slogan "From the closet to the living room." Three years later, public opinion had changed in response to the mostly favorable media exposure.

The SPPR was established in 1975 by a handful of courageous gay rights pioneers. Four years later, when the Fourth International Conference of Gay and Lesbian Jews was held in Israel, and nobody wanted to rent space to the organization for the meetings, the first public protest took place, with the participation of some twenty lesbians and gay

I men, mostly from overseas. It was still dangerous to be out and proud because sodomy was still a felony. Before that conference, extensive fund-raising took place to ensure the planting of a gay grove of three-thousand trees in the Lahav Forest near Beersheba. The Jewish National Fund (JNF), which is responsible for planting forests in Israel, refused to place a sign noting the donors and their sexual orientation. It took thirteen years, but finally in 1992 the plaque was put in place and was the site a picnic heralding Israel's first gay pride week the next year. Interestingly, in 1994, when the next picnic took place there, this time hosted by the local representative of the JNF, it was noticed that the plaque was no longer in place. So ironically, later that summer, the LGB community held the festive commemorative ceremony that had been denied them in 1979.

In 1988, Shulamit Aloni, the founder and chair of the Citizen's Rights Movement in Israel, introduced a bill to rescind the sodomy law and, in the absence of the religious parties, steered it through three readings in as many minutes to overturn one of the relics of the British Mandate (1922–1948). Hadar Namir, an SPPR activist who later became the first open lesbian activist on national television on a late-night news program, immediately organized Otzma, an advocacy group determined to pursue other legal rights for the (still closeted) LGB community. The five-year plan called for a change in the labor code to ensure the rights of lesbians and gay men; the change was effected in eighteen months. On January 2, 1991, the law went into effect and was instrumental in helping flight attendant Jonathan Danilovich win a court case against his employer, El-Al Airlines, which was told to grant his longtime lover free airline tickets, a perk given all spouses. El-Al appealed the ruling twice—to the National Labor Court and later to the Supreme Court—and lost twice. Gay men and lesbians are now assured of equal protection under the law in all work-related instances.

The appearance on prime-time television, with her partner and mother, was important not only because it introduced a lesbian couple into every living room via the small screen for the first time, nor because the white-haired mother was proudly supportive, but also because a homophobic guest, a prominent singer, changed her mind during the show—thus modeling changes that would slowly transform a family-based society into a more pluralistic one. Today, lesbians and gay men are routinely featured in the media.

Moreover, in 1992, the SPPR opened the first Lesbian and Gay Community Center in the Middle East, thanks to a generous contribution from an anonymous donor (in 1997, the SPPR officially changed its name to Agudah [Association of Gay Men, Lesbians, and Bisexuals in Israel]). The center hosts board meetings, a variety of support groups (for parents, youths, young lesbians, married bisexuals, gay men, HIV-positive men, AIDS support network, etc.), and cultural events. In 1993, the SPPR received official recognition and some financial support from the Tel Aviv Municipality for the Community Center and its youth activities, as well as for the White Line telephone information and help line (the White Line has expanded to include services in Haifa and Jerusalem, as well as a separate help line for lesbians).

The legal advances in Israel over the past few years have been tremendous, and more changes are likely soon, including the right of nonbiological parents to adopt their same-sex partner's child(ren) and inheritance rights for pensions. A test case involving Adir Steiner and the Israeli Defense Forces (IDF) was settled out of court but nevertheless moved negotiations forward on this issue. The country's courts already routinely use the same criteria to adjudicate domestic issues for same-sex and two-sex couples, adding to the sense of mainstreaming. The media have been extremely helpful in publicizing both the struggles and the results in a generally sympathetic manner. Thus, a special session of the Knesset subcommittee on homosexuality, spearheaded by Yael Dayan, daughter of the late Moshe Dayan, brought one hundred gay men and lesbians, as well as many members of the national and international media, who helped spread word of the concerns of Israel's LGB community all over the world. Several activists spoke, as well as public figures who ranged from neutral to supportive; the religious opposition that had threatened to disrupt the "abominable" session stayed away instead. That spring, gay pride week established the first annual outdoor "happening" in the heart of Tel Aviv, sanctioned by the mayor. The 1993 event, emceed by actress Idit Teperson, drew huge crowds and wide media coverage; almost overnight, it seemed, public opinion shifted from disgust to a shrug to reluctant acceptance.

During that Knesset session a former high-ranking army officer turned scientist, Uzi Even, publicly came out and told of his summary dismissal from the IDF after it found out he was gay.

That dramatic story resulted in a review of IDF policy and, pressured by Prime Minister Yitzhak Rabin, by May 1993 the IDF had revised its standing orders and declared that gay men and lesbians would be enlisted, posted, and promoted on their merit rather than their sexual orientation. This change had great impact on the LGB community (and little on the IDF), galvanizing young gay and lesbian soldiers to establish social and political groups all over the country. Because every Israeli Jew, at eighteen, is conscripted into an army that serves not only as a military system but also as a means of socialization, gay men and lesbians had been exempted routinely as unfit and thus stigmatized for life. Israeli Arabs are not conscripted but may volunteer; they are thus as isolated from the mainstream of Israeli society and culture today as openly gay soldiers had been in the past. The nation's Declaration of Independence imagines an egalitarian society, but this cannot be accomplished while Israel and its Arab neighbors have not (with the exception of Egypt and Jordan) signed a peace treaty. The continuing security concerns of all peoples in the region often trumps individual and civil rights.

For the region's gay men and lesbians, the tense political climate that fostered suspicion and even hatred between nations has not been translated into similarly alienated groupings. Instead, whenever possible, Israeli and Palestinian gay men and lesbians meet wherever they can; although its boundaries and ownership are hotly contested, Jerusalem serves as a magnet for Israelis, Arabs, and Palestinians. The city's Independence Park is aptly named to describe the premier cruising borderland for gay men, while Women in Black peace vigils in Paris Square draw a wide cross section of lesbians.

In the twentieth century, since Jews began to migrate to what they call the Land of Israel and considered their ancestral home through two millennia of exile, Israel has been seen by its Arab and Palestinian neighbors as a colonial power. Israel, no larger than the state of New Jersey, was blamed by the Arab world for most of their woes. Those Palestinians who chose to live in Israel after its creation in 1948 were first subjected to military rule until the 1960s, while hundreds of thousands of exiled Palestinians were herded into refugee camps in Lebanon, Syria, Jordan, and the Gaza Strip by the Arab nations to which they had fled. After the Six-Day War of 1967, Israel occupied the West Bank in Jordan, the Golan Heights in Syria, and the Sinai Peninsula in Egypt, and the Gaza Strip, along with 1.5 million

Palestinians; thirty years of occupation of these territories, only half of which have been returned by the summer of 1998, is a serious source of tension despite the Oslo Peace Accords signed in 1993 that established the Palestinian Authority in the Gaza Strip and parts of the West Bank.

Thus, there are three groups in Israel and the parts of the territories still not under the aegis of the Palestinian Authority (PA): Arabs, Jews, and Palestinians. There are Israeli Jews and Israeli Arabs, some of whom self-identify as Palestinian and some of whom do not, and all of whom constitute nearly 20 percent of Israel's population; they are Muslim or Christian, as are the Palestinians who live in the territories. Palestinians living under the PA's jurisdiction are either Muslim or Christian. Jews live in Israel, where they form the undisputed majority, as well as in the territories, where they are a fringe but firebrand minority.

From 1967 to 1993 Israeli, Arab, and Palestinian gay men and lesbians met regularly in bars, discos, and private parties (men also met in pick-up parks). Some formed lasting relationships. In 1993, the Palestinian partner had to choose whether to live under PA or Israeli jurisdiction. In one publicized case, a gay Palestinian petitioned Prime Minister Rabin for the right not only to live with his lover in Israel but also to visit his family in Gaza; permission was granted.

For lesbians in the Arab world and in PA areas, life is dangerous; they must keep a low profile and remain closeted to survive. Gay Palestinian and Arab men marry and raise families but come up with creative ways to meet other gay men and elude the police. The rise of fundamentalism in the world of Islam has made life for gay men and lesbians much more dangerous than before; the romantic British homoerotic literature involving sensuous Arab youths of previous centuries cannot be replicated today. And there is no public cultural output by gays and lesbians living in the Arab/Palestinian Middle East.

Israel is the only gay-friendly country in the region, but this statement is largely true only for Jewish gays and lesbians; Arab/Palestinian ones, especially Muslims, live in fear of discovery. For males, this means derision and ostracism; for females, it may even lead to death to avenge the family honor. A case in point is the case of a Bedouin teenager from Rahat, a town in the Israeli desert, who dared to come out on the Arab-language television channel; his teachers, peers, and family members, as well as Muslim politicians, denounced and shamed him. A national (and progressive) Arab-language newspaper refused to publish his personal ad. He finally moved to Tel Aviv to live openly as a gay man. More recently, a young Arab man from a city in central Israel that is half-Jewish, half-Muslim, claimed that his life was threatened there; he moved to Jerusalem, the only place where Arab men can live a full gay life that includes both Israelis and Arabs/Palestinians.

Jewish Israeli writers and filmmakers have been increasingly prolific, visible, and embraced in recent years. Yotam Reuveni was the first openly gay writer; Elisheva was an openly lesbian poet; Yona Wallach was the first outspoken bisexual poet; and Amos Gutman was the first gay filmmaker. In 1993, a mainstream press published Dana Amir's first book of homoerotic poetry; recently, another press published Noga Eshed's collection of lesbian-themed stories, *Queen-Bees' Nectar*. Poet Ilan Sheinfeld's poetry has been well received from the start and garnered him a prestigious prize as well as loyal readers. Eytan Fox's forty-five-minute film *Time Off* (1990) was the first to deal with gays in the military; Amos Gutman's *Amazing Grace* (1992) was the first to deal with AIDS. In 1994 two stage shows energized the community: the gay-themed *He Has Words of His Own*, which has since toured abroad in English translation; and *Laila Lohet* (Hot Night), a lesbian cabaret. In 1997, the amateur Zoo Show premiered a series of vignettes of lesbian life and lore. Israel's most successful comedy group, Pessia's Daughters, billed as "the first Zionist drag show," had its first gig at the 1995 gay pride event sponsored by CLAF (Israeli lesbian-feminist association, established in 1987) to celebrate its new nonprofit status and reorganization. Punk rocker Shez (Efrat Yerushalmi), who was the first out lesbian performer in Israel, used Laila Lohet to launch a comeback as a poet-songwriter. Although rumor and proof abound about the "lesbigayness" of some of Israel's most successful singer-songwriters, they have chosen not to come out while performing on Israeli soil. There is no local Ellen, Elton, or Melissa.

Diva Dana International is the exception. Headlining the 1994 Israel Gay Pride Month, she sang "those who want me must accept me for who I am," and has never looked back. Interestingly, she is an icon for the entire Middle East, where her bootlegged CDs outsell all others as she offers up a stew of syllables from Hebrew, Arabic, and a handful of European languages to create her own lavender lingo in such songs as "Saida Sultana" and "Danna International." She adopted this latter as her public name, later dropping one *n*—much like Barbra Streisand, who dropped an unuttered *a*—to become "Dana." Her Eurovision win signaled a proud victory over the fundamentalists who were becoming increasingly powerful in the region: "I delivered a knock-out to the religious establishment."

Paradoxically, the rise of gay pride and fundamentalist fervor seems to coincide in the Middle East, where East meets West but neither acknowledges the other.   *Liora Moriel*

Bibliography

Gluzman, Michael, and Gil Nader. *Milon Akher* (Other Dictionary). Private printing. Tel Aviv, Israel, 1996.

Moriel, Liora. *Laila Lohet* (Hot Night). Private printing. Beersheba, Israel, 1994.

http://www.poboxes.com/asiron.

http://www.geocities.com/WestHollywood/5515.

See also Activism, International; Islam; Judaism; Parenting; Politics: Global

Israel, Frank (1945–1986)

Frank Israel was one of the most versatile designers to practice in Los Angeles in the 1980s and 1990s. Combining an interest in film, interior design, and urban culture with a classical training in architecture, Israel designed structures whose vivid colors and strong forms acted as condensations of the urban collage that makes up Southern California.

Israel was a native of Long Island in New York and was trained at the University of Pennsylvania and Columbia and Yale Universities. After working for several New York offices, he moved to Los Angeles in 1978, where he also became a highly influential teacher at the University of California, Los Angeles. He worked as a set designer and critic, and in 1983 he opened his own architecture office. His earlier work consisted mainly of residential additions and remodelings. Between 1988 and 1992, he also designed a series of offices for film-related companies that were like abstracted stage sets. He then began to receive commissions for larger civic institutions, such as a library at UCLA and the University of California, Riverside Arts complex, both of which remained unfinished at the time of his death.

A master at condensing historical references into simple and enigmatic shapes, Israel created forms that made much of simple activities, places, and sequences of space. Fragmented geometries, bright colors, and a sense of monumentality helped forge his disparate compositions into coherent structures. By the end of his life, he was "folding" his forms into increasingly complex and dense shapes meant to echo the contours of both the natural and man-made landscape. His last completed structure, the 1996 Drager House, in Oakland, California, remains a masterful monument to his never fully realized abilities.   *Aaron Betsky*

Bibliography

Betsky, Aaron. *Queer Space: Architecture and Same-Sex Desire.* New York: Morrow, 1997.

See also Architecture; Los Angeles

Italian Literature

Michelangelo Buonarroti (1475–1564) and Pier Paolo Pasolini (1922–1975) are perhaps Italy's two most noted homoerotic writers. Separated by four

The Goldberg/Bean residence, Frank Israel's design for a gay couple. Courtesy of Israel Callas Shortridge Associates. Photo by Grant Mumford.

hundred years, the supreme artist of the Renaissance and the Marxist intellectual might seem at first glance to have little in common. In the sonnets dedicated to the young nobleman Tommaso Cavalieri, Michelangelo agonized over a love, the purity of which he constantly defends, while more visibly Pasolini deployed his homosexuality as a weapon against church and state. Parallels, however, can be drawn. Both knew the isolation of the sexual transgressor as someone who stands outside society's moral or religious codes. Both recognized that same-sex relations also disrupted the social order by creating affinities across class boundaries. In this the work of Michelangelo and Pasolini can be said to characterize the ways in which homosexuality has been represented in the Italian context as a phenomenon whose consequences are social and political, and above all public.

Dante in *The Divine Comedy* follows the view of the church in that sodomites are sinners and as such condemned to Hell. The poet, however, is more interested in commenting on the fact that those sodomites he encounters are typical of the new rising classes in contemporary Florence. The political disruption they cause is exemplified by their tendency to indulge in sodomy; there is a fine boundary set up between religious and social transgression. Pietro Aretino in his comedy *The Stablemaster* (1533) adopts a different genre and a very different moral tone to cover similar ground. The homosexual stablemaster is tricked into believing that he has been ordered to get married. Much of the humor of the play derives from the conversations he has trying to justify his wish to remain single. What emerges is that marriage has less currency as a moral institution than as a means of taming unruly men and placing women in a state of permanent servitude. Marriage is a moral condition only inasmuch as it is politically expedient for the conservative needs of the state.

The view that homosexuality is more significant as a social indicator than as an individual phenomenon occurs also in much twentieth-century literature. Left-wing writers such as Vasco Pratolini and Alberto Moravia have used the figure of the homosexual to symbolize the moral depravity of the fascist regime. In doing so they play on the fascist rhetoric of virility that promoted a normative heterosexual masculinity on the sports field and in the marriage bed. Unwittingly they adopt the same rhetoric to validate the moral uprightness of the antifascist working class. Women writers such as Natalia Ginzburg and Elsa Morante have also employed the figure of the homosexual as a metaphor of the indifferent relations between men and women in contemporary society. Giorgio Bassani gives a different emphasis to the idea in *Gli occhiali d'oro* (Glasses with Golden Frames, 1958), where he uses the vicious marginalization of a homosexual man by the bourgeoisie of Ferrara as a prism through which to view attitudes to the Jews under fascism.

Homosexual writers have not notably freed themselves from this way of thinking. Pasolini's early works paint an idyllic portrait of pastoral homosexual encounters, but more typically in his writing the homosexual is represented as a middle-class predator who buys sexual favors from working-class youths. The youths remain heterosexual in essence, merely exploiting the needs of a decadent class. Homosexuality spills over easily into narratives of class also in the work of Umberto Saba (1883–1957) and of Giovanni Comisso (1895–1969), whose sexual adventuring in the Middle East is reminiscent of Pasolini's late work without sharing the latter's political dimension.

In recent years writers with a more affirmative "gay" political outlook and sensibility have modified this pattern without abandoning it altogether. The work of Pier Vittorio Tondelli (1955–91) traces this movement. His first novel, *Altri libidini*, is a collection of short stories loosely woven together whose central characters are united only in that they are marginalized from society. Here the homosexuality of some characters functions in much the same way as the drug taking of some of the others. Neither activity is glamorized; both are metaphors of social dissidence. In *Pao pao*, his next novel, Tondelli explores the proximity of homosexual relations and heterosexual male bonding in the context of national military service. His final novel, *Camere separate*, deals with the conflicting emotions aroused by love, absence, illness, and death. Although AIDS is never mentioned by name, the clear parallels invoked make this text perhaps the most resonant piece of recent Italian gay fiction to an international readership.

The work of Aldo Busi (1948–) is in some respects more challenging. Busi's writing is iconoclastic in content and innovative literary form, combining novelistic elements with travel writing, personal reminiscence, and baroque fantasy. The strong sexual element in his work is neither lyrical nor gratuitously shocking but is a compelling metaphor for the brute reality of human relations in all their forms.

Although gay writing in Italy has yet to burgeon in quite the way it has elsewhere, an increasing number of gay writers are coming to the fore, presenting a range of concerns that add significant complexity to gay literature in general. The autobiographical work of Nico Naldini reflects on a culture in which homosexual relations between men were commonplace yet never discussed. Ivan Teobaldelli's *Esercizi di castità* is a humorous account of an erotic triangle but raises significant questions about the nature of gay transvestite culture in Italy and the diaspora of gay men from the provinces to the large cities.

While contemporary gay writing is more attentive to the specific qualities of homosexual experience than in the past, it has tended to cling to the persistent notion of the homosexual as outsider and upsetter of social conventions. Unlike much gay writing in English, homosexuals are not bedeviled by an aesthetic sensibility, and scant attention has been paid to the negotiation of homosexuality and family life. Conversely, the enormous success in Italy of writers such as E. M. Forster and David Leavitt in recent years suggests that such concerns are not entirely alien to contemporary Italian culture.

Derek Duncan

Bibliography

Baranksi, Zygmunt G., and Lino Pertile, eds. *The New Italian Novel*. Edinburgh: Edinburgh University Press, 1993.

Mieli, Marco. *Homosexuality and Liberation: Elements of a Gay Critique*. London: Gay Men's Press, 1980.

The Poetry of Michelangelo: An Annotated Translation. New Haven: Yale University Press, 1991.

Saslow, James M. *Ganymede in the Renaissance: Homosexuality in Art and Society*. New Haven: Yale University Press, 1986.

Siciliano, Enzo. *Pasolini*. London: Bloomsbury, 1987.

See also Alighieri, Dante; Busi, Aldo; Forster, E. M.; Italian Renaissance; Italy; Michelangelo Buonarroti; Pasolini, Pier Paolo; Penna, Sandro; Saba, Umberto; Tondelli, Pier Vittorio

Italian Renaissance

It would be incorrect to depict a uniform attitude toward homosexual behaviors in the Italian Renaissance. First, it is necessary to distinguish between the social view of same-sex relationships and the literary and artistic masterpieces of the fifteenth and sixteenth centuries. Since the end of the thirteenth century, in every Italian state sodomitic practices, rather strictly interpreted as the sexual encounter between two men, were considered a serious crime, and many natural plagues were attributed to this allegedly widespread "vice." In 1432 the Florentine authorities created the so-called Office of the Night, a special commission charged with the persecution of homosexuality. In four famous sermons delivered in Florence between 1424 and 1425, Franciscan preacher Bernardino of Siena gave a horrifying description of the sodomitic "homicide," whose "stench had reached heaven." Bernardino understood that homosexual encounters (in taverns, private places, parks, public streets) were rather com-

Donatello (c.1386–1466), David. *Museo Nazionale del Bargello, Florence. Alinari/Art Resource, NY.*

mon in Florence and throughout Italy. As Michael Rocke reminds us, "With as many as 15,000 individuals incriminated and 2,500 convictions for homosexual acts in little more than the last forty years of the fifteenth century, sodomy was no 'deviant' behavior of a distinct sexual minority but a common part of male experience." Contradicting an old view on Renaissance homosexuality, sodomy was not limited to the upper classes but involved every stratum of Florentine society. Reminiscent of the Greek tradition, sexual roles tended to be quite defined. Young men were supposed to be mere recipients of older men's active desire. In the well-known *Alcibiade fanciullo a scola* (Alcibiades boy at school), libertine friar Antonio Rocco speaks of the infamous *bardasse*, boys who had sex with older men for money. Particularly telling is the contradictory portrait of homosexual activities during the era of Lorenzo the Magnificent (1469–1492). On the one hand, under Lorenzo's government the Office of the Night condemned almost a thousand men, the harshest repression of homosexuality in Florentine history. On the other, it is a fact that many of Lorenzo's friends had homosexual tendencies. For instance, the great writer Luigi Pulci, author of *Il Morgante*, the first major epic poem of the European Renaissance, was repeatedly accused of being a sodomite. It is almost superfluous to mention other important artists, such as Donatello, Michelangelo, Benvenuto Cellini, Angelo Poliziano, and Leonardo da Vinci.

If we examine the Italian Renaissance from a strictly cultural perspective, we may say that in the fifteenth and sixteenth centuries Italian literature and visual arts were imbued with homoerotism. The study of classical literatures certainly played a major role in the "revival" of homosexuality. In particular, homosexuality, or better yet, homosexual desire, acquired a philosophical status with the birth of Florentine Neoplatonism, thanks to Marsilio Ficino's groundbreaking interpretations of Plato's dialogues. It is no exaggeration to state that Ficino and his Neoplatonic Academy molded the European Renaissance. In his texts, Ficino theorized the supremacy of same-sex desire and thus created a rhetoric that influenced every aspect of Renaissance culture, both in Italy and in every other European country. Thanks to Ficino, homosexual desire became a legitimate topic of artistic and philosophical investigation. Ficino created a new philosophical genre, the so-called treatises on love, which analyzed love's controversial aspects and meanings. Following Ficino, other Renais-

I sance philosophers spoke of the "male Venus," a neologism referring to a man's desire for another man. Contemporary psychoanalysts believe that Ficino discovered the subconscious. In the graphic *Cazzaria* (Treatise on the dick), Antonio Vignale parodized Ficino's highly theoretical works. Vignale imagined a dialogue between two men who, sitting on a bed, praised the male member's infinite qualities. The two friends tried to define the most suitable shape, length, and color of a penis, along with its innumerable "applications." Another masterpiece of Italian late Renaissance is "L'Adone," by Giovanbattista Marino. In Marino's work, the beautiful Adonis expresses an ambiguous sexual identity. Marino's well-crafted verses often have the metrical shape of a male member.

A landmark of Renaissance literature is Michelangelo's collection of verses. In recent years, thanks to Eugenio Montale, the major Italian poet of the twentieth century, Michelangelo's poetry has been reevaluated. Montale stated that Michelangelo's "rough" verses and fragmented sonnets had been one of his major sources of inspiration. Michelangelo expressed a tormented view of love, divided between homosexual desire and Catholicism's denial. Elaborating a typically Neoplatonic poetics, Michelangelo theorized the necessity of transcending carnal desire to attain a glimpse of divine love. Tommaso Cavalieri, Michelangelo's handsome and younger beloved, thus becomes a means through which the poet comes in touch with his agonizing desire for immortality. Another man's beautiful "forms" trigger an inherently painful desire, which forces the lover to question his whole identity. In this way, a homosexual drive is a fundamental source of self-investigation. Rather than denying its reality, Michelangelo and Ficino dissect their homoerotic desire in an extraordinarily modern manner.

Homoerotic undertones are present in most of the epic poems written in the fifteenth and sixteenth centuries, such as Boiardo's *Orlando innamorato*, Ariosto's *Orlando furioso*, and Tasso's *Gerusalemme liberata*.   *Armando Maggi*

Bibliography

Canosa, Roberto. *Storia di una grande paura: La sodomia a Firenze e a Venezia nel Quattrocento*. Florence: Bonechi, 1991.

Dall'Orto, Giovanni. "'Socratic Love' as a Disguise for Same-Sex Love in the Italian Renaissance." In *The Pursuit of Sodomy*. K. Gerard and G. Hekma, eds. New York: Harrington Park Press, 1989, 33–65.

Rocke, Michael. *Forbidden Friendships: Homosexuality and Male Culture in Renaissance Florence*. New York: Oxford University Press, 1996.

See also '*Alcibiade fanciulloa Scola;* Art History; Catholicism; Cellini, Benvenuto; Florence; Leonardo da Vinci; Michelangelo Buonarroti; Renaissance Neoplatonism; Rome

Italy

According to a poll recorded in 1987, homosexuals are the most "disliked" social group (48 percent) in Italy, followed by gypsies (45 percent) and foreigners (43 percent), that is, immigrants from North Africa, eastern Europe, and the Philippines. This result is an eloquent description of the general condition of Italian gays and lesbians. Despite important improvements, Italy still fails to accept people expressing a different identity, primarily gays and "non-Italians." However, whereas immigrants sometimes become the object of philanthropic concern, homosexuals are radical "others." It is important to remember that the notorious "Codice Rocco" (Rocco's Civil Law), in force during the fascist era, does not mention homosexuality at all. This apparent omission does not reflect an open-minded attitude toward homosexual practices. Given that fascist legislation did not consider the "sodomitic crime," homosexuals were prey of public officials' indisputable and totally personal decisions. Moreover, to mention sodomy would have meant to recognize its existence. This is why, for instance, today a homosexual is still discharged from military service not because of "perversion" but "mental imbalance." As a group of leftist intellectuals (among them Umberto Eco and Alberto Moravia) wrote in the journal *Critica Sociale* in 1968, "In Italy political Fascism still survives in the form of sexual Fascism."

F.U.O.R.I. (OUT), the first homosexual organization, was founded in 1968 by Angelo Pezzana. Pezzana owned a bookstore in Milan that carried alternative and foreign titles. With a group of friends, Pezzana also created the first gay magazine, *Fuori*. He himself sold it in the traditional cruising places, such as parks and train stations. Other gay papers are *Rome Gay News*, published both in Italian and in English, and *Babilonia*, one of the most interesting and culturally engaged gay periodicals in Europe.

Arcigay and Arcilesbica are the two most important political groups. Franco Grillini, who founded Arcigay in 1980, is extremely visible in the Italian political arena. Arcigay and Arcilesbica tend to be closer to the lefist parties, primarily the so-called Party of the Left (PDS). Since the early eighties several cities, run by leftist coalitions, have elected openly gay activists, in most cases as "counselors" to the mayor. A gay parade is held every year in one of the major cities, such as Bologna, Rome, or Naples. Particularly pro-gay is the actual mayor of Naples, Antonio Bassanini, who in 1996 marched in the streets of his city holding hands with gay men and women.

In Italy gay social groups are rare and financially unstable. For instance, Circolo Mario Mieli in Rome is one of the few social organizations in the capital. In most cases, gays and lesbians can meet only in discos, bars, saunas, and the bushes. In recent years the first gay coffee shops have become visible in Rome, Milan, and Florence. Babele is the sole Italian gay bookstore, opened in Milan in the mid-eighties. A second Babele has opened in Rome. In Milan gay people speak with pride of their "gay street," via Sammartini, with its two bars, a porn shop, and the Babele bookstore.

From a legal standpoint, some Italian cities have recently decided to recognize gay couples. In June 1996, Pisa introduced the Civic Union (*unione civile*) which legalizes gay and lesbian couples. In southern Italy, however, the situation for gay people is strikingly different. On the two major islands, Sicily and Sardinia, several cases of attempted suicide were reported in 1994 and 1995. Young gay couples, who see no future for their relationship, have chosen to die together.

Italy remains a country where homosexuality is still seen as a marginal and thus unthreatening phenomenon. Gays are objects either of contempt or of irony. The traditional machismo is still a central aspect of Italian culture. Yet both cinema and literature often investigate homosexual themes. The problem is that, when an Italian writer or filmmaker speaks about homosexuality, Italian critics interpret homosexuality as a metaphor for the artist's malaise. In other words, homosexuality is almost never read per se. For instance, although Pier Paolo Pasolini's texts (*A Violent Life*, *The Ragazzi*, *The Dream of Something*, *Theorem*) revolve around sodomy, practically no critic broaches this difficult theme. In a recent conference in Milan on Pasolini's posthumous *Petrolio*, no scholar mentioned its heavily homosexual connotation. In fact, Italian literature has a long tradition of homosexual authors. Sandro Penna (1906–1977) was an openly gay poet who described in detail his sexual encounters. His evocative verses were often criticized for their sexual content. Only in recent years Penna has finally acquired the stature of one of Italy's major poets. In *Ernesto*, poet Umberto Saba recounts the story of a young man who comes to grips with his homosexual desire. In his numerous novels Alberto Arbasino (b. 1930) describes the intellectual milieus of the capital with a distinct sense of irony. Giovanni Comisso, Carlo Emilio Gadda, novelist, playwright, and filmmaker Giuseppe Patroni Griffi (*Death of Beauty*), poet and playwright Giovanni Testori, and Aldo Palazzeschi are other important writers whose pages have a clearly homosexual subtext. Pier Vittorio Tondelli (*Separate Rooms*), Aldo Busi (*Seminar on Youth*), and Mario Fortunato (*Blood*) represent a new phase in Italian gay literature. In their novels homosexuality becomes a visible and "normal" practice. Their style, especially Busi's, does not avoid graphic descriptions of sexual encounters. Busi appears frequently on the most popular Italian talk shows, speaking freely about his sexual identity and his private life. Homosexuality is also the major theme of important novels written by "non-gay" authors. *Gli occhiali d'oro* (The glasses with golden frames) by Giorgio Bassani, for instance, narrates the story of a homosexual Jew during the fascism period. Bassani investigates his character's isolation and repressed sexuality with rare sensitivity. *L'isola d'Arturo* by Elsa Morante and *La città e la casa* (The house and the city) by Natalia Ginzburg examine different aspects of male homosexual identity. Luchino Visconti and Pier Paolo Pasolini are two filmmakers who considered homosexuality the core of their cinema.

Armando Maggi

Bibliography

Scalise, Daniele. *Cose dell'altro mondo: Viaggio nell'Italia gay*. Milan: Zelig Editore, 1996.

See also Busi, Aldo; Florence; Italian Literature; Italian Renaissance; Mediterranean; Pasolini, Pier Paolo; Renaissance Neoplatonism; Penna, Sandro; Rome; Saba, Umberto; Tondelli, Pier Vittorio; Visconti, Luchino

J

James I (1566–1625)

The son of Mary, Queen of Scots, and Lord Darnley, James VI of Scotland inherited the English crown on the death of Elizabeth I on March 24, 1603, and reigned as James I. Best remembered for the translation of the Bible undertaken during his reign, James was an able politician and gifted scholar. His own works included a treatise on statecraft, *Basilicon Doran* (1599), and numerous theological writings. Many of his earlier writings are concerned with demonology.

Initiated out of political and economic necessity, James was married to Anne of Denmark in Oslo on November 23, 1589. The marriage was not a happy one. James and Anne were often quarrelsome with each other as both spouses as well as king and queen. James seems to have shown little remorse on her death in 1619. They had a son, Henry, on February 19, 1594, of whom James was very fond, but the prince died at age eighteen. His daughter, Elizabeth, born on August 19, 1596, was married to the Elector Palatine in 1613, moved to Bohemia, and was never seen in England again. His other son, Charles, was born on November 19, 1600.

Elizabeth, the "Virgin Queen," seems to have vested much of her political power in her gender and inaccessible sexual status. James reconfigured courtly politics along homosocial codes. As historian Bruce R. Smith has noted, "James' homosexuality may be the equivalent of Elizabeth's virginity: the erotic seal of men's transactions with one another." Certainly James, who was said to have "loved young men, his favorites, better than women," mixed his political and sexual preferments.

In September 1579, James entered into his first recorded male romance, with his French cousin Esmé Stuart. The clergy charged that Esmé "foully misused his [James's] tender age" with "delights and disordinant desires." Esmé was by accounts a handsome and amusing man, some twenty-four years older than the king. James showered his love with titles and preferment. Esmé was first created earl, then duke of Lennox and given the offices of the Lord Chamberlain and First Gentleman of the Chamber. He helped to dress and undress the king and had first option in sleeping in the royal bedchamber.

James's greatest love seems to have been George Villiers, whom the bishop of Gloucester called "the handsomest man in England." As with Lennox, James was generous in his preferment. In 1616, Villiers was made a viscount and the First Master of the Horse and a Knight of the Garter; in 1617 he was made earl of Buckingham; in 1618 his title was upgraded to marquis, in 1623 to duke. The king had him marry Lady Katherine Manners, the only surviving child of the earl of Rutland, one of the richest men in England. It is said that after his marriage Buckingham became even more familiar with the king. The king's letters to him are often addressed to his "Sweetheart," or "Sweet Steenie gossip," or "Sweet wife and child." The last address may indicate that the relationship was not entirely sexual. James had lost his favorite son, Henry, to illness and his daughter, Elizabeth, had become queen of far-off Bohemia. Buckingham, who often addressed James as "Dear Dad" in letters, seems to have also filled their filial positions.

Although James cautioned Prince Henry against acts of sodomy, no one dared question his own conduct openly. One criticism that has survived is Sir Simonds D'Ewes's recorded conversation with

J

a friend, in which he mentions that the king is infected with the "sin of sodomy" and his whole court filled with "great personages prostituting their bodies." It was written in cipher.

Even D'Ewes, who clearly disapproved of James's sexual politics, highly approved of James as a man, whom he described as full of "virtues and learning" and theological doctrines that were "pure and sound." James died on March 27, 1625. His funeral at Westminster was "the greatest indeed that was ever known in England." He was succeeded by his son, Charles I, under whose reign England descended into civil war.   *Jeffrey Kahan*

Bibliography

Bergeron, David M. *Royal Family, Royal Lovers: King James of England and Scotland.* Columbia, Mo.: University of Missouri Press, 1991.

Houston, S. J. *James I.* 2d ed. London: Longman, 1995.

Smith, Bruce R. *Homosexual Desire in Shakespeare's England: A Cultural Poetics.* Chicago: University of Chicago Press, 1991.

See also England; English Literature; Shakespeare, William

James, Henry (1843–1916)

Son of Henry Sr., a Swedenborgian philosopher, and brother to William, founder of pragmatism, Henry James dedicated his life to belles lettres and the pursuit of European aesthetics. Born in New York City, Henry benefited from an excellent education and much travel abroad. He not only abandoned the traditional law education at Harvard to pursue his writing but left his homeland to establish himself in Europe. By 1871, he had set up residence in London and proceeded to become one of the greatest practitioners and theoreticians of English fiction. His sympathy for the Allied cause and his anger at American isolation led James to assume British citizenship in 1915.

To read James is to follow what critic Lyall Powers calls "a short course in the history of the novel," for James's work encompasses three main phases, and moves from the influence of Hawthornesque romance to the wave of realism, naturalism, and then into the modern. The work of his "major phase" (1897–1915), featuring such works as *The Ambassadors*, produced a literature that explored the possibilities of internal monologue, limited per-spective, and developing consciousness. James's first period (1876–1885) set the ground for his invention of the international novel of which Isabel Archer in *Portrait of a Lady* is often cited as the paradigmatic character of the American adrift in Europe. The middle phase (1885–1897) featured an exploration of the social novel, styled after the French novelists, and includes James's foray into theater.

His two autobiographical volumes, *A Small Boy and Others* and *Notes of a Son and Brother*, explore this life of sensation, yet reveal little about his romantic affairs. James felt a tension between his public self and his private self. No decisive evidence on his sexual orientation exists, but James was certainly attuned to the friction in himself. A contributor to the *Yellow Book*, a publication of decadent poetry that came to be associated with a number of famous homosexuals including Lytton Strachey and Oscar Wilde, James is linked with the fin-de-siècle aesthetes even as he keeps his distance.

In a letter to close friend Hendrick Anderson of February 9, 1902, James expresses his desire to "touch" and "hold close" his male friend. Such a seemingly homoerotic expression of emotion is rare in James's writing; his characters are typically sexually unfulfilled. As with Lambert Strether's fascination with Chad Newsome, "a fair young man," in *The Ambassadors*, James creates characters with ambiguous sexual orientation.

Eve Kosovsky Sedgwick, with her analysis of James's tale "The Beast in the Jungle," brought the protagonist, John Marcher, and by extension, the puritanical James, out of the closet. Instead of diagnosing James as homosexual, Sedgwick masterfully reveals the discursive subterfuge of the piece, suggesting how James hid "the love that dare not speak its name." For a writer who urges William Dean Howells to take people and characters "on what they do and allow them absolutely and utterly their conditions," James suggests that by submerging these questions, a larger art may be saved.   *Kylie Hansen and Robert Rhyne*

Bibliography

Edel, Leon. *Henry James: A Life.* New York: Harper and Row, 1985.

Sedgwick, Eve Kosofsky. *Epistemology of the Closet.* Berkeley: University of California Press, 1990.

See also Aestheticism; Strachey, Lytton; Wilde, Oscar; U.S. Literature

Japan

The first, however debatable, instance of what has been interpreted as male homosexuality in Japanese history dates back to ancient times. It concerned a priest being buried after having committed suicide with another man whose death was supposed to be the reason for the suicide in the *Nihongi* (*Chronicles of Japan*, A.D. 720). Other early writings contain similar vague descriptions of matters that might be interpreted as homosexuality but also as friendship, such as the Manyôshû (*Collection of Thousand Leaves*, ca. 750), the *Ise monogatari* (Tales of Ise, 951) and the famous *Genji monogatari* (Tale of Genji, ca. 1010) by the female courtier Murasaki Shikibu, with its passage in which the hero, Prince Genji, seeks solace in the arms of a boy after having been rejected by his older sister. In the Heian period (794–1185), we find the first more explicit allusions to homosexuality in diaries of court nobles. For instance, Fujiwara Yorinaga (1120–1156) wrote about his sexual adventures with dancers. He, like other courtiers, wrote also about handsome boys that were kept by emperors for sexual pleasures. Further, there existed a clear interest in cross-dressing and a high value attached to feminine beauty in men.

In the same period homosexuality in the context of Buddhist monasteries appears on the scene. Kôbô Daishi, alias Kûkai (774–835), founder of the Shingon sect, has even posthumously been attributed the introduction of homosexuality to Japan from China and with a refined discourse on how it was to be practiced. The extent to which these so-called *Chigo monogatari* (Acolyte Tales) related to the actual practice of homosexuality in monasterial contexts has been questioned, but there is little doubt that monks engaged in homosexuality. In the Muromachi period (1333–1573), the ruling Ashikaga family maintained close relations with the masters of the Buddhist Zen sect and the tea ceremony, the most famous example being Zeami's relationship with Shogun Ashikaga Yoshimitsu. Already during the Kamakura period (1185–1333), Zen had become very much the sect of the warrior class, which gained paramount powers during the later part of Muromachi period, known also as the period of Warring States (Sengoku Jidai, 1467–1573). In this period what came eventually to be called *wakashudô* or *shudô* (the way of the youth) developed. Love relationships between samurai and younger men came to be much idealized, which is attributed to the low regard in which women were held combined with the fact that warriors were away

from their wives for prolonged periods during long campaigns. Many famous warriors and shoguns are known to have engaged in relationships with young men.

In Japanese history homosexuality was seen more as an activity people could choose to engage in than a characteristic of particular individuals. In Tokugawa Japan (1603–1868), two major constructions of homosexuality existed simultaneously: that of a difference in gender role, in which one of the partners assumed the feminine role and the other the masculine, and the transgenerational construction, in which the age of the partners differed greatly. Historical discourses tended to concentrate on the bodies into which masculine men may stick their penis, while ignoring those into which their penis is actually stuck, neglecting the position of the younger or feminine passive men who are essentially positioned on a par with young women, in particular the other object of sexual desire outside marriage. *Danshoku* or *nanshoku* (male colors, i.e., love of men for persons of the male sex) was placed on a par with *joshoku* or *nyoshoku* (female colors, i.e., love of men for persons of the female sex), and both forms of sex for pleasure were characterized by prostitution. This led one authority to claim that in Tokugawa Japan, bisexuality was "the norm" among townspeople, which seems to be an exaggeration, given that there were many more brothels where women worked than where men worked. Male homosexuality as viewed in twentieth-century Japan was determined mainly by the concept of *okama* (literally a type of cooking pot), a term stemming from the Tokugawa era and used mostly to refer to effeminate gay men who are cast as sexually passive and sometimes more specifically to the anus, as in "*okama ga horareta*" (I/you/he/we/they was/were fucked in the ass), a phrase still common in gay pornography today. In the Japanese-English dictionary *Kenkyûsha*, okama is explained as synonymous with *danshô*, or male prostitute. It appears that active, masculine men were not necessarily seen as homosexual, even if this may have been their major sexual activity. Thus, only passive, effeminate, and/or younger men were regarded as homosexual, as was by and large the case in the historical constructions above. This is supported by the fact that the general understanding of the term *gei* (the Anglo-Japanese pronunciation of the English term "gay") was that it meant transvestite man, male-to-female transsexual, or a person born as a man who has acquired breasts, who may refer to himself as

J *nyû-hâfu* (new-half) or *shii-mêru* (she-male). In addition, homosexuality was still viewed in the framework of prostitution and crime until from about 1990, when gay and lesbian people began coming out and gaining in media interest.   *Wim Lunsing*

Bibliography

Childs, Margaret H. "Chigo Monogatari: Love Stories or Buddhist Sermons." *Monumenta Nipponica* 35, no. 2 (1980): 127–51.

Furukawa, Makoto. "Sekushuariti no henyô: Kindai Nihon ni okeru dôseiai no mittsu no kôdo." *Nichibei Josei Jânaru* (Japan America Women's Journal) 17 (1994): 29–55.

Leupp, Gary P. *Male Colors: The Construction of Homosexuality in Tokugawa Japan.* Berkeley: University of California Press, 1995.

Lunsing, Wim. *Beyond Common Sense: Negotiating Constructions of Sexuality and Gender in Contemporary Japan.* London: Kegan Paul International, forthcoming.

Masuda, Koh, ed. *Kenkyûsha's New Japanese-English Dictionary.* Tokyo: Kenkyûsha, 1988.

Schalow, Paul Gordon. "Kûkai and the Tradition of Male Love in Japanese Buddhism." In *Buddhism, Sexuality and Gender.* José Ignacio Cabezón, ed. Albany: State University of New York Press, 1985, 215–30.

———. "Male Love in Early Modern Japan: A Literary Depiction of the 'Youth.'" In *Hidden from History: Reclaiming the Gay and Lesbian Past.* Martin Bauml Duberman, Martha Vicinus, and George Chauncy, eds. New York: New American Library, 1989, 118–28.

Watanabe, Tsuneo, and Iwata, Junichi. *La Voie des éphèbes: histoire et histoires des homosexualités au Japon.* Paris: Éditions Trismégiste, 1987.

See also Japanese Literature; Kabuki

Japanese Literature

There are works of Japanese literature that might be interpreted as portraying homosexual themes from its very beginnings, but it is not until the Heian period (794–1185) that writings of court nobles in particular become more explicit. Following these autobiographical writings are the so-called *Chigo Monogatari* (Acolyte Tales), which have been produced and reproduced from the fourteenth century onward. Essentially stories about young men who study at monasteries to become monks and the attraction older monks feel toward them, they not only romanticize these transgenerational relationships but also describe how such love is to be consumed, reminiscent of its classic Greek counterpart.

Famous is the collection of stories by Ihara Saikaku, *Nanshoku Ôkagami* (The Great Mirror of Male Love, 1687), which deals with homosexuality in contexts varying from warriors to Buddhist priests and Kabuki actors. A novel by Natsume Sôseki, *Kokoro* (Heart, 1914), dealt with intimacy between a mentor and his student. It has been much discussed as presenting sensitivities that are thought to be particular for Japanese men. In the West, the best-known Japanese author dealing with homosexuality is Mishima Yukio, author of *Kamen no Kokuhaku* (Confessions of a Mask, 1949) and *Kinjiki* (Forbidden Colors, 1953). During the 1970s a genre of girls' comics (*shôja manga*) developed that dealt with male homosexual characters, one of the most famous being *Hiizuredokoro no Tenshi* (The Angel That Came from the Sun), by Yamagishi Ryôko. It is a serial, published from 1980 onward, comprising eleven volumes, loosely based on the life of Shôtoku Taishi, the introducer of Buddhism to Japan. Another is *Kaze to Ki no Uta* (Poem of the Wind and the Trees), by Takemiya Keiko, a seventeen-volume serial on the relationship between two schoolboys in France, published from 1976 onward. From the early 1990s a virtual boom of novels dealing with male homosexuality developed in the wake of increased media attention to homosexuality. Written by gay men themselves, they are marked by realism and often appear to be autobiographical. Some examples are Hiruma Hisao's *Yes, Yes, Yes* (1989) and *Happy Birthday* (1990); Nishino Kôji's *Nichôme de Kimi ni Attara* (When I Meet You in Nichôme [an area with many gay bars in Tokyo], 1993) and *Tisshu* (Tissue, 1995); and Hashiguchi Ryôsuke's *Hatachi no Binetsu* (A Touch of Fever, 1994) and *Nagisa no Shindobaddu* (Sindbad on the Beach, 1995), both of which have also been the bases for films.   *Wim Lunsing*

Bibliography

Lunsing, Wim. " 'Gay Boom' in Japan: Changing Views of Homosexuality?" *Thamyris: Mythmaking from Past to Present* 4, no. 2 (1997): 267–93.

Schalow, Paul Gordon. "Introduction." In *The Great Mirror of Male Love.* Ihara Saikaku. Paul Gordon Schalow, trans. Stanford, Calif.: Stanford University Press, 1990.

—. "Introduction." In *Partings at Dawn: An Anthology of Japanese Gay Literature*. Stephen D. Miller, ed. San Francisco: Gay Sunshine Press, 1996.

See also Buddhism; Japan; Kabuki

Jarman, Derek (1942–1994)

Denouncing deliberate passivity, Britain's Derek Jarman actively, purposefully, and constantly challenged heterosexual society on many fronts. Born in 1942 into what he called a "typical suburban family," Jarman fought homophobia with films and books until his death from AIDS. Ever the controversial filmmaker and writer, Jarman spoke as an individual representative for collective causes: the liberation of homosexuals and the rights of people with AIDS. Demanding that we "break the circle of death" that has been so persistently and conspiratorially associated with homosexuality and that claimed such figures as Wilde, Tchaikovsky, and Marlowe, Jarman infused his works with his experience as a gay man to create a "shared language" to enunciate the struggles of the right-less. As a leading independent filmmaker, he created visual worlds that gave a homoerotic look to the martyred saint in *Sebastiane* (1976), his first film, and explored with serious attention the tragic fates of gay lovers in later films like *The Garden* (1990) and *Caravaggio* (1986). Jarman fought for what he thought was an "indigenous British cinema" in very unconventional and visually arresting ways. Although his efforts to raise funds for his films were frequently frustrated, a fact he attributed to what he believed was the government's disdain for homosexuality and independent film-making, Jarman produced enough films to secure him a solid cult following. His three autobiographical diaries about his experience with AIDS—*Modern Nature* (1991), *At Your Own Risk: A Saint's Testament* (1992), and *Dancing Ledge* (1984)—also endeared him to readers still willing to challenge the heterosexual establishment. Like his work *Chroma*, much of his writing revolved around experiments with color: how to historicize its homoerotic transformations and how to use it to memorialize the loss of one's self to AIDS. In one of his last films, *Blue* (1993), Jarman innovatively combined the visual potency of film and the poignancy of poetry to produce a disturbing and thoughtful analysis of the uses and meanings of color as it relates to and embodies the observations of a gay man ill with AIDS. In this work he abandons visual action altogether. For nearly eighty minutes the screen remains an unchanging blue; poetry and an apocalyptic musical score call us to witness the author's struggle with the disease. This work more than anything else represents an oeuvre of experimental films and books that survive as boldly confrontational and positively homoerotic.

Craig McCarroll

Bibliography

Lippard, Chris, ed. *By Angels Driven: The Films of Derek Jarman*. Westport, Conn.: Greenwood Press, 1996.

Wollen, Roger, Introduction. In *Derek Jarman: A portrait*. With contributions by James Cary Parkes et al. New York: Thames and Hudson, 1996.

See also Activism, International; AIDS; AIDS Performance; Film; Film: New Queer Cinema; Marlowe, Christopher; Tchaikovsky, Pyotr Ilich; Wilde, Oscar

Jewel Box Revue

The Jewel Box Revue, the longest-running touring drag show in America, had its beginning in 1939 in a gay Miami nightclub, Club Jewel Box. Produced by Danny Brown and Doc Benner, the Jewel Box Revue was a unified production, not a string of solo drag acts. In addition to lavish gowns and opulent sets for the production numbers, the show featured original music, dance routines, and comic sketches—but no lip-sync. By 1942, Doc and Danny began limited tours of the Jewel Box Revue, booking it into "straight" nightclubs and theaters, eventually touring the United States, Mexico, and Canada continuously for more than thirty years. In addition to producing the Jewel Box, Doc and Danny—who were lovers—also performed; Doc sang and Danny was the master of ceremonies. The show was run as a family business; Danny's brother-in-law was the revue's musical director, and both Doc's and Danny's mothers traveled with the show. During the 1950s Danny's mother, Bertha, managed a "cub" version of the Jewel Box Revue. With a dozen performers, the "junior" company toured clubs too small for the main troupe and also served as a training ground for performers who aspired to be hired by the senior company.

The Jewel Box Revue billed itself as "Twenty-Five Men and a Girl"—a gimmick that encouraged audiences to locate the "real" woman among the female impersonators. From 1955 to 1969, the "girl"

Jewel Box Revue performers Mr. Lynn Carter and Miss Stormé De Laverié. Photo courtesy of Jewel Box Revue.

For over thirty years, the concept and content of the Jewel Box Revue remained relatively the same, a lavish production dedicated to the glamour and mystique of the consummate showgirl. A reviewer for *Variety* (November 10, 1961) marveled at the "hermaphroditic musical variety" created by the Jewel Box Revue, those "boy-ological experts" who excelled in the "freud-ulent 'art' of fem-mimicry."

Bud Coleman

Bibliography

Coleman, Bud. "Jewel Box Revue: America's Longest-Running Touring Drag Show." *Theater History Studies* 17 (1997): 79–92.

Paulson, Don, with Roger Simpson. *An Evening at the Garden of Allah.* New York: Columbia University Press, 1996.

See also Cabaret, Variety, and Revue Entertainment; Drag Balls; Harlem Renaissance, Musical Theater; Transvestism

of the show was the emcee, male impersonator Stormé De Laverié. Other headliners who performed with the company included Gita Gilmore, Lynne Carter, and T. C. Jones. The Jewel Box was immortalized in the Broadway smash hit *A Chorus Line* (1975), in which the character Paul relates Nicholas Dante's experiences as a "chorus girl" in the revue.

As nightclubs across the country closed, victims of the television age, the Jewel Box found a lucrative market on the "chitlin' circuit," but the progress of the civil rights movement made the cross-dressing revue an unwelcome guest in many black theaters. In the late 1960s, residents of Harlem began to picket the Apollo Theater when the Jewel Box was in residence, complaining that the "dregs and drags of society" were polluting their community. The last gasp of the Jewel Box Revue occurred in 1975, when the stars of the show presented a brief run at New York's Bijou Theater, after which Doc and Danny retired to Florida.

The Jewel Box Revue was so well known that it inspired several rip-off companies. Dorian Corey was the star of the Pearl Box Revue for twenty-seven years (1955–1982), and during the 1950s, another traveling troupe of female impersonators billed themselves as the Powder Box Revue.

Joffrey Ballet

From the Joffrey Ballet's inception in 1956, male dancers were elemental to the company founder's aesthetic. Robert Joffrey and his artistic associate, Gerald Arpino, gradually and without an articulated plan to subvert ballet's "old" gender order, helped revolutionize and empower male identity by providing roles for men that were of equal weight to the ones for women. Joffrey concentrated mainly on the classroom, where he made male virtuosity a priority, building men's confidence by asking them to execute combinations before the women (an unheard-of practice) and holding all-men's classes (a rare but not unprecedented occurrence in the fifties). Arpino choreographed works for the dancers Joffrey trained that stressed their individual values. Joffrey and Arpino lived together and worked collaboratively like this for over forty years.

For Joffrey, the accomplishment of gender equality in ballet emerged as one of his strongest and earliest impulses. Growing up in Seattle, Washington, he saw many Ballets Russes de Monte Carlo performances and remembered vividly the disappointment of Michel Fokine's ethereal, romantic *Les Sylphides,* because the leading man had "nothing to do." With the realization that men were shunted to the background in traditional classical ballets, where they partnered ballerinas as essentially invisible shadows, Joffrey determined that he would help men move into the foreground. He then cast himself as a dancer and choreographer in the image of his hero, Vaslav Nijinsky, committed to an almost scientific comprehension of the sheer physicality of dance and to making and presenting works that showed the power of the male form engaged fully in body, mind, and spirit.

For three years (1965 to 1968), the Joffrey Ballet contained more males than females during a time when most companies were in short supply of men. At the New York City Ballet, the great choreographer George Balanchine had proclaimed, "Ballet is woman." The dictum left a deep mark on the psyches of American choreographers. Joffrey, who was a traditionalist by nature and uncomfortable as a rebel, responded intuitively with his unstated, "Ballet is also man." At first he created all the company's works, but in 1965, realizing that he was not a born dance maker, he appointed Arpino to be official house choreographer. Arpino's whiz-bang, sexy, high-powered, romantic works distinguished the troupe and captured a broader audience than perhaps for any other American ballet company up to that time.

Without causing mainstream alarm, Arpino shaped the "ballet is also man" image, presenting in 1966 his all-male tribute to athletics, *Olympics,* that incorporated a suggestive, fleshy, "groin-to-groin" pas de deux that escaped the notice of all but the gay press and the most astute liberal critics. In *The Relativity of Icarus* (1974), Arpino recast the mythological story as incestuous by creating vividly sensual, emotional movement for the half-naked father and son. His *Round of Angels* (1983) evolved into one of the first anthems for victims of AIDS. Arpino has repeatedly denied the presence of homoerotic content in his work.

In 1988, Joffrey died of AIDS-related illness (he and Arpino had ceased being lovers around 1949). By 1996, twenty dancers, who were at some time affiliated with the company, had also succumbed to the AIDS virus. This represented more AIDS victims than for any other American ballet troupe.

The Joffrey Ballet today is directed by Arpino and his associate, Ann Marie de Angelo, from its home base in Chicago, and the repertoire reflects a continuing interest in gender equality and gender bending.   *Sasha Anawalt*

Bibliography

Anawalt, Sasha. *The Joffrey Ballet: Robert Joffrey and the Making of an American Dance Company*. New York: Scribner, 1996.

Biddle, Livingston. *Our Government and the Arts: A Perspective from the Inside*. New York: ACA Books, American Council for the Arts, 1988.

Gruen, John. *The Private World of Ballet*. New York: Viking, 1975.

Siegel, Marcia B. *At the Vanishing Point*. New York: Saturday Review Press, 1972.

———. *The Shapes of Change: Images of American Dance*. Boston: Houghton Mifflin, 1979. Paperback printing, Berkeley: University of California Press, 1985.

———. *Watching the Dance Go By*. Boston: Houghton Mifflin, 1977.

Solway, Diane. *A Dance Against Time: The Brief, Brilliant Life of a Joffrey Dancer*. New York: Pocket Books, 1994.

See also Ballets Russes; Dance and AIDS; Nijinsky, Vaslav Fomich

Johns, Jasper (1930–)

Perhaps the most critically and commercially successful artist in the history of American art, Jasper Johns emerged to immediate acclaim. Three paintings from his first solo show in 1958 went to the Museum of Modern Art, one graced the cover of a leading art magazine, while another won an important prize. More remarkable still, his images of everyday banalities like American flags, numbers, maps, and targets were manifestly unabstract and unexpressionist in an era dominated by the work of a group of painters called abstract expressionists. Yet his use of seemingly simple, everyday icons had a complex philosophical charge, for Johns's signs were themselves in essence abstractions made into representations. A flag is, after all, merely a two-dimensional abstract design accorded representational status by virtue of its place within our common social contract. Is a painted flag an actual flag or simply a picture of a flag? Johns's work thus embraced the ambiguities of identity, asking profound questions about the nature of things and how we label them.

Johns was born and raised in small towns in Georgia and South Carolina and moved to New York after briefly attending the University of South Carolina. While working at a bookstore and debating whether he wanted to become an artist or a poet, Johns met painter Robert Rauschenberg, and under the senior artist's tutelage quickly began to paint in earnest. Theirs was an intensely emotional and creative exchange lasting from the winter of 1953 until 1961, and a number of paintings of this period reveal the depths of their partnership.

While Johns's trademark imagery of iconic forms like flags and targets may seem profoundly impersonal, his work has great expressive immediacy, engendered by layer upon layer of buried collage elements within thick, waxy paint animated by evocative brushwork. In a series of paintings created in the fifties, Johns obscured everyday objects like books, newspapers, window shades, and drawers with thick paint. Each of these objects functions only when opened, and in each instance, Johns offered it to the viewer painted shut. In this regard, there is a probable symmetry between these works and the dynamics of the closet within the Cold War period, especially seen against the then-dominant codes of abstract expressionist art and its aesthetic of self-revelation.

Following his breakup with Rauschenberg, Johns began to explore even more expressly autobiographical themes, often using collage techniques made famous by his ex-lover. Referencing the work of gay poets like Hart Crane and Frank O'Hara, Johns found a way to encode his love and loss in paintings that on the surface seem meditative, literary, cool, and abstract. As late as the 1980s, Johns made a group of images called *Ventriloquist,* which thematized the now familiar Johnsian notion of throwing the authorial voice by speaking through objects. While never publicly acknowledging his homosexuality, Johns used his art repeatedly to play with the theme of what can and cannot be seen and/or said. So it is not so much in what Johns expresses as in what he could or did not that we find the authentic revelation of sexuality in his art.

Jonathan Katz

Bibliography

Crichton, Michael. *Jasper Johns.* New York: Harry N. Abrams, 1977.

Francis, Richard. *Jasper Johns.* New York: Abbeville, 1984.

Katz, Jonathan. "The Art of Code: Jasper Johns and Robert Rauschenberg." In *Significant Others.* Whitney Chadwick, ed. New York: Thames and Hudson, 1993.

Orton, Fred. *Figuring Jasper Johns.* Cambridge, Mass.: Harvard University Press, 1994.

Silver, Ken. "Modes of Disclosure: The Construction of Gay Identity and the Rise of Pop Art." *Hand Painted Pop: American Art in Transition: 1955–1962.* Exhibition Catalog Los Angeles: Museum of Contemporary Art, 1993.

See also Art History; Crane, Hart; O'Hara, Frank; Rauschenberg, Robert

Johnson, James Weldon (1871–1938)

Born in Jacksonville, Florida, James Weldon Johnson is today perhaps best remembered as the first black executive secretary of the NAACP and the author of what remained his single novel, *The Autobiography of an Ex-Colored Man,* published in 1912. While nothing in Johnson's own life suggests that he himself was gay, he is included in this encyclopedia because of the rich suggestiveness of his novel. Though a fictional work, the book's autobiographical mode allows Johnson to tell the story through the voice of a deeply complex and often contradictory protagonist. The protagonist, son of a prominent Southern white man and his well-kept mistress, is never named and finally crosses the color line and passes for white. His clearly ambiguous racial identity is complicated by an attendant, though never directly explicit, equally ambivalent sexual identity suggested both in his feminized descriptions of himself and in his relationship with a white millionaire who becomes his patron. Johnson's treatment of sexual identity is important because it may have influenced later writers of the Harlem Renaissance in whose work such themes enjoyed frank and open treatment, and because it raises important questions about the complicated interrelationship between racial and sexual identity.

Nimisha Ladva

Bibliography

Kinnamon, Kenneth. "James Weldon Johnson." In *Dictionary of Literary Biography: Afro-American Writers from the Harlem Renaissance to 1940.* Trudier Harris and Thadious M. Davis, eds. Vol. 51. Detroit: Gayle Research Company, 1987.

See also African American Gay Culture; Harlem Renaissance

Johnson, Philip C. (1906–)

Philip Johnson is the best-known openly gay architect in America. His coming out in 1993 capped a sixty-year career of great influence, and sometimes celebrity status, in American design.

Johnson began as a historian of and propagandist for radical architecture. The Harvard-educated young millionaire discovered avant-garde art in the early 1930s in the New York gay subculture around Lincoln Kirstein and the Museum of Modern Art (MoMA). His 1932 "Modern Architecture" exhibition for the museum (usually called the "International Style" show after the accompanying book Johnson coauthored) set the terms through which the American design world encountered European modernism. After a short, disastrous career in fascist politics, Johnson trained at Harvard under émigré modernist Marcel Breuer.

In 1946 Johnson entered practice while continuing to mount shows for MoMa, like his seminal 1947 show on German modernist Mies van der Rohe. The architectural landmark of this period is Johnson's house for himself, the Mies-derived Glass House, in New Canaan, Connecticut. This structure, a single steel-and-glass framed room, helped to make Mies's steel-frame aesthetic a norm in American design. After the mid-1950s, Johnson broke with the functionalist International Style to play with different forms, moods, and historical styles. As a big-budget commercial architect in the firm Johnson & Burgee, Johnson combined historical reference with ironic pop art motifs in his AT&T (now Sony) Building on New York's Madison Avenue, a landmark of postmodernism. As a practitioner, he continued to encourage new ideas and forms in design, acting as a gadfly in an often conformist profession. His devotion to architecture as a fine art earned him the American Institute of Architect's Gold Medal in 1978.

As a propagandist or a builder, a modernist or a postmodernist, Johnson has always made the same claim: architecture has no moral or social mission beyond beauty. He has been unusually articulate about the ways in which architecture's pleasures are sensual, not intellectual or practical. Johnson has also insisted, pointing to his countless shifts in style over the decades, that change is the only constant in art and life; modernism's search for one functionalist method of building is thus inhuman.

In the 1960s, Johnson's aestheticism earned him the label of camp architect. Since his coming out, some critics have praised Johnson in terms closer to queer theory, calling his subversions of accepted styles and functions an embrace of radical indeterminacy. While it is true that Johnson admires the subversive camp of Andy Warhol, whom he befriended, his freedom as a designer has been limited by his preoccupation with rules in architecture—variously the rules of modernism or historical styles, his clients' demands, or the supposed imperatives of fine art as his moods shift. However, the free, anti-Euclidean shapes of his post-1993 work, like his Visitor's Center for the Glass House and the proposed Cathedral of Hope for a gay and lesbian church in Dallas, may forecast Johnson's invention of an architecture of bodily freedom.

M. David Samson

Bibliography

Schulze, Franz. *Philip Johnson: Life and Work.* New York: Knopf, 1994.

See also Architecture; Art History; Kirstein, Lincoln; Postmodernism; Warhol, Andy

Jones, Bill T. (1952–)

African American dancer and choreographer Bill T. Jones was born William Tass Jones in Bunnell, Florida, the tenth of twelve children. Jones attended Wayland Central School in Wayland, New York, where his family had settled after working as migrant farmers. He began to study dance as a college student at the State University of New York at Binghamton in 1970 and quickly distinguished himself by his use of autobiographical storytelling in his performances.

Jones began a seventeen-year partnership with Arnie Zane in 1971. Zane, a student of art history and a practicing photographer, joined Jones in dance, where their collaboration fascinated audiences as a study in contrasts. In early duets, Zane, a small man of Jewish and Italian descent, born and raised in Queens, New York, would easily lift and support tall, brown-skinned Jones. The duo formed Bill T. Jones/Arnie Zane & Company in 1982, and their unlikely appearance and outspoken commitment to each other onstage and off galvanized the downtown art world. They achieved prominence with the full-length *Secret Pastures*, which premiered at the Brooklyn Academy of Music's Next Wave Festival in 1984 with costumes by Willi Smith, sets by Keith Haring, and music by Peter Gordon. As the company's acclaim grew, Jones continued to work as a soloist. His powerful performances sometimes included improvised movement layered with freely associated autobiographical text; in 1981, he danced an untitled solo built on spoken oppositional statements such as "I love women; I hate women" and "I love white people; I hate white people."

Jones and Zane were both diagnosed as HIV-positive in 1986, and Zane succumbed to AIDS in 1988. After Zane's death, Jones continued to make large-scale work that addressed themes of racial identity, sexuality, and cultural memory, as in the epic *Last Supper at Uncle Tom's Cabin/The Promised Land* (1990), a four-part, three-hour fantasia loosely based on the Harriet Beecher Stowe novel, which included an intergenerational cast, rap poetry, and scores of nude dancers in its final utopian vision. In 1994, he conducted a series of movement and discussion workshops with survivors of life-threatening illnesses that led to the landmark work *Still/Here* (1994). A full-length work concerned with the divide between sick and well, the dance ranked among the first large-scale works to deal soberly with impressions of premature death.

Working with passionate abandonment of propriety and a firm belief in the multifaceted aspects of human personality, Jones accepted his identity as a gay African American man as an important attribute of his work. In 1981 he explained his motive to *Village Voice* reporter Burt Supree as the

> revealing of a person. Revealing something that is normally hidden. Because in this dance scene there aren't many people like myself, that is, black people from poverty backgrounds, who have been educated in a university, and now, instead of being doctors and lawyers, which is the usual trajectory of improvement—have instead become downtown artist types. I feel that if I can reveal the process that has brought me here, that's a social bridge. I feel like a map of the aspirations of the '60s.

His eclectic, ten-member company achieved international acclaim for its artistry as well as its provocative variety of physical types. Peopled by rotund, tall, and petite dancers of varied complexions, the company consistently included openly gay, straight, and bisexual artists who collectively challenged conventional assumptions of who could be a dancer and how that dancer might look. Jones received many awards and honors throughout his career, including two Bessie performance awards and a 1994 MacArthur "Genius" Fellowship; he created work for many companies, including the Alvin Ailey American Dance Theater, the Boston Ballet, and the Lyon Opera Ballet, where he was resident chore-

ographer from 1994 through 1996. As a whole, his work addressed the complexities of contemporary life with bold, provocative strength, delicacy, and spirituality.   *Thomas DeFrantz*

Bibliography

Dunning, Jennifer. "A Partner Exits, a Solo Begins." *New York Times*, November 4, 1990.

Gates. Henry Louis. "The Body Politic." *New Yorker*, November 28, 1994.

Jones, Bill T., and Peggy Gillespie. *Last Night on Earth*. New York: Pantheon, 1995.

Supree, Burt. "Any Two Men on the Planet." *Village Voice*, March 18–24, 1981.

See also African American Gay Culture; Ailey, Alvin; Dance and AIDS; Haring, Keith; Zane, Arnie

Jorgensen, Christine (1926–1989)

The first internationally known transgender personality of the twentieth century, Christine (née George) Jorgensen was not only a pioneer in the field of sex reassignment surgery but provided an unprecedented example for the thousands of gender-dysphoric individuals who would follow in her footsteps.

George Jorgensen was born to working-class parents of Danish descent in the Bronx, New York. In her autobiography, Jorgensen described her early years of solitude and confusion as "the no man's land of sex." After graduating from high school in 1944, Jorgensen entered the army and served as a clerk at Fort Dix, N.J. With money from the GI bill passed for World War II veterans, Jorgensen studied at photography school in New Haven, Conn., with the intent of becoming a professional photographer.

In 1948, Jorgensen read Paul de Kruif's *The Male Hormone* and wondered whether his own gender confusion might be the result of a deficit of testosterone or a surfeit of estrogen in his body. Jorgensen had heard about endocrinologists in Denmark who could chemically "correct" natural hormonal imbalances. In 1950, Jorgensen sailed to Copenhagen to undergo experimental estrogen therapy and, later, sex reassignment surgery, and rechristened herself in tribute to the supervising physician, Christian Hamburger.

In late November 1952, while recovering from surgery, the story of her transformation leaked to the New York *Daily News*, which launched the Jorgensen phenomenon with the spectacular headline "Ex-GI Becomes Blonde Beauty." On her return to

Christine Jorgensen arriving in Miami after a nightclub engagement in Havana, 1953. UPI/Corbis-Bettmann.

Jorgensen was an early advocate for transgender rights and often used her position to defend not only herself but the nascent homophile rights movement. By the late 1960s, however, the momentum of the sexual liberation movement, as well as the acceptance of gender dysphoria and sex reassignment surgery in professional medical circles, made Jorgensen's femme version of the 1950s glamour queen seem dated, if not reactionary. In 1967, Jorgensen published her memoirs to great acclaim, which spurred on the transsexual autobiography as a literary genre that many emulated throughout the 1970s. Except for a few brief public appearances—including *Good Morning America*, the *Tom Snyder Show*, and some cabaret performances in the early 1980s—Jorgensen spent her remaining years quietly, a self-described "old maid." She died at home of bladder cancer on May 3, 1989, just weeks before her sixty-third birthday. *David Serlin*

Bibliography

Jorgensen, Christine. *Christine Jorgensen: A Personal Autobiography*. New York: Paul S. Ericksson, 1967.

Serlin, David Harley. "Christine Jorgensen and the Cold War Closet." *Radical History Review* 62 (Spring 1995): 136–65.

See also Gender; Transgender; Transsexualism

the United States in February 1953, Jorgensen became an international media celebrity and was known shortly thereafter as "the most talked about girl in the world." Because there were no precedents for Jorgensen's transformation, she was understood alternately as an ex-soldier, a glamorous femme fatale, and an upwardly mobile success story. While she rejected film contracts, Jorgensen did accept an offer to perform in Las Vegas at the regal salary of $12,000 per week. She suffered a minor setback in April 1953 when the media announced that she was not a "real woman" but instead only a "castrated male" (surgeons did not construct a vagina for Jorgensen until 1954). However, she continued to be a star attraction, and throughout the 1950s and early 1960s she toured the United States, Hawaii, the Philippines, Cuba, and Europe.

In 1956, Jorgensen made headlines again when the New York City Board of Licenses refused to issue a marriage license to her and her then-fiancé, Howard Knox, on the grounds that Jorgensen's birth certificate still read "male." During the intervening weeks while they contested the order, she and Knox broke up. Despite a continuous stream of suitors and proposals, Jorgensen never married.

Josephus Flavius (c.37–c.100 C.E.)

Joseph, Son of Matthias, Jewish historian, better known under his Roman name, Josephus Flavius. An educated man of noble priestly descent, he became a commander of the Jewish army in the revolt against Rome (66–70 C.E.). He surrendered, went over to the Roman side, and ingratiated himself with Roman general Vespasian (soon to become emperor). After the war, he followed the Roman troops back to Rome, where he lived until his death, receiving Roman citizenship and an imperial pension. He wrote an account of the war (*The Jewish War*), a lengthy history of the Jewish people from the time of creation (*Jewish Antiquities*), as well as two shorter works (*Life*; *Against Apion*). In his historical work, he also attempted to explain Jewish law and customs to what was probably a largely Roman audience. Josephus is one of our main sources for Jewish shistory during the late Hellenistic and early Roman period.

Josephus makes only occasional comments in relation to male same-sex acts. Like other contemporary Jews and Christians, he generally condemns such relations. He implicitly acknowledges that in his cultural context male youth can be sexually attractive to older men (Ant. 1.200, 15.25) but insists that the only sexual relation legitimated by the Torah is of a husband with his wife for the procreation of children (Josephus always writes from the perspective of the man): sex "with males" is punishable by death (Ap. 2.199). He seems to place sex with men on a par with sex with animals or menstruating women, all of which are "in pursuit of lawless pleasure" (Ant. 3.275). Elsewhere, more explicitly in defense of Jewish life, he maintains that Jewish laws and customs are superior to those of "other nations" inter alia because those nations practiced sex "with males" and excused their "unusual and unnatural pleasure," attributing its origins to the gods (Ap. 2.273–275). Finally, while Josephus's interpretation of the biblical Sodom narrative (Genesis 19; cf. Ant. 1.194–201) still mentions greed, arrogance, and the lack of hospitality as the reason for Sodom's iniquity, he begins to shift the focus to the sexual aspect of the story (similar to Philo of Alexandria). In contrast to Philo, Josephus offers too little material for the analysis of the motives for his condemnatory stance of male erotic same-sex acts, although it can be surmised that it is comparable to Philo's.

Josephus was largely ignored by the Jewish community. Instead, his works were preserved by Christians, who copied them frequently. His historical works filled the Christian need for appropriating Jewish history as they began to regard themselves as "the new Israel." His occasional condemnation of sex among men was surely appreciated by the church fathers.   *Holger Szesnat*

Bibliography

Boswell, John. *Christianity, Social Tolerance, and Homosexuality.* Chicago: University of Chicago Press, 1980.

See also Christianity; Philo of Alexandria; Rome, Ancient

Journalism

In January 1943, feature article in the Washington, D.C., *Evening Star* described "How the Navy's 'Mind Detectives' Seek Men of Sound Nerve for Warfare" by trying to weed out homosexuals and other "unde-

sirables." Similar stories appeared in newspapers and magazines nationwide. "To screen out this undesirable soldier-material," *Newsweek* reported in 1947, "psychiatrists in induction-station interviews tried to detect them (1) by their effeminate looks or behavior and (2) by repeating certain words from the homosexual vocabulary and watching for signs of recognition."

The media image of gays and lesbians had emerged from the depths of an unacknowledged conspiracy of silence that prevailed throughout the major news media before World War II. But the dark and dreary picture of gay life grew even darker during the witch-hunts of the 1950s. Homosexuals were easy prey for Senator Joseph McCarthy and other politicians eager to capitalize on the nation's postwar paranoia. In newspapers and magazines, "undesirable" homosexuals became traitors and criminals. A *New York Times* headline blared: "Perverts Called Government Peril." One in the Washington *Times-Herald* said: "Reds Entice Women Here in Sex Orgies."

Network television did not approach the subject until 1967, when "CBS Reports" broadcast an hour-long documentary. Narrator Mike Wallace intoned: "The average homosexual, if there be such, is promiscuous. He is not interested in nor capable of a lasting relationship like that of a heterosexual marriage. . . . The pickup—the one night stand—these are characteristics of the homosexual relationship."

Media images from the 1940s through much of the 1960s was a reflection of society's understanding of homosexuality. Reporters like Wallace based their description on what they had been told by psychiatrists, who classified homosexuals as sick; police, who considered them criminals; and clergy, who saw them as a moral menace. Even though they did not create this image, the media reinforced such stereotypes, and through repetition their depiction became fact.

In September 1969, gays began to challenge what the media were saying about them. Angry that in its reporting of the Stonewall riots, New York's *Village Voice* had referred to them as the "forces of faggotry," they picketed the newspaper's editorial offices. While the paper refused to print an ad from the Gay Liberation Front, it permitted landlords to specify "no gays" in apartment rental ads. Eventually the publisher agreed to change the advertising policy but vowed to retain the right to call gays whatever his writers pleased.

Heartened by their partial success at the *Voice* and their efforts in the early 1970s to convince the American Psychiatric Association to drop homosexuality from its list of mental illnesses, gays stepped up their challenges against media inaccuracies. Confronted with protests at *Time, Harper's,* the *San Francisco Examiner,* the *Los Angeles Times,* the New York *Daily News,* and ABC Television, the media for the first time began to listen to their complaints.

But by 1977 the adoption of antidiscrimination legislation in a host of American cities touched off an antigay backlash. Anita Bryant in Florida, for one, sparked a rash of negative publicity nationwide. Even so, journalists began to delve more deeply into the gay culture, without the help of "experts" who had biased coverage in the past. While the coverage remained spotty and uneven at best, there were major breakthroughs. At a few print and broadcast outlets, reporters explained gay life in terms that began to reflect accurately who gays were and what they wanted from the rest of society.

Coverage turned darker again beginning in 1982 with the onset of AIDS. Some journalists ignored the epidemic altogether because they did not consider the death of homosexuals relevant to their largely heterosexual audiences. Where the mainstream media did address the illness, gays often became synonymous with death and disease. In the *National Review,* for instance, conservative publisher William F. Buckley urged a crackdown on people with AIDS, including mandatory tattooing.

But gay activists quickly rallied again. By the mid-1980s, AIDS and the negative publicity surrounding it became an organizing tool to rally the community. In creating the Gay and Lesbian Alliance Against Defamation in 1985, gays and lesbians had their first organization exclusively dedicated to challenging negative depictions of gays throughout the media.

The case for fair and accurate depictions of gay life was also being made by an increasing number of open gay and lesbian journalists. Randy Shilts became the first open gay reporter at a major mainstream American newspaper when he was hired by the *San Francisco Chronicle* in 1981. After *New York Times* deputy national editor Jeffrey Schmalz contracted AIDS and revealed his homosexuality to his colleagues at the *Times* in 1990, he became the highest-ranking openly gay editor in American journalism. Similarly, Linda Villarosa at *Essence* and Andrew Sullivan at the *New Republic* rose quickly through the ranks.

In increasing numbers, gay and lesbian journalists were willing to make their sexuality known within their newsrooms and to serve as resources on stories about the gay community. In 1992, former *Washington Post* editor Leroy Aarons formed the National Lesbian and Gay Journalists Association (NLGJA). Within three years its membership roles had swelled to more than one thousand. In growing numbers, gays who would have been considered too biased to write on the subject in an earlier era were routinely reporting on their own community, sometimes from their own personal experience.

"It is a history of seismic change in the way American journalism treats gay subjects and in the openness so many of us now enjoy in our newsrooms," Leroy Aarons told the NLGJA's fifth annual convention in 1996. But he also sounded a note of caution. Pointing out that heightened visibility often sparks vicious backlash, he urged gay journalists to work even harder to assure fair, accurate coverage of the gay community. "The issue of how our nation treats homosexuality is more at center stage than ever before," he said. "We need more vocal strength in this army of journalists, more people who do ask and do tell the honest and true story of one of the profound social trends of our time."   *Edward Alwood*

Bibliography

Buckley, William F, Jr. "AIDS: And Then, What?" *National Review,* May 22, 1987, 56.

"Homosexuals in Uniform," *Newsweek,* June 9, 1947, 54.

Ottenberg, Miriam. "How the Navy's 'Mind Detectives' Seek Men of Sound Nerve for Warfare." *Evening Star,* January 10, 1943, B-5.

"Perverts Called Government Peril." *New York Times,* April 19, 1950, 25.

"Reds Entice Women Here in Sex Orgies." *Times-Herald,* March 29, 1950, 1.

Teal, Donn. *The Gay Militants.* 1971. New York: St. Martin's Press, 1995.

Transcript. "The Homosexuals." *CBS Reports,* March 7, 1967.

See also AIDS; AIDS in the Media; Gay Liberation Front; Gay and Lesbian Press; Gay and Lesbian Alliance Against Defamation (GLAAD); McCarthyism; Psychological and Psychoanalytic Perspectives on Homosexuality; Shilts, Randy's; Stonewall

Juan de la Cruz, San (1542–1591)

Spanish poet and visionary San Juan de la Cruz (Saint John of the Cross) was born in Fontiveros, near Avila in central Spain, in 1542. He was ordained a priest in 1567. He and Saint Teresa of Avila initiated a reform

J of the Carmelite order, resulting in his arrest in December 1577, followed by eight months' confinement in the convent of the Calzados in Toledo and his escape down a rope. During this period, he is thought to have composed two of his best-known works, *Noche oscura* (Dark Night) and *Cántico espiritual* (Spiritual Canticle). These two and *Llama del amor viva* (Living Flame of Love) are San Juan's most important works. Besides poems, he wrote, at the request of his readers, commentaries on his poetry, which was nearly incomprehensible to them. He died on December 15, 1591, in the convent of Ubeda in Andalucía. Since 1593, his remains have been in Segovia. He was beatified in 1675, canonized in 1726, and proclaimed a doctor of the Roman Catholic Church in 1926 and the patron saint of Spanish poets in 1952.

Renaissance neoplatonists like Marcello Ficino and Pico Della Mirandola began a style of interpretation of Christian mysticism that assimilated the mystic's experience of God to the Platonic direct knowledge of eternal forms or ideas, and earthly love, no matter how erotic, into an intimation of direct experience of the divine. San Juan's highly erotic poetry is usually interpreted according to this tradition, as dealing with three principal themes: the path toward union with God, the joys of marriage, and the delights of divine love. San Juan's commentaries, and the vast majority of later criticism, follow this line. But anyone who had not been informed previously that these were mystical poems would read them as carnal, erotic, and sensual.

The poetic voice (*la amada*: the beloved, interpreted by San Juan as the believer's soul) is, on the surface, a woman; the grammatical gender of *alma* (soul) is feminine. She (or it) speaks directly and sincerely of her pleasure in love, with no sense of transgression or sin, not at all the feminine type of the sixteenth century. Without diffidence or caution in matters concerning her honor, she is autonomous and liberated, psychologically androgynous from a sixteenth-century perspective. Not a word in the poems, in contrast with the commentaries, suggests a platonic ascent to a higher plane. On the contrary, the divine Beloved (*el Amado*) and the beloved make love among the white lilies that grow in the meadow at the foot of the fortress. It was completely inconceivable at that point in the Western literary tradition that an ascetic Carmelite brother, the founder of an order, would make a woman the protagonist of his poems, and that, moreover, this woman would not represent the image of stereotypically feminine passivity, of the devotional or sexual object resigned to wait patiently until her lover arrives via the secret ladder. In her place, San Juan introduces a woman with a "masculine" attitude toward love—free, unafraid to acknowledge herself burning with passion, going into the dark night to meet her lover.

Nothing is known about the sexual aspect of San Juan's life, and we will never know whether his own earthly desires are reflected in those of the woman who speaks in his poems. Nevertheless, it does not seem completely unreasonable to conjecture that Saint John uses a poetic strategy familiar to that of Federico García Lorca. Like the latter's play, *El público* (The public), San Juan's poems were composed in secret, and he had no plan to publish them, especially the *Noche oscura*. His work was not in fact published during his lifetime but circulated only in manuscript among a small group of his aristocratic friends in the Spanish court.

Juan M. Godoy,
translated by Bruce Vermazen

Bibliography

Nieto, José C. *San Juan de la Cruz, poeta del amor profano*. Madrid: Editorial Swan, S. L. Avantos & Hakeldama, 1988.
San Juan de la Cruz, Poesía completa y comentarios. Raquél Asún, ed. Barcelona: Planeta, 1996.

See also Lorca, Federico García; Love Poetry; Renaissance Neoplatonism; Spain; Spanish Literature

Juan II of Castille (1405–1454)

In 1406, when Juan II of Castille was just an infant, his father, Enrique III, died on Christmas Day. Juan succeeded him, at first under the regency of his mother, Catalina, and his uncle, Fernando de Antequera. Juan officially ascended to the throne in 1419.

As king, Juan lacked interest in governing, preferring to rule through his favored minister, Álvaro de Luna (1385–1453). Luna served the king for forty years—as page, soldier, statesman, and confidant—progressively achieving total control over Juan's will and the realm. His unparalleled power angered other feudal lords, ensuring conspiracies and strife throughout Juan's reign.

In 1453, at the behest of his second wife, Isabel of Portugal, Juan had Luna arrested and publicly beheaded. The charges against Don Álvaro were treason, murder, and "bewitching" the king. According to legend, Juan's hand trembled so that he was unable to sign Luna's death warrant without the aid of the queen. Juan was mortified over what he had done and died only a year later.

Antonio Mira de Amescua's golden age play, *The Prosperous Fortune of Don Álvaro de Luna and the Adverse Fortune of Ruy López de Ávalos,* shows young Juan immediately attracted to Luna, his page, and telling his sister of his strong inclination toward him. The king vows eternal devotion to Luna, and other attendants note Juan's compulsive attachment to the page.

Juan II is also renowned for his refined court, which became a literary center and inaugurated the Renaissance in Spain. *María Dolores Costa*

Bibliography

Haliczer, Stephen. *The Comuneros of Castile: The Forging of a Revolution, 1475–1521.* Madison, Wis.: University of Wisconsin Press, 1981.

MacCurdy, Raymond R. *The Tragic Fall: Don Álvaro de Luna and Other Favorites in Spanish Golden Age Drama.* Chapel Hill, N.C.: North Carolina Studies in Romance Languages and Literatures, 1978.

See also Spain; Spanish Literature

Judaism

Judaism is both a religion and a way of life. Moreover, since Jews, at least since the Diaspora (the destruction of Jerusalem in the first century of the modern era), have lived and interacted with—and been influenced by—a wide variety of other cultures. The practices of Chinese Jews, for example, differ from those of India or Ethiopia or for that matter from American Jews. In America, Judaism is divided into three major religious communities: Orthodox, Conservative, and Liberal or Reform. The Orthodox hold that the Torah (or Pentateuch) is word for word and letter for letter the word of God, and they seek strict conformity to its words. Reform Jews hold, that while the Torah might be divinely inspired, it is the work of human beings, and so as a group it reserves the right to evaluate, criticize, and modify the book and to change or even dispense with some of the laws based on it. The Conservatives, while allied with the Reform in their view of the Torah, tend to seek a somewhat greater degree of conformity to traditional observations. There are also lesser communities within Judaism that are both more liberal (such as Humanistic Judaism) and more traditional (such as the Hassidism). While most American Jews are descended from the Ashkenazi or Yiddish-speaking community, most of those in the Third World and in southern Europe came from the Sephardic or Ladino-speaking community.

Inevitably any discussion of Jewish attitudes toward homosexuality has to be selective, and not every view can be presented. In general, however, Jewish attitudes toward sex throughout most of Jewish history have been positive, that is, sex is considered both for procreation and for pleasure and is seen as a blessing to be used wisely.

In general, there is not very much in the early scriptures about homosexuality, and what there is has often been overemphasized by the Christian West. Homosexual cultic practices were common in biblical times, and, inevitably, the Jewish writers of the time viewed both the cults and practices with hostility. The Pentateuch legislation or Holiness Code as preserved in Leviticus condemns homosexual practices and calls for those found guilty to be stoned. In the sections incorporated into the Christian Bible, believers are told: "Thou shall not lie with mankind as with womankind: it is abomination" (Leviticus 18:22). This is later amplified:

> If a man also lie with mankind, as he lieth with a woman, both of them have committed an abomination: they shall be put to death; and their blood shall be upon them. (Leviticus 21:13)

Earlier scholars believed that the Holiness Code dated from the period of exile in Babylon, but scholars today do not agree because some of the references seem to date from a later period, including possible references to Greek homosexual practices. Some writers believe the anxiety over homosexuality dates form much earlier, and that the scriptural hostility to nudity is a veiled fear of homosexuality. It is argued that only such a deep seated homoerotic activity could account for the reaction of Noah in cursing his son Ham for not covering his father's nakedness (Genesis 9:22–24). Interestingly, the equation of the destruction of Sodom and Gomorrah with homosexuality (Genesis 19:1–11), so prominent in Christian thinking, has little place in the Jewish commentators who usually interpret the sin of Sodom to be pride, unwillingness to aid the poor and needy, and violence.

Lesbianism is known in Jewish law and condemned prior to the modern period, but it seldom

J

Members of Shaíar Zahar gay synagogue light Chanukah candles, 1987. Photo by Marc Geller.

posed the legal problems to Jewish commentators that homosexuality did, and so it was generally ignored. In post-biblical law, in which conditions that Judaism faced were different from those in the earlier period, homosexuality was considered a moral failure rather than an illness or alternative lifestyle. In spite of this, because the biblical penalty had been stoning, an accusation of homosexuality could result in a homosexual case being treated the same as a murder case. Because of fear of miscarriage of justice in such cases, however, there were all kinds of requirements to be met before sentence was imposed, and there is no record in which a person was accused and convicted of homosexual acts and stoned to death.

Many of the biblical stories can be interpreted as having a homoerotic theme and have been so interpreted by many modern writers. Drawing the most attention are the love between David and Jonathan and Ruth and Naomi. The scriptures state that David's love for Jonathan surpassed the "love of women" (II Samuel 1:26). Parts of the statement attributed to Ruth in speaking of her devotion to Naomi, in fact, have often been incorporated into the modern marriage ceremony, an indication of just how deep some same-sex affection ran:

Intreat me not to leave thee, or to return from following after thee: for whither thou goest, I will go, and whither thou lodgest, I will lodge; thy people shall be my people, and thy God is my God. (Ruth 1:16–17)

Although the first redaction of the Babylonian Talmud took place in the fifth century of the modern era, commentaries continued to be made by the heads of the four yeshivas (or Talmudic academies) near Baghdad until well into the tenth century. Other sections of the Jewish community, following the Diaspora in the first century, continued to comment on and interpret the Jewish tradition, and such commentary continues today. Unfortunately, much of later commentary remains comparatively unexplored. Jews, in their interaction with non-Jews, wrote for non-Jewish audiences in their adopted languages, and when writing in Ladino or Yiddish incorporated secular concepts. There is, for example, a Hebrew secular-love literature from Muslim Spain. Probably the most notable was the tenth-century author Samuel Ibn Naghrillah, who was also prime minister of Granada and commander in chief of its army. His love poems feature both women and boys as love objects. All the Hebrew poets of this era wrote similar poems, and whether these poems reflect actual practices or simply erotic figments of the author's imagination is a question much debated. No matter how modern commentators look upon these writings, they are highly erotic and powerful vehicles for their authors' fantasies about boy love.

In the twentieth century, homosexuality and lesbianism have come to be understood in different ways, if only because Jewish thinking mirrors the changes taking place in the secular world and, in fact, is often in the front ranks of those demanding change. There are gay and lesbian congregations often led by gay or lesbian rabbis. Those who belong to them are considered, even by the most Orthodox authorities, to be no less Jewish than other Jewish congregations. Though there still might be some stigma associated with homosexuality or lesbianism, it is no more than exists in the Christian community. It is important to note, however, that while Reform Jewish theology has gone far to emphasize that homosexuality and lesbianism is not a moral failing or an illness, this cannot be said about the more rigidly Orthodox who like their rigidly orthodox fellow Christians hold to more traditional views.   *Vern L. Bullough*

Bibliography

Bullough, Vern L. *Sexual Variance in Society and History.* Chicago: University of Chicago, 1976.

Ehrman, A. *The Talmud, with English Translation and Commentaries.* Jerusalem: el Am, 1965.

Epstein, Soncino. *The Babylonian Talmud.* London: Soncino Press, 1933.

Freehof, S. *Reform Jewish Practice and Its Rabbinic Background and the various editions of the* Responsa. Cincinnati: Hebrew Union College, 1944–.

Podet, Allen Howard. "Judaism and Sexuality." In *Human Sexuality: An Encyclopedia.* Vern L. Bullough and Bonnie Bullough, eds. New York: Garland, 1994, 325–30.

Roth, C., and C. Wigoder, eds. *Encyclopedia Judaica.* Jerusalem: Keter, 1972.

Roth, Norman. "A Note on Research into Jewish Sexuality in the Medieval Period." In *Handbook of Medieval Sexuality.* Vern L. Bullough and James Brundage, eds. New York: Garland, 1996, 309–18.

See also Bible; David and Jonathan; Israel and Palestine; Nazism and the Holocaust; Religion and Religiosity; Sodom

Jung, Carl Gustav (1875–1961)

The predominance of psychoanalysis and behaviorist thinking in psychology for most of the twentieth century consigned Jung's theories to the fringes of psychology. Though often seen, inaccurately, as a disciple of Freud, Jung was well on the way to developing his own psychology of the unconscious before meeting Freud in 1907, a psychology that Jung continued to refine for nearly fifty years following his formal break with Freud in 1912. The concept responsible in part for their break—Jung's notion of a collective unconscious, common to all human beings, organized into typical patterns of psychological experience that he called archetypes—remains his best-known theoretical contribution, and Jung consistently refused to place sexuality at the center of psychological development, insisting on psychological growth as a life-long process, not one ending with childhood.

As might be expected, therefore, Jung had little to say concerning homosexuality, nor was he especially motivated to find its "explanation" or "cure." Nevertheless, what he did say on the topic reveals a number of progressive attitudes. He felt, with others, that homosexuality ought not to be a concern of legal authorities, and he consistently acknowledged the universal nature of homosexuality across time and culture. His reports of work with homosexual patients show him to be intent on discerning both the positive and negative meanings homosexuality held for the individual in question, and Jung always took care to appreciate the individual's sexuality in the context of the person's whole personality.

As for etiological theories, Jung considered that homosexuality might well be constitutional and could function as a sort of natural birth control. He also put forth the idea that homosexuality might result from an identification with the archetype of the androgyne, an image of wholeness which for any given individual could function both progressively—as a union of opposites—or regressively—as an undifferentiated, chaotic experience of self. However, these two potentially more affirmative etiologies were largely ignored by Jung's followers in favor of his third and most frequent explanation: that homosexuality, male and female, results from an unhealthy attachment to the feminine, personally and archetypally.

Only recently in analytical psychology has the underlying homophobia and sexism of this view been challenged by clinicians who have sought to develop a more affirmative approach to

J homosexuality. This newer generation of practitioners and writers has explored a variety of issues: for example, the effects of homophobia inside and outside of Jungian psychology, the importance of the archetypal masculine in gay men's development, the essential role of the feminine in lesbian development, and the symbolic rituals to be found in gay communities. With the presumption that homosexuality is an archetypal phenomenon, Jung's ideas have thus allowed contemporary clinicians to approach such diverse phenomena in the contemporary gay community as sadomasochism, the popularity of certain films and film stars, spiritual and religious attitudes, and patterns of gay male relationships, with a great deal of symbolic insight and understanding.

Robert H. Hopcke

Bibliography
Hopcke, Robert H. *Jung, Jungians and Homosexuality.* Boston: Shambhala, 1989.
Hopcke, Robert H., Karin Lofthus Carrington, and Scott Wirth. *Same-Sex Love and the Path to Wholeness.* Boston: Shambhala, 1993.

See also Androgyny; Freud, Sigmund; Masculinity; Psychological and Psychoanalytic Perspectives on Homosexuality; Sadomasochism

K

Kabuki

Kabuki, a traditional form of Japanese theater, is characterized as an all-male theater where female personification is considered as an art form. Kabuki, as is true of much Japanese culture, was of religious origin. In the medieval period, members of a Buddhist sect started dancing in ecstatic frenzy, chanting in praise of Amitabha Buddah, praying to fend off evil spirits or to send the souls of the deceased to their resting places; in the fifteenth century, the dancers were often cross-dressed. As its religious significance gradually faded, the dancing became a central attraction in its own right. By the end of the sixteenth century, this type of dance had caught fire among every class; the participants wore eccentric costumes and accessories, with cross-dressing frequently practiced, and were called *Kabukimono,* "people of Kabuki."

The Chinese characters applied to the word *Kabuki* today indicate "song, dance, and skill": in the Edo period (1603–1868), another set of characters was widely used, signifying "song, dance, and female dancer/prostitute." However, etymologically, *Kabuki* meant otherwise: *Kabuki* was a noun derived from the verb *kabuku,* which connoted for instance, to recline one's head; by extension, to deviate, stray from the norm in appearance and behavior; further derivations were to be eccentric, self-willed, wild, and playful. Hence, a person whose appearance or behavior was stylishly unconventional was called *Kabuki-mono.* The people who danced in outlandish fashion were rightfully so.

Toward the end of the sixteenth century, Izumo no Okuni, a legendary female dancer, organized a professional dancing troupe. In 1603, she caused a sensation with her performances in Kyoto. She is said to have been a priestess of the Great Izumo Shrine before she became the first pop icon in Japanese history. In the first part of her dance revues, she appeared in a monk's costume, indicating the religious vestige of her dancing; in the second part, she changed to a man's kimono, wearing her hair short, a headband, a sword, a dagger, and a sake container at her waist—all men's properties. She also wore an imported cross pendant and other foreign objects to emphasize the distance of her entity from everyday reality and sexual stereotypes. Her theater was frequently called "Kabuki dancing." For this reason, she is considered the originator of present-day Kabuki.

The main attraction of Okuni's performance was a dance set in a tea- or bathhouse (which was also a brothel) between a male customer and the madame. Okuni impersonated the dandified customer, and a male transvestite performed the role of the madam. The first professional Kabuki thus was a cross-dressing dance.

Many all-female troops, hence called "female Kabuki," comprising bathhouse women or courtesans, followed the pack. In 1629, however, the government banned female dancers from public performance for their licentiousness, because after the performances they sold their services in private. Thereafter pubescent male performers took over Kabuki performances. The all-young-male theater had previously existed alongside the all-female theater, but the banning of the latter brought the former into the spotlight. Their performances were provocatively homoerotic. These boys also prostituted themselves after hours, and again the shogunate prohibited them both on and off the stage in 1652. Thereafter, only adult males were allowed to perform in Kabuki. The government at the same time

K prohibited sensuous song-and-dance revues, and Kabuki had to shift its focus to dramatic quality.

The banning of actresses was fortuitous to the art of transvestism. Adult male actors, facing the limits of mimicry, were compelled to cultivate femininity from a nonmimetic perspective: their solution was to distill the supposed essence of femininity from the male's viewpoint and to codify it artfully through a man's body. In this way, the *onnagata*, a female impersonator, was created as an embodiment of abstract femininity, and yet surpassing the "real" woman in femininity.

During the seventeenth and eighteenth centuries, Kabuki evolved into several genres: dance, one-act and full-length plays, historical and domestic, fantastic and realistic plays, or a combination of all. The structure of the Kabuki stage, at first an imitation of the Noh stage, gradually developed its own system: the *hanamichi* (raised corridor) running on the left side of the orchestra seats was invented to provide intimacy with the audience, and the stage turntable was for spectacular effects. As to scripts, in Kabuki's early stage, it often adapted Noh, Kyogen (comic interludes for Noh), and Bunraku (puppet) plays. These adaptations remain integral in the repertoire of Kabuki today. In the late seventeenth century, dramatist Chikamatsu Monzaemon (1653–1724) provided original Kabuki plays, using current as well as historical events. Kabuki plays were generally written for specific actors; the audience tended to attend the performances for the dramatic skill of the actors rather than for the plays' own merits. Frustrated, Chikamatsu stopped writing for Kabuki in the early eighteenth century.

Kabuki was primarily a culture for commoners. It interacted intimately with the citizen's everyday life: the actors' on- and offstage fashion often became a vogue among people; actor portraits in woodblock prints often formed an important genre in Edo art. To playwrights, consequently, Kabuki was not a private aesthetic but spoke to a public culture; they dramatized people's lives and thoughts, realities and fantasies. In the confined atmosphere of Tokugawa society after Japan was closed to the rest of the world in 1641, people's daily lives were circumscribed by multiple political and social laws. Consequently, people felt the stagnation and boredom brought on by the homogeneous, enclosed society, and their lives became little more than a series of mannerisms. Kabuki provided an outlet.

In Kabuki's early and middle stages, actors were divided into male-role specialists and female-role specialists. But toward the end of the Edo period, female impersonators started to explore their hitherto suppressed masculinity. There arose a singular theater genre: it entailed the rewriting of famous plays with the male title roles now transferred to heroines. The result was the creation of the masculine-type woman, who was antithetical to the shy, obedient, weak woman. Simultaneously plays were written in which an *onnagata* was required to perform multiple-gender roles: "she" was at once a man, a woman, and both in a single play. On the other hand, some male-role specialists also started to invade the realm of the *onnagata* roles. The actors presented both masculine and feminine sides, as well as multiple personalities, residing in a single person.

Once the conventional gender images were overturned, it was easy to cause a chain reaction of subversions within the existing social decorum and laws. Evil became glamorous, grotesqueness attractive, the unexpected pleasurable, and taboos were ignored. Tsuruya Namboku (1755–1829) and Kawatake Mokuami (1816–93) were the representative dramatists in this vein.

Tsuruya Namboku's plays were full of provocative and antisocial elements such as the use of the femme fatale figure, incest, glorified vice, and alluring grotesqueness. Namboku captured a panorama of society that was undergoing dramatic changes beneath its controlled surface: social uneasiness deriving from the financial impoverishment of the ruling classes, the frustration of masterless samurai, natural disasters, and political corruption. His femmes fatales and irresistible villains were the embodiments of the gradual transformation of class and moral structures.

Kawatake Mokuami's career spanned Japan's transitional period from feudal to modern society: the arrival of the Black Ships led by Commodore Perry in 1853, the downfall of the Tokugawa shogunate, the opening of Japan, the establishment of the Meiji government in 1868, and the modernization of Japan. His aim was to translate people's feelings and concerns onto the stage: pessimism originating from the suffocating social structure, a mounting foreign threat, and the collapse of the old world order. Androgyny, homoeroticism, incest, and moral anarchy in his plays were the vicarious representations of the social paralysis and general bewilderment of the people.

After Japan opened its gates to the rest of the world, Kabuki confronted modernism from the West and was influenced by Western dramaturgy, acting, and production methods. However, Kabuki as a contemporary drama failed, largely because the majority of the successful plays written by modern writers are set in premodern Japan. As such, Kabuki found its present identity in following its traditional form, style, and materials. Audiences have also chosen to preserve Kabuki as a heritage of Edo culture. Therefore, by distancing itself from modern Japan, Kabuki has augmented its magical, unworldly glamour, as Izumo no Okuni did with her male impersonation and outrageous costumes. Amid this glamour the *onnagata* is its central magnet: "she" is pivotal to creating a world of make-believe by transcending sexual binarism and, by extension, banal reality.

Seigo Nakao

Bibliography

Brandon, James R., trans. and ed. *Kabuki: Five Classic Plays*. Honolulu: University Press of Hawai'i, 1992.

Ernst, Earl. *The Kabuki Theater*. Honolulu: University Press of Hawai'i, 1974.

Gunji, Maakatsu. *Kabuki*. John Bester and Janet Goff, trans. Tokyo: Kodansha International, 1985.

See also Androgyny; Buddhism; Japan; Japanese Literature; Transvestism

Kama Sutra

The Kama Sutra by Vatsyayana is probably the best-known Sanskrit book in the world. It consists of 1,250 verses divided into seven parts ranging from the rights and duties of a wife to the practices of courtesans. While it has long been famous as a source of esoteric heterosexual sexual positions, few know that in its efforts to cover all the sexual mores of its time, it also presents detailed accounts of same-sex sexual activity. Kama Sutra was written by the sage Vatsyayana around the fourth century A.D. But the English-reading world first became aware of it through an 1883 translation by explorer-diplomat Sir Richard Burton and British India civil servant F. F. Arbuthnot. In deference to Victorian notions of morality, the book was severely bowdlerized and abridged, and as a result many were not aware of the extent to which it treated same-sex sexual practices. Gay French Indologist Alain Danielou published what was described as the "first unabridged modern translation" of the Kama Sutra in 1994, which shed new light on this facet of the treatise.

One of the most famous sections of the Kama Sutra deals with *auparishtaka*, or what Burton describes as "oral congress." Burton describes two kinds of eunuchs—those who disguised themselves as females and led the life of courtesans and those who chose the role of men and led the life of shampooers. Danielou simply says that "people of the third sex are of two kinds, according to whether their appearance is masculine or feminine." In each case, the Kama Sutra goes on to describe step by step how the shampooer or the courtesan performed oral sex. Eight steps are indicated, each of which has a name like "biting the sides" and "inside pressing" and "sucking a mango fruit." The Kama Sutra indicates that male citizens who knew each other well also practiced *auparishtaka*, as did male servants with their masters. It also says that women, when they were amorous, placed their mouths on the *yoni* (vagina) of each other. The Kama Sutra has a whole chapter on "virile behavior" in women, in which Vatsyayana recommends that when a man is spent after repeated intercourse, the woman can lie on top of him and penetrate him with a dildo.

Danielou claims that the Kama Sutra states that there are also "urban sophisticates" of the same sex, "greatly attached to each other and with complete faith in one another, who get married together." Other scholars claim that the text indicates only that they "embrace one another," indicating consensual sex rather than marriage. Be that as it may, it clearly indicates that there were egalitarian, same-sex relationships between urban males in premodern India. For the modern reader what is most astonishing is the tenor of Vatsyayana's Kama Sutra. It describes homosexual practices as just another facet of human sexuality—without condemnation or moral proscriptions.

Sandip Roy

Bibliography

"Kama Sutra": The Complete Kama Sutra. Alain Danielou, trans. Rochester, Vt.: Park Street Press, 1994.

Less Than Gay: A Citizens' Report on the Status of Homosexuality in India. New Delhi: AIDS Bhedbhav Virodhi Andolan, 1991.

"A New Translation of the Kama Sutra: Perceptions and Misperceptions of Ancient Indian Sexuality" *Trikone Magazine* 10, no. 1 (1995).

"Virtue and Pleasure." *Outlook Magazine,* September 11, 1996.

See also Burton, Sir Richard Francis; *Hijras* of India; India; Hinduism; Third Sex

Kant, Immanuel (1724–1804)

Eighteenth-century philosopher Immanuel Kant was born in Königsberg, East Prussia (today part of Russia). The son of a soldier, Kant went on to become professor of logic and metaphysics. Kant remained unmarried. His most relevant works are *Critique of Practical Reason*, *Critique of Pure Reason*, *Critique of Judgment*, *Religion Within the Bounds of Mere Reason*, *Metaphysics of Morals*, and the influential *Groundwork of the Metaphysics of Morals*. The *Groundwork* as well as his *Lectures on Ethics* provide the primary sources for Kant's ethical thinking in general and his condemnation of homosexuality in particular. In the paragraph *Crimean carnis* (Sins of the Flesh) in the *Lectures*, Kant argues that certain deeds are "against the ends of humanity" and "consist in the abuse of one's sexuality." To Kant, whose ethical applications are compatible with a Catholic tradition rooted in Aquinas's *vita contra naturum* (contrary to nature), every form of sexual intercourse outside marriage is an abuse of sexuality. He considers homosexuals (along with onanists and practicers of bestiality) guilty of committing crimes "contrary to the natural instinct and to animal nature" because their acts are contrary to the "ends of humanity." The purpose of humanity in respect to sexuality (following this deontological ethics) is to preserve the human species (reproduce) without "debasing the person." Kant believes that sexual acts among members of the same sex dishonor humanity, and that they degrade themselves below the level of nonhuman animals. Erroneously assuming that homosexual acts do not occur between other animals, Kant considers homosexuality to be "unnatural."

Kant's ethics is based on a principle laid out in the *Groundwork*, the categorical imperative. Its second formulation states: "An action done from duty has its moral worth *not in the purpose* to be obtained by it, but in the maxim in accordance with which it is decided upon." The categorical imperative is a purely formal ethical principle. It is impossible to deduce the practical conclusions Kant draws in his *Lectures* on homosexuality from the categorical imperative. Sex and the categorical imperative are certainly in an uneasy relation. Kant states in another formulation of this principle that we always ought to treat other human beings as ends not as means. Since sexual desires often lead to the use of another (consenting) person's body as a means to reach certain ends (e.g., pleasure), in this interpretation of the categorical imperative, sexual desires would be immoral. However, as Arthur Schopenhauer persuasively pointed out, Kant's definition of a human being as an end in itself is an *Ungedanke* (unthinkable thought), a contradiction in terms.   *Udo Schüklenk*

Bibliography

Kant, Immanuel. *Eine Vorlesung über Ethik.* Paul Menzer, ed. Berlin: 1924; *Lectures in Ethics.* Louis Infield, trans. London: Methuen, 1930.
———. *Groundwork of the Metaphysics of Morals.* H. J. Paton, trans. New York: Harper & Row, 1964.
Schopenhauer, Arthur. *Preisschrift über das Fundament der Moral.* Hamburg: Felix Meiner Verlag, 1979. *On the Basis of Morality.* E. F. J. Payne, trans. Indianapolis, Ind.: Bobbs-Merrill, 1965.

See also Schopenhauer, Arthur; Aquinas, Thomas

Kenya

"When I was in Primary Six in a boarding school in my native Yimbo District, some boy in our dormitory attempted to deflower another sexually. All hell broke loose. The following day, prayers were organized for the soul of the pervert, before he was sent away to be purified by a traditional healer. It was not until I visited San Francisco, some 20 years later, that I came across men who kissed and took each other to bed! Was I shocked? You bet I was!"

In an article published on April 27, 1997, by Nairobi's leading newspaper, the *Sunday Nation*, renowned Kenyan scholar William Ochieng was commenting on the national political culture and morality when he painted a telling picture of male homosexuality (or the lack of it) in the East African nation.

"Kenyans, the Sleaze Factor and Public Opinion" was the headline. "Homosexuality, lesbianism and other sexual perversions were unheard of in Africa (except on a few patches along the coasts). In Kenya, as in the rest of black Africa, we are still very largely governed by tradition and superstition. These traditions and fetishes are still devoid of hypocrisy and have a lot of influence on the ordered life in the teeming African villages," wrote the Maseno University College principal.

"For example, a man who went after married women was frowned upon, but the man who married many wives and conquered many girls was (and still is) a hero. A thief who stole locally was frowned on, but the man who robbed, or stole from, 'foreigners' was a hero.

"The obvious question is, why would the sexually perverted American society hound Bill Clinton over his alleged sexual transgressions? Is America not the heartland of homosexuals, lesbians, and broken homes? How do the Americans get away with their public moral nerve?"

Ochieng argued that "what is interesting in Britain (as in the United States of America) is that these are societies that are morally depraved—societies where men kiss and sleep with one another, where marriage as an institution has virtually collapsed, and where single parent families are the order of the day, owing to chaotic sex and divorces. I am convinced that our society is still morally healthier than those sin-infected Western societies."

Most of Kenya's twenty-five million people would agree. To them, especially the rural folk and the schoolchildren age eighteen and below, *homosexuality* is just a dictionary word that does not apply in their lives in any way at all. They would not believe there are real humans, grown men, who use the penis and the anus for sexual pleasure. To them, this is an abomination too grotesque to imagine.

There is no registered or covert organization of homosexuals anywhere in the country—not even in Mombasa, the chief seaport city, where more activity is recorded. Overt sexual perversion is illegal, but it's the social and cultural traditions of the people, rather than the law, that make it so rare.

Statistics are hard to come by in this field, which is regarded as so insignificant that no one cares to know or keep a tally of the homosexuals or their activities. I have come across more instances of men defiling domestic animals—especially cows, goats, sheep, and poultry—than sex between men and boys or between boys and each other. And virtually unheard of is the case of a man having anal sex with his wife or girlfriend. Such blatant sacrilege would break the marital bond irredeemably.

In my mother tongue, Embu, as well as most of Kenya's indigenous vernacular languages (there are more than forty of them), there is no word for *homosexual* or *homosexuality*. That means traditionally the experience was either unheard of or so rare it did not etch a mark in either the vocabulary or social life. Of the Kikuyu (eight million), Luhya (five million), Luo (four million), Kamba (four million)—none of them have this word in their native languages.

It was not until I, at age sixteen, left my home in central Kenya for Shimo-la-Tewa High School in Mombasa, five hundred miles away on the Indian Ocean, that I came to believe there were men who actually slept with others as sexual partners. Not that I saw anyone do this, but the language and talk of it were so rampant and convincing that I suffered a cultural shock.

Swahili, a blend of ancient Arabic and Bantu (African) dialects, is the main language used in Mombasa. I had no problem with that since I was studying it as a major subject, but the school lingo was profaned by constant use of such epithets as *shoga* (homo), *kufira mkundu*, *kutia mkundu* (fuck in the arse), and *kinyocho* (your shit, or excreta). Innocent words *nisukume* (push me) and *nyuma* (behind, rear) had been wrenched out of their meaning and tagged with obscenity.

The language seemed to point an accusing finger at male homosexuality. Frequently you would hear a boy shout at another: "*Nitakufira wewe kinyocho*" (I'll fuck your arse, you shit). I got the impression that homosexuality was despised even more than it was practiced and that the man who played the woman's role during the act was badly looked down upon—perhaps even by his partner.

An indigenous resident explained to me that *kufira mkundu* was not alien to the largely Muslim city of 1.5 million people, because religion bars sex with women until marriage. The girls must remain virgin, and this is put to the test on their wedding day. Failing the test may abort the marriage. So the boys are inclined to seek sexual comfort from each other. If a girl must have sex before she's married, then it has to be anal, the Mombasa resident explained. "That's why 'I'll fuck your arse' is such a common epithet here," in East and Central Africa's chief port city.

Visiting European and American tourists, sailors, and naval officers exacerbate matters. "Many of these male visitors solicit sex from the beach boys, and they pay generously in cash for that service. So there are beach boys who make a living out of it, and the pecuniary incentive is very damaging." Mombasa's sunny beaches and classy tourist resorts attract a lot of visitors the year round, but the indigenous population is roughly half Arabs and Asians and half Africans.

However, a tour operator says this sex business has declined by more than half since the 1980s, when AIDS came to the fore and was blamed on homosexuality. "But there are the few diehards who never changed their sex style except that now they use condoms."

K The female prostitutes frown at male competition. "This seems to push the shit up the arses of the female prostitutes. They get pissed and are willing to bend over backwards twice to make up and accommodate the homosexual tourists' demands," the operator explains. "Most insist on use of the condom and then they will open both the front and rear doors at the same time for the tourist who so requests . . . it's starting to gain currency here in Mombasa."

Such things are rarely heard of among Nairobi's three million people—of whom 90 percent are Africans, while Asian and white settlers and visitors and expatriates make up the balance. Like most parts of central and upcountry Kenya, the capital city is predominantly Christian (about 85 percent), with mainly Muslims and Hindus making up the balance.

To most Nairobians, sodomy is an outrageous taboo, and it is rare to hear talk of it or the mention of words that denote it—such as *shoga, gay, homo, kufira,* or *nyuma*—even in boys' dormitories.

A former male prostitute who works as a receptionist in a popular city restaurant says the emergence of AIDS has reduced homosexuality to a mere trace: "In the late 1970s and early 1980s, I was one among a good number of male prostitutes who frequented the top clubs. These days I don't see any. AIDS has wiped out that business. Both demand and supply have fizzled out for the players' fear of catching the disease."

In Nairobi's nightclubs, you occasionally hear the twilight girls whisper the names of gays who sometimes give them business. Mostly they are white or Asian middle-aged expatriates or the settler community members. But there is no registered roll or club of homosexuals anywhere in Kenya, and you never know whether the whispers are based on truth or falsehood, hearsay or proven fact.

Mbogo Murage

Bibliography

Murray, Stephen O., and Will Roscoe, eds. *Boy-Wives and Female-Husbands: Studies in African Homosexualities.* New York: St. Martin's Press, 1998.

See also Africa Precolonial sub-Saharan Africa; Colonialism; South Africa; Zimbabwe

Kertbeny, Karl Maria (1847–1882)

The most significant professional contributions made by this Vienna-born German Hungarian writer were undoubtedly his translations of the works of Hungarian poets into the German language. Despite his tremendous productivity, Kertbeny never managed to become a successful writer in his own right and suffered financially throughout his life.

His crucial and most influential contribution to sex research is his coining of the terms *homosexuality* in 1868–1869 and *heterosexuality* in 1880. Kertbeny's views of (homo)sexuality are today available only in fragments and may well never have existed in the form of a coherent theory. He differentiated the direction of sexual instincts into three possible objects, "monosexuals" (i.e., onanists), "homosexuals," and "normalsexuals." Our sexual instincts are inborn and not chosen, in his view. Homosexuals are "physically and mentally unable to maintain a normal erection, because of the direct horror they feel towards the other sex," while at the same time they are unable "to escape the influence of the impression [that] individuals of the same sex have of them." He suggested a number of subcategories for homosexuals, which included those who only masturbate each other, those who attempt the "natural coitus between man and woman in an unnatural manner," those who are "active" and "passive," and "Platonists," who love the company of people of the same sex without wanting to have sex with them.

Early historians of homosexuality such as Ferdinand Karsch-Haack suggested that Kertbeny was homosexual himself, but there is no historical evidence as to Kertbeny's sexual orientation.

Udo Schüklenk

Bibliography

Herzer, M., and J.-C. Féray. "Karl Maria Kertbeny." In *Homosexualität: Handbuch der Theorie- und Forschungsgeschichte.* R. Lautmann, ed. New York: Campus Verlag, 1993, 42–47.
Kertbeny, K. M. *§143 des Preußischen Strafgesetzbuches vom 14. April 1851.* Leipzig: Anonymous, 1869.

See also Ellis, Havelock; Freud, Sigmund; Hirschfeld, Magnus; Homosexuality; Sexology; Sexual Orientation

Keynes, John Maynard (1883–1946)

John Maynard Keynes was the most influential economist of the twentieth century. As the author of *The Economic Consequences of the Peace* (1919) and

The General Theory of Employment, Interest, and Money, Keynes helped shape the Anglo-American recovery from the Great Depression of the 1930s by showing how governments could manage capitalist economies to achieve stability with low unemployment.

Although much studied, Keynes's economics is rarely considered in relation to his sexuality. Until recently, commentators ignored the issue, an oversight enabled by Keynes's marriage at the age of forty-two. Biographies citing Keynes's affection for his wife overlooked clear evidence of his homosexual affairs, including his long-term relationship with painter Duncan Grant. Only since the 1980s have biographers acknowledged Keynes's homosexuality, chronicling the anxiety it caused him as he became an increasingly public figure. As early as 1910, Keynes wrote to Grant after a conversation with his family that he "had practically to admit to them what I was! . . . The sooner we can become womanizers the better." In the teens, Keynes was twice threatened with blackmail and worried that rumors about his sex life could end his career. His romances with women began around 1920 and culminated with his 1925 marriage to Lydia Lopokova, a dancer with the Russian Ballet. Skidelsky's definitive biography identifies this period as "a new beginning" for Keynes in which his private association with the Bloomsbury group gave way to a public role as a statesman with a celebrity wife.

On a basic level, Keynes's radical critique of various nineteenth-century economic conventions can be linked to his sense of himself as an outsider. In "My Early Beliefs," an autobiographical essay prepared in 1938 for his Bloomsbury friends, Keynes cited as a definitive component of his thought Bloomsbury's repudiation of any obligation to "obey general rules." Though in retrospect—and on the brink of World War II—Keynes criticized the utopian naïveté of this drive to challenge authority, he concluded, "So far as I am concerned, it is too late to change."

More specific connections between Keynes's homosexuality and his economics have been proposed by right-wing proponents of laissez-faire capitalism, who link the Keynesian focus on money circulated as spending rather than hoarded as savings to a penchant for "immediate and present satisfaction" that they see as typical of the "childless" homosexual. Divorced from their reactionary origins, such ideas are intriguing. Keynes's sexuality may well have enabled him to reject the Victorian fixa-

tion on dynastic accumulations of static capital in favor of a broader goal of wealth and productivity for all of society. As was true for other gay men in Bloomsbury, Keynes's sexual experience provoked in him a Whitmanesque belief in the nobility of working-class men, whose good cheer and resourcefulness deeply impressed him. It is possible that Keynesian economics—which aims to distribute the benefits of capitalism beyond the upper classes without requiring a highly scrutinized central planning that inhibits individual self-determination—was materially affected by the conditions of homosexuality in the early twentieth century.

Christopher Reed

Bibliography

Hession, Charles H. *John Maynard Keynes: A Personal Biography of the Man Who Revolutionized Capitalism and the Way We Live*. New York: Macmillan, 1984.

Himmelfarb, Gertrude. *Marriage and Morals Among the Victorians*. New York: Knopf, 1986.

Keynes, John Maynard. "My Early Beliefs" (1938). In *Two Memoirs*. London: Rupert Hart-Davis, 1949, 78–106.

Moggridge, D. E. *Maynard Keynes: An Economist's Biography*. London: Routledge 1992.

Skidelsky, Robert. *John Maynard Keynes*. London: Macmillan. Vol. 1, 1983; Vol. 2, 1992.

See also Bloomsbury; The Bloomsbury and Art; Class; Grant, Duncan

Khanith (also Xanith)

In Oman and the eastern Arabian peninsula, the term *khanith* (also *xanith*) denotes the gender role ascribed to men who function sexually, and in some ways socially, as women. From the Arabic word meaning "effeminate" or "soft," *khanith* is closely related to *mukhannath*, the effeminate male of classical Arabic literature. While possessing both female and male traits, the *khanith* is considered neither. He occupies a distinct gender space, one not so much defined in terms of "maleness" and "femaleness" as in contrast to them. The primary determining characteristic of the *khanith* is the "female," or exclusively passive, role he plays during sex with other males. By allowing himself to be penetrated, the *khanith* renounces any claims to "masculinity" and is thus not perceived as a sexual threat to women. As a result, the *khanith* is al-

K lowed to move freely among women (an impossibility for "real" men in this sexually segregated society), and he typically undertakes what is considered "women's work," e.g., cooking, cleaning, singing, dancing, and prostitution. His mannerisms and voice patterns are viewed as female, and his attractiveness is judged by feminine standards. Nevertheless, as a "biological male," the *khanith* possesses certain male traits. Unlike women, he does not require male guardianship, and he is not subject to the movement restrictions that constrain women. He is known by a male name, his clothes are predominantly male in style, and he is considered male for legal and religious purposes.

Richard McKewen

Bibliography

Garber, Marjorie. *Vested Interests: Cross Dressing and Cultural Anxiety.* New York: Routledge, 1992, 348–52.

Wikan, Unni. *Behind the Veil in Arabia: Women in Oman.* Chicago: University of Chicago Press, 1982, 168–86.

See also Arabic Literature; *Hijras* of India; India; *Mukhannath*

Kinsey, Alfred C. (1894–1956)

Alfred Kinsey was an American zoologist and sexologist who, after writing a detailed study of the gall wasp, researched and produced two of the most influential American texts on sexuality, *Sexual Behavior in the Human Male* (1948) and *Sexual Behavior in the Human Female* (1953). Each volume was enormously successful commercially and made Kinsey something of a celebrity. Coming as they did at the height of American conventionalism, the books astonished their contemporaries and have enormously influenced American attitudes on sexuality.

One of the more unusual things about both studies was Kinsey and his associates' methodology in collecting their data. They performed ten thousand face-to-face interviews with white middle-class Americans, collecting their erotic histories with amazing detail. (In his autobiography, Gore Vidal claims to be one of those interviewed.) Written in a dry, scientific style, the volumes presented graphs of sexual behavior including statistics on adultery, masturbation, sodomy, and homosexuality. Kinsey sought to keep the findings free of any moral content, and, in fact, periodically argued against American moralism, particularly when faced with the sheer amount of "sexual perversion" to which his informants admitted.

It was perhaps on the topic of homosexuality that Kinsey's statistics challenged conventional wisdom the most. Fifty percent of men, he discovered, admitted to some erotic responses to men, and 37 percent admitted to at least one postadolescent homosexual experience. Four percent were exclusively homosexual. For women, the proportions were lower but revealed extensive lesbian activity; 28 percent responded erotically to other women, 13 percent had achieved orgasm with another woman, and 2 percent were exclusively homosexual. The numbers astounded his contemporaries, and Kinsey was widely vilified by prominent Americans for his supposed moral ineptitude. A 1954 congressional committee singled out the reports as examples of scientific research that produced "extremely grave" social effects.

Perhaps the most important aspect of Kinsey's work is what we now call the "Kinsey scale." Kinsey pointed out that with the amount of people who engaged in some sort of homosexual activity, it was senseless to assume that all were either exclusively homosexual or exclusively heterosexual. Instead he postulated a seven-point scale, with exclusivity at either end but with many gray areas in between, a continuum of sexual experiences and identities. This idea of a continuum of sexual identities has informed gay rights and lesbian feminist arguments in which the continuum is used to argue that homophobia is an "unnatural" denial of the pervasiveness of homosexual experiences. It has also given bisexual activists crucial evidence of the pervasiveness of bisexuality in humans. The most profound effect of Kinsey's work, however, could be that at a crucial time in the history of homosexuality in America, it offered proof that homosexuals and bisexuals were not alone and suggested that they were actually part of a group. His findings are still disputed, but their effects have been long-lasting.

Douglas Eisner

Bibliography

D'Emilio, John. *Sexual Politics, Sexual Communities: The Making of a Homosexual Minority in the United States, 1940–1970.* Chicago: University of Chicago Press, 1983, esp. 33–37.

Halbersam, David. "Discovering Sex (Sexual Revolution and Discovery of the Birth Control Pill in the 1950s)." *American Heritage* 44, no. 3 (1993): 39–54.

Jones, James H. *Alfred C. Kinsey: A Public/Private Life.* New York: Norton, 1997.

Kinsey, Alfred C., Wardell B. Pomeroy, and Clyde E. Martin. *Sexual Behavior in the Human Female.* Philadelphia: W. B. Saunder, 1953.

———. *Sexual Behavior in the Human Male.* Philadelphia: W. B. Saunder, 1948.

Morantz, Regina Markell. "The Scientist as Sex Crusader: Alfred C. Kinsey and American Culture." *American Quarterly* 29 (1977): 563–89.

Pomeroy, Wardell. *Dr. Kinsey and the Institute of Sex Research.* New Haven: Yale University Press, 1972.

See also Homosexuality; Sexology; Sexual Orientation

Kirstein, Lincoln (1907–1996)

Easily one of the most astonishing and influential figures in twentieth-century American culture, Lincoln Kirstein was at the same time full of contradictions and a visionary with a focused goal: that of changing Western art. Convinced that modern art was infected with "cancerous self-indulgence," he wrote over thirty books and hundreds of articles on painting, sculpture, photography, film, architecture, and dance that helped shape modernism in the twentieth century. A Jew who converted to Catholicism, a homosexual who married, this Renaissance man's primary passion was ballet. With his stewardship, money, and behind-the-scenes maneuvering, Kirstein literally made New York the dance capital of the Western world.

This philosopher was not just interested in ideas for their own sake; he devoted his life to realizing them. While a sophomore at Harvard, with family money he founded a literary journal, *Hound & Horn* (his father was Filene's department store chief executive). As a junior, young Kirstein cofounded the Harvard Society for Contemporary Art, a forerunner of the Museum of Modern Art. Remarkably versatile, Kirstein wrote the librettos to several ballets, including Lew Christensen's *Filling Station* (1938) and Eugene Loring's *Billy the Kid* (1938), helped plan Rockefeller Center and Lincoln Center, was managing director of City Center from 1953 to 1955, produced a twelfth-century play, *The Play of Daniel*, in 1958, produced a tour of *Gagaku* from Japan, and taught directing

and arts administration for the Yale School of Drama in 1977.

At the age of twelve Kirstein was first exposed to live dance when he saw Anna Pavlova perform in Boston in 1920. Numerous trips to Europe allowed him to indulge in his fascination with classical ballet. After seeing several ballets by George Balanchine, Kirstein met him in London and promptly invited the twenty-nine-year-old choreographer to come to New York, where they would build an American ballet tradition. Balanchine's famous response was, "But, first a school." The School of American Ballet opened in 1934, with Kirstein as president, a position he would hold until his retirement in 1989.

Convinced that ballet was moribund in Europe, Kirstein reasoned it would be easier to resuscitate it in America, a country with no stultifying dance traditions of its own. Balanchine and Kirstein would establish four different companies before New York City Ballet was begun in 1948: American Ballet Company (1934–1935), Ballet Caravan (1936–1940), American Ballet Caravan (1941), and Ballet Society (1946–1948). Invited to become the resident company at City Center, New York City Ballet was established with Lincoln Kirstein as general director, a post he held until 1989.

In 1937, Kirstein met painter Paul Cadmus and surprised everyone by proposing marriage to Cadmus' sister, Fidelma. Married in 1940, the union lasted until she was institutionalized for mental illness many years later; she died in 1991. Regardless of his marital status, Kirstein had heterosexual and homosexual affairs throughout his life. In autobiographical writings, he described one of his early lovers, merchant seaman Carl Carlsen, a former lover of poet Hart Crane.

George Balanchine would have created choreographic masterpieces for any ballet company, but without Lincoln Kirstein's backing there would not have been a New York City Ballet. The school and company the two men established became to many the preeminent ballet group perhaps in the world and assured the continuation of a vital ballet tradition with the twenty-first century.

Bud Coleman

Bibliography

Kirstein, Lincoln. *Mosaic.* New York: Farrar, Straus & Giroux, 1994.

Weber, Nicolas. *Patron Saints: Five Rebels Who Opened America to a New Art, 1928–1943.* New York: Knopf, 1992.

K

See also Ballet Russes; Cadmus, Paul; Dance: Concert Dance in America

Kissing

Kisses are semiotic acts: "A kiss may signify betrayal as easily as love. . . . there are culturally specific codes of display for kissing . . . [and they] are always highly coded according to existing sociocultural, historical and political systems for both performers and observers" (Hartley 4).

In Western culture, kisses have signified romantic love, and linked to this (although not the same thing), the eruption of the private realm of sexuality into the public sphere of politics. Popular culture is saturated with kisses. In movies, television programs, magazine advertisements, and postcards, they are exchanged as betokening the contract of romantic heterosexuality that structures our culture, our ambitions, and our dreams. "In classical Hollywood cinema, the classic kiss . . . conventionally represents sexuality. The power of this kiss derives from its dual metaphoric and metonymic function. It both stands for sexual activity and begins it . . . [thus comes the] metonymic power of the kiss to suggest both romance and sexuality" (Straayer 44).

Gay kisses are a problem. Some homophobes have asserted that homosexuality is fine so long as it stays in the (private sphere of) the bedroom; and so the possibility that kisses might bring gay expression into the public sphere is a shocking one. And so, while heterosexuals have been provided with the relevant identity-forming materials to swoon at the possibility of what they know to be impossible (true love), gay men have been denied these in a variety

Kissing as protest: Queer Nation "Kiss-In," 1990. Photo by Marc Geller.

of ways. While it is no longer true that gay men are absent from popular culture, gay kisses still are.

1. No kissing

In most gay relationships on television, men do not kiss. Their sexuality is performed in other ways. Steven Carrington in *Dynasty*, for example, demonstrates his affection for lovers in manly hugs and knowing smiles. His homosexuality is performed in other ways. Although he could say, "I am gay," he could not perform it.

2. Invisible kissing

The 1994 season finale of *Melrose Place* featured gay character Matt trying to kiss a lover. The program broke into slow motion, and cut away to a shot of his friend Billy watching the kiss. It is too terrifying to be seen.

3. Straight "gay" kissing

In *Star Trek: The Next Generation*, "The Outcast"—the program's self-proclaimed "gay episode"—a central character, Commander William T. Riker, kisses an androgynous alien in a narrative about tolerance of different sexualities. The androgynous alien is (visibly) played by a woman. This is as close as the program can get to a gay kiss.

4. Comic kissing

In an episode of *Seinfeld*, "The Kiss Hello" (1995), Kramer kisses Jerry. Jerry is shocked and gesticulates wildly. George walks in and does an elaborate double take. The audience laughs hysterically. The possibility that men's lips might meet is not literally unimaginable, but that it might signify what heterosexual kisses have signified—the romantic and the sexual, the validation of the private in the public sphere—is rejected with self-conscious, rather too hysterical laughter.

5. Nostalgic kissing

In the miniseries *Tales of the City* two attractive men kiss. They are gay, they are lovers, their lips meet, and the audience gets to see it. But as the video cover has it, this is a fantasy story, set in a fairy-tale land of 1970s San Francisco. (San Francisco in 1976 is a city where the unlikely always seems to happen, whether by coincidence or fate, and where true love comes in unexpected ways. It's a city buzzing with innocent but naughty fun, orgies, and therapy sessions. This is obvious in every detail of the text: tie-dye, sideburns, old-fashioned dancing. This is not reality.)

Hopeful signs

There are hopeful signs. In Australia, for example, a soap opera called *GP* has centered the gay male kiss as offering the same possibilities as heterosexual kissing. In the episode "Out" (1995), the gay central character, Dr. Martin Dempsey (Damien Rice), begins a relationship with a patient. On the second date, after a short flirting scene, they kiss. The kiss is shown. It is not structured as something shocking, surprising, unbelievable, unseeable. Both characters are men. They are placed as part of the everyday milieu. Nobody laughs or screams. The kiss expresses tenderness, sexual attraction, the possibility of romance, the possibility of that romance being celebrated in a public sphere. This is the potential of gay kissing. This is what has previously proved so difficult in popular culture.   *Alan McKee*

Bibliography

Finch, Mark. "Sex and Address in *Dynasty*." *Screen* 27, no. 6 (1986): 24–43.

Frutkin, Anne. "Family Outings." *Advocate* 62, (1995): 30–31.

Fuqua, Joy V. "There's a Queer in My Soup!: The Homophobia/AIDS Storyline of *One Life to Live*." In *To Be Continued . . . Soap Operas Around the World*. R. C. Allen, ed. London: Routledge, 1995, 199–212.

Gross, Larry. "Out of the Mainstream: Sexual Minorities and the Mass Media." In *Remote Control: Television, Audiences, Cultural Power*. Ellenb. Seiter, H. Borcher, G. Kreutzner, and E. M. Warth, eds. London: Routledge, 1989, 130–49.

Hartley, John. *Popular Reality: Journalism, Modernity, Popular Culture*. London: Edward Arnold, 1996.

Straayer, Chris. Redressing the 'Natural': The Temporary Transvestite Film. *Wide Angle* 14, no. 1 (1992): 36–55.

Torres, Sasha. "Television/Feminism: *Heartbeat* and Prime Time Lesbianism." In *The Lesbian and Gay Studies Reader*. Henry Abelove, Michèle Aina Barale, and David M. Halperin, eds. London: Routledge, 1993.

See also AIDS in the U.S. Media; Television

Klein, Calvin (1942–)

As American ready-to-wear designers achieved unprecedented recognition in the 1970s, one of the youngest and most successful was Calvin Klein. His spare, luxurious sportswear was popular, but the designer became a household name through body-conforming "designer" jeans. Klein and Richard Avedon created a 1980 print and media campaign using Brooke Shields saying seductively, "Nothing comes between me and my Calvins." From this first flirtatious double entendre, Klein has sustained avant-garde frisson, sexual assertion, and immense recognition, especially for his most ineffable products, jeans, underwear, and fragrance.

In the summer of 1995, one campaign was withdrawn owing to controversy over the use of young models, but the consistency of hedonistic imagination is a flaunted pleasure in the body, sexuality, and fantasy. Simulated vangardism is one co-opting advertising strategy, effecting "edge" or social/aesthetic risk. Even more important is Klein's homoeroticism throughout the ads that feature his wares. Ads in 1986 posed male-female interaction but more suggestively, clusters of shirtless men. In 1987 ads for Obsession featured callipygian models (male and female) disconcertingly oblivious to one another. A *Vanity Fair* supplement (October 1991), photographed by Bruce Weber, suggested a narrative of homosexual attractions and activity. The model's penis is clearly visible within boxer shots in an ad in *Spin* (December 1995). Employing advertising for social provocation as well as for consumer desire, Klein has skillfully merged illicit homoeroticism with that of a consumption model. Even Klein's critics acknowledge the compelling force of the homoerotic. His advocates find heroes and dreams on every package, in countless magazines, and perhaps even fulfilled (if only in the mind) in the garment itself.   *Richard Martin*

Bibliography

Martin, Richard. "Out and In Fashion." *Artforum* (May 1995).

———. "The Gay Factor in Fashion." *Esquire Gentleman* 1, no. 1 (Spring 1993): 135–40.

See also Fashion; Weber, Bruce

Kleist, Heinrich von (1777–1811)

During the course of a short and troubled writing career, Kleist composed dramas and novellas utterly different from any previously composed in German. Most of Kleist's contemporaries, in particular the classicists Wolfgang von Goethe and Friedrich von Schiller, dismissed the writer's freakish uses of

K structure and subject matter. But now, Kleist is recognized as a harbinger of modernism and a major influence on such high modernists as Franz Kafka, as well as on renowned gay filmmaker Rainer Werner Fassbinder.

In such dramas as *Amphitryon*, *Prince Friedrich of Homburg*, and *Penthesilea*, the author traces circuits of desire that subtly transgress and challenge emerging myths of heterosexuality. In the novellas *The Marquise of O*, *The Engagement in Santo Domino*, and *The Earthquake in Chile*, Kleist explicitly links sexual desire with gendered power relations within the family, colonial and racial tensions, and the violence of war. In *Michael Kohlhaas*, the author undertakes a profoundly ironic parable of the emergence of the modern bureaucratic state.

Kleist's life and career were overshadowed by the Prussian state and value system, where military discipline and national allegiance were valued over individual desires and predilections. Accordingly, he began his adult life as an officer in the Prussian army in 1792. Kleist requested a voluntary discharge in 1799 to follow an odd assortment of pursuits: university studies in Frankfurt; travel in Germany, France, and Switzerland; an engagement to Wilhelmine von Zenge (broken off in 1802) as well as a writing career in the theater. Having attempted in vain to join Napoleon's armies in northern France, Kleist returned to Berlin and sought a position in the Prussian civil service. When the Prussian court moved to Königsberg to escape Napoleon's troops, Kleist followed, but when he attempted to return to Berlin on his own, he was arrested by French officials on a charge of espionage and imprisoned for six months. After this traumatic experience, Kleist founded a literary journal, *Phoebus*, which ran for twelve issues, and founded the newspaper *Berlinabendblätter* (Berlin Evening Pages), which ran for six months, and applied unsuccessfully for permission to publish a patriotic journal, *Germania*. During this time his play *The Broken Jug* was performed in Weimar but was not well received, and his stories were collected and published in two volumes between 1810 and 1811. In the fall of 1811, Kleist became intimate friends with Henriette Vogel, and the two made a suicide pact, carried out at the Wannsee lake in Berlin on November twenty-first of that year. *Stephanie Hammer*

Bibliography

Allen, Sean. *The Plays of Heinrich von Kleist: Ideals and Illusions*. Cambridge: Cambridge University Press, 1996.

Greenberg, Martin, intro. and trans. *Kleist: Five Plays*. New Haven: Yale University Press, 1988.

See also Fassbinder, Rainer Werner; German Literature; Germany; Goethe, Johannes Wolfgang von

Kliuev, Nikolai (1887–1937)

Russian poet Nikolai Kliuev came from a peasant family belonging to the Old Believer splinter sect Khlysty. (The name of this sect is often translated as "Flagellants," but it is actually a distorted plural form of *Christ;* the sect split off from the mainstream Old Believers in the eighteenth century and had recognizable homosexual and sadomasochistic features in its religious lore and ritual.) Kliuev was actually involved with the sect and its affairs throughout his life. He spent his childhood in his native Olonets region of the Russian far north. Love of his native landscape and of the peasant folk arts, such as wood carving, icon painting, and the religious poetry of the Khlysty, permeates everything he wrote. Several poems written when he was seventeen suggest that Kliuev's first love was a sailor who lost his life in the Russo-Japanese War of 1904.

When he was about twenty, Kliuev began publishing his bookish, or literary, poetry, written in the rather trite vein of standard civic protest doggerel typical of Russian provincial publications of the time. But then he became aware of the new versification and imagery introduced into Russian poetry by the symbolist poets. Study of their work and personal contact with some of them enabled Kliuev to combine his native Khlysty religious poetry with the literary culture of the symbolists. The results were his two collections of verse, both published in 1912, *Chiming Pines* and *Brotherly Songs*, the latter containing openly gay themes. These two books created a sensation and made Kliuev a celebrity. His admirers included literary and political figures as diverse as the great symbolist poet Alexander Blok, the Empress Alexandra, the Greek novelist Nikos Kazantsakis, and, with reservations, Leon Trotsky.

After Kliuev's talent was acclaimed, he became the leader of a group of peasant poets, two of whom—Aleksand Shiriaevets and Sergey Esenin—were at different times his lovers. These peasant poets were opposed to importing Western political institutions into Russia, advocating instead a kind of peasant separatism. Kliuev's group saw the reformist and socialist parties of prerevolutionary Russia as noblemen plotting to impose foreign ways on the Russian people. In Lenin's autocratic rule after the

Russian Revolution of 1917, Kliuev saw a restoration of a new peasant-oriented monarchy. Between 1917 and 1919, Kliuev sang Lenin's praises and celebrated the demise of landowners and the gentry.

By 1922, however, Kliuev was alarmed by the Soviet government's militant atheism and its persecution of the religious sects he had hoped it would protect. He was also apprehensive that its crash industrialization program might pollute the pristine countryside of his native Olonets region and destroy its wildlife. Most of all, he was concerned with the new government's disapproval of his sexual identity. In two magnificent long poems written in 1922, "The Fourth Rome" and "Mother Sabbath," Kliuev proclaimed his gay pride with a fervor unprecedented in Russian poetry. For voicing such sentiments in print, he was soon branded a *kulak* in the Soviet press, someone who did not understand the meaning of industrialization and communism. After 1925, he found it hard to get his work published. In the late 1920s he wrote a powerful epic poem, "Burned Ruins," about village life under Soviet rule. This work survives because Kliuev gave a copy to an Italian scholar who took it out of the country. In 1933, a violent diatribe in which Kliuev denounced the cruel persecution of the poet Anna Akhmatova, which he read only to a few close friends, led to his arrest.

Kliuev was sentenced to four years of hard labor. He survived those years, but his sentence expired at the height of Stalin's purges. The camp authorities, not sure whether they should release him, kept transporting him back and forth across Siberia in jammed trains bound for the Gulag until he solved their problem by dying of a heart attack in August 1937. Kliuev's unpublished poems and his correspondence, which were preserved by his last lover, Nikolai Archipov, disappeared without a trace when Archipov was in turn arrested and sent to a labor camp, where he died.   *Simon Karlinsky*

Bibliography

Kliuev, Nikolai. *Poems*. John Glad, trans. Ann Arb, Mich.: Ardis, 1977.

See also: Esenin, Sergey; Russia; Russian Literature

Kohs, Ellis Bonoff (1916–)

American composer Ellis Kohs was born into a cultured musical family. His mother was an accomplished violinist, and after he learned to play the piano Kohs often accompanied her. His peripatetic family moved from Chicago to San Francisco and then made a further move in 1928 from California to New York, where the young Kohs studied piano at the Institute of Musical Art. In 1933, he enrolled as a composition student at the University of Chicago. Upon graduation, he studied at the Juilliard School of Music in New York and later matriculated at Harvard University, where he studied musicology with Willi Apel and composition with Walter Piston. While at Harvard, Kohs attended a composition seminar given in 1940–1941 by Igor Stravinsky, who was favorably impressed by his work. During World War II, Kohs initially served in the U.S. Army, playing the organ and assisting a chaplain; later he was transferred to the air force as a bandmaster, holding the rank of warrant officer. While in the service, Kohs composed *The Automatic Pistol* (1943) for unaccompanied male chorus, a witty setting of a text drawn from an army manual on the care and maintenance of handguns. After his discharge from the service in 1946, Kohs held a variety of academic appointments: Wesleyan University (1946–1948); the College of the Pacific (1948–1950); Stanford University (1950); and the University of Southern California (1950–1985). Compositions by Kohs have been performed by such organizations as the San Francisco Symphony, the Los Angeles Philharmonic, and the Paganini String Quartet. Kohs's music reconciles the serial techniques of Arnold Schoenberg with the extended tonality of Igor Stravinsky's neoclassic scores. This formidable accomplishment allowed Kohs to forge an inimitable style characterized by elegiac lyricism, dark expressive power, and, at times, wry humor. In 1955, Kohs completed *Lord of the Ascendant* for chorus, soloists, dancers, and large orchestra, a resplendent homoerotic treatment of the Gilgamesh legend with a libretto by Dexter Allen. At the shimmering conclusion of his highly dramatic work, Gilgamesh and his companion, Enkidu, are blissfully united in a fragrant nocturnal garden; their union is delineated by music that rises to an uncanny and sensuous eloquence. Homoeroticism is also present in Kohs's setting of Gertrude Stein's *Men* (1984), for narrator and three percussionists, as well as in his *Lohiau and Hiiaka* (1987), a "Hawai'in legend" for narrators, flute, cello, percussion, and dancers. Kohs's most extended score is *Amerika* (1960), an opera in three acts with a libretto by the composer after Kafka's unfinished novel.   *Byron Adams*

See also Gilgamesh; Music and Musicians 1: Classical Music

K

Krafft-Ebing, Richard von (1840–1902)

With the seemingly modest aim to collect, present, and clarify, Krafft-Ebing, a physician and later a professor of psychiatry, produced a volume of immodest proportions. This is the compendium of case histories known as *Psychopathia Sexualis* (1886). For all its heavy use of Latin in its first editions, directed as it was at scientific and medical readers, later, less Latinate editions came to have a life of their own on the mail-order circuit of the late 1960s: "Monstrous, strange, almost unbelievable sex acts. For mature adults only!" Presumably, Krafft-Ebing's lack of extended, theoretical explanations allow for the striking descriptions of anomalies that make for such compelling reading. For though he lent an obviously shaping hand to his sources—patients' narratives, letters from sufferers, colleagues' collections of cases and their considered opinions, even court proceedings—Krafft-Ebing always remained more taxonomic than explanatory.

With an eye to curing patients, he condemned all sexual acts outside of heterosexual intercourse. Masturbation was especially singled out for contributing so powerfully to pathology and standing so clearly as its sign. It weakened inclination toward the opposite sex, Krafft-Ebing believed, and even drained the masturbator of the physical strength to accomplish coitus. And yet, though he deemed masturbation a cause of same-sex relations, he stressed the largely "congenital" nature of homosexuality (which he called "antipathic sexual instinct," after Otto Westphal's designation). In this way, what appeared an "acquired anomaly" probably indicated "a latent homosexuality" that required "accidental exciting causes to rouse it from its dormant state." For all his talk of "anomaly," "taint," "pathology," and "degeneration," Krafft-Ebing admitted that "the majority" of homosexuals are happy—"unhappy only insofar as social and legal barriers stand in the way of the satisfaction of their instinct toward their own sex."

Kathryn Bond Stockton

Bibliography

Krafft-Ebing, Richard von. *Psychopathia Sexualis: A Medico-Forensic Study*. New York: Putnam, 1965.

See also Masturbation; Sexology; Westphal, Carl Friedrich Otto

Kramer, Larry (1935–)

Larry Kramer was born in Bridgeport, Connecticut. He grew up in Connecticut and Washington, D.C. and received a B.A. from Yale. After serving in the army, he embarked on his first career, as a screenwriter, a vocation he began as a clerk in the William Morris Agency that extended to production. Based in London, he was a production executive for Columbia Pictures. Then, in 1967, as an assistant to the president of United Artists, he became associate producer of the modestly successful film *Here We Go Round the Mulberry Bush*. The culmination of this experience was his commissioning, writing, and coproducing the film *Women in Love*, based on the novel by D. H. Lawrence. Directed by Ken Russell and starring Glenda Jackson, Oliver Reed, and Alan Bates, the 1969 film garnered several academy award nominations, including one for Kramer's screenplay. Released at the same time as *Boys in the Band*, some in the gay community felt that both films fit within older, pre–gay pride (pre-Stonewall) traditions of exploring and representing homosexuality as covert, repressed, and unhappy. In any event, there could be no denying the film's legendary nude wrestling sequence involving Bates and Reed as a landmark in the history of what Vito Russo called "the celluloid closet."

Kramer's additional work in film included an unproduced version of Yukio Mishima's *Forbidden Colors* and a musical remake of *Lost Horizon*, a critical and popular disaster that, however, gave Kramer enough financial independence to pursue writing full-time. In 1978, Random House published *Faggots*, a fiercely satirical exposé of gay life as Kramer felt he saw it being lived in the sex- and self-obsessed fantasy environments of Manhattan and Fire Island. The novel is still the funniest, most controversial and dazzling evocation in all of gay literature, and has become an American classic. At the time of its publication, however, such was the furor it provoked that it was banned from Craig Rodwell's Oscar Wilde Memorial Bookshop in New York. Much of the outrage in the gay press centered around Kramer's lending fuel to enemies who in fact did utilize the book as by-their-own-testimony proof of gay decadence and unworthiness of the civil liberties considerations that were pending, initiatives in which Kramer himself had not participated.

Whatever the arguments for and against *Faggots*, as they have continued unabated, there can be no question of its atmosphere of a community on the brink, a precipice that turned out to be more than figurative. With the first press reports of AIDS in 1981, Kramer for the first time directly entered the arena of gay community political activism. Weather-

Larry Kramer in Washington, 1987. Photo by Marc Geller.

ing criticism that this involvement was a way of say-ing "I told you so" to the community in which he had sustained so much rejection, culminating in the widespread condemnation of his novel, Kramer be-came the driving force behind what would become the first and what has remained the largest AIDS in-formation and service agency in the world, Gay Men's Health Crisis (GMHC). But his position as a prophet without honor in his own land continued as his visionary and severe criticism of the community and its efforts to confront AIDS intensified. Eventu-ally, Kramer found himself at such odds with what he perceived to be its conservatism that he resigned from GMHC, an experience that became the subject of his next major endeavor, his play *The Normal Heart*. Earlier attempts at playwriting had included a biographical work, *Sissies' Scrapbook*, which be-came the basis of a play called *Four Friends*, a groundbreaking work that was so savagely reviewed by Clive Barnes that it closed after one perfor-mance. As produced by Joseph Papp, *The Normal Heart*, which premiered in 1985, has had six hun-dred productions around the world and is the most successful play in the history of New York's Public Theater.

As Kramer's battles with GMHC continued, some critics observed that what was necessary was

not the destruction or even the wholesale transfor-mation of GMHC so much as a new organization to do the political work, the street fighting and demon-strations, that GMHC was never set up to do. In 1987, with his own realization of this, Kramer founded ACT UP, which would revolutionize not only AIDS research but the way activists worldwide now look at medical research. After a period of lead-ership in ACT UP, Kramer again withdrew from the front lines of organizational activism to pursue his principal means of expression, his writing. In 1988, *Just Say No*, Kramer's savage farce of the Reagan and Koch years, premiered in New York. Though it was not a success, the published edition included a scathing rebuttal to Barnes within its analysis of the state of the theater in New York and the rest of America.

Within the same time frame, Kramer wrote two other important works: a collection of essays and speeches called *Reports from the Holocaust*, which was republished several years later in an expanded edition, and *The Destiny of Me*, Kramer's autobio-graphical sequel to *The Normal Heart*. Other no-table writings include a short story, "Mrs. Tefillin." For some years now, he is paid to be at work on an epic novel, *The American People*. Whatever one's reservations about Larry Kramer, he has been indis-

K putably the leading figure of the AIDS epidemic and, quite possibly, of the post-Stonewall gay liberation era as well. *Lawrence D. Mass*

Bibliography

Kayal, Philip M. *Bearing Witness: Gay Men's Health Crisis and the Politics of AIDS*. Boulder, Colo.: Westview Press, 1993.

Kramer, Larry. *Reports from the Holocaust*. New York: St. Martin's Press, 1994.

See also Activism; ACT UP; AIDS; AIDS Literature AIDS Performance; Gay Men's Health Crisis (GMHC)

Kreis, Der (The Circle)

With a publication history of more than thirty-five years, the gay Swiss journal *Der Kreis* sets a record for gay and lesbian media. Founded in 1932 as a mixed gay and lesbian journal with the title *Schweizerisches Freundschafts Banner*, it changed its name to *Menschenrecht* in 1937. In 1942, the same year in which homosexuality between adults became legal in Switzerland, lesbians on the editorial staff left. One year later, the now exclusively gay journal, was published in German and French and was named *Der Kreis/Le Cercle*. In 1954 an English section and the title *The Circle* were added. Circulation grew from 200 copies in 1942 to 1,900 in 1957, including 700 subscribers in the rest of Europe and the United States. During World War II, *Der Kreis* was, thanks to Swiss neutrality, the only available gay magazine in Europe.

The moving spirit behind the success of *Der Kreis* was Rolf, pen name for Karl Meier (1897–1974), a cabaret performer, actor, and radio play artist who was chief editor for thirty-three years. Meier, for whom *Der Kreis* was his life's work, kept his two careers and circles of friends almost completely separate.

Der Kreis offered its readers membership of "Der Kreis-Club," which held weekly evenings in Zürich. In the club, men could meet, listen to lectures, dicuss current affairs, get advice, buy books, and use a library. Every year international parties were organized that attracted hundreds of gay men. Der Kreis-Club inspired others in Switzerland to found similar clubs like Isola in Basel and Ursus in Bern. The model of combining a journal with a reader's circle got an international response. One of the editors of the Dutch magazine *Levensrecht*, Nico Engelschman, took the initiative to found a reader's circle after he visited Meier and Der Kreis-Club in the summer of 1946. This circle developed into the future COC (Center for Culture and Recreation).

With its mixture of culture and information, Meier wanted *Der Kreis* to be a journal for a wide gay audience, with readership restricted to adults. *Der Kreis* included short stories, poems, pictures, news flashes, and reports on scientific research. It encouraged individual readers to accept their homosexuality and to develop a positive gay identity. Although full integration of homosexuality in society was its ultimate goal, *Der Kreis* advised gay men to restrict their coming out to an inner circle of friends and relatives. The value of a permanent "marriage-like" relationship was emphasized, and promiscuity, sex with minors, and prostitution were rejected. In the tradition of prewar magazines like *Der Eigene* and *Die Insel*, *Der Kreis* propagated a masculine image of homosexuality and the male body. Meier and his fellow editors followed Freud's idea of a universal bisexual predisposition, which they saw confirmed in the Kinsey reports.

Meier didn't affiliate with the moral liberalization of the 1960s. *Der Kreis*, with its editorial formula of the 1950s, failed to attract a younger audience that was already used to Scandinavian magazines containing explicit nudes and pornography. The closing of the last Kreis-Club in 1967 also meant the financial downfall of the magazine. Karl Meier never got over his disillusionment and, after suffering several periods of serious depression, died in 1974. *Maurice van Lieshout*

Bibliography

Hohmann, Joachim S., ed. *Der Kreis. Erzählungen und Fotos*. Frankfurt am Main: Foerster Verlag, 1980.

Löw, Thomas. "Der 'Kreis' und sein idealer Schwuler." *Männergeschichten. Schwule in Basel seit 1930*.

Steinle, Karl-Heinz, 'Der Kreis. Entwicklungshilfe aus der Schweiz'. In *Goodbye to Berlin? 100 Jahre Schwulenbewegung*. Berlin: Verlag Rosa Winkel, 1997, 238–42.

See also *Advocate*; Amsterdam; Bisexuality; COC; Freud, Sigmund; Journalism; Kinsey, Alfred; *Lampião*

Kupffer, Elisar von (1872–1942)

Elisar von Kupffer, an aesthete of Baltic aristocratic ancestry, gained popularity in homosexual circles around 1900 with his anthology of homoerotic literature from antiquity to his own time, *Lieblingminne und Freundesliebe in der Weltliteratur* (1899). With his anthology, poet and painter Kupffer hoped to create a counterbalance to medical theories of homosexuality, especially those of Richard von Krafft-Ebing and Magnus Hirschfeld. He rejected the terms *homosexuality* and *uranism* because to him they were loaded with the stigma of sickly deviation and effeminacy. Instead, he introduced the words *Lieblingminne* (Chivalric love) and *Freundesliebe* (Love of friends) to indicate that same-sex love should be viewed not as a biomedical issue but as a cultural and historical one. As he explained in the highly polemical introduction to his anthology, which was also published in Adolph Brand's *Der Eigene*, Greek boy-love, pedagogical eros, and the cult of romantic friendship in eighteenth- and nineteenth-century Germany had been discredited by medical interference with same-sex love. Advocating a cultural-aesthetic and masculine-nationalist approach to homoeroticism, Kupffer set the tone for Brand's *Gemeinschaft der Eigenen*. In light of his ardent plea for masculinity at the beginning of the century, it is remarkable that, as a painter, Kupffer later elevated androgyny as the state of human perfection. Eros would span the gulf between the masculine and the feminine. Together with his friend Eduard von Mayer, he contrived an esoteric doctrine called *Klarismus*, for which he built the Sanctuarium Artis Elisarion in Minusio (Locarno) in Switzerland. The walls of this temple and museum in one consisted of a monumental painting by Kupffer of eighty-four strikingly similar naked ephebic youths in various positions. *Harry Oosterhuis*

Bibliography

Ekkehard, Hieronimus. *Elisar von Kupffer (1872–1942)*. Basel: Kunsthalle, 1979.

Keilson-Lauritz, Marita. "Vorwart." In *Lieblingminne und Freundesliebe in der Weltliteratur*. Berlin: Verlag Rosa Winkel, 1995.

See also Brand, Adolph; Hirschfeld, Magnus; Krafft-Ebing, Richard von

Kushner, Tony (1956–)

The author of the celebrated two-part play *Angels in America* was born in New York's Manhattan in 1956 and raised in Lake Charles, Louisiana. He returned to New York City to attend Columbia University, where he majored in medieval studies. After college he enrolled in the graduate theater program at New York University and received an M.F.A. in directing.

Angels in America is subtitled "A Gay Fantasia on National Themes." Set in the United States during the Reagan years, Kushner sets out to contextualize the gay and lesbian liberation movement within the larger canvas of American politics. The play's central protagonist, Prior Walter, is a white gay man with AIDS. There are four other major characters who are gay—Louis, Prior's Jewish lover; Belize, Prior's best friend; Joe, a closeted Mormon; and the historical figure Roy Cohn. While much of the play takes place throughout various locations in New York City, it includes scenes set in such diverse locales as Salt Lake City, Antarctica, and Heaven. Part one, *Millennium Approaches*, portrays a world where the kinship structures and ideological beliefs of the various characters fail them. Part two, *Perestroika*, portrays the restructuring these characters must undergo to survive.

Although Kushner's work bears the influence of his Jewish background and his homosexuality, it cannot be easily reduced to these identity categories. His plays are informed by a variety of progressive intellectual, cultural, and political movements. He himself identifies his work as a "theater of the fabulous," a phrase that incorporates both his own queer political identifications and the overt theatricality of his plays.

Angels in America was commissioned in 1987 by Oskar Eustis for San Francisco's Eureka Theatre, where *Millennium Approaches* premiered in 1991 and *Perestroika* was given a staged reading. In 1992, the Mark Taper Forum in Los Angeles staged the first full production of the complete play. *Millennium Approaches* opened on Broadway at the Walter Kerr Theatre in 1993. *Perestroika* opened on Broadway later that year, and the two parts were performed in repertory through 1994. *Angels in America* went on to win the Pulitzer Prize for drama (1993), Tony awards for best play (*Millennium Approaches* in 1993, *Perestroika* in 1994), and the *Evening Standard* Award (Great Britain, 1992). *Angels in America* has since been staged throughout the world.

With the success of *Angels in America*, Kushner has emerged as a tireless spokesperson for various progressive causes including lesbian and gay issues and AIDS activism. He lectures widely on these topics and others throughout the United States and abroad. His early plays include *A Bright Room Called Day* and *Hydriotaphia*. His more recent

K

plays include *Slavs!* and adaptations of Brecht's *The Good Person of Sezuan*, Ansky's *A Dybbuk*, and Corneille's *The Illusion*. In the late 1990s he was working on the play *Henry Box Brown or the Mirror of Slavery*. His published works include *A Bright Room Called Day*, *Angels in America*, and *Thinking About the Longstanding Problems of Virtue and Happiness: Essays, A Play, Two Poems, and A Prayer.*   *David Román*

Bibliography

Geis, Deborah, and Steven Kruger, eds. *Approaching the Millennium: Essays on Angels in America*. Ann Arbor, Mich.: University of Michigan Press, 1997.

Vorlicky, Robert, ed. *Tony Kushner in Conversation*. Ann Arbor, Mich.: University of Michigan Press, 1997.

See also Activism, U.S.; AIDS; Cohn, Roy M.; McCarthyism; Theater: Premodern and Early Modern

Kuzmin, Mikhail (1872–1936)

Russian poet, novelist, playwright, and composer, Mikhail Kuzmin was born in the ancient town of Yaroslavl into a large family of minor gentry. During Kuzmin's childhood, his family moved to another provincial town, Saratov, where he went to school and was introduced to homosexuality by one of his older brothers. When Kuzmin was thirteen, he was taken to St. Petersburg and at once felt at home. He was enrolled in a traditional classical gymnasium.

His closest school friend was George Chicherin (1872–1936), who after the Russian Revolution became famous as Lenin's commissar of foreign affairs. During their school years, Chicherin was already self-assuredly gay, thus helping Kuzmin to come to terms with his own budding orientation. Their mutual interests also included music (Kuzmin, whose family was very musical, grew up knowing operas by Rossini, Weber, and Verdi from performances by family members), philosophy, and the history of religion. Early in life, Kuzmin became attracted to various religious sects that had splintered off from the Russian Old Believers, an interest that later found an important reflection in his poetry.

After graduating, Kuzmin enrolled at the St. Petersburg Conservatory to study composition. Among his teachers were Nikolai Rimsky-Korsakov and Anatoly Liadov. Kuzmin composed art songs and began several fragmentary operas in the manner

of, as he later admitted, Delibes, Massenet, and Bizet. He dropped out of the conservatory after three years but continued to set various texts to music. When he had a musical idea but could not find a suitable text, he would write the poem himself. These poems were at first derivative, but they gradually matured, pointing the way to Kuzmin's later literary career.

At the age of twenty-one, Kuzmin entered into a major love affair with a somewhat older, wealthy cavalry officer, mentioned in his confessions (first published in 1990) only as "Prince Georges." The relationship culminated in a joint trip they took to Athens, Constantinople, and Egypt, which Kuzmin recalled as the happiest and most fulfilling period in his life. But shortly after that journey, "Prince Georges" died suddenly of heart failure. Kuzmin sought oblivion in private music studies with Vasily Kühner and in his friendship with Chicherin, which was then at its peak. He also went on pilgrimages to Old Believer religious retreats in the north of Russia, at which times he affected lower-class dress and let his beard grow. Kuzmin was diminutive in stature, with a swarthy face dominated by his huge black eyes. Poet Marina Tsvetaeva, who wrote a wonderful memoir about Kuzmin, described her first impression of him thus: "His eyes and nothing else. His eyes and the rest of him. There was very little of the rest of him: almost nothing."

A number of people who had admired the words Kuzmin wrote for setting to music, among them major symbolist poet Valery Bryusov, urged Kuzmin to devote himself to writing poetry. He finally made his literary debut at the age of thirty-three when he published his dramatic poem (or, perhaps, an opera libretto) *The History of the Knight d'Alessio*, a sort of gay variation on Mozart's *The Magic Flute*, in a literary miscellany in 1905. One year later came his novel *Wings*, which brought him both genuine success and a *succès de scandale*; and two years after that, in 1908, came his first collection of verse, *Nets*.

In publishing these three works, Kuzmin launched what his biographer John Malmstad has described as "a project without precedent in Russian and, for that matter, European literature: living an openly gay life, making it the central subject of his art, and writing about it with absolute candor." Scorning all the subterfuges so common in the underground gay world of his time (think only of Wilde or Proust), Kuzmin invited the reader's complicity by the frankness with which he dedicated his works to his male lovers—and through the direct references to himself and his family and friends. The liberalization of the government censorship of books and periodicals after the revolution of 1905 facilitated this openness. While the gay love story in *Wings* was attacked and denounced by the critics of the far right and far left of the political spectrum, the leading symbolist and acmeist poets and critics, who were then in the vanguard of Russian literary life, acclaimed Kuzmin as a major new figure. His example of depicting gay life in prose and poetry was soon followed by the major symbolist poet, Vyacheslav Ivanov, by Ivanov's wife, novelist Lydia Zinovieva-Annibal, who introduced lesbian themes into Russian literature, and also by fiction writers Yevdokia Nagrodskaya and Sergey Auslender.

Between the turn of the century and World War I, Kuzmin published several other novels, such as *Travellers by Land and Sea* (1915), and numerous short stories, such as the famous "Aunt Sonya's Sofa" (where the sofa itself is the narrator that tells the story of a gay love affair). He also wrote many stage plays on gay themes, such as *Dangerous Precaution* (1907) and *Venetian Madcaps* (1914). But his fiction and drama, although significant historically and important as phenomena of cultural development, seem (except for a few really excellent short stories) both faded and lightweight now. It is as a lyrical poet that Kuzmin retains his major place in Russian literature. From the very first poem in *Nets*, which sang of iced Chablis, splashing bodies at the beach, the glories of Mozart's music, and the sly and enticing glance of the poet's male lover, Kuzmin's poetry struck his contemporaries by the unprecedented precision and intimacy with which it reflected life. Amid the metaphysics and mysticism that typified the poetry of his symbolist contemporaries, Kuzmin's poetry reminded the reader of the joys of here and now, of the concrete beauty of this world, which other poets of his time tended to forget or overlook. Even after his literary position was established, Kuzmin went on composing music: operettas and incidental music for the production of plays, the best known of which was his score for Vsevolod Meyerhold's staging of Alexander Blok's fantastic comedy *The Fairground Booth* (1907).

Of all the Russian writers to deal with gay themes, Kuzmin was the least interested in politics. He welcomed the democratic revolution in February 1917 and was, at first, highly enthusiastic about the October revolution of the same year, seeing in the Bolsheviks' seizure of power a promise of greater freedom and social justice and calling the Bolsheviks' opponents "animals and scum." In the early postrevolutionary years, he maintained his position on the literary scene and published some of his most interesting verse. But the clarity for which his earlier poetry was particularly admired disappeared, and his writings became more cryptic and surrealistic in the 1920s. His recently published correspondence with literary impresario Vladimir Ruslov mentions mass arrests of gay men in Moscow in 1924 and the gay community's fear of attending his public readings. After about 1925, Kuzmin had difficulty publishing, though by some miracle he managed to publish his last collection of verse, *The Trout Breaks Through the Ice*, in 1929. This book, Kuzmin's masterpiece and one of the finest achievements of Russian poetry in this century, came out in a minuscule printing and was ignored by Soviet critics. After this Kuzmin was no longer allowed to publish any of his original work and had to devote himself to translation, mostly of Shakespeare. After his death in 1936, several of his close friends and his longtime lover, Yuri Yurkin, were arrested and shot.

Kuzmin's name became unmentionable in the Soviet Union from the 1930s to the 1970s. His work was brought to light again in the 1970s by literary scholars who live and work in the West, such as John Malmstad, Vladimir Markov, and Michael Green. With the coming of Gorbachev's *glasnost*, Kuzmin was rediscovered and revived in Russia.

Simon Karlinsky

Bibliography

Green, Michael. "Mikhail Kuzmin and the Theater." *Russian Literature Triquarterly* 7 (Winter 1974).
Karlinsky, Simon. "Kuzmin, Gumilev, and Tsvetayeva as Neo-Romantic Playwrights." In *Russian Theatre in the Age of Modernism*. Robert Russell and Andrew Barratt, eds. London: Macmillan, 1990.

See also Opera; Russia; Russian Literature

L

Lambda

Lambda is the Greek letter *L* for liberation. Originally, it was a pictographic symbol for the scales of justice, and, in time, it began to represent the concept of balance. Spartan soldiers painted a lambda on their shields as a symbol of unity and as a representation of the delicate balance they believed must exist between the demands of the state and the freedom of the individual. Romans borrowed the lambda from the Greeks, using it as a symbol for *lampas,* the Roman word for "torch." In 1970, without knowing of the historical significance of the letter, the Gay Activists Alliance of New York designated the orange lambda on a blue field as a symbol of gay liberation. In December 1974, the lambda was adopted as the international symbol for gay and lesbian rights by the International Gay Rights Congress meeting in Edinburgh, Scotland.

See also Author; Gay Activists Alliance (GAA); Gay Liberation; Sparta; Lamda Rising Bookstore, Washington, D.C.

Lampião

In Brazil the term *lampião*, in addition to the general meaning, "lantern," is the name of Virgolin Lampião (1900–1938), the most important bandit in the nation's history. This controversial figure employed extremely violent methods to kill his opponents, and, at the same time, he used perfumes, silk handkerchiefs, and rather unorthodox jewelry, given the predominant standards of machismo at the time.

O Lampião was the name chosen for the first and until the present time the most important homosexual newspaper in Brazil. It was founded in 1978 by eleven gay journalists, intellectuals, and artists from Rio de Janeiro and São Paulo, including Jono Antonio Mascarenhas, a senior figure in the Brazilian gay movement; and writers Jono Sivério Trevisan, Gasparino da Matta, Peter Fry, Jean Claude Bernadet, Darcy Penteado, and Agnaldo Silva. Several months after the newspaper was founded, when Brazil was still under a military dictatorship, the editors underwent a police investigation headed by the military police of Rio de Janeiro, who accused the publication of defending homosexuality.

O Lampião was principally an innovator for addressing homosexual topics with language closely identified with the gay subculture, although it also opened its pages to subjects related to the black, feminist, and environmental movements. Its first issue set as a proposal "to say no to the ghetto and come out. We are interested in destroying the standard image of the homosexual as someone who lives in the shadows, who prefers the night, who considers his sexual preferences as a kind of curse, and who is inclined to use exaggerated gestures." *O Lampião*, which was sold in major newsstands and alternative book stores in most of Brazil's state capitals, was a sixteen- to twenty-page tabloid with a two-color front page and many photos and illustrations.

Its creation coincided with the emergence of the first homosexual groups throughout the country and served as a place to publicize the addresses and proposals of the recently founded Brazilian Homosexual Movement. Yet when the first gathering of the Brazilian Homosexual Movement took place in São Paulo in 1980, the publication radicalized the ideological differences between its editors and gay and lesbian leaders, especially over the newspaper's use of expressions considered vulgar when referring to homosexual militants, such as *bichas* (fairies), *veados* (fag-

L gots), and *sapatonas* (dykes), and the overemphasis on the camp subculture of transvestites to the neglect of other sectors of the gay community.

Some issues of *O Lampião* covered specific topics, such as Carnival, male prostitution, the life of homosexuals in Cuba, love between women, the murder of gays, the homophobia of the Catholic Church, and transvestites, as well as interviews with national celebrities, such as labor leader Lula, television personality and clothing designer Clodovil, romance writer Cassandra Rios, and the transvestite Rogéria. Many articles translated from European and U.S. lesbian and gay magazines allowed the readership to be aware of the latest events and victories achieved in the Northern Hemisphere. These were exclusive news stories because during the military dictatorship, the Brazilian press censored information about the international homosexual movement.

After thirty-seven monthly issues, *O Lampião* ceased publication in July 1981 from lack of an infrastructure for advertising and the almost exclusive reliance on newsstand sales, as well as an internal crisis among its editors. Its rich archive, the first documented collection of the Brazilian homosexual press, was unfortunately discarded by its last editor-in-chief, Agnaldo Silva.

Luiz Mott, translated by James N. Green

Bibliography

Trevisan, Jono S. *Perverts in Paradise*. London: Gay Men's Press, 1986.

See also *Advocate; Brazil; Journalism; Kreis, Der*

Laughton, Charles (1899–1962)

British American actor Charles Laughton made his professional debut at the relatively late age of twenty-six, but his success was almost immediate—within eighteen months he was starring on stage in London's West End. In 1931 Laughton made his New York debut when *Payment Deferred*, in which he had starred in London, transferred to Broadway. In 1932 he made his Hollywood film debut in James Whale's comedy-horror film, *The Old Dark House*. During the 1930s, Laughton received international acclaim for his film roles. Among these were the title character in *The Private Life of Henry VIII* (1933)—a role in which his corpulent body suited him and for which he won the Academy Award for best actor—and Captain Bligh in *Mutiny on the Bounty* (1935). After becoming a Hollywood star, Laughton settled in California and spent most of his career in the United States, becoming a U.S. citizen in 1950.

After starring as Quasimodo in *The Hunchback of Notre Dame* (1939), Laughton appeared in films less frequently, often in supporting roles, and his performances were less consistently successful. Perhaps this change came about because he had found other, more personally satisfying outlets for creative expression. Beginning in the 1940s, he directed for the theater and taught acting classes. He collaborated with German playwright Bertolt Brecht on an English-language adaptation of Brecht's *Galileo*, in which Laughton starred in 1947. Laughton toured the United States in one-man shows in which he read from the Bible and works by American authors. In 1951–1952, he directed and toured in a staged reading of Shaw's *Don Juan in Hell*. He compiled two anthologies of readings, *Tell Me a Story* (1957) and *The Fabulous Country* (1962). Laughton also directed one film, *The Night of the Hunter* (1955). Though initially this murder story was unsuccessful with critics and audiences, it has since come to be admired among film historians and enthusiasts. Laughton's last performance in a play was in 1959, when he gave a controversial portrayal of King Lear at Stratford, England. Despite the change in his career's focus, Laughton continued to create satisfying performances. Among his film roles of this period were Sir Wilfred Robarts in *Witness for the Prosecution* (1957) and the homophobic Senator Seabright Cooley in *Advise and Consent* (1962).

In 1929 Laughton married actress Elsa Lanchester. Their marriage was marked by emotional distance, frequent separations, and extreme competition, yet it was important to both and endured until Laughton's death. Though Laughton was guilt-ridden about his homosexuality during much of his life, he came to feel pride in it. In 1960 he and Lanchester bought a house in Santa Monica, next door to novelist Christopher Isherwood and artist Don Bachardy, because of Laughton's wish to live among his "own people." Four years before his death, Laughton began a lasting romantic relationship with a young aspiring actor, Terry Jenkins.

In his best performances, Laughton combined a flamboyant acting style, emotional intensity, an expressive voice and face, remarkable physical grace, and a sexual presence at once attractive and disturbing to create brilliant portrayals of a variety of characters.

Charles Krinsky

Bibliography

Callow, Simon. *Charles Laughton: A Difficult Actor*. London: Methuen, 1987.

Higham, Charles. *Charles Laughton: An Intimate Biography*. Garden City, N.Y.: Doubleday, 1976.

Lanchester, Elsa. *Elsa Lanchester Herself*. London: Michael Joseph, 1983.

See also Film; Isherwood, Christopher; Whale, James

Lautréamont, Comte de (born Isidore Ducasse, 1846–1870)

Isidore Ducasse, one of the more mysterious figures of French literature, used the name Lautréamont as his pseudonym. Born in Montevideo, Uruguay, of French parents who had emigrated to South America, Ducasse was sent to the south of France to be educated in 1859. From 1859 to 1865 he attended secondary school in Tarbes and Pau. He seems to have made a return trip to Montevideo in 1867, during which he apparently convinced his father to allow him to set himself up in Paris for a literary career. He lived in Paris from 1867 until his mysterious death in November 1870. The cause of his death remains obscure.

He is the author of two works, *Les Chants de Maldoror* (The Song of Maldoror) and *Poésies*, both written during his Paris years. The first of the six songs was published anonymously in 1868 and again in 1869. Ducasse would arrange for the publication of the complete edition of the six songs in 1869 but never convinced his publisher to distribute the copies once they were printed. (They finally went on sale in 1874.) Ducasse further arranged in 1870 for the publication of *Poésies*.

Almost entirely unknown during his short life, Ducasse would become increasingly important throughout the twentieth century. He became a favorite of the surrealists and other members of a variety of avant-garde movements. *Les Chants de Maldoror*—six cantos with varying numbers of stanza—is a difficult work of great poetic virtuosity, full of violent metamorphoses among human, animal, and divine; it experiments with collage and textual borrowings in ways that became standard in future modernist moments; it is strongly critical of the moralism of its time.

Stanza 5 of the fifth song of Maldoror begins, "O pédérastes incompréhensibles, ce n'est pas moi qui lancerai des injures à votre grande dégradation; ce n'est pas moi qui viendrai jeter le mépris sur votre anus infundibuliforme" (O incomprehensible pederasts, I shall not cast insults at your great degradation; I shall cast no scorn on your funnel-shaped anus). The stanza continues as an odd and explicit apologia for the important transgressive beauty of the "pederast." There are many other implicit references to male homosexuality throughout the six songs, including the story, told in the last song, of Maldoror's fascination with the beautiful adolescent, Mervyn, whom he lures away from his perfect English family toward a bizarre sacrificial death.

Michael Lucey

Bibliography

Ducasse, Isidore. *Lautréamont's Maldoror*. Alexis Lykiard, trans. New York: Crowell, 1972.

Lautréamont. *Oeuvres complètes*. Pierre-Olivier Walzer, ed. Paris: Gallimard [Pléiade], 1970.

See also French Literature

Lawrence, T. E. (1888–1935)

Thomas Edward Lawrence, known as "Lawrence of Arabia," is one of the most celebrated and enigmatic heroes of World War I. His memoir concerning the Arab revolt, *Seven Pillars of Wisdom,* is one of the great adventure stories of modern literature. Lawrence was a private, elusive figure, and many aspects of his life continue to be controversial, including his sexual identity.

Born to Anglo-Irish parents on August 15, 1888, the second of five illegitimate sons, Lawrence attended the City of Oxford High School for Boys and won a scholarship to Jesus College at Oxford University. While a student, he worked at the Ashmolean Museum for archaeologist D. G. Hogarth, and from 1909 to 1914, assisted Hogarth in the Middle East, not only with excavations but also with intelligence operations for the British government. In Charchemish, Syria (now part of Turkey), he became deeply attached to a youth of about sixteen known as Dahoum, "the little dark one." For at least three years, the two were intimate friends, and several Arab observers considered them to be lovers. They parted when World War I broke out and Lawrence was assigned to the British intelligence office in Cairo. In 1915, the British government decided to encourage an Arab revolt against Turkey, ruler of the region since 1512 and Germany's ally in the war. Lawrence, acting without official sanction, joined with Prince Faisal, son of Sharif Hussein of Mecca, to lead a Bedouin expedition across the

L harsh terrain of the Hejaz desert and take the vital port of Aqaba by land. They triumphantly entered the city on July 6, 1917, and subsequently, Lawrence led guerrilla-style strikes aimed at disabling the Turkish supply line. But for Lawrence personally, a decisive turning point occurred when he stole into the Turkish-occupied town of Deraa undercover. He was captured, viciously tortured by Turkish soldiers, and sexually abused by the bey. In *Seven Pillars,* Lawrence wrote: "In Deraa that night the citadel of my integrity had been irrevocably lost" (447). Lawrence's desolation deepened when he learned on the way to Damascus that Dahoum had fallen ill and died.

At the end of the war, Lawrence and Faisal participated in the Paris Peace Conference and helped to produce a settlement in the Middle East. Although Lawrence became world-famous when American journalist Lowell Thomas publicized his feats in the desert, he shunned public adulation. Seeking anonymity, Lawrence secretly enlisted in the air force and the tank corps under assumed names, Ross and Shaw. With a strong tendency toward masochism, perhaps exacerbated by the torment of Deraa, during this period Lawrence retained a fellow soldier, John Bruce, to flagellate him regularly with a birch rod. In 1926 he published *Seven Pillars of Wisdom* in a private edition of three hundred copies. It opens with a love poem, "To S. A."—a figure who has been variously identified but was likely Dahoum, whose real name, according to one source, was Salim Ahmed. For the time, the description in the first chapter of the homosexual practices of the desert tribesmen is daring but consistent with British notions of "Oriental" culture. A shorter, less risqué version, *Revolt in the Desert* (1927), was published for mass circulation.

Lawrence was killed in a motorcycle accident in 1935. *The Mint,* an iconoclastic memoir of his experiences in the Royal Air Force, was published in 1955.   *Matthew Parfitt*

Bibliography

Lawrence, T. E. *Seven Pillars of Wisdom: A Triumph.* Garden City, N.Y.: Doubleday-Anchor, 1935.

Meyers, Jeffrey. *The Wounded Spirit: T. E. Lawrence's Seven Pillars of Wisdom.* New York: St. Martin's Press, 1989.

Wilson, Jeremy. *Lawrence of Arabia: The Authorized Biography of T. E. Lawrence.* New York: Atheneum, 1989.

See also Arabic Literature; Colonialism; Turkey; War

Leander, Zarah (1907–1981)

Zarah Leander, the Swedish diva of the German musical film, represents something of a German Judy Garland. Introduced to German audiences as both the new Garbo and the new Dietrich of German film, Leander became the main star of the Nazi-era musical, repeatedly cast as the maternal singing vamp.

A year after her most successful film, *The Great Love* (1942), Leander left Germany for Sweden. After the war, Leander's career became a series of comebacks in the German Federal Republic. In stark contrast to her career as a Nazi diva, Leander's postwar career was characterized more than anything by failure. It was also during the 1950s that Leander began to serve as a gay icon. Appearing in the press as "unbelievable groups of young men" or "whole groups of beautiful men in black silk suits," the "bachelors" around Leander became an integral part of her star system in the decades of its decay.

The gay male fascination with Leander can be attributed especially to her voice. A perversely deep alto, almost baritone in range, was her trademark: this, as well as her film roles and their tendency to feature outrageous costumes, made Leander a spectacle of the version of heterosexuality and femininity available to gay political performativity. As Rosa von Praunheim put it: "Zarah looked like a drag queen: strong body, big hands, big feet, little breasts, and a fabulous male voice" (Praunheim 158).   *Brian Currid*

Bibliography

Lowry, Stephen. *Pathos und Politik: Ideologie im Spielfilmen des Nationalsozialismus.* Tübingen: Niemeyer, 1991.

Praunheim, Rosa von. "Die Baßamsel singt nicht mehr." *Der Spiegel* 35, no. 27 (1981): 158–59.

Rentschler, Eric. *The Ministry of Illusion: Nazi Cinema and Its Afterlife.* Cambridge, Mass.: Harvard University Press, 1996.

Seiler, Paul. *Zarah Leander.* Berlin: Albino Verlag, 1982.

See also Cabaret, Variety, and Revue Entertainment; Film; Film Stars; Germany

Leathermen

In Hollister, California, during the summer of 1947, a group of drunken motorcycle riders terrorized the town and shocked the nation by fighting and doing wheelies up and down the main drag. In the summer of 1997, the town welcomed thousands of bikers from all over the world for a fiftieth anniversary celebration of the incident. Between those two events lie the birth and maybe the death of a modern icon, the leatherman, the black-clad loner with special significance for a segment of the gay community.

Outlaw heroes—Spartacus, Robin Hood—have always had admirers, but they were really the Good Guys; the Sheriff of Nottingham was the villain. The leatherman, however, was purely an outlaw, and that was new. Defying "good" society, his real-life prototypes just wanted to drink, carouse, and ride their bikes. During the fifties, early physique photographers such as Chicago's Charles Renslow, himself a motorcycle champion, found that shots of half-naked men in leather bending over Harleys were wildly popular.

Homosexuals who felt demonized by society's rejection developed a mystique around the leatherman. They wanted to have sex with him, but they also wanted to be him—protest and pleasure combined. By the mid-sixties, a network of leather bars existed; the Tool Box in San Francisco, the Coleherne in London (still popular), and any bar anywhere called the Eagle. The Stonewall riots, started by street drags and hustlers, were quickly augmented by leathermen from the bars farther west on Christopher Street.

Through the seventies, the leather lifestyle grew, documented by writers like Larry Townsend, serenaded by the Village People, and lived by thousands of men in gay ghettos mushrooming from West Berlin to West Hollywood.

Outsiders tended to assume "leatherman" meant heavy-duty sex. Some celebration organizers tried to ban them from Pride celebrations as undesirables. In truth, those who enjoyed extreme sex practices seldom wore leather and leathermen seldom practiced extreme sex. Sex was at the heart of the leather lifestyle, of course, but its philosophy demanded honesty above all, being oneself, never pretending. This hostility to all pretense led to signs: "No cologne—smell like a man" in many leather establishments. Like all ideals, it was seldom fully realized and easily satirized.

Inevitably, codes of conduct developed, often in exhaustive detail: "yellow hanky in the right pocket = I like to be pissed on." However, just as a leather establishment was arising, AIDS brought fear, confusion, and the death of many of the most socially active of its members. Gradually realization spread that most behavior favored by leathermen was not unsafe if practiced sensibly, but the community had been decimated.

Meanwhile, the leatherman became a victim of his own charisma. His iconography was preempted by the mainstream, beginning with the warbling hoods of *West Side Story* and *Grease*. By the late eighties, suburban matrons cruised the mall with their toddlers wearing mother-and-daughter black leather jackets. The swaggering biker outlaw was in danger of being hugged to death.

The leatherman, a gay iconoclastic icon, sprang forth with mythic suddenness to join the pantheon of male idols—warrior, lumberjack, cowboy. Whether he is to be a permanent member or just a twentieth-century aberration has yet to be determined.   *F. Valentine Hooven III*

Bibliography

Duberman, Martin. *Stonewall*. New York: Dutton, 1993.

Muller, Heino, and Ralf Marsault, eds. *Athletic Model Guild*. Amsterdam: Intermale, 1987.

Preston, John. *Mr. Benson*. New York: Masquerade, 1992.

Townsend, Larry. *Leatherman's Handbook*. New York: Freeway Press, 1974.

See also Athletic Model Guild; Body Image; Disco and Dance Music; Mapplethorpe, Robert; Preston, John; Sadomasochism

Legal Organizations

From the earliest days of the post–World War II movement for lesbian and gay rights in the United States, organizational participants have recognized the need to address legal issues. Many of the early organizations, such as the Mattachine Society, had legal committees. But open participation by lawyers in homosexual rights organizations was problematic, because standards for admission to practice law focused on the "moral character" of applicants, and homosexuality was considered a disqualifying moral attribute in many jurisdictions. In addition, prior to 1961 every state in the United States criminalized the commission of homosexual sex acts, and most jurisdictions also made solicitation of homosexual acts a crime. These statutes certainly had a deterrent effect on lawyers becoming openly involved with lesbian and gay rights organizations.

Consequently, before the 1970s, organized efforts to advance the legal interests of lesbian and gay people were necessarily carried on "behind the scenes." A rare example of the existence of a gay rights legal organization surfacing in print is a reference to an amicus curiae brief being filed by the Homosexual Law Reform Society of America in the historic U.S. Supreme Court case of *Boutilier v. Immigration and Naturalization Service* (1967). One suspects that this may have been an ad hoc group of lawyers formed expressly to file a brief in the case, in which the Supreme Court rejected a challenge to the federal statute barring immigration to the United States by homosexuals. Working behind the scenes, a group known as the National Committee for Sexual Civil Liberties (and later known as the American Association for Personal Privacy) coordinated work on court challenges to solicitation and sodomy laws and legislative reforms in several states.

Two decisions issued on July 3, 1973, by the New York Court of Appeals (that state's highest court) made it possible for homosexual lawyers to form organizations to advocate for lesbian and gay rights. In the first decision, *In re Kimball*, the court reversed a lower-court decision and ruled that Harris Kimball, who had been disbarred in Florida for homosexual activities in 1957, could be admitted to practice law in New York. The court ruled that an openly gay man did not automatically lack the necessary good moral character to practice law, even though the New York Penal Code made consensual homosexual sex a misdemeanor at that time.

In the second decision, *In re Thom*, the court reversed a lower-court decision and ruled that the Lambda Legal Defense & Education Fund, Inc., cofounded by William J. Thom and E. Carrington Boggan, formed specifically to advance lesbian and gay legal rights, could be chartered by the state of New York. (The lower court had ruled that an association to advance the legal rights of homosexuals did not serve the public interest and should not be authorized to practice law as a public interest firm.)

Lambda Legal Defense & Education Fund was the first public interest law firm established specifically to advance the legal rights of lesbians and gay men. Soon afterward, lesbian and gay advocates began to establish similar organizations in other cities: Gay Rights Advocates (subsequently known as National Gay Rights Advocates) and the Lesbian Rights Project (subsequently the National Center for Lesbian Rights) in San Francisco, and Gay & Lesbian Advocates & Defenders in Boston were the most prominent and long-lasting of these organizations. (National Gay Rights Advocates ceased operations in the late 1980s.)

In addition to Thom and Boggan, other attorneys active in Lambda Legal Defense during its early years were Margot Karle, Michael Lavery, and William J. Gardner. During the 1980s, Lambda employed as executive directors Rosalyn Richter, Timothy Sweeney, and Thomas B. Stoddard; Abby Rubenfeld and Paula Ettelbrick served as legal directors. Among the West Coast attorneys who played leading roles at (National) Gay Rights Advocates (NGRA) and the Lesbian Rights Project included Leonard Graff, Donna Hitchens, Mary Dunlap, and Roberta Achtenberg. Jean O'Leary served for many years as NGRA's executive director. The early leadership of Gay and Lesbian Advocates and Defenders in Boston included Richard Burns, John Ward, Kevin Cathcart, and Katherine Triantafillou.

During the 1980s, the main focus of these young organizations was to attack sodomy laws, pursue discrimination claims, and fight for the rights of lesbian and gay parents. The emergence of the AIDS epidemic presented new challenges but at the same time began to open the door to financial assistance from mainstream foundations for lesbian and gay public interest firms. The volume of work led all the surviving lesbian and gay public interest firms to expand greatly during the 1990s, with Lambda Legal Defense becoming truly national in reach, establishing branch offices in Los Angeles, Chicago, and Atlanta, to become one of the few national lesbian and gay organizations with a physical presence in several parts of the country.

Because of the small size of lesbian and gay public interest law firms during the early years of the gay liberation movement, litigants occasionally relied on the American Civil Liberties Union (ACLU) for representation. The ACLU at first hesitated to get involved in gay rights litigation but by the mid-1960s had begun to bring such cases and through the 1970s became one of the most significant participants in the struggle. During the mid-1980s, the ACLU established a Lesbian and Gay Rights Project and a jointly administered AIDS and Civil Liberties Project, both under the direction of Nan Hunter. The ACLU Projects quickly emerged as major participants in the movement, being in the position of coordinating activities by ACLU affiliates in most of the states, and thus having a reach that none of the other gay and lesbian legal organizations could equal.

The major lesbian and gay legal organizations attempted to coordinate their work by forming a roundtable that met periodically beginning in the mid-1980s and arranged for the exchange of information through telephone conference calls and document exchange, as well as face-to-face conferences. These organizations have also established regular consulting relationships with political associations such as the National Gay and Lesbian Task Force and the Human Rights Campaign.

In addition to forming public interest law firms, lesbian and gay lawyers began during the 1970s to form professional associations. The earliest were formed in New York, Los Angeles, and San Francisco. Major impetus to such local organization stemmed from the formation of a National Lesbian and Gay Law Association (NLGLA) at a national meeting of lawyers coordinated by the roundtable group during the National March on Washington for Lesbian and Gay Rights in 1987. By the mid-1990s, the NLGLA's "lavender law" conferences had become an established national event, and NLGLA had become an affiliate organization of the American Bar Association (ABA). Lesbian and gay bar associations had been formed in most major cities, some with statewide aspirations. In addition, many large mainstream bar associations had begun to form committees to deal with lesbian and gay legal issues, or to focus on the particular problems encountered by lesbian and gay lawyers and law students within the legal profession. The earliest such committee was probably the committee on the rights of homosexuals formed by the American Bar Association Section on Individual Rights and Responsibilities in the late 1970s.

Within legal education, organizational efforts began late in 1982, with a Section on Lesbian and Gay Legal Issues being formed at the January 1983 annual meeting of the Association of American Law Schools (AALS). Accorded official recognition in 1984, the section undertook surveys of law school discrimination policies and curricula, and encouraged the first AALS-sponsored workshop on sexual orientation in law schools in 1996. In 1990, the AALS amended its bylaws to require member law schools to ban sexual-orientation discrimination. In 1995, the ABA amended its law school accreditation standards to include a similar requirement.

Arthur S. Leonard

Case Reference

In re Kimball, 33 N.Y.2d 586, 347 N.Y.S.2d 453 (1973).

In re Thom, 33 N.Y.2d 609, 347 N.Y.S.2d 571 (1973).

See also Civil Rights (U.S. Law); Crime and Criminality; Human Rights Campaign; Immigration, U.S.; Mattachine Society; National Gay and Lesbian Task Force; Stoddard, Thomas B.; Thom, William J.; U.S. Law: Equal Protection

Leonardo da Vinci (1452–1519)

Leonardo da Vinci, painter of the *Mona Lisa*, has long been held up as the epitome of the universal genius for his achievements in numerous branches of the arts and sciences and is one of the most written-about figures from the Italian Renaissance. The reconstruction of Leonardo's sexual orientation and its consequences for both his artistic and scientific work has been relatively short on facts and long on speculation. Central to most accounts are a set of archival documents recording anonymous accusations of sodomy lodged twice in 1476 against him while he was an apprentice in Andrea del Verrocchio's workshop in Florence. Both charges—which implicated Leonardo and several other Florentine citizens, some from prominent families, with one Jacopo Saltarelli, an artist's model whose name appears in at least one other sodomy case prosecuted by the Office of the Night, a special magistracy set up to police homosexual activity—were dismissed.

Softer, more oblique evidence has been mined by Leonardo's interpreters in his family history, fragmentary notebook jottings, his apparent distaste of sexuality, his choice of shop assistants, the androgyny of some of the figures he painted, and his reputation among his contemporaries. That same-sex attractions were constitutive of Leonardo's reputation (and that of Florentine men in general) already by the sixteenth century is indicated—indeed, writ large—by a derisive sonnet from 1568 by art theorist Gian Paolo Lomazzo on the subject of *l'amore masculino,* which ventriloquizes Leonardo as boasting of sodomizing his beautiful, teenage apprentice "many times." The assistant in question, whose androgynous features and curly hair may have served Leonardo as a model for his *St. John the Baptist,* was Gian Giacomo de' Caprotti, whom Leonardo nicknamed "Salai" (little devil) in his notebooks because of his petty crimes. Only ten years old when Leonardo took him in 1490, Salai remained until 1516 with his master, who lavished fine clothes and jewelry on him and took him on his various travels about Europe. It is surely to Salai

L

Leonardo's Bacchus. *Louvre, Paris. Art Resource, NY.*

that we owe the cliché about Leonardo's preference for beautiful looks over talent in the selection of his assistants.

The first major study to stress the significance of Leonardo's sexuality to an understanding of his work was Sigmund Freud's *Leonardo da Vinci and a Memory of His Childhood* (1910), which argued that Leonardo was an "ideal" (sublimated) homosexual. Freud's account has received much critical attention since its publication. It was established early on that Freud had jeopardized his interpretation of Leonardo's childhood fantasy—and, by extension, of the artist's entire personality—by basing it on a mistranslation of the Italian word *nibbio*, which means "kite," not "vulture." Some scholars have found Freud's conclusions inconsistent with the intellectual history and art history out of which Leonardo was working, while others have pointed up slippages in Freud's psychoanalytic logic. Still others have questioned the whole validity of Freud's enterprise, deeming the " 'psychological' interpretation . . . a supreme irrelevance when it comes to understanding in historical terms" why a particular image by Leonardo took the form it did (Kemp 341).

Studies like Saslow's are predicated on the opposite view. 						*William B. MacGregor*

Bibliography

Beltrami, Luca. *Documenti e memorie riguardanti la vita e le opere di Leonardo da Vinci*. Milan, 1919.

Freud, Sigmund. *Leonardo da Vinci and a Memory of His Childhood*. Alan Tyson, trans. New York: Norton, 1964.

Gilman, Sander L. "Leonardo Sees Himself: Reading Leonardo's First Representation of Human Sexuality." *Social Research* 54, no. 1 (1987): 149–71.

Jackson, Earl, Jr. "The History of an 'Ideal' Homosexual: Freud's *Leonardo*." In *Strategies of Deviance: Studies in Gay Male Representation*. Bloomington, Ind.: Indiana University Press, 1995.

Kemp, Martin. *Leonardo da Vinci: The Marvellous Works of Nature and Man*. Cambridge, Mass.: Harvard University Press, 1981.

Lomazzo, Gian Paolo. *Il libro dei sogni*, in *Scritte sulle arti*. Roberto Ciardi, ed. 2 vols. Florence: Marchi and Bertolli, 1973–1974.

Rocke, Michael. *Forbidden Friendships: Homosexuality and Male Culture in Renaissance Florence*. New York: Oxford University Press, 1996.

Saslow, James M. *Ganymede in the Renaissance: Homosexuality in Art and Society*. New Haven: Yale University Press, 1986.

Schapiro, Meyer. "Leonardo and Freud: An Art-Historical Study." *Journal of the History of Ideas* 17 (1956): 147–78.

See also Florence; Freud, Sigmund; Italian Renaissance; Michelangelo Buonarroti

Leopold and Loeb

The "thrill murder" of fourteen-year-old Bobbie Franks by two brilliant and wealthy Chicago youths, Nathan Leopold Jr. and Richard Loeb, has long fascinated the American public. The 1924 "crime of the century" has been the basis for a Broadway play and a film, both drawn from Meyer Levin's novelization of the events (*Compulsion*, 1956), and at least two additional films: Alfred Hitchcock's *Rope* (1948) and Tom Kalin's impressionist film noir *Swoon* (1993), which more explicitly depicts the killers' sexual relationship.

Leopold, at eighteen, was a law student, having graduated from the University of Chicago. Enamored of the philosophy of Friedrich Nietzsche, who had theorized that the evolutionary struggle would produce an idealized, superior, dominating man, Leopold found that superman in nineteen-year-old Loeb, who at seventeen had reputedly been the youngest graduate of the University of Michigan. According to the terms of their secret pact, Leopold would serve as an accomplice to Loeb's criminal activities, which had begun at the age of eight or nine, if Loeb would submit to Leopold's erotic advances.

To seal their relationship and prove their superiority to society, the two plotted the "perfect" crime. They kidnapped fourteen-year-old Bobbie Franks at random. It was their intention to jointly strangle their victim, but he was accidentally bludgeoned to death in an effort to keep him quiet, almost certainly by Loeb. After pouring acid on the body to thwart identification, they hid it in a culvert. It was found before they could collect the ransom. Moreover, they left a host of clumsy clues that led to their apprehension. Each made a full confession, blaming the other for the fatal blow.

Their frantic parents quickly engaged renown defense attorney Clarence Darrow to save their sons from the gallows. Darrow, drawing on the new psychological theories of Sigmund Freud, put up a novel defense, declaring his clients' guilt to be mitigated not by insanity but by mental illness. Defense experts, pointing to the sexual and emotional abuse the two had suffered as children, claimed the teenagers were fixed at the emotional age of seven. Darrow, using Leopold's homosexual tendencies—and Loeb's tolerance of those tendencies—to shore up his case, concluded that his clients were weak and diseased and therefore not fully responsible for their crimes. The judge cited the youth of the defendants in his decision to forgo the death penalty in favor of a sentence of life plus ninety-nine years.

Loeb was slashed to death by a fellow inmate, James Day, in 1936. Although later studies disprove Day's claims that he was defending himself against Loeb's sexual advances, his story was widely believed at the time in accordance with prevailing stereotypes concerning homosexual aggression. Leopold was present at Loeb's deathbed and wrote openly of his continued love and admiration for Loeb in his 1957 autobiography, *Life Plus Ninety-Nine Years*, despite admonitions that such declarations would diminish his chances for parole. Leopold was nonetheless paroled the following year at the age of fifty-three, having served thirty-three years. He lived out his life in Puerto Rico. Unhap-pily married to an American widow, he always kept prominently displayed a photograph of the consuming love of his life, Richard Loeb. Leopold died of natural causes on August 30, 1971.

Nancy C. Unger

Bibliography
Fass, Paula S. "Making and Remaking an Event: The Leopold and Loeb Case in American Culture." *Journal of American History* 80 (1993): 919–51.
Higdon, Hal. *The Crime of the Century: The Leopold and Loeb Case*. New York: Putnam, 1975.

See also Film; Hitchcock, Alfred; Psychological and Psychoanalytic Perspectives on Homosexuality

Lewd and Lascivious Conduct

Public lewdness laws are different from laws prohibiting sodomy in that the gravamen of the latter is the specific sex act itself, which often has attached to it a severe moral—if not religious—judgment and, usually, a felony punishment. While many states still criminalize private consenting-adult acts of sodomy, most now make it a crime only when minors, force, or prisoners are involved. On the other hand, virtually all states have public lewdness laws designed to protect the public from being accosted by offensive behavior in a public location, and the crime is usually a misdemeanor.

Early public lewdness laws ran afoul of the constitutional right to due process by being couched in terms so vague that people of normal intelligence would not know what to refrain from doing in order to avoid arrest. This "vagueness" test became a primary vehicle for invalidating many such laws.

For example, California Criminal Code section 647, subdivision (a), prohibited anyone from engaging in "lewd" conduct, without defining the term at all. Various cases suggested that lewd meant "lascivious," "wanting in morals," or other descriptions of equal vagueness. The idea was to give broad and unfettered discretion to police to cast their nets widely to catch anyone they personally deemed undesirable. In effect, this made each officer a mini-legislature, deciding which acts violated the law in each circumstance. Under that vague law, thousands of gay men were arrested for such varied conduct as kissing, holding hands, dancing, and inviting someone to go home with them. If convicted, they were

L forced to register as sex offenders for life alongside child molesters and rapists.

In *Pryor v. Municipal Court*, a 1979 landmark decision from the California Supreme Court, defense attorney Thomas F. Coleman successfully challenged the lewd conduct law on vagueness grounds. Instead of totally invalidating the law, however, the court redefined the criminal act, supplying the specifics the legislature had left out. Thereafter, in California, the elements of the offense were (a) touching the genitals, buttocks, or female breast; (b) with the specific intent to sexually arouse, annoy, gratify, or offend; (c) in a place exposed to public view; (d) when the actor knows or should know that there is someone present who may be offended. Further, basing its decision largely on an amicus brief filed by Arthur C. Warner of Princeton, New Jersey, the court severely limited those circumstances in which speech about future sexual conduct would be a crime.

The following year, the high court in Massachusetts adopted the same definition (*Commonwealth v. Sefranka*). Other states responded to the vagueness problem in various similar ways through their courts or legislatures.

Even after judicial and legislative redefinition has cured most wording deficiencies, several major problems remain with the practical application of public lewdness laws. First, gay men are usually the only objects of arrest. When police happen upon straight couples engaged in sexual activity in a public place, the usual procedure is merely to admonish them to move on, with a wink and a nod. In addition, vice officers are often the only contact gay men have with police, setting up an unhealthy adversarial relationship between the entire gay and lesbian community and local police departments.

Moreover, the attraction, or at least vulnerability, of some gay men to anonymous sex with strangers remains a complex sociological and/or psychological issue, sometimes (but not always) involving problems of self-esteem and societal discrimination, for which the criminal justice system is often not well suited to finding just and appropriate solutions. The gay guidebooks and magazines that describe public cruising areas in various cities exacerbate the problem and bring potential danger to unwary travelers.

The most intractable problem has always been the enforcement of public lewdness laws by undercover vice officers. The actions, manner, and appearance of such officers are often intentionally se-

ductive and enticing, designed to lure gay men into a sexual encounter. This brings into question the legitimacy of the police action, since it encourages rather than discourages criminal conduct. A related problem in these cases is the absence of any objective test of credibility, since the very vice officers who encourage the conduct are usually the only witnesses, leaving innocent gay men at the mercy of a seemingly stacked deck.

The impact of an arrest and conviction can be unnecessarily harsh. While jail time, if imposed at all, is usually negligible under such laws, a minor or momentary indiscretion can easily lead to collateral disabilities created by other state and local laws for sex offenses, such as loss of a teaching credential or some other professional license, resulting in a penalty that does not fit the crime.

Finally, all the issues raised above have never been adequately reconciled with the legitimate objective of the criminal law, which is to protect people—and especially children—from being affronted with public sex acts.   *Jay M. Kohorn*

Bibliography
Pryor v. Municipal Court, 25 Cal.3d 238 (1979).
Commonwealth v. Sefranka, 382 Mass. 108 (1980).

Case References
Achtenberg, Roberta, ed. *Sexual Orientation and the Law*. New York: Clark Boardman Callaghan, 1996.

See also Civil Rights (U.S. Law); Homosexual Panic; International Law; Tearooms; U.S. Law: Discrimination; U.S. Law: Equal Protection; U.S. Law: Privacy

Leyendecker, J. C. (1874–1951)
Arguably the most effective illustrator in twentieth-century America, J. C. Leyendecker created such advertising icons as the Arrow Collar Man and covers for *Boys' Life*, *Collier's*, and *Saturday Evening Post*. His advertising for Gillette, Coopers (later Jockey) Underwear, and Kellogg's peaked in the 1920s, but he continued to create covers for *Saturday Evening Post* and the Hearst Sunday magazine *The American Weekly* into the 1940s. For many years, he created a Baby New Year for *Saturday Evening Post*. His illustrations were narratives of heroic men, perfect family life, and traditional American values embodied in pristine WASP indi-

viduals. Leyendecker's lifetime companion was Charles Beach, reputedly the model for the Arrow Collar Man. This fictional idol received thousands of letters a month at his peak in the early 1920s, including proposals of marriage. Behind Leyendecker's all-American men of sartorial elegance and ever-victorious athletes was implicit homoerotic desire. His athletes for magazine covers are peerless fantasies in stalwart perfection, including a heroic team for the August 6, 1932,*Saturday Evening Post* and an athlete in tank top (falling away to expose a nipple) for the June 24, 1916, *Collier's*. His tackling football players on the cover of the November 1909 *Century Magazine* interlock with the blond's head diving into the center of the ball carrier with Whitmanesque virility and physical joy. His 1910 men in Kuppenheimer tailored clothing are regularly juxtaposed with partially nude football players and swimmers, suggesting more than mere collegiate fellowship.   *Richard Martin*

Bibliography

Martin, Richard. "Gay Blades: Homoerotic Content in J.C. Leyendecker's Gillette Advertising Images." *Journal of American Culture* 18, no. 2 (Summer 1995): 75–82.

Schau, Michael. *J. C. Leyendecker*. New York: Watson-Guptill, 1974.

See also Fashion; Photography; Whitman, Walt

Lezama Lima, José (1910–1976)

Lezama, born in Havana, Cuba, was one of the most important Latin American literary figures of the twentieth century. He was a poet, essayist, novelist, and cultural promoter of legendary stature, as well as the author of elaborate neobaroque poetry and prose; his works include the collections of verse *Muerte de Narciso* (The Death of Narcissus, 1937), *Enemigo rumor* (Enemy Whisper, 1941), *La fijeza* (Fixity, 1949), *Dador* (Giver, 1960), and the posthumous *Fragmentos a su imán* (Fragments in Search of His/Their Magnet, 1977); the collection of essays *La expressión americana* (The American Expression, 1957), *Tratados en La Habana* (Treatises in Havana, 1958), and *La cantidad hechizada* (The Enchanted Portions, 1970); and two novels, *Paradiso* (1966) and the unfinished *Oppiano Licario* (1977). Director and cofounder of one of the most important Latin American journals of its time, *Orígenes* (1944–1956), Lezama began to write with the decline of the literary avant-garde and the collapse of the Cuban revolutionary movement of the 1930s. His joyful, optimistic writing, in which fragments are recycled to create new possibilities both for literature and for social life (he makes no distinction between the two), may be seen as a response to the pessimism of the era. In his writings, the secondariness of Latin American culture is embraced, and terms such as "echo," "incorporation," and "receptiveness" are reclaimed as primary. A supporter of the Martí legacy of the Cuban revolution, Lezama was appointed, with the advent of the revolution, to several posts, including that of vice president of the National Union of Cuban Writers and Artists in 1962.

In 1966, Lezama published the bildungsroman *Paradiso,* his masterpiece. A summa of Lezama's poetics, the novel reappropriates Catholic allegories of salvation, discourses on *cubanía* (Cubanness), and the development of the novel in high modernists such as Proust and Joyce to create a total text. It is as unabashedly corporeal as it is mystical, and it contains the most explicit and literarily allusive figurations of homosexuality in all of Latin American literature. The novel's Catholicism, homoeroticism, and refusal to make a distinction between reality and literature went against the ideological grain of the revolution. Published at a time when Cuban society was becoming increasingly militarized and "internal enemies" were either being purged or "rehabilitated" in concentration camps on the basis of religious or sexual "deviations," *Paradiso* caused a scandal and was briefly removed from circulation. As the 1960s came to a close with a cultural policy, as officially sanctioned by the Congress on Culture and Education of 1971, that became intolerant of ideological diversity, Lezama was increasingly marginalized in Cuban culture.

Since his death, he has been rehabilitated as the greatest modern exponent of Cubanness: important collections of his essays have been published, major conferences have been devoted to his work, and his home has been turned into a cultural center. Even a recent movie, *Strawberry and Chocolate (Gutiérrez Alea and Tabío,* 1944), which critiques revolutionary homophobia, features Lezama as the twentieth-century master of Cubanness. Initially, the debate over the status of homosexuality in Lezama's oeuvre was provoked by scandalized reactions to *Paradiso* in and out of Cuba. A polemic ensued about homosexuality as a theme in *Paradiso*. Because homosexuality in *Paradiso* is generally presented not unlike in other homosexual writers such as Proust, in an abject manner, *Paradiso* was considered by some to be a moral treatise against homosexuality and the excesses associated with it (the narcissistic narrative of postmodernism, for example). Other critics have argued that *Paradiso* transgresses its own ethical discourse. From this perspective, it is striking to note that in *Paradiso* and its sequel, *Oppiano Licario,* homosexuality infuses every discourse, even those of everyone who is, within the logic of the novel's own ethical judgments, homosexuality's others: the languages of the father, the family, Cubanness, the nation. Lezama had hoped that *Paradiso* would initiate a rereading of his earlier work. In this sense, the effeminate, emasculated condition of the neocolonial Cuban nation and of the dependent Latin American writer, inscribed in his earlier works in the figures of Narcissus, of the impotent mule, and of the receptive island, also becomes, from the perspective of *Paradiso*, a trope for homosexuality. It is Lezama's achievement to reclaim that abject condition. This rereading of Lezama, which would make him not a gay but certainly a queer writer, is just beginning.   *Arnaldo Cruz-Malavé*

Bibliography

Cruz-Malavé, Arnaldo. *El primitivo implorante.* Amsterdam: Rodopi, 1994.

Lihn, Enrique. "*Paradiso*, novela y homosexualidad." *Hispamérica* 7, no. 22 (1979): 3–21.

Pellón, Gustavo. "The Ethics of Androgyny: A Sexual Parable." In *José Lezama Lima's Joyful Vision.* Austin, Texas: University of Texas Press, 1989, 28–44.

Pérez Firmat, Gustavo. "Descent into *Paradiso*: A Study of Heaven and Homosexuality." *Hispania* 59 (May 1976): 247–57.

Rodríguez Monegal, Emir. *Narradores de esta América.* Buenos Aires: Alfa Argentina, 1974, 141–55.

See also Cuban Literature; Cuban Writing in Exile

Libertines and Libertinism

The terms *libertine* and *libertinism* are related to personal freedom and the development of modern concepts of the self. *Libertinism* originated in France in the sixteenth century; the word was initially used to describe religious nonconformism but came to encompass other forms of social misbehavior. Libertines were particularly associated with sex-ual misconduct—they were represented as rakes who corrupted married women and ruined virgins. Libertinism was also linked to fashion, the stage, and the rise of pornography; it emphasized consumption, whether of risqué plays, erotic prints, or expensive clothes. The theater's place in libertine culture suggests another important aspect of libertinism, namely, its playful, performative qualities.

Rather than endorsing serious moral values, libertines posed in a variety of scandalous roles, using these to signal their dissatisfaction with existing cultural norms. The blasphemy and sexual freedom associated with libertinism can therefore be seen as a challenge to a restrictive feudal society that emphasized class obligations over individual pleasure. Instead of being constrained by social conventions and traditional morality, libertines followed their own "will"—a broad term indicating various forms of self-gratification, including sexual pleasure; in doing so, they asserted the individual's right to forge an identity centered on personal inclinations. This more than anything else connects libertinism to the evolution of modern homosexuality. One can certainly find instances of homosexual behavior in libertine culture—for example, in 1680 the earl of Rochester wrote a poem beginning "Love a woman? You're an ass!" in which he praised a "sweet, soft page of mine" who is "worth forty wenches," while the mid-1700s saw the formation of the Hell-Fire Club, whose meetings may have included group masturbation.

Although specific libertines may be classed retrospectively as homosexual or bisexual, some of the same-sex behavior associated with libertinism probably originated from a desire to repudiate middle-class respectability rather than from a true alliance with homosexual subcultures. Moreover, the freedoms that libertines claimed were available only to a small minority. Far from being egalitarian, their stance was reliant on their class position and their gender—libertines were aristocratic men, not working-class women. Working-class women were frequently their victims, and the language used in libertine texts—such as the Rochester poem cited above—is often misogynistic. Nevertheless, libertinism flourished in sixteenth- and seventeenth-century France and England, encouraged by the rise of atheism in France and by the restoration of the English monarchy in 1660, which ushered in an era of consumption that contrasted strongly with the Puritan rule of Oliver Cromwell.

The late eighteenth century produced libertinism's most famous advocate—the Marquis de

Sade—but by then the age of the libertine was almost over. Besides decimating the aristocracy, the French Revolution marked an irreversible trend toward democracy and middle-class values. Romantics such as Byron and Shelley owed much to the libertine tradition (including its homosexual aspects), but as the nineteenth century progressed, libertinism faded and was displaced by the urban dandyism of the new bourgeoisie.   *Vincent Quinn*

Bibliography

Sade, Marquis de. *The One Hundred and Twenty Days of Sodom, and Other Writings*. Compiled and translated by Austryn Wainhouse and Richard Seaver, and with introductions by Simone de Beauvoir and Pierre Klossowski. London: Arrow Books, 1990.

Trumbach, Randolph. "London's Sodomites: Homosexual Behavior and Western Culture in the Eighteenth Century." *Journal of Social History* 11 (1977): 1–33.

Weber, Harold. " 'Drudging in Fair Aurelia's Womb': Constructing Homosexual Economies in Rochester's Poetry." *The Eighteenth Century: Theory and Interpretation* 33 (1992): 99–118.

Wilmot, John. *The Poems of John Wilmot, Earl of Rochester*. Keith Walker, ed. Oxford: Blackwell, 1984.

See also Dandy; Mollies; Rochester, John Wilmot, Earl of; Sade, Marquis de

Librarians

The central if largely neglected role of U.S. lesbian and gay librarians in the gay rights struggle results in part from the unique American public library philosophy. The belief in education as a cornerstone of democracy, the U.S. Constitution's First Amendment protecting freedom of speech, and the American Library Association (ALA) Code of Ethics, which is implicitly inclusive, have all contributed to the importance of librarians as gatekeepers of knowledge. At the same time, the successes and failures of lesbian and gay librarians in promoting their own professional case mirror to a large extent the ebb and flow of the struggle for equality on the part of persons of different sexual orientations. Only in New Zealand, where lesbians and gays have been protected by law since 1986, have lesbian and gay librarians played such a central role, notably in the establishment of the National Gay and Lesbian Archives, now part of the National Library of New Zealand.

Librarianship as a profession presents peculiar problems in the study of lesbian and gay professional issues, primarily because of the gender dynamics within the field. Librarianship, like nursing, social work, and teaching—the other so-called feminine semiprofessions with which it is often identified—since about 1890 has been 78 to 90 percent female. Recent research suggests that many male librarians feel that they are stereotyped as gay, and a belief among librarians generally persists that large numbers of male librarians are gay, although no statistical evidence supports such beliefs. Moreover, the corollary assumption that a large proportion of lesbians occupy the field has never been raised, much less tested—further witness to the fact that women are discounted, even as a suspect minority.

Lesbian and gay library issues are particularly poignant because of the tension created by the ambiguity of critical professional documents, one of which, the ALA Code of Ethics, would seem to require strict neutrality of professional public librarians with respect to discrimination against clients and client information requests, and the ALA Intellectual Freedom Statement, which would seem to call for a more proactive stance by librarians with regard to users, and by implication, social issues generally. Some librarians have construed the ALA Code of Ethics to defend a stance of denial in the refusal to honor discussion of lesbian and gay professional issues, even while the information requests of lesbian and gay library clients are honored. Such an argument is somewhat disingenuous, because the works of lesbian and gay writers occupy a central place in the canon of many cultures (hence in the library), and because similar arguments were used to rationalize endorsement of separate-but-equal racial policies in the Jim Crow South until 1964 (including segregated professional meetings).

Librarians formed the first gay professional organization in the world at the 1970 ALA annual meeting in Detroit. Known originally as the Gay Liberation Caucus, the organization now operates under the ALA Social Responsibilities Round Table as the Gay, Lesbian, and Bisexual Task Force (GLBTF). Israel Fishman of the Upsala College Library provided the idea for the group's founding, as well as the organizing genius for early programs and activities. Although membership records for the early years are scanty, fifty librarians attended the first Detroit meeting. Some early task force members placed themselves and their job security at risk by braving the generally conservative organizational temper of the profession. Michael McConnell, for example, lost his job at the University of Minnesota library after he applied for a marriage license with his lover, Jack Baker. He appealed to the ALA for several years for censure of the university for its action, but ALA's position was equivocal, although a gay support resolution was adopted in 1971 and an equal employment policy in 1974.

When Fishman left the profession in 1974, the task force leadership was turned over to Barbara Gittings, a nonlibrarian lesbian activist who advocated for the dissemination of accurate information about lesbians and gays through better gay literature in libraries. Gittings headed the task force until 1986, when leadership was turned over to elected male and female cochairs. During those years, Gittings regularly updated annual bibliographies of lesbian and gay literature (for several years, the only such bibliographies in existence), fostered a gay and lesbian book award (supported by task force members until the ALA finally assumed the award in 1986), and organized programs on a variety of themes ranging from literature for gay teenagers to images of gays and lesbians in art and film. It is probably not overstating the case to say that the growth of gay and lesbian literature, the abandonment of pejorative gay and lesbian subject headings in library catalogs, and the creation of lesbian and gay libraries and archives in the past quarter-century owes a great debt to the activities and efforts of Gittings and other GLBTF pioneers as well as to grassroots activism such as that of Jim Kepner, founder of the Gay and Lesbian Archives. Notable gay and lesbian collections include community-based groups such as the HerStory Archives (New York) and the Gebner-Hart Archives (Chicago), as well as institutional collections such as the Human Sexuality Archives (Cornell University) and the James C. Hormel Gay and Lesbian Center of the San Francisco Public Library. Recent surveys indicate, however, that lesbian and gay collections in small and medium-sized public libraries are underrepresentative, if they exist at all, no doubt owing in part to the conservatism of many county and municipal governments and populations, retrenchment, and lack of lesbian and gay–supportive curricula in library education programs. Nevertheless, great progress has been made in the past quarter-century; lesbian and gay librarians in the United States now publish a newsletter, sponsor a listserv, march in host cities'

gay day parades (usually coinciding with the national summer conferences), and publish professional articles reflecting the challenges of serving diverse clientele in an increasingly censorious climate, particularly as regards literature for younger clients.

Although dampened by the conservative backlash of the 1980s, activism among lesbian and gay librarians increased in the 1990s, perhaps as a result of the reactionary social climate. At the same time, research (as opposed to polemic) about lesbian and gay librarians, as well as substantive research on gay client issues, remains sparse, because of the conservatism of social sciences methodology in the academy as well as to the job security and information infrastructure concerns of some librarians.

James V. Carmichael Jr.

Bibliography

Carmichael, James V., Jr. "The Gay Librarian: A Comparative Analysis of Attitudes Towards Professional Gender Issues." *Journal of Homosexuality* 30, no. 2 (1995): 11–57.

Carmichael, James V., Jr., and Marilyn L. Shontz. "The Last Socially Acceptable Prejudice: Gay and Lesbian Library Issues, Social Responsibilities, and Coverage of these Topics in M.L.S./M.L.I.S. Programs." *Library Quarterly* 66 (January 1996): 21–58.

Cough, Cal R., and Ellen Greenblatt, eds. *Gay and Lesbian Library Service.* New York: McFarland, 1990.

Thistlethwaite, Polly J. "Gays and Lesbians in Library History." In *The Encyclopedia of Library History.* Wayne A. Wiegand and Donald J. Davis Jr., eds. New York: Garland, 1990.

See also Libraries and Archives; New Zealand; Stereotype

Libraries and Archives

One of the earliest and most prodigious collections of gay and lesbian materials took shape around the Institute for Sexual Science, founded in Berlin in 1919 by sexologist Magnus Hirschfeld. The institute was formed to serve as a center for research into sexual phenomena, primarily homosexuality and transvestism. The institute quickly developed a library and archive that became a repository for all kinds of anthropological, biological, ethnological, and statistical data and documentation, which attracted writers and scientists from around the world. But the institute came to an abrupt and tragic end with the rise of Nazism in Germany. Luckily, Hirschfeld's onetime lover and curator, Karl Giese, was able to rescue a portion of the library, parts of which found their way eventually to the Kinsey Institute Collection at Indiana University and to the Humanities Research Center at the University of Texas, by way of the British Sexological Society.

This dark chapter in gay, lesbian, and bisexual history illustrates both the precarious position of libraries and archives that choose to collect lesbian and gay materials and the important role that such collections play in securing the positions of gays, lesbians, and bisexuals in society. Fortunately, similar collections of materials have flourished around other gay, lesbian, and bisexual organizations.

The Institute for Sex Research was founded in 1947 by Alfred C. Kinsey of Indiana University as an interdisciplinary center for the study of human sexuality, gender, and reproduction. The institute swiftly began amassing a large collection with a strong focus on social and behavioral science materials dealing with sexual behavior and attitudes. A recent estimate of the institute's holdings reported that the collection contained 80,000 books and journals, 7,000 original works of art, 75,000 photographs, 6,500 reels of film, as well as a 55-cabinet archive of institutional and personal papers. Although the Kinsey collection includes gay, lesbian, and bisexual materials, it does not collect in this area exclusively.

Jim Kepner of the ONE Institute of Hollywood, California (the oldest ongoing gay and lesbian organization in the United States), formed the International Gay and Lesbian Archives in 1975. In 1994 ONE and the IGLA merged and affiliated themselves with the University of Southern California to form the ONE Institute International Gay & Lesbian Archives—which is reputedly the largest research collection in the world devoted to gay, lesbian, bisexual, and transgendered heritage and concerns. The collection includes some 15,000 books, pamphlets and scripts; 4,000 periodical titles; a clipping file with over one million items; 800 videos; hundreds of audio recordings, as well as personal and organizational papers (including those of the Mattachine Society). The institute also houses the Lesbian Legacy Collection and a museum of posters, buttons, T-shirts, and objets d'art.

Similarly in the early 1970s the Mariposa Education and Research Foundation started collecting and preserving periodicals, pamphlets, books, films, artwork, legal briefs, erotica, and diaries concerned with gay life since World War II. This collection was then donated to Cornell University in 1988, which, with an endowment from *Advocate* publisher David B. Goodstein, allowed the creation of the Human Sexuality Collection.

Barbara Grier began collecting lesbian literature in 1946 at the age of thirteen, and went on to form the Naiad Press in 1973. The Naiad Press Archives had grown to 26,000 items in 1982, and was donated in 1996 to the James C. Hormel Gay & Lesbian Center at the San Francisco Public Library. Among the great variety of materials in this collection are the personal correspondence of authors such as May Sarton, Jane Rule, and Mary Renault— as well as a large collection of unpublished manuscripts.

Another example of collections growing up around lesbian and gay organizations was the collection of the Gay Activists Alliance in New York City. After a fire in 1982 the GAA archive found its way to the International Gay Information Center (IGIC); in 1988 more than 100 boxes of materials documenting the gay rights movement in the United States from 1958 to 1969 were donated by the IGIC to the New York Public Library.

These examples are by no means the only collections of gay, lesbian, and bisexual materials available—there are hundreds of such library and archival collections around the world. The above collection histories illustrate the symbiotic relationship between archives and libraries when it comes to gay, lesbian, and bisexual materials. Often gay, lesbian, and bisexual organizations amass collections that are later incorporated into the larger collections of research or university libraries. If it were not for the efforts of these organizational and often grassroots archives, much of the material currently available would have been lost.

The Lesbian HerStory Archives of New York City has resolved not to bequeath its extensive holdings in lesbian history to a public or academic library in the conviction that only lesbian archivists supported by the lesbian community can be expected to "identify, preserve and protect the richness of our cultures with the knowledge, passion and integrity required." There are advantages of using a focused collection like the Lesbian HerStory Archive, the Gerber-Hart Archive in Chicago, the Canadian Gay Archives in Toronto, or the Bisexual Resource Center in Boston, since their focused col-

L lections allow researchers to locate easily additional pertinent information that they may not know existed. The large sexuality collection at the University of Indiana's Kinsey Institute or Cornell's Human Sexuality Collection do not provide this focus. However, since most archives are volunteer-run and community-based, large academic and research libraries can provide the institutional support and funding necessary to guarantee the long-term preservation of these research materials.

With the growth of queer studies in academia, many academic libraries have established collection development policies to regularly and aggressively acquire gay, lesbian, and bisexual publications. Among the academic libraries that currently stand out for their collections of books and/or serials are at the following universities: Harvard, Brown, Princeton, Cornell, Michigan, Northwestern, Stanford, and California, Berkeley.

Even with the explosion of gay, lesbian, and bisexual publishing in the decades since Stonewall, some libraries fail to develop collections in this area. A recent survey of 250 academic and public libraries revealed that 14 percent of the respondents carried no materials with gay or lesbian themes. Furthermore, of the 86 percent who did collect in this area, 50 percent had no more than 30 titles—a minuscule number in view of the approximately 1,000 gay, lesbian, and bisexual titles published annually; in 1992 alone there were 300 gay and lesbian magazines and 9,000 gay and lesbian books in print. Another study in 1988 found that the Library of Congress owned fewer than half the 375 titles randomly selected from a dozen gay and lesbian publishers.

The reasons for this blind spot in many library collections are complex and can be the result of several situations. Often librarians are unaware that gay, lesbian, and bisexual patrons exist in their communities. When they are aware, some librarians have difficulty choosing materials for an unfamiliar clientele. But the most common reason for not collecting such materials has been the tightening materials budgets of most libraries—as well as the fear that bad press could reduce their budgets even more.

Even once libraries have acquired gay, lesbian, and bisexual materials, access to these materials has often been hindered and restricted. Extreme examples include the British Library (then Museum), which segregated gay literature into a private case and omitted bibliographic records from their public catalog; the U.S. Library of Congress, which separated erotica into their Delta Collection; and the French Bibliothèque Nationale with its L'Enfer (Hell) Collection. Noncirculating and sometimes locked collections are often used to discourage vandalism, theft, or controversy—but often discourage and embarrass researchers who encounter them.

Access to gay, lesbian, and bisexual materials in libraries is further hampered by a lack of thorough indexing for such periodical literature. Kilpatrick found that only 22 percent of a core list of gay, lesbian, and bisexual periodicals were indexed—and only 19 percent of them were held by a reasonable number of libraries. *The 1990 Gay and Lesbian Periodicals Index* was an attempt to remedy this situation by indexing some 29 gay, lesbian, and bisexual periodicals, but it has not been published since.

The Library of Congress Subject Headings (LCSH) are the standard tool used to provide subject indexing in library catalogs and have been available to the public since 1898. Despite the first use of the word *homosexuality* in 1869 and its entry into the terminology of mainstream publications by the 1920s, this term was not approved as a subject heading until 1946. Similarly, the terms *lesbian* and *lesbianism* began to be used in 1870, but *lesbianism* did not appear in the LCSH until 1954—with *lesbians* having to wait until 1976. Sanford Berman of Hennepin Public Library and the Gay, Lesbian, and Bisexual Taskforce of the American Library Association continues to petition the Library of Congress to update the LCSH to reflect current usage.

Considering the history of library collections in regard to homosexuality, it is understandable why archives such as the Lesbian HerStory Archives would want to maintain their independence from large university and research collections. Nevertheless, the tremendous cooperative work that continues to be done around the world by gay, lesbian, and bisexual archives with libraries greatly improves the chances that gay, lesbian, and bisexual research materials will survive, for both present patrons and future scholars.   *Edward Summers*

Bibliography

Bryant, Eric. "Pride and Prejudice." *Library Journal* 120, no. 11 (1995): 37–39.

Embardo, Ellen E. "Gay and Lesbian Special Collections Libraries." In *Voices from the Underground*. Vol. 2. Ken Wachsberger, ed. Tempe, Ariz.: Mica Press, 1993.

Gough, Cal, and Ellen Greenblatt, eds. *Gay and Lesbian Library Service*. Jefferson, N.C.: McFarland, 1990.

Gough, Cal, Dee Michel, and Stephen Kline, eds. *Gays & Lesbians, Libraries & Archives: A Checklist of Publications, 1970–1990.* Chicago: American Library Association, 1991.

Greenberg, Alan M. *The 1990 Gay and Lesbian Periodicals Index.* Charlotte, N.C.: Integrity Indexing, 1992.

Kester, Norman G., ed. *Liberating Minds: The Stories and Professional Lives of Gay, Lesbian, and Bisexual Librarians and Their Advocates.* Jefferson, N.C.: McFarland, 1997.

Kilpatrick, Thomas. "A Critical Look at the Availability of Gay and Lesbian Periodical Literature in Libraries and Standard Indexing Services." *Serials Review* 22 (Winter 1996): 71–81.

Miller, Alan V. *Directory of the International Association of Lesbian and Gay Archives and Libraries.* Toronto: Canadian Gay Archives, 1987.

Tsang, Daniel C. "Homosexuality Research Collections." In *Libraries, Erotica, and Pornography.* Martha Cornog, ed. Phoenix, Ariz.: Oryx Press, 1991.

See also Gay Activists Alliance (GAA); Germany; Hirschfeld, Magnus; Homophile Movement; Kinsey, Alfred; Librarians; Mattachine Society; *One Magazine*

Ligon, Glenn (1960–)

Glenn Ligon was born in the Bronx, in New York City. He landed his first one-person show, "How It Feels to Be Colored Me," at an alternative art space in downtown Brooklyn in 1989. In the relatively brief period of time since that exhibition, he has emerged as one of the leading contemporary American artists working on issues of race, language, and desire. Ligon is best known for his black-on-white paintings in which appropriated texts are stenciled onto door-size canvases. In these works, the artist often repeats an especially charged sentence (e.g., Zora Neale Hurston's "I feel most colored when I am thrown against a sharp white background") until it verges, through the force of excess paint, on illegibility. The resulting paintings set up a visual, and almost visceral, tension between black identity and its forced invisibility.

In his recent work, Ligon has begun to address issues of gay desire while still attending to the specificity of African American experience. In *A Feast of Scraps* (1994–1998), for example, he inserts pornographic shots of black men, complete with invented captions ("Mother knew," "I fell out," "It's a process") into albums of family snapshots, some of which include the artist's own family. Ligon thus renders visible that which must be kept hidden, left unspoken, or otherwise repressed within traditional records of domestic and familial life. In *A Feast of Scraps*, unbidden erotic fantasies and sexual stereotypes suddenly—and altogether spectacularly—take their place beside graduation photographs, vacation snapshots, pictures of baby showers, birthday celebrations, and baptisms.

Like almost all of Ligon's art, this project draws out the secret histories and submerged meanings of inherited texts and images.   *Richard Meyer*

Bibliography

Conner, Kimberly Rae. "To Disembark: The Slave Narrative Tradition." *African American Review* (May 1996): 35–57.

Golden, Thelma, et al. *Black Male: Representations of Masculinity in Contemporary American Art.* Exhibit Catalog. New York: Whitney Museum of American Art, 1994.

A Feast of Scraps, 1994–1998, *photographs and text (detail). From Glenn Ligon,* Unbecoming. *Used with permission of Glenn Ligon.*

Ligon, Glenn. *Unbecoming*. Exhibit Catalog. Philadelphia: Institute of Contemporary Art, 1998.

Meyer, Richard, "Glenn Ligon: The Limits of Visibility." *Art/Text* (August–October 1997): 32–35.

See also African American Gay Culture; Art History

London

Gay communities have developed most strongly in Britain, as elsewhere, in large urban centers. London has been the largest city in Britain since the earliest rise of urbanization under the Roman occupation, from the mid-first century. Roman London is estimated to have had a population of perhaps fifty thousand at its peak, a level not recovered, after the collapse of the Roman Empire, until the high Middle Ages. It is only from that later period that the first written sources survive to tell us of what had most likely been true before, that London was a major center of sexual diversity. We cannot speak of gay culture in that period, unless dandified fashions are seen as having been the specialty of people of homosexual leanings, as was the accusation of Archbishop Anselm, against many of the courtiers of King William Rufus in the late eleventh century. Male prostitution would have developed in the context of London's being a major center for commodities and services of all kinds. Moreover, in London there were nobles free from family life on estates, as well as merchants with money to spend on luxuries. In this context we can envisage a gay subculture emerging through the operation of money in the context of city anonymity. Through the ensuing centuries opportunity flickered in a repressive social climate.

A typically ambiguous product of this world was Christopher Marlowe's play *Edward II* (1594), which has been held up, for example, by Derek Jarman, as the witness of one gay man to the tragedy of another. John Boswell and others working on premodern periods have preferred to talk of same-sex activity or affection, and this we can identify even if the modern gay self-identity was not to be created until the last one hundred years. From the late sixteenth century come references to "male stews." We should not imagine these as being brothels in the modern sense, but rather "low" taverns where clients could be entertained by rent boys, or where men who had picked each other up could have sex. The sodomite in contemporary satire was a rich, debauched man about town with a mistress on one arm and a catamite on the other. Buggery was mentioned in tracts along with other abominations of sexual excess, such as incest and rape. The aristocracy was particularly associated with such acts as part of a popular critique of luxury. By the eighteenth century the population of London had begun to expand substantially as had its prosperity. Men made assignations in parks and coffeehouses as well as attending "molly houses" for sex. Individuals might make only occasional visits to this clandestine world. The dangers of public exposure were great, ranging from the pillory to hanging, for capital punishment had been established for buggery since the time of Henry VIII. Nevertheless, those involved in selling sexual services in particular began to develop their own subculture, prominent features of which were a specialized argot, together with distinctive effeminacy involving the use of feminine terms of self-reference.

The fundamentals of this culture survived intact in essence to the 1950s, because while London's extent and wealth grew steadily, repression remained constant. Although the penalty for sodomy was reduced to imprisonment in 1861, the advent of an organized police force increased the chances of arrest, while public opinion had grown distinctly more censorious in all sexual matters. The tensions among luxury, knowledge of the wider world, and the prevailing moral code were intense. The downfall of the glitteringly fashionable playwright Oscar Wilde came about in these conditions. The main feature of the ensuing period was silence. Homosexuality was the love that dare not speak its name. The publication and televising of Quentin Crisp's autobiography, *The Naked Civil Servant,* was one of the more dramatic signs of changed mores in the late twentieth century. Crisp described taunts, flaunts, and haunts from pre– to post–World War II life in Soho, together with his brushes with authority, much as could a molly of a previous generation. The Wolfenden Report of 1957 advocated limited legalization of homosexual acts in private between men aged twenty-one or over. The aim was to bring the "problem" to the surface and address it by the medical profession. Yet the report was greeted as a "buggers' charter" by the popular press. Decriminalization was not to take place until 1967, when Parliament passed a private bill on the subject by just one vote.

Gay life in London today was made possible by this legislation. The Gay Liberation Front could organize, and in 1972 the first London gay pride "carnival" took place, attended by around one thousand people. *Gay News* and other publications such as *Come Together* were on sale. Despite such new openness, however, police activity continued to target cottaging (sex in public toilets), as well as cruising in the open. Paradoxically, the 1980s saw both the emergence of a more hostile political climate, after the liberalism of the 1970s, and the development of a large commercial gay scene in London. The government of Margaret Thatcher took increasingly draconian control of the public sector, including the imposition of clause 28 of the Local Government Act (1988), banning local "promotion" of homosexuality. But the same free-market government relaxed the operation of the private sector. London saw a commercial boom from which many young, upwardly mobile gay men in the financial and other service industries were ideally placed to benefit. At the same time, more late licenses began to be granted to venues, and the rave scene revivified clubs. London today has 150 or so gay bars, shops, and cafes.

On the other hand, vice laws ensure that pornography remains heavily censored, and prostitutes who advertise openly must call themselves "escorts." Tragically, along with the large concentration of gay men in London has come a high proportion of Britain's HIV cases. Nevertheless, the backlash that appeared to halt the shift in public opinion with the advent of AIDS seems to have abated. The age of consent has been lowered from twenty-one to eighteen. A large Labour majority in Parliament, including the first out gay cabinet minister, together with helpful judgments in the European courts, should, it is hoped, see Britain move toward equality for homosexuals. Public opinion in London is rather ahead of much of the rest of country in this, largely because there are so many gay people living in the capital that they, their fashions, and attitudes are familiar not just in such traditional strongholds as Soho, Earls Court, and Islington but all across central and inner-city London. *Dominic Janes*

Bibliography

Bray, Alan. *Homosexuality in Renaissance England.* London: Gay Men's Press, 1982.

Crisp, Quentin. *The Naked Civil Servant.* London: Cape, 1968.

Higgins, Patrick. *Heterosexual Dictatorship: Male Homosexuality in Postwar Britain.* London: Fourth Estate, 1996.

Power, Lisa. *No Bath but Plenty of Bubbles: An Oral History of the Gay Liberation Front, 1970–73.* London: Cassell, 1995.

Sanderson, Terry. *Mediawatch: The Treatment of Male and Female Homosexuality in the British Media.* London: Cassell, 1995.

Trumbach, Randolph. "London's Sodomites: Homosexual Behaviour and Western Culture in the Eighteenth Century." *Journal of Social History* 11 (1977–1978): 1–33.

See also Crisp, Quentin; Gay Liberation Front; Jarman, Derek; Marlowe, Christopher; Molly Houses; Sodomy Trials; Tearooms; Wilde, Oscar; Wolfenden Report

Lorrain, Jean (1855–1906)

Novelist, essayist, and poet, Jean Lorrain was born August 9, 1855, to haute bourgeoise parents in provinical Fécamp, France. After Catholic schooling, he moved to Paris, pursued literature, and soon became a leading French decadent.

His first book, *Le Sang des dieux* (1882), contains a section "Les Éphèbes" (dedicated to Flaubert) that celebrates classical love with poems for Ganymede, Alexander, Narcissus, Patroclus, and Antinöus and others. Gustave Moreau provided a frontispiece with Salome holding John the Baptist's head.

Lorrain became known as French Ambassador from Sodom and as such greeted Oscar Wilde on the Englishman's 1883 Paris visit. Lorrain's *Mousier de Phocas* (1901) parallels Wilde's *The Picture of Dorian Gray* (1891). Lorrain's bibliography is vast: seven books of poetry, twenty-five novels, seven plays, and hundreds of magazine articles. Lorrain wrote accounts of his travels to North Africa (1892–1893), the Pyrenees (1894–1895), Spain (1896), and Italy (1898). In his final years he retired to Nice, where he died June 30, 1906.

Sailors in Nice inspired two of his most homoerotic and greatest works: *Monsieur de Phocas* and *Le Vice errant.* Published in 1901, both combine homoerotic themes with necrophilia, drugs, flowers, perfume, and other lush artifacts. *Le Vice* celebrates the erotic tattoos of nude sailors, who become centerpieces for an elegant banquet.

Lorrain's presence may have exceeded his other creations. Partying with Rachilde ("La Marquise de Sade"), he wore leopard skin wrestler's trunks. He used English, German, or Russian nobles for the most decadent roles in his novels and poked fun at ideas of Aryan supremacy in his post-humously published *L'Aryenne* (1907). Lorrain avoided politics but his views tended to be conservative, as he opposed Zola and the Drefuysards.

Collette admired his outrageous artifice of cheap jewelry, red-white-green hair dye, scarves, and makeup. Philippe Jullian writes that "between Baudelaire and Cocteau, Lorrain was the drug writer; before Genet, he was the 'écrivain' pédéraste." (13).

Charles Shively

Bibliography

Birkett, Jennifer. *The Sins of the Fathers, Decadence in France, 1870–1914*. London: Quartet, 1986.

Jullian, Philippe. *Jean Lorrain ou le satiricon 1900*. Paris: Fayard, 1974.

Kingcaid, Renee A. *Neurosis and Narrative: The Decadent Short Fiction of Proust, Lorrain, and Rachilde*. Carbondale, Ill.: Southern Illinois University Press, 1992.

See also Alexander the Great; Decadence; Flowers and Birds; French Literature; Ganymede; Sade, Marquis de; Wilde, Oscar

Los Angeles

Not until after the Civil War did gay life blossom in Los Angeles. In the wake of Oscar Wilde's 1882–1883 Western lecture tour, many young men took to swaying about in fur coats, yellow gloves, and green carnations. But Wilde's later trials shocked a naive public into taking a closer look at these amusing young men, and gay life went back in the closet.

In 1910, Cecil B. DeMille made *The Squaw Man* in a quiet, somewhat "arty" L.A. suburb called Hollywood. Within two years, Hollywood's Prospect Avenue was a grand place to cruise. Out-of-work cowboys lined up there, hoping to be extras in the movies. By the time Prospect Avenue was paved and renamed Hollywood Boulevard, the city was world famous for sin, including the one that dared not speak its name. Rudolph Valentino was called a "Pink Powder Puff" for wearing wigs and beauty patches and, perhaps more shocking, a wristwatch in the modern-dress *Camille*. Even George O'Brien, all-American boy, posed stark naked for publicity stills, although on screen the Hays Office made him keep his pants on in such classics as *Sunrise* for gay director F. W. Murnau. In 1929 a fad for drag shows swept Hollywood, packing gays and straights into BBB's and other clubs.

But such antics clashed with the grave years of the Depression. By 1933 all but La Boheme had closed, and the more openly gay celebrities of the now "talking" movies, like wisecracking Billy Haines, had to leave film. For George Cukor, Cary Grant, Cole Porter, and others, it was back into the closet. Cary Grant portrayed Cole Porter in 1938's *Night and Day*, but with nary a hint of lavender.

Gay life in L.A. at this time ranged from the sleazy waterfront bars of Long Beach to the bedrooms of the very wealthy, which could be even sleazier, as when the heir to the Teapot Dome fortune shot his handsome valet and then himself, although (after large sums of money had been dispersed) the police report stated just the opposite. Gay taste and great wealth could combine to create the sublime; the male heir to the Oviatt fortune built a splendiferous art deco penthouse, which had a reverse step pyramid ceiling in the library and, opposite the bathroom, a wall of 8 x 10 glossies signed by everyone who was anyone in the gay Hollywood of the thirties.

No American city was changed more by World War II than Los Angeles. The entire county became one huge military-industrial complex; San Pedro swarmed with shipbuilders and servicemen waiting to depart for the South Pacific; and, of course, there was all that jiving at the Hollywood Canteen, just off the cruising circuit which ran several blocks along Selma Avenue. Police were reluctant to arrest boys here, since they were considered to be out for a last fling before being shipped to battle. It wasn't all fun, however. Wartime clashes in downtown L.A. between enlisted men and Mexican youths in zoot suits entailed a strong homophobic element, with Hispanic teenagers being stripped of their "draped shapes" and left naked in the street.

Postwar L.A., seemingly all sunshine and surfer boys, epitomized the American dream. Many a gay serviceman moved to L.A. or San Francisco instead of going back to his hometown. Gay bars sprang up everywhere, especially in the then unincorporated area known as West Hollywood. They were easy to find if you were in on the code: any bar named for a color and an animal—the Blue Parrot, the Golden Bull, the Red Raven—was almost guaranteed to be gay. However, police entrapment was common, although it was not until the fifties that such bars were numerous enough to merit broader attention. Self-awareness paralleled police awareness.

Los Angeles also pioneered the efforts of homosexuals to be taken seriously. The first meetings of the Mattachine Society were in L.A. living rooms where Harry Hay, Jim Kempner, Morris Kight, and Rudy Gernreich variously made early moves toward acceptance, or at least tolerance. They battled McCarthyism, which hated "homos" second only to "commies," and Hollywood's attempts to eradicate them were second only to Washington's.

But widespread gay awareness came about through the physique magazines. The earliest one, *Physique Pictorial*, started by photographer Bob Mizer, sold its first issues from the World Newsstand at the historically homosexual corner of Hollywood and Cahuenga in 1951. By the mid-fifties the "muscle mags" were sending out upwards of a million copies every year, filled with images clearly aimed at a gay male audience, by L.A.-based artists and photographers such as Bruce of Los Angeles. The homoerotic pictorial and later pornography industries have remained centered in L.A. throughout the second half of the twentieth century, with much of it moving to the San Fernando Valley in recent years.

For twenty years after World War II, Southern California gay life focused on the beaches. Laguna Beach's "Tournament of the Masters" recreated famous works of art using live people and always included well-built men posing as, for example, *The Thinker,* wearing nothing but a coat of bronze paint or, without the paint, as Adam or Hercules. Further up the coast was the gay epicenter, Muscle Beach, flanked by Venice Boardwalk and Santa Monica Pier, where bodybuilders flexed their muscles and party givers handed out invitations on the sand. L.A.'s palm trees and lifeguards drew gay men from all over, both lesser known people and celebrities. David Hockney and Christopher Isherwood came from England; John Rechy and James Dean from "the rest" of the United States. A few, like detective novelist Joseph Hanson, actually grew up there.

The 1969 Stonewall revolution started in Greenwich Village, but Los Angeles carried it forward with the first Gay Pride parade, held in 1970 over the objection of Police Chief Ed Davis, who felt it would be like "permitting a parade of thieves and burglars." But one community of L.A. gay men was already substantially well organized before Stonewall—the leather community. Local queer motorcycle clubs began in the late fifties, formed by gays rebelling against the cashmere sweater set. By the sixties they had their own bars, such as the Explorer in Silverlake, a neighborhood preferred by many leathermen.

Gay bars diversified as L.A. grew. Bars where blacks and whites could cruise each other, like the Jupiter, were popular until the 1965 Watts riots, which caused a temporary rift among black and white gays. But by the seventies they were back, along with salsa bars for the Latino crowd and bars catering to Asians of all nationalities. The bars may have been specialized, but the clientele could vary. In the late seventies, the notorious leather hangout Ten-Seventy was on Western, just around the corner from Faces, a drag show bar on Route 66 (Santa Monica Boulevard) with a high percentage of minority patrons. Many men would alternate between the bars.

The seventies, spanning the period between Stonewall and AIDS, was the "break-out" decade. Angelenos took their shirts off and danced to disco far into the night at glitter clubs like Studio One, where even the toilets were dazzling (the main urinal was a circular trough surrounding a glowing fish tank). Then they would head to the sex clubs, where they took their pants off for even closer physical contact with a roomful of men. It wasn't all about sex, however. Openly gay businesses now ranged from the predictable clothing stores, book stores, health clubs, and restaurants, to banks and auto repair shops. By the end of the decade, West Hollywood was incorporated, becoming in 1984 the first "gay" city (though even in West Hollywood gay men and women only make up a large constituency, not a majority), with Steve Schute, a former nude model, as the new city's first mayor. TV helicopter views of the tens of thousands who attended the Gay Pride parades and Halloween celebrations of WeHo were beamed worldwide.

As one of the three largest gay communities in the world, Los Angeles was hit hard by AIDS. Unlike other cities, the local government never closed the sex businesses, but it was slow to respond to the stricken. L.A.'s gay community was more geographically diffuse and ethnically diverse than elsewhere, so it never generated the intensity of demand for action that was created by such groups as ACT UP, Radical Faeries, and Queer Nation. But, being home to Cedar/Sinai Hospital, UCLA Medical, and a number of other large hospital complexes, the city specialized in experimental treatments, helping to pioneer the AZT cocktail approach. Meanwhile, gay social life, which had imploded during the first years of AIDS shock and fear, slowly began to reinvent itself with many calling for a community less reliant on drugs and orgasms.

AIDS-related deaths of celebrities like Rock Hudson and Liberace made gay men more visible to many Americans, and such losses helped to break taboos, even in Hollywood. At the Academy Awards, gay winners began publicly thanking same-sex partners and, after William Hurt and Tom Hanks won Oscars for gay roles, a horde of gay characters began appearing on the screen. Many gay and lesbian performers came out off screen as well as on.

Los Angeles is currently undergoing further cultural shifts which affect its gay inhabitants. The aerospace and defense industries have recently been displaced by the entertainment industry as the number one employer in Los Angeles County. Now, even family-oriented Disney offers generous domestic partnership terms to its gay employees and holds Gay Nights at its theme parks in the face of fundamentalist boycotts.   *F. Valentine Hooven III*

Bibliography

Anger, Kenneth. *Hollywood Babylon*. New York: Dell, 1975.

Duberman, Martin, Martha Vicinus, and George Chauncey, Jr., eds. *Hidden From History: Reclaiming the Gay and Lesbian Past*. New York: Penguin Books, 1990.

Friedrich, Otto. *City of Nets: A Portrait of Hollywood in the 40s*. New York: Harper & Row, 1986.

Hooven, F. Valentine, III. *Beefcake*. Cologne: Benedikt Taschen Verlag, 1995.

Kammerman, Roy. *L.A. Superlatives*. New York: Warner Books, 1987.

Mann, William J. *Wisecracker: The Life and Times of William Haines*. New York: Viking Penguin, 1998.

Marcus, Eric. *Making History*. New York: Harper Collins, 1992.

This entry was possible thanks to personal interviews with Ken Bartley, Mark Bramlette, Miles Evrett, Jim Kempner, Bob Mizer, and Donald E. Watson.

See also Athletic Model Guilds; Bathhouses and Sex Clubs; Bruce of Los Angeles; Chicano and Latino Gay Cultures; Circuit Party Scene; Cukor, George; Film; Film Stars; Hay, Harry; Hockney, David; Homophile Movement; Isherwood, Christopher; Leathermen; Marches and Parades; Mattachine Society; Mizer, Bob; Rechy, John

Love Poetry, the Petrarchan Tradition

The poetry of Francesco Petrarca (1304–1374) stands in a tradition that reaches from Ovid to Dante and the medieval troubadours. Petrarch, as he came to be known in the English-speaking world, gave to the ancient traditions of writing about love and sex a new twist with far-reaching consequences. His cycle of poems entitled *Il Canzoniere* (1374) became the most influential single work in the history of Western love poetry. From the fourteenth century onward up to and including our own time, he has been imitated, expanded upon, borrowed from, and contradicted by the most distinguished poets writing in any European language. Petrarca's theme is the anguish of an unfulfilled desire for a beautiful and chaste beloved. A basic paradox that inspires both the *Canzoniere* and all poetry in its wake lies in the fact that the urges of both the lover's soul and his body are constantly and simultaneously addressed in a most masochistic way: the beloved's chastity and purity are admired; at the same time, every single part of her or his body is described minutely in an attempt to possess her or him sexually, if only in a fantasy. The lover's futile hopes find expression in a great variety of metaphorical expressions, all of which illustrate the paradoxical experience that there is pleasure in pain. There is thus a sado-masochistic quality inherent in most poetry in the Petrarchan strain. Sonnet No. 14 from Samuel Daniel's *Delia* cycle, for instance, reads like an extended scenario for a sadomasochistic play session. Images of cruelty, violence, war, sexually inspired hurting and healing, hunting and killing (i.e., provoking orgasm), and bringing back to life again (i.e., arousing sexually) abound in many poems from the sixteenth and seventeenth centuries. In an obsessive attempt at incorporating one's beloved, the detailed description of his or her body often entails physical torture, anatomical dissection, and surgery.

Both Petrarca's *Canzoniere* and most of the poetry in its wake are heterosexual—at least on the surface—but there are notable exceptions: Richard Barnfield's "Sonnets" and his "Affectionate Shepherd" openly celebrate homosexual love and sex, and Shakespeare's sonnets are the most distinguished example of openly homoerotic—if not outright homosexual—verse, a fact that has been played down by heterosexist literary criticism throughout the centuries.

In recent years critics writing from a position sympathetic to the gay and lesbian cause have changed that bias considerably. In the overall project of queering heterosexual writing, many critics have now started to look at older poetry in new ways to make it available for gay or lesbian interpretations. Such new gay and lesbian readings offer themselves easily in the case of Petrarchan poems, as a substantial number of them do not specify gender grammatically: "I" and "you" are used far more frequently than "he" or "she." On the other hand, the fantasies displayed by those poems and the imagery they draw on are often explicitly homosexual: images of a polymorphously perverse (in the Freudian sense) sexuality inspire the poems of Edmund Spenser (*The Fairie Queene*), John Donne (*Holy Sonnets*), or Richard Crashaw, whose devotional lyrics depict the naked body of Christ on the cross in language that resembles twentieth-century gay pornography.

Bruce R. Smith provides the as yet most substantial and judicious rereading of English Renaissance literature from a gay perspective. Joseph Pequigney writes about Shakespeare's sonnets on the assumption that they depict a homosexual relationship. Eve Kosotsky Sedgwick shows how heterosexual Petrarchan poetry served as a currency for the establishing of homosocial bonds between men in the English Renaissance. Jonathan Sawday discusses Petrarchan conventions of poetic praise of the body of the beloved in terms of medical anatomy, geographical discovery, and colonial expansion and its function as a form of homosocial mediation among men. Carol Siegel traces the male masochist throughout English literary history, and Gregory Woods—a distinguished gay poet himself—writes uncompromisingly about the functions of the male body in twentieth-century English and American poetry, supplying detailed analyses of the poetry of D. H. Lawrence, Hart Crane, W. H. Auden, Allen Ginsberg, and Thom Gunn, all of whom explore the paradox of body and soul in gay love and do it in the best Petrarchan tradition of giving pride of place to the body. The Petrarchan imagery of pleasure-in-pain is conspicuously present in a substantial part of that poetry, among whose immediate forerunners are the French poets Arthur Rimbaud and Paul Verlaine, who both individually and together wrote a number of openly gay poems in praise of the most intimate parts of the male body and the significance of sexual love. Their jointly written "Le Sonnet du trou du cul"—the octet is by Verlaine, while Rimbaud contributed the concluding sestet—is a tour de force of gay poetry in the Petrarchan tradition: both a parody and a new enactment of the blazon (i.e., an inventory of the physical attractions of one's beloved), it reuses standard Petrarchan language in an attempt to identify the act of poetry with the act of sex. Such is the concern also of their American contemporary Walt Whitman in

his long poem entitled *Leaves of Grass*. In this most famous American poem Whitman extensively inventories body parts ("I Sing the Body Electric"), explores their vulnerability ("The Sleepers"), and in the Calamus section expresses his conviction that spiritual gay relationships can be achieved only through the sensations of the body. Whitman can safely be considered the one major innovator of Petrarchism, a "Petrarch of a newly ritual poetics," as Roland Greene calls him. Whitman's poetry is still an example for many contemporary gay poets. The 1993 edition of *The New Princeton Encyclopedia of Poetry and Poetics* (s.v. "Love Poetry") provides succinct and judicious information on twentieth-century love poetry from a decidedly gay-friendly perspective.   *Christian A. Gertsch*

Bibliography

Dubrow, Heather. *Echoes of Desire: English Petrarchism and Its Counterdiscourses.* Itahca, N.Y.: Cornell University Press, 1995.

Greene, Roland. *Post-Petrarchism: Origins and Innovations of the Western Lyric Sequence.* Princeton, N.J.: Princeton University Press, 1991.

Pequigney, Joseph. *Such Is My Love: A Study of Shakespeare's Sonnets.* Chicago: University of Chicago Press, 1985.

Preminger, Alexander, and T.V.F. Brogan, eds. *The New Princeton Encyclopedia of Poetry and Poetics.* Princeton, N.J.: Princeton University Press, 1993, 705–10.

Rambuss, Richard. "Pleasure and Devotion: The Body of Jesus and Seventeenth Century Religious Lyric." In *Queering the Renaissance.* Jonathan Goldberg, ed. Durham, N.C.: Duke University Press, 1994.

Rimbaud, Arthur, and Paul Verlaine. *Lover's Cock and Other Gay Poems.* San Francisco: Gay Sunshine Press, 1979.

Sawday, Jonathan. *The Body Emblazoned: Dissection and the Human Body in Renaissance Culture.* London: Routledge, 1995.

Sedgwick, Eve Kosofsky. *Between Men: English Literature and Male Homosocial Desire.* New York: Columbia University Press, 1985.

Siegel, Carol. *Male Masochism: Modern Revisions of the Story of Love.* Bloomington, Ind.: Indiana University Press, 1995.

Smith, Bruce R. *Homosexual Desire in Shakespeare's England: A Cultural Poetics.* Chicago: University of Chicago Press, 1988.

L

Woods, Gregory. *Articulate Flesh: Male Homo-eroticism and Modern Poetry*. New Haven: Yale University Press, 1987.

See also Auden, W. H.; Barnfield, Richard; Crane, Hart; English Literature; French Literature; Ginsberg, Allen; Gunn, Thom; Italian Literature; Rimbaud, Arthur; Sadomasochism; Shakespeare, William; U.S. Literature; Verlaine, Paul

Ludlam, Charles (1943–1987)

Actor, playwright, director, producer, and dramatic theorist Charles Ludlam is one of the key figures in contemporary American theater and in queer theater. Ludlam's life has been well documented in the posthumous collection of his essays and opinions, *Ridiculous Theatre: Scourge of Human Folly* (1992).

Born of Catholic parents in Floral Park, Long Island (New York), raised across from a movie theater, Ludlam claimed to have been converted to theater at the age of six, when he got lost at the Mineola Fair and wandered into a Punch and Judy show. Ludlam studied theater at Hofstra University, where his acting teachers did not know what to do with his pre-1960s long hair and flamboyant personality. He did not fit into the mold of naturalistic acting, which was de rigueur in the American theater in the 1950s: "I had to create a theatre where I could exist."

After Hofstra, Ludlam moved across the East River to lower Manhattan. He had been inspired as a teenager by the early poetic, imagistic work of Julian Beck and Judith Malina at the Living Theatre, an antidote to the naturalism of Broadway, television, and serious American film of the time. Within a year of graduating from Hofstra, Ludlam joined the troupe at the Play-House of the Ridiculous, run by playwright Ronald Tavel and director John Vaccaro. Tavel's work, involving a camp theatricality, drag, parody, and satire, was the perfect environment for Ludlam to find himself as performer and writer. When Tavel and Vaccaro split up, Ludlam became writer as well as actor for the Play-House. During rehearsals for Ludlam's second play, *Conquest of the Universe* (1967), the temperamental Vaccaro fired him. Over half of the rest of the actors left in protest and joined Ludlam to found the Ridiculous Theatre Company, opening with *When Queens Collide*, which was *Conquest of the Universe* under another title.

From the founding of the Ridiculous Theatre Company in 1967, Ludlam became impresario (he was a gifted fund-raiser), playwright, director, and star of a stable theater company, writing at least one play a year. The company had its first tour of Europe in 1971, its first permanent theatrical home in 1974. By 1978, the company was based in its permanent home in Greenwich Village.

Meanwhile, as Ludlam's company became a highly respected, if never respectable, theatrical institution, Ludlam emerged as a theatrical sage, publishing articles and manifestos in major dramatic publications and teaching playwriting at Yale and New York Universities. Ludlam and his Ridiculous Theatre were taken seriously. He was invited to direct at the Santa Fe Opera and the New York Shakespeare Festival (*Titus Andronicus*). *The Mystery of Irma Vep* (1984) won critical plaudits and awards and has become a staple of regional and university theater. At the height of his career, Ludlam died of AIDS-related infections in 1987. The Ridiculous Theatre continues under the directorship of Ludlam's lover and colleague, Everett Quinton.

Ludlam's theater is above all theatrical. Built from bits of pop culture (old movies, Victorian penny dreadfuls) and high classics (*Camille, Hedda Gabler, Medea*), it giddily mixes serious elements with hilarity. Drag has been a crucial aspect of the work of Ludlam and his theater, but never merely for its own sake: "I pioneered the idea that female impersonation could be serious acting, an approach to character." When Ludlam played Marguerite Gautier in *Camille*, his low-cut gown revealed a hairy chest. Ludlam was not attempting a convincing drag act but was on one level a man trying honestly to portray a female character, while acknowledging the physical absurdity of the travesty. Such duality was the essence of Ludlam's theater.

The Ridiculous Theatre Company was unapologetically, in-your-face queer, a crucial antidote to the solemnity of so much gay drama and to the bland picture of gayness offered in film and television. Ludlam was totally uninterested in the problems of gay men fitting into the mainstream—he was uninterested in the mainstream. "It's the theater that is queer," he claimed, and his theatrical work was for everyone.

Ludlam's death was a front-page story in the *New York Times*. At the age of forty-four, he was a theatrical eminence. Since Ludlam's death all his plays and writings on the theater have been published.
John M. Clum

Bibliography

Ludlam, Charles. *Theatre of the Ridiculous: Scourge of Human Folly*. New York: Theatre Communications Group, 1992.

See also AIDS Performance; Camp; Theater: Premodern and Early Modern

Ludwig (Louis) II, King of Bavaria (1845–1886)

Ludwig II was born on August 25, 1845, at Nymphenburg Palace, Munich, the elder son of King Maximilian II of Bavaria and Marie of Prussia. After his succession to the throne in 1864, he worked for a reconciliation between Austria and Prussia and was instrumental in the creation of the German Empire following the Franco-Prussian War of 1870–1871.

Disappointed with the cultural and political situation of his time, Ludwig, a sentimental dreamer and a man of extravagant tastes, soon began to create an eccentric world of his own. Chancellor Otto von Bismarck's financial concessions, granted in return for support of his greater political plans, allowed Ludwig to pursue the construction of several elaborate castles (Linderhof 1869–1878; Neuschwanstein, 1869–1886; Herrenchiemsee, 1878–1885), despite a vast and ever-growing personal debt.

Rumors about the king's homosexuality surfaced even during his brief engagement to his cousin, Princess Sophie, daughter of Duke Max of Bavaria. Lacking desire for women and even disliking their company, Ludwig behaved excessively coldly toward his fiancée as his panic grew at the thought of marriage. Though haunted by an acute sense of guilt, he made little secret of his infatuations with men, including his lifelong worship of the composer Richard Wagner, his love for the younger actor Josef Kainz, and his need for an entourage of menservants who more and more became his closest companions.

On June 9, 1886, following a medical evaluation, Ludwig II was declared insane, arrested, and removed to Schloss Berg. Four days later, he drowned in Lake Starnberg together with his psychiatrist, Bernhard von Gudden, who tried to save his life.   *Christoph Lorey*

Bibliography

Blunt, Wilfrid. *The Dream King: Ludwig II of Bavaria*. London: Hamish Hamilton, 1970.
McIntosh, Christopher. *The Swan King: Ludwig II of Bavaria*. London: Allen Lane, 1982.
Prinz, Friedrich. *Ludwig II. Ein königliches Doppelleben*. Berlin: Siedler, 1993.

See also Germany; Wagner, Richard

Lully, Jean-Baptiste (1632–1687)

French composer, born Giovanni Battista Lulli, arrived in France from his native Tuscany in March 1646. On February 23, 1653, at age twenty, he danced for the first time with the fourteen-year-old Louis XIV, who appointed him royal "composer of instrumental music" three weeks later. On May 16, 1661, he became superintendent of music at court and was granted French nationality seven months later, changing his name officially (and rewriting his humble family background). His marriage on July 24, 1662, to Madeleine Lambert, the daughter of court composer Michel Lambert, temporarily calmed rumors concerning his "Italian tastes." They had six children: three sons, who all became mediocre musicians, and three daughters.

Lully was the leading French composer from 1655 until his death, exercising a profound influence over all musical activities at court: theater, opera, ballet, concerts, religious services in the royal chapel, and the publication of music. His skills as a violinist, dancer, and organizer allowed him to discipline the famous group of "24 violins" (along with his own elite musicians, the "Little Band") into the most rigorous and competent orchestra in Europe, thereby providing endless dance music and theatrical entertainments for the king. He is also credited with having single-handedly created French opera. His musical skills enabled him to find the exact mixture of pompous simplicity, melodic elegance, and French grace that pleased the king, and that mix became politically significant as "the French style" was increasingly imitated all over Europe.

Nevertheless, Lully's scandalous private life was always the subject of gossip. He seems not to have taken pains to hide his homosexual behavior. This led to many intrigues against him. Assessment of these attacks is now particularly difficult since professional jealousies led easily to such calumnies and played into the hands of the powerful conservative religious group, headed by Madame de Maintenon (the king's morganatic wife from late 1683 onward). In 1685, a major scandal broke out, confirmed by various documents. It now appears to be the high point of a moral crusade, a concerted attempt to break up the influence of *les sodomites* at court. The Abbé Bourdaloue had preached a sermon at Versailles against the dangers to youth of "vice." Several of the most notorious homosexuals (the duc de Vendôme, the duc de Gramont, the comte de Guise, the chevalier de Tilladet, the marquis de Biran, and the comte de Tallard) had, around 1678, founded a secret confraternity of sodomites. The young Prince de Conti and the eighteen-year-old Comte de Vermandois (one of Louis XIV's sons with Louise de la Vallière) had joined the group around 1681. In 1682, when Louis XIV found out, the prince was exiled; the frail young Vermandois, however, was publicly whipped in front of the court and died shortly after.

Lully, known in his lifetime as "Baptiste," had been careful never to join the secret society, but his preferences were an open secret, as is shown by the following quatrain: "Un jour l'Amour dit à sa mère / Pourquoi ne suis-je pas vêtu? / Si Baptiste me voit tout nu / C'en est fait de mon derrière" (One day Cupid said to his mother / "Why am I not wearing any clothes? / If Baptiste sees me naked / My backside will be lost"; in Bibliothèque nationale de France Ms. fr 12644, p. 191). In January 1685, Lully was accused of impropriety with one of the royal music pages, a boy named Brunet, who lived in Lully's house. (An earlier page with whom he seems also to have had a relationship was called Lafarge.) Brunet was exceptionally handsome, according to contemporary street ballads, which comment with a certain malicious glee on how attractive he was from behind. Louis XIV (whose younger brother was openly homosexual) now told Lully that he could no longer count on his protection. A police raid ended up with "little Brunet" being taken away and (according to the *Journal* of the marquis de Dangeau, January 16, 1685) confined to the Saint-Lazare monastery. There, the "good fathers" were instructed to flog him into submission. As a result, he named many other sodomites with whom he had associated. Brunet was saved from a worse fate only by the fact that one of the boys whose name was thus disclosed turned out to be the son of the head of police. A surviving vaudeville commemorates this incident: "Monsieur de Lully est affligé / De voir son Brunet fustigé; / Il est jaloux qu'un Père (eh bien!) / Visite son derrière, / Vous m'entendrez bien" (Monsieur de Lully is all worked up / To see his Brunet beaten up; / He's jealous that a Father (heigh ho!) / Should pay a visit to his [Brunet's] backside, / If you get my meaning").

A surviving poem by Saint-Evremond likens Lully to Orpheus, but comments that "if Lully one day went down into the underworld, with full powers to release and forgive, a young man who was a criminal would be freed from his chains, while Euridice would keep hers."

Lully's last two stage works, *Acis et Galatée* (1686) and *Achille et Polyxène*, both had librettos written by Jean Galbert de Campistron (1656–1723), a protégé of the duc de Vendôme and also a member of the same "infamous" circle. These works would therefore appear to be among the first that might be considered as a kind of gay collaboration between two major artists of their age.

Lully had been ennobled in 1681. A contemporary description mentions that he was "of dark complexion, had little eyes, a large nose and his mouth was large and good-looking; he was very nearsighted and was of small, stocky build." He died ten weeks after hitting his toe with his conducting baton on January 8, 1687; an abscess formed and, because he refused to allow the surgeon to remove the toe, gangrene spread rapidly. He died an extremely rich man, the owner of five Parisian houses, two country properties, and a vast amount of cash.

Davitt Moroney

Bibliography

Levy, Maurice. *Les Bûchers de Sodome*. Paris: Fayard, 1985.

Masson, Chantal. "Journal du marquis de Dangeau, 1684–1720." *Recherches sur la musique française classique* 2 (1961–1962).

Prunières, Henry. "La Vie scandaleuse de Jean-Baptiste Lully." *Mercure de France* 115 (1916).

See also France; Music and Musicians 1: Classical Music; Orléans, Monsieur Philippe, duc d'

Lynes, George Platt (1907–1955)

Pale, delicate, and smitten with celebrity, George Platt Lynes partied his way to fame as one of the most important gay photographers of the twentieth century.

As if he knew he had less lifetime than most, Lynes rocketed out of New Jersey to Paris in 1925, befriending Gertrude Stein, Jean Cocteau, and anyone else who was a cultural icon of the time. He was eighteen and, being the son of a minister who had scrimped to send him to expensive private schools, he was a very naive eighteen at that, but he was not going to let anything stand in his way of becoming a major writer. He returned to the United States to attend Yale University, but by 1928 he was back in Paris. No longer so naive, this time he traveled in a *ménage à trois* with Glenway Wescott and Monroe Wheeler, actually a *ménage à quatre*, since he also brought his camera and began the first of his celebrity portraits by shooting Stein and Alice B. Toklas.

Back in the States, he started a bookstore and publishing house in Englewood, New Jersey, which published Hemingway and other top authors to great success. But Lynes was discovering that his real love was not the word but the image, so he settled in New York's Greenwich Village and opened a photography studio. In exhibitions of the early thirties, Lynes's highly stylized photographs hung alongside Cecil Beaton, Man Ray, and Alfred Stieglitz. His dramatic combination of expressionistic lighting with surrealistic props and settings soon had a large clientele coming to him for portraits (Christopher Isherwood), advertising shots (Saks Fifth Avenue), and fashion layouts (*Harper's Bazaar*). "But the theater, especially modern dance and ballet, gave Lynes his most important commissions during the thirties and forties, particularly Lincoln Kirstein's New York City Ballet, for whom he did some of his most unforgettable photographs. Though he had already begun to photograph the nude male, those were not on public display.

Lynes seemed content with various sexual encounters rather than with true lovers, and many of his short-lived passions metamorphosed into long-term friendships. Then, early in World War II, he met George Tichenor, a Jersey boy with sultry dark looks. Tichenor became the photographer's studio assistant, posing nude for him but resisting his sexual advances. In 1942, he joined the ambulance corps and was killed in North Africa. Lynes never quite regained his prewar high spirits after that, though he took George's more amenable brother, Jonathan, to bed briefly.

In fact, after the war nothing seemed right for Lynes. He was bored with fashion, turning down more and more projects. Abstract expressionism and International-style architecture were rapidly become "the new look" of the fifties, sweeping aside the dated Art Deco and surrealism epitomized by the work of Lynes. He tried a major change by becoming the head of *Vogue*'s new Hollywood division, but it was a disaster. Never one to pay the slightest heed to financial matters, Lynes was forced to declare bankruptcy, and in 1949 he returned to Manhattan.

In 1950, he had a final triumph, shooting the dancers of George Balanchine's *Orpheus* wearing nothing but the masks and props of Isamu Noguchi. However, the board of directors was offended by Lynes's nude photos of the dancers and, after his old friend Lincoln Kirstein was angered by his demand for more money, even the New York City Ballet dropped him.

Living on money borrowed from relatives and friends, Lynes continued to lavishly decorate cheap apartments, where he gave one flamboyant party after another, working hard to live up to his own self-description: "I don't have an unpretentious bone in my body." His myriad friends ranged across the arts from Paul Cadmus to Katherine Ann Porter. His strenuous efforts to get to know the artistically prominent names of his time may look on the surface like celebrity scalp hunting but, from Gertrude and Alice on, they unanimously remained his friends as long as he and they lived.

Toward the end of his life, especially after being diagnosed with lung cancer, Lynes reached an unexpected decision for a man of his generation by concluding that his future reputation was in his male nudes. He destroyed many of the negatives of his carefully staged fashion and art photographs, and he helped Alfred Kinsey choose two hundred of his nudes for the Kinsey Institute's famed archives, emphasizing his later work, when his often heavy-handed stylizing had been gradually abandoned. By the early fifties, he was photographing naked men so simply and uncompromisingly that the images still look shockingly modern.

But he was wrong to think his once-secret nudes were his only lasting creations. Today his portrait, fashion, and art photographs are widely appreciated for wit and style, but the unsung portion of his legacy was his fostering of friendship and community among all manner of artists from the late twenties to the mid-fifties. By his enthusiastic fomenting of the fun and freedom of bohemian Greenwich Village, who knows how many works of art in how many fields are indirectly the gift of George Platt Lynes?

F. Valentine Hooven III

Bibliography

Crump, James. *George Platt Lynes, Photographs from the Kinsey Collection*. Boston: Little, Brown, 1993.

Ellenzweig, Allen. *The Homoerotic Photograph*. New York: Columbia University Press, 1992.

L

Green, J., and J. Friedman. *American Photography*. New York: Harry Abrams, 1984.

Leddick, David. *Naked Men, Pioneering Mail Nudes, 1935–1955*. New York: Rizzoli International, 1997.

Sternweiler, A., and H. G. Hannesen. *Good-bye to Berlin? 100 Jahre Schwulenbewegung*. Berlin: Verlag Rosa Winkler, 1997.

Waugh, Thomas. *Hard to Imagine*. New York: Columbia University Press, 1996.

See also Cadmus, Paul; Cocteau, Jean; Fashion; Isherwood, Christopher; Kinsey, Alfred C.; Kirstein, Lincoln; Photography

M

Machismo

From the Spanish *macho* (male) and the Latin *ismo* (doctrine, or tradition of thought). In Latin America *machismo* refers to the ideology that informs the practices of the *macho* man. To be *macho* is to assume a particular position in the gender order. It is, therefore, a historical and socially determined position, constructed in relation to other positions available to men and women. Among some Latin American scholars and others who work in Latin America, *machismo* has been used to mean "a field of productive relations" (Lancaster 19) among men and between men and women, a definition close to the notion "patriarchy" or "gender order."

In Mexico, the word *macho* had positive connotations in the past, meaning a good provider and a responsible father. According to some academics, the word broadened its meaning during the golden age of Mexican filmmaking in the 1940s and 1950s. That cultural production depicted Mexican male heroes who used to boast about their masculinities and their "Mexicanness." A poetics of manhood expressed in a particular set of practices became associated with the word *macho*: heavy drinking, womanizing, passionate loving, homosociality, emotional closure, risk taking, and homophobia.

The conflation of these poetics and Mexican nationalism in cultural production gave birth to a stereotype of Mexican and, by extension, Latin American males that still persists outside and inside the region. Many reductionist essays have been written in order "to account for" this character. Most of them have traced its "origin" to the traumatic experience of the Spanish conquest (symbolized by the rape of Indian women by Spanish soldiers) in the *mestizo* descendant (of mixed origin). In general, the *macho* is presented in this (mainly philosophical or psychoanalytic) literature as a man with a deep sense of inferiority and even with unconscious homosexual tendencies, but never as the normal and functional product of a pervasive patriarchy. Very soon, the stigma became associated with working-class people. Later on (the 1970s and 1980s), the scholarly approach to *machismo* was complemented with the "opposite" term, *marianismo*: a gender ideology that coerces women to adopt the virtues epitomized by the Virgin Mary.

Contrary to some Latin American societies, in Mexico the word *macho* has negative connotations nowadays, which can include "beating, alcoholism, gambling, the abandonment of children and bullying behavior in general." It is considered a "premodern" and backward identity, and it is used as a stigma for regionalist purposes: some people in Mexico City consider *machismo* a "rural phenomenon," some people in the northern states think of it as "more common in the south" (Gutman 15).

In Mexican society the *macho* coexist in the gender order with some other male social personas: the *mandilón* (user of the apron, or female-dominated man) and the *sólo hombre* (just man). Each of these words is loosely defined, and its respective semantic fields are used in daily life to negotiate and inform subjectivities, practices (like child care), and power relations. Their wide presence in popular cultural production (songs, films) and male-to-male interactions, as part of a continuous mockery over their gender status, signals the importance of the gender transformations now occurring in Mexican society.

Gabriel Nuñez-Noriega

Bibliography

Gutmann, Matthew C. *The Meanings of Macho: Being a Man in Mexico City.* Berkeley: University of California Press, 1996.

Lancaster, Roger N. *Life Is Hard: Machismo, Danger, and the Intimacy of Power in Nicaragua.* Berkeley: University of California Press, 1992.

See also Argentina; Brazil; Cantina Culture; Chicano and Latino Gay Cultures; Masculinity; Mexico

Mahlsdorf, Charlotte von (1928–)

Born male as Lothar Berfelde on March 18, 1928, in a small village on the outer edge of Berlin, Charlotte von Mahlsdorf's unusual life story seems almost to mirror the entire German gay history of this century. Although her abusive father tried to raise his son according to Prussian and fascist male standards, Mahlsdorf rebelled, even refusing to join the Hitler Youth. Encouraged by a lesbian aunt, Mahlsdorf read Magnus Hirschfeld's book *The Transvestites* at the age of fifteen. While working at a secondhand furniture store in Berlin at the beginning of World War II, Mahlsdorf started not only to collect furniture from the design period Gründerzeit (1870–1900) but also to buy and wear female clothes on a regular basis. She was caught wearing them and escaped imprisonment in a concentration camp only because she was too young and the police judged it as a young boy's joke. In February 1944, Mahlsdorf killed her father, who threatened to shoot the "dysfunctional" son and the rest of the family. During her resulting imprisonment, Mahlsdorf was observed and given a psychiatric evaluation by Robert Ritter. (Ritter was responsible for the racist elimination of Romanies in Germany during World War II.) Mahlsdorf was freed in April 1945 as Soviet soldiers were marching into Berlin. The same day, owing to a bombing of the site, she miraculously survived an execution by the SS, who were hunting and shooting any men out on the street not serving in the German army during the last days of the war. After the war, Mahlsdorf reconstructed two old mansions, collected furniture, and founded a *Gründerzeit* museum that soon became the biggest of its kind in Europe. She had to defend the museum several times against the East German government: not only did it want to sell the antiques for hard currency, but it also wanted to shut down a meeting place for gay men and lesbians. Even though Mahlsdorf was accused after the reunification of the country of voluntary collaboration with the

Charlotte von Mahlsdorf in her museum. Photo by Erwin Bode.

East German intelligence service, she received the Bundesverdienstkreuz (one of the most prestigious decorations given by the German government) in 1992 for her preservation of cultural values. Mahlsdorf published her biography under the title *Ich bin meine eigene Frau* (*I Am My Own Woman*) in 1995 and starred in a film of the same title by Rosa von Praunheim. Still shaken from a bashing by skinheads in 1991, and facing increasing financial difficulties with her museum in Berlin, Mahlsdorf left Germany in 1997 for Polarbrunn, Sweden, where she opened a new Gründerzeit museum.

Jens Richard Giersdorf

Bibliography

Mahlsdorf, Charlotte von. *Ich bin meine eigene Frau.* Munich: Deutscher Taschenbuch Verlag, 1995.

See also Germany; Hirschfeld, Magnus; Nazism and the Holocaust; Rosa von Praunheim

Malouf, David (1934–)

Winner of the first International IMPAC Dublin Literary Award in 1996 for his novel *Remembering Babylon*, also shortlisted for the 1993 Booker Prize, David Malouf is one of Australia's most critically successful writers. Malouf works in several forms, including poetry, the novel, libretto, and drama. His fiction appeared in *Australian Gay and Lesbian Writing* (1993) and *The Faber Book of Gay Short Fiction* (1991). Malouf says, "If I were to name the people who have been most influential on me as a poet, I would have to say Rilke, and Stevens, and, in a very different way, Auden."

Malouf's first novels, *Johnno* (1975) and *An Imaginary Life* (1978), are both known for their homoeroticism. *Remembering Babylon* (1993) enters the mythology of the white invasion of Australia, while *Conversations at Curlow Creek* (1996) details aspects of colonial Australia. Other novels include *Harland's Half Acre* (1984) and *The Great World* (1990). His novellas are *Fly Away Peter* (1981), *Child's Play* (1981), *Eustace* (1982), and *The Prowler* (1982). Now acclaimed internationally as a novelist, Malouf is also of major national significance as a poet, and as a playwright he is known among gay audiences for *Blood Relations* (1988). Malouf's work is characterized by a lyrically intense preoccupation with the anxieties of masculinity and their relationship to epic forms; consequently, we might constitute it as a sustained exploration of aspects of national culture.

Michael Hurley

Bibliography

Duwell, M., M. Ehrhardt, and C. Heatherington, eds. *The ALS Guide to Australian Writers: A Bibliography, 1963–1995.* St. Lucia: University of Queensland Press, 1997.

Indyk, Ivor. *David Malouf.* Melbourne: Oxford University Press, 1993.

Malouf, David. *Poems 1959–89.* St. Lucia: University of Queensland Press, 1992.

———. *12 Edmonstone Street.* London: Chatto & Windus, 1985.

See also Auden, W. H.; Australia; Australian Literature

Mann, Thomas (1875–1955)

Thomas Mann's writings have always both flaunted homosexuality and allowed it to be disavowed. In *Tonio Kröger* (1903), the first love affair of the eponymous protagonist is with blond and blue-eyed Hans Hansen. *Death in Venice* (1912) famously depicts Aschenbach's crumbling resistance to his decadent desire for the beautiful Polish youth Tadzio. In "Mario and the Magician" (1929), a grotesque male illusionist causes a hypnotized Italian man to kiss him in full view of a large audience. In *The Magic Mountain*, Hans Castorp's love for Claudia Chauchat, a seriously ill female patient in a sanitarium, is presented as a resurgence of his first schoolboy love for the young male Pribislav Hippe. And in *Doktor Faustus*, the composer Adrian Leverkühn falls for the charismatic and handsome Rudiger Schwerdtfeger. Mann also explicitly addressed the subject of homosexuality in a number of essays, including "The German Republic," "Platen," and "On Marriage."

At the same time, many readers have found it easy to ignore or discredit this homosexuality. Even today, critics may claim that the homosexuality in Mann's works had nothing to do with his life, or was basically irrelevant to the larger themes of his writing, or was depicted as purely negative. Such interpretations find a certain resonance in Mann's texts, which do link male homosexuality with sickness, decadence, authoritarianism, and even National Socialism. In Mann's essays on Platen and Michelangelo, as well as his depictions of Aschenbach and Leverkühn, the importance of homosexuality in the creative process lies in its repression—rather than its celebration.

As problematic as some of the underlying conceptions of homosexuality in Mann's works are, one

M issue has been resolved since the late seventies. Those biographers who maintained that Mann had no personal experience of homosexuality have had to retract their claims ever since Mann's diaries started coming out. The diaries, covering the years 1918–1921 and 1933–1955, make clear that Mann had a series of passions for young men. Traces of many of these men appear in the descriptions of the characters involved in homosexual relationships in Mann's works: Armin Martens is the model for Hans Hansen, Willri Timpe for Pribislav Hippe, and Paul Ehrenberg for Rudiger Schwerdtfeger. Even though Mann was married and had six children, two men—Paul Ehrenberg and Klaus Heuser—show up in his diaries as the loves of his life. Anchoring homosexual desire in Mann's life has eliminated some of the controversy over the presence of homosexuality in his writing. The interpretation of that homosexuality remains unclear. Perhaps Mann wanted it that way, for now his readers confront the issue that troubled him the most: how to evaluate the homosexuality that affected his writing so strongly.   *Robert Tobin*

Bibliography
Heilbut, Anthony. *Thomas Mann: Eros and Literature*. New York: Knopf, 1996.

See also German Literature; Germany; Michelangelo Buonarroti; Platen-Hallermund, August Graf von Hallermund

Manrique Ardila, Jaime (1949–)
Jaime Manrique Ardila, born in Barranquilla, Colombia, resides in New York City. He was awarded the Colombian National Poetry Award, "Eduardo Cote Lamus," in 1975 for his collection of poems *Los adoradores de la luna*. Since moving to the United States, he earned a B.A. in English literature from the University of South Florida and participated in the Spanish Workshop at Columbia University in 1977 under the direction of Manuel Puig. Also, he has participated in several creative writing workshops and has taught creative writing and literature in several colleges and universities in the United States. His additional poetry collections are *Scarecrow* and *My Night With Federico García Lorca*. He has written four works of fiction to date: *El cadaver de papá* (My Father's Corpse), *Colombian Gold, Latin Moon in Manhattan,* and *Twilight at the Equator. Latin Moon in Manhattan* was a finalist for a Lambda Literary Award in 1993.

Manrique's literary works have evolved greatly since the appearance of his first poems and novel. *El cadaver de papá* and *Colombian Gold* focus on the political situation of his native Colombia. With *Latin Moon in Manhattan*, the author moves away from violence to examine more closely the problem of the integration of his Colombian heritage and that of his gay orientation into the United States. His latest narrative, *Twilight at the Equator*, centers on the search for his Colombian roots in the face of AIDS. This novel highlights Manrique's narrative growth; gone is the sexual violence of the earlier works and in its place is a main character satisfied with himself as a gay Colombian living in New York City.

Stephen Du Pouy

Bibliography
Foster, David William, ed. *Latin American Themes: A Bio-Critical Sourcebook*. Westport, Conn.: Greenwood, 1994.

See also Chicano and Latino Gay Cultures; García Lorca, Federico; Puig, Manuel

Mapplethorpe, Robert (1946–1989)
The work—and very name—of Robert Mapplethorpe have become synonymous with the issues of censorship and homosexuality. In June 1989, the Corcoran Gallery of Art in Washington, D.C., canceled a planned retrospective of Mapplethorpe's photography entitled The Perfect Moment. The cancellation, which occurred in the midst of Republican attacks on both Mapplethorpe's work and the National Endowment for the Arts (which had partially funded The Perfect Moment), provoked a national controversy over artistic freedom and the representation of homosexuality. That controversy led, in turn, to content restrictions on federally funded art and to the (still ongoing) dismantling of the NEA.

Mapplethorpe died of AIDS-related causes in March 1989, some three months prior to the Corcoran cancellation. By the time of his death, he had emerged as one of the most successful American art photographers of the postwar era. His elegant prints commanded critical attention (if not always praise) and high-end prices within the burgeoning market for art photography in the 1980s. Mapplethorpe often presented his photographs as luxury objects, whether by printing them on linen, by surrounding them with fabrics such as silk, velvet, and leather, or by enclosing them in mirrored frames of his own design.

Two contrasting images. © The Estate of Robert Mapplethorpe. Used by permission.

Throughout his career, Mapplethorpe organized his photography around three major themes: still lifes, portraits, and homosexuality. Each of these themes was filtered through a signature style that emphasized formal symmetry, intricate gradations of black and white, and the utter clarity of texture and visual detail. Mapplethorpe delighted in offering wildly different subjects as equally stylized—and sensual—pictorial forms. "I don't think there's that much difference," he told an interviewer in 1979, "between a photograph of a fist up someone's ass and a photograph of carnations in a bowl." Mapplethorpe's pictures of gay sadomasochism were no less aestheticized than his still lifes, and, correspondingly, his photographs of flowers sometimes seemed nearly as suggestive as those of leathermen.

In the 1978 portrait of Helmut, Mapplethorpe offers the elegant (if unlikely) display of a squatting leatherman atop a pedestal. Even as it reveals Helmut's buttocks, boots, and leather harness, the portrait also emphasizes the spare, art studio setting—the pedestal, the white walls, that framing swath of fabric. Mapplethorpe's formalist play with light and shadow is insistent and unapologetic here, the leather jacket becoming blackest, for instance, when it overlaps the white muslin fabric behind it. Mapplethorpe's use of a central pedestal and background drapery recall nineteenth-century photographs of still lifes and classical statuary. Toward the end of his career, Mapplethorpe would, in fact, photograph neoclassical busts and statues in much the same way as he portrayed Helmut.

While considered strictly a photographer, Mapplethorpe had studied painting, sculpture, and drawing (though not photography) at Pratt Institute in Brooklyn, New York, from 1963 to 1969. As a student, he favored psychedelic paintings and drawings loosely based on French surrealism and the engravings of William Blake. In 1967, Mapplethorpe met Patti Smith, an aspiring poet and singer, and the two moved in together in an apartment near Pratt. Smith quickly became one of Mapplethorpe's closest friends and favorite models. In 1969, Mapplethorpe dropped out of Pratt and moved, with Smith, into the Chelsea Hotel in Manhattan.

At this time, Mapplethorpe was creating collages and mixed-media objects, many of which incorporated images of gay pornography appropriated from commercial sources. These works, which bore titles such as *Ah Men*, *Cowboy*, and *Untitled (Blow Job)*, sexualized the male body while simultaneously suggesting, through the use of obscuring bars and spray paint, the censorship to which that body had historically been subject. For all their visual wit, Mapplethorpe's collages were not considered commercially viable by the galleries he approached in the early 1970s. Perhaps because of this, he moved away increasingly from collage and mixed media and toward the production of his own photographic images.

In 1972, Mapplethorpe met Sam Wagstaff, a wealthy art collector and curator who would become his mentor and, more briefly, his lover. Wagstaff supported Mapplethorpe financially, encouraged his interests in photography, and introduced him to

M prominent figures in the art and museum worlds. With Wagstaff's help, Mapplethorpe landed his first one-man show at the Light Gallery in New York in 1973. The exhibition featured Polaroid photographs, several of which were self-portraits. Following the show, Mapplethorpe turned to a large-format press camera and finally, to a Hasselblad.

In 1975, Smith signed a contract with Arista records and Mapplethorpe shot the cover for her first album, *Horses*. Mapplethorpe's stark portrait of the singer in a man's shirt and suspenders, standing against a blank white wall, marks one of the aesthetic highpoints of his early career. Between 1977 and 1979, he produced a series of intense, impressive photographs of sadomasochism, of its practitioners and paraphernalia, while also continuing to create photographs of flowers and portraits of celebrities. During this time, Mapplethorpe was taken on by the prestigious Robert Miller gallery in New York and developed an international reputation. Relatively quickly, he was given one-man shows in Chicago, San Francisco, Houston, and Los Angeles, as well as in Paris, Amsterdam, and Brussels.

Around 1980, Mapplethorpe began to photograph black men, some of whom he had met at gay bars. Unlike the (mostly white) men portrayed in the S/M pictures, Mapplethorpe's black male nudes are, without exception, muscular, youthful, and well endowed. The nudes have been cut to the very pattern of Mapplethorpe's desire and thus reveal more, perhaps, about the photographer than about the men portrayed. In 1986, *The Black Book*, a collection of Mapplethorpe's black male nudes, was published to both acclaim and controversy. Later that same year, Mapplethorpe was diagnosed with AIDS. In 1988, his health on the decline, he established the Robert Mapplethorpe Foundation, a charitable organization that funds both AIDS research and photography projects such as museum exhibitions and catalogs.

Even as Mapplethorpe's photographs now command record prices at auction, they continue to spark controversy worldwide. In March 1998, British police seized a copy of a book entitled *Mapplethorpe* from the University of Central England in Birmingham, declaring two of its photographs obscene. The university's vice chancellor, who has refused to excise those pictures from the book, remains under the threat of imprisonment. Part of Mapplethorpe's legacy, it seems, will be to test the limits of artistic freedom and creative expression wherever his photographic images are seen.

Richard Meyer

Bibliography

Bolton, Richard, ed. *Culture Wars: Documents from the Recent Controversies in the Arts*. New York: New Press, 1992.

Fritscher, Jack. "The Robert Mapplethorpe Gallery." *Son of Drummer* (1978): 14.

Hodges, Parker. "Robert Mapplethorpe: Photographer." *MANhattan Gaze* (December 10, 1979): 5.

Kardon, Janet, David Joselit, Kay Larson, and Patti Smith. *The Perfect Moment*. Exhibition Catalog. Philadelphia: Institute of Contemporary Art, University of Pennsylvania, 1988.

Mapplethorpe. With essay by Arthur Danto. New York: Random House, 1992.

Marshall, Richard, Richard Howard, and Ingrid Sischy. *Robert Mapplethorpe*. Exhibition Catalog. New York: Whitney Museum of American Art in association with the New York Graphic Society Books and Little, Brown, 1988.

Mercer, Kobena. "Skin Head Sex Thing: Racial Difference and the Homoerotic Imaginary." In *How Do I Look?: Queer Film and Video*. Bad Object-Choices, ed. Seattle: Bay Press, 1991, 169–222.

Meyer, Richard. "Robert Mapplethorpe and the Discipline of Photography." In *The Lesbian and Gay Studies Reader*. Henry Abelove, Michèle Aina Barale, and David Halperin, eds. New York: Routledge, 1993, 360–80.

See also Censorship; Leathermen; Photography; Pornography; Sadomasochism

Marais, Jean (1913–1998)

French actor Jean Marais was born Jean-Alfred Villain-Marais. During the 1940s and 1950s, he was one of the most popular stars of the French screen and stage. Marais first determined to become a movie star when, as a child, he was taken to see Pearl White in *The Exploits of Elaine*. Yet despite his blond, classical good looks, the progress of his career was at first slow.

Marais's career improved when in 1937 he met Jean Cocteau and was given a small role in the poet's play *Oedipe Roi* (*Oepidus Rex*). From 1937 to 1950, the two were partners in their personal and professional lives and their relationship was creatively enriching for both. In 1938, both enjoyed a great success when Marais starred in Cocteau's play *Les Parents terribles*, based on Marais's own family relationships. Cocteau, who had previously directed an avant-garde film, returned to filmmaking when, at

Marais's instigation, he wrote a screenplay for the actor to star in, *L'Éternel retour* (*The Eternal Return*, 1943, directed by Jean Delannoy). Cocteau subsequently directed Marais in several films, most notably *La Belle et la bête* (*Beauty and the Beast*, 1946).

Marais became an accomplished and versatile actor, worked with a number of directors, and starred in a wide variety of roles on stage, screen, and television. He continued his acting career during the German occupation of France in World War II, but later served in General Leclerc's division of the Third American Army, receiving the Croix de Guerre for his war service. *Charles Krinsky*

Bibliography

Marais, Jean. *Histoires de ma vie*. Paris: A. Michel, 1975.

Steegmuller, Francis. *Cocteau*. Boston: Little, Brown, 1970.

See also Cocteau, Jean; Film; France; French Literature

Marches and Parades

While certainly not unique to lesbian and gay/queer community, parades and marches have played, and continue to play, a central role in the formation and presentation of gay community and identity. A parade and a march share the same basic structure—a conglomeration of people moving together through a public space on a route with a fixed beginning and end—but a distinction can be drawn as to the purpose of this movement. A parade is generally a celebratory ritual through which a community (however constituted) creates of itself a spectacle for itself, thus making visible its characteristics, cohesion, and commonalties. This ritual celebration also makes the community visible within the larger social domain.

Generally sharing the same form as the parade, the march differs mostly in function: whereas a parade is largely a celebratory ritual, a march is largely a ritual of social demonstration and a format for protest. The focus of a march is an attempt by the participants at effecting social change through a ritualized display of collective power. Furthermore, to participate in a march, one must "march," whereas in a parade, one may also participate as a spectator. Though it is assumed that participants and spectators at a parade share some common racial, ethnic, or national identity (Irish for the St. Patrick's Day parade; American for the Memorial Day parade; lesbian and gay/bisexual/transgender for a pride parade), no such assumption necessarily underlies a

The Provincetown Contingent at the March on Washington. Photo courtesy of Lisa Nelson.

M march. Participants at a given march are primarily drawn together through common ideologies rather than common identities. It is necessary to keep in mind these general distinctions of the parade as celebration and the march as demonstration, but it is also important to be aware of how these distinctions are blurred within gay community.

The gay community has a history of both marches and parades. The most visible marches have been the "marches on Washington," the first of which predated the Stonewall riots (the 1969 mythological origin of gay liberation to be discussed below) by four years. In 1965 a "homophile march" was organized by the Mattachine Society and the Daughters of Bilitis (a gay and lesbian group, respectively). Approximately fifty demonstrators were bused to Washington, D.C., where they picketed the White House on July 4 to protest federal employment discrimination. The next large-scale Washington march took place in 1987, and the most recent one was in 1993. The Washington march projected for the year 2000 will be called the "Millennium March."

Unlike marches, pride parades have developed into a distinctive yearly phenomenon in most American cities, in many towns, and even in other countries. The pride parade is commonly held in conjunction with a community's gay pride celebration, often as the culmination of a week of events. Like other civic parades, the pride parade has developed a more or less standard format. The parade is almost always led by a contingent of Dykes on Bikes (if not the actual club, then a facsimile) and typically contains floats provided by local commercial gay establishments, particularly bars and clubs; marching contingents of gay and gay-friendly organizations such as ACT UP and P-FLAG; contingents from gay religious and erotic organizations such as DIGNITY and S/M leather organizations; and even gay musical organizations such as the Gay Men's Chorus. More and more, the parade is becoming a venue for advertising gay-friendly segments of straight culture to gay audiences: waving politicians in convertibles and loud, brightly painted radio station vehicles are quickly becoming standards. Typically, the parade route ends at a civic park or in a gay neighborhood, where after-parade parties are held.

Although the parade and the march are distinctive rituals in gay community, the terms are sometimes used synonymously. This "confusion" is not only a result of conflicts of opinion as to the purpose of any one event but is embedded in the origin of the pride parade tradition itself. The historical marker for the mythological birth of the gay liberation movement is the 1969 Stonewall riots: three days of rioting following the June 27 raid by the New York police on the Stonewall Inn, a Greenwich Village bar. Stonewall is also taken as the mythological origin of the pride parade, generally conceived as a yearly commemoration of the community's origin, history, and struggles. New York City's commemoration of the event began in June 1970, and has taken place every year since.

Three important qualifications must be made to this national narrative of Stonewall as the origin of gay liberation and the event ritualized as the pride parade/march. First, while Stonewall, as mythologized in gay histories, provides a historical marker around which histories can be organized, the histories of individual communities (in both senses: as local and as subculture) are often obscured by this New York narrative.

On a local level, many are aware of Stonewall as mythologized, but they remain unaware of their own civic histories equally if not more relevant to the production of local pride celebrations. In Chicago, for example, a 1970 protest march evolved into that city's pride parade. Gay Liberation, Mattachine Midwest, and the Women's Caucus organized the city's first Gay Pride Week in June 1970, the celebrations to culminate in a protest march on June 27. Unable to obtain a permit, the approximately 150 protesters marched along city sidewalks, producing "the city's first open demonstration for gay rights" (Rinella). Thus, as Rinella goes on to say, while the Stonewall riots "energized activists nationally," the 1970 demonstration itself "grew out of the [city's] activism of the late 1960s." The following year the 150-person demonstration had turned into a 1,200-person parade and has been held every year since, with current attendance estimated at 200,000.

There is an overlapping but distinct sense in which community history can be and has been obscured by the gay liberation/Stonewall narrative. It was largely what would today be called the transgender community that was responsible for and the heroes of the Stonewall riots. As Laura Mansnerus wrote in a June 26, 1994, *New York Times* article, "Under Many Banners," the riots "were carried out by the very people who are looked down upon now: drag queens, effeminate gay men and diesel dykes, most of whom were people of color." These communities, however, have historically been erased, excluded, and repressed from the gay and lesbian and feminist communities organizing pride parades and celebrations.

E. J. Graff of the *Progressive* wrote in his June 1994 article, "Pride and Prejudice: New York Gay Pride Demonstration," that "pride parades [have been] policed by a PR patrol," from the beginning. The policing practices, which Graff calls "image skirmishing," go beyond the attempts to dictate proper attire for celebrants (shirtless Lesbian Avengers a recent target example), and into the realm of dictating which identities should be considered abhorrent to the community itself. More often than not, transgender communities have been the objects of this policing. As early as June 1973 at a rally following New York's parade, Sylvia Rivera, a drag queen who participated in the Stonewall riots only four years earlier, was forced from the podium by feminists who argued that drag itself was misogynistic. This simultaneous appropriation of transgender activist history and erasure of the transgender activist continues today and is discussed below.

A third qualification concerns the relationship between the highly political nature of pride's origins as riots and demonstrations and the arguably depoliticized and commercialized event that has evolved into the yearly parade form. This relationship came to the fore in 1994 during the twenty-fifth commemoration of the Stonewall riots, dubbed "Stonewall 25." Organized by several international organizations, Stonewall 25 was intended to celebrate gay unity and to draw attention to the abuse of gay and lesbian rights worldwide. The main event of Stonewall 25 was a march up New York's First Avenue, past the United Nations (as part of the international focus), and then on to a rally in Central Park.

From the outset, Stonewall 25 was a demonstration of how pride parades and marches have remained and/or become both a site and a forum for community conflict and change. First, in deference to Stonewall 25, a march for international gay rights, New York's Heritage of Pride canceled its annual gay pride parade, but arguments soon arose regarding the exclusion of local organizations from the planning of the event. Other conflicts arose regarding the organizers' of Stonewall 25's treatment of the transgendered community. First, the organizers did not include any of those present at the riots in their planning of the commemoration. Second, while the Gay Games '94 were held to coincide with the commemoration, game organizers required trans-women to provide documentation as to why they should be allowed to compete as women (this

policy, however, was rescinded before the games began). Third, and most heinous, was Stonewall 25's refusal to include "transgender" in the commemoration's title, dubbed a "Gay, Lesbian, and Bisexual Event." Though challenged for this exclusion by Transexual Menace, It's Time America!, Transgender Nation, and the Transgender Law Conference, among other organizations, the organizers of Stonewall 25 refused to alter their title, claiming that Stonewall 25 was an international event and that the term *transgender* was not translatable. These factors, along with the perceived commercialization and conservative focus of the event, led to the staging of countermarches or demonstrations.

Besides the official Stonewall 25 march on First Avenue, a second march was scheduled to take place simultaneously on Fifth Avenue. This countermarch, organized largely by ACT UP, was intended to focus attention on the fight against AIDS, following a route from the Stonewall up Fifth Avenue and past St. Patrick's Cathedral. Though a second permit was requested on the basis that the two marches, expressing vastly divergent ideologies, required distinct venues, the city turned down the second request, citing financial constraints. Permit or not, however, the countermarch was held without interference, the police closing Fifth Avenue to vehicular traffic. This countermarch drew support from a wide range of gay, lesbian, queer, and transgender organizations as well as from individuals dissatisfied with the official march and was led by drag queen Sylvia Rivera (the same original Stonewall rioter forced from the 1973 rally platform by feminists who insisted that her transgendered identity was offensive to women).

The inability of a single event/march/parade to provide a forum for all segments of the community is further underscored by the recent development of other distinctive pride forums. For instance, the final weekend of May 1998 in New York featured the fourth annual People of Color Pride Weekend, dubbed United Voices/United Visions. The event first materialized as a people of color hospitality suite organized by the Lesbian and Gay People of Color Steering Committee during the 1994 Stonewall 25 celebration, then a People of Color Pride Day in 1995, growing into a weekend in 1996.

Another recently evolving pride forum is the Dyke March. Besides the unofficial Fifth Avenue march during Stonewall 25, a Dyke March was also held, though scheduled separately so as not to conflict with the official march. The Dyke March is simultaneously a protest of the historical sexism in the gay community and a celebration of lesbian-identified women and their particular histories and activism. Dyke marches are becoming more and more common components of pride events; they figured in the 1994 New York celebration and the 1993 March on Washington, for example, and even local pride celebrations are beginning to feature them (e.g., the 1997 Chicago pride celebration).

What arises from this schematic exploration into the seemingly simple topic of "Parades and Marches" is not simply a history and format for community celebration and demonstration but a nexus of concerns and conflicts surrounding the construction of history, community, and, ultimately, identity itself. Thus, parades and marches are not simply rituals of celebration and demonstration enacted by lesbian and gay/bisexual/transgender community but dynamic forums for the construction of community itself. *Lisa Nelson*

Bibliography

Goldstein, Richard. "The Coming Crisis of Gay Rights: At the Very Moment When Our Pride Is at Its Peak, Our Political Agenda Is in Jeopardy." *Village Voice* (June 28, 1994): 25.

Graff, E. J. "Pride and Prejudice: New York Gay Pride Demonstration." *Progressive* (June 24, 1994).

Heiwa, Jesse. "Fourth People of Color Celebration Launches Pride Month." *Lesbian & Gay New York* (June 4, 1998): 10.

Herrell, Richard K. "Chicago's Gay and Lesbian Pride Day Parade." In *Gay Culture in America: Essays from the Field*. Gilbert Herdt, ed. Boston: Beacon Press, 1993.

Mansnerus, Laura. "Under Many Banners: Varied Voices in Gay Life Not Always in Chorus." *New York Times,* June 26, 1994.

McKinley, James C., Jr. "Gay Rights Group Suing to March on Fifth Ave." *New York Times,* September 24, 1994.

Rinella, Jack. "For 28 Years, Parade Has Brought Gay Pride 'Out in the Daylight.' " *Chicago Tribune,* June 27, 1997, Tempo 1.

Rose, Rita. " 'Stonewall' Focuses on Games and Diversity of Gay Community." *The Indianapolis Star,* October 7, 1994, C09.

Trejo, Frank. "Thousands March in NY for Gay Rights Participants in Stonewall Event Optimistic but Say Work Remains." *Dallas Morning News,* June 27, 1994, News 1A.

Wilchins, Riki Anne. *Read My Lips: Sexual Subversion and the End of Gender.* Ithaca, N.Y.: Firebrand, 1997.

See also Activism, U.S.; ACT UP; Bisexuality; Choruses and Marching Bands; Homophile Movement; Leathermen; Marches on Washington; Mattachine Society; Parents and Friends of Lesbians and Gays (PFLAG); Politics, Global; Stonewall; Transgender; Washington, D.C.

Marches on Washington

The lesbian, gay, bisexual, and transgender rights movement has grown enormously since the late 1970s, perhaps best demonstrated by the success of the three national marches held in Washington, each of which has been much larger and more diverse than the previous one. Coming in the wake of the lenient jail sentence given to Dan White for the assassination of openly gay San Francisco supervisor Harvey Milk, the 1979 March on Washington for Lesbian and Gay Rights, the first national demonstration of its kind, drew more than 100,000 people from around the country. Despite the fear of established lesbian and gay groups that the march would spawn a right-wing backlash similar to Anita Bryant's "Save Our Children" campaign, it had the opposite effect, helping to solidify a national lesbigay rights movement. The march also featured the first National Third World Gay and Lesbian Conference, which was attended by hundreds of people of color, and spurred the creation of the National Coalition of Black Lesbians and Gays.

On October 11, 1987, more than a half million people (between 500,000 and 650,000 according to organizers) descended on Washington to participate in the second national March on Washington for Lesbian and Gay Rights. Many were angry over the government's slow and inadequate response to the AIDS crisis and the Supreme Court's 1986 decision to uphold sodomy laws in *Bowers v. Hardwick*. The march brought national attention to the impact of AIDS on gay communities with the first display of the NAMES Project AIDS Memorial Quilt; in the shadow of the U.S. Capitol, a tapestry of 1,920 fabric panels offered a powerful tribute to the lives of some of those who had been lost in the pandemic. The march also drew unprecedented media coverage to antigay discrimination as approximately 800 people were arrested in front of the Supreme Court two days later in the largest civil disobedience action ever held in support of

Hundreds of thousands in support of gay rights at the 1987 March on Washington. Photo by Marc Geller.

the rights of lesbians, gay men, bisexuals, and transgendered people.

Although the 1987 March on Washington sparked the creation of BiNet U.S.A. and the Latino/a Lesbian and Gay Organization, the first national groups for bisexuals and lesbigay Latinos, respectively, the most lasting effect of the weekend's events might have been felt on the local level. Energized and inspired by the march, many activists returned home and established social and political groups in their own communities, providing even greater visibility and strength to the struggle for lesbian, gay, bisexual, and transgender rights.

The resulting growth of the movement was shown six years later when close to a million people attended the 1993 March on Washington for Lesbian, Gay, and Bi Equal Rights and Liberation, making it the largest demonstration in U.S. history. The event was also groundbreaking for receiving the unanimous endorsement of the board of the NAACP—the first time that direct institutional ties had been made between the lesbigay rights movement and the civil rights movement—and for explicitly including bisexuals. In addition to the march, participants could take part in more than 250 related events, ranging from conferences and workshops, to protests and congressional lobbying, to dances, readings, and religious ceremonies.

Brett Beemyn

Bibliography

Thompson, Mark, ed. *Long Road to Freedom: The Advocate History of the Gay and Lesbian Movement*. New York: St. Martin's Press, 1994.

Vaid, Urvashi. *Virtual Equality: The Mainstreaming of Gay and Lesbian Liberation*. New York: Doubleday, 1995.

See also Activism, U.S.; Bisexuality; Marches and Parades; Milk, Harvey; NAMES Project AIDS Memorial Quilt; Politics, Global; San Francisco; Voting Behavior Washington, D.C.

Marketing

Marketing is the discipline of fulfilling customers' needs with offerings provided by entrepreneurs or commercial enterprises. According to the marketing concept, organizations may attain objectives such as long-term profitability and customer satisfaction by researching customer needs and preferences and providing superior goods and/or services relative to their competitors. This statement is both a prescrip-

M tion for businesses and an ideology for competent business practice and resulting success.

Given the aggressive and enterprising nature of the business culture, it is rather surprising that it was not until the late 1980s that a sufficient number of American, British, and Canadian commercial enterprises "discovered" the gay and lesbian market to the extent that it was noteworthy to report in the mainstream journalistic press. Gay men particularly have been described as a stereotypical "dream market" for marketers: well educated, sophisticated, discerning, intelligent, and (perhaps most important) willing to spend their supposedly higher-than-average disposable incomes to acquire the best of everything. In 1993, the Yankelovich *Monitor* sample found that the mean household income in the United States was $37,400 for gay men and $34,800 for lesbians. Overlooked Opinions, a market research firm based in Chicago, reported in its *Gay Market Report* that nearly 20 percent of gay men and lesbians earned over $75,000 annually versus 11 percent of the general population.

The myth of the affluent gay male consumer has been debunked, however. The market research on which this stereotype was founded is grievously flawed, as it is based predominantly on nonrepresentative or convenience samples of magazine or print readers, a group with higher than average disposable incomes. In fact, as reported by the Yankelovich Research Company survey of 1995, gay men and lesbians have slightly (but not statistically significantly) lower household incomes than heterosexual Americans. Also, when one considers the physical, emotional, and economic devastation that the AIDS crisis has precipitated within gay men's communities, the big spender stereotype becomes harder to sustain.

Another important contribution made by the Yankelovich report is that it provides the first reliable, statistically sound measure of the size of the gay and lesbian market. Previous market studies have relied on sex research such as the 1948 Kinsey study (the now famous "10 percent" rule). The Yankelovich report asserts that 6 percent of those surveyed self-identified as gay or lesbian. Yet a strong social acceptability bias is involved in this form of self-reporting; while out gay and lesbian individuals would presumably be willing to make such a form of disclosure, many closeted ones may have lied or been unsure about their appropriate status.

Yet large and small companies have found compelling reasons to focus marketing resources on the gay male population if not the lesbian. First, given that men earn significantly more than women,

two cohabiting males may have significantly higher disposable income and thus form economies in living together. Second, given that many unmarried gay men do not have wives or children to support, they may have more money for luxuries such as travel, leisure, furniture, fine wines, self-improvement activities, and upscale clothing.

Marketing as a managerial process has been traditionally conceptualized around four activities usually dubbed the "marketing mix" or "the four P's": pricing, product development, place (i.e., channels of distribution), and promotion (advertising, public relations, and other activities to make the product more attractive to consumers such as contests or special offers). Most businesses that have targeted the gay or lesbian populations have focused their marketing efforts on consumer advertising. It is not unusual for large, mainstream companies to advertise regularly in the gay and lesbian press, attempting to win product trial and continuing brand loyalty. Absolut Vodka, Molson beers, Digital Equipment Company, Saturn car dealerships, Toyota car dealerships, and AT&T are only a partial list of companies that have at one time or another placed advertisements in gay and lesbian magazines, newspapers, or pride day souvenir guides.

Still, the decision to target gay and lesbian consumers is often a difficult one for mainstream businesses. Their chief concern is whether heterosexual audiences in general and the religious right in particular will subsequently perceive their firm as immoral, less desirable, and promoting an antifamily, pro-gay agenda. Thus, advertising to gays and lesbians in mainstream media such as broadcast television is quite rare as to be remarkable. The one remarkable example of this is that of furniture retailer Ikea, which aired a television spot in 1994 featuring two gay men in a relationship looking for a dining room table. This advertisement is believed to be the first mainstream television commercial to feature a gay relationship.

In spite of IKEA's foray into gay marketing, most promotional effort directed toward gays and lesbians is done within the gay media. Mulryan Nash, an advertising agency based in New York City, estimated in 1994 that $53 million per year was spent on advertising in the American gay press. The largest spending categories were bars and clubs (almost 20 percent of advertising spending), phone services (12.6 percent), professional services (10.8 percent), and social events (6.3 percent). At the time, the gay press in the United States consisted of nine national magazines (such as *Out* or *Advocate*) and sixty-seven regional magazines and newspapers.

The development of programs that specifically target gay and lesbian consumers may be viewed as part of the larger phenomenon of niche marketing. A popular stream of marketing thought contends that while mass marketing is in decline, more focused and sophisticated efforts aimed at serving smaller but potentially profitable groups of consumers should fare successfully. This marketing trend itself is part of a larger societal trend that incorporates identity politics, valuing human diversity, and the fragmentation of general market demand into more particular taste cultures, subcultures, and ethnic groups, among many other interests, calling for fine-tuned and well-honed marketing mixes that are more sensitive to the needs and lives of different types of consumers in pluralistic countries.   *Steven M. Kates*

Bibliography

Gluckman, Amy, and Betsy Reed. "The Gay Marketing Moment: Leaving Diversity in the Dust." *Dollars and Sense* (November/December 1993): 16.

Nash, Mulryan. "Advertising Spending in the Gay Press." *Marketing* (June 1994).

Pelñaloza, Lisa. "We're Here, We're Queer and We're Going Shopping: A Critical Perpective on the Accommodation of Gays and Lesbians in the U.S. Marketplace." In *Gays, Lesbians, and Consumer Behavior: Theory, Practice, and Research Issues in Marketing*. Daniel L. Wardlow, ed. New York: Haworth Press, 1966, 9–42.

"Stirring Up the Marketing Mix." *Marketing* (June 10, 1991): 1.

See also Boycott; Business

Marlowe, Christopher (1564–1593)

Christopher Marlowe was born in Canterbury, England. Little is known of his early life except that he was the son of a cobbler and earned a scholarship to Cambridge University. He received a B.A. and an M.A. in 1584 and 1587, respectively. Like many other students, Marlowe originally intended to receive holy orders in the church. Instead he found fame as a playwright and also probably was an espionage agent for Elizabeth I. He was a politically controversial figure and found himself accused in 1593 of libel and treason. An untimely stabbing death in a bar in Deptford that same year eliminated the need for a trial.

One of the most famous texts associated with Marlowe—the one most responsible for figuring him within gay history—is not one that he wrote but one written about him. The so-called Baines libel, written shortly after Marlowe's murder and probably designed to remove its author from culpability in some crime of scapegoating, claims that Marlowe professed that "St. John the Evangelist was bedfellow to Christ and leaned alwaies in his bosome, that he used him as the sinners of Sodoma." It also gives rise to perhaps the most famous quote attributed to Marlowe—although there is absolutely no proof Marlowe ever said it—"All they that love not Tobacco & Boies were fooles."

While Marlowe produced a large and enduring canon of writing, one text deals overtly and extensively with homoeroticism. *Edward II* is Marlowe's most famous text to deal with homoeroticism. The play depicts the fall of Edward II, a king of England, and the role that the king's love for Pierse Gaveston, a courtier and boyhood friend, played in that downfall. The play is particularly notable for its unwillingness to offer easy, moralistic answers to the questions posed by the king's downfall. No character, either homosexual or heterosexual, is given an entirely noble portrayal. And while at the end of the play sympathy tends to rest with the king—a remarkable stance in a country and at a time where sodomy was punishable by death—the monarch's own culpability as a love-torn, immoderate leader is never erased.

Homoeroticism also enters topically in other Marlowe texts. *Dido, Queen of Carthage*, begins with a comic vignette that shows Jupiter toying erotically with the young Ganymede. In the fragmentary drama *The Massacre at Paris*, there are strong intimations that Henry III is sexually obsessed with his male minions. *Hero and Leander*, an epyllia (a genre also known as the brief epic or the Ovidian erotic narrative), tells the mythical story of Hero—locked in a tower to preserve her chastity—and Leander—the amorous young suitor who almost dies trying to save her. In the story, Neptune, in the form of the water of the Hellespont in which Leander swims, confuses the young man with Ganymede. The god grabs the boy, plays with his hair and genitals, and kisses him. Only when the god realizes Leander does not share his affection does he release him and give him safe passage to Hero's tower.   *Gregory W. Bredbeck*

M

Bibliography

Bredbeck, Gregory W. *Sodomy and Interpretation: Marlowe to Milton.* Ithaca, N.Y.: Cornell University Press, 1991.

Goldberg, Jonathan. *Sodometries: Renaissance Texts, Modern Sexualities.* Stanford, Calif.: Stanford University Press, 1992.

Shepherd, Simon. *Marlowe and the Politics of Elizabethan Theatre.* New York: St. Martin's Press, 1986.

Smith, Bruce R. *Homosexual Desire in Shakespeare's England: A Cultural Poetics.* Chicago: University of Chicago Press, 1991.

Summers, Claude J. "Sex, Politics and Self-Realization in *Edward II.*" In *"A Poet and a Filthy Playmaker": New Essays on Christopher Marlowe.* Kenneth Friedenreich, Roma Gill, and Constance B. Kuriyama, eds. New York: AMS, 1988, 211–40.

Woods, Gregory. "Body, Costume, and Desire in Christopher Marlowe." In *Homosexuality in Renaissance and Enlightenment England: Literary Representations in Historical Context.* Claude J. Summers, ed. New York: Haworth Press, 1992, 69–84.

See also Barnfield, Richard; Beaumont and Fletcher; English Literature; Shakespeare, William; Theater: Premodern and Early Modern

Masculinity

For many gay men there seems to be a simultaneous embracing of sociocultural definitions of masculinity and varied attempts either to challenge or to deny the efficacy of those definitions. Tending to vacillate between acquiescing to exterior definitions of what it means to be a man and flagrantly denying those same paradigms, gay men are in a precarious position when it comes both to understanding masculinity and to adopting its tenets, partially or wholly, for their own lives. An examination of how society defines manliness and the homosexual place within (or outside) masculinity could perhaps shed light on the rather tenuous position gay men appear to occupy in relation to masculinity.

In its simplest terms masculinity is defined by attributes or characteristics that have come to be associated with being a man and have come to define what might be called "traditional masculinity." To be successfully considered a man under this rubric, a person of the male sex must demonstrate that he is ever rational and in control, possessed of a competitive and aggressive spirit, ambitious, and able to solve problems and to complete tasks, especially those that require physical toughness or strength. Finally, and perhaps most important where gay men are concerned, the traditionally masculine man must be ardently heterosexual. Conversely, overly emotional men who are submissive to the demands of others or dependent on them and men who fail to demonstrate an aggressive and competitive nature do not measure up to these standards. Traditionally, gay men have been included in this latter category, their sexuality being both reason for and cause of their inability to enact a successful manhood.

But the forces that deny gay men their rightful place in the masculine realm also exist in language, which has set up binary oppositions in terms of sex, gender, and sexuality that serve to establish a "place" for homosexuals in opposition to men and masculinity. These binaries are as follows: in terms of sex, male as opposed to female; in terms of gender, masculine as opposed to feminine; and in terms of sexuality, heterosexuality as opposed to homosexuality. By virtue of these incontrovertible oppositions, the male sex is linked with masculine gender and heterosexuality, while the homosexual automatically becomes associated with both the female and the feminine, and is already removed from the possibility of full masculine function by virtue of the structure of language.

This removal from masculine function via language subtends the vacillation many gay men feel between the desire to accept and the desire to disavow such societal configurations. On the one hand, they may enjoy the connection to the feminine, whether through ritualistic or merely celebratory drag where the guise of the female is willingly taken on or through taking pride in being emotional, compassionate, nurturing, and understanding in a traditionally feminine manner. They may even further embrace the connection to the feminine, either through overtly feminine mannerisms or the use of feminine names and/or pronouns in reference to members of their own group (and, sometimes, disparagingly, to those outside), such as "Mary," "Nancy," or merely "she," "her," or "girl."

On the other hand, these types of displays, or verbal utterances, while they may be misconstrued to demonstrate an essential or literal connection between gay men and the feminine, they may also be utilized to show that gay men understand the constructs of gender as merely constructs. Much gender theory introduced in the last decade or two indicates that gender attributes are not ingrained but selected and performed by individuals who understand the workings of language and of a culture that deems it necessary for people to demonstrate "traditional" gender norms. Ironically, it appears as though all adoptions of feminine attributes or characteristics on the part of gay men have been entered upon to demonstrate the real performative aspects of gender, especially of masculinity, for it is seldom doubted that gay men, regardless of how feminine they appear or act, are anatomically male.

For this reason, some theorists feel that gay men have long understood masculinity's performative nature. Their claims encompass many ideas about masculinity. While ostensibly about the competition for the female prize in the most basic "survival of the fittest mode," for example, masculinity actually entails competition between men with the female only as an auxiliary. In this case, masculinity is all about men, concerned only with men, and is therefore homoerotic. Along these same lines, gender theorists have also postulated that homosexuality, while once thought to preclude a man from successful enactment of masculinity, rather serves to buttress his masculinity because homosexuality, and homoerotic desire, thrive in a realm devoid of both desire for and dependence on the female, if not in her nearly complete absence. These theorists note that in its traditional definition, masculinity shrinks from any imputation of the feminine.

A few short forays into gay culture may prove true many of the theories of gender, for it seems as though gay culture has long known what it means to enact masculinity—witness the Levi and leather subculture or the pervasiveness of gay bodybuilding. The attire and bodies of the men involved in these activities certainly show how gender norms can be put on, rather than being simply innate. In addition, many gay fashion trends have in the last quarter-century seen their way into straight culture to become dominant modes of masculine dress, including suede and leather work boots, flannel shirts, with or without sleeves, decorative goatees and sideburns, even ear and body piercings and tattoos. While these co-optations by mainstream straight culture may merely signal the gay finger on the pulse of style, they also interrogate the validity of gender norms created and maintained through judgment by appearance as what once "looked" gay (feminine) now appears straight (masculine).

The burgeoning schools of gender theory have fomented a cultural reconsideration of gender norms. Though perhaps last to the cutting board,

masculinity, too, has met with some redefinition through feminism and male reactions to it. One such redefinition has come through the mythopoetic men's movement. However corny such phrases as "sensitive new age guy" once were, new and different expectations concerning what it means to be a man have emerged. Because these definitions call for an inculcation of feminine virtues and attributes, gay men are no longer so stringently viewed as failing to meet standards of masculinity. In the future, gay men might even teach those standards.

Jon Robert Adams

Bibliography

Savran, David. *Taking It Like a Man: White Masculinity, Masochism, and Contemporary American Culture*. Princeton, N.J.: Princeton University Press, 1998.
Silverman, Kaja. *Male Subjectivity at the Margins*. New York: Routledge, 1992.

See also Body Image; Clone; Feminism; Gender; Homosexuality; Machismo; Physical Culture; Sexual Orientation; Sports; Transsexualism

Mass, Lawrence (1946–)

A gay physician, Lawrence Mass was responsible for the gay press providing American journalism's first coverage of the AIDS epidemic. Born in Macon, Georgia, Mass earned his medical degree from the University of Illinois and came to Manhattan in 1979, where he worked for the Greenwich House substance abuse program.

Mass received the tip for his historic first AIDS article when a friend overheard a doctor talking about an unusually large number of gay men being in the intensive care unit of a New York hospital. The friend called Mass that night, and after Mass investigated the tip, he published a story in the *New York Native*, a biweekly gay tabloid founded in 1980.

That first article appeared on May 18, 1981—a month and a half before the new disease was mentioned in the *New York Times* on July 3, 1981. Mass's story was of singular importance because it alerted gay New York—where the disease would do fully half its killing for the next two years—that a deadly phenomenon was lurking in its midst.

Mass remained far ahead of the *Times* news staff on July 27, 1981, when he pushed what others were calling, to Mass's dismay, "gay cancer" to page one of the *Native*, whereas the *Times* did not give

M the disease that much prominence for another two years. The huge headline on Mass's story in the *Native* bluntly announced: "Cancer in the Gay Community." Mass reported that sexually active gay men in several cities were suffering from a relatively rare cancer called Kaposi's sarcoma. Mass's July article ran for an exhaustive 170 column inches, allowing room for a question-and-answer interview with a doctor from New York University Medical Center as well as two close-up photos of cancerous lesions designed not only to show readers what to look for but also to scare them.

Even more remarkable was that Mass informed readers what experts suspected regarding how the deadly disease was being spread. To save the lives of his readers, Mass—unlike reporters working for mainstream news organizations—did not hesitate to use graphic sexual terms. Mass told readers that "traumatic sex," such as anal intercourse and fist fucking, caused microscopic cuts that medical experts believed played a major role in the rapid spread of the disease. For a gay writer to challenge these sacrosanct sexual activities was both bold and courageous.

In 1982, Mass joined activist Larry Kramer and a handful of other concerned men to found Gay Men's Health Crisis, a New York organization created to fight AIDS—as well as the government's lukewarm response to the disease.

After Mass, who received no payment for his work in the *Native*, began to realize in 1982 that the disease might decimate the gay male population, he tried to persuade larger-circulation newspapers that the disease merited more coverage. But he was rebuffed by both the *Times* and the *Village Voice*.

Mass continued his pioneering AIDS coverage until 1983. But after two years of leading American journalism's tracking of the disease, Mass, a sensitive man who became overwhelmed by the human devastation of AIDS combined with the complexities of his personal life, suffered from anxiety and exhaustion that became so severe he had to be hospitalized for depression and ceased writing about AIDS.   *Rodger Streitmatter*

Bibliography

Streitmatter, Rodger. *Unspeakable: The Rise of the Gay and Lesbian Press in America*. Boston: Faber and Faber, 1995.

See also Activism, U.S.; AIDS; Gay and Lesbian Press; Gay Men's Health Crisis (GMHC); Journalism; Kramer, Larry; Sexually Transmitted Diseases

Masturbation

Masturbation is the stimulation of one's own or another's genitals, usually to orgasm and ejaculation, by manipulation or methods other than sexual intercourse. The word derives from the Latin *manustupration* (pollution by the hand). Christian cultures, in particular, have traditionally condemned it on moral and medical grounds. Its archaic synonyms *self-pollution* and *self-defilement* distinguished solitary or autoerotic masturbation from "conjugal onanism." The eighteenth-century term *onanism* alludes to the biblical story of Onan, who "spilt his seed on the ground" rather than conceive an heir by his widowed sister-in-law, Tamar. For this violation of Levirate law, God punished Onan with death (Gen. 38:7–10). Although Onan's action seems to have been *coitus interruptus* rather than masturbation, this biblical passage has served as the foundation for the Roman Catholic censure of *manustupration*.

Medieval theologians, particularly Thomas Aquinas (1225–1274), first singled out masturbation as a "vice against nature" and a mortal sin in which "pollution is provoked in order to obtain sensual pleasure without carnal union." Aquinas distinguished "voluntary pollution" from involuntary, "nocturnal pollution" since he considered the latter sinful only because of the lascivious thoughts that might accompany it and not because of the seminal emission itself. Medieval penitential manuals also associated masturbation with the Pauline condemnation of *mollities*, softness or effeminacy, which in turn could also refer to homosexuality.

Classical physicians believed that male and female seed or semen was the product of a complex distillation of the blood. They claimed that it took forty ounces of blood to yield one ounce of semen. Excessive expulsion of this "precious essence"—whether through coitus or masturbation—could lead to humoral imbalance and illness. The Hippocratic texts describe under the term "consumption of the back" a disease most common in newlyweds and the libidinous. They lose semen during coitus, urination or defecation, and nocturnal emissions. This leads to softening of the spinal cord and eventual bodily wasting. Yet most doctors, such as Galen (second century A.D.), were far more concerned with the morbid effects of *retained* semen in celibate people. Some medieval doctors even recommended the employment of specialized midwives to rub the genitals of hysterical women to expel their corrupt seed. Involuntary seminal loss was referred to as *gonorrœa* because of the white, genital discharge accompanying this venereal disease. These humoral models of "spermatorrhœa" are similar to those in traditional Chinese, Indian, Native American, and other medical systems, where excess seminal loss is blamed for weakness, consumption, and insanity.

Serious medical concern about masturbation per se began in the early eighteenth century with the publication in London of "Onania," a quack doctor's pamphlet advertising various patent medicines for treating the evils of self-pollution. "Onania" blamed masturbation for almost every conceivable illness, from pimples to consumption and death. These fears were given full medical credence and a firm physiological basis thanks to Swiss physician Samuel-Auguste Tissot (1728–1797). His treatise on *Onanisme* (1760) specially highlighted the ill effects of masturbation in children, who required all their humoral strength for normal, healthy growth.

Later medical writers continued to expound on Tissot's antimasturbatory teachings. Nineteenth-century physicians particularly warned that masturbation exhausted the nervous system, thereby producing neurasthenia (nervous weakness), neurosis, and hysteria. Furthermore, the masturbator's thinned semen spawned feeble, degenerate offspring. Aside from these physiological effects, doctors feared that the "solitary vice" encouraged antisociality and "unnatural" erotic attachments. For these reasons, masturbation was often conflated with a variety of sexual deviations including homosexuality. Masturbation posed a danger to the imagination because it allowed associations between sexual pleasure and objects other than people of the opposite sex. "Autophilia," as a form of self-loving or narcissism, was portrayed as a starting point for same-sex love. Physicians also viewed mutual masturbation as a common form of homosexual sex, particularly in lesbians or "tribades" (women who rub their genitals together).

The medical condemnation of masturbation was waning by the early twentieth century; however, Sigmund Freud and his psychoanalytic followers continued to portray autoeroticism as infantile or arrested sexuality. But the extensive sexual surveys by Alfred C. Kinsey and his colleagues published in 1948 and 1953 demonstrated that masturbation was an almost universal aspect of sexual behavior among Americans. The Kinsey studies thus justified a tidal change in medical attitudes toward masturbation, whereby the absence of autoeroticism, particularly in adolescence, came to be taken as a symptom of psychosexual abnormality or stunted develop-

ment. Nevertheless, the Catholic Church continues to consider masturbation sinful, and vestiges of its medical pathologization persist as folk beliefs and cultural taboos.   *Vernon A. Rosario*

Bibliography

Bennett, Paula, and Vernon Rosario, eds. *Solitary Pleasures: The Historical, Literary, and Artistic Discourses of Autoeroticism.* New York: Routledge, 1995.

Bottéro, Alain. "Consumption by Semen Loss in India and Elsewhere." *Culture Medicine and Psychiatry* 15 (1991): 303–20.

*Onania, or the heinous sin of self-pollution and all its frightful consequences, in both sexes considered.... * 8th ed. London, 1776. Facsimile reprint, New York: Garland, 1986.

Stengers, Jean, and Anne Van Neck. *Histoire d'une grande peur: La masturbation.* Brussels: Éditions de l'Université de Bruxelles, 1984.

See also Catholicism; Christianity; Freud, Sigmund; Kinsey, Alfred; Mollies; Sexology; Thomas Aquinas

Mattachine Society

One of the first gay rights organizations, the Mattachine Society was founded in Los Angeles in 1951 by Henry (Harry) Hay, Chuck Rowland, and Bob Hull. The three were members of the Communist Party, and their understanding of the society's goals and ideology was deeply influenced by their party experience. An instructor in the history of music at the party-sponsored People's Education Center, Hay took the name of the society from an obscure medieval fraternity of musicians who wore masks to conceal their identities when performing in public. He and the other founders were eager to build a mass movement of homosexuals capable of militant, collective action. They identified three objectives: The society would seek to mobilize and unify homosexuals, teach them to conceive of themselves as an oppressed minority with their own distinct culture, and provide them with leadership in their struggle for emancipation.

Membership remained small until February 1952, when the society publicly protested the entrapment of one of its members by a plainsclothes police officer. As membership grew, the society's secretive structure, modeled on that of the Communist Party, became a divisive issue, threatening to split it apart. In March 1953 Paul Coates, a columnist for the Los Angeles *Mirror*, reported that the

M

society's lawyer, Fred Snider, had taken the Fifth Amendment when appearing before the House Un-American Activities Committee. Worried that the society might be a front for the Communist Party, several of the members called on Hay, Rowland, and Hull to abandon their secrecy and make themselves known. Although the three had already broken with the party, they wanted to avoid a confrontation, and in April they convened a conference to draft a constitution, adopt bylaws, and elect officers. At the conference, opposition to the founders' political vision mounted. The militantly anticommunist leaders of the San Francisco delegation introduced a motion requiring a loyalty oath. The Laguna Beach delegation raised questions about the founders' minoritarian understanding of homosexuality. Convinced that homosexuals did not differ significantly from heterosexuals, the delegation urged the society to promote assimilation into the mainstream rather than the building of a separate homosexual culture.

Although the delegates sided with the founders and rejected these views, the opposition gained control of the society at a conference the following November. Under the new leadership, the society's priorities shifted dramatically. Rather than protesting entrapment and other oppressive police practices, it sponsored blood drives and other charitable activities intended to show that homosexuals were solid, patriotic citizens. It also sought the support of medical professionals, discouraging members from engaging in practices that reinforced negative stereotypes (cruising in parks, frequenting gay bars, engaging in butch-femme role-playing). This shift in priorities was costly. Membership declined precipitously, even as new chapters formed in other cities. In 1961 the society was forced to dissolve the national structure, although the New York, San Francisco, and Los Angeles chapters remained active until the late sixties, when they proved unable to compete with more confrontational gay liberation organizations.   *Robert J. Corber*

Bibliography

Adam, Barry D. *The Rise of a Gay and Lesbian Movement*. Boston: Twayne, 1987.

D'Emilio, John. *Sexual Politics, Sexual Communities: The Making of a Homosexual Minority in the United States, 1940–1970*. Chicago: University of Chicago Press, 1983.

Katz, Jonathan Ned. *Gay American History: Lesbians and Gay Men in the U.S.A.* Rev. ed. New York: Meridian, 1992.

Marotta, Toby. *The Politics of Homosexuality: How Lesbians and Gay Men Have Made Themselves a Political and Social Force in Modern America*. Boston: Houghton Mifflin, 1981.

Timmons, Stuart. *The Trouble with Harry Hay: Founder of the Modern Gay Movement*. Boston: Alyson, 1990.

See also Activism U.S.; Assimilation; Gay Left; Gay Liberation; Hay, Harry; Homophile Movement; McCarthyism

Matthiessen, F. O. (1902–1950)

One of the most influential literary critics of his era, Francis Otto Matthiessen was born in Pasadena, California. He spent most of his childhood in Illinois with his mother, who had been abandoned by his father. As an undergraduate at Yale University, he edited the literary magazine, organized a Bible study group, and was a member of the Liberal Club, activities that foreshadowed his later career. After graduating from Yale, he studied at Oxford on a Rhodes Scholarship, where he was active in the Labour Party. In 1925, he returned to the United States and began graduate work at Harvard. After receiving his Ph.D., he taught briefly at Yale before accepting a position at Harvard, where he taught English and American literature until his death.

In 1924, while sailing for England, Matthiessen met and fell in love with the painter Russell Cheney. Cheney, who was twenty years older than Matthiessen, was less comfortable with his homosexuality, which he associated with his alcoholism, and he discouraged Matthiessen from telling his friends about their relationship. Nevertheless, the two pioneered a new form of gay relationship, drawing support from Whitman's ideas about comradeship. They remained lovers until Cheney's death in 1945.

Matthiessen's renown as the author of *American Renaissance: Art and Expression in the Age of Emerson and Whitman* (1941), one of the founding texts of American studies, has obscured his other achievements. He was an exemplary scholar/activist who managed to bridge the divide between the university and the larger community. Although his religious convictions prevented him from joining the Communist Party, he was a prominent fellow traveler. The political organizations in which he was most active were the Harvard Teachers' Union, which he helped found in 1935, and the Progressive Party. Moreover, he courageously refused to disavow his commitment to socialism, despite the postwar backlash against literary leftism, and he campaigned actively for Henry Wallace, the 1948 Progressive Party presidential candidate.

Matthiessen maintained fairly rigid boundaries between his personal and professional lives, leading some to speculate that authorizing the American Renaissance required him to suppress his homosexuality. What influence his sexuality had on his literary criticism was necessarily subtle and indirect. His book on Sarah Orne Jewett, published in 1929, sympathetically portrayed Jewett's struggles against Victorian ideals of femininity and celebrated her relationship with Annie Fields. *American Renaissance* located Walt Whitman at the pinnacle of the American literary canon. Still, he was hostile to more openly gay colleagues, and former students complained that he avoided addressing homoerotic themes in his American literature classes.

The Cold War threatened to drive Matthiessen still further into the closet. Because of the connection between communism and homosexuality in Cold War ideology, he was especially vulnerable to Red-baiting. On April 1, 1950, shortly before he was to appear before the House UnAmerican Activities Committee, he jumped out the window of a Boston hotel. His suicide note did not mention the growing persecution of communists and homosexuals, but it expressed despair over the increasingly reactionary political climate.   *Robert J. Corber*

Bibliography

Bergman, David. "F.O. Matthiessen: The Critic as Homosexual." In *Gaiety Transfigured: Gay Self-Representation in American Literature*. Madison, Wis.: University of Wisconsin Press, 1991, 85–102.

Sweezy, Paul M. "A Biographical Sketch." In *F.O. Matthiessen (1902–1950): A Collective Portrait*. Paul M. Sweezy and Leo Huberman, eds. New York: Henry Schuman, 1950, ix–xii.

See also McCarthyism; U.S. Literature: Contemporary Gay Writing; Whitman, Walt

Maupin, Armistead (1944–)

For historical purposes one might call Armistead Maupin "Rita Mae Brown in drag." Both writers are products of the South and of the post-Stonewall seventies; they share down-to-earth wit, mainstream aspirations, liberal politics, and the highest royalty earnings of any out-of-the-closet scribes. Like John Rechy, Paul Monette, and (arguably) Edmund White, Maupin and Brown are stars in their own rights, instantly recognizable outside marginalized gay circles.

But they differ in one crucial respect: Brown queered the individual's rite of passage in *Rubyfruit Jungle* (1973), but Maupin charted the serendipitous passages traveled by communities, queer and straight, in his most famous work, *Tales of the City*. Maupin first serialized *Tales* in the *San Francisco Chronicle*, then published them in six volumes between 1978 and 1989. As executive producer, Maupin brought volume one of *Tales* to the television screen in a Peabody-winning PBS miniseries in 1994. Despite critical raves for the TV adaptation, the subsequent tales of hapless Mary Ann Singleton, unlucky-in-love Michael (Mouse) Tolliver, and mystery woman Anna Madrigal took four years to reach the airwaves. (The Showtime cable network aired *More Tales of the City* in June 1998.) Maupin has made no secret about the difficulty of filming gay-friendly teleplays in a homophobic, right-wing era.

Although Maupin is best known for *Tales*, he published *Maybe the Moon* (1992), a best-selling story of a has-been "little person" who miraculously improves the lives of those around her. Maupin's prose has invited comparisons to P. G. Wodehouse, E. F. Benson, and Charles Dickens. "Still," as Barbara Kaplan Bass writes of Maupin, "critics insist upon labeling Maupin as merely a translator of pop culture rather than a serious mainstream satirist, emphasizing the local-color aspect of his writing and noting his popular success" (Bass 258). Harper-Collins has published the following titles in Maupin's *Tales of the City* Series: *Tales of the City* (1978), *More Tales of the City* (1980), *Further Tales of the City* (1982), *Babycakes* (1984), *Significant Others* (1987), and *Sure of You* (1989).

John M. Ison

Bibliography

Bass, Barbara Kaplan. "Armistead Maupin (1944–)." In *Contemporary Gay Novelists: A Bio-Bibliographical Critical Sourcebook*. Emmanuel S. Nelson, ed. Westport, Conn.: Greenwood, 1993, 254–59.

See also Benson, E. F.; Fiction; Monette, Paul; Rechy, John; San Francisco; U.S. Literature: Contemporary Gay Writing; White, Edmund

M

McAlmon, Robert (1896–1956)

"There are no real homos, male or female," wrote Robert McAlmon, "but there is the bi-sex, and in more people than know it about themselves. Personally the types I object to are the female who droops female sex appeal or the male who swaggers with virility. They are the real abnorms" (Smoller 216). McAlmon delighted in exposing latent homosexuality of people who hysterically insisted on their unimpeachable heterosexual masculinity. He was also openly critical of the egotistic self-mythicizing of some writers of his generation. His dislike of sham provoked revengeful tarnishing of his artistic reputation and contributed to his neglect by the mainstream press and a fall into virtual oblivion.

McAlmon was a key figure among American expatriate artists in Paris in the 1920s and 1930s. As a publisher, he helped promote the careers of several crucial modernist authors, most of whom highly praised his own writings. Although a prolific poet, McAlmon excelled in fiction, in which he depicts, in a direct and unaffected manner, a great variety of characters and experiences. In most of his works homosexuality is subterranean, though the collection of short stories, *Distinguished Air* (1925), describes with candor the sexual underground of Berlin in the 1920s.

In 1921 McAlmon married English writer Bryher, whose family's wealth enabled his career. The marriage was asexual and served as a respectable screen for Bryher's lesbianism, but it is unclear whether McAlmon married for similar reasons. He rarely referred to his marriage, terminated by divorce in 1927, or to his emotional and sexual life. Various guesses about his love affairs remain unconfirmed, and it seems likely that McAlmon's restlessness and increasing bitterness caused not only his excessive drinking and almost compulsive traveling but also his inability or unwillingness to commit himself sexually or romantically to only one man or woman.   *Dejan Kuzmanovic*

Bibliography

McAlmon, Robert, and Kay Boyle. *Being Geniuses Together, 1920–1930*. San Francisco: North Point Press, 1984.

Smoller, Sanford J. *Adrift Among Geniuses: Robert McAlmon, Writer and Publisher of the Twenties*. University Park, Pa.: Pennsylvania State University Press, 1975.

See also Bisexuality; Paris

McCarthyism

McCarthyism is the name for the politically repressive campaign in the 1940s and 1950s to expunge communism from American political and cultural life. Historians usually trace the beginning of McCarthyism to Wisconsin Republican Senator Joseph McCarthy's speech on February 9, 1950, to the Women's Republican Club of Wheeling, West Virgina, in which he announced dramatically that he held in his hand a list of communist spies in the State Department. McCarthy's charges of communist subversion were nothing new; opponents of the New Deal had been making similar charges since the 1930s. What distinguished McCarthy was his willingness to back up his charges with names and numbers, although the names and numbers varied, depending on the context of his speeches and the skepticism that he encountered in reporters.

McCarthy was also more adept than other anticommunist politicians at manipulating the media. He waited to release his charges until shortly before evening deadlines, guaranteeing sensational news coverage the following day. He also positioned himself as the "common man," mythologized by countless liberal Hollywood films of the thirties and forties, who had come to the nation's capital from the American heartland to clean it up. McCarthy's frequent appearances on such television shows as *Meet the Press,* in which he addressed reporters by their first names and responded to their aggressive questions with seemingly guileless humor, helped to persuade audiences that he had no desire to trample on the Constitution, as his critics asserted, but only to expose an elite group of Ivy League–educated intellectuals who despite their contempt for ordinary Americans determined the policies and programs that governed them. In this way, he skillfully recaptured the political terrain occupied by the Communist Party since the Popular Front era, when it emerged as the representative of the "common man."

Although McCarthy embodied the excesses of the Cold War era more fully than did the many other politicians who built their careers on anticommunism, the use of his name to refer to the anticommunist fervor of the forties and fifties has led to some serious distortions. First, it has deflected attention from the equally important roles played by FBI director J. Edgar Hoover and President Truman. It was Truman, after all, who in 1947, some three years before McCarthy's notorious Wheeling speech, issued an executive order requiring loyalty oaths of government employees. It was also Truman who initiated the criminal prosecutions and deportation proceedings directed against Communist Party leaders that effectively outlawed party membership.

But a more serious problem with the term *McCarthyism* is that it obscures the relation between Cold War political repression and earlier episodes of anticommunist hysteria. McCarthy's fanaticism has enabled many scholars to treat the anticommunist crusade of the 1950s as a political aberration. Yet underlying McCarthy's demonization of communists were attitudes and beliefs deeply rooted in American political culture. The McCarthy witch-hunts followed a pattern first set by the Palmer raids of the 1920s, in which Attorney General A. Mitchell Palmer ordered the FBI to round up foreign-born Communist Party members and detain them for deportation.

Where the Red scare of the 1920s differed from that of the 1950s was in its exploitation of the nativist fervor that gripped Anglo-Americans following the great strike wave of 1919 and that culminated in passage of legislation restricting immigration from eastern and southern Europe. The majority of activists deported by the FBI in the 1920s were eastern European Jews. The Nazi Holocaust prevented anticommunists of the 1950s from deploying a similar strategy, which would have been seen as anti-Semitic. Instead, they exploited fears that there was no way to tell gay men from straight men. These fears can in part be traced to the 1948 publication of the first Kinsey report, which challenged the stereotype of the effeminate homosexual with statistical evidence showing that gay men did not differ significantly from straight men. The report's controversial findings enabled anticommunists to demonize communism by indirectly linking it to homosexuality. For if gay men were virtually indistinguishable from straight men, then like the communists allegedly conspiring to overthrow the government, they could infiltrate the nation's political and cultural institutions without being detected. In positioning gays as national-security risks, anticommunists not only helped to contain the report's explosive impact but also identified communism as a form of psychopathology. What is most troubling about this aspect of McCarthyism is that many of those responsible for it (Hoover, McCarthy, Roy Cohn, the Wisconsin senator's infamous chief counsel) participated in the gay male subculture, although they did not conceive of themselves as gay.

Historians often emphasize McCarthyism's detrimental impact on American politics. With the decline of the Communist Party, the possibility that serious alternatives to the status quo would become a topic of debate in the political public sphere grew increasingly dim. For this reason, the development of the American welfare state lagged well behind that of other industrialized nations. Afraid of arousing controversy, Congress abandoned the unfinished agenda of the New Deal, allowing measures such as national health care, once supported by Truman, to fall by the wayside. Less frequently acknowledged by historians is McCarthyism's impact on the postwar gay rights movement. Henry (Harry) Hay, Chuck Rowland, and Bob Hull, were all members of the Communist Party when in 1951 they founded the Mattachine Society, one of the first gay rights organizations. Inspired by the party's position on the "Negro question," which argued that African Americans comprised a nation within a nation, they conceived of gays and lesbians as an oppressed minority with their own distinct culture. Although their affiliation with the party was a carefully guarded secret, their militancy aroused the suspicions of anticommunist members who urged them to abandon their secrecy and reveal themselves. The anticommunists' attempts to Red-bait the founders alienated the other members of the society. But their justifiable concerns about the founders' confrontational tactics were widely shared, and the anticommunists were eventually able to gain control of the society. A radical alternative to the accommodationist approach pursued by the new leadership did not emerge until the gay liberation movement of the 1960s. *Robert J. Corber*

Bibliography

Caute, David. *The Great Fear: The Anti-Communist Purge Under Truman and Eisenhower.* New York: Simon and Schuster, 1978.

Corber, Robert J. *Homosexuality in Cold War America: Resistance and the Crisis of Masculinity.* Durham, N.C.: Duke University Press, 1997.

D'Emilio, John. *Sexual Politics, Sexual Communities: The Making of a Homosexual Minority in the United States, 1940–1970.* Chicago: University of Chicago Press, 1983.

Kazin, Michel. "A Free People Fight Back: The Rise and Fall of the Cold War Right." In *The Populist Persuasion: An American History.* New York: Basic Books, 1995, 165–93.

Rogin, Michael. "Political Repression in the United States." In *Ronald Reagan, the Movie, and Other Episodes in Political Demonology.* Berkeley: University of California Press, 1987, 44–80.

M

Schrecker, Ellen. *The Age of McCarthyism: A Brief History with Documents*. Boston: Bedford Books, 1994.

See also Cohn, Roy M.; Gay Left; Hay, Harry; Hoover, J. Edgar; Mattachine Society

McKay, Claude (1889–1948)

A writer and important figure of the Harlem Renaissance, Festus Claudius McKay was born into a relatively prosperous farming family in Clarendon Parish, Jamaica, in 1889. In 1912 he published two volumes of poetry, *Songs of Jamaica* and *Constab Ballads*, that established him as one of the brightest lights in Jamaican literature, while his use of Jamaican dialect was considered revolutionary.

Perhaps the most important influence on McKay's early work and his later decision to make writing his career was his friendship with British expatriate Walter Jekyll. The Cambridge-educated Jekyll, generally believed to have been homosexual, may also have introduced McKay to the early writings on homosexuality that accounted for the surprisingly untroubled acceptance of his own sexual preferences that McKay displayed throughout his life. Although he does not explicitly deal with homosexuality in any of his published works, he seems to have made little effort to conceal his bisexuality.

After his emigration to the United States in 1912, McKay went on to become one of the premier poets and fiction writers of the Harlem Renaissance. His best-known work is his novel *Home to Harlem* (1928). The first work of fiction by a black writer to make the best-seller list, the book's unvarnished depictions of the lives of the black underclass earned McKay undying hostility from the more conservative members of the black intelligentsia, most notably Alain Locke and W.E.B. Du Bois. McKay died in relative obscurity in 1948.   *Terry Rowden*

Bibliography

Cooper, Wayne. *Claude McKay: Rebel Sojourner in the Harlem Renaissance*. Baton Rouge: Louisiana State University Press, 1987.

See also African American Gay Culture; Harlem Renaissance

McNally, Terrence (1939–)

Terrence McNally is one of America's pioneering gay playwrights. Over a career spanning more than three decades, he has been successful artistically and commercially in moving gay characters onto mainstream stages and screens.

In the sixties, McNally was seen as a young countercultural playwright whose work did not belong on the Broadway stage. His first Broadway play, *And Things That Go Bump in the Night* (1964), was considered too radical and adventurous and died a quick death. McNally moved to the more congenial environment of Off-Broadway and had considerable success with the saga of a sixties countercultural figure, *Where Has Tommy Flowers Gone* (1971), which in its surreal, dark comedy has much in common with the early works of McNally's contemporary, John Guare. With the two one-act plays produced off and on Broadway as *Bad Habits*, McNally showed his talent at writing screwball comedy. The plays also contained gay characters among their galleries of eccentrics.

The Ritz (1975), a hilarious farce set in a gay bathhouse, put urban gay culture of the time on the commercial Broadway stage with considerable success. In a move that would become typical of McNally's work, the tables were turned and, within the gay world of the bathhouse, the heterosexual characters were the endangered outsiders. McNally uses the same tactic in his hit *Lips Together, Teeth Apart* (1991), in which two heterosexual married couples stay in a summer house in a gay community on Fire Island. McNally's work is rooted in a philosophy of assimilation. He has been for years the house playwright of the Manhattan Theatre Club, whose audience is predominately well-heeled heterosexuals. His interest is in showing that audience their similarities to and differences from their gay neighbors. When he writes a play about a heterosexual couple, *Frankie and Johnny in the Claire de Lune* (1987), their names suggest that the two lovers could be any gender. And in the screen version, he opened out the script to include a gay couple.

McNally's work has been daring in its candid presentation and critique of gay life, incurring wrath from all sides. *The Lisbon Traviata* (1985) and *Love! Valour! Compassion!* (1994) offer the darker and lighter sides of contemporary middle-class, urban gay life. The former depicts opera queens who hide in their obsession with Maria Callas and other doomed divas. Stephen and Mendy live hermetic lives. One hides from contact with everyone but the salespeople at Tower Records, while the other elevates his failure in personal relationships to the level of grand opera. *Love! Valour! Compassion!* dramatizes the summer holiday interactions of a group of gay men who form a loving alternative to the traditional nuclear family. As the hyperbolic title suggests, these men manage to inject small but significant forms of heroism into their battles with disease and mortality and their ability to rise above petty behavior. The eight characters are the rebuttal to the bitchy, self-hating characters of Mart Crowley's *The Boys in the Band* (1968). If Crowley's play shows how gay men of a certain generation were taught self-hating, self-destructive behaviors, McNally's shows how far gay men have come in three decades. It is ironic that *Love! Valour! Compassion!* has received the most vitriolic attacks not from heterosexuals but from queer radicals who see the play as hopelessly bourgeois. McNally's most recent play, *Corpus Christi* (1998), a daring attempt to reclaim Christianity for gay men, inspired threats of violent retaliation from conservative Christian groups.

McNally has also had considerable success as the writer of books for Broadway musicals, including the award-winning hit adaptation of Manuel Puig's *Kiss of the Spider Woman*.

John M. Clum

Bibliography

Clum, John M. *Acting Gay: Male Homosexuality in Modern Drama.* New York: Columbia University Press, 1994.

Zinman, Toby Silverman, ed. *Terrence McNally: A Casebook.* New York: Garland, 1997.

See also Opera Queens; Puig, Manuel

McPhee, Colin (1900–1964)

The music of this Canadian composer and pianist is enjoying a small revival as the result of art music's unreflected admiration of Orientalism in the work of (straight) minimalist composers like Steve Reich and Philip Glass. McPhee's most ambitious work, *Tabuh-Tabuhan* (1936), is "a celebration of the Balinese gamelan" (Oja 103). The composer's reflection on this phenomenon focuses on the degree of originality in the Occidental composer rather than on the politics of exploiting "a so-called primitive music" (Oja 116), which remain largely unexamined in the music world to the present day. McPhee's life is not the best advertisement for the arty homosexual of his day.

His long period in Bali in the thirties was financed entirely by his wife, Jane Belo, whose support is not even mentioned in *A House in Bali*. After their divorce, McPhee told Mrs. Cowell that Jane had turned into a prig, largely, it seems, because having the Balinese man with whom he was "in love" continually around "was too much for her vanity" (Oja 142). On returning to the States in 1939, he became depressed, took to drink, and sponged off his friends (Cesar Chávez, Aaron Copland, Henry Cowell, Oliver Daniel). His psychiatrist was William Mayer, whose wife, Elizabeth, was very good to gay artists like W. H. Auden and Benjamin Britten—the younger English composer befriended McPhee only to be rewarded by enormously patronizing reviews of his music. A letter from McPhee to Mayer is interesting about the concatenation of homosexuality, creativity, and Orientalism in his own case: "Many times there was a decision to be made between some important opportunity and a sexual (homosexual) relationship which was purely sensual. I never hesitated to choose the latter. This I did deliberately and would do again and again, for it seemed the only thing that was real. The Balinese period was simply a long extension of this" (Mayer Collection, Britten-Pears Library, Aldeburgh). In 1960, McPhee landed a job at UCLA, whose ethnomusicology library contains his papers.

Philip Brett

Bibliography

Brett, Philip. "Eros and Orientalism in Britten's Operas." In *Queering the Pitch: The New Gay and Lesbian Musicology.* Philip Brett, Elizabeth Wood, and Gary C, Thomas eds. New York: Routledge, 1994, 235–56.

McPhee, Colin. *A House in Bali.* New York: John Day, 1946, reprinted New York: AMS Press, 1980; New York: Oxford University Press, 1987.

———. *Music in Bali.* New Haven: Yale University Press, 1966; reprinted New York: Da Capo, 1976.

Oja, Carol. *Colin McPhee: Composer in Two Worlds.* Washington, D.C.: Smithsonian Institution Press, 1990.

See also Auden, W. H.; Britten, Benjamin; Copland, Aaron; Cowell, Henry

Media

The history of the depiction of gays and lesbians in the mainstream U.S. media is a story of suicide, murder, and evil. Vito Russo in an appendix to *The Celluloid Closet* (1987), under the heading "Necrology," lists over forty examples of the ways in which gay or lesbian characters in films have died. The rest of his book depicts the numerous ways gay men were portrayed as effeminate and sissy stereotypes, lesbians as butch and aggressive women, and all homosexuals as victims and villains.

For years, gays and lesbians had to depend on their own media to tell their stories. As early as 1924, a Chicago gay newsletter called *Friendship and Freedom* was published, as was, among others, a 1934 newsletter the *Chanticleer,* and *Vice Versa*, a 1947 Los Angeles lesbian publication. But with the beginning of the modern homophile movement in the early 1950s in Los Angeles, *ONE* became the first widely circulated homosexual magazine, selling two thousand copies a month. Along with the *Ladder*, published by the Daughters of Bilitis from 1956 to 1970, and the *Mattachine Review*, published from 1955 to 1964, these early and important gay and lesbian media contributed to a growing sense of community identity. The tradition carries on today with such widely circulated national magazines as the *Advocate* (the longest continuously published gay magazine, since 1967), *Lesbian News*, and *Out*, along with a large number of less commercialized local newspapers, underground 'zines, independent films, cable TV shows, and computer Web sites on the Internet, produced by and for gay and lesbian audiences.

But these media have often been in response to mainstream films, newspapers, radio, and television that were much slower in recognizing gay and lesbian lives. From 1930 to the late 1960s, the Motion Picture Production Code was the major form of self-regulation of Hollywood movies, and it developed a list of forbidden topics, including "any inference of sexual perversion," i.e., homosexuality. Before 1930, many pre-Code films had explicit references to homosexuals and numerous depictions of cross-dressing, but it was not until 1961 that the subject of homosexuality was allowed on-screen so overtly. The Code era's images of the humorous, innocent sissy of failed masculinity typical of the 1930s and 1940s then gave way in the 1960s and 1970s to gay characters who were shown as lonely, predatory, and pathological.

Television was also slow in responding to accurate and fair depictions of gays and lesbians. Partly in response to pressure from a growing gay activists' movement, the American Broadcasting Company (ABC) in 1973 became the first U.S. network to air a made-for-TV movie about gay men, *That Certain Summer*. Within a few years, most major situation comedies, drama shows, and talk shows addressed gay topics, typically as a special issue, rarely in terms of a continuing character or plot. By the mid-1980s, any attention to gay issues was almost always framed in terms of AIDS, and then with gays as victim or villain.

One of the explanations for the negative media images and the relative invisibility of gays and lesbians historically can be traced to social, economic, and political forces that structure the entertainment industry and the ways it constructs images of people. As profit-making business corporations, media organizations reflect the economic marketplace and political climate of the culture. Targeting the "typical viewer" who purchases sponsors' goods, the media tailor their products so as not to offend the least common denominator.

With the rise of an increasingly active gay movement in the 1970s, pressure against the media began when the Gay Activists Alliance (GAA) in New York City confronted executives at ABC-TV in 1973 about unfavorable treatment of homosexuality. A group of GAA members split to form the National Gay Task Force (NGTF), which then formed a Gay Media Task Force (GMTF) in Los Angeles, under the direction of Newt Deiter. The Association of Gay and Lesbian Artists (AGLA) also started in the early 1980s as a support group of gay media people to lobby the industry, consult on projects, and present awards for positive depictions of gays and lesbians.

In 1975, NGTF called for a boycott of sponsors of the *Marcus Welby* TV show. These early attempts at organizing resistance, the later street protests against the filming of such movies as *Cruising* in 1979 and *Basic Instinct* in 1991, and the visibility of the Gay and Lesbian Alliance Against Defamation (GLAAD) have all contributed to significant changes in the media's presentations. Although GMTF and AGLA no longer exist, their efforts led to the formation of GLAAD in New York in 1985, then in Los Angeles in 1988. Today, GLAAD is the largest and most influential national gay organization, with chapters around the country devoted to monitoring the media's portrayals of gays and lesbians.

Some argue that the new images are nothing more than assimilationist forms of incorporation, however, in which the dominant culture accommodates the radical perspective into its view and perpetuates an image of a mostly white and mostly middle-class gay community, often one without networks of friendships and typically desexualized and apolitical.

One way of analyzing the media's images of gays and lesbians is to consider four possible depictions: overt homophobic and negative stereotypic characterizations; heterosexist forms of stereotyping; invisible and ignored; and accurate, fair, and balanced images.

Overt Homophobic and Negative Stereotypic Characterizations

Combating overtly homophobic images has dominated a good deal of the energies and time of many lesbian and gay activists. Although some of the early strategies of protest and lobbying have resulted in a significant decline of overtly negative characterizations, the repeated use of epithets such as "faggot," "dyke," "queer," "homo," and "fruit" continues in many media. When these words are used, they often signify a way of establishing evil or marginality about the character so labeled, although occasionally they demonstrate the ignorance of the person using them. These words become a shorthand for indicating the villain or underlining the pathology of the character. Linking the villains with homosexuality has been another common way of signaling their evilness, even when explicit epithets are not used.

While the use of overtly homophobic expressions in movies and on television dramas and situation comedies has declined significantly in recent years, ad campaigns and videos created and marketed by radical right groups fighting to overturn antigay discrimination ordinances and to pass repressive legislation against gays and lesbians depend primarily on presenting the most stereotypical images in sensational and negative ways. Many conservative religious programs consistently attack gays and lesbians with bogus research data, misinformation, and fear.

Heterosexist Forms of Stereotyping

When the media do decide to include gay and lesbian voices and perspectives, the techniques and words used often end up reinforcing the dominance of the heterosexual perspective and the outside status of the gay viewpoint. So, for example, referring to gays' and lesbians' lives as "lifestyles," calling a lesbian an "avowed homosexual," or describing nongay people as the "general population" perpetuates the "otherness" of the gay person without using traditionally negative stereotypes or epithets. Although these phrases are not overtly homophobic, certain heterosexist assumptions are indicated by them.

In addition to language, the subtle forms of heterosexual dominance can be seen in the ways gays and lesbians are depicted, even fairly. The images are almost exclusively white, middle or upper class, disproportionately male, and desexualized. Many gays and lesbians also appear in sitcoms usually isolated from other relationships, or in real newspaper obituaries without reference to romantic partners, thereby reinforcing some stereotypes about gay people being alone or separate from the ways in which others lead lives embedded in networks of family and friends.

Invisible and Ignored

Nonreporting of major gay events is one form of distortion that seriously affects lesbian and gay images in the news media. Overt cases of omission are also matched by routine exclusion from the everyday discourse of entertainment television, movies, newspapers, and magazines. Hence, a feature story in a newspaper on the elderly in America typically excludes the problems facing older lesbians; a TV documentary on youth suicide ignores gay teenagers; and a movie located in some large city rarely shows gay people as neighbors, lead characters, or part of the urban environment.

Although appearances of gay characters occur on many more television shows today, they tend to show up once or irregularly, thereby emphasizing their invisibility throughout the rest of the series. And along the way, they have been depoliticized, desexualized, and made nonthreatening to the status quo. Thus, they achieve a form of invisibility by looking and acting just like every other character. Historically, it was also not unusual for movies, plays, poetry, and other forms of writing to alter gay and lesbian characters into heterosexuals or to remove any reference about their homosexuality (as in the movie versions of *A Streetcar Named Desire*, *Cat on a Hot Tin Roof*, and *The Color Purple*).

Accurate and Balanced Portrayals

While invisibility continues to characterize media images, there has been an increase in the media representation of gays and lesbians in recent years and a trend toward more accurate and fair images. Some of this is the result of to an increase in the production of media by gays and lesbians themselves. But nongay media are also increasingly devoting more attention to gay images, especially in light of major social, legal, and political issues that have focused on gays and lesbians. Attention by the news media on issues related to gays in the military and "gay marriage" have generated many magazine cover stories and radio and TV feature stories without the disparaging and distorted language that once would have been the norm.

Similarly, TV sitcoms and dramas have increasingly included continuing characters who are gay or lesbian and stories with gay or lesbian themes. No longer have these become forbidden topics or ones used to generate a laugh at the expense of the gay character. However, the price paid has been depictions of people who look no different from everyone else on TV, thereby minimizing the more political, sexual, and social differences that may arise from having to live in a society where people continue to discriminate and commit violence against gays and lesbians.

The more accurate and balanced portrayals are also in part because of an increasingly more tolerant climate in the media workplaces that allow gay and lesbian employees to have domestic partner benefits; to be visibly present, organized, and open with their comments and creative skills; and to work with less fear of job discrimination. Thus, creating environments in which gays and lesbians can openly live their lives becomes a salient strategy in the development of accurate media portrayals of the complexity and diversity of lesbian and gay people and their worlds.

Peter M. Nardi

Bibliography

Alwood, Edward. *Straight News: Gays, Lesbians, and the News Media*. New York: Columbia University Press, 1996.

Gross, Larry. "What Is Wrong with This Picture? Lesbian Women and Gay Men on Television." In *Queer Words, Queer Images*. R. J. Ringer, ed. New York: New York University Press, 1994, 143–56.

Hantzis, Darlene, and Valerie Lehr. "Whose Desire? Lesbian (Non)sexuality and Television's Perpetuation of Hetero/sexism." In *Queer Words, Queer Images*. 107–21.

Moritz, Marguerite. "Old Strategies for New Texts: How American Television Is Creating and Treating Lesbian Characters." In *Queer Words, Queer Images*. 122–42.

Nardi, Peter M. "Changing Gay and Lesbian Images in the Media." In *Overcoming Heterosexism and Homophobia: Strategies That Work*. James Sears and Walter Williams, eds. New York: Columbia University Press, 1997, 427–42.

———. "AIDS and Obituaries: The Perpetuation of Stigma in the Press." In *Culture and AIDS*. D. Feldman, ed. New York: Praeger, 1990, 159–68.

Russo, Vito. *The Celluloid Closet: Homosexuality in the Movies*. Rev. ed. New York: Harper & Row, 1987.

See also *Advocate;* AIDS in the Media; Business; Film; Gay Activists Alliance (GAA); Gay and Lesbian Press; Gay and Lesbian Alliance Against Defamation (GLAAD); Journalism; Mattachine Society; *ONE Magazine;* Stereotype; Talk Shows; Television

Medieval Latin Poetry

Through the bulk of the European Middle Ages (which is summarily defined here as the seventh through the fourteenth centuries), most literary activity, and virtually all literary activity in Latin, took place in conjunction with one church institution or another, from monastic scriptorium to cathedral school, from papal chancery to bishop's court. While this might not seem to promise much scope for poetry with gay and/or lesbian interest (antisodomitical verse apart), the traditional and requisite instruction in "classical" Latin language, particularly Latin poetry, familiarized medieval clerics—"cleric" (whence English "clerk") says more about learning than piety—with themes such as Jupiter's abduction of Ganymede, just as the cultural prestige of reproducing classicizing verse provided opportunities for developing such topics. Sodomy was condemned, but quite often, and perhaps surprisingly, poets could risk appearing to voice more positive personal sentiments, for the excuse could always be given that one was merely indulging in a literary game. However, medieval Latin poetry served as a ludic space in a deeper sense—a space where men (and occasionally women) could assume other roles. The language and often forms and themes of this other culture could liberate them from the strictures of their own day. By "making believe," they could begin to remake their own world. In other words, Latin poetry was a site of resistance and, potentially, renegotiation.

The classical "cover" is already employed by the English monk Alcuin (735–804), who uses names such as "Daphnis" and "Menalcas" in his verses for the beloved Dido. This establishes both a cover and gestures to a subtext known to be homoerotic, for (as medieval lives of Virgil report) Virgil's own love for the boy Alexander was concealed beneath/revealed by the passion of Corydon for Alexis in Eclogue 2. (Virgil's other boyfriend's name was Cebes.) The eleventh and twelfth centuries witnessed a remarkable efflorescence of learning and, in its wake, of poetry with homoerotic interests, even sensibilities. Baudri of Bourgueil (France, 1046–1130), ultimately an archbishop, wrote thousands of verses in the style of (and often in tribute to) Roman poet Ovid. He exchanged verse epistles with women religious but wrote many more poems to and about boys and men. "Love" could always, in the end, be religious—we are enjoined, after all, to love one another—but Baudri revels in the possible erotic construction of his verse. Peter Abelard, a great student of human and divine love, penned a memorable lament for David to sing for Jonathan (it is interesting that in a case where the personification is not personal, at least not as far as the same-sex aspect is concerned, the poet found a biblical, not classical, precedent). We are now increasingly in the world of cities and universities, and Abelard's pupil, Hilary the Englishman, writes completely unambiguous songs in celebration of handsome boys. One begins "Ave, puer speciose" ("Hail, lovely boy") and claims that given the choice, Jupiter would replace Ganymede with this young man. Increased prominence meant increasingly virulent attacks, such as those by Bernard of Cluny and Alain of Lille (the latter's *De planctu naturae* is a mixture of prose and verse). Also from the late twelfth or early thirteenth century come actual poetic debates about the relative virtues (not to mention propriety) of the love of women and the love of boys. In "Ganymede and Helen," Helen wins, and Ganymede is vanquished. But sodomy had its champions, too, and a rejoinder was prepared; the rematch pits Ganymede against Juno's daughter Hebe, whom Ganymede replaced as the gods' wine pourer, and this time Ganymede has the last word. If the above poems, and the debates, consider love strictly from the male perspective, there are at least two female-female love letters, from a twelfth- or thirteenth-century manuscript written in the Bavarian monastery of Tegernsee. Though Tegernsee was a noted classicizing center, these letters draw on the erotic vocabulary of the Song of Songs and the love poetry, both religious and frankly sexual, inspired by that biblical book. By the fourteenth century, most poets developing popular themes were writing in one or another of the emerging vernaculars. Though the actual date is uncertain, the short late medieval Latin skit *De Cavichiolo*, in which a woman threatens to leave her nonperforming-because-boy-crazy husband until the two agree to share their boys, repre-

sents in classicizing Latin the increasingly popular, and brutal, world of the fabliaux.

Ralph Hexter

Bibliography

Boswell, John. *Christianity, Social Tolerance, and Homosexuality: Gay People in Western Europe from the Beginning of the Christian Era to the Fourteenth Century.* Chicago: University of Chicago Press, 1980.

Stehling, Thomas, collector and trans. *Medieval Latin Poems of Male Love and Friendship.* New York: Garland, 1984.

Wilhelm, James J., ed. *Gay and Lesbian Poetry. An Anthology from Sappho to Michelangelo.* New York: Garland, 1995.

See also Alan of Lille; Bible; Catholicism; David and Jonathan; Elegiac Poetry; Ganymede; Love Poetry, the Petrarchan Tradition; Sodomy

Mediterranean

For generations, homosexuals found a historical antecedent and cultural legitimation for their sexuality in the Mediterranean region, especially by recalling ancient Greece. Plato's dialogues, Sappho's poetry, and other works of antiquity lauded same-sex love, and classical statuary provided a representation of ideal beauty. Yet the very centrality of antiquity in Western culture owed much to several homosexuals who themselves journeyed to southern Europe on a cultural and sexual pilgrimage. The Greek ideal of beauty, for instance, was promoted most notably in the neoclassical movement of the eighteenth century by Johann Joachim Winckelmann (1717–1768), a German scholar who spent much of his life working at the Vatican and who is considered the father of art history. Winckelmann's *History of Classical Art,* published in 1764, extolled the beauty of such classical sculptures as the *Apollo of the Belvedere* in terms that mixed art criticism with barely disguised homosexual lust. His own sexual interest in men was documented, and he died, perhaps killed by a hustler, in suspicious circumstances.

Throughout the nineteenth and early twentieth centuries, northern Europeans visited Italy to admire the ruins of antiquity and the art of the Renaissance. Writers, a number of whom were homosexuals, left accounts of their impressions and experiences. Romantic poets Lord Byron and August von Platen numbered among them as did, somewhat later, John Addington Symonds and A. E. Housman. The latter had sexual liaisons with gondoliers, Platen enjoyed encounters with various men in Florence and other cities, and Byron's last poem was addressed to a youth with whom he fought in the Greek war of independence. Arcadian images of the Mediterranean, both classical and modern, appeared in the works of a host of European authors known to have homosexual tendencies, including the verses of the British Uranian poets, Walter Pater's manifestos of aestheticism, defenses of homosexuality written by Symonds and Adolph Brand, stories by E. M. Forster, novels by Louis Couperus and Mikhail Kuzmin, and, perhaps most famously, the novella *Death in Venice* (1911), by Thomas Mann. Until well into the twentieth century, study of the classics was at the heart of elite education, and universities were suffused with a Greek-inspired homosociality. A visit to modern Italy, whether it delighted or disappointed, was a complement to the study of antiquity.

Homosexual visual artists, such as German painter Hans von Marées, were also drawn to the Mediterranean. The best known for his homoerotic images was probably Wilhelm von Gloeden (1856–1931), scion of a German noble family who moved to Taormina, Sicily. He took hundreds of photographs of peasant youths, often in a state of undress or posed with togas or other classical accoutrements. Gloeden saw his subjects as the flesh-and-blood heirs of antiquity, available for artistic inspiration and sensual enjoyment. Others followed in his wake and took similar photographs of comely ephebes in which peasant Italy harked back to what viewers perceived (often in rather simplistic fashion) as the glories and pleasures of antiquity.

The activities of such expatriates contributed to the growth of homsexual subcultures in Florence, Rome, Venice, and Taormina, where, for instance, a number of celebrities visited Gloeden. Capri also became a notable center of expatriate male homsexual and lesbian life, centered around eccentic French novelist and poet Jacques d'Adelswärd-Fersen (1880–1923). A wealthy poet who fled Paris after a scandal involving schoolboys, he built a luxurious villa in Capri. His elaborate parties, complete with sexual escapades, were chronicled in Roger Peyrefitte's factually accurate novel about the "exile of Capri" (*L'Exilé de Capri*). Capri was also a favorite holiday spot for German arms dealer Friedrich Krupp. Revelations about his homosexual life on the island led to Krupp's ruin and death.

Italy was attractive not only for its climate and its cultural riches. Homosexuality was not illegal in Italy, as it remained in Britain, Germany, and various other northern countries, and a number of northern homosexuals—including Oscar Wilde and German sexologist Karl Heinrich Ulrichs—found refuge there. Expatriates from northern Europe had the leisure and wealth to indulge their whims in Italy, still beset with poverty and unemployment. Many of the youths of men who became their sexual partners received some financial compensation in return. Casual encounters verged on prostitution and sexual tourism. Yet some resulted in longer-term arrangememts; Pancrazio Bucini, "Il Moro," served as Gloeden's loyal protégé and companion for several decades.

The sexual mores prevalent in the Mediterranean, where a blind eye was generally turned to homosexual encounters between unmarried youths and older men, was congenial to such arrangements. A traditional easygoing sexual openness among teenagers was still described in the novels of Pier Paolo Pasolini in the 1950s, and there is much evidence of homosexual subcultures in Italy dating as far back as the fifteenth century.

The emergence of new homosexual gathering places and associations in London, Paris, and Berlin, the waning of justification of homosexuality through reference to antiquity, and changed socioeconomic and political conditions in Italy largely displaced the Mediterranean as the central myth in homosexual culture by the 1930s. The continued appeal of the south of Europe, both for its cultural treasures and for its climate and style of life, has nevertheless been obvious in more recent literary and visual works, some inspired by earlier versions, such as *Death in Venice*, turned into an opera by Benjamin Britten and a film by Luchino Visconti in the 1970s. The development of Mykonos, Ibiza, and Sitges as gay tourist resorts produced a new sort of migration to southern Europe, but this odyssey was almost entirely emptied of its classical and Renaissance links.

Robert Aldrich

Bibliography

Aldrich, Robert. *The Seduction of the Mediterranean: Writing, Art and Homosexual Fantasy.* London: Routledge, 1993.

Dowling, Linda. *Hellenism and Homosexuality in Victorian Oxford*. Ithaca, N.Y.: Cornell University Press, 1994.

Peyrefitte, Roger. *L'Exilé de Capri*. Paris: Flammarion, 1959.

Potts, Alex. *Flesh and the Ideal: Winckelmann and the Origins of Art History*. New Haven: Yale University Press, 1994.

See also Art History; Brand, Adolph; Britten, Benjamin; Byron, George Gordon, Lord; Couperus, Louis; Florence; Forster, E. M.; Gloeden, Baron Wilhelm von; Greece, Ancient; Housman, A. E.; Italian Renaissance; Italy; Kuzmin, Mikhail; Mann, Thomas; Pasolini, Pier Paolo; Peyrefitte, Roger; Platen, August Graf von Hallermund; Rome, Ancient; Symonds, John Addington; Visconti, Luchino; Wilde, Oscar; Winkelmann, Johann Joachim

Melanesia

The anthropological and cultural history of Melanesia is now well documented in the scope and symbolic significance of same-gendered relations and customary erotic relations between boys and men. The cultural practices in question have been reported since the nineteenth century and were generally referred to as "sodomy" or "homosexuality," or later as "ritualized homosexuality." As evidence mounted and theory changed, however, an awareness of the pejorative meanings of the early categories, together with an understanding of the differences between "homosexual" as a nineteenth-century identity category and the Melanesian practices, gradually led to a divergent cultural formulation: boy-inseminating practices. The stipulated purposes of these social practices was to "grow" and "masculinize" the younger male, preparing him for social and reproductive competence, and thus implicating desires, ontologies, and roles within the same institutional package.

Approximately sixty distinct societies—notably the Marind-anim, Big Nambas, East Bay, Sambia, Baruya, and Gebusi, among others—practiced these boy-inseminating rites in precolonial times. These societies existed on the margins of Highlands Papua New Guinea but were also scattered among certain off-lying islands of the larger area of Melanesia. It has been suggested by anthropologists from the turn-of-the-century writings of Sir Alfred Haddon, Paul Wirtz, Jan Van Baal, and later by Gilbert Herdt in the 1980s, and Bruce Knauft in the 1990s, that institutionalized same-gendered practices were distinctive of a cultural migration of waves of non-Austronesian or Papuan language groups issuing from ten thousand years ago or later. Linguistic and fragmentary cultural evidence, primarily in the form of word lists, diffusion of ritual practices, morphological structural parallels of myths and legends of origin, hints that prehistoric hunter-gatherer groups entered Melanesia with an ancient ritual complex of semen beliefs and practices not unlike those known from the anthropological reports. Semen, in this cultural model, is regarded as an elixir of life, a vital constituent of growth and well-being, and the necessary ontological means for the production of masculinity and warriorhood personality, according to the world view of such peoples as the Marind-anim and the Sambia. Thus, semen is treated on a par with blood and milk and is believed to have the magical power to transform itself into mother's milk, fetal tissue, muscles, and other elements of physical and spiritual development. It follows that in a number of these societies, including the Sambia, it is believed that only insemination will produce the desired outcomes, since this body fluid does not "naturally" occur in the human body, but must be exchanged and acquired through the proper moral and social relations of ritual.

In all reported cases from Melanesia, boy-inseminating practices are hierarchical, such that the older male is the penetrator and semen donor, and the younger male is always the semen recipient. In return for the gift of semen, the older male receives the gift of pleasure and no doubt the expressive social confirmation of having achieved manhood in the eyes of the community. The hierarchical nature of age-structured relations is mirrored in male/female marriage and sexual relations as well. The possible exceptions to this principle of nonreciprocal or nonmutualistic sexual relations between man and boy, as reported by Davenport for East Bay society and Tobias Schneebaum for Asmat society, have recently been analyzed by Herdt, who suggests that these are postcolonial products of social change, leaving intact the structural principle of hierarchy in all same-gendered traditional sexual relations. Woman/girl sexual relations in Melanesia, as elsewhere in the world, are rare; Herdt cites two or three tentative and sketchy reports of institutionalized same-gender relations between females, of which the most reliable report concerns the famous

M Big Nambas society of the New Hebrides (now Vanuatu).

Several characteristic themes are widely reported for the man/boy practices throughout Melanesia. First, boy-inseminating relationships are implemented through initiation or puberty rites of a collective, rather than individualized, form. Second, religious sanctification through ancestral spirits or beings attending or blessing the proceedings is omnipresent; hence, the homoerotic is indelibly linked to the sacred and to spiritual development and afterlife in the whole person. Third, same-gendered erotic relations are rationalized in social roles, usually age-graded, that involve entry into hierarchical secret societies or at least into semisecret practices excluding all women and uninitiated children. The lawful nature of these roles is specified by cultural roles about who may occupy a status or advance up the status ladder. Fourth, ritual beliefs motivate and rationalize insemination as *the* masculine elixir vital to physical growth, social maturity, and reproductive competence, but no necessary opposition is created between semen for growth or reproduction, suggesting the significance of both practices in the male cycle. Fifth, kinship and marriage and their related rights and prohibitions govern the formation of man/boy relationships always; for example, incest taboos mirror those of male/female bonds, forbidding sexual intercourse with certain relatives (i.e., brothers and fathers). That these cultural ideals are sometimes broken, as they are in heterosexual incest taboos, but only between cousins and distant relatives, has been documented for the Sambia of Papua New Guinea. Sixth, cultural ideals prescribe that the male inseminator should be a structurally identified mentor, often the boy's brother-in-law, sometimes metaphorically referred to as mother's brother, which suggests that the boy's sister is exchanged on the condition that the older male provides the gift of semen and "growth" as a compensation for the loss of female reproductive resources to the donor group. Seven, the erotic techniques known from Melanesia are largely confined to oral sexual relations (fellatio) and anal sex—about equally divided in sheer number of tribes—with two or three reported practices of masturbation used to rub semen on the younger boy's body. In all known cases, these forms of sexual practice are mutually exclusive, such that fellatio and anal sex never occur within the same society, or within its customary man/boy relations.

The cultural history of these practices suggests the spuriousness of reducing the whole meaning system to the sexual act; nor should we imagine eliminating the erotic element and suggesting that the practice is concerned only with the social production of the political economy of gender or power. Homosexuality in Melanesia was a traditional form of social economy, the desires, ontologies, and passions of which were every bit as complex and variegated as the system of age-structured same-gender relations that occurred in Homeric Greece or later in feudal Japan. In these places, the body fluids and honor and spirit of the partners were constantly implicated in a ritual and warrior complex of sufficient antiquity and cultural totalism that we are justified in thinking of these as parallel ritual traditions and desires.

Gilbert Herdt

Bibliography

Allen, M. R. *Male Cults and Secret Initiations in Melanesia.* Melbourne: Melbourne University Press, 1967.

Davenport, W. H. "Sexual Patterns and Their Regulation in a Society of the Southwest Pacific." In *Sex and Behavior*. F. A. Beach, ed. New York: Wiley, 1965, 164–207.

Deacon, A. B. *Malekula: A Vanishing People in the New Hebrides.* London: George Routledge, 1934.

Godelier, M. *The Production of Great Men.* Cambridge: Cambridge University Press, 1986.

Herdt, Gilbert. "Father Presence and Ritual Homosexuality: Paternal Deprivation and Masculine Development in Melanesia Reconsidered." *Ethos* 18 (1989): 326–70.

———. *Guardians of the Flute: Idioms of Masculinity.* New York: McGraw-Hill, 1981.

———. "Ritualized Homosexuality in the Male Cults of Melanesia, 1862–1982: An Introduction." In *Ritualized Homosexuality in Melanesia.* Gilbert Herdt, ed. Berkeley: University of California Press, 1984, 1–81.

———. ed. *Ritualized Homosexuality in Melanesia.* Berkeley: University of California Press, 1984.

———. *The Sambia: Ritual and Gender in New Guinea.* New York: Holt, Reinhart and Winston, 1987.

Knauft, Bruce. "Homosexuality in Melanesia: The Need for a Synthesis of Perspectives." *Journal of Psychoanalytic Anthropology* 10 (1987): 155–91.

———. *South Coast New Guinea Cultures.* New York: Cambridge University Press,1993.

Layard, J. "Homo-Eroticism in a Primitive Society as a Function of the Self." *Journal of Analytical Psychology* 4 (1959): 101–15.

———. *Stone Men of Makkula.* London: Chatto and Windus, 1942.

Murray, Stephen O. *Pacific Homosexualities.* New York: Garland, 1984.

Schieffelin, E. L. *The Sorrow of the Lonely and the Burning of the Dancers.* New York: Martin's Press, 1976.

Van Baal, J. *Dema, Description and Analysis of Marind-Anim Culture.* The Hague: Martinus Nijhoff, 1966.

———. "The Dialectics of Sex in Marind-anim Culture." In *Ritualized Homosexuality in Melanesia.* Gilbert Herdt, ed. Berkeley: University of California Press, 1984, 128–66.

Williams, E. E. *Papuans of the Trans-Fly.* Oxford: Oxford University Press, 1936.

See also Anthropology; Greece; Japan

Melville, Herman (1819–1891)

American novelist, short story writer, poet, and social critic Herman Melville was born into a comfortable New York City family with ties to Revolutionary War heroes and early Calvinist and Dutch settlers. Melville dropped out of Albany Academy to save money shortly after his father's bankruptcy and subsequent death in 1832. As early as 1839, while still struggling to find gainful employment, he published "Fragments from a Writing Desk," a collection hinting at an early awareness of society's impingement on individual freedom and identity. *Typee* (1846) was his first novel, one containing a biting commentary on Western civilization. Partway through *Mardi* (1849), he turned to more subversive social criticism: book sales plummeted. Even *Moby-Dick* (1851), now a classic, sold fewer than three thousand copies in America during its first fifteen years. Yet for the rest of his life, Melville sharpened his critique of patriarchal, heterosexist society, despairing in his later years of remedying cultural ills through writing. After achieving neither financial security nor literary acclaim, he died in near obscurity.

Not until the early twentieth century did readers in any number revisit his writing. Not until the middle of the twentieth century did his use of "antisocial" desire register to any extent with critics. In 1960, Leslie Fiedler, in *Love and Death in the American Novel*, noted that homosexual desire "threatens to take over" *Moby-Dick*. But by the mid-1980s, critics saw Melville's use of desire as something other than a discomfiting, adolescent evasion of heterosexuality.

For Melville, expressions of antisocial desire are the standard by which society is judged as well as the site of visionary social possibilities. He investigates the connection between expressions of sexuality that position the individual self in society and the makeup of social power. From his earliest work to his last, his always male heroes are made more socially aware by desiring another male who is generally nonwhite, non-Christian, non-American. With such expressions of desire Melville subverts the hegemonic social order in a manner that is at times homosexual, at times "pansexual."

Disconsolate over the fate of the individual in society, especially in such works as *Pierre* (1852), *Timoleon* (1891), and *Billy Budd* (1924), Melville illustrates how the overarching society classifies the homosexual as a minoritizing signifier within a more universal homophobic discourse. In fact, as his literary career draws to a close, his work reveals more clearly society's paranoid need to exert its power and safeguard its perspective by denoting the homosexual as clearly recognizable and easily manipulated.

Perhaps anticipating his own lack of social acceptance, Melville at times turns to a homosexual semiotics in which to encode the full meaning of his social critique for more attuned readers. His reliance on homosexual desire and narrative deviousness can be seen as an effort to educate his readers and induce at least some knowing few into a complicity of socially alienated understanding of social ills and alternatives.

Although critical perspectives vary, Melville's social criticism is almost always presented as "experimental expressions of self-perception," what we today call queer performance.   *Jerome Buckley*

Bibliography
Bryant, John. *Melville and Repose.* New York: Oxford University Press, 1993.

Creech, James. *Closet Writing/Gay Reading.* Chicago: University of Chicago Press, 1993.

Fiedler, Leslie. *Love and Death in the American Novel.* New York: Criterion Books, 1960.

Leverenz, David. *Manhood and the American Renaissance*. Ithaca, N.Y.: Cornell University Press, 1989.

Martin, Robert K. *Hero, Captain, and Stranger: Male Friendship, Social Critique, and Literary Form in the Sea Novels of Herman Melville.* Chapel Hill, N.C.: University of North Carolina Press, 1986.

See also Fiction; U.S. Literature

Merrill, James (1926–1995)

Born into wealth, James Merrill enjoyed the genteel upbringing of an East Coast blue blood, except for the glitch caused by the divorce of his parents when he was twelve. His father was the cofounder of the Merrill/Lynch stockbroking firm. There is every evidence that his poetic talents were encouraged early on as his father himself collected some of the boy's poetry and had it published under the title *Jim's Book.* Merrill interrupted college studies to serve in World War II, returned to Amherst College, from which he graduated in 1947, and published *First Poems* in 1951. A bout with writer's block ensued, and Merrill sought psychiatric help in Rome. By 1959 he had published his first novel, *The Seraglio,* and another volume of poems, *The Country of a Thousand Years of Peace.*

His home base became Stonington, Connecticut, where he lived on Walter Street, above a row of shops. He spent half of each year, however, in Greece until 1979, when he switched to Key West. His lover, David Jackson, began to figure in Merrill's poetry as early as 1969 in *The Fire Screen,* but the relationship became literally overt in Merrill's long poem "The Book of Ephraim" at the end of his *Divine Comedies* (1976). The poem describes Ouija board experiments that purportedly began with Jackson's wife, Doris, in 1955. Two more installments of the poetic experiments appeared as *Mirabell: Books of Number* and *Scripts for the Pageant* before Merrill combined all three into one volume called *The Changing Light at Sandover* (1982). The work is over five hundred pages long and remains one of the most ambitious single-frame works in modern American poetry.

For the Ouija board poems, lines were elicited by means of a teacup from various dead people, chief among them W. H. Auden, who chat merrily about life beyond life. The peacock Mirabell is a key player as well as the God Biology, but more important than the fantasies of the voices is the underlying motif that gay people are the true creative force of the universe. The work uses various orthographic tricks, and throughout is Merrill's beautifully controlled meter and rhyme. He is one of the finest craftsmen of traditional verse forms in the last quarter of the century. In 1992 he published his selected poems, and a final volume of verse, *A Scattering of Salts,* appeared after his death. He died in Tucson. During his life, in addition to twelve books of poetry, he published two novels, two plays, a book of essays, and a memoir. In 1966 he was named the first poet laureate of Connecticut. Awarded two National Book Awards for poetry, Merrill was also awarded a Pulitzer Prize for *Divine Comedies* and the first Bobbitt National Prize for poetry from the Library of Congress in 1988 for *The Inner Room.*

George Klawitter

Bibliography

Lehman, David, and Charles Berger, eds. *James Merrill: Essays in Criticism.* Ithaca, N.Y.: Cornell University Press, 1983.

Moffett, Judith. *James Merrill: An Introduction to the Poetry.* New York: Columbia University Press, 1984.

See also Auden, W. H.; Love Poetry, the Petrarchan Tradition; U.S. Literature: Contemporary Gay Writing

Metropolitan Community Church

The Metropolitan Community Church was founded in Los Angeles in 1968 by the Rev. Troy D. Perry (1940–). It was established originally as a Pentecostal congregation openly welcoming homosexuals and lesbians. In a sense, its organization represented the solution to the problems that Perry had with his own homosexuality. At that time, Perry, a dedicated and believing Pentecostal, had in his own words "received the call" to minister as a teenager. He worked briefly as a paid teenage evangelist, and at eighteen married the daughter of a fellow minister in the Church of God. While married, he attended an unaccredited Bible college for two years, all the time working at another job and preaching to a small community of believers in the Church of God. By the time he left the college, the congregation had grown enough that Perry began planning a building campaign for a church. Shortly before the planned opening of his fund-raising campaign, he was excommunicated because of same-sex relations with a young man in his father-in-law's congregation.

With his wife's support, Perry made an effort to live the life of a heterosexual (and he fathered two children), but at heart he knew he was homosexual. He still retained a belief in his calling as a minister but, unable to preach in the Church of God, he joined the Church of God in Spirit, which shared a common background but was a separate church. Shortly after this his employer transferred him to Los Angeles, where fortuitously a Church of God in Spirit congregation also called him to be its minister. Realizing by now that he was truly a homosexual, Perry decided to tell the officials in his church of his sexual desires before taking over the congregation, and was immediately forced to vacate his ministry in his new church.

Perry still kept his faith but increasingly moved in gay circles and eventually separated from his wife. Drafted into the U.S. Army in 1965, he served in Germany, where he often preached in Pentecostal churches and became convinced that God loved gays as much as he did the nongay. In the words of one of his friends that Perry often repeated: "God knows that I am a homosexual. God made me the way I am, and God loves." After his return to Los Angeles, Perry became increasingly concerned with police harassment of gays, as well as the rejection by many churches of their gay members.

His solution was to advertise the opening of a new church, the Metropolitan Community Church, in the *Advocate*, a gay newspaper, emphasizing that gays and lesbians were welcome. Some twelve people attended the first meeting held in the house in which Perry was living. In his first sermon, entitled "Be True to You," Perry outlined the three principles of his new church:

SALVATION—God so loved the world that God sent Jesus to tell us that whoever believes shall not perish but have everlasting life; and "whoever" included me as a gay male, unconditionally, because salvation is free—no church can take it away.

COMMUNITY—for those who have no families who care about them, or who find themselves alone or friendless, the church will be a family.

CHRISTIAN SOCIAL ACTION—We would stand up for all our rights, secular and religious, and we would start fighting the many forms of tyranny that oppressed us.

Perry summarized:

If you believe in yourself, then God will help you. God cares about you. He created you. He wants you to survive. I found out the hard way, but now I know—and I want you to know! And I don't want you to ever forget: God really cares!

Perry was a charismatic leader and growth of the church was rapid, so rapid that other congregations sought affiliation with the Los Angeles congregation. Although he says he initially believed that the purpose of his congregation was to force other churches to examine their treatment of gays and lesbians, members early on became organized for the long term. In the second year, the Universal Fellowship of Metropolitan Community Church was formed with Perry as moderator, and new congregations accepted.

By 1972, at the third general conference of the Metropolitan Community Church, which then had twenty-three affiliated churches, a call to become a new prophetic voice to the world was enunciated by an ex-Mormon missionary, James E. Sandfort, and accepted by the members in attendance in traditional Pentecostal fashion with visions, glossalia, miracles of healing, and prayer. It was also decided to give new emphasis to women and minority groups, and to openly welcome heterosexuals, in the process moving to becoming an ecumenical faith. In the aftermath, one congregation withdrew, upset over the Pentecostal tenor of the meeting.

Growth was not always easy. By 1990 seventeen sites where churches stood or church meetings had been held had been intentionally burned. One of the worst fires took place in New Orleans, where twenty-nine congregants died. Still the church continued to grow, but as it did, it redefined itself as a church embodying elements from many faiths: Catholic, Anglican, Baptist, and others, as well as Pentecostal. One of the first Pentecostal traditions abandoned was the male-dominant tradition of the ministry. Women have been ordained since 1973, and numerous congregations now have women ministers. As of 1997, the church had forty-two thousand members in three hundred congregations in nineteen countries. Many of the foreign congregations are in Africa, particularly Nigeria, where the first overseas congregation was established; interestingly, it was a heterosexual congregation. Within the United States there are 250 churches with the

M largest congregation, one of two thousand members, in Dallas, Texas. The church has observer status in the World Council of Churches. It applied for membership in the American Council of Churches in 1981, but in 1983 the council officially postponed a decision, setting up a study commission. In effect the application was denied since no action has since been taken.   *Vern L. Bullough*

Bibliography

Perry, Troy D. *The Lord Is My Shepherd and He Knows I'm Gay.* Reprint. Los Angeles: Fellowship Press, 1997.

Perry, Troy D., with Thomas L. Swicegood. *Don't Be Afraid Anymore: The Story of Reverend Troy Perry and the Metropolitan Community Churches.* New York: St. Martin's Press, 1990.

See also Christianity; Religion and Religiosity; Religious Organizations

Mexico

The entry "Mexico" in an encyclopedia of homosexuality poses questions about the word *homosexual* in Mexico. How is it used? How does it take part in the organization of sexual discourses, sexual subjectivities, and power? And, more important, how is homoeroticism experienced? These questions have only been partially answered by recent social research. At the same time, it brings about another important discussion regarding the presumed homogeneity of Mexican culture. In Mexico, the open discussion of both subjects came to the forefront in the same cultural context: the years that followed the 1968 massacre by state forces of a popular student movement. Thus, the Mexican gay movement started in 1978, when a group of gays from the political left took part with other nongay groups in the parade that commemorated the massacre. The gay movement is marginal. Nevertheless, the public debates on sexuality, homoeroticism, and Mexican society continue to gain ground, although they are very much restricted to intellectual and artistic spaces. One exception is the Zapatistas' indigenous rebellion in the state of Chiapas, which included "the homosexuals" as an oppressed group (along with Indians, women, and peasants) in a proclamation to the nation.

The terms *homosexual* and *gay* are relatively recent in mainstream Mexican society and still (but less and less) circumscribed to mass-media and urban spaces. Other terms are used more; the most common ones for men are the highly offensive *puto* and *maricón* (with implications of effeminacy), and the supposed less offensive and widely used *juto*. There are also some regional variants: *leandro, lilo, mariposón,* and *puñal,* among many others. For women the usual names are *marimacha* and *machorra.*

This scarcity of names for women in comparison to men indexes the social visibility of both groups in society. Although the first openly "Mexican lesbian novel" was published eight years ago (*Amora*), a lesbian character (and not a gay man) was the first to be included in a recently popular Mexican soap opera, *Nada Personal* (Nothing Personal). In this program, the positive image of homosexuality goes along with a major criticism of the Mexican political system. Up to now, no major study has been done regarding how female homosexuality or homoeroticism is being experienced in Mexico. Pioneering essays are being produced by activist and intellectuals organized in the group El Clóset de Sor Juana in Mexico City.

The use of the terms *homosexual, lesbiana,* and *gay* has to do with the enactment of "proper" ways of referring to sexual practices and social identities by specialists, or other persons, in places that require a language of respectability, including a middle- and upper-class urban gay community that claims for itself a U.S. urban gay lifestyle. In Mexico, therefore, these words say more about the politics of enunciation and "proper public discourse" and less about the conceptual territory they have in that country.

Contrary to current opinion among U.S. scholars, the Mexican male homoerotic landscape cannot be obtained easily by the well-known "active-passive" dichotomy either. Although it is an important and explicit frame for signifying certain sexual experiences, such as anal or oral penetrations, and a current basic meaning of what it means "to be *puto*" (as an interviewee said: '*Puto*' is the guy who is fucked"), it is a limited explanatory device for understanding the complexities of many intimate sexual encounters. First of all, to be *puto* in Mexico, one has to enjoy being penetrated. At the same time, a male who engages in homoerotic relations as "active" is not necessarily considered a "normal" guy if he does it continuously, exclusively, and for pleasure. Second, in the cultural imagery, the words *joto* and *puto* involve something more than anal receptivity, including a whole economy of desire, somewhat expressed in "feminine behavior"; "normality" (the word *heterosexuality* is reserved almost exclusively for highly educated people) is also associated with something more than the inserter role; it involves an economy of desire and pleasure expressed in a minimum of heteroerotic practices and "masculine" appearance.

The anus and the mouth (to a lesser degree) are objects of major concerns as potentially disruptive of the "normal" economy of desire. In the context of homosexuality, men joke about the danger of "effeminacy" and pleasure if being touched in the anus (by a doctor, a female partner, or other men). In the same way, the anus and the act of being penetrated are used as metaphors for describing the experience of disempowerment in daily social interactions with more powerful people or institutions ("My boss fucked me up"; "The cop got his dick inside me"). The anus (and other openings like the vagina) being an index of the boundaries of subjectivity, it is not surprising that *putos* (and women) are represented as people "anxious" about being "fucked up," with an "uncontrollable anus" (or vagina), "unstable" subjectivities (*loca,* or "mad," is a major word for referring to *putos*), and weak, disempowered people. The phallocentricity of culture is rooted in a particular way of reading the bodies and in the organization and contention of desires in the body of *normal* and *putos* people.

Nevertheless, in this cultural context, besides the sexual practices between "gay people," there is an underground homoeroticism practiced by "normal" males who escape social stigma and elude the *homosexual* or *puto* identity (the word *bisexual* is scarcely known or used), because it shares the "normal" public presentation of the body and the "normal" economy of desire (as exhibited in a poetics of masculinity and the co-presence of heterosexual practices). There are many negotiations and subversions in male-to-male encounters that make the "active-passive" distinctions insufficient and studies on the semiotics of the body and desire, and the negotiations of subjectivity, more interesting.

These and other variables like gender role, level of involvement, and reason for engagement (money or just love and pleasure) configure a wide array of social personas according to *gente de ambiente* (a common expression that refers to people who continuously engage in homoerotic encounters and share a set of symbols and knowledge): the *loquitas,* or transvestite; the *obvious,* or lightly effeminate people; the *jotos tapados,* or masculine homosexual types; the *bisexuales* (usually married

people); the *mayates* or *chichifos* (males who prostitute themselves as "active" and who do not consider themselves "homosexuals"); *jaladores* ("normal" males who engage in homoerotic relations for pleasure, who do not consider themselves "*homosexuals,*" and tend to be friendly with gay people); and even the *normales* ("straight"), people who once or occasionally had a homoerotic encounter but do not engage in same-sex activities anymore. According to informants, the number of *jaladores* is "just amazing," and is part of the daily scenario of streets and cantina culture.

Secrecy (as well as guilt and homophobia) crosses this erotic landscape in Mexico and involves both male and female "homosexuals." Although there is no legal regulation or prohibition of homoeroticism in the country, they are the object of social stigma and discrimination by many people including civil servants who can make use of the local codes of "police and good government" to make charges of "immoral behavior" or "scandal" (terms never defined by local authorities) against same-sex public expressions of love and eroticism.

Guillermo Nuñez-Noriega

Bibliography

Careaga, P. Gloria, and Patricia Jiménez. "Mexico." In *Unspoken Rules: Sexual Orientation and Women's Human Rights*. Rachel Rosenbloom, ed. International Gay and Lesbian Human Rights Commission, USA, 1995.

Carrier, Joseph. *De Los Otros: Intimacy and Homosexuality Among Mexican Men*. New York: Columbia University Press, 1995.

Nuñez-Noriega, Guillermo. *Sexo entre varones. Poder y resistencia en el campo sexual*. Hermosillo, Sonora, Mexico: Universidad de Sonora y El Colegio de Sonora, 1994.

See also Cantina Culture; Chicano and Latino Gay Cultures; Machismo

Miami

The most populous city (373,000) and county (Miami-Dade 1.9 million) in Florida, Miami was incorporated in 1896. While some notable figures in Miami history, such as industrialist John Deering, are thought to have been homosexual, no written accounts about homosexual life in Dade County exist prior to World War II. The first mention of homosexuals in Miami newspapers ap-

M

Miami Beach Art Deco District in 1992. Photo courtesy of the Greater Miami Convention and Visitors Bureau.

peared in the early 1940s, with military officials advocating the closing of those Miami and Miami Beach bars that featured "lewd" shows with "admitted homosexuals."

In the years prior to and just after the war, Miami was home to two or three highly visible female impersonator shows catering to mostly straight audiences. Particularly the Las Vegas–style shows of the Jewel Box Review earned notices in local and national nightlife columns of the early 1940s (though without mention of the sexuality of the performers).

As throughout the country, the 1950s brought a chilling of attitudes toward what visible signs of gay life there were in Miami. In 1954 the molestation and murder of a young girl and the brutal murder of an airline steward were dangled before the press by Miami politicians as evidence of a town overrun by sexual "deviates." After an aggressive campaign of bar raids, in 1957 the city of Miami passed an ordinance banning bars from employing or serving drinks to known homosexuals. Beginning in 1959 and lasting until 1964, the Florida legislature's infamous Johns Commission (named after Florida state senator Charlie Johns) conducted a witch-hunt against homosexuals throughout Florida, including Miami.

In 1966 Richard Inman became the first individual in South Florida to openly discuss his homosexuality in the media when he appeared on Miami's channel 4 TV's special program, "The Homosexual." A virtual one-man band for gay rights, Inman had just founded the Mattachine Society of Florida, which, like Mattachine chapters around the country, advocated that society show tolerance toward homosexuals.

Shortly after the Stonewall riots in New York, Miami's first gay church, the Metropolitan Community Church, opened in Coconut Grove in 1970. The first organized gay pride week was celebrated in Miami Beach in early June 1972 with a march on Lincoln Road protesting a city law banning cross-dressing. Two weeks latter, the law was struck down by a federal court. In August of that year, hundreds of gays and lesbians joined thousands of protesters at the 1972 Republican National Convention in Miami Beach.

More than any other event, the 1977 fight over gay rights in Dade County put the spotlight on gays and lesbians in Miami. On January 18, 1977, the Metro Dade Commission approved a human rights ordinance banning discrimination in housing and employment based on sexual orientation. Entertainer and Florida Citrus Commission spokeswoman Anita Bryant was urged by her minister and husband to lead an effort to have the ordinance repealed by voter referendum. The six-month campaign waged both by gay and antigay groups brought the issue of homosexuality to the forefront in mainstream society via intense media coverage as never before. By a two-to-one margin, the ordinance was repealed by voters on June 7, 1977. An attempt one year later by gay activists to reinstate the ordinance was again defeated by voters.

Fifteen years after the defeat of the Dade ordinance, in 1992 Miami Beach passed a human rights law that includes protection against discrimination based on sexual orientation. The key role played by gay and lesbian residents and tourists in the fast-paced urban revitalization of Miami Beach's booming South Beach neighborhood is cited as an example of a nascent new gay power base in Dade County. Yet when a new human rights ordinance was brought forward to the Metro-Dade County Commission on June 17, 1997, commissioners voted it down by seven to five. *Eugene Patron*

Bibliography

Alwood, Edward. *Straight News: Gays, Lesbians, and the News Media*. New York: Columbia University Press, 1996.

Patron, Eugene. *Miami-Dade County Gay and Lesbian History Research Guide*. Ft. Lauderdale, Fla.: Stonewall Library and Archives, 1997.

———. *Once Upon a Queer Time: The Gay Days of Old Miami*. TWN, Miami, Vol. 18, issue 4, October 5, 1994.

Weiss, Susan. *Miami Bibliography*. Miami: Historical Association of Southern Florida, 1995.

See also Jewel Box Review; Mattachine Society; Metropolitan Community Church; Resorts and Beaches

Michals, Duane (1932–)

More than any other photographer, Duane Michals is obsessed with the passage of time and, in his quest to portray in pictures such an essentially nonpictorial concept, he breaks most of the rules of "high art" photography. His most striking individualisms, his blurred figures in motion, his storytelling photograph sequences, his addition of text in the margins are all related to the attempt to carry the image beyond the moment, to "unfreeze" still pictures. Even his use of handwritten text furthers that purpose because we tend to be subliminally conscious of the time it takes to handwrite something, whereas typeset text seems to leap full-blown into existence. All these characteristic Michals-isms are generally frowned on in formal photography, which subscribes to the concept "A photograph, like any work of art, should stand on its own without requiring outside references to be understood." Michals disagrees.

After spending the Korean War in the army, he finished his higher education in New York City, then spent the next fifteen years in the main field for ambitious photographers, fashion journalism. Not until the late sixties did Michals's work begin to be his own. Wanting to prevent the viewer from focusing on the photograph as an art object in itself, he began to avoid all the tricks of commercial photography, for example, no dramatic compositions or lighting effects. Backgrounds were kept simple and models were used who, though often handsome and muscular, were never in the supermodel category of Calvin Klein ads or Colt Studios calendars.

In sequence works like *Paradise Regained* (1968), in which a very "mod" couple are gradually stripped of their fashionable clothes while the art and furnishings of their chic apartment are replaced by tropical plants, Michals creates a witty paean to the natural life, but he is seldom so lighthearted. Perhaps more typical is the *Fallen Angel,* who succumbs to sexual desire, loses his wings, and falls into despair. Even in single-image works, the photographer's use of blurred action and added text encourage the viewer to surmise what has already happened and conjecture what will next come to pass.

It has been mistakenly suggested that Michals take his narratives the final step and go on to film or video as his medium. But those media are creatively parallel with the narrative of novels and short stories. Michals's sequences follow a narrative that is much more like that of poems or perhaps songs. There is no need for him to delineate what occurs between his images; the intervening moments are superfluous. In fact, filling in those time gaps would dissipate rather than resolve the intensity. To actually portray the passing of time in his work would defeat the purpose because Michals's ultimate subject is not time's passage but its effects—anxiety, regret, and sweet melancholy—on the human heart.

F. Valentine Hooven III

Bibliography

Ellenzweig, Allen. *The Homoerotic Photograph: Male Images from Durieu/Delacroix to Map-*

M

plethorpe. New York: Columbia University Press, 1992.

Waugh, Thomas. *Hard to Imagine.* New York: Columbia University Press, 1996.

See also Photography

Michelangelo Buonarroti (1475–1564)

Michelangelo is one of the supreme figures of history whose place in the pantheon of Western art is preeminent. Considered a genius as sculptor, painter, and architect, he was also a prolific poet of grace and power. Along with certain well-documented circumstances of his long life, it is his verse—lyrical, passionate, self-revealing—that supports most convincingly an argument for his homoerotic nature.

Born in 1475 into a Florentine family of bankers and government officials, Michelangelo Buonarroti in his youth was recognized as a sculptor of exceptional abilities, no small feat in a city that was at the time the center of European art. Early on, he enjoyed the patronage of Lorenzo de' Medici (Lorenzo the Magnificent), whose family was to play an important role throughout his life. Up to 1508, Michelangelo lived alternately in Bologna, Rome, and Florence (the return of Leonardo to Florence in 1500 after a long absence was a significant event in the artistic life of Michelangelo, without question spurring his creativity and influencing the power of his style). It was during these years that he created several of his masterpieces, including the *Pièta,* numerous renderings of Madonnas, the *Bacchus,* and the mammoth statue of David, the archetype of the Renaissance ideal of the male form.

In 1508 Michelangelo left Florence once again for Rome, where he worked under the patronage of Julius I on a variety of projects at the Vatican, culminating in perhaps his most celebrated work, the paintings on the ceiling of the Sistine Chapel (1508–1612). By now regarded as the most illustrious of living artists, Michelangelo was not yet forty when this mammoth project was completed (the "Last Judgment" panels were added during the years 1534–1541).

After the naming of Leo X, son of Lorenzo de' Medici, to the papacy in 1513, Michelangelo returned to Florence, where he created the magnificent Medici Chapel. In 1534 he returned once again to Rome, where he remained for the rest of his life. His creative powers unabated, Michelangelo designed in his later years the Capitoline Square and

Michelangelo's David, *detail of right side, head, and shoulder. The Academy, Florence. Corbis-Bettmann.*

the dome of St. Peter's Basilica. He died in 1564, shortly before his eighty-ninth birthday.

In 1532, before his final departure for Rome, Michelangelo made the acquaintance of one Tommaso Cavalieri, a much younger aristocrat and politician (Michelangelo was fifty-seven at the time, Cavalieri, twenty-three). Cavalieri is generally believed to represent the most important emotional attachment of Michelangelo's life. It is to Cavalieri that he wrote much of his most impassioned poetry, as well as several letters notable for their intense declarations of affection. Michelangelo also presented Cavalieri with a series of drawings highly symbolic in their erotic overtones (Ganymede, a naked young Trojan prince, is depicted in a passive position, a powerful eagle—Zeus/Jupiter—mounted behind him). Although Cavalieri subsequently married, it is he who was present at Michelangelo's deathbed, thirty-two years after their initial meeting.

Despite an inclination to assume a homosexual connection between the two men, one can only speculate on its precise nature. Robert S. Liebert writes in *Michelangelo: A Psychoanalytic Study of His Life* and *Images*: "As to whether he had an overt sexual relationship with Tommaso or other young men, it must be stated . . . that there is no documentary evidence which provides an answer; . . . [however,] all the early correspondence, the presentation drawings, the sharing of feelings by both men with intermediaries and their making the drawings public bespeak their love for each other in the first few years of their relationship" (Liebert 294).

Michelangelo's poetry provides further speculative evidence of his feelings for Cavalieri. The poems, approximately three hundred of them written over his lifetime but mostly during a twenty-year period between 1530 and 1550, have had a circuitous history. In 1623, fifty-nine years after Michelangelo's death, they received their first publication, by his great nephew. In that edition, the text was altered to indicate that the recipient of certain love sonnets was a woman, an obfuscation perpetuated for hundreds of years; only in the past century has the authentic voice of the poet been restored.

Even with a clarified rendering of his verse, there remains controversy and ambiguity as to the exact nature and direction of Michelangelo's sexuality as expressed in the poetry. In his later writing, many poems were created for Vittoria Colonna, marchioness of Pescara, whose deep friendship with the artist is extensively documented. At the same time, a variety of young men besides Cavalieri were the recipients of impassioned poems and letters, including the youth Cecchino de' Bracci, whose early death occasioned a great deal of intense verse; Gherardo Perini, about whom little is known; and especially Febo di Poggio, possibly a model, to whom Michelangelo wrote a series of passionate letters and sonnets.

It is Tommaso Cavalieri, nevertheless, to whom Michelangelo directed his finest poems that securely place him among the preeminent poets of the sixteenth century. The verse ranges in subject from death and grief to passionate exaltation, with the intense love of the speaker for the beloved everywhere present. In a poem believed to have been written in 1533, soon after they met, Michelangelo expresses in verse feelings similar to those written in a letter to Tommaso on January 1 of the same year:

> . . . Hence if I approach, my heart cannot support
> Such infinite beauty which, dazzling, blinds the eyes,

> Nor from afar assures me or trust instill.
> What will become of me? What guide or escort
> Might ever shield or solace me against surprise
> If I draw near, you burn me; if I depart, you kill.
> (Alexander 1991, 88)

More universally celebrated over the centuries as painter, sculptor, and architect, Michelangelo the poet now speaks to us with equal power and beauty—and from a perspective that places him persuasively within the canon of gay literature.

David Garnes

Bibliography

Alexander, Sidney, ed. *Complete Poetry of Michelangelo*. Athens, Ohio: Ohio University Press, 1991.

Liebert, Robert S. *Michelangelo: A Psychoanalytic Study of His Life and Images*. New Haven: Yale University Press, 1983.

Mays, Stedman. "Michelangelo." In *Gay and Lesbian Literary Heritage*. Claude Summers, ed. New York: Holt, 1995.

See also Art History; David and Jonathan; Ganymede; Italian Literature; Italian Renaissance; Italy; Leonardo da Vinci

Military

Sexuality is intimately linked to military identity and practice. The U.S. military constructs itself in opposition to homosexuality, insisting on a heterosexual, hypermasculine identity. The cultural and legal battle to maintain this military self-image by narrowly defining homosexuality as sexual desire and sexual conduct is ongoing. But historical and cultural expressions of homosexuality undermine this military self-image. Homosexuals always have served in the military. Broadening the definition of homosexuality even slightly to include cultural practices, one sees that individual and institutional military practices mark the military as among the queerest of U.S. public institutions.

The military is the organ of government charged with protecting a polity from internal and external security challenges. It is the expression of a modern nation-state's presumed monopoly on its legitimate uses of violence. As such, the military is the institution that promises to make a man out of any recruit. It offers a rite of passage into heterosexually configured manhood. This popular image of

M

Tom of Finland's view of the military. Photo courtesy of the Tom of Finland Foundation.

the military and of service people leaves little room for homosexuality. The homoeroticism created by the military's encouragement of same-sex emotional bonds and the realities of close physical contact are channeled into a love and defense of country. Homosexual subtexts like obsessions with uniforms are fetishized into drag shows. In these ways, military institutional and individual identities are defined in contrast to homosexuality, even in queer contexts. What homosexual elements cannot be heterosexually channeled are either silenced or purged. This allows military institutions to claim that there are no homosexuals in the military while tolerating the presence of vast numbers of known homosexuals who do not disrupt the straight, masculine public perception of the military.

Since its inception, the U.S. military has battled to maintain its masculinity by excluding or denying equal status to what are deemed to be nonmasculine elements—homosexuals, women, and, until 1948, African Americans. The form of homosexual exclusion and the degree of its enforcement have varied. Homosexual acts by military personnel were first criminalized during World War I. By World War II, regulations governing the recruitment of military

personnel embodied the norms of psychiatry that deemed those with "homosexual tendencies" unfit for military service. By 1943, the ban on homosexuals serving in any branch of the armed services was in place. The persistent arguments for the ban are that the presence of known homosexuals in the military would make heterosexual service people uncomfortable and threaten the efficient functioning of the armed services.

While the ban historically has produced witch-hunts for homosexuals, two notable trends emerge in the ban's selective implementation. First, the ban is relaxed during wartime, thereby contradicting the military's argument that homosexuals interfere with military performance. Second, the ban has resulted in more dismissals of women than men, and it fuels the environment of sexual discrimination and sexual harassment for military women. The ban encourages straight and homosexual women to accept unwanted sexual advances from male military personnel to avoid charges of lesbianism.

In his presidential campaign of 1992, Bill Clinton promised to lift the military ban on homosexual service. President Clinton could have followed the example of President Harry Truman, who issued an executive order racially integrating the armed services. The Rand Corporation—a conservative American think tank—concluded in its government-commissioned report that "[a] policy that ends discrimination based on sexual orientation can be implemented in a practical and realistic manner." Instead Clinton implemented the "don't ask, don't tell, don't pursue" policy—don't ask recruits or personnel about their sexual orientation, don't tell if you are a homosexual or bisexual service person, and don't pursue charges against service people who engage in acts that are no longer labeled "homosexual conduct" (reading homosexual literature, going to gay bars, and associating with known homosexuals).

The "don't ask" policy is the most explicit expression of the U.S. military's queer contradiction. The policy neither removes gays and lesbians from the military nor acknowledges that they are there. It simply offers the military deniability of the presence of homosexual personnel at the price of individual freedoms for homosexual service people. But because the military's institutional practices queer it, a policy that denies homosexual identities the right to speak their names is seemingly essential. The cultural effects of this policy evidence this. The policy in no way challenges the U.S. cultural representation of military masculinity, thereby protecting both U.S. masculinity generally and military masculinity specifically from any queer contents. Furthermore, the policy withholds legitimacy from homosexuals. Unlike Truman's executive order that gave African American service people equal status in the military and sent the message that institutionalized racism would not be tolerated, Clinton's "don't ask" policy attempts to erase inequality toward homosexuals by erasing them. In the process, it encourages an environment of homophobia within and beyond the military. Military discharges of homosexuals continue under this policy.

The American Civil Liberties Union (ACLU) charges that the "don't ask" policy violates the First Amendment right to free speech and the Constitution's equal protection clause. Court challenges have met with mixed results. While some lower courts have ruled in favor of the ACLU position, as of May 1997 the U.S. Supreme Court has declined to hear any cases that challenge the policy and let stand one case that upheld the policy's constitutionality (*Thomasson v. Perry*).

U.S. policy on homosexuals serving in the military differs from that of most of its European allies. Besides the United States, Greece, Portugal, and the United Kingdom are the only other NATO members to ban homosexuals explicitly from military service. These bans are expected to fall when challenges pending in the European Court of Human Rights are heard. *Cynthia Weber*

Bibliography

Office of the Secretary of Defense. Rand Corporation report. "Sexual Orientation and U.S. Military Personnel Policy: Options and Assessment." MR-323-OSD, 1993.

Shilts, Randy. *Conduct Unbecoming: Gays and Lesbians in the U.S. Military*. New York: St. Martin's Press, 1993.

See also European Commission of Human Rights; U.S. Law: Equal Protection

Milk, Harvey (1930–1978)

Harvey Milk is the first martyr of the modern gay movement, felled by an assassin's bullet in 1978. Known as the "mayor of Castro Street," Milk was instrumental in transforming the burgeoning gay enclave in San Francisco's Eureka Valley in the 1970s into the socially, politically, and economically unique gay community of the Castro, recognized internationally as the symbolic heart of the gay community.

Milk was born to a Jewish family on Long Island, N.Y., and experienced the cultural and subterranean homosexual milieus of Manhattan. He trained as a teacher at Albany State Teachers' College (later SUNY, Albany), served a tour of duty in the navy, worked on Wall Street, and grew into a conservative, closeted gay everyman of the 1950s.

Milk also had a passion for theater, and his contact with the stage musical *Hair* (in which he had invested)—as well as the Stonewall riots—would begin his dramatic political transformation. After spending a year driving around California and with funds exhausted, Milk settled down to the practical matter of generating income. He was also possessed of an as yet unfocused vision, and in 1972, decided to move to Castro Street, with his then-lover, Scott Smith, and open a camera shop. The business would prove no commercial success but served well as a storefront from which Milk could pursue his newly emerging gay politics and his vision of the Castro transformed into a real gay community.

In the late 1960s and early 1970s gays began "invading" the Castro in unparalleled numbers, while the city of San Francisco systematically harassed homosexuals with the intent of dissuading them from "homosexualzing" the city. A homophile political establishment already existed, but Milk threw his lot in with the radical new "gay" populace migrating to Castro Street. Milk created the first alliance between gays and San Francisco's blue-collar unions, organizing a boycott of Coors Beer because of their homophobic policies. While mingling with Marxist-oriented gay liberationists and using the fiscal conservatism of the Republican Party of his youth, he mobilized as a coalitionist Democrat.

After two unsuccessful bids, Milk was elected to the Board of Supervisors in San Francisco's first district-based elections in 1977. He represented the gay community of District 5 as well as the spirit common to many of the city's long disenfranchised neighborhoods. (Milk's political generation in San Francisco was the first to seriously bring the disparate and politically overlooked ethnic communities together and to table at City Hall.) Milk held office less than a year when fellow supervisor and ex-cop Dan White (who, ironically, represented the Excelsior District, composed of the very same con-

M servative blue-collar Irish Catholics who had fled the Castro during the 1950s–1970s) shot first Harvey, then the liberal mayor, George Moscone, before turning himself in.

The infamous "twinkie" defense, i.e., diminished mental capacity owing to eating inordinate amounts of junk food, was invented to secure White a very mild prison sentence. The "White Night Riots" erupted spontaneously when gays gathered at City Hall on the evening following the announcement of White's conviction on a charge less than murder. San Francisco police responded with a retaliatory raid on the Castro, smashing the Elephant Walk bar and attacking gay men in their own neighborhood.

In the end, dramatically improved relations with City Hall, the police, and business associations ensued. The Castro became galvanized as a bona fide gay neighborhood, and Harvey Milk entered the realm of legend as the myth of his martyrdom to the gay cause rose to a level of historical significance on a par with the Stonewall riots.   *Les Wright*

Bibliography

Shilts, Randy. *The Mayor of Castro Street: The Life and Times of Harvey Milk*. New York: St. Martin's Press, 1982.

The Times of Harvey Milk. Rob Epstein, director. Video. 1984.

See also Boycott; Politics, Global; San Francsico; Stonewall

Mineo, Sal (1939–1976)

Filmstar Sal Mineo questioned the social definition of American masculinity in the 1950s without toppling the hegemony of the he-man. Like his *Rebel Without a Cause* (1955) costar James Dean, as well as the young Montgomery Clift and Marlon Brando, Mineo found social acceptance by playing a professional antisocial. Born in the Bronx on January 10, 1939, Salvatore Mineo Jr. was a child performer on Broadway. As a film character-actor or as an aging teen pinup, Mineo won stardom. He earned supporting Oscar nominations for *Rebel* and 1960's *Exodus*, in which Mineo moaned, "They used me as you would use a woman!" A victim of the sexually repressive fifties, Mineo was also its product; his sensitive-but-tough man-child persona had no outlet in permissive post-sixties cinema. In 1971, five years before a robber stabbed him to death, Mineo buried his famous face, with its olive skin and baby-doll features, in chimp makeup for *Escape from the Planet of the Apes*.

He fed the gay liberationist fervor, rising since Stonewall, with his sexually explicit staging of the prison play *Fortune and Men's Eyes* (1969). Mineo the director gave the public its first hard glimpse of actor Don Johnson. But Mineo the actor spent his career simultaneously fleeing and flaunting signs of homosexuality. Robin Wood writes that "*Rebel* is the only film in which Mineo's character is clearly coded as gay . . . [but it] achieves a resonance that escapes the film's glib sociologizing" (Wood 681).

John Ison

Bibliography

Russo, Vito. *The Celluloid Closet: Homosexuality in the Movies,* rev. ed. New York: Harper and Row, 1987.

Wood, Robin. "Sal Mineo." In *International Dictionary of Films and Filmmakers: Actors and Actresses*. Nicholas Thomas, ed. Detroit: St. James, 1992, 680–81.

See also Film; Film Stars

Minority Standing

It is a commonplace of contemporary American politics that if gays are counted as a "legitimate" minority, then they deserve rights, and if not, then they do not. The rights in question are of two types: rights against private-sector discrimination in housing, employment, and public accommodations and rights against the government burdening members of a group in virtue of their group membership.

But what constitutes a legitimate minority is less than clear from the discourses of the political scene itself. Those on the political Right take race, understood narrowly as a biological or genetic characteristic, as the standard for minority status and hold that a legitimate minority is any group defined by an immutable characteristic, one over which an individual has no control and for which the individual is not responsible. They then move on to claim both that white people, as defined by an immutable, genetic characteristic, are a legitimate minority and that affirmative action programs that burden whites are therefore unconstitutional violations of minority rights to equal protection of the law.

The political Right is correct here to the limited extent that the "minority" in "legitimate minority" is not a statistical notion. It is defined by norms, not numbers. The expression now found in job advertisements encouraging "women and other minorities to apply" shows that the statistical sense of minority—less than 50 percent—is not a necessary condition for the correct application of the term when it is used to invoke rights. Women are considered—now without contestation—a minority properly protected by both civil rights statutes and constitutional law, even though women, like whites, constitute a statistical majority in the country.

But just as minority status does not turn on numbers, neither does it turn on immutable characteristics. In the nation's considered moral opinions, immutability is neither a necessary nor a sufficient condition for right-invoking minority standing. Consider cases.

On the one hand, immutable characteristics are not necessary conditions for a group having minority status in a morally relevant sense. Among star cases of minorities that have properly invoked civil and constitutional equality protections are religious minorities, even though one's religion is a matter of choice. A person's religious values are morally meaningful in one's life—fit subjects for making sacrifices of one's interests—only if they are a matter of choice, not compulsion. And the law treats the physically challenged as a protected minority even when the challenge in question is the result of actions for which the disabled individual is personally responsible, as in a negligently caused car accident or a botched suicide.

On the other hand, immutability is not a sufficient condition for invoking moral minority status. Sometimes drawing moral distinctions with respect to nonchosen properties is morally acceptable, even morally to be expected. For example, "grandfathering provisions" are not, on their own, considered unjust. A law with a grandfathering provision blocks future access to a privilege but allows those currently with the privilege to maintain it (say, a vendor's license or a past land use in the face of newly restrictive zoning). If grandfather exceptions do not front for some illegitimate goal (for example, perpetuating racial oppression in the post-Reconstruction era), then they are not felt to be substantially unjust, even though they create closed classes of people with privileges to which others, sometimes as a matter of when they were born, can have no access no matter what they do—and so ruled the Supreme Court in 1975 in *City of New Orleans v. Dukes*. Or again, a law that lowers the inheritance tax rate will disadvantage a person whose parents have already died compared with people whose parents have not yet died. Still, this disadvantage is not an inequitable treatment, even though its falling on that individual is not a consequence of anything that he or she has done.

If a law disadvantaging members of a group marked by an immutable characteristic has some legitimate public purpose, then it does not, without more, violate equality and may employ immutable characteristics in its design. Affirmative action programs favoring women and blacks, then, are not automatically violations of any rights of whites and males.

But if statistics and immutability do not determine what counts as a minority for the purposes of rights, what does? The account that best captures America's considered experience in this matter is that a minority is a group that has historically been treated inequitably, and an inequitable treatment of a group is one that holds members of the group in morally lesser regard—either as less than fully human or as worth less than other groups—independently of their actions. Individuals may be held in lower regard, even contempt, because of some action they perform—say, lying, thieving, murdering—which both permits and warrants censure and punishment. But individuals may not legitimately be held in lower regard because of some status they have, some membership in a group independent of any action that puts them in the group.

A minority, then, is a group whose members are held to have a degraded status independently of anything they do. And so America in constitutional law and civil rights legislation has considered blacks, ethnic groups, women, illegitimate children, legal aliens, religious groups, and the disabled as minorities. An immutable characteristic invokes minority standing only if in addition it is culturally viewed as a degraded status, as has historically been the case for blacks, but not the blue-eyed.

On this understanding of minority status, gays too should be added to the list of groups considered legitimate minorities and given strong equal protection rights. An examination of history and culture, especially jokes, invective, stereotypes, health policy, military policy, and symbolic legislation (like unenforced sodomy laws), indicates that gays are held in morally lesser regard independently of what they do. To take but one example: current military policy, despite its claims to the contrary, discriminates purely on the basis of the despised status of gay people rather than on the basis of any actions

M that gay individuals perform. For, on the one hand, a person caught performing homosexual acts can still be retained by the armed forces if he claims simply to have been drunk or skylarking rather than performing the acts because he is a homosexual. On the other hand, a person will be thrown out of the armed forces if he claims or is thought to have a homosexual identity, even if he has never performed a homosexual sexual act. So in the army's eyes, homosexual acts are neither necessary nor sufficient conditions for treating gays less well than others, indeed for throwing them out of the very institution by which the nation has traditionally taken the measure of full civic personhood.

Whether gays are or are not in their "nature" objectively like a highly distinctive ethnic group, that is how society views and threats them—as a despised ethnic group and not as a pack of criminals. When actions *are* ascribed to gays as grounds for discrimination, the actions are mere stand-ins for presumed degenerate status, just as accusations of Jews being messiahs and killers of babies are morally retrofitted to the group to justify treatments of the group motivated by considerations that have nothing to do with individuals' actions. When gay men are put down as "cocksuckers," it is the same cultural gesture as when Catholics are put down as "mackerel-eaters"—the attributed action merely echoes degenerate status. We know this because there are lots of people who suck cock and eat mackerel who yet are not subject to invective for doing so.

It is society's classification and treatment of gays, not gay's "nature," that is relevant to whether they are deserving of rights on a par with blacks. Studies about gay twins, fetal hormones, hypothalamus sizes, and genetic markers—though they grab headlines—are morally irrelevant to whether gays' should be treated as a legitimate minority deserving strong rights to equal protection of the law.

In its May 1996 decision, *Romer v. Evans*, the Supreme Court took a big step in the direction of adopting this model of minority status as applied to gays. The Court struck down, as a violation of the equal protection clause of the U.S. Constitution, a Colorado state constitutional provision—Amendment 2—that barred gays from getting civil rights protections through any means but further state constitutional amendment. Nowhere in the Court's opinion were the actions of gays or acts of "homosexual sodomy" the focus of analysis. And Amendment 2 was as clear an example as one could find of a classification that burdened a group based solely on its perceived status rather than on any actions of its members. The Court exclusively focused on society's classification and treatment of gays. It held that laws motivated by animus against some group cannot stand. Thus the Court found society's treatment of gays to be irrational, even given the Court's own broad past understanding of what counts as rational. Implicit in the case, as the three-judge dissent warily noted, was the view that gays have historically been held in lesser moral regard independently of what they do and so are deserving of the same strong protections as are held by women, blacks, and historically persecuted religious groups.

Richard D. Mohr

Bibliography

Halley, Janet E. "The Politics of the Closet: Towards Equal Protection for Gay, Lesbian, and Bisexual Identity." *UCLA Law Review* 36 (1989): 915–76.

Koppelman, Andrew. *Antidiscrimination Law and Social Equality*. New Haven: Yale University Press, 1996.

LeVay, Simon. *Queer Science*. Cambridge, Mass.: MIT Press, 1996.

Mohr, Richard D. *A More Perfect Union: Why Straight America Must Stand Up for Gay Rights*. Boston: Beacon Press, 1994.

See also Gay Rights in the United States; U.S. Law: Equal Protection

Mishima, Yukio (1925–1970)

Yukio Mishima was a prolific Japanese writer of various genres: novels, plays, literary and theater criticism, and diaries. At the same time, he ventured to be a singer, actor, stage director, and boxer. He produced many best-sellers, especially those that were inspired by real stories, combining scandalous value with literary merit; some caused a sensation for their subversive sexual topics such as homoeroticism and incest; some puzzled the reader with their right-wing overtones; while other books fascinated for their dazzlingly ornate stylish classicism. His plays, fraught with ironies, spanned the gamut from traditional Kabuki to Western motifs. Some of his works were made into films, in which he occasionally appeared in a cameo role. He posed as a model for *Barakei* (1963), a collection of seminude photographs. On another occasion, he was photographed as St. Sebastian, pierced by arrows and ecstatic with pain. In 1965 he wrote, directed, and performed in the film *Patriotism*, which became a sensation for the bloody seppuku/hara-kiri scene of the protagonist: the movie projected and predicted Mishima's idealized life and death.

Mishima lamented the disappearance of traditional Japanese values, which were becoming more and more anachronistic in post–World War II Japan—elitism, aristocratic aestheticism, and samurai machismo and asceticism. At the same time, he was fascinated by modernism and the energetic vulgarity of the middle and lower classes as materials for his novels. He took pride in his paternal grandmother's samurai family line and disciplined himself to live up to the Bushido (the way of samurai), organizing his own private military group in 1968 and eventually staging a coup d' état and dying the death of a samurai by seppuku/hara-kiri in 1970.

Mishima's childhood was ironically far removed from the image of the samurai. He was born Kimitake Hiraoka in 1925. Soon after his birth, he was virtually taken hostage by his grandmother, Natsu; his mother was allowed to see her son only when she was summoned to breast-feed him. Mishima was effeminate as a child, picking up feminine patterns of speech. His hostage state continued until he was twelve. He was infirm, and his school peers nicknamed him the "pale one." Mishima's background formed his misogyny and misanthropy, as well as his longing for a powerful male image. His life demonstrated a desperate pursuit of masculinity.

Mishima's literary talent was already manifest when he was in elementary school; his precociously stylish compositions amazed his teachers. He made his commercial literary debut at nineteen with a collection of his earlier works, which were strongly colored with Japanese classicism. Although his earlier works attracted some attention among critics and readers, it was *Confessions of a Mask* (1949) that established his fame.

Confessions caused a stir for its excessively homoerotic subject, intertwined with sadomasochism and necrophilic images. Mishima's intention was to cover his sexuality by overexposure. His homoeroticism was introverted and manifested itself as a narcissistic cult of masculinity; bodybuilding became his obsession when he was thirty years old. At the same, he took up martial arts and boxing, wrapping

himself in leather jackets or military uniforms. He described the re-creation of himself from the "pale one" into a paragon of masculinity in *Sun and Steel* (1968), in which he asserted that splendidly muscled bodies achieved perfection only when accompanied by tragic beauty—by slashing and bleeding: muscle, blood, and tragedy were the prerequisites for a "romantic death." The destruction of beauty had been one of the recurring themes in his works, and he tried to live up to his credo in real life.

Seigo Nakao

Bibliography

Mishima, Yukio. *Confessions of a Mask.* Meredith Weatherby, trans. New York: New Directions, 1958.

Stokes, Henry Scott. *The Life and Death of Yukio Mishima.* New York: Farrar, Straus and Giroux, 1974.

See also Japan; Kabuki; Machismo; Sadomasochism; Samurai

Misogyny

Hatred of women has been linked to male homosexuality in a variety of ways, each homophobically asserting a different stereotype of gay men. In one view, misogyny is seen as constitutive of homosexuality, such as when Freud, in his 1940 essay "The Medusa's Head," linked male homosexuality to a horror of the female genitals. Such efforts to view homosexual men as innately misogynistic attempt to shift the interpretive emphasis surrounding same-sex desire between men away from love and attraction of one man for another toward a paradigm of fear of, or disgust for, women. This homophobically posits heterosexual desire as natural and same-sex desire as a deviation from the norm. Homosexuality is not considered in its own light but as failed heterosexuality.

This negative stereotype is often countered by a positive stereotype in which gay men are portrayed as the perfect companions for heterosexual women: dramatic, witty, and sexually unthreatening. Though there may be a degree of truth to this stereotype (as with all stereotypes), and though a positive stereotype is more flattering than a negative one, this view oversimplifies the complexity and variety of gay male existence. In actuality, gay men are neither more nor, unfortunately, less misogynistic than their straight counterparts.

The third, and by far most common, form of misogyny linked to gay men is not hatred of women per se but hatred of femininity, or rather, effeminacy. Gay men are currently most likely to express misogynistic feelings not toward women but toward signs of effeminacy in other gay men, and effeminate gay men face homophobia (closely linked, as it is, to misogyny and anxieties about "proper" gender roles) from men both outside of and within the gay community. What Quentin Crisp said of men in the 1920s, that they "searched themselves for vestiges of effeminacy as though for lice," is still largely true in our day. This fear is typified by the "no fems" declarative so often found in personal ads for gay men in magazines and newspapers. Gay men, sensitive to normative culture's coding of them as already feminized, can be especially intolerant of community members who display feminine characteristics. A flamboyant drag queen will be tolerated and laughed at as mere theater, while a man who dresses in men's clothing but displays "feminine" mannerisms is treated with disdain or outright hostility. Ultimately, this behavior derives from a rigid conception of essential gender traits and behaviors. Its link to internalized homophobia is demonstrated in personal ads, by the frequency with which "no fems" is linked with "straight acting." To act or appear gay is, to some, always a failure of proper masculine conduct.

Some feminist critics have charged that drag is misogynistic, claiming it makes fun of or exaggerates feminine appearance or behavior. These charges have been met most effectively by other feminists, who have pointed out that drag adopts as its target not women themselves but the rigid gender roles that construct male and female as essential, timeless categories that demand strict adherence. *Scott Speirs*

Bibliography

Crisp, Quentin. *The Naked Civil Servant*. New York: Penguin, 1983.

Freud, Sigmund. "The Medusa's Head." In *The Standard Edition of the Complete Psychological Works of Sigmund Freud*. Vol. 18. James Stratchey, trans. London: Hogarth Press, 1955.

See also Crisp, Quentin; Effeminacy; Freud, Sigmund; Gender; Homphobia; Masculinity; Stereotype

Mizer, Bob (1921–1992)

When the U.S. Post Office cleaned up the men's magazines of the late forties, the first things to go were ads offering images of naked men "[s]uitable for artists! Inspiring for body builders!" Los Angeles photographer Bob Mizer talked a group of those physique artists and photographers into combining ads and mailing lists. Eventually, he hit on the idea of stapling them all together and suddenly realized, "What's a bunch of pages stapled together and issued periodically?—A magazine!"

Mizer took a sample to the largest Hollywood newsstand, got an order, and thus was born *Physique Pictorial*, the first and longest-lasting (1951–1990) of the little "muscle magazines" that contributed so much to burgeoning gay culture before Stonewall, not just by introducing George Quaintance and Tom of Finland, Ed Fury and Joe Dallesandro, but by being the first gay consumer products.

But Mizer was not just publisher of the magazine; he was the main photographer as well. Since each issue was crammed with over a hundred new faces (and other body parts), he was forced to photograph almost any man or boy who showed up and took his clothes off, not that Mizer ever complained. He never had a lover and only once took a vacation (and hated it); his life was photographing naked men. Documenting a spectacular range of men and styles, from outright campy to studiedly artful to charmingly candid boy next door, he left a legacy of several hundred thousand negatives. Bruce of Los Angeles and George Platt Lynes get higher critical acclaim, but no one did more than Bob Mizer to celebrate the naked male. *F. Valentine Hooven III*

Bibliography

Muller, Heino, and Ralf Marsault, eds. *Athletic Model Guild*. Amsterdam: Intermale, 1987.

Stanley, Wayne, ed. *The Complete Reprint of Physique Pictorial*. Cologne, Germany: Benedikt Taschen, 1997.

Waugh, Thomas. *Hard to Imagine*. New York: Columbia University Press, 1996.

See also Athletic Model Guild; Bruce of Los Angeles; Los Angeles; Lynes, George Platt; Photography; Physical Culture; Pornography; Tom of Finland

Moffett, Donald (1955–)

Artist Donald Moffett blurs the line between art and activism. Born in San Antonio in 1955 and the recipient of a B.A. in art and biology from Trinity University in 1977, he first reached large audiences in New York City with the street-graphic *He Kills*

Me (1987). This manifestolike protest against the Reagan administration's lack of response to the AIDS crisis proposed the street as a potent venue for politically inflected art. Moffett's agitprop approach would be expertly mined by Gran Fury, ACT UP's semiofficial propaganda office, of which Moffett was a founder in 1988.

His gallery-bound art also coupled words and images. Works such as *You* (1990)—a light box of a porno still emblazoned with a repeated "YOU"—utilized the postfeminist style of artists such as Barbara Kruger and Jenny Holzer to address queer audiences directly. He blended issues of social and personal identity in works like *Gays in the Military #3* (1990), on which he inscribed the phrase "brilliant war strategist, fierce bottom" to a nineteenth-century engraving of U.S. Grant.

Moffett's distinctly postmodern assault on the modernist dichotomies of gallery/street, public/private, and high/low art forms characterizes not only his art but also his establishment, in 1989, of the "trans-disciplinary studio" Bureau. In partnership with queer artist Marlene McCarty, Bureau has been awarded commissions including the credits for the film *I Shot Andy Warhol* (1996).

Robert Atkins

Bibliography

Crimp, Douglas, with Adam Ralston. *AIDS demo graphics*. Seattle: Bay Press, 1990.

See also Activism; ACT UP; AIDS; Gran Fury; Postmodernism

Moix, Terenci (1942–)

Currently Spain's best-selling novelist, Terenci Moix was the first openly gay Spanish author. His emergence onto the literary scene in the 1960s (first in Catalan, later alternating Catalan and Spanish) was perceived by critics and public alike as a turning point in Spanish culture, for he introduced a radically new interest in pop culture and homosexuality. In novels like *El día que va morir Marilyn* (The Day Marilyn Died, 1969), *La increda consciéncia de la raça* (The Uncreated Conscience of the Race, 1972), and *El sexs dels ángels* (The Sex of Angels, 1992), Moix produced realist narratives that bring Catalonia's history and identity together with homosexual desire. Other books display Moix's interest in sadomasochistic fantasies, camp, and the myths of pop culture, as in *Món Mascle* (Muscle World,

1971), *La caiguda de l'imperi sadomita* (The Fall of the Sodomite Empire, 1976), his Egyptian melodrama *No digas que fue un sueño* (Don't Say It Was a Dream, 1986), and his high camp parody of lesbian life, *Carras de astracán* (Astrakhan Claws, 1991). In 1990 he began to publish his autobiography, *El peso de la paja* (The Burden of Masturbation).

Josep-Anton Fernández

Bibliography

Fernández, Josep-Anton. "Perverting the Canon: Terenci Moix's *La caiguda del l'imperi sodomita*." In *Proceedings of the First Scottish Conference on Contemporary Catalan Studies*. Chris Doxon, ed. Oxford: Dolphin, forthcoming.

Smith, Paul Julian. *Laws of Desire: Questions of Homosexuality in Spanish Writing and Film, 1960–1990*. Oxford: Oxford University Press, 1992.

See also Spanish Literature

Moll, Albert (1862–1939)

Although virtually unknown today, Albert Moll was the preeminent neurologist and sexologist at the turn of the century before being eclipsed by Freud. The son of a Jewish merchant, Moll gained a medical degree under the supervision of Rudolf Virchow from the University of Berlin in 1885 and then did two years of postgraduate work in Vienna. Highly influential on the work of Krafft-Ebing, his studies include *Die konträre Sexualempfindung* (1891), *Untersuchungen über die Libido Sexualis* (1897), and *Handbuch der Sexualwissenschaften* (1911). Moll considered homosexuality a disease.

Moll argued that two factors lead to homosexuality: an inborn disposition for it and environmental influences. This reasoning, which supported to some degree innate theories of homosexuality, ran along the lines of suggesting that since biological organs and functions are susceptible to variation and anomalies, why should sexual instinct be any different. As his ideas developed, though, he gradually became more critical of the concept of innate homosexuality, until in his autobiography of 1936, *Ein Leben als Arzt der Seele,* he roundly attacked those (such as Magnus Hirschfeld) who believed that homosexuality was inborn rather than acquired. Moll developed an "association therapy" for homosexuality that attempted to convert homosexuals into heterosexuals by changing the environmental influences that combined with the inborn disposition to cause homosexuality.

He was extremely critical of the psychoanalysts' position that early sexual activity is an important correlate of later perversions, and as a result the psychoanalytic community turned against him.

The guiding theoretical orientation in his *Libido Sexualis* is of a neo-Darwinian evolutionary approach, with perversion interpreted as a congenital weakness in one or more of a complex set of elements that go to make up normal heterosexual reaction capacity in humans; among the defects he cited were the use of clothing (removing visual sexual stimuli) and the reduced human sense of smell. Moll, consistent with his interpretation of homosexuality as an illness, argued against the prosecution of consenting homosexual adults who engage in homosexual acts because sick people deserved compassion and help rather than persecution.

Adam Hedgecoe

Bibliography

Moll, Albert. *Der Hypnotismus*. Berlin: Fischer, 1889.
———. *Die konträre Sexualempfindung; mit Benutzung amtlichen Materials*. 2., verm. Aufl. Berlin: Fischer, 1893

See also Evolution; Freud, Sigmund; Hirschfeld, Magnus; Krafft-Ebing, Richard von; Scientific Approaches to Homosexuality; Sexology

Mollies

In northwestern Europe during the late seventeenth and eighteenth centuries, urbanization went hand in hand with the development of a male homosexual subculture. By the first decade of the eighteenth century in England, participants and opponents had begun regularly to employ the term *molly* to signify male sodomites who sought out and engaged in sex with other men. Prior to this period, there had been places where men met and had sex. But the taverns, back rooms, inns, and private houses that made up London's numerous "molly houses" are the first locales (outside of the royal court) known to have provided a consistent network of like-minded individuals and relatively secure access to erotic gratification. The mollies who socialized in these places were crucial to the formation of a modern homosexual identity. While the name *molly* has disappeared from the current gay male lexicon, related terms such as *Mary Ann, girlfriend,* and *sister* along with queeny camp behavior reflect cultural continuities across time.

Most of the extant information about mollies' experiences is derived from satirical attacks and published trial records. Despite the negative light shed by these documents, scholars have been able to reconstruct much of what transpired during mollies' nights out. Prostitution seems not to have been a major component in their community. By and large, mollies were working-class men who, in addition to sex, came together for gossip, merriment, and drink. One informer's testimony at a sodomy trial gives a likely accurate picture of popular nonsexual entertainment among these men: "In a large Room there we found one a fiddling, and eight more a dancing Country Dances" (*Trials* 2.368).

According to *Hell Upon Earth*, a tract published in 1729, London possessed twenty "Houses of Resort" (43) at which mollies regularly gathered. George Whitle, for instance, ran an establishment called the Royal Oak at the corner of St. James's Square and Pall Mall; Thomas Orme had one called the Red-Lyon in Crown Court, Knaves Acre; Mr. Jones operated the Three Tobacco Rolls house in Drury Lane; Thomas Wright's was located in Beech Lane, near the Sodomites' Walk; and, most famous of all, Margaret "Mother" Clap was the proprietor of an eponymous pleasure den in Field Lane, Holborn. Thirty to fifty mollies are reported to have visited Mother Clap's house each night (Sunday seems to have been most popular; a tea dance ancestor, perhaps?) (*Trials* 2.362; 3.37). Outside of the pubs and houses, popular spots for mollies' sexual assignations included public cruising zones such as the south side of St. James's Park, the "Bog-Houses" at Lincoln's Inn, the Covent Garden piazzas, the Sodomites' Walk in the Moorfields, St. Clement's churchyard, and the Royal Exchange.

Some of the most distinguishing and notorious features of molly activities were frequent sartorial and behavioral travesty. There is probably some truth in *Hell Upon Earth*'s glimpse of a molly soirée:

They assume the Air and affect the Name of *Madam* or *Miss, Betty* or *Molly,* with a chuck under the Chin, and *O you bold Pullet I'll break your Eggs,* and then frisk and walk away to make room for another, who thus accosts the affected Lady, with *Where have you been you saucy Queen? If I catch you Strouling and Cat-*

erwauling, I'll beat the Milk out of your Breasts I will so. (42–43)

Frequently regarded by outsiders as a damnable degeneration from upright masculinity, molly effeminacy was a "common coinage" that contributed to group identification (Bray 86–88). So-called maiden names—such as Moll, Mary, Margaret, Fanny, and Sukey—were the general rule among participants. Mollies would often further distinguish their sobriquets by adding titles such as Madam, Miss, Countess, or Queen; because he sold citrus fruit, Martin Mackintosh called himself "Orange Deb" (*Trials* 3.36).

While Rictor Norton is justified in cautioning against the assumption that mollies cross-dressed and acted effeminately all the time, their penchant for role-playing (and its public vilification) provides important information about eighteenth-century conflicts over, and reorganization of, gender roles. In his *History of the London Clubs*, for instance, Edward "Ned" Ward describes a ceremony in which a man, disguised as a pregnant woman and surrounded by other men dressed up as midwives and nurses, gave birth to a "wooden Offspring" which was later christened (28). Such a performance makes sense when it is considered in the context of establishments that contained a "Chappel" in which couples were, euphemistically, "married" (see *Trials* 2.370). As these examples illustrate, molly travesty went beyond mere effeminacy to involve the parodic performance of heteronormative experiences and institutions.

No single answer, however, can adequately explain molly customs. In certain cases, appropriating stereotypical female garb and mannerisms might have been just campy (if at times misogynist) fun. Norton also suggests that it may have been a way of alleviating fears over social persecution. Randolph Trumbach and others have argued that by 1700 a shift in public attitudes had occurred toward gender and sexuality, such that masculinity was henceforward largely defined by the desire for, and performance of, sex with women; effeminacy, in turn, became linked with homosexual sodomy. Mollies' behavior may represent an internalization of this equation. A more likely explanation is that their practices frequently involved a deliberate, transgressive flouting of conventions and, as Alan Bray suggests, a willfully ironic dislocation of heterosexual norms. On this account, John Dunton's satiric blast against mollies, in which he rails that "He-

Whore! The Word's a Paradox," (95), makes sense if one considers molly travesty as a threat to supposedly essential gender identification. Ward's description of mollies' activities as "preternatural polotions" (29)—by which he likely means that they demonically pollute society—suggests that at least some observers recognized, though overexaggerated, the dissident gender politics embedded in molly amusements.

Mollies were attacked not only in print but also by the police, who often worked in concert with the Societies for the Reformation of Manners. While mollies were often left alone, periodic raids and mass arrests subjected participants to fines, pillorying, imprisonment, and death. In 1726, for instance, Gabriel Lawrence, William Griffin, and Thomas Wright were convicted of sodomy and hanged at Tyburn (*Trials* 2.362–366; 367–369). Mollies did not, however, always acquiesce meekly to homophobic pogroms. On December 28, 1725, twenty-five masquerading mollies caught in a house in Covent Garden aggressively fought back against the London constabulary; their defiant clash foreshadowed events on another continent over two centuries later: New York's Stonewall riots. The molly subculture's resilience testifies to the ongoing ability of marginalized and demonized people to survive and even flourish in the context of malevolent attitudes and violent acts.

Michael M. Holmes

Bibliography

Bray, Alan. *Homosexuality in Renaissance England*. London: Gay Men's Press, 1982.

British Journal 120 (January 2, 1725/6): 3; 123 (January 23, 1725/6): 3.

Dunton, John. "The He-Strumpets: A Satyr on the Sodomite-Club." In *Athenianism: or, the New Projects of Mr. John Dunton*. 2 vols. London: 1710.

Hell Upon Earth: or the Town in an Uproar. 1729. *Hell Upon Earth: or the Town in an Uproar and Satan's Harvest Home*. Facsimile reprint. New York: Garland, 1985.

Norton, Rictor. *Mother Clap's Molly House: The Gay Subculture in England, 1700–1830*. London: Gay Men's Press, 1992.

Select Trials at the Sessions-House in the Old Bailey. 4 vols. 1742. Facsimile reprint. New York: Garland, 1985.

Trumbach, Randolph. "Sodomitical Assaults, Gender Role, and Sexual Development in Eighteenth-Century London." In *The Pursuit of*

M

Sodomy: Male Homosexuality in Renaissance and Enlightenment Europe. Kent Gerard and Gert Hekma, eds. New York: Harrington Park Press, 1989, 407–29.

———. "Sodomitical Subcultures, Sodomitical Roles, and the Gender Revolution of the Eighteenth Century: The Recent Historiography." In *'Tis Nature's Fault: Unauthorized Sexuality During the Enlightenment*. R. P. Maccubbin, ed. Cambridge: Cambridge University Press, 1987, 109–21.

Ward, Edward. "The Mollies' Club." 1709. In *The History of the London Clubs*. Fred Marchmont, ed. nd. 28–29.

See also Camp; Effeminacy; Molly Houses; Sodomy

Molly Houses

Public houses in eighteenth-century England that catered to a predominately or exclusively male homosexual clientele were known as "molly houses" or "molly clubs" (the term *molly*—which appears originally to have been a pet form of the name Mary—was initially applied early in the period as a contemptuous slang term for female "wenches" and prostitutes; the word soon came similarly to be used to designate effeminate men and boys as well). By the mid-1720s civic authorities in London claimed to have identified at least twenty such clubs or houses operating in and around the city and Westminster. Some of these houses were elaborate and carefully run professional operations. The notorious house kept by one Margaret "Mother" Clap in Holborn, for example, could accommodate as many as forty men on any given evening (Sunday nights were popular), and boasted a back room containing beds so that customers could engage in sexual activity on the premises. Providing as they did a welcome alternative to approaching and making advances to potential partners in considerably more indiscreet public rendezvous such as the brothels near Covent Garden, Birdcage Walk in St. James's Park, or the so-called Sodomites' Walk in the Moorfields, such houses presented a comparatively safe space within which homosexual encounters could take place. Other molly houses were quite limited in their facilities, amenities, and resources; it was probably not all that unusual for a single, enterprising individual to volunteer to entertain several homosexual "clients" and customers simultaneously in the privacy of his or her own room. Behavior in molly houses appears often deliberately and self-consciously to have mimicked and parodied both the rituals and the rhetoric of heterosexual relationships and marriages. Patrons drank ale and danced together, and often addressed one another in specifically female terms (e.g., "Miss," "Madam," "Your Ladyship," etc.). As Randolph Trumbach has observed: "Sometimes they enacted heterosexual responsibility. Then they mimicked childbirth and spoke of their husbands and children. They referred to intercourse as 'marrying,' and the room in the molly house where the beds were was called 'the Chapel'" (Trumbach, "London's Sodomites," 17). Cross-dressing was apparently a common activity in the houses, some of which reflected the growing popularity of the masquerade as a form of entertainment and social intercourse by encouraging an aggressive transvestism. The molly clubs of early-eighteenth-century England were described in some detail by journalist (and innkeeper) Edward "Ned" Ward, who wrote the popular contemporary chronicle *The London-Spy* (1698–1709). A famous—and, in many eighteenth- and nineteenth-century editions, omitted—passage in John Cleland's *Memoirs of a Woman of Pleasure* (1748–1749) describes a chance homosexual encounter witnessed by the novel's heroine, Fanny Hill, in a roadside public house somewhere between London and Hampton Court. Fanny is counseled to forget the encounter, since such "unsex'd male-misses" are "scarce less execrable than ridiculous in their monstrous inconsistency, of loathing and contemning women, and all at the same time aping their manner, airs, lisp, and scuttle." It is noteworthy that the habitual cross-dressing of the molly house and adult male transvestism in general were likewise often dismissed as satirically destructive and misogynistic—"an expression of the sodomites' hatred of women" (Trumbach, "London's Sodomites," 18).   *Robert L. Mack*

Bibliography

Rousseau, G. S. "The Pursuit of Homosexuality in the Eighteenth Century: 'Utterly Confused Category' and/or Rich Repository?" *Eighteenth Century Life* 9 (1985): 133–68.

Trumbach, Randolph. "London's Sodomites: Homosexual Behavior and Western Culture in the Eighteenth Century." *Journal of Social History* 11 (1977): 1–33.

See also Camp; Effeminacy; London; Mollies; Sodomy

Monasticism, Christian

In Christian history, *monasticism* refers to very different attempts to establish ways of life that would mirror the ideals of the Gospel while bringing about more immediate union with God. The commonest form of Christian monasticism is a single-sex community in which the members renounce sexual activity and private property so as to dedicate themselves to prayer, study, manual labor, and ascetic practices. Homosexual activity has been a concern in Christian monasteries from the beginning. The earliest stories of desert monasticism warn against letting beautiful young men into the monastic enclosure. The earliest monastic "rules," or constitutions, in western Europe prohibit monks from sharing beds or having tempting contacts in private. Monastic spiritual writers describe in detail how homoerotic desires might arise and how they should be resisted. The warnings, prohibitions, and counsels did not stop sexual activity within monastic houses. Medieval penitential codes and collections of church law consider many cases in which monks copulate with each other or with "boys," and historical records relate a number of such cases. Although there is less evidence for lesbian activity, we do know of late medieval women's houses in which there was sexual activity. Certainly the popular literature of Christian countries is filled with stories of homosexual monks and nuns. At present, many Catholic monasteries are being challenged to accept members who want to live in community as celibates but who also want to identify themselves as gay and lesbian. The response to these challenges has varied widely from house to house.

Mark D. Jordan

Bibliography

Boswell, John. *Christianity, Social Tolerance, and Homosexuality: Gay People in Western Europe from the Beginning of the Christian Era to the Fourteenth Century*. Chicago: University of Chicago Press, 1980.

See also Catholicism; Christianity; Clergy; Religion and Religiosity

Monette, Paul (1945–1995)

American novelist, poet, and essayist. Monette's greatest claim to fame are his two memoirs, *Borrowed Time* (1988), the first AIDS narrative to become a best-seller, and *Becoming a Man* (1992), a National Book Award–winning autobiography of his childhood and coming-out experience. For the American popular media and general public, Monette single-handedly brought the AIDS pandemic home, humanizing it in a way that no one had been able to do before. Similarly, his coming-out memoir was crucial in allowing the general reading public to enter the life of a gay man and experience coming out firsthand.

Monette began his writing career in 1979 as a novelist, writing popular fiction with openly gay men who have come to terms with their homosexuality. He uses popular generic styles—melodrama, romance, western, mystery—but manipulated to allow for gay men and their lives. The early novels are often witty and to a certain extent apolitical. They tend to be escapist and popular, but they never stray from Monette's desire to portray gay men as three-dimensional, comfortable characters whose main problems often derive from homophobic expectations.

The advent of the AIDS pandemic and its effects on his own life transformed Monette's writing, and with the publication of *Borrowed Time*, his writing attained an urgency and political stridency not evident in his earlier work. *Borrowed Time* tells the story of the AIDS diagnosis of Monette's lover, Roger Horwitz, the medical battles that ensued, and his illnesses and death. Told in an intensely urgent tone, often with shades of hysteria and self-remorse, the memoir is brutally honest in its portrayal of the disease's ravages on Roger and the ways in which his illnesses change their relationship. The memoir shares with his other work a conviction of the worth of gay men's lives, and although it often spills over into melodrama, it is a profound statement of the strength of love even in the most dire circumstances.

Monette's other major autobiographical work, *Becoming a Man*, is unique in Monette's oeuvre in the sense that it addresses a coming-out experience, a subject Monette generally avoids. Monette's story of being a lower-middle-class white child in New England who attains much privilege by going to the right schools is countered by his increasing anxiety over his sexuality and how to express it. The memoir is fairly consistent with other pre-Stonewall coming-out stories in that without an active gay rights movement, Monette must find his own way of being gay without any models or any support. It explains to a certain extent Monette's commitment to writing stories about self-respecting gay men who

M

have found their own way but who can also serve as models for younger generations.

Monette's remaining work, both poetic and fictional, explores the ways in which gay men who survive AIDS must change their lives to accommodate the loss. *Afterlife* (1990) tells the story of three AIDS widowers who become friends while waiting in a hospital during their lovers' illnesses and deaths, and the ways these deaths transform their friendships. The importance of the novel is its message that gay men can live meaningful, productive lives even in the midst of the AIDS pandemic. *Halfway Home* (1991) is the story of a gay man living with AIDS and reconciling with his straight brother; the novel explores the complexities of gay men's lives deriving from heterosexist family structures. Monette also published two volumes of poetry and a number of movie novelizations. *Douglas Eisner*

Bibliography

Clum, John M. "'The Time Before the War': AIDS, Memory, and Desire." *American Literature* 62, no. 2 (1990): 648–67.

Eisner, Douglas. "AIDS and Limits of Melodrama in Monette and Weir." *College Literature* 24, no. 1 (1997): 213–24.

Román, David. "Paul Monette." In *Contemporary Gay American Novelists: A Bio-Bibliographical Critical Sourcebook.* Emmanuel S. Nelson, ed. Westport, Conn.: Greenwood Press, 1993.

See also AIDS Literature; Fiction; Love Poetry, the Petrarchan Tradition; U.S. Literature: Contemporary Gay Writing

Montaigne, Michel de (1533–1592)

Michel de Montaigne, the great French humanist, politician, and author of the *Essays*, is most often mentioned in considerations of homosexuality for his friendship with Étienne de la Boétie. Three years his senior, La Boétie was a member with Montaigne of the Parliament of Bordeaux and is himself best known for his friendship with Montaigne and for his political treatise, *The Discourse of Voluntary Servitude*, which explores the reasons for political servitude. The two men met in Bordeaux around 1558 and quickly became friends; in a moving letter to his father, Montaigne tells how their relationship ended tragically only a few years later with La Boétie's premature death in 1563. (Montaigne is also signifi-

cant for his mention of marriages performed for male couples in Rome. For the most complete listing of references to homosexuality in Montaigne's works, see Beck.)

Despite the critical attention the friendship has received, we know virtually nothing about their relationship except what Montaigne tells us in his various writings. From these writings, it is impossible to know whether or not the two shared a sexual relationship, and indeed in most ways it doesn't matter. Montaigne describes a relationship with La Boétie in many ways typical of celebrated male friendship in periods where women were largely excluded from intellectual or political pursuits, sometimes using memorable—and strikingly passionate—language: "[I]t is I know not what quintessence of this mixture, which, having seized my whole will, led it to plunge and lose itself in his; which, having seized his whole will, led it to plunge and lose itself in mine, with equal hunger, equal rivalry" (*Essays* I:28, 139). Proclamations such as these in the context of intellectual or spiritual friendship may or may not have served in part as screens for a physical relationship; in any case, they emerge from an erotic context markedly different from that of contemporary homosexuality.

In terms of relating Montaigne to contemporary homosexualities, rather than finding in the sixteenth-century author a Renaissance protohomosexual, it may be more productive to look for certain conceptual continuities between his work and more recent writings. For example, André Gide, defending pederasty in his *Corydon*, cites Montaigne's discussion of the arbitrariness of custom to support his argument that what is commonly called "natural" is in fact a product of custom. Perhaps more strikingly, Montaigne's insistence on the radical equality of ideal friends (rather than the constitutive imbalance characteristic for him both of pederasty and of relationships between men and women) shares much with some modern views of homosexuality, as does his paradoxical insistence on ideal friendship's lack of use value and its potential for promoting liberty. Although Montaigne's classically inflected rhetoric of male friendship is far from identical with the liberatory models of male homosexuality developed in the early 1970s by such figures as Guy Hocquenghem that would conceive of homosexuality in resistance to capitalism and the family, certain similarities between the two do suggest undertheorized continuities between the pre- and early-modern discourses of male friendship and those that treat con-

temporary homosexuality. Attention to these similarities in such figures as Montaigne may lead to a more
nuanced appreciation of the implications of homosexuality's conceptual patrimony.   *Marc Schachter*

Bibliography

Beck, William. "Montaigne face à l'homosexual-
      ité." *Bulletin de la Sociéte des Amis de Mon-
      taigne* 9–10 (1982): 41–50.
Gide, André. *Corydon.* Richard Howard, trans. New
      York: Farrar, Straus and Giroux, 1983.
Hocquenghem, Guy. *Homosexual Desire.* Introduc-
      tion by Michael Moon; preface by Jeffrey
      Weeks. Daniella Dangoor, trans. Durham,
      N.C.: Duke University Press, 1993.
La Boétie, Étienne de. *The Politics of Obedience:
      The Discourse of Voluntary Servitude.* Intro-
      duction by Murray N. Rothbard. Harry Kurz,
      trans. Montreal: Black Rose Books, 1997.
Montaigne, Michel de. *The Complete Works of Mon-
      taigne: Essays, Travel Journal Letters.* Donald
      M. Frame, trans. London: Hamish Hamilton,
      1957.
Stambolian, George, and Elaine Marks, eds. *Homo-
      sexualities and French Literature: Cultural Con-
      texts, Critical Texts.* Preface by Richard Howard.
      Ithaca, N.Y.: Cornell University Press, 1979.

See also French Literature; Friendship; Gide, André; Hocquenghem, Guy; Pederasty

*Proust's friend the French poet Robert de Montesquieu,
1855–1922. Corbis-Bettmann.*

Montesquieu, Count
Robert de (1855–1921)

Robert de Montesquieu, a descendant of prominent
French nobility with valid claims to prerevolutionary aristocratic origins, is best recognized as a close
acquaintance of writer Marcel Proust and as the
model for the baron de Charlus, a main character of
Proust's magnum opus, *À la Recherche du temps
perdu* (Remembrance of Things Past). Like his literary counterpart, Montesquieu was a most visible
member of Parisian high society, manifesting an
erudite knowledge of history and literature as well
as a taste for the direction and control of that society's activities. Montesquieu wrote and published
his poetry sometimes to great effect. He could often
make or break the careers of nascent writers
and artists introduced to his entourage by Proust or
others.

      As seen through the literary character of Char-
lus, this gradually closer acquaintance of Proust's
narrator lives a secretly promiscuous life of sexual
pursuits the objects of which range from servants
and secretaries to fellow aristocrats as his preferences take him from artistic salons to the underworld of male brothels. It is quite clear that Mon-
tesquieu/Charlus had tremendous influence on the
greater part of Proust's work, both as an inspiration
for character and as a literary critic. Montesquieu
himself manifested an enormous self-importance
and an exclusive snobbism with an incisive edge for
those who displeased him. His inherited station in
society not always manageable, he could often be
seen transporting a family heirloom for sale in Paris
when funds ran short. An elegant manner in speech
and self-presentation as well as a striking style of
dress became the most recognizable traits of this
outstanding member of both Parisian and Proustian
society.   *Steven Infantino*

Bibliography

Hayman, Ronald. *Proust: A Biography.* New York:
      HarperCollins, 1990.
Painter, George D. *Proust.* 2 vols. Boston: Little,
      Brown, 1959–1965.

M

Proust, Marcel. *À la Recherche du temps perdu.* Paris: Gallimard, 1954.

See also France; Proust, Marcel

Montherlant, Henry de (1896–1972)

French writer Henry de Montherlant was antifeminist, bisexual, and sometime fascist. Feeling out of step with what he considered to be an increasingly feminine and democratic age, he made a career of writing masculinist, aristocratic protests against the twentieth century. His criteria of moral excellence were centered in purity and patriotism. This did not stop him, in a characteristic moment of arrogance, welcoming the German victory over France in 1940.

Montherlant made a virtue of the egocentricity he derived from his noble Catholic background. He saw himself as a pagan Christian, and was much attracted to both Spain and the Orient. An apologist for sports and violent masculinity, he regarded vigorous action as the solution to the ills of stagnation, and exercised a haughty disdain for what he regarded as the middle-class sentimentality that fears violence. All these views made him a ripe target for Simone de Beauvoir's feminist attack on him in *Le Deuxième sexe* (The Second Sex, 1949).

His main gay texts are the play *Le Ville dont le prince est un enfant* (1951, reworked in 1967), set in a French Catholic college in the mid-1930s, and the autobiographical novel *Les Garçons* (written 1929, published 1969), which is based on the same materials. He writes of Jesuit schools as, at the same time, havens of pederastic Hellenism and the forges of moralistic asceticism. When boys fall in love in such an atmosphere, their love must be sweet but doomed.

Montherlant committed suicide in 1972, fearing the onset of blindness.   *Gregory Woods*

Bibliography

Robinson, Christopher. *Scandal in the Ink: Male and Female Homosexuality in Twentieth-Century French Literature.* London: Cassell, 1995.

Beauvoir, Simone de. *Le Deuxième sexe.* Paris: Gallimard, 1949.

See also Feminism; France; French Literature; Masculinity; Pederasty

Moran, Robert (1937–)

Robert Moran is an American composer particularly known for his stage and mixed-media works.

He studied in Vienna with Hans-Erich Apostel, in the United States with Luciano Berio and Darius Milhaud, and also briefly with Roman Haubenstock-Ramati. Although he has worked as a conductor, broadcaster, and lecturer on contemporary music, since the late 1970s he has been a full-time composer. A self-professed opera fanatic, many of his compositions display a pronounced theatrical bent, often employing mixed-media and improvisational techniques. The work *39 Minutes for 39 Autos* (1969), for example, was written for auto horns and lights, synthesizers, skyscrapers, radio stations, dancers, and airplanes. Recently, Moran has undergone a stylistic shift from the avant-garde, electronic, and aleatoric techniques used in his earliest works toward the more neoromantic idiom seen first in his collaboration with Philip Glass, *The Juniper Tree* (1985). Moran has written several operas, including *Desert of Roses* (1989) and *The Dracula Diary* (1994). His 1995 chorus opera, *Night Passage* (libretto by James Skofield), was commissioned by the Seattle Men's Chorus, and movingly chronicles the flight of six hundred gay men across the English channel on the night of Oscar Wilde's arrest. Its concluding ballad, "Let Love Lead," was originally written for the *AIDS Quilt Songbook* tour. Moran has described his recent *Requiem: Chant du Cygne* as "somewhat of an AIDS requiem." Many of his works have been recorded on the Decca and Argo labels.

Stephen McClatchie

Bibliography

Ruppenthal, Stephen. "Moran, Robert." In *The New Grove Dictionary of American Music.* H. Wiley Hitchcock and Stanley Sadie, eds. New York: Grove's Dictionaries of Music, 1986.

Stiller, Robert. "Moran, Robert." In *The New Grove Dictionary of Opera.* Stanley Sadie, ed. London: Macmillan, 1992.

See also AIDS Quilt Songbook; Choruses and Marching Bands; Music and Musicians 1: Classical Music; Opera; Wilde, Oscar

Morocco

Located only nine miles from Europe on the northwestern coast of Africa across the Strait of Gibraltar, Morocco has always occupied a significant position within the Orientalist imagination. A gateway to the Middle East, it has often been the first stop on the itinerary of Westerners seeking exotic experiences and the fulfillment of erotic fantasies. The region's perceived sexual plenitude coupled with a local ambivalence to male-male sex acts has attracted prominent Western artists, thinkers, and writers for almost two centuries. Those who have visited and/or lived in Morocco include Camille Saint-Saëns, Paul Bowles, William S. Burroughs, Truman Capote, Jean Genet, Tennessee Williams, and Joe Orton. Capitalizing on Western desires, a thriving sex tourist trade (centered in the city of Tangier) peaked during the 1970s and early 1980s, but has been in decline in recent years owing to the resurgence of religious conservatism, the advent of AIDS, and increased anti-Western sentiment.

Morocco, Algeria, Tunisia, and Libya together form an area known as the Maghreb (Arabic for "west"). Originally settled by Berber tribes, the region was invaded by Arabs in the seventh century C.E., converting the vast majority of the populace to Islam. In 1990, more than two-thirds of Moroccans were of Berber descent; Arabs make up the second-largest ethnic group, followed by black Africans. Considerable intermarriage among the three groups makes determining precise ethnic boundaries difficult, though. Smaller numbers of Europeans and Jews make up the remainder of the population. Most Moroccans speak Arabic as a first language, although Berber languages are still in widespread use, particularly in rural areas. Many people also speak French, the language of Morocco's former colonial rulers. Morocco achieved independence from France in 1956, and its government is a constitutional and secular monarchy.

Same-sex eroticism among males has had a long history in the Maghreb. During the premodern era (as far back as Roman times), a thriving slave trade provided the ruling classes with both young males and females for concubinage. In the eighteenth and early nineteenth centuries, the Barbary (i.e., Berber) Coast pirates dominated the slave trade and sold captured youths to the courts of North African and eastern Mediterranean rulers. The region also has had a long tradition of male dancers and performers. In a culture where belly dancing and singing in public have been equated with prostitution, such careers were deemed unfit for women. These roles were therefore frequently assumed by boys and young men. Often attired in women's clothing, they would perform in cafés and cabarets that doubled as brothels. When French colonial rule began, shocked colonial administrators closed many of these performance venues. Forced underground, the practices nevertheless continued, and the tradition of the homosexual male singer/dancer remains to this day.

The Moroccan conception of homosexuality differs significantly from that of the West. Morocco shares with the rest of Arab-Islamic society an understanding of sexuality that centers around the act of penetration: when two people engage in sex, there is always an active partner (i.e., someone who penetrates) and a passive partner (i.e., someone who is penetrated). In this highly patriarchal society, activity is considered a positive and male trait, while passivity a negative and female one. Through penetration the active partner reaffirms his own "maleness" and maintains his claim to patriarchal privilege, even if the object of his penetration is another male. Conversely, the passive partner disavows his own maleness by allowing himself to be penetrated. Relegated symbolically to womanhood and to the sexual and social margins, he loses his place within the matrix of patriarchal power. It is only this passive partner who could possibly be viewed as "homosexual." Playing the active role during sex carries little if any stigma, while the passive role invites scorn. Therefore, a man when asked will almost inevitably deny having ever been the passive partner during sex. Masturbation is frowned upon as a means of sexual gratification because there is no penetration and no sexual object other than the self. Fellatio, considered an unclean practice, likewise denies activeness to the insertive partner.

While the criminal code prohibits "acts against nature with a person of the same sex," observers have noted that homosexual activity is considered a normal part of a young man's sexual development in Morocco. In many ways Morocco is still a sexually segregated society. Unless a young man is willing to hire a female prostitute, opportunities for premarital sex with women are rare. Thus prepubescent boys are often obliged to serve as sexual outlets for older male friends and relatives. However, after a boy reaches puberty and becomes a man, he is expected to assume the passive role no longer, or at least to deny it. The active partner's masculinity is never called into question. The passive partner, to protect his masculinity, denies his receptive role. Despite religious and legal injunctions against male-male eroticism, such activity does not cast social obloquy on the participants so long as it is carried out according to this schema. In fact, some Western anthropologists have written of a practice in Morocco

M called *baraka* (from the Arabic word for "blessing") whereby religious knowledge and virtue are believed to be transmitted from a saintly man to a younger pupil via anal intercourse.

In Morocco it is common for male friends to hold hands or kiss on the cheek in public. Friendly affection such as this is often misread by Westerners as being sexual in nature. Homosexual activity, while perhaps not uncommon, is something that does not typically manifest itself in open view. Since "homosexuality" is equated with sexual passivity and looked on with disdain, an openly "gay" identity is almost unheard of except within a highly Westernized subset of the population. Nevertheless, within each community there are men who are known to be *hassas* or *pédés* (passive homosexuals). A close relative of the king is widely acknowledged as one. Yet those so labeled almost always deny it publicly. In the distant past male-male eroticism may have been tolerated and even celebrated in poetry and song. Perhaps as a result of French colonial rule and the adoption of Western biases, same-sex eroticism is now considered shameful, and current prospects for a gay rights movement and a change in cultural attitudes are poor at best.

Richard McKewen

Bibliography

Chebel, Malek. *L'Esprit de sérail: perversions et marginalités sexuelles au Maghreb*. Paris: Lieu Common, 1986.

Murray, Stephen O., and Will Roscoe, eds. *Islamic Homosexualities: Culture, History, and Literature*. New York: New York University Press, 1997.

See also Anthropology; Arabic Literature; Bowles, Paul; Burroughs, William Seward; Capote, Truman; Colonialism; Dancing Boys; Genet, Jean; Islam; Orton, Joe; Saint-Saëns, Camille; Tourism and Travel; Williams, Tennessee

Morris, Jan (1927–)

Born James Humphrey Morris in Somerset, England, award-winning travel writer Jan Morris is probably best known for her account in *Conundrum* of her journey between the sexes. First published in 1974, two years after Morris's sexual reassignment surgery in Casablanca, it was reprinted in 1986 as mass culture's interest in transsexualism reached new heights. Morris was one of the first of the public transsexuals, famous for being transsexual rather than trying to disappear into their altered legal sex identities. Morris and others like her—Christine Jorgensen, Mario Martino, Renee Richards, and, more recently, Caroline Cossey (the model Tula), Kate Bornstein, and Sandy Stone—have focused popular attention on the issue of "sex change." In doing so, they may not have changed sexes but rather helped construct a new, "transgender" sexual identity outside the West's sexual binary opposition, which the very possibility of sex change destabilizes. Nevertheless, Morris's writing is not radical in its discussion of sex or gender, reproducing a great many stereotypes about what it means to be a man or a woman, even as her life demonstrates the difficulty of assigning traits or individuals to a fixed category. As transsexualism became more common in the 1970s, many feminists critiqued it just because it seemed to confirm sexist stereotypes, arguing that transsexuals were not women but a man's idea of a woman—and "the idea of a man not nearly so intelligent as James Morris used to be," as Rebecca West wrote in her *New York Times* book review of *Conundrum* (April 14, 1974, p. 5).

Carole-Anne Tyler

Bibliography

Bornstein, Kate. *Gender Outlaw: On Men, Women, and the Rest of Us*. New York: Routledge, 1995.

Morris, Jan. *Conundrum: An Extraordinary Narrative of Transsexualism*. New York: Henry Holt, 1974.

Raymond, Janice. *The Transsexual Empire*. Boston: Beacon Press, 1979.

See also Jorgensen, Christine; Richards, Renee; Transgender; Transsexualism

Morris, Mark (1956–)

U.S. dancer and choreographer Mark Morris is thought by many to be one of the greatest U.S. choreographers of the twentieth century. Renowned for both his choreography and his brash style, Morris was influenced by early modern dance pioneers and folk dance styles. His dances demonstrate a respect for tradition and a concern with form. One of the remarkable aspects of Morris's work is his attention to music. Mark Morris Dance Group is rare among modern dance companies in that they often tour and perform with live musical accompaniment. His approach to choreography is often called "musical visualization"—the movement makes visual the form of the music. Notoriously crass and openly gay, Morris has long held a reputation as an enfant terrible. His work is tremendously popular with mainstream modern dance audiences titillated by his reputation. While there are certainly choreographers who more fully address gay issues in their choreography, no one reaches as large an audience as Morris. In his restaging of the familiar narrative of *The Nutcracker*, called *The Hard Nut* (1991), Morris explores cross-dressing in different ways, at times for camp appeal, at times intentionally blurring gender distinctions perpetuated by ballet. In his frankly erotic *Dido and Aeneas* (1989), Morris himself dances the role of Dido, Queen of Carthage. Other dances are more subtle in their references to sexuality. For example, in *Going Away Party* (1990), danced to western swing music by Bob Wills and His Texas Playboys, one section is reminiscent of a traditional square dance. Morris has no partner but dances alone among the male-female couples. There is no limit to what becomes source material for Morris's dances; his early training in flamenco, essays by Roland Barthes, music by the Violent Femmes, poetry by Milton, and American Sign Language all have merited Morris's choreographic attention. What remains constant is Morris's celebration of the human body's performing unexpected rhythms with lusty physicality   *Maura Keefe*

Bibliography

Acocella, Joan. *Mark Morris*. New York: Farrar, Straus and Giroux, 1993.

See also Dance: Concert Dance in America

Mujûn

"Libertinism" or "profligacy" in classical Arabic. According to Ibn Manzûr's (d. 1311) dictionary *Lisân al-'Arab*, the verb *majana* means "to be solid and coarse." The Egyptian lexicologist adds "and therefrom derives the term *mâjin* (libertine), because of his solid [unabashed] face and his absence of modesty," thus analyzing the common use of the notion as a metaphor. The definition of the *mâjin* as one who "commits vile acts and shameful scandals, indifferent to the blame of blamers and the withering of witherers" underlines an essential dimension: *mujûn* is an open and public transgression of moral norms, and a remorseless scorn of those. Both poetry and prose were to reflect the word of the *mâjin*, although it is not clear whether literary *mujûn* corresponds to a ritualized genre, highly fashionable from the Abbasid era until the first half of the nineteenth century, or is the true reflection of a space of freedom in a strictly regulated society. *Mujûn* is closely associated in literature with *hazl* (jest), since amusement is a most natural function of literature, as ascertained in his *Book of Maids and Lads* by the famous writer al-Jâhiz (d. 868): the soul must be soothed with jest, for an excess of seriousness would burden it. This author adds that "some of those who flaunt piety and asceticism, express embarrassment and revolt at the mention of vulva, penis and coit. But such people are most often of little knowledge, devoid of elevation and dignity if only in this affectation of theirs." Among the most famous collection of *mujûn*-related anecdotes (*akhbâr*), judges and men of religion are to be found both as authors and actors. *Mujûn* is also close to two other notions: *khalâ'a* and *sukhf* (ribaldry). Whereas *khalâ'a* seems to designate a free attitude toward moral and social restraints, especially those connected with sexual codes, *sukhf* seems to qualify outright obscenity, whether sexual or scatological, although most often in piquant anecdotes or witty lines by the lowest orders of society or marginals like open passive homosexuals or effeminates (*mukhannath*). The possible moral outcome of the anecdote is not necessarily relevant, for a *denunciation* is primarily an *enunciation*.

Sexual irregularity is not the sole indecency classified as *mujûn* in classical literature: wine drinking and disrespect toward religion are also part of the notion, but the mention of sexual activities, particularly illicit, whether masturbatory, heterosexual, or homosexual, is central. In the sixteenth night of his "*al-imtâ' wa-l-mu'ânasa*" (Book of Pleasure and Nice Company), a night wholly devoted to *mujûn*, Abû Hayyân al-Tawhîdî (d. 1010) provides a *mâjin*'s definition of life:

> security and health, slapping the bald spots on their heads, shamelessly scratching one's scabies, eating prime pomegranate in the summer, having pure thick wine delivered every two months, mounting silly women and beardless youths, walking without pants before those you do not fear, behaving as a wag with the heavy-spirited, never disagreeing with friends, enjoying the company of idiots so as to glean anecdotes, getting acquainted with people of trust, and deserting the vile.

M

Poets qualified as *mâjins* generally claim to be adulterers or lovers of boys, as "one is unlikely to claim to be a catamite, since in this society . . . even the desire for such an activity is thought to be both pathological and shameful" (Rowson 91). Listen to Mus'ab al-Kâtib (nineth century, lived under the reign of the caliph al-Mutawakkil, a *mujûn*-friendly sovereign):

> ana l-mâjinu l-lûtiyyu dîniya wâhidun
>> wa-'inni fi kasbi l-ma'âsî la-râghibu
> alûtu wa-lâ 'aznî, fa-man kâna lâ'itan
>> fa-'inni lahu hatta l-qiyâmati sâhibu

(I am the libertine, the ass-fucker, I have only one religion
Performing what is forbidden is my only desire
I fuck male asses and never touch a woman, and all ass-fuckers
Are my companions until the day of the Judgment)

or Amr al-Warrâq (ninth century, died in the days of al-Ma'mûn):

> ayyuha s-sâ'ilu 'anni
>> lastu min ahli s-salâhi
> ana 'insânun murîbun
>> ashatahî nayka l-milâhi
> qad qasamtu d-dahra yawmay—
>> —ni, li-fisqin wa-li-râhi
> la 'ubâli man lahânî
>> la 'utî'u d-dahra lâhî

(If you ask about me
You will learn I am not a righteous man
I'm a dubious character
Who loves fucking good-looking lads
My days are of two sorts:
days of illicit pleasures and days of wine
I do not mind whoever blames me:
I shall never obey the orders of censors!)

Few poets, with the exception of ninth-century Jahshawayh, evoke passive homosexuality other than in biting satire, as in those verses by Abû al-'Aynâ' (ninth century):

> ishtakâ diqqata l-'uyûri ilayna
>> fa-agabnâhu, wa-l-gawâbu 'atîdu
> lam tadiqqa l-'uyûru ya-bna lûlû
>> innamâ 'istuka-ttisâ'an yazîdu

(He complained to us about the small size of cocks

so we answered on the spot:
Cocks haven't shrunk, my little pearl
Your asshole just went sloppier!)

or in the usually playful Ibn al-Rûmî's (d. 896) satire of a certain Ibn Surayj:

> Ibnu Surayjin qâla lî marratan
>> wa-qad ra'â ramhi fi tursihi:
> 'ayruka hâdha nâhilun jismuhu
>> ka'annahu l-mayyitu fi ramsihi
> fa-ghâzani dhâka wa-'akhrajtuhu
>> minhu wa-ta'mu n-nayki fi darsihi
> fa-qâla min hammin wa-min hasratin
>> wa-qad ra'â l-ma'tama fî 'ursihi:
> ma yablughu l-a'dâ'u min jâhilin
>> ma yablughu l-jâhilu min nafsihi!

(Ibn Surayj told me once,
While my spear was up his shield
This cock of yours is awfully thin
It looks like a dead man in his coffin
I was so outraged I took it out of him
while in his mouth remained the taste of fucking
So he said out of sorrow and desolation
Having seen a burial at his wedding
Enemies will never hurt an ignorant
As he himself might be hurting.)

Frédéric Lagrange

Bibliography

Badawi, Mustafa. "Medieval Arabic Drama: Ibn Dâniyâl." *Journal of Arabic Literature* 13 (1982).

Pellat, Charles. "Mudjûn." In *Encyclopedia of Islam*. Leiden: Brill.

Rowson, Everett K. "The Categorization of Gender and Sexual Irregularity in Medieval Arabic Vice Lists." In *Body Guards: The Cultural Politics of Gender Ambiguity*. Julia Epstein and Kristina Straub, eds. New York: Routledge, 1991.

———. "Two Homoerotic Narratives from Mamlûk Literature: al-Safadî's *Law'at al-Shâkî* and Ibn Dâniyâl's *al-Mutayyam*." In *Homoeroticism in Classical Arabic Literature*. New York: Columbia University Press, 1997.

See also Arabic Literature; Libertine and Libertinism; Mukhannath; Persian (Iranian) Literature and Culture

Mukhannath

The word *mukhannath* means "effeminate" in Arabic. Etymologists derive *khinâth* (effeminacy) and the passive participle *mukhannath* from the verb *khannatha* ("to bend"). The common meaning is thus explained by the effeminate's "pliability" and "languidness" (*takassur*), for suppleness and lack of firmness both in gestures and moral standards are seen as feminine. Indeed, much of the arguments used by al-Tawhîdi (d. 1010) against his foe, the Vizir Ibn al-'Abbâd, in order to establish his effeminacy and passiveness are based on the latter's extravagant gesturing while speaking and his unmanly whims. The *mukhannath* is a commonplace of medieval literature, whether as an object of satire in polemic poetry or of jest in *mujûn* literature. Literature also reflects "a form of publicly recognized and institutionalized effeminacy ... in pre-Islamic and early Islamic Arabian society" (Rowson, 1991), as well as in many pre-modern Muslim societies.

In the first century of Islam, the *mukhannaths* of Mecca and Medina were allowed to visit high-ranking women freely, including the wives of the Prophet, for no risk was taken with such "men of no desire." A famous *hadîth* (saying of the Prophet) tells of Hît the Effeminate's banishment from Mecca after the Prophet overheard him praise the desirable body of a woman. It is not clear, however, whether Muhammad feared in him a man attracted to the other sex or disapproved of the crudeness of his tone. During the first half of the Ummayad caliphate (seventh century), when Mecca and Medina became cities of leisure and pleasure, the effeminates were renowned as talented musicians and singers, encouraging the development of love poetry and often working as go-betweens for lovers. Tuways (the small peacock), whose name has remained in books of proverbs as a reference in effeminacy, is said to have been the first learned musician in the history of Arabs. Some of those men sported feminine nicknames such as *bard al-fu'âd* (delightment of hearts) and *Nawmat al-Duha* (slumber of the morning). The golden age of the effeminates in Hijâz was to end tragically when the Umayyad caliph Sulaymân ordered their castration. Although historically dubious, an anecdote explains that the caliph had merely asked his governor to establish a census of the town's effeminates (in Arabic *ahsi*), but a dot of ink fell on the letter *h*, turning it into a *kh* and the governor read *akhsi* (castrate). The effeminates' reaction, as reported by Hamza al-Isfahânî (d. ca. 970) a few centuries later in a typical *adab* style, offer a good example, if most probably imaginary, of "queer humor" at its tragic best. Tuways is said to have answered, "This is simply a new circumcision which we must undergo again"; Nawmat al Duha added, "We have become women in truth"; and Zill al-Shajar (shade of the tree) concluded, "What would we do with an unused weapon, anyway" (Rowson, 1991, 691).

In his article "The Effeminates of Early Medina," Rowson has defended the hypothesis that the effeminacy described in seventh-century Arabia is essentially an attitude, reflected in softness of gesture and voice, and the use of feminine clothing, perfumes, and habits, such as the use of henna, but argued that it is not proved those *mukhannaths* necessarily engaged in homosexual intercourse. Anecdotes found in later compilations, however, explicitly mention the homosexuality of famous seventh-century *mukhannaths* such as "Musaffar Istuhu" (he who has coated his anus with saffron) and Dalâl. When caught with a young servant in the desert, Dalâl was condemned by the caliph to the lash. He answered, "What will your lashes do to me, for I am receive lashes everyday."

The caliph asked "Who lashes you?"
"The cocks of the believers."
"Lay him face down."
"I gather the Commander of Believers desires to witness how I am fucked?"
"Raise him, may God curse him, and exhibit him around the town with the young servant."
When asked by the people of Medina what was happening, Dalâl answered :
"The Commander of Believers wanted to associate two lovers, so he joined me to this young man, showed us all around town, but he loses his temper when called a pimp." The governor ordered his releasing, fearing more scandals from the *mukhannath*'s sharp tongue.

The term *mukhannath* became in later times specifically attached to the most obvious passive homosexuals. The last and longest chapter of al-Tîfâshî's (d. 1253) anthology of sexual deviances *Nuzhat al-albâb* (The Promenade of Hearts) is devoted to effeminacy and the effeminates, but it is clear that the real subject of the chapter is rather passive sodomy, seen as the most obvious expression of effeminacy. *Khinâth* is thus considered as a synonym of *ubna* (bending of a stick, metaphorically the illness of bending before other men) and *bighâ'* (desire for illicit sexual relationship.) The word *baghiyy* is de-

M scribed in the conservative thirteenth-century dictionary *Lisân al-'Arab* to be feminine in essence and applied to the adulteress (*zâniya*), although the usual meaning, from ninth-century until premodern literature, is a man who has an irrepressible desire to be penetrated.

Mujûn (libertine) literature in the Abbasid period (eighth to thirteenth centuries) insists on the *mukhannaths'* shamelesness, which offers matter for countless anecdotes, but also underlines their wit and sharpness, which demand a perfect command of the language. *Khinâth* is a consequence of urbanity, as opposed to bedouinity. Remarkably, the profession most frequently associated with effeminacy is of the *kâtib,* the secretary in caliphal chancellery, a man of great knowledge and extreme refinement (*zarf*). The description of the perfect *zarîf,* the delicate courtesan, as found in the *Kitâb al-Muwashsha* by al-Washshâ' (d. 936), seems quite ripe with effeminacy of manners, if no allusion to sexuality is made. The languid and effeminate servant boy also appears to be a fad during the late seventh and eighth centuries in court poetry, just when the *ghulâmiyyât,* slave girls who cut their hair short and dress as boys, are all the rage: the caliphal court of Baghdâd patronized and almost institutionalized, for purposes of entertainment, transvestism and gender-crossing.

The effeminate boy will remain a cliché in poetry, and forms of institutionalized effeminacy managed to live through the centuries. In eighteenth- and nineteenth-century Egypt, the *khawals,* male dancers performing dressed as women, were a common sight in cafés and a source of shock or delight for European travelers, such as Gérard de Nerval. They even replaced female dancers (*ghawâzî*) when "the presence of public women might have detracted from the respectability of the event or its sponsors" (Dunne 1996, 112), and were the only available entertainers after Muhammad Ali Pacha ordered in 1836 a ban on female prostitutes and dancers, which did not extend to male prostitutes and performers. There is no doubt the *khawals* were available to rich patrons, and in modern colloquial Egyptian, the term *khawal* has lost its technical signification, simply meaning (passive) homosexual. The normalization of sexuality according to European standards in the nineteenth century put an end to the *mukhannath's* role in Arab societies. In the modern world, institutionalized gender-crossing is an exception, solely encountered in periphercal societies; as late as the 1980s *khanîths* (the local colloquialism for

mukhannath) could be found in Sohar, on the northeastern coast of Oman, the status of whom reminds one of the pre-Islamic effeminates of Mecca and Medina (Murray 1997, 244–55).

Frédéric Lagrange

Bibliography

Dunne, Bruce W. "Sexuality and the 'Civilizing Process' in Modern Egypt." Ph.D. diss., Georgetown University, Washington D.C. 1996.

Murray, Stephen O., and Will Roscoe, eds. *Islamic Homosexualities.* New York: New York University Press, 1997.

Rowson, Everett K. "The Effeminates of Early Medina." *Journal of the American Oriental Society* 111(1991): 671–93.

See also Arabic Literature; Dancing Boys; Effeminacy; *Mujun;* Persian (Iranian) Literature and Culture; Transvestism

Müller, Johannes von (1752–1809)

This Swiss historian and politician was born January 3, 1752, in Schaffhausen, the oldest son of a pastor. After attending the local gymnasium, Müller studied theology at the University of Göttingen. Following a brief period of lecturing and tutoring in his hometown, Müller held various positions as adviser, councillor, and diplomat at German courts in Kassel, Mainz, Vienna, and Berlin. Müller was knighted in 1791 by Emperor Leopold II.

The publication in 1772 of an essay on the Cimbri, an ancient Germanic tribe, confirmed his talent as a scholar of history. But it was the first volume of the five-part *History of the Swiss Confederacy* (1780), a brilliantly composed account of the country's struggle for freedom and independence, that won Müller the admiration of Europe's foremost intellectuals and the hearts of German-speaking people. His endeavor "to present historical developments objectively and truthfully" set an example for many future historians. Through Müller's intriguing characterization of folklore, the heroic tale of William Tell entered the popular consciousness. J. W. Goethe, J. G. Herder, Georg Forster, Jacob Grimm, Alexander von Humboldt, Mme de Staël, and Grand Duchess Anna Amalia were among Müller's over two thousand correspondents.

He was only twenty when, "like a flash of lightening" (Müller 33), Müller fell in love with Karl Victor von Bonstetten, who, for the next twelve years, would remain his greatest inspiration. The collection of their love letters, *Briefe eines jungen Gelehrten an seinen Freund* (1798; 1802), fascinated the early romantics in Jena and Berlin. Müller's epistolary confessions of his love for another man brought back memories of Johann Joachim Winckelmann, to whom Müller was now compared by many. However, his lifelong yearning for a lover and companion later resulted in scandal and financial ruin, when Müller—a lonely but trusting and generous man who fell in love easily—fell victim to a vicious fraud instigated by his pupil Fritz von Hartenberg. Although many personal friends showed solidarity and also lent financial support, Müller had to give up his post at the Austrian court. He had not recovered from the emotional scars caused by this affair when he died in 1809.

Christoph Lorey

Bibliography

Craig, Gordon A. "Johannes von Müller: The Historian in Search of a Hero." *American Historical Review* 74 (1969): 1487–1502.

Derks, Paul. *Die Schande der heiligen Päderastie: Homosexualität und Öffentlichkeit in der deutschen Literatur, 1750–1850*. Berlin: Verlag Rosa Winkel, 1990, 295–369.

Jamme, Christoph, and Otto Pöggeler, eds. *Johannes von Müller—Geschichtsschreiber der Goethezeit*. Schaffhausen, Switzerland: Meili, 1986.

Schib, Karl. *Johannes von Müller, 1752–1809*. Thayngen-Schaffhausen, Konstanz, Switzerland: Augustin, 1967.

See also Germany; Goethe, Johannes Wolfgang von Winckelmann, Johann Joachim

Music and Musicians 1: Classical Music

It is no accident that, for more than a century, the best way of asking whether someone was gay was: "Is he . . . musical?" It is often difficult to clearly define composers before the twentieth century as gay or lesbian; for many, we have little record of their private lives, and for others there are only suggestive circumstances. However, we can identify certain composers as probably having had same-sex romantic or erotic relationships.

As for the music itself, unlike certain popular genres such as disco, there has been no type of art music that can be considered essentially gay or lesbian. Homosexual composers have produced entertaining and socially successful music, and many of the most sentimental composers are known to have been gay. But some of the most uncompromisingly rarefied and experimental music has also been by gay composers.

It has been claimed that twelfth-century Notre Dame polyphony—by composers that include Leonin, Perotin, and Philippe le Chancelier—may have been written in a homosexual subculture symbolized in the music. In the Renaissance, homosexual behavior was not uncommon; probable gay composers include Guillaume Dufay, Nicolas Gombert, and Orlando Lasso. In baroque and classical music, several figures appear to have had same-sex relationships, although the evidence in some cases is no more than suggestive: Johann Rosenmüller, Jean-Baptiste Lully, Arcangelo Corelli, George Frideric Handel, Nicola Porpora, and Domenico Cimarosa.

In the nineteenth century, with gender patterns providing a more familiar context, identifications get somewhat clearer. We cannot be sure about Ludwig van Beethoven, although the composer's feelings for his nephew were intense and confused. The case of Franz Schubert, however, seems clear—letters and journals indicate that he was part of a distinctly gay circle. People have been suspicious about the complex, but probably unconsummated, relationship between Robert Schumann and Johannes Brahms; but we are sure of the bisexual Frédéric Chopin's interest in other men. Pyotr Ilich Tchaikovsky is acknowledged as gay, while Modest Mussorgsky and Ernest Chausson were apparently gay and Aleksandr Scriabin was bisexual. And toward the end of the century, Camille Saint-Säens proclaimed to a journalist: "But no, Madame, I am not a homosexual, I am a pederast!"

In the twentieth century, in the wake of the first waves of homosexual liberation movements, composers became more open about their private lives. A number of European composers were reputedly gay, including Maurice Ravel, Reynaldo Hahn, Karol Szymanowski, and Francis Poulenc; the avant-garde had a large share of gay composers, including Wolfgang Fortner, Hans Werner Henze, Sylvano Bussotti, Peter Maxwell Davies, Karel Goeyvaerts, Jean Barraqué, Konrad Boehmer, and Pierre Boulez. English composers who were reputedly gay include Roger Quilter, John Ireland, George Butterworth, Arthur Benjamin, Eugene Goosens, and Noël Coward; two of the most important English composers, Benjamin Britten and Michael Tippett, both

M achieved particular notoriety for being openly gay (although each handled it very differently).

Among Americans the list of reputedly gay composers becomes quite long: songwriters such as Stephen Foster, Cole Porter, Lorenz Hart, George Gershwin (possibly), and Stephen Sondheim; and composers such as Daniel Gregory Mason, Charles Tomlinson Griffes, Colin McPhee, and Paul Bowles. Gay composers at the forefront of musical experimentation included Henry Cowell, Harry Partch, Virgil Thomson, John Cage, Lou Harrison, Charles Wuorinen, and "Blue" Gene Tyranny. Other twentieth-century composers who have tended toward a neoclassical or neoromantic aesthetic include Aaron Copland, Samuel Barber and Gian-Carlo Menotti (who were lovers), Marc Blitzstein, David Diamond, Leonard Bernstein, Daniel Pinkham, Ned Rorem, Conrad Susa, David Del Tredici, John Corigliano, Thomas Pasatieri, and David Conte. The rise of gay and lesbian musical ensembles in America and western Europe has led to an explosion of new commissioned works and recordings; organizations for gay and lesbian composers include the Society of Gay and Lesbian Composers in San Francisco (founded in 1981), which continues to hold concerts and competitions.

There are also many gay and lesbian performers. As Vladimir Horowitz once said, "There are three kinds of pianists: Jewish pianists, homosexual pianists, and bad pianists." Major gay conductors include Dmitri Mitropoulos, Seiji Ozawa, and Michael Tilson Thomas; and there are internationally acclaimed gay and lesbian opera stars, instrumental virtuosi, and every other variety of classical performer.

The establishment by Philip Brett of a Gay and Lesbian Study Group in the American Musicological Society in 1990 has greatly encouraged scholarship on historical figures who may have been gay or lesbian. Public arguments, especially those over Handel and Schubert, show that the relative conservatism of both scholarly and amateur music circles presents a great deal of resistance to that scholarship; but the rapidly increasing publication of gay and lesbian music studies indicates that the discussion is no longer taboo.

But why should we care about a musician's sexual preference? Perhaps the best answer is in the music. Some think that, although gay men and lesbians are individuals with different backgrounds, it is possible to understand and enjoy gay or lesbian sensibilities in art. It may seem problematic to project homosexual identities onto historical figures; but perhaps we've been projecting heterosexual identities for too long onto those who cannot protest.   *Paul Attinello*

Bibliography

Brett, Philip, Elizabeth Wood, and Gary Thomas, eds. *Queering the Pitch: The New Gay and Lesbian Musicology.* New York: Routledge, 1994.

Koestenbaum, Wayne. *The Queen's Throat: Opera, Homosexuality, and the Mystery of Desire.* New York: Vintage, 1993.

Kopelson, Kevin. *Beethoven's Kiss: Pianism, Perversion, and the Mastery of Desire.* Stanford, Calif.: Stanford University, 1996.

See also Bernstein, Leonard; Blitzstein, Marc; Bowles, Paul; Britten, Benjamin; Cage, John; Corigliano, John; Cowell, Henry; Del Tredici, David; Gay American Composers; Griffes, Charles Tomlinson; Handel, George Frideric; Harrison, Lou; Henze, Hans Werner; Lully, Jean-Baptiste; McPhee, Colin; Partch, Harry; Poulenc, Francis; Rorem, Ned; Saint-Säens, Camille; Schubert, Franz Peter; Susa, Conrad; Szymanowski, Karol; Tchaikovsky, Pyotr Ilich; Thomson, Virgil; Tippett, Sir Michael Kemp

Music and Musicians 2: Popular Music

Although it is certain that gay men and members of other sexual minorities were active in the popular music industry from its beginnings in the nineteenth century, clear documentation of such involvement strongly emerges first in blues and vaudeville during the 1920s. "Sissies" were both a topic of blues lyrics as well as occasional performers. During the Prohibition era "Pansy Craze" of New York's speakeasies, effeminate performers were enormously popular as cabaret acts. The revocation of Prohibition and the onset of the Great Depression, however, sent such out performance styles for the most part back to the urban underground, and gay involvement in the production of popular music during the mid-twentieth century tended to be closeted. Gay jazz performer and composer Billy Strayhorn, for instance, worked in collaboration with Duke Ellington and tended to avoid the spotlight; other figures such as Cole Porter and particularly Noël Coward took refuge in wordly and epicene personas. All in all, the world of jazz and Broadway was a place populated with homosexual artists who could win a measure of space for themselves mostly by half-concealing their sexual orientation within the trappings of urbanity. Evidence of gay identity in such music was invariably heavily coded. In a similarly vicarious fashion, the cult of the diva was particularly important among audiences of gay men in winning a measure of subjective space for themselves as popular music listeners; it is from this time that the fans of singers like Judy Garland could become the pop music equivalent of opera queens.

U.S. society after World War II was particularly determined to suppress sexual nonconformity, but its desire not to see evidence of homosexuality led to an astonishing spate of outrageous performance styles in some popular artists of the 1950s. Liberace's glitzy closetedness was ultimately maintained by perjury, of course, but the most remarkable thing about his reception among audiences was surely their blindness to his deliberate, relentless campiness; and this campiness was not simply a matter of costume and the chat between songs; it was inherent in his gaudy, arch arrangements of classical and popular standards. Similarly, Little Richard's flamboyant effeminacy, apparent in dress, makeup, and exhilarating performance shrieks, at once protected and marginalized him. (Aspects of these styles were imitated by straight performers as well, as a look at any of Elvis Presley's Vegas performances instantly reveals.) Rock and soul traditions, then, were powerfully imbued with the sensibility of some gay artists from their very inception, and the problem of performance and ambiguity of gender and sexuality has continued to be an issue in reception and criticism.

Reaction to the Beatles and the Rolling Stones attested to the unease that many mainstream audiences felt about the sexually transgressive potential of rock. But the Velvet Underground (formed 1965) took the lead in introducing songs explicitly portraying gay experience, particularly the kind surrounding the Warhol circle in New York City. The Velvet Underground was immensely influential, and the band's music and image inaugurated the marked and unmarked transvestism characteristic of glitter or glam rock as well as early heavy metal during the 1970s. But from the point of view of mainstream audiences, the most important gay and bisexual presence in popular music at this time came from performers like David Bowie and Elton John. Both singers were notable for coming out surprisingly early, in 1972 and 1976, respectively; in each case, the bisexuality they acknowledged seemed continuous with the elaborate artifice of their stage personas and so it could be dismissed to some extent by straight audiences. Bowie's career seemed if anything made more intense by his declaration, but Elton John's career soon stagnated, and in the press this was often attributed to his coming out.

Within gay communities, the 1970s were a time of phenomenal institutional/cultural development that nourished several important musical styles and genres. Disco was created largely at the intersection of urban gay, African American, and Latino communities within the United States; the genre also quickly proved itself hospitable to influences from continental Europe as well. Established at the beginning of the 1970s, by the middle of the decade disco had become increasingly popular among straight audiences as well, and the surge in disco clubs across the continent was one of the primary conduits for what Dennis Altman would call "The Homosexualization of America." Despite disco's powerful roots in urban gay sensibilities, most of its visible performers were African American straight women. Out gay performers became important only near the end of the decade, with the rise of the Village People (a special case, since mainstream audiences tended not to realize that the characters were mostly gay stereotypes) and particularly Sylvester. The straight backlash against disco (the racist and homophobic "disco sucks" campaign) and diminished mainstream interest sent dance music back to the gay clubs, and the disco era was over by 1980.

An important new source of gay involvement in popular music came by 1978 with the formation of the San Francisco Gay Men's Chorus (first performance at the memorial service for Harvey Milk and George Moscone). Gay and lesbian choruses quickly formed in other large urban centers of North America as well, and by 1982 there were enough active groups to see the formation of an organization, the Gay and Lesbian Association of Choruses (GALA). The gay and lesbian choral movement has continued to expand, including groups from less urbanized areas of North America as well as from abroad. In this process, as well, choruses frequently came to commission works from living composers and to broaden their repertories; CDs of various groups are increasingly available.

In mainstream rock and soul traditions there had been little room for out performers. (The success of the 1977 song "Glad to Be Gay" by the English group Tom Robinson Band was exceptional for its time.) By the 1980s, however, pop music was becoming more hospitable to openly gay and bisexual

M artists, as well as to complex representations of sexuality in individual songs. The popularity of New Wave in the late 1970s and early 1980s introduced a number of groups informed by gay sensibilities, most notably the B-52s and German performance artist Klaus Nomi. The early days of MTV featured the introduction of several British gender-bending artists to North America, most notably Boy George. The most important out bands to achieve widespread commercial success in the later eighties were British as well. Bronski Beat, formed in 1984, had an important hit in 1985 with the song "Smalltown Boy." Bands formed by the mid-1980s included the Pet Shop Boys and Erasure, each with a significant number of hits in North America and the United Kingdom. A crucial figure at this time was the singer Morrisey, who as lead singer in the Smiths promulgated sexual ambiguity, celibacy, and vegetarianism, among other things. In less mainstream venues, music by gay artists with gay content included the work of singer-songwriter and AIDS activist Michael Callen, David Lasley, gay duo Romanovsky and Phillips, and the a cappella trio the Flirtations.

Gay dance music at the beginning of the 1980s was largely derived from disco and fused with New Wave dance music. Styles such as house (and later, techno) moved from gay African American clubs to Europe and back to North America. More mainline dance hits continued to enjoy limited mainstream popularity. The return of disco (part of the 1970s revival) was joined to a new straight interest in dance music, which became important on the charts by the early 1990s. The success of RuPaul's single "Supermodel" (1993) was a significant symbol for gay dance music as a whole. More recently, drag performer Pussy Tourette has released significant dance music as well.

The mainstream interest as well in alternative rock at the beginning of the 1990s was accompanied by increasing identification across orientations as well as explicitly antihomophobic activity. This extended in the case of some artists to the projections of bisexual or gay content. Michael Stipe, lead singer of the alternative group R.E.M., came out as bisexual in late 1995; but there was already strong evidence of gay-friendly focus in R.E.M.'s video for "Losing My Religion" (banned in Ireland for undue homoeroticism). Kurt Cobain of Nirvana repeatedly gave gay-positive interviews and identified himself strongly with gay subject positions. Gay Punk Rock and allied styles, often described as "queercore,"

have been central to an important underground scene that dates back to the early 1980s and includes groups and artists like God Is My Co-Pilot, Vaginal Davis, Mukilteo Fairies, and Los Crudos. (An important source for reviews and information about such bands and an important aspect of the underground scene are the self-published 'zines that appear in gay bookstores or on-line.) Of the widely known queercore bands, the most mainstream attention has been paid to Pansy Division. More recent bands such as Extra Fancy and Slojack continue to negotiate with major record labels, with mixed success.

A number of institutions have developed in support of out gay and bisexual popular music. Record labels include Michael Callen's Significant Others Records, Chainsaw Records, and Fresh Fruit Records. The recently instituted Gay and Lesbian American Music Awards (GLAMA) are also likely to prove important in reinforcing the continuing productivity of gay musicians.   *Mitchell Morris*

Bibliography

Attinello, Paul. "Authority and Freedom: Toward a Sociology of Gay Choruses." In *Queering the Pitch: The New Gay and Lesbian Musicology*. Philip Brett, Elizabeth Wood, and Gary C. Thomas, eds. New York: Routledge, 1993, 315.

Chauncey, George. *Gay New York: Gender, Urban Culture, and the Making of the Gay World, 1890–1940*. New York: Basic Books, 1994.

Dyer, Richard. "In Defence of Disco." In *Only Entertainment*. New York: Routledge, 1992, 149.

Gill, John. *Queer Noises*. London: Cassell, 1995.

Hajdu, David. *Lush Life: A Biography of Billy Strayhorn*. New York: Farrar, Straus & Giroux, 1996.

Larry-bob. *Holy Titclamps*. San Francisco: 1989–.

Morris, Mitchell. "It's Raining Men: The Weather Girls, Gay Sensibility, and the Erotics of Excess." In *Audible Traces*. Elaine Barkin and Lydia Hammesley, eds. Zurich: Carcifoli Press, 1998.

Studer, Wayne. *Rock on the Wild Side: Gay Male Images in Popular Music of the Rock Era*. San Francisco: Leyland, 1994.

See also *AIDS Quilt Songbook*; Altman, Dennis; Cabaret, Variety, and Revue Entertainment; Camp; Choruses and Marching Bands; Coward, Noël; Disco and Dance Music; Epstein, Brian; Musical Theater; Opera Queens; Porter, Cole Albert;

Somerville, Jimmy; Strayhorn, Billy; Sylvester; Transvestism; Voguing

Musical Theater

What has become known as "musical theater" in the late twentieth century—the integrated book musical associated with New York City's Broadway theaters—came about as a hybrid of earlier musical and dramatic forms. Drawing on eighteenth- and nineteenth-century European traditions of ballad and comic opera, operetta, ballet, and pasticcio, as well as American types of musical entertainment such as minstrel shows (using black performers or white actors in blackface), vaudeville, and burlesque, the modern musical theater synthesized these forms into a new standardized technique. Historians of the musical theater generally trace its origins to John Gay's *The Beggar's Opera* (1728), a popular, satirical ballad opera that offered light entertainment and "low" subject matter, in contrast to opera; by the end of the nineteenth century, Gilbert and Sullivan had honed the traditions of "light" opera into a definitive and highly successful genre that would be further developed in America by Victor Herbert, Sigmund Romberg, and Rudolf Friml. Concurrent with the popularization of light opera in America in the decades before and after the turn of the twentieth century, theatrical productions called "spectacles" and "extravaganzas" began to reach an increasingly large audience. These revues offered very large casts, elaborate and expensive sets and costumes, much music, and little or no story; the form reached its pinnacle in Florenz Ziegfeld's *Follies*, annually produced from 1907 until its final edition in 1931.

The American book musical would integrate, transform, and ultimately supplant these various types of musical theater, achieving its greatest popularity from the late 1930s through the 1960s. The most significant individual productions that heralded the transition from an old set of forms to a new integration of them were *Show Boat* (Kern/ Hammerstein, 1927), the operatic *Porgy and Bess* (Heyward/Gershwin/Gershwin, 1935), *Pal Joey* (Rodgers/Hart, 1940), *Lady in the Dark* (Weill/ Ira Gershwin/Moss Hart, 1941), and *Oklahoma!* (Rodgers/Hammerstein, 1943). The older revue shows had offered a series of entertaining but unrelated set pieces; the new, integrated form subordinated songs, dances, comedy, and spectacle to the book's narrative. The new musical required an "organic" structure, and all the elements of the show now had to propel the story. Richard Rodgers and Oscar Hammerstein II were largely responsible for defining the new genre in such shows as *Carousel* (1945), *South Pacific* (1949), and *The King and I* (1951), and other standouts of the new type were *West Side Story* (Laurents/Bernstein/Sondheim, 1957) and *Gypsy* (Laurents/Styne/Sondheim, 1959). Later, Stephen Sondheim ushered in the "concept musical" with *Anyone Can Whistle* (with Arthur Laurents, 1964), *Company* (with George Furth, 1970), and *Follies* (with James Goldman, 1971); the concept musical retained the "organic," book-oriented focus of the Rodgers and Hammerstein type, but did away with plot in favor of a meditative, lyrical structure. Sondheim's successors in this mode include, among others, *Chicago* (Fosse/Kander/Ebb, 1975), *A Chorus Line* (Hamlisch/Kirkwood/Dante/ Kleban, 1975), and *Rent* (Larson, 1996).

Given this account of the development of the modern musical, the historical relationship between musical theater and homosexuality appears both self-evident and nonexistent. Perhaps no other modern art form succeeds so thoroughly in appealing, at the level of reception, to a gay (and implicitly male) "sensibility," and in refusing, at the level of denotation, gay content. Several musicals have included gay characters, plots, and settings—notably *Cabaret* (Masteroff/Kander/Ebb, 1966); *Applause* (Comden/Green/Strouse/Adams, 1970); *A Chorus Line*; William Finn's trilogy of one-acts, *In Trousers* (1979), *March of the Falsettos* (1981), and *Falsettoland* (1990); *La Cage aux Folles* (Fierstein/ Herman, 1983); *Kiss of the Spider Woman* (McNally/ Kander/Ebb, 1992); and *Rent*—but these productions, in the history of musical theater, have been exceptions to the rule. Because musical theater has traditionally cultivated a middle-class audience, its status as popular entertainment has given it a "reputation of being unbearably conservative, frequently misogynist, and ragingly heterosexual" (Wolf 52).

Despite the apparent paucity of gay content in musicals, however, "It was Broadway where the threat and the promise of toleration for homosexuals found a sort of social truce" in twentieth-century America (Bronski 110). Though homosexuality has been virtually erased from the musical stage thematically, the mythical and actual affinity of many gay men for musical theater has contributed in shaping modern conceptions of gay subculture. Almost always refusing to stage gay men's lives fictionally, the musical theater nonetheless provides two critical points of entry for gay male participation: as audience and as creators.

Public access to the theaters, though mitigated by sometimes exclusionary prices and the general confinement of major theatrical productions in urban centers, admits gay men and lesbians along with the rest of the population, and the recording and wide distribution of original cast albums, which became common practice by the end of the 1940s, likewise enables mass consumption of musical theater. Moreover, the clichéd love of musicals by the "theater queen," however insufficient and illusory in offering a distinct mark of gay identity in general, has given many gay men a route through which to understand and organize their sense of sexual identity; having entered the cultural imagination, the conjunction of gay men and musical theater affords one crucial mode of gay identity formation within a heterosexist culture that has offered precious few.

Recently, gay critics have begun to explore in detail the pleasures and problems associated with gay male and lesbian spectatorship in the musical theater. In the work of Michael Bronski, Stacy Wolf, and D. A. Miller, among others, the apparently "heterosexual" tradition in musicals finds its homosexual answer: Michael Bronski, for example, notes the gay "code" underlying Noël Coward's 1933 lyric to the ostensibly heterosexual "Mad about the Boy" (113), and D. A. Miller displays with musical alacrity the process of transforming "straight" songs through gay appropriation so that, in the gay piano bar, "every lyric now becomes a figure for present-day metropolitan homosexuality, which no lyric has ever cared, or dared, literally to mention." Similarly, Stacy Wolf's close analysis of Mary Martin and *The Sound of Music* (Rodgers/Hammerstein, 1959) demonstrates the usually unremarked capacity of musicals to allow for lesbian readings; for Wolf, that musical's overarching question—"How do you solve a problem like Maria?"—invokes the social "problem" of the tomboy/dyke. The power to be tapped in musical theater, these authors suggest, lies in its availability for gay interpretation; the musical, like much popular culture, can be consumed and rearticulated, camped and made to affirm rather than deny gay existence.

The very structure of theatrical presentation encourages mobile desiring relations between spectator and spectacle; as does the cinema, the musical theater relies on presenting images of interacting bodies to an audience in the dark, and the spectator therefore can engage in private fantasies in this otherwise very public domain. The parade of male and female bodies, typically styled to adhere to conventions of beauty, offers the spectator seemingly endless "eye candy": a chorus line of barely clad female dancers, for example, or the eroticized body of a hero (Joey in *Pal Joey*; Billy Bigelow in *Carousel*) or a whole corps of male dancers (the baseball team singing "Heart" in the Abbott/Wallop/Adler/Ross *Damn Yankees*, 1955). Performers, music, choreography, lighting, and costumes all work to create an atmosphere of erotic plenitude for the spectator, and the "escapist" function of the musical thereby bespeaks an escape into fantasy. Gay desire, that is, may require no thematization on the stage for it to be present during the show; desires instead move in every direction in the musical theater, engendered by the visual delights enclosed by the proscenium. The musical theater has therefore provided an arena conducive to gay spectatorship.

Of perhaps greater importance than the gay audience for musical theater (and unlike much of popular culture), the gay men involved in its development in the twentieth century represent a rare instance of gay power over artistic production. Present not only as actors and actresses but also as costume designers, choreographers, book writers, composers, lyricists, directors, and producers, gay people (mostly men) have had a pervasive influence on the creation of both individual shows and the entire genre. Though tracing a gay genealogy of the musical is a difficult task—sexual secrecy has held sway throughout its history—even a short list of gay and bisexual contributors reveals the extraordinary impact they have had: Lorenz Hart (lyricist), Cole Porter (composer/lyricist), Leonard Bernstein (composer), Arthur Laurents (director), Michael Bennett (choreographer/director), Jerry Herman (composer/lyricist), William Finn (composer/lyricist), Harvey Fierstein (librettist), Howard Ashman (lyricist), and Jonathan Larson (composer/lyricist/librettist). Unlike other popular forms cherished by gay subculture, "the Broadway musical, with 'disproportionate numbers' of gay men among its major architects, is determined from the inside out by an Open Secret" (Miller 275): "everyone knows" that gay men not only enjoy musical theater but also produce it.

Hence the emergence since the 1960s of self-identified gay characters in musicals; the generation that produced the Stonewall rebellion and the subsequent wave of "coming out" created a new language of sexual identity that could then be articulated in Broadway musicals. Two visual modes of representing gay men on the stage—kissing and drag—already had a history in nonmusical plays and were incorporated into Broadway musicals in the form, for example, of the drag queen Albin in *La Cage aux Folles* and the gay male and lesbian kisses in *Rent*. Also, new—homosexual—interpretations alter the context of old lyric forms: the defiant first-act anthem becomes Albin's furious gay manifesto "I Am What I Am"; the (heterosexual) lovers' quarrel in song becomes Maureen and Joanne's "Take Me or Leave Me" in *Rent*; and the love duet appears in *La Cage*'s "Song on the Sand" and *Rent*'s "I'll Cover You." Mama Morton, the prison matron in *Chicago*, sings "When You're Good to Mama (Mama's good to you)," both a stereotypical sadist-dyke threat (familiar to Hollywood audiences) and a knowing, post-Stonewall send-up of that same figure. Introducing out gay and lesbian desire to the Broadway stage thus alters radically the terms of the musical theater and, paradoxically, alters them not at all; the post-Stonewall production of gay individuals and gay identity on the musical stage may in fact operate to support the (heterosexual, bourgeois) structure of the musical genre. Because musical theater occupies a peculiar cultural place—both resoundingly middle-class and provocatively desiring—it continues to pose the questions of political action and pleasure that are central to lesbian and gay community and identity.

In particular, in the late 1980s and 1990s, musicals began to address HIV and AIDS. William Finn's *Falsettoland*, the third installment of the Marvin trilogy, narrates the seroconversion and death of Whizzer, the main character's lover, and Jonathan Larson's *Rent* offers three major characters who are HIV-positive (a straight couple, Mimi and Roger, and a gay transvestite, Angel). *Falsettoland* represents a unique instance of musical theater's grappling with a social concern. Its predecessors in the series, *In Trousers* and *March of the Falsettos*, introduced the character Whizzer and were initially staged before AIDS became publicized; when *Falsettoland* appeared in 1990, the intervening years provided a virtual mandate that AIDS be integrated thematically into the progression of the trilogy's narrative, and in killing off Whizzer, Finn killed off a character that audiences had "met" before AIDS became a current event (*March of the Falsettos* and *Falsettoland* appeared together on Broadway as *Falsettos* in 1992). Another example of a "gay" musical, *Kiss of the Spider Woman*, based on Manuel Puig's 1976 novel *El beso de la mujer araña*, displays the evolving relationship between two prisoners, the homosexual Molina and the heterosexual Valentin, in an Argentine penitentiary;

with its depictions of blood, incontinence, and the embodiment of deathly desire in the Spider Woman, *Kiss* has been interpreted as an AIDS allegory, with its activist's anthem "The Day after That." These musicals' response to and addressing of the AIDS crisis—while representing a small minority of major musical productions—incorporate the militant gay and lesbian rights movement organized and strengthened by AIDS activism, drawing on the media iconography of people with AIDS, activists, and the disease itself.

The relation between homosexuality and musical theater alternately frustrates and exhilarates, provides evidence of a gay history and too often erases that history, guarantees pleasure and withholds it from its gay audiences. But more songs remain to be sung—theatrical, interpretive, rafter-ringing.

Matthew Bell

Bibliography

Bordman, Gerald. *American Musical Comedy: From* Adonis *to* Dreamgirls. New York: Oxford University Press, 1982.

Bredbeck, Gregory W. "The Ridiculous Sound of One Hand Clapping: Placing Ludlam's 'Gay' Theatre in Space and Time." *Modern Drama* 39, no. 1 (Spring 1996): 64–83.

Bronski, Michael. *Culture Clash: The Making of Gay Sensibility*. Boston: South End Press, 1984.

Clum, John. *Acting Gay: Male Homosexuality in Modern Drama*. New York: Columbia University Press, 1992.

Kislan, Richard. *The Musical: A Look at the American Musical Theater*. New York: Applause Books, 1995.

Mates, Julian. *America's Musical Stage: Two Hundred Years of Musical Theater*. Westport, Conn.: Greenwood Press, 1985.

Miller, D. A. "The Piano Bar." In *Stud: Architectures of Masculinity*. Joel Sanders, ed. New York: Princeton Architectural Press, 1996, 268–77.

Mordden, Ethan. *Broadway Babies: The People Who Made the American Musical*. New York: Oxford University Press, 1983.

Román, David, and Alberto Sandoval. "Caught in the Web: Latinidad, AIDS, and Allegory in *Kiss of the Spider Woman, the Musical.*" *American Literature,* 67, no. 3 (1995): 553–85.

Rosenberg, Bernard, and Ernest Harburg. *The Broadway Musical: Collaboration in Commerce and Art*. New York: New York University Press, 1993.

Wolf, Stacy. "The Queer Pleasures of Mary Martin and Broadway: *The Sound of Music* as a Lesbian Musical." *Modern Drama* 39, no. 1 (1996): 51–63.

See also Activism, U.S.; AIDS; AIDS Performance; Bennett, Michael; Bernstein, Leonard; Cabaret, Variety, and Revue Entertainment; Fierstein, Harvey; Film; Music and Musicians 2: Popular Music; Opera; Opera Queens; Puig, Manuel; Sondheim, Stephen Joshua; Stonewall, Theater; Wagner, Richard

Mystery and Detective Fiction

From its earliest years, mystery and detective fiction has been preoccupied with intimate male-male relationships. In Edgar Allan Poe's short story "The Murders in the Rue Morgue" (1841), detective Auguste Dupin shares with the male narrator a life of seclusion and togetherness, and in Englishwoman Mary Elizabeth Braddon's near-contemporary novel, *Lady Audley's Secret* (1862), the character Robert becomes an amateur detective not out of a desire to bring his masquerading aunt to justice but out of a need to be reunited with his longtime friend, George Talboys.

The opening decades of the twentieth century offer many instances of particularly British women keeping with this tradition and equipping their detectives with male companions. But Nero Wolfe and Archie Goodwin's slightly ambiguous domestic relationship—first presented in Rex Stout's *Fer-de-Lance* (1934) and developed in the long series of novels that followed—raised eyebrows among contemporary reviewers; audiences had become increasingly familiar with homosexuality through psychology, literature, and the burgeoning gay subcultures, and fictional partnerships such as the one created by Stout were not above suspicion. Stout's series also remains notable for the manner in which it bridges with its two main characters the wide gap between the British aesthete-detective and the pistol-toting wisecracker prominent in much of American detective fiction.

This representative American detective is a tough man of action, working alone, rarely confined to legal means of investigation, and frequently defining himself in opposition to women and homosexual men. In the first novels of Dashiell Hammett (*The Maltese Falcon*, 1930) and Raymond Chandler (*The Big Sleep,* 1939), there is no tolerance of male homosexuality: Joel Cairo is repeatedly targeted with pointed slaps and kicks from Sam Spade and others in Hammett's work, and Chandler's Philip Marlowe is pleased to learn that the pornographer, Mr. Geiger, has been fatally shot and that Geiger's boyfriend, Carol, is so easily rendered unconscious and taken into custody.

Gore Vidal, publishing under the pseudonym Edgar Box his first murder mystery, *Death in the Fifth Position* (1952), had certainly read Hammett and responded to these negative representations of male homosexuality. In Vidal's novel, the heterosexually active narrator Peter Sargeant is aggressively pursued by the deep-voiced, handsome ballet dancer, Louis Giraud, and is taken first to a drag show and then to a crowded gay bathhouse. Despite his cultivation and Harvard education, Sargeant tries to strike the cool pose of a Spade or Marlowe in the face of this adversity, but the reader can delight in the character's increasing lack of certainty:

> Standing by the pool in a strong light, I was very embarrassed not only by what was going on but by Louis who was staring at me, taking inventory. "Where'd you get those muscles, Baby?" he asked, in a low husky voice.
>
> "Beating up dancers," I said evenly. But I wasn't too sure of myself. Louis looked like one of those Greek gods with his clothes off, all muscle and perfect proportions. (Box 203)

A second and more recent example of the continuing influence of hard-boiled fiction is Geoffrey Miller's first novel, *The Black Glove* (1981), in which the protagonist, Terry Traven, goes so far as to dress and speak like a detective right out of Chandler or Hammett, even as he rejects the racism, misogyny, and homophobia informing those earlier works. Of the two, however, Vidal's novel is the more significant and memorable, particularly for its denunciation of the Red scare politics of midcentury Britain and America.

Although anticipated as early as Arthur Conan Doyle's *The Red-Headed League* (1892), a mystery recently shown to be suggestive of homosexual conspiracy, the portrayal of the "homosexual menace" reached its heyday in America and England in the 1950s and early 1960s and was fueled by scandals of spies and defectors to the Soviet Union. These decades witnessed a spate of fictional representations of the homosexual as murderer, among them Patricia Highsmith's *Strangers on a*

Train (1950), Hampton Stone's *The Murder That Wouldn't Stay Solved* (1951), Roy Fuller's *Fantasy and Fugue* (1954), and Colin Wilson's two novels, *Ritual in the Dark* (1960) and *The Glass Cage* (1966).

More recent gay mystery and detective fiction demonstrates the widening range of roles open to gay characters. Alongside the continued stories of homosexual murderers and victims, gay characters have also emerged as the protagonist in many stories, often in an official role. George Baxt's police character, Pharoah Love, first appears in *A Queer Kind of Death* (1966); Joseph Hansen's insurance investigator, Dave Brandstetter, is introduced in *Fadeout* (1970); and Michael Nava's lawyer, Henry Rios, makes his debut in *The Little Death* (1986).

This widening of roles has no doubt been made possible through the rise of lesbian and gay publishing houses as well as the mainstreaming of much gay literature. Alyson has published a number of quality stories, and St. Martin's Press now offers an extensive Stonewall Inn series of gay mystery and detective fiction. With mainstreaming, of course, come a new set of problems as writers find themselves having to negotiate between the expectations of a variety of readers. For example, the first of the Tom and Scott mysteries by Mark Richard Zubro, *A Simple Suburban Murder* (1989), offers a modern twist on the tradition of the detective and his companion, for here the reader is introduced to high school teacher Tom Mason and his lover, professional baseball player Scott Carpenter. Yet while Tom and Scott make investigative excursions into a graphically described homosexual Chicago underworld, any direct treatment of sexual expression between the two of them back in their suburban homes is to be found, if anywhere, within sets of ellipses or in the breaks between paragraphs.

James Kelley

Bibliography

Box, Edgar (pseud. Gore Vidal). *Death in the Fifth Position*. 1952. New York: Armchair Detective Library, 1991.

Slide, Anthony. *Gay and Lesbian Characters and Themes in Mystery Novels: A Critical Guide to Over 500 Works in English*. Jefferson, N.C.: McFarland, 1993.

See also Fiction; Film; Hitchcock, Alfred; McCarthyism; Vidal, Gore

Mythology

Greek (and Roman) mythology is essentially literary, embedded in texts composed almost exclusively by male authors in or for specific contexts, ranging from religious and dramatic festivals to Greek symposia—all-male drinking parties at which poems were performed by male poets.

Studies of poetry composed in societies dominated by an oral tradition have demonstrated that the audience plays a role in shaping the poem's content and the values of the poet. Similarly, in classical antiquity, when society was at best never more than five percent literate, the myths—the traditional tales of the community containing some moral or social application—were shaped in the interactive process between singer-poet and audience. Furthermore, if the poet and audience were almost always exclusively male, it is reasonable to assume that the myths would construct gender and sexuality from a "masculinist" perspective.

The myth of the Amazons is an excellent example of a myth about women transmitted by male authors. In this myth, the female in power is dangerously destructive; she subverts the "natural" order by rejecting patriarchal marriage and maiming her male children. The Amazons are defeated by Theseus, one of the Rambos of mythology, who, in one version of the myth, sexually humiliates their queen, Hippolyta. That the myth should illustrate the triumph of the male and the subjugation of the female clearly indicates how male Greek authors constructed masculinity and femininity, by enshrining in the myth what the "natural" roles and behavior of each sex should be. The didactic function of this myth is further emphasized by its representation in public places, such as on the metopes of the Parthenon.

As myths construct gender, so they construct sexuality. Sexual relations between men and women are often characterized by violence and rape. Gods rape mortal women at will, and goddesses often rape young men of surpassing beauty. The father of the gods, Zeus, arranges for his daughter, Persephone, to be raped by her uncle, Hades; she becomes queen of the underworld and her mother, Demeter, the powerful goddess of agriculture, is forced into a compromise that establishes her role in a patriarchal pantheon. In the mythological world, heterosexual relations are characterized by dominance and submission, reflecting the roles of women in an arranged marriage system where women, who were not citizens, like children and slaves, were more often than not pawns in dynastic, political, or financial alliances.

M Similarly, male same-sex sexual relations in mythology reflect the society that created the myths. Zeus kidnaps the beautiful Trojan prince Ganymede to be his cupbearer and, in later sources, his catamite (derived from Ganymede): the gap in age and status reflects the inequalities in the relationship between "lover" and "beloved" in classical Athenian society. The sexual object choice in the myths is irrelevant, but sexual relations reflect the power hierarchies that structure Greek society.

In a society without divinely sanctioned moral authority, such as the Bible, mythology serves to construct, legitimize, and transmit the society's values, from a gendered perspective.   *Michael Lambert*

Bibliography

Sergent, B. *Homosexuality in Greek Myth*. London: Athlone, 1967.

See also Bible; Ganymede; Greece, Ancient; Homer; Rome, Ancient

N

NAMBLA: North American Man/Boy Love Association

The North American Man/Boy Love Association (NAMBLA) was founded on December 2, 1978, to support consensual intergenerational relationships between men and teenage boys. Two dozen men and boys attended the first meeting, amid public hysteria over a sex scandal in nearby Revere, MA. NAMBLA soon became the gay movement's most controversial group, but it continued to march in gay pride parades until the early 1990s.

Over the years, NAMBLA, whose headquarters are in New York City, sprouted chapters in Boston, New Haven, Los Angeles, San Francisco, and Toronto, although its actual membership was never much more than one thousand. Allen Ginsberg, the group's most famous member and defender, whose poems extolled the love of boys, spoke at NAMBLA's November 1989 membership conference in New York City. Another notable supporter was cultural critic Camille Paglia, who criticized the "narrow political focus of gay activism" in banning NAMBLA from marches in her 1994 bestseller, *Vamps & Tramps*.

NAMBLA argued that age-of-consent laws (varying across states) were arbitrary and unfair and should be abolished. It sought to win over an increasingly hostile public through its publications, including the monthly *NAMBLA Bulletin*, an irregular *NAMBLA Journal* (formerly *News*), and assorted topical pamphlets. NAMBLA also published *A Witchhunt Foiled: The FBI vs. NAMBLA* (1985), a case study of how the disappearance of six-year-old Etan Patz in New York City was used to attack NAMBLA, which insisted it had nothing to do with it. But law enforcement interest in NAMBLA stayed

constant, as state and federal laws punishing sex crimes involving children were toughened, and a new bogeyman, the "pedophile," entered the vocabulary. NAMBLA did not focus its attention on sexual rights alone. It advocated a comprehensive program to liberate and empower youth, opposing circumcision, corporal punishment, and any coercion of youth. Its Web site (www.nambla.org) has proclaimed its support for greater economic, political, and social opportunities for young people and its denunciation of the "rampant ageism that segregates and isolates them in fear and mistrust."

NAMBLA's meetings were routinely kept under surveillance by undercover agents, and dossiers were compiled on its members. Over the years, a few steering committee members went to jail as the result of sex-crime convictions. The FBI conducted a coordinated national investigation, and Congress held hearings on pedophilia and child pornography that, in the end, exonerated NAMBLA itself from any involvement in criminal activities. A Senate investigation did not find NAMBLA to be a serious threat: "It is the pedophile with no organized affiliations who is the real threat to children," it concluded, citing a detective who testified before the committee.

NAMBLA also came under attack over its very right to exist. The Massachusetts state legislature failed in an early attempt to outlaw NAMBLA, but in 1996, New York state enacted a law dissolving a nonprofit agency, Zymurgy, set up by three NAMBLA steering committee members intending to use it to further NAMBLA's nonprofit activities.

Individuals linked to NAMBLA, especially educators, also faced scrutiny. In 1993, Peter Melzer, a physics teacher at Bronx High School of Science for over thirty-one years, who served on NAMBLA's steering committee, was fired by the New York City Board of Education after WNBC-TV in Manhattan publicized his NAMBLA ties. Pending an appeal, Melzer was given a desk job away from the classroom. Alone among the press, the *New York Times* editorialized in his support.

The media, however, caused NAMBLA's San Francisco chapter to stop holding meetings at the Potrero Hill branch of the public library, after a crusading local television station, KRON-TV, in 1992, found that out. NAMBLA's core leadership comprised seasoned 1960s gay antiwar activists, such as Tom Reeves and David Thorstad, who viewed NAMBLA as a gay organization fighting for rights of an oppressed group. The group soon embraced the defense of pedophilia, not just man/boy love.

Another key figure was Bill Andriette, who joined NAMBLA at age fifteen. Elected to the steering committee, he later assumed editorship (1990–1996) of its bulletin, becoming the group's chief theoretician. Andriette even appeared on CNN's *Larry King Live* to defend NAMBLA's membership in the Brussels-based International Lesbian and Gay Association (ILGA).

ILGA, reversing its 1985 call for the abolition of age-of-consent laws, voted in 1994 to expel NAMBLA, ironically its first U.S. gay member, and began screening out other ILGA members for any support of "pedophilia." The U.S. Congress approved an amendment, proposed by Senator Jesse Helms, that drastically cut (by some $119 million a year for two years) U.S. funding of the United Nations, unless the United Nations cut its ties to any group that condoned pedophilia. Despite the internal purge, ILGA lost its consultative status with the UN's Economic and Social Council in September 1994.

The ILGA move mirrored assimilationist tendencies elsewhere, as mainstream gay and lesbian organizations rushed to dissociate themselves from NAMBLA, arguing that NAMBLA was not a gay organization. Undeterred, NAMBLA continued to seek new frontiers to propagate its message. In the 1990s, NAMBLA went electronic, first linking its gopher site through the Gay Resources Directory Web site, and eventually creating its own. In 1997, NAMBLA's Web site came under attack by crusaders against child abuse.

Mired in controversy in what may be America's worst nightmare come true, NAMBLA became practically a household word beginning in the 1980s, given its advocacy of taboo sex between men and youth. But it was not just news accounts that gave the group its notoriety. In 1995, *Chicken Hawk*, a sixty-minute documentary on NAMBLA by an independent filmmaker, Adi Sideman, which premiered at film festivals and was later distributed by video outlets, helped popularize the group.   *Daniel C. Tsang*

Bibliography

Andriette, Bill. "Dumbed Out and Played Out: The Gay Movement and the Liquidation of Boy-Love." In *Taking Liberties*. Michael Bronski, ed. New York: Masquerade Books, 1996, 145–74.

Boys Speak Out on Man/Boy Love. NAMBLA Topics #4. 4th ed. New York: NAMBLA, 1996.

Chicken Hawk: Men Who Love Boys. Adi Sideman, director. Los Angeles: Film Threat Video, 1995.

Clendinen, Dudley. "Group Promoting Man-Boy Love the Focus of Police Inquiry." *New York Times*, January 1, 1983, A5.

Lowenthal, Michael. "The Boy-Lover Next Door." *XY Magazine* no. 6 (February–March 1997): 36–39.

Not Fade Away: Selections from the NAMBLA Bulletin. NAMBLA Topics #6. New York: NAMBLA, n.d.

Tsang, Daniel, ed. *The Age Taboo*. Boston: Alyson, 1981.

"North American Man-Boy Love Association." In *Child Pornography and Pedophilia*. U.S. Senate. Committee on Government Affairs, Permanent Subcommittee on Investigations (Senate Report 99-537). Washington, D.C.: Government Printing Office, 1986.

"Weighing a Teacher's Rights." *New York Times*, October 9, 1993, A22.

A Witchhunt Foiled: The FBI vs. NAMBLA. New York: NAMBLA, 1985.

See also Assimilation; Crime and Criminality; Ginsberg, Allen; Pederasty; U.S. Law: Discrimination

Nameless Sin (or Crime)

Homosexual acts came to be called the "nameless sin" through a misreading of a passage in the Christian Bible. In Ephesians 5:3–4, Paul lists certain sins that are not even to be spoken of among Christians, much less committed by them. The list of six terms contains three sexual terms, two of which (*akatharsia*, uncleanness; *aischrotês*, shamefulness) might refer to same-sex activity or masturbation. Among medieval theologians, the passage was taken as saying that homosexual acts were to remain "nameless" in the sense that they should never be spoken. This strange misreading of Ephesians was connected with other biblical misreadings and with larger regimes for controlling speech about homosexuality. According to a popular medieval etymology, "Sodom" meant "mute" or "mute herd." It was argued that "sodomy" made those who practiced it animal-like, depriving them of the human capacity for speech. Again, and more important, many medieval theologians professed the fear that to speak of homosexual acts in any but the most indirect way was to encourage them. By the end of the Middle Ages, same-sex acts are generally mentioned in sermons, moral treatises, and canonistic texts simply as the "unspeakable" sin or vice. This usage passes into English civil law not later than the sixteenth century. By the end of the nineteenth century, most notably with Alfred Douglas and Oscar Wilde, the phrase was transformed into the "love that dare not speak its name."

Mark D. Jordan

Bibliography

Boswell, John. *Christianity, Social Tolerance, and Homosexuality: Gay People in Western Europe from the Beginning of the Christian Era to the Fourteenth Century.* Chicago: University of Chicago Press, 1981.

See also Aelred of Rievaulx; Alan of Lille; Albert the Great; Augustine of Hippo; Catholicism; Christianity; Paul, Saint; Thomas Aquinas; Wilde, Oscar

NAMES Project AIDS Memorial Quilt

The NAMES Project AIDS Memorial Quilt has proven to be one of the most visible and powerful memorials to those who have died of AIDS-related illnesses. More than just a memorial, it incorporates processes of public mourning, remembrance, action, education, and fund-raising for AIDS/HIV causes. It is also commonly recognized as the world's largest community artwork, perhaps in all history. Its success is largely owed to a collaborative and democratic nature and its ability to make known the enormity of AIDS losses by retaining the specificity of individual lives and deaths. Unlike so many other memorial artworks, the NAMES Quilt subverts our admiration of its vast size when we realize that each addition symbolizes another loss to AIDS.

The quilt consists of various arrangements of individual three-by-six-foot cloth panels, each of which remembers the life and person of someone who has died of AIDS. They are put together by friends, loved ones, or others who cared about the deceased. The panels are adorned with every conceivable sort of personal effects, mementos, and ephemera: glitter, fabric paint, clothing, photographs, embroidery, stuffed animals, and the like can all be found on the quilt panels. After a panel has been made, it is sent to the San Francisco offices of the NAMES Project, where it is hemmed and stored.

Portions of the quilt have been seen in venues as small as school gymnasiums and as large as football stadiums. For display, the panels are sewn together in groups of eight and arranged on an ordered grid. At every display of the quilt, volunteers carefully unfold the panel sections in an emotional and moving ceremony, while the names of the dead are read aloud. Celebrity panels like Rock Hudson's and Willi Smith's are shown alongside those of the less-well-known who might be identified only by a name, a picture, or a message of love from the panel makers.

The AIDS Quilt in Washington. Photo Mike Theiler, Reuters/Corbis-Bettmann.

N The originator of the NAMES project was Cleve Jones, a San Francisco gay rights activist. Jones conceived the idea at a 1985 candlelight march to remember the 1978 assassinations of San Francisco Mayor George Moscone and openly gay city supervisor Harvey Milk. The number of AIDS deaths in San Francisco had passed one thousand, and Jones asked marchers to write the names of the dead on placards, which were taped to the front of the San Francisco Federal Building after the march. The display reminded Jones of a patchwork quilt. A year later he created the first quilt panel to honor his friend Marvin Feldman, and in June 1987 a small group of strangers gathered in a San Francisco storefront to document the lives of those who might otherwise be lost to history. Eventually the group formed the NAMES Project Foundation, which manages and displays the quilt as a fund-raising and educational device.

Rapidly the NAMES Project drew national and international interest, and panels were sent to San Francisco for inclusion in the memorial. In October 1987, more than 500,000 people viewed the quilt's 1,920 panels displayed on the National Mall in Washington, D.C. A subsequent tour of twenty U.S. cities in 1988 raised over $500,000 for AIDS charities. Contributions along the tour expanded the quilt to over 6,000 panels. In October of 1988, 8,288 panels were displayed on the Ellipse in front of the White House when the tradition of reading names aloud was begun. It returned to Washington in 1989, and again in October 1992, when the entire quilt was displayed between the Washington and Lincoln Memorials. By 1992, the AIDS Memorial Quilt included panels from every U.S. state and twenty-eight countries. The Washington, D.C., displays of October 1987, 1988, 1989, and 1992 are the only ones to have featured the quilt in its entirety.

By 1997 the quilt included over 43,000 panels from countries around the world yet represented only 12 percent of U.S. AIDS deaths. Today there are forty-four NAMES Project chapters in the United States and thirty-nine international Quilt affiliates. Since 1987, over 9 million people have visited the quilt at displays worldwide. The NAMES Project foundation has raised over $1.7 million for AIDS service organizations throughout North America. The quilt will be displayed until the epidemic is over.

In 1989 the NAMES Quilt was nominated for a Nobel Peace Prize. That same year a film, *Common Threads: Stories from the Quilt,* won an Oscar for best feature-length documentary from the Academy of Motion Picture Arts and Sciences. A number of books have been published that highlight panels from the quilt and the stories of those the quilt remembers.

As memorial and art, the quilt serves as a quiet counterpart to the cacophonous yet important street activism of Gran Fury, Queer Nation, and ACT UP, fulfilling Douglas Crimp's observation that what is needed is "mourning and militancy" (Weinberg 39). The quilt is a "visual metaphor" of the AIDS epidemic conveying the enormity of the loss, not through medical statistics but as a personal and immediate experience. It is often compared to Maya Lin's equally moving Vietnam memorial, which similarly records each name of the remembered dead. In its avoidance of abstraction, the quilt benefits from feminist artists' emphasis on the personal-as-political, collaboration over individuality, and process over product. The quilt inherits an undeniably American folk tradition of activist quilting by women, which contributes to its accessibility and general comprehensibility.

Finally, the quilt is unfailingly democratic. The NAMES Project gives privilege to no one panel as it is shuffled and reordered with every display, never remaining the same. Rather than privilege the few celebrity panels, the NAMES Project insists that each life that has been lost is worth remembering. The result has proven to be a touchstone of grief and mourning, but also hope and beauty, in the midst of an epidemic that has had few public spaces for any of these.

Michael J. Murphy

Bibliography

Crichton, E. G. "Is the NAMES Quilt Art?" In *Critical Issues in Public Art.* Harriet Senie and Sally Webster, eds. New York: HarperCollins, 1992, 287–94.

NAMES Project Web site: http://www.aidsquilt.org.

Weinberg, Jonathan. "The Quilt: Activism and Remembrance." *Art in America* 80 (December 1992): 37–39.

See also Activism, U.S.; AIDS; in the Media; AIDS Literature; AIDS Performance; AIDS Quilt Song book; Gran Fury; Queer Nation

National Gay and Lesbian Task Force

The National Gay and Lesbian Task Force (NGLTF) is an activist organization and resource center for the gay and lesbian civil rights movement. The Task Force focuses its political efforts in four areas: lobbying, media and public information, support for grassroots organizations, and direct action. Bruce Voeller and other associates in the Gay Activists Alliance (GAA) formed the National Gay Task Force (NGTF) in 1973 after becoming dissatisfied with the direction of the GAA. The NGTF was modeled on the American Civil Liberties Union, with a board of directors and a paid professional staff. Toby Marotta noted: "The organizers of the Task Force wanted to synthesize the old homophile and the reformist gay and lesbian approaches into a new hybrid with broader appeal."

The NGTF had 2,500 members by the end of its first year and was a major player in the decision of the American Psychiatric Association to remove homosexuality from the list of mental illnesses the following year. Under the direction of Voeller and Jean O'Leary, co-executive directors, in its formative years NGTF also courted support for gay and lesbian rights from mainstream organizations, challenged media portrayals of gays and lesbians, and began a concerted lobbying effort for changes in laws that discriminated against gays and lesbians. O'Leary coordinated the first meeting of openly gay and lesbian leaders with representatives of the Carter White House on March 26, 1977.

The next decade was a period of growth and change for the Task Force. It abandoned the co-executive director structure, moved the offices from New York to Washington, D.C., and formally became the National Gay and Lesbian Task Force (NGLTF). In the 1980s, NGLTF redirected its initiatives, as the AIDS epidemic and the gains of the religious right altered the national climate for gays and lesbians.

In 1991, NGLTF moved its educational and organizing areas to a separate organization, the NGLTF Policy Institute. Membership passed thirty thousand. Lobbying and other legislative initiatives remained within the purview of NGLTF. During the 1990s, NGLTF reemerged as a national leader in the gay and lesbian civil rights movement. Lobbying efforts remained at the forefront of the organizations activities, including a first-ever meeting with a sitting president, "lobby days," and an organized AIDS lobbying program.

Other NGLTF initiatives also receive national recognition. The Anti-Violence Project maintains statistics and promotes legislation designed to curb violence against lesbians and gays. The Creating Change Conference, part of the grassroots support offered by the Task Force, provides annual training and networking for activists. The media and public information programs provide commentary and resources for mainstream media organizations, the gay and lesbian press, and the public. The Task Force recently increased its electronic presence, maintaining a site on the World Wide Web (www.ngltf.org) and making much of its information available in electronic form.

By 1996, the NGLTF had thirty-five thousand members and an annual income approaching $2.5 million.

Mel Netzhammer

Bibliography

Marotta, Toby. *The Politics of Homosexuality: How Lesbians and Gay Men Have Made Themselves a Political and Social Force in Modern America*. Boston: Houghton Mifflin, 1981.

See also Activism; Gay Activists Alliance (GAA); Human Rights Campaign; Politics, Global

Natural Law

In Christian theology, the "natural law" is that part of God's moral teaching knowable to all human beings apart from any special revelation or grace. This natural law is opposed to "divine" or religious law not because it is about nature, but because it is taught by nature in the sense that it can be learned by rational beings through their natural experience. The Christian doctrine had many sources, especially in Roman law and later Stoic philosophy, but it was also based in scriptural passages that suggested some universal knowledge about God. The doctrine was developed fully in medieval theology and canon law. Its formulation by Thomas Aquinas was to become particularly influential. From Thomas, the doctrine passed both into later theology and into European jurisprudence, where it served as the foundation both for criminal legislation and for international law. A number of Christian theologians have taught that homosexual acts violated natural law. They meant not only that the acts were wrong, but that they could be known to be wrong apart from religious revelation. The acts could be known to be wrong, they claimed, by reasoning on the purposes of sexual differentiation and its relation to reproduction. Unfortunately, this claim about natural law was regularly confused with the very different claim that homosexual acts were "against nature." The confusion is encouraged by an authoritative scriptural passage, Romans 1:18–32. Paul there argues that homosexual behavior followed as a consequence or punishment on the idolatrous rejection of what could be learned from creation about God as creator. But Paul also asserts in the passage that the same-sex behavior is "against nature." He seems to mean by this last phrase that same-sex acts undo the "natural" subordination of passive-female to active-male or that they contravene the "natural" purposes of genital organs and reproductive powers. Whatever it means, the phrase does not capture what later theologians meant by "against the natural law." A theological claim about nature is a claim about God's creative purposes. A theological claim about natural law is a claim about the extent to which those purposes can be known apart from revelation. Claims of the second sort have traditionally been more common in Catholic theology than in Protestant, where they have sometimes been attacked quite sharply. Specific claims that homosexual activity violates natural law are repeated in the 1975 Vatican documents on sexuality and in the 1992 Catechism of the Catholic Church.   *Mark D. Jordan*

Bibliography

Pronk, Pim. *Against Nature? Types of Moral Argumentation Regarding Homosexuality*. Grand Rapids, Mich.: Eerdmans, 1993.

See also Aquinas, Thomas; Catholicism; Christianity; Paul, Saint; Rome, Ancient

Nava, Michael (1954–)

Michael Nava's detective fiction represents an effective, "gay" marriage of the conventional techniques of the genre and the kinds of innovations its contemporary practitioners have brought to it. Like his precursors, Raymond Chandler and Joseph Hansen, Nava has strung a series of novels involving the exploits of a single detective-protagonist, gay Chicano investigative attorney Henry Rios, whose character and story lines have evolved and improved with the skills and talents of the author. From the earliest of the Rios series, *The Little Death* (1986), through *Goldenboy* (1988), *How Town* (1990), *The Hidden Law* (1992), and *The Death of Friends* (1996), Nava has managed to cover such unconventional topics (for "classical," Chandleresque noir fiction) as Chicano social and political history, AIDS's impact on both the Chicano and gay communities, and the complicated sexual and cultural politics among gay men in the 1990s, while at the same time spinning suspenseful, compelling plots worthy of any of his precursors and contemporaries in the genre. Nava,

born in Stockton, Calif., raised in Sacramento, and educated in law at Stanford University, has been a practicing attorney in Los Angeles as well as a writer; in addition to his Rios series, Nava has edited a collection of gay detective stories (*Finale*, 1989) and co-written with Robert Dawidoff a book-length political essay, *Created Equal: Why Gay Rights Matter to America* (1994). Nava's work is an important contribution not only to his chosen genre but also to the ongoing, general development of literary writing by U.S. Latino and gay writers; the parallels between Nava's life and that of his hero Henry Rios also suggest that Nava is writing the (albeit highly fictionalized) autobiography of a complicated and fascinating gay man.   *Ricardo Ortiz*

See also Chicano and Latino Gay Cultures; Mystery and Detective Fiction

Navarre, Yves (1940–1994)

The French writer Yves Navarre produced of over thirty published novels and nearly thirty stage works, many of which deal directly with homosexuality. In 1992 he was awarded the prize of the Académie Française, in recognition of his literary output. Navarre worked for various advertising agencies until the appearance of *Lady Black* (1971), his seventeenth novel but the first to be published. Subsequent books dealt regularly with the ambiguities, or horrors, of a gay man's position inside his family, notably *Le Jardin d'acclimatation* (*Cronus's Children*, 1979), which won France's most prestigious literary prize, the Prix Goncourt.

Navarre was handsome, large, and boyish-looking. Navarre's slow physical gestures, gentle voice, slightly malicious sense of humor, and eloquence in interviews gave France's emerging gay movement a modern, positive face. His center-left political views led to an early involvement in the fight for greater visibility of openly gay writers. In 1974, he participated, with Roger Peyrefitte and Jean-Louis Bory, in the first debate on French television involving openly gay writers. He was an enrolled member of France's Socialist Party, and as such, in March 1981, delivered presidential candidate François Mitterand's written message to the gay electorate, two months before Mitterand's election. Nevertheless, he always rejected the idea of being a "gay writer," finding such a concept absurd.

Perhaps the most significant of his earlier books are *Le petit Galopin de nos corps* (*Little*

Rogue in Our Flesh, 1979), an extraordinary celebration of the lifelong passion of Roland and Joseph (taking place between 1899 and 1936, thereby scrupulously avoiding any trace of modern gay jargon) and *Le Temps voulu* (Our Share of Time, 1979), which opens with an attempted suicide and goes on to present the enigmatic encounter between Pierre and Daniel (Duck) that provides a redeeming lifeline for Pierre by way of a short-term relationship. (This is presented as bittersweet, but Navarre, always extremely precise with word order and nuance, would no doubt have preferred the French expression "sweet-bitter.") In a different vein, the heroine of *Louise* (1986) is shown through a subtle and affectionate portrait that brought Navarre a wider audience; irritated by what he saw as a pervasive misogyny in the works of some gay French writers, he considered this novel to be his homage to women.

After several years of living in Canada that he later characterized as an attempt to run away from black reality while more and more of his friends were dying, Navarre published the violent *Hôtel Styx* (1989). His change of direction resulted from an increasing sense of despair, culminating in *Ce Sont amis que vent emporte* (*Friends Carried Away by the Wind*), possibly the finest French novel to date dealing with AIDS. His last published novel was *Poudre d'or* (*Gold Dust*, 1993).

One of his favorite phrases was "*J'écris comme j'appellerais au secours*" (I write in the same way I would cry for help). Toward the end of his life, especially when resentful of the lost freedoms that came with fame, he was more blunt: "*Yves n'aime plus Navarre*" (Yves no longer loves Navarre). To say "he took his own life" would be to rob his last act of both its sense and its cultural context. The phrase in French is "he gave himself death," a gesture prefigured several times in his novels, where death is rarely perceived as being worse than the horrors that life can hold. He left behind a host of beautifully written letters, much unpublished early work, and a body of distinguished published novels and plays that have earned him a firm place in modern French literature.   *Davitt Moroney*

Bibliography

Anon. "Yves Navarre." *Libération*, January 25, 1994.
"Fonds Yves-Navarre" (the Yves Navarre collection). http://www.biblinat.gouv.qc.ca/t0157
Marsan, Hugo. "Yves Navarre." *Le Monde*, January 26, 1994.

See also AIDS Literature; France; French Literature; Paris; Peyrefitte, Roger

Nazism and the Holocaust

Gays were not victims of the Holocaust. This awful title belongs only to the Jews and, according to more recent historical research, the Gypsies. Gays were, however, victims of Nazism. They, along with others such as Jehovah's Witnesses and political dissidents, refused to conform to Nazi ideological strictures and thus were termed "undesirable" beings within the Third Reich.

In understanding this history, it is useful to divide the years of the Third Reich into three eras as they reflect Nazi attitudes toward homosexuality. The first, lasting from the takeover of power on January 30, 1933, until 1935, might be called "exclusion." During the Weimar Republic (1919–1933), gays and lesbians had led increasingly more open lives and developed a vibrant subculture of social and political organizations, publishing venues, and bar life. But beginning in February 1933, the Nazis set about destroying gay and lesbian cultural and social institutions. On May 6, the Institute for Sexual Science, home of the chief fighter for homosexual rights, the Scientific-Humanitarian Committee, was plundered and its vast library added to the bonfires of the book burnings a few days later.

Two further major steps toward exclusion ensued. On June 30, 1934, members of Heinrich Himmler's SS murdered almost three hundred leaders of the SA, the unofficial Nazi army of "Brown Shirts" that had helped bring the Nazi Party to power through street battles in the early Depression years. The assassinated leader of the SA was Ernst Roehm. His homosexuality had become well known because of a campaign against the Nazi Party, launched by the leftist press, especially in the electoral battles of 1930. Hitler had known from the beginning of their close friendship that Roehm was homosexual, but now he needed the generals of the German army firmly on his side and they were threatened by Roehm's call for the SA to take the army's place. Homosexuality provided one convenient cover for assassination. Hitler's address to the nation on the following day defended the murders as acts of defense against a scourge threatening Germany's manhood. In the ensuing months, raids on bars and other public meeting places intensified.

One year later, on June 28, 1935, the sodomy law (paragraph 175) was changed. Previously, only intercourselike acts were punishable. The new statute criminalized "unnatural vice" or "criminally indecent activities" between two males. These broad terms were interpreted to mean not just any specifically sexual act but even homosexual intent. Worse still, the new law was often applied retroactively, thus criminalizing such previously legal acts as mutual masturbation and kisses. With this law, the conviction rates for those accused of homosexuality more than doubled in 1935 and did so again in 1936.

Why did the Nazis pursue those who engaged in homosexuality so vigorously? Male homosexuals were seen as weak, degenerate, even diseased creatures. Their acts of sexual deviance would spread their contagion to the healthy majority through their insatiable lust to seduce males, preying especially on teenaged boys. Reflecting in some ways the differing explanations offered by German sexologists as to the origin of homosexuality, Nazi policy would sometimes differentiate between various "categories" of men who had been accused under the expanded paragraph 175. Some were defined as homosexual by nature. They would later be subject to medical experimentation and to castration in concentration camps. Others, however, had been led astray by seduction or improper experimentation. Since their actions were not the product of an innate identity, these men could, according to Nazi belief, more easily be saved for the nation and might be less harshly punished.

No matter the source of homosexuality, National Socialist policy was aimed at eradicating all homosexual *acts*. That homosexuals per se were not targeted for extermination may seem a dubious point when we know that thousands of them were killed, but it is important to remember the difference between persons and acts. The Nazis viewed some individuals as salvageable for the Reich, if they would conform to the new ideological dictates of the state (e.g., homosexuals, political dissidents). Others, however, had no place in the new nation simply because of who they were, most notably the Jews.

In the years 1936 through 1939, persecution intensified. Homosexual men came into the Nazi legal machinery by the thousands. For example, between 1937 and 1939, almost 95,000 men were taken into custody by the Gestapo through raids on bars, parks, and other meeting places, as well as through denunciations or forced "confessions" that often implicated others. The story of this persecution is difficult to follow solely through statistics. Only 36 percent of those arrested were brought to trial (about 34,000 men), and 72 percent of those (26 percent of those originally taken into custody) were sentenced (just under 25,000 men). Being sentenced carried with it harsh penalties (a prison sentence, possible internment in a concentration camp). But even being taken into custody and questioned often served as enough of a scare tactic to achieve the goal of eliminating homosexual acts. In addition, one's name was probably added to the lists that were being kept by the Federal Department for Combating Homosexuality and Abortion, founded in 1936.

During this period, the Nazis also used homophobia as a weapon against those who might thwart their domination within the Reich. First, they went after leaders from the various youth groups that had to be forcibly integrated into the Hitler Youth between 1933 and 1936. In some of those groups, homoerotic, even homosexual relationships had existed, and this strengthened the Nazis' hand in their propaganda battle. Next, the Nazis attacked the Catholic Church, claiming that monks, nuns, priests, and teachers were corrupting "Aryan" youth. Despite a long series of often sensational trials between 1936 and 1939, few convictions were won in court.

Finally, one could characterize the war years, 1939–1945, as a period of "eradication" of homosexual behavior, homosexual identity, and, at times the homosexual person. The Germans pursued this policy most vigorously against so-called Aryans, i.e., German citizens and citizens of present or future provinces of the Reich: Austrians, Dutch, Alsatians, and Czechs. They also persecuted non-Aryans (e.g., Poles) who engaged in homosexual behavior with Aryans.

Through analysis of police records, court cases, and concentration camp lists, German scholars (led by the work of Rudigar Lautmann) have been able to offer a reasonably accurate estimate of the number of men convicted and interned for sodomy. Of the approximately fifty thousand to sixty thousand males convicted, they estimate that between five thousand and fifteen thousand were assigned the pink triangle in concentration camps between the mid-1930s and 1945. (Others were placed in prisons.) Because the records were incomplete and in part destroyed, precise figures do not exist. Nor will we ever know of those homosexuals who wore other triangles, much less those who committed suicide for fear of persecution. We also know little about the involvement of homosexuals in acts of resistance or about the lives of those who went into exile.

Nonetheless, we do know quite a bit about the experience of homosexual men in the camps. Prisoners wearing pink triangles occupied one of the lowest places in the social hierarchy. As such, they were often subjected to vicious beatings by the guards and even other prisoners simply because they were identified as homosexual. Out of fear and homophobia, they were isolated not only from friends and family but from other prisoners and often from one another.

Homosexual prisoners were often simply worked to death. Some examples from the research and from first-person accounts include draining the moorland in northwestern Germany, where prisoners often stood in knee-deep water all day; testing synthetic soles for shoes by walking back and forth for hours on end on a variety of demanding surfaces; or excavating tunnels in the Harz Mountains and then assembling V-1 and V-2 rockets in the dank conditions there.

Homosexuals also became subjects of medical experimentation. Some were injected with typhus to observe the disease's effects and to test possible treatments. Two experiments sought to eradicate homosexuality through medical intervention. Some of the Reich's medical and legal personnel believed that castration would eliminate this unwanted sexual desire or at least the ability to act on what desire might remain. Thus, homosexuals were sometimes offered the choice of castration or further internment. At other times, if they were already incarcerated, castration was simply ordered.

The second experiment for attempted eradication of homosexuality was carried out in 1944 by Carl Vaernet, a Danish physician who volunteered for the SS. He chose about a dozen homosexual prisoners in Buchenwald concentration camp as the subjects of his experiments at "reversing" homosexuality into heterosexuality. Believing that homosexuality was caused by a hormonal imbalance, he implanted a device to release large doses of male hormones into the victim.

From this variety of persecutions, the chances of survival were significantly lower for homosexuals than for other comparable groups. According to one researcher, pink triangle prisoners experienced a 53 percent death rate (compared with 40.5 percent for politicals and 34.7 percent for Jehovah's Witnesses). Some 63 percent died within the first eighteen months (compared with 40.2 percent and 24.8 percent, respectively), with three of four dying within the first year. Contrary to the myth that young homosexuals could survive by serving as sexual partners to prisoners who held power positions, those age twenty-six to thirty had the greatest chance of surviving (29.7 percent of this age group died).

The persecution of homosexuals did not end with liberation from the camps in 1945. The Nazi version of the sodomy law remained on the books until 1949 in the Soviet Occupation Zone (later the German Democratic Republic, or East Germany), 1969 in West Germany, and 1971 in Austria. In fact, prosecutions and convictions in West Germany's first twelve years exceeded those during the twelve years of the Third Reich. Not only did stigmatization and incarceration of homosexuals continue, but West German courts expressly ruled that homosexuals did not belong to that class of persons who had been "unjustly" persecuted and were thus eligible for restitution payments from the government. In 1987, the West German government created a special fund for "forgotten victims," a category that can apply to homosexuals. However, very few of the small number of survivors have had the courage, energy, and necessary "documentation" to make their way through the bureaucratic maze. *James W. Jones*

Bibliography

Grau, Günter, ed. *Homosexualität in der NS-Zeit. Dokumente einer Diskriminierung und Verfolgung*. Frankfurt am Main: Fischer Taschenbuch, 1993. Published in English as *Hidden Holocaust? Gay and Lesbian Persecution in Germany, 1933–45*. Patrick Camiller, trans. London: Cassell, 1995.

Heger, Heinz. *Die Männer mit dem rosa Winkel. Der Bericht eines Homosexuellen über seine KZ-Haft von 1939–45*. Hamburg: Merlin, 1972. Published in English as *The Men with the Pink Triangle: The True, Life-and-Death Story of Homosexuals in the Nazi Death Camps*. David Fernbach, trans. Boston: Alyson; London: Gay Men's Press, 1980.

Jellonek, Burkhard. *Homosexuelle unter dem Hakenkreuz. Die Verfolgung von Homosexuellen im Dritten Reich*. Paderborn, Germany: Schöningh, 1990.

Lautmann, Rüdiger. "Categorization in Concentration Camps as a Collective Fate: A Comparison of Homosexuals, Jehovah's Witnesses and Political Prisoners." *Journal of Homosexuality* 19, no. 1 (1990): 67–88.

——. ed. *Seminar: Gesellschaft und Homosexualität*. Frankfurt am Main: Suhrkamp, 1977.

Oosterhuis, Harry. "The 'Jews' of the Antifascist Left: Homosexuality and Socialist Resistance to Nazism." In *Gay Men and the Sexual History of the Political Left*. Gert Hekma, Harry Oosterhuis, and James Steakley, eds. New York: Haworth Press, 1995, 227–57. This is the publication in book form of *Journal of Homosexuality* 29, no. 2, 3 and 4 (1995).

Plant, Richard. *The Pink Triangle: The Nazi War against Homosexuals*. New York: Henry Holt, 1986.

Röll, Wolfgang. "Homosexual Inmates in the Buchenwald Concentration Camp." *Journal of Homosexuality* 31, no. 4 (1996): 1–28.

Seel, Pierre. *I, Pierre Seel, Deported Homosexual: A Memoir of Nazi Terror*. Joachim Neugroschel, trans. New York: Basic Books, 1995. Also published as *Liberation Was for Others: Memoirs of a Gay Survivor of the Nazi Holocaust*. New York: Basic Books, 1997. Originally published *Moi, Pierre Seel, déporté homosexuel*. Paris: Calmann-Lévy, 1994.

Stümke, Hans-Georg, and Rudi Finkler. *Rosa Winkel, Rosa Listen: Homosexuelle und "Gesundes Volksempfinden" von Auschwitz bis heute*. Reinbek bei Hamburg, Germany: Rowohlt Taschenbuch, 1981.

van Dijk, Lutz. *"Ein Leben—Trotzdem . . ." Erinnerungen Homosexueller, 1933–1945*. Reinbek bei Hamburg, Germany: Rowohlt Taschenbuch, 1992.

——. *Verdammt starke Liebe: Eine wahre Geschichte*. Reinbek bei Hamburg, Germany: Rowohlt Taschenbuch, 1991. Published in English as *Damned Strong Love: The True Story of Willi G. and Stefan K.* Elizabeth D. Crawford, trans. New York: Henry Holt, 1995.

See also Germany; Hirschfeld, Magnus; Judaism; Sexology

Neighborhoods: Gay Neighborhoods in the United States

In the latter decades of the twentieth century in the United States, the disparate collection of personal sexual awakenings born of the labor demands of armed conflict across the globe became the eventual beneficiary of many declarations of cultural independence in the 1960s. These awakenings were nurtured by intimate explorations more ancient in provenance than nation-states themselves. The most signal transformations came from an appreciation that "gay" meant a wholesome validation not just of lifestyle but of *raison d'être*. This was in sharp contrast to the dark ideology of a majoritarian society that at midcentury viewed homosexuality as evil, criminal, and insane. In the 1970s and early 1980s, cultural consciousnesses that had previously been furtive and desperate, vulnerable to all sorts of phobias and prejudices, found increasingly firm allies in the social philosophy of liberation and the dramatic abandonment of the medicalization of homosexuality in 1973 by the American Psychiatric Association.

The notion of "gay pride" not only spawned separatist enclaves—urban gay ghettos, rural lesbian feminist homesteads, Radical Faerie retreats, and the like—but also came to permit more generic membership in an assertive *perceived* community united primarily by sexual imperatives at odds with the heterosexual norm. This cultural mélange of incredible diversity and strength was not uniformly present or discoverable across the country. Legal and religious strictures continued to challenge these new presences in varying degrees and helped explain why recognizable "gay" neighborhoods could emerge early on in the tolerant atmosphere of New York and San Francisco but not as readily in the more conservative heartland. Migration from less tolerant to more tolerant sites continues to occur not just on the grand scale of a coastal megalopolis but also from one rural township to another.

In the latter part of the 1980s and thereafter, two scenarios have had profound impacts on these nascent settlement patterns: the emergence of the AIDS pandemic and the information explosion brought about by the widespread introduction of digital communication systems. AIDS—first known as the "gay disease"—has brought stark tragedy, but the fight against AIDS has created enormous community of effort. The irreversible proliferation of accurate and expressive information about sexual diversity and allied communities of interest via the Internet has diminished social isolation and the likelihood of high-risk behavior as the perceived price of admission to a "gay" world.

Approaching the end of the century, gay neighborhoods are experiencing diffusion effects from new understandings about diversity. In 1975, to be gay meant not to be cursed with the semiotic drawbacks of homosexuality. Two decades later, by the end of the millennium, the *understood* nuances of sexual diversity and novel family structures only begin to suggest the range of intricacies involved. Popular attitudes have begun to move away from a discredited binary heterosexual/homosexual hegemony, and the notion of neighborhood has acquired greater latitude as life opportunities expand to include job choices, homeownership, and family structures previously attainable only to persons ostensibly congruent to the dominant heterosexual mode of sexuality.   *Fredric Markus*

Bibliography

Barber, Judith. *Bodies That Matter*. New York: Routledge, 1993.

Estrikin, J. Nicholas. *The Betweenness of Place*. Baltimore: Johns Hopkins University Press, 1991.

Harris, Daniel. *The Rise and Fall of Gay Culture*. New York: Hyperion, 1997.

Jackson, Peter. *Maps of Meaning*. London: Unwin Hyman, 1989.

Sedgwick, Eve Kosofsky. *The Epistemology of the Closet*. Berkeley: University of California Press, 1990.

Vaid, Urvashi. *Virtual Equality*. New York: Doubleday, 1995.

See also AIDS; Castro; Gentrification; Los Angeles; Marches and Parades; New York City; Radical Faeries; San Francisco

Neoclassicism

Neoclassicism is the name given to a movement of classical revival that arose in European art, architecture, and interior design from the mid-eighteenth to the early nineteenth century. The movement was encouraged by the discovery of a wealth of well-preserved artifacts excavated from the ancient ruins of Herculaneum (first excavated in 1709) and Pompeii (excavation began in 1748) in Italy. Both cities had been buried under volcanic ash from the eruption of Mount Vesuvius in A.D. 79. The cache of art and other remains uncovered exerted a profound impact on European taste.

The interest in classical revival soon spread to numerous countries throughout western Europe, and each nation added its own unique signature to the movement. In England, neoclassicism was associated with British self-confidence and the building of empire. In France, it was linked with political and moral considerations arising from the revolution

and was embodied in the severe art of Jacques-Louis David (1748–1825). David's most famous neoclassical paintings include *Belisarius Begging for Alms* (Musée des Beaux-Arts, Lille, 1781), *Oath of the Horatii* (Louvre, Paris, 1784), *Death of Socrates* (Metropolitan Museum of Art, New York, 1787), and *Leonidas at Thermopylae* (Louvre, 1814). All these works have in common an identifiable approach to subject matter and style. Regarding subject matter, most works of neoclassicism focus on literary subjects centered around the heroic and stoic deeds of men, with a sharp division between the roles and attitudes of men and women. Males, shown in public roles, are given the qualities of heroism, unwavering resolve, and physical and moral strength. Conversely, females and femininity are relegated to the realm of the private, domestic, and passive. These sharp divisions in the function and role of the sexes are also underscored in terms of style. Neoclassical works of art are characterized by a stress on linearity, direct lighting, rational and mathematical composition, and sharp, acidic coloration. Male figures are given hard, angular, sculptural qualities, while females are typically rendered in soft, melting, curvilinear forms. Neoclassicism is often referred to as a masculine art form obsessed with the deeds and expectations of males and set in distinct opposition to the period of light and frivolous "feminine" preoccupations and style that preceded it called the rococo. In neoclassicism, it is the male body (nude and clothed) as well as masculine deeds and desires that are put forth as the critical site for a variety of important meanings ranging from the political to the sexual.

The neoclassical program, although not precisely defined, adhered to approaches to nature and the antique as part of the education of the male artist. The artist's studio became the primary locale for the understanding, development, and dissemination of neoclassicism. Male homosexuality and its erotic currents played a major role in much of the formation and content of neoclassicism as an aesthetic. David's studio, for example, was an all-male environment in which young men in their late teens and early twenties not only developed a strong moral, intellectual, and erotic bond with one another but also competed with one another for the attention and love of the master painter, who, in his role as art patriarch, functioned as father figure. The pedagogical and erotic intimations of man-boy coupling as practiced in ancient Greece were transplanted to and imitated in the artist's studio. In no other painting are the dynamics of neoclassicism, the artist's studio, and homoerotic desire more explicitly represented than in David's *Death of Socrates*. This is a work in which the issue of homosexuality (more specifically, pederasty as practiced in antiquity) and the homoerotic are part of the story being told. The philosopher Socrates, condemned to death by the democratic assembly for the corruption of youth, is shown unflinchingly reaching for the cup of hemlock as he engages in a metaphysical monologue and as his disciples, gathered around him, lament what is about to occur. All the elements required for a neoclassical picture are here: an all-male environment, heroic action, sculptural form, intense linearity, rational composition, strong lighting, and an intensely homoerotic subtext.

An important influence in developing the homoerotic aesthetic of neoclassicism was the noted scholar and librarian Johann Joachim Winckelmann (1717–1768), who, in his writings on ancient painting and sculpture (published in 1755 and 1764), gave intellectual justification and an international reputation to the homoerotic dimensions of neoclassicism. In his writings on Greek art, Winckelmann sublimated his homosexuality into intense erotic and sensual descriptions of male Greek sculptures. This was most noticeable in his famous description of the *Apollo Belevedere* (Vatican Museums, Rome, c.fourth century B.C.), whose corporeal beauty was described as the realization of "an eternal springtime like that which reigns in the happy fields of Elysium, [that] clothes his body with the charms of youth and softly shines on the proud structure of his limbs."

Neoclassical subject matter and style were not confined to the medium of painting. Of the most famous neoclassical sculptors, Italian Antonio Canova (1757–1822) and Dane Bertel Thorvaldsen (1770–1844) created works of male beauty and sensuality based on classical statuary. Such works as *Theseus and the Centaur* (Kunsthistorisches Museum, Vienna, 1804–1819) by Canova and *Jason* (Thorvaldsen Museum, Copenhagen, 1802–1803) by Thorvaldsen rely on stock mythological themes of Greek gods and heroes as one way to focus on the sensuous aspects of the male body. The suspension of action—the frozen contemplation of heroic deed and male bodily beauty—is reinforced by the smooth and polished marble surfaces that heighten the sensual quality of the figures. The figures tend to feel light and airy, underscoring the combination of ideal perfection and spirituality that derive from Neoplatonic ideas. There is an attempt in these and other neoclassical works to elicit the viewer's emotional response to the concept of the *beau idéal* (beautiful ideal). This idea in neoclassical sculpture was the result of an ongoing debate during the period between successful imitation versus rote copying of the art of the ancient Greeks. The most successful sculpture was required to piece together the most beautiful parts of antique statuary with the most beautiful aspects of the living model. The result—the *beau idéal*—was based on a combined intellectual and erotic need to forge in art a representation of the ultimate beautiful male body.

Neoclassicism as a style and movement in art was not restricted to reliance solely on the male form. Painter J.A.D. Ingres (1780–1867) applied the vestiges of neoclassical purity of line, voluptuous form, and the quality of grace to women. Landscape painter Pierre-Henri de Valenciennes (1750–1819) put to use the neoclassical principles of line and rational form to depict the landscape, while Claude-Nicolas Ledoux (1736–1806) and Étienne-Louis Boullée (1728–1799) did the same for architecture in France. In England, Robert Adam (1728–1792) revived classical motifs in his approach to architecture, interior design, and the decorative arts. In the area of illustration, the works of Englishman John Flaxman (1755–1826) became the prime exponent of a neoclassical trait in which line replaced sculptural form and color.

For obvious reasons related to homophobia and the conservative nature of art history as a discipline, the role of homosexuality and homoerotic desire in forging the content and dissemination of neoclassicism in western Europe has been downplayed, denied, and rejected. This is slowly changing as postmodern culture considers the profound impact of gender, race, and multiple sexualities on the forging and consumption of art in both the past and the present.   *James Smalls*

Bibliography

Crow, Thomas. *Emulation: Making Artists for Revolutionary France*. New Haven: Yale University Press, 1995.

Honour, Hugh. *Neo-Classicism*. New York: Penguin, 1977.

See also Art History; Greece; Winckelmann, Johann Joachim

Netherlands

Little is known of same-sex relations in the Netherlands before 1700. A hundred cases of sodomy have been uncovered until now. Half of them concern same-sexual acts among men, many but not all pederastic. Some women have been persecuted for entering a marriage with another female. In the arts, same-sex desire seems to have been largely absent, although little research has been instigated. Sodomy appears not to have been high on the agenda of either religious or political authorities until 1730. That year marked an important change when a major persecution of sodomites started in Utrecht. In the years 1730–1732, one hundred sodomites were sentenced to death, all for anal sex between men. Many more men were convicted in their absence. During the eighteenth century, several waves of smaller-scale persecutions took place. Another one hundred capital punishments were executed. After the Batavian Revolution of 1795, the Dutch copy of the French Revolution, the number of persecutions increased but the severity of the punishments decreased. Sodomy became a major concern during the Enlightenment, the period in which greater tolerance would have been expected. In 1777 the first tract that pleaded for less severe punishment of sodomy was published anonymously. Nevertheless, persecutions stepped up. This ambiguous situation has been explained as a revolution shaking northwestern Europe that gave rise to new gender and sexual roles and to a sodomitical subculture defined by illicit pleasures and secret places, by blackmailers and police persecutions. The subculture consisted of networks of friends and lovers, of rich men and the menservants and soldiers who served their sexual interests, of some bars and several public cruising places (the English word *cruising* stems from the Dutch *kruysen* used by Dutch sodomites for their sexual quests).

The Netherlands became under Napoléon a part of France. In 1811, the French *Code Pénal* was introduced that decriminalized sodomy but penalized public indecency. As privacy was largely reserved for heterosexual males, most criminal cases of public indecency concerned homosexual acts during the nineteenth century. After the defeat of Napoléon in 1813, several proposals were brought to parliament to recriminalize sodomy but did not materialize. With the criminal law of 1886, sodomy remained licit. The age of consent, before not well defined, was brought to sixteen years. In the sex law of 1911, it was raised to twenty-one years for homosexual acts. The nineteenth century in the Netherlands had been in political terms a liberal age. Homosexual acts were unspeakable sins, severely punished only when public. At the end of the century, Christian and socialist parties with a moral agenda took over from liberals and participated in framing ideologies that opposed sexual pleasures beyond the bounds of nuclear family and monogamy.

Notwithstanding rising conservative ideologies, the Netherlands witnessed in the period 1880–1911 a sort of sexual revolution. In arts, scholarship, and politics new topics were raised and fresh demands made. Poetry and literature harbored gay and lesbian themes. Jacob Israël de Haan produced *Pijpelijntjes* (1904) on gay life in Amsterdam and Louis Couperus *De berg van licht* (1905) on Roman Emperor Heliogabal. Medical doctors wrote apologies for homosexuality and demanded pity for the poor homosexual. Arnold Aletrino and Lucien von Römer were the first to do so and defied their opponents, ranging from socialists and medical professors to the Calvinist prime minister. After the new sex law passed parliament in 1911, squire Jacob Anton Schorer founded in 1912 the first homosexual movement in the Netherlands, the Dutch section of the Wissenschaftlich-humanitäre Komitee (NWHK), largely a private enterprise. Persecution of homosexuals was on the rise because of the new law. Until 1971 some five thousand men and fifty women were brought to court under this law, most of them in the period 1930–1960. From the late 1930s to the 1960s, castration could be demanded of convicted "sex criminals," often homosexuals, while others went under social pressure to doctors to request this operation to heal themselves of unwholesome desires.

The German occupation of the Netherlands (1940–1945) brought stricter laws, but they were rarely enacted. The new homosexual monthly *Levensrecht,* which began publication in January 1940, shut down after the invasion, while the house of Schorer, center of the NWHK, was raided. This important library was dragged off to an unknown destination, never to be recovered. Although the war years brought misery and death to the Dutch people, it offered gay men special attractions under the darkness of curfew. After the war the situation for homosexuals did not improve much. The *Levensrecht* group started a movement in 1946, the Shakespeare Club, that changed its name soon after to Centre for Culture and Recreation (COC). It lobbied to change political, police, and medical attitudes while offering culture and recreation for homosexuals.

The COC contributed to a major breakthrough in national politics in the sixties. In 1964 it renamed itself Society of Homophiles COC. At that time both Catholic and Calvinist psychiatrists and clergymen successfully requested compassion for homosexuals. The Dutch Society for Sexual Reform (NVSH) made major inroads in society with demands of social tolerance for pre- and extramarital sex, contraception, abortion, pornography, prostitution, and homosexuality. The growing self-consciousness of gays and lesbians was matched by a growing acceptance of their existence by the general public. The sexual revolution encouraged, in the Netherlands even more than elsewhere, a liberation not only of gays and lesbians but also of straights of all persuasions. The image of the homosexual changed from a promiscuous invert seducing boys to a homophile desirous of stable friendships. As a psychiatrist close to the COC stated, the homosexual was simply the same as any other human being. The COC fared well with the sexual revolution and its attendant normalization of homosexuality. In 1971 parliament voted for decriminalization, and in 1973 gays and lesbians were allowed to enter the army while legal recognition was given to the COC; it had been withheld heretofore, because, it was feared, the organization would endanger marital life.

Most of the political struggle happened behind doors. The first demonstration was held in 1969 before parliament to demand the same age of consent for gay and straight. In 1971, gays interrupted the national Commemoration of the Second World War to call for attention to the gay victims. Since 1977 Pink Saturday is celebrated annually following the Stonewall example. Parades started in Amsterdam, and since 1980 they have come every year to another city. The number of participants is in general quite low, averaging fifteen thousand in a population of fifteen million, and declining.

When in 1983 in Amersfoort, the center of the Dutch Bible Belt, the parade faced gay and dyke bashing from local youth, the national press and politicians were alarmed. The government and local councils decided to start homosexual emancipation programs. The police force was requested not to raid gay places but to protect them. Gays and lesbians organized self-defense groups. The eighties represented a watershed. Political action had abolished in the seventies the mainstays of homosexual discrimination, and in the next decade, gay and lesbian emancipation was stimulated by political means. With the appearance of AIDS, preventive measures were taken by health authorities in close cooperation with the gay community. In 1993 an equal rights bill was enacted after sixteen years of fierce debate. In 1998 the right to adopt was accorded to lesbian and gay couples, while the last scrimmages on opening up marriage are taking place. About 5 percent of the members of parliament and of many city councils are openly gay or lesbian, but gay and lesbian topics are rarely on their agenda. The emancipatory efforts of the state erode a stagnating gay and lesbian movement that does not succeed in going beyond dated slogans of discrimination "that still exists in the provinces" and in formulating attractive and promising queer politics for the next century. Neither does it succeed in breaking open the straight ghetto that Holland still remains.   *Gert Hekma*

Bibliography

Hekma, Gert. "Amsterdam." In *Queer Sites. Gay Urban Histories since 1600.* David Higg, ed. New York: Routledge, 1999.

———. *Homoseksualiteit, een Medische Reputatie: De Uitdoktering van de Homoseksueel in Negentiende-eeuws Nederland.* Amsterdam: SUA, 1987.

Hekma, Gert Dorelies Kraakman, Maurice van Lieshout, and Jo Radersma, eds. *Goed verkeerd. Een geschiedenis van Homoseksuele Mannen en Lesbische Vrouwen in Nederland.* Amsterdam: Meulenhoff, 1989.

Ossewold, Jurriënne, and Paul Verstraeten. *Two of a Kind.* Amsterdam: Amsterdams Historisch Museum, 1989.

Tielman, Rob A. P. *Homoseksualiteit in Nederland. Studie van een Emancipatiebeweging.* Meppel: Boom, 1982.

van der Meer, Theo. *Sodoms Zaad in Nederland: Het Ontstaan van Homoseksualiteit in de Vroegmoderne Tijd.* Nijmegen: SUN, 1995.

van Naerssen, A. X., ed. *Interdisciplinary Research on Homosexuality in the Netherlands.* New York: Haworth, 1987.

See also Amsterdam; COC; Couperus, Louis; Crime and Criminality; France; Haan, Jacob Israël de; Psychological and Psychoanalytic Perspectives on Homosexuality; Sodomy; Stonewall

New York City

In 1646 the colony of New Netherland convicted "Jan Creoli, a negro," on charges of sodomy and ordered him "choked to death, and then burnt to ashes." Creoli's young sexual partner, Manuel Congo, was flogged. When the English took possession of New Netherland, changing its name to New York, they retained the death penalty for sodomy. After the American Revolution, New York reformed its legal code; homosexual behavior, while no longer a capital offense, remained illegal. Despite these inauspicious beginnings, New York City has emerged as an international center of gay culture and life.

In the nineteenth century, New York became the nation's largest metropolis, drawing hundreds of thousands of immigrants from the rural hinterland and abroad. Walt Whitman's poetry, filled with passionate praise of New York's workingmen, gives a vivid picture of the city's erotically charged landscape. Walking the streets of Brooklyn and Manhattan, Whitman reveled in the "frequent . . . swift flash of eyes offering me love"; his diary records his sexual encounters with the city's available men.

Among the city's large, unmarried male population homosexual activity seems to have been fairly common, though not necessarily connected to a gay identity. Only those men whose gender identity and performance were distinctly effeminate—men commonly known as "fairies"—were conceived of as constituting a sexual minority. Earl Lind, a self-described "androgyne" known as "Jennie June," claimed that "two-thirds" of New York's workingmen "would accommodate him provided their sexual needs were not fully met by normal intercourse—which is generally the case." For Lind and most of his contemporaries the world was divided into women, "normal" men, and "fairies," identities having more to do with gender than with same-sex behavior per se.

By the turn of the twentieth century the Bowery, a working-class entertainment district, had several dance halls where "fairies" and their sexual partners congregated. Eventually Greenwich Village, Times Square, and Harlem eclipsed the Bowery as the center of gay life in New York. The Village, where anarchist Emma Goldman gave the first public lectures on the subject of gay rights, attracted men who associated it with free love and wild living. The work of such writers as Claude McKay, whose novel *Home to Harlem* contains a vivid scene of a bar where "luxuriating under the little colored lights, the dark dandies were loving up their pansies," documents the sexual culture of the Harlem Renaissance.

Increasingly, and especially among middle-class men influenced by psychological theories of sexual identity, a new sense of self, one dependent on same-sex desire and not necessarily on gender inversion, developed. Rather than having sex with "normal" men or "fairies," these men coupled among themselves. Writing to his lover, F. O. Matthiessen spoke movingly of his embrace of this sense of difference: "Oh, the majesty," he wrote, "of knowing what you are . . . of having admitted that you and I are born unlike the majority and yet have found . . . love." The distinction Matthiessen makes between a "homosexual" minority, which includes both him and his lover, and a "heterosexual" majority assumed to have no interest in other men has gained increasing salience.

World War II acted as a precipitating agent in the construction of a gay community in the city. New York was flooded with men. Bob Ruffing recalls gay parties that "got to be a little wild, because the war spirit was starting to invade everything." Along with new freedoms came new forms of regulation. World War II was the first time that the armed forces instituted a policy of "screening" homosexuals from service. In the postwar period, President Eisenhower extended this ban to all government employees and contractors.

In the 1950s and 1960s, a rapid increase in the number of gay bars was paralleled by the growth of a political consciousness among gay men. The government's homophobic regulations meant that gay rights activists had clearly discriminatory policies to protest against. In 1955, a local branch of the Mattachine Society was formed in New York. By the mid-1960s the group had about 450 members. Despite these advances, bars were subjected to periodic police raids and many men hid themselves in the closet. Gay men, as Martin Duberman remembers, lived an "active *underground* . . . life" bound by a homophobic climate of intimidation and social opprobrium.

The Stonewall riots of June 1969 mark the symbolic end to the reign of the closet. "For me," Edmund White recalls, "New York Gay life in the seventies came as a completely new beginning." Over the next two decades, the illicit economy of the preliberationist period shed its cultivated invisibility. Gay activists facilitated this transformation by challenging and overturning discriminatory laws and practices. Changes in obscenity laws meant that pornography and gay literature became widely available and sex clubs could operate openly. Organizations such as the Lambda Legal Defense Fund and the Gay and Lesbian Alliance Against Defamation were formed, and by 1984 a Gay Community Services Center opened, offering meeting space to hundreds of affinity groups and political clubs.

Following changes in immigration policy in the mid-1960s, gay life in New York was greatly transformed by the arrival of large numbers of people from the Caribbean, Asia, and Latin America. While some of these men identified themselves with the gay community, many immigrants did not share the same sexual cultural values as assimilated, native-born citizens. Some Filipino men, for example, used sexual terminology and self-identifiers from their birth culture. The founding of organizations such as Kambal sa Lusog, a Filipino group organized in 1991, the name of which can be translated as "comrades in the struggle," reflects the way in which different populations in New York have carved out identities that bridge their ethnicity and their place in the city's gay social world.

In 1981 AIDS hit the gay male community with deadly force, and grassroots organizations developed to serve the needs of New York's HIV-positive men and women. The Gay Men's Health Crisis and ACT UP (AIDS Coalition to Unleash Power) both agitated for increased resources to meet the epidemic. The militant spirit of AIDS activists transformed local politics, leading to the election of gay and lesbian officials and the establishment of city agencies like the Office of Gay and Lesbian Health Concerns. By the 1990s improved medical treatment and the adoption of safe-sex practices offered new hope for New York City's gay community.   *Terence Kissack*

Bibliography

Berube, Allan. *Coming Out Under Fire: The History of Gay Men and Women in World War Two*. New York: Free Press, 1990.

Chauncey, George. *Gay New York: Gender, Urban Culture, and the Makings of the Gay Male World, 1890–1940*. New York: Basic Books, 1994.

Duberman, Martin. *Cures: A Gay Man's Odyssey*. New York: Dutton, 1991.

Kaiser, Charles. *The Gay Metropolis, 1940–1996*. New York: Houghton Mifflin, 1997.

Katz, Jonathan Ned. *Gay and Lesbian Almanac: A New Documentary*. New York: Harper and Row, 1983.

Manalansan, Martin F. IV. "Searching for Community: Filipino Gay Men in New York City." In *Asian American Sexualties: Dimensions of the Gay and Lesbian Experience*. Russell Leong, ed. New York: Routledge, 1996.

White, Edmund. "Fantasia on the Seventies." In *The Christopher Street Reader*. Michael Denneny, Charles Ortleb, and Thomas Steele, eds. New York: Coward-McCann, 1983.

See also ACT UP; AIDS; Bathhouses and Sex Clubs; Colonial America; Gay Men's Health Crisis (GMHC); Gay and Lesbian Alliance Against Defamation (GLAAD); Mattachine Society; Matthiessen, F.O.; McCarthyism; McKay, Claude; Stonewall; United States; White, Edmund; Whitman, Walt

New Zealand

Aotearoa—"Land of the Long White Cloud"—comprises two main islands and is situated in the South Pacific, with a population of 3,428,000 and a temperate climate. It is known for its rugged and varied geographic terrain; the friendliness of its people; and its clean, green, nonnuclear image.

Its first inhabitants were the Maori (*tangata whenua*), who arrived centuries before the European explorers. The subsequent partnership between the races was recognized in the Treaty of Waitangi, signed in 1840. Pre-European history shows no animosity toward same-sex relationships.

New Zealand's Maori record the legend of Hinemoa, who swam across Lake Taupo to take Tutanekai from his lover (*takataapui*), Tiki. The first recorded incidents of Europeans involving same-sex relationships were often sensational. In 1836 the Reverend William Yate was expelled from New Zealand for "scandalous practices" (*tiitoitoi*) with young Maori men. Most often, because of severe criminal penalties, the subject was surrounded by fear and silence.

The first punitive legislation affecting gay men was brought from England when the colony was established in the early 1800s. The death penalty for buggery was abolished in 1861. The Labouchère Amendment criminalized all same-sex male activity but left women out of the legislative provisions because it was believed that they were incapable of committing such acts. It specified up to ten years imprisonment with hard labor—along with flogging and whipping—for any indecency.

The law remained largely unchanged and unchallenged until 1957, when the British Wolfenden Committee, after two years' study, recommended the "decriminalization of homosexual acts between consenting adults in private." This report intensified the demand for changes in the New Zealand law.

The brutal murder of a gay man, Charles Aberhart, in a Christchurch Park in 1963 by six young men later acquitted of manslaughter provided the impetus for public debate necessary to increase public support.

Active supporters of change were the New Zealand Homosexual Law Reform Society, founded in Wellington in 1967; Gay Liberation Groups in the three main cities in 1972; and the National Gay Rights Coalition, networking throughout the country in 1977. These groups, as well as prominent individuals, worked vigorously for over two decades before a Labour member of Parliament, Fran Wilde, introduced the Homosexual Law Reform Bill in 1985.

A bitter struggle followed, and a national petition opposing the decriminalization, primarily organized by conservative religious groups, was presented with 810,000 signatures (only 350,000 of which were finally validated). Despite this, the law was passed 49 to 44 on July 9, 1986, with an age of consent of sixteen with no exemptions. The antidiscriminatory human rights legislation was defeated, but when reintroduced in July 1993, it passed with no special exemptions—in education or for the army or the police force.

Consequential changes in the law now allow New Zealand citizens to bring their same-sex de facto partners into the country, and the continuing national debate centers on the legal recognition of same-sex marriages, parental status, and the creation of positive learning and working environments for gay men.

The 1996 election brought a center coalition and a divided country. Gay-friendly parties gained significant support, and the number of "friendly" members of Parliament increased greatly. Despite a hostile campaign from the Christian Coalition (a right-wing fundamentalist group), it gained only 4 percent of the vote and failed to break the 5 percent threshold to elect any members of Parliament.

There are only a few specialist national gay organizations but a large number of local social and activist groups. Several individuals are prominent in these gay rights groups. One of the most influential groups is the New Zealand AIDS Foundation, a publicly funded government health body that played an important role in promoting and supporting antidiscriminatory changes since its foundation in 1984.

Legislative changes have brought an improved social climate for gay men and lesbians, and the gay community is thriving in major urban areas. The established commercial scene is expanding, and there is an increasing alternative culture. A wide range of services and special-interest and support groups exist to cater to the increasingly visible numbers of gay partners.

Auckland, situated in the subtropical north, is nationally known as the "Queen City." With over a million people, it has the largest and most prominent gay community in the country. Its focus is the suburb of Ponsonby, in the central city, where large numbers of gays live and where the clubs and bars are most active and most heavily concentrated. Their major festival, parade, and dance party, called Hero, is held in early February to link with other New Zealand lesbian and gay festivals and the Sydney, Australia, Mardi Gras.

The "Windy City" is Wellington, with a quarter of a million people. It is also the political capital, with a circular parliamentary building popularly described as "The Beehive." The city is home to a large number of civic, government, and business networks. The smaller but active gay community enjoys a city often at the forefront of many of the political changes that have occurred. Their major festival is Devotion, also held in February.

Christchurch, the "Garden City," on the banks of the Avon River, is the only other major urban center. It has a quarter of a million people, is situated on the South Island, and is the most English of New Zealand cities, with its own cathedral. It is also an active political and social center. Freedom, the southern festival, is a February celebration.

Robin Duff

Bibliography

Millett, A.P.U. *Bibliography on Homosexuality in New Zealand*. Hamilton, New Zealand: University of Waikato Library, 1995.

See also Australia; Sydney Gay and Lesbian Mardi Gras; Wolfenden Report

Nicolson, Harold (1886–1968)

Harold Nicolson's life was more decisively defined by his diplomatic career, his writing, and his marriage than by his homosexual experience. Nicolson entered the Foreign Office in 1909 and served with brilliance at various overseas posts and several international peace conferences, but his independent thinking and distaste for the more coercive side of politics prevented him from reaching the top ranks of diplomacy, which he abandoned in 1929. He held a seat in Parliament between 1935 and 1945, and later dedicated himself entirely to his marriage and writing. Nicolson published over 125 books, including biographies of poets and politicians, political essays, travel accounts, memoirs, and fiction, but none of them dealt substantially with homosexuality. He was knighted in 1953 for his official biography of George V, and his books on diplomacy and European politics between the world wars are still considered among the best of their kind.

Nicolson married Vita Sackville-West in 1913, but their marriage was based on shared values and mutual support, rather than sexual fidelity. According to one of their two sons, for them the marriage was "a harbor," and love affairs "mere ports of call." Nicolson had many "ports of call" among men of his own class as well as with men of the lower classes. He was apparently never bothered by his homosexual activity, believing that it should not be taken too seriously, but he was strongly repulsed by gender deviations, such as effeminacy and transvestism. His biographer's homophobic dismissal of Nicolson's "casual flings" with men that "meant no more to him than a bee's pollination of a foxglove" (Lees-Milne 58) is not entirely inaccurate, because Nicolson was a man for whom same-sex affinities and experiences never amounted to a homosexual identity and were no cause for political engagement.

Dejan Kuzmanovic

Bibliography

Lees-Milne, James. *Harold Nicolson: A Biography.* 2 vols. Hamden, U.K.: Archon Books, 1982.
Nicolson, Nigel. *Portrait of a Marriage.* New York: Atheneum, 1980.

See also Bloomsbury Group

Nijinsky, Vaslav Fomich (1889–1950)

Nijinsky was a Russian-trained dancer and choreographer whose technical prowess and exotic stage presence made him a star of early Ballets Russes seasons in Paris and London (1909–1913), and whose four choreographic works blazed new artistic trails in an atmosphere of scandal and invention on the eve of European modernism. Born in Kiev to itinerant Polish dancers, Nijinsky was trained at the Imperial Theatre School in St. Petersburg before joining the Maryinsky (later Kirov) Ballet, where he had early successes partnering the company's highest-ranking ballerinas. In his subsequent work with the Ballets Russes, a troupe taken to the West by impresario Sergey Diaghilev, Nijinsky first became known for his spectacular leap and his enigmatic and powerful sensuality in such roles as the Spirit of the Rose in *Le Spectre de la Rose* and the Golden Slave in *Schéhérazade.*

Encouraged to become a choreographer by Diaghilev, his mentor and lover, Nijinsky produced radically new ballets that shocked audiences of the time with their departures from classical ballet vocabulary and themes. In his two most famous pieces, meticulously reconstructed from historical evidence since the late 1980s, Nijinsky did away with balletic virtuosity in favor of mood: *Prélude l'Après-midi d'un Faune* (1912, Debussy) explored voyeurism and sexual awakening in dreamlike tempo and profile positions that recalled Greek vases or Egyptian reliefs; and *Le Sacre du Printemps* (1913, Stravinsky) evoked volatile primeval forces and human sacrifice using angular and turned-in postures, shivers, foot stamping, and blank-faced circling. The less spectacular *Jeux* (1912, Debussy), a trio of two women and one man, combined the idea of playing sexual games and tennis at the same time.

The sexual ambiguity found in many of Nijinsky's performances and choreographies has been related to his private life. For Diaghilev scholar Lynn Garafola, *Faune* showed "Nijinsky the overt homosexual" declaring himself "a covert heterosexual," before the autoerotic final gesture confirmed that he was "torn between the power of his lust and the fear of its consequences [opting for] the safe haven of self-gratification" (Garafola 57). In *Sacre*, which premiered just months before Nijinsky unexpectedly married a woman he barely knew, Garafola sees the Chosen Maiden's death as a representation of the demise of Nijinsky's own "ambisexual youth" (Garafola 71). Audiences could draw their own conclusions. During Nijinsky's lifetime, dance scholar Ramsay Burt points out, Nijinsky's "heterodox representations of masculinity" could appeal to radical and conservative factions alike, since his genius and presumed exotic "Russian-ness" exempted him from prevailing gender norms of the time, and his sensual charisma attracted viewers of various sexual persuasions.

Nijinsky's great period of creativity came to an end with his marriage in 1913 to Polish socialite Romola de Pulszky, his subsequent dismissal from the Ballets Russes, and his deteriorating mental health. He briefly rejoined the Ballets Russes in 1916, making his last ballet, *Tyl Eulenspiegel,* on an American tour. Advancing schizophrenia debilitated him until his death from kidney failure in a London hospital on April 8, 1950. His legend has, if anything, grown since then: Burt points to Nijinsky's key role in bringing the male dancer back to European stages after an era of decline and setting a standard of dynamic technical dancing for all male dancers who followed. Burt also notes that the many images of Nijinsky in revealing costumes inspired a new genre of homoerotic visual art. His ballets have now been considered forerunners of both modernism and postmodernism in dance, as well as prototypes for ballet neoclassicism. As Garafola notes, Nijinsky had shown "that ballet could generate styles of expression as powerfully imagined, deeply personal, and vitally contemporary as those of the other arts."

Jennifer Fisher

Bibliography

Burt, Ramsay. *The Male Dancer: Bodies, Spectacle, Sexualities.* London: Routledge, 1995.

Garafola, Lynn. *Diaghilev's Ballets Russes.* New York: Oxford University Press, 1989.

See also Ballets Russes; Dance: Concert Dance in America; Diaghilev, Sergey; Russia

Novo, Salvador (1904–1974)

Poet, playwright, and essayist Salvador Novo was born in Mexico City. Fleeing the 1910 revolution, his family returned in 1916, but soon after his father died. Novo enrolled in the National Preparatory School and rented a downtown apartment with fellow students; nicknamed "The Girls of Donceles Street," they raised money hustling.

Novo wrote his first poem at eleven. *Ulysis*, a magazine he edited, published a group known as Contemporaneos. Novo's first poetry book, *XX poemas* (1925), disguised his homosexuality: "so sad this mascarade." He soon opened up: *Espejo, Poemas antiguos* (1933): "Loving's this timid silence." *Nuevo amor* (1933) led to a friendship with Federico García Lorca, who provided drawings for *Seamen Rhymes* (1934), celebrating a merchant marine named Buster. Novo's *Romance de Angelillo y Adela* (1934) compared Lorca to a little eagle and Novo to Adela, whose love overcomes her.

Openness about his sexuality brought dismissal from the Department of Education. Proletarians denounced his homosexuality, and Novo responded with *Poemas proletarios* (1934), celebrating working men. Novo favored taxi drivers and brought Jean Genet to the Mexican stage. He wrote travel books on Hawai'i (1928), Mexico (1933, 1947), South America (1935), and other journeys (1951). His novel *El joven* (1928) attempted to do in short scope for Mexico City what Joyce had done for Dublin; some of that spirit went into his popular *New Grandeur* (1946).

In 1946 Novo received appointment as Fine Arts Institute theater director. In 1928, he and Xavier Villaurrutia had operated an experimental theater that for two seasons stunned Mexico with translations of Ibsen, O'Neill, Wilde, Cocteau, and others. Novo himself wrote many plays: *The Woman Cult* (1951), *Eight Columns* (1956), *Yocasta, o casi* (Yo Virgin, or almost, 1961), *Cauhtémoc* (1962), *The War of the Fatties* (1963), and *The Enchanted Mirror* (1966). His gayest play, *Faust, Part III,* was published by the 69 Press (Paris, 1934).

Named official chronicler of Mexico City and elected to the Mexican Academy, Novo received a literary prize from President Díaz-Ordaz in 1967. For the Olympic Games in 1968, Novo designed a light show at the Tenochtitlán archaeological site. The government, however, lost credit after killing between forty and four hundred demonstrators at a student demonstration in Tlatelolco. Novo publicly defended the president, but in "Adam Nude," one of his last poems, he privately supported the students. Novo died January 13, 1974; a "Memoir" of his gay life first appeared in 1979, published by the Gay Sunshine Press, and was reprinted in July 1980 in the Mexican gay periodical *Nuestro cuerpo.* A museum is now dedicated to Novo in Mexico City, and a conference in 1994 marked publication of the first three volumes of his complete works.

Charles Shively

Bibliography

Acero, Rosa María. "Novo Ante Novo: Un Novisimo Personaje Homosexual." Ph.D. diss., University of California, Santa Barbara, 1998.

Novo, Salvador. *The War of the Fatties and Other Stories from Aztec History.* Trans. with introduction and bibliography by Michael Alderson. Austin, Texas: University of Texas Press, 1994.

See also García Lorca, Federico; Genet, Jean; Mexico; Villaurrutia, Xavier; Wilde, Oscar

Nureyev, Rudolf Hametovich (1938–1993)

Rudolf Nureyev was a Russian-trained dancer and choreographer of Tartar background whose brilliant

N and often stormy international career in the West also included restaging ballet classics for many major companies, as well as the artistic directorship of the Paris Opera Ballet from 1983 to 1989. He faced strong obstacles on his way to becoming one of the most famous dancers of this century. Raised in poverty in Ufa, a town in the Ural Mountains far from the dance mecca of Leningrad (St. Petersburg), Nureyev first began dancing in a folk troupe, despite the strong protests of his father, a government worker. At seventeen, with little ballet training and a lot of nerve, he circumvented bureaucratic red tape and on his own managed to gain admittance to the Vaganova Choreographic Institute, the school of the Kirov Ballet. A talented and sometimes brutish loner in a rush to improve his skills, Nureyev was not popular with his fellow students or the faculty—with the important exception of his most influential teacher, the renowned Alexander Pushkin.

Nureyev joined the Kirov Ballet as a soloist in 1958. His ascent was meteoric but nearly catastrophic: as a singularly gifted individualist who did not deal diplomatically with the ballet hierarchy or with Communist Party officials, Nureyev regularly clashed with authorities of all stripes. His homosexuality, which then would have been punishable by internal exile or death, was providing his enemies with as much ammunition as they needed. Recently available KGB files indicate that when Nureyev defected in 1961 at a Paris airport, there was more at stake for him than just artistic freedom.

In the West, Nureyev's dramatic escape and brooding sensuality, paired with his virtuosic technique and daring style, almost immediately launched him into a kind of pop star status. His defection and subsequent partnership with the Royal Ballet's reigning ballerina, Margot Fonteyn, first got him into the public eye, and his constant globe-trotting guest appearances with major ballet companies kept him there, as did his many television appearances on variety shows, dance specials, and on one occasion, the news, when he and Fonteyn were arrested while attending a party at which marijuana was found. Like Nijinsky, Nureyev seemed to have had a sexual allure that seduced many audiences. With his animal-like athleticism and legions of female fans, he was said to be making the dance world safe for ballet-phobic men, while at the same time his icon status in the gay community grew. His rampant libido and visits to the baths were an open secret to insiders, so much so that a biography published after his death features a chapter called "The Great Gay Myth: 'I Slept with Nureyev'" (Stuart).

Nureyev's legacy to the ballet world is multifold. He is credited with improving the lot of male ballet dancers significantly, first by inspiring them to more bold characterizations with his dancing (he ate up the scenery with his signature solo from *Le Corsaire* and left burning impressions of characters from princes to fools), and eventually with new stagings of classics (such as *The Sleeping Beauty* and *The Nutcracker*). His gifts to the many ballet companies with which he worked were improved standards, visibility, inspiration, and repertoire; they were much appreciated, even when tempered with his often blunt manner and legendary temper tantrums. Though he branched out into choreography (*Washington Square*, a version of *Cinderella*), acting on film (*Valentino*) and stage (*The King and I*), and even conducted an orchestra toward the end of his life, he could not bring himself to leave dancing and performed long past the time when he could have gracefully stopped. Nor could he bring himself to admit that he was mortal, denying his diagnosis of AIDS until the end. Nureyev died in Paris on January 6, 1993.   *Jennifer Fisher*

Bibliography

Stuart, Otis. *Perpetual Motion: The Public and Private Lives of Rudolf Nureyev*. New York: Plume/Penguin, 1996.

See also Ballet (British); Dance and AIDS; Dance: Concert Dance in America; Nijinsky, Vaslav Fomich; Russia

O'Hara, Frank (1926–1966)

Born in Baltimore, Frank O'Hara moved with his family to Grafton, Massachusetts, in 1927 and was educated in private schools there until 1944. He served a two-year term in the navy and then began college at Harvard University as a music major. After changing his degree to English and receiving a B.A. in 1950, he completed an M.A. at the University of Michigan in 1951. At Michigan O'Hara's writing career began to coalesce. He won the university's prestigious Hopwood Award in Creative Writing and also crafted two plays, *Try! Try!* and *Change Your Bedding*, which were mounted at the Poet's Theatre in Cambridge, Massachusetts.

O'Hara's early national reputation was secured as art critic, not poet. After graduation he gained a position at the Museum of Modern Art (MoMA) in New York City. From 1953 to 1954 he left the museum to serve as associate editor of *Art News*, but then returned as special assistant to the MoMA International Project. In 1960 he was promoted to curator of painting and sculpture. O'Hara's influence in the art world is widely credited with drawing international attention to the abstract expressionists of the 1960s, and in particular Jackson Pollock. O'Hara's study of Pollock for George Braziller's Great American Artists Series is still generally considered to be the central work about the artist. Other artistic studies O'Hara published during this period covered the topics of contemporary Spanish art, Robert Motherwell, David Smith, and Nakian.

O'Hara's career as a poet is interwoven with his career in the art world. His first major collection, *A City Winter and Other Poems* (1952), was published by the Tibor de Nagy Gallery. His poetry manifests a profound concern with issues of surrealism and with techniques of dadaist collage and montage. *Stones* (1958) is a series of poems that elucidate original lithographs by the artist Larry Rivers. *Odes* (1960) is a joint presentation of O'Hara's poems and Mike Goldberg's serigraphs. In his role as champion of the New York avant-garde, O'Hara also coproduced two experimental films with Al Leslie, *The Last Clean Shirt* (1963) and *Philosophy in the Bedroom* (1965).

O'Hara's reputation grew from his ties with the art world, but his continued popularity and importance have been due mostly to his early embrace of pop culture as an inspiration for poetry. His topics and imagery frequently derive from the daily life of urban gay male culture. "The Day Lady Died," one of O'Hara's most famous poems, depicts the precise instant when O'Hara heard that singer Billie Holiday had died. The title is a pun on Holiday's popular name, "Lady Day." "Biotherm (For Bill Berkson)," a long collage poem, combines images of Fire Island, a popular gay retreat near New York City, with things as varied as classical music, Hollywood cinema, and restaurant menus. The title "Biotherm" was a brand of popular sun screen.

O'Hara died on July 25, 1966, the result of a freak dune buggy accident on Fire Island. Although he is largely unknown today, O'Hara's influence lives on. John Ashbery, Kenneth Koch, Ned Rorem, and Allen Ginsberg, to name a few, all acknowledge their debt to O'Hara's poetry. *Gregory W. Bredbeck*

Bibliography

Altieri, Charles. "The Significance of Frank O'Hara." *Iowa Review* 4 (Winter 1973): 90–104.

Berkson, Bill, and Joe LeSueur, eds. *Homage to Frank O'Hara*. Bolinas, Calif.: Big Sky, 1988.

O

Bredbeck, Gregory W. "B/O—Barthes's Text/ O'Hara's Trick." *PMLA* 108 (1993): 268–82.

Elledge, Jim, ed. *Frank O'Hara: To Be True to a City*. Ann Arbor, Mich.: University of Michigan Press, 1990.

Gooch, Brad. *City Poet: The Life and Times of Frank O'Hara*. New York: Knopf, 1993.

Holahan, Susan. "Frank O'Hara's Poetry." In *American Poetry Since 1960: Some Critical Prespectives*. Robert B. Shaw, ed. Cheadle Hulme: Carcanet Press, 1973, 109–22.

Perloff, Marjorie. *Frank O'Hara: Poet Among Painters*. Austin, Texas: University of Texas Press, 1977.

See also Art History; Ashbery, John; Ginsberg, Allen; Rorem, Ned; U.S. Literature

ONE Magazine

The first widely distributed gay publication in the United States was *ONE* magazine, founded in Los Angeles in 1953. The monthly publication was produced by a group of gay men who had begun meeting to discuss gay issues and then decided to broaden their conversation to a larger audience. The idea of publishing the magazine is generally attributed to Dale Jennings, and Martin Block was the first editor. The driving force behind *ONE*, however, was W. Dorr Legg, the magazine's business manager and major financial benefactor. The editors opted not to work directly with the Mattachine Society, the country's first gay organization, also based in Los Angeles, but created ONE, Inc., to oversee the magazine as well as operate a library of material about homosexuality. By the end of the decade, *ONE* boasted a national circulation of five thousand.

Personal essays dominated *ONE*'s editorial content, with topics including such provocative issues as gay marriage and the ethics of promiscuity. *ONE*'s tone was best described as progressive rather than radical. In addition to essays, the magazine contained short stories, poems, book reviews, and descriptions of research projects that pertained to gay men. The editorial mix did not include homoerotic images or "four-letter" words. News content initially was minuscule, as the editors had no national network of gay-oriented news to tap into. As the magazine became established, however, news editor Jim Kepner encouraged readers to send him relevant news items that he then reprinted.

From its first issue, *ONE* was typeset and well designed, highlighted with clean, modern drawings. The magazine measured five and a half inches by eight and a half inches and generally contained twenty to thirty pages.

ONE magazine's most historic accomplishment began in October 1954 when postal officials confiscated that month's issue, calling it obscene and lascivious. Legg and the other editors hired a lawyer and fought to continue their publication. Even though they lost in appeals court, they took their case to the U.S. Supreme Court. In January 1958, the justices unanimously reversed the decision of the lower courts. The landmark decision established that gay publications had the right to be distributed through the mail, giving the fledgling gay liberation movement its only major victory of the decade.

By the mid-1960s, however, *ONE* began to suffer from internal disputes among its editors as well as a failure to embrace the movement's new militancy. From the founding of ONE, Inc., Legg had been primarily interested not in publishing the magazine but in building the organization's library. In 1965, Don Slater, then *ONE*'s editor, began publishing a second and competing version of the magazine, also titled *ONE*. Legg went to court and, as director of the corporation, won the exclusive right to the name. Slater then renamed his magazine *Tangents*.

The ideological stances of both magazines were eclipsed by those of a new generation of gay magazines founded in the 1960s. *ONE* ceased publication in December 1969, and *Tangents* folded a few months later.   *Rodger Streitmatter*

Bibliography

Streitmatter, Rodger. *Unspeakable: The Rise of the Gay and Lesbian Press in America*. Boston: Faber and Faber, 1995.

See also Gay and Lesbian Press; Homophile Movement; Mattachine Society

Opera

The generic term for musical dramas that, with few exceptions, are entirely sung. Invented within the milieu of Neoplatonic Italian Renaissance humanism, opera from its beginning has accorded an important place to various kinds of sexual complexity; Monteverdi's *Orfeo*, for instance, closes with a homoerotic duet between Orpheus and his father,

Apollo. But the most important documented source of queerness in seventeenth-century opera came from the participation of the castrati, male sopranos and altos who had been castrated before puberty and trained rigorously as virtuoso singers. The operation, normally involving only a minor incision in the back of the scrotum, produced unusual physical characteristics, including enlarged chest and lungs and disproportionately long limbs. The castrati were said to have voices of enormous range and power; their intense training ensured immense vocal athleticism as well, and many accounts stress the stunning impact of their performances. Castrati were used in opera by the mid-seventeenth century for both male and female roles in Italian opera (male roles being written preferentially for soprano voice); this gender-bending was cause for complaint by morally anxious critics but unquestionably contributed heavily to the popularity of opera. By the eighteenth century, the greatest castrati became international sensations on the order of modern rock stars, commanding adulation and vast salaries. During the entire period the castrati were in vogue, an elaborate sexual mythos circulated around them. (Modern conceptions of the castrati tend to speculate even more on their sexual nature.)

Baroque opera in general strikes modern listeners as abstract and ceremonial; its characteristic dramaturgies emphasized discrete numbers strung together to create a plot. The genre of opera seria, where the castrati were most extensively employed, usually depended on a strong contrast between recitative, speechlike music with minimal melodic character and accompaniment that served to advance plot, and aria, expansively melodic and ornate numbers that explored in depth emotional states. Plots were vaguely based on ancient history or mythology and the conflict between love and politics. The genre of opera buffa, which grew up during the eighteenth century, by contrast, seldom used castrati, favored musical ensembles as well as solo arias, and often explored domestic comic plots.

The sexual attachments of most important seventeenth- and eighteenth-century opera composers are mostly obscure. Jean-Baptiste Lully, the dominant figure of French baroque opera, was so publicaly involved in homosexual relationships that he was censured by Louis XIV (Lully lost none of his terrifying control over French musical life, however). Recent research suggests ever more strongly that George Frideric Handel associated with aristocratic homosexual circles in Rome and England.

Although the castrati virtually disappeared from the operatic stage by the beginning of the nineteenth century, much of their glamour was transferred to the figure of the diva. The various romantic styles that largely superseded opera seria and opera buffa tended to place female figures in fraught sexual situations. Sexual transgressions such as incest, miscegenation, rape, and adultery call forth striking displays of vocal virtuosity so that the singers, their roles, and their music become sources of the transport earlier associated with the castrati. The cultural power of this style of opera, intertwined with a host of sexual ambiguities, is amply attested to by innumerable writers, and much of the style as well as the habits of its listeners continues to the present day. It is likely, for instance, that the kind of fanship associated with modern-day opera queens dates from the listening habits of nineteenth-century audiences.

Although little is known about the sex lives of nineteenth-century opera composers, much research remains to be done. Richard Wagner, although extravagantly involved with women, exhibited such strong homosocial ties to other men as to make his sexuality questionable to contemporaries as well as later writers.

Of indubitably gay opera composers, the most significant are Modest Petrovich Mussorgsky and Pyotr Ilich Thaikovsky. The documented number of gay, bisexual, and otherwise homophile opera composers increased dramatically in the twentieth century, whether because of greater ability to be out, simple accessibility of information, or the various shifts in musical life that occurred over the course of the century. Heading the list is Benjamin Britten, most of whose works take complex approaches to issues raised by sexual identity. Other more or less openly gay composers of opera in the twentieth century include Samuel Barber, Marc Blitzstein, Lou Harrison, Hans Werner Henze, Thomas Pasatieri, Francis Poulenc, Karol Szymanowski, and Michael Tippett.   *Mitchell Morris*

Bibliography

Blackmur, Corinne E., and Patricia Juliana Smith. *En Travesti: Women, Gender Subversion, Opera.* New York: Columbia University Press, 1995.

Disch, Thomas. *On Wings of Song.* New York: Carroll and Graf, 1988.

McClary, Susan. "Gender Ambiguities and Erotic Excess in Seventeenth-Century Venetian Opera." In *Actualizing Absence: Performance, Visuality, Writing.* Mark Franko and Anne Richards, eds.

O

Hanover, N.H.: Wesleyan University Press, forthcoming.

Rees, David. *Words and Music*. Brighton, U.K.: Millivres Books, 1994.

Rice, Ann. *Cry to Heaven*. Reprint. New York: Pinnacle, 1995.

See also Barber, Samuel; Blitzstein, Marc; Britten, Benjamin; Handel, George Frideric; Harrison, Lou; Henze, Hans Werner; Lully, Jean-Baptiste; Poulenc, Francis; Szymanowski, Karol; Tchaikovsky; Tippett, Sir Michael Kemp; Wagner and Wagnerism

Opera Queens

Opera queen is originally a camp term for a gay opera fan of a notably extravagant type. Opera has a long history of standing in a strikingly queer relationship to other high musical genres, particularly with respect to English-language traditions of musical commentary. Dr. Johnson's eighteenth-century description of opera as "an exotick and irrational entertainment" is but the most famous example. And much opera displays a high degree of nonconformity with respect to gender relations and sexual expression—for example, the long vogue for castrati in baroque opera, a variety of gender-bending roles appearing throughout the genre's history, the common presence of sexual transgressions such as miscegenation, incest, and prostitution in nineteenth- and twentieth-century opera—suggesting that opera has nearly always been available as potential cultural support to sexual dissidents among its audience.

The stereotypical opera queen has usually been held to be obsessed with all aspects of opera to a degree bordering on mania, and particularly mad for sopranos; the cults surrounding such figures as Maria Callas and Joan Sutherland are prime locations for hunting opera queens, although canvassing the fandom of most sopranos will certainly turn up at least a few of them. These diva cults share many features with those surrounding Hollywood figures like Bette Davis and Joan Crawford, as well as popular music icons such as Judy Garland and Barbra Streisand. While the attitudes of stars and fans owe an incalculable debt to nineteenth-century styles of opera worship, their histories in the twentieth century have in turn molded the attitudes of opera queens to the extent that all three forms of diva worship tend to share the same stances.

Until the 1970s, opera queens were chiefly known through gay oral tradition. With the rise of post-Stonewall gay publications, literary representations emerged in journalism as well as fiction and theater. Some gay critics, such as "Tessi Tura" in the *Advocate*, began to write music reviews from points of view associated with opera queens. Ethan Mordden's books on opera also display opera-queenish attitudes. Albert Innaurato's play *Gemini* (1977) featured as its main character a young opera queen in the making, and his short story "Solidarity" follows a small circle of opera queens through various clashes with more mainstream gay culture. Charles Ludlam based his play *Galas* (1983) on a carnivalesque interpretation of Maria Callas. But Terrence McNally's play *The Lisbon Traviata* (1989) was the most responsible for bringing the figure of the opera queen into general view from a literary standpoint. Since then, opera has taken on increasing resonance as a trope for gay male sexuality: the most widely known example of this is Tom Hanks's interpretation of a performance by Maria Callas in the 1993 film *Philadelphia*. The term *opera queen* has also in recent years become an active site of speculation on the cultural work performed by representations of gay male subjectivity.   *Mitchell Morris*

Bibliography

Bronski, Michael. "Opera: Mad Queens and Other Divas." In *Culture Clash: The Making of Gay Sensibility.* Boston: South End Press, 1984, 134–43.

Innaurato, Albert. "Gemini." *In The Best Plays of Albert Innaurato*. With an introduction by the author. New York: Gay Presses of New York, 1987.

———. "Solidarity." In *Men on Men 2*. George Stambolian, ed. New York: New American Library, 1988, 87–118.

Koestenbaum, Wayne. *The Queen's Throat: Opera, Homosexuality, and the Mystery of Desire.* New York: Poseidon Press, 1993.

Ludlam, Charles. "Galas." In *The Complete Plays.* New York: Harper and Row, 1989.

McNally, Terrence. "The Lisbon Traviata." In *Three Plays by Terrence McNally*. With an introduction by the playwright. New York: Plume, 1990, 1–88.

Mordden, Ethan. *Demented: The World of the Opera Diva.* New York: Franklin Watts, 1984.

———. *Opera Anecdotes.* New York: Oxford University Press, 1985.

Morris, Mitchell. "Admiring the Countess Geschwitz." In *En Travesti: Women, Gender Subversion, Opera.* Corrine E. Blackmur and Patricia Juliana Smith, eds. New York: Columbia University Press, 1995, 348–70.

———. "On Gaily Reading Music." *Repercussions* 1, no. 1 (1992): 48–64.

———. "Reading as an Opera Queen." In *Musicology and Difference: Gender and Sexuality in Musical Scholarship*. Ruth A. Solie, ed. Berkeley: University of California Press, 1993, 184–200.

Robinson, Paul. "The Opera Queen: A Voice from the Closet." *Cambridge Opera Journal* 6, no. 3 (1994). 283–91.

See also Camp; Film Stars; Ludlam, Charles; McNally, Terrence; Musical Theater; Opera; Theater

Oppression

The concept of oppression was strongly associated with the leftist analyses that became central to gay liberation movements from the end of the 1960s on and that signaled an emphasis on social structures as distinct from psychological maladjustment. Gay liberation argued that there was no inherent problem in homosexuality but rather that its stigma was the result of certain social institutions and ideologies that required direct political confrontation. As Rosa von Praunheim put it (in a film of that name): "It is not the homosexual who is perverse, but the society in which he lives."

Oppression takes a number of forms, ranging from direct physical attacks on those who are—or are perceived to be—homosexual, through much more subtle means whereby homosexuality is presented as less acceptable than homosexuality. There is a clear difference between vigilante attack on "fags" and the 1996 Defense of Marriage Act, yet both result from a set of social beliefs that maintain the ideology of heterosexuality as the norm against which homosexuality is seen as deviant, less acceptable, and undesirable.

Oppression has a somewhat different meaning from *repression*, more accurately used in its psychoanalytic meaning, and *suppression*, which in psychological language implies a conscious rather than unconscious action, although the three terms overlap in common usage. Gay liberation theorists such as Guy Hocquenghem, Dennis Altman, and Mario Mieli drew on psychoanalytic concepts and theorists such as Marcuse to link individual repression and social oppression. As Mieli wrote:

> The monosexual Norm . . . is based on the mutilation of Eros, and in particular on the condemnation of homosexuality. It is clear from this that only when we understand why the homoerotic impulse is repressed in the majority, by the whole mechanism of society, will we be able to grasp how the exclusive or at least highly predominant assertion of heterosexual desire in the majority comes about.

(A not dissimilar argument was developed by feminist theorists such as Adrienne Rich when she spoke of "compulsory heterosexuality.")

Politically, the concept of oppression was used to include oppressive actions directed against those who are or seem to be homosexual as well as hostility to homosexuality as a possible form of human sexuality; thus it encompassed both ideology and actions, the state and the individual.

There is a long history in diverse societies, most notably those in the Western Christian tradition, of punishing people found guilty of homosexual acts, but the oppression of homosexuals depends on the creation of a homosexual identity, whose origin is more recent and less universal. Thus oppression often seems to be a response to the creation and affirmation of homosexual identities, as in frequent attacks on lesbian and gay bars, on individuals seen as butch (if women) or effeminate (if men), and on gay political and social organizations. The most famous example is the police raid on the Stonewall Inn, which led, at least in myth, to the emergence of the modern gay movement. In countries such as Brazil and Thailand, often regarded in the West as particularly nonoppressive of homosexuality, there is often considerable hostility toward overt expressions of homosexual identity.

One of the crucial insights of a politicized homosexuality was that oppression once internalized helped explain the apparent unhappiness of many homosexuals. The self-loathing associated with at least some readings of plays like *Boys in the Band* (Matt Crowley, 1968) and *The Killing of Sister George* (Frank Marcus, 1965) was explained as the result of social attitudes turned inward. Thus one of the major agendas of the radical gay and lesbian movement became to work through internalized oppression and to become aware of the extent to which it needed to be combated in the public arena.

Self-oppression was an important concept that drew on the political insights of black and feminist movements, as well as on the anticolonial writings of people like Franz Fanon and Jean Genet, to provide both an analysis and a program for the gay liberation movement. It continues to be a contested concept, as in arguments by some gay radicals that to seek the right to marry, or to serve in the armed forces, represents an internalization of heterosexual norms that perpetuates oppressive structures.

The term tended to fall into disuse, at least in English-speaking countries, as the gay movement became more mainstream during the latter part of the 1970s and gay liberation movements gave way to more institutionalized political lobby groups. The coining of the word *homophobia* by American psychologist George Weinberg provided a term that seemed to be more attractive to the more moderate language of the gay movement as it evolved within societies where the New Left radicalism of the early 1970s has largely disappeared.

However, *oppression* remains a useful term in societies where there is systematic and brutal treatment of homosexuals and deep ideological opposition to homosexuality, and the word remains, for example, in neo-Marxist attempts to analyze the link between political and cultural power. Elsewhere it is an important term precisely because it combines the social and the personal, emphasizing the extent to which prejudice and discrimination are related to larger structures. Unlike *homophobia,* it reminds us that there are both social and psychological dimensions to the ways in which homosexuality is managed in different times and places.   *Dennis Altman*

Bibliography

Adam, Barry. *The Survival of Domination.* New York: Elsevier, 1978.

Altman, Dennis. *Homosexual: Oppression and Liberation*, rev. ed. New York: New York University Press, 1992.

Hocquenghem, Guy. *Homosexual Desire.* London: Allison and Busby, 1978.

Mieli, Mario. *Homosexuality and Liberation.* London: London Gay Men's Press, 1980.

Weinberg, George. *Society and the Healthy Homosexual.* New York: St. Martin's Press, 1972.

See also Altman, Dennis; Brazil; Christianity; Effeminacy; Gay Left; Gay Liberation; Genet, Jean; Hate Crimes; Hocquenghem, Guy; Homophobia; Rosa von; Praunheim; Thailand; Politics; Psychological and Psychoanalytical Approaches

Orléans, Monsieur Philippe, duc d' (1640–1701)

The second son of Louis XIII and Anne of Austria, Philippe, at the accession of his brother Louis XIV in 1643, was given the title Monsieur. In 1661 he wed Henriette-Anne of England, and a year after her death under mysterious circumstances in 1670 he took as his second wife the prolific writer of letters, Charlotte Elizabeth of Bavaria, Princess Palatine.

In addition to being renowned for his military prowess, Monsieur was also known for his theatricality, flamboyant dress, and love of men. Of his lovers, the chevalier of Lorraine held the highest position. The memorialist Saint-Simon records that the power exercised by him over Monsieur was on more than one occasion used by the Sun King to persuade his younger brother to accede to his political wishes.

Monsieur did not even try to hide his lack of interest in women, and his love for the chevalier of Lorraine, who dominated him all his life, suggests a different taste. The chevalier had been a beautiful youth, and Monsieur had him painted in his adolescence "*en Ganymède.*" While the chevalier was not Monsieur's only lover, he was clearly the most powerful erotic influence in the latter's life. The two were often seen together at parties where the duke, dressed in women's clothes, was escorted by his lover. Their relationship was a sadomasochistic one insofar as Monsieur took great pleasure in being dominated and treated cruelly, especially when in drag. Because he was passive in sexual matters, all his lovers were young, virile noblemen by whom he permitted himself to be abused. This behavior prompted the count of Tournon to call him "the craziest woman in the world."

Philippe's first wife and his lovers had a mutual hatred for one another that ended in the death by poisoning of the duchess. Monsieur's relations with his second wife produced three children, among whom Philippe II would become regent at the death of Louis XIV. Princess Palatine showed little interest in her husband's personal life and spent most of her time occupied with her correspondence.

Although his relationship with his older brother the king was severely strained, in part because of his sexual preference, in part because of his financial irresponsibility, Louis always insisted that Philippe's title be respected. When Monsieur lay dying, the king spent the entire night at his bedside and wept when given the news sometime later of Philippe's death at St. Cloud.   *Todd Black*

Bibliography

Barker, Nancy. *Brother to the Sun King, Philippe, Duke of Orléans.* Baltimore: Johns Hopkins University Press, 1989.

Saint-Simon, Duc de (Louis de Rouvroy). *Mémoirs.* Paris: Éditions Gallimard, 1992.

See also France; French Literature; Sadomasochism

Orpheus

Orpheus was a mythical singer, poet, and musician, the power of whose music could entrance tigers and attract rocks and oak trees. Usually regarded as the son of the Greek god Apollo and one of the Muses, he eventually (like his father) became associated with healing, oracles, and rites of initiation.

Apollonius Rhodius (third century B.C.E.) relates that Orpheus was the son of the Muse Calliope and her Thracian lover, Oeagrus, and that he joined the voyage of the Argonauts in search of the golden fleece (1.23–34). Orpheus's lyre playing saves the Argonauts from the seductive songs of the Sirens, melodic enchantresses who lured men to their doom (4.891–919).

The texts attributed to Orpheus are largely theogonies, which deal with the creation of the gods and humans, and hymns in honor of Dionysus. Many Dionysiac mystery cults were influenced by Orphic beliefs, especially those about the afterlife; the latter connects Orphism with Pythagoreanism and its teachings regarding the transmigration of the soul.

The myth of Orpheus and the Underworld is central to the Orphic emphasis on the afterlife. Roman poets Virgil (70–19 B.C.E.) and Ovid (43 B.C.E.–C.E. 17) are the chief sources for the myth of Orpheus's love for his wife, Eurydice. According to Virgil, Eurydice died of snakebite, while fleeing from an attempted rape. Orpheus then braved the Underworld, charmed Cerberus and the Furies with the music of his lyre, and negotiated the return of his wife, on the condition that she follow behind and that he not look back. Orpheus looked back, Eurydice returned to the Underworld, and, overcome with grief, he wandered over the frozen northern wastes, singing of his woe; eventually, a band of Thracian women, considering themselves despised by his excessive devotion to Eurydice's memory, dismembered him during a nocturnal Bacchic orgy. His head then floated down the Thracian river Hebrus, calling "Eurydice! Poor Eurydice!" (*Georgics* 4.453–527).

Ovid adds the detail that many women became enraged because they were scorned by Orpheus, who, after the death of his wife, transferred his af-fections to young men and was the first man to introduce this custom to the Thracians (*Metamorphoses* 10.78–85). Interestingly, after the women murder Orpheus, he is reunited with Eurydice in the Underworld (*Met.* 11.63–66) and Bacchus, deprived of the poet who had sung of his mysteries, punished the Thracian women by turning them into trees (*Met.* 11.67–84).

Orpheus's influence over nature, his journey to the underworld to recover a "stolen soul," and his sexual ambiguity have led some scholars to regard him as a shamanistic figure, rather like the Scythian men-women.

The prophetic, mystical aspect of Orpheus and the Orphic hymns were especially popular in Neoplatonic circles in Renaissance Florence, and the myth of Orpheus and Eurydice is intimately connected with opera's origins, illustrated by Peri's *Euridice* (1600) and Monteverdi's *Orfeo* (1607). Both opt for the heterosexual ending (being reunited with Eurydice), although the Ovidian version of the myth had been revived by the great humanist Politian more than a century earlier.   *Michael Lambert*

Bibliography

Burkert, Walter. *Greek Religion.* Cambridge, Mass.: Harvard University Press, 1985.

Innes, M. M., trans. *The Metamorphoses of Ovid,* reprint. Harmondsworth, U.K.: Penguin, 1968.

See also Dionysus; Florence; Greece Mythology; Renaissance Neoplatonism; Scythia

Orton, Joe (John Kingsley) (1933–1967)

Joe Orton's short, notorious life and literary career achieved neither the squalid infamy of Jean Genet's nor the aesthetic influence of Oscar Wilde's. Yet a combination of the sensibilities of these two writers suggest with some accuracy the tenor and impact of Orton's work. Before being bludgeoned to death with a hammer by his companion, Kenneth Halliwell, Orton wrote nine plays (one unpublished), three novels (two with Halliwell, both unpublished), and a screenplay for the Beatles, and kept a brilliant and viciously funny diary. Orton began writing for the stage when sexual subjects still were only touched on gingerly; by the time his last play, *What the Butler Saw*, was produced, the climate in Britain had changed remarkably. Homosexual acts, in 1967, finally were deemed legal (though only between two people over the age of twenty-one), and the lord chamberlain's censorship office was on its way out—a change perhaps precipitated by the candor with which Orton among others travestied Britain's upstanding institutions—church, monarchy, army, civil service.

Orton was born to working-class parents in Leicester, attended Clark's College (a private vocational school) until the age of sixteen, where he learned shorthand and typing, and then held a number of low-paying clerical positions until 1951. That year, he received a grant to attend the Royal Academy of Dramatic Art in London, where he studied acting for two years and met Halliwell (a fellow student seven years his senior). The two remained lovers for the next fourteen years. Halliwell, by far the more bookish of the two, became Orton's mentor, pushing him to read widely and to write. Whether or not they read Genet then is a matter of conjecture, but the two embarked on a similar life of petty crime and were finally imprisoned in 1962 for inserting lewd marginalia in library books and ripping out countless hundreds of plates from art books—with which they decorated the walls of their small apartment—replacing these with pornographic pictures and drawings. While in prison, Orton wrote his first-produced play, *The Ruffian on the Stair*, and sent it off to the BBC. It aired eventually in 1964.

This first one-act (later combined with his television play *The Erpingham Camp*, 1966, produced on the stage as a double bill entitled *Crimes of Passion*, 1967) sets the tone and style for all his subsequent work—the hint of illicit homo sex; a superbly chaotic, farcical plot; a Wildean playfulness with syntax; a Genetesque explosion of repressed sex, crime, and lust; graphic, violent, extraordinary statements delivered in the most ordinary way. Orton's genius lies in the way he connects Wilde's and Shaw's ability to manipulate commonly held moral beliefs into their exact opposites with plots that celebrate criminal sexuality, including homosexuality.

Many critics, like Orton's chief biographer, John Lahr (*Prick Up Your Ears*), read the plays through Orton's life as documented in his diaries—the quick, promiscuous encounters in public lavatories and parks, the homosexual posing (tight T-shirt, blue jeans, black leather jacket, leather boots—almost as much a coded wardrobe as Wilde's dandyism), Halliwell's growing irritation and jealousy, and his commercial success on the London stage, leading to even more flagrant attempts to shock his public. These critics find in this behavior a deliberate affront to societal codes and conventions, trans-

lated into the plays as a sequence of anarchic events and grotesque sexual relationships designed specifically to outrage and insult.

Orton did as much as possible to fan the scandal his work generated, creating an alter ego of sorts, Edna Welthorpe (Mrs.), in whose voice he wrote numerous letters to the press objecting to what most audiences registered as the immorality of his own plays. His life, in this sense, was simply an extension of his work, a performance in itself, filling in the nastiest crevices of the role—criminal homosexual—that others assigned to him but also assuming the moral high ground through his letters as Aunt Edna, mocking the very sensibilities that condemned him in the first place. His work and his life were groundbreaking in that with neither did he attempt to hide, or to convey through coded behavior, his own polymorphous sexuality or that of his characters.

Orton wrote at a moment of transition—between the more closeted handling of homosexual subject matter by such writers as Tennessee Williams and Terrence Rattigan and the more explicitly gay work by Mart Crowley and Colin Spencer. Orton's work, as Alan Sinfield argues, engages exactly this movement toward self-identification—toward an unashamed, unequivocal affirmation of queer sex.   *Framji Minwalla*

Bibliography

Bigsby, C.W.E. *Joe Orton*. London: Methuen, 1982.

Charney, Maurice. *Joe Orton*. London: Macmillan, 1984.

Esslin, Martin. "Joe Orton: The Comedy of (Ill) Manners." In *Contemporary English Drama*. C.W.E. Bigsby, ed. New York: Holmes & Meier, 1981, 93–107.

Lahr, John. *Prick Up Your Ears: The Biography of Joe Orton*. New York: Knopf, 1978.

Lucas, Ian. *Impertinent Decorum*. London: Cassel, 1994, 38–44.

Orton, Joe. *The Orton Diaries*. John Lahr, ed. London: Methuen, 1986.

Sinfield, Alan. "Who Was Afraid of Joe Orton?" *Textual Practice* 4, no. 2 (Summer 1990): 259–97.

See also Dandy; Genet, Jean; Queer; Wilde, Oscar; Williams, Tennessee

Outing

Outing, the involuntary revelation of a public figure's homosexuality by movement activists, has a long past, if only a short history. The issue, although not the term, arose at the very dawn of modern gay consciousness, as homosexual emancipation crusaders and movements emerged in England and Germany at the end of the nineteenth century. These pioneers saw themselves as persons for whom homosexual behavior was as "natural" as heterosexual behavior was for heterosexuals. The idea that homosexuals constitute a "people" set apart from the society they live among, however invisibly, led inevitably to the question of what obligations they have to this "community." In 1897 Magnus Hirschfeld founded the first homosexual emancipation organization, the Scientific-Humanitarian Committee. When imperial Germany was rocked by accusations that many of the Kaiser's associates were homosexual, the committee decided that exposure of prominent homosexuals would not be an effective or moral strategy and promised that "the frequently suggested 'path over corpses' will not be taken by us under any circumstances." But another wing of the movement took the initiative.

Adolph Brand, founder of the first homosexual periodical, *Der Eigene*, published a pamphlet claiming that an antireform leader was secretly homosexual. Under threat of libel action Brand printed a retraction, yet many viewed the incident as a tactical success. The United States in the 1990s is not the Germany of Hirschfeld and Brand. The tactical debate today takes place against a very different backdrop. A lesbian and gay community has emerged with all the institutional complexity of an ethnic minority: political, religious, social, and cultural organizations of all stripes. Publicly lesbian and gay people exist in sufficient numbers to discredit the claim that exposure will invariably lead to ruin, and that we must therefore under all circumstances protect one another's secrets.

Were it not for AIDS, outing might have remained the road not taken by the gay movement. Communities have always been willing to sacrifice some members in times of crisis, drafting often unwilling recruits in the common interest. For many gay people, AIDS is a war and outing became a weapon wielded against lethal complacency and hypocrisy. For the ACT UP/Queer Nation generation, the "path over corpses" had a new and dreadful meaning after over 100,000 deaths from a plague made more deadly by government, media, and public indifference and hostility.

In 1989, Michelangelo Signorile unleashed the militant anger of ACT UP in New York's *OutWeek*

magazine, dissecting New York's and Hollywood's celebrity elite. Signorile outed Hollywood moguls Barry Diller and David Geffen and movie star Jodie Foster, but his most frequent targets were the media, attacked for failing to pay enough attention to AIDS, for pretending that lesbian and gay celebrities are heterosexual, and for flattering politicians "who are keeping us down at best, murdering us at worst." The gay journalists and activists who broke the code of silence grew up in an age in which gay people were a part of the public landscape. They also grew up in an age drenched in gossip and "news" about celebrities of all sorts, and became impatient with the double standard by which the media granted gay private lives an exemption from the "public's right to know," thus protecting the closets of the rich and famous and leaving unchallenged the distaste of the media—and the public—for facing the reality of lesbian and gay existence.

Gay author Armistead Maupin began challenging the gay press to name names: "If the gay press has any function at all," Maupin stated, "it's to tweak the conscience of famous people who are in the closet; and certainly we shouldn't continue to lionize those among us who are making a success of themselves in the mainstream while remaining so determinedly in the closet. . . . I'm taking the hard line on it and saying homophobia is homophobia." Maupin's disclosures were printed in many gay papers, and mainstream media joined in playing the game while simultaneously debating the rules. *Time* critic William Henry described and condemned outing: "It claims an unjustifiable right to sacrifice the lives of others."

In 1990, *OutWeek* ran Signorile's cover story, "The Secret Gay Life of Malcolm Forbes," which concluded with a defense of outing. First, "All too often history is distorted," and the fact that one of the most influential men in America was gay should be recorded. Second, "It sends a clear message to the public at large that we are everywhere." The Forbes outing set off another round of debate in the mainstream and gay press, with most journalists condemning the tactic even as many were eager to be "first to be second" by reporting that someone else had accused a public figure of being homosexual.

In the *Village Voice* gay activist and writer Vito Russo pointed out, "Signorile is saying that if being gay is not disgusting, is not awful, then why can't we talk about it? After all, it's not an insult to call someone gay. Is it?" The effectiveness of outing as a political strategy was demonstrated when Signo-

Orile's outing of Assistant Secretary of Defense Pete Williams in August 1991 placed the issue of military antigay discrimination on the public agenda, generating articles and editorials sympathetic to the gay cause.

Congressman Steve Gunderson (R.-Wis.) had never supported gay causes in his eleven years in office. After activists made his homosexuality public, Gunderson began to be more supportive of gay issues and more open about his sexuality. A 1994 *New York Times* profile headlined him as "Congressman (R) Wisconsin. Fiscal Conservative. Social Moderate. Gay." The furor over outing shifted the news media toward a greater willingness to include someone's homosexuality when it is relevant to a story. In 1995 the *Wall Street Journal* reported that *Rolling Stone* founder Jann Wenner "left . . . his wife and three young children and began a relationship with a young male staffer at Calvin Klein." Former *Out-Week* editor Gabriel Rotello commented, "If *Out-Week*'s Forbes article ignited the outing war with a bang, the *Journal*'s piece on Wenner . . . symbolically ends it with a whimper."

The war might have ended, but outing remains a tactic in activists' arsenals, as closeted legislators Senator Barbara Mikulski (D.-Md.) and Congressman Jim Kolbe (R.-Ariz.) discovered after they voted for the Defense of Marriage Act in 1996. Kolbe beat the *Advocate* to the punch by coming out himself, telling a reporter, "I feel a tremendous burden lifted. It's a relief." After confronting Mikulski at a New York book signing, Signorile and media activist Ann Northrop proposed October 10 as National Outing Day: "From this day forward, the day before National Coming Out Day will be National Outing Day," Signorile said. "It's a day to out a favorite public figure to everyone you know, through e-mail messages, voice mail messages, notes and letters in the mail, and in casual conversation throughout the day. And if there happens to be an elected official who voted anti-gay and who is making a public appearance, it's a day to go and confront that person."

Like many other innovations of the post-Stonewall movement, outing spread to other countries. In 1994 the British group OutRage wrote to Anglican church leaders, urging them to come out voluntarily, and followed up two months later by publicly naming ten bishops. Shortly afterward two bishops came out and a third, soon to be appointed archbishop of York, described his sexuality as "a gray area." At the same time the Church of England entered into discussions with the lesbian and gay community for the first time. OutRage raised the stakes in March 1995 by urging twenty unnamed members of Parliament to come out. Although few individuals have actually been outed by activists, more public figures have publicly acknowledged their homosexuality, and the Parliament elected in 1997 includes four openly gay members.

Larry Gross

Bibliography

Gross, Larry. *Contested Closets: The Politics and Ethics of Outing*. Minneapolis: University of Minnesota Press, 1993.

Johansson, Warren, and William Percy. *Outing: Shattering the Conspiracy of Silence*. Binghampton, N.Y.: Haworth Press. 1994.

Mohr, Richard. *Gay Ideas: Outing and Other Controversies*. Boston: Beacon Press, 1992.

Murphy, Timothy, ed. *Gay Ethics: Controversies in Outing, Civil Rights, and Sexual Science*. Binghampton, N.Y.: Haworth Press, 1994.

Signorile, Michelangelo. "The Other Side of Malcolm." *OutWeek* (March 18, 1990); reprinted in Gross, 1993, 207–16.

———. *Queer in America: Sex, the Media, and the Closets of Power*. New York: Random House, 1993.

See also Activism, U.S.; ACT UP; Brand, Adolph; Community Centers; Gay and Lesbian Press; Hirschfeld, Magnus; Maupin, Armistead; Media; Queer Nation

Owen, Wilfred (1893–1918)

Wilfred Edward Salter Owen is widely considered the most accomplished of modern war poets. Almost all the poems that established his reputation were written in the last year of his life; he was killed in action just a week before the end of World War I.

Owen was born in Shropshire, England, to lower-middle-class parents. As a youth he shared his mother's evangelical Christian piety, and after leaving the Shrewsbury Technical School, he became lay assistant to the vicar at Dunsden, Oxfordshire. But after a crisis of faith in September 1913, he left England to begin work as a tutor in Bordeaux, France. A full thirteen months after World War I broke out, Owen finally returned to England and joined the Artists' Rifles. The following year he received a commission to the Manchester Regiment, and in December 1916, he sailed to France to suffer the experience of the front lines for the first time. After leading his platoon through severe fighting in positions near Beaumont-Hamel and Savy Wood, the blast from a shell threw him into the air and shattered his nerves, though he suffered no physical injury. As a victim of shell shock, he was transferred to Craiglockhart War Hospital for Neurasthenic Officers in Edinburgh, Scotland, in June 1917. It was here that his craftsmanship as a poet developed with extraordinary speed, as he discovered a fresh, distinctive poetic voice, so that within a few months of his arrival he was writing some of the finest poems of the war, including "The Dead-Beat," "Anthem for Doomed Youth," and "Dulce et Decorum Est."

These poems are suffused with tenderness for the soldiers who had to endure the horrors of the war, a "pity" that controls and validates the anger to which they also give voice. In a draft of a preface for the volume he was planning, Owen declared: "I am not concerned about Poetry. / My subject is War, and the pity of War. / The Poetry is in the pity." His poems directly contradict the facile notions of "glory" and "honor" that war poetry typically celebrated up to that time. In "Dulce et Decorum Est," for example, Owen rejects the hackneyed Latin tag meaning "It is sweet and honorable to die for one's country," calling it "the old lie." Instead, the poem vividly describes a soldier's ghastly death during a gas attack. Owen also developed an unusual system of consonantal rhyme: "escaped/scooped," "groined/groaned," "bestirred/stared" ("Strange Meeting"). But he published only four poems during his lifetime, the first in the magazine of Craiglockhart War Hospital and the rest in the pacifist journal the *Nation*.

Before the war, Owen had met Laurence Tailhade, a French symbolist poet, but the chief influence on his verse was Siegfried Sassoon, who arrived at Craiglockhart shortly after Owen. Owen greatly admired Sassoon's biting, satirical verse, but the student soon surpassed his mentor. Through Sassoon, Owen won the encouragement of Robbie Ross, Oscar Wilde's old friend, and became a member of the circle of homosexual writers who gathered around Ross at his home in Mayfair. He became particularly close to C. K. Scott Montcrieff (Proust's translator) and influenced his translation of *The Song of Roland*.

In early September 1918, Owen returned to France on active duty. He was awarded the Military Cross for gallantry in action on October 1, 1918, and was killed at the Sambre Canal on November 4.

Matthew Parfitt

Bibliography

Hibberd, Dominic. *Wilfred Owen: The Last Year, 1917–1918*. London: Constable, 1992.

Owen, Wilfred. *The Collected Poems of Wilfred Owen*. C. Day Lewis, ed. New York: New Directions, 1965.

Stallworthy, Jon. *Wilfred Owen*. London: Oxford University Press, 1974.

See also English Literature; War; Wilde, Oscar

Owens, Craig (1950–1990)

An art critic who lived and worked in New York City during the 1970s and 1980s, Craig Owens was senior editor of *Art in America*, where many of his essays and reviews appeared. He also contributed important writing to the journal *October*, anthologies of art and cultural criticism, and various exhibition catalogs. Although his professional career spanned little more than fifteen years, Owens was a compelling voice of political dissent in his day, proffering astute and often trenchant criticism of the dominant fine art establishment. His legacy of criticism and teaching has continued to have an impact on art production and criticism in the years since his death.

In the late 1970s Owens played a crucial role in introducing postmodern theory to the critical dialogue surrounding contemporary art in the United States. His early criticism drew heavily on the thoughts and writings of Michel Foucault. Like Foucault, Owens advocated a postmodernist examination of how visual representation is directly linked to mechanisms of power in society. He believed that modernism falsely claimed that an art object could be free of external associations and could correctly represent a single, fixed subject or possess a universal truth. Rejecting this idea as a fiction, Owens sought "to expose the particular interests which all representations serve, their affiliations with classes, offices, institutions" (Owens, *Beyond Recognition*, 91). He ultimately equated representation with domination and subjugation, claiming that representation is "the founding act of power in our culture."

Having sufficiently developed this critical stance, Owens turned to the work of an emerging group of artists in the early 1980s. His commentary on the work of several female artists at this time—notably Barbara Kruger, Sherrie Levine, and Cindy Sherman—was extremely influential. These artists utilized photography and media-derived images (frequently of women) to expose the very act of rep-

O resentation as an instrument of sexual power and mastery. Owens's critical support of this art was an effort "to introduce the issue of sexual difference into the modernism/postmodernism debate," which had previously been neglected. Essays like "The Discourse of Others: Feminism and Postmodernism" asserted that sexual inequality was primarily the product of dominant representational practices in contemporary culture.

Expanding upon this feminist consciousness, Owens's later writing continued to examine the links between representation and subordination and their effects on other marginalized social groups, including gay men. In the late 1980s, he began to teach courses that specifically analyzed images of the AIDS epidemic produced by the media and legal and medical discourse. He sought to reveal the homophobia, sexism, racism, and class bias that surfaced in such imagery. These pedagogical efforts, and the bulk of Owens's critical corpus, helped lay a crucial intellectual foundation for various activist responses to the AIDS epidemic. His work informed the way activist groups such as ACT UP confronted oppositional representational strategies. Owens himself died of AIDS-related complications at the age of 39.   *Matthew Nichols*

Bibliography

Owens, Craig. *Beyond Recognition: Representation, Power, and Culture.* Berkeley: University of California Press, 1992.

See also ACT UP; AIDS and Art; Art History; Foucault, Michel

Owles, Jim (1946–1993)

After being discharged from the Air Force for circulating anti–Vietnam War materials, Jim Owles came to New York City from his native Chicago and joined the Gay Liberation Front (GLF), which supported many nongay causes. He was twenty-three years old in December 1969 when he and eleven other GLF members split off to form the single-issue Gay Activists Alliance (GAA), which quickly outgrew GLF to become the largest militant gay rights organization in the United States, with hundreds of members attending its weekly meetings. Owles was elected the founding president, a post he held for two years until the end of 1972.

He led GAA through its early "zaps"—nonviolent confrontations with police, politicians, media representatives, and others—during which he was frequently arrested and on one occasion severely beaten. He made fiery speeches to advance the cause of gay liberation while presiding over the establishment of GAA's headquarters, "The Firehouse," and he initiated legislation for the protection of gay men and lesbians in the areas of employment and housing, which was ultimately approved by New York's City Council after a battle of fifteen years.

In 1973 he declared his own candidacy for the New York City Council. Although he lost the election to the long-term incumbent, he became the first open homosexual to run for public office in the nation's largest city. In 1974, he became the founding president of Gay and Lesbian Independent Democrats (GLID), New York's liberal political club, and in 1986 he was a founding member of the Gay and Lesbian Alliance Against Defamation (GLAAD).

Owles died of AIDS in New York on August 6, 1993.   *Arnie Kantrowitz*

Bibliography

Teal, Donn. *The Gay Militants.* New York: Stein & Day, 1971; reprint St. Martin's Press, 1995.
Tobin, Kay, and Randy Wicker. *The Gay Crusaders.* New York: Paperback Library, 1972.

See also Activism, U.S.; Gay Activists Alliance (GAA); Gay and Lesbian Alliance Against Defamation (GLAAD); Gay Liberation Front; New York City

P

Papacy

Homosexuality can be considered in two very different relations to the papacy. The first is the role of various popes or their agents in constructing Christian teaching and church policy on homosexuality. The second relation is the extent to which certain popes or prominent members of their courts expressed same-sex desire or engaged in same-sex activities. The first relation is easier to establish, though it is diffused throughout the history of the European churches. Over the centuries, papal power has expanded and contracted in various cycles, but the underlying trend has been toward greater claims of doctrinal and legal authority. Various popes have been instrumental in codifying and extending church law on sexual matters. Thus the prohibitions of sodomy in canon law and the punishments meted out for it have been backed by papal power. There have also been particular papal actions and decrees. For example, Gregory I (reigned 590–604) ordered that a sodomite priest be removed from his ministry. At the other end of the Middle Ages, Pius V (1566–1572) issued two constitutions, *Cum primum* and *Horrendum*, which reaffirmed the traditional defrocking of clerics guilty of habitual sodomy and which handed over some classes of sodomites to secular authorities for punishment. The papacy had also played an increasingly active role in policing sexual practices through regular sacramental confessions (from the thirteenth century) and through the courts of the Inquisition (from the fifteenth century). In modern times, popes and their agents have also supported secular laws against homosexuality. Most recently, the Vatican has denounced efforts to extend equal rights to lesbians and gays.

On the other hand, and to turn to the second relation, a number of popes have themselves been accused of homosexual acts. John XII (955–964) was accused by one chronicler of various debaucheries, including sex with men and boys. Very detailed testimony was given against Boniface VIII (1294–1303) in a "trial" arranged by his French adversaries. Boniface was alleged to have sexually harassed male servants and to have remarked that homosexual acts were no more immoral than rubbing one's hands together. Paul II (1464–1471) was ridiculed with feminine epithets for his love of ecclesiastical costume and beautiful young men. By contrary logic, Julius II (1503–1513), known more for his military acumen than for his patronage of the arts, was also accused of sodomy. This list, which could easily be extended, says more about the use of homosexuality as an insult than it does about the sexual tastes of the popes mentioned. Other kinds of internal evidence, if genuine, would suggest that the papal court was sometimes quite tolerant of same-sex desire. For example, a letter purporting to be written by one of his clerical assistants describes the inner court of Innocent III as a sort of gay club. But this sort of document should be treated with skepticism, for it might well be a bit of clever satire. The historical evidence does not permit anyone to reconstruct a comprehensive account of the sexual lives of high members of the Catholic clergy.   *Mark D. Jordan*

Bibliography

Kelly, J. N., ed. *Oxford Dictionary of Popes*. London: Oxford University Press, 1989.

McBrien, Richard P. *Lives of the Popes: The Pontiffs from St. Peter to John Paul II*. San Francisco: Harper, 1997.

See also Canon Law; Catholicism; Clergy; Inquisition; Sodomy

P

Paragraph 175

On June 11, 1994, the German government eliminated paragraph 175, a law that had made sex between two men punishable by imprisonment, from the German law books. This brought an end to over 124 years of legal discrimination against gay men. Punishment for gay sex had been carried out by the German state long before paragraph 175 was officially established on May 31, 1870, in most parts of Germany. By January 18, 1871, the law became applicable in all parts of the newly created German Empire. Although Prussia was the third European country, after Austria (1778) and France (1791), that finally removed the death penalty for sodomy, Prussia's law still demanded imprisonment, physical punishment, and exile for any gay sexual activities. In all of Germany, only the Bavarian kingdom, influenced by the postrevolutionary French *Code Pénal,* renounced any punishment for homosexual activity entirely in its law from 1813 until the kingdom's unification with Prussia by a peace settlement in 1867. The paragraph of the German Empire's law that finally achieved in 1871 the number 175 preserved nearly in its entirety the existing paragraph 143 of Prussian law. The wording of paragraph 175 defined any sexual activities between men or between men and animals as a perverse sexual offense, and demanded imprisonment for up to four years in conjunction with the dispossession of citizenship.

Paragraph 175 and its predecessors met with great resistance by many gay activists. German lawyer Karl Heinrich Ulrichs (1825–1895) was fired from his government position for his homosexuality by the Hanoverian government. Beginning in 1864, he published several brochures in defense of homosexuality, or what he termed "Uranismus." He also tried to initiate a movement against the anti-gay law. In 1867, physicist and scholar of sexual science Magnus Hirschfeld (1868–1935) founded the Scientific-Humanitarian Committee, the gay political organization formed to protest discrimination against gay men in history. It also served as the first group organized to reform paragraph 175 in Germany. Between 1897 and 1907 the committee proposed five petitions to alter paragraph 175. The committee petitioned to have paragraph 175 reworded so as the law would apply only in three situations: cases of nonconsensual sex between two persons of the same sex, homosexual contact with minors under the age of sixteen, and same-sex activity in public. The German government not only denied all the petitions but also canceled a revision to the law that followed the committee's proposals before World War I in 1914. Nonetheless, Hirschfeld continued his fight for emancipation by founding the Institute for Sexual Science in Berlin in 1919. In 1933, the Nazis plundered the institute and, in 1935, strengthened paragraph 175, which ultimately allowed the Nazis to imprison and murder thousands of gay men before and during World War II. The elimination of Nazi legislation after World War II brought a short period of liberation for homosexuals in Germany, but the founding of the Federal Republic of Germany (FRG) in 1949 reestablished paragraph 175 as it was used by the Nazis before the end of World War II. The FRG finally dismantled the paragraph in 1969, though it was still illegal to have same-sex contact with minors under the age of twenty-one. In 1949 the German Democratic Republic (GDR), or East Germany, reinstated paragraph 175 as it was used before 1935 but substituted the entire paragraph in 1968 with paragraph 151, which punished adults who engaged in same-sex activities with minors under the age of eighteen. In the summer of 1989, two months before the fall of the Wall, the GDR eliminated paragraph 151. With the reunification of Germany in 1990, the new government intended to expand paragraph 175 to apply to the newly unified country. It was not until 1994 that paragraph 175 was finally abolished from German law.

Jens Richard Giersdorf

Bibliography

"Freunde eines Schwulen Museums in Berlin e.V. in Zusammenarbeit mit Emanzipation e.V. Frankfurt am Main." In *Die Geschichte des Paragraph 175: Strafrecht gegen Homosexuelle.* Katalog zur Ausstellung in Berlin und Frankfurt am Main 1990. Berlin: Verlag Rosa Winkel, 1990.

Sternweiler, Andreas, and Hans Gerhard Hannesen, eds. *Homosexuelle in Deutschland: Eine politische Geschichte.* Munich: Verlag C. H. Beck, 1989.

See also Activism, International; France; Germany; Hirschfeld, Magnus; Nazism and the Holocaust; Sodomy; Ulrichs, Karl Heinrich; Uranianism

Parenting

Openly gay parenting is a relatively new phenomenon. Nevertheless, it is useful to remember that throughout history there have been many men, such as Oscar Wilde, who had important homosexual relationships yet became fathers through heterosexual intercourse. Today it is difficult to estimate how many gay men are parents. Figures from large-scale surveys in the gay community have been used to extrapolate that nearly one in ten gay men have children of their own, but it is likely that many more gay men are involved in parenting in some capacity.

Diversity of Gay Parenting Experiences

Clearly there are many family forms headed by a gay parent. Children can be parented by a single gay man or by a couple, and additional parenting also may be provided by ex-partners and friends. Considering this in relation to other important contextual factors such as ethnicity, class, (dis)ability, and the timing of parenthood in relation to the life cycle means that there is a wide diversity of experience of parenthood among gay men.

A major consideration in relation to gay father families is whether the child has been brought up in a gay environment from his or her earliest memories, or whether there has been a period of transition during which the father has developed his gay identity. At the present time most gay or bisexual men who become parents have had children in a heterosexual relationship, which may or may not be ongoing. A number of studies estimate that between 2 and 4 percent of married men have homosexual relationships alongside their marital relationship. Not all these men will develop and integrate their gay identity with fatherhood. Bozett and Miller both outline several different identity possibilities, depending on the extent to which the father acknowledges his gay relationships to himself and to his heterosexual family, and the extent to which he acknowledges his role as a father when socializing in the gay community.

Most gay fathers sooner or later decide to end their previous heterosexual relationship. However, if their ex-wife contests their continued relationship with their children, gay fathers mostly find that the courts dismiss their previous parenting involvement and do not allow their children to reside with them. Furthermore, it is not unusual for courts to place restrictions on the father's visits with his children (e.g., prohibiting a child from meeting his or her father's new partner), which have no parallels in court orders issued to heterosexual fathers. Moreover, in recent times gay fathers appear to be even more vulnerable than lesbian mothers within the legal context.

Becoming a parent as a gay man or as a gay couple is often a difficult process. Gay men some-

times become involved in parenting in a limited capacity through fathering children conceived via donor insemination to lesbian parents. Achieving full parental responsibility, or coparenting, through surrogacy is an option for some men. Many complicated issues are raised in any surrogacy arrangement, yet having children through such an agreement may not necessarily be a more difficult option for gay men than other routes to parenthood. In the United States the legality of commercial and noncommercial surrogacy, and indeed access via surrogacy agencies, varies among states. In Great Britain and elsewhere commercial surrogacy is illegal, and while noncommercial surrogacy is not illegal, it is often extremely difficult to arrange.

Gay parents may also become involved in parenting through fostering or adopting a child. However, there is wide divergence among states in policy on adoptions by lesbians and gay men, ranging from specific prohibition in New Hampshire to recognition in neighboring Vermont. In other states and countries there are some barriers to fostering and adoption; for example, in Great Britain gay men can adopt only as individuals, not as a couple. Even under more liberal jurisdictions many prospective gay parents feel that they have been discriminated against by particular agencies.

Gay Men as Effective Parents

In comparison with the wider media coverage and growing number of research studies on lesbian motherhood, relatively little attention has been given to gay men and parenting. As the father's role in parenting is generally marginalized compared with that of the mother, so gay men are often rendered invisible as parents through gender as well as sexual identity. When socializing in the gay community, many gay men feel that their identity as a parent is not recognized. If gay fatherhood is acknowledged in the heterosexual community, it is often denounced with considerable hostility based on the homophobic confusion of homosexuality and pedophilia.

The available evidence suggests that gay men are often parenting in somewhat different circumstances from those faced by lesbian mothers. Fewer gay fathers live with their children, and possibly for this reason are less likely than lesbian mothers to be out to their children about their sexuality. Compared with previously married lesbian mothers, gay men are more likely to report having been aware of homosexual feelings prior to marriage, although many remembered hoping that these would end. Gay fathers surveyed tend to have relatively higher incomes than most lesbian mothers. The few research studies that ask comparable questions of both lesbian mothers and gay fathers also suggest that approaches and attitudes toward parenting not surprisingly differ between the two groups. In comparison with the more feminist lesbian mothers surveyed by Harris and Turner in the early 1980s, gay fathers were more likely to report that they encouraged their children to play with sex-typed toys. Gay fathers in this research also reported fewer disagreements with their partner over discipline than did lesbian mothers, and greater satisfaction with parenting. On the other hand, while most lesbian mothers and gay fathers saw some benefits and few problems for their children as a result of their sexual orientation, lesbian mothers perceived more benefits relative to the gay fathers surveyed. However, given the changes in gay culture during the 1990s, many new gay parents might have quite different attitudes toward child rearing were Harris and Turner's survey to be repeated today.

The vast majority of gay fathers represented in the research literature have had children in the context of previous heterosexual relationships. Gay men who have become involved in parenting their partner's children are not represented, nor are men who planned to parent as gay fathers. Furthermore, published research on gay fatherhood generally draws on the experiences of well-educated, high-earning, white, North American gay parents. Last but not least, research to date suffers from serious methodological limitations. The two in-depth studies of gay fathers cited here lack comparison groups of heterosexual fathers, without which it is difficult to conclude how gay identity influences the experience of fatherhood. Studies that do examine both gay and heterosexual men's parenting often are restricted by their small sample size. Finally, much of the data on children with gay fathers are provided by the fathers only (many of whom have little contact with their children), while only a few investigators have surveyed the children directly.

Paralleling research conducted on children with lesbian mothers, studies of children growing up with gay fathers have tended to examine the topics that are the focus of the main arguments raised in legal cases; namely, gay men's parenting, children's gender development, and children's emotional and social development. Comparing previously divorced gay fathers with divorced heterosexual fathers where both groups of fathers were now nonresidential parents, Bigner and Jacobsen concluded that gay fathers generally seemed to be more responsive to their child's real needs and yet also were able to set more consistent limits for their children. Similarly, the gay fathers in Harris and Turner's survey reported positive relationships with their children, rating communication, cooperation, enjoyment, and discipline of their children all as being important. Interviews with the same gay parents revealed the ways in which they helped to create positive relationships with their children and maintained a stable home environment. Moreover, other research suggests that for both gay fathers and their children, the factor most associated with family satisfaction was the extent to which the father's gay partner was integrated into family life.

Contrary to the fears often expressed in legal cases, there is no evidence that gay men are more likely than heterosexual men to commit sexual crimes against children. Understandable concern over homophobic prejudices in fact may have influenced gay fathers in Bigner and Jacobsen's study to be more cautious than heterosexual fathers in expressing physical affection to their partners in front of their children. These same pressures also present extra difficulties for many gay fathers in coming out to their children. Many gay fathers do not disclose their sexuality unless they feel some compelling reason to do so, such as divorce, the development of a long-term gay relationship, fear of exposure, the realization of having HIV, or the advent of a serious illness. In these situations children therefore have several issues to come to terms with simultaneously. Both Bozett and Miller suggest that most children regardless of their age or gender respond positively to a sensitively timed disclosure.

Research has tended to focus on the sexual identity of the sons and daughters of gay fathers, rather than consider the gender development of younger children (the issue most often considered in research on children raised in lesbian-led families). Bailey and colleagues surveyed both gay fathers and their sons to find that the majority of sons were heterosexual, with only 9 percent identifying as gay or bisexual, a percentage that the authors argue is congruent with evidence of slight genetic inheritance. Other studies of both sons and daughters of gay fathers find that most identify as heterosexual.

With regard to the emotional and social development of the children of gay fathers, one study showed that a majority of gay fathers report considerable concern that their children would be stigmatized at school because of having a gay father. However, in the same survey, only a fifth of the gay fathers reported that any of their children had actually experienced discrimination. Bozett outlines a number of strategies that the gay fathers and children he interviewed successfully used to deal with or avoid the possibility of homophobia. But in many cases, this involved the potential strain of keeping aspects of family life secret, for example, Crosbie-Burnett and Helmbrecht found that over half of their sample of adolescents in gay stepfamilies were not open with heterosexual friends about their family background. No study has yet focused directly on the well-being of children raised by gay fathers; nevertheless, there are no indications either from fathers' reports or from interviews with children of implications for mental health. Barret and Robinson conclude from reviewing their interviews with the children of gay fathers: "They are like all kids. Some do well in just about all activities; some have problems, and some are well adjusted" (Barret and Robinson 168).

Conclusion

Parental access is generally refused to gay fathers on the grounds that they would not be effective parents, that the children would experience difficulties in peer relationships and would develop behavioral and emotional problems as a result, and that the children would show atypical gender development. These same arguments are raised when decisions are made on gay men as suitable foster carers, prospective adopters, or parents of children conceived through surrogacy arrangements. Yet the limited research to date clearly challenges these assumptions and suggests the general warmth of father-child relationships, despite the prejudice and discrimination often faced by gay father families.

Little research has been shaped by the interests and concerns of gay parents themselves. No research has yet investigated the likely distress felt by both child and gay father in losing a previously close relationship because of restrictions placed by the child's mother or court orders. Finally, research has yet to fully consider family dynamics within gay father families, including the important role of male coparents or the impact of homophobia on the context of gay parenting.   *Fiona Tasker*

Bibliography

Bailey, J. Michael, David Bobrow, Marilyn Wolfe, and Sarah Mikach. "Sexual Orientation of Adult Sons of Gay Fathers." *Developmental Psychology* 31 (1995): 124–29.

Barret, Robert L., and Bryan E. Robinson. *Gay Fathers*. Lexington, Ky.: Lexington Books, 1990.

Bigner, Jerry J., and R. Brooke Jacobsen. "Parenting Behaviors of Homosexual and Heterosexual Fathers." In *Homosexuality and the Family*. F.W. Bozett, ed. London: Harrington Park Press, 1989, 173–86.

Bozett, Frederick W. "Gay Fathers." In *Gay and Lesbian Parents*. F. W. Bozett, ed. London: Praeger, 1987, 3–22.

Bryant, A. Steven and Demian. "Relationship Characteristics of American Gay and Lesbian Couples: Findings from a National Survey." *Journal of Gay and Lesbian Social Services* 1 (1994): 101–17.

Crosbie-Burnett, Margaret, and Lawrence Helmbrecht. "A Descriptive Empirical Study of Gay Male Stepfamilies." *Family Relations* 42 (1993): 256–62.

Harris, Mary B., and Pauline H. Turner. "Gay and Lesbian Parents." *Journal of Homosexuality* 12 (1986): 101–13.

Miller, Brian. "Gay Fathers and Their Children." *Family Coordinator* 28 (1979): 544–52.

Strasser, Mark. "Fit to Be Tied: On Custody, Discretion, and Sexual Orientation." *American University Law Review* 46 (1997): 841–95.

Wyers, Norman L. "Homosexuality in the Family: Lesbian and Gay Spouses." *Social Work* 32 (1987): 143–48.

See also Children's Books; Gay Families; Homophobia; Pederasty

Parents and Friends of Lesbians and Gays (PFLAG)

Parents and Friends of Lesbians and Gays (PFLAG) is the national organization formed in the United States in 1981, although smaller, regional support groups for parents had been forming for at least two years prior to that time. Jeanne Manford, who marched in 1972 with her son Morty, formed the first support group in New York City. Soon after, she helped Adele and Larry Starr form a similar group in Los Angeles. Now PFLAG has 389 affiliates nationwide with 55,000 member households, located in more than 390 communities in the United States, as well as in 11 countries outside the United States.

P

PFLAG members in the March on Washington, 1993. Photo by Marc Geller.

PFLAG is a grassroots organization with chapters all over the nation. Its primary goals are support programs, educational projects, and advocacy. One of PFLAG's ongoing educational campaigns, Project Open Mind, is meant to inform the public about the truth regarding gay, lesbian, and bisexual people and to dispel the myths put out by antigay groups. They began a $1 million newspaper and television ad campaign in 1995 aimed at confronting hatred toward bisexuals, lesbians, and gays, and have even made a thirty-minute broadcast on television addressing violence and harassment of gays, bisexuals, and lesbians. PFLAG aims to support lesbians, gays, and bisexuals as well as their families and friends, to help them learn to cope with homophobia in their lives, and to advocate equal rights for them.

PFLAG aims to counter harmful images in the mainstream media as well as within scientific journals and standard religious doctrine regarding bisexuals, gays, and lesbians, who are often portrayed on television as engaging in criminal activity.

PFLAG also puts out many publications that help parents deal with their children's coming out as well as for counselors and educators to help provide information and counter misconceptions.

As with many organizations that try to present the truth about lesbian, bisexual, and gay people, PFLAG has met with resistance from antigay groups as well as from the general public. Project Open Mind ads have been rejected by television stations in certain places, such as Missouri; elsewhere, their advertisements aimed at confronting antigay violence have been allowed only after 10:00 P.M. Also in recent years, groups within the ex-gay movement have formed to counter PFLAG's effectiveness, primarily sponsored by antigay and right-wing religious organizations. *Robert W. Anderson*

Bibliography

Aarons, Leroy. *Prayers for Bobby: A Mother's Coming to Terms With the Suicide of Her Gay Son.* New York: HarperSanFrancisco, 1995.

Bernstein, Robert A. *Straight Parents/Gay Children: Keeping Families Together.* New York: Thunder's Mouth Press, 1995.

Durgin-Clinchard, Jean. *Characteristics of Selected Local Chapters of Parents and Friends of Lesbians and Gays That Have Been Identified as Strong or Successful.* Lincoln: University of Nebraska Libraries, 1993.

Gallagher, John. "Making Airwaves: Gay Groups Declare TV the New Battleground for Tangling with Religious Right." *Advocate*, 720 (1996): 30–32.

Gibson, Mike. "TV Stations Refuse to Run PFLAG Ads (Parents and Friends of Lesbians and Gays)." *St. Louis Journalism Review*, 27, no. 192 (1996): 7.

See also Activism, U.S.; Community Centers; Gay Families; Parenting

Paris

"He who is convicted of sodomy shall be castrated; if convicted a second time, he shall lose the whole member; after a third conviction he shall be burned." In medieval France, the legal penalties for sodomy were thus clearly established. Reconstructing a gay history of this period is particularly difficult, however, since medieval French law insisted that when a man was burned for sodomy, all the documents concerning the case should be burned with him.

During the Renaissance, male homosexuality ("Italian vice," as the French called it) and lesbianism are documented in artistic and court circles around Catherine de Medici and above all her son

Henry III, of whom Agrippa d'Aubigné asked whether he was "a female king or indeed a male queen?" In Ronsard's words "the King embraces, kisses, and licks the fresh faces of his *mignons*, night and day while they, in return for money, one by one lend him their plump asses, and put up with the assault."

While homosexuality was often tolerated among the French aristocracy, it was usually punished among the lower classes, although in Paris there were fewer executions than in the provinces. A famous anecdote by Tallemand des Réaux describes in his *Historiettes* (c.1659) what appears to have been Louis XIII's first orgasm. One day when the sixteen-year-old Louis got out of his bath in front of Blainville (who was in charge of his wardrobe and had just got back from England), the king was seen to have an erection. "Indeed, Sire! Are you often troubled in this way?" asked the eighteen-year-old Blainville. "I will show you what they do in England," and he applied a few rapid wrist movements to the royal body, bringing the story to a rapid end to the king's great pleasure. Tallemand des Réaux puts down to this first encounter the king's fondness for handsome young men. The list of his favorites is long, starting with the well-named Saint-Amour and ending with the tragic case of the eighteen-year-old Henri d'Effiat, marquis de Cinq Mars, executed four years later, in 1642.

Louis XIV was not homosexual, unlike his brother Philippe, known as Monsieur, under whose princely patronage many homosexual poets (Campistron) and musicians (Lully) thrived. Saint-Simon describes him acerbically as "a small man with a big belly, walking on stilts since his heels were so high, always dressed like a woman, with many rings and bracelets and precious stones, with a long black powdered wig, ribbons everywhere he could put them, and covered in perfume." He nevertheless married twice. The letters of the Princesse Palatine (his tolerant second wife) to her sister in Germany give many insights into homosexual life at court: "Where have you been to know so little of the world? If one wanted to detest all those men who love males there would be very few people left to like. Here one finds all sorts. There are those who hate women like death and can only love men. Others only like young boys 10 or 11 years old; but most of them prefer boys between 17 and 25" (letter of 3 October 1705).

It is in this context that, in about 1678, one of the first-known societies of sodomites, a "*confrater-*

nité," was created, as described at the time by Bussy-Rabutin. It included many members of the nobility, including the prince de Conti, all under thirty. New applicants had to follow the statutes of the society:

> Article 3: Members will be received into the Order without regard to their social status . . . ; Article 5: The Order shall be divided into four groups so that the four Grand Masters shall have equal numbers; any new member must first submit himself to all four Grand Masters in turn, in order to avoid jealousies. Article 9: Anyone who brings a new member into the Order shall have the same rights as the Grand Masters during two days, it being understood that they will have their fill only after the Masters have been served.

Louis XIV decided to intervene when his eighteen-year-old son, the duc de Vermandois, joined the group. The young man was publicly whipped in front of the court and died shortly afterward. Other members of the group went into exile.

In 1720, the Paris police set up a special brigade to deal with sodomites. As a result, many detailed eighteenth-century reports concerning homosexual activity survive (Bibliothèque Nationale de France, collection Clairambault 983–986; another important collection of reports concerning arrests of sodomites between 1723 and 1749 is found in the Bibliothèque de l'Arsenal, Archives de la Bastille, 10254–10260). From these documents Lever shows that it is also possible to build up a list of nearly forty bars and cabarets where homosexuals met, usually in an upstairs room. In several of them it was possible for two men (or more) to hire a room with a bed for one hour. Many of the bars have evocative names: La Tour d'Argent, La Grande Pinte, Au Franc Bourguinon, Le Jardin des Coeurs. One was even called, ironically, Au Bon Chrétien (The Good Christian).

In 1725 a police report estimated the number of Parisian sodomites at twenty thousand (about 4 percent of the population), and lists were kept of known or suspected sodomites. The earliest dates from 1725 (113 names), but by 1783 there was a "great book where the names of all the pederasts were noted, about 40,000 of them." The police employed *agents provocateurs*, either paying them money or, in the case of handsome boys whom they had arrested, offering to drop all charges if they would work for the police. These boys were known as *mouches* (flies), and they could earn up to fifty pounds for each conviction. Thus in 1724 a *mouche* named Jallan provided a list of over twenty names (including the son of the painter Largillière). Lever shows that the names are known of over thirty such *mouches*, who seem to have worked specifically at entrapping eighteenth-century Parisian homosexuals. The most notorious was Simonnet, who worked regularly for the police from when he was about twenty, in 1704 (having been first arrested having sex with another man in a public park) until about 1740; another named Haymier worked (1715–1740) mostly in the royal gardens such as the Palais Royal, the Tuileries, and the Luxembourg. They were followed by Louis-Alexandre Framboisier, who was named inspector "in charge of the execution of the king's orders against sodomites."

From the reports of the *mouches,* it is also possible to reconstruct the known pickup areas in eighteenth-century Paris. The royal gardens were particularly favored since it was not possible to arrest anyone in them. The *mouche* therefore had to lead his prey out of the garden before he could be arrested. The Luxembourg Gardens were preferred by those looking for younger boys out of school. The royal Tuileries Gardens were the most popular (and had been since at least the seventeenth century), especially for noblemen looking for soldiers; the Tuileries have in fact attained an almost mythical status in Parisian gay history (Proust's Baron de Charlus visits them at night), and they are still very popular today.

Men also met under the bridges of the Seine (where it was socially acceptable for men to urinate publicly into the river). When Bernard Girardot was arrested (1737), the report by the *mouche* describes a strikingly modern scene:

Near the sand of the Pont Neuf, I found Girardot who looked at me as he walked close by, giving me the signal known to sodomites, and he then went on to the next arch where he looked back to see if I was following. Since all his signals made it impossible for me not to see him, I followed and walked close by him, but looking in the other direction. He then came over and started up a conversation. . . . There were young men in the water, and he said "You see, they look young, but they are well built and well membered." And seeing a young man come out of the water he said "He's beautiful! You see how he puts me in form?" . . . I said to him "So you like men?" And he said "Everyone has his weakness. Will you come into the water with me?" . . . I agreed to bathe my feet, and when he saw my legs he cried "Oh! You have hairy legs! . . . You see the state I'm in? I used to manipulate myself in the water. Shall we go somewhere else?" I walked him to the Petit Châtelet, where he was arrested.

The punishment for those caught in the act varied from brief imprisonment to twenty-five years in jail or exile, in extreme cases or repeated offenses. Execution resulted only in cases where violence was also involved, in particular on a young child. The last Parisian execution for sodomy occurred on October 10, 1783; Jacques-François Pascal had been found guilty not merely of sodomy but also of brutally murdering the fourteen-year-old delivery boy who had tried to resist his advances.

The police reports were usually drawn up by the *mouches* and are thus written in everyday language. They provide a wealth of details about the terminology, coded language, social habits, sexual practices, and attitudes of Parisian homosexuals at the time. Many men were clearly quite without guilt and defended their actions by referring to "pleasure" and to their emotional bond with the other man. After the French Revolution, the first Code Pénal (1791) did not mention homosexuality at all. The Code Napoléon (1810) likewise refrained from introducing specific antihomosexual measures. The various revisions of this code brought in small changes: in 1832 consensual sex, without violence, between two males was deemed legal as long as both were over the age of eleven; the age was raised to thirteen in 1863; under the Nazi-inspired Vichy regime, in 1942 it was raised to twenty-one. In 1982 this was again lowered to fifteen.

During the nineteenth century, Paris became a haven especially for homosexuals fleeing the more repressive British laws (Oscar Wilde died and is buried there). The work of writers such as Marcel Proust and later André Gide established Paris's reputation for tolerance and sexual freedom. During the 1930s a strong feminist lesbian movement was also formed. Writers have always been at the center of Parisian gay life, and their meeting places on the Left Bank such as the Café Flore or the Deux Magots became world famous. Many American homosexuals settled in Paris. The homosexual movement was intimately tied with the group of French "intellectuals," including heterosexual freethinkers such as Jean-Paul Sartre and Simone de Beauvoir, who supported many gay writers, protected them, and helped them financially (notably Jean Genet).

After World War II, the center of Paris gay life moved to the Right Bank, closer to the Opéra, to the rue Sainte-Anne, but gay life was still led behind closed doors. The main homosexual rights group was Arcadie. In the 1970s, with the arrival of a French gay liberation movement, the center of gravity moved into the Marais, near the Town Hall. The first bars appeared that refused to hide what they were but had open plate-glass windows and doors wide open. The Marais is now the center of a thriving gay commercial area. During the 1980s the gay press was dominated by the *Gai Pied*, founded by Michel Foucault. There has been a full-time gay radio station, Fréquence Gaie, since 1981. The main association for helping AIDS victims, AIDES, was founded by Daniel Deffert, Foucault's lover.

Since French law has protected the concept of "privacy" ever since the Code Napoléon, the modern gay movement has had difficulty in getting over the psychological hurdle of defining homosexuality as a purely private matter. The first elected public officials to come out as openly gay did so only in 1998.   *Davitt Moroney*

Bibliography

Courouve, Claude. *Les Origines de la répression de l'homosexualité*. Paris, 1978.

Coward, D. A. "Attitudes to Homosexuality in 18th-century France." *Journal of European Studies* 10 (1980): 231–55.

Daniel, Marc. *Hommes du grand siècle. Études sur l'homosexualité sous les règnes de Louis XIII et de Louis XIV*. Paris, Arcadie, 1957.

Lever, Maurice. *Les Bûchers de Sodome*. Paris: Fayard, 1985.

See also Code Napoléon; Foucault, Michel; France; French Literature; Gay and Lesbian Press; Genet, Jean; Gide, André; Henri III; Lully, Jean-Baptiste; Orléans, Monsieur Philippe, duc d'; Proust, Marcel; Wilde, Oscar

Parnell, Peter (1953–)

Peter Parnell was born in New York City, the only child of Sol and Pearl (née Bogen) Parnell. His father was an executive in the textile industry. Parnell grew up and received his primary and secondary education in Queens, New York. He began writing plays while a student majoring in theater and English at Dartmouth College (B.A., magna cum laude, 1975). He was three times the winner of the Frost Playwriting Competition at Dartmouth and received a Reynolds Fellowship to live in London and write in 1975–1976.

His short play *Scooter Thomas Makes It to the Top of the World* was workshopped at the O'Neill Playwrights Conference in 1977, and he joined the Playwrights Unit of the Actors Studio the following year. His play *Sorrows of Stephen* was then workshopped at the Actors Studio and produced by Joseph Papp at New York's Public Theater in 1979. His next play, *The Rise and Rise of Daniel Rocket*, was produced at Playwrights Horizons in 1982, and Parnell shortly joined Playwrights Horizons' Artistic Board. Subsequently, he had four more plays produced at Playwrights Horizons: *Romance Language* (1984), *Hyde in Hollywood* (1989), *Flaubert's Latest* (1992), and *An Imaginary Life* (1993). *Daniel Rocket* and *Hyde* in Hollywood were taped by American Playhouse and broadcast nationally on PBS. *Romance Language* also played at the Mark Taper Forum in Los Angeles in 1985–1986. His stage adaptation of John Irving's 1985 novel *The Cider House Rules* was presented at the Lincoln Center Theatres in the 1996–1997 season and the Mark Taper Forum in 1998–1999. He has received fellowships from the National Endowment for the Arts and from the Guggenheim and Ingram Merrill Foundations and was playwright in residence at the Denver Center Theatre Company in 1983–1984.

Daniel Rocket can be read as having a gay subtext. Its plot centers around a boy marginalized by his peers because he is different—he can fly. Certainly the play's depiction of childhood cruelties and isolation is familiar to queer children. *Hyde in Hollywood* tells the story of a fictional gay film director from the golden age of Hollywood. *Flaubert's Latest* and *An Imaginary Life* at their very center feature openly gay characters, with a character in the earlier play suffering from AIDS. A gay character in the later play constantly reinvents his life after being diagnosed with a serious disease. Parnell is a leading theatrical innovator, with each new play breaking dramaturgical grounds and experimenting with storytelling techniques and dramatic structure. Many of his plays could be described as theatrical magic realism. In this respect, only Edward Albee among his contemporaries exceeds his importance.

D. S. Lawson

P

Bibliography

Bennetts, Leslie. "A Literary Cast Populates *Romance Language*." *New York Times*, November 21, 1984, C14.

Blau, Eleanor. "He Calls Sorrow a Comic Ache." *New York Times*, January 6, 1980, sec. 2:3f.

Gusso, Mel. "The Return to *Romance*." *New York Times*, January 6, 1980, sec. 2:3f.

Harris, William. "The Evening that *Flaubert* Came to Stay." *New York Times*, June 14, 1992, sec. 2:8.

Levy, Laurie M. "A Partnership for the Theater." *Theater Week* (December 18–24, 1989): 32–34.

"Peter Parnell." In *Contemporary Authors*. Vol. 143. Donna Olendorf, ed. Detroit: Gale, 1994, 329–30.

Sheehy, Catherine. "A Life in the Theatres." *Village Voice*, December 14, 1993, 105f.

Stuart, Jan. "Stars and Stripes Forever." *American Theatre* (April 1985): 12–18.

See also Albee, Edward; McNally, Terrence

Partch, Harry (1901–1974)

An extreme individualist in both his musical style and personality, Partch witnessed three quarters of the twentieth century from a position at the margins of American society. Like several other West Coast experimental composers, Partch was influenced by a wide variety of musics. In his late twenties, he developed a system of microtonal just intonation and began a long career of inventing unique instruments of great sculptural beauty. His works from the 1930s represent a devotion to bardic, monophonic music. In 1935, Partch entered on a period that has been mythologized as his "hobo years," during which he produced a prose-music journal entitled *Bitter Music*. This work, which Partch assumed he had destroyed, offers insights into his experiences as a homosexual living in transient shelters during the Great Depression.

Partch's *Oedipus* (1951, revised 1952–1954) signaled a transition from a bardic ideal to a vision of totally integrated music theater based on his standards of "corporeal" performance. Partch spent much of 1955–1962 at the University of Illinois, where he created several of his major music theater works, including *The Bewitched* and *Revelation in the Courthouse Park*. *Revelation* is concerned with individual integrity, turning on issues of nonconformity and ambiguous sexuality within an emphatically heterosexual and hostile society.

The quintessential loner, Partch proved ill-suited for collaboration and was satisfied with a production only when he had designed every element himself. Many of his professional and personal relationships collapsed under the weight of his demanding temperament. While essential to Partch's composition and fundamental concept of theatrical performance, his unconventional intonation system and massive instruments continue to impede the dissemination of his music. Partch and his singular creations remain somewhat isolated within a private realm of bitter music.

W. Anthony Sheppard

Bibliography

Gilmore, Bob. *Harry Partch: A Biography.* New Haven: Yale University Press, 1998.

Partch, Harry. *Bitter Music: Collected Journals, Essays, Introductions, and Librettos.* Thomas McGeary, ed. and intro. Urbana, Ill.: University of Illinois Press, 1991.

———. *Genesis of a Music.* New York: Da Capo, 1974.

See also Music and Musicians 1: Classical Music

Pasolini, Pier Paolo (1922–1975)

Pasolini was an Italian poet, novelist, filmmaker, playwright, and essayist whose vast and compelling production makes him one of the most important European intellectuals of this century. Pasolini saw both his writings and his films as forms of political intervention in Italian society, defining himself as a Marxist deeply influenced by Catholicism. His complex relationship with his homosexuality, however, is the actual core of his poetics. Expelled from the Communist Party because of his sexual diversity, Pasolini considered himself an outcast both from an ideological and a personal standpoint. Referring to Giovanbattista Vico's philosophical theories, Pasolini believed that Western culture had detached itself from a mythic golden age, characterized by "natural," spontaneous, and thus "honest" relationships with oneself and others. According to Pasolini, only marginalized, poor, and/or working-class individuals still had an unconscious connection with nature and "normalcy." But after World War II, Italy's transformation into a modern, wealthy society irremediably corrupted those social classes that still maintained some form of "authenticity." Italy, Pasolini believed, had turned into a bourgeois, and thus "inauthentic," dishonest society. He was aware that he himself belonged to that bourgeois milieu he abhorred and was torn between the awareness of his intrinsic "corruption" and his visceral attraction toward that lost naturalness. His "corruption" had also, and primarily, a sexual connotation. Pasolini's desire was essentially directed toward men who contrasted with his own identity. Poor and unlettered men were the objects of his sexual fantasies. Since for Pasolini to be aware meant to be aware of one's moral and intellectual corruption, self-awareness signified everything that was marred by unnaturalness, homosexuality included. Yet Pasolini also considered his "deviancy" an expression of opposition to the Italian bourgeoisie. On the one hand, his homosexuality manifested his being a product of middle-class culture; on the other, his sexual "scandal" showed the fundamental abnormality of that very culture.

Pasolini wrote his first verses in the dialect of Friuli, the region in northern Italy where he grew up. *Le ceneri di Gramsci* (1957), his first collection of poetry written in Italian, established him as one of the most influential poets of his time. *La religione del mio tempo* (1961), *Poesie in forma di rosa* (1964), and *Transumanar and organizzar* (1971) are among his other books of poetry. *Ragazzi di vita* (*The Ragazzi*, 1955) and *Una vita violenta* (*A Violent Life*, 1959), written in the dialect of Rome, and the posthumous *Petrolio* (1992) are Pasolini's most interesting novels. His theater work, albeit fascinating, has not been the object of much attention. *Affabulazione*, *Porcile*, and *Orgia* are three provoking plays.

His films have always had a controversial reception because of their unconventional, disturbing contents. *Accattone* (1961), *La ricotta* (1963), *Il vangelo secondo Matteo* (1964), *Teorema* (1968), *Porcile* (1969), *Medea* (1969), *Il decameron* (1971), and *Salò o le centoventi giornate di Sodoma* (1975) are only some of Pasolini's most accomplished and compelling films. Particularly significant are Pasolini's essays on film theory contained in *Empirismo eretico* (*Heretical Empiricism*, 1972).

Armando Maggi

Bibliography

Rohdie, Sam. *The Passion of Pier Paolo Pasolini*. Bloomington, Ind.: Indiana University Press, 1995.

See also Film; Italian Literature; Italy; Renaissance Neoplatonism

Pastoralia and Penitentials

"*Pastoralia*," or Christian pastoral writings, are intended to help priests or pastors in ministering to the needs of their congregations. The term is applied particularly to medieval Christian writings in a number of different genres, including summaries of church law or doctrine, handbooks for confessors, and preaching manuals. The medieval pastoral writings are unanimous in denouncing same-sex activity, which some of them consider more serious than murder or maternal incest. The texts are also anxious to prevent the spread of homosexuality, so they speak of it quite indirectly, with few details. Penitentials represent an earlier and much franker genre of pastoral writing. They are lists of penances to be assigned by confessors for specific sins, which they catalogue in great detail. Originating in the practice of the Celtic monasteries, the penitentials were widely diffused throughout Europe, where they continued to exert influence well into the twelfth century. The penitentials refer many times to same-sex activities, between both men and women. The penances assigned for these acts vary so widely from one list to another that it is not possible to summarize them. But it is generally true that male homosexuality is penalized more severely than female, adults more severely than children or adolescents, and clerics more seriously than laypeople. In their categorization of different kinds of sexual activity, the penitentials set the groundwork for later systematization of moral theology.

Mark D. Jordan

Bibliography

Payer, Pierre J. *Sex and the Penitentials*. Toronto: University of Toronto Press, 1984.

See also Catholicism; Monasticism, Christian; Clergy

Pater, Walter Horatio (1839–1894)

Walter Horatio Pater's *Studies in the History of the Renaissance* (1873) was the first coherent embodiment of the tenets and homoerotically coded discourse that define aestheticism. Pater was educated at King's School, Canterbury, and Oxford, where he became a fellow of Brasenose College in 1864. From 1869 onward, he lived with his sisters Hester and Clara. In *The Renaissance*, his most famous and influential work, Pater, who was attracted to men, often encourages a reading of his aesthetic views as supporting unconventional desires. His essay on "Winckelmann," for example, defends a rare type of person who is shunned by the status quo but whose passion and "moral sexlessness" (a concept also discussed in his essay "Diaphaneité") are conjoined with insight and heroism. Pater's frequently recurring image of a man learned in aesthetic appreciation being attracted to, and wishing to instruct, a young man whose heightened sensuality is signified by his physical beauty echoes the Hellenic model of *paiderastia*. This classic discourse of male friendship offered Pater a sanctioned context for voicing the view, for example, that Winckelmann's affinity with Hellenism is proven to be more than intellectual by his "romantic, fervent friendships with young men" (1:191). The context also encouraged Pater and his audience to join Winckelmann as he "fingers those pagan marbles" of physical beauty without any sense of shame (1:222).

The Renaissance became the "golden book," as Oscar Wilde called it, for many of Oxford's young male undergraduates. Conversely, Margaret Oliphant condemned the collection for its "Greekness," while W. H. Mallock caricatured Pater in *The New Republic* (1877) as Mr. Rose, a self-absorbed hedonist attracted to young men. Ironically, at least one person, Charles Edward Hutchinson, author of *Boy Worship* (1880), read Mallock's parody as confirmation that others besides himself experienced same-sex desire.

Pater described his novel *Marius the Epicurean* (1885) as an elaboration of the views that he first presented in the infamous conclusion to *The Renaissance*, which encourages readers "to burn always with this hard, gemlike flame" (1:236), "to be for ever curiously testing new opinions and courting new impressions, never acquiescing in a facile orthodoxy" (1:237). Set in the days of Marcus Aurelius, the novel follows its hero, Marius, as he explores various philosophies and religions only to die believing that "the unclouded and receptive soul [should quit] the world finally, with the same fresh wonder with which it had entered the world still unimpaired" (2:220). The novel also echoes *The Renaissance* in combining its advocacy of wonder and exploration with homosensuality, most notably in the hero's relations with other men such as Flavian, a beautiful young schoolmate who lives a life of sensual pleasure.

Pater's other publications include *Imaginary Portraits* (1887), a collection of historical and mythological fantasies; *Plato and Platonism* (1893); *Greek Studies* (1895); *Gaston de Latour* (1896), an unfinished novel set in sixteenth-century France; and *Appreciations: With an Essay on Style* (1889), a highly respected collection of essays on English literature.
Dennis Denisoff

Bibliography
Pater, Walter. *Works*. 10 vols. London: Macmillan, 1920–1927.

See also Aestheticism; Art History; Greece; Pederasty; Plato; Wilde, Oscar; Winckelmann, Johann Joachim

Patrick, Robert (1938–)

The theater, although always a haven for gay people backstage, did not portray an onstage gay character as if he were normal until Robert Patrick's brilliant triple monologue, *Kennedy's Children*. This American work made it to Broadway in 1976 only after success in London. Beginning in the late sixties, Patrick developed his skills Off-Off Broadway, especially at the Caffe Cino, a hotbed of revolution of all sorts. His ability to create believably natural and yet theatrically entertaining dialogue carried him through a series of increasingly gay plays culminating in the first gay "everybody takes his clothes off" opus, *T-Shirts* (1980), which was wildly popular. But by that date, the dynamic Off- and Off-Off Broadway scene was collapsing, harassed by unions, the FBI, and lack of money. Patrick moved to Los Angeles, where he turned to short stories and novels, carving out a second career in film and television with his unfailing sense of what's funny, both about being gay and about being human.
F. Valentine Hooven III

Bibliography
Duberman, Martin. *About Time*. New York: Sea Horse Press, 1986.

See also Caffe Cino; Ludlam, Charles

Paul, Saint (c.5–c.60 C.E.)

Probably born in Tarsus, in present-day Turkey, and trained in the Pharisaic tradition, the erstwhile enemy of the Jewish Christian movement joined that very group after a revelatory experience, becoming one of the main "missionaries" to non-Jews, and apparently dying as a martyr in Rome. His letters, part of this "missionary" endeavor and his only literary remains, form an important and historically influential part of the Christian canon of scriptures.

Erotic same-sex acts did not feature prominently in Paul's letters; only three passages are of interest: Romans 1:26–27, 1 Corinthians 6:9–10, and 1 Timothy 1:10. The Timothy passage (very similar to 1 Cor. 6:9–10) can be ignored for our purposes as it is usually taken as having been written by Paul's followers in his name. The Corinthians text translates as "Neither the sexually immoral, nor idolaters, nor adulterers, nor *malakoi*, nor *arsenokoitai*, nor thieves, nor the greedy . . . will inherit the kingdom of God." Such "catalogs of vices" (popular contemporary rhetorical devices) were designed to castigate people in wholesale fashion. Paul's intention here is to remind the Corinthian Christian community to abstain from "unrighteousness" (e.g., marrying one's stepmother; suing each other in law courts). The meaning of the italicized Greek words in this context is disputed. *Arsenokoites* is likely to be related to sex for economic exploitation, not necessarily male same-gender sex only. *Malakos* may refer to a man taking on culturally defined female gender characteristics (e.g., being penetrated; desiring "too much sex"; even beautifying himself to attract women). Yet modern translations have consistently rendered these terms with reference to "effeminacy" and "abusers of themselves with mankind," and since the mid-twentieth century (following the ideological revolution of sexual science) as "sexual perverts," "homosexuals," and the like.

Probably more important in the history of interpretation is the passage from Romans. Here Paul maintains that all humankind was able to perceive God in the created world but refused to do so (Rom. 1:18–32): "For this [reason] God handed them over to dishonorable passions, for also their females exchanged natural [sexual] intercourse with the one against nature, and likewise also the males, leaving the natural [sexual] intercourse with the females, were inflamed in their lust toward each other: males effecting shamelessness in males, receiving the retribution among themselves which is due on account of their delusion." Many scholars interpret verses 26–27 in the context of Jewish Hellenistic wisdom theology, ultimately arguing that Paul understood "against nature" as "against the divinely created order." Perhaps more appropriately, it could be seen as Paul using a popular Greek stock argument concerning certain sexual acts "against nature" (*para physin*), similar to the argument of 1 Cor. 11:14–15. "Nature" (*physis*), however, is a culturally loaded word incorporating elements of what the modern West calls "nature" as well as "culture": "nature" is

socially constructed. Paul's words are ultimately based on culturally constructed gender conceptions that were seen as "natural facts," ordering society in Mediterranean antiquity. However, as Christian canonical scripture, Paul's use of the "nature argument" would prove to be fateful in the history of the condemnation of erotic same-sex relations.

Holger Szesnat

Bibliography

Countryman, L. W. *Dirt, Greed and Sex: Sexual Ethics in the New Testament and Their Implications for Today.* Philadelphia: Fortress Press, 1988.

Martin, D. B. "*Arsenokoites* and *Malakos*: Meanings and Consequences." In *Biblical Ethics and Homosexuality: Listening to Scripture.* R. L. Brawley, ed. Louisville, Ky.: Westminster John Knox, 1996, 117–36.

See also Alan of Lille; Bible, Canon Law; Christianity; Natural Law

Pears, Sir Peter (1910–1986)

Although this English tenor and life partner of composer Benjamin Britten, worked as a professional singer in the 1930s, it was not until his return from America with Britten in 1942 that his long career really began. Not unexpectedly, he was particularly associated with Britten's music: he created tenor roles in all of Britten's operas, from *Peter Grimes* (1945) to *Death in Venice* (1973), and gave the first performances of most of Britten's song cycles, beginning with the *Serenade for Tenor, Horn, and Strings,* op. 31. Pears also sang, and often commissioned, music by other composers, and was a notable Evangelist in both of Bach's passions.

Pears and Britten were a famous recital pair, performing at home and abroad songs by Schubert, Schumann, Purcell, and others, as well as Britten's own. Their partnership ceased only with Britten's ill health. Pears also performed with guitarist Julian Bream and harpist Ossian Ellis, and Britten wrote works for these ensembles. Later in his life Pears devoted considerable time to teaching, mostly at the Britten-Pears School for Advanced Musical Studies in Snape.

With Britten, Pears was among the founders of the English Opera Group in 1946; his 1947 suggestion led to the establishment of the Aldeburgh Festival, the annual presentation of music and other arts in their hometown, which began in 1948. His literary talent is evinced by his collaboration with Britten on the libretto of *A Midsummer Night's Dream*, his choice of the texts for Britten's *Songs and Proverbs of William Blake*, op. 74, and the diaries, articles, and notes about his career, singing, and repertoire that he contributed to the Aldeburgh Festival program books and other publications.

After Britten's death in 1976, Pears became more vocal about his sexuality, speaking frankly about their relationship in an interview in the *Advocate* (July 12, 1979) and in Tony Palmer's 1980 documentary about Britten, *A time there was. . . .* Theirs was a true partnership in every respect, and one is hard-pressed to imagine one without the other, so closely were their lives and careers intertwined.

Stephen McClatchie

Bibliography

Headington, Christopher. *Peter Pears: A Biography*. London: Faber & Faber, 1992.

Reed, Philip, ed. *The Travel Diaries of Peter Pears*. Woodbridge, Suffolk: Boydell Press/Britten-Pears Library, 1995.

Thorpe, Marion, ed. *Peter Pears: A Tribute on His 75th Birthday*. London : Faber Music in association with the Britten Estate, 1985.

See also Britten, Benjamin; Music and Musicians 1: Classical Music; Opera; Schubert, Franz Peter

Pederasty

Cross-culturally and transhistorically, homosexual relations have most often been structured through some form of either age-grading or gender-grading. *Pederasty* may be taken to refer either to the most widely recognized forms of age-graded male homosexuality or age-graded male homosexuality in general, with the caveat that use of the term generally is limited to relations in which the younger partner is in some sense not fully mature. This may in some instances include relations between an older man and a younger man in his late teens or early twenties, but more commonly it is reserved for those relations where the younger partner is under eighteen. The term has sometimes been used to denote all-male homosexuality, or specific sexual acts between males, probably owing to the close association of the idea of male homosexuality with traditionally recognized forms of age-graded male relationships. Other terms that have been used to denote age-

graded male homosexual relationships include man/boy love, boy-love (*Knabenliebe* in German literature), Greek love, ephebophilia, and pedophilia. Standard definitions of *pedophilia* specify that the younger partner be prepubertal, whereas pederasty is generally taken to apply when the younger partner is pubescent or postpubertal. As it is used here, pederasty is not taken necessarily to exclude relationships between prepubertal boys and older partners, as the idea of puberty is culturally constructed from a complex and interactive set of independently varying factors, and is not recognized in many of the cultures and periods under consideration. The word is also not taken here necessarily to include or exclude any specific sexual practice.

Cultural Variations of Pederasty

Age-graded male homosexuality has enjoyed widely varying degrees of tolerance, integration, and institutionalization in different cultures and historic periods, and has been conceived and expressed in an equally wide variety of ways. Two well-known examples of institutionalized pederasty have frequently been employed to illustrate the socially constructed nature of human eroticism and the cultural structuring of patterns of sexual interaction. In classical Athens, age-graded male relationships were considered essential as the means by which a beardless male youth could best be socialized into a responsible and ethical citizen. Accordingly, pederastic relations in Athens tended toward long-term one-on-one relationships, with the youth eventually marrying and adopting the role of mentor to a youth of the next generation. Among the Sambia of Papua New Guinea, age-graded male homosexual eroticism has also traditionally been institutionalized, but the Sambia ascribe greater importance to specific erotic behaviors and emphasize certain magical powers attributed to semen. The Sambia believe that ingesting semen orally, via fellatio, is essential for a boy's proper masculine development. This insemination is provided to boys by older bachelors during ritualized and kinship-structured nocturnal sex play in the bachelor's quarters. The boys are inseminated from around age eight to around age fifteen, when they switch roles and serve as inseminators until they are married, at which point they cease regular homosexual contacts. What is important in these examples is the variability they represent in conceptualizations and structuring of sexuality, and the links they demonstrate between social organization and the organization of eroticism. Sociologist

Barry Adam has noted that institutionalized forms of age-structured male homoeroticism often follow the same kinship rules and sometimes even the same conventions as heterosexual marriages (including, for example, complex incest prohibitions, bride prices, and the mourning of a deceased partner), and that the relationships that are socially prescribed tend also to be perceived by participants as sexually attractive.

Examples of institutionalized or well-integrated cultural forms of pederastic eroticism are abundant in both the ethnographic and the historical literature. According to Adam, "[E]thnographic evidence, drawn from all continents except North America, suggests a special propensity for homosexual relations among unmarried male youths." Some instances include medieval Persia, classical Tibet and Southeast Asia, imperial China and Byzantium, feudal Japan, numerous Islamic and Berber societies of North Africa (e.g., the Siwa in the Libyan desert), the Nyakyusa of eastern Africa, the Azande and the Mossi of the Sudan, most of the indigenous tribes of the South Pacific region including Australia, and the Hellenic and Roman empires. In general, pederasty may be said to flourish where sexual expression is not generally met with extreme fear and hostility, or where such fears are directed principally toward heterosexual contacts.

Pederasty in Western History

Historically, pederasty has been the predominant form of same-sex eroticism in Europe as well as in most of the non-European cultures to which we look for the roots of Western culture. Bullough considers the Jewish prohibition of homosexuality to have been an effort to distinguish Jews from non-Jews, since pederastic traditions were widely observed among all the other groups with whom they had extensive contact, including Assyrians, Phoenicians, Persians, Egyptians, and Greeks. Social historians have noted the widespread observance of pederastic traditions and the forms they have taken in many regions of Europe throughout most of the succeeding generations since ancient times. These include not only the classic Greek pedagogical tradition but also the traditions of temple prostitution practiced in Greece, Rome, Egypt, and elsewhere; the Christian monastic and pedagogical traditions; various traditions based in apprenticeship; traditions based in recreation, such as at swimming holes, urban hustling, and cruising traditions; and, more recently, traditions based in modern ideas, such as the "scout-

ing" tradition with which Lord Baden-Powell is associated, or the "democratic" tradition of Walt Whitman's "comradely love," also associated with Edward Carpenter.

It is possible to see these traditions played out in narrative history, which records the relationships of many leading historical figures, particularly those well known for their homosexuality. The earliest of these was the Egyptian pharaoh Akhenaton, who appointed the youth Smenkhare as his coregent. Not counting the Greeks, other notable figures whose life stories incorporate participation in pederastic traditions include Roman emperor Hadrian; Christian theologian Augustine; major figures of the Renaissance such as Leonardo da Vinci, Michelangelo, Shakespeare, and Marlowe; philosophers such as Erasmus and Francis Bacon; romantic writers such as Goethe and Byron; such modern figures as Walt Whitman, Oscar Wilde, and André Gide; and later twentieth-century figures such as Paul Goodman, William S. Burroughs, and Allen Ginsberg.

Pederasty Today

The rise of industrialism and capitalism have brought rapid and remarkable changes in ideas and social organization to the West in recent centuries. Although these changes have led to a withdrawal of cultural approval, and indeed vehement rejection, of traditional pederastic forms, these forms have not been entirely suppressed. The regular occurrences of scandals over eruptions of pedagogical eros, overly devoted apprenticeships, overly "adhesive" comradely love between unequals who refuse to act as unequals, priests partying with acolytes, "inappropriate" cruising, heretical hustling, and boys "being boys" serve as apt confirmation that the traditions linger on. Further confirmation is offered by Bell and Weinberg, who found in the late 1970s that 25 percent of their large sample of 3,538 gay white men and 16 percent of 316 gay black men from the San Francisco Bay Area had had at least one sexual partner under age sixteen when the respondents were over age twenty-one. The traditional character of many of these contacts may be surmised from a wide array of more or less fictionalized accounts available in most libraries and gay bookstores.

What was once a vaunted tradition, or a common practice, is now seen as a subversive act that threatens the authority of the parent over the child and the state over the citizen, and so it goes underground. Because of the new subversive status of pederasty—complete with lengthy mandatory minimum prison sentences, state and national registries, indefinite psychiatric incarceration statutes, and mandatory antiandrogen injections—accurate information about it is not as well disseminated as it might be. It has become standard practice for mainstream researchers to lump together all sexual interactions between legal adults and legal minors—including rape, father-daughter incest, and various forms of literal molestation as well as consensual pederastic, heterosexual, and lesbian relations—and then imply (usually by means of a simple correlation containing a gross statistical aggregation bias) that the predictably negative aftereffects of some of these experiences are characteristic of all of them. But many available studies avoid this approach and provide instead a clearer picture of the range and nature of childhood and youthful sexual experiences.

The picture of pederasty that emerges from this literature contrasts sharply with present-day media hyperbole but is not inconsistent with the ethnographic and historic records of pederasty in other times and places. In general terms, contrary to the view promoted in some quarters (and unlike heterosexual contacts between comparably aged persons, according to most studies), the majority of pederastic relationships do not involve force or coercion and are not perceived by the younger male partner to be either qualitatively negative or to have negative effects—this is clear from the results of many studies, including studies by researchers who have issued ardent moral condemnations of pederasty. In closer perspective, Sandfort has found that the most common affective reactions indicated by his self-selected sample of twenty-five boys (age 10–16) to their ongoing relationships with older men (age 26–66) were "nice," "happy," "free," "safe," "contented," and "proud." These boys' relationships with their older friends were based on a variety of mutual recreational activities aside from sex, and also typically included some mentoring, including help with schoolwork and advice regarding difficult decisions. The relationships were also typically characterized by a feeling on the part of the boy that he could speak openly with his partner without fear of condemnation. Some of the boys felt they needed this kind of understanding, because of troubles with their parents, but in just as many cases, the boys were happy with their families and appreciated the man as an additional asset in their lives. Tindall, using a smaller but probably more representative sample, found that nine boys he counseled in school as young teens and who at that time had been involved in pederastic relations, tended—two to three decades later—to be well adjusted, successful in their lives, and contributors to their communities. In several cases, the boys had entered the same line of work as their older lovers. Tindall found that a majority of the boys felt an erotic attraction to the man at the time of the relationship, even though all of them later married and raised families relatively unproblematically. Only one of the nine boys took a mildly negative view of his relationship later in life, while several of the boys maintained close friendships with their former lovers. Larger studies and literature reviews, such as that of Bauserman and Rind, have confirmed in general outline the findings of these and several similar qualitative studies of consensual pederastic relationships. Bauserman and Rind also include a useful bibliography for the study of outcomes of sexual interactions between children or adolescents and adults. *David Menasco*

Bibliography

Adam, Barry D. "Age, Structure, and Sexuality: Reflections on the Anthropological Evidence on Homosexual Relations." *Journal of Homosexuality* 11 (1985): 19. (Also published in E. Blackwood, ed. *The Many Faces of Homosexuality: Anthropological Approaches to Homosexual Behavior.* New York: Harrington Park Press, 1985.)

Bauserman, Robert, and Bruce Rind. "Psychological Correlates of Male Child and Adolescent Sexual Experience with Adults: A Review of the Nonclinical Literature." *Archives of Sexual Behavior* 26 (1997): 105–41.

Bell, Alan P., and Martin S. Weinberg. *Homosexualities: A Study of Diversity Among Men and Women.* New York: Simon & Schuster, 1978.

Brongersma, Edward. *Loving Boys: A Multidisciplinary Study of Sexual Relations between Adults and Minor Males.* Vols. 1 and 2. Elmhurst, N.Y.: Global Academic Publishers, 1986.

Bullough, Vern L. *Sexual Variance in Society and History.* Chicago: University of Chicago Press, 1976.

Eglinton, J. Z. *Greek Love.* New York: Oliver Layton Press, 1964.

Jones, Gerald P. "The Social Study of Pederasty: In Search of a Literature Base." *Journal of Homosexuality* 8 (1982): 61–95.

Percy, William Armstrong III. *Pederasty and Pedagogy in Archaic Greece.* Urbana, Ill.: University of Illinois Press, 1996.

Sandfort, Theo G. M. "Sex in Pedophiliac Relationships: An Empirical Investigation Among a Non-representative Group of Boys." *Journal of Sex Research* 20 (1984): 123–42.

Tindall, R. H. "The Male Adolescent Involved with a Pederast Becomes an Adult." *Journal of Homosexuality* 3 (1978): 373–82.

Tsang, Daniel. "Resources: An Annotated Guide to the Literature." In *The Age Taboo: Gay Male Sexuality, Power and Consent.* Daniel Tsang, ed. Boston: Alyson, 1981.

See also Beloved; Dancing Boys; Education; Gay Relationships; Gide, André; Greece; Judaism; Melanesia; Morocco; NAMBLA; North American Man/Boy Love Association

Penna, Sandro (1906–1977)

Sandro Penna, an Italian poet and native of Perugia, spent his life from the age of sixteen in Rome. Often kept out of school by illness, he developed early patterns of isolation that, nevertheless, allowed for abundant contact with the passing flesh of adolescent boys. This way of life gave him both the time to write and the theme to write about.

In 1929, Penna sent a batch of his poems to the distinguished poet Umberto Saba, who encouraged him to continue writing. Three years later he met Saba, and the older man did him the honor of privately circulating some of his poems. For all his isolation, Penna nevertheless managed to enlist the aid—and friendship—of many of the luminaries of modern Italian literature. In 1935 the poet Eugenio Montale helped him compile a collection of his poems. He made lasting friendships with novelists Elsa Morante, Alberto Moravia, and Natalia Ginzburg, but above all with Pier Paolo Pasolini. Penna met Pasolini after the latter reviewed his 1950 collection *Appunti*. The two men's friendship developed around their shared interests, not only in poetry and boys but also in the relationship between these two great sources of beauty.

In 1956, the year of the collection *Una strana gioia di vivere*, Penna met Raffaele Cedrino, then age fourteen, with whom he formed a relationship that lasted until 1970. In 1957, the year of Saba's death, Penna brought out his collected poems, *Tutte le poesie*, and was joint winner of the literary prize The Premio Viareggio. The 1970s saw a period of extreme poverty and intermittent illness, during which Penna had to be financially helped by his literary friends.

Like many of the boys they are about, his poems are small, sinewy, and perfectly formed. Like some of the boys, they are ill-behaved and outspoken but nonetheless elegant for all that. (However, he never uses "bad" language.) Like Pasolini's fiction and some of his films, Penna's poetry tends not to be located in the classical center of the city of Rome but in its scarred hinterlands, where proletarian boys are observed in their natural surroundings, cycling, playing football, urinating against trees or walls, and just plain loafing about.

While a lot of the poetry celebrates the mere sight of boys, as much is informed by the touch and taste of them. Their physicality requires no aesthetic transformation by the poet's art to freight it with spiritual worth. Penna does not seek to transform an already consummate beauty; he merely records it. Moreover, nothing else interests him. To those who demanded that he write about some topic more wholesome than boys, he replied: "*Ma io non so parlare d'altre cose. / Le altre cose son tutte noiose*" (I don't know how to write about anything else; everything else is just boring).   *Gregory Woods*

Bibliography

Garboli, Cesare. *Penna Papers.* Milan: Garzanti, 1984.

Pecora, Elio. *Sandro Penna: Una cheta follia.* Milan: Frassinelli, 1984.

Vaglio, Anna. *Invito alla lettura di Penna.* Milan: Mursia, 1993.

See also Italian Literature; Pasolini, Pier Paolo; Saba, Umberto

Penteado, Darcy (1926–1987)

The Brazilian artist, writer, and gay activist Darcy Penteado published three collections of stories, a novel, some childhood recollections, and numerous book illustrations and helped found the pioneering gay newspaper *Lampião* (1978–1981).

Many of Penteado's stories are lighthearted, humorous anecdotes of urban gay life, though with references to the darker aspects of homophobia, poverty, and social inequality. A recurrent character is the self-confident middle-class gay man. The most successful stories are "*Jarbas o imaginoso*" (Jarbas the imaginative), about a young fantasist and his admirers, and "*Bofe a prazo fixo*" (Part-time hustler) in which a factory worker secures his family's future through his relationship with a homosexual man. These are available in English translation.

Penteado's optimistic outlook appears clearly in his two longer works. The novella *Espartanos* (Spartans, 1977), depicts an idyllic relationship among three generations of gay men in a positive story that nevertheless lacks tension and drama. The full-length novel *Nivaldo e Jerônimo* (1981) is Penteado's most ambitious work, with its portrait of romantic gay love between a left-wing guerrilla and a young student during the military dictatorship of the 1970s. It attempts to bridge the gap between class and sexual politics by showing a gay man who combines political commitment with an emotional relationship. The novel is artistically flawed by sentimental dialogue, weak characterization, and a melodramatic plot, but is noteworthy because of its unusual utopian vision. The lovers survive but are defeated not because of their sexuality but by the political repression that affected all Brazilians at the time.   *Robert W. Howes*

Bibliography

Foster, David William. *Gay and Lesbian Themes in Latin American Writing*. Austin, Texas: University of Texas Press, 1991.

Leyland, Winston, ed. *My Deep Dark Pain Is Love: A Collection of Latin American Gay Fiction*. San Francisco: Gay Sunshine Press, 1983.

———. *Now the Volcano: An Anthology of Latin American Gay Literature*. San Francisco: Gay Sunshine Press, 1979.

See also Brazil; *Lampião*

Perlongher, Néstor (1949–1992)

When the Argentinian Néstor Perlongher died from AIDS, he had spent over fifteen years in exile in São Paulo, Brazil, where he worked as a social anthropologist, publishing in Portuguese the first professional examination of male prostitution, *O negócio do michê; prositituição viril em São Paulo* (The Hustler's Trade: Male Prostitution in São Paulo; 1987). Although the scientific bases of the study have been seriously questioned, it is important for the characterization of public aspects of homosexuality and fetishizing of rough trade. Perlongher, who had been involved with the first homosexual-rights movements in Argentina in the 1970s, left Argentina at the time of the neofascist military coup of 1976. Although Brazil at the time was also under military dictatorship, São Paulo was much more propitious for the pursuit of gay culture than almost anywhere else in Latin America.

Yet Perlongher violated the taboo of explicit reference to homosexuality in a country where sexual morality is elastic but public decency is strictly maintained, with the result that his monograph still stands essentially in bibliographic isolation. It is regrettable, especially since such hustlers are responsible for at least 25 percent of gay killings in São Paulo, that Perlongher's work on male prostitution perpetuates the "taxi boy" myth of male homosexuality: essentially masculine men dallying with boys and preserving their own sexual integrity by staking a claim for, or pretending to prevail in, the active penetrator role that guarantees macho integrity. In this record, the gender-bending drag queen and the sexual agent who represents a sliding shifter of sexual identity disappear, even when the former is, typically, the public face of homosexuality in the Latin American metropolis.

Perlongher's poetry in Spanish is another thing. Subscribing to the proposition that language is the ground zero of social transgression, Perlongher published a half dozen brilliant collections of texts in which the subversion of fixed meanings—semantic, syntactic, referential—promotes a queer aesthetics in which meaning is accessible only for the individual willing and able to evade the multiple straight ideologies that dominate Argentine/Brazilian/Latin American cultures. Moreover, Perlongher also understood that the personal is political, and political oppression is not only the most immediate mask of homophobia, but the strut of the screaming queen, if "only" a neobaroque poet, is the foremost gesture of institutional subversion.   *David William Foster*

Bibliography

Echevarren, Roberto. "Um Fervor Neobarroco." Néstor Perlongher, *Lamê*. Campinas, São Paulo, Brazil: Editoria da Universidadae Estadual de Campinas, 1994, 5–14.

Torres, Daniel. "Néstor Perlongher." In *Latin American Writers on Gay and Lesbian Themes: A Bio-Biographical Sourcebook*. David William Foster, ed. Westport, Conn.: Greenwood Press, 1994, 321–22.

See also Activism; Argentina; Brazil; Hustlers

Persian/Iranian Literature and Culture

Sexual intercourse between Persian men was observed by foreigners from early times. The Greek father of history, Herodotus, noted in his description of the customs of the Persians that had learned pederasty from the Greeks, and Richard Burton (1821–1890), famous traveler and translator of the *Thousand and One Nights,* linked the frequency of pederasty with the climatic zone in which Persia and other countries of the same propensity were located. The literature of Persia (modern Iran) fairly abounds in references to male intercourse and infatuation, typically of an older man for a younger man or a boy. Not surprisingly, a clear distinction is always made between the active and the passive partner: the former loses little if any of his masculinity in the act, while the latter is an object of contempt and ridicule.

Pre-Islamic Persia

The pre-Islamic religion of Persia was Zoroastrianism, so called after its prophet, Zarathustra/Zoroaster, whose followers are today found mainly in Iran, India, and America. Zoroastrianism is a dualistic religion, according to which the universe is divided into two warring camps, those of good and evil. The good and evil aspects of the world were regarded as having been created by two spirits. One of the duties of the partisans of the good spirit being to produce offspring, the barrenness of homosexuality clearly qualified it for the camp of evil; according to some texts, the practice itself was instituted by the evil spirit when he performed sodomy on himself to create demons, lies, and other abominations. In the oldest Zoroastrian text, the Avesta, homosexuality is mentioned as an instance of sinful behavior that is to be punished. Thus, both sodomized and sodomizing males are regarded as demons. The punishment for a man who is sodomized against his will is 1,600 whiplashes, the same as for killing a sheepdog), but if he does it willingly his sin is inexpiable. In one text, active and passive sodomites are said to be the only ones that can be killed without the permission of high priests or kings. Interestingly, laws like these are still being practiced by Iran's current Islamic regime.

In the *Book of Arda Wiraz,* a *Divine Comedy*–type of visionary text written in the ninth century C.E. but with older precursors, the soul of Wiraz, who has taken a narcotic, travels to heaven and hell and is shown the rewards and punishments of men and women for sins, among them passive and active same-sex sodomy, but also heterosexual sodomy. On the whole, however, Zoroastrian literature is more preoccupied with stressing family values, among which were marriages between close relatives such as father and daughter or mother and son, practiced in historical times, for instance, by the Achaemenid kings (Darius, Xerxes, etc.), and still regarded in the third century C.E. as one of the supremely pious acts of a true believer.

Islamic Iran/Persia

In the Islamic period, we regularly find the theme of homosexuality in Persian literature. It usually takes the form of love for boys but is also the subject of rougher, pornographic prose and poetry and satire, often coupled with disparaging remarks about women and heterosexual love and intercourse. The youths are invariably depicted as hairless, as facial hair is said to spoil them. The situation described by Sadi below is probably typical: as long as boys are young, smooth, and hairless, they are insolent and hard to get, but when they become rough and hairy they also become much more accessible; but, then, who would want them?

Homosexuality is represented in wisdom literature from early times onward. Thus, in the *Qabus-name* (1083), a book in which a father advises his son about sex, the importance of trying both forms of sexuality is stressed, as sometimes one is better than the other: intercourse with women is healthier in winter, with young men in summer. When it comes to choosing a lover, however, intelligence is just as important as good looks.

A sometimes disturbing feature of the Persian language (which is also true to some extent of Arabic) is the absence of grammatical gender; there is only one pronoun in the third person, which means that "he," "she," and "it" are not distinguished, nor do words such as *beloved* or *friend* have different forms according to whether they refer to males or females. This aspect of the language has frustrated those who have wanted to find evidence for same-sex relationships and eased the task for translators and commentators who have aimed at obliterating any such references. Moreover, in most classical Persian poetry, the love of a beautiful boy or youth is used by the poet as a means to focus on the Divine Beloved, which makes it difficult to determine to what extent the poems express actual physical love or desire. This mystical interpretation, intentional or not, cannot hide the often extreme sensuality and eroticism of the poetry. The descriptions of the beloved in this poetry can often apply only to the human beloved, as it contains features that would be ridiculous to attribute to the Divine Beloved: lying, ogling, and promiscuously giving favors to rivals are not plausible attributes of an omnipotent, omniscient God. In much other poetry, the rose, a recurrent metaphor for the beloved object of the yearning poet's phallic nightingale, is really God and not a boy's anus. In the poetry of Turkish Mehemmed Ghazali, the anus is explicitly compared to a rose.

Several classical Persian poets were known or reputed to have been interested in boys, the earliest being Ahmad al-Ghazzali (d. 1126), whom later writers described as seeing the Divine Beloved in the form of beautiful boys. There are other poets in this tradition. Awhad-ud-Din Kermani (d. 1237), who was accused of unseemly behavior with young men during the sama, but maintained he treated the love of boys as a metaphor for divine love, although his famous contemporary Shams-e Tabriz advised him to the effect that he would be better off concentrating directly on God rather than the boys. Fakhr-ud-Din Eraqi (d. 1289), whose writings were almost entirely of a mystical and erotic character, was known for falling in love with handsome young men, among them a cobbler's son in Cairo. Ruzbehan-e Baqli (d. 1209) is reported to have had extraordinary visions, such as dancing with God, or having his tongue sucked by angels and the Prophet.

Famous mystic Farid-ud-Din Attar (d. 1220) wrote about love between males, such as the love of dervishes for their princes and the Sufis for their youths as a symbol of the love of God. The best-known male love story used by Attar is that of Sultan Mahmud of Ghazna and his slave boy Ayaz. In fact, under the Turkish Ghaznavid, Seljuq, and Khwarazmshah rulers of Iran (eleventh and twelfth centuries), pederasty was quite common in courtly circles, and the story of the king and his slave came to be included among other famous, mostly unhappy, love stories in Persian literature, while Ayaz became a symbol of purity in mystic literature.

Two of the most famous Persian poets who used the theme of love of young men were Sadi and Hafez, both from Shiraz, in southern Iran. Sadi (Mosleh-ud-Din Abdollah, c.1213–1292) was one of the best-known classical Persian authors. His most famous works are his *Golestan* (The Rose Garden), a collection of short stories interspersed with poetry, and *Bustan* (The Garden), a long poem. His complete works also include *qasidas* (elegies or odes), *ghazals* (lyric poems), and *robais* (quatrains), as well as less serious poems, among them a number with explicit sexual references, the *hazliyat*. Several of Sadi's works are concerned with the theme of love of young men by men. Thus, chapter 5 of *Golestan* and chapter 3 of *Bustan* are devoted to the theme of love of youths, most of them male, some female, and some indeterminate. Sadi's sexually explicit poems exhibit the same skill as his other work. Like other Persian mystics, Sadi used the theme of the love of a beautiful boy as a means to focus on the Divine Beloved, which, however, cannot and should not blind us to the sensuality of the poems. Sadi's poems are characterized by a mixture of otherworldly and worldly concerns, the refined orthodox sentiments of the religious writings or the refined passion of the mystical poems on the one hand, and the lustful, pornographic pieces on sodomy and seduction of boys on the other, which must have been appreciated by his contemporaries but has disconcerted modern editors. In the pornographic pieces, love between men is exalted above that between men and women, and the references to heterosexual relationships in the love chapters of *Golestan* and *Bustan* deal with marital discord.

Hafez (Shams-ud-Din Hafez, c.1320–1389), one of the most popular Persian authors of all time, left thousands of manuscript copies of his work. Together with the Koran, his poems are still used for divining. The collected works contain his *ghazals* (lyric poems), a short *masnavi* (couplets), the *Saqiname* (poem about the saki, or wine pourer), *qetes* (short, light pieces), *robais* (quatrains), and a few satirical verses (*malhaqat*), the attribution of which to Hafez often remains uncertain. It is for his *ghazals* that Hafez is best known. Here we find the famous poem about his unfulfilled yearning for the young Turk from Shiraz, for whom he would give all the treasures of the fabled cities of Samarkand and Bukhara. The absence of grammatical gender in the language usually leaves the gender of the beloved unspecified; there are indications that the beloved is a male, although there is no tradition that Hafez himself practiced pederasty. Hafez's beautiful poems are mostly about unrequited love, wine drinking, and music, but their scope is universal and transcendent. His beloved is not as clearly symbolic of the Divine Beloved as in the poems of the great Persian mystic Jalal-ud-Din Rumi. It is a human beloved but one who raises the poet and his poems to the stars.

One of the last great mystical Persian poets in this tradition is Nur-al-Din Jami (d. 1492), from eastern Iran, reputed to have practiced pederasty. In his most famous work, *Baharestan* (The Spring Garden), he depicts a monastery spellbound by a particular youth, who is admonished by the prior not to let all and sundry sample his bodily charms.

A poet of a different kind was Obeid-e Zakani (Nezam al-din Obeid-allah Zakani, d. c.1370), the greatest Persian writer of erotic satire, partly in verse and partly in prose. He also mastered the other forms of classical Persian poetry, and his *ghazals*, *masnavis*, and *robais* have considerable literary merit. Among the *masnavis* is the long *Tale of Lovers*, in which the poet falls in love with a handsome creature of undefined sex. At first his advances are spurned, then they are encouraged; there is a delightful meeting, but finally the lovers are parted. Obeid-e Zakani's satire takes the form of longer poems, among them *Ode of the Mouse and the Cat* and *Story of the Beard*, which revolves around the theme of the beardlessness of attractive youths as opposed to older, bearded, men, but also of short anecdotes or jokes. Obeid-e Zakani's parody on the Persian national epic poem, *Shahname* (Book of Kings), written by Abu 1-Qasem Mansur Ferdousi in the second half of the tenth century, is of special interest, because it provides a rare example in Persian literature of adult male sex in which reciprocity is emphasized. The story of Rostam, the main protagonist of Ferdousi's epic and the national hero of Iran, is given an interesting twist when one of his duels with his opponent Homan is turned into an erotic tryst. Laying aside their weapons, the two heroes attack each other with their natural equipment, alternating as bottom and top. The poet concludes: Know that eternal bliss is in intercourse, but only he obtains bliss who also gives.

A modern poet who included the theme of pederasty in his writings is Iradj Mirza (1874–1926). Some of his poems describe the author's infatuation with young men, such as one in which he sodomizes the son of one of his friends after getting him drunk.

Descriptions of lesbians and lesbian love are fairly rare in Persian literature, although the seclusion of women from men was bound to foster female relationships, as indeed frequently observed by Western travelers in the East, and references to leather dildos is found throughout Persian literature.

There never was a gay liberation movement in Iran, though under the preceding regime of the Shah, with the surge of the Western entertainment culture, there developed a gay subculture in some of the larger cities. In Tehran male prostitution was common in the red-light district (the Red City), hustlers and their customers frequented the city parks, and escort services were available for the wealthy. With the return to power of Islamic orthodoxy, any openly gay person who commited sodomy, as defined by Islamic penal law as sexual intercourse with a male, faced immediate execution, and lesser offenses brought severe lashings. The stoning to death of a member of the Khaksarie sect of Dervishes was reported in the Islamic Republic News Paper of Nov. 14, 1995. Among Iranians abroad, however, some progress is now being made, and a Persian gay magazine, *Homan*, published by the Group to Defend the Rights of Iranian Gays and Lesbians and receiving much of its financial support from Scandinavia, is already well established.

Oktar Skjaervo

Bibliography

Arberry, Arthur J., ed. *Classical Persian Literature*. London: Macmillan, 1958.

———. *Fifty Poems of Hafiz*. Cambridge: Cambridge University Press, 1962.

Browne, Edward G. *A History of Persian Literature*. 3 vols. New York: Cambridge University Press, 1920.

Murray, Stephen O. "Corporealizing Medieval Persian and Turkish Tropes." In *Islamic Homosexualities: Culture, History, and Literature*. Stephen O. Murray and Will Roscoe, eds. New York: New York University Press, 1997, 132–41.

The Sacred Books of the East. translated by various scholars and edited by F. Max Müller. Oxford University Press; reprinted Motilal Banarasidas, Delhi, 1879–1883.

Sadi. *The Gulistan, or, Rose Garden of Sadi*. W. G. Archer, ed. E. Rehatsek, trans. New York: Putnam, 1965.

Skjaervo, Peter J. "Middle Eastern Literature: Persian." In *The Gay and Lesbian Heritage: A Reader's Companion to the Writers and Their Works*. Claude J. Summers, ed. New York: Henry Holt, 1995, 485–86.

Smith, Pail. *Divan of Hafiz*. Melbourne: New Humanity Books, 1986.

Southgate, Minoo S. "Men, Women, and Boys: Love and Sex in the Works of SADI." *Iranian Studies* 17, no. 4 (1984): 413–52.

Sprachman, Paul. *Le beau garçon sans merci: The Homoerotic Tale in Arabic and Persian. Homoeroticism in Classical Arabic Literature.* J. W. Wright, Jr., and Everett K. Rowson, eds. New York: Cambridge University Press, 1997, 192–209.

Summers, Claude J., ed. *The Gay and Lesbian Literary Heritage: A Reader's Companion to the Writers and Their Works, From Antiquity to the Present.* New York: Henry Holt, 1995.

Wafer, Jim. "Persian Mystical Literature." In *Islamic Homosexualities: Culture, History, and Literature.* Stephen O. Murray and Will Roscoe, eds. New York: New York University Press, 1997, 117–31.

Wright, Jim, Jr., and E. K. Rowson, eds. *Homoeroticism in Classical Arabic Literature.* New York: Cambridge University Press, 1997.

See also Arabic Literature; Beloved; Burton, Sir Richard Francis; Dancing Boys; Greece; Islam; Pederasty; Sodomy

Perversion

Perversion literally means "a turning away or about"; in relation to sexuality, it refers to a deviation from what is considered normal, natural, or true. Within medicine, perversion has historically been synonymous with *sexual deviation*, or any sexual act that deviates from the normal or uses abnormal means to achieve orgasm. Many types of sexual perversion have been described, including homosexuality, fetishism, pedophilia, transvestism, exhibitionism, voyeurism, sadism, masochism, and necrophilia. While homosexuality is no longer officially considered to be a type of sexual deviation, throughout much of the past 150 years homosexual behavior was considered to represent a form of perversion.

Shortly after the American Psychiatric Association removed homosexuality from its list of mental disorders in 1973, the term *sexual deviation* was replaced in the diagnostic classification by *paraphilia*, defined in the *Diagnostic and Statistical Manual of Mental Disorders,* fourth edition, as "recurrent, intense sexually arousing fantasies, sexual urges, or behaviors generally involving 1) nonhuman objects, 2) the suffering or humiliation of oneself or one's partner, or 3) children or other nonconsenting persons, that occur over a period of at least 6 months" (pp. 522–523). To be diagnosed as a mental disorder, the paraphilia must also be accompanied by

"clinically significant distress or impairment in social, occupational, or other important areas of functioning." Sexologist John Money has defined perversion as "the pejorative and also the legal term for paraphilia" (p. 217). Thus, *perversion* and *sexual deviation* have been replaced in the psychiatric and medical literature by the supposedly more objective term *paraphilia.*

Historically the concept of perversion has been closely related to notions of sin, immorality, and degeneracy, and until recently, homosexuality has been the most abhorrent and, at the same time, the most interesting of the perversions. The pervert has been religiously condemned, legally punished, and medically diagnosed, all of which serve as mechanisms for social control and regulation of individual behavior. Thus, through labeling deviance, which itself signifies only variation or difference and implies no evaluation, as perversion, a wide range of nonconforming individual behaviors and beliefs can be restricted, discouraged, eliminated, and punished.

While any type of activity or idea can be described as perverse, the term became inextricably linked to the sexual realm through the elaboration of theories of the sexual perversions within the field of psychoanalysis. Freud presented a complex and ambiguous view of homosexuality and rejected the distinction between homosexuality as a form of inversion, or an innate or congenital characteristic, and as a type of perversion acquired as the result of a developmental corruption. While Freud posited the notion of an infantile state of polymorphous perverse sexuality, he also described homosexuality as the product of a developmental arrest and heterosexuality as the outcome of normal psychosexual development. Later psychoanalytic writers, particularly those in the United States, such as Rado, Bergler, Bieber, and Socarides, invariably described homosexuality as a perversion and viewed it as an expression of severe and primitive psychopathology. Stoller has described perversion both as any habitual sexually stimulating act that is not genital heterosexual intercourse and, more recently, as "the erotic form of hatred," or erotic behavior motivated by hostility.

Ultimately, a perversion, whether it is considered within the moral, legal, or medical discourse, is defined by both deviance and derogation. Homosexuality is no longer technically a perversion in Western culture, but the perverse act, belief, or feeling exists in a sociocultural context that fluctuates in its tolerance for variation and selectively categorizes and proscribes behaviors and people. The boundaries of perversion with respect to same-sex desire and behavior will undoubtedly continue to reflect changes in social attitudes and customs.

Terry S. Stein, M.D.

Bibliography

American Psychiatric Association. *Diagnostic and Statistical Manual of Mental Disorders,* 4th ed. Washington, D.C.: American Psychiatric Association, 1994.

Money, John. *Gay, Straight, and In-Between: The Sexology of Erotic Orientation.* New York: Oxford University Press, 1988.

Stoller, Robert J. *Perversion: The Erotic Form of Hatred.* Washington, D.C.: American Psychiatric Press, 1986.

See also Counseling; Freud, Sigmund; Homosexuality; Inversion; Psychological and Psychoanalytic Perspectives on Homosexuality; Sadomasochism; Sexology; Transvestism

Pessoa, Fernando (1888–1935)

Fernando Pessoa is the greatest Portuguese poet since Vax de Camoes, of the Renaissance. He established modernism in Portugal and deeply influenced the language. It is said that even Lisbon chambermaids speak differently from their grandparents because of him. He was born in Lisbon, but he grew up in Natal, South Africa, where he had an English education, attending the University of Cape of Good Hope, Cape Town. At fifteen, he published a number of virtuosic English sonnets modeled on Shakespeare's. In 1905, he returned to Portugal, where for the rest of his life he earned his living as a business correspondent, writing letters for export companies in foreign languages, and was also an habitué of literary cafés. He was briefly connected with the nationalist movement in poetry called *saudosismo* and edited two short-lived journals. Like his near contemporary Langston Hughes in the United States, he was essentially a reclusive though dandyish person. His sexuality is at best a guess, for no certain relationship with a man or a woman has been documented, but homoeroticism is important to his poetry.

Like Cavafy, another near contemporary, he developed a style based on multiple voices and distinct personae. He wrote and published under many names, each of whose work grew from competing traditions and some of whom engaged in literary rivalries with one another in journals and had biographies and even horoscopes attached to their publications. For these distinct personalities, he invented the term *heteronym*; the most important are Alberto Caeiro, Alvaro de Campos, Ricardo Reis, and the writer of English poetry, published under his own name. Each received intense critical scrutiny; each is acclaimed to have established specific developments in modern Portuguese writing. The English poetry exhibits the best of a high Edwardian style, steeped in Elizabethanisms, similar to but perhaps better than the poetry of Rupert Brooke or Sacherville Sitwell. Many of the English poems have a homoerotic explicitness that Pessoa's post-Wilde English counterparts scarcely dared. The long poem "Antinous," published with *35 Sonnets* (1918), is singled out as the finest of his English style. It also has provoked speculation about his sexuality, for it luxuriates over the Hadrian-Antinous story in the grand style of an Elizabethan mock epic.

In contrast, Alvaro de Campos writes in the tradition of Whitman. His work founded a Whitmanesque school in Portuguese, much as Pablo Neruda's did in Spanish. Campos's "Salutation to Walt Whitman" is an ecstatic love song across time, with lines like these:

> . . . And just as you felt everything, so I feel everything, and so here we are clasping hands
> Clasping hands, Walt, clasping hands with the universe
> doing a dance in our soul.

It ends with Campos embracing Whitman as mentor/father/lover, imagining a psychic insemination of the spirit:

> Goodbye, bless you, live forever, O Great Bastard of Apollo
> Impotent and ardent lover of the nine muses and of the graces
> Cable-car from Olympus to us and from us to Olympus.

Lines like these call to mind Hart Crane's similar stance in *The Bridge.*

Pessoa's *heteronyms* have provided a field day for psychoanalytically inclined critics, such as Roditi, Hamburger, and Paz, who see them as the work of a schizophrenic uniquely articulated as art. Rothenberg and Joris, who place Pessoa among a select group of seminal modernist innovators, reverse Paz's position,

P

seeing the *heteronymic* habit as neither an instability of identity nor a search for a lost one, but rather "a questioning of all that such identity might mean." Recent trends in queer theory, especially interrogations into essentialism and performativity, might inspire a new generation of readers to discover in Pessoa's unprecedented virtuosity not the psychosis of failed identity, nor a mere questioning of it, but the powerful expression of a ventriloquistic "poetic drag" that deconstructs the very notion of a straightforward adult unitary self.   *Donald N. Mager*

Bibliography

Hamburger, Michael. "Multiple Personalities." In *Truth of Poetry*. New York: Methuen, 1982.

Monteiro, George, ed. *The Man Who Never Was: Essays on Fernando Pessoa*. Providence, R.I.: Gavea-Brown, 1982.

Pessoa, Fernando. *Selected Poetry*. Edwin Honig, trans. Octavio Paz, intro. Chicago: Swallow Press, 1971.

Roditi, Edouard. "Fernando Pessoa: Outsider Among English Poets." *Literary Review* 6 (1963): 372–85.

Rothenberg, Jerome, and Pierre Joris. *Poems for the Millennium: Volume One: From fin-de-siècle to Negritude*. Berkeley: University of California Press, 1995.

See also Cavafy, Constantine P.; Crane, Hart; Hughes, Langston; Portugal; Whitman, Walt

Peter Damian (1007–1072)

Peter Damian was a monastic leader who rose to prominence as an adviser to the papacy on church reform. His chief preoccupations were clerical celibacy and the selling of church offices. One of his earliest polemics is the *Book of Gomorrah* (*Liber gomorrhanus*, c.1050), in which Peter calls on the pope to stop the spread of "sodomitic vice" among the clergy. Peter defines the vice as including male masturbation, mutual masturbation, interfemoral intercourse, and anal intercourse. These activities are already widespread in the clergy, on Peter's testimony. He claims that there are groups of sodomitic clergy who sin together and then absolve each other in confession. There are also "incestuous" relations between sodomitic bishops and their priests. Peter urges the pope to remove all sodomites from clerical office and to send them into a life of penance. Yet Peter shows himself skeptical about the possibility of reforming the vice. He considers it not only a violation of nature but something akin to madness and demonic possession. Peter insists that the sodomite is already dead to the clergy world, a traitor to family and city, an enemy of God. Peter's treatise is an attempt to reorganize and systematize the confused prescriptions of the early-medieval penitentials (or penance books). The treatise may also contain the first appearance of the abstract term *sodomia* (sodomy) in theological literature.   *Mark D. Jordan*

Bibliography

Jordan, Mark D. *The Invention of Sodomy in Christian Theology*. Chicago: University of Chicago Press, 1997, 45–66.

See also Monasticism, Christian; *Pastoralia* and Penitentials

Petronius (first century C.E.)

According to Roman historian Tacitus (*Annales* 16.18–19), Caius Petronius was favored at Nero's court until his standing as the emperor's acknowledged arbiter of elegance (*arbiter elegantiae*) aroused the envy of other courtiers. Falsely accused and arrested, Petronius commited suicide in 66 C.E., but not before detailing Nero's sexual peccadilloes. Though Tacitus does not mention the *Satyricon*, this Petronius certainly sounds like the man who could have written the Latin novel attributed to "Petronius Arbiter," a text that we do not possess complete. If the indications of one manuscript are to be believed, the whole would have been five or six times as large as the portion(s) we now read, and potentially even larger.

Although neither its form nor its milieu is unparalleled among ancient texts (form: largely prose with an admixture of verse [*prosimetrum*, or so-called Menippean satire]; milieu: roguish, known from some satire and mimes), the *Satyricon* is remarkable for the length to which it goes to represent the underbelly of life. Its presentation, for example, of characters speaking less-than-standard classical diction is astonishing. The action takes place in a variety of locations along the Tyrrhenian coast, from Marseilles down through Naples to the bottom of the Italian peninsula (Crotona). The characters are not heroes or historical figures but fictional versions of everyday contemporary types—free youths, slaves, freedmen, urban poor, parvenus. The main character (and narrator) is one Encolpius, punished with recurrent impotence for an (unwitting?) offence to Priapus, Roman god of the phallus. His beloved is Giton, a young man roughly sixteen (Encolpius is likely in his twenties, possibly his thirties), who does not always seem worthy of the affection Encolpius accords him. Encolpius at times travels in tandem with Ascyltos, a sometime rival for Giton, and at times with Eumolpus, a roguish older poetaster who would also gladly jump Giton. However, all the characters have occasional relations (sometimes coerced) with women, though this quartet would seem to be more interested in same-sex activity than anything else, at least in the existing portions of the text.

It is hard to be confident about an overarching interpretation given the fragmented state of the text. Some scholars, pointing to the literary nature of the parody—not only of specific contemporary works (Lucan, Nero's own poetry) but of the epic conceit of the hero dogged by an angry deity, as well as to the fact that no other extant ancient novel, Greek or Latin, has a male-male couple front and center—regard the whole as totally satirical and nothing more absurd, or contemptible, than Encolpius and his boyfriend Giton. A more nuanced reading is called for. Much is satirized mercilessly, for example, the extravagance and cultural pretensions of the nouveaux riches freedmen whose elevation in the empire galled the more established Roman families. But their perspective is hardly all that matters. Encolpius is more, not less, sympathetic for his self-dramatizing, fecklessness, and charmingly quixotic idealization of Giton. The text presents situations, and a context, that permit us to see those ideals themselves as misplaced; Giton is one of those characters who (with apologies to Cole Porter) is "always true to" Encolpius "in his way," and there appears to be real affection between the two. The lovers' speeches when they believe they are about to drown at sea are affecting, and when the female Circe comes on to Encolpius and would like a liaison, she recognizes the significance of his relationship with Giton and does not seek to displace it.

The effect of Petronian realism is to convince us we are seeing snatches of early imperial sensibilities—the plural is important—from the noble infidelity of the widow of Ephesus to the wacky and often self-serving machinations of all and sundry involved in the cult of Priapus. In Eumolpus's tale of his seduction of the boy of Pergamum, he rips the veil off the ancient conceit (shared by some modern scholars) that the passive youth merely suffers penetration; by the time the story ends, an exhausted Eumolpus has to threaten to tell the boy's father unless he leaves off his voracious demands. The various scenes in the baths as well as the commotion that the sight of the well-hung Ascyltos causes seem familiar and replicable today, though the world of Petronius is more honest: where we might whisper in admiration and envy, his bathers break into a round of applause.

Italian director Federico Fellini filmed an idiosyncratic *Satyricon* (1969) memorable for its atmospheric decadence, but the camp sensibilities of American director John Waters might better capture the madcap absurdity of the Roman novel.

Ralph Hexter

Bibliography

Müller, Konrad, ed. *Satyrica Schelmenszenen*. 3d rev. ed. Munich: Artemis Verlag, 1983.
Petronius. *Satyrica*. R. Bracht Branham and Daniel Kinney, trans. London: J. M. Dent, 1996.

See also Camp; Priapus; Rome, Ancient; Waters, John

Peyrefitte, Roger (1907–)

French novelist Roger Peyrefitte was educated by Jesuits in a privileged milieu designed to produce urbane and untroubled acolytes of the upper reaches of the national establishment. Yet not long into his expected career, Peyrefitte proved far too scandal-prone to be a successful diplomat. He left the service under a cloud in 1944 and turned himself into a scandalous novelist.

The writing of *Les Amitiés particulières* (1945, filmed by Jean Delannoy in 1964) was an act of defiance, rejecting the values of the establishment in which Peyrefitte had failed to make his career. It tells the story of a love affair between two boys, Georges de Sarre and the younger Alexis, in a Jesuit school. True to the period of its composition, it ends with the tragic death of the younger boy. After this book's publication François Mauriac made the mistake of publicly attacking Peyrefitte on moral grounds. Peyrefitte responded in style, by outing him.

Georges de Sarre, a character largely based on the author himself, returns as the central figure in two later novels, *Les Ambassades* (1951) and *La Fin des ambassades* (1953). Peyrefitte's decision to send him into the diplomatic service gives him scope for extensive satire on the pretensions, extravagances, and hypocrisies of the French ruling class. Much of the meat of this satire is to be found in their sexual lives.

There followed several satires on the Roman Catholic Church, past and present—*Les Clés de Saint Pierre* (1955), *Chevaliers de Malte* (1957), and *La Nature du prince* (1963). In these narratives, Peyrefitte is always at his most cheerful when exposing to public view, even while changing names to stay within the law, some sexual scandal that demonstrates that, far from being merely as human as the rest of us, clerics are likely to be far more so.

From a gay point of view Peyrefitte's most cheerfully readable and celebratory book must be *L'Exilé de Capri* (1959), a gossipy but dignified fictional biography of Baron Jacques d'Adelsward Fersen. It is virtually a cultural history of a period (1897–1927) when rich northern Europeans used to escape south for their pleasures but when northern society and its bourgeois respectability rarely failed to catch up with them.

In *Roy* (1979), with characteristic audacity, Peyrefitte studies 1970s California through the eyes and orifices of a fourteen-year-old boy. Supposedly corrupted more by capitalism than by sexual abuse at the hands of adult men, Roy is never regarded as being at any risk from prostituting himself as much to the reader's gaze as to his clients.

Peyrefitte has shown great stamina as a long-term campaigner for homosexual rights. Moreover, he has worked tirelessly as a historian and custodian of homosexual culture, particularly that derived from ancient Greek pederasty. His satires can now seem leaden and dated. At their best, however, they successfully deflate upper-class pomposity.

Gregory Woods

Bibliography

Robinson, Christopher. *Scandal in the Ink: Male and Female Homosexuality in Twentieth-Century French Literature*. London: Cassell, 1995.

See also France; French Literature

Phallus

Phallic cults usually centered on the god Liber, who was associated with the seeds of plants and animals, and more generally with fertility. St. Augustine refers to the immodest and licentious worship of the male genitals in *The City of God*. In pagan cults the rites of Liber were often celebrated at crossroads; the phallus was often used as a charm or amulet against evil (particularly infertility). The phallus was sometimes placed above shops to represent prosperity. In addition, Pliny recorded that the phallus protected not only generals but children. At Lanuvium, an entire month was dedicated to the phallic festival. In the course of the ceremonies the phallus was ritually "disgraced" before being carried across the marketplace and wreathed by women of honor to suggest its renewal.

The phallus has played an important role in psychoanalysis. In the work of Freud and Lacan, phallus is separated from penis. The phallus is deployed as a signifier of desire or the lack of it. The phallus at best merely symbolizes the penis. The penis functions with the narrative known as the Oedipus, or castration, complex. The symbolic order is generated as a moment of having, and a defining fear of losing, the penis. Because desire cannot be fully and permanently satisfied (if it were, desire would cease), the phallus becomes a kind of unobtainable prototype of the desired object; it is the signifier of an idea; it is an impossible identity.

Modern feminist scholarship has begun to criticize the way in which Freud prioritizes the male genitals over the erotogenic zones. The phallus is treated in Freud as a privileged asexual signifier, and it acts accordingly as a structuring center. The phallus symbolized the penis, which as a body part is elevated or erected over others. In this synecdochical logic, the part stands up for the whole. Could that body part be substituted? Why does the phallus require that specific body parts be used in order to symbolize, rather than others? Psychoanalytic theory works on the assumption that the body is initially a collection of pieces and that only later, as one matures, does it become a totality, with a center, and the possibility of control. The phallus becomes an ordering device that militates against the danger of proliferation, diversity, or fragmentation. Some critics have argued that insofar as writing represents essential divisions in gender, women's writing is more accommodating, celebrating diversity, difference, mutability, and contradiction.

For feminists, the priority of the phallus is symptomatic of a male bias. The phallus is itself the signifier of a patriarchal order that must be deprivileged and decentered. The word *phallocentric* has been coined to explain how psychoanalysis and, more generally, our cultural and social organization is the result of patriarchy. A pressing feature of the effort to overturn the patriarchal order has been the need to show that the phallocentric outlook is socially constituted rather than a natural or essential product of biology or genetics. Controversially it has been argued that homosexuality is a kind of phallus fetishism. Tough, muscular males are set at a premium by delicate homosexuals, who simply project their own "lack" onto the desired person. Eugene Monick has argued that we need to rethink the phallus as a harmonious combination of the rational, the ideal, the primeval, and the sexual. For Monick the homoerotic is opened up between masculine affirmation and sexual desire.

Ian McCormick

Bibliography

Keuls, Eva C. *The Reign of the Phallus: Sexual Politics in Ancient Athens*. New York: Harper and Row, 1985.

Lacan, Jacques. "The Signification of the Phallus." 1958. In *Feminine Sexuality: Jacques Lacan and the Ecole Freudienne*. London: Macmillan, 1982.

Monick, Eugene. *Phallos: Sacred Image of the Masculine*. Toronto: Inner City Books, 1987.

See also Augustine of Hippo; Feminism; Freud, Sigmund; Rome, Ancient

Philo of Alexandria (Philo Judaeus) (c.20 B.C.E.–c.50 C.E.)

This Jewish philosopher and interpreter of Jewish sacred writings was born to a wealthy family of considerable social standing and political influence in the large Jewish community of ancient Alexandria, Egypt. He was asked to participate in a political mission to Rome, interceding on behalf of Alexandrian Jews with Emperor Gaius "Caligula." A prolific writer of approximately sixty books, all in Greek (about forty are extant), he was well versed in the Greco-Roman philosophical and cultural currents of his time. His chief aim lay in interpreting the Jewish sacred writings in relation to Greek philosophy.

For Philo, the only legitimate sexual intercourse was between husband and wife, and strictly for the purpose of procreation. Anything beyond this constituted illicit pleasure, and pleasure in general had to be carefully avoided. In this, Philo links certain Greek philosophical trends that stress procreation as the aim of sex with biblical proscriptions. Like other ancient male authors, Philo wrote entirely from a man's point of view, thought in terms of an active/passive, penetrator/penetrated scheme of sexual acts, and implicitly regarded the male as capable of being attracted to human beauty in its male and female form. But he held the harshest view of male same-gender sexual relations, combining the restrictions of the Torah (e.g., Leviticus 18:22) with the Greek philosophical tradition that began to criticize such relationships (e.g., by utilizing the notion of acts "against nature"). He typically writes about a slave boy/adolescent in a passive sexual role who turns into a "man-woman" or is reduced to the status of a girl, and acquires the "female disease," using cosmetics and other artifices to beautify himself. The lover of such boys wastes away in body, soul, and property, growing sterile and causing the desolation of cities. The biblical death penalty, claims Philo, applies to both the boy and his lover. Only sex with animals is worse. Primarily at the root of this outlook lies Philo's fear of gender boundary transgression. In general, he regarded female characteristics as negative and male as positive; hence the taint of female characteristics on a man horrified Philo, a view not unusual in ancient Mediterranean cultures.

In his interpretation of the biblical Sodom narrative (Genesis 19), Philo, like the biblical prophets, stresses gluttony and luxury resulting from excessive wealth as the root of the sin of Sodom. Yet he also begins to emphasize the sexual nature of the crime of Sodom's men. Philo's historical significance lies in the widespread use of his writings by the theologians of the early church (he was largely ignored in the Jewish community). His allegorical exposition of the Greek version of the Hebrew Bible, together with his utilization of philosophy as well as his austere views on sex, were quite amenable to their purposes. Philo's move to combine biblical proscriptions with certain Greek philosophical notions such as "natural law" was important (achieving a certain universalization of prescribed behavior), as was the procreationist principle, which acquired a significant role in parts of later Christian tradition.

Holger Szesnat

Bibliography

Gaca, Kathy L. "Philo's Principles of Sexual Conduct and Their Influence on Christian Platonist Sexual Principles." *Studia Philonica Annual* 8 (1996): 21–39.

Szesnat, Holger. "'Pretty Boys' in Philo's *De Vita Contemplativa*." *Studia Philonica Annual* 10 (1998).

See also Bible; Christianity; Judaism; Natural Law; Sodom; Sodomy

Phone Sex

The consumer of phone sex—a highly commodified form of homoerotic interaction—faces many options. He (the industry seems directed primarily to men) may talk with paid actors or other amateurs like himself. He may engage in live conversation or opt for recorded messages—either sexually explicit monologues or personal ads from other callers. He may speak to one person at a time or choose a group chat room. He may pay for the call through his local telephone bill or use a credit card. Since about 1984, phone sex ads have run in everything from local "alternative" newspapers to gay skin magazines reaching an international audience.

The cost of phone sex is often quite high, recently averaging about $3.00 a minute. As a result, people often try to meet one another in a group chat room, exchange telephone numbers, then hang up and call each other back, paying only the usual phone fees. Chat rooms may also contain men engaged in casual conversation. There is often lots of heavy breathing, too—callers waiting to hear sexually explicit conversation but unwilling to speak or unable to divulge their phone numbers.

A caller to a chat room usually begins with "hello." If other callers are present, the greeting may be returned. This is followed by an exchange of social pleasantries that usually lead to a series of questions: What are you into? What do you look like? Do you want to give me a call? Some participants will skip the pleasantries and simply ask, "Anyone interested in a hot bottom?" or something similar.

Once callers have connected, each partner usually describes what he would like to do with or to the other; this is sometimes transformed into a fantasy in which the activities are spoken about as if they were actually occurring. Reference is often made to the actual bodily responses of the participants, the scenario moving back and forth between fantasy and the actual. Expressions of pleasure are also voiced. Sometimes, the conversation is controlled by one of the parties. At other times, discussion is more reciprocal. Discussion is accompanied by masturbation, actual or simulated, to orgasm.

Given the prohibitive cost of phone sex (if one has not yet exchanged phone numbers), people often try to arrange for simultaneous orgasms. The call usually ends with a thank you, a compliment, and sometimes a request to speak again. It is considered bad form simply to hang up after one's orgasm.

Michel Foucault called homosexuality a historic occasion for the formation of alternative relationships. Given the isolation, fear, and guilt felt by some men, phone sex provides a safe means whereby to secure homoerotic connections. These encounters are not exclusively sexual: some people call simply to talk to someone else; regulars meet, as if in a bar. Phone sex is a highly codified ritual. While a series of rules operate, no single individual is responsible for these rules. Rather, they develop out of the attempt to thwart heteronormativity.

Like adult bookstores and pornography, phone sex alters us to the contradictions of capitalism that both craves gay subjects (as consumers, as producers) and deploys and relies on homophobia. In pursuit of the commodification of sexuality, capitalism makes possible "subversive" behaviors such as phone sex. But to say that homosexuals attempt to maneuver within capitalism is not necessarily to endorse capitalism. "Transgressive" activities like gay phone sex are a response to some of the contradictions of capitalism; they are not a mastering of those contradictions. If phone sex is to be valorized, it is as a testament to the historically contingent abilities of homosexuals to thwart, if only provisionally, heteronormativity, and not a dome kind of liberatory practice.

John Champagne

Bibliography

Barbadette, Gilles. "The Social Triumph of the Sexual Will: A Conversation with Michel Foucault." Brendan Lemon, trans. *Christopher Street* 64 (May, 1982): 36–41.

See also Adult Bookstores; Foucault, Michel; Pornography

Photography

One of the latest genres of the visual arts, photography has had a close association with gay and lesbian culture since its inception in the nineteenth century. Besides its potential for homoerotic expression in the works of Wilhelm von Gloeden (1856–1931) and others, the development of photography led to the documentary works of artists such as Berenice

Abbott, who photographed gay, lesbian, and bisexual Parisians in the 1920s. Most important, it also enabled artists to depict the global development of a gay and lesbian identity.

The concept of gay photography is enigmatic. While a person can be described as homosexual by sexual preference or gay consciousness, an inanimate object such as a photograph cannot. The photos exhibited by a homosexual photographer may be declared as "gay photography," but not every image is imbued with a gay sensibility. In some cases gay photography may consist of the documentation of gay events, cultural affairs, or behavior. Gay photography may best exemplify the ideal where photographic images evoke conscious or unconscious associations, either homoerotic or not, shared mutually by the viewer and the artist.

Photography in its earliest form was not considered an art form but a machination to record reality in service to art or science. This provided the impetus for the development of homoerotic images in the form of "etudes," nude studies of men and boys for artists unable to obtain live models. In the study of the nude, the camera provided a stock of images from which artists could work. It also served as a tool for complex experiments designed to learn more about the human anatomy and its fluid movements, by artists such as Thomas Eakins (1844–1916) and Henry Scott Tuke (1858–1929).

Wilhelm von Gloeden was the first to treat photography as an independent art form. A German living in Sicily, von Gloeden captured the beauty of the young male nude form, mirroring the aesthetics learned in his academic school of painting education. Photography as an art did not follow von Gloeden's academic aesthetics. A new conception in pictorial photography was initiated by prominent American homosexual photographer F. Holland Day (1864–1933).

Day was a proponent of photography as a fine art and was one of the few Americans elected to the prestigious Linked Ring Brotherhood in England. Day also founded the New American School of Photography and introduced the works of its artists to patrons in the United States and Europe. After a disastrous studio fire in 1904 and a prolonged rivalry with Alfred Stieglitz, Day's reputation was diminished and he ceased photographic endeavors in 1915.

Following the acclaim of F. Holland Day, Cecil Beaton moved from amateur status to celebrated professional. Beaton was completely disinterested in the technical aspects of photography, his objective being to make his models look beautiful. By the end of the 1920s he was recognized as an established society portrait and fashion photographer. Subtle but persistent homoerotic elements gave his portraits of friends such as Noël Coward and Rex Whistler an overt theatrical air.

During the 1920s, photographer George Platt Lynes (1907–1955) began studies with Lincoln Kirstein in Paris. With a camera acquired in 1927, he began to take photos of friends and gay celebrities such as Gertrude Stein and Jean Cocteau. Following the death of his father, he opened a commercial studio in 1933 and garnered a reputation as an accomplished fashion photographer. At the same time he made detailed studies of the male nude. The erotic, very private themes were formally and edifyingly presented, with the carefully arranged theatrical devices of the studio. Each image had a minimum of props and presented the figure as an object to be admired and worshiped.

Disillusioned with commercial photography and the death of his friend George Tichenov, Lynes moved to Los Angeles in 1942. His documentary photographs of Christopher Isherwood, Igor Stravinsky, Thomas Mann, and Aldous Huxley reflected the new social circles he moved in. A decade later Lynes befriended Alfred Kinsey, director of the Institute for Sexual Research. Shortly before his death he started contributing photographs of nude men to the Swiss homosexual magazine *Der Kreis* under the pseudonym Roberto Rolf and Robert Orville.

Another key artist in gay photography, Minor White (1908–1976), refused to accept that his personal life could be separated from his art, and his art from his existence. Energy was poured into his artistic endeavors as a sublimation for his homosexual desires. White's studies of the figure took a celebratory theme. The natural setting continues the idea of the "wholeness of man," understanding the restrained, sensitive, homoerotic element. Men are shown in images of a sparely expressed love, which is unemotional and intellectual rather than sexually involved. White's portraits of men have been described as "seductive idols" of masculinity, staring out of the photograph, tempting but untouchable. White established a highly respected reputation after World War II, teaching at the California School of Fine Art in 1946 and later joining the staff of the Rochester Institute of Technology. In 1953, he helped found *Aperture* magazine.

P

With the exception of homoerotic elements, the photographic documentation of gay life remained sparse until late in the twentieth century. Following the Stonewall riots of 1969, a number of documentary photographers emerged—Robert Girard, John Gettings, Steve Ziffer, Rich Wandel, Sunil Gupta. The portraits and visual representations of gay life by Indian photographer Gupta symbolized the move toward documentary reporting in gay photography that neither sensationalized nor glamorized the gay scene. His series "Ten Years On" of lesbian and gay couples is an intimate picture of gay life and sensibilities. Unquestionably the impact of early photojournalism by gay newsmagazines such as the *Advocate* also had a profound impact on the development of gay photography.

With the climate of sexual liberation beginning in the 1960s, gay photographers became unfettered to explore homoerotic and documentary themes, without the necessary excuses and covers previously employed. Artists were free to explore their personal visions of gay life and society. Thus arose a distinct link between the photograph and gay photography, which paralleled the development of the photograph and the development of a homosexual identity .

Michael A. Lutes

Bibliography

Cooper, Emmanuel. *The Sexual Perspective: Homosexuality and Art in the Last 100 Years*. New York: Routledge, 1994.

Waugh, Thomas. *Hard to Imagine: Gay Male Eroticism in Photography and Film From Their Beginnings to Stonewall*. New York: Columbia University Press, 1996.

See also *Advocate;* Beaton, Cecil; Cocteau, Jean; Coward, Noël; Day, F. Holland; Eakins, Thomas; Gloeden, Baron Wilhelm von; Isherwood, Christopher; Journalism; Kinsey, Alfred; Kirstein, Lincoln; *Kreis Der;* Lynes, George Platt; Mann, Thomas; Mediterranean; White, Minor

Physical Culture

Since the history of homosexuality is a history of the body and desire, it could be said that it is essentially the history of the production of physical culture—the organization of meaning in the body. This entry treats physical culture as it pertains to the deliberate shaping of gay male bodies in those parts of the world in which globalizing (post)modern gay culture has a presence. As other articles in this encyclopedia suggest, the construction of homosexuality is historically contingent. The focus is on developments over the last quarter century, since this is a period in which there has been great interest in the shape and meaning of the male body in global gay culture.

Until the mid-1970s, bodybuilding was socially marginalized among the middle classes of both mainstream and gay cultures. For the mainstream middle and upper classes, the specter of men devoting themselves to the aesthetics of hypertrophic masculine bodies aroused suspicion that there was a homoerotic undercurrent in physical culture. In homosexual circles, on the other hand, the ostensible masculine and heterosexual significance of highly developed musculature played to gay ironic sensibilities that were part of the covert gay milieu before modern gay liberation. Gay attitudes to overt musculature were mediated by class sensibilities, which reflected the wider history of the significance of the muscular body: from the rise of the bourgeoisie in the seventeenth century up until the 1970s, highly developed musculature was a sign of physical labor, which thus signified working- rather than middle- or upper-class status. Middle- and upper-class men thus eschewed having muscular bodies themselves. Bourgeois gay men who cared about their class status, and thus did not want to embody muscular working-class bodies themselves, could still be interested in such bodies in their sexual partners or sexual fantasies. Until fairly recently, middle- and upper-class homosexual desire for musculature brought to that already transgressive propensity the added frisson of violating prohibitions against interclass intimate relations.

Class sensibilities regarding musculature began to change in the 1970s and 1980s. The hard, muscled body was resignified as the sign of bourgeois discipline and productivity in the midst of a consumer culture that beckoned all to indulge in conspicuous consumption and relax. But the muscular body also became a sign of erotic hedonism— the male body intentionally and conspicuously intensifying its masculine erotic appeal. As a number of critics of the body in consumer culture have argued, the body that can signify indulgence and discipline is the body that most thoroughly embodies the bourgeois consumer culture that demands the strategic ability to produce and indulge maximally. Added to this is the centrality of youthfulness to the culture of consumption: only by purchasing clothes, beauty aids, and the services of the physical fitness

Physique Competition, Gay Games II, San Francisco, 1986. Photo by Marc Geller.

industry can one achieve and maintain that youthful appearance, which signifies the capacity both to produce and to consume vigorously. The muscular body, therefore, economically produced in these *consumer* logics of physical culture has become ever more fully the subject, in a Foucaultian sense, of an economic regime.

Gay male bourgeois culture participated fully in this consumer logic of the body, adding its own tendency toward camp productions of gender. Erotic images of muscular masculine excess abound at all levels of gay consumer culture, in fashion, political magazines, local community newspapers, movies, pornography, dance clubs, and bathhouses. By the late 1990s, the highly produced muscular male form became omnipresent in gay culture. While some representations of the gay male body do not fit the muscular mode, hegemony at the time of writing belongs to the commercialized image of the buff gay man. Representation and the life-world find their symbiosis in the fact that going to the gym became through the 1980s and 1990s a central part of the social and personal lives of many urban bourgeois gay men.

The advent of exaggerated masculine musculature in gay society in the 1970s also reflected changing and conflicting currents of masculine gender in gay male physical culture. From the late nineteenth century onward, homosexual culture was identified with effeminacy: heroes of that form were such men as Oscar Wilde and, more recently, Quentin Crisp. That image was characterized negatively by some American gay liberationists as an "effeminate homosexual stereotype" that needed to be overcome if gay men were to be liberated. Such moderate gay liberationists argued that gay men gaining traditionally masculine bodies was proof of the fallacy of the effeminate homosexual stereotype and the normalcy of gay men who thus deserve acceptance in the mainstream of American culture. Other, more radical liberationists maintained that bodybuilding changed only the appearance of gay men, allowing them to fulfill their erotic fantasies of gay men embodying traditionally masculine forms, while retaining an ironic appreciation of both the futility and the interpersonal and political undesirability of traditional masculinity for men who love men.

It could be argued that the muscular gay physical culture of the late twentieth century is a form of drag, engaging in camp sensibilities not dissimilar to the queenly forms of drag; it merely substitutes muscles for makeup, a new bouffant, as it were. But the effects of these two forms are quite dissimi-

P

lar in the content if not in the volume of their excess. Judith Butler has argued, quite influentially, that the content of drag is not the accomplishment of one set of gender signs replacing another but the process by which drag reveals the embodiments of all signs of gender as imitation; they are performances of cultural power that are pure simulation. In this interpretation, the final effect of drag is to disrupt the perception of masculine and feminine cultural forms as somehow natural to men and women, respectively. It is first and foremost an ironic exercise that liberates the dominant gendered perceptions of reality and expectations of others. Does the hypertrophic musculature of gay physical culture invite the same kind of perceptive disruption of the naturalness of gender?

Pronger has argued that gay muscles are ironic: musculature, traditionally the sign and the physical instrument of patriarchal and heterosexual power, useful in subjugating women and *repelling* other men, within a gay ironic sensibility signifies the subversion of such power by acting as homoerotic *enticements* to other men. Although that subversive irony may still be part of the formal logic of the homoerotic desire for muscular men, the omnipresence of the buff body in the consumer logic of gay culture suggests that there may be no more subversive power here than in the fetishization and acquisition of any other object of consumption—where the consumption of hegemonic cultural artifacts (such as the buff body) functions to support, rather than subvert, cultural dominance. The imperative in gay physical, which is to say *erotic*, culture to acquire and maintain such a body even into late middle age to be desirable in the marketplace of sexual consumption may be more oppressive than emancipating.   *Brian Pronger*

Bibliography

Bersani, Leo. *Homos.* Cambridge, Mass.: Harvard University Press, 1995.

Bordo, Susan. *Unbearable Weight: Feminism, Western Culture and the Body.* Berkeley: University of California Press, 1993.

Butler, Judith. *Gender Trouble.* New York: Routledge, 1990.

Featherstone, Mike. "The Body in Consumer Culture." In *The Body: Social Process and Cultural Theory.* M. Featherstone, M. Hepworth, and B. S. Turner, eds. London: Sage, 1991, 170–97.

Foucault, Michel. *Discipline and Punish: The Birth of the Prison.* New York: Vintage, 1979.

Levine, Mike. "Gay Ghetto." In *Gay Men: The Sociology of Male Homosexuality.* M. Levine, ed. New York: Harper and Row, 1979, 183–203.

Pronger, Brian. *The Arena of Masculinity: Sports, Homosexuality and the Meaning of Sex.* New York: St. Martin's Press, 1990.

Vaid, Uvashi. *Virtual Equality: The Mainstreaming of Gay and Lesbian Liberation.* New York: Anchor, 1995.

See also Bathhouses and Sex Clubs; Body Image; Gay Games; Sparta; Sports

Piñera, Virgilio (1912–1979)

The literary career of Cuban writer Virgilio Piñera embodies the worst consequences of the Cuban revolutionary government's cultural policies. A protégé of Jorge Luis Borges and already a prominent playwright and critic in his own right by the time of the 1959 revolution, Piñera marshaled his considerable cultural influence to support the revolution in its first years. He worked alongside Guillermo Cabrera Infante, Severo Sarduy, and others as a contributor to and editor of *Lunes de revolución*, the cultural supplement to the government's news daily. Rumors both of his growing skepticism about the regime's policies and of his homosexuality led to his arrest in 1961 for "assault on revolutionary morality"; Piñera remained a persona non grata in Cuba, even after his release, until his death in 1979.

Born in 1912 to a middle-class family in Cárdenas, Cuba, Piñera frequently traveled abroad in the decades before the revolution, meeting Borges and Witold Gombrowicz in Argentina and developing with their encouragement his own signature literary style, which combines elegant minimalism with absurdist irony. By 1959, Piñera had collected his major theatrical works and composed his major novel, the explicitly gay-themed *René's Flesh.* Piñera remained a key literary influence in Cuba well into his years of internal exile, representing an important counter both to the elaborate aestheticism of "baroque" writers like José Lezama Lima and to the reductive program of socialist realism sanctioned by the government. The surest measure of Piñera's lasting influence may be determined by the extent to which he is featured in literary memoirs by such prominent fellow writers as Reinaldo Arenas, Guillermo Cabrera Infante, and Heberto Padilla, writers who could tell his story only in leaving Cuba.   *Ricardo Ortiz*

Bibliography

Quiroga, José. "Fleshing Out Virgilio Piñera from the Cuban Closet." In *¿Entiendes?: Queer Readings, Hispanic Writings*. Emilie Bergmann and Paul Julian Smith, eds. Durham, N.C.: Duke University Press, 168–80.

See also Arenas, Reinaldo; Cuban Literature and Culture; Cuban Writing in Exile; Lezama Lima, José; Sarduy, Severo

Pink Triangle

From about the latter 1930s through early 1945, the pink triangle was the symbol sewn to the concentration camp uniform of prisoners who had been convicted of offenses against the German Reich's sodomy law, whose paragraph 175 prohibited sexual acts or, from mid-1935 on, acts with a sexual intent, e.g., a kiss or possibly even a look, between adult males or between an adult and a minor.

At first, men convicted under this statute were marked by other identification symbols such as a badge imprinted with "175" or an insignia bearing a large letter *A* (for "ass-fucker"). As the system of Nazi concentration camps spread from about 1937 onward (camps existed as early as 1933), a spectrum of colored triangles was created as a means of identification. Prisoners were classified according to the reason they did not conform to Nazi racial and political ideals: two yellow triangles sewn to form a Star of David for Jews; violet for Jehovah's Witnesses; brown for Gypsies (Roma or Sinti); red for political prisoners; green for criminals; blue for illegal emigrants; and black for "asocials."

Several of these colors were chosen because of specific cultural associations with the groups so marked (e.g., red had long connoted leftist politics). The choice of pink may have arisen from the long tradition in Western culture of linking male homosexuality and effeminacy. Long before the Nazis, males who engaged in sexual acts with other males had been defined as effeminate creatures who had abandoned their masculinity. In German culture, the color pink had been associated with femininity, but the specific reason for the Nazis' choice of pink as the insignia for homosexuals remains to be explained.

The black triangle encompassed almost anyone who refused to conform to the dictates of Nazism. Some lesbians were assigned this badge, but research has so far found relatively few women who were prosecuted solely for their lesbianism. Those who were interned were more likely to have been arrested under some other charge (lesbian acts were not illegal under German law), although they may have been denounced or come under suspicion because of their love of women.

Research into the persecution of homosexual men in the Third Reich is still relatively young with most of the work done in the 1980s and 1990s. Based on the number of convictions for paragraph 175 and on detailed records from some of the camps, it is estimated that between five and fifteen thousand men were assigned the pink triangle.

The Nazis differentiated between those who were deemed "unworthy of life" (all Jews and Gypsies and many Slavs) and those who might be "reeducated" and thus made useful to the *Volk*. Generally, the former were sent to extermination camps (e.g., Auschwitz, Treblinka) and the latter to concentration camps (e.g., Buchenwald, Sachsenhausen). In such camps homosexuals were often worked to death through assignment to the harshest work details. Research shows that a larger percentage of pink triangle prisoners died within the first year than other prisoners, such as Jehovah's Witnesses and politicals, and that, on the whole, homosexuals had the highest mortality rate in these camps.

In addition, some of these men were subjected to medical experiments. Many were castrated, some "voluntarily" in the hope of being released. Such hopes were just as often crushed as fulfilled. Some pink triangle prisoners at Buchenwald became the objects of hormonal experiments by Carl Vaernet, a Danish physician who had joined the Nazi SS. He believed that male homosexuality was caused by a deficit in male hormones.

When scholars in the 1970s began writing about the Nazi persecution of homosexuals, several icons were being used as symbols of gay liberation, e.g., the lambda, interlocked male or female symbols, or the color lavender. Yet the pink triangle resonated most deeply among gays and lesbians. It has become a symbol of gay remembrance and a sign of gay pride. Perhaps its best-known use is in the "Gay Monument" in Amsterdam, one block from the Anne Frank House. Three pink granite triangles representing the past, the present, and the future combine to form one large triangle that has become a central site for gay and lesbian life. In the late 1980s, the AIDS activist group ACT UP sought to reshape the meaning of this symbol. As an emblem of queer resistance, the pink triangle was reversed,

P so that it pointed up, thus marking a proactive, defiant stance against AIDS discrimination and homophobia. As an international symbol of gay and lesbian people, it would seem that the pink triangle has most recently been replaced by the rainbow flag, perhaps owing to its more celebratory character and, in contrast to the triangle, its unmarked past.

James W. Jones

Bibliography

Lautmann, Rüdiger. "Categorization in Concentration Camps as a Collective Fate: A Comparison of Homosexuals, Jehovah's Witnesses and Political Prisoners." *Journal of Homosexuality,* 19, no. 1 (1990): 67–88.

Plant, Richard. *The Pink Triangle: The Nazi War against Homosexuals.* New York: Henry Holt, 1986.

Röll, Wolfgang. "Homosexual Inmates in the Buchenwald Concentration Camp." *Journal of Homosexuality,* 31, no. 4 (1996): 1–28.

See also ACT UP; Activism, International; Amsterdam; Germany; Nazism and the Holocaust; Paragraph 175

The infamous Captain Bartholomew Roberts. From A General History of the Lives of the Most Famous Highwaymen, Murderers, Street Robbers, etc. *London, 1736. Courtesy of McMaster University Library.*

Piracy and Pirates

The evidence that pirates were sodomites is scant. The "truth" of pirate sexuality—barring discovery of new primary sources—is impossible to determine. Truth and legend have become hopelessly entangled. More significant to the history of sexuality is the way that pirates have been constructed as both cultural transgressors and economic criminals. The modern perception of the pirate—the romantic figure of legend—comes from piracy's "golden age," the years approximately 1695 to 1725. In fiction and popular history the myth and the reality of the pirate have merged to create the romantic antihero, recognizable by his outlandish costume, profane language, excessive violence, drinking, and carousing—all performed within a world of homosocial camaraderie. European law deemed the pirate *hostis humani generis,* "the common enemy against all mankind," because of his crimes at sea. All the pirate's cultural transgressions suggest how the "brethren of the sea"—who lived outside the boundaries of conventional society—can be represented as sexually deviant as well.

There is a crucial distinction between "golden age" pirates and earlier maritime figures such as the Corsairs of the Barbary Coast, mid-seventeenth-century buccaneers, and Sir Francis Drake. These marauders—like the privateers who sailed during wartime—were sanctioned by their governments. The golden-age pirate declared himself "at war against all mankind." He worked for no official government but only his own illicit profit. His self-declared outlaw status becomes the basis for his heroic status as well. Because of violations of cultural norms, over the last three hundred years the pirate has been the subject of hundreds of novels, plays, and popular histories. He is almost invariably portrayed as a masculine, violent, pleasure-seeking man whose desires are not repressed by the conventions of society. Curiously, women are nearly always absent from the historical representations—and many of the fictional works as well—raising the specter of masculine and passionate men "at war against all mankind" with no outlet for their sexual desires. The absence of explicit sexuality in pirates' behavior begs the question: How did pirates, who spent months at sea without the benefit of female companionship, relieve the sexual tensions implicit in a world of men?

B. R. Burg attempts to answer this question in *Sodomy and the Pirate Tradition* (1982), the only history that seriously looks at maritime sexuality. He argues that sodomitical behavior was rampant on board seventeenth-century buccaneer and pirate vessels. His argument is undermined by a lack of hard evidence. There are few records that can illuminate the sexual proclivities of the pirates. A pirate might have a companion with whom he shared his work and his "estate." Sodomitical accusations can be found in a few of the travelogues written by privateers in the early eighteenth century, but none of these cases particularly condemn the accused for their sexual proclivities. Rather, their incompetence as privateer captains is the reason for the condemnation in the first place.

The earliest and still most important pirate history, Charles Johnson's *A General History of the Robberies and Murders of the Most Notorious Pyrates* (1724–1728), offers tantalizing suggestions of piratical sodomy. The articles for Captain Roberts's crew forbid "women and boys among" the pirates (212). Johnson implies a suggestive relationship between the fictional Captain Misson and his mentor, "a lewd Priest" named Caraccioli (383–419). Reading between the lines, however, is not hard evidence and precludes arguing for rampant sodomy on board pirates ships in traditional scholarship. Burg further undermines his argument because he ahistorically takes twentieth-century prison statistics and places these findings of homosexual behavior on seventeenth-century pirate ships. Nonetheless, he offers an important correlative to piratical history precisely because he does point out the possibilities of the sodomitical pirate.

At the height of the pirates' power, their threat was economic. At the end of the seventeenth century and the early years of the eighteenth, Madagascar, off the southeast coast of Africa, was an important pirate stronghold. Rumors abounded throughout London that the pirates had set up a democratic "kingdom." Pamphlets were written to urge Parliament to action. One of Daniel Defoe's earliest novels, *The King of Pyrates* (1719), is in fact a fictional "autobiography" of the great pirate Captain Avery. In a pirate coup that infuriated the English government and the East India Company, Avery captured the Great Mogul's treasure-laden ship in 1695. But the political and economic repercussions had a counterpoint: the public's fascination with Avery's audacity. Avery became the first great pirate antihero, and the legends surrounding his act quickly grew. Ballads and contemporary pamphlets say that Avery also kidnapped the Mogul's granddaughter and left progeny on Madagascar, although the kidnapping is left out of court records or newspaper accounts. Interestingly, Defoe's version of Avery's life downplays the sexual aspects of the story. In fact, Defoe's Avery specifically denies having any sexual relations with the Mogul princess. He is aroused by her jewelry, not her desirability as a sexual object.

Fiction and popular history, finally, are where pirate sexuality becomes emphasized. Defoe, who may or may not be "Charles Johnson," author of the *General History*, is the most important influence for understanding the pirate. He constructs a pseudolibertine figure in such works as *Captain Singleton* (1720). Singleton brags about his violent, transgressive behavior, but women are absent from the narrative. Instead, Defoe emphasizes the romantic relationship between Singleton and his closest friend, a Quaker pirate. The novel ends with the two characters spending their days in England in private domesticity.

Other "real" pirates such as Blackbeard reflect the age in which they were written about. In the *General History*, Blackbeard is a ferocious brute with enormous sexual appetites who had fourteen wives. As the centuries pass, however, Blackbeard's violent nature, as well as the representations of other pirates, is either softened or emphasized. In the 1850s Blackbeard and other pirates are portrayed in several novels as effeminate criminals with no interest in women. In the 1890s, when many boy's adventures were published, Blackbeard and his ilk are the bloodthirsty pirates we picture today, but the stories emphasize piratical cruelty rather than other cultural transgressions like Blackbeard's polygamy. By the 1970s, a biography of Blackbeard tries to make him into both a ferocious pirate and a gentleman around women, a sort of hairy Hugh Hefner.

At the end of the eighteenth century, the pirate was no longer portrayed in literary representations as the economic threat to commerce that he had been earlier in the century. The antiheroic, romantic qualities of the pirate became paramount. In these plays, novels, and histories, however, the pirate almost always lives in homosocial camaraderie with other pirates. As notions of sexuality change and as a people are defined and define themselves by their sexual orientation, so does the pirate become defined by his transgressive life at sea in a world devoid of women. Many of the most famous pirates

P

are entirely fictional. By the twentieth century, the distinction between real and fictional pirates had been erased. Blackbeard, Bonnet, Kidd, and Avery have merged with Captain Hook, who kidnaps boys, or Long John Silver or Zap Comics' fellatiating Captain Pissgums, and the reader imagines a homoerotic brotherhood that defies the customs of conventional society.   *Hans Turley*

Bibliography

Burg, B. R. *Sodomy and the Pirate Tradition*. New York: New York University Press, 1982.

Defoe, Daniel. *The King of Pirates: Being an Account of the Famous Enterprises of Captain Avery, The Mock King of Madagascar, with his Rambles and Piracies; wherein all the Sham Accounts formerly publish'd of him, are detected*. London: 1720.

———. *The Life, Adventures, and Pyracies, of the Famous Captain Singleton* (1720). Shiv K. Kumar, ed. Oxford: Oxford University Press, 1990.

Johnson, Charles (Daniel Defoe?). *A General History of the Pyrates* (1724–1728). Manuel Schonhorn, ed. Columbia, S.C.: University of South Carolina Press, 1972.

See also Comic Strips and Books; English Literature; Libertine and Libertinism

Platen, August Graf von Hallermund (1796–1835)

Platen, a German poet, was born into an aristocratic family in Ansbach. Following cadet school and four years of service as royal page at the Bavarian court in Munich, Platen entered the University of Erlangen. His studies in languages and Oriental cultures led him to experiment in foreign verse forms, particularly the Persian *ghasel*. The poems of his first collection, *Ghaselen* (1821), clearly inspired by personal relationships and the result of Platen's aestheticized same-sex desire, were praised for their ingenuity in handling the most complicated meters and rhyme schemes.

Transformed by a journey to Italy in 1824, Platen produced some of the most beautiful poetry in German: the *Sonette aus Venedig* (Sonnets from Venice, 1825). A set of twenty sonnets (the so-called "Sonnets to Jonathan," a term coined by Platen's editor, Max Koch), addressed to his friend Karl Theodor German, gives testimony to the joy and burden of the poet's search for a love relationship considered sinful at the time. His best-known but also most disputed poem, "Wer die Schönheit angeschaut mit Augen, / Ist dem Tode schon anheimgegeben" (He who's seen beauty with his eyes, / has been touched by death already), has frequently been used to describe Platen's divided inner self in his battle against his homosexual feelings. Thomas Mann—for whom Platen was a source of inspiration and a model for the protagonist in his novella *Death in Venice*—saw in Platen a combination of Tristan, the knight who encounters death in his search for love, and Don Quixote, who hides in a world of self-illusion.

In 1826, driven by his growing estrangement from Germany's literary scene and several failed attempts to find a lover, Platen returned to Italy, where he spent most of his remaining life. To the chagrin of many friends, his homosexuality was openly attacked in a satire by the poet Heinrich Heine in 1830, who took offense at Platen's play *Der romantische Ödipus* (1829). Count August von Platen died in Syracuse, Sicily, from self-prescribed overdoses of medicine against cholera.   *Christophe Lorey*

Bibliography

Derks, Paul. *Die Schande der heiligen Päderastie: Homosexualität und Öffentlichkeit in der deutschen Literatur, 1750–1850*. Berlin: Verlag Rosa Winkel, 1990, 479–613.

Heck, Werner. "August von Platen: *Tristan*. Ein Gedicht und seine (Be-) Deutung." *Forum Homosexualität und Literatur* 11 (1991): 1–52.

Mann, Thomas. "August von Platen." In *Schriften und Reden zur Literatur, Kunst und Philosophie*. Frankfurt: M. Fischer, 1960, 33–43.

Williams, W. D. "August von Platen." In *German Men of Letters*. Vol. 5. *Twelve Literary Essays*. Alex Natan, ed. London: Oswald Wolff, 1969, 131–52.

See also Arabic Literature; German Literature; Mann, Thomas

Plato (c.429–347 B.C.E.)

Plato was an Athenian teacher and writer. What can be known with certainty of his life beyond that is very little. Even the chronology or sequence of the dialogues, his principal writings, is a matter for guesswork. Plato's importance lies not in what he did or when he did it, but in what he wrote. All of Western philosophy has been called a footnote to him. If that is an exaggeration, it is no exaggeration to say that he exceeds in influence all but a few philosophic writers and that he equals any of them.

No one can be so widely influential without suffering contradictory interpretations. So there are dozens of versions of Plato, dozens of Platonisms, spread across ancient, medieval, and modern philosophy. One of the few characteristics shared by most of them is embarrassment over Plato's depictions of erotic passion between men. This embarrassment carries forward into contemporary translations and commentaries, many of which become unreliable or explicitly homophobic as soon as the Platonic text turns to male-male sex.

Even when the texts are left to speak for themselves, it is no easy thing to understand what they teach about same-sex desire. Plato's dialogues narrate imaginary and ironic conversations in which he himself never participates. So they cannot be read as offering his straightforward prescriptions for sexual behavior, much less as giving neutral or objective evidence for a social history of Greek homoeroticism.

Many passages in the Platonic dialogues do describe male-male love vividly. They describe it, in the form best known to Athenians, as *paiderasteia*—the erotic, active love of an adult man for a beautiful, passive adolescent. Many of the dialogues presume a society in which *paiderasteia* is a principal means of education and socialization, not to say the most intense form of erotic expression. The Platonic Socrates is depicted as one of the most famous players of the game of courting adolescents. Three of the dialogues—*Lysis*, *Charmides*, *Euthydemus*—have as their backdrop the public admiration of "boys" (*neoi*) or "beauties" (*kaloi*) in the Athenian *palaestras*, the wrestling grounds that had become general schools. In the *Lysis*, Socrates confesses that he was seized by an animal hunger, was set on fire, when he caught a glimpse of the body inside a young beauty's loose-fitting robe. These various depictions of Socrates as pursuer of adolescent beauty are summed up masterfully in the *Symposium*, which tells of an all-night drinking party devoted to speeches about Eros, the god or demigod of passionate love. Before the speeches begin, Socrates claims that the only thing he knows is *Eros*. In the speech of the drunken Alcibiades, a former beauty, Socrates is said to be famously fickle in chasing after all the most beautiful young men. Moreover, in his own speech, Socrates pretends to repeat a discourse in which Eros appears with many of Socrates' own features and habits. Socrates is more than an expert in erotic matters; he is the very embodiment of the god who presides over male-male couplings.

Here Plato's ironies begin to complicate things, because if Socrates adopts the attitudes of Athenian *paiderasteia*, he seems always to transform them. He wants to persuade Lysis that a perfect body, no matter how inflaming, is less valuable than wisdom. More poignantly, Alcibiades reveals that Socrates had refused to have sex with him because he thought Alcibiades' sought-after body a poor exchange for wisdom. The refusal can be appreciated only when one realizes how much it reversed Athenian expectations—or modern American ones. Socrates was older, unattractive, not wealthy, and apolitical (as politics are usually understood). Alcibiades was young, beautiful, wealthy, and powerful. Yet Socrates rebuffed each of Alcibiades' carefully arranged seductions at the *palaestra* and over dinner. He went so far as to spend a night beside him, the two alone, without touching him sexually.

Socrates' reversals of Athenian expectations cannot be interpreted as a condemnation of male-male relations in favor of male-female sex. They are rather condemnations of prevailing notions about the relative value of bodily beauty—and wealth, social status, and political power. Socrates is not attacking "homosexuality," a category that had no equivalent in ancient Greek. He is not even attacking Athenian *paiderasteia*. He judges it as one of many sociopolitical arrangements that typically encourage sophistry rather than philosophy, pleasure rather than excellence, power rather than wisdom—which is to say, lies in place of truth. That is why Socrates can mix his reversals or rejections of paiderastic conventions with indulgent appropriations of sexual attitudes between males. In the *Phaedrus*, for example, Socrates not only plays out a seduction drama with a young man in a secluded place; he offers an allegory of the soul's ascent from the body that is powered by homoerotic love. According to Socrates, the best form of that love will not enact itself sexually, but he recognizes immediately that the next-best love will involve sexual relations. He does not suggest replacing male-male erotic relations with male-female ones. For the parallel allegory that Socrates rehearses at second hand in the *Symposium*, the soul can attain a vision of the good itself only by beginning from devotion to beautiful boys. If there is a single Socratic teaching,

P it is that *Eros* is the necessary beginning for philosophy—and that *paiderasteia* is an excellent instance of *Eros*.

There are other views of male-male love in the Platonic dialogues, as there are other voices. Socrates himself is perfectly willing to call up the darker prejudices of Athenian society. In the *Gorgias*, for example, he reminds his interlocutors that they consider the pleasures of passive anal intercourse disgusting in an adult—at least officially. Socrates no more endorses this prejudice than he endorses the hundreds of others that he quotes in his dialectical arguments. Nor is Plato endorsing all the contradictory views about male-male love that appear in the speeches of the *Symposium*. Comic poet Aristophanes tells a myth according to which the human race is divided by different origins into men who seek men, women who seek women, and men or women who seek the opposite sex. Some readers want to make this into a Greek anticipation of modern views of the biological causality of sexual orientation. They forget that they are reading a myth in a dinner speech by a writer of comedies—as invented by his longtime opponent, who happens to be a master ironist.

A similar skepticism is required by passages in Plato's *Laws* where the institutions of *paiderasteia* seem to be condemned as "against nature"—a phrase that will go on to have a long history in Christian moral theology. Here, as in many Christian arguments, male-male relations are condemned along with masturbation, fornication, and adultery as being purely for pleasure's sake, unjustified by orderly social arrangements for procreation. Of course, these words are spoken not by Socrates but by a nameless "Athenian," who makes them as one small piece of an immense legislative hypothesis—or game. They cannot be attributed to Plato—they cannot even be understood—without decoding the ironic complexities of this most complex dialogue.   *Mark D. Jordan*

Bibliography

Halperin, David M. "Why Is Diotima a Woman?" In *One Hundred Years of Homosexuality and Other Essays on Greek Love*. New York: Routledge, 1990.

Percy, William Armstrong III. *Pederasty and Pedagogy in Archaic Greece*. Urbana, Ill.: University of Illinois Press, 1996.

See also Greece, Ancient; Pederasty; Renaissance Neoplatonism

Political Asylum

Political asylum is imprecisely used to refer to any number of permanent or semipermanent legal statuses in a country to which a refugee has fled for fear of persecution in her country of residence. Although its historical roots date back some 3,500 years, the modern system of international protection is a result of and a response to the plight of the Jews in Nazi Germany, compounded by the failure of other countries to protect them during that period.

In 1954, the new office of the United Nations High Commissioner for Refugees (UNHCR) promulgated a consolidation of the patchwork of existing refugee agreements in the Convention Relating to the Status of Refugees and its 1967 Protocol, which both direct contracting states to grant asylum to those who will suffer persecution on account of race, religion, nationality, political opinion, or membership in a particular social group. Signatories to this convention are to implement its norms in their domestic legal systems.

People who engage in same-sex behavior face persecution in many forms, some of which do not match the traditional conception of what constitutes refugee persecution: examples include homophobic mob violence by groups or individuals that the government cannot control (Brazil); state-perpetrated torture in the form of forced psychiatric confinement and treatment (Russia); imprisonment, "shock therapy," or even execution (Iran); or tremendous societal discrimination. Legally, penal codes (often remnants from a colonial period) generally condemn men to prison for consensual sodomy; women, when homoerotic behavior is noticed at all in the law, are defined as mentally ill or are subject to vague charges of "vagabondism" that local police use to harass them where they meet each other.

There is no one way attorneys and activists came to use the international law of refugee protection for those fleeing homophobic persecution in their homelands. Anecdotal evidence suggests that some claims of asylum on the grounds of sexual orientation were made and granted in the late 1970s, but certainly by the 1980s it became possible to claim that "membership in a particular social group" includes those who are gay men, lesbians, bisexuals, the transgendered, and/or the HIV-positive. This is gradually becoming the norm in the developed world. Most countries, however, arrived at the inclusion of these groups in their domestic refugee systems through case law, and so comprehensive data regarding this phenomenon are unavailable, as most of these cases are not published (and naturally include confidential information).

For instance, in *Matter of Inaudi* (1992), an Argentine man was granted asylum in Canada by the Refugee Division of the Immigration and Refugee Board on deciding that eight years of antigay harassment by officials and military authorities in Argentina constituted persecution of the type protected by refugee law. The court noted that the modern international system was designed to protect those groups targeted by Hitler and Stalin, including homosexuals.

In the United States, 1986 saw the grant of "withholding of deportation" (a slightly different legal status) to a Cuban in the case *Matter of Toboso*. The administrative court's decision was based both on antigay persecution suffered by Toboso at the hands of the Cuban authorities and on the Cuban government's attempts to dissuade people from living openly as lesbians or gay men through public humiliation and harassment. The Immigration and Naturalization Service appealed this ruling unsuccessfully in 1990, and Attorney General Janet Reno elevated the Board of Immigration Appeals decision, upholding his grant to precedent in 1994. The federal Ninth Circuit heard arguments in the sexual orientation asylum claim of a Russian lesbian in late 1996.

Other countries known to have granted these kinds of claims include the Netherlands, Great Britain, Sweden, Australia, New Zealand, Denmark, Finland, Belgium, and Ireland.

Furthermore, the UNHCR has interpreted the refugee definition in the convention to include sexual minorities. As the UNHCR *Handbook* to the 1951 convention states, " '[A] particular social group' normally comprises persons of similar background, habits or social status" and that "membership in a social group may be at the root of persecution . . . because the very existence of the social group as such . . . is held to be an obstacle to the Government policies." That is certainly the case for lesbians, gay men, bisexuals, the transgendered, and the HIV-positive, because they are, more often than not, seen to be a threat to dominant social and moral norms.

Accordingly, attorneys who have sought advisory opinions in refugee claims from the UNHCR to present as evidence in proceedings have received favorable consideration.

These new developments in international law, although taking place in vastly different social and political contexts throughout the world, face some common challenges. Documentation of human rights abuses perpetrated against these groups is difficult to obtain. The world's major human rights agencies are only beginning to appreciate fully the depth and complexity of antigay violence as a human rights problem. Recently, the San Francisco–based International Gay and Lesbian Human Rights Commission and its Asylum Project have emerged as the leading voice for inclusion of gay concerns in international human rights and as a one-stop documentation center.

These claims are often highly controversial, and so despite their infinitesimal number compared with the world's millions of refugees, the related publicity can contribute to the anti-immigrant backlash sweeping the developed West. Fear of the spread of AIDS is particularly exacerbated in these cases.

Lesbian asylum seekers face considerable problems: even less documentation of human rights conditions specific to lesbians is available than for gay men; women generally have less money to leave their country of residence or to use for counsel in the country of asylum; and lack of specific legal penalties against female-female sexual activity (despite severe social sanction) can make adjudication of claims murky at best. These developments are related to the deepening understanding of gender-based persecution around the world and the issuance of guidelines for granting asylum to women in several countries.

The significance of these developments in refugee law is only now being understood. Scholars, attorneys, students, and activists are beginning to explore how international law can be used to coerce governments to better human rights conditions worldwide.   *Mark J. Harris*

Bibliography

Anker, Deborah. "US Immigration and Asylum Policy: A Brief Historical Perspective." *Harvard Law Bulletin* 38, no. 4 (1987).

Goldberg, Suzanne. "Give Me Liberty or Give Me Death: Political Asylum and the Global Persecution of Lesbians and Gay Men." *Cornell International Law Journal* 26, no. 3 (1993).

Office of the United Nations High Commissioner for Refugees. *Handbook on Procedures and Criteria for Determining Refugee Status Under the 1951 Convention and 1967 Protocol Relating to the Status of Refugees*, 1979.

P

See also Australia; Activism, International; Denmark; European Commission of Human Rights; Finland; Immigration, U.S.; Ireland; Nazism and the Holocaust; Netherlands; New Zealand; Sweden

Politics, Global

Although there was limited contact between small gay and lesbian circles, primarily in western Europe, from the late nineteenth century on, it was only in the post–World War II period that one could speak of an international gay movement, and much more recently that there existed any meaningful movement that extended beyond the North Atlantic region.

The emergence of gay organizations in countries of western Europe after 1945 meant some limited contact, but it was only in the 1970s, with the rapid growth of overt gay social, economic, and political organizations, that a genuine international movement could be created. Ten years after the student revolutions of 1968, which helped create new radical homosexual movements in parts of western Europe, the International Lesbian and Gay Association (ILGA) was established, largely on the initiative of established groups from the Netherlands, Scandinavia, and Britain. (It is revealing that its 1985 survey of "Lesbian and Gay Oppression and Liberation" was confined to chapters on eight European countries plus Israel and Cuba, the latter two written by two Dutch observers.)

ILGA continues to exist, with its administrative offices in Brussels and about three hundred member organizations, mainly European but with significant numbers from elsewhere, especially Latin America. It acts as a lobby, working to achieve the incorporation of gay and lesbian issues into international human rights agendas and seeking to influence national governments and international agencies. With a shoestring budget and one staff member, its achievements have been largely symbolic, depending heavily on individual commitment.

Although the United States has by far the largest and best-organized gay movement, it has been a relatively small contributor to international gay politics. In 1991 the International Gay and Lesbian Human Rights Commission (IGLHRC) was established in San Francisco; it has increasingly close ties with both ILGA and international HIV/AIDS networks. IGLHRC seeks to monitor antihomosexual activities across the world and to sponsor protests, as does Amnesty International.

American influence, through publications and cultural production, has been considerable, however, in expanding the sense of a global gay and lesbian culture and community. It was Stonewall in 1969 rather than Paris in 1968 that became the model for gay movements in other parts of the Western world, and later in the developing world. The increasing reach of the American media and the constant expansion of movement of both people and images have played their roles: in a cover story on the global spread of gay identities the *Economist* wrote, "In effect, what McDonald's has done for food and Disney has done for entertainment, the global emergence of ordinary gayness is doing for sexual culture."

It would appear that organizing around a common gay identity demands a liberal political culture, and the expansion of liberal democratic institutions in the past decade, with the collapse of European communism and South American military dictatorships, has been reflected in the growth of gay organizations in both areas of the world. But there are small gay groups even in countries such as China, despite constant uncertainty about police reactions.

Gay groups have a history in Latin America dating back to the early 1970s. In a number of countries, they experienced very severe repression during the military dictatorships that took power in that decade. The late 1980s saw a new wave of organizing, partly in response to HIV/AIDS, which opened up new opportunities—and urgency—to the development of links between homosexual men worldwide. Groups such as Pink Triangle in Malaysia and Gays and Lesbians of Zimbabwe (GALZ) show both the influence of a global gay culture and the possibilities for developing specific political actions by local gay communities.

The 1990s have seen an unprecedented awareness of gay issues internationally and a push to bring them within the framework of international human rights discourses. Thus after many years of lobbying (mainly by ILGA), Amnesty International adopted imprisonment on the grounds of homosexual behavior as one of the issues it would protest. And in 1994 the United Nations Human Rights Commission upheld a complaint by Australian Nick Toonen against the sodomy laws of his home state, Tasmania, which led Australia to override the state's laws. Other governments have bitterly opposed making gay rights part of international human rights, insisting that this is morally and culturally inappropriate.

It is now possible to speak of an international gay movement, and to find groups in over fifty countries on all continents that share a common language of gay identity and opposition to antigay prejudice. Yet such groups represent only a small part of those who have a conscious political identity based on their homosexuality, and these in turn are only a relatively small proportion of those who engage in some form of same-sex acts.

Gay communities worldwide have experienced growing awareness of the vulnerability of those involved in homosexual acts to infection by HIV, and despite some reluctance on the part of international AIDS agencies, the global response to the epidemic has been significant in developing a sense of commonality among gay groups. The various International AIDS conferences and NGO networks have provided important opportunities for international networking among gay organizations.

Dennis Altman

Bibliography

Adam, Barry. *The Rise of a Gay and Lesbian Movement*. Boston: Twayne, 1987.

Altman, Dennis. "It's Normal to Be Queer." *Economist*, January 6, 1996.

———. "Rupture or Continuity: The Internationalization of Gay Identities." *Social Text* 14, no. 3 (Fall 1996): 48.

ILGA Pink Books. London: Cassell, 1985, 1988, 1993, 1998.

McKenna, Neil. *On the Margins*. London: Panos, 1996.

See also Activism, International; AIDS; AIDS Organizations, U.S.; Argentina; Australia; Brazil; China; Civil Rights (U.S. Law); Czech Republic; Denmark; England; European Commission of Human Rights; France; Gay Rights in the United States; Germany; Identity Politics; Immigration; India; International Law; Ireland; Italy; Japan; Kenya; Paragraph 175; Political Asylum; Slovenia; South Africa; Sweden; Thailand; Yugoslavia; Zimbabwe

Pomo Afro Homos

From 1991 until the ensemble disbanded in 1995 (though the company is still active), the theatrical collective Pomo Afro Homos (Post Modern African-American Homosexuals) reigned as one of the most important performance groups in the country.

Noted for the entertaining candor of their performances, the Pomo Afro Homos illuminated a

Members of Pomo Afro Homos, 1998. Photo by Marc Geller.

uniquely black *and* gay space, created in part by the racism of white gays that, on the political level, expects gay African Americans to toe the "mainstream" (white) gay party line, and on the personal level, eroticizes racial difference in such a way as to orientalize black men, viewing them as the dark and exotic objects of white pleasure, and also created by the neoconservatism of a religiously fervent African American community that views homosexuality as inherently "white" and attempts to silence all discourse on black queerness. Thus, the Pomo Afro Homos used this double-edged sword of marginalization to create a liberatory space that affirmed a voice that was both culturally unique and an affirmation of same-gender desire, and they did so in a way that did not romanticize sexual and ethnic oppression but viewed gay African American identity as dynamic and inclusive.

The Pomo Afro Homos debuted in 1991 at Josie's Cabaret and Juice Joint in San Francisco's Castro district with the performance piece *Fierce Love*, which toured the United States and also played at the Drill Hall in London. The height of the short-lived fame of the Pomo Afro Homos was when *Dark Fruit* played Lincoln Center, in New York City, in 1993 and 1994 and the International Black Arts Festival in Atlanta, Georgia. They have also been involved in a number of video productions, most notably Marlon Riggs's *Tongues Untied*, for which Brian Freeman was associate director.

Fierce Love and *Dark Fruit* were written by Brian Freeman, Marion K. Wright, and Djola Branner; other major works include *Black and Gay: A Psycho-Sexual Study*, *Doin All Right*, and *Chocolate City, USA*, all by Brian Freeman. They have been anthologized in *Coming Out Laughing*, *Staging Gay Lives*, and *Colored Contradictions*. The body of critical writing on the Pomo Afro Homos is still in its nascency, though their major pieces have been anthologized in *Staging Gay Lives*, edited by John Clum. *Matthew Williams*

Bibliography

Clum, John, ed. *Staging Gay Lives*. Boulder, Colo.: Westview Press 1996.

Elan, Harry, ed. *Colored Contradictions*. New York: Penguin, 1997.

See also Activism, U.S.; African American Gay Culture; AIDS Performance; Black and White Men Together, National Association of; Riggs, Marlon

Pontormo, Jacopo da (1494–1556)

Jacopo da Pontormo is considered to have been the preeminent painter and draftsman of mid-sixteenth-century Florence and was the principal innovator of the mannerist style, which drew heavily on Michelangelo's language of the body. He was eccentric and reclusive. Giorgio Vasari, Renaissance art historian and Pontormo's contemporary, described him as a "frugal and sober man, and in his dress and manner of life he was rather miserly than moderate; and he lived almost always by himself" (181). Although his religious works, with their mannerist distortions, are arguably what most distinguishes his achievement as a painter, Pontormo is probably best known in the United States for his *Portrait of a Halberdier*, widely thought to be a portrait of Duke Cosimo I de' Medici from circa 1537, which hangs in the J. Paul Getty Museum in Los Angeles. The figure has been invested with a peculiar eroticism. One scholar of Renaissance portraiture has characterized it, with his pinched waist and bulging codpiece, as "sexually ambiguous," and describes the pouting expression in terms of "orgasmic vacancy" (Campbell 9).

Pontormo, Three Men Walking. *Musée des Beaux-Arts, Lille. Giraudon/Art Resource, NY.*

While nothing about Pontormo's reputation would indicate either an articulated, much less dissimulated, homosexual identity or same-sex erotic relations, two kinds of document, both by Pontormo's own hand, recommend themselves to the historian of early-modern homosexuality. The first is the diary Pontormo kept during the final three years of his life (1554–1556), in which he records in meticulous (one might almost say neurotic) detail the daily vicissitudes of his body, frail health, and diet. His food intake was carefully and habitually measured out to the ounce. Though Pontormo socialized little, several figures from his restricted, virtually all-male circle of friends and workshop are given regular mention. Pontormo's most frequent dinner companion was Agnolo Bronzino (1503–1572), the painter's devoted pupil and junior by nine years, who is often referred to in the diary with affectionate diminutives, like "Bro" and "Bronzo." About their lasting friendship, Vasari notes that "above all others, and always supremely beloved by him was Bronzino, who loved him as dearly" (182). Pontormo also seems to have been on close terms with Benedetto Varchi (1503–1565), the Florentine poet and orator whose outspoken and explicit defense of the idea of Socratic (i.e., homoerotic) love was a source of scandal to his contemporaries. That Varchi regularly dined with Pontormo, wrote a sonnet to him, and delivered the oration at the painter's funeral all suggest that Pontormo could have been no stranger to some of the more high-profile sodomitical circles in the already intensely homosocial world of sixteenth-century Florence that Michael Rocke has investigated in his recent historical study, *Forbidden Friendships*.

The second, and more suggestive, set of documents are visual: Pontormo's sizable corpus of drawings of the male nude. A perceptible homoerotic sensibility seems to inform many of his academy studies and preparatory drawings featuring single and sometimes multiple male nude figures, done primarily in red or black chalk. Pontormo favored extreme rotational poses that allow the viewer to savor simultaneously a figure's muscular chest, curving back, and (especially) buttocks, or else seated or recumbent positions that invariably privilege a crotch view. Pontormo's interest in the male nude included his own body, which he drew on at least one occasion reflected in profile in a mirror, with the singular and intriguing addition of underwear.

William B. MacGregor

Bibliography

Campbell, Lorne. *Renaissance Portraits: European Portrait-Painting in the 14th, 15th and 16th Centuries*. New Haven: Yale University Press, 1990.

Cox-Rearick, Janet. *The Drawings of Pontormo*. 2 vols. Cambridge, Mass.: Harvard University Press, 1964.

Dall'Orto, Giovanni. "Socratic Love as a Disguise for Same-Sex Love." *Journal of Homosexuality* 16 (1988): 33–64.

Pontormo, Jacopo da. *Pontormo's Diary*, Rosemary Mayer, ed. and trans. New York: Out of London Press, 1982.

Rocke, Michael. *Forbidden Friendships: Homosexuality and Male Culture in Renaissance Florence*. New York: Oxford University Press, 1996.

Vasari, Giorgio. "Jacopo da Pontormo." In *Lives of the Most Eminent Painters, Sculptors and Architects*. Vol. 7. Gaston duc de Vere, trans. London, 1912–1914.

See also Art History; Bronzino, Agnolo; Florence; Italy; Michelangelo Buonarroti

Pornography

In common parlance, pornography refers to sexually explicit images consumed in a particular context—one in which the possibility of arousal is deemed "appropriate," if still the object of some censure. Part of pornography's appeal is that it provides an illicit pleasure. "Soft-core" porn is usually defined by what it prohibits—no erections, no split beavers, no ejaculation, and no oral, anal, or vaginal penetration—though these prohibitions are subject to revision and depend on particular historical conventions and contexts. For example, while soft-core magazines increasingly feature erections, not a single boner can be spied on late-night cable TV. "Hardcore" usually designates representations of penetration in particular. Pornography is often further subdivided according to its perceived audience—gay, lesbian, straight, bi—and particular acts that it represents or tastes to which it appeals.

It is somewhat misleading to speak of homosexual versus heterosexual pornography. While a given text is usually advertised as featuring heterosexual, homosexual, or bisexual activity, there is no necessary correspondence between the images and the audiences who consume them. For example, in an adult theater, two men may have sex with each other while ostensibly watching images of straight sex. Pornography follows the lead of sexuality in its pursuit of the polymorphously perverse. (Is masturbation, for example, a homosexual act?) Given pornography's mandate to arouse, and to arouse a variety of spectators, it is sometimes difficult to separate gay from straight pornography—even on the level of the images. For example, one straight porno star is noted for his ability to perform autofellatio. Many "heterosexual" porno films feature lesbian scenes, though these seem to be constructed for the eyes of heterosexual male spectators, as a kind of warm-up to heterosexual activity. Such films also often feature orgies. Even when the men do not touch one another, these images suggest the potential pleasure of looking at another man's erection. This not to imply that "anything goes"; it is rare, for example, for men to touch each other in a "straight" porno film. Nonetheless, in its inability to withhold a visual knowledge of both male and female bodies, hard-core pornography is particularly "perverse."

Much recent criticism had attempted to explain how visual pornography manages to arouse. This question is often answered with recourse to psychoanalytic theories of desire in general, and to accounts of scopophilia (the sexualizing of the drive to see) and voyeurism (a perverse pleasure in looking) in particular. These debates have followed the trend of related debates in film theory. Does the spectator of pornography identify primarily with the camera as pure protection—a sexuality reduced to a hypertrophy of the visual? If spectators identify secondarily with characters, do they do so as the active partner, the passive partner, or some shifting combination of the two? The problem with these debates is that they take as their model the spectator of commercial film—a specious analogy, given pornography's modes of reception. The typical account of the film spectator offered by psychoanalytic theory—silent, immobile, repressing his "exhibitionism," engaging in covert, yet authorized, forms of "voyeurism," isolated, experiencing "displaced" forms of sexual gratification—is laughably inadequate to an understanding of gay pornography in particular. As important as the porno images themselves are the contexts in which they are received. Pornography is consumed both publicly and privately—in bars, adult bookstores, at parties, within the home, and so forth—in situations in which genital activity occurs and does not occur, and in which spectators pay different kinds and levels of attention to the images.

For some time, both critics and consumers have often assumed that men enjoy pornography more than women; male sexuality is said to be more "visually oriented." A number of women have challenged this assumption, suggesting at the very least that if men are more aroused by visual images, it is the result of cultural conditioning and not nature. Recently there has been an increase in literary and film pornography made by women for women, straight and lesbian.

Objections to pornography are often concerned about the relationship between pornographic images and the real. Such arguments warn that consumers will be encouraged by pornography either to act out in their lives fantasies deemed by some to be "unhealthy"—fantasies that involve some measure of violence, defined in a variety of ways, either to the self or to one's partner—or at the very least will be led to treat their sexual partners as "objects" rather than as "full" human beings. Both these objections seek on some level to redeem sex from its threat to confuse the boundaries of self and other, and to purge from it any hint of power. Other critics have argued that the value of pornography is its very refusal to sanitize the sexual.

Rather than consider pornography as chiefly a representation of the real, we might instead think of pornography as a discourse. This discourse does not simply "reflect" current sexual fantasies and practices; it simultaneously "implants" them. There is thus an interanimating relationship between pornography and the real. It is neither a simple reflection of reality nor "pure" fantasy. This is not to suggest that pornography is anything the individual desires it to be. Even without recourse to concepts like the unconscious, we can acknowledge that individuals do not "choose" what turns them on. Pornography necessarily structures sexuality, and vice versa. It does so, however, in ways that are often difficult to describe.

Many critics have noted the particular importance of pornography to gay men's lives. In a culture that denigrates homoeroticism, pornography provides some of the only "positive" representations of gay sexuality. In its refusal to obey the strictures of procreative heterosexuality, homosexuality represents as desirable an inappropriate and undisciplined use of the body. Gay and lesbian pornography is a discourse about that undisciplined use. It advertises, conveys, and implants the pleasures of polymorphous perversity.

Pornography is also, however, a commodity. Some critiques of pornography are directed toward the deleterious working conditions under which porno actors suffer. A discussion of the value of pornography also necessarily engages the vexing relationship of capitalism to modern gay culture. While capitalism has played a role in the formation of a gay identity, it has done so in its own interests, and often in opposition to those of real human beings. It is thus impossible simply to embrace pornography as one of capitalism's positive contributions to gay culture.   *John Champagne*

Bibliography

Bersani, Leo. "Is the Rectum a Grave?" In *AIDS: Cultural Analysis, Cultural Activism*. Douglas Crimp, ed. Cambridge, Mass.: MIT Press, 1988, 197–222.

Bright, Susie. *Susie Sexpert's Lesbian Sex World*. Pittsburgh: Cleis Press, 1990.

Champagne, John. *The Ethics of Marginality: A New Approach to Gay Studies*. Minneapolis: University of Minnesota Press, 1995.

———. "Homo Academicus." In *Boys: Masculinity in Contemporary Culture*. Paul Smith, ed. Boulder, Colo.: Westview Press, 1996, 49–79.

D'Emilio, John. *Making Trouble: Essays on Gay History, Politics, and the University*. New York: Routledge, 1992.

Faludi, Susan. "The Money Shot." *New Yorker*, October 30, 1995, 64–87.

Kimmel, Michael S., ed. *Men Confront Pornography*. New York: Crown, 1990.

Snitow, Ann, Christine Stansell, and Sharon Thompson, eds. *Powers of Desire: the Politics of Sexuality*. New York: Monthly Review Press, 1983.

Waugh, Tom. *Hard to Imagine: Erotic Gay Male Photography and Film from the Pre-Stonewall Underground*. New York: Columbia University Press, 1996.

———. "Men's Pornography, Gay vs. Straight." *Jump Cut* 30 (1985): 30–36.

Williams, Linda. *Hard Core: Power, Pleasure, and the "Frenzy of the Visible."* Berkeley: University of California Press, 1989.

See also Adult Bookstores; Athletic Model Guild; Bruce of Los Angeles; Films; Masturbation; Photography

Porter, Cole Albert (1891–1964)

One of the most famous American composers of Broadway shows and popular songs of his era, Cole Porter is probably best remembered for famous hit songs such as "Night and Day," "Let's Do It, Let's Fall in Love," "You Do Something to Me," and "Begin the Beguine." Porter's musicals include *Fifty Million Frenchmen* (1929), *Anything Goes* (1934), *Jubilee* (1935), *DuBarry Was a Lady* (1939), and *Kiss Me, Kate* (1948).

Born in Peru, Indiana, to a prosperous Midwestern family, Porter married wealthy divorcée Linda Lee Thomas in 1919, and with her led a life replete with world travel and the constant company of theatrical and other celebrities. Since his death, Porter's homosexuality has been openly acknowledged in biographies and documentaries, and the marriage to Linda is now most often described as a relationship of companionship. The heterosexual version of Porter's life portrayed in the 1946 film musical biography *Night and Day* demonstrates that his homosexuality, as would be expected in this pre-Stonewall era, was not commonly recognized by Porter's public during his life. It is said that Porter loved to laugh about the absurdities of this Hollywood version of his life, telling his friends that "none of it is true."

Porter's music has always had a certain resonance with queer listeners. Unlike many of his peers, Porter wrote both lyrics and music for virtually all his songs and is especially noted for his wry, sophisticated, often bawdy musical and verbal puns. The degree to which his lyrics point to a sexual dimension while maintaining a morally conventional surface level ("Let's Do It, Let's Fall in Love" and "My Heart Belongs to Daddy" are good examples) is one explanation for this affinity. The biting camp in songs like "Thank You So Much, Mrs. Lowsborough—Goodby," in which the singer lays waste to a hostess for an unhappy weekend through a deadly sarcastic thank-you note, is undoubtedly another reason for his gay following.

In the 1990s, Porter became a frequently recurring icon as a gay American composer. A 1990 rock album entitled *Red, Hot and Blue* featured Porter songs as interpreted by various contemporary rock artists as part of an AIDS relief fund-raising campaign. Moreover, a number of gay male choruses, including both the Seattle Men's Chorus and the San Francisco Gay Men's Chorus, have performed the musical *Swellegant Elegance* by David Maddux. Maddux's show is a revue of selected Porter songs for the purpose of celebrating both Porter's music and his homosexuality.   *Alan Mason*

P

Bibliography

Gill, John. *Queer Noises: Male and Female Homosexuality in Twentieth-Century Music.* London: Cassell, 1995.

See also Camp; Choruses and Marching Bands; Music and Musicians II: Popular; Musical Theater

Portugal

Portugal is the oldest country in Europe within its present borders. Although it shares a common origin with Spain and both countries now form part of the European Union, Portugal has its own distinct history and culture.

During the Middle Ages, sodomy was expressly condemned by successive legal codes, which prescribed severe penalties such as castration, burning at the stake, confiscation of possessions, and banishment. Later codes, known as *Ordenações*, also contained measures to encourage informers to denounce homosexuals. The legislation covered women as well as men. Besides the secular authorities, the Inquisition, or Holy Office, also pursued sodomites. The records of these cases survive and give a rare glimpse of gay life in the sixteenth through eighteenth centuries, which flourished despite the threat of persecution. Relatively few of the sodomites caught were actually executed in an auto-de-fé. A more common punishment was torture and banishment, either to other parts of Portugal or to the colonies of Angola and Brazil, or forced labor. These draconian laws were replaced by a more liberal criminal code in 1852, which omitted all mention of homosexuality, although it continued to regulate sexual behavior in public. In the late nineteenth and early twentieth centuries, doctors and specialists in legal medicine introduced contemporary European theories about homosexuality to Portugal. Today, the law generally ignores homosexuality except for an explicit prohibition of homosexual relations between adults and minors age fourteen to sixteen, while the age of consent for most heterosexual acts is fourteen.

There is little active hostility to homosexuality in Portugal but the influence of the conservative countryside, the Catholic religion, family pressures, and the fear of gossip and ridicule tend to encourage a discrete attitude among gays. Nevertheless, there is a thriving gay scene in Lisbon centered on the night-life area of the Bairro Alto, with bars, discotheques, and saunas, and various gay beaches visited by Portuguese and foreign tourists. Changing social values and increased opportunities to travel since the 1970s have liberalized attitudes, particularly in Lisbon, encouraging the creation of a number of gay groups and publications, such as the Gay International Rights group in Braga and the magazine *Órbita Gay Macho* (Macho Gay Orbit). ILGA-Portugal, a group that aims to increase the visibility of gays as well as provide social and counseling services, was formed in 1995. It has its own Web site (http://www.ilga-portugal.org) and publishes a newspaper, *Trivia*, which was launched in 1996. Other organizations include the lesbian group Lilás (Lilac) and the left-wing Grupo de Trabalho Homossexual (Homosexual Working Group).

Homosexual themes have a long pedigree in Portuguese literature, beginning with some of the satirical medieval troubadour poems known as *Cantigas de escárnio e mal dizer*, which castigate in the crudest language named men and women for same-sex relations. A few minor gay characters appear in the classic nineteenth-century novels of Eça de Queirós (1845–1900), but the most remarkable work is the novel *O Barão de Lavos* (The Baron of Lavos), by Abel Botelho (1855–1917), published in 1891. This naturalist novel with decadent overtones tells the story of the three-way sexual relationship between a Lisbon aristocrat, his wife, and his young male lover. Although hostile in tone, it is important as one of the earliest European novels to have homosexuality as its overt and central theme. The subject was also exploited by popular novelist Alfredo Gallis (1859–1910) in *O Sr. Ganymedes* (Mr. Ganymede) (189?, 2d ed., 1906), in which an heiress discovers that her elegant husband is a transvestite with a male lover.

In the early twentieth century, a group of modernist writers published several works with homosexual themes. *A confissão de Lúcio* (The Confession of Lúcio, 1913–1914), by Mário de Sá-Carneiro (1890–1916), is an enigmatic novel dealing with sexual ambiguity and gender confusion. The poem "Antinous" (1918), written in English by Fernando Pessoa (1888–1935), now recognized as Portugal's greatest modern poet, contains some thinly disguised descriptions of the physical love-making between the emperor Hadrian and his young lover. In a second, revised edition, which he published in 1921 through his own publishing house, Olisipo, Pessoa systematically removed all the words expressing shame in the relationship. Pessoa is most famous for his invention of heteronyms as authors of his poetry in Portuguese, an elaborate system of masks that has many resonances for gay readers. Olisipo also published *Canções* (Songs, 1922), a book of love poems by the openly gay António Botto (1897–1959). This caused a famous polemic with some Catholic students in which Botto was defended by Pessoa and by Raul Leal (1886–1964), who wrote an inflamed pamphlet entitled "*Sodoma divinisada*" (Sodom Exalted, 1923), also published by Olisipo. The latter, because of the subject matter of the works it published, was effectively a gay imprint.

In the novel *Sedução* (Seduction, 1937), by José Marmelo e Silva (1913–1991), the narrator describes his sister's lesbian relationships, providing a complex critique of notions of masculinity and the hypocritical conventions governing sex before marriage. Among contemporary novelists who have written openly about homosexuality, journalist Guilherme de Melo's *A sombra dos dias* (The Shadow of the Days, 1981) gives a vivid account of the life of a white middle-class gay man in the Portuguese colony of Mozambique before, during, and after its war of independence. His later novels *Ainda havia sol* (There Was Still Sunshine, 1984) and *O que houver de morrer* (He Who Should Die, 1989) describe gay relationships set in Portugal. A relationship between conscript soldiers during the colonial wars is depicted by Álamo Oliveira (1945–) in the novel *Até hoje* (Until Today, 1986).

A number of writers have made an increasingly overt gay contribution to the tradition of Portuguese love poetry. Among poets with a particular appeal to gay readers are Eugénio de Andrade (1923–) and surrealist Mário Cesariny de Vasconcelos (1923–) of the older generation and Joaquim Manuel Magalhães (1945–), Gastão Cruz (1941–), and Luís Miguel Nava (1957–1995) of the younger. Contemporary poets who have published verse with an explicit homoerotic content include João Miguel Fernandes Jorge (1943–), some of whose poems are addressed to a male lover, and Al Berto (Alberto Pidwell Tavares, 1948–), who, besides a novel, *Lunário* (1988), has published a number of erotic gay poems.

In recent years a number of foreign plays about homosexuality have been staged in translation. In the cinema, *Onde bate o sol* (Where the Sun Beats Down, 1989), directed by Joaquim Pinto (1957–), deals with homosexual desire in a rural setting. A gay newsmagazine entitled *Korpus* began publication in 1996.
Robert Howes

Bibliography

Aguiar, Asdrúbal António d'. *Evolução da pederastia e do lesbismo na Europa: contribuição para o estudo da inversão sexual*. Lisbon: Arquivo da Universidade de Lisboa, 1926, no. 11, 335–620.

Gomes, Júlio. *A homossexualidade no mundo*. 2 vols. Lisbon: Ed. do Autor, 1979–1981.

Melo, Guilherme de. *Ser homossexual em Portugal*. Lisbon: Relógio d'Água Editores, 1983.

Monteiro, Arlindo Camilo. *Amor sáfico e socrático: estudo médico-forense*. Lisbon: Instituto de Medicina Legal de Lisboa, 1922.

ILGA-Portugal Web site: http://www.ilga-portugal.-org

See also Brazil; Inquisition; Pessoa, Fernando; Spain

Postmodernism

Postmodernism is simultaneously a form of criticism, a description of generic post–World War II modes of existence, and a label applied to specific dimensions of culture and cultural objects in recent and contemporary history. In each instance, postmodernism refers to a number of wide-ranging and differing phenomena. Of particular significance to any consideration of postmodernism from the perspectives of gay men, lesbians, and other sexually dissident communities and identities are the following characteristics: emphasis on multiplicity; skepticism of the utility of culturally sanctioned binary divisions; decolonization of the "Third World"; antiracist and feminist critiques of Eurocentrism; the flourishing of the new social movements of the 1960s; the electronic communications boom; the recession of the nation as a unit of analysis; the technologies of the Internet and the domain of cyberspace; the global economy and its offshore productions and investments; cross-cultural influences; and, perhaps most obviously germane, a "constructivist" framework for understanding sexuality and gender apart from biogenetic or transhistorical explanations.

What is postmodernism? What is postmodern? There are countless ways to answer these questions, which are always under interrogation. In dictionary terms, *postmodernism* is usually identified within the terms of architecture or the decorative arts. Given that the formulation of postmodernism as a field of criticism has taken place within the acad-

Pemy, it might be appropriate to gauge at least some of its effects on an epistemological level. Postmodernism as a cultural and historical process can be said to have attacked modernism on the following counts: by emphasizing the capillary, microphysical functioning of power as well as the violence necessarily inherent in the production of "truth" (Foucault); by proclaiming the death of the author (Barthes) and the lack of authority within authorial presence (Derrida); by instigating mimetic readings of "master" texts to demonstrate their many limitations (Irigaray); by arguing the coercive inevitability of state violence lying just below the surface of public consensus (Althusser); by demonstrating the nonexistence of the "original" in an age of the "simulacra" (Baudrillard); and by emphasizing the centrality of colonialist categories at the heart of Western culture (Fanon and Hall).

Also central to discussions of postmodernism has been Frederic Jameson's *Postmodernism, or, The Cultural Logic of Late Capitalism* (1984). Jameson examines postmodernism across many cultural fields—architecture, culture, ideology, film, video, space, and economics among others. Judith Butler's *Gender Trouble* has also been key to discussions of sexuality within a postmodern framework. Among other assertions made in *Gender Trouble*, Butler insists that "sex," far from serving as the foundation of "gender," is itself founded on the notion of gendered division. Other important perspectives on postmodernism's many forms and functions have been written by Katie King and Chela Sandoval, who have both mapped the postmodern in their theoretical and historical considerations of U.S. feminist movements. While King has examined canon formation within feminism and the "globalization" of gay identities, Sandoval has investigated forms of feminism written by women of color as emblematic of an "oppositional consciousness" possible only under postmodernism.

Within academic circles, various manifestations of "postmodern" thinking have animated a critical edge of intellectual chic for several decades. And while different disciplines find different ways of channeling the varied energies of postmodernism, interdisciplinary fields like cultural studies, English and literary studies, ethnic studies, women's studies, and gender studies, lesbian and gay studies and queer theory have all been relatively friendly to the intellectual contributions made by postmodern theories and practices. Though postmodernism has found a home in the social sciences as well as the humanities, it is within humanities departments—at least in North America—that postmodernism has had the widest range of influence.

Central to the postmodern turn in lesbian, gay, and queer thought, politics, and culture are a number of specific orientations. From a postmodern perspective, homosexuality is not understood as individual or essential truth. Instead, there is an effort in postmodern thinking toward conceptualizing homosexualities, as plural as the cultures, generations, and people shaping them. Following this turn in thinking, there is in postmodern gay, lesbian, and queer cultural politics a concomitant strike against *identity* as the most productive mode for describing and denoting these homosexualities, as well as a related assault on narratives of "coming home" into a gay identity. This trope, which is typically featured in the coming-out story, is rejected within a postmodern framework as forcing from individual varied experiences a formula of containment. Lastly, there is an unwillingness within postmodern thinking to identify a given sexuality across temporal and cultural contexts to particular, enduring, and fixed meanings. In place of such ascriptive reasoning, postmodern lesbian, gay, and queer thought often argues in favor of affinity-based politics of sexual dissidence against identity-anchored attempts to justify political mobilizations and cultural judgments.

Heavily indebted to a deconstructive opposition to binary models of social organization, postmodern lesbian, gay, and queer thought opposes any practice of "gay reading" or "lesbian writing" as necessarily caught in the heteronormative trap of reducing a wide range of sociosexual positions to two—"heterosexual" and "homosexual"—arranged hierarchically, with the former term advantaged materially and symbolically over the latter. The very idea of "lesbian reading" or "gay writing" in this analysis confuses the need to undo sexual hierarchies with the desire to superimpose a set of lesbian and gay/queer–affirmative definitions onto dominant culture. A postmodern or deconstructive lesbian, gay, or queer literary strategy refuses this kind of activity precisely because it limits the possibility of queer criticism while it reinscribes the binary it has failed in the first place either to critique or to subvert.   *Alex Robertson Textor*

Bibliography

Butler, Judith. *Gender Trouble: Feminism and the Subversion of Identity*. New York: Routledge, 1990.

Jameson, Frederic. *Postmodernism, or, The Cultural Logic of Late Capitalism.* Durham, N.C.: Duke University Press, 1989.

King, Katie. *Theory in Its Feminist Travels: Conversations in U.S. Women's Movements.* Bloomington, Ind.: Indiana University Press, 1994.

Sandoval, Chela. *Oppositional Consciousness in the Postmodern World.* Minneapolis: University of Minnesota Press, 1998.

See also Architecture; Barthes, Roland; Coming Out; Deleuze, Gilles; Essentialist-Constructionist Debate; Foucault, Michel; Identity Politics; Queer; Queer Theory

Poulenc, Francis (1899–1963)

French composer Francis Poulenc shamelessly embraced the paradoxes inherent in his nature and by so doing created some of the most durable and entertaining music of the twentieth century. A devout Roman Catholic, he was also an irrepressible epicure with a refined taste in cuisine, poetry, interior decoration, and susceptible gendarmes. Poulenc was one of the most eclectic composers of his era, borrowing from Mozart, Stravinsky, and a host of other composers, yet he developed an inimitable style. By fearlessly expressing his individuality, Poulenc attained an enduring position in the history of French music; his songs rank with those of Fauré, Ravel, and Debussy.

Poulenc was born into a family of pharmaceutical manufacturers. His Parisian mother encouraged his musical talent, but his provincial father insisted that he attend the Lycée Condorcet rather than the Paris Conservatoire. Aside from piano lessons with Ricardo Viñes and some harmony lessons with Charles Koechlin, Poulenc was essentially self-taught as a composer. Influenced during this period by the music of Satie and the aesthetics of Cocteau, Poulenc became a member of a loose confederation of composers known as "Les Six." His early music reflects the high spirits of Paris in the 1920s, admirably exemplified by his ballet *Les Biches.* Written in 1924 for the *Ballets Russes,* *Les Biches* repeatedly confounds the audience's gender expectations, as in the tender *pas de deux* between an athlete and a ballerina dressed as a messenger boy.

While Poulenc never repudiated his frothy side, the expressive content of his music deepened throughout the 1930s. A series of sacred choral works, beginning with the *Litanies à la vierge noire* (1936), eventually led to the creation of the religious opera *Les Dialogues des carmélites* (1954). At the same time, he began to accompany baritone Pierre Bernac, for whom he composed many of his finest songs. (Unlike Peter Pears and Benjamin Britten, to whom they have been compared, Poulenc and Bernac were not lovers.)

After serving in the French Resistance during World War II, Poulenc resumed his comfortable, productive existence, commuting between Paris and his house in Touraine. His music continued to expand in technical resource and emotional intensity, including such scores as the solo scena *La Voix humaine* (1958), the *Gloria* for soprano, chorus, and orchestra (1959), and the Sonata for Oboe and Piano (1962). Poulenc died of a heart attack a few weeks after his sixty-fourth birthday; with him died the last vestiges of grace and charm in twentieth-century French music.

Byron Adams

Bibliography

Daniel, Keith W. *Francis Poulenc: His Artistic Development and Musical Style.* Ann Arbor, Mich.: UMI Research Press, 1982.

Poulenc, Francis. *Diary of My Songs.* Winifred Radford, trans. Foreword by Graham Johnson. London: Victor Gollanz, 1985.

See also Ballets Russes; Britten, (Edward) Benjamin; Cocteau, Jean; France; Music and Musicians 1: Classical Music; Pears, Sir Peter; Ravel, (Joseph) Maurice

Preston, John (1946–1994)

When John Preston died of AIDS in Portland, Maine, he had single-handedly turned that town into a Mecca of gay publishing. For thirty years, the Boston-born writer and editor was in the forefront of the development of gay media. During that vital period, when the gay community was making such strides in self-awareness and organization, its writers and editors tended to fall into one of two categories: apolitical writers, both literary (such as Edmund White) and pornographic (such as Lars Eighner), or political activists whose writing and editing was a means to an end, such as Larry Kramer and Michelangelo Signorile. Preston carved out for himself an intermediary position with a foot in both camps. Though he was only briefly editor for publisher Robert McQueen's *Advocate* magazine during its 1970s rise from local California newspaper to national news magazine, his policies of responsible gay reporting, facing issues squarely but without being shrill or polemical, remains influential today. Between him and McQueen, Liberation Publications quickly became a gay publishing organization that treated its contributors as well as, and often better than, the mainstream press, with standards as high as any in the industry.

But it is Preston's fiction that has had the greatest effect on gay society. After leaving the *Advocate* in 1975, Preston began to write what he himself liked to call pornography. By that time, censorship barriers had fallen and homoerotic writers were pretty much letting it all hang out in print. Some of them, like Sam Steward, writing as Phil Andros, did it quite well. But Preston not only wrote well, he chose subjects—S/M, bondage, dominance, submission—that when they weren't being ignored were negatively portrayed, but he wrote about them approvingly. He did in print what Tom of Finland was doing in pencil, portraying heavy-duty sex between healthy, happy homosexuals. His stories developed a devoted following. When *Mr. Benson*, his novel eulogizing the perfect master, was serialized in *Drummer* magazine, T-shirts appeared in leather bars stating "Looking for Mr. Benson" or asking "Looking for Mr. Benson?" Eventually it was published in book form (1983), followed by other novels and short story collections (*I Once Had a Master*, 1984; *Tales of the Dark Lord*, 1992; and others). Master/slave stories were not his only oeuvre; he wrote a series featuring Alex Kane, a gay avenging hero, and even Franny, the Queen of Provincetown.

In 1986, Preston was diagnosed as HIV-positive. "The news had been devastating. I had stopped writing for quite a while," he said. But he eventually returned to the keyboard. To the end, he wrote and edited works both sociopolitical (*Personal Dispatches, Writers Confront AIDS*) and erotic (*Flesh and the Word*, Vols. 1 and 2). In the year preceding his death, no fewer than five volumes of his writings were published. *F. Valentine Hooven III*

Bibliography

Preston, John, ed. *Flesh and the Word 2*. Introduction. New York: Penguin, 1992.
———. *Mr. Benson*. New York: Masquerade, 1992.
———. *My Life as a Pornographer*. New York: Masquerade, 1993.
Townsend, Larry. *Leatherman's Handbook*. New York: Freeway Press, 1974.

See also Advocate; Kramer, Larry; Leathermen; Pornography; Sadomasochism; Sex Practice; Tom of Finland; White, Edmund

Priapus

For the ancient Romans, Priapus was a kind of garden god, a deterrent of thieves and birds (rather like a scarecrow). He was characterized by an enormous genital organ and can therefore be linked with the phallic cults that also tended to exaggerate the size of the male member. The Priapus was often an ornamental figure. According to Petronius, there were priapi of pastry as well as ones made of gold, silver, and glass. In 1834 great quantities of phallic amulets were discovered at Xanten on the Rhine, presumably brought there by the Roman legions.

Otto Kiefer has argued that the Priapus cult originated in Asia Minor and was combined with other kinds of celebrations of the phallus. Many of these cults began to be challenged in the eleventh century. Popular worship of Priapus figures was reflected in pagan festivals and local fetes. The existence of secret societies perpetuated older forms of worship. Often the medieval church had not considered them as heresies but ignored them. Increasingly, the church sought to exercise its authority. The Bolgres (also known as Bougres) were charged not only with doctrinal waywardness but also with indulging in unnatural vices. Some critics and antiquarians such as William Payne Knight have argued that the name Bulgarus (heretic) came to be identified with sodomy and buggery.

The deployment of Priapus as a literary figure is nowhere more evident than in the Carmine Priapea, an obscene anthology of doggerel verse much of it collected from inscriptions and graffiti on Priapic statues. This Latin verse provides important insights into the nature of humor and satire but also of Roman attitudes to a range of sexual practices. Priapus was usually presented as a threatening or violent male figure. He frequently boasts his strength and his virility, yet the reader is encouraged to identify with these traits. Roman humor and sexual practice were both active and aggressive in these terms. Moreover, Priapus's victims were generally described in the vilest terms. The representations of women, for instance, are frequently misogynistic by modern standards.

Priapus sometimes threatens his victims with punishment. This usually involves the attack on an orifice, irrespective of one's sex. Many of the poems deal with pueri, pathics, or homosexuals, in a satirical manner. Priapus was sometimes himself satirized, finding himself engaged in unwholesome, foul, or disgusting acts.   *Ian McCormick*

Bibliography

Kiefer, Otto. *Sexual Life in Ancient Rome*. London: Abbey Library, 1934.

Knight, William Payne. *A Discourse on the Worship of Priapus, and its connexion with the Mystic Theology of the Ancients*. London, 1786–1787.

Richlin, Amy. *The Garden of Priapus: Sexuality and Aggression in Roman Humor*. Oxford: Oxford University Press, 1992.

Rousseau, G. S. "The Sorrows of Priapus: Anticlericalism, Homosocial Desire, and Richard Payne Knight." In *Sexual Underworlds of the Enlightenment*. G. S. Rousseau and Roy Porter, eds. Manchester, England: Manchester University Press, 1987.

See also Christianity; Petronius; Phallus, Rome, Ancient

Price, Reynolds (1933–)

Novelist, dramatist, poet, and Duke University professor Edward Reynolds Price was born on February 1, 1933. Profiling her former instructor in *Vanity Fair*, Pulitzer Prize–winning novelist Anne Tyler remarked that Price has "the great good fortune to know his place, geographically speaking." That place is the American South. Although comparisons to Faulkner have dogged him since his first novel, *A Long and Happy Life* (1962), won the William Faulkner Foundation award, Price's greatest influence was Eudora Welty and her gentle, spare romanticism.

Feminine influence, usually maternal, remains a major theme of Price's fiction: "My mother nearly died when I was born. Or, as I saw it, I killed her." Many of his characters lived with this tragic legacy, including those featured in *The Surface of the Earth* (1975). Phoebe-Lou Adams commented that this novel "contained the largest number of deaths in childbirth ever packed into a single novel." Price himself survived cancer of the spine that confined him to a wheelchair. During his recovery, he finished *Kate Vaiden* (1986) and won the National Book Critics Circle Award for his achievement.

He also wrote the novel *The Tongues of Angels* (1990) and *The Promise of Rest* (1994), which tells the story of a man with AIDS. In *Conversations with Reynolds Price* (1991), he said that "literature is not a slice of life, and it shouldn't be. Life is horrendous enough . . . literature shows us life in a far more organized and controlled way" (282).

John Ison

Bibliography

Humphries, Jefferson, ed. *Conversations with Reynolds Price*. Jackson: University Press of Mississippi Press, 1991.

See also Fiction; U.S. Literature: Contemporary Gay Writing

Prisons, Jails, and Reformatories

The earliest known document addressing homosexuality in the American prison system is a letter written by Louis Dwight on April 25, 1836, to a government official. After visiting prisons in various states, Dwight documents the practice of prisoners forcing boys to engage in sodomy. Dwight uses this evidence to argue that juvenile delinquents should be separated from hardened offenders. Although most minors are now housed in separate facilities, the problem of forced sex in prison continues.

While studies analyzing sexual activity in jail and prison should be examined with caution, contemporary research has resulted in the following generalizations. A significant amount of sexual activity in prisons is consensual, yet rape is still a serious problem for inmates. The typical profile for victims of sexual aggression in prison is a young, white inmate of smaller physical stature who has entered the institution within sixteen weeks of the incident. Gays, lesbians, and bisexuals are more likely than heterosexuals to engage in consensual sexual activity in prison. Male heterosexual inmates are more likely to be the aggressor in and recipient of sexual acts than the provider.

The use of slang is common in prisons to describe the nature of sexual activity. A *kid* or *punk* refers to an inmate who was *turned out* or forced to perform sexual acts on another inmate. A *jocker* or *stud* is an inmate who has sexual activity with either a punk or a known gay inmate. The jocker views this sexual act as a sign of his masculinity, not as a homosexual encounter. A *queen* or *sissy* is a gay inmate who assumes a submissive sexual role and effeminate mannerisms. A queen may be known in the prison as an inmate who will provide sexual services for a payment. A *homosexual* or *gay* inmate engages in a variety of sexual roles. In addition, the terms *catcher* and *pitcher* are used to distinguish sexual roles in prison. A catcher is the recipient of a sexual act, such as the person being satisfied by oral or anal copulation. The pitcher is the person providing oral or anal copulation to the catcher. These roles provide inmates with a social structure that allows them to carry out a modified version of their sexual identity in a controlled environment.

In addition to being victimized by inmates, gay and lesbian inmates have been subjected to many injustices by guards, wardens, and other government employees. For example, in 1955 the local government in Boise, Idaho, engaged in an extensive anti-gay witch-hunt. One of the targets (X) of this witch-hunt was given a jail sentence for violating the state's sodomy law. Local government officials in the prosecutor's office and sheriff's office conspired and entrapped X into engaging in consensual sex while in jail. They offered other inmates plea bargains in exchange for enticing X to engage in sex and taking a photograph of the incident. The prosecuting attorney owned the camera. As a result, X was sentenced to a seven-year prison term.

Many jails and prisons have adopted and enforced policies targeting gay and lesbian inmates. These policies have often been upheld by courts reasoning that these policies are necessary to maintain security and to "protect" gays and lesbians. For example, gays and lesbians have been assigned to solitary cells and have had their privileges restricted in an effort to "protect" them from abuse from other inmates. In addition, the decision by penal institutions to refuse to allow the Metropolitan Community Church, a Christian church ministering to gays and lesbians, to participate in group worship services in prison has been upheld by the courts. Prisons have also enforced discriminatory visit policies that allow for noncontact visits for heterosexual couples and preclude gay and lesbian inmates from visiting with their partners. Gay, lesbian, and heterosexual inmates who have HIV/AIDS have been subjected to mental abuse, physical segregation, and denial of privileges and medical treatment. These abuses are being slowly litigated in the courts.

While gay and lesbian inmates continue to face abuse and discrimination, advocacy and support groups have helped to improve prison life for gays and lesbians. Some inmates will have access to books, magazines, newsletters, Web sites, and support groups while incarcerated. There is a critical need to continue research, support, and advocacy for gay and lesbian inmates. *Christine A. Yared*

Bibliography

Barnes, H. E., and N. K. Teeters. *New Horizons in Criminology*. 3d ed. Englewood Cliffs, N.J.: Prentice-Hall, 1959.

Katz, Jonathan Ned. *Gay American History*. Rev. ed. New York: Meridian, 1992.

Stojkovic, S., and R. Lovell. *Corrections: An Introduction*. 2d ed. Cincinnati: Anderson Publishing, 1997.

Cases

Brown v. Johnson, 743 F.2d 408 (6th Cir. 1984).
Doe v. Sparks, 733 F. Supp. 227 (1990).
Moore v. Mabus, 976 F.2d 268 (5th Cir. 1992).

See also Gay Rights in the United States; Sexual Abuse

Proust, Marcel (1871–1922)

Marcel Proust's best-known work, the multivolume novel *À la Recherche du temps perdu* (*Remembrance of Things Past*) has become one of the most celebrated works of European literature. The author grew up in a prosperous bourgeois Parisian family. His father was a successful doctor; his mother was from a wealthy and cultivated Jewish background. As much of his famous novel recounts the life of the narrator (named Marcel) from early childhood to a moment in his adult life when he undertakes to write a novel about his life, Proust's biographers have frequently used the novel as a source of biographical information. In parallel fashion, many critics of the novel have spent a great deal of time documenting sources in the real world for various characters in the novel.

Remembrance of Things Past constitutes a remarkable portrait of French society from the late nineteenth century through the first two decades of the twentieth, and encompasses many themes from Proust's own life. It portrays an ongoing battle for cultural prestige among a variety of rich bourgeois circles and aristocratic circles. It portrays the intense internal psychological dynamics of a rich bourgeois family such as Proust's. It traces the vexed place of Jewishness and anti-Semitism in French society at the time of the Dreyfus affair. It dwells in magnificent detail on the forms of aesthetic experience as theorized and practiced in the music, painting, and writing of the time. It also gives a major place to the exploration of both male and female practices and cultures of homosexuality of the time.

Marcel Proust. Corbis-Bettmann.

The first volume of this magnum opus, *Du Côté de chez Swann* (*Swann's Way*), was published in 1913, when Proust was already in his forties and had as yet no reputation as a novelist. He had had a traditional French education, although his school attendance had been rendered problematic since the age of about nine by very serious bouts of asthma. He studied both law and political science but was more interested in pursuing a social life that would allow him to move in the highest Parisian society and in following various literary interests. In 1892 he and some of his former schoolmates founded a literary journal, *Le Banquet*, for which Proust did some of his earliest writings.

In school, Proust had formed romantic attachments to various of his schoolmates and wrote several of them ardent letters. To Daniel Halévy he wrote, for instance, "I know some very intelligent boys of—and I pride myself on this—a high moral refinement, who once had a good time with another boy they knew. That was when they were very young. Later they turned back to women" (quoted in Rivers, p. 58). Proust's pursuit of his desires and also his efforts to conceal them would be juxtaposed throughout his life. He would have friendships and affairs with numerous men, yet would often speak and write disparagingly of "sodomists." In 1897 he fought a duel with Jean Lorrain (they both apparently fired a pistol shot into the air) after Lorrain published a review of a book of Proust's short stories, *Les Plaisirs et les jours*, in which he intimated that Proust was intimate with Lucien Daudet, an insinuation biographers assume to be correct. Proust had also been involved with the pianist and composer Reynaldo Hahn, who would remain a lifelong friend. He had a somewhat rocky friendship with the famous dandy Robert Montesquieu, who lived with his male secretary and companion, Gabriel d'Yturri, for twenty years. Montesquieu is taken to be one of the most important models for the character of the Baron de Charlus in *Remembrance of Things Past* (as well as for Des Esseintes, the protagonist of the novel *À Rebours* (*Against Nature*), by Joris-Karl Huysmans).

Over the next decade, Proust would undertake a number of literary projects, as well as writing society columns on Parisian salons for *Le Figaro*. He translated a number of books by English art critic John Ruskin and worked on a novel he never published, *Jean Santeuil*. (It would be published in fragmentary form in 1952 and is often read as a first draft of *Remembrance*.) He formulated and began writing a long essay, *Contre Sainte-Beuve* (*Against Sainte–Beuve*; again, only to be published in fragmentary form in 1954, long after his death). He also began writing and publishing a series of well-received "pastiches," imitations of authors such as Balzac, Flaubert, Renan, and the Goncourt brothers, stylistic exercises that investigated the individuality of a writer by miming the forms of that writer's sentences.

Over the course of these years, Proust also became more and more of an invalid, continually subject to his asthma. He withdrew almost entirely from social life around 1910, occasionally receiving nighttime visits from friends, occasionally taking trips out at night, and once in a while taking excursions out of Paris. At about this moment, all his writing projects coalesce into work on his novel, a merging of his various critical and literary endeavors. It was to be about the experience of time, about modes of aesthetic appreciation; it would encompass psychological analysis, a portrait of his particular social world, and an investigation of homosexuality.

The size of the novel grew enormously as Proust worked on it from 1910 until his death in

P 1922. The experience of World War I caused him to make substantial modifications and extensions of his original plan. At the time of his death from complications of pneumonia, he had not yet brought the closing volumes into final form. From the first moment he started corresponding with publishers about his novel, Proust insisted that it was centrally concerned with homosexuality, even though in published form it was not until the fourth volume that homosexuality comes to occupy a large place. *Swann's Way* contains one lesbian scene that shocked a number of its first readers and contains veiled references to the past or present sexual activities of several other characters.

Several publishers refused to publish *Swann's Way*, finding its style and subject matter—including digressive, detailed accounts of aesthetic experiences and their psychological ramifications—somewhat inscrutable. With the second volume, *À l'Ombre des jeunes filles en fleurs* (*Within a Budding Grove*, 1919), Proust achieved clear recognition. *Swann's Way* had been refused by the publication house of the *Nouvelle Revue Française,* a decision for which André Gide was apparently largely responsible. Gide came to regret his decision on reading the published novel and convinced Proust to switch to the NRF house with his second volume, which won the prestigious Goncourt prize for best novel of the year. Proust was winning recognition as a "moralist," a painter of detailed psychological portraits of characters, investigating inner sources of their behaviors. His reputation continued to grow with the publication of the next installment, *Le Côté de Guermantes* (*The Guermantes Way*, 1920).

But the following installment, published in 1921, included not only the conclusion of the *Guermantes* section, but also the opening of the next volume *Sodome et Gomorrhe* (*Cities of the Plain*), Sodom being the world of male homosexuality and Gomorrah the world of lesbianism. In particular, that volume opens with an essay, "Introduction to the Men-Women," which presents a theory of gender inversion as the basis for homosexuality. The rest of *Cities of the Plain* devotes a great deal of attention to the world of the Baron de Charlus (Sodom) and the world of a band of girls (Gomorrah), including, in particular, Albertine, the main love interest of the narrator. The final volumes of the novel—*La Prisonnière* (*The Captive*, 1924), *Albertine disparue* (*The Sweet Cheat Gone*, 1925), and *Le temps retrouvé* (*The Past Recaptured*, 1927)—continue this focus. (The text and the title

of the penultimate volume are particularly disputed; it is also sometimes entitled *La Fugitive* and exists in several versions.) In fact, as the novel continues, more and more characters are slowly discovered to be inhabitants of the two cities of the plain. The final volume contains a scene of the Baron de Charlus being flagellated in a male brothel in wartime Paris.

Unlike his contemporary Gide, Proust shielded his own sexual identity fairly successfully from public knowledge. Thus even though the later volumes of the novel were attacked on publication for their subject matter, the attacks were not personalized as they often were in the case of Gide's writings. It is also the case that the tone of the narrator varies from sympathetic to medicalizing to pathologizing in his analysis of the inhabitants of Sodom and Gomorrah—this, paradoxically, in a novel whose brilliance and subtlety have made it a watershed in literary investigations of same-sex sexuality. As rumors of Proust's sexuality spread more widely after his death, a discussion began as to whether or not he had merely transposed the gender of various characters, whether Albertine in particular might not have been based on a man, perhaps an Albert. Subsequent researchers have shown that the introduction of the character Albertine into the novel corresponded with a moment in Proust's life when he was deeply in love with a man named Alfred Agostinelli, whom Proust employed as his chauffeur and who died in a plane crash in 1914. The vexed question of the relation between a writer's life and work here combines in complex ways with the ramifications of conceptualizing same-sex sexuality through paradigms of gender inversion, as well as with the confusions created by the strategies of concealment that have historically surrounded homosexuality. These interrelated questions, combined inextricably with Proust's concern with the nature of the experience of time and the nature of aesthetic experience, contribute to the intense richness of his novel.   *Michael Lucey*

Bibliography

Ahlstedt, Eva. *La Pudeur en crise: un aspect de l'accueil d'A la recherche du temps perdu de Marcel Proust, 1913–1930.* Göteborg, Sweden: Acta Universitatis Gothoburgensis, 1985.

Hayman, Ronald. *Proust: A Biography.* New York: Carroll & Graf, 1990.

Rivers, J. E. *Proust and the Art of Love: The Aesthetics of Sexuality in the Life, Times, and Art of Marcel Proust.* New York: Columbia University Press, 1980.

Sedgwick, Eve Kosofsky. *Epistemology of the Closet*. Berkeley: University of California Press, 1990.

See also French Literature; Gide, André; Montesquieu, Count Robert de; Sodom

Psychiatry and Homosexuality

Psychiatry, the medical specialty concerned with the study, diagnosis, treatment, and prevention of disorders of the mind and behavior, reflected and defined Western societal attitudes toward homosexuality for much of the nineteenth and twentieth centuries. Beginning in the mid-nineteenth century with the first scientific attempts to determine the causes of homosexual behavior, the biomedical sciences began a process leading to the reification of a type of person defined by his or her participation in same-sex sexual relations. Originally focused almost exclusively on men, this work eventually led to the description of categories of persons known as gay men, lesbians, and bisexuals. Physicians, sexologists, and jurists all played a role in the medicalization of same-sex behavior; but by the early part of the twentieth century, psychiatrists began to locate what was viewed then as the "problem of homosexuality" primarily within the purview of their discipline. While researchers in other fields, particularly the biological sciences, continued to seek a cause for homosexuality in anatomical, endocrinological, and neurological aberrations, psychiatry and the allied fields of psychoanalysis and psychology gradually claimed dominion over the "disease" of homosexuality and increasingly focused on developmental and familial disturbance as the basis for the "malady."

Originally considered to be an ideologically liberal field, as psychiatry's influence grew in Europe and the United States during the middle part of the twentieth century and as psychiatrists became more integrated into institutions of social control, such as the military, prisons, and the government, the discipline began more and more to reflect middle-class norms, and psychiatrists often served to enforce societal standards of behavior. With respect to sexuality, these standards required a "compulsory heterosexuality" that was to be enacted within a monogamous marriage relationship between a man and a woman. Thus, while Freud could state, in 1935 in his famous "Letter to an American Mother" whose son was homosexual: "Homosexuality is assuredly no advantage; but it is nothing to be ashamed of, no

vice, no degradation; it cannot be classified as an illness," by the 1950s, psychiatrists, psychologists, and psychoanalysts had become increasingly extreme and vitriolic in their description of homosexuality. Psychologist Albert Ellis stated, "[M]ost homosexuals, I am convinced, are borderline psychotic or outrightly psychotic," and psychiatrist and psychoanalyst Edmund Bergler claimed that "though I have no bias . . . homosexuals are essentially disagreeable people. . . . Like all psychic masochists, they are subservient when confronted with a stronger person, merciless when in power, unscrupulous about trampling on a weaker person . . . you seldom find an intact ego . . . among them."

Homosexuality was first formally defined as a mental disorder in the 1930s as a type of psychopathic personality disorder, and the American Psychiatric Association (APA) in its first *Diagnostic and Statistical Manual of Mental Disorders (DSM)*, published in 1952, included a category called sexual deviation as a subtype of sociopathic personality disturbance. Homosexuality was mentioned as one example of the sexual deviations. In the second edition (*DSM-II*), published in 1968, the reference to homosexuality continued to be included under the heading for personality disorders, as a type of sociopathic personality disorder, and specifically as one of the sexual deviations. In *DSM-II* the description for sexual deviations was expanded to include a larger number of types of sexual deviations, and each type was given a separate code. The code for the "disease" of homosexuality was 302.0.

The publication of the studies by Kinsey and his colleagues on sexual behavior in men (1948) and women (1953) and the findings of later researchers in the 1950s and 1960s challenged the prevailing psychiatric view of homosexuality as a form of psychopathology and began to undermine the hegemony of the medical model in defining the social status of gay men and lesbians. The formation of homophile organizations and the development of a nascent gay culture in the United States during and following World War II led to the first political activities on behalf of lesbians and gay men. These early gay rights activists helped to clarify how psychiatry and medicine had, during the nineteenth century and the first half of the twentieth century, moved conceptualizations of homosexuality away from morality and toward disease, but had at the same time retained and reinforced a negative view of homoerotic behavior and of gay men and lesbians. By the end of the 1960s, these scientific and political forces began to confront the psychiatric profession to reevaluate its theories about homosexuality.

Conclusions about homosexuality derived from observations of persons receiving psychiatric treatment were challenged as unrepresentative of the general population of gay men and lesbians and viewed as no more valid than conclusions about heterosexuality would be if based solely on observations of heterosexual persons seeking psychiatric help. Gay rights groups began to protest at psychiatric meetings, and the APA reviewed the findings from more recent research on gay men and lesbians. Following a period of intense political engagement and of considerable scientific evaluation, the Board of Trustees of the APA voted in December 1973 to remove homosexuality from its list of mental disorders. Through this historic decision, the psychiatric profession officially altered the status of homosexuality from a condition of abnormality to one of normality and, as a result of the simultaneous approval of a position paper opposing criminal sanctions against homosexual behavior and endorsing civil rights for homosexual persons, moved the political rhetoric of the gay rights movement to the mainstream of American politics. Remnants of the diagnosis of homosexuality as a type of disease, applied only to persons who were disturbed about being gay or lesbian, were finally removed from the official list of diagnoses in 1986, and currently sexual orientation is not a consideration in defining mental health or illness in American psychiatry.

Hostility toward homosexuality persisted among some psychiatrists after the nomenclature change and is maintained today by groups of psychiatrists and other mental health professionals who continue to advocate an illness model of homosexuality and offer treatment for it. These professionals do not represent the official view of American psychiatry regarding homosexuality and gay men and lesbians, but they continue to practice antigay and antilesbian approaches to treatment and to place many gay men and lesbians and persons uncertain about their sexual orientation at risk for further harm when seeking help for emotional and mental problems.

Feeling significant risk of discrimination and stigmatization from disclosure of their sexual orientation, gay, lesbian, and bisexual psychiatrists and other mental health professionals were largely in the closet until the late 1960s and 1970s. When their homosexuality was discovered, gay and lesbian students were often forced to undergo treatment and expelled from medical schools, graduate training programs, and residencies. Psychoanalytic institutes continued to exclude gay and lesbian trainees into the 1990s. Since the 1970s, however, openly gay, lesbian, and bisexual psychiatrists, psychologists, and social workers have led the way in changing negative attitudes toward homosexuality within their respective disciplines, and they have formed support, advocacy, and research groups within their professional organizations.

The paradigm shift in views of homosexuality away from disease and toward normality has encouraged a broader range of study and discourse about sexual orientation in a wide variety of fields within and outside of psychiatry and the other mental health disciplines, and has led to a burgeoning in knowledge about the topic. This growth in understanding has helped to alter psychiatric approaches to working with gay men and lesbians and to redefine the primary impact of psychiatry on them from pathologizing and stigmatizing to acknowledging, accepting, and affirming their attractions, behaviors, and identities.   *Terry S. Stein, M.D.*

Bibliography

American Psychiatric Association. *Diagnostic and Statistical Manual of Mental Disorders*. Washington, D.C.: American Psychiatric Association, 1952.

———. *Diagnostic and Statistical Manual of Mental Disorders*, 2d ed. Washington, D.C.: American Psychiatric Association, 1968.

Bayer, Ronald. *Homosexuality and American Psychiatry: The Politics of Diagnosis*. Princeton, N.J.: Princeton University Press, 1987.

Bergler, Edmund. *Homosexuality: Disease or Way of Life?* New York: Collier Books, 1956.

Cabaj, Robert P., and Terry S. Stein. *Textbook of Homosexuality and Mental Health*. Washington, D.C.: American Psychiatric Press, 1996.

Ellis, Albert. *Homosexuality: Its Causes and Cures.* New York: Lyle Stuart, 1965.

Jones, Ernst. *The Life and Work of Sigmund Freud.* Vol. 3. *The Last Phase: 1919–1939*. New York: Basic Books, 1957.

Kinsey, Alfred C., Wardell B. Pomeroy, and Clyde E. Martin. *Sexual Behavior in the Human Male*. Philadelphia: W. B. Saunders, 1948.

———. *Sexual Behavior in the Human Female.* Philadelphia: W. B. Saunders, 1953.

Krajeski, James. "Homosexuality and the Mental Health Professions." In *Textbook of Homosexuality and Mental Health*. Robert P. Cabaj and

Terry S. Stein, eds. Washington, D.C.: American Psychiatric Press, 1996, 17–31.

Weeks, Jeffrey. *Coming Out*. London: Quartet Books, 1983.

See also Freud, Sigmund; Homophile Movement; Kinsey, Alfred C.; Psychological and Psychoanalytic Perspectives; Psychotherapy; Sexology

Psychological and Psychoanalytic Perspectives on Homosexuality

Psychology, the behavioral science dealing with the mind, mental processes, and behavior, and psychoanalysis, the theory of psychology developed by Freud and his followers and applied to the study and treatment of mental and emotional problems, have elaborated theories concerning homosexuality since the latter part of the nineteenth century, when medicine and psychiatry first began to study homosexual behavior scientifically. By the early part of the twentieth century, psychological views of homosexuality were firmly embedded within the medical model of disease.

Historically, psychological and psychoanalytic perspectives on homosexuality can be divided into three periods: prior to 1950, when homosexuality was almost universally considered to be a disease; from 1950 until 1973, a period of transition when studies began to be published that challenged the view of homosexuality as illness; and after 1973, when homosexuality was no longer considered to be an illness, and a range of studies about the lives of lesbians and gay men became available. During these periods, various objectives and themes underlay the psychological discourse on homosexuality, including attempts to identify the cause of homosexuality; transformation in the locus of study from homoerotic behavior to gay, lesbian, and bisexual persons; evolution of an understanding of development from defining the etiology of a pathological condition to describing the development of gay, lesbian, and bisexual identities; and modification of psychological approaches to treatment from attempts to cure a disease to efforts to support healthy development and to identify and respond to special concerns and needs of lesbians, gay men, and bisexual persons.

Freud elaborated the first psychoanalytic theories of homosexuality, maintaining both that heterosexuality was the normal outcome of development and that homosexuality was not in itself a sign of degeneracy. Freud posited an innate bisexuality in hu-

mans and believed that aspects of homosexual love motivated aspects of adult relationships even among heterosexual persons. Freud stated that exclusive homosexuality represents a developmental arrest and formulated a number of causes for this arrest, but he also maintained that, in the absence of other problems in behavior or adaptation, adult homosexuality was not a sign of mental illness. While Freud identified both environmental and constitutional factors that could produce homosexuality, he never isolated a single cause for it and maintained that psychoanalytic treatment was unlikely to cure homosexuality.

Later psychoanalysts, including Sandor Rado, Irving Bieber, and Charles Socarides in the United States, rejected Freud's notion of innate bisexuality; believed that heterosexual development was the only normal developmental pathway and that homosexuality was invariably an illness; and, as a result of adherence to a disease model, thought that homosexuality could be cured through psychological approaches to treatment. Locating the etiology of homosexuality in various dynamic and familial sources, these psychoanalysts viewed homosexuality as a sign of neurotic and even psychotic conflicts that began in early childhood and as an adaptation to a fear of women and of being heterosexual. Psychoanalytic writers focused almost exclusively on homosexuality in men. Maggee and Miller identify two assumptions that have until recently permeated the psychoanalytic literature that has been published on homosexuality in women: "I. A woman who loves a woman must be a man, or be like a man, or must wish to be a man," and "II. A relationship between two women must always remain incomplete compared to the complementarity of a heterosexual relationship." (76).

In contrast to psychoanalytic theories, early conceptualizations of homosexuality by behavioral psychologists focused less on identifying the cause of same-sex desire and behavior and more on attempts to extinguish them—often by aversive techniques—and to replace them with heterosexual attraction and relationships. Attempts to cure homosexuality or to transform it into heterosexuality—whether behavioral or psychoanalytic—were rarely effective, but throughout much of the twentieth century these pathologizing psychological views of homosexuality served both to reflect and to support the prevailing negative social views of homosexuality and to reinforce legal and religious sanctions on homosexual behavior. Thus, same-sex sexual behavior was condemned not only as a sin and a crime but

P also as a type of mental illness. During this period, lesbians and gay men almost universally learned to experience shame about their sexual feelings and behaviors, and if they entered into any type of psychological treatment, efforts were routinely made to eliminate or alter their homosexuality.

The second, transition period in psychological views of homosexuality began in the 1950s and ended in 1973, when homosexuality was removed from the official list of mental disorders. During this period, the results of several studies demonstrated that homosexuality was not in itself associated with any type of mental disturbance, that same-sex feelings and behaviors were widespread in society, and that homosexuality occurred in different forms in many societies. The transition period was marked by advocacy of often contradictory psychological views toward homosexuality, some continuing to adhere to a pathological perspective on homosexuality and others recommending a variant or normal model of a range of sexual orientations. Psychological perspectives also began to be influenced by the growing political activism of the gay rights movement and the increasing visibility of lesbians and gay men, who openly challenged the still prevailing illness model of homosexuality. The expanded and open presence of gay men and lesbians increasingly focused the attention of psychology on gay and lesbian persons and less on the condition of homosexuality.

After 1973, when homosexuality was no longer officially considered to be a mental disorder, interest in the topic within psychology and psychoanalysis began to shift to include a broad range of issues relevant to understanding the lives of gay men and lesbians and the types of problems they encounter because of their unique developmental pathways and as a result of societal discrimination and stigmatization. In the postmodern era of psychology, sexual orientation is understood to be multifactorial, consisting at least of sexual desire, behavior, and identity, and studies of homosexuality focus on an enormous range of topics. Sexual orientation is viewed both as a central aspect of individual and group identity for some persons and, at the same time, as a factor that does not determine or predict other aspects of personality, identity, or behavior. Contemporary psychological views of homosexuality must consider both psychosocial dimensions of development, such as acquisition of a gay, lesbian, or bisexual identity, and contextual issues, such as the influence of culture, gender, and age on the expression of sexuality. Psychological and psychoana-

lytic views of homosexuality are increasingly shaped by openly gay and lesbian researchers and clinicians who have published an enormous amount of information about contemporary forms of same-sex desire and behavior. *Terry S. Stein, M.D.*

Bibliography

Bayer, Ronald. *Homosexuality and American Psychiatry: The Politics of Diagnosis*. Princeton, N.J.: Princeton University Press, 1987.

Davuson, Gerald C. "Constructionism and Morality in Therapy for Homosexuality." In *Homosexuality: Research Implications for Public Policy*. John C. Gonsiorek and James D. Weinrich, eds. Newbury Park, Calif.: Sage, 1991, 137–48.

Isay, Richard A. *Being Homosexual: Gay Men and Their Development*. New York: Farrar, Straus and Giroux, 1989.

Lewes, Kenneth. *The Psychoanalytic Theory of Male Homosexuality*. New York: Simon and Schuster, 1988.

Maggee, Maggie, and Diana Miller. "'She Foreswore Her Womanhood': Psychoanalytic Views of Female Homosexuality." *Clinical Social Work Journal* 20, no. 1 (1992): 67–87.

Ruse, Michael. *Homosexuality*. Oxford: Basil Blackwell, 1988.

Silverstein, Charles. "Homosexuality and the Ethics of Behavioral Intervention." *Journal of Homosexuality* 2 (1977), 205–11.

See also Counseling; Freud, Sigmund; Psychiatry and Homosexuality; Psychotherapy; Sexology

Psychotherapy

Psychotherapy is defined as a psychological form of treatment for mental illness and behavioral problems involving a relationship in which a trained professional helps to remove, modify, or alleviate symptoms in a person suffering from emotional or mental distress. There are a variety of types of psychotherapy, including psychoanalysis, supportive psychotherapy, short-term psychotherapy, counseling, guidance, group therapy, and family therapy, all of which employ primarily verbal and expressive techniques to accomplish change and to promote positive personality growth and development. Practitioners of psychotherapy, or psychotherapists, may be trained as psychiatrists, psychologists, social workers, counselors, marriage and family therapists, or other mental health professionals.

The goals of psychotherapy in general reflect the desired treatment outcomes for a particular mental or emotional disturbance. A dramatic shift in the goals of psychotherapy in work with lesbians and gay men occurred following the elimination of homosexuality from the list of mental disorders by the American Psychiatric Association (APA) in 1973. Before that time, when homosexuality was still diagnosed as a form of mental illness, most psychotherapists attempted to eliminate patients' same-sex attractions and sexual behaviors and to achieve heterosexual relationships. The goals of psychotherapists at that time were often similar to what patients, who had been socialized to deny and to denigrate their homoerotic feelings, sought when they entered treatment; however, other patients entered treatment involuntarily, having been forced to seek psychotherapy by their families, the courts, training institutions, or other coercive agents. Some persons who were subjected to such treatment achieved a heterosexual adaptation, though change in underlying sexual orientation or attraction was rarely accomplished.

Many individuals who underwent psychotherapy that was aimed at eliminating or suppressing their same-sex attraction reported negative outcomes, such as lowered self-esteem, development of furtive or unsafe outlets for their sexual feelings, difficulty in establishing healthy relationships of any type, and appearance of symptoms such as depression and anxiety. Portrayals of gay men and lesbians in the psychotherapy literature helped to foster denigrating stereotypes of these men and women and to perpetuate beliefs that homosexuality was associated with a wide range of negative personality characteristics. Often the sexual orientation of the gay and lesbian patient became the central issue during therapy, even when the patient was not troubled by it or when it was not related to the reason the individual had sought treatment in the first place.

Since 1973 a new body of professional literature about psychotherapy with lesbians and gay men has been published, based on the assumption that homosexuality is a normal variation of sexual desire and behavior. This literature defines a set of approaches that have been labeled *gay and lesbian affirmative psychotherapy*, described by Alan Maylon as a "theoretical position [that] regards homosexuality as a non-pathological human potential. The goals of gay- (and lesbian)-affirmative psychotherapy are similar to those of most traditional approaches to psychological treatment and include both conflict resolution and self-actualization." Such therapy recognizes the centrality of sexual attraction, behaviors, and identity in a person's life but also appreciates that sexual orientation is only one aspect of personality and, depending on the patient's need and goals, may or may not be a central focus of therapeutic work.

In spite of the development of these gay and lesbian affirmative approaches to psychotherapy, lesbians and gay men are still at risk for encountering negative reactions to their sexuality and identities within psychotherapy. A study conducted by the American Psychological Association in 1990 identified twenty-five ways in which bias currently affects psychotherapy with lesbians and gay men. Inappropriate and negative assumptions made by psychotherapists about patients based on their sexual orientation may be a reflection of outdated and inaccurate information but may also result from personal prejudice. Two of the most detrimental contemporary negative approaches to psychotherapy with lesbians and gay men are the religious conversion and the so-called reparative therapies. Both approaches arise from the erroneous beliefs that homosexuality results from disturbances in masculine and feminine gender role characteristics and that it is a type of mental illness. These approaches have not been shown to be effective, and they place vulnerable patients who are uncertain about their sexual orientation or are struggling with the effects of *internalized homophobia*—which occurs when the developing gay or lesbian person incorporates negative societal views of homosexuality and then experiences these feelings and beliefs in the form of a negative self-evaluation—at risk for further psychological damage. Reports from persons who have been the subjects of such attempts to suppress or change sexual orientation demonstrate their negative effects in encouraging self-defeating behaviors, maintaining lack of self-acceptance, and prolonging or terminating struggles to achieve a healthy gay or lesbian identity.

Effective work in psychotherapy with gay men and lesbians requires the acceptance, acknowledgment, and affirmation by the therapist of their same-sex desire, relationships, and identities, in contrast to the denial and derogation with which these aspects of the patient have often been met by their families, peers, and the larger society. Ultimately, as with any patient, the psychotherapist working with gay and lesbian patients should maintain a position of neutrality and not advocate for any specific type of sexual feeling or behavior, but the therapist must

P also convey a recognition of the ongoing negative impact of societal prejudice against gay men and lesbians.

Gay men and lesbians enter psychotherapy with the same concerns as other patients, seeking help with the full range of mental disorders and adjustment to interpersonal, work, and social situations. In many cases, the sexual feelings, behaviors, or identity of the patient may be incidental to treatment; in other cases, these issues may be central in the treatment. In addition, there are several special treatment issues relevant to psychotherapy with lesbians and gay men, including developmental problems related to growing up gay and lesbian, coming out, and acquiring a gay or lesbian identity; dealing with the effects of heterosexism and antigay and antilesbian attitudes, including violence and internalized homophobia; concerns about relationships, families, and parenting; and special physical and mental problems, including increased rates of alcohol and substance abuse, higher rates of suicidality in gay and lesbian youth, and particular types of sexual dysfunction. The nature of these concerns associated with sexual orientation will be influenced as well by whether the patient is a man or a woman, and by the patient's race, age, and other personal and social characteristics.

Historically, psychotherapy was used as a tool for reinforcing societal prohibitions on same-sex desire, relationships, and identities; in contrast, contemporary approaches to psychotherapy with lesbians and gay men generally are employed to support the healthy expression of these feelings and experiences, to help overcome the effects of internalized homophobia, and to achieve healthy identities. In the past, lesbian and gay psychotherapists could not openly disclose their sexual orientation without risk of losing their professional standing, but today, lesbian and gay therapists are at the forefront of the field helping to define helpful clinical approaches to working with gay men and lesbians within psychotherapy.   *Terry S. Stein, M.D.*

Bibliography

American Psychological Association, Committee on Lesbian and Gay Concerns. *Bias in Psychotherapy with Lesbians and Gay Men.* Washington, D.C.: American Psychological Association, 1990.

Cabaj, Robert P., and Terry S. Stein, eds. *Textbook of Homosexuality and Mental Health.* Washington, D.C.: American Psychiatric Press, 1996.

Falco, Kristine L. *Psychotherapy with Lesbian Clients.* New York: Brunner/Mazel, 1991.

Maylon, Alan K. "Psychotherapeutic Implications of Internalized Homophobia in Gay Men." *Journal of Homosexuality* 7 (1982): 59–70.

Silverstein, Charles, ed. *Gays, Lesbians, and Their Therapists.* New York: Norton, 1991.

Stein, Terry S., and Carol J. Cohen, eds. *Contemporary Perspectives on Psychotherapy with Lesbians and Gay Men.* New York: Plenum, 1986.

See also Alcohol and Drugs; Counseling; Psychiatry and Homosexuality; Psychological and Psychoanalytic Perspectives; Suicide

Puig, Manuel (1932–1990)

Latin American literature has been consistently a culture of exile, and Manuel Puig was no exception. Although he lived in Brazil and died in Mexico, he got his literary start while living in New York City, and, except for brief visits, he never returned to live in his native Argentina during his literary lifetime. The result of this circumstance was that Puig was able to break out of the Mediterranean legacy of homosexual identity to which Argentina, including the highly sophisticated capital, Buenos Aires, continues to subscribe. According to this code, one is a homosexual only if one is penetrated by another man and if this condition of feminized insertee is marked by a public behavior characteristic of the *maricón* (queer, fag, fairy).

Puig in his writing denied this scheme in two senses. In the first place, he viewed homoeroticism as a free-floating erotic pulsation of the body that led the individual into all sorts of erotic combinations. Second, Puig rejected the identity politics characteristic of modernity, whereby individuals were obliged to cultivate fixed declarations of unswerving cultural and political affiliation. Moreover, as part of the rejection of the latter configuration, Puig underscored the eminently feminist principle whereby the "personal is political," and he was one of the first Latin American authors to demonstrate how projects of erotic transgression were intimately related to projects of prerevolutionary politics. In the context of the Latin American macho left of the 1960s and 1970s (typified by the swaggering military machos Fidel Castro and Che Guevara, who was an Argentine), Puig sought to underscore how political liberation meant nothing if it did not bring with it personal, including sexual, liberation.

It is for this reason that Puig's most famous novel is *El beso de la mujer araña* (*Kiss of the Spider Woman*), published in 1976 and made into an Oscar-winning film in 1985. *Kiss* details the relationship between a paradigmatic swishy interior decorator incarcerated with a paradigmatic severe revolutionary. The assumption by the former of a political commitment and the transformation of the latter into a gay lover (although apparently always the penetrator) constituted a narrative formula that was exceptionally audacious for Latin American culture at the height of stern male-dominated guerrilla movements. Moreover, Puig peppered his novel with extensive footnotes demonstrating his intensive readings in what was at that time the available bibliography of sexuality and homoeroticism.

Prior to *Kiss*, Puig had published *La traición de Rita Hayworth* (*Betrayed by Rita Hayworth*, 1968), which, echoing Rita Hayworth's famous "Put the Blame on Mame" routine in Charles Vidor's gay-marked *Gilda* (1946; set and filmed in Buenos Aires), models the way in which sexual inferiors are the scapegoats of the failures of heterosexist masculinism. Probably the first truly gay novel in Argentina and Latin America, in the sense of displaying a subversion of masculinist order rather than (typically, superficially) detailing the comings and goings of homosexual stereotypes, *Betrayed* put sexual transgression, gender troubles, and masculinist pathos on the agenda of Latin American fiction. Moreover, the fact that, unlike a more writerly author such as Cuba's Severo Sarduy, Puig was able both to correlate his vision of a gay Latin American with popular culture (films, music, soap operas, and newsstand culture in general) and to perceive how popular culture, in addition to reinforcing heterosexuality, has the subversive potential for, as Alexander Doty has claimed, "making things perfectly queer," ensuring him a place as one of Latin America's first truly postmodern writers.

David William Foster

Bibliography

Muñoz, Elías Miguel. *El discurso utópico de la sexualidad en Manuel Puig*. Madrid: Pliegos, 1987.

———. "Manuel Puig." In *Latin American Writers on Gay and Lesbian Themes: A Bio-Biographical Sourcebook*. David William Foster, ed. Westport, Conn.: Greenwood Press, 1994, 339–45.

Titter, Jonathan. *Manuel Puig*. New York: Twayne, 1993.

See also Argentina; Film; Gay Left; Guevara, Ernesto "Che"; Machismo; Sarduy, Severo

Purdy, James (1923–)

American novelist James Otis Purdy first wrote fiction as a child, but he did not find a commercial publisher for his work until 1957, when, on the recommendation of poet Edith Sitwell, his book comprising short stories and a novella, *63: Dream Palace*, was published in England. The stories had been censored by his publisher, but the book's success with British critics resulted in the publication of an unexpurgated edition in the United States, entitled *Color of Darkness* (1957). Among critics, Purdy's early books were controversial as well as acclaimed.

Some of Purdy's earlier writings had contained homosexual themes and characters, but *Eustace Chisholm and the Works* (1967) was his first book to center on gay characters. Reviewers were outraged by the depiction of homosexuality in this novel, and their reaction confirmed Purdy's disaffection with commercial publishing and corporate America. Nevertheless, he has continued to write novels, short stories, plays, and poetry and has retained an appreciative readership.

Purdy's fiction portrays, affectionately and with dark humor, people who are marginalized in American society. He satirizes that society and sympathetically depicts those who are invisible within it. His characters are social outsiders, lonely and alienated people who are afraid to love or be loved. They sometimes remain alone, never finding personal satisfaction. In other instances, two isolated people find incomplete solace when they begin to love each other. Purdy writes in a naturalistic but idiosyncratic version of Midwestern speech, echoing its rhythms and idioms.

Charles Krinsky

Bibliography

Chupack, Henry. *James Purdy*. Boston: Twayne, 1975.

Purdy, James. "James Purdy." In *Contemporary Authors: Autobiography Series*. Vol. 1. Dedria Bryfonski, ed. Detroit: Gale Research Company, 1984, 299–305.

Schwarzschild, Bettina. *The Not-right House: Essays on James Purdy*. Columbia, Mo.: University of Missouri Press, 1968.

See also Fiction; U.S. Literature: Contemporary Gay Writing

Q

Quaintance, George (1900?–1957)

George Quaintance died in 1957, cutting short a career that was hardly more than a spectacular beginning. His work appeared on the earliest covers of the popular new physique magazines, but that was only in 1951. In those few years, Quaintance became the first "name" in physique art. His studio produced original oils, photographs, lithographs, greeting cards, even ceramic wall plaques (aqua-green swimmers and mermen—very fifties), all spotlighting handsome naked men.

It was not his first career. He began in the twenties as an adagio dancer (a popular combination of dance and acrobatics) in New York vaudeville. In the thirties, he did a stint as a designer of hairstyles for rich matrons. By the forties, he had became a minor society portraitist, but for special clients, he began to do male nudes, such as *The Crusader* (1942).

Late in the forties, he moved to Los Angeles and concentrated on his first love, the naked male, especially naked Hispanic and Native American males. Quaintance's paintings conjure up a Southwest Never-Neverland, where the Lost Boys were all muscular men who loved to strip down and frolic in waterfalls and horse troughs. In the fifties, he briefly lived the life he fantasized, on a spread in Arizona with a Mexican lover. He had his artistic shortcomings—notably, poor composition and a palette as garish as a Technicolor movie set—but when it came to making male muscle look as mouth-watering as marzipan, nobody excelled George Quaintance.

F. Valentine Hooven III

Bibliography

Hawkins, Richard. "George Quaintance, First Gay Superstar." *Dispatch* (Spring 1997).

Quaintance, George. "My Autobiography." *Grecian Guild Pictorial* (Winter 1956).

Stanley, Wayne, ed. *The Complete Reprint of Physique Pictorial*. Cologne, Germany: Benedikt Taschen, 1997.

Waugh, Thomas. *Hard to Imagine*. New York: Columbia University Press, 1996.

See also Athletic Model Guild; Photography

Quakers

The Religious Society of Friends, more commonly referred to by the originally derogatory term *Quakers*, is the name of the church structure that developed among the followers of George Fox (1624–1691), an English mystic and religious reformer. Highly distrustful of the then-existing Church of England with its university-trained clergy, Fox argued that "Christ has come to teach His people" through the process of continuing revelation. In contrast to the Ranter movement, Fox taught that individuals should not trust their "leadings" as being from God unless they were also seen as being from God by other members of the group and in line with the spirit of revealed scripture (the Bible). This seventeenth-century teaching remains the basis for contemporary Quaker decisions on homosexuality, as on other matters.

To understand the contradictory and conflicting attitudes of contemporary Quakers toward homosexuality, it is necessary to look more closely at the history and administrative structure of the Religious Society of Friends. The basic Quaker unit, a worship group, is generally referred to as a Meeting or Church. Meetings/Churches are generally gath-

Q ered into progressively larger units (often called Monthly, Quarterly or Regional, and Yearly Meetings [though terminology varies in different parts of the world]), which are themselves loosely joined together under the umbrella of the Friends World Committee for Consultation, whose administrative offices are in London. This basically Meeting/Church—an autonomous, lay-run structure—has led to the existence and acceptance of a great variety of theological beliefs and worship practices among contemporary Quaker groups, though most remain broadly Christian while not practicing baptism or communion.

Of particular importance for Quaker views on homosexuality is the fact that U.S. Quakerism underwent several splits as some groups joined in the revival and evangelistic movements sweeping the country and others did not. It is predominantly from within the former groups that Quakerism was carried by missionary effort to East Africa and Latin America. Thus contemporary Quaker attitudes toward homosexuality are based on a variety of theological positions, ranging from the fundamentalist Christian belief of (some) Evangelical Friends that the (1611 English) Bible is a direct and unambiguous revelation of God's will to the Universalist position that the Bible—like the sacred texts of other religions—offers fallible human interpretations of Divine will that should be understood in their "spirit" rather than according to their "letter." In addition to this, Quakers (like others) are influenced in their views on homosexuality by local (secular) attitudes and customs.

Following what they and the members of their Meeting/Church perceive to be Divine "leadings," individual members of the Religious Society of Friends have traditionally played an active role in social reform, being leaders of (among other causes) the antiwar, reconciliation, prison reform, antislavery, birth control, and civil rights movements. It is in this light that one should view the first statement of what might be called the "liberal Quaker position on homosexuality" in *Towards a Christian View of Sex*—authored by a committee of British Quakers in 1963—that "one should no more deplore homosexuality than left-handedness."

Among "liberal" Quaker groups in the mid-1990s, particularly those in North America, discussion of homosexuality is generally centered on the issue of same-sex marriage (or commitment ceremonies). Following normal Quaker procedures for marriage, a number of same-sex Quaker couples have asked that a meeting for worship be organized in their Meeting/Church to witness their marriage/commitment. Since Quaker procedure requires that such "called" meetings for worship be approved by the Meeting/Church, this has over and over again led to usually lengthy discussions at the local level that have tended to moved up the scale of Quaker organization over a period of sometimes years before agreement is reached that it is (or is not) the will of God that same-sex couples should be joined in this particular Meeting/Church. While such a procedure can seem painfully slow (particularly to a couple anxious to gain religious sanction for their relationship), it is in line with the traditional Quaker practice of testing Divine leadings first at the lowest organizational level and then progressively at higher levels.

Among Evangelical Quakers in North America and the majority of Quakers in Africa and Latin America, the very notion of acting on homosexual impulses remains anathema, and the question of same-sex commitment is not open for discussion. To simplify somewhat, it is generally the First World Quakers of Europe and North America (numerically a minority but privileged by virtue of greater economic power, generally better education, and longer historical contact with Quakerism) who favor holding homosexual persons to the same moral standards required of heterosexuals, and the small group of Evangelical Quakers in the United States, together with the largest group of world Quakers—those in the Third World—who continue to view homosexuality itself (or at least its expression) as a sin.

Since it is clear to all Quakers that the conditions set by George Fox for determining the will of God for the Society of Friends as a whole on the issue of homosexuality have not yet been met, homosexuality remains a continual topic of discussion (often at the unofficial as well as the official level) at the Triennial World Conferences of the Society and other international gatherings. Though it seems unlikely that the Religious Society of Friends will soon have a consistent teaching on homosexuality, it is encouraging that Quakers who feel they are following different Divine leadings on the subject appear to have been developing a greater sensitivity to one another's views (or at least a willingness to hear one another out) during the 1980s and 1990s.

Gay, lesbian, and bisexual Quakers and their friends and families have formed "interest group" organizations in North America and in Britain. Both groups organize local and regional gatherings, and each publishes a newsletter. Both are members in good standing in the "world family" of Quakers and are invited to organize meetings for worship at national and international gatherings. Members of the North American group have traditionally taken on much of the responsibility for child care at the yearly meetings of Friends General Conference (one of the North American Yearly Meetings). There is also an e-mail network of gay, lesbian, and bisexual Quakers and their supporters open to all.

James Haines

Bibliography

Cooper, William, and Bob Fraser, eds. *Sexual Ethics: Some Quaker Perspectives*. Greensboro, N.C.: Quaker Theological Discussion Group, 1990.

Heron, Alastair, et al. *Towards a Quaker View of Sex*. London: British Friends Home Service Committee, 1979.

Leuze, Robert, ed. *Each of Us Inevitable: Some Keynote Addresses Given at FLGC Annual Mid-Winter (and Other) Gatherings, 1977–1989*. Sumneytown, Pa.: Friends for Lesbian and Gay Concerns, 1989.

Punshon, John. *Portrait in Grey: A Short History of the Quakers*. London: Quaker Home Service, 1984.

See also Bible; Christianity; Religious Right; Same-Sex Marriage

Queen

This camp term is used primarily within the gay community, and in that context it carries a pejorative but often comic or gently satiric ring. Though it can refer to any male homosexual, it principally connotes an effeminate gay male, especially one given to theatrical or flamboyant behavior. That the term signifies an attitude rather than a physical type is evidenced by its use as both an adverb/adjective (queeny) and a verb (to queen out). The word descends from two roots in Old English, *cwen* or *cwene*, both from the common root *gwen*, meaning "woman." *Queen* became elevated, used to refer to the companion of a king, or serving more generally as a term of endearment or honor for any woman, whereas *quean* acquired a lower usage, typically referring to a woman of low morals, an "impudent, or ill-behaved woman; a jade, hussy," especially a harlot. How the word began to designate effeminate homosexuals is not clear, although one avenue may have been the extravagant costume balls that became one of the main forms of social interaction for urban homosexuals throughout the twentieth century. In balls, the precursor to modern drag shows, men dressed in traditionally "female" costumes, glamorous attire that perhaps led to the use of a word like *queen*, with connotations of wealth, royalty, and power. That homosexual men appropriated the word for themselves is further suggested by Partridge's *Dictionary of Slang and Unconventional English*, which gives the following definition of "Quean, a rejection of": "incorrectly Queen, a homosexual, especially one with girlish manners or carriage." *Queen* may therefore represent a radical reappropriation of the derogatory *quean*, a rejection of the pejorative phrase in favor of its more elevated cousin.

Queen may also be coupled with another noun, a compound that indicates a particular interest: "drag queen," a man who dresses in "women's" clothing; "seafood queen," a man whose primary erotic interest is sailors; "size queen," men with a fondness for large penises; "rice queen," someone attracted solely to Asians; and so on. These terms (with the exception of *drag queen*, which has attained a level of chic over the past decade, along with a degree of mainstream acceptance) are typically used derogatorily, suggesting a too narrow fixation or fetishistic attachment.

Scott Spears

Bibliography

Grahn, Judy. *Another Mother Tongue: Gay Words, Gay Worlds*. Boston: Beacon, 1984.

See also Camp; Faggot; Fairy; Gay Language; Queer

Queer

A word that originally denoted difference or otherness, *queer* has undergone fluctuations in usage that range from the pathological to the politically charged. Besides *gay,* perhaps no other word designating homosexuality—particularly male homosexuality—has been such a catalyst for challenging and refashioning attitudes both inside and outside the gay community. A word with multiple appropriations by various persons and groups, including Queer Nation and scholars in the humanities and social sciences, *queer* has become a watchword of today because of its explicit statement of identity politics that is at once a challenge to the boundaries of the heterosexual/homosexual dichotomy and is, at

Q

the same time, representative of a move toward greater inclusiveness of all nonheterosexual persons and categories.

As early as the first two decades of the twentieth century, *queer* was used as a term to designate male homosexuality. In *Gay New York*, George Chauncey notes that as early as the 1910s, some gay men applied *queer* to themselves with the particular intention of separating themselves from other homosexual males who displayed feminine characteristics, the latter being termed "fairies" and "faggots" (15–17). Thus, even in the emerging gay male culture of the twentieth century, the notion of acceptable behavior was coded by language. At the same time, the word was also being employed by medical and governmental agencies to denote pathological behavior. The *Oxford English Dictionary* notes a 1922 U.S. Department of Labor publication on juvenile delinquents who were pathologized further with the label "queer." And it is, of course, the latter use that took hold in American culture and turned *queer* into a label of ostracism. As American culture became more tolerant of gay men after the 1950s, *queer* fell into disuse and was replaced by *gay*.

The decade of the 1990s, however, has witnessed a revival and reappropriation of *queer*. Part of the change dates from the establishment of Queer Nation in June 1990. Believing that gay culture had adopted an assimilationist mode, Queer Nation members sought to revive the spirit of activism from the 1970s after Stonewall. An article appearing in the April 6, 1991, issue of the *New York Times* about the organization even suggested that *queer* would replace *gay*, which would disappear as did the word *Negro*. But the word *queer* was adopted by the group for its shock value; it was also used to show the attempt of gay men in particular to reinvent an identity from a word associated with oppression. The chant "We're here, we're queer, get used to it" became the cry of a new group of gay men. Much discussion arose throughout the gay community, often with older gay men rejecting *queer* and younger gay men appropriating it. Such reception can be seen in remarks quoted in the *Bay Times* in reaction to the theme of the 1993 San Francisco Lesbian/Gay Freedom Day Parade: "The Year of the Queer."

David J. Thomas notes that "[q]ueer is less personal, more political. *Queer* politicizes sexuality in a new way" (90). Not only is there a politics of usage in gay culture, but a similar approach can be found in academic circles, particularly in the re-

placement of gay and lesbian studies with queer studies. The real significance of the change, however, is more than semantic; it reflects a move toward greater inclusion of all nonheterosexualities and, thus, is a far less precise term than *gay, lesbian*, or *bisexual*. Behind the entire queer versus gay and lesbian labeling is the debate between essentialism and social constructionism (nature and nurture) of sexual identity. From the 1940s on, *gay* has been employed to normalize same-sex desire in a culture that has long sought to see it as deviant. Biology and genetics have been enlisted to support this position of normality in a deterministic way. *Queer*, on the other hand, has forced a reopening of the nature of identity politics with more attention given to the social construction of same-sex desire and with the intention of showing the complexity of any sexual category. The word *queer* can and has been applied to a range of nonheterosexual desire. At the same time, such an umbrella term has limitations. For many in the gay community, while a desire for inclusiveness at some level exists, there remains a feeling that differentiation among *gay, lesbian, bisexual*, and *transgendered* needs to be made. Using *queer* in some ways refuses that need. In addition, the blurriness of the term forces writers, speakers, and readers into the continual preoccupation with definitions.

Throughout written history, linguistic designations have privileged the male gender, and so the reappropriation of *queer* has raised questions about the gender bias in the word, which from its earliest history has been identified with males. Not all are convinced that *queer* is an inclusive term for both men and women. The pronouncements in the early 1990s that *queer* could provide a quick, shorthand way of writing the more cumbersome *lesbian, gay, bisexual* labeling has been challenged, particularly by lesbians who noted the same problem earlier with the term *gay*.

The revival of *queer* in the late twentieth century shows the continuing process of identity definition not only for gay men but for all sexualities. How long *queer* will remain in use is open to speculation. What does seem clear is that gay men have sought to liberate themselves at the same time that they have been freeing themselves from a language of oppression. In this case, language helps to shape a present and future reality. *Daniel F. Pigg*

Bibliography

Chauncey, George. *Gay New York: Gender, Urban Culture, and the Making of the Gay Male*

Queer Nation protests the inauguration of Pete Wilson as governor of California in 1991. Photo by Marc Geller.

World, 1890–1940. New York: HarperCollins, 1994.

Gamson, Joshua. "Must Identity Movements Self-Destruct?: A Queer Dilemma." In *Queer Theory/Sociology.* Steven Seidman, ed. Oxford: Blackwell, 1996, 395–420.

Signorile, Michelangelo. *Queer in America: Sex, the Media, and the Closets of Power.* New York: Doubleday, 1993.

Thomas, David J. "The 'Q' Word." *Socialist Review* 25, no. 1 (1995): 69–93.

See also Essentialist-Constructionist Debate; Gay; Gay Language; Gay Studies; Homosexuality; Queer Nation; Queer Theory

Queer Nation

Queer Nation constituted perhaps the high-water mark of lesbian/gay/bisexual/transgender activism in the late 1980s and early 1990s. Born in late 1989 as a subcommittee of ACT UP, New York, it was charged with the specific mission of fighting homophobia. Queer Nation soon proved immensely popular, offering an opportunity for AIDS activists to turn their attention and newly honed civil disobedience skills to other pressing social issues equally close to home. Within months, chapters were founded in a number of other American cities. The San Francisco chapter, the first such satellite, soon grew larger and more active than the parent chapter, attracting over four hundred people at weekly open meetings and organizing as many as three different actions a week.

An anonymously circulated manifesto entitled "I Hate Straights"—which suddenly appeared in stacks at lesbian and gay pride marches all over America—sowed the seeds for the rapid proliferation of Queer Nation–style activism. Fearing that the gay and lesbian rights movement had grown accommodationist, Queer Nation sought to reinvent gay activism along the lines of guerrilla politics and street theater, choosing a name that was deliberately provocative and antiassimilationist. The Queer Nation catch phrase "We're here, we're queer, we're fabulous" accurately captures the flavor of Queer Nation's mix of 1960s-style resistance and high camp.

Derided by some AIDS activists as an ACT UP for HIV-negatives, Queer Nation was nonetheless very much a product of ACT UP's confrontational, headline-grabbing approach. Organized like its parent organization according to a consensus system of governance, it too formed affinity groups or committees, each targeting a specific issue or population. For example, Queer Nation, San Francisco, hosted

Q

the Suburban Homosexual Outreach Program (SHOP). SHOP activists organized demonstrations called actions at various Bay Area shopping centers in an attempt to take queer activism outside the largely safe haven of San Francisco local politics. Hundreds of colorfully dressed Queer Nation activists would suddenly descend on a suburban shopping center in joyous parade, float banners to the ceiling on helium balloons, redecorate with stickers and crepe paper, pass out leaflets, host a cruising fashion show, pause for a kiss-in, and suddenly depart. Through great visuals and calculated outrageousness, media-savvy Queer Nationals ensured that a queer protest would be seen on TV again that night.

Protests against Hollywood or homophobic politicians were as much a part of Queer Nation as attempts to turn tough, straight bars queer through an infusion of hundreds of queer activists in locked-lip political fervor. Women, people of color, Jews, and bisexuals, among others, all hosted weekly Queer Nation organizational meetings, seeking to educate the group about their communities and identities. Organized according to the model of a 1960s-style grassroots organization with no centralized control, Queer Nation was hamstrung by constant debates over process and procedure. A consensus decision-making system and open meetings proved increasingly unwieldy as the organization grew in size and sophistication. Queer Nation chapters had largely disbanded by 1992.

Jonathan Katz

Bibliography

Abelove, Henry. "From Thoreau to Queer Politics." *Yale Journal of Criticism* 6, no. 2 (1993): 17–27.

Doty, Alexander. *Making Things Perfectly Queer.* Minneapolis: University of Minnesota Press, 1993.

Duggan, Lisa. "Making It Perfectly Queer." *Socialist Review* 22 (1992): 11–31.

Warner, Michael. *Fear of a Queer Planet.* Minneapolis: University of Minnesota Press, 1993.

See also ACT UP; Assimilation; Queer; Queer Politics; Queer Theory

Queer Politics

In June 1990, a plethora of as yet unidentified activists distributed a leaflet entitled "Queers Read This: I Hate Straights." This tract defines *queer* as

an opposition to traditional assumptions of gender: "We use queer as gay men loving lesbians and lesbians loving being queer. Queer, unlike GAY, doesn't mean MALE." It further defines *queer* as a term for those who favor radical political actions: "I[t] is easier to fight when you know who your enemy is. Straight people are your enemy. They are your enemy when they don't acknowledge your invisibility and continue to live in and contribute to a culture that kills you." By striking a line of opposition between straights and queers, the leaflet attempts to incite militancy. It calls for something akin to all-out war:

> [H]eterosexual culture is too fragile to bear up to the admission of human or sexual diversity. Quite simply, the structure of power in the Judeo-Christian world has made procreation its cornerstone. Families having children assures consumers for the nation's products and a work force to produce them, as well as a built-in family system to care for its ill, reducing the expense of public health care systems.
>
> ALL NON-PROCREATIVE BEHAVIOR IS CONSIDERED A THREAT, from homosexuality to birth control to abortion as an option. It is not enough, according to the religious right, to consistently advertise procreation and heterosexuality. . . . it is also necessary to destroy any alternatives.

"Queers Read This" is sometimes cited as the inaugural tract of queer politics, or of queer activism, a brand of in-your-face activism that has become popularized briefly in the early 1990s and that found its apotheosis in the political activism of Queer Nation. Although virtually every chapter of Queer Nation has now dissolved, the group is still vividly remembered for a series of activities designed to capture media attention through shocking and confrontational behavior. One strategy was the widespread dissemination of "crack-and-peels" fluorescent stickers with bold, black, shocking slogans that usually incorporated puns. One such sticker read simply "Fuck Your Gender." On the one hand, the sticker rebelled against the conformity of gender roles, prompting people to resist the norms of gendered identity; on the other hand, the sticker promoted homosexual behavior, prompting people to engage in sexual activity with others of the same gender.

Queer Nation's effective adoption of a "sound bite" tactics indicates another important aspect of the brief queer politics movement: it was above all media-savvy. Queer Nation was one of the first groups to stage what it called "virtual" demonstrations, judging the success of their actions not by actual attendance or political effects but by the extent to which their images were disseminated electronically via television and computer. Unlike civil rights organizations, which seek intervention in the legal system, Queer Nation primarily sought intervention in systems of information and images. For this reason, Queer Nation was also frequently referred to as a *postmodern* political group.

Gregory W. Bredbeck

Bibliography

Sedgwick, Eve Kosofsky. *Tendencies*. Durham, N.C.: Duke University Press, 1993.

Warner, Michael, ed. *Fear of a Queer Planet: Queer Politics and Social Theory*. Minneapolis: University of Minnesota Press, 1993.

See also Civil Rights (U.S. Law); Gay Liberation; Gender; Postmodernism; Queer; Queer Nation

Queer Skinheads

The early 1990s saw the formation of a number of youth-based music subcultures that give voice and expression to a variety of queer identities. Falling under the larger category of punk rock or DIY (Do It Yourself, i.e., music produced by independent labels) music, these subcultures—indie, punk, hardcore, queercore, emocore—have created a liberatory queer space through a variety of constructions of sexuality, and maintain this space through cultural products in print, electronic, and audio media. The most notable example of constructed sexuality among these subcultures are queer skinheads, as Murray Healy noted in his *Gay Skins* (1996). Healy's work has been heavily criticized by many skinheads as a fetishization of skin masculinity, though Healy defends his work as only reporting on the hypersexualized construction of masculinity skins present, noting that when homosexual activity occurs in a completely homosocial milieu, masculinity automatically becomes fetishized as the object of same-sex desire. The queer skinhead movement is in part a response to the unspoken classism of the urban gay meccas, an environment where a supposedly progressive vision of middle- and upper-middle-class urban life has been infused with gay politics and a clearly homoerotic, but still somewhat genteel, aesthetic that privileges upper- and middle-class values and allegiances over those of the working classes. Thus, the queer skinhead movement sees its goal as articulating a traditional vision of male power while also challenging the dictum of uniform heterosexuality generally associated with homosocial spaces.

Originally appearing as a subcultural identity among working-class youth in 1960s Britain in response to the feminization of the male form presented by the hippie and mod identities, queer skinheads exist today globally along with other subcultures held together by common musical aesthetics and political values, all of which fall into the larger punk category. The skin movement revolves around working-class class politics—which can be the small minority of neonationalist or white supremacist skins who are most often recognized by the mainstream media, or, more often, a less confrontational articulation of class-based socialism—and Oi! punk or ska musics.

In a flyer distributed at the 1997 pride parade in New York City, the Queer Skin Brotherhood—an Internet-based coalition of gay and bisexual skinheads—described itself as

The Last Real Men: Being a skinhead is not about shaving your head! Nor is it about politics. BEER AND BROTHERHOOD, OI! and SKA, DEFEND THE WORKING CLASS! STAND BY YOUR MATES RIGHT OR WRONG! be real, loyal, and reliable * love music, hate politics, work hard * and sport the look . . . from shorn head to steel-tip toe! it's not just the attitude that makes you [sic] skin its [sic] the lack of it!"

The QSB is being forged as an . . . international crew. Skinheads of all crews . . . are welcome here–left, right, red, black, Asian, Latin, whitepower, neonazis, toy–nazis, SHARPs [Skinheads Against Racial Prejudice], liberal, masochistic, Jewish, anarchist, nationalist, sadist, vanilla, Traditional Skins, Hammerskins, "first Skin, then gay/first gay, then skin," bootboys, punks. . . . We endorse none of the above. We endorse honesty.

"Queer" and "Skinhead" both mark revolts. Add the words and multiply the revulsion. You can't pretend all skins are straight, and the gay movement can no longer tell you what it means if a man lusts for another man.

Matthew Williams

Q

Bibliography

Healy, Murray. *Gay Skins: Class, Masculinity, and Queer Appropriation*. London: Cassall, 1996.

Queer Skinhead Brotherhood: http://www.geocities.com/WestHollywood/6136/

See also Disco and Dance Music; Music and Musicians 2: Popular Music

Queer Theory

Queer theory on the simplest level refers to an ensemble of strategies of reading and interpreting texts (whether literary or social) that has emerged in the last decade and has been profoundly influenced by poststructural theory. In contradistinction to criticism, which explicates facts about texts and instructs readers as to *what* a text means, theory attempts to explain *how* a text makes meanings. Russian critic Mikhail Bakhtin has been influential in the evolution of theory through his conception of *heteroglossia*. As Bakhtin states, at any given time, a number of cultural determinants allow a text, phrase, word, or event to have meaning. These forces may be social, historical, psychological, political, or even personal. But a text must have relevance in relation to these conditions to have meaning; theory, in turn, generally takes as its task the *delimitation* or exposition of these conditions.

Queer theory typically examines the role of desire in the heteroglossia of a text, exposing the ways in which homoeroticism and heteroeroticism function, intermingling and mutually confusing modes of expression within a text. Queer theory has evolved as an eclectic and diffuse ensemble of practices influenced by the contestatory realms of psychoanalysis, Marxism, cultural materialism, semiotics, social constructionism, structuralism, and feminism. Eve Kosofsky Sedgwick's *Between Men: English Literature and Male Homosocial Desire* (1985) is frequently cited as the germinal text of queer theory. Sedgwick examines the ways in which homosexuality and "homosociality" inflect texts of English literature. Homosociality represents the bonds of sublimated desire between men that are necessary to maintain a culture, especially those that represent lines of transmission of power through women—marriage, birth, and so on. Homosocial bonds through women are posited by Western culture as being antithetical to homosexual bonds, in which men bond directly without the mediating figure of women. But Sedgwick proceeds to demonstrate how the terms continually collapse into each other in practice and in literature. Hence Sedgwick finds the origin and reflection of homosexuality within heteroerotic practices themselves.

Queer theory is a plural and diffuse set of practices, not a unified field. A brief glance at two important texts can begin to suggest the polymorphousness of the topic. Judith Butler's *Gender Trouble* (1990) begins by reading a number of contemporary theorists, including Jacques Lacan, Michel Foucault, Monique Wittig, Julia Kristeva, and Luce Irigiray, to demonstrate how gender functions as both a solidifying and unintentionally destabilizing assumption within their arguments. Her own theory then proposes that a number of subversive "performative" strategies, including parody and drag, can be used to "overplay" the codes of gender and thereby foreground identity in its most subversive and denaturalized forms. Jonathan Dollimore's *Sexual Dissidence* (1991) begins by contrasting the homosexual writings of André Gide and Oscar Wilde. Gide symbolizes for Dollimore a sort of acceptance of identity troubled or altered by sexual difference, whereas Wilde symbolizes a full embrace of difference that, in its extremity, calls into question the very possibility of identity. These two positions become theoretical polarities that Dollimore traces through both the Renaissance and contemporary culture. What should be apparent from these two reductive summaries is the intense postmodern skepticism toward determinant identities that is perhaps the only unifying hallmark of queer theory as a practice.

Although queer theory is generally thought of as an invention of the modern academy, it has a distinct history within the separate lines of gay and lesbian criticism and theory. Lesbian theorist and anthropologist Gayle Rubin forcefully introduced some of the basic premises of queer theory in 1975 in two germinal essays, "The Traffic in Women: Notes on the 'Political Economy' of Sex" and "Thinking Sex: Notes for a Radical Theory of the Politics of Sexuality." In the two essays Rubin elaborates a radical and now central theory: that gender difference and sexual difference are related but are not the same. Gender difference refers to those governed by the binary *man/woman*, while sexual difference refers to those governed by the binary terms *homosexual/heterosexual*. Typically, sexual difference is expressed *through* gender difference; hence the common stereotypes of the feminine gay man and the masculine lesbian, wherein a deviance in relation to sexuality is made meaningful through a deviance in gender identification. Although sexual difference and gender difference are almost inextricable from each other in Western cultures, it should theoretically be possible to separate them and to examine the interplays between and within them. Moreover, how gender and sexual difference interact in any given text can provide clues about the ways in which power operates in the culture producing it. Clearly, this formulation paves the way for much of the queer theory to follow, and especially that of Sedgwick.

Even earlier than Rubin, Guy Hocquenghem's *Homosexual Desire* (1968) also presages and paves the way for dominant nodes of queer thought. Strongly influenced by the French leftist rebellions of 1968 and also deeply indebted to the theory of "schizoanalysis" proposed by Gilles Deleuze and Félix Guattari in *Anti-Oedipus*, Hocquenghem's Marxist revision of Freudian analysis examines the historical and psychological construction of "the homosexual" as a displacement and repression of society's own homosexual desire. Arguing that desire is an unbroken and polyvocal phenomenon, *Homosexual Desire* suggests that the establishment of exclusive homosexuality is a way of isolating and expelling those segments of desire that do not imitate the productive and reproductive goals of capitalism. Sexuality, therefore, is not a "natural" phenomenon but is the effect of the economic relations of a given culture—a conclusion that, again, clearly leads to the domain currently negotiated by queer theorists.

Although the representative authors mentioned here can be seen as exemplifying certain key ideas in the formation of queer theory, it is also true that a multitude of other theorists could just as easily have been invoked. One of the happiest aspects of queer theory is that its intensely dissolute form and luxurious volume suggest that it shall remain widely and deeply resonant for some time to come.

Gregory W. Bredbeck

Bibliography

Abelove, Henry, Michèle Aina Barale, and David M. Halperin. *The Gay and Lesbian Studies Reader*. New York: Routledge, 1993.

de Lauretis, Teresa. "Sexual Indifference and Lesbian Representation." In *Performing Feminisms: Feminist Critical Theory and Theatre*. Sue-Ellen Case, ed. Baltimore: Johns Hopkins University Press, 1990, 17–39.

Deleuze, Gilles, and Félix Guattari. *Anti-Oedipus: Capitalism and Schizophrenia*. Robert Hurley, Mark Seem, and Helen R. Lane, trans. Minneapolis: University of Minnesota Press, 1983.

Dollimore, Jonathan. *Sexual Dissidence: Augustine to Wilde, Freud to Foucault*. Oxford: Clarendon Press, 1991.

Foucault, Michel. *The History of Sexuality: An Introduction*, Vol. I. Robert Hurley, trans. New York: Random House, 1978.

Fuss, Diana. *Inside/Out: Lesbian Theories, Gay Theories*. New York: Routledge, 1991.

Hocquenghem, Guy. *Homosexual Desire*. Daniella Dangoor, trans. London: Allison and Busby, 1968.

Irigiray, Luce. *This Sex Which Is Not One*. Catherine Porter with Carolyn Burke, trans. Ithaca, N.Y.: Cornell University Press, 1985.

Sedgwick, Eve Kosofsky. *Between Men: English Literature and Male Homosocial Desire*. New York: Columbia University Press, 1985.

See also Deleuze, Gilles; English Literature; Foucault, Michel; Freud, Sigmund; Gay Studies; Gender; Gide, André; Hocquenghem, Guy; Queer Politics; Wilde, Oscar

R

Rabe, David (1940–)

Born in Dubuque, Iowa, to parents William, a high school history teacher turned meatpacker, and Ruth (McCormick), a department store worker, David William Rabe's early ambitions included the desire to become a professional football player. While pursuing an undergraduate degree in theater, however Rabe began to write his first plays. Today, Rabe is an accomplished author, playwright, and screenwriter who has won numerous accolades for his work, including a 1970 Associated Press Award for a serial piece he wrote while in the employ of the New Haven Register, a 1971 Obie for Best Play for the Off-Broadway production of *The Basic Training of Pavlo Hummel*, a Tony for *Sticks and Bones* for best play of the 1971–1972 season, and a New York Drama Critics Circle Award for the Best American Play for the 1976 production of *Streamers*. In addition, Rabe has authored *The Orphan*, *In the Boom Boom Room*, *Crossing*, *Goose and TomTom*, *Hurlyburly,* and *Those the River Keeps*. Rabe has also written screenplays for Barbara Gordon's *I'm Dancing as Fast as I Can* and Daniel Lang's *Casualties of War*.

Perhaps of greatest concern for this volume is Rabe's play *Streamers*, one of four plays Grove Press has collected and published in two volumes entitled *The Vietnam Plays*. The plays are concerned with the human reactions to the circumstances of war and the violence fueled by it, in Rabe's words, an attempt to "embrace a portion of that inherently unembraceable subject" of the Vietnam War. They serve as Rabe's means of comprehending the travesty to which he was subjected during his eleven-month assignment as part of a hospital support unit at Long Binh, South Vietnam, in 1966–1967.

Streamers in particular addresses social tensions, both racial and sexual, and presents a range of both verbal and physical violence as its characters attempt to accommodate their impending departure for Vietnam from the barracks they have come to call home. The four principal soldiers in *Streamers* are Roger, an intelligent and highly motivated black man; Billy, a blond and trim midtwenties Midwesterner; Richie, the homosexual privileged New Yorker; and Carlyle, the second black soldier whose introduction to the barracks of the previous three causes the tensions between races and sexualities to attain their climax, resulting in the stabbing deaths of Billy and of Sergeant Rooney, a Korean veteran soldier in charge of the boys.

Much like actual combat in Vietnam, which remains always suspended in an unknown future, homosexuality exists in Rabe's play not as a predetermined and static self-claimed identity but in the many fissures in masculine desire and action that belie true heterosexuality, from defensive male posturing to the conflation of sex and exercise, to heterosexual challenge, and, finally, to the violence that results from reduced inhibitions owing to the consumption of alcohol. But, in *Streamers*, homosexuality remains unconstituted in actions that would define it, for even Richie's statement of gay identity remains unbelieved by Roger until after the death of Billy. In this manner, Rabe confronts the issue of the presence and absence of homosexuality in the military, or in any male collectivity, years before the debate over service eligibility for the military's gay personnel would reach its fevered pitch. Ironically, in terms of that debate, what matters in Rabe's play is not what one says but what one does. *Jon Adams*

R

Bibliography

Rabe, David. *The Vietnam Plays*. Vol. 2. New York: Grove Press, 1993.

See also Military; War

Radical Faeries

How do you define a group of people whose favorite saying is: "Ask four Faeries what a Radical Faerie is, and you'll get five different answers"? Well, you simply don't.

This is not a definition—just one Faerie's perspective on the movement. Faeries have been described variously as a neo-pagan spiritual group, a gay tribe, a new religious/social movement, a bunch of hippy-faggot-farmers, gender-fuck activists, queer community anarchists. The number of different definitions of faerie is synergistically greater than the number of queer men and women who self-identify as part of the movement.

Some would say radical faeries have always existed, that their ancestors were the witches burned during the Inquisition and the faeries of myth who survived through the camouflage of glamour. Some would point to a gathering of gay men in Arizona in 1979 where two hundred men met for a gay spirituality conference. Yet others would locate their beginnings in an amalgam of the feminist men's movement, the "hippy" back-to-the-land movement, and the gay liberation movement. A whole heap of others would say: "Who cares?" For a lot of Faeries (but by no means all), there are some common ideas, approaches, and behaviors that are integral to a definition of the movement.

Faeries sometimes gather to celebrate the link between their queer sexuality and their spirituality, believing the ability to mediate between the masculine and the feminine gives them a unique, *queer window* to the world of spirit. By donning a dress they can *become* the Goddess in ritual. Although a large number are witches and pagans, there is no formal Faerie dogma. At Gatherings one can find Jewish, Buddhist, Christian, and agnostic Faeries. Some Faeries think spirituality is irrelevant and ignore it.

There are Faerie sanctuaries in the United States, Canada, and Australia where Faeries can live close to the land through self-sufficiency. Sanctuaries also host Faerie gatherings, where members gather to network, ritualize, "recharge our batteries," and experience the joy of a queer safe space. At gatherings, Faeries send out a cry of "YOOOO-HOOOO" and meet in circles to *listen* to one another. As the talisman is passed around the circle, each person has the opportunity to share feelings, frustrations, dreams, and desires. Faeries sometimes also network in cities by meeting at regular "circles" or irregular "gatherettes." Recently, some have found Faerie community through networking electronically on the Internet.

Some Faeries would say that most important, they are an activist movement. They are walkers between the worlds—shamanistic gender-fuckers in chiffon and army boots who challenge the stereotypes of the mainstream—whether straight or queer mainstream. Faeries can be found at pride marches, environmental rallies, and pro-choice demonstrations. They can also be found at home composting their vegetable scraps in silent activism.

> We are an old people
> We are a new people
> We are the same people
> Different from before
> (Conner 13)   *Willow Fey*

Bibliography

Conner, Randy P. *Blossom of Bone—Reclaiming the Connections between Homoeroticism and the Sacred*. New York: HarperCollins, 1993.

See also Activism, U.S.; Berdache; Effeminacy; Masculinity

Radiguet, Raymond (1903–1923)

Raymond Radiguet was born to a father with alleged descent from Mme de Pompadour, the favorite of Louis XV, and a creole mother with family ties to Empress Josephine Bonaparte. In contrast to the destinies of those femmes fatales, the family suffered financial difficulties. A desire for an independent life led Raymond eventually to quit school. He preferred to read French literature on his own. Consequently, the heroic years of World War I were, in Radiguet's antinationalistic view, "four years of summer vacation." This nonchalant attitude toward the war distinguishes him from his disillusioned contemporaries and underscores his originality as a writer.

While the postwar period found inspiration in dada and surrealism, Radiguet invented his own political and esthetic conservatism to which he partially converted his lover, Jean Cocteau. From the age of sixteen until Radiguet's untimely death from typhoid four years later, the two maintained a relationship, as well known as that of Rimbaud and Verlaine. Their influence on each other is an example of how two literary styles can become intertwined.

His first novel, *Devil in the Flesh*, a semiautobiographical story of a teenager who seduces a young housewife while her husband is away at the front and drives her to madness and death, earned him instant and lasting success. His second novel, *The Ball of Count Orgel*, posthumously published, told the story of an ambiguous relationship between two men and a woman. Prevarication and love triangles are major themes in Radiguet's life and work. Although often compared to Rimbaud and his tragic genius, Radiguet was sweetly sentimental in his poetry volume, *Cheeks on Fire*, a neoclassicist whose advice to poets was "to be banal" (*Oeuvres complètes*, 1:464–465). Radiguet did not hide his disdain for modernism and its obsession for stylistic and technical innovation.   *Robert Rhyne*

Bibliography

McNab, James. *Raymond Radiguet*. Boston: Twayne, 1984.
Radiguet, Raymond. *Oeuvres complètes*, Vol. 10. Geneva: Slatkine Reprints,1978.

See also Cocteau, Jean; French Literature; French Symbolism; Rimbaud, Arthur; Verlaine, Paul

Raffalovich, Marc-André (1864–1934)

Although Marc-André Raffalovich is remembered today primarily as the devoted lifelong companion of poet and priest John Gray, he was, in his own time, a poet of some distinction and an important contributor to the developing field of sexology. A Russian Jew born in Paris, Raffalovich moved to England in 1882, settling in London to make a name for himself as a wealthy young writer and socialite. His first published book, *Cyril and Lionel and Other Poems* (1884), was followed by four other books of vaguely homoerotic verse, including *Tuberose and Meadowsweet* (1885), considered by recent critics to be his best work. Raffalovich also wrote two novels and several plays, some co–authored with Gray, whom he met in 1892.

In 1895, the year of Oscar Wilde's trials, Raffalovich published two sexology essays in France: the unsympathetic "L'Affaire Oscar Wilde" and

"L'Uranisme: Inversion Sexuelle Congénitale," a study of "Uranianism," or "sexual inversion." He incorporated these into the larger study, *Uranisme et Unisexualité* (1896), which Havelock Ellis praised, and which deserves renewed attention for its attempts to legitimize homosexuality as congenital and natural—neither sin nor diseaase—at a time of increasing medicalization and persecution.

Despite his belief in morally neutral congenital orientation, Raffalovich urged homosexuals toward a "superior" emotional but nonphysical expression—the type of relationship some biographers insist he had with Gray. Following Gray's example, Raffalovich converted to Catholicism in 1896. After Gray finished studies for the priesthood in Rome, Raffalovich moved to Edinburgh, Scotland, in 1905 to live near him, spending the last thirty years of his life there as a generous benefactor to church construction and young literary talents.   *Ed Madden*

Bibliography

McCormack, Jerusha Hull. *John Gray: Poet, Dandy, and Priest*. Hanover, Mass.: Brandeis University Press, 1991.
Smith, Timothy d'Arch. *Love in Earnest: Some Notes on the Lives and Writings of English "Uranian" Poets from 1889 to 1930*. London: Routledge and Kegan Paul, 1970.

See also Ellis, Havelock; Inversion; Sexology; Uranianism; Wilde, Oscar

Rainbow Flag

The Rainbow Flag, probably the most popular symbol of pride in gay and lesbian communities, originated in San Francisco in the late 1970s. San Francisco had seen earlier incarnations of rainbow flags during the hippie movement in its own Haight-Ashbury district. One early example included red, white, black, brown, and yellow stripes, celebrating racial unity.

While planning San Francisco's 1978 Gay Freedom Day Parade, gay rights activist Artie Bressan and artist Gilbert Baker suggested using the Rainbow Flag as a symbol that could be flown each year at the parade. Baker designed a flag with eight horizontal stripes in the following colors: hot pink, red, orange, yellow, green, turquoise, indigo, and violet. Two gigantic flags flew that first year. The image of the Rainbow Flag became popular in the gay community in San Francisco almost immediately.

R

Baker also designed a Rainbow Flag based on the American flag; he called it New Glory. This flag replaced the familiar thirteen stripes of Old Glory with the eight colors of the first Rainbow Flag.

During this time, Steve Tyson, who worked for the Paramount Flag Company's flag store in San Francisco, found at the store some old rainbow flags originally made for a Masonic organization. The flag store quickly sold the flags, which featured seven colors: red, orange, yellow, green, blue, indigo, and violet.

For the 1979 Gay Freedom Day Parade, Baker and the Paramount Flag Company developed a six-stripe version of the Rainbow Flag. Consisting of red, orange, yellow, green, blue, and violet, this version became immensely popular in San Francisco and beyond. Gay and lesbian organizations across the country began to produce various versions of the Rainbow Flag. Some used different colors and different widths; others added a lambda or a pink triangle. AIDS activist Leonard Matlovich led an unsuccessful movement that wanted to add a black stripe to the Rainbow Flag as a somber reminder of the AIDS crisis. Matlovich intended for the black stripes to be removed and burned in Washington, D.C., when a cure was found.

The Rainbow Flag's popularity grew throughout the 1980s. By the end of the decade, the symbol was prominently displayed in front of gay households throughout the United States, especially in San Francisco. The flag was also used as a symbol of hope in health care facilities that treated persons with AIDS. In the 1990s, a new and extremely popular incarnation of the Rainbow Flag has come about. Today, many people display bumper stickers with the Rainbow Flag, often with the catch phrase "Celebrate diversity" printed on it.   *William DeGenaro*

Bibliography

Ferrigan, James J. "The Evolution and Adoption of the Rainbow Flag in San Francisco." *Flag Bulletin* 130 (1989): 116–22.

See also AIDS; Lambda; Marches and Parades; Pink Triangle; San Francisco

Ramos Otero, Manuel (1948–1990)

The most important gay writer in Puerto Rican letters, Manuel Ramos Otero could be considered the author who took Puerto Rican contemporary homosexual literature out of the closet. He wrote both narrative and poetry. The titles of his narrative works include *Concierto de metal para un recuerdo y otras orgías de soledad* (Concert of One Brass Instrument for a Memory and Other Orgies of Loneliness, 1971), *La novela bingo* (The Bingo Novel, 1976), *El cuento de la mujer del mar* (The Story of the Woman from the Sea, 1979), *Página en blanco y staccato* (A Blank Page and Staccato, 1987), and *Cuentos de buena tinta* (Short Stories on Good Ink, 1992). His books of poetry are *El libro de la muerte* (The Book of Death, 1985) and *Invitación al polvo* (Invitation to Dust, 1991). In his work, Ramos Otero sees the deconstruction of gender as necessary to the creation of a true sexual liberty. The poem "Nobleza de sangre" (Nobility of Blood) from *Invitación al polvo* attacks hypocritical religious attitudes toward AIDS by thanking God for sending the disease. Apart from the identification between the homosexual and the feminine as related phenomena, Ramos Otero uses a seemingly perverse discourse that he endows with poetic status. The lyric speaker experiments with the baroque sources of the love poem, recontextualizing the lyric and sublime into the limits of the perverse. It is a reading that codifies the sensual and sexual possibilities of the metaphysical sonnet as one of the greatest institutions of Hispanic poetry.   *Daniel Torres*

Bibliography

Foster, David William. *Latin American Writers on Gay and Lesbian Themes: A Bio-Critical Sourcebook.* Westport, Conn.: Greenwood, 1994.

"Interview with Manuel Ramos Otero." *The Dispatch: Newsletter of the Center for Hispanic Studies, Columbia University* 5, no. 1 (Fall 1986): 14–16.

See also AIDS; AIDS Literature; Chicano and Latino Gay Cultures; Lezama Lima, José; Love Poetry, the Petrarchan Tradition; Zapata, Luís

Rauschenberg, Robert (1925–)

Restlessly creative American painter, sculptor, theatrical designer, and conceptual and performance artist, Robert (born Milton) Rauschenberg pioneered a number of the most influential tendencies in postwar American art. His striking combinations of painting and assemblage were so original a medium that he coined a new word, *combine*, to describe them. His art employs a wide range of materials: from stuffed and mounted animals to Coke bottles, mud, comic strips, and family photos.

While the rich synergy of objects, gestural paint, and collage in the combines established his international reputation in the early 1960s, Rauschenberg began his career some ten years before with a very different kind of work—pared down, intensely introverted, and largely monochromatic pure abstraction. These early works, which included images made of growing grass, crumpled tissue paper, and the erased drawing of another artist, tended to explore the rich possibilities of an unexpressive art at the time of expressionism's ascendancy. In this sense, they are very much the work of a closeted gay artist.

A short marriage to fellow painter Susan Weil, which produced a son, Christopher, ended in divorce in 1952—owing in part to Rauschenberg's deepening involvements with a group of gay men who would shortly prove to be among the leading figures in the Cold War art world. Rauschenberg's first male lover was the artist Cy Twombly, while both were still students at the avant-garde academy Black Mountain College. They traveled together extensively, subsequently sharing a studio in New York. At Black Mountain, Rauschenberg also began a lifelong friendship with composer/philosopher John Cage and his lover, choreographer Merce Cunningham. Rauschenberg would become set and later costume designer for the Merce Cunningham Dance Company for many years.

The art Rauschenberg created prior to meeting Jasper Johns tended toward black-and-white minimal forms, erasure, and large empty canvases. He achieved widespread notoriety with a series of all-white paintings that John Cage acknowledged as predecessors for his equally notorious *4'33"*. The White Paintings, flat white paint on a flat white surface, were conceived in opposition to the then-dominant mode of abstract expressionist art, with its aesthetics of flung paint and aggressive self-assertion. Amid such macho posturing, Rauschenberg's White Paintings were deliberately self-effacing, so without autographic content of any kind that Rauschenberg decreed they were to be painted by others.

Only after meeting Jasper Johns and inaugurating a six-year personal and professional association did Rauschenberg begin what is now recognized as his mature style. He and Johns worked together every day, carrying on a kind of pictorial dialogue in their paintings. The resulting combines are dense amalgams of interpersonal codes, sly humor, and worldly observation. Some paintings coyly reference gay culture through their use of autographed photos of Judy Garland or a tie cascading through the open fly of a pair of men's pants, captioned "What You Want." In place of the rigorous negation so characteristic of the earlier work, there is instead an abundance of those expressive effects that Rauschenberg had so long avoided. On meeting Johns, it seems, Rauschenberg finally felt free to become himself.   *Jonathan Katz*

Bibliography

Hopps, Walter. *Rauschenberg: The Early 1950s*. Houston: Houston Fine Art Press, 1991.

Katz, Jonathan. "The Art of Code: Jasper Johns and Robert Rauschenberg." In *Significant Others*. Whitney Chadwick, ed. New York: Thames and Hudson, 1993.

Kotz, Mary Lynn. *Rauschenberg/Art and Life*. New York: Abrams, 1990.

Rauschenberg, Robert. *Rauschenberg*. Interview by Barbara Rose. New York: Vintage, 1987.

Tomkins, Calvin. *Off the Wall: Robert Rauschenberg and the Art World of Our Time*. New York: Penguin, 1980.

See also Art History; Cage, John; Cunningham, Merce; Johns, Jasper; Postmodernism; Twombly, Cy

Ravel, (Joseph) Maurice (1875–1937)

It cannot be stated with confidence that the French composer Maurice Ravel was gay, although his sexuality has been the subject of ongoing speculation. He was never linked to Parisian gay subculture, but numerous traits place him in a field of homosexual connotation: a lifelong bachelor, his most important emotional attachment was to his mother. Intensely guarded about his personal life, the public identity he proudly claimed was that of a dandy of refined tastes. Pianist Ricardo Viñes, also a bachelor and dandy, was Ravel's close friend; both recorded enigmatic statements of profound social nonconformity. Even if we cannot be sure what he was guarding, his status as recluse, dandy, and sexual enigma suggests some sort of queer identity.

Ravel is best known for his piano, vocal and orchestral music of sensuous textures, harmonic subtlety, and highly polished surfaces. While his structures are always classical in clarity and proportion, he worked with various styles from archaic to impressionistic, often incorporating exotic elements.

He had a fondness for evocative titles. The only overtly queer moment in Ravel's oeuvre is found in the third song, "L'Indifférent" (The Indifferent One), of the orchestral song cycle *Schéhérazade,* in which the (originally) male narrator sings the praises of an aloof, androgynous youth. But his overall musical rhetoric is shaped by relations of the closet: the glittering surfaces create an impeccable facade, maintaining an exquisite distance from sincere expression; eroticism is everywhere haunted by irony. Through modernist detachment Ravel creates an inscrutable, evasive aesthetic space.

Chip Whitesell

Bibliography

Larner, Gerald. *Maurice Ravel.* London: Phaidon, 1996.

Marnat, Marcel. *Maurice Ravel.* Paris: Fayard, 1986.

See also Dandy; French Symbolism; Music and Musicians 1: Classical Music

John Rechy, in a photo taken for the jacket of Numbers, *1967. Photo courtesy of John Rechy.*

Rechy, John (1934–)

U.S. writer John Rechy made a significant and lasting literary impression with the publication of his first novel, *City of Night* (1963). An unlikely bestseller, *City of Night* exploded the conventions of stories, like Jack Kerouac's *On the Road*, of existential exploration and drift by casting the existential drifter as a male hustler whose majority of sexual contacts are with other men. Rechy succeeded in *City of Night* in combining a brutally direct account of life in America's sexual underground with a prose style that rivals and at times exceeds Kerouac's for lyrical power. Largely autobiographical, *City of Night* features a nameless young male protagonist who, like Rechy himself, leaves his hometown of El Paso, Texas, and the troubled home life he knew as a child to undertake a simultaneously spiritual and erotic quest. Rechy's parents, Mexican immigrants of mixed-ethnic ancestry, raised their son in an emotionally volatile setting, leaving him as deeply ambivalent about his cultural identity as about his sexual identity.

Rechy's novels following *City of Night*, though generally less commercially successful, clearly document the author's creative and personal evolution. Novels like *Numbers* (1967), *This Day's Death* (1969), and *Sexual Outlaw* (1977) foreground Rechy's primary interest in the complex dynamics of male homosexual desire in a world at once increasingly more tolerant of homosexuality in the abstract but still deeply repressive of it in the concrete. Each of these novels also maintains some focus on matters of ethnic identity; their protagonists are typically, like their author, made more exotic by their own mixed-race ancestry. With the simultaneous emergence in the last two decades of scholarly work on both Chicana/o and lesbian/gay literature, all of Rechy's work, which since the 1970s has included the novels *Rushes* (1979), *Marilyn's Daughter* (1988), and *The Miraculous Day of Amalia Gómez* (1991), has come under critical scrutiny focused around issues of ethnic and sexual identity. Most notably, Juan Bruce-Novoa has devoted serious attention to Rechy's status in the Chicano literary tradition, arguing in favor of Rechy's positive contribution to the diversity and complexity of that tradition. Rechy himself has participated in this debate, arguing both for the legitimacy of his simultaneous explorations of gay and Chicano experience and against the kind of cultural ghettoization that can result from classifying writers and texts according to any overly categorical terms of identity.

Since the publication of *Amalia Gómez*, his most sustained treatment of Chicana/o experience,

Rechy has continued to expand the limits of his art; in *Our Lady of Babylon* (1996), he constructs an elaborate meditation on gender by retelling world history from the perspectives of its most infamously "fallen" women, and in 1997 he continues to work on a project that promises to reverse the generic dynamic of his previous fictions, an autobiography he plans to subtitle "A Novel." More than thirty-five years after the publication of *City of Night*, John Rechy continues to unsettle his own unquestionable literary reputation by reinventing himself as both a writer and a character.   *Ricardo Ortíz*

Bibliography

Ortíz, Ricardo L. "John Rechy and the Grammar of Ostentation." In *Cruising the Performative: Interventions into the Representation of Ethnicity, Nationality and Sexuality*. Sue-Ellen Case, Philip Brett, and Susan Leigh Foster, eds. Bloomington, Ind.: Indiana University Press, 1995, 59–70.

Rechy, John, with Debra, Castillo. "Interview with John Rechy." *Diacritics: A Review of Contemporary Criticism* 25 no. 1 (Spring 1995): 113–25.

See also Beat Generation; Chicano and Latino Gay Cultures; Fiction; Hustlers; Pornography

Recruitment Myth

The myth of recruitment refers to the misconception that gay men and lesbians seduce heterosexuals, particularly children, in order to convert them to homosexuality. The supposed motivation for this program of conversion is that, since gay people cannot reproduce, they must conscript others to create new generations of gay men and lesbians. Variations of this myth contend that teaching gay issues to children, or the mere presence of gay men and lesbians among impressionable young people, will persuade them to become homosexual.

The recruitment myth rests on several false premises. It asserts that gay people cannot reproduce, but gay men and lesbians can and do become fathers and mothers—although their children are no more inclined to be gay than are the children of heterosexuals. It assumes that it is possible to seduce unsuspecting heterosexuals into becoming homosexual, whatever their desires or social identities. It suggests that gay people, because they must enlist converts, have a greater motivation to molest children than do heterosexuals, while in fact heterosexual men are the group most likely to commit such abuse. The myth also contends that gay people must take action to ensure the continued existence of homosexuality, although homosexual behaviors have been common throughout history and across cultures.

The myth of recruitment has been used to support local, state, and national efforts—often successful—to deny gay men and lesbians their civil rights. For example, in 1997 a resolution passed by the county government in Charlotte, North Carolina, cut funds for "any and all activities by private agencies that promote, advocate, or endorse . . . behaviors . . . that . . . undermine . . . the traditional American family," and denounced gay people for thinking "they have a right to recruit children for experimenting sexually." In 1996 fear of homosexual recruitment led the Utah state legislature to ban gay high school student groups from meeting on campus. In 1995 the school board of Merrimack, New Hampshire, adopted a policy that forbids teaching gay issues in a positive light because this would supposedly encourage homosexuality among students. The policy statement repeated word-for-word language used in a failed amendment, championed by Senator Jesse Helms (R.-N.C.), to the federal Elementary and Secondary Education Act of 1994. Both the amendment and the policy stated that schools "shall neither implement nor carry out any program or activity that has either the purpose or effect of encouraging or supporting homosexuality as a positive life-style alternative." In 1984 in an effort to demonstrate that gay parents cannot serve their children's best interests, the Family Research Institute sponsored a study that unsuccessfully sought to prove that children of gay parents are especially likely to become gay themselves. The Boy Scouts of America have used the myth of recruitment to justify their policy, implemented in 1990, of excluding "avowed homosexuals" as leaders or members, arguing that the presence of gay adults or youths interferes with the beliefs of some (presumably heterosexual) boys. In 1995 the Subcommittee on Oversight and Investigations of the House Economic and Educational Opportunities Committee held hearings to investigate recruitment and promotion of homosexuality in schools.

In these and other campaigns to deny gay people their civil rights, opponents of gay rights argue that it is necessary to limit gay people's freedoms to protect children from the sexual and moral threats

R posed by homosexual recruitment. Yet the myth of recruitment harms both gay people and heterosexuals, because the fear it engenders and the exclusion it justifies hinder the ability of gay teachers, counselors, and parents to meet the needs of young people—whether gay or straight—by exposing them to facts about gay people and homosexuality and by presenting them with positive role models.

Charles Krinsky

Bibliography

Rowe, Robert N. "Are We Educators Who Are Homosexual Recruiting Youth?" *Education* 113, no. 3 (Spring 1993): 508–10.

Smolowe, Jill. "The Unmarrying Kind." *Time* 147, no. 18 (April 29, 1996): 68–69.

See also Boy Scouts; Civil Rights (U.S. Law); Education: Theory and Pedagogy

Religion and Religiosity

Humans have been said to be incurably religious. Some have called it the transcendental temptation, the will to believe in something outside of themselves, although technically religion does not require a supernatural deity, and if modern humanism can be called a religion (some argue that it cannot), it can simply be a way of life. Usually religion involves worship but it also involves moral conduct, right belief, and participation in religious institutions. The issue of moral conduct is the most relevant to any discussion of religion and homosexuality.

Though it is possible to separate worship from moral conduct, it is difficult to do so because worship tends to imply being in touch or in adjustment with the object of worship. The religious person is usually thought of as one who follows a certain path of life, which is one of the definitions for religiosity.

In modern society, whether or not one is a believer, religious tradition exercises great influence on the way one thinks and acts. One of the great sources of information on the past is religious literature, and religion tends to incorporate into itself the standards by which its adherents should live, long after they may have abandoned a particular church or faith. Norms for sexual conduct can be found in religious literature of most of religions: Buddhism, Christianity, Confucianism, Hinduism, Islam, Jainism, Judaism, Sikhism, and Taoism, to name several.

A good illustration of this in terms of sexual issues is the Western Christian tradition. Sexual attitudes in Christianity are influenced by the Jewish scriptures, the teachings and sayings of Jesus and their interpreters in the Christian Testament, the writings of the church fathers, and various conciliar decisions. One issue, often misinterpreted, is the story of Onan detailed in Genesis 38:7–10. Onan is struck dead by the Hebrew God for spilling his semen on the ground instead of impregnating his sister-in-law. Although biblical scholars might well argue whether spilling the seed or ignoring the command of the Lord was the issue, the story came to be the basis for condemnation of masturbation and making masturbation a sin in Christianity.

This condemnation of masturbation ran so deeply in Christian thinking that it came to be accepted as part of popular wisdom. In the eighteenth century, when medicine turned to new theories to explain illness, this idea was incorporated into the medical teaching emphasizing masturbation's disease- and even death-causing capabilities. Interestingly, homosexuality was also defined as a form of masturbation, especially among women, and among men as well unless penetration was involved. This, then, brought in the sin of Sodom, in which the Lord destroyed Sodom because of its evilness, (Genesis 19:11), namely the desire of males to lie with other males. Again, biblical scholars argue over the story of Sodom, but the popular image remains.

Popularizing the health dangers of these traditional sins was the eighteenth-century Swiss physician S.A.D. Tissot, who condemned the loss of any semen not used for procreative purposes as masturbation and implied that it weakened and ultimately destroyed the individual. It was not until the twentieth century, when investigators could prove masturbation was not necessarily harmful, that change in thinking on the subject could come about. Each successive broadening of human horizons through exploration, discovery, and research tends to force a redefinition of religion to include the new elements; but change does not come easy, particularly in the hierarchical churches such as the Catholic, where new developments have been regularly condemned from the replacement of the geocentric worldview with a heliocentric one to the theory of evolution replacing the idea of a special creation some five thousand years ago. Often the changing views are accepted under new definitions only long after the controversy over them has disappeared. The same is true of moral codes. Many of the bitterest controversies in the history of religion have been fought by strict constructionists who adhered to traditional prescriptions of moral authority in their struggle against revisionists who sought to adopt both moral and ceremonial requirements to the changing conditions. Judaism is a good example of these changes with the emergence of several varieties of Judaism—from Humanistic to Reform to Conservative to Orthodox to Hasidic—with separate seminaries and heated disagreements, particularly in Israel, where the different versions of Judaism are not recognized by the Orthodox Rabbinic Council.

The religiosity of the ultra religious tends to be particularly difficult to overcome. In the Islamic world, similar struggles have broken out in Iran, Algeria, and Egypt. In the United States, Southern Baptists and Missouri Synod Lutherans have been conflicted over key biblical statements. The list goes on, but even more difficult are the struggles between competing religions which have different moral codes. Today the United States is witnessing this as many Asian immigrants arrive with a traditional moral code somewhat different from the American one derived in large part from the Judeo-Christian tradition.

Sexual conduct is one of the most controversial issues among different religious groups, and homosexuality and lesbianism in particular have served as tinder for the fires of hate.   *Vern L. Bullough*

Bibliography

Bullough, Vern L. *Sexual Variance in Society and History.* Chicago: University of Chicago Press, 1976.

Lopez, Enrique Hank. *Eros and Ethos: A Comparative Study of Catholic, Jewish and Protestant Sex Behavior.* Englewood Cliffs, N.J.: Prentice-Hall, 1979.

Parrinder, Geoffrey. *Sex in the World's Religions.* New York: Oxford University Press, 1980.

See also Bible; Buddhism; Catholicism; Christianity; Hinduism; Islam; Judaism; Masturbation Metropolitan Community Church; Quakers; Sodom and Gomorrah; Sodomy

Religious Organizations

Gayellow Pages, the most comprehensive annual directory for the gay community, lists hundreds of gay religious organizations in Canada and the United States. The national listing for 1995–1996 includes organizations of and for gay Mormons, Jews, Methodists, Baptists, Quakers, Eastern Orthodox, Brethren, Mennonites, Catholics, Christian Scientists, Disciples of Christ, Episcopalians, Unitarian-Universalists, Lutherans, Pentecostals, Presbyterians, Seventh-Day Adventists, Witches, Pagans, and members of the Reformed Church and the United Church of Christ.

Inter- or nondenominational groups include Christian Lesbians Out Together (CLOUT), Evangelicals Concerned, and the largest predominantly gay denomination in the world, the Universal Fellowship of Metropolitan Community Churches. Local lists include organizations of and for Buddhists, atheists, and humanists. Gay Muslims and Hindus associated with the other major religious groups in North America seem not yet to have organized, or are not yet listed.

Although established religious institutions, at least those originating in Western and Middle Eastern cultures, have traditionally been antigay, religion plays the same role in the lives of gay people as for anyone else, addressing the major questions of life and providing guidance through the high and low points of living. In most Christian and Jewish denominations or groupings, gay members and their supporters have gathered together because they have been excluded by the main body. The characteristics of these gay religious organizations depend, in large part, on their relations with the larger group and the nature of the larger organization.

Gay groups associated with denominations having a democratic form of government, in which it is fairly easy for gays to participate in the political process, tend to focus on education, lobbying, and political strategizing aimed at changing antigay policies. The Presbyterian Church is a prime example. At the other extreme, there are groups like Dignity, in the Roman Catholic Church, which has been banned from meeting in Roman Catholic churches by the church hierarchy. Instead, Dignity has created what constitutes nearly a parallel denomination for many gay and lesbian Catholics. Integrity, in the Episcopal Church, falls in between these two extremes. In some dioceses, Integrity is not allowed to meet in Episcopal churches, while in others, bishops have ignored the national policy banning ordination of lesbian and gay priests, so that the Episcopal Church is one of the few mainline denominations in which numerous lesbian and gay clergy have been openly ordained. Like Presbyterians, gay Episcopalians have been extraordinarily active in the politics of the Episcopal Church.

In the United Methodist Church, the principal focus of efforts on behalf of gay members has been at the congregational level, led by its Reconciling Congregations Program, the strongest such program

R

among all denominations, with several full-time staff members. Similar "welcoming congregation" movements are active among Presbyterians, Baptists, Lutherans, Mennonites, Brethren, Unitarian-Universalists, and the United Church of Christ.

The more intolerant churches have tended to "disown" their gay groups. Examples are the Church of Jesus Christ of Latter-Day Saints (Mormons) and Seventh-Day Adventists. The Seventh-Day Adventist Church actually went to court to try to prevent its lesbian-gay group, SDA Kinship International, from using the words "Seventh Day Adventist" or the initials SDA. The United Pentecostal Church expelled gay and lesbian members, after telling them it would be better to commit suicide than to be gay, so these outcasts began a new, inclusive Pentecostal denomination.

The first denomination with a special ministry for lesbians and gay men and their families, the Universal Fellowship of Metropolitan Community Churches (UFMCC), began in a similar way, founded in 1968 by another Pentecostal who had been expelled from his denomination, the Reverend Troy Perry. It is now an international, ecumenical denomination, drawing its members from every segment of the larger Christian community.

Groups like Emergence, lesbian and gay Christian Scientists, have given up or lost interest in trying to change the attitudes or policies of their denominations. Instead they focus on support and education for their own members and friends.

Gay and lesbian Jewish synagogues flourish in most major U.S. and Canadian cities. Most are independent or are associated with the more liberal Reform or Reconstructionist movements within Judaism. Congregation Beth Simchat Torah, with more than one thousand members, is the largest lesbian-gay synagogue in the world and one of the largest synagogues in New York City. Similar gay religious organizations flourish around the world.

James D. Anderson

Bibliography

Comstock, Gary David. *Unrepentant, Self-Affirming, Practicing: Lesbian/Bisexual/Gay People within Organized Religion*. New York: Continuum, 1996.

Gayellow Pages, the National Edition. New York: Renaissance House, 1995.

See also Metropolitan Community Church; Religion and Religiosity

Religious Right

The term *religious right* has been coined to cover a segment of the U.S. population, composed largely but not exclusively of evangelical and fundamentalist Christians, that has mobilized into a major political force during the 1980s and 1990s.

On a left-to-right political spectrum, the religious right is roughly situated to the right of the mainstream Republican Party yet still to the left of white supremacist groups such as the Ku Klux Klan and various neo-Nazi factions. In both style and substance, the religious right is distinct both from the libertarian-minded Old Right and from traditional American fundamentalist and evangelical Protestants, who rejected involvement in politics as well as even tactical alliances with Roman Catholics, Mormons, Orthodox Jews, and others they perceived as not among the "saved."

The religious right actively promotes a sociopolitical agenda whose cornerstone is the concept of "traditional values." As such, individuals and organizations associated with the religious right assume positions that they characterize as "pro-family" but that their opponents perceive as retrogressive and intended to roll back the gains of the movements for women's, gay, and ethnic/racial minority rights. The religious right also tends to take a minimalist view of the separation of church and state, arguing that the First Amendment prohibits the congressional establishment of any specific state religion but not religious expression in the public arena.

Although a wide variety of divergent organizations are associated with the religious right, two of the most prominent have been the Moral Majority, led by Baptist minister Jerry Falwell, and the Christian Coalition, led by Pentecostal minister Pat Robertson. The Moral Majority was founded in 1979 and disbanded in 1989. Subsequently, the Christian Coalition emerged as the premier institution of the religious right, quickly swelling by 1996 to include some two million members and over a thousand chapters.

Although theoretically nonpartisan, the Christian Coalition and other groups of the religious right have been major players in state and national Republican Party politics, and both the Reagan and Bush administrations were openly solicitous of them.

The condemnation of homosexuality is a key concern of the religious right. In condemning homosexual activity, members typically rely on biblical prohibitions (notably Leviticus 18:22 and 20:13, and Romans 1:27), as well as notions of "traditional morality" that regard sexual abstinence before marriage and lifelong monogamy inside heterosexual marriage as behaviorally normative and morally compulsory. The more extreme branches of the religious right regard homosexual behavior as deliberately chosen moral evil; less extreme branches may regard it as akin to a personal shortcoming like alcoholism or drug addiction. Almost all members of the religious right regard homosexuality as an aberrant and socially destructive force deserving of repression and punishment by the government and by society at large.

Individuals and groups associated with the religious right have been among the most vehement opponents of gay rights on the national, state, and local levels. At the national level, religious right groups have lobbied Congress and pressured executive agencies to block explicit HIV/AIDS education, outlaw same-sex marriage, and prohibit gays from serving in the military. At the state and local level, they have led the drive for anti/gay ordinances and constitutional amendments, claiming that homosexuals were seeking "special rights." Most notably, religious right forces led the campaign for a 1992 amendment to the Colorado state constitution prohibiting any state laws designed to prevent discrimination on the basis of sexual orientation. (The amendment was passed by the voters but overturned as blatantly unconstitutional by the U.S. Supreme Court in 1996.) At the lowest levels of government, representatives of the religious right have used their positions on school boards, town councils, and other municipal bodies to promote their putatively pro-family agenda by, for instance, censoring school curricula and libraries.

Across the board, political forces aligned with the religious right have forced the gay rights movement to abandon most hopes of further progress and simply fight a rearguard action to preserve the gains of the past few decades. Fed by deep differences rooted in profoundly incompatible worldviews, the culture war between the religious right and the gay movement shows no signs of abating. Occasional attempts at bridge building between the two sides have been notably unsuccessful, and extreme polarization and hostility remain the general rule.

Raymond A. Smith

Bibliography

Berlet, Chip. *Eyes Right! Challenging the Right Wing Backlash*. Boston: South End Press, 1995.

Bull, C., and J. Gallagher. *Perfect Enemies: The Religious Right, the Gay Movement, and the Politics of the 1990s*. New York: Crown, 1996.

Herman, Didi. *The Antigay Agenda*. Chicago: University of Chicago Press, 1997.

Martin, William. *With God on Our Side: The Rise of the Religious Right in America*. New York: Broadway Books, 1996.

See also Bible; Christianity; Religion and Religiosity

Renaissance Neoplatonism

Italian philosopher and translator Marsilio Ficino (1433–1499) is the key figure of Renaissance Neoplatonism. Ficino's influence on early-modern theories on love and sexuality is crucial. His commentaries and interpretations on Plato's dialogues, primarily the *Commentary on Plato's Symposium on Love* (1484) and his *Platonic Theology* (1482), had an incredible impact in France, Spain, and England, where Ficino's *De amore* was known as early as 1500, when a copy of Ficino's Latin *Opera Platonis* was found at Cambridge University. In his commentary on Plato's *Symposium*, Ficino develops a complex theory concerning the relationship among desire, sexuality, and religious contemplation. Analyzing each speech contained in Plato's dialogue, Ficino comes to formulate a complex, and apparently contradictory, philosophical discourse. Following Plato, Ficino states that love is desire for beauty. Sight and hearing are our two major senses. By gazing at and listening to the beloved, the subject may ascend to a profound contemplation with the divinity. Desire, brought about by beauty, has thus a strongly religious connotation. However, for Ficino a man is naturally drawn more toward another man than toward a woman. Man "naturally" desires another man because the male other reminds him of the "idea" of his own inner beauty. If divine contemplation is spurred by the other's beautiful forms, a man cannot help but fall in love with another man. In particular, Ficino strongly defends the so-called Socratic love—the love relationship between a mature man and a young man. In Ficino's philosophical structure sexuality plays a complex role. As he writes in chapter 14 of the sixth speech of the *Commentary*, "Since the reproductive drive of the soul, being without cognition, makes no distinction between the sexes, nevertheless, it is naturally aroused for copulation whenever we judge any body to be

R beautiful; and it often happens that those who associate with males . . . copulate with them." In other words, although any physical encounter is inherently negative because it disturbs the subject in his contemplative ascent toward God, sexuality is unavoidable. Therefore, he who feels more interested in a person of his own gender ends up copulating with him. According to Ficino, male friendship is superior to any other form of union. Two male friends come to exchange their own souls and nurture each other's wisdom. Male friendship is the noblest expression of love.

Ficino's Neoplatonism is one of the central features of Renaissance culture. In Italy innumerable books were written in response to *De amore*, creating a literary genre called *trattati d'amore* (treatises on love), among others Pietro Bembo's *Asolani* (1505), Leo Hebreo's *Dialoghi d'amore* (1501), and Giordano Bruno's *Degli eroici furori* (1585).

Renaissance poetry is molded by Neoplatonic ideas. It suffices to mention Michelangelo's and Shakespeare's sonnets, dominated by homoerotic themes. Theater as well is influenced by Neoplatonism. For instance, in *Erophilomachia* (The Battle between Friendship and Love, 1605) Italian playwright Sforza Oddi depicts male bonding as far more important than heterosexual love. Similar concepts are present in many early-modern plays and tragedies. *Armando Maggi*

Bibliography

Ficino, Marsilio. *Commentary on Plato's Symposium on Love.* J. F. Sears, trans. Woodstock, N.Y.: Spring Publications, 1985.

See also Friendship; Italian Renaissance; Love Poetry, the Petrarchan Tradition; Michelangelo Buonarroti; Plato

Renault, Mary (1905–1983)

Historical novelist Mary Renault was born Eileen Mary Challans into a middle-class London professional family. Her father, Frank Challans, a doctor, and her mother, Mary Clementine Newsome Baxter, fought throughout their long marriage and were not much interested in their eldest daughter. Renault was educated at private schools and St. Hugh's College, Oxford, where she studied English literature, graduating in 1928. She drifted through a series of temporary jobs until 1933, when she entered training as a nurse. While in training she met Julie

Mullard, with whom she established a relationship that was to last until her death. Renault and Mullard both worked as nurses while Renault began to write.

Renault's first novel, *Purposes of Love* (1939), was a critical and popular success. She produced five more contemporary novels, each containing characters unsure of their sexual orientation and/or their place in relation to conventional understandings of gender, including her only lesbian novel, *The Friendly Young Ladies* (1944). Renault continued nursing as well as writing through World War II. After the war, when *Return to Night* (1947) won an MGM prize of $150,000, she and Mullard decided to leave England and emigrate to South Africa, which they did in 1948. Renault's last contemporary work, *The Charioteer* (1953), which focused on a young soldier in an English hospital during the war, was her first gay novel.

With *The Last of the Wine* (1956), she moved on to the Greek novels for which she is best known. Apart from her two studies of Theseus, *The King Must Die* (1958) and *The Bull From the Sea* (1962), her historical fiction generally focused on men in same-sex relationships and/or told the stories of famous male couples. She wrote a trilogy about Alexander the Great, *Fire From Heaven* (1969), *The Persian Boy* (1972), and *Funeral Games* (1981); Socrates and Alcibiades appear in *The Last of the Wine* (1956), Plato and Dion in *The Mask of Apollo* (1966), and Harmodios and Aristogeiton in *The Praise Singer* (1979). Women were necessarily marginal figures in the social worlds she described in the second half of her career.

Renault's Greek novels, based on meticulous research, were international best-sellers. They continue to be popular after her death, although her critical reputation has suffered from the marginalization of historical fiction as well as gay subjects.

Julie Abraham

Bibliography

Abraham, Julie. *Are Girls Necessary?: Lesbian Writing and Modern Histories.* New York: Routledge, 1996.
Sweetman, David. *Mary Renault: A Biography.* New York: Harcourt Brace, 1993.

See also Alexander the Great; Greece; Plato

Resorts and Beaches

Whether offering sun and surf or snow and skiing, those resorts and beaches that are popular with homosexuals each provide some level of opportunity to interact openly in public without fear of negative consequence. This relative safety of space and association is as much an attraction of a locale as its natural setting. Fire Island (New York), Key West (Florida), Provincetown (Massachusetts), South Beach (Florida), Palm Springs (California), Aspen (Colorado), and the Russian River (California) are among the best known of American resort towns and beach communities.

The growth of the American middle class in the latter part of the nineteenth century made it possible for far more people than ever to afford leisure as an escape from work and routine. As an ideal, this meant escaping from the confines and rigid social dictates of the city to the "wilds" of nature. Homosexuals were no different from most other Americans in their desire to vacation away from the rapidly industrializing cities. But because most vacationers still carried with them an ample supply of middle-class morality as cultural baggage, the most popular resorts did not offer homosexuals a true escape.

The initial places that did were a handful of islands and towns geographically farther removed than the destinations to which most vacationers traveled. Often these fairly remote locales, such as Provincetown and Key West, first attracted artists (a number of whom were homosexual) also seeking relief from the spatial and social confines of the city. In each locale, older homes, near secluded beaches or remote countryside were available to rent or buy and renovate, and they were.

While far less secluded, sections of popular city beaches were also (and continue to be) appropriated by homosexuals as places to congregate and socialize. This has been particularly true for working-class homosexuals who could not afford to leave the city on extended vacations.

Homosexual social networks helped spread information by word of mouth about these resorts and beaches, and in turn, homosexuals who visited these sites strengthened their social network by making new contacts and friends. The growing body of gay and lesbian pulp novels in the 1950s and 1960s, followed by the evolution of serious gay and lesbian literature, also popularized these resorts and beaches by often including them as settings for their plots.

Many of these resort and beach towns have developed a prominent community of homosexual residents, and gay and lesbian visitors are recognized as an important contributor to the local economy.

Yet the homosexual residents often have trouble developing community organizations and avenues for association beyond commercial enterprises such as bars and guest houses, which cater to gay and lesbian visitors.

In recent years these resort and beach towns have become home to a growing number of HIV-positive residents, who come presumably seeking a higher quality of life. This in turn has challenged local homosexual communities to establish AIDS service organizations and other support services in geographic locales mostly without any formal social services infrastructure. Alcoholism and drug use are also a problem in places like Key West, South Beach, and Palm Springs, where the emphasis on providing a hedonistic vacation experience for visitors becomes an influence on the resident community's cultural and behavioral norms. *Eugene Patron*

Bibliography

Kolber-Stuart, Billy, and David Alport. *Out & About Gay Travel Guides: USA Resorts and Warm Weather Vacations*. New York: Hyperion, 1997.

Miller, Neil. *In Search of Gay America*. New York: Harper and Row, 1989.

Newton, Esther. *Cherry Grove, Fire Island: Sixty Years in America's First Gay and Lesbian Town*. Boston: Beacon Press. 1993

Rofes, Eric. *Reviving the Tribe: Regenerating Gay Men's Sexuality and Culture in the Ongoing Epidemic*. New York: Harrington Park Press, 1996.

See also Circuit Party Scene; Community Centers; Neighborhoods: Tourism and Travel.

RFSL (Riksförbundet för sexuellt likaberättigande—Swedish Federation for Lesbian and Gay Rights)

RFSL was founded in 1950, originally as the Swedish branch of the Danish Federation for Gays and Lesbians (Forbundet af 1948), by Allan Hellman. Hellman, an engineer by profession, became the symbol of the early organized homosexual rights movement as he was the first person in Sweden to declare publicly that he was homosexual. Because of very strong antigay currents at the time, manifested by two major public scandals, the first ten years of RFSL's existence were filled with political struggle involving the comprehensive writing of petitions in legal and social issues.

During the sixties the emphasis was on consolidating the organization and the social welfare of the members; a wide range of lectures and entertainment was organized. In 1964, the organization for the first time opened its own premises in Stockholm.

Inspired by the Stonewall rebellion in New York in 1969 and the emergence of the gay power movement, a new generation of gay activists joined the RFSL in the early 1970s with the aim of radicalizing the organization and moving it toward becoming an open and updated political movement. The first political marches in Sweden soon followed. The first of the annual gay pride marches in Sweden was organized in Stockholm in 1977. The main political struggle of the RFSL now became to demand the same age of consent for homosexual and heterosexual consenting adults. This symbolic struggle was carried to victory in 1978, when the Swedish parliament approved an equal age of consent of fifteen years.

Mainly owing to the spectacular method used, the occupation of the premises of Socialstyrelsen (National Board of Health and Welfare) in 1979 had profound symbolic implications. The occupation led to the immediate abolition of the listing of homosexuality in Socialstyrelsen's classification of diseases. During the 1970s a number of new local branches of the RFSL were founded.

The 1980s brought about a professionalization of the work of the RFSL, through the new possibility of employing people. In part this was made possible as a side effect of the AIDS epidemic, which made it necessary for cooperation among the state powers, the authorities for the prevention of infection, and the gay community. At the end of the decade the RFSL could also start collecting a subsidy for its strictly political work.

Through the struggle for the domestic partnership law, protracted over several years and finally brought to victory in 1994, the RFSL established its name as a strong and respected lobby organization in the eyes of the national mass media and public opinion. This is said to be one reason why RFSL membership increased considerably by the end of the 1990s. Another explanation was its skill in maintaining the interest of both the mass media and the gay community through constantly refreshing its fields of activities.

In 1998 the RFSL had 5,500 members in twenty-eight local branches, eight local radio stations, one of Sweden's ten most popular Web sites (http://www.rfsl.se), and a widely read national magazine.   *Greger Eman*

Bibliography
Kom Ut no 5. 1990. The Archives of RFSL, Stockholm.

See also Denmark; Domestic Partnership; Gay Liberation; Marches and Parades; Politics, Global; Same-Sex Marriage; Stonewall; Sweden

Rhodes, Cecil John (1853–1902)

British imperialist, southern African politician, mining magnate, and financier, Rhodes was arguably the most powerful figure in southern Africa during the 1880s and 1890s. He built a large personal fortune through his two diamond companies, De Beers Mining Company (founded 1880) and its successor, De Beers Consolidated Mines (founded 1888); his British South Africa Company (founded 1889), which through its concessions claimed the territory subsequently renamed Rhodesia after him; and his gold-mining company, Consolidated Gold Fields of South Africa (founded 1892). Rhodes also served as prime minister of the Cape Colony between 1890 and 1896.

Of Rhodes's homosexual inclinations there can be little doubt, though little direct evidence exists to prove that his male friendships were anything more than platonic. All his close emotional attachments were to men, usually his social or intellectual inferiors. He surrounded himself with male secretaries and servants, many of whom were treated as confidants rather than employees, and who were dubbed his "lambs." The closest of these was Neville Pickering, his secretary from 1881 until his death at age twenty-nine, in October 1886, and with whom he shared a house for four years, enjoying, in the words of a contemporary, an "absolutely lover-like friendship." Others replaced Pickering in Rhodes's affections, though he was never as passionately attached to any of them. He also shared a dwelling with a bachelor surgeon, Leander Starr Jameson, who in the early 1890s looked after Rhodes's interests in Rhodesia, and who led a small force that invaded the Transvaal at the end of 1895. This incident, known as the Jameson Raid, led to Rhodes's downfall as premier of the Cape; some historians have plausibly argued that the emotional bonds between Jameson and Rhodes clouded the latter's political judgment in one of the most notorious incidents that led to the outbreak of the South African War in 1899.

Nick Southey

Bibliography

Rotberg, Robert I. *The Founder: Cecil Rhodes and the Pursuit of Power*. New York: Oxford University Press, 1988.

See also South Africa; Zimbabwe

Richards, Renee (1934–)

Star tennis player, coach, and ophthalmologist, Dr. Renee Richards is the best-known public transsexual, among them Christine Jorgensen, Jan Morris, Caroline Cossey ("Tula"), and Kate Bornstein, who have sparked discussion in the mass media about transsexual and gender identities. Born Richard Raskind in New York City in 1934 and reborn in that same city in 1975 as Renee (literally "reborn") Richards several years after backing out of surgery in Casablanca, Morocco, Richards was exposed as a transsexual while competing in an amateur tennis tournament in La Jolla, California, in 1976. She was politicized by the flood of supportive mail she received in response to the press about her, two-thirds of it from other members of minority groups, as she reports in her memoir, *Second Serve*. Realizing that she was part of a small but growing sexual minority whose rights were not secure and who needed a public advocate, Richards coauthored (with John Ames) the autobiography that was later made into a television movie starring Vanessa Redgrave. It is almost a textbook illustration of the psychoanalytic account of transsexualism, which sanctioned transsexual surgery. But Richards's first action on behalf of transsexuals was her highly publicized battle to compete as a woman in professional tennis, with legal representation from Roy Cohn and his partner. Although she won her case, the result was the kind of paradox associated with transgender: as far as the world of tennis was concerned, she was a woman in North and South America but a man in Europe (where the legal decision was not binding). *Carole-Anne Tyler*

Bibliography

Birrell, Susan, and Cheryl Cole. "Double Fault: Renee Richards and the Construction and Naturalization of Difference." *Sociology of Sport Journal* 7 (1990).

Bornstein, Kate. *Gender Outlaw: On Men, Women, and the Rest of Us*. New York: Routledge, 1995.

Richards, Renee, with John Ames. *Second Serve*. New York: Stein and Day, 1983.

See also Cohn, Roy M.; Jorgensen, Christine; Morris, Jan; Transgender

Riggs, Marlon (1957–1994)

Most famous for his controversial 1988 documentary, *Tongues Untied*, filmmaker Marlon Riggs spent his life giving honest voice to the experiences of black gay men and is noted for work that exists outside the framework of minority voices being mediated by a white privileged gaze. Funded by a National Endowment for the Arts grant, *Tongues Untied* became a central part of the fight for cultural freedom and congressional attempts to micromanage American culture because of the film's forthright depictions of the experiences of black gay men as a subculture marginalized by both the homophobia of the Afro-American community and the racism of the white gay mainstream. *Tongues Untied* broke many conventions of the documentary genre by replacing the invisible omniscient narrator with the first-person experiences of a number of black gay men, including the author himself and his own candid discussion of his HIV-positive status. Senator Jesse Helms (R.-N.C.) lobbied in Congress to end NEA support for Riggs's work, while Christian fundamentalists campaigned unsuccessfully against the 1990 national public television broadcast of *Tongues Untied*. This film went on to win Best Documentary at the Berlin Film Festival.

Born into a Fort Worth, Texas, military family, Riggs moved with his family to Augusta, Georgia, in seventh grade; in both cities he suffered the racism he would examine in his films. Later his family moved to Germany, where he attended high school. Riggs graduated magna cum laude from Harvard University, with a bachelor's degree in history in 1978, and earned a master's degree in journalism from the Graduate School of Journalism at the University of California at Berkeley in 1981. He wrote a large body of essays challenging the identity politics of a white liberal gay mainstream espousing a doctrine of antiracism but making few concrete steps toward realizing racial equality within the gay community. Riggs received numerous fellowships and began teaching in the Graduate School of Journalism at U.C. Berkeley, becoming one of the youngest tenured professors in 1992. He founded *Signifyin' Works* in 1991 to produce educational materials about blacks and was working on *Black Is Black Ain't*, a documentary examining how racist stereotypes are propagated by mass media—a se-

Black activist and filmmaker Marlon Riggs. Photo by Marc Geller.

quel to his 1987 *Ethnic Notions* and 1990 *Color Adjustment*—at the time of his death.

Riggs is remembered for the clarity and truthfulness of his portrayal of racism and homophobia as being both maintained by homo- and heterosexual blacks and whites in a quadrangle of multilayered complicity and co-optation. In his own words, "Silence kills the soul; it diminishes its possibilities to rise and ply and explore. Silence withers what makes you human. The soul shrinks, until it is nothing."   *Matthew Williams*

Bibliography

White, Evelyn C., and Teresa Moore. "Film Maker Marlon Riggs Dies of AIDS." *San Francisco Chronicle*, April 6, 1994, A13.

See also African American Gay Culture Film; Film: New Queer Cinema

Rimbaud, Arthur (1854–1891)

Along with Charles Baudelaire and Stéphane Mallarmé, Arthur Rimbaud is usually considered one of the most influential poets of the second half of the nineteenth century in France, helping to transform modern French poetry and influencing poetry outside of France as well. He has also offered many avant-garde figures or marginally positioned artists and poets a powerful image of a poet in radical revolt against various stifling forces typical of modern societies. Formally speaking, Rimbaud broke with traditions of rhyme structure and syllable count. He mixed registers of language in startling ways; much of his later work was written as prose poems. In a letter many take to be his poetic credo, he claims that the poet's task is to "make oneself a *seer*" (*se faire voyant*), and that this is to be achieved "by a long, immense, carefully thought out *disruption of all the senses*" (*un long, immense et raisonné dérèglement de tous les sens*). Much of his poetry records a quest for extreme forms of experience that violate traditional social concepts of acceptability and disrupt the stability of an individual psyche. Rimbaud was interested in the intensification of sensual (including erotic) experience to the point where that experience might reshape psychic structure, thereby altering political and social forms of subjectivity as well.

In 1870 and 1871, the teenage Rimbaud made numerous attempts to escape his provincial home for Paris. His attempts were complicated by lack of money as well as by the political turmoil of the time. France was suffering defeat and invasion in the Franco-Prussian War (July 1870–January 1871). The spring of 1871 would see the fateful Parisian political uprising known as the Commune, quelled brutally in May 1871. Rimbaud's poems are marked by political sympathy for the radicals of the moment, and literary historians wonder whether he spent time in Paris during the Commune.

Having been in correspondence with a number of Parisian poets, Rimbaud was invited to Paris in September 1871 by the more established poet Paul Verlaine, recently married and ten years older than Rimbaud. Rimbaud and Verlaine began a turbulent, erotic, and sentimental relationship, which included traveling to London and setting up house together there in 1872. They separated and reunited a number of times in 1872 and 1873. In a violent episode in Brussels in July 1873, Verlaine fired a revolver at Rimbaud and wounded him in the wrist. Verlaine would be condemned to two years in prison.

Most of Rimbaud's verse poetry dates from 1870 to 1872, and most people believe *Illuminations* and *Une Saison en enfer* (A Season in Hell, collections of prose poems) to have been composed in 1872 and 1873. Rimbaud himself arranged only for the publication of one of his works, *Une Saison en enfer* (1873) and even in this case, as he apparently didn't pay the printers, the work was not distributed at the time. While this collection of nine prose poems was for a long time thought to be his last poetic writing, some scholars believe some of the prose poems in the collection *Illuminations* might postdate *Une Saison*. An edition of *Illuminations* appeared in 1886, put together by others than Rimbaud. His collected poems, prefaced by Verlaine, appeared only in 1895, after his death. A trio of homoerotic sonnets, called *Les Stupra*, apparently written in collaboration with Verlaine, including the "Sonnet of the Ass Hole," was first published in 1926 in the surrealist journal *Littérature*.

Through his literary writing, Rimbaud remains a poet of youth, an advocate for youthful rebellion, a poet in pursuit of erotic, social, and political liberation. His life from 1874 until his death from cancer at the age of thirty-seven, by contrast, seems resolutely antiliterary, though he left behind a substantial correspondence. During these years he traveled widely in Europe and then around the world. In 1878, he established himself in Egypt and then Ethiopia as a trader of a variety of goods, ultimately of arms. He was forced to return to France in 1891, owing to difficulties with his leg, which had to be amputated because of the cancer to which he succumbed shortly thereafter.   *Michael Lucey*

Bibliography

Michon, Pierre. *Rimbaud le fils*. Paris: Gallimard, 1991.

Rimbaud, Arthur. *Complete Works*. Paul Schmidt, trans. New York: Harper and Row, 1976.

Ross, Kristin. *The Emergence of Social Space: Rimbaud and the Paris Commune*. Foreword by Terry Eagleton. Minneapolis: University of Minnesota Press, 1988.

See also France; French Literature; French Symbolism; Verlaine, Paul

Ritts, Herb (1952–)

Fame came early to Herb Ritts. Before he was out of his twenties, he was one of the best-known fashion photographers, a special favorite with the newer breed of designers who wanted an edgier, pseudo-street look to the photos of their clothes. Celebrities also appreciated his ability to make almost any subject look dramatic and interesting, as opposed to just attractive. Handsome coffee-table books such as

1982's *Notorious* resulted from his multifaceted work in fashion, advertising, and celebrity portraiture, culminating in the best-selling *Men Without Ties*, in which he and Richard Avedon, among others, documented the career of Gianni Versace.

For gay men, the name Ritts will probably evoke his nudes. While they are not the photographer's main focus, he has produced quite a few, both male and female, usually formally posed and glamorously lit in Retro-Neo-Deco style, but the image that probably leaps first to mind when his name is mentioned is only half-naked: *Fred with Tires* is a 1984 photograph that became a runaway hit as a poster.

The photographer deserves the acclaim. Despite the perfection of the model, Ritts's photographic skills are what make the image unforgettable. First, he devotes an inordinate amount of space to the background, creating the surprise of finding Fred's beauty in the midst of all that sludge and grunge. A lesser photographer would have cropped away much of the "empty" background, mistakenly focusing the photo on the man instead of allowing him to be discovered by the viewer. Though the model is wearing too much makeup to be a real grease monkey, Ritts has given him a simple pose—work shoes squarely on the ground, hands hooked into old tires. As a black-and-white composition, the picture is a masterful balancing act between the gleam of Fred's sweat-slicked muscles and the matte black of worn-out rubber. The converging lines of his torso counterpoise the exuberantly diverging lines of his arms and tires, and all of it meets not at his face, which appears to be only the center of the picture, but on the subtly highlighted, intricately detailed, oversized zipper of his crotch. Even Fred's partially bared rump forms a pale crescent pointing toward his groin.

Consequently, underneath the workaday surface, all is seduction; the rounded, soft yet firm forms of the tires, the smears of oil and perspiration, the steadiness with which the model stares directly into the camera, much too intense to be thinking just "You call me, boss?" Then there's the more-than-half-naked body. If his belt were to slip another inch lower, those overalls would drop from his hips, leaving Fred naked from the ankles up. It's a masterful demonstration of the photographer's greatest strength, his ability to take mere surfaces and imbue them with an intensity that makes them unforgettable.

Fred with Tires, like a C. P. Cavafy poem, documents a fleeting moment of male perfection and the

R swelling ache of desire it generates. "I never had you nor, I suppose, will I ever. . . . But we who serve art can sometimes create pleasure that is almost physical." *F. Valentine Hooven III*

Bibliography

Ellenzweig, Allen. *The Homoerotic Photograph: Male Images from Durieu/Delacroix to Mapplethorpe.* New York: Columbia University Press, 1992.

Ritts, Herb. *Notorious.* Boston: Little, Brown, 1992.

Waugh, Thomas. *Hard to Imagine.* New York: Columbia University Press, 1996.

See also Fashion; Photography; Versace, Gianni

Rochester, John Wilmot, Earl of (1647–1680)

Rochester is a figure of sexual carnival who transgressed as brilliantly in letters as in life. The only issue of a Cavalier father and Puritan mother, he came of age following Charles II's restoration to the English throne, the emptiness behind whose rich court facade Rochester delighted in satirically skewering both by his actions and in his poems. A portrait of him crowning a monkey (rather than a bust of Aristotle or Virgil, as a philosopher or man of letters was traditionally depicted doing) demonstrates iconographically his genius for satiric self-fashioning and cultural deconstruction, a genius applied in numerous recorded events. Disguised as a London merchant, he lived for several days in bourgeois society, where he joined in reviling the licentious behavior of the court, especially his own. On another occasion he dressed as a physician newly arrived in town who, as one memoirist of the period reports, achieved great success in the treatment of women's venereal diseases. So sharp was his sense of the theatrical illusion of social life that through his coaching, his mistress, Elizabeth Barry, became one of the premier stage actresses of the age, and he himself earned dramatization as Dorimant in his friend George Etherege's *Man of Mode.* Even his 1680 deathbed repentance, made famous in a narrative published by Gilbert Burnet, later bishop of Salisbury, is liable to have been a piece of theater.

Rochester's poetry, notes A. J. Smith, projects a world "animated by sex but racked by metaphysical anxiety" (208); Rochester, says Smith, manifests a "radical questioning of an existence which we can never pin down long enough to call our own." Poems like "A Ramble in St. James's Park," "Signior Dildo," and "Mistress Knight's Advice to the Duchess of Cleveland in Distress for a Prick" undercut Elizabethan and Cavalier poets' idealization of courtly mistresses, revealing women to be animated by their insatiable desire for sexual satisfaction, more concerned with reputation than hygiene. Conversely, in poems like "The Imperfect Enjoyment" and "The Disabled Debauchee," he reveals men—including, in the notorious "Verses for which he was Banished," the king himself—to be led by "the savory scent of salt-swoln cunt," but often incapable of sustaining an erection. People in his world are driven to bestial excess by their hunger for sensation because, as Barbara Everett notes, they fear that "nothing" lies at the heart of human existence. The hauntingly beautiful lyric "Love and Life" elegizes what Rochester remarks in a letter to his wife is the great misfortune of human existence, that there is "so great a disproportion t'wixt our desires and what . . . has [been] ordained to content them."

The poetry and a play attributed to him celebrate the sexual polymorphous perverse. "Love a woman!" exclaims the exasperated speaker of the lyric of that title, who cannot justify "Drudg[ing]in fair Aurelia's womb" when "There's a sweet soft page, of mine, / Does the trick worth forty wenches." Likewise, "The Disabled Debauchee" reminds his mistress of the night that, striving to enjoy "the well-looked [handsome] link-boy,"

> . . . the best kiss was the deciding lot:
> Whether the boy fucked you, or I the boy.

And in *Sodom, or the Quintessence of Debauchery,* a play in which Rochester had a major hand if he was not the primary author, King Bolloxinion's kingdom erupts into a sodomical sexual carnival after he decrees vaginal intercourse to be illegal. The king's anal nihilism reverses the heterosexual creationism of the biblical book of Genesis, Bolloxinion persevering in it despite signs of impending divine chastisement because homosexual sodomy provides the strongest physical sensation possible, a male's best escape from the threat of "nothing."

If not a direct influence on Lord Byron or Joe Orton, Rochester is—as the first great English-language creator of sexual carnival—their cultural progenitor, defining in his work and his life a zone of ambivalent sexual identity that undercuts the forces of presumptive morality.

Raymond-Jean Frontain

Bibliography

Everett, Barbara. "The Sense of Nothing." In *Spirit of Wit: Reconsiderations of Rochester*. Jeremy Treglown, ed. Hamden, Conn.: Archon Books, 1982, 1–41.

Frontain, Raymond-Jean. "Bakhtinian Grotesque Realism and the Subversion of Biblical Authority in Rochester's *Sodom*." *Journal of Homosexuality* 33, no. 3–4 (1997): 71–95.

Rochester, John Wilmot, Earl of. *Complete Poems and Plays*. Paddy Lyons, ed. and intro. London: Dent, 1993.

Smith, A. J. *Metaphysical Wit*. Cambridge: Cambridge University Press, 1991.

Thormählen, Marianne. *Rochester: The Poems in Context*. Cambridge: Cambridge University Press, 1993.

Weber, Harold. " 'Drudging in Fair Aurelia's Womb': Constructing Homosexual Economies in Rochester's Poetry." *The Eighteenth Century: Theory and Interpretation* 33 (1992): 99–117.

See also Byron, George Gordon, Lord; English Literature; Libertine and Libertinism; Orton, Joe

Rodríguez Matos, Carlos A. (1949–)

Puerto Rican poet Carlos Rodríguez Matos, who lives in New Jersey, has published two collections of poetry, *Matacán* (1982) and *Llama de amor vivita, Jarchas* (Flame of Living Love. Jarchya, 1988), as well as poems in various anthologies. A serious researcher, Rodríguez Matos has also published several articles of literary criticism and is the author of *El narrador pícaro: Guzmán de Alfarache* (The Picaresque Narrator: Guzmán de Alfarache, 1985). He is the editor of *Simposio: Clemente Soto Vélez* (Symposium on Clemente Soto Vélez, 1990) and *POESÍdA: An Anthology of AIDS Poetry from the United States, Latin America and Spain* (1995). Since 1979, he has been a professor of Spanish and Spanish literature in the Department of Modern Languages at Seton Hall University (South Orange, New Jersey).

For Rodríguez Matos, the impact of societal repression on homosexuality is revealed in the inevitable guilt that accompanies the act of writing. To deal with this repression, in *Matacán* he develops several textual strategies. One of them is the creation of an Arcadian ideal that permits the free expression of same-sex love. In these beautiful poems, the Puerto Rican landscape is part of an offering of gifts included in the symbolic rituals for the Arcadian who seeks to overcome obstacles to liberate the beloved. From this ideal space, the prejudices of a homophobic society are challenged and subverted. The use of a ludic and humoristic tone challenges the conventions of poetry by depriving it of its traditional solemnity.

In *Llama de amor*, the poetic space is created through the image of a house that gives form to the intimate values of an interior space. These poems thus convey a transcendental preoccupation: how to live in a society that does not allow same-sex love, developing the power of creativity, in particular, that of writing.

The eradication of a false life in which society reduces homosexuals to a marginal existence, and its substitution for one in which the erotic will be experienced as a transforming desire that leads to freedom, is the objective of Rodríguez Matos's work.

Ana Sierra

Bibliography

Fone, Byrne R. S. "This Other Eden: Arcadia and the Homosexual Imagination." In *Essays on Gay Literature*. Stuart Kellog, ed. New York: Harrington Park Press, 1983.

Rodríguez Matos, Carlos A. *POESÍdA: An Anthology of AIDS Poetry from the United States, Latin America and Spain*. New York: Ollantay Press, 1995.

———. "To Be Gay, Puerto Rican, and a Poet." *ANQ* 10, no. 3 (Summer 1997).

See also Love Poetry, the Petrarchan Tradition; Ramos Otero, Manuel

Röhm, Ernst (1887–1934)

The German Social Democrat Party (SPD) started a monthlong campaign in April 1931 against famous homosexual members of the National Socialist Democratic Labor Party (NSDAP) and the Sturmabteilung (SA). Ernst Röhm, the reestablished leader of the SA, was one of the most renowned Nazis to be accused of being a homosexual. Born in Munich, Röhm pursued a military career early in life and received honors in World War I. He met Adolf Hitler in 1919 and became one of his closest political companions. With the SA, Röhm founded a paramilitary organization that helped enable Hitler to achieve political power in Germany. In so doing, however, he turned increasingly into a tactical problem for Hitler. Röhm not only tried to incorporate the German army (Reichswehr) into the SA, thus centralizing all military power in the SA, but also lived openly as a homosexual. Hitler decided to move against Röhm and the SA to eliminate their threat to his power. On the evening of June 30, 1934, the entire SA elite and many of Hitler's other political enemies were murdered. Röhm was imprisoned and executed on July 1. After Röhm's execution, Hitler explained that he needed to "cleanse" the German nation of the homosexual SA leader and his companions. He also fabricated a lie about an intended rebellion by the SA. Röhm's elimination enhanced Hitler's power and provided him with the leverage he sought to control the Reichswehr. For homosexuals in Germany, the Röhm execution meant the beginning of an unrestricted hunt that was two years later further supported by a law that led to imprisonment in concentration camps and death for thousands of gay men. *Jens Richard Giersdorf*

Bibliography

Plant, Richard. *Rosa Winkel*. Frankfurt: Campus Verlag, 1991.

Stümke, Hans-Georg, and Rudi Finkler. *Rosa Winkel, Rosa Listen: Homosexuelle und 'Gesundes Volksempfinden' von Auschwitz bis heute*. Reinbeck, Germany: Rowohlt, 1981.

See also Germany; Nazism and the Holocaust; Paragraph 175

Rolfe, Frederick William ("Baron Corvo") (1860–1913)

Frederick William Serafino Austin Lewis Mary Rolfe, who later used the pseudonym "Baron Corvo," was an eccentric figure of the English decadent movement, known for his ornate and mannered style, his obsession with the Catholic priesthood and the beauty of adolescent males, and his tendency to make enemies out of almost every friend and benefactor. Called by W. H. Auden a "homosexual paranoid," Rolfe is perhaps better known for his life, artfully depicted in A. J. A. Symons's *The Quest for Corvo*, than for his literary work, which includes poetry, novels, short fiction, and journalism.

Rolfe was born in Cheapside, London, the eldest of five sons in a poor and strict Protestant family. After a profound religious experience at about age fourteen, Rolfe left school and home in 1875 to spend ten years working as a schoolmaster. In 1885 he converted to Roman Catholicism and sought to enter the priesthood. Twice he was dismissed from seminaries, first from St. Mary's College at Oscott, near Birmingham, in 1888, and later from Scots College in Rome. His desire to become a priest, as well as his resentment and anger over his rejection by the church, colored much of his later writing. He began referring to himself as Fr. Rolfe, a disingenuous abbreviation for "Frederick," not "Father."

After his expulsion from Scots College in 1890, Rolfe lived briefly in Italy as the guest of an Englishwoman, Duchess Sforza-Cesarini, who he claimed granted him the (landless) title of Baron Corvo. Moving back to England, first to Christchurch then London, he tried several occupations—painting (including church murals), photography, furniture design, journalism, teaching, tutoring—and often lived beyond his means, scrounging from friends and acquaintances as he would throughout his life. In 1895 and 1896, Rolfe published six stories in John Lane's *Yellow Book*, which he later published as *Stories Toto Told Me* (1898), with additional stories in *In His Own Image* (1901). These retold legends of saints are narrated by Toto, a peasant boy Rolfe had befriended and photographed in Italy.

In his painting, photography, and poetry, Rolfe took a special interest in boy saints and boys swimming. Bathing or swimming boys became a popular theme in late Victorian homoerotic art, and Rolfe was a friend of the Uranian poets Charles Kains-Jackson and John Gambril Nicholson. Rolfe's first book was *Tarcissus: The Boy Martyr of Rome* (1880), a long poem that fuses the Uranian romantic worship of adolescence with religious devotion. He published "Ballade of Boys Bathing" in the *Art Review* in 1890 (published in book form in 1972). Although he took a vow of celibacy in connection with his hopeless dreams of priesthood, the romance of adolescent boys seems a fantasy writ large in his art. In the summer of 1908, Rolfe traveled to Venice, where he would remain, sometimes homeless, often living on the money of others, until his death in 1913. There the gondolieri replaced bathing boys in his romantic fantasies, and from there, in 1910, he wrote a series of letters to Charles Mason Fox, later published as *The Venice Letters* (1974), which made clear his sexual and romantic attraction to young men.

Among his other works, Rolfe published a noted historical study, *Chronicles of the House of*

Borgia (1901), and a historical novel, Don *Targuinio* (1905). His two most significant novels were fictionalized autobiographical fantasies, *Hadrian the Seventh* (1904) and *The Desire and Pursuit of the Whole* (1934). Rolfe imagined in Hadrian a failed priest named George Rose not only readmitted to the priesthood but elected pope, then blackmailed by a rejected female suitor and eventually assassinated by a socialist agitator. In the posthumously published *The Desire and Pursuit of the Whole*, Rolfe tells the story of Nicholas Crabbe, a writer living a miserable existence in Venice who falls in love with his androgynous servant, Zildo. An emphatically boyish girl, Zildo-turned-Zilda saves Crabbe's life and fortune at the end, and he falls in love with her—transforming this tale of homoerotic romance and penniless existence into a fantasy with a heterosexual and wealthy conclusion. *Ed Madden*

Bibliography

Auden, W. H. "Foreword." In *The Desire and Pursuit of the Whole*. Frederick Rolfe. New York: New Directions, 1953, v–ix.

Benkovitz, Miriam J. *Frederick Rolfe, Baron Corvo: A Biography*. New York: Putnam, 1977.

Gilsdorf, Jeanette W., and Nicholas A. Salerno. "Frederick W. Rolfe, Baron Corvo: An Annotated Bibliography of Writings about Him." *English Literature in Transition* 23 (1980): 3–83.

Reade, Brian, ed. *Sexual Heretics: Male Homosexuality in English Literature from 1850–1900*. New York: Coward-McCann, 1970.

Symons, A. J. A. *Quest for Corvo: An Experiment in Biography*. 1934. Harmondsworth, U.K.: Penguin, 1966.

Weeks, Donald. *Corvo*. London: Michael Joseph, 1971.

Woolf, Cecil. *A Bibliography of Frederick Rolfe, Baron Corvo*. London: Rupert Hart-Davis, 1957. Revised and enlarged edition, 1972.

Woolf, Cecil, and Brocard Sewell, eds. *New Quests for Corvo: A Collection of Essays by Various Hands*. London: Icon, 1961.

See also Auden, W. H.; Decadence; Fiction; Italy; Papacy; Photography; Uranianism

Rome, Ancient

The vocabulary of Roman male same-sex sexual relationships contains many Greek loan words that suggest that "Greek love," along with various other vices, was imported into Rome by returning armies of conquest. That the Greeks exported same-sex sexual activity abroad is as credible and misguided as the notion that the Dorians "exported" their mode of loving to the rest of Greece.

By the late republic, Rome was the largest Greek city in the world. The process of Hellenization, begun in the third century B.C.E., had extended to art, literature, religion, dress, and language, especially among the upper classes, where it was considered highly fashionable to litter one's speech with Greek loan words, rather as French was the European language of intellectual fashion in the eighteenth century. The well-educated writers of Roman literature, almost exclusively male and from either the patrician or equestrian classes, were steeped in Greek literature and chose to imitate or at least advertise their knowledge of it in every way possible.

One such author was the love poet Catullus (c.84–54 B.C.E.), whose passionate love poetry to his mistress, Lesbia, and to his boyfriend, Juventius, seems a subtle blending of the tradition of Greek love poetry with the freshness of real-life affairs.

Whether Lesbia was really the pseudonym for Clodia Metellia, a femme fatale from the highest circles, and whether Juventius really existed, is of marginal interest. What is interesting is that Catullus portrays himself as capable of sexual passion for both sexes (in common with other poets, such as Tibullus and Martial), yet at the same time he uses highly derogatory Greek loan words for the man in a same-sex relationship who allows himself to be anally penetrated. Julius Caesar, whom the muckraking palace chronicler Suetonius regarded as "every woman's husband and every man's wife," is lambasted by Catullus with the insults *cinaedus* and *pathicus*, both of which mean that he was buggered, although there is evidence to suggest that *cinaedus* could be applied to both penetrator and penetrated. The greatest insult that Catullus can muster for two *cinaedi* is "*pedicabo . . . vos et irrumabo*," meaning "I shall sodomize you and make you suck my cock" (Poem 16.1). In fact, Catullus uses *irrumator* (cocksucker) to tarnish the reputation of his tightfisted boss, while serving in the province of Bithynia (Poem 10.12).

In common with attitudes to male same-sex sexual relationships in ancient Egypt and ancient Greece, Roman attitudes are also inextricably linked with power relations and concepts of gender. A real man can happily penetrate either sex, but when he allows himself to be passive, submissive, and penetrated, he transgresses gender and power boundaries, thereby associating himself with the unmasculine categories of women, slaves, and perhaps the subculture of the *cinaedi* themselves. It is unclear whether such a subculture, comprising transvestite, castrated priests of foreign cults, and bathhouse/brothel pathics, actually existed. The characters in Petronius's *Satyricon* might reflect the sort of real-life *cinaedi*, who presumably frequented the House of Jupiter and Ganymede at Ostia Antica, where homoerotic wall painting suggests the existence of a "gay" hotel or brothel. Depictions of scenes of male same-sex lovemaking on Arretine pottery and on the lovely silver Warren cup from the Augustan period imply that Romans from a variety of classes bought and used vessels that resonated with their fantasies or with real-life situations. If such a subculture of *cinaedi* existed, it might have been dangerous for free Roman citizens to belong to or be associated with it. The controversial Scantinian law (the *lex Scantinia*), the text of which does not survive, may well have criminalized passive "homosexuality" by free men, as Richlin has claimed (570), but was clearly infrequently used, as it is first mentioned in 50 B.C.E. by Caelius and is thereafter alluded to by the poet Juvenal more than a century later; more significantly, the crime of *stuprum* included not only adultery but also the rape of a freeborn youth and perhaps even the penetration of a freeborn male with or without his permission.

Catullus Juventius and Tibullus Marathus are both probably examples of *pueri delicati* (long-haired, pretty boy slaves), whose short-lived beauty and mercenary wiles seem to have resulted in brief, intense relationships, without commitment or the pressure of sociocultural taboos surrounding the position of the younger partner (as was the case in classical Athens). Such taboos, of course, disappear when the younger partner is neither a citizen nor in fact, technically, a human being (slaves were things, *res*, under Roman law).

The position of women in Roman society and changing attitudes toward marriage during the imperial period seem to have affected Roman attitudes toward male same-sex sexual relationships. During the late republic, memorable Hellenistic role models improved educational opportunities for upper-class women, and the political influence of many of these women behind the scenes (for women were still, legally, voteless minors) resulted in the development of the respected and formidable matrona Romana. Roman love poets of the late republic and early empire extol the learned mistress at whose feet they grovel.

Catullus attempts to define a real love relationship with a woman outside the confines of the loveless arranged marriage. The change in the political system during the empire seems to have placed less importance on arranged marriages, as there was then not much point in making politically advantageous marriages in a system in which there was little political mobility for anyone outside the imperial circle. Consequently, the institution of marriage became characterized more by choice and love, rather than the reverse.

In an ancient society in which the lot of women is generally ameliorated, as it was in particular by the "right of three children," which freed Roman women with three free-born children from the necessity of male guardianship, and in which marriage for love becomes more and more of a possibility, the likelihood of same-sex relationships of the classical Athenian kind decreases. Furthermore, the development of the concepts of reciprocity and fidelity within the marriage relationship, especially during the late imperial and early Christian periods, tended to result in the contrasting construction of male same-sex relationships as increasingly hierarchical and fruitless, as the example of the emperor Hadrian's obsession with the young Antinous suggests.   *Michael Lambert*

Bibliography

Foucault, Michel. *The Care of the Self. The History of Sexuality*. Vol. 3. New York: Random House, 1986.

Richlin, Amy. "Not Before Homosexuality: The Materiality of the Cinaedus and the Roman Law Against Love Between Men." *Journal of the History of Sexuality* 3, no. 4. 523–573.

See also Egypt, Ancient; Etruscans; Greece, Hadrian; Italy; Petronius

Rorem, Ned (1923–)

Ned Rorem was the first and has remained the best known of openly homosexual American composers, though the music of other gay American composers who were not openly gay in their own lifetimes (e.g., Aaron Copland, Virgil Thomson, Leonard Bernstein) is more widely known, and the music of some composers, such as Lou Harrison and David Diamond, who were openly gay but not as well known, has garnered more consistent critical acclaim. Despite winning a Pulitzer Prize and a Grammy for his compositions, being declared by *Time* magazine to be "since the death of Poulenc . . . the world's greatest composer of art song," and notwithstanding the commissioning of his pieces by some of the country's leading orchestras and other musical institutions, Rorem's music, heavily influenced by twentieth-century French, Russian, and American masters, has not sustained the popularity, critical stature, and influence that his writing has. The author of many books, mostly journals and essay collections, Rorem may be thought of as succeeding Virgil Thomson as perhaps the premier commentator on musical culture of his generation and communities.

Rorem was born in Richmond, Indiana, formally and self-educated in America, France, and Morocco, and has lived much of his life in New York City and Nantucket with his life partner, composer and choir director James Holmes. Much of Rorem's output and recognition has been in the realm of song, and it was for his achievements in that realm that he was awarded a Pulitzer. But he has also written an array of symphonies, concerti, other orchestral pieces, and a number of one-act or otherwise small-scale operas (Rorem appropriately resents the use of the subtly belittling characterization of these works as somehow not "full-length"). Of these, *Miss Julie*, recently revised, continues to assert its place as a work of singular character and resonance.

Although Rorem was a pioneering and heroic figure of the post-Stonewall gay liberation movement in America, publicly standing up to bigoted individuals and institutions when virtually no one else in the world of serious music was, his characteristic scrappiness, so unwaveringly democratic, likewise extends to the gay movement and its values. Rorem is fond of observing that he has had a much more difficult journey as a contemporary composer and artist in America than as a gay man, and that homosexuality is no more interesting, per se, than heterosexuality. Beyond the exigencies of the gay liberation movement, which he respects, he views recent efforts of gay and lesbian studies to establish subcultural differentiation and specificity as misguided in the realm of music, which he sees as an art form that should transcend such approaches.

Lawrence D. Mass

Bibliography

Mass, Lawrence D. "Homosexuality, Music and Opera: A Conversation With Ned Rorem." In *Queering the Pitch: The New Gay and Lesbian Musicology*. Philip Brett, Elizabeth Wood, and Gary Thomas, eds. New York: Routledge, 1994, 85–112.

Rorem, Ned. *Dear Paul, Dear Ned: The Correspondence of Paul Bowles and Ned Rorem*. New York: Elysium, 1997.

———. *Knowing When to Stop: A Memoir*. New York: Simon and Schuster, 1994.

———. *The Nantucket Diary*. San Francisco: North Point Press, 1987.

———. *The Paris and New York Diaries of Ned Rorem: 1951–1961*. San Francisco: North Point Press, 1983.

See also Bernstein, Leonard; Copland, Aaron; Gay American Composers; Harrison, Lou; Poulenc, Francis; Thomson, Virgil

Rosa von Praunheim (1942–)

Openly gay enfant terrible of the New German Cinema, film director Rosa von Praunheim was born Holger Mischwitzky in Riga. He grew up in West Berlin and in the Praunheim district of Frankfurt. Rosa pursued training as a painter but became interested in theater and filmmaking as a young man. When he realized he was gay, he assumed his trademark gender-fuck name, Rosa, for his favorite color (pink) and Praunheim after the neighborhood in which he had lived. The drag name belies his typically hypermasculine black leather dress. The mix of camp, self-irony, and seriousness is the signature of his work.

Rosa's first notable success, *Bettwurst* (1970), was immediately eclipsed by one of the seminal films of New German Cinema, *Nicht der Homosexuelle ist pervers, sondern die Situation in der er lebt* (*The Homosexual Is Not Perverse, But Rather the Situation in Which He Lives*, also 1970). Such highly controversial work highlighted Rosa's cinematic roots in American underground film and his role as a founding auteur director of the New German Cinema. The film was originally made for German TV and, despite great resistance, eventually aired nationwide in 1970, except in Bavaria, where broadcast was blacked out.

The pseudodocumentary film tells the story of a young man from the provinces who comes out in Berlin gay subculture, encounters a catalog of gay stereotypes along the way, and, the film implies, ultimately finds salvation when he joins a gay commune whose members teach him to publicly acknowledge his homosexuality and to value his

R

personal worth by realizing that the *real* problem is socially sanctioned homophobia. During the production of this film Rosa was unaware of the gay liberation movement developing in the United States at the same time. When the film was originally released for general distribution, it played in art movie houses and Rosa required that he or another member of the film production crew be present to answer questions and engage discussion. This led directly to the establishment of an organized *schwulenemanzipatorisch* (gay liberationist) movement in West Germany in the early 1970s.

Despite growing resistance by conservative gays in Germany to Rosa's self-critical analyses, he has remained faithful to his social and political values. His films place minorities (gays, women, foreigners) or eccentric individuals at the story's center to expose reigning middle-class conventions and show how they contribute to social oppression. Calling his own approach "dilettante," Rosa relies on camp, bombast, and parody to make serious socially critical observations in documentary and pseudo-documentary films.

Many, but certainly not all, of Rosa's films document gay social history. *Armee der Liebenden, oder Aufstand der Perversen* (Army of Lovers, or Revolt of the Perverts, 1975) documents the gay movement in 1970s America. *Ein Virus Kennt Keine Moral* (A Virus Knows No Morals, 1985) is a scathing satire of AIDS hysteria, a pseudodocumentary set in West Germany. Two later noted AIDS films, *Positive* (1990) and *Silence = Death* (1990), capture AIDS activism in New York City. *Ich bin meine eigene Frau* (I Am My Own Woman, 1993) and *Transgender Menace* (1995) foreground gender radicals. The autobiographical parody *Neurosia* (1995) finds everyone trying to murder Rosa.

Les Wright

Bibliography

Bryan, Bruce. "Rosa von Praunheim in Theory and Practice." *CineAction!* 9 (Summer 1987): 25–31.
Rosa von Praunheim (Reihe Film 30). Munich: Carl Hanser Verlag, 1984.

See also Film; Film: New Queer Cinema; Germany

Rousseve, David (1961–)

The choreography of U.S. dancer and choreographer David Rousseve is frequently charged with passion and a commitment to social themes, like racism, the AIDS epidemic, and women's issues. He draws on his experience as a gay black man in making his often autobiographical work. Rousseve has commented that the more he delves into his cultural legacy as an African American and the struggle against racism, the more intersections he has found with the legacy of gay culture. Finding those points of intersection has been critical for Rousseve in his battle against homophobia within the African American community. A postmodernist, Rousseve uses a movement vocabulary for his dance company, REALITY, that includes his African American roots, street and pop culture, and a robust physicality. His dances frequently incorporate spoken text, sometimes in the form of complete stories, sometimes as fragments, sometimes for rhythmic accompaniment. In his critically acclaimed *Urban Scenes/Creole Dreams* (1992), Rousseve entwines the contemporary experience of AIDS with an old woman's account of love thwarted by racism. By bringing together the stories his grandmother told him about her youth as a sharecropper and his own stories as an urban youth, Rousseve finds recurring themes of love and desperation, discovering moments of kindness in the midst of alienation. While his topics are challenging, Rousseve does not wallow in despair, as he tempers his stories with humor and irony. However personal his dances are in plumbing his own past as source material, his stories resonate with our own, touching what Rousseve considers universal issues of the heart. *Maura Keefe*

Bibliography

Sadownick, Doug. "Clash Consciousness." *Advocate,* August 27, 1991.

See also African American Gay Culture; Dance and AIDS

Rudoph, Paul (1918–1997)

Paul Rudolph belonged to the brilliant postwar generation of American designers (including his friend and rival Philip Johnson) that wiped historical styles out of American practice and naturalized functionalist modernism in the United States. Rudolph's unique contribution was to demonstrate how modernist forms could express drama, power, and personal emotion. The Kentucky native received graduate training at Harvard University in the 1940s under the leading German émigré modernist in

America, Walter Gropius. Unlike Gropius, Rudolph insisted that architecture was an art form as much as (or more than) the making of useful buildings. Beginning in the 1950s, and especially in his Art and Architecture Building at Yale University (1963), Rudolph turned modernism's functionalist method into experiments with strong, rough forms and complex, layered spaces. Rudolph headed Yale's architecture school in the 1960s and was considered a leader of the so-called New Brutalist cadre of modernists. However, most of his post-1970 work was in Asia, as American architects distanced themselves from the uncompromising, heroically scaled vision of modernism that Rudolph espoused.

As an artist, Rudolph emphasized how space and form can please and excite the senses. He once said that he was concerned above all with the "psychology of space, both interior and exterior." Rudolph's spaces are pinwheeling, often ambiguous in their scale and depth cues, and shaped by exaggeratedly powerful walls with dramatic effects of light and shadow. His New York penthouse (1976–1997) was an ongoing experiment in the creation of gleaming abstract spaces in dizzying horizontal and vertical layers. But Rudolph's major concern after 1970 was to realize the play of form and space at the scale of the city itself. In complexes like the Burroughs Wellcome headquarters in North Carolina (1982) and his many commercial projects in Southeast Asia, especially the Concourse, Singapore (1970–1994), Rudolph provocatively related the scale of the body to the scaleless forms of skyscrapers, highways, and high-tech engineering. He showed how modernist architects could embrace cities as they really were, in all their messy vitality, without trying to impose a purified utopian grid on them.

Rudolph's work has suggestive but ambiguous implications for an architecture of the gay body. Critics have described his style in terms that suggest exaggerated masculinity: "heroic," "aggressive," "arrogant." His devotion to architecture as an expressive art was labeled "camp" in the 1960s for its emotionalism, at a time when the concept of camp was implicitly understood to refer to homosexuals. A more sympathetic critic, Joseph Giovannini, called Rudolph's penthouse, with its spectacular but unreadable plays of transparency and reflection, "a window onto the architect's subconscious." A private and intensely professional figure, Rudolph resisted seeing his work discussed in a gay context. His strongest legacy is his insistence on the architect's freedom to express the complexity and dynamism of human experience, unfettered by rules and patterns. As Rudolph said of his work in 1966, the architect must "celebrate the differences in our life, not nullify them."   *M. David Samson*

Bibliography

Moholy-Nagy, Sybil. *The Architecture of Paul Rudolph.* New York: Praeger, 1970.
Schmertz, Mildred. "Resolutely Modernist." *Architectural Record* 177, no. 1 (January 1979).

See also Architecture; Camp; Israel, Frank

Russia

Medieval Russia was apparently very tolerant of homosexuality. There is evidence of homosexual love in some of the lives of the saints from Kievan Rus dating to the eleventh century. Homosexual acts were treated as a sin by the Orthodox Church, but there were no legal sanctions against them at the time, and even churchmen seemed perturbed by homosexuality only in the monasteries. Foreign visitors to Muscovite Russia in the sixteenth and seventeenth centuries repeatedly express their amazement at the open displays of homosexual affection among men of every class. Sigismund von Heberstein, Adam Olearius, Juraj Krizhanich, and George Turberville all write about the prevalence of homosexuality in Russia in their travel and memoir literature. Nineteenth-century historian Sergey Soloviev writes that "nowhere, either in the Orient or in the West, was this vile, unnatural sin taken as lightly as in Russia."

The first laws against homosexual acts appeared in the eighteenth century, during the reign of Peter the Great but only in military statutes that applied exclusively to soldiers. Not until 1832 did the criminal code include Article 995, which made *muzhelozhstvo* (men lying with men, which the courts interpreted as anal intercourse) a criminal act punishable by exile to Siberia for up to five years. Even so, the legislation was applied only rarely, especially among the upper classes. Many prominent intellectuals of the nineteenth century led a relatively open homosexual or bisexual life. Among these were memoirist Philip Vigel, explorer Nikolai Przhevalsky, critic Konstantin Leontiev, and composer Pyotr Tchaikovsky.

The turn of the century saw a relaxation of the laws and a corresponding increase in tolerance and

Russian activist Roman Kalinin being interviewed by the Baltic press, 1991. Photo by Marc Geller.

visibility. In 1903 Vladimir Nabokov, father of the writer and a founder of the Constitutional Democrat Party, published an article on the legal status of homosexuals in Russia in which he argued that the state should not interfere in private sexual relationships. The period between the revolutions of 1905 and 1917 was the Silver Age in Russian literature but something of a golden age for Russian homosexuals. Many important figures led openly gay lives, including several members of the imperial court. Sergey Diaghilev and many of the members of the World of Art movement and the Russian ballet were gay. In 1906 Mikhail Kuzmin published his semiautobiographical coming-out novel *Wings*, which became the talk of literary circles in Russia.

Scholars disagree about the effect of the Russian Revolution on homosexual rights. Some argue that the Soviets were at the forefront of humanity in decriminalizing gay sex; others that the Bolshevik asceticism and distaste for sexuality of any kind set the movement back. In fact, the revolution of 1917 did away with the entire criminal code, and the new Russian criminal codes of 1922 and 1926 eliminated the offense of *muzhelozhstvo* from the law. Unfortunately, decriminalization in the early Soviet period did not mean an end to persecution. The modern So-

viet fervor for science meant that homosexuality was now treated as a subject for medical and psychiatric discourse, an illness to be treated and cured. Furthermore, in the popular mind, homosexuality was still associated with bourgeois and aristocratic values, with the prerevolutionary bohemian elite.

The sexual liberation that accompanied the revolution was short-lived. The egalitarian and pro-women policies that had liberalized divorce and marriage laws and promoted abortion gave way by the early 1930s to Stalinist pro-family policies. It was in this context that the Soviet Union recriminalized homosexuality in a decree signed in late 1933. As an article by writer Maxim Gorky demonstrates, it was also a context in which homosexuality was connected with Nazism at a time when German-Soviet relations were strained; Gorky writes, "Eradicate homosexuals and fascism will disappear." Of course, the Nazis themselves criminalized homosexuality only a year later.

The new article 121, which punished *muzhelozhstvo* with imprisonment for up to five years, was followed by raids and arrests at the height of the Stalinist terror. The numbers of men arrested is not known, but by the 1980s there were about one thousand every year. The Soviet Union had the largest population of incarcerated men in the world, and given the importance of prison culture for Soviet culture as a whole, it is likely that prison homosexuality played a part in forming Soviet gay culture. In Soviet prisons a class of men called *opushchennye* (degraded) were required to fulfill the sexual needs of the rest. On the one hand, they were at the lowest rung of the social ladder, but they were sometimes protected by their lovers. Not only men charged with article 121 were *opushchennye*: any prisoner could be degraded by ritualized rape—for losing at cards, over an insult, or even because his beauty made him an attractive sex object.

Article 121 was often used throughout the Soviet period to extend prison sentences and to control dissidents. Among those imprisoned were film director Sergey Paradjanov and poet Gennady Trifonov. Threat of prosecution was also used to blackmail homosexuals into informing for the police and the KGB. Accordingly, gay men kept a low profile during the Soviet period, many restricting their gay activities to small circles of proven friends. Still, there were public cruising areas in the larger cities and one or two bars known to be popular with gay men, though the threat of arrest or blackmail always loomed. Another threat by the 1980s was the gangs of gay bashers who robbed and beat gay men, often with the encouragement of the police. They knew that if they were brought to court, their victims would be put in jail.

In 1984 a handful of gay men in Leningrad attempted to form the first organization of gay men. They were quickly hounded into submission by the KGB. It was only with Mikhail Gorbachev's *glasnost* that such an organization could come into existence, in 1989–1990. The Moscow Gay and Lesbian Alliance was headed by Yevgeniya Debryanskaya, and Roman Kalinin became editor of the first officially registered gay newspaper, *Tema*. Organizations and publications proliferated. The summer of 1991 saw the first international conference, film festival, and demonstrations for gay rights in Moscow and Leningrad. This was followed almost immediately by the attempted coup. Reversion to a more conservative regime would clearly have threatened homosexuals' recent gains, and legend has it that many gay activists manned the barricades protecting the Russian White House and that Yeltsin's decrees were printed on the Xerox machines of the new gay organizations.

The collapse of the Soviet Union that soon followed the failed coup only accelerated the progress of the gay movement. Occasional gay discos opened, more gay publications appeared, and gay plays were staged. In 1993 a new Russian Criminal Code was signed without article 121. Men who had been imprisoned under that article began to be released. Gay life in Russia today is in the process of normalization. Capitalism has brought the first gay businesses—bars, discos, saunas, a travel agency. While life in the provinces remains hard for gay men, gays in Russian cities are beginning to create a community.

Kevin Moss

Bibliography

Gessen, Masha. *The Rights of Lesbians and Gay Men in the Russian Federation*. San Francisco: IGLHRC, 1994.

Healey, Daniel. "The Russian Revolution and the Decriminalisation of Homosexuality." *Revolutionary Russia* 6 no. 1 (June 1993): 26–54.

Karlinsky, Simon. "Russia's Gay Literature and Culture: The Impact of the October Revolution." In *Hidden from History. Reclaiming the Gay and Lesbian Past*. Martin Bauml Duberman, Martha Vicinus, and George Chauncey, Jr., eds. New York: New American Library, 1989, 348–64.

Kon, Igor. *The Sexual Revolution in Russia: From the Age of the Tsars to Today*. James Riordan, trans. New York: Free Press, 1995.

Poznansky, Alexander. *Tchaikovsky. The Quest for the Inner Man*. Boston: Schirmer, 1991.

Tuller, David. *Cracks in the Iron Closet: Travels in Gay and Lesbian Russia*. Boston: Faber & Faber, 1996.

See also Ballets Russes; Diaghilev, Sergey; Kuzmin, Mikhail; Russian Literature; Tchaikovsky, Pyotr Ilich

Russian Literature

Some of the oldest original writing in the Russian tradition portrays gay love. The eleventh-century "Legend of Boris and Gleb" tells of George the Hungarian, who was "loved by Boris beyond all reckoning." George's brother, who was canonized as St. Moses the Hungarian, inspired part of the *Kievan Paterikon*, which dates to the 1220s. Moses refuses the advances of the Polish noblewoman who has bought him as her slave, preferring the company of her other male slaves. Most of the writing in Kievan Rus and Muscovite Russia was done by churchmen, and when they mention homosexuality, it is usually to condemn it as a sin.

R Modern Russian literature and the Russian literary language date to the beginning of the nineteenth century. The undisputed greatest figure of this period is Alexander Pushkin (1799–1837), who set the standard for prose, poetry, and drama in Russian. Pushkin himself was not gay, but he was what we would call gay-friendly, confident enough to write to his gay friend Philip Vigel about the relative merits of the latter's potential male bedmates. Pushkin's references to homosexuality are light and humorous, but not disapproving. The second great writer of Russia's Golden Age, Mikhail Lermontov (1814–1841), also had some familiarity with gay sex. In two bawdy poems written when he was twenty, he describes the sexual antics of his fellow classmates in the Cavalry Cadet School.

A third major literary figure of the nineteenth century, Nikolai Gogol (1809–1852), was exclusively gay, but as a religious man he never acted on his desires and spent his life repressing his sexuality. Gogol's stories and plays are full of his fear of marriage and of any kind of sexuality involving women, while his diary describes his strong romantic attachments to men. In his later years, Gogol fell under the spell of a religious fanatic who eventually induced him to fast and pray until he starved to death.

Another literary giant, Leo Tolstoy (1828–1910), also had homosexual attractions, which he describes both in his diary and in his autobiographical *Childhood, Boyhood*, and *Youth*. He repressed these urges not only because his views on sex were Victorian but also because he was attracted to men for their physical beauty and to women because of their spiritual attributes. Descriptions of the physical attraction between men appear in *The Cossacks* and *Anna Karenina*. By the time Tolstoy wrote his last novel, *Resurrection*, he had turned against all sexuality and portrayed homosexuality as one more symptom of society's moral decay.

The reforms and mood that accompanied the revolution of 1905 prompted Russia's first real flowering of gay literature. The most open and prolific of the gay writers of this period, the Silver Age, was Mikhail Kuzmin (1872–1936). Kuzmin wrote carefully crafted poetry on gay themes, setting his works sometimes in contemporary Russia, sometimes in the classical world of ancient Greece and Rome. In 1906 he published the first Russian coming-out novel, *Wings*, in which a young man learns to accept his sexuality; this makes him feel as if he had grown wings. Kuzmin's poetry on gay themes was praised by the greatest poets of his day, and he also wrote plays and short stories about gay love.

Other gay or bisexual poets who wrote about gay love include Vyacheslav Ivanov (1866–1949), Nikolai Kliuev (1887–1937), Sergey Yesenin (1895–1925), and Ryurik Ivnev (1891–1981). The Russian Revolution of 1917 eventually reversed the gains of the previous decade. While gay writers continued writing, gay-positive work was not encouraged under the Soviet regime, and after 1933, when Stalin recriminalized homosexuality, no gay-themed works were published in the Soviet Union. The Soviet regime controlled every aspect of the publishing industry, and persecution of homosexuals was at an all-time high. This accounts for the half century of silence in Russian gay writing.

There were émigré gay writers, however, among them memoirist Georgy Ivanov (1894–1958) and poet Anatoly Steiger (1907–1944). One of the most prolific gay poets, Valery Pereleshin (1913–1992), emigrated to China and eventually to Brazil. Pereleshin's classically composed poems express his multicultural background; he translated from Chinese and wrote poetry in Portuguese. His verse memoirs, "Poem Without an Object," describe his gay love affairs, and he warns readers, "My chronicle will not be to the tastes of uncles and aunts—for half a century we haven't gotten on, the breeders and I." Pereleshin's tour de force, *Ariel* (1976), contains 169 sonnets, a poetic epistolary romance with a married man in Moscow.

At the same time, Soviet writers risked persecution and arrest. Leningrad poet Gennady Trifonov spent four years in jail in the 1970s for circulating gay poetry. Yevgeny Kharitonov (1941–1981) was harassed by the authorities even though he never published his work during his lifetime. Kharitonov, who wrote experimental postmodern prose, was highly respected by his straight writer-colleagues, even as they disapproved of his open treatment of homosexuality. Not only does Kharitonov show a surprising celebration of his sexuality (given the times), he also claims it is a kind of divine gift directly related to his genius as a writer. Kharitonov was the first Russian writer to use gay slang in his work.

The relaxation of censorship and proliferation of gay journals that began with *glasnost* and accelerated with the breakup of the Soviet Union meant that émigré and underground writers could be rediscovered and new writers could be published as well. Unexpurgated editions of Kuzmin and the first publication of Kharitonov's work appeared in the early 1990s. At the same time, straight writers who had exhausted the shock value of heterosexual sex often turned to the topic of homosexuality to titillate their readers and boost their sales. Such writers include Zufar Gareev, Viktor Erofeev, and Vladimir Sorokin. A few serious gay writers have appeared on the Russian literary scene as well. Among these, the most noteworthy are poets Dmitry Kuzmin and Yaroslav Mogutin, and Alexei Rybikov ("Werewolf"), who writes fantasy fiction and humorous verse. Trifonov, who continues to write, has turned to prose. Thus far little writing has been published chronicling the recent boom in gay life in Russia, but such work may well appear in the coming years.

Kevin Moss

Bibliography

Karlinsky, Simon. *The Sexual Labyrinth of Nikolai Gogol*. Cambridge, Mass.: Harvard University Press, 1976.

Kuzmin, Mikhail. *Selected Prose and Poetry*. Ann Arbor, Mich.: Ardis, 1980.

Moss, Kevin, ed. *Out of the Blue: Russia's Hidden Gay Literature: An Anthology*. San Francisco: Gay Sunshine Press, 1997.

See also Gogol, Nikolai; Kliuev, Nikolai; Kuzmin, Mikhail; Russia

Russo, Vito (1946–1990)

Vito Russo—author, journalist, lecturer, and activist in the gay and AIDS movements—was born in Manhattan. He earned a master of arts in film studies from New York University and worked for a time in the film department of the Museum of Modern Art.

He brought his expertise in film to the gay liberation movement when he joined the Gay Activists Alliance (GAA) in 1970 and arranged all-night screenings at GAA's "Firehouse," whose all-gay and lesbian audiences inspired the first gay film festivals.

This work lead to his lecture on the images of gay men and lesbians in film, which he delivered at over two hundred colleges, universities, museums, and theaters in the United States, Europe, and Australia, including Harvard, Yale, Princeton, Columbia, the American and Swedish film institutes, the Chicago and Berlin film festivals, and New York's Public Theatre and Museum of Modern Art. Eventually his work grew into a book, *The Celluloid Closet*, published in 1981 and revised in 1987. In the late 1980s he taught two courses—the Celluloid Closet and Gay Liberation in the Media—at the University of California, Santa Cruz.

His essays, reviews, and interviews appeared in magazines and newspapers such as *New York*, *Esquire*, *Newsday*, *Rolling Stone*, *Village Voice*, *New York Native*, and *Advocate*. In 1983, he wrote, produced, and cohosted the gay and lesbian show *Our Time* on cable station WNYC-TV.

Diagnosed with AIDS in 1985, he became a founding member and leading activist of ACT UP. His story was recorded in the Academy Award–winning documentary *Common Threads*. In 1986, he became a founding member of the Gay and Lesbian Alliance Against Defamation. Russo, whose courage served as inspiration to many, died in New York. *The Celluloid Closet* was made into a documentary film by Rob Epstein and Jeffrey Friedman in 1995.

Arnie Kantrowitz

Bibliography

Russo, Vito. *The Celluloid Closet*. San Francisco: HarperCollins, 1981, 1987.

See also Activism, U.S.; ACT UP; AIDS; Film; Gay Activists Alliance (GAA); Gay and Lesbian Alliance Against Defamation (GLAAD)

Rustin, Bayard (1912–1987)

U.S. political activist Bayard Rustin was born in West Chester, Pennsylvania, into a family of black Quakers. This upbringing would ground his interest in nonviolent forms of social protest to which he would be committed for most of his public life. Initially torn between a career as a singer (he was for a time a member of a singing group with acclaimed black folk singer Josh White) and one of political activism, Rustin devoted himself to the latter after making his choice with indefatigable energy. Almost from the beginning he was welcomed into the upper echelons of the pacifist, antiwar, and civil rights struggles.

Although never a spokesperson for gay rights nor publicly affiliated with gay organizations, Rustin did not attempt to disguise his sexual preferences. His career was almost destroyed when in 1953, after a speaking engagement as a representative for the pacifist organization Fellowship of Reconciliation (FOR), he was discovered in a parked car engaging in sexual acts with two young men. Arrested on a morals charge, he was sentenced to sixty days in the county jail. Circulation of this incident in the media led to his dismissal from the FOR and haunted Rustin for the rest of his life.

R Another occasion when Rustin's sexuality would become a political issue was black Congressman Adam Clayton Powell Jr.'s threat to announce to the media that Rustin and Martin Luther King Jr. were sexually involved with each other unless King fired Rustin as one of his advisers and called off a demonstration at the 1960 Democratic National Convention. King gave in to Powell's threat and dismissed Rustin but unofficially continued to rely on his advice.

The major political accomplishment of Rustin's career and the one for which he is best known is his organizing of the landmark 1963 March on Washington. Even this achievement was tainted by homophobia, however, when Senator Strom Thurmond attempted to discredit the march by charging publicly that its chief organizer was a "communist, draft dodger, and homosexual."

Despite the setbacks and controversy that public knowledge of his sexuality created, Rustin survived politically. By the early 1960s he was recognized as one of the major strategists and theoreticians for the civil rights movement and eventually became the chair and president of the A. Philip Randolph Institute. Soon, however, Rustin's commitment to nonviolence and his cosmopolitan investment in issues that went beyond the civil rights struggle brought him into conflict with the Malcolm X–inspired black militants of the late 1960s, and he drifted to the margins of African American political life while still remaining very active on other fronts. Rustin died in New York City.   *Terry Rowden*

Bibliography

Anderson, Jervis. *Bayard Rustin: Troubles I've Seen*. New York: HarperCollins, 1997.

See also Activism; African American Gay Culture; Black Power Movement; Marches on Washington

S

Saba, Umberto (1883–1957)

Italian poet Umberto Saba was brought up by his mother and aunts in the Jewish quarter of the city of Trieste. After a year's military service in Italy in 1908, he returned to Trieste, where he married. His wife, Carolina (Lina), bore a daughter, Lina (Linuccia), in 1910.

In 1919 Saba bought a bookstore from which he published *Il canzoniere* (*The Songbook*, 1921), a collection of his poems. The book went through successive editions and expansions in 1945, 1951, and 1961. Its most famous, anthologized poems are addressed to his wife or his daughter. But the collection also contains paeans to the attractions of boyhood—not an idealized boyhood of classical spirituality but the rough-and-tumble of real creatures who enjoy such profane pursuits as football and masturbation. From memories of his first affair to affectionate encounters in old age, Saba records his love of boys with a clarity of focus that makes no excuses for desires he regards as self-explanatory.

In 1953, at age seventy, Saba began a short novel, *Ernesto*, based on his adolescence. It is a rite-of-passage narrative, fully dedicated to the concept of the passing phase: Ernesto has a sexual affair with a man for whom he works, then allows a prostitute to relieve him of his heterosexual virginity, then meets and starts to love a younger boy, and finally catches sight of the young woman who will eventually become his wife. *Ernesto* was posthumously published in 1975, and Salvatore Samperi's film version was released in 1983.   *Gregory Woods*

Bibliography

Aymone, R. *Saba e la psicoanalaisi*. Naples: Guida, 1971.

Pinchera, A. *Umberto Saba*. Florence: Nuova Italia, 1974.

See also Italian Literature; Italy; Love Poetry, the Petrarchan Tradition

Sade, Donatien-Alphonse-François, Marquis de (1740–1814)

The Marquis de Sade produced four major novels, many short stories, dialogues, plays, pamphlets, letters, journals, and a number of still unpublished works. Still more has been lost, as many of Sade's unpublished papers fell into the hands of the Nazis and were destroyed during the German occupation of France in World War II.

Damned by both royal and revolutionary authorities, Sade's writing is now recognized as crucial to the development of erotic discourse. The inventor of a philosophical system based on perversion, Sade took the values of the Anglo-European Enlightenment to their ultimate extreme. Profoundly anti-Christian, as was the earlier writing of Diderot and Voltaire, Sade wrote vast novels that functioned as exhaustive and exhausting catalogs of sexual deviance. In his fictional worlds, virtue is always punished and vice rewarded; self-interest and the will to power alone guarantee a human happiness that approaches a Zen-like serenity. Sade's successful libertine is no frenzied sensualist but a perverse stoic, a man (and sometimes a woman) who uses sadomasochism as a means to achieve detachment from others and from the self. She or he achieves apathetic sovereignty, and this status is open to any who can achieve such emotional, ideological self-mastery.

S Sade was born in Paris and was raised primarily by his grandmother and educated by his uncle, a worldly abbot, who openly kept two mistresses—a mother and daughter—in his house. At ten, he attended a Jesuit lycée, and at fourteen he joined the Light Horse regiment of the king. At twenty-three, he married Renée-Pelagie de Montreuil, a match arranged by his father. He engaged in a series of increasingly violent orgies that resulted in scandal, complaints, and eventual imprisonment. While Sade enjoyed the cooperation of his wife in these schemes, it was his mother-in-law who had him incarcerated in 1777 under a *lettre de cachot,* a system that sanctioned imprisonment without trial. Escaping from an escort bringing him to his appeal in 1778, Sade was discovered, rearrested, and remained imprisoned for the next eleven years.

Sade wrote his most important work during his many incarcerations. It was in Vincennes and then at the Bastille that he composed *One Hundred Days of Sodom, Justine,* and *Aline and Valcour.* Released in 1790, Sade was rearrested in 1793 as a suspected enemy of the revolution; he wrote *Philosophy in the Bedroom* during this time and was subsequently released in 1794. In 1801 he was apprehended at the office of his publisher, Masse, where police found illustrated editions of *The New Justine* and *Juliette.* He was imprisoned again and transferred to Charenton Asylum in 1803, where he died.

Stephanie Hammer

Bibliography

Allison, David, Mark Roberts, and Allan Weiss, eds. *Sade and Narrative Transgression.* Cambridge: Cambridge Uni, 1995.

Blanchot, Maurice, intro. *The Marquis de Sade: The Complete Justine, Philosophy in the Bedroom and Other Writings.* New York: Grove Press, 1965.

Crosland, Margaret, trans. and ed. *The Passionate Philosopher: A Marquis de Sade Reader.* London: Peter Owen, 1991.

See also France; French Literature; Sadomasochism

Sadomasochism

The abbreviation S/M points to both sadist/masochist and slave/master, while the slash indicates for some that the two roles are in general not exclusive but reversible. The term *sadomasochism* was coined by Richard von Krafft-Ebing in his *Neue Forschungen auf dem Gebiet der Psychopathia sexualis* (1890). He defined it as mostly imaginary pleasure in pain. The word has noble ancestry as it derived from the names of Donatien-Alphonse-François, Marquis de Sade (1740–1814), and Sir Leopold von Sacher-Masoch (1836–1895).

Perhaps because most sexual relations in history had been unequal and exploitative, sadomasochism found shelter in normal sexuality and came to the fore only in the late nineteenth century when equality and democracy became erotic ideals. But unlike homosexuality, sadomasochism did not produce an important subculture, movement, or press until after World War II. It was seen by psychiatrists as well as by the general public as a major and dangerous perversion that in the end would lead to lust murder.

Since the fifties a gay and since the seventies a lesbian leather scene developed in which S/M played an important part. The connection with leather was accidental; Sacher-Masoch's favorite fetish was fur, and Sade liked satin for boys. Fetishes like high heels, uniforms, slave collars, and brandings express relations of inequality. S/M is often linked not only to fetishes but also to other "perversions" like bestiality, golden showers, scat, exhibitionism, voyeurism, and so on. All kinds of bondage are used in S/M.

Contemporary advocates have come up with a series of claims. S/M should be a consensual game that has little to do with cruelty or violence. The abuse should often be more psychical than physical. According to them, the masochist is the master of the game who sets the rules that the sadist subsequently applies for mutual pleasure. When limits are transgressed, the masochist indicates with a code word that the game has to be interrupted or ended. This conventional apology may be functional to disclaim criticisms that S/M is harmful and abusive, racist, patriarchal, and homophobic, but it does not fit the excesses of desire that become apparent in S/M.

Leo Bersani criticizes apologetic work because he believes S/M does not undermine but repeats social structures of dominance and submission, masculinity and femininity, active and passive roles, penetrating and unclosing, power and subservience. He suggests that S/M will not "survive an antifascist rethinking of power structures." Notwithstanding his firm critique, he points to Freud's concept of "self-shattering" that would apply to masochism and enable nonidentitarian politics.

Gilles Deleuze in his book on Sacher-Masoch eulogized earlier male masochists as exemplary outlaws who have given up their prerogatives and annihilated the figure of the father. According to him and Anita Phillips, sadist and masochist are not complementary but very different figures. If the masochist indeed sets the rules of the sex game, he needs not a sadist but a simulacrum of a sadist.

Sade, Georges Bataille, and other writers have focused not on rules for desire but on desirable transgressions. Annie LeBrun has pointed to the abyss of desire that Sade disclosed. He has been presented most often as a sadistic torturer while his foremost interests were masochistic—to be fucked and whipped. His loss of self in literary and real scenes of rape and torture might well be analyzed as a corporal revolution against the dictates of religion that suffocated sexual desire. Masochism could be considered at the historical conjunction of Sade's and still of our time as a way to experience sexual desire in its extremes of torture and filth.

A century before Nietzsche, Sade went beyond good and evil by delving into abysmal pleasures. These were not any longer the forbidden and unmentionable vices excoriated by Christianity but lustful transgressions that should be stimulated by sexy stories and practical philosophy. Passion offered Sade in the eighteenth century a way beyond restraints and denials of his time. He desired not so much destruction of self but of the *ancien régime* to create new political configurations and sexual pleasures. His utopia were castles, boudoirs, and bordellos devoted to a surrender to sexual abjection.

Sade's work offers a persuasive alternative for contemporary culture that remains confined by limits set on sex by ideas of chastity, love, and normalcy. Sadian philosophy goes beyond concepts of identity and community, volition and consensus, private and public, male and female, and so forth. Such dichotomies are under postmodern attack because they fix sexuality in closets of paralyzed preferences and stagnant practices.

Sadism and masochism have different forms that separate and intermingle, have different backgrounds and perspectives, need specific explanations, and work within certain social and historical contexts. Nowadays they represent desires, lifestyles, and cultures that seem to be on the rise. The question will become not so much whether S/M can withstand an antifascist inquiry but what desires we lust for.

Gert Hekma

Bibliography

Bersani, Leo. "The Gay Daddy." In *Homos*. Cambridge, Mass.: Harvard University Press, 1995.

Deleuze, Gilles. *Présentation de Sacher-Masoch*. Paris, 1967. Translated as *Coldness and Cruelty*. New York: Zone Books, 1991.

LeBrun, Annie. *Soudain, un bloc d'abîme, Sade*. Paris, 1986.

Mains, Geoff. *Urban Ab Originals. A Celebration of Leather Sexuality*. San Francisco: Gay Sunshine Press, 1984.

Phillips, Anita. *A Defence of Masochism*. London: St. Martin's, 1998.

Samois. *Coming to Power. Writings and Graphics on Lesbian S/M*. Boston: Alyson, 1981.

Thompson, Bill. *Sadomasochism*. London: Cassell, 1994.

Townsend, Larry. *The Leatherman's Handbook*. New York: Masquerade, 1972.

Weinberg, Thomas, and G. W. Levi Kamel, eds. *S and M. Studies in Sadomasochism*. Buffalo: Prometheus, 1983.

See also Freud, Sigmund; Krafft-Ebing, Richard von; Leathermen; Sade, Donatien-Alphonse-François, Marquis de; Sex Practice: Watersports and Scat; Sexual Violence

Safer Sex

The concept of safer sex was introduced in the early 1980s in response to

- suspicions that what came to be called Acquired Immunodeficiency Syndrome (AIDS) has a viral causal agent. This was later confirmed and the agent was discovered to be the Human Immunodeficiency Virus (HIV)
- empirical epidemiological information about the rapid spread of AIDS
- alarming and tragic numbers of illnesses and deaths from AIDS among gay men in the United States and heterosexuals in Africa

These factors led people to believe that what came to be called HIV, and therefore AIDS, could be spread through sexual behaviors. The task, then, was to identify which behaviors are risky and what measures can be taken to reduce this risk. The results are what we know as safer sex. Safer-sex programs include informational meetings, social gatherings, journal and periodical articles, social skills

S

Buzz Bense in his safe sex club in San Francisco, 1989. Photo by Marc Geller.

training, theater and visual arts, and media campaigns.

Philosophies underlying safer sex include belief in

- social obligation to educate about sexual behaviors and their risks
- social obligation to provide access to condoms as a means of reducing risk
- individual responsibility for implementing safer-sex practices

HIV can be transmitted via the following bodily fluids:

- semen
- blood, including menstrual blood
- breast milk
- vaginal fluids

While the phrase "safer sex" is in common usage, we are speaking of risk reduction, not absolute safety. In addition, the level of risk for any behavior is situational. A behavior that may be relatively safe, for example, when neither partner has cuts, broken skin, or bleeding gums may be high risk when one has these conditions.

These behaviors are *unsafe*:

- anal intercourse without a latex condom
- sharing needles
- vaginal intercourse without a latex condom
- exchanging blood

These behaviors are thought to be low or moderate risk:

- vaginal oral sex
- penile oral sex
- deep kissing

Given the potentially devastating results of HIV transmission, it is recommended that one err on the side of safety.

Because of the risk of reinfection, or infection with a different strain of HIV, it is considered important that people who have tested positive for HIV practice safer sex when they are having sex with other people who have tested positive for HIV.

The National Institutes of Health (NIH) Consensus Panel has determined that focus on safer sex is effective in reducing risky sexual behavior in adolescent and adult populations. The effectiveness of safer sex is demonstrated by reduction in the growth of HIV infection rates and by reductions in other sexually transmitted diseases. Joseph Sonnabend, one of the first to stress safer sex and a prominent AIDS physician, states, "The striking reduction of all sexually transmitted diseases among gay men and the correlation of reduced HIV transmission with the adoption of safer-sex practices found in many studies attest to the success of safer sex."

All populations are at risk for HIV infection. Providing culturally appropriate and culturally competent preventive measures is a key facilitator of safer-sex practice. Thus, understanding the demographics of HIV infection detail is necessary for program development.

Globally, HIV/AIDS is primarily a heterosexual disease, with an estimated 70 percent of all HIV infections worldwide acquired through heterosexual sex. Globally, including in the United States, the rate of HIV infection is rising faster in women than in men and in some countries women are the group at greatest risk of acquiring HIV.

In the United States, men who have sex with men have the highest percentage of HIV infections, though this is fewer than half of all infections. In all countries, sex workers (both men and women) have high rates of HIV acquisition owing to economic and social issues making it difficult for sex workers to demand safer sex. African Americans and Latinos are overrepresented compared with their representation in the population at large. For women, the age at acquisition of the HIV virus is greatest in ages 15–15; for men, it is greatest at ages 25–35.

Barriers to practicing safer sex range from individual social and psychological makeup to macro processes. Safer-sex education addresses the individual issues.

Macro processes that militate against safer-sex practices include institutionalized and structural causes such as conflict, economic crises, migrant labor flows, economic relations, and power differences between men and women. In the midst of war or famine, for example, education on safer sex has a very low priority for governments and for individuals. For many, health care itself is a luxury, and purchase of condoms—even when these are available—is not possible.

In both developing and industrial nations, lack of information, misinformation, cultural and religious beliefs, and government failure to fund and promote safer sex are critical barriers. In the United States, there is an egregious lack of government leadership and even opposition to making information and condoms available, especially to the young men and women who may be most in need of them. The NIH Consensus Panel has endorsed youth education on safer sex and called on the U.S. government "to reverse policies that place the public at risk and to take the lead in implementing proven, lifesaving public health strategies." In Uganda and Thailand, government leadership has resulted in reducing rates of new infections, so it is known that such leadership can save lives.

Given the efficacy of safer sex in preventing HIV transmission, government, religious, and other institutions that have opposed or failed to support, fund, and promote safer sex must take responsibility for many cases of HIV transmission and for consequent deaths from AIDS.

Safer sex is about specific sexual behaviors. Some suggest that having multiple partners or having public sex is in itself high risk. There does not appear to be scientific support for this view. Sonnabend concludes, "The most effective way to combat AIDS and prevent a second wave [of AIDS epidemic] is intensive and well-crafted targeted safer-sex education, not telling people with whom they should or should not have sex."

AIDS is a preventable disease, with safer-sex education a key to its prevention. If current trends are allowed to continue, however, the Global AIDS Policy Coalition predicts, between sixty and seventy million adults will have been infected with HIV by the end of the year 2000. To reverse this trend, safer-sex education programs must be continued and expanded. Government policies of sabotage and neglect must end and be replaced by government leadership, including promotion and funding for safer-sex education and condoms. A successful U.S. and global campaign to reduce HIV acquisition must also address the economic and social issues that stand in the way of the practical application of safer-sex measures.   *Jackie Thomason*

Bibliography

Division of HIV/AIDS Prevention, National Center for HIV, STD, and TB Prevention (NCHSTP). Available on the World Wide Web at http://www.cdc.gov/nchstp/hiv_aids/dhap.htm

Gay Men's Health Crisis (GMHC) on the Web. Available on the World Wide Web at http://www.gmhc.org/

Long, Lynellyn D., and E. Maxine Ankral, eds. *Women's Experiences with AIDS: An International Perspective.* New York: Columbia University Press, 1997.

McIlvenna, Ted, ed. *The Complete Guide to Safer Sex.* Fort Lee, N.J.: Barricade Books, 1992.

Sonnabend, Joseph, and Richard Berkowitz. "Safer-Sex Panic." Available on the World Wide Web at http://www.geocities.com/~sexpanicnyc/safe.htm

U.S. Department of Health and Human Services, Public Health Services, Centers for Disease Control and Prevention. *HIV/AIDS Surveillance Report: U.S. HIV and AIDS Cases Reported Through June 1997.* Midyear Edition, Vol. 9, no. 1. Available on the World Wide Web at http://www.cdc.gov/nchstp/hiv_aids/stats/hasrlink.htm.

See also AIDS; AIDS Organizations, U.S.; Gay Men's Health Crisis (GMHC); Sexually Transmitted Diseases; Sisters of Perpetual Indulgence

Saint, Assotto (1957–1994)

U.S. writer and performer Assotto Saint was born Yves Lubin in Haiti and emigrated to New York

S City in 1970 to be with his mother, who had moved there. He attended Queen's College but left to pursue his interests in dance and theater. In the early 1980s he established himself as one of the founding members of the gay black men's writing collective Other Countries, serving as poetry editor of their anthology *Other Countries: Black Gay Voices.* Saint quickly became one of the best-known figures in the gay black scene and, because of his appearances in Marlon Riggs's landmark documentaries on black gay life, one of the best-known gay black figures in the country.

His poetry and theatrical performances are uncompromisingly direct, reflecting issues related to his transgendered identity and his and his partner's struggles with AIDS and the AIDS bureaucracy. Much of Saint's poetry was incorporated into the performance pieces that constitute his best work; individual poems often take on a startling new life when placed in that context. As Saint expressed his aesthetic, "Right from the start, my writings, especially my plays . . . became what I call a necessary theater. I was cognizant of the wants and needs of our emerging community; my writing needed to serve its visibility and empowerment." Saint also wrote essays condemning homophobic practices in his native Haiti and in other areas of the African diaspora.

In addition to producing his own work, Saint established Galiens Press, which published two major collections of gay black men's poetry, *The Road Before Us: 100 Gay Black Poets* and *Here to Dare: 10 Gay Black Poets,* as well as Saint's own collections *Stations* (1989) and *Wishing for Wings* (1994). Saint died of an AIDS-related illness.   *Terry Rowden*

Bibliography

Saint, Assotto. *Spells of a Voodoo Doll.* Michele Karlsberg, ed. New York: Masquerade Books, 1996.

See also African American Gay Culture; AIDS Literature; AIDS Performance; Riggs, Marlon; Transgender

Saint-Saëns, Camille (1835–1922)

The career of French composer Camille Saint-Saëns was a long journey from a progressive youth to a reactionary old age. The young Saint-Saëns defied the complacent French musical establishment of his day by defending the work of such composers as Berlioz and Liszt, both of whom were considered dangerous radicals. Rather than compose trivial ballets and for-mulaic operas, like most of his French contemporaries, Saint-Saëns cultivated the unpopular genres of symphony, concerto, and symphonic poem. His symphonic poem *Danse macabre,* op. 40 (1874) was considered so avant-garde that there was a riot at the premiere. By the end of his life, however, he had turned musically conservative, bitterly criticizing the music of Debussy and Stravinsky.

Saint-Saëns was a child prodigy, rivaling the precocity of his beloved Mozart. Nurtured by his vigilant mother, Saint-Saëns became an accomplished pianist and organist, as well as a prolific and versatile composer. Despite opposition from envious rivals, Saint-Saëns career developed an inexorable forward momentum that brought him early fame. At twenty-one he was appointed to the influential post of organist at the fashionable Church of the Madeleine in Paris. As a teacher at the École Niedermeyer, he influenced such gifted students as André Messager and Gabriel Fauré. Saint-Saëns was a frequent visitor to the salon of the great soprano Pauline Viardot, where he entertained fellow guests by performing coloratura arias in drag, his full beard adding a touch of absurdity to the proceedings.

In 1875, Saint-Saëns abruptly married the young Marie Truffot, perhaps trying to still the gossip then circulating in Paris about his sexual predilections. This uneasy union was riven by tragedy in 1878 when both of the couple's children died within the same month. The composer left his wife three years later. After the death of his mother in 1888, Saint-Saëns began a nomadic existence, frequently traveling to Algeria and other exotic locales. Like his younger contemporary André Gide, Saint-Saëns was drawn to North Africa as much to assuage his craving for Arab boys as for the evocative sun-drenched landscape. Saint-Saëns recorded his African impressions in several entertaining scores: the Suite Algérienne, op. 60 (1880), the fantasy for piano and orchestra *Africa,* op. 89 (1891), and the remarkable Fifth Piano Concerto, op. 103 (1896), known as the "Egyptian." Despite fame and honors, Saint-Saëns's became increasingly waspish in old age, raging against the latest musical developments with a venom born of despair at his own irrelevance. He died in his beloved Algiers at the age of eighty-six, a solitary, weary man.   *Byron Adams*

Bibliography

Harding, James. *Saint-Saëns and His Circle.* London: Chapman and Hall, 1965.

Stegemann, Michael. *Camille Saint-Saëns and the French Solo Concerto from 1850 to 1920*. Ann C. Sherwin, trans. Portland, Oreg.: Amadeus Press, 1991.

See also France; Gide, André; Music and Musicians 1: Classical Music

Saki (Hector Hugh Munro, 1870–1916)

English short story writer and novelist Saki is best known today as a master of the well-crafted story. He modeled his style on that of Oscar Wilde, and was, along with Wilde, Ronald Firbank, and Frederick Rolfe (Baron Corvo), an early practitioner of the camp flamboyance often associated with gay culture. The stories in *Reginald* (1904) exemplify Saki's epigrammatic style but lack the careful attention to plot that is now seen as one of his trademarks; these stories consist largely of witty, aimless dialogues between the twenty-two-year-old Reginald and an unnamed admirer called "the Other." After a stint as a foreign correspondent (1904–1909), Saki took up fiction again but dispensed with the dialogue form; instead, he began to hone his skill for the story line with an unexpected twist, developing the breathtaking plot as the narrative analog of the stunningly brilliant epigram. *Reginald in Russia* (1910) was quickly followed by *The Chronicles of Clovis* (1911), dedicated "to the lynx kitten, with his reluctantly given consent." This collection introduced Clovis Sangrail, the complacent, young, urbane dandy who would continue to silence philistines and embarrass slow-witted conformists in many of the stories Saki published over the next few years. During that period, he also wrote two novels—*The Unbearable Bassington* (1912), which describes the gloomy fate of one of his narcissistic heroes, and *When William Came* (1913), about an imaginary invasion of England by Germany. At the outbreak of World War I, Saki enlisted and returned to journalism, writing editorials in which he disparaged the beautiful, petulant boys who had been the heroes of his short stories. He was killed in combat in 1916.

Though usually classified as a social satirist, Saki generally chooses his targets less because of their urgency than because they lend themselves to his technique of exploding the reader's expectations. Thus he draws on heterosexual romance, patriotism, philanthropy, and religion as tools that his heroes can exploit for their own sybaritic ends. Only rarely does sexuality figure explicitly in Saki's fiction, and when it does—as in "Gabriel-Ernest" and "The Music on the Hill"—its effects are savage and uncontrollable.

Simon Stern

Bibliography

Langguth, A. J. *Saki: A Life of Hector Hugh Munro, with Six Short Stories Never Before Collected*. New York: Simon and Schuster, 1982.

Stern, Simon. "Saki's Attitude." *GLQ: A Journal of Lesbian and Gay Studies* 1 (1994): 275–98.

See also Dandy; English Literature; Firbank, Ronald; Rolfe, Frederick William; Wilde, Oscar

Salinas, Pedro (1892–1951)

The issue of rereading Pedro Salinas's work cannot be a discursive operation inspiring the desire of "outing" an insider. As far as is known, no specific documentation or evidence of (un)veiled homosexuality could be attributed to him and presented as a proof to validate a reading focusing a gay sensibility as such. On the contrary, what seems possible to achieve is a way of reading Salinas's poetry, narrative, and theater beyond the parameters of compulsory heterosexuality imposed on him by most of his critics. Many of the poems in Salinas's famous erotic poetry included in *La voz a ti debida* (1933) and *Razón de amor* (1936) reveal the avoidance of gendered pronouns. Though some critics have pointed out the ambiguity or, rather, the flotation of the meaning, they promptly refer to other poems in which the "*yo*" (I) speaks of or to a woman. What seems to be problematic is not only the consistency of this woman (always defined as a double and even as a proxy), but the sexual identity of the "I" when it is not read as a representative of Salinas himself. Salinas, who was born in Madrid, but exiled in the United States, seems to favor more the concept of gender as drag (mask, shadows of shadows), that is, as a subject position, than the essentialist perspective of sexual identity. An alternative reading appears when we pay attention simultaneously to the distinctive poetic procedure that opposes a mundane woman to an abstract, phallic, or conceptual one. This insistent homoerotic triangle can also be easily discovered in many stories in *El desnudo implacable y otras narraciones* (1951) and in many plays. Salinas's work has been unexplored from the perspective of sexual dissidence. His works include *Seix Barral* (1975), *Teatro completo* (1957), *Narrativa completa* (1976),

S and *Ensayos completos* (1981). The one work available in translation is *Prelude to Pleasure* (*Véspera de gozo,* trans. Noel Valis, 1993). *Gustavo Geirola*

Bibliography

Debicki, Andrew P. *Pedro Salinas*. Madrid: Taurus, 1976.

See also Spanish Literature

Same-Sex Marriage

In his 1994 book *Same-Sex Unions in Pre-Modern Europe*, John Boswell recounts his discovery of medieval liturgy for the priestly blessing of same-sex couples in church ceremonies. The liturgy is found in many collections of prayers from the eighth to at least the twelfth century in both the Western and Eastern Orthodox traditions. Boswell interprets the ceremonies as weddings and the couples' relationships as marriages. But the content of the prayers is thin and the known social context for the ceremonies nearly nonexistent. Other scholars have interpreted the ceremonies not as marriages but as blood-brother rites, aimed at sealing dynastic alliances or ending blood feuds, and have viewed the commitments that the ceremonies bless as more a matter of politics and economics than of intimacy and love.

Some modern liberal churches have begun offering ceremonies to same-sex couples that are explicitly understood as wedding ceremonies and have endorsed state recognition of same-sex marriages. These denominations include the Unitarian-Universalists, the United Church of Christ, and Reconstructionist Judaism.

The effort to gain legal recognition of same-sex marriages, however, has proven highly volatile. During the 1970s and early 1980s, gay couples in four states (Kentucky, Minnesota, Pennsylvania, and Washington) tried to get the courts to acknowledge their relationships as marriages. In all four cases the couples lost. But in 1993 Hawaii's supreme court ruled that the state's law requiring different-sex partners for legal marriage is a presumptively unconstitutional violation of the state's Equal Rights Amendment barring sex discrimination. The court, though, remanded the case to the lower courts to give the state a chance to prove that the law is necessary to a compelling state interest and thus constitutional after all. In its opinion, the court already entertained and dismissed the standard sort of moves the state might make along these lines. The struggle

Happily ever after. Photo by Marc Geller.

for gays' access to legal marriage continues in Hawaii, although in 1998, a public referendum against gay marriages was passed.

This prospect spurred a nationwide backlash in the summer of 1996. As preemptive strikes against the common law tradition and possible constitutional requirement (under Article IV's full faith and credit clause) that states acknowledge each other's marriages, around a dozen states passed legislation making explicit prohibitions against in-state same-sex marriages and barring recognition of any out-of-state same-sex marriages. In addition, Congress passed and the president signed a so-called Defense of Marriage Act, which bars recognition of same-sex marriages for federal purposes (taxation, Social Security, and immigration) and permits the states to bar recognition of out-of-state same-sex marriages.

These legal moves against gay marriage all operate by definitional fiat. They all define marriage as "the legal union of one man and one woman as husband and wife." But this definition tells one nothing whatever of the content of marriage, for the definition is unhelpfully circular. Since "husband" and "wife" *mean* people who are in a marriage with each other, the definition presupposes the very thing to be defined. In consequence, the definition does no positive work in explaining what marriage is and so simply ends up rawly assuming or stipulating that marriage must be between people of different sexes.

To avoid this difficulty, some legislators and courts have tried to establish a requirement for gender disparity in access to marriage by giving marriage a functional definition that appeals to reproduction. They take "the procreation and rearing of children" as essential to married life. But the legally acknowledged institution of marriage in fact does not track this functional definition. All states allow people who are over sixty to marry each other, with all the rights and obligations that entails, even though by natural necessity such marriages will be sterile. The functional definition is too broad as well. If the function of marriage is to bear and raise children in a family context, then the state should have no objection to the legal recognition of polygamous marriages. And in any case, lots of gay and lesbian couples do have children—by prior marriages, through adoption, artificial insemination, or surrogacy. It might well be asked what conceivable purpose can be served for these children by barring to their gay and lesbian parents the mutual cohesion, emotional security, and economic benefits that are ideally promoted by legal marriage.

If legal and functional definitions of marriage all fail, how should marriage be defined? To put it somewhat poetically, marriage is intimacy given substance in the medium of the everyday life, the day-to-day. Marriage is the fused intersection of love's sanctity and necessity's demand.

Not all loves or intimate relations count or should count as marriages. The culture is disinclined to think of Great Loves as marriages. Antony and Cleopatra, Tristan and Isolde, Catherine and Heathcliff—these loves burn gloriously but too intensely to be manifest in a medium of breakfasts and tire changes. Neither are roommates nor mere "domestic partners" who regularly cook, clean, tend to household chores, and share household finances considered as married, even though they "share the common necessities of life." Marriage requires the presence and blending of both necessity and intimacy. And life's necessities are a mixed fortune: on the one hand, they frequently are drag, dross, and cussedness, yet on the other hand, they can constitute opportunity, abidingness, and prospect for nurture.

The required blend of intimacy and the everyday explains much of the legal content of marriage. For example, the required blend means that for the relationship to work, there must be a presumption of trust between partners; and, in turn, when the relationship *is* working, there will be a transparency in the flow of information between partners—they will know virtually everything about each other. This pairing of trust and transparency constitutes the moral ground for the legal right against compelled testimony between spouses and explains why this same immunity is not extended to (mere) friends.

The remaining vast array of legal rights and benefits of marriage equally well fit this matrix of love and necessity—chiefly by promoting the patient attendance that such life requires (by providing for privacy, nurture, mutual support, persistence) and by protecting against the occasions when necessity is cussed rather than opportune, especially when life is marked by crisis, illness, and destruction. First and foremost, marriage changes strangers-at-law into next of kin with all the rights that this status entails, including the right of access to hospitals, jails, and other places restricted to "immediate family," the right to obtain "family" health insurance, the right to live in neighborhoods zoned "single family only," the right to make medical decisions in the event a partner is injured or incapacitated, the right to bring wrongful death suits, the right to make funeral arrangements for one's deceased partner, to inherit in cases of intestacy, and rights to bereavement leaves and survivors' benefits.

The portraits of gay and lesbian committed relationships that emerge from ethnographic studies—like Kath Weston's 1991 *Families We Choose*—suggest that in the way they typically arrange their lives, gay and lesbian couples fulfill the definition of marriage in an exemplary manner. In gay relationships, the ways in which the day-to-day demands of necessity are typically fulfilled are themselves vehicles for the development of intimacy. Both the development of intimacy through choice and the proper valuing of love are interwoven in the day-to-day activities of gay couples. Choice improves intimacy; it makes sacrifices meaningful and gives love its proper weight.

Starting with Denmark in 1989, the Scandinavian countries plus Holland have legalized gay unions, giving them all the rights and obligations of heterosexual marriages with the exception of rights to adopt and rights to weddings in churches of the state religion. In the United States, social resistance to such reform has been enormous. The issue is an emotional, which is to say, symbolic, one. The intensity of the issue does not derive from the role marriage plays as an institution operating in people's daily lives; after all, gay marriage would take away nothing—no legal right or material benefit—from any heterosexual couple. Rather, the issue is supercharged because of the role marriage plays as a value-laden concept or social ideal.

To put it bluntly, marriage, viewed as a symbolic event, enacts, institutionalizes, and ritualizes the social meaning of heterosexuality. The rituals of marriage are the chief means by which culture maintains heterosexuality as a social identity. It is not sexual behavior but marriage—the ritual plus the status—that is the social essence of heterosexuality. Don Juan, Casanova, and Lothario are now cultural tropes not for robust heterosexuality but for homosexual denial. In consequence, on the plane of social symbols and identities (whatever biology might say), if one did not marry, one would not be fully heterosexual. Further, if others were allowed to get married, one wouldn't be fully heterosexual either, for then the ideal and source of one's heterosexuality would not be pure. This analysis explains why the courts, the president, and Congress can claim that marriage *by definition* is the union of one man and one woman as husband and wife, even though this definition is circular, lacks any content, and explains nothing. Its function is not to clarify or explain; its function is to assure heterosexual supremacy as a central cultural form.

Richard D. Mohr

Bibliography

Boswell, John. *Same-Sex Unions in Premodern Europe*. New York: Villard Books, 1994.

Hayden, Curry, and Denis Clifford. *Legal Guide for Lesbian and Gay Couples*, 8th ed. Berkeley, Calif.: Nolo Press, 1994.

Eskridge, William N., Jr. *The Case for Same-Sex Marriage: From Sexual Liberty to Civilized Commitment*. New York: Free Press, 1996.

Mohr, Richard D. *A More Perfect Union: Why Straight America Must Stand Up for Gay Rights*. Boston: Beacon Press, 1994.

Weston, Kath. *Families We Choose: Lesbians, Gays, Kinship*. New York: Columbia University Press, 1991.

See also Couples; Denmark; Domestic Partnerships; Gay Families; Gay Relationships; Gay Rights; Netherlands; Parenting

Samurai

During the twelfth century, the emperor and nobility of Japan gradually lost control over the country owing to successive political upheavals in the court as well as riots in the provinces. Fierce strife among political factions, family members, and clans in the ruling classes invited chaos and made it impossible for the emperor and court to rule. In their place, a warrior class rose to power toward the end of the twelfth century. Warriors or samurai (also called *bushi*) thereafter controlled Japan under a feudal system until 1867.

Among samurai, homosexuality was viewed positively, in contrast to heterosexuality. Women were principally considered as breeders of heirs to ensure the continuation of the family line, and they were looked down upon as inferior to men. Indeed, some sects of Buddhism in Japan taught that women were by nature more sinful and less likely to attain enlightenment than men, while menstruation was viewed as a sign of tainted karma. The Chinese idea of yin and yang also contributed to this belief—male sexuality was primarily yang, while female was primarily yin, and a yin element in man was thought to be exposed through physical contact with a woman. Consequently, association with women was considered a feminization of the male self, except for the purpose of impregnation or the mundane gratification of one's carnal lust.

For spiritual uplift and enhancement of their masculinity, warriors were encouraged to associate with other men. Male bonding helped raise morale and engender camaraderie among warriors, especially on the battlefield. And it was common for the focus on the spiritual side of homosexuality to advance into homoeroticism: physical relationships between samurai came to be considered as a reinforcement not only of masculinity but also of one's spirituality. Homosexuality thus came to be widely accepted without moral or ethical stigma. During the long civil war period (1467–1603), homosexuality was celebrated as the flower of *Bushido* (the way of the samurai).

Throughout the feudal period, marriage between a man and a woman in the samurai class was exclusively based on politics. In a strict sense, samurai were bisexual. However, it was generally believed that since heterosexuality was necessary for producing heirs, homosexuality was exempt from such utilitarian purposes and was therefore considered more spiritual—men found pure love only with other men.

Writings of the feudal period document many homosexual episodes between lords, between lords and vassals, or between vassals. Some foreign missionaries from Europe and Korea recorded shock at the general tolerance toward open homosexuality in Japan in the seventeenth and early eighteenth centuries.

During the civil war period, the *kosho,* or "page" system, was established. Kosho, who were mostly in their teens, served their lords as attendants and in many cases also as sexual partners. Those who won great and lasting love from their lords later attained positions of authority. Takeda Shingen, Oda Nobunaga, Tokugawa Leyasu, and other warlords have left written records of their homosexual relations with their *kosho*.

As Japan became politically stable during the Tokugawa Shogunate (1603–1868), homosexuality, which had been prevalent only among priests, nobles, and warriors, became widespread among the bourgeoisie as well. With the rise of bourgeois capitalism, economic and cultural centers shifted from the samurai to the bourgeoisie, and male homoeroticism became a commodity, losing its original spiritual side. Pubescent male actors in the newly established Kabuki performance theater attracted both male and female audiences with their talent and androgynous beauty, and they sold sex after the performances. Their popularity spawned a class of professional male prostitutes, some of whose clients included samurai. The Tokugawa Shogunate repeatedly attempted to ban male prostitution as a cause of social disturbance, but to no avail.

At this time, male homoeroticism was called *nanshoku* (love or sex between men) or *shudo* (way of young men). Both terms generally refer to love between an adult and a pubescent boy, although they could be applied to love between men of any age.

Although homosexuality flourished during the civil war and early Tokugawa periods, it gradually dwindled in the latter half of the eighteenth century among the samurai. Many causes contributed to this decline. For one thing, the government repeatedly discouraged homosexuality because partners tended to be suicidal when their lovers died from disease, *seppuku (hara-kiri),* or accident. Love triangles often incited bloody incidents, and there were many cases of bloody retribution when one partner was slandered, humiliated, or killed by a third party. Moreover, within the government, some Tokugawa shoguns' infatuation with *kosho* and vassals invited political uneasiness. Other reasons can be put forth for this decline, but its principal cause was ironically the peace Japan attained: during peacetime, warriors receded, surrendering their role as moral, ethical, and cultural leaders to the financially predominant bourgeoisie. Consequently, the spiritual uplift engendered by homosexuality and the celebration of masculinity lost its attraction, resulting in the dwindling of the significance and the glamour of homosexuality. *Seigo Nakao*

Bibliography

Ihara, Saikaku. *The Great Mirror of Male Love.* Paul Gordon Schalow, trans. Stanford: Stanford University Press, 1990.

Leupp, Gary P. *Male Colors: The Construction of Homosexuality in Tokugawa Japan.* Berkeley: University of California Press, 1995.

Mishima, Yukio. *The Way of Samurai: Mishima Yukio on Hagakure in Modern Life.* Kathryn N. Sparling, trans. New York: Basic Books, 1977.

See also Androgyny; Buddhism; Japan; Japanese Literature; Kabuki; Mishima, Yukio; Transvestism

San Francisco

Civic devotion, it has been written, is the most noticeable characteristic of San Francisco's residents. Taking the phoenix as its symbol, the city (founded in 1835 and with a current population of more than 700,000) has been rebuilt seven times, the last following the fires caused by the 1906 earthquake. Long inhabited by Native Americans, the first European settlements (1776) include the Spanish military outpost at the Presidio and the Franciscans' Mission Dolores. In 1821 the land passed into Mexican hands and in 1846 was conquered by Americans. Two years later, the California Gold Rush transformed the enclave of one hundred people into a port city of some ten thousand. By the end of the nineteenth century, San Francisco had become the city of its legends—rough-and-ready, tolerant, and cosmopolitan cultural capital of the Wild West. Not until after World War II, when San Francisco served as the major point of embarkation for the Pacific theater of war, would the city be eclipsed by Los Angeles.

Early History (Through World War II)

Same-sex and cross-gender activities have always been present here. California Indian tribes valued the berdache—men who dressed as women, filled women's roles in their tribe, and maintained emotional and sexual relationships with men. As a port city and preeminent frontier town, it is not surprising that after 1849 same-sex encounters occurred in the notorious Barbary Coast, where male prostitution abounded, and reports of women passing as men made the newspapers. An account of genteel, prequake San Francisco is captured in Charles Warren Stoddard's *For the Pleasure of His Company*

(1903). Reputedly the first identifiably gay bar in San Francisco was the Dash (1908). With the disappearance of the Barbary Coast by 1917, gay cruising spaces migrated to the sailors' hangouts, by the piers along the Embarcadero and along the middle stretch of Market Street during the 1920s, 1930s, and 1940s.

With the repeal of Prohibition in 1933, gay bars (mostly in North Beach) became the central social space of gays and lesbians. The most famous of them include the Black Cat, Mona's (the first lesbian bar), and the Big Glass (the first black gay bar, located on Fillmore Street). Finocchio's, founded in the 1930s, was the first Bay Area nightclub to feature female impersonators (e.g., Ray Bourbon, Walter Hart, and Lucian Phelps), remaining a popular spot for gays and lesbians throughout World War II. Mobilization for war brought unprecedented numbers of gay men and lesbians from all across the country into contact with one another in San Francisco. Although not openly tolerated, many gays and lesbians decided to settle permanently in the Bay Area, particularly in the Nob Hill/Polk Gulch area, after being discharged from the military (see Allan Berube's *Coming Out Under Fire*). This set the stage for social and political homophile organizing for the first time.

1950s and 1960s

Under the crossed shadows of the McCarthy-era House Un-American Activities Committee and the first Kinsey report, reformist political organizing began, with a branch of the Mattachine Society in 1953 and the Daughters of Bilitis in 1955. By the mid-1950s the bohemian literary scene in North Beach had attracted Beat writers, including bisexual Jack Kerouac and homosexual poets Robert Duncan, Jack Spicer, and Allen Ginsberg. The 1957 obscenity trial against Ginsberg's *Howl* (which included homoerotic content) and a 1959 scandal in which one mayoral candidate accused the incumbent of turning San Francisco into "the national headquarters of organized homosexuals in the US" reinforced San Francisco's freewheeling image. In the 1960s the homophile movement and the bar subculture converged. In the spring of 1960 the "gayola" scandal broke, with gay bar owners reporting to the district attorney's office a long history of extortion by the police.

In the end all cops were acquitted, but the department and city administration were seriously embarrassed. A police crackdown of gay bar patrons followed, leading to arrests and bar closings and much public discussion about homosexuality. In protest José Sarria, noted drag personality from the Black Cat, ran for the Board of Supervisors in 1961. In 1962 the Tavern Guild was formed as a defense organization to resist attacks from the state, and in 1964 SIR (Society for Individual Rights) began as an alternative social outlet to the bars. In December 1964, in response to police harassment, the Council on Religion and the Homosexual was formed, and a New Year's Eve dance for homosexual men and women was planned. Police harassed and arrested patrons as they entered California Hall on Polk Street. Eric Garber notes that, "The well-publicized court cases gave the gay community its first taste of power and radically redefined its relationship with the police."

In the 1960s Polk Street/Tenderloin rose to prominence as a gay neighborhood, and Folsom Street became the legendary Miracle Mile of leather bars (such as Febe's) and bathhouses; the Toolbox was featured in a *Life* magazine article (June 26, 1964). Annual gay events were established: the Beaux Arts Ball in 1964 and the CMC (California Motorcycle Club) Carnival in 1966. By the late 1960s the hippie movement of the Haight-Ashbury, the Oakland-based Black Panther movement, the Berkeley free speech movement, and the national women's and antiwar movements were radicalizing San Francisco homosexuals. "By the late 1960s mass magazines were referring to San Francisco as the gay capital of the U.S.," writes John D'Emilio, so, when the Stonewall riots sparked a gay liberation movement, San Francisco was primed for assuming a social leadership role.

The Castro Clone Era (1970s to Early 1980s)

In the 1970s and early 1980s, waves of gay and lesbian immigrants found a gay infrastructure within the social structure of the city's political, commercial, and cultural realms. Women settled in the Duboce Triangle, Noe Valley, and Upper Mission, and men in the Haight, Folsom, and especially Castro Street neighborhoods. The new "liberated look" of the Castro clone style, a mainstream masculine image of gay men, contrasted with the drag style of Polk Street or the leather style of Folsom Street. The transformation of the city was documented in Armistead Maupin's *Tales of the City*, which attracted even more immigrants in search of "gay Mecca." The new community celebrated itself in the Gay Freedom Day parade (1970, 1972). In 1975 it became the largest gay parade, superseding New York City's, with 82,000, and draws (contrary to official police estimates) an average 300,000 visitors annually.

The seminal gay political moment in San Francisco's history began with Harvey Milk's 1977 election to the city's Board of Supervisors as the first openly gay public official in the United States (chronicled in Randy Shilts's *The Mayor of Castro Street*). Three events soured advances for gay rights, however. Anita Bryant's successful campaign to repeal a gay civil rights ordinance in Dade County, Florida, in 1978; the 1978 Briggs Initiative in California (which attempted to dismiss gays or those who supported gays from teaching jobs in California); and the assassination of Milk a year after his election. In 1978, Dan White, a political maverick and homophobic supervisor, shot and killed Milk and Mayor George Moscone. White was let off with a light, seven-year prison sentence. Following the obvious injustice of this sentence and just days after the stunning news of the Jonestown massacre (Jim Jones's ministry was San Francisco–based), gays massed in front of City Hall to protest. The gathering erupted into the White Night Riots. The police retaliated the following nights by storming the Castro, smashing several gay bars on Castro Street, and beating up people on the street. For all its liberal polish, homophobic intolerance lay just below the surface in nongay San Francisco.

The Age of AIDS, 1980s–1990s

While gay San Francisco was recouping from these political setbacks, a silent killer was stalking the gay community. Along with New York and Los Angeles, San Francisco was ground zero for the epidemic. The density of the city's gay demographic and geographic parameters made the epidemic most visibly seen and felt here. By 1983, gay San Francisco was reeling from the impact. Following heated debate, then-mayor Dianne Feinstein closed the city's bathhouses, fanning fears of serious suppression of gays' civil rights. Cleve Jones, successor to Harvey Milk, conceived the NAMES Project and the AIDS Memorial Quilt as a way to embrace, contain, and communicate the community's grief. The San Francisco model (Shanti Project, San Francisco AIDS Project) for coping with medical, practical, and emotional needs of people with AIDS (PWAs) was nationally acclaimed.

Health, recovery, and community became the bywords of the generation to follow AIDS. In 1983, Tom Waddell founded the Gay Olympics (later changed to Gay Games owing to a lawsuit from the U.S. Olympic Committee). The proliferation of twelve-step pro-grams in the gay community in the 1980s brought many segments of the community together through a mixture of Eastern, Western, and New Age spiritual philosophies. Multiculturalism, transgenderism, bisexuality, and even the "bear movement" were adopted into the political agenda, as ACT UP and queer nationalism at the grassroots level, and gay and lesbian studies and queer theory at the academic level, struggled to articulate changing social perceptions. The first Department of Gay and Lesbian Studies was established at City College of San Francisco in 1989.

In San Francisco the gay community had become a specific place with a complete infrastructure, truly a city within a city. Serialized in the *New Yorker*, Frances Fitzgerald's "The Castro" took up where Maupin had left off. A new generation of gay authors captured this spirit in novels such as *Some Dance to Remember* (Jack Fritscher), *As If After Sex* (Joseph Torchia), *Longing* (Paul Reed), and *Jack the Modernist* (Robert Glück). By 1990, San Francisco had a whole calendar of "gay holidays," including the AIDS Candlelight March, Milk/Moscone Memorial March, Gay Freedom Day Parade, Folsom Street Fair, Castro Street Fair, Dore Alley Fair, and Halloween.

Les Wright

Bibliography

D'Emilio, John. "Gay Politics and Community in San Francisco Since World War II." In *Hidden From History: Reclaiming the Gay and Lesbian Past*. Martin Duberman et al., eds. New York: Meridian, 1990, 456–73.

Fitzgerald, Frances. "The Castro." In *Cities on a Hill*. New York: Touchstone, 1987, 25–119.

Garber, Eric. "Finocchio's: A Gay Landmark." SFBAGLHS Newsletter 3, no. 4 (1988): 1ff.

Shilts, Randy. *The Mayor of Castro Street*. New York: St. Martin's, 1982.

See also Activism, U.S., ACT UP; AIDS; Bathhouses and Sex Clubs; Beat Generation; Berdache; Castro; Clone; Gay Games; Ginsberg, Allen; Hay, Harry; Marches and Parades; Mattachine Society; Maupin, Armistead; McCarthyism; Milk, Harvey; NAMES Project AIDS Memorial Quilt; Neighborhoods; *ONE Magazine*; Queer Nation; Queer Theory; Shilts, Randy

Sánchez, Luís Rafael (1936–)

Puerto Rican playwright, novelist, and essayist, Luís Rafael Sánchez is best known for his 1976 novel, *La guaracha del Macho Camacho*. Sánchez's own *guaracha,* or stylistic "beat," marks his novel, set in Puerto Rico and enlivened by a playful use of language and an unconventional narrative structure, as an exemplary text in the larger Latin American postmodern literary movement. Set during a severe traffic jam in San Juan to the frenetic rhythm of radio disc jockey "Macho" Camacho's Caribbean musical repertoire, Sánchez's story allows for the collision of numerous disparate characters' lives, from the most to the least privileged and powerful in Puerto Rican society. Among these are sexually marginalized characters whose experiences directly challenge the repressive machismo and heterosexism of that society.

Sánchez's interest in gender politics and the sexual attitudes ingrained in his culture were already apparent in his considerable literary output predating *La guaracha*; this body of work includes a long list of dramatic works, notably his classic *The Passion According to Antigone Pérez* (1968) and his collection of short fiction, *En cuerpo de camisa* (The Shirt Body, 1966). Critical and scholarly work on Sánchez, who has continued to produce significant literary material (like his novel *The Importance of Being Daniel Santos*, 1988) into the 1990s, has typically focused on his status as one of Puerto Rico's premier literary figures. Only since the early 1990s, however, have scholars begun to pay specific attention to queer content and queer effects in Sánchez's work, especially *La guaracha* and the short story "!Jum!" It will certainly determine Sánchez's cultural legacy in and out of Puerto Rico that he successfully integrated all aspects of Puerto Rican society into his expansive, complex literary and social vision. *Ricardo Ortiz*

Bibliography

Cruz-Malavé, Arnaldo. "Toward an Art of Transvestism: Colonialism and Homosexuality in Puerto Rican Literature." In *¿Entiendes?: Queer Readings, Hispanic Writings*. Emilie Bergmann and Paul Julian Smith, eds. Durham, N.C.: Duke University Press, 137–67.

See also Chicano and Latino Gay Cultures

Sandow the Magnificent (1869–1925)

At the 1893 World's Fair in Chicago, on the same Midway where the formerly infamous Little Egypt did the hootchy-kootch, a German strongman displayed an even more spectacular body in sandals and a scrap of fake leopard skin. In the P. T. Barnum world of nineteenth-century entertainment, strongmen were so popular that competition incited them to the most outrageous claims. Posters showed them stopping cannonballs with their abdomens and lifting teams of Clydesdales overhead. Eugen Sandow was indeed strong, but in his show he shifted the emphasis from what he could do to how he looked doing it, claiming to be "the world's most perfect man."

The young Florenz Ziegfeld, who saw box office gold in that difference because it gave the act appeal to women as well as men, made Sandow his first client. Thanks to the showman's genius for ballyhoo, "Sandow the Magnificent" became a household phrase before the turn of the century, touring the country and then the world with his own orchestral accompaniment (whose handsome Italian conductor shared his quarters on the road).

A cast was made of his body in gilded bronze, and his photographs sold by the thousands, especially in his favorite guise as Hercules, but exhaustive touring broke his health. Ziegfeld went on to glorify the other sex. Sandow returned to his wife and daughter in London and opened a luxurious institute of physical culture, still posing nude into his fifties, the first physique superstar.

F. Valentine Hooven III

Bibliography

Chapman, David. *Sandow the Magnificent*. Urbana-Champagne, Ill.: University of Illinois, 1994.

Ellenzweig, Allen. *The Homoerotic Photograph: Male Images from Durieu/Delacroix to Mapplethorpe*. New York: Columbia University Press, 1992.

Waugh, Thomas. *Hard to Imagine*. New York: Columbia University Press, 1996.

See also Body Image; Photography; Physical Culture; Sports

Sarduy, Severo (1936–1993)

Severo Sarduy was a Cuban writer and publisher. Despite his considerable literary and critical output, Sarduy may have left his chief mark on literary and cultural history through his work as editor of the Latin American division of France's influential publishing house Éditions du Seuil. In this capacity, Sarduy oversaw the French critical and popular reception of the "boom" in Latin American fiction, which began in the late 1960s with the publication of major novels like Gabriel García Marquez's *One Hundred Years of Solitude*. Sarduy, who was born in Camagüey, Cuba, of mixed Hispanic, African, and Chinese ancestry, left Cuba in 1961 under a government fellowship to study literature in Paris. An early strong supporter of Cuba's revolutionary government, Sarduy worked in Havana before 1961 as editor of the cultural supplement, *Lunes*, of the régime's daily newspaper, *Revolución*.

Once in France, however, Sarduy grew disillusioned with the regime's increasingly authoritarian policies and decided to remain abroad in exile, and to turn his intellectual attention to the work in critical theory and semiotics conducted by Roland Barthes, François Wahl, and others involved in the publication of the influential journal *Tel Quel*. Sarduy, who continued to write his many volumes of literary and critical work in Spanish, became one of the most innovative and experimental figures in Latin American letters from his base in France. He provided the most direct link between French semiotic and poststructural theory and the growing body of literary work by primarily Latin American novelists who were revolutionizing the very form of the novel as quickly as the French were devising strategies to analyze it.

While little has been biographically documented of Sarduy's sexual orientation, homosexual issues, effects, and sensibilities are everywhere inscribed in his work. Sarduy's prose style is typically described as "baroque," elaborate to the point of impenetrability. In this respect he exhibits the influence of José Lezama Lima, the gay Cuban novelist whose masterwork, *Paradiso,* Sarduy helped to publish in France. In his own fiction, Sarduy regularly draws his images from practices of cross-dressing, sex-changing, and tattooing to ground erotic pleasures derived from writing and from reading as nevertheless bodily pleasures. Such effects appear across the course of Sarduy's literary work, from early novels like *From Cuba With a Song* (1967) and *Cobra* (1972), to later work like *Colibrí* (1984) and *Daiquiri* (1980), his collection of explicitly homoerotic sonnets.

Since Sarduy's death from AIDS, his work has commanded increasing attention outside European and Latin American cultural circles. Novels like *From Cuba With a Song* and essay collections like *Written on a Body* appeared in English translation in the early 1990s, and other major works have been slated for translation as well. Sarduy's cultural and intellectual legacy promises thus to deepen and to grow. As much for his work as a theorist and critic as for his work as an editor, novelist, and poet, Sarduy's contribution to a queer sensibility in world letters remains to be measured. *Ricardo Ortiz*

Bibliography

Sarduy, Severo. *Written on a Body*. Carol Maier, trans. New York: Lumen Books, 1989.

See also AIDS Literature; Barthes, Roland; Cuban Writing in Exile; Lezamo Lima, José

Sargent, John Singer (1856–1925)

John Singer Sargent's sexuality is more a function of posthumous interpretation of his art than documentation from his life. Although his biography reads like a *New York Times* obituary of a 1950s closet queen, there is little hard evidence to support a claim of homosexuality. He enjoyed a stellar public career as a society portraitist, yet remained a lifelong bachelor with a private personal life. Sargent's papers were destroyed by his family at his death, and little is known about the artist's twenty-five-year relationship with Italian model-turned-valet Nicola d'Inverno. Sargent was an associate of notorious aesthetes and dandies like Oscar Wilde, Robert de Montesquieu, and Henry James, and it is known that he kept an overstuffed photo album of photographs of "primitive" male nudes. If Sargent was homosexual, his mastery of social proprieties served as well to obscure the nature of his affections as to produce his often insightful, sometimes scandalous artwork.

Although American by birth, Sargent spent most of his life in Europe—Venice, Paris, London—sharpening his acute awareness of the limits of social acceptability and the thin line separating public and private domains. His awareness was often manifest in carefully calculated artistic transgressions producing momentary infamy and notoriety and enduring success and renown. With *El Jaleo* (1879, Museum of Fine Arts, Boston), Sargent voyeuristically profited from the erotic potential of the exotic other in the climactic dance of a Spanish Moorish woman. The famous full-length *Portrait of Madame X* (New York, Metropolitan Museum of Art, 1884) was a strategic puncturing of the artifice and pretense of French society by revealing the erotic sensuality of the American arriviste and "professional beauty" Virginie Gautreau. Both works catapulted Sargent to international renown and produced hundreds of portrait commissions. Sargent's

Sargent's portrait of W. Graham Robertson, 1894. Tate Gallery, London/Art Resource, NY.

viewing angle emphasizing intertwined legs and male groins transformed the figures' easy familiarity into a sensual one, the viewer's position into that of voyeur, and the artist's brush into an unwelcome intruder. Images of nude male youths are sprinkled throughout Sargent's oeuvre, but they are concentrated in the innumerable drawing studies for the unfinished Boston Public Library mural *Triumph of Religion* (1890–1919). So erotic was Sargent's jumbling of male bodies in a study for the mural's Hell scene that Andy Warhol asked whether it was a "gang-bang" when he saw it in a 1986 exhibition.

Michael J. Murphy

Bibliography

Fairbrother, Trevor. "Sargent's Genre Painting and the Issues of Suppression and Privacy." *Studies in the History of Art* 37 (1990): 29–49.

———. "Warhol Meets Sargent at Whitney." *Arts Magazine* 61 (February 1987): 64–71.

Hills, Patricia, et al. *John Singer Sargent*. Exhibition catalog. New York: Whitney Museum of American Art, 1986.

See also Art History; Dandy; James, Henry; Montesquieu, Count Robert de; Warhol, Andy; Wilde, Oscar

Sargeson, Frank (1903–1982)

Frank Sargeson, who was born Norris Davey, is acclaimed as one of New Zealand's most accomplished writers. Sargeson grew up in Hamilton, where his father was a leader in the Methodist Church. He qualified as a solicitor and traveled to England and Europe before establishing himself as a writer in Auckland from 1931 until his death.

He was the first major New Zealand writer to remain in the country, and in the 1930s he established a new direction in New Zealand letters by publishing short stories that shaped the language and rhythm of colloquial speech into an art form. His later plays and novels were less restrictive than his earlier works. Although he was honest about most things, every aspect of his life and writing was touched by his overwhelming desire to conceal his homosexuality. This was initiated by a traumatic court case when, at the age of twenty-six and with the threat of "ten years imprisonment with hard labour" he testified against an older man—who got five years jail—and promised the judge to never again participate in "such activities." He was or-

exquisite surfaces and fluid brushwork were much admired, but his unsparingly candid brush eventually scared off all but the most fearless sitters. Far from depicting the beau monde as they wished to be seen, Sargent often depicted them as whom he perceived them to be: uncomfortable, insecure, awkward, or small. It is ironic that an artist sought after for his ability with the painted surface was so talented at peering beneath that of his sitters.

The most homoerotic aspects of Sargent's work are found in his genre paintings and in his preparations for a large-scale mural commission. The artist's European vacation travels with family and friends produced a series of spontaneous and intimate works of slumberous picnickers. Sargent's dered to come up for sentence—and jail—if called upon within two years. This was profoundly to affect his relations with society for the rest of his life.

Sargeson rejected his family and their puritanism while maintaining a fanatical commitment to his calling as a writer. He genuinely suffered poor health as well as hypochondria. Though at times he was argumentative and even nasty, he could also be generous and compassionate. He was a mentor to younger writers—notably Janet Frame—and cared for many social misfits and drifters.

Sargeson's writing was prodigious; his most admired works include *"That Summer" and Other Stories* (1946), *Memoirs of a Peon* (1965), *Once Is Enough* (1973), *More Than Enough* (1975), and *Never Enough* (1977). The finest stories are in *Collected Stories 1935–1963* (1964). Sargeson examines how the emotional needs of New Zealand men are met or thwarted. He writes about men surviving in hostile or cramped circumstances/environments. He is essentially subversive in that the irony and symbolism is evident to the reader while the narrator remains largely inarticulate.   *Robin Duff*

Bibliography

Copland, R. A. *Frank Sargeson*: Oxford: Oxford University Press, 1976.

King, Michael. *Frank Sargeson: A Life*. Harmondsworth: Penguin, 1995.

See also New Zealand

Schlesinger, John (1926–)

Openly gay British director John Schlesinger has produced social or "issue" dramas (*A Kind of Loving,* 1962), taut suspense dramas (*Marathon Man,* 1976), eerily disturbing thrillers (*The Believers,* 1987), and deliciously wicked satire (*Cold Comfort Farm,* 1995). But he is perhaps best known for his affecting, literate character studies, often set against a backdrop that perfectly captures the zeitgeist of a particular time and culture.

Of all his films, two are gay in theme: *Midnight Cowboy* (1969) and *Sunday Bloody Sunday* (1971). *Midnight Cowboy* can be viewed today as a museum piece, a look at the underbelly of 1960s Manhattan. But its view of homosexuality is ambiguous: the hero, Joe Buck (Jon Voight), offers sexual services to men but assaults his johns out of contempt; at the same time, however, his romantic involvement with his streetwise mentor, Ratso Rizzo (Dustin Hoff-

man), lingers below the surface for the duration of the movie.

Sunday Bloody Sunday provides an antidote to such ambiguity. An unusual triangle provides the focus for the story: a straight woman (Glenda Jackson), a gay man (Peter Finch), and a younger bisexual man (Murray Head), whose ego basks in the adoration of the two older people. Schlesinger orchestrates a fervent kiss between the two men, a kiss that makes up in thirty seconds for all the decades of tortured and lonely gay characters that have ever appeared in film. A poignant, genteel drama, *Sunday Bloody Sunday* is not about sexualities but about adults falling in love with the wrong people.

Many of Schlesinger's other films have gay content as a matter of course. Several have gay characters at their periphery: in *Darling* (1965), a gay waiter loses the object of his desire to Julie Christie's character; Madame Souzatska, in the film of the same name, has a gay neighbor. In two of his later films, Schlesinger also treats the homosexualities of his characters as a priori facts; the British spies Guy Burgess and Sir Anthony Blunt are major characters in *An Englishman Abroad* (1985) and *A Question of Attribution* (1992), respectively, and the homosexuality of each is established without fanfare. In 1996, Schlesinger signed on to direct the film adaptation of Larry Kramer's *The Normal Heart.*   *J. A. White*

Bibliography

Brennan, Mary. "John Schlesinger: Comfortable with Controversy." *The Mr. Showbiz Interview Archive* (May 23, 1996). (http://web3.starwave.com/features/interviews/greenroom/schl esinger.html)

Brooker-Bowers, Nancy. *John Schlesinger: A Guide to References and Resources.* Boston: G. K. Hall, 1978.

Phillips, Gene D. *John Schlesinger.* Boston: Twayne, 1981.

See also Bisexuality; Blunt, Anthony; Film; Kramer, Larry

Schools

Schools have functioned throughout the twentieth century as sites of anxiety and danger—as well as opportunity and achievement—for boys and young men experiencing same-sex attractions. During this century, adult gay men employed as teachers, coaches, principals, librarians, and other school-workers have experienced a gradual shift in both legal status and social acceptance. At the close of the twentieth century, schools remain one of the primary public institutions where lesbians, gay men, bisexuals, and their allies grapple with the organized religious right over issues as diverse as student clubs, AIDS education, school safety, curriculum, and teacher rights.

Autobiographies of gay men are filled with accounts of alienation, ostracism, and abuse at the hands of school bullies who prey on nonathletic or nontraditional boys. Writers as diverse as Paul Monette, Michelangelo Signorile, and John Preston have captured the isolation and suffering of young gay boys from different white ethnic perspectives. A separate narrative, best captured in John Reid's *The Best Little Boy in the World*, reveals how some boys construct identities focused on scholastic achievement in reaction to their growing sense of difference from other boys. While many argue that the progress of the gay movement has radically altered the social and cultural position of homosexuals, schools appear to be a site where gay youth continue to be vulnerable and face increasing harassment from peers and occasionally school officials.

In 1996, Jamie Nabozny successfully sued administrators at a middle school and high school in Wisconsin for failing to protect him from repeated antigay abuse by classmates over a period of several years. Nabozny had suffered verbal taunts, been spit upon, assaulted, and urinated upon by local students, and he dropped out of the public school system because of violence and harassment. This landmark legal case produced a federal court finding that officials could be held accountable for failing to protect gay students in their schools. Coming on the heels of court cases that found that female students had a legal right to protection from sexual harassment in schools, the Nabozny case resonated powerfully for school officials throughout the nation.

Gay male teachers in American schools have experienced a long history of discrimination, harassment, and persecution. Throughout the early part of the century, Karen Harbeck writes, "the most common scenario is one of a person living an exemplary life in fear of discovery." Teachers discovered to be homosexual would quietly resign from their position and get on the next bus out of town. This shifted in the 1940s and 1950s when changing social views of consensual adult sexual conduct emboldened gay male teachers arrested for public sex and charged with lewd conduct. Increasingly these men successfully fought criminal charges, yet were nevertheless fired from their jobs because their reputation made them supposedly unfit to work with children.

The situation for teachers again shifted in 1969, when the California supreme court, in *Morrison v. State Board of Education,* ruled that teachers could successfully challenge dismissals for a variety of "personal indiscretions" occurring outside the workplace. This provided an opening for a number of gay male teachers to fight to retain their jobs after coming out, being "outed," or being caught in public sex situations. The late 1970s and 1980s saw changes in state laws about sex between consenting adults, sodomy, and gay employment rights that resulted in a dramatic change in the social climate and legal status of gay male teachers.

During the 1980s, the religious right's obsession with homosexuality was increasingly focused on public schools. This has resulted in a wide range of local battles involving gay and lesbian issues in schools, including censorship of books from libraries; silencing of gay, lesbian, and bisexual teachers; and banning all student clubs in Salt Lake City after gay students formed a support group. Penny Culliton, a heterosexual English teacher in a rural school in New Hampshire, received national acclaim from the gay community when she asserted her right to utilize books including gay characters in her high school classroom. Over a two-year period, Culliton was fired and won reinstatement, insisting that discussions of gay issues belonged in public classrooms.

Similar progress was evident throughout the rest of the nation. Massachusetts Governor William Weld sponsored a highly visible safe schools program that resulted in the training of school personnel throughout the state on issues of homophobia and access and the creation of dozens of gay/straight alliances in high schools. New York City's Harvey Milk School, Project 10 in Los Angeles, and additional programs in cities such as San Francisco, Seattle, and St. Paul continue to provide public school–based academic and support services for queer youth. It is clear that public schools will continue to emerge as a primary site for the assertion of the civil rights of gay people over the next decade.

Eric Rofes

Bibliography

Harbeck, Karen M., ed. *Coming Out of the Classroom Closet: Gay and Lesbian Students,*

Teachers, and Curricula. Binghamton, N.Y.: Harrington Park Press, 1992.

Jennings, Kevin, ed. *One Teacher in 10: Gay and Lesbian Educators Tell Their Stories.* Boston: Alyson Publications, 1994.

Rofes, Eric. "Making Our Schools Safe for Sissies." In *The Gay Teen.* Gerald Unks, ed. New York: Routledge, 1995.

See also Education: Theory and Pedagogy; Lewd and Lascivious Conduct; Monette, Paul; Preston, John; Religious Right; Sex Education

Schopenhauer, Arthur (1786–1860)

Different from many of his contemporary colleagues, the neo-Kantian philosopher Arthur Schopenhauer enjoyed financial independence, thanks to a large inheritance from his father. His ethic of compassion, which was fully developed in his critique of Kant's ethics, *On the Basis of Morality,* commands respect even today. Schopenhauer published his evaluation of homosexuality in his magnum opus *The World as Will and Representation* in 1859 as an extension to a paragraph on the metaphysics of sexual love. Social constructionists will criticize this claim on the basis that the term *homosexuality* had not entered the public or scientific debate at the time; Schopenhauer actually used the term *pederasty.* However, it seems beyond doubt that Schopenhauer tried to discover what the origin of homosexuality is, and whether homosexuality is, ethically speaking, a good or a bad thing. He concluded his historical survey by pointing out that same-sex love and activity had occurred at all times during recorded history and among all ethnic groups living on earth, hence, the basis for his argument that homosexuality cannot possibly be described as unnatural.

This goes very much against the Kantian condemnation of homosexuality as unnatural. In his teleological interpretation of nature, Schopenhauer makes of male homosexual behavior turns a "stratagem of nature," as Oskar Eichler suggested in 1926. Schopenhauer's explanation of the causes of homosexuality makes use of Aristotle's idea that both male adolescents and old men (above the age of fifty-four) are unlikely to generate healthy offspring, because of the supposedly inferior quality of their semen. Schopenhauer preferred Lamarck's concept of evolution to Darwin's theory. Schopenhauer specialist Christopher Janaway comments that

Schopenhauer's explanation of nature, which forces young and old men to be attracted to each other in order to perfect the human species, is "desperate," yet it is worth pointing out that at the time, Lamarck's school of evolutionary thought was not completely discounted. Schopenhauer, who was eighty-three years of age in 1859 and could have been attracted to younger men, was concerned about the possibly harmful consequences of the "seduction" of minors by elderly homosexual men.

In his view, homosexuality as such is not ethically problematic, but the seduction of adolescents is. Schopenhauer biographer Bryan Magee argues quite persuasively that Schopenhauer was a homosexual who systematically suppressed his same-sex desires. Very much like Goethe and other writers of the time, Schopenhauer not only admired writers like Lord Byron but also shared Goethe's views of women. Schopenhauer gained notoriety with his remark that "only the male intellect, clouded by the sexual impulse, could call the undersized, narrow-shouldered, broad-hipped, and short-legged sex the fair sex." In one of many letters written to his admirer, Julius Frauenstädt, Schopenhauer stressed that women's "faces are nothing alongside those of handsome boys." No wonder that this and similar comments led to the commonly accepted view of Schopenhauer as a misogynist.   *Udo Schüklenk*

Bibliography

Eichler, Oskar. *Die Wurzeln des Frauenhasses bei Arthur Schopenhauer: eine psychanalytische Studie.* Bonn: Marcus & Weber, 1926.

Janaway, Christopher. *Schopenhauer.* Oxford: Oxford University Press, 1994.

Magee, Bryan. *The Philosophy of Schopenhauer.* Oxford: Oxford University Press, 1983.

Schüklenk, Udo. "Arthur Schopenhauer und die Schwulen." *Münchner Zeitschrift für Philosophie* 16–17 (1989): 100–16.

See also Byron, George Gordon, Lord; Evolution; Kant, Immanuel; Pederasty

Schubert, Franz Peter (1797–1828)

One of the pillars of the German art music tradition, Schubert was constructed as a composer in opposition to Ludwig van Beethoven (1770–1827) by the composer-critic Robert Schumann (1810–1856) in a review in his journal *Neue Zeitschrift für Musik:* "Schubert is a more feminine character compared to the other . . . for he pleads and persuades where the man commands." In contrast to Beethoven's career at court and in public concerts, Schubert's activities as a musician took place within the domestic sphere of Biedermeier Vienna, the venue for performances of his compositions being typically the *Schubertiade,* at which he accompanied Johann Michael Vogl in his incomparable songs, or played duets or chamber music. His circle of friends was almost exclusively male and included (besides Vogl, his "second father") an older school friend, Josef von Spaun; a classicizing poet, Johann Mayrhofer, who was eight years his senior and with whom he lived for some time; a sensualist rich boy, Franz von Schober, who is ominously referred to as having led him astray; and, toward the end of his short but enormously productive life, several younger men who cheered him from the depressive effects of the sexually transmitted disease—apparently syphilis—that he contracted in 1822. Not a clearly identified pederast like August von Platen (whose poems he set interestingly) or William Beckford, Schubert nevertheless partook fully in the language and customs of intense male friendship and seems because of his bohemian lifestyle and antiauthoritarian views hardly the sort to have censured physical relations of any kind.

Schubert's homo- or bisexuality, a long-established rumor in gay circles, was first openly broached by Maynard Solomon in an article for a psychoanalytic readership on a veiled autobiographical statement called "Schubert's Dream." It was not until Solomon published a full-scale consideration of the historical and circumstantial evidence in *19th Century Music* that controversy occurred far more intense than the subject warranted. Susan McClary's attempt to read alternative models of subjectivity into the *Unfinished Symphony* was pilloried by the music critics of the (otherwise) recently reformed *New York Times* in 1992. One disturbed Schubertian compared the Nazis' treatment of the composer with his "promotion" as a homosexual composer in the correspondence columns of the *New York Review of Books* (October 20, 1994). Gay scholars held their peace, realizing how great were the stakes of the "classical music" canon in transcendence, autonomy, and (therefore) compulsory heterosexuality. Middlebrow culture, however, has begun to accept the queer Schubert: the sound track of Christopher Hampton's *Carrington* (British, 1995), for instance, uses the slow movement of the late String Quintet in C to signal not only Lytton Strachey's homosexuality but also Carrington's idealized view of him and of their life together. Further explorations of Schubert's music in relation to sexuality seen inevitable.

Philip Brett

Bibliography

Brett, Philip. "Piano Four Hands: Schubert and the Performance of Gay Male Desire." *19th Century Music* 21 (1997): 149–176.

Kramer, Lawrence, ed. "Schubert: Music, Sexuality, Culture." *19th Century Music* 17 (1993): A special issue with articles by Rita Steblin, Maynard Solomon, Kristina Muxfeldt, David Gramit, Kofi Agawu, Susan McClary, James Webster, and Robert S. Winter.

McKay, Elizabeth Norman. *Franz Schubert: A Biography*. Oxford: Clarendon Press, 1996.

Muxfeldt, Kristina. "Schubert, Platen, and the Myth of Narcissus." *Journal of the American Musicological Society* 49 (1996): 480–527.

Solomon, Maynard. "Franz Schubert and the Peacocks of Benvenuto Cellini." *19th Century Music* 12 (1989): 193–206.

———. "Schubert's 'My Dream.'" *American Imago* 38 (1981): 147–54.

See also Beckford, William; Music and Musicians 1: Classical Music; Platen, August Graf von Hallermund; Strachey, (Giles) Lytton

Schuyler, James (1923–1991)

Although born in Chicago, U.S. poet James Schuyler will always be associated with Manhattan as one of the so-called New York poets. He made his name as a writer in a relatively narrow social group that included John Ashbery and Frank O'Hara, but did not really achieve wider recognition until the 1970s.

He and Ashbery wrote a collaborative novel, *A Nest of Ninnies*, in the 1950s. It started out as a private joke long before the possibility of publication was ever considered. Like Schuyler's later novel, *What's for Dinner?* (1979), it makes ruthless fun of the values of American suburban life.

Like O'Hara, Schuyler worked on the staff of the Museum of Modern Art in New York City and also served as W. H. Auden's secretary in Italy for a while. From Auden he seems to have learned a certain lightness of tone, masking seriousness, which is identifiably gay.

Schuyler's life was increasingly interrupted by schizophrenic intervals that do not, however, unduly disturb the calm surfaces of the poetry, which is less flashy than that of Ashbery and O'Hara, and consequently more underrated.

His fourth collection, *The Morning of the Poem* (1980), which won a Pulitzer Prize, contains a number of particularly touching, reminiscent passages celebrating loves that have taken on new value in the living museum of memory. His newly confident and expansive Whitmanesque line proves to be the perfect medium for making personal history a matter of national cultural concern.   *Gregory Woods*

Bibliography

Woods, Gregory. *Articulate Flesh: Male Homoeroticism and Modern Poetry.* New Haven, Conn.: Yale University Press, 1987.

See also Ashbery, John; O'Hara, Frank; Whitman, Walt

Scientific Approaches to Homosexuality

Scientific research on homosexuality cannot be understood without reference to the history of this research and in particular to the history of the concept of homosexuality. Of significance are ideas proposing that homosexuals constitute a third and fourth sex, a theory put forward by Karl-Heinrich Ulrichs in the mid-nineteenth century. Ulrichs believed that the cause of sexual orientation was to be found in our minds. In his view, homosexual men have a female soul, and homosexual women a male soul. Using the Platonic term *urning,* he suggested that homosexuals are a distinct group of people with a different nature from heterosexuals. This idea was later taken up and developed further by another German sex researcher, Magnus Hirschfeld. The cause of homosexuality, he believed, was to be found not in the mind, as Ulrichs believed, but in the glands. Both Hirschfeld and Ulrichs argued that homosexuals should not be persecuted, because their sexual orientation was not deliberately chosen, and they interpreted it as a natural occurrence similar to heterosexuality. Modern sexual orientation researchers, such as neurobiologist Simon LeVay, are strongly influenced by these models, as discussed below.

Recent Developments

Recent studies concerning the biological basis of homosexuality have basically taken two avenues of investigation: one involving physiology and anatomy, and another involving endocrinology and genetics. Both approaches are scientifically flawed.

The brain is a logical place to look when we ask, Is homosexuality biological? and it has been one of the specific areas where investigations on the biological basis of homosexuality have focused. To understand behavior, including sexual behavior, we must begin to understand the brain. We are only at the very beginning of understanding how the brain is responsible for behavior. This is no less true when we talk about sexual behavior. A variety of problems have plagued this research. To understand the role of the brain in human sexual behavior, we need to look carefully at the assumptions of the researchers. This has been a common critique of science in general of late, and it applies just as well to this field.

To investigate the role of the brain in homosexuality in humans, two approaches have been taken: a neuroendocrinological approach, and an approach that looks at the anatomy of specific regions of the brain. Both these approaches have focused on the hypothalamic region of the brain.

The neuroendocrinological approach seeks to look at the interrelationship of hormonal responses and influences of hormones on the brain. The hypothalamus is thought to be the part of the brain that is the most involved in sexual differentiation, and control of sex hormones, sexual behavior, and reproduction. The hypothalamus secretes a variety of releasing factors, which control the release of specific hormones in the pituitary gland. These hormones released from the pituitary then go on to cause the release of hormones from the gonads, or testes and ovaries. In women, injection of estrogen results in an increased level of a hormone called leutinizing hormone (LH) in the blood. This hormone is important for female reproductive function. A few studies have suggested that homosexual men display an increased level of LH in the blood in response to estrogen and heterosexual men do not. Thus, it is hypothesized that a release of LH from the pituitary in response to estrogen is the female differentiation of the hypothalamic-pituitary system. Therefore, according to this hypothesis, the brains of homosexual men have differentiated in a more female direction.

Neuroendocrinological studies have also considered the possible influence of hormones prenatally. The hypothesis put forward here is that the possible reason that homosexual men show this differentiation pattern is androgen (or male hormones) insufficiency during an important developmental stage of the hypothalamus. This hypothesis has been supported solely by research on the development of this system in rats.

The second approach has been to investigate possible associations between differences in brain anatomy and homosexuality. The best known of these studies was done by Simon LeVay, published in *Science* in August 1991. He investigated the size of specific areas of the brain in different men. These areas, which have been investigated in some detail to determine their possible function, have been implicated in sexual arousal and male-typical sexual behavior, almost entirely by studies in rats. There is little knowledge of the function of these areas of the hypothalamus in humans, but the theory is that they function in the same ways as those areas in rats. In his study, LeVay found that one specific area of the hypothalamus, called INAH 3, was significantly smaller in gay men than in heterosexual men. The size of this area in gay men had values that were closer to the values of women (who were not differentiated in terms of sexual orientation).

Other biological studies have focused on genetics. Recently, research into a variety of "undesirable" behavioral traits such as homosexuality, alcoholism, violent behavior, and the like have taken this tack. Pillard's group has been interested primarily in familial relationships. Pillard and Weinrich, in 1986, presented work that suggested an increased rate of homosexuality in brothers of homosexual and bisexual men. Bailey and Pillard, in a fairly classic 1991 twin study, look at male twins. They find that identical twins have the highest rate of homosexuality (52 percent of identical twins of homosexual men were also homosexual), fraternal twins were next, with 22 percent of brothers being homosexual or bisexual, and adoptive brothers at 11 percent. Interestingly enough, only 9.2 percent of nontwin biological brothers of homosexuals were themselves homosexual. This conflicts with the earlier study and is also lower than the rate for fraternal twins and adoptive brothers. Similar studies have been done on female homosexuals, and the data seem to follow the same patterns.

These studies, like all familial and twin studies, have a variety of weaknesses. Although they may suggest some genetic component to homosexuality, they suffer from probable ascertainment bias (that is, individuals with homosexual siblings or twins would be more likely to be "recruited"). Although they attempt to deal with this question, they are unable to eliminate it as a potential bias. In addition, their sample sizes are quite small, and even twin studies can't eliminate the effect of environment. Although the environment of siblings is similar,

twins share different environments than nontwin brothers because of temporal factors. Identical and fraternal twins are often treated differently.

Hamer's group followed up this work with a study that purports to map DNA markers for homosexuality. This study was carried out in 76 male homosexuals from one geographic location. It offers statistical evidence that genes influencing sexual orientation may reside in the q28 region of the X chromosome. Females have two X chromosomes, but they pass a copy of only one to a son. The likelihood of two sons receiving a copy of the same Xq28 from their mother is thus 50 percent. They found a region of the X chromosome that was shared in 33 pairs of siblings. Hamer's finding is often misinterpreted as showing that all 66 men from these 33 pairs shared the same Xq28 sequence. But what Hamer really demonstrated was that each member of the 33 concordant pairs shared his Xq28 region with his brother but not with any of the other 64 men. No single specific Xq28 sequence was common to all 66 men.

A Canadian research team has been unable to duplicate the finding using a comparable experimental design. Furthermore, Hamer confined his search to the X chromosome on the basis of family interviews. These interviews reveal a disproportionately high number of male homosexuals on the mothers' side of the family. Women could be more likely to know details of family medical history, rendering these interviews less than objective in terms of directing experimental design.

All these studies, from the neuroendocrinological to the neuroanatomical to the genetic have the same fundamental flaw: how homosexuality is defined. The bias of the researchers is that homosexuality is a simple, two-dimensional trait (you have it or you don't). There are serious problems of definition, and without concrete and unbiased ways to define homosexuality (a potentially impossible task), it is absolutely impossible to determine a biological cause.

Many studies have equated the presence of female-typical sexual behavior (specifically, a behavior called lordosis, which is a behavior that facilitates copulation) in male rats to homosexuality in male humans. They have completely oversimplified the issue of human sexual orientation and have been unable to include the complexities present in human behavior; they have also ignored years of research on human sexuality. The human studies are similarly flawed. A major problematic feature of those studies is their categorization of individual subjects by sexuality. The definition of homosexuality found in these studies generally does not (or cannot, as in the case of LeVay's postmortem study) take the complexities of behavior into account.

Second, it is clear that the assumption that "gay men are like women" (and the concomitant assumption "lesbians are like men," although there has been very little research on lesbians) underlies much of this research. Yet that assumption is really based on societal biases and is problematic in the investigation of the possible "biological basis" for homosexuality. These assumptions produce biases in the way the questions are asked, the way the research is carried out, and the manner in which the data are analyzed. It may well be impossible to come to a balanced perspective on this field because of the intense and deeply imbedded societal bias that exists.

In addition, these anatomical and physiological studies can in no way distinguish between effects that are due to "innate" factors or those related to pre- or postnatal development or experience. Of necessity, these studies look at adults. The brain is quite plastic throughout the life span. There is absolutely no evidence that changes in either neuroanatomy or neuroendocrine function are not a result of experience.

Another issue is that the question really being asked is What is the biological basis for homosexuality? rather than Is there a biological basis for homosexuality? Researchers thus assume that homosexuality is biological, which is far from proven. We perhaps have a few clues, but the research to date has not led to even the beginnings of an answer to the question Is homosexuality biological?

Ethical Considerations

Biologic sexual orientation research serves no immediate medical purpose because homosexuality is not considered a disease by bodies such as the World Health Organization or the American Psychiatric Association. Hence, there is no immediate medical need to conduct biological sexual orientation research simply because no human pain is supposed to be alleviated. Previous research into the causes of homosexuality emerged from a desire to eradicate homosexuality. Conversion therapies, including electroshock treatment, hormonal therapies, genital mutilation, and brain surgery, were in most Western countries a consequence of etiologic sexual orientation research. The Chinese Psychiatric Association in the 1995 edition of the *Chinese Classification of Mental Disorders* still considers homosexuality a mental disorder. In China, people believed to be homosexuals are regularly subjected to police harassment and prison sentences. Homosexual "therapy" involving drugs, acupuncture, and electroshocks is still common in major hospitals such as the Nanjing Psychiatry Research Institute. A National University of Singapore psychiatrist asks in an article published in 1995 whether "pre-symptomatic testing for homosexuality should be offered in the absence of treatment," thereby accepting the idea that homosexuality is something in need of a cure. Given the obvious danger of widespread abuse of the results of sexual orientation research, it comes as no surprise that there has been debate about the ethical merits of etiologic sexual orientation research.

Arguments in favor of research into the causes of homosexuality have been proposed most notably by U.S.-based researchers trying to further a domestic political agenda. Very much like Ulrichs and Hirschfeld their motive is to demonstrate that homosexuality is immutable and not a matter of choice. It has been suggested that a biological cause of homosexuality would lead to the recognition of homosexuals as a distinct group of people comparable to ethnic minorities. This, in turn, would improve the legal situation of gays and lesbians because they could claim equal opportunity protection based on an amendment of the U.S. Constitution. This position has been criticized by legal scholars. Other arguments suggest that when homosexuality is considered destiny rather than choice, heterosexuals would be less inclined to discriminate against gays and lesbians. Stein has pointed out that this argument ignores that what needs to be protected is (not only) sexual orientation as such, because it is possible to conceal one's homosexuality, but the conscious decision of homosexuals to come out and live readily identifiable by society as homosexuals without fear of discrimination.

Sexual orientation researchers without sufficient competence in ethics mistakenly believe that a genetic cause of homosexuality would have a number of normative implications. Dean Hamer, for instance, thinks that it would demonstrate that homosexuality is "normal." He and his associates have suggested that a possible future genetic probe should not be used to "try to assess or alter a person's current or future sexual orientation, either heterosexual or homosexual, or other normal attributes of human behavior."

Hamer's argument is philosophically unsound, constituting a good example of a naturalistic fallacy.

Hamer et al. believe that a major genetic factor contributes to homosexual orientation. This makes it in their interpretation a normal attribute of human behavior. They argue that it follows from this that homosexuality is a normal attribute of human behavior. They argue that it would be unethical to use this information to select a child's sexual orientation because they assume that whatever is genetically influenced or determined therefore ought to be. Of course, this is not so. Nature cannot provide us with any moral guidance about how we ought to live our lives. Genetic information may be a determining factor in a variety of human behaviors. Whether we should try to use this information to assess or alter a person's behavior is a decision that must be based on a normative evaluation of that behavior, whatever its cause.

The reasons for the early attempts by Hirschfeld and Ulrichs and the reasons for Hamer's preoccupation with demonstrating that homosexuality is "natural" or "normal" have much to do with another set of mistaken beliefs, in this case mistaken ideas about the normative implications of normality and naturalness. These scientists seem to think that nature has a prescriptive normative force such that what is deemed natural or normal is necessarily good and therefore ought to be. Everything that falls outside these terms is interpreted as unnatural and abnormal, and it has been argued that this constitutes sufficient reason to consider homosexuality worth avoiding. Arguments that appeal to "normality" to provide us with moral guidelines also risk committing the naturalistic fallacy. This fallacy is committed when one mistakenly interprets the way things in fact are as the way they ought to be. For instance, Hamer and colleagues commit this error in their *Science* article when they state that "it would be fundamentally unethical to use such information to try to assess or alter a person's current or future sexual orientation, either heterosexual or homosexual, or other normal attributes of human behavior." Hamer et al. believe a major genetic factor contributing to sexual orientation. From this they think it follows that homosexuality is normal, and thus worthy of preservation. Thus they believe that genetics can tell us what is normal, and that the content of what is normal tells us what ought to be. This is a typical example of a naturalistic fallacy.

Normality can be defined in a number of ways, but none of them directs us in the making of moral judgments. Normality should always be defined in a scientific, *descriptive* sense as a statistical average. Appeals to what is usual, regular, and/or conforming to existing standards ultimately collapse then into statistical statements. For an ethical evaluation of homosexuality, it is irrelevant whether homosexuality is normal or abnormal in this sense. All sorts of human traits and behaviors are abnormal in a statistical sense, but this is not a sufficient justification for a negative ethical judgment about them. Second, "normality" might be defined in a functional sense, where what is normal is something that has served an adaptive function from an evolutionary perspective. This definition of normality can be found in sociobiology, which seeks biological explanations for social behavior. But even if sociobiology could establish that certain behavioral traits were the direct result of biological evolution, no moral assessment of these traits would follow.

Positions holding the view that homosexuality is unnatural, and therefore wrong, also inevitably develop incoherences. They fail to explicate the basis on which the line between natural and unnatural is drawn. More important, they fail to explain why we should consider all human-made or artificial things as immoral or wrong. These views are usually firmly based in a nonempirical, *prescriptive* interpretation of nature rather than a scientific *descriptive* approach. They define arbitrarily what is natural and have to import other normative assumptions and premises to build a basis for their conclusions. For instance, they often claim that an entity called "God" has declared homosexuality to be unnatural and sinful. Unfortunately, these confused analyses have real-world consequences. In Singapore, "unnatural acts" are considered a criminal offense, and "natural intercourse" is arbitrarily defined as "the coitus of the male and female organs." A recent high court decision there declared oral sex "unnatural," and therefore a criminal offense, unless it leads to subsequent reproductive intercourse.

Bioethical analyses of the normative implications of the human genome project was quick to point out that a contextualization of genetics research is crucial. Genetics sexual orientation research takes place in the United States primarily because those homosexuals who conduct it believe it will help further the political agenda of gays and lesbians. The problem is that the consequences of such research (i.e., a possible probe) won't be confined to the United States. Their research results will be interpreted quite differently in different parts of the world, and with some likelihood more often than not they would be used in a manner that would be considered unethical not only by Western bioethicists but also by those responsible for the development of such devices.

Conclusion

There is no persuasive evidence that sexual orientation is biological. Historically, much of the research that has been undertaken served primarily the political agendas of those conducting it. This holds true even for ongoing research. The ethical and political question is whether etiologic sexual orientation research should be undertaken in homophobic societies. The debate in this regard takes place primarily in Western societies and disregards the implications of possible research results in non-Western societies.

Udo Schüklenk
Michelle Murrain

Bibliography

Bailey, J. Michael, and Riçhard. C. Pillard. "A Genetic Study of Male Sexual Orientation." *Archives of General Psychiatry* 48 (1991): 1089–96.

Byne, William. "Why We Cannot Conclude That Sexual Orientation Is Primarily a Biological Phenomenon." *Journal of Homosexuality* 34 (1997): 73–80.

Chinese Psychiatric Assoc. and Nanjing Medical University Teaching Hospital. *The Chinese Classification of Mental Disorders*. Nanjing, 1995.

Halley, Janet E. "Sexual Orientation and the Politics of Biology: A Critique of the Argument from Immutability." *Stanford Law Review* 46 (1994): 503–68.

Hamer, Dean H., et al. "A Linkage Between DNA Markers on the X Chromosome and Male Sexual Orientation." *Science* 261 (1993): 21–327.

Hirschfeld, Magnus. *Die Homosexualität des Mannes und des Weibes*. Berlin: Ulrich Marcus, 1914.

Katz, Jonathan Ned. *Gay American History*. New York: Thomas Cromwell, 1976.

LeVay, Simon. "A Difference in Hypothalamic Structure between Heterosexual and Homosexual Men." *Science* 253 (1991): 1034–36.

———. *Queer Science: The Use and Abuse of Research into Homosexuality*. Cambridge: MIT Press, 1996.

Levin, Michael. "Why Homosexuality Is Abnormal." *Monist* 67 (1984): 251–83.

Lim, L.C.C. "Present Controversies in the Genetics of Male Homosexuality." *Annals Academy of Medicine Singapore* 24 (1995): 759–62.

Pillard, Richard C., and James D. Weinrich. "Evidence of Familial Nature of Male Homosexuality." *Archives of General Psychiatry* 43 (1986): 808–12.

Rice, G., et al. "Male Homosexuality: Absence of Linkage to Microsatellite Markers on the X Chromosome in a Canadian Study." Presented at the 21st Annual Meeting of the International Academy of Sex Research, Provincetown, Mass., 1995.

Schüklenk, Udo, and David Mertz. "Christliche Kirchen und AIDS." In *Die Lehre des Unheils*. Edgar Dahl, ed. Hamburg, Germany: Carlsen, 1993, 263–79, 309–12.

Schüklenk, Udo, and Michael Ristow. "The Ethics of Research into the Causes of Homosexuality." *Journal of Homosexuality* 31, 3/4 (1996): 5–30.

Ulrichs, Karl H. (aka Numa Numantius). "*Vindex. Social-juristische Studien über mann-männliche Liebe.*" Pamphlet. Leipzig, 1864.

Vines, Stephen. "Singapore Court Blows Away Passion." *Independent* (London), February 22, 1997, A1.

See also Animal Sexual Behavior; Evolution; Hirschfeld, Magnus; Natural Law; Sexology; Third Sex

Scythians

Defining the barbarian "other" is a common feature of the ideology of classical Greek and Roman authors, who construct other peoples in terms of their own cultural prejudices. *Scythians* is a loose term for one such people, "barbarian" nomads speaking an Indo-European tongue and inhabiting inhospitable northern climes somewhere between the rivers Danube and Volga.

According to Herodotus (6.84), to drink in Scythian style means to drink wine without mixing it with water, a sign to the Greeks of an almost indecent lack of refinement. Other barbarian practices, such as making cloaks out of human scalps and drinking out of gilded skulls, were also attributed to the Scythians.

After coming into contact with Greek colonies in the Black Sea area, the Scythians seem to have opted for the advantages of a more settled life and established a kingdom on the Russian steppes, which reached its zenith in the fourth century B.C.E. and then declined in the wake of frequent incursions by peoples like the Sarmatae (of Iranian origin).

Herodotus also records that soldiers in the Scythian army, which had been prevented from invading Egypt by the Egyptian king Psammetichus, looted the temple of Aphrodite Urania, while retreating through the town of Ascalon in Syria. For this act of sacrilege, the goddess inflicted the robbers with what Herodotus calls the "female disease," a disease that was transmitted to the descendants of these men, whom the Scythians called *enarees* (1.105).

Elsewhere, Herodotus records that the enarees (whom he categorizes as *androgunoi,* or menwomen) used a particular form of divination taught to them by Aphrodite. Scholars have thus suggested that the *enarees* were seers of the shamanistic sort who, like the Greek seer Tiresias, transgressed gender boundaries and so occupied marginal positions in Scythian society.

But the author of the Hippocratic text *Airs, Waters, Places* claims that the majority of Scythian men, especially among the upper classes who rode horses frequently, became impotent (*eunouchiai*) and subsequently dressed and lived like women; the author attributes this disease to the development of swellings in the joints, which the Scythians attempted to cure by severing the veins behind each ear and so destroying the semen essential for sexual potency (22). As is assumed by both the Hippocratic authors and Aristotle, loss of the capacity to produce semen is responsible for the change of state from male to female.

In perhaps the most interesting tale involving the Scythians, Herodotus relates that the Amazons found the Scythians willing sexual partners and eventually settled down with them. There was clearly no problem with sexual impotence. Rather than adopt the sedentary lifestyle of the Scythian women, the Amazons retained their customs, one of which was wearing men's clothes. This gender reversal, in the case of both the Scythians and the Amazons, is indicative of the manner in which Greek ethnographers constructed the foreign "other," and is not really evidence of the existence of a race of congenital transvestites, however attractive such a possibility may be.   *Michael Lambert*

Bibliography

de Selincourt, A., trans. *Herodotus: The Histories.* Reprint. Harmondsworth, U.K.: Penguin, 1968.
Hall, Edith. *Inventing the Barbarian.* Clarendon, U.K.: Oxford University Press, 1989.

See also Egypt, Ancient; Etruscans; Greece; Rome, Ancient

Settembrini, Luigi (1813–1876)

Neapolitan Luigi Settembrini was one of the great patriots of nineteenth-century Italy. From a young age, he opposed the oppressive Bourbon regime that then ruled the southern part of Italy. His inflammatory political tracts led him to be sentenced to death, but he won a late reprieve and spent instead nearly all the decade leading up to Italian unification in prison. He subsequently took up the chair of Italian literature at Naples University before his election to the senate.

As a writer, Settembrini is largely remembered for his memoirs, yet it was the posthumous publication in 1977 of a novella, *I Neoplatonici,* written during his imprisonment, that gives him a place in the history of homosexual literature. Settembrini presents *I Neoplatonici* as a translation from a Greek manuscript. It is the tale of the "platonic" love of two youths and vaunts the superiority of male homosexuality over heterosexual relationships as something heroic and less economically wasteful. Interestingly, although both boys later marry, they still sleep together occasionally for the remainder of their lives. The association of Hellenism and homosexuality in the figure of Settembrini implicitly taints the myth of Italian masculinity that was promulgated at the time of unification. This in part explains the text's very late publication. In the early twentieth century, philosopher Benedetto Croce and his associates agreed to silence this unexpected paean to Greek love by one of democratic Italy's most stalwart advocates to protect the author's memory and the integrity of the nation.   *Derek Duncan*

Bibliography

Settembrini, Luigi. *I Neoplatonici.* Milan: Rizzoli, 1977.

See also Italian Literature; Italy; Renaissance Neoplatonism

Sex Education

We have no choice as to whether children are sexually educated because they acquire sex education from birth. Our choices concern the extent to which this education is systematic, comprehensive, and accurate. Children most often want their parents to be their primary source of information about sexuality. Most parents want the schools to provide sex education, and most want programs to begin in elementary school.

Currently, formal sex education varies from a few hours of instruction on anatomy and menstruation to a semester-long course. Few students are exposed to systematic and comprehensive programs. Those who argue that sex education is ineffective fail to realize that we have not yet tried comprehensive sex education programs.

Inclusion of information about sexual orientation in sex education programs has sparked controversy across the United States and attracted national attention after the defeat of the New York City public schools' "Children of the Rainbow" curriculum. The importance of discussing same-sex sexual behavior has also been highlighted by the HIV disease epidemic.

The extent to which homosexuality is discussed in school-based programs and at what ages varies widely. Those who oppose including sexual orientation in sex education programs often argue that providing any information amounts to promoting an alternative lifestyle. Control over these decisions has been, for the most part, at the local and state levels. Although few states prohibit discussion of homosexuality, state-approved guidelines for sex education often omit discussion of sexual identity and orientation.

Sex education programs rarely present homosexuality as a normal variation in sexual orientation. When students are presented with information concerning sexual orientation, it most often occurs during one, or at most two, class periods in a health class and is rarely integrated into the curriculum. Discussion is often limited to simple definitions of homosexuality, heterosexuality, and bisexuality. Affirming messages concerning sexual identity and orientation are exceedingly rare.

Teachers claim to be ill-prepared to teach about homosexuality. Many rely on the mass media for information and perceive their schools as being unsupportive of gay, lesbian, and bisexual students. Some teachers fear for their own job security should they be supportive of gay, lesbian, and bisexual students or oppose antigay harassment.

Attempts have been made by the U.S. Congress to limit discussion of homosexuality in an affirming climate by attempting to prohibit schools from receiving federal funds if they encourage or support "homosexuality as a positive lifestyle." Yet policies that ban discussion of positive views on homosexuality have been challenged in court.

Generally, there are two varieties of sex education programs: abstinence-only programs and postponement and protection programs. Abstinence-only programs typically prohibit discussion of masturbation, homosexuality, birth control, and abortion. Evaluation data from these programs show that they are not effective in postponing or decreasing sexual activity and that they may increase sexual behavior by stimulating rebellion rather than decreasing sexual behavior by inspiring responsibility.

Postponement and protection programs do not withhold information. They promote the ideal that adolescents should postpone sexual behavior but should be knowledgeable about protection from disease and pregnancy, so that when they decide to become sexually active they will be prepared. These programs have been successful in decreasing the likelihood of participation in sexual activity, particularly for those who are not already sexually active. The programs also increase the likelihood of use of appropriate birth control and disease protection when youths choose to become active. Such programs are more effective at reaching the goal of decreasing sexual behavior among adolescents than the "just say no" approach. There is no evidence from evaluations of sexuality education programs that comprehensive programs lead to the early initiation of sexual activity, to increased sexual activity, or to experimentation with homosexuality or bisexuality.

Data from college students suggest that discussion of homosexuality can decrease antigay prejudice but has no effect on the incidence of homosexual behavior. In other words, discussions about homosexuality can lead students to be more accepting of homosexual behavior in others but do not lead them to experiment with same-sex behavior themselves. There are no data as yet on precollege students.

Taken together, these findings suggest that the "don't tell" approach or the "just say no" approach may lead to rebellion among adolescents and greater experimentation, whereas talking openly and honestly about the varieties of sexual behavior and identities, including homosexuality, is likely to lead to less experimentation and greater acceptance. Such discussion could also decrease prejudice, victimization, and perhaps even the suicide rate, given that a considerable number of adolescent suicides are associated with confusion about sexual identity.

Sexual identity is the process through which people come to understand their sexual attractions and behaviors and incorporate them into their self-concepts. Most people grow up with expectations of sexual interest in members of the other sex and most find confirmation of these expectations. Therefore,

S most adopt a heterosexual role, rarely questioning the social expectations of heterosexual attraction, courtship, marriage, and parenthood. Others find that they are uncomfortable in these roles and perhaps that they enjoy or desire to participate in sexual or gender behaviors that are contradictory to these role expectations. Without accurate knowledge and information about sexual orientations and identity, these thoughts and feelings can lead adolescents to engage in risky behavior including unsafe sexual activities, which in turn can lead to pregnancy, infection from sexually transmitted diseases, substance abuse, even suicide. Coupled with isolation, discrimination, and harassment experienced in school, these risk behaviors can be pronounced among gay and lesbian youth as they cope with sexual feelings thought to be "unacceptable" to parents. Open discussion of homosexuality and bisexuality would be particularly beneficial for these children.

Michael Stevenson

Bibliography

Gambrell, Alan E., and Debra Hafner. *Unfinished Business: A SIECUS Assessment of State Sexuality Education Programs.* New York: Sex Information and Education Council of the U.S., 1993.

Parents, Schools and Values: Hearings before the Subcommittee on Oversight and Investigations of the House Committee on Economic and Educational Opportunities. 104th Congress, 1995. Testimony of the American Psychological Association.

See also Children's Books; Community Centers; Education: Theory and Pedagogy; Schools

Sex Practice: Anal Sex

Gay porno director Matt Sterling's film *Heatwave* contains a sequence remarkable for what it suggests about anal pleasure and its complicated and sometimes contradictory relationship to genital sexuality. Following an extended orgy staged in and beside a swimming pool, seven men—young, muscular, and, as is typical of Sterling's films, white—kneel on hands and knees along the edge of the pool, their asses facing the water. Using mammoth squirt guns, two actors swimming in the pool spray these asses with water. The seven men cover their flaccid penises and testicles with their hands while gleefully thrusting their asses in the air. The camera cuts

in to reveal their anuses in extreme close-up, some of which react to the blasts of water by contracting, as well as to show us their facial responses to the blasts: they laugh and flinch. The action is accompanied by a sprightly contrapuntal tune played on a synthesizer, the music emphasizing the playfulness of the scene and signaling its almost baroque excess. Eventually, the seven men jump into the pool, capture their two buddies, then use the same squirt guns to pump water up their asses. The scene ends with a kind of perverse inversion of the boyhood peeing contest: as their companions cheer them on, the two men see who can expel their water farther. How might one make sense of such a sequence in the context of a porno film, given its lack of the usual signifiers of homoerotic visual pleasure—erect penises, oral or anal intercourse, come shots?

Although researchers insist that anal sex is far from universally practiced among even self-identified gay men, it remains today in the West perhaps the act most often symbolically equated with male-to-male eroticism. To cite just one perhaps idiosyncratic example: a recent episode of the popular comedy series *Saturday Night Live* guest-hosted by gay icon David Duchovny featured a cartoon depicting the exploits of two "Ambiguously Gay Superheroes." The cartoon was filled with numerous (humorous) visual references to anal eroticism, including one repeated image of the two heroes flying through the air, one mounted atop the other. There were virtually no visual references, however, to any other kind of homoerotic sexual activity.

A number of physiological factors might account for the pleasure of so-called receptive anal sex among men, including "nerve distribution, proximity to the genitals, muscular relationship to other pelvic muscles and anal contractions during sexual activity" (Morin 8), stimulation of the prostate, and the pleasurable sensations associated with the emptying of the bowels. The so-called active partner in anal sex receives pleasure from having his penis stimulated by his lover's anus and rectum. Common sense suggests that the affective and emotional appeal of anal sex resides in the desire for intensely intimate physical contact with another human being, romantic fantasies of either "submitting to" or "conquering" one's object of affection, and the myth of the lovers' fusion. It is thus not unheard of for some gay men to "save" anal sex for partners for whom they feel particularly strong sensations of love and trust. For at least some gay theorists, however, these accounts do not sufficiently explain the profound phantasmic appeal of anal intercourse, particularly given the virulence of the cultural taboos against the act. One of the many consequences of HIV disease has been the intensification of this anal taboo, such that some gay men today prefer to avoid anal sex altogether rather than risk the possibility of HIV infection. At the same time, some of the more determined now sport stickers that proclaim "Buttfucking is fun."

In different but related ways, both Michel Foucault and Leo Bersani have relied on the concept of the human subject to explain the pleasures and dangers of anal sex. Briefly, to be a subject means both to be autonomous, independent, sovereign, and in possession of a consciousness—as opposed to an object—and to be subjected or subjugated to an "other," whether that other be God, a king, the law (parental or juridical), or a more dispersed set of rules, practices, and procedures that ensure the maintenance of (Western) culture. Both theorists see anal sex as embodying both a radical potential for the dissolution of the self as we know it and an assault on dominant forms of subjectivity.

For Foucault, the practices that ensure the production of our contemporary subjectivity are associated with what he terms disciplinary society. According to Foucault, the nineteenth century in particular saw the emergence in the West of a "meticulous control of the operations of the body" (137). Through military, medical, educational, and industrial institutions, as well as practices of colonization, slavery, and child rearing, a number of processes of normalization and disciplinarity coalesced to inaugurate an "uninterrupted, constant coercion" of the subject. This coercion "assured the constant subjection of [the body's] forces and imposed upon them a relation of docility-utility" (137).

Although Foucault rarely spoke of anal sex per se, his work suggests compelling ways to think about the meaning of this sexual practice. In an interview in a French gay magazine, Foucault notes the historical potential in gay sexuality to make of the body "a field of production for extraordinarily polymorphous pleasure" (Le Bitoux 33). For Foucault, anal sex, as well as other "monstrously counterfeit" pleasures such as fist fucking, seeks both to eroticize areas of the body other than the penis while simultaneously attempting to desexualize physical pleasure itself, creating, through the negation of sexual pleasure, new forms of physical pleasure. Foucault is particularly interested in gay sex as it might make possible "the affirmation of non-

identity" (Le Bitoux 36). According to Foucault, certain sexual practices common to gay men—we might assume anal sex to be among them—contain the potential for "de-subjectifying" oneself, for "de-subjugating oneself to a certain point, perhaps not radically, but significantly."

Foucault's account of the disciplined body also suggests that anal sex might represent a kind of willful thwarting of disciplinary society, which understands anal sex as a dangerous "misuse" of the anus—and it is no coincidence that both the religious right and the medical establishment sometimes cast the act in these terms, as evidenced most recently by what Paula A. Treichler has termed the "epidemic of signification" surrounding AIDS. Anal sex makes a phantasmic, noneconomical use of the body's forces, squandering energy (and sperm) on nonreproductive sexuality and threatening to dissolve the body's "integrity" by reducing it to a hole that can never be sufficiently filled. Unlike the penis, the anus does not require any period of "recovery" following orgasm. It is potentially insatiable. Some men can actually achieve orgasm simply from anal penetration, and the failure to achieve an erection while being penetrated is not always evidence that the act is void of pleasure. And in anal sex, the roles of penetrator and penetrated are easily reversed; anal sex advertises the pleasure of an unabated series of reversals of "active" and "passive" pleasures.

Bersani's "Is the Rectum a Grave?" remains one of the most engaging if controversial psychoanalytic accounts of why gay men have anal sex. Working from a sometimes implicit neo-Freudian perspective, Bersani sees the taboo against anal pleasure as necessitated by the cultural demand to negotiate the oedipal triangle, with its insistence that anatomical males take up a properly masculine, "active" subject position, and females a properly feminine, "passive" one. According to patriarchal, phallocentric culture, a "successful" resolution of the Oedipus complex is marked by a genital organization of sexuality appropriate to one's gender; for the boy child, this means (temporarily) abandoning one's "active" desire for the mother (and accompanying "passive" desire for the father) in order to preserve one's penis from the father's threat of castration; for the girl child, it means forsaking both the "active" pleasure of clitoral masturbation and its object—the mother—and adopting the properly "feminine," "passive" pleasures of vaginal sex and the desire to receive a child from the father as com-

S pensation for being "castrated." On its journey from the small human animal to the human subject, the child is thus required to abandon its constitutional bisexuality, and the "polymorphously perverse" pleasures of what Freud termed the oral stage and the sadistic anal stage—the latter characterized by the psychic and physiological pleasures associated with the giving and withholding of feces. Such an abandonment is never absolute, however, and traces of this "pre-genital organization of the libido" remain in a repressed or sublimated form even in so-called normal (heterosexual) adult sexuality.

For Bersani, anal sex symbolically represents the ecstasy of the dissolution of the self. Through a careful rereading of Freud, Bersani argues that "sexual pleasure occurs whenever a certain threshold of intensity is reached, when the organization of the self is momentarily disturbed by sensations or affective processes somehow 'beyond' those connected with psychic organization" (217). According to Bersani, gender as a culturally and historically inscribed subject position is an eroticized phantasmic account of the subject's bodily experience of mastery and subordination, masculine "activity" representing a kind of self-hyperbole, feminine "passivity" a kind of self-annihilation. Phallocentrism is the excessive privileging of the former and devaluing of the latter. According to phallocentrism's logic, one must be "either" masculine "or" feminine; there is no place "between" genders—or at least no place sanctioned by culture. Phallocentric culture thus "reworks" the physiology of heterosexuality in such a way as to bind the body's experience of sexual pleasure to a social script in which men are valued for and find pleasure in their ability to be "on top," women "on the bottom." It ties "anatomy" to "destiny" by reserving the pleasure of self-hyperbole exclusively for males, and self-annihilation for females.

For Bersani, "sex as self-hyperbole is perhaps a repression of sex as self-abolition" (218). The reverse, however, is not the case; self-abolition may be rather a tautology for sexual pleasure, "at least in the mode in which it [sexuality] is constituted": again, rereading Freud, Bersani suggests, "the sexual emerges as the jouissance of exploded limits, as the ecstatic suffering into which the human organism momentarily plunges when it is 'pressed' beyond a certain threshold of endurance" (217).

The penetrated gay man thus re-presents, to himself, to his partners, and to his culture at large, the "murderous" pleasure of a deliberate abandonment and annihilation of the masculine, active self.

He is a dangerous reminder to phallocentric culture of the fact that the (masculine) self is nothing more than a necessary evolutionary evil, a "practical convenience" that makes human survival possible. Bersani suggests that "the rectum is the grave in which the masculine ideal (an ideal shared—differently—by men and women) of proud subjectivity is buried" (222). According to Bersani, the rectum "should be celebrated for its very potential for death," owing to the fact that it "never stops representing the internalized phallic male [again—internalized by both men and women, given the constitutional bisexuality of the subject, as well as phallocentric culture's linking of the possession of the self with the possession of a penis] as an infinitely loved object of sacrifice."

Both theorists are working from the assumption that the anus represents a site where the division between self and non-self is particularly problematic, not "essentially" but in terms of what we might clumsily call the cultural construction of the organ. Unlike the genitals, the excretory functions of the anus are not "redeemed" by procreative sexuality. The anus is a troubling reminder of our animality, and all the surplus repression of culture cannot erase our awareness that we shit to live. Anal sex is a celebration of the possibility of undoing our subjectivity, of rewriting culture's repressive and restrictive understanding of gender and sexuality, and of opening up new possibilities for bodily pleasure.

John Champagne

Bibliography

Bersani, Leo. "Is the Rectum a Grave?" In *AIDS, Cultural Analysis, Cultural Activism*. Douglas Crimp, ed. Cambridge: MIT Press, 1988, 197–222.

Foucault, Michel. *Discipline and Punish*. Alan Sheridan, trans. New York: Vintage Books, 1979.

Freud, Sigmund. *Sexuality and the Psychology of Love*. New York: Macmillan, 1963.

———. *Three Essays on the Theory of Sexuality*. James Strachey, trans. New York: Basic Books, 1975.

Halperin, David M. *Saint Foucault: Towards a Gay Hagiography*. New York: Oxford University Press, 1995.

Hocquenghem, Guy. *Homosexual Desire*. Daniella Dangoor, trans. 1978. Reprint. Durham, N.C.: Duke University Press, 1993.

Le Bitoux, Jean. "Michel Foucault, le gai savoir." *Mec* 5 (June 1988): 32–36.

Morin, Jack. *Anal Pleasure & Health*, 2d ed. Burlingame, Calif.: Yes Press, 186.

Treichler, Paula A. "AIDS, Homophobia, and Biomedical Discourse: An Epidemic of Signification." *AIDS, Cultural Analysis, Cultural Activism* Cambridge, Mass.: MIT Press, 1988, 31–70.

See also AIDS; Foucault, Michel; Pornography; Sadomasochism; Sex Practice: Fisting; Sex Practice: Watersports and Scat

Sex Practice: Fisting

Fisting, also called "handballing" or "fist fucking," is the insertion of the hand, wrist, and even forearm of the active partner (fister) into the rectum and sigmoid colon of the passive partner (fistee). It is primarily a male-male activity, although lesbians and other women sometimes practice it both anally and vaginally. Fisting by an inexperienced or overenthusiastic partner can be dangerous, owing to risks of tearing internal tissues and of infection. Nonetheless, experienced practitioners claim it provides pleasure, fulfillment, and spiritual tranquillity.

Although many people involved in S/M practice fisting, some of them say it is not real S/M activity because its object is pleasure, based on intense trust, intimacy, and physical awareness, rather than erotic pain. Fistees say its sensuality stems from stimulation of tissues not usually stimulated and from pressure on internal organs. For men fisting offers unique prostate contact. Since internal body temperature is warmer than skin, fisters also experience intense feelings of intimacy.

A fistee must be prepared through anal stretching and relaxation. The bowel of the fistee is first cleansed with a series of enemas. The fisting is accomplished by inserting fingers into the anus; once they have passed through the sphincter the hand can slowly be formed into a fist and moved backward and forward in the body of the fistee or used, by carefully forming the fingers into a cone, to push further into the bowel. Insertion, hand movements, and withdrawal should be slow for the fistee's pleasure and to avoid damage to the colon or rectum.

Fisting raises health concerns. In earlier days of the AIDS crisis fisting was suspect as a primary means of spreading HIV because of its promiscuous occurrence in bathhouses; but practiced with proper hygiene, it can be considered a safer-sex practice since no exchange of fluids occurs. Large quantities of lubricant are required, and inexpensive Crisco was once commonly used. Even though a condom is not involved, safer-sex advisers now recommend that only water-based lubricants be used, since oil-based lubricants may coat a virus and protect it from the body's immune system. Safety also requires that even protected anal intercourse occur before, not after, fisting.

Fisters clip their nails very short and file them to avoid scratching. Most fisters wear latex gloves to avoid passing or contracting infections through minute cuts in the skin or abrasions in the rectal tissue. A separate, clearly identified lubricant container for each fistee is essential to avoid spreading hepatitis, various amoebas, giardiasis, shigellosis, salmonellosis, campylobacter, or other diseases.

Enemas and fisting disrupt and remove bacterial flora in the bowel; for HIV-positive fistees this is a problem. They should consult their physicians about replacement supplements. In rare cases, bacteria natural to the rectum and colon can be pushed up into the intestinal tract, causing peritonitis. Because there are no neurological pain receptors in the bowels, fisting can cause unrealized ruptures, leading to dangerous internal hemorrhaging with no external signs. Any visible sign of internal bleeding demands immediate urgent medical attention.

Despite the risks, fisting seems to be widely practiced without serious consequences, and at least one organization, Fist Fuckers of America (FFA), exists for devotees.   *James A. Eby*

Bibliography

Herrman, Bert. *TRUST/The Hand Book: A Guide to the Sensual and Spiritual Art of Handballing*. San Francisco: Alamo Square Press, 1991.

See also AIDS; Sadomasochism; Sex Practice: Anal Sex

Sex Practice: Oral Sex

Dividing homosexual practice into oral, anal, and genital emphasizes the sexual pleasure of using the mouth, anus, or genitals. Homosexual "oral sex" usually implies the meeting of a mouth and a penis but can also include a mouth and anus or incorporate other species (bestiality). Sucking toes, ears, fingers, nipples, testicles, or other body parts exercises the mouth. Kissing represents the only sexual intercourse joining the same parts of both partners. In oral masturbation, some particularly nimble males can fellate themselves.

Oral sexual practices comprise talk itself. Talking about oral sex exercises analogies: lick, suck, eat, nurse, milk, or taste. Sexual talking (as in "phone sex") concentrates on oral communication. Talk and action don't necessarily correspond; thus within male slang, use of the word *cocksucker* is more common than the practice itself.

Studies of sexual practice rely on interviews and self-reports that reflect views of the literate (and oral). English speakers have connected oral sex with the French. Urban dwellers couple anal sex with the country. Many countries link North Americans with fellatio. Whether particular groups practice different amounts of oral/anal or other sexual activities are loaded questions. In Micronesia, Gilbert Herdt interviewed a group where prepubescent boys consumed semen for passage through puberty. They then fed younger boys until they married a woman.

Fellatio manners vary widely. Occasionally partners fellate simultaneously in the sixty-nine position; sometimes they trade off; and some men (the "passive" partners) only fellate and others (the "active" partners) only receive fellation. Certain fellators will only fellate reciprocally; others would never fellate someone who would fellate another man. Some remain completely still while being fellated; others actively pursue the mouth of their partner. Gershom Legman calls the latter "irrumation" (*Oragenitalism* 255).

The technique of fellatio comes naturally and requires little experience. Different parts of the mouth and throat come into play. Some prefer to use only their lips; others "swallow" everything. Controlling his gagging, a fellator can take any size penis deep into his throat. Protocol for swallowing the ejaculate has varied. Masters and Johnson found, "The only appreciable difference between homosexual and heterosexual fellatio was in the practice of swallowing the ejaculate."

While oral sex has seldom spread AIDS, semen (like blood and mother's milk) carries the virus in infected individuals. Thus some partners prefer coming outside their partner's body. Protocol dictates that the fellated inform the fellator of coming ejaculation. Teeth raise another question. Some men have no teeth (or have removable false teeth). Those with teeth need to gauge their partner's feelings. Some dislike biting or scraping; others seek it out. Another remarkable practice appears in the "glory hole." Here (often in a toilet wall) a hole allows one man to insert his penis for a man on the other side to suck.

Oral male homosexual practice has varied geographically, historically, and socially. Some habits originate in social custom, other responses (semen production, arousal, ejaculation, anatomy) have biological/genetic roots. The differences across class, gender, race, history, geography, age, and other variations remain largely unexplored. Talk about such questions has varied as widely as oral sexual practices.

Charles Shively

Bibliography

Legman, Gershom. *Oragenitalism: Oral Techniques in Genital Excitation*. New York: Julian Press, 1969.

Masters, William H., and Virginia E. Johnson. *Homosexuality in Perspective*. Boston: Little, Brown, 1979.

Silverstein, Charles, and Felice Picano. *The New Joy of Gay Sex*. Preface by Edmund White. New York: HarperCollins, 1992.

See also Kissing; Melanesia; Phone Sex; Sadomasochism; Safer Sex; Sex Practice: Anal Sex; Tearooms

Sex Practice: Watersports and Scat

"*Inter fæces et urinam nascimur* is an ancient text which has served the ascetic preachers of old for many discourses on the littleness of man and the meanness of that reproductive power which plays so large a part in man's life," observed Havelock Ellis in his volume *Erotic Symbolism*. Ellis, however, considered the possibility that such a paradox might also serve to eroticize the excretory functions: "From the standpoint of ascetic contemplation eager to belittle humanity, the excretory centers may cast dishonor upon the genital which they adjoin. From the more ecstatic standpoint of the impassioned lover . . . it is not impossible for the excretory centers to take on some charm from the irradiating center of sex which they enclose" (Ellis 47–48). In fact, Ellis asserted that the idealization and eroticization of the excremental functions associated with the sexual organs were inevitable consequences of anatomy and sexual ardor.

For his own part, Freud maintained that a childhood fascination with scatological processes initiated both scopophilia and erotic desire:

Small children whose attention has once been drawn—as a rule by masturbation—to their own genitals usually take the further step without help from the outside and develop a lively interest in the genitals of their playmates. Since opportunities for satisfying curiosity of this kind usually occur only in the course of satisfying the two kinds of need for excretion, children of this kind turn into *voyeurs*, eager spectators of the processes of micturition and defæcation. (58)

Thus Freud connects some of the earliest sexual impulses to the erotic pleasure that the excremental functions offer, providing an even stronger basis for Ellis's suspicions about the inherently normal fascinations with the body's capacity for producing waste. French librarian, pornographer, and philosopher Georges Bataille would further explore the erotics of waste in both his intellectual writings and his famous pornographic novel, *The Story of the Eye*.

Both Freud and Ellis built their theories of human sexuality on the foundations laid by German sexologists like Richard von Krafft-Ebing, whose nineteenth-century inquiries into sexual behavior were largely driven by a desire to catalog the wide variety of "perversities" that appeared to mark human sexual behavior the world over. Works like John G. Bourke's 1891 *Scatologic Rites of All Nations: A Dissertation upon the Employment of Excrementitious Remedial Agents in Religion, Therapeutics, Divination, Witchcraft, Love-Philters, etc., in All Parts of the Globe. Based upon Original Notes and Personal Observation, and upon Compilation from One Thousand Authorities* attempted to combine anthropological curiosity and sexological interest with Victorian predilections for sexual prurience. Such works cannot be easily separated from the sensationalized images of fecal stains on hotel bed sheets that circulated during Oscar Wilde's sodomy trials. Thus a connection between gay male "perversity" and the excremental, and nonproductive—indeed wasteful—human body was forged in the Western imagination at the fin-de-siècle.

Freud's attempt to link burgeoning childhood sexuality with excremental functions has served both to explain and to condemn much of gay male behavior in the West. For example, the emergence of the public rest room as a favored location for gay male sexual liaisons vividly illustrates the collapse of sexual and excremental functions. In such a context the dual functions of the male sexual organs are brought into relief. A strong fascination with and eroticiza-tion of the male excretory functions characterizing much of the gay male sexual subcultures (especially the leather, kink, and fetish communities) can partly be explained through such associations.

On the other hand, the connection of gay male sexual behavior with scatology has served pointedly conservative attempts to deny lesbians and gay men equal rights. For example, to promote their antigay Proposition 9 in 1992, the Oregon Citizens Alliance provided sensational and bogus propaganda to convince voters that "homosexual men on average ingest the fecal material of 23 different men per year" (qtd. in Signorile 338). Such reactions have understandably encouraged many lesbian and gay activists to disavow any suggestion that homosexuals may be prone to eroticize urinary and excremental activity. Indeed, nothing suggests that the eroticization of these functions is particularly more prevalent among gay men and lesbians than among heterosexuals.

Nevertheless, in recent years some gays have chosen to foreground their sexual fascinations with the excremental, much in the way that leather folk have been "outing" their kinky desires for the last twenty years or so. The Waterboys, based in San Diego, California, entails a global network of over one thousand men interested in the various erotics of urine. Apart from maintaining a Web site with many personal ads, the organization publishes a glossy quarterly, sells merchandise, and sponsors a variety of beer busts and other events, including a yearly weekend-long party in Palm Springs that attracts hundreds of men from around the world. The Internet has proved to be a particularly useful resource for gay men into watersports, or "golden showers," and other groups of like-minded men such as Water Buddies in Washington, D.C., and Rainmakers of South Florida maintain Web sites devoted to erotic art, photography, and fiction, as well as personal ads.

While men who are interested in watersports are more and more becoming a visible presence among the gay community's many subcultures, men into scat—the desire to ingest or play with shit—have far fewer resources available to them. Many states in the United States have stringent laws against erotic art that depicts such activity, and so long as the long-standing homophobic associations of gay men with the excreting anus continue, many gay men and women will continue to regard the erotic uses of shit as reprehensible and politically counterproductive.

Many aficionados of watersports and scat are concerned about the health risks associated with these activities. Feces can contain blood as well as harmful bacteria and parasites, and thus the ingestion of fecal matter can pose serious health risks; scat play that doesn't entail its ingestion, however, can be markedly safer. The risks involved in watersports are less certain. Popular opinion among watersports practitioners maintains that urine is sterile and therefore a much less dangerous bodily fluid than semen in terms of transmitting HIV or other sexually transmitted pathogens. Nevertheless, medical professionals have been reluctant to provide detailed studies on the effects that consuming urine and/or feces might have on one's health.

John Beynon

Bibliography

Bourke, John G. *Scatalogic Rites of All Nations.* Washington, D.C.: W. H. Lowdermilk, 1891.

Ellis, Havelock. *Erotic Symbolism.* In *Studies in the Psychology of Sex*, Vol. 2. New York: Random House, 1936.

Freud, Sigmund. *Three Essays on the Theory of Sexuality.* Trans. and rev. by James Strachey. New York: Basic Books, 1975.

Signorile, Michelangelo. *Queer in America: Sex, Media, and the Closets of Power.* New York: Random House, 1993.

See also Ellis, Havelock; Freud, Sigmund; Krafft-Ebing, Richard von; Leathermen; Sadomasochism; Sex Practice: Anal Sex; Tearooms; Wilde, Oscar

Sexology

Sexology refers, however loosely, to the practices of studying sex prior to the establishment of psychoanalysis as a dominant and regularized sexual vocabulary. Sexological theory, which is almost exclusively considered to be the domain of the nineteenth century, divided into two primary schools of thought: degeneration theory and dysphoric theory.

Degeneration theory found its fullest explication in the work of Richard von Krafft-Ebing. His early editions of *Psychopathia Sexualis* helped to establish the common model of homosexuality as a hereditary, pathological degeneration. Generally stated, Krafft-Ebing's thesis is that "perverse" sexual impulses result from the increasing nervous susceptibility of later generations—much like purebred dogs, in which each generation amplifies the weaknesses of the preceding one—which in turn is augmented by the overly refined lifestyles of modern culture. This combination focuses an inordinate degree of psychical and physical attention on the "sexual spheres" and leads to "the manifold abuse of organs of generation" and "monstrous aberrations of the sex impulse." In an article of 1877, which later was included almost verbatim in the *Psychopathia Sexualis*, Krafft-Ebing makes his case explicitly:

> Conspicuous in these [homosexual] neuropsychopathic individuals are symptoms and groups of symptoms which are adduced by the observers as belonging in general to conditions of psychical degeneration, in particular to the hereditary degenerative condition. . . . From all of this it results with probability that the contrary sexual feeling [i.e., homosexuality], where it occurs as inborn, is to be regarded clinically as a partial occurrence of a neuropsychopathic, mostly hereditary condition, and it has the significance of a functional sign of degeneration.

This idea returns in a more succinct form in the early pages of *Psychopathia Sexualis*: "such functional anomalies" are "frequently symptoms of a diseased condition—mostly hereditary—of the central nervous system."

Although ideas of gender dysphoria, the second major branch of sexology, can be traced throughout the entire history of Western civilization, its most important sexological theorist is Karl Heinrich Ulrichs. Ulrichs, born in 1825 to German parents of considerable means, is almost exclusively remembered today for coining the pithy aphorism to describe male homosexuality, "a woman's soul in a man's body," and the alternative model, "a man's soul in a woman's body," to describe lesbianism. The easy quotability of these phrases has tended to obscure their complicated contexts. Ulrichs's concern with homosexuality arose originally from his own experiences. His friendships in gymnasium, the German equivalent of high school, were almost exclusively remembered by him as ones of homosexual passion, and by 1862 he had already confessed his desire for men to his own family. Ulrichs's comprehension of his own homosexuality as a type of congenital identity is evident in the fact that one of his primary contributions to the history of liberation theory is literally the construction of a language of identity. Drawing on Plato's *Symposium*, Ulrichs coined the term *urning* to refer to what is currently called a gay male and *urinde* for a lesbian. In many ways, dysphoric theory emerges as Ulrichs's own defense of his homosexual identity. It can be seen as a political resistance to the pathologizing tendency of degenerative theory.

As sexual theory progressed toward a psychoanalytic model—one that would culminate with the publication of Freud's *Three Essays on the Theory of Sexuality*—the early models of sexology diminished in terms of scientific importance. Yet in many ways they continue to constitute the basis of popular thought about sex. Images of the effeminate gay man and of the mannish lesbian obviously derive from dysphoric thought, while the all-too-common notions of the homosexual as sick or depraved derive from a degenerative model.

Gregory W. Bredbeck

Bibliography

Foucault, Michel. *The History of Sexuality,* Vol. 1. *An Introduction.* Robert Hurley, trans. New York: Random House, 1980.

Kennedy, Hubert. *Ulrichs: The Life and Works of Karl Heinrich Ulrichs, Pioneer of the Modern Gay Movement.* Boston: Alyson, 1988.

Krafft-Ebing, Richard von. *Psychopathia Sexualis.* Stuttgart, Germany, 1898.

See also Freud, Sigmund; Homosexuality; Inversion; Kertbeny, Karl Maria; Krafft-Ebing, Richard von; Moll, Albert; Sexual Orientation; Third Sex; Uranianism; Westphal, Carl Friedrich Otto

Sexual Abuse

Nominally a sexual act, sexual abuse occurs when the intent of the act is harmful or the meaning behind it has a harming effect on a partner, or when such a situation "must be kept secret." Abuse may be overt (openly sexual and transparent), as in rape, certain forms of incest, or sex with an inebriated person; or covert (the sexual nature of the activity disguised as nonsexual), as in verbal or emotional abuse of a sexual nature or seduction of a child. The effects of sexual abuse are multiple and may be lifelong: physical (bodily injury, dissociative response, a sense that one is not in charge of his or her body), mental (one's thoughts and perceptions are not to be trusted, heightened sense of paranoia, development of personality disorders, development of victim or offender mentality), emotional (increased sense of fear, guilt, shame, profound loneliness, omnipresent anger), behavioral (self-mutilation, addictive disorders, abusive relationships, sexual problems), and spiritual.

Males are the target of sexual abuse far more often than has been supposed. Western society tends to view men as categorically "not-victim." Research into sexual abuse of gay men began in the 1970s, growing out of grassroots efforts by victims of sexual abuse and their therapists and drawing on more extensive research by and about female victims and their therapists. Only in the 1990s have broader sociological investigations been initiated. To understand the dynamics of sexual abuse specifically relevant to gay men, several myths must first be dispelled—that gay men are sexual predators who seduce children, that adult homosexuality is caused by homosexuals' seduction of children, that children seduce adults, that males *cannot* be sexually victimized, and that there are no female perpetrators of sexual abuse.

A male child may be victimized if he is perceived as being gay by the adult (usually) heterosexual male perpetrator. A man known or suspected of being gay may be targeted for rape, particularly in a prison setting, by a heterosexual male. Despite the decriminalization of homosexuality in many places, the current U.S. military's "Don't ask, don't tell" policy and other legal arrangements continue to provide blame-the-victim social dynamics conducive to sexual abuse of gay males and the threat of blackmail.

Women may seduce a male child, and Western society has tended to believe the male child is not negatively affected, indeed that the male child is responsible or even that he is being done a favor by being introduced to adult heterosexuality. The myth of gay male misogyny may find a kernel of truth in the discounting of female perpetrators (forced assault, "baby-sitter" abuse, incest).

Because alcohol and recreational drug use may play a more central role in gay male socializing, the risk of chemical dependency and the development of sexually abusive patterns (both as victim and perpetrator) may be correspondingly greater. Alcohol abuse may lead to sexually abusive behavior or may be consumed as a pretext for the behavior, or past sexual abuse may make the individual more prone to develop a chemical dependency in response to the long-term traumatic effects, such as a capacity for *only* anonymous sex, extreme social withdrawal into

S an exclusive primary relationship, or emotional problems arising from unresolved self-esteem issues (internalized homophobia), played out in its most extreme in a batterer/battered spouse dynamic.

Les Wright

Bibliography

Hunter, Mic. *Abused Boys: The Neglected Victims of Sexual Abuse*. New York: Fawcett Columbine, 1990.

Renzetti, Claire M., and Charles Harvey Miley, eds. *Violence in Gay and Lesbian Domestic Partnerships*. New York: Harrington Park Press, 1996.

See also Alcohol and Drugs; Homophobia; Incest; Recruitment Myth; Suicide

Sexual Orientation

According to most dictionaries, the word *sexual* arises from the Latin *sexus,* and means "pertaining to sex or the sexes" or alternately, "pertaining to the genital organs." The word *orientation* is from the Latin *oriens* (rising), which originally meant "the act of turning to, or determining, the east or the rising sun" (hence *Oriental*). More generally, it signifies "sense of direction" or "the act of determining one's position, literally or figuratively." The term therefore implies a private realization of gender direction of the erotic impulse (rather than a public one as for "coming out"). The term now describes an affectional erotic direction that does not necessarily involve sexual erotic contact. The latter behavior for same sexes is traditionally labeled as "homosexual." By analogy, the erotic sexual contact of persons of different gender is traditionally "heterosexual" behavior.

From Aristotle to the Enlightenment

The Greek philosopher Aristotle (384–322 B.C.), tutor of Alexander the Great (356–323 B.C.) and student of Plato (c.429–347 B.C.), wrote *History of Animals, Parts of Animals,* and *Generation of Animals,* which many scholars believe to be the beginning of the Western civilization sciences of zoology and sexology. Aristotle classified animals (equivalent to our more general term *organisms*) into those that propagated by sexual means, asexually, and by spontaneous generation. These views held sway throughout the Roman Republic and Empire (290 B.C.–A.D. 476), the Byzantine Empire (395–1453),

and the lands of the Middle East conquered by Alexander the Great, and were co-opted by Christian and Islamic civilizations up to the end of the Renaissance in 1514. After this period, the observational techniques of Aristotle were used gradually to subvert his own theories during the reemergence of the modern experimental and observational sciences. Even so, the most widely used source of information about sex in the English-speaking world from the seventh through the nineteenth centuries was *Aristotle's Masterpiece* (Bullough), dubiously attributed to Aristotle. Aristotle believed that the male was the major factor in reproduction, and that females contributed "material for the semen to work upon." Aristotle postulated that semen contained microscopic babies, and that the female was a passive incubator, a view that did not upset his patriarchal society. This was a variation of the theory of *On Generation* by the group of Greek physicians under Hippocrates of Cos (469–399 B.C.), in which two seeds were postulated, one in the male semen and the other in the female vaginal secretions, with the female incubating the resulting product. Their views did not upset their mixed matriarchal and patriarchal society. The Hippocratic writers were reputed to have gained their knowledge from Egypt (the first Egyptian dynasty was founded about 3000 B.C.), which had accumulated the wisdom also of Persia (Susa was founded in 4000 B.C.), Sumeria (founded 3500 B.C.), Minoan civilization (Crete: 3000–1400 B.C.), Troy (2870–1200 B.C.), Babylon/Hittites/Assyria (1700–538 B.C.), Africa, and the Jews (1300–1230 B.C.). Galen (131–201), Greek physician to Roman Emperor Marcus Aurelius (121–180), supported both notions. Galen postulated the existence of "coagulative power" and "receptive capacity," with the male stronger in the former and the female stronger in the latter, from the data of animal experiments.

Christianity became the official religion of the Roman Empire in 381 under Theodosius the Great (346–365), though it had been tolerated from 313 after the Edict of Milan. The Leviticus 20:13 death penalty for male same-sex acts was first imposed in 342 by Emperors Constantine (274–338) and Constans, and again by the Theodosian Code of 390. Lesbian behavior was similarly proscribed in the Middle Ages through an A.D. 287 law of Diocletian (245–313) and Maximianus, as well as the law of A.D. 342. All these were incorporated into the Byzantine Code of Justinian I (lived 483–565) in A.D. 529, 534, 538, and 544, which was resurrected in the West beginning in the eleventh century at Bologna. The 1267–1273 *Summa Theologica* of Thomas Aquinas (1224-1225–1274) reinforced the Pauline strictures (Romans 1: 27) against same-sex behavior. The death penalty was not repealed in civil law until Josephine of Austria in 1787, revolutionary France in 1791, post–Frederick the Great (1712–1786) Prussia in 1794, and pre-Victorian England in 1835.

The Advent of Modern Science

William Harvey (1578–1657) in *Anatomical Exercitations Concerning the Generation of Living Creatures*, of 1651, showed by observation that semen had to fertilize the female-produced ovum to produce a fertilized egg that developed later into a baby creature in chickens and deer. The invention of the microscope by van Leeuwenhoek (1632–1723) was soon followed by publication of his group's observation of spermatozoa in semen in the 1678 *Proceedings of the British Royal Society*. Linnaeus (1707–1778) in 1771 formulated his organism taxonomy scheme based on the means of reproduction as well as morphology. The scheme was not generally accepted until 1838 until support by results from the new science of cytology founded by Schleiden and Schwann. The mammalian egg was discovered in 1827, but it was not until 1875 that Hertwig observed the fertilization of a transparent sea urchin egg, and not until 1879 that Fol saw the spermatozoa contribute the second nucleus within the female egg, confirming the function of chromosomes discovered in 1873 by van Beneden. The actual ova of humans were not observed until the twentieth century. The experimental work on human hormones also began only at the end of the nineteenth century.

The association of syphilis and other sexually transmitted diseases with sexual activity, the biblical prohibitions against homosexuality and adultery, and the antisexual bent of the doctrines of the Roman Catholic and the Protestant churches (1517 was the start of the Reformation) were the starting points for the many medical systems that attempted to make science, religion, societal constructs, and philosophy compatible after Vesalius. One popular feature was to blame excess sexual activities outside of marriage for illness and pathology. French physician Tissot (1728–1787) in his *Onanism: Or a Treatise Upon the Disorders of Masturbation* of 1766 particularly blamed nonprocreative sexual activity including masturbation, homosexuality, and use of contraceptives. Tissot attributed lesbian behavior to clitoral masturbation. He thought madness in youth and thereafter was associated with prepubertal masturbation. He postulated that syphilis was caused by promiscuity that caused excess loss of semen. Many of Tissot's ideas are still current, even among medical professionals. As church was gradually separated from state, the legal and public health codes of countries had to deal practically with secular problems associated with sexual activity and behavior. For example, an 1802 Paris law provided public facilities to examine prostitutes for venereal diseases. The posthumous publication of *De la Prostitution dans La Ville de Paris* by Parent-Duchatelet (1790–1836) occurred in 1836 on a study of the 3,558 registered prostitutes of Paris, one of the first Western public health investigations that involved sexuality. Prussian forensic physicians advised the court, including on issues of pederasty as detailed in *A Handbook of the Practice of Forensic Medicine Based on Personal Experience* of Casper (1796–1864) of 1863. In addition, the Christian notion of procreative sex as duty only (no pleasure) began to erode as a societal norm. Industrialization and urbanization from the eighteenth century onward brought sexual behavior under closer scrutiny, since it influenced production rate and workforce morale. Some outcomes were the formulation of the concept of the urban nuclear family in place of the preindustrial village or tribe concept, the enhanced segregation of the sexes when not in the nuclear family abode, the formulation of socialist and communist theories in reaction to imperialism and capitalism, and the beginning of emancipation movements. The last brought to bear increasing pressure for equality for females and their roles in laws, institutions, education, and norms.

Homosexuality Becomes the Medical Term

Against this historical backdrop, the lawyer Ulrichs (1825–1895) sought to preserve the civil freedom originally conferred by the Code Napoléon to his Germanic Hanover homeland relative to homosexual behavior against impending change wrought by Prussian hegemony (Kennedy). In February 1862 he deposited in the Free German Foundation for Science, Art and General Culture in Frankfurt a sealed statement on the necessity of researching and propagandizing on same-sex love. The latter was to be attained by making one's nature known publicly, and then campaigning for civil rights. This is still the strategy of the present civil rights movement. He defended same-sex love as "natural" and God-given.

Males showing sexual attraction to the same sex were termed *urning* or *Uranian,* and the female analogs *urningin* or *Urinde* (from Plato's *Symposium*), bodies born with the souls of the opposite sex, just as hermaphrodites were born with both sets of sexual organs. He thought that the sexes were indeterminate up to a specific stage of embryonic development, whereupon specialization into male, female, and the "third sex" occurred before birth. He subdivided urnings into a spectrum with *Männlinge* (the masculine) and *Weiblinge* (the feminine) as extremes. Bisexuals he classified as *Urano-Dioning* and similarly subclassified between "conjunctive" (tender and passionate toward men) and "disjunctive" (tender toward men but passionate only toward women) extremes. Heterosexuals were *dioning,* which had the same extremes as *urning.* He wrote twelve booklets on the subject, the first five under his pseudonym, Numa Nemantius. After he unsuccessfully addressed the Munich Assembly of Jurists on the topic on August 29, 1867, he used his own name for the other booklets, from 1868 through 1879. Ulrichs's ideas influenced physician Krafft-Ebing (1840–1902) and scientist Westphal (1833–1890). The terms *homosexuality* and *heterosexuality* were coined by the first person to quote Ulrichs, the novelist Karl Maria Benkert (Karl Maria Kertbeny, 1824–1882), in a letter draft to Ulrichs dated May 6, 1868. He also used the terms in two anonymous pamphlets he published in 1869 to urge repeal of section 143 of the Prussian legal code and its adoption as section 152 of the new North German Confederation (Herzer).

Krafft-Ebing in 1886 popularized the term *homosexuality* and postulated that male homosexual behavior was the result of multiple hereditary flaws, based only on observations of abnormal homosexuals. His ideas formed the basis of the medical model of homosexuality as a mental illness and genetic disease that flourished until 1973, when homosexuality was no longer designated as a mental illness by the American Psychiatric Association. Freud (1856–1939), Ellis (1859–1939), and Hirschfeld (1868–1935), all physicians, based their theories of sexual behavior on psychology and biology, still further strengthening the disease medical model.

Hirschfeld, a Jewish homosexual, took up Ulrichs's mission to research homosexuality and to gain civil rights for homosexuals. He defined a ten-point scale of development of sexuality, postulated people to be basically bisexual at birth, and proposed that homosexuals constituted a third sex. He founded the Wissenschaftlich-Humanitäres Komitee (Scientific-Humanitarian Committee) in 1897 to carry on the civil rights struggle to repeal paragraph 175 of the German Imperial Code, and the Ärtzliche Gesellschaft für Sexualwissenschaft in 1913 to press worldwide sexual reform. He published the first journal on homosexuality, *Jahrbuch für Sexuelle Zwischenstufen* (Yearbook for Sexual Intermediates), from 1899 to 1923, as well as the first scientific journal on sexology, *Zeitschrift für Sexualwissenschaft,* in 1908, which merged with another journal to become *Zeitschrift für Sexualwissenschaft und Sexual Politik* in 1909 that was published intermittently with seventeen volumes up to 1929. His first sexual behavior survey was published in 1903, in which he posited that 2.2 percent of respondents were homosexual. He published several books and 187 articles, and created the Institute of Sexual Science in 1919 in Berlin, the first research institute devoted to sexology. The contents of the library were burned by the Nazis in 1933. Hirschfeld was the moving force behind the international sexology congresses that began in 1921, and the World League for Sexual Reform, which became the Congress of the World League for Sexual Reform in 1928. Other congresses in Hirschfeld's lifetime took place in 1929, 1930, and 1932. The Nazis destroyed his organizations, but he inspired many, notably in the United States, Britain, Scandinavia, the Soviet Union, Japan, China, and Argentina. The science of the day was not sufficiently advanced to prove his hypotheses relative to the importance of endocrinology and genetics in sexuality. It was only after World War II that Kallman, in his seminal 1952 study of identical twins, showed that genetics had to be involved.

The debate between adherents of "nature" versus "nurture," or the "genetic" versus "environmental" causation, or the "essentialism" versus "social constructionism" concepts of sexual orientation and homosexuality continues as in many other areas of behavior and biology as it has from Ulrichs onward. Although male homosexuality appears to have some genetic basis, there is no such evidence for lesbianism. And while there are apparent physiological differences between male heterosexuals and male homosexuals, when and how these differences arose is as yet unknown (LeVay).

Homosexuality has been recorded in all known ancient human cultures and in all known vertebrate animals (Kirsch and Weinrich). Other entries in this encyclopedia should be consulted for examples of cross-cultural homosexual roles and animals showing homosexual behavior. Its occurrence or frequency is natural and "essential," and must therefore serve a biological function. If "survival of the fittest" (the 1859 theory of evolution in *Origin of Species* of Darwin, 1809–1882) is the criterion, then the homosexual trait has stood the test of time. The extent to which homosexuality occurs in human societies, however, is a function of social mores, but there is no question as to its existence or ubiquity. The correct answer relative to the polar opposites ("dimorphisms") mentioned above is a mixture of the above alternatives in an operative dynamic sense rather than a causative sense, meaning sexual behavior is flexible for a given person over time, with a somewhat fluid but not immutable sexual orientation. Interpersonal sexual behavior itself must be learned, but is an extension of autoeroticism (masturbation) that has been observed to begin soon after birth. The interaction of time and growth with the biochemical biological clock encoded into deoxyribonucleic acid (DNA) for each individual causes the most active awareness of erotic impulses during puberty on through adolescence, even though earlier and later realizations of sexual orientation occur.

Modern Reasons for Homosexual and Heterosexual Sexual Orientations

Two major reasons have been advanced as to why evolution has favored the survival of the homosexual trait: balancing gene pools to enhance survival fitness (balanced polymorphism) and selection of emotional altruistic traits associated with homosexuals (Wilson). In the latter, release from the cares and responsibilities of breeding and caring for the young may cause human procreative energies to be funneled into other creative paths like the arts, theater, sciences, leadership, and visionary thinking, all these being to the ultimate good of human society. Heterosexuality is currently necessary to propagate the species. The advent of artificial insemination, cloning, and test-tube babies is likely to change that.

Post–World War II Measurements of Sexual Orientation

Epidemiological Markers

The earliest measurements of American homosexuality or heterosexuality measured sexual contact behavior and sexual fantasy only. The Kinsey scale of 1948 (males) and 1953 (females) described sexual behavior and fantasy via a continuum, with 0 being exclusively heterosexual and 6 exclusively homosexual, and 3 being perfectly bisexual currently (Table 1). The scale of Kinsey (1894–1956) resembles the cojoined three scales of Ulrichs. The instrument of measurement in these epidemiology studies was the face-to-face confidential interview. Over 20,000 subjects were interviewed between 1938 and 1963. Information has now been gained through telephone interviews and self-answered questionnaires. That American literature is too extensive to summarize here and is usually of poorer scientific quality than the Kinsey statistics from the perspective of number of subjects and design of the questions. Relative to a 1995 cross-cultural study with 5,700 subjects age 16–50 years in the United States, France, and the United Kingdom, the self-reported categories were lesbian, 11.6 percent; gay male, 7.8 percent; and bisexual, 11.6 percent. Within the most recent five years, these categories relative to homosexual behavior were lesbian, 10.8 percent; gay male, 4.7 percent; and currently bisexual, 6.3 percent. Within the last five years for the three countries, the percentage reporting no sexual contact was 9.2–13 percent; 80.1–88.1 percent for heterosexual contact; and 4.5–10.7 percent male homosexual and 2.1–3.6 percent lesbian contact (Table 2). More recent reviews are also available. All these investigations relied on study participant replies.

Homosexual behavior has also been defined as sexual arousal by the same gender or sex, whereas heterosexuality has been defined as sexual arousal by the opposite gender or sex (Freund). Bisexuals have it both ways. The measuring device of sexual arousal for men is the plethysmograph, which fits over the penis and measures its blood volume. The female instrument measures female genital blood flow. Subjects are shown photographs of nude people of various ages, appearances, and sexes. The technique is impractical for large populations, especially if they are reluctant.

Shively and De Cecco have advocated the use of two continuous Kinsey-type scales for each sex, one for sexual behavior and the other for sexual orientation. Others have advocated three such scales for each sex for sexual behavior, sexual fantasy, and affectional orientation. There is no end in sight to the subdivisions proposed. Thus, the current thinking is that sexual orientation requires multivariables for definition rather than just the single answer of a questionnaire respondent (Gonsiorek and Weinrich; Sell et al.). Some of the mental health variables have been discussed extensively in a recent book (Cabaj and Stein).

Research on sexual orientation and homosexuality by American nonphysicians became "safe" after homosexuality was officially declassified as a

Table 1. A Summary of the Kinsey Statistics on American Homosexuality

Category	% >16 Years	
	Men	Women
Homosexual activity before puberty	47–57	30–43
Homosexual fantasy during recent masturbations	8–11	5–6
Five same-sex partners or twenty-one orgasms during homosexual relations	10–17	3–5
Admitted likelihood of future homosexual relations	6–12	2–4
During most recent homosexual orgasm was:		
Never married	10–49	2–11
Currently married	0–5	0–2
Separated/Widowed/Divorced	0–18	0–8

The above ranges are for the second-lowest and second-highest figures for that category combining all education/race/age classifications.

mental illness in 1973 by the American Psychiatric Association. This ushered in an era of learned journals devoted to research on homosexuality, the chief being the *Journal of Homosexuality* (first published in 1974) and the *Archives of Sexual Behavior* (first published in 1971). The 1970s and 1980s were focused mostly on epidemiology and hormonal influences. In the 1990s, genetics and brain/hypothalamus anatomical studies gained in importance, with endocrinological studies still significant. The advent of AIDS resulted in studies that attempted to consider sexual orientation and AIDS simultaneously. The appropriate negative control for AIDS studies is the age-, race-, gender-, and occupation-matched healthy homosexual. Few AIDS studies have included such cohorts.

Endocrinological Markers

Since embryos start out as female, it can be argued that the female trait is the fundamental one. Sustaining the male identity after birth is basically under endocrine control. This has been verified by the effects of physical and chemical castration and effects of temperature on the production of sperm (De Cecco and Parker). Thus environment (defined here as nonendogenous factors) can exert effects over behavior in spite of biology, even with intact genitalia. The simple picture of a male having androgens and a female having estrogens does not explain maleness and femaleness. While explanations in terms of estrogen/androgen ratio have better validity, this concept also has problems. If there is no objective chemical description of male and female identity, such a description of sexual orientation is even more difficult using a dimorphic model of sex. In fact,

there is no correlation between sexual orientation and adult hormonal constitution (Meyer-Bahlburg, "Psychoendocrine research"). Hormonal therapies do not change sexual orientation either, nor is the latter shifted by changes in hormone levels resulting from gonadal malignancies, trauma, or surgical removal (Gooren). Hormonal changes in animals at specific early stages of development in the womb (the prenatal hormonal hypothesis) do cause more male mounting behavior in treated female rats relative to untreated controls. Castration of in-utero rats at the same stage also causes less male mounting behavior and more female mounting posture. The extrapolation to humans is problematic. Regardless of their genetic sex or the nature of their prenatal hormonal exposure, such affected humans usually become heterosexual in accordance with the sex they are assigned as long as the assignment is made unambiguously and early (before eighteen months of age) (Meyer-Bahlburg, "Gender").

Brain/Hypothalamus Markers

Relative to the four candidate interstitial nuclei of the human anterior hypothalamus, one labeled INA3 has been claimed by LeVay to be smaller in females and homosexuals than in males. The suprachiasmatic nucleus of the brain is also reported to be larger in homosexuals with AIDS than in heterosexuals but does not vary with sex. The anterior commissure of the brain is similarly larger for women and homosexual men with AIDS than for heterosexual men (Allen and Gorski). These findings have not been confirmed, and the homosexual patients all suffered from AIDS, a condition that affects androgen secretion and the brain itself.

Table 2. Cross-Cultural Comparison of Homosexual Attributes (% of persons age 16–50 years) from the United States (U.S.), United Kingdom (U.K.), France (Fr.), and Range. The numbers for the three countries are about equal, with males approximately equal to females.

Homosexual Attribute		U.S.	U.K.	Fr.	Range
Sexual contact within 5 years:					
	Male	6.2	4.5	10.7	4.5–10.7
	Female	3.6	2.1	3.3	2.1–3.6
	Overall	3.6–4.2	2.1–4.5	3.3–10.7	2.1–10.7
Some homosexual attraction/contact since age 15:					
	Male	20.8	16.3	18.5	16.3–20.8
	Female	17.8	18.6	18.5	17.8–18.6
	Overall	17.8–20.8	16.3–18.6	18.5	16.3–20.8
Homosexual attraction without sexual contact since age 15:					
	Male	8.7	7.9	8.5	7.9–8.7
	Female	11.1	8.6	11.7	8.6–11.7
	Overall	8.7–11.1	7.9–8.6	8.5–11.7	7.9–11.7

Behavioral Markers

Behavioral markers are those that involve human reactions to stimuli or tasks. The literature is large and typically studies have few participants. Reproducibility is difficult for such studies.

The extent of rough-and-tumble play is a reliable animal behavioral marker for maleness that is affected by prenatal androgen exposure (Ehrhardt and Meyer-Bahlburg), while aversion to this is postulated by some to be a marker of homosexual orientation in humans (Bell et al.). This could be a predisposing factor given reinforcement, but may not affect sexual orientation at all given no reinforcement.

Lesbians and bisexual females appear to be intermediate in cochlear response to click sounds between heterosexual women (higher response) and heterosexual men. Male homosexuals did not differ relative to heterosexual men. The study needs to be reproduced.

The Kinsey data indicate there is no correlation between sexual orientation and handedness, birth order for women, height, and paternal age. Male homosexuals have a later birth order, an earlier onset of puberty, and a lower body weight.

Chemical Markers

One type of male pseudohermaphroditism in humans involves 4-steroid 5-alpha reductase deficiency (Imperato-McGinley et al.). The enzyme converts testosterone to dihydrotestosterone, the prenatal mediator of masculinization of external genitalia. The syndrome is rare and occurs in males who appear genetically normal and is inherited as an autosomal recessive trait. The bifid scrotum appears labialike. The penis may be absent or clitorislike. The testes may be undescended. There may be evident hermaphroditic traits. Virilization occurs at puberty. The original interpretation of the original study in the Dominican Republic was that biological sex overwhelmed the sex of rearing. The tribe had a specific term for these hermaphrodites—*guevedoche* (woman then man). Herdt criticized the investigators for not asking the tribe whether they treated *guevedoche* any differently from females, and if they had special tribal roles tantamount to a third sex, as do the Sambia of New Guinea for such pseudohermaphrodites.

Family Studies

Kinsey found from his questionnaires that homosexuality appeared to run in families. The seminal identical twin studies of Kallman in 1952 began the modern study of the influence of genetics on heredity showing higher rates of homosexuality in identical twins. The major paper after 1952 probably is that of the National Institutes of Health, which showed a family disposition for male homosexuality on the long arm of the X chromosome (Xq28), but not for lesbianism (Hamer and Copeland). Sexual orientation appears to correlate with the number of older brothers, each additional older brother increasing the odds of homosexuality by about 33 percent. About 50 percent of the variance in sexual orientation can be explained by heritable components (Pillard and Bailey).

Modern Redefinition of Terms

In many questionnaires, often terms are not defined. Thus in answer to the question What sexual orientation do you consider yourself to be? It is unclear whether the answer relates to gay or lesbian identity, sexual orientation, or sexual behavior. Some scholars have tried to clarify the above situation by defining the following terms relative to sexual identity.

Biological sex: determined by the presence or absence of the Y chromosome on chromosome 46 (XX: female; XY: male). XXY males are also known.

Gender identity: the psychological sense of being male or female. This allows people who are biologically male to think like females, and vice versa. Preoperational transsexuals fit into this classification.

Social sex role: adhering to the behaviors and attitudes defined culturally for males and females. This allows a person who recognizes the biological gender to live nevertheless in the cultural role of the opposite gender. An example is the North American Indian berdache (a term dating from before 1726). The case of transient role playing is transvestism (a term coined by Hirschfeld in 1910).

Sexual orientation: erotic and/or affectional disposition to the same and/or opposite sex, as alluded to above.

The first three categories may have nothing to do with sexual orientation. Thus a person can exhibit behavior that is homosexual but not self-identify as a gay person. An example is "straight trade." Another example occurs when homosexual behavior is manifested as culturally sanctioned power dominance, as in male homosexuality between older and younger men in Islamic countries, the raping of boys by conquering male soldiers, and male prison rape, all men not having to have a distinct gay identity.

Gay males and *lesbians* are people who define themselves as homosexual.

Queers are people who define themselves publicaly as proudly homosexual.

Straight is the term used by gay people to describe heterosexuals, but it is also used by heterosexuals for other contexts, for example, to describe behavior after an addiction.

The term *sexual preference* connotes deliberate choice of behavior rather than mental realization, and so does not describe the coming-out process for most gay people. It is also arguable whether sexual preference applies to bisexuals. This term was popular between 1970 and 1980 but is not used by gay people now to describe their coming-out process, or what they realize about themselves after that process.

Older terms like *sodomy, sexual inversion, buggery,* and *onanism* are in disfavor since they have been defined in different ways by too many people, causing confusion.

The Future

The tendency of researchers to allow respondents to define "sexual orientation" subjectively has led to ambiguity as to how to interpret much data related to sexual orientation.

Researchers should define their terms in questionnaires and in face-to-face interviews. The advent of cloning, artificial insemination, and test-tube babies will mean that heterosexuality may not be crucial to propagation of the human species but is merely an option like homosexuality. This will cause a revolutionary change in social dynamics and in the validity of arguments used against homosexuality. Furthermore, the unlocking of the genetic code of the human genome may allow embryos that show markers of homosexuality to be aborted, not cloned, or excluded as candidates for test-tube babies or artificial insemination. The questions of ethics have still to be thought through (Byne and Stein).

One thing is certain: progress in science is inexorable whether one likes the changes or not. The challenge is to be always informed and vigilant.

Shane S. Que Hee

Bibliography

Allen, Laura S., and Roger A. Gorski. "Sexual Orientation and the Size of the Anterior Commissure in the Human Brain. *Proceedings of the National Academy of Science USA* 89 (1992): 7199–7202.

Bell, Alan P., and Martin S. Weinberg. *Homosexualities: A Study of Diversity Among Men and Women.* New York: Simon and Schuster, 1978.

Bell, Alan P., Martin S. Weinberg, and S. K. Hammersmith. *Sexual Preference: Its Development in Men and Women.* Bloomington, Ind.: Indiana University Press, 1981.

Blanchard, Ray, and Peter Klassen. "H-Y Antigen and Homosexuality in Men." *Journal of the Theory of Biology* 185 (1997): 373–78.

Brecher, Edward M. *The Sex Researchers*. Boston: Little, Brown, 1969.

Bullough, Vern L. *Science in the Bedroom: A History of Sex Research*. New York: Basic Books, 1994.

Byne, William, and Edward (Terry) Stein. "Ethical Implications of Scientific Research on the Causes of Sexual Orientation." *Health Care Analysis* 5 (1997): 136–48.

Cabaj, Robert P., and Terry S. Stein, eds. *Textbook of Homosexuality and Mental Health*. Washington, D.C.: American Psychiatric Press, 1996.

Crompton, Louis. "The Myth of Lesbian Impunity: Capital Laws from 1270 to 1791." In *The Gay Past: A Collection of Historical Essays*. Salvatore J. Licata and Robert P. Peterson, eds. New York: Harrington Park Press, 1985, 11–25.

De Cecco, John P., and David A. Parker, eds. *Sex, Cells, and Same-Sex Desire: The Biology of Sexual Preference*. New York: Harrington Park Press, 1995.

De Cecco, John P., and Michael G. Shively, eds. *Origins of Sexuality and Homosexuality*. New York: Harrington Park Press, 1985.

Ehrhardt, Anke A., and Heino F. L. Meyer-Bahlburg. "Effects of Prenatal Sex Hormones on Gender-Related Behavior. *Science* 211 (1991): 1312–18.

Ellis, Havelock. *Studies in the Psychology of Sex*. 7 vols. New York: Davis, 1900–1928.

Ford, Clennen S., and Frank A. Beach. *Patterns of Sexual Behavior*. New York: Harper and Row, 1951.

Freud, Sigmund. *Standard Edition of the Complete Psychological Works of Sigmund Freud*. James Strachey, ed. London: Hogarth, 1953–1974.

Freund, Kurt W. "Male Homosexuality: An Analysis of the Pattern." In *Understanding Homosexuality: Its Biological and Psychological Bases*. John A. Loraine, ed. New York: Elsevier, 1974, 25–81.

Gebhard, Paul H., and Alan B. Johnson. *The Kinsey Data: Marginal Tabulations of the 1938–1963 Interviews Conducted by the Institute for Sex Research*. Philadelphia: Saunders, 1979.

Gonsiorek, John C., and James D. Weinrich, eds. *Homosexuality: Research Implications for Public Policy*. Newbury Park, Calif.: Sage, 1991.

Gooren, Louis. "Biomedical Theories of Sexual Orientation: A Critical Examination." In *Homosexuality/Heterosexuality: Concepts of Sexual Orientation*. David P. McWhirter, S. A. Sanders, and John M. Reinisch, eds. New York: Oxford University Press, 1990, 71–87.

Goy, Robert W., and Bruce S. McEwen. *Sexual Differentiation of the Brain*. Cambridge, Mass.: MIT Press, 1980.

Hamer, Dean, and Peter Copeland. *The Science of Desire: The Search for the Gay Gene and the Biology of Behavior*. New York: Simon & Schuster, 1994.

Herdt, Gilbert. "Mistaken Sex: Culture, Biology and the Third Sex in New Guinea." In *Third Sex, Third Gender: Beyond Sexual Dimorphism on Culture and History*. New York: Zone Books, 1994, 419–45.

Herzer, Manfred. "Kertbeny and the Nameless Love." *Journal of Homosexuality* 12 (1985): 1–26

Hirschfeld, Magnus. "Homosexuality." In *Encyclopedia Sexualis*. Victor Robinson, ed. New York: Dingwall-Rock, 1936, 321–24.

Hutchinson, Geoffrey E. "A Speculative Consideration of Certain Possible Forms of Sexual Selection in Man." *American Naturalist* 93 (1959): 81–91.

Imperato-McGinley, Julliane, L. Guerrero, T. Gautier, and R. E. Peterson. "Steroid 5-Alpha-Reductase Deficiency in Man: An Inherited Form of Male Pseudohermaproditism." *Science* 186 (1974): 1213–15.

Kallman, Franz J. "Comparative Twin Study on the Genetic Aspects of Male Homosexuality." *Journal of Nervous Mental Disease* 115 (1952): 283–98.

———. "Twin and Sibship Study of Overt Male Homosexuality." *American Journal of Human Genetics* 4 (1952): 136–47.

Kennedy, Hubert C. "The 'Third Sex' Theory of Karl Heinrich Ulrichs." In *The Gay Past: A Collection of Historical Essays*. 103–111.

Kinsey, Alfred C., Wardell B. Pomeroy, and Clyde E. Martin. *Sexual Behavior in the Human Female*. Philadelphia: Saunders, 1953.

———. *Sexual Behavior in the Human Male*. Philadelphia: Saunders, 1948.

Kirsch, John A.W., and James D. Weinrich. "Homosexuality, Nature, and Biology: Is Homosexuality Natural? Does It Matter?" Gonsiorek and Weinrich, 13–43.

Klein, Fritz, Barry Sepekoff, and Timothy J. Wolf. "Sexual Orientation: A Multivariable Dynamic Process." *Journal of Homosexuality* 12 (1985): 35–49.

Krafft-Ebing, Richard von. *Psychopathia Sexualis.* Reissued. New York: Paperback Library, 1965.

LeVay, Simon. *The Sexual Brain.* Boston: MIT Press, 1994.

McFadden, D., and E. G. Pasanen. "Comparison of the Auditory Systems of Heterosexuals and Homosexuals: Click-Evoked Otoacoustic Emissions." *Proceedings of the National Academy of Science USA* 95 (1998): 2709–13.

Meyer-Bahlburg, Heino F. L. "Gender Development in Intersex Patients." *Child and Adolescent Clinic of North America* 2 (1993): 501–12.

———. "Psychoendocrine Research on Sexual Orientation: Current Status and Future Options." *Program for Brain Research* 71 (1984): 375–97.

Pillard, Richard C., and John M. Bailey. "Human Sexual Orientation Has a Heritable Component." *Human Biology* 70 (1998): 347–65.

Sell, Randell L. "Defining and Measuring Sexual Orientation: A Review." *Archive of Sexual Behavior* 26 (1997): 643–59.

Sell, Randell L., and Christian Petrulio. "Sampling Homosexuals, Bisexuals, Gays, and Lesbians for Public Health Research: A Review of the Literature from 1990 to 1992." *Journal of Homosexuality* 30 (1996): 31–48.

Sell, Randell L., James A. Wells, and David Wypij. "Prevalence of Homosexual Behavior and Attraction in the United States, the United Kingdom and France: Results of National Population-Based Samples." *Archive of Sexual Behavior* 24 (1995): 235–49.

Shively, Michael G., and John P. De Cecco. "Components of Sexual Identity." *Journal of Homosexuality* 3 (1977): 41–48.

Steakley, James D. "Sodomy in Enlightenment Prussia: From Execution to Suicide." In *The Pursuit of Sodomy: Male Homosexuality in Renaissance and Enlightenment Europe.* Kent Gerard and Gert Hekma, eds. New York: Harrington Park Press, 1989, 163–75.

Swaab, D. F., and M. A. Hoffman. "An Enlarged Suprachiasmatic Nucleus in Homosexual Men." *Brain Research* 537 (1990): 141–48.

Weinberg, Martin S., and Alan P. Bell. *Homosexuality: An Annotated Bibliography.* New York: Harper and Row, 1972.

Weinrich, James D., and Walter L. Williams. "Strange Customs, Familiar Lives: Homosexualities in Other Cultures." In Gonsiorek and Weinrich, 44–59.

Wilson, Edward O. *Sociobiology: The New Synthesis.* Cambridge, Mass.: Harvard University Press, 1975.

See also AIDS; Alexander the Great; Animal Sexual Behavior; Berdache; Bible; Civil Rights in the U.S.; Code Napoléon; Egypt, Ancient; Ellis, Havelock; Essentialist-Constructionist Debate; Freud, Sigmund; Gender; Germany; Greece; Hermaphroditism; Hirschfeld, Magnus; Homosexuality; Inversion; Islam; Kertbeny, Karl Maria; Kinsey, Alfred; Krafft-Ebing, Richard von; Masturbation; Persian (Iranian) Literature and Culture; Plato; Queer; Rome, Ancient; Scientific Approaches to Homosexuality; Sexually Transmitted Diseases; Sodomy; Third Sex; Thomas Aquinas; Uranianism, Westphal, Carl Friedrich Otto

Sexual Orientation Therapy

For various medical and social reasons, health professionals have sometimes attempted to control and change sexual orientations, especially same-sex attractions. Efforts of this kind are of relatively recent origin. Across the vast span of Western history, biomedical or psychological interventions to correct homosexuality were virtually unknown. When same-sex attractions were judged sinful or immoral, their "remedy" was sought in spiritual, moral, or legal methods. However, nineteenth-century attempts to achieve scientific status for the study of sexuality fostered a trend to treat homoerotic desire and behavior as pathological. This assumption of pathology formed the basis for most attempts to discover a psychotherapeutic or biomedical "cure." Fortunately, the heyday of sexual orientation therapy—sometimes known as conversion therapy—has passed.

Historian Vern Bullough dates the modern era of pathological interpretations of homosexuality as beginning with the work of German physician Carl Westphal (1833–1890), who believed that "contrary sexual feeling" was a mostly congenital condition. Many physicians and researchers who came after him believed that homosexuality was either congenital or acquired but that in either case it ought to be treated. The tradition that pathologized homosexuality peaked in 1952, when the American Psychiatric Association (APA) declared that adult homosexuality was necessarily a sociopathic personality disturbance. That broad declaration and the implied need for sexual orientation therapy prevailed in U.S. psychiatry, however, for only about twenty years. During that time, though, any number of remedies were sought for homosexuality. Attempts to extinguish homoerotic desires and behaviors have been pursued through techniques that reflect the science of their times.

Behavioral Remedies

Some of the earliest forms of conversion therapy tried to redirect sexual orientation by effecting change in behavior. Exercise and strenuous activities out of doors were recommended. One U.S. physician in the late 1880s recommended fatiguing exercise on a bicycle as a way to subdue same-sex desires. The "cure" of homosexuality through exercise and work had a grisly climax in the Nazi German concentration camps. In the expectation of altering their sexual orientation, men and women incarcerated for homosexual "crimes" were often worked to exhaustion and death. In contrast to theories favoring robust living and physical exertion, some nineteenth-century researchers thought homosexuality reflected the damaging effects of urban life on the nervous system. Consequently, those therapists prescribed rest in the hope that relaxation would restore men and women to sexual equilibrium, i.e., to heterosexuality.

Some researchers believed that homosexuality resulted from fear of the opposite sex. In 1893, German physician Albert Moll counseled men to engage in sex with female prostitutes and claimed this method as successful with his patients. Another German physician, Albert von Schrenck-Notzing (1872–1919), also advised men to visit brothels after consuming large amounts of alcohol. Researchers cleaving to a more conventional moral standard sometimes recommended marriage as a means of overcoming homosexuality, on the theory that contact with prostitutes encouraged a debased and repellent view of women. Other researchers, less optimistic about the benefits of marriage, condemned marriage as any sort of effective remedy. They noted the stain a spouse's homosexuality would put on the marriage, with no guarantee that sexual orientation would change. Theories that homosexuality represents a phobic reaction to members of the opposite sex have remained attractive to many therapists. For example, the Masters and Johnson sexual orientation therapy that began in the 1970s tried to restore or inaugurate heterosexuality through a series of encounters with a sexual "surrogate" of the opposite sex who encouraged sexual exploration and encounters in a nonthreatening way.

Other behavioral therapies focused on masturbation. In "orgasmic reconditioning," therapists advised male clients to masturbate in familiar ways but then in the moments just before climax to shift attention to pictures of women. Over time, it was claimed, the man would generalize the pleasures of orgasm under these circumstances to actual encounters with women. Behavioral conversion therapy focused not only on discovering the sexual rewards of heterosexuality, but also attempted to drive persons from homosexuality by making it repulsive and intolerable. Electroshock therapy punished subjects for responding to homoerotic stimuli and rewarded them for sexual response to images of the opposite sex. In 1961 two British researchers even designed an electroshock device that patients could use at home should they be tempted by forbidden sexual desires when away from their physician. Aversion therapy has seen many variants: harsh chemicals, water deprivation, and threats of beating. All these techniques reflect the view that behavioral modifications are capable of molding desire. Because sexual orientation is a complex amalgam of biopsychological predispositions and experiences, it is not clear that behavior modifications can mold sexual desire in any simple or decisive fashion.

Psychodynamic Theories

One of the most historically dominant efforts at conversion therapy grew out of the psychoanalytic tradition. Sigmund Freud (1856–1939) himself denied that homosexuality in adults was any grave psychic or social disability and did not generally advocate conversion therapy. He did nevertheless regard homosexuality as in some ways an inferior sexuality, suggesting that conversion therapy might be possible for some, even if he was not convinced that psychoanalysis could offer much help. Yet many U.S. analysts after Freud did hold the view that homosexuality is a psychological disorder driven by anxiety. In 1975, physician-analyst Irving Bieber said, "[R]epetitive behavior in adult life between same-sex members is always pathological. It is never normal. There is no such thing as homosexuality being a normal sexual variant." Treatment for this disorder required, according to many analysts, the years of intensive self-examination and interpretation that are the hallmarks of psychoanalysis.

Other schools of psychotherapy also perceived homosexuality as psychologically maladaptive and sought to repair the deficits of homosexuality through various techniques of psychic interventions. The technique of fantasy satiation, for example, involved barraging a subject with homoerotic images

S and language. According to the theory, after time the subject would become numb to these images and seek sexual arousal in heteroeroticism. Hypnotic suggestion was also enlisted against homosexuality, but to no avail. In one of the more inventive theories, homosexuality was said to be the result of a faded aesthetic appreciation of the world. It was believed that correction and instruction in the beauty and worth of the world would have the result of revealing the attractiveness of the opposite sex. Psychodynamic therapies investigated for their potential to control sexual orientation run the gamut. Assertiveness training and primal screaming, to name two examples, were also advocated for their potential to alter a given sexual orientation. Like the therapies tried before them, efforts in these areas have come to nothing. But some psychoanalysts do claim to have success in sexual orientation therapy, though these claims are often vigorously criticized.

Biomedical Interventions

While many therapists put their hope for a clue of homosexuality in psychodynamic techniques, others sought more direct biological interventions. One nineteenth-century U.S. physician used cocaine, bromides, and "saline cathartics" to cure a woman of lesbianism. Other physicians tried extracts derived from animal organs and glands such as the pituitary. The discovery of hormones in the late 1800s was still young when medical practitioners sought to discern their influence on sexual orientation. Homosexuality in men was once hypothesized to be the consequence of androgen deprivation, and some men were treated with testosterone. Karl Freund injected men with testosterone while they watched sexually explicit movies featuring women. It was found that while such treatments did not redirect sexual orientation, ironically they did have the effect of heightening sex drive. This outcome led other physicians to treat men with estrogen, expecting that such treatment would at least minimize the urgency of homoerotic drives, and courts sometimes imposed this treatment on persons convicted of sexual crimes. The most famous person to receive court-ordered estrogen therapy was British mathematician Alan Turing who was instrumental in the development of computers and the decoding of secret German communications during World War II. After his conviction for consensual relations with another man, Turing received estrogen injections. As a result, he experienced a certain amount of breast enlargement and was impotent for a time. He never-

theless soon afterward sought sexual adventures with men again. All these forms of drug therapy consistently proved incapable of changing sexual orientation.

Surgery has also been used in various campaigns against homosexuality. Castration was sometimes used against homosexuality and other forms of sexuality, and the Nazis seem to have availed themselves freely of this technique. But controlled studies in the area have shown that while castration diminishes sexual drive and causes changes in skin and hair as well as fatty deposits in mammary regions, it does not alter sexual orientation. Testicle transplants, cauterizations of the body, clitoridectomies, and even lobotomies have also proved incapable of altering sexual orientation.

In the early 1990s, a number of reports appeared that offered anatomical and genetic characterizations of homosexual men and women. If these studies are replicated and prove well founded, some researchers may attempt to control sexual orientation through genetic intervention. Because the exact nature of genetic contributions to expression of sexual orientation is unknown, and because genetic experimentation is only in its earliest stages, it is difficult to predict whether such efforts could be successful. Nevertheless, there have already been discussions whether it would be ethical to attempt to control the sexual orientation of children by either identifying genetic markers characteristic of sexual orientation or through more direct interventions during embryonic or fetal development. Though such control is not at present possible, the question of a child's sexual orientation—and its implications for abortion choices—was nevertheless taken up dramatically as the subject of Jonathan Tolins's 1993 play, *Twilight of the Golds*.

Religion

Rites of religion have also been employed in conversion therapy, though these attempts do not usually consider homosexuality to be pathological. Such approaches typically stress the need to reject the sin of homosexuality, to shun all sin generally, and to strive toward union with God. In 1980 two U.S. researchers reported that eleven of thirty men had converted to heterosexuality by participating in religious services and group Bible study, by socializing with like-minded believers, and through religious conversion experiences. Like many other studies of this kind, imprecisions of methodology make it difficult to ascertain that durable changes in sexual orientation in fact have occurred.

Assessment

Sexual orientation therapy has proved controversial both on scientific and moral grounds. There have always been skeptics about the possibility of and need for conversion therapy. A 1955 report from the British Medical Association, for example, concluded: "It must be admitted with regret that some of the advice given to homosexuals in the name of treatment is often useless, simply defeatist, or grossly unethical." Even though some medical practitioners thought homosexuality to be pathological, they nevertheless thought it incurable.

Gay men and lesbians—and their allies in the sciences—often objected to sexual orientation therapy on the grounds that homosexuality could not and should not be treated because it is not in fact pathological. Faced with mounting scientific evidence about the normalcy of "homosexuals" and with growing political resistance to its view of homosexuality as disordered, in 1973 the APA repudiated its 1952 declaration about homosexuality. Since then, the APA has removed all specific mention of homosexuality from its nomenclature of pathologies. All that remains in the current nomenclature is "sexual orientation distress," the suffering associated with an unwanted sexual orientation. This classification does not single out homosexuality—it applies to anyone with any unwanted sexual orientation and therefore does not ostensibly stigmatize homosexuality. As psychologist John Money has pointed out, it therefore follows that "today the fact of an erotic encounter or partnership between two people of the same genital anatomy is not considered pathological, nor a sickness." There is, therefore, no justification in reigning theories of psychic disorder to seek a cure for homosexuality. Because of this view, fewer and fewer researchers take seriously the investigation of sexual orientation therapy. Some researchers do, though, try to modify atypical gender behavior in children as a way of avoiding homosexuality in them as adults.

At present, there is no generally confirmed, reliable, replicated, or effective method of extinguishing homoerotic orientation and putting heterosexuality in its place. Virtually every study reporting success in conversion therapy contains serious methodological flaws. It is thus impossible to tell whether reported "successes" belong to the charm of the therapist, to the self-deception of the subject, to the failure to conduct long-term studies, or to psychosexual change unrelated to the therapy. This is not to say that there cannot be a successful, empirically confirmable change in sexual interests. It is to say that despite considerable efforts—often at considerable emotional cost to people who have tried—there has not yet been one. One may expect that advances in biomedical and psychological research will open up new avenues for attempted controls of homosexuality, even if demand for such services decreases owing to greater social acceptance and accommodation of homosexuality in personal and public life. The 1978 study *Homosexualities*, by Alan P. Bell and Martin Weinberg, showed that some gay men and lesbians did at some point in their lives try to alter their sexual orientation. One may expect though that fewer men and women will seek therapeutic help if society increasingly accepts and accommodates people with homosexual interests and identities. Most psychiatrists, for example, now counsel gay and lesbian patients on how to cope with the sexual orientation they have, rather than proposing shifts to heteroerotic identities. For a large segment of the population, therefore, sexual orientation therapy has been discredited both on scientific and social grounds.

Future Prospects

Attempts to articulate a comprehensive and scientifically sound theory of psychosexual development in human beings will of necessity require inquiry into the origins of specific erotic orientations and interests. Such study is not necessarily aimed at controlling sexual orientation, only understanding how it develops. In describing mechanisms of development, however, such study may raise anew questions of control over sexual orientation. Many contemporary efforts that do continue to investigate sexual orientation therapy do not any longer justify themselves in the name of curing disease or disorder. Adopting a neutral language, they claim to be respecting patient/client preferences in much the same way that cosmetic surgery responds to patient preferences about nose or ear size and shape. In fact, these latter-day therapists contend that it would be wrong to abandon patients who find their sexual inclinations at odds with their religious or moral values. It may be, though, that in treating men and women for unwanted sexual orientations, therapists have lost sight of the reasons people suffer from homoerotic sexual orientation to begin with. If men and women seek out sexual orientation therapy to escape invidious and unjust social treatment, it may be society, and not individual men and women, that ought to be "treated" for its disorders.

Timothy F. Murphy

S

Bibliography

Bayer, Ronald. *Homosexuality and American Psychiatry*, 2d ed. Princeton, N.J.: Princeton University Press, 1987.

Bell, Alan P., and Martin S. Weinberg. *Homosexualities: A Study of Diversity among Men and Women*. New York: Simon & Schuster, 1978.

Decco, John P., and John P. Elia. *If You Seduce a Straight Person, Can You Make Them Gay?: Issues in Biological Essentialism Versus Social Constructionism in Gay and Lesbian Identities*. Binghamton, N.Y.: Haworth Press, 1993.

Isay, Richard. *Being Homosexual: Gay Men and Their Development*. New York: Farrar, Straus and Giroux, 1990.

Murphy, Timothy F. "Redirecting Sexual Orientation: Techniques and Justifications." *Journal of Sex Research* 29 (1992): 501–23.

See also Counseling; Freud, Sigmund; Homosexuality; Masturbation; Moll, Albert; Nazism and the Holocaust; Psychiatry and Homosexuality; Psychological and Psychoanalytic Perspectives on Homosexuality; Psychotherapy; Religion and Religiosity; Scientific Approaches to Homosexuality; Sexual Orientation; Turing, Alan; Westphal, Carl Friedrich Otto

Sexually Transmitted Diseases

Sexually transmitted diseases (STDs) are diseases transmitted during or through sexual contact: that is, vaginal, anal, penile, clitoral, pubic hair, digital, body fluids, breast, or oral means. Symptoms may arise at the site of contact or distant from those sites, or there may be no symptoms ("asymptomatic"). STDs with symptoms (pain, painful urination, abnormal discharge, itching, burning, irritation, unpleasant odor, sores, and visible abnormalities) include urethritis, epididymitis, vulvovaginitis, cervicitis, pelvic inflammatory disease, proctitis, genital/anal ulcers, genital/anal warts, intestinal infections, skin lesions, and systemic diseases. The suffix *-itis* signifies "swelling or inflammation of." STDs are a subset of communicable diseases, the latter also including diseases spread by touching, breathing infected breath, or surfaces touched recently by humans, for example, exposure to bubonic plague, influenza, and biocides.

Causes and Treatments

People at high risk of STDs have the following general characteristics in decreasing order of frequency: under age thirty; single; multiple sexual partners; frequent unsafe sex practices; women who have had previous inflammatory diseases; women who have had no children; women who use contraceptive devices; and smokers. Unsafe sex practices include, in decreasing order of seriousness, activities that bruise or tear internal tissues of the vagina, anus, throat, or mouth; sexual intercourse or oral sex without a condom; wet or open kissing; masturbating on broken skin or sores; and lesbian oral sex. Safer-sex practices include masturbating, massaging, hugging, holding hands, and dry kissing.

Many STDs are caused by microbes (bacteria, fungi, and actinomycetes), protozoa, or viruses. Table 1 summarizes the major STDs that are not Acquired Immune Deficiency (AIDS)–related, their causative agent(s), and the most effective drugs. Some causative STD agents not in the table include for bacteria, *Mycoplasma hominis*, *Calynnatobacterium granulomatis*, *Shigella* spp (treated by Ampicillin or Trimethoprim-sulfamethoxazole), *Campylobacter* spp (treated by Erythromycin); for the human pubic louse, *Phthirus pubis* (treated with Permethrin and piperonyl butoxide); for the arthropod, the human scabies, *Sarcoptes scabiei* (treated with Lindane); for viruses, cytomegalovirus (there is no effective treatment, but Ganciclovir and Foscarnet are the best), Hepatitis B virus (immunization is the best preventive measure), *Molluscum contagiosum* virus, and HIV. The infections that characterize full-blown AIDS arise through symbiotic organisms ordinarily controlled by a healthy immune system, rather than organisms that have invaded from animals or other humans. Overgrowth of *Candida* symbionts in the mouth (thrush) and in the vagina, cervix, urethra, and bladder of females occurs in mild cases of immunosuppression. Drug dosages for any STD are the legal responsibility of a certified physician.

Prevention

Patients should find out as much information as possible about their STD and their prescribed drugs. Two excellent textbooks about STDs are *Sexually Transmitted Disease*, by T. F. Mroczkowski (New York: Igaku-Shoin, 1990) and *Sexually Transmitted Disease: Problems in Primary Care*, by R. M. Fish, E. T. Campbell, and S. R. Trupin (Los Angeles: Practice Management Information Corporation, 1992). The most recent edition of *The Physician's Desk Reference* is the indispensable source about specific drugs. It can be consulted at public and university biomedical libraries. A person should also be aware of how the body works and have some basic knowledge of what occurs to chemicals within the human body after exposure, whether as medicines or after inadvertent chemical exposure.

Self-education as above is the most important personal preventive measure against STDs. Asking intelligent questions before sex ranks next in importance. Each participant before sexual play or intercourse should ask about the partners' sexual history relative to STDs and be more careful with people who have had many prior sexual contacts. The next personal mechanisms to prevent STDs are by using condoms or other prophylactic barriers during sex, and then douching after sex. Condoms should be of the correct size and employ nonoil-based lubricants and spermicides like nonoxynol-9. Douching involves washing the body areas that have contacted genitalia, feces, urine, or saliva with aqueous solutions of mild disinfectant or, failing that, tap water that has been chlorinated or ozonated. Douching should consist of at least three separate washings. Showering can substitute for douching as long as contacted body parts are also washed thoroughly with soap and water. The best preventive measures involve both condoms and douching/showering. People should self-inspect themselves regularly with a mirror and flashlight, at least once a week, and note any bumps that get bigger or painful areas. The next important stratagem is to visit a nearby STD clinic regularly but at least once a year, even if the individual feels healthy. Many STDs can be diagnosed only through laboratory testing. People must take responsibility for themselves since prevention is better (and much less costly) than cure.

History and Statistics

The term *venereal disease* has been the major English-language word to describe STDs from the sixteenth century up to the 1970s. Some other terms that were used include "French disease" and the "French pox." Traditional "VD" treatments before the advent of sulfanilamide in 1936 and penicillin in 1941 (especially for treatment of syphilis) consisted of treatment with mercury and arsenic compounds, all very toxic. The advent of AIDS since 1981 and the Human Immunodeficiency Virus (HIV) since 1985 has increased the incidence of other STDs, independent of gender, sexual orientation, race, or ethnicity. In 1992, STD clinics reported 14,532 positive non-HIV-related STD test results to the Centers

for Disease Control and Prevention in the United States (Division of STD/HIV Prevention). The true rate of STD prevalence is underreported because many STDs do not have diagnostic tests, many STD clinics do not have the full complement of STD tests, or test results are simply not recorded for various reasons. Many STDs are also asymptomatic or have nonspecific symptoms and require laboratory diagnosis. A recent Centers for Disease Control and Prevention journal paper reported that of the one thousand laboratories selected for survey in 1994 the percentage that tested for specific STDs were as follows: syphilis, 86.9 percent; *Chlamydia trachomatis* infection, 71.1 percent; gonorrhea, 81 percent; and chancroid (*Hemophilus ducreyi*), 7.9 percent. The Herpes Simplex Virus-2 (HSV-2) and the human papillomavirus virus infections in the general U.S. population were prevalent to the extent of 20 to 25 percent and 20 to 40 percent, respectively. The major chronic (long-lasting) persistent STDs in the U.S. heterosexual population are genital herpes, hepatitis, human papillomavirus, and HIV infections. Heterosexual users of intravenous illicit drugs and crack cocaine are known to be at high risk for the acquisition and transmission of STDs. The STD prevalence in the Midwest of the United States between 1992 and 1995 was Caucasian men, 29 percent; Caucasian women, 55.9 percent; black men, 53.6 percent; and black women, 64.7 percent, from a study of 1,046 individuals.

Types of STDs
Gonorrhea

Gonorrhea can be asymptomatic ("carriers"), but it can cause a painful urethral discharge with dysuria (difficulty in passing urine) and frequent urge to urinate. Gonorrhea in males spreads to the small glands around the urethra, then the prostate, seminal vesicles, vas deferens, and epididymis. This spread can cause lower abdominal and pelvic pain, fever, scrotitis, and urine retention. In women, the uterine cervix is the most frequent initial location, and spreads by ascending to the uterus, the lymphatic system, the fallopian tubes, and into the peritoneal cavity, giving rise to pelvic peritonitis. *Chlamydia trachomatis* and *Ureaplasma urealyticum* infections (see Table 1) frequently accompany gonorrhea, and treatment must be for the ensemble by Ceftriaxone followed by Doxycycline. In women genital mycoplasmas and anaerobes are also associated with gonorrhea. The risk factors for gonorrhea are smoking, being younger than thirty, multiple sex partners, and men-

S

Table 1. Some Non-AIDS Related STDs, Their Causative Agents, and Treatment Drugs

Disease	Causative Agent	Treatments
Amebiasis	*Entamoeba histolytica* (Protozoan)	Metronidazole, tetracycline, Paromomycin Chloroquine (liver)
Balantidiasis	*Balantidium coli* (Protozoan)	tetracycline
Cervix and Throat Infection	*Actinomyces israelii* (Actinomycetes)	Penicillin G, ampicillin, tetracycline, erythromycin
Chancroid	*Haemophilus ducreyi*	Trimethoprim-sulfamethoxazole, erythromycin Ceftriaxone, Rifampin, sulfonamide, tetracycline
Genital and Throat Infection	(1) *Chlamydia trachomatis* and *psittaci*	tetracycline, erythromycin, sulfonamide, Chloramphenicol
	(2) *Candida* spp	Nystatin, Ketoconazole, Fluconazole
Genital Infections	(1) *Fusobacterium nucleatum* (gram-negative bacterium)	Penicillin G, Clindamycin, Metronidazole, cephalosporin; erythromycin, tetracycline, Chloramphenicol, Cefoxitin,
	(2) Herpes simplex virus	Acyclovir
Giardiasis	*Giardia lamblia* (flagellated protozoan)	Quinacrine, Metronidazole
Gonorrhea	*Neisseria gonorrhoeae* (gram-negative gonococcus)	Parenteral penicillin G + Probenecid, Amipicillin+ Probenecid, Amoxicillin + Probenecid, tetracycline, Cefttriaxone, erythromycin, Spectinomycin, Ciprofloxacin penicillin-insensitive: Ceftriaxone, Cefuroxime, Cefoxitin, Spectinomycin, Ciprofloxacin, topical eyedrops (silver nitrate or antimicrobial) to newborn infants of infected mothers for prophylaxis
HPV	Human papilloma virus	Alfa interferon
Meningo-coccal	*Neisseria meningitidis* (aerobic gram-negative meningococcus)	Rifampfin, Ceftriaxone, Minocycline, Ciprofloxacin in carrier state; Infection: penicillin G, Cefuroxime
Pyorrhea	*Entamoeba gingivalis* (protozoan)	Metronidazole, tetracycline, Paromomycin
Syphilis	*Treponema pallidum* (spirochete)	Penicillin G, Ceftriaxone, tetracycline
Trichomoniasis	*Trichomonas vaginalis* (flagellated protozoan)	Metronidazole
Urethritis (nonspecific)	*Ureaplasma urealyticum*	tetracycline, Erythromycin
Urinary tract infections consistently after sex	Microbial overgrowth	Trimethoprim-sulfamethoxazole Nitrofurantoin
Urinary tract infections	(1) *Candida* spp (yeast)	Flucytosine, Amphotericin B

Table 1. Continued

Disease	Causative Agent	Treatments
	(2) *Chlamydia trachomatis*	tetracycline, Erythromycin, sulfonamide
	(3) *Enterobacter* spp	Cephalosporin, aminoglycoside, penicillin, Aztreonam, Trimethoprim-sulfamethoxazole
	(4) *Enterococcus* spp	Ampicillin, penicillin G, Vancomycin, Ciprofloxacin, Norfloxacin, Nitrofurantoin
	(5) *Escherichia coli*	Ampicillin + aminoglycoside, Trimethoprim-sulfamethoxazole, sulfonamide, Norfloxacin, Nitrofurantoin, tetracycline
	(6) *Enterobacter aerogenes*	Cefamandole, Cefuroxime, cephalosporin, aminoglycoside, broad-spectrum penicillin
	(7) Herpes simplex virus	Acyclovir (Zovirax)
	(8) Human papilloma virus	Podophyllin/Benzoin; Trichloracetic acid; 5-Fluorouracil; Bleomycin
	(9) *Klebsella pneumoniae*	cephalosporin + aminoglycoside, Mezlocillin, Piperacillin, Trimethoprim-sulfamethoxazole
	(10) *Neisseria gonorrhoeae*	See gonorrhea entry
	(11) *Proteus mirabilis*	Ampicillin, Amoxicillin, aminoglycoside, cephalosporin
	(12) Other *Proteus* spp	Aminoglycoside, cephalosporin, broad-spectrum penicillin, Aztreonam
	(13) *Pseudomonas aeruginosa*	broad-spectrum penicillin, Norfloxacin Ciprofloxacin, aminoglycoside, Aztreonam
	(14) *Streptococcus bovis*	Penicillin G, Streptomycin, Gentamicin Cephalosporin, Vancomycin
	(15) *Streptococcus faecalis*	Ampicillin, PenicillinG, Vancomycin, Nitrofurantoin
Vaginitis	(1) *Candida albicans*	Imadazole (Clotrimazole, Monistat, Miconazole), Nystatin, Gentian violet, boric acid, potassium sorbate
	(2) *Candida glabrata*	As for *Candida albicans*
	(3) *Candida tropicalis*	Butoconazole
	(4) *Enterobius* (pinworm)	Pyrantel pamoate
	(5) *Escherichia coli*	tetracycline, Sulfisoxazole, Ampicillin Trimethoprim-sulfamethoxazole, Doxycycline, Nitrofurantoin, Cephradine
	(6) *Gardnerella vaginitis*	Metronidazole, Ampicillin, Cepradine, tetracycline, Cephalexin
	(7) *Trichomonas vaginalis*	Metronidazole, Tinidazole, Ornidazole

The order of the drugs is the order of preference, beginning with most preferred; drugs with lowercase initial letters denote one of that drug class; drugs with uppercase initial letters are specific.

Note that Metronidazole interacts with alcohol taken within 24-hours (alcoholic beverages and alcoholic mouthwashes) to cause nausea; it is never prescribed for pregnant women unless the mother's life is in danger. Other drugs with the same caveat for the latter are tetracycline, Doxycycline, and Trimethoprim-sulfamethoxazole.

S struation. Menstruating and prepubertal females are especially susceptible to gonorrhea, as are those who use intrauterine contraceptive devices and tampons and those who have had hysterectomies. The rates of gonorrhea increased worldwide since 1974 up to the mid-1980s, because some gonococci produced penicillinase, which deactivates penicillin G, the major antibiotic used to treat the disease. Spectinomycin, Cefoxitin, Cefotaxime, or Trimethoprim-sulfamethoxazole are the major alternatives for these resistant strains, and have succeeded in causing decreased infection rates. In 1988, 719,536 civilian cases of gonorrhea were reported to the Centers for Disease Control and Prevention, and it is still the most common notifiable disease in the United States. In the late 1980s in the United States, though gonorrhea rates decreased, syphilis prevalence increased, showing that not all STDs need increase or decrease together. The gonorrhea and syphilis trends for heterosexuals appear to apply to homosexuals also.

Chlamydial infections

These are the most common STD in the world and also in the United States, and are often asymptomatic. In women, their genital tract infections can cause severe or chronic pain and sterility, with added risk of pelvic inflammatory disease and ectopic pregnancy (development of fetus outside the uterus). In men, epididymitis and proctitis occur. Chlamydia are parasites as well as being gram-negative bacteria. The major symptom of chlamydia infection is ulcer formation. It is implicated in lymphogranuloma venereum, trachoma (in infants and in the adults of underdeveloped countries), inclusion conjunctivitis ("pink eye"), urethritis, perihepatitis, cervicitis, pelvic inflammatory disease, and neonatal pneumonia. It has the same risk characteristics as gonorrhea.

Syphilis

Syphilis is still a major STD. It can seriously damage the brain, spinal cord, heart, and joints. Since 1988 in the United States, syphilis has decreased among homosexual and bisexual males, but it has increased in heterosexual males and females. The genital lesions of syphilis have been correlated with increased incidence of HIV infection potential. The spirochete *Treponema pallidum*, the causative agent, is very slowly dividing, and has a prolonged incubation time within the body of from thirty to ninety days. It enters the body through mucous membranes (leaving a chancre at its first entry site) and through skin abrasions during sexual intercourse, kissing, nonsexual body contact, blood transfusions, being stuck with a contaminated needle, and being passed from the mother to the fetus during the first trimester of pregnancy. Wearing condoms therefore cannot be a fully effective preventative measure. It is not a very contagious disease, being transmitted in only about 10 percent of contacts. The major risk factors include urban adolescents with poor body hygiene, multiple sex partners, drug abusers, and partners of intravenous drug users or bisexuals. The time period that the chancre persists is called *primary syphilis* and is often asymptomatic. The time when the spirochete spreads from its initial entry area is called *secondary syphilis,* which may also be asymptomatic but is often characterized by skin rashes, patchy loss of hair, condyloma lata (slow-growing, wartlike protruberances of the genitals and skin), mucous patches, flulike symptoms, and enlarged lymph nodes. Latent syphilis up to four years after the initial infection may lead to tertiary syphilis in about half the cases from ten to forty years after the initial infection. Skin, bone, and soft tissue effects involve the appearance of lesions called *gummas*; heart valves and the aorta may become damaged; central nervous system damage may cause brain damage, delusions, hallucinations, impaired memory, blurred vision, and personality changes. Tertiary syphilis can also cause tabes dorsalis, spinal cord degeneration leading to a clumsy mode of walking with widely spaced steps. Impotence is also common, and sensitivity to sensation and temperature is also impaired.

Chancroid

Chancroid was first described in 1852 and is most reported now among prostitutes. Men usually get one ulcer, while women often have four to five, both with swelling of the lymph nodes. The incidence of *Hemophilus ducreyi* has increased, owing to resistance to penicillin, sulfonamides, trimethoprim-sulfamethoxazole, and tetracycline. Amoxicillin/clavulanic acid and Ceftriaxone are presently the most effective therapies.

Herpes simplex

These virus lesions are usually painful and unsightly, though 75 percent of those infected are asymptomatic. It is predominantly found in prostitutes and adults of lower socioeconomic status.

Herpes zoster

This causes shingles, a painful infection of nerves as a result of mild immunosuppression and is also common in the elderly. Acyclovir is the major chemotherapy for both. Herpes infection in the eyes is relieved through application of Trifluridine eye drops and Vidarabine ointment. Steroid therapy for other ailments (for example, prednisone for asthma) makes the herpes infection worse.

Human papillomavirus

This virus causes condylomata acuminatum (venereal warts), first described in A.D. 25 by Celsus. The viral agent was recognized in 1907 by Ciuffo, but the first pathological examination was by Ayre in 1949. This virus is thought to be the causative agent for cervical and penile cancers. Its infections are enhanced by immunosuppression, vitamin A deficiency, and smoking. It appears to be a symbiont. The Pap smear is the major form of diagnosis.

Hepatitis

Hepatitis has many "types": A, B, non-A non-B, C, D, or E, and a mild form accompanying mononucleosis. It can be caused by cytomegalovirus, herpes simplex virus, and other viruses. Chemically induced hepatitis from drug reactions, industrial chemical exposure, inherited metabolic disorders, alcoholism, blood transfusions, uncooked shellfish (types A and C), drug abuse, and liver-attacking infections may be indistinguishable from a viral causation. Antibody tests to detect types A, B, and C are available but not non-A non-B. Often flulike symptoms precede jaundice (yellow eyes and skin). When jaundice does not appear, low-grade fever, malaise (bodily discomfort), fatigue, joint pains, loss of appetite, decreased desire to smoke, nausea, vomiting, and skin rash may occur. The interferons have shown some promise in alleviating some of the symptoms of hepatitis. Human immune serum globulin protects against hepatitis A, and in the already infected, immune serum globulin IM. People with hepatitis B are usually asymptomatic. Risk factors for hepatitis B include intravenous drug users, homosexual males, workers or patients in institutions for the mentally retarded, household contacts with infected individuals, health-care workers exposed to blood, number of sex partners, nurses who needle-stick, and patients on hemodialysis. Vaccines are available for prophylaxis. Infected individuals should be given immune serum globulin, which also protects against A, B, and non-A non-B hepatitis. The most effective postinfection therapy for the B type is hepatitis B immune globulin. Alpha-interferon has proved helpful also. Hepatitis D can occur only in patients who have recovered from hepatitis B. Hepatitis E occurs mostly in India and Mexico, usually through a contaminated water supply. The non-A non-B type is associated with hepatitis C, the predominant hepatitis after blood transfusions. The only prophylaxis is immune serum globulin.

Bacteriuria

The pH of the urine of women is more likely to support *Escherichia coli* growth than that of men, excepting sexually active male homosexuals. Bacterial growth often migrates from the vagina, into the urethra, and from there into the bladder. Women (especially pregnant ones) are more likely to suffer from the upper urinary tract STD pyelonephritis, which is characterized by fever (temperatures above 102°F), chills, tender flanks, and back pain. Men beyond the age of fifty are likely to experience bacteriuria usually related to prostatic disease. Medical conditions like diabetes, sickle cell disease (blacks especially), and gout (the elderly) are also associated with susceptibility to urinary tract infections. Vaginitis can give rise to cervicitis, urethritis, bladder infection, pyelonephritis, and kidney infection.

Special Homosexual Concerns

Rimming, or *fecal-digital-oral* sexual contact, may result in diarrhea caused by mouth ingestion of fecal *Entamoeba histolytica* (causes amoebic dysentery; the incidence is about 2 to 4 percent in the United States), the flagellated protozoan *Giardia lamblia* (may also cause weight loss through malabsorption of nutrients), or *Balantidium coli* (ciliated protozoan of the large intestine). Diarrhea can also be caused by microbial infection: enterotoxigenic *Escherichia coli, Vibrio cholerae, Campylobacter, Salmonella, Shigella,* and *Yersina enterocolitica.* Among those with AIDS who have diarrhea, the causative organisms may be in order of decreasing frequency *Candida, Cryptosporidium, Cytomegalovirus, Salmonella,* herpes simplex virus, and *Mycobacterium avium.* Among those with enteritis who have diarrhea, the causative organisms may be *Campylobacter, Chlamydia trachomatis, Clostridium difficile, Entamoeba, Giardia,* and *Shigella.* Among those with proctitis (inflammation of the anus and rectum) who have diarrhea, the causative organisms are similarly *Campylobacter, Chlamydia trachomatis,* herpes simplex virus, *Neisseria gonorrhoeae,* and *Tre-*

S *ponema pallidum.* The above behavior may also cause the following diseases in decreasing order of frequency: enteric infections, shigellosis, *Campylobacter* infection, enterotoxigenic *Escherichia coli* infection, all the hepatitis types but especially the A type, amebiasis, giardiasis, salmonellosis, Enterobius vermicularis, Strongyloides stercoralis, oral infections, oral warts, oral gonorrhea, syphilis, lymphogranuloma venereum, oral donovanosis, oral chancroid, herpes simplex virus, and anorectal meningococcal infection.

Receptive fellatio causes in descending order of frequency physical abrasions, oral gonorrhea, oral herpes simplex virus infection but especially HSV-2, nongonococcal throat infection but especially *Chlamydia*, oral condylomata acuminata, syphilis, hepatitis B, enteric infections, lymphogranuloma venereum, oral donovanosis or granuloma inguinale, and oral chancroid.

Insertive fellatio has caused in decreasing order of frequency physical abrasions, bites, genital herpes simplex virus but especially HSV-1, and nongonococcal urethritis.

Kissing and *French-kissing* can transmit *Entamoeba gingivalis,* which is associated with pyorrhea (pus from the gums around the roots of teeth), candida albicans (thrush), hepatitis A, Epstein-Barr virus (infectious mononucleosis), syphilis, HSV-1 and -2 virus, and *Chlamydia.*

Bestiality has as its risk factors all the vectors of animal-borne diseases, many being common with humans, for example, *Campylobacter.*

Homosexual men who are sexually active can have a high incidence of *acute urinary tract infection* characterized by pyuria (pus in urine), symptoms of cystitis, bacteriuria (usually *Escherichia coli*), a urethral discharge on squeezing the penis shaft, and a nongonococcal urethritis on gram stain. *Proctitis* is prevalent in homosexual men, and is treated with drugs for any gonorrhea infection first (see Table 1), and then tetracycline for the *Chlamydia* infection that is the root cause of the proctitis. Syphilitic chancre on the penis, lips, anus, and rectum is often seen in homosexual men with syphilis. Hepatitis B is more common among homosexual men than heterosexual men. Even artificial insemination can spread hepatitis B, an important consideration for lesbian mothers-to-be. Vaginitis in women and urethritis in men can both be caused by *Trichomonas vaginalis,* a flagellated protozoan.

The HIV I and II viruses can be sexually transmitted, and the eventual breakdown of the immune system brings forth full-blown AIDS. Some drugs developed against chemotherapy of protozoal infections by nonhuman causes have proved effective for some AIDS-related infections. For example, aerosolized pentamidine for lung *Pneumocystis carinii* is used parenterally also to treat trypanosomiasis and leishmaniasis. Toxoplasmosis caused by the intracellular protozoan *Toxoplasma gondii* is treated with pyrimethamine and a sulfonamide, the usual treatment for chloroquine-resistant falciparum malaria. This illustrates how treatments for AIDS-related infections can differ from human-transmitted STDs.

Of those who are HIV infected, a high proportion also have other classic STDs. For example, at four Florida STD clinics, the rates for HIV+/HIV− patients were (in percentages) gonorrhea (30/36), primary or secondary syphilis (8/4), chancroid or lymphogranuloma venereum (1/1), gonorrhea contact or epidemiological treatment (32/42), and syphilis contact or epidemiological treatment (29/17). Homosexual men with HSV-2 showed higher rates of HIV infection than those not infected with HSV-2. The same was found for genital ulcers, and also for heterosexuals.

Demographic Variables for Antibiotic Therapy

Some variables to remember about STD treatment antibiotics are provided below.

1. Be an Informed Patient: One should always refer to the current edition of *The Physician's Desk Reference* for basic information on type of drug; side effects; interactions; and age-related, behavioral, genetic sensitivity, and allergy information for one's medicine. Patients are the final quality control for their own health, and the physician will be a better doctor for the individual who is an informed patient.

2. Age Effects: Elderly patients and newborn/premature children may have slower rates of drug metabolism, and if the original compound is the molecule that is actually therapeutic, the average dose may be too high. However, if metabolism is necessary to generate the therapeutic molecule, the dose may be too low. Ear problems for aminoglycosides may also be experienced. The elderly on antacid therapy and young children/elderly suffering from achlorhydria may also have increased absorption of penicillin G and decreased absorption of Ketoconazole.

3. Genetic Sensitivity: The sulfonamides, Nitrofurantoin, and Chloramphenicol may cause he-

molysis (red blood cells leak their contents) owing to a glucose-6-phosphate dehydrogenase deficiency. The condition is often found in blacks but is occasionally found in Caucasians as well. Clinical anemia (insufficient red blood cell iron) may be present also. Isoniazid doses may need to be higher in Asian Americans and some Caucasians because of "fast" acetylating capacity, and liver problems may be seen as evidenced by nonreference range blood enzyme activities.

4. Pregnancy: Pregnant lesbians who are being treated with streptomycin may transmit this to the fetus with hearing loss or impairment in the newborn. Tetracyclines in pregnant women may cause maternal liver damage, pancreatitis, and kidney damage, as shown by the appropriate markers in the blood enzyme panel and urine markers. Penicillins cross the placenta, so doses need to be higher to treat maternal STDs. Raising doses may put the fetus at risk. Lactating mothers may transmit sulfonamides and nalidixic acid to their suckling child and cause hemolysis in those children who have glucose-6-phosphate deficiency, which, as mentioned above, is much more common in blacks than in Caucasians. Sulfonamides also sensitize the nursing child to kernicterus (inability to glucuronidate bilirubin).

5. Drug Allergies: Any antibiotic may cause an allergic reaction at some time or another during therapy. The beta-lactam drugs are especially notorious for this. Sulfonamides, trimethoprim, Nitrofurantoin, and erythromycin may cause skin rash, and those who are infected with Epstein-Barr virus (mononucleosis) often have rashes after ampicillin and amoxicillin treatments. Patients who have anaphylaxis (immediate skin rash responses on chemical exposure), laryngitis (swollen vocal cords and windpipe), hives (poxy skin eruptions), hypersensitivity to stinging nettles, or other hypersensitivities preclude the use of penicillins in all but life-threatening situations. Because they attack the symbiotic microflora and microfauna within the body, the antimicrobial agents may also cause "drug fever," which is a mild allergy and can be mistaken for continued infection.

6. Behavioral Effects: High doses of penicillin G can cause seizures (local or general motor) in susceptible patients. The penicillin and the beta-lactam antibiotics often cause neurological problems in patients with kidney disease. Patients with myasthenia gravis (neuromuscular paralysis from an autoimmune process leading to ineffective neuromuscular

nerve junctions) or other muscle–nervous system disorders are susceptible to the neuromuscular blocking effects of the aminoglycosides, polymyxins, and Colistin. Sexual performance may also be affected. Patients undergoing general anesthesia who are taking a neuromuscular blocking agent like these are susceptible to antibiotic toxicity, and deaths have occurred from this cause.

7. Individual Sensitivity: Drug doses often have to be titrated to have a compromise between therapeutic effect and adverse side effects. Patients must tell their physicians if they feel any side effects, or they may suffer needlessly. Such effects may be even more important in multidrug therapy. This is especially important for drug cocktail treatments containing protease inhibitors for treating people with AIDS (PWAs).   *Shane S. Que Hee*

Bibliography

Beck-Sague, C. M., J. R. Cordts, K. Brown, S. A. Larsen, C. M. Black, J. S. Knapp, J. C. Ridderhof, F. G. Barnes, and S. A. Morse. "Laboratory Diagnoses of Sexually Transmitted Diseases in Facilities within the United States." *Sexually Transmitted Diseases* 23 (1996): 342–49.

Division of STD/HIV Prevention. *Sexually Transmitted Disease Surveillance, 1992.* Atlanta: Centers for Disease Control and Prevention, 1993.

Gilman, A. G., T. W. Rall, A. S. Nies, and P. Taylor. *Goodman and Gilman's The Pharmacological Basis of Therapeutics*, 8th ed. New York: Pergamon, 1990.

Holmberg, S. D., J. A. Stewart, A. R. Gerber, et al. "Prior Herpes Simplex Virus Type 2 Infection as a Risk Factor for HIV Infection." *Journal of the American Medical Association* 259 (1988): 1048–50.

Leenaars, E. *Prevention and Early Detection of Sexually Transmitted Diseases*. Amsterdam: Thesis Publishers, 1994.

Nahmias, A .J., F. K. Lee, and S. Beckman-Nahmias. "Sero-Epidemiological and -Sociological Patterns of Herpes Simplex Virus Infections in the World." *Scandinavian Journal of Infectious Diseases* 69 (1990): 19–36.

Osewe, P. L., T. A. Peterman, R. L. Ransom, A. A. Zaidi, and J. E. Wroten. "Trends in the Acquisition of Sexually Transmitted Diseases among HIV-Positive Patients at STD Clinics, Miami 1988–1992." *Sexually Transmitted Diseases* 23 (1996): 230–33.

S

Que Hee, Shane S. *Biological Monitoring: An Introduction.* New York: Van Nostrand Reinhold, 1993.

Siegel, H. A., R. S. Falck, J. Wang, and R. G. Carlson. "History of Sexually Transmitted Diseases Infection, Drug-Sex behaviors, and the Use of Condoms among Midwestern Users of Injection Drugs and Crack Cocaine." *Sexually Transmitted Diseases* 23 (1996): 277–82.

Stamm, W. E., H. H. Handsfield, A. M. Rompalo, et al. "The Association Between Genital Ulcer Disease and Acquisition of HIV Infection in Homosexual Men." *Journal of the American Medical Association* 260 (1988): 1429–33.

See also AIDS; AIDS Organizations, U.S.; World Health Organization/WHO Global AIDS Programme

Sexual Violence

There are two general categories of sexual violence: nonconsensual and consensual. The former usually garners more attention with its screaming headlines and frightening statistics. Whose interest is not aroused by priests who violate their vows? For instance, in 1989, two Roman Catholic priests named Harold McIntee and Glenn Doughty were convicted of multiple abuse of male youngsters. Who is not horrified by the details of a serial killing? Jeffrey Dahmer not only confessed to killing seventeen boys and mutilating some of their bodies; he also admitted to having anal sex with most of his victims, some after they were dead. Statistics are equally attention-getting. In 1994, there were about 4,890 rapes of males age twelve and over in the United States. Almost as many boys as girls are sexually abused before they reach eighteen, and one in six males will be sexually victimized in his lifetime.

This attention has resulted in easily available information about nonconsensual sex or rape. This article focuses on consensual sexual violence, more commonly called sadomasochism, or S/M.

In spite of John K. Noyes's objection that S/M wants to be understood as a form of role-playing—not an act of violence, but a metacommunicational act about violence and sexual stereotyping—for purposes of this article, consensual sexual violence and S/M are synonymous.

More specifically, this article focuses on S/M between or among gay males. This presents several problems. First, S/M scenes often involve more than two partners and the participants may include

women (Joseph 30–67). Second, the self-disclosed sexual orientations of sadomasochists show a significant percentage of bisexuals: 30 percent exclusively heterosexual, 31 percent bisexual, and 38 percent exclusively homosexual. Of the 31 percent bisexual, 16 percent said they were bisexual but more homosexual (Spengler 59). Finally, the validity of self-disclosure in surveys has been questioned. Males apparently tend to be more influenced than females by variation in item wording, interviewer gender, and respondent control (Cabania et al. 345). For all these reasons, this article includes, rather than excludes, any male sadomasochist who engages in consensual sexual violence with other males, regardless of his self-identified sexual orientation.

Inclusion is important in a group that is sometimes a despised minority within a despised minority. S/M practitioners have not always been welcome by other gays. In 1985, for example, some of the 300 members of London's Lesbian and Gay Centre objected to allowing S/M groups use of the center. Additionally, many feminists object to S/M. Feminists like Alexandra Symonds, Natalie Shainess, Paula J. Caplan, and Deborah Franklin object for a variety of sociological, legal, and psychiatric reasons. For instance, they point out that Helene Deutsch's concept of the biological foundation of women's masochism "could easily be used to condone domestic violence. [In the past] this worked . . . in courts of law" (Noyes 142).

Welcome outside the gay community has often been just as wanting. According to Gloria Brame et al., in 1980, the movie *Cruising* portrayed the leather (S/M) scene as inherently sordid and violent. That same year, PBS aired "Gay Power, Gay Politics," which incorrectly stated that 10 percent of all gay deaths in San Francisco were S/M-related (quoted in Hart 40). A decade later, the National Endowment for the Arts reacted to S/M themes in the works of Robert Mapplethorpe and other artists by drafting a clause that requires recipients of grant money to guarantee they will not use the money for depictions of S/M or homoeroticism. There have also been legal attacks. In 1992, the voters of Oregon considered Measure 9, which would have banned the use of state money to promote, encourage, or facilitate homosexuality, pedophilia, sadism, and masochism. The measure also mandated the teaching of all four as abnormal, unnatural, and wrong. Even though the measure was defeated, "No on 9" tacticians won by projecting homosexuals as clean-cut, tax-paying professionals whose rights should not be violated. Such winning tactics, however inadvertent, distanced normal gays from S/M gays. Finally, the mental health industry has often been less than kind. In December 1986, the American Psychiatric Association added self-defeating personality disorder (masochism) and sadistic personality disorder (sadism) to its *Diagnostic and Statistical Manual of Mental Disorders*, revised third edition *(DSM-III-R),* the Bible of psychiatric ailments. Psychiatrists like John Gunderson, Laura Brown, and Lenore Walker criticized these additions. Gunderson believed there was not enough literature, Brown believed the self-defeating personality disorder actually described a traditional good woman, and Walker concurred with Brown and as well accused other psychiatrists of using this description to increase the number of potential patients. Still other mental health professionals noted that when hatred and sensuality condense, aggression is absorbed by libido, hatred by love. S/M practitioners are in greatest danger when two or more of these unwelcoming fields intersect. Even before the *DSM-III-R* additions, an American sadist's legal defense was that his partner consented in a 1967 case. The court disallowed this defense, saying a person with all his mental faculties would never consent to being injured in this manner.

The field of psychology, however, is not always unwelcoming. Using Jung's theory that archetypal ideas survive in the ancestral subconscious stratum of the human mind as well as in legends, myths, rites, dreams, and delusions, Robert Eisler proposes that all crimes of violence derive or evolve from prehistory. This seems confirmed by the creation of contemporary legends. In Berlin shortly after the Wall fell, S/M studios offered customers simulated experiences of interrogation by East German police. Some psychologists and psychiatrists also offer a more positive explanation for masochism. In the United States, Germany, and probably South Africa, S/M practitioners are disproportionately high-income earners and well educated. In Germany, for instance, Wetzstein found a 63.1 percent sample of high-income, well-educated practitioners (qtd. in Noyes 138). Psychologist Roy F. Baumeister notes, "The rich, powerful, and successful, the people with the heaviest burdens of selfhood . . . need the escape of masochism" ("An Inside Look" 47; Noyes 141). Masochists, then, are taking a breather from their heavy burden of selfhood. Even as early as 1981, psychologist Samuel Janus and psychiatrist Barbara

Bess, interviewing eighty call girls, found that 60 percent of the prostitutes' 7,645 clients were politicians and power brokers, most of whom requested bondage, humiliation, and pain. Regrettably, there are no such studies on or explanations of sadists.

The field of literature provides some of the warmest welcome. Perhaps the foremost American writer of gay S/M is Dennis Cooper. Cooper writes novels about gay teenage sexual turmoil, drug abuse, and obsessive violence in signature spare and meticulous narrative style. In *Closer* the angelic, drugged-out George Miles is seduced by an older man who injects his lovers with novocaine and dissects them. In *Frisk*, published shortly before Jeffrey Dahmer's arrest, the adolescent Dennis moves to Amsterdam and pens a letter home describing a series of ritualistic murders, which turn out to be imaginary. In *Try*, Ziggy is sexually brutalized in excruciating detail by his two gay fathers. Although critics contend Cooper's work is sadistic and politically irresponsible, Cooper is admired for his prose style, which has been called American pop writing because the characters speak as Americans do. Cooper is also admired for his awareness of S/M history. He knows that the Marquis de Sade had sexual orgies that included whipping prostitutes and forcing them to whip him. Cooper is also aware of French dramatist Henry Bataille, who wrote plays with sexual and scandalous themes, influencing later playwrights. Cooper is aware of Baudelaire, who wrote in *My Heart Laid to Bare* that there are three pursuits worthy of respect: to know, to kill, and to create. Cooper's writing even reflects Baudelaire. For Cooper, sex as the ultimate intimacy is not enough. Thus, in all Cooper's writing, sex contains transcendent possibilities in the form of a metaphysics of desire punctuated by death. S/M practitioners seem to confirm this transcendence. In *Leatherfolk,* practitioners finally speak for themselves, and some claim S/M as a spiritual journey.

Considering all the negatives from inside and outside the gay community, the greatest irony is that S/M has become fashionable. Today, it is so trendy that it is used to sell everything from beer (Bass Ale) to designer products (Gucci); it is shown on TV (*Friends*) and records (Janet Jackson's *Rope Burn*). It has given rise to S/M-themed restaurants (New York's La Nouvelle Justine) and nightclubs (San Francisco's Bondage Go-Go). There are even seminars at universities with titles like Safe, Sane, and Consensual S/M: An Alternate Way of Loving. As American society approaches the millennium, maybe Americans—gay,

S straight, bisexual, transgender—will conclude that consensual sexual violence or S/M really is just another way of loving.

Rae N. Watanabe

Bibliography

Bing, Jonathan. "Dennis Cooper: Adolescent Rebellion Propels His Dystopian Vision." *Publishers Weekly,* March 21, 1994, 48.

Birnie, Lisa Hobbs. "Sins of the Father." *Saturday Night* (February 1994): 37.

Boxer, Sarah. "The Parable of the Cheek-Turners and the Cheek-Smiters." *Discover,* August 1987, 80f.

Cabania, Joseph, et al. "Effects of Interviewer Gender, Interviewer Choice, and Item Wording on Responses to Questions Concerning Sexual Behavior." *Public Opinion Quarterly* (Fall 1996): 345.

Chancer, Lynn C. *Sadomasochism in Everyday Life: The Dynamics of Power and Powerlessness.* New Brunswick, N.J.: Rutgers University Press, 1992.

Donaldson, Stephen. "Rape of Males." In *Encyclopedia of Homosexuality.* Wayne R. Dynes, ed. New York: Garland, 1990.

Durrell, Anna. "Uproar over Violent Images." *New Statesman,* June 14, 1985, 16.

Eisler, Robert. *Man into Wolf: An Anthropological Interpretation of Sadism, Masochism and Lycanthropy.* New York: Greenwood Press, 1951.

Hart, Lynda. *Between the Body and the Flesh: Performing Sadomasochism.* New York: Columbia University Press, 1998.

Hochberg, M. J. "Police Negligence Delayed End to the Milwaukee Murder Horror." *Advocate,* September 10, 1991, 56–58.

"An Inside Look at S and M." *Psychology Today* (November–December 1995): 47.

Joseph, Edward D. "Beating Fantasies." In *The Kris Study Group of New York Psychoanalytic Institute Monograph I.* New York: International Universities Press, 1965.

Kernberg, Otto. "Hatred as Pleasure." In *Pleasure Beyond the Pleasure Principle.* Robert A. Glick and Stanley Bone, eds. New Haven: Yale University Press, 1990.

Leo, John. "Stomping and Whomping Galore." *Time,* May 4, 1981, 73f.

Linden, Robin Ruth, et al., eds. *Against Sadomasochism: A Radical Feminist Analysis.* Palo Alto, Calif.: Frog in the Well, 1982.

Male Rape Bibliography. On-line. April 29, 1998.

Mannes-Abbot, Guy. "Try." *New Statesman and Society,* September 30, 1994, 56.

Marin, Rick, and Nadine Joseph. "Lick Me, Flog Me, Buy Me!" *Newsweek,* December 29, 1997, 85.

Myths and Facts about Rape. On-line. April 29, 1998.

The National Victim Center. Male Rape. On-line. April 29, 1998.

Noyes, John K. "S and M in South Africa." *American Imago* (Spring 1998): 135f.

"Perversity, Adversity: Oregon." *Economist,* October 10, 1992, A31.

Red Wing, Donna. *Address to Hawai'i Community Activists on Same-Gender Marriage Strategies.* Honolulu: Ward Warehouse, February 28, 1998.

Spengler, Andreas. "Manifest Sadomasochism of Males: Results of an Empirical Study." In *S and M: Studies in Sadomasochism.* Thomas Weinberg and G. W. Levi Kamel, eds. New York: Prometheus Books, 1983, 59f.

Thompson, Mark, ed. *Leatherfolk: Radical Sex, People, Politics, and Practice.* Boston: Alyson, 1991.

Weir, John. "Dark Man: The Mad, Mad World of Writer Dennis Cooper." *Advocate,* March 8, 1994, 59f.

See also Fiction: New Queer Narrative; Germany; Jung, Carl Gustav; Leathermen; Mapplethorpe, Robert; Sade, Donatien-Alphonse-François, Marquis de; Sadomasochism; South Africa

Shakespeare, William (1564–1616)

On several fronts—as an actor, as a poet/playwright, as a cultural icon—William Shakespeare stands in a complicated relationship to homosexuality. "Homosexual" may not have existed as a concept in early-modern England, but Shakespeare's contemporaries associated theater in general with the one word they did have for aberrant sexual behavior: sodomy. Philip Stubbes speaks for a host of antitheatrical controversialists when he imagines that members of the audience, inflamed by "bawdy speeches" and "wanton gestures," leave the theater and take each other home, where "in their secret conclaves (covertly) they play *the Sodomites,* or worse." In sixteenth- and seventeenth-century usage, *sodomy* could refer to outrageous behavior of all kinds (including bestiality, heresy, and treason), but Stubbes and his ilk clearly have in mind sexual acts between males. Citing Deuteronomy's warning about men putting on women's apparel (22:5), John Rainolds finds the real abomination in early-modern theater to be, at bottom, boy actors who assume women's parts. Shakespeare's scripts, true to the Puritans' charges, seem to play up the homoerotic possibilities whenever a boy playing a girl is asked by the fiction to play a boy—as, for example, when Rosalind in *As You Like It* disguises himself/herself as "Ganymede" or Viola in *Twelfth Night* as "Cesario." There may have been something subversive and sodomitical about the whole theatrical enterprise, but Shakespeare as playwright and poet goes far beyond the specific situation of boy actors playing women's parts. One effect of casting boys in women's roles was to separate gender from anatomy. *Gender* roles and *sexual* roles may or may not coincide; erotic desire can operate *within* gender as well as *across* gender.

Populating Shakespeare's scripts from beginning to end, in tragedy and history as well as in comedy and romance, are same-sex pairs who express their affections for each other in bodily terms. Helena and Hermia in *A Midsummer Night's Dream* ("a double cherry," in Helena's image, "two lovely berries moulded on one stem") are the most notable in a series of female pairs, most of whom are ultimately set apart by men. Other such pairs include Portia and Nerissa in *The Merchant of Venice*, Rosalind and Celia in *As You Like It*, Cleopatra and Iris in *Antony and Cleopatra*, and Emilia and Flavina in *The Two Noble Kinsmen*. Male friends who express a similarly physical attachment include Valentine and Proteus in *The Two Gentlemen of Verona*, York and Suffolk in *Henry V*, Antonio and Bessanio in *The Merchant of Venice*, Sebastian and Antonio in *Twelfth Night*, Achilles and Patroclus in *Troilus and Cressida*, and Leontes and Polixines in *The Winter's Tale*. Like their female counterparts, most of these same-sex pairs must come to terms with intruders of the other gender. The rivalry and violence that complicate male bonds—violence that sometimes approaches sadomasochistic spectacle in its staging— is particularly strong in the cases of Mercutio and Romeo, Iago and Othello, Aufidius and Coriolanus. The fact that homoerotic rhetoric in all these plays is deployed within the framework of patriarchal marriage suggests that the modern dichotomy of homosexual/heterosexual may be anachronistic. In Shakespeare's sonnets, as in his narrative poem *Venus and Adonis*, readers are invited to entertain erotic desire for both male and female objects. Instead of either/or, Shakespeare's plays and poems imply a paradigm of both/and. Shakespeare criticism since the eighteenth century has struggled to reconcile this early-modern construction of sexuality with the supposedly transcendent values that have made Shakespeare an icon of Western culture.

Bruce R. Smith

Bibliography

Bray, Alan. *Homosexuality in Renaissance England.* 1982. Reprinted with new afterword. New York: Columbia University Press, 1995.

Bredbeck, Gregory W. *Sodomy and Interpretation: Marlowe to Milton.* Ithaca, N.Y.: Cornell University Press, 1991.

Goldberg, Jonathan. *Sodometries: Renaissance Texts, Modern Sexualities.* Stanford: Stanford University Press, 1992.

Orgel, Stephen. *Impersonations: The Performance of Gender in Shakespeare's England.* Cambridge: Cambridge University Press, 1996.

Smith, Bruce R. *Homosexual Desire in Shakespeare's England: A Cultural Poetics.* 1991. Reprint with new foreword. Chicago: University of Chicago Press, 1994.

Traub, Valerie. *Desire and Anxiety: Circulations of Sexuality in Shakespearean Drama.* London: Routledge, 1992.

See also English Literature; Ganymede; Sodomy; Theater: Premodern and Early Modern

Shilts, Randy (1951–1994)

Randy Shilts became the first openly gay journalist to cross over into mainstream print and television journalism. He parlayed his position with the gay news magazine *Advocate* into television news beats covering the gay community and local politics in San Francisco for KQED, San Francisco's PBS TV affiliate, and KTVU, a local independent station. Shilts established his fame, in the tradition of Truman Capote's *In Cold Blood*, penning three massive books in which he merged journalism with novelistic technique. In *The Mayor of Castro Street: The Life and Times of Harvey Milk* (1982), Shilts examined the development of Milk's charismatic leadership and the unique situation of district electoral politics that established the gay community as a dominant political power in 1970s San Francisco. Shilts's freelance local coverage of a strange new disease led to *And the Band Played On: Politics, People, and the AIDS Epidemic* (1987), the definitive study of the epidemiology and politics of AIDS in the Reagan era. Shilts's last work, *Conduct Unbecoming: Lesbians and Gays in the U.S. Military, Vietnam to the Persian Gulf* (1993), was influenced by Allan Bérubé's groundbreaking *Coming Out Under Fire*, bringing documentation of the U.S. military's homophobic policies and practices up to the 1990s "Don't ask, don't tell" ruling.

Randy Shilts was born in Davenport, Iowa, grew up in a conservative Methodist family in suburban Chicago, and came out to his family while a student at Portland (Oregon) Community College in 1971. He majored in English and then journalism, and received a B.S. from the University of Oregon at Eugene in 1975. He began working for the *Advocate* (located in suburban San Francisco at that time) as their Northwest correspondent, then moved to San Francisco and served as staff writer on the magazine. Shilts resigned from the *Advocate* in 1978 over various differences with its owner and publisher, David Goldstein. He then worked as a freelance reporter covering both the gay community and local politics for KQED (1977–1980) and KTVU (1979–1980). Income from his TV journalism and freelancing for prominent national newspapers and magazines afforded Shilts the independence to research and write his first book, *The Mayor of Castro Street*. The book was critically acclaimed in gay and mainstream media, catapulting him from local to national fame. In 1981 the *San Francisco Chronicle* hired Shilts as a staff reporter, making him the first openly gay journalist at a major daily newspaper. Shilts began reporting on the strange new pneumonia and skin cancer striking gay men in San Francisco. He went on to expose the homophobically induced resistance by government, medicine, and the scientific community to addressing the emergent AIDS epidemic as a serious health threat. While being the first to bring AIDS to national media attention, Shilts found himself under scathing and bitter attack by the San Francisco gay community for criticizing the practices of anonymous and promiscuous "bathhouse sex."

In 1986 Shilts himself tested positive for HIV antibodies. He rejected the gay community's defensive strategy to frame the epidemic in political rather than public health terms. As a result Shilts was seen by much of the San Francisco gay community as a traitor and was vilified for his assimilationist stance. He compiled his investigative journalism in *And the*

Band Played On, which was widely praised and received several prestigious awards. The book was adapted for an HBO film, which first aired in 1993.

Shilts's third work, *Conduct Unbecoming*, exposed the selective, systematic mistreatment of gays and lesbians in the U.S. military, foregrounded the homosexuality of many of America's most celebrated soldiers, and documented the development of a gay subculture within the military structure. The book received positive reviews and was on the *New York Times* best-seller list for six weeks. The gay community attacked Shilts again, this time for failing to "out" his sources within the military.

While completing *Conduct Unbecoming* in 1992, Shilts developed full-blown AIDS and died from its complications two years later in the resplendent surroundings of his ten-acre Russian River ranch in the gay resort town of Guerneville, California.   *Les Wright*

Bibliography

Streitmatter, Rodger. *Unspeakable: The Rise of the Gay and Lesbian Press in America*. Boston: Faber and Faber, 1995.

See also Advocate; AIDS; Assimilation; Bathhouses and Sex Clubs; Capote, Truman; Gay and Lesbian Press; Military; San Francisco

Sims, Jon Reed (1947–1984)

Jon Reed Sims, American conductor, teacher, and founder of several gay and lesbian instrumental and vocal ensembles, was born in Smith Center, Kansas. He studied piano (from 1957) and horn, and was drum major of his high school band. He attended Wichita State University (B. Mus. in horn and B.A. in theory and composition, 1969), and Indiana University (M. Mus. in horn, 1972). He studied widely, including eurythmics at the Dalcroze School, New York; arts administration at Golden Gate University, San Francisco; dance in New York, Chicago, and San Francisco; and private studies in horn and composition (with Darius Milhaud). He taught at schools in Chicago (1972–1974) and San Francisco (1974–1978). In June 1978 he founded the San Francisco Gay Freedom Day Marching Band and Twirling Corps, the first lesbian and gay musical organization in the world, which made its first public appearance that month at the Gay Pride Day parade. He then founded in rapid succession the San Francisco Gay Men's Chorus (November 1978), Golden

Gate Performing Arts (an administrative organization, March 1979), the orchestra Lambda Pro Musica, and the San Francisco Lesbian and Gay Men's Community Chorus. Sims directed the San Francisco band until January 1982, including concerts at Louise Davies Symphony Hall (November 9, 1980), Grace Cathedral, and the famous disco Dreamland. From the beginning, Sims intended to create a nationwide network of gay and lesbian instrumental and choral ensembles; the success of that network, both during his lifetime and after, remains an astonishing legacy. Sims died in San Francisco from the complications of AIDS.   *Paul Attinello*

Bibliography

"Sims, John." In *Baker's Biographical Dictionary of Musicians.* New York: Schirmer/Macmillan, 1992.

See also Choruses and Marching Bands; Marches and Parades

Singapore

Situated in Southeast Asia, Singapore is a small island city-state with an entirely urban population of 2.9 million. Beginning as a simple fishing village in the nineteenth century, then growing into a British port, postcolonial Singapore is now a modern, multicultural society, consisting of Tamils, Malays, Javanese, Arabs, Bugis, and Filipinos but with the majority (77 percent) being overwhelmingly Chinese. The government of Singapore has been led by the People's Action Party (PAP) since 1959, Lee Kuan Yew being its most famous leader. Singapore has been described variously as a dictatorship, a hegemonic state, a corporatist state, and a technocratic state. As one of the most successful Asian economies, Singapore is the confluence of the global and technological while retaining traditional Confucian ethics bound up with responsibility to the family and duty to the community.

Homosexuality, in the context of Singapore's highly socially engineered society, is not only illegal but suffers from immense social stigmatization, fear, and deception. Singapore is prudish when it comes to sexuality and morality. Strong cultural prohibitions exist against homosexual behavior. Legal sanctions against homosexuality have been inherited from British colonial law (enacted 1872). Sections 377 and 377a of the Penal Code both outlaw homosexual activity for males and females. Arrests are made sporadically and offenders may incur imprisonment (up to ten years), caning, or humiliation (by being named in newspapers).

Homosexuality, in terms of gay and lesbian identity, is viewed by the ruling elite as a Western-derived, decadent, and immoral lifestyle. Singapore's leaders have been loud in their rhetoric about cultural differences between the West and Asia, using homosexuality as a focus of difference. Hence, a statement by Singaporean foreign minister Wong Kan Seng, in 1993, that "homosexual rights are a Western issue." In the battle lines drawn between perceived Asian family and community values in contrast to the individualist, Western ways, homosexuality has become an ideological pawn in a crude clash of cultures.

For homosexuals in Singapore, the regulated social and cultural life is entrenched in institutions such as heterosexual, monogamous marriage; bearing of descendants; personal subjection to family cohesion, social habits and religious rituals; and closed role choice. The approach by many gay Singaporean men is to go "softly, softly." Lesbians go even more quietly.

Despite the difficulties of homosexual identity, many gay Singaporeans are happy to remain in Singapore, where, with discretion, and in a nonconfrontational way, they live their lives within social and cultural parameters. In this sense, the gay and lesbian Singaporean lives with a burden of identity. Some gays have sought asylum in other, more tolerant societies.

In 1993, a group called People Like Us (PLU) was formed with a mandate to assist gays, lesbians, and bisexuals through mutual support. Recent attempts to register the group legally with the government were, however, rejected without explanation. In 1997, PLU continues to exist informally through its homepage and discussion list, where Singaporean homosexuals can communicate, post news items, and organize social events.   *Baden Offord*

Bibliography

Aart Hendricks, Rob Tielman, and Evert van der Veen, eds. *The Third Pink Book.* New York: Prometheus, 1993.

Erik, Paul. *Obstacles to Democratisation in Singapore.* Working Paper 78. Centre of Southeast Asian Studies, Monash University, Clayton, 1992.

See also China; Indonesia; Politics, Global; Thailand

S

The Sisters of Perpetual Indulgence enjoy their moment in the sun. Top: Sr. Vicious Power Hungry Bitch. Bottom, clockwise from left: Sr. Salvation Armee, Sr. Lilly White Superior Posterior, Sr. Julia Sunbeam, Sr. There's No Place Like Rome (Roma!), Sr. Luscious Lashes, Sr. Marquesa de Sade. Photo by Jean Baptiste Carhaix, courtesy of the Sisters of Perpetual Indulgence.

Sisters of Perpetual Indulgence

On Holy Saturday, 1979, three men left their homes in San Francisco wearing habits borrowed from a convent in Cedar Rapids, Iowa. That day, Sister Missionary Position, Sister Adhanarisvara, and Sister Roz Erection set in motion a series of events that would change the face of queer activism in cities like San Francisco, Seattle, London, and Paris. The Order of the Sisters of Perpetual Indulgence was established in the fall of that year to expiate stigmatic guilt and promulgate universal joy, and became an incorporated entity in 1986. Through the years, the Sisters have internationally spread their mission and goals, establishing orders and missions in Australia, France, the United Kingdom, Germany, Scotland, Amsterdam, Thailand, Colombia, New Zealand, Belgium, Switzerland, and Vancouver.

Originally founded as an Order of Gay Male Nuns, today the group includes gay, lesbian, bisexual, heterosexual, and transgendered men and women. The Sisters do not subscribe to any specific religious doctrine. Many of their rituals and ceremonies are loosely based on Hinduism, Buddhism, Radical Faeryism,

and Roman Catholicism. Their doctrine is one of spreading joy and eradicating guilt; they do not participate in actions that invite guilt or shame, and the idea of sin is not one they espouse.

While the Sisters work with many causes, they are best known for their work surrounding the AIDS epidemic. In 1982, the San Francisco Sisters published the first safer-sex pamphlet called "Play Fair," using plain language and Sisterly humor to address the issues of STDs, including what was then known simply as the "gay cancer." The Sisters throughout the world remain committed to bringing an end to the epidemic. Some houses focus on direct intervention, distributing prophylactics to those in need, while others focus on outreach to the ill and raising funds for needy organizations.

The Sisters of Perpetual Indulgence are readily identifiable by their habitual manifestation: the clothing they wear. Sisters in different cities manifest differently, much in the same way that each cultivates its own political and spiritual focus. In San Francisco, Sisters wear wimples fashioned after those worn by fourteenth-century Danish ladies-in-waiting, and white face makeup adorned with elaborate lashes, jewels, and glitter. In Australia and England, the Sisters wear more simple garb and no makeup. French and Colombian Sisters don a malleable coronet that bends to a Sister's will and whimsy. Seattle nuns sport large, rigid coronets, and Los Angeles nuns wear wimples affectionately said to resemble the Hollywood Bowl. Each order has a traditional, formal look, but individuality and freedom of interpretation is always strongly encouraged. *Sr. Ann R. Key and Sr. Phyllis Stein the Fragrant, Mistress of Sistory*

Bibliography

Stryker, Susan, and Jim Van Buskirk. *Gay by the Bay: A History of Queer Culture in San Francisco*. San Francisco: Chronicle, 1986.

See also Activism, International; Activism, U.S.; AIDS; AIDS Performance; Catholicism; Radical Faeries; San Francisco; Transgender

Slovenia

There is no mention of homosexuality in Slovenian culture before modern times. In fact, one cannot begin to discuss an independent Slovene culture before the beginning of the nineteenth century. During the fourteenth century, Slovenia was part of the Holy Roman Empire, whose leader, Charles IV, authored a law in 1353 that punished homosexual sexual acts with death. This regulation remained in effect until 1787, when Joseph II, as ruler of the Hapsburg Empire of which Slovenia was a part, removed it from the books. Nevertheless, there are no records of anyone actually being punished by this rule. This silence about homosexuality continued during the period when Slovenia was part of the Kingdom of Yugoslavia, from 1918 to 1941. After World War II, Slovenia became part of the Socialist Federal Republic of Yugoslavia, under the leadership of Josip Broz Tito. Homosexuality was again criminalized and punished with a year's imprisonment, although this measure was never used against anyone as far as is known. As part of Tito's Yugoslavia, Slovenia retained its historic nature as an industrious, conservative people who clung to their Roman Catholic roots.

It is somewhat surprising, then, that of all the former Yugoslav republics, Slovenia became the first to initiate a modern gay rights movement. In 1974, the Slovene legislature, which could act independently in some areas of Yugoslavia's federal parliament, legalized homosexuality. In 1984, a student gay rights group, MAGNUS, was formed under the auspices of SKUC, a student organization from the University of Ljubljana, which organized the first gay pride event, including a festival of international gay-themed films, an exhibition of gay publishing, and lectures and discussions about gay culture, and included such notable speakers as F. Arnal, A. Avanzo, and Guy Hocquenghem. During this year, MAGNUS also began to publish its own journal titled *VIKS*, about the cultural and social problems of homosexuality.

In 1986, MAGNUS issued a manifesto demanding the immediate abolition of all antihomosexual laws in all the Yugoslav republics that still retained such statutes—Serbia, Bosnia-Herzegovina, Macedonia, and Montenegro—and that antidiscrimination laws be introduced into the Yugoslav constitution. Their demands were not met, and the following year, authorities prevented MAGNUS from holding its annual festivities. Despite these problems, MAGNUS continued in its efforts to change Slovene attitudes about same-sex relationships, and by 1993 succeeded in establishing a sister organization for lesbians, sponsored several international congresses on gay and lesbian issues, held in Croatia and Slovenia, started a highly visible AIDS awareness campaign, and assisted in establishing several gay and lesbian newspapers and magazines, as well as several discos, cafés, and restaurants in Ljubljana. *Revolver Magazine*, one of MAGNUS's many offspring, was refused funding by the Ljubljana city government in 1991, because its content was considered pornographic.

In 1994, the Slovene gay and lesbian rights movement celebrated its tenth anniversary, despite the Ljubljana city government's attempts to stop the festivities, with a week of lesbian and gay films and a special exhibition about Slovene gay and lesbian pride, entitled Tu smo (We are here). First in March 1993 and again in 1995, gay rights leaders presented initiatives to the Slovene government to pass legislation legalizing same-sex partnerships. Both initiatives were predictably refused, but the movement remains optimistic that these laws will indeed be instated within the next two years. *Zoran Milutinović and Will Petersen*

Bibliography

Brzek, Antonín, and Jaroslava Pondělíčková-Mašlová. *Třetí Pohlaví (The Third Sex)*. Prague: Scintia Medica, 1992.

Silber, Laura, and Allan Little. *The Death of Yugoslavia*. London: Penguin, 1995, rev. ed. 1996.

See also Activism, International; Czech Republic; Politics, Global

Smith, Jack (1932–1989)

Jack Smith was an American filmmaker, performance artist, writer, and visual artist. From the early 1960s through most of the 1980s, he was a key figure in American avant-garde film and theater. His works, marked by a deceptively playful camp sensibility, combine a flamboyant style with radical social and political criticism. They both evoke Hollywood glamour and indict capitalist exploitation, racism, and normative ideas about gender and sexuality.

Smith's first feature-length film, *Flaming Creatures* (1961), remains his best-known work. Shot in a setting reminiscent of the *Arabian Nights,* it employs transgendered actors and intercuts nearly abstract images of breasts and penises to undermine conventional distinctions between genders. His second feature, *Normal Love* (1963), is a paean to Maria Montez, star of 1940s Hollywood Arabian fantasies who inspired much of his work.

A performer as well as a filmmaker, by 1970 Smith began to use his films in his live performances. He spontaneously reedited his films in front of the audience, creating a unique version for each performance. As this technique suggests, Smith continually experimented with his work, aiming for an "aesthetic delirium" that would transcend formal limitations, narrative coherence, and prevailing standards of good and bad taste.

Partly because of Smith's unfaltering commitment to his idiosyncratic creative vision, he was not as celebrated or commercially successful as some of the artists he inspired. The films of Andy Warhol and John Waters and the performance pieces of Cindy Sherman and Charles Ludlam are among the works that show his influence. Smith died of AIDS-related complications.   *Charles Krinsky*

Bibliography

Hoberman, J., and Edward Leffingwell, eds. *Wait for Me at the Bottom of the Pool: The Writings of Jack Smith*. New York: High Risk Books, 1997.

Suárez, Juan A. *Bike Boys, Drag Queens, and Super Stars: Avant-garde, Mass Culture, and Gay Identities in the 1960s Underground Cinema*. Bloomington, Ind.: Indiana University Press, 1996.

Tartaglia, Jerry. "Program Notes: Jack Smith Film Preservation Benefit." New York: Millennium Film Workshop, 1997.

See also Camp; Film; Ludlam, Charles; Transgender; Warhol, Andy; Waters, John

Soccer

There is little doubt that homosexual behavior and homosocial desire are common in the soccer world. Fans routinely suspect or accuse players (usually on opposing clubs) of being gay, soccer stadium chants are filled with homosexual imagery, and soccer scholars routinely read soccer fans' passion as latently homosexual. Few players, however, openly identify themselves as gay. Brazilian Pelé, for example—considered the greatest soccer player of all time—does not identify himself as homosexual or bisexual, but he has said he and most of his teammates were sexually initiated by older men. There are indications that Pelé's experience is typical. Argentine soccer coach Jorge Solari said that it is common in Argentina for older players to sodomize younger players, yet neither the penetrator nor the penetrated is identified as homosexual.

Leandro and Renato—two of Pelé's teammates on Brazil's national team—did identify themselves in public as a homosexual couple, and when Leandro was cut from the team, Renato resigned in protest. The Surinamer-Dutch player Ruud Gullit—who was named the best soccer player in the world in 1987 and 1989—left his wife to live with his gay lover, saying, "I care for my wife and my children very much, but I am in love with him." Justin Fashanu, a Premier League player in England, not only came out of the closet but also said that 25 percent of the first division players in England are gay.

The late Carlos Jáuregui—director of Argentina's Gays por los Derechos Civiles (Gays for Civil Rights)—started a national scandal in Argentina in July 1995, when he announced that there were many gays in the soccer world, including a gay player on Argentina's junior national team and another gay (perhaps a coach) on the senior national team. Jáuregui's claims were supported by Cris Miró, a transvestite *vedette*. Though she declined to name any of her lovers and deflected questions about her rumored affair with Diego Maradona,

Sebreli, Juan José. *Fútbol y Masas*. Buenos Aires: Editorial Galerna, 1981.

Simpson, Mark. *Male Impersonators: Men Performing Masculinity*. New York: Routledge, 1994.

Suárez-Orozco, Marcelo Mario. "A Study of Argentine Soccer: The Dynamics of Its Fans and Their Folklore." *Journal of Psychoanalytic Anthropology* 5, no. 1 (1982): 7–28.

Tobin, Jeffrey. "A Question of Balls: The Sexual Politics of Argentine Soccer." In *Decomposition: Post-Disciplinary Performance*. Sue-Ellen Case, Philip Brett, and Susan Leigh Foster, eds. Bloomington: Indiana University Press, 2000.

See also Gay Games; Physical Culture; Sports

"Goal!" Pastel on paper by Jorge Azar, Buenos Aires, 1991. The painting was featured in the 1995 exhibit "Angeles y Chongos" at Buenos Aires's Centro Cultural Lola Mora. The term chongos *refers to men who sodomize other men. (Photo courtesy of the artist)*

then a player for Boca Juniors, Miró said suggestively that "many Boca Junior players have my autograph in their T-shirts." Maradona—who was named the best soccer player in the world in 1986—does not identify himself as gay, but he expressed his support of civil rights for gays by kissing his teammate Claudio Caniggia on the lips after each goal so that fans would learn tolerance for displays of homosexual affection.   *Jeffrey Tobin*

Bibliography

Bianco, Marcelo. "No al miedo, sí a la prevención." *Goles* 35, no. 1801 (1994): 3–7.

Jáuregui, Carlos. "En el fútbol tambien hay homosexuales." *El Gráfico* 3954 (July 18, 1995): 27.

Olivera, Daniel. "Diego es muy especial . . ." *Noticias* 19, no. 1024 (August 1996): 92–94.

Sociology of Gay Life

In the mid-1980s, Stacey and Thorne questioned prevailing sociological practice by noting the discipline's "missing feminist revolution." This issue remains relevant to sociological research on gay and lesbian issues, particularly when weighed against the corresponding body of gay and lesbian scholarship in history, literature, musicology, and art history. Although Stacey and Thorne's question has been answered in part by the growing influence of feminist theory in sociology, the impact to date of the gay and lesbian movement on sociology has been unremarkable, even though "the challenge to hegemonic heterosexuality from lesbian and gay movements is logically as profound as the challenge to men's power from feminism."

Teaching

One measure of the incorporation of gay and lesbian issues into mainstream sociology is their treatment within the classroom. Undergraduate texts often cover gay and lesbian issues poorly. For example, eminent sociologist Anthony Giddens discusses homosexuality only in the context of sexual practice, in between sections on sexual identity and prostitution.

Survey Research

Social surveys have systematically excluded items on sexual orientation because of funding restrictions and other factors. This has led sociologists studying gay and lesbian issues to employ other methodologies and sociological traditions. More recently, items on sexual orientation have appeared in at least three U.S. national probability surveys, the General Social Survey, the National Health and Social Life Survey (University of Chicago), and the National Longitudinal Survey of Adolescent Health (North Carolina, Chapel Hill). The reliability and interpretation of such data are controversial, given concerns both about the validity of responses about sexual behavior and the sensitive nature of sexual orientation. Although little is known empirically, one might reasonably expect responses to these and other questions to vary under alternative modes of item administration and by race and ethnicity, age, geographic area, social class, and educational attainment. But increases in gay and lesbian visibility mean that individuals are increasingly willing to disclose details relevant to their sexual orientation. Projecting these trends forward suggests that survey data on sexual orientation may improve in quality with time.

Gender, Sexuality, Marriage, and the Family

The influence of gay and lesbian scholarship both within and outside of sociology is most clear in the areas of sexual behavior, intimate relationships, and gender. Risman and Schwartz note that much research on gay relationships contains an implicit critique of traditional assumptions concerning the gender-based division of labor, assumptions that pervade much of the theoretical literature on gender, marriage, and the family. For example, their review of the psychological literature of the effects of partner homogamy and egalitarianism on relationship satisfaction and stability leads them to conclude that "gay [and therefore] heterosexual couples do not need to organize their roles around culturally defined masculine or feminine tasks or traits to function well." Rust explicitly questions pervasive assumptions concerning stable sexual identities by documenting the fluidity of sexual orientation among bisexual men and women. Connell draws on life history data to advance the argument that conventional masculinity is both integral to gay desire but also the site of a key difference between gay and straight men. "Hegemonic masculinity" is thus the object of, but also subverted by, the process by which same-sex desire unfolds over the life course of both gay-identified and nongay-identified males. At the macrolevel, it stands to reason that state and political institutions incorporate the social, political, and economic interests of the heterosexual majority in much the same way that these institutions reflect

interests encoded in the prevailing gender regimes. Consider, for example, a 1996 U.S. decision on same-sex marriage by the Hawaiian Second Circuit Court in *Baehr v. Lewin,* which, if upheld, could carry implications for the social institution of marriage beyond extending the rights, benefits, and obligations accompanying legal marriage to same-sex couples.

Social Movements and Social Activism

Adam's social history of the gay and lesbian movement argues that the emergence of a specific gay social identity distinguishes the modern gay movement from precursors such as the Mattachine Society and homophile movements of the 1950s. Although drawing mainly on resource mobilization theory, his account also mirrors the recent emphasis on identity politics in sociological research by tracing how social expressions of gay and lesbian identity evolved from affirmations of same-sex emotional attachments, coming-out stories, public expressions of pride, to the development of shared cultural symbols (the Rainbow Flag, the pink triangle, the letter lambda) and specific gay and lesbian subcommunities. Epstein notes that resource mobilization arguments assume a relatively unambiguous and uncontested collective identity shaped by the shared social and political interests of gays and lesbians; by contrast, scholars stressing issues of identity politics argue that the contested process shaping collective identities plays a primary role in shaping gay and lesbian social and political interests. Queer theorists (see, for example, Bravman; Epstein; Stein and Plummer) influenced by Foucault and deconstructionists challenge these assertions: sexual identity and sexual desire are the social products of historically specific cultures, and discourse concerning the fixed nature of sexual identities reveals the repressiveness of the majority sexual regime. Gamson proposes a more contextually specific research agenda emphasizing "for whom, when, and how are stable collective identities necessary for [or, conversely, oppressive of] social action and social change?"

Sociological Theory

Underlying much of the above is the observation by Sedgwick and others on the pervasive nature of "compulsory heterosexuality" as revealed, for example, in individual behavior, social norms, and large-scale societal institutions. Because sociological theory and research typically lag behind actual social behavior, gay and lesbian praxis can be seen as providing an implicit critique not only of the specific research activities of sociologists but more generally of major foundational issues underpinning sociological theory. The insights so generated carry the potential for significant creative developments in sociological theory.

Lawrence L. Wu
and Mathew Sloan

Bibliography

Adam, Barry D. *The Rise of a Gay and Lesbian Movement*. Boston: Twayne, 1987.

Bravman, Scott. "Postmodernism and Queer Identities." In *Queer Theory/Sociology*. Steven Seidman, ed. Cambridge, Mass.: Blackwell, 1996, 333–61.

Connell, R. W. *Masculinities*. Berkeley: University of California Press, 1995.

Epstein, Steven. "Gay Politics, Ethnic Identity: The Limits of Social Constructionism." *Socialist Review* 17, no. 3–4 (1987): 9–54.

Gamson, Joshua. "Must Identity Movements Self-Destruct? A Queer Dilemma." *Social Problems* 42, no. 3 (1995): 390–407.

Giddens, Anthony. *Introduction to Sociology*. New York: Norton, 1991.

Risman, Barbara J., and Pepper Schwartz. "Sociological Research on Male and Female Homosexuality." *Annual Review of Sociology* 14 (1988): 125–47.

Rust, Paula C. " 'Coming Out' in the Age of Social Constructionism: Sexual Identity Formation among Lesbian and Bisexual Women." *Gender and Society* 7, no. 1 (1993): 50–77.

Sedgwick, Eve Kosofsky. *Epistemology of the Closet*. Berkeley: University of California Press, 1990.

Seidman, Steven, ed. *Queer Theory/Sociology*. Cambridge, Mass.: Blackwell, 1996.

Stacey, Judith. *Brave New Families*. New York: Basic, 1991.

Stacey, Judith, and Barrie Thorne. "The Missing Feminist Revolution in Sociology." *Social Problems* 32, no. 4 (1985): 301–16.

Stein, Arlene, and Ken Plummer. "I Can't Even Think Straight: 'Queer' Theory and the Missing Sexual Revolution in Sociology." *Sociological Theory* 12, no. 2 (1994): 178–87.

See also Activism, U.S.; Alcohol and Drugs; Assimilation; Coming Out; Couples; Essentialist-Constructionist Debate; Foucault, Michel; Gay Families; Gender; Homophile Movement; Lambda; Mattachine Society; Neighborhoods: Gay Neighborhoods; Pink Triangle; Queer Theory; Rainbow Flag; Same-Sex Marriage

Sodom

Like many of the narratives found in Genesis, the Sodom text is structured around multiple etiological folk tales regarding the origin of the "Abrahamic Blessing," the meaning of the name of Abram's son, Isaac ("laughter"); the existence of a region near the Dead Sea called Sodom (literally "burned" in Hebrew—leaving us to ask why it was ostensibly called that even before it was burned); odd geological formations near the Dead Sea; and the origins of two tribes (the Moabites and the Ammonites) who were inhospitable to the Israelites escaping from slavery in Egypt (see Deuteronomy 23:3–4).

Given the prosperity of well-watered Sodom and its subsequent inhospitality to strangers, its story was inextricably linked to that of the Abrahamic Blessing as a reminder for Abram's descendants to do *mishpat* (social justice) in the midst of their prosperity. Importantly, it is in the Sodom text that Yahweh first explains that social justice is a stipulation for receiving the Blessing. Abram was told twice before by Yahweh that he would be blessed with innumerable posterity, but no stipulations were mentioned then.

Several scholars have recently pointed out that the Sodom story, found in Genesis 18 and 19, is a seminal narrative in our understanding of Western civilization. Interpretations of this story currently range from the antihomosexual rhetoric of conservative religious movements to calls for reclaiming Sodom as an idyllic Queer Arcadia.

In the words of theorist Robert Alter, Sodom is a "great monitory model, the myth of a terrible collective destiny antithetical to Israel's," that is meant to warn readers "of the ghastly possibility that Israel can turn itself into Sodom" (Alter 39). For Jewish scholar Harold Bloom, the story of Sodom is the literary pinnacle of biblical narrative, from which we learn J Source's still unequaled depiction of a (rather Freudian) "psychology" of the Hebrew god Yahweh, with J being, in Bloom's fascinating hypothesis, a royal Lady of the Davidic house who composed the earliest text of what we now call Genesis as part of a literary competition. Australian "Sodom/olog/ist" Michael Carden moves away from homosexualizing this "text of terror" by examining the extensive post-J commentary on Sodom and its meaning for biblical writers, readers, and commentators (including midrashic, patristic, apocryphal, pseudepigraphic, Qu'ranic, and medieval Christian traditions), and trying to pinpoint the move from a warning against inhospitality to one against sexual license, and thence to homosexuality. Jonathan Goldberg finds that sodomy is immensely useful because it is "that utterly confused category" (in Foucault's words); by the very nature of its vagueness (found even in its biblical "founding document"), sodomy refuses regulation and referential designation.

In *Cities of the Plain*, Proust argued that the locus of Sodom is too shameful to reclaim. More recently, however, others have called for a reclamation of that space (much as black Americans have Africa, Chicanos have Aztlan, and lesbians have the Isle of Lesbos as [meta]physical loci) for healing and empowerment: "[T]hey always give us wastelands and we always turn them into music and gardens." Sodom, collapsed upon itself, is become a postmodern paradise for queer men, ironically at the very moment that we challenge Western civilization to remember social justice. *Connell O'Donovan*

Bibliography

Alter, Robert. "Sodom as Nexus: The Web of Design in Biblical Narrative." In *Reclaiming Sodom*. Jonathan Goldberg, ed. New York: Routledge, 1994.

Carden, Michael. "Sodom, Gomorrah, Gibeah." http://student.uq.edu.au/~s101014

Goldberg, Jonathan. Introduction. *Reclaiming Sodom*. Jonathan Goldberg, ed. New York: Routledge, 1994.

O'Donovan, Rocky [Connell]. "Reclaiming Sodom." In *Reclaiming Sodom*. Jonathan Goldberg, ed. New York: Routledge, 1994.

Rosenberg, David, and Harold Bloom. *The Book of J*. New York: Grove Weidenfeld, 1990.

See also Bible; Christianity; Foucault, Michel

Sodoma, Il (Giovanni Antonio Bazzi) (1477–1549)

Renaissance painter Giovanni Antonio Bazzi, as his nickname indicates, has traditionally been more noted for his scandalous homosexual proclivities than for his artistic prowess. Born in the Piedmontese town of Vercelli, he completed his artistic apprenticeship in the region before moving to Siena at the beginning of the sixteenth century. Sodoma is widely credited with revitalizing painting in Siena and of introducing to the Tuscan city the more cosmopolitan lessons first of Leonardo and then Raphael. Although he also spent significant periods of the first two decades of the century in Rome, he settled in Siena after 1518 and it is with Siena that his more mature work is associated.

Art historians have tended to view Sodoma as a minor figure and as someone who never mastered fully the influences and ideas of his many illustrious contemporaries. The sure knowledge of his homosexuality has also affected assessments of his achievements. For the contemporary gay audience the attraction of Sodoma's work is clear. His depiction of the male figure is bold and realistic. In *Cristo alla colonna*, one of his better-known works currently housed in the Pinacoteca in Siena, the center of the canvas is filled with the muscular and perfectly formed torso of the bound Christ. Christ's head is slightly tilted back and in shadow, ensuring that the spectator's eye settles immediately on the masculine frame and creating an erotic charge that exceeds the conventional religious context.

Derek Duncan

Bibliography

Hayum, Andrée. *Giovanni Antonio Bazzi, 'Il Sodoma.'* New York: Garland, 1976.

See also Art History; Italian Renaissance

Sodomy

In contemporary American English, *sodomy* has no agreed meaning. But then it has never had an agreed meaning. It is and has always been "that utterly confused category," to use Foucault's phrase. To say that the term's meaning is confused is not to say that its rhetorical force is weak. *Sodomy* has also always been a term of powerful condemnation. Whenever it appears, whatever acts it seems to name, it means to bring exemplary judgment and unique punishment on them. *Sodomy* and *sodomite* are not terms of neutral description but of hate speech. A great part of their usefulness in hate speech comes from their being so unclear.

Two cautions must be kept in mind before tracing any part of the history of this hate term. First, because *sodomy* is an essentially unstable term that blurs acts and identities, it cannot be equated with *homosexuality, homosexual acts,* or any similar modern expression. Second, because *sodomy* is essentially a Christian term, it cannot function easily (if at all) in secular contexts. The history of the category shows how deeply embedded it is in religious speaking and thinking.

The category "sodomy" (Medieval Latin *sodomia*) was coined in the Middle Ages as a term of stigma within Christian moral theology. It fixed and summarized a string of previous terms. Before there was "sodomy," there had been the "sins" of "Sodomites." According to the Hebrew Bible, the crimes of the inhabitants of Sodom were so horrible that God was provoked to its complete destruction (Genesis 18–19). Genesis does not specify these crimes. Other writers in the Hebrew Bible typically understood them as pride, greed, luxury, and inhospitality (e.g., Ezechiel 16:49–50). The crimes of Sodom were first restricted to sexual sins much later, in rabbinical writings from the period just before the appearance of Christianity. The new interpretation is registered in some New Testament epistles—though not in the Gospels, which never explicitly mention male-male sex (compare 2 Peter 2:6–10 and Jude 7–8).

For several centuries of Christian writers, the sexual interpretation of the sin of the Sodomites was only one of several interpretations. The evidence from St. Augustine (354–430) is typical. On the one hand, there are passages in which he understands Sodom as a symbol of human depravity generally, of "the pernicious society of humankind." On the other hand, Augustine can be quite clear that Sodom was a place where "debaucheries of men" flourished by custom. Writers after Augustine came increasingly to assume this second, sexual reading of Genesis 19, though they also left the exact kind of male-male sex unclear.

The coining of the category "sodomy" depends partly on this fixation of a sexual interpretation of the story of Sodom. It also depends on the early medieval books of penances, first compiled before the seventh century in Irish and Anglo-Saxon monasteries for the use of confessors. These penitentials typically arrange and describe certain sins in order to assign penances for each kind. They name a particular kind of sexual intercourse as "fornication in the sodomitic manner" or simply as "the sodomitic sin." If these phrases sometimes seem to refer to anal intercourse between men, at other times they are entirely unclear.

The more abstract and durable term *sodomy* seems to have been coined around 1050 by Peter Damian (1007–1072), a hermit-cardinal famous as a reformer of priestly morals. He coined it in a treatise, the *Gomorran Book*, devoted to sodomitic sins in the Christian clergy. It is worth emphasizing this: the category of sodomy made its first decisive appearance in a polemical attack on failures of clerical discipline. Peter Damian also provided the first official definition of *sodomy*: masturbation, mutual masturbation, copulation "between the thighs," and copulation "in the rear." Note that the definition includes masturbation, applies only to men, and makes no mention of oral sex.

Peter Damian's term passed into the tradition, but his frankness in defining it did not. Succeeding generations of theological writers made the term both vaguer and wider. They further combined it with other categories, such as the category of the "sin against nature." For example, in Thomas Aquinas (1224/1225–1274) "sodomy" is one of a number of sexual acts that violate nature by frustrating reproductive purpose. These acts include every kind of genital activity except vaginal intercourse between a man and a woman in something like the missionary position.

Alongside the high medieval articulation of theological categories, there is the development of agencies of enforcement, both ecclesiastical and civil. From the twelfth century on, most dioceses in Europe possessed some kind of ecclesiastical court charged with the hearing of cases brought under church law, including cases of sodomy. At roughly the same time, and certainly by the first quarter of the thirteenth century, the papacy began to build international agencies for punishing those who dissented from its doctrinal or moral teachings. These agencies included the new religious orders, chiefly the Dominicans and Franciscans, but also (from the 1230s) the papal Inquisition. The systematization of the theological treatment of sodomy went hand in hand with the growth of bureaucracies charged with pursuing sodomites and other deviants.

The church was not the only persecutor. With the growth of national and regional powers, there was competition between ecclesiastical and civil courts for jurisdiction over sodomy cases—which is to say, for control of the extremely potent charge of sodomy. It remained a term of violent accusation or denunciation often associated with blasphemy, bestiality, murder, and treason. From the fourteenth century, many civil governments began to pass sodomy statutes and to establish special agencies to prosecute the crime, so that they, too, could have some profit from this political weapon. Accusations

S of sodomy were used by kings against noblemen, by popes against kings, by kings against popes. They were also used, more locally, to motivate campaigns of civic repentance. Popular preachers, such as Bernardino of Siena (1380–1444), could whip up local populations to chase down sodomites—along with heretics, witches, and Jews. They could also move local governments to adopt antisodomy statutes. Of course, these statutes were enforced unevenly. Leaving aside instances of discoverable religious zeal or political ambition, the surviving sodomy cases often contain aggravating circumstances, such as rape, child abuse, or connection with other crimes. Some cities did attempt more systematic regulation by special courts or offices charged with extirpating sodomy. Venice established such an office in 1418, Florence in 1432, Lucca in 1448. But these offices also pursued accusations of sodomy with greater or lesser vigor, depending on transient conditions. In their energetic periods, they often clashed with local church courts when it came to pursuing sodomitic clergy. Moreover, while the civic ordinances were written to include both men and women, the civic officers seem to have understood sodomy mostly as a crime between men.

The Reformation changed many things, but it did not abolish the mechanisms for projecting and persecuting sodomy. On the contrary, it led, in both Catholic and Protestant countries, to more intense forms of regulation. In the wake of the Council of Trent (1545–1560), Catholic moral theology developed an elaborate categorization of sodomitic acts, including rationales for minutely distinguishing and ranking them. Complete or "perfect" sodomy required the intent to penetrate and/or ejaculate inside the body of a partner of the same sex—a man using his penis, a woman some instrument (such as a dildo) or some (unspecified) technique for injecting her "seed" inside another woman. These distinctions and others like them were enforced by various kinds of ecclesiastical courts, such as the branches of the Spanish Inquisition.

If Protestant nations rejected much of the foundation of Catholic moral theology, they tended to carry over its horror at sodomy. So far as Protestant theologians emphasized the moral obligations of local and national rulers, they encouraged vigilance over sexual sins by civic magistrates. So, for example, sodomy entered English statutory law as part of efforts to reform monastic communities. In 1534, the "Reformation Parliament" under Henry VIII adopted a statute that criminalized "the detestable and abominable vice of buggery committed with mankind or beast." The statute's linking of male-male intercourse and bestiality recalls the biblical authority of Leviticus 18, but its effect was to move sodomy cases from ecclesiastical to civil jurisdiction. As elsewhere in Europe, English sodomy legislation seems to have been enforced infrequently. Where sodomy cases appear in the surviving historical sources, they typically involve some other factor—political scheming, racial or religious or class prejudice, personal enmity.

When the English colonists came to North America, they brought with them the complex of religious and legal attitudes toward sodomy. The Virginia Colony's Articles of 1610 prohibit "the horrible, detestable sins of Sodomie" on pain of death. The context makes it seem that these "sins" are committed by men, and a male ship's captain was indeed executed for sodomy in Virginia in 1624. In New England, in the Puritan theocracies, religious reasoning is more evident both in the legal language and in the surveillance of daily life. In 1636, the Plymouth colonists adopted a list of capital crimes including "Sodomy, rapes, buggery," but did not specify their meaning. The Massachusetts Bay colony adopted in 1641 a more extensive list of fifteen crimes punishable by death. The printed version of this list (1643) describes male-male intercourse with the Levitical language: "a man [who] lyeth with mankind, as he lyeth with a woman." Similar language was enacted in Connecticut (1642), New York (1665), and New Jersey (1668). Because these lists do not use *sodomy,* that word's meaning was still undetermined—and was the source of ongoing public disagreement between theologians and judges. Rhode Island's legislation of 1647 does speak of "sodomy" and refers to the laws of Henry VIII and Elizabeth I, buttressed with Romans 1, but it does not specify which acts are prohibited between which sexes. New Haven in 1656 passed a statute filled with allusions to the Old and New Testaments. It specifically included women who commit acts "against nature," but it did not say what those acts might be.

Whatever the confusion or disagreements, sodomy prosecutions went forward. Early colonial cases cover a wide range of charges. Sometimes sodomy is distinguished by penetration—anal, vaginal, or bestial. Sometimes it is run in with a large number of "lewd" or "obscene" acts, such as mutual masturbation or fondling. At other times, the specific acts are left entirely unspecified. This confused and yet dangerous body of legislative and case law was left largely unchanged when the colonies separated from England. As the new states laid their legal foundations, they typically adopted "English common law" as a whole, understanding this to include the prohibitions of sodomy, even though these had actually been statutory and not common law. In the following decades, a number of states went on to enact specific statutes against sodomy, without defining it. While the nineteenth century did bring movements to disestablish various Christian churches and to give real freedom of religion, they left the essentially religious sodomy laws untouched. In fact the last decade of the nineteenth century gave the old sodomy statutes new force. Until then, American courts tended to interpret sodomy between human beings as anal intercourse—regardless of the sexes of the parties performing it. It was only after Oscar Wilde's trials in London in 1895 that American courts suddenly began to extend sodomy statutes to cover fellatio and cunnilingus.

Organized efforts to revoke American sodomy statutes began with the first lesbian and gay liberation organizations of the 1950s. Illinois was the first state to revoke them, in 1962, when adopting a new legal code. By 1986, about half the states had revoked or significantly amended their statutes. In that year, however, the U.S. Supreme Court declared that statutes against "homosexual sodomy" were indeed constitutional. *Mark D. Jordan*

Bibliography

Halley, Janet E. "Reasoning about Sodomy: Act and Identity in and after *Bowers v. Hardwick*." *Virginia Law Review* 79 (1993): 1721–80.

Jordan, Mark D. *The Invention of Sodomy in Christian Theology*. Chicago: University of Chicago Press, 1997.

Katz, Jonathan Ned. *Gay and Lesbian Almanac*. New York: Harper & Row, 1983.

Rocke, Michael B. *Forbidden Friendships: Homosexuality and Male Culture in Renaissance Florence*. New York: Oxford University Press, 1996.

See also Augustine of Hippo; Bible; *Bowers v. Hardwick* and *Romer v. Evans*; Buggery; Christianity; Colonial America; England; Florence; Foucault, Michel; Inquisition; Nameless Sin (or Crime); Papacy; *Pastoralia* and Penetentials; Peter Damian; Sex Practice: Anal Sex; Sex Practice: Oral Sex; Sodom; Sodomy Trials; Thomas Aquinas; Wilde, Oscar.

Sodomy Trials

The eighteenth century saw several waves of sodomy trials; most of these resulted from large-scale surveillance operations, but there were also some one-off prosecutions, such as that of Richard Branson in 1760. Most of our information about these trials comes from antisodomy propaganda and contemporary court reports. These, by definition, do not present a positive view of homosexual activity; instead they set out to vindicate state prosecutions by representing such behavior as unnatural. Records of sodomy prosecutions are nonetheless useful as guides to eighteenth-century attitudes to sexuality. A series of trials in 1726 is especially interesting, since they may have been initiated when the police came under pressure from crusading groups such as the Societies for the Reformation of Manners. During this period, an informer known as P took constables undercover to popular molly houses, such as those run by Margaret Clap and Thomas Wright, while other officers patrolled well-known cruising grounds. The evidence that the police gathered through P and others led to several much-publicized trials in April and July 1726. Court reports from these show that cross-examinations usually focused on the need to uncover what had happened during, and just before, the alleged sexual activity. Here the empirical resources of the legal system can be seen grappling unsuccessfully with wider philosophical issues such as consent, pleasure, and the individual's right to privacy. For example, when William Brown was entrapped by an *agent provocateur* in 1726, he insisted, "I thought I knew him, and I think there is no crime in making what use I please of my own body." Brown was sentenced to the pillory, plus a fine and a year's imprisonment, but his statement still has enormous force as a complaint against the state's unwarranted interference in the lives of its private citizens. Just as important, Brown's comments provide a rare insight into the interior life of an eighteenth-century sodomite. His desire to organize his sexual life in his own way reflects a wider rejection of existing sexual models combined with a growing insistence that sexual activity could be about individual pleasure as well as procreative duty. This is borne out by the way that witness statements in sodomy trials dwell negatively on kissing, fondling, and mutual masturbation, as well as on anal sex. Such activities yield bodily pleasure without leading necessarily to orgasm, so it is hard to escape the conclusion that eighteenth-century sodomy prosecutions were not just concerned with punishing a supposedly inappropriate form of penetrative intercourse but were also a way of regulating sexuality in its widest sense. Although these court reports make grim reading, some comfort can be gleaned from accounts of eighteenth-century sodomy trials. After all, the high number of prosecutions is related to the increased visibility of homosexual meeting places such as public houses, male brothels, and open-air cruising grounds, and although the trials were intended to inhibit the spread of such facilities, this trend toward openness was ultimately irreversible.

Vincent Quinn

Bibliography

Bray, Alan. *Homosexuality in Renaissance England.* London: Gay Men's Press, 1982.

McCormick, Ian. *Secret Sexualities: A Sourcebook of Seventeenth and Eighteenth Century Writing.* London: Routledge, 1997.

Norton, Rictor. *Mother Clap's Molly House: The Gay Sub-Culture in England, 1700–1830.* London: Gay Men's Press, 1992.

See also Buggery; England; English Literature; Mollies; Molly Houses; Sodomy

Solomon, Simeon (1840–1905)

English painter, illustrator, and author Simeon Solomon was born into comfortable circumstances in London, a respected member of the Jewish community. After study at the Royal Academy Schools (1855–1858), Solomon distinguished himself as an active exhibitor at the Royal Academy (15 paintings), the Dudley Gallery (35 paintings), and the French Gallery (7 paintings) from 1858 to 1872. His early work (1855–1863) develops Old Testament and pre-Raphaelite themes, in particular Solomon's depictions of biblical subjects of same-sex attraction—David and Jonathan, David and Saul—were suffused with homoeroticism yet within the safe bounds of religious narrative. In his mature work (1863–1873), Solomon depicted classical subjects, often resonating with the theme of sorrowful love, yet set safely within the distant past.

Solomon's ten-year friendship with poet Algernon Charles Swinburne resulted in the artist's most innovative and morally daring work. In *Sappho and Erinna* (1864), *Love Relating Tales to Boys* (1865), the flagellation rites of the cult of Diana Orthia (1865), or the decadent boy-emperor *Heliogabalus, High Priest of the Sun* (1866), for example, Solo-

mon explored his own forbidden desires and found a means of subverting the conventions of Victorian respectability. Solomon also challenged the hegemony of Victorian heterosexual marriage in numerous works from the 1860s, such as *The Bride, the Bridegroom and Sad Love*, works that offer the possibility of male-male desire beyond the bounds set by matrimony.

Gradually over the course of the 1860s, Solomon became a part of the homosexual subculture of Victorian London, which included such men at Walter Pater, George Powell, and Oscar Browning. In March 1871, Solomon published his major literary work of his career, a prose poem entitled *A Vision of Love Revealed in Sleep*. This spiritual allegory, which is the key to the complex iconography of many of the motifs in Solomon's paintings, may be read as Solomon's statement of commitment to representing male-male desire as morally and aesthetically acceptable. By the early 1870s Solomon was aware that his paintings were looked on by some—Robert Browning, Sidney Colvin, Robert Buchanan—with suspicion, yet rather than remove that impression he increased the hermaphroditic traits of his figures and more and more enjoyed sexual and emotional ties with other men. In 1871 Solomon, along with Rossetti, Swinburne, and others, came under public attack for immorality in their works in what would be known as the "Fleshly School of Poetry" controversy. This was but a premonition of the catastrophe of February 1873, when Solomon and a sixty-year-old stableman, George Roberts, were arrested in a public washroom in central London and charged with "buggery, against the order of nature." Roberts was sentenced to eighteenth months at hard labor; Solomon was set free, owing to the influence of the artist's wealthy first cousin, Meyer Salaman, on a suspended sentence after serving two weeks in the Clerkenwell House of Correction. Solomon's intimate friends, most notably Swinburne, immediately turned their backs on him, fearing the effect on their own reputations of being associated with the artist.

Solomon's fall from grace was symptomatic of a wider public hostility and a subsequent tightening of the laws against homosexuals in the late nineteenth century following a series of public scandals. After 1873 Solomon lived the life of a pariah, and as the century progressed, his name became more and more associated with deviancy and deranged behavior. While the last twenty-eight years of Solomon's life are poorly documented, records of his being an occasional inmate of the St. Giles and St. George Endell Street Workhouse reflect a man suffering from alcoholism, poverty, and homelessness. Nonetheless, Solomon was remarkably productive during this period, creating over five hundred drawings and paintings, evidence that he was intermittently sober and responsible. He died of heart failure aggravated by alcoholism in the St. Giles Workhouse.

Gayle M. Seymour

Bibliography

Morgan, Thais E. "Perverse Male Bodies: Simeon Solomon and Algernon Charles Swinburne." In *Outlooks: Lesbian and Gay Sexualities and Visual Cultures*. London: Routledge, 1996.

Seymour, Gayle M. "The Art and Life of Simeon Solomon." Ph.D. diss., University of California, Santa Barbara, 1986.

———. "Simeon Solomon and the Biblical Construction of Marginal Identity in Victorian England." In *Reclaiming the Sacred: the Bible in Gay and Lesbian Culture*. New York: Haworth, 1997.

See also Art History; Buggery; David and Jonathan; Pater, Walter Horatio

Somerville, Jimmy (1964–)

Born in Glasgow, Scotland, Somerville gained prominence in 1984 as vocalist for the pop group Bronski Beat. Their first single, "Smalltown Boy," chronicling the rejection of a gay adolescent leaving his provincial hometown, reached the number-three position on the British music charts and was a hit throughout Europe. Despite a number of other hit songs, Somerville left Bronski Beat in 1985 and a year later formed the Communards with Richard Coles. After a string of several hits from two albums, the Communards disbanded in 1988. Somerville worked afterward as a solo artist. His career has been characterized by a mixture of his own music—a blend of pop, blues, and commentary on social issues—and covers of traditional disco classics, such as Donna Summers's "I Feel Love" (a duet with Marc Almond), Thelma Houston's "Don't Leave Me This Way," and Sylvester's "You Make Me Feel (Mighty Real)." Somerville even covered Judy Garland's "Zing Went the Strings of My Heart" while with the Communards. He achieved perhaps his greatest exposure to an American audience with his contribution to the AIDS awareness album *Red,*

Hot and Blue, for which he contributed a cover of Cole Porter's "From This Moment On." Throughout his career, the combination of Somervilles infectious falsetto, commitment to political issues, and candor regarding his own sexuality has made him an icon for young gay men in both Europe and the United States, setting a standard of personal honesty for other artists in the music industry to follow.

Scott Speirs

Bibliography

Gill, John. *Queer Noise: Male and Female Homosexuality in Twentieth-Century Music*. London: Cassell, 1995.

See also Disco and Dance Music; Music and Musicians 2: Popular Music; Porter, Cole; Sylvester

Sondheim, Stephen Joshua (1930–)

"Now . . . there are perhaps as many as ten seventeen-year-old honor students who are crazy about Stephen Sondheim and heterosexual as well, but nothing in Leo's bearing led me to suspect that he was among them," comments the narrator in Joe Keenan's novel *Blue Heaven*. Sondheim, who writes the music and lyrics but not the spoken dialogue (the "book") for the Broadway shows on which he collaborates, can be considered the greatest living exponent of the American musical, for with his canon of thirteen shows, plus three more for which he wrote lyrics only, he has outdistanced his competitors and critics and remains loyal to a genre whose future is as uncertain as his mastery of it is undeniable. Yet, while a formidable name to conjure with, he has never been a truly popular figure. He used to describe his following as a cult. Has it been a gay cult, and if so, to what extent and why?

There are various considerations. Until the mid-1990s, Sondheim was not completely "out"— or rather, for a showbiz celebrity he was shy, private, self-contained, sometimes abrasive, apparently a confirmed bachelor, and at the same time extraordinarily approachable (for instance, as a correspondent), all of which must have intrigued followers until, at the time of *Passion* (1994), word got out that he had fallen powerfully in love for the first time, a relationship (with one of the approachers, Peter Jones) now chronicled in Meryle Secrest's biography. But while musical theater has always attracted gay men as practitioners and Sondheim is no exception, his teacher and mentor, Oscar Hammerstein II, was straight, as have been several of his close collaborators. Nor are his audiences unmixed, and it is easiest to claim that he appeals to a constituency with the leisure or experience to examine personal relationships, as well as historical will, with critical introspection.

Yet the question of a gay voice and a specifically gay response remains. One seam of material is of sadomasochism, only indirectly touched on by Secrest but felt by many to be a crucial ingredient in *Sweeney Todd* (though curiously the role-playing of barber and customer is far more overt and integral in Austin Roper's 1970s version of the nineteenth-century melodrama than in the play text by Christopher Bond that served Hugh Wheeler and Sondheim). Camp, on the other hand, is generally absent—compare, for instance, its apotheosis in Jerry Herman (*Hello, Dolly!*; *La Cage aux Folles*). Nevertheless, where it comes into its own in Sondheim's work, above all in *Follies* (1971), it is transcendent. Listen to the 1985 *Follies in Concert* recording of "Beautiful Girls." Not being allowed to applaud other numbers on this disc was described as "faggot torture" by the invited audience. No character in a Sondheim musical is purposively gay, and the nagging doubt that something more than fear of heterosexual commitment is amiss with bachelor Bobby in *Company* (1970) has led to persistently revisionist directors wishing to have the show rewritten; perhaps the problem is that whenever creative vision in song exceeds a certain level of intensity, it is bound to be received as autobiographical. (Bobby's final song, "Being Alive," has become something of a gay anthem at AIDS benefits.) Nevertheless, some of the most searing insights come from the married partners in *Company*, who are "always sorry . . . always grateful . . . always wondering what might have been / [when] she walks in." Profound ambivalence over personal relationships is no special prerogative of gays.

Why, then, are so many gays so convinced that Sondheim's voice speaks particularly and personally to them? Perhaps it has something to do with his musical techniques, for his noble ironies are always couched in the great traditions of harmonic expression that he inherited from Kern and Gershwin (with an admixture of Copland and the modernists), yet forged into a unique voice. This lends them something of a tragic view of history, the view of a person who fully understands and accepts the family crucible yet pursues the lonely imperative of self-sufficiency through difference—an unfashionable and perhaps outmoded view of gay identity or even of artistic creation, but a deeply moving and challenging one for those who still have ears to hear.

Stephen Banfield

Bibliography
Secrest, Meryle. *Stephen Sondheim: A Life*. New York: Knopf, 1998.

See also AIDS Performance; Camp; Copland, Aaron; Musical Theater

South Africa

At the end of the twentieth century, South Africa is the only country in the world that guarantees protection for gays and lesbians in its constitution. As members of one of the world's newest democracies (1994), South Africans had the unique opportunity to negotiate a constitution that reflected the respect for the rights and dignity of all men and women, which the legislation of the previous apartheid government so painfully denied.

To entrench the "equality clause" with explicit reference to "sexual orientation" in the final version of the constitution, gays and lesbians campaigned on a national level, bombarding members of parliament with carefully prepared arguments to counter the propaganda generated by many fundamentalist Christian and Islamic South Africans, who bitterly opposed the inclusion of the equality clause in the constitution. Able lobbying by representatives of the National Coalition for Gay and Lesbian Equality (NCGLE) eventually contributed to the retention of the clause, which reads:

> The state may not unfairly discriminate directly or indirectly against anyone on one or more grounds, including race, gender, sex, pregnancy, marital status, ethnic or social origin, color, sexual orientation, age, disability, religion, conscience, belief, culture, language and birth. (Constitution of the Republic of South Africa, *Bill of Rights, Act 108 of 1996*, Chapter 2, 9 [3])

However, constitutional protection for gays and lesbians does not mean that South Africa is now a homosexual paradise. Legislation from the apartheid era, still on the statute books, criminalizes male same-sex sexual relationships; what is important is that this legislation can now be challenged in terms

South African gay activist Simon Nkoui. Photo by Marc Geller.

of the constitution, which outlaws any form of discrimination against gays or lesbians.

Consequently, the NCGLE in 1998 challenged sections of the Sexual Offences Act of 1957, which criminalized sodomy and, notoriously, any man who committed it with another man at a party, defined as an occasion at which more than two persons are present, any act "calculated to stimulate sexual passion or to give sexual gratification." Effectively, private gay social gatherings and gay clubs could be, and were, subjected to police surveillance and raids on these grounds, especially during the 1970s and 1980s. The NCGLE was victorious: sodomy is now legal and gay parties, at least in the Gauteng province where the judgment was made, can happily occur without fear of harassment.

Other victories for the NCGLE include a nondiscriminatory defense force policy, gay rights in the workplace entrenched in the Labour Relations Act, and the adoption in 1997 of a resolution by the fiftieth conference of the ruling African National Congress Party that inter alia, supported the equal right to marry and parliamentary representation for gays and lesbians. In 1998, the NCGLE launched its "Equal Right to Marry" campaign, which involves challenging and negotiating the amendment of the existing marriage laws.

Ripple effects of the equality clause have been experienced in both the public and private sectors, where institutions, like some universities, for example, now recognize gay and lesbian partnerships for the purposes of medical aid and housing subsidies; and some companies, for instance, those selling insurance, dare not discriminate against HIV-infected gay men, usually because of the fear of messy, public litigation.

Constitutional protection does not mean the end of homophobia, but it has entailed the throwing open of the closet doors, arguably the best way of ensuring its eventual demise. Gays and lesbians are in the public eye more significantly than ever before.

The first gay pride march was held in Johannesburg in 1990; national television has regularly covered the annual parade since then. The gay press, represented by tabloids and glossy magazines such as *Exit* (1985), *Outright* (1994), and *Gay SA* (1996), the Out in Africa Gay and Lesbian Film Festival (screened in Cape Town, Johannesburg, and Pretoria); intermittent screening of gay and lesbian films on national TV and on the general circuit; and TV coverage of the participation of a large South African contingent at the Gay Games in Amsterdam in 1998 have all raised the awareness of gay and lesbian issues publicly, on a scale unthinkable twenty years ago.

Gay travel agencies and gay bed-and-breakfasts can now be found in the major cities; Cape Town was voted the most preferred destination for gay men by *Out and About Magazine* in 1998 (winning the designation over London). Gay bars and clubs, catering for most tastes, exist in the major cities (Johannesburg, Cape Town, Pretoria, Durban, Port Elizabeth), as do video and bookstores, many of them specializing in the kind of pornography banned by the censors of the apartheid era, during which gay men were often deliberately confused with child molesters in the political (and moralistic) rhetoric of the ruling National Party.

In most areas of South African life, profound divisions still exist along racial and class lines. The gay community is no exception to this; gay clubs and bars are urban phenomena rather than rural, and the clientele tends to be drawn largely from the white, Indian, and colored (mixed-race) middle classes.

In some circles, the argument, fueled by mindlessly homophobic utterances, for example, by members of the African Christian Democratic Party and of President Robert Mugabe of Zimbabwe, persists that homosexual behavior is "un-African" and is a pernicious, Western import, along with colonialism and venereal disease. Where it exists among African men, it is suggested, homosexuality is institutionally shaped through necessity (as in prisons or

S
in the mine hostels, where same-sex "mine marriages" between older black miners and younger men existed).

However, studies of African gay and lesbian individuals and communities (e.g., in Gevisser and Cameron) reveal that homosexuality is as African as it is European, although the struggle for acceptance in African society is made even tougher by the rigidly patriarchal and heterosexist nature of traditional African society.

A recent study of the constructions of masculinity among gay Zulu men in Pietermaritzburg (Natal University, 1999) reveals a community in which gay relationships are modeled along traditional heterosexual lines, with strict demarcation between active and passive partners extending even to marriage ceremonies, where the "female" partner is adorned as a traditional heterosexual bride. Such communities have evolved their own rich vocabularies revealing English, Afrikaans, and Zulu hybrids.

In a country as racially and culturally diverse as South Africa (the "rainbow nation," in Archbishop Desmond Tutu's words), which has eleven official languages, it is evident that homosexuality and gay masculinity are constructed and perceived in many different ways, which will result in ever more interesting combinations, especially as the artificial racial barriers erected during the apartheid era begin to disappear and power relations, affected by political and socioeconomic realities, alter.

Michael Lambert

Bibliography

Gevisser, Mark, and Edwin Cameron, eds. *Defiant Desire: Gay and Lesbian Lives in South Africa.* Johannesburg: Ravan Press, 1994.

Moodie, Dunbar. "Migrancy and Male Sexuality on the South African Gold Mines." *Journal of Southern African Studies* 14 (1988): 228–56.

Reddy, Vasu. "Negotiating Gay Masculinities." *Agenda* 37 (1998): 65–70.

See also Africa: Precolonial and sub-Saharan Africa; Colonialism; Politics: Global; Same-Sex Marriages; Zimbabwe

Spain

There are literary indications that suggest the existence of a homosexual subculture in medieval Spain. The city of Granada, in the south, has historically been considered a symbol of homosexual activity (which the Spaniards equate with Moorish Spain). The book burnings of the Inquisition ensure that much information on homosexuality in earlier ages has been lost forever, but it is believed to have been common among Granada's nobility, as evidenced in some eleventh-century poetry.

Enrique IV (1454–1474), uncle of the famed Queen Isabel, was known for his intimate liaisons with young men. Isabel and Fernando (1474–1516) changed the thirteenth-century penalty for male homosexuality from castration and stoning to burning at the stake. The Inquisition (begun in 1480) focused a fair amount of attention on sexual deviation. There are recorded accounts of executions for sodomy in Sevilla, Valencia, Zaragoza, and Barcelona from 1566 to 1620. Many of those accused were not killed but sentenced to forced labor. This leniency was believed to have resulted from the high incidence of homosexuality among priests and monks, and it was not in the interest of the inquisitors to decimate its clergy. In sixteenth-century Granada, women accused of lesbianism were whipped, not killed.

A recent theory proclaims that Don Juan Tarsis y Peralta, count of Villamediana (1580–1622)—the historical figure who inspired the Don Juan of literature and myth—may have been murdered because of his homosexuality. The investigation of his death exposed a network of practitioners of sodomy who were later burned alive. Many of the references cited as evidence of this claim have vanished, perhaps to help sustain the legend of Don Juan as the great seducer of women.

The word *homosexual* was introduced into Spanish in the late nineteenth century, but Spanish criminal law, derived from the Napoleonic Code of the nineteenth century, did not designate homosexuality as a crime. It was the Penal Code of the Spanish Republic that made homosexuality illegal, provided it involved "public scandal" or "corruption of minors." Under the Franco regime (1939–1975), homosexual activity was often blamed on foreigners and artistic celebrities who recruited young Spanish men to their cause. Homosexual penal camps were established in Madrid in the 1960s. The "Law of Social Hazard" of 1970 set a three-year prison sentence for those accused of homosexual conduct. In 1976, the sodomy law was repealed except in the military. That year also saw the first gay march in Barcelona. Film director Eloy de la Iglesia, who has made a number of gay-themed films, claims it was the banning of his motion picture *Hidden Pleasures* (1976) that precipitated this uprising.

Gay demonstration in Barcelona, Spain, 1979. Photo by Marc Geller.

With the transition to democracy and progressive liberalization after Franco, gays and lesbians were theoretically granted equal rights with heterosexuals. The current age of consent for both male and female homosexual acts in Spain is twelve, which, along with Portugal and the Netherlands, is the lowest in Europe.

Overall, the gay and lesbian movement is not as appreciable in Spain as in the United States, and Spanish gays and lesbians are much less likely than their U.S. counterparts to classify themselves by sexual orientation. The English terms *being in the closet, queer,* and *to come out* have no Spanish-language equivalents. Many Spaniards view the gay and lesbian movement as an Anglo-American phenomenon that is beginning to make its way into Spanish culture. It is evident that many Spanish gay and lesbian groups model themselves after American groups.

There is a distinct gay subculture in Spain today, most notably in the urban centers that are more accessible to outside influences. Colectivo de Gays y Lesbianas de Madrid (COGAM) is the most prominent gay and lesbian group in the capital. Other Spanish cities—Barcelona, Valencia, Seville—are better known for their gay communities than Madrid. Coordinadora Gai-Lesbiana (formed in 1986) and Casal Lambda (1976) are powerful gay and lesbian groups based in Barcelona. Since 1995, Barcelona has hosted an annual International Gay and Lesbian Film Festival. Sitges, a town south of Barcelona, has been called the gay tourist capital of Europe.

In 1994, the Basque town of Vitoria became the first to create a Register of Civil Unions, which affords gay and lesbian couples the same rights as married heterosexuals. Other towns quickly followed this lead. The problem for gays and lesbians is that, in Spain, marriage and family matters are regulated at the federal level, and thus require a national (rather than city-by-city) commitment. In January 1995, a new Spanish law acknowledging the rights of de facto couples, regardless of marital status or sexual orientation, went into effect. The law is being applied sporadically and often unwillingly. Allowing for gay and lesbian adoption is proving more controversial. In 1997, gays and lesbians throughout Spain marched in what was described as the largest demonstration since the 1976 march. The Madrid demonstration was timed to coincide with the discussion of a comprehensive partnership law in the Spanish parliament.

Currently, there are many slang terms—mostly pejorative—to designate gay men: *marica, afeminado, loca* (crazy woman or hedonist), and *maricón* (distinguished from the *marica* by his virility). Fewer terms denote lesbians, and those that do participate in food metaphors. *Bollera* (buns maker) and the more common *tortillera* (omelet maker) are two such terms. Among Spanish gay and lesbians, it is customary to ask whether one "understands" or is a "member of the union" to indicate a gay or lesbian identity.

There are a number of prominent homosexual artists from Spain, including Manuel de Falla

S (1876–1946), a composer of ballets and operas; director Eloy de la Iglesia; and flamboyant writer/director of outlandishly melodramatic comedies Pedro Almodóvar. Almodóvar is, to date, the most popular Spanish filmmaker of all time, and his *Women on the Verge of a Nervous Breakdown* (1988) is the top-grossing Spanish movie to date.

María Dolores Costa

Bibliography

Alas, Leopoldo. *De la acera de enfrente: Todo lo que se debe saber de los gays y nadie se ha atrevido a contar.* Madrid: Ediciones Temas de Hoy, 1994.

Bergmann, Emilie L., and Paul Julian Smith, eds. *¿Entiendes? : Queer Readings, Hispanic Writings.* Durham, N.C.: Duke University Press, 1995.

"Casal Lambda Gay and Lesbian Centre." http://www. redestb.es/lambda/inici7.htm (May 8, 1997).

"COGAM: Colectivo de Gays y Laesbianas de Madrid." http://www.ctv.es/USERS/cogam/quescog.htm (May 20, 1997).

"Coordiinadora Gai-Lesbiana." http://www.pangea.org.org/cgl/indc.htm (May 23, 1997).

Crapotta, James F. "Hispanic Gay and Lesbian Issues." In *Gay and Lesbian Themes in Hispanic Literatures and Cultures.* http://www. columbia.edu/cu/libraries/events/sw25/case9.html (May 8, 1997).

DeStefano, George. "Post-Franco Frankness." *Film Comment* 22 (May–June 1986): 58–60.

Haro Ibars, Eduardo. "La homosexualidad como problema socio-político en el cine español del postfranquismo." *Tiempo de Historia* 52 (March 1979): 88–91.

Murphy, Ryan. "A Spanish Fly in the Hollywood Ointment: Gay Director Pedro Almodóvar Refuses to Be Tied Up by Censorship." *Advocate* (June 19, 1990): 37–40.

Pérez Cánovas, Nicolás. *Homosexualidad, homosexuales y uniones homosexuales en el derecho español.* Granada: Editorial Comares, 1996.

Reborias, Ramón F. "Bisex: El tercer sexo, último tabú del milenio." *Cambio* 16 (April 26, 1996): 22–25.

Smith, Paul Julian. *Laws of Desire: Questions of Homosexuality in Spanish Writing and Film, 1960–1990.* Oxford: Clarendon Press, 1992.

Soriano Gil, Manuel. *Homosexualidad y represión: Iniciación al estudio de la homofila.* Madrid: Zero, 1978.

Stradling, Robert. "The Death of Don Juan: Murder, Myth and Mayhem in Madrid." *History Today* 43 (May 1993): 11–17.

See also Almodóvar, Pedro; Cernuda, Luís; Christianity; Code Napoleón; Coming Out; Falla, Manuel de; García Lorca, Federico; Inquisition; Monasticism, Christian; Queer; Spanish Literature

Spanish Literature

When discussing gay and lesbian literature from Spain, it is wise to remember that Anglo-American critical theories do not always apply, and that homosexuality has not been treated as extensively in Spanish literature as in some other national literatures. There are now a number of studies on this topic—many of them originating among scholars in the United States and Britain. Since the gay identity is such a recent phenomenon, most of these studies approach modern and contemporary works.

Federico García Lorca (1898–1936) is undoubtedly the best-known Spanish homosexual author. In fact, along with Miguel de Cervantes and Benito Pérez Galdós, he is one of the most distinguished Spanish writers of all time. This poet, dramatist, musician, and illustrator was born in Granada and killed by a Falangist firing squad early in the Spanish Civil War. In Madrid's highly regarded Residencia de Estudiantes, Lorca first became aware of his sexuality. There he developed an intimate friendship and, some suspect, infatuation with Spanish painter Salvador Dalí. A later affair with sculptor Emilio Aladren brought on a serious depression that Lorca's family hoped to remedy by sending the young Federico to the United States in 1929. While in New York, Lorca discovered Walt Whitman's *Leaves of Grass*, which had a powerful impact on him. From 1933 until his death, Lorca maintained a relationship with Rafael Rodríguez Rapún.

Lorca's poetry and plays are characterized by the combination of Andalusian folklore and surrealist techniques. His work is laden with hopeless, uneasy relationships—mostly heterosexual. Common themes in his work—often explained by reference to the author's sexuality—include darkness, concealment, disappointment, grief, and barrenness. "Cancíon del mariquita" (Song of the Faggot) is Lorca's first apparent literary treatment of homosexuality. The poem is an ironic description of an effeminate Andalusian male. Homosexuality also occurs vividly in his "Ode to Walt Whitman," in which Lorca seizes on the American poet as a model of gay virility. The poem seemingly condemns certain homosexual types by using a string of Spanish epithets, but because of its complex nature, the poem has inspired contrary readings. Lorca's *Sonnets of Dark Love*—not published until 1983—are believed to be fairly autobiographical. Here the author depicts unfortunate clandestine relationships. Lorca's play, *The Public*, also approaches issues of homosexuality and gender crossing. Two incomplete outlines for dramatic projects—*The Destruction of Sodom* and *Blackball*—also address gay themes. The first of these was to be a dramatic presentation of the biblical story of Sodom; the latter was to depict the story of a young man denied membership in a local club because of his homosexuality.

The Generation of 1927, a group of young poets that included Lorca, boasted other gay writers: Nobel Prize winner Vicente Aleixandre, the all but forgotten Emilio Prados, and poet, critic, and educator Luís Cernuda. Of these, Cernuda most directly appeals to his sexuality in his writing.

Luís Cernuda (1902?–1963) clearly viewed himself as a member of a persecuted minority. At the age of fourteen, he began writing poems to men he found attractive. Later, he would use his poetry to verbalize the oppression suffered by gays in Spain and record the social abyss between heterosexual and homosexual identities during his time. Though not always regarded as such by literary critics, his is a discourse of social protest in which love and sex become revolutionary, liberating forces. At the time of its publication, Cernuda's openly homoerotic poetry posed a problem for many readers, so critics often chose to quiet the gay voice within these works. Cernuda's anthologies include *Prohibited Pleasures* (1931) and *Reality and Desire* (1936).

Cernuda, who staunchly supported the Spanish Republic, went into exile in 1938, once it was clear that Franco's forces would win the civil war. The poet, who taught Spanish literature at Mount Holyoke College in Massachusetts, also published literary criticism. He died in Mexico.

Novelist Juan Goytisolo (1931–) is perhaps the most prominent contemporary Spanish novelist (let alone gay novelist). His work often focuses on the linguistic, social, and sexual struggle to achieve an authentic subjectivity through textual (and often violent) expression. In the author's narrative trilogy, homosexuality is associated with the act of writing. His more recent book, *The Virtues of the Solitary Bird* (1988), deals with the AIDS issue. More than celebrating gay identity, Goytisolo, like a number of Spanish authors, examines it attentively. His work customarily explores dissident voices within Spanish history.

The work of openly gay novelist Terenci Moix (1943–) is known for its outrageous camp style. The author delights in the frivolous aspects of popular culture, especially cinema. He frequently employs anachronisms and incongruities in his novels, which are also distinguished by this amoral and apolitical bent.

Luís Antonio de Villena (1951–) tackles gay subject matter in his poetry. Villena is a prolific writer and media celebrity who has produced essays, short stories, novels, and poetry. He started his literary career during the period of transition from the Franco dictatorship to democracy—a period marked by the transition in literature from sociopolitical dilemmas to aestheticism.

Lesbianism is, overall, less visible in Spanish letters than male homosexuality. Ana María Troix (sister of Terenci) deals with immobility that can result from the quelling of lesbian desire in her novel, *Julia* (1970). Her short story "Las virtudes peligrosas" presents two women who, mysteriously and for years, love each other from afar. Unlike her brother, Ana María does not publicly discuss her own sexual orientation.

Esther Tusquets (1936–) is the author of a trilogy of novels in which the theme of lesbianism is linked to an ironic critique of the upper middle class. Tusquets is considered to have produced the first substantive treatment of lesbianism in Spanish literature. Her literary production, which relies heavily on archetypes, myths, and seemingly endless sentences, can be connected to the theories of Monique Wittig. Like Moix and other Spanish writers, Tusquets refuses to publicly discuss her own sexuality. *María Dolores Costa*

Bibliography

Bartlett, Neil. *The Uses of Monotony.* London: Birkbeck College, 1994.

Bellver, Catherine G. "The Language of Eroticism in the Novels of Esther Tusquets." *Anales de la Literatura Española Contemporánea* 9 (1984): 13–27.

Bergmann, Emilie L., and Paul Julian Smith, eds. *¿Entiendes?: Queer Readings, Hispanic Writings.* Durham, N.C.: Duke University Press, 1995.

S

Binding, Paul. *Lorca: The Gay Imagination.* London: Gay Men's Press, 1985.

Ellis, Robert R. *The Hispanic Homograph: Gay Self-Representation in Contemporary Spanish Autobiography.* Urbana, Ill.: University of Illinois Press, 1997.

Epps, Bradley S. *Significant Violence: Oppression and Resistance in the Narratives of Juan Goytisolo.* Oxford: Clarendon Press, 1996.

García Lorca, Federico. *Ode to Walt Whitman and Other Poems.* San Francisco: City Light Books, 1988.

Real Ramos, César. *Luís Cernuda y la Generación del 27.* Salamanca: Universidad de Salamanca, 1983.

Sahuquillo, Ángel. *Federico García Lorca y la cultura de la homosexualidad masculina.* Alicante: Instituto de Cultura, 1991.

Smith, Paul Julian. *García Lorca/Almodóvar: Gender, Nationality, and the Limits of the Visible.* Cambridge: Cambridge University Press, 1995.

———. *Laws of Desire: Questions of Homosexuality in Spanish Writing and Film, 1960–1990.* Oxford: Clarendon Press, 1992.

Thomas, Patricia Corcoran. " 'La verdad su amor verdadero': Gay Love and Social Protest in the Poetry of Luis Cernuda." *DAI* 52 (1991): 3306A. University of Minnesota.

See also AIDS; Cernuda, Luís; García Lorca, Federico; Goytisolo, Juan; Moix, Terenci; Salínas, Pedro; Sodom; Spain; Whitman, Walt

Sparta

Sparta, leading Dorian Greek city-state in the Peloponnese, which, after the war with Athens (431–404 B.C.E.), enjoyed brief hegemony in Greece. Sparta was a highly conservative community that relied on the enslavement of a neighboring people, the Helots of Messenia, to free its male citizens for intensive training as warriors (Spartiates).

The Spartan constitution, attributed to the legendary lawgiver, Lycurgus, probably evolved between the seventh and fifth centuries B.C.E. One of its features was the *agoge,* the training of boys and young men, an institution that endured until the third century B.C.E.

From the age of seven, healthy boys were removed from their families and reared by the state. The boys were grouped in age squadrons, or *agelai,* which received a thorough initiation into Spartan ideals of masculinity, which embraced deprivation and cunning. The boys were given one rough cloak a year and were encouraged to steal their food and murder Helots at night. To inculcate deception and endurance, brutal public flogging was inflicted on them if caught stealing. Through attendance at the communal messes, where the boys and younger men listened to the conversations and jokes of their seniors, they were socialized into Spartan *mores,* until they became full members of the messes at thirty. This prolonged initiation was further strengthened by rituals and festivals, characterized by competition.

According to Plutarch, Spartan marriages were extraordinary affairs in which the eighteen-year-old bride, hair close-cropped and dressed as a man for the occasion, was "introduced" to the groom in a darkened room at night. The groom, who continued to spend his nights in the barracks, would persist in visiting his wife by stealth, until she became pregnant; only then would he live with his bride, while continuing to dine in the communal mess until the age of sixty.

This ritual may well have arisen to ease the groom's transition from an all-male environment, in which same-sex sexual relations were the norm, into a heterosexual one, designed not for love but breeding. Significantly, Plutarch also records that, at the age of twelve, the boys received lovers chosen from among the respectable young men. Thus the prolonged process of Spartan initiation seems to have included an erotic or sexual element. Some Athenian writers even referred to same-sex love as "doing it the Spartan way" and invented derogatory words like *kusolakon* (Spartan-arsed). The Dorian Greek word for the male lover (*eispnelas*) could mean something like the "blower-in" or "breather-in" (of semen?), suggesting that anal intercourse was the preferred means of copulation.

The notion that Greek same-sex relations originated in Dorian military structures, whence they were exported to the rest of Greece, was current in antiquity and has been resurrected by modern scholarship. Yet there is no convincing evidence for this. The exclusively male socialization of Spartan men obviously fostered same-sex relations and contributed to the relatively "liberated" lot of Spartan women, who, freed from their sons and often their husbands (away on endless campaigns), enjoyed an economic power rare in antiquity.

Michael Lambert

Bibliography

Dover, Kenneth J. *Greek Homosexuality,* 2d ed. London: Duckworth, 1989.

See also Athens; Greece

Sports

Homosexual men have been and continue to be active in both mainstream and gay community sports. Their experience in sports is in many respects the same as that of their heterosexual counterparts: experiences such as physical exertion, team camaraderie, and competition.

Athletics and Masculinity

Since the ancient Olympic Games began, athletic participation has been considered a sign of masculinity. Women, until the twentieth century, had been excluded from athletics; they were prohibited from participation in the Sacred Games of Olympia and from the activities of the gymnasia of ancient Greece. There is evidence, however, that in ancient China, upper-class women played a version of the game of soccer with men. The modern Olympics prohibited the participation of women until 1928. Sports continue to be dominated by men. Women's sports receive little coverage in the mainstream sports media; at the Olympic Games in Atlanta, only one-third of the participants were women.

In nineteenth-century Europe, theories of homosexuality were developed that saw it as a symptom of gender confusion—homosexual men were considered to be essentially feminine. The nineteenth-century expansion of the British Empire and its sphere of cultural and economic influence, the ascendancy of the bourgeoisie, the rise of the British public school system, and the central role that sports played in that system made a cumulative contribution to the twentieth-century Western cultures of sports. Athletics became the quintessential expression of capitalist masculine values, the values of model citizenship: aggression, competition, racism, elitism, militarism, imperialism, sexism, and heterosexism. That athletic image is dramatically unlike the dominant religious, medical, and legal models of homosexuality that categorized homosexuals as effeminate, sinful, pathological, and criminal. The culture of mainstream sport has thus been overwhelmingly homophobic. Consequently, for many years many homosexual men have refrained from athletic participation. Among those gay men who did participate, many, especially professionals, have found it difficult to acknowledge publicly their homosexuality. At the time of writing there are not three dozen elite athletes who have come out publicly. Consequently it is difficult to know which high-performance athletes are homosexual. Among those who are now known to be are the following:

John Menlove Edwards (mountaineering), David Kopay (football), Rudy Galindo (figure skating), Mark Leduc (amateur boxing), Greg Louganis (diving), Ian Roberts (professional Australian rugby), and Tom Waddell (decathlete and founder of the Gay Games).

Gay Community Sports

Since athletic participation offers a subjective feeling of physical, emotional, and spiritual power, homosexual men who have felt powerless because of the low social position of their sexuality can, in gay-positive environments, find athletics and sports particularly empowering. Indeed, they can derive intense satisfaction from excelling in sports knowing that as "faggots" they are beating "macho men" at their own game. Gay liberation encouraged gay athletes to come out. Coming out has made it possible for some to become gay athletes.

One of the products of the gay liberation movement has been the creation of specifically gay political and social organizations. Gay athletic clubs, which can be found in major cities in Europe, Australia, New Zealand, North America, and parts of South America and Africa, constitute an important part of gay community life. The common purpose of gay sports groups is essentially twofold: to promote social interaction and to provide athletic opportunities for people who share a way of life. The roster of gay community sports clubs is extensive; space affords only a brief sampling of this significant facet of gay culture. In many places the largest gay organizations are sports clubs. There are outing clubs associated with the International Gay and Lesbian Outdoor Organization with names like the Out and Out Club and organize activities such as camping jamborees, bicycle tours, cross-country and downhill skiing, hiking, canoeing, parachuting, and white-water rafting. Included in the list of organized gay community sports are groups such as Spokes, a cycling club in Vancouver; Gruppo Pesce, a swimming group in Milan; Paris Lutte Amateur Groupe, a wrestling club in Paris; and the Penguins, a San Francisco hockey team.

There are many gay sports governing bodies. For instance, the North American Gay Amateur Athletic Alliance is a nonprofit organization dedicated to promoting amateur softball for all persons, with a special emphasis on gay participation; like similar bodies in other sports, it also establishes uniform playing rules and regulations. Other governing bodies include the International Gay Bowling Association, the Interna-

S tional Gay and Lesbian Aquatics Association, and the International Gay and Lesbian Hockey Association.

The ideological significance of gay sports is noteworthy. Since the early 1980s, there has been a shift in focus in gay culture from the dialectic of oppression and liberation to the experience of gay pride. An important expression of gay pride can be found in sports: in many cities the most important annual gay event is pride day, which often includes in the celebrations athletic events such as ten-kilometer runs and swim meets. The most prestigious international gay pride event is the Gay Games. Gay activists have seized on athletics as an ideological instrument of gay politics. Taking advantage of the common association of sports with healthy normality, sporting events are promoted to counteract the image of homosexuals as unhealthy deviants. This has been especially the case in the context of the AIDS epidemic.

Conclusion

The participation of homosexual men in sports is extensive. Their presence in mainstream sports is often not visible because they frequently pass as heterosexual. Their experience in that milieu can be unique and is intimately related to the history of homosexuality and sport. The modern gay liberation movement has brought with it a flourishing of gay culture that has produced a plethora of gay teams, clubs, and sports governing bodies around the world.   *Brian Pronger*

Bibliography

Kopay, David, and Perry Young. *The David Kopay Story: An Extraordinary Revelation*. New York: Donald I. Fine, 1988.

Louganis, Greg, and Eric Marcus. *Breaking the Surface*. New York: Random House, 1995.

Messner, Mike. *Power at Play*. Boston: Beacon, 1992.

Messner, Mike, and Don Sabo. *Sex, Violence and Power in Sports: Rethinking Masculinity*. Freedom, Calif.: Crossing Press, 1994.

Pronger, Brian. *The Arena of Masculinity: Sports, Homosexuality and the Meaning of Sex*. New York: St. Martin's Press, 1990.

Simpson, Mark. *Male Impersonators: Men Performing Masculinity*. New York: Routledge, 1994.

See also Boy Scouts; Colonialism; Coming Out; Gay Games; Gay Liberation; Greece; Masculinity; Physical Culture; Soccer

Stereotype

The notion of stereotyping was developed in communications theory to describe the use of endlessly repeated figures to represent social groups. Such typifications are achieved through character construction (e.g., dandified or overfastidious dress, pursed lips and makeup, wittiness and misogyny to signify gay men) and recurrent narrative structures (e.g., gay men's lives end in death, they are killers, they are lonely). Though always recognized to be simplistic and reductive, communications theory has also generally assumed that stereotypes will always be necessary in some form to make sense of the sheer complexity and multiplicity of social life. In principle, they need not be value-laden, but in practice, the term has come to mean negative typifications. This is the sense in which gay activists have used it, pointing to the remorseless deployment in the arts and media of such types as the screaming queen, the neurotic fag, the self-pitying closet case, and the predatory pederast. Gay scholarship has extensively catalogued such images in most media and most countries, and has explored the role of stereotypes in establishing ideas of sexual normality. These ideas are not only about sexual activity but also about gender, since gay stereotypes most often link gay men with notions of effeminacy or, more recently, exaggerated masculinity—in either case, gay men do not quite fit the male gender role, probably because of their incorrect relation to women within heterosexuality and male domination.

Objection to stereotyping as negative images of gay men remains a cornerstone of gay rights thinking. However, the issue is far more complex than may at first sight appear. To begin with, stereotypes are an immensely strong mode of communication that cannot simply be argued away. They have formal values of economy, directness, and instant recognizability, while also often conveying complex information about, for instance, the nature of sexuality and gender; this combination is especially valuable within mass communications. Second, they perform a precious ideological function in the reinforcement of majority sexuality. Third, and most difficult to come to terms with, they are in practice valued by gay communities. Their visibility (as well as their general mass communicative value) recommends itself to the gay rights strategy of coming out, of making gay men present in the arts and media. Gay activism still calls for "positive images" that, on inspection, are positive stereotypes (evident in the anodyne representations in 1990s prime-time

Stoddard (left) strategizing. Photo courtesy Robert Murphy.

television). Gay culture has devoted itself to living stereotypes such as the clone and the guppie, and queer activism has often sought to embrace the sexual nonconformity recognized in the queen and the leather types. There is a logic to all this. If gays were to abandon all kinds of typical representations of themselves, then "they" as a recognizable category would no longer exist. This might be where they want to get to, but it is not clear that the psychological comfort or political effectiveness of recognizable representations is something gays are quite ready to do without.   *Richard Dyer*

Bibliography

Champagne, John. *The Ethics of Marginality: A New Approach to Gay Studies*. Minneapolis: University of Minnesota Press, 1995.

See also Activism, U.S.; Coming Out; Effeminacy; Film; Gay Left; Homophobia; Masculinity; Queen; Queer; Queer Nation; U.S. Law: Discrimination

Stoddard, Thomas B. (1948–1997)

Lobbyist, litigator, teacher, writer, and public spokesperson, Stoddard was the most broadly accomplished advocate of gay rights for much of the 1980s and 1990s. His gay rights career is more gen-erally significant as promoting an individualistic, civil-libertarian vision of the movement.

Stoddard first became prominent as a lobbyist for the New York Civil Liberties Union, where he fought for freedom of speech and religion, criminal justice, reproductive rights, and gay rights. Even his adversaries respected his lobbying genius, and his clear, passionate articulation of civil liberties issues made Stoddard a fixture in the *New York Times* and on national television.

Stoddard drafted New York City's gay rights bill in 1986, and taught a profession-transforming course in gay rights law at New York University Law School for over fifteen years.

Recruited as executive director of Lambda Legal Defense and Education Fund in 1986, Stoddard catapulted Lambda into its modern role as a highly effective, national legal organization. Under Stoddard's direction, Lambda managed to combat burgeoning AIDS discrimination, even while expanding its gay rights mission. During these perilous, post-*Hardwick* years, Stoddard was the movement's most visible and articulate spokesperson in the national media.

Stoddard left Lambda in 1992, in part because of concern over the progress of his HIV disease. Nonetheless, in 1993 he led the Campaign for Military Service, providing Bill Clinton with legal and

S lobbying support for his pledge to end the ban on gays in the military but ultimately failing to persuade the president not to renege on that promise.

In 1993, Stoddard married Walter Rieman. Despite worsening HIV disease, Stoddard remained active as a teacher, lawyer, and vice chair of the American Foundation for AIDS Research until his death at age forty-eight.   *Robert Murphy*

Bibliography

Kaiser, Charles. *The Gay Metropolis, 1990–1996.* Boston: Houghton Mifflin, 1997.

See also Bowers v. Hardwick *and* Romer v. Evans; Civil Rights in the U.S.; Gay Rights; Lambda; Military United States Law: Equal Protection

Stonewall

In the early morning of June 28, 1969, Martha Shelley was showing two women from Boston the bars of New York City's Greenwich Village. Shelley was president of the city's chapter of the Daughters of Bilitis, a lesbian rights organization founded in San Francisco in the 1950s. During their tour the three women walked into a riot. "What's going on here?" asked one of the women. Shelley, adopting the voice of a jaded New York activist, responded, "Oh, it's a riot. These things happen in New York all the time. Let's toddle away and do something else" (Marcus 180). Wrapping up her tour, Shelley dropped her guests off at a friends' and headed over to New Jersey to see her lover.

The next morning Shelley learned that the riot she had led her friends away from was prompted by a police raid of a gay bar called the Stonewall Inn, one of the Village's most popular bars. The Stonewall, though not, as is sometimes thought, a hangout for transvestites, drew "a magical mix of patrons ranging from tweedy East Siders to street queens" (Duberman 182). Like many gay and lesbian bars of the time, the Stonewall was run by the mob and was subject to periodic police raids. These raids were often prompted by the failure of the bar's owners to make their regular payoffs to the local precinct or by crusading politicians who cherished the opportunity to wear the voter-appealing mantle of "family values." Though it is likely that at least some of the Stonewall's patrons had had previous experience with police raids, on June 28 they did not go quietly into the night. Rather than comply with the forces of oppression, the bar's patrons,

joined by the people who called the streets of the Village their home, fought back against the police in riots that continued for the better part of a week.

For Shelley and her activist comrades in and out of the gay and lesbian rights movement, the Stonewall riots were a turning point. By the end of the summer, Shelley was helping to organize the Gay Liberation Front (GLF), a gay and lesbian rights group named after the South Vietnamese National Liberation Front. Within a year, Gay Liberation Fronts had sprung up in Austin, Texas; Berkeley, California; and London, England; the inspiring story of the Stonewall riots spread with them. In 1970 the first Stonewall commemoration parades were held. Today hundreds of thousands of people gather at the end of June in powerful displays of unity. Increasingly Stonewall marches are held overseas, helping to bind together an international gay and lesbian movement. In the years since 1969, the story of Stonewall has been told and retold in manifestos, in bars, on the streets, and in encyclopedias. What had been to Shelley "just another riot" has been transformed into the mythic origin of the modern gay and lesbian movement.

Though accounts often depict Stonewall as an unprecedented event, the riots were not the first acts of resistance against police harassment of gays, lesbians, and transgendered peoples. Countless acts of individual defiance are recorded in police records, personal documents, and memory. Events on the scale of Stonewall had also occurred. In August 1966, for example, a riot erupted at Crompton's Cafeteria in San Francisco. The local police had tried to arrest a "street queen," who, rather than accept the officer's authority, threw coffee at her tormentors. Fighting broke out and the next day Crompton's was picketed. Many of Crompton's clientele, like the Stonewall rioters three years later, were people whose access to bars and other "protected" spaces was restricted by their lack of class, gender, race, and ethnic privilege.

Unlike Stonewall, however, the Crompton's Cafeteria riots are not commemorated each year by hundreds of thousands of people intent on celebrating gay pride. Though separated by only three years, the two incidents occurred in a radically different context. In 1969 the anti–Vietnam War movement was reaching its height; Martin Luther King Jr. and Robert Kennedy had been assassinated; liberal reform had been discredited for partisans on both the left and the right; and hundreds of thousands of people had "dropped out" and joined the counterculture. Many Americans—some with trepidation, some with anticipation—felt that a revolution was imminent. By the second half of the 1960s, the hundreds of gay men and lesbians who had been organized by the Daughters of Bilitis (DOB) and other homophile groups were becoming increasingly radicalized. The rhetoric of many homophile activists had begun to resemble that of antiwar, black power, radical feminist, and New Left spokespersons. Shelley acquired her political savvy in the DOB and put it to good use in the GLF.

By 1969, the stage was set for a dramatic confrontation. Only one year before Stonewall, the 1968 Democratic national convention was the scene of televised riots where demonstrators yelling "The Whole World Is Watching!" were charged by the police. After Stonewall, gay and lesbian activists were ready to make sure that the whole world was watching once again. Sexual dissidents creating a life in the counterculture were ready to hear their cry and rally around the banner of gay liberation. Stonewall was but a spark that set aflame a bonfire waiting to happen.

Stonewall has become a symbol of enormous power. Like all symbols, Stonewall sometimes obscures as much as it reveals. Transgender, gay, and lesbian resistance did not begin in 1969; countless acts of spontaneous and organized acts of resistance preceded that year. And the men and women who were swept up into gay liberation and lesbian feminism after Stonewall were not necessarily the same people who had fought on the streets of New York City. Street queens and butch lesbians have not held many positions of power in mainstream gay and lesbian political organizations. To truly appreciate the power and the ideals that Stonewall has come to symbolize, we need to construct historical accounts that reflect the complexity of the past. We need accounts that acknowledge the many struggles that preceded and followed the night of June 28, 1969.

Terence Kissack

Bibliography

Anderson, Terry. *The Movement and the Sixties: Protest in America from Greensboro to Wounded Knee.* New York: Oxford University Press, 1995.

D'Emilio, John. *Sexual Politics, Sexual Communities: The Making of a Homosexual Minority in the United States, 1940–1970.* Chicago: University of Chicago Press, 1983.

Duberman, Martin. *Stonewall.* New York: Dutton, 1993.

Feinberg, Leslie. *Transgender Warriors: Making History From Joan of Arc to RuPaul.* Boston: Beacon Press, 1996.

Kennedy, Elizabeth Lapovsky. "Telling Tales: Oral History and the Construction of Pre-Stonewall Lesbian History." *Radical History Review* 62 (Spring 1995).

Marcus, Eric. *Making History: The Struggle for Gay and Lesbian Rights, An Oral History 1945–1990.* New York: HarperPerennial, 1993.

Stryker, Susan, and Jim Van Buskirk. *Gay by the Bay: A History of Queer Culture in the San Francisco Bay Area.* San Francisco: Chronicle Books, 1996.

See also Activism; Gay Liberation; Gay Liberation Front; Marches and Parades; New York City; San Francisco

Strachey, (Giles) Lytton (1880–1932)

Lytton Strachey is justly famous for revolutionizing English biography. His father, General Richard Strachey, was an important official in British India, and his mother, Jane (née Grant), produced thirteen children. Strachey was named for a viceroy of India, the earl Lytton. Considered to be a "funny little creature" by his siblings, he grew up in poor health in a huge London house that his parents could barely afford to maintain. He was educated mainly at home, though he did study briefly at Abbotsholme and at Leamington College, where he was frequently bullied. His precocity and articulate speech were first appreciated at University College, Liverpool, where he studied under Walter Raleigh, whose theatrical lecturing style appealed to Lytton. Strachey often had crushes on other boys, but his homosexual impulses would not be fully explored until he entered Trinity College, Cambridge, in 1899.

As an undergraduate, Strachey became a sensation. His long, thin, ungainly body, his prim and limpid manner, his squeaky voice, and his pince-nez inspired the head porter of Trinity to exclaim, "You wouldn't think he was a general's son." Strachey's intimidating, otherworldly manner gained him both enemies and friends. The latter group included G. E. Moore, Bertrand Russell, E. M. Forster, Leonard Woolf, Clive Bell, and John Maynard Keynes, most of whom were, like Strachey, members of the Apostles, a secret Cambridge society that championed the "higher sodomy." After graduation, Strachey fell

S

Duncan Grant's portrait of Lytton Strachey reading State Trials, *1909. Tate Gallery, London/Art Resource, NY.*

in love with his cousin Duncan Grant; as that passion cooled, he became attached to the core of the early Bloomsbury group, the Stephenses: Thoby, Adrian, Vanessa (later Bell), and especially Virginia (later Woolf).

Strachey was a pacifist during World War I; when asked what he would do if he saw a German soldier trying to rape his sister, he famously replied with characteristic wit and double entendre, "I should try and come between them." During this period he became close to society hostess Lady Ottoline Morrell; he also met painter Dora Carrington, with whom, despite his strong homosexual proclivities, he developed an intense romantic friendship that lasted for the rest of their lives. He lived with Carrington more or less continuously beginning in 1917, for a time in a complicated domestic arrangement—a *ménage*—with her husband, Ralph Partridge. Strachey had numerous lovers, notably Roger Senhouse, but his relationship with Carrington would always be the central emotional bond in his life. She killed herself within days of his death from cancer.

Strachey published only one book before World War I, *Landmarks in French Literature* (1912), which did not bring him the fame that he sought. But he became famous and notorious with the publication of *Eminent Victorians* (1918), a suite of biographical portraits that form a witty attack on Victorian values and culture. His other important books are the more stately and sympathetic *Queen Victoria* (1921) and the salacious *Elizabeth and Essex* (1928). Strachey's "Mandarin camp" biographical style is firmly in the tradition of Oscar Wilde. His emphasis on fun over facts and his flair for the dramatic and the use of *le mot juste*, sometimes to the detriment of historical truth, have influenced biographers from Virginia Woolf (particularly her *Orlando*) to Kitty Kelly.　　　　*George Piggford*

Bibliography

Holroyd, Michael. *Lytton Strachey: The New Biography*. New York: Farrar, Straus and Giroux, 1994.
Spurr, Barry. *Diabolical Art: The Achievement of Lytton Strachey*. New York: Edwin Mellen, 1994.

See also Bloomsbury Group; Forster, E. M.; Grant, Duncan; Keynes, John Maynard

Strayhorn, Billy (1915–1967)

Billy Strayhorn is the composer of such standard jazz works that were not only important as songs in their own right but also as the basic building blocks of the jazz genre, the melodies of which form the foundations on which jazz musicians expound to create improvisations—like "Satin Doll," "Take the 'A' Train," "Lotus Blossom," "The Star Crossed Lovers," "Lush Life," and "Chelsea Bridge." He spent the formative years of his life in Pittsburgh, summering with his paternal grandparents in Hillsborough, N.C. His initial interests in music were cultivated by his grandmother, who played the piano for the choir of her church. Strayhorn began composing at a very early age, writing the uniquely structured "Lush Life" while still in his teens.

In his biography of Strayhorn, David Hadju documents how, in 1938, the brash youngster originally cemented his lifelong creative partnership with the already old master Duke Ellington by first playing a tune on the piano for Ellington, demonstrating Ellington's own voicing, and then playing the same tune again in his own style. Ellington, immensely impressed by Strayhorn as a composer of similar artistic vision, brought Strayhorn into the Ellington organization, where he continued to create until his alcohol-related death from cancer. Having studied the works of composers like Stravinsky, Strayhorn is credited with having helped jazz from the more lyrically based and rhythmically static bebop style to a more complexly orchestrated form, paving the way for later avant-garde artists like Miles Davis.

One of the central questions of Strayhorn's life is why the possessor of such formidable talent allowed Ellington to take credit for so much of his work. Hadju posits that Strayhorn, as an introverted gay man who was never apologetic about his homosexuality living in 1940s America, preferred working in Ellington's shadow to the possibility of enjoying his own limelight, as it allowed him to move freely through closed but private circles.

Matthew Williams

Bibliography

Hadju, David. *Lush Life: A Biography of Billy Strayhorn.* New York: Farrar, Straus and Giroux, 1997.

See also Music and Musicians 1: Classical Music; Music and Musicians 2: Popular Music; Musical Theater

Student Organizations

Lesbian and gay student organizations play significant roles within the developing cultures of lesbian and gay identities and communities. Historically, several campus groups in Australia, the United States, and Europe were strongly affiliated with or responsible for founding some of the major lesbian and gay political rights groups during the late 1960s and early 1970s. The Student Homophile League (U.S.) was founded by Rita Mae Brown in 1968; Australia's first lesbian and gay activist organization, CAMP Inc., maintained strong links with student organizations at the University of Sydney and Macquarie University.

Today student organizations, though frequently politically active, play a different role within universities and other student institutions. Recent research has suggested that debates over the advances in gay rights have tended to cause campus tensions that include homophobic attitudes and antigay violence. Three areas of sexuality-related student organization activity can be identified.

The first is the provision of a social network for lesbian and gay students and university staff. By providing social and emotional support for students in the process of coming out and developing a non-heteronormative sexual identity, these organizations have facilitated what has been identified as a necessary source of support and affirmation for students questioning their sexuality. High rates of sexuality-related suicide have increased the need for organizations that redress feelings of isolation and alienation and furnish ways for students to discuss or explore their sexuality, an important element in their sexual development. The failure of attempts in recent years to reduce sexuality-related suicide among students is perhaps an indication of the failure of student organizations to provide appropriate support.

A secondary function of campus organizations is the promotion of an awareness of lesbian and gay issues on campuses and a concentrated increase in the visibility of nonheteronormative sexualities. Frequently lesbian and gay students have been left to educate campus communities about issues relating to the oppression of and discrimination against these students. By prompting student affairs administrators to improve the environment and "safety"

A student activist. Photo by Marc Geller.

resulted in their perceived marginalization, student organizations have been in a position to promote a social and cultural questioning of values, assumptions, and belief systems both on campus and in the wider community. Frequently student organizations have highlighted concerns of heterosexism in course and textbook content, library resources, and graduate career opportunities.

The histories of gay and lesbian student organizations in Britian and the United States illustrate both tensions and successes. In Britain, most higher education institutions (HEs), a number of further education institutions (FEs), and sixth-form colleges (age sixteen and over) have lesbian, gay, and bisexual (LGB) student groups and societies. The LGB student groups are formed by students often with the support of student unions or student services of the institutions. The National Union of Students (NUS) accommodates an LGB campaign to support LGB students and staff in educational institutions. The NUS LGB campaign provides advice and resources for students to set up their LGB societies at further and higher education colleges.

NUS and Stonewall are the two main organizations that incorporate equal rights for LGB students into their campaigns. NUS LGB campaign integrates the efforts of individual LGB student groups by providing networking and training support and organizing biannual LGB conferences. The activists participating in the NUS LGB conferences set the policies and priorities of the campaign and elect the National Committee and convenors. The LGB campaign of NUS was formed with the motivation gained from the wider gay liberation movement in the early 1970s, but it acquired its current formal structure in the mid-1980s. Stonewall, on the other hand, incorporates "equality at school" in its national campaign, Equality 2000.

Both national campaigning groups of LGB student activists aim at dealing with homophobia, discrimination, and hate crime. The student campaigns focus on two of the most infamous aspects of legal inequality in Britain: equalizing the age of consent for lesbian and heterosexual sex (currently sixteen years of age) with gay male sex (currently eighteen years of age), and repeal of Clause 28 (Section 28) of 1988, which banned the local authorities from intentionally promoting homosexuality, publishing material with the intention of promoting homosexuality, and recognizing homosexual partnerships as a form of "pretended" family relationship as part of the teaching in any maintained schools. The politi-

for lesbian, gay, bisexual, and transgender students, student organizations have encouraged several university administrations to institute campus regulations that provide protection against discrimination of nonheterosexual students. By coordinating coming-out rallies, educational programs, speakers panels, and, on many university campuses worldwide, "pride week" activities, student organizations have been instrumental in raising the visibility of nonheterosexual students, which has been seen as a necessary step toward changing societal perceptions of lesbian and gay people. A perceived frequency of "open" contact between heterosexual and nonheterosexual students has been correlated with increased levels of tolerance among university populations, and such activities facilitate further development of visibility and cross-sexually-identified contact.

The increased visibility of lesbian and gay students and faculty members has promoted social change and acceptance of lesbian and gay sexualities—the third function of student organizations. By organizing around the part of their identity that has cal campaign gained acceleration with recent changes in the British political scene. The 1997 general election resulted in a change in government from the Conservative to the Labour Party. Many people believe that the new Labour government will lift the legal restrictions put into place by the previous government. At the general election, over one hundred Conservative MPs who had voted against an equal age of consent lost their seats, mostly to Labour or Liberal Democrat candidates who support equal age of consent. This political change has raised hopes for legal equality for lesbians, gays, and bisexuals in Britain.

In the United States, the original gay student organizations formed in the months following Stonewall in 1969; groups at Columbia University, University of California at Berkeley, University of Kansas, and New York University were among the first. Many of the original groups were born from, or as, efforts of the Gay Liberation Front (GLF), and reflected the liberation politics and social activism of the GLF.

Gay student organizations in the 1970s were dominated by two themes: litigation and social activity. Colleges and universities disallowed recognition of such groups, while students filed suits to force campuses to accept them (and their meetings and dances) on campus. Many of the cases, particularly those concerning the University of Kansas, University of New Hampshire, Virginia Commonwealth University, University of Missouri, and University of Oklahoma, established important precedents for nondiscrimination, equality of access, and funding opportunities for all student organizations.

By the early 1980s, the legal climate had calmed, and student organizations began focusing on social services as well as social activities. Support groups, speaker bureaus, lending libraries, and community outreach programs (particularly public dances in schools not in metropolitan areas) became staples of the organizations.

In the late 1980s, university communities increasingly accepted gay student groups, while the organizations showed indications of returning to earlier activism. Spurred by the actions of social movements ACT UP and Queer Nation, gay students fought against personal discrimination on campus, as well as continued general discrimination. Many worked to include sexual orientation in institutions' nondiscrimination statements, and, when successful, argued that ROTC activity on campus violated those statements, since ROTC would not accept any gay or lesbian student/recruit into its program. Occasionally, these activities resulted in campuswide reviews of quality of life for gay students, faculty, and staff; as is the nature of higher education, committees were established to assess campuses and to recommend changes. The committees issued reports, but, with a few notable exceptions (particularly Rutgers University and the University of Massachusetts at Amherst), little lasting climatic or academic change resulted from these efforts. Gay students did become more aware of higher education governance processes, however, and more out students became involved in student politics and campus governance.

The return to activism was met by a return to litigation. By the early 1990s, conservative student governments protested, and occasionally rescinded, student fee funding for gay student organizations. State legislatures, such as Alabama's and Colorado's, reflected conservative values and initiatives, passing antigay legislation aimed at student organizations (particularly in the case of Alabama, where state senators were angered when the administration of Auburn University overturned the student government's ban on funding Auburn's gay student organization). These initiatives were eventually overturned by the courts as examples of illegal discrimination.

In fewer than thirty years, the number of gay student organizations in higher education grew from a handful in 1968 to over two thousand in 1996. The University of Michigan alone boasted over twenty gay student organizations, including groups based on ethnic origin, religious affiliation, and academic major. Such diversity in organizations reflects the changes of interest and activities, as well as the diversification of the gay student population, on college campuses at the end of the twentieth century.

Rob Cover (Australia)
Patrick Dilley (United States)
Fatih Ozbilgin (United Kingdom)

Bibliography

Baker, Judith A. "Gay Nineties: Addressing the Needs of Homosexual Community and Junior College Students and Faculty." *Community/Junior College* 15, no. 1 (1991): 25–32.

D'Emilio, John. *Making Trouble: Essays on Gay History, Politics, and the University*. New York: Routledge, 1992.

Gose, B. "The Politics and Images of Gay Students." *Chronicle of Higher Education* 42, no. 22 (February 9, 1996): A33–A34.

MacKay, A., ed. *Wolf Girls at Vassar: Lesbian and Gay Experiences, 1930–1990.* New York: St. Martin's Press, 1993.

Marotta, T. *Sons of Harvard: Gay Men from the Class of 1967.* New York: Quill, 1983.

McClintock, Mary. "Sharing Lesbian, Gay, and Bisexual Life Experiences Face to Face." *Journal of Experiential Education* 15, no. 3 (1992).

National Union of Students Information Pack, 1997.

Rhoads, Robert A. "The Cultural Politics of Coming Out in College: Experiences of Male Students." *Review of Higher Education* 19, no. 2 (1995): 1–22.

———. "Implications of the Growing Visibility of Gay and Bisexual Male Students on Campus." *NASPA Journal* 34, no. 4 (1997): 275–86.

Sanford, Michele, and Catherine McHugh Engstrom. "Attitudes Toward Gay and Lesbian Students: An Investigation of Resident Advisers." *Journal of College and University Student Housing* 25, no. 2 (1995): 26–30.

Stonewall Newsletter: Equality 2000 5, no. 3 (August 1997): 4.

Thompson, Denise. *Flaws in the Social Fabric: Homosexuals and Society in Sydney.* Sydney: Allen & Unwin, 1985.

Suicide

Suicide is the act of an individual, or group, voluntarily ending their own life or lives. This may be in response to the individual's having exhausted her or his own ability to tolerate grief or disappointment. Alternatively suicide may be a response to unbearable pain or humiliation.

There are five commonly advanced explanations for suicidal behavior. The first sees it as linked to experiences in the early family, such as acute love withdrawal, being the firstborn child or an only child, or to the suicidal behavior of relatives. The second type of explanation focuses on cultural factors, such as the demand within Western societies that men should be strong, which may lead to men being less able to cope with grief and emotional distress than women. The social explanation focuses on the potential for conflict between the interests of the individual and the interests of the group, such as an individual who feels social pressure to subordinate his or her own feelings or needs to those of the larger group. This explanation is most relevant to the position of members of sexual, racial, or other minorities stigmatized by the wider society. The fourth avenue of exploration recognizes the higher rate of suicide among the unemployed and economically disadvantaged. This economic explanation stresses the relative fall in suicide rates among elderly males as social security systems improve. The fifth type of explanation sees suicide as a response to the pressures of modernization. Urbanization, industrialization, and the decline in community spirit all contribute to a rise in suicide.

Suicide is known to occur in both genders and across the age range. Different types of explanations would be more appropriate in different age ranges. Suicides among children are not likely to be a response to economic pressures; that is a more convincing explanation among older men. It is also clear that many of these explanations could be linked. Gay, lesbian, or bisexual people, for example, may have experienced the withdrawal of love from members of their family as a result of their sexuality. This may be linked to the cultural and social pressures to conform to dominant cultural values and social norms. This can lead to feelings of social isolation, poor feelings of self-worth, and difficulties in terms of self-acceptance. Such stigma and isolation could well lead to thoughts of suicide or to actual suicide attempts.

Cultural differences also manifest themselves in terms of attitudes to suicide. Some societies, such as Japan, have had an appreciation of the noble suicide as a way of self-sacrifice in favor of the interests of the group or the notion of suicide as preferable to a loss of personal honor. This contrasts with an overwhelmingly negative view of suicide in the West, where it has been traditionally seen as an offense against religious law that could prevent the individual from receiving a religious burial. In many societies attempted suicide has also been a criminal offense.

Gay men, lesbians, bisexuals, and transgendered people are sometimes prone to suicidal feelings or attempts. In studies by Rofes, it is reported that 40 percent of gay or bisexual men and 39 percent of women had attempted or considered suicide. At least half these individuals identified their sexual orientation as being a contributory factor to these feelings.

Suicide prevention and intervention programs are important to prevent suicidal feelings from turning into reality. Prevention is longer-term and involves eliminating stigma, homophobia, and social rejection and marginalization that could lead individuals to feel isolated and suicidal. Intervention is focused more on working with individuals at risk and ensuring that individuals with suicidal feelings might seek support and/or counseling.

Reducing the rate of suicide among lesbian, gay, and bisexual people must be a priority for the gay community and for society at large.

Robert J. Buckley

Bibliography

Rofes, Eric E. *"I Thought People Like That Killed Themselves": Lesbians, Gay Men and Suicide.* San Francisco: Gay Fox Press, 1983.

See also Community Centers; Counseling; Homophobia; Samuraí

Susa, Conrad (1935–)

The music of American composer Conrad Susa possesses a remarkably expressive power born of a fierce and authentic individuality. The first composer ever commissioned by a gay men's chorus, Susa incorporates his experience as a gay man into his work as a matter of course, without becoming constrained by a specific gender ideology. Indifferent to the reigning fashions, Susa has forged an inimitable style based as much on his love of the music of Handel and Purcell as on his study of twentieth-century composers such as Stravinsky and Shostakovich. Susa is concerned with the relationship of composers to their communities, and has reached a wide community of performers and listeners by creating many beautifully crafted choral works. Several of these works have become indispensable additions to the choral repertory: *Chanticleer's Carol,* for male chorus (1983); the Magnificat and Nunc Dimittis, for mixed chorus and organ (1987); and *Carols and Lullabies From the Southwest,* for chorus, guitar, harp, and percussion (1992).

The heart of Susa's achievement is his five operas. His first, *Transformations* (1973), is one of the most frequently performed operas by an American composer. Based on poems by Anne Sexton, *Transformations* is a lively and disquieting meditation on the creative process that contains a memorable scene of lesbian seduction. Two years later, Susa finished the first version of *Black River: A Wisconsin Idyll* (revised 1993), with a libretto by the composer and his partner, librettist Richard Street. Later revised and reorchestrated, *Black River* takes as its subject the triumph of the human spirit over defeat and loss; the on-stage immolation with which it closes rises to a grandeur comparable to the final scene of Janáček's *Makroupoulos Case.* Susa's third opera, *The Love of Don Perlimplin* (libretto by Susa and Street after Lorca, 1984) is a dashing tragicomic tale of Spanish honor and thwarted love, while his fourth opera, *The Wise Women* (libretto by Susa and Phillip Littell, 1994), is a Christmas pastoral filled with luminous warmth tempered by a tough and irrepressible wit. Susa's latest opera, *The Dangerous Liaisons* (libretto by Susa and Littell after Laclos, 1994; revised 1996–1997), is a masterly study of the destruction wrought by devouring passion and habitual self-deception.

Born in rural Pennsylvania, Susa attended Carnegie Mellon University, where he studied with Lopatnikoff, and the Julliard School, where his teachers included Bergsma and Persichetti. After a hectic period of activity in New York, Susa moved to San Francisco in 1971. He subsequently held posts as resident composer for the Old Globe theater in San Diego and as dramaturge for the O'Neill Center in New London, Connecticut; in 1988 he joined the faculty of the San Francisco Conservatory. Susa has received various honors and awards, including the George Gershwin Memorial Scholarship, the Gretchaninoff Prize, a grant from the Ford Foundation, and two grants from the National Endowment for the Arts.

Byron Adams

Bibliography

Humphrey, Mary Lou. "Conrad Susa." In *The New Grove Dictionary of Opera,* Vol. 4. New York: Macmillan, 1992.

Jackson, Gilbert Otis. "The Choral Music of Conrad Susa." Ph.D. dissertation, Michigan State University, 1984.

See also Handel, George Frideric; Music and Musicians 1: Classical Music; Opera

Sweden

Sweden, a country of almost nine million inhabitants, has a record of liberal social relations. Many of the controversies on the labor market and concerning the distribution of wealth have been solved peacefully by negotiations between the parties concerned. The struggle for equality has been hard, but fairly successful until the 1990s, when a change in social climate could be noticed. The same could be said regarding sexual relations. A long tradition of liberal and free sex makes Sweden the third country

S

to adopt a law of partnership between adult homosexuals. All the Scandinavian countries except Finland now have the same laws.

Medieval Times

One of the first recorded instances of same-sex love in Sweden is found in the revelations of Sankta Bridget. She accuses King Magnus Eriksson (ruled 1332–1363) of unnatural intercourse with a nobleman, Bengt Algotsson. Bridget accuses the king of "loving men more than God or your own soul or your own spouse." His queen was Blanche of Namur. Sankta Bridget was a powerful person in the political intrigues of these years. She had a political purpose in her way of presenting her religious ideas.

Seventeenth Century

Not much is known about sex crimes in Sweden during the seventeenth century. But there was an addendum to the law in 1608 that specified the death penalty for same-sex sexual relations between adult males. The law was copied from the Mosaic Law in the Old Testament. There was no prohibition against women having sex with each other. A few cases of same-sex love crimes are known from this period. Punishment was severe. One of the most prominent instances of same-sex love in the seventeenth century concerns Queen Christina (reigned 1632–1654). She reportedly fell in love with one of her best friends, Ebba Sparre—*"la belle comtesse"*—and abdicated in 1654.

Eighteenth Century

There is one recorded case of cross-dressing and marriage between two persons of the same sex in eighteenth-century Sweden, where one of the two participants dressed and lived like a man. A woman named Ulrika Eleonora Stålhammar changed dress and became Wilhelm Edstedt. She joined the armed forces and worked in the artillery between 1715 and 1726. She married Maria Lönman in April 1716. After she was dismissed from the military ranks, she wanted to return to womanhood. The case was brought before a court of law, which sentenced her to one month in prison; then she was sent to a relative to live like the lady of the nobility she was.

The law code of 1734 did not contain any reference to same-sex love crimes. Some researchers believe that the law commission recommended that same-sex love not be criminalized on the theory that ignorance would be much better than the publicity that would arise around these questions in a trial. Yet

there were trials concerning same-sex love. In 1761 farmhand Arvid Arvidsson was condemned to death for trying to commit sodomy, but the verdict was later changed.

During the reign of Gustav III (1772–1792), there was much talk about same-sex love. The king himself was accused of loving men, and gossip had it that he had help in producing an heir to the throne. Gustav III loved opera and the arts, and his reign is a golden age of cultural achievements.

Nineteenth Century

After the French Revolution the influence of the Code Napoléon on legislative assemblies in Europe was important. The code did not state any punishment against these kind of crimes. Though Sweden was never conquered by Napoleon, it took a new royal family from one of the Marshals de France, the Bernadotte family, which rules Sweden today. Not until 1864 was there any law against same-sex love. Sweden here followed many of the German states, which around the same time reintroduced laws regulating "unnatural behavior." This was partly due to Prussia's domination of the German states.

Erik Sjöberg Vitalis (1794–1828) was a romantic poet not well known today but important in his own time. He held a romantic friendship with another young poet, Karl August Nicander (1799–1839). Vitalis is known for his *Sånger till mannen i månen* (Songs to the Man in the Moon), poems with a strong sentiment of same-sex love. He exploited the Greek tradition in literature for his own purpose, like so many other romantic poets. Wilhelm Erik Svedelius (1816–1889) was professor of history and political science and became a member of the Swedish Academy. He has written about his own romantic affair, in his youth, with Gustaf Sebastian Leijonhufvud, who died at the age of sixteen. A prominent figure in philosophy during the last decades of the nineteenth century was Pontus Wikner (1837–1888). He presented a speech called *"Kulturens offerväsen"* (The Sacrificial Nature of Culture, 1880), in which he develops, in a veiled fashion, the same thoughts as in a posthumous work *Psykologiska självbekännelser* (Psychological Confessions) from 1879. The *Confessions* were published in 1971, almost a century after his death. In them he describes his longing for men and the almost carnal worship of Jesus that became a part of his religion. This sexual yearning is filled with agony because of the ignorance of society at large.

He advocates marriage between members of the same sex. Wikner died young, having been a professor of philosophy in Kristiania, Norway, for only four years. Another writer with a longing for young men was Viktor Rydberg (1828–1895). He was a prominent liberal journalist in Gothenburg for a period of his life. After having gone to Italy in 1874 to get over a crisis, he was inspired by the antique statues in Rome. *Romerska kejsare i marmor* (Roman Emperors in Marble) includes a story called "Antinous" (1875), in which Rydberg paints the life of Emperor Hadrian's lover. In his youth Rydberg was a private tutor to and possibly also lover of Rudolf Ström. One of the most prominent figures in Swedish literature, Selma Lagerlöf (1858–1940), famous writer of novels and fairy tales, member of the Swedish Academy, lived the life of a lesbian, as is well known after the publication of her correspondence with fellow writer Sophie Elkan (1853–1921). Valborg Olander was another important woman in the life of Selma.

During the late nineteenth century the decadent movement was a strong force in cultural life. Ola Hansson (1860–1925) was one of the exponents of this literary current. His collection of short stories, *Sensitiva amorosa* (1887), contained a story on a same-sex love theme, although he himself was not gay.

The Twentieth Century

The newspapers reveled in a scandal involving homosexuals in 1907. This was the first time the word was used with a wider audience. The scandal involved Nils Santesson, factory owner and designer, and created a lively discussion of the subject of homosexuality. Many intellectuals spoke openly after the scandal. Painter Eugène Jansson (1862–1915) changed his lifestyle radically and displayed a flamboyant attitude after 1907. From this time on his paintings are filled with naked men who are bathing, exercising, or just posing in the studio. Vilhelm Ekelund (1880–1949) was a poet with a flair for Greek love. He adored the young boy's body in his lyrics, for instance in *In Candidum* (1905), and had many friends among the well-known gay writers of his time. He is still regarded as an outstanding Swedish poet. He later married and had children.

An outstanding painter was Gösta Adrian-Nilsson, called GAN (1884–1965), who painted in cubist style where strong colors and strength of composition is predominant. He favored sailors as models both in real life and on the canvas. His contemporary

Nils Dardel (1888–1943), bisexual painter of class, was more of a dandy who painted *Den döende dandyn* (The Dying Dandy), which today could be viewed as an emblem of gay sensibility.

Finland has produced many fine Swedish-language poets. Gunnar Björling (1887–1960) wrote excellent poetry in a very reduced syntax. His small apartment in the cellar of a villa at Brunnsparken in Helsinki saw many young men pass through. Björling was known for his modesty and discretion. Another well-known Finnish-Swedish writer is Tove Jansson (1917–), who has lived her life with Tuulikki, a person who enters into her children's fairy tales about *Mumintrollet* (The Mumin Troll) in the name of Too-tikki. Another woman she shared part of her life with was Vivica Bandler (1917–), a well-known theater manager and intellectual in her own right. Already in 1925 Mauritz Stiller (1883–1928), another Swede of Finnish origin, and Greta Garbo (née Gustafsson) (1905–1994), from Stockholm, went to America to find their future in filmmaking in Hollywood. Stiller rented a villa by the ocean. There they met silent film star Nils Asther (1897–1981), who played a secondary role in one of Stiller's movies, *Vingarne* (The Wings, 1916), probably the first same-sex love movie in the world, based on a story by Danish writer Herman Bang. Garbo went on to achieve iconic status as perhaps the most beautiful woman of the century, at least in film, and was known to have had numerous affairs with women and men. The theater in Stockholm held a historian of outstanding quality in Anders De Wahl (1869–1956). A true diva who never could stand an equal, he was known to favor military men. And there was only one actor to equal him, Gösta Ekman (1890–1938), a bisexual dandy who set the standard for how young men should behave in the Roaring Twenties.

One of the most celebrated poets of her time was Karin Boye (1900–1941), admired for the force of her poems and her skill. She was also an influential intellectual during the 1930s. In an attempt to resolve her lesbianism, she went to Berlin, where she met Margot Hanel, who followed her back to Sweden. But life was never calm for Boye. In 1941 she committed suicide. An outstanding and discriminating literary critic was Klara Johanson (1875–1948), who preferred writers of an inclination toward same-sex love. She appreciated young writers Ivar Conradson (1884–1968) and Gustaf Otto Adelborg (1883–1965), an eccentric couple of the times. And she held high esteem for Emil Kléen

S (1868–1898), a poet of Baudelairian tastes. Klara Johanson had a crush on Lydia Wahlström (1869–1954), an outstanding figure in the Swedish feminist movement, and they lived together for some years. Wahlström was also part of an influential group of women called Fogelstadgruppen (Fogelstad Group).

Karl Gerhard (1891–1964) played an important role as leader of vaudeville shows during the 1920s and 1930s. He also acted in his own shows and became popular because of his songs. He lived together with another man and adopted a girl whom they called Fatima.

The early 1950s represented the worst period of repression of homosexuals during the twentieth century in Sweden. The so-called Haijby and Kejne affairs drew attention to blackmail and prostitution that was said to flourish in the wake of legalizing homosexuality in 1944. Involvement at the very highest levels of society was indicated. A cabinet minister, Nils Quensel, was named and a thorough investigation followed. A writer of gay erotic stories, Nils Hallbeck (Jan Hogan, 1907–), wrote a number of books from the 1940s to the present. *Grabb på glid* (Boy Going Astray) and *Brinnande blomma* (Burning Flower, both 1949) started his writing career. Another writer of deeper artistic value, Bengt Söderbergh (1925–), started his career with a novel in existentialist fashion, *Den förstenade* (The Petrified, 1948), with faintly homosexual themes, but he became known to a larger audience in 1977 when he published *En livslång kärlek* (A Lifelong Love). Eva Alexandersson (1911–1994) wrote *Kontradans* (Counterdance) with a lesbian theme. She developed a long career in publishing firms and as an author. Paul Andersson (1930–1976) was a bisexual poet inspired by Rimbaud in his life and his writing. His life became legend, but his poetry does not touch upon the subject of homosexuality. Gösta Carlberg (1909–1973), a friend of his, wrote a number of books, some of which had a homosexual theme, such as *Den sparade ynglingen* (The Saved Young Man, 1954). Birgitta Stenberg (1932–) became one of the most celebrated lesbian writers in the 1980s with her novels based on her own experiences in Europe in the 1950s, together with Paul Andersson. *Kärlek i Europa* (Love in Europe, 1981) and *Apelsinmannen* (The Orange Man, 1983) became a huge success. They are part of four novels delineating the life of the author. Barbro Alving (Bang) (1909–1987) was a famous journalist from the thirties to the sixties. She lived with another woman, and they raised a child together.

Allan Hellman (1905–1983) was an engineer living in Lysekil, on the west coast of Sweden. He can be called the founding father of the Swedish gay movement. He came in contact with the Danish group Forbundet af 1948 and decided to start a parallel section of the group. In 1950 he founded the Swedish section, which became the Riksförbundet för sexuellt likaberättigande (RFSL, Swedish Federation for Lesbian and Gay Rights). Discretion was the word of the day; people went by pseudonyms and had to be recommended by two members to be accepted into the organization. The smaller local groups of RFSL make up the backbone of the movement. Hellman gave his name to the café in RFSL of Gothenburg. He was honored by many young activists in the seventies and eighties.

During the sexually liberal 1960s a series of books was published called *Kärlek* (Love, 1965–1970), in fourteen parts. It caused a storm of media interest. Anna-Karin Svedberg (1934–) became famous when she cowrote in this series. Before that she published a book called *Vingklippta* (Clipped Wings, 1962), which had a few descriptions of lesbian love and of gay milieus. There were a few attempts to discuss homosexuality openly; in 1968, one televised program, *Storforum* (Big Forum), brought Bengt Martin (1933–) into every household. He became, at the time, the foremost spokesman for homosexuals, together with his partner, Hans. They became *the* homosexual couple in Sweden. Martin had published a book about a young man who came to know his gay side, what today would be called a coming-out story, *Sodomsäpplet* (Apple of Sodom, 1968).

After founding new branches of the old RFSL and working openly under their actual names, during the early 1970s, as a result of the upheavals of the late 1960s, a new kind of research into gay history began. Now was the time to unveil all that had been previously hushed. One of the most prominent researchers during this period was Fredrik Silverstolpe (1947–), who worked for some time with two important books, *En homosexuell arbetares memoarer* (The Memoirs of a Homosexual Worker, 1981) and *Fångarna med rosa triangel* (Pink Triangle Prisoners, 1984). Both set a standard for the future of how to write gay history. The homosexual worker concerned was Eric Thorsell (1899–1980), who was an indefatigable writer on homosexual themes during a time when the law prohibited explicit homosexuality.

During the 1990s there has been an outspoken attitude toward gay themes in literature as never before. Jonas Gardell (1963–) worked in that genre more as a stand-up comedian than as an author. His books include *En komikers uppväxt* (The Growth of a Comedian, 1992). He has cohabitated with Mark Levengood, director of children's programs in the state television. A new genre was the coming-out story. Hans Olsson (1962–) made his debut in this genre with the novel *Spelar roll* (Plays a Role, 1993). Another writer to come out in the open with a story about same-sex love was Louise Boije af Gennäs (1961–). She wrote a story copied on life, "Stjärnor utan svindel" (Stars without Dizziness, (1996), in which she describes, in a fictitious way, how she fell in love with her partner, Mian Lodalen, journalist and feminist.

Other writers who exploited the theme of gay experiences were Malin Backström (1961–), with a book of prose poems called *Berättelser som inte får vidröras* (Stories Not to Be Touched Upon, 1997); Eva Leijonsommar, with the novels *Stilla Tiger* (Still Silent, 1991) and *Att älska henne* (To Love Her, 1995); and Anna Karin Granberg (1959–), with the novel *Där ingenting kan ses* (Where Nothing Can Be Seen, 1992).

A new phenomenon was the attention that the mass media gave to gay celebrities. Eva Dahlgren, a popular singer, started living openly with Efva Attling, and they were closely followed by media. Jonas Gardell lived with Mark Levengood, and what they did was recorded in the tabloid press. Well-known hair dressers and other gay people were also followed by the evening papers.

Gay Periodicals

An early information periodical was *Revolt mot sexuella fördomar* (Revolt Against Sexual Prejudice, 1971–86), edited by Michael Holm (1933–). It started in the seventies, a time of freedom fighting from all repressed groups in the West. Holm also published a book called *Udda Eros* (Queer Eros, 1971). *Revolt* had a drawback in its appearance of a porno magazine. During the eighties and nineties gay periodicals became more like house publications in defense of a repressed group. Jon Voss (1959–) and Dodo Parikas (1956–) started *Magazine Gay* (1983–84) and went on to publish *Reporter* in 1986–1995, an influential publication. Later Voss started the free magazine *QX* (from 1995 onward). *Kom Ut* (Come Out, 1980–) is the name of the membership periodical of RFSL. It has flourished under Greger Eman (1952–), who has maintained a high standard. Research in the area of ho-

mosexuality can be found in *Lambda Nordica* (1989 and 1995–), a magazine inaugurated by distinguished researcher Benny Henriksson (1947–1995) and continued by Göran Söderström (1934–). These magazines all have an outspoken, activist attitude toward nonhomosexuals.

The Partnership Law

A persistent effort to legalize same-sex unions started in the eighties but had a long prehistory. An important victory for the political gay movement struggle came in 1979. Socialstyrelsen (State Authority on Social and Medical Affairs) decided to ban the sickness label for homosexuality. A thorough state investigation into the questions of homosexuality led to an official report in 1984 called *Homosexuella och samhället* (Homosexuals and Society). From this investigation on, the goal for the political gay movement was to legalize same-sex unions. For some time it seemed as if Sweden was to become the first country in the world to adopt a law of marriage between members of the same sex. However, both Denmark (1989) and Norway adopted the partnership law before Sweden did. In 1994 the law was accepted and from January 1, 1995, it was in force. The partnership law made an exception for children; gay couples cannot adopt children or take each others' children from earlier marriages into custody. The struggle continues to equalize heterosexual and homosexual married life.

Jan Magnusson

Bibliography

Andreasson, Martin. *Öppenhet och motstånd: Om homosexualitet i massmedia 1990–1994* (Openness and Resistance: On Homosexuality in the Media 1990–1994). Stockholm: Folkhälsoinstitutet, 1996.

Bergenheim, Åsa, and Lena Lennerhed, eds. *Seklernas sex: Bidrag till sexualitetens historia* (Sex of the Centuries: Contributions to the History of Sexuality). Stockholm: Carlssons, 1997.

Eman, Greger. *Nya himlar över en ny jord—om Klara Johansson, Lydia Wahlström och den feministiska vänskapskärleken* (New Heavens Over a New Earth: About Klara Johansson, Lydia Wahlström, and the Feminist Friendship Love). Stockholm, Sweden: Ellerströms, 1993.

Gustafsson, Barbro K. *Stenåker och ängsmark: Erotiska motiv och homosexuella skildringar i Tove Janssons senare litteratur* (Stone Field and Meadowland: Erotic Motifs and Homosexual

S

Depictions in Tove Jansson's Later Literature). Uppsala Studies in Social Ethics, 13. Uppsala, Sweden: Almqvist & Wiksell, 1992.

Hammarström, Camilla. *Karin Boye*. Stockholm, Sweden: Natur och Kultur, 1997.

Homosexuella och samhället: Betänkande av utredningen om homosexuellas situation isamhället (Homosexuals and Society: From the Official Report on the Situation of Homosexuals in Society). Stockholm, Sweden: Liber/Allmänna förlaget, 1984.

Johannesson, Lechard. *Pontus Wikner: Dagböckerna berättar* (Pontus Wikner: The Diaries tell). Doxa, 1982.

Lambda nordica: Tidskrift om homosexualitet (Lambda Nordica: Journal on Homosexuality). Stockholm, Sweden, 1989–1995.

Rydström, Jens. *Översikt: Homosexualitetens historia—ett försummat forskningsfält* (Survey: The History of Homosexuality—A Neglected Field of Research). *Historisk Tidskrift* 3 (1995): 338–54.

Silverstolpe, Fredrik. *En homosexuell arbetares memoarer: Järnbruksarbetaren Eric Thorsell berättar* (The Memoirs of a Homosexual Worker: The Ironworks Worker Eric Thorsell Tells). Stockholm, Sweden: Barrikaden, 1981.

Sympatiens hemlighetsfulla makt: Stockholms homosexuella 1860–1960 (The Secret Power of Sympathy: The Homosexuals of Stockholm 1860–1960). Stockholm, Sweden: Stockholmia förlag, 1998.

See also Activism, International; Bang, Herman; Code Napoléon; Coming Out; Denmark; Domestic Partnership; Film Stars; Finland; Papacy; Politics, Global; RFSL, Rimbaud, Arthur; Rome, Ancient; Same-Sex Marriage; Transvestism

Switchboards, Gay

Gay switchboards—telephone counseling and information services staffed by gay and lesbian volunteers—proliferated in the 1970s in North America and western Europe, and now exist in many large cities around the world. In a world before the Internet, the World Wide Web, commercialized sex phone lines, and glossy gay magazines, switchboards disseminated the messages of gay liberation to a wider audience than coming-out groups and small press publications, concentrated in metropolitan centers, could reach.

Pre-Stonewall homophile groups made limited use of the telephone as a tool for education and organization, with certain noteworthy exceptions, such as San Francisco Daughters of Bilitis leader Del Martin's "Citizens' Alert" (1965), a hotline for victims of police brutality, or Holland's COC (Center for Culture and Recreation, a homophile self-help organization). Before the 1970s the lines of communication in lesbian and gay communities were chiefly confined to informal friendship networks and to subscriptions to newsletters and physique magazines.

Patterned after phone counseling services aimed at other social groups, the first British gay line, London Gay (now Lesbian & Gay) Switchboard was established in 1974 in the old offices of the Gay Liberation Front. In its first year it took 20,000 calls and grew in the 1980s to a five-line, 150-volunteer, 5,000-calls-a-week organization, one of the strongest gay groups in the country. It now operates a computerized information service from its own premises in the same Islington district. Since 1975 it has operated a 24-hour, 7-days-a-week schedule, attracting calls not only from London but from all over the United Kingdom and the rest of the world. Switchboards soon appeared in Britain's smaller cities, operating on a more limited scale and schedule; similar expansion took place in western Europe, Canada, and the United States.

The late 1970s and early 1980s also saw an expansion in lines run for and by lesbians, paralleling the general trend of these years toward separate women-run institutions. Callers bring a wide range of questions to switchboard volunteers: dealing with coming out, family, isolation, and housing; finding entertainment; and getting gay-friendly legal and medical assistance. London's switchboard devised the first gay-positive responses to the AIDS crisis in Britain, in the process sponsoring the development of the National Aids Manual for counselors, and serving as the model for the government's own AIDS hotline. Switchboards often operate in cooperation with coming-out groups that meet and counsel callers in person, such as Icebreakers and Friend in the UK.

Commercialized phone lines and many other media have taken over some of the first switchboards' entertainment, housing, and even advice functions. The revenue generated by gay and lesbian voice mail and other phone services has sponsored a fresh increase in queer print media, some of it owned by phone lines in search of new advertising venues. Canada's nonprofit Pink Triangle Press uses the proceeds from its gay commercial phone lines to subsidize a national chain of queer magazines. Despite these technological and financial shifts, the sympathetic human ear is still in demand, as the continued expansion of specially targeted services like queer youth lines, lines for ethnic communities, HIV and PWA hotlines, and dedicated services for people with disabilities demonstrate.   *Dan Healey*

Bibliography

D'Emilio, John. "Gay Politics, Gay Community: San Francisco's Experience." In *Making Trouble: Essays on Gay History, Politics and the University*. John D'Emilio, ed. New York: Routledge, 1992.

Faderman, Lillian. *Odd Girls and Twilight Lovers: A History of Lesbian Life in Twentieth-Century America*. New York: Penguin, 1991.

Weeks, Jeffrey. *Coming Out: Homosexual Politics in Britain from the Nineteenth Century to the Present*. London: Quartet Books, 1990.

See also Activism, International; AIDS; AIDS organizations; COC; Coming Out; Community Centers; Counseling; Gay and Lesbian Press; Gay Liberation; Gay Liberation Front; Homophile Movement; Phone Sex; Stonewall; Suicide

Sydney Gay and Lesbian Mardi Gras

In just under twenty years, the Sydney Gay and Lesbian Mardi Gras has developed from a humble, ad hoc beginning into a highly organized and extensively promoted monthlong festival of art, theater, film, and dance. Every February, these cultural activities are accompanied by sporting, community, and academic events that culminate in the Mardi Gras parade and party through inner-city Sydney. The evening parade down Oxford Street, which lies in the heart of Sydney's gay precinct, has become one of Australia's most popular cultural events, attended by half a million spectators, and, recently, televised nationally by the Australian Broadcasting Corporation. In many ways, the transformation and success, as well as the controversies and failures, of the Sydney Gay and Lesbian Mardi Gras have reflected the broader development of homosexual politics, culture, and communities in Australia and the West.

The first Mardi Gras was organized for June 24, 1978, by a small group of Sydney gay activists to mark the ninth anniversary of the Stonewall riots. There was, as Graham Carberry has pointed out in his informative *History of the Sydney Gay and Lesbian Mardi Gras*, some resistance to the idea of a fancy dress parade from activists more accustomed to traditional forms of protest and demonstration. From its conception, then, there were anxieties about the "fun" side of Mardi Gras outweighing its more serious and political message. These debates would reappear over the years, though more often within academic and feminist circles than among the participants themselves. The organizers of the first Mardi Gras need not have worried about the lack of overt politics. That problem, if it was one, was solved when police moved in to arrest and jail fifty-three women and men for unauthorized procession. In turn, these arrests led to a series of demonstrations by gay activists with more arrests following. These events garnered considerable publicity, and all charges were eventually dropped.

The arrest and police brutality of 1978 ensured that the Mardi Gras held to mark the tenth anniversary of Stonewall had a particularly local resonance. In its second year, the street parade was preceded by a week of cultural and social activities, opening with a large dance party. By 1981, however, the link with Stonewall, and perhaps a history of gay rights, was weakened as the Mardi Gras was shifted from June to late summer. This moved Mardi Gras away from its radical activist origins into a broader event that was to represent and entertain Sydney's increasingly confident and visible gay community. In many ways, this objective has underpinned the growth of Mardi Gras.

The expansion and depth of the Mardi Gras festival and the national and international appeal of the street parade and the Mardi Gras party—which immediately follows the parade and attracts up to twenty thousand revelers—has required a professionalization and organization somewhat at odds with Mardi Gras's radical beginnings. Now a company, Mardi Gras Ltd. wields considerable political, cultural, and financial clout within the Sydney gay and lesbian community and beyond. Members of the Mardi Gras organizing bodies have become the unofficial leaders and spokespeople of Sydney's gay and lesbian communities. A former president of Mardi Gras was preselected as an Australian Labor Party candidate in the 1995 state election, because the party hoped that her public profile would win votes in an electorate with a high percentage of gay constituents.

The growth of Mardi Gras as a popular cultural event has mirrored an increasing Australian acceptance of gays and lesbians as political players, and perhaps even more so, as consumers. In recent years, messages of support for Mardi Gras have been received—and published in the *Festival Guide*—from the governor general of Australia, former Prime Minister Paul Keating, and the premier of the state of New South Wales. Major corporations, most notably Qantas, Smirnoff, and Australia's foremost communications company, Telstra, have become major sponsors of the festival. This commercialization of Mardi Gras has not been without controversy. Some have worried that by courting the corporate dollar, Mardi Gras has lost touch with its community roots and that an oppositional politics is being traded for consumerism. Mardi Gras organizers have replied that sponsorship has enabled the festival to expand and better represent the diverse interests of gay and lesbian communities. A sponsorship offer from Playboy condoms in 1993 brought some of these tensions to the surface. Amid some dissent, Mardi Gras president Susan Harben rejected a lucrative arrangement—which would have seen the Playboy logo featured prominently throughout the festival and parade—on the grounds that Playboy represented "heterosexual misogyny" (Carberry 172).

The Playboy controversy drew upon a troubled history of Mardi Gras gender relations. Although men and women had been involved in the first Mardi Gras, by the early 1980s, Mardi Gras had become overwhelmingly a gay male event. In this, Mardi Gras reflected the separatism of gay and lesbian politics of the period. During the mid-1980s, there was no female representation on the Mardi Gras boards. As coalition politics reemerged in the late 1980s, however, so too did Mardi Gras begin to change. To reflect this shift, the Sydney Mardi Gras became the Sydney Gay and Lesbian Mardi Gras. Female membership in Mardi Gras increased, as did lesbian representation on the Mardi Gras boards. This was not without some opposition. When a lesbian was elected president in 1989, there were some disgruntled murmurs from gay men about a lesbian takeover. But generally relations between men and women have improved remarkably. Real efforts are now made to appeal to both lesbian and gay male constituencies. Organizationally, a rough gender parity prevails.

The very success of Mardi Gras has created tensions around questions of ownership and participation. Some gays and lesbians are worried that the appeal of the parade to a nonhomosexual audience may dilute Mardi Gras's function of strengthening homosexual communities. The presence of heterosexuals—men in particular—at the post-parade party has generated heated debate, with some gays calling for the effective exclusion of all heterosexuals. Alternatively, the emergence of a queer politics and sensibility has cast doubt over the coherence of the categories "lesbian" and "gay." For some queers, Mardi Gras, and in particular the Mardi Gras party, has lost an earlier sense of adventure and transgression. From outside homosexual and queer communities, the 1996 defeat of the federal Labor government has ushered in a conservative government suspicious of public expressions of sexual difference. Unlike his predecessor, the new prime minister declined to send a message of support to the 1997 Mardi Gras festival. In this new political culture, the more transgressive and oppositional elements of Mardi Gras might become more evident to both its critics and its supporters.

Robert Reynolds

Bibliography

Carberry, Graham. *A History of the Sydney Gay and Lesbian Mardi Gras.* Melbourne, Australia: Australia Lesbian and Gay Archives, 1995.

See also Activism, International; Australia; Business; Circuit Party Scene; Marches and Parades; Politics, Global; Stonewall

Sylvester (1947–1988)

Sylvester James was born in Los Angeles and died of AIDS in San Francisco. He started singing at the age of five and became a child star on the national gospel circuit; in his teens he moved to live with his grandmother, who was the first to encourage his flamboyant side. Sylvester became an openly gay transvestite disco star at a time when gay liberation and disco were receiving their greatest publicity. In the late sixties and early seventies, he sang with the Cockettes, a gay theater troupe; he also sang a drag show for eight years under the name Ruby Blue at the Rickshaw Lounge in San Francisco. He made a film appearance as a drag Diana Ross in Bette Midler's *The Rose* (1979). Sylvester's first album was *Sylvester and the Hot Band* (1972), a glitter-rock album on the Blue Thumb label with Sylvester in drag on the cover, which included the song "Why Was I Born." His first backup singers were the Pointer Sisters, four sisters from Oakland who had also moved from gospel to disco. In February 1976, Sylvester met Izora Rhodes and Martha Wash, two large women with large voices who sang backup for him as Two Tons o' Fun. They worked with Sylvester until 1983 and later produced the single "It's Rainin' Men" (1984) as the Weather Girls. Until 1981, Sylvester's songs were written by Victor Orsborn (1953–1990) and Eric Robertson. Sylvester established a contract with Fantasy Records of Berkeley, California, producing the albums *Step II* (1977), with the long-running hits "Dance (Disco Heat)" and "You Make Me Feel Mighty Real"; the Fantasy Records contract ended in 1981, but the company produced a compilation, *Sylvester's Greatest Hits* (1983). Sylvester then met Patrick Cowley (who died of AIDS in 1982) of Megatone Records, San Francisco, a songwriter/producer who created a new sound for Sylvester, allowing him to make a comeback in the postdisco era. With Megatone, Sylvester recorded *All I Need* (1982), with "Do You Wanna Funk"; *Call Me* (1984), with "Trouble in Paradise"; and *M-1015* (1985), with "Rock the Box" and "Take Me to Paradise." Sylvester's last album, *Mutual Attraction* (1986), was recorded for the major label Warner/Elektra and included "Living for the City," a duet with Stevie Wonder. Megatone later produced various posthumous collections and singles, of which the most important is "Immortal" (1989).

Paul Attinello

Bibliography

Diebold, David. *Tribal Rites: San Francisco's Dance Music Phenomenon 1978–1988*. Northridge, Calif.: Time Warp, 1986.

See also African American Gay Culture; Camp; Disco and Dance Music; Music and Musicians 2: Popular Music; Somerville, Jimmy; Transvestism

Symonds, John Addington (1840–1893)

Late-Victorian man of letters, art historian, classicist, literary critic, poet, aesthete: Symonds served as midwife during the birth of "the homosexual" in late-nineteenth-century England. He collaborated with Havelock Ellis on the ground-breaking study *Sexual Inversion* (1897), which includes his own case history. He helped to popularize the inversion theory in England, which characterizes male homoerotic desire as the love resulting from a woman's soul trapped in a man's body. He was one of the first people to use the term *homosexual* in the English language. Symonds privately published and circulated "A Problem in Greek Ethics" (1883), on Hellenic same-sex practices, and "A Problem in Modern Ethics" (1891), on contemporary homosexuality, which he discusses in psychological, juridical, and literary terms (with a section on Walt Whitman). His lengthy correspondence with Whitman ended when Symonds finally asked the poet if the manly love of comrades included physical intimacies; Whitman famously replied that such "morbid inferences . . . are disavowed by me and seem damnable." Symonds's *Memoirs* published in 1984, provide a remarkably candid account of the frequently tormented homosexual life of a Victorian gentleman. When at Harrow, Symonds discovered that Dr. Vaughan, the master at the school, was carrying on a love affair with one of the students; he told his father, who forced Vaughan to resign. He discovered and idealized his own homosexuality through passionate readings of Plato and Whitman, refusing to participate in the sex play rampant in the English boarding school as he found it coarse and vulgar. He confided his secret desires to his father, who urged him to marry. He did, and fathered two daughters, but eventually (after his father's death) acted on his feelings for men once he moved from England to Switzerland for health reasons in 1877. He began making regular visits to Italy and enjoyed relationships ranging from platonic admiration to sexual intimacy with Swiss peasants and Venetian gondoliers.

Besides his classic seven-volume study *Renaissance in Italy* (1875–1886), Symonds wrote about Christopher Marlowe, Plato, and Michelangelo, discreetly suggesting their homoerotic inclinations. Much of what is now known about Michelangelo's love for young men is the result of Symonds's research. The brief mention of Greek love in his *Studies of the Greek Poets* (1873) was, he believed, the reason he was not offered the Chair of Poetry at Oxford. He was often associated in people's minds with Oscar Wilde due to the interest in aestheticism they shared, but Symonds was a moralist not a decadent, and he anguished about the ethical questions raised by past and present homosexual practices. In his later years he became a vigorous campaigner for homosexual rights and frequently discussed the subject in his wide-ranging correspondence with the important literary men of the day. He died in Rome in 1893.

Leland Monk

Bibliography

Grosskurth, Phyllis. *John Addington Symonds: A Biography*. London: Longmans, 1964.

See also Aestheticism; Carpenter, Edward; Ellis, Havelock; Greece; Homosexuality; Inversion; Marlowe, Christopher; Michelangelo Buonarroti; Plato; Whitman, Walt; Wilde, Oscar

Szymanowski, Karol (1882–1937)

Born of an aristocratic and artistic Polish family living in the Ukraine, Szymanowski became the central figure in Polish music of the first half of the twentieth century. He traveled a path not unfamiliar among homosexual composers in reacting against the initial, mostly German, influences upon his style (largely Wagner, Reger, and Strauss, though his early piano music draws upon Chopin, naturally). After travels in Italy and North Africa, his own individual style emerged (with elements from Ravel, Skryabin, and others) as a brand of ecstatic Orientalism. Later, inspired by the liberation of Poland in 1919, he turned to a nationalism based in what he saw as the inherent qualities present in Polish folk and traditional music. He was unusual, however, in writing a homosexual novel, *Ephebos*, which was unfortunately lost in the Warsaw fires of 1939. This literary episode occurred just before the composition of his most famous work, the opera *King Roger* (1918–1924), which is clearly autobiographical, centering on a struggle in the title role between conventional authority and Dionysian abandon (personified by a wild, attractive Shepherd) from which he emerges as a Nietzschean man "strong enough for freedom." The reaction against modernism has stimulated growing interest in Szymanowski's music.   *Philip Brett*

Bibliography

Palmer, Christopher. *Szymanowski*. BBC Music Guides. London: British Broadcasting Corporation, 1983.

See also Music and Musicians 1: Classical Music; Opera; Ravel, (Joseph) Maurice

T

Taiwan

"Because people in Taiwan refrain from talking about male homosexuality," said Pai Hsien-Yung, the author of *Niezi (Crystal Boys)*, the first modern Chinese novel on male homosexuality in Taiwan, "the homosexuals have to struggle in their inner worlds like helpless orphans." Published in an interview in the late 1970s, Pai's words rightly characterize the dominant social attitude toward homosexuality in modern Taiwan. Same-sex sexual acts or love could be thought of only as a psychic disorder or an unnatural habit that disrupts social order and public morality. Apart from murders or criminal cases involving or supposedly caused by homosexuality, homosexuality was seldom if ever represented in the media. Such conspicuous silence around homosexuality indicates that it was feared and repudiated in Taiwanese society in such a way that silencing became the only way to "talk about" it in the media in the 1960s and 1970s, lest people would learn to acquire this pathetic "cut-sleeve quirk." Strangely enough, even though regulation around homosexuality was (and still is) totally absent from Taiwanese laws, the police could still abuse their power. In the defense of morality and the so-called virtuous custom (*shanliang fengsu*) under martial law (imposed in 1949 by the Chiang Kai-shek regime), which was strictly antisex, the police constantly arrested gay people cruising in the New Park, the gay Mecca of Taiwan,—and cracked down on gay bars and saunas. Homophobia operating in this repressive mode underwent a drastic change in 1985 when social anxiety over the emergence of AIDS in Taiwan finally brought homosexual panic to the fore. Suddenly great social concern triggered a proliferation of discourses on homosexuality at various institutions such as psychiatry, medicine, and the educational establishment. For the first time straight society was consumed by a desire to understand this incomprehensible human species known to be on the one hand "universal," historically as well as geographically, and yet on the other hand a product of decadent "western" influence. In the AIDS crisis, precisely because of cultural ignorance, what the locals called the "glass community" needed urgently to be unveiled and studied, so that social and national "health" could be secured.

A term that circulated originally among gangsters, "glass" was denigrating slang for "ass" that referred to homosexuals during the 1960s in Taiwan. The mainstream culture was equally fascinated by the ideogrammatic signs of "No. 0" and "No.1" used by the glass community: "No. 0" is said to play the bottom and feminine role in contrast to the top and masculine role played by "No. 1." What could have been inventive linguistic terms that designate the performative nature of anal intercourse was later essentialized as the core of homosexual gender identity. Within the heterosexual economy, No. 0 and No. 1 naturally can be thought of only as a gender "dysphoria" that violates the harmony of yin and yang. Punishment for transgressing the heterosexual gender norm is manifest in the violence of language, which stigmatizes the homosexual as culturally unintelligible *renyao* (literally specter-like human beings).

A further examination of the notion of "virtuous custom" previously defended so righteously by the Taiwanese government would bring to light the mechanism of homophobia and explain what it means to be gay in Taiwan. The illegitimacy of homosexual desire, despite its absence in any Tai-

Twanese laws, lies in the fact that it manifestly deviates from the kind of patriarchal familialism prescribed by neo-Confucianism—a state philosophy notably and thoroughly implanted by Chiang Kai-shek in his attempt to construct "real" Chinese-ness (ideological war against the Communist regime in China). Modern neo-Confucianism reinforces the notion of "the relational self" in regard to the "traditional" hierarchical matrimonial family according to one's gender (husband-wife) and generation (parents-children). Children's submission to parents (*xiao*, filial piety) in particular is analogized to the citizen's relation to the state. In addition, Taiwanese folk beliefs and ritual practices—a hybridized religious system of Confucianism, Taoism, and Buddhism—heavily emphasize marriage, procreation, and the continuation of family as filial duties. Such heterosexualization of a society bespeaks the specific kind of homosexual oppression in Taiwan. It is by no means incidental that Pai Hsien-Yung's literalization of Taiwanese homosexuality is titled *niezi*, (extremely unfilial son).

It is therefore meaningless to talk about "coming out" in view of the structural problem of Taiwanese familialism on an island with one of the highest population densities in the world. Since the lifting of martial law in 1987 and the onset of democratization, gays and lesbians have also broken silence and begun to speak out. Most significant of all was the enunciation of the concept of *Tongzhi* (or comradeship) in the early 1990s. This parodic reappropriation of nationalist rhetoric signifies for Taiwanese gays and lesbians a collective will to claim political agency against heterosexual subordination. In recent years, the emergence of the *Tongzhi* movement and proliferation of various gay-themed cultural production have given Taiwan a new face in the 1990s. *Tongzhi* groups have launched several campaigns and demonstrations for antidiscrimination laws and same-sex marriage. As the New Park under the new city plan was to be "reoriented," in 1995, the allied *Tongzhi* groups waged a war with the Taipei city mayor to assert their rights as gay citizens for using public space. The year 1996 saw the celebrated Taiwanese film *The Wedding Banquet* restaged featuring a gay couple. Since 1995, there have been more than five radio *Tongzhi* programs all over the island, and gays and lesbians can now easily find *Tongzhi* publications in bookstores. With all this cultural change, one even hears the government and political parties congratulating themselves for their increasingly liberal attitudes toward homosex-

uality. As Taiwan embraces liberalism and celebrates its pluralistic, democratic society, social attitudes toward homosexuality have been transformed: from a kind of unspeakable taboo to tolerance. But tolerance does not mean acceptance. Today, Taiwanese gay men pay taxes and, like straight men, get conscripted into the military for two years, but as yet no law protects gays from discrimination. The fact that gay citizenship is not recognized and that *Tongzhi* is usually treated in patronizing humanistic terms in mainstream culture shows that homosexuality in Taiwan is still not legitimized enough. Indeed, *Tongzhi* issues remain to be more politicized. As *Tongzhi*'s favorite motto by Sun Yat-sen, father of the Republic of China, goes, "Since our revolution is not yet accomplished, lo, comrades (*Tongzhi*), efforts still need to be made!"

Hans Tao-Ming Huang

Bibliography

Ni, Jiazhan. "Discourse and Agency in Lesbian and Gay Movement in Taiwan." Paper delivered in "Sex Education, Sexology, Gender Studies and Gay and Lesbian Studies" International Conference, Taipei, June 29–30, 1996.

Pai, Hsien-Yung. *Crystal Boys*. Howard Goldblatt, trans. San Francisco: Gay Sunshine Press, 1995.

See also Buddhism; China; Politics: Global

Takahashi, Mutsuo (1937–)

Born in Japan and educated at Fukuoka University of Education, Mutsuo Takahashi is one of Japan's major poets. His frank exploration of gay life in his poems and plays has gained him an audience all over the world. His prize-winning work has garnered him awards such as the Reketei Prize (1982), the Yomiuri Prize, and the Takami Jun Prize.

Of the volumes of poetry that Takahashi has published, including *You Dirty Ones, Do Dirtier Things* (1966), *Poems of a Penisist* (1975), *The Structure of the Kingdom* (1982), *A Bunch of Keys* (1984), *Practice/Drinking Eating* (1988), *The Garden of Rabbits* (1988), and *Sleeping Sinning Falling* (1992), the role of sexuality and a quest to understand more deeply the nature of desire are common themes.

In drama, in 1987, Takahashi won the Yamamoto Kenkichi Prize for his *Princess Medea* stage script. He has adapted W. B. Yeats's play *At the Hawk's Well* to Japanese, and Georges Bataille's *Le Procès de Gil de Rais* inspired him to write a Noh play.

Takahashi's work challenges prevailing cultural attitudes in Japan about the homosexual—who he really is as opposed to what the culture considers him to be. Often the homosexual is culturally an outsider because he does not bind himself to rituals associated with Japanese family life. For Takahashi, this outsider status offers the homosexual an opportunity to critique culture. More free of the rules that govern it, the homosexual can revel in it, both finding and losing himself in it.

Poems such as "The God Status I Love" celebrate an attraction to a body "made of lily and sex." In "Legend of a Giant," a poem dedicated to Che Guevara, the speaker claims:

> The two pure materials from which the entire you derives,
> your scrotum and your thought—I separate them on two pans of a balance.

The sexual and the intellectual engage in both battle and blossom. The speakers are often clandestine lovers, men who have met in men's rooms or other forbidden places. His poem "Ode" employs Christian religious language, blurring the lines between the supposedly sacred and the supposedly profane. The "holy fluid" is semen, not the Holy Spirit. Sexual encounters give the speaker an identity—he is saved by the grace of touch. For the speaker, love must be turned into flesh.

Takahashi's *Poems of a Penisist* is one of the world's great books of erotic poetry. The personae in this collection are not interested in being "tolerated" by the rest of society. They will find their way, touch by touch, not needing to ape heterosexual conventions. The queen (*okama*) may be mocked by society, but this mocking only gives the *okama* greater strength. In "Ode," the speaker says he presses

> my lips
> To the camelia, to the alembic, to the
> wide-mouthed jar—
> Joyous glitter.

Desire itself unites the memories of the young gay man with the older gay man. In an essay printed after "Ode" in *Poems of a Penisist*, Takahashi describes the speaker as a saint of desire.

Takahashi's work celebrates erotic longing, but it also celebrates lives that cannot be subsumed by prevailing cultural mores. He is ultimately a freedom poet, stripping down life of its multilayered rules so that a real, more alert self can emerge.

Kenneth Pobo

Bibliography

Takahashi, Mutsuo. *Poems of a Penisist*. Heroaki Sato, trans. Chicago: Chicago Review Press, 1975.

———. "The Searcher." In *Partings at Dawn: An Anthology of Japanese Gay Literature*. Steven D. Miller, ed. San Francisco: Gay Sunshine Press, 1996, 207–19.

See also Guevara, Che; Japan; Japanese Literature; Love Poetry, the Petrarchan Tradition

Talk Shows

The talk show is a television and radio genre that emerged strongly in the late 1960s, notable for its emphasis on audience participation in discussion of social and personal topics, often including homosexuality, transgender issues, and sexual politics. Rooted in earlier radio and television genres, talk shows variously combine audience participation, discussion of social issues, sensational conflict, and information. Talk radio, with a predominantly male audience, has generally been more receptive to conservative political expressions, while television talk programming, aimed primarily at an audience of women, has been more receptive to liberal perspectives on social issues. (Although they have been especially significant in the United States, radio and television talk shows, both indigenous ones and those imported from the United States, are found worldwide.)

Beginning with the *Donahue* show in 1967, followed by *Oprah* in 1986 and numerous others subsequently, daytime television talk shows in particular became early and ongoing media sites in which nonconforming sex and gender populations, identities, and issues were publicly visible and openly discussed. In their single-topic, controversy-driven "talk/service" format (as opposed to other talk formats such as celebrity chat), television talk shows for a time were among the only spots on national television where gay men, lesbians, bisexuals, and transgendered people were invited to appear as themselves, to speak about, sometimes argue about and defend, their lives. In particular, *Donahue* and

T

Talk show host Phil Donahue puts on a skirt for a show on cross-dressing, 1988. A/P Wide World Photos.

his followers in the 1980s and 1990s tapped into and contributed to a shift in the boundaries between public and private partly attributable to the entry of women into key arenas of society and politics. The shows have publicly aired many issues—ones related to sexuality and gender, in particular—previously considered inappropriate for public discussion. Homosexuality and gender-crossing, as taboo and controversial subjects, were both prominently included in these new discussion areas.

In the mid-1990s, talk show production companies, led by *Ricki Lake* and its imitators (many of them short-lived), began successfully targeting a younger, less middle-class audience than their predecessors and effected a shift in the tone, content, and methods of guest recruitment. Many programs became faster-paced and included more guests per program, focused on interpersonal relationships rather than social issues, and recruited individuals through toll-free call-in numbers rather than through organizations. Some programs also began strategies of "surprising" guests. (The most notorious case of this "ambush" strategy came in 1994 when, after allegedly being surprised on *Jenny*

Jones by a male admirer, John Schmitz murdered the admirer, Scott Amedure. The show's producers contend that Schmitz was informed in advance of the taping that his secret admirer could be male.) Although participation of gay men, lesbians, bisexuals, and transgendered people continues in these newer programs, guests tend less often to be affiliated with political organizations and have shorter speaking times, and studio audiences tend to be more emotionally expressive. At the same time, guests—including gay, lesbian, bisexual, and transgendered guests—tend to be from a greater diversity of racial, geographical, and socioeconomic backgrounds than those on earlier programs.

Criticisms of daytime talk shows as exploitative or individually and socially damaging have been continuous, reaching a peak in a 1995 campaign by former Secretary of Education William Bennett and Connecticut Senator Joseph Lieberman, with the political action group Empower America, to clean up the "cultural rot" of daytime television. In particular, talk shows have been criticized as "freak shows" that promote stereotypes, on the one hand, and as parades of dysfunction and deviance that "define deviance down" and normalize the abnormal, both claims of particular relevance to sex and gender nonconformists.   *Joshua Gamson*

Bibliography

Empower, America. *Press Conference*. Washington, D.C.: Federal Document Clearing House, October 26, 1995.

Kurtz, Howard. *Hot Air: All Talk, All the Time*. New York: Times Books, 1996.

Rose, Brian G. "The Talk Show." In *TV Genres: A Handbook and Reference Guide*. B. G. Rose, ed. Westport, Conn.: Greenwood Press, 1985.

Signorile, Michelangelo. "The *Jenny Jones* Murder: What Really Happened?" *Out*, June 26–29, 1995, 142–46.

See also Censorship; Media; Television; Transgender; Transsexualism

Taylor, Paul (1930–)

American dancer and choreographer Paul Taylor is a seminal figure in the history of modern dance. From his early career as a dancer with Martha Graham, to his work as a choreographer of more than one hundred dances, to his mentorship of and influence on a whole generation of dance makers, Taylor spans four decades. As a choreographer, he first received notoriety in 1957, when in response to his concert at the 92nd Street YM-YWHA, *Dance Observer* published critic Louis Horst's review, four square inches of blank space. His choreographic range is quite broad, with early works tending toward everyday movements with long periods of stillness, and later works becoming increasingly lyrical. Some of his work is humorous and even sardonic; other pieces revel in the pleasure of movement, like *Esplanade*, in which dancers only run, skip, and jump. Unlike that of the first generation of modern dance choreographers, Taylor's work is rarely solemn or overtly political; instead, he uses a lightheartedness to point subtly to darker themes. The tremendously popular *Company B* (1992) is danced to music sung by the Andrews Sisters and portrays scenes of military life in World War II. At times, the bubbly music is in direct contrast to the dancers, as they dodge bullets or fall to their deaths. Although his movement vocabulary is performed with a weightedness unfamiliar to most ballet choreography, several ballet companies have added his modern dance works to their repertory. The lyrical style, large ensemble casts, and male-female partnerings make his work accessible to a ballet audience.

In his autobiography, *Private Domain*, Taylor is much more open about his sexuality than is readily apparent in his choreography. One glimpse of gay sexuality appears in a section of *Company B*, in a section loosely resembling a social dance at an officer's club. In a shadowed area of the stage, two men move together with longing, secretly touching. Taylor's dances are instilled with a sense of humanity and dignity. It is in that same spirit that members of the Paul Taylor Dance Company started the fundraising organization Dancers Responding to AIDS (DRA).   *Maura Keefe*

Bibliography

Taylor, Paul. *Private Domain*. San Francisco: North Point Press, 1987.

See also Dance: Concert Dance in America; Dance and AIDS; Joffrey Ballet

Tchaikovsky, Pyotr Ilich (1840–1893)

This great Russian composer was the author of eleven operas; three full-length ballets; six symphonies; numerous concerti, orchestral, chamber, and choral works; and a large body of art songs.

Tchaikovsky's musical gifts were manifested in his childhood, spent in a small town in the Ural Mountains, where his father managed the ironworks. From the age of twelve to nineteen, Tchaikovsky stayed as a boarding student at the School of Jurisprudence (a combination of high school and junior college that prepared its students for a career in law), taking music lessons on the side. Numerous memoirs depict that school as a hotbed of homosexuality, where the angelic beauty of the young Pyotr brought him numerous admirers.

Upon graduation, he obtained a job with the Ministry of Justice and for a few years lived the life of a man about town, moving mostly in gay circles. But at the age of twenty-three, he gave up the job and enrolled as a full-time student of theory and composition at the St. Petersburg Conservatory. This conservatory training later led to much invidious commentary about Tchaikovsky's music lacking Russian authenticity, as opposed to such supposedly self-trained contemporaries as Mussorgsky and Borodin. In fact, Tchaikovsky is an essential link in the Russian musical tradition of high Westernized culture that leads from Glinka to Stravinsky.

Tchaikovsky's great originality, his unique musical language, was already manifest in his First Symphony (1866, revised 1875) and the overture-fantasy *Romeo and Juliet* (1869). In 1877, after completing the ballet *Swan Lake* and just before undertaking the opera *Eugene Onegin*, the composer became alarmed over the rumors about his private life. This led to the ill-advised marriage to an unbalanced woman, Antonina Miliukova. The marriage quickly brought on a nervous breakdown; after his recovery, Tchaikivsky wrote: "There is nothing more fruitless than not wanting to be what I am by nature." The composer had gay liaisons with, among others, his classmate Ivan Klimenko, his valet Aleksey Sofronov, and violinist Iosif Kotek. His greatest love was his gay nephew Vladimir ("Bob") Davydov, to whom the Sixth Symphony was dedicated. According to an oral tradition among Russian gays, this symphony depicts a homosexual's search for love. Some of his art songs, such as "So Soon Forgotten" and "A Terrible Moment," op. 28, no. 6, are settings of gender-neutral texts that might well refer to same-sex love.

Tchaikovsky's death from cholera is reliably documented. Around 1970, his biography was taken over by extremely homophobic musicologists such as Edward Garden, David Brown, Alexandra Orlova, and more recently, Anthony Holden. They believe that homosexuals cannot have lovers or friends and lead lives of unrelieved misery. On the basis of unverifiable rumors, they assert that Tchaikovsky was forced to commit suicide by his onetime fellow students at the School of Jurisprudence. The publication of Alexandre Poznansky's books reestablishes the facts of the composer's life and discredits his homophobic biographers.

Simon Karlinsky

Bibliography

Poznansky, Alexandre. *Tchaikovsky: The Quest for the Inner Man.* New York: Schirmer, 1991.

———. *Tchaikovsky's Last Days: A Documentary Study.* Oxford: Clarendon Press, 1996.

See also Homophobia; Music and Musicians 1: Classical Music; Russia; Russian Literature

Tchelitchew, Pavel (1898–1957)

Neoromantic painter, sculptor, and stage designer Pavel Tchelitchew was born outside Moscow of aristocratic parents. He fled during the Russian Revolution to Kiev in 1918, where he studied at the academy and later joined the White Army. With its defeat in 1920, he ended up in Berlin, focusing on set designs in a constructivist style. There he became lovers with pianist Allen Tanner. Encouraged by Sergey Diaghilev, he moved to Paris in 1923, where he later designed for Diaghilev's Ballets Russes.

In Paris he abandoned constructivism. His *Basket of Strawberries* (1925) exhibited at the Salon d'Automne caught the interest of Gertrude Stein. Tchelitchew's elongated and moody male nudes, acrobats, and dancers, such as *Two Nude Boys* (1929) and *Rose Necklace* (1931), were heavily influenced by Picasso's rose period, examples of which he saw at Stein's salon. He later exchanged Stein's patronage for that of Dame Edith Sitwell.

In wire sculptures of heads and in paintings in which skin becomes transparent to reveal hidden figures and anatomy, he tried to suggest the psyche of his subjects. Although Tchelitchew rejected the surrealist label, his merging of highly illusionistic objects and figures in composite images, distorted perspectives, and incongruous landscapes—for example, the epic *Phenomena* (1936–1938)—parallels the art of Salvador Dalí. As happened to Dalí, Tchelitchew's narrative illusionism fell out of favor with modern art critics with the advent of abstract expressionism.

Tchelitchew's most famous painting, *Hide and Seek* (1942), is a garish fire-red picture of an enormous tree that reveals itself to be made up of body parts and the translucent faces of children. For many years, this painting was New York City's Museum of Modern Art's most popular work. Although it does not deal with homosexuality per se, the painting's quality of sexual disjunction and its emphasis on masquerade suggest aspects of queer experience.

Tchelitchew expressed his attraction to the nude body in portraits like *Tattooed Man* (1934) and *Lincoln Kirstein* (1937), in which Kirstein figures as a nude boxer. He illustrated Charles Henri Ford and Parker Tyler's gay novel, *The Young and the Evil* (1933; these watercolors, executed on blank pages of a copy of the book, were not published with the text until 1988).

But arguably, Tchelitchew's most interesting gay works are his private, ostensibly pornographic pen and ink sketches, several of which are in the Kinsey Collection. Here Tchelitchew dispenses with his usual distortions simply to record erotic desire. For example, a wash drawing of a half-naked sailor, lying in bed with an erection, is remarkable for showing the male body as passive love object—here the erect penis is as much a sign of vulnerability as power.

Tchelitchew was based in the United States throughout the forties and fifties (he became a citizen in 1952), where he collaborated with George Balanchine. After World War II, he traveled extensively with his lover, Charles Henri Ford, in Europe. He died in Frascati, Italy.

Jonathan Weinberg

Bibliography

Kirstein, Lincoln. *Tchelitchew.* New York: Foundation for Modern Art, 1964.

Tyler, Parker. *The Divine Comedy of Pavel Tchelitchew.* New York: Fleet Publishing Corporation, 1967.

See also Ballets Russes; Diaghilev, Sergey; Ford, Charles Henri; Kinsey, Alfred; Kirstein, Lincoln; Tyler, Parker

Tearooms

Perhaps no single issue polarizes gay political activists as dramatically as that of tearoom, or cottage, sex. According to some, it is a source of embarrassment for the gay community and its efforts to achieve political and social legitimacy. To others, it is a form of sexual expression that ought to be defended, even championed. Still others take a position between these two. They find the practice relatively harmless, a victimless crime, but they argue that because it is illegal and because its decriminalization is a cause not likely to receive much support (even among gays and lesbians), it should be discouraged. Pop star George Michael's arrest in a Beverly Hills tearoom in 1998 has reanimated in the gay press a debate at least as old as Stonewall.

The term *tearoom* refers to a public restroom that has gained a reputation as one in which men have sex with one another. (Women do not seem particularly interested in tearoom sex.) Tearooms are located in parks, libraries, highway rest areas, department stores, college campuses, and adult movie theaters. An Internet Web site currently advertises the location of popular tearooms, along with other places—beaches, streets, parking lots— where men cruise other men for sex. (Also included are warnings concerning police entrapment.) In his watershed study of public sex entitled *Tearoom Trade*, Laud Humphries offers a possible origin of the word *tearoom*; according to Humphries, "tea" is British slang for urine.

The debate over tearoom sex circles around the question of how to interpret this behavior. Those who oppose it see it as either an unfortunate and anachronistic residue of a time when cultural prohibitions against homosexual behavior made it particularly difficult for urban men to find male sex partners or as a symptom of pathology—sexual addiction, simple hedonism, or even immaturity. The discussion is complicated because some men who engage in tearoom sex do not self-identify as homosexual and are married or in relationships with women. Critics believe the activity encourages the stereotype of gay men as sex-crazed, promiscuous, and eager to seduce "innocent" and unwilling straight men and possibly children. Larry Kramer frets that this "childish" behavior evidences our suicidal "determination to celebrate our promiscuity" (quoted in Zonaran). In similarly moralizing tones, Al Rantel worries, "For too long," gays and lesbians "have sat quietly, appearing to approve of public sex and outright pedophiles within our community. They have done nothing but make it harder for the majority of us to be seen as good and moral citizens." "Scorn the perverts!" he urges.

Those who take an opposing view argue that tearoom sex is a form of resistance to a repressive regime of the normal, sometimes termed "heteronormativity." Such writers take their cue from Michel Foucault, who argued that, since the nineteenth century, in the West, military, medical, religious, educational, and industrial institutions, as well as practices of colonization, slavery, and child rearing, have instituted a "meticulous control of the operations of the body," an "uninterrupted, constant coercion" that Foucault terms "discipline." Discipline is a historical form of power that "categorizes the individual, marks him by his own individuality, attaches him to his own identity, imposes a law of truth on him which he must recognize and which others have to recognize in him" ("The Subject and Power," 212). Writers influenced by Foucault argue that homosexual behavior represents one attempt to thwart this discipline. It makes an "inappropriate" and "wasteful" use of sex and the body, and offers alternative forms of relating to one another, forms not based on the model of heterosexual monogamy. With its transgression of laws, its blurring of the lines between homosexual and heterosexual identities (any man who enters the rest room is at least theoretically a possible participant), and its potential to promote and facilitate group sexual encounters, tearoom sex seems a particularly charged response to what Foucault terms "disciplinary society."

Another way to describe tearoom sex is what Michel de Certeau terms a "tactic," an attempt by the dominated to make an illegitimate use of a space in which they are held captive—and to avoid detection in the process. The heteronormative restricting of gender mobility represented by the sex-segregated washroom is significant here. Given the tendency in the Western world to equate same-sex desire with gender nonconformity, it is no surprise that the oppressively hypermasculine space of the men's room would be a place for covert homoerotic encounters.

Some supporters of tearoom sex question whether sexual addiction or compulsion even exists; they see such terms as symptoms of a cultural fear of the erotic. And as for the charge that tearoom denizens prey on the unsuspecting and unwilling, Humphries's study details some of the practices and rituals that attempt to ensure that those engaging in tearoom sex do not encroach on or approach the unwilling. Humphries mentions in particular the distance of many tearooms from other public spaces and details some of the codes of behavior that operate in securing sex partners.

Obviously, the consequences of being caught with one's pants down or approaching the wrong man are profound, ranging from humiliation, to arrest, to gay bashing, to murder. David Woodhead has noted that the tearoom "may pretend safe-space status, yet it encloses the very same men it serves to protect, leaving them open to attack just at the moment they enjoy their safety." Tearooms can be the site of fag bashing and police stings. It is not unusual for the news media to report the names of those charged with public sex. Such men have been known to kill themselves in response. Nor is it unheard of for murders to occur in tearooms.

Recent media accounts of tearoom sex seem caught up in the poles of the debate that surrounds it. While they warn of some of its dangers, they simultaneously advertise its potential pleasures. As Art Greenwald gushes in an article ostensibly critical of tearoom sex, "Quick, easy and free of emotional entanglements. The thrill of contact with a stranger. An adrenaline rush of the hunt and the risk of being caught. No feeling or commitment required." Similarly, a cover story in the *Advocate* on sexual addiction is illustrated by a series of photos of a tearoom encounter that look like stills from a porno film. Both pieces reveal something of the complicated relationship of capitalism to gay identity and tearoom sex. Tearoom sex flourishes under conditions made possible by capitalism—the dissolution of the nuclear family, the migration of single adults to urban spaces, and the development of a modern gay identity. Magazines like the *Advocate* take advantage of these conditions, advertising to a niche market looking to express its gayness through the purchasing of rainbow flags, vodka, and trips to the Caribbean. But as homosexuality comes further out of the closet, it also threatens to interfere with capitalist commodity production and distribution. Greenwald's story in particular details the efforts of a Fort Lauderdale hardware store to crack down on tearoom sex to "give our customers back a feeling of comfort about going in an [*sic*] taking their kids to the restroom." It is not surprising that the *Advocate* can't decide whether to be for or against tearooms; Home Depot might decide to advertise in its pages some day.

As homosexuality becomes more culturally acceptable, behaviors such as tearoom sex are transformed and take on new meaning. What was once a survival strategy for some men who sought erotic attachments to other men is today perhaps a way of contesting the emergent normative sense of a gay identity.

John Champagne

Bibliography

Bell, David. "Perverse Dynamics, Sexual Citizenship and the Transformation of Intimacy." In *Mapping Desire*. David Bell and Gill Valentine, eds. London: Routledge, 1995, 304–17.

de Certeau, Michel. *The Practice of Everyday Life*. Berkeley: University of California Press, 1984.

Foucault, Michel. *Discipline and Punish*. Alan Sheridan, trans. New York: Vintage, 1979.

———. "The Subject and Power." In *Michel Foucault: Beyond Structuralism and Hermeneutics*. Hubert Dreyfus and Paul Rabinow, eds. Chicago: University of Chicago Press, 1983.

Gideonse, Ted. "Addicted to Sex." *Advocate* (May 26, 1998): 24–38.

Greenwald, Art. "Tearoom Sex, Home Depot Says Enough!" *Scoop* 7, no. 20 (May 20, 1998).

Greyson, John. *Urinal*. 1989. Distributed by Frameline. San Francisco.

Humphries, Laud. *Tearoom Trade*. Chicago: Aldine, 1970.

Rantel, Al. "The Right Side." *Scoop* 7, no. 20 (May 20, 1998).

Woodhead, David. " 'Surveillant Gays': HIV, Space and the Constitution of Identities." In Bell and Valentine. 231–44.

Zonanan, Victor. "Kramer vs. the World." *Advocate* 617 (December 1, 1992): 47.

See also Adult Bookstores; Foucault, Michel; Lewd and Lascivious Conduct; Phone Sex; Sodomy Trials; Trick

Television

On American television, the various forms of visibility of gays and lesbians—as persons, as part of a minority group, as a political constituent, or merely as caricatures displaying stereotypical behavior—have increased over time. Yet these visibilities have paradoxically rendered them "invisible," owing to television's consistent lack of nuanced treatment of gay, lesbian, and queer lives and experiences. Visible myths are nonetheless myths.

In general, audience research repeatedly suggests that television remains the most influential form of mass medium affecting people's social consciousness. Being primarily a domestic medium, and in recent years having to compete for audience ratings and advertising revenue because of the vast proliferation of the cable industry, the mainstream television networks have treated homosexuality with caution, even as they have included more and more gay characters in sitcom and dramatic programs and in gay-themed documentaries.

Controversial events abound on American television trying to come to terms with homosexuality. As did the cinema, television in the 1950s and 1960s presented mostly gay male caricatures mainly for comic effects, as in *The Jack Benny Show, Mister Peepers,* and *I Love Lucy.* The limp wrist, the high-pitched voice, and the flamboyant clothing were clichéd signifiers for effeminized gayness. Occasionally, dramatic programs, such as *Alfred Hitchcock Presents,* cast a homosexual as a villain. The nation's first television documentary on homosexuals, "The Rejected," was produced in 1961 by KQED, a public television station in San Francisco. The program was made with a budget of less than $100. In 1967, CBS aired the controversial program "The Homosexuals," hosted by Mike Wallace. Forty million viewers tuned in to watch this bigoted portrayal of urban gay males, whom Wallace called "promiscuous," "not interested in nor capable of a lasting relationship," and trapped in "chance encounters at the clubs and bars."

The 1970s saw the battle between a television industry reluctant to change and a developing gay political movement demanding change. The emergence of media watchdog groups monitoring the treatment of gays and lesbians on television (e.g., the National Gay Task Force, Gay Media Task Force, Alliance of Gay and Lesbian Artists) and the handful of "TV raids" of live programs by young activists (such as Mark Segal in the early 1970s) forced the industry to address its biases, insensitivity, and ignorance. In 1972, ABC aired the made-for-TV movie *That Certain Summer,* which concerned a father (Hal Holbrook) forced to explain his relationship with his live-in lover (Martin Sheen) to his fourteen-year-old son. It was the first serious treatment of a gay domestic relationship on television. Yet the same network produced two episodes of *Marcus Welby* in the 1973 and 1974 seasons, depicting a self-loathing gay father and a gay rapist in a junior high school, respectively. In the mid- to late 1970s, playful gay or gay-suggestive characters on sitcoms (e.g., *Three's Company, Soap, Laverne and Shirley*) and dramatic characters in TV movies and docudramas (e.g., *A Question of Love, Sgt. Matlovich vs. the U.S. Air Force*) appeared on prime-time television. The somewhat uncertain treatment of homosexuality on television perhaps mirrored the social ambivalence resulting from the depathologization of homosexuality by the American Psychiatric Association in 1973 and traumatic events such as the assassination of Harvey Milk in 1978.

By the 1980s, homosexuality was no longer closeted on television. In fact, trends suggested that it might even be a topic with commercial value. Occasional and regular gay and lesbian characters appeared in a number of sitcoms (e.g., *Taxi, Cheers, Kate & Allie, The Golden Girls, Designing Women, The Kids in the Hall*), dramatic series (e.g., *Sidney Shorr, Heartbeat, thirtysomething*), and made-for-TV movies (e.g., *Consenting Adults, The Women of Brewster Place*). In addition, PBS aired several American and British productions in the 1980s and 1990s based on literary and theatrical adaptations (e.g., *Brideshead Revisited, Fifth of July, The Lost Language of Cranes, Oranges Are Not the Only Fruit,* Armistead Maupin's *Tales of the City*).

Two significant phenomena in the 1980s forever changed the representation of gays and lesbians on television: the AIDS crisis and the emergence of the MTV generation. The AIDS crisis brought forth many issues regarding homosexuality that television had effectively ignored. NBC's *An Early Frost,* the first treatment of AIDS on prime-time television, depicted the torment of a gay son returning to his middle-class family when he found out that he was HIV-positive. Made-for-TV movies focusing on family dramas involving mother-son conflicts and reconciliation became a dominant genre (e.g., *An Early Frost, Our Sons, Andre's Mother, In the Gloaming*).

Over the 1980s and into the 1990s, MTV has become a steadily queer-friendly space on mainstream television, albeit a space limited to "hip" youth culture. Dance music videos often contain images of gender-bending and sexual crossover (most notably Madonna's videos). Likewise, fashion-oriented programs and specials, such as *House of Style,* feature gay fashion designers and queer haute couture. Taking the "supermodel" as an iconic cue, RuPaul launched her career on MTV, blending queer-styled fashion consciousness with the tradition of black female impersonation. *The RuPaul Show* debuted on VH1 (owned by MTV) in 1996. In addition, MTV Music Video Awards shows have increasingly served as a haven for queer-friendliness, accommodating scandal-ridden stars such as Michael Jackson and Paul Reuben (Pee Wee Herman). Finally, one of

MTV's most popular programs, *The Real World*, has featured a gay or bisexual character in every season from 1992 to 1997 (except the 1995 London season). The 1993 season in San Francisco featured Pedro Zamora, a young gay Cuban-born AIDS educator who was HIV-positive. Zamora's activism, romantic life, and death from AIDS complications were dramatically displayed, offering one of the most unusually moving depictions of homosexuality and AIDS on television.

Both daytime and prime-time television in the 1990s continue to promote a commodified visibility of homosexuality. Daytime talk shows incorporate sensational depictions of queer lives to compete for ratings, while prime-time programs present gay and gay-suggestive characters usually with a self-congratulatory tone, thereby generating well-publicized "TV controversies" that feed back into ratings gain (e.g., the "kiss" on *Roseanne*, the "kiss" on *L. A. Law*, the lesbian "founders" of Cicely in *Northern Exposure*, the lesbian wedding in *Friends*, and the comical ranting about gay tolerance in *Seinfeld*). The highly orchestrated publicity of the coming-out episode on *Ellen* on April 30, 1997, nonetheless presented American television with the first lesbian lead character in a prime-time program. A 1997 poll by Gay and Lesbian Alliance Against Defamation (GLAAD) found thirty "out" characters on television in the fall lineup, which represented a 23 percent increase of coverage compared with 1996.

One notable issue is the wholesale invisibility of gay and lesbian people of color on television, pointing to the industry's inability to address the intersection of sexual and racial identities. The example of the censorship of black video maker Marlon Rigg's *Tongues Untied* by various PBS-affiliated stations in 1991, on the one hand, and the example of the hysterical "black queen" characters in *In Living Color*, on the other hand, suggest network television's bifurcated fear of black queer sexuality: the fear of black queer politicization and the fear of nonnormative black masculinity.

Overall, the intersection of American television and homosexuality remains an awkward—yet increasingly commodified—cultural phenomenon. The basic set of treatments remains relatively unchanged: (1) quantity substitutes for quality; (2) homosexuality is seen through the framework of heterosexuality, as a disruption of heterosexuals' lives and expectations; (3) gays and lesbians are desexed and without affection; and (4) except on the news, they are not depicted as part of a community; their sense of belonging is rarely considered and thus rendered unimportant.   *John Nguyet Erni*

Bibliography

Alwood, Edward. *Straight News: Gays, Lesbians, and the News Media*. New York: Columbia University Press, 1996.

Fejes, Fred, and Kevin Petrich. "Invisibility, Homophobia and Heterosexism: Lesbians, Gays and the Media." *Critical Studies in Mass Communication* 10, no. 4 (1993): 395–422.

GLAAD. " '97 Television Lineup Includes Record Number of 'Out' Characters." Press release. August 13, 1997.

Goldstein, Lynda. "Revamping MTV: Passing for Queer Culture in the Video Closet." In *Queer Studies: A Lesbian, Gay, Bisexual and Transgender Anthology*. Brett Beemyn and Mickey Eliason, eds. New York: New York University Press, 1996, 262–79.

See also AIDS; AIDS in the U.S. Media; Censorship; Gay and Lesbian Alliance Against Defamation (GLAAD); Journalism; Kissing; Maupin, Armistead; Media; Milk, Harvey; Music and Musicians 2: Popular Music; National Gay and Lesbian Task Force; Pschychiatry and Homosexuality; Riggs, Marlon; Talk Shows; Wilson, Lanford

Tennyson, Alfred (1809–1892)

Alfred Tennyson was born at Somersby, Lincolnshire, and educated at Trinity College, Cambridge, where he joined the intellectual society of the Apostles and came in contact with Arthur Hallam's views on the poetry of sensation and the benefits of a feminine sensibility to a male poet. Critics first took note of Tennyson with the publication of his *Poems, Chiefly Lyrical* (1830) and *Poems* (published 1832; dated 1833), which were followed by a roughly ten-year hiatus from publishing collections, brought on in part by the death of his dear friend Hallam. It is also likely that the harsher reviews of his work made Tennyson hesitant to publish again, and revisions to the poems republished in 1842 reflect critics' comments. The collection that broke the relative silence contains texts from the previous publications as well as some new pieces, including "The Vision of Sin," which encourages a reading of same-sex male passion, as well as "Mort d'Arthur," which incorporates an erotically tinged relationship between the king and his attendant, Sir Bedivere.

The Princess (1847) depicts the affections between a princess who advocates women's rights and separatism and an effeminate, cross-dressing prince who imagines a future in which the male and female sexes become more similar.

Tennyson's most complex presentation of same-sex male love and attraction, and one of the most powerful elegies in English is *In Memoriam, A.H.H.* (1850). The poet started work on the elegy the year after Hallam's death, but he took over two decades to complete it. *In Memoriam* depicts Tennyson's loneliness, dejection, and doubt after the loss of his friend and his gradual sense of reconciliation. The sense of hope toward the end of the elegy is encapsulated in a depiction of his sister's marriage. Tennyson himself seemingly remains wed to the memory of Hallam, having referred to himself as "widow'd," and to the deceased as his "mate," "love," and "lost desire." Ironically, Tennyson married Jane Sellwood in the same year that the elegy was published, and he may have chosen to publish it anonymously to avoid raising any conflict between these two celebrations of love. A number of reviewers did not hesitate to note the actual author, but others claimed, either naively or coyly, that the elegy was written by a woman.

In Memoriam was followed by a collection of poems entitled *Maud, and other Poems* (1855), its title poem depicting a male narrator who acknowledges a physical attraction to the heroine's brother, "that dandy-despot." Stimulated by a chivalrous battle song that he once heard Maud sing, the speaker muses, "Ah God, for a man with heart, head, hand, / Like some of the simple great ones gone . . . and ah for a man to arise in me, / That the man I am may cease to be!" Frustrated by the limited available roles within his cultural context, the narrator ultimately leaves Maud for the all-male realm of the battlefield.

Depictions of androgyny and ambiguous same-sex attraction wane in Tennyson's later work, while his 1889 snipe at "One Who Affected an Effeminate Manner" makes clear his own discomfort with the ways in which some critics were interpreting his poetry. After excising references to same-sex male attraction from his father's letters, Hallam Tennyson published them in a biography in 1897, the same year that Havelock Ellis, in *Sexual Inversion*, was recommending *In Memoriam* as a form of release for his homosexual patients.   *Dennis Denisoff*

Bibliography

Nunokawa, Jeff. "*In Memoriam* and the Extinction of the Homosexual." *ELH* 58 (1991): 427–38.

Sinfield, Alan. *Alfred Tennyson*. Oxford: Basil Blackwell, 1986.

Tennyson, Alfred. *The Poems of Tennyson*. Christopher Ricks, ed. London: Longman, 1969.

See also Androgyny; Elegiac Poetry; Ellis, Havelock; English Literature; Love Poetry, the Petrarchan Tradition

Thailand

The popular culture of Thailand has a rich history of transgenderism and homoeroticism that has underpinned the emergence in contemporary Bangkok of the largest and most visible gay subculture in Asia outside Tokyo.

Historically Thai discourses have not distinguished the categories of gender and sexuality, with one term (*phet*) denoting biological sex, gender, and sexuality. One should therefore speak of a complex of Thai sex/gender discourses rather than of distinct discourses of gender and sexuality. Until the emergence of gay-identified men in the 1960s, homoeroticism and transgenderism were conflated in a single category, the *kathoey*, which variously denoted hermaphrodites, transvestites, transsexuals, as well as effeminate and masculine homosexual men. *Kathoeys* remain prominent in the Thai subculture, but today the term is restricted to cross-dressing men and male-to-female transsexuals.

Since the 1960s the Thai sex/gender system has diversified considerably, with new gay and bisexual identities emerging from the old categories of the feminine/effeminate *kathoey* and masculine *phuchai* (man), which historically were the only recognized identities a Thai male could assume. Nevertheless, masculine/feminine gender oppositions remain important in the construction of all-male identities, both new and old. While the term *gay* has been borrowed to describe masculine-identified homosexual men, the distinction between insertive "gay kings" and receptive "gay queens" is important within the subculture, with "kings" being considered more masculine than "queens" and the ideal gay relationship being between a king/queen couple. More recently, the notion of sexual versatility has been described by the neologism *gay quing*, that is, a gay man who combines the sexual potentials of both the feminine queen and the masculine king.

The Thai sex/gender regime is generally tolerant of both transgenderism and homosexuality. While the dominant religion, Theravada Buddhism, demands celibacy of its renunciate monks, the only religious controls over lay sexuality are a prohibition against adultery and an injunction to restrain all passions. Homosexual and cross-dressing behaviors are not interdicted, although they are considered inferior to heterosexuality, with homoerotic and transgender desires being explained as the karmic consequence of having committed adultery in a previous life; that is, within traditional discourses homosexuality results from heterosexual sin rather than itself being sinful, with condescending pity rather than condemnation being the prevailing religious attitude toward gay men and *kathoeys*.

Current Thai law criminalizes neither crossgender nor homosexual behavior. In modernizing the criminal code along European lines in the early 1900s, King Chulalongkorn did criminalize both male and female homosexuality as being "against human nature," but the irrelevance of this law in the Thai context is indicated by the fact that it never once led to a prosecution and the antihomosexual clause was abolished after a review of the criminal code in 1956. Institutional tolerance also extends to the domain of everyday life, with homophobic violence and gay "hate crimes" being all but unheard of. Whether cross-dressing *kathoeys* may, like women, be the victims of sexual attack and misogynistic violence in the society has long been an issue of public debate.

While tolerated, homosexuality and cross-gender behaviors are not accepted as appropriate and are often subjected to intense criticism in popular and formal discourses. Indeed, it is in the domain of discourse, not practice, that the strongest sanctions against nonnormative sex/gender behavior operate. The problematic status of gay men, in particular, is revealed in Thai academic studies, which overwhelmingly define homosexuality as a "problem" (*panha*) to be "treated/cured" (*raksa*) or "solved" (*kae-khai*). Thai gay men and *kathoeys* do not confront homophobic legal, religious, or other interdictions. Nevertheless, they do conduct their lives within a domain of highly charged condemnatory discourses that denounce their sex/gender deviance as disgraceful (*nabatsi*), shameful (*na-ap-ai*), disgusting (*man-sai*), and perverted (*wiparit*, *witthathan*). Furthermore, while enjoying informal tolerance, gay men and *kathoeys* receive no formal recognition. Thailand lacks antidiscrimination legislation on the basis of sexuality, and neither gay relationships nor the changed gender status of transsexuals is recognized in law.

As in many other countries, the local press and media demonized gay men as the supposed "source" of HIV when the first AIDS cases were reported in the mid-1980s. But although the first infections were among gay men, by the late 1980s the epidemic was spreading quickly among heterosexual intravenous drug users and female prostitutes and their clients. This refocused public anxieties toward these latter "risk groups" and led to an almost complete "heterosexualization" of Thai HIV/AIDS discourses in which gay men and *kathoeys* all but disappeared. Paradoxically, the intense press and media coverage of gay issues and the increased visibility of gay men during the brief period that they were labeled the "source" of AIDS appear to have contributed to a further liberalization of attitudes since the late 1980s. In the mid-1990s gay issues are commonly reported straightforwardly in the media, with none of the sensationalism that until recently characterized most reporting. But the belief that heterosexuals are more at risk of HIV infection has led to a neglect of gay men in safe-sex programs, with still unclear consequences for the spread of infection within the gay subculture.

In the mid-1990s gay men and *kathoeys* are much less marginalized and stigmatized than they were only a decade ago, with a discernible trend toward mainstreaming and no organized homophobic opposition such as the moralistic religious groups found in Western countries. Thailand thus presents a contrast to the histories of the gay and transgender communities in most Western societies. The emergence of large numbers of gay-identified men and of a significant commercial scene in Bangkok and other cities has occurred entirely as a cultural movement with no accompanying gay political movement, no institutional or legal support, and almost none of the community organizations or activist networks found in Western gay centers.

Yet this increasingly liberal environment is contrasted with a dearth of publicly identified gay men. Coming out and identifying openly as gay, whether at home or at work, remains extremely uncommon—although there are exceptions among a handful of gay media personalities. Thai homosexual men are leading increasingly visible gay lifestyles, but few are prepared to reveal their sexuality to anyone but other gay men. This reflects the continuing power of antigay popular discourses, which lead to shame, loss of face, and a "damaged image" (*sia phap-phot*) for homosexual men whose sexuality is revealed explicitly. The Thai sex/gender system, which is tolerant in practice but discursively unaccepting of homosexuality, has produced the contemporary form of the Thai gay subculture in which it is increasingly easy for homosexual men to live their sexuality but where it remains difficult to speak of it publicly.   *Peter A. Jackson*

Bibliography

de Lind van Wijngaarden, Jan Willem. "The Variety of Homosexual Experience in the Context of HIV/AIDS in Chiang Mai, Northern Thailand." In *Gender and Sexuality in Modern Thailand.* Peter Jackson and Nerida Cook, eds. Chiang Mai, Thailand: Silkworm Books, 1997.

Jackson, Peter A. *Dear Uncle Go: Male Homosexuality in Thailand.* Bangkok: Bua Luang, 1995.

———. *The Intrinsic Quality of Skin.* Bangkok: Floating Lotus Books, 1994.

———. "*Kathoey* < > Gay < > Man: The Historical Emergence of Gay Male Identity in Thailand." In *Sites of Desire/Economies of Pleasure: Sexualities in Asia and the Pacific.* Margaret Jolly and Lenore Manderson, eds. Chicago: University of Chicago Press, 1997.

———. "Tolerant But Unaccepting: Correcting Misperceptions of a Thai 'Gay Paradise.'" In Jackson and Cook.

Jonathan, David, trans. *The Dove Coos II: Gay Experiences by the Men of Thailand.* Bangkok: Floating Lotus Books, 1994.

Miller, Neil. "Thailand I: City of Angels" and "Thailand II: Mr Minami Dances." In *Out in the World, Gay and Lesbian Life from Buenos Aires to Bangkok.* London: Penguin Books, 1992.

Morris, Rosalind C. "Three Sexes and Four Sexualities: Redressing the Discourses on Gender and Sexuality in Contemporary Thailand." *Positions* 2, no. 1 (1994): 15–43.

Nukul Benchamat and Somboon Inpradith, trans. *The Dove Coos: Gay Experiences by the Men of Thailand.* Bangkok: Bua Luang Publishing, 1992.

Werasit Sittitrai, Chuanchom Sakondhavat, and Tim Brown. *A Survey of Men Having Sex with Men in a Northeastern Thai Province*, Research Report No. 5. Bangkok: Thai Red Cross Society Program on AIDS, 1992.

Wiresit Sittitrai, Tim Brown, and Sirapone Virulrak. "Patterns of Bisexuality in Thailand." In *Bisexuality and HIV/AIDS: A Global Perspective.* Rob Tielman, Manuel Carballo, and Aart Hendriks, eds. Buffalo, N.Y.: Prometheus Books, 1991.

See also AIDS; Bangkok; Bisexuality; Buddhism; Coming Out; Effeminacy; Gay; Gender; Masculinity; Melanesia; Politics, Global; Tourism and Travel; Transgender; Transexualism

Theater: Premodern and Early Modern

What is gay theater? Does "gay" denote an aesthetic sensibility, an identity, a sexual preference, a life, a lifestyle, a politics? And what falls under the label "theater"—written dramas, religious rituals, any staged event? What happens when the two terms collide, as they do here? Can, say, an ACT UP protest or an S/M encounter in a sex club be called "gay theater"? Do plays written or produced before the middle of the twentieth century qualify, even though "gay" had yet to signify male-male erotic desire (Mae West's *Pleasure Man*, Cosmo Manuche's *The Loyal Lovers*, John Wilmot, Earl of Rochester's *Sodom, or The Quintessence of Debauchery*, Euripides's *The Bacchae*)? Is it more appropriate to call these "homosexual," despite (or because of) all the clinical, pejorative assumptions that cling to this taxonomic classification? If so, how would works like Shakespeare's *Coriolanus* and Middleton and Dekker's *The Roaring Girl* fit the category—plays written by allegedly heterosexual men, but which allude to decidedly sodomitical acts and relationships? The list of such work encompasses almost the entire classical cannon: Aeschylus's *The Myrmidons*, Aristophanes' *Thesmophoriazusae*, Hrotswitha's *Paphnutius*, the Wakefield *Second Shepherd's Play*, Nicholas Udall's *Ralph Roister Doister*, all of Shakespeare's cross-dressed comedies, Ben Jonson's *Epicene*, Aphra Behn's *The Town Fop*, John Gay's *Achilles*, Byron's *Sardanapalus*, Bulwer-Lytton's *Not So Bad as We Seem*, and the Kabuki dramas crafted to be performed by *onnagatas* (female impersonators who often doubled as male prostitutes), or even those nontraditional performances by Yoruban shaman (thought to have spiritual powers because they either were effeminate, hermaphroditic, or homosexual), or Indian *hijras* (eunuchs whose power to bless or condemn swells entirely from the fact of an absent phallus). Perhaps, as scholar Carl Miller suggests, "Theater and homosexuality are inseparably companions, intimately involved for as long as anyone can tell."

If theater begins, as Arthur Pickard-Cambridge asserts in *Dithyramb, Tragedy and Comedy*, with men dressing up as maenads (Dionysian bacchantes) to perform fertility rites, then the very nature of performance is already inflected with an anxiety about gendered identity. Such an anxiety opens quite readily into the paranoia surrounding male-female, male-male, and female-female relations inscribed in Greek tragedy and comedy, and etches this history into all subsequent western drama from the Roman idealization of pater familias in Plautus, Terence, and Seneca to current fascinations with pants and skirts in musicals like Blake Edwards's *Victor/Victoria*, Jonathan Larson's *Rent*, John Cameron Mitchell's *Hedwig and the Angry Inch*, and even an unconscionably heterosexist melodrama like David Mamet's *Oleanna*. While much contemporary queer performance has worked hard to take apart assumptions about sexuality and gender—assumptions embedded in the moral and cultural fabric of the twentieth century—an equal number of plays still sustain a prevalent antipathy toward gay sex, an antipathy that extends at least as far back as Greek attempts to contain the cult of Dionysus and that figures in the rhetoric of Renaissance Puritans and in contemporary conservative moralizing. The history of "gay theater," then, is as much a history of deeply rooted antitheatrical prejudices as it is a record of a gradually codified homophobia.

Writing about gay theater requires making some arbitrary distinctions, for example, where, historically, to fix a meaningful point of departure; what kinds of plays, and/or performances to include; and who, in the pantheon of men and women writing about homosexual and homosocial identity and desire, to canonize? The most contentious narrative would start with the Greeks, the least contentious with the development of an Off-Off Broadway theater movement in the late 1950s. Neither seems wholly useful or accurate. Nor does the notion that gay theater (as Jill Dolan, also resisting the lure of chronology, once put it) "is closeted, then comes out, then gets avant-garde, then looks queerly, then goes Vegas, or something." Certainly Marlowe's provocative evocation of Edward II's obsession with Gaveston—imagined a little less than four hundred years before that torch-bearing play, *The Boys in the Band*, was hailed as the first "out" gay play—already stands as a classic monument to homoerotic desire.

Sodomites, buggers, ingles, inverts, catamites all abound in drama. What follows is an attempt to put this history into an albeit brief context, one that demonstrates how the very nature and function of theater is implicated in the way cultures, especially in the Western world, have thought about, categorized, maligned, outlawed, and celebrated male-male desire.

Classical Antiquity: Greece and Rome

For the Greeks, sex between men was as commonplace as breathing, but only those relationships where an older man (*erastes*, or the lover) served as sexual and spiritual mentor for a younger boy (*eromenos*, or the beloved) were deemed legitimately praiseworthy. Sex between men of the same age was frowned at, though not legally outlawed. Even so, of the extant Greek tragedies we have, none represent homosexual love, though, a handful of fragments from lost plays—Aeschylus' *The Myrmidons* (about the love between Achilles and Patroclus), Sophocles' tragedy *Niobe* (also known as *Paiderastria*), his satyr play, *The Lovers of Achilles*, and Aeschylus' *Laius*, Sophocles' *Chrysippus*, and Euripides' *Chrysippus* (about the abduction and rape of the eponymous son of Pelops by Oeidpus's father, Laius)—suggest that the subject was overtly represented in the dramas of the period. The historical record contains numerous salacious anecdotes about Sophocles' many affairs with boys and about Euripides' love for Agathon (reputedly as talented a playwright as the big three and the chief advocate of homosexual love in Plato's *Symposium*) after they both left Athens in 406 B.C. None of this is particularly surprising given the Greek celebration of male physical beauty and its fundamental position in aesthetic and educational thinking of the period.

What is odd is that so little of the extant drama reflects themes and representations of same-sex eroticism and desire explicitly present in so much of the extant prose, poetry, and art of the period. One possible explanation for this almost complete erasure is the way these works were transmitted: they were preserved by Christian monks who painstakingly copied and recopied the works of classical writers. Undoubtedly, the church engaged in as much censorship then as it does now. Even so, transcribers could not excise all homoerotic instances from these texts, the most obvious gender-bending, of course, bleeding through the male enactment of female roles—a conventional practice emulated by the Elizabethans, but with greater self-conscious wit and queer resonance—and through the destabilizing presence of plot-driven transvestism in plays like *The Suppliants*, *The Bacchae*, and *Thesmophoriazusae*.

The extant comedies of Aristophanes contain numerous explicit representations—mostly satirical and disparaging—of effeminacy, buggering, and pederasty. Aristophanes was a noted social conservative, and not surprisingly championed the lyric heroism of Aeschylus's verse while attacking, in both *The Frogs* and more caustically in *Thesmophoriazusae*, Eurpides' and Agathon's moral characters and dramatic talents. His work revels in the grotesque deflation of martial pomp, often making his satirical point by casting emasculated men as passive recipients of phallic penetration—a strategy not very different from Euripides' own when he shows that archconservative, Pentheus, dressed in female garb as he goes out to spy on the revels of the bacchantes. Aristophanes, however, does not question the legitimacy of the *erastes-eromenos* relationship, but rather draws comparisons between those adult Athenian men who place themselves at the receiving end of foreign thrusts. The Aeschylean tragedy Aristophanes most liked was *The Myrmidons* (he cites the play frequently in his own work), and Plato, in the *Symposium,* portrays him as an advocate for the love of the male body.

Roman dramatists inherited from Greek texts both the lyric celebration of male love and a deeply felt cultural anxiety about all sexual behavior. Roman society, even more misogynist than its Greek predecessor, developed a sexual system where both women and slaves were male property, denied even those meager freedoms meted out by Athenians and Spartans. While most same-sex love was confined to encounters between masters and their slaves, and while many philosophers cautioned against pederasty, especially where male citizens serviced those below their class, same-sex love and even marriage were common enough to be documented by historians and biographers. It is commonly held that all Roman emperors, except perhaps Claudius, were sexually ambivalent, none more so than Nero who, in publicly lavish ceremonies, married two men, and often also performed in women's clothing to the mandatory applause of his court.

Even the very orators—Cicero, for example—who railed against "Greek" love engaged in the very acts they publicly condemned. Most mentions of homosexuality in the drama uphold a firm Roman belief in the value of maintaining social decorum. Plautus' plays reflect this. Though allusions to homosexuality occur in many of his works, the satirical bantering that surrounds these sexual acts castigates both partners—passive and active. Terence's work, even more so than Plautus', aspires to a pandering conventionality that merely confirms cultural

stigmas against the corrupting influences of sodomy, an attitude that passed from Roman lawmakers and moralizers directly to their Christian heirs.

The Middle Ages and the Renaissance

The eroticized bonds between men so celebrated in almost all Greek and some Roman poetry, philosophy, and song comes, in the medieval period, under the chastising influence of the Christian church. The immediate effect of this shifts aesthetic representations of male-male attachments away from the sexual and toward the purely platonic—male friendships, however much eroticized in medieval epic and lyric poetry, remain mostly homosocial, a metaphoric imitation of the ideal, spiritual bond between man and God epitomized in the love Christ demonstrated for his spiritual brothers. In a culture that exalted celibacy and deemed any sexual behavior sinful (even if, in some cases, necessary), sex between men became gradually one of the worst imaginable religious offenses and was finally proscribed by Justinian in the sixth century A.D.

Medieval performances, when they touched on homosexual acts at all, personified sodomy as a Vice that would undoubtedly lead Mankind or Everyman immediately to hell. In the later medieval period, scatological humor abounds in the work of writers like Hans Sachs in Germany and Angelo Beolco in Italy, and in the more farcical cycle plays written by the anonymous Wakefield master (*The First Shepherd's Play*, *The Second Shepherd's Play*, and *The Killing of Abel*, for example). This focus on the anus as the satirical butt of religious humor, while not explicitly homosexual, embeds into the metaphoric fabric of Western thinking the notion that any kind of ass-play is sinful, disgusting, and automatically evil. John Bale's play, *The Three Laws of Nature, Moses and Christ Corrupted by the Sodomites, Pharisees, and Papists,* in which a character aptly named the Law of Nature triumphs over Idolatry, Infidelity, and Sodomy, typifies the kind of moralizing commentary visited on the idea of homosexuality by Catholics, and later, Puritans.

While the stage, because of its licentious display of all kinds of human behavior, had always been associated with sin and vice, this connection gained considerable authority in the twelfth, thirteenth, and fourteenth centuries, especially after the enactment of sumptuary laws forbade men to dress in women's clothing—a regular practice in the theater, one that continued throughout Europe well into the Renaissance. As John Franceschina puts it, "[B]etween 1150 and 1350, same sex behavior appears to have changed in the eyes of the public from the personal preference of a prosperous minority, satirized and celebrated in popular verse, to a dangerous, antisocial, and severely sinful aberration."

The religious condemnation of homosexual acts did not, though, extend to a similar attitude toward metaphysical bonds between men. In fact, such bonds church leaders encouraged such intimate friendships, and, as John Boswell argues, often led to marriage ceremonies spiritually uniting affectional same-sex couples. This is not surprising given the social codification of patriarchal privilege and its consequent adulation of phallic power. Women—deemed untrustworthy, unchaste, and generally unclean—could not, so the popular wisdom would have us believe, merit the kind of attention reserved by men for their biological fellows.

Sodomy, in early biblical commentary, specifically signified bestiality, and not until the eleventh and twelfth centuries did the definition expand to include all nonprocreative acts. By the start of the 1400s, even procreative sex between non-Christians was considered venial. In the theater, this meant coupling Jews, Moors, Arabs, and homosexuals as similarly corrupt enemies of all Christendom. This, then, is the sensibility the Renaissance inherited. The ambivalence toward homosexual sex acts that emerges in the drama of the period comes from a dissonant clash between orthodox church proselytizing and the recovery and assimilation of a classical art, poetry, and philosophy that often celebrated male beauty and the carnal pleasures of same-sex love.

To make matters more complicated, medieval and Renaissance assumptions about sodomitical behavior get bound up in a misogynist discourse that continually calls attention to male anxieties about lineage and inheritance. So many of the comedies and tragedies end with the reaffirmation of marriage and male authority, where marriages actually consolidate authority (*Taming of the Shrew* and *The Alchemist* are representative examples), and where the upholding of an economy of patriarchal transaction among genders becomes a moral imperative, that any subversion (through the attempt to defeat or betray marriage vows) is the most extreme heresy. The clearest example of the complicated and contradictory relationship of authority, morality, marriage, and sodomy occurs of course in the most celebrated of all homosexual tragedies of the period, Marlowe's

Edward II. Here, Edward's publicly displayed love for Gaveston, his refusal to give ground to the nobles who find his offense indefensible, and, more important, his obsessive fawning at the expense of governing England, all conspire against him, leading to that nightmare in the dungeon when Lightborn, his assassin, shoves a red hot poker into his anus. The symbolism, I'm sure, was not lost on anybody.

The Renaissance, especially in England, has received perhaps as much if not more scholarly attention from queer academics than even the twentieth century. While Shakespeare's plays and poems still maintain a central position in the scholarship of writers like Jonathan Dollimore and Jonathan Goldberg, Alan Sinfield, Lisa Jardine and Stephen Orgel, the ambiguous valences of gendered identity in the plays of many of his contemporaries have increasingly received serious critical attention. Cross-dressed boy actors playing tantalizing ganymedes and the many plot complications such performances provide were ingeniously exploited by Marlowe, Jonson, Marston, Dekker, Heywood, and of course Beaumont and Fletcher. Though some critics still claim that the conventional fact of boys dressed as women allowed Elizabethan and Jacobean audiences to ignore, or look past, the gender-doubleness performed on stage, this seems an attempt to get past the crucial role homoeroticism played in the rhetoric of age. Many of these playwrights, especially Jonson and Shakespeare, call explicit attention to the cross-dressed actors by centering their comic plots on female characters who disguise their "true" identities by assuming male garments. That the number of such comedies increased exponentially after James I, that supremely effeminate king, rose to the English monarchy suggests not only the greater license playwrights enjoyed, but also an increased anxiety focused on the hermaphroditic body of James himself.

No play betrays this anxiety better than Ben Jonson's *Epicoene*, whose very first exchange makes explicit satirical reference to the practice of men using their pages to satisfy their sexual urges, and whose plot revolves around the disguising of a boy as a girl to trick an old man into a false marriage. Similar episodes occur in almost all Elizabethan and Jacobean comedies—*As You Like It*, *Twelfth Night*, *The New Inn*, *Antonio and Mellida*, *Philaster*. The relationships among boy actors and older mentors received much derisive name calling by Puritan crusaders; their rhetoric found proof-positive of seditious, heretical intent in the master-apprentice arrangement of the acting troupes, especially given the obviously effeminizing public display of boys in women's dress. Of course, the very act of putting on garments belonging to members of the opposite sex was in itself a violation of the sumptuary laws enacted during the medieval period that prohibited such cross-dressing entirely. The Puritan Phillip Stubbes, whose *Anatomie of Abuses* piles charge upon damnation against the theater, captures the more extreme rhetoric best: "Mark the flocking and running to theater and curtains, daily and hourly, night and day, time and tide to see plays and interludes, where such wanton gestures, such bawdy speeches . . . such kissing and bussing: such clipping and culling: such winking and glancing of wanton eyes, and the like is used. . . . Than these goodly pageants being done, every mate sorts to his mate, every one brings another homeward of their way very friendly, and in their secret conclaves (covertly) they play the Sodomites or worse." That such statements rang true also finds evidence in the plays themselves—Cleopatra's infamous line, "boy my greatness in the posture of a whore" undoubtedly reflects the popular belief that boy actors did indeed spend their hours offstage prostituting themselves to men and women alike.

Less obvious, but equally apparent in the plays, is the euphuistic language of courtly allegiance which walks a thin line between platonic love and full-blown arousal. The innumerable male friendships in Shakespeare's plays—Aufidius and Coriolanus, Romeo and Mercutio, Antonio and Bassanio—Clermont and the Duke de Guise in Chapman's *Bussy D'Ambois*, Alexander and Hephestion in Lyly's *Campaspe*, and even (in a gross, satirical inversion) Ithamore and Barabas in Marlowe's *The Jew of Malta* all testify to a language that, while not explicitly sexual, achieves its erotic effect because audience's understood the inherent tensions among gendered and sexual signifiers these playwrights exploited to achieve their complicated ends. Homoeroticism that refused to spill from language into act retained an almost holy aura, while base displays of physical affection—Edward for Gaveston, Zeus for Ganymede, Falstaff for Hal, Tiberius for Sejanus—almost always become the object of contempt.

The most famous example from the Renaissance Italian stage comes in Pietro Aretino's *The Stablemaster*, produced in 1533. The play's title character, who clearly expresses his sexual desire for members of his own sex, is made the butt of a se-ries of vicious jokes, the central one being that his master wants him to marry a rich woman. That the play does not overtly condemn male-male love comes clear in the resolution when the "bride" turns out to be a page in disguise. Yet the play does manage to rehearse a penetrating catalog of epithets leveled at men who prefer other men. The sentiments expressed here seem remarkably different from Michelangelo's anguished love poetry, where homosexual need is sublimated in the very act of writing.

The entertainments performed by commedia dell'arte troupes across Europe seem closer in spirit to Aretino's and Jonson's comedies than to Shakespeare's. Many of the *lazzi* that come down to us reveal an obsession with scatological humor almost as perverse as Bale's fervent denunciations of sodomites. The main interest of these plays center not on the narrative, but rather the invariably comic digressions in which servants play tricks on their masters, often with gender-bending effects. One famous description of a variation on the "lazzo of delivering an enema" reads, "analyzing zanni's urine, the doctor announces that the zanni requires an enema, after which zanni discovers he is pregnant." The mixing of genders, the pandering to an audience's "baser" instincts by playing with and through stereotypes typifies this more popular, physical comedy, and in many instances, forms the basis for many of the jokes—both implied and apparent—that revolve around moral and social prejudices surrounding the practice of male-male sex.

Finally, it is not so much what the plays do say as what they do not say. There is no clearer example of revisionary historiography (some would call it dramatic license) than Racine's political thriller, *Britannicus*. Though almost all Roman historians knew of Nero's sexual attachment to Britannicus, Racine chooses—perhaps wisely given that any such overt statement would have carried him straight to stake—to expunge this fact entirely; and, as Roland Barthes astutely comments, discussing yet another of his plays, that he gives Hippolytus a female love interest to make sure his audience did not construe misanthropy as sexual inversion. The sin that dare not speak its name remains, for the most part, disguised, masked in plots that close only to reaffirm the procreative status quo.

Framji Minwalla

Bibliography

Bray, Alan. *Homosexuality in Renaissance England.* London: Gay Men's Press, 1982.

T

Cantarella, Eva. *Bisexuality in the Ancient World.* Cormac O Cuilleanain, trans. New Haven: Yale University Press, 1992.

Clum, John M. *Acting Gay: Male Homosexuality in Modern Drama.* New York: Columbia University Press, 1994.

Curtin, Keir. *We Can Always Call Them Bulgarians.* Boston: Alyson Publications, 1987.

de Jongh, Nicholas. *Not in Front of the Audience: Homosexuality on Stage.* London: Routledge, 1993.

DiGangi, Mario. *The Homoerotics of Early Modern Drama.* Cambridge: Cambridge University Press, 1997.

Dolan, Jill. "Building a Theatrical Vernacular: Responsibilities, Community, Ambivalence, and Queer Theater." *Modern Drama* 39 (1996): 1–15.

Ferris, Lesley ed. *Crossing the Stage: Controversies in Cross-Dressing.* London: Routledge, 1993.

Franceschina, John. *Homosexualities in the English Theater: From Lyly to Wilde.* Westport, Conn.: Greenwood Press, 1997.

Furtado, Ken, and Nancy Hellner. *Gay and Lesbian American Plays: An Annotated Bibliography.* Metuchen, N.J.: Scarecrow Press, 1993.

Goldberg, Jonathan. *Sodometries: Renaissance Texts, Modern Sexualities.* Stanford: Stanford University Press, 1992.

Halperin, David M. *One Hundred Years of Homosexuality and Other Essays on Greek Love.* New York: Routledge, 1990.

Lucas, Ian. *Impertinent Decorum: Gay Theatrical Manoeuvres.* London: Cassell, 1994.

Miller, Carl. *Stages of Desire: Gay Theater's Hidden History.* London: Cassell, 1996.

O'Connor, Sean. *Straight Acting: Popular Gay Drama from Wilde to Rattigan.* London: Cassell, 1998.

Sinfield, Alan. *The Wilde Century: Effeminacy. Oscar Wilde and the Queer Moment.* New York: Columbia University Press, 1994.

Stubbes, Phillip. *Anatomie of Abuses.* London, 1583.

Summers, Claude J. ed. *The Gay and Lesbian Literary Heritage.* New York: Henry Holt, 1995.

Woods, Gregory. *A History of Gay Literature: The Male Tradition.* New Haven: Yale University Press, 1998.

Thebes

Thebes, in central Greece, became the chief city-state of Boeotia. In myth, the city was founded by Kadmos, a Phoenician immigrant; this has been controversially regarded as proof of West Semitic settlement in Greece. The archaeological record does not confirm such settlement, but reveals considerable Mycenaean influence. Thebes is particularly renowned as the setting for Aeschylus' tragedy *Seven Against Thebes* and for the Oedipus cycle of myths, powerfully dramatized by Sophocles in his great Theban trilogy.

Historically, Thebes supported the Persians during the Persian Wars and eventually joined its old enemy, Athens, to resist the growth of Spartan power. After the defeat of the Spartans at the battle of Leuctra in 371 B.C.E., Thebes enjoyed a brief period of hegemony in Greece under the general Epaminondas, but it fell to the ambitions of Philip II of Macedon at the battle of Chaeronea in 338 B.C.E.

Of special interest during these battles was the role of the "Sacred Band of Thebes," a battalion composed of 150 pairs of male lovers, maintained at state expense, who were stationed on the battlefield in couples, thus establishing a noble precedent for homosexuals in the military. Established by Gorgidas in 378 B.C.E., after the liberation of Thebes from the Spartans, this battalion contributed to Thebes' military prestige until its heroic end at Chaeronea. Epaminondas died at Mantineia (362 B.C.E.) with his beloved, Asopikhos, beside him. Plato stresses the fact that same-sex relations in Boiotia were customary and uncomplicated, in contrast to Athens (*Symposium* 182b1-6).   *Michael Lambert*

Bibliography

Dover, K. J. *Greek Homosexuality*, 2d ed. London: Duckworth, 1989.

See also Alexander the Great; Athens; Greece; Persian / Iranian Literature and Culture; Sparta; Plato

Théophile de Viau (1590–1626)

Born near Agen into a Protestant family, Théophile de Viau, or simply, Théophile, as he would come to be known as both playwright and poet, became famous with the performance of his play *Pyrame et Thisbé* in 1621. Shortly thereafter, however, he was forced into a life of exile and imprisonment since he was chosen the unwilling representative of France's libertine movement of the early seventeenth century.

Around the same time of the publication of his play, Théophile also participated in a collection of satirical poems called *Le Parnasse satyrique* (1622), published in his name, which resulted in his being condemned by parliament and burned in effigy. To add to his misfortune, in 1623 he was vehemently attacked by a Jesuit priest named Garasse in his book *Doctrine curieuse des beaux esprits de ce temps*. The priest accused the poet of, among other things, sodomy and atheism. These accusations were based on certain pieces found in *Le Parnasse* signed by Théophile. In one, entitled simply "Satire" the poet speaks of his bad luck, which includes venereal disease and getting "fucked by fate":

> L'on ne me voit point rire aux farces,
> Je n'aime ni bals ni chansons,
> Foutre des culs et des garcons,
> Maugrébieu, des cons et de garces.
> (I can no longer be seen laughing at farces,
> I like neither dances nor songs,
> Fucking asses and boys,
> Damn it, cunts and girls.)

In a sonnet from the same collection, Théophile complains to his mistress Philis about his impotence and his regret of their sexual relationship. He concludes with the prayer:

> Mon Dieu, je me repens d'avoir si mal vécu:
> Et si votre courroux à ce coup ne me tue,
> Je fais v u désormais de ne foutre qu'en cul.
> (My God, I repent for having lived so badly:
> And if your wrath spares me this time,
> I promise henceforth to only fuck in the ass.)

Apart from the turmoil created by some of his poetry, Théophile's personal life was also attacked. He was known to have had a number of homosexual relationships, including one with a pimp/prostitute named Louis Sageot and another with an old school friend, Guez de Balzac. Both of these relationships came back to haunt him during his trial, but the testimony of Guez proved to be the most damning.

Théophile's trial and banishment in 1625 brought to an end the visibility of the libertine movement. The poet spent the last year of his life with the wealthy and powerful friends who had supported him throughout his career. The time spent prison had ruined his health, and he died one year after being released during a stay in Paris. He was buried in the church cemetery of St. Nicholas des Champs.   *Todd Black*

Bibliography

Théophile de Viau. *Oeuvres poétiques*. Guido Saba, ed. Paris: Bordas, 1990.

Lever, Maurice. *Les Bûchers de Sodome*. Paris: Fayard, 1985.

See also France; French Literature; Libertine and Libertinism; Sodomy Trials

Third Sex

In the West, the notion of a third sex that combines elements of male and female finds its roots in classical antiquity. Plato's *Symposium* refers to a period in prehistory during which the existence of man, woman, and a union of the two (or man-woman) mirrored the tripartite nature of the sun, earth, and moon. The three sexes were doubly embodied: each was two-headed and eight-limbed. After these early humans tried to defeat the gods, the gods separated them into halves; thus, love begins when halves seek to restore their original wholeness. The inclusion of a third sex in this myth of origin already presupposes the possibility of same-sex love. Subsequent literary allusions to a third sex occur fairly frequently, for instance in works by Mary Wortley Montagu and Johann Winckelmann in the eighteenth century and in modernist novels by Djuna Barnes and Thomas Mann in the twentieth century.

In 1860s, Karl Heinrich Ulrichs drew from Plato's work to develop a sexological theory of the Urning, or male homosexual. His *Riddle of Man-Manly Love* calls for the acceptance of the Urning, relying on complex distinctions among sex organs, secondary sexual characteristics, gendered behaviors, and drives. Not an inherently degenerate being, the Urning was, rather, a woman's soul trapped in a man's body. While Ulrichs's third-sex theory concerns mostly the male homosexual, he also proposed the existence of a fourth sex, in which masculine souls are similarly trapped inside women's bodies.

The world-renowned sexologist Magnus Hirschfeld reworked Ulrichs's theory later in the nineteenth-century, listing various types of intermediaries, including the hermaphrodite, the transvestite, and the homosexual. Like Ulrichs, Hirschfeld challenged the notion of a pathological homosexuality, actively working toward tolerance of the third sex and critiquing rigid distinctions between male and female. Prefiguring the discovery of estrogen and testosterone, Hirschfeld suggested that hormones were responsible for the congenital nature of the in-

T termediary. Though he, like Ulrichs, challenged polarized sexual binarisms, his theory proves paradoxical, for it relied on fixed notions of masculinity and femininity even as it suggested that "absolute representatives of their sex are . . . abstractions, invented extremes" (Hirschfeld 220).

In the early twentieth century, Edward Carpenter expounded on the third-sex theory to argue that intermediary types were more highly evolved than males and females. Carpenter suggested, for example, that intermediaries were uniquely suited to religious or military endeavors. By mid-century, however, the third-sex theory was abandoned by scientists and sexologists, many of whom overlooked the ambiguities this theory allows.

As both Ulrichs and Hirschfeld's formulations indicate, the introduction of a third term to the male/female binary seems to produce a dizzying array of reconfigurations of heteronormative gender roles and object choices: Hirschfeld himself hypothesized the existence of over 43 million classes of intermediaries. Recent critiques of sexual dimorphism use the concepts of third sex and third gender fruitfully to challenge static categorizations of male, female, masculine, and feminine, arguing that such dimorphism is neither inescapable nor universal. Notably, Gilbert Herdt's anthology *Third Sex, Third Gender* discusses the ways in which the Native American Indian berdache, the Indian *hijra,* the eunuch, the transsexual, the sapphist, and the sodomite challenge, cross culturally and transhistorically, the myth of "normal" heterosexuality.   *Nancy San Martin*

Bibliography

Herdt, Gilbert, ed. *Third Sex, Third Gender: Beyond Sexual Dimorphism in Culture and History.* New York: Zone, 1994.

Hirschfeld, Magnus. *Transvestites: The Erotic Drive to Cross Dress.* 1910. Trans. Michael A. Lombardi-Nash. Buffalo: Prometheus, 1991.

See also Berdache; Carpenter, Edward; *Hijras* of India; Hirschfeld, Magnus; Homosexuality; Inversion; Mann, Thomas; Melanesia; Plato; Sexology; Sexual Orientation; Transsexualism; Winckelmann, Johann Joachim

Thom, William J. (1941–)

William J. Thom's appointment by Mayor Edward I. Koch as New York City's first openly gay judge capped an important career as a gay legal activist.

Born in 1941 and educated at Princeton and Yale Law School, Thom was a junior attorney at a New York law firm by day and a member of the Gay Activists Alliance by night, working on the successful effort to get the American Bar Association to condemn consensual sodomy laws.

He founded the Lambda Legal Defense and Education Fund, the world's first gay rights public interest law firm, in 1973. *In re Thom,* 33 N.Y.2d 609 (1973), the case in which his application to allow Lambda to practice law was approved by New York's highest court, was a landmark decision establishing associational rights for gay people. Thom served as a Lambda board member and cooperating attorney while practicing in partnership with E. Carrington Boggan in one of the few openly gay law firms in the United States during the 1970s.

Beginning in 1979, Thom submitted his name to judicial screening panels and three times campaigned in primary elections for a Democratic nomination to the New York Civil Court. Although he never won election, his efforts and qualifications earned him interim appointments to Civil Court for four years beginning in 1984, after which he joined the New York City Law Department, specializing in appellate litigation until 1994.

Thom received Lambda's "Liberty Award" at its twentieth anniversary celebration in 1993. He currently practices law in New York City.

Arthur S. Leonard

Bibliography

Leonard, Arthur. "Empowering Sexual Minorities Through Legal Organization." In *Sexuality and the Law: An Encyclopedia of Major Legal Cases.* New York: Garland, 1993, chap. 41.

See also Gay Activists Alliance (GAA); National Gay and Lesbian Task Force; U.S. Law: Discrimination; U.S. Law: Equal Protection

Thomas Aquinas (1224/1225–1274)

Thomas Aquinas was a preeminent teacher of Christian theology at the University of Paris and the schools of his religious order, the Dominicans. Although his teachings were often controversial during his lifetime, they came to be adopted first by the Dominicans then by the papacy in the centuries after his death. From the Counter-Reformation on, Thomas's terminology and doctrine were frequently incorporated in the official documents of the

Catholic Church, and his writings were widely used as textbooks for theological and philosophical instruction. Thomas himself mentions same-sex desire or intercourse in a number of texts, but he never discusses it at any length. He treats it most carefully when analyzing sins of *luxuria*, or sexual self-indulgence. One category of these sins Thomas names with the traditional term "vices against nature." They comprise any genital activity other than penile-vaginal intercourse in an approved position: masturbation, mutual masturbation, oral sex, any same-sex activity, bestiality. Thomas counts the worst of these bestiality, but he treats none of them in this passage as particularly heinous. Elsewhere, however, Thomas seems to endorse stronger condemnations. He singles out same-sex activity as a special denial of God's plan to the extent that it violates the fundamental purposes for animal reproduction. On these grounds, he sometimes likens it to murder. At the same time, and by misreading Aristotle, Thomas describes the sin as bestial, since it degrades human beings to the level of animals.

Mark D. Jordan

Bibliography

Jordan, Mark D. *The Invention of Sodomy in Christian Theology*. Chicago: University of Chicago Press, 1997, 136–58.

See also Alan of Lille; Albert the Great; Augustine of Hippo; Canon Law; Catholicism; Christianity Natural Law

Thomson, Virgil (Garnett) (1896–1989)

The Missouri-born composer and critic was celebrated for his collaboration with Gertrude Stein and for his literary skill as music critic of the *New York Herald Tribune* from 1940 to 1954. Thomson was trained by French-oriented teachers at Harvard and in France by the legendary Nadia Boulanger, though he was critical of her and more influenced by the music of Erik Satie. If other homosexual Euro-American composers often looked to the exotic for inspiration, Thomson based his modest diatonic style for the most part on the Baptist hymns and other vernacular idioms of his childhood and cultivated a careful approach to musical prosody. Combined with the Stein collaboration (besides the two operas, *Four Saints in Three Acts* and *The Mother of Us All*, her influence also led to a series of "musical portraits"), this should have been a winning combi-

nation for America. It didn't work. Copland captured the middle ground with his urbanely bucolic All-American-Boy ballets, the younger John Cage (a Thomson protégé who provided musical commentary for the first biography) took over the avant-garde, and the "complexity boys" (as Virgil called them), headed by the straight Roger Sessions, appropriated the university faculties and foundation grants—but not the Pulitzer Prize (which Thomson won in 1949 for his score for the film *Louisiana Story*). "We all loved his music and rarely performed it," said Leonard Bernstein in grand elegiac mood (Tommasini 6).

Thomson's retort was simple and lethal: he practiced music criticism. Smarter, wittier, and more stylish than almost anyone (the Constant Lambert of *Music Ho!* dimly compares), he laid waste around him in prose that exhilarates with its perceptions and tires with its too frequent malice. He was the model of musical subversion in his day, and has influenced all trenchant music critics since (e.g., Joseph Kerman, John Rockwell, Susan McClary)—not least in refusing to acknowledge the artificial barriers set up around "classical music" by both the music and "music appreciation" industries, which he understood and pilloried. His pontificating was accepted by a readership conditioned to egocentricty from composers since Beethoven started striking attitude in the early 1800s—Virgil could not escape this debt to the Teutonic tradition he loathed. As a homosexual he belonged to the deeply closeted and much ashamed variety: few in the music world were less closeted, however, and fewer still had his experience of being arrested in a police raid on a gay brothel (1942). In his later years, despite his mean-spiritedness, racism, and homophobia, Thomson was surrounded by a circle of young (mostly) gay men, who put up with his cantankerousness for the sake of his celebrity, charm, and cleverness (and perhaps something more), and catered to his every need. One of them, Anthony Tommasini, has published a warts-and-all biography, a brilliant, compassionate application of modern gay-male sensibility to the life of a historic homosexual/musical figure that may belatedly gain for Thomson what his own rigorous self-advertising campaign never seemed fully to achieve.

Philip Brett

Bibliography

Thomson, Virgil. *A Virgil Thomson Reader*. Boston: Houghton Mifflin, 1981.

———. *Virgil Thomson*. New York: Knopf, 1966; reprinted by Dutton, 1985.

Tommasini, Anthony. *Virgil Thomson: Composer on the Aisle.* New York: Norton, 1997.

See also Bernstein, Leonard; Cage, John; Copland, Aaron; Music and Musicians I: Classical Music

Thurman, Wallace (1902–1934)

Born into a middle-class family in 1902 in Salt Lake City, Utah, Wallace Thurman was one of the most promising and, ultimately, tragic figures of the Harlem Renaissance. Generally recognized by his peers as perhaps the most intellectually brilliant and ambitious of their number, his career never fulfilled its promise because of Thurman's ambivalence about his own sexual desires and the often abrasive manner and self-destructive lifestyle he adopted in an attempt to camouflage them. An arrest for "indecency" in a men's room soon after his arrival in New York City made his sexual proclivities a matter of public record in a way from which he never fully recovered.

After attending the University of Utah for two years and graduating from the University of Southern California, Thurman arrived in New York City in 1925, determined to make a name for himself. As Thurman's friend, the novelist Dorothy West, wrote of Thurman's position within the "Negro literary renaissance": "He wanted to get in on the ground floor, and not get off the crowded lift till it banged the roof and skyrocketed him and such others as had his ballast of self-assurance and talent, to a fixed place in the stars" (West 77).

Although Thurman's production was wide-ranging (plays, film scripts, novels, essays, and innumerable book reviews), he revealed his ambition most notably in his creation and editing of two short-lived journals—*Fire!!* (1926) and *Harlem, A Forum of Negro Life* (1928). As Langston Hughes described *Fire!!*, its purpose was "to burn up a lot of the old, dead conventional Negro-White ideas of the past, *épater le bourgeois* into a realization of the existence of the younger Negro writers and artists, and provide us with an outlet for publication not available in the limited pages of the small negro magazines then existing." Thurman's contribution, the short story "Cordelia the Crude," an account of a teenage girl's relatively untraumatic embracing of a life as a prostitute, was particularly representative of this aesthetic. This story later became the basis for Thurman's most financially successful effort, the Broadway play (coauthored with white playwright William Jourdan Rapp) *Harlem* (1929).

Thurman's major works, however, are the novels *The Blacker the Berry* (1929), an examination of black interracial prejudice, and *Infants of the Spring* (1932), a roman à clef and satire of the Harlem Renaissance offering thinly disguised depictions of most well-known members of the Harlem intelligentsia. In this novel, he comes closer than in any of his other published works to explicitly acknowledging and narratively working through issues related to his homosexuality, most strikingly with the character Paul Arbian, based on Richard Bruce Nugent. As West wrote of Thurman, "He wanted to be thoroughly male and was afraid that he was not" (West 80).

Thurman died from "liquor, T.B., and despair" (Walden 207) in the charity ward of City Hospital.

Terry Rowden

Bibliography

Walden, Daniel. "The Short Promising Life of Wallace Thurman." In *The Harlem Renaissance Re-examined.* Victor Kramer, ed. New York: AMS Press, 1987.

West, Dorothy. "Elephant's Dance: A Memoir of Wallace Thurman." *Black World.* 20, no. 1 (November 1970): 77–86.

See also African American Gay Culture; Harlem Renaissance; Hughes, Langston

Tippett, Sir Michael Kemp (1905–1998)

This English composer is known particularly for his operas, string quartets, symphonies, and vocal music. After studies at the Royal Conservatory of Music with Charles Wood and C. H. Kitson, Tippett made composition his primary vocation, while supporting himself through conducting amateur choirs and teaching. His most important teaching post was at Morley College in London (1932–1951). Tippett's works, full of harmonic and rhythmic complexities, intricate counterpoint, and extended, ornate melodies, took a long time to gain acceptance by the musical establishment. His success since the 1960s may be measured by the many commissions he has received, most recently by the Toronto, London, and Boston symphony orchestras for *The Rose Lake.*

Tippett believed that all an artist's activities nourish his inner creative life and are directed to the ends of the art that he produces; thus, an artist's social and personal awareness is crucial. For Tippett, this necessary self-awareness was reached after completing a course of Jungian analysis and self-analysis in the late 1930s. Jungian mythological and psychological symbols proliferate in Tippett's operas, particularly *The Midsummer Marriage* (1946–1952), whose libretto, as in many of Tippett's works, is by the composer. A longtime pacifist, Tippett spent two months in jail in 1943 rather than comply with the terms imposed by the tribunal adjudicating his status as a conscientious objector. His social and political consciousness is also reflected in operas like *A Child of Our Time* (1939–1941) and *The Knot Garden* (1966–1969, premiered 1970). Mel and Dov, the interracial couple in the latter opera, are most likely the first modern gay characters in opera.

Several collections of essays by Tippett, encompassing a wide variety of subjects, have been published: *Moving into Aquarius* (1958-1974), *Music of the Angels* (1980), and *Tippett on Music* (1995); the last two were edited by Tippett's companion, Meirion (Bill) Bowen, who has also written a short study of the composer.

Stephen McClatchie

Bibliography

Bowen, Meirion. *Michael Tippett*. London: Robson Books, 1981.

Kemp, Ian. *Tippett: The Composer and His Music*. London: Eulenburg Books, 1984.

Theil, Gordon. *Michael Tippett: A Bio-bibliography*. New York: Greenwood Press, 1989.

Tippett, Michael. *Those Twentieth-Century Blues: An Autobiography*. London: Hutchinson, 1991.

See also Jung, Carl; Music and Musicians 1: Classical Music; Opera

Tom of Finland (c.1925?–1991)

In the winter of 1939–1940, Touko Laaksonen, a first-year art student in Helsinki, was drafted into the Finnish Army. Although a truce was declared while he was still in officer training camp, the war was not over. For the next five years, Touko and every able-bodied man in Finland wore military gear. For most of that time, they had nothing to do but admire each other by day and fondle whomever they met in the blackouts at night. That sounds like a perfect training camp for turning out an artist infatuated with men in boots and uniforms. Actually, since Touko grew up in semirural Finland, he was surrounded practically from birth by burly farmhands and lumberjacks. Even his school bus

A classic image from Tom of Finland. Photo courtesy of the Tom of Finland Foundation.

driver wore a uniform with a peaked cap and knee boots. His earliest extant drawings form a cartoon storybook. At its climax, big, strong policemen in boots and uniforms come to the rescue. It was done when he was five years old.

Thirty-two years later, the cover of the spring 1957 issue of the popular American muscle magazine *Physique Pictorial* featured a laughing lumberjack balancing on a floating log. His bare chest was broad, his hips narrow, and his thighs strained the fabric of his pants, but it was the smile on his face that made every gay man who saw that first published Tom of Finland drawing remember it forever after. For seven years, the little physique magazines had been extolling the charms of the undraped male. Artists had been doing that at least since Michelangelo and Caravaggio, but these periodicals went at it with an openness that was new and some of their contributors, George Quaintance in particular, were quite good at it.

So why was Tom of Finland's work so memorable? His drawings began being published right at a watershed time for homosexuals, a change symbolized by the shift in terminology that occurred during those years: the harried homosexual men of the fifties had begun to coalesce into the gay communities of the sixties, a movement that would blossom into full gay pride in the seventies. Twelve years before Stonewall, when the term *out* had not yet been coined, the artist now called Tom of Finland quite consciously decided that not only would the men in his drawings be as masculine and sexy as he could make them but they would also be openly, proudly, and happily gay. A figure in the background of that debut drawing is often overlooked, a second logger on a log behind the first. It is clear that the first lumberjack has removed his shirt and is smiling for him. Even the censors knew that, but what could they do? Smiling was not on the list of censurable acts.

As an artist, Tom of Finland had his finger on exactly what made homo hearts beat faster. Each of his men was a walking (sucking, fucking) compendium of everything that was sexiest about a man. Other homoerotic artists of the time (Quaintance, Étienne, Harry Bush) drew some very arousing male figures as well, but what made Tom's work unforgettable to the gay men who saw it was the subliminal message of pride and affirmation. That took it beyond what any heterosexual erotic art could ever be for straight viewers (who did not need the reassurance). By the later drawings, the extra meaning was no longer subliminal. Tom's men demonstrated for all to see that it was okay, it was even fun, to be gay.

By the mid-sixties, Tom was the most famous Finnish artist in the world, but the financial rewards were not what they would have been had his field been female nudes, or even landscapes. Not until the early seventies did he begin to see his work decently printed, and not until sixteen years after his first publication did Tom have his first gallery exhibition in Hamburg, Germany. In the late seventies, financial security finally arrived in the person of Durk Dehner, a Canadian American who became not just his business partner but briefly his lover as well (after the death of Veli, Tom's Finnish lover of twenty-nine years, in 1983), and who remained one of his favorite models for his drawings for over ten years.

Tom was a household name in the gay world but the straight world was largely unaware of his pneumatically muscled, meticulously rendered, monster-donged icons of masculinity until shortly before his death, when the Finnish Cartoonist League named him Cartoonist of the Year (1990), and a documentary of his work, *Daddy and the Muscle Academy,* was seen on Finnish TV, won a Finnish Emmy in its category, and was featured at film festivals worldwide. Tom died on November 6, 1991, but his acclaim continued to grow. His biography went briefly to number one on the Finnish bestseller list, and a monograph of his works, published by Benedikt Taschen, the largest art book publisher in the world, proved so popular that a second, larger volume was created.

But Tom himself was proudest of the Tom of Finland Foundation, which he and Dehner formed in 1985, originally to preserve his own numerous works but that even before his death had became a haven for erotic art of all sorts, eventually sponsoring exhibitions and contests, and planning for a museum of erotic art.

Through the seventies, eighties, and into the nineties, society became less and less oppressive to gay men, but there was still more than enough guilt and repression to make each man's first sighting of a Tom of Finland a memorable event, titillating his libido with incredibly sexy sailor boys, leathermen, and cops and at the same time soothing his ego with the message: be proud, be happy, be gay.

F. Valentine Hooven III

Bibliography

Sternweiler, A., and H. G. Hannesen, eds. *Goodbye to Berlin? 100 Jahre Scheulenbewegung.* Berlin: Verlag Rosa Winkler, 1997.

Townsend, Larry. *The Leatherman's Handbook.* New York: Freeway, 1974.

See also Caravaggio; Leathermen; Michelangelo Buonarroti; Physical Culture; Quaintance, George; Sadomasochism

Tondelli, Pier Vittorio (1957–1992)

This Italian novelist never became a political activist, yet he embodied a new attitude in Italian gay culture. He spoke openly about his sexual orientation and supported other young gay authors by editing anthologies of homosexual writings. *Altri libertini* (1980), his first collection of short stories about identities "on the edge," such as drag queens, druggies, and sexually confused teenagers, is now a classic of contemporary Italian literature. *Pao Pao* (1982), his first novel, recounts the experiences of a gay man during his military service. An involving and melancholic monologue in the form of "stream of consciousness," the novel confirmed Tondelli as a remarkable and accomplished narrator interested in depicting marginal, unconventional situations. *Rimini* (1984), a much less convincing text, was a best seller for several months. This novel, set in one of the most touristy beaches in northern Italy, is Tondelli's attempt to write a postmodern narration. Postmodernism is also the central theme of *Un weekend postmoderno* (1986), a sort of anthology of the author's meditations, travel narrations, and essays on contemporary Italian and American literature and art. Tondelli's masterpiece is *Camere separate* (Separate Rooms, 1985). Considered "a gay Romeo and Juliet," the novel is Tondelli's most convincing meditation on the nature of gay love, commitment, and remembrance. Leo, and Italian writer in his early thirties who constantly travels from Milan to Paris and London, remembers his love story with Thomas, who died of AIDS months after their separation. While having new sex encounters, Leo cannot help but question the reasons they slowly drifted apart. Both graphic and poignant, *Camere separate* is undoubtedly the most passionate gay novel ever written in Italian.   *Armando Maggi*

See also AIDS Literature; Italian Literature; Italy; Postmodernism

Tourism and Travel

The tradition linking travel and homosexuality is long and venerable (arguably reaching back far beyond even such peripatetic nineteenth-century celebrities as Oscar Wilde and Lord Byron to the likes of Friedrich and Alexander the Great). But as the twentieth century draws to a close, never before in history have so many gay men and lesbians throughout the world been so mobile in their holiday choices. U.S. marketing studies, for example, have shown that nearly 90 percent of all American homosexuals have recently traveled within their own country and nearly half abroad; this business has recently been valued at more than $70 billion annually.

Many travel to the same destinations—both well-trod and out-of-the-way—as the general public, while a significant percentage prefer to patronize specific cities and resort areas that have attracted large homosexual followings. Prerequisites for such popularity usually include a significant and vibrant local gay and lesbian community, culture, and/or social scene (or, in a few cases, a critical mass of young males catering to sex tourists).

North American cities that are the most popular with gays include New York, San Francisco, Miami Beach, Los Angeles, Washington, D.C., and Montreal, while top overseas magnets are London, Amsterdam, Berlin, Sydney, and Bangkok. Recognizing

its economic potential, many localities and even countries have begun specifically promoting themselves to the gay market.

Parallel to them are a handful of resort towns—many of which started out as artists' colonies in the early years of the twentieth century—whose tourism has become significantly or even largely homosexual. The best-known U.S. examples are Fire Island, on New York's Long Island; Key West, Florida; Provincetown on Massachusetts's Cape Cod; and Palm Springs in southern California. On the next tier are a handful of regional gay-popular resorts such as Rehoboth Beach, Delaware; the Lake Michigan communities of Saugatuck and Douglas; and the Russian River area north of San Francisco. Abroad, such vacation oases exist mostly but not exclusively in western Europe; examples include the town of Sitges in Spanish Catalonia as well the islands of Mykonos in Greece and Ibiza off Spain's Mediterranean coast.

Special events such as the international Gay Games (held quadrennially), lavishly produced gay pride celebrations, and annual "gay days" at theme parks like Walt Disney World play a significant part in drawing homosexual tourists at certain times of year. In addition, many American and increasing numbers of foreign destinations have since the 1980s hosted annual "circuit parties," hedonistic and often drug-filled events that have created a core of men who regularly spend thousands of dollars every year just to attend; among the highest profile are the White Party in Palm Springs, the Winter Party in Miami Beach, Fire Island's Morning Party, New York City's Black Party, and Montreal's Black and Blue. The highest-profile lesbian counterpart is the Dinah Shore Weekend, scheduled around the eponymous women's golf tournament held each March in Palm Springs.

As the number of openly homosexual men and women has grown, and as many of these make travel a regular part of their lives, a gay-oriented travel industry that barely existed just a decade or so ago has grown to cater to them. Pioneered in 1972 by tour operator Hanns Ebensten (now based in Key West), the field of tours designed specifically for homosexuals began burgeoning particularly in the late 1980s, with the RSVP gay cruise operator (founded in 1987) in the forefront. Since its founding in 1983, the International Gay Travel Association has grown from a handful of gay-owned travel enterprises to a 1998 membership of 1,310 companies and organizations in 30 countries (in addition to travel agents and tour operators, they include airlines, publishers, cruise lines, and city tourism boards). In 1997 it became the International Gay and Lesbian Travel Association and moved from Key West to Fort Lauderdale, Florida—itself an up-and-coming gay destination. Member companies such as Advance Damron Vacations, Alyson Adventures, L'Arc en Ciel, Men on Vacation, and Our Family Abroad provide a wide range of products for various budgets, geared to everything from cultural offerings to adventure travel to sports, and in just about every conceivable part of the world.

Europe and Australia also boast a growing gay travel industry; German-based Mantours has an international reputation, and Australia has its own Australian Gay and Lesbian Travel Association. A few tours have specifically homosexual-identified themes, from one that retraces the Outback route of the popular film *Priscilla, Queen of the Desert* to a dungeons-and-leather excursion through Europe. Mainstream companies from American Express to British Airways have also gotten into the act, devoting ever more advertising to and creating travel products aimed at the gay market.

A booming subset of gay travel vendors are companies specializing in cruises and all-inclusive resort vacations predominantly aimed at homosexuals. RSVP (more popular with men) and Olivia (for women) are two of the better-known companies that charter ships for regular gay cruises, while Atlantis has made something of a specialty of booking Club Meds in Mexico and the Caribbean for exclusively gay vacations.

Accompanying this boom has been an ever-growing selection of media geared to the gay traveler. The pioneer was Germany's Bruno Gmünder, who began publishing the worldwide *Spartacus* guide in Berlin in 1970; it now claims annual sales of more than 78,000. In the United States, the best-known resources for many years were the male-oriented *Damron's Address Book*, *Gayellow Pages*, and the Ferrari guides for women, which, like *Spartacus*, were originally a mix of addresses and advertisements with minimal description. In the 1990s, major publishers like Random House, Hyperion, and HarperCollins have joined smaller presses in capitalizing on the increasing interest in gay travel by bringing out their own gay guidebooks, sometimes under well-known brand names like Access and Fodor's. Foreign language phrasebooks came on the market as well, such as *Hot! International/Gay* and *Hot! International/Lesbian*.

Somewhat less crowded is the field of periodicals devoted primarily or exclusively to gay travel. The oldest, *Our World* (circulation 50,000), has been publishing monthly since 1988, the same year that Boston's four-year-old *The Guide* (current circulation 30,000) went national and began extensive domestic and international travel coverage. They were followed in 1992 by the respected newsletter *Out & About* (circulation 16,500). American gay publications such as *Out* and *Genre* regularly run travel articles, as do many local gay newspapers and magazines and overseas publications. Outnumbering both books and periodicals are the multiplicity of on-line resources, based both on the Internet and on commercial services like America Online, Compuserve, and Prodigy, dealing with some aspect of gay travel. Varying widely in quality and currency, they number in the tens of thousands.

Even as major issues of discrimination and homophobia remain worldwide and in many areas of life, gay and lesbian travelers still face discrimination, particularly in much of Asia, Africa, and Latin America. The Caribbean has proved a notoriously homophobic region, as illustrated most recently in 1998 by the refusal of the Cayman Islands to permit a previously scheduled port call by Norwegian Cruise Lines Leeward, chartered by Atlantis, claiming they could not count on this group to uphold the standards of appropriate behavior expected of visitors. Substituting a stop in Belize, even there passengers were confronted by hundreds of picketers. While the world of travel certainly offers today's homosexuals opportunities beyond the wildest dreams of earlier generations, incidents such as these are reminders that tolerance unfortunately is often a distinctly limited and precious commodity throughout the world.   *David Appell*

Bibliography

Andrusia, David. *Gay Europe*. New York: Perigee, 1995.

Appell, David, and Balido, Paul. *Access Gay USA*. New York: HarperCollins, 1998.

Chestnut, Mark. *The Gay Vacation Guide*. Secaucus, N.J.: Citadel Press, 1997.

Ebensten, Hanns. *Volleyball with the Cuna Indians and Other Gay Travel Adventures*. New York: Penguin, 1987.

Newton, Esther. *Cherry Grove, Fire Island: Sixty Years in America's First Gay and Lesbian Town*. Boston: Beacon Press, 1993.

Sullivan, Andrew. *Fodor's Gay Guide to the USA*. New York: Random House, 1996.

See also Alexander the Great; Amsterdam; Bangkok; Berlin; Business; Byron, George Gordon, Lord; Circuit Party Scene; Gay Games; London; Los Angeles; Marketing; Miami; Resorts and Beaches; San Francisco; Washington, D.C.; Wilde, Oscar

Townsend, Prescott (1894–1973)

Born into a prominent Boston family, Prescott Townsend claimed direct descent from twenty-three passengers on the *Mayflower*. One of his revolutionary heroes was his ancestor, Roger Sherman, the only signer of the Declaration of Independence, the Articles of Confederation, and the Constitution. Prescott graduated from Harvard University (1918) and served in the U.S. Navy during World War I.

During the Roaring Twenties, he traveled to Paris and was a moving force in the bohemian underground of Boston's Beacon Hill and Provincetown. He backed theater productions, experimented with new architecture, encouraged authors, and played an active part in the city's gay life.

Even in the 1920s, he examined ways of legalizing sodomy and was active in the Mattachine Society. He opposed their desire for respectability (they wanted to legalize sex only for those over twenty-one) and soon formed his own Demophile Union of Boston. From the beginning, he was something of a hippie and became a flower person in the 1960s. Underground filmmaker Andy Meyer's *An Early Clue to the New Direction* featured Townsend propounding his snowflake theory of sexuality. He argued that people, like snowflakes, are unique, but that all sexual relations fit into a hit, miss, or submit pattern. Unfortunately, all his papers were destroyed in a fire in 1971; his publications survive only in the Kinsey Institute Library. In his final years, his work was taken up by Boston's anarchist *Fag Rag*, which held a celebration in Townsend's honor a month before his death.　　　　　*Charles Shively*

Bibliography

History Project. *Improper Bostonians: Lesbian and Gay History from the Puritans to Playland.* Boston: Beacon, 1998, 194–97.

See also Gay Left; Gay Liberation; Journalism; Kinsey, Alfred; Mattachine Society

Trade

Trade refers, either individually or collectively, to nonreciprocal sexual partners, usually considered to

be heterosexual or bisexual. The term gained currency among female prostitutes in the late eighteenth century before it migrated to the emerging homosexual subculture. Besides self-identifying (or being identified) as heterosexual, trade are expected to engage solely in the active or penetrative role during sex, reflecting an attitude that has persisted in various cultures throughout the ages—with roots in ancient Greece—by which only the passive or penetrated position in homosexual sex was considered shameful for adult males, a violation of normative gender roles. Additionally, trade's designates are required to assume a convincingly masculine demeanor. Failures in any of these particulars risk being judged a closet case, one with an inadequately convincing grasp of heterosexual identity. *Commercial trade* refers to seemingly heterosexual hustlers serving a gay clientele. *Rough trade* designates men who turn violent either during or after a sexual encounter. This could entail a much appreciated sadistic streak or an unwanted gay bashing. Trade, as a category, flourished in the earlier decades of the century, pre-Stonewall, and before the hetero-homo binarism gained its current hegemonic currency. As the century progressed, and as knowledge of homosexuality increasingly penetrated America's cultural consciousness, the category of trade became increasingly restricted as individuals were compelled to attach a sexual identity to their sex acts.

Increasingly, trade became aligned with those venues that were to some degree anonymous, or allowed surreptitious contact between men, such as locales for public cruising like parks, public rest rooms, or tearooms, or in situations in which women are absent or the sexes are highly segregated, such as the military, boarding schools, and prisons.

It is difficult to gauge the frequency of trade as a phenomenon, as those who fit the category of trade are unlikely to designate themselves by this term. Nor are they likely to admit or broadcast their activities. Hence, most evidence of trade is anecdotal and/or apocryphal. It should not be assumed, however, that trade does not exist, or exists only as a fantasy among gay men. Sufficient evidence exists of the disjunction between sex acts and sexual identity in many countries and cultures for us to accept trade as an actual phenomenon. It must be acknowledged, however, that trade depends on perception, not essence, and the prevalence of trade as a transitional category—in which men having sex with other men initially refuse to adopt a label like gay, as a prelude to fully coming out—is evidence of the

T increasingly narrow nature of that gap in the modern cultural climate.

Scott Speirs

Bibliography

Chauncey, George. *Gay New York: Gender, Urban Culture, and the Making of the Gay Male World, 1980–1940.* New York: Basic Books, 1994.

Grahn, Judy. *Another Mother Tongue: Gay Words, Gay Worlds.* Boston: Beacon, 1984.

Humphries, Laud. *Tearoom Trade.* Chicago: Aldine, 1970.

See also Coming Out; Greece; Hustlers; Relationships; Sex Practice: Anal Sex; Sex Practice: Oral Sex; Sexual Orientation; Tearooms; Trick

Transgender

Transgender, like *queer*—with which it has much in common—is a concept and emergent identity of the 1980s and 1990s. The term is said to derive from *transgenderist,* coined in the 1960s by male-to-female cross-dresser and early transgender researcher Virginia Prince as an alternative to the stigmatizing and objectifying medical category of the "transvestite." She applied it to those like herself who chose to cross-live as the "opposite sex" without seeking the body-altering treatments of hormone therapy and surgery that the medical community had established as normative and necessary for the transsexual, an equally stigmatized diagnostic category. For many in the gender community *transgender* and *transgenderist* are synonyms. However, others employ *transgender* as an umbrella term for all those who might challenge the West's sex and gender binary oppositions, including not only occasional cross-dressers and full-time "transgenderists" like Prince but also drag kings and drag queens, pre-, post-, and nonoperative transsexuals, intersexuals, she-males, gender-benders, and gender-fuckers, to name just a few of an ongoing proliferation of identities in an increasingly visible and vocal gender community, which now has its own lobby in Washington, D.C. (GenderPAC, directed by Riki Anne Wilchins, cofounder of Transsexual Menace). As the transgender symbol developed by Holly Boswell, Wendy Parker, and Cambridge, Mass., GenderTalk Radio host Nancy Nangeroni suggests, transgender represents a third alternative to the two sexes the West recognizes and legitimates, which in what queer theorist and philosopher Judith Butler and others have termed the "natural attitude" are usually understood as binary opposites based in a biology that expresses itself in quite distinct but complementary gender roles, whose occupants are naturally (hetero)sexually attracted to one another. For some, transgender is a "third sex" that, as in one vision of androgyny, combines male and female, masculine and feminine, to transcend the limitations of any single sex, a notion conveyed by the portion of the symbol that melds the signs for male and female. But the transgender "third" can equally signify the confounding of the West's bipolar structure of sex, gender, and sexuality, in which each serves as a support for the other, as queer theorist and literature scholar Marjorie Garber argues of transvestism in *Vested Interests* (1992). Through the refusal to identify with or assimilate to either sex or gender, transgender calls into question sexual orientation, which depends on identifying the sex of partners. Such transgender subversion is signified by the symbol as a whole, which maps together in novel fashion lavender, pink and blue, and male and female elements pointing in multiple directions, providing no compass for those who would locate themselves at the poles of sex-gender sexuality binaries.

The desire of trans activists and theorists to define the transgendered as transgressive in this fashion—"warriors" in the battle against oppressive gendering, to echo the title of Leslie Feinberg's book about the history of transgender—is strong. To "pass" is to risk being labeled an assimilationist gender defender. For that reason, some argue, transgender excludes transsexuals, whose orientation to a sex reassignment surgery (SRS) that is at the heart of that medical diagnostic category makes them complicit with the system their very existence also throws into crisis. Others use transgender as if it were a synonym for transsexualism, whether pre-, post-, or nonoperative, just because transsexualism does unsettle assumptions about sex, gender, and sexuality, however briefly, particularly the foundational role of biological sex. Transsexualism and SRS are therefore at the center of debates in the gender community about gender politics. Some of the debates focus on whether medical professionals should continue to act as gatekeepers determining who qualifies for SRS, but many of them question whether SRS should take place at all. If the history of sexuality comprises the consolidation of a homo/hetero binary in the modern era, together with a specification of other "perversions," it also encompasses the constitution of a distinction between sex, understood as an essential and unchanging biology, and gender, a psychology and set of social roles once thought to be a direct expression of sex but now theorized as an identification in no way contingent on sex and potentially at odds with it. SRS has played a key role in this articulation of "gender," as well as in the structure of transgender subcultures, in which the desire for it has differentiated—and hierarchized—transsexuals and transvestites as those who are more and less identified with the gender of the "opposite sex" and therefore more or less "real" men or women. SRS helped establish gender as the core of identity that sex once was thought to be, what did not change even when sex did. The process of distinguishing and stabilizing gender began with nineteenth- and early-twentieth-century inversion theories of homosexuality, which defined it as "psychic hermaphroditism." Gay men, therefore, really were "feminine spirits" in men's bodies, and their attraction to other men was essentially heterosexual—an explanation that anticipates the contemporary definition of the transsexual as "trapped in the wrong (sexed) body." It was not until the 1910 publication of *Transvestites*, by gay cross-dresser, sexologist, and activist Magnus Hirschfeld, that crossdressing was distinguished from homosexuality, instead of being considered a symptom of it—a distinction still tenuous today in the minds of much of the heterosexual public. "Transsexualism" was not widely recognized as different from transvestism until the 1960s, although Hirschfeld used the term as early as 1923. Hormonal and surgical treatments were as central to the consolidation of the transsexual diagnosis and identity as the psychoanalytic and sexological discourses that had earlier specified and treated transvestism. Endocrinologist Harry Benjamin, the "father of transsexualism," was convinced that if psychotherapies could not adjust the transsexual's mind to the body, as seemed only too clear, then the body had to be altered to fit the mind. In altering the body to fit the mind, however, SRS ensured that Westerners did not have to alter their minds about the sex-gender binary to fit the fact of the "transsexual" bodies that troubled it. For many, SRS offers an individual—and pathologizing—solution to what is a political problem requiring a social revolution: limiting and oppressive gender roles.

Radical lesbian feminist Janice Raymond was one of the first to note this in her antitranssexual thesis, *The Transsexual Empire* (1979), recently reprinted with a new foreword on transgender, about which she is equally suspicious. Raymond argues that transsexuals are artifactual rather than real women because no one can change sex. Demanding an end to SRS, she makes it clear that chromosomes determine not only sex but also gender as an expression of sex because that sex determines how one is treated in the world; those with Y chromosomes are treated as men. Raymond's argument resorts to the older, essentialist worldview in which sex and gender were not distinct, although her calls for feminist gender role change are congruent only with social constructionist theory, since essentialism precludes significant change. While Kate Bornstein agrees that sex change is impossible, she neither rejects SRS nor endorses essentialist theories of gender. "I've no idea what a 'woman' feels like," she writes in *Gender Outlaw* (1994). "I never did feel like a girl or a woman; rather, it was my unshakable conviction that I was not a boy or a man" (24). Illogically, Raymond advocates critiquing gender while at the same time living out a gender congruent with the sex assigned at birth. Bornstein instead calls for the deconstruction—and destruction—of gender difference. In addition, she urges transgender play, "the ability to freely and knowingly become one or many of a limitless number of genders," also endorsed in the International Bill of Gender Rights adopted by the International Conference on Transgender Law and Employment Policy in 1993, printed in full in an appendix of *Transgender Warrior*. It is not clear whether Bornstein's two goals are compatible, nor how SRS is consistent with either, which Bornstein admits she found necessary for her "comfort" and believes should remain available because other transsexuals might too, even if the demand for it is "largely . . . a result of the cultural genital imperative," the "natural attitude" about sex-gender-sexuality. However, other trans activists and theorists have been much more critical of SRS, including Terri Webb and Gordene MacKenzie, who argue that one can live as a man or a woman without SRS; we therefore should change society, not sexes, cure bipolar culture, not its sex-gender transgressors.

Anthropologist Anne Bolin, author of a well-received scholarly book on transsexualism, suggests that three factors have made transgender identity increasingly possible. The closing of the university-affiliated, research-oriented gender identity clinics in the 1980s has meant that "gender dysphoric patients" have become "clients" at clinics that have to be more consumer-oriented to survive. It is no longer necessary to reproduce the stereotypes of transsexualism to qualify for hormonal therapy or SRS, nor is treatment with hormones seen only as a prelude to SRS, rather than an end in itself. Client-centered clinics, free from the necessity of studying a "condition" and compelled to cater to consumers for financial reasons, have tended to accept a greater diversity of gender presentations and sexual orientations as part of the treatments they offer, encouraging those who come to them for help to explore their gender and sexuality. Another key factor in the explosive growth of transgender is the appearance of new models of femininity besides traditional somatic frailty or pinup girl curves, which have enabled a greater number of people to identify and pass as a woman. Finally, the rise of trans activism has meant other options for transgender besides passing and "coming out" only within the "safe" spaces of the gender community or to encourage public acceptance of transsexual assimilation into a reassigned sex or better medical care. Trans activism is inspired by the lesbian and gay liberation movements, feminism, and struggles for racial equality, as well as by other New Left movements of the postwar era. Though Bolin does not mention it, trans activism also owes much to the media fascination with transsexualism and, to a lesser extent, cross-dressing and intersexuality, which has enabled a forum for publications ranging from autobiographies to "how to" books, and opportunities to reach a mass audience through television appearances, even if one simultaneously functions as exotic spectacle. In addition, trans activism and theory is indebted to the parallel explosion of queer activism and theory, in which genderqueer performances such as drag and camp have figured importantly, as have cross-cultural studies of gender and sexuality that suggest that the West's hierarchical binary oppositions are neither universal nor natural.

Bolin, Bornstein, Feinberg, and others clearly view transgender as both the cause and the effect of a renewed gender and sexual revolution. Not everyone shares their view, however. Some transsexuals are proud of having changed sexes, rather than confounding them, and reject the transgender identity for erasing their own. "Every application of the term transgender to me is an attempt to mask what I've done and as such co-opts my life, denies my experience, violates my very soul. I changed my sex . . . and proved that anatomy is not destiny," Margaret Deidre O'Hartigan has emphatically asserted. A few lesbian and gay activists believe the transgendered are really closet queens who need to acknowledge their homosexuality (ignoring the large number of transhomosexuals and gay or lesbian cross-dressers). Others worry that the transgendered, like drag queens and street fairies, will damage the gay movement's respectability or will waste activist time and energy better spent on the "core" constituency, which seems to be why the Human Rights Campaign initially opposed including gender in still-pending national hate crimes legislation for which it lobbied. But most critiques of transgender echo those made of androgyny and queer theory. Raymond argues that all too often, the transgendered "see masculinity and femininity as entities in and of themselves, to be preserved and grafted onto one another" either through combining or switching between them, rather than recognizing gender as an oppressive social construct whose roles must be dismantled, not reproduced. She claims that most transgenderists are men who add a little bit of traditional femininity to their traditional masculinity or adopt a "hyperfeminine and hypersexual" style, like RuPaul, who, she believes, simply recycles sexist feminine stereotypes. Finally, she suggests that transgender offers an individual solution to social and political problems: it "reduces resistance to wardrobes, hormones, surgery, and posturing," and by doing so, becomes yet another example of liberal humanist expressive individualism. Bernice Hausman, author of the most recent scholarly book on transsexualism, concurs with this conclusion, pointing out that much of Bornstein's language of consensual gender play assumes complete self-determination, as if social constraints did not operate at the deepest level of the psyche, constituting even our desires, including their gendered expression. Though Bornstein argues that identity is performative, rather than "essential" and based on biology, she writes as if there were an "I" prior to and apart from the gender acts said to socially construct it. Feminists have argued for years that such neuter identities, like "mankind," are inevitably masculine and masculinist; activists and scholars also have drawn our attention to how the supposedly "unmarked" naturalizes what serves the interests of the heterosexual, white, and middle class. Not surprisingly, critics are suspicious of the claim to an unmarked identity or transcendent position. Raymond is troubled by the FTM (female-to-male) transgendered protagonist of Feinberg's *Stone Butch Blues* (1993), who, she says, repudiates her lesbian womanhood and her critique of sexism and homophobia to identify with an "otherness" beyond both masculinity and femininity. In a similar vein, Biddy Martin critiques queer theory's desire to transcend the limitations of having a sex or gender and argues that femininity in particular is demonized as the constraining alternative to queer liberation. Pat Califia, too, asserts that gender is more than a prison and notes that Bornstein would not argue for the elimination of race as the solution to racism. She worries that the transgender call for the dissolution of gender will precipitate new "sex wars" like those that, in the past, have divided the feminist community, as gendered expressions of sexuality such as lesbian *butch* and *femme* again become suspect.

Carole-Anne Tyler

Bibliography

Bolin, Anne. "Transcending and Transgendering: Male-to-Female Transsexuals, Dichotomy, and Diversity." In *Third Sex, Third Gender: Beyond Sexual Dimorphism in Culture and History.* Gilbert Herdt, ed. New York: Zone Books, 1994, 447–85.

Bornstein, Kate. *Gender Outlaw: On Men, Women, and the Rest of Us.* New York: Routledge, 1994.

Bullough, Bonnie, Vern Bullough, and James Elias, eds. *Gender Blending.* Amherst, N.Y.: Prometheus Books, 1997.

Butler, Judith. *Gender Trouble: Feminism and the Subversion of Identity.* New York: Routledge, 1990.

Califia, Pat. *Sex Changes: The Politics of Transgenderism.* San Francisco: Cleis Press, 1997.

Feinberg, Leslie. *Transgender Warriors: Making History from Joan of Arc to RuPaul.* Boston: Beacon Press, 1996.

Garber, Marjorie. *Vested Interests: Cross-Dressing and Cultural Anxiety.* New York: Routledge, 1992.

Hausman, Bernice. *Changing Sex: Transsexualism, Technology, and the Idea of Gender.* Durham, N.C.: Duke University Press, 1995.

Israel, Gianna, and Donald E. Tarver, eds. *Transgender Care: Recommended Guidelines, Practical Information, and Personal Accounts.* Philadelphia: Temple University Press, 1997.

MacKenzie, Gordene Olga. *Transgender Nation.* Bowling Green, Ohio: Bowling Green State University Press, 1994.

Martin, Biddy. "Extraordinary Homosexuals." *Differences* 6, no. 2–3 (Summer–Fall 1994): 100–25.

Raymond, Janice. "The Politics of Transgenderism." In *Blending Genders: Social Aspects of Cross-Dressing and Sex-Changing.* Richard Ekins and Dave King, eds. London: Routledge, 1996, 215–23.

Webb, Terri. "Autobiographical Fragments from a Transsexual Activist." In *Blending Genders*, 190–95.

Wilchins, Riki Anne. *Read My Lips: Sexual Subversion and the End of Gender.* Ithaca, N.Y.: Firebrand Books, 1997.

See also Androgyny; Assimilation; Drag Balls; Effeminacy; Essentialist-Constructionist Debate; Gay Left; Gender; Hermaphroditism; Hirschfeld, Magnus; Homosexuality; Inversion; Masculinity; Queer; Sexual Orientation; Third Sex; Transsexualism; Transvestism

Transsexualism

In the West, transsexualism is understood as a conflict between gender, or psychology and social role, and sex, or biology, whose conformity is assumed in a culture that naturalizes the former as a product of the latter in the service of heterosexual procreation. That conflict is explained as an instance of "TITWB," as Riki Ann Wilchins, cofounder of Transsexual Menace and executive director of GenderPAC, disparagingly abbreviates it, the claim that some people are "trapped in the wrong body," which can be corrected by "sex change." "No one is trapped in the wrong body," Wilchins asserts, "although many of us are trapped in the wrong culture" (230). As Michel Foucault and others have argued, the modern West has pathologized and medicalized "misalignments" of the binary oppositions structuring sex, gender, and sexuality. Although *transsexualism* was not included in the health industry's bible, the American Psychiatric Association's *Diagnostic and Statistical Manual of Mental Disorders (DSM)*, until 1980 (nor in general dictionaries until the late 1980s), it was by then well established in the medical world as an illness. It appeared as a subject heading in the *Index Medicus* in 1967 after forty years of transsexual surgeries and medical essays about transsexual treatment, earlier listed under *transvestism* or *sexual perversions*, even though the term *transsexualism* had been introduced in 1923 by German sexologist and gay activist Magnus Hirschfeld. In the late 1940s and early 1950s David Cauldwell reintroduced it in medical articles and lay pamphlets about it and transvestism, but it was popularized in mainstream medical and national media usage by endocrinologist Harry Benjamin, the so-called father of transsexualism.

The revised third edition of the *DSM* (*DSM-III-R,* 1987), grouped *transsexualism* with *gender identity disorders* and specified it by its symptoms:

> Persistent discomfort and sense of inappropriateness about one's assigned sex. Persistent preoccupation for at least two years with getting rid of one's primary and secondary sex characteristics and acquiring the sex characteristics of the other sex. The person has reached puberty (before that the diagnosis of Gender Identity Disorder of Childhood is used).

However, just as lesbian and gay activism led to the dropping of *homosexuality* from the *DSM* in 1974, agitation to depathologize transsexualism resulted in its replacement in the fourth edition (*DSM-IV,* 1994) by *gender dysphoria*. The possible effects of this replacement have been much debated. Many see it as dehistoricizing, as it privileges the concept of "gender" invented in part to account for transsexualism (as well as intersexuality) and to justify surgical interventions. Benjamin rationalized SRS by arguing that if the mind could not be harmonized with the body, as suggested by the failure of psychoanalysis to cure transsexualism, then the body would have to be changed. His reasoning was based on a gender/sex distinction consolidated by the other three major medical figures in the history of transsexualism, psychologist John Money and psychiatrists Richard Green and Robert Stoller. Like Benjamin, they saw the body as more amenable to change than the mind, finding in transsexual and intersexual case histories proof that a fixed "core gender identity" was established very early in a child's life, regardless of sex—a paradoxical use of social constructionist theory, as that which was said to be culturally created, rather than natural, was nevertheless viewed as impossible to change. *Gender dysphoria* substantiates the centrality of gender as an explanatory concept and has no immediate resonance with *transvestism, intersexuality,* and *homosexuality* as "psychic hermaphroditism," the whole family of "intermediate sex" identities from which *transsexualism* was gradually distinguished in the twentieth century and to which its name indicates its ties (even Christine Jorgensen, the first of the "public transsexuals," made headlines in 1953 as a "transvestite with sex change surgery," while her Danish doctors viewed her as a homosexual).

Gender dysphoria may depoliticize as well as dehistoricize. As Foucault has shown, the history of sexuality involves a specification of "perverse" individuals, such as transsexuals, whose whole being was determined by their sexuality, as the modern world made formerly singular sinful or criminal acts into the expression of perverted identities to be medically disciplined or regulated. It is on behalf of those assigned identities, however, that activists have made demands or expressed pride through acts of civil disobedience or celebratory parades and festivals, instances of what Foucault terms "reverse discourses." By naming a condition rather than an identity, *gender dysphoria* deconstitutes subjects, confusing the only recently crystallized distinction between transvestites and transsexuals and rendering more difficult the production of reverse discourses by and about a sexual "type." *Gender dysphoria* also is not oriented to a single therapy, hormonal and sex reassignment, which were conceptually central to transsexualism, since it was specified only with the advent of its cure through endocrinology and advanced genital plastic surgery techniques developed in the treatment of intersexuals and casualties of the two world wars. The demand for these new therapies became the definitive symptom of the transsexual, as opposed to the transvestite or drag queen, as part B of the definition in *DSM-III-R* suggests. While some transgender activists believe that *gender dsyphoria* encourages gender clinics to foster the exploration of gender expression, rather than channel clients into treatments with SRS and assimilation to the gender system as the inevitable outcome, others fear that SRS will not be covered by health insurance, since transsexualism is no longer an officially recognized illness (it was only rarely covered in any case), and may not be recommended even for those who desperately desire it. Many in the medical community, on the other hand, worry that the new diagnosis is a license to recommend SRS for those who are not transsexual and will not benefit from it, as screening for SRS ceases to be a key function of gender clinic professionals. They are concerned about any potential growth of a treatment that has always been hotly contested and never conclusively proven a success. In fact, questions about its effectiveness, as well as about the ethics of amputating "healthy genitals," led to the closing in the 1980s of most of the university-affiliated and research-oriented gender identity clinics, including the one at Johns Hopkins, home to Money and Green and the first to be established, in 1965 (thanks to the Erickson Foundation, which also helped fund Benjamin's research and was endowed by a female-to-male transsexual in the 1950s).

Debates about the ethics and politics of SRS and transsexualism have involved not only the medical and gender communities but also feminists, lesbian and gay activists and theorists, and others in the New Left. Because phalloplasty is not as successful aesthetically or functionally as vaginoplasty, there is a disparity in the outcomes of female-to-male (FTM) and male-to-female (MTF) reassignments, although surveys of client satisfaction seem to suggest that FTMs are overall somewhat happier than MTFs with their results. However, Lothstein, MacKenzie, Millot, and others have argued that the success rate for both is low, with unacceptable numbers of what doctors literally term necessary surgical "revisions" and demands for more and other surgeries, including breast augmentation, voice augmentation, rhinoplasty, tracheal shave, false rib removal, orbital rim contouring, angle of the mandible surgery, knee shaves, cheek and chin implants, electrolysis, and liposuction. All of these "are designed to help enhance an individual's physical presentation," according to *Transgender Care*, a recent volume coauthored by doctors, therapists, and members of the gender community that not only expands on the Benjamin Standards of Care developed in 1979 to ensure good treatment of transsexuals but also offers information about procedures and issues. It is hardly surprising that many cultural critics are suspicious of the sexing of every element of the body and the endorsement of a drive to measure up to a sexual ideal—a feminine ideal, since most of the ancillary "aesthetic" surgeries are for MTFs—derived from the commodified, fetishized bodies on display in the mass media and entertainment industries. Raymond, Billings and Urban, Hausman, and MacKenzie have all emphasized that transsexualism is a creation of capitalist medical technology, which supports the belief in gender and sexual dimorphism by literally selling assimilation to what its very existence puts in question, offering a personal solution to the political problem of patriarchal and rigid gender roles presumed to be expressions of naturally "opposite" sexes. SRS protocols also legislated heterosexuality, since transhomosexuality was for years a counterindication for SRS. For that reason, Kate Bornstein, Sandy Stone, Susan Stryker, and others have "come out" as transsexual lesbians, refusing to pass. Increasingly, transsexual activists and theorists are advocating not only coming out but also identifying as "transgender," rather than as a man or woman, and living in role without SRS so as to destabilize sex/gender binaries. Yet even transgender has come under fire, often for the same reasons as transsexualism, as critics argue it too is apolitical and individualist or a doomed and misguided effort to evade the limitations of having just one sex, the explanation of transsexualism advanced by Lacanian psychoanalysts such as Millot.

Carole-Anne Tyler

Bibliography

Benjamin, Harry. *The Transsexual Phenomenon.* New York: Julian Press, 1966.

Billings, Dwight, and Thomas Urban. "The Socio-Medical Construction of Transsexualism: An Interpretation and Critique." *Social Problems* 29, no. 3 (February 1982): 266–82.

Bornstein, Kate. *Gender Outlaw: On Men, Women, and the Rest of Us.* New York: Routledge, 1994.

Green, Richard, and John Money, eds. *Transsexualism and Sex Reassignment.* Baltimore: Johns Hopkins University Press, 1969.

Hausman, Bernice. *Changing Sex: Transsexualism, Technology, and the Idea of Gender.* Durham, N.C.: Duke University Press, 1995.

Israel, Gianna E., and Donald E. Tarver II, eds. *Transgender Care: Recommended Guidelines, Practical Information, and Personal Accounts.* Philadelphia: Temple University Press, 1997.

King, Dave. *The Transvestite and the Transsexual: Public Categories and Private Identities.* Aldershot, U.K.: Avebury, 1993.

Lothstein, Leslie Martin. *Female-to-Male Transsexualism: Historical, Clinical and Theoretical Issues.* Boston: Routledge and Kegan Paul, 1983.

Mackenzie, Gordene Olga. *Transgender Nation.* Bowling Green, Ohio: Bowling Green State University Popular Press, 1994.

Millot, Catherine. *Horsexe: Essay on Transsexuality.* 1983. Kenneth Hylton, trans. New York: Autonomedia, 1990.

Raymond, Janice. *The Transsexual Empire.* Reprint. New York: Teacher's College Press, 1994.

Stoller, Robert. *Sex and Gender.* Vol. 2. *The Transsexual Experiment.* New York: Jason Aaronson, 1976.

Stone, Sandy. "The Empire Strikes Back: A Post-Transsexual Manifesto." In *Body Guards: The*

Cultural Politics of Gender Ambiguity. Julia Epstein and Kristina Straub, eds. New York: Routledge, 1991, 280–304.

Stryker, Susan. "My Words to Victor Frankenstein above the Village of Chamounix: Performing Transgender Rage." *GLQ* 1, no. 3 (1994): 237–54.

Wilchins, Riki Anne. *Read My Lips: Sexual Subversion and the End of Gender.* Ithaca, N.Y.: Firebrand Books, 1997.

See also Foucault, Michel; Gender; Jorgensen, Christine; Morris, Jan; Richards, Renee; Scientific Approaches to Homosexuality; Sexual Orientation; Transgender; Transvestism

Transvestism

Derived from the Latin for "cross" and "dress," the term *transvestism* was coined by German sexologist Magnus Hirschfeld in a 1910 volume of case studies of people who regularly wore the clothing of the opposite sex. Over the years, a number of other names have been proposed for what Hirschfeld analyzed, as people have argued about the nature and meaning of cross-dressing (the term the transvestite community prefers, since it has fewer connotations of pathology).

Anthropologists, historians, and some transvestites have pointed out that in other places and times, cross-dressing has not been associated with sexual deviance; for example, it has been frequently used in religious rituals as a source of androgynous power. Furthermore, what are today regarded as very different phenomena may involve cross-dressing: transsexualism, fetishism, butch-femme role playing, drag, camp, burlesque, sadomasochism, exhibitionism, gender dysphoria, transgendering, and intersexuality.

Cross-dressing itself ranges from appropriating a single piece of clothing of the opposite sex to wearing an entire outfit, or, by extension, altering the body with hormones and engaging in gender-stereotyped activities. It may be an occasional fantasy, a weekly compulsion, or a fact of daily life for those who live "in role" all the time, with or without hormone treatments or sex reassignment surgery. Cross-dressers themselves may "pass" or may seem to parody the gender they "put on," and they may experience a range of sensations, from a pleasant sense of relaxation to a powerful eroticism, or nothing at all out of the ordinary. They may be asexual, autoerotic, heterosexual, homosexual, or bisexual—and their orientation may vary with the gender of their clothing, so that what some would label gay sex might be considered heterosexual by a male participant who was dressed and identifying as his feminine alter ego.

Cross-dressing may make relatively little difference to personality and behavior, or it may radically change them, enabling cross-dressers to do things, both sexual and nonsexual, which they would not permit themselves in their "straight" roles, from having sex with others of the same sex or participating in sadomasochism to washing dishes or discussing emotions. Cross-dressing may express—and evoke—sexual desire, identification, admiration, envy, anxiety, hostility, tranquillity, shock, deception, escapism, transcendence, or a combination of all of these.

Given the range of what psychoanalysts call sexual "object choices" and "aims" or activities with which cross-dressing has been associated, as well as the variety of causes adduced for it and explanations given of it, both sexual and nonsexual, it is hardly surprising that there has been serious doubt about the utility of identifying any instance of it as transvestism. What Hirschfeld first conceptualized as a distinct sexual phenomenon has been subject to the increasing differentiation of sexual "dysfunctions" that has characterized Western modernity since the beginning of the seventeenth century, with once sinful acts being interpreted as crimes and then as symptomatic expressions of deviant identities.

Hirschfeld's book participated in this interpretive process, distinguishing transvestism from homosexuality—with which it was confused by earlier sexologists such as Westphal and Krafft-Ebing because of theories of homosexuality as "inversion" or "psychic hermaphroditism." Although Hirschfeld too thought lesbians and gays were "sexual intermediaries," he asserted that what was distinctive about homosexuals was their inverted sex drive, whereas transvestites were characterized by inverted emotional characteristics, feeling and acting like "the opposite sex," and were often in fact heterosexual. Contrary to Krafft-Ebing, who discussed some of his cases of cross-dressing as "dress fetishism," Hirschfeld maintained that transvestism and fetishism were quite different. The transvestite focused on the self, rather than on the love object the fetish replaced and supplemented, and therefore wanted to wear new clothes, while the fetishist wanted clothing worn by the object of desire. Hirschfeld also was the first to note that cross-dressing often involved elements of masochism, such as pleasure in tight corsets or in being forced into transvestism. While British sexologist Havelock Ellis agreed with many of Hirschfeld's observations, he thought the term *transvestism* incorrectly implied that only clothes were at stake. He argued that for many, cross-dressing was not "an erotic impulse to disguise," as Hirschfeld had glossed it, but an expression of the real self; for such individuals, sex-appropriate fashions and activities, and not transvestism, felt like the masquerade. Ellis therefore proposed renaming transvestism *eonism,* after the famous eighteenth-century French cross-dressing spy and courtier, the Chevalier d'Eon de Beaumont (his term never caught on with the medical community).

Later theorists, including endocrinologist Harry Benjamin, the "father of transsexualism," argued for a continuum of transvestic behaviors based on the feelings that Ellis had emphasized. The degree of discomfort with the clothes and social roles associated with the cross-dresser's biological sex suggested a new diagnostic category for those who felt most alienated from their sex: transsexualism.

Although *transvestism* and *transsexualism* continued to be used interchangeably until the late 1960s, after Christine Jorgensen's 1953 sex-change surgery the medical community increasingly sought to refine the criteria for distinguishing candidates for similar treatment. As they did so, they consolidated the distinction between sex and gender first adumbrated in the early work on homosexuality and transvestism and established transsexualism as a new sexual identity and research focus, one that largely displaced interest in transvestism. Not until the closing of the university-affiliated gender identity clinics in the 1980s and the recent growth of queer theory and activism did a belief in the progressive possibilities of cross-dressing resurface.

While some queer theorists, such as Marjorie Garber, still use "transvestism," as Hirschfeld did, to refer to a range of cross-dressing practices (although Garber attempts to underline their common potential for subverting fixed gender roles), the mental health community today defines transvestism very narrowly, as indicated by the entry for "transvestic fetishism" in the revised third edition of the industry's bible, the American Psychiatric Association's *Diagnostic and Statistical Manual of Mental Disorders* (*DSM-III-R,* 1987):

Over a period of at least six months, in a heterosexual male has recurrent intense sexual urges and sexually arousing fantasies involving cross-dressing.

The person has acted on these urges or is markedly distressed by them.

Does not meet the criteria for Gender Identity Disorder of Adolescence or Adulthood, Nontranssexual Type or Transsexualism.

The fact that cross-dressing is classed as an instance of fetishism testifies to the influence of psychoanalysis, whose explanations of the phenomenon owed more to Krafft-Ebing than to Hirschfeld and Ellis. Although Freud himself never discussed transvestism, classic psychoanalytic essays such as that by Fenichel describe it as a fetishistic defense against castration anxiety through the construction of and identification with a fantasy phallic woman. This accounts for *DSM*'s exclusion of female cross-dressers. (Historically, more women than men have cross-dressed, but there is little evidence suggesting they have experienced sexual and fetishistic pleasure from it). The *DSM* definition also excludes any male cross-dressers for whom the activity is not erotic—up to 10 percent of the nontranssexual population, according to reviews of transvestite research by Vern and Bonnie Bullough, who also note that older transvestites in particular emphasize they cross-dress for relaxation, to escape what they describe as a restrictive and oppressive masculinity.

Perhaps what is most unexpected about the *DSM* definition, however, is the fact that transvestism is only heterosexual (or the transvestism that counts as mental illness is only heterosexual). Given (a) the early history of conflating cross-dressing and homosexuality; (b) the psychoanalytic explanations of transvestism not just as fetishistic but as a latent expression of homosexuality or of "homosexual panic"; and (c) the social science research suggesting that a significant percentage of cross-dressers are gay or have sex with men (or fantasies about it) when they are dressed as their feminine personae, the elimination of homosexual transvestism from the *DSM-III* is surprising. Arguably, its omission is the effect both of gay activism (which led to the removal of homosexuality from the manual in 1973) and of organized transvestism—clubs, publications, and fairs—whose de facto head for twenty or more years was biochemist, transvestite activist, and researcher Virginia (Charles) Prince, who since 1964 has lived as a "transgenderist" (her neologism)—a transgendered woman who has no plans for sex reassignment surgery (and in her case, no longer takes hormones). From the late 1950s onward, Prince worked to gain public acceptance for transvestism by trying to normalize it, excluding homosexuals and sadomasochists from the transvestite clubs she helped found or charter (including the famous Phi Pi Epsilon sorority, or FPE, for "full personality expression") and the fantasy literature and journalism in the Chevalier Publications newsletters and magazines she started and then edited for many years. Prince has also advocated "good taste" in clothing, eschewing the more obviously fetishistic fashions, which she believes are low-class and unlikely to enable a transvestite to "pass" as a woman. Such clothes also signify the eroticism she has sought to downplay as another part of her strategy for "cleaning up" transvestism for the public. She has asserted that "one doesn't get cross-dressed to get aroused," adding, "The point to be made is that the clothes are merely a means to an end, which is that of the feeling of unification, participation, and identity with womanliness" (474), a claim Benjamin disputes when he writes that "to take sex out of transvestism is like taking music out of opera" (37). Indeed, some of Prince's statements seem to be directed specifically to feminists who disapprove of transvestism because of the stereotypical and fetishistic feminine style associated with it—a critique also made of male-to-female transsexualism (which Prince does not condone because she believes gender has nothing to do with anatomy). According to Prince, the chief manifestation of "women's liberation" has been the adoption of masculine occupations, attitudes, and clothes. Transvestism is "men's liberation," "the retreat from the former masculine stereotype" (476) and a step toward "full personality expression." Some self-identified feminist sex radicals also espouse this view, such as Veronica Vera, who runs a transvestite "finishing school" in New York. Queer theorists, too, often have argued that transvestism calls into question rigid sex and gender binaries.

Many feminists, however, are critical of transvestism for the same reasons they have been wary of androgyny, transgender, and the queer. Transvestism is a personal and individual solution to inflexible gender roles, which it may in fact help to perpetuate by compartmentalizing and alternating between a masculinity and femininity it treats as fixed, unchangeable, and distinct, with little overlap—just as do those who advocate preventing transvestism itself by exacting compliance with traditional gender

identities from genderqueer children and their parents. Furthermore, transvestites are "fantastic women," as Annie Woodhouse phrases it, whose idea of femininity is literally a fantasy having little to do with women's day-to-day experience of it, a fantasy which may disrupt marriages and families, whose suffering she believes has not been taken as seriously as the transvestite's own by transvestite advocates or researchers. The transvestite who finds femininity relaxing because he imagines it is free of oppressions does not have a feminist understanding of gender as not only rigidly dimorphic but hierarchical—and he also has the benefit of being able to return to a masculine role when he tires of playing a woman. It would seem he has little incentive to change society's gender roles when he can simply change his own gender role.   *Carole-Anne Tyler*

Bibliography

Allen, J. J. *The Man in the Red Velvet Dress: Inside the World of Cross-Dressing.* Secaucus, N.J.: Carol Publishing, 1996.

Benjamin, Harry. *The Transsexual Phenomenon.* New York: Julian Press, 1966.

Bullough, Bonnie, Vern Bullough, and James Elias, eds. *Gender Blending.* New York: Prometheus Books, 1997.

Bullough, Vern L., and Bonnie Bullough. *Cross Dressing, Sex, and Gender.* Philadelphia: University of Pennsylvania Press, 1993.

Ekins, Richard, and Dave King, eds. *Blending Genders: Some Aspects of Cross-Dressing and Sex-Changing.* New York: Routledge, 1996.

Fenichel, Otto. "The Pyschology of Transvestism." *International Journal of Psychoanalysis* 11 (1930): 212–37.

Hirschfeld, Magnus. *The Transvestites: An Investigation of the Erotic Drive to Cross Dress.* 1910. Michael Lombardi-Nash, trans. Buffalo, N.Y.: Prometheus Books, 1991.

King, Dave. *The Transvestite and the Transsexual: Public Categories and Private Identities.* Aldershot, U.K.: Avebury Press, 1993.

Prince, Virginia. "Seventy Years in the Trenches of the Gender Wars." In *Gender Blending*, Bullough, Bullough, and Elias, eds., pp. 469–76.

Vera, Veronica. *Miss Vera's Finishing School for Boys Who Want to Be Girls.* New York: Doubleday, 1997.

Woodhouse, Annie. *Fantastic Women: Sex, Gender, and Transvestism.* New Brunswick, N.J.: Rutgers University Press, 1989.

See also Androgyny; Ballets Trockadero de Monte Carlo; Drag Balls; Ellis, Havelock; Freud, Sigmund; Gender; Hirschfeld, Magnus; Inversion; Jorgensen, Christine; Kabuki; Krafft-Ebing, Richard von; Sadomasochism; Sexology; Transgender; Transsexualism; Westphal, Carl Friedrich Otto

Tress, Arthur (1940–)

Born into a Jewish household in Brooklyn, New York, Arthur Tress was encouraged by his parents to pursue his intellectual and artistic interests. After graduating from Bard College with a degree in painting and art history, he studied film in Paris and his father helped him fund a world tour that encompassed Egypt, Italy, Mexico, India, and Japan. His travels brought him into contact with Japanese gardens, Buddhism, African tribal culture, documentary filmmaking, and hepatitis—all of which influenced his mystical and mystifying photographic aesthetic. Tress recorded haunting and surreal locales and those who inhabited them during his travels, but having immersed himself in non-Western rituals, he determined "to start a project soon on American myths and rituals, to find the primitive shades of darkness in our modern life with its ceremonies of violence and sex" (qtd. in Weiermair 10).

In his early work, Tress's commitment was unqualifiedly to the urban decay characterized by the industrial wastelands of New Jersey and New York and their denizens. He also documented the surreal quality to everyday relationships between mothers and sons, daughters and fathers, people and animals. His project eventually led him to explore the sexualized power dynamics between men in his late 1970s "homosexual fantasies." Here he created scenarios in which a nude man attempts to saw his ass in two with a lumberjack's saw, another appears on all fours with his head in a bucket and boot on his back, and a man in a welder's mask is poised to plunge a railroad wrench into the anus of his male partner. In these, Tress stages eerie scenarios between men that investigate the impulses and meanings behind oral sex, anal sex, sadomasochism, and athletic competition between men. Unlike the glossy and overtly phallic depictions of gay male life by Robert Mapplethorpe, Tress concentrates on the metaphoric, even cartoonlike aspects of gay male sexuality, while emphasizing the anus and the excremental. Many of these photographs were taken amid the detritus of New York's decaying piers.

Since the late 1970s, Tress has stopped photographing human models and has continued his exploration of magical, surrealistic environments in miniatures, still lifes, and collages. *John Beynon*

Bibliography

Ellenzweig, Allen. *The Homoerotic Photograph: Male Images from Durieu/Delacroix to Mapplethorpe.* New York: Columbia University Press, 1992.

Livingston, Marco. *Arthur Tress: Talisman.* London: Thames and Hudson, 1986.

Weiermair, Peter, ed. *Arthur Tress: A Retrospective.* Zurich: Edition Stemmle, 1995.

See also Buddhism; Mapplethorpe, Robert; Photography

Trevisan, João Silvéro (1944–)

This Brazilian writer, script writer, film director, playwright, translator, and journalist was born in Ribeirno Bonito, a small city in the countryside of the state of São Paulo. He studied at the Diocese of Aparecida Seminary and graduated in philosophy from the Catholic Pontificate University of São Paulo. During some of the years of the military dictatorship, he lived in the United States, Mexico, and Germany.

Returning to Brazil, in 1976 he tried to form a group of gay activists. In 1978 he joined with other gay writers and journalists from Rio de Janeiro and São Paulo to participate actively in the founding of *O Lampião*, the first and most important homosexual newspaper in Brazilian history, remaining a part of the editorial board until 1981. In 1979 he was one of the founders of *Somos*, the first homosexual group organized in Brazil, and always defended the independence of the gay movement from political parties.

Recognizing the influences of Constantine Cavafy, Marquerto Yourcenar, James Baldwin, and Thomas Mann on his work, in 1976 he published *Testamento de Jônatas a David* (Jonathan's Testament to David), his first collection of short stories with homoerotic subjects. This was followed by the play *Em nome do desejo* (In the Name of Desire), and his principal nonfiction work, *Devassos no Paraiso* (Perverts in Paradise), a 1986 essay on the ethnohistory of homosexuality in Brazil. His literary work was a masters in literature thesis topic from the Federal University of Paraná. In the opinion of S. Grootendorst from the University of Utrecht, "Trevisan should be seen as one of the most informed

T

and important persons when it comes to homosexual tradition and literary production in Brazil" (*Literatura Gay no Brasil?*).
Luiz Mott
Translated by James N. Green

Bibliography

Ventureli, Paulo C. "A Carne Embriagada: Uma leitura em torno de João Silvéro Trevisan." A. thesis, Federal University of Paraná, 1993.

See also Baldwin, James; Brazil; Cavafy, Constantine P.; *Lampião*; Mann, Thomas; Yourcenar, Marguerite

Trick

This slang term can function as both a noun, referring to a casual, often anonymous sexual encounter or partner, or as a verb, referring to the act of obtaining such an encounter. The phrase originated in the argot of female prostitutes and migrated into the urban, gay male lexicon near the turn of the twentieth century. It was most likely first used by those transvestite male prostitutes who occupied the same milieu, indeed, often different rooms in the same residences as female sex workers, dressing in women's clothing and catering almost exclusively to a straight, or at least nonhomosexual-identified clientele, referred to as *trade*. The word probably derives from the Old French *trichier*, meaning to "deceive" or "cheat," as in games of chance—especially cards—or sleight of hand; the word continues to carry the attendant connotations of risk, deception, competition, and gambling, though usually in a less pejorative sense.

The use of such slang was a necessary component of the often dangerous and underground gay existence emerging in the late nineteenth and early twentieth centuries. The double entendre allowed one to communicate with other individuals in the know while excluding the uninitiated, an act of cultural resistance that fostered a sense of communal and individual identity decidedly outside the normative. Its use has continue post-Stonewall, broadening to refer to any casual sexual liaison, not just those in exchange for money, as a means of asserting the solidarity of gay communities and insisting on gay male cultural uniqueness.
Scott Speirs

Bibliography

Grahn, Judy. *Another Mother Tongue: Gay Words, Gay Worlds*. Boston: Beacon, 1984.

See also Hustlers; Stonewall; Trade

Tune, Tommy (1939–)

Tommy Tune, born in Wichita Falls, Texas, is Broadway's reigning tall tapper from Texas, and so much more. Tune won his first Tony award as featured actor in a musical for his portrayal of an openly gay character in Michael Bennett's *Seesaw* in 1974. Since then, he has won eight more Tonys, receiving acclaim as a director, choreographer, actor, and dancer. He won Obies for his direction of Eve Merriam's *The Club* in 1976 and for *Cloud 9* in 1981. His first Broadway musical was *The Best Little Whorehouse in Texas*, in 1977. Other award-winning theatrical achievements include *Nine* (1982), *My One and Only* (1983), *Grand Hotel* (1989), and *The Will Rogers Follies* (1991).

At the age of five, the young part-Shawnee enrolled in tap, acrobatics, and ballet classes. In his teens, Tune's early love of dance grew into a special appreciation of musical comedy; from his early education he went on to earn a B.F.A. in drama from the University of Texas at Austin and an M.F.A. in directing from the University of Houston. He was taught by and has collaborated with Mike Nichols, Michael Bennett, Jule Styne, Carol Channing, and Peter Stone. Though he has received notice for his direction of nonmusical theater, it is in the style of the glitzy Broadway musical that Tune is thought to be a virtuoso. His very "out" autobiography, *Footnotes,* was published in 1997, and includes tales of many theatrical escapades.
Rebecca Rugg

Bibliography

Lassell, Michael. "Tommy Towers Over Broadway." *Dance Magazine* (November 1991): 26–40.
Pikula, Jona. "Tommy Tune." *Dance Magazine* (September 1982): 53–57.

See also Bennett, Michael; Dance: Concert Dance in America; Musical Theater

Tunisia

Located across the Mediterranean Sea from Italy, Tunisia occupies the northernmost point of Africa and is less than ninety miles from Sicily. Originally settled by Berber tribes, the region has been ruled by a succession of outsiders. Phoenician traders colonized the area during the ninth century B.C.E. and founded the city of Carthage (the ruins of which are located near the modern capital, Tunis). Following the Punic Wars, the area fell under Roman control only to be subsequently conquered by the Vandals. After a second period of Roman rule, Arabs overran the region in the seventh century C.E. and converted the population to Islam. Arab rule continued until the sixteenth century when, after a brief period of Spanish control, Ottoman Turks assumed hegemony over Tunisia. As a result of European expansion during the nineteenth century, Tunisia was occupied by France and made a French protectorate in 1881. In 1957 Tunisia declared itself a sovereign republic, and the last French forces were expelled in 1963.

A warm climate, an exotic locale, and a local ambivalence to male-male sex acts have made Tunisia a popular site for Westerners wanting to explore Orientalist fantasies. André Gide, Oscar Wilde, and Isabelle Eberhardt (masquerading as a man) all sojourned in the area. Michel Foucault worked and taught in Tunisia during its drive for independence after World War II. A supporter of the anticolonial movement, he sheltered Tunisian dissidents from French forces. As a result of its colonial past, many Tunisians speak French. The country's official language is Arabic, spoken by 98 percent of the population.

In ancient times, Carthage was known throughout the Mediterranean for its male courtesans. In the thirteenth century C.E. Tunisian author Ahmed al-Tifashi compiled a collection of tales and poems about love and sex in which male-male eroticism figures prominently. In the eighteenth and early nineteenth centuries, the Barbary (i.e., Berber) Coast pirates sold captured youths to North African and eastern Mediterranean rulers for concubinage.

Tunisia, Algeria, Libya, and Morocco together comprise the Maghreb (Arabic for "west"). European observers since the nineteenth century have noted that homosexual activity is considered a normal part of a young man's sexual development throughout the region. In the absence of available women, prepubescent boys are often obliged to serve as sexual outlets for older male friends and relatives. While a youth may allow himself to be sodomized, once he reaches puberty and becomes a man, the practice is expected to cease. So long as one denies having been sodomized, there is no stigma attached. And there is little or no shame in being the penetrative partner. In fact, it is considered an expression of one's masculinity. But the owning of a "homosexual" identity invites scorn.

In Tunisia it is common for male friends to hold hands or kiss on the cheek in public. Affection such as this is often misread by Westerners as being sexual in nature. Homosexual activity, while perhaps not uncommon, does not typically manifest itself openly. The criminal code prohibits sodomy between consenting adults, and the authorities have routinely targeted tourist areas for policing. In the distant past, male-male eroticism may have been tolerated and even celebrated in poetry and song. Perhaps as a result of French colonial rule and the adoption of Western biases, a homosexual identity is now considered shameful, and prospects for a gay rights movement and a change in cultural attitudes are poor at best.   *Richard McKewen*

Bibliography

Chebel, Malek. *L'Esprit de sérail: perversions et marginalités sexuelles au Maghreb*. Paris: Lieu Common, 1986.

al–Tîfâchî, Ahmed. *Les délices des cœurs, ou Ce que l'on ne trouve en aucun livre*. René R. Khawam, trans. Paris: Pocket, 1993.

See also Arabic Literature; Colonialism; Foucault, Michel; Gide, André; Islam; Politics: Global; Resorts and Beaches; Tourism and Travel; Wilde, Oscar

Turing, Alan (1912–1954)

Alan Turing was a Cambridge-educated mathematician, wartime cryptanalyst, and pioneering theorist of digital computer technology. His early paper "On Computable Numbers with an Application to the *Entscheidungsproblem*" (1937) outlined a universal Turing machine capable of calculating any resolvable algebraic problem. The Turing machine would become the essential model for the programmable computer. Turing joined the British Government Code and Cypher School in 1939 to work on cracking the Enigma machine the German military used to encipher its communications during World War II. Through his efforts, England possessed practically current deciphering of German communications by June 1941. Also during the war years, Turing developed techniques for enciphering speech communications and pursued early speculations on computer automation of chess play.

After the war Turing began turning his universal machine to a practical application. It would become the modern computer, an electronic digital machine capable of storing its instructions internally (as programs in memory) and performing a countless variety of tasks. He worked first at England's National

Physical Laboratory and then at Manchester University, where the first internally stored program was run on a digital computer on June 21, 1948. His 1948 report "Intelligent Machinery" imaginatively anticipated many contemporary research programs in robotics and artificial intelligence. In 1950 he proposed what has come to be called the Turing Test for judging computer intelligence. A human interrogator communicates with a concealed human and a computer through written questions and answers. If the interrogator cannot determine which respondent is human and which computer, the computer should be accorded a thinking intelligence. For his work in the fields of mathematics and computer design, Turing was elected a fellow of the Royal Society in 1951.

Turing introduced the Test scenario with a male interrogator trying to determine which of two humans is a man and which a woman, while the concealed man pretends to be a woman. This gender-bending fantasy would not have surprised Turing's closest friends, for he had been open about his homosexuality since the early 1930s. He was engaged briefly in 1941 but broke off the engagement out of sympathy for his fiancée. In late 1951 Turing met and became involved with a young man on a Manchester street. Their affair continued for several months until an acquaintance of the man burgled Turing's home. Turing reported the incident to the police, who inferred the nature of the relationship between Turing and the young man. After imprudently offering a confession, Turing was charged with "gross indecency." He pled guilty at trial and was placed on probation on the condition that he submit to an estrogen therapy aimed at suppressing the male homosexual libido. Turing's probation and the estrogen treatments ended in April 1953, by which time he was impotent and had grown breasts. He committed suicide by cyanide poisoning in June 1954, in the midst of a Cold War "moral crisis" that targeted homosexuals as state security risks.

Andrew Hodges's 1983 biography of Turing recovered his profound accomplishments from the obscurity of public silence. Hugh Whitemore's 1986 play *Breaking the Code* celebrates Turing, whose cryptanalytical work helped save England from defeat during World War II, only to be persecuted for violating the conventions of a homophobic Cold War state apparatus. *Kirk Pillow*

Bibliography

Hodges, Andrew. *Alan Turing: The Enigma.* New York: Simon & Schuster, 1983.

See also Hoover, J. Edgar; McCarthyism; Sexual Orientation Therapy

Turkey

In early Ottoman times Turks discovered the sensuality of boy love. Bayezid I (1360–1403) dispatched soldiers into conquered lands to capture beautiful boys for his harem. Seizing boys for sexual purposes became widespread practice in the military, government, and nobility. Owing to the hierarchical social structure, sultans could not form intimate relationships with those of similar social status and were forced to seek pleasures with boys, eunuchs, and women.

The Ottoman practice of man-boy love continued for five centuries. The most highly prized items were European boys because of their capacity for affection and sensuality. When Mehmed II captured Constantinople in 1453 troops were dispatched immediately to capture the most beautiful boys of the Christian aristocracy for him. Some boys captured were sold as catamites or male prostitutes. Since the homoerotic side of Turkish life was omnipresent, many young men viewed this as an opportunity to climb the social ladder and achieve success.

When the Turkish state became Islamic, homosexuality was punished by torture, burning, or beheading. The Hanefi and Sufi sects of Islam held less strict positions on homosexuality. The Era of Tulips flourished in the 1920s sparked by modernization programs of Kemal Atatürk, the founder of modern Turkey. Islamic teachings were overlooked by Atatürk's strong convictions concerning human rights and freedoms enabling him to not legislate against homosexuality. Further Westernization of Turkey inhibited the historically free expression of homosexuality.

Turkish language stereotypes a gay man as either *ibne* (*laco*) or *kulampara* (*lubunya*). An *ibne* is an effeminate man predisposed to the passive role during sex, spurned by Turkish society. The *kulampara*, who is frequently over sixteen and often married, has an active role in sex. The *kulampara* does not fit stereotypes as does the *ibne*. To have sex with an *ibne* does not incur derision. Societal research indicates that many Turkish men believe male-male sexual play performs a crucial role in a Turkish young man's development.

For individuals to develop the role and identity of a gay man and for society to accept it requires a conducive social climate. In Turkey this occurs primarily in Istanbul and other larger cities. Istanbul, like other international cities, attracts many gay people from the rural areas and smaller towns, where conservative Islamic beliefs are oppressive. Some cities have started to develop a gay subculture replete with bars and other amenities. But a gay identity is still lacking, with the roles of *ibne* and *kulampara* slowly fading.

Under the Turkish constitution homosexuality is not illegal, but police oppression and brutality are often directed toward homosexuals based on morals statutes. Police harassment is often targeted against effeminate men, transvestites, and transsexuals. During the late 1970s the underground press frequently announced the establishment of a gay organization. But the military coup d'état halted all attempts. Reacting to ongoing instances of police brutality and a crackdown on 1993 Christopher Street celebrations, a number of gay men and lesbians founded Lambda Istanbul. The organization is the largest gay liberation group in the nation. It produces its own magazine and radio show, 100% GL, and operates an AIDS Awareness campaign.

Michael A. Lutes

Bibliography

Murray, Stephen, and Will Roscoe. *Islamic Homosexualities: Culture, History, and Literature.* New York: New York University Press, 1997.

Schmitt, Arno, and Jehoeda Sofer, eds. *Sexuality and Eroticism Among Males in Moslem Societies.* New York: Haworth Press, 1992.

Second ILGA Pink Book: A Global View of Lesbian and Gay Liberation and Oppression. Utrecht, Netherlands: Interfacultaire Werkgroep Homostudies, Rijkeuniversiteit Utrecht, 1988.

See also Arabic Literature; Beloved; Islam; Tourism and Travel

Twombley, Cy (1928–)

American painter Cy Twombly, born Edwin Parker Twombly Jr., is best known for quirky, graffitilike paintings and drawings that seem to cross innocence with experience and idealism with scatology. Using melted crayon and house paint, Twombly built up a dense, varied surface into which he carved pencil lines with a childlike fluidity. Like a window into the subconscious, the resulting stains, swirls, and scratches appear and disappear into the thick, pale ground.

Born in Lexington, Virginia, Twombly showed early talent and attended art schools in Boston and New York City. While at the Art Student's League in New York, he met Robert Rauschenberg, and the two men moved together to Black Mountain College in North Carolina, where they became lovers. They traveled extensively together in Europe and North Africa, where Twombly studied and drew the remains of Roman and North African cultures. Resonances of this ancient imagery found its way into his work, as did references to Greco-Roman mythology. In these early works, erudite and obscure classical references jostle erect, ejaculating penises and defecating anuses to create a sensual tapestry that privileges neither body nor mind, but instead projects them both as seamless unity.

Following the dissolution of his relationship with Rauschenberg, the two men shared a studio and remained close. Twombly's hand can be seen in a number of Rauschenberg's classic combines, and, likewise, Twombly's work abounds with references to Rauschenberg, Jasper Johns, and male sexuality in general. Three-dimensional oblong brown globs resembling nothing so much as excrement share the surface with a weird calligraphy of lovers' names, body parts, and fluids; painting, writing, shitting, and ejaculating are presented as contiguous processes of mark-making.

In Twombly's work, the presumptive transcendence of abstract expressionist gestural painting is specified, gendered, and sexualized, in essence literalizing the terms of abstract expressionist macho discourse and concretizing its operative dynamics. Yet for all the import of the American context on his work, in 1957 Twombly moved to Italy, married, and fathered a child. He continues to reside in Italy, maintaining a patrician reserve belied by his creation of some of the most sensuous painting in contemporary art.

Jonathan Katz

Bibliography

Bastian, Heiner. *Cy Twombley: Catalogue Raisonné of the Paintings.* Vols. 1–3. Munich: Schirmer/ Mosel, 1992, 1993, 1994.

Norden, Linda. "Not Necessarily Pop: Cy Twombley and America." In *Hand Painted Pop: American Art in Transition, 1955–1962.* Exch. Exhibit Catalog. Los Angeles: Museum of Contemporary Art, 1993.

Varnedoe, Kirk. *Cy Twombley: A Retrospective.* Exhibit catalog. New York: Museum of Modern Art, 1994.

T *See also* Art History; Greece; Johns, Jasper; Rauschenberg, Robert

Tyler, Parker (1904–1974)

Born Harrison Parker Tyler in New Orleans, Louisiana, Tyler is best remembered for his film criticism, but he was also an art and literary critic, novelist, poet, biographer, magazine editor, and dramatist. He wrote more than twenty-five books, ten of which were about some aspect of film.

Tyler was open and unapologetic about his homosexuality, both in his work and in his life. Sexuality, particularly his own homosexuality, formed a recurrent theme in his poetry and other writings. In 1933 he collaborated with poet Charles Henri Ford on *The Young and Evil*, one of a small handful of English-language gay novels published during the decade. *The Divine Comedy of Pavel Tchelitchew* (1966) is an early example of a biography that recounts its subject's homosexuality with some candor. His *Screening the Sexes* (1972) was the first book-length survey of gay characters and themes in films. In 1945 Tyler met Charles Boultenhouse, and the two were life partners until Tyler's death.

As a film critic, Tyler championed the American avant-garde, but he also loved the hallucinatory qualities he found in some Hollywood films. He believed that film constitutes a modern mythology—a symbolic system that is created by, and communicates to, humanity's central moral concerns. He argued that great artists are social outsiders who, motivated by their inner "scandals," challenge the social order. In his writings Tyler attempted to identify the universal principles and inmost emotions that underlie both art and life.   *Charles Krinsky*

Bibliography

Boultenhouse, Charles. "Parker Tyler's Own Scandal." *Film Culture*, no. 77 (Fall 1992): 10–23.

Ford, Charles Henri, ed. *View: Parade of the Avant-garde 1940–1947*. New York: Thunder's Mouth Press, 1991.

Tyler, Parker. *The Granite Butterfly*. Orono, Me.: National Poetry Foundation, 1994.

See also Film; Ford, Charles Henri; Tchelitchew, Pavel

U

United States

Homophobia in the United States has deep roots. From their arrival in the New World, Europeans treated sexuality as a socially destructive force that needed to be contained. Although they understood sodomy primarily in religious terms, defining it as a sin, they increasingly criminalized it. As early as 1642 Richard Bellingham, the governor of the Massachusetts Bay Colony, queried Puritan elders about which sodomitical activities could be punished by death. Citing the Bible as their authority, the elders responded that sex between men, whether or not it included penetration, constituted a capital offense. Although the growing influence of Enlightenment thought in the colonies eventually led to the reform of sodomy laws, sodomites continued to face persecution. Between 1777 and 1779, when the Virginia legislature was redrafting the state constitution, Thomas Jefferson and other "enlightened" reformers advocated castration as a more humane punishment than death for sodomitical activities.

European attempts to eliminate the love that dare not speak its name from the New World were not confined to the colonies. American Indians who engaged in cross-dressing and other forms of sex-role reversal, called *berdaches* by French explorers, scandalized Christian missionaries who tried to persuade them to abandon their practices, which may or may not have included sodomy. Such Indians occupied an institutionalized and, in some cases, a highly respected position in their tribes, performing religious and ceremonial functions. But missionaries considered these functions a crime against nature, and conversion to Christianity was contingent on their eradication.

The colonial persecution of sodomites foreshadowed the increasingly important role homopho-bia would play in the formation of American national identity. Until the rise of the medical professions in the late nineteenth century, the strategies for suppressing sodomitical practices remained virtually unchanged in the republic. Men convicted of sodomy, who included laborers, soldiers, clergymen, lawyers, and civil servants, were pilloried, imprisoned, or otherwise publicly humiliated. One notable case involved Horatio Alger Jr., whose enormously popular stories for boys in the 1870s and 1880s propounded the myth of the self-made man so central to American capitalism. In 1866 the Unitarian Church where Alger officiated as minister expelled him when it discovered that he had sexually molested two boys.

A paradox of nineteenth-century American society is that it was at once deeply homophobic and homoerotic, a function perhaps of the segregation of the sexes into separate spheres. As Leslie Fiedler scandalously pointed out in his classic study *Love and Death in the American Novel*, first published in 1960, homoerotic friendships between men of different races occupied a central place in nineteenth-century American literature. Canonical examples include Natty Bumppo and Chingachgook in James Fenimore Cooper's Leatherstocking Tales, Ishmael and Queequeg in Herman Melville's *Moby-Dick*, and Jim and Huck in Mark Twain's *Huckleberry Finn*. But nowhere was this homoeroticism more pronounced than in the work of the quintessentially American poet, Walt Whitman. Whitman's poetry and essays profoundly influenced how many homosexuals saw themselves. For Whitman, homoerotic male bonding represented one of the deepest expressions of American democracy and was crucial to its survival. "Democracy infers such loving comradeship," he asserted in a famous essay, "Democratic Vistas," published in 1871, "as its most inevitable twin or counterpart, without which it will be incomplete, in vain, and incapable of perpetuating itself." Such views inspired two pioneers of the homosexual emancipation movement then emerging in England, the writers John Addington Symonds and Edward Carpenter. Both Symonds and Carpenter saw themselves as embodying Whitman's ideal of manly love in the service of democracy. In a famous correspondence carried on for nineteen years, Symonds repeatedly asked Whitman whether the male bonds celebrated in his poetry and essays included sex, and Whitman repeatedly avoided answering him directly. Finally, in 1890 when Symonds grew more pressing and solicited Whitman's support for the cause of homosexual emancipation, Whitman wrote back emphatically denying Symonds's construction of his ideas.

With the emergence of the social-purity movement in the 1870s and 1880s, attempts to eradicate homosexuality intensified. Sensationalistic accounts of the homosexual underworld began to appear in newspapers, dime novels, and reports commissioned by state legislatures. Organizations such as the Anti-Saloon League and the Women's Christian Temperance Union mobilized support for their antivice campaigns by describing in lurid detail saloons where male prostitutes solicited customers; drag balls organized by African Americans; and parks and Turkish steam baths where men cruised other men for sex. In response to a growing public outcry, the police began to target this underworld. Judging from prison records, the victims of these antivice campaigns were disproportionately black and foreign-born. Meanwhile, the medical professions were developing more subtle strategies for regulating sodomitical practices. Doctors argued that homosexuality constituted a mental illness that required treatment rather than imprisonment or moral condemnation. These claims not only helped to solidify their professional status but contributed to the emergence of homosexuality as a distinct form of personhood. Although a few dissenting doctors conceived of homosexuals as an intermediate, or "third," sex, and argued that their desires were not perverted but natural, the majority regarded homosexuality as a form of gender inversion that through therapy could be reversed.

Despite the growing authority of medical expertise, the older conceptions of homosexuality as sin or crime persisted, standing in contested and disruptive relation to the newer one. Doctors, lawyers, and ministers competed with one another throughout the twentieth century over the authority to define homosexuality. In the 1920s and 1930s, acknowledgment of the homosexual underworld by two of the nation's most influential institutions of mass culture, Broadway and Hollywood, provoked religious organizations to intervene aggressively in the public sphere. In 1926, when a series of plays opened on Broadway that exploited the public's fascination with the sexually exotic and portrayed homosexuals in a positive light, these organizations urged the New York legislature to enact legislation banning the production of plays with homosexual themes and characters. Shortly after Mae West announced plans for a Broadway production of her play *The Drag*, which opened with a doctor decrying the criminalization of homosexuality, the controversy reached a head. On February 9, 1927, the police raided the plays and arrested members of their casts. Soon after, the New York legislature passed the Padlock Law, which prohibited the production of plays that dealt explicitly with homosexuality.

Despite this prohibition, however, Broadway soon reemerged as one of the few official spaces in American society where homosexuality received sympathetic treatment. Beginning in 1934, Lillian Hellman's play *The Children's Hour*, which implicitly compared the persecution of two teachers accused of lesbianism to the persecution of Jews in Nazi Germany, ran for 691 performances. This relative openness played a particularly important role in the 1950s, when the homophobia of American society was unusually intense and homosexuality was understood primarily as a form of psychopathology that threatened the nation's security. Dominated by gay male playwrights such as Tennessee Williams and William Inge, Broadway helped counteract this understanding of homosexuality by constructing alternative narratives of gay male experience. Williams's plays in particular dramatized, albeit indirectly, the devastating impact of homophobia on homosexuals.

Because it sought to reach a mass audience that cut across racial, ethnic, gender, and class lines, Hollywood was even more susceptible to outside censorship than was Broadway, whose audience was increasingly limited to the upper middle class. In 1915 the Supreme Court ruled that movies were a form of commercialized speech and thus were not protected by the First Amendment. As censorship pressures mounted, Hollywood created a Production

Code to which all the studios were subject. But the Catholic Church and other religious and civic organizations were skeptical of the industry's ability to regulate itself and pressured the studios into strengthening the code. In 1934, the studios issued a new version of the Code, which prohibited, among other things, the explicit treatment of homosexuality. Despite this prohibition, however, homosexual themes and characters did not disappear from the silver screen; they simply became more ambiguous, thus allowing audiences to fill in the blanks however they chose. Hollywood further appeased its critics by having characters coded as homosexual turn out to be the villain and/or die ignominiously in the final scene.

Following World War II, the relation between homophobia and American national identity solidified. During the McCarthy witch-hunts, homosexuals were compared to communists who were allegedly conspiring to overthrow the nation. The "homosexual menace" can in part be traced to the publication of the first Kinsey report in 1948, which showed that homosexuals did not differ significantly from heterosexuals. Although Kinsey, who was probably homosexual, hoped the report would undermine the medical model of homosexuality, his findings contributed to fears of a homosexualization of American society. Forty percent of the men interviewed by Kinsey had engaged in homosexual activity, indicating that sexual identity was not fixed but could shift over the course of a person's lifetime. But if sexual identity was not fixed, then homosexuals might be able to convert heterosexuals to their "perverted" practices. Kinsey's findings further contributed to the "homosexual menace" by calling into question the stereotype of the effeminate gay man. The report showed that "persons with homosexual histories are to be found in every age group, in every social level, in every conceivable occupation in cities and on farms, and in the most remote areas of the country." Thus homosexuals could infiltrate the nation's centers of power without being detected and thus were akin to communists. In 1950, in response to mounting hysteria, Congress held widely publicized hearings on whether homosexuals constituted a security risk. As a consequence of these hearings, more gays and lesbians were expelled from the federal government than were suspected communists.

Gay men first began to challenge the homophobic construction of American national identity in the 1920s. Inspired by the German homosexual emancipation movement, which he learned about while stationed in Germany after World War I, Henry Gerber founded the Chicago Society for Human Rights in 1924. Gerber's political and rhetorical strategies foreshadowed those of later gay rights activists. He hoped to promote the reform of sodomy laws through the dissemination of scientific knowledge. He justified these goals by invoking the nation's founding principles. According to its charter, issued by the state of Illinois, the society sought to protect "the interests of people who by reasons of mental and physical abnormalities are abused and hindered in the legal pursuit of happiness which is guaranteed them by the Declaration of Independence." When a sensationalistic account of the society's activities appeared in the Chicago *Examiner* in 1925, the police raided Gerber's apartment and arrested the society's officers.

With the emergence of the homophile movement in the 1950s, gay male activism grew more effective. In 1951, Edward Sagarin published an influential study of homosexual oppression, *The Homosexual in America*, under the pseudonym Donald Webster Cory. Inspired by the civil rights movement, Sagarin was the first to argue that homosexuals constituted an oppressed minority and therefore deserved the same legal protections as other oppressed minorities. Like Gerber, he thought that the dissemination of scientific knowledge would eventually lead to the acceptance of homosexuals by showing that they did not differ significantly from heterosexuals. Meanwhile, in 1950 three former members of the Communist Party, Henry Hay, Chuck Rowland, and Bob Hull, founded the Mattachine Society. Unlike Sagarin, they were not interested in promoting the assimilation of homosexuals into mainstream American society. Rather, they argued that as an oppressed minority, homosexuals had their own distinct history and culture, which they should struggle to preserve. As anticommunist hysteria spread, their former ties to the Communist Party began to alarm members, and they were forced to resign from the society. Following their departure, the society grew more conservative, causing membership to decline precipitously.

Following the Stonewall rebellion of 1969, gay men began to mobilize on a mass scale. Gay rights organizations proliferated and achieved significant gains. Perhaps the most notable of these was the formation of a public culture centered around sex in which gay men participated without fear of police harassment. But the onslaught of the AIDS epidemic in the early 1980s threatened to reverse these gains. And when viewed from the perspective of the AIDS crisis, the 1980s bore an uncanny resemblance to the 1950s. Gay men once again emerged as the enemy within. As carriers of HIV, the virus that causes AIDS, they allegedly threatened to contaminate the nation as a whole. Hysteria over this possibility led to a remedicalization of the gay male body that overturned one of the most important achievements of the 1970s, the refutation of the medical model of homosexuality. Compounding the resemblance between the 1980s and the 1950s was the discovery that many of the figures who had helped to orchestrate the Cold War persecution of gays and lesbians such as Roy M. Cohn, J. Edgar Hoover, and Francis Cardinal Spellman were themselves homosexual. Deploying a homophobic tactic that they themselves had pioneered, the media depicted these figures as maladjusted, self-hating homosexuals who had undermined the nation's security. They had supposedly infiltrated that nation's centers of power undetected and embarked them on a campaign of political and sexual repression they would otherwise not have undertaken.

The movement experienced another major setback in 1986 when in a landmark decision, *Bowers v. Hardwick*, the Supreme Court upheld the Georgia sodomy law, ruling that homosexuals had no constitutional right to privacy or to engage in consensual sex. Following the rise of the New Right in the 1970s, activists had all but abandoned the legislative arena, where support for gay rights had evaporated. Adopting a strategy of the civil rights movement, they began to petition the courts for equal protection. But in the wake of *Bowers v. Hardwick*, the lower courts refused to extend civil rights laws to gays and lesbians. In a series of rulings that justified antigay discrimination, the courts held that sexual orientation could not be compared to race or gender because it was supposedly undetectable unless gays and lesbians themselves made it known. As a consequence of these rulings, state and local initiatives excluding sexual orientation from civil rights laws proliferated.

Despite these setbacks, the AIDS crisis helped to revitalize the gay rights movement. In the 1970s, many activists repudiated the militancy and sexual utopianism of the gay liberation movement. Instead, they tried to show that gays and lesbians did not differ significantly from other Americans. As a result, gays and lesbians gradually emerged as a special interest comparable to other special interests (labor, women, and racial and ethnic minorities). Activists began to

lobby Congress for civil rights legislation and to pressure the media for more balanced and "objective" coverage of gay and lesbian issues. President Jimmy Carter even appointed a liaison to gay rights groups, thereby ensuring that they had access to the White House. But when Congress and the media failed to respond to the AIDS crisis, activists grew more militant, forming groups such as ACT UP, which adopted more confrontational strategies. These groups organized mass demonstrations against the lack of government funding for medical research and sexually explicit AIDS-education materials. They also disrupted medical conferences, pressuring researchers to alter scientific methods and protocols. Through these strategies, they gradually transformed how medical research is conducted in the United States.

Another important development was the formation of Queer Nation, a short-lived spin-off of ACT UP. Frustrated by ACT UP's exclusive focus on AIDS but inspired by its militancy, Queer Nation rejected the goal of assimilation and adopted an "in-your-face" approach to gay rights that made no apologies for the gay and lesbian subcultures. The group aggressively appropriated public space through Queer Nights Out and Kiss-Ins, forms of street theater in which same-sex couples scandalously made out in sports bars, shopping malls, and other places where gays and lesbians were expected to remain invisible. It also outed closeted celebrities such as Malcolm Forbes and Jodie Foster to expose the homophobia of the dominant media, which treated their homosexuality as a shameful secret. Despite their achievements, however, both ACT UP and Queer Nation were hampered by a limited understanding of the politics of identity. They underestimated the degree to which gay and lesbian experience are determined by race, class, and gender. As a consequence, they alienated gays and lesbians unable or unwilling to privilege their sexuality over other aspects of their identities.

Although in 1996 in another landmark decision, *Romer v. Evans*, the Supreme Court held that antigay initiatives violated the equal protection clause of the Constitution, new obstacles to gay liberation arose. In 1997 Congress passed the Defense of Marriage Act, which allowed states to bar same-sex marriages. Moreover, deep divisions opened up within the gay rights movement. In the wake of the AIDS crisis, some activists repudiated the ethics of pleasure pioneered by the gay liberation movement. Alarmed by studies showing that a growing number of younger gay men were having unprotected anal sex, even though they knew that in so doing they risked exposing themselves to HIV, these activists met secretly with public health officials in New York City, urging them to crack down on the institutions that traditionally formed the foundation of gay culture, such as bathhouses and porn shops, because they allegedly promoted the spread of AIDS. For these activists, one of the most important goals for gays and lesbians was to acquire the right to marry. This shift in priorities reflected a desire that simultaneously had galvanized and hindered the gay rights movement from its inception: the assimilation of gays and lesbians into mainstream American society. But the inextricable link between homophobia and American national identity ensured that this goal would continue to elude and divide the movement.

Robert J. Corber

Bibliography

Chauncy, George. *Gay New York: Gender, Urban Culture, and the Making of the Gay Male World 1890–1940.* New York: Basic Books, 1994.

Fiedler, Leslie. *Love and Death in the American Novel,* rev. ed. New York: Anchor, 1992.

Katz, Jonathan Ned. *Gay American History: Lesbians and Gay Men in the U.S.A.,* rev. ed. New York: Meridian, 1992.

Russo, Vito. *The Celluloid Closet: Homosexuality in the Movies,* rev. ed. New York: Harper & Row, 1987.

See also ACT UP; Adult Bookstores; African American Gay Culture; AIDS; Alger, Horatio; American Indian / Alaska Native Gender Identity and Sexuality; Bathhouses and Sex Clubs; Berdache; *Bowers v. Hardwick* and *Romer v. Evans*; Carpenter, Edward; Censorship; Chicano and Latino Gay Cultures; Cohn, Roy M.; Colonial America; Cory, Donald Webster; Film; Gay Liberation; Gay Rights in the United States; Harlem Renaissance; Hay, Harry; Homophile Movement; Hoover, J. Edgar; Inge, William; Kinsey, Alfred; Los Angeles; McCarthyism; Melville, Herman; Miami; New York City; Outing; Pornography; Queer Nation; Same-Sex Marriage; Stonewall; Symonds, John Addington; U.S. Government; U.S. Law: Equal Protection; U.S. Literature; Washington, D.C.; Whitman, Walt; Williams, Tennessee

Uranianism

Uranianism, a term coined by Karl Heinrich Ulrichs, was one of many terms used during the nine-teenth century to denote homosexuality. Even though Ulrichs's sexual terminology did not survive in the work of most subsequent sexologists, his theories of congenital homosexuality influenced a number of writers, and the term *Uranian* was adopted by poets in late-nineteenth-century England to designate homosexual—and, more specifically, pederastic—love.

Ulrichs derived the term *Uranian* from the speech of Pausanias in Plato's *Symposium,* in which Pausanias proposes that there are two goddesses of love, the earthly or common Aphrodite, daughter of Zeus and Dione, connected with heterosexual love for women, and the heavenly or Uranian Aphrodite, motherless daughter of Uranus, connected with the love of young men. In a series of pamphlets that he began publishing in 1864, Ulrichs developed a theory of "Uranian" love, or sexual love of men for men. He called men who loved men *Urnings,* and men who loved women *Dionings,* after the two Aphrodites.

Ulrichs believed that Urnings constitute a "third sex" distinct from male and female. Because he understood love directed toward a male as an essentially female drive, he imagined the male homosexual as a kind of psychological hermaphrodite, or, as he expressed the idea, a feminine soul trapped in a masculine body, *anima muliebris virile corpore inclusa.* Building on his theory that sexual drives are innate, Ulrichs argued that Uranian love is a natural form of sexual oppression that should be neither stigmatized nor criminalized. Ulrichs also proceeded to delineate further sexual identities: homosexual and heterosexual women (with the equivalent terminology of *Uringin* and *Dioningin*), masculine and feminine types of Urnings, and combined types or bisexuals, as well as those of either type who, through force of habit or circumstance, act like the opposite.

Ulrichs's complex terminology and system of classification were never fully adopted by other theorists of sexuality, but the term *Uranian* continued to appear alongside other terms for same-sex love through the turn of the century. Marc-André Raffalovich, Magnus Hirschfeld, and Xavier Mayne (pseudonym of Edward Irenaeus Prime Stevenson)—and later in America Edward Perry Warren (using the pen name Arthur Lyon Raile)—all published defenses of "Uranian" love, though they did not fully utilize the systemization of sexual identity that Ulrichs proposed. Ulrichs's theory of congenital homosexuality was adopted by Raffalovich, Edward

U Carpenter, John Addington Symonds, and others to argue for the naturalness of homosexuality, but other sexologists, such as Richard von Krafft-Ebing, adapted his biologism to explain homosexuality as a disease rather than an innate condition or acceptable version of human love.

The term *Uranian* was used by a number of homoerotic poets in late-nineteenth- and early-twentieth-century England and America, including John Leslie Barford (*Ladslove Lyrics,* 1918), Edwin Emmanuel Bradford, Ralph Nicholas Chubb, George Cecil Ives, Charles Kains Jackson, Edmund John, John Gambril Nicholson, and others discussed in Timothy d'Arch Smith's important study of the Uranian poets, *Love in Earnest.* Influenced by German sexology (through Symonds and Havelock Ellis) but inspired by their appropriation of classical literature as a culture through which to explore erotic desire for male youth, they wrote homoerotic verse dedicated specifically to the love of adolescent males.   *Ed Madden*

Bibliography

Kennedy, Hubert C. *The Life of Karl Heinrich Ulrichs: Pioneer of the Modern Gay Movement.* San Francisco: Alyson, 1988.

———. "The 'Third Sex' Theory" of Karl Heinrich Ulrichs." *Journal of Homosexuality* 6 (1980–81): 103–11.

Reade, Brian, ed. *Sexual Heretics: Male Homosexuality in English Literature from 1850–1900.* New York: Coward-McCann, 1970.

Smith, Timothy d'Arch. *Love in Earnest: Some Notes on the Lives and Writings of English 'Uranian' Poets from 1889 to 1930.* London: Routledge and Kegan Paul, 1970.

Ulrichs, Karl Heinrich. *The Riddle of "Man-Manly" Love: The Pioneering Work on Male Homosexuality.* Michael A. Lombardi-Nash, trans. Buffalo, N.Y.: Prometheus Books, 1994.

See also Carpenter, Edward; Ellis, Havelock; Hirschfeld, Magnus; Krafft-Ebing, Richard von; Pederasty; Plato; Raffalovich, Marc-André; Sexology; Symonds, John Addington

U.S. Government

The effort to prohibit discrimination on the basis of sexual orientation started at the federal level in 1975. Early proposals attempted to prohibit discrimination in employment, housing, public accommodations and facilities, public education, and federally assisted programs. Although bills have been introduced in some form in each succeeding Congress, none of the broad-based bills received serious attention. The Employment Nondiscrimination Act (ENDA) of 1995 was limited to prohibiting discrimination in employment. It covered hiring, firing, promotions, and compensation by public and private employers. Religious organizations, the military, and employers with fewer than fifteen employees were exempt. It did not require employers to provide partner benefits, and it specifically prohibited quotas or preferential treatment.

Congress passed the Defense of Marriage Act (DOMA) in 1996. DOMA exempts states from recognizing marriages between same-sex couples contracted in other states and defines marriage for purposes of federal law. Under DOMA, "marriage" is a legal union between one man and one woman, and "spouse" refers to a person of the other sex who is a husband or a wife.

The sponsors argued that DOMA was necessary because of a Hawaii court case. In 1988, three same-sex couples sued the state of Hawaii, arguing that denying them the right to marry violated the state's constitutional ban on sex discrimination. The state supreme court sent the case back to the lower court, indicating that the state must demonstrate a compelling interest in denying marriage to these couples. Even though the final decision in this case was not expected until well into the next legislative session, and the Hawaiian legislature could delay enforcement and could amend the state constitution before same-sex marriages become legal, DOMA supporters insisted that this bill must pass "before it was too late."

Never before had Congress enacted legislation dealing purely with domestic relations. Family law, including regulations concerning who can marry whom, has always been left to the states on constitutional grounds. In spite of arguments that DOMA was unnecessary, if not unconstitutional, DOMA passed the Senate on September 10, the same day the Hawaii court case began. President Clinton signed it soon thereafter, some said under the strain of his reelection campaign. The law will be challenged in court and opponents of this policy will continue to work toward introducing some form of domestic partnership legislation.

Ironically DOMA provided advocates of gay civil rights an opportunity to educate Congress and the general public about discrimination against gay, lesbian, and bisexual people by threatening to offer ENDA as an amendment to DOMA. Eventually, separate votes were cast on the bills. DOMA passed overwhelmingly. ENDA achieved a high-water mark for civil rights legislation in this area but was defeated in the Senate with a 49–50 vote.

In addition to these major civil rights bills, repeated attempts have been made to add antigay language to federal legislation. On various occasions, amendments have been offered that would prohibit the federal government from recruiting employees on the basis of sexual orientation and from providing interventions that might reduce antigay prejudice. Attempts have also been made to limit discussion of homosexuality in sex education programs.

Michael R. Stevenson

Bibliography

Eddy, M. "Sexual Orientation Discrimination in Employment: Legislation and Issues in the 104th Congress." *CRS Report for Congress*. Washington, D.C.: Congressional Research Service, 1995.

Eddy, M. "Defense of Marriage Act." *CRS Report for Congress*. Washington, D.C.: Congressional Research Service, 1996.

See also Gay Rights; Gay Rights in the United States; Same-Sex Marriage; Sex Education; United States; U.S. Government Surveillance; U.S. Law

U.S. Government Surveillance

The implementation of government surveillance of homosexuals in the United States predates the beginning of the homophile movement. At the federal level, as early as 1919, the U.S. Navy conducted sting operations in which young male informants were ordered to have sex with naval personnel to expose them as homosexual. And in 1937, J. Edgar Hoover, director of the Federal Bureau of Investigation (FBI), directed his agents to create dossiers on alleged homosexuals. These files, labeled "Sex Degenerates and Sex Offenders," "Sex Offenders Foreign Counterintelligence," and "Sex Perverts in Government Service," would by 1977, when they were eventually closed, amount to some 300,000 pages and take up almost 100 cubic feet of storage space. The dossiers were ordered destroyed with the approval of the National Archives, but before their destruction, information from them was used to smear countless Americans and destroy their livelihoods.

A related FBI surveillance effort mandated the creation, from March 1925, of an "Obscene" file. Hoover ordered his agents to collect pornographic films, literature, and other published materials, eventually including homophile and, later, gay liberation magazines. During the McCarthy period, the FBI made much use of these files, aided by Executive Order 10450, signed by President Dwight D. Eisenhower, that allowed federal employees to be discharged for "sexual perversion." The FBI was given the task of supplying the Civil Service Commission with background information. Thousands of federal workers were fired after being accused of homosexuality in "loyalty" investigations. These files contained unverified allegations of same-sex or adulterous behavior, where fact was conflated with fiction. They became political fodder for Hoover, a master manipulator of presidents and members of Congress. Damaging information was leaked to favored reporters or shown discreetly to politicians to ensure their cooperation with the bureau and to prevent them from criticizing Hoover or the bureau.

The homosexual smear became an art. In 1952, the then governor of Illinois, Adlai E. Stevenson (who would later become an ambassador to the United Nations), was labeled a "sex deviate" in FBI records, which accused him of engaging in "sexual perversion." In 1969, Hoover approved the creation of a "Pick the Fag" poster with prizes (such as 500 rolls of red toilet paper—with Mao's Tse-tung's picture—or a free trip to Hanoi) going to the winner correctly identifying one of four antiwar leaders as homosexual. The FBI also tried to discredit Black Panther leader Huey Newton after he publicly supported gay liberation. It faked letters from supposed members questioning Newton's masculinity. Ironically, Hoover also made his agents investigate anyone who accused Hoover himself of homosexuality.

The files show that the FBI relied on informants, infiltrated activist groups, wiretapped phone calls, opened personal mail, and even paid sources to have sex with targets of surveillance. The FBI also kept files on America's literary establishment. Allen Ginsberg, Tennessee Williams, James Baldwin, and Truman Capote were among those whose files have become public.

The rise of the homophile movement led the FBI to create dossiers on such groups as the Mattachine Society, the Daughters of Bilitis, and ONE, Inc. With the advent of gay liberation, the FBI wondered how to name its new dossiers. "Fag Liberation Movement" was the caption of one 1969 file in the

U New York City field office. Groups such as the Gay Activists Alliance became targets of surveillance.

Alleged criminal violations of law often became the rationale for compiling files on homosexuals. Thousands of pages of files resulted from the FBI's "Homex" investigation of individuals accused of extorting money from accused homosexuals, with whom they would have sex. Those extorted included high government and military officials. With the U.S. Post Office, obscenity codes were used as a rationale for surveillance of recipients of homosexual physique magazines. Infiltrating homosexual clubs, postal inspectors reported suspected homosexuals to their employers, who promptly fired them.

By the 1980s, as homosexuals became more assimilated into mainstream society and the FBI itself began allowing its agents to come out, the FBI's attention turned more toward investigating more taboo behavior: males suspected of being attracted to adolescent boys. A full-scale FBI investigation of the North American Man/Boy Love Association (NAMBLA) would result in police raids, arrests, and the creation of thousands of pages of FBI dossiers from local field office to FBI headquarters, as the agency compiled dossiers on almost anyone associated with the activist group. Using newly enacted child pornography laws as their rationale, the U.S. Customs Service, as well as postal authorities, mounted numerous sting operations, using computer-generated magazines, to lure suspected pedophiles by offering to sell them outlawed magazines and videos.

The U.S. Department of Defense has long resisted the integration of homosexual personnel into its services. The 1919 scandal at the Newport, Rhode Island, naval training station cast an aspiring assistant secretary into the limelight. Franklin D. Roosevelt, later to become president, was reprimanded by the Senate for authorizing the sting operation that sent young men to be fellated by naval personnel. Over the years, thousands of homosexuals were kicked out of the military, although they were more likely to be discharged administratively or through resignation than by court-martial. The rate of involuntary homosexual discharges went from about one thousand per year to three thousand by the early 1960s, with the rate in the 1990s back to about one thousand a year. Not all instances involved criminal offenses; criminal investigations were conducted only half the time. Of the three services, the Navy seemed the most aggressive in investigating homosexuals; two-thirds of all criminal naval investigations involved homosexuality.

Homosexuals within the military have continued to face investigations and courts-martial, despite the "Don't ask, don't tell" policy in place during the Clinton administration in the 1990s. With the new policy, these interrogations were supposed to have been stopped. But data from activist groups show that military personnel have continued to be investigated and expelled from the service because of their sexual orientation. And during the Persian Gulf War (1991), there were charges that homosexuals about to be discharged were sent to the front while their paperwork was being processed.

State and local "Red Squad" police dossiers also included unverified rumors about the sex lives of suspected homosexuals. Release of these files led to an interesting dilemma: should they be destroyed or not? In Michigan, subjects of the Michigan State Police files were able to obtain their own files prior to their being preserved in an archive. But in San Francisco, with the concurrence of the American Civil Liberties Union (ACLU), Red Squad files from the Sheriff's Department were destroyed to prevent further ruining of lives. Surveillance of public restrooms and parks, which peaked in the 1950s and 1960s, has nonetheless continued, often with youthful-looking police officers entrapping homosexuals. By the 1990s, sting operations were more likely to be high tech, utilizing digitalized images and electronic communication targeting vulnerable individuals within electronic chat rooms.

Legislative attempts to curtail political surveillance had mixed results. Grassroots coalitions in various cities, including Detroit, were able to put an end to Red Squad surveillance. But nationally, although Congress in 1974 enacted the Privacy Act in the wake of FBI and other agency abuses from the Vietnam War period, its provision barring the collection and retention of information relating to First Amendment–protected activities of Americans and permanent residents did not appear to be faithfully observed by intelligence and law enforcement agencies.

In the 1990s, the FBI successfully argued in court that it could collect political information on Americans despite the Privacy Act provision. And the Central Intelligence Agency, in *Tsang v. CIA*, maintained that the National Security Act of 1947, which established the spy agency, allowed it to do whatever was necessary to fulfill its mission. It refused to agree not to spy on all Americans but made one exception. In settling *Tsang v. CIA*, in which the CIA admitted to collecting information on Daniel Tsang, a gay activist librarian, his publication *Gay Insurgent* and his Lavender Archives, the CIA agreed to release a redacted copy of his dossier, never to spy on Tsang again, and to pay his ACLU lawyers $46,000. In late 1997, the CIA revised its Web site to delete an earlier assertion that it does not spy on Americans. *Daniel C. Tsang*

Bibliography

Bérubé, Allan. *Coming Out Under Fire: The History of Gay Men and Women in World War Two*. New York: Free Press, 1990.

D'Emilio, John. *Sexual Politics, Sexual Communities*. Chicago: University of Chicago Press, 1983.

Government versus Homosexuals. New York: Arno Press, 1975. Reprints "Alleged Immoral Conditions at Newport (R.I.) Naval Training Station: Report" (1921), "Employment of Homosexuals and Other Sex Perverts in Government" (1950), and "Homosexuality and Citizenship in Florida" (1964).

Gregory-Lewis, Sasha. "Jack Davis: Using the Sexuality Connection." *Advocate* (May 4, 1977): 7–9, 45.

———. "Revelations of a Gay Informant," Part 1. *Advocate* (February 23, 1977): 12–15; and Part 2: *Advocate* (March 9, 1977): 13–14, 16, 38.

Mitgang, Herbert. *Dangerous Dossiers: Exposing the Secret War against America's Greatest Authors*. New York: Donald I. Fine, 1988.

Murphy, Lawrence R. *Perverts by Official Order: The Campaign against Homosexuals by the United States Navy*. New York: Harrington Park Press, 1988.

Robins, Natalie. *Alien Ink: The FBI's War on Freedom of Expression*. New York: Morrow, 1992.

Shilts, Randy. *Conduct Unbecoming: Lesbians and Gays in the U.S. Military: Vietnam to the Persian Gulf*. New York: St. Martin's Press, 1993.

Silberman, Steven. "Librarian Follows FBI's Anti-gay Trail." *Orange County Register*, October 10, 1990, B1, B7.

Stanley, Lawrence A. "The Hysteria over Child Pornography and Paedophilia." *Paidika* (Amsterdam), no. 2 (Autumn 1987): 13–34.

Theoharis, Athan G., ed. *From the Secret Files of J. Edgar Hoover*. Chicago: Ivan R. Dee, 1991.

Tsang, Daniel C. "A CIA Target at Home in America." *Los Angeles Times*, January 18, 1998, M2.

U.S. General Accounting Office. *Defense Force Management: DOD's Policy on Homosexuality*. Washington, D.C.: The Office, 1992.

U.S. General Accounting Office. *Defense Force Management: Statistics Relating to DOD's Policy on Homosexuality*. Washington, D.C.: The Office, 1992.

A Witchhunt Foiled: The FBI vs. NAMBLA. New York: North American Man/Boy Love Association, 1995.

See also Baldwin, James; Black Power Movement; Capote, Truman; Gay Activists Alliance; Gay Liberation; Ginsberg, Allen; Homophile Movement; Hoover, J. Edgar; Mattachine Society; McCarthyism; Military; NAMBLA: North American Man / Boy Love Association; *ONE* Magazine; Pederasty; Pornography; Tearooms; U.S. Government; U.S. Law: Discrimination; Williams, Tennessee

U.S. Law: Discrimination

U.S. law derives from a common law tradition that allows individuals the freedom to select their personal and business associates. In the absence of specific constitutional provisions or statutes dictating otherwise, discrimination based on personal preferences is presumptively lawful. The only exception recognized by the common law was that businesses providing important public services, such as transportation systems (known as "common carriers"), could not arbitrarily exclude particular individuals from using their services.

The U.S. and state constitutions place restrictions on the ability of government to discriminate. The Fourteenth Amendment to the Constitution requires that state governments afford "equal protection of the laws" to all persons within their jurisdiction. The Supreme Court has ruled that the Fifth Amendment, through its due process clause, imposes the same requirement on the federal government.

Additionally, the due process clauses of the Fifth and Fourteenth Amendments require all levels of government to observe fair procedures in dealing with individuals.

Statutes, ordinances, regulations, or executive orders may abridge the discretion of both governmental and nongovernmental actors to discriminate in their public or commercial activities. The federal government has not directly legislated against sexual orientation discrimination, but a 1990 statute forbidding discrimination against persons with disabilities—the Americans With Disabilities Act (ADA)—forbids discrimination against persons who are regarded as having a disability. This may protect homosexuals who encounter discrimination because a discriminator believes that they may have or present a risk of Acquired Immune Deficiency Syndrome (AIDS). The ADA provides that homosexuality, bisexuality, or transsexuality, as such, may not be considered disabilities. Proposals for a direct ban on sexual orientation discrimination as a provision of federal law have been introduced in Congress for more than twenty years. In 1996, the Senate rejected one such proposal to housing and public accommodations.

At the local level, some of the laws apply only to governmental employment and services, but most also apply to private businesses. Some private businesses (including a substantial portion of the five-hundred largest U.S. corporations) have voluntarily adopted internal policies of nondiscrimination, which may be enforceable in most states as part of the contract of employment if they are incorporated in employee handbooks, personnel manuals, or other written products of the employer. Some labor organizations have won protection against such discrimination in their legally enforceable collective bargaining agreements with employers.

The list of such laws and policies changes so frequently that its inclusion in this work is impractical. (The Lambda Legal Defense and Education Fund, a national legal organization, attempts to maintain a current list.) By the end of 1996, however, a majority of all employees in the United States worked in jobs subject to such nondiscrimination policies, and similar protection existed for many employees in Canada, Australia, South Africa, and many countries in western Europe.

Disputes over the interpretation and application of laws banning sexual orientation discrimination have most frequently concerned claims of religious exemption or personal privacy rights by discriminators. For example, Georgetown University, a Catholic (Jesuit) university in the District of Columbia, claimed a religious exemption from compliance with a District ordinance banning sexual orientation discrimination. The District's highest court ruled that the ordinance should be interpreted to allow the university to observe its religious precepts to the extent compatible with protecting lesbian and gay students from discrimination. Thus, it refused to order the university to extend "official recognition" to lesbian and gay student organiza-

tions but required the university to allow such organizations to meet on campus and use university facilities to the same extent as other students are allowed to do so.   *Arthur S. Leonard*

Bibliography

"Sexual Orientation and the Law, III. Employment Law Issues Affecting Gay Men and Lesbians." 102 *Harvard Law Review* 1508, 1554 (May 1989).

See also Business; Education; International Law; Stoddard, Thomas B.; Student Organizations; U.S. Law: Equal Protection

U.S. Law: Equal Protection

The U.S. Constitution's Fourteenth Amendment provides that no state may deprive any person of equal protection of the laws. The Supreme Court has interpreted the Fifth Amendment's due process clause to impose the same obligation on the federal government. State constitutions have their own equal protection requirements. Constitutional equal protection requirements are binding solely on the government, not private actors, and apply only to intentional discrimination.

Equal protection has never imposed a rigid requirement of absolute equality of treatment. The courts recognize that the government may have legitimate reasons to classify individuals according to personal characteristics. The Supreme Court has developed an equal protection analysis that presumes the validity of government policies unless they discriminate either on the basis of a constitutionally "suspect" classification or concerning a "fundamental" right. A government action or policy presumed to be valid can be successfully challenged only by proving that the policy has no "rational relationship" to achieving a "legitimate state interest."

If a policy discriminates based on a suspect classification or concerning a fundamental right, the burden of justifying the policy falls on the government, which must prove that the policy is necessary to achieve a "compelling state interest" and is "narrowly tailored" to achieve that interest without more discrimination than necessary. In such cases, the court engages in "strict scrutiny" of the challenged policy. Examples are policies that discriminate on the basis of race, or in the right to vote.

The Supreme Court has recognized circumstances where a classification is somewhat (quasi)

suspect or where a policy abridges an important, albeit not fundamental, right. In such cases, "heightened scrutiny" will apply, requiring the government to prove that its policy was adopted to achieve important governmental interests. Examples are policies that discriminate on the basis of sex, or in access to public education.

In cases challenging government policies alleged to discriminate against homosexual persons, most courts have ruled that sexual orientation is not a suspect classification, which means that unless the particular governmental discrimination against homosexuals involves a fundamental right, the burden is entirely on the challengers of the government action or policy to prove that it bears no rational relationship to a legitimate end.

The Supreme Court has never ruled directly on whether sexual orientation is a suspect classification, although it ruled in *Bowers v. Hardwick* (1986) that homosexuals do not have a fundamental right to engage in sodomy (which was defined in the challenged Georgia statute as anal or oral intercourse). The Court said that the presumed moral disapproval of homosexuality by the state's citizens, reflected in the action of their elected legislators, provided a rational relationship between a law banning homosexual sodomy and achieving legitimate state interests. (The statute challenged in *Bowers* applied to *all*, not just homosexual, sodomy, but the Court held that the challenger, as a gay man, could challenge only the statute's application to his own conduct.) Because the theory Michael Hardwick used to challenge the Georgia sodomy law was "privacy," a fundamental right under the due process clause, the Court did not address the question whether a state ban on homosexual sex would violate equal protection. In subsequent cases, however, lower courts relied on *Bowers v. Hardwick* to deny claims of heightened or strict scrutiny in equal protection cases brought by homosexual litigants, reasoning that a class of people defined by conduct that carries no constitutional protection could not obtain "special protection" under equal protection theories.

In 1996, the Supreme Court ruled in *Romer v. Evans* that animus against homosexuals does not provide a rational justification for a state policy that broadly disfavors homosexuals. Striking down a Colorado constitutional amendment that barred the state or its subdivisions from adopting policies affording homosexuals redress against discrimination, the Court held that "sexual orientation" is a cognizable classification for purposes of the equal protec-

tion clause, and that the breadth of the discrimination imposed by the amendment rendered insufficient the weak policy justifications the state articulated in its defense. Indeed, the Court said that the amendment seems to have been adopted for no better reason than dislike of homosexuals, which could not be a legitimate justification for discriminatory legislation.

Because the Court found no rational basis for such sweeping discrimination, it did not determine whether a more demanding level of judicial review needed to be imposed in cases concerning sexual orientation discrimination. The dissenters argued that the result was inconsistent with *Bowers v. Hardwick*, and a subsequent lower court decision, *Nabozny v. Podlesny*, suggested that *Romer* would "eclipse" *Bowers* in future equal protection cases. *Romer v. Evans* marked the first time the Supreme Court had ever invalidated a government policy disfavoring homosexuals using an equal protection analysis.

Nabozny may herald a renewed emphasis on equal protection theories in vindicating the rights of lesbians and gay men. Jamie Nabozny charged that while he was a public school student in Wisconsin, he was subjected to severe harassment by other male students but was denied help by teachers and school administrators, even though the school had a sexual harassment policy and the state had a law banning sexual orientation discrimination. Although a lower court dismissed his case, the U.S. Court of Appeals for the 7th Circuit found that if, as Nabozny alleged, the school applied its policy to protect female students from harassment by male students but would not apply the policy to protect male students from such harassment, or would not apply the policy because the student was gay, then the equal protection requirement might be violated. The court opined that it was hard to conceive of any rational state interest that would be advanced by denying such protection to a student because he was male and/or gay, and ordered that a trial be held to determine the truth of Nabozny's charges. The Nabozny decision shows how claims involving antigay discrimination may sometimes be conceptualized as sex discrimination claims, bringing them within the umbrella of the "quasi-suspect" status accorded to sex-based discrimination.

Equal protection theories may also be used under the various state constitutions. In *Baehr v. Lewin*, for example, three same-sex couples in Hawaii challenged that state's failure to grant them marriage licenses. The Hawaii supreme court ruled in 1993 that denying marriage licenses because of the gender of the applicants would violate the state's equal protection clause, under which sex is a suspect classification, unless the state could prove a compelling justification for such denial. A referendum held in November 1998 resulted in an amendment to the Hawaii constitution that gives the ultimate authority to determine whether same-sex couples can marry to the state legislature. Shortly after the referendum, the Hawaii Supreme Court asked the parties to submit briefs on whether the case is moot because of the constitutional amendment.

In December 1998, the Oregon Court of Appeals became the first state appellate court to rule that government discrimination on the basis of sexual orientation was "suspect" under the state constitutional equal protection clause, in a case involving the domestic partnership benefits for same-sex partners of state employees.

A significant test for equal protection theory is the continued exclusion of openly lesbian, gay, or bisexual people from military service. Because the courts are normally deferential to personnel decisions by the armed forces, and military leaders adamantly assert that the presence of openly lesbian or gay members would destroy the morale and unit cohesion of nongay members, all legal challenges to the exclusionary policy have been unsuccessful. However, the *Romer* decision seriously undermines these justifications, which are based on the presumed animus of nongay service members toward homosexuals.   *Arthur S. Leonard*

Case References

Baehr v. Lewin, 852 P.2d 44 (Haw. 1993).
Bowers v. Hardwick, 478 U.S. 186 (1986).
Nabozny v. Podlesny, 92 F.2d 446 (7th Cir. 1996).
Romer v. Evans, 116 S.Ct. 1620 (1996).

See also *Bowers v. Hardwick* and *Romer v. Evans*; Civil Rights in the U.S.; Education; Gay Rights in the United States; Same-Sex Marriage; U.S. Government; U.S. Law: Discrimination

U.S. Law: Privacy

The legal concept of privacy in U.S. law derives from various strands of constitutional and common law.

The main text of the U.S. Constitution, adopted in 1789, provides in article VI that "no religious Test shall ever be required as a Qualification to any Office or public Trust under the United States," and the Bill of Rights, adopted in 1791, includes in the First Amendment protection for religious and political belief by forbidding Congress from making any law "respecting an establishment of religion, or prohibiting the free exercise thereof; or abridging the freedom of speech, or of the press." Thus, from the earliest period of U.S. history, the federal government has been formally excluded from regulating the innermost beliefs of individuals.

In the Fourth Amendment, the Bill of Rights identifies a "right of the people to be secure in their persons, houses, papers, and effects, against unreasonable searches and seizures," which "shall not be violated, and no Warrants shall issue, but upon probable cause, supported by Oath or affirmation, and particularly describing the place to be searched, and the persons or things to be seized," and the Third Amendment prohibits quartering soldiers in private homes without the owner's consent during peacetime, and in wartime only pursuant to legislative action. The Fifth Amendment forbids requiring people to testify against themselves in criminal proceedings and guarantees that the government will not deprive individuals of life, liberty, or property without due process of law. The Ninth Amendment states that the listing of rights in the Constitution is not exclusive or exhaustive; "others retained by the people" are no less valued or protected just because they are not explicitly enumerated in the document.

Before the Civil War (1861–1865), the Supreme Court construed the provisions of the Bill of Rights as imposing restrictions only on the federal government. After the Civil War, the Fourteenth Amendment extended to the states the obligations of the due process requirement, as well as imposing a requirement of "equal protection of the laws" and forbidding the states from abridging the "privileges or immunities of citizens of the United States." By the 1930s, the Supreme Court had begun to construe the due process clause as making binding on the states the particular guarantees of provisions of the Bill of Rights, and by the 1970s, virtually all the significant individual rights of the Bill of Rights had been "incorporated" into the Fourteenth Amendment as binding the state governments and their local subdivisions.

At the same time, state and federal judges began to give credence to proposals that the common law of torts (a body of judge-made law generated primarily through private litigation concerned with personal injuries) should be extended to compensate injuries to personal dignity, such as invasions of the privacy of the individual. Perhaps the most persuasive advocates of this view were Louis D. Brandeis and Joseph Warren, Boston lawyers who coauthored an article in an early issue of the *Harvard Law Review* arguing that private citizens whose lives had been exposed to public scrutiny by sensationalistic newspaper reports should be able to claim damages for violation of their "right of privacy" in civil lawsuits. Brandeis later became a justice of the Supreme Court and authored a famous dissenting opinion in *Olmstead v. United States* (1928), a Fourth Amendment wiretapping case that included perhaps the most famous summation of the right of privacy in American law:

> The makers of our Constitution undertook to secure conditions favorable to the pursuit of happiness. They recognized the significance of man's spiritual nature, of his feelings and of his intellect. They knew that only a part of the pain, pleasure and satisfactions of life are to be found in material things. They sought to protect Americans in their beliefs, their thoughts, their emotions and their sensations. They conferred, as against the government, the right to be let alone—the most comprehensive of rights and the right most valued by civilized men.
>
> To protect that right, every unjustifiable intrusion by the government upon the privacy of the individual, whatever the means employed, must be deemed a violation of the Fourth Amendment. And the use, as evidence in a criminal proceeding, of facts ascertained by such intrusion must be deemed a violation of the Fifth.

While Brandeis discussed this right of privacy in the context of use of evidence obtained through wiretapping in a criminal proceeding, the concept of privacy gained broader currency as the Court confronted attempts by the state to regulate sexuality. In 1961, dissenting from the Court's refusal to rule on the merits of a constitutional challenge to a Connecticut law criminalizing the use of contraceptives to prevent pregnancy, Justice John Marshall Harlan argued in *Poe v. Ullman* that a broader concept of privacy might be derived from the protection of liberty in the Fourteenth Amendment. Harlan identified personal privacy as a "fundamental" component of liberty, which meant that state policies invading privacy would be unconstitutional unless narrowly tailored to achieve a compelling state interest.

When the Court subsequently struck down the Connecticut law in 1965 in *Griswold v. Connecticut*, Justice William O. Douglas found an even more diverse grounding for the right of privacy, mentioning all the constitutional provisions previously discussed in this essay and finding in them a pervasive concern with personal privacy that gave rise to a constitutionally protected zone of privacy violated by the state law, at least as it was applied to the married couple who challenged the statute. Thus was privacy enshrined as a "fundamental right" protected from federal or state abridgment by the due process clauses of the Fifth and Fourteenth Amendments. In a separate concurring opinion, Justice Harlan reiterated his narrower view of the theoretical basis for constitutional privacy, and in another opinion, Justice Arthur J. Goldberg suggested that the Ninth Amendment's insistence on respect for "unenumerated" rights could provide the basis for a right of privacy without specific resort to other constitutional language.

Writing for the Court in 1972 in *Eisenstadt v. Baird*, Justice William J. Brennan Jr. took the analysis further, asserting: "If the right to privacy means anything, it is the right of the *individual*, married or single, to be free from unwarranted governmental intrusion into matters so fundamentally affecting a person as the decision whether to bear or beget a child." Thus, Brennan suggested that the right of privacy was actually a broad right of personal autonomy on "matters" that "fundamentally affect" a person's life. In 1973, the Court ruled in *Roe v. Wade* that the right of privacy was broad enough to prohibit the government from totally outlawing abortions or imposing restrictions for reasons other than the health of the mother during the period prior to fetal viability. In subsequent cases, the Court extended the privacy right to entitle adolescents to obtain contraceptives and to require states to provide judicial mechanisms by which adolescents could obtain abortions without the consent of their parents.

Emphasizing the locational aspect of privacy derived from the Fourth Amendment, the Court also found that the constitutional right of privacy would shelter the private possession and use of sexually explicit materials that might otherwise lack protection under the First Amendment, owing to their "obscene" nature. In this case, *Stanley v. Georgia* (1969), Justice Thurgood Marshall wrote: "Our whole constitutional heritage rebels at the thought of giving government the power to control men's minds."

Taking heart from these constitutional developments, which suggested a broad privacy right that could potentially extend to all private, consensual sexual activity between adults, lesbian and gay activists sought to use the right of privacy to challenge laws criminalizing homosexual activity. During the 1950s, legislative reform efforts in the United Kingdom and the United States had led to proposals that such sexual activity be decriminalized. Partial reform occurred in England in 1967, and individual American states began to repeal sodomy laws in 1960, but more than half the states still retained such laws by the early 1970s. The first attempt to litigate against sodomy laws using the privacy theory, undertaken by the American Civil Liberties Union (ACLU) in Virginia, was unsuccessful, as the Supreme Court summarily affirmed (without hearing oral arguments or receiving full briefs on the merits) a decision by a federal court in Virginia rejecting the challenge in *John Doe v. Commonwealth's Attorney for City of Richmond* (1976). The Virginia court noted that Justice Harlan's dissent in *Poe v. Ullman* had specifically identified homosexuality as a form of intimacy that the state could prohibit, and found nothing in *Griswold* that contradicted this.

Rebuffed by the Supreme Court, gay rights advocates turned their attentions to state courts and achieved privacy-based victories in New York to join earlier victories in Massachusetts and Pennsylvania. A return to the federal court system in Texas and Georgia produced contradictory federal appellate rulings by the mid-1980s, when the Court granted review to the Georgia case brought by the ACLU on behalf of Michael Hardwick, in which a three-judge panel of the U.S. Court of Appeals for the Eleventh Circuit ruled that Georgia's sodomy law, which outlawed all anal or oral sex regardless of the genders of the participants or the degree of privacy and consensual nature of their conduct, potentially violated the right of privacy.

The resulting Supreme Court decision in *Bowers v. Hardwick* marked a significant defeat for the privacy theory. Dividing 5–4, the Court rejected a broad view of privacy suggested by the language of Justices Harlan, Douglas, and Brennan in the contraception cases and instead clung to a narrow conception articulated for the majority by Justice Byron R. White. Justice White characterized the issue in the case as "whether the Federal Constitution confers a fundamental right upon homosexuals to engage in sodomy" and largely ignored the rhetorical sweep of the privacy precedents, asserting that actually the earlier cases were not about a broad, general right of privacy, which is not explicitly mentioned in the Constitution. Instead, White viewed each of the prior cases as a holding that the particular activity at issue implicated a fundamental right, such as the right to engage in reproductive activity. Rejecting the notion that the right to engage in homosexual intimacy bore any resemblance to the rights protected in prior cases, White characterized the constitutional privacy challenge in this case as "facetious." Finding that no fundamental right was at stake, White concluded that the sodomy law could be sustained if there were some rational basis for its enactment, and concluded that the presumed moral disapproval of homosexuality among Georgians provided such a basis.

Despite a passionate dissenting argument by Justice Harry Blackmun, White's opinion stood for the Court as a deterrent to future federal challenges to sodomy laws on privacy grounds. Further signaling its discomfort with privacy theory, the Court began to back away from the broad protection of women's right to abortion, sustaining various state regulations that had previously been struck down under the privacy theory. In 1992, this trend appeared to come to a halt with the Court's decision in *Planned Parenthood of Southeastern Pennsylvania v. Casey*, in which a three-judge plurality made up of Justices Anthony M. Kennedy, David Souter, and Sandra Day O'Connor rested support for a continued right of abortion on the "liberty" guarantee in the Fourteenth Amendment without reference to any privacy theory, with Justices Blackmun and John Paul Stevens concurring. Blackmun specifically noted that the plurality opinion departed from the privacy approach he had used in his opinion for the Court in *Roe v. Wade*, and mourned its apparent passing.

However, under the dual federal/state system, state courts may construe their state constitutions independently from the U.S. Supreme Court's construction of the federal constitution, and the reasoning of *Bowers v. Hardwick* proved unpopular with many state judges. Subsequent attempts to use a privacy theory to attack sodomy laws in the state courts have produced favorable appellate decisions in Kentucky, Tennessee, and Texas, while unfavorable decisions in Louisiana and Georgia did not specifically reject the privacy theory so much as declare its irrelevance to the facts of the particular cases, which involved public solicitation rather than direct prosecution for private sexual conduct.

About a year after the *Hardwick* ruling, Justice Lewis F. Powell, a member of the *Hardwick* majority who subsequently retired from the Court, stated publicly that he now disagreed with the decision. And in 1996, the Supreme Court's decision in *Romer v. Evans*, finding unconstitutional a popularly enacted Colorado state constitutional amendment that banned the state from protecting gays from discrimination, appeared to undermine at least one important aspect of the *Hardwick* decision: Justice White's contention that majoritarian moral judgments about homosexuality were sufficient to justify the criminalization of homosexual conduct. Indeed, dissenting Justice Antonin Scalia argued that the Court's decision in *Romer* was inconsistent with *Hardwick*. These developments encouraged some gay rights advocates to hope that the privacy theory might still be used in the future to challenge state laws penalizing private homosexual activity in federal court.

Meanwhile, the concept of privacy has taken hold among the general public and has begun to flourish in other contexts, although in many instances courts and legislatures are tentative about embracing them. A new body of law has emerged around the issue of HIV/AIDS testing and confidentiality, with many states passing laws specifically protecting the privacy of HIV-positive individuals from disclosure of their status. Drug-testing cases spawned two bodies of case law, one affecting public employees and another affecting private-sector employees (relying primarily on common law concepts). The right of intimate association, an offshoot of the privacy concept, emerged as a possible source of protection for nonmarital relationships.

Concerns about intrusive employer inquiries into the off-duty lives of their employees led to laws protecting employees from discrimination based on lawful off-duty conduct, restrictions on employment testing (especially polygraph testing, but also including psychological and genetic testing), and inquiries about mental or physical disabilities. Some of these developments emerged at the state level, while others found expression in federal legislation, such as the Americans With Disabilities Act of 1990. Clearly, the notion of a right of privacy, regardless of how it fares in the Supreme Court in cases involving homosexual conduct, has won a strong foothold in public and legal consciousness.   *Arthur S. Leonard*

Case References

Bowers v. Hardwick, 478 U.S. 186 (1986).
Doe v. Commonwealth's Attorney for City of Richmond, 403 F.Supp. 1199 (E.D.Va. 1975), summarily affirmed, 425 U.S. 901 (1976).

Eisenstadt v. Baird, 405 U.S. 438 (1972).
Griswold v. Connecticut, 381 U.S. 479 (1965).
Olmstead v. United States, 277 U.S. 438 (1928).
Planned Parenthood of Southeastern Pennsylvania v. Casey, 505 U.S. 112 (1992).
Poe v. Ullman, 367 U.S. 497 (1961).
Roe v. Wade, 410 U.S. 113 (1973).
Romer v. Evans, 116 S.Ct. 1620 (1996).
Stanley v. Georgia, 394 U.S. 557 (1969).

See also AIDS; *Bowers v. Hardwick* and *Romer v. Evans*; Crime and Criminality; Homosexual Panic; Legal Organizations; Sodomy; U.S. Law: Discrimination; U.S. Law: Equal Protection

U.S. Literature

Leslie Fiedler famously commented in 1960 that American fiction was marked by what he called "the failure . . . to deal with adult heterosexual love and [a] consequent obsession with death, incest, and innocent homosexuality." Fiedler took an observation—the lingering impact of the Gothic in American literature—and made it the basis for a condemnation ("failure") of what he took to be a prominent characteristic of the literature as a whole. While Fiedler's comment has had lasting critical power, it lacks historical grounding and ignores what we would now take to be the necessary precisions of categories of male relations. The adoption of the term *homosocial*, promoted by the work of Eve Kosofsky Sedgwick, has enabled us to see that by no means are all male-male relationships homosexual, and homosocial relationships are not necessarily homosexual. It seems unlikely that American literature as a whole is any more or less homosexual in subject than French literature (from Balzac to Proust to Gide) or German literature (from Goethe to Platen to Mann). On the other hand, it does seem likely that the relative absence of a settled and historically continuous community encouraged the kind of male comradeship that could sometimes be transformed into sexual and erotic relations between men. What is striking is the extent to which the authors generally associated with the American Renaissance—Melville, Hawthorne, Whitman—in different ways made relations between men central to their work.

The generation of transcendentalists, who immediately preceded the Renaissance, was also concerned with same-sex relations (in the case of its most significant woman, Margaret Fuller, as well as the men) but derived its treatment of such themes from a platonic tradition that emphasized the ideal over the real. Although Ralph Waldo Emerson (1803–1882), the most important of the transcendentalists, accorded great significance to friendship and devoted a major essay to the subject in 1839, he continued to insist platonically that love "transcends the unworthy object." His friend Henry David Thoreau (1817–1862) pursued male friendships, sometimes modeled on classical friendship but containing a strong element of disgust at the body, represented in part by the "bottom" of Walden Pond. With his friend he feels "a more than maiden modesty," a phrase that has led some of his biographers to imagine foolishly that the friend in question is a woman. The transcendentalists' successors found the object of love less unworthy.

Although of the same generation as the transcendentalists, Nathaniel Hawthorne (1804–1864) maintained a philosophical distance. The transcendentalists' optimism offered no place for evil. Hawthorne's works, rooted in New England history, saw cruelty and intolerance in place of ideal love. Relations between men are charged since they incorporate a drive to power alongside an idyllic friendship. The most obvious manifestation of this troubled relation may be seen in the two men of *The Scarlet Letter* (1850), the minister Dimmesdale and the physician Chillingworth, whose struggle for power takes place over the stigmatized body of Hester Prynne. The patterns of this struggle are repeated and rendered more explicit in *The Blithedale Romance* (1850), a dystopian novel based on the Fourierist community at Brook Farm. The passive poet, Coverdale, is cared for by the blacksmith Hollingsworth (the names echo those of the men in *The Scarlet Letter*) in a relation that is ultimately resolved by the victory of a new masculinity. Hawthorne's work thus uses a contest over the nature of the masculine as a source of both suggesting and containing homosexual relations.

Hawthorne's friend Herman Melville (1819–1891) was more direct in his treatment of homosexuality. His early travel writings, *Typee* (1846) and *Omoo* (1847), use the cultural difference of the South Seas just at the moment of their colonization as the source of an exploration of a male sexuality in social context. Melville found a kind of sexual freedom in the South Seas not available at home. Resisting the negative categories of sodomy and buggery, he celebrated an ideal of male friendship grounded in the body and integrated into social custom. This would become one of the major themes of his masterpiece, *Moby-Dick* (1851). Before setting out on their journey on the *Pequod,* the narrator, Ishmael, and the South Sea islander Queequeg must share a bed at the inn. Their night together constitutes a kind of male marriage, a "honeymoon" that overcomes Ishmael's panic at intimacy with another man. The relation between the two men breaks racial as well as sexual boundaries and proclaims a democratic spirit at odds with Captain Ahab's mad mission of vengeance and with the economic role of the whale hunt. Once on board the ship, the two men must take their place in a hierarchy of authority (always an obstacle to male friendship in Melville's work). Even in the factorylike environment of the ship, though, Ishmael finds an opportunity, in the "Squeeze of Hand" chapter, to celebrate mutual masturbation.

As his work increasingly lost its audience, Melville grew increasingly bitter about the apparent impossibility of friendship between men. In his long poem *Clarel*, Melville ascribes to the character Vine, based on Hawthorne, the thought that the "dream of love / In man toward man" is impossible; physical "non-cordialness" rules out spiritual intimacy. Melville's final work, left unfinished at his death, is the long story *Billy Budd*, which once again reflects on the possibility of male desire on board ship. The military context provides an instance of the social control of a revolutionary spirit expressed in the body. Billy, a failed version of the "handsome sailor," is unable to speak in his own defense and thus strikes his accuser, the evil Claggart. Frustrated desire leads to violence in this brilliant analysis of homophobia.

By the time of Melville's last work, homosexuality had been constructed as an identity, subject to political and medical control. Much of the nineteenth century was marked by the fraught creation of a sexual identity that would at once provide a new subjectivity and allow for its policing. The crucial figure in America for the creation of a homosexual identity is Walt Whitman (1819–1892), whose first edition of *Leaves of Grass* (1855) was the first major American work to celebrate sexuality between men. Whitman was directly influenced by Emerson and his call for a national democratic poetry. He put into practice what Emerson had preached: the liberation of verse from meter. Like Emerson, Whitman placed emphasis on a visionary poetry based on the experience of nature. But unlike the older poet, Whitman retained a strong sense of the corporeal.

His mystical experiences were grounded in actual experience of physical and sexual contact. "Song of Myself," Whitman's most important poem, which opens the first edition, is founded on the erotic experience of section five, which stresses the equality of body and soul. Calling on the "you" to "loaf with me on the grass," the speaker recalls a sexual encounter, where "you . . . plunged your tongue to my barestript heart," that gives rise to a mystic experience of unity. Whitman reclaims the body for the source of transcendence.

If "Song of Myself" is open about the physical experience of male love, it does not introduce the question of sexual identity. In the second edition (1856), however, Whitman introduced a new term, *adhesiveness*, adopted from phrenology, that could express a social construction: the new urban homosexual. Whitman's new, or "unfashioned," word, gives voice to the experience of cruising: "Do you know what it is as you pass by to be loved by strangers?" Whitman recognizes the hidden, or closeted, homosexual everywhere, and calls on his lover, or "Camerado," to join him on the "open road" (a call that would be taken up by Jack Kerouac) away from convention, to "love more precious than money." The dream of male lovers who "stick by each other as long as we live" was not to survive long, given the pressure from without and within. In the third edition (1860), Whitman devoted a major section of his poem to male love, the "Calamus" poems. Whitman's idea for a section in celebration of "athletic love" derives from his desire to represent the totality of experience and from his own need to tell the "secret of my nights and days." The earliest version of these poems were gathered around the figure of the "live oak with moss," a symbol of lasting affection, but in revision that earlier cycle was transformed into the "Calamus" cycle, with its central symbol of the aromatic plant that represented the male genitals. The poems range considerably in mood and tone. Some, such as "When I Heard at the Close of the Day," are idyllic expressions of personal love, while others, such as "Hours Continuing Long" (excluded from later editions), present the "torment" that comes from the lack of a community, the fear that one's desires might be shared by no one. Whitman must come to terms with himself ("I am ashamed—but it is useless—I am what I am") through the assertion of a sexual identity. "Calamus" becomes a source of support and community for American and English writers of the late nineteenth century.

One of the most interesting of Whitman's followers is Charles Warren Stoddard (1843–1909). Stoddard sent Whitman a copy of his Melvillean *South-Sea Idylls* (1873), addressing him "in the name of CALAMUS!" Like Melville, Stoddard used the travel narrative as the occasion for the celebration of sexual difference (as well as an opportunity for sexual experiences). The best-known travel writer of the period, Bayard Taylor (1825–1878), also used his many works as the basis for exploring male relations. The orientalism of these works, like a generalized appeal of the "primitive," offered an escape from the limits of compulsory heterosexuality. Like Melville, Taylor was married, but his poems celebrate the lads of the East. His novel, *Joseph and His Friend* (1870), is set in America, with California functioning as the dreamed-of "other" place. The love between the two men, Philip and Joseph, is seen as the result of something fundamental in their nature. They feel "a manly love, rarer, alas! but as tender and true as the love of women." No disciple of Whitman's, George Santayana (1863–1952), engaged for many years in an intense artistic struggle with Whitman, acted out in terms suggestive of mixed attraction and repulsion. His "Walt Whitman: A Dialogue" (1890) dramatizes the two voices of form and feeling. A later essay, "The Poetry of Barbarism" (1900), offers a troubled account of Santayana's relation to what he perceives as formlessness. Whitman can only be "a welcome companion" "when intellect is in abeyance." Santayana's work is highly formal, even when he is celebrating male love, as in the sonnet sequence "To W.P." (Warwick Potter). Potter's early death permits the expression of love in these elegies: his "virgin body" is forever "untainted." Santayana is the last great flowering of the platonic tradition in American literature.

Santayana was not the only homosexual writer to be troubled by Whitman's "barbarism." Henry James (1843–1916) was still a young man when he reviewed "Drum-Taps"(1865) in harsh terms. For the young James, Whitman is "monstrous" because he does not know how to put "the masculine" in "worthy form." James's tone was remarkably different in 1898 when he reviewed *Calamus: Walt Whitman's Letters to Peter Doyle*. For the mature James the meeting of the poet and the tram conductor is "Charming," and the collection of letters testifying to this friendship "positively delightful." James's own work had also grown franker in its treatment of sexuality, although the foundation was laid many years before. *Roderick Hudson* (1875) is the story of

U an older man's love for the young sculptor Roderick, whom he takes under his wing and brings to Europe. The two men enjoy an idyllic time together, but their relationship is interrupted by the intervention of a woman. Such mentor/pupil relations are frequent in James and always imbued with an erotic tint; however, they are by no means ensured of success. The pupil in the story of that name ("The Pupil," 1890) dies when his tutor is unable to accept the boy's challenge to free him from his manipulating family. In "The Author of 'Beltraffio' " (1884), based on John Addington Symonds, a mother lets her child die rather than be subject to the influence of her husband. The best-known of the pupil stories is *The Turn of the Screw* (1898), in which a governess tries to wrest control of young Miles from the ghost of the servant Quint.

James's fullest exploration of homosexuality comes in *The Bostonians* (1886), situated in the feminist movement of the nineteenth century, with deliberate echoes of Hawthorne's *The Blithedale Romance*. Wealthy reformer Olive Chancellor uses her fortune to gain control over the attractive Verena Tarrant, whom she wants to employ as the public spokeswoman for the movement. Verena is also the subject of the desire of Basel Ransom, a Southerner who is Olive's cousin. Ransom's reactionary politics win out over the passionate embrace of victimization on the part of Olive. James's ironic ending, in which Basel carries off Verena, promises much unhappiness, for the couple as for the nation. Although many critics have criticized James for his negative portrayal of the women's movement, his concern was primarily with the nature of power and desire; he remained a steadfast opponent of marriage as a suppression of the individual, and the "Boston marriage," or monogamous lesbian union, is no exception.

James kept a discreet distance from Oscar Wilde at the time of the latter's trial (1895) and expressed his homosexual themes in a guarded manner. Nonetheless, by the 1890s homosexuality had become a topic of public discussion, and James's works, like his letters and passionate friendships, became more explicit. "The Beast in the Jungle" has been interpreted by Eve Kosofsky Sedgwick as a study of suppressed homosexuality by a man who has been afraid to live. James may have been making up for lost time as he engaged in a romance with several young men, especially sculptor Hendrick Andersen. Although James numbered many openly effeminate and gay men among his friends, he could

not risk his reputation by speaking too frankly. The modernist generation would attempt to break that silence.

The most important American modernist, Hart Crane (1899–1932), began his career under the influence of the symbolists and decadents. His first published poem, "C 33," in 1916, is a tribute to Wilde in melodramatic terms. Crane's identification with the suffering artist would continue throughout his career, sometimes expressed as masochism, sometimes as an exploration of the "feminine." Crane's move from his native Ohio to New York City enabled him to experience the vibrancy and sexuality of the city, a Manhattan inherited from Whitman. A poem such as "Possessions" (1924) records the "thousand nights" of the flesh and the desire to transform lust into love. Crane's characteristic style is dense and metaphoric, as he attempts to join the tight opacity of modernism with the expansive spirit of Whitmanian America. His cycle of love poems, *Voyages* (1921–1926), written for Emil Opffer, can arguably be counted among the most beautiful in the English language. The poems follow a love affair from its inception to its ultimate failure and transformation through the power of art. The third poem addresses the distant lover at sea, as the waves create a movement similar to the interplay of the two bodies. There is an ecstatic moment when the language of the poem enacts the penetration of the beloved: "Star kissing star through wave on wave unto / Your body rocking." Love is defeated by time and space, what Crane calls a "tidal wedge," as the speaker feels a "flagless . . . piracy." The last two sections of the sequence see the transformation of love into "the imagined Word," a process at once spiritual and poetic. Art alone has the ability to offer an "unbetrayable reply."

Crane's most famous work, *The Bridge* (1923–1929), is his response to T. S. Eliot's *The Waste Land*. Against the Spenglerian pessimism of Eliot's poem, Crane sought to identify a Whitmanian optimism. Unlike many of his contemporaries of the 1920s, Crane did not turn primarily to Europe for his inspiration; he sought to find it instead in a native mythology, such as that depicted in "The Dance." This decision gave Crane access to a new body of thought and imagery and enabled him to explore the American land for its mythic possibilities, but he felt that it insisted on a heterosexual pattern of rebirth from the soil. Alongside his fertility myth, Crane thus placed the dance of the narrator and the chief Maquokeeta, a dance that passes through an ecstatic overcoming of self in a masochistic celebration of change that ultimately leads the two men "beyond their farms." For Crane, the Indian past needed reclaiming as part of a project to undercut idealism, by insisting, in the tradition of Whitman, on the body as a means to transcendence. Crane was not ready to abandon his sexuality: love was at once "a burnt match skating in a urinal" and "Deity's glittering page."

Eliot's treatment of homosexuality in *The Waste Land* is largely satirical, a sign of the decay of Western culture, as in the attempted seduction of the narrator by Mr. Eugenides, "Who asked me in abominable [altered to "demotic"] French, / To luncheon at the Cannon Street Hotel / Followed by a weekend at the Metropole." But the context is important as well: the lines following invoke the hermaphroditic Tiresias, Sappho, and Tennyson's "In Memoriam." James Miller has suggested that a somewhat more balanced portrayal of homosexuality in *The Waste Land* emerges from a reading of the "hyacinth girl" passage. Hyacinth is, of course, a figure of male desire, and the passage as a whole seems to evoke a recollection of Eliot's friend Jean Verdenal, to whom *Prufrock* was dedicated. A text related to *The Waste Land*, "The Death of St. Narcissus," was published only after Eliot's death but is strikingly similar to Crane's "The Dance." Narcissus is an androgynous figure related to the iconography of the "gay saint" Sebastian, whose "white skin surrendered itself to the redness of blood, and satisfied him." Given such traces, many readers have suggested that Eliot's denial of the personal in poetry had its own motivations.

The work of white primitivists such as Crane remained a project by and for whites. It was paralleled by similar developments within black culture in the Harlem Renaissance. There were, of course, white promoters of black culture, such as photographer and novelist Carl Van Vechten (1880–1964), whose motives were often a mixture of the cultural and the erotic. *Nigger Heaven* received the most attention of his novels, partly because of the provocative title. Many of the Harlem, or New Negro, writers were gay or bisexual, and Alain Locke (1886–1954) worked hard to promote them, but few of them were very open in their texts, judging perhaps that belonging to a racial minority offered enough of a disadvantage. Both Langston Hughes (1902–1967) and Countee Cullen (1903–1946) had relations with other men, but neither of them wrote very openly about the subject. Cullen represented his sexuality through the themes of brotherhood and

difference, and Hughes took an apparently documentary position in his account of a raid on a gay bar, "Café 3 A.M." Hughes's "Port Town" continues the tradition of the homoerotic sailor but is "safe" since it could be read as spoken by a woman.

Later generations of black writers were more open about their sexuality. The most important figure is James Baldwin (1924–1987), born in Harlem. Baldwin's story "Outing" (1951) deals with the emerging recognition of a gay identity between two boys, Johnny and David (the allusion to the biblical David and Jonathan was frequent in Baldwin's writing, including the David and Giovanni of *Giovanni's Room,* 1956). Baldwin's first novel, *Go Tell It on the Mountain* (1953), continues the theme of sexual recognition in a context where the erotic and the spiritual are interwoven in a lush language drawing from biblical cadences. For *Giovanni's Room* Baldwin moved away from his native landscape to Paris and presented a novel about homosexual love and betrayal in which the race of the major characters is not insisted upon. The American David is in flight from his sexuality, which reemerges when his fiancée leaves him in Paris while she travels in Spain. Caught up in the claustrophobic space of Giovanni's room, David flees once more, abandoning Giovanni and ultimately causing his death (or so the reader is directed to believe through the guilty narrative voice of David), thus reiterating Baldwin's major theme that the failure to love is the source of most unhappiness. Echoing Henry James in *The Ambassadors,* Baldwin insists that the "great difficulty is to say Yes to life." Tennessee Williams (1911–1983), one of America's greatest playwright, although writing about the South, shared with the Harlem writers a sense of the intricate connections between passionate desire and history. In this he shared his concerns with one of the most important American novelists of the twentieth century, William Faulkner (1897–1962). For Faulkner the South was preoccupied with its sense of an hereditary curse with its origins in slavery. *Absalom, Absalom!* (1936) employs his intense and obsessive language to depict the interracial and homosexual love between Henry Sutpen and Charles Bon. While this fatal attraction can be understood as a metaphor for racial issues, it is but one of several themes of homosexuality in Faulkner's work. Williams's play *The Glass Menagerie* (1945) is an autobiographical story of a family living increasingly in its dreams and illusions. Tom escapes into films to avoid his sister's withdrawal into herself and concludes the play by searching for companions,

U for the "nearest stranger." *Cat on a Hot Tin Roof* (1955) depicts a quarrel over Big Daddy's inheritance, the plantation that he himself inherited from Jack Straw and Peter Ochello. The heterosexual couple, Gooper and Mae, believe they deserve the property since they have bred children, while lame Brick is the unacknowledged and apparently sterile homosexual, despite his marriage to Maggie. Brick's betrayal of his friend Skipper led to Skipper's death. Compulsory heterosexuality in the play leads to a denial of desire, perhaps the greatest example of what Big Daddy calls "mendacity." Self-identified homosexuals are absent in Williams's plays, although they haunt the world that has destroyed them. In *A Streetcar Named Desire* (1947), Blanche represents herself as a woman of manners and breeding, but she is clinging to a lie about herself and her relation to the lost plantation, Belle Rive. The play eventually reveals that her first husband shot himself when Blanche confronted him with his homosexuality. Blanche's condemnation of Stanley as vulgar and aggressive could be said to conceal her own desire for him. Her final departure for the mental hospital is an instance of Williams's repeated metaphor for the social control of difference.

Until the arrival of the Beats in the 1950s, gay American poetry was not as forthright or as political as Williams's writing. Poetry of these years was dominated by W. H. Auden (1907–1973), who emigrated to the United States from England in 1939. Auden was an enormously talented formal poet with a mordant sense of humor and a vast knowledge of the world. Some of his poems from the late 1930s (just before his emigration) are particularly moving, including the extraordinary and much appreciated "Stop All the Clocks" (1936):

> He was my North, my South, my East and West
> My working week and Sunday rest,
> My noon, my midnight, my talk, my song;
> I thought that love would last forever: I was
> wrong.

Auden's poetry, such as "Lay Your Sleeping Head" (1937), is typically lyric and reflective at once. In America he entered into a long-term relationship with Chester Kallman, who became his collaborator as well as his lover. A number of poems, including "The Common Life," record the bittersweet reality of their companionship. Auden has often been criticized as too cerebral and too strict in form, but he is arguably the only worthy successor to W. B. Yeats

and the mediator between Yeats and more recent poets including Adrienne Rich, James Merrill, and Richard Howard.

The passage of time has reduced the general assessment of Auden's stature. A postmodern reader may well prefer Frank O'Hara (1926–1966), as gay liberationists once favored Allen Ginsberg (1926–1997). O'Hara's light, witty, campy poems capture urban gay life of the 1950s. Whitman is, as O'Hara says, his precursor, in his exuberance and his love for the insignificant detail, but O'Hara's tone shifts away from Whitman's declarativeness. In "At the Old Place," O'Hara evokes the lively mood of an excursion to a gay bar with friends including poet John Ashbery ("Wrapped in Ashes' Arms I glide"). The parenthetical asides mark this as a typical O'Hara poem—conversational, outrageous, joyful. Ginsberg, a descendant of the romantics, is strongest in his earliest poems, where the anger at injustice is the most powerful. (In the later, more overt political poems there is something almost programmatic about the protest.) "Howl" (1956) makes its mark through an accumulation of accusation and an ecstatic vision that had passed out of the language after Blake. Ginsberg's frank vocabulary announced a new openness, a breaking down of boundaries of taste. At the same time, he was aware of the destruction of the American dream, depicted vividly in the moving "Kaddish" (1959), which he wrote for his mother, whose paranoia echoes that of the nation. Ginsberg and the Beats made poetry popular and gave it a public forum. They introduced homosexuality both as a record of their sexual freedoms and as a means of challenging American conformity of the 1950s. Calling for liberation, they remained obsessed by guilt. Other poets were subject to different influences. James Merrill, like so many twentieth-century writers, was deeply influenced by the Greek poet of Alexandria, Constantine Cavafy, and his combination of eros and domesticity, in a poem such as "Days of 1964." Merrill's "The Friend of the Fourth Decade" displays his flair for social comedy that suddenly turns real. All illusions fail and are absolutely necessary, he seems to say. Merrill's work points to a new sophistication in American poetry, an ironic voice that would be sorely challenged within a few years by a new political activism and the reality of disease.   *Robert K. Martin*

Bibliography

Austen, Roger. *Playing the Game: The Homosexual Novel in America*. Indianapolis: Bobbs-Merrill, 1977.

Bergman, David. *Gaiety Transfigured: Gay Self-Representation in American Literature.* Madison, Wis.: University of Wisconsin Press, 1991.

Fiedler, Leslie A. *Love and Death in the American Novel.* Cleveland: World, 1962.

Martin, Robert K. *The Homosexual Tradition in American Poetry.* Austin, Texas: University of Texas Press, 1979.

Miller, James C. *T.S. Eliot's Personal Waste Land.* University Park, Pa.: Penn State University Press, 1977.

Sarotte, Georges-Michel. *Like a Brother, Like a Lover: Male Homosexuality in the American Novel and Theatre from Herman Melville to James Baldwin.* Richard Miller, trans. Garden City, N.Y.: Doubleday, 1978.

Sedgwick, Eve Kosofsky. *Between Men: English Literature and Male Homosocial Desire.* New York: Columbia University Press, 1985.

Woods, Gregory. *Articulate Flesh: Male Homoeroticism and Modern Poetry.* New Haven: Yale University Press, 1987.

See also Ashbery, John; Auden, W. H.; Baldwin, James; Beat Generation; Cavafy, Constantine P.; Crane, Hart; Cullen, Countee; Decadence; English Literature; French Literature; French Symbolism; Friendship; German Literature; Gide, Andre; Ginsberg, Allen; Goethe, Johannes Wolfgang von; Harlem Renaissance; Homophobia; Howard, Richard; Hughes, Langston; James, Henry; Mann, Thomas; Masculinity; McCarthyism; Melville, Herman; Merrill, James; New York City; O'Hara, Frank; Platen, August Graf von Hallermund; Plato; Proust, Marcel; Symonds, John Addington; Tennyson, Alfred; Van Vechten, Carl; Whitman, Walt; Wilde, Oscar; Williams, Tennessee

U.S. Literature: Contemporary Gay Writing

Contemporary gay writing has been written under the shadow of AIDS. Such writers as Andrew Holleran, Larry Kramer, and Edmund White have assumed the role of éminences grises while still in their fifties because so many writers of their generation have died. Given the foreshortening of life expectancies because of AIDS, few writers can be said to be in midcareer. David Leavitt is a notable exception, having published his first book of stories, *Family Dancing*, in 1984. Yet Leavitt shows the problems of developing a career as a gay writer. The books have followed without either developing a central core of concerns or exhibiting a mercurial power of continual self-invention. As a writer and gay man who has come out under the specter of AIDS, Leavitt has dealt directly with the pandemic only sparingly. Of course, not all gay writing deals with AIDS or needs to deal with it, but even when it is absent from a work—perhaps most when it is absent from a work—the silence is itself significant. In this regard contemporary gay writing differs markedly from the writing of heterosexuals.

Other poets in midcareer include Frank Bidart, Alfred Corn, J. D. McClatchy, and Mark Doty. All these writers have produced work that places language under the pressure of intense emotion and formal rigor. Bidart and Doty have channeled their experience with AIDS into a metaphysical and sometimes mystical awareness of time and nature. Corn's work is more anchored in traditional forms of religious observance. All four poets are particularly interested in exploring longer lyrics and lyric sequences. In Corn, Whitman has been a clear influence. For McClatchy, Merrill is a strong presence.

Younger poets include Raphael Campo, Cyrus Cassells, David Brendan Hopes, Michael Klein, Wayne Koestenbaum, Timothy Liu, Richard McCann, Carl Phillips, and Reginald Shepherd. The intensity of their lyricism is particularly striking about these poets. It is not that the somewhat older poets are not lyrical—both Bidart in his later work and Doty can be as rhapsodic as Cassells, perhaps the most purely lyrical of the group. But there appears to be an unrestrained and uncompromised lyricism in the works of many of these younger poets. Yet before making so sweeping a generalization, one should invoke Justin Chin, whose sassy book, *Bite Hard* (1997), is not especially lyrical but filled with the manic urban energy of much performance poetry. Nevertheless, Chin—like Campo, Cassells, Liu, Phillips, and Shepherd—is committed to incorporating issues of race and ethnicity into his work in no programmatic yet insistent way.

Koestenbaum, whose second book of poetry, *Rhapsodies of a Repeat Offender* (1994), in its very title suggests the thrust of these younger poets' work, is nevertheless best known for his prose—*The Queen's Throat* (1993) and *Jackie under My Skin* (1995). These works represent a rebirth of a belletristic tradition that has been somewhat dormant in earlier gay writing with the exception perhaps of Quentin Crisp's and Andrew Holleran's essays. In addition to Koestenbaum, Hilton Als has published the extraordinary collection of autobiographical es-

U says, *The Women* (1996), and Bernard Cooper the memoir *Truth Serum* (1996). Although they do not fit exactly under the self-imposed restriction of this entry, David Wojnarowicz's *Close to the Knives* (1991) and David B. Feinberg's *Queer and Loathing* (1994) are essay collections whose quality transcends the moment for which they were written.

Gay fiction is an enormously vital field, and it is difficult to characterize it generationally, thematically, or stylistically. Several recent novels deal with gay life in the seventies as a period definitively closed. These include Edmund White's *The Farewell Symphony* (1997), Allen Gurganus's *Plays Well with Others* (1997), and Felice Picano's *Like People in History* (1995). That these books feel so much like historical novels indicates how clear a wall divides pre- and post-AIDS experience.

Another historical work is Mark Merlis's stunning debut novel, *American Studies* (1994), which is concerned with the 1950s. Christopher Bram in virtually all his novels has a keen eye for the way history and politics affect the lives of gay men. Of particular note are *Almost History* (1992) and *The Father of Frankenstein* (1995).

West Coast writers seem in general to be less concerned with the strictures of realism. Among the most important are Tom Spanbauer, whose *The Man Who Fell in Love with the Moon* (1991) is often overlooked; Matthew Stadler; and the writers of the New Narrative group, which includes Robert Glück, Bruce Boone, and Kevin Killian. Among the most challenging writers formalistically is James McCourt, whose work has a very East Coast complexity.

Two writers of about the same age who have emerged from the Midwest, Scott Heim and Dale Peck, indicate how difficult it is to make generalizations. Peck's interest in formal experimentation is very different from Heim's exploration of psychology. Yet both writers are connected by an interest in blue-collar lives—which stands in marked contrast to the work of earlier generations of gay writers. Among the writers in midcareer who have written about working-class life are Bruce Benderson, whose fiction centers on the disappearing world of New York's 42nd Street hustlers and sex workers, and Jim Grimsley, whose concern has been with the rural Southern poor. Along with Heim and Peck are such younger writers as Lee Williams, who has written about runaways in his novel *After Nirvana* (1997) and Keith Banner, who writes about working-class life along the Ohio valley. Thomas Glave

has penned a beautiful series of stories about a Jamaican community that has taken root in the fictional Sound Hill neighborhood of the Bronx, in New York City, and Randall Kenan has written about African Americans in rural North Carolina. Harder to place are writers such as Michael Lowenthal, Michael Cunningham, William Mann, and Paul Russell, all of whom have written novels of note. John Weir, who wrote an exceptional first novel, *The Irreversible Decline of Eddie Socket* (1989), has fallen into silence after a promising start.

Comic novels have been particularly popular, and contemporary gay writers have shown a flair for the light touch. Stephen McCauley's work is humorous despite its darker tone. Joe Keenan, before becoming the head writer for the TV sitcom *Frasier*, wrote several wonderful novels.

Two writers who have crossed over to a large number of straight readers are the very different David Sedaris and E. Lynn Harris. African American women seem to be especially entranced by Harris's romantic novels about bisexual upwardly mobile black men, and David Sedaris's darkly comic pieces have won a following that began with their broadcast on National Public Radio.   *David Bergman*

Bibliography

Nelson, Emmanuel S., ed. *Contemporary Gay American Novelists: A Bio-Bibliographical Sourcebook.* Westport, Conn.: Greenwood Press, 1993.

Woodhouse, Reed. *Unlimited Embrace: A Canon of Gay Fiction, 1945–1995.* Amherst: University of Massachusetts Press, 1998.

See also AIDS Literature; Autobiographical Writing; Crisp, Quentin; Doty, Mark; Fiction: New Queer Narrative; Kramer, Larry; Merrill, James; Violet Quill; White, Edmund; Wojnarowicz, David

Usury

While *usury* has come to mean lending money at excessive rates of interest, it was originally employed by Christian churchmen and theologians to condemn any charging of interest on loans. The Christian condemnations go back to passages in the Old Testament that attack the greed of moneylenders, especially with regard to the poor. These passages found echoes in the teachings of some Greek and Roman philosophers and to a lesser extent in various bodies of ancient law. The Christian churches began to legislate against the taking of interest as early as the fourth century and continued to do so well into the modern period. Usury was counted a sin against nature. One of the oldest arguments against usury is that interest is unnatural because money is infertile and cannot reproduce itself. Because similar arguments were used against same-sex copulation, usury and sodomy were often linked in the theological imagination. Alan of Lille consistently describes sexual "deviations" with monetary images, and he gives greed as the principal motive for same-sex activity by young men. Dante Alighieri places the sodomites alongside the usurers in hell, although in purgatory he locates penitent sodomites alongside others saved from sins of lust. The connection between sodomy and usury is equally explicit in medieval commentators on canon law. A rather different link between illicit moneymaking and sodomy is made by Peter Damian, who links sodomy with simony, that is, the buying and selling of church offices.

Mark D. Jordan

Bibliography

Noonan, John T., Jr. *The Scholastic Analysis of Usury*. Cambridge, Mass.: Harvard University Press, 1957.

See also Alan of Lille; Canon Law; Dante Alighieri; Natural Law; Peter Damian; Sodomy

V

Vampires

Vampires are countless, and so are the laws informing both their extravagant powers and their stringent limitations. Not only have the last two centuries witnessed an extraordinary textual proliferation of vampires (novels, stories, poems, films, television, comic books, etc.), but the very figure of the vampire itself is marked by an overproduction of meanings: so many diverse, even contradictory fantasies have been projected upon vampirism that it cannot plausibly be assigned a single or definitive signification. These projections include fantasies of life and death, power and impotence, appetite and control, transformation and stasis, gender and its mobility, and most insistently of all, sexuality and its manifold "perversions." Because the vampire's body is polymorphic, it can readily bear all these significations, and more. No single interpretive framework can exhaust the possibilities of vampirism because vampiric meanings proliferate as vampires do—promiscuously.

It is nonetheless inarguable that a persistent linkage joins vampirism to homosexuality, both male and female. Some of the reasons for this are intrinsic to the vampire metaphor itself; others are purely historical. The intrinsic reasons may be specified as follows: (1) *The vampire embodies an allegory of perverse or disordered desire.* The mode of that desire is emphatically oral (vampires bite and suck), and its object is a bodily fluid: "The blood is the life," says Dracula in a parodic quotation of Christ. The vampire hungers for its victim only because that victim possesses, in his or her blood, an available quantity of life (or undeath) that will enable the vampire to continue repeating its interminable cycle of desire/satisfaction/renewed desire. (2) Because blood is a universal element of life, *vampiric desire in its pure state ignores all distinctions of species, person, and sex.* The vampire's human victim may be male or female, and indifferently so: it is the volume of blood, not the shape of its human container, that propels the vampire toward its victim. (3) Whether using outright violence or subtle seduction (the "evil eye") to dominate its prey, *the vampire imposes on its victim a mandatory passivity suffused with a desire to be penetrated*; however terrified he or she may be, the vampire's victim nonetheless wants to be vamped. The violence of this penetration always bypasses the body's natural openings; arrogant in his entry, the vampire makes her own holes. (4) *The gender identity of the vampire itself is mobile and indeterminate.* Although anatomically either male or female, the vampire confuses and undermines the traditional organization of masculine and feminine roles. When, for instance, "female" vampires employ their enlarged canines to enter another body, they effectively usurp the "masculine" offices of penetration; conversely, "male" vampires assume the "feminine" offices of nurturance when they compel their victims to drink blood from (in Dracula's case) an open wound in the breast—an obvious inversion of maternal nursing. (5) *Vampirism performs a brutal parody of generative sexuality.* By forcing selected victims to consume tainted vampiric blood, vampires engender a demonic progeny—children of the night—who will endlessly repeat the very act that brought them into monstrous existence. Precisely these aspects or qualities of vampirism (and still others could be adduced) enable the vampire metaphor to transmit or convey homosexual signification that might otherwise remain repressed. The very displacement of sex into sanguinary violence empowers vampirism to function as a formal literary model capable of both

V *expressing and filtering* an otherwise unspeakable content.

Vampirism and homosexuality are conjoined for historical reasons as well. The regime of modern sexuality and the rise of vampirism as cultural metaphor are contemporaneous events, unfolding over time. Both have their antecedents in the eighteenth century, both develop variously throughout the nineteenth, and both find their definitive elaborations in the last decades of the nineteenth century and in the first of the twentieth. Michel Foucault and others have persuasively argued that the modern notion of "the homosexual," dating roughly from the 1880s, marks an important shift in ways of conceptualizing and regulating same-sex desire, a shift that moves away from the already established category of "sodomy." "As defined by the ancient civil or canonical codes," Foucault writes, "sodomy was a category of forbidden acts; their perpetrator was nothing more than the juridical subject of them. The nineteenth-century homosexual became a personage, a past, a case history, and a childhood, in addition to being a type of life, a life form [with] . . . a mysterious physiology. . . . Nothing that went into his total composition was unaffected by his sexuality. . . . The sodomite had been a temporary aberration; the homosexual was now a species" (Foucault, 43). This historical specification of the homosexual as *a species apart*, as a determinate class of beings whose singular identity was defined by a "perversion" in sexual object-choice, strongly resembles the figure of the vampire: an "unnatural" creature hidden in our midst and driven by an overwhelming desire that threatens to undermine the health and vitality of the dominant ("normal") order. Both figures are marked by a powerful conjunction of desire and fear, *philia* and *phobia*. This irreducible ambivalence is important because it enables the vampire metaphor to express a contradictory relation to homosexual desire, i.e., a relation characterized on the one hand by a desire for perversion and on the other by a repudiation of that very desire. This capacity for double articulation helps explain the historical "fit" between vampirism and modern configurations of homosexual desire. Probably the clearest expression of this ambivalence occurs in Bram Stoker's *Dracula* (1897) as a central male character, Jonathan Harker, awaits the "kiss" offered by three of Dracula's vampiric daughters: "All three had brilliant white teeth, that shone like pearls against the ruby of their voluptuous lips. There was something about them that

made me uneasy, *some longing and at the same time some deadly fear*. I felt a wicked, burning desire that they would kiss me with those red lips" (51; italics added). If this passage openly expresses a male's passive longing for penetration, much of the rest of *Dracula* will work furiously to expel this "wicked, burning desire" by destroying, with great violence, the monsters who incite it. In *Dracula* this work of destruction is performed as a ritual counter-penetration, the extermination of the vampire (here, Lucy), requiring first staking through the heart, then a reassuring decapitation. Only through such recuperative violence is the "proper" function of the phallus restored.

Critics almost universally agree that the vampire metaphor finds its definitive articulation in *Dracula*. Certainly the oscillation between homophilia and homophobia is most discernible there, and certainly the many recapitulations of Stoker's novel (print, film, television) confirm it as the most influential of all vampire texts; thus Dracula the novel fulfils the ambition of Dracula the monster: to become "the father or furtherer of a new order of beings" (360). But Dracula's way was prepared by other literary vampires. The vampire proper enters English literature with John Polidori's story "The Vampyre" (1819), which presented its revenant as Byronic outcast, itself already a figure of problematic sexuality; Polidori's story was almost immediately rendered for the stage in J. R. Planché's *The Vampire; or, the Bride of the Isles* (1820). Some critics prefer to locate the advent of vampirism in Samuel Taylor Coleridge's poetic fragment "Christabel" (1816). True perhaps, and all the more interesting because Christabel narrates a tale of desire and possession between two women, a clear eruption of lesbianism in a literary tradition that has largely preferred to ignore it; yet at no point in Coleridge's poem is the dominant female, Geraldine, ever identified specifically as a vampire, though the relationship is surely vampiric. By midcentury James Malcom Rymer's serial novel *Varney the Vampire; or, The Feast of Blood* (1847) offered vampirism in installments to a mass-market audience. And in 1872 Joseph Sheridan Le Fanu published his compelling novella *Carmilla*, a tale of lesbian vampirism; one critic even identifies Carmilla as "one of the few self-accepting homosexuals in Victorian or any literature." (Auerbach, 41). With *Carmilla*, certainly, the association of vampirism and sexuality becomes explicit and self-conscious: "The vampire," writes Le Fanu, "is prone to be fascinated with an engrossing vehemence, resembling the passion of love"; further, it will "husband and protract its murderous enjoyment with the refinement of an epicure, and heighten it by the gradual approaches of an artful courtship" (337). Here the language of marriage and husbandry—the language, that is, which founds and sustains the heterosexual order—is used to explain the vampire's manifestly homosexual liaison, Carmilla's seduction of Laura. Twenty-five years after *Carmilla*, and clearly influenced by it, Stoker publishes *Dracula*, with its insistent conjunction of monstrosity and homosexual desire. A parable of blood and penetration, it has never since been out of print.

All twentieth-century vampires are *Dracula's* children, prodigal or dutiful, and this because Stoker's novel provides the twentieth century with its lexicon of vampirism. Of the myriad cinematic adaptations, three at least deserve mention here: F. W. Murnau's German expressionist *Nosferatu* (1922), a silent masterpiece with Max Shreck in the vampire's role; Todd Browning's black-and-white American classic *Dracula* (1931), with Bela Lugosi's definitive performance as the vampiric count (tuxedoed immobility, hypnotic gaze, unearthly intonation); and Terence Fisher's *Horror of Dracula* (1958), the first and best of the many color Dracula films starring Christopher Lee and emanating from England's Hammer Studios. Nor has there been any shortage of vampires in twentieth-century literature, where proliferation is again the rule. A single example will have to suffice here: Anne Rice's extraordinarily popular *The Vampire Chronicles* (six volumes as of this writing) offers its readers the postmodern American vampire. Chatty, fashionable, and ultimately bored by their own perversity, Rice's vampires titillate but fail to frighten. In doing so, they implicitly raise a question about the continued viability of the vampire metaphor: Which repetition is one repetition too many? Perhaps the next volume will tell.   *Christopher Craft*

Bibliography

Auerbach, Nina. *Our Vampires, Ourselves*. Chicago: University of Chicago Press, 1995.

Foucault, Michel. *The History of Sexuality: An Introduction*. Vol. 1. Robert Hurley, trans. New York: Vintage, 1978.

Le Fanu, Joseph Sheridan. *Carmilla. Best Ghost Stories of J.S. Le Fanu*. E. F. Bleiler, ed. New York: Dover, 1964.

Stoker, Bram. *Dracula*. 1897. New York: Penguin, 1979.

See also Byron, George Gordon, Lord; Film; Foucault, Michel; Gender; Homophobia; Homosexuality; Sex Practice: Oral Sex; Sexology

Van Sant, Gus (1953–)

Whatever one thinks about the advisability of redoing *Psycho,* it makes sense that Gus Van Sant directed the remake of Hitchcock's 1960 thriller. Though the story does have queer content, it is anything but clear-cut: something like the director's own position regarding his work. Refusing to be labeled a "gay director," Van Sant nonetheless fills his films with queerness, even those without obvious gay and lesbian elements. Under Van Sant's direction, for example, *To Die For* (1995) became a campy dark comedy in which Nicole Kidman seduces three teenagers into helping her kill her conventional husband so she can have a career in TV news. Perhaps it is not surprising that the director's attempt to camp it up in *Even Cowgirls Get the Blues* (1994), a film with lesbian and gay content, fell flat. Van Sant seems to work best when everything—narrative, character, tone—isn't so clearly queer.

Most often Van Sant interjects queerness into the proceedings of "straight" films like *Drugstore Cowboy* (1989) and *Good Will Hunting* (1997) through his tender and loving treatment of nubile young men—a quality that links these films to his other works. Matt Damon and Ben Affleck, the scriptwriters and stars of *Good Will Hunting*, were shrewd in their choice of Van Sant to direct the project. He enriched the careers of fresh-faced young actors like Matt Dillon (*Drugstore Cowboy*, 1989), Keanu Reeves (*My Own Private Idaho*, 1991), River Phoenix (*My Own Private Idaho*), and Joaquin Phoenix (*To Die For*) by making them tantalizing, pansexual erotic objects.

But connected to the adoring treatment of young men in Van Sant's films is the sense that part of what makes them such powerful figures of desire is their inaccessibility. *Mala Noche* (1985), the director's first feature film, concerns a character who becomes obsessed with a straight sixteen-year-old Mexican immigrant even while he has sex with the teenager's equally attractive friend. In *My Own Private Idaho*, River Phoenix's Mike spends his time mooning over his uninterested "gay for pay" friend Scott (Keanu Reeves). For queer male audience members, Van Sant's films likewise can

V

Keanu Reeves (left) and River Phoenix in Gus Van Sant's My Own Private Idaho, *1991. UCLA Arts Library, Special Collection.*

be fraught as they offer up pretty young men for erotic delectation who are either coded straight in the narrative or who are already engaged in the same game of frustrated desire that has captured the viewer.

The erotics of Van Sant's films are just one aspect of a "non-positive" or "non-politically correct" approach to queer representation that has often drawn criticism from journalists and the public. But whether his subject matter and characters are straight or queer (or somewhere in between), Van Sant has consistently been unconcerned with straight or queer mainstream attitudes, with *Good Will Hunting* as the exception to date. Van Sant has been drawn to projects that allow him to combine ironic humor with provocative material, a predilection he shares with gay filmmakers (or, as Van Sant would probably prefer, filmmakers who happen to be gay) John Waters and Todd Haynes. Consider the skid row setting for *Mala Noche*'s wry tale of obsessive queer love; or the nonjudgmental, often comic tone taken to tell the story of young junkies in *Drugstore Cowboy*; or *My Own Private Idaho*'s alternately romantic and *Dolce Vita*–like approach to presenting the life of male prostitutes.

The huge critical and box-office success of *Good Will Hunting* finds Van Sant poised at a career crossroads. Will he continue to make more palatable, less quirky, and less troubling films, or will he bring his sometimes disturbing queerness into Hollywood filmmaking? What he does with *Psycho* is a good indication of what to expect.

Alexander Doty

See also Film; Film: New Queer Cinema; Haynes, Todd; Hitchcock, Alfred; Waters, John

Van Vechten, Carl (1880–1964)

Born in Cedar Rapids, Iowa, to a solidly middle-class family, writer and critic Carl Van Vechten would go on to become one of the most versatile and well-known cultural critics, novelists, and photographers of the first three decades of this century. The best of his criticism was collected in six volumes that he published between 1915 and 1920. In addition to being this country's first professional dance critic, Van Vechten's championing of avant-garde artists and writers, most notably Ronald Firbank and Gertrude Stein, was largely responsible for the success that they achieved in the United States.

Van Vechten was also a tireless promoter of black writers and artists. He was certainly the primary white influence on the black cultural movement called the Harlem Renaissance. His involvement with black culture was, in fact, so great and so personalized that artist Miguel Covarrubias once caricatured Van Vechten in blackface and called the drawing "A Prediction." His novel *Nigger Heaven* (1928), one of the major best-sellers of the decade, sparked a firestorm of controversy over its depiction of black life.

Van Vechten, an inveterate collector, was also responsible for establishing a number of research archives, most notably the James Weldon Johnson Memorial Collection of Negro Arts and Letters at Yale University, one of the best of its kind in the world. In the 1930s, after the success of his novels and an inheritance from a wealthy brother left him financially independent, Van Vechten turned his creative energies to photography. This "hobby," in which he photographed an astonishing number of the great and near-great cultural figures of his time, dominated his life until his death in 1964.

Although married to actress Fania Marinoff for over fifty years, Van Vechten maintained an active homosexual life. Despite his refusal to "come out," the seven Firbankian novels that he wrote during the 1920s (*Peter Whiffle: His Life and Works*, *The Blind Bow-Boy*, *The Tattooed Countess*, *Firecrackers*, *Nigger Heaven*, *Spider Boy*, and *Parties*) quite obviously revealed his familiarity with "the life" for those in the know.

Van Vechten later created a sexual autobiography of sorts with the series of homoerotic scrapbooks that he put together in the 1950s. Although interest in Van Vechten's work declined quickly after the 1930s, given the changes that have taken place in the critical landscape over the last twenty years, few figures seem as ripe for rediscovery and reappraisal.

Terry Rowden

Bibliography

Kellner, Bruce. *Carl Van Vechten and the Irreverent Decades*. Norman, Okla.: University of Oklahoma Press, 1968.

Weinberg, Jonathan. "'Boy Crazy': Carl Van Vechten's Queer Collection." *Yale Journal of Criticism*, 7 no. 2 (1994): 25–49.

See also African American Gay Culture; Firbank, Ronald; Harlem Renaissance; Johnson, James Weldon

Vere Street Coterie

The early 1800s saw several antihomosexual prosecutions, but the most notorious of these was the trial of the so-called Vere Street coterie. This was the name given to the regular customers of the White Swan, a male brothel and homosexual meeting place in Vere Street, London. The police staged a raid on the White Swan on July 8, 1810, fewer than six months after it opened as a brothel. During that period it had become popular with a range of men, including artisans and aristocrats; some of its customers wore drag, and the premises had a fake chapel for homosexual marriages. The police operation resulted in the detention of almost thirty men, most of whom were released after questioning. On September 22, however, the landlord, James Cook, was found guilty of running a disorderly house and was sentenced to two years in prison, plus an hour in the pillory. Six other men were found guilty of attempted buggery. One of them was given a year's imprisonment, while the other five were sentenced to the pillory plus terms of between two and three years' imprisonment. At a later trial two men who had not been present in the White Swan that night but who were implicated by the testimony of an informer were found guilty of buggery and were sentenced to death. Apart from the scale of the police offensive, the most notable feature of the Vere Street episode was the ferocity with which the accused men were treated by the public. Such outrage was not unprecedented. A man found guilty of homosexual acts had died in 1780 after he was hit by a stone while being pilloried. After this case, Edmund Burke called for the abolition of the pillory, but it was still in use in 1810, and the Vere Street coterie experienced its full horrors. After being led from the jail on September 27, Cook and the others were faced by a horde of onlookers armed with "offal, dung, [. . .] apples, potatoes, turnips, cabbage-stalks, and other vegetables, together with the remains of divers dogs and cats." The men were covered with excrement after their journey through London in an open cart. Once in the pillory they were assaulted with "mud, dead cats, rotten eggs, potatoes, and buckets filled with blood, offal, and dung" (*The Trying and Pilloring* [sic] *of the Vere Street Club*, 1810; cited in Crompton, 163 ff.). Unsurprisingly, they began their sentences with serious injuries. Astonishingly, there were complaints in the press that this rough justice was insufficient, and several commentators called for the introduction of the death penalty for homosexual soliciting. Of

V

course, capital punishment was already in place for anyone guilty of buggery, and this sentence was duly carried out on Thomas White and John Hepburn, who were hanged on March 7, 1811, in front of a crowd rumored to include several lords who had escaped punishment because of their rank. Of the nine men prosecuted in the scandal, all were lower middle class.

Vincent Quinn

Bibliography

Crompton, Louis. *Byron and Greek Love: Homophobia in Nineteenth-Century England.* London: Faber and Faber, 1985.

Hyde, H. Montgomery. *The Other Love: An Historical and Contemporary Survey of Homosexuality in Britain.* London: Heineman, 1970.

Norton, Rictor. *Mother Clap's Molly-House: The Gay Subculture in England, 1700–1830.* London: Gay Men's Press, 1992.

See also England; London; Mollies; Molly Houses; Sodomy Trials

Verlaine, Paul (1844–1896)

Decadent French poet Paul Verlaine's bittersweet lyricism, through the use of musical rhyme and innovative verse, evokes the ineffable temperaments of the soul. His subtle, harmonious style contrasts with his tumultuous life: periods of bourgeois stability alternating with drunken, violent, and sexual excesses. After publishing *Poèmes saturniens,* a reference to the "evil sign" under which he claimed to have been born, and *Fêtes galantes* (1869), a collection illustrating Parnassian theory, Verlaine, a government employee, married seventeen-year-old Mathilde Mauté, to whom he dedicated *La Bonne Chanson* (1870). In 1871, Mathilde gave birth to a son; the same year Verlaine began a romance with teenage poet Arthur Rimbaud. The notorious lovers escaped to London, then Brussels, where, in 1873, an intoxicated and enraged Verlaine was jailed for shooting Rimbaud. *Romance sans paroles* (1874) evokes episodes of their brief yet legendary literary convergence. While in prison, Verlaine experienced a religious awakening that inspired *Sagesse* (1880). Over the next decade, he published *Jadis et naguàre* (1885), a collection of previously written works, *Amour* (1888), personal poems dedicated to a favorite male student, and *Parallèlement* (1889), a poetic attempt to reconcile conflicting spiritual and sensual tendencies. Verlaine's last texts, *Femmes/Hombres*, are explicitly erotic poems that celebrate the fulfillment of homo- and heterosexual desire. Often hospitalized, the poet spent his final years in the company of male and female prostitutes. Rejected by the prestigious Académie Française, he was, nonetheless, honored by his peers as *"prince des poètes"* before dying of a leg ulcer in 1896. While earlier studies do not emphasize the role of sexuality in his work, recent scholarship now recognizes Verlaine's pioneering contribution to bisexual poetics.

David Aldstadt

Bibliography

Minahen, Charles D. "Homosexual Erotic Scripting in Verlaine's *Hombres.*" In *Articulations of Difference.* Dominique Fisher and Lawrence R. Schehr, eds. Stanford, Calif.: Stanford University Press, 1997, 119–35.

Richardson, Joanna. *Verlaine.* New York: Viking, 1971.

Rimbaud, Arthur, and Paul Verlaine. *A Lover's Cock and Other Gay Poems.* J. Murat and W. Gunn, trans. San Francisco: Gay Sunshine Press, 1979.

Total Eclipse (film). Dir. Agnieska Holland. Writ. Christopher Hampton. With David Thewlis and Leonardo Dicaprio. Fine Line Features, 1995.

Troyat, Henri. *Verlaine.* Paris: Flammarion, 1993.

Verlaine, Paul. *Œuvres poétiques complètes.* Y. G. le Dantec, ed. Revised and completed by Jacques Borel. Paris: Gallimard "Pléiade," 1962.

———. *Selected Poems.* C. F. MacIntyre, trans. Berkeley: University of California Press, 1948.

———. *Women/Men (Femmes/Hombres): The Erotic Poetry of Paul Verlaine.* William Packard and John D. Mitchell, trans. Illustrated by Michael Ayrton. 2d ed. New York: IASTA Press, 1977.

See also French Literature; French Symbolism; Love Poetry; The Petrarchan Tradition; Rimbaud, Arthur

Versace, Gianni (1946–1997)

Fashion designer Gianni Versace lived a vivid, majestic life, rising from modest beginnings in Reggio Calabria, Italy, to global renown before being murdered by gay spree-killer Andrew Cunanan outside Versace's extravagant South Beach, Miami, residence. First a contract designer, working for other labels such as Callaghan and Genny, Versace established his womenswear label in 1978, immediately followed by a menswear line in 1979. Audacious in sensuality and sexuality, Versace transformed vulgarity into elegance, prostitute into style ideal. Sleek dresses clung to the body; bright silks risked sleazy seduction but discovered and delighted in tantalizing glamour. Versace abjured decorum; he understood desire and he expressed a candor in clothing's eroticism. He also enjoyed spectacle and lifestyle, coming to personify an opulent gay Gatsbyesque life. In menswear, torsos were conspicuous in blouselike silk shirts, often accompanied by leather jeans. His was the first mainstream gay menswear, but he purveyed it to men as varied as Mike Tyson, Sylvester Stallone, and Elton John.

His 1992 "bondage" collection was clearly S/M inspired, but the fetish style was rendered as supple lattice on the body. By 1995, Versace was manifestly a world-famous mainstream designer when Claudia Schiffer appeared on the cover of *Time* magazine (April 17, 1995) wearing a white Versace suit. Thus, ladies who lunch and ladies of the street were united in their admiration for Versace. After Versace's death, in an unprecedented gesture, New York's Metropolitan Museum of Art presented a Gianni Versace exhibition in 1997. A front-page *New York Times* article (July 16, 1997) the day after Versace's murder extolled him as "the fashion designer who rejuvenated the industry by tapping the energy of popular culture," but even that tribute was insufficient.

The key to Versace's fashion is his unabashed sexuality. An out gay man, he expressed sex honestly as a form of individual and cultural dynamic. For Versace, sex and homosexuality were predicates to beauty. *Richard Martin*

Bibliography

Hannah, Barry N., et al., eds. *Men Without Ties.* New York: Abbeville Press, 1995.

Martin, Richard. *Versace.* New York: Vendome Press, 1997.

Versace, Gianni. *The Art of Being You.* New York: Abbeville Press, 1997.

See also Fashion; Sadomasochism

Vidal, Gore (1925–)

American novelist, essayist, and dramatist Gore Vidal is a member of one of the most established political families in America (he is distantly related to Vice President Al Gore). When he published his first novel, *Williwaw* (1946), he was widely considered one of the most important World War II–era novelists. But his reputation was shattered with the publication in 1948 of *The City and the Pillar*, the first gay-themed novel to be a best-seller. The literary establishment was so appalled that their World War II novelist had written about homosexuality that for all practical purposes it drove Vidal out of novel writing and into writing for television, film, and the stage in the 1950s, including *Visit to a Small Planet*, *The Best Man*, and the filmed version of *Suddenly, Last Summer*. He wrote mystery novels during the same period under the name Edgar Box. He also began writing essays for various magazines, including the *New York Review of Books*, and has continued to do so; these have been collected in seven volumes.

Vidal returned to novel writing with the publication of *Julian* in 1964. This work showed Vidal's interest in history, which he would continue to explore in novels like *Washington, D.C.* (1967), *Burr* (1973), *1876* (1976), *Lincoln* (1984), and *Hollywood* (1990). These novels did much to improve his reputation and were commercially successful. He also returned to exploring issues of sexuality in *Myra Breckinridge* (1968), *Myron* (1974), and *Duluth* (1983). Vidal is also noted for his pointed political commentaries, most famously rendered in a series of television appearances in 1968 with William F. Buckley Jr., which culminated in Chicago when Vidal accused Buckley of being a "crypto-Nazi" and Buckley called Vidal a "queer." In 1996, Vidal contradicted his recurrent statements that he would never write an autobiography by publishing the widely acclaimed *Palimpsest*, in which he admitted that he has been in love only once, with a boy he knew at school in the 1940s, and that this relationship was the model for the one presented in *The City and the Pillar*. Vidal's understanding of sexuality has been consistent throughout his career. He believes that all people are by nature bisexual, that people would have sex with anyone if they had the time and the inclination, and that desire is a form of power. These tropes come up over and over in all his writing, whether or not sexuality is a main theme.

It is possible to underestimate the importance of *The City and the Pillar* in both the American literary tradition and in the development of American gay culture. Although other novels had been written about homosexuality by Americans prior to 1948, Vidal's reputation guaranteed that the novel would be taken seriously, if finally rejected, by literary crit-

V ics, and its success encouraged the publication of other "homosexual"-themed novels in the 1950s and early 1960s, particularly the lesbian pulp fiction boom. The novel stands out in that Vidal works hard to make the characters of Jim Willard and Bob Ford as "normal" as possible. The main character, Jim, is ordinary to the point of blandness, and the novel traces his entrance into gay culture without losing any of his blandness. Counterposed to Jim are the many gay characters that he meets who resemble many different "types" of people: actors, authors, scientists, professors, soldiers; their ubiquity underscores the communal feel of the novel as it progresses. Jim avoids gay men who are flamboyant or effeminate so that the novel undercuts American understanding of gay men as not properly performing their gender. Finally, the sex scene between Jim and Bob may be the first such representation in American literature. Vidal understands true love and sexuality as appealing to the Aristophanic understanding of two halves searching for each other, and homosexuality as a twinning in which two men find themselves in each other. *Douglas Eisner*

Bibliography

Dick, Bernard F. *The Apostate Angel: A Critical Study of Gore Vidal*. New York: Random House, 1974.

Kiernan, Robert F. *Gore Vidal*. New York: F. Ungar, 1982.

Summers, Claude J. *Gay Fictions: Wilde to Stonewall, Studies in a Male Homosexual Literary Tradition*. New York: Continuum, 1990.

Vidal, Gore. *The City and the Pillar Revised: Including an Essay, "Sex and the Law" and "An Afterword."* New York: Dutton, 1965.

———. "On Pornography." *New York Review of Books*. 6–7 (March 3, 1966): 4–10.

———. *Palimpsest: A Memoir*. New York: Random House, 1995.

See also Fiction; Film; Mystery and Detective Fiction; Williams, Tennessee

Villaurrutia, Xavier (1903–1950)

Mexican writer Xavier Villaurrutia belongs to a generation that could not openly write gay literature. He and other avant-garde writers endured prosecution and gay bashing by different revolutionary governments, which led to the loss of their bureaucratic jobs. He developed a poetic modern language using models like Luís de Góngora, Marcel Proust, and Walt Whitman to describe desire for other men.

Villaurrutia belongs to the avant-garde group Los Contemporáneos. He attempted to renew Mexican theater with societies like *Ulises* (1928) and *Orientación* (1932), which trained new actors, translated European and American plays, and implemented the most advanced stage techniques. In his plays he wrote about queer men and urbane women who transcended the characters of honor dramas—cosmopolitan, upper-class melodramas. He cowrote *La mulata de Córdoba* (1939) with his lover, painter Agustín Lazo. *Mulata* is a Freudian text that goes beyond the character of the devilish woman to create a triangle that puts together a father and his son. The manipulation of the Oedipus complex helps to form a queer couple out of the relationship of father and son. An interesting secondary character is the hunk, El Cuadrado. As a poet, his most important collection is *Nostalgia de la muerte* (1938), of which a representative poem is "Nocturno de los ángeles," about the promiscuity of gay sailors in Los Angeles. In prose a key text is *Variedad* (c.1930), where Villaurrutia used André Gide as the model to explain the closet. *Cartas de Villaurrutia a Novo* (1960) are the letters sent to his friend, the gay poet Salvador Novo, while Villaurrutia was a student at Yale. *Salvador A. Oropesa*

Bibliography

Dauster, Frank. *Xavier Villaurrutia*. New York: Twayne, 1971.

Villaurrutia, Xavier. *Obras*. 2d ed. Miguel Capistrán, Alí Chumacero, and Luís Mario Schneider, eds. Mexico City: Fondo de Cultura Económica, 1966.

See also Gide, André; Mexico; Novo, Salvador; Proust, Marcel; Whitman, Walt

Violet Quill

The Violet Quill was one of the most important coteries of gay writers in the early eighties who met to read one another's works in progress and discuss the problems of writing gay fiction. Its seven members were Edmund White, Andrew Holleran, Felice Picano, Robert Ferro, George Whitmore, Michael Grumley, and Christopher Fox. Although they met formally only eight times—between March 31, 1980, and March 2, 1981—their informal association extends to the present day. Holleran met Ferro and Grumley, who became lovers, at the Iowa Writers' Workshop, where they were all students in the midsixties. White had been the lover of both George Whitmore and Christopher Cox. The social and sexual connections among the group were as important as their literary affinities.

The Violet Quill emerged at a crucial moment in the development of several of its authors. White, Ferro, and Picano began by publishing novels in which homosexuality was either suppressed or highly encoded. By the time Violet Quill was formed, they had published or started writing works that were explicitly gay in content. Yet only as the group was coalescing did they begin to address specifically gay readers as their central audience in order, in White's words, to "get beyond the See-Dick-Run level and apologetic tone" of most previous gay writing.

By writing for gay readers, the Violet Quill could stop representing gay men as exotic creatures from the sexual underworld. Instead, the works that Violet Quill writers produced during their most intense period of association—White's *A Boy's Own Story* (1982), Ferro's *The Family of Max Desir* (1983), Holleran's *Nights in Aruba* (1983), Grumley's posthumously published novel *Life Drawings* (1991), as well as the short stories of Whitmore and Picano—featured middle-class or lower-upper-class men in recognizable urban bourgeois society. Such unremarkable characters contrasted strikingly with earlier representations in which, according to White, gay authors "could choose only among the same three metaphors for homosexuality—as sickness, crime, or sin." One of the achievements of the Violet Quill was to produce a body of work in which being gay became a journey, a way of getting on with life, rather than an obstacle to overcome.

The dissolution of the group foreshadowed by months the first announcements of a disease that came to be called AIDS. Of the seven writers, four—Cox, Ferro, Grumley, and Whitmore—have died from the disease. The final legacy of the Violet Quill has been the way that, as a group, they responded to AIDS. Ferro's *Second Son* (1988) is arguably the first novel about AIDS; Holleran wrote a memorable collection of essays about the pandemic, *Ground Zero* (1988). Picano has produced a saga-like novel of gay life framed by AIDS. White, who was a founder of the Gay Men's Health Crisis, has written about it in the stories collected in the *Darker Proof* (1988) and in *The Farewell Symphony* (1997), and Whitmore wrote not only one of the most stirring early books on the subject, *Someone Was Here* (1988), but he initiated one of the first lawsuits to provide equal medical treatment to persons infected with HIV.   *David Bergman*

Bibliography

Bergman, David. *The Violet Quill Reader*. New York: St. Martin's, 1994.

Mordden, Ethan. Introduction. *Waves: An Anthology of New Gay Fiction*. New York: Vintage, 1994.

Woodhouse, Reed. *Unlimited Embrace*. Amherst, Mass.: University of Massachusetts Press, 1998.

See also AIDS Literature; Fiction; Gay Men's Health Crisis (GMHC); U.S. Literature: Contemporary; White, Edmund

Visconti, Luchino (1907–1976)

Luchino Visconti was a leading opera, theater, and film director, primarily in Italy, from the early 1940s through the mid-1970s. His work has many of the hallmarks of the stereotypically gay: an emphasis on exquisitely elaborate costume and decor (especially when he worked with gay designer Piero Tosi), a devotion to divas (notably Maria Callas and Anna Magnani), the needless stage/screen presence of handsome young men (most often Teutonic, in line with two of his longest relationships, with photographer Horst and actor Helmut Berger), and the recurrence of gay characters and situations. The last are most evident in the films. There are extensive treatments of gay characters and situations in *La caduta degli dei* (*The Damned*, 1969), in which Nazi SS troops slaughter Nazi SA Brown Shirts at the end of a night of homoerotic pleasure; *Morte a Venezia* (*Death in Venice*, 1971), in which an elderly, hitherto heterosexual composer becomes obsessed with a young man at the Venice Lido; and *Ludwig* (1972), about the mental disintegration of the king of Bavaria, played by Helmut Berger. Even more glancing ones occur in *Ossessione* (1942), based on *The Postman Always Rings Twice* and including a sequence where the hero temporarily leaves his adulterous and fatal heterosexual liaison and shacks up with a traveling salesman known as "Lo Spagnolo"; *Rocco e i suoi fratelli* (*Rocco and His Brothers* 1960), about a family of brothers, one of whom sleeps for pay with and eventually beats up his boxing manager; and *Gruppo di famiglia in un interno* (*Conversation Piece*, 1974), in which a family

V

Silvana Mangano, Bjorn Andresen, and Dirk Bogarde in a scene from Luchino Visconti's film Death in Venice (1971). *UCLA Arts Library (Special Collection).*

moves in on a reclusive, retired intellectual who finds himself drawn to the wife's lover, again played by Berger. Yet despite these gay elements, often remarkable for their time, Visconti's work is neither unambiguously gay-affirmative nor yet unsettlingly queer. The very privilege and respectability that permitted such gay expression (his aristocratic background, his involvement with high culture, and, not least, his closeness to the Italian Communist Party) also formed and limited it. Sexuality of any kind is viewed as corrosive, often to the point of destruction; at the same time, there is a cultural longing for a manly homoeroticism, free of guilt and the violence of lust. This is evident in the physically charged relations between the brothers in *Rocco*, the frolicking boys on the beach in *Morte a Venezia*, and even the dreamy repose before the massacre in *La caduta degli dei*, but perhaps most effectively in the "Lo Spagnolo" sequence in *Ossessione*, where the relation between the two men is both obviously erotic yet not expressed in sex, and where a striking contrast is drawn with the delirious violence of the

hero's heterosexual lovemaking. Openly homoerotic yet physically restrained longing also marks the underrated *Gruppo di famiglia* and is the core of *Morte a Venezia*, a film consisting almost entirely of the camera and Aschenbach (Dirk Bogarde) gazing after unsullied masculinity. Visconti's work is not pro-gay but neither is it of the closet; it is rather an open and always superbly realized exploration of the dynamics of homosexual respectability in a homophobic culture.   *Richard Dyer*

Bibliography

Nowell-Smith, Geoffery. *Visconti*. London: British Film Institute, 1973.

See also Friendship; Film; Italy; Mann, Thomas

Voguing

Voguing is a style of dance born in Harlem's gay scene during the 1980s. The cousin of Chicago's jacking, voguing is often thought of as the gay "version" of breakdancing. Made popular by Madonna's hit song "Vogue" and Jenny Livingston's documentary *Paris Is Burning,* this subcultural practice had a kind of heyday in the American mainstream in the early 1990s. From Madonna's highly stylized video for the song, an archaeology of voguing's mass cultural "roots," to Malcolm Maclaren's video for his song "Deep in Vogue," featuring New York's star voguer, Willi Ninja, this dance form took on a highly visible public presence throughout the world.

The dance is dominated by the use of poses derived from film stars and models, as well as stylizations of the practices (fashion shows, makeup) that connote beauty and glamour in mass culture. Danced to the beat of house music, voguing takes apart the production of heterosexual white body norms by revealing their stylized quality. "[B]lending the sultry flair of an Imam working the runways of Europe with the butch cool of the GQ look, voguers sweep the dance floor striking picture perfect poses around/behind/alongside—but never strictly on top of—the cross rhythms of house music" (Goldsby 34). While voguing can be performed independently, it can also be a part of a competition, or "ball," where the goal is to use the dance to upstage your opponent.

Voguing complicates our notion of what subcultural resistance might be. How can this practice, which seems so thoroughly commodified and appropriated by Madonna, be read as a mode of queer resistance? Cindy Patton offers a powerful reading of the resistant potential of voguing that rethinks the framing of this question. In the tradition of cultural studies, on which queer studies' approach to popular culture is largely based, resistance is often seen in stark contrast to appropriation. Patton takes voguing as an example of a subcultural practice that refuses this dichotomy: using the concept of "subaltern memory," Patton suggests that "it is no longer useful to view recirculation and dislocation of cultural critique as a result of appropriation." But rather, the style of voguing, even in its mass mediated forms, embodies a kind of critique; while this moment of queer/black/Latino critique is not immediately visible or audible in something like the "Vogue" video, "reembodiment by club dancers unpredictably adds to and reinterprets the critique, retracing or reconnecting memories of resistance" (Patton 83). By dramatizing the performative nature of both heterosexuality and whiteness in the space of the dancer's body, Patton suggests that voguing also refuses the minoritizing model of dominant ways of imagining gay identity in late capitalism, that is, identity and

dramatizes the relational place of subalternity to the production of the dominant and the history of those relations.   *Brian Currid*

Bibliography
Goldsby, Jackie. "All About Yves." *Outlook* (Summer 1989): 34–35.
Patton, Cindy. "Embodying Subaltern Memory: Kinesthesia and the Problematics of Gender and Race." In *The Madonna Connection: Representational Politics, Subcultural Identities and Cultural Theory.* Cathy Schwichtenberg, ed. Boulder, Colo.: Westview Press, 1993.

See also African American Gay Culture; Disco; Fashion; Music and Musicians II: Popular Music; Transvestism

Voting Behavior

"Voting behavior" refers to patterns of participation in elections by both individuals and distinct sociopolitical groups. Since the formation of the "New Deal" coalition in the 1930s, electoral politics in the United States has frequently been analyzed in terms of voting blocs defined along lines of race, gender, religion, income, education, ethnicity, and other factors. Since at least the beginning of the 1990s, some voter polls have attempted to add sexual orientation to that list by including it on the demographic portions of voter surveys and other forms of electoral analysis.

Through the mid-1990s, however, these analyses have mostly run aground of two serious methodological problems. The first problem is how self-identification as lesbian, gay, or bisexual (LGB) is properly to be understood: as a measure of sexual attraction, sexual behavior, political identity, or as some combination of these factors. The second problem is that a substantial number of respondents are probably unwilling to identify as lesbian, gay, or bisexual (whatever they take that designation to mean), owing to the stigma attached to such an identification or because they are themselves deeply closeted.

Given these two problems, the results of various voter surveys have varied widely, and none can be said to be empirically reliable. Nonetheless, much anecdotal information suggests that gay men and lesbians can sometimes constitute a significant electoral force on the national, state, and local levels, as well as within the Democratic Party. In the

V 1992 elections, for instance, some survey data suggested that strong LGB support for Bill Clinton may have helped him win Michigan and New Jersey and certainly buffered his popular vote margins in the key electoral college states of California and New York. Similarly, on a local level, the reality of the LGB vote has been acknowledged by the creation of distinct voting precincts around gay enclaves in cities such as San Francisco, Los Angeles, New York, Houston, Philadelphia, and Washington, D.C. LGBs have also established a sizable presence in the Democratic Party, with particular impact in primary races in the larger cities and states and at the Democratic National Convention.

The available evidence on the characteristics of the so-called lavender vote confirms much of what would intuitively be expected: LGB voters tend to be highly liberal on social issues, most lesbians hold strongly feminist views, and LGBs are more engaged by elections in which their issues figure prominently. One somewhat counterintuitive finding has been that LGBs do not always vote the Democratic Party line but tend to vote for the most pro-gay candidate regardless of party; this is particulary the case if the candidate is him- or herself LGB.

In all, the combined analytical and anecodal evidence suggests that the LGB vote can be critical in the nation's major urban centers and in several coastal states. The clearest figures available place the national LGB vote at between 3 and 5 percent (the percentages from, respectively, the 1992 and 1996 presidential elections). This estimate indicates that the LGB vote is larger than the Asian American vote, is comparable to the Latino vote, and may reach the size of the Jewish vote. The LGB vote is also skewed toward younger voters, suggesting that over time its size will continue to grow as more individuals come out and openly self-identify as gay or lesbian.

While much remains to be empirically established, the gay and lesbian vote (as well as the anti-gay vote) is likely to remain a moderately but not overwhelmingly important element in American electoral politics. The intense politicization of sexual orientation issues helps to forge a comparatively high level of group consciousness and mobilization among gay men and lesbians, resulting in larger contributions of time and money to political candidates and a higher voter turnout rate. But if LGBs continue to become integrated into the American mainstream, their coherence as a voting bloc may decline, much as the coherence of earlier voting blocs of ethnic European immigrants, Roman Catholics, and others did in the past.

Raymond A. Smith

Bibliography

Hertzog, Mark. *The Lavender Vote: Lesbians, Gay Men, and Bisexuals in American Electoral Politics.* New York: New York University Press, 1996.

See also Civil Rights (U.S. Law); Gay Rights in the U.S.; Human Rights Campaign; National Gay and Lesbian Task Force; Queer Politics

Wagner, Richard (1813–1883)

The German composer and theorist of opera Richard Wagner was notorious in his lifetime for his violations of nineteenth-century bourgeois moral codes. The most egregious of these was his long-term adulterous affair with Cosima von Bülow, daughter of Franz Liszt as well of wife of Wagner's friend and supporter Hans von Bülow. Wagner had several illegitimate children by Cosima before finally marrying her in 1870. Almost as important to Wagner's dubious moral image in public life was his close connection to the eccentric homosexual King Ludwig II of Bavaria. Upon Ludwig's accession to the throne in 1864, he summoned Wagner to Munich, settled the composer's debts, and offered him substantial patronage. Since Wagner had spent the years 1849–1860 in exile from Germany for political subversion, his later incarnation as a defender of royalty seemed insincere at best. The press criticized his voluptuous or peculiar personal habits, which included wearing finely made satin dressing gowns, indulging in scented baths, opposing vivisection, and propounding vegetarianism. Publishing a set of letters in which Wagner gave his seamstress instructions on the precise colors and styles of his robes, Viennese journalist Daniel Spitzer juxtaposed Wagner's tastes in ornament with his written texts in praise of manliness and German national identity to imply that they had a common source in Wagner's own sexual irregularity. Several of philosopher Friedrich Nietzsche's attacks on Wagner also hint at a sexual source for Wagner's flaws of character.

Wagner's scandalous way of life resonated in the minds of many of his audience with the subject matter of his operas, which presented a near-constant spectacle of feverish, transgressive love, including several cases of incest, adultery, and miscegenation, as well as a focus on extravagantly suffering male characters. The riskiness of such representations found even greater expression in Wagner's music, which carried the sublime poetics of the works of composers such as Beethoven to the point of shock. There was no doubt in Wagner's audiences that an excessive and unrestrained sexual desire was the fundamental topic of a work such as *Tristan und Isolde* (1859), and even in as ostensibly sexually restrained a work as *Parsifal* (1882), the presence of actual and symbolically castrated characters could suggest latent unconventional turmoil.

The appeal of Wagner's work to potentially homosexual audiences found further support in the atmosphere of the Wagner festivals in Bayreuth in the years following Wagner's death. Wagner's son Siegfried, who ran the annual festivals with his mother, enjoyed an extensive international circle of homosexual acquaintances, many of whom seem to have attended the festival with some regularity. His own homosexual behavior was an open secret. Given Wagner's status as a sexually transgressive culture hero and the strong homoerotic associations of Wagnerism both in and out of Bayreuth, it is no wonder that Wagnerian elements form a strong part of the background to late-nineteenth-century discourses of sexuality. Wagnerism appears in a number of homosexual apologetics at the turn of the century, most dramatically in the work of German writer Hanns Fuchs, who was involved in the German homophile group Die Gemeinschaft des Eigenen. Fuchs not only authored a study on "spiritual homosexuality" in Wagner's life and work but also made homosexual Wagnerism a central theme of his melodramatic novel *Eros zwischen Euch und uns*

W (1909). Wagnerian scenes also figure prominently in Mikhail Kuzmin's early gay liberationist novel, *Krïlya* (Wings, 1906).

Wagner's cultural force was substantially diminished during the twentieth century, first by the antiromantic reaction that followed World War I, then by widespread revulsion after World War II over the ease with which his work was adopted by Nazi Germany as propaganda. Recent work on Wagner has been interested mostly in the nature and extent of anti-Semitism in his creations; but studies of Wagner's representations of gender and sexuality are beginning to be published as well.

Mitchell Morris

Bibliography

Fuchs, Hanns. *Eros zwischen euch und uns* (Eros Separating Us and You). Berlin: 1909.

———. *Richard Wagner und der Homosexualität.* Leipzig: Verlag H. Barsdorf, 1903. Reprint. Berlin: Janssen Verlag, 1992.

Kuzmin, Michael Alekseyevich. *Krïlya* (Wings). 1906. Translated and edited by Neil Granoien and Michael Green as *Wings: Prose and Poetry.* Preface by Vladimir Markov. Ann Arbor, Mich.: Ardis, 1972.

Mohr, Richard D. " 'Knights, Young Men, Boys': Masculine Worlds and Democratic Values." In *Gay Ideas: Outing and Other Controversies.* Boston: Beacon Press, 1992, 129–218.

See also Brand, Adolph; German Literature; Germany; Kuzmin, Mikhail; Ludwig (Louis) II, King of Bavaria; Music and Musicians I: Classical Music; Nazism and the Holocaust; Opera

Walpole, Horace (1717–1797)

Horace Walpole is best known as the author of *The Castle of Otranto* (1764) and the occupant of Strawberry Hill, a villa outside London that he redesigned to showcase medieval and oriental styles of decoration. Often described as the first Gothic novel, *Otranto* showed that nonrealist fiction could explore taboo themes more freely than the mainstream eighteenth-century novel could. Walpole's use of supernatural effects in an archaic setting had an incalculable influence on writers such as Byron and "Monk" Lewis, who were more overt than Walpole in their representations of homosexual desire. Walpole's father, Sir Robert Walpole, was prime minister of England from 1721 to 1742 and was created first Earl of

Orford in 1742; Walpole himself was a member of Parliament for over twenty years and became fourth Earl of Orford in 1791, after the death of his nephew. As one might expect, Walpole's letters and *Memoirs* are an invaluable source of detail on eighteenth-century political life. His correspondence (collected in forty-eight volumes) also charts his close friendships with Thomas Gray and Henry Seymour Conway, both of whom he was in love with. Walpole's most overtly sexual letters were addressed to Henry Clinton, Lord Lincoln; although these letters valorize Lincoln's heterosexual promiscuity, Walpole's praise of his friend's potency has a strongly homoerotic component. Walpole's interest in paintings, architecture, garden design, and chinoiserie helped shape late-eighteenth-century taste, while his letters—with their biting wit and superb irony—provide the most entertaining of guides to upper-class British life in the 1700s.

Vincent Quinn

Bibliography

Mowl, Timothy. *Horace Walpole: The Great Outsider.* London: John Murray, 1996.

Walpole, Horace. *The Yale Edition of Horace Walpole's Correspondence.* W. S. Lewis, ed. 48 vols. New Haven: Yale University Press, and Oxford: OUP, 1937–1983.

Walpole, Horace. *The Castle of Otranto* (1764). W. S. Lewis, ed. Oxford: Oxford University Press, 1964.

See also English Literature; Gray, Thomas

War

In Western history, wars have typically had a twofold effect on the experience of gays and lesbians. On the one hand, wars often throw males together into a situation where women are excluded, where privacy is strictly limited, and where extraordinary emotional stress and cramped living quarters intensify personal relations. For these reasons, war can awaken and promote homosexual feeling, whether conscious or unconscious. On the other hand, war tends to encourage the persecution of individuals believed to threaten the "moral health" of the state, and so, particularly in the modern West, homosexuals have often suffered even more severe repression during wartime than in peacetime. Since the seventeenth century, the rise of nationalism has been accompanied by heightened anxieties concerning the moral health of the body politic and fostered the notion that "degenerate" activities—particularly those that might adversely affect the birthrate—weaken the nation-state as a whole. During the Napoleonic wars, for example, prosecutions against "sodomites" increased sharply in England, while prosecutions for other crimes fell. And toward the end of World War I, an intensified concern for public morals focused attention in England on homosexual coteries. Noel Pemberton-Billing, an eccentric member of Parliament, created a sensation in January 1918 by alleging that the enemy possessed a "black book" listing forty-seven thousand English homosexuals, at all levels of society, who were being systematically used for extortion and blackmail. Though purely fictitious, the story played to a widespread fear.

Since before recorded history, a certain homoerotic aspect or potential has marked the exceptionally close relationships that typically develop between comrades in arms. The literature of the ancient world frequently celebrated friendships between heroes or between a hero and his lesser "pal." These friendships are generally described not as sexual but as exceptionally passionate and exclusive. For the West, the archetypal "comrade lovers" are Achilles and Patroclus in Homer's *Iliad*, but a similar relationship may be discerned between David and Jonathan in the Hebrew scriptures (Samuel I and II) and between Gilgamesh and Enkidu in the Babylonian Epic of Gilgamesh. The Greeks of the classical period held that erotic feeling between soldiers enhanced their courage and resolve, and Athenians attributed the salvation of their democracy to the lovers Harmodius and Aristogiton. In 378 B.C., Gorgidas of Thebes formed a corps composed entirely of pairs of lovers. Known as the Sacred Band, it brought Thebes military supremacy until Philip II of Macedon overwhelmed it in the Battle of Chaeronea (338 B.C.). Perhaps the more lasting legacy of the Greeks for the history of warfare was the very institution of pitched battle through the invention of the phalanx, a formation in which citizen soldiers were arranged in a tight rectangle rather than a loose line. This type of warfare relied on the willingness of ordinary citizens to stand shoulder to shoulder against the enemy in a clash of arms that was brief and terrifying, but in almost all cases decisive. Victory no longer required merely raw strength or superior numbers but the discipline and courage to stay in formation, qualities that the presence of comrade lovers enhanced. This basic concept of pitched battle between armies in dense formations would remain "the Western way of war" for two millennia. Recognizing this in the first century A.D., Roman military historian Onasander concluded that soldiers fought best when "brother is in rank beside brother, friend beside friend, lover beside lover."

The role that rank-and-file homosexuals have played in wars throughout history cannot be estimated, though many important generals seem to have been homosexual, including Alexander the Great of Macedon (356–323 B.C.), Roman emperor Hadrian (A.D. 76–138), Richard I of England (1157–1199), Frederick the Great of Prussia (1712–1786), Frederick William Steuben (1730–1794; he was inspector general of the American forces in the Revolutionary War), and T. E. Lawrence (1888–1935), popularly known as Lawrence of Arabia. There may have been some grounds for the charge of homosexuality (as well as heresy and sorcery) against the Knights Templar by the pope in 1312.

It was not until shortly after World War I that the first serious attempt was made to study homosexuality in wartime, when German sexologist Magnus Hirschfeld devoted chapter 7 of *The Sexual History of the World War* to "Homosexuality and Transvestitism." His unparalleled archives were completely destroyed when marauding Nazi German youths demolished his Institute for Sexual Research in Berlin on May 6, 1933. The Nazis included homosexuals among the "degenerate" populations that were to be eliminated under their rule. Hitler's troops arrested perhaps fifty to sixty thousand homosexuals between 1933 and 1944, and killed perhaps five thousand to fifteen thousand in the concentration camps. The pink triangle badge used to distinguish homosexuals in the camps has subsequently become a widely recognized symbol of the gay rights movement.

Only since the decriminalization of homosexual acts and the emergence of gay and lesbian identities in the later twentieth century has it been possible to raise the question of whether gays and lesbians may serve openly in the military. The armed forces of most nations still consider homosexuality to be a psychological disorder that renders soldiers both unreliable in combat and vulnerable to blackmail. Yet ironically, the screening procedures that the Allied nations developed during World War II to exclude gays and lesbians from active service helped to define a homosexual identity and so to launch the modern gay rights movement.

In the last two decades, the military ban on homosexuals in the armed forces has became a subject of national debate in several countries. While several countries, including Israel and the Netherlands, now admit gays and lesbians into the service, others either continue to exclude them or, like the United States, permit them to serve only so long as their sexual identity remains hidden.   *Matthew Parfitt*

Bibliography

Bérubé, Allan. *Coming Out Under Fire: The History of Gay Men and Women in World War Two*. New York: Free Press, 1990.

Gilbert, Arthur N. "Sexual Deviance and Disaster During the Napoleonic Wars." *Albion* 9 (1977) 98–113.

Halperin, David M. "Heroes and Their Pals." In *One Hundred Years of Homosexuality and Other Essays on Greek Love*. New York: Routledge, 1990, 75–87.

Hanson, Victor David. *The Western Way of War: Infantry Battle in Classical Greece*. New York: Knopf, 1989.

Hirschfeld, Magnus. *The Sexual History of the World War: Three Volumes in One*. New York: Panurge Press, 1934.

Mosse, George L. *Nationalism and Sexuality*. New York: Harold Fertig, 1985.

Plant, Richard. *The Pink Triangle: The Nazi War Against Homosexuals*. New York: Henry Holt, 1986.

Shilts, Randy. *Conduct Unbecoming: Lesbians and Gays in the U.S. Military, Vietnam to the Persian Gulf*. New York: St. Martin's Press, 1993.

See also Alexander the Great; David and Jonathan; Friendship; Gilgamesh Epic; Greece; Hadrian; Hirschfeld; Magnus; Lawrence, T. E.; Military; Nazism and the Holocaust; Owen, Wilfred; Pink Triangle; Rabe, David; Sodomy Trials; Sparta; Thebes

Warhol, Andy (1928–1987)

"I'm sure I'm going to look in the mirror and see nothing. People are always calling me a mirror and if a mirror looks into a mirror, what is there to see?"

Andy Warhol

Andy Warhol constantly warned people not to look any deeper than the surface of his art and life—and he insistently connected the two. He aggressively advertised his superficiality in both spheres in a carefully deadpan performance of innocent unconcern. But a person whose work reflects us back to ourselves is more often termed social critic than superficial. Here, as in so much of what Warhol said and did, there is an air of disingenuousness. Andy Warhol carefully constructed Andy Warhol, and the figure he invented was a screen behind which he hid.

No American artist in history has ever been as famous or as influential as Andy Warhol. "Artist" is only one of his many titles, for he was also a leading filmmaker, author, magazine publisher, music promoter, collector, and cultural critic. No matter what his chosen medium, the works of Andy Warhol generally shocked, outraged, and influenced public opinion like that of no other cultural figure in modern America. No other artist has ever been more "American," and in many respects his life's work has come to epitomize success in post–World War II American consumer culture.

Yet despite the breadth and scope of his art, Warhol's chief creative endeavor was always himself. He succeeded in making himself into a priceless commodity, a kind of cultural brand name with powerful cachet. Embracing paradox, he self-consciously crafted an image at once immensely sophisticated and unbelievably naive, part debutant and part social critic. He controlled through passivity, commanded attention through shyness, attended church as religiously as he attended the nightclub Studio 54, and loved his mother as much as he loved pretty boys and drugs. He collected first-rate Art Deco furniture and kitschy, mass-produced cookie jars. He seemed to be trying to level all hierarchies of value, yet he shamelessly sucked up to whichever celebrity ruled at the moment. To many he was a mass of contradictions, and even his pale, wan figure capped by a white wig seemed at once calculated to fade into the woodwork and to make an indelible impression.

Warhol turned himself into a cipher, a vacuum of signification for recording, blatantly and unmediated, the ebb and flow of American life. He has been called, famously, a Rorschach blot of our society (typically, he did a series of paintings of Rorschach inkblots).

Warhol was born Andrew Warhola on August 6, 1928, in Pittsburgh to Czech immigrant parents, and he grew up a sickly kid in working-class neighborhoods. He was the only member of his family to attend college, graduating from Carnegie Tech with a degree in design in 1949, and shortly thereafter moving to New York City to try his at hand at commercial illustration. Commissions came fairly readily, and within a few years he became a commercial success, one of the leading fashion illustrators in New York and winner of a number of design industry awards.

Early in his career, he drew everything from shoe ads for tony department stores to homoerotic male nudes. In 1957 Warhol self-published a series of one hundred bound books entitled *A Gold Book*. The book contained such images as a comely nude youth pictured from the rear and a beautiful boy with a rose between his teeth. The choice of these images is a remarkably open statement of identity for what was an enormously repressive era, especially considering the book's prospective audience of ad agency art directors and its purpose as a form of advertisement. Significantly, only a year earlier he had attempted to exhibit a series of drawings of boys passionately kissing one another.

Even after achieving art world success, Warhol never tried to hide his homosexuality. In his book *POPism* he refers to himself as "swish." In distinct contrast to the previous generation of American artists who were almost exclusively heterosexual and often aggressively macho, the art world into which Andy Warhol emerged was very gay yet equally very closeted. Warhol, in contrast, surrounded himself with drag queens, produced films with titles like *My Hustler* and *13 Most Beautiful Boys*, and "swished" his way through interviews, sometimes referring to himself as "Miss Warhol."

Yet for all his overt camping, Warhol still carried an air of reserve, as if he were holding something back. Paradoxically, this cool reserve, this refusal to engage, made him acceptable in all his swishiness. He may have been a queen, but he wasn't a political, or worse, sexual, being—or so at least he wanted people to think. In combination with this indifferent mien, Warhol's sexuality became unthreatening to dominant culture; it was but another aspect of the Warhol mystique, in which he was a court jester, an exotic, not a "queer."

A continuous theme in Warhol's art was the disjunction between public and private life. He repeatedly painted celebrities who came to embody this split like Marilyn Monroe and Elizabeth Taylor, whose famously fractious private lives warred with their commodified public images. As a gay man, Warhol perhaps saw something he recognized in these women's uncomfortable maintenance of a disingenuous identity for public consumption. In retrospect, that disjunction of public and private became Warhol's leitmotif. Despite his open sexuality and documented swishiness, there is much about Warhol that remains utterly mysterious. For all his obsessive recording of the minutiae of his daily life (as revealed in his posthumously published diary) and in spite of nearly thirty years in the public eye, we know next to nothing about what Warhol actually felt, what his opinions were, how he understood himself. In a sense, his work—which included his life—can be understood as an instantiation of a great paradox, the closet on parade, the public revelation of a lack of revelation.

For those who would persist in ignoring Warhol's words of warning to look only at his surfaces, the artist left behind a final tease. Shortly before his death in 1987 following gallbladder surgery, he completed a set of gigantic self-portraits in various guises, all covered with a military pattern in bright colors. The self-portrait, traditionally the most self-revelatory subject in the history of Western art, is in Warhol's hands turned against itself. In his self-portraits, he simultaneously proffers and refuses identity, using camouflage to create an image of his own self-closeting, a fitting totem for a man who made a trademark out his refusal to speak out and surely laughed as he then became the most widely quoted artist in the world.   *Jonathan Katz*

Bibliography

Bourdon, David. *Warhol*. New York: Abrams, 1989.

De Salvo, Donna, ed. *"Success Is a Job in New York. . ."* New York: Grey Art Gallery and the Carnegie Museum of Art, 1989.

Katz, Jonathan. *Andy Warhol*. New York: Rizzoli, 1993.

Koch, Stephen. *Stargazer: Andy Warhol's World and His Films*. New York: Marion Boyars, 1985.

Smith, Patrick. *Andy Warhol's Art and Films*. Ann Arbor, Mich.: UMI Research Press, 1981.

———. *Warhol: Conversations About the Artist*. Ann Arbor, Mich.: UMI Research Press, 1988.

Warhol, Andy. *The Philosophy of Andy Warhol*. San Diego: Harvest/HBJ Book, 1975.

Warhol, Andy, and Pat Hackett. *POPism: The Warhol '60s*. New York: Harcourt Brace Jovanovich, 1980.

See also Art History; Film; Film Stars; Postmodernism

Washington, D.C.

The U.S. capital has a rich gay history, dating back at least to the early 1890s, when black men in "womanly attire" held an annual "drag dance," and eighteen men, the majority of them African American, were arrested for engaging in oral sex in Lafayette Square across from the White House during a brief period in 1892. The city's parks were one of the few places where blacks and whites interested in same-sex sexual relationships interacted with each other across racial lines. The gay communities that developed in Washington in the early twentieth century were divided by race, with white lesbians, gay men, and bisexuals socializing primarily in predominantly gay bars, and black lesbians, gay men, and bisexuals entertaining primarily at home or in bars with straight African Americans. Even after segregation in the capital's public institutions was ruled unconstitutional in 1953, African Americans were often not welcomed in many of the city's gay bars; as a result, they began to form their own, including the Nob Hill, perhaps the oldest continuing black gay bar in the country. African American lesbians, gay men, and bisexuals in Washington have continued to make history, establishing the first Black Lesbian and Gay Pride Weekend in 1991.

Besides its vibrant black community, the capital stands out in gay history for being the site of one of the worst crackdowns against gays in the twentieth century. Responding to the increased visibility of lesbians, gay men, and bisexuals in the streets and bars of Washington after World War II, the city's park police launched a "Sexual Perversion Elimination Program," and the district police formed a special morals squad; together they arrested more than a thousand gays per year in the late 1940s and early 1950s. The persecution culminated with Senator Joseph McCarthy's (R.-Wis.) witch-hunt against suspected gays in the federal government, which led to the firing of 381 people from the State Department alone between 1950 and 1953. Although the number of dismissals declined in subsequent years, it was not until the 1990s that federal agencies began instituting antidiscrimination policies to protect the rights of lesbians, gay men, and bisexuals.

Brett Beemyn

Bibliography

Beemyn, Brett. "A Queer Capital: Lesbian, Gay, and Bisexual Life in Washington, D.C., 1890–1955." Ph.D. diss., University of Iowa, 1997.

See also African American Gay Culture; Marches and Parades; Marches on Washington; McCarthyism; U.S. Government

Waters, John (1946–)

John Waters is one of the great subversive, radical film directors of the twentieth century. A nephew of President Nixon's undersecretary of the Interior, he produced several short films starring his boyhood friend, Divine, before directing the transvestite actor in the extraordinary trilogy *Multiple Maniacs* (1970), *Pink Flamingos* (1972), and *Female Trouble* (1974). These amazing films were followed by *Desperate Living* (1976), starring Edith Massey; *Polyester* (1978), the first odorama movie, complete with scratch-and-sniff card; and his recent, more mainstream films—*Hairspray* (1988, Ricki Lake and great dance sequences), *Cry-Baby* (1990, Johnny Depp and juvenile delinquency), *Serial Mom* (1994, Kathleen Turner and suburban mayhem); and *Pecker* (1998, Edward Furlong and the New York art scene).

Waters's films are populated by outsiders proud to be different and by events that celebrate the gross and antisocial. In *Pink Flamingos*, Edie the Egg Lady (Edith Massey) eats eggs all day, Crackers (Danny Mills) and his female date (Cookie Mueller) have sex with live chickens between their bodies, the Marbles send Divine a turd in the mail, a partygoer does tricks with his asshole, party guests cannibalize the police, a real-life male-to-female pre-op transsexual flaunts her breasts and penis, and Divine eventually eats (real) dog excrement.

Waters' dialogue is bold, memorable, and even musical. In *Pink Flamingos*, Connie Marble (Mink Stole) speaks to a prospective employee in a legato drone: "I guess there's just two kinds of people, Miss Sandstone: my kind of people and assholes. It's rather obvious which category you fit into. Have a nice day." The response is delivered in a staccato outburst: "Eat the bird, bitch!" Perhaps the greatest line in film history is heard in *Female Trouble* when Taffy (Mink Stole) responds to her stepfather's request for oral sex by telling him: "I wouldn't suck your lousy dick if I was suffocating and there was oxygen in your balls."

Filled with baroque excess (*Pink Flamingos*: "He's been castrated! HIS PENIS IS GONE!"), expressionist fury, and Rabelaisian energy, the trilogy seems like Bosch's *Garden of Earthly Delights* come to life. Although characters express mock outrage at homosexuality and at extraordinary events, it is clear that this kind and generous director revels in their presentation. "Oh honey, I'd be so happy if you'd turn nelly," says Aunt Ida (Edith Massey) in *Female Trouble*. "Queers are just better. I'd be so proud if you was a fag and had a nice beautician boyfriend." "I worry that you'll work in an office, have children, celebrate wedding anniversaries. The world of [a] heterosexual is a sick and boring life."

Doug DiBianco

Bibliography

Ives, John G. *John Waters*. New York: Thunder's Mouth Press, 1992.

Waters, John. *Crackpot: The Obsessions of John Waters*. New York: Macmillan, 1986.

———. *Shock Value*. New York: Dell, 1981.

———. *Trash Trio: Three Screenplays*. (*Pink Flamingos*, *Desperate Living*, *Flamingos Forever* [not produced]). New York: Vintage, 1988.

See also Camp; Divine; Film

Weber, Bruce (1946–)

The eroticization of the male body during the late twentieth century has numerous causes, and the photography of Bruce Weber is definitely one of them. When he graduated from New York's New School in the early 1970s, sex appeal was a popular advertising ploy, but the sex was invariably female. Supposedly, men were "sexy" by being smart, rich, powerful—Henry Kissinger was the country's ideal bachelor.

Of course, male movies stars and sports figures were sexy physically, but they had only begun to bare their bodies. Early examples like Ken Russell's film *Women in Love*, with its nude wrestling scene, and Joe Namath's BVD ads started a trend on which Weber expanded. Many photographers helped to make men exploitable as sex objects, but the trend crystallized in Weber's photography for the fashion industry. His unpretentious style in a field not known for it helped focus attention on the daring of his presentation of men as physically desirable, which might have been somewhat disguised if he had opted for more drama in his lighting and composition. Instead, interior backgrounds are featureless; lighting is carefully presentational; the range of grays in his work is subtly modulated and he rarely utilizes extreme blacks and whites—imparting a simplicity to his style that highlights the subject.

The real breadth of the revolution spearheaded by Weber is seen not in a shot of Marky Mark wearing little more than a sneer but in a book such as *Bear Pond*, which becomes a top-selling Christmas gift item because of the boys in the photos, who wear nothing more than their dogs. Critics have argued that Weber is selling a fascist image; others claim that these images of male perfection beckon across gender and sexuality barriers. Allen Ellenzweig says that Weber's photographs "mirror their time; they are surface deep, their reflections are shallow, they throw back at us shimmering mirages of man-to-man sex, illusory material comforts, and illusive physical perfection" (Ellenzweig 167).

F. Valentine Hooven, III

Bibliography

Ellenzweig, Allen. *The Homoerotic Photograph: Male Images from Durieu/Delacroix to Mapplethorpe*. New York: Columbia University Press, 1992.

Weber, Bruce. *Bear Pond*. New York: Little, Brown, 1991.

———. *Gentle Giants*. New York: Little, Brown, 1994.

See also Body Images; Fashion; Klein, Calvin; Photography, Physical Culture

Westphal, Carl Friedrich Otto (1833–1890)

German psychiatrist Carl Westphal was considered one of the new generation of German psychiatrists of his time. The prior mainstream of psychiatry was philosophically oriented. Doctors regarded mental disturbances as emotional disorders that resulted because the contact between soul and reason had broken down owing to a sinful way of life. From the middle of the nineteenth century onward, scientifically orientated psychiatrists supported instead the thesis of the physical causes of mental diseases. Mental illness from then on was regarded as a disease of the brain. In 1886, this new profession founded the Archives of Psychiatry and Mental Diseases, creating an appropriate forum in which to discuss their clinical observations.

Westphal, a founding member of the archives, published his first article on homosexuality under the characteristic title *Conträre Sexualempfindung*, The Contrary Sexual Emotion). His contribution illustrates the swing in opinion that was taking place within psychiatry by using the example of homosexual behavior. Homosexuality was no longer considered sinful and bad but a symptom of illness brought on by neuropathic disorders of the central nervous system. Westphal reported, for the first time in the professional literature, the clinical case of a woman whose sexual inclinations were aimed at someone of her own sex. The contrary sexual emotion could occur equally among men as among women, and gender confusion was the cause of same-sex desire. To argue this point, Westphal refers to reports by court doctors

Johann Ludwig Casper and Ambroise Tardieu and to jurist and author Karl Heinrich Ulrichs.

Psychiatry had followed jurist Ulrichs in establishing the association between gender and sexuality, which became the basis for later theories on homosexuality. Gender characteristics were thought to change within a sexual inclination toward the same sex. According to this, homosexual feeling was possible only under the conditions of a reversal of gender, as Westphal's definition commentary verifies: "I chose the term 'contrary sexual emotion' from a suggestion by an admirable and in the field of philology and archeology most distinguished colleague, after failing to find shorter and more appropriate terms. What shall here be expressed is that it is not always simultaneously the sexual urge as such with which we are dealing but rather also merely the feeling of the complete inner being, being alienated from its own sex" (Westphal 107).

With this contribution, Westphal was able within the field of psychiatry to establish the idea of same-sex sexual behavior as an expression of the essential character in a person. In its time, this idea was controversial within medical circles. In the same year, the whole of the medical faculty at the then University of Berlin, the Deputation of Medical Matters, had rejected the theory in a specialist report for the Prussian Ministry of Justice on the grounds that congenital sexual predisposition in a person was completely without scientific foundation. The medical deputation referred to publications by Ulrichs, which had nonetheless spoken of a physiological basis for homosexual feelings. The idea of congenital predisposition gained acceptance only with Westphal's publication and became the prevailing opinion. The pathology of homosexuality, however, remained unchanged. *Jörg Hutter*

Bibliography

Hutter, Jörg: "Westphal." In *Homosexualität, Handbuch der Theorie und Forschungsgeschichte*. Rüdiger Lautmann, ed. Frankfurt: Campus, 1993, 39–41.

Westphal, Karl Friedrich Otto. "Die conträre Sexualempfindung, Symptom eines neuropathischen (pychopathischen) Zustandes." *Archiv für Psychiatrie und Nervenkrankheiten* 2, no. 73 (1869): 108.

See also Homosexuality; Psychiatry and Homosexuality; Sexology; Uranianism

Whale, James (1889–1957)

This English director of Hollywood films was born into a poor family in the Midlands of England. After serving in World War I, Whale began his career as an actor and set designer in the British theater. His initial professional success came when he directed R. C. Sherriff's play about World War I, *Journey's End*, in London and New York. This success led Whale to move to California in 1929 to direct films. Soon after arriving in Hollywood, he met assistant producer (later producer), David Lewis, and they lived together until they separated in 1953.

Several of Whale's best films manifest a camp sensibility and expressionistic technique far different from the realism of Sherriff's drama. A series of gothic horror films that he directed—including *Frankenstein* and its sequel, *The Bride of Frankenstein*—are remarkable for their black humor, barely suppressed sexuality, and stylized acting and direction.

Except for one film that was not commercially released, Whale's career as a film director ended in 1941. One reason for this may have been that he became tired of producers' interference and no longer wanted to work in the medium. Another reason may have been that his homosexuality, which he refused to hide, alienated coworkers.

Whale had become financially comfortable, but after his retirement from filmmaking his health declined and he was often depressed. Whale, who could not swim, committed suicide by jumping head-first into his swimming pool. *Charles Krinsky*

Bibliography

Curtis, James. *James Whale*. Metuchen, N.J.: Scarecrow Press, 1982.

Kemp, Philip. "James Whale." In *World Film Directors*. Vol. 1: 1890–1945. John Wakeman, ed. New York: H. W. Wilson 1987, 1197–1202.

See also Camp; Film

White, Edmund (1940–)

Of all gay writers to emerge in the seventies in the United States, Edmund White is surely the most famous. He has won the National Book Critics Circle Award for his biography *Genet* (1993), a Lambda Literary Award, and a Guggenheim Fellowship. He has been made a member of the American Institute of Arts and Letters as well as a Chevalier de l'Ordre des Arts et Lettres by the French government. His

Ed White, 1988. Photo by Marc Geller.

behaviors of people around him. Only at the end does he recover his memory and recall that he is the deposed prince who once ruled the land. Although the book won critical praise, White did not achieve popular recognition with the gay reading public until he published *The Joy of Gay Sex* (with Charles Silverstein) and the nonfiction book *States of Desire: Travels in Gay America* (1980). An indefatigable journalist and essayist, White has had his short nonfiction pieces collected in *The Burning Library* (1994).

In 1978, White published his second novel, *Nocturnes for the King of Naples,* his first explicitly gay novel. Like *Forgetting Elena,* it is a highly poetic work in which White exhibits the style for which he is justly regarded. In the novel an unnamed narrator addresses his older dead lover. Like so much of White's work, it concerns initiation into manhood, an initiation that requires the betrayal of loved ones. *Caracole* (1985), his fourth novel, is also in a highly elaborate style that shuns the conventions of literary realism.

Under the influence of Christopher Isherwood and about the time he was active in the Violet Quill Club, White experimented with a somewhat plainer style in the first two volumes of his trilogy of autobiographical novels, *A Boy's Own Story* (1982) and *The Beautiful Room Is Empty* (1988), and in his short story collection, *Skinned Alive* (1995). Several of the stories and *The Farewell Symphony* (1997), the final volume of his trilogy, concern AIDS. One of the founding members of the Gay Men's Health Crisis (GMHC), White, who is infected with HIV, watched his partner, artist and architect Hubert Sorin, die from its consequences even as they were completing *Our Paris: Sketches from Memory* (1994), a compilation of Sorin's whimsical drawings and White's charming essays about his adopted city.   *David Bergman*

Bibliography

Bergman, David. "Edmund White." In *Contemporary Gay American Novelists.* Emmanuel Nelson, ed. Westport, Conn.: Greenwood Press, 1993, 386–94.

See also AIDS Literature; Fiction; Gay Men's Health Crisis (GMHC); Isherwood, Christopher; U.S. Literature: Contemporary Gay Writing; Violet Quill

reputation may be greater in Europe than in his own country; there, he is frequently interviewed on radio and television. This attention has not been achieved by downplaying his homosexuality. Throughout his career, he embraced the label of "gay" writer even as he attempted to break down the barriers that have led to the ghettoization of much gay writing.

White was born and raised in an upper-class suburb of Cincinnati. After his parents' divorce, he lived alternately with his mother in Chicago and his father in Cincinnati. For high school he was sent to the Cranbrook School, then he graduated from the University of Michigan, where he majored in Chinese and won a Hopwood Award in play writing. After graduating, he went to New York City, where he worked for Time/Life and had his play *The Blueboy in Black* produced Off-Broadway. White has never abandoned playwriting, but his theater work has been overshadowed by his novels and essays.

White's first novel, *Forgetting Elena* (1973), concerns a young man who wakes up with amnesia in an imaginary island country (to some degree modeled on Fire Island's Pines Community). Unwilling to let anyone know his condition, he tries to figure out the rules of society by closely observing the manners and

White, Minor (1908–1976)

When nearly forty years old, Minor White returned from World War II with a Bronze Star and a new mission in life. As a self-taught photographer, during the Depression he earned critical attention photographing buildings and landscapes for the WPA, but in 1947 he assembled an exhibition that focused on the soldiers he had photographed, coupled with haiku-like poems. On the eve of its opening at San Francisco's Palace of the Legion of Honor, the show was canceled for being "too personal" and "not patriotic," at least not patriotic enough for an America just entering the McCarthy era.

This setback failed to divert White from his mission. He continued to create photographs out of step with the mainstream, commenting on the very popular "Family of Man" show in 1955, "How quickly the milk of human kindness turns to schmaltz." White was a postwar bohemian, a proto-beatnik—Jack Kerouac with a camera. Like Kerouac, he had great difficulty dealing with his homosexual feelings, which is understandable for the times. He converted to Roman Catholicism, then to Zen Buddhism, and finally to the teachings of Gurdjieff. He enlisted his camera in his search for spiritual depth, attempting to fuse into his photographs a spirituality that would deflect, or rather, transform life's carnality. This is most evident in his male nudes. He almost invariably shied away from fully confronting their eroticism, either by heavy cropping or by having the model turn away or hide his face. The best of these achieve an extra aesthetic power but the results are sometimes annoyingly coy or schmaltzy.

Friend of Ansel Adams and Dorothea Lange, among others, White was firmly in the American naturalism school of photography but more than any of them, he used the camera to evoke the depths he perceived beneath the surface details, an almost direct parallel with Kerouac's prose efforts. He made that elusive goal even more difficult for himself by avoiding the photographic playacting of F. Holland Day or Baron von Gloeden and the visual tricks of George Platt Lynes's surrealism, though he occasionally used dramatically expressionistic lighting.

Despite his bohemianism (his male students often lived with him, though they did not necessarily sleep with him), White attained a respectability that enabled him to edit the influential photography magazine *Aperture* through the fifties and teach at the Rochester Institute and M.I.T., where he espoused his highly personal, even mystical approach to photography.

In many ways, he is the direct opposite of later gay photographers such as Robert Mapplethorpe,

who was a master at forcing the viewer to look for the universal in extremely personal gay imagery. Minor White used his genius to entice universal images—a winding road, a starched white shirt—into conveying a very personal (gay) sensibility.

F. Valentine Hooven III

Bibliography

Bunnell, Peter, ed. *Minor White: The Eye That Shapes*. Princeton, N.J.: Princeton University Art Museum, 1989.

Doty, Robert, ed. *Photography in America*. New York: Greenwich House, 1974.

Ellenzweig, Allen. *The Homoerotic Photograph: Male Images from Durieu/Delacroix to Mapplethorpe*. New York: Columbia University Press, 1992.

Waugh, Thomas. *Hard to Imagine*. New York: Columbia University Press, 1996.

See also Beat Generation; Day, F. Holland; Gloeden, Baron Wilhelm von; Lynes, George Platt; Mapplethorpe, Robert; Photography

White, Patrick (1912–1990)

In the Routledge *Encyclopedia of Post-Colonial Literatures in English*, Veronica Brady describes Patrick White as "a classic example of the writer as suspended man, suspended between belonging and alienation, the aesthetic and the civic, the national and international." Yet a central element of that "suspension," his sexuality, is mentioned only in an enigmatic reference to his lifelong partner, "Manoly Lascaris, the Greek friend who was to become the 'central mandala in my life's hitherto merry design.'" This is a typical Australian reaction to this most Australian of writers, who was always an alien. It began with his birth to Australian parents visiting England, White's first perverse reversal of colonization. His Nobel Prize for literature in 1973 remains the only one awarded to an Australian. In his modesh suburb of Sydney, it led to streets named "White" and "Nobel." But it also led to another famous writer lamenting that a "poofter" should so represent Australia.

White's fiction ranges widely but often centers on that alienation, of the individual who sees the errors of society but has neither the power nor the will to change them. Often the specific situation reflects his sexuality, as in *Voss* (1957). The title character represents German scientist Ludwig Leichhardt, lost while exploring Australia. The homosociality of the men on the expedition is thwarted by their Nietzschean obsessions, yet all are molded by their love for the primary superman, Voss. As they travel, Voss's thoughts mingle with those of his fiancée, Laura, left in Sydney, but their spiritual connection actually reinforces their gendered isolation, as the spinster wanders through a similarly homosocial desert of women. Neither of them fits the usual heterosexual mix: each must be with his or her gender, and yet who of the heteronormal can understand? In his autobiography, *Flaws in the Glass* (1981), White states, "Ambivalence has given me insights into human nature, denied, I believe, to those who are unequivocally male or female."

In *Memoirs of Many in One* (1986), this gender flux shapes the autobiography of a very strange woman, but it is *The Twyborn Affair* (1979) that can be seen as White's contribution to the brief list of classic homosexual texts. It begins with an exotic young woman, Eudoxia, living in France before World War I with her elderly Greek husband. By the second part Eudoxia has become the Australian war hero Eddie Twyborn, returning to be Australian gentry in the outback. In the finale, once again transformed and transported, the hero(ine) is Eadith, owner of a brothel in London. The time frame is the space of the greatest disruptions of Europe and the coming of age of white Australia. The journeys provide the back-and-forth experience of Australia's relationship with the Old World of Europe and of White himself. The sexuality morphs with the gender, from the monogamous young wife in France through the vitally homo- and heterosexual man in Australia, back to the celibate bawd in England.

These are but four of White's many complex works, most notably novels, but also stories and plays. None of the critical works to date sums up this oeuvre, but there is a sparkling biography by David Marr, who demonstrates that White, the acknowledged homosexual who rejected the ideology of gay liberation, had his own manner of not being in the closet: "Homosexuality was lived not debated by him" (526).   *Terry Goldie*

Bibliography

Marr, David. *Patrick White: A Life*. Sydney: Random House Australia, 1991.
White, Patrick. *Flaws in the Glass: A Self Portrait*. New York: Viking, 1981.

See also Australia; Australian Literature

Whitman, Walt (1819–1892)

Extending from one end of the nineteenth century to the other, Walt Whitman's long life can serve cultural historians of sexuality and "homosexuality" as a particularly sensitive barometer of changes in the sex-gender systems of the United States. Whitman grew up in and around New York City, the second-oldest son in a large and patriotic family, as the names of three of his brothers suggest: Thomas Jefferson Whitman, George Washington Whitman, Andrew Jackson Whitman. This may seem a relatively trivial detail about the family background of a figure so central not simply to American gay history but to American literary history as well. But we do well in thinking about Whitman's sexuality to recall that the first word in the first edition of *Leaves of Grass*—the poetic collection that became his forty-year, continuously revised magnum opus after its initial publication around July 4, 1855—is "America." Tracing a genealogy for Whitman's distinctly homoerotic American poetics, we might then usefully place ourselves around the Whitman supper table, where a glance in any direction would have driven home a reminder of the glorious pantheon of the young nation's greatest democratic heroes. And driving this political point "home" is precisely the point, for this conjunction of the nation's history at the domestic site of the family reminds us how Whitman's writings everywhere trouble our notions of the borders between the public and the private, between the national and the familial.

Written before recognizably modern sexualities coalesced around the now familiar binary homo-/hetero-, Whitman's poems register the broadest engagement with the world beyond the merely private, where "sexuality" and especially "homosexuality" will by century's end come to be situated. To begin by recalling the (to us) curiously public nature of Whitman's brothers' names may prepare us to uncover in his writings this same insistent linking of the public with the (ostensibly) private. This is, indeed, the most salient feature of the "Calamus" cluster of poems that Whitman first published in the 1860 (third) edition of *Leaves of Grass*, poems that virtually from the time of their appearance have been touchstones for a recognizably gay male literary heritage (though tellingly in England and Europe before the United States).

Published at the outset of the Civil War, "Calamus" chronicles the relationship between the speaker and his male "lover," and includes passages that portray explicitly erotic touching and kissing between two men for perhaps the first time in American literature. The poems are as concerned with these portrayals as with figuring the relations between this couple and other male couples and collectivities ("friends," "brothers," and "comrades") with which they might be allied, including the political bonds of comity and mutuality between the union of "States" just then coming apart. Thus sexual expression and "homosexuality" as figured in "Calamus" are insistently, simultaneously *public*: "It shall be customary in all directions, in the houses and streets, to see manly affection, / The departing brother or friend shall salute the remaining brother or friend with a kiss" ("Calamus No. 5" [1860]). The poems draw their most important consequences from these public dimensions.

This link between the sexual and the public is made only clearer when, in 1865, Whitman reshuffles sections and lines from "Calamus" into *Drum-Taps*, his Civil War poems. "[A]ffection shall solve the problems of freedom yet": this is one of the lines Whitman adapts from the earlier poetic cluster to the later one by adding the final, qualifying adverb to "Over the Carnage Rose Prophetic a Voice." The addition marks how the bloodiest war in history (to that time) has made nonsense out of any presumptions about the immediate saving power of comradeship, but leaves untouched the essential, overriding "orientation" that inextricably links the homosocial and homoerotic to the national, the political to the poetic.

The logic of all this mixing is precisely the same logic that makes it impossible simply to affix the label "homosexual" to either Whitman the man or his writings. Without question these writings reflect an urgent, desiring, and affectionate bond between men—the same bond evinced in the numerous ("marriage") photographs taken of Whitman and a range of "boy friends," starting in the 1860s (see Folsom in *Breaking Bounds*). But in their publicness, their insistence on a political dimension for these relationships and bonds, we see something different from what we might expect to find when Whitman's life and writings are aligned by calling either simply "homosexual." It is a difference we would not want to overlook.

Whitman's reply to Englishman John Addington Symonds's questions about the "Calamus" series, written near the end of his life, urges us in another way to pay attention to the kinds of chronological shifts inscribed by that adverb "yet." Here is the crux of the many questions Symonds asked the poet: "In your conception of Comradeship, do you contemplate the possible intrusion of those semi-sexual emotions and actions which no doubt do occur between men? I do not ask, whether you approve of them, or regard them as a necessary part of the relation? But I should much like to know whether *you are prepared to leave them to the inclinations and the conscience of the individuals concerned?*" (*Letters* 3:482; italics in original).

In Whitman's reply, the vigor of his apparent denial is matched by a curious temporal precision. Speaking of the "Calamus" cluster, Whitman writes: "I am fain to hope the pages themselves are not to be even mention'd for such gratuitous and quite at the time entirely undream'd & unreck'd [unreckoned] possibility of morbid inferences—wh'[ich] are disavow'd by me & seem damnable" (*Correspondence* 5:72–73). If Whitman seems eager to deny Symonds's "gay" reading of his poetry, what seems crucial here is his insistence—his awareness—about how much had changed even over the thirty years since "Calamus" first appeared. In this reading, Whitman denounces not the "intrusion of those semi-sexual emotions & actions" but rather the "morbid inferences" that have subsequently been attached—by Symonds, among others—to these affectionate, sustaining, and erotically charged bonds between men. Rather than a denunciation of his own or others' "homosexuality," Whitman's reply is best read as the poet's rejection of the new medical and legal models of same-sex affection that are by the time of his reply in 1890 increasingly prominent, and within which "morbidity" and "homosexuality" come to be synonymous. When "Calamus" was first composed and published, Whitman insists, such inferences were "at the time entirely undream'd & unreck'd."

Walt Whitman was indeed a pioneer—the father (the mother?) with Emily Dickinson of a modern idiom and form for American poetry, and a crucial starting place (among many) for writing the dignity and the possibility of gay men's lives. But he was also something different from the various "homosexual" progenies he nevertheless engendered, and with our eye set upon ongoing, "unreck'd possibilities," those differences seem as important as many similarities, imagined or otherwise.   *Jay Grossman*

Bibliography

Dowling, Linda. *Hellenism and Homosexuality in Victorian Oxford*. Ithaca, N.Y.: Cornell University Press, 1994.

Erkkila, Betsy. *Whitman the Political Poet*. New York: Oxford University Press, 1989.

Grossman, Jay, and Betsy Erkkila, eds. *Breaking Bounds: Whitman and American Cultural Studies*. New York: Oxford University Press, 1996.

Lynch, Michael. " 'Here is Adhesiveness': From Friendship to Homosexuality." *Victorian Studies* 29 (Autumn 1985): 67–96.

Martin, Robert K. *The Homosexual Tradition in American Poetry*. Austin: University of Texas Press, 1979.

Moon, Michael. *Disseminating Whitman: Revision and Corporeality in* Leaves of Grass. Cambridge, Mass.: Harvard University Press, 1991.

Shively, Charley, ed. *Calamus Lovers: Walt Whitman's Working-Class Camerados*. San Francisco: Gay Sunshine Press, 1987.

Symonds, John Addington. *Letters*. Herbert M. Schueller and Robert L. Peters, eds. 3 vols. Detroit: Wayne State University Press, 1967–1969.

Whitman, Walt. *The Correspondence*. Edward Haviland Miller, ed. 6 vols. New York: New York University Press, 1961–1977.

———. *Leaves of Grass*. 3d ed. Boston: Thayer and Eldridge, 1860. Facsimile ed. Ithaca, N.Y.: Cornell University Press, 1984.

See also Friendship; Sexology; Symonds, John Addington; United States; U.S. Literature; War

Wilde, Oscar Fingal O'Flahertie Wills (1854–1900)

Little would perhaps be remembered of Oscar Wilde were he not convicted for being a sodomite. Wilde's canon of writing, while not without merit, hardly merits the reverence paid by gay and lesbian history to this Irish writer. His theatrical oeuvre consists of nine plays, only one of which, *The Importance of Being Earnest,* receives regular performance. Of his prose, only a single novel, *The Picture of Dorian Gray,* and a few critical essays have sustained much discussion. Judged by his canon, Wilde probably deserves a place as a critic more than an artist. Popular in his own day, Wilde nonetheless seems like a minor canonical figure in retrospect. Yet the celebrated trial of 1895 that resulted in his conviction has solidified him as a key figure in a certain history of both homosexual identity and homophobic persecution. And thus while near his death, they serve as a fitting starting place for a discussion of his life.

The "trial" that resulted in Wilde's conviction was but one of three. The legal proceedings began on April 3, 1895, when the trial of Lord Queensberry for libel of Wilde began. Queensberry, dismayed at his son Alfred Douglas's association with Wilde, accused the playwright of "posing as a somdomite," in a famously misspelled note. The written note provided Wilde with a basis for a libel suit—probably more a means of ending the lord's longstanding harassment of him and Douglas than as a means of defending his honor. Wilde lost the trial, and Queensberry was exhonerated. But the tremendous public attention led to the crown's prosecution of Wilde. In effect, the inability of Wilde to prove that the accusation of being a sodomite was false opened the door for the crown to prove it was true. The second trial, which commenced on April 19, resulted in a hung jury; but a third trial, undertaken on May 22, resulted in a conviction on the charge of commission of acts of gross indecency in private with members of his own sex and the legally mandated punishment of two years at hard labor—a fate the trial judge described as "totally inadequate for a case like this."

What is particularly important in the Wilde trials is the state's active intervention in what began as a civil matter. The Queensberry libel case carried precious little reverberation for state safety. Only the public outcries resulting from the trial motivated state prosecutors to capitalize on the scenario. And in this sense, Wilde's trials mark a dubious milestone in legal history, for they in many ways denote one of the primary modern examples of the government capitalizing on public homophobia to win political clout.

But there is actually a great deal more to Wilde's life, much of which remains underexamined owing to the eclipsing power of his trials. Wilde was born October 16, 1854, at 21 Westland Row, in Dublin, Ireland. Although he is frequently described as an English writer, Wilde sprung from a strong tradition of Irish nationalism. His father, Sir William Wilde, was a doctor well respected for his charitable work. He was unusually well-to-do for a physician and devoted much of his free time to the study of science and archaeology. He blended his considerable academic talents with his passion for Ireland and specialized in producing descriptive illustrations of contemporary and historical Ireland from a scientific standpoint. Wilde's mother was the notoriously free-spirited Jane Francesca Agnes Lady Wilde, who wrote passionate nationalist verse and prose under the pen name Speranza. Like Sir Wilde, she was a student of Irish folklore, and she also was an early figure in the women's rights movement. She was the grandniece of the Reverend Charles Maturin, author of *Melmoth the Wanderer*—a lineage that later prompted Oscar to take on the name Sebastian Melmoth when he left England after the trials.

Wilde's early indoctrination in socialism and politics is clearly visible in his writings, yet these themes are frequently overlooked because of his subsequent infamy as a sodomite. One of Wilde's earliest and most serious essays is "The Soul of Man Under Socialism," in which he advocates the abandonment of private property as a means of alleviating what he perceives to be the greatest social evil, property. Probably while at Trinity College, Dublin, he wrote an award-winning essay, "The Rise of Historical Criticism," which examines the role of classical scholarship in pointing the way to new directions of thought and social order. Clearly the intellectual pursuits of his parents were of no small importance to Wilde, for both these early inquiries directly parallel those of his parents.

The Wilde most remembered by modern readers—the Wilde most congruent with the sodomite—is the aesthetician. And this Wilde finds his genesis at Oxford. After immigrating to England, Wilde matriculated at Magdalen College, Oxford, in 1878. In his course of studies Wilde found himself deeply influenced by two conflicting doctrines—the moral precepts of John Ruskin and the epicurean aestheticism of Walter Pater. Wilde's own eventual stance, as witnessed in critical tracts such as "The Critic as Artist" and "The Decay of Lying," is that the aesthetic itself is a moral stance, as it can produce pure beauty unencumbered by the exigencies of the current moment. In a sort of utopian style, Wilde eventually posited the beautiful object as the disembodied point that enables thought outside of the imperfections of today. To paraphrase one of his famous epigraphs, art can create the perfection that life can then imitate. Even in his "purely" aesthetic phase, vestiges of his family's social activism are present.

Wilde's life after college progressed quickly. He married Constance Lloyd in 1884 and sired two sons. In 1886 he began what appears to be his first significant homosexual relationship with a young Canadian, Robbie—who eventually became his literary executor after his death. In 1891 he met Lord Alfred Douglas, the young man who eventually led to his court trials. In 1888 Wilde began his primary period of literary achievement and in a scant five years produced all his major works except for *An Ideal Husband* and *The Importance of Being Earnest,* both of which he wrote in 1895. Unfortunately, his decline was as quick as his rise, and in 1900, exiled in Paris, physically decimated from his hard labor and practically alone, he died.

Gregory W. Bredbeck

Bibliography

Cohen, Ed. *Talk on the Wilde Side: Toward a Genealogy of Discourse on Male Homosexuality.* New York: Routledge, 1993.

Ellman, Richard. *Oscar Wilde.* New York: Viking, 1987.

———. *Oscar Wilde: A Collection of Critical Essays.* Englewood Cliffs, N.J.: Prentice-Hall, 1969.

Gagnier, Regina. *Idylls of the Marketplace: Oscar Wilde and the Victorian Public.* Stanford, Calif.: Stanford University Press, 1986.

Hyde, H. Montgomery. *The Trials of Oscar Wilde.* New York: Dover, 1962.

See also Aestheticism; Dandy; Decadence; England; English Literature; Ireland; Pater, Walter Horatio; Sodomy; Sodomy Trials

Williams, Tennessee (Thomas Lanier) (1911–1983)

Although Tennessee Williams is known primarily as a playwright, one can fully understand him as a gay writer only if one also knows his fiction and poetry. Williams's dramas of the 1940s and 1950s demonstrate the playwright's courageous but cautious insertion of "the love that dare not speak its name" into his plays, from Blanche's description of her discovery that her husband was "a degenerate" in *A Streetcar Named Desire* (1948) to the Baron Charlus in *El Camino Real* (1953) to Brick's discovery that his best friend, Skipper, loved him in *Cat on a Hot Tin Roof* (1955) to Sebastian's pederasty in *Suddenly Last Summer* (1958). Except for the Baron Charlus in the fantastic *El Camino Real*, the gay characters in Williams's major plays are relegated to the exposition, dead before the opening curtain. He inserted homosexuality into mainstream Broadway drama without putting gay characters on stage. It was easy, if clumsy, for the film studios to excise homosexuality altogether in their film versions, making the plays safe, if somewhat incoherent (though it was the films that made Williams a millionaire). The short stories written during this period offer vivid glimpses into the ways in which Williams's homosexuality merged with his other major obsessions: death, devouring, delinquency, defiance of social convention. Some of them, particularly "One Arm," "Desire and the Black Masseur," "Hard Candy," and "The Mysteries of the Joy Rio," are among the classics of gay short fiction. And the poetry often depicts the loneliness of anonymous homosexual encounters.

Williams's life and work merge in complex ways. He was fond of asserting that he was his central female characters: Alma (*Summer and Smoke, Eccentricities of a Nightingale*), Blanche (*A Streetcar Named Desire*). Anyone who has studied biographies of Williams could also assert that his neurotic but powerful women, the most fascinating, complex female characters created by an American playwright, are projections of his mother and sister, the two most important personal forces in Williams's life.

Williams was born in his grandfather's Episcopal rectory in Columbus, Mississippi. His mother was a powerful if prim woman who found sex to be a traumatic event. Even when she lived in Ohio during her teenage years, she affected an exaggerated version of the Southern belle. His father, C. C. Williams, was a hard-drinking Southern "good ol' boy" driven off in part by the mother's frigidity and in part by his own love for long distances. When the parents were together, turbulence was inevitable. C.C. did not care much for his firstborn, Rose (b. 1909), nor for Tom, whom he called "Miss Nancy." His affection was saved for the more conventional younger son, Dakin (b. 1919). The rectory provided much happier memories for Tom and Rose than their parents' home. The unhappiness was exacerbated when the family moved north to St. Louis in 1918 when C.C. was made a sales manager of the International Shoe Company. The family was not suited to apartment dwelling in a big city and the children suffered mockery for the exaggerated Southern mannerisms they learned from Edwina.

Tom began writing as a teenager and his first story was published in *Weird Tales* magazine when he was sixteen. From then on he saw writing as a salvation and an outlet for his obsessions and fantasies. He began studying journalism at the University of Missouri, but his father pulled him out during his junior year and put him to work at the shoe company. Tom's grades were mediocre, but C.C. may have been forced to bring Tom home because of the Depression. The five years of life at home and in the International Shoe Company (1932–1937) are depicted in Williams's first great success, *The Glass Menagerie* (1945), with one significant change from biographical fact: the father is merely a picture on the wall rather than a harsh presence. Thanks to some financial assistance from his grandparents, Tom began studying drama at the University of Iowa in 1937. At the same time, his sister, Rose, began her descent into madness and institutionalization and, in 1943, she had a lobotomy. Tom's close identification with his sister may have been because of his own crippling anxiety attacks and extreme hypochondria. In his grand neurotic women, his and Rose's psychological pathologies merge. The ultimate horror is institutionalization (*Streetcar*) or lobotomy (*Suddenly Last Summer*).

Williams claims to have remained a virgin until he was twenty-seven, the year he finished his formal education. From that point on (1938), he led an itinerant life as one of "the fugitive kind" and an active sex life filled with the hustlers he wrote about in his short stories, "the kindness of strangers," and the exploitation of cynical young men on the make. His one serious relationship was with Frank Merlo, a loyal companion to the less steadfast writer for over a decade.

Williams's peak years as a writer were from 1945 until 1961. While not all of the plays he wrote during those years were artistic or commercial successes, he did give the American theater some of its greatest plays, from *The Glass Menagerie* to *The Night of the Iguana*.

After the early 1960s Williams's life and writing deteriorated. Merlo, whom Williams had left years before, died of lung cancer in 1958. The guilt and grief signaled an end to what was left of the writer's personal and artistic control. He continued to write, but the plays lacked artistic discipline or were such odd expressions of the writer's psychic state that audiences were baffled and critics enraged. To some extent Williams's loss of his audience and hostility from his critics was the result of his rejection of psychological realism, the dominant mode of American drama at the time, for a freer, more poetic, at times absurdist theatrical expression. Williams always had an uneasy relationship with realism and was always more of a dramatic poet. Some of the plays written during his later years bear close examination, particularly the first version of *The Milk Train Doesn't Stop Here Anymore* (1963). Some of the other works merely show how addled the playwright had become.

The excessive drug use during this period exacerbated Williams's tendency to paranoia. In 1969, his suicidal state led his brother to institutionalize him. The withdrawal from the drugs led to two heart attacks. Williams lived on, continually attempting a comeback as a playwright at a time when serious Broadway theater was no longer economically viable. In the years following the Stonewall rebellion (1969), Williams tried to be part of gay liberation by coming out in public statements and in his *Memoirs* (1972). Anyone who had read his nondramatic work written twenty years before was not surprised. Nor had Williams ever tried to hide his homosexuality. But his post-Stonewall expressions lacked the genius of his earlier fictional work.

Williams died at the age of seventy-three in a New York hotel room from choking on the plastic cap of a medicine bottle. Since then, his work continues to be revived and a generation of gay scholars and critics have studied Tennessee Williams as one of America's foremost gay writers.   *John M. Clum*

Bibliography

Leverich, Lyle. *Tom: The Unknown Tennessee Williams*. New York: Crown, 1995.

Roundané, Matthew. *The Cambridge Companion to Tennessee Williams*. New York: Cambridge University Press, 1997.

Savran, David. *Communists, Cowboys, and Queers: The Politics of Masculinity in the Work of Arthur Miller and Tennesee Williams*. Minneapolis: University of Minnesota Press, 1992.

Spoto, Donald. *The Kindness of Strangers: The Life of Tennessee Williams*. Boston: Little, Brown, 1985.

See also Film; U.S. Literature

Williams, William Carlos (1883–1963)

In answer to the question Why do you go on living? posed by *The Little Review*, Williams replied, "Because I have an enjoyable body for my pleasure." At age forty-six, Williams was affirming the guiding principle of his writing that can be found in his early Imagist lyrics all the way through to his last major work, Book Five of his epic poem *Paterson* (1958), with its famous injunction: "Paterson, / keep your pecker up / whatever the detail!"

Born of scrupulously Victorian parents and growing up in the suburban normalcy of Rutherford, New Jersey, Williams's life-affirming belief in the pleasures of the body did not come easily. Many critics trace his poetics of the body to his career as a pediatrician, which he practiced in Rutherford for most of his life. However, he was ambivalent toward his hometown and his chosen career, viewing them in the obscurity of his youth and middle age as obstacles to his writing, then viewing them more positively with recognition and old age.

A vital influence and support to his early writing was the bohemian community of New York's nearby Greenwich Village. The Village provided a unique community of artists, freethinkers, and political radicals united against what they saw as a common enemy, America's puritanical middle class. In this context, Williams's early poetics of the body takes shape in works with tellingly belligerent titles, such as *Tempers* (1913), *Al Que Quiere!* (To Him Who Wants It, 1917), and *Sour Grapes* (1921). Then, in 1923, Williams's art takes a dramatic turn with a prose-and-poetry hybrid, *Spring and All*. Transcending the relatively limited politics of antipuritanism and imagism, *Spring and All* eloquently expresses Williams's theory of "contact"—a call for the American artist to put a thorough familiarity with the materials of his or her local environment before (European) theories of art. *Spring and All* shows how Williams's notion of contact could subtly comprehend America's political, environmental, sexual, and artistic forces, while arguing for their full release.

Williams moved on to other terms (most notably, objectivism in the 1930s and the variable foot in the 1950s), but whatever the terms or the genre, his best writing reflects a Whitmanian appreciation of the body's joys caught within a political complex. As early as 1917, and steadfastly thereafter, Williams was telling American poets that "we cannot advance until we have grasped Whitman and then built upon him." Not until the Beat revival of Whitman in the 1950s would a significant number of American poets and readers be able to appreciate Williams's advice. Williams's modernist revision of Whitman was a crucial aspect of the support and guidance he gave to post–World War II American poets. In particular, his relationship with Allen Ginsberg has had a lasting impact on the history of American poetry. Through their respective modernist and postmodernist revisions of Whitman, American poetry is left with a Whitmanian tradition that cannot be ignored.   *Sergio Rizzo*

Bibliography

Williams, William Carlos. "America, Whitman, and the Art of Poetry." *Poetry Journal* 8, no. 1 (November 1917): 27–36.

———. *Paterson.* New York: New Directions, 1963.

———. "Questionnaire." *Little Review* 12, no. 2 (May 1929): 87–88.

See also Ginsberg, Allen; U.S. Literature: Contemporary Gay Writing; Whitman, Walt

Wilson, Sir Angus (1913–1991)

One of Sir Angus Wilson's triumphs was to pioneer an open, truthful depiction of homosexuals within society without special pleading, at a time when his sexual temperament made him technically still a criminal. He was the first openly to depict a homosexual subculture in Britain, yet he is much more than a gay novelist.

He was the youngest of five sons, born a Johnstone-Wilson to a lowlands Scottish father living off steadily dwindling rents and his South African wife's money. Two of his brothers worked for a time as homosexual prostitutes. Middle-class poverty and elements of raffish psychological risk and danger fill his work. At the British library where he worked in 1945, he met Tony Garrett. They became partners in an exemplary, stable relationship for nearly fifty years. In 1960 homophobic gossip forced Garrett's resignation from the Probation Service, and Wilson campaigned thereafter for homosexual law reform. Many younger writers profited from their help.

His first novel, *Hemlock and After* (1952), depicted English life as dominated by a comically grotesque blackmailing procuress dealing in underage children of both sexes. Bernard Sand is the Socratic fifty-seven-year-old novelist of the title, and though he appears a "respectable" father of two, his marriage is troubled. Late in life he has started to have homosexual love affairs, first with stage designer Terence Lambert, who is socially on the make. Terence's *arrivisme* is benignly focused; but the degrading spite, jealousy, and cruelty of the "butterfly-spiv" world he formerly moved in is not. Sand's current ephebe is the innocent, kindly Eric Craddock. Bernard undergoes a moral and spiritual crisis when he witnesses the arrest of a young man who tries to pick him up in Leicester Square. He feels a deep, sadistic excitement that unsettles his self-image and causes his breakdown, despair, and, later, death. Fifteen years before homosexuality was decriminalized, Wilson deals with homosexuality with courageous assurance and innovative moral relaxation in a book concerned throughout with the necessary dangers of truth telling.

In *The Middle Age of Mrs. Eliot* (1958) and *Late Call* (1964), he aims to look directly at the psychological effects of loss of caste and status, and within the sex that starts at a disadvantage, the "poor bitch-sex that had been for ever pushed around by brute force." Homosexuality is incidental to this major theme. Both Mrs. Eliot and her gay brother, David, have to cope with losing their partners, and Meg is to cope with greater courage and openness. In *Late Call* the apparently well-adjusted Ray moves to London, where he can express his homosexuality with less fear of legal prosecution. This excellent novel predates the 1967 liberalization of laws against homosexuality, and Ray's gay friend Wilf Corney is to gas himself, probably because of blackmail.

No Laughing Matter (1967) has a huge cast and range. Its presentation of Marcus Matthews, flamboyant aesthete and picture collector, embattled with his cruel and spiteful mother, whom he partly resembles, is remarkable. The play debates escaping the past as a condition for staying open for change, and Marcus gains in moral stature throughout. "How novelists do love to romanticize pansies!" Marcus comments. Against type, Marcus has a good war as an adjutant, and learns both political and business acumen. *As If by Magic* (1973) has a leading gay character in Hamo Langmuir, and Wilson depicts his sexual utopianism, as well as that of his goddaughter, engaged in a ménage à trois. Pedophilia is used as a figure for neocolonialism in this ambitious and innovative work.

Margaret Drabble depicted Wilson as a role model, both in life and letters. "If some men weren't really 'men,' then, thank God, maybe women didn't have to be women. Angus extended the map of the human. . . . Angus's redefinition of the homosexual and his exploration of homosexual society were to lead to a redefinition of society at large" (Drabble 182–183).

Peter J. Conradi

Bibliography

Conradi, Peter. *Angus Wilson.* London: Northcote House, 1997.

Drabble, Margaret. *Angus Wilson: A Biography* London: Secker and Warburg, 1995. Reprint London: Minerva, 1996.

Wilson, Angus. *No Laughing Matter*. 1967. Harmondsworth U.K.: Penguin, 1969.

See also Colonialism; English Literature; Fiction; Pederasty

Wilson, Lanford (1937–)

Lanford Wilson was born in Lebanon, Missouri, the town that would later become the setting for his Talley trilogy. His parents divorced when he was five. In 1956, Wilson went to San Diego to visit his father, who had resettled and started another family there. This ill-fated visit was later dramatized in Wilson's play *Lemon Sky* (1970). Wilson briefly attended classes at San Diego State and University the University of Chicago before moving to New York City in 1962. He soon connected with the Greenwich Village theater scene, and his earliest plays were produced at the Caffe Cino and the La Mama Experimental Theater Club.

He cofounded the Circle Repertory Company in 1969 with Marshall Mason, Rob Thirkield, and Tanya Berezin. Mason has directed the premieres of Wilson's plays ever since, constituting one of the longest, most successful, and celebrated collaborations between playwright and director in the history of American theater. Wilson's first work to appear on Broadway was *The Gingham Dog* (1968), and his plays have continued to appear there regularly ever since. Wilson won the Pulitzer Prize in 1980 for *Talley's Folly.*

Wilson is an exceptionally prolific playwright who has taken on a variety of subjects. Thus, direct depictions of the lives and situations of gay men have been only a small part of his dramatic oeuvre. *The Madness of Lady Bright* (1964) featured a lonely, demented drag queen as its title character. Several gay characters can be found in the large cast of *Balm in Gilead* (1965). The one-act *A Poster of the Cosmos* (1987) has as its only character a gay man who is interrogated by an offstage policeman.

Wilson's earliest full-length play to focus on gay concerns is *Lemon Sky,* an autobiographical play that tells the story of a young man who must come to grips with rejection by his father as both become aware of the son's homosexuality. *Lemon Sky* is a memory play indebted to Tennessee Williams's *The Glass Menagerie*, told in retrospect by Alan, whose life is much like Wilson's own. (As a young man, Wilson performed the role of Tom Wingfield in a production of *The Glass Menagerie*.)

Fifth of July (1978), Wilson's only other major play to focus on the lives of gay men, is the last part of Wilson's trilogy about the Talley family. In *Fifth of July*, a gay Vietnam veteran and his lover host a weekend reunion of family and friends. *Fifth of July* is influenced by two of Anton Chekhov's plays, *The Cherry Orchard* and *Uncle Vanya,* and its plot involves Ken Talley's efforts to get on with his life in the aftermath of his terrible injuries from the war and his disappointment in the failure of the social activism of the 1960s to create appreciable improvement in the world of the 1970s. Though the play presents a nostalgic view of the 1960s as a time of great hope and progress—in contrast to the materialistic and aimless 1970s—the play ends on a hopeful note as Ken returns to work as a teacher and as the family unit reasserts itself as a vehicle for caring and support of its members.

Though gay characters occasionally appear in Wilson's other plays (e.g., Larry in *Burn This*, 1987), the majority of Wilson's plays center on other topics that confront the American middle class.

D.S. Lawson

Bibliography

Barnett, Gene A. *Lanford Wilson*. Boston: Twayne, 1987.

Bryer, Jackson R. *Lanford Wilson: A Casebook.* New York: Garland, 1994.

Busby, Mark. *Lanford Wilson.* Boise, Idaho: Boise State University Press, 1987.

Dean, Anne M. *Discovery and Invention: The Urban Plays of Lanford Wilson.* Rutherford, N.J.: Fairleigh Dickinson University Press, 1994.

Lawson, D. S. "Lanford Wilson." In *The Gay and Lesbian Literary Heritage.* Claude J. Summers, ed. New York: Henry Holt, 1995, 754–55.

See also Caffe Cino; Williams, Tennessee

Winckelmann, Johann Joachim (1717–1768)

Art historian, archaeologist, and chief librarian of the Vatican, German scholar Johann Joachim Winckelmann infused his influential vision of Greek antiquity with all the telltale signs of homoerotic desire. Born in Stendal, he overcame penurious conditions to become a prominent European intellectual. After a haphazard university education, he took a position as a private tutor until he was appointed headmaster of a Latin school in Seehausen (1743–1748). His classical erudition won him acclaim and he was appointed librarian to Count von Bünau near Dresden. It was in Dresden that he encountered for the first time plaster casts of the ancient statues about which he would soon write with passion and flair. It was here also that he became acquainted with Vatican representatives who enticed him to Rome, where both his aesthetic aspirations and his erotic desire might more readily be satisfied. Of course, the condition for enjoying Roman patronage was conversion to Catholicism.

Winckelmann's first publication, *Reflections on the Imitation of the Greek Works in Painting and Sculpture*, appeared a few months before he left Germany for Rome in 1755. *Reflections* became a manifesto that inspired artistic production, aesthetic theory, and a consuming enthusiasm for Greece in Germany for the next fifty years. At the center of this vision of Greek antiquity stood the figure of Laocoön, the statue he would soon see in the Belvedere Courtyard in the Vatican. Once in Rome, Winckelmann became acquainted with German painter Anton Rafael Mengs, who introduced him to much of the painting and sculpture to be seen there. He enjoyed the support of a succession of patrons and particularly thrived in the company of Cardinal Albani. The culture of Rome allowed him an unusual degree of aesthetic and erotic liberty. His published letters give plentiful evidence of romantic friendships and liaisons with Italian castrati and other youths. His closest German and Roman friends were in no doubt with respect to his sexual preferences, and, at times he even boasted of his conquests. Winckelmann's major work, *History of the Art of Antiquity*, was published in 1764. Showing the fruits of his sustained daily engagement with ancient artifacts and texts, *History* is a compendium of numerous individual artworks, placing them in the service of aesthetic, art-historical, and cultural observation and theorization. Whereas *Reflections* featured Laocoön as its centerpiece, *History* more openly describes an eroticized ideal of male beauty. Among the new works he discusses is a fresco of Zeus kissing Ganymede, a perfect instance of his homoerotic aesthetics—too perfect, for he was still to discover that the Ganymede was a forgery specifically designed to deceive him. By 1768 Winckelmann had achieved the pinnacle of fame. Many luminaries and dignitaries made a point of visiting him. The royal courts in Venice and Berlin had long invited him to receive their acknowledgment of his service, and he finally agreed. Once north of the Alps, Winckelmann was stricken by paranoia and parted company from Casanova's brother, an artist who would become director of a German art academy.

While returning to Rome, Winckelmann was murdered in Trieste. A novella by Gerhart Hauptmann offers a splendid if speculative interpretation of the event. For many, beginning after his death and continuing to the present, Winckelmann has been a model for gay identification. In both the manner and incidents of his life, as narrated in early accounts such as Goethe's "Winckelmann" and in the lush prose describing favorite statues, gay men found a language for their desire. At the same time, many informed gays and probing scholars have long known that the basis of the classical aesthetics inspired by Winckelmann and deemed central to Western cultural traditions is crucially inflected by Winckelmann's own homoerotic gaze.　　　　　　　　　*Simon Richter*

Bibliography

Potts, Alex. *Flesh and the Ideal: Winckelmann and the Origins of Art History*. New Haven, Conn.: Yale University Press, 1994.

Richter, Simon, and Patrick McGrath. "Representing Homosexuality: Winckelmann and the Aesthetics of Friendship." *Monatshefte* 86 (1994): 45–58.

See also Art History; Ganymede; German Literature; Goethe, Johannes Wolfgang von; Greece; Mediterranean

Wittgenstein, Ludwig Josef Johann (1889–1951)

Born to wealthy Austrian parents of Jewish ancestry, Wittgenstein grew up in a milieu of privilege in a family that cultivated the society of artists and musicians. At the age of fourteen, Wittgenstein was sent to the Realschule in Linz, where Adolf Hitler was also a pupil. He went on to study engineering in Berlin before moving to Manchester, England, in 1908, where he became immersed in research into aerodynamics. Developing an interest in mathematics, he became aware of the work of Bertrand Russell on mathematical logic. This led to a move to Cambridge, where Russell was based; the older man soon became convinced that Wittgenstein would make the next big step in logic.

At Cambridge, Wittgenstein was introduced to the Apostles, who at that time included John Maynard Keynes and Lytton Strachey, but he was never comfortable with the elitism of the group. Moreover, despite his obvious brilliance, he felt unable to write down his theories. Feeling incapable of work-

Wing at Cambridge, he retreated to Norway to continue his work in isolation.

At the outbreak of World War I, however, he enlisted for active service. During the war, Wittgenstein developed his ideas on logic, which now took a more mystical turn, and his *Tractatus Logico-Philosophicus* was published in Germany in 1921 and in London the following year.

After giving away his private fortune and working as an elementary schoolteacher, he was eventually persuaded to return to Cambridge, where, in 1939, he became professor of philosophy. During World War II he worked as a hospital porter. In 1947 he resigned his chair, and he died of cancer in 1951.

At the time of its publication, Wittgenstein believed that the *Tractatus* solved the problems of philosophy and, therefore, represented its end. Over time, however, he began to adopt a different position. These changes are recorded in *The Blue and Brown Books* and *Philosophical Investigations*.

The *Tractatus* was concerned with the limits of language. It argued that the world consists of simple facts, and that language states those facts pictorially. Any other use of language—including that of philosophy and the *Tractatus* itself—leads to nonsense. But later, Wittgenstein conceded that there is a variety of language purposes, or "games," apart from picturing. He also questioned the tendency to seek the common feature of all things called by the same name, contending that there need be only a family resemblance. Wittgenstein's influence on modern philosophy has been considerable.

The question of Wittgenstein's sexual life has been controversial. A storm followed the publication of a biography by W. W. Bartley III in 1973, which claimed that during 1919 Wittgenstein regularly consorted with "rough young men." In an afterword to the second edition, Bartley discusses the controversy, accusing Wittgenstein's executors of a cover-up and the academic establishment of prudishness and homophobia. A later biographer, Ray Monk, while doubting Bartley's evidence, has established that Wittgenstein's notebooks reveal his love for David Pinsent, Francis Skinner, and Ben Richards, and that his love for men was sexually consummated. Indeed, he and Skinner lived together as a couple for more than a year.

Some have attempted to link Wittgenstein's philosophy and his sexuality. His emphasis on the limits of speech, for instance, could be connected to the idea of the love that dare not speak its name.

Russell Crofts

Bibliography

Bartley, W. W. III. *Wittgenstein*. London: Open Court, 1985.

Monk, Ray. *Ludwig Wittgenstein: The Duty of Genius*. London: Jonathan Cape, 1990.

See also Keynes, John Maynard; Strachey, (Giles) Lytton

Wittman, Carl (1943–1986)

Carl Wittman—activist, folk dancer, red-diaper baby—was born in New Jersey and attended Swathmore College. As a campus leader, he spent summers in Tennessee supporting black civil rights, wrote for the student newspaper and organized antisegregation demonstrations in Chester, Pennsylvania, and Cambridge, Maryland. After student and faculty arrests, the dean called Carl into her office on the afternoon of November 22, 1963, to expel him but was distracted by news of the assassination of President Kennedy. Wittman graduated in June 1964.

The Swathmore Political Action Committee provided a model for the Students for a Democratic Society (SDS). Joining the national council in 1963, Wittman played a prominent role in SDS until his departure in 1966. In September 1963, SDS established the Economic and Action Research Project (ERAP), based on his paper "Students and Economic Action," which was further elaborated with Tom Hayden in "An Interracial Movement of the Poor?" They called for nonhierarchical organizing: "We are people and we work with people." Wittman joined the Newark SDS project and recalled that "Tom Hayden confidently announced that there was to be no homosexuality or marijuana on our community organizing project, and then proceeded to borrow my room to bed down with his latest woman, leaving me stunned and terrified." In 1965, Wittman began another SDS project in Hoboken.

While listed as a speaker for the SDS-affiliated Radical Education Project during 1967, Wittman went to the West Coast and settled into a mixed San Francisco commune of Resistance (an antiwar group), enjoyed the psychedelic revolution, and raised money hustling. During 1968 he organized war resistance events in British Columbia, Oregon, and Washington state.

Although closeted about his love for other men, Carl had begun an active homosexual life at fourteen. "Kids can take care of themselves," he wrote, "and are sexual beings way earlier than we'd like to admit. Those of us who began cruising in early adolescence know this, and we were doing the cruising, not being debauched by dirty old men." Wittman came out in an antiwar magazine ("Waves of Resistance"), where he held that resisting heterosexuality was related to resisting war.

Wittman was part of a gay contingent at a San Francisco demonstration in May 1969 against the States Steamship Line, a Vietnam war supply carrier. His essay "Refugees from Amerika: A Gay Manifesto" was written after the steamship demonstration—but before Stonewall (June 27–28, 1969)—and was first published late in 1969. Providing an ideology for radial gay males and widely reprinted by gay and left movement groups, the manifesto never became dogma: "The gay liberation movement is in its polymorphous, unbureaucratic, anarchistic form," Wittman wrote gleefully in 1970.

In 1969 Wittman acquired land in Wolf Creek, Oregon, with his lover Stevens McClave, who committed suicide in 1974. Between 1973 and Wittman's death, he and Allan Troxler were lovers. In autumn 1974, the first issue of *RFD* appeared with a cover by Troxlor and an article by Wittman. *RFD* promised "to build some sense of community among rural gay people."

Believing in "the transcendent importance of art in social change," Wittman followed his interest in English and Scottish country dance and music, which he taught at Rogue Community College in Oregon and at Duke University in North Carolina. In 1978 he wrote "A Report on One Group's Pursuit of English Dancing in a Non-Sexist Context." *Sun Assembly* is a posthumous collection of his teachings about teaching and dancing gender-free seventeenth- and eighteenth-century Scottish and English dances.

In 1981 Wittman moved to Durham, North Carolina, where he worked in the Durham Food Co-Op; was a leader in Citizens for a Safer East Durham, which closed the Armageddon Chemical plant; and helped write Durham's *Convention Center: In Whose Interest?* while codirector of the N.C. Public Interest Research Group in 1981–1982. He was one of the founders of the Durham Lesbian and Gay Health Project and was active in AIDS work. He himself died January 22, 1986, after he rejected hospital AIDS treatment and chose to end his life in dignity among friends at home. In choosing the time of his death, he demonstrated his 1963 principle that people must be "confident that they have some control over the decisions which affect their lives."

Charles Shively

Bibliography

Wittman, Carl. "Us and the New Left." *Fag Rag* 22/23 (Fall 1978): 22.

———. "Waves of Resistance." *Liberation* 13 (November 1968): 29–33.

See also Gay Left; Gay Liberation; Journalism; Stonewall; Student Organizations

Wojnarowicz, David (1954–1992)

David Wojnarowicz was a New York City photographer, painter, film and video maker, writer, and activist who died of complications from AIDS. Despite having been an abused child and living on the streets, Wojnarowicz became a highly educated, well-read, and talented artist who directly invested his art with the personal and public politics of an angry gay man who was dying of AIDS. Wojnarowicz refused to separate his desire from his illness, his personal life from public politics, and his artwork from governmental and religious homophobia. He was a close friend of many notable New York City artists of the 1980s and 1990s. In 1986 he collaborated on a film with Karen Finley (*You Killed Me First,* directed by Richard Kern), and was close to author Fran Lebowitz, photographer Peter Hujar, performance artist Kiki Smith, and photographer Nan Goldin.

Wojnarowicz is perhaps best known for his part in the fight against religious conservative attacks on the funding decisions of the National Endowment for the Arts. In 1990, at the height of battles about funding of the federal agency, Wojnarowicz and the Center for Constitutional Rights sued Donald Wildmon and the American Family association for illegally appropriating Wojnarowicz's artwork from the *Tongues of Flame* catalog. Wildmon had taken the artist's photographs out of context and distributed them to the media and members of Congress as examples of publicly funded "pornography." The artist was awarded only token damages of $1.00 but scored a moral victory over specious attacks by religious conservatives on contemporary gay and lesbian art.

Demonstrating an uncanny sense of the postmodern and mythopoetic, Wojnarowicz juxtaposed explicitly sexual photography, anatomical diagrams, animal imagery, and institutional symbols in his photography, collages, paintings and multimedia works. Rather than merely chronicling or recording his life as a gay man with AIDS, Wojnarowicz developed a highly personal iconography that engaged illness, politics, and homophobia in a poetic and visceral imagery. The resulting works resonate far beyond his individual life and articulate the anger and frustration of an entire generation of gay men whose sexual desires ran up against AIDS, ignorance, homophobia, and unfeeling religious and governmental institutions.   *Michael J. Murphy*

Bibliography

"David Wojnarowicz: Brush Fires in the Social Landscape." *Aperture* 137 (Fall 1994).

David Wojnarowicz: Painting and Sculptures. Exhibition catalog. Philadelphia: Institute of Contemporary Art, University of Pennsylvania, 1986.

Rose, Matthew. "David Wojnarowicz: An Interview." *Arts Magazine* 62 (May 1988): 60–65.

See also AIDS; AIDS Literature; Censorship; Fiction; Hujar, Peter; Photography

Wolfenden Report

The Wolfenden Report, officially the *Report of the Committee on Homosexual Offences and Prostitution* (1957), was a British government report that recommended the limited decriminalization of male homosexual acts committed by consenting adults in private. It was commissioned in 1954 amid rising public concern, especially in the popular press, about the perceived social problem of homosexuality and "vice" in general. Meanwhile, a number of high-profile court cases in the early 1950s, including the convictions for homosexual offenses of Lord Montagu of Beaulieu and the actor Sir John Gielgud, had increased pressure for law reform.

Under the chairmanship of John Wolfenden, vice-chancellor of Reading University, a committee made up of academics, lawyers, doctors, politicians, and clergymen met over a period of three years and took evidence from more than 200 individuals and organizations, including the police, the prison service, women's organizations, the probation service, and churches. The Committee's mandate was to review the law and its operation relating to homosexuality and prostitution and to recommend any changes it thought desirable. As the law stood, prosecution was possible under a number of statutes for any same-sex acts committed by males in public or private, making homosexual men vulnerable to blackmail and police harassment. Female homosexuality was not in itself a criminal offense and was therefore outside the scope of the committee's investigation.

The committee's final proposals were driven by its overall view that the function of the criminal law was to protect vulnerable members of society, including the young, and to preserve public order. Matters of private morality should not be the law's business. Its main recommendations, therefore, were that private homosexual acts between consenting males over the age of twenty-one be decriminalized and that the maximum penalties for homosexual offenses be amended. On prostitution, the report also drew a distinction between public decency and private morality, suggesting that the penalties for so-called "street offenses" be increased to reduce soliciting in public places. New offenses to criminalize male prostitution were also proposed.

On publication, the report generated widespread controversy, dividing press and public opinion. One newspaper columnist, furious at the proposed changes to the laws on homosexuality, described it as "The Pansies' Charter." However, although the report's recommendations were in some respects liberalizing, its stated aim was not to condone homosexual activity but rather to regulate it more effectively and, in the case of private sexual behavior, by means other than the criminal law. Thus the report condemned homosexuality as immoral and damaging to individuals and urged continued research into its causes and potential cures, such as psychiatric treatment and hormone therapy. Nevertheless, the report proved too bold for the government of the day. Although many of the proposals on prostitution were implemented almost immediately, most of the Wolfenden recommendations on homosexual law reform were not enacted until the Sexual Offences Act of 1967.   *Stephen Rooney*

Bibliography

Higgins, Patrick. *Heterosexual Dictatorship.* London: Fourth Estate, 1996.

Moran, Leslie J. *The Homosexual(ity) of Law.* London and New York: Routledge, 1996.

Report of the Committee on Homosexual Offences and Prostitution. London: HMSO, 1957.

See also England; International Law; Politics, Global

Womack, H. Lynn (1923–1977?)

Herman Lynn Womack was perhaps the first gay man to head a publishing house dedicated solely to gay men's literature and photography. Despite considerable resistance from homophile organizations and continued prosecution from the federal government, Womack's publishing empire extended from the early 1950s into the 1970s.

Womack was born in Hazelhurst, Mississippi. He attended the University of Mississippi before World War II and graduated from George Washington University in 1949. He received a Ph.D. in philosophy from the Johns Hopkins University in 1955. He married and fathered a daughter before coming out. Womack was a striking figure—240 pounds, according to the *New York Times*—and an albino. It has not been established when he died.

Starting in the 1950s, he took over the Guild Press, which at its height published ten journals, including *Grecian Guild Pictorial*, one of the most popular physique magazines of the time. The Grecian Guild also hosted national conferences celebrating the male body and may have been the largest, most popular organization of the 1950s. The Guild Press published books including the landmark work of gay erotic artist Phil Andros titled *$tud*.

In the early 1960s Womack won a Supreme Court ruling that allowed him to distribute nude male photographs through the postal system, but in 1971, he was convicted of selling pornography. An activist, he printed the pamphlet "Gay, Proud and Healthy" and other materials for the 1972 campaign within the American Psychiatric Association to remove homosexuality from its list of mental illnesses. His papers are in the Human Sexuality Collection at Cornell University.   *David Bergman*

Bibliography

Hatton, Jackie. "The Pornographic Empire of H. Lynn Womack." *Thresholds: Viewing Culture* 7 (Spring 1993): 9–32.

Waugh, Thomas. *Hard to Imagine*. New York: Columbia University Press, 1996.

Womack, H. Lynn. *Papers, 1951–1977*. In *Human Sexuality Collection*. Cornell University Library.

See also Athletic Model Guild; Censorship; Gay and Lesbian Press; Pornography

World Health Organization/WHO Global AIDS Programme

The international cooperative efforts of the Ministry of Health, World Health Organization, and the United States Centers for Disease Control enabled the serodiagnoses of the HIV virus in 1985. When the Special Programme on AIDS of the World Health Organization (WHO) was established in January 1987, three objectives were proposed: mobilization of education and resources: mutual support for programs, promotion of research, and intervention.

At the official launching of the Global AIDS Programme on February 1, 1987, the organization resolved on prevention of HIV and reduction of AIDS morbidity and mortality as its highest priorities. A distinguishing characteristic of the GAP program was concern not only for the toll of human suffering and death, but also for the social burden of the stigma and resulting discrimination of AIDS victims. The response time for the agency was remarkable. Within fifteen months the organization had brought AIDS programs to more than 120 nations. The massive effort was modeled on successful strategies from the smallpox eradication campaign of the 1960s and 1970s. It focused on the need for planning and coordination on a worldwide scale, and demonstrated the necessity for a multinational approach for handling the AIDS crisis. The climate of world opinion regarding HIV/AIDS seemed to respond almost instantly. Many nations began to recognize that the disease was prevalent in their citizens.

An October 1987 resolution of the United Nation General Assembly created an alliance between the WHO and the United Nations Development Programme. The alliance, titled the WHO/UNDP Alliance to Combat AIDS, brought together the UNDP's experience in socioeconomic development with the health policy and scientific knowledge of WHO to help governments establish and analyze national AIDS programs.

By year's end the needs of national AIDS committees made it increasingly noticeable that there was a big need for social and behavioral information to formulate local AIDS policies. Information and data were especially lacking among underdeveloped and developing nations, where the virus was spreading. The organization quickly mobilized to control the spread of AIDS in these countries. It provided support for national AIDS programs through leadership and assistance in biomedical, behavioral, and epidemiological research, health education, monitoring, and forecasting the impact of AIDS on the populace.

A major accomplishment of the WHO/GAP activities has been the establishment of an AIDS database covering infection and mortality, which serves as a resource for creating national reporting

W systems and AIDS policies. Maintaining a world profile enables nations to prepare an analytical frame of reference for target populations and collaborating institutions. The World Bank can also assess the data, observe future trends and courses of the epidemic, and take appropriate action.

The Global AIDS Programme has developed into a large organization with sections devoted to program support, surveillance, health education, social and behavioral research, and biomedical and epidemiological research. Through collaborative efforts the WHO Global Programme on AIDS has brought a multitude of resources to effectively battle the pandemic of AIDS.   *Michael A. Lutes*

Bibliography

Cleland, John, and Ferry Benoit, eds. *Sexual Behavior and AIDS in the Developing World*. Bristol, Pa.: Taylor & Francis, 1995.

Global Impact of AIDS. Proceedings of the International Conference of the Global Impact of AIDS. London, 1988. Alan Fleming et al., eds. New York: Alan R. Liss, 1988.

Sills, Yole. *AIDS Pandemic: Social Perspectives*. Westport, Conn.: Greenwood Press, 1994.

See also AIDS; AIDS Organizations, U.S.; Politics: Global; Sex Education; Sexually Transmitted Diseases

Y

YMCA

The Young Men's Christian Association (YMCA) is an international network of health clubs and gymnasiums founded in 1844 by George Williams, a clerk in a London drapery. Industrialization had led to a population explosion in cities; young men filled London for the jobs that new industries offered. Williams wanted to provide these young men with centers that promoted Christian values in the context of leisure activity. These early YMCAs, which usually consisted of dormitories, libraries, and sitting rooms, quickly spread first to other draperies, and then to other industries. The centers put forth a nondenominational Protestant philosophy and prided themselves on peer evangelization. Even overt religious activity like Bible study was most often led by the laity.

The YMCA's reputation spread to North America, which was experiencing similar population growth in urban areas. Boston and Montreal saw the founding of the first North American YMCAs in the early 1850s. The spread of the YMCA was rapid. By 1900, there were nearly 1,500 YMCAs in operation in the United States alone. Most were in downtown areas of large cities, usually in rented space above buildings and shops. By World War I, nearly all major cities had YMCAs, and they now occupied their own buildings in many instances. The facilities began to include gymnasiums, hoping to improve the conditions of its members' minds, spirits, and bodies. The gymnasiums were also a tool for recruiting members who could then be evangelized.

YMCAs in urban centers were often filled with single young men available for sexual experimentation. George Chauncey argues in *Gay New York* that "by World War I, the YMCAs in New York and elsewhere had developed a reputation among gay men as centers of sex and social life. . . . The reputation only increased in the Depression with the construction, in 1930, of two huge new YMCA hotels, which soon became famous within the gay world as gay residential centers" (*Gay New York* 155). Chauncey says that this reputation "became a part of gay folklore in the 1930s, 1940s, and 1950s, when the extent of sexual activity at the Ys—particularly the 'never ending sex' in the showers—became legendary in the gay world" (*Gay New York* 156).

This goes some way to explain the resonances behind the 1979 pop song "YMCA" by New York disco group the Village People. The group dressed in outlandish, macho outfits and were tremendously successful with both gay and straight audiences. "YMCA," in all its blatantly homoerotic glory ("You can hang out with all the boys at the YMCA"), climbed to number two on the pop charts and can still be heard at baseball games, roller rinks, weddings, and in both gay and straight dance clubs.

The gymnasiums of ancient Greece were, in many ways, predecessors to the modern YMCA. The ancient gyms were meeting places where males gathered for swimming, exercise, and massage—all in the nude. They spread to most parts of the Hellenistic empire, including Rome. After Christianity became the official religion of the Roman Empire, however, homosexuality, pederasty, public bathing, and nudity began to be seen as sinful. The influential model of education based on English public schools began in the sixteenth century to incorporate physical fitness into the overall development of youth. Thus playing fields, sports games, and gymnasiums began to spring up.

These modern gymnasiums, like their Hellenistic counterparts, were mostly for the rich, until the YMCA, which offered membership to the middle and working classes. These modern gymnasiums were sometimes gathering places for gays. However, gymnasiums specifically for gays have appeared more recently, particularly in large cities, and have enjoyed large membership. This is probably because involvement in athletics can be such a source of gay pride, as gays can often gain confidence by athletic superiority over straights.   *William DeGenaro*

Bibliography

Chauncey, George. *Gay New York: Gender, Urban Culture, and the Making of the Gay Male World, 1890–1940*. New York: Basic Books, 1994.

Hopkins, Howard. *History of the Y.M.C.A. in North America*. New York: Association Press, 1951.

Pronger, Brian. *Irony and Ecstasy: Gay Men and Athletics*. Toronto: Summerhill Press, 1989.

Zald, Mayer N. *Organizational Change: The Political Economy of the YMCA*. Chicago: University of Chicago Press, 1970.

See also Bathhouses and Sex Clubs; Greece; New York City; Physical Culture; Sports

Yourcenar, Marguerite (1903–1987)

Born Marguerite de Crayencour to a family of Belgian origin, Marguerite at age eighteen took as her pen name Yourcenar, an anagram of her actual name, which also became her legal name when she moved to the United States. Although Yourcenar never earned a university degree, she was trained in classics from an early age and knew Latin and Greek. In 1937, after meeting Virginia Woolf concerning a translation of Woolf's novel *The Waves*, Yourcenar met Grace Frick in Paris. After moving to the United States in 1939, Marguerite and Grace lived together until the latter's death in 1979. Grace translated many of Marguerite's works into English, and her connections with Sarah Lawrence College procured for her companion the position of part-time professor of French and art history in 1942.

While the word *homosexual* never appears in her novels, male homosexuality is present in many of them, and her first, *Alexis* (1929), took the subject as its main theme. Alexis, based on a personal friend of Yourcenar's, is a young musician who tells his wife in a long letter—the novel—that he cannot stay with her because he desires men. It is Yourcenar's direct response to André Gide's *Corydon*.

Yourcenar rejected the use of scientific vocabulary where sexual orientation was concerned, preferring an archaic style that reflected more authentically, in her view, the complex nature of human sexuality. Her most famous novel, about the emperor Hadrian, *Memoirs of Hadrian* (1951), portrays candidly the bisexuality of the third ruler of the Antonin dynasty. Although the main character speaks of his many lovers, the novel's primary love interest is between Hadrian and his young Greek slave, Antinous.

In addition to her many novels, Yourcenar was also a prolific writer of essays, and in "Bleue, Blanche, Rose, Gaie," from a collection called *Le Tour de la prison* (1991), she takes as her subject the gay community of San Francisco in the early 1980s. Yourcenar preferred the term *gay* because of its similarity to the Gaya Scienza of the troubadours and the poets of the court of Frederick II. She concludes with some reflections on AIDS and a call to tolerance with the saying "Il faut de tout pour faire un monde."

In 1980 Yourcenar was elected to the Académie Française, the first woman of letters to be honored in this way by the ultraconservative institution. She continued writing and lecturing until her death.   *Todd Black*

Bibliography

Yourcenar, Marguerite. *Essais et mémoires*. Paris: Éditions Gallimard, 1991.

———. *Oeuvres Romanesques*. Paris: Éditions Gallimard, 1982.

See also French Literature; Gide, André; Greece; Hadrian; Renault, Mary

Yugoslavia

No written documentation reveals anything of a gay Serbian history from the period of an independent Serb state of the tenth century until the modern era. Throughout this period, homosexual behavior was neither regulated nor explicitly prohibited. Nevertheless, the dominant patriarchal culture forbade, as it still does, public discussion of personal matters and, especially, sexual activities of any kind.

After the fall of the Kingdom of Yugoslavia, which existed from 1918 to 1941, and following World War II, Josip Broz Tito formed the Socialist Federal Republic of Yugoslavia. During his rule, the communist government implemented a law affecting all six Yugoslav republics prohibiting gay sex, which was punishable by a yearlong prison sentence. There is no known instance that this law was enforced. The invisibility of a homosexual society was caused by the combination of a dominant macho-Mediterranean culture paired with communist control of all public discourse, which prevented public discussion of sexual topics. One could freely mock or make fun of lesbians and gays, but there are no documented instances of discrimination against them because of their sexuality. Thus, sexual identities were kept private; Serbia's urban centers tended to be tolerant, and in rural areas, taunting of gays and lesbians was about the worst offense against them.

After the death of Tito in 1980, the entire social climate of Yugoslavia began to open up. The media gained more independence from the government and public discourse about all aspects of life began. For example, during the mid-1980s, Jovan Ćirilov, a Serbian writer and director of the Yugoslav Dramatic Theatre, demanded the abolition of the Yugoslav antigay law at a Communist Party convention, though to no avail. A few people began to publish magazines and journals dealing with gay issues, but with little success.

Following the breakup of Tito's Yugoslavia and the formation of the new Federal Republic of Yugoslavia in 1992, comprising the republics of Serbia and Montenegro, this lack of discourse about same-sex relationships continued. One can only speculate as to what the reasons are. One explanation is that during this period of breakup, with a war raging nearby in Bosnia and the nation living under severe economic hardships, more fundamental issues were at stake, specifically those of basic human rights, the absence of an independent media, and the problems of establishing a civil society. Since no public institution keeps records of gay rights violations, it is impossible to say whether such rights are respected or not. This can mean either that gays and lesbians are accepted and tolerated in this society and only lack visibility, or that there is still a great deal of homophobia.

One organization that subscribes to the latter explanation is the gay activist group Arkadija (Arcadia), formed in 1990 by a group of students dedicated to increasing the visibility of gay men and lesbians in Serbian society as well as to ending all discrimination based on sexual preference. Until July 14, 1994, however, the very existence of such a gay activist group was illegal. The Serbian Criminal Law Article 110/3, which criminalized homosexual sex since the time of Tito, was finally replaced with a new one that does not mention gay behavior at all. Arkadija's main point of contention is the continued harassment of gays by the police, who are notorious for overstepping normal procedures in general. One can find examples of this in the book *Serbian Diaries*, published in English by a Serb writing under the pseudonym Boris Davidovich. It is the author's account of his sex life during the last two decades, from which one can see many examples of police harassment toward gays, notably toward men who engaged in having sex in public places.

Yet there are other instances where gay men and lesbians have been visible in positive and healthy ways. In 1995, the Yugoslav movie *Marble Ass*, directed by Želimir Žilnik, was awarded a Golden Bear at the Berlin Film Festival for the best international gay-affirmative film. In what is essentially an antiwar film, Belgrade's underground gay culture, portrayed as peace-loving and nonaggressive, is contrasted with the macho, war-loving outer world. Dragoslav Srejović, a late professor of archaeology and vice president of the Serbian Academy of Sciences who is famous for discovering Lepenski Vir, a prehistoric settlement in Serbia, openly discussed his gay love life in his last book of interviews. Perhaps the strongest positive influence has come from gay-themed international mass culture available in records stores, on television, and in movie houses. It would appear that attitudes toward gays and lesbians are changing slowly increased acceptance and tolerance, despite a continuing lack of visibility.

Zoran Milutinović
and Will Petersen

Bibliography

Davidovich, Boris L. *Serbian Diaries*. Dragan Vujanic, trans. London: Gay Men's Press, 1996.
Silber, Laura, and Allan Little. *The Death of Yugoslavia*. London: Penguin, 1995, rev. ed., 1996.

See also Politics, Global; Slovenia

Z

Zane, Arnie (1948–1988)

Born in New York City, Arnie Zane entered the State University of New York at age sixteen to study biology, graduating in 1970 with a degree in art history. In 1971, Zane took up photography as his "vehicle of expression" and began his lifelong artistic collaboration with Bill T. Jones. In 1972, he accompanied Jones to Amsterdam. In 1973, following their return to the United States, Zane, Jones, and Lois Welk formed the American Dance Asylum in Binghamton, New York. Initially more involved as a visual artist producing slide and text projections for performances, Zane later became involved as a dancer and choreographer, receiving a Creative Artists Public Service (CAPS) Fellowship in 1973. In the mid-1970s, Zane's photography was exhibited at New York's prestigious Light Gallery. Zane received a second CAPS Fellowship for choreography in 1981 and two choreographic fellowships from the NEA in 1983 and 1984. In 1980, Zane and Jones were co-recipients of the German Critics Award for Blauvelt Mountain. In 1982, the Bill T. Jones/Arnie Zane Dance Company was formed. Commissioned by the Alvin Ailey American Dance Theatre to create a new work, *How to Walk Like an Elephant* premiered at Wolftrap (a Washington, D.C., area outdoor theater) in 1985. In 1988, Zane died of AIDS.

Although more widely known for his work in dance, Zane's photography is equally significant. His photography, which focuses on the human body, is influenced primarily by experimental cinema and his early involvement in dance. His work concerns itself with a physicality, sexuality, variations in body types, and the ravages of disease and age, reflecting the same concerns with theatrical framing, time and timelessness, flux and stasis that provide the orga-

Arnie Zane, "Self Portrait" c.1975. Photo courtesy of the Arnie Zane Archive, UCR/California Museum of Photography, University of California, Riverside. Gift of Bill T. Jones.

nizing principles of his choreography. While by no means derivative, Zane's work relates on the one hand to the theatrical and metaphorical work of Minor White, and on the other to the unflinching portraiture of Diane Arbus.   *Cynthia Morrill*

Bibliography

Green, Jonathan, ed. *Continuous Replay: The Photographs of Arnie Zane.* Cambridge, Mass.: MIT Press, 1999.

Pichini, Christine. "Corpus Delecti: A Scrapbook of Arnie Zane's Remembrance." B.A. thesis, Wesleyan University, 1995.

Zimmer, Elizabeth, and Susan Quasha, eds. *Body Against Body: The Dance and Other Collaboration of Bill T. Jones & Arnie Zane*. Tarrytown, N.Y.: Station Hill Press, 1989.

See also Ailey, Alvin; Dance: Concert Dance in America; Dance and AIDS; Jones, Bill T.; Photography; White, Minor

Zapata, Luis (1951–)

Over the past two decades Luís Zapata has become Mexico's most celebrated gay writer, mixing influences from abroad with Mexican views on family, gender, and sex to produce an original and memorable collection of characters and texts. His first two works helped usher in the 1980s boom of gay literature in Mexico, during which he published three more novels, two collections of short stories (*De amor es mi negra pena*, 1983; *Ese amor que hasta ayer nos quemaba*, 1989), and a translation of Adolfo Caminha's *Bom-Crioulo* (*Bon Criolho*, 1987). His first publication, *Hasta en las mejores familias* (1975), concerns the difficult relationship between a campy, rebellious son and his closeted homosexual father. In it, Zapata reworks Mexican literature's earlier presentation of homosexuals as either pederasts or conversely lovers of father figures by suggesting that repressed father-son sexual desires underpin both the social order and the modern family. His second work, the commercially and critically successful *Las aventuras, desventuras y sueños de Adonis García el vampiro de la colonia Roma* (1979), derived from Zapata's taped interviews with a hustler. It chronicles and celebrates Adonis's picaresque adventures and offers information on the emerging gay lifestyle of Mexico City. His next two works were *Melodrama* (1983), a short, camp novel about an affair between a handsome youth and a married detective, and *En jirones* (1985), a diary of an obsessive relationship between two young professionals. In 1989, he published *La hermana secreta de Angélica María*, the story of a hermaphrodite who believes he is the famous Mexican actress's secret sister. More recently, Zapata has published *De cuerpo entero* (1990), memories of his youth spent going to movies, and *Por qué mejor no nos vamos?* (1992) and *Paisaje con amigos* (1995), both reflections, one fictionalized and the other journalistic, of a middle-aged gay man on the road. His literary trajectory is one of increasing personalization and self-exposure, of his own coming out.

Zapata, technically gifted and adventurous in both form (stream of consciousness, heavy use of pastiche and intertextuality) and content (hermaphroditism, hustling, graphic descriptions of sex acts), has opened up spaces for other writers by presenting "unacceptable" content in established literary forms. He has presented both mainstream and marginalized homosexual types, and has allowed each his own dignity and voice. Characters and characterization drive the action and themes, and the personal and psychological is privileged over the social. The body is a source of knowledge, the medium through which truth is revealed, and fantasy is a tool for liberation. Playfulness and camp, narrative tease, and "pornography" all reflect Zapata's desire to entertain, to show the reader a good time. Humor, vitality, and optimism mitigate tragedy. Recurrent themes include the influence of cinema and mass culture on personal identity, the role of family in postmodern society, and conflicting conceptualizations of homosexuality. Female characters rarely appear outside of the role of mother or screen star.

Zapata grew up in Chilpancingo and currently lives in Cuernavaca. *Maurice Westmorland*

Bibliography

Schaefer-Rodríguez, Claudia. "Luis Zapata." In *Latin American Writers on Gay and Lesbian Themes: A Bio-critical Sourcebook*. David William Foster, ed. Westport, Conn.: Greenwood Press, 1994, 460–70.

Teichmann, Reinhard. Interview with Luís Zapata. In *De la onda en adelante: Conversaciones con 21 novelistas mexicanos*. Mexico City: Posada, 1987, 355–74.

See also Barba Jacob, Porfirio; Calva Pratt, José Rafael; Caminha, Adolfo; Camp; Fiction; Machismo; Mexico; Villaurrutia, Xavier

Zimbabwe

Homosexuality in Zimbabwe (formerly Rhodesia), an independent nation since 1980, is wrapped up in the vicissitudes of postcolonialism. If we take seriously the arguments that homosexuality is historically (Foucault) and culturally (Blackwood) specific, understanding homosexuality in Zimbabwe today means recognizing that gay and lesbian histories must encompass precolonial sexual practices of the Shona and Ndebele, the forms of (hetero-)sexual regulation introduced and maintained by colonizers and Christian missionaries in Rhodesia, and the nationalist rhetoric of contemporary Zimbabwean life.

Little research has been done on traditional same-sex practices of the Shona and Ndebele peoples, and even less has been published in English. However, most agree that in polygamous Shona societies, same-sex relations were practiced, even though their cultural meanings may not be clear. Much work remains to be done in this area, and the excavations must proceed carefully to disentangle traditional Shona and Ndebele cultures from the residue of Christian colonization, which codified sexual relationships into conjugal, monogamous heterosexuality.

Paradoxically, some of colonization's economic structures have made same-sex relations visible. During the early twentieth century Rhodesian mines, relying on migrant labor in all-male environments, produced man-boy marriages along the lines of those better documented in South Africa. In these relationships, an older worker would take on a younger as his "wife." The older partner enjoyed sexual access to his younger partner (though apparently the sex was not mutual), and the younger member of the dyad usually received money and gifts that would enable him to purchase a homestead in his community after he finished working in the mines. In addition, the younger partner would often procure a better job through his "marriage." Frequently a young man would serve as a "wife" to an older worker for a few years before setting himself up as a "husband" and acquiring a "boy" of his own.

As usual, less is know about same-sex practices among women in this industrially produced, sex-segregated society, although Judith Gay's investigation of "mummy-baby" relationships in Lesotho suggests tantalizing directions for research. Basotho women established households with each other, nurturing each other materially, emotionally, and sexually. As with mine marriages among men, a central feature of mummy-baby relationships is the disparate ages of the participants; again like the men's mine marriages, the older partner undertakes to provide for the younger, who may eventually graduate to a senior role in another mummy-baby relationship. Sometimes these relationships, which are not necessarily monogamous, coexist with heterosexual relationships, especially the mummy's.

The most prominent lesbian and gay advocacy group in Zimbabwe today is Gays and Lesbians of Zimbabwe (GALZ). Founded in 1989 with a relatively low profile, GALZ sought to provide a network for gays and lesbians to exchange information and socialize. Increasingly, however, it has been called to political activism and now maintains close links with AIDS organizations, women's advocacy groups, and human rights struggles. Gay and lesbian activism in Zimbabwe was kicked into high gear in 1995, after President Robert Mugabe disallowed GALZ from participating in the Zimbabwe International Book Fair in Harare. His homophobic comments on this occasion (among them that lesbian women and gay men were "worse than dogs and pigs" and deserved "no rights at all") sought to solidify a narrow view of nationalism. Framing his homophobic remarks as "a question of protecting and guaranteeing the cultural health of Zimbabwe," Mugabe suggested that homosexuality represents a form of Western decadence that has no historical basis in "authentic" Zimbabwean culture. Barred from the book fair in 1995, GALZ was reinstated at the 1996 event on a court order that banned interference with the organization in the future. In addition to sparking resistance within Zimbabwe, Mugabe's remarks incited international outrage, prompting a letter from U.S. congressional representatives and protests in New Zealand, the Netherlands, and England.

Ironically, Mugabe's narrow view of authentic Zimbabwean culture reasserts as "natural" and "traditional" what Christian missionaries earlier in the century instituted by force. These two constituencies, Mugabe's nationalism and Christian morality, came to a head in December 1998 during the World Council of Churches' meeting in Harare. Archbishop Desmond Tutu, speaking from South Africa, which is the only country to explicitly protect sexual orientation in its constitution, issued a strong challenge to the WCC, calling on Christians to take a positive stand on homosexuality. When asked why he has taken on this controversy, he responded, "The answer is straightforward. It's a matter of ordinary justice." However, neither local Zimbabwean churches nor the WCC agreed to endorse homosexuality.   *Heather Zwicker*

Bibliography

Blackwood, Evelyn. "Breaking the Mirror: The Construction of Lesbianism and the Anthropological Discourse on Homosexuality." In *The Many Faces of Homosexuality*. New York: Harrington Park Press, 1986.

Desai, Gaurav. "Out in Africa." *Genders* 25 (1997): 120–43.

Foucault, Michel. *The History of Sexuality,* Vol. 1. New York: Vintage, 1978.

Z Gay, Judith. "'Mummies and Babies' and Friends and Lovers in Lesotho." *Journal of Homosexuality* 11, no. 3–4 (Summer 1985): 97–116.

Harries, Patrick. "Symbols and Sexuality: Culture and Identity on the Early Witwatersrand Gold Mines." *Gender and History* 2, no. 3 (Autumn 1990): 318–36.

Moodie, T. Dunbar, with Vivienne Ndatshe and British Sibuyi. "Migrancy and Male Sexuality on the South African Gold Mines." In *Hidden from History: Reclaiming the Gay and Lesbian Past.* Martin Duberman, Martha Vicinus, and George Chauncey Jr., eds. New York: Meridian, 1989, 411–25.

See also Africa: Precolonial sub-Saharan Africa; Kenya; Politics, Global; South Africa

Index

Spanish, 838–840
Swedish, 852–856
U.S., 917–924
Living End, 66
Livingston, Jennie, 19, 261
Living Theater, 108, 109
Llama de amor (Rodríguez Matos), 749
Loeb, Richard, 536–537
London, 546–547
Long and Happy Life, A (Price), 709
Long Day Closes, The (Davies), 246
Longest Journey, The (Forster), 336
Looking Queer (Atkins), 131
Lord of the Ascendant (Kohs), 521
Lorrain, Jean, 547–548
Los Angeles, 548–550
Los Angeles Gay and Lesbian Community Services Center, 214
Lost Generations (Bang), 95
Love Alone (Monette), 32
Love Paintings, 442, 443
Love poetry, 550–552
Love's Coming of Age (Carpenter), 172
Love's Instruments (Dixon), 257
Love! Valour! Compassion! (McNally), 579
Loving v. Virginia, 387
Lubovitch, Lar, 238
Ludlam, Charles, 552–553, 650
Ludwig II, 67, 553
Lully, Jean-Baptiste, 553–554
Luther, Martin, 191–192
Lynch, Michael, 32
Lynes, George Platt, 554–556, 687–688

MacCarthy, Desmond, 127
Machismo, 557–558
Mademoiselle de Maupin (Gautier), 14–15
Magic Mountain, The (Mann), 559
Mahlsdorf, Charlotte von, 558–559
Malcolm (Albee), 42
Male Figure, The, 146
Mallarmé, Stépane, 350
Malouf, David, 84, 559
Mann, Thomas, 312, 559–560, 584
Manrique Ardila, Jaime, 183, 560
Mantegazza, Paolo, 389
Mapplethorpe, Robert, 74, 560–562
Marais, Jean, 562–563
Marching bands, 189–190, 563–566
Marches on Washington, 121, 566–567
Mardi Gras, 261
Marketing, 567–569
Marlowe, Christopher, 119, 281, 360, 546, 569–570
Marriage, 768–770
    domestic partnership, 258–259
Marvel, 209
Masculinity, 570–571
Mass, Lawrence, 571–572
Massine, Léonide, 92
Masturbation, 572–574
Mattachine Review, 366
Mattachine Society, 120, 124, 381, 400, 432, 446, 455, 574

Matthiessen, F. O., 76, 574–575
Maupin, Armistead, 575–576, 655, 772
Mayor of Castro Street, The (Shilts), 773, 819, 820
McAlmon, Robert, 576
McCarthyism, 204, 376, 432, 446, 456, 576–578
McClatchy, J. D., 923
McFarlane, Rodger, 384
McKay, Claude, 426, 578, 641
McNally, Terence, 27, 38, 578–579, 650
McPhee, Colin, 579–580
Media
    censorship, 178–179
    coverage of AIDS by, 28–29
    coverage of gays by, 502–503, 580–582
Medieval Latin poetry, 582–584
Mediterranean, 584–585
Melanesia, 585–587
Melville, Herman, 76, 311, 312, 587–588, 918
Merchant of Venice, The (Shakespeare), 282, 819
Merino, Chuck, 140
Merrill, James, 588–589
Metropolitan Community Church, 589–590
Mexico, 590–592
    cantina culture, 169
Miami, 592–593
Michals, Duane, 593–594
Michaels, Dick, 13
Michelangelo, 73, 243–244, 360, 485, 488, 594–595
Midnight Cowboy, 777
Migrant Souls (Islas), 182
Migrations to Solitude (Acosta-Posada), 3
Mikaël (Bang), 95
Military, 596–597
Milk, Harvey, 10, 367, 566, 597–598, 630, 773
Milstead, Harris Glenn. *See* Divine
Mineo, Sal, 598
Minority standing, 598–601
Mirgorod (Gogol), 409
Mishima, Yukio, 601
Misogyny, 601–602
Miss Julie, 753
Mizer, Bob, 80–81, 146, 602–603
Moby-Dick (Melville), 587
Moffett, Donald, 603
Moix, Terenci, 603, 839
Moll, Albert, 388–389, 603–604, 805
Mollies, 604–605
Molly houses, 282, 284, 606–607
Monasticism, 607
Monette, Paul, 31–32, 315, 607–608
Montaigne, Michel de, 357, 608–609
Montesquieu, Robert de, 609–610
Montheriant, Henry de, 610
Moore, Charles, 67
Moral Majority, 740
Moran, Robert, 610–611
Morocco, 611–612
Morris, Jan, 612
Morris, Mark, 237, 612–613
Morrison v. State Board of Education, 778
Moscone, George, 630, 773
Motley, Willard, 19
Movies. *See* Films/movie industry